Samuel L. Wright

THEOLOGICAL DICTIONARY

OF THE

NEW TESTAMENT

EDITED BY

GERHARD FRIEDRICH

Translator and Editor

GEOFFREY W. BROMILEY, D. LITT., D. D.

Volume VII

Σ

WM. B. EERDMANS PUBLISHING COMPANY

GRAND RAPIDS, MICHIGAN

THEOLOGICAL DICTIONARY OF THE NEW TESTAMENT

Translated from
THEOLOGISCHES WÖRTERBUCH ZUM NEUEN TESTAMENT
Siebenter Band: Σ, herausgegeben von Gerhard Friedrich

Published by
W. KOHLHAMMER VERLAG
Stuttgart, Germany

Reprinted, May 1975

8/99

PHOTOLITHOPRINTED BY CUSHING - MALLOY, INC.
ANN ARBOR, MICHIGAN, UNITED STATES OF AMERICA

K. Lincoln

Preface

After an interval of five years another volume of the Theological Dictionary has been concluded and published for service in research and preaching. In letters and publications many wishes, proposals and criticisms have in the meantime been uttered, whether in relation to individual articles or to questions of method and scientific accuracy. Even on the same problem the voices have not been harmonious but diametrically opposed. For some the articles are too broad, for others they cannot be explicit enough with a view to sermon preparation. Some think too much attention is paid to Judaism, since the New Testament is a Greek book for Greek readers and discontinuity is a stronger feature in the relation to Judaism than continuity. Others think they discern anti-semitic tendencies in the Dictionary because Paul's reforming attitude to the Law gives a false picture of the Judaism of his day. It has been suggested that the Dictionary falls short of critical exactitude in virtue of its attempt to expound the abiding spirit of the Old Testament and the New. On the other hand it has been proposed that articles should not be entrusted to two different authors since the unity of the Bible is not set forth in the Dictionary if one part is done by an Old Testament scholar and the other by a New Testament scholar. Some want a strict lexical account of the meaning of words while others are asking for express discussions of the broader concepts which deal with the matter and not just the term. Many like etymology; others think the meaning of a word should be determined, not from its history, but from individual sayings. If publishing the Dictionary entails much labour, it has its humorous side when articles which theologians dismiss as complete failures receive the highest praise from philologists, or articles which are subjected to the sharpest criticism by philologists are extolled as most significant by theologians.

The opposing judgments and wishes show that the Dictionary is on the right path. The editor tries to do justice to all justifiable criticism and to remedy all real mistakes. Articles in the later volumes do not draw far-reaching theological conclusions from the etymology of a word and keep almost too expressly to the meaning in individual sayings, so that stringent abbreviation has been required. On material grounds the history of a word cannot be ignored. Words are not lifeless stones which always remain the same and which can be put together in a mosaic. They are living things which develop or decline. As in a tree branches die off and new twigs grow in other places, so old meanings of words disappear and new ones emerge. It is certainly a mistake if conclusions about a people are over-hastily drawn from the presence or absence of a word in its vocabulary. On the other hand, one can hardly deny that the way of thinking is different in different peoples and that this thinking finds expression in language. Whether this is due to ethnological, historical, or cultural causes, it certainly exists. From this difference arise certain problems when two peoples with different languages are in contact. The author of the preface to Jesus Sirach says already that it is hard to transmit the expressions of one language into another in such a way that the meaning remains the same. Most of the New Testament authors were Jews who were passing on in Greek what they had received in part in Aramaic. To understand them, it is important that we know what the relevant word means in the Greek world, in the Old Testament, in the Septuagint, in the Rabbis, in the New Testament, and in the early Church. This is the task of the Theological Dictionary.

Our thanks are extended to the many scholars without whose help in the reading of manuscripts and correction of proofs the articles of the Theological Dictionary would not be as reliable as they are. In gratitude for services of different kinds I mention H. Balz, G. Bertram, A. Böhlig, P. Boendermaker, E. Dammann, A. Dihle, G. Egg, G. Fohrer, E. P. D. Gooding, A. Hiller. W. Kasch, P. Katz, H. Kleinknecht, H. Krämer, W. Lohse, C. F. D. Moule, E. Nestle, C. H. Peisker, K. Reinhard, K. H. Rengstorf, E. Risch, K. H. Schelkle, G. Schlichting, W. Schneemelcher, S. Schulz, K. Staab, H. Traub and K. Zimmermann. A special word of appreciation is due to H. Riesenfeld, who has placed his comprehensive catalogue and bibliography at our disposal, and K. H. Rengstorf, who has allowed us to use his Josephus concordance in so far as it is applicable.

Buckenhof bei Erlangen, June 16, 1964.   *G. Friedrich*

Editor's Preface

The post-war volumes of the Theological Dictionary of the New Testament are distinguished from the first four by many special features. Gerhard Friedrich succeeds Gerhard Kittel as editor. The fall of Hitler has made possible wider international contacts, especially with scholars of the English-speaking world. The series begins to benefit not only from newer developments in biblical and theological studies but also from exciting discoveries like the Dead Sea Scrolls.

These changes have certain important implications for the Dictionary. Some of the judgments in earlier articles have had to be reconsidered. A place has had to be found for additional material. Points not originally thought to be significant have had to be discussed. In a work extending over so many decades some of this would have been inevitable in any case. The break between the Kittel and the Friedrich volumes, however, has made an even more imperious demand, even at the risk of adding to the final size of the work.

Naturally the purpose, design and structure of the Dictionary remain the same. Nor is there any change in either its proper use or its enduring value. Added interest is imparted, however, by the fact that the post-war volumes bring us increasingly into the sphere of modern research and debate. Readers of the present version will also profit by the fact that few of even the most important articles in these later volumes have ever been offered previously in English translation.

A great debt is again owed to Professor F. F. Bruce of Manchester University for his invaluable and indefatigable labours in proof reading. If some errors still slip through the net — and we are grateful to readers who call attention to these — there is the consolation that Dr. Bruce in particular has been able to correct not a few errors in the original German.

The English version of Volume VII has been more than usually subject to the changes and chances of this mortal life. Originally planned to appear in January, 1971 it was first delayed by the relocation and reorganisation of the printers and then the final proofs were held up again by the British postal strike. We beg the indulgence of our readers for the tardy publication and also for any extra errors that might have crept into especially the closing sections.

Pasadena, California, 1971.   *G. W. Bromiley*

Contents

Contents

Contributors

Editor:

Gerhard Friedrich, Erlangen.

Contributors:

Otto Bauernfeind, Tübingen.
Friedrich Baumgärtel, Erlangen.
Georg Bertram, Giessen.
Otto Betz, Tübingen.
Werner Bieder, Basel.
Günther Bornkamm, Heidelberg.
Hans Conzelmann, Göttingen.
Gerhard Delling, Halle.
Gottfried Fitzer, Vienna.
Werner Foerster, Münster.
Georg Fohrer, Erlangen.
Ernst Fuchs, Marburg.
Heinrich Greeven, Bochum.
Walter Grundmann, Jena.
Günther Harder, Berlin-Zehlendorf.
Claus-Hunno Hunzinger, Hamburg.
Joachim Jeremias, Göttingen.
Wilhelm Kasch, Kiel.
Helmut Köster, Harvard.
Friedrich Lang, Tübingen.
Eduard Lohse, Göttingen.
Ulrich Luck, Bethel.
Christian Maurer, Bethel.
Rudolf Meyer, Jena.
Wilhelm Michaelis, Bern.
Otto Michel, Tübingen.
Gottfried Quell, Berlin.
Karl Heinrich Rengstorf, Münster.
Knut Schäferdiek, Bonn.
Johannes Schneider, Berlin.
Wolfgang Schrage, Tübingen.
Siegfried Schulz, Zürich.
Eduard Schweizer, Zürich.
Gustav Stählin, Mainz.
Konrad Weiss, Rostock.
Ulrich Wilckens, Berlin-Zehlendorf.

> σάββατον, σαββατισμός,
> παρασκευή

† σάββατον, παρασκευή.

Contents : The Sabbath in the Old Testament : 1. The Origin of Israel's Sabbath ; 2. The Sabbath in the Pre-Exilic Age ; 3. The Sabbath in the Post-Exilic Age ; 4. The Sabbatical Year. B. The Sabbath in Judaism : 1. The Development of the Sabbath in Judaism : a. The Usage in Palestinian and Hellenistic Judaism ; b. The Sabbath from the Maccabean Period to the Editing of the Mishnah ; 2. The Prohibition of Work on the Sabbath : a. The Regulations in the Book of Jubilees and the Damascus Document ; b. The Regulations in Rabbinic Literature ; c. The Superseding of the Sabbath Law in Special Cases ; 3. The Celebration of the Sabbath : a. Celebration at Home ; b. Worship on the Sabbath ; c. The Jewish Celebration of the Sabbath in the Judgment of Non-Jews ; 4. The Sabbatical Year : a. Fallow Ground and the Remission of Debts each Seventh Year ; b. The Cosmic Week and Cosmic Sabbath. C. The Sabbath in the New Testament : 1. The Jewish Sabbath in the New Testament ; 2. The Sabbath Conflicts of Jesus : a. The Sabbath Stories in Mark and their Parallels in Matthew and Luke ; b. The Sabbath Stories Peculiar to Luke ; c. The Sabbath Stories in John's Gospel ; 3. The Sabbath in the Christian Churches. D. The Sabbath in the Early Church : 1. Sabbath and Sunday; 2. The Jewish Week in the Christian Church ; 3. The Sabbath in Jewish Christianity.

σάββατον. On A.: J. Wellhausen, *Prolegomena z. Gesch. Israels*³ (1886), 113-121; H. Zimmern, "Sabbat," ZDMG, 58 (1904), 199-202; also "Nochmals Sabbat," *ibid.*, 458-460; J. Meinhold, "Sabbat u. Woche," FRL, 5 (1905); W. Lotz, Art. "Sabbath u. Sabbathjahr," RE³, 17 (1906), 283-295 with older bibl.; J. Hehn, "Siebenzahl u. Sabbat bei d. Babyloniern u. im AT," *Leipziger Semitistische Stud.*, 2, 5 (1907); E. Mahler, "Der Sabbat," ZDMG, 62 (1908), 33-79; G. Beer, *Schabbath* (1908); J. Meinhold, "Sabbat u. Sonntag," *Wissenschaft u. Bildung*, 45 (1909); J. Hehn, "Der isr. Sabbat," *Bibl. Zeitfragen*, II, 2 (1909); J. Meinhold, "Die Entstehung des Sabbats," ZAW, 29 (1909), 81-112; B. Landsberger, "Der kultische Kalender d. Babylonier u. Assyrer," *Leipziger Semitistische Stud.*, 6, 1-2 (1915); E. Mahler, *Hndbch. d. jüd. Chronologie* (1916); J. Meinhold, "Zur Sabbatfrage," ZAW, 36 (1916), 108-110 (= Sabbatfrage I); J. Hehn, "Zur Sabbatfrage," BZ, 14 (1917), 198-213; G. Beer, Art. "Sabbat" in Pauly-W., 1a (1920), 1551-1557; W. Nowack, *Schabbat* (1924); B. D. Eerdmans, "Der Sabbath" in *Vom AT, Festschr. K. Marti* (1925), 79-83; P. Volz, *Die bibl. Altertümer*² (1925), 81-90; F. H. Colson, *The Week* (1926); O. Eissfeldt, Art. "Feste u. Feiern, II" in RGG², II, 552-554; K. Budde, "Sabbath u. Woche," *Chr. W.*, 43 (1929), 202-208, 265-270 = "The Sabbath and the Week," JThSt, 30 (1929), 1-15; J. Meinhold, "Zur Sabbathfrage," ZAW, 48 (1930), 121-128 (= Sabbathfrage II); K. Budde, "Antwort auf J. Meinholds 'Zur Sabbathfrage,'" ZAW, 48 (1930), 138-145; W. W. Cannon, "The Weekly Sabbath," ZAW, 49 (1931), 325-327; E. G. Kraeling, "The Present Status of the Sabbath Question," *American Journ. of Semitic Languages and Literatures*, 49 (1932), 218-228; S. Langdon, *Babylonian Menologies and the Semitic Calendars* (1935); J. and H. Lewy, "The Origin of the Week and the Oldest West Asiatic Calendar," HUCA, 17 (1942/43), 1-152; H. Cazelles, *Études sur le Code de l'Alliance* (1946), 92-95; O. Procksch, *Theol. d. AT* (1950), 543-545; N. H. Torczyner, "Sabbat u. Woche," *Bibliotheca Orientalis*, 8 (1951), 14-24; H. H. Rowley, "Moses and the Decalogue," *Bulletin of the John Rylands Library*, 34 (1951), 81-118; M. Buber, *Moses*² (1952), 95-102; G. J. Botterweck, "Der Sabbat im AT," *Theol. Quart.*, 134 (1954), 134-147, 448-457; W. Bienert, *Die Arbeit nach d. Lehre d. Bibel* (1954), 21-39; R. North, "The Derivation of Sabbath," *Biblica*, 36 (1955), 182-201; G. Yamashiro, *A Sudy of the Hebrew Word Sabbath in Biblical and Talmudic Literatures*, Diss. Harvard (1955); E. Jenni, "Die theol. Begründung des Sabbatgebotes im AT," *Theol. Studien*, 46 (1956); Eichr. Theol. AT, I⁵, 76-78. On B.: F. Bohn,

A. The Sabbath in the Old Testament.

1. The Origin of Israel's Sabbath.

The Sabbath commandment, whose content changed in the course of the centuries, is found in all the sources of the Mosaic Law, Ex. 34:21 (J); Ex. 23:12 (E); Ex. 20:8-11 and Dt. 5:12-15 (Decalogue); Lv. 23:1-3; 19:3; 26:2 (H); Ex. 31:12-17; 35:1-3 (P).[1] This broad witness is not available for any other OT command, so that the great age of the Sabbath commandment may be deduced from this alone. But where is its origin to be sought?

In spite of much discussion the historical problem is still much debated. Some par. to the OT commandment have been found in Babylon, where the 7th, 14th (19th), 21st and 28th days of the months Elul and Marcheshwan are bad days and the following rules have to be observed in respect of them: "The shepherd of the great peoples shall not eat flesh cooked on coals or baked bread. He shall not put on clean (clothes). He shall not bring an offering. The king shall not travel by chariot. He shall not speak as ruler. At the place of the mystery the one who views the sacrifices shall not utter a word. The physician shall not lay his hands on a patient. (The day) is not suitable for carrying out plans. At night the king shall bring his gift to the great gods; he shall offer a sacrifice; the lifting up of his hands is then acceptable to the god."[2] In ancient Babylon a feast of the full moon was also held on the 15th day of the month. On this day work was stopped because it was an unlucky day and as ûm nuḫ libbi, "a day of pacification of the heart (i.e., of the gods)"[3] it was to be spent in penitence and prayer. This day of the full moon was called shapattu; the etym. and meaning are still obscure.[4] Are there connections between the Bab. shappatu and Israel's Sabbath?

In distinction from Israel's Sabbath the Babyl. shappatu is not held every week, its dating is connected with the cycle of the moon, and its character, like that of the

Der Sabbat im AT u. im altjüd. religiösen Aberglauben (1903); E. G. Hirsch *et al.,* Art. "Sabbath, Sabbatical Year and Jubilee," Jew. Enc., X (1905), 587-608; Schürer, II, 551-560, 574-576; M. Wolff, "Het oordeel der Heleensch-Romeinsche schrijvers over den oorsprong, naam en viering van den Sabbath," ThT, 44 (1910), 162-172; I. Elbogen, "Eingang u. Ausgang des Sabbats nach talmudischen Quellen" in *Festschr. zu I. Lewy's 70. Geburtstag* (1911), 173-187; Bousset-Gressm., 126 f. and Index, *s.v.* "Sabbat"; Moore, II, 21-39; Str.-B., II, 610-630 and Index, *s.v.* "Sabbat"; I. Elbogen, *Der jüd. Gottesdienst in seiner geschichtlichen Entwicklung*[3] (1931), 107-122; W. O. E. Oesterley, *Le Sabbat* (1935); M. Zobel, *Der Sabbat, sein Abbild im jüd. Schrifttum, seine Gesch. u. seine heutige Gestalt* (1935); S. M. Segel, *The Sabbath Book* (1942); A. J. Heshel, *The Sabbath* (1951); J. Z. Lauterbach, *Rabbinic Essays* (1951), 437-472; D. Correns, *Die Mischna Schebiit* (*vom Sabbatjahr*), Diss. Göttingen (1954); F. Landsberger, "Ritual Implements for the Sabbath," HUCA, 27 (1956), 387-415; H. Braun, *Spätjüd.-häret. u. frühchr. Radikalismus,* I (1957), 116-120. On C.: I. Abrahams, *Studies in Pharisaism and the Gospel,* I (1917), 129-135; G. Schrenk, "Sabbat oder Sonntag?" Judaica, 2 (1946/47), 169-189; J. Bauer, "Vom Sabbat zum Sonntag," *Bibel u. Liturgie,* 23 (1955/56), 106-110; D. Daube, *The NT and Rabb. Judaism* (1956), 67-71; J. Nedbal, *Sabbat u. Sonntag im NT,* Diss. Vienna (1956); W. Grundmann, *Die Gesch. Jesu Christi* (1957), 134-142; H. Braun, *Spätjüd.-häret. u. frühchr. Radikalismus,* II (1957), 70-72; E. Lohse, "Sabbat u. Sonntag im NT," *Verlorener Sonntag? Kirche im Volk,* 22 (1959), 25-36; A. Szabó, "Sabbat u. Sonntag," Judaica, 15 (1959), 161-172; H. Riesenfeld, "Sabbat et Jour du Seigneur," *NT Essays in Memory of T. W. Manson* (1959), 210-217; E. Lohse, "Jesu Worte über den Sabbat," ZNW, 51 (1960). On D.: E. Schürer, "Die siebentägige Woche im Gebrauch d. chr. Kirche d. ersten Jhdt.," ZNW, 6 (1905), 1-66; C. W. Dugmore, *The Influence of the Synagogue upon the Divine Office* (1944), 26, 37.

[1] Cf. Budde Sabbath, 203.

[2] AOT, 329.

[3] This is the pacification of the heart of the gods by sacrifice and prayer, cf. Hehn Sabbatfrage, 201.

[4] Cf. T. G. Pinches, "Sapattu, the Babyl. Sabbath," *Proceedings of the Society of Bibl. Archaeology,* 26 (1904), 51-56; Zimmern, 199-202, 458-460; Jenni, 11, n. 19.

seventh days, is that of a day of penance marked by taboos and prohibitions. Israel's Sabbath, on the other hand, comes regularly every seven days irrespective of the cycle of the moon, [5] and it is more than a *dies nefastus* laden with taboos. Hence one cannot assume that there is a direct connection between it and the Babyl. *shappatu*. It is possible, however, that by links not now known the Sabbath took its name from the *shappatu*, though שַׁבָּת always means "day of rest" in the OT. [6] The name must have been adopted by the tribes of Israel in very ancient and probably pre-Mosaic days. [7] The idea that they might have taken over the Sabbath from the Canaanites [8] is ruled out by the fact that no trace of the Sabbath has been found among the latter. [9] Conjectures that they adopted it from the Kenites are also hazardous. [10] The meaning and content of the OT Sabbath certainly cannot be explained in terms of Babyl. or other non-Israelite models. They are exclusively controlled by Israel's faith in Yahweh. [11]

2. The Sabbath in the Pre-Exilic Age.

Absolute rest from work is enjoined by the Sabbath commandment. This order does not necessarily presuppose agricultural conditions [12] such as obtained in Israel only after the conquest. It could well have been observed by nomads. Hence the keeping of the Sabbath goes back to the very first beginnings of Yahweh religion. [13]

The commandment is firmly rooted in both forms of the Decalogue which have come down to us. One may assume, then, that it was at first formulated negatively like the others. It forbade all work on the Sabbath. [14] The prohibition of work was then changed into a positive sanctifying of the Sabbath [15] and later express reasons were given, cf. Ex. 20 and Dt. 5. The argument in Ex. 20:8-11, which echoes Gn. 2:2 f., pts. out that Yahweh made heaven and earth and all that therein is in 6 days, and then rested on

---

[5] Meinhold's repeated attempts to try to make the pre-exilic Sabbath into a feast of the full moon have been answered by Budde and may be regarded as unsuccessful. "In no single OT passage does 'sabbath' mean the day of the full moon," Budde Antwort, 145. Ex. 34:21 (J) and 23:12 (E) bear undisputed testimony to a recurrent seventh day Sabbath at an early date, for in both שבת is used denominatively "to keep the Sabbath"; cf. Budde Antwort, 143.

[6] Cf. B. Stade, *Bibl. Theol. d. AT*, I² (1905), 178. The verb שבת originally means "to cease activity." Cf. Köhler-Baumg., *s.v.* שבת; Jenni, 28.

[7] Cf. Procksch, 544.

[8] So F. Delitzsch, *Babel u. Bibel*⁵ (1905), 65; also *Die grosse Täuschung*, I (1920), 99 f.; Eissfeldt, 553.

[9] Cf. Budde Sabbath, 205.

[10] Eerdmans, 79-83; Budde Sabbath, 268-270; L. Köhler, "Der Dekalog," ThR, NF, 1 (1929), 180 f. Cf. also Rowley, 109-114; North, 198 f. In the uncertain state of the text Am. 5:26 (= day or worship of Saturn ?) cannot be adduced. Ex. 35:3 (cf. also Nu. 15:32), which forbids lighting fires on the Sabbath, is from P, so that no conclusions as to the earliest days can be drawn from it. Jenni, 12 f., following H. Webster, *Rest Days* (1911), tries to derive the Sabbath from regular market days, but he has to admit that there is no evidence for such days in the area, 13. Am. 8:4 f. also shows that in ancient Israel trade was forbidden on the Sabbath, so that the Sabbath could not possibly have been a market day.

[11] Torczyner, 14-16 rejects any connection between the Sabbath and the Babyl. *shappatu* and thinks "the noun *šapattu* in its use as the name of a specific day was adopted into the Babyl.-Assyrian calendar from a dialect close to Heb.," 15.

[12] So Wellhausen, 115; B. Stade, *op. cit.* (→ n. 6), 176 f. *et al.*

[13] Rowley, 117 also thinks that Sabbath might well have been pre-Mosaic.

[14] Cf. A. Alt, "Die Ursprünge d. isr. Rechts," *Kleine Schriften z. Gesch. d. Volkes Israel*, I (1953), 317-321. The unconditional prohibitions of apodictic as distinct from casuistic law suggest that the Sabbath commandment cannot have been taken over from the Canaanites, Alt, 323, 330.

[15] Cf. A. Alt, *op. cit.*, 321, n. 1; 331, n. 1.

the 7th day, thus blessing and sanctifying the Sabbath, v. 11.[16] In the par. Dt. 5:12-15[17] (1) it is emphasised more clearly than in Ex. 20 that the benefit of Sabbath rest is not just for the Israelite and his family but also for slaves and domestic animals: "Thy slave and thy maidservant shall rest as well as thou," v. 14 cf. Ex. 23:12. The social element discernible elsewhere in Dt. comes to expression here.[18] (2) In Dt. 5:15 the Sabbath is not based on Yahweh's work of creation and His resting on the 7th day but a reminder is given that Israel was a slave in Israel and Yahweh brought it out with a mighty hand and stretched out arm.[19] "Therefore the Lord thy God commanded thee to keep the sabbath day," v. 15. The Sabbath is thus grounded in the history of Israel in which Israel experienced the redemption wrought by Yahweh. As Yahweh liberated the people from slavery in Egypt, so the slave is to be freed from work on the Sabbath.[20] Duties to God and neighbour are thus fused together to form an indissoluble unity.[21]

Acc. to the cultic Decalogue of J the Sabbath commandment expressly includes the times of ploughing and reaping in which it is esp. difficult to interrupt work, Ex. 34:21. The Book of the Covenant lays down that every Israelite, his ox and ass, the son of his slave, and also the alien shall rest and be refreshed every seventh day, Ex. 23:12.

In the oldest OT accounts outside the legal corpus the Sabbath and the new moon are often mentioned together, since they are the only festivals to recur regularly throughout the year, Am. 8:5; Hos. 2:13; Is. 1:13; 2 K. 4:23.[22] On both business is to stop, Am. 8:5. Gifts and sacrifices are to be brought to the sanctuary, Is. 1:13. There is to be a joyous feast, Hos. 2:13. The day of rest offers a good opportunity for consulting the man of God, 2 K. 4:23. On a Sabbath Jehoiada the high-priest in a temple revolt in Jerusalem broke the tyranny of Athaliah and set Joash on the throne, 2 K. 11:5, 7, 9. The narrator does not object to the desecration of the Sabbath incurred thereby, 2 K. 11.[23] At an earlier time, then, the prohibition of work was not taken as strictly as later. One can only say with certainty that already in the pre-exilic period the Sabbath was kept at the end of every week as a day of rest ordained and sanctified by Yahweh.[24]

3. The Sabbath in the Post-Exilic Age.

Banished in the exile, the community of Yahweh made the necessary separation from those of other faiths by ascribing special significance to the two remaining features which ensured its adherence to God. From now on the Sabbath, along with circumcision, acquired enhanced importance. In distinction from the Gentiles Israel alone kept the Sabbath every seventh day as a day holy to its God. Ez. can thus call the Sabbath

---

[16] The verb here, of course, is נּוּחַ rather than the שָׁבַת of Gn. 2:2 f. Heaven, earth and sea are the works of creation; the sea is not mentioned in Gn. 2:1.

[17] The supporting argument in Dt. 5:15 is plainly in the same style as Dt., so that there is no reason to isolate the Sabbath commandment or the Decalogue as a whole from Dt. and to put it in the post-exilic age, so Meinhold Sabbat u. Woche, 38, but cf. Budde Antwort, 128 etc. Compare "remember" in 7:18; 8:2, 18; 9:7; 16:3; 24:9; 25:17; "that thou wast a bondman in the land of Egypt," 15:15; 16:12; 24:18, 22; "by a mighty hand and by a stretched out arm," 4:34; 6:21; 7:8, 19; 9:26, 29; 11:2; 26:8; "Yahweh, thy God, has commanded," 1:19; 2:37; 4:5, 23; 5:32 (29); 6:1, 20; 13:6; 20:17. Cf. Rowley, 85, n. 2.

[18] Cf. Dt. 12:12, 18; 16:11 f., 14 etc.; slaves, too, are to take part in the feasts of the community of Yahweh.

[19] This is common in Dt., → n. 17.

[20] Jenni, 15-19.

[21] Eichr. Theol. AT, I⁵, 38.

[22] The new moon and the Sabbath are often mentioned together later as well, Is. 66:23; Ez. 45:17; 46:1; Neh. 10:34; 1 Ch. 23:31; 2 Ch. 2:3. This sheds no light, however, on the origin of the Sabbath, since the Sabbath mentioned along with the new moon cannot possibly be the full moon, cf. → n. 5.

[23] Cf. Meinhold Entstehung, 84; Meinhold Sabbathfrage, II, 123.

[24] For examples cf. Cannon, 325-327.

a sign between Yahweh and Israel: "that they might know that I am the Lord that sanctify them," 20:12 cf. v. 20. For the prophet, then, the desecration of the Sabbath is the reason why disaster has overtaken the people, Ez. 20:13, 16, 20, 24; 22:8, 26; 23:38; cf. 2 Ch. 36:21. There is thus impressed on the community with particular urgency the obligation to observe the feasts and to keep the Sabbath holy, Ez. 44:24. Detailed rules are given concerning the numbers and kinds of sacrifices to be offered on the Sabbath when offerings can again be made in the temple, Ez. 45:17; 46:4 f.

The priestly legislation also ascribes special significance to the Sabbath commandment. It calls the Sabbath a sign between Yahweh and Israel, Ex. 31:13, 17. It categorically forbids work with very severe penalties: he who desecrates the Sabbath is to be put to death, Ex. 31:14 f.; 35:2. The Sabbath is to be kept holy by Israel as a perpetual ordinance (בְּרִית עוֹלָם), Ex. 31:16. "For in six days the Lord made heaven and earth, and on the seventh day he rested, and was refreshed," Ex. 31:17. Yahweh blessed and sanctified the seventh day, Gn. 2:1-3. [25] The Sabbath is not just based on the manna incident in the wilderness, Ex. 16:22-30 P. It corresponds to the divine will from creation. This was declared to Israel at Sinai. The Sabbath is given to Israel as a sign that it is Yahweh who has sanctified the people, Ex. 31:13. The Sabbath is thus a divine blessing which constantly keeps alive the recollection that Yahweh has chosen and sanctified the people of God. [26]

The strict prohibition of work on the Sabbath is now set forth in greater detail. Fires are not to be kindled (Ex. 35:3) nor burdens carried (Jer. 17:21 f., 24, 27) nor trade carried on (Neh. 10:32) nor the winepress trodden nor beasts laden nor markets held (Neh. 13:15-22) nor highways traversed nor business pursued (Is. 58:13) nor is the Sabbath to be desecrated in any other way (Is. 56:2). A warning example is given to underline the seriousness of the commandment; in the wilderness a man gathering sticks on the Sabbath was executed as Yahweh ruled, Nu. 15:32-36 P. What is needed on the Sabbath must be collected and prepared the day before (Ex. 16:22-26, 29), for the Sabbath is Yahweh's most holy day of rest (Ex. 35:2) to be celebrated in the sanctuary (Lv. 23:32 cf. Ez. 46:1). Each Sabbath the show-bread is renewed (Lv. 24:8; 1 Ch. 9:32) and two one-year-old lambs without blemish are offered along with the food and drink offerings, Nu. 28:9 f. Temple singers strike up the 92nd psalm (title Ps. 92). [27]

In the post-exilic community the Sabbath commandment is indeed the most important part of the divine Law. That Yahweh gave the Law and that He commanded the sanctifying of the Sabbath mean much the same thing. He who keeps the Sabbath holy and calls it his delight is pleasing to Yahweh, Is. 58:13 f. He who observes the covenant and does the will of Yahweh will be careful not to defile the Sabbath, Is. 56:1-7. Love of Yahweh and loyalty to His covenant are shown in zealous and scrupulous fulfilment of the Law, whose supreme commandment is the keeping holy of the Sabbath.

4. The Sabbatical Year.

As each week ended with the Sabbath after six days, so the OT speaks of a Sabbath which is to be kept after each six years. [28] In the seventh year the whole land is to lie fallow and there is to be neither ploughing nor harvest. This rule applied after the conquest and originally included a complete remission of all legal or financial obligations

---

[25] Whereas Gn. 2:2 HT says that Yahweh completed His works and rested from them on the seventh day, acc. to the LXX God finished creation on the sixth day, so that there cannot be the slightest suspicion that the day of rest might have been marred by any work. Cf. also Jub. 2:16.

[26] The unconditional command to keep the sanctity of the day by not doing any work applies to the Day of Atonement (שַׁבַּת שַׁבָּתוֹן, Lv. 23:32) as well as the Sabbath.

[27] On the Sabbath sacrifices cf. also 1 Ch. 23:31; 2 Ch. 2:3; 8:13; 31:3.

[28] On the Sabbatical yr. cf. Correns, with bibl.; H. Wildberger, "Israel u. sein Land," Ev. Theol., 16 (1956), 404-422; E. Kutsch, Art. "Erlassjahr," RGG³, II, 568 f.; also "Erwägungen z. Gesch. d. Passafeier u. des Massotfestes," ZThK, 55 (1958), 25-28.

each seventh year and a redistribution of the land by lot to the various families. [29]
The oldest version of the law of the sacred fallow is to be found in Ex. 23:10 f. Each seventh year the fruits of the land are not to be gathered "in order that the poor of thy people may eat," as an explanatory note puts it. In Dt. a statute of ancient divine law [30] commands that "at the end of every seven years thou shalt make a release," Dt. 15:1. This commandment is then expounded in hortatory fashion. All loans to the poor are to be remitted in the seventh year, 15:2-11. The short rules about leaving the land fallow in Ex. 23:10 f. were later defined more closely in the Holiness Code and linked with rules concerning the Sabbath, Lv. 25:1-7. The whole land was to keep a Sabbath to Yahweh in the seventh year, 25:4. Sowing and reaping were to cease entirely. What the land produced of itself in this year of rest was to be for the nourishment of the Israelites, their slaves, their labourers, and aliens, Lv. 25:6. [31]

In the Holiness Code instructions concerning the year of the jubilee [32] are added to the law of the sabbatical year, Lv. 25:8-55. This year comes in the fiftieth year when seven times seven years have passed. All Israelites sold into slavery are to be freed during this year, and they have all to get back their land. These rules are based in part on traditions relating to the sabbatical year but they seem to have been theoretical only, since a year of jubilee was never actually celebrated.

B. The Sabbath in Judaism.

1. The Development of the Sabbath in Judaism.

a. The Usage in Palestinian and Hellenistic Judaism.

Palestinian Judaism and the Judaism of the Diaspora agree that Israel corresponds to its divine selection from among the peoples by scrupulous keeping of the divine Sabbath commandment, and that even when scattered it is hereby reminded of the covenant of God with His community. Everywhere the traditional name שַׁבָּת is used for the seventh day. [33] Of course, this does not mean only "Sabbath." It can also denote the period between two Sabbaths, i.e., the whole week. [34] The Aram. שַׁבְּתָא is used for the single Sabbath or for the whole week. [35] The day of preparation is עֶרֶב שַׁבָּת, "the evening before the Sabbath." [36] The night of the Sabbath on the first day of the week, and the first day itself, are מוֹצָאֵי שַׁבָּת, "the termination of the Sabbath." [37] The other days of the week are then numbered consecutively. [38]

---

[29] Cf. Alt, op. cit., 327 f.

[30] Cf. G. v. Rad, "Deuteronomiumstudien," FRL, 58 (1947), 10.

[31] There are also ref. to the Sabbatical yr. in Neh. 10:32; 2 Ch. 36:21.

[32] On the year of jubilee cf. A. Jirku, "Das isr. Jobeljahr," R. Seeberg-Festschr., II (1929), 169-179; N. M. Nikolskij, "Die Entstehung des Jobeljahres," ZAW, 50 (1932), 216; Alt, op. cit., 328, n. 1; C. H. Gordon, "Sabbatical Cycle or Seasonal Pattern?" Orientalia, 22 (1953), 79-81; R. North, "Sociology of the Biblical Jubilee," Analecta Biblica, 4 (1954).

[33] Cf. Str.-B., I, 610 f.

[34] Ibid., I, 1052 f.: כל ימות השבת "all the days of the week," Gn. r., 11 (8b) on 2:3; בכל השבת, "throughout the week," Ned., 8, 1. Cf. also S. Krauss, Talmudische Archäologie, II (1911), 422 f.

[35] Cf. Dalman Gr., 247 f. for examples.

[36] E.g., Shab., 2, 7; 19, 1 etc. Aram. ערובת שובא or ערובתא; cf. the examples in Str.-B., I, 1052 f.

[37] Gn. r., 11 (8a) on 2:3. Examples in Str.-B., I, 1052 f.

[38] Cf. the terms for the days of the week in bShab., 156a : בחד בשבא (on the first day of the week); בתרי בשבא (on the second day of the week); בתלתא בשבא (on the third day of the week); בארבעא בשבא (on the fourth day of the week); בחמשא בשבא (on the fifth day of the week); במעלי שבתא (on the preparation for the Sabbath); בשבתא (on the Sabbath). Cf. also the examples in Dalman Gr., 247 f.; Str.-B., I, 1052; Schürer Die siebentägige Woche, 3-8.

The Greek-speaking Judaism of the Dispersion retained the Heb. word and gave it the Gk. form σάββατον. In explanation of the meaning of the Heb. term ἀνάπαυσις was used as a transl.: τὸ μὲν γὰρ σάββατον κατὰ τὴν τῶν Ἰουδαίων διάλεκτον ἀνάπαυσίς ἐστιν ἀπὸ παντὸς ἔργου, Jos. Ap., 2, 27; cf. also Philo Cher., 87; Abr., 28. The plur. τὰ σάββατα [39] can have three meanings: 1. several Sabbaths, e.g., ἐν τοῖς σαββάτοις καὶ ἐν ταῖς νουμηνίαις, Ez. 46:3 LXX cf. also Is. 1:13 LXX; 2 Ch. 31:3; Jos. Ant., 3, 294; 12, 276 f.; 13, 252; 2. one Sabbath (in spite of the plur.), e.g., τῇ δὲ ἡμέρᾳ τῇ ἑβδόμῃ σάββατα κυρίῳ τῷ θεῷ σου, Ex. 20:10 LXX; τὴν γὰρ ἑβδόμην ἡμέραν σάββατα καλοῦμεν, Jos. Ant., 3, 143 cf. also Ant., 1, 33; 3, 237; 11, 77 etc.; another name for the Sabbath is ἡ ἡμέρα τῶν σαββάτων, Ex. 20:8 LXX; 35:3; Dt. 5:12; Ἰερ. 17:21 f.; Jos. Ant., 7, 305; 12, 259 and 274; 13, 12; 14, 226 etc.; 3. the whole week as in Heb. usage (also sing. τὸ σάββατον), [40] e.g., in psalm titles in the LXX: τῆς μιᾶς σαββάτων ψ 23:1; δευτέρᾳ σαββάτου ψ 47:1; τετράδι σαββάτων ψ 93:1. [41] The preparation is προσάββατον in Jdt. 8:6, ἡ πρὸ τοῦ σαββάτου in Jos. Ant., 3, 255 f., παρασκευή in Jos. Ant., 16, 163. The Sabbath itself is often simply the seventh day, so that ἡ ἑβδόμη (ἡμέρα) often means the same as σάββατον, cf. Gn. 2:2 f. LXX; Ex. 16:26 f. etc.; κατὰ δὲ ἑβδόμην ἡμέραν, ἥτις σάββατα καλεῖται, Jos. Ant., 3, 237 cf. 3, 143; τὴν ἑβδόμην, ἣν Ἑβραῖοι σάββατα καλοῦσιν, Philo Abr., 28 cf. also Mut. Nom., 260; Spec. Leg., II, 41 and 86; also Vit. Mos., II, 209, 215, 263. ἡ ἑβδομάς is used for the Sabbath as well as the week, 2 Macc. 6:11; 15:4; Jos. Ant., 14, 63; Bell., 1, 146; 2, 147 and 517. Keeping the Sabbath, in usage close to that of the OT, is φυλάσσειν (φυλάσσεσθαι) τὸ σάββατον, Ex. 31:13 f. LXX; Lv. 19:3 etc. [42] But a new verb σαββατίζειν also occurs: σαββατιεῖτε τὰ σάββατα ὑμῶν, Lv. 23:32 LXX cf. also Ex. 16:30 LXX; Lv. 26:35; 2 Macc. 6:6 etc. [43]

Judaism thus follows a consistent usage for the Sabbath in which the term derived from the Law is common to both Palestine and the Diaspora. It thus demonstrates that the scattered Jewish communities felt themselves to be linked and united by the divine Sabbath commandment. [44]

---

[39] "σάββατα was not originally a plur.; it is simply the Heb. šabbāt or šabbat; the -α is from the outset a purely vocal addition to reproduce the Heb. -t in Gk.," E. Schwyzer, "Altes u. Neues zu [hbr.-]griech. σάββατα [griech.-]lat. sabbata usw.," Zschr. f. vergleichende Sprachforschung, 62 (1935), 10. In practical usage, however, τὰ σάββατα was then assimilated to the comprehensive plur. of Gk. festivals, Schwyzer, Griech. Grammatik, II, 43 with n. 5. For the dat. we find τοῖς σάββασιν in 1 Macc. 2:38; Jos. Ant., 13, 337; 16, 163; Vit., 279 and τοῖς σαββάτοις in Nu. 28:10 LXX; 2 Ch. 2:3 and commonly in the LXX, also in Jos. Ant., 3, 294; 11, 346; 12, 4 and 276 f.; 13, 252; Bell., 1, 146; cf. Str.-B., I, 610 f.; Pr.-Bauer⁵, s.v.

[40] ἡ ἑβδομάς is also used for week in the LXX, cf. Lv. 23:15 f.; 25:8 etc.

[41] Cf. also Lv. 23:32 LXX σάββατα σαββάτων "the day of atonement," also Philo Spec. Leg., II, 194.

[42] Cf. also τὸ σάββατον τηρεῖν in Jn. 9:16 and παρατηρεῖν τὴν τῶν σαββάτων ἡμέραν in Jos. Ant., 14, 264. Cf. Schl. J. on 9:16.

[43] In Jos. we also find σαββατεῖον, Ant., 16, 164 = "place appointed for keeping the Sabbath" (cf. on this S. Krauss, Synagogale Altertümer [1922], 25 f.; P. Katz, "Das Problem des Urtextes d. Septuaginta," ThZ, 5 [1949], 5 f., n. 6) and σαββατικός in Ant., 14, 202; Bell., 7, 99 = "having a sabbatical nature."

[44] The Samaritans, whose Bible is the Pentateuch, also retained circumcision and the Sabbath as covenant signs. Small Jewish groups exposed to syncretistic influences in the Dispersion and thus far removed from orthodox Judaism tried to maintain their link with Israel by keeping the Sabbath. Thus on an inscr. from the neighbourhood of Elaiussa in Cilicia (Ditt. Or., II, 573) we find the name Σαββατισταί for a group or society whose God is called ὁ θεὸς ὁ Σαββατιστής, Krauss, op. cit. (→ n. 43), 27. This society of "Sabbath-keepers" (ἡ ἑταιρεία τῶν Σαββατιστῶν) was probably a heretical Jewish group which also worshipped the god Sabazios, cf. H. Lietzmann, Gesch. d. alten Kirche, I² (1953), 166. It was thus on the very margin of Judaism, if not outside, cf. J. Leipoldt, "Das Ev. der Wahrheit," ThLZ, 82 (1957), 829. The small Asia Minor sect of the Hypsistarians (4th cent.) also came out of the same syncretistic Judaism of the Dispersion. They combined their Jewish legacy with Parsee views, worshipping the supreme God,

b. The Sabbath from the Maccabean Period to the Editing of the Mishnah.
The weekly Sabbath is for Judaism a sign of divine election, for no people apart from Israel has sanctified God in keeping the Sabbath, Jub. 2:19, 31; 50:9 f. The day of the rest which the patriarchs celebrated [45] grants a foretaste already of eternal glory, which will be an unending Sabbath. [46] The wonderful power of the Sabbath is so great that on the seventh day even the ungodly in Gehenna may rest from their torment. [47] For this reason the Sabbath commandment is as urgent as all the other commandments of the Torah put together, jBer., 1 (3c, 14 f.). The reward which God's grants for keeping it is also especially great. [48] If Israel would only keep two Sabbaths as ordained redemption would come. [49]

The Sabbath commandment is thus the heart of the Law. [50] The Syrian king Antiochus Epiphanes attacked it when he not only banned the sacrificial cultus in Jerusalem but also forbade observance of the Sabbath and therewith the public profession of Judaism, 1 Macc. 1:39 f., 44. From now on this meant: ἦν δ' οὔτε σαββατίζειν, οὔτε πατρῴους ἑορτὰς διαφυλάττειν, οὔτε ἁπλῶς 'Ιουδαῖον ὁμολογεῖν εἶναι, 2 Macc. 6:6. In fact many Jews fell away, "sacrificed to the gods and desecrated the sabbath," 1 Macc. 1:43. On the other side, however, the passionate resistance of the pious was kindled by this decree of the king. To the very last they defended confession of the Law and protected the sanctity of the Sabbath. Finally, after savage conflict, they secured the official recognition of the Syrian kings for their festivals and days of rest, 1 Macc. 10:34.
In the older Halachah fighting was brought under the prohibition of work, Jub. 50:12. In obedience to this some pious Jews at the beginning of the Maccabean revolt were killed without offering any resistance on the Sabbath, 1 Macc. 2:32-38. [51] Due to this terrible event, however, it was decided that in future weapons might be lifted in self-defence even on the Sabbath, 1 Macc. 2:39-41. [52] Attack, however, was still forbidden, [53]

---

keeping the Sabbath and dietary laws, but rejecting circumcision, cf. Greg. Naz. Or., 18, 5 (MPG, 35 [1857], 991 f.); G. Bornkamm, "Die Häresie d. Kol," *Das Ende des Gesetzes*[2] (1958), 153-155. Peculiar ideas about the Sabbath are finally found among the Ethiopian Falashas, cf. J. Halévy, *Tĕʾĕzāza Sanbat, texte éthiopien publié et traduit* (1902), who single out esp. the seventh Sabbath. For them Sanbat, the personified Sabbath, is a divine being, God's own son, who has his dwelling in heaven and is incorruptible and eternal. Each week he comes down to men in exercise of his office. On Friday evening he gets up from his throne, comes down to earth with the angelic hosts, and remains there to the joy of the righteous until early on Sunday. The Gnostic myth of the descent of the redeemer undoubtedly had some influence here, as also on Mandaean ideas concerning Habšābbā, the first of the week, and his descent as a messenger from the realm of light, cf. L. Troje, "Sanbat, Beigabe, III" in R. Reitzenstein, *Die Vorgeschichte d. chr. Taufe* (1929), 328-377; A. Adam, "Die Ps. d. Thomas u. d. Perlenlied als Zeugnisse vorchr. Gnosis," Beih. z. ZNW, 24 (1959), 79.
[45] Cf. Jub. 2:19-24; Gn. r., 11 (8c); Str.-B., I, 200.
[46] Cf. the examples in Str.-B., IV, 839 f. and Volz, 384 f. bBer., 57b can say more precisely that the Sabbath is a sixtieth part of the future world.
[47] bSanh., 65b; Gn. r., 11 (8b); cf. also Str.-B., IV, 1082 f.
[48] Acc. to R. Eli'ezer (c. 90) keeping the Sabbath holds off three punishments: the woes of the Messiah, the day of Gog and the day of the great judgment, M. Ex., 16, 29 (59a). For other Rabb. passages on the reward for exact observance of the Sabbath cf. Str.-B., I, 614 f.; IV, 497, 950, 1067.
[49] So R. Shim'on b. Jochai (c. 150); bShab., 118b, Bar.
[50] The gt. importance of the Sabbath for Judaism may be seen also from the fact that the Mishnah has three tractates dealing exclusively with Sabbath questions: Shabbat, Erubin and Beza, and that in addition Shebiit deals with the sabbatical year.
[51] Cf. also 2 Macc. 6:11; Jos. Ant., 13, 377.
[52] Cf. also 1 Macc. 9:34, 43 f.; Jos. Ant., 13, 12 f.; 18, 318-324; Bell., 1, 146.
[53] When Judas Maccabeus won a victory on a Friday, he broke off pursuit of the enemy on the Sabbath, 2 Macc. 8:26 f.; cf. also Jos. Ant., 14, 63 and Schl. Theol. Judt., 127.

Jews in foreign armies refused to take the offensive on the Sabbath, 2 Macc. 15:1-5. The Romans would not enlist Jews for this reason. [54] Later, however, it was sometimes regarded as permissible to attack invading Gentiles on the Sabbath. [55] The Rabb. gave general recognition to the principle that when life was in danger the Sabbath commandment might be broken and one could either take to arms [56] or flee. [57]

The development of other Sabbath rules is not so easily followed as this one since there is not the same literary attestation. It may be stated, however, that the older Halachah was stricter than the later exposition in the Mishnah. Pious Judaism expounded the Law and the Sabbath commandment strictly in self-defence against invading Hellenistic influences. Thus Jub. 2:29 f. and Damasc. 11:4 f. (13:13 f.) will not allow any carrying or erub. Jub. threatens death for drawing water (2:29 cf. 50:8), travelling by ship (50:12), hunting (50:12) and even marital intercourse (50:8). [58] A Sabbath journey must not be more than 1000 cubits in Damasc. 10:21 (13:7). [59] One is not to beat or lead obstinate cattle on the Sabbath, Jub. 50:12; Damasc. 11:6 f. (13:15 f.). No service must be asked of a slave, Damasc. 11:12 (13:21). If an animal falls into a pit, one is not to lift it out acc. to Damasc. 11:13 f. (13:22-24). Sacrifice is restricted to the indispensable minimum, the offering of the Sabbath burnt offerings, Damasc. 11:17 f. (13:27); Jub. 50:10 f. If many other rules of the older Halachah were taken over more or less unchanged by the Rabb., in the cases mentioned they were always judged much less strictly than earlier. [60] But the more close-knit groups of the pious, who like the loyal Jews of the Maccabean period sought to protect the sanctity of the divine commandment and to represent the true community of Israel, espoused and followed a strict exposition of the Sabbath Torah acc. to which undivided obedience was demanded. [61] The Essenes kept the Sabbath more conscientiously than other Jews, doing no work, not lighting fires, moving no vessels and not even relieving themselves throughout the day. [62] Whereas the Sadducees also sought to keep to a stricter exposition of

---

[54] Cf. the edicts in Jos. Bell., 14, 223-240.

[55] When the Romans approached Jerusalem the Jews did not hesitate to attack and repel them on the Sabbath, Jos. Ant., 2, 517 f.

[56] T. Er., 4, 5-8 (142) regards it as permissible in some cases to go out armed against invading Gentiles on the Sabbath, cf. Str.-B., I, 626 f.

[57] Str.-B., I, 952 f. for examples.

[58] The later rules in the Mishnah are milder. Under certain circumstances one may draw water acc. to Er., 10, 7. Travelling by ship does not seem to be forbidden in Shab., 16, 8, nor does hunting, cf. the permitted exceptions in Shab., 1, 6; 13, 5 f.; 14, 1. Prohibition of marital intercourse is nowhere found in the Mishnah.

[59] Damasc. 11:5 f. (13:14 f.) allows cattle to be driven to pasture not more than 2000 cubits from the town. Perhaps, then, one should read אלפים for אלף at Damasc. 10:21 (13:7). Cf. Braun, I, 117, n. 1.

[60] Cf. → n. 58 and the comparative tables in Braun, I, 117-120.

[61] Cf. Damasc. 3:14 f. (5:2 f.); 6:18 f. (8:15). That Jub. and Damasc. were read and accepted in the Qumran community seems fairly certain in view of the fragments from the two books found in the Qumran Caves. O. Eissfeldt, Einl. in d. AT² (1956), 751, 804-807 and bibl. There is no mention of the Sabbath in 1 QS. 1 Qp Hab. 11:8 refers to שבת מנוחתם, "the sabbath of their (sc. the righteous) rest." New moons and Sabbaths occur together in 1 QM 2:4. In the "words of Moses" it is said that the Israelites will infringe every holy convocation and the sabbath of the covenant and the feasts, 1 Q 22 I 8 (DJD, I, 92). Finally the word שבת occurs in the fragment 1 Q 27 Fr. 4 (DJD, I, 106). In connection with strict Sabbatarian practice in pious circles one should mention the note in bNidda, 38a, Bar. that even in conceiving children the Chassidim rishonim tried to avoid a time which would make birth on a Sabbath likely. Cf. K. Schubert, Die Gemeinde vom Toten Meer (1958), 36.

[62] Jos. Bell., 2, 147. Acc. to Philo Omn. Prob. Lib., 81 the Essenes marked off the Sabbath by using it for teaching, avoiding all work, and assembling in the synagogue. Cf. Braun. I, 74, n. 2. In Vit. Cont. Philo tells of the related society of the Therapeutae who lived as hermits but gathered on the Sabbath to hear an address by an elder, Vit. Cont., 30 f. They gave special emphasis to the seventh Sabbath, on the eve of which they assembled in white

the Sabbath commandment, [63] the Pharisees and scribes tried to avoid rigorism in order to bring the Sabbath laws as far as possible into harmony with practical situations and requirements, and hence not to destroy joy in the Sabbath. The regulations collected in the Mishnah tractate Shabbat are thus the provisional result of a longer development, [64] and this was continued in the discussions of Amoraean scholars. [65]

Hellenistic Jews, like their brethren in Palestine, realised that they were pledged to obedience to the Torah and observance of the Sabbath. In the Diaspora, however, it was not thought enough to base the Sabbath simply on God's command. Under the influence of Orphic-Pythagorean speculations concerning the number seven an attempt was made to invest the Sabbath with philosophical significance and in this way to expound and justify it to the Hell. world around. Aristob. in the 2nd cent. B.C. said that the Sabbath, because it is the seventh day, is different from all other days, ἣ δὴ καὶ πρώτη φυσικῶς ἂν λέγοιτο φωτὸς γένεσις, ἐν ᾧ τὰ πάντα συνθεωρεῖται· μεταφέροιτο δ᾽ ἂν τὸ αὐτὸ καὶ ἐπὶ τῆς σοφίας· τὸ γὰρ πᾶν φῶς ἔστιν ἐξ αὐτῆς, Eus. Praep. Ev., 13, 12, 9 f. The Sabbath is thus called "the first production of light wherein all is seen together; the same might be said of wisdom, for all light derives from it." God wanted us to keep this day διασεσάφηκε δ᾽ ἡμῖν αὐτὴν ἔννομον ἕνεκεν σημείου τοῦ περὶ ἡμᾶς ἑβδόμου λόγου καθεστῶτος, ἐν ᾧ γνῶσιν ἔχομεν ἀνθρωπίνων καὶ θείων πραγμάτων, 13, 12, 12. As everything in the cosmos moves acc. to the number seven, so the seventh day is brought in by God as a day of rest, 13, 12, 13, ἣ δὴ καὶ πρώτη τῷ ὄντι φωτὸς γένεσις, ἐν ᾧ τὰ πάντα συνθεωρεῖται καὶ πάντα κληρονομεῖται, Cl. Al. Strom., VI, 138, 1. Philo of Alex. [66] calls the Sabbath the birthday of the world, Spec. Leg., II, 59 and 70. It is significant for him that σάββατα corresponds to the Gk. ἀνάπαυσις, ὅτι τῷ ὄντι ὁ ἕβδομος ἀριθμὸς ἔν τε τῷ κόσμῳ καὶ ἐν ἡμῖν αὐτοῖς ἀεὶ ἀστασίαστος καὶ ἀπόλεμος καὶ ἀφιλόνεικος καὶ εἰρηνικώτατος ἁπάντων ἀριθμῶν ἐστι. Proof of this is to be found in the seven δυνάμεις which work in man and among which the seventh is ἡ περὶ τὸν ἡγεμόνα νοῦν, so that ἀνάπαυσις as the point of the Sabbath corresponds to it, Abr., 28-30. The Sabbath is ordained that one might dedicate it to φιλοσοφεῖν and thus share in the θεωρεῖν of God in which He contemplated creation on the seventh day, Decal., 100. [67]

This historical review of the development of the Sabbath commandment from the age of the Maccabees to the editing of the Mishnah has shown that all Judaism was aware of its commitment to the demands of the Law but that its understanding of these changed during the centuries and could take different forms in the home-land and the Dispersion.

---

clothes for common worship and a common meal (65-82) to which was annexed the sacred nocturnal feast παννυχίς (83).

[63] The Sadducees rejected Pharisaic rules concerning the permissibility of an erub, Er., 6, 2; cf. Damasc. 11:4 f. (13:13). They also thought it wrong to offer the Passover on a Sabbath. Hillel taught that the Passover takes precedence of the Sabbath, T. Pes., 4, 1 f. (162), cf. Str.-B., II, 819 f. But the Sadducees did not share the Essene view that the requirement of the Law is a claim to total obedience. Cf. Braun, I passim.

[64] Cf. Moore, II, 27; Str.-B., II, 819: "One is often forced to conclude that in the days of Jesus there was greater rigour in sanctifying the Sabbath than in the time from which the regulations of the Mishnah come."

[65] In the course of centuries not only did the rules about the prohibition of work on the Sabbath change but the way in which the Sabbath was celebrated was also subject to change. The biggest break came with the destruction of the temple in 70 A.D., since this put an end to celebration in the temple and the Sabbath offerings. On observance → 15, 10 ff.

[66] Cf. also Troje, op. cit. (→ n. 44), 343-346.

[67] These "philosophical" considerations of Hell. Judaism concerning the Sabbath were later adopted by Chr. Gnosticism (e.g., Cl. Al Strom., VI, 137, 4-145, 7) and syncretistic Jewish Christianity (→ 33, 12 ff.) and developed in various ways.

2. The Prohibition of Work on the Sabbath.

To be able to obey the commandment Judaism had to discuss and answer the question what detailed rules were to be deduced therefrom. The statutes had to be worked out in an ever more complicated casuistry and applied to all conceivable cases. [68]

a. The Regulations in the Book of Jubilees and the Damascus Document.

The oldest lists of prohibited activities are in Jub. [69] Here the version of the bibl. story of creation culminates in the story of the divine founding of the Sabbath and the exposition of its symbolical meaning, 2:17-33. [70] Within the broader expositions there is a more precise development of the prohibition of work whose violation carries the death penalty, 2:25-27. On the Sabbath the Israelites are not allowed "to do their (own) will, to prepare anything to eat or drink, to draw water, to bring in or out of their doors anything that has to be carried, which they have not prepared in the six days of work in their dwellings. And in this day they shall not fetch and carry from house to house," Jub. 2:29 f. At the end of Jub. the laws relating to feasts and times are stated even more sharply, and the significance of the Sabbath is esp. emphasised, 50:6-13.

The prohibition of work is expounded no less strictly in Damasc. than in Jub. [71] It is worked out in 28 individual halakot in 10:14-11:18 (13:1-27). [72] Under the heading עַל הַשַׁבָּת in 10:14 (13:1) there is a series of apodictically formulated prohibitions. [73] Each is introduced by אַל, all are terse, and only occasionally are they extended by exposition or closer definition. [74] The rules lay down among other things that one is not to go more than 1000 (2000 ?) [75] cubits on the Sabbath, there is to be no erub, [76] one is not to drive cattle more than 2000 cubits, lift cattle out of a pit, help men out of a pit with

---

[68] Cf. Moore, II, 30.

[69] "As regards the sub-division into individual cases Damasc. is closer to the Rabb. and Jub. is thus obviously older than Damasc." Braun, 120.

[70] The Dead Sea Scrolls, Jub. and Damasc. lay special stress on correct observance of feasts and times. The priests in Jerusalem were accused of following an incorrect calendar. Thus Damasc. 3:14 f. (5:2) numbers Sabbaths and feasts among the hidden things in which all Israel fell into error, 1 Qp Hab. 11:8; 1 Q 22 I 8 (DJD, 92). The rigorous view of the Sabbath in Jub. and Damasc. is to be connected with the general significance of the calendar in the pious communities to which these works belong. We need not pursue here the difficult special problems relating to calculating the calendar presupposed in Jub., Damasc. and the Dead Sea Scrolls. Cf. on this A. Jaubert, "Le calendrier des Jub. et de la secte de Qumran," VT, 3 (1953), 250-264; also "Le calendrier des Jub. et les jours liturgiques de la semaine," VT, 7 (1957), 35-71; J. Morgenstern, "The Calendar of the Book of Jubilees, Its Origin and Its Character," VT, 5 (1955), 34-76; J. Obermann, "Calendaric Elements in the Dead Sea Scrolls," JBL, 76 (1956), 285-297; J. Milik, "Le travail d'édition des manuscrits du Désert de Juda," VT, Suppl. Vol. 4 (1957), 17-26; E. Kutsch, Art. "Chronologie, III," RGG³, I, 1813.

[71] Damasc. is milder than Jub. only in not threatening death for desecration of the Sabbath. The person guilty of desecration can be received back into the community after seven yrs., Damasc. 12:3-6 (14:6 f.). Cf. Braun, 113; 129, n. 2.

[72] Some of the rules in Jub. have no counterpart in Damasc., e.g., the forbidding of marital intercourse, lighting fires, and travelling.

[73] As the stylistic form shows, the list was not composed ad hoc but derives from legal decisions which must often have been given in the community, cf. v. Rad, op. cit. (→ n. 30), 11-14.

[74] The positive principle in 11:1 (13:10) breaks the sequence: "On the way when one goes down to wash a man may drink where he stands."

[75] → n. 59.

[76] Damasc. 11:4 f. (13:13); read יתערב and cf. Braun, I, 118, n. 1. The conjecture יתרעב would yield a prohibition of fasting and thus soften the rigour of the commandment in Damasc.

a ladder, rope, or instrument, [77] nor offer sacrifices apart from the statutory Sabbath burnt offerings. [78] All Israelites belonging to the saved community are pledged by these detailed directions to undivided obedience and strict observance of the Sabbath.

b. The Regulations in Rabbinic Literature.

The many detailed regulations of the Rabb. concerning the prohibition of work on the Sabbath are gathered into lists in the Mishnah. [79] The most important of these is in Shab., 7, 2 : "The main tasks prohibited are forty save one : he who sows and ploughs and reaps and binds ; he who threshes and winnows and fans ; he who sifts and kneads and bakes ; he who shears wool and bleaches it and combs and dyes and spins ; he who weaves and draws and twists and separates two threads ; he who ties and unties a knot and sews two stitches and tears apart to sew two stitches ; he who hunts and kills and skins a gazelle ; he who salts it and dresses its skin and scrapes and cuts it ; he who writes two letters and rubs out again to write two letters ; he who builds and pulls down ; he who lights a fire and puts it out ; he who strikes with a hammer ; he who carries from one place to another. These are the main tasks, forty save one." If 39 main jobs are mentioned in this list, this means that with the help of the schematic number 40 less 1 [80] an attempt is made to give a systematic summary of the individual Sabbath prohibitions. Many scholars explained the choice of these particular tasks by saying they were the jobs which had to be done in making the tabernacle. [81] Other rabb. later tried to derive the number 40 save 1 from the value of the letters of אלה הדברים in Ex. 35:1. [82] This list of forbidden tasks was later greatly extended by bringing six subsidiary jobs under each main one. Thus harvesting would include reaping, making wine, plucking, cutting and taking out olives, and plucking figs, jShab., 7 (9c 1-7). [83] Nevertheless, the list of 39 chief activities and their subsidiaries is not complete and is not regarded as such, for there are other important tasks which are in no circumstances to be performed on the Sabbath, e.g., trade or the administration of justice. Thus we find in the Mishnah at Beza, 5, 2 another list which is by no means the same as that in Shab., 7, 2 : "On account of the following activities (one incurs guilt on the Sabbath or feasts) by reason of the Sabbath rest : one is not to climb a tree, nor ride on an animal, nor swim in water, not clap the hands, nor slap the hips, nor dance. On account of the following activities one incurs guilt even though they are legitimate as such : one is not to administer justice, [84] nor become engaged to a woman,

---

[77] But cf. Braun, I, 118. Cf. also, however, the review of K. Schubert, BZ, NF, 3 (1959), 122.

[78] Cf. also Jub. 50:10 f.; Braun, I, 119.

[79] In Rabb. works we also find lists of activities with no ref. to the Sabbath, e.g., T. Ber., 7, 2, where Ben Zoma praises God that He has created other men that they might serve Him with their works. Cf. also the list of jobs forbidden on feast days in T. Beza (Yom tob), 4, 4 (207); Str.-B., II, 815 f.

[80] Cf. Dt. 25:3 and Moore, II, 27 f.

[81] For the making of the tabernacle cf. Ex. 35:4. Since the Sabbath commandment comes just before in 35:1-3 the Rabb. linked the passages and based the list of 39 jobs on the fact that these were all necessary in making the tabernacle, cf. bShab., 49b, 73b, 96b; bBQ, 2a; Str.-B., I, 616 f.

[82] Rabbi acc. to bShab., 97b, Bar.: the plur. דברים = 2 things, הדברים with art. 3, אלה yields a value of 36, hence 36 + 3 = 39. R. Abbahu (c. 300 A.D.) counted differently: אלה = 36; דבר (sing.) 1; דברים (plur.) 2, thus 36 + 1 + 2 = 39. The Rabb. of Caesarea : א = 1; ל = 30; ה (= ח) = 8, thus 1 + 30 + 8 = 39, jShab., 7, 2 (9b, 72-76); cf. Str.-B., I, 617.

[83] Cf. Str.-B., I, 617 and v. also Philo Vit. Mos., II, 22 : οὐ γὰρ ἔρνος, οὐ κλάδον, ἀλλ᾽ οὐδὲ πέταλον ἐφεῖται τεμεῖν ἢ καρπὸν ὁντινοῦν δρέψασθαι.

[84] Acc. to Jewish law it was forbidden to conduct a case on the Sabbath or a festival. Cf. on this Str.-B., II, 815-822. This Halakah is to be taken into account in assessing the

nor go through the ceremony of casting off the shoe (in refusing Levirate marriage), nor contract Levirate marriage. On account of the following activities one incurs guilt even though they are based on a commandment : one is not to sanctify anything, nor make an evaluation, nor bring under the ban, nor separate heave offerings and tithes." [85] Even when the two lists are put together, we still do not have a complete list of all the statutes relating to the Sabbath, for such important matters as engaging in business and healing the sick, etc. are not mentioned. How far such things are allowed or forbidden is laid down in individual judgments. The deciding principle is that anything is prohibited which can take on the character of work. [86]

To keep pious Jews from inadvertently transgressing the Halakah has some preventive rules, e.g.: "A tailor is not to start with his needle at dusk lest he forget and do so (after the beginning of the Sabbath); similarly a writer is not to start with his reed," Shab., 1, 3. This building of a fence around the Sabbath was designed to prevent any possibility of doing any work on the Sabbath. If nevertheless someone broke the Sabbath accidentally, he was to bring a sin-offering, Sanh., 7, 8. Intentional desecration of the Sabbath, however, was to be punished by stoning to death, Sanh., 7, 4.

Particular care was taken by the Rabb. to exegete exactly those OT passages which gave more precise instructions regarding the prohibition of work on the Sabbath. Acc. to the Law animals were also subject to the Sabbath, Ex. 20:10; Dt. 5:14. More detailed legislation was thus required as to the leading out and watering of beasts. [87] Acc. to Ex. 35:3 no fire was to be kindled on the Sabbath. Hence the Sabbath lamp had to be lit before the Sabbath began (Shab., 2, 7 etc.), and no lamp had to be put out on the Sabbath (2, 5). [88] In Ex. 16:29 the Israelites were forbidden to go out of the camp on the Sabbath. The deduction was thus made : οὐκ ἔξεστι δ' ἡμῖν οὔτε τοῖς σαββάτοις οὔτ' ἐν τῇ ἑορτῇ ὁδεύειν, Jos. Ant., 13, 252, and the Rabb. restricted a permissible Sabbath journey to 2000 cubits. [89] Incisive elucidations develop the rule against bearing burdens on the Sabbath, Jer. 17:21 f.; Shab., 7, 2. The minute quantities which may be carried are carefully fixed : "(He is guilty) who carries enough wine for the mixing of a cup, milk enough for a sip, honey sufficient to put on a wound ... (He is guilty) who carries enough cord to make a handle for a basket ... enough ink to write two letters," Shab., 8, 1-4. One may carry on the body only clothing and necessary adornment, all else being forbidden, Shab., 6, 1-9. [90] It was forbidden to move something from one place to another, 7, 2. [91] All kinds of evasions were attempted to escape the

---

Gospel account of the trial of Jesus. Cf. also J. Jeremias, *Die Abendmahlsworte Jesu*² (1949), 44. The Jews did not come before Gentile courts on the Sabbath ; this privilege was expressly granted them by Augustus, Jos. Ant., 16, 163; cf. also 16, 168.

[85] Cf. Str.-B., I, 617; II, 915. Philo Migr. Abr., 91 has the following list : πῦρ ἐναύειν ἢ γεωπονεῖν ἢ ἀχθοφορεῖν ἢ ἐγκαλεῖν ἢ δικάζειν ἢ παρακαταθήκας ἀπαιτεῖν ἢ δάνεια ἀναπράττειν ἢ τὰ ἄλλα ποιεῖν, ὅσα κἂν τοῖς μὴ ἑορτώδεσι καιροῖς ἐφεῖται.

[86] It is not possible to give all the detailed rules here, but only some typical examples. Specific casuistical decisions mentioned in the NT are dealt with in the NT section.

[87] Shab., 5, 1-4; on watering cf. Er., 2, 1 f. and Str.-B., II, 199 f.

[88] A further rule is that it is forbidden to tilt the lamp a little to get more oil to the wick, T. Shab., 1, 13 (110); cf. Str.-B., IV, 936.

[89] Cf. Sota, 5, 3; Er., 4, 3 etc.; also Hier. Ep., 121, 10 : *Solent ... dicere. Barachibas et Simeon et Helles, magistri nostri, tradiderunt nobis, ut duo milia pedes ambulemus in sabbato.* Since this distance was often not enough, ways were sought to extend it. Thus the place of Sabbath observance, which was not supposed to have a radius of more than 4 cubits, was extended to an enclosed locality, so that one might walk about freely in a town, T. Er., 4, 12 f. (142), cf. also Str.-B., II, 592 f. Another form of extension was the "mixing of boundaries" (עֵירוּב תְּחוּמִין): to be able to travel more than 2000 cubits one would on the preparation day deposit food for two meals at the end of the Sabbath journey and thus have a second Sabbath centre from which one might travel another 2000 cubits, cf. Er., 4, 7-9; 8, 2 etc.; Str.-B., II, 591, 593 f.

[90] Cf. Str.-B., II, 457.

[91] Different kinds of places were distinguished : רְשׁוּת הָרַבִּים the public place ; רְשׁוּת הַיָּחִיד,

burden of this prohibition of carrying. Thus two persons may carry something which one might have removed quite easily, 10, 5. [92] It was also permissible to carry something in an unusual way, e.g., with the foot or mouth, 10, 3. Or an object could be passed along the street from one person to another so long as no one carried it more than the statutory radius of 4 cubits from the Sabbath place, Er., 10, 2. The rule that nothing was to be carried from a private place to a public place (e.g., the street) or *vice versa* was overcome by making an erub : On Friday those who lived in houses opening on a common court held a common meal in one of the houses. In this way the whole court was made into conjointly owned private property and it was permissible to carry objects in it, [93] cf. Er., 3, 1; 6, 1-3, 8-10 etc. This "mixing of courts" (עֵירוּב חֲצֵרוֹת) led to the possibility of a "mixing of the alley" (עֵירוּב מָבוֹי). i.e., the closing of an alley, or of a space with walls on three sides, by erecting a barrier and eating in the enclosure, so that things might be carried here too, cf. Er., 1, 1-7 etc. [94] In this way the Rabb. tried to keep to the letter of the Law while bringing its demands as much as possible into harmony with practical necessities.

c. The Superseding of the Sabbath Law.

Though the prohibition of work on the Sabbath was taken very comprehensively, [95] in special cases the Rabb. saw that the Sabbath commandment was necessarily superseded by an unescapable obligation. Thus even on the Sabbath the priests had to make the necessary arrangements for the Sabbath offerings, Jub. 50:10 f. In Damasc. 11:17 f. (13:27) only the offering of the Sabbath burnt offerings is allowed. Acc. to the Rabb., however, the temple ministry (bShab., 132b) and the Passover sacrifice (Pes., 6, 1) supersede the Sabbath, though the rule of R. 'Aqiba is kept that any work which can be done on the preparation day is not to be done on the Sabbath, Pes., 6, 2. [96] If a Jew was in mortal danger he could break the Sabbath. [97] This is why taking to arms could be allowed in the days of the Maccabees. [98] The Rabb. accepted this, and also declared that it was permissible to save oneself by flight on the Sabbath. [99] When someone was mortally ill on the Sabbath help could be brought and the Sabbath infringed, Yoma, 8, 6. [100] The superseding of the Sabbath by the saving of life is dealt with in a saying of R. Shim'on bMenasya (c. 180 A.D.): "The Sabbath is given over to you and not you to the Sabbath." [101] But this does not apply when there is no acute danger to life. In that case one must wait until the Sabbath ends to tend the sick. If child birth begins on the Sabbath midwifery is permitted (Shab., 18, 3) to save human life. If a fire breaks out, the most urgent rescue operations are permitted, Shab., 16, 1-7. Finally, the Sabbath is superseded by the commandment that every male Israelite be circumcised on the eight day after birth, Gn. 17:10-12; Lv. 12:3. The circumcision is to

---

the private ; כַּרְמְלִית, the intermediary with features of both ; מָקוֹם פָּטוּר, free, not forbidden territory, T. Shab., 1, 1 (110); cf. Strack Einl., 37; Str.-B., II, 455.

[92] Cf. Str.-B., IV, 412.

[93] *Ibid.*, 349. On the various ways of escaping the prohibition of carrying by making an erub cf. the tractate Erubin, also Schürer, II, 574-576.

[94] Damasc. (→ n. 76) and also the Sadducees (→ n. 63) would not allow an erub.

[95] Typical of the comprehensive understanding of the commandment is the discussion whether or not one may eat an egg laid by a hen on the Sabbath, cf. Beza, 1, 1; Ed., 4, 1.

[96] Cf. Str.-B., IV, 47. The Sadducees, of course, would not allow the slaying of the Passover lamb on the Sabbath, → n. 63.

[97] On this ground some scholars excused David's eating of the shew-bread at Nob on a Sabbath, cf. bMen., 95b; Str.-B., I, 618 f. and → 22, 7 ff.

[98] 1 Macc. 2:39-41, cf. → 8, 22 ff.

[99] Tanch. מסעי 245a; Str.-B., I, 952 f.

[100] Cf. the examples in Str.-B., I, 623-629; II, 533 f. → 24, 6 ff.

[101] M. Ex., 31, 12 (109b); cf. Str.-B., II, 5.

proceed even if this day is a Sabbath, Shab., 18, 3; 19, 1-3.[102] Here, too, the rule formulated by 'Aqiba and generally accepted is still to be kept, namely, that only things which cannot be done on the day of preparation may be done on the Sabbath, Shab., 19, 1.

All these instances in which the Sabbath is superseded are exceptions in which the indispensability of what is to be done justifies infringement of the Sabbath. If there is doubt as to the need or danger, the Sabbath should not be desecrated and no work should be done.[103]

3. The Celebration of the Sabbath.

After six days of work the Sabbath was hailed with joy as a queen and bride, bShab., 119a. Devoted exclusively to rest and refreshment, this day was to be celebrated at home and in gatherings for worship. R. Joshua (c. 90) enjoined that one half of the Sabbath should be given to eating and drinking and the other half to the house of instruction, bPes., 68b.[104]

a. Celebration at Home.

All things were to be made ready for the Sabbath on the preparation day. The tithing of Sabbath food was to be seen to (Shab., 2, 7), the meal prepared (bShab., 119b) and kept warm, since no fire was to be lit on the Sabbath and there was to be no cooking (bShab., 4, 1), the lamps arranged and an erub made, Shab., 2, 7. The beginning of the Sabbath was indicated when the priests in the temple[105] or the servants of the synagogue in the country blew three blasts on the trumpet and declared the distinction between the profane and the holy.[106] Now one had to put off the phylacteries (bSanh., 68a),[107] light the Sabbath lamps (Shab., 2, 7) and put on good clothes to begin the festal day worthily.[108]

In general the evening meal was taken at dusk on the day of preparation, T. Ber., 1, 1. The commencing Sabbath was thus introduced festively with the "dedication of the day."[109] If there was enough wine available for two cups, the first cup was mixed first and grace pronounced over it, Ber., 6, 1. The head of the house would then pronounce over the second cup the consecration of the day, the so-called Qiddush, T. Ber., 5, 4. R. El'azar bar Zadoq (end of the 1st cent. A.D.) supplied the following words for this: "My father used to say over the cup: [Blessed be He] who has sanctified the Sabbath (קידש את יום השבת).[110] bBer., 49a has a longer formula: Blessed be He who in love has given Israel the Sabbaths for rest as a sign and a covenant. Blessed be He who has sanctified the Sabbath.[111] If the meal lasted from Friday mid-day to the beginning of the Sabbath the meal was first ended and then the Qiddush was put in the concluding grace.[112]

---

[102] For further examples cf. Str.-B., II, 487 f.; IV, 24 f.

[103] Tanch. Β לך לך § 20 (38b); Str.-B., I, 624.

[104] Cf. Str.-B., I, 611.

[105] Jos. Bell., 4, 582; Sukka, 5, 5.

[106] T. Sukka, 4, 11 f. (199); bShab., 35b; Tanch. פנחס (243b); cf. Str.-B., I, 580; IV, 140-142.

[107] Cf. also jShab., 5b, 61-63; Str.-B., IV, 315 f.

[108] Rabbi said: "Sanctify the Sabbath with the garment," Pesikt. r., 23 (117b). Cf. also Str.-B., I, 611, 615.

[109] Cf. Elbogen Eingang, 173-187.

[110] T. Ber., 3, 7. Cf. Jeremias, op. cit. (→ n. 84), 23; Moore, II, 36.

[111] Cf. Str.-B., IV, 632 f.

[112] Jeremias, op. cit., 23 f. with examples. The Qiddush was originally part of the meal but in Amoraean days was moved to the synagogue when the practice grew up of holding

The day of rest was to be characterised by good eating, Jub. 2:21, 31; 50:9 f.; bShab., 119a etc. [113] Whereas two meals were normally eaten on week-days, there were to be three on the Sabbath. [114] To be able to enjoy the Sabbath properly at these meals it was advised that little should be eaten the day before and one should begin the Sabbath hungry, T. Ber., 5, 1. [115] The main meal was usually held at mid-day after worship, Jos. Vit., 279. On the Sabbath guests were often invited so that they could be entertained lavishly, Shab., 23, 2; T. Shab., 17, 5 (137). [116] Fasting on the Sabbath was not allowed lest the enjoyment of the feast be hampered, Jdt. 8:6; bBer., 31b. [117]

When the day ended, the distinction between the profane and the holy was again denoted by a special blessing. [118] At evening prayer a distinction was inserted into the fourth benediction or it was pronounced alone at the end of the last meal when another cup of wine might be taken. Acc. to bPes., 103b the so-called Habdala ran : "[Blessed be He] who distinguishes between holy and profane, between light and darkness, between Israel and the Gentiles, between the seventh day and the six working days, between unclean and clean, between sea and dry land, between the waters above and the waters below, between the priests and the Levites and Israelites," and in conclusion "[Blessed be He] who orders creation," bPes., 104a. With this distinction the Sabbath was solemnly ushered out and the new week begun.

b. Worship on the Sabbath.

The appointed offerings were made each Sabbath in the temple : two lambs without blemish and two tenth ephahs of flour mingled with oil as meat offerings along with the appropriate drink offerings, Nu. 28:9 f. [119] More priests were need for these additional offerings than on week-days, Yoma, 2, 3-5. Two extra priests were also appointed on the Sabbath to set the bowls of incense on the table of the shew-bread and to renew the shew-bread, Lv. 24:8; 1 Ch. 9:32; Men., 11, 7. [120] The change in the rota of officiating priests was always made on the Sabbath so that the outgoing course offered the morning sacrifices and the incoming course the evening sacrifices, Jos. Ant., 7, 365; T. Sukka, 4, 24 f. (200); Sukka, 5, 7 f. [121] The 92nd Psalm was appointed for the Sabbath, Ps. 92:1. [122]

Throughout the land and in the Dispersion [123] services were held in the synagogues on the Sabbath. [124] The morning service consisted of the same parts as the weekly services on Monday and Thursday : [125] recitation of the sch^ema, the t^ephilla, Scripture

---

a service at the beginning of the Sabbath. Cf. Elbogen Gottesdienst, 111; Jeremias, *op. cit.,* 24, n. 2.

[113] For further Rabb. examples cf. Str.-B., I, 611-615, 825.

[114] Shab., 16, 2; Str.-B., I, 611-615.

[115] Cf. Str.-B., I, 612 f.

[116] *Ibid.,* II, 202 f.

[117] Even when the 9th Ab, the day of the destruction of Jerusalem, fell on a Sabbath, there was to be no fasting but one was to eat and drink as much as required, T. Taan., 4, 13 (221), cf. Str.-B., IV, 89. Only in exceptional circumstances could one fast on the Sabbath, e.g., if one had had a bad dream, bShab., 11a; cf. E. L. Ehrlich, "Der Traum im Talmud," ZNW, 47 (1956), 141. Cf. also the examples in Taan., 3, 7.

[118] Cf. on this Str.-B., IV, 236 f.

[119] Cf. Jub. 50:10. Acc. to Damasc. 11:17 f. (13:27), however, only the burnt offerings were to be made on the Sabbath. On the Sabbath offerings cf. also Jos. Ant., 3, 237.

[120] Cf. J. Jeremias, *Jerusalem zur Zeit Jesu,* II A² (1958), 64.

[121] Cf. Schürer, II, 336.

[122] bRH, 31a tells how at the musaf offering the Song of Moses (Dt. 32) was sung and at the mincha offering Ex. 15:1-10, 11-18; Nu. 21:17 f. Cf. Elbogen Gottesdienst, 116 f.

[123] Examples from Philo and Jos. in Schl. Theol. d. Judt., 101 f.

[124] Cf. Str.-B., IV, 153-188; Elbogen Gottesdienst, esp. 107-122.

[125] Elbogen Gottesdienst, 112.

reading and the related exposition. [126] The passages constituting the sch^{e}ma (Dt. 6:4-9; 11:13-21; Nu. 15:37-41) were recited as on week-days, but with some additions on the Sabbath. [127] The t^{e}philla was spoken as a sevenfold prayer, i.e., the 13 middle petitions were left out and between the first three and the last three benedictions the consecration of the day (קדושת היום) was interpolated, T. Ber., 3, 12. [128] For the readings from the Torah, which were held as in the morning and mincha service on Monday and Thursday, the Pentateuch was divided into pericopes. Palestine followed a three-year cycle with 154-175 sections, while Babylon read the whole Torah each year and thus divided it into only 54 sections. [129] In the Mishnah it is laid down that at morning service on the Sabbath there should be a reading from the prophets as well as the Torah, but there were no fixed passages for this. [130] Since the reading from the prophets came at the end of the service it was called Haphtarah, [131] i.e., that the service should conclude herewith and the congregation should be dismissed after the reading from the prophets. [132] An exposition might be annexed to the Haphtarah if someone was present at the service who had the necessary abilities and knowledge for expounding the text and instructing the congregation. [133]

c. The Jewish Celebration of the Sabbath in the Judgment of Non-Jews.

"There is no city either among the Greeks or the barbarians or anywhere else, nor is there any people, where the custom of the seventh day, which we keep, has not reached and where fasting and the lighting of lamps and many of our prohibitions of meats are not observed," writes Jos. Ap., 2, 282. This is an exaggeration, yet it is true that throughout the Hell. Roman world there were Jewish congregations which enjoyed the protection of *religio licita* and kept the Sabbath unhindered. Their worship was also noted by Gentiles so that many non-Jews adopted Jewish customs and practices. To be sure the Jewish Sabbath was often ridiculed by Gk. and Latin authors. [134] It was simply regarded as a day of inactivity which the Jews spent in idleness and sloth. [135] Seneca blamed the Jews for squandering one seventh of their lives in inactivity. [136] One could explain their avoidance of work every seventh day only by supposing that it was for them a taboo, the Sabbath being like the day of Saturn, which was regarded everywhere as an unlucky day, Tac. Hist., V, 4. [137] Acc. to Dio C. the capture of Jerusalem by Pompey, by Herod, and later by Titus took place on the unlucky day of

---

[126] Cf. the succinct account of synagogue worship in Midr. Cant., 8, 13 (134a): "If the Israelites are occupied with work the six (week-)days, they stop on the Sabbath and come to the synagogue and recite the sch^{e}ma and come (in prayer) before the ark (to pray the Prayer of Eighteen Petitions) and read from the Torah and conclude with the reading from the prophets (read the Haphtarah)," cf. Str.-B., III, 323; IV, 153.

[127] Elbogen Gottesdienst, 114.

[128] *Ibid.*, 109. On the musaf prayer on the Sabbath cf. W. Staerk, "Altjüd. liturgische Gebete," Kl. T., 58^2 (1930), 21 f., 26 f.

[129] Cf. Meg., 3, 4-6; cf. also Str.-B., IV, 155 f.; Moore, I, 297 f., 300; III, 98 f.; Elbogen Gottesdienst, 155 f.

[130] Meg., 4, 5; Elbogen Gottesdienst, 176.

[131] Cf. הפטיר "to release"; cf. Str.-B., IV, 166.

[132] Cf. Str.-B., IV, 165-171.

[133] *Ibid.*, 171-188.

[134] Cf. the material in Wolff, 162-172.

[135] Cf. Ovid Ars Amatoria, I, 76 and 416; Remedia Amoris, 219 f.; Juv. Sat., 14, 95-106; Persius Satira, V, 179-184.

[136] In Aug. Civ. D., VI, 11. Horat. Sat., I, 9, 69 is to be punctuated: *hodie tricesima, sabbata,* "to-day is the new moon, hence the Sabbath rest."

[137] The Rabb., too, sometimes connected the seven-day week of the Jews with the planetary week and hence the Sabbath with Saturn, bShab., 156a. Naturally these were later comparisons and no conclusions should be drawn from them as to the origin of the Sabbath.

Kronos (= Saturn), 37, 16, 4; 49, 22, 4; 66, 7, 2. Thus the observance of the Sabbath must have seemed superstitious to the Gks. and Romans. Seneca seems to think that Jewish worship consisted primarily in the lighting of the Sabbath lamp at the right time, Ep., 95, 47. Plut., explaining the Jewish Sabbath to Gk. readers, equates the Asia Minor god Sabazios-Dionysus with Yahweh Sabaoth, Quaest. Conv., 2 (II, 671e-672a). In this explanation, as in the statement of Mart., IV, 4 and 7 that the Jews fasted on the Sabbath, one sees that the Graeco-Roman world had only a superficial knowledge of Judaism and its observance of the Sabbath. [138]

To gain understanding and perhaps acceptance for their religion Jewish apologists tried to find support for the Sabbath in non-Jewish authors, though they usually quoted them incorrectly. Thus Aristobul. pts. out that observance of the seventh day is mentioned in sayings of Hes., Hom. and Linus, Eus. Praep. Ev., 13, 12, 9-16. Though the Jews were ridiculed, their apologetic and esp. their strict keeping of the Sabbath commandment made a deep impression in many non-Jewish circles, so that some even adopted Jewish customs, resting on the Sabbath, following the rules about food, fasting, and lighting the lamps. Witness is borne to this not only by the apologetically slanted statement of Jos in Ap., 2, 282 (→ 17, 18 ff.) but also by non-Jewish authors who refer to the influence of the Sabbath on the Gentile world. Suet. tells how in the days of Tiberius there lived on Rhodes a grammarian called Diogenes who used to dispute only on the Sabbath. Even when the emperor visited him he would not depart from this custom but let the emperor come to see him only on the Sabbath, Caes., III, 32. Tert. tells of Gentiles who in acc. with the Jewish practice observed the seventh day as a day of rest, Nat., 13. [139] Beyond the circle of the Jewish communities which everywhere in the Diaspora sanctified the Sabbath to the God of Israel many god-fearers and proselytes also kept the Sabbath as a day of rest.

4. The Sabbatical Year.

a. Fallow Ground and the Remission of Debts each Seventh Year.

From the 2nd cent. B.C., and perhaps earlier, [140] the statutes of the Torah concerning the sabbatical year were kept in Palestine. [141] From 1st Tishri on the land was left fallow, RH, 1, 1. The results of the lack of harvest must have been very severe in times of war and distress. There are many ref. to such times. [142] 1 Macc. 6 tells us that during the siege of Bethzur and Jerusalem (163 B.C.) there was famine among the besieged ὅτι σάββατον ἦν τῇ γῇ (v. 49) or διὰ τὸ ἕβδομον ἔτος εἶναι (v. 53, cf. also Jos. Ant., 12, 378). A sabbatical year is also mentioned in the account of the siege of the

---

[138] Jos. has to correct the allegations of Ap. that after the exodus all the Jews fell sick and had swellings on their secret parts, and that the term Sabbath derives from this sickness called σαββάτωσις (or σαββώ), Ap., 2, 20-27. Ap. had obviously picked up in the alleys of Alexandria an abusive expression designed to make fun of the Jewish Sabbath. Cf. M. Scheller, "σαββώ u. σαββάτωσις," Glotta, 34 (1955), 298-300.

[139] Cf. Schürer, III, 166 f.

[140] Cf. Neh. 10:32.

[141] Cf. Schürer, I, 35-37, 214, 258 f.; Mahler Chronologie, 103-115, 410-419; J. Jeremias, Jerusalem z. Zeit Jesu, II A² (1958), 57-61; also "Sabbatjahr u. nt.liche Chronologie," ZNW, 27 (1928), 98-103; Schl. Theol. d. Judt., 128 f.; Dalman Arbeit, II, 136-139; III, 183-185; R. North, "Maccabean Sabbath Years," Biblica, 34 (1953), 501-515; Correns ; H. Wildberger, "Israel u. sein Land," Ev. Theol., 16 (1956), 411-416; E. Kutsch, Art. "Erlassjahr" in RGG³, II, 568 f.

[142] One can no longer say for certain whether the sabbatical year was kept regularly, since records are scanty. On the chronology cf. Correns, 25-33, though North, op. cit. (→ n. 141), esp. 511-514 takes a different view.

fortress of Dagon by Hyrcanus (135 B.C.), Jos. Ant., 13, 234; Bell., 1, 60. [143] When Herod had invested Jerusalem in 37 B.C. the inhabitants suffered particular distress τὸν γὰρ ἑβδοματικὸν ἐνιαυτὸν συνέβη κατὰ τοῦτ' εἶναι, Jos. Ant., 14, 475, cf. also 15, 7. A sabbatical year preceded the capture of Jerusalem by Titus (70 A.D.) and this increased unbearably the distress in the city. [144] Acc. to Jos. Ant., 11, 338 Alexander the Gt. had already excused the Jews from taxes each seventh year. [145] That the Jews were permitted to keep the sabbatical year by the Romans may be seen from an edict of Julius Caesar to the effect that no taxes are to be collected in the seventh year, Jos. Ant., 14, 202 and 206. How seriously the regulations of the Torah were taken may be seen from the ref. to the sabbatical year in the Dead Sea Scrolls [146] and from the precise instructions which the Rabb. give in the tractate Shebiit concerning the fallow year. Agriculture must stop in the sabbatical year, though life proceeds normally in other respects. The main concern of the Rabb. is to fix the boundary between what may and may not be done in the sabbatical year. [147]

Instructions had also to be given concerning the remissions of debts required by the Law. [148] A consistent observance of this provision (Dt. 15:9) would have brought with it a general refusal to lend money at all. Hence Hillel (c. 20 B.C.) issued the so-called prosbol by which a lender could stipulate that he might press his claim at any time, even in a sabbatical year, Shebi., 10, 3-7. [149] In this way an attempt was made to reduce the severity of the Law so that economic life might be kept going in spite of the sabbatical year.

b. The Cosmic Week and Cosmic Sabbath.

Apocalyptic speculates a good deal about the course of world history in successive periods. [150] In these attempts to calculate the duration and end of the world the number seven plays an important part, → II, 627 ff. [151] Thus Da. 9:24-27 speaks of seventy weeks of years which begin when Jerusalem is destroyed (by Nebuchadnezzar) and proceed until wickedness is complete and the measure of sin is full. After seven days the aeon which now sleeps will awake and the past will vanish acc. to 4 Esr. 7:31. [152] In Slav. En. 33:1 f. the world is to last seven millennia. In this difficult passage [153] the apocalyptist is probably saying that the new aeon will be a completely new creation.

---

[143] Jos. is wrong, of course, when in analogy to Sabbath observance he says of the sabbatical year: ἐνίσταται τὸ ἔτος ἐκεῖνο, καθ' ὃ συμβαίνει τοὺς Ἰουδαίους ἀργεῖν· κατὰ δὲ ἑπτὰ ἔτη τοῦτο παρατηροῦσιν, ὡς ἐν ταῖς ἑβδομάσιν ἡμέραις, Ant., 13, 234, cf. Bell., 1, 60; Correns, 19 f.

[144] T. Taan., 4, 9 (220); jTaan., 4, 8 (68d, 28 f.); bTaan., 29a; bAr., 11b.

[145] Acc. to Jos. Ant., 11, 343 the Samaritans sought the same favour. The decree of Alexander is not authentic. Cf. Jeremias Sabbatjahr (→ n. 141), 98, n. 2.

[146] In the "words of Moses" in 1 Q 22, III, 1-7 (DJD, I, 94 f.) we find instructions about the sabbatical year demanding that the land be completely fallow. 1 QM II, 6-9 lays down that there is to be no arming or military service in the year of release, "for it is a sabbath of rest for Israel."

[147] On the sabbatical yr. cf. also 1 Εσδρ. 1:55; Jub. 50:3; Philo Spec. Leg., II, 86-109; Tac. Hist. V, 4.

[148] On the remission of debts there are just a few regulations in the last chapter of Shebiit; it was no longer practised in the days of the editing of the Mishnah.

[149] Cf. Str.-B., I, 718. Hillel was simply legalising a practice which had long since been accepted. Cf. Correns, 24 f. An agreement in acc. with Hillel's prosbol has perhaps been preserved in an Aram. fr. from Qumran. Cf. J. T. Milik, "Le travail de l'édition des manuscrits du Désert de Juda," VT Suppl. IV (1956), 18.

[150] Cf. Bousset-Gressm., 246 f.; Volz Esch., 141-145.

[151] Cf. the division into "jubilees" in Jub.

[152] Cf. also the 70 shepherds in Eth. En. 89:59; the 70 generations in Eth. En. 10:12.

[153] In interpretation cf. Volz Esch., 35, 339.

After 6000 years of world history the 7th millennium will be one gt. Sabbath, so that there is a pause before the 8th day dawns as the beginning of the new creation. [154] In bSanh., 97a the Rabb. teach that the world will last 6000 yrs. and be destroyed 1000 yrs., or that it will lie fallow 1000 yrs. in 7000 yrs. [155] In the course of world history, then, a gt. sabbatical year was expected before the new aeon could begin. [156]

C. The Sabbath in the New Testament.

1. The Jewish Sabbath in the New Testament.

NT usage is in full agreement with Jewish, → 6, 21 ff. Heb. שַׁבָּת is transl. τὸ σάββατον [157] in Mk. 2:27 f., 6:2; Mt. 12:8; Lk. 6:5 etc., ἡ ἡμέρα τοῦ σαββάτου in Lk. 13:14, 16; 14:5 etc., or τὰ σάββατα for single Sabbaths in Mk. 1:21; 2:23, 24 and par.; 3:2, 4 and par. [158] In Hb. 4:4 the Sabbath is simply ἡ ἑβδόμη (sc. ἡμέρα); there are Jewish models for this too, → 7, 15 ff. In acc. with Jewish usage (→ 7, 11 ff.) σάββατον in the sing. (Lk. 18:12 : δὶς τοῦ σαββάτου cf. also Mk. 16:9; 1 C. 16:2) and the plur. (Mk. 16:2 : τῇ μιᾷ τῶν σαββάτων cf. also Lk. 24:1; Mt. 28:1; Jn. 20:1, 19; Ac. 20:7) can also mean "week."

The picture of the Sabbath gained from Jewish sources is confirmed and amplified by the NT writings. All necessary arrangements for the Sabbath were to be made on the day of preparation [159] (→ 15, 16 ff.) so that the day of rest might be free from all work. Hence the body of Jesus had to be taken down from the cross on the preparation so as not to desecrate the Sabbath, Mk. 15:42-47 and par.; Jn. 19:42. [160] The sanctity of the day is protected by a strict prohibition of work. All harvesting (→ 12, 7 f.; 12, 24 f.), including the plucking of ears, is forbidden, Mk. 2:23 f. and par. Help and healing are not to be brought (→ 14, 31 ff.) to a sick person not in danger of death, Mk. 3:1 and par.; Lk. 13:14; 14:3 f.; Jn. 7:23; 9:14. The carrying of all kinds of objects (→ 12, 14 f.; 13, 26 ff.) is also

---

[154] Cf. also Barn., 15, 4 f. → 31, 27 ff. For other examples from Chr. apocalyptic cf. Wnd. Barn., 385 f.

[155] Cf. PREl, 18 (9d): "Seven aeons has God created, and of them all He has chosen only the seventh aeon. Six are for the coming and going (of men) and one (the seventh) is wholly Sabbath and rest in eternal life." Cf. Str.-B., III, 687. On the idea of the cosmic Sabbath cf. also Str.-B., IV, 969, 976, 990 f.

[156] The idea of the cosmic week and expectation of an intervening kingdom are used by John the Divine in his doctrine of the millennial kingdom, Rev. 20:1-10. Cf. A. Wikenhauser, "Die Herkunft d. Idee des tausendjährigen Reiches in d. Apk.," Röm. Quartalschrift, 45 (1937), 1-24; also "Weltwoche u. tausendjähriges Reich," Theol. Quart., 127 (1947), 399-417; H. Bietenhard, Das tausendjährige Reich² (1955).

[157] Plur. τὰ σάββατα Ac. 17:2 etc. Dat. plur. τοῖς σάββασιν Mk. 3:2; Mt. 12:10 etc. or τοῖς σαββάτοις Mt. 12:1, 12 vl. Cf. → n. 39; Pr.-Bauer⁵, s.v. for a full list of NT ref.

[158] Mt. 28:1 has ὀψὲ δὲ σαββάτων, τῇ ἐπιφωσκούσῃ εἰς μίαν σαββάτων. ὀψὲ σαββάτων corresponds to the Rabb. מוֹצָאֵי שַׁבָּת (→ 6, 29 ff.) and thus means the night from the Sabbath to the first day of the week or the first day of the week itself. Cf. Str.-B., ad loc.; P. Gardner-Smith, "ΕΠΙΦΩΣΚΕΙΝ," JThSt, 27 (1926), 179-181.

[159] Preparation = παρασκευή Mt. 27:62; Jn. 19:31, 42; Lk. 23:54. Here we have : καὶ ἡμέρα ἦν παρασκευῆς, καὶ σάββατον ἐπέφωσκεν. The ref. is obviously to the shining of the first star as the Sabbath comes. An explanation is given for the Hell. reader in Mk. 15:42 : παρασκευή, ὅ ἐστιν προσάββατον. Jn. 19:14 refers to the παρασκευὴ τοῦ πάσχα.

[160] Jn. 19:31 says of the Sabbath after the preparation : ἦν γὰρ μεγάλη ἡ ἡμέρα ἐκείνου τοῦ σαββάτου. It is gt. because acc. to John's chronology it coincides with the first day of the feast of the Passover and Unleavened Bread. Cf. Str.-B., II, 581 f.

forbidden, Jn. 5:9 f. One may only go the prescribed journey on the Sabbath (→ 13, 24 ff.), Ac. 1:12. [161]

The rules prohibiting work on the Sabbath may be overruled only in special cases by urgent obligations; thus the priests must do what is necessary to make the statutory offerings on the Sabbath (→ 14, 19 ff.), Mt. 12:4 f. If a man or beast is in mortal danger (→ 14, 27 ff.), assistance may be given, Mt. 12:11 f.; Lk. 14:5. The Law which requires all Israelite boys to be circumcised the eighth day after birth (→ 14, 35 ff.) is also to be kept even on the Sabbath, Jn. 7:22 f.

The Sabbath is regarded as a day of rest (→ 15, 10 ff.), Lk. 23:56. On it guests may be invited to the house (→ 16, 6 f.), Lk. 14:1; good may thus be done to others, cf. Mk. 3:4 and par. Each Sabbath the Law of Moses and the prophetic writings (→ 17, 5 ff.) are read in the synagogues, Ac. 13:15, 27; 15:21; Lk. 4:16-20. Like all the righteous in Israel Jesus and His disciples go to the synagogue on the Sabbath to take part in worship (→ 16, 30 ff.) and to avail themselves of the right of every male Israelite to append a sermon or instruction to the reading of Scripture, Mk. 1:21 f. and par.; [162] 6:2 and par.; Lk. 4:16-21; 13:10; Jn. 6:59 vl. In the same way the early Christian missionaries attend the synagogue on the Sabbath, teach in the service, and proclaim the glad tidings of Jesus the Christ, Ac. 13:14 f., 42, [163] 44; 16:13; 17:2.

2. The Sabbath Conflicts of Jesus.

a. The Sabbath Stories in Mark and their Parallels in Matthew and Luke.

At the end of a series of confrontations between Jesus and the Pharisees and scribes (Mk. 2:1-3:6 and par.) the Evangelist Mark tells of two conflicts regarding the Sabbath. On the way through a field of grain the disciples pluck the ears, Mk. 2:23-28 and par. [164] Though the Law allowed ears to be plucked from a field in case of hunger (Dt. 23:26), the Pharisees object [165] that by doing this on the Sabbath the disciples were engaging in work, [166] ὃ οὐκ ἔξεστιν (= אָסוּר, v. 24). Jesus answers the objection by referring to David, who on his flight from Saul came to Ahimelech the priest, [167] who at his request gave him the shew-bread to eat, 1 S. 21:2-7. As David's men also ate, Jesus justifies in this way the conduct of His disciples, → VI, 19, 16 ff.

---

[161] Cf. also Mt. 24:20, ad loc. → 29, 10 ff.

[162] In the pericope in Mk. 1:21-28 the Evangelist combines two motifs: the authoritative teaching of Jesus and the demonstration of His ἐξουσία by miracles, cf. Bultmann Trad., 223 f. In the story of the miracle there is nothing to suggest that it took place on the Sabbath. The witnesses are astonished at Jesus' ἐξουσία (v. 27). No one objects that the healing is on the Sabbath.

[163] τὸ μεταξὺ σάββατον Ac. 13:42 = "the following Sabbath"; cf. Ac. 13:44: τῷ δὲ ἐρχομένῳ σαββάτῳ.

[164] On the story cf. the comm. and the somewhat arbitrary interpretations of K. Born-häuser, "Zur Perikope vom Bruch des Sabbats," NkZ, 33 (1922), 325-334 and B. Murmelstein, "Jesu Gang durch die Saatfelder," Angelos, 3 (1930), 111-120.

[165] In Mk. and Mt. the Pharisees complain to Jesus, while in Lk. they criticise the disciples themselves.

[166] Plucking ears of grain is a subsidiary work under harvesting, one of the 39 forbidden tasks, → 12, 22 f.

[167] Abiathar in Mk. 2:26, though he succeeded only after his father's death, 1 S. 22:20 etc. Mt. and Lk. omit the name.

The relation between the OT story and the present instance of infringement of the Sabbath by the disciples of Jesus is obviously that righteous people are in both cases doing what is forbidden. [168] The point of comparison comes out even more clearly, however, when one considers that the example of David was adduced in learned discussions of the Sabbath. [169] Some rabb. took the view that David received the shewbread on the Sabbath when the old bread was always replaced by the new, Lv. 24:8. [170] His breaking of the Sabbath was justified because on his flight from Saul he was in sorry straits and mortal danger supersedes the Sabbath. [171]

In this debate between Jesus and the Pharisees it is not just a single act on the part of the disciples which is being defended. The practice of the Christian community, which has freed itself from the Jewish Sabbath, is being supported and vindicated from Scripture. [172]

This attitude of the community towards the Sabbath is expressed in two sayings attached to the story. The first in v. 27 is that "the sabbath was made for man, and not man for the sabbath." Now Judaism has similar-sounding sayings. [173] But in such sayings the Rabbis are not in any way attacking the Sabbath commandment. They are simply saying that in exceptional cases the Sabbath may be infringed to save human life. [174] In Mk. 2:27, however, man and his needs are said to be of greater value than the commandment. [175] The absolute obligation of the commandment is thus challenged, though its validity is not contested in principle. The second saying in v. 28 goes much further: "The Son of man is Lord also of the sabbath." This is not a deduction from the first saying by which man is granted lordship over the Sabbath. [176] In this originally independent saying the Christian community is confessing Jesus, the Son of Man, who as the κύριος decides concerning the applying or transcending of the Sabbath. [177] In His lordship Sabbath casuistry comes to an end. In this final statement, then, the Christian community formulates a conclusion which it draws from the story of the Sabbath conflict. [178]

---

[168] Cf. Loh. Mk., 64.

[169] Cf. the examples in Str.-B., I, 618 f. and Murmelstein, op. cit., 112 f.

[170] So R. Shim'on (c. 150) acc. to bMen., 95b and the tradition in Jalqut Shim'oni on 1 S. 21:5 (§ 130) from the Midrash Jᵉlammᵉdenu.

[171] So the opinion in the passages → n. 170. Cf. Str.-B., I, 619.

[172] The objection of the Pharisees is to the action of the disciples, not Jesus. The debate which follows is along the lines of disputations between the primitive community and the Jews. Hence some regard the form of the story in Mk. 2:23-28 and par. as the work of the community, cf. Bultmann Trad., 14. Nevertheless, the fact that Jesus Himself before the community was engaged in conflict regarding the Sabbath regulations is to be regarded as one of the best established parts of the tradition, even though one cannot reconstruct all the details. Cf. Braun, II, 70-72.

[173] Cf. (→ 14, 29 ff.) the saying of R. Shim'on bMᵉnasya.

[174] Cf. Str.-B., II, 5.

[175] Mt. and Lk. perhaps left out the saying in Mk. 2:27 because it did not seem to be so adequately supported as v. 28. Cf. Braun, II, 70, n. 1.

[176] So already H. Grotius, Annotationes in NT, I (1755), ad loc. With others Wellh. (Mk., 20) esp. would refer υἱὸς τοῦ ἀνθρώπου to man. T. W. Manson, "Mk. II, 27 f.," Conj. Neot., 11 (1947), 138-146 takes the opposite view and refers both v. 27 and v. 28 to the Son of Man = the people of the Most High of Da. 7:27, i.e., Jesus and His community.

[177] As against E. Käsemann, "Begründet der nt.liche Kanon die Einheit der Kirche?" EvTh, 11 (1951/52), 18, who finds in v. 28 an addition of the community qualifying v. 27: "The community could ascribe to its Master what it dare not claim for itself. Its qualifying addition shows that it was afraid of the freedom conferred on it and took refuge in a Christianised Judaism."

[178] Cf. Loh. Mk., 66 : "Hence the 'therefore' too is justified ; it denotes the conclusion

In the par. in Matthew's Gospel (Mt. 12:1-8) [179] the debate between Jesus and the Pharisees is extended by two additional OT references. First, the Evangelist points out that the sacrifices which are to be offered by the priests on the Sabbath according to Nu. 28:9 f. necessarily entail a violation of the prohibition of work. [180] But if the sacrificial laws already take precedence of the Sabbath, even more so may the Sabbath rules be broken now ὅτι τοῦ ἱεροῦ μεῖζόν ἐστιν ὧδε, v. 6. [181] To underline the fact that one greater than the temple is here Hos. 6:6 is then appended: ἔλεος θέλω καὶ οὐ θυσίαν; this had been used already by Matthew in the discussion with the Pharisees in 9:13. [182] The commandment of love is above Sabbath casuistry. If the Pharisees had understood the saying of the prophet they would not have condemned the innocent disciples, v. 7. But why are the disciples innocent when they have transgressed the Sabbath commandment? As a final reason — not a conclusion — Matthew uses the statement that the Son of Man is Lord of the Sabbath, v. 8. His disciples are thus released from the absolute obligation of the Sabbath commandment; their supreme command is that they exercise mercy. In Lk. the story is shortened and the tension is thus heightened, 6:1-5. [183]

Cod D puts the concluding saying only at the end of the second incident and in v. 5 adds another story instead : On the same day that Jesus went through the fields with His disciples He met someone who was working on the Sabbath and said to him that he was blessed if he knew what he was doing but accursed and a transgressor of the Law if he did not. This antithetically formulated saying suggests a Palestinian provenance. [184] Yet it is hardly conceivable that the historical Jesus should actually have met a man working on the Sabbath. [185] The saying is rather making the suspension of the Sabbath commandment in the Chr. community dependent on the εἰδέναι. Only those

---

which the community draws from the deeds and words of Jesus."

[179] Mt. 12:1 says that the disciples plucked the ears because they were hungry.

[180] This example from the Torah takes on gter. significance in the discussion than the story of David's transgression of the Law. Mt. adds a halachic conclusion to the haggadic argument. Cf. Daube, 67-71.

[181] "If the priests break the Sabbath, even more so may He who is the Lord of the sanctuary, the Messianic High-priest." G. Friedrich, "Beobachtungen z. messianischen Hohepriestererwartung in d. Synpt.," ZThK, 53 (1956), 289.

[182] On the quotation of Hos. 6:6 cf. K. Stendahl, *The School of St. Matthew* (1954), 128 f.

[183] At Lk. 6:1 we are to read ἐν σαββάτῳ δευτεροπρώτῳ with ACD Θ φ 𝔎 vg. This can only mean the second Sabbath in a series beginning with the first. The Sabbath is mentioned in 4:16. 4:31 introduces the first Sabbath pericope from Mk. Cf. on this Jn. 2:11 ἀρχὴ τῶν σημείων, Jn. 4:54 δεύτερον σημεῖον. There is no corresponding enumeration of Sabbaths in Judaism. Str.-B., II, 158 pts. out that acc. to Lv. 23:15 f. the days and weeks were numbered from the offering of the first-fruits to Pentecost, so that the second sabbath after the first would be the second between the Passover and Pentecost. *Preaching of Peter* mentions a σάββατον τὸ λεγόμενον πρῶτον, Cl. Al. Strom., VI, 5, 41; this obviously presupposes an enumeration of Sabbaths. Cf. E. Klostermann, *Apocrypha*, KlT, 3 (1933), 14. E. Vogt, "Sabbatum 'deuteroproton' in Lc. 6:1 et antiquum Kalendarium sacerdotale," Biblica, 40 (1959), 102-105, thinks the word δευτεροπρώτῳ is a very old gloss and interprets it as an *indicationem liturgico-chronologicam.* The Sabbath *ante oblationem spicarum* in Lv. 23:11, 15 is the *sabbatum primum post azyma et secundum post pascha.* The deduction is thus made : *Antiquus igitur glossator, cum post vocem 'sabbato'* (Lk. 6:1) *alteram 'deuteroproto' inseruit, videtur voluisse significare discipulos spicas vulsisse sabbato ante diem oblationis spicarum,* 103 f.

[184] Cf. J. Jeremias, *Unbekannte Jesusworte* (1951), 49-53.

[185] There is no suggestion that the man was supposed to be doing a work of love, Jeremias, *op. cit.,* 52.

who know what they are about may break the Sabbath. [186] Others are accursed as transgressors of the Law, cf. Nu. 15:35 f. This is probably a product of the Jewish Chr. community justifying violation of the Sabbath for those who know what they are doing.

The conflict between Jesus and His opponents becomes even more acute in a second loosely related incident, Mk. 3:1-6 and par. [187] Jesus enters a synagogue [188] and He there comes across a man with a withered hand. [189] According to a generally accepted Halakah it was permissible to help a sick man on the Sabbath only when there was imminent danger of death, → 14, 27 ff. [190] The double question which Jesus puts to His opponents, however, leaves no place for casuistical considerations. It is obviously imperative to do good on the Sabbath, [191] to save life and not to kill. Jesus heals the sick man and thus demonstrates that the Son of Man is Lord of the Sabbath. [192] The healing is briefly mentioned at the end of the story, v. 5. [193]

In the version in Matthew the second Sabbath conflict is more closely linked to the preceding story [194] and there is again increased emphasis on the discussion. [195] In this the Evangelist uses an independent Sabbath logion which has also been transmitted by Luke in another context, 14:5 → 26, 7 ff. In this saying [196] man is again set above the casuistical demands of the Law. [197] To the initial question of His opponents Jesus replies with a counter-question which requires an affirmative answer: If someone has a sheep which falls into a pit on

---

[186] One may compare the significance of "knowing" in the Dead Sea Scrolls. Cf. F. Nötscher, "Zur theol. Terminologie der Qumrantexte," *Bonner Bibl. Beiträge,* 10 (1956), 38-63.

[187] Lk. notes that the incident happened ἐν ἑτέρῳ σαββάτῳ, 6:6.

[188] Since the synagogue is that at Capernaum Mt. 12:9 and Lk. 6:6 add the art.: εἰς τὴν συναγωγήν.

[189] Ev. Hebr. adds further details to the story. The sick man says to Jesus : *caementarius eram, manibus victum quaeritans ; precor te, Jesu, ut mihi restituas sanitatem, ne turpiter mendicem cibos,* Hier. Comm. in Mt. 12:13. Cf. E. Klostermann, *Apocrypha,* II³, KlT, 8 (1929), 8; Hennecke³, I, 96. Mk., however, confines himself to the few details which are absolutely necessary for an understanding of the story.

[190] Cf. the comprehensive material in Str.-B., I, 622-629. In this case the decision would be that "since the withered hand presents no immediate threat to life healing on the Sabbath is not permitted," *ibid.,* I, 623.

[191] Cf. the story of the pious Abba Tachna who rated works of mercy toward a leper higher than correct observance of the Sabbath rules, Midr. Qoh., 9, 7 cf. Str.-B., I, 391. Again the Rabb. view was that the joy of the Sabbath is not adversely affected by comforting the mourning or visiting the sick, cf. the examples in Str.-B., I, 630.

[192] The interest of the story is not in the healing, for which there are various par. (1 K. 13:1-6; Philostr. Vit. Ap., III, 39), but in the conflict, in which the authority of Jesus is demonstrated.

[193] V. 6 does not end the pericope but the whole cycle of conflicts from 2:1-3:6.

[194] The new pericope does not begin, as in Mk. 3:1, with the indefinite πάλιν but Jesus moves on from the field to the synagogue.

[195] The form of the stories in Mt. is an obvious sign that the community of Mt. was still engaged in debates with the Synagogue about the Sabbath. Cf. on this G. D. Kilpatrick, *The Origins of the Gospel according to St. Matthew* (1946), 116 and cf. on Mt. 24:20 → 29, 10 ff.

[196] There are no Rabb. par. to the sayings introduced by τίς ἐξ ὑμῶν. This logion thus goes back to Jesus Himself. Cf. H. Greeven, "Wer unter euch ...," *Wort u. Dienst, Jbch. d. Theol. Schule Bethel,* NF, 3 (1952), 86-101; G. Bornkamm, *Jesus v. Nazareth³* (1959), 63, 124.

[197] The saying of Jesus is obviously used quite often in Sabbath debates and has come down in several versions, of which that in Mt. 12:11 f. is the oldest. On Lk. 14:5 → n. 203.

the Sabbath he will help it out, v. 11. [198] A deduction is then made *a minori ad maius* : how much more is a man worth than a sheep ! Hence one should do good on the Sabbath, v. 12. In this saying the thought in the double question of Mk. 3:4 is taken up and the end of the debate is reached. The commandment of love rather than casuistical requirements is set at the heart of the demand made by the divine commandment. The question εἰ ἔξεστιν τοῖς σάββασιν θεραπεῦσαι (v. 10) finds an answer which goes beyond the exception and announces a general principle which shapes the attitude of the community to the Sabbath : ὥστε ἔξεστιν τοῖς σάββασιν καλῶς ποιεῖν, v. 12. The short account of the healing of the sick man then forms a relevant conclusion to the successful debate. [199]

The Lucan version follows in essentials that of Mk. (Lk. 6:6-11).

b. The Sabbath Stories Peculiar to Luke.

In addition to the two Sabbath stories taken from Mk., Lk. has two additional accounts of healing on the Sabbath (13:10-17; 14:1-6). In Lk. 13:15 the argument again moves from the less to the greater; anyone will take an ox or ass from its stall on the Sabbath and water it, v. 15. [200] With a stress on the word λύειν the conclusion is thus drawn : How much more should this daughter of Abraham be loosed from her bond on the Sabbath, v. 16 !

In the story of the healing of the bowed-down woman in Lk. 13:10-17 a noteworthy pt. compared with Mk. 3:1-6 and par. is that the healing comes first and the debate with the ruler of the synagogue follows. For this reason the account is regarded by some as a later product based on the originally independent logion in 13:15. [201, 202] On this view the Evangelist took the story from his tradition and by a concluding

---

[198] In the Law it is laid down that help should be given an animal, Ex. 23:5; Dt. 22:4. The only question is whether it should be given on the Sabbath. Damasc. 11:13 f. (13:22-24) is against this, → 11, 22 f. The Rabb. were not so definite. The stricter school among scholars allowed the animal to be fed but not helped out. Less strict scholars, however, permitted help to be given and the animal brought out. Cf. the discussion in bShab., 128b (Str.-B., I, 629). Mt. 12:11 presupposes an extension to animals of the principle that danger to life supersedes the Sabbath.

[199] In the final statement, which speaks of the resolve to put Jesus to death, Mt. 12:14 mentions only the Pharisees and not the Herodians too (Mk. 3:6). A possible reason for this is that there were no longer any Herodians when Mt. was written. It was the Pharisees whose views exclusively shaped the life of the Synagogue after 70 A.D. and who in debate with Christians, in this matter of the Sabbath too, brought about the final breach between the Synagogue and the Church. There is also a ref. to this breach in the days of Mt. when at the beginning in v. 9 we read that Jesus went εἰς τὴν συναγωγὴν αὐτῶν, i.e., into the synagogue from which He and His disciples had already parted.

[200] Acc. to Shab., 7, 2 the tying and untying of knots is one of the 39 chief tasks forbidden on the Sabbath, → 12, 10 f. The scribes could, of course, make exceptions. R. Me'ir (c. 150) said : "One is not guilty on account of a knot which can be tied with one hand," Shab., 15, 1. Cattle naturally had to drink on the Sabbath. But only what was absolutely necessary for this was allowed. Thus bEr., 20b Bar. rules : "One is not to pour in water and set it before the animal on the Sabbath ; but one may pour in water so that the animal drinks for itself." There are regulations about the use of fountains in Er., 2, 1 f. Cf. the examples in Str.-B., II, 199 f.

[201] In comparison with Mt. 12:11 f. par. Lk. 14:5 this is less Jewish in form ; the pt. of the comparison is no longer the saving of animal and man but the fundamentally literary one of the loosing of the animal from the stall and of man from sickness, cf. M. Dibelius, *Die Formgesch. d. Evangeliums*³ (1959), 94.

[202] Cf. Bultmann Trad., 10.

editorial observation in v. 17b wove it into the chosen context, in which the Sabbath incident serves as an example of the impenitence of the Jews, 13:1-9, cf. v. 15 : ὑπο-κριταί.

Lk. 14:1-6 is also taken by some to be a later product analogous to Mk. 3:1-6 and par. Whereas in Mk. 3:4 the question to the opponents is so phrased that they cannot answer it (→ 24, 8 ff.), Lk. 14:3 echoes this in a way which suggests that the Sabbath problem was no longer acute for the community. But the second question which Jesus puts to His opponents undoubtedly comes from the tradition : τίνος ὑμῶν υἱὸς ἢ βοῦς εἰς φρέαρ πεσεῖται, καὶ οὐκ εὐθέως ἀνασπάσει αὐτὸν ἐν ἡμέρᾳ τοῦ σαββάτου; v. 5, cf. Mt. 12:11 f. [203] This leads necessarily to the conclusion that if an animal is to be helped on the Sabbath, even more so should aid be given to a man. [204] The pericope Lk. 14:1-6 is based on the saying in v. 5, for which the story forms a suitable frame. [205] The Evangelist seems to have taken the incident from the tradition, provided an introduction in v. 1, and then used the scene of the meal for the sayings and parables which follow, 14-1-6, 7-11, 12-14, 15-24.

If Luke uses Sabbath stories in other contexts in this way, the question must be faced as to why he tells us more about the Sabbath conflicts of Jesus than the other Evangelists. For him and his community the Sabbath was no longer such an urgent problem. [206] But the stories show what course the fulfilment of salvation history had taken. [207] The public ministry of Jesus in Luke no longer opens with proclamation of the imminent kingdom of God, Mk. 1:15. Jesus now teaches in the synagogues of Galilee, Lk. 4:15. On the Sabbath He goes as His custom was to the synagogue and opens His preaching with a Sabbath sermon in which He sets out His intentions, 4:16-30. He continues to teach in the synagogues, 6:6; 13:10. But He is rejected. Similarly His messengers go first to the synagogues, Ac. 13:14 f., 42, 44; 16:13; 17:2; 18:4; as pious Jews they were in the habit of doing this, Ac. 17:2. Only when their message was continually rejected by the Jews did they turn to the Gentiles. It was thus that the Gospel took its course into all the world.

c. The Sabbath Stories in John's Gospel.

In two healings in the Fourth Gospel we are told that they took place on the Sabbath and that they brought Jesus into sharp controversy with the Jews. The command of Jesus that the lame man of Bethesda should arise, take up his bed and walk (Jn. 5:1-9), was a public violation of the Sabbath and consequently a challenge to the Jews. [208] For carrying an object was among the 39 chief tasks

---

[203] M. Black, *An Aram. Approach to the Gospels and Acts*[2] (1954), 126 has shown that the saying contains a pun in Aram. : υἱός = בְּרָא, βοῦς = בְּעִירָא, φρέαρ = בֵּירָא. A noteworthy pt. in the Lucan version is the ref. to the son, which is not in Ex. 23:5; Dt. 22:4, nor Mt. 12:11 f. Black considers the explanation that through misunderstanding the Aram. בְּעִירָא (beast) became בְּרָא (son) and this could lead to the various renderings πρόβατον, ὄνος and βοῦς. Cf. also J. Jeremias' review of Black in GGA, 210 (1956), 9 : בְּרָא is "a genuinely oriental extension of the original pun be'ira/bēra in the course of oral transmission to beᵉra be'ira/bēra."

[204] On the Jewish halakah in such a case → n. 198.

[205] Cf. Bultmann Trad., 10.

[206] As it was in Mt. → n. 195.

[207] Cf. on this E. Lohse, "Lk. als Theologe d. Heilsgeschichte," EvTh, 14 (1954), 256-276, esp. 266 f., and on the whole complex of problems H. Conzelmann, *Die Mitte d. Zeit*[3] (1959) (E.T. *The Theology of St. Luke* [1960]).

[208] In the healing in vv. 1-9a there is no mention of the Sabbath ; only in v. 9b does the

forbidden on the Sabbath, Shab., 7, 2.[209] It was natural, then, that this infringement of the Sabbath should kindle the opposition of the Jews. Jesus defends
Himself [210] by attack : ὁ πατήρ μου ἕως ἄρτι ἐργάζεται, κἀγὼ ἐργάζομαι,
v. 17. The first clause refers to the much debated question of Judaism whether
God Himself was bound in the same way as the Israelites by the Sabbath commandment which He had given, and hence whether He had to break off His work
on the day of rest. A negative answer was given to this question both by Hellenistic Judaism and also by the Rabbis. [211] God never ceases to make and to work,
says Philo. [212] In different ways the Rabbis also argued that God's work goes
on on the Sabbath and that He is uninterruptedly active as Sustainer and Judge
of the world. [213] On the basis of these considerations the saying of Jesus stresses
the constancy of the divine work, which is not affected even by the Sabbath. [214]
But Jesus then continues that as the Father works, so do I. He thus claims that as
the Father works unceasingly, so does Jesus, that divine authority is given to
Him as the Son, and hence that His work cannot tolerate any interruption, even
by the Sabbath. [215] The Jews grasp what is being said: Jesus has not just broken
the Sabbath but is abolishing it. He calls God His Father, making Himself equal
to God, v. 18. [216] The story of the breaking of the Sabbath thus raises the decisive
question whether the authority of Jesus as the One whom God has sent is recognised or not. The address which follows deals with this question, 5:19-47. [217]
The Sabbath conflict, however, is pursued in a short debate between Jesus and
the Jews in 7:19-24. [218] Jesus puts to the ὄχλος the question: ἓν ἔργον (sc. the

---

Evangelist add the note : ἦν δὲ σάββατον ἐν ἐκείνῃ τῇ ἡμέρᾳ.

[209] For a survey of the materials relating to detailed Rabb. rulings cf. Str.-B., II, 454-461.

[210] The imperfects ἐδίωκον (v. 16) and ἐζήτουν (v. 18) express the enduring hostility
of the Jews to Jesus ; similarly His own permanent attitude and conduct are expressed by
the ἐποίει (v. 16) and ἔλυεν τὸ σάββατον (v. 18).

[211] Cf. Str.-B., II, 461 f.; Bau. J., 82; C. H. Dodd, *The Interpretation of the Fourth Gospel*
(1953), 320-328.

[212] It is true that God brings created powers to rest οὐ παύεται δὲ ποιῶν αὐτός,
Leg. All., I, 6. Cf. also Aristob. in Eus. Praep. Ev., 13, 12, 11 = Cl. Al. Strom., VI, 141 f.

[213] Acc. to R. Hoshaya (c. 225) God on the seventh day rested from His work on the
world but not from His work on the ungodly on whom He visits judgment and retribution,
Gn. r., 11 (8c) on 2:2. Rabban Gamaliel II (c. 90) has a deduction *a minori ad maius* :
If man on the Sabbath may carry to and fro in his private domain, how much more may
God work on the Sabbath when the whole world is His private domain, Ex. r., 30 (89d).
Cf. Str.-B., II, 461 f.; H. Odeberg, *The Fourth Gospel* (1929), 202.

[214] In explanation of ἕως ἄρτι cf. C. Maurer, "Steckt hinter Joh. 5:17 ein Übersetzungs-
fehler ?" *Wort u. Dienst, Jbch. d. Theol. Schule Bethel*, NF, 5 (1957), 130-140. Following
a conjecture in Bultmann J., 183, n. 6 Maurer makes the interesting proposal that ἕως ἄρτι
goes back to a Semitic עוֹד, which can denote duration as well as end. Since there is no ref.
to an end in Jn. 5:17, the words must be expressing duration = ἀεί, so that the unceasing
nature of God's work is emphasised.

[215] One can hardly detect any liturgical interest on the part of the Evangelist here, for
there is no suggestion of a replacing of the Sabbath by Sunday. But cf. O. Cullmann,
"Sabbat u. Sonntag nach d. Joh.-Ev.," *In Memoriam Ernst Lohmeyer* (1951), 127-131; also
*Urchr. u. Gottesdienst*³ (1956), 89.

[216] The relation between Church and Synagogue towards the end of the 1st cent. is
reflected here.

[217] V. 17 is also the theme of the ensuing address of Jesus in 5:19-47. Like the Father,
Jesus does a work of salvation and judgment. Cf. Maurer, *op. cit.,* 139 f.

[218] Jn. 7:15-24 seems indubitably to belong to the end of c. 5; probably confusion of pages
put it in the present context, where it is simply an example of Jesus' διδάσκειν (Jn. 7:14).
Cf. E. Schweizer, "Ego Eimi," FRL, 56 (1939), 108-111; Bultmann J., 177 f., 205-209;
R. Schnackenburg, "Die 'situationsgelösten' Redestücke in Joh. 3," ZNW, 49 (1958), 98.

healing on the Sabbath) ἐποίησα καὶ πάντες θαυμάζετε διὰ τοῦτο; v. 21 f. [219]
Circumcision, which God ordained and the fathers practised (Lv. 12:3; Gn. 17:10-
12), constantly demands a breaking of the Sabbath, since the command that it
be given the eighth day after birth has to be followed even when the eighth day
falls on a Sabbath, v. 22 f. [220] A deduction a minori ad maius is then made: If a
man may receive circumcision on the Sabbath in order that the Law of Moses may
not be broken, how can people be angry at Jesus because He has made the whole
man well on the Sabbath (v. 23)? There are similar-sounding statements in the
Rabbis which allow the infringement of the Sabbath in special cases in order
that help may be given without delay to those in danger of death. [221] If the
argument of Jesus is not cogent for His Jewish audience it is because the healing
did not save a man from death but was an expression of the claim of Jesus that
God had sent Him. This claim is thus brought to the fore once again. The end of
the Sabbath conflict makes it plain that for the Christian community the Sabbath
commandment had already been set aside definitively by the end of the 1st century. Jesus had abolished it, 5:18. His work is thus an expression of His divine
majesty. The community which confesses Him is freed from the Sabbath as He is.

In the story of the healing of the man born blind (Jn. 9:1-41) we read that on
a Sabbath [222] Jesus spat on the ground, kneaded the spittle into clay, and put this
on the eyes of the blind man to restore his sight, v. 6 f. Kneading, however, is
listed expressly among the 39 chief tasks forbidden on the Sabbath, Shab. 7, 2.
Since Jesus obviously does not keep the Sabbath, [223] He can only be a sinner in
the eyes of the Pharisees, v. 16. But others ask whether a sinner can do such
works, so that a σχίσμα arises among the Jews, v. 16. Here, too, Jesus' act on
the Sabbath is an expression of His work as the One whom God has sent and
who is the φῶς τοῦ κόσμου, 9:5; 8:12. Face to face with Him the decision is
made as to who is blind and who sees, 9:39-41. Thus the works of God are
manifest in the healings of Jesus on the Sabbath, 9:3. Church and Synagogue are
separated from one another by confession of Him on the one side and on the
other a passionate rejection of His work which sets aside the Law. [224]

3. The Sabbath in the Christian Churches.

Acc. to the unanimous witness of all four Evangelists Jesus was crucified on a Friday,
Mk. 15:42; Mt. 27:62; Lk. 23:54; Jn. 19:31, 42, [225] and rose again from the dead the

---

[219] On the division of the saying cf. Bultmann J., 208.
[220] On the superseding of the Sabbath by circumcision → 14, 35 ff. and the material in
Str.-B., II, 487 f.
[221] Cf. the saying of R. El'azar b'Azariah (c. 100): "If circumcision, which affects one
of the 248 members of a man, supersedes the Sabbath, how much more must his whole body
(when in mortal danger) supersede the Sabbath." bYoma, 85b, cf. Str.-B., II, 488 and the
Rabb. par. there.
[222] The observation that the healing took place on the Sabbath is again made later in
v. 14. Cf. → n. 208.
[223] The Rabb. discussed what eye ailments might be treated by ointment on the Sabbath,
bAZ, 28b. But they always kept to the principle that healings were permissible only where
there was acute danger, cf. Str.-B., II, 533 f.
[224] Cf. L. Goppelt, "Christentum u. Judt. im ersten u. zweiten Jhdt.," BFTh, II, 55
(1954), 46 f. For the Jews Jesus was sabbati destructor, Tert. De Spectaculis, 30.
[225] Cf. Jeremias, op. cit. (→ n. 84), 10. The Synoptists and Jn. seem to vary as to the
date of this Friday.

first day of the week, Mk. 16:2; Mt. 28:1; Lk. 24:1; Jn. 20:1, 19. [226] The Chr. community gathers for worship the first day of the week (1 C. 16:2; Ac. 20:7) to keep the day of the resurrection as the κυριακὴ ἡμέρα, Rev. 1:10. [227] Sunday, whose origin reaches back into the very earliest days of the Church, [228] is everywhere celebrated in the Gentile churches.

The Jewish Christian churches, which still remained within Judaism, clung at first to observance of the Law and the Sabbath. The discussions in Matthew's Gospel with their biblical quotations and dominical sayings show that the Sabbath question was by no means irrelevant for Jewish Christian congregations, → n. 195. Furthermore Mt. 24:20 offers an example of the keeping of the Sabbath by Jewish Christians. Whereas in the Synoptic apocalypse Mk. 13:18 says that in the dreadful events of the last time believers should pray that the disaster will not strike in winter, the corresponding saying in Mt. 24:20 reads: προσεύχεσθε δὲ ἵνα μὴ γένηται ἡ φυγὴ ὑμῶν χειμῶνος μηδὲ σαββάτῳ. It is true that the Rabbis regarded flight as legitimate on the Sabbath when there was danger to life. [229]

---

[226] The very oldest confession in 1 C. 15:3-5 already has the note: ὅτι ἐγήγερται τῇ ἡμέρᾳ τῇ τρίτῃ. This τῇ ἡμέρᾳ τῇ τρίτῃ can hardly have been taken from the proof from Scripture, since Jon. 2:1 occurs for the first time only in the later Mt. 12:40 and is not in Lk. 11:30; Mk. 8:12; Mt. 16:4, nor is Hos. 6:2 adduced anywhere at all in the NT. Hence κατὰ τὰς γραφάς in 1 C. 15:4 refers to the resurrection rather than the third day, cf. Ps. 16:8-11 in Ac. 2:25-28. In spite of differences in dating the Passover the Synoptists and John agree that the crucifixion was followed by the day of rest and the resurrection of Christ took place on the first day of the week. Here, then, we must have a very old chronological sequence which is in accordance with the historical facts. Jesus was crucified on a Friday, and the first appearance of the Risen Lord was on the Sunday following. Cf. also H. Lietzmann, *Gesch. d. alten Kirche,* I² (1953), 60 f. On the dating of the three days → II, 948-950; H. Grass, *Ostergeschehen u. Osterberichte* (1956), 127-138; B. M. Metzger, "A Suggestion concerning the Meaning of 1 C. 15:4b," JThSt, NF, 8 (1957), 118-123.

[227] → III, 1096, 16-36. In the Talmud (bAZ, 6b, 7a) there is ref. to a יוֹם נוֹצְרִי, the "day of the Nazarene," a Jewish transl. of κυριακὴ ἡμέρα. Cf. W. Bacher, "Ein Name des Sonntags im Talmud," ZNW, 6 (1905), 202.

[228] In this context we cannot go into the development of the Chr. observance of Sunday, for which Barn., 15, 9; Did., 14, 1; Ign. Magn., 9, 1; Just. Apol., I, 67, 3 and 7; Dial., 24, 1; 41, 4; 138, 1 and Pliny (the Younger) Ep., X, 96, 7 are also early witnesses. A contributory factor was undoubtedly the fact that from the 1st cent. B.C. the seven-day week named after the planets had been increasingly adopted in the Hell.-Roman world. The Day of Saturn was generally regarded as an unlucky day, while the Sunday which followed it was a particularly good day. Cf. on this Schürer, 1-66; F. Boll, "Hebdomas," Pauly-W., 7 (1912), 2547-2578; Colson. On the development of the Chr. Sunday cf. T. Zahn, "Gesch. d. Sonntags, vornehmlich in d. alten Kirche," *Skizzen aus dem Leben d. alten Kirche*² (1894), 196-240; Deissmann LO, 304-309; S. V. McCasland, "The Origin of the Lord's Day," JBL, 49 (1930), 65-82; J. Boehmer, *Der chr. Sonntag nach Ursprung u. Gesch.* (1931); P. Cotton, *From Sabbath to Sunday* (1933); F. J. Dölger, "Die Planetenwoche d. griech.-röm. Antike u. d. chr. Sonntag," Ant. Christ., VI (1950), 202-238; P. Carrington, *The Primitive Christian Calendar* (1952), 38; Lietzmann, *op. cit.* (→ n. 226), 60 f.; Cullmann Gottesdienst, 14 f.; Bauer, 106-110; J. Nedbal, *Sabbat u. Sonntag im NT,* Diss. Vienna (1956); H. Riesenfeld, "Sabbat et Jour du Seigneur," *NT Essays in Memory of T. W. Manson* (1959), 210-217. Riesenfeld tries to explain the development of the Chr. Sunday by saying that the first Christians mostly took part first in the observance of the Jewish Sabbath and then went on to meet as the Chr. congregation in their homes. This worship was held on the night of the Sabbath and the first day, so that Christians were keeping Sunday rather than the Sabbath. But there is not the necessary support in the sources for this hypothesis. On the ethical question of keeping Sunday holy cf. K. Barth, K.D., III, 4 (1951), 51-79 (C.D., III, 4 [1961], 47-72).

[229] Cf. Tanch. מסעי 247a, Str.-B., I, 952 f. → 14, 24 ff.

But if desecration of the Sabbath was required in face of the terrors of the last time, this could only mean an escalation of the catastrophe. [230] As Jewish Christians still sacrificed in the temple (Mt. 5:23) and paid the temple tax (Mt. 17:24-27), so they kept the Sabbath holy in obedience to the Law. [231]

On the other hand, in the Gentile Christian churches, which arose out of the Hellenistic Christian and Pauline mission, the Sabbath commandment was no longer regarded as binding.

> Judaisers who came into the Galatian churches from without tried to convince Gentile Christians that only by joining Israel and accepting circumcision and the yoke of the Law could they receive full salvation. The apostle Paul passionately resisted these efforts and in relation to the Jewish calendar of feasts [232] he argued that if the Galatian Christians pledged themselves to observe it they would be relapsing into the paganism in which they were enslaved to the demonic powers which rule in the cosmos, Gl. 4:8-10. To be ὑπὸ νόμον (Gl. 4:5) means the same as bondage ὑπὸ τὰ στοιχεῖα τοῦ κόσμου (Gl. 4:3). If, however, Christ is the end of the Law (R. 10:4), this implies the end of the Sabbath commandment whose observance was necessary to salvation.

A peculiar combination of Gnostic ideas and Jewish legalism is to be found in the teaching of the "philosophers" in Colossae, cf. Col. 2:8. [233] The → στοιχεῖα τοῦ κόσμου to which man is subject by birth and destiny are to be served not only in the θρησκεία τῶν ἀγγέλων (Col. 2:18 → III, 157, 18 ff.) but above all in the scrupulous observance of ascetic dietary regulations, of new moons, and of Sabbaths (Col. 2:16). [234] When these days are singled out and their laws carefully kept, the course of nature is followed as determined by the movement of the stars. But this means that the Sabbath is subordinate to worship of the στοιχεῖα τοῦ κόσμου from which the particular days and times receive their content and significance. [235] Face to face with this syncretistic heresy the apostle reminds the Colossian Christians that they are dead with Christ to the elements of the world. It is thus impossible to desire to keep the laws and demands of these elements, Col. 2:20. With liberation from bondage to the στοιχεῖα τοῦ κόσμου the δόγματα (→ II, 231, 22 ff.) are also set aside, so that the Christian community is definitively freed from the Sabbath commandment — no matter whether this is based on the supposed necessity of the Law to salvation or on the controlling power of cosmic forces. [236]

---

[230] There is little to be said for the conjecture of K. Boll, *Aus d. Offenbarung d. Johannes* (1914), 134, n. 1 that the idea of the Day of Saturn as an unlucky day lies behind Mt. 24:20.

[231] Cf. also Braun, II, 69, n. 4. That Jewish Christians considered how they ought to keep the Sabbath as Christians may be seen clearly from the debates in Mt. 12:1-11. The commandment of love and mercy is higher than the legal ordinance, Mt. 12:7.

[232] The ἡμέραι of Gl. 4:10 are in the first instance Sabbaths, though they include other days too, e.g., the Day of Atonement.

[233] Cf. Bornkamm, *op. cit.* (→ n. 44), 139-156; Dib. Gefbr.³, Exc. on Col. 2:23; Goppelt, *op. cit.* (→ n. 224), 137-140.

[234] ἑορτή, νεομηνία and σάββατα: cf. Hos. 2:13; Ez. 45:17; 1 Ch. 23:31; 2 Ch. 2:3; 31:3; Jub. 1:14; T. Ber., 3, 11; Just. Dial., 8, 4.

[235] Bornkamm, *op. cit.,* 148.

[236] Cf. R. 14:5 f. The Roman church obviously included both Jewish Christians who clung to the Sabbath and Gentile Christians who did not keep it. Sabbath observance can be allowed by the apostle when it is not viewed as if obedience to the Law were necessary to salvation.

D. The Sabbath in the Early Church.

1. Sabbath and Sunday.

In the Chr. Churches Sunday was observed as the day of the Lord's resurrection : κατὰ κυριακὴν δὲ κυρίου συναχθέντες κλάσατε ἄρτον καὶ εὐχαριστήσατε, Did., 14, 1; διὸ καὶ ἄγομεν τὴν ἡμέραν τὴν ὀγδόην εἰς εὐφροσύνην, ἐν ᾗ καὶ ὁ Ἰησοῦς ἀνέστη ἐκ νεκρῶν καὶ φανερωθεὶς ἀνέβη εἰς οὐρανούς, Barn., 15, 9. [237] Celebration of the first day of the week was in conscious opposition to the Jewish Sabbath, which had now been completely abandoned : μηκέτι σαββατίζοντες, ἀλλὰ κατὰ κυριακὴν ζῶντες, Ign. Mg., 9, 1. [238] Jewish περὶ τὰ σάββατα δεισιδαιμονία, with prohibition of foods, circumcision, fasting and observance of the new moon, was regarded by Chr. polemics as among the things which are καταγέλαστα καὶ οὐδενὸς ἄξια λόγου, Dg., 4, 1. Indeed, is it not blasphemy to maintain that God forbids us ἐν τῇ τῶν σαββάτων ἡμέρᾳ καλόν τι ποιεῖν, Dg., 4, 3 ? [239] Orig. rejects the Jewish Sabbath because it cannot possibly be kept lit. οὐδενὸς ζῴου δυναμένου δι' ὅλης καθέζεσθαι τῆς ἡμέρας καὶ ἀκινητεῖν ἀπὸ τοῦ καθέζεσθαι, Princ., IV, 3, 2. Acc. to the apocr. Acts the apostles emphasise in their missionary preaching that the Sabbath is done away. Thus in *Preaching of Peter* the apostle says of the Jews that without true righteousness they worshipped angels and archangels, the month and the moon. But ἐὰν μὴ σελήνη φανῇ, σάββατον οὐκ ἄγουσι τὸ λεγόμενον πρῶτον οὐδὲ νεομηνίαν ἄγουσιν οὔτε ἄζυμα οὔτε μεγάλην ἡμέραν. [240] Paul disputing with the Jews said : *Christus enim, in quem patres vestri manus inmiserunt, et sabbatum eorum dissolvebat et ieiunia et ferias et doctrinas hominum dissolvebat et ceteras traditiones.* [241]

Efforts were made to prove the superiority of the Lord's Day over the Sabbath with the help of Scripture. Thus Barn., 2, 5 quotes Is. 1:11-13 to show that God cannot endure new moons and Sabbaths and does not want the sacrificial cultus. It is deduced from this that the cultus and sacrifices are rightly abolished in order that the καινὸς νόμος τοῦ κυρίου ἡμῶν Ἰησοῦ Χριστοῦ may replace the old Law, 2, 6. Yet the OT Sabbath commandment is more positively evaluated in c. 15 of Barn., where its content is reinterpreted with the help of apoc. speculations, → 19, 23 ff.: [242] What does it mean that God accomplished the creation of the world in six days and finished it on the seventh [243] (Gn. 2:2)? τοῦτο δὲ λέγει, ὅτι ἐν ἑξακισχιλίοις ἔτεσι συντελέσει κύριος τὰ σύμπαντα, for one day is for Him a thousand yrs., 15, 4. And how are we to understand the statement καὶ κατέπαυσεν τῇ ἡμέρᾳ τῇ ἑβδόμῃ (Gn. 2:3)? τοῦτο λέγει· ὅταν ἐλθὼν ὁ υἱὸς αὐτοῦ καταργήσει τὸν καιρὸν τοῦ ἀνόμου καὶ κρινεῖ τοὺς ἀσεβεῖς καὶ ἀλλάξει τὸν ἥλιον καὶ τὴν σελήνην καὶ τοὺς ἀστέρας, τότε καλῶς καταπαύσεται ἐν τῇ ἡμέρᾳ τῇ ἑβδόμῃ, 15, 5. As God's creating and resting are referred to the cosmic week and the Sabbath which concludes it, so the commandment to keep the Sabbath holy is to be fulfilled in the future age of con-

---

[237] On Sunday → n. 228 and the examples in Wnd. Barn., 384 f.

[238] Probably Ign. is arguing against false teachers who wanted to restore the Sabbath. Cf. Bau. Ign., 226, ad loc.; also *Rechtgläubigkeit u. Ketzerei im ältesten Christentum* (1934), 92.

[239] Cf. Mk. 3:4 and par.

[240] Cl. Al. Strom., VI, 5, 41; cf. Klostermann, op. cit. (→ n. 183), 14. On τὸ σάββατον τὸ λεγόμενον πρῶτον → n. 183.

[241] Act. Verc., 1. Acc. to Act. Phil., 15 the high-priest accused Philip of believing in Jesus who καὶ τὸν νόμον καὶ τὸν ναὸν κατέλυσεν, καὶ τὸν καθαρισμὸν τὸν διὰ Μωσέως κατήργησεν καὶ τὰ σάββατα καὶ τὰς νεομηνίας, ὅτι φησὶν οὐκ εἰσὶν ὑπὸ θεοῦ τεταγμέναι.

[242] Cf. Wnd. Barn., 381-385. Cf. also J. Daniélou, "La typologie millénariste de la semaine dans le christianisme primitif," *Vigiliae Christianae*, 2 (1948), 1-16.

[243] Acc. to Gn. 2:2 LXX God finished creation on the sixth day (→ n. 25), but Barn. thinks nothing of letting Him finish His work on the seventh day.

summation. Now no one can genuinely keep holy the day which God has sanctified, 15, 6. But we shall hallow it in genuine rest when there is no ἀνομία and everything is established anew by the κύριος, τότε δυνησόμεθα αὐτὴν ἁγιάσαι, αὐτοὶ ἁγιασθέντες πρῶτον, 15, 7. In contrast to this positive apoc. interpretation is the sharp repudiation of the present Sabbath on the basis once again of Is. 1:13 : τὰς νεομηνίας ὑμῶν καὶ τὰ σάββατα οὐκ ἀνέχομαι. From this one must deduce : οὐ τὰ νῦν σάββατα ἐμοὶ δεκτά but only the beginning of the eighth day is pleasing to God, which He will make as the beginning of another world, 15, 8. Thus Christians keep the eighth day, i.e., the beginning of the new week, as the dawning of the new creation at whose commencement Jesus rose from the dead and after His appearances ascended up to heaven, 15, 9. [244]

2. The Jewish Week in the Christian Church.

Although the Chr. Church freed itself from the Sabbath it adopted the Jewish week [245] and kept almost unchanged the Jewish system of enumeration, counting the days up to the Sabbath [246] and giving special prominence only to the Lord's Day. Thus in the writings of the ancient Church we often find σάββατον/σάββατα in the sense of "week," and Friday is called the day of preparation even though it no longer has significance as such. In a statement designed to emphasise the distinction from Jewish fasting, for example, the Jewish division of the week is presupposed : αἱ νηστεῖαι ὑμῶν μὴ ἔστωσαν μετὰ τῶν ὑποκριτῶν· νηστεύουσι γὰρ δευτέρᾳ σαββάτων καὶ πέμπτῃ· ὑμεῖς δὲ νηστεύσατε τετράδα καὶ παρασκευήν, Did., 8, 1. It is said that Polycarp suffered martyrdom on a σάββατον μέγα, [247] Mart. Pol., 8, 1; 21, 1. One might also mention as instances of the common usage : τὰ δικαστήρια ὑμῶν γινέσθω δευτέρᾳ σαββάτων in Const. Ap., II, 47; δευτέρᾳ σαββάτων ... τῇ τρίτῃ τοῦ σαββάτου ... τῇ δὲ τετράδι ... τῇ πέμπτῃ ... παρασκευῆς οὔσης, ibid., V, 14; οἶδεν αὐτὸς καὶ τῆς νηστείας τὰ αἰνίγματα τῶν ἡμερῶν τούτων, τῆς τετράδος καὶ τῆς παρασκευῆς λέγω, Cl. Al. Strom., VII, 12, 75. [248] The sixth day is also called προσάββατον, Epiph. Haer., 70, 12, 3; 75, 6, 2, and the seventh is the Sabbath. Thus the Church Order of Hippolytus, c. 45 f. lays down that catechumens approaching the day of baptism should bathe on the fifth day of the week, fast on the day of preparation, assemble on the Sabbath to spend the night in fasting, and then receive baptism early on Easter Day. [249]

3. The Sabbath in Jewish Christianity.

Jewish Christian groups clung to the Sabbath and appealed to Jesus Himself in support. He is said to have taught that only by fasting can one find entry into the kingdom of God, καὶ ἐὰν μὴ σαββατίσητε τὸ σάββατον, οὐκ ὄψεσθε τὸν πατέρα. [250] When

---

[244] The special distinction of the eighth day and its superiority to the seventh are often stressed by Just. in Dial., and circumcision on the eighth day is seen as a type pointing to the Lord's Day, Dial., 24, 1; 41, 4-7. 138, 1-5 says of the eight members of Noah's family saved from the flood, σύμβολον εἶχον τῆς ἀριθμῷ μὲν ὀγδόης ἡμέρας, ἐν ᾗ ἐφάνη ὁ Χριστὸς ἡμῶν ἀπὸ νεκρῶν ἀναστάς, δυνάμει δ' ἀεὶ πρώτης ὑπαρχούσης. Trypho, however, demands of Just.: πρῶτον μὲν περιτεμοῦ, εἶτα φύλαξον, ὡς νενόμισται, τὸ σάββατον καὶ τὰς ἑορτὰς καὶ τὰς νεομηνίας τοῦ θεοῦ, Dial., 8, 4.

[245] Schürer, passim.

[246] Already in the NT : 1 C. 16:2; Ac. 20:7; Mk. 16:2 par.; Jn. 20:1, 19.

[247] On the "great Sabbath" → n. 160 and A. Strobel, "Die Passaerwartung in Lk. 17:20 f.," ZNW, 49 (1958), 184, n. 103.

[248] Schürer, 8-13 for further examples.

[249] Hennecke², 578 f.; H. Achelis, "Die ältesten Quellen d. orientalischen Kirchenrechtes," TU, 6, 4 (1891), 93.

[250] P. Oxy., I, 1 = Klostermann, op. cit. (→ n. 189), 19. Cf. W. Bauer, Das Leben Jesu

Jesus had to break the Sabbath (→ 21, 20 ff.), acc. to Jewish Chr. thought there were cogent reasons which justified His action. Thus Ev. Hebr. touches up the story of healing in Mk. 3:1-6 and par. The sick man alludes expressly to his urgent need and asks Jesus for help on the Sabbath.[251] To be obedient to the Law Jesus could not deny this request. In distinction from this account the apocr. Gospels which arose in Gentile Chr. circles pay no heed to the Sabbath commandment. In the childhood story in Thomas 2:2-5[252] the boy Jesus makes twelve sparrows of moist clay on a Sabbath. When a Jew complains to Joseph that Jesus is desecrating the Sabbath and Joseph takes Him to task, Jesus unconcernedly claps His hands and tells the sparrows to fly off. The birds fly away noisily and the Jews are terrified.[253]

The ideas of Jewish Chr. groups which keep the Sabbath are influenced and moulded to a large degree by syncretistic Gnostic notions. In the teaching of these sectarian societies Sabbath observance is usually subordinate to the worship of angels and constellations whose course fixes human destiny and thus demands the careful observance of special days. The fathers tell us little about this Jewish Chr. view of the Sabbath. Orig. says that Dositheus of Samaria ordered ἐπὶ τοῦ σχήματος, οὗ ἂν καταληφθῇ τις ἐν τῇ ἡμέρᾳ τοῦ σαββάτου, μένειν μέχρις ἑσπέρας, Princ., IV, 3, 2. Filastrius says of Cerinthus : *Docet autem circumcidi et sabbatizari et Christum nondum surrexisse a mortuis, sed resurrecturum adnuntiat,* Haereses, 36 (CSEL, 38, 19). In Ps.-Clem. Hom., 2, 35, 3 there is ref. to a Sabbath festival of the Simonians which they were oddly supposed to hold only every eleven days.[254] Acc. to Eus. Hist. Eccl., III, 27, 5 the Ebionites kept the Sabbath as a day of rest but celebrated Sunday too.[255] Epiph. Haer., 30, 2, 2, however, ref. only to their keeping of the Sabbath along with the Jews : ἐν τῷ νόμῳ τοῦ Ἰουδαϊσμοῦ προσανέχειν κατὰ σαββατισμὸν καὶ κατὰ τὴν περιτομὴν καὶ κατὰ τὰ ἄλλα πάντα, ὁσάπερ παρὰ Ἰουδαίοις καὶ Σαμαρείταις ἐπιτελεῖται, Haer., 30, 2, 2.[256] The position of the Nazoraeans between the Jews and the Christians is defined by Epiph. as follows : ἐν τούτῳ δὲ μόνον πρὸς Ἰουδαίους διαφέρονται καὶ Χριστιανούς, Ἰουδαίοις μὲν μὴ συμφωνοῦντες διὰ τὸ εἰς Χριστὸν πεπιστευκέναι, Χριστιανοῖς δὲ μὴ ὁμογνωμονοῦντες διὰ τὸ ἔτι νόμῳ πεπεδῆσθαι, περιτομῇ τε καὶ σαββάτῳ καὶ τοῖς ἄλλοις, Haer., 29, 7, 5. Another product of syncretistic Jewish Christianity was Elchasai who in a teaching composed of very different elements adopted from Judaism the demand for circumcision and sanctifying of the Sabbath, cf. Epiph. Haer., 29, 3, 5. He enjoined his followers : ἔτι δὲ τιμήσατε τὴν ἡμέραν σαββάτου, because the Sabbath is one of the days which must be observed carefully on account of the movement of the stars, Hipp. Ref., IX, 16, 3. For the

---

im Zeitalter d. nt.lichen Apkr. (1909), 352; Jeremias, *op. cit.* (→ n. 184), 19 and in Hennecke³, I, 67. This saying is also found in the Coptic Gospel of Thomas, cf. J. Leipoldt, "Ein neues Ev. ?" ThLZ, 83 (1958), 486, though Saying 28 here is probably to be taken fig., *ibid.,* 496; Hb. 4:9.

[251] Klostermann, 8 and → n. 189. Cf. also H. J. Schoeps, *Theol. u. Gesch. d. Judenchristentums* (1949), 144.

[252] Hennecke³, I, 293 f.

[253] In the Gospel of Philip found in Nag-Hamadi Saying 8 speaks of fruits coming forth daily and "on the Sabbath too [the power (of growth)] is [not] unfruitful." Cf. H. M. Schenke, "Das Ev. nach Phil.," ThLZ, 84 (1959), 6. There is also ref. to the Sabbath in Codex Jung (32:18-25), though it is fig. the day of redemption : On a Sabbath Jesus rescued a sheep which had fallen into a pit "that ye may know what the Sabbath is on which it is not seemly that salvation should be idle." Cf. H. M. Schenke, *Die Herkunft d. sogenannten Evangelium veritatis* (1959), 48.

[254] "The par. in Recg., I, 20 has been altered and the expression removed. The Hom. text is thus primary and goes back to the original. It is possible that the original author (c. 260) took the idea from a Simonian tradition" [G. Strecker in a letter]. σάββατον occurs elsewhere in Ps.-Clem. only at Hom., 19, 22, 4.

[255] If they keep Sunday they are probably orthodox rather than heretical Jewish Christians. Cf. Schoeps, *op. cit.* (→ n. 251), 139.

[256] Cf. also Schoeps, *op. cit.* (→ n. 251), 137.

same reason one should not begin anything the third day after the Sabbath, *loc. cit.*
As the Chr. community parted from the Synagogue on the question of the Sabbath,
so the Catholic Church parted from heretical Jewish Christianity which clung to the
Sabbath. The Catholic Church kept Sunday as the day of the Lord's resurrection and
warned Jewish Christians not to set the Sabbath above this, Didasc., 27.[257] As Judaism
both in the homeland and in the Diaspora was united in keeping the Sabbath, so the
whole Church of Jesus Christ kept the Lord's Day as a day of joy and jubilation : τὴν
δὲ τοῦ ἡλίου ἡμέραν κοινῇ πάντες τὴν συνέλευσιν ποιούμεθα, ἐπειδὴ πρώτη
ἐστὶν ἡμέρα, ἐν ᾗ ὁ θεὸς τὸ σκότος καὶ τὴν ὕλην τρέψας κόσμον ἐποίησε, καὶ
Ἰησοῦς Χριστὸς ὁ ἡμέτερος σωτὴρ τῇ αὐτῇ ἡμέρᾳ ἐκ νεκρῶν ἀνέστη, Just. Apol.,
I, 67, 7.

† σαββατισμός.

The word σαββατισμός, which occurs in non-biblical writings only in Plut.
Superst., 3 (II, 166a), is not found in the OT and is used only once in the NT
at Hb. 4:9. In connection with the exposition of Ps. 95:7-11 in Hb. 3:7-4:13 the
author learns from Ps. 95:11 that the wilderness generation did not enter into
κατάπαυσις. Rest was denied them because of unbelief and disobedience, though
there was rest as a blessing of salvation from the time that God rested from His
work of creation, Hb. 4:3-5. By combining Ps. 95:7 and 11 the writer shows that
the promise of κατάπαυσις is still outstanding and thus applies to the people of
God. The word κατάπαυσις in the LXX denotes on the one side the gift of
God which Israel would experience in the land as rest from all its enemies round
about (Dt. 12:9 f. cf. also Dt. 25:19; Jos. 21:44[42]; 3 Βασ. 8:56; ψ 94:11)[1] and
on the other the Sabbath rest which is to be observed as a cessation from all work
on the seventh day (Ex. 34:21; 35:2; 2 Macc. 15:1). Thus in a kind of deduction
Hb. 4:9 can speak, not of κατάπαυσις, but of the σαββατισμός which still remains for the people of God and which will bring a perfect Sabbath when man
can cease from all his works as God did from His after completing creation,
Hb. 4:10.[2] This rest of which Hb. speaks is related, however, neither to possession
of the land nor to the Sabbath of the OT and Jewish Law. It is a purely heavenly
blessing towards which the pilgrim people of God moves.[3] This eschatological
understanding of σαββατισμός is not reached by exegesis of Ps. 95. Expectation
of heavenly rest is rooted in apocalyptic and Gnostic ideas which make perfect
rest the goal of the way to redemption.[4] The author of Hb. bases this hope of
heavenly rest on his exposition of Ps. 95:7-11 and Gn. 2:2 and he gives his discussion a hortatory thrust. Since the people of God is moving towards the σαββα-

---

[257] Cf. H. Achelis-J. Flemming, "Die syr. Didaskalia," TU, 25, 2 (1904), 136 f.

σαββατισμός. [1] = מְנוּחָה, cf. G. v. Rad, "Es ist noch eine Ruhe vorhanden dem
Volke Gottes," ZdZ, 11 (1933), 104-111; also *Theol. d. AT,* I (1957), 223.

[2] Cf. שַׁבּוּת for perfect Sabbath rest, Shab., 10, 6; cf. Ab. R. Nat., 1 (1c): "The day of the
Sabbath in Ps. 92:1 — this is the day which is wholly Sabbath (rest), in which there is no
eating or drinking, buying or selling ; but the righteous will sit there with crowns on their
heads and delight in the radiance of the shᵉkhina" (Str.-B., III, 687). Part of this future
blessing of salvation is experienced by Israel already on the Sabbath. Cf. the statement in
the Sabbath prayers (W. Staerk, *Altjüd. Liturgische Gebete²,* KlT, 58 [1930], 27):
וְגַם בִּמְנוּחָתוֹ לֹא יִשְׁכְּנוּ עֲרֵלִים כִּי לְיִשְׂרָאֵל עַמְּךָ נְתַתּוֹ בְּאַהֲבָה.

[3] Cf. E. Käsemann, "Das wandernde Gottesvolk," FRL, 55³ (1959), 40-45.

[4] Cf. Rev. 14:13 : ἀναπαήσονται ἐκ τῶν κόπων αὐτῶν, PRE1, 18 (9d) → 20, n. 155.

τισμός prepared for it, no one must fall away in unbelief or disobedience, but : σπουδάσωμεν οὖν εἰσελθεῖν εἰς ἐκείνην τὴν κατάπαυσιν (4:11), for the promise is given : εἰσερχόμεθα γὰρ εἰς τὴν κατάπαυσιν οἱ πιστεύσαντες (4:3).

Lohse

---

† Σαδδουκαῖος   → Φαρισαῖος.

Contents : A. Usage. B. Sadduceeism in Judaism : I. Origin of the Term Σαδδουκαῖος : 1. Zadokites and Sadducees ; 2. Zadok and Boethos ; 3. Sadducee as the Term for a Political Group ; II. The Sadducees of Jerusalem : 1. Sadducees and Hasmoneans ; 2. The Sadducees under the Herods and the Romans ; III. Sadduceeism as a Religious Phenomenon : 1. Sadducean Dogmatics ; 2. The Sadducean View of the Law. C. The Sadducees in the New Testament : I. The Synoptic Gospels ; II. Acts.

A. Usage.

Σαδδουκαῖος occurs in the NT and Jos. only in the plur. Σαδδουκαῖοι. [1] It presupposes what is obviously a linguistically late Heb. construct in the form of an adj.

In Act. Phil., 148 the goal of the way of redemption is stated : θέλετε ἀναπαῆναι ἐν τῇ ἀναπαύσει τοῦ θεοῦ, cf. Barn., 15 → 31, 27 ff. Cf. also L. Troje, "Sanbat" in R. Reitzenstein, *Die Vorgeschichte d. chr. Taufe* (1929), 328-377; E. Käsemann, *op. cit.* (→ n. 3), 40-45.

Σ α δ δ ο υ κ α ῖ ο ς. Bibl.: V. Aptowitzer, *Die Parteipolitik d. Hasmonäerzeit* (1927); Bousset-Gressm., Index, *s.v.* "Sadduzäer"; G. H. Box, "Who were the Sadducees ?" Exp., 8, 15 (1918), 19 ff.; also "Scribes and Pharisees in the New Testament," *ibid.*, 401 ff.; A. E. Cowley, Art. "Sadducees" in EB, IV, 4234-4240; D. Eaton, Art. "Sadducees" in Hastings DB, IV, 349-352; B. D. Eerdmans, "Farizeën en Sadduceën," ThT, 48 (1914), 1-16; A. Geiger, *Urschrift u. Übers. d. Bibel²* (1928), 101-158; G. Hölscher, *Der Sadduzäismus* (1906); also Art. "Levi" in Pauly-W. 12 (1925), 2169-2208; J. Jeremias, *Jerusalem zur Zeit Jesu*, II B³ (1958), 95-100; J. Klausner, *Jesus v. Nazareth³* (1952); K. Kohler, Art. "Sadducees" in Jew. Enc., 10 (1909), 630-633; J. Z. Lauterbach, "The Pharisees and Their Teachings," HUCA, 6 (1929), 69-139; also "The Sadducees and Pharisees," *Rabbinic Essays* (1951), 23-48; also "A Significant Controversy between the Sadducees and the Pharisees," HUCA, 4 (1927), 173-205; R. Lescynsky, *Die Sadduzäer* (1912); J. W. Lightley, *Jewish Sects and Parties in the Time of Jesus* (1925); T. W. Manson, "Sadducee and Pharisee — The Origin and Significance of the Name," *Bulletin of the John Rylands Library*, 22 (1938), 144-159; Meyer Ursprung, II, 290-319; Moore, Index, *s.v.* "Sadducees"; H. Oort, "De oorsprong van den naam 'Sadduceën,'" ThT, 10 (1876), 605-617; H. Rasp, "Flavius Josephus u. d. jüd. Religionsparteien," ZNW, 23 (1924), 27-47; H. J. Schoeps, "Die Opposition gg. die Hasmonäer," ThLZ, 81 (1956), 663-670; K. Schubert, "Die jüd. u. judenchr. Sekten im Lichte d. Handschriftenfunde von 'En Fešḫa," *Zeitschr. f. kath. Theol.*, 74 (1952), 1-62; Schürer, II⁴, 475-489 (Bibl. 447-449); M. H. Segal, "Pharisees and Sadducees," Exp., 8, 13 (1917), 81 ff.; F. Sieffert, Art. "Pharisäer u. Sadduzäer" in RE³, 15, 264-292; E. Stauffer, "Probleme der Priestertradition," ThLZ, 81 (1956), 135-150; J. Wellhausen, *Die Pharisäer u. Sadduzäer* (1874).

[1] Pr.-Bauer⁵, *s.v.*

of origin or relation [2] צָדוֹקִי[3] though this occurs traditionally as צָדוֹקִי with the plur. צְדוֹקִים, fem. צְדוֹקִית plur. צְדוֹקִיוֹת.[4] The apocr. and pseudepigr. lit. known to us does not have Σαδδουκαῖος or צָדוֹקִי, though it occurs in the Rabb., mostly in the plur., e.g., Jad., 4, 6 f.;[5] Mak., 1, 6; Para, 3, 7; Nidda, 4, 2; bYoma, 19b. The rare sing. is found, e.g., in Er., 6, 2 and T. Para, 3, 7.[6] Jos. mentions the Σαδδουκαῖοι in Bell., 2, 119, 162-166; Ant., 13, 171 ff.; 293-298; 18, 11 and 16 f.; 20, 199; Vit., 10. The distribution in the NT is as follows : Mk. 12:18; Mt. 22:23; Lk. 20:27 (common to the Synoptics); Mt. 22:34; 3:7; 6:1; 16:6; 16:11 f. (peculiar to Mt.); Ac. 4:1; 5:17; 23:6 ff. Thus far Σαδδουκαῖος has not been found outside Jewish and Chr. writings. Its interpretation is complicated by the fact that it is obviously referred to different Jewish groups and used polemically and disparagingly not only in the NT but also in Jos. and Rabb. sources.

B. Sadduceeism in Judaism.

I. Origin of the Term Σαδδουκαῖος.

1. Zadokites and Sadducees.

a. The term Σαδδουκαῖος, צָדוֹקִי goes back to the proper name צָדוֹק LXX Σαδδουκ [7] and can be replaced by an equivalent בֶּן צָדוֹק "son of Zadok," "Zadokite." The compound בְּנֵי צָדוֹק "sons of Zadok" or "Zadokites" corresponds in sense to the plur. צְדוֹקִים [8] The question is constantly put, therefore, whether the Sadducees are in some form historically related to the Zadokites already known to us from the OT. [9]

b. The Zadokites derive from Zadok, one of the ruling priests under David, cf. 2 S. 15:24, 27, 29, 35; 17:15; 19:12. In the battle of David's succession Zadok was one of the supporters of Solomon and with the latter's victory in 965 B.C. he became the chief priest in Jerusalem, 1 K. 1:32 etc.;[10] his rival Abiathar, who opposed the new king and supported Adonijah, was banished, 1 K. 2:35. Like their royal masters, the descendants of Zadok seem to have established a priestly dynasty in Jerusalem which was able during the cultic reforms under Josiah (c. 623 B.C.) to gain a hierarchical and ideological victory over the priests outside Jerusalem, the later Levites → IV, 239 ff. This is the historical starting-pt. for the demand of Yahweh in Ezekiel's reconstruction :

---

[2] On the nature of this construct cf. G. Beer-R. Meyer, *Hbr. Grammatik*, I (1952) § 41, 4.

[3] There is a secondary gemination in צַדּוּקִי, *ibid.* § 28, 3.

[4] T. Nidda, 5, 3 with בנות הצדוקין, 5, 2.

[5] In Jad., 4, 8 צדוקי גלילי "a Galilean Sadducee" is a censorious emendation for מין גלילי "a Galilean heretic," cf. on this Schürer, II, 452, n. 5; G. Lisowsky, *Jadajim* (1956), 79 f.

[6] In T. Para, 3, 7 צדוקי is par. to כוהן גדול and denotes the high-priest by Sadducean appointment, → 53, 15 ff.

[7] For the Tiberian *ṣāḏōq* the pronunciation *saddūq* is attested by LXX, Jos., and Asc. Is. 2:5; the Cod de Rossi also has the form צָדוּק or צָדוֹק in Pea, 2, 4; Ter., 10:9; Shab., 24, 5; Pes., 3, 6; 7, 2; 10, 3. Cf. Schürer, II, 477, n. 13.

[8] → n. 2. The older view that Σαδδουκαῖος derives from Heb. צָדִיק "righteous" — cf. already Epiph. Haer., 14, 2, 1 (GCS, 25, 207) — has now been generally abandoned, cf. Schürer, II, 477, n. 10 f.

[9] The historical connection between the Zadokites and the Sadducees was first argued in 1857 by A. Geiger ; Wellhausen, 45-51 took up the same idea with better arguments ; cf. also Hölscher Sadduzäismus, 102-104; Schürer, II, 477-480; Schl. Gesch. Isr., 165, n. 151; Str.-B., IV, 339; M. Noth, *Gesch. Isr.*[2] (1954), 335, n. 2. The connection is contested by Meyer Ursprung, II, 290 f., and H. J. Schoeps, *Urgemeinde, Judenchristentum, Gnosis* (1956), 71 does not think the pre-exilic Zadokites had any influence on later Judaism.

[10] Cf. P. Gaechter, "Petrus u. seine Zeit," *Nt.liche Studien* (1958), 64-74 [G. Bertram].

"But the levitical priests, the sons of Zadok (בְּנֵי צָדוֹק), that kept the charge of my sanctuary when the children of Israel went astray from me, they shall come near to me to minister unto me" (44:15). [11] In the same context the former priests of the sanctuaries outside Jerusalem, because of their transgression, are degraded to a lower class as Levites, Ez. 44:10-14 cf. 40:46; 43:19; 48:11. In fact it was a son of Zadok, Joshua ben Josedech, who filled the reconstituted office of high-priest in Jerusalem after the exile. [12] Nevertheless, it would seem to be only in Babylon in the 5th cent. B.C. that there arose a true priestly hierarchy expressed esp. in a corresponding genealogy, and this established itself in Jerusalem only after Ezra, i.e., in the 4th cent. [13] The priestly aristocracy, which appoints the high-priest for life, now claims to consist of the sons of Aaron. [14] Within them are two genealogical strands, the one deriving from Ithamar and the other from Phinehas, the son of Eleazar and grandson of Aaron. [15] The Zadokites descended from Phinehas acc. to 1 Ch. 5:29-34. [16] We do not know how the two groups divided the priestly rule of Jerusalem in the 4th and 3rd cent. [17] It may be said with certainty, however, that c. 200 the Zadokites were at the head of the hierocracy. There is an excellent witness to their position in Jesus bEleazar bSirach, c. 190 B.C. The son of Sirach includes Phinehas, the ancestor of the Zadokites, alongside David in his praise of famous men, Sir. 45:25. The sons of David are the legitimate holders of secular power, the sons of Aaron the legitimate holders of spiritual power. The position of the Zadokites is esp. clear when one realises that the whole panegyric culminates with the high-priest Simon, in whose praise and honour it was manifestly composed, 50:1-21. Furthermore, the Heb. text of Sir. contains in an appendix a song of thanksgiving which was probably part of the liturgical heritage of the time and which extols God for the priestly rule of the Zadokites: "Praise him who elects the sons of Zadok to the priestly office; for his grace endureth for ever." [18]

---

[11] Ez. 44:15; on this and what follows cf. G. Fohrer-K. Galling, *Ez., Hndbch. AT,* I, 13 (1955), on 44:4-31.

[12] Hag. 1:1 cf. 1 Ch. 5:40 f. and W. Rudolph, *Ch., Hndbch. AT,* I, 21 (1955), ad loc.

[13] Many argue, perhaps correctly, that Ezra came after Nehemiah. He can only have worked under Artaxerxes I Longimanus (465-424 B.C.) or Artaxerxes II Mnemon (404-358 B.C.). Acc. to W. Rudolph, *Esr. u. Neh., Hndbch. AT,* I, 20 (1949), on Ezr. 7-10; M. Noth, *op. cit.* (→ n. 9), 288 f., he probably came on the scene under Artaxerxes I. W. F. Albright, "From Ezra to the Fall of the Persian Empire," *The Biblical Archaeologist,* 9 (1946), 13 suggests a date as early as 428 B.C. On the other hand, A. van Hoonacker, "Néh. et Esdras," *Le Muséon,* 9 (1890), 151-184, 317-351, 389-401 supports a later date under Artaxerxes II in the yr. 398 B.C.; cf. on this also E. G. Kraeling, *The Brooklyn Museum Pap.* (1953), 109. C. H. Gordon, *Geschichtliche Grundlagen d. AT* (1956), 278, n. 1 returns to the traditional view that Ezra precedes Neh. On the problem and bibl. cf. H. H. Rowley, "The Chronological Order of Ezra and Nehemiah," in *The Servant of the Lord and Other Essays on the OT* (1952), 129-159. Irrespective of the order it is important in our sketch that Ezra is presented as the first post-exilic Zadokite in Jerusalem, Ezr. 7:1 ff. cf. also Ezr. 8:2 and Rudolph, *op. cit.* on 8:1-14.

[14] Cf. the P passages Ex. 28:1; 40:12-14; Nu. 3:4, 10, 38; 18:1, 7, also 1 Ch. 23:13 and the stress on the Aaronic claim in 2 Ch. 26:16-21.

[15] Cf. the list of the 24 priestly classes in 1 Ch. 24:1-19 which acc. to v. 7 can only have attained its definitive form in the Hasmonean period, Rudolph, *op. cit.,* ad loc. with bibl.

[16] Rudolph, *ad loc.*

[17] 1 Ch. 24:4 ff. shows that there was rivalry between the Eleazar and Ithamar branches and that the priests of the former claimed precedence; at the beginning of the 2nd cent. B.C. the Zadokites, who belonged to this, were in power.

[18] Sir. 51:12 i (Heb.) הודו לבוחר בבני צדוק לכהן כי לעולם חסדו. Cf. on this Stauffer, 138 f. and P. Kahle, "Zu den Handschriftenrollen in Höhlen beim Toten Meer," *Das Altertum,* 3 (1957), 34-46, who rightly emphasises that the Zadokite psalm in Sir. 51:12a-r was not transl. into Gk. because the rule of the Zadokites in Jerusalem had long since collapsed in the days of the grandson of Sirach. Hölscher Sadduzäismus, 103, n. 1 fails to appreciate the true nature of this ps. when he sees in it a later stylisation.

c. With Simon II the dominion of the Zadokites in Jerusalem reached its height. [19] His likeminded son and successor Onias III could not withstand the "hellenising" reform movements; he was deposed by Antioches IV Epiphanes in 175 B.C. and was the victim of assassination in Antioch in 170 B.C. Further battles for the high-priestly office led not merely to the elimination of the Zadokites [20] but to the loss of a leading role by the sons of Aaron with the death of Alkimos in 159 B.C. After this the throne of the high-priest was vacant for 7 yrs. [21]

In 152 B.C. Alexander I Balas appointed the Hasmonean Jonathan high-priest at the Feast of Tabernacles, 1 Macc. 10:18-21. In the late summer of 140 B.C. Simon received the hereditary high-priesthood by popular decision, 1 Macc. 14:25-49. In the course of the successful battle against "reforming" Judaism and the Seleucid royal house small village priests had come to power. [22] As upstarts these men had all the marks of illegitimacy and their legal connection with the Jerusalem priesthood was doubtful. [23] One must not make the mistake of thinking that a new priestly ideology was forged with the new dynasty or that the Hasmoneans tried to root out or at least to discredit the Zadokite traditions in Jerusalem. [24] The sons of Zadok and their supporters were far from dead. At the same time that Alkimos replaced Menelaos and thus restored a legitimate, though not a Zadokite, high-priest in Jerusalem, the Zadokite Onias IV, son of Onias III, fled to Egypt, Jos. Ant., 12, 237 and 387. With the support of Ptolemy VI Philometor he established a Jewish temple in Leontopolis and set up a new temple community, 12, 388; 13, 62-73; Bell., 1, 33. Though the literary tradition is disconnected, there can be little doubt but that Egypt thus became a centre of Zadokite traditions. [25]

d. The dispossession of Onias III seems to have had yet another result. Acc. to 1 Macc. 2:29-48 even before the Maccabean revolt and independently of it Jews faithful to the Law moved off into the surrounding deserts. Among them we read esp. of the Ασιδαῖοι (חֲסִידִים), who were only loosely connected with the Maccabees. [26] The

---

[19] On the evaluation of Simon II cf. also Jos. Ant., 12, 43 : Σίμων ... ὁ καὶ δίκαιος ἐπικληθεὶς διά τε τὸ πρὸς τὸν θεὸν εὐσεβὲς καὶ τὸ πρὸς τοὺς ὁμοφύλους εὔνουν (incorrectly ref. by Jos. to Simon I), cf. also Ab., 1, 2.

[20] After Onias III his "reforming" brother Jason ruled for a short time (with the name Joshua acc. to Jos. Ant., 12, 239), 2 Macc. 3:1 ff.; 4:1-6, 7 ff., 33 ff. Already in 173 or 172 B.C. he was replaced by the usurper Menelaos (originally Onias acc. to Jos. Ant., 12, 239), who held power until 162 B.C., 2 Macc. 4:26; 5:1-10; 13:1-8; Jos. Ant., 12, 385; 20, 235. Cf. on this E. Bickermann, *Der Gott der Makkabäer* (1937), 85.

[21] 1 Macc. 7:1-5; 9:54 ff. In spite of the pro-hasmonean depiction there can be no doubt as to the Aaronic legitimacy of Alkimos-Eliakim; hence Bickermann, *op. cit.*, rightly emphasises that under him the temple state was restored as it had been prior to Antiochus Epiphanes. Part of the legal status was that the high-priest was appointed and supported by the king, though cf. M. Noth, *op. cit.* (→ n. 9), 335. On this whole matter cf. also Meyer Ursprung, II, 245-252.

[22] So rightly Stauffer, 140.

[23] 1 Macc. 2:1; 14:29 says the Hasmoneans belonged to the priestly aristocracy in the form of the priestly order Jojarib (→ n. 15), but this group does not belong to the temple priesthood since it was late in coming back from exile, cf. bTaan., 27b par., where Jojarib is an appendage of Jedaiah. This priestly family, originally outside the temple priesthood in Jerusalem, undoubtedly owes its rise to the emergence of the Hasmonean branch which goes back to a priest Hasmon — Jos. Bell., 1, 36; Ant., 12, 265 : Ἀσαμωναῖος = חַשְׁמוֹן — and which, in spite of Jos., had its seat in the town Modein. Cf. on this Schoeps, 663 f.

[24] Schoeps, 664 rightly emphasises that with the naming of Simon as ἀρχιερεύς, στρατηγὸς καὶ ἐθνάρχης (ἡγούμενος) τῶν Ἰουδαίων by the priests and the popular assembly in 140 B.C. (1 Macc. 14:41 ff.) the Zadokites and their claims were officially set aside.

[25] Cf. Schl. Gesch. Isr., 122-127.

[26] 1 Macc. 2:42 : Ασιδαῖοι Heb. חֲסִידִים, are in the first instance the "righteous" who go into opposition as loyal champions of the Law and high-priestly legitimacy. Their strong

hostility of these groups to "reforming" movements suggests that they were on the side of the ousted Zadokites. [27]

We learn from the Damascus Document and the Dead Sea Scrolls that the Aaronic-Zadokite traditions displayed a remarkable resilience outside the temple state in Jerusalem and independently of the political changes there. Ez. 44:15, which speaks of the cultic personnel of the future temple in Jerusalem, is quoted in Damasc. 4:2 ff. (6:1 ff.) in a form ("priest and levites and sons of Zadok") which is adapted to Zadokite interests, [28] and the following exposition is given: "The priests are those who turned back in Israel [and] went forth out of the land of Judah[, and the levites are those] who attached themselves to them, and the sons of Zadok are the elect of Israel, those who are called by name and who will come forth at the end of the days." [29] Damasc. here presupposes a strict priestly community in which the Zadokites will obviously be the leaders. Since they are already divinely ordained to rule, it is expected that one day they will grasp high-priestly power in all its fulness. If Damasc. presupposes a later stage in the development of the community, [30] the claims of the Zadokites suggest that this priestly expectation ultimately has its roots in a period when the Zadokites were expelled from Jerusalem. [31] Damasc. is now supplemented by, e.g., 1 QS 5:2, 9, where the Zadokites are called "the priests who keep the covenant." [32] To the sons of Aaron alone is thus granted the right to exercise judgment in the community and to control the common possessions until the time when "a prophet comes forth and the anointed of Aaron and

---

connection with the temple state may be seen in 1 Macc. 7:13, where they are ready to make peace when Alkimos, a son of Aaron and hence a legitimate claimant, takes power as high-priest, → n. 21.

[27] A basic question is whether the συναγωγή 'Ασιδαίων = עֲדַת חֲסִידִים (1 Macc. 2:42) is a "party" which later became that of the Pharisees (→ Φαρισαῖος), cf. Noth, op. cit., 335, n. 1. It is more likely that the chasidim were unrelated groups more or less strongly opposed to the dominant trend in the Jerusalem hierocracy. This helps us to see why acc. to 1 Macc. 7:13 some Chasidim could make peace with the high-priest while others continued their opposition. It should also be noted, as perceived by H. Ewald, Gesch. d. Volkes Israel, IV (1864), 483-494, cf. also Wellhausen, 78, n. 1, that the Heb. plur. חסידים corresponds to the Syr.-Aram. plur. abs. ḥasên or plur. emphaticus ḥasaiyā (Gk. 'Εσσηνοί or 'Εσσαῖοι), and that Philo Omn. Prob. Lib., 13 rightly renders 'Εσσαῖοι <'esaiyā <ḥasaiyā by ὅσιοι. It thus seems likely that the Essenes as well as the Pharisees derive from the chasidim of the 2nd cent. B.C. The later Essenes, treated as a philosophical school by Jos. and Philo, also seem to have kept their varied character acc. to recent finds, cf. Schoeps, 85. The source material quoted in what follows shows, however, that the Zadokite traditions had an established place in Essene circles.

[28] HT: והכהנים הלוים בני צדוק, "but the levitical priests, the sons of Zadok"; Damasc.: הכהנים והלוים ובני צדוק.

[29] הכהנים הם שבי ישראל היוצאים מארץ יהודה והלוים] הנלוים עמהם ובני צדוק הם בחירי ישראל קריאי השם העמדים באחרית הימים; for the text cf. L. Rost, Die Damaskusschrift, KIT, 167 (1933), ad loc.

[30] Cf. O. Eissfeldt, Einl. in d. AT² (1958), 806 f.

[31] To be distinguished from the first suppression of the Zadokites under Onias III is that under Alexander Jannaeus. Acc. to 4 QpNah 2:12 f. (J. M. Allegro, "Further Light on the History of Qumran," JBL, 75 [1956], 89-95) there is a strong probability that the Teacher of Righteousness of 1 QpHab c. 90 B.C. raised Zadokite claims in the anti-hasmonean disorders. Like other opponents he was defeated and put to flight, cf. Jos. Ant., 13, 383; Ps. Sol. 17:15-23. It is possible that bQid., 66a (→ 43, 21 ff.) contains a final reminiscence of Zadokite charges against the priest-kingship of Jannaeus when legend has Jehuda bGedidiah say: "King Jannaeus, be content with the kingly crown and leave the priestly crown to the sons of Aaron."

[32] בני צדוק הכוהנים שומרי הברית; cf. 5:21, where the sons of Aaron are referred to as those "who have pledged to set up his covenant and adopt all his statutes"; cf. also Stauffer, 140, n. 27.

Israel." [33] In keeping is the leading role of the Zadokites in 1 QSa 1:2, 2, 24; 2:3 and 1 QSb 3:22 f. In the latter passage the sons of Zadok are called the priests "whom God has chosen that they should make strong his covenant for (ever and) apply all his statutes among his people." [34] These statements seem to be supplemented by the fact that the Qumran community gives evidence of a hierarchical structure in the liturgy. [35, 36]

e. From the standpt. of the history of religion an important role is played in the Zadokite tradition by a this-worldly eschatology which is in full correspondence with the older post-exilic hope of salvation. [37] The concept of the resurrection, which is so heavily stressed in Pharisaic teaching from the 1st cent. A.D., is here a motif which does not have the character of what is necessary to salvation, [38] so that those who belong to the Zadokite group might seem to be denying it. [39] On the other hand we

---

[33] 1 QS 9:7: ‏עד בוא נביא ומשיחי אהרן וישראל‎; line 11: ‏רק בני אהרון ימשלו במשפט ובהון‎. Though the text is fragmentary, the plur. constructus ‏משיחי‎ is materially established by 1 QSa 2:12, 14, and the par. which offer the sing. in Damasc. 12:23 (15:4) ‏עד עמוד משוח‎; 19:10 f. (9:10): ‏משו[ח אהרן וישראל‎; and ‏בבוא משיח אהרן וישראל‎, 14:19 (18:8): ‏אהרן וישראל‎; 20:1 (9:29): ‏עד עמוד משיח מאהרן ומישראל‎, are due to later mediaeval emendation. For bibl. cf. Stauffer, 136, n. 6; K. G. Kuhn, "Die beiden Messias Aarons u. Israels," NT St, 1 (1954-1955), 159-179; DJD, I, 121 f.; also F. Nötscher, "Zur theol. Terminologie d. Qumran-Texte," Bonner Bibl. Beiträge, 10 (1956), 50 f.

[34] ‏בני צדוק הכוהנים אשר בחר בם אל לחזק בריתו ל[עולם ולב]חון כול משפטיו בתוך עמו‎; cf. DJD, I, 124 f.

[35] Cf. M. Weise, Kultzeiten u. kultischer Bundesschluss in d. "Ordensregel" von Qumran, Diss. Jena (1956), esp. 73-112.

[36] How strongly the Qumran community was influenced by older ideas of priestly legitimacy may be seen from Ass. Mos. (1st cent. A.D.), a work which fairly certainly belongs to the Qumran circle. This contests the illegitimate high-priesthood of the Hasmoneans (6:1 cf. 5:4 : qui non sunt sacerdotes, sed servi de servis nati), the kingship of Herod (6:2 : rex petulans, qui non erit de genere sacerdotum, homo temerarius et improbus) and the rule of his sons (6:6 f.). In a form which reminds us of Rabb. polemics against the Boethusians (→ 41, 29 f.) Ass. Mos. 7:7 f. describes the priests of the time : in scelere pleni et iniquitate ab [sole] oriente usque ad occidentem, dicentes : Habebimus discubitiones et luxuriam edentes et bibentes, et potabimus nos tamquam principes (= ‏נשיאים‎) erimus ; Ass. Mos. also rejects the Pharisaic Rabbinate, 5:5; 7:3, 6, and it does so in a way wholly similar to Damasc. 8:13 f. (9:22), cf. 4:19 (7:1). Materially cf. Stauffer, 137 f., 141 f.; P. Kahle, "Die Gemeinde d. neuen Bundes u. d. hbr. Hdschr. aus d. Höhle," ThLZ, 77 (1952), 401-412; for bibl. cf. Eissfeldt, op. cit. (→ n. 30), 770 f.

[37] Cf. the coming of the Teacher of Righteousness, possibly in the time of the gt. revolt under Alexander Jannaeus (→ n. 31), and esp. 1 QM with its unambiguously this-worldly expectations. For texts and bibl. cf. Eissfeldt, 807-810.

[38] Acc. to 1 QH 6:29 f. all the sons of his truth will rise up at the time of judgment : ‏כול בני א[מ]תו יעורו‎, while in 6:34 those who rest in the dust will set up the signal and the inhabitants of the grave (lit. the worm of the dead) will raise the banner : ‏ושוכבי עפר הרימו תרן ותולעת מתים נשאו נס‎. This does not go beyond Da. 12:2.

[39] Schoeps, op. cit. (→ n. 9), 72 f. pts. to two venerable traditions which show that the recollection of a group called Sadducaei not related to the Σαδδουκαῖοι of Jos. and the NT, though denying the resurrection for all its piety, persisted for a long time : a. Ps.-Clem. Recg., I, 53 f.: In multas etenim iam partes populus scindebatur initio sumto a Johanne baptista ... Erat ergo primum schisma eorum, qui dicebantur Sadducaei, initio Johannis iam pene temporibus sumpto. Hique ut caeteris iustiores segregare se coepere a populi coetu, et mortuorum resurrectionem negare idque argumento infidelitatis asserere, dicentes non esse dignum ut quasi sub mercede proposita colatur deus ; b. Ephr. Syr., Arm. Text. Corp. Script. Christ. Or., 137 (1953), 351; Lat. transl. by L. Leloir, Evangelii concordantis expositio, ibid., 145 (1954), 249 : Sadducaei (in) diebus Johannis initium habuerunt, quasi iusti separantes seipsos, et resurrectionem mortuorum negant, confidentes in seipsis, quia non convenit, aiunt, ob mercedem gratiae adorare et colere Deum. Cf. → n. 46.

find very ancient forms of thought which possibly come from the Canaanite heritage of Israel and which in the priestly circle find expression in the polarity of antithetical concepts. [40] This world of antitheses perhaps contributed to the notable development of dualism at Qumran and to the fact that, historically, Iranian elements among others could make an entry and be worked out theologically. [41]

f. In so far as one can follow the story of the Zadokites to-day, one may say that from the very outset this group could never make peace with the temple government in Jerusalem. For this reason one cannot simply equate them with the Sadducees of Jerusalem known to us from Jos. and the NT. Another pt. is that one part of the Zadokite literature survived after the destruction of the second temple. When rediscovered c. 800 A.D., it had such an impact on the Karaites, who for a time exerted a decisive influence on the intellectual development of Judaism, that they saw themselves as genealogically related to the Sadducees, → 42, 26 ff. [42]

2. Zadok and Boethos.

In a Rabb. tradition the Sadducees and the Boethusians, who are often referred to along with them, are traced back to two Pharisaic-Rabb. figures of the 2nd cent. B.C.

a. Acc. to Ab. R. Nat., 5 Antigonos of Soko, active at the beginning of the 2nd cent. B.C., had two pupils named Zadok and Boethos. To them he passed on the central principle : "Be not as servants who serve their master to get a gift but as servants who serve their master without prospect of getting a gift, and the fear of the Lord be upon you." [43] In the next generation but one after Zadok and Boethos the question of payment was raised in relation to this principle : "Why did our fathers say this ? Is it possible for a labourer to work all day without receiving a reward in the evening ? If our fathers had known there is another world and a resurrection of the dead they would not have spoken thus." Since acc. to the view of the pupils of Zadok and Boethos belief in the coming aeon, which naturally included hope of recompense, was excluded by the principle of Antigonos along with the doctrine of the resurrection of the dead, they supposedly broke away from the Torah and founded two sects which were named the Sadducees and the Boethusians after Zadok and Boethos. Because of their purely this-worldly focus they were also thought to have looked for compensation in this life. [44]

---

[40] Thus we find in Ass. Mos. 10:1 the name Zabulus for the devil, rightly equated with διάβολος by Stauffer, 142, n. 37. Now the same term zbl = *zabūlu, "prince," "lord," occurs already in the mythological texts of Ugarit, partly as a title for Baal (zbl b'l = "prince Ba'al," or zbl b'l 'arṣ "prince, lord of the earth," also written zblb'l, cf. Βεελζεβουλ → I, 605 f.), but in the main an epithet for jm = *jammu "sea" (zbl jm = "prince sea," like ṭpṭ nhr "judge river," expresses the chaotic power of water, which is in polar tension to Ba'al or Alijan Ba'al and hence to blossoming nature). There can be no doubt that in the occasionally used Zabulus we have a relic of the priestly tradition of ancient Canaan. On the examples cf. G. D. Young, "Concordance of Ugaritic," Analecta Orientalia, 36 (1956), s.v. b'l, zbl, ṭpṭ.
[41] Cf. Nötscher, op. cit. (→ n. 33), 79-104; Stauffer, 137.
[42] → n. 51; on the Karaites cf. P. Kahle, The Cairo Geniza² (1959), 17-28.
[43] So acc. to Ab. R. Nat. Rec. B and Ab., 1, 3. Rec. A offers a correction along the lines of Rabb. dogmatics when it adds : "That your reward may be double in the world to come" (כדי שיהיה שכרכם כפול לעתיד לבוא). To get the original sense this should be left out, as against J. Goldin, The Fathers acc. to Rabbi Nathan (1955), 39, n. 2. On the character of the legend cf. Hölscher Sadduzäismus, 16 f.; Meyer Ursprung, II, 291.
[44] Thus the conclusion of Ab. R. Nat., 5 runs : "Hence all their life long the Sadducees and Boethusians used vessels of silver and gold — not because they were high-minded, but the Sadducees said : The following tradition is abroad among the Pharisees, namely, that they (the Sadducees) strive greatly in this world but have nothing at all in the world to come." Cf. the polemic in Ass. Mos. 7:7 f. (→ n. 36).

b. Under the governor Quirinius in 6/7 A.D. the then Pharisee Zadok founded the Zealot party along with the Galilean guerilla leader Judas, → II, 884 f. This act probably meant that both existing national-religious groups adopted a programme of eschatological salvation. According to this the kingdom of God was to be set up in this world by an eschatological war against the Romans and Jewish collaborators.[45] In this case one might well say that Zadok left Pharisaic Rabbinism and founded a new school, the main difference from Pharisaism of at least the Hillel type being that the Rabb. in relative neutrality vis-à-vis current events made future salvation independent of the dawn of the new aeon (→ I, 206, 7 ff.), whereas the Zealots accepted the ancient this-worldly hope of the future and expected God's kingdom to come through the personal exertions of believers.[46] In this respect legend makes Zadok the eponymous hero of the Sadducees[47] by making him a pupil of Antigonos or, which is equally possible, identifying him with such a pupil. This was all the easier because the Sadducees connected with the temple government were in the last resort eschatologically oriented for all their political cleverness, → 45, 43 ff.

c. Alongside this Zadok tradition mentions a Simon bBoethos or Boethos of Alexandria who founded the dynasty of the Boethusians.[48] Among the high-priests of this house Joazar bBoethos is important since, at the time when Zadok was uniting with Judas against the census of Quirinius, he tried to persuade the people not to oppose the measures of the Roman governor.[49] Thus in Joazar we find a Boethos along with a Zadok, not in close relation, but in absolute opposition. The fact that such dissimilar figures were linked may be due to the fact that Rabb. tradition for the most part equates the Sadducees and Boethusians (→ 46, 8 ff.), though one has to reckon with the possibility that the Alexandrian Boethos came ultimately from Zadokite circles in Leontopolis (→ 45, 22 ff.), so that on this basis, too, legend associated Joazar bBoethos, as "Boethos," with Zadok.[50] The interfusion of various motifs may explain why the same legend which the Rabb. use polemically against the Sadducees and Boethusians plays a positive role in the Karaite tradition;[51] the Karaites find their spiritual ancestor in the Zadok of

---

[45] Jos. Ant., 18, 4 ff., 23 ff.; Bell., 2, 118, 151 ff.; cf. R. Meyer, Der Prophet aus Galiläa (1940), 74 f., n. 169; Schl. Gesch. Isr., 261-264.

[46] Ab., 1, 3 may be taken in the sense of unselfish sacrifice for God in this world. It is thus conceivable that Zadok followed Antigonos and adopted Ab., 1, 3 as a programme. He could thus join a mixed coalition in opposition to Jerusalem and the Romans; the Qumran sect obviously belonged to this coalition too. If Ps.-Clem. Recg., I, 53 f. and Ephr. (→ n. 39) say that in the day of John the Baptist the Sadducees separated themselves from the rest of the Jews as the righteous, the ref. can only be, not to the ancient Zadokites, nor to the Sadducees of the temple government, but to the followers of Zadok the spiritual leader of the Zealots. Hence there is perhaps more than apologetic when Jos. in Ant., 18, 9 says that Zadok was with Judas the founder of a "fourth philosophy." The fact that Rabb. tradition relates Zadok directly to Antigonos and says the schism broke out only in the second generation may be due to a secondary extension of the chain of tradition for chronological reasons. It is still an open question whether this Zadok was related to the Zadokite circles in Qumran, though spiritual kinship is evident.

[47] For the Rabb. the ref. is obviously to the temple Sadducees; the older Zadokites and more recent followers of Zadok play no part in the Rabb.

[48] Acc. to Jos. Ant., 19, 297 Boethos himself rather than Simon bBoethos was the father-in-law of Herod. On Simon cf. Ant., 15, 319-322; 17, 78; 18, 109.

[49] Jos. Ant., 18, 3: οἱ δὲ καίπερ τὸ κατ' ἀρχὰς ἐν δεινῷ φέροντες τὴν ἐπὶ ταῖς ἀπογραφαῖς ἀκρόασιν ὑποκατέβησαν τοῦ μὴ εἰς πλέον ἐναντιοῦσθαι πείσαντος αὐτοὺς τοῦ ἀρχιερέως Ἰωζάρου, Βοηθοῦ δὲ οὗτος υἱὸς ἦν.

[50] Schl. Gesch. Isr., 231, n. 211 rightly pts. out that the acc. to the sources the legitimacy of the house of Boethos was not in question like that of the Hasmoneans, → 43, 21 ff.

[51] Cf. Ja'qub al-Qirqisani, Kitab al-Anwar wal-Maraqib, ed. L. Nemoy (1939), I, 2, 7; also L. Nemoy, "Al-Qirqisani's Account of the Jewish Sects and Christianity," HUCA, 7 (1930), 326. If Al-Qirqisani regards Boethos as well as Zadok as a forefather of the Karaites, this shows his dependence on Rabb. tradition (Ab. R. Nat., 5) but does not explain

Ab. R. Nat., 5. This passage sheds no light at all, however, on the story of the Sadducees associated with the temple government.

3. Sadducee as the Term for a Political Group.

The final pre-Hasmonean high-priest of legitimate descent, Alkimos the son of Aaron, brought the Aaronic priesthood into disrepute among the "righteous" by his harsh "reforming" rule.[52] Since among the sons of Aaron the sons of Zadok were esp. firmly anchored in the tradition, the historical picture could easily change slightly so that the unfavourable outcome of the sons of Aaron could be summarily attributed to the "sons of Zadok" and the members of the other priestly classes with a dubious past could be described as those of "Zadokite" persuasion, i.e., as Sadducees. Here, too, an important self-contradiction resulted, for whereas in Leontopolis and on the cultural borders of Palestine the true Zadokites and their supporters were in opposition to developments in Jerusalem, the priestly majority remaining in the temple was polemically described as Zadokite too.

II. The Sadducees of Jerusalem.

1. Sadducees and Hasmoneans.

The story of the political group which Jos. and the Rabb. tradition call Sadducees in close connection with the temple government in Jerusalem cannot be fully written because of lack of sources. Only at a few points does the historical darkness lift somewhat. The Sadducees are first mentioned by Jos. as a party or school under Hyrcanos I (135-104 B.C.). Acc. to Jos. Ant., 13, 288-296, in a floating anecdote linked with Alexander Janneus (103-76 B.C.) in bQid., 66a, John Hyrcanos I was at first a pupil and friend of the Pharisees. At a feast which he gave to the whole Pharisaic society, however, the Pharisee Eleazar, to the horror of all, accused him of illegitimacy in respect of the high-priesthood. Though the parting was amicable, the Sadducee Jonathan succeeded in enraging John so that he broke with the Pharisees and went over to the Sadducees. The result was an official persecution of strict adherents of the Law and a resultant hatred of the Hasmoneans.[53] The historical core of this anecdote, which is based on school rivalries and may well belong to the 1st cent. A.D., is probably to be sought in the underlying question how it came about that John Hyrcanos I, whose house finally owed its rise to the resistance movement of those faithful to the Law, should make alliance with men of a dubious past.[54] The only possible answer to this question, however, is not to be sought in Ant., 13, 288-296 but along the following lines. If the Hasmoneans were to retain power in the hierocracy of the time, they had of necessity to align themselves with the ancient priestly aristocracy in so far as this still lingered on in Jerusalem, i.e., with the "Zadokites."[55] They alone by virtue of their

how or how far the Karaites did in fact have genuine Zadokite traditions at their disposal, cf. E. Bammel, "Kirkisanis Sadduzäer," ZAW, 71 (1959), 265-270.

[52] Cf. 1 Macc. 7:13-18; characteristically 1 Macc. does not say why Alkimos had 60 chasidim executed.

[53] Soon after Hyrcanos is described enthusiastically by Jos. as a charismatic ruler having the office of ruler, the dignity of high-priest and the gift of prophet (→ VI, 825, 20 ff.), Ant., 13, 299; Bell., 1, 68.

[54] This alliance was regarded as apostasy, bBer., 29a: "The high-priest Jochanan discharged the high-priestly office for 80 yrs.; but finally he became a Sadducee" (יוחנן כהן גדול שמש בכהונה גדולה שמנים שנה ולבסוף נעשה צדוקי); cf. the prototype of Solomon, who fell away in old age, 1 K. 11:1-8.

[55] The murder of Simon and his sons Mattathias and Judas by Ptolemaios, his son-in-law, shows the instability of the Hasmonean regime in spite of 1 Macc. 14:25-46, though cf.

descent could remove from the Hasmoneans the stigma of illegitimacy. [56] The Zadokites for their part had to make peace with the Hasmoneans and forge an alliance with them if they were not finally to be destroyed by inner dissension. [57] In the priestly genealogy, however, this meant that at the latest under Hyrcanos I the class of Jojarib, which ranked last, was officially put first. [58] This automatically stirred up the opposition of the "righteous" against the Hasmonean house when they could not prevent this "apostasy."

The union between the new priestly house and the "Zadokites" or Sadducees made sense historically and politically, for the Hasmonean wars of expansion were in keeping with the ancient particularist eschatology [59] and the rulers pursued this policy, in spite of many reverses, [60] up to their overthrow. If, then, we would categorise the school which supported the Hasmoneans, with both the priestly and secular aristocracy at its head, the following definition might serve. To have the mind of the Zadokite or Sadducee is to be sustained by the concept of a particularist temple state which along the lines of traditional eschatological hopes is the seed for the purification of the Holy Land, its liberation from all Gentiles and semi-Gentiles, and the restoration of the idealised kingdom of Israel as David once reigned over it; [61] all this, of course, with the proviso that the actual historical epoch stood under the sign of the priest-princely rule of the Hasmonean house.

2. The Sadducees under the Herods and the Romans.

When Herod in 37 B.C. established his rule with the capture of Jerusalem and the Hasmonean Antigonos was beheaded by the Romans, acc. to Jos. Ant., 15, 6 forty-five leading Jews lost their lives. Another tradition in Ant., 14, 175 says that when Herod seized power all the members of the Council (→ συνέδριον) except the Pharisee Samaios were deposed. It is a natural conjecture that both accounts refer to the same event, namely, the overthrow of the Hasmonean-inclined Council by Herod. [62] It would

---

16:13. Whether and how far the attempt to remove the Hasmoneans is due to legitimist opposition (→ n. 24) 1 Macc. naturally does not tell us. That John Hyrcanos I had domestic problems is indicated by Jos. Ant., 13, 288; Bell., 1, 67 (drawing on Nicolaos of Damascus).

[56] A sign that Jos. Ant., 13, 288-296 par. is late is that the charge of the Pharisees against Hyrcanos that his mother was for some yrs. a prisoner of war and hence would not be a virgin would affect only his personal qualifications to be high-priest and not the legitimacy of the whole house of Hasmon-Jojarib. Primarily, however, the fundamental concern is not just observance of a law regarding the personal fitness of a priest, as Schl. Gesch. Isr., 139 thinks, but the upholding of an attained position in face of Zadokite opposition outside the temple government.

[57] The moment the alliance cracked, disaster smote, Jos. Ant., 13, 405-417.

[58] → n. 23.

[59] Cf. the war against the Samaritans and their sanctuary, Jos. Ant., 13, 275 ff.; Bell., 2, 64 ff. with Sir. 50:26; Jub. 30:18, 28; R. Meyer, op. cit. (→ n. 45), 63 f.; Noth, op. cit. (→ n. 9), 346 f. The annexation of Galilee is part of the suppression of Hell.-Gentile elements, Jos. Ant., 13, 280, 318 f., cf. A. Alt, "Galiläische Probleme, 5: Die Umgestaltung Galiläas durch d. Hasmonäer," Kleine Schriften z. Gesch. d. Volkes Israel, II (1953), 407-423. The same is true of the subjugating of Idumaea with Hebron, the ancient coronation city of David (→ VI, 78), Jos. Ant., 13, 257. Obviously on the same assumptions Aristobulos I (104-103 B.C.) even forced the Ituraeans to accept circumcision, Jos. Ant., 13, 318 f.

[60] Alexander Jannaeus was acting in acc. with the same particularist eschatology when he destroyed Pella, Jos. Ant., 13, 397. The popular revolt unleashed by the "righteous" and fought out by foreign mercenaries on both sides should not deceive us in this regard, Jos. Ant., 13, 372 ff. Cf. on this Schl. Gesch. Isr., 143-146; Noth, op. cit., 349 f.; Schoeps, 666 f.

[61] There is in the Hasmoneans and their priestly and secular followers no trace of universalism or friendliness to the Gentiles such as later sources ascribe to the Sadducees; this is correctly pointed out by Hölscher Sadduzäismus, 89 f. If their family history shows that the Hasmoneans also paid tribute to the forms of life of the surrounding Hell. world, this does not alter their basic conception or that of their "Zadokite" followers.

[62] Cf. Wellhausen. 106.

be wrong to see in this bloody happening no more than the terrible revenge of an upstart who had finally come to power. One is rather to see in it an expression of the fact that with Herod a system triumphed which was diametrically opposed to that of the Hasmoneans and fundamentally hostile in outlook to ancient Sadduceeism. The hierocracy of the Hasmoneans was based on religious and national particularism, and the obstinate defence of Jerusalem by Antigonos is enough to show that the population, apart from the Pharisees, was animated by the same mind. [63] In contrast Herod was a universalist. His kingdom was to be an integral part of the Roman Empire. There was to be room for anyone, whether Jew or Gentile, within it. As king he had a concern for all. [64] Though he felt himself a Jew, [65] he could never accept the idea, self-evident to the Hasmoneans, that the Holy Land should be purged by forced conversions or expulsions of non-Jews. From a purely external standpt. the fall of the Hasmoneans had decisively affected the older Sadduceeism too ; it had certainly lost its vital force. Herod abolished the privilege of high-priesthood for life and put men of his own choosing in the office. This not only initiated the last phase in the history of the high-priesthood but also ushered in the new and final section in the story of what remained of Sadduceeism.

The first high-priest after the execution of Antigonos was Chananel. There are two accounts of his origin. Acc. to Jos. Ant., 15, 22 he came from Babylon, but M. Para, 3, 5 calls him an "Egyptian." If the latter is true, one might suppose that for the sake of legitimacy Herod appointed a priest of Leontopolis who as the bearer of true Zadokite traditions would supplant the Hasmonean high-priesthood ideologically. [66] Herod's aims are even clearer in the choice of Simon bBoethos as high-priest. [67] The house of Boethos, to which Simon belonged, was from Alexandria. Acc. to Jos. Ant., 15, 319 f. and 322 Herod appointed Simon high-priest because he wanted to marry his beautiful daughter Mariamne II and also because he wanted a father-in-law of equal status. It is possible, however, that this is just a fictional version of a political act on the king's part. For it could well be that the house of Boethos — though Jos., a scion of the Hasmoneans, conceals this for obvious reasons — had at its command Egyptian Zadokite traditions and thus brought with it the presuppositions of a new and legitimate high-priesthood in Jerusalem. [68] If so, Simon sold out to the universalism of Herod and abandoned the older line of opposition to his family and person.

The house of Boethos remained very closely connected with Herod's dynasty and its policies. In the eyes of the "righteous" of varying types this compromised severely the high-priestly house. Since the house of Boethos had gt. influence among the other high-ranking priests, in the general opinion the verdict necessarily applied to the whole priestly caste in Jerusalem. Moreover, the Sadducees and Boethusians were often mentioned together. Thus the concept "Sadducees" sank even further in esteem even to the pt. of meaning "semi-Gentile" or "apostate." This may well be the starting-pt. for the further fact that towards the end of the 1st cent. A.D. Jos. and the Rabb., aware of the victory of Pharisaic dogma over other Jewish movements, linked the Sadducees and Boethusians with beliefs which no longer corresponded to the dominant mood in the Synagogue. In spite of the situation created by Herod, the older Sadduceeism was not completely destroyed in the priesthood or secular aristocracy, and even in the 1st cent.

---

[63] Cf. Jos. Bell., 1, 347; Ant., 14, 470; Schl. Gesch. Isr., 230. On the opposing views of the Pharisees Pollion and Samaia cf. Jos. Ant., 15, 3.

[64] On the reign of Herod cf. Schürer, I, 360-418; Schl. Gesch. Isr., 230-241; Noth, *op. cit.*, 369-376.

[65] Cf. the consistent acceptance of circumcision by Herod and his relatives, → VI, 78.

[66] Cf. Schl. Gesch. Isr., 429, n. 211.

[67] Jesus, son of Phiabi, officiated between Chananel (whose term was briefly interrupted by Aristobulus) and Simon, Jos. Ant., 15, 322.

[68] It is worth noting that for all the hatred of the Boethusians by the opposition they were never charged with illegitimacy, → n. 50.

A.D. there lived on a Sadducean outlook which rested ultimately on a particularist eschatology. Not the Pharisees, but the priestly and secular aristocracy attempted with sagacity and energy, and not without success, to keep alive the temple state within the Empire. When finally disaster overtook Jerusalem under Vespasian in 66 A.D., it was the priestly nobility which did not falter, but went down with the temple and the idea of a holy city as the source of Israel's life. [69] This is still reflected in Rabb. legend. [70]

III. Sadduceeism as a Religious Phenomenon.

In addition to what has been said thus far. Jos. and the Rabb. use Sadducees and the Rabb. tradition uses Boethusians to describe Jews who patently do not conform to the dogmatic and ethical norm set up in the Synagogue after the destruction of the Jerusalem hierocracy and the resultant victory of Pharisaism. Rabb. tradition lays special stress on the fact that Sadduceeism or Boethusianism is to be regarded as apostasy, perversion and splintering from the dominant orthodoxy.

1. Sadducean Dogmatics.

a. In Sadducean dogmatics, [71] which Jos. sketches at some pts. though with plain disapproval, ref. should be made first to the view of God. In contrast to the Pharisees, God's working and man's action are balanced synergistically. [72] The Sadducees acc. to Jos. Bell., 2, 164 f. rule out *heimarmene* in the form of divine providence. God neither intervenes in history at large nor cares for the individual in particular. Similarly, good and evil, prosperity and adversity, have their origin solely in the free will of man. [73] Sadduceeism thus seems to be a teaching which, while it does not dispute God's existence theoretically, amounts to atheism in practice. [74] It is worth noting that Jos., who compares the Pharisees with the Stoics and the Essenes with the Pythagoreans, i.e., with "pious" philosophical schools (Jos. Vit., 12; Ant., 15, 371), refers to the Sadducees in the same way as to the Epicureans. The latter are mistaken in thinking that there is no providence and that God is in no way concerned about the self-existent all, Jos. Ant., 10, 278. [75] A similar comparison between the Sadducees and the Epicureans is to be found in the Rabb. tradition (→ 47, 19 ff.), though there is here no proper understanding of the world of Epicurean thought.

b. Sadducean anthropology corresponds to the Sadducean idea of God. Acc. to Jos. Ant., 18, 16 the Sadducees deny the existence of an immortal soul, [76] cf. also Ab. R. Nat., 5 (→ 41, 17 ff.), where the luxurious life of the Sadducees and Boethusians

---

[69] This is plain when, e.g., one compares the flight of the Pharisaic leader from the besieged city (bGittin, 56a/b; Meyer, *op. cit.*, 56) with the martial role of the priesthood, or at least a section of it, Hölscher Sadduzäismus, 73-77.

[70] Acc. to a secondary legend in bTaan., 29a, Bar. relating to the destruction of Solomon's temple the flower of the priesthood handed back the keys of the sanctuary to God in the hour of its fall and then plunged into the flames.

[71] For material cf. Str.-B., IV, 344 f.

[72] Cf. e.g., Ab., 3, 15; R. Meyer, "Hellenistisches in d. rabb. Anthropologie," BWANT, IV, 22 (1937), 69-74.

[73] Σαδδουκαῖοι ... τὴν μὲν εἱμαρμένην παντάπασιν ἀναιροῦσιν καὶ τὸν θεὸν ἔξω τοῦ δρᾶν τι [κακὸν] ἢ ἐφορᾶν τίθενται, φασὶ δ' ἐπ' ἀνθρώπων ἐκλογῇ τὸ δὲ καλὸν καὶ τὸ κακὸν προκεῖσθαι καὶ τὸ κατὰ γνώμην ἑκάστου τούτων ἑκατέρῳ προσιέναι, Jos. Bell., 2, 164 f.

[74] Hölscher Sadduzäismus, 4 f.

[75] Θεὸν οὐκ ἀξιοῦσιν ἐπιτροπεύειν τῶν πραγμάτων, οὐδ' ὑπὸ τῆς μακαρίας καὶ ἀφθάρτου πρὸς διαμονὴν τῶν ὅλων οὐσίας κυβερνᾶσθαι τὰ σύμπαντα, ἄμοιρον δὲ ἡνιόχου καὶ ἀφρόντιστον τὸν κόσμον αὐτομάτως φέρεσθαι λέγουσιν, Jos. Ant., 10, 278.

[76] Σαδδουκαίοις δὲ τὰς ψυχὰς ὁ λόγος συναφανίζει τοῖς σώμασι, Jos. Ant., 18, 16.

is causally related to the restriction of life to this world. There is thus no belief in individual survival after death or in a future judgment, which acc. to Jos. Bell., 2, 165 is to take place in Hades.

c. In eschatology in the strict sense the Sadducees reject the tenet of the resurrection of the dead. In contrast to the Pharisees they have no place for the "refreshing of rising to life again," which is the materially sound transl. of the Middle Heb. תְּחִיָּה in Jos. Ant., 18, 14. For the Rabb. this is a leading characteristic of Sadducean thought. Thus bSanh., 90b records the following debate between the Sadducees and Rabban Gamaliel II (c. 90 A.D.): "The Sadducees asked Rabban Gamaliel whence (it could be proved) that the Holy One, blessed be He, makes the dead alive again. He said to them : From the Law, the Prophets, and the Writings. But they would not accept this." Acc. to this account the Sadducees were obviously of the opinion that there is no adequate bibl. proof of the resurrection and that Rabban Gamaliel could not persuade them to the contrary. In other words, they reject the dogma on theological grounds, as the Sadducees and Boethusians do in Ab. R. Nat., 5 (→ 41, 19 ff.). This attitude comes under the condemnation of Sanh., 10, 1: "But these have no part in the coming aeon : He who says there is no resurrection of the dead, and the Torah does not come from God, i.e., the Epicureans." The term "Epicureans" here is used for "free-thinkers" and characterises Sadduceeism. Hence the Sadducees can be grouped with traitors, hypocrites and Epicureans in Seder Olam r., 3. It is said of them that they spread terror abroad in the land of the living, do not believe in the resurrection of the dead, and contest the divinity of the Torah. This group of offenders, among whom are those Jews who despise the words of the wise, is going to sure punishment in hell. [77] Of the motifs mentioned the denial of the resurrection and the despising of the words of the wise, which undoubtedly means rejection of the oral tradition of the Rabb., are quite certainly to be regarded as the principal marks of Sadduceeism. In Rabb. Pharisaic eschatology the dogma of the resurrection finds a relevant counterpart in the hope that one day this world will be replaced by the coming aeon (→ I, 206, 7 ff.) of consummated salvation. Hence acc. to Ab. R. Nat., 5 (→ 41, 22 ff.) the Sadducees and Boethusians reject this part of eschatology, and in Ber., 9, 5 the Sadducees are expressly said to be corrupt because they espouse the view that there is only one aeon. [78]

d. If we are to get a proper understanding of the polemical statements of Jos. and the Rabb. about the Sadducees we must first investigate the religious and historical setting of the ideas which are used as a norm by which to judge Sadducean dogmatics. The main pt. here is that from the 2nd cent. B.C. Judaism was gradually undergoing a deep change in inner structure. On the soil of Hell. and in part ancient oriental and Iranian thought-forms such as are found throughout the Eastern Mediterranean from Egypt to the Euphrates and the Tigris, there gradually developed among the Jews dispersed in this area an anthropology and eschatology which no longer corresponded to ancient ideas but transcended and theologically expanded the traditional concept of God. This process of change, which is also of decisive importance in the development of early Chr. theology, obviously had its point of origin in the Synagogue of the Dispersion. In Israel itself however, and esp. in the Jerusalem hierocracy, the traditional

---

[77] אבל מי שפרשו מדרכי צבון הצדוקין (מינין .vl) והמסורות המשומדין והאפיק רוסים ושנתנו חתם בארץ החיים ושכפרו בתחיית המתים והאומרים אין תורה מן השמים ...... והמלעיגין על דברי חכמים גיהום נגעלת בפניהם ונידונין בתוכה לעולמי עולמים ed. B. Ratner (1897), 17.

[78] All who ended praises in the temple used to say : "From eternity" (מן העולם; vl. עד העולם "to eternity"). But when the Sadducees (Cod Monacensis, 95 : מינין "heretics") went astray and said there is only one aeon (עולם אחד), the order went forth to say : "From aeon to aeon" (מן העולם ועד העולם).

theology of the temple was for a long time a powerful bulwark [79] which from the larger historical standpt. even the interlude of "reforming" efforts under Antiochus IV Epiphanes could not essentially shake. [80]

Eth. En. 103:2 ff. might be adduced as an example of the understanding of man hitherto alien to Judaism. Here we find the fully developed new anthropology with an established individual hope for the world to come such as is found in Jos. and the Rabb. tradition. Man has an earthly body and an eternal soul, here usually described as "spirit," which is moving forward either to heavenly felicity or to torments in hell acc. to its earthly walk. [81] When this view of man came into Pharisaic theology and was espoused by the Rabb. it is hard to say. If the Ps. Sol., which are sustained by a strong hope of salvation though they are not uniform, are at least in part Pharisaic in spirit, [82] we have here some instances from the second half of the 1st cent. B.C. which show that acc. to the Pharisaic teaching of the time death is not the end of human existence but that a future life brings blessedness or eternal damnation. [83] The oldest relatively certain Rabb. instance of belief in an immortal soul is in Lv. r., 34, 3 on 25:25. Here Hillel, who lived at the turn of the epochs and came from the Babyl. *diaspora*, tells in anecdotal form how he regarded the soul as a guest in the house of life. [84] After the destruction of the temple there are many more instances of the new understanding of man. One may pt. to bBer., 28b, which tells us that Jochanan b. Zakkai wept at the end of his life because he feared the incorruptibility of the last Judge who has the power to assign man either to everlasting life in the Garden of Eden or to everlasting death in Gehinnom. Roughly contemporary is 4 Esr. 7:78-99; at the moment of death souls part from their mortal bodies and return to the God from whom they come, some to sevenfold felicity in the heavenly chambers of rest and others to sevenfold torment in unceasing wandering to and fro. [85] From the end of the 1st cent. A.D. body-soul dualism in this sense prevailed in Rabb. anthropology, so that it may be regarded as a dogma from this time.

Things are much the same in eschatology. Faith in the resurrection or revivifying of the dead (תְּחִיַּת הַמֵּתִים), which is only intimated in the canonical writings, [86] may be found for sure in the B.C. period only in 2 Macc., En. and Ps. Sol., [87] so that one can hardly say that it is generally held. Thus one reads in Ps. Sol. 3:12 : "But those who fear the Lord will rise again to eternal life, and their life (is spent) in light, and (this) will never be exhausted." Only in the A.D. period do we find more numerous instances in the pseudepigr. and the Rabb.; decisive here is that belief in the resurrection is now embedded in the liturgy. [88]

Expectation of a coming aeon (→ I, 206, f.) obviously developed out of eschatological ideas which sought to view the course of history in the form of successive epochs. But this is found only comparatively late in the history of Jewish religion. [89] In the 1st cent. one may refer to Eth. En. 48:7, which speaks of "this world of unrighteousness," and Eth. En. 71:15, which alludes to the "future world." Qumran, too, shows acquaintance with the schema of two worlds ; thus in 1 QS 3:13-4:26 the present with its conflict

---

[79] The most obvious source for this is the book of proverbs of the son of Sirach.

[80] Bousset already perceived that the new sense and understanding first developed in circles which were in opposition to the dominant orthodoxy or which were not acknowledged by its leading representatives ; Bousset-Gressm., 189 f.; Schoeps, *op. cit.*, 85.

[81] Meyer, *op. cit.* (→ n. 72), 14.

[82] Cf. Eissfeldt, *op. cit.* (→ n. 30), 754-758.

[83] Cf. Ps. Sol. 3:11; 13:11; 14:9 f.; 15:10; 16:2; Volz Esch., 27.

[84] Meyer, 49.

[85] For instances Str.-B., IV, 1016-1168.

[86] Is. 26:19; Da. 12:2.

[87] Cf., e.g., 2 Macc. 7:9 ff.; 12:43 ff.; 14:46; En. 22 etc.; on this whole subject *v.* Volz Esch., 229-256.

[88] Cf. Sh. E., 2; bBer., 60b.

[89] Cf. R. Meyer, Art. "Eschatologie, III (Judt.)" in RGG³, II, 662-665.

between light and darkness is replaced by a new creation. [90] The oldest Rabb.-Pharisaic example seems to be jBM, 2, 5 (8c, 25 f.), where Simon b. Shetach (c. 90) presupposes the concept of a coming aeon. Only during the course of the 1st cent., however, do we get a real development in Rabb. theology, not only of belief in the resurrection, but also of the dogma of the coming aeon as a period of the absolute consummation of salvation at what is in part a transcendental level.

Since the polemical statements about Sadduceeism obviously belong to a later stage of dogmatic development they cannot be used as a standard to evaluate Sadducean thought. [91] Sadduceeism is not a strand of belief apart from orthodoxy but one which was not interwoven into ongoing dogmatic development. It may thus be described as conservative. [92]

In fact it may be shown quite easily that the statements about Sadduceeism attack the official theology of the Jerusalem hierocracy which was in the ascendant when the new anthropology and eschatology began its gradual development apart from the main line. Sir. 17:27 f. may be adduced as a testimony to this official theology c. 190 B.C. : "Who will praise the Most High in the underworld in place of those who now live and render thanks to Him by their songs of praise ? The song of praise has ceased in the dead who is not (any more); he who lives and is healthy praises the Lord." For the son of Sirach, an enthusiastic supporter of the Zadokites (→ 37, 15 ff.), man is exclusively a creature of this world. Law and wisdom are the pillars on which the world in which he lives rests. But this world is once and for all. God and man meet in it. It is also the place where man is rewarded or punished for his conduct. Hades, on the other hand, is eternal death or a shadowy existence in which there are no relations with God. This orthodox post-exilic thinking continues, so far as we can now see, in two forms. First are the genuine Zadokites and their followers who acc. to the present evidence from Qumran preserved a this-worldly view of man. As may be learned already from Damasc., which always viewed future salvation immanently within the framework of dominant eschatological hopes, it appears esp. on the basis of 1 QS 3:13-4:26 that where man is regarded as a single being in the conflict between the angel of light and the angel of darkness there is no room for belief in the individual life of the soul in the world to come, and in the Qumran texts thus far known to us the motif of resurrection is at best attested only as one which is not necessary to salvation, → n. 38.

The same strand is then found in the official theology of the Jerusalem hierocracy. The older orthodoxy is most clearly set forth in the utterances of opponents, e.g., En. 103:2-6. These also emphasise that the ruling authorities or leading strata are its champions. But one may also see from, e.g., Ps. Sol. 4-6 that in circles radically opposed to the Hasmonean policies of the 1st cent. B.C. the thought still lives on that the individual and society are limited to this life and that there is only this-worldly recompense. [93] This is esp. evident where on the soil of the older orthodox view of the world and God optimism has given way to profound pessimism. Thus recognition of the relatively of all human existence (e.g., Qoh. 2:12 ff.; 3:19 ff.; 8:14) leads the author of Ecclesiastes, not to surrender, but on the contrary to increased activity. He sees it as his task to rejoice in his brief allotted span and to get the best out of it before the eternal night of death falls, Qoh. 9:1-10. In the main it is thus true that what Jos. and the Rabb. see and attack as Sadduceeism or Boethusianism is simply the older dogmatic orthodoxy of Judaism which, on the basis of the Torah and wisdom, is championed by the ruling strata of the Jerusalem hierocracy and their scattered supporters, and which

---

[90] Acc. to present evidence it must be left open or questioned whether this division into periods in Qumran extends beyond the sphere of this world ; cf. Nötscher, op. cit. (→ n. 33), 149-153.

[91] Cf. Hölscher Sadduzäismus, 105 f.

[92] Cf. Bousset-Gressm., 185-187.

[93] Cf. Volz Esch., 27.

was regarded from now on fundamentally as heresy and apostasy, since its supporters perished with the fall of Jerusalem and Pharisaic Rabbinic dogmatics with its new understanding of life and the world achieved ascendancy.

2. The Sadducean View of the Law.

The old-fashioned aspect of Sadduceeism as a religious trend in Judaism is confirmed by statements which speak about the relation of the Sadducees or Boethusians to the Law. Acc. to both Jos. and Rabb. tradition a principal feature of the Sadducees is their rejection of the Pharisaic tradition, the so-called oral law. Thus in Jos. Ant., 13, 297 "the Pharisees gave the people from the tradition of the fathers many injunctions not found in the Law of Moses. On this ground, however, the school of the Sadducees repudiates them, saying that only what is written [in the Law of Moses] is to be regarded as an injunction and there is no need to keep that which comes from the tradition of the fathers." [94]

A decisive element in the Sadducean understanding of the Law is that rejection of the oral tradition of the Rabb. may sometimes work out positively, esp. in discussions of difficult legal decisions. Thus in bSanh., 33b the question is ventilated whether and how far wrong verdicts may be revised in criminal cases. On the basis of a tradition deriving from R. Ishmael (middle of the 2nd cent. A.D., cf. bHor., 4a b) the Palestinian Amoraean Chiyya bar Abba (c. 280 A.D.), following Jochanan bar Nappacha (d. 279 A.D.), asserts that a distinction must be made between verdicts which are based on Rabb. halachah not recognised by the Sadducees and those which the Sadducees also accept because they are based on a corresponding Mosaic law. In the former case there can be revision only in favour of the accused, whereas in the latter revision must also be undertaken even when reopening of the case may be to his disadvantage. The radical seriousness of the Sadducean view of law is acknowledged in bSanh., 33b: A verdict acc. to the basic Sadducean principle must always be in acc. with the legal norm. Hence "grace for law" does not apply even when revision works against the accused. For the Sadducean judge there is no "hedge about the Torah," since he always stands directly on the Mosaic Law. [95]

The difference in the conception of law seems to be the true reason why the Pharisee appears to be a mild judge and the Sadducee a stern judge, as emphatically stressed in Jos. Ant., 13, 294; 20, 199 f. The "hedge about the Torah" enables the Pharisee to apply the Law of God to everyday life. The opponents of Pharisaism or the Pharisaic Rabbinate did not see in this a deepening of piety. On the contrary they saw a dissolution and weakening of the true understanding of the Law. Hence genuine Zadokites (→ n. 36) attack the Pharisaic "hedge about the Law," and for the same reason the Sadducees or Boethusians connected with the temple government reject the oral tradition of the Pharisees, and several centuries later the Karaites bring the same charge against the Rabbinate. [96]

In the cultic sphere the distinctiveness of Sadduceeism may be seen in T. Sukka, 3, 1. In the post-exilic period a popular custom on the 7th day of the Feast of Tabernacles and in the course of the great willow procession was to smite the earth around the altar with twigs. The meaning and derivation of this originally magical rite are no longer

---

[94] Νόμιμά τινα παρέδοσαν τῷ δήμῳ οἱ Φαρισαῖοι ἐκ πατέρων διαδοχῆς, ἅπερ οὐκ ἀναγέγραπται ἐν τοῖς Μωυσέως νόμοις, καὶ διὰ τοῦτο ταῦτα τὸ Σαδδουκαίων γένος ἐκβάλλει, λέγον ἐκεῖνα δεῖν ἡγεῖσθαι νόμιμα τὰ γεγραμμένα, τὰ δ' ἐκ παραδόσεως τῶν πατέρων μὴ τηρεῖν, Jos. Ant., 13, 297, cf. 18, 16 (→ n. 76).

[95] In itself, of course, this does not rule out a Sadducean or Zadokite halachah; for the latter cf. J. T. Milik, Dix ans de découvertes dans le désert de Juda (1956), 36, who emphasises that the halachah of Qumran is more practical than the purely theoretical Pharisaic law codified in the Mishnah, → Φαρισαῖος.

[96] Cf. on this Kahle, op. cit. (→ n. 42), 81.

known. But the practice was so deeply embedded in the ritual of Tabernacles that the Pharisees declared it to be a halachah of Moses from Sinai and approved of it even when the 7th day fell on a Sabbath. The Boethusians, however, took the view that the Sabbath has precedence and tried to get the better of pilgrims by hiding the willows under stones on the evening of the Sabbath. But the participants were not so easily cheated and still practised the rite. [97] This is important because it shows that the Boethusians took a very strict view of the Sabbath, whereas the Pharisees, on the basis of the their doctrine of oral law, could easily incorporate a popular custom of this kind into their system. It may be noted that the story of the Tabernacles ritual in the Synagogue shows that the ancient Boethusian view was still very much alive later. [98]

T. Sukka, 3, 17 offers another example. At the morning sacrifice on the Feast of Tabernacles there was a libation of water. Now a Boethusian once poured the water, not on the altar, but beside it "on his feet." Hereupon the people pelted him with the festal fruits in such a way that a corner of the altar broke off and the rite had to stop until the damage could be repaired with a piece of salt. From Jos. Ant., 13, 372 we learn that this man was the notorious enemy of the Pharisees, Alexander Jannaeus. [99] Acc. to both Jos. and T. Sukka, 3, 16 the officiating high-priest was a scoffer at sacred practices and a foe of true piety. But the historical truth behind the accounts seems to be quite different. There is no basis in the priestly legislation of the Pent. for a cultic libation even in connection with Tabernacles. Libation of water is a popular custom under David in 2 S. 23:16 (cf. 1 S. 7:6), but we do not know when in the post-exilic period a similar rite made its way by right of custom into the festal liturgy. If the high-priest, whether Alexander Jannaeus or an unknown Boethusian, poured out the water without directing it to its sacral purpose, this is evidence, not of a supposed impious mind, but of the fact that he represented a different and older priestly tradition which he tried to carry out in opposition to current practice. The attempt to depart from established popular practice does, of course, evoke the protest of the masses, and the unequivocal position of the Rabb. shows that at this pt. Pharisaism was on the side of the people.

Both examples illustrate the contention of Jos. Ant., 18, 15 that all religious actions take place acc. to the exposition of the Pharisees. If this assertion rests on anti-Sadducean polemic at a time when the Rabbinate had already gained the victory and the Sadducees were only a minority, [100] it is undoubtedly true that with the help of their view of the Law the Pharisees were then in a position to legalise popular practices irrespective of their origin, whereas Sadduceeism was too strongly tied to the priestly tradition to be able to achieve popularity in this way.

C. The Sadducees in the New Testament.

I. The Synoptic Gospels.

A peculiarity of the NT tradition is that the complicated relationships of contemporary Judaism are reflected in it only on the margin. It is not surprising, then, that Sadduceeism is not depicted in its varied character and complexity. [101] The

---

[97] On the term עַמֵּי הָאָרֶץ for the festal pilgrims in T. Sukka → V, 589, 19 ff.

[98] Since processions on the Sabbath were in agreement with the Boethusian but not the Pharisaic halachah care was taken that the 7th day of Tabernacles should not fall on a Sabbath, I. Elbogen, *Der jüd. Gottesdienst in seiner geschichtlichen Entwicklung*[3] (1931), 219.

[99] Cf. Schl. Gesch. Isr., 144 f.

[100] This is clear, e.g., in a discussion about the ritual cleanness of a Sadducean woman in Nidda, 4, 2; T. Nidda, 5, 2 f. In bNidda, 33b it is expressly stated that for fear of the Pharisees she follows their halachah, which shows that Sadduceeism no longer had any power.

[101] In Chr. writings outside the NT it is worth noting that there is no ref. to the

NT documents limit themselves in the main to the one point that the Sadducees deny the doctrine of the resurrection (→ 47, 4 ff.). In the common Synoptic story of the question of the Sadducees (Mk. 12:18-27) [102] the Sadducees are introduced as representatives of a group hostile to Jesus, "which say there is no resurrection." [103] From the structure of Mk. 12:18-27, which culminates in the description of the Sadducees as false teachers (πολὺ πλανᾶσθε), it may be seen that Mark is rooted in the same academic tradition as Josephus (→ n. 76) and the Rabbis (→ 41, 17 ff.), though it is better not just to deduce the content from the form nor to see in Mk. 12:18-27 no more than a bit of community theology. When one realises that what is later depicted as Sadducean heresy is older Jewish orthodoxy, it is not only historically possible, but seems to be the fact that Jesus had to take issue with the representatives of the official theology of the temple government.

Matthew uses the term "Sadducee" more often than Mark. Nevertheless, his use does not show any greater familiarity with Sadduceeism. Indeed, one has the impression that he is even further from the historical reality. In the transition from the story about the resurrection to that of the question concerning the great commandment the Sadducees are said to be worsted (22:34) and the Pharisees are pleased at their discomfiture. There is nothing of this, however, in Mk. 12:28, which simply speaks of one of the scribes being pleased at the fine answer given by Jesus and putting his own question as to the chief commandment. The mention of the Pharisees and Sadducees together at the baptism of John in Mt. 3:7 is stereotyped; Lk. 3:7 refers only to the multitude and thus seems to be closer to the source. The same applies in Mt. 16:1, where in contrast to Mk. 8:11 the Sadducees as well as the Pharisees are said to ask Jesus for a sign from heaven. Finally, in the address on the leaven in Mt. 16:5-12 Jesus tells His disciples to beware of the leaven of the Pharisees and Sadducees, whereas Mk. 8:15 has the leaven of the Pharisees and Herod in this connection. In Mt. 16:11 f., which is peculiar to Mt., the Evangelist not only mentions the Pharisees and Sadducees together but also finds a parallel between their teachings. [104] The distinctive aspects of the two groups are thus ignored.

II. Acts.

Luke rests on a more solid tradition. He does not make stereotyped use of the term "Sadducee" either in the Gospel, where the only instance in Lk. 20:27 sticks close to Mk. 12:18, or in Acts. The Sadducees are mentioned only three times in Ac., and each time here again in connection with belief in the resurrection.

Ac. 4:1-22 tells of the imprisonment of the apostles Peter and John after their address in the temple (3:12-26) and of the ensuing trial. [105] The temple guard,

---

Sadducees apart from a single mention in Just. Dial., 80, 4. This passage simply presents them in traditional guise as deniers of the resurrection. It does not appear, then, that Just. has any real acquaintance with them [W. Schneemelcher].

[102] Cf. Mt. 22:23-33; Lk. 20:27-40 and the comm., ad loc.

[103] The debate, which M. Dibelius, Formgeschichte d. Ev.³ (1959), 40, 54, 56, categorises as a "paradigm," proceeds along the same lines as similar debates between the Rabb. and the Sadducees. Thus it bears a strong affinity to bSanh., 90b, where Rabban Gamaliel II (c. 90 A.D.) is asked by the Sadducees to support the resurrection from Scripture, → 47, 7 ff.

[104] Τότε συνῆκαν ὅτι οὐκ εἶπεν προσέχειν ἀπὸ τῆς ζύμης τῶν Φαρισαίων καὶ Σαδδουκαίων, ἀλλὰ ἀπὸ τῆς διδαχῆς τῶν Φαρισαίων καὶ Σαδδουκαίων, Mt. 16:12.

[105] Cf. Haench. Ag. on 4:1-12.

A. Origin and Meaning.

σάκκος is one of the terms for objects of civilisation common to the whole world of antiquity, both Semitic and Indo-Europ. [1] It comes from Babylon (Accadian šaqqu) by way of Palestine (Heb. שׂק) [2] into the Gk. and Lat. world (saccus) [3] and thence into modern Europ. languages ("sack," "Sack," "sac" etc.). Phoenician trade probably played a decisive part in the transition from the Semitic to the Indo-Europ. tongues. [4]

The original meaning [5] is not "sack" in the current sense but 1. "hair-cloth," i.e., a coarse fabric (not felt), [6] mostly of goats' hair, [7] though also camels' hair, cf. Mt. 3:4 (→ n. 54) etc. It was made in several lands around the Mediterranean, but esp. in Cilicia, [8] which exported a good deal of the stuff for tent-making. [9] This is how the material came to be known as cilicium, [10] e.g., Plin. Hist. Nat., 6, 143 : [tabernacula] quae ciliciis metantur, "tents pitched of awnings of goats' hair." In Lat., esp. the Lat. Bible, this is synon. with saccus. Since the hair of goats in these countries was mostly dark brown or black (cf. Cant. 4:1; 6:5), the material made from it and the tents, [11] sails, carpets, clothes etc. manufactured from this material were dark or black, cf. 1 S. 19:13, 16; Cant. 1:5; Sir. 25:17 Cod B; Rev. 6:12 (→ 61, 7 ff.); 1 Cl., 8, 3 (→ 63,

_Is. 50:3_

---

riten (1932), 48 f., 58 f. etc.; B. Poschmann, Paenitentia secunda. Die kirchliche Busse im ältesten Christentum bis Cyprian u. Orig. (1940); also Die abendländische Kirchenbusse im Ausgang des chr. Altertums (1928), 18 f., 89 f., 148 f., 168.

[1] Cf. O. Schrader-A. Nehring, Art. "Sack" in Reallex. f. idg. Altertumskunde², II (1929), 270.

[2] Cf. KAT, 603, 650; H. Zimmern, Akkadische Fremdwörter als Beweis f. bab. Kultureinfluss² (1917), 67; Köhler-Baumg., s.v. שׂק; Schwally Miscellen, 174 : perhaps it is Egyptian.

[3] Cf. H. Lewy, Die semitischen Lehnwörter im Griech. (1895), 87; Walde-Hofmann, II, 459.

[4] Cf. T. K. Cheyne, Art. "Sack" in EB, IV, 4182.

[5] In Gk. it is written either in Attic fashion with one κ (e.g., Aristoph. Ach., 822; Eccl., 502) or in Doric with double κκ (e.g., Aristoph. Ach., 745 on the lips of a man from Megara); cf. Phryn. Ecl., 229 and other grammarians of antiquity, esp. Thes. Steph., s.v. Both forms occur in inscr. and pap., cf. esp. the instances in Pass., Liddell-Scott, Preisigke Wört., s.v. The same vacillation may be seen in the diminutive σακ(κ)ίον. σάκκος prevailed, it alone being found in LXX and NT. The Hexapla transcribes שׂק as σεκκι in ψ 29:12 col b.

[6] So erroneously Schürer, II, 80, n. 219; that it was woven may be seen plainly from S. Lv., 11, 32 (214a) cf. Str.-B., II, 746, n. 1 and S. Nu., 157 on 31:20.

[7] Cf. Hesych., s.v. σάκος αἴγειος, Nu. 31:20; S. Nu., 157 on 31:20; Cook, 4182; Hauck, 216; Hermann, 127; Hindringer, 967; Leclercq, 1623; Lesêtre, 760; Mau, 2545; Nowack, 614; Thomsen, 390; H. B. Tristram, The Natural History of the Bible⁷ (1883), 66; Dalman Arbeit, V, 17 f., 163 with n. 1, 165, 175 f.; Blümner, 204. R. J. Forbes, Studies in Ancient Technology, IV (1956), 58, cf. 63, disregards cloth of goats' hair as economically insignificant.

[8] Cf. Plin. Hist. Nat., 8, 203; J. Finegan, Light from the Ancient East (1946), 255 : "Goats living on the Taurus Mountains, where the snow lies until May, grow magnificent coats whose hair has long been famous for strength and durability. This is spun into thread and woven into a tough fabric which anciently was known from the name of the province as cilicium. This fabric, in turn, is made into tents and other necessities."

[9] It is debated whether there is a connection between Paul's belonging to Tarsus, where the fabric is still used, and his being a σκηνοποιός, Ac. 18:3. Schürer, II, 80, n. 219 and Str.-B., II, 746 f. think there is, but most ancient expositors took → σκηνοποιός to mean "leather-worker," "saddler," and many modern exegetes agree, cf. Zn. Ag. on 18:3 with n. 10; Jackson-Lake, I, 4, 223 on Ac. 18:3; Haench. Ag. on 18:3, n. 3.

[10] Cilicium is found as a loan word in the Rabb.: קילקי e.g., S. Lv., 53b; bShab., 64a; cf. Schürer, II, 80, n. 219; Dalman Arbeit, V, 163, n. 1; Krauss, 534, n. 111; Levy Wört., IV, 293, s.v.

[11] Cf. Dalman Arbeit, VI, 29 f. with Ill. 18a. The tabernacle was made of this dark hairy fabric, cf. Ex. 26:7; 35:6, 23, 26; 36:14.

12 ff.). The term שַׂק-σάκκος then came to be used not merely for the material but also for things made of it, esp. 2. the "sack," [12] e.g., Gn. 42:25, 27, 35; [13] Jos. 9:4; Hdt., IX, 80; Aristoph. Lys., 1209; Poll. Onom., 10, 64, 3; 3. the "carpet," e.g., Est. 4:3 cf. also 2 S. 21:10; Jos. Ant., 19, 349; Eus. Hist. Eccl., II, 10, 5; Thdrt., 1, 24, 1 (→ n. 47), 4. the "hair-clothing" [14] used specifically for mourning and penitence (→ lines 10 ff.) though also as a working apron, cf. Herm. s., 8, 4, 1: περίζωσαι ὡμόλινον [15] ... ἐκ σάκκου γεγονὸς καθαρόν, also things made of hair, 5. the "strainer," "sieve," [16] P. Hamb., 10, 39 : σάκκοι τρίχινοι, or like sackcloth, 6. a great "beard," [17] Aristoph. Eccl., 502, or resembling sacks, 7. "hair-sack," "hair-net," "hair-band." [18]

B. Use and Meaning of Hair-Clothing (Sackcloth) [19] in Antiquity and especially the Old Testament.

1. σάκκος as a Garment of Hair-Cloth. From the cultural and religious standpt. and esp. in relation to the NT, σάκκος is most important in the sense of a garment of hair-cloth. As a garment of mourning (→ 59, 3 ff.) and penitence (→ 59, 11 ff.; 61, 21 ff.) it seems to be an ancient institution in the Semitic world; [20] it is also found quite early as a prophetic garment, → 62, 9 ff. It is probably an ancient form of human clothing (cf. Gn. 3:7, 21) [21] preserved as a garment for times and situations of mostly religious significance. [22] Originally it was perhaps no more than a loin-cloth [23] but later became bigger. [24] It was then fastened with a girdle (cf. Mk. 1:6 and par.) or cord (Is. 3:24) on the hips, cf. Gn. 37:34; 1 K. 20:31 f.; Is. 20:2; Jdt. 4:14; 8:5 etc. and was usually

---

[12] Cf. Hug, 1622 f. Derived from it are σακκίζω "to felt" (Hesych., s.v.: ἐπὶ τοῦ ἐκκενῶσαι διὰ κλοπὴν τοὺς σάκκους); σακκοφόρος (σακοφόρος), σακκηγός, σακκᾶς (nick-name for the philosopher Ammonius Sakkas from his former work), Lat. saccarius; cf. A. H. Hug, Art. "Saccarius" in PaulyW., 1a (1914), 1620; E. Ziebarth, Art. "σακκοφόρος" Pauly-W. Suppl., 7 (1940), 1200, also Lesêtre, Art. "Sac" with many instances and 2 ill. On σάκκος as a measure = the load of an ass cf. F. Preisigke, "Kornfrachten im Faijûm," APF, 3 (1906), 45-54, esp. 47, n. 1.

[13] J has אַמְתַּחַת for שַׂק in Gn. 42-44; for this (and once for שַׂק in 42:27) LXX uses μάρσιππος "bag"; elsewhere LXX always has σάκκος for שַׂק (only ψ 29:12 in 'ΑΣ, also ψ 34:13 in the Quinta) [Bertram].

[14] In full לְבוּשׁ שֵׂעָר (Est. 4:2), "garment of (fabric of) goats' hair," Gk. τρίχινον ἔνδυμα, e.g., Athanasius Vita Antonii, 91 (MPG, 26 [1857], 972 B), Lat. saccea tunica, Hier. in Is. 20:1 (MPL, 24 [1845], 188 D). Hence σακκοφόρος (→ n. 12) can also be one who wears a hairy garment, e.g., Plut. Instituta Laconica, 37 (II, 239c); cf. also Just. Dial., 107, 2 (σακκοφορέω and σακκοφορία); on the later ascetic groups of σακκοφόροι → 64, 14 ff.

[15] This naturally does not mean "shoulder-cloth" (from ὦμος, so H. Weinel in Hennecke[2] ad loc.) but "coarse apron" (from ὠμός, Dib. Herm., ad loc.: "a kind of apron made of [goats'] hair material").

[16] Cf. Hug, 1624, hence σακεύω, σακίζω, σακελίζω "to sift."

[17] Cf. the use of קילקי (→ n. 10) in Miq., 9, 2.

[18] Cf. Hug, 1623 f., hence σακκοπλόκος, σακχυφάντης, saccarius (→ n. 12) "maker of hair-bands"; cf. also V. Ryssel, Sir. in Kautzsch Apokr., 360 on 25:17.

[19] In the narrower sense of the robe made of sackcloth.

[20] Cf. Emonds, 812; Schrank, 69 f., 61, n. 1.

[21] Cf. among others Benzinger, 75.

[22] Cf. Schwally Leben, 12; Kittel, 159; Cook, 4183; → IV, 551, n. 16; M. Jastrow, "Baring of the Arm and Shoulder as a Sign of Mourning," ZAW, 22 (1902), 117-120. Perhaps it was a return to an older form of clothing, cf. Thomsen, 390 f. Ref. is often correctly made in this connection (e.g., Schwally Miscellen, 174 f.) to the related iḥrâm, a kind of leather apron worn by pilgrims to Mecca.

[23] Schwally Leben, 12; Benzinger, 75; Cook, 4182; Dalman Arbeit, V, 202.

[24] Cf. Grüneisen, 64. A larger size is suggested by its use as a covering or an under-blanket (cf. 2 S. 21:10) or a penitential mat → n. 47.

worn as the only garment over the naked body. [25] The upper half hung down over the lower half [26] and left the upper part of the body uncovered. [27]

2. Sackcloth as Mourning Garb. This way of wearing sackcloth was significant in relation to its use for mourning, [28] since it left the breast free for κόπτεσθαι, e.g., Is. 32:11 f. → III, 831, 11 ff., 833, 7 ff., 837, 37 ff., 842, 12 ff. The black colour of the cloth was also important here as the ancient colour of mourning among many peoples. [29] The custom of wearing sackcloth, like other mourning rites, came from nations around Israel. [30] It established itself both for personal mourning (e.g., Gn. 37:34, Jos. Ant., 2, 38; 2 S. 21:10; Jl. 1:8; Jdt. 8:5) and also national mourning (e.g., 2 S. 3:31, Jos. Ant., 7, 40; cf. Is. 3:24; Jer. 6:26; 48:37).

3. Sackcloth as Penitential Garb. In earlier times in the East sackcloth was worn not only as mourning garb but also as penitential garb before both gods and men; the motifs of grief and self-abasement are the common inner root of the two uses. Babylon was probably the first home of the penitential use, [31] and from there it quickly spread to Israel. [32] The putting on of sackcloth was a sign

---

[25] Sometimes sackcloth is worn under the upper garment, next to the skin, so 2 K. 6:30 (in later antiquity, Hermann, 134) or over the usual garment, so Jon. 3:6; cf. esp. Jos. Ant., 5, 37: σάκκους ἐπενδύντες ταῖς στολαῖς, where Jos. projects the practice of his own day back into earlier times. Cf. Jdt. 9:1, where sackcloth is combined with widows' weeds. But cf. Grüneisen, 79 : sackcloth is a cloak worn over the undergarment.

[26] Cf. AOB, Ill. 198.

[27] Cf. Jer. 48:37; 2 Macc. 3:19 (ὑπεζωσμέναι ... ὑπὸ τοὺς μαστοὺς αἱ γυναῖκες σάκκους); Galling, 337; AOB, Ill. 665 and 198; cf. expressions like ἐπὶ πάσης ὀσφύος σάκκος in Ιερ. 31(48):37.

[28] Cf. Benzinger, 75 and 78; also Art. "Kleider u. Geschmeide," RE³, 10, 519 f.; on mourning rites in gen., Grüneisen, 61-104 (with bibl.); Benzinger, 134; A. Bertholet, *Kulturgesch. Israels* (1919), 139; → III, 837, 34 ff. Several explanations have been advanced for wearing sackcloth as mourning attire : 1. it is originally part of the cult of the dead ; one gets closer to the dead in sackcloth in the attitude of humble supplication, Schwally Leben, 12; 2. it has its origin in the belief in spirits of the dead against which there has to be protection, hence a minimum of clothing or complete nakedness in mourning lest the spirit lodge somewhere in the clothes ; 3. it is based on respect for the power of death, "the house of death" being "a temple of death," cf. H. J. Elhorst, "Die isr. Trauerriten," *Festschr. f. J. Wellhausen*, ZAW Beih., 27 (1914), 117-128. This explanation is perhaps on the right track. On the frontier of death man wears the simplest garb which is that of his forefathers and also expresses respect for the powers to which he is subject.

[29] Eur. Alc., 440; Or., 458; Hel., 1088; cf. Diod. S., 19, 106 : εἰώθασι ... ἐπειδὰν μείζων τις ἀτυχία γένηται περὶ τὴν πόλιν, μέλασι σάκκοις κατακαλύπτειν τὰ τείχη, → μέλας, IV, 549, 9 ff. and n. 4; 550, 28 ff. and n. 11. F. Delitzsch, Art. "Farben in d. Bibel," RE³, 5, 759 f.; Dalman Arbeit, V, 214; Herzog-Hauser, 1226-1230; G. Radke, *Die Bdtg. d. weissen u. d. schwarzen Farbe in Kult u. Brauch d. Griechen u. Röm.*, Diss. Berlin (1936), 69-73; P. Stengel, *Opfergebräuche d. Griechen* (1910), 135; Wettstein, II, 775.

[30] Cf. AOB, 64 with Ill. 198 (Egypt); 191 with Ill. 665 (Byblos), also Galling, Ill. 7. Among the early Gks. we do not find sackcloth but only ashes etc. as a sign of mourning, Hom. Il., 18, 22-27; 24, 164 f., though Plut. Instituta Laconica, 37 (II, 239c): σακκοφόρον ἀνεῖλον διότι παρυφὴν εἰς τὸν σάκκον ἐνέβαλε, records a Spartan practice in the class. age.

[31] Cf. Schrank, 69 f.; KAT, 393 (with examples); H. Winckler, *Altorientalische Forschungen*, II, 1 (1898), 29, 35, 44.

[32] Originally the Gk. world had no special penitential garb, → n. 30; known penitents in the underworld (cf. Nilsson, I², 690 f., 825) did not wear such. σάκκος came into the Hell. world with Semitic cults, e.g., those of Sabazios and Dea Syria, cf. Menand. Deisidaimon in Porphyr. Abst., IV, 15 of the Syrians and Plut. Superst., 7 (II, 168d) probably with ref. to an adherent of Phrygian-Syrian cults, cf. Emonds, 813, who also refers to the

or parabolic action [33] which actualised what it signified. Self-disfigurement by sackcloth and often by ashes (→ n. 48) and cutting the hair or beard (cf. Sir. 25:17 vl.) represents profound self-humiliation [34, 35] before God (e.g., 2 K. 19:1; [36] 1 Ch. 21:16) and before men (e.g., 1 K. 20:31 f.) [37] with a view to attaining favour and reconciliation and thus warding off impending disaster. [38] To stress the mood of penitence sackcloth was often worn at night too, 1 K. 21:27; Jl. 1:13. It was worn esp. in times of national emergency (2 K. 6:30; Da. 9:3; 1 Macc. 3:47) or threatened danger for the people (Est. 4:1 f.; Is. 22:12; Jer. 6:26; Jon. 3:5 f., 8), [39] above all when eschatological destruction seemed imminent (Jl. 1:13; cf. Am. 8:10; Ez. 7:18). Sackcloth was also put on in personal crises to support the plea for help, cf. Ps. 30:11; 35:13; 69:11; Jos. Ant., 7, 154.

As religious practices were ritualised, sackcloth became a definite penitential rite, cf. Neh. 9:1; Job 16:15; Jon. 3:5-8; Da. 9:3. With other penitential ceremonies which had become mere forms it thus fell under the condemnation of the prophets, cf. Is. 58:5. Nevertheless, it remained an established custom in Judaism. It was often worn during fasts, cf. already Ps. 35:13 (→ n. 48). Indeed, theurgic efficacy was ascribed to it as an aid in prayer, [40] → n. 38.

---

cult of Hermes Trismegistos ; F. Cumont, *Die orientalischen Religionen im röm. Heidentum*[4] (1959), 37 with n. 41; texts (esp. Catal. Cod. Astr. Graec., VIII, 4, 148, 2; 165, 16) also in Steinleitner, 72 f., cf. 113 f., also Pr.-Bauer[5], *s.v.* σάκκος.

[33] Cf. G. Fohrer, *Die symbolischen Handlungen d. Propheten* (1953), esp. 91-97; also C. A. Keller, *Das Wort Oth als "Offenbarungszeichen Gottes,"* Diss. Basel (1946); G. Stählin, "Die Gleichnishandlungen Jesu," *Kosmos u. Ekklesia, Festschr. f. W. Stählin* (1953), 9-22.

[34] Sackcloth can also symbolise humiliation by others, i.e., as the garb of prisoners of war, cf. Is. 3:24 with branding. This perhaps explains the conduct of Benhadad's men in 1 K. 20:31 f.; they pretended to be prisoners of war before Ahab. Cf. Grüneisen, 64 f., 86, 88, who suggests that prisoners of war were originally under the ban and thus wore mourning garb.

[35] Cf. the Rabb. interpretation in bTaan., 16a (Str.-B., IV, 84, n. 4): "Why clothe oneself with raiment of sackcloth? R. Chiyya bAbba (c. 300) has said it is meant to express : 'Lo, we are made like cattle' " (with ref. to sackcloth being made of coarse animal hair → n. 59). Not very likely is the explanation considered by Schwally Leben, 12 that as originally the garb of slaves sackcloth represents the attitude of the slave both before God and men, whom one approaches with humble supplication, and also before the dead.

[36] Par. (v. 2) is the sending of messengers in sackcloth to the prophet Isaiah with the request for intercession, cf. also Est. 4:17 k.

[37] Cf. the much reproduced relief of Sennacherib in Nineveh showing the capture of Lachish (between Hebron and Gaza), e.g., in A. Legendre, Art. "Lachis" in *Dict. Bibl.,* IV, 23, Ill. 11; G. E. Wright, *Bibl. Archaeol.* (1957), 164 ff., Ill. 116 and 117: The inhabitants of Lachish are arrayed in penitential garb — the meaning is much debated — before the conqueror.

[38] Cf. the incidents with μέλαινα ἐσθής in Jos. Vit., 138; Ant., 14, 172; Krauss, I, 550, n. 211; for later antiquity Hermann, 134. Obviously sackcloth was supposed to have magical efficacy in relation to those upon whom the wearers called, Jos. Bell., 2, 237 → n. 40.

[39] In such cases, then, the whole nation, including domestic animals (Jon. 3:8), take part in the penitential acts of fasting and sackcloth ; cf. the place of animals in mourning, which is common in history and national customs, e.g., Plut. Aristides, 14 (I, 327): shaving horses and mules ; cf. E. F. C. Rosenmüller, Scholia in Vetus Testamentum, 7, 2² (1827), 394 f. on Jon. 3:8. Jon. depicts the genuine repentance of the Ninevites in terms of the established ceremonies of his day.

[40] Cf. the saying of R. Chelbo (c. 300) in Str.-B., IV, 103 : "He who puts on sackcloth and fasts, let him not lay it aside until what he prays for has been granted"; cf. Jalqut Reubeni, 55d on Gn. 33:1 (Str.-B., I, 605): "The valuable thing about putting on sackcloth is that the prayer of man does not return empty."

4. Sackcloth as Prophetic Garb. For sackcloth as prophetic garb → 62, 9 ff.

C. σάκκος in the New Testament.

In the NT σάκκος occurs only 4 times, always as a garment of hairy fabric
(→ 58, 12 ff.), once (Mt. 11:21 = Lk. 10:13) as penitential garb, once (Rev. 11:3)
as prophetic garb, and once (Rev. 6:12) in a comparison with the colour black
as the point of comparison.

1. σάκκος as an Example of Dark Things. Rev. 6:12 : καὶ ὁ ἥλιος ἐγένετο
μέλας ὡς σάκκος τρίχινος. Apart from roughness and simplicity, which are a
mark of humility, the colour black (→ 59, 5 ff. with n. 29) is also a basic characteristic of σάκκος. Hence the eschatological darkening (→ σκοτίζω) of the sun [41]
etc. can be depicted under the image of garbing with sackcloth, → IV, 551, 6 ff. [42]

> The direct model is Is. 50:3. The theme of the darkening of the sun, which can be
> traced back to the omens of the Bab. time of cursing, [43] is a common one in OT, later
> Jewish and pre-Chr. eschatology, [44] cf. Am. 8:9; Is. 13:10; Jl. 2:31 = Ac. 2:20, whence
> also Ass. Mos. 10:5; Jl. 3:15; Qoh. 12:2; En. 102:2; Sib., 3, 801 f.; 5, 476-482; Mk. 13:24
> par.; Lk. 21:25, also 23:44 f.; Rev. 9:2 from Jl. 2:10.

In Rev. 6:12 the darkening of the sun is one of the events with which the
opening of the next to the last seal introduces the ἡμέρα μεγάλη τῆς ὀργῆς
(v. 17 → V, 401, 10 ff.; 430, 13 ff.); [45] in the Synoptic Apocalypse it comes immediately before the *parousia* of the Son of Man, Mk. 13:24 ff.

2. σάκκος as Penitential Garb. σάκκος is a sign of conversion and repentance
in the saying of Jesus to the cities of Galilee which reject Him, Mt. 11:21 =
Lk. 10:13 (Q): εἰ ἐν Τύρῳ καὶ Σιδῶνι ἐγένοντο (Lk. ἐγενήθησαν) αἱ δυνάμεις
αἱ γενόμεναι ἐν ὑμῖν, πάλαι ἂν ἐν σάκκῳ καὶ σποδῷ (Lk. + καθήμενοι)
μετενόησαν. By adding καθήμενοι to σποδῷ in a saying which otherwise is almost literally the same, Luke shows clearly that his understanding is slightly
different from that of Matthew. For Matthew σάκκος is a garment and ashes
are carried on the head, but Luke seems to have sitting [46] in view as a gesture
of grief → III, 443, 13 ff., so that σάκκος is the penitential mat [47] and σποδός

---

[41] This is not due to the earthquake which comes just before (Bss. Apk., *ad loc.*) nor is
the sun obscured by a dark cloud as in Ez. 32:7; Jl. 2:2; cf. on this F. Boll, *Aus d. Offenbarung Joh.* (1914), 17 with n. 5; also Clemen, 391.

[42] Cf. bSuk., 29a : If the sun has the appearance of a sack, arrows of hunger come on
the world, cf. Str.-B., I, 955 on Mt. 24:29. Acc. to Hier. Pelag., II, 3 (MPL, 23 [1883],
589 C D) all heaven will be covered by a σάκκος (*cilicium*) on the Day of Judgment.

[43] Cf. KAT, 393.

[44] Cf. Clemen, 142-144; Bss. Apk. on 6:12.

[45] Cf. J. Behm, *Die Offenbarung d. Joh., NT Deutsch,* 11⁷ (1956), *ad loc.*: The storm of
the great day of wrath has come.

[46] Later we find standing on σάκκος, e.g., in baptismal exorcism, cf. F. J. Dölger, *Der
Exorzismus im altchr. Taufritual* (1909), 114-118; J. Quasten, "Theodore of Mopsuestia on
the Exorcism of the Cilicium," HThR, 35 (1942), 209-219; Hermann, 131.

[47] In the OT and Judaism, too, sackcloth sometimes has the form of a penitential mat,
cf. Is. 58:5; Est. 4:3; Jos. Ant., 19, 349, also Eus. Hist. Eccl., II, 10, 8 : the whole multitude
with women and children on the death of Herod Agrippa I (cf. Ac. 12:23) ἐπὶ σάκκων
(Eus. σάκκον) καθεσθεῖσα (Rufin. *supra cilicia strati*) τῷ πατρίῳ νόμῳ τὸν θεὸν
ἱκέτευον ὑπὲρ τοῦ βασιλέως. Jos. often (cf. Ant., 10, 11; 12, 300) stresses the motif of
faithfulness to the Law in wearing sackcloth, though it is not commanded in the Torah.
Cf. Schl. Mt., 379; jTaan., 4, 8 (68d, 53 f.); Jos. Ant., 7, 154 (which distinguishes between the
mourning garment, μέλαινα ἐσθής, and the penitential mat, σάκκος).

the place where the penitents sit. [48] According to both conceptions σάκκος and σποδός are the outer signs of humiliation and grief, and hence of inner μετάνοια, though Jesus was not necessarily saying that such signs were essential for those around Him. [49] On His view the important thing is not sackcloth and the like, but conversion. [50] In His saying He probably had in mind the depiction of the μετάνοια of the Ninevites in Jon. 3:4 ff.; the same image occurs shortly after in a related saying in Mt. and Lk. (Mt. 12:41; Lk. 11:32). In both instances the Gentiles are contrasted with impenitent Israel. [51]

3. σάκκος as Prophetic Garb. Οἱ δύο μάρτυρες, who are introduced abruptly in Rev. 11:3 as though they had been referred to before, are described as prophetic figures (→ IV, 495, 10 ff.; VI, 853, 22 ff.): καὶ προφητεύσουσιν ... περιβεβλημένοι σάκκους; in v. 10 they are then expressly called οἱ δύο προφῆται. The depiction is based generally on Moses (v. 6b) and Elijah (v. 5, 6a). [52] The σάκκοι in which they are clothed [53] bear allusion to the prophetic garb of Elijah, though

---

[48] Cf. Schl. Mt. on 11:21. Elsewhere σάκκος is often found with σποδός or fasting, e.g., Taan., 2, 1 (→ n. 50); Gn. r., 84 (154a), cf. E. K. Dietrich, *Die Umkehr (Bekehrung u. Busse) im AT u. im Judt.* (1936), 369-371; Str.-B., IV, 103 f., or with both, Da. 9:3; Barn., 7, 5. Sometimes the use of σάκκος and σποδός corresponds to the idea in Mt., so Est. 4:1 f.: 1 Macc. 3:47; Test. Jos. 15:2; cf. Jos. Ant., 20, 123 : μετενδυσάμενοι σάκκους καὶ σποδοῦ τὰς κεφαλὰς ἀναπλήσαντες, Bell., 2, 237: σάκκους ἀμπεχόμενοι καὶ τέφραν τῶν κεφαλῶν καταχέοντες, jShebi., 6, 4 (37a, 7) in Schl. Mt. on 11:21; Dt. r., 11 (207c) in Str.-B., III, 688 on Hb. 5:7; PREl, 43 in Str.-B., I, 647, sometimes to that in Lk., so Is. 58:5 : οὐδ' ἄν ... σάκκον καὶ σποδὸν ὑποστρώσῃ, also Just. Dial., 15, 4 (in Barn., 3, 2 ἐνδύσησθε is added); Est. 4:3 : σάκκον καὶ σποδὸν ἔστρωσαν ἑαυτοῖς jTaan., 4, 8 (68d, 54): יוֹשֵׁב עַל הַשַּׂק וְעַל הָאֵפֶר, also Barn., 7, 5 : τοῦ λαοῦ νηστεύοντος καὶ κοπτομένου ἐπὶ σάκκου καὶ σποδοῦ. The same combination of σάκκος καὶ σποδός = *cinis et cilicium* is common later in penitential practice (→ 63, 19 ff.) so already Tert. De Paenitentia, 9, 4 (CSEL, 76, p. 163, 11); cf. → IV, 1008, 11 ff.; Jungmann, 48, 43, 58 f., and sometimes they are put on the penitent's head, sometimes he lies on sackcloth strewn with ashes, so Nilus Ep., III, 243 (MPG, 79 [1860], 497 C): ... σάκκου καὶ σποδοῦ ὑποστρώσεως, esp. when he is sick, cf. Jungmann, 114, 122, n. 438, 131, n. 18.

[49] In the early Church, however, σάκκος became one of the necessary signs (→ 63, 18 ff.) indispensable to express penitence, humility, or sorrow for sin, e.g., Nilus Ep., III, 243 (MPG, 79 [1860], 497 C): κάλλιστον ... καὶ μάλα πρέπον ... δι' ἔργων ποιεῖσθαι τὴν ἐξομολόγησιν, οἷον δὲ νηστείας καὶ ἀγρυπνίας τε καὶ σάκκου καὶ σποδοῦ ὑποστρώσεως καὶ ἐλεημοσύνης ἀφειδοῦς καὶ ἱλαρᾶς καὶ τῶν ἄλλων καρπῶν τῶν κεχρεωστημένων τῇ ἀκριβεῖ μετανοίᾳ, cf. the examples in Hermann, 135 f. In some sense this was retrogressive as compared with the insights of many Rabb. → n. 50.

[50] Cf. Taan., 2, 1: It is not said of the men of Nineveh : God saw their penitential garb and fasting, but Jon. 3:10. Cf. also bTaan., 16a (→ n. 35), on this Dietrich, *op. cit.* (→ n. 48); → IV, 998, 1 ff.

[51] Cf. Bultmann Trad., 118 who ascribes both logia to the community, but 1. mention of the otherwise unnamed towns of Chorazin and Bethsaida as the sites of Jesus' work suggests very early tradition ; 2. there is little more typical of the real Jesus than the self-understanding and the evaluation of the miracles in these sayings, cf. J. Schniewind, *Das Ev. nach Mt., NT Deutsch,* 2⁸ (1956), ad loc.

[52] Probably the two prophets are meant to be Moses and Elijah, → II, 939, 17 ff.; IV, 327, 7 ff. with n. 28; IV, 863, 21 ff. with n. 189. There are many other conjectures : Enoch and Elijah (Bss. Apk.; ad loc.; W. Bousset, *Der Antichrist* [1895], 134-139; → II, 939, 2 ff., 940, 12 ff.); Ezra and Baruch (cf. 4 Esr. 6:26); also Peter and Paul (J. Munck, *Pt. u. Pls. in d. Off. Joh.* [1950]); John and James. The OT colouring is an argument against apostles, cf. Clemen, 144-146; Bss. Apk. on 11:3; Bousset-Gressm., 122, 233; O. Cullmann Pt. (1952), 94-96.

[53] The dark σάκκοι are also a counterpart to the δόξα which surrounded the companions of Jesus on the Mt. of Transfiguration, Lk. 9:31.

in 2 K. 1:8 this is a skin rather than a garment of hair.[54] The verse is an important example of σάκκος as prophetic garb. As in the case of mourning or penitential raiment (→ 58, 16 ff.) an archaic style of clothing is probably adopted,[55] and here too (→ 59, 13 f.) it is natural to suppose that there is a connection between the task of the prophets and their "professional dress."[56] Especially in Rev. 11:3 the σάκκοι of the witnesses probably signify their task of preaching and threatening punishment, just as the raiment of the Baptist (Mk. 1:6 par.) may be regarded as a parabolic action (→ 59, 15 ff.) which accompanied his preaching of repentance.[57]

D. σάκκος in the Post-New Testament Period.

1. In the post-apost. fathers and early Apologists the use of σάκκος is definitely coloured by the OT, cf. 1 Cl., 8, 3 in an otherwise unknown quotation : ἐὰν ὦσιν αἱ ἁμαρτίαι ὑμῶν ... πυρρότεραι κόκκου καὶ μελανώτεραι σάκκου (cf. Is. 1:18); Barn., 3, 2 (Is. 58:4 f.); 7, 5 (Lv. 23:26-32); Just. Dial., 15, 4 (Is. 58:4 f.); 107, 2 (Jon. 3:5 ff.). Only Herm. s., 8, 4, 1 mentions a garment of hair-cloth as a working garment, → 58, 6 f. with n. 15.

2. Not much later the σάκκος τρίχινος — saccus (cilicium) is an established part of the practice of penance as found already in Tert. De Pudicitia, 13 (conciliciatus et concineratus, "covered with the penitential robe and ashes") and Cyprian De Lapsis, 35 (in cilicio et sordibus volutari, "to wallow in the mire in the penitential robe"), → n. 48. This practice was enjoined by several synods, e.g., Toledo, 400 and 589; Agde, 506. During penance the cilicium had to be worn and it could be put off only on remission.[58] Often the symbolical roughness of the garment is emphasised;[59] it signifies sorrow for sin and self-abasement, e.g., Ps.-Ambr. De Lapsu virginis, 8 (MPL, 16 [1880], 394): totum corpus ... cinere aspersum et opertum cilicio perhorrescat ...,[60] and its effect is

---

[54] What is said about the "professional dress" of the prophets in the OT (cf. Kittel, 183) is not uniform : 1. a skin in 2 K. 1:8; cf. Hb. 11:37; also Mk. 1:6 D : δέρρις; 2. a hairy mantle in 1 S. 28:14; 2 K. 2:8, 13 f.; Zech. 13:4; 3. sackcloth in Is. 20:2, cf. also the instructive ref. in Mart. Is. 2:10 to the secessio of prophets clothed in sackcloth, and esp. the garment of the Baptist, ἔνδυμα ... ἀπὸ τριχῶν καμήλου, Mt. 3:4; cf. E. Nestle, "Zum Mantel aus Kamelshaaren," ZNW, 8 (1907), 238; Wbg. Mk., 41, n. 15 on 1:6; → VI, 838, 9 ff.

[55] Cf. Schwally Miscellen, 174.

[56] Cf. Dillmann in Kittel, 183; F. Düsterdieck, Die Offenbarung Johannis, Krit.-exeget. Komm. z. NT, 16⁴ (1887) on 11:3; Dalman Arbeit, V, 165 and 248.

[57] Later many preachers of repentance themselves wear sackcloth. The early Church found in John the Baptist a NT model of the wearer of sackcloth, cf. Ps.-Chrys. Opus imperfectum in Mt., Hom. 3 (MPG, 56 [1859], 648).

[58] Hermann, 131; cf. C. J. v. Hefele, Conciliengesch., II² (1875), 653, 779; M. Férotin, Le Liber Ordinum, Monumenta Ecclesiae Liturgica, V (1904), 87 f. → n. 61.

[59] E.g., Ps.-Isidore De Officiis Ecclesiasticis, II, 17, 4 (MPL, 83 [1862], 802 C): bene ergo in cilicio et cinere poenitens deplorat peccatum, quia in cilicio asperitas est et punctio peccatorum etc. Cf. Bas. Ep., 45, 1 (MPG, 32 [1857], 365 C): σάκκῳ δὲ τραχεῖ τὸ σῶμά σου διανύττων, also the saying from the Liturgy of St. Caecilia : cilicio Caecilia membra domabat (Leclercq, 1623), also Hier. Ep., 23, 2; 24, 4. 3 (MPL, 22 [1854], 426 and 428). There is a symbolical evaluation of the material (goats' hair) in Aug. Civ. D., 15, 20, 4 (CSEL, 40, 2, p. 104, 27 ff.) on the basis of the goats in Mt. 25:32 f.; cf. also Caesarius Sermo, 261, 1 (MPL, 39 [1865], 2227); Ps.-Isidore, op. cit., 802 B etc.; cf. Poschmann Kirchenbusse, 285; Jungmann, 49, n. 175; Hermann, 135 f., here also other symbolical interpretations of σάκκος, and cf. the symbolical interpretations of sackcloth in the Rabb., bTaan., 16a → n. 35.

[60] In the M. Ages preachers of repentance as well as penitents wore sackcloth, cf. Grupp, V, 173, and already Mt. 3:4 par.; Rev. 11:3 (→ 62, 9 ff.); cf. also Bas. Ep., 44, 1 (MPG, 32 [1857], 361 D).

readmission to the worshipping fellowship. [61] Increasingly, however, sackcloth became a mere rite, [62] esp. and necessarily in the case of the sick, when it was laid over them, or over their heads if they were very seriously ill. [63] Alongside the ecclesiastical use we also find from ancient times a varied private use ; sackcloth was esp. worn in preparation for death and as the garb of death. [64]

3. Temporary penitence and a transitory wearing of the penitential garment was replaced in the case of monks, and later in that of religious of the third order, by a permanent *vita paenitentium* in which the wearing of sackcloth was also permanent. [65], [66] It is true that the nature of the Egyptian deserts first suggested this attire for monks, cf. Pachomius Ep., 8 (MPL, 23 [1883], 102A B): *ad fratres, qui tondebant in deserto capras, de quarum filis texuntur cilicia.* Later voices were raised against σάκκος as a means of vanity and a hindrance to the work which monks were commanded to do, [67] but these did not prevail, as may be seen, e.g., from the rule of Benedict of Nursia. [68]

4. As final off-shoots [69] of the movement sketched here we may refer on the one side to the Eastern and Western σακκοφόροι (Bas. Ep., 199 [Canonica secunda] Canon 47, MPG, 32 [1857], 730 C) or *saccophori* or *fratres saccati* (suspected of heretical tendencies), also the *saccariae,* nuns wearing sackcloth, [70] and on the other side to a remarkable Byzantine σάκκος which was the very opposite of a penitential garment, namely, the ornate (purple) garment of patriarchs and metropolitans, or the black but festive garment which East Roman emperors and empresses wore as a diadem. [71]

Stählin

---

[61] Cf. the play on words in Can. 2 of the Council of Toledo (400): *sub cilicio divino ... reconciliatus altario,* F. Lauchert, *Die Kanones d. wichtigsten altkirchlichen Concilien* (1896), 178, 7.

[62] Cf. Jungmann, 58, n. 199.

[63] Jungmann, 130 f.; Férotin, *op. cit.,* 91; → n. 48.

[64] Hermann, 132 f.; Grupp, II³, 365, 367; IV², 118 f., 120; VI, 99.

[65] Sometimes very literally, cf. Hier. Vita Hilarionis, 10 (MPL, 73 [1883], 33 B): *Saccum quo semel fuerat indutus nunquam lavans et superfluum esse dicens munditias in cilicio quaerere* (sc. since it was dark-brown); cf. also with ref. to another hermit Vita Abrahae, 18 (MPL, 73 [1883], 292).

[66] Cf. P. R. Oppenheim, "Das Mönchskleid im chr. Altertum," *Röm. Quartalschr.,* Suppl. 28 (1931).

[67] Cf. Cassianus De Institutis Coenobiorum, I, 2, 3 (CSEL, 17, 10, 13 ff.); Epiph. Haer., 80, 6, 6 : ἀλλότριον γάρ ἐστι τῆς καθολικῆς ἐκκλησίας σάκκος προφανής ("the penitential garment worn publicly for show," cf. Mt. 6:1, 16); Pall. Hist. Laus., 28; for further examples cf. K. Holl on Epiph. Haer., 80, 6, 5 (GCS, 37, 491).

[68] Cf. H. Leclercq, Art. "Cénobitisme," DACL, 2 (1910), 3188.

[69] Another off-shoot is the use of the *cilicium* described by J. Mast, Art. "Cilicium" in H. J. Wetzer-B. Welte, *Kirchen-Lex.,* II (1848), 546 : "An instrument of mortification of plaited hair or wire usually worn around the loins."

[70] Cf. O. Zöckler, Art. "Sackbrüder" in RE³, 17, 327.

[71] Cf. the ref. in Thes. Steph., VIII, 29, *s.v.*; cf. H. Leclercq, Art. "Vêtement," 27, 6 in DACL, 15 (1953), 3005.

---

† σαλεύω, † σάλος

σαλεύω, σαλ-εύω, "to shake," "to cause to totter," and σάλος, of uncertain etym., perhaps from the Indo-Eur. root *tw-el* "to swell"[1] (not phonetically related), denote the restless movement of the sea with its rise and fall, whether from the standpt. of inconstancy suggesting transitoriness or of peril suggesting destruction. In sense the word is related to σείω, κινέω and derivates, also to ταράσσω, and it also has points of contact with words which express the inner emotion of fear, astonishment, or surprise.

A. The Word Group in Profane Greek.

Found from Aesch., the word is relatively common in the tragedians, of the tossing sea in Eur. Hec., 28; Or., 994; Iph. Taur., 1443; Soph. Phil., 271; an earthquake in Eur. Iph. Taur., 46. Acc. to Aristot. the phenomena of rise and fall, becoming and perishing, may be viewed differently, but they belong to nature and mechanics, Meteor., II, 2, p. 356a, 3; Mechanica, 26 and 27, p. 857a, 7-26. Ps.-Aristot. Mund., 3, p. 392b, 33 f. argues for the basic solidity, immovability and unshakability of the earth within the cosmos[2] — an idea which dominated the ecclesiastical view of the world up to Giordano Bruno (d. 1600). The ref. in Soph. Oed. Tyr., 23. 24 and Ant., 162 f. is to political unrest, and in Soph. El., 1074 f. to man's conduct. In the uncertainty of everything earthly reflection alone can guarantee unshakability, Eur. Ba., 386-393. In itself human nature is vacillating and is impelled by vacillating desires, Plut. De Amore Prolis, 1 (II, 493d). Epict. Diss., III, 26 contains a warning against letting oneself be unsettled by sophisms ; the warning is similar to those against false teachers in the NT. Vacillation also characterises man's corporeality in so far as it is subject to normal change (Plat. Tim., 79e) and threatened by sickness and old age (Plat. Leg., XI, 923b). Hence the Hell. world seeks true impregnability in the world beyond death. In that world there is no trouble, aging, or conflict ; unshakable (ἀσάλευτος) rest is enjoyed, Ps.-Plat. Ax., 370d. On the other hand astrological texts[3] refer to eschatological shakings of the earth whether in relation to the political situation, the *pax Romana,* or to natural events, Lydus De ostentis,[4] 89, 3 and 8; 92, 26; 111, 1. In P. Lond., I, 46, 462 (4th cent. A.D.) there is invocation of the Shaker of heaven.[5]

B. The Word Group in the Greek Old Testament.

There is no fixed Heb. original for σαλεύω in the Gk. transl. of the OT, esp. the LXX. In canonical books with a Heb. basis the word is used 61 times for 23 Heb. roots. This extends considerably the range of the Gk. word and even causes shifts of sense. Whereas the Gk. term has in view the natural movement typical of the sea, the Heb.

σ α λ ε ύ ω.   Pr.-Bauer[5], Liddell-Scott, Moult.-Mill., *s.v.*; Helbing Kasussyntax, 320.

[1] Boisacq, 850; Walde-Pok., I, 710; Hofmann, II, 303 f. [Debrunner].
[2] Acc. to Manetho Apotelesmatica, II, 22 (ed. C. A. M. Axtius-F. A. Rieger [1832]) the poles are unshakable.
[3] F. Boll, *Aus d. Offenbarung Johannis* (1914), 135.
[4] Ed. C. Wachsmuth (1897).
[5] Preisigke Wört., II, 449. Only the verb is found in the pap. and with some extension and refinement of meaning : of indissoluble agreements, P. Lips., I, 34, 18 (4th cent. A.D.), "to depend," Ditt. Or., II, 515, 47 (3rd cent. A.D.); P. Oxy., III, 472, 50 (2nd cent. A.D.), "to move," P. Oxy., III, 528, 12 (2nd cent. A.D.), "to stir," P. Greci e Latini, 4, 299, 4 (2nd cent. A.D.).

root מוט, which is the original in a third (20) of the instances, refers esp. to the sudden, unexpected and disastrous shaking of the solid earth, ψ 81:5. With another Heb. original Jon. 1:15 refers to the raging of the sea. But Heb. terms for "to stagger," "to tremble," "to quake," "to be afraid or agitated," which denote movements of an uncertain or aimless kind, also of anxiety, unrest, anger, or even joy, are also rendered by σαλεύω by the translators. In so far as there is a material ref., it is to God's work or man's conduct. All inconstancy or shaking is against the order of creation. Thus the tossing of the sea in Jon. 1:15 indicates God's wrath, and it is God who stills the raging of the waves ψ 88:10; 106:27. God's wrath and power are revealed when He shakes the earth, ψ 59:4; cf. Ez. 12:18; Job 39:24; Is. 63:19 (64:1) and Θ Is. 54:10. Israel's liberation from Egypt involves a cosmic battle in which all creation shares and the earth quakes, ψ 76:19. In Mi. 1:4, too, the manifestation of God is accompanied by the shaking of the mountains and other destructive natural phenomena, cf. Na. 1:5; Am. 9:5; Hab. 3:6. The reverent quaking (→ II, 459, 22 ff.) and joyful trembling of creation in the presence of its Creator is also expressed thus. The LXX also speaks of the heaving of the sea (ψ 95:11; 97:7) when the Heb. original refers to its roaring as part of the song of praise of all creation. The ref. in ψ 32:8; 95:9b (cf. 1 Ch. 16:30a); 96:4; 98:1; 113:7 is also to the reverent worship of the Creator by the works which He has made. ψ 17:8 speaks of the quaking of the earth and the mountains at the revelation of the God of wrath, and ψ 45:6, 7 refers to the unshakableness of the city of God in contrast to the confusion of the nations, the fall of kingdoms and the quaking of the earth itself. In Job 9:6 again God, the Creator of the universe, reveals Himself in the shaking of heaven and earth, and His might is destructively declared in history. 'A uses the term in the threat that the walls of Babylon will shake and fall (Jer. 51[28]:58), and Θ uses it in relation to the destruction of the city-ship of Tyre (Ez. 27:28). Zech. 9:14 says similarly that the Lord shall stride in with quaking at His threatening (Mas. with the storms of the south). [6] At Jer. 10:10 Θ takes the revelation of God's wrath in the quaking of the earth to be a threatening of the nations. Materially relevant here is also the image of the staggering of the drunken man which Jer. (23:9) uses for his inner agitation when he has the revelation of God's words → II, 227 f. The figure of the wine of reeling is also used in Σ ψ 59:5 and Θ Is. 51:17. Acc. to Zech. 12:2 Jerusalem is made by Yahweh a cup of staggering for all the surrounding nations. Through misunderstanding (or on the basis of another reading?) the LXX has here the thought of a "shaken tower" [7] which is important in Chr. interpretation. Materially relevant is Hab. 2:16 [8] where the wrath of Yahweh is manifested in the cup of reeling, → VI, 149, 25 ff. Like Jerusalem in Zech. 12:2, Babylon in Jer. 51(28):7 is a golden cup in the Lord's hand, a cup of staggering from which the nations must drink and thus fall into vacillation. The same term is used elsewhere for the destructive work of God in history which shakes man. Thus the watchers and inhabitants of Jerusalem are shaken when the city is captured, Lam. 4:14, 15, [9] and men are shaken and flee when Babylon falls, Jer. 50(27):3 'A (no LXX), cf. also Da. 4:14 Θ; 2 K. 17:20; 21:8 = 2 Ch. 33:8. Acc. to Na. 3:11 the strong cities of Nineveh are like ripe figs which are shaken down and fall into the mouth of the enemy. The idea of the journey of the king of Babylon into Hades (Is. 14:9) which

---

[6] For the text cf. F. Wutz, *Die Transkriptionen v. d. Septuaginta bis zu Hieronymus* (1933), 234 f., 318 f.

[7] Cf. Mt. 27:51; Ev. Hebr. in Hier. Ep., 120, 8, 2 (*superliminare templi ... corruisse*); on this W. Bauer, *Das Leben Jesu im Zeitalter d. nt.lichen Apkr.* (1909), 232 f.; Str.-B., I, 1046, who also refers to Ps. 104:32; Jer. 25:30; 51:29; Zech. 14:5; G. Bertram, *Die Leidensgesch. Jesu u. der Christuskult* (1922), 90-92. With a ref. to Am. 8:3 Prot. Ev. Jc. 24:3 has a similar account of the death of Zacharias. The earthquake motif is related to the descent of Jesus into Hades in Pist. Soph., 3, 4 (6, 7); cf. also Rev. 11:12 f.

[8] F. Horst, *Kleine Propheten, Hndbch. AT,* 14[2] (1954), ad loc. emends the Mas. on the basis of J. Wellhausen, *Die kleinen Propheten*[2] (1898), ad loc. and with appeal to 1 Qp Hab and LXX, cf. BH K[10], ad loc.

[9] Cf. Θ Is. 24:20 with ref. to eschatological judgment.

caused the whole underworld to quake (Σ uses the verb here) was important in depictions of the descent of Christ into Hades. [10] Sir. 16:18 speaks of the shaking of the earth when God visits it, though the true ref. is to the heart of man which experiences God's working in a wonderful way, cf. Sir. 43:16. [11] God is not always the direct author when the OT refers to shaking, cf. Qoh. 12:3; Ez. 12:18 ΣΘ; Job 39:24. What is meant is the anxiety and unrest of the human heart, as in Sir. 40:1-5; [12] the shaking is linked to confusion, fear of death, and other human afflictions. Lam. 1:8 sees an express connection between sin and shaking such as is implicit in other OT sayings. The verb can thus embrace numinous awe, and along with it the translators use terms for astonishment (→ III, 29 ff.), confusion and horror (→ III, 4 f.), ψ 47:6 cf. 2 K. 7:15; ψ 30:23; 115:2; 103:7 etc. The righteous, too, is in danger of stumbling ψ 72:2 — cf. the confession of stumbling in ψ 93:18 — in the certainty of God's mercy. Acc. to ψ 14:5 unshakableness seems to rest on achievement along the lines of the doctrine of retribution. But when the righteous boasts of this, he immediately retracts, ψ 29:7, 8. The ungodly however, stubborn in his arrogance, falls under God's wrath, ψ 9:27.

In all this the concept of shaking characterises anthropological and theological statements concerning the world and man without God, under God's wrath. In contrast, σαλεύω is fairly often used with a negative in the LXX for unshakableness. This is not merely so in eschatological sayings. [13] Even with the future the ref. may be to the direct experience of the righteous. In particular, faith in God the Creator leads to a statement of confidence that the world cannot be shaken. The beginning of Yahweh's rule means that the earth wobbles no more, ψ 92:1; 95:10; 1 Ch. 16:30. [14] All who belong to Yahweh share this unshakableness: Jerusalem, the hill of Zion and its inhabitants, the king and the righteous ψ 15:8; 16:5; 29:7; 45:6; 54:23; 61:3; 65:9; 111:6; 120:3; 124:1 cf. Prv. 10:30 ΣΘ; Prv. 12:3 Σ and also 2 S. 22:37; Ps. 26:1. In the praise of famous men in Sir. 48:12 the unshakableness of Elisha, the spirit-endowed prophet and bearer of revelation, is extolled.

The LXX view of the world and concept of God find expression in its use of σαλεύω. Within the sphere of natural life the divine revelation works itself out as shaking. This is transferred to historical life and in the eschatological threats of the prophets shaking depicts God's judgment on the chosen people, its enemies, and the ungodly. Man is always in danger of wavering, and it is sinful arrogance for him to think he can stand fast. In nature the apparent unshakableness of the solidly grounded earth is in contrast to shaking in many natural processes. To this there corresponds a tension in both the individual and mankind. The righteous esp. lives in this tension. He is in danger of stumbling when he tries to walk in his own strength. Yet he knows that he has the divinely given unshakableness which keeps him both inwardly and outwardly from all stumbling and gives him the sure confidence of faith and hope in all the shattering experiences of life and the world.

C. The Word Group in Philo of Alexandria.

In Philo the essentially theological use of the LXX is replaced or reduced by a psychological use. Philo does not proclaim directly the God revealed in the OT who

---

[10] LXX "to find bitter." The ref. is to difficulty in digesting : hell and death cannot swallow the Redeemer, cf. Od. Sol. 42:16, 17; H. Schmidt, *Jona* (1907), 172-184; J. Kroll, *Gott u. Hölle* (1932), Index, *s.v.* "Verschlingung"; G. Bertram, Art. "Höllenfahrt Christi," RGG², II, 1968-1970.

[11] For the text cf. R. Smend, *Die Weisheit d. Jesus Sirach* (1906), *ad loc.* and F. Wutz, *op. cit.* (→ n. 6), 222 f. (confusion of ר and ר).

[12] This takes up ideas from Qoh. 1:13, cf. G. Bertram, "Hbr. u. gr. Qoh.," ZAW, 64 (1952), 44 f.

[13] As creation statements, these have, of course, an eschatological orientation in so far as they speak of the participation of the righteous in God's unshakableness.

[14] For the eschatological exposition of these enthronement songs cf. H. Gunkel, *Die Ps.,*

powerfully intervenes in world events and human life with natural force and in personal freedom. For him the work, reality, and efficacy of God are comprehended in the concept of omnipotence and totality as this is already developed in the LXX → V, 890, 35 ff. Thus the element of shaking is less prominent in God's revelation, and in Philo one sees an inclination, which almost leads him to statements that sound like dualistic Gnosticism, to define the divine as the unshakable. This applies first to the Law as the unshakable cosmic order, Vit. Mos., II, 124; it also applies to the Law as the national order imparted through Moses to Israel : the laws of all nations are variable, only those of the Jewish people are sure, unshakable and unshaken as though stamped by the seals of nature itself, Vit. Mos., II, 14. The cosmic order rests on the unshakable balance of the elements, Aet. Mund., 116. On this rests the idea of the order and regularity of the movements of the elements, esp. the heavenly bodies. The present verb is used in relation to the balance of these movements, and it hereby receives a basically new and different content, cf. Plat. Tim., 79e → 65, 21 f. In addition to its original use for the heaving of the sea it now indicates, not the wild and disorderly tossing but the regular and harmonious movement of the heavenly forces whereby the divine order is wonderfully represented. In the human sphere reason corresponds to this. Reason has weight and is steadfast in contrast to unreason, which is easily swept away, Omn. Prob. Lib., 28 cf. Eur. Ba., 386-393 → 65, 17 f. Firmness in both the cosmic and the human world is ultimately grounded in God, who sets the seal of unshakableness on such of His creatures as He chooses, Som., I, 158. God is the only one to stand fast ; all else is confused and vacillating, Leg. All., III, 38. Uncertainty and vacillation are thus characteristics of all that is earthly, esp. of man. Along the lines of changeableness and variability Philo allegorically [15] expounds OT names like Canaan (Sacr. AC, 90; Sobr., 44 and 55), Nod (Gn. 4:16; Cher., 12 and 13; Poster. C., 22 and 32), and Timna (Gn. 36:12; Congr., 60). The name of Timna means that the soul is weak and helpless against passion so that under the influence of the body it shifts and vacillates. The Stoic basis of this doctrine of the soul, which through the movement of the emotions comes to the peace or haven of virtue with the help of understanding and wisdom, is plain in the passages already quoted from Sacr. AC, 90 and Deus Imm., 26, cf. Conf. Ling., 31 and 32. [16] The philosopher, who is also the free man, is described accordingly in Omn. Prob. Lib., 24. The wise man belongs to God's side in acc. with God's unshakable and unchangeable nature. If human reason is thus solidly grounded in divine reason, it can offer an antithesis to all who rejoice in vacillation. The servant of God who keeps to the truth stands opposed to those who have no sure basis of knowledge and are thus at the mercy of the tossing sea of life, Sacr. AC, 13. Joseph by his conduct shakes his brothers, who are representatives of physical love, Migr. Abr., 22. Abraham was at first the victim of vacillation, but he freed himself from all enticements, ibid., 150. This corresponds to the nature of the man who is still bound fast to sin ; Adam is described thus in Leg. All., III, 53. The opposite may be seen in Leg. All., II, 90. σάλος is used more positively in Spec. Leg., IV, 139 : the legal statutes should always be before us in vibration and movement to make us attentive. When Philo expounds the law of the tefillim (Dt. 6:8) along these lines, he seems to be reading σαλευτά and not ἀσάλευτα in the Gk. OT. [17] In Cher., 36-38 the fig. of the wind which whips up the waves of the sea is used for the changes and chances of life.

Handkomm. AT (1926), ad loc.; also Einl. in d. Ps. (1933), 329-347.
    [15] Philo's explanations are arbitrary and are taken from the Jewish tradition of allegorical exposition of the OT. Cf. L. Cohn, Die Werke Philos v. Alex., III (1919), 250, n. 2.
    [16] W. Völker, Fortschritt u. Vollendung bei Philo v. Alex. (1938), 318-321; E. R. Goodenough, The Politics of Philo Judaeus (1938), 76-85.
    [17] Cf. Field on Ex. 13:16. The ᾽Α and Σ renderings adduced there, and the various attempts at emendation, are no help.

D. The Word Group in the New Testament.

In the NT the verb is often used in a transferred sense. In Ac. 17:13 it denotes the agitators who follow Paul from Thessalonica and stir up the people of Berea against Paul. [18] σαλεύω is a term used to describe the vacillation of the crowd both here and in many other stories, Mt. 21:10; Ac. 17:13; 2 Th. 2:2. But the word can also be used to characterise the individual. In Jesus' image of the reed in the wind [19] (Mt. 11:7; Lk. 7:24) the steadfastness of John the Baptist is presupposed. Neither his proclamation as Messiah by some of his followers, nor the persecution which he endured, nor the threat of death, have caused him to become uncertain or ambivalent in his outlook or conduct. [20] Paul uses the word in a similar way. He warns the Thessalonians (2 Th. 2:2) that in their eschatological expectation they should not let themselves be shaken or unsettled by deceitful apocalyptic preaching. [21]

σαλεύω occurs in Ac. 2:25 ff. in a quotation from ψ 15:8. For the righteous man of the OT the word expresses a religious awareness bordering on arrogance. Here, however, it is used eschatologically and christologically and in the context it is part of the prophetic proof of the resurrection of Christ. [22] If the statement in Ac. 2:25 f. refers to the earthly life and death and resurrection of the Lord, the idea is in tension [23] with the dereliction expressed in the word from the cross (Mt. 27:46; Mk. 15:34 → I, 627, 11 ff.) and Hb. 2:9 [24] reading χωρὶς (θεοῦ). [25] In reality, however, ψ 15 proves, not the resurrection, but the exaltation from the cross, [26] and the statement of steadfastness attributed to Christ (2:25) seems to contradict the passion story, especially the incident in Gethsemane. In this connection Jn. 12:27 can even use the word ταράσσειν, which in the light of the usage of the Greek OT seems to be a synonym of σαλεύω.

In Lk. 6:48 σαλεύω is used in the parable of the fall of a house not built on a proper foundation, while the raging flood cannot shake the house built on the rock. In Lk. 6:38 three popular terms are used in a crescendo — the measure which is pressed down, which is shaken and which overflows — to bring out the

---

[18] σαλεύοντες (καὶ ταράσσοντες left out by p⁴⁵ ℵ E al); perhaps the second verb was added in elucidation. Cf. A. C. Clark, *The Acts of the Apostles* (1933), ad loc. In the LXX the two verbs are sometimes found together or as alternative renderings of the same Heb. roots.

[19] In 3 Macc. 2:22 it is God Himself who shakes like a reed in the wind the wicked persecutor of the Jews, Ptolemy Philopator. The image also occurs in Luc. Hermot., 68.

[20] Cf. Titus of Bostra, ad loc. acc. to Cramer Cat., II, 58.

[21] Paul's preaching, the message of the cross, is not concerned with the eschatological advent but bears witness to the death and resurrection of the Lord. Apocalyptic presentation of eschatological expectation is fundamentally a part of the gnosis which is falsely esteemed, 1 Tm. 6:20, 21 → ματαιολογία, IV, 524; → μωρολογία, IV, 844 f.; → πολυλογία, VI, 545 f.

[22] The scene in Act. Phil. 60 seems to be a par. to the revelation of the Risen Lord, though the concluding sentence refers to the inner shaking of those who live in the house rather than to an earthquake which hits the house.

[23] Haench. Ag., ad loc.

[24] A. v. Harnack, "Zwei alte dogmatische Korrekturen im Hebräerbr.," SAB (1929), 62-73.

[25] W. Hasenzahl, *Die Gottverlassenheit des Christus nach dem Kreuzeswort bei Mt. u. Mk. u. das christologische Verständnis d. griech. Psalters* (1937), 103-145.

[26] G. Bertram, "Die Himmelfahrt Jesu vom Kreuz aus u. d. Glaube an seine Auferstehung," *Festgabe f. A. Deissmann* (1927), 187-207; also "Der religionsgeschichtliche Hintergrund d. Begriffs der 'Erhöhung' in der Septuaginta," ZAW, 68 (1956), 57-71.

fulness and indeed the superabundance of the divine gift in terms of the good measure which goes beyond any concept of repayment, → IV, 634, 4 ff. [27]

The NT reference to earthquakes is partly historical and partly eschatological-apocalyptic. In Ac. 4:31 the place where the community prays is shaken. According to the view of antiquity this is a sign of the God invoked and signifies that the prayer is heard. [28] In the story of Paul in Ac. 16:26 the strong earthquake is again a sign that prayer is heard. The direct result is the freeing of the apostles and the accreditation of their mission to the pagan guards. As in 4:31 the earthquake is a shaking of the place where those who make the prayer are. [29] In the Synoptic Apocalypse, the Revelation of John and Hebrews shakings of the earth and the cosmos are signs of the last time. σάλος is used of eschatological threatening by the sea in Lk. 21:25, 26. [30] It is not clear how far apocalyptic quakes are a pre-condition of the renewal of heaven and earth. But the shaking of the world in Hb. 12:26 is certainly taken in this sense. The reference, however, is to change, not destruction. What is made is subject to change, cf. 1 C. 7:31. σαλεύω is to be construed thus. What cannot be shaken remains, v. 27. This is the kingdom of God which the Christian community has received. In spite of this statement about the present, which has a Hellenistic ring, the Christian community holds fast to the eschatological hope. Thus patristic exegesis [31] of the phrase "un-shakable kingdom" (Hb. 12:28) notes that we are not to be content with what God gives us in the present but are to give Him the greatest thanks for what is to come. Nevertheless, cosmological influence on the usage largely robbed the verb of its eschatological content. Thus in 1 Cl., 20, 1 it is used for the regular course of the heavenly powers which are subject to God in peace. The Hellenistic view adopted by Philo (→ 68, 10 ff.) is expressed here in the Christian view of things. The heavens pursue their course according to God's ordinance.

Theologically the verb σαλεύειν and cognates have no great significance in the NT, especially as the eschatological concept of the shaking of the cosmos is more commonly linked with σείειν and derivates, → σεισμός. The distinctive sense of the verb derives from its link with the OT concept of God. In the OT creation stands under the threat of divine shaking and the promise of divinely given unshakability. Hence NT eschatology is based on the eschatologically oriented OT belief in the Creator.

Bertram

---

[27] Hck. Mk., *ad loc.* would apportion the explanatory terms between giver and repayment; H. J. Holtzmann, *Mk.* (1892), *ad loc.* emphasises the superabundance of the repayment, which does not quite seem to fit in with the equivalence in the continuation and in Mk. 4:24.

[28] The closest par. is the thunder when Jesus prayed in Gethsemane, cf. Jn. 12:28-30. Here, too, an answer is given by heavenly means; those concerned can understand it in human terms, whereas others perceive only a natural phenomenon and at most can only surmise that this is a voice from heaven.

[29] Haench. Ag., *ad loc.*, who also points out the relation to 2 Th. 2:2.

[30] In Mt. 8:24 σεισμός is used of the storm; Mk. 4:37 and Lk. 8:23 have λαῖλαψ.

[31] Chrys. Hom. in Hb. 33 (MPG, 63 [1862], 225) cf. also Theod. Mops. acc. to Staab, 211.

† σάλπιγξ, † σαλπίζω, † σαλπιστής

Contents: A. The Word Group in the Greek World: I. Meaning: 1. σάλπιγξ;
2. σαλπίζω; 3. σαλπιστής; II. Origin and Use of the Trumpet: 1. Origin of the Trumpet;
2. The War Trumpet; 3. The Significance of the Trumpet in Peace; 4. The Trumpet as
a Musical Instrument. B. The Word Group in the Old Testament: I. Hebrew Equivalents:
1. σάλπιγξ: a. שׁוֹפָר; b. חֲצֹצְרָה; c. קֶרֶן; d. יוֹבֵל; e. תְּרוּעָה; f. תָּקֹעַ; 2. σαλπίζω; 3. σαλπιστής; II. Use and Significance of the Horn and the Trumpet: 1. The Horn and the
Trumpet in War; 2. The Horn and the Trumpet on Solemn Occasions in Peace; 3. The
Cultic Significance of the Trumpet and the Horn; 4. The Sounding of Horns at Theophanies;
5. The Eschatological Significance of the Horn; 6. The Horn and the Trumpet as Musical
Instruments. C. The Word Group in Judaism: I. The Individual Words: 1. שׁוֹפָר; 2. חֲצוֹצְרָה;
3. קֶרֶן; 4. סַלְפִּינְגָס; II. The Significance of Horns and Trumpets in Judaism: 1. As Signals
in War; 2. Trumpets and Horns on Special Occasions in Peace; 3. Trumpets and Horns
in the Jewish Cultus; 4. The Eschatological Significance of the Sound of Horns; 5. The
Horn and the Trumpet as Musical Instruments. D. The Word Group in the New Testament:
I. The Individual Words: 1. σάλπιγξ; 2. σαλπίζω; 3. σαλπιστής; II. The Significance
of the Blowing of Trumpets: 1. In War; 2. On Solemn Occasions; 3. The Trumpet in
Theophany and Vision; 4. The Eschatological Significance of the Trumpet; 5. The
Trumpet as a Musical Instrument.

σάλπιγξ κτλ. I. Abrahams, Art. "Trumpet," Hastings DB, IV, 815 f.; C. Adler,
"The Shofar, Its Use and Origin," *Annual Report of the Board of Regents of the Smithsonian
Institution* (1893), 437-450; F. Behn, *Musikleben im Altertum u. frühen Mittelalter* (1954),
Index, *s.v.* "Trompete," "Salpinx," "Tuba"; A. Büchler, "Zur Gesch. d. Tempelmusik u. d.
Tempelpsalmen," ZAW, 19 (1899), 96-133; 20 (1900), 97-114; I. M. Casanowicz, Art.
"Trumpet" in Jew. Enc., XII, 268; F. L. Cohen-I. D. Eisenstein, Art. "Shofar" in Jew. Enc.,
XI, 301-306; C. H. Cornill, "Music in the OT," *The Monist*, 19 (1909), 240-264; S. B.
Finesinger, "Musical Instruments in the OT," HUCA, 3 (1926), 56-63; also "The Shofar,"
HUCA, 8-9 (1931/32), 193-228; F. W. Galpin, "The Music of the Sumerians and their
Immediate Successors, the Babylonians and Assyrians," *Sammlung musikwissenschaftlicher
Abh.*, 33 (1955), 20-25; E. R. Goodenough, *Jewish Symbols in the Greco-Roman Period*, III
(1953); IV (1954), 167-194; H. Gressmann, *Musik u. Musikinstrumente im AT* (1903);
H. Hickmann, "La trompette dans l'Égypte Ancienne," *Annales du service des antiquités de
l'Égypte*, Suppl., 1 (1946); K. v. Jan, "Signal- u. Schlaginstrumente," in A. Baumeister,
Denkmäler d. klass. Altertums, III (1888), 1657 f.; B. Kohlbach, "Das Widderhorn," *Zschr.
d. Vereins f. Volkskunde*, 25 (1915), 113-128; E. Kolari, *Musikinstrumente u. ihre Ver-
wendung im AT* (1947), 39-54; S. Krauss, *Talmudische Archäol.*, III (1912), 83 f., 96-99;
F. Lammert, Art. "Tuba" in Pauly-W., 7a (1948), 749-752; A. Maecklenburg, "Über d.
Musikinstrumente d. alten Hebräer," ThStKr, 101 (1929), 196-199; R. Maux, Art. "Salpinx"
in Pauly-W., 1a (1920), 2009 f.; K. O. Müller and W. Deecke, *Die Etrusker*, II (1877),
206-213; J. Parisot, Art. "Trompette," Dict. Bibl., V, 2322-25; Art. "Corne," *ibid.*, II, 1010-
12; J. D. Prince, Art. "Music," EB, III, 3230 f.; T. Reik, "Probleme d. Religionspsychologie,
I: Das Schofar," *Internationale psychoanalytische Bibliothek*, V (1919), 178-235; A.
Reinach, Art. "Tuba," Daremb.-Saglio, V, 522-528; H. Riemann, *Hndbch. d. Musikgesch.*[3]
(1923), 115 f.; E. C. A. Riehm, Art. "Musik" in HW, II, 1052 f.; H. Seidel, "Horn u.
Trompete im alten Israel unter Berücksichtigung d. 'Kriegsrolle' v. Qumran," *Zschr. d.
Karl-Marx-Univ. Leipzig, Gesellschafts- u. sprachwissenschaftliche Reihe*, 6 (1956/57), 589-
599; O. R. Sellers "Musical Instruments of Israel," *Biblical Archaeologist*, 4 (1941), 42;
N. H. Snaith, *The Jewish New Year Festival* (1947), 150-176; M. Wegner, *Das Musikleben
d. Griechen* (1949), 60 f.; J. Weiss, *Die musikalischen Instrumente in d. hl. Schriften d. AT*
(1895), 89-98; E. Werner, "Musical Aspects of the Dead-Sea-Scrolls," *The Musical Quarterly*, 43 (1957), 21-37; Wetzstein, "Schofar," *Verhandlungen d. Berliner Gesellschaft f.*

A. The Word Group in the Greek World.

I. Meaning.

1. σάλπιγξ.

a. σάλπιγξ, Lat. *tuba*, is mostly a specific wind instrument [1] in distinction from the *bucina*, Gk. βυκάνη, the coiled metal horn, and κέρας, Lat. *cornu*, the twisted instrument originally made from animal horn. [2] The σάλπιγξ is made of iron or bronze, the mouthpiece of horn. At the end the long pipe broadens out into a megaphone, Poll. Onom., IV, 85. b. σάλπιγξ can denote not merely the instrument but also the sound produced by it, σάλπιγμα in Poll. Onom., IV, 86. It is the "sound of the trumpet," Xenoph. Eq., 9, 11; Arrianus Anabasis Alexandri, I, 14, 7; [3] Aristot. Rhet., III, 6, p. 1408a, 9; Paus., III, 17, 5; the "signal" given by a trumpet, Thuc., VI, 32, 1; Xenoph. Eq. Mag., 3, 12; Polyb., 4, 13, 1; Arrianus Anabasis Alex., III, 18, 5; πρώτη σάλπιγξ, the "first trumpet signal," Ael. Arist. Or., 34, 22 (Keil), cf. also σάλπιγγος ἀκούειν, Aristoph. Ra., 1042; Ael. Arist. Or., 37, 27 (Keil), ἡ σάλπιγξ παρακαλεῖ, Arrianus Anab. Alex., V, 23, 7, τῇ σάλπιγγι κελεύειν, Xenoph. Hist. Graec., V, 1, 9. σάλπιγξ can also be used for "trumpet playing," Dio C., 57, 18, 3. c. Fig. Διὸς σάλπιγξ in Nonnus Dionys., 2, 558, οὐρανίη σάλπιγξ in Tryphiodorus Excidium Ilii, 327, [4] or οὐρανίη Διὸς σάλπιγξ in Nonnus Dionys., 6, 230 f. means "thunder." Men are also called trumpets. Pindar is Πιερικὰ σάλπιγξ in Anth. Graec., 7, 34, 1 cf. 16, 305, Demosthenes is δημηγόρος σάλπιγξ in Anth. Graec., 2, 23. In a negative sense Antisthenes is called a σάλπιγξ in Dio Chrys. Or., 8, 2. There is a fig. use in Achill. Tat., VIII, 10, 10 : αὕτη οὐχ ὑπὸ σάλπιγγι μόνον ἀλλὰ καὶ κήρυκι μοιχεύεται.

2. σαλπίζω.

a. Corresponding to the deriv. the aor. of σαλπίζω is at first ἐσάλπιγξα, Xenoph. An., I, 2, 17. Later we find ἐσάλπισα, Jos. 6:13; Athen., 4, 5 (130b), fut. σαλπιῶ Nu. 10:8, or σαλπίσω 1 K. 15:32; b. The verb means "to produce a blast on the trumpet," "to trumpet," "to give a signal with the trumpet," Artemid. Onirocr., I, 56; Athen., 4, 5 (130b), "to blow the trumpet," Dio. C., 57, 18, 3. The subj. denoting the one who blows does not have to be given, since the common subj. σαλπικτής is contained in the verbal concept σαλπίζω, Xenoph. An., I, 2, 17. σαλπίζω can sometimes have the gen. sense "to blow," "to play an instrument," *ibid.*, VII, 3, 32. c. Like the noun (→ lines 16 ff.) the verb can be used fig., e.g., of heaven when it thunders, Hom. Il., 21, 388, cf. Eustath. Thessal. Comm. in Il., 21, 388, or of the crowing of the cock, Ps.-Luc. Ocyp., 114.

Anthropologie, Ethnologie u. Urgeschichte (1880), 63-71; J. G. Wilkinson, *Manners and Customs of the Ancient Egyptians,* II (1887), 260-265; Y. Yadin, *The Scroll of the War of the Sons of Light against the Sons of Darkness* (1962), 87-113 (Eng.).

[1] But cf. Poll. Onom., IV, 85. Ill. in C. Sachs, *Geist u. Werden d. Musikinstrumente* (1929), Plate 23, Ill. 154; Wegner, Plate 26. Etym. uncertain ; σάλπιγξ is usually linked with Lithuan. *švilgiù* "pipe with the lips," cf. Boisacq, 850 f.; Hofmann, 304. But cf. P. Chantraine, *La formation des noms en grec ancien* (1933), 398. On the suffix -ιγγ cf. Schwyzer, I, 498 [Risch].

[2] Later the κέρας was often understood as the Phrygian flute with a horn affixed. In Eustath. Thessal. Comm. in Il., 18, 219 and MS T (Townleyana) of Schol. on Hom. Il., 18, 219 (ed. E. Maass, II [1888], 253) 6 different trumpets are described : 1. the large Hellenic ; 2. the round Egypt.; 3. the medium Galatian ; 4. the very large Paphlagonian ; 5. the medium with reed pipe ; 6. the Tyrrhenian with doubled back horn. Probably these are different brass instruments rather than different kinds of trumpets.

[3] Ed. A. G. Roos (1907).

[4] Ed. W. Weinberger (1896).

3. σαλπιστής.

The noun for the trumpeter takes different forms.[5] The expected σαλπιγκτής occurs in CIG, I, 1583, 5 (2nd cent. B.C.); IG, 7, 3195 (1st cent. B.C.) etc. cf. Thuc., VI, 69, 2; Polyb., 4, 19, 12; 14, 3, 6. σαλπικτής is attested earlier in inscr., Ditt. Syll.[3], I, 153, 68 f. (4th cent. B.C.); Ditt. Or., I, 51, 64 (3rd cent. B.C.); Ditt. Syll.[3], II, 667, 44 (2nd cent. B.C.); cf. Polyb., 1, 45, 13; 2, 29, 6 etc. Both readings often occur in MSS, cf. Xenoph. An., IV, 3, 29, 32; Dio C., 36, 49, 1 cf. 47, 43, 1; 56, 22, 3; Appian. Bell. Civ., I, 105 (494). Later, in accordance with ἐσάλπισα for ἐσάλπιγξα (→ 72, 24 f.) we find σαλπιστής in Ditt. Syll.[3], III, 1058, 4 (2nd-1st cent. B.C.); IG, 7, 4147, 6 (2nd-1st cent.); Ditt. Syll.[3], III, 1059 col. II, 20 (c. the time of Christ's birth); cf. Theophr. Char., 25, 5.

II. Origin and Use of the Trumpet.

1. Origin of the Trumpet.

The trumpet was not a typical Gk. instrument. It is hardly mentioned in the earliest writings. Hom. is acquainted with it (Il., 18, 219; 21, 388) but in his day it does not seem to have been used in the Gk. army. On the other hand, it was common in the Orient. In a Mari temple (c. 2700 B.C.) two figures hold in their hands bent objects which might be horns. Trumpets are mentioned on the cylinders of Gudea (2400 B.C.) and in temple accounts. Miniature trumpets of gold have been found on the mounds of Tepe Hissar and Astarabad in Persia (2nd millennium B.C.).[6] Trumpets are depicted on a Hittite Carchemish relief[7] and a relief from the palace of Sennacherib.[8] Tušratta, king of Mitanni, sent two trumpets as a gift on the occasion of the marriage of his daughter with Amenophis III (1380 B.C.).[9] This shows how highly the instrument was valued. In Egypt it is found on many depictions from 1550 B.C. onwards.[10] In Tutankhamon's tomb two well-preserved examples were found, one of silver, the other of copper (c. 1350 B.C.).[11] The expression Τυρσηνικὴ σάλπιγξ in Aesch. Eum., 567 f.; Eur. Heracl., 830 f.; Phoen., 1377 f.; Rhes., 988 f. also pts. to the oriental origin of the Gk. trumpet. The Tyrrhenians are supposed to have invented it in Lydia, Diod. S., 5, 40, 1; Athen., 4, 82 (184a); Poll. Onom., IV, 85; Paus., II, 21, 3, to make themselves better understood by wind, Isidorus Etymologiae, 18, 4, 2 f.[12]

2. The War Trumpet.

In antiquity the trumpet was not much used as a musical instrument; its main task was to give signals. Hence there is frequent ref. to the σημαίνειν of the trumpet or trumpeter, Xenoph. An., IV, 2, 1; Polyb., 14, 3, 5; Diod. S., 15, 55. 3; Polyaen. Strat., IV, 3, 26, cf. also τὸ σημεῖον σαλπίζειν, Athen., 4, 5 (130b); τὰ παρακλητικὰ τοῦ πολέμου ἐπισημαίνειν, Dion. Hal. Ant. Rom., 4, 17, 3. In the main it was used as σάλπιγξ πολεμία (Athen., 10, 59 [442c]) in the army. It is an ὄργανον πολέμου, Philo Spec. Leg., II, 190, an ὄργανον πολεμιστήριον, Artemid. Oniroer., I, 56, or

---

[5] Phryn. Ecl., 167 cf. W. G. Rutherford, The New Phrynichus (1881), 279 on 167.
[6] Galpin, 21-23, 78 Plate XI, 19.
[7] BR, 390; C. Sachs, Musik d. Altertums (1924), Plate 5; J. B. Pritchard, The Ancient Near East in Pictures (1954), 63, Ill. 201; Galpin, Plate III, 1.
[8] Behn Musikleben, Ill. 37.
[9] Galpin, 23 f.
[10] Trumpets from the time of Thotmes IV (c. 1400 B.C.) in M. Wegner, "Die Musik-instrumente d. alten Orients," Orbis Antiquus, 2 (1950), Plate 14a; for further pictures from the age of the Egypt. kings cf. W. Wreszinski, Atlas z. altägypt. Kulturgesch., II (1935), Plate 24 f., 110 f., 127 f., 134 f., 151, 161 f., 169 f., 185, 191 f., 199 f.; Hickmann, 4-16.
[11] H. C. Carter, Tut-ench-Amun, II[10] (1938), Plate 2 B; Hickmann, Plate I.
[12] Ed. W. M. Lindsay (1911).

ὄργανον πολεμικόν, Hesych., s.v., εὐχρηστοτάτη εἰς τοὺς πολέμους, Diod. S., 5, 40, 1. The χαλκοκώδων σάλπιγξ sounds forth πολεμῖαν ἀοιδάν, Bacchyl., 18, 3 f. When the Gks. depict Nike with a trumpet in hand, [13] this shows the importance of the trumpet in attaining victory. Originally the Spartans went to battle, not with trumpet signals, but with the sound of flutes, marching in step, Thuc., V, 70; Plut. Lycurgus, 22 (I, 53); Polyb., 4, 20, 6; Paus., III, 17, 5; Cl. Al. Paed., II, 42, 2. The flute also gave them the signal for battle, Luc. Salt., 10. The Cretans used the lyre as well as the flute, Strabo, 10, 4, 20. Later the trumpet replaced the other instruments, Plut. De musica, 26 (II, 1140c). It served to pass on various commands, Asclepiodotus Tactica, 12, 10; Ael. Tact., 35, 1, [14] esp. when communication was difficult in any other way, Arrianus Tactica, 32, 5. [15] By means of the trumpet signals were given to prepare for battle and to attack, Sept. c. Theb., 394; Eur. Phoen., 1377 ff.; Xenoph. An., IV, 2, 7 f.; IV, 3, 29; Diod. S., 20, 51, 2. It strengthened the war-cry of the soldiers (Arrianus Anabasis Alexandri, I, 14, 7), fired the courage of the attackers (Thuc., VI, 69, 2; Plut. Aem., 33, 1 [I, 272 f.]; Plut. Crass., 23, 9 [I, 557d]; Polyaen. Strat., IV, 3, 26; Dio C., 47, 43, 2; Eustath. Thessal. Comm. in Il., 21, 388), terrified the foe and brought confusion to their ranks (Xenoph. An., VII, 4, 19; Polyb., 2, 29, 6). The trumpet was also used to signal the retreat (Polyb., 3, 69, 13; 10, 13, 11; 15, 14, 3), to end the battle (Xenoph. An., IV, 4, 22; Diod. S., 15, 87, 2), to gather the scattered (Artemid. Onirocr., I, 56), and for the march back to camp (Philo Spec. Leg., II, 190; Poll. Onom., IV, 86). Trumpet signals were often used as feints to deceive the enemy as to the true situation, Dio C., 56, 22, 3. Among the Romans the guards were summoned by trumpet to take up their posts at the time of the evening meal, Polyb., 14, 3, 6. Jos. Bell., 3, 86 says of the Roman army that "the trumpet gives the signal for sleeping and watching and getting up. Nothing is done without a command." Like the standard-bearer etc. the trumpeter is one of those in the company who is available for special tasks outside the ordinary, Asclepiodotus Tact. (→ n. 14), 2, 9; 6, 3; Ael. Tact., 9, 4; 16, 2.

3. The Significance of the Trumpet in Peace.

Apart from the military use trumpets were employed on various occasions. Shepherds gathered their flocks by trumpet signals, Polyb., 12, 4, 2 f. Acc. to Aesch. Eum., 566 ff. the herald silenced the people by a trumpet at the beginning of a trial. A trumpet also ordered silence before prayer, Thuc., VI, 32, 1. The trumpet summoned the people to sacrifice, Poll. Onom., IV, 86; Eustath. Thessal. Comm. in Il., 18, 219; Schol. on Hom. Il., 18, 219 → n. 2. In distinction from the war trumpet the cultic trumpet is called ἱερά in Artemid. Onirocr., I, 56 or ἱερατική in Lydus De Mensibus, IV, 73. [16] The cultic trumpeter is ἱεροσαλπικτής (CIG, II, 1969, 4; 2983, 4 f.) or ἱεροσαλπιστής (IG, IV, 617, 6). In a mural from Herculaneum which depicts a scene from the cult of Isis a trumpeter may be seen alongside the officiating priest. [17] In the Dionysus cult, too, the trumpet had a place, Plut. Quaest. Conv., IV, 6, 2 (II, 671e). As is stated in Plut. Is. et Os., 35 (II, 364 f.) Dionysus in a spring rite is summoned out of the water by a trumpet blast.

---

[13] Wegner, Plate 26b. Further ill. of war trumpets A. Furtwängler-K. Reichhold, Griech. Vasenmalereien, II (1909), 113 and Plate 82; P. Hartwig, Die griech. Meisterschalen d. Blüthezeit des strengen rothfigurigen Stiles (1893), 276, esp. n. 1 with references to other ill.
[14] Asclepiodotus and Ael. ed. H. Köchly and W. Rüstow, Griech. Kriegsschriftsteller, II (1855).
[15] Ed. R. Hercher and A. Eberhard (1855).
[16] Ed. R. Wünsch (1898).
[17] J. Quasten, "Musik u. Gesang in d. heidnischen Antike u. chr. Frühzeit," Liturgie-geschichtliche Quellen u. Forschungen, 25 (1930), Plate 24. On the cultic use of the trumpet cf. also A. Frickenhaus, "Der Schiffskarren d. Dionysos in Athen.," Jahrbuch d. deutschen Archäol. Institutes, 27 (1912), 65, App. 1, Ill. 4 : A youth blowing a trumpet is at the head of the sacrificial procession.

Already in Egypt. drawings trumpeters take part in festal processions. [18] In the Gk. and Roman period, too, they are mentioned in both mourning processions and triumphs. At the head of the procession to the grave of those who fell at Plataeae marched the trumpeter who blew the war signal, Plut. Aristides, 21, 3 (I, 332a) cf. Arrianus Anabasis Alex., VII, 3, 6. Originally the task of mourning music was to secure for the dead a friendly welcome among the gods of the underworld. Later it was merely for display, Appian. Bell. Civ., I, 105 (494 f.); Persius Satura, III, 103; [19] Horat. Serm., I, 6, 44. In Sen. Apocolocyntosis, 12, 1 we read in an account of the burial of Claudius that many trumpeters made such music that the deceased could hear; all were gay and cheerful. A Roman relief has a vivid depiction of a funeral procession with its musicians. [20] The triumph, too, was opened by trumpeters, Plut. Aem., 33, 1 (I, 272 f.); Appian. Libyca, 66 (293). It is reported of a woman: ἐσάλπισεν ... ἐν τῇ πρώτῃ ἀχθείσῃ μεγάλῃ πομπῇ ἐν Ἀλεξανδρείᾳ τὸ πομπικόν, Athen., 10, 7 (415a), cf. Eustath. Thessal. Comm. in Il., 21, 388; Poll. Onom., IV, 89; Ael. Var. Hist., 1, 26. At the games the trumpeter summoned competitors, gave the signal to start, and fired the contestants, Poll. Onom., IV, 89; Soph. El., 711; Martianus Capella De Nuptiis Philologiae et Mercurii, IX, 925. [21] Though only a few notes can be played on the trumpet (→ lines 35 ff.), blowing the trumpet was regarded as an art since a very strong blast was needed to make it sound. [22] Trumpet competitions were held at the games, CIG, I, 1585, 5; IG, 7, 1760, 11; Ditt. Syll.³, II, 667, 44 etc. Strength of sound was apparently a factor. The strong lungs of the not very big Herodorus were praised: ἐσήμαινε δὲ σαλπίζων μέγιστον. He is supposed to have been able to play on two trumpets at the same time, Athen., 10, 7 (414e); Eustath. Thessal. Comm. in Il., 21, 388. It is said of the blowing of Aglais σάλπιγγι ὑπερερρωμένως ἐχρήσατο ἀγωνιστηρίῳ τε καὶ πομπικῇ, Poll. Onom., IV, 89. Acc. to Porphyrius Comm. in Ptolemaei Harmonica, 4 [23] the hours were announced by trumpet signals, cf. Petronius Satirae, 29, 6. At gt. festivities trumpets indicated the end of the meal, Athen., 4, 5 (130b).

4. The Trumpet as a Musical Instrument.

Whether the trumpet was used as a musical instrument is doubtful. In Xenoph. An., VII, 3, 32 it is mentioned with other instruments in the description of an orchestra at a gt. feast, but the fact that it is called σάλπιγξ ὠμοβοεία shows that the ref. is not to the usual metal trumpet. When we read in Dio C., 56, 22, 3 οἱ σαλπικταί ... τροχαῖόν τι συμβοήσαντες, this does not mean that the trumpeters played a march but that they blew the signal or gave the step for the advancing troops. The trumpet was not well adapted to serve as a musical instrument. The Egypt. trumpets which have been preserved (→ 73, 23 ff.) have fundamentally only two notes, the basic note and the tenth. With gt. effort a third note two octaves above the basic sound can be produced. [24] The situation is much the same with other trumpets. [25] Such instruments are useful for giving signals and setting rhythms, but not for playing real music. The notes produced by the Egypt. trumpets are harsh and strong and not very pleasing to

---

[18] Wreszinski, op. cit. (→ n. 10), Plate 185, 191 f., 199 f.; Hickmann, 8 f.
[19] Ed. W. V. Clausen (1959).
[20] Quasten, op. cit., Plate 31. Cf. also Ant. Christ., II, 2 f., 316. Tert. De Corona 11, 3 (CCh, 2 [1954], 1056) objects that Christians waiting to be awakened by the trumpet of the archangel will be disturbed after death by the trumpet of the musicians.
[21] Ed. A. Dick (1925).
[22] Hickmann, 33 f.
[23] Ed. I. Düring (1932).
[24] R. Kirby, Ancient Egypt. Trumpets, Music Book, 7 (1952), 250, though cf. Hickmann, 31, who refers to the basic tone, the octave and the upper fifth.
[25] If a modern mouthpiece is attached to the ancient Egypt. trumpets the skilful player can get other notes too; Hickmann, 32.

the ear. [26] The Gks. called the sound of trumpets ἀρίζηλος "very clear," "loud," Hom. Il., 18, 219, διάτορος "penetrating," "shattering," Aesch. Eum., 567; Ael. Var. Hist., 2, 44 and τραχύς, Ael. Var. Hist., 2, 44. Because of the loud and penetrating tone the Egypt. police ordered that trumpets should be blown only in barracks outside the city. The sound of the trumpet was compared to the braying of an ass (→ 85, 6 ff.), Plut. Is. et Os., 30 (II, 362 f.). On a tablet in the temple of Enki in Eridu (2200 B.C.) it is said that the trumpet makes a noise like a bull. [27]

B. The Word Group in the Old Testament.

I. Hebrew Equivalents.

1. σάλπιγξ.

a. שׁוֹפָר.

In the LXX σάλπιγξ is most often (over 40 times) used for שׁוֹפָר, which is also transl. 20 times, and better, by κερατίνη. Thus far no satisfactory etym. has been found for שׁוֹפָר. The word probably derived from the Accad. *sapparu,* but underwent a shift of meaning, the wild goat becoming the horn of the goat. [28] שׁוֹפָר is then the wind instrument made of ram's horn. Hence שׁוֹפָר should not be transl. by trumpet or trombone but by "horn." [29] Later the specific sense of "ram's horn" broadened out and שׁוֹפָר is a general term for various animal horns, or horns generally, or wind instruments. In contrast to σάλπιγξ in Gk. (→ 72, 8 ff.) שׁוֹפָר does not mean the sound of the horn. For this we find קוֹל שׁוֹפָר Ex. 19:16; Jos. 6:20; 2 S. 6:15; Jer. 4:19 etc.

b. חֲצֹצְרָה.

This occurs some 30 times in the OT, always plur. except at Hos. 5:8. The etym. is difficult. [30] The word is probably connected with the Arab. *ḥṣr,* [31] whose basic sense is "narrow," so that the חֲצֹצְרָה is a narrow and shrill instrument. This corresponds to the description in Jos. Ant., 3, 291 f., which says that the tube was narrow, a little thicker than a flute. [32] The depiction on the triumph arch of Titus agrees with this. [33] It is a long, narrow, straight instrument of metal, made from silver (Nu. 10:2), to be distinguished from the שׁוֹפָר, the curved ram's horn, → lines 15 ff. In contrast to the latter it is an express cultic instrument which is always in the hands of the priests except in the accounts of the coronation of Joash in 2 K. 11:14 and 2 Ch. 23:13. Nu. 10:8 ordains explicitly that the priests are to blow it. Acc. to Nu. 10:2 Moses is charged by God to make two silver trumpets. In the course of time the no. of priestly trumpets

---

[26] Hickmann, 33.
[27] Galpin, 23.
[28] Kolari, 42 f.
[29] It is not possible to give an exact def. distinguishing the trumpet from the horn, cf. C. Sachs, *Reallex. d. Musikinstrumente* (1913), 189 f., 395. Trumpets are normally taken to be wind instruments in cylindrical form with a megaphone, while the horn is bent with a conical form, Hickmann, 23.
[30] Kolari, 49.
[31] Gressmann, 30 f.
[32] εὗρε δὲ καὶ βυκάνης τρόπον ἐξ ἀργύρου ποιησάμενος, ἔστι δὲ τοιαύτη· μῆκος μὲν ἔχει πηχυαῖον ὀλίγῳ λεῖπον, στενὴ δ' ἐστὶ σύριγξ αὐλοῦ βραχεῖ παχυτέρα, παρέχουσα δὲ εὖρος ἀρκοῦν ἐπὶ τῷ στόματι πρὸς ὑποδοχὴν πνεύματος εἰς κώδωνα ταῖς σάλπιγξι παραπλησίως τελοῦντα· ἀσώσρα καλεῖται κατὰ τὴν Ἑβραίων γλῶσσαν, Jos. Ant., 3, 291.
[33] Cf. Cornill, Plate VI; Behn, Ill. 83; AOB, Ill. 509 etc.

was increased. At the dedication of Solomon's temple 120 priests blew trumpets, 2 Ch. 5:12 f. Since the bibl. חֲצֹצְרָה bears some similarity to Egypt. trumpets, [34] it has been conjectured [35] that the Israelites brought them out of Egypt at the exodus. But this is unlikely. The חֲצֹצְרָה is mentioned only in later writings, and it probably came into use by the Israelites at a later stage. Since it was a more costly and a better instrument than the שׁוֹפָר, it tended to supplant the latter. [36] The priestly blowers of חֲצֹצְרוֹת had an established place in Solomon's temple, 2 Ch. 5:12. In connection with the reforms of Hezekiah the trumpets of the priests are important cultic instruments, 2 Ch. 29:26 ff. Where the שׁוֹפָר used to be blown, the ref. later is to the חֲצֹצְרוֹת. The שׁוֹפָר is sounded at a coronation in 2 K. 9:13, but חֲצֹצְרָה are mentioned in 2 K. 11:14; 2 Ch. 23:13. Comparison of the two accounts of bringing up the ark yields the same result: 2 S. 6:15 speaks of the שׁוֹפָר, 1 Ch. 13:8; 15:24, 28 of the חֲצֹצְרוֹת. חֲצֹצְרוֹת are mentioned in war in 2 Ch. 13:12, 14, שׁוֹפָר in Ju. 7:16 etc. Both instruments occur in Hos. 5:8; Ps. 98:6; 1 Ch. 15:28; 2 Ch. 15:14. In the OT as a whole there is no discernible distinction in the use of the two instruments.

c. קֶרֶן.

In the Heb. part of the OT the only ref. to קֶרֶן as a wind instrument is in Jos. 6:5. The Aram. form occurs 4 times in Da. 3:5, 7, 10, 15. Like שׁוֹפָר it is an animal horn. It is not a specific instrument as compared with שׁוֹפָר and חֲצֹצְרָה. שׁוֹפָר and קֶרֶן are synon. in Jos. 6:5 ff. In Da. it is one of the instruments in Nebuchadnezzar's "orchestra." It is never a cultic instrument.

d. יוֹבֵל.

Nothing certain is known about the origin of this word. [37] It has been conjectured that the vocalisation is wrong and the instrument has been connected with Jubal, the inventor of music, Gn. 4:21. If the instrument is identical with the name of the first musician, יוֹבֵל is the "trumpet" in person. [38] More probably יוֹבֵל is originally the leader of the flock, the "bell-wether." [39] From this developed the various senses: "ram's horn," "trumpet" made of the horn of the ram, "trumpet signal," and finally the "feast" announced by this signal. [40] יוֹבֵל again is not a specific instrument as compared with שׁוֹפָר and חֲצֹצְרָה. In the sense of "horn" it occurs only in Ex. 19:13, where the long sound of the יוֹבֵל is obviously identical with the קוֹל הַשֹּׁפָר of Ex. 19:19, cf. 16. Elsewhere it occurs only along with קֶרֶן or שׁוֹפָר. קֶרֶן הַיּוֹבֵל is found in Jos. 6:5, שׁוֹפְרוֹת הַיּוֹבְלִים in Jos. 6:4, 6, 8, 13. In the relevant passages יוֹבֵל probably denotes the material from which the horn is made.

e. תְּרוּעָה.

Once at Lv. 23:24 (cf. also Ιερ. 30:2 Σ) σάλπιγξ is in the LXX the transl. of תְּרוּעָה. But תְּרוּעָה is not a musical instrument; it is the "noise," "tumult" [41] (Jos. 6:5;

[34] Behn, Ill. 63, 65; C. Sachs, "Altägypt. Musikinstrumente," AO, 21, 3 f. (1920), Ill. 14; Hickmann, Plate I; H. Hickmann, "Musicologie Pharaonique," Sammlung musikwissenschaftlicher Abh., 34 (1956), 35.
[35] A. W. Ambros, Geschichte d. Musik, I² (1880), 166 and Kirby, op. cit. (→ n. 24), 255.
[36] Finesinger Shofar, 210; Seidel, 593.
[37] On the difficult etym. and the many theories suggested cf. R. North, "Sociology of the Biblical Jubilee," Analecta Bibl., 4 (1954), 100-102.
[38] Gressmann, 2 f., 31.
[39] Ibid., 31; M. Noth, Das Buch Josua, Hndbch. AT, 7² (1953) on 6:4.
[40] G. Lambert, "Jubilé Hébreu et Jubilé Chrétien," Nouvelle Revue Théol., 72 (1950), 235.
[41] P. Humbert, La "Terou'a," Analyse d'un rite bibl. (1946).

1 S. 4:5 f.) or "alarm" (Nu. 10:5). When LXX uses σάλπιγξ for it, σάλπιγξ bears the Gk. sense of "sound of the trumpet" or "signal" (→ 72, 11 ff.), though elsewhere the LXX has two words for this in lit. correspondence to the Heb. original, → 76, 18 ff. In Nu. 29:1, which corresponds to Lv. 23:24, the LXX rightly uses σημασία for תְּרוּעָה.

f. תָּקוֹעַ.

At Ez. 7:14 LXX has σαλπίσατε ἐν σάλπιγγι for תִּקְעוּ בַתָּקוֹעַ. It obviously takes תָּקוֹעַ to be a wind instrument. Since there is no other instance of the noun, and the verb תָּקַע means "to blow" abs. only in Nu. 10:7 (→ line 15 f.), textual corruption has been suspected. Usually the word is turned into an inf. abs. by the omission of the בּ. This yields תִּקְעוּ תָקוֹעַ and the ref. is simply to blowing, not to an instrument. [42]

2. σαλπίζω.

a. Heb. formed a verb from only one of the different words for horn, trumpet. As σαλπίζειν arose out of σάλπιγξ, so did חצר out of חֲצֹצְרָה. This the LXX renders by σαλπίζω in 1 Ch. 15:24; 2 Ch. 5:12 f.; 7:6; 13:14; 29:28. Elsewhere σαλπίζω is used for other Heb. words and expressions. b. Most commonly we find תָּקַע "to beat," "to thrust" (cf. the Germ. "ins Horn stossen"). In the abs., however, this is rare, Nu. 10:7 cf. Ez. 7:14 (→ lines 6 ff.). The expression תָּקַע בַּשּׁוֹפָר is very common, e.g., Ju. 3:27; 1 S. 13:3; Is. 27:13; Zech. 9:14, cf. also תָּקַע שׁוֹפָר, e.g., Ps. 81:3; Is. 18:3; Hos. 5:8; Jl. 2:1. With חֲצֹצְרָה we sometimes find תָּקַע בַּחֲצֹצְרָה, Nu. 10:8; 2 K. 11:14; 2 Ch. 23:13. תָּקַע תְּרוּעָה "to blow the alarm" occurs in Nu. 10:5 f., LXX σαλπίζειν σημασίαν. On תָּקַע בַּתָּקוֹעַ at Ez. 7:14 → lines 6 ff. c. רוּעַ hi "to make a noise," "to cry," is combined with חֲצֹצְרָה in Nu. 10:9 cf. 2 Ch. 13:12 : "to make a noise on the trumpet." At Nu. 10:9 the LXX MSS vacillate between σημανεῖτε and σαλπιεῖτε ταῖς σάλπιγξιν. Though no instrument is mentioned with רוּעַ at Nu. 10:7, it is to be transl. "to blow" here too, corresponding to תָּקַע תְּרוּעָה in Nu. 10:6. At Is. 44:23 the LXX has σαλπίζειν for רוּעַ, though here the word means "to exult" rather than "to blow." d. Apart from the 3 verbs mentioned other Heb. words mean "to blow" in combination with horns, e.g., מָשַׁךְ "to draw," "to draw the note out," "to produce a long-drawn out note," מָשַׁךְ הַיּוֹבֵל Ex. 19:13 and מָשַׁךְ בְּקֶרֶן Jos. 6:5. e. עָבַר hi "to cause to go through," "to push air through the wind instrument," "to sound forth," occurs in Lv. 25:9 : הַעֲבִיר שׁוֹפָר. f. Probably שָׁמַע hi is also a verb of blowing in 1 Ch. 16:42 : "to cause to hear," "to sound," "to play."

3. σαλπιστής.

The noun σαλπιστής does not occur in the LXX. The OT has no special term for those who blow on trumpets. The instrument חֲצֹצְרָה is used for the player in 2 K. 11:14; 2 Ch. 23:13; 29:28. The trumpeter is הַתּוֹקֵעַ בַּשּׁוֹפָר ("the one who blows the trumpet") in Neh. 4:12. There are also many ref. to priests with trumpets, 2 Ch. 29:26; Ezr. 3:10; Neh. 12:35, 41.

II. Use and Significance of the Horn and the Trumpet.

1. The Horn and the Trumpet in War.

In Palestine as in Greece (→ 73, 30 ff.) the horn is an important instrument in war. On the borders and here and there throughout the country guards were posted who warned the inhabitants of threatened danger, esp. from invasion, Jer. 4:5; 6:1, 17; Hos.

---

[42] W. Zimmerli, Ez., Bibl. Komm. AT, 13, ad loc.

8:1; Am. 3:6; Ez. 33:3 ff.; Neh. 4:12. Horn signals summoned the young men to the holy war, Ju. 3:27; 6:34; 1 S. 13:3; Jer. 51:27; Ez. 7:14. How much the gathering of the tribes by the שׁוֹפָר was a religious rather than a purely secular affair may be seen from the note in Ju. 6:34 : "But the Spirit of the Lord came upon Gideon, and he blew a trumpet." In revolts, too, horn signals were used to alert the conspirators, 2 S. 15:10; 20:1. For the Jews as well as the Gks. (→ 74, 11 f.) the horn was a signal to attack, Job 39:24 f.; 1 Macc. 4:13; 9:12 f.; with the battle-cry the host would fall on the enemy and the horn would give added strength to the noise of the charge, Jos. 6:20; Ju. 7:18 ff.; 2 Ch. 13:14 ff.; Jer. 4:19; 1 Macc. 5:31. But the horn was not just a signal to pass on orders (Nu. 10:2 ff.), to inspire courage, or to terrify the foe (→ 74, 16 f.) cf. Ju. 7:18 ff. In war, too, it had religious significance for the Israelites. God was invoked by the sounding of the horn. It was meant to remind Him (Nu. 10:9), so that the blast of the trumpets was a calling upon God. Thus the sounding of the trumpets before battle is often mentioned along with prayer : "They cried unto the Lord, and the priests sounded with the trumpets," 2 Ch. 13:14; "they cried aloud to heaven ... How can we stand before them, if thou dost not help us ? And they blew the trumpets and cried with a loud voice," 1 Macc. 3:50 ff.; "they fell on their faces to the earth and blew the trumpets and cried to heaven," 1 Macc. 4:40; "he attacked them in the rear with three companies, and they blew the trumpets and cried in prayer," 1 Macc. 5:33 cf. 2 Macc. 15:25 f. The horn was also a signal to break off the pursuit and end the battle (→ 74, 17 ff.), 2 S. 2:28; 18:16. The trumpet sounded forth with other instruments when the army returned home after victory and went to the temple, 2 Ch. 20:28. As the horn summoned the host, so it was dismissed and sent home by the trumpet, 2 S. 20:22.

2. The Horn and the Trumpet on Solemn Occasions in Peace.

At a royal coronation the heralds blew the horn and the people cried : Long live the king ! 2 S. 15:10; 1 K. 1:34, 39, 41; 2 K. 9:13; 11:14; 2 Ch. 23:13. Since God is the real King and His enthronement corresponds to the rite of political coronation, trumpets are also mentioned in the enthronement psalms : "God is gone up with a shout, the Lord with the sound of a trumpet," Ps. 47:5; "With trumpets and sound of cornet make a joyful noise before the Lord, the King," Ps. 98:6. The horn was also blown on other special occasions. When Solomon's temple was dedicated, 120 priests blew on trumpets, 2 Ch. 5:12; 7:6, and when the foundation of the new temple was laid the trumpets of the priests sounded forth again, Ezr. 3:10 cf. 1 Εσδρ. 5:57, 59, 62 f. As among the Gks. (→ 75, 1 ff.) the Israelites also blew the instruments in festal processions. Thus the ark was brought up to Jerusalem to the sound of horns (2 S. 6:15) and trumpets (1 Ch. 13:8; 15:24, 28). In the solemn procession at the dedication of the wall each of the two groups had seven priests with trumpets, Neh. 12:35, 41. When in the cultic reformation under Asa the men of Judah declared that they were ready to cleave to God with all their hearts and all their souls they swore by the Lord to the sound of trumpets and horns, 2 Ch. 15:14.

3. The Cultic Significance of the Trumpet and the Horn.

The cultic significance of the trumpet and the horn has already come to light in the preceding section. It was blown at the burnt offering and peace offerings, Nu. 10:10. When the trumpets sounded at the burnt offering, the whole congregation cast itself at once to the ground to worship, 2 Ch. 29:27 f.; Sir. 50:16 f. The purpose of the blast, as at the beginning of battle (→ lines 10 ff.), is that God should not forget them but keep them in mind, Nu. 10:10; Sir. 50:16. When the trumpets and other instruments sounded at the dedication of the temple, and a song of praise was struck up to the Lord, God came with His shechinah into the temple and the glory of God filled the house, 2 Ch. 5:13 f. The use of the trumpet at the various feasts was important, Nu. 10:10; 2 Εσδρ. 18:15. It was blown at the new moon, Nu. 10:10; Ps. 81:3. The horn announced the New Year's feast, which was a day of commemoration with the sound of trumpets,

Lv. 23:24; cf. Nu. 29:1. The year of release was proclaimed with the horn on the Day of Atonement, Lv. 25:8 f. When fasts were ordained, they were proclaimed by signals, Jl. 2:15.

4. The Sounding of Horns at Theophanies.

It is not possible to differentiate strictly between the secular, the cultic and the theological significance of the horn. In the use in war, as a warning of invasion (→ 78, 41 ff.), at the commencement of battle (→ 79, 5 f.), or at the coronation of a king in peace (→ 79, 24 ff.), there is always a relation to God. If the horn often seems to be a secular signal, in most cases it stands in a strict relation to God. The sound of horns accompanies the divine theophany, Ex. 19:16 ff. Who blows it is not stated in Ex. 19. Perhaps God Himself does. He does so in Zech. 9:14. At theophanies the blast of the horn does not simply announce God's coming. Nor is it just a figure of speech for thunder as among the Gks., → 72, 16 ff. For thunder and the sound of horns are differentiated in Ex. 19:16 and 20:18. The sound of horns probably denotes the inexpressible voice of God. [43] This seems to be so in Ex. 19:19 : "The voice of the trumpet sounded long, and waxed louder and louder. Moses spake, and God answered him by a (loud) voice." Dt. 5:22 confirms the correctness of this exposition : "These words the Lord spake unto all your assembly in the mount out of the midst of the fire, of the cloud, and of the thick darkness, with a great voice."

5. The Eschatological Significance of the Horn.

As the horn sounded when God was revealed at Sinai, so it will sound at the events of the last time. The day of Yahweh will be announced by the sound of the horn, Jl. 2:1; Zeph. 1:16. The same signal will usher in the Last Judgment. As it announced the approach of enemies and thus caused anxiety and terror (→ 78, 42 ff.), so God's eschatological judgment is proclaimed by it. It also proclaims the beginning of the age of salvation. There follows the gathering of Israel and the return of the dispersed to Zion. "And it shall come to pass in that day, that the great trumpet shall be blown," Is. 27:13. God Himself shall blow the horn and bring about the return and liberation of the Jews, Zech. 9:14

6. The Horn and the Trumpet as Musical Instruments.

In Da. 3:5, 7, 10, 15 the horn is with the pipe, the zither, the seven-stringed lute and the trapezoid zither one of the instruments in the court orchestra of Nebuchadnezzar. 2 Ch. 5:13 says that the music of the trumpeters and singers is to be heard as a voice in praise of Yahweh. Ps. 150:3 mentions the horn first among the temple instruments. This might suggest that in Palestine the horn and trumpet were blown like wind instruments in a modern orchestra. But this is impossible, since there was no valve or keyhole and hence only a few notes could be blown, → 75, 35 ff. On the ram's horn, as may be seen from the customary instruments in synagogues to-day, only two notes in addition to the basic note could be produced at the distance of a fifth and an octave. [44] A varied sound and rhythm could be achieved, however, by sustained and even blowing on the one hand or short blowing on the other. Various signals are differentiated in

---

[43] Reik, 204; A. Weiser, "Zur Frage nach den Beziehungen d. Psalmen zum Kult : Die Darstellung d. Theophanie in d. Psalmen u. im Festkult," Festschr. A. Bertholet (1950), 523; Seidel, 589.

[44] Kirby, op. cit. (→ n. 24), 254.

Nu. 10:3 ff. One may simply blow the trumpet (10:3 f.) or sound an alarm (10:5 f. cf. v. 7). Possibly the verbs תָּקַע (→ 78, 15 ff.), מָשַׁךְ (→ 78, 27 ff.) and רוּעַ (→ 78, 21 ff.) denote different ways of blowing. תָּקַע may be brief, staccato blowing, מָשַׁךְ sostenuto with longer notes, רוּעַ the shattering blast. In the temple the priests did not accompany the Levites but filled in the intervals between the stanzas with loud blasts. If later trumpets are mentioned with other instruments or the singers (1 Ch. 15:28; 2 Ch. 15:14; Ps. 98:6; 150:3), this was not because they played a melody but because they emphasised the rhythm and like modern fanfares strengthened the sound of loud, popular music.

C. The Word Group in Judaism.

I. The Individual Words.

1. שׁוֹפָר.

The שׁוֹפָר is usually curved (RH, 3, 4), though it could be straight. It was blown at the New Year feast, RH, 3, 3a. It was used in the temple with the חֲצוֹצְרוֹת (RH, 3, 3b) and also in the synagogue. In Qumran the horns were blown by the Levites and all the people, 1 QM 7:13 f.; 8:9 ff.; 16:7 f.; 17:13 f., whereas the חֲצוֹצְרָה was strictly a priestly instrument. The significance of the שׁוֹפָר for the Jews may be seen from the fact that it is often depicted on grave-stones, glasses, lamps, pillars, coins, mosaics, rings and amulets. [45]

2. חֲצוֹצְרָה.

The חֲצוֹצְרָה was a typical instrument in the temple cultus. "There were no trumpets outside the temple," jRH, 3, 3 (58d, 30). How fully it was identified with the ministry of the priests may be seen from the observation that he who does not have a חֲצוֹצְרָה is not a priest, T. Sota, 7, 15. Trumpets were exclusive to the priests in Qumran, → 82, 11 f. After the temple with its cultus was destroyed and the trumpets were sent to Rome with the other sacred vessels, the חֲצוֹצְרָה went out of use and the שׁוֹפָר again swept the field, so that the two became interchangeable (bShab., 36a) and no distinction was seen between them (bSota, 43a; bSukka, 34a).

3. קֶרֶן.

As in the OT, so in Judaism קֶרֶן is a more general term. It can denote an instrument made from the cow's horn, whereas שׁוֹפָר is made from the ram's horn, RH, 3, 2 and bRH, 26a. Elsewhere we read of horns with metal mouthpieces made up of various parts, Kelim, 11, 7.

4. סַלְפִּינְגֵּס.

The Gk. word σάλπιγξ came into the vocabulary of Judaism as a loan word. [46] It is found in various forms : סלפינגס (= σάλπιγγας) Qoh. r. on 8:8; סלפירגסי Lv. r., 29, 4 on 23:24; סולפירים Gn. r., 99 on 49:26; סרפינוס Lam. r. Intr., 23; סרפיניסם Qoh. r. on 12:7.

---

[45] Cf. the ill. in A. Reifenberg, *Denkmäler d. jüd. Antike* (1937), Plate 44, 54, 57 f., 62 f.; also *Ancient Jewish Coins*² (1947), Ill. 174, 182, 186; Goodenough, III, Ill. 334 ff., 346, 444, 478, 565 f., 571 ff., 580 ff., 592, 624, 632, 639, 647, 651 f., 666, 671, 696, 715 ff., 768 f., 787, 806, 808, 817, 837, 846 ff., 872 f., 878, 891, 983, 928, 941, 958, 961 ff., 1010 ff., 1023, 1026, 1034.

[46] Krauss Lehnw., II, 395 f., cf. Jastrow, *s.v.* סַלְפִּינְגֵּס.

II. The Significance of Horns and Trumpets in Judaism.

1. As Signals in War.

The book of *The War of the Sons of Light against the Sons of Darkness* gives explicit rules for the army in which the significance of the trumpet is clearly set forth. [47] At the sound of the trumpet of summons חצוצרות מקראם the soldiers get ready to go out of the gates to battle, 1 QM 3:1, 7; 7:13, 15; 8:3; 9:3. The trumpets of battle array חצוצרות סדרי give the sign for the formation of the ranks. At a second signal the army approaches the enemy, 1 QM 3:1, 6; 8:5-8; 16:5 f.; 17:10 f. The signal for battle (→ 79, 5 ff.) is given by the trumpets of the smitten חצוצרות החללים 1 QM 3:8; 8:8 f.; 9:2; 16:7, 9; 17:13, also called the alarm trumpet of the smitten חצוצרות תרועות החללים 1 QM 3:1, or briefly the alarm trumpet שופרות היובל 1 QM 7:13. A group of six priests blew these trumpets, 1 QM 8:8; 16:6 f. The blast of the trumpets united with the horns of the Levites to sound the alarm, 1 QM 8:9; 16:7 f.; 17:13. The trumpets of the smitten accompany the battle with their cry (1 QM 9:1 f.; 16:9) "to cause the heart of the enemy to melt" (1 QM 8:10). The task of the trumpets of ambush חצוצרות המארב (1 QM 3:1 f., 8) cannot be stated, since they are not mentioned in accounts of individual battles. Their inscription: "The mystery of God for the destruction of wickedness," is worth noting (3:9). The trumpets of pursuit חצוצרות המרדף (3:2, 9; 9:6) lead the troops when the enemy is defeated. Their inscription reveals their purpose: "God has overthrown all the sons of darkness. He does not turn aside His wrath until they are destroyed," 3:9. The trumpets of retreat חצוצרות המשוב (8:2, 13) are identical with those of assembly חצוצרות המאסף (3:2). The trumpets of homecoming חצוצרות דרך משוב are mentioned only in 3:10 f. They sound when the army returns from the battlefield to the community at Jerusalem. The signals are differentiated by different ways of blowing. Mostly the verb תקע is used, → 78, 15 ff. In the actual battle when the trumpets of the smitten and the horns of the Levites are blown, we find רוע (→ 78, 21 ff.), 1 QM 8:1, 8 f., 12, 15; 9:1 f.; 16:7 f.; 17:12 f. Sometimes the way of blowing is esp. noted. A sustained blast is sounded as the signal of battle array (8:5), a quiet, firm note as the second signal to advance (8:7), short, sharp blasts in the battle itself (the trumpets of the smitten, 8:9; 16:7), and then again a quiet, sustained note as the signal to retreat, 8:14.

2. Trumpets and Horns on Special Occasions in Peace.

A summons to a general fast was blown (→ 80, 2 f.) in special emergencies such as blight, pestilence, plagues of locusts or wild animals (Taan., 3, 5), or drought (1, 6; 3, 2 f.). On such occasions the two trumpeters were flanked by horn-players who had curved ram's horns with silver coated mouthpieces. Since the trumpets were the main instruments, they blew longer than the horns, RH, 3, 4. A horn signal was given to intimate a death, bBM, 59b; bMQ, 27b. The imposing and lifting of excommunication were also announced by signals, bMQ, 16a, 17a; bShebu., 36a. In this way God was reminded of the iniquity of the transgressor that He might punish him, bMQ, 17b.

---

[47] The text as we have it, of course, presents no single system, since it was probably composed of various elements, cf. C. H. Hunzinger, "Fragmente einer älteren Fassung d. Buches Milhama aus Höhle 4 von Qumran," ZAW, 69 (1957), 131-151. Various overlappings and discrepancies may be noted, cf. J. Carmignac, *La règle de la guerre* (1958), 110; J. van der Ploeg, "Le rouleau de la guerre," *Studies on the Texts of the Desert of Judah,* II (1959), 14 f., 18, 118. The no. of trumpets and the language varies. 1 QM 3:6-11 speaks of 7 trumpets, 7:12 of 6 priests with trumpets, 7:13 of only 5 trumpets. 1 QM 7:13 distinguishes between the trumpets of summons and those of remembrance, 1 QM 3:1, 7 and 8:3 give the former the same task as that of the latter in 16:3 f., and the trumpets of re-

3. Trumpets and Horns in the Jewish Cultus.

The true significance of these wind instruments may be seen from their regular use in worship and at feasts. On ordinary days there were at least 21 trumpet blasts in the temple, and more on special occasions, though never more than 48. Three blasts were sounded in the morning when the temple gates were opened, nine at the morning sacrifice, nine at the evening sacrifice, Sukka, 5, 5. At the morning sacrifice the Levites gave the signal for the choir of Levites to strike up, and during intervals in the singing the trumpets sounded again. When they did so, the people prostrated themselves in worship (→ 79, 44 f.), Tamid, 7, 3. Acc. to Damasc. 11:21-23 (14:2 f.) one was not to enter the place of worship once the trumpet of assembly had been blown. Probably this began the act of worship, which was not to be disturbed by coming and going. [48] Apart from the war trumpets (→ 82, 2 ff.) 6 different trumpets for times of peace are mentioned in 1 QM 3:2-11. These call the community together and regulate its life. [49] The commencement of the Sabbath is intimated by a threefold blast (→ 15, 19 ff.), T. Sukka, 4, 11 f.; Sukka, 5, 5; Shab., 35b; Jos. Bell., 4, 582; bAZ, 70a. With trumpet signals the college of scribes proclaimed the new moon, bNidda, 38a. On New Year's Day the blast was that of the horn. For this the straight horn of the goat was used, its mouthpiece overlaid with gold. To emphasise the importance of the שׁוֹפָר on this day, it was flanked by two trumpeters, RH, 3, 3b. The same applied at the Feast of Jubilees, RH, 3, 5b. At Tabernacles the trumpets sounded when the willow branches were laid on the altar, Sukka, 4, 5. At the dispensing of water the priest was received by a blast of the trumpet when he came from the well of Shiloah to the Water Gate, Sukka, 4, 9a. At cockcrow trumpet signals ended the nightly feast of lights in the court of women, Sukka, 5, 4c. At Passover blasts were blown on the trumpets before the slaying of the lambs, Pes., 5, 5. [50]

This liturgical blowing was not just an intimation of liturgical acts. It had its own efficacy. As in the OT (→ 79, 12 ff.; 79, 45 ff.) it was an act of prayer; God was reminded by it, bShab., 131b. "Why blow on horns? To say: Look on us as though we lowed like cattle before thee," jTaan., 2, 1 (65a, 30 f.). If God judges the world on the four feasts of Passover, Ingathering, New Year and Tabernacles, then He is reminded by the sound of horns: "Blow before me with the ram's horn, that I may be mindful of the offering of Isaac, the son of Abraham, and so I will impute it to you as if you had offered yourselves for me," bRH, 16a. The ram caught by its horns in the thicket (Gn. 22:13) was linked with the saying about the ram's horn in Zech. 9:14:

---

membrance replace those of battle array in 1 QM 3:1, 6. In 1 QM 18:4 the trumpet of remembrance gives the signal for rallying to pursue the defeated foe, so that it seems to correspond to the trumpet of pursuit. Perhaps this trumpet of remembrance has no fixed place in the battle but as a trumpet of prayer (→ 79, 12 ff.) may be blown in different phases of the battle. In 1 QM 7:13 the alarm trumpet is obviously that of the smitten, but it corresponds to that of battle array in 1 QM 16:6.

[48] H. Kosmala, "Hebräer, Essener, Christen," Studia Post-Biblica, 1 (1959), 359.

[49] Acc. to N. Müller, Art. "Glocken" in RE³, 6, 704 a trumpet blast was the signal for Chr. monks in Egypt to commence the gathering for worship. It is usually assumed that the monks took the custom from the OT. Acc. to Kosmala, op. cit., 359 they took it from the Essenes. But perhaps they were adopting an Egypt. practice, for the trumpet had played a big role there from an early time, → 73, 22 ff. From Lidz. Joh., 104, 4 ff. one gets the impression that Christians used horns in missionary preaching and in worship: "Thou hast deceived them by horns and spread abroad shameful things by the shofar." But for lack of other testimony one must assume that the author was confusing Judaism and Christianity.

[50] The following rule of blowing is given in RH, 4, 9: 3 notes are blown 3 times. The measure of a תקיעה corresponds to that of 3 תרועות, and that of a תרועה to that of 3 יבבות. We find תרועה, תקיעה and שברים in bRH, 34a. The תקיעה must have been a sustained note equal to 3 תרועות and 9 יבבות. Eisenstein, 306 and P. Fiebig, Rosch haschana, Giessener Mischna, II, 8 (1914), 105 give examples from current synagogue practice.

"In every generation thy children shall be seized by sins and snared in afflictions, but at the last they shall be redeemed by the horns of this ram," jTaan., 2, 4 (65d, 10 ff.) cf. Lv. r., 29, 10 on 23:24. Naturally other peoples, too, have various kinds of horns and trumpets, Lv. r., 29, 4 on 23:24. The difference is that Israel can evoke the grace of the Creator by blowing the horn, bRH, 16b. "In the hour when God sits and mounts the throne of justice, He mounts it with righteousness. What does it mean that He mounts it with the sound of jubilation ? (Ps. 47:5). In the hour when the Israelites take the horn and blow before the Holy One, blessed be He, He leaves the throne of justice and mounts the throne of mercy, as it is said : the Eternal One with the sound of horns (Ps. 47:6), and He is filled with mercy toward them, and has pity on them and turns punishment into mercy," Lv. r., 29, 3 on 23:24 cf. Pesikt., 151b. As the blast of the horn makes God merciful, it confuses Satan. When Satan hears the sound of the horn for the first time, he becomes anxious, and when he hears the second blast he knows the time has come to be swallowed up, and so he withdraws, bRH, 16a. Thus blowing has more than external significance ; it has a profound meaning.

4. The Eschatological Significance of the Sound of Horns.

a. The trumpet proclaims the end (→ 80, 21 ff.): "The trumpet will sound out loud, and all men will hear it suddenly and quake," 4 Esr. 6:23; for the hour of judgment draws near just as the trumpet blast of Michael announced God's sentence on Adam in Paradise : "When we heard the archangel's trumpet, we said : Lo, God comes to Paradise to judge us," Apc. Mos. 22 cf. 37. The trumpet blast has a place in the description of judgment along with cosmic disasters, Sib., VIII, 239. A gt. sign with swords and trumpets appears before the end, IV, 173 f. b. But salvation also begins with a trumpet blast : In Tišri they will one day be redeemed. This may be deduced from the word horn, for it is said : Blow the horn on the new moon (Ps. 81:3); also : In that day a great horn shall be blown (Is. 27:13), bRH, 11b. The exiled are brought back by the signal of the great horn, Midr. Qoh. 1:7. Acc. to Apc. Mos. 22 the archangel Michael blows the trumpet, and in Apc. Mos. 38 trumpets are part of the equipment of the angels who accompany God. On the basis of Zech. 9:14, however, God is usually said to blow the horn Himself, S. Nu., 77 (20a) on 10:10. "Then will I blow the trumpet from the winds and send forth mine elect ... he then summons my despised people out of all nations," Apc. Abr. 31:1 f. Prayer is thus made : "Blow the great trumpet for our liberation, and raise a banner for the gathering of our exiles," Sh. E., 10. At the time the trumpet shall be blown in Jerusalem in order that its inhabitants may be ready to receive those who come back home, Ps. Sol. 11:1. c. The dead, too, are raised to the sound of the horn : "God will take a great horn in his hand, ... he will blow it and its note will go from one end of the earth to the other. At the first blast the whole earth shakes ; at the second the dust is sifted out ; at the third the bones are brought together ; at the fourth the limbs are warmed ; at the fifth their skin is put on ; at the sixth the spirits and souls enter their bodies ; at the seventh they come to life and stand on their feet in their clothes, as it is said : The almighty Yahweh will blow the horn (Zech. 9:14)," Alphabet-Midr. of R. Aqiba, 9. [51]

5. The Horn and the Trumpet as Musical Instruments.

In Judaism, too, the horn and the trumpet are not wind instruments in an orchestra. At the nocturnal feast of lights during Tabernacles a distinction is made between the Levites with zithers, harps, cymbals and other musical instruments [52] and the priests with the 2 trumpets who proclaim the end of the feast, Sukka, 5, 4. In bRH, 28a and TRH, 3, 5 it is said that the duty of blowing is discharged when a song is blown. But

---

[51] Beth-ha-Midrash (ed. A. Jellinek[2] [1938], III, 31, 28 ff.).
[52] Cf. H. Bornhäuser, *Sukka, Giessener Mischna,* II, 6 (1935) on 5:4b.

at best the horn and trumpet can only have given the signal or note for striking up the song. They cannot have been instruments to accompany the song or play the melody, → 81, 4 ff. Probably this passage in the Talmud bears some other sense, since the text is uncertain. [53] The tone of these instruments was more loud than it was beautiful. On New Year's Day the sound of the horns was so strong that one could not hear one's own voice at prayer, bRH, 30a. The blowing could be confused with the braying of an ass (→ 76, 4 f.), bRH, 28b. The Romans thought the blowing of the Jewish horns at New Year was a signal for revolt and fell on the Jews, jRH, 4, 8 (59c, 41 ff.). This indicates the nature of liturgical blowing.

D. The Word Group in the New Testament.

I. The Individual Words.

1. σάλπιγξ.

As in Gk., σάλπιγξ in the NT denotes both the instrument (→ 72, 4 ff.) — so in most instances, 1 C. 14:8; Hb. 12:19; Rev. 1:10; 4:1; 8:2, 6, 13; 9:14 — and also the note produced (→ 72, 8 ff.), the "sound of the trumpet," "signal," Mt. 24:31; 1 C. 15:52; 1 Th. 4:16.

2. σαλπίζω.

The verb σαλπίζω occurs mostly in Rev. In 1 C. 15:52 it is used impersonally as in profane Gk. → 72, 28 ff. We are not told who blows the trumpet.

3. σαλπιστής.

The only instance of σαλπιστής in the NT is in Rev. 18:22 in connection with the musicians of Babylon, → 88, 5 ff.

II. The Significance of the Blowing of Trumpets.

1. In War.

In his discussion of tongues Paul uses the metaphor of the military trumpet (1 C. 14:8) to show that proclamation in the congregation must be clear, → II, 770, 20 ff. If the trumpet does not give a definite signal the troops will not prepare for battle.

2. On Solemn Occasions.

The point of what is said about blowing trumpets at the giving of alms (Mt. 6:2) is plain : One is not to do good visibly before all men (v. 1 and 3) for one's own glory (v. 2). Not so clear is whether σαλπίζω is to be taken metaphorically "to blaze abroad" or whether there is reference to a specific custom in Judaism. Neither view can produce concrete illustrations.

A mistake in translating from Aram. to Gk. has been conjectured. [54] The 13 offering chests in the temple (Mk. 12:41) were called שׁוֹפָרוֹת because they were horn-shaped to prevent theft, narrow at the top and broad at the bottom, Sheq., 6, 1. 5. There were similar collection horns in the provinces, 2, 1. Perhaps, then, Jesus in Mt. 6:2 was

---

[53] Finesinger Shofar, 227.
[54] G. Klein, "Mt. 6:2," ZNW, 6 (1905), 204.

warning against putting alms in the שׁוֹפָר. The transl., however, did not understand this sense of שׁוֹפָר. and hence used σαλπίζω. But this suggestion falls to the ground because putting money in the שׁוֹפָר could not be misunderstood as σαλπίζειν. Nor can one suppose that the rich blew a trumpet in the streets and squares to summon the poor in order that they might give them alms. [55] In the synagogues, esp. at fasts when in serious crises worship was held in open places in the city (Taan., 2, 1), specific sums were often pledged publicly for the poor chest by individuals (bBer., 6b) because it was thought that alms, like penitence and prayer, could avert disaster, jTaan., 2, 1 (65b, 3). But blowing the horn also played an important part in fasts. Taan., 2, 5 tells us that at the end of each of the benedictions used there was a summons after the prayer : "Blow, priests, blow ; sound, sons of Aaron, sound." We are also told that the givers of greater amounts were specially honoured by being allowed to sit alongside the rabbis at worship, jHor., 3, 7 (48a, 39. 54. 57). Sir. 31:11 says : "The community will proclaim his alms." [56]

It is against this background that the saying of Jesus in Mt. 6:2 is to be construed. Probably when particularly generous gifts were given, as the opposite of excommunication (→ 82, 38 ff.), the horn was blown in the synagogue to stir up others to similar acts and to bring the donors to remembrance before God, → 83, 27 ff. Jesus objects that this is to give things before men for one's own glory. God's attention does not need to be directed to good works by a horn, for He sees what is hidden, v. 4.

3. The Trumpet in Theophany and Vision.

At Sinai acc. to Hb. 12:19 the sound of the trumpet is not, as in Ex. 19:16 ff. (→ 80, 15 ff.), a term for the voice of God, for the words which the hearers will not receive are mentioned separately. The sound of the trumpet is with the cloud and darkness and storm one of the accompanying phenomena of the theophany. This is not so, however, in Rev. 1:10 and 4:1. In his vision the divine hears a voice like the sound of a trumpet. There is no reference to a trumpet blast as in Hb. 12:19, but the sound which John hears is compared to a trumpet. What is indicated is the loudness and the indescribability of the tone. We are not told who the speaker is. It can hardly be the voice of an angel as in Rev. 5:2; 17:1; 21:9. Only twice at the beginning of the vision (Rev. 1:10; 4:1) is the voice compared to a trumpet, while in the further course of Rev. it is an angel who speaks to the seer. In the light of Rev. 1:12 ff. one might conjecture that the voice is that of the Son of Man, but this is described differently in 1:15. The voice which has a sound like that of a trumpet is surely that of God Himself (cf. Rev. 16:1, 17) as in the OT (→ 80, 15 ff.), though one may see from Rev. 1:1 and 22:6, 16 that no essential distinction need be made between God and Christ. In Rev. 1:10 the great voice introduces the revelation of the epistles, while in 4:1 it introduces the visions in the true sense.

4. The Eschatological Significance of the Trumpet.

Eschatological trumpet sayings in the NT correspond to those in the OT and Judaism.

---

[55] J. Calvin, Comm. in Harmoniam Evangelicam on Mt. 6:2 (Corp. Ref., 73 [1891], 191).
[56] Cf. Str.-B., IV, 546-554.

a. The trumpet proclaims the great judgment at the end of the time, → 84, 17 ff. In Rev. 8:2 it is not just the archangel Gabriel who blows the trumpet as at the condemnation of Adam; since judgment is now passed on the whole world 7 angels hold the trumpets. The number 7 is connected with the significance of this number in the structure of the book (→ II, 632, 14 ff.) but also with references to 7 trumpeters elsewhere. [57] The first blasts bring down divine judgments in the form of natural disasters upon the four areas of creation, thus attacking the dwelling-place of man: the earth (Rev. 8:7), the sea (8:8 f.), the rivers (8:10 f.), and the stars (8:12). These judgments are the final warning of God, His summons to repentance; they are not the last punishment. For the plagues are not yet directed against man. Nor is the whole cosmos destroyed, only a third part, so that the possibility of life still remains for man. The fifth blast (9:1) brings suffering on man himself (9:4 f.). Plagues come on him such as were never known before. The hound of the abyss comes forth (9:2) and the king of demonic powers (9:11) falls on man with his tormenting spirits. The aim of these judgments, too, is not yet definitive destruction (9:5); they are a call to conversion. But men seek death rather than God, destruction rather than forgiveness (9:6). The sixth trumpet (9:13) brings further intensification. The invading cavalry host has the direct task of slaying men. Even this, however, is not yet the last judgment, for in the first instance only a third part of the race is destroyed, 9:15, 18. That these penal judgments are at root judgments of grace is emphasised in Rev. 9:20 f. The aim of God in sending the plagues is that men should be converted from idolatry. They are meant to drive men to repentance before it is too late. But men will not be warned. The seventh trumpet is depicted very differently from the six which precede it. One would expect the third and final woe, 9:12; 11:14. But the last judgment and the punishment of the ungodly are not described. Instead the divine speaks of the fulfilment of God's counsel to save, 10:7. He tells us, not about events on earth, but about the effect of the seventh trumpet in heaven. There a song of triumph is heard because God and His Christ have now assumed unrestricted dominion over the whole earth for all times, 11:15 ff.

b. With a loud blast of the trumpet which reaches to the remotest corner of the earth the angels at the end of the age gather the elect from all quarters, Mt. 24:31 → 84, 26 ff.

c. The transforming of the living and raising of the dead (→ 84, 35 ff.) take place to the sound of the trumpet, → 84, 35 ff. The ἐσχάτη σάλπιγξ (1 C. 15:52) is not the last in a series of trumpets. It is the eschatological signal which sounds forth at the end of the age, → 84, 17 ff. Descending from heaven, Christ gives a command (→ III, 657, 37 ff.) to dead Christians which is sounded forth by the voice of the archangel (→ I, 87, 23 ff.) and the trump of God (1 Th. 4:16). Neither 1 C. 15:52 nor 1 Th. 4:16 says who blows the trumpet. [58] Whether the

---

[57] Jos. 6:4, 8, 13; Neh. 12:41; 1 Ch. 15:24; 1 QM 7:14; 3:6-11. The seven angels with trumpets are perhaps the archangels (Tob. 12:15), though cf. Apc. Mos. 38 : "All angels came, some with censers, the others with trumpets."
[58] In Descensus Mariae, 3 (ed. H. Pernot, "Descente de la Vierge aux enfers," *Revue des Études Grecques,* 13 [1900], 240), Mary says to Michael : χαῖρε, Μιχαὴλ ἀρχιστράτηγε, ὁ μέλλων σαλπίζειν καὶ ἐξυπνίζειν τοὺς ἀπ' αἰῶνος κεκοιμημένους. But this work, of course, is only 8th or 9th cent.

reference is to the μεγάλη σάλπιγξ (Mt. 24:31), the ἐσχάτη σάλπιγξ (1 C. 15:52), or the σάλπιγξ θεοῦ (1 Th. 4:16), what is meant is always the trumpet-signal at the end of the age which no human instrument can give.

5. The Trumpet as a Musical Instrument.

Only once is there a hint the trumpet might be a musical instrument. In Rev. 18:22, in connection with the judgment on Babylon which puts an end to everything, silent trumpeters are mentioned along with harpists, flautists and other musicians. The trumpet is significantly regarded as one of the instruments which may be heard at pagan feasts and ceremonies. At first it played no part in the Christian cultus, → n. 49.

Friedrich

| Σαμάρεια, Σαμαρίτης, † Σαμαρῖτις |

Contents : A. The Samaritans in the New Testament Period : 1. The Samaritan Religion ; 2. Jews and Samaritans : a. The Story of Relations up to 300 A.D.; b. The Attitude of the Jews to the Samaritans in the Days of Jesus. B. The Samaritans in the New Testament : 1. Hostility between the Jews and the Samaritans ; 2. Jesus' Attitude to the Samaritans ; 3. The Mission of the Primitive Community in Samaria.

Up to the days of Herod the Gt. the word Σαμάρεια had two meanings. It denoted the territory called Samaria and was also the name of its capital. When in 27 B.C. Herod gave the capital the name Σεβαστή (Augusta), it continued in use for the territory alone, as always in the NT. In the NT period Samaria embraced central West Palestine from Megiddo (tell el-mutesellim) in the North to Borkeos (near el-lubban) in the South, and from 6 A.D. it constituted with Judea and Idumea the Roman province of Judea. Samaria had its own senate (Jos. Ant., 18, 88) which corresponded to the Sanhedrin in Judea. The nomen gentile is Σαμαρίτης, fem. Σαμαρῖτις, Heb. שֹׁמְרֹנִי (in the OT only 2 K. 17:29 plur.), Aram. שָׁמְרָאָה; the Mishnah always has for this the contemptuous כּוּתִי, "Cuthean," cf. 2 K. 17:24, 30.

Σ α μ α ρ ί τ η ς κτλ. On A.: For comprehensive Rabb. material Str.-B., I, 538-560; J. A. Montgomery, *The Samaritans. The Earliest Jewish Sect. Their History, Theology and Literature*, Bohlen Lectures, 1906 (1907); Schürer, II, 18-23, 195-198, 522; A. E. Cowley, *The Samaritan Liturgy* I and II (1909); A. Merx, "Der Messias oder Ta'eb der Samaritaner," Beih. ZAW, 17 (1909); J. E. H. Thomson, *The Samaritans. Their Testimony to the Religion of Israel*, Alexander Robertson Lectures, 1916 (1919); M. Gaster, *The Samaritans. Their History, Doctrines and Literature*, Schweich Lectures, 1923 (1925); also *The Samaritan Oral Law and Ancient Traditions*, I : *Samaritan Eschatology* (1932) (suspiciously inclined to early dating); J. Jeremias, "Die Passahfeier d. Samaritaner u. ihre Bedeutung f. d. Verständnis d. at.lichen Passahüberlieferung," Beih. ZAW, 59 (1932); Schl. Theol. d. Judt., 75-78; D. Rettig, *Memar Marqa. Ein Samaritanischer Midrasch z. Pentateuch* (1934); J. Jeremias, *Jerusalem z. Zeit Jesu*, II B² (1958), 224-231; E. Haenchen, "Gab es eine vorchr. Gnosis ?" ZThK, 49 (1952), 316-349. B.: K. Bornhäuser, "Die Samariter d. NT," ZSTh, 9 (1932), 552-566; M. S. Enslin, "Luke and the Samaritans," HThR, 36 (1943), 277-298;

A. The Samaritans in the New Testament Period.

1. The Samaritan Religion.

In the two centuries of Persian rule over Palestine (538-332 B.C.) Jerusalem and district were gradually detached from the Persian province of Samaria.[1] The schism, however, resulted from the establishment of a Samaritan centre of worship at Gerizim rather than from the achievement of administrative autonomy by the province of Judah. Since the Pentateuch alone is the Bible of the Samaritans, the final break must have taken place after its editing was complete and prior to the canonisation of the other OT books.[2]

The two main differences between the Jewish and Samaritan religions have thus come to light already. 1. For the Samaritans even to this day Gerizim rather than Zion is the "chosen place," the Moriah of the offering up of Isaac, the place where "our fathers worshipped," Jn. 4:20. The fact that from the time of its destruction by John Hyrcanos (c. 128 B.C.) the temple at Gerizim lay in ruins (→ 90, 16 ff.) did not alter in the least the high estimation of the sacred mountain. 2. To this day the Samaritans recognise as Holy Scripture only the Pentateuch, and this in an ancient version which deviates from the Masoretic text at some 6000 points.[3] The Talmud itself admits that the Samaritans kept scrupulously the statutes of the Law of Moses.[4] In NT days the Samaritans still rejected the hope of the resurrection, which is not found in the Pentateuch.[5] Their Messianic hope, which is clearly attested for the first time in Jn. 4:25, is based solely on the Pentateuch and hence has nothing to do with the house of David. The Samaritans await as the Messiah the prophet like Moses promised in Dt. 18:15-19 (→ IV, 858, 15 ff.) and they call Him Ta'eb (→ I, 388, 22 ff.), the "restorer," because they expect Him to re-establish the cultus.[6] How much alive this hope was in the days of Jesus (→ VI, 826, 28 ff.) may be seen from the fact that in 36 A.D. "a man summoned (the people) to go with him up Mt. Gerizim ... and promised he would show those who came with him the buried sacred vessels which Moses himself had put there," Jos. Ant., 18, 85.

O. Cullmann, "La Samarie et les origines de la mission chrétienne. Qui sont les "ΑΛΛΟΙ de Jean IV, 38 ?" École Pratique des Hautes Études. Section des Sciences Religieuses, Annuaire 1953-54 (1953), 3-12; J. Jeremias, Jesu Verheissung f. d. Völker, Franz Delitzsch-Vorlesungen² (1959); J. Bowman, "Samaritan Studies," Bulletin of the John Rylands Library, 40 (1958), 298-327; J. Macdonald, The Theol. of the Samaritans (1964).

[1] A. Alt, "Die Rolle Samarias bei d. Entstehung d. Judt.," Festschr. O. Procksch (1934), 5-28; also "Zur Gesch. d. Grenze zwischen Judäa u. Samaria," PJB, 31 (1935), 94-111.

[2] Exact dating is not possible. The OT does not mention the Samaritan sanctuary. The Samaritan chronicles, which date only from the Middle Ages, put the building of the temple in the 5th cent. B.C. (ref. in Jeremias Jerusalem, 225, n. 2), the unreliable account of Jos. in 332 B.C. (Ant., 11, 324 cf. 13, 256). Some scholars put the schism in the Hasmonean period (W. F. Albright, From the Stone Age to Christianity). For a survey of the discussion cf. H. H. Rowley, "Sanballat and the Samaritan Temple," Bulletin of the John Rylands Library, 38 (1955/56), 166-198.

[3] Apart from Samaritan alterations this version lived on in Judaism too. We know the text from the Dead Sea Scrolls, cf. the Exodus MS found in Cave 4 (c. 100 B.C., 4 QExᵃ, cf. P. W. Skehan, "Exodus in the Samaritan Recension from Qumran," JBL, 74 [1955], 182-187). For an ed. of the Samaritan Pent. cf. A. v. Gall, Der hbr. Pent. d. Samaritaner (1914-18).

[4] bBer., 47b. The strictly conservative attitude of the Samaritans may be seen in the rules for the slaying of the Passover lambs, Jeremias Passahfeier, 66-106.

[5] Str.-B., I, 551 f.

[6] Cf. Merx, 28, 17 ff.

In the days of the primitive Church a *goet* called Simon (→ IV, 359, 9 ff.) from Gitta (dshett) [7] gained quite a following in Samaria, Ac. 8:9 f. Unfortunately we have little reliable information about him and his teaching, since the patristic accounts of the Gnostic system of Simon reflect a later development of the movement. [8] But the view that we know only his existence and his name [9] is too sceptical, for the statement in Ac. (→ IV, 540, 23 ff.) that his followers saw in him the incarnation of the "great power" (8:10), [10] and that they thus honoured him as a revealer, has the ring of truth. [11] Justin, who settled in Palestine and can hardly have been making it up, tells us that Simon was accompanied by a former harlot of Tyre called Helena, and that she was described by his sect as the first *ennoia* (idea) to emanate from Simon. [12] If this is true we have in this movement the beginnings of a pre-Christian Gnosticism. [13]

2. Jews and Samaritans.

a. The Story of Relations up to 300 A.D.

The very different judgments on the Samaritans in Rabb. works is due to the strong fluctuations in relations between the Jews and the Samaritans. [14] The tensions which followed the schism reached a climax when John Hyrcanos destroyed the temple on Gerizim (c. 128 B.C.), Jos. Ant., 13, 255 f. The fact that Herod married a Samaritan woman (Malthake, Jos. Ant., 17, 20; Bell., 1, 562) is perhaps an indication that he wanted to ease the situation. But when in the days of the procurator Coponius (6-9 A.D.) the Samaritans defiled the Jerusalem temple by human bones which they scattered by night (Jos. Ant., 18, 29 f.) the old hatred became more implacable than ever. Only in the 2nd cent. under the leadership of R. Aqiba (d. 135 A.D.) did a milder trend set in. But relations were embittered again before the end of the 2nd cent., and by 300 A.D. the break was complete and from now on the Samaritans were regarded as Gentiles. [15]

b. The Attitude of the Jews to the Samaritans in the Days of Jesus. [16]

The 1st century was thus a time of very strained relations between Jews and Samaritans. The old antithesis of North and South, of Israel and Judah, was revived in all its sharpness. Whereas the Samaritans laid gt. stress on their descent from the patriarchs (Jn. 4:12), the Jews called them "Cutheans" (→ 88, 25) and would not accept them

---

[7] Just. Apol., I, 26, 2. On the identifying of Gitta as dshett (18 km. S.E. of Caesarea Philippi) cf. A. Alt, "Das Institut im J. 1924," PJB, 21 (1925), 47 f.

[8] The most important sources are Just. Apol., I, 26, 1-3; Iren. Adv. Haer., I, 23; Hipp. Ref., VI, 9-20.

[9] E. de Faye, *Gnostiques et gnosticisme*[2] (1925), 429-432.

[10] οὗτός ἐστιν ἡ δύναμις τοῦ θεοῦ ἡ καλουμένη μεγάλη. The gen. τοῦ θεοῦ may be an explanatory addition, cf. Jackson-Lake, I, 4, *ad loc.*; Haenchen, 345.

[11] G. Kretschmar, "Zur religionsgesch. Einordnung d. Gnosis," *Ev. Theol.*, 13 (1953), 358.

[12] Just. Apol., I, 26, 3: Ἑλένην τινά, ... πρότερον ἐπὶ τέγους σταθεῖσαν, τὴν ὑπ' αὐτοῦ ἔννοιαν πρώτην γενομένην λέγουσι. The doubts of G. Quispel, *Gnosis als Weltreligion* (1951), 69 f. and Haenchen, 341 ("Helena does not belong to the oldest form of the teaching of Simon") are not very convincing, cf. H. Jonas, *The Gnostic Religion* (1958), 104.

[13] G. Quispel, "Simon en Helena," *Nederlands Theol. Tijdschr.*, 5 (1950/51), 345: Haenchen, 349.

[14] Jeremias Jerusalem, 224-227.

[15] Str.-B., I, 552 f.

[16] Jeremias Jerusalem, 228-231.

as blood-relations. [17] Another charge was that they worshipped the gods of the five Gentile peoples which had settled in Samaria, 2 K. 17:30 f. The legitimacy of their current worship of Yahweh was also questioned. [18] This basic judgment entailed their exclusion from the Jerusalem cultus, [19] the prohibition of *connubium* with them, [20] and the restriction of dealings by many detailed regulations. [21] For "they have no law, not even the remnants of a commandment, and are thus suspect and degenerate." [22] This means that in practice the Samaritans were put on a level with the Gentiles in the 1st cent. [23]

B. The Samaritans in the New Testament.

Though they are not mentioned in Mk. and only once negatively in Mt. at 10:5, Lk. shows gt. interest in them (Lk. 9:51-56; 10:30-37; 17:11-19; Ac. 1:8; 8:1-25; 9:31; 15:3 and so, too, does Jn. (4:4-42). It is no accident that all the three Samaritan stories in Lk. are peculiar to this Gospel, which is generally concerned to depict Jesus as turning to the despised and lowly.

1. Hostility between Jews and Samaritans.

More than once the Gospels reflect the fierce hatred between the two peoples, → 90, 20 ff. On the part of the Jews Σαμαρίτης is used as a term of bitter contempt, Jn. 8:48. [24] The Jewish scribe avoids the word, preferring a circumlocution, Lk. 10:37. National animosity is also evident in the just indignation of the sons of Zebedee at the inhospitable Samaritan village upon which they would call down eschatological fire, Lk. 9:54. The astonishment of the Samaritan woman at Jesus' request for a drink from her vessel (Jn. 4:9) confirms the fact that in NT times the Jews in practice put the Samaritans on the same level as the Gentiles, for the materially pertinent observation of the Evangelist on the woman's astonishment : οὐ γὰρ συγχρῶνται 'Ιουδαῖοι Σαμαρίταις, "for the Jews do not use (vessels) in common with the Samaritans" (4:9b), [25] presupposes that Samari-

---

[17] Jos. Ant., 11, 341; 12, 257; cf. Lk. 17:18 : ἀλλογενής.

[18] For the Rabb. charge that the Samaritans practised idolatry cf. Str.-B., I, 538, 549, 553. Whether Jn. 4:18 may be cited in this connection is very doubtful in view of v. 19; for the allegorical significance of the 5 husbands cf. Cullmann, 6 f. (bibl.).

[19] Pledges and gifts alone were taken from them, as from the Gentiles, Sheq., 1, 5. Some offerings were included, but not obligatory ones, cf. Str.-B., II, 549-551; Schürer, II, 357-363.

[20] The prohibition is found in many places, Qid., 4, 3; TQid., 5, 1 f.; bQid., 74b-76b; Tractate Kuthim, 1, 6; 2, 9 etc.; cf. Jeremias Jerusalem, 230.

[21] Jews were not to eat what was slaughtered for a Samaritan, Chul., 2, 7 (Str.-B., I, 538), nor their Passover Maҫҫoth, bQid., 76a Bar.; bChul., 4a, Bar.; TPes., 1, 15 (cf. Str.-B., I, 543); their drinking vessels were not to be used, Jn. 4:9 (→ lines 21 ff.) etc.

[22] jPes., 1 (27b, 51) (R. Shim'on bJochai [c. 150], who represents an older tradition in relation to the Samaritans).

[23] The many milder rules in the Mishnah may not be adduced in depiction of 1st cent. relations.

[24] Rather strangely there are no Talmudic instances up to bSota, 22a (Str.-B., II, 524 f.), where *kuthi = bur* ("boor"). But cf. Sir. 50:26; Test. L. 7:2. The context of Jn. 8:48 equates Samaritan and demon-possessed : Σαμαρίτης εἶ σὺ καὶ δαιμόνιον ἔχεις, though cf. Bowman, 308, n. 1: "Thou speakest as though thou wert a Samaritan."

[25] That συγχρᾶσθαι in Jn. 4:9b means "to use the same vessel" is noted by D. Daube, *The NT and Rabbinic Judaism,* Jordan Lectures, 1952 (1956), 373-382. The absence of 4:9b from ℵ* D it hardly justifies our assuming that it is a later gloss but might be simply due to a slip in copying.

tan vessels were regarded as unclean by the Jews.[26] That the Samaritans repaid the Jews in the same coin may be seen in Lk. 9:53, where Jesus is refused lodging because He is on the way to the hated temple at Jerusalem.

Only against the background of this reciprocal implacable hatred can one understand the NT account of the attitude of Jesus and the primitive community to the Gentiles.

2. Jesus' Attitude to the Samaritans.

a. For Jesus, too, the mixed population of Samaria is not part of the community of Israel, but confronts Israel in company with the Gentiles. The Samaritan leper is an ἀλλογενής (Lk. 17:18) and an ancient tristich based on the Aramaic tradition[27] forbids the disciples to work among either Samaritans or Gentiles : "Go not to[28] the Gentiles / and enter not into the land[29] of Samaria / but go (only)[30] to the lost sheep of the house of Israel," Mt. 10:5 f.

b. Yet even though Jesus basically shares the judgment of His time on the Samaritans, His attitude to them is quite different from that of His contemporaries. To be sure, it is not very important that he takes the road through Samaria when on pilgrimage to Jerusalem,[31] for this direct route was the usual one.[32] More important is the fact that Jesus rebukes His disciples for their hatred (Lk. 9:55), that in spite of the danger of defilement He asks the Samaritan woman for a drink from her vessel (Jn. 4:7), that He extends help to a Samaritan leper (Lk. 17:16), that He holds up a Samaritan before the eyes of the members of God's people as a humbling example of the unselfish love of neighbour which overcomes hatred (10:30-37) and of the gratitude which honours God (17:11-19), and that

---

[26] The basic rule was probably that from the cradle on (continually) Samaritan women were regarded as menstruous women and their husbands as men defiled by menstruous women (cf. Lk. 15:24), Nidda, 4, 1; TNidda, 5, 1, cf. Str.-B., I, 540. But this rule, acc. to bShab., 16b, 17a, came into force only through the so-called "loft" resolutions composed in the loft of Chananiah bChizqiyya bGaron 65/66 A.D. (perhaps prior to 48 A.D., Jeremias Jerusalem, 230, n. 44; P. Billerbeck by word of mouth), though they could have been practised earlier, cf. Daube, op. cit., 373 f. Yet there might be a ref. to the rule that the Samaritans were guilty of defilement by dead bodies because they were supposed to dispose of miscarriages in the "unclean rooms" (toilets), Nidda, 7, 4 (cf. Str.-B., I, 541; Jeremias Jerusalem, 230, n. 45).

[27] For details cf. Jeremias Verheissung, 16 f., with a discussion of authenticity.

[28] εἰς ὁδόν does not mean "on a way" but == Aram. לְאוֹרַח == "to."

[29] εἰς πόλιν Σαμαριτῶν. The lit. "into a city of the Samaritans" makes no sense. Absence of the art. before πόλιν hints at an underlying st. c. Transl. back into Aram. yields לִמְדִינַת שֻׁמְרָיִין. This st. c. had two senses : in Palest. Aram. מְדִינָא (indefinite) "province," מְדִינְתָּא (definite) "city." The original meaning of εἰς πόλιν Σαμαριτῶν "into the province of Samaria." For the mistransl. as "city" cf. also Lk. 1:39 (cf. Ac. 8:5). Jeremias Verheissung, 17, n. 66 (bibl.).

[30] The Semitic omits "only" even where indispensable in other tongues, cf. Jeremias Gl., 29, n. 1.

[31] This fact is confirmed by Lk. 9:51-56 (cf. Jn. 4:4 : ἔδει). W. Gasse, "Zum Reisebericht d. Lk.," ZNW, 34 (1935), 293-299 does not think Lk. 9:51 ff. presupposes a journey through Samaria, since εἰς ἑτέραν κώμην might be used for a non-Samaritan village. He misses the pt., however, that then, as now, there were in Palestine districts friendly to strangers as well as those notoriously fanatical.

[32] Jos. Ant., 20, 118 : ἔθος ἦν τοῖς Γαλιλαίοις ἐν ταῖς ἑορταῖς εἰς τὴν ἱερὰν πόλιν παραγινομένοις ὁδεύειν διὰ τῆς Σαμαρέων χώρας, cf. Bell., 2, 232.

at least on a two-day journey (Jn. 4:40, 43) He offers the Gospel to the Samaritans too (4:4-42). If one may ask whether all the details are historical, e.g., in Jn. 4:4-42, taken together they present a uniform picture. This is wrongly interpreted if one regards the attitude of Jesus as that of a great-hearted man who had broken free from the prejudices of His fanatical countrymen and was far in advance of His times, for on this view the forbidding of a mission to the Samaritans in Mt. 10:5 f. is quite unintelligible. Rather the attitude of Jesus to the Samaritans in its apparent contradictoriness may be understood only in the light of His sense of majesty and His proclamation of the eschatological turning-point. The prohibition of a Samaritan mission on the part of the disciples is to be seen in relation to His attitude to non-Jews. Jesus fundamentally restricts the work of His disciples to Israel because the promise to the fathers that salvation will be offered to Israel must first be fulfilled before there can be the eschatological incorporation of the Gentiles, including the Samaritans, into the people of God. [33] But Jesus was also certain that with His sending the time of salvation had already come. Already there breaks into the present world the royal dominion of God in which the uncleanness of the Gentiles is taken away and they are granted a share in the salvation of God. This hour of fulfilment is proleptically and symbolically manifested in the attitude of Jesus to the members of this despised and hated mongrel people which is equated with the Gentiles.

3. The Mission of the Primitive Community in Samaria.

a. Acts opens with the promise of the Risen Lord that the disciples are to be His witnesses in Jerusalem, Judea, Samaria and to the ends of the earth, 1:8. Acc. to 8:4-25 Philip, a leader of the Hellenists driven out of Jerusalem by the Stephen persecution, is the first to do missionary work in Samaria. [34] His preaching reached several Samaritan villages (8:25) and even Simon was baptised (8:13) → 90, 1 ff. Justin, however, says that around the middle of the 2nd century almost all the Samaritans worshipped Simon as the supreme God, [35] so that one is well advised not to overestimate the results of the Christian mission, [36] especially as the contacts of Simon with the missionaries were only fleeting. [37] The significance of the preaching of the Gospel in Samaria does not lie in its numerical success but in the fact that this first crossing of the frontiers of Israel was the transition to the Gentile mission. The taking of this step can be understood only in the light of the fact that the eschatological turning-point came with Easter, for the preaching of the good news to the nations is a sign of the eschatological hour. [38]

b. John's Gospel (4:4-42) uses a single incident from the ministry of Jesus, His conversation with a Samaritan woman at Jacob's well, [39] to show that the

---

[33] Jeremias Verheissung, 61 f.
[34] On κατελθὼν εἰς τὴν πόλιν τῆς Σαμαρείας (8:5) → n. 29.
[35] Just. Apol., I, 26, 3; Dial., 120, 6.
[36] Acc. to primitive Chr. usage in R. 15:26; 2 C. 9:2 the saying "Samaria had received the word of God" (8:14) means no more than that Chr. congregations had arisen there, Haench. Ag., ad loc.
[37] This is shown by Ac. itself, 8:18-24.
[38] Jeremias Verheissung, 63.
[39] The story rests on sound tradition, for it shows good knowledge both of the geographical data (cf. on Jacob's well and Joseph's tomb J. Jeremias, *Heiligengräber in Jesu Um-*

Samaritan mission goes back to Jesus Himself [40] and to bring out its significance for the Church. This consists in the fact that the introduction of half-castes into the saved community is an anticipation (v. 23 : νῦν; v. 35 : ἤδη) of the time when the strife about temples ends, and the religious separation of the peoples is set aside, because "the true worshippers worship the Father in spirit and in truth," v. 23.

J. Jeremias

σανδάλιον → V, 310, 33 ff.

---

† σαπρός, † σήπω

1. In basic meaning both words relate to the process of "decay." [1]

a. σήπω act. "to cause to decay" (from Aesch.), more commonly pass. "to decay," "to rot" (from Hom. → n. 2), usually lit. [2] It is to be noted that with the exception of fire there is no material of which it may not be said that it is exposed to σήπεσθαι. [3] In view of this breadth of range of the lit. use it is natural that complete destruction should not always be meant. The word may even be used for material changes which are necessary to life, [4] e.g., the rising of sap in the vine, [5] though this sense is rare. In transf. use the word always means "to rot away," "to perish." [6]

b. σαπρός "rotting" (from Hipponax. Fr., 32a [Diehl³, III, 90]) corresponds in its lit. use [7] to the verb σήπω from which it derives (→ n. 1); but the transf. sense is more common and varied. Both the offensiveness of the process of decay (→ n. 2) and the

---

welt [1958], 31-36) and also of the Samaritans (cf. the aor. προσεκύνησαν in v. 20; there was no cult on Gerizim at the time of Jesus, Jeremias Passahfeier, 58 and → 90, 16 ff.).
[40] Cullmann, 5 f., 12.
σ α π ρ ό ς, σ ή π ω. C. Lindhagen, "Die Wurzel ΣΑΠ im NT u. AT," *Uppsala Univ. Årsskrift,* 1950, 5 (1950), 27-69.
[1] Root *ksap* "rotten," cf. Walde-Pok., I, 500; Boisacq⁴, 857 f.; E. Zupitza, "Etymologien," *Beiträge z. Kunde d. idg. Sprachen,* 25 (1899), 92-95. On nominal suffixes in -ρο (σαπρός -σήπω like ἁβρός -ἥβη) cf. Schwyzer, I, 481b, 2.
[2] In living bodies, Hom. Il., 24, 414; Aesch. Choeph., 995; in corpses Hes. Scutum Herculis, 152; of wood, Aristoph. Eq., 1308, rain-water, Hippocr. De aere aquis locis, 8 (CMG, I, 1, p. 62, 25 f.). The stench of decay is ref. to in Theophr. Fr., 4, 2 : ἅπαν γὰρ τὸ σηπόμενον κακῶδες but → n. 13.
[3] Aristot. Meteor., IV, 1 esp. p. 379a, 14 : διὸ σήπεται πάντα τἄλλα πλὴν πυρός.
[4] Hippocr. Morb., I, 6, 28 (Littré, VI, 152 and 196); Aristot. Meteor., IV, 1, p. 379b, 6 f.: καὶ ζῷα ἐγγίνεται τοῖς σηπομένοις, "living creatures arise in rotting materials," cf. IV, 3, p. 381b, 9-11.
[5] Emped. Fr., 81 (Diels, I⁸, 340, 32): οἶνος ... σαπὲν ἐν ξύλῳ ὕδωρ (challenged by Aristot. Topica, IV, 5, p. 127a, 17-19).
[6] Plat. Theaet., 153c : αἱ μὲν ἡσυχίαι σήπουσι καὶ ἀπολλύασι, "peace brings decay and destruction," cf. Dion. Hal. Ant. Rom., 11, 37; Menand. Fr., 23, 6 (Koerte, 22): σήπεσθαι ὑπὸ τῆς ἡδονῆς; Ps.-Luc. Philopatris, 20 : σηπόμενον γερόντιον.
[7] Fish : Alexides-Fr., 125, 8 (CAF, II, 342); fruit : Theophr. Hist. Plant., IV, 14, 10-18;

fact imply that rotting objects are old and usually, though not always, of little worth or even quite unserviceable. Sometimes the domination of one of these elements is so strong that the possibilities of use deviate considerably from the basic sense and from one another. [8]

Though what is lit. σαπρόν offends only sight or smell (→ n. 2) the word can be used less strictly even when, e.g., it is hearing which is affected, Theopompus Comicus Fr., 50 (CAF, I, 746): αὐλεῖ γὰρ σαπρὰ αὕτη γε κρούματ᾽ ("unpleasant sounds of flutes"); M. Ant., 11, 15 : ὡς σαπρὸς καὶ κίβδηλος ὁ λέγων, "how contrary and wrong is one who says ..." Similarly, as a par. to the use of σαπρός to denote the offensive and menacing character of the ravages of disease in the human body (Hippocr. Morb., I, 13 [Littré, VI, 160]) the word can be used fig. for an unfavourable horoscope (Vett. Val., I, 21 [Kroll, 36, 30 ff.]) or adverse fate (Preis. Zaub., II, 13, 636 : ἀναλυσόν μου τὴν σαπρὰν εἱμαρμένην).

A man is called σαπρός when he can also be called old. If γέρων is added (Aristoph. Pax, 698), σαπρός denotes the wasting of strength and beauty associated with old age. [9] If σαπρός stands alone, the idea of "old" is comprised within it, Aristoph. Eccl., 884 : σαπρά, old woman, slut, cf. Vesp., 1380. In relation to food and drink, too, σαπρός denotes old commodities, though these do not have to be unpalatable. The pious σαπροπωμάριος in Inscr. No. 760 from Korykos [10] did not buy spoiled but preserved apples or cider. The θρῖον ταρίχους σαπροῦ ("cabbage leaf with pickled meat") of Aristoph. Ach., 1101 is to be eaten, not thrown away. In Lat. saprus came to be used for a kind of cheese which Pliny in Hist. Nat., 28, 132, though he does not mention the taste, [11] describes as a remedy. [12] If some decay (→ n. 4, 5) is desirable in certain foods, σαπρός can take on a positive sense as in the case of "ripe" cheese and esp. wine, → 94, 15 f. → n. 5. If σαπρός is usually the opp. of γλυκύς, Antiph. Fr., 125, 3 and 6 (CAF, II, 61), in the judgment of wine it is often found with an approving γέρων, Alexis Fr., 167, 3 f. (CAF, II, 358): ἔσται καὶ μάλα ἡδύς γ᾽, ὀδόντας οὐκ ἔχων ἤδη σαπρὸς λέγων (?), γέρων γε δαιμονίως. [13] Already quite early σαπρός could lose its sinister ring and become almost synon. with ἡδύς. [14] Eupolis Fr., 442 (CAF, I, 367) offers the following explanation of σαπρός : οὐ τὸ μοχθηρὸν καὶ φαῦλον, ἀλλὰ τὸ παλαιόν. [15]

---

corpse : Dio Chrys., 5, 27; clothes : BGU, III, 846, 9; decaying stone : Ditt. Syll.², II, 587, 24. Cf. esp. H. Jacobi, Comicae dictionis Index, s.v., Fr. Comicorum Graecorum (ed. A. Meineke, V, 2 [1857], 931).

[8] The deviation is sometimes so gt. that inaccurate transmission of the text has been suspected : F. H. Bothe, Aristophanis comoediae, 1 (1828), 340 on Aristoph. Pax, 554 → n. 15; A. Dieterich, Abraxas (1891), 178 on Preis. Zaub., II, 13, 636 → line 12 f.; Liddell-Scott, s.v. III on Theopompus Comicus Fr., 50 (CAF, I, 746) → line 6 f. But σαπρός can hardly have been so attractive a word that copyists substituted it for more suitable terms in very different contexts. Each of the conjectures is helpful in itself, but together they simply show that the term has a breadth of use which takes even the expert by surprise.

[9] Cf. the judgment on the dated greeting by a mere χαίρειν in Aristoph. Plut., 323 : ἀρχαῖον καὶ σαπρόν. On the enigmatic verdict of Stratonicus on the actor Simycas (μέγας οὐδεὶς σαπρὸς ἰχθύς) in Athen., 7, 40 (348a) cf. Lindhagen, 29, n. 2.

[10] Ed. J. Keil-A. Wilhelm, Monumenta Asiae Minoris Antiqua, III (1931), 207, 210.

[11] Cf. Mart., 3, 77, 10 saprophagere for too plentiful fare.

[12] Diosc. Mat. Med., I, 84, 2 : σαπρία (→ n. 23) as a remedy.

[13] On σαπρίας in Hermippus Fr., 82, 6 (CAF, I, 249) cf. aging wine. Cf. also Schol. on Aristoph. Pax (ed. F. Dübner [1842] 554): σαπρὸν οἱ παλαιοὶ ἔλεγον τὸ σεσηπὸς διὰ τὸν χρόνον, χρῶνται δ᾽ αὐτῷ καὶ ἀντὶ τοῦ ἀρχαίου καὶ παλαιοῦ. That a usage in which the noun σαπρότης does not refer to a bad odour is possible, though rare, may be seen from the continuation of Theophr. Fr., 4, 2 (→ n. 2): ... εἰ μή τις τὴν ὀξύτητα λέγει τοῦ οἴνου σαπρότητα.

[14] Later σαπρός and καλός were only opposites even in the case of wine, cf. P. Greci e Latini, 6, 718, 12 : σαπρὸν οἶνον ποιῆσαι καλόν.

[15] Relevant here is the singular verse ὡς ἅπαντ᾽ ἤδη 'στὶ μεστὰ τἀνθάδ᾽ εἰρήνης

Acc. to the general rule elsewhere σαπρός thus contains a critical and adverse but not very precise judgment with a sinister overtone : "unserviceable," "of little worth." [16] Sometimes the context pts. to a special sense. Thus a σαπρὸν ὄνομα (Preisigke Sammelbuch, III, 5761, 23) is not just of little worth but "notorious," and σαπρὰ δόγματα (Epict. Diss., III, 22, 16 cf. 16, 7) are "harmful," "dangerous." [17] On the other hand the φάρμακα called σαπρά in P. Lond., II, 252 are thus described because they are no good for selling in a city like Alexandria, i.e., they are not valuable enough. The word does not mean that they are old or offensive or rotten.

2. In the LXX we find

a. the act. σήπω once fig. "to destroy" at Job 40:12 : σῆψον δὲ ἀσεβεῖς παραχρῆμα (Heb. הדך). [18] In the lit. sense the pass. refers to the rotting flesh in the living body of Job (αἱ σάρκες), 19:20 (Heb. דבק [רקב?]); 33:21 (Heb. כלה), cf. ψ 37:6 : ἐσάπησαν οἱ μώλωπές μου (Heb. מקק). The process of physical dissolution is also at issue in Job 16:7: κατάκοπόν με πεποίηκεν, μωρόν, σεσηπότα → IV, 836, 5 ff. Ez. 17:9 speaks fig. of a decaying root and fruit (Heb. יקם), Ep. Jer. 71 of purple clothing which rots. [19] Fig. πᾶν ἔργον σηπόμενον in Sir. 14:19 means every "perishable" work. [20] Prv. 10:7 'ΑΣ also says fig. that the name of the ungodly shall perish (Heb. רקב, LXX σβέννυται). Lit. Σ also has the act. at Qoh. 10:1: "to make sweet-smelling oil stink," LXX : σαπρίζω or σαπριόω, Heb. באש hi. [21]

b. The Gk. transl. of the Samaritan Tg. Lv. 27:14 has σαπρός for רע (opp. טוב), also an "Αλλος [22] (Field, 218) in the similarly constructed v. 33 of the same c., both in the sense "of poor quality" (LXX : πονηρός ~ καλός). In the other transl. in-

---

σαπρᾶς in Aristoph. Pax, 554. εἰρήνης σαπρᾶς is meant to raise a laugh, perhaps by association with the vocabulary of wine, and also as an exaggeration (in the context the state of peace has only just arrived). But Aristoph. was obviously not thinking of a decayed peace. Here too, then, σαπρός is close to παλαιός in a good sense, and remote from μοχθηρόν καὶ φαῦλον → 95, 29 f. This exception, which is related to that mentioned → 94, 16, but not derived solely from this, is restricted both materially (→ 95, 22 f.) and chronologically (→ n. 14).

[16] Cf. Chrys. Hom. in 1 Tm. 4 (MPG, 62 [1862], 525): πᾶν γὰρ ὃ μὴ τὴν ἰδίαν χρείαν πληροῖ σαπρὸν λέγομεν. The adv. σαπρῶς in Epict. Diss., II, 21, 14 refers to useless baths.

[17] Also an official statement against someone, P. Greci e Latini, 6, 717, 4 : [ἐὰν] κατ' ἐμοῦ καταψηφίσηταί τι σαπρόν.

[18] Where the Heb. original is not given, it is uncertain.

[19] Cf. ἄσηπτον (ξύλον) for לֹא יִרְקָב Is. 40:20 : The maker of idols needs wood that will not decay. Ἄσηπτος is common in Ex. 25-37 with ref. to the materials in making the tabernacle, esp. wood in its erection, and cf. also the ark in Dt. 10:3. Everything is to be made of ξύλα ἄσηπτα. There are additional examples here in Θ. An anon. transl. at Gn. 6:14, with ref. to Noah's ark, has ἐκ ξύλων ἀσήπτων for עֲצֵי־גֹפֶר (conifer wood), cf. also Lindhagen, 39, n. 1 [Bertram].

[20] Here רקב is rendered by ἐκλείπειν as well as σήπεσθαι, cf. Lindhagen, 38.

[21] Of derivates of σήπω, σήπη and σῆψις are used only once each in the LXX at Sir. 19:3 and Is. 14:11, both times in the sense "mould" (Is. 14:11 Heb. רִמָּה). In 'Α σήπη is used for רִמָּה at Job 17:14; 21:26 "worms in rotting matter" (LXX σαπρία → n. 23). 'ΑΣ have σῆψις at Hos. 5:12 for "decay" (LXX κέντρον Heb. רקב). Finally σηπεδών is used for רקב at Σ Job 13:28 "rot" (LXX ἀσκός for רקב?).

[22] σαπρός in the marginal reading of LXX Cod M may go back to this, A. Rahlfs, "Verzeichnis d. gr. Hdschr. d. AT," Mitteilungen d. Septuagintaunternehmens, 2 (1914), 183, cf. also Lindhagen, 40 f.

cluding the LXX, and also in Philo and Jos., σαπρός does not occur. Since the word combines bluntness with a certain imprecision, this can hardly be an accident. [23]

3. In Jm. 5:2 (→ III, 335, 24 ff.) we find the extended basic sense of σήπω (→ 94, 14 f.): ὁ πλοῦτος ὑμῶν σέσηπεν, "your riches go the way of everything earthly, they decay," but with no reflection on the quality of the riches in question. [24] The meaning of σαπρός in Eph. 4:29a may be seen from 4:29b : ἀλλὰ εἴ τις ἀγαθὸς πρὸς οἰκοδομὴν τῆς χρείας, "but that which is good for edifying where needed." A λόγος σαπρός does not serve the needs of the community. Hence it is not to be regarded as an adiaphoron ; it is unprofitable ("idle gossip"). We are led to the same conclusion by comparison with v. 28, which is similarly constructed : The λόγος σαπρός is related to the λόγος ἀγαθός as stealing is to helping Christians in need. [25]

In the parable of the drag-net in Mt. 13:47-50 it is palpable that the defect which causes one part of the netted fish to be called τὰ ... σαπρά is that they are no good as food. Biologically they may be quite normal. The same applies in the parabolic sayings in Mt. 7:17-19; 12:33; Lk. 6:43. The bad fruits and trees are "useless," "of no value," irrespective of their biological condition. [26] No application is made, but the reader is led himself to transfer the blunt word from the image to the christocentric or theocentric application. Should not a judgment nourished by faith in Jesus be able to see through a false prophet, no matter how impressive, with the same certainty as valueless fruit is recognised and the tree estimated accordingly (Mt. 7:15, 20)? Can man avoid perceiving that he himself for all his supposed advantages is seen by the eye of God, and might be σαπρός ? Thus the NT uses σαπρός only in a very general transferred sense (→ n. 16), but the context makes it very concrete.

4. In Herm. s., 2, 3 f. the verb and adj. are used lit. of the "decaying" fruit of the vine (→ n. 2, 7) which has no support (from the elm); here again (→ 97, 17 f.) there is no specific application of either word. Again lit. 1 Cl., 25, 3 speaks of the "rotting" flesh of the phoenix from which — a μεγαλεῖον τῆς ἐπαγγελίας, 26, 1 — new life arises. Dg., 2, 2 refers to decaying idols which are not immune to common (→ 94, 14 f.) σήπεσθαι, 2, 4 → n. 19. When Herm. s., 9, 6, 4 describes the ποικιλίαι τῶν λίθων τῶν σαπρῶν, it is apparent that in spite of s., 9, 5, 2 the sense is the general one of "useless" rather than the strict one of "decayed." But the continuation in s., 9, 8 shows that there is hope for some of the useless stones, even though the word is not used again.

Bauernfeind

---

[23] It is also no accident that often when the adj. σαπρός might be used we find the noun σαπρία, which is not attested before the LXX and only rarely later. In a sense close to the original, LXX uses this noun at Jl. 2:20 for בְּאֹשׁ "musty smell" (cf. 2 Macc. 9:9), and 4 times in Job for רִמָּה "worms in decaying or decayed matter," 7:5; 17:14; 21:16; 25:6; cf. 2:9c. At Job 8:16 πρασιᾶς "(through) his garden" would make sense as a transl. of גַּנָּתוֹ, H. M. Orlinsky, "Some Corruptions in the Gk. Text of Job," JQR, NS, 23 (1935/36), 134 f.; the idea behind σαπρίας in the text is probably "decaying stone" → n. 3; Lindhagen, 43. B has σαπρία for πικρία (Heb. נְכֵרִיָה) at Is. 28:21; Lindhagen, 47-53 suggests an *alienum opus* and recalls Preis. Zaub., II, 13, 636 (→ 95, 12 f., → n. 8). 'A has σαπρία at Am. 4:10 "stink" and at Is. 5:2 "wild grapes."

[24] Cf. Dib. and Hck. Jk., *ad loc.*

[25] In view of the fact noted → 97, 1 ff. it is unlikely that an OT or Rabb. expression lies behind this (as against Str.-B., III, 640 f.) or that σαπρός is to be transl. "infamous." Eph. 5:3 (μηδὲ ὀνομαζέσθω) is hardly to be presupposed.

[26] Cf. the φάρμακα of → 96, 5 f. On the origin of the metaphor cf. M. Black, *An Aramaic Approach to the Gospels and Acts*[2] (1954), 148 f.

σάρξ, σαρκικός, † σάρκινος

Contents : A. σάρξ in the Greek World : 1. σάρξ as the Muscular Part of the Human or Animal Body ; 2. The Origin of Flesh ; 3. σάρξ as Body ; 4. Special Meanings ; 5. σάρκινος ; 6. The Corruptible σάρξ in Distinction from the Incorruptible Part of Man ; 7. σάρξ as the Seat of Emotions in Epicurus ; 8. The Influence of Epicurus. B. Flesh in the Old Testament: 1. בָּשָׂר : a. Flesh in the Strict Sense; b. In an Extended Sense; c. כָּל־בָּשָׂר ; d. As a Term for Blood-Relationship ; e. Euphemistically ; f. In a Transferred Sense ; g. Metaphorically; 2. שְׁאֵר : a. Flesh in the True Sense; b. As a Term for Blood-Relationship; c. In a Transferred Sense ; 3. Translation of the Hebrew Terms in the Septuagint ; 4. Texts not in the Hebrew Canon. C. Flesh in Judaism : I. The Concept in the Dead Sea Scrolls : 1. The General Concept ; 2. A Term for the Person ; 3. The Collective Use ; 4. Man's Corruptibility; 5. The Relation to Sin ; 6. Flesh and Spirit ; II. The Usage in the Targums ; III. Flesh and Body in the Talmud and Midrash ; IV. The Apocrypha and Pseudepigrapha ; V. Philo and Josephus. D. Historical Summary. E. The New Testament : I. The Synoptic Gospels and Acts : 1. The Synoptics ; 2. Acts ; II. Paul : 1. σάρξ = Body; 2. σάρξ as the Earthly Sphere ; 3. σάρξ καὶ αἷμα, πᾶσα σάρξ ; 4. σάρξ as an Object of Trust ; 5. κατὰ σάρκα with Verb ; 6. σάρξ as the Subject of Sin ; 7. The Vanquished σάρξ ; 8. Summary; III. Colossians, Ephesians, Pastorals : 1. Colossians ; 2. Ephesians ; 3. Pastorals ; IV. John : 1. The Gospel ; 2. The Epistles ; V. Hebrews ; VI. The Catholic Epistles ; VII. σάρκινος, σαρκικός. F. The Post-New Testament Period : 1. The Post-Apostolic Fathers ; 2. Apocryphal Acts ; 3. The Apologists ; 4. Gnosticism.

σ ά ρ ξ. E. de W. Burton, *Spirit, Soul and Flesh ... in Greek Writings and Translated Works from the Earliest Period to 180 A.D. ... and in Hebrew Old Testament* (1918); P. Daubercies, *La condition charnelle* (1959); W. D. Davies, "Paul and the Dead Sea Scrolls : Flesh and Spirit" in K. Stendahl, *The Scrolls and the NT* (1957), 157-182; O. Kuss, *Der Römerbrief* (1959), 506-540; Pr.-Bauer[5], *s.v.*; J. A. T. Robinson, *The Body* (1952), 17-26; W. Schauf, *Sarx* (1924); E. Schweizer, "Die hell. Komponente im nt.lichen σάρξ-Begriff," ZNW, 48 (1957), 237-253; H. H. Wendt, *Die Begriffe Fleisch u. Geist im bibl. Sprachgebrauch* (1878). On A.: D. Dimitrakos, *Lex. Hellenikes Glosses*, VIII (1950), *s.v.*; Liddell-Scott, *s.v.*; R. B. Onians, *The Origins of European Thought about the Body, the Mind, the Soul, the World, Time and Fate* (1954); Pass., *s.v.*; Thes. Steph. *s.v.* On C.: Bousset-Gressm., 399-409; D. Flusser, *The Dead Sea Scrolls and Pre-Pauline Christianity,* 9. *Flesh and Spirit* (Scripta Hierosolymitana, IV [1958], 252-263); H. Huppenbauer, "Basar 'Fleisch' in d. Texten v. Qumran," ThZ, 13 (1957), 298-300; J. P. Hyatt, "The View of Man in the Qumran 'Hodayot,' " NTSt, 2 (1955/56), 276-284; R. Meyer, "Hellenistisches in d. rabb. Anthropologie," BWANT, IV, 22 (1937); Moore, 445-496; S. Schulz, "Zur Rechtfertigung aus Gnaden in Qumran u. bei Pls.," ZThK, 56 (1959), 160-163; W. D. Stacey, *The Pauline View of Man in Relation to its Judaic and Hellenistic Background* (1956), 85-117, 154-180; Str.-B., I, 730 f.; III, 330-332, 400; IV, 466-483. On E.: Bultmann Theol., 228-241 (§ 22 f.); Cr.-Kö., *s.v.*; W. P. Dickson, *St. Paul's Use of the Terms Flesh and Spirit* (1883); E. Käsemann, *Leib u. Leib Christi* (1933), 100-118; C. H. Lindijer, *Het begrip Sarx bij Paulus,* Diss. Amsterdam (1952); E. Lohmeyer, "Probleme paul. Theol., III : Sünde, Fleisch u. Tod," ZNW, 29 (1930), 1-59; E. Schweizer, "R. 1:3 f. u. d. Gegensatz v. Fleisch u. Geist vor u. bei Pls.," *Ev. Theol.*, 15 (1955), 563-571.

A. σάρξ in the Greek World.

1. σάρξ as the Muscular Part of the Human or Animal Body.

In older speech [1] the plur. σάρκες is mostly used, and exclusively for the flesh of the human body in Hom. It is first used in Hes. Theog., 538 for animal flesh in connection with sacrifice, apparently on the basis of Hom. Od., 9, 293. Then it is used for the flesh of fish and small animals, Diosc. Mat. Med., II, 4; Poll. Onom., V, 51. Flesh and bones are mentioned together in Hippon. A, 13 (Diels, I, 386, 41); an anon. Pythagorean Fr., 25 (I, 457, 10); Anaxag. A, 45 (II, 18, 22); Pind. Fr., 168 [2]; Eur. Hec., 1072; Plat. Phaed., 96d; Aristot. Hist. An., III, 2, p. 511b, 5 ff.; Part. An., II, 9, p. 655b, 23; Alex. Aphr. An., 98, 10. [3] The sinews νεῦρα, ἶνες, φλέβες often occur too, Hom. Od., 11, 219; Anaxag. A, 45 (Diels, II, 18, 15); Democr. A, 141 (II, 123, 32); Plat. Tim., 74b, 82c, 84a; Aristot. Part. An., I, 5, p. 645a, 29; II, 1, p. 646b, 25, and other parts may be mentioned too; Epict. Diss., IV, 7, 32 cf. II, 9, 18; Alex. Aphr. De Mixtione, 15 (p. 235, 4 f.), the blood being mentioned too. Sometimes we have a ref. to the entrails, Hom. Od., 9, 293; Hes. Theog., 538. There is a whole list of other parts in Poll. Onom., II, 232 f. Flesh (σάρκες) and blood as the perishable part of man occur as par. in Eur. Fr., 687, 1 f. (TGF, 575). In Polyaen. Strat., III, 11, 1 men having αἷμα καὶ σάρκας are contrasted with the gods. [4] As muscle flesh protects the limbs or bones against cold and heat, Plat. Tim., 74b; Aristot. Probl., 27, 4, p. 966a, 37; Part. An., II, 9, p. 654b, 27 and p. 655a, 30; cf. already Hom. Od., 18, 77. It may be separated from them, Eur. Med., 1200, 1217; Nicand. Theriaca, 404. It is the layer between the skin and the bones, Aristot. Hist. An., III, 16, p. 519b, 26. As a tt. in medicine the word means "muscle" in Hippocr. De Arte, 10 (CMG, I, 1, p. 15, 21); De Carnibus, 1 (Littré, VIII, 584). [5] But the eroticist Charito De Chaerea et Callirrhoe, II, 2, 2 [6] can also rave about the τρυφερὰ σάρξ of a woman. Thus the σῶμα consists of bones and sinews, flesh and skin, Plat. Phaed., 98c d, of hair, flesh, bones and blood, Plat. Symp., 207d, of αἷμα καὶ πνεῦμα as also of flesh, bones and sinews, Dio Chrys., 30, 15. In this sense σάρξ as matter is distinguished from the fashioned σῶμα, Eur. Ba., 1130, 1136 f. (the flesh is torn from the body, cf. 607); Aristot. Gen. Corr., I, 5, p. 321b, 19; [7] Dio Chrys., 39, 5; Poll. Onom., V, 80. This is already an advanced stage of thought. The idea that Hom. did not view the body as a unity [8] is hardly tenable in this sharp form. [9] Yet he undoubtedly describes the body predominantly in plural concepts. [10] This is in keeping with early plastic depictions in

---

[1] Probably from τϝαρκ- *twṛk- (cf. Ael. σύρκες) and perhaps most closely related to the Hittite tuekkaš "body," "person," plur. "limbs," if this comes from *twerka. It is also connected with the θwarəs- of the Avesta, "to cut," better "to shape," "to fashion," cf. Boisacq, s.v.; with reservations Hofmann, s.v.; on the Avesta cf. M. Leumann, "Der indo-iranische Bildnergott Twarštar," Asiatische Studien, 8 (1954), 79-84 [Risch].
[2] Ed. B. Snell² (1955).
[3] Cf. also the def. Poll. Onom., II, 233.
[4] Cf. Gk. → 102, 7 f., 31 f.; n. 56; Jewish → 109, 27 ff.; 120, 6 ff.
[5] The σάρκες consist of σάρξ Hippocr. De Carnibus, 9 (Littré, VIII, 596, 3 f.). Plat., too, speaks only of σάρξ, not μῦς, cf. F. M. Cornford, Plato's Cosmology (1952), 298; Gal. Definitiones Medicae, 80 (Kühn, 19, 367) makes the distinction: μύες are σώματα νευρώδη with which σάρξ is mixed, cf. Alex. Aphr. An., p. 98, 12 f.: the σῶμα of the heart muscle is something between σάρξ and νεῦρον.
[6] Ed. W. E. Blake (1938).
[7] It is ὕλη, cf. also Aristot. Part. An., III, 4, p. 429b, 13 f.; 7, p. 431b, 15.
[8] B. Snell, "Die Auffassung d. Menschen bei Hom.," Die Entdeckung d. Geistes³ (1955), 21-25.
[9] R. Hirzel, "Die Person," SA Mün., 1914, 10 (1914), 5-7; H. Rahn, "Tier u. Mensch in d. homerischen Auffassung der Wirklichkeit," Paideuma, 5 (1954), 431-443; H. Köller, "Σῶμα bei Homer," Glotta, 37 (1958), 278-281 → σῶμα.
[10] Cf. → σῶμα.

which the individual parts are esp. emphasised and differentiated. [11] Perhaps the plur. σάρκες, predominant in Hom. [12] and the older tragedians, is also related hereto. At first the sing. denoted only the individual part [13] or the substance. [14] This usage dropped out later. [15] Yet the plur. continued to hold the field even where the word took over the function of σῶμα (→ lines 34 ff.) and Dio Chrys. uses the plur. exclusively. Connected with this plur. is the idea of a mass of flesh, esp. in stout people, Dio Chrys., 39, 5; Luc. Nec., 10, 5; but this is true of the sing. too, Eur. Cyc., 380; cf. εὔογκος σάρξ in the physician Aret., VIII, 6, 1 (CMG, II, 165, 11); πολλὴ σάρξ in Soranus Gynaecia, IV, 2, 3 (CMG, IV, 131, 24). The σάρκες ἀλλότριαι in Plat. Resp., VIII, 556d denote the corpulence of the rich man won at the expense of others. Flesh is something proper to man in a special way, Antiphon Fr., 53 (Diels, II, 361, 8).

Σάρξ can also denote the flesh which is eaten, though κρέας is preferred for this. [16] It is the flesh which the dog eats, Antiphanes Fr., 326 (CAF, II, 134) or the roasted or cooked flesh which man eats, Eur. Fr., 467, 3 (TGF, 503); Gal. Comm. on Hippocr. Vict., IV, 98 (CMG, V, 9, 1, p. 348, 2 ff.) in alternation with κρέας; Nicand. Alexipharm., 573 f.; cf. Aesch. Ag., 1097; Eur. Tro., 775. Orpheus is supposed to have warned against ἐδωδὴ σαρκῶν, Orph. Fr., 215 (Kern, 62) cf. Plat. Leg., VI, 782c.

2. The Origin of Flesh.

The pre-Socratics were already discussing the development of flesh out of the four elements, Emped. Fr., 98 (Diels, I, 346, 23) cf. Ps.-Heracl. C, 1 (I, 185, 9) and Emped. A, 78 (I, 299, 5 f.) [17] or out of female seed, the bones, soul and faculty of perception coming from male seed, Hippon. A, 13 (I, 386, 41); an anon. Pythagorean Fr., 1a (I, 450, 4). But perhaps flesh and bone are themselves elements, since flesh cannot arise out of non-flesh, Anaxag. A, 43 (Diels, II, 17, 19); Fr., 10 (II, 37, 7). The next to be mentioned is blood, Emped. Fr., 98 (I, 346, 23), which is absorbed by the fleshy parts, the σαρκώδη, Diogenes of Apollonia Fr., 6 (II, 65, 13). Plato teaches that flesh and sinews arise out of blood, Tim., 82c d cf. 80e. Hippocr. De natura infantis, 14-17 (Littré, VII, 492-498) has the same doctrine : The σάρξ of the child originates in the blood of the mother. It is πνέουσα, absorbs the blood, and grows through the πνεῦμα, cf. Gal. Definitiones medicae, 80 f. (Kühn, 19, 367); Alex. Aphr. De Mixtione, 16, p. 238, 13 f. Aristot. Gen. An., II, 6, p. 743a, 10 ff. cf. 744b, 23 seeks its origin in moisture, while on the other hand thick blood arises out of flesh, Aristot. Hist. An., III, 2, p. 512b, 9.

3. σάρξ as Body.

The sense broadens out. When Hom. Od., 18, 77 speaks of the trembling of the σάρκες he has expressly in view the muscular part surrounding the limbs. One may ask how far this usage still affects the examples which follow. [18] It is plain, however, that in the

---

[11] Snell, op. cit. (→ n. 8), 21-25.
[12] Od., 19, 450 is the only exception.
[13] IG, 12, 7, No. 237, 17; 12, 2, No. 498, 16; Nicand. Fr., 74, 49; also Ditt. Or., 78, 16; Ditt. Syll.³, III, 1047, 7; 1171, 5.
[14] Hes. Scutum Herculis, 364 and 461 → n. 5, 15.
[15] The plur. is used for the substance in Plat. Phaed., 96d, cf. Eur. Hipp., 1239, 1343; Ba., 1130. Aristot. Gen. Corr., I, 5, p. 321b, 21 f. says expressly that ὕλη as well as εἶδος is σάρξ or ὀστοῦν, though cf. p. 321b, 32; Meteor., IV, 12, p. 390a, 2-b, 22.
[16] Hom. Od., 9, 293; Theocr. Idyll., 25, 224 and 230, where σάρξ is the flesh of the living lion ; Philetaerus Fr., 10 (CAF, II, 233) where a piece of pork is σαρκὸς ὑείας κρέας. In Dio Chrys., 8, 30 the bodily fulness of the athlete is σάρκες, the flesh he needs for food κρέας. But Hom. Od., 9, 293, 297 uses σάρξ with κρέας for the human flesh which Cyclops eats → n. 21.
[17] Cf. also Alex. Aphr. Quaestiones, II, 24 (p. 75, 13 f.).
[18] So, e.g., Aesch. Choeph., 280; Fr., 253 (TGF, 81), where illness consumes the σάρκες; similarly the Furies in Soph. Trach., 1054.

use of σάρξ there is a growing understanding that the body is a whole. Where σάρξ sing. or plur. embraces this totality it is esp. the physical body, which may be young or ageing, Aesch. Ag., 72; Sept. c. Theb., 622; Eur. Herc. Fur., 1151, 1269, [19] and which can be torn and destroyed, Eur. Hipp., 1239, 1343; Med., 1189; Soph. Phil., 1157; Trach., 1054; Poll. Onom., IV, 179. [20] Eur. Fr., 201 (TGF, 421) speaks of the well-being of the σάρξ. The dead body can also be called σάρκες, Eur. Hipp., 1031. [21] When Philemon Fr., 95 (CAF, II, 508) stresses that the slave has the same σάρξ as the free man, the concept is physical, for the argument is that none is born a slave φύσει. The same applies to the saying about the unresisting softness of the human σάρκες, Dio Chrys., VI, 26, and the θνηταὶ σάρκες. [22]

4. Special Meanings.

Since the skin is only dried up σάρξ (Aristot. Probl., 10, 27, p. 893b, 33; Gen. An., II, 6, p. 743b, 6; cf. Plat. Tim., 75e-76a), the inner part of the skin can be called σάρξ. [23] This helps us to understand the use of σχοινίων σαρκίνων (P. Lond., III, 1177, 169 and 172) for leather thongs or catgut. ὕδρωψ ἀνὰ σάρκα is a medical tt. for dropsy of the skin, Aret., IV, 1, 4, cf. Gal. Comm. on Hippocr. Acut., IV, 106 (CMG, V, 9, 1, p. 352, 6-24). Swellings can also be called σάρκες, Hippocr. De regimine, I, 2 (Littré, VI, 470, 5). Finally the word is used for the flesh of fruits, e.g., the olive or the poppy-head, Theophr. De causis plantarum, III, 14, 6; VI, 8, 5 f.; Hist. Plant., I, 11, 1; IV, 15, 1; Aret., V, 10, 10; VI, 1, 2; VIII, 2, 3.

The ref. in Aristot. De Plantis, I, 4, p. 819a, 35, cf. p. 818a, 33 is to the veins and flesh of a tree, and in p. 820a, 37 to the fruits. Finally note should be taken of the fabulous idea of a monster with "iron flesh" in Theocr. Idyll., 22, 47. The expression εἰς σάρκα πημαίνειν [24] means "to hurt to the flesh, to the quick."

5. σάρκινος. [25]

It is no surprise that the adj., too, denotes the material flesh, Plat. Leg., 906c; "consisting of flesh" σώματα Dio C., 38, 21, 3 : the σῶμα is σάρκινον; Philodem. Philos. De Signis, 27, 24 f. (→ n. 28); Max. Tyr., 29, 7g : φύσις σαρκίνη. From the idea of bulky flesh comes the sense "corpulent," Aristoph. Fr., 711 (CAF, I, 565); Eupolis Fr., 387 (CAF, I, 359); Aristot. Eth. Nic., III, 12, p. 1117b, 5; Polyb., 38, 8, 7. But there is an interesting development of usage. On the one side the word comes to mean "real," e.g., a fish of flesh as distinct from one seen only in a dream, Theocr. Idyll., 21, 66. On the border are σάρκινοι θεοί in distinction from statues of the gods, Artemid. Onirocr., II, 35. But when Plut. De Profectibus in Virtute, 8 (II, 79c) uses τὸ σάρκινον τῶν

---

[19] The flesh is the part of the body where age and sickness are most clearly seen, Plat. Gorg., 518d; Dio Chrys., 19, 5, cf. 39, 5.

[20] Cf. also Eur. Ba., 746 : The skin is the husk of the flesh of the dying bull. Bathing the σάρκες or σάρξ = the body, Nicand. Alexipharm., 462; Plut. Quaest. Conv., 8, 9 (II, 734a).

[21] Cf. Emped. Fr., 137, 6 (Diels, I, 367, 21): φίλαι σάρκες are one's children. Hom. Il., 8, 380; 13, 832 speaks of the fat and σάρκες of men given to the dogs and birds to eat.

[22] Apollodorus of Athens Bibliotheca, I, 5, 1 (2nd/1st cent. B.C.), ed. J. G. Frazer, I (1954).

[23] Cf. the pipes of flesh under the skin, Emped. Fr., 100, 1 f. (Diels, I, 347, 14).

[24] Philodem. Philos. De Epicuro, II, Fr. 6, col. IV, 2 (ed. A. Vogliano [1928]).

[25] σαρκικός is not attested for certain before Paul : Sotades Collectanea Alexandrina (ed. J. U. Powell [1925], 244); Aristot. Hist. An., XI, 3, p. 635a, 11; Probl., 5, 7, p. 881a, 16; after Paul Max. Tyr., 11, 10e; Chr.: Anth. Graec., 1, 107.

λόγων for the πραγματική καὶ ὑλική sense [26] which serves the end of philosophical instruction the word is used already in a transf. sense. Acc. to Fr. Philodem. [27] the same applies to the noun σάρξ when it denotes the reality which the image does not have. On the other side, however, the adj. has the nuance of corruptibility. Men are θνατοί καὶ σάρκινοι with their easily destroyed σῶμα and the afflictions and sorrows of their ψυχή, Ps.-Democr. C, 7 (Diels, II, 228, 25). [28] The σάρκινον is subject to φθορά acc. to Epicurus. [29] Hence being σάρκινος differentiates man from the gods, Aesch. Fr., 464, 2 (TGF, 127); Epic. [30] → 99, 17 f. No fleshly or earthly πάθος affects the gods (Epict. Gnom. Stob., 4) or the soul which mounts up above the stars (Max. Tyr., 11, 10e). [31] There are, of course, those who regard the gods as σάρκινοι, Philodem. Philos. De Pietate, 59, 21 f.; De Deis, III, Fr., 6 → n. 29. But the decisive question is what is the opposite of this corruptible being of man.

6. The Corruptible σάρξ in Distinction from the Incorruptible Part of Man.

Hom. Od., 11, 219-22 states already that flesh and bones are destroyed in death but the θυμός and ψυχή escape. Similarly Eur. Med., 1200, 1217, 1219 mentions the ψυχή, the vital force, along with the σάρκες which loose themselves from the bones. Even a great amount of flesh is no help for one must put it off when getting aboard the skiff of death and cross over "naked," Luc. Nec., 10, 5. In the Pythagorean school the body of flesh and bones stands in contrast to the ψυχή and αἴσθησις, Anon. Fr., 1a (Diels, I, 450, 4). Aristot. mentions the material σάρξ and the ψυχή, Part. An., III, 4, p. 429a, 10 ff. [32] Acc. to Chrysippus Fr., 1152 (v. Arnim, II, 322, 30 f.) the ψυχή, the vital force which protects against corruption, is mixed like salt even in the σάρξ of swine.

The situation is different, however, when the opposite is not the vital force but the spirit or understanding of man. Thus Aesch. Sept. c. Theb., 622 refers to the aged νοῦς and the youthful σάρξ, while in the pregnant formulation in Eur. El., 387 αἱ σάρκες κεναὶ φρενῶν are foolish men who have nothing to say. Here σάρκες is used for the whole man, but man without understanding, and hence not man in the full sense. [33] Later one may refer, e.g., to Philodem. Philos., [34] who says that undisturbed διάνοια and unbroken σάρκες are needed for ataraxy. Epict. Diss., IV, 7, 32 opposes to flesh and bones and sinews that which uses and rules these and has conscious ideas. Hence the gods are not of σάρξ (→ 99, 17 f.); they are νοῦς, ἐπιστήμη, λόγος, II, 8, 2.

More important, however, are views which set an incorruptible part of man in antithesis to the corruptible σάρξ. [35] Most pregnant here is the much quoted saying in

---

[26] Dimitrakos, s.v.

[27] Philodem. Philos. Volumina Rhetorica, 4 Fr., 1, col., 5, 11 (ed. S. Sudhaus, I [1892], 149). The εἴδωλον is μακρῷ τῇ καθαπερεὶ σαρκὶ διαφέρον, obviously from the thing denoted, and certainly not toto corpore differens as supposed by C. J. Vooijs and D. A. Krevelen, Lex. Philodemeum (1934-1941), s.v. Cf. Cl. Al. Strom., I, 48, 4.

[28] The saying comes from the Neo-Pythagorean Hipparchus. Cf. also Philodem. Philos. De Signis, 33, 30-34, 5 (ed. P. H. de Lazy [1941], 100 f.) → 120, 28.

[29] Philodem. Philos. De Deis, III, Fr. 8, 7 (ed. H. Diels, AAB, 1916, 4 [1916], 45), though cf. De Pietate, 59, 21 f. (ed. T. Gomperz, Herkulanische Studien, II [1866], 31). σάρκες for the earthly body, Epigr. Graec., 650, 8 (→ 103, 13 ff.).

[30] Philodem. Philos. De Deis, III, Fr., 6, 6 → n. 29. The Aesch. Fr. is not genuine.

[31] ὕλης πάθος Max. Tyr., 11, 11e. Cf. Schweizer Hell. Komponente, 239, n. 12.

[32] σάρξ as αἰσθητήριον Part. An., II, 1, p. 647a, 20; 8, p. 653b, 24 cf. II, 3, p. 650b, 5; 5, p. 651b, 4; 10, p. 656b, 35; An., III, 2, p. 426b, 15; the αἰσθητικὴ ψυχή in the σάρξ Gen. An., II, 5, p. 741a, 10 cf. II, 1, p. 734b, 25 f.

[33] Cf. Horat. Ep., I, 4, 6 : non tu corpus eras sine pectore ; also Eur. Fr., 1052 (TGF, 693): Hair only and flesh and no deeds ; Philo Vit. Mos., I, 54 : long hair and flesh, no men → 109, 5; 145, 6 f.

[34] De Deis, I, 17, 25 f. (Diels, AAB, 1915, 7 [1916]).

[35] We are limiting ourselves strictly to passages which use σάρξ; → σῶμα; → ψυχή.

Emped. Fr., 126 (Diels, I, 362, 5) about "the alien garb of the flesh," the ἀλλογνὼς χιτὼν σαρκός, which Plut. Carn. Es., 4 (II, 998c) and Porphyr. (Stob. Ecl., I, 49, 60) adopt in discussing παλιγγενεσία or μετακόσμησις. [36] For Plat. Symp., 211e again the vision of divine beauty is free from "any taint of human flesh." The ὄγκος σαρκῶν which is buried is not the true being; the immortal ψυχή is much more than the σῶμα, Leg., 959a-c. What is mortal about the ψυχή [37] belongs with the σάρξ, Tim., 61c, 69c. In the 4th cent. one may refer to Epigr. Graec., 90, 1: The earth has the bones and flesh (σάρκας), but the soul of the righteous wanders in the θάλαμος. [38] Acc. to a dream book of the 2nd cent. B.C. someone dreams that he sloughs off the σάρκες as a snake does its skin, because his soul is about to leave the σῶμα. [39] Instead of σῶμα and ψυχή (Quaest. Conv., V, 1 [II, 672d]; Col., 20 [II, 1118d]) Plut. sometimes has σάρξ and ψυχή as the two components of man (De Exilio, 1 [II, 599c]), for the imperishable soul is sown in the perishable flesh (Ser. Num. Pun., 17 [II, 560c]). He also refers to the fleshly (σάρκινα) impediments of the soul in Quaest. Conv., IX, 14, 7 (II, 745e f); Col., 27 (II, 1122d). [40] In Epict. Diss., I, 3, 5 f.; 29, 6 the σαρκίδιον is contrasted with the λόγος, the true I. Dio C., 38, 21, 3 also declares that the σῶμα, being σάρκινον, needs much help from deity, but reason is more divine by nature, → 99, 17 f. Eur. Fr., 971 (TGF, 674) offers a formal par. to the NT antithesis of σάρξ and πνεῦμα: "Swollen with σάρξ he expired, releasing the πνεῦμα to the aether," → 116, 31 ff.

7. σάρξ as the Seat of Emotions in Epicurus.

It is early seen that stimuli affect the σάρξ. The fearful quiver and shake, Hom. Od., 18, 77; Eur. Ba., 607. Once σάρξ comes to denote the whole body (→ 101, 1 ff.) it can be said to be filled with pity, Eur. Phoen., 1285 f. [41] It is soon observed, too, that the flesh experiences, e.g., heat and cold, and various theories are advanced in explanation, e.g., that of Aristot. that the αἰσθητικὴ ψυχή has its seat in the σάρξ, → n. 32. Similar ideas are found in the later period which is so important for the NT. Acc. to Philodem. Philos. De Pietate, 116, 13 f. (→ n. 29) feeling is embraced by the παραίσθησις σαρκίνη. In Sext. Emp. Math., VII, 290 the fleshly substance (σάρκινος ὄγκος) is the seat of emotions, and Alex. Aphr. discusses in An., 56, 14-58, 5 whether it is the flesh which feels or something in it. [42]

From the NT standpoint this is especially important in Epicurus and above all his opponents. If Plato once referred to ἐπιθυμίαι κατὰ σῶμα (e.g., Phaed., 82c → σῶμα), Epic. has ἡ κατὰ σάρκα ἡδονή. [43] In him the σάρξ is in particular the seat of desire, ἡδονή, Sententiae selectae, 4 and 18 (→ II, 915, 30 ff.). Since

---

[36] Cf. Ev. Veritatis, 20, 30: Putting off of mortal clothes and putting on of immortality.
[37] On this cf. Cornford, op. cit. (→ n. 5), 284-286; L. Gernet, "L'anthropologie dans la religion grecque," in C. J. Bleeker, Anthropologie religieuse (1955), 55-59.
[38] Cf. Epigr. Graec., 225, 1 where the soul shares in aethereal rotation.
[39] Artemid. Onirocr., V, 40.
[40] Without the insatiable σάρξ life would be easier, Plut. Sept. Sap. Conv., 16 (II, 160bc).
[41] With Schol. on Eur. Phoen., 1285 διὰ σάρκα is to be construed as "through," as in Hom. Il., 10, 297 f.
[42] For Stoicism cf. L. Stein, Die Erkenntnistheoroie d. Stoa (1888), 133-153 and → VI, 354, 32 ff., also → σῶμα.
[43] Philodem. Philos. De Epicuro (→ n. 24), II, Fr., 6, col., II; H. Diels, "Ein epikureisches Fr. über Götterverehrung," SAB, 37 (1916), 903, II, 5: αἱ συγγενεῖς κατὰ σάρκα ἡδοναί. σῶμα is for him the total conglomeration of the atoms which includes the soul; C. Bailey, The Greek Atomists and Epicurus (1928), 487, n. 3; N. W. De Witt, Epicurus and His Philosophy (1954), 197 f., 225.

the genesis of desire is explained by a mechanical intrusion of atoms, [44] the desire experienced in the σάρξ takes first place as the most evident. "The beginning and root of all good is the desire of the belly," Fr., 409. If the voice of the flesh calls : Do not hunger, thirst, or freeze, the soul will not miss the admonition of nature, Fr., 200. If man has this, he is as happy as Zeus. [45]

This does not mean at all that Epic. is simply calling for the satisfying of every desire and the avoiding of all pain. On the contrary he demands conscious choice and prudent evaluation. [46] διάνοια [47] knows the ends and limits of the σάρξ with its infinite desire. It is thus essential for wise restriction, Sentent. selectae, 20. It should also be remembered that what is necessary for happiness is not the present well-being of the σάρξ but expectation of this in the future, Fr., 68. Thus the ἡδοναί of the ψυχή are greater than those of the σάρξ, Diog. L., X, 137. [48] The σάρξ is also the seat of sorrow, Epic. Fr., 40 (Diano); Sentent. selectae, 4. In the long run, however, pleasure surpasses sorrow (Sentent. sel., 4, 18) and the soul is responsible for much greater evils, Fr., 445; Diog. L., X, 137.

8. The Influence of Epicurus. [49]

One has to realise how widespread were the ideas of Epicurus. [50] In the process of popularisation it was inevitable that the finer distinctions should be quickly forgotten. Epic. himself had to resist the view that he was teaching unbridled lust, an unceasing series of revellings and of orgies with boys and women, Diog. L., X, 131 f. He was charged with sanctifying the desire and itch of the body, fornication, and similar vices, Fr., 414. It should not be forgotten that his opponents belonged to a tradition which from the time of Plato [51] had regarded the desires and cravings of the body as the means whereby the soul was bewitched, stained, and polluted. In NT days, then, the catchword ἡδονὴ σαρκός was an anti-epicurean slogan, esp. popular in Hell. Judaism. [52] It was constantly regarded as a summons to the crudest forms of pleasure. Animals knew nothing better than ἡδονή, no divine righteousness; all things served ἡδονὴ σαρκός and the fulfilment of their desire. The Epicurean Metrodor. acts thus when he declares that everything beautiful and wise and excellent in the soul is simply τῆς κατὰ σάρκα ἡδονῆς ἔνεκα, Plut. Col., 30 (II, 1125b). The Epicureans fed their souls with the pleasures of the body like pigs ; they spat at the beautiful and found the good in the flesh and its lust, Plut. Suav. Viv. Epic., 14 (II, 1096d). How abhorrent this was may be seen from the fact that the man who wants to sleep with a hetaira waits for

----

[44] Examples and bibl. Schweizer Hell. Komponente, 240, n. 20. Cf. also De Witt, op. cit., 201 f.

[45] Fr. 35 (ed. C. Diano [1946], 53). Epic. seems here to be summoning to moderation, cf. Diano, 140 on Fr., 50. On ἡδονή as the true goal of life before and in Epic. cf. E. Schwartz, Ethik d. Griechen (1951), 97-100, 151-154, 179-191.

[46] Examples and bibl. Schweizer Hell. Komponente, 241, n. 27.

[47] This is not just reason but includes understanding, will and sensibility, Diano, op. cit. (→ n. 45), 121 f. and Sententia, 18, 8.

[48] On this cf. Schwartz, op. cit. (→ n. 45), 180 f.

[49] Cf. Schweizer Hell. Komponente, 241-246. Only the most significant statements are mentioned here.

[50] Diog. L., X, 9; Lucretius De Rerum Natura, VI, 8; Cic. Fin., I, 13, 25; De Witt, op. cit., 328-331.

[51] Phaed., 81b; cf. 79c; Leg., VIII, 835c. On the resurgence of these ideas in Pos. and others cf. K. Holl, Ges. Aufsätze z. Kirchengeschichte, II (1928), 259 f.

[52] Epic. → n. 43; Cic. Fin., I, 23 : voluptas in corpore, cf. Tusc., III, 37 and 50; Plut. De Virtute et Vitio, 3 (II, 101b); αἱ τῆς σαρκὸς ἡδοναί (cf. II, 1087 f.); Suav. Viv. Epic., 14 (II, 1096c): αἱ τῆς σαρκὸς ἐπιθυμίαι, Cons. ad Apoll., 13 (II, 107 f.): πάθη τῆς σαρκός, Max. Tyr., 33, 7a: ἴδιον σαρκῶν ἡδοναί, 4 Macc. 7:18 : τὰ τῆς σαρκὸς πάθη, Philo

the obscurity of night to do so, Plut. Lat. Viv., 4 (II, 1129b). [53] Epict., who uses σάρξ only in controversy with Epic., [54] refers to him as a κιναιδολόγος, one who teaches licentiousness, and Timocrates tells how twice a day he was sick through overeating, Diog. L., X, 6. In Alciphr. Ep., III, 19, 8 the Epicurean is depicted embracing the nearest dancing-girl and saying with damp and half-closed eyes that this is the necessary rest of the flesh and concentration of pleasure, of ἡδόμενον. Even so eminent a polemicist as Cic. calls the followers of Epic. *voluptarii* (Tusc., III, 40) who put obscene lusts in the centre (V, 94); indeed, Epic. himself preferred the lusts of the lower part of the body to the delights of the eyes and the ears, Or. in Pisonem, 66. Thus σάρξ is increasingly regarded as the source of ἡδονή and esp. of uncontrolled sexuality and immoderate gluttony. [55] It makes the freedom of the soul impossible. [56] Hell. Judaism drank all this in eagerly.

Schweizer

B. Flesh in the Old Testament.

This art. deals only with the linguistic material. Theological aspects are discussed along with the other terms in OT anthropology (רוּחַ, נֶפֶשׁ, לֵב etc.) in the art. → ψυχή.

The Heb. equivalents to the Gk. σάρξ in the LXX are [57] בָּשָׂר (273 times in the Heb. text) and שְׁאֵר (17 times). [58]

1. בָּשָׂר. [59]

Etym. Arab. *bašar* orig. meaning "skin," then sing. and plur. for "man," "men," "human race." Accad. *bišru* "flesh and blood." Ugaritic *bšr* "flesh."

a. Flesh in the Strict Sense.

In man *passim*; עוֹר הַבָּשָׂר Lv. 13:2 ff.; בָּשָׂר חַי "wild flesh" [60] Lv. 13:10 ff.; בָּשָׂר עָרְלָתוֹ Gn. 17:11 ff.; Lv. 12:3; עָרֵל־בָּשָׂר (par. עָרֵל־לֵב) Ez. 44:7, 9; par. דָּם Ez. 39:17 f. For the

---

Deus Imm., 143 and Rer. Div. Her., 57: σαρκὸς ἡδονή, cf. Gig., 40; Agric., 97. Rer. Div. Her., 268 : πάθη σαρκὸς ἐκπεφυκότα, Leg. All., II, 49 (cf. III, 158): μία σάρξ καὶ ἕν πάθος), cf. Diog. L., X, 145; 1 QH 10:23 : יֵצֶר, = "impulse" ? = "construct" ? (→ 132, 30; 137, 14 ff.; 140, 23; 147, 5 ff.).

[53] But cf. Plut. De Tuenda Sanitate Praecepta, 8 (II, 126c) for the influence of the real Epic.: the sexual impulse attains ἡδονή better in the peace and quietness of the σάρξ.
[54] A. Bonhöffer, *Epict. u. d. NT* (1911), 160 f.
[55] The view that in Gk. the σάρξ is never the root of evil (Burton, 135 f.) must be modified in the light of these passages.
[56] → n. 31, 52; also Plut. Quaest. Conv., IX, 14, 6 (II, 745e f): Music reminds the soul of divine and heavenly things, but the ears are usually stopped up with carnal hindrances and πάθη so that the soul cannot free itself from the body. M. Ant., 12, 1: No αἴσθησις of the flesh which has grown up around us should hamper us. Cic. Tusc., III, 50 disagrees with Epic. and thinks the supreme good is spiritual not physical, virtue not pleasure. Seneca, too, can occasionally use *caro* instead of *corpus*, seeing in it that which chains the *anima*, bearing the same relation to it as matter to God, Ep., VII, 3 (65), 16. 22. 24. Many opt for Epic. to excuse their vices. Hence his school is called the teacher of vice, Dialogus ad Gallionem de Vita Beata, 12, 3-5; 13, 2; cf. Ep., II, 9 (21), 9 and Dialogus ad Marciam de Consolatione, 24, 5.
[57] The difficult לְחוּם (cf. the lex. and comm.), which LXX transl. σάρξ at Zeph. 1:17, may be left out of account.
[58] Including שְׁאֵרָה in Lv. 18:17 → n. 82.
[59] On the gender cf. K. Albrecht, "Das Geschlecht d. hbr. Hauptwörter," ZAW, 16 (1896), 72; on the use cf. A. H. Cremer, Art. "Fleisch" in RE³, 6, 99 f.
[60] Acc. to Köhler-Baumg., *s.v.* "raw flesh."

sense "skin" (Arab. *bašar*) cf. דָּבְקָה עַצְמִי לִבְשָׂרִי ("my bones cleave to my skin") in Ps. 102:5. The same expression [61] is possibly used in Job 19:20 (if we eliminate בְעוֹרִי). [62] Cf. also Ex. 4:7. [63]

In animals: דַּקּוֹת בָּשָׂר or פָּרוֹת בְּרִיאֹת בָּשָׂר Gn. 41:2 f.; בָּשָׂר פִּגּוּל "unclean flesh" Ez. 4:14; food for the bird of prey Da. 7:5; as meat for man *passim*; of the sacrifice בְּשַׂר־קֹדֶשׁ Jer. 11:15 *passim*.

b. In an Extended Sense.

Body of man *passim*; par. עֶצֶם Gn. 2:23; par. עֲצָמִים Ps. 38:3; par. עַצְמוֹת Job. 33:21; par. בְּרָכַיִם Ps. 109:24; par. עוֹר Job 7:5; par. כּוֹחַ Job 6:12; נֶפֶשׁ הַבָּשָׂר Lv. 17:11; כָּל־בְּשָׂרוֹ "his whole body" Lv. 13:13; "the naked body" Lv. 6:3 and 16:4 (עַל־בְּשָׂרוֹ) on the naked body); [64] 1 K. 21:27; 2 K. 6:30; בְּרִיאֵי בָשָׂר "well-nourished" Da. 1:15; "dead body," "corpse," 1 S. 17:44; 2 K. 9:36; בְּשַׂר חֲסִידֶיךָ par. נִבְלַת עֲבָדֶיךָ Ps. 79:2; par. רְמוּת [65] Ez. 32:5. A special use of בָּשָׂר (cf. נֶפֶשׁ) is for "self": אֹכֵל אֶת־בְּשָׂרוֹ "the fool consumes himself" Qoh. 4:5; לַחֲטִיא אֶת־בְּשָׂרֶךָ "to make thyself guilty" Qoh. 5:6; then "a person," "someone" Lv. 13:18.

Body of animals Lv. 17:11, 14; Job 41:15, also the cherubim Ez. 10:12.

c.   כָּל־בָּשָׂר.

כָּל־בָּשָׂר "all living creatures," men and animals Gn. 6:17; [66] 9:11 ff.; Nu. 18:15; Ps. 136:25; Da. 4:9. כָּל־בָּשָׂר "all men," the whole race, Is. 40:5, 6; Jer. 25:31 etc.; par. כָּל־חַי Job 12:10; par. אָדָם (collective) Job 34:15; אֱלֹהֵי כָל־בָּשָׂר Jer. 32:27; אֱלֹהֵי הָרוּחֹת לְכָל־בָּשָׂר (→ VI, 361, 3 ff.); Nu. 16:22; 27:16; "everybody" Is. 66:23, 24; Jer. 12:12; מִי כָל־בָּשָׂר "where is there any human being?" Dt. 5:26 (23). Special senses are the whole population of the land in Ez. 21:4, 9 [67] and the whole cultic community of Israel in Jl. 2:28; Ps. 65:2.

כָּל־בָּשָׂר "the whole animal kingdom" Gn. 6:19; 7:15, 16, 21; 8:17.

d. As a Term for Blood-Relationship. [68]

בָּשָׂר מִבְּשָׂרִי Gn. 2:23; עַצְמִי וּבְשָׂרִי "my blood-relation" Gn. 29:14; 2 S. 19:13, 14; cf. Ju. 9:2; 2 S. 5:1; 1 Ch. 11:1; כִּבְשַׂר אֲחֵינוּ בְּשָׂרֵנוּ Neh. 5:5; שְׁאֵר בְּשָׂרוֹ "his closest relative" Lv. 18:6; 25:49; אָחִינוּ בְשָׂרֵנוּ הוּא [69] "he is our flesh and blood" Gn. 37:27. In a broader sense בְּשָׂרֶךָ "thy fellow-countryman" Is. 58:7.

---

[61] But hardly Job 4:15 (in spite of H. Gunkel, *Die Psalmen, Komm. AT* [1926] on Ps. 102:6b) or Ps. 119:120 (Gunkel, *loc. cit.* and Köhler-Baumg., *s.v.* בשׂר); in both verses "body" is more natural.

[62] Cf. G. Beer, *Der Text d. Buches Hi.* (1897), 121; C. J. Ball, *The Book of Job* (1922), ad loc.; G. Hölscher, *Das Buch Hi.*, Hndbch. AT, I, 17² (1952), ad loc.

[63] Cf. B. Baentsch, *Ex., Lv. u. Nu.*, Hndkomm. AT (1903), ad loc.

[64] Unless a euphemism for the *membrum virile*.

[65] The original reading is perhaps רִמָּה, cf. the comm.

[66] Whether animals are also meant in Gn. 6:12, 13 is doubtful (as against A. Dillmann, *Die Genesis, Kurzgefasstes exeget. Hndbch. z. AT* [1892], ad loc. and O. Procksch, *Die Genesis, Komm. AT*², ³ [1924], ad loc.).

[67] Unless v. 9 refers to general world judgment, cf. A. Bertholet, *Hesekiel, Hndbch. AT*, I, 13 (1936), ad loc.

[68] Also Accad. *bišru* = blood-relationship.

[69] Read with LXX etc. וּבְשָׂרֵנוּ.

e. Euphemistically.

In the man בְּשַׂר עֶרְוָה Ex. 28:42; the woman Lv. 15:19. The *membrum virile* Gn. 17:13; [70] Lv. 15:2, 3; perhaps also 6:3 and 16:4 → n. 64; Ez. 23:20; 44:7, 9 : גִּדְלֵי בָשָׂר Ez. 16:26. With ref. to circumcision בְּשַׂר עָרְלָה praeputium Gn. 17:11 ff.; Lv. 12:3; עֲרֶל־בָּשָׂר (par. עֲרֶל לֵב) Ez. 44:7, 9.

f. In a Transferred Sense.

(a) For all man's external life : בְּשָׂרִי יִשְׁכֹּן לָבֶטַח Ps. 16:9; the words of the teacher of wisdom are life (חַיִּים) and medicine לְכָל־בְּשָׂרוֹ Prv. 4:22; הַעֲבֵר רָעָה מִבְּשָׂרֶךָ "keep evil from thy flesh" Qoh. 11:10; "to satisfy oneself with someone's בָּשָׂר" Job 19:22 or to eat his בְּשָׂר Is. 9:19; [71] 49:26; Zech. 11:9; Ps. 27:2, i.e., to destroy his whole existence ; all existence par. עֶצֶם Job 2:5; חַיֵּי בְּשָׂרִים [72] "success in life," par. רְקַב עֲצָמוֹת "caries," i.e., the destruction of existence Prv. 14:30; בְּשָׂרִי וְעוֹרִי par. עַצְמוֹתַי Lam. 3:4; בְּשָׂרִי par. נַפְשִׁי "body and life" Job 13:14; בְּשָׂרְךָ וּשְׁאֵרֶךָ Prv. 5:11.

(b) Expressing the whole inner attitude : בָּשָׂר and נֶפֶשׁ yearned after God Ps. 63:1; לֵב, נֶפֶשׁ and בָּשָׂר in their longing for God Ps. 84:2.

(c) Expressing human frailty and impotence (opp. the eternal God): man is בָּשָׂר, i.e., he is mortal Gn. 6:3; מַה־יַּעֲשֶׂה בָשָׂר לִי, "what can men who are impotent do to me ?" Ps. 56:4; עָמּוֹ זְרוֹעַ בָּשָׂר וְעִמָּנוּ יְהוָה אֱלֹהֵינוּ Is. 31:3; מִצְרַיִם אָדָם וְלֹא אֵל וְסוּסֵיהֶם בָּשָׂר וְלֹא רוּחַ 2 Ch. 32:8; שָׂם בָּשָׂר זְרֹעוֹ who relies on feeble human help Jer. 17:5; mortal men Da. 2:11; הַעֵינֵי בָשָׂר (אֱנוֹשׁ par.) לָךְ "are thine eyes like those of a mortal man ?" Job 10:4; par. רוּחַ הֹלֵךְ Ps. 78:39.

g. Metaphorically.

לֵב בָּשָׂר (opp. לֵב הָאֶבֶן) "a living heart," i.e., open to God's will, Ez. 11:19; 36:26; כְּבוֹד יַעֲקֹב par. מִשְׁמַן בְּשָׂרוֹ might and prosperity Is. 17:4; מִנֶּפֶשׁ וְעַד־בָּשָׂר "root and branch" Is. 10:18. [73]

2. שְׁאֵר. [74]

Etym. Arab. ṯa'r, "blood," then "blood-revenge," hence שְׁאֵר orig. "inner bloody flesh" as distinct from בָּשָׂר = "skin with flesh." Accad. šîru "flesh." Ugaritic šurt "flesh."

a. Flesh in the True Sense.

In man, not used (though this is accidental, cf. under b. and c.). In animals, as food for man Ex. 21:10; Ps. 78:20, 27.

---

[70] Cf. E. König, *Stilistik, Rhetorik, Poetik in Bezug auf die bibl. Literatur* (1900), 37 f.
[71] For זְרֹעוֹ read רֵעוֹ cf. BHK, *ad loc.*
[72] On the plur. (only here) cf. E. König, *Historisch-komparative Syntax d. hbr. Sprache* (1897) § 259e; Ges.-K. § 124d.
[73] On the difficult Job 14:22 (par. נֶפֶשׁ) and Job 19:26 (perhaps one should read מִבְּשָׂרִי) cf. the comm.
[74] On the gender → n. 59.

b. As a Term for Blood-Relationship. [75]

שְׁאֵר "blood-relation" Lv. 18:12 f.; 20:19; שְׁאֵר בְּשָׂרוֹ Lv. 18:6; 25:49 or שְׁאֵרוֹ הַקָּרֹב אֵלָיו Lv. 21:2; Nu. 27:11 "his nearest relative."

c. In a Transferred Sense.

For all man's external existence: בְּשָׂרְךָ וּשְׁאֵרֶךָ Prv. 5:11; שְׁאֵרִי וּלְבָבִי Ps. 73:26; חֶמְסִי וּשְׁאֵרִי par. דָּם = destroyed existence Jer. 51:35; [76] to eat the שְׁאֵר of the people Mi. 3:3; to tear it from the bones of the people Mi. 3:2; עֹכֵר שְׁאֵרוֹ אַכְזָרִי "the cruel man disorders his whole existence" (par. נֶפֶשׁ) Prv. 11:17. [77]

3. Translation of the Hebrew Terms in the Septuagint.

a. For בָּשָׂר σάρξ is used 145 times, [78] κρέας 79, [79] σῶμα 23, [80] and χρώς 14. [81] Other renderings are ἄνθρωπος at Gn. 6:13, πνεῦμα παντὸς ἀνθρώπου for רוּחַ כָּל־בְּשַׂר אִישׁ at Job 12:10, βροτός at Job 10:14, τὰ πίονα τῆς δόξης αὐτοῦ for מִשְׁמַן בְּשָׂרוֹ at Is. 17:4, μεγαλόσαρκος for גְּדָל בָּשָׂר at Ez. 16:26, σάρκινος at Ez. 11:19; 36:26; 2 Ch. 32:8, ἀπὸ τῶν οἰκείων τοῦ σπέρματός σου for מִבְּשָׂרְךָ at Is. 58:7, πραΰθυμος ἀνήρ for חַיֵּי בְשָׂרִים at Prv. 14:30. For שְׁאֵר we find οἰκεῖος 7 times, [82] σάρξ 5 [83] and σῶμα 4. [83] Also found are τὰ δέοντα at Ex. 21:10, οἰκειότης at Lv. 20:19, τράπεζα at Ps. 28:20, ταλαιπωρία (LXX probably read שָׁאתִי or שִׁבְרִי → n. 76) at Ιερ. 28(51):35.

Baumgärtel

b. Certain special points [84] should be noted. [85] The LXX shows no inclination to link σάρξ esp. with sexuality, but rather avoids this usage. [86] On the other hand, in

---

[75] Also Accad. *šīru* = "blood-relation."

[76] חֶמְסִי (or דָּם following) would elucidate שְׁאֵר as "flayed and bloody flesh" ("chair déchirée," A. Condamin, *Le livre de Jérémie* [1920], ad loc.). Other readings for שְׁאֵרִי are שִׁבְרִי, יָשֹׁב, שָׁאתִי, cf. the comm. On the textual situation cf. P. Volz, "Studien z. Text d. Jer.," BWANT, 25 (1920), ad loc.

[77] Unless the meaning is "he himself" as with בָּשָׂר → 106, 13 f., cf. C. H. Toy, *The Book of Proverbs*, ICC⁴ (1948), ad loc.; B. Gemser, *Sprüche Salomos*, Hndbch. AT, I, 16 (1937), ad loc.

[78] Including Da. Θ and Sir. While σάρκες is used 17 times for human flesh delivered up to be consumed (κρέας only at Zech. 11:16), it is used for animal flesh only in ψ 77:27 for the living quails from heaven, in Zech. 11:9, where the sheep are the Israelites, and in Mi. 3:3, where two words are demanded by the parallelism.

[79] Including Da. Θ; κρέας does not occur in Sir.

[80] Including Sir.; σῶμα - בָּשָׂר does not occur in Da. Θ.

[81] There is no original in Da. Θ and Sir.

[82] The reading שָׁאֲרָה or (with LXX) שְׁאֵרָךְ is presupposed for שַׁאֲרָה in Lv. 18·17. There is no original in Sir.

[83] Including Sir.

[84] The plur. is very common, regularly used when the ref. is to the consuming of flesh (→ n. 16, 21, 78, 168 → 124, 11 f.; 145, 9 f.), also to denote relationship, or muscle as distinct from bone, or the whole body, in an individual ψ 118:120. Apart from πᾶσα σάρξ the plur. is always used in Job, Ez., 4 Macc. except for Job 16:18 (αἷμα τῆς σαρκός μου = דָּמִי); Ez. 11:19; 36:26 ("stony heart from your flesh"); 44:7, 9 (ἀπεριτμήτους σαρκί), and 4 Macc. 9:28 (τὴν σάρκα πᾶσαν).

[85] Cf. further Cr.-Kö., *s.v.* σάρξ.

[86] Only in Ez. 23:20 (cf. 16:26) is there ref. to the sexual member, while χρώς or σῶμα is used for בָּשָׂר in Ex. 28:42; Lv. 15:2 f., 7, 19.

connection with circumcision there is common ref. to the foreskin σάρξ even where there is no Heb. equivalent, Gn. 34:24; Jer. 9:25 [87] → 109, 22; 119, 12; 129, 28 f. σάρξ is never used for the flesh of sacrifice. [88] The interrelating of σάρξ and ψυχή does not go beyond the Heb. text at Gn. 9:15 f.; Lv. 17:11, 14; Is. 10:18. A new point, however, is the Gk. possibility of distinguishing between σάρξ and the whole → σῶμα and of speaking of the σάρκες τοῦ σώματος, Prv. 5:11; Job 41:15. [89] The combination τρίχες καὶ σάρκες in Job 4:15 [90] had obviously been developed already in Gk. → n. 33 and 145, 9 f.

The most important point is the LXX distinction of the cosmos into two spheres, that of spirits and that of flesh. The Lord of the spirits of all flesh in Nu. 16:22; 27:16 becomes in the LXX the Lord of spirits and of all flesh, and it is as such that it comes into the Gk. speaking Jewish Chr. world. [91] Ez. 10:12 LXX avoids speaking of the flesh of the cherubim. [92] This cosmic dualism is not the Gk. antithesis between the divine νοῦς and the material σῶμα. [93] The underlying thought is not that man unites both spheres in himself. It is the Persian conception of a spiritual world above the earthly world. The only difference is that there the only essential distinction, that between good and evil, cuts right across the two worlds as an ethical dualism, → VI, 389, 34 ff. In Judaism, however, cosmic dualism is increasingly influenced by the OT distinction between Creator and sinful creature [94] → 110, 1 ff.; 119, 20 ff.; 126, 22 ff.; 138, 25 ff.; n. 377.

4. Texts Not in the Hebrew Canon.

a. It is not surprising to find the use of πᾶσα σάρξ (→ 106, 17 ff.) for animals in Sir. 17:4; 13:16, men in 1:10; 45:1, or both in 40:8, [95] ref. to the flesh of circumcision in Jdt. 14:10; Sir. 44:20 → 108, 21 ff., or employment for the muscular part of the body generally in Sir. 19:12; 38:28; 4 Macc. 9:20, 28 etc., often with the bones as in Ps. Sol. 4:19; 13:3; 4 Macc. 9:20 f. That the whole body in its corruptibility (→ 107, 16 ff.) is σάρξ in Sir. 31:1, or woman ἰδία σάρξ of man in Sir. 25:26 → 106, 26 ff.; 119, 16 ff., is also no surprise. New, however, are the description of man as flesh and blood in Sir. 14:18; 17:31 → 110, 23 f.; Wis. 12:5 [96] → 99, 17; 116, 4 ff.; 119, 10 ff.; 139, 5 ff.; 144, 33 ff.; 148, 27; n. 205, 361, and also the expression σῶμα σαρκός in Sir. 23:17 → 110, 33; 120, 19 f.; 136, 19 f.; n. 176. [97]

---

[87] Cf. Ez. 44:7, 9 (→ 107, 4 f.).

[88] Cr.-Kö., s.v. (p. 975). Cf. only Lv. 4:11. Cf. also → 106, 5 f.; 110, 31.

[89] Not MS S. HT בְּשָׂר וּשְׁאֵר or מַפְּלֵי בְשָׂרוֹ.

[90] HT quite different. Cf. Apc. Elias 16:11-13.

[91] Jewish : Jub. 10:3; Philo Virt., 58; Preisigke Sammelbuch, 2034, 2; Chr.: ibid., 3901, 2; 4949, 3; 5716, 4; 5826, 2; 1 Cl., 59, 3. Cf. also Preis. Zaub., I, 5, 460; II, 13, 797 f. S. Aalen, Die Begriffe Licht u. Finsternis im AT, im Spätjudt. u. im Rabbinismus (1951), 96-102 shows how spatial thinking becomes stronger in Judaism.

[92] [I owe this ref. to H. W. Huppenbauer.]

[93] This is perhaps confirmed by the fact that the LXX disturbs the juxtaposition of σάρξ and πνεῦμα (Is. 31:3).

[94] Hell. statements which refer to the macrocosm are related. But "God" and "divine" mean something very different for Jews as compared with Hellenists, who find the same power microcosmically in themselves. Persian and Gk. thought helped to develop the ideas. The later development of Gnosticism (→ VI, 394, 7 ff.) is apparent already at the outset. But the knowledge which the Jews expressed thus is ever more clearly the awareness of God's transcendence rooted in the OT message of God's holiness and man's sin.

[95] In Sir. 14:17 σάρξ is used for man along with ψυχή in v. 16. Cf. also Bel and the Dragon 5 "dominion over all flesh" → 138, 8 f. πᾶσα σάρξ is used with a plur. at Jdt. 2:3.

[96] ψυχή in v. 6 refers to the whole man.

[97] For interpretation cf. V. Ryssel in Kautzsch Apkr. u. Pseudepigr., ad loc. and Lindijer, 77 f.

b. Cosmic dualism (→ 109, 9 ff.; 117, 40 ff.) may be seen in the contrast between the βασιλεὺς σάρκινος and the βασιλεὺς τῶν θεῶν in Est. 4:17 p. But there is worked out here a view which also distinguishes flesh and spirit anthropologically → 102, 33 ff. This is weakly expressed in Ps. Sol. 16:14 which describes earthly life as life ἐν σαρκί. Jdt. 10:13 has the formulation οὐ ... σάρξ μία οὐδὲ πνεῦμα ζωῆς. Here the two expressions are par. Both describe man as a whole as in the OT, and they are fully equal. Yet it is apparent that for the author man consists of both, so that he is not to be viewed from one side alone.[98] This dualism is most pronounced, however, in the writings more strongly influenced by Hellenism. Here sexuality is also suspected as such. Acc. to Wis. 7:1 f., 7 man is mortal, fashioned from σπέρμα and ἡδονή, formed as σάρξ in the womb, the πνεῦμα σοφίας being added only later, → II, 912, 5 f.; VI, 371, 3 ff. Acc. to 4 Macc. 7:13 man is made up of flesh, tendons, and muscles, to which the πνεῦμα of reason is added, → VI, 369, 21 ff. Here one finds the typical expression πάθη τῆς σαρκός → n. 52. On the basis of later Hell. hostility to the body, there is thus approximation to an understanding of σάρξ which combines the passions (and hence also sin) with it, → II, 916, 30 ff. But the same process has a different nuance in Sir. If σάρξ in Sir. 40:8 stamps man as frail and a victim of sickness[99] and distress, this is still wholly along the lines of the OT.[100] Hard to understand is Sir. 28:5 : "He himself, who is flesh, keeps his anger ; who shall expiate his sins ?" But here, too, the OT antithesis is the starting-pt. If he himself, limited and fallible man, keeps his anger against his fellows, why should not God, who has a much greater right to do so, do the same in relation to him ? Once again, then, the antithesis is simply between the infallible God and fallible man with his limited insight.[101] In Sir. 17:31 the text is unfortunately very unreliable.[102]

Schweizer

C. Flesh in Judaism.

I. The Concept in the Dead Sea Scrolls.

1. The General Concept.

"Flesh" is used with no theological or anthropological significance in 1 QS 9:4, where the ordinances of the Qumran community are said to be more efficacious than the flesh of burnt offerings and the fat of sacrifices. A similar general use with ref. to man is in 1 QpH 9:2, where the wicked priest suffers vengeance in his body of flesh ; the underlying thought is that the body is particularly vulnerable to sickness and blows. The same idea is plain in 1 QSa 2:5 f. where "everyone who is smitten in his flesh"[103] or who has a visible bodily defect is excluded from the assembly.[104]

---

[98] Sir. 16:17, however, presupposes the resurrection of the flesh, → 120, 33 f.; 146, 6 ff.; 147, 13 ff.

[99] Cf. σάρξ as the seat of sickness in Ps. Sol. 4:6.

[100] Sinners here are simply one group within mankind.

[101] Cf. Lindijer, 79 f.: "although he is flesh."

[102] If one reads with LXX : "So he has regard to the evil that he is flesh and blood," this simply means that man is mortal. If one prefers the Syr.: "Man who does not tame his mind because he is flesh and blood," lack of control is a mark of flesh and blood. More developed views are found if V. Ryssel gives a correct reconstruction in Kautzsch Apkr. u. Pseudepigr.: "... whose יֵצֶר is but flesh and blood."

[103] וכול מנוגע בבשרו (note the Mishnah form מנוגע rather than the bibl. נגוע; cf. DJD, I, 117). On "body of flesh" cf. M. Philonenko, "Sur l'expression 'corps de chair' dans le Commentaire d'Hab.," Semitica, 5 (1955), 39 f.

[104] In QSa 2:8 f. the priestly rule of freedom from bodily defect is based on the presence of the holy angels (מלאכי קודש) in the assembly, cf. 1 K. 11:10 and DJD, I, 117, *ad loc.*

2. A Term for the Person.

In the sense of body as a term for the total human person (→ 106, 12 ff.) flesh occurs in 1 QS 3:8 f.: "In that his soul subjects itself to all the commands of God his flesh becomes pure." Here soul and flesh are used in the same sense and both denote the person concerned.[105] Similarly flesh can mean the true ego. Thus "I have no fleshly refuge"[106] in 1 QH 7:17 means acc. to the very fragmentary context "I can no longer rely on myself."[107] The annihilation of one's own flesh means the destruction of one's own power in 1 QH 8:31.[108] The description of the crippling horror which the poet experiences is introduced by the words: "Then my heart flowed like water and my flesh melted like wax," 1 QH 8:32 f.[109]

3. The Collective Use.

The collective use of flesh for men or mankind (→ 106, 17 ff.) occurs in 1 QS 11:7 where those outside the community are called a "gathering of flesh" (סוד בשר); in the same context (line 6) the expression "sons of Adam" or "children of men" (בני אדם) can be used instead. In the same sense we also find "all flesh" in 1 QSb 3:28: "May the plan of all flesh be blessed by thy hand,"[110] cf. also 1 Q 34 Fr., 3, col., 1, 3 (DJD, I, 153): "a disgrace for all flesh."[111] In both instances all flesh is the same as all men or everybody.

4. Man's Corruptibility.

Flesh can also be used to emphasise the corruptibility of man and the lowliness of the creature over against the Creator, → 107, 16 ff. There may be here an echo of man's sinfulness. 1 QH 4:29 f.: "Who that is flesh is worthy, and what creature of clay can do great wonders, living in sin from the womb?"[112] Esp. common is the motif of man's powerlessness in relation to God, e.g., 1 QH 15:21: "What is he then that is only flesh, that he should have understanding ... and the creature of dust ... how can it direct its steps?"[113] Similarly the poet says on the basis of a divinely given insight

---

[105] ובענות נפשו לכול חוקי אל יטהר בשרו להזות דמי נדה; confession of sin and acknowledgement of God's commands are needed if the purity and holiness of the whole man are to be restored in the sacral act of washing.

[106] ומחסי בשר אין לי; on מחסי instead of the expected מחסה cf. J. Licht, *The Thanksgiving Scroll. A Scroll from the Wilderness of Judaea. Text, Introduction, Commentary and Glossary* (1957), 125.

[107] Cf. Licht, 125; also A. Dupont-Sommer, "Le Livre des Hymnes découvert près de la mer Morte," Semitica, 7 (1957), 59. H. Bardtke, *Die Handschriftenfunde vom Toten Meer*, II (1958), 244: "and my refuge was flesh. Neither full mercy nor righteous deeds were present with me," hardly corresponds to the material context.

[108] On להתם כוח לקצים ולכלות בשר עד מועדים cf. Licht, 139; Dupont-Sommer, 68. Bardtke, 246: "to perfect power for the last times," does not take into account the parallelism of the two inf. לכלות pi and להתם pi. One may agree with Licht, 139 that behind 1 QH 8:31 lies the idea of the visitation of the elect at ordained seasons (למועדים, לקצים).

[109] וינגר כמים לבי וימס כדונג בשרי. As against Huppenbauer, 298 and in part Bardtke, 258, 1 QH 18:14 should not be cited here, since מבשר means "messenger of good news" and לבשר ענוים "to bring good news to the afflicted," cf. Licht, 216; Dupont-Sommer, 101.

[110] ועצת כול בשר בידכה יברך, 1 QS b 3:28.

[111] חרפה לכל בשר, 1 Q 34 f. 3, col., 1, 3.

[112] מי בשר כזאת ומה יצר חמר להגדיל פלאות והוא בעוון מרחם; cf. Licht, 95 and Dupont-Sommer, 44; for a different view Bardtke, 239.

[113] ומה אף הוא בשר כי ישכיל....[ויצר] עפר איך יוכל להכין צעדו; cf. Licht, 198, also Dupont-Sommer, 93 and Bardtke, 255.

(1 QH 15:12 f.) that "it does not lie in the hand of flesh (ביד בשר) or with man (אנוש, אדם) to determine his way or to establish his steps," and that the "striving of every human spirit (יצר כל רוח) is in God's hand." [114] An important point historically is that flesh, man and spirit are on the same level and are simply synonyms for the human creature as subject to the divine will. The same is true in 1 QH 9:15 f., where "flesh," "human being" (אנוש), "man" (גבר), "[creature of] dust" (יצר [עפר])[115] and "spirit" (רוח) are used together to express the fact that all relative human distinctions are removed in face of God's righteousness and omnipotence. Finally, the rhetorical question : "What is flesh ?" (מה בשר) occurs where this flesh is honoured with special insight. Thus acc. to 1 QH 18:21-24 the heavenly "host of knowledge" [116] is charged "to proclaim (God's) mighty acts to flesh and eternal (?) laws to that which is born (of woman)." [117]

5. The Relation to Sin.

In what they say about the fleshly or corruptible existence of man the examples given in no way go beyond that which the writings of the Rabb. canon link with the idea of flesh. But there is also in the Scrolls a series of ref. in which flesh is very closely related to sin and hubris. This raises the question whether and how far the Qumran community found in the term flesh an embodiment of the world which is hostile to God. Since a strongly positive answer has been given to this question, and flesh as an anthropological concept has been assigned to the ungodly sphere within the dualism of Qumran, [118] the material thus far available needs to be examined on this point. [119]

Flesh is negatively evaluated in Damasc. 1:2 (1:2): "For God has a controversy with all flesh, and exercises judgment on all who scornfully reject him." [120] Here flesh is obviously arrogant humanity. The word has the same sense in the description of the destruction of the generation of the flood on the basis of Gn. 7:22 f.: "All flesh which was on dry land died and they were as though they had never been; for they had asserted their own will and not kept the commands of their Creator until his wrath was kindled against them." [121] Flesh is used in the same way in 1 QM 4:3, which says that the standards of the hundreds which fight against the sons of darkness are to bear the device : "From God comes the strength to war against all the flesh of evil." [122] Again, in the priestly war-prayer in 1 QM 12:10 f. we read : "For thy sword shall consume guilty flesh." [123] No special sense attaches to the term here, for, as above, it can be

---

[114] Cf. Licht, 196.

[115] 1 QH 9:16 : יכבד [עפר] ובשר מיצר transf.: "The one corruptible creature is honoured more than the other ..."; on the emendation on the basis of 1 QH Fr., 3, 5 and in interpretation cf. Licht, 145; Bardtke, 247, but for a different view Dupont-Sommer, 71.

[116] Cf. on this 1 QH 3:22 f., where there is ref. to the "host of the saints" (צבא קדושים) and the "spirits of knowledge" (רוחות דעת).

[117] 1 QH 18:23 f. לספר לבשר גבורות וחוקי נכונות לילוד [אשה]; on the singular חוקי נכונות cf. Licht, 217.

[118] K. G. Kuhn, "πειρασμός — ἁμαρτία — σάρξ im NT u. die damit zusammenhängenden Vorstellungen," ZThK, 49 (1952), 200-222.

[119] It must be emphatically pointed out that theological and anthropological statements can be made about Qumran only with great reserve so long as merely a part of the findings has been critically edited.

[120] Damasc. 1:2 (1:2). כי ריב לו עם כל בשר ומשפט יעשה בכל מנאציו

[121] כל בשר אשר היה בחרבה כי גוע ויהיו כלא היו בעשותם את רצונם ולא שמרו את מצות עשיהם עד אשר חרה אפו בם Damasc. 2:20 f. (3:6 f.).

[122] מאת אל יד מלחמה בכול בשר עול; cf. Y. Yadin, *The Scroll of the War of the Sons of Light*[2] (1957), 278 f.

[123] וחרבכה תואכל בשר אשמה; Yadin, 330 f.

interchanged with other words. Again, 1 QM 14:7 runs: "Through those who walk perfectly the nations of unrighteousness are destroyed,"[124] and cf. 1 QS 11:9, where those outside the community are described with the righteous or elect as "men of ungodliness" or "the fellowship of the flesh of iniquity" (סוד בשר עול) → 119, 23 ff.

Other instances seem to go further anthropologically when they refer to the nature of the elect. Thus we read in 1 QS 4:20 f.: "God ... will purify the figure (?) of man when he expunges the spirit of evil from the inner part (?) of his flesh and cleanses him by the Holy Spirit."[125] Here we find an eschatological view in which flesh is not opposed to spirit but the spirit of evil to the Holy Spirit.[126] Flesh is man's total being which the Holy Spirit will one day take in complete possession. Hence the thought of the ungodly nature of flesh is not to be deduced from 1 QS 4:20 f. Yet there is an antithesis between the righteous or elect and flesh to the degree that he is exalted above it; 1 QH 15:16 f.: "And thou hast lifted up his (the righteous') glory over flesh; but offenders hast thou created for the times of thine anger."[127] In this instance flesh is not all creation in its corruptibility[128] but the ungodly part of man. Hence the concept "flesh" has here a negative connotation as compared with 1 QS 4:20 f.

The same idea is found where the righteous comes before God in prayer and either reckons himself among sinners or differentiates himself from carnal being. In 1 QS 11:9 the elect calls himself a sinner in the words: "But I belong to the men of ungodliness and the fellowship of the flesh of iniquity." In other words, the elect is in his whole being an ungodly man or an erring creature. For this reason he may stumble. But he is certain of the divine pardon: "When I stumble through the sinfulness of the flesh, my pardon remains for ever through the righteousness of God," 1 QS 11:12.[129] Here the sinfulness of the flesh is simply the sinfulness of human life. Since sinfulness is identical with defective insight into the divine mysteries, it can be said of man in his creatureliness that he is a "carnal spirit," 1 QS 13:13 f.: "and the spirit of flesh cannot understand all this."[130] As a carnal spirit man is also "born of woman" (ילוד אשה), a "creature of dust" (מבנה עפר), a "thing of water" (מגבל מים), one over whom the "corrupt spirit" (רוח נעוה) rules, → 114, 9 ff. Only through God's goodness is man justified and saved, and the Spirit God gives the elect or the servant imparts the awareness that God's works are right and His Word stands fast irrevocably, → lines 8 ff. The member of the community is thus grateful that God has not planted "carnal

---

[124] ובתמימי דרך יתמו כול גויי רשעה; Yadin, 340 f.; cf. also 1 QM 15:2: "destruction for each nation of ungodliness."

[125] וזקק לו מבני (= מבנה) איש להתם כול רוח עולה מתכמו בשרו ולטהרו ברוח קודש. On the above interpretation, which in its rendering of the difficult תכמי בשרו as "the inner part of his flesh or body" relies on Y. Yadin "A Note on DSD, IV, 20 (= 1 Q 4:20)," JBL, 74 (1955), 41-43, cf. Licht, 106; 1 QH 5:28; also F. Nötscher, "Zur theolog. Terminologie d. Qumran-Texte," Bonner bibl. Beiträge, 10 (1956), 85, n. 17. But cf. for a different view J. T. Milik, DJD, I, 139 f. on 1 Q 36, Fr., 14, 2: בתכמי בשר; on מבני איש = איש מבנה איש cf. 1 QH 13:15: מבנה עפר "thing of dust" for corruptible man.

[126] Cf. 1 QH 5:14 f.: רק אתה]ברא[ותה צדיק; Licht, 196.

[127] ותרם מבשר כבודו ורשעים בראתה לוקצי חר]ונכה; cf. Licht, 197.

[128] So Huppenbauer, 299, who relates בשר to corruptible creatures and thus overlooks the material context.

[129] ואם אכשול בעוון בשר משפטי בצדקת אל תעמוד לנצחים; cf. Schulz, 158-167.

[130] ול]וא רוח בשר להבין בכול אלה; cf. Licht, 182, but for a different view Dupont-Sommer, 86: ... . ומה הוא]ה רוח בשר. But Sukenik, Plate 47 favours Licht's reconstruction. On רוח בשר cf. also 1 QH 17:25.

striving" within him, 1 QH 10:22 f.: "thou hast not permitted that I rely on gain, and my heart [does not desire] wealth [attained by violence], and thou hast not given me the striving of the flesh," [131] → 121, 9 ff.

6. Flesh and Spirit.

The situation thus far may be summed up as follows. Apart from passages in which the concept flesh is neutral, man both collectively and individually is flesh in his total creaturely existence. Bound up with this term is his creatureliness, his sinfulness, and his defective understanding of God's saving acts and plan of election. But nowhere is it even probable that the flesh is in conflict with the spirit. Denoting man's total personality, the flesh is rather the field of battle between the Holy Spirit and the spirit of iniquity. Only at the end of the days will this conflict between light and darkness, graphically depicted in 1 QS 3:13-4:24, be decided. Only then will the man whom God has chosen be finally purified in his totality. The material thus far available does not justify us in saying that the flesh belongs in principle to the ungodly sphere, nor that the flesh or the body is a prison for the human soul which keeps man back from true knowledge of God or ecstatic experience. All the indications are that the anthropological ideas of the Qumran community follow the ancient paths. [132] The thinking in antitheses, e.g., spirit of evil and Holy Spirit, need not be traced back to Iranian influence alone. It finds a precedent in the priestly thinking of Israel, → VI, 389, 30 ff.

II. The Usage in the Targums.

Recent discoveries have made it more than likely that the oldest parts of the Targumic literature are pre-Chr. [133] and in the first instance are not related at all to Pharisaic Rabbinism. Since this means that the theology and anthropology found here bear some features which do not correspond exactly to the dogmatic ideas which established themselves as normative in the Synagogue from the 2nd cent. A.D. onwards, [134] it seems advisable to treat the Tg. separately rather than within the context of the Rabbinic writings.

In the Tg. [135] the term flesh (בשרא, בסרא) is used in the same way as in the Qumran texts thus far available. The anthropology does not advance beyond the then Heb. original. Thus neutrally the word means "all living creatures" (כל בשרא Pal. Tg. N. I

---

[131] ולא נתתה משעני על בצע ובהון [חמס לא יאוה ל]בי ויצר בשר לא שמתה לי; Licht, 156.

[132] So rightly Nötscher, op. cit. (→ n. 125), 85 f.; cf. also Huppenbauer, 299 f.

[133] Thus there is ancient Targumic material on Gn. 14:1-15:4 in the Gn. Midrash from Cave 1 of Qumran, col., 2, 19-22 (N. Avigad-Y. Yadin, A Genesis Apocryphon [1956]), which in its present form is to be put in the 1st cent. B.C., but which is undoubtedly based on one or more older versions. Linguistically cf. P. Kahle, The Cairo Geniza[2] (1959), 198-200.

[134] To understand the Targumic literature it should be noted that Tg. O., which is from Babylon, is in its present normative form the end-product of a long, dogmatically controlled process, and that it made its way definitively into the Targumic lit. of Palestine only from about 1000 A.D.; cf. Kahle, op. cit., 191-195. Our knowledge of the latter was decisively enriched when A. Diez Macho found in the Vatican Library a complete 16th cent. MS of the Palestinian Tg. on the Pent. Thanks to the generosity of P. Kahle I have had at my disposal a photostat of this significant find which is called Pal. Tg. N. I in what follows (Palestinian Targum Neofiti I). On this cf. provisionally Kahle, op. cit., 201 f.

[135] Cf. on what follows Str.-B., III, 331.

[→ n. 134], Tg. O. on Gn. 7:21: כָּל־בָּשָׂר) or "all men" (כל בני בסרא) Tg. Pro. on Is. 40:3 : (כָּל־בָּשָׂר) → 111, 1 ff. Yet it carries a stress on man's mortality and his creaturely distance from God, usually along the lines of the Heb. original → 107, 16 ff.; cf. Tg. Ps. 78:39, where "sons of flesh" or "fleshly" is used for "merely mortal men," [136] or Tg. J. I on Dt. 5:26 (23): "For where is any son of flesh (הי דין כל בר בישרא) who could hear the voice of the memrah of the living God out of the midst of the fire as we have, and remain alive?" [137] Since flesh denotes man or mankind in general, it is possible to take the term in different ways acc. to the individual hermeneutical situation. Thus Is. 40:6 : "All flesh (כָּל־הַבָּשָׂר) is as grass," is rendered in Tg. Pro., ad loc. by "all the ungodly (כל רשיעיא) are as grass," [138] but Is. 66:24: "They will be a scandal to all flesh" (לְכָל־בָּשָׂר) is paraphrased: "Until the righteous (צדיקיא for כָּל־בָּשָׂר) shall say with reference to them, We have seen enough." [139] On the other hand, flesh can also be used primarily for man in his nature as a sinful and arrogant creature. Thus Gn. 6:3 bases the restriction of man's life to 120 years quite factually on his being only flesh or a creature, [140] but Pal. Tg. N. I says: "Since they are flesh and their works are evil, lo, I will give them a life-span of 120 years." [141] The establishment of this maximum of 120 years [142] is thus presented as a divine judgment on the flesh and its sinful acts. In this case, too, the flesh is the whole man. It is unlikely that there is in the Tg. any distinction of flesh and spirit along the lines of anthropological dichotomy → 117, 40 ff. Nor is there any assigning of the flesh specifically to the sphere of hostility to God.

III. Flesh and Body in the Talmud and Midrash.

1. In the Talmud and Midrash, as in the Dead Sea Scrolls and the Targums, the concept flesh (בשר, בסרא, בשרא), apart from its other functions, refers to man in his collective and individual existence. The 'Alenu prayer is an instance of the collective use: [143] "Thus we hope in thee ... that ... the world may be ordered by the kingly rule of the Almighty, and that all men (וְכָל־בְּנֵי בָשָׂר) may call upon thy name." [144] Flesh is used in the sense of bodily ego or person in bBB, 17a, Bar., where Ps. 16:9 : "My flesh (בְּשָׂרִי) also shall dwell secure," is quoted to show that David, too, is one of the righteous over whom the worm and corruption have no power. [145]

---

[136] HT בָּשָׂר, whose meaning is established by what follows: "a breath which passes away and does not return."

[137] HT מִי כָל־בָּשָׂר cf. Tg. O.: מָן כָּל בִּשְׂרָא "who among all men." Cf. also Tg. J. I on Nu. 23:19, where the unchanging nature of God's works is contrasted with the fickle works of the sons of flesh (בני בשרא), Str.-B., II, 423 f.

[138] Cf. also Tg. Pro. on Zech. 2:17: the passing away of all the ungodly (כל רשיעיא), HT of all flesh (כָּל־בָּשָׂר).

[139] Str.-B., III, 331 shows emphatically that כל בשר is "ethically absolutely neutral" in the above context.

[140] לֹא־יָדוֹן רוּחִי בָאָדָם לְעֹלָם בְּשַׁגַּם הוּא בָשָׂר וְהָיוּ יָמָיו מֵאָה וְעֶשְׂרִים שָׁנָה; in the Targums and LXX the form בְּשַׁגַּם is always construed as a conjunction "because."

[141] מן בגלל דאינון בשר ועובדיהון בישין; cf. on this Tg. J. II (ed. M. Ginsburger [1899], 7) and Tg. O. ארכא מאה ועשרין שנין (for לכון דאינון בשר ועובדיהון בישין הא יהיבת להון).

[142] Reaching this age is dependent on man's repentance; hence Pal. Tg. N. I, ad loc.: דילמא דיעבדון תתובה ולא עבדו and cf. Tg. J. II; Tg. O. only אִם יְתוּבוּן.

[143] On this prayer, traced back to the Bab. Rab (d. 247 A.D.), cf. J. Elbogen, Der jüd. Gottesdienst in seiner geschichtlichen Entwicklung³ (1931), 8 f., 143; cf. also Dalman WJ, I, 307 and Str.-B., III, 331.

[144] Cf. Siddur Oṣar ha-Tefillot (1914), 435 f.

[145] Str.-B., I, 755; on the idea of the existence of the dead in the grave or sheol, which rests on ancient anthropological notions, cf. Meyer, 1-13.

2. Especially characteristic of Rabbinic usage is the fact that on the one side man is called flesh and blood but on the other flesh in the sense of body or person is replaced by the term גּוּף.

a. The description of man as "flesh and blood" is older than Rabbinism. It is rooted in the widespread Semitic tendency to express complex phenomena by two complementary terms. In illustration one might refer in Old Canaanite-Ugaritic to "ruler sea" and "judge river" for water as the ancient power of chaos, [146] and in Hebrew to "heaven and earth" for the cosmos (Gn. 1:1) or "waste and void" for chaos (Gn. 1:2). "Flesh and blood" as an expression for man refers to man's external life and also to his existence as a living creature, which is guaranteed by blood (→ I, 173, 13 ff.) as the sap of life. From the very outset, then, the idea of mortality and creatureliness seems to be especially bound up with the phrase, cf. Sir. 14:18 (Heb.): "Like the buds on a sprouting tree, of which one decays and the other opens, so are the generations of flesh and blood ; the one perishes and the other grows up." [147]

In the same way the Rabb. use the expression "flesh and blood" chiefly where the corruptible nature of man — usually in a conclusion *a minori ad maius* — is compared with the eternity and omnipotence of God : jBer., 9 (13b, 1): "If he who depends on flesh and blood (i.e., another man) is delivered, how much more he who depends on God." Well-known are the many royal parables in which an earthly king (מלך בשר ודם) is the counterpart of God as the heavenly king, [148] → 109, 27 f.

b. It is significant for the development of Jewish anthropology, however, that the word flesh, used alone, gives place to גּוּף, which is to be regarded as a derivate of the root *gup*, found in Arab. and meaning "to be hollow." [149] Found in the OT only in 1 Ch. 10:12 as גּוּפָה* "corpse," [150] *guf* acquires an extraordinarily wide range of meaning in Middle Hebrew and Aram., e.g., "cavity," "hollow place," [151] "body." [152] Hence גּוּף can mean "person," cf. bQid., 37a f., where a legal religious duty which is connected with the person and is to be discharged everywhere (חובת הגוף) is distinguished from that which is bound exclusively to Palestine (חובת הארץ). Like נֶפֶשׁ and בָּשָׂר in the OT and עֶצֶם "bone" in Middle Heb. גּוּף can also be used as a pronoun : גופה של פתילה "the wick itself," jShab., 2 (5a, 23).

3. From all that may be said on the basis of the examples, the transition from the older "flesh" to the later "body" is connected with the change in anthro-

---

[146] Cf., e.g., Text 68, 7 and 14 etc. (*Gordon Manual*, 150); cf. also G. D. Young, *Concordance of Ugaritic, Analecta Orientalia*, 36 (1956), s.v. zbl I (594). ṯpṭ (2061).

[147] כפרח עץ רענן... כן דורות בשר ודם אחד גוע ואחד גומל; cf. Sir. 17:31 f. and Wis. 12:5.

[148] Cf. Str.-B., I, 730 f.

[149] Cf. Arab. ğauf "hollow," "belly"; Ges.-Buhl, Köhler-Baumg., s.v. גּוּף, גּוּפָה.

[150] גְּוִיָּה is used for this in 1 S. 31:12. גּוּף does not yet seem to be attested in Qumran ; cf. K. G. Kuhn, *Rückläufiges Hbr. Wörterbuch* (1958), s.v.

[151] The idea of a "hollow place" in the sense of the Gk. κοιλία (→ III, 786-789), "stomach," "womb," may underlie bJeb., 62a f., which says that pre-existently created souls wait for their embodiment in the heavenly chamber *guf* : "The Messiah will not come until all the souls in *guf* are brought out" : עד שיכלו כל הנשמות שבגוף. To the *guf* in which souls live before their earthly sojourn correspond the heavenly chambers of rest (4 Esr. 7:78 ff.) or the chamber of rest אוצר in Qoh. r. on 3:21 (ed. Vilna [1887], 12c.), which after the completion of their life on earth preserve the souls of the righteous from the "naked" disembodied existence of the wicked, who must roam about the world as spirits which can find no rest, Meyer, 53-56, 61, n. 6.

[152] On this whole question, and on the many transf. meanings such as "essence," "main point," "capital," "cardinal doctrine," "male member," cf. Levy Wört., s.v.

pological ideas observable from about the 2nd century B.C. Whereas flesh as used from the canonical writings to the Dead Sea Scrolls and the Targums normally embraces man as a total person, body carries with it from the very first the idea of something hollow or empty and needing to be filled. But according to later anthropology, whose presuppositions are to be found in the Hellenistic-Oriental world around Judaism, the body is filled by a soul (→ ψυχή) which, though thought of corporeally and personally, is at any rate invisible to the human eye. From the standpoint of religious history it is especially significant that the Pharisaic Rabbinic wise men were the ones who adopted the new anthropology which stood in antithesis to ancient traditions, and who organically integrated it into their theological system (→ Φαρισαῖος).

One is not to think of the new body-soul anthropology as a complete break from the older idea of man as a unity. This idea remains, and there can still be speculation on the concept of flesh and its creaturely corruptibility and ethical ambivalence. Thus R. Jochanan b. Nappacha (d. 279 A.D.) breaks up the corresponding terms אָדָם "man" and בָּשָׂר "flesh" as follows : aleph = אֵפֶר "dust," daleth = דָּם "blood" and mem = מְרָה "recalcitrance"; beth = בּוּשָׁה "shame," samech (for schin) = סְרוּחָה "corruption" and resh = רִמָּה "worm." [153] Another tradition in the same context regards the schin in בשר as an abbreviation for שְׁאוֹל "underworld" as the place to which all flesh finally goes → 120, 31.

But the decisive anthropological speculations are connected with גּוּף, which in relation to בָּשָׂר represents only the muscular part → 99, 2 ff.; 105, 23 ff.

In this connection גּוּף is also related to the "drop which reeks of decay" (טִפָּה סְרוּחָה), i.e., the male seed as the germ cell of the body. Thus in the probably Tannaitic Haggada jKil., 8, 3 (31c, 40-42) there is the following speculation on the constitution of man as body and soul : "The white comes from the male, for from him are the brain, skeleton and sinews. The red comes from the woman, for from her are the skin, the flesh and the blood. But the spirit, the breath and the soul come from the Holy One, blessed be He. All three have a share in Him." [154] The elements thus shown to be necessary form an earthly portion which the parents pass on to the new individual and a heavenly and lifegiving part which is given by God Himself. If in accordance with the poetic form of the haggada the latter is divided into spirit, breath and soul, the reference is simply to the personal soul. Speculation about the basic materials of the body, in which flesh and blood belong to the feminine part, come down from the pre-Socratics (→ 100, 19 ff.) through Gk. philosophy, and it may be assumed that the Rabb. are dependent here on the surrounding intellectual world. The same applies to the rise of man from a "drop" which acc. to the Rabb. view has from the very first the character of corruption. This idea, first intimated in Job 10:10, [155] goes back to Aristot. acc. to our sources. [156]

This body, however, does not merely stand in cosmic-dualistic tension to God by reason of its creatureliness, like flesh on the older view. By nature it is also different from the soul. Man is thus a dichotomy → VI, 377, 33 ff.; he is so in

---

[153] ;א״ר יוחנן אד״ם אפ״ר ד״ם מר״ה בש״ר בוש״ה סרוח״ה רמ״ה, איכא דאמרי שאול דכתיב בשין bSota, 5a.
[154] Meyer, 15-25.
[155] Cf. Wis. 7:1; Meyer, 34 and n. 2.
[156] Cf. J. Preuss, Bibl.-talmudische Medizin (1911), 448.

such a way that by nature soul and body belong to two different and antithetical spheres. [157] This is particularly well stated in S. Dt., 305 on 33:2 : "All creatures created from heaven derive both soul and body from heaven, and all creatures created from earth derive both soul and body from earth. Man is an exception : his soul derives from heaven and his body from earth. If, then, man keeps the law and will of his Father in heaven, lo, he is as the upper creatures ... But if he does not keep the law and will of his Father in heaven, lo, he is as the lower creatures." [158] By nature, then, man belongs to both the upper and the lower world. Hence he has the qualities both of ministering angels on the one side and cattle on the other, bChag., 16a Bar. If he does not keep the divine will he sinks to the level of lower creatures and is carnally minded, even though the expression is not used. [159]

There thus arises an antithesis between the pure heavenly soul [160] and the body, which on the basis of its earthly character inclines to ungodliness. To the ethical dualism of body and soul, which is common in the Hellenistic-Oriental world around Judaism, corresponds on the other side the idea that by night the soul brings man new powers from above : "This soul fills the body, and in the hour when man sleeps it rises up and fetches him life from above." [161] According to this view it is also the soul which in dreams gives men knowledge of future events, since it leaves the body by night and wanders about in the world. [162]

From what has been said, however, it should not be concluded that uncontested acceptance of Hellenistic ideas in Rabbinic anthropology led to a consistent dualism such as that found in Alexandrian theology. [163] Traditional unitary thinking obviously had a decisive influence on Rabbinic speculation. According to this the world is the only theatre of the crucial encounter between God and man. This idea, along with the strong eschatological expectation that the final goal, whether for salvation or eternal perdition, is the reuniting of body and soul after a period in the intermediate state, [164] sets a limit to the popular dualism rooted in the Hellenistic-Oriental world. [165] In the Last Judgment man receives sentence as a total person according to his acts in the life of the body. The body may belong to the lower world and the soul to the upper world. The soul, when embodied in earthly life and put to the test in the body, may in its quality as

---

[157] Meyer, 25-31. Cf. → 109, 8 ff.

[158] The author is the Tannaite Simai (c. 200 A.D.); cf. Bacher Tannaiten, II, 544; Meyer, 27 f.

[159] The rare adj. בְּשָׂרָנִי "fleshy" is used in the sense of "stout"; cf. bKet., 61a and Levy Wört., s.v. No adj. was formed from גּוּף.

[160] Cf. on this Meyer, 63-68.

[161] The author is R. Meïr (c. 150 A.D.) Gn. r., 14, 9 on 2:19 par.; cf. Bacher Tannaiten, II, 64; Meyer, 51.

[162] PREl, 24; cf. on this already Jos. Bell., 7, 343 ff.; Meyer, 50 f.

[163] Meyer, 31 f., 145 f.

[164] An aphorism of Aqabiah b. Mahalalel in Ab., 3, 1 refers to judgment directly after death : "Direct your attention to three things and you will not come under the power of transgression. Know whence you have come and before whom you must give account : Whence do you come ? From a drop reeking of corruption. Whither do you go ? To the maggots and worms. Before whom must you give account ? Before the King of all kings, blessed be He"; cf. Meyer, 33.

[165] Cf. the illustrated interpretation of Ez. 37 in the synagogue of Dura-Europos (3rd cent. A.D.); R. Meyer, "Betrachtungen zu drei Fresken d. Synagoge v. Dura-Europos," ThLZ, 74 (1949), 35-38; The Excavations at Dura-Europos. Final Report VIII, Part I : C. H. Kraeling, The Synagogue (1956), 178-202.

a pure heavenly being start back in horror from the "drop" which sends forth corruption. [166] Nevertheless, in the Last Judgment the two will have to render an account in concert. Thus in bSanh., 91b, at the end of a debate between "Antoninus" and the patriarch Jehuda II (c. 190 A.D.), we read : "The holy One, blessed be He, will fetch the soul and set it in the body and then judge them both together." [167]

Meyer

IV. The Apocrypha and Pseudepigrapha.

1. The usage found in the LXX still occurs. [168] Man is made of bones and flesh, Test. S. 6:2; Joseph and Asenath, 16 (→ n. 168), p. 64 → 124, 27. The expression "flesh and blood" occurs in Jub. 7:14; 21:10, at sacrifice, 7:28, in description of the human body, → I, 172, 18 ff. → 109, 27 f.; 120, 28 f.; 121, 23 f. We read of circumcision of the flesh in Jub. 15:13 f. → 108, 21 ff. The phrase "all flesh" is common in Jub.; [169] Eth. En. 1:9; 61:12; Test. Jud. 24:4 [?]; Test. G. 7:2; Apc. Eliae 18:10; Apc. Esr. 7:7 (p. 32). In this lit., too, we do not at first find any negatively tinged linking of the word with sexuality or the pleasures of eating. A wife is her husband's "own flesh," Vit. Ad. 3 → 109, 26; 122, 31 f. In Jub. 16:5 illicit sexual intercourse with "one's own flesh" is condemned. [170] Perhaps for the first time in Apc. Mos. sexual union generally is evaluated as ἁμαρτία τῆς σαρκός. [171]

2. But a development seen already in the LXX (→ 109, 8 ff.; 120, 21 ff.) is more clearly discernible here. God and man are distinguished with increasing strength, and indeed in such a way that this distinction seems to be linked with the cosmological one between heaven and earth, the sphere of spirits and that of flesh. In Eth. En. the situation is at first exactly the same as in the OT. The fact that all flesh is judged by God (1:9) [172] does not mean that all flesh is sinful, for in the similitudes all flesh can also be said to praise God (61:12). When it is said in 14:21 that no flesh can see God, this goes beyond the OT only to the degree that the same is also said of angels. This shows that while man as flesh is distinguished from non-fleshly beings he is also with them set in the antithesis of creature to Creator. The distinction between carnal and spiritual beings is thus made, but it is not decisive. The limitation of man does not rest

---

[166] Cf. Tanch. פקודי 3 (1927), 344 ff. par.; Meyer, 88-93.

[167] Cf. on this whole question, Str.-B., I, 581.

[168] Purely neutral "human flesh" Eth. En. 7:5; Jub. 3:5; 4 Esr. 15:58 (carnes); Test. Job (ed. M. R. James, TSt, V, 1 [1897]) 13 (σάρκες); Apc. Elias Heb. p. 21, 2 (בשר and דם) "Animal flesh" Test. Jud. 21:8 (σάρκες); cf. Sib., 3, 790 f.; κρέας in Test. Abr. A 6 (83, 12); Demetrius in Eus. Praep. Ev., IX, 21, 14; Ezekiel, *ibid.*, 29, 12; Jos. and Asenath 10 (ed. P. Batiffol, *Studia patristica*, 1/2 [1889/90] 52, 14); Ps.-Phocylides, 137. Everywhere except in Jub. 3:5 = Gn. 2:21 the ref. is to flesh which is consumed.

[169] Note should be taken of 7:32 : "Give not the soul to eat with blood, that your own blood be not demanded by the hand of all the flesh which it spills on the earth." This abbreviated statement can be understood only in the light of Gn. 9:4-6. As a punishment for eating blood death threatens at the hand of the murderer, who for his part is then punished by God. "All flesh," then, does not mean the whole human race but is defined by the relative clause. Is the choice of expression also influenced by the closeness of flesh and sin ? Or is it an accidental echoing of phrases from Gn. 9:5 ?

[170] Acc. to 20:5 this cannot be "with their body" (E. Littmann in Kautzsch Apkr. u. Pseudepigr.) but must refer to the homosexuality characteristic of the inhabitants of Sodom and Gomorrah (Str.-B., III, 785 f.) or to sexual intercourse within the forbidden degrees (→ 122, 30 f.), of which 16:8 is a blatant example, cf. Damasc. 5:7-9 (7:9-11).

[171] But this interpretation is by no means certain, Lindijer, 79.

[172] Also transmitted in Gk. Cf. Damasc. 2:20 (3:6).

on his materiality. [173] One may see the same in the visions, 84:4-6. Here it is certainly said that the flesh of man provokes God's wrath. But it is also said that the angels in heaven are sinful. The tendency, then, is to emphasise God's uniqueness in relation to the world of both men and angels, to contrast Him as the only pure One with the fallen world, [174] though not to drop the ethical distinction between sinners and righteous.

The situation is very different in the angelological section 15:4-16:1. The sin of the "watchers of heaven" is that as "holy and eternal spirits" they defiled themselves with the blood of women and with the blood of flesh gave birth to flesh and blood, 15:4 → 109, 27 f. [175] Hence the giants who arose from them were born "of spirits and flesh" (15:8) and spirits proceed from the "soul of their flesh" (16:1). [176] In the Gk. text of 106:17 the giants born of the union of angels with the daughters of men are described as οὐχ ὅμοιοι πνεύμασι ἀλλὰ σάρκ<ιν>οι. [177]

Anthropological dualism may also be seen here. Acc. to the Eth. text of 17:6, which is probably original, Hades is the place where all flesh goes → 117, 19 f. But in the Gk. version we read : "... where no flesh goes." Here the expression "all flesh" is no longer understood as a Semitism for humanity but is taken as a substantial statement — a typical example of the change of meaning in transl. For the translator Hades is thus a sphere which is distinct from that of flesh. In death man sets aside his flesh, → 102, 13 ff. This is stated explicitly in 102:5. ψυχαί go to Hades while the σῶμα τῆς σαρκός characterises the earthly period. [178]

3. The cosmological antithesis is esp. clear in Jub., where the realm of spirits is distinct from that of carnal beings. [179] The two spheres are now plainly equated with heaven and earth. [180] In later writings the distinction between the two realms becomes ever sharper. Pure spirits have no body, Apc. Abr. 19. They are πνεῦμα, man is σάρκινος, Test. Job 27. Flesh is essentially defined by its substantiality. To be flesh is to belong to the earth, to dust, not to heaven, ibid. 38; 36; Sib. Fr., 1, 1 (θνητοὶ καὶ σάρκινοι), 13 f. → 102, 1. Bearing σάρξ, man cannot see what a spiritual being sees, Apc. Esr. 3:1 (p. 27); 4:4 (p. 28). Since he is σάρξ καὶ αἷμα (→ 109, 27), he cannot bear the δόξα of a ὑψηλὸν πνεῦμα which is not of this world, i.e., of death, Test. Abr. B 13 (117, 26). Hence one cannot see God with eyes of flesh but must see Him in the spirit, 4 (5) Esr. 1, 37 → 124, 20 f.; 148, 31 f., 10 f.

4. The last passage again mingles cosmic dualism with an anthropological dualism which is more strongly rooted in Gk. thought. Where OT influence is powerful, there is hope of the resurrection of the flesh → n. 98. [181] Acc. to Paral. Jer. 6:6 the σάρξ

---

[173] Cf. 61:12 : "every spirit of light ... and all flesh shall praise God"; 81:2 : "those born of flesh."

[174] Cf. statements like S. Bar. 44:9; 4 Esr. 7:11 f., 20-24, 46-48, 68, 116-126; 8:17, 35; Apc. Esr. 5 (p. 30), though "flesh" is not used.

[175] Acc. to 15:7 the spirits dwell in heaven where there are no women, cf. Mk. 12:25. On the text cf. the apparatus and notes in R. H. Charles, The Apocrypha and Pseudepigr. of the OT (1913), ad loc.

[176] A Gk. MS alters to "from their soul as from flesh." In 15:9 it reads : ἀπὸ τοῦ σώματος τῆς σαρκὸς αὐτῶν. Soul of σάρξ (as of bones, sinews etc.) also in Apocr. Johannis 49:15 (ed. W. Till, Die gnostischen Schriften d. kopt. Pap. Berolinensis 8502, TU, 60 [1955]).

[177] The Eth. text (G. Beer in Kautzsch Apokr. u. Pseudepigr.: "begot giants not acc. to the spirit but acc. to the flesh") is secondary.

[178] Eth. text : soul and body. Cf. also 108:11: the spirits of the good which are not rewarded in their flesh.

[179] Jub. 2:2, 11: Spirits are created on the first day, the first fleshly creatures on the fifth.

[180] Jub. 2:30 : "They kept sabbath in heaven before it was shown all flesh to keep sabbath on earth."

[181] Cf. Apc. Mos. 13 (πᾶσα σάρξ); Apc. Elias Heb. 22:6 ff. (based on Ez. 37); S. Bar. 50; also Ezekiel in Epiph. Haer., 64, 70, 6 : judgment on body and soul → 119, 2 ff.

remains incorruptible, [182] though the body is regarded in 9:11-13 as the σαρκικὸς οἶκος of the καρδία from which this is removed, 6:3. We find an intermediate view in Apc. Eliae 35:7 f.; 42:12 f.: the flesh of the body is put off, the spiritual flesh (σάρκες πνεύματος → 148, 31 f.) is put on. [183] The idea gains in strength that man is a dual creature consisting of flesh and spirit; alongside the μέλη belonging to the σάρξ (→ n. 284) is the πνεῦμα of man, Test. Abr. A 20 (103, 6 f.). [184] Indeed, the soul can be thought of as enclosed in the body (Apc. Shadrach 11 [185] → 103, 12 f.; 122, 21 ff.) and loosed from it at death (Vit. Ad. 43; 4 Esr. 7:78, 100; cf. 88 [186] → 117, 40 ff.; 123, 10).

5. A few indications may be found of the combining of flesh and sin. In this respect two different roots are to be distinguished. Where anthropological dualism holds sway, we find ascetic tendencies aimed at binding the flesh to achieve freedom for the spirit. Renunciation of bodily enjoyment may be combined with the idea that in the last time, as in the first, purely vegetarian nourishment suffices. [187] Abstinence from meat and wine is, of course, a rejection of luxury. [188] Along these lines sexual intercourse as such possibly becomes sin → 119, 18 f. The situation is different in Test. XII. The radical antithesis between the divine and heavenly sphere on the one side and the human and earthly on the other leads to the according of a central position to statements like Gn. 6:12; Job 4:17 ff.; 15:14 ff.; 25:4 ff. Mankind as a whole has fallen. It is not just weak, mortal, or limited. [189] It is also delivered up to the seducing of spirits which as non-bodily beings are stronger. "They are flesh and the spirits of seduction mislead them," Test. Zeb. 9:7. [190] Hence the limitation of human knowledge is also connected with sin: "ignorant like a man and corrupted in sins like flesh," Test. Jud. 19:4 → 112, 15 ff. Later writers put it even more strongly: "I am a thing of flesh and blood (→ 109, 27 f.), I know my filth and my sin," Test. Isaac (→ n. 188), Fol. 14 recto.

V. Philo and Josephus.

1. Philo is not easy to assess, since different traditions mix in him. He is pulled hither and thither between the OT and Gk. philosophy. [191], [192] In spite of some restraints

---

[182] *The Rest of the Words of Baruch,* ed. J. Rendel Harris (1889). Cf. also E. König, "Der Rest d. Worte Baruchs," ThStKr, 50 (1877), 327 f. Cf. the idea in Test. Abr. B 7 (112, 3): πᾶσα σάρξ ἐγερθήσεται, but the σῶμα is put off in the intermediate state.
[183] Cf. the transl. of Steindorff, p. 169. But cf. Apc. Eliae 36:18-37:1: The Lord takes to himself spirit and soul, the flesh becomes (stone?).
[184] In the underworld the Egypt. sun-god bears only his "flesh" without his soul, H. Bonnet, *Reallex. d. ägypt. Religionsgesch.* (1952), 19.
[185] ὦ ψυχή, τί γάρ σε ἐνέβαλεν εἰς τὸ ταπεινὸν καὶ ταλαίπωρον σῶμα, ed. J. A. Robinson, TSt, II, 3 (1893), 134, 33 f.
[186] *Exibit anima de corpore, recedente inspiratione* (Syr. "breath"?) *de corpore, (animae) separatae de corporibus.* If P. Riessler, "Jos. u. Asenath," *Theol. Quart.,* 103 (1922), 8 f. is right, we have in Jos. and Asenath an allegory on the soul imprisoned in the body.
[187] Cf. H. Bardtke and K. G. Kuhn, Art. "Askese," RGG³, I, 641 f.; Is. 11:6 ff.; Gn. 1:29 f.; 9:2 ff.
[188] 4 Esr. 9:24 to prepare for revelation; T. Schermann, "Propheten- u. Apostellegenden," TU, 31, 3 (1907), 95, 16 (κρέας); Test. Isaac, ed. J. A. Robinson, TSt, II, 2 (1892), Folio 13 verso. But bSanh., 59b (Str.-B., I, 138) says the angels cooked meat and strained out wine for the first man in Paradise. Cf. also Jub. 49:6, 12, 20; Test. R. 1:10.
[189] Gn. 6:3 (→ 115, 13 ff.) is also important. It flesh is taken to mean sinful being here, this may be due to the influence of the reading "on account of their aberrations." There is an echo of this in the adj. carnales in Ps.-Philo Antiquitates Biblicae, 3, 2 (ed. G. Kisch [1949]).
[190] MS α: "... and they are misled."
[191] On his dependence on Gk. tradition cf. A. J. Festugière, *La révélation d'Hermès Trismégiste,* II (1949), 533-544; W. Bousset, *Jüd.-chr. Schulbetrieb in Alexandria u. Rom* (1915), 47 f., 56 thinks the positive estimation of πάθη and ἡδονή is a tradition of the schools.
[192] Cf. Jonas Gnosis, II, 1, 74; S. Sandmel, *Philo's Place in Judaism* (1956), 1-29. Neither

due to his Jewish origin, he has for the most part a negative view of σάρξ. [193] For him, too, it is the seat of αἴσθησις, Rer. Div. Her., 71; Agric., 97; Leg. All., II, 41; Abr., 164, closely related to the πάθη and ἡδονή, Leg. All., III, 158; Gig., 35 and 40. These are ignoble and irrational and enslave the νοῦς. [194] Yet he is cautious in tracing back sin to the σάρξ. [195] Philo can take the fall to mean that the bodily desire kindled by the woman led to sin, Op. Mund., 151 f., 155 f., 164 → n. 195. He can say that the body with its passions inclines man to sin, Plant., 43; Rer. Div. Her., 296. Egypt is the embodiment of the desire and lust which enter through the senses, Congr., 81. Hence Philo, like the opponents of Epicurus (→ 104, 16 ff.), can refer to gluttony and sexual indulgence as the causes of evil. [196] Yet Philo is also aware that it is the soul which has ἄλογα πάθη and which gives rise to evil, though only when the flesh has power over it. [197] The σάρκινος ὄγκος, like sandals on the feet, can also be impressed into service, Sacr. AC, 63. This is simply to say that Philo's anthropology is much more complicated than the original antithesis of σῶμα and ψυχή. [198] The decisive thing for him is to maintain the freedom of the will to choose between good and evil and not to find an excuse in the physical constitution of man. [199] This is connected with the insight that in some sense the soul, too, belongs to the body [200] and that the true union of God and man takes place beyond body and soul [201] → VI, 396, 2 ff. At this pt. good OT insights exert an influence.

Yet a second strand of thought may be seen which is to be understood more against the background of cosmic (→ 109, 8 ff.) rather than anthropological dualism. God is for Philo a non-fleshly, non-corporeal being. [202] Hence He may be known only by friends of the soul who can set aside the husk of the flesh; for the soul, too, is non-fleshly and non-corporeal. [203] Thus the body or the flesh is for the soul a burden, bondage, coffin, or urn. It is a corpse which it lugs around with it. [204] Hence it must come out of Egypt, the body; this is possible for man in ecstasy, Migr. Abr., 14; Som., II, 232. Here the flesh is simply the physical part of man which hampers the flight of the soul and the growth of wisdom. Thus the servants of the spirit must become pale and as it were non-corporeal beings who are almost skeletons, setting aside everything that is dear to the flesh, Spec. Leg., IV, 114; Gig., 30; Mut. Nom., 32 f. Freeing from the flesh in ecstasy is essential, not because the flesh leads to sin, but because it prevents the non-material soul from soaring up to the heavenly heights of God. If, then, the

---

the Rabb. nor the Jewish apocr. tradition seems to have any essential influence on him, *ibid.*, 198 f., 210 f.

[193] For ref. cf. Schweizer *Hell. Komponente*, 246-250.

[194] Rer. Div. Her., 268; Leg. All., II, 49 f.; for further examples W. Völker, *Fortschritt u. Vollendung bei Philo v. Alex.* (1938), 80-84.

[195] Cf. W. Knuth, *Der Begriff der Sünde bei Philon v. Alex.*, Diss. Jena (1934), 23-32. Thus sexual intercourse is in Philo's view good if for procreation but bad if for desire, cf. Helmut Schmidt, *Die Anthropologie Philons v. Alex.*, Diss. Leipzig (1933), 37 f.

[196] Leg. All., III, 143 and 159; Op. Mund., 152 and 157 f., where he takes issue with Epic. (160-162). Cf. Spec. Leg., I, 192 : Eating and drinking stir up the belly and the lower desires, cf. H. A. Wolfson, *Philo* (1947), 108 f. Cf. also Leisegang, *s.v.* "Epikur."

[197] Deus Imm., 52; Rer. Div. Her., 295; Leg. All., I, 106; cf. also Knuth, *op. cit.*, 23. Sen. thinks the power of thought plays a big part in the rise of sin, Knuth, 25 f.

[198] Cf. E. R. Goodenough, *An Introduction to Philo Judaeus* (1940), 151-153.

[199] Völker, *op. cit.*, 73-79. Hence Philo never says directly that ὕλη is bad, Burton, 163-166.

[200] Det. Pot. Ins., 15 speaks of the friendship of soul and body. The senses are also viewed positively when brought under the mastery of the spirit, cf. Schmidt, *op. cit.*, 34, 70-73.

[201] Cf. Jonas Gnosis, II, 1, 103-106, 113 f.

[202] So also Epict. Diss., II, 8, 2, → 148, 23.

[203] Deus Imm., 52-56; Gig., 31. The heavenly man is non-corporeal, cf. H. Willms, *Eikon* (1935), 82 f.

[204] Gig., 31; Rer. Div. Her., 268; Migr. Abr., 16; Agric., 25; Deus Imm., 2. Cf. also the collection of examples in Schmidt, *op. cit.*, 34-36.

flesh is opposed to all piety, and carnal desire to all knowledge of God, [205] the physical antithesis is in view. Flesh is not the total man who is condemned by God, as in the OT, but the physical constitution of man which acts as a drag on the flight of the soul. Only when remaining in this physical state and refusing the flight of the soul is regarded as guilty, does this antithesis become ethically significant. [206]

2. In Joseph. σάρκες means animal flesh (Ant., 6, 120 with αἷμα; 12, 211 f. with ὀστᾶ) [207] or human flesh, Ant., 6, 186 = 1 S. 17:44. Intrepidity is manifested in the unaltered colour of the σάρξ, Ant., 15, 236. The vulnerable σάρξ is par. to σῶμα in Bell., 3, 274. The ἴδιαι σάρκες at which a raging beast flies out are its kin, Bell., 5, 4 → 109, 26. An important idea is that the ψυχή parts from the σάρξ in death, Ant., 19, 325; Bell., 6, 47. [208] Free from corruptible σώματα and passing ὕλη, ψυχαί are unencumbered by κατὰ σάρκα δεσμοί, Bell., 2, 154 f. Here Joseph. adopts a purely Gk. view and vocabulary, → 102, 33 ff. [209]

D. Historical Summary.

Completely different possibilities of understanding man presented themselves.

1. Man as a composite being may be understood in terms of his parts, → 99, 30. The problem of his unity arises afresh, e.g., in Plato (→ 103, 3 ff.), in the question as to the relation of body and soul → σῶμα, ψυχή. The Stoic attempt (→ σῶμα) to think of the soul corporeally but to distinguish between *regens* and *rectum* gives evidence of the same problem. This attempt leads directly to the terminology of Epicurus, who distinguishes the non-spiritual parts of the body as σάρξ from the διάνοια, and seeks to bring these into a rightly balanced relation, → 104, 6 ff. All these answers are at one in the fact that they try to understand man in terms of himself. He is to be grasped in terms of his nature or super-nature, of his individual parts, of the conflict of soul and body, of the intellectual centre which governs the whole, or of the feelings of the σάρξ. At any rate he is a self-contained microcosm. Here σάρξ describes the nature or substance which determines the nature of man.

2. Very different is the understanding of man in the OT sphere. Here man is seen from the very first in his relation to God. As creature of God he is flesh, always exposed to death. God's breath is his life, his soul. The will of his heart is Yes or No to God's commandment. Man is understood in terms of his relationship, not his nature. He is what he is in relation. Thus flesh is his situation before God. When he is viewed in this way, he can no longer be split up into a divine part and an earthly part. If there is to be a distinction, it can only be between God and man, heaven and earth. That is, only cosmic dualism is conceivable.

---

[205] Som., II, 67; Deus Imm., 143; Rer. Div. Her., 57 (αἷμα καὶ σαρκὸς ἡδονή).
[206] Cf. Leg. All., III, 152 : the soul which leaves the sacred houses of virtue turns to the ὕλαι.
[207] Here par. to κρέας, which [acc. to a communication from P. G. Fritz] is used 17 times (once sing.) for animal flesh which is consumed (cf. also Ant., 10, 261 f.; 12, 194).
[208] Here both terms in the plur.
[209] Flesh, however, is not connected with sin : H. Braun, *Spätjüd.-häretischer u. frühchr. Radikalismus*, I (1957), 88.

3. In Hellenism this OT-Oriental dualism (→ VI, 392, 30 ff.; 417, 17 ff.) combines with that of Greek naturalism. The sphere is a datum of nature. Man belongs to it by destiny, not by decision. Man is what he is in virtue of the sphere to which he belongs. He is enslaved and bound so long as he lives below, free and whole when he manages to get up above. Ecstasy, consecration, secret formulae and insights are designed to help him leave the sphere of the flesh → VI, 391, 18 ff.

E. The New Testament.

How strongly the OT thought of totality influences the NT may be seen even externally from the fact that the plural σάρκες, which is common in the LXX and the Jewish apocrypha (→ n. 84), occurs only in Jm. 5:3; Rev. 17:16; 19:18, 21, which in OT terms speak of the consuming of human flesh. σαρκίον, which tends to be contemptuous, does not occur at all (→ 151, 2), and the antithesis σάρξ-πνεῦμα is found in Gk. only in the reference → 103, 19 f.

I. The Synoptic Gospels and Acts.

1. The Synoptics.

Apart from two quotations from the OT in Mk. 10:8 and par.; Lk. 3:6, and one instance of πᾶσα σάρξ in Mk. 13:20 and par., σάρξ is used only three times.

In Mt. 16:17 "flesh and blood" (→ 109, 27 f.) denotes man in his limitation *vis-à-vis* God. The reference is not to his mortality but to his inability to know God → 109, 8 ff.; 120, 27 ff. Flesh and blood are not parts of man. They include his intellectual, religious and mystical capacities. The opposite is God. The OT concept of wholeness (→ 107, 7 ff.) is fully maintained. In Mk. 14:38 (→ VI, 396, 24 ff.) [210] the statement comes close to anthropological dualism. But as in Judaism (→ 113, 5 ff.) and Philo (→ 122, 3 ff.) the antithesis of the flesh is not a human possibility; it is God's act. In Lk. 24:39 (→ VI, 415, 21 ff.) "flesh and bones" (→ 99, 6 ff.; 102, 14 ff.; 119, 9) denotes the substance of earthly man. The contrast is between the corporeal and the non-corporeal worlds. [211] Account is taken of both possibilities, but they do not qualify man, since transition to incorporeality is not salvation → 121, 7 ff.

2. Acts.

Apart from two quotations (2:17, 26) the only reference is in 2:31, [212] which deduces the incorruptibility of the σάρξ of Jesus from the quotation in 2:26, → 120, 34. It should be noted that the ψυχή of v. 27a is not mentioned again here. The author thus avoids what might seem to be the obvious division of man

---

[210] Excised as a later gloss by Braun, *op. cit.* (→ n. 209), 115, n. 4.
[211] → 108, 20 ff.; Hell. Philostr. Vit. Ap., VIII, 12 in Kl. Lk. and esp. Luc. Vera Historia II, 12 : The blessed are invulnerable and without flesh and bones, though one can establish their incorporeality only by touch.
[212] A secondary reading at 2:30 corresponds verbally to R. 1:3 or 9:5 → 126, 22 ff.

into the complementary rather than antithetical parts σάρξ and ψυχή. "He" is used instead of the ψυχή of the quotation. As in the OT ψυχή and σάρξ are thus regarded as terms for the whole man.

II. Paul.

1. σάρξ = Body.

σάρξ can simply denote the muscular part of the body (→ 99, 2 ff.) as in the image of the thorn in the flesh in 2 C. 12:7. [213] In Paul, however, we never get such combinations as "flesh and bones" → 124, 26 f. Even when used in the customary sense, σάρξ always denotes the whole of man's physical existence. [214] Thus in 1 C. 15:39, in spite of the "substantial" form of thought, the reference is not to the muscular part of the body → VI, 421, 3 ff. [215] In Gl. 4:13 the ἀσθένεια τῆς σαρκός would seem to be a weakness of the body, a sickness, [216] and σάρξ μου (v. 14) is Paul's sick body, the outward form of his appearance, → VI, 32, 13 ff. [217] In R. 6:19, however, the same expression is used for weakness of perception. Hence σάρξ does not just include the mental capacities; on occasion it can be used almost exclusively for them as elsewhere for physical powers. [218] According to 2 C. 7:5 ἡ σάρξ ἡμῶν = ἡμεῖς, and it expressly embraces inner anxieties too (→ VI, 435, 3 ff.), though external affliction is primary here (but not in 2:13). Similarly in 1 C. 7:28 σάρξ denotes the whole man exposed to both physical and spiritual θλῖψις. 2 C. 7:1 is perhaps a gloss, [219] though a popular combination like πνεῦμα καὶ σάρξ is not impossible in Paul → VI, 390, n. 335. At any rate, a better part of man is not distinguished from a worse. Both are threatened by pollution and both may be cleansed. [220] θνητὴ σάρξ in 2 C. 4:11 describes the earthly existence of Paul.

---

[213] Even if with P. Menoud, "L'écharde et l'ange satanique," *Studia Paulina, Festschr. J. de Zwaan* (1953), 163-171, one sees here sorrow at the unbelief of Israel and not a sickness which afflicts the body, σάρξ is to be understood in terms of the figure rather than the transfer of use. O. Glombitza, "Gnade — das entscheidende Wort," Nov. Test., 2 (1959), 281-290 takes σάρξ to refer to Paul's existence (= his earlier persecuting activity).
[214] The ref. is always to the living man; κρέας is used for dead flesh, R. 14:21; 1 C. 8:13 → 100, 12; n. 16, 168, 207.
[215] J. Héring, *1 Corinthiens, Comm. du NT, 7* (1949), ad loc.: "chemical" use of the term (alongside the moral, genealogical, biological and social). Paul avoids the term with ref. to plants or heavenly bodies, since σάρξ also includes the idea of earthly, muscular corporeality ↦ 129, 3 ff. Hence we find σῶμα in relation to plants and δόξα in relation to stars. Though Paul might at a pinch use this term for earthly bodies too (v. 40b), he could not, like later writers (→ 120, 32 ff.), speak of heavenly σάρξ, nor could the community be called this as the body of Christ → 137, 4 ff. But Robinson, 17, n. 2 emphasises that there is no essential distinction here between σάρξ and σῶμα.
[216] Probably with Moulton, 172; Bl.-Debr. § 223, 3 App. we are to transl. "on account of weakness" rather than "in weakness" (Vg, fathers); it kept him among the Galatians.
[217] Two constructions are fused: "You did not scorn me" and "you did not yield to the temptation to scorn me" (Ltzm. Gl., ad loc.).
[218] Schl. R., ad loc. sees moral weakness here: "I say what is human" = the impotence of the flesh does not bring it to pass. But ἀνθρώπινον λέγω is surely not to be construed in terms of 3:5.
[219] The passage 6:13-7:2 has obviously been tampered with at the two points of juncture. Βελιάρ for σατανᾶς is not Pauline. In content the warning is also completely unexpected, 1 C. 5:10. But the content and form are in keeping with the group discussed in → VI, 391, 2 ff. Cf. Bultmann Theol., 202, n. 1 (§ 18, 3).
[220] Cf. 1 C. 5:3; 7:34; Col. 2:5 (σάρξ only here) → VI, 434, 32 ff.

Is the point that the power of the resurrection of Jesus is manifested in it after death ?[221] If so, this can only mean that it disappears under the new state and is swallowed up by it[222] → 128, 27 ff. But this thought comes up for the first time only in v. 14. As may be seen from v. 12, v. 11 is saying that the life of Jesus is revealed precisely in the present mortal form of the apostle's existence, and that it is so in such a way that his very affliction procures this life of Jesus for the congregations. Apart from the weakness of the messenger his proclamation lacks its ultimate power. This is not a Philonic flight from corporeality, → 121, 26 ff. On the contrary, Paul accepts this, for he knows that only through it will his message carry conviction. He can think along these lines because fundamentally he does not regard man as a self-enclosed microcosm but realises that man is what he is in his relation to God and to those whom God has given him, i.e., the community. Hence one must stress creatureliness more strongly than physical materiality, which merely describes the manner of creatureliness.[223]

In 2 C. 10:3; Gl. 2:20; Phil. 1:22, 24 (ἐν) σαρκί simply denotes the earthly life in its totality.[224] It is not in any way disparaged. In it man has the possibility of not living after the flesh (→ 130, 24 ff.), of dying to the Law and living for God in faith, rendering service for Christ. Ultimately, then, the σάρξ which is given up to destruction in 1 C. 5:5 denotes earthly being as a whole → VI, 435, 20 ff. For this reason σάρξ (Gn. 2:24) can be adopted with σῶμα in 1 C. 6:16, → VI, 419, 11 ff.; 420, 17 ff.

2. σάρξ as the Earthly Sphere.

As R. 1:3 f. shows (→ VI, 416, 32 ff.), Paul adopts a usage — cf. Is. 31:3 and Judaism → 109, 8 ff. — which contrasts the earthly sphere as that of σάρξ with the heavenly sphere as that of πνεύματα or πνεῦμα. The sphere of σάρξ is viewed here, not as sinful and hostile to God, but simply as limited and provisional. It is characterised by the natural sequence of the generations. Within this sphere Jesus is the Davidic Messiah. But the decisive thing comes only in the sphere of the Spirit.[225] If σάρξ describes the earthly sphere in respect of the interconnection of the generations, this is a natural use, since the word is employed for "relationship" in Judaism → 106, 26 ff. In R. 11:14, too, the singular denotes the totality of earthly and national Israel. In a series of passages referring to this national unit σάρξ has a wider sense. In R. 9:3 the term συγγενεῖς denotes relationship and the addition κατὰ σάρκα (→ 127, 9 ff.; 136, 3 f.)[226] distinguishes

---

[221] So Ltzm. K.⁴, ad loc.
[222] Cf. Kümmel in Ltzm. K.⁴, ad loc.: πνεῦμα is in any case not a "core" of the earthly man.
[223] K. Stalder, Das Werk des heiligen Geistes in d. Heiligung nach d. Lehre d. Ap. Paulus. Unpubl. Diss. Berne (1959), n. 394.
[224] Bultmann Theol., 231 f. (§ 22, 2) concludes from the unusual ἐν that here the (Gnostic, Käsemann, 103-105) idea of the sphere is new (par. to ἐν πνεύματι) → lines 21 ff.; but there is Jewish precedent for the expression → 110, 4; n. 178; 145, 29 f.
[225] One may even ask whether σάρξ does not carry with it the nuance of lowliness. If so, David is understood in OT terms as God's servant, cf. E. Schweizer, Erniedrigung u. Erhöhung bei Jesus u. seinen Nachfolgern (1955), 56. But Son of David seems to denote a provisional stage of exaltation. There is a remote analogy in the subordination of the Davidic Messiah to the high-priestly Messiah in the Dead Sea Scrolls, cf. K. Schubert, "Zwei Messiasse aus dem Regelbuch von Chirbet Qumran," Judaica, 11 (1955), 234; J. Liver, "The Doctrine of the Two Messiahs in Sectarian Literature in the Time of the Second Commonwealth," HThR, 52 (1959), 149-185.
[226] It is not wholly true that κατὰ σάρκα and ἐν σαρκί are peculiar to Paul (Lohmeyer, 31) → n. 177, 224; 123, 12.

this as an earthly and human relationship from a relationship of a different kind. σάρξ stands for the sphere of man. This is not viewed negatively, but it is also not the decisive sphere for salvation. The same applies to R. 4:1; [227] 9:5 (→ n. 238); [228] 9:8. Here one may ask whether both σάρξ and ἐπαγγελία do not denote generating power. [229] It should be considered, however, that in the par. Gl. 4:23, 29 (→ 131, 13 ff.) we have the formula διὰ τῆς ἐπαγγελίας but not the parallel διὰ τῆς σαρκός, → VI, 429, 3 ff. Nor is σάρξ ever used elsewhere by Paul for generative power. Hence the genitive in R. 9:8 indicates the sphere to which the children belong. [230] ὁ Ἰσραὴλ κατὰ σάρκα in 1 C. 10:18 is the earthly nation (→ III, 387, 24 ff.) to which each belongs by natural descent. But here, as distinct from R. 9:5, [231] another Israel stands side by side with this, Gl. 6:16; cf. R. 2:29; Gl. 3:29; 4:29; Phil. 3:3. The expression carries with it an evaluation; this is the Israel which understands itself only in terms of descent. In the context, however, this is not the point at issue, and it is no accident that we do not find the antithesis ὁ Ἰσραὴλ κατὰ πνεῦμα. [232] Here too, then, σάρξ is the intrinsically neutral earthly and human sphere of which Paul says that it does not mediate salvation. κατὰ σάρκα is truly negative only in association with a corresponding verb → 130, 24 ff. Similarly the σοφοὶ κατὰ σάρκα in 1 C. 1:26 are those in the earthly world who are wise according to human categories. This does not in itself exclude the possibility that they may also have God's wisdom. It is quite possible to be wise in both spheres. But in the community there are only a few wise according to the flesh. [233] Phlm. 16 is the only verse where σάρξ and κύριος are linked by a καί. [234] Here, too, σάρξ denotes the circle of purely human relations irrespective of the fact that the slave and his master are also believers in the Lord's kingdom. [235] The reference is to social relations rather than kinship. Here it is especially plain that the two spheres are not mutually exclusive. But the sphere of σάρξ is not the decisive one. It embraces the whole of human

---

[227] It is perhaps stressed that Abraham is the apostle's national ancestor too, since proselytes were denied the right to call him father acc. to many Rabb. (Mi. R., ad loc.), and this distinction is set aside in what follows. κατὰ σάρκα makes no sense when taken with the verb unless one conjectures εἰργάσθαι, R. R. Williams, "A Note on R. 4:1," Exp. T., 63 (1951/52), 91 f.

[228] τὸ κατὰ σάρκα is formulated to restrict the closer definition to ἐξ ὧν ... and to avoid the misunderstanding that Jesus is the Messiah only κατὰ σάρκα. The possibility of another view is thus implied, Robinson, 21.

[229] So C. H. Dodd, The Epistle of St. Paul to the Romans (1932), ad loc.; Ltzm. R., ad loc.

[230] So Mi. R., ad loc.; but his paraphrase "who simply think in terms of natural descent," is too strongly influenced by Gl. 4:23, 29. Nothing is said here about their inner attitude. Paul's thought is that they are the children of God, not as physical descendants of Abraham, but as those who stand under the promise.

[231] No τό here.

[232] v. 18 is a connecting thought which is simply designed to clarify the idea of κοινωνία. v. 19 introduces a new idea connected with the problem taken up in v. 14. For Israel in v. 18 is the same as οἱ πατέρες ἡμῶν in v. 1, so Héring, op. cit. (→ n. 215), ad loc.; also H. v. Soden, "Sakrament u. Ethik bei Pls." in Urchr. u. Gesch., I (1951), 246, who relates v. 18 to the incident of the golden calf (which is most unlikely). The contrast to the Israel of God is stronger if contemporary Israel is in view.

[233] σάρξ is never used for the relative value of human attributes; σοφός occurs alone in 1 C. 6:5, Wendt, 171. σάρξ occurs when there is an explicit or implicit contrast with God's sphere as the one which is truly decisive.

[234] Loh. Phlm., ad loc.

[235] Dib. Gefbr., ad loc. with Ltzm. R. Exc. on R. 8:11: "as man and Christian."

existence, both its bodily and its intellectual functions, though apart from the
gracious gift of faith in the κύριος. The event of revelation is understood as
something which is not to be thought of in terms of the life-circle of man but
which breaks into this from without.

This usage corresponds to a large extent to that of the OT → 109, 8 ff. This
may be seen in the fact that the distinction between physical and intellectual
plays no part whatever. We do not even have the distinctions above and below
→ n. 302. Instead we find temporal definitions. In 1 C. 2:6; 3:18 f. this aeon or
κόσμος can be used for what is called σάρξ in 1 C. 1:26. [236] The demonic spiritual
powers belong to the realm of the σάρξ, → n. 174, 302; 137, 14 ff. [237] As in the
OT, however, the decisive antithesis is between God and man. As κατὰ κύριον
can be used for κατὰ πνεῦμα in 2 C. 11:17, so κατὰ ἄνθρωπον can replace κατὰ
σάρκα in 1 C. 3:3. Again, in 1 C. 1:24-26 the wisdom of God is contrasted with
that of the σάρξ (cf. 2 C. 1:12), and in 2 C. 10:4 the power of God is the antithesis of σαρκικὰ ὅπλα. In R. 9:8; Gl. 4:23, 29 the promise is the opposite of
σάρξ, [238] → 130, 19 f. As for Paul the coming aeon already breaks into this aeon
in the community, so here the sphere of God can invade that of man. This is to
be understood in the light of the OT antithesis between the omnipotent Creator
and the feeble creature. But it is already apparent that there is a radical underlying distinction which goes beyond this contrast → 129, 27 ff.; VI, 428, 23 ff.;
430, 8 ff.

3. σὰρξ καὶ αἷμα, πᾶσα σάρξ.

a. What has been said is proved by the way in which Paul uses these formulae.
In Gl. 1:16, as in Mt. 16:17 (→ 124, 19 ff.), σὰρξ καὶ αἷμα (→ 109, 27 f.) means
man as such, the man who can pass on theological insight, religious experience,
or ecclesiastical tradition. But here again God as the Revealer is the opposite.
The nuance of that which is sinful is completely absent. 1 C. 15:50, however, is
much harder to assess.

Are σὰρξ καὶ αἷμα to be differentiated from φθορά? This would be so if v. 50
were to be taken with vv. 51-55. [239] vv. 36-49 would then be answering the question
"with what body?" (v. 35b) and vv. 50-55 the question "how?" (v. 35a). σὰρξ καὶ
αἷμα would refer to men alive at the time of the *parousia*, φθορά to those who are
dead. [240] But this distinction in v. 51 is no longer possible in v. 53 f. [241] μυστήριον in
v. 51 (→ IV, 823, 6 ff.) heralds a new mystery not previously mentioned. This being

---

[236] Cf. also → VI, 422, 17 ff. For further par. between σάρξ and κόσμος cf. Bultmann
Theol., 231 (§ 22, 2).

[237] They are never, of course, called σάρξ, though → 143, 20 f. Hence the idea of
corporeality is not lost → n. 215.

[238] If θεός in R. 9:5 refers to Christ (cf. O. Cullmann, *Das Christologie d. NT* [1957],
321 [E.T. 312 f.]; Cr.-Kö.), then the character of the exalted Lord as God is also contrasted
with the σάρξ of the earthly Lord. Now this is not impossible in Paul. But since he never
styles Christ thus, it is more probable that the doxology refers to God.

[239] ἀδελφοί may be used at the beginning of a section, but also in the summary at the
end, e.g., 1 C. 7:24; 11:33; 14:39.

[240] So J. Jeremias, "Flesh and Blood cannot Inherit the Kingdom of God," NTSt, 2
(1955/56), 151-159.

[241] In R. 1:23, at any rate, φθαρτός is used, not for the dead man, but for the living
= θνητός.

so, σάρξ καὶ αἷμα stands in parallelism to φθορά and is thus to be construed as the conclusion to vv. 36-49 → 125, 9 f. Having to deal here with adversaries who think wholly in substantial categories, Paul in this v. links σάρξ καὶ αἷμα (→ 141, 12 ff.) with the thought of substance. [242] σάρξ is the quality of the earthly as distinct from the heavenly, v. 48 f. But this is for him only a thought-form. Unlike Gk. thought, he is not distinguishing an incorruptible part of man from a corruptible. On the contrary, Paul's whole concern is to present the new state as an absolutely different and unimaginable gift of God, as a miracle, → VI, 421, 10 ff. Paul does not deny that it will be → σῶμα, but he does not speak of σάρξ καὶ αἷμα in the sense of a being which man can conceive of and which stands in understandable continuity with the present state. [243]

In 1 C. 15:50, then, σάρξ καὶ αἷμα denotes the whole man with all his functions. [244] It should be noted, however, that βασιλείαν θεοῦ κληρονομεῖν is a formula [245] which occurs elsewhere only in 1 C. 6:9 f. and Gl. 5:21 in traditional ethical contexts, and in Gl. 5:21 in a statement about the works of the σάρξ. We may thus surmise that in 1 C. 15:50, too, σάρξ carries with it the thought of man's vulnerability to temptation as well as corruption, → 113, 17 ff.; 121, 18 ff.; 133, 15 ff. Yet this is not actually stated, and hence it cannot be proved.

b. A fresh nuance may be detected in the use of πᾶσα σάρξ. This occurs in R. 3:20 and Gl. 2:16 in a quotation from ψ 142:2 as a substitute for πᾶς ζῶν, [246] and also in 1 C. 1:29. [247] In all three passages we are told that πᾶσα σάρξ is not justified or cannot boast before God. ἐνώπιον τοῦ θεοῦ or αὐτοῦ is expressly added in R. 3:20; 1 C. 1:29 and assumed in Gl. 2:16. The expression thus suggests itself to Paul when he views mankind as under God's judgment and unable to boast before Him. The influence of the saying in Gl. 6:12 (→ n. 246) may be seen here. As already in Judaism (→ 112, 21 ff.; 121, 5 ff.), the contrast between the two spheres thus acquires a new emphasis.

4. σάρξ as an Object of Trust.

In R. 2:28 σάρξ is in the first instance no more than the bodily member on which circumcision takes place, → 108, 21 ff.; 145, 1 f. The opposite, however, is the καρδία rather than the πνεῦμα. On this takes place the true and decisive circumcision — cf. the OT and Jewish expression. [248] But this antithesis, in which σάρξ is simply the outside of man and does not touch him inwardly, is given by

---

[242] Bultmann Theol., 189 (§ 17, 1). Cf. → n. 215.
[243] The distinction in Schauf, 56-58 that the resurrection body is fleshly in substance in continuity with the earthly body, but no longer fleshly in quality, is true only in respect of the negation.
[244] This may be seen also in the originally sing. form of the verb, cf. Jeremias, op. cit., 151.
[245] Elsewhere Paul always has ἡ βασιλεία τοῦ θεοῦ.
[246] HT כָּל־חָי; cf. Gn. 6:2; Philo Deus Imm., 140-142 and esp. M. Philonenko, "L'origine essénienne des cinq psaumes syriaques de David," Semitica, 9 (1960), 38 : III, 10 : "sans justice est devant Toi toute chair."
[247] = τις Eph. 2:9 (Robinson, 18).
[248] For the contrast between σάρξ and καρδία in circumcision cf. Jer. 9:25 LXX; Ez. 44:9; cf. ψ 72:26. On circumcision of the heart → VI, 77, 17 ff.; 79, 18 ff. and 1 Qp Hab. 11:13; cf. Lv. 26:41. Jub. 1:23 expects it as an eschatological phenomenon. Cf. criticism of purely bodily circumcision : Ptolemaeus ad Floram, Epiph. Haer., 33, 5, 11 (GCS, 25) and → n. 347.

Paul a wholly new twist which adapts it to his own peculiar concern.[249] When the σάρξ as the φανερόν[250] is set in contrast with the κρυπτόν, this is not just a variation on the stock formula, for with the φανερόν man seeks praise among his fellows. This means that σάρξ takes on a negative aspect from the fact that it is the object which man can display and of which he can boast, v. 17, 23. The idea of the γράμμα (→ I, 765, 15 ff.; VI, 428, 38 ff.) also comes in here, v. 27, 29. What is sinful is not the σάρξ but confidence in it. Gl. 6:12 f. should probably be mentioned in this connection. The ὑμετέρα σάρξ of which the false teachers boast can only be the flesh of circumcision,[251] which again plays a negative role as the object of boasting. Paul seems to have the same thing in view in v. 12 too,[252] though it is possible that what he means by this expression is simply "before men"[253] or "within the sphere of the σάρξ," i.e., earthly, non-divine considerations.[254] Paul chooses the phrase because he already has v. 13 in mind, but the expression as such may still be taken generally.

Phil. 3:3 f. is especially important. Here again (→ 126, 26 ff.) σάρξ embraces in the first instance the natural descent of the Israelites, but also Pharisaism, zeal for the Law, legal righteousness,[255] and hence the intellectual and religious functions of men in particular. These things are not bad in themselves, but trust in them is wrong. Hence the direct opposite of σάρξ here is Χριστὸς Ἰησοῦς → 128, 11 ff. The revelation of the righteousness which is of God in Christ makes all other things ζημία, vv. 7-9 (→ II, 890, 33 ff.). They are not bad, but they can no longer be considered as objects of confidence, as the foundation of life. Even the new trust is God's act,[256] → VI, 428, 23 ff.

5. κατὰ σάρκα with Verb.

What has been said is particularly apparent in 2 C. 10:2 f. ἐν σαρκὶ περιπατεῖν means quite simply "to live on earth, in the body as a man," → 126, 26 ff. This applies to Paul as to everyone else. The only wrong thing is the orientation of thought to the σάρξ, a life which is no longer lived neutrally in the σάρξ but which regards this as its norm: κατὰ σάρκα περιπατεῖν or στρατεύεσθαι.[257] What Paul means by this may be seen in 2 C. 11:18 : such a life is a καυχᾶσθαι

---

[249] Hb. 9:9 f.; 10:22; 1 Pt. 3:21 are also based on the current antithesis between outward cleansing and that of the heart or conscience. This is also developed, but in a typically new way, in Hb. 9:10, → 142, 7 ff.

[250] H. Sahlin, "Einige Textemendationen zum R.," ThZ, 9 (1953), 95 f. cuts out the second ἐν τῷ φανερῷ.

[251] Ltzm. Gl., ad loc. sees a twofold sense : "an outward victory over you" and "the operation on your body." In view of the many par. (→ 108, 21 ff.) the first rendering is unlikely.

[252] So Schlier Gl., ad loc., who also thinks there may be a twofold sense.

[253] Cf. Pr.-Bauer⁵, s.v. εὐπροσωπεῖν.

[254] Cf. Ltzm. Gl., ad loc.

[255] σάρξ is in the last analysis anything outside Christ, cf. J. Calvin, Corp. Ref., 80 (1895), ad loc. On the par. with 2 C. 11:18, 21 cf. W. Schmithals, "Die Irrlehrer d. Phil.," ZThK, 54 (1957), 316, n. 4.

[256] Naturally one is to read θεοῦ, not θεῷ, cf. Loh. Phil., ad loc.

[257] This antithesis between ἐν and κατά does not occur elsewhere in Paul, cf. W. Schmithals, Die Gnosis in Korinth (1956), 80. But it is not to be explained as a particularly emphatic rejection of Gnostic enthusiasm which seeks to do away with ἐν σαρκί (loc. cit.), for materially one finds the same antithesis in Gl. 2:19 f., and ἐν σαρκί is often used neutrally for earthly life, while κατὰ σάρκα with verb always denotes a wrong orientation of life. Here, as the continuation shows, the special ref. is to trust in weapons which are too weak and which fail, cf. Robinson, 20.

κατὰ σάρκα, → III, 650, n. 39. [258] It is a boasting in which man has regard only to what may be seen and what counts with men. The opposite is speaking κατὰ κύριον (v. 17) which pays heed to what pleases the Lord and is accepted by Him. Similarly βουλεύεσθαι κατὰ σάρκα in 2 C. 1:17 is a planning which takes note only of human and earthly circumstances and not the Lord's will. The same applies to the much debated verse 2 C. 5:16. κατὰ σάρκα goes with the verb γινώσκειν, not the noun Χριστός. [259] In the context Paul is defending himself against those who boast ἐν προσώπῳ, [260] i.e., of qualities which are on the surface and which may be asserted by anyone, v. 12. [261] He himself will no longer judge anybody in this way. v. 16b shows how absurd this would be. [262] γινώσκειν κατὰ σάρκα denotes a knowledge of Christ which judges Him by human standards, i.e., by what may be known of the historical Jesus considered as one figure among others. [263] Finally γεννᾶν κατὰ σάρκα in Gl. 4:23, 29 (→ VI, 429, 3 ff.) is a generation which takes place only with regard to human possibilities and not with regard to the promise. If this means that there are two διαθῆκαι for Paul (→ II, 130, 29 ff.), this brings out a new aspect of Paul's view, namely, that the decision to orientate one's life to the σάρξ or to the Lord and His promise and Spirit is obviously not just the single decision of a moment but a fundamental decision which affects the whole of life. This may also be seen in R. 8:4, 12 f., where newness of life is described as renunciation of περιπατεῖν or ζῆν κατὰ σάρκα. When the formula τὰ τῆς σαρκὸς φρονεῖν is used in v. 5, this shows that what is involved is the conscious spiritual orientation of life on the earthly level. [264] But here, too, it is apparent that this is not an individual decision resting in the free will of man. It arises out of the basic orientation of all life. Thinking develops out of an εἶναι κατὰ σάρκα, → 134, 14 ff.

6. σάρξ as the Subject of Sin.

In Phil. 3:3; R. 8:13 f.; Gl. 4:23; 5:18 an instructive observation may be made on the text. The πνεῦμα or ἐπαγγελία of God is introduced in the instrumental

---

[258] As always in Paul (17 times + 1 each in Col. and Eph.) κατὰ σάρκα without art. (as against MS B ℵ).

[259] The question is not crucial, cf. Bultmann Theol., 234 (§ 22, 3), but it would be the only instance of a negative evaluation of κατὰ σάρκα with a noun. The arrangement is also against this combination, and Paul seems to avoid Χριστὸς κατὰ σάρκα → n. 228. So also A. Oepke, "Irrwege in d. neueren Paulusforschung," ThLZ, 77 (1952), 454; O. Michel, " 'Erkennen dem Fleisch nach,' " Ev. Theol., 14 (1954)́, 22-29. It is not impossible that the readers took κατὰ σάρκα with the noun because they understood it substantially (Schmithals, op. cit., [→ n. 257], 69), but this is most unlikely, since σάρξ does not play any gt. part elsewhere in 1 Cor.

[260] ἐν σαρκί R. 2:28 f., both times opp. καρδία. Similarly κατὰ σάρκα in 2 C. 11:18 takes up the κατὰ πρόσωπον of 10:7.

[261] The ref. would seem to be to the gift of free inspired speech, which was regarded as a sign of the gift of the divine Spirit in Corinth. In v. 13 Paul says that he is acquainted with an ἐξίστασθαι but only to God, his σωφρονεῖν being for them, 1 C. 14:1 ff.; the love of God keeps him from the enthusiasm his adversaries think they may boast of, so R. Bultmann, "Exegetische Probleme d. 2 K.," Symbolae Biblicae Upsalienses, 9 (1947), 12-20.

[262] W. Schmithals, "Zwei gnostische Glossen im 2 K.," Ev. Theol., 18 (1958), 552-564 regards this as unbelievable since it is not actually said, 554. He thus regards it as a later gloss, like 2 C. 3:17. But Paul often speaks impulsively.

[263] This does not mean that Paul knew the earthly Jesus. He regarded him as a purely historical figure, a false Messiah, when he first learned of him after his death. But in the νῦν of salvation this is impossible in the community, cf. J. Dupont, Gnosis (1949), 180-186.

[264] Paul can use τὰ ἐπίγεια for τὰ τῆς σαρκός in Phil. 3:19.

dative or with an instrumental διά, but Paul avoids this in the case of the anti-thetical σάρξ. The σάρξ, then, is not a power which works in the same way as the πνεῦμα. The σάρξ never occurs as the subject of an action where it is not in the shadow of a statement about the work of the πνεῦμα, [265] while the πνεῦμα on the other hand is often presented as an acting subject with or without σάρξ in the context. The typical line for Paul is thus that considered → 129, 27 ff. It is shaped by the OT and corresponds to what has been said elsewhere, → II, 215, 23 ff.; III, 648, 17 ff. Paul is misunderstood if the starting-point is seen in two-sphere thinking, though this was undoubtedly familiar to him. [266] Later Judaism (→ 109, 8 ff.) and Hellenism (→ 99, 17 ff.) think in this category. Paul uses the ideas of his time to express his own thought. But he does not understand this schema in a mythological sense in which the spheres represent powers con-trolling man. The typical Pauline conjunction of flesh and sin is the same as that already found in the OT → 107, 18 ff. Man's building on the flesh is sinful. This is called sowing to the flesh in Gl. 6:8. If the σάρξ brings φθορά, it is in the first instance a comprehensive expression for all that in which man puts his trust. In antithetical parallelism to πνεῦμα, however, σάρξ approximates to the idea of a power which works on man and determines his destiny even beyond life on earth.

Here one may see a second line of thought which goes beyond what is found in the OT. Paul adopts it only hesitantly and as a counter-formulation to state-ments about the πνεῦμα. As in the case of πνεῦμα the meaning of power leads to that of norm (→ VI, 428, 14 ff.), so in the case of σάρξ that of norm leads conversely to that of power. The norm σάρξ by which a man directs his life becomes a power which shapes him. Paul's obvious concern here is to show the bondage of man to the σάρξ, from which only the power of God's Spirit can free him. Flesh and Spirit are not two forces between which man can always choose freely → VI, 436, 21 ff. Gl. 5:19 speaks of the ἔργα τῆς σαρκός and uses a traditional list of vices to describe these. Sexual sins come first, then eating and drinking, hate and strife. In v. 16 Paul also mentions the ἐπιθυμία σαρκός. [267] In a similar context R. 13:14 has much the same formulation. [268] This usage is undoubtedly influenced in part by the Hellenistic expressions listed in → n. 52, which passed into the Jewish polemic against paganism. But in a manner which is not at all Greek Paul can equally well speak of the ἐπιθυμίαι τῶν καρδιῶν, R. 1:24 → 137, 17 ff. Yet this reveals only the one way in which the fall of man

---

[265] The formulae in 1 C. 1:29; 15:50; also 2 C. 7:5 are naturally no exception. The absence of σάρξ is esp. striking in R. 5:12-21 (Mi. R., 121). But πνεῦμα is not used there either. The same applies to the first chapters of R. Cf. Kuss, 514, 539 f.

[266] Hence Paul is not directly dependent on Qumran, → 112, 15 ff. The usage attested there merely facilitates the development mentioned → 132, 20 ff. Cf. Davies, 171 and H. Braun, "R. 7:7-25 u. d. Selbstverständnis des Qumran-Frommen," ZThK, 56 (1959), 15-18. This also applies against Schauf, 194-198, who regards Gn. 6:3 (→ 115, 13 ff. and Ps.-Philo Antiquitates Biblicae [→ n. 189], 3, 2) and esp. Wis. as the earlier stages of a physico-eschatological dualism which Paul changed into an ethical dualism. But he also notes that Paul develops the σάρξ concept par. to what he says about the πνεῦμα, 199. Acc. to Käsemann, 105 the flesh is a kind of Gnostic aeon *in* which man lives.

[267] Cf. Schauf, 158-163; Käsemann, 8-16. The alternation of σάρξ and σῶμα in R. 8:13 shows that Paul can also have in view bodily relations and impulses, Mi. R., *ad loc.* σάρξ is *also* the physical flesh whose end is the end of exposure to temptation too, Schauf, 84-86. But this is not the essential thing for Paul.

[268] Luther's transl., which relates the negation only to εἰς ἐπιθυμίας, would demand σῶμα for σάρξ, as against Lohmeyer, 34.

may manifest itself. Gl. 3:3 uses σαρκὶ ἐπιτελεῖσθαι [269] to describe the attempt of legalism, and Gl. 4:8-10 evaluates the pious observance of days as equivalent to the former paganism. It is only in R., however, that the guilt of the legalistically righteous is truly revealed. Bondage to the σάρξ finds expression in the legalism of the Pharisee no less than the immorality of the pagan. [270] But in his case the post-Epicurean history of the term (→ 104, 16 ff.) cannot be the decisive one. σάρξ is for Paul everything human and earthly, which includes legal righteousness, → 130, 5 ff., 15, 2 f. But since this entices man to put his trust in it, to find security and renown thereby, it takes on for Paul the character of a power which is opposed to the working of the Spirit. The sharpest formulation is in Gl. 5:13, 17, where σάρξ is an independent force superior to man. [271] Paul realises, of course, that this power which entices away from God and His Spirit is not just a power alien to man. It belongs to man himself. The Gnostic answer that the divine core of man has been tragically overpowered by the sinister forces which seduce the senses is not Paul's answer. OT man regarded himself as flesh when he experienced subjection to sickness and death, to the inscrutability of his destiny, to the hiddenness of God. Paul is aware of the subjection to things which take the place of God for him. But this is not just tragic fate; it is his guilt. The same applies in R. 8:1-13 → 131, 19 ff.; VI, 429, 29 ff.; 430, 29 ff.; 433, 2 ff. [272] A life orientated to the σάρξ is also a life which serves the σάρξ (v. 12) and carries out its thinking (v. 6 f.). This is not the thinking of a mythological power. For Paul can just as well regard man himself as the subject of φρονεῖν τὰ τῆς σαρκός. [273] It is the thinking which is proper to pre-Christian man, which rejects God and consequently reaps death. This is also the reason for repudiation of the Law, v. 3. [274] If on this account the Son of God comes ἐν ὁμοιώματι σαρκὸς ἁμαρτίας (→ V, 195, 28 ff.) and God condemns sin ἐν τῇ σαρκί, Paul has in view the corporeality of the earthly Jesus who was crucified. But this embraces man with all his physical and mental functions. Its opposite, then, is not the spiritual; it is God. [275]

R. 7:18, 25 seems to contradict this → II, 359, 8 ff. We see here the influence of Hellenistic usage, which understands man in terms of his nature and hence also of his cleavage into body and spirit (νοῦς). [276] But what Paul is trying to say is very different. Behind R. 7 stands the experience of the fallenness of the pre-Christian man. This includes his cleavage into what he really is in life and

---

[269] Dat. modi; cf. Bl.-Debr. § 198, 5. Schlier Gl., ad loc. takes it more instrumentally.

[270] Mi. R. on 2:28, n. 4 sees in the antithesis of πνεῦμα and σάρξ a polemical thesis against the Rabbinate, but this is to take it too narrowly in view of Gl. 5:13-24. The antithesis is correctly understood in terms of → 129, 27 ff. Cf. → 124, 13 f.

[271] Here already, however, it must be said that Paul expressly declares that he who walks in the Spirit, though under the temptation of the σάρξ, does not fulfil its desires → 134, 14 ff.

[272] Cf. J. Huby, "La vie dans l'esprit," Recherches de science religieuse, 30 (1940), 5-39.

[273] Cf. τὰ ἐπίγεια φρονεῖν Phil. 3:19.

[274] In the first instance Paul has in mind the man who misuses the Law to establish his own righteousness; only secondarily is he thinking of the moral transgressor of the Law.

[275] For this reason Paul can choose ὁμοίωμα with no thought whatever of Docetic misunderstanding. Cf. Kuss, 491-496, 498, though he emphasises that the flesh of Christ, and hence flesh generally, is not destroyed.

[276] Mi. R. on 7:14 sees a Hell.-Jewish basis. Cf. ibid., on 7:22, n. 2; Ltzm. R. on 7:13 f. Exc.; Kuhn, op. cit. (→ n. 118), 211; as against Wendt, 111-114; cf. Schauf, 103-105. But one has to consider whether 7:25b is not a later gloss, cf. R. Bultmann, "Glossen im Römerbrief," ThLZ, 72 (1947), 198 f.; also E. Fuchs, Die Freiheit des Glaubens (1949), ad loc.

what he ought to be or would like to be. A difference from Greek thought is that the νοῦς (→ IV, 958, 9 ff.) is not here a power which can temporarily or totally rule or restrain the σάρξ. On the contrary, it is an impotent spectator. [277] This is so true that only the believer knows the cleavage in retrospect. The point of these sayings, then, is simply that the pre-Christian man, even with the best will in the world, falls into acts which are contrary to God. Paul is thinking primarily of the Pharisee who wants to be obedient to God and for this very reason commits the real sin, namely, that of establishing his own righteousness. [278] For it is especially clear that the right desire of man to please God is perverted at once into his own carnal action, so that it is no longer possible to distinguish between moments of pure will and moments of wrong action. [279] Only in retrospect is the will the ascertainable opposite of the work of the σάρξ, which makes this work both responsible and guilty.

7. The Vanquished σάρξ.

According to R. 7:5; 8:8 f.; Gl. 5:24 the believer no longer lives in the σάρξ; he has crucified it. This message is new and typical of Paul. It stands behind all the formulations in which there is reference to the victory of God and of His promise and Spirit. Paul certainly does not mean that by ascetic or mystical practices man can escape his corporeality. 2 C. 10:3 and Gl. 2:19 f. state expressly that the believer always lives physically ἐν σαρκί → 126, 14 ff. In the latter passage Paul says at the same time that he is crucified with Christ. The σάρξ of Gl. 5:24 is not, then, a part of man which he may put off or overcome. It is the man himself. Where σάρξ is understood in a full theological sense as in Gl. 5:24, it denotes the being of man which is determined, not by his physical substance, but by his relation to God → 123, 29 ff. The opposing concept in Gl. 2:20 makes this plain : the life of the Christian is life in faith in Christ. The sayings R. 7:5; 8:8 f.; Gl. 5:24 certainly do not mean that, although a man does the works of the flesh listed in Gl. 5:19-21, he knows that that they are no longer imputed to him by God. Paul indisputably says that the believer no longer does these works. Yet at the same time he can speak of hatred and contention and the like in the community and issue a constant summons to put off these deeds of the

---

[277] Schauf, 105, 189-192 refers to R. 2:10-16. But νοῦς is not used there, nor is there any other indication of anthropological dualism. Only καρδία (→ III, 612, 27 ff.) and → συνείδησις occur. For Paul's purpose here is simply to shame the Jews. The fact that the Gentile also does τὰ τοῦ νόμου does not mean that he keeps the Law in such a way as to be just before God, for he, too, lives in the strife of conscience like the man of R. 7. With Schauf, 105 and against B. Weiss, Lehrbuch d. bibl. Theol.⁷ (1903), 248-253 one may say that σάρξ does not denote the sinful nature of man. But it is incorrect to say either that all the work of non-believers is corrupt and wrong or that there is a purely quantitative lack. The wrong thing is to insist on one's ποιεῖν, even one's good ποιεῖν (Gl. 3:12), and to see self as the goal of life. Paul is certainly not concerned to glorify or perfect an intrinsically good νοῦς (Schauf, 118) → VI, 430, n. 648; 436, 8 ff. On σάρξ cf. also Kuss, 454.

[278] So Bultmann Theol., 260-264 (§ 27, 2); G. Bornkamm, "Sünde, Gesetz u. Tod" in Das Ende des Gesetzes² (1958), 51-69. At this pt. Paul parts company with the Jewish concept of the evil impulse to which C. K. Barrett, A Comm. on the Epistle to the Romans (1957), ad loc. refers, and also with Qumran, cf. Braun, op. cit. (→ n. 266), 15-18.

[279] It is precisely thus that the γνόντες τὸν θεόν of R. 1:21 turns at once into the perversion of idolatry.

flesh. For Paul acts of this kind are illogical. He calls for fresh faith. From what has been said (→ 131, 23 ff.; 132, 20 ff.) it is apparent that for Paul orientation to the σάρξ or the πνεῦμα, and hence life in the power of the σάρξ or the πνεῦμα, is a total attitude which determines everything. The man ruled by the Spirit must no longer secure his life by the σάρξ, whether by wealth or by good works. But this means that the splitting of life into thousands of individual acts, which is typical of legalists and scrupulous penitents, is quite impossible. Life is determined as a totality by σάρξ or πνεῦμα. It does not consist of many ἔργα; it is a single ἔργον. [280] In the splintered view of Pharisaic pride or a sense of religious worthlessness σάρξ occupies the central point. But the man who has come to faith in the Son of God is no longer in the σάρξ, for he believes, and he has thus ceased to build his life on the σάρξ, which is to sin. That Paul is very far from being a perfectionist is due to his realisation that man has to receive and to practise his faith afresh each day.

8. Summary.

a. Man is not essentially determined by his nature, whether by his bodily constitution [281] or by the material world which is about him. He is finally qualified by his relation to God and hence to his fellow-man. b. Salvation does not lie in a retreat from corporeality (e.g., sexuality) to the spiritual (e.g., study of the Law or asceticism). [282] Bodily and mental functions are viewed in comprehensive unity as a common expression of human life. Both can separate man from God and both can be put in the service of God. c. Hence the flesh is not a sphere which is to be differentiated from other earthly things and which is intrinsically bad or especially dangerous. It becomes bad only when man builds his life on it. Sexuality on the one side and Pharisaic religiosity on the other are particularly blatant examples of this false orientation of human life. But everything else human and earthly can also be flesh. d. Where man understands himself as flesh, this describes his subjection to that which would draw him away from God. [283] It may be felt so strongly that the flesh seems to be a power which controls man. Yet it is his own wrong disposition. e. Redemption, then, is not a physical or metaphysical event which abolishes corporeality. [284] The σκάνδαλον of the Cruci-fied, who attained neither legal righteousness nor riches, becomes salvation for him who lets himself be caught up by Him into a life which is lived by the gift of God and which is thus liberated from bondage to those goals.

---

[280] 1 C. 3:13 f.; Gl. 6:4; 1 Th. 1:3. In Gl. 5:22 καρπός (sing.) replaces plur. ἔργα and φανερά is not used. In 2 C. 5:10 ἀγαθόν and φαῦλον embrace all individual acts as they appear before God's judgment. Cf. also → II, 643, 13 ff. Except in the quotation at R. 2:6 (but cf. v. 7) the plur. is used only for wicked works, though cf. Eph.; Past. Kuss on R. 8:5 : There are two categories of men : those who belong absolutely to the sphere of the flesh and those who belong absolutely to the sphere of the pneuma, but cf. *ibid.,* on R. 8:12, 17.

[281] Cf. Schauf, 16-21, also 186 f., but in contrast cf. Dickson, 311-315.

[282] This does not mean that study of the Law and asceticism might not be necessary. But if so, it is for the sake of Christ, not for their own sake, R. 3:21; 1 C. 9:27. Cf. Schauf, 95-98.

[283] This is not just the OT subjection to trouble and death.

[284] In view of R. 8:12 f.; Gl. 5:17; 1 C. 3:3 it is hardly possible to maintain that in the redeemed the σῶμα or μέλη is the seat of sin rather than the σάρξ, Schauf, 106 f. On μέλη as the seat of sin cf. S. Bar. 49:3; R. 7:5, 23; Jm. 4:1 and → 121, 5; 149, 14, n. 401.

III. Colossians, Ephesians, Pastorals.

1. Colossians.

σάρξ is used neutrally for external and visible corporeality (2:1 → 126, 21 ff.; 2:5 → VI, 435, 1 ff.). κατὰ σάρκα with noun in 3:22 denotes the sphere of human relations [285] → 126, 26 ff. In the difficult v. 1:24 (→ V, 933, 8 ff.) [286] the reference is to the physical existence of the apostle as this is exposed to affliction. [287] As in 2 C. 4:11 what is said here is that through the sufferings to which he is subject in the body Paul is an authentic witness of the Gospel and thus fulfils the work of salvation in so far as proclamation is part of this, 2 C. 5:19 f. In the very obscure expression in Col. 2:23 σάρξ presumably denotes the man who measures by his own standards and not by God's. [288] In 2:13 (→ 129, 27 ff.) the opposite number is the Gentile rather than the Jew. His sin shows itself in licentiousness rather than trust in circumcision, 3:5. Thus the expression ἀκροβυστία τῆς σαρκός, which in the first instance is used quite simply for the Gentile in his bodily distinction from the Jew, becomes a term for those who have not yet experienced the circumcision of 2:11. Hence σάρξ describes the nature of the man who is alienated from God, but with a distinctive nuance which derives from Hellenistic usage. [289]

A new expression is σῶμα τῆς σαρκός → 109, 29 f. In 1:22 this is used for the crucified body of Jesus (→ 133, 26 f.), so that σάρξ is simply physical corporeality. But in 2:18 there is reference to the νοῦς τῆς σαρκός, [290] and 2:11 declares that the man who comes to faith [291] should put off the σῶμα τῆς σαρκός in the circumcision of Christ. The passage is thus to be construed in the same way as 2:13 (→ lines 11 ff.). [292] Pauline usage is echoed but modified here. This is not so elsewhere.

---

[285] Added because κύριος is otherwise the heavenly Lord.

[286] Bibl. in Schweizer, op. cit. (→ n. 225), 140, n. 635; J. Kremer, Was an den Leiden Christi noch mangelt (1956); G. Le Grelle, "La plénitude de la parole dans la pauvreté de la chair d'après Col. 1:24," Nouvelle Revue Théol., 81 (1959), 232-250 has the paraphrase: "I compensate fully the poverty of Christ's anguish (suffered) in my flesh."

[287] Close by σῶμα is used for the body of Christ, Schauf, 101; → 137, 4 f.

[288] For various possibilities cf. Dib. Gefbr.³; C. F. D. Moule, The Epistles of St. Paul the Apostle to the Colossians and to Philemon (1957), ad loc. and → VI, 133 f. The simplest is a conjecture not mentioned in these works, namely, that of P. L. Hedley, "Ad Colossenses 2:20-3:4," ZNW, 27 (1928), 211-216: Χρῆσθε οὖν αὐτοῖς, ἀλλ' οὐκ ... Otherwise σάρξ in the vicinity of 2:18 is to be understood as σῶμα as above. The meaning is either: "is worth nothing, serving only to satisfy the flesh," or v. 22b and 23a are to be taken as a parenthesis and combined: "to destruction in use ..., not to the satisfaction of the flesh through the fact that honour is done them (by asceticism)."

[289] This is not impossible for Paul → 132, 28 ff. 2:16 shows that the danger of legalism is also seen, cf. E. Percy, Die Probleme d. Kolosser- u. Epheserbriefe (1946), 79, n. 27.

[290] Gen. of relationship; materially → 134, 1 ff.

[291] Hardly to be distinguished from baptism itself as a preparatory stage.

[292] Materially → 134, 14 ff. The figure of putting off the σῶμα τῆς σαρκός is even more vivid in connection with circumcision. It is also true that this means liberation from the demonic powers behind the Law (Percy, op. cit., 80). But the fact that σῶμα τῆς σαρκός can denote the physical body like the man of 3:5 shows that there is no approximation here to the Hell. derivation of sin from the physical σάρξ. Does not the Law of 2:14 threaten only the immoral? It is typical that Col. and Eph. no longer refer to temptation by the σάρξ → 133, 10 ff. πειράζειν and πειρασμός are not used, cf. Bultmann Theol., 520 (§ 58, 3k). Things would be different if we were to agree with J. Moffatt, The New Testament (1913) that the ref. is to a mere cutting off of the flesh from the body, or with Moule,

2. Ephesians.

The use of σάρξ is much simpler in Eph. In 5:31 (→ IV, 823, 12 ff.) we find the same quotation as in 1 C. 6:16. This leads to the description of the wife as σάρξ (= σῶμα v. 28) ἑαυτοῦ (the husband) in v. 29. The use of this concept for the Church as the body of Christ, presupposed in v. 32, is a distinctive one.[293] On 6:5 = Col. 3:22 → 136, 4 ff. 2:14 refers to the crucified body of the earthly Jesus → 133, 26 f.; 136, 19 f. In 2:11 (→ VI, 83, 5) the influence of the common statement about circumcision in the flesh (→ 108, 21 ff.) is only linguistic, since περιτομή is a name for Israel corresponding to ἔθνη. Hence ἐν σαρκί shows that the distinction between Jew and Gentile is provisional cf. → n. 248. It holds good within the earthly human world to which religion also belongs, but does not apply to membership of the community of Jesus. Hence there is also no reference to the uncircumcised → n. 87. The same reservation is expressed by the addition of λεγόμενος.[294] If one notes in 2:2 the parallel concept to 2:3 (→ 132, 30 ff.; III, 61, 9 ff.), one sees how σάρξ can take on an increasingly personal demonic character. What was among the Gentiles the aeon of this world or the prince of the power of the air was σάρξ among the Jews.[295] The division of man into σάρξ and διάνοιαι is surprising → 102, 29; 104, 8. The OT legacy may be seen, however, in the fact that the διάνοιαι (Nu. 15:39 LXX → IV, 966, 21 ff.) are just as corrupt as the σάρξ, cf. also → n. 297. 6:12 is distinctive.[296] Materially the statement corresponds to the later Jewish thinking which differentiates the sphere of non-corporeal spirits from that of the flesh → 109, 8 ff.[297]

3. Pastorals.

While echoing R. 8:3 (→ 133, 25 ff.); Col. 1:22 (→ 136, 19 f.) and Eph. 2:14 (→ 137, 6 f.), 1 Tm. 3:16 (→ VI, 416, 34 ff.) differs from all else thus far by saying that the appearing of Christ in the flesh (→ 139, 9 ff.; 140, 14 ff.; 147, 22 ff., 148, 1 ff., 39 ff.), i.e., in the earthly sphere, is already as such the event of

---

op. cit., ad loc. that it is to the death of Christ as a putting off of the body of flesh. Against the former it must be asserted that the negation in ἀχειροποιήτῳ cannot control what follows, and against the latter the main argument is the difficulty of the image of the circumcision of Jesus, esp. when one notes the par. to the baptism of the believer (not Jesus) and to v. 13a. In v. 15 the interpretation that Christ has put off His fleshly body (Robinson, 41 f., cf. C. A. A. Scott, *St. Paul* [1936], 75, 113, 262) is refuted by the fact that this object is not mentioned (J. B. Lightfoot, *St. Paul's Epistles to the Colossians and to Philemon* [1876] and Moule, ad loc.). W. Schmithals, "Die Häretiker in Galatien," ZNW, 47 (1956), 46 f. thinks there may be a Gnostic background.

[293] H. Schlier, *Religionsgeschichtliche Untersuchungen zu d. Ignatiusbr.* (1929), 91-93; cf. also E. Best, *One Body in Christ* (1955), 182. The *koine* reading in 5:30, however, is a correction on the basis of Gn. 2:23. On the Jewish tradition cf. P. Winter, "Sadokite Fragments, IV, 20, 21," ZAW, 68 (1956), 82. On the historical scheme of the heavenly and earthly syzygies cf. Schlier Eph. on 5:32 f. Exc. (276) → 147, 20 f. and → σῶμα.

[294] v. 12 sounds a different note. On the absence of the art. cf. Bl.-Debr. § 272, Radermacher, 117.

[295] This division with Dib. Gefbr.³, ad loc.; Schlier Eph., ad loc. (in spite of the alternation in vv. 5-8). Otherwise the par. would be even closer.

[296] αἷμα comes first as → 99, 17 f.; 141, 12; 147, 31; 148, 13 and 32 f.; n. 205, where the ref. is to substances which man "has."

[297] Acc. to Test. Sol. 20:12, too, the demons dwell in the firmament. In Eph. 2:2 f. the desire of the σάρξ corresponds to that of the prince of the power of the air, to the πνεῦμα which works in the disobedient. This cosmic distinction between earth and air, flesh and

salvation. The presupposition of the statement is the Hellenistic idea of the spheres → 124, 1 ff. Christ is viewed as a heavenly being whose entry into the world of men is already a miracle.[298] Characteristically this concept is not found at all elsewhere (→ VI, 445, 13 ff.).

IV. John.

1. The Gospel.

The usage here is quite different from that of Paul. This may be seen already in the comparative rarity of σάρξ. The use of πᾶσα σάρξ (17:2) is traditional → 106, 17 ff. The only new point is that the Father gives power over all flesh to the Son.[299] For the rest, apart from 6 instances in the contested section 6:51-58, σάρξ occurs in only 5 passages.

In 8:15 Jesus brings against His opponents the accusation: ὑμεῖς κατὰ τὴν σάρκα κρίνετε. The article shows that we are not simply to expound this in Pauline terms → n. 258. According to v. 14 such judgment is an expression of the blindness of man which has no knowledge of the whence and whither of Jesus. The same antithesis is mentioned in 7:27. Because the people of Jerusalem think they know whence Jesus comes they do not recognise Him as the Messiah. But before this statement comes the warning: μὴ κρίνετε κατ’ ὄψιν, 7:24. 6:42 makes it plain that the reference is to Jesus’ descent from parents who were known to the hearers. σάρξ, then, denotes that which is externally visible regarding the person of Jesus, and especially His descent → 126, 26 ff.; 136, 4 f. This is a wrong judgment, but not in the pregnant Pauline sense → 130, 25 ff. It is wrong only in relation to Jesus. It is quite right to assess a man by his genealogy and descent. But as far as Jesus is concerned these statements say nothing about whence He comes. σάρξ is thus the earthly sphere which is quite appropriate for the judgment of earthly things but which is wholly inadequate when one is assessing Him who comes from another sphere. The nuance of that which is sinful or which entices to sin is quite absent. 3:6 is related. This says of mankind and all that is born thereof that it is σάρξ. The term acquires its content from the antithetical parallelism in which it stands. Alongside the σάρξ is the πνεῦμα → VI, 438, 19 ff. σάρξ is the human earthly sphere which has no knowledge of God and hence cannot mediate such knowledge → 109, 8 ff.; 141, 21 ff.; n. 308 cf. I, 681, 30 ff.[300] This does not mean that as such it stands in sin. It is expressly declared in 15:22-24 that only the coming of Jesus makes the cosmos sin. In its being as σάρξ the world does not find, of course, anything that can save it from a state marked out for lostness. To that degree σάρξ as the earthly lower sphere[301] determines

---

spirit, is thus quite different from the qualified antithesis of σάρξ and πνεῦμα in Pl., which is echoed at most in 2:3 but not found elsewhere in Eph., cf. D. E. H. Whiteley, "Eph. VI. 12," Exp. T., 68 (1956/57), 100-103.

[298] Cf. Schweizer, op. cit. (→ n. 225), 132 f. and on the schema of the hymn the fivefold chiasmus in Prv. 10:1-5.

[299] Presumably at the incarnation acc. to the second half of the v. Cf. → n. 95.

[300] We do not have here, then, the later Jewish view that events in heaven and on earth correspond, Test. Sol. 20:15; cf. Schl. J. on 3:31. To relate 3:31 to the Baptist (C. K. Barrett, The Gospel acc. to St. John [1955], ad loc.) is thus difficult. Cf. R. Schnackenburg, "Die 'situationsgelösten' Redestücke in Joh. 3," ZNW, 49 (1958), 94, who refers 3:31 to Nicodemus as the representative and type of all.

[301] Cf. 3:3, 7, 12; 8:23, 44, where ἐπίγεια and κάτω are par. concepts → VI, 390, 20 f.;

the one who simply lives in it, and it almost takes on the character of a power
(→ 113, 17 ff.), especially as it is also the principle of conception and birth
→ 106, 26 ff. But the world acquires its sinful character only through unbelief,
not through the σάρξ. It is never called σάρξ after the decision for unbelief. [302]
In 1:13 σάρξ is the principle of natural birth as distinct from birth of God. To
the σάρξ is ascribed a will, so that it is parallel to ἀνήρ rather than αἵματα
→ 109, 27 f.; 141, 12 ff. and n. 296. It thus embraces, not an anatomically distinct
part of the body, but the whole man as the one who stands over against God,
not possessing salvation. σάρξ ἐγένετο (1:14) does not mean that the Logos
took upon Himself the sin of the world. [303] Nor is it merely a geographical note
on the place where revelation came to pass. It tells us that the self-revealing
took the form of man [304] and did not merely bear it as a vesture but became
identical with it in order that those born of God might see the δόξα of the
Father [305] both in the patent if misunderstood miracles and also in the obedience
of Jesus even to the cross. [306] The theological basis of the incarnation is thus to
be found in the fact that in the cosmic controversy of God with the world which
accuses Him faith can be created only by a μαρτυρεῖν (→ IV, 497, 34 ff.) which
includes the full committal of the whole person and not by a mere impartation
of divine *gnosis*. How different the theology is here from that of Paul may be
seen from the fact that, while Paul certainly knows the pre-existent Christ, he
never speaks of His descent or indeed of His incarnation.

Finally the antithesis of σάρξ and πνεῦμα occurs again in 6:63 → III, 741, 22 ff.

If 6:51c-58 is excised as an ecclesiastical redaction, [307] the antithesis can be understood as in 3:6. There, too, the mystery of the descent and ascent of the Son of Man

---

E. Schweizer, "Der Kirchenbegriff im Ev. u. d. Briefen d. Joh.," Studia Evangelica, TU,
73 (1959), 373.

[302] Jn.'s starting-pt. is thus two-sphere thinking. But unlike Paul he does not get essentially
beyond these categories. Yet this does not include "substantial" thinking, neither in the
sense that the believer gets a share in the spiritual substance of Jesus and thus loses his
σάρξ, nor in the sense that after death he is set in an upper sphere in which the substance
of the flesh ceases. Asceticism is quite alien. The decisive thought-form is that of controversy between God and man (T. Preiss, "Die Rechtfertigung im joh. Denken," *Ev. Theol.*,
16 [1956], 293-303) in which the πνεῦμα, not as substance but as the witness of the upper
world of God, represents God's case and convinces the world.

[303] This is first said only in 1:29. In a Chr. hymn underlying the Prologue (without
vv. 6-8, 12b, 13, R. Schnackenburg, "Logos-Hymnus u. johann. Prolog," BZ, NF, 1 [1957],
69-109) what preceded v. 14 was probably a ref. in the language of Wisdom literature to
the presence of the as yet non-incarnate Logos in the world. John, however, focuses
everything on the attitude to Jesus. For him, then, everything from v. 5 on is related to the
incarnate Logos (E. Käsemann, "Aufbau u. Anliegen d. johann. Prologs," *Libertas Christiana* [1957] 79-82, though cf. Cullmann, *op. cit.* [n. 238], 269). For him σάρξ is once
again the sphere which has no knowledge of God but which becomes God's enemy only
by rejecting Jesus. Cf. also S. Schulz, "Die Komposition d. Johannesprologs," Studia Evangelica, TU, 73 (1959), 351-359.

[304] Perhaps σάρξ is used instead of ἄνθρωπος because the idea of the heavenly man
is still at work, J. Héring, "Kyrios Anthropos," RevHPhR, 16 (1936), 207-209.

[305] v. 14b c may be the Evangelist's own addition → n. 303.

[306] Schweizer, *op. cit.* (→ n. 225), 56 f.

[307] For the best arguments cf. G. Bornkamm, "Die eucharistische Rede im Joh.-Ev.,"
ZNW, 47 (1956), 161-169; cf. Bultmann J., *ad loc.*; H. Koester, "Gesch. u. Kultus im
Joh.-Ev. u. bei Ign. v. Antiochien," ZThK, 54 (1957), 62. W. Wilkens, *Die Entstehungs-
geschichte d. vierten Ev.* (1958), 28 f., 75 f. tries to show that the author himself added an
original eucharistic pericope.

is related to it, 3:13 f.; 6:51a, 62. Natural knowledge cannot grasp this. [308] If, however, 6:51c-58 is regarded as an original part of the Gospel, [309] 6:63 says exactly the same as is said in a similar debate in 8:15.

6:63 means, then, that he who considers the σάρξ of Jesus, His outer appearance, is not helped at all. Only the preaching of Jesus, who proclaims Himself to be the Son of the Father, is πνεῦμα and ζωή → VI, 441, 7 ff. The verse is thus warning against a sacramentalism which misunderstands the σάρξ eaten in the Supper as the "medicine of immortality," [310] for the sixfold σάρξ, combined with αἷμα (→ 109, 27 f.), is to be referred to the Eucharist. If here the believer eats [311] the σάρξ of Jesus, he is told that nothing less than the coming of the Son of God into the σάρξ was necessary for his salvation. At the same time he confesses herewith that he accepts this and will live by this gift. [312]

2. The Epistles.

The confession (→ VI, 209, 28 ff.) of Jesus' coming "in the flesh" [313] (→ 137, 25 ff.) is regarded in 1 Jn. 4:2; [314] 2 Jn. 7 as the point of division. We now find not merely faith and unbelief but also the new phenomenon of a false faith in Jesus. The danger is obviously not that there will be too strong a stress on His humanity but rather that there will be too strong a stress on His deity. [315] This is connected with Hellenistic cults of divine saviours. The assertion that the Son of God took σάρξ increasingly became a central one in early dogmatics (→ 145, 25 ff.) but at the same time the Johannine root of the assertion (→ 139, 9 ff.) became more and more blurred. In 1 Jn. 2:16 we find the expression ἐπιθυμία τῆς σαρκός → n. 52. [316] Parallel to this is ἐπιθυμία τῶν ὀφθαλμῶν. The preceding warning not to love the world might be taken in an OT sense as a warning

---

[308] In 3:6, as in 1:13, the σάρξ is, of course, only the principle of natural birth which does not mediate salvation. There is no ref. to this here. H. Becker, Die Reden d. Joh.-Ev. (1956), 68, n. 4 ascribes 3:6 to the source and 6:63 to the Evangelist.

[309] Apart from what is said in E. Schweizer, "Das joh. Zeugnis vom Herrenmahl," Ev. Theol., 12 (1952/53), 353-363, ref. may be made to S. Schulz, Untersuchungen z. Menschensohnchristologie im Joh.-Ev. (1957), 114, 135-139, who shows that 5:28 f. is a tradition used by the Evangelist and thinks the same may be true of 6:51-58 (54b). This is supported by W. Nauck, Die Tradition u. der Charakter d. 1. Joh.-briefes (1957), 23. Cf. also W. Wilkens, "Das Abendmahlszeugnis im vierten Ev.," Ev. Theol., 18 (1958), 354-370. ὑπέρ in v. 51c also occurs in 10:11, 15; 11:50 ff.; 18:14 (17:19). The ref. to Jesus' death in vv. 51-58 leads to schism in v. 61 as in 10:17-19. The meaning of σάρξ is exactly the same as in 8:15, where the same discussion precedes as in 6:42. There is ref. to καταβαίνειν both in 6:51a and 6:58, which is not just a redactional repetition of v. 51. Finally, since σάρξ is so rare in Jn., its use in 6:63 would be strange if unrelated to a later addition in vv. 51-58.

[310] Ign. Eph., 20, 2 → III, 23, 16 ff.

[311] τρώγειν does not mean "to chew," for Jn. 13:18 has τρώγειν for the ἐσθίειν of Ps. 41:9 and cf. Mt. 24:38 and Lk. 17:27.

[312] Par. 13:6-10 where there is a ref. to baptism. 15:3, too, refers to the Word of Jesus (Barrett, op. cit. [→ n. 300], ad loc.). Is σάρξ Syr. usage (Bultmann J., 175, n. 4)? But the Syr. transl. make no distinction as compared with the Synoptic σῶμα, J. H. Bernard, St. John I, ICC (1928), CLXIX.

[313] The expression is broader than Jn. 1:14. Obviously the misunderstanding that a divine being might appear in the flesh as a vesture is no threat.

[314] Acc. to some witnesses repeated in 4:3.

[315] Cf. also Nauck, op. cit., 124 f.

[316] The thought here is that of sin as well as physical dissatisfaction, J. Chaine, Les épitres catholiques (1939), ad loc.

not to put one's trust in the world. But the term "to love" shows that the reference is to a subjection which goes beyond what the OT has in view, → III, 895, 24 ff. Furthermore v. 16 says that the desire of the flesh, like everything in the cosmos, comes from the cosmos and not from the Father. Here, then, we have the dualistic thinking in which man is determined by the sphere which surrounds him. σάρξ, as the parallel terms show, is regarded as the organ of sense impressions which stimulate desire. [317] If this is typically Hellenistic, there are good Jewish models for the warning against seductive glances. [318]

V. Hebrews.

As in 1 Jn. 4:2 σάρξ can denote the earthly existence of Jesus. The expression "the days of his flesh" [319] (5:7) shows that Jesus is regarded as a heavenly being whose earthly life was only for a period. [320] Similarly αἷμα καὶ σάρξ (2:14 → n. 296) is plainly viewed as that which Jesus assumed. The Jewish legacy (→ 109, 27 f.) is retained to the degree that the concept embraces the whole of human nature including the intellectual functions. But the "substantial" character, which is not excluded in the Jewish expression, is now much more prominent (→ 99, 17 f.), since it is said here that a heavenly being assumed flesh and blood. [321] In this way he who is subject to death, and thus stands in need of redemption, is distinguished from the angels, v. 16. [322] Related is 12:9, where the "fathers of our flesh" are differentiated from the "Father of spirits." This is hardly an anthropological dualism in which the spirits are the souls of men. The saying is rather to be understood in terms of the two-sphere thinking which is so characteristic of Hb. [323] The Father of spirits is the Almighty to whom the upper world is also subject (→ 109, 8 ff.), while the fathers who belong to the sphere of flesh are earthly fathers. The addition of ἡμῶν [324] shows, of course, that the thought of generation is also present → 106, 26 ff. δικαιώματα σαρκός (9:10) is almost always understood as a term for statutes relating to the flesh. [325] This is

---

[317] → 103, 22 ff. What is meant is primarily though not exclusively sexual desire, cf. Schnackenburg J., ad loc. Cf. Reitzenstein Ir. Erl., 25 : "Consider the world ... which is all desire." For the further development → n. 368.

[318] Gn. 39:7; Nu. 15:39; Job 31:7; Ez. 6:9; Sir. 23:4-6; Test. R. 2:4; Mt. 5:29; (2 Pt. 2:14). Chaine, op. cit., ad loc. refers to Qoh. 2:10; Prv. 27:20 (which acc. to him refer to fornication); 1 K. 20:6; Qoh. 4:8 (with a ref. to avarice).

[319] σῶμα is first used for this in 10:5, 10, where it is taken from LXX and denotes the sacrificial body, Mi. Hb. on 10:10, n. 1.

[320] Mi. Hb., ad loc. refers to Gn. 6:3, 5; 9:29; 10:25; 35:28; Dt. 30:20; Lk. 1:7, which help us to understand the expression.

[321] Wnd. Hb. on 5:7 thinks Jesus set aside the flesh at His exaltation but took the blood with Him, 9:14. But this is only a concrete way of saying that the crucifixion retains its atoning power. Hence one cannot make any essential distinction between the two substances.

[322] H. Strathmann, Der Brief an d. Hb., NT Deutsch, 9⁷ (1957) on 2:14-16. But the saying differs from Paul. The train of thought connected with the expression σάρξ καὶ αἷμα culminates in redemption from death, which is characteristic of earthly creatures. The "forerunner" (6:20) overcomes death when He takes the substance flesh and then lays it aside again. With this schema is linked a thought which is important for the author of Hb., namely, that of the atoning sacrifice of the High-priest which remits sins, v. 17. Here the taking of flesh and blood is important in order that He may have compassion and make true intercession.

[323] Cf. the contrasting of ὁ θεός and ἄνθρωποι in 6:16 f.

[324] Only with σάρξ, not πνεύματα, Mi. Hb., ad loc.

[325] Mi. Hb., also Wnd. Hb., Strathmann, op. cit. C. Spicq, L'épître aux Hb., II² (1953),

supported by 9:13 f., where the cleanness of the flesh is contrasted with the cleansing of the → συνείδησις [326] → VI, 982, 19 ff.

The ref. is undoubtedly to cultic purity. [327] The prophetic saying in Hos. 6:6; 1 S. 15:22, which also plays a part in primitive Christianity (Mt. 9:13; 12:7), [328] exerts an influence here. But this external cleanness is also a sign of the earthly sphere in general. Purity of conscience is found only in the priest of the temple not made with hands, which does not belong to this creation, 9:11. [329] One may ask, then, whether the phrase in 9:10 does not mean "statutes of the earthly sphere." [330] At any rate, the external aspect is not contrasted with an inner aspect which denotes a possibility of man's own. It is contrasted with man as he stands before God and is judged by Him. Hence only the heavenly Priest has this inner purity.

Hard to understand is 10:20, where the σάρξ of Jesus is the veil through which He has made a new and living way.

Is the σάρξ of Jesus the crucifixion? But apart from the fact that σῶμα is used for σάρξ in this sense (→ n. 319), one would then have to take the διά, first locally, then instrumentally, and the curtain would have to be regarded as a possibility of entry rather than a hindrance. The last two arguments still apply if σάρξ is taken in the broader sense of the human nature of Jesus. [331] Should one say, then, that the flesh of Jesus had to be destroyed, as the curtain had to be torn, in order that blood might be offered in sacrifice, [332] or in order that Jesus might attain to full divine sonship? [333] Or is σάρξ the place where the heavenly and the earthly worlds meet, but in such a way that the heavenly world is concealed thereby, and hence the σάρξ of Jesus both conceals and opens access to heaven? [334] If the clause is not a gloss [335] the most likely interpretation is that the way to heaven leads the believer alone past the σάρξ of Jesus, but in such a way that he goes through it to the heavenly High-priest, who on the far side of everything earthly intercedes for him with God, [336] → V, 76, n. 124.

In all these passages σάρξ denotes the earthly sphere which is separated from the world of God. But the thought of sin is never linked with it. Like the cultic Law in relation to the new covenant, the earthly sphere in relation to the heavenly is the inadequate and provisional sphere which is threatened by death but which

---

ad loc. and already John of Damascus, Comm. on Hb. on 7:16 (MPG, 95 [1864], 964).
[326] Cf. 10:22, where the συνείδησις located in the heart and the σῶμα are complementary, → 143, 16 ff. But in Hb. 9:13 f., too, the σάρξ stands in a certain contrast to the sphere of the πνεῦμα, → VI, 446, 13 ff.
[327] Acc. to the OT relations of soul are to be set in order too, Wnd. Hb., ad loc.
[328] Cf. also Plat. Crat., 405b.
[329] The δικαιώματα of 9:1 are related to the sanctuary in the κόσμος in contrast to that not made with hands, 9:11, 24.
[330] This finds support also in 7:16 (→ 144, 3 ff.), and, with a different theological slant, cf. R. 2:28 f. → 129, 28 ff.
[331] So Spicq, op. cit., ad loc.
[332] So W. Manson, The Epistle to the Hb. (1951), 67 f. and J. Moffatt, To the Hb., ICC (1924), ad loc.
[333] This is considered by Strathmann, op. cit., ad loc., but he pts. to the ἡμῖν as an argument against it.
[334] N. A. Dahl, "The Approach to God acc. to Hb. 10:19-25," Interpretation, 5 (1951), 405.
[335] C. Holsten, Exegetische Untersuchung über Hb. 10:20 (1875), 15.
[336] Cf. E. Käsemann, "Das wandernde Gottesvolk," FRL, 55² (1957), 146 f.: Ordered to the sphere of the earthly, the σάρξ is a hindrance on the way to God → VI, 446, 13 ff.

is never rebellious and does not revolt against God. [337] Hb. thus occupies a place in the history of the term as it developed outside Paul and found clearest expression in R. 1:3 f. (→ 126, 22 ff.) and John (→ 138, 7 ff.).

VI. The Catholic Epistles, → 140, 14 ff.

1. On James 5:3 → 124, 11.

2. The usage in 1 Pt. lies for the most part within the confines of what has been said already. The OT πᾶσα σάρξ (→ 106, 17 ff.) occurs only in the quotation in 1:24. 3:18 and 4:6 contain two-sphere thinking, but they are traditional → VI, 447, 11 ff. (ἐν) σαρκί in 4:1 f. simply denotes the time of life on earth, → 126, 14 f. Worth noting, however, is the twofold addition to παθεῖν, since no one can think of other than earthly suffering. Since this occurs first in connection with Christ, it goes back to formulae like 3:18. [338] If 4:1b is to be expounded as in → V, 922, 19 ff., then σαρκί is to be understood along the lines of Col. 2:11 → 136, 21 ff. More likely, however, is a reference to bodily suffering in persecution, with a conscious assimilation to v. 1a. [339] Here too, then, we have the contrast of the earthly and heavenly spheres. In 3:21, as in Hb., we also find the use which differentiates σάρξ as the external aspect from the συνείδησις → 142, 1 f.

3. Jd. 7 is of interest. Fornication with "strange flesh" refers to the lust of the Sodomites for the angels who visited Lot, [340] → 109, 26; 119, 16 ff.; 123, 9 f. σάρξ is thus "corporeality," which is different in men and angels, → n. 215. This is the object of sexual desire. But sexual desire is not wicked as such; it is wicked only in its perversion. The v. is adopted in 2 Pt. 2:10, but ἑτέρα is dropped and ἐν ἐπιθυμίᾳ μιασμοῦ added; 2 Pt. regards carnal lust itself as sinful. A decisive step is thus made towards the ascetic despising of the flesh. The Hellenistic catch-word ἐπιθυμίαι σαρκός (→ n. 52) is also introduced in 2:18 in place of the simple ἐπιθυμίαι of Jd. 16. The verses Jd. 6, 23 (→ IV, 692, 38 ff.) are very obscure. In both σάρξ denotes man in his concrete outward existence, polluted by (unnatural sexual?) sin, → 125, 22 f.; 147, 6 ff. The fact that even the coat he wears is infected shows how strong the view is. Yet there is no thought whatever of an intellectual or spiritual core which is not affected by this pollution. The statements are too brief, however, to allow of any sure interpretation.

VII. σάρκινος (→ 101, 25 ff.), σαρκικός (→ 121, 1).

a. The use of the adjective yields no new insights as compared with that of the noun. The common Greek σάρκινος occurs in a neutral sense only in 2 C. 3:3 in an OT quotation. The fleshly tables of the heart [341] are viewed favourably in

---

[337] Mi. Hb. on 7:26 ff.
[338] One should perhaps read ἔπαθεν here too.
[339] πέπαυται ἁμαρτίας then means that with His resolve to suffer He radically rejected the way of sin.
[340] Hence angels have flesh or at least appear to have it, but → 109, 12 f.; 120, 21 ff.
[341] Do Roman inscr. lauding officials in the East form the antithesis, M. Smith, Conference of the Society for Biblical Literature and Exegesis (1959)? Is Paul the bearer of a letter in the sense of 1 Th. 1:7 f. (W. R. Baird, loc. cit.)?

contrast with the stony tables of the Law. [342] They denote the inward part of man, which is set in antithesis with the externality of purely legal fulfilment of the commandments, → 107, 22 ff. On the other hand, the ἐντολὴ σαρκίνη of Hb. 7:16 (→ 142, 7 f.) is the Law which belongs to the earthly sphere. This does not have the power of indestructible life, as heavenly things have. [343] The oath of the living God Himself stands in contrast to this, v. 21. In Paul the word occurs twice apart from the quotation already mentioned. Except for the fact that in both cases it refers to man, [344] it differs in no way from σαρκικός. In 1 C. 3:1-3 it is used in alternation with this for the Corinthians, who show by their contentiousness that they are still men and not πνευματικοί, → VI, 424, n. 605. In R. 7:14 Paul calls himself σάρκινος in his pre-Christian days. The antithesis here, then, is νόμος πνευματικός, and "sold under sin" is said in interpretation, → VI, 160, 29 ff. Thi confirms the fact that σάρξ here does not embrace only one side of man but the whole man inasmuch as he is not in faith or under grace, → 133, 32 ff. In both passages, then, σάρκινος is used in the full Pauline sense. It qualifies the man who in pugnacious desire for glory or Pharisaic fulfilment of duty builds his life only within the σάρξ and pays no heed to the ἐπαγγελία.

b. σαρκικός is used 6 times in Paul but elsewhere only in 1 Pt. 2:11. Formally this use depends on Paul, but in content it is plainly Hellenistic. [345] If fleshly lusts war against the soul, anthropological dualism is present. The soul is the better part against which the flesh, which evokes desires, is fighting, → 104, 16 ff. [346] In R. 15:27; 1 C. 9:11, however, σαρκικά is used neutrally of outward things such as means of sustenance, clothes etc., while πνευματικά denotes the Gospel. This corresponds to the usage → 128, 6 ff. On 1 C. 3:3 → 144, 9 ff., on 2 C. 1:12; 10:4 → 128, 15 f. σαρκικός means what is inadequate, what is not decisive before God, but in such a way that it tempts man to be satisfied with it and hence to lose God.

F. The Post-New Testament Period.

1. The Post-Apostolic Fathers.

Here the term σάρξ is increasingly Hellenised. The Semitic expression πᾶσα σάρξ occurs only as a formula in 1 Cl., 59, 3; 64 (→ n. 91) and in a quotation in 2 Cl., 7, 6; 17, 5. "Flesh and blood" is not used for man at all, → 109, 27 f.; 145, 20 f.; it occurs only with ref. to the crucifixion of Jesus or the Eucharist, → 109, 2; 148, 2 ff. In

---

[342] Flesh contains a ref. to what is living, Käsemann, 6.

[343] Cf. 9:10 : A commandment which has to do with the flesh of men (cultic purity) (Mi. Hb., ad loc.); or : A commandment which demands fleshly things (descent from Levi) (Wnd. Hb., ad loc.). At any rate the ref. is not to a commandment which derives from the flesh or provokes to sin.

[344] Mi. Hb. on 7:15.

[345] F. W. Beare, The First Epistle of Peter (1948), ad loc. refers to Plat. Phaed., 82c → n. 51. It is typical that in 1 Pt. sin consists merely in a wicked life, Bultmann Theol., 524 § 58, 31.

[346] H. Preisker in Wnd. Kath. Br.³, ad loc. refers to the fact that in 3:18; 4:1 f., ὁ σάρξ comprises the whole man. But the adj., adopted from Paul, can have a different sense from the noun (→ ψυχή and ψυχικός). Furthermore 3:18; 4:6 and probably 4:1 f. are traditional. Finally the cosmic dualism of 3:18; 4:6 and esp. the ἐν σαρκί of 4:1 f. are releated to the Hell. idea of a soul which comes from the upper sphere and dwells in the flesh. It is possible

traditional style σάρξ is the place of circumcision (Barn., 9, 4; Dg., 4, 4 → 108, 2 ff.), [347] a term for the earthly Jesus ("Christ after the flesh" or the like, 1 Cl., 32, 2; Ign. Sm., 1, 1; Eph., 20, 2; Mg., 13, 2), and also a term for human life gen. (2 Cl., 8, 2). [348] 2 Cl., 5, 5; 9, 2-4 refer characteristically to "this flesh" because there is also risen flesh → 146, 8; 147, 8; 148, 3 f., 19 ff. Thus σάρξ can denote the human "body" (Barn., 7, 9; 8, 6; Herm. v., 3, 9, 3) or simply the "person," Ign. R., 2, 1. The Gk. combination of "flesh and hair" (→ n. 33) is found in Herm. v., 3, 10, 4; 12, 1. In particular the body which Jesus sacrificed on the cross is called His σάρξ, Barn., 5, 1. 12 f.; [349] 6, 3; 7, 5; Ign. Sm., 1, 2. Here, then, σάρξ is used for σῶμα, → n. 319, 361. Barn., 10, 4 has an older usage when it speaks of the consuming of σάρκες → n. 84. Barn., 5, 13; 1 Cl., 6, 3; Pol., 7, 2 (= Mk. 14:38) are quotations.

New here is the problem of the hierarchy of flesh and soul or flesh and spirit, whether in Jesus or in man gen. Even where the answer is not Gk., the question can be understood only in Gk. terms. There is no marked emphasis in 1 Cl., 49, 6: "He gave his flesh for our flesh and his soul for our souls." [350] Only the two together constitute the whole man, but both are offered up. The soul is not the part which survives. If a strong body is necessary to receive revelation acc. to Herm. v., 3, 10, 7; s., 9, 1. 2, this certainly does not reflect any hostility to the body. Hell. dualism is clearest in Dg., 6, 5 f.: "The flesh hates the soul ... because it hinders it from yielding to lusts." Lusts are plainly seen here as a function of the flesh, against which the soul battles → 144, 20 ff. Yet it is also stated that the soul loves the flesh and members, [351] and this ought to be an example to believers to do the same towards those who persecute them. In Herm. s., 5, 7, 4 both spirit and flesh are stained, and acc. to m., 3, 1; 10, 2, 6 the spirit dwells in the flesh, → VI, 391, 10 ff.

This problem is worked out most fully in Ign. [352] In the first place he stands in the dogmatic tradition for which the incarnation of the Pre-existent is the decisive saving event → 137, 26 f. Thus Pol., 7, 1 adopts the dogmatic norm of 1 Jn. 4:2 f. Since men would not otherwise know Him, Christ had to reveal Himself in the flesh, Barn., 5, 6, 10 f.; 6, 7. 9. 14. [353] David was His ancestor in the flesh, Barn., 12, 10. At first πνεῦμα, He became σάρξ, 2 Cl., 9, 5. [354] The most interesting notion is in Herm. s., 5, 6, 5-7: The flesh of Jesus served the indwelling spirit so well that as a reward it made it participant in the resurrection too. [355] This antithesis to the πνεῦμα, which is not found in Jn. 1:14 or 1 Jn. 4:2 f., shows that σάρξ is understood much more strongly as substance here. This is also true in Ign. Jesus is ἐν σαρκὶ γενόμενος θεός, Eph., 7, 2, σαρκοφόρος,

---

that for 1 Pt. σάρξ is the total nature of the unredeemed man (Beare, op. cit., ad loc.) and the ψυχή is God's Spirit. But even so, Hell. terminology is used with no sense of distinction.

[347] This circumcision seems to be disparaged in 4(5) Esr. 1:31 → n. 248.
[348] Similarly the "way of the flesh" in Ign. R., 9, 3 is the earthly journey of Ignatius.
[349] Barn., 5, 13 in the plur.
[350] The choice of σάρξ here is partly influenced by the preceding αἷμα.
[351] No longer, then, is this the whole man, but the lower part abandoned to lusts, → 109, 27 f.
[352] Cf. on this Schlier Ign., 131-135; C. C. Richardson, The Christianity of Ign. of Antioch (1935), 48-50; H. W. Bartsch, Gnostisches Gut u. Gemeindetradition bei Ign. v. Antiochien (1940), 104, 119-122; T. Rüsch, Die Entstehung d. Lehre vom Hl. Geist bei Ign. v. Antiochien, Theophilus v. Antiochien u. Iren. v. Lyon, Diss. Zürich (1952), 50-54, 59-65; H. v. Campenhausen, Kirchliches Amt u. geistliche Vollmacht (1953), 106, n. 3; Bultmann Theol., 535-540 (§ 38, 3 o); Köster, op. cit., 56-69.
[353] The Chr. addition to Test. B. 10:8 also speaks of the "God who has appeared in the flesh."
[354] Acc. to 14, 3 f. the same is true of the Church. As pre-existent, it is spiritual. It appeared in the σάρξ of Jesus, and remains His σάρξ after His death, while He is πνεῦμα. The incarnation of the Spirit-Christ thus continues in the Church → n. 372.
[355] Cf. Dib. Herm. Exc. on s., 5, 6, 7; Schlier Eph. on 5:32 f., Exc. (269 f.).

Sm., 5, 2. [356] Thus the two substances [357] which characterise the two spheres became one in Him. He is σαρκικός τε καὶ πνευματικός, Eph., 7, 2; cf. Mg., 1, 2. Hence heaven and earth and God and man [358] are brought together again. Not what Jesus did or preached is important, but His being as such. [359]

This is a Hellenistic approach. Yet the answer is quite different. The point is not the saving of a divine kernel in man from the fleshly husk. Hence the real incarnation of Christ is emphasised and it is also maintained that the unity of flesh and spirit continues in the Risen Lord. [360] This is also mediated to the believer, perhaps in the sacrament, [361] but esp. in an appropriation in life. [362] The believer, too, is fleshly and spiritual, Ign. Tr. inscr.; 12, 1; Sm., 1, 1; Pol., 2, 2, [363] and is summoned to work out this unity ethically, e.g., to take pleasure in his spouse in both "flesh and spirit," Pol., 5, 1; Mg., 13, 1; R. inscr., adj. Eph., 10, 3; Mg., 13, 2; Pol., 1, 2. The sign of the reconciled man is not then, as in Pl. (→ 133, 8 ff.), the assailing of the spirit by the flesh or the overcoming of the flesh by the spirit. It is the union of the two. To be sure, a positive evaluation of σάρξ is possible only in virtue of this union. σάρξ is simply the corporeality which only demons and heretics lack, Sm., 3, 2; 2 (→ 120, 27 ff.; 124, 24 ff.). But it can become a power which takes man captive. As such it can be opposed to God or Christ (as in Paul), i.e., when man lives κατὰ σάρκα, Mg., 6, 2; R., 8, 3. [364], [365] In this sense it is true that the spirit does not tolerate the erring of the flesh, Phld., 7, 1. In all these passages, and even more plainly in Phld., 7, 2; Mg., 3, 2, we do not find anthropological

---

[356] Cf. Sib., 1, 325; Ep. apostolorum, 19, 21 (ed. C. Schmidt and J. Wajnberg, "Gespräche Jesu mit seinen Jüngern nach der Auferstehung," TU, 43 [1919], 66, 72 f.; cf. 294 f.) → 149, 3 ff.

[357] R., 6, 2; 7, 2 calls the ὕλη a characteristic of the earthly sphere.

[358] Jesus is θεὸς ἀνθρωπίνως φανερούμενος, Eph., 19, 3.

[359] Hence the Redeemer remains silent here, Köster, 60 f.

[360] He is ἐν σαρκί, σαρκικός, Sm., 3; 12, 2. On the other hand, the supraterrestrial angels are subject to judgment, Sm., 6, 1.

[361] It is debated whether Ign. is a magico-sacramentalist (→ III, 743, 8 ff.) or not (Rüsch, 60-62; C. Maurer, Ign. v. Antiochien u. d. Joh.-Ev. [1949], 88-99). Note should be taken of the passages which contain σάρξ (cf. → I, 543, 34 ff.). If in Eph., 7, 2 Christ can be a physician in His unity of flesh and spirit, this may be linked with 20, 2 → III, 23, 16 ff. But if one reads there the more difficult ὅ for ὅς (Maurer, 93 f.), as in Tr., 8, 1, the relation to the sacrament disappears. The Eucharist is called the σάρξ of Jesus in Sm., 7, 1. But it is an open question whether Ign. has in mind the substantial appropriation in the sacrament of the union of flesh and spirit in Christ (Köster, 61), since this is not elsewhere linked with the Eucharist. In R., 7, 3; Phld., 4, 1 we find the association of flesh and blood typical in sayings about the death of Jesus (→ 144, 32 ff.), Sm., 1, 1; 12, 2; Tr., 8, 1. Bartsch, op. cit., 119-122 finds the sacramentally mediated πάθος of Jesus in Sm., 12, 2 and Tr. inscr. But Phld., 5, 1 calls the Gospel rather than the Eucharist the σάρξ of Jesus. Cf. → n. 362.

[362] The Eucharist also typifies the fellowship with Christ attained in martyrdom (R., 7, 3) or the fashioning of a life in faith and love, Maurer, op. cit. 88-92; Bultmann Theol., 537 f. (§ 58, 3 o).

[363] It is debated whether the ref. is to the Spirit as donum superadditum or to a purely anthropological ἔσωθέν τε καὶ ἔξωθεν, R., 3, 2, as Richardson, op. cit., 48 f., with appeal to the LXX, is inclined to think. Since Ign. speaks only of believers it is hard to decide. The question was probably not so sharp for Ign. since the Holy Spirit renews the human spirit. One can hardly regard the antithesis as purely anthropological since LXX dualism is cosmological (→ 109, 8 ff.) and this predominates in Judaism and the NT too.

[364] σάρξ, then, is not just sensuality but the earthly sphere which can acquire power, though in distinction to Paul it is seen as corruptibility rather than sin, R. Bultmann, "Ign. u. Pls.," Studia Paulina, Festschr. J. de Zwaan (1953), 45 f. In Eph., 16, 2 the tearing down of houses κατὰ σάρκα is probably about fornication. But even so σάρξ is the earthly-corporeal sphere confronting the higher sphere of faith, though without the theological significance of Mg., 6, 2; R., 8, 3.

[365] Dg., 5, 8 corresponds even more clearly to Pauline usage in 2 C. 10 : 3 : Christians are in the flesh but do not live after it.

dualism but the antithesis between God and man.[366] The two views of the σάρξ are united in Eph., 8, 2. Spiritual men, i.e., those ruled by God's Spirit, are in absolute opposition to carnal men, i.e., those ruled by the flesh.[367] But for this very reason their fleshly being, i.e., their external, bodily life, becomes spiritual.

This leads to increasing suspicion of the flesh as such. Did., 1, 4 warns against "carnal and physical desires," the ref. being to the human egoism castigated in the Sermon on the Mount.[368] The "desire of the flesh," which in Barn., 10, 9 keeps the Jews from true understanding, is taken sexually.[369] Pol., 5, 3 has the sexually tinged ἐπιθυμία for σάρξ in a quotation. Sexual continence is clearly preached in 1 Cl., 38, 2. Yet, unmistakable though the ascetic features may be, the Hell. flight from the flesh is not taught. The admonition to keep the flesh[370] like a temple and not to pollute it is quite common, Herm. s., 5, 7, 1-4; m., 4, 1, 9; Ign. Phld., 7, 2; Pol., 5, 2; 2 Cl., 8, 4 and 6; 9, 3; cf. 14, 3-15, 1; for this flesh will be raised up and judged, 2 Cl., 9, 1 and 5; cf. 1 Cl., 26, 3.[371] Esp. interesting is the statement in 2 Cl., 14, 5 that it becomes immortal only by union with the Holy Ghost. Strictly this contradicts what is said about the resurrection, but the author is not aware of this. Already one sees the problem caused by the fusion of a bibl.-hbr. acceptance of the flesh and a Hell. depreciation of it. The solution is often found in the fact that real life consists only in a union of spirit and flesh (as corporeality). This can easily be taken to mean that the union is possible only when the flesh gives place to the spirit, whether in a flawless marriage or in asceticism. Christ is the true example of this union of spirit and flesh.[372]

2. Apocryphal Acts.

Here, too, the virgin birth is a σαρκωθῆναι, Act. Phil. 141 (p. 76, 9). In it a πνεῦμα δυνάμεως is sent into the σάρξ, namely, Mary.[373] Only this can redeem our flesh so that it can be raised again.[374] σάρξ is used for earthly life gen. in Act. Thom. 66 (p. 183, 5), 159 (270, 15).[375] It is what man carries and what differentiates him from spiritual beings, 66 vl. (183, 10), cf. 45 (162, 20). The σαρκικὸν εἴδωλον is not the true ego, Act. Joh. 28 (p. 166, 13) → 124, 26 ff. Ascetic suspicion of the σάρξ is esp. strong in Act. Thom. ἡ τῆς σαρκὸς κοινωνία[376] is marital fellowship, 103 vl. (215, 21 ff.); it is ἐπιθυμία σαρκός, 7 vl. (110, 19) and belongs to the ἀσθένεια τῆς σαρκός, 1 (100, 7). But this leads already to Gnosticism, → 148, 38 ff.; VI, 393, 18 ff.[377]

---

[366] In this sense (→ n. 358) ἄνθρωπος or ἀνθρώπινος can be used in place of σάρξ, Tr., 2, 1; R., 8, 1; Eph., 5, 1. But only the man freed from ὕλη is true man, R., 6, 2.

[367] The πιστοί and ἄπιστοι correspond to these, Mg., 5, 2.

[368] Orientation to this world is always more suspect, orientation to the next world more laudable, Ign. R., 7; Barn., 4, 1; Pol., 9, 2; Herm. v., 1, 1, 8; 2 Cl., 5, 6; 6, 6; cf. Ab., 5, 21.

[369] Just before there are three allegorical interpretations which refer the OT commandment to homosexuality, adultery and fornication.

[370] Not the σῶμα as in 1 C. 6:19.

[371] Also Ep. apostolorum, 22, 26 (op. cit. [→ n. 356], 74 f., 82 f. etc., cf. 196, 199 f., 314).

[372] Cf. the passages in Ign. and Herm. In 2 Cl., 14 and Ign. Pol., 5, 2, unless the ref. is to the celibate Christ, the union of Christ and the Church serves as a model. Eph. 5:32 (→ 137, 4 f.) and similar verses can easily suggest this further step. The widespread idea of the ἱερὸς γάμος may have had some influence, though a developed syzygy teaching is more doubtful, cf. Schlier Eph. on 5:32 f. (esp. 268-271) and → σῶμα.

[373] Act. Pl. 8:25 f. (ed. C. Schmidt, Veröffentlichungen d. Hamburger Staats- u. Universitätsbibliothek, II [1936]).

[374] 3 C. 3:5 f. in Act. Pl. 48:22 ff. (Copt. text, ed. C. Schmidt² [1905]).

[375] Here with the addition of αὕτη par. τὸ κόσμος οὗτος.

[376] Xenoph. Oec., 10, 4 f.: τοῦ σώματος. Cf. J. Doresse, Les livres secrets des gnostiques d'Egypte (1958), 238, 260.

[377] Cf. the further influence of cosmic dualism, e.g., Stob. Ecl., I, 275, 21-276, 11; 277, 8-16 (Corp. Herm., 11, 2).

3. The Apologists.

σάρξ becomes increasingly important in designation of the incarnation → 137, 26 f. [378] The σάρξ καὶ αἷμα of Jesus are dispensed in the Eucharist to nourish our αἷμα καὶ σάρκες, Just. Apol., 66, 2. In the criticism of pagan ideas of God in Athenag. Suppl., 21, 1. 4 the incarnation of Jesus is a difficulty, but the author has to allow that God can take σάρξ and be σαρκοειδής. But since for him the concept of a δοῦλος ἐπι-θυμίας, subject to eros and suffering, is elsewhere linked herewith, he declares expressly that it is unworthy of a God. In Just. Dial. σάρξ is often used for external [379] circumcision or uncircumcision (→ 109, 1 ff.), τὴν σάρκα (10, 1), κατὰ σάρκα (16, 2 f.; 18, 2 f.; 19, 3 f.; 43, 2), περὶ τὴν σάρκα (92, 3 f.), σαρκική (23, 5), baptism (14, 1), descent (43, 7; 44, 1; 66, 4; 140, 2), σαρκικὸν σπέρμα (125, 5). σαρκικῶς νοεῖν in 14, 2 no longer has a Pauline ring but simply denotes Jewish attachment to the cultic and national. Similarly αἷμα καὶ σάρξ is the natural principle of generation, πίστις καὶ πνεῦμα the divine, 135, 6. There is an echo of Paul only in 12, 3, where it is said of the outwardly circumcised that they ἐπὶ τῇ σαρκὶ μέγα φρονεῖν. The use is quite different when Aristid. Apol., 15, 7 refers to brothers κατὰ ψυχήν as well as κατὰ σάρκα. The Gk. contrast between the outer and the inner has here replaced that between God and man.

σαρκὸς ἀνάστασις, which does not occur in the NT, is plainly taught in Just. Dial., 80, 5. Tat. Or. Graec., 13, 1 f. contests the idea of an immortal soul; the soul dies with the σάρξ (= σῶμα) and with it the σαρκίον is made immortal (25, 2) so that both rise again, 15, 1. The difficulty of the apologist is that he thinks in Gk. terms acc. to which God is ἄσαρκος and man is σάρξ. That ψυχή and σάρξ belong together and are ruled by the πνεῦμα does not fit in with this. The resurrection of the σάρξ and the fact that demons, who are not demi-gods but evil forces, have no σαρκίον poses serious problems, 14, 1; 15, 1-3. σαρκικὴ ὕλη is a sign of earthly existence, 6, 2. Similarly in Athenag. αἷμα καὶ σάρξ is the earthly and material in contrast to the heavenly, to the pure πνεῦμα which the soul ought to be, Suppl., 27, 1. Sexual intercourse is the union of σάρξ and σάρξ, 33, 2. To serve σάρξ καὶ αἷμα is to serve earthly desires (31, 2) and the fallen angels are subject to the σάρξ i.e., to lust after virgins, 24, 5. In the world to come man will have flesh but will live as heavenly spirit rather than flesh, 31, 3. Such passages help us to understand why the Church had to teach the resurrection of the flesh when it allowed access to the Gk. way of looking at things. [380] This does at least form an awkward rampart as the NT σῶμα could no longer do. [381]

4. Gnosticism, → VI, 390, 13 ff.

Gnostic usage is best seen from → σῶμα. Here just a few instances of σάρξ will be adduced.

Christologically it is stressed that the Redeemer appeared only "in a flesh (σάρξ) of likeness," Evang. veritatis, 31, 5 f. [382] Thus acc. to the Valentinians only the σάρξ

---

[378] The earthly Lord "has" flesh, Just. Dial., 48, 3; cf. Aristid. Apol., 15, 1, He is σαρκο-ποιηθείς Just. Apol., 32, 10; 66, 2, obviously traditionally linked with the virgin birth, Dial., 45, 4; 84, 2; 100, 2 → 147, 23 ff.

[379] Cf. 69, 6: invalids κατὰ τὴν σάρκα were cured by Jesus; 23, 5: the form of the σάρξ (= sexual member or body?) is different in women and so they cannot be circumcised.

[380] W. Bieder, "Auferstehung d. Fleisches oder des Leibes?" ThZ, 1 (1945), 105-120.

[381] For patristic ref. relating to the eating of flesh cf. the Bibl. d. Kirchenväter, General Index, I (1931), 205. Cf. J. Haussleiter, "Der Vegetarismus in d. Antike," RVV, 24 (1935), 35-41.

[382] Ed. M. Malinine, H. C. Puech, G. Quispel (1956).

of the ψυχικός Χριστός was crucified, Cl. Al. Exc. Theod., 62, 2.[383] In keeping is the idea that the πνεῦμα first descended on the σάρξ of the Logos in the form of the dove, ibid., 16; cf. Iren. Haer., I, 7, 2; Hipp. Ref., VI, 35, 6. On the other hand the Gospel of Thom.[384] speaks unreservedly of the appearance of Jesus in the flesh.[385] The coming into being of flesh for the sake of the spirit is the miracle which is to be adored.[386] The Manicheans are no less unreserved.[387] But Cl. Al. Exc. Theod., 1, 1 is very different; here the σπέρματα (the ἐκκλησία) represent the σάρξ which the Redeemer assumes → σῶμα Χριστοῦ.

Anthropologically σάρξ is mostly the evil principle. But it played no very gt. part in the earliest systems,[388] and other terms are used.[389] Sometimes it is neutral, if subordinate, e.g., in the statement that "tongues of flesh" cannot declare the divine mystery.[390] The Gospel of Phil. takes a middle position:[391] "Do not fear the flesh, but do not love it either," Logion, 62; "Overcome the carnal mind," 104. An unstained marriage has nothing to do with the σαρκικόν, 122. Circumcision of the σάρξ means the destruction of the σάρξ of the members (→ n. 401) of the world, 123. Resurrection as such does not mean divestiture of the flesh, 63. But Jesus has the true flesh of which ours is only a copy, namely, the Logos, 72 and 23, so that the Church's doctrine of the resurrection of the flesh can be retained. A strange logion is that in the Gospel of Thom., Logion 112 (Plate 99, 10 ff. → n. 384): "Woe to the flesh which clings to the soul; woe to the soul which clings to the flesh." Here division of flesh and soul is obviously to be sought, and the flesh can perhaps be given a provisional positive role of service as in Logion 29 (→ line 4 f.). Acc. to Corp. Herm., 3, 3 f. the ψυχή lives in the ἔμψυχος σάρξ. For the Valentinians the divine soul is concealed in the σάρξ or in the material soul which serves it as σάρξ or σῶμα, Cl. Al. Exc. Theod., 51, 1 f. First the ψυχικὸν σῶμα is formed, then the added male σπέρμα mingles with ψυχή and σάρξ, 2, 1 f., cf. 5, 3. The σαρκικόν naturally comes from ὕλη, Iren. Haer., I, 5, 6;

---

[383] Only the soul of the suffering σῶμα gives itself into the hands of the Father; the Redeemer Himself saves His πνευματικόν, ibid., 62, 3, cf. also 1, 1; 26, 1; also Iren. Haer., I, 6, 1.

[384] Cf. J. Leipoldt, "Ein neues Ev. ?" ThLZ, 83 (1958), 481-496.

[385] Logion 28 (Plate 86, 22) = P. Oxy., I, 13 f.

[386] Logion 29 (86, 31 f.). An even greater miracle is the coming into being of spirit for the sake of the body (= σῶμα), probably that of the Pre-existent with a view to the coming incarnation.

[387] Kephalaia, Manichäische Hndschrften. d. staatlichen Museen Berlin, I (1940), 61, 23 : He came into the πλάσμα of the σάρξ; 89, 26 f.; 95, 3 f.: The light-νοῦς passes into the body of the flesh and puts it on. Apostles also appear in the flesh, 101, 33.

[388] Neither σάρξ nor σῶμα seems to play any part in Simon Magus apart from the ref. to the journeying of ennoia from body to body, Iren. Haer., I, 23, 2 and the use of πᾶσα σάρξ in the OT sense, Hipp. Ref., VI, 9, 8; 10, 2. The story in Ps.-Cl. Hom., 2, 26 that Simon changed πνεῦμα into water, then blood and finally flesh presupposes transition (→ 100, 26 ff.) rather than antithesis of substances. Corp. Herm., 1; 10; 13 uses only → σῶμα cf. → lines 22 ff.; 150, 26 ff.

[389] Among the 3 classes of men (→ VI, 395, n. 384) we find in the Valentinians the ὑλικός or χοϊκός instead of the σαρκικός, Iren. Haer., I, 5; 6, 1; 7, 5; 8, 3; Orig. Comm. in Joh., 10, 33. 37; 20, 24; cf. the Gnostic Justin in Hipp. Ref., V, 26, 32; 27, 3 and the Naassenes, ibid., V, 7, 30. 36; 8, 14. 22 → 150, 12 ff. On ὑλικός cf. also Corp. Herm., 1, 24; 10, 10 f., on γήϊνος 10, 17-19. In Apocr. Johannis (→ n. 176) 55:7-13 ὕλη, darkness, ἐπιθυμία and ἀντικείμενον πνεῦμα are a chain and grave for the body. But only in 16:9 f. do we find the kingdom and foolish cleverness of the flesh along with other forms of the "fourth power" which meets the soul on its ascent. Acc. to 58:4-7 (cf. 63:5 f.; 74:1-75:7) the dragon of Gn. 3 teaches the generation of ἐπιθυμία, but with no ref. to the flesh → 150, 1 ff. Cf. also Doresse, op. cit. (→ n. 376), 183.

[390] Koptisch-gnostische Schriften, ed. C. Schmidt-W. Till, GCS, 45 (1954), 341, 27; 359, 33. Cf. → 120, 29 ff. Acc. to Sophia Jesu (Till [→ n. 176], 79, 2-5) mortal σάρξ cannot see the Risen Lord, only that which is pure and perfect.

[391] Cf. H. M. Schenke, "Das Ev. nach Philippus," ThLZ, 84 (1959), 5-26.

cf. 6, 1, and the ἐκ ψυχῆς κρεμαμένη σάρξ is the ὕλη created by the demiurge, Hipp. Ref., VI, 37, 7 f. In the Apocr. Joh. souls come out from the flesh and are not sent back into it when redeemed. [392] Among the Manichees we once find the comparison of the σάρξ of men with the oyster which holds the pearl (= the soul), Kephalaia (→ n. 387), 204, 8 f. 14. [393] But 220, 6 f. shows that body is better here, while hatred is proper to the flesh of sin. [394] The bond is the σάρξ of εἱμαρμένη which man escapes when he leaves the body. [395] Hence when σάρξ is used typically it denotes a sphere of power to which man is subject. [396] A Gnostic understanding is reflected here. But it can be regarded as a further development of two-sphere thinking (→ 109, 9 ff.); Gk. ideas of substance have taken over what was originally a very different schema. The Gnostic Redeemer myth does not have to be presupposed as yet.

Similarly the re-born τέλειος ἄνθρωπος of the Naassenes or of the Phrygians who followed them is no longer σαρκικός but πνευματικός, ἀθάνατος, Hipp. Ref., V, 7, 40; 8, 7. 18. 23. 36 f.; 9, 4. [397] He has left the σῶμα, 8, 23 and no longer exercises the ἐπιθυμία τῆς σαρκός (→ n. 52), 8, 31. [398] Carnal birth is one of the little mysteries; one must break free from it like the castrated Attis, 8, 40. No ψυχικός or σαρκικός [399] enters heaven, 8, 44. [400] Among the Manicheans it is esp. the carnal body which gives birth to demons and is the root and origin of all evil. [401] Sin lives in it, Kephalaia, 94, 26 cf. 151, 9. It chains the mind to the flesh (95, 18 f.) and at redemption the mind of the soul which is bound to the flesh [402] is released from it, but not the mind of sin, 95, 25; 96, 18 f. ἡδονή dwells in the five worlds of the σάρξ or the male and female σάρκες, 26, 33 f.; 27, 3 f. 7 f.; cf. 151, 30. Thus the flesh corresponds to the "vehicle of darkness," 170, 15. It is fashioned by the sent one through the power of sin (54, 4 f.; 56, 23 f.; 138, 10 ff.) and ὕλη has put its stamp on it (179, 4 f.). Hence one should not taste "flesh and blood," 192, 12, cf. 229, 21. [403] One day the flesh = body will be destroyed, Manich. Homilies (→ n. 393), 8, 11, cf. 11, 28; 39, 23-25. [404] The Hermetic Stob. Ecl., I, 461, [405] where souls are dipped (βεβαπτισμέναι) in flesh and blood, combines Hell.

---

[392] Apocr. Joh. 68:2; 70:8. Acc. to the uncertain reading supplied at 65:20 the σάρξ is the exterior of man which he uses but which does not affect his inner being.

[393] Cf. also H. J. Polotsky, Manich. Homilien (1934), 14, 10; Doresse, 209.

[394] Cf. Books of Jeû, op. cit. (→ n. 390), 259, 30-260, 4 : "Flesh" does not mean corporeality but the "flesh of ignorance."

[395] Cf. Books of Jeû, op. cit. (→ n. 390), 315, 4-7. In the Psalms of Thomas (ed. C. R. C. Allberry, A Manichaean Psalm-Book, II [1938], 219, 6; cf. 204, 22) σάρξ carries no stress.

[396] Käsemann, 57: "The body 'has' us" (not we it), cf. also Doresse, 172, 238, 244.

[397] Cf. the Sethians in Hipp. Ref., V, 21, 6.

[398] Saul perished with the demon of σαρκικὴ ἐπιθυμία, ibid., V, 9, 22.

[399] Ibid., V, 8, 45, where, with a ref. to the virgin birth, we find σωματικός and μακάριος for πνευματικός, → n. 389.

[400] Cf. the Valentinians : the χοϊκὴ σάρξ does not enter Paradise, Cl. Al. Exc. Theod., 51, 1 f.; cf. Iren. Haer., I, 7, 1 of the ψυχικόν; acc. to I, 6, 3 they practise the ἡδοναὶ τῆς σαρκός because they feel superior to them.

[401] E. Waldschmidt-W. Lentz, "Die Stellung Jesu im Manichäismus," AAB, 1926, 4 (1926), 100 f. (19b, 23a b). 106 (49a). 121 (15, 15). 123 (394). In 112 (2 recto 1a) we find corporal members and prisons which increase desire, cf. Kephalaia, 95, 17 → n. 284. But in 110 (76c) the believer asks that his carnal body may attain lasting rest and joy, and in Kephalaia, 151, 9; 169, 31 body of flesh is used neutrally.

[402] Cf. also Polotsky, op. cit. (→ n. 393), 86, 12; cf. 27, 7.

[403] At the same time Cl. Al. himself is not far from his adversaries. For the linking of σάρξ and ἐπιθυμία cf. Strom., II, 41, 4; 115, 3; III, 87, 2; IV, 137, 3; V, 67, 4; VII, 33, 6; for trichotomy (σάρξ, ψυχή, πνεῦμα) III, 68, 5 (acc. to the view of others); for the idea of a σαρκικὸν (σωματικὸν) πνεῦμα which wars against the ψυχή or higher πνεῦμα, VI, 52, 2; 134, 1; 135, 3; 136, 1 f.; VII, 20, 4 (σάρκινον occurs only in Quis Div. Salv.). Finally he distinguishes the σάρκες (nominal Christians) from the πνευματικὸν σῶμα, VII, 87, 3 f.

[404] Pist. Soph., p. 24, 17 speaks of the "flesh of the archons."

[405] Corp. Herm., 25, 8.

anthropology and Jewish terminology. σαρκίον is used contemptuously among the Valentinians. [406]

There is unquestionably a distinct Gnostic usage in these statements. Yet inasmuch as it does not express the simple hostility of later antiquity to the body, or a feeling of subjection to it, it hardly stands in primary antithesis to the NT. In both, later Jewish and oriental cosmological dualism (→ 109, 8 ff.) had an influence. But in so far as Jn. had any obvious effect the negative evaluation of σάρξ was quite weak (→ 138, 7 ff.), and the power of the σάρξ in Paul is not to be explained in terms of the Gnostic myth or even two-sphere thinking (→ 132, 6 ff.). The negative role of the σάρξ in Gnosticism, [407] as to some degree in the later NT, may be traced back to the ideas mentioned → 104, 16 ff., a misunderstanding of Paul, and above all a two-sphere thinking increasingly affected by "substantial" categories, → VI, 392, 30 ff.

Schweizer

| † σατανᾶς |

→ δαίμων, II, 1, 1 ff.; → διάβολος, II, 72, 23 ff.; → ἐχθρός, II, 814, 37 ff.; → κατήγορος, III, 636, 1 ff.; → ὄψις, V, 566, 8 ff.; → πεῖρα, VI, 24, 16 ff.; → πονηρός, VI, 558, 27 ff.

Contents : A.: Qumran and Later Jewish Satanology : 1. Qumran ; 2. Later Judaism. B.: Satan in the New Testament : 1. The Accuser and His Fall ; 2. Satan Sayings in the Synoptists ; 3. Satan Sayings in the Epistles ; 4. The Prince of This World in John's Gospel and the Johannine Epistles. C.: Satan in the Post-Apostolic Fathers : a. Linguistic Data ; b. General Material ; c. Satan and the Church ; d. Satan and the Martyr ; e. Satan and the Individual Christian.

Since the art. on → διάβολος, II, 72, 1 ff. was published, the finding of the Dead Sea Scrolls has enlarged our knowledge of later Jewish Satanology and at many points brought the NT data into sharper focus. This art. discusses passages which contain διάβολος and related terms as well as σατανᾶς.

---

[406] Cl. Al. Exc. Theod., 52, 1-53, 1; also 1, 1; 26, 1; Stoic M. Ant., II, 2; Apologists Tat. Or. Graec., 6, 2 (though → 148, 19 ff.), the only one to use the word. Positive evaluation, Mart. Pol., 17, 1. For the Gk. use Liddell-Scott, *s.v.*

[407] "'Discarnate' man is the heretical answer to the 'incarnate God,'" E. Peterson, "Der Hass wider das Fleisch, Versuchung u. Fall durch die Gnosis," *Wort u. Wahrheit*, 7 (1952), 9.

σ α τ α ν ᾶ ς. → διάβολος, II, 69 f.; J. Turmel, *Histoire du diable* (1931); *Satan, Études carmelitaines*, 27 (1948), esp. A. Frank-Duquesne, "En marge de la tradition judéo-chr.," 181-311; E. Langton, *Essentials of Demonology* (1949); K. L. Schmidt, "Lucifer als gefallene Engelmacht," *ThZ*, 7 (1951), 161-179; S. V. MacCasland, *By the Finger of God* (1951), 72-75; K. G. Kuhn, "πειρασμός, ἁμαρτία, σάρξ im NT u. die damit zusammenhängenden Vorstellungen," *ZThK*, 49 (1952), 200-222; G. Piccoli, "Etimologie e significati di voci bibliche indicanti Satana," *Rivista di filologia classica*, NS, 30 (1952), 69-73; A. Roets, "De duivel en de stichting van het godsrijk," *Collationes Brugenses et Gandavenses*, 2 (1956), 145-162; also "De duivel en de kristenen," *ibid.*, 300-321; J. Duchesne-Guillemin, Art. "Dualismus B II. III. C I" in RAC, III, 342-347. On A.: A. Lods, "La chute des anges," *RevHPhR*, 7 (1927), 295-315; J. Wochenmark, "Die Schicksalsidee im Judt.," *Veröffentlichungen d. oriental. Seminars d. Universität Tübingen*, 6 (1933), 71-77; M. Burrows, *The Dead Sea Scrolls* (1955), 257 ff. (= Burrows I); *More Light on the Dead Sea Scrolls* (1958), 277-289 (= Burrows II); H. W. Huppenbauer, "Belial in d. Qumrantexten,"

A. Qumran and Later Jewish Satanology.

1. Qumran.

The Dead Sea Scrolls have many special sayings about the figure of Satan, mostly called Belial, which differ from those in the pseudepigr. and Rabb. Judaism. Acc. to 1 QS 3:13-4:26 God has set for man "two spirits to walk therein" (→ VI, 389, 35 ff.), the רוח האמת and the רוח העול; "in the dwelling [1] of light are the origins of truth and from the source of darkness are the origins of wickedness. In the hand of the prince of lights is dominion over all the sons of righteousness ...; in the hand of the angel of darkness is all dominion over the sons of wickedness," 1 QS 3:18-21. It is later said of the two spirits that "up to now they strive in the heart of a man," 4:23. This passage is in many respects isolated in the Scrolls, for the two spirits are not mentioned in them elsewhere [2] nor do we find the antithesis of the prince of lights and the angel of darkness at any other pt. The ref. to the source of darkness also raises the question whether there is not a kingdom which precedes and embraces the angel of darkness, so that the angel also has an origin. Again it is nowhere said expressly that God created this angel. These open questions are connected with the fact that here Iranian ideas are adopted [3] which linguistically do not harmonise with other sayings in the Scrolls and materially have not been integrated into a dogmatically consistent system. But from the section 1 QS 3:13-4:26, esp. when taken with 1 QH, 1 QM and Damasc., one may see with tolerable certainty what is in view here. After a kind of preface the exposition proper begins in 1 QS 3:15 with the statement that everything comes from the "God of knowledge," that He fixed the whole purpose of things before they came into being, so that there is no alteration. This absolute sovereignty of God over all creatures, including man and his way, is emphasised in the strongest terms in the concluding psalm

---

ThZ, 15 (1959), 81-89 (= Huppenbauer I); also "Der Mensch zwischen zwei Welten," AbhThANT, 34 (1959) (= Huppenbauer II). On B.: Bultmann Theol.[3], 258 f., 368 f., 376 f., 500 f.; Stauffer Theol. § 13-15, 28, 36, 53; L. Bouyer, 'Le problème du mal dans le christianisme antique," Dieu vivant, 6 (1947), 17-42; B. Noack, Satanás u. Soteria (1948); E. Fascher, "Jesus u. d. Satan," Hallische Monographien, 11 (1949); R. Leivestad, Christ the Conqueror (1954), 40-61, 85-92, 224-228; G. B. Caird, Principalities and Powers. A Study of Pauline Theology (1956); J. M. Robinson, "Das Geschichtsverständnis d. Mk.-Ev.," AbhThANT, 30 (1956); S. Lyonnet, "De natura peccati quid doceat Novum Testamentum," Verbum Domini, 35 (1957), 204-221, 271-278, 332-343; G. Baumbach, "Qumran u. d. Joh.-Ev.," Aufsätze u. Vorträge zur Theol. u. Religionswissenschaft, 6 (1958).

[1] Or from the source, מְעוֹן or מַעְיִן, 1 QS 3:19; A. Dupont-Sommer, "L'instruction sur les deux Esprits dans le 'manuel de Discipline,' " RHR, 142 (1952), 17 f.; P. Wernberg-Møller, The Manual of Discipline (1957), 70, n. 58.

[2] They are to be supplied only in 1 QS 1:17; H. Bardtke, "Die Loblieder v. Qumran," ThLZ, 81 (1956), 151; cf. A. Dupont-Sommer, "Le Livre des Hymnes," Semitica, 7 (1957), 27.

[3] K. G. Kuhn, "Die Sektenschrift u. d. iranische Religion," ZThK, 49 (1952), 296-316; A. Dupont-Sommer, The Jewish Sect of Qumran and the Essenes (1954), 118-130; K. Schubert, "Der Sektenkanon u. d. Anfänge d. jüd. Gnosis," ThLZ, 78 (1953), 495-506; H. Wildberger, "Der Dualismus in d. Qumranschriften," Asiatische Stud., 8 (1954), 163-177; A. Dupont-Sommer, "Le problème des influences étrangères sur la secte juive de Qumran," RevHPhR, 35 (1955), 75-92; F. Nötscher, "Zur theol. Terminologie d. Qumrantexte," Bonner bibl. Beiträge, 10 (1956), 79-92; E. Schweizer, "Gegenwart d. Geistes u. eschatologische Hoffnung bei Zarathustra, spätjüd. Gruppen, Gnostikern u. Zeugen d. NT" in The Background of the NT and Its Eschatology, Studies in Honour of C. H. Dodd (1956), 482-508; Burrows I, 260-262; G. Widengren, "Quelques rapports entre Juifs et Iraniens à l'époque des Parthes," Suppl. VT, 4 (1957), 197-241; Duchesne-Guillemin, 342-347; also "Le Zervanisme et les manuscrits de la mer morte," Indo-Iranian Journal, 1 (1957), 96-99; S. Wibbing, "Die Tugend- u. Lasterkataloge im NT," Beih. ZNW, 25 (1959), 64 f.; O. J. F. Seitz, "Two Spirits in Man," NT St, 6 (1959/60), 82-95.

of 1 QS and again and again in 1 QH. There is no place here for an autonomous angel of darkness ; one may thus conclude that God created him too and as such. Nor is the source of darkness a sphere independent of God. The men of Qumran might learn from Is. 45:7 that it was created by God. Since the same things are said of the angel of darkness and of Belial, one must equate the two. Since again both spirits are referred to in personal categories, the spirit of wickedness is personal as in the view of Zoroaster, which has left its mark here, and it is the same as the angel of darkness and Belial. [4]

The ref. to the conflict of the spirits in the heart of a man reminds us of the Rabb. doctrine of the two impulses with which God created man from the very first, [5] → VI, 552, 12 ff. In fact, however, there is only one ref. to this. Acc. to 1 QS 3:21-25 the angel of darkness causes the children of light to go astray, and "the spirits of his lot are there to cause the children of light to stumble, but the God of Israel and the angel of his truth help all the children of light." There is nowhere any ref. to a par. work of the angel of light on the children of light. Hence the doctrine of the two spirits has a different sense here from the Rabb. doctrine of the two impulses between which man can and must decide. The thinking of the Dead Sea Scrolls is predestinarian ; in them the prevenient and absolute sovereignty of God extends over men too.

God has created Belial, the angel of darkness, the spirit of evil, and both the just and the unjust. The world and men are under the sway of Belial, whom God and the righteous hate and who hates God and the righteous. God calls forth the righteous out of the mass of the children of Belial and so prepares them by His leading that they gives themselves up freely to His will. Belial tries to overthrow the children of light ; he oppresses and persecutes them, 1 QS 3:24; 1 QH *passim*. The spirits of punishment are also under Belial's command, 1 QS 4:12; Damasc. 2:6 (2:4), cf. Eth. En. 56:1-4; Jub. 49:2. Belial has put forth his power against God's electing, which is seen in the whole history of Israel, Damasc. 2:11 f. (2:9), Damasc. 5:17-19 (7:19). But the prince of lights protects the children of light. What strengthens both the whole community and also individuals within it in the fight against Belial is not the Law, which is for the Rabb. *the* remedy against the evil impulse (S. Dt. § 45 on 11:18), but God and the angel of light, [6] hence the reminder of God's pity and His tokens of grace in 1 QH 1:31 f.; 2:25, 28; 4:31-40; 6:9 f.; 7:18; 9:12 f.; 10:17; cf. 1 QS 1:21 f. As God created the spirit of wickedness, so He has appointed an end for the being of wickedness, 1 QS 4:18; then Belial, his angels, and the hosts of men who belong to his "lot" will fall under judgment. In a last violent battle Belial's end will come and then truth will reign on the earth. God will create something new, the return of Paradise and a life of men with the angels, 1 QS 4:20-25; 1 QH 3:21 f.; 6:13; 7:14 f.; 11:12 f., 25-27; 15:16.

Naturally there are some open questions. If God is to create something new (1 QS 4:25), has the old become imperfect or corrupt ? In the texts there is no trace of a union of Belial with the evils of the world or the dominion of death. If God created the wicked and appointed them for the day of battle, this was because he knew their works, 1 QH 15:17-19; Damasc. 2:7 f. (2:6 f.). Does not this reduce predestination to foreknowledge ? But these questions only make it the plainer that the men of Qumran were concerned to solve the problem of evil by tracing back to God even that which He hates and rejects. In the role played by the concept of mystery in Qumran one may detect a feeling that this solution cannot answer all questions.

---

[4] This is the common view, cf. J. T. Milik, *Dix ans de découvertes dans le désert de Juda* (1956), 77 f.; Burrows II, 287 f.; F. M. Cross, *The Ancient Library of Qumran* (1958), 157; K. Schubert, *Die Gemeinde vom Toten Meer* (1958), 58 f.; with qualifications Huppenbauer I, 85; II, 35 f., 53. It should be noted that the spirit of wickedness derives from darkness, whereas the angel of darkness, Belial, is its lord, cf. Wernberg-Møller, *op. cit.* (→ n. 1), 70, n. 56.

[5] Str.-B., IV, 466-483; Moore, I, 479-493.

[6] 1 QS 3:24 f.; 1 QH 7:6; 9:28 f. "I flee to thee before the ranks of Belial" (H. Bardtke, *Die Handschriftenfunde am Toten Meer*, II [1958], 17, 21-23; 18, 9. 24 f.).

That this Qumran conception held a place of its own within the development of the later Jewish world of thought may be seen from the fact that the most common name for the devil here is בליעל, but this does not occur in the Rabb. writings. [7] משטמה seems to be used in the Scrolls only as an abstr.; 1 QS 3:23; 1 QM 13:4, 11; Damasc. 16:5 (20:2); it is a proper name in Jub. 10:8; 11:5, 11; 17:16; 18:9, 12; 19:28; 48:2; 49:2; it does not occur in Pharisaic writings. שטן is found only 3 times in the Scrolls in obscure connections, so that one cannot be sure whether it is a proper name or an appellative ("the enemy"). [8] Sammael, the Rabb. name for the devil, is not used. [9]

2. Later Judaism. [10]

The OT work of the devil, accusation before God, [11] is found in Jub., the symbolical addresses of Eth. En. (plur.), Apc. Eliae 4:4, 9; 10:19 f. etc., [12] and the Rabb. → II, 76 f., n. 31, 37, 39, 41. Angels who report all sins in heaven and earth to God also figure in Jub. 4:6. [13] Ref. to the accusations of the wicked one raises the acute question how they can be met. In Jub. 48:15, 18 Satan is bound so that he cannot accuse ; in Eth. En. 40:7 the archangel Phanuel, who is set over repentance, resists the satans. In the Rabb. Michael or good works are our advocates, → II, 77, n. 37-39. Demons are never said to accuse. [14]

If in the OT Satan is one of the sons of God and as such has access to God, the Qumran doctrine of the two spirits created by God might have been linked with this (→ 152, 5) in such a way that one of them, Belial, could bring accusations. But this idea does not occur in the Scrolls, a sign that the whole concept of the two spirits was not developed on the basis of OT statements concerning Satan. It is also quite patent that the view of the devil as a fallen angel has no place in the basic Qumran teaching. Hence we do not find this in the pseudepigr. discovered in the caves of Qumran ; it occurs for the first time in the Rabb. (→ II, 78, n. 44), Slav. En. 29:4 f.; 31:4 f., also Vit. Ad. 12-16, though it is presupposed in Wis. 2:24. Nor is there any place for the idea that Belial brought sin into the world by seducing Adam or that sin first came into the world through the fall of Adam. Nor do we find this view in Jub., Test. XII, or Eth. En. [15] The decisive significance of Adam's fall is stated in Sir. 25:24,

---

[7] Str.-B., III, 521 f. בליעל is not always a proper name but often an appellative as in the OT, "wickedness," "corruption," Huppenbauer I, 81-84; II, 35 f., 53. Βελιαρ is a proper name in prophecy, cf. C. C. Torrey, The Lives of the Prophets, JBL Monograph, I (1946).

[8] 1 QH Fr. 4:6 : בכל שטן משחית; ibid., 45:3 : כל שטן ומשחית; 1 QSb 1:8 : שטן; cf. Huppenbauer I, 83, n. 21. Satan is a proper name in Jub. 10:11; 23:29; 50:5. 40:9 and 46:2 are uncertain. Σατανᾶς occurs 5 times in Test. XII and is common in Test. Job, ed. M. R. James, TSt, V, 1 (1897).

[9] Sammael occurs 8 times in Asc. Is. (Beliar 13 times, Satanas 6) and also in Gr. Bar. 4:9.

[10] If there is any Satanology at all in the Dead Sea Scrolls it is in 1 QS, 1 QM, 1 QH, cf. also Damasc. At some distance from these are Jub.; Eth. En.; Test. XII, of which some fr. have been found in Qumran. Close in time to these are Ass. Mos. and Ps. Sol. Most of the little pseudepigr. apocalypses are later. On this cf. W. Foerster, Nt.liche Zeitgeschichte, I³ (1959), 78-80.

[11] A. Lods, "Les origines de la figure de Satan, ses fonctions à la cour céleste," Mélanges syriens offerts à R. Dussaud, II, Bibliothèque archéologique et historique, 30, 2 (1939), 649-660, points out that there were no state police in the Orient and conjectures that the model for the OT Satan was the mobile inspector known as the "eye" or "ear of the king."

[12] Cf. also Sophonias Apc. 1:13, ed. G. Steindorff, TU, 17, 3 (1899), 111, 170.

[13] Cf. also → II, 77, n. 41 for a Rabb. par., similarly jQid., 1, 10 (61d, 32-51) cf. Str.-B., II, 560.

[14] But cf. the angel princes of the nations in Cant. r., 2, 1, Str.-B., III, 49.

[15] Eth. En. 98:4 (men created sin themselves) is not thinking of the fall, as the plur. shows. Nor is there ref. to the fall in the vision of the 70 shepherds or the 10 week apoc. of Eth. En. 85-90; 93; 91:12-17. Acc. to Huppenbauer II, 90-93 the fallen angels are perhaps

presupposed in Wis. 2:24, and expressed in 4 Esr., S. Bar., Vit. Ad. and the Rabb. [16]
Here the biblical story, which does not teach the doctrine of the two spirits, is adopted
and developed.

On the other hand the story of the fall of the angels in Gn. 6:1-4 was already playing
a big part in the older pseudepigr. [17] The doctrine of the two spirits left no room for
this either. It is worth noting that Damasc. 2:18-21 (3:4-7) mentions the fall of the
watchers, but does not ascribe to this the fundamental significance of having brought sin
into the story of mankind ; it is simply compared to the sin of the sons of Noah, the
sons of Jacob in Egypt, the Exodus generation in the wilderness, and the children of
Israel in Palestine, 3:1-12 (4:1-10). In the vision of the 70 shepherds in Eth. En. the
fall of the angels is again an episode of no more than passing importance for the history
of man. [18] The situation is already somewhat different in Jub., where the fallen angels
of Gn. 6 are bound, their children are destroyed and God creates a new and righteous
nature for all His creatures, 5:1-12, but where unclean demons seduce the grandchildren
of Noah after the flood. Inconsistently these are called the "children of the watchers"
in Jub. 10:5 and the "spirits of Mastema" in 19:28. When they are destroyed on the
petition of Noah, Mastema, the prince of spirits, secures the survival of a tenth of them,
since otherwise he could not exercise the dominion of his will over the children of men,
10:8. Very obviously different strands of thought have been artificially interwoven here.
The same applies to the pertinent statements in Eth. En., where paganism, war, luxury
and betrayal of the secrets of God are connected with the fall of the angels — things
which since then have been the vogue amongst men. [19] Adam's fall is not mentioned
in Test. XII, and in Test. R. 5:6 f.; N. 3:5, as in Jub., the fall of the ἐγρήγοροι is used
only in exhortation. Rabb. writings contain only weak and late reminiscences of these
apoc. speculations ; [20] there is here deliberate rejection. [21]

Acc. to Test. XII man is confronted by choice : "Know that two spirits strive for
man, that of truth and that of error," Test. Jud. 20:1. Man must choose between light
and darkness, the Law of the Lord and the work of Belial, L. 19:1. Quite unmythologi-
cally Sir. 15:17 says that "before men lies life and death, and what he wills will be
given him." Acc. to 4 Esr. each man must fight and receive the fruits of his victory
or defeat, 7:127 f. etc. Aqiba compares the situation of man to a buyer who purchases
from a merchant on credit but who will necessarily have to pay one day, Ab., 3, 16. To
resist evil, whether it be Sammael or the evil impulse, the weapon of the Law has been
given to man, S. Dt. § 45 on 11:18 (the Law is God's requirement here). This was not
the view of Qumran. Here man has no free choice. The relation between God's election
and the founding of the Qumran community, between the membership of the individual
in it and the attacks and hostilities of Belial, is less prominent in the pseudepigr. found

---

the authors of corruption in Fr. 27, Col. I, 5 (DJD, I, 103). But the Gn. apocryphon of
Qumran I seems to allude not at all or only briefly to the fall of the angels in Gn. 6:1 ff.,
Huppenbauer II, 94.

[16] Str.-B., III, 227 f.; Moore, I, 474-479.

[17] Lods, 295-315.

[18] In Eth. En. 86:1-88:3 the fallen angels are chained. After the flood the earth is not
invaded again by demonic powers, 89:9.

[19] The different names of the leaders of the fallen angels, esp. Shemyaza and Aza(z)el,
are already a pointer to the presence of different speculations. This is also apparent in the
fact that in Jub. 69:6 the temptation of Eve is attributed to Gadreel but a few vv. later it
is said that death would not have touched men, who are made like angels, if they had not
learned writing through Penemue, 69:11. In 54:6 the hosts of Azazel are subject to Satan
and seduce the dwellers on earth.

[20] Str.-B., III, 780-783.

[21] Earlier than the few Rabb. echoes of the Enoch tradition is the view in the Tg. and
the Tannaitic period that the sons of God of Gn. 6 are the sons of great men on the earth,
Str.-B., III, 783. Worth noting is the fact that in S. Bar. 56:5-11 Adam's fall was a danger
to the angels (not vice versa), an allusion to Gn. 6. Cf. Bousset-Gressm., 253.

in Qumran, as also in Rabb. Judaism (along with predestinarian ideas). Here election is again referred to all Israel and is weakened, since in the long run it is overshadowed by the idea that Israel is elected because it freely accepts the Law. The individual struggle to keep the Law now comes to the forefront. Often interwoven are the concepts of the fall and of human sinfulness. Satan's activity, broadly depicted along the lines of Gn. 3, is either explained and thereby weakened or it fades into the background altogether, as in 4 Esr. → II, 76, 11 ff.; 78, 6 ff. Thus the influence of a transcendental factor is more or less eliminated and man is left with a free choice either for or against the Law of God.

In the history of later Judaism the only more or less consistent view of Satan is that developed in the Dead Sea Scrolls. In the divinely created dualism between light and darkness, the angel of darkness, Belial, is the one sovereign prince in the kingdom of darkness, beside whom there can be no other autonomous powers of evil. The battle between light and darkness is the theme of world history. There is no "middle group" between the sons of light and the sons of darkness. [22] Though men are not unwilling instruments in the hands of the two spirits, the view of Qumran is that God gives to men their "lot" in good or evil. Thus a whole series of statements from the OT and other sources is set aside. Nothing is said about Satan as the accuser before God, about the fall of Adam or his seduction by the serpent or Satan, about the fall of the angels as an invasion by evil and by demonic powers, or about Lucifer. These ideas made their way into the pseudepigrapha found at Qumran and even more so into other pseudepigraphical writings and into Pharisaism, but in such a way that we find little but scattered remnants of such concepts in the works of the Rabbis. [23] In place of election comes free decision on the basis of the Law, and this crowds out the figure of Satan. Only at one point is later Judaism united, namely, that in the last time the power of evil, no matter how it is envisaged, will be destroyed. [24] The gaze of Qumran is primarily fixed on the end of iniquity, but the last time, as a life with the angels (1 QH 3:21 f.; 6:12 f.; 11:11 f.), will also bring with it the end of "trouble and sighing" (1 QH 11:26). The latter point is also made in the pseudepigrapha : *tum zabulus finem habebit et tristitia cum eo abducetur*, Ass. Mos. 10:1, cf. Jub. 23:29; 4 Esr. 7:11-13; 8:54a. It is always found when there is reference to a new heaven and a new earth. [25]

B. Satan in the New Testament.

1. The Accuser and His Fall.

The distinctiveness of the Satan sayings of the NT is to be found in the special use of the motif of Satan's fall from heaven. This works out the familiar OT idea that as accuser Satan has access to God, but it does so in a new way. The

[22] On the "middle group" cf. Moore, I, 495 f.; II, 318; jQid., 1, 10 (61d, 32-51) cf. Str.-B., II, 560a (Aqiba); bRH, 16b and T. Sanh., 13, 3 cf. Str.-B., IV, 1043 f., 1178 (school of Shammai and Hillel); Test. Abr. A. 12 (p. 90, 23-25).
[23] Satan as angel of death, world ruler, → II, 77, 17 ff.; Str.-B., I, 144-149; identified with the evil impulse, bBB, 16a (Resh Laqish).
[24] 1 QS 4:18-23; Jub. 23:29; 50:5; Eth. En. 69:29; 91:8; 4 Esr. 6:27; 7:113 f.; 8:53; Str.-B., IV, 482 f.; → II, 78, n. 43; Volz Esch., 309-320, 332-340.
[25] Jub. 1:29; 4:26; Eth. En. 10:7, 17, 22; 45:4 f.; 91:16; 4 Esr. 13:26; S. Bar. 51:8; Sl. En. 65:6-9; Gn. r., 12, 5 on 2:4 (Str.-B., I, 19) cf. Volz Esch., 338-340. Satan and his angels harm men outwardly → II, 76 f., n. 32, 33; Ex. r., 20, 8 on 13:17.

situation in Lk. 22:31 is similar to that in the prologue to Job, → I, 194, 14 ff.; Satan requests that he may have the disciples to sift them like wheat. The goal of the sifting is that the unwillingness of each disciple may be brought to light and Satan may thus be able to accuse them; but the accusation is opposed by the intercession of Jesus. [26] Jesus thus assigns Himself the role which angels, and esp. Michael, play in Judaism → 154, 14 ff. Related is Rev. 12:7-12, where Michael fights with Satan, the great serpent. The reference here is to a definitive fall of Satan from heaven, so that he no longer has any access to God as accuser, 12:10. This fall of Satan from heaven and its point in time (v. 12), i.e., its conjunction with the coming of Jesus (v. 5), separate the NT from Judaism → 154, 22. Both are to be found in Lk. 10:18 (peculiar to Lk.): ἐθεώρουν τὸν σατανᾶν ὡς ἀστραπὴν ἐκ τοῦ οὐρανοῦ πεσόντα → VI, 163, n. 11. ἐθεώρουν here is certainly not to be referred to pre-existent vision, → IV, 130, n. 220. Nor is it the proleptic seeing of an event at the Last Judgment. Once again, then, the fall from heaven denotes primarily the end of the possibility of accusing before God. [27] The context shows, however, that though Satan's activity in general is not ended, with the total cessation of the ability to accuse he has also lost his power to harm wherever the power of Jesus is at work. We are not told to what specific point in time ἐθεώρουν refers. [28] If it is presupposed in Lk. 22:31 f. that Satan still has access to God, this is not an argument against the present understanding of Lk. 10:18, since the life of Jesus is a unity. It is worth noting that in none of the epistles ascribed to Paul, including those which some do not regard as authentic, is any use made of the image of the fall of the accuser.

Ref. might be made, however, to Jn. 12:31, though the reading βληθήσεται κάτω is undoubtedly secondary. The place from which the prince of this world is cast out (→ I, 489, n. 5) can only be the place of judgment, i.e., heaven. [29] In Jn. 16:11: ὁ ἄρχων τοῦ κόσμου τούτου κέκριται, the judgment on him is not so manifest that the world does not have to be persuaded of it. In all these passages which speak of the fall of the devil or of judgment on him an Already is combined with a Not yet. This is the characteristic feature of NT sayings about Satan. The mythological concept of a pre-cosmic fall of Lucifer cannot be united with the idea of a fall of Satan in time, [30] and the basic principle of Qumran, the doctrine of two divinely created spirits (→ 152, 5 ff.), is also abandoned. Jd. makes use of a legend about the devil whose literary source is unknown. [31] The more surprising it is, then, that the NT does not refer to a primal fall of Satan and related motifs. [32] Quite apart from Pl., the Johannine

---

[26] So Schl. Lk., ad loc.; W. Foerster, "Lukas 22:31 f.," ZNW, 46 (1955), 129-133; most comm. take a different view; cf. Bultmann Trad., 287 f., Suppl., 39; Noack, 101 f.

[27] Zn. Lk.; Schl. Lk.; K. H. Rengstorf, Das Ev. nach Lk., NT Deutsch, 3⁸ (1958), ad loc.; cf. also M. Zerwick, "Vidi satanam sicut fulgur de caelo cadentem," Verbum Domini, 26 (1948), 110-114.

[28] We are certainly not to think merely of the temptation, Zn. Lk., ad loc.

[29] Schl. J., ad loc., but not Bultmann J., ad loc.

[30] We do find in the NT speculations about the fall of the angels; Jd. 6 and 2 Pt. 2:4 adopt the pseudepigr. doctrine of the provisional punishment of the fallen angels of Gn. 6, and there is perhaps an echo of this in Lk. 8:31 though not 1 Pt. 3:19 (→ III, 707, 15 ff.; VI, 447, 25 ff.), cf. the comm. and B. Reicke, "The Disobedient Spirits and Christian Baptism," Seminarii Neotest. Upsaliensis, 13 (1946). Cf. also Rev. 9:1-11; 12:4a.

[31] V. the comm., ad loc.

[32] The only possible NT allusion to this is in Phil. 2:6: οὐχ ἁρπαγμὸν ἡγήσατο τὸ εἶναι ἴσα θεῷ. Perhaps Pl. has in view here the antithesis of a devilish striving to be equal with God and hence a pre-cosmic fall of the devil. But since the section as a whole

writings also say nothing about this. We read there, not ἐν ἀρχῇ ὁ διάβολος ἥμαρτεν, but ἀπ' ἀρχῆς ἁμαρτάνει, 1 Jn. 3:8. The same ἀπ' ἀρχῆς occurs in Jn. 8:44 too. [33] The equation of Satan with the serpent of Paradise is made in Rev. 12:9 (→ V, 580, 40 ff.), as previously in Paul (→ V, 581, 18 ff.). But Paul did not make use of Jewish speculations about a sexual seduction of Eve by the serpent/Satan (→ V, 581, 1 ff.). When Jn. 8:44 calls the devil a murderer from the beginning, this presupposes the same equation with the serpent. [34] On the other hand, we do not find in the NT the later Rabb. equation of Satan with the angel of death or the evil impulse (→ II, 77, 17 ff.; 78, n. 43). Hb. 2:14 is closest to the first equation but does not make it. Both Paul and Rev. plainly differentiate between death and Satan, 1 C. 15:26; Rev. 20:10, 14.

2. Satan Sayings in the Synoptists.

Linguistic Data. Mk. (1:13; 3:23, 26; 4:15; 8:33) and the material peculiar to Lk. (10:18; 13:16; 22:3, 31) apart from Lk. 10:19 (→ ὁ ἐχθρός) use only ὁ σατανᾶς (no art. only Mk. 3:23; Lk. 22:3, as vocative Mt. 4:10; Mk. 8:33 = Mt. 16:23), which is derived from the Aram. אָטְנָס. In Mt. apart from 4:10 and elsewhere in Lk. ὁ σατανᾶς occurs only in the Beelzebul pericope (par. to Mk.) and Mt. 16:23 = Mk. 8:33. In the story of the temptation (Q) Mt. (apart from 4:3 ὁ πειράζων and 4:10 σατανᾶ) and Lk. use ὁ διάβολος, found elsewhere only in Mt. 13:39; 25:41. Mt. also uses → ὁ ἐχθρός and → ὁ πονηρός quite commonly. Mt. 13:19 has ὁ πονηρός and Lk. 8:12 ὁ διάβολος for the ὁ σατανᾶς of Mk. 4:15.

In the primitive Christian tradition transmitted in the Synoptists there are few references to Satan, but these are enough to enable us to trace the basic outlines of the NT view of Satan. [35] The overcoming of the temptation by Jesus (→ VI, 34, 13 ff.) is more than a negative act. It is a victory which proves who is the stronger. [36] The one who handed down the temptation story regarded the devil as a conscious will which sought to prevent the coming of the kingdom of God through Jesus' way of life and suffering and which also had the power of this world at its command. In the saying to Peter (Mk. 8:33 par. Mt. 16:23) it might at first seem most natural to take σατανᾶ as an appellative in the sense "opponent." [37] Yet the tradition would hardly have retained the Aram. word except

---

considers only Christ's work and does not even mention men as those who are to be redeemed, it is unlikely that the Lucifer motif forms the background. Stauffer, 47 thinks the vv. mentioned above (Lk. 10:18; Rev. 12:9; Jn. 12:31) prove that Jewish traditions about a pre-human disaster in the volitional life of creation were known and accepted in the primitive Church. esp. in Paul ; but the passages hardly support this, nor does Rev. 9:1-11. In 2 C. 11:14 Pl. does not write : ὁ σατανᾶς μετεσχηματίσατο εἰς ἄγγελον φωτός, but chooses the pres. This leads Wnd. 2 K., ad loc. to the precarious theory that Paul was acquainted with many such Satanic transformations. Ltzm. K., ad loc. and Langton, 138 and 191 also see a ref. to Jewish myths about the fall.

[33] Jn. 8:44a seems to refer to a father of the devil. In good Gnostic terms this could only mean that the Jews derive from the demiurge as the father of the devil. But for the Gnostics the demiurge is characterised more by ignorance and pride than by lusts. The resultant tripartite division of the world would also contradict the total view of Jn.

[34] Another possibility is a ref. to the story of Cain, Hirsch J., 218 f.; Hirsch Studien, 78-80, but rightly this is for the most part rejected, cf. the comm. and Noack, 86-90; J. H. Bernard, Comm. on the Gospel acc. to St. John, ICC (1928), ad loc. leaves it an open question.

[35] Even if the formulation of the Synoptic pericopes discussed is to be traced back more or less to the primitive Palestinian or Hell. community, the basic spiritual attitude goes back to Jesus Himself. How else could it have arisen in distinction from Judaism ?

[36] As against Leivestad, 50-53.

[37] Noack, 86 also considers this possibility, but rightly rejects it.

as a term for the one opponent. But then all kinds of other difficulties arise. Peter is called Satan because he thinks in human terms ; Satan, however, thinks in satanic rather than human terms. Thus what is human is so much opposed to God that it can be called satanic, and this because it is set against the way of God for the salvation of men. The situation at the temptation is seen again for a moment here. [38] Only at this point and in the εἰσῆλθεν δὲ σατανᾶς εἰς 'Ιούδαν of Lk. 22:3 (peculiar to Lk.) do the Synoptists mention Satan in the passion story ; in particular there is no reference in the Gethsemane pericope. [39] In the main it is astonishing how little the Synoptists depict the life and passion of Jesus as a battle against Satan, or how seldom Satan is mentioned at all in them. At any rate it is not stated that the evil one stands behind the questions which were put to Jesus to tempt Him, [40] → VI, 28, 17 ff.; 35, 16 ff. Nevertheless, one should not overlook the light which the temptation story casts on the life of Jesus. The whole life and suffering of Jesus are a Yes to God and consequently a No to the tempter.

Only once is there reference in the Synoptists to a conflict with Satan, namely, in the Beelzebul pericope in Mk. 3:22 ff. and par. With this account the primitive community has handed down a whole set of important sayings. In place of the current ambivalence of Judaism concerning demons (→ 155, 4 ff.; I, 605, 23 ff.; II, 13, 35 ff.; 15, 28 ff.) one notes first the unequivocal unity of the kingdom of evil under the single head, Satan. Furthermore the possessed are not men who are summoned to decision by the message of Jesus ; they are men whom Jesus' word of power liberates from a force which enslaves them in their personal life. These are sick people of a particular kind, and their sickness is a work of the power of the evil one, → II, 822, 7 ff. A sickness which does not have the features of possession (→ II, 18, 38 ff.) can also be attributed to Satan, Lk. 13:16. [41] It is worth noting, however, that not every sickness is hereby regarded as due to satanic influence. But no balance or clear-cut distinction is attempted between natural and Satanic ailments ; the "murderer from the very beginning" is secretly behind the phenomenon of sickness. Hence Ac. 10:38 : ('Ιησοῦς) ὃς διῆλθεν εὐεργετῶν καὶ ἰώμενος πάντας τοὺς καταδυναστευομένους ὑπὸ τοῦ διαβόλου, can represent all the cures of Jesus as exorcisms of the devil. [42] A third basic statement in the Beelzebul story is the parable about the strong man and the stronger, Mk. 3:27 and par. This is a justification of the work of Jesus and alludes to an episode in His own life. It is usually assumed that the binding of the strong man took place in the temptation, → III, 401, 19 ff. This is correct so long as one perceives that the cross and the resurrection were germinally present in the temptation. Only in this indissoluble interrelationship can one see clearly what it was all about. The disarming of Satan is not just a matter of power ; it is a

---

[38] The same is true of Lk. 22:53 : αὕτη ἐστὶν ὑμῶν ἡ ὥρα καὶ ἡ ἐξουσία τοῦ σκότους, where the "hour of men" is also the "power of darkness" and the ἄχρι καιροῦ of Lk. 4:13 is taken up again.

[39] Hb., which is closely akin to the primitive tradition, probably offers the key when in 4:15 it stress the πεπειρασμένον κατὰ πάντα καθ' ὁμοιότητα.

[40] But cf. Fascher, 35-38; Robinson, 37 f., 58.

[41] Langton, 169 thinks the πνεῦμα ἀσθενείας (v. 11) pts. to a case of possession, but neither the word of healing (v. 12) nor the laying on of hands (v. 13) is in keeping with this, cf. also Str.-B., IV, 524-526.

[42] So Noack, 75 f.; Bau. Ag., ad loc.; Zn. Ag., ad loc., but not Langton, 182. Robinson, 30 calls Ac. 10:38 a commentary on Mk. 3:27.

matter of right. The binding of the strong man and the fall of the accuser from heaven refer to the same thing. Mk. 3:27 and Lk. 10:17 f. elucidate one another.

Two further important statements are passed down in interpretations of parables. In the parable of the sower the fact that some seed falls on the path (Mk. 4:4) decides its fate. In the interpretation, which does not make the parable an allegory, [43] there corresponds to this falling on the path only the μὴ συνιέντος which is found in Mt. alone at 13:19. The plur. "birds" is against a reference to the work of the devil, and so, too, is the fact that one might just as well think of the activity of the evil one in relation to persecutions or the deceitfulness of riches. The work of Satan, which is mentioned only in Mk. 4:15 and Lk. 8:12, is the supernatural factor which is beyond man's comprehension. It is not in keeping with the parable to find in the μὴ συνιέντος of Mt. the prior guilt of man and in the work of Satan the consequences, nor to see in the work of Satan [44] the view of the Evangelists and in Mt. 23:37 the meaning of Jesus Himself. [45] The juxtaposition of what sound like predestinarian statements with the "he that hath ears to hear, let him hear" must not be evaded in any way. [46] If in the parable of the wheat and the tares the mixed state of the community is ascribed to the devil (Mt. 13:28, 39), this is not an explanation; basically it is an even greater enigma, for how is it possible for the enemy to sow his tares in the community? In sowing, he does not sow semi-christians, but sons of iniquity in the community. Rejection of the ideal of a pure community is accompanied in Mt. by the demand for Church discipline, Mt. 18:15-17. Obviously the two belong together and protect one another against misunderstanding.

The traditions preserved in the Synoptic Gospels do not offer any fully developed Satanology but they do show what the primitive community regarded as important and worth keeping and passing on with respect to the work of the evil one. No attempt whatever is made to depict the devil's being, origin, or work, and the solution of 1 QS 3:13-4:26 is not adopted. Here is a mystery which no effort is made to solve. [47] The power of evil is regarded as a single power working towards a specific objective. This objective is the destruction of man in every respect. In particular, there is war against Jesus of Nazareth as the bringer of the redeeming lordship of God. Through His way of obedience even unto death, which the devil sought in vain to disrupt, Jesus has broken the power of the evil one, though He has not completely destroyed it or made it irrelevant. In virtue of this work He differs from the prophetic Teacher of Righteousness of the Qumran community. The Jewish world of thought is plain to see in the Synoptists; it is also radically transcended.

3. Satan Sayings in the Epistles. [48]

Linguistic Data. Paul never uses ὁ διάβολος in the older epistles including 2 Th. but mostly ὁ σατανᾶς, R. 16:20; 1 C. 5:5; 7:5; 2 C. 2:11; 11:14; 12:7; 1 Th. 2:18; 2 Th. 2:9 (without art. only 2 C. 12:7); ὁ πειράζων 1 Th. 3:5 (→ VI, 32, 1 ff.); ὁ πονηρός

---

[43] Jülicher GlJ, II, 537.
[44] A. M. Brouwer, De gelijkenissen (1946), 140.
[45] Noack, 111.
[46] The position is the same in Paul, who in 2 C. 4:4 speaks of the ἄπιστοι whose thoughts have been blinded by the "god of this aeon."
[47] Cf. → II, 75 ff. with n. 26, 30, 32, 45; also Vit. Ad., 9:12-16; Apc. Mos. 7:17-19.
[48] Apart from the Johannine Epistles but including Ac. and Rev.

2 Th. 3:3 (→ VI, 561, 19 ff.); Βελιάρ 2 C. 6:15 (→ I, 607, 1 ff.). ὁ σατανᾶς also occurs in 1 Tm. 1:20; 5:15; ὁ διάβολος in Eph. 4:27; 6:11; 1 Tm. 3:6, 7; 2 Tm. 2:26; ὁ πονηρός in Eph. 6:16. Other terms are used in 2 C. 4:4; Eph. 2:2. Ac. has ὁ σατανᾶς in 5:3 and 26:18 and (ὁ) διάβολος in 10:38 and 13:10. The Catholic Epistles use only διάβολος, Jm. 4:7; Hb. 2:14; 1 Pt. 5:8; Jd. 9. Rev. has ὁ σατανᾶς in 2:9, 13, 24; 3:9; 20:7; ὁ διάβολος in 2:10; 12:12; 20:10; both together in the emphatic 12:9; 20:2. ὁ κατήγωρ occurs in 12:10 (→ III, 636, 7 ff.), and we also find the fig. ὁ ὄφις (→ V, 580, 40 ff.) and ὁ δράκων (→ II, 281, 2 ff.). On Johannine usage → 162, 27 ff.

In the NT Epistles the devil is mentioned predominantly in connection with his attack on the community. This takes place first in persecutions, Rev. 2:10; 12:17; 13:7; 1 Pt. 5:8.[49] Active hostility to the Christian community is also the reason why Rev. 2:9; 3:9 call the Jewish communities synagogues of Satan.[50] Specifically, however, the devil works against the community in temptations. 1 Th. 1-3 is written out of a concern μή πως ἐπείρασεν ὑμᾶς ὁ πειράζων (3:5), i.e., lest the community might be put off by the fate of the apostle, who was hounded from city to city (→ VI, 32, 1 ff.). In 1 C. 7:5 it is ἀκρασία which can offer Satan the chance to tempt. Paul refers in 2 C. 2:11 to the νοήματα of Satan, who seeks to outwit him, and in Eph. 6:11 he speaks of the μεθοδεῖαι (→ V, 103, 11 ff.) of the devil. 1 Tm. 3:7 also refers to a snare of the devil (→ II, 81, 10 ff.) and so, too, does 2 Tm. 2:26 (→ III, 61, 18 ff.). Paul finds a particularly dangerous and misleading work of Satan in libertinistic ideas, whose champions pretend to be apostles of Christ and whose appearance shows how dangerous Satan is when he transforms himself into an angel of light, 2 C. 11:14. The same danger, which is present throughout the primitive congregations, is also brought into connection with Satan in R. 16:20. This seducing activity of Satan finds its climax in the work of antichrist, 2 Th. 2:3-12; Rev. 13, 17; cf. 3:10.

Temptations are warded off by the blood of the Lamb (Rev. 12:11), by putting on the armour of God (Eph. 6:11), i.e., by faith (Eph. 6:16), or often by avoiding situations in which temptation comes (1 C. 7:5; 1 Tm. 3:6 f.; 5:14 f.; cf. Eph. 4:27; R. 16:17). Ὁ δὲ θεὸς τῆς εἰρήνης συντρίψει τὸν σατανᾶν ὑπὸ τοὺς πόδας ὑμῶν ἐν τάχει (R. 16:20) is Paul's call to the Roman church. God will do it, but He does it through the community.

Satan tries to work against the community in other ways too. He prevents Paul from making the very necessary journey to Thessalonica (1 Th. 2:18) and his angel buffets Paul (2 C. 12:7; → 159, 25 ff.).[51] Paul does not connect every

---

[49] In view of the following v. the work of Satan is to be related to persecutions in v. 8.

[50] That the Jews were for a long time the main force behind persecution may be seen from 1 Th. 2:15, also from Ac. and cf. Mart. Pol., 12, 2; 13, 1; 17, 2; Just. Dial., 16, 11; cf. also H. J. Cadbury, The Book of Acts in History (1955), 91 f. In detail the reason why Pergamon is called Satan's seat in Rev. 2:13 is either because of the emperor cult (Bss. Apk., ad loc.; R. H. Charles, The Revelation of St. John, ICC [1950], ad loc.) and the great altar to Zeus (I. Birt, "Der Thron des Satans," Philol. Wochenschr., 52 [1932], 1203-1210), or because of the cult and temple of Aesculapius (Bss. and Had. Apk., ad loc.; K. H. Rengstorf, "Die Anfänge der Auseinandersetzung zwischen Christusglaube u. Asklepiusfrömmigkeit," Schriften d. Gesellschaft zur Förderung d. Westfälischen Wilhelms-Universität, 30 [1953], 26-28), or because of the local synagogue. Or did Pergamon with its castle hill have for the seer the appearance of a giant's throne on which Satan sat, ruling over all the busy religious life of the town?

[51] Whatever the thorn in the flesh may be (→ σκόλοψ, also Langton, 191 and G. Thils, "De 'stimulo carnis' in 2 K. 12:7," Collectanea Mechliensia, 31 [1946], 160-163), it is at any rate a hindrance to missionary work.

illness of Christians or fellow-workers with the devil (Phil. 2:25-30), nor does he attribute every blocked journey to Satan (R. 1:13 ἐκωλύθην). One can only say that in his ministry the apostle thought he could detect the hampering of Satan as well as the guidance of God, though he never tried to interrelate the two in any logical manner. Most striking is Satan's work in 1 C. 5:5 and 1 Tm. 1:20. Later Judaism, apart from its equation of Satan with the angel of death, occasionally stated that Satan and his hosts can harm and even kill men (→ n. 25, cf. also Lk. 13:16). Nor is it unheard of in later Judaism for the angel of destruction to execute the judgment of God. In 1 C. 5:5, however, the sentence which Satan himself carries out is for a purpose of salvation. Later Judaism did not dare venture this bold thought. Can Paul write thus because the hour of darkness was for the salvation of the world? The angel of Satan (→ II, 17, 1 ff.; III, 819, 12 ff.), the thorn in the flesh, is "given" to Paul lest he should exalt himself (2 C. 12:7).

There are far fewer references to Satan's work outside the community than to his battle against it. In the world outside he holds undisputed sway except in so far as the witness of the community contests it. The task which the Risen Lord gives to Paul on the Damascus road is to open the eyes of the Gentiles τοῦ ἐπιστρέψαι ἀπὸ ... τῆς ἐξουσίας τοῦ σατανᾶ ἐπὶ τὸν θεόν, Ac. 26:18. In paganism magic is thought to be particularly associated with the evil one, cf. Ac. 13:10 : υἱὲ διαβόλου.

The only direct references to the final destruction of the devil are in Mt. 25:41 and Rev. 20:10. Naturally it may be presupposed in Paul, but it is worth noting that in 1 C. 15:24-26 Paul speaks of the end of every ἀρχή and ἐξουσία, and also of the end of death, but not of the end of Satan — or of sin.

4. The Prince of This World in John's Gospel and the Johannine Epistles.

In the Johannine writings four terms are used for the devil. a. διάβολος is not a proper name but is the true designation (7 times); the children of God and the children of the devil stand opposed to one another, 1 Jn. 3:10. b. σατανᾶς occurs only once in the decisive saying about Judas Iscariot in Jn. 13:27: τότε εἰσῆλθεν εἰς ἐκεῖνον ὁ σατανᾶς. [52] c. ὁ πονηρός, which cannot always be distinguished for certain from the neuter τὸ πονηρόν, occurs in Jn. only at 17:15 but then 6 times in 1 Jn. (→ VI, 559, 6 ff.). d. ὁ ἄρχων τοῦ κόσμου τούτου is a final name for Satan in Jn. 12:31; 14:30; 16:11.

The crucial point about the devil is made in Jn. 8:44. The relation of the devil to man is that of father to child (cf. 1 Jn. 3:10), i.e., he determines man's whole being. For this we also find ἔκ τινος εἶναι (without the image of the father) in 1 Jn. 3:12. Essentially the Rabbis did not think in this way; [53] for them the will of man fixes his religious relation. There is a special form of this determination of man's nature by Satan in Jn. 6:70 : ἐξ ὑμῶν εἷς διάβολός ἐστιν, which reminds us of the Satan saying to Peter in Mk. 8:33 (→ 158, 28 ff.), and also in Jn. 13:27, where Satan entered into Judas, Lk. 22:3 being a parallel here. For neither statement is there any analogy in later Judaism, where neither the

[52] The other ref. to the betrayal by Judas use only διάβολος. In the solemn designation of the devil in Rev. 12:9; 20:2 σατανᾶς is used.
[53] Schl. J. on 8:44. "The children of darkness" and "the men of the lot of Belial" in the Dead Sea Scrolls are similar, cf. also Wis. 2:24b.

devil nor Belial, but only one of their spirits, enters into man. [54] Three things are said about Satan in Jn. 8:44. The saying that he was a murderer ἀπ' ἀρχῆς reminds us of the fall → n. 34. The statement which follows (ἐν τῇ ἀληθείᾳ οὐκ ἕστηκεν) is none too certain textually. What it means is that at no time can one speak of truth in connection with the devil. This is made plain by the third assertion that when he speaks lies he speaks from what is his own. The meaning is not that by creation the devil stood in the truth and that the fall and lying are of himself, not created by God. Only the second point is made. In fact the saying forbids us to ask what the devil was before he became the devil. What it says is that the devil is determined by the fact that he is the devil. Whether wittingly or unwittingly the ideas expressed by later Judaism, including Qumran, about the being, nature and origin of the devil, are here rejected.

A distinctive aspect of the Johannine writings is the role played in them by ontic statements : to be born of God or the devil, or to be the children of God or the devil. He who commits sin is for this reason ἐκ τοῦ διαβόλου, 1 Jn. 3:8. Conversely, because Cain was ἐκ τοῦ πονηροῦ he slew his brother, 1 Jn. 3:12. He who is born of God does not sin, the evil one does not touch him, 1 Jn. 5:18. This is in different terms exactly the same thing as Jesus said about the tree and its fruits [55] and Paul makes the same point with his interrelation and juxtaposition of indicatives and imperatives. When John cries to the νεανίσκοι : You are victors over the wicked one (1 Jn. 2:13 f.), this is not meant either in the sense of what is self-evident by nature or in that of a rigid predestinarianism ; otherwise the petition of Jesus in the high-priestly prayer : ἐρωτῶ ... ἵνα τηρήσῃς αὐτοὺς ἐκ τοῦ πονηροῦ (Jn. 17:15), would have no point. The imperative is enclosed in the ontic sayings of John.

Foerster

C. Satan in the Post-Apostolic Fathers.

a. Linguistic Data.

The term σατανᾶς (appellative as in the NT) occurs in the post-apost. fathers only 4 times : Barn., 18, 1; Ign. Eph., 13, 1; Pol., 7, 1; Mart. Pol. Ep., 3. διάβολος is the most common word (32 times, 25 in Herm., who uses only this): 2 Cl., 18, 2; Ign. Eph., 10, 3; Ign. Tr., 8, 1; Ign. R., 5, 3; Ign. Sm., 9, 1; Pol., 7, 1; Mart. Pol., 3, 1; Herm. m., 4, 3, 4. 6; m., 5, 1, 3; 9, 9. 11; 11, 3. 17; 12, 2, 2; 4, 7; 5, 1. 4; 6, 1. 4; s., 8, 3, 6; 9, 31, 2 (= *diabolus*), and twice each in m., 7, 2. 3; 12, 4, 6; 5, 2; 6, 2. ἄρχων is also used with various qualifying terms : πονηρὸς ἄρχων, Barn., 4, 13; ἄδικος ἄρχων, Mart. Pol., 19, 2, ἄρχων καιροῦ τοῦ νῦν τῆς ἀνομίας, Barn., 18, 2 and ἄρχων τοῦ αἰῶνος τούτου, Ign. Eph., 17, 1; 19, 1; Mg., 1, 2; Tr., 4, 2; R., 7, 1; Phld., 6, 2. ἀντικείμενος is used in the abs. in 1 Cl., 51, 1 and with the addition τῷ γένει τῶν δικαίων in Mart. Pol., 17, 1. The obscure ἐνεργῶν of Barn., 2, 1 also seems to be relevant here ; the Lat. has *contrarius*. [56]

---

[54] The closest par. is Test. A. 1:9 : ὁ θησαυρὸς τοῦ διαβουλίου πονηροῦ πνεύματος πεπλήρωται, for acc. to the context the evil spirit is not one of many possible spirits but it denotes being radically filled by evil.

[55] In the expression used by Jesus the image of the tree and its fruits finds no par. in later Judaism.

[56] A. Hilgenfeld, NT extra canonem receptum² (1876 ff.), ad loc. thus suggests ἀντενεργῶν.

Other terms are πονηρός in Barn., 2, 10; 21, 3, with ἀντίζηλος and βάσκανος, Mart. Pol., 17, 1, μέλας, Barn., 4, 10; 20, 1, and ἄνομος in Barn., 15, 5. The relation between Satan and the antichrist called κοσμοπλανής in Did., 16, 4 is not clear.

b. General Material.

In the post-apost. fathers as in the NT the existence and activity of Satan are pre-supposed and there is no independent reflection or speculation about this. The centre of concern is salvation, and Satan calls for consideration only in relation hereto. He is the one who has been deprived of his power by Christ. Ign. speaks of this in terms which betray Gnostic influence. The rule of the ἄρχων τοῦ αἰῶνος τούτου, which is characterised by μαγεία, δεσμὸς κακίας, ἄγνοια [57] and death, has to be regarded as παλαιὰ βασιλεία, Ign. Eph., 19, 3. For it has been shattered by the event of salva-tion, by the birth and death of the Redeemer, which were concealed from the ἄρχων τοῦ αἰῶνος τούτου (19, 1) and were revealed to the αἰῶνες only by the ascension which accompanied His death (19, 2). In an apocalyptic statement Barn., 15, 5 speaks of the ending of the καιρὸς τοῦ ἀνόμου, cf. 21, 3. Yet in the main Satan is viewed in antithesis to the way of salvation rather than to the Bringer of salvation. In accordance with differing views of the actualising of salvation, whether in the Church, martyrdom, or the keeping of the new Law, he is seen primarily from the standpt. of his opposition to the Church, the martyr, or the individual Christian.

c. Satan and the Church.

For Ign. salvation is by sacramental union with the Church, which as such is union with Christ and the Father, ἐν ᾧ ὑπομένοντες τὴν πᾶσαν ἐπήρειαν τοῦ ἄρχοντος τοῦ αἰῶνος τούτου καὶ διαφυγόντες θεοῦ τευξόμεθα, Mg., 1, 2. Where this union is achieved in the assembling of the Church εἰς εὐχαριστίαν θεοῦ καὶ εἰς δόξαν, the δυνάμεις τοῦ σατανᾶ are destroyed and his corruption is ended, Ign. Eph., 13, 1. On the other hand, where the unity of the Church is threatened, the κακοτεχνίαι and ἐνέδραι of the ἄρχων τοῦ αἰῶνος τούτου are at work, Ign. Tr., 8, 1; Phld., 6, 2, and the man who leaves the unity of the Church in schism, or in heresy, or by evading the moral control of life by the new being mediated through the Church, falls back into the sphere of Satan's dominion, Sm., 9, 1; Eph., 17, 1; 10, 3 cf. Pol., 7, 1; Mart. Pol. Epil., 3. The hostility of Satan to the Church is presented more externally when Mart. Pol., 17, 1 blames him for the refusal to hand over the body of Polycarp to the local church.

d. Satan and the Martyr.

The martyr's passion is a wrestling with Satan which achieves victory in martyrdom, Mart. Pol., 3, 1; 19, 2. So long as the battle has not been fought out Ign. sees himself still ὑπὸ κίνδυνον (Eph., 12, 1; Tr., 13, 3) and hence he must exercise πραότης because the ἄρχων τοῦ αἰῶνος τούτου who is at work in the ζῆλος which oppresses him is defeated thereby, Tr., 4, 2. As the martyr's passion, i.e., the sign of this conflict with the ἄρχων τοῦ αἰῶνος τούτου who seeks to break the divinely orientated will of Ign. and thus to win him over (R., 7, 1), the torments are then called κολάσεις τοῦ δια-βόλου, R., 5, 3. The martyr's passion is also a battle with the devil in Herm. s., 8, 3, 6, though a pt. worth noting is that here it is not *imitatio Christi*, as in Ign. and Mart. Pol., but suffering for the Law.

---

[57] H. Schlier, *Religionsgeschichtliche Untersuchungen zu den Ignatiusbriefen*, Beih. ZNW, 8 (1929), 18, n. 1 links κακίας with ἄγνοια rather than δεσμός.

e. Satan and the Individual Christian.

For Barn. Christians are τῇ πίστει ἐπαγγελίας καὶ τῷ λόγῳ ζωοποιούμενοι (6, 17), but they live in the present age over which Satan has ἐξουσία (2, 1) as ἄρχων καιροῦ τοῦ νῦν τῆς ἀνομίας (18, 2 cf. 15, 5). The means of exercising this dominion is the possibility of the way of darkness over which the ἄγγελοι τοῦ σατανᾶ are set, 18, 1 cf. 20, 1. Not to perceive the resultant situation is to incur the danger of falling under the rule of the "black one" or the "wicked one" (4, 10. 13 cf. 2, 1. 10) and thus forfeiting salvation.

Satan is the tempter in 1 Cl., 51, 1; 2 Cl., 18, 2 (the only ref. to the devil in these two works), and esp. in Herm. m., 4, 3, 6; s., 9, 31, 2, which finds in the weakness of man and the πολυπλοκία of the devil the reason why God gives a chance of new repentance, m., 4, 3, 4. 6. If we set aside m., 11, 3, which says that when a false prophet occasionally speaks the truth the devil has filled him with his spirit in order to deceive the righteous, this πολυπλοκία τοῦ διαβόλου or ἐκπειρασθῆναι ὑπὸ τοῦ διαβόλου represents the possibility of sin entailed by man's freedom of choice. Herm. uses various motifs and ideas to depict this possibility of choice between good and evil. These are only imperfectly harmonised and developed, if at all. In the main they rest on demono- logical dualism, but only partially and unsystematically are they linked to the figure of the devil. Thus the two-angel teaching of m., 6, 2, 1-9 stands in no relation whatever to the devil. For Herm. himself, however, it is in each case the διάβολος who posits, and leaves open, and seeks to actualise the possibility of the choice of evil. This is plain in the expressions ἐντολαὶ τοῦ διαβόλου in m., 12, 4, 6 and ἔργα τοῦ διαβόλου (obj. gen.) in m., 7, 3. In this function the devil acquires a power which he can exercise only in relation to those who do not have the moral resolution of the servants of God, whereas this power is broken by those who make use of the opportunity given by the angel of repentance, m., 7, 1-3; 12, 4, 6-6, 5. Like martyrdom, this struggle can be called a conflict with the devil, cf. m., 12, 5, 2 with s., 8, 3, 6.

Schäferdiek

---

† σβέννυμι

σβέννυμι [1] and σβεννύω, [2] except in the pres. from Hom., Hell. often ζβέννυμι, e.g., P. Lond., I, 121, 364, [3] means basically "to quench."

A. The Greek World.

The verb is found from Hom. to the pap. in both the lit. and the transf. sense.

1. Literal Use.

a. Mostly of fire or burning objects trans. (fut. σβέσω, aor. ἔσβεσα) "to quench" (in Hom. only compounds): τὸ καιόμενον, Hdt., II, 66; κεραυνόν, Pind. Pyth., 1, 5;

σ β έ ν ν υ μ ι. Liddell-Scott, Pape, Pass., Moult.-Mill., Preisigke Wört., Diels, III; Hatch-Redp., Leisegang, Pr.-Bauer[5], *s.v.*; not in v. Arnim, Ditt. Syll.[3], Cr.-Kö., or Trench.

[1] Etym. Indo-Eur. *sgᵘes-neu-mi, cf. Boisacq, 856; Hofmann, 307 f.

[2] Cf. Bl.-Debr. § 92; Schwyzer, I, 698 f.

[3] On the widespread Hell. ζβ for σβ cf. Bl.-Debr. § 10.

φλόγα, Thuc., II, 77, 6; intr. (pass. fut. σβεσθήσομαι, aor. ἐσβέσθην, also act. aor. 2 ἔσβην and perf. ἔσβηκα), "to be extinguished," "to go out" : πῦρ ... ὑπὸ τοῦ ἐναντίου φθείρεται σβεννύμενον, Aristot. Cael., III, 6, p. 305a, 10; οὐδέ ποτ᾿ ἔσβη πῦρ, Hom. Il., 9, 471 f. b. Of fluids trans. "to suck dry" : ἡ Μηδικὴ πόα ... σβέννυσι τὸ γάλα, Aristot. Hist. An., III, 21, p. 522b, 25 f., intr. "to dry up" : γάλα τ᾿ αἰγῶν σβεννυμενάων, "goats whose milk goes dry," Hes. Op., 590, πηγαί, Anth. Graec., 9, 128; αἶμα, Plut. Adulat., 2 (II, 49c). c. Of men, plants and cities, only pass. "to die," "perish" : ὁ δὲ θάνατός ἐστι σβεσθῆναι, Luc. Verae Hist., 1, 29; δένδρον, Poll. Onom., 1, 231; ῾Ρόδος, Anth. Graec., 9, 178. d. Of foods in cooking "to steam" ἰχθύων ᾠὰ μεθ᾿ ἁλῶν σβεσθέντα, Athen., III, 121c. e. Gen. trans. "to still," "to damp down," "to restrain" : κύματα, Aristoph. Av., 778; τὴν αὔξην τε καὶ ἐπιρροήν, Plat. Leg., VI, 783b; ὁ βορέας ... σβέννυσι τὴν θερμότητα, Aristot. Meteor., I, 10, p. 347b, 4; ὕδατι δίψαν, Apoll. Rhod., 3, 1349; ὄφεων ἰόν, Orph. Lithica, 49 (Abel, p. 110), intr. "to rest," "to lie down," "to abate," of the wind, Hom. Od., 3, 182 f., of sound, Tryphiodorus Excidium Ilii, 10; medically of the disappearing of a carbuncle, Hippocr. Acut., 26 (Kühlewein, I, 159).

2. Transferred Use.

a. Esp. of emotions and moods trans. "to still," "to calm ᾿ : χόλον, Hom. Il., 9, 678; ἀνθρώπων ... μένος, ibid., 16, 621; ὕβριν, Heracl. Fr., 43 (Diels, I, 160, 12); Plat. Leg., VIII, 835e; τὸν θυμόν, ibid., X, 888a; ἀγηνορίην, Anth. Graec., 5, 300; εὐφροσύνην, ibid., 9, 375. b. Gen. act. "to suppress," "to restrain" : τὸ καλὸν χρόνος ἔσβεσεν, Anth. Graec., V, 62; κλέος, 9, 104; τυραννίδα, Plut. De Lycurgo, 20 (I, 52e); φόνον, Eur. Herc. Fur., 40; πεῖραν, Soph. Ai., 1057; δυνάμεις, Plot. Enn., VI, 4, 10, pass.: "to fade," "to die out," "to disappear" : of the influence of a personality, ἐσβέσθη Νίκανδρος, Anth. Graec., 12, 39; of a speaker ἀπαγορεύοντα καὶ σβεννύμενον, Plut. Praec. Ger. Reip., 9 (II, 804c); of fighting strength τὸ μάχιμον ... σβεννύμενον ὑπὸ γήρως, Plut. Pomp., 8 (I, 622e); of the magic of love ἐσβέσθη τὰ φίλτρα, Anth. Graec., 7, 221.

B. Hellenistic Judaism.

1. In the LXX the word occurs some 45 times, almost always for Hbr. כבה and דעך. כבה is transl. by σβέννυμι 21 times and once by ἀποσβέννυμι at Prv. 31:18. Only twice at 1 S. 3:3 (᾿ΑΣ σβέννυμι) and Prv. 26:20 are other words used. דעך is transl. by σβέννυμι 6 times; ἐκκαίω (᾿ΑΣ ἀποσβέννυμι) is used in ψ 117:12 and twice the LXX is abbreviated. Other Hbr. equivalents for σβέννυμι are rare. נכא ni (a secondary form of נכה) occurs in Job 30:8. In the LXX we find the lit., fig. and transf. senses.

a. Lit. the ref. is mostly to fire and burning objects trans.: blazing fire πῦρ φλογιζόμενον ἀποσβέσει ὕδωρ, Σιρ. 3:30; "to extinguish" lamps, 2 Ch. 29:7; but also "to scorch" sprouting meadows ἀποσβέσει χλόην ὡς πῦρ, Sir. 43:21; intr. "to go out" : fire on the altar, Lv. 6:5 f.; flame, Ez. 21:3; sparks Σιρ. 28:12; the lamp of the virtuous woman οὐκ ἀποσβέννυται, Prv. 31:18; glowing coals, 4 Macc. 9:20;[4] but also of the destruction of the mountains ἀποσβεσθήσεται τὰ ὄρη, Is. 10:18 LXX. There is ref. to the unquenchable fire of judgment in Am. 5:6; Is. 1:31; 34:10; 66:24; Jer. 17:27; Ez. 21:4; Sir. 28:23.

b. Fig. the light (φῶς Job 18:5; Prv. 13:9), or lamp (λύχνος Jos 21:27; cf. 18:6) or candlestick (λαμπτήρ Prv. 24:20; cf. 20:20 [LXX 20:9a]) of the wicked will "go out," i.e., they will not last and are under judgment. The putting out of a spark can denote

---

[4] σβέννυσθαι of the sun in Test. L. 4:1.

the extinction of posterity, 2 S. 14:7; cf. 21:17; the extinguishing of fire is a figure for the expiation of sins, Sir. 3:30. The phrase "a smoking flax will he not quench" in Is. 42:3 illustrates the turning of the Servant of the Lord to the smitten with help and pardon.

c. In a transf. sense the verb is used of God's wrath (my anger ... will not be extinguished, 2 K. 22:17; 2 Ch. 34:25; cf. Jer. 4:4; 21:12), of passions in bonam and malam partem (love in Cant. 8:7; fire-eating boldness in 3 Macc. 6:34, desire in Sir. 23:17, flames of ardour in 4 Macc. 3:17, contention μακρόθυμος ἀνὴρ κατασβέσει [ʊʾpʰʲ] κρίσεις Prv. 15:18a; cf. 26:20; emotions τῷ λογισμῷ τῆς εὐσεβείας κατέσβε-σεν τὰ ... πάθη ἡ μήτηρ, 4 Macc. 16:4) and also of the destruction of man (the un-godly in Job LXX 34:26; 40:12; ὄνομα ... ἀσεβοῦς, Prv. 10:7).

2. Philo and Joseph. are acquainted with the multiple use of the word. Philo has it lit. of fire (Plant., 10) and eyesight (Deus Imm., 78), fig. of the flame of passions (Sacr. AC, 15) and in a transf. sense of the soul of the dying (Som., I, 31) and of reason (οὐ ... σβέννυται ... ὁ ὀρθὸς λόγος, Leg. All., I, 46). Joseph. speaks of the extinction of fire (πῦρ Bell., 7, 405) and also of the damping dowₐ of joy (τὴν χαράν, Bell., 6, 31) or of sorrow (τὸ λυποῦν, Ant., 11, 40).

C. The New Testament.

In the NT the word occurs 6 times altogether (4 times transitively and 2 in-transitively) and it is used three times in a literal sense, twice figuratively, and once in a transferred sense.

1. Literal Use.

Mk. 9:48 [5] (καὶ τὸ πῦρ οὐ σβέννυται) quotes Is. 66:24, the central Jewish passage depicting the torments of hell under the twofold image of the worm and the fire. The quotation deviates from the LXX, which in accordance with the Hebrew reads καὶ τὸ πῦρ αὐτῶν οὐ σβεσθήσεται. The context in Mk. makes it clear that the reference is to the unquenchable fire of hell, cf. v. 43 → I, 658, 8 ff.; VI, 945, 33 ff. In Mt. 25:8 the foolish virgins, awaking out of sleep, suddenly find that they are short of oil (cf. v. 3) and their lamps are going out (αἱ λαμπάδες ἡμῶν σβέννυνται). An allegorical interpretation of this is not intended in the original parable. Hb. 11:34 (ἔσβεσαν δύναμιν πυρός) alludes to the three friends of Daniel who by God's help were not harmed at all by the fire in Nebuchad-nezzar's burning fiery furnace, Da. 3:23-25; cf. 1 Macc. 2:59; 1 Cl., 45, 7.

2. Figurative Use.

In Mt. 12:18-21 the saying about the Servant of the Lord in Is. 42:1-4, which is also taken Messianically in the Targum, is referred to Jesus. The quotation follows exactly neither the LXX (λίνον καπνιζόμενον οὐ σβέσει, Is. 42:3) nor the Hebrew. In v. 20 Jesus is depicted as the Helper of the down-trodden and oppressed. [6] Figuratively Eph. 6:16 says that with the shield of faith Christians can quench all the fiery darts of the wicked, → I, 608, 25 ff. In this metaphor σβέσαι describes the final result rather than the direct effect. Arrows encased in blazing tow and pitch (→ VI, 950, 9 ff.; V, 300, 20 ff.) strike against the shield

---

[5] Textually v. 44 and v. 46 (Western and Syr. MSS) are a later assimilation to v. 48.
[6] Loh. Mt., ad loc.

(→ V, 313, 37 ff.) and fall to the ground, where they go out ineffectively. Materially the image expresses the victorious superiority of God's power, which is appropriated in faith, against all the onslaughts of the devil.

3. Transferred Use.

In 1 Th. 5:19 Paul admonishes the community : τὸ πνεῦμα μὴ σβέννυτε. πνεῦμα (→ VI, 332, 12 ff.) is here a master concept which embraces several special forms, e.g., prophecy (v. 20) and tongues, and which has reference to extraordinary manifestations of the Spirit, → VI, 422, 26 ff. In a transferred sense (→ 166, 21 ff.) σβεννύναι means "to suppress," "to restrain" [7] (opp. ἀναζωπυρεῖν in 2 Tm. 1:6). This does not take place through an impure walk (Chrysostom) or through sloth (Calvin). [8] Paul is rather warning against a deliberate suppression of the extraordinary operations of the Spirit in the congregation, cf. also 1 C. 14:28 ff. There does not have to be any particular cause for this warning in Thessalonica, since the whole section is a short church order.

D. The Post-Apostolic Fathers.

In the post-apost. fathers the word occurs only in bibl. quotations or in echo of bibl. ideas. In 2 Cl., 7, 6 and 17, 5 Is. 66:24 is quoted lit. from the LXX (in contrast to Mk. 9:48). Did., 16, 1 (οἱ λύχνοι ὑμῶν μὴ σβεσθήτωσαν) echoes Lk. 12:35 and Mt. 24:42, 44; 25:8. Mart. Pol., 11, 2 contrasts earthly fire which is temporal and extinguishable (τὸ πρὸς ὥραν καιόμενον καὶ μετ᾽ ὀλίγον σβεννύμενον) with the eternal and unquenchable fire of hell, cf. 2, 3 : τὸ αἰώνιον καὶ μηδέποτε σβεννύμενον. Behind this lies Is. 66:24 and the bibl. concept of the πῦρ ἄσβεστον, Job 20:26 vl.; Mk. 9:43; Mt. 3:12; Lk. 3:17.

Lang

σέβομαι, σεβάζομαι, σέβασμα,
Σεβαστός, εὐσεβής, εὐσέβεια,
εὐσεβέω, ἀσεβής, ἀσέβεια,
ἀσεβέω, σεμνός, σεμνότης

Derivates of the stem σεβ- are used very commonly in Gk. and are a typical expression of Greek piety. In marked contrast is the LXX, which, if it does not avoid the group altogether, is very restrained in its use of it. This is particularly

---

[7] For the combination with πνεῦμα there are par. in the Gk. world (τοῦ πνεύματος παντάπασιν ἀπεσβεσμένου, Plut. Pyth. Or., 17 [II, 402c]; τὸ πνεῦμα τὸ κατασβεννύμενον, Ps.-Plut. Vit. Poes. Hom., 127; cf. Gal. De Theriaca ad Pisonem, 17 [Kühn, 14, 286]), though πνεῦμα here is the natural vital spirit, → VI, 336, 13 ff.; 357, 37 ff.

[8] J. Calvin, Comm. on 1 Th., ad loc., Corp. Ref., 80 (1895), 175; Chrys. Hom. in 1 Th., ad loc., MPG, 62 (1862), 461.

σ έ β ο μ α ι. K. Kerényi, *Die antike Religion*² (1952), 87-90; D. Loenen, "Eusebeia en de cardinale deugden," *Mededelingen der Koninklijke Nederlandse Akademie van Wetenschappen, Afdeeling Letterkunde*, NR, 23, 4 (1960), 7-9.

noteworthy in respect of εὐσεβής, εὐσέβεια and εὐσεβέω. These important Greek terms are used extensively only in 4 Macc. The LXX is not so restrained in relation to ἀσεβής, ἀσέβεια and ἀσεβέω, though most of the instances are in the Wisdom literature. Almost more surprising is the usage of the NT, for here the whole group, apart from ἀσεβέω etc., is used in a Christian sense, with one exception, only in the Pastoral Epistles, Jude and 2 Peter. In the post-apostolic fathers σεβ- does not occur at all in Ign. or Did. These facts demand explanation.

σέβομαι.

A. σέβομαι in the Greek World.

1. Homeric Usage in the Light of the Basic Meaning of the Stem σεβ-.

The stem σεβ- means originally "to fall back before."[1] In what sense this is used may be seen in Hom. and Hom. Hymn., where σέβομαι occurs once, σεβάζομαι twice, and σέβας 9 times. This is in the first instance falling back in the sense of shrinking from. In Hom. Il., 4, 242 Agamemnon summons the Argives to battle : οὔ νυ σέβεσθε, "Do you not shrink from being cowardly," cf. 18, 178, where Iris calls to Achilles : σέβας δέ σε θυμὸν ἱκέσθω, "shrinking should come over you," i.e., at the thought that the body of Patroclus might fall prey to the dogs of Troy. σεβάζομαι is used similarly : Proitos shrinks from smiting Bellerophon in Il., 6, 167 and Achilles from despoiling Eetion of his armour : σεβάσσατο γὰρ τό γε θυμῷ, 6, 417. The idea is rather different in the common expression which speaks of someone being seized by a σέβας on seeing something, σέβας ἔχει (εἰς)ὁρόωντα : Nestor on seeing Telemachus because of his similarity to Odysseus, Od., 3, 123, cf. 4, 142, also Odysseus on seeing Nausicaa, Od., 6, 161, Telemachus in Sparta on seeing the greatness of the palace of Menelaus, Od., 4, 75, the immortals on seeing Athene, Hom. Hymn. ad Minervam, 6. To see the meadow which Gaia made to bloom to deceive Kore was a σέβας for gods and men, Hom. Hymn. Cer., 10; it is worth noting that the word stands close to θαυμαστός here. In the same hymn there is a description in v. 190 of how Demeter stood in the hall of Keleos and touched the rafters with her head : the mother was seized by αἰδώς, σέβας and χλωρὸν δέος. Here astonishment is mingled with fear. σεβ- always denotes awe whether at a great mistake or at something lofty and sublime.

The broader development of the group σεβ- was in association with the latter. The bodily movement expressed an inner attitude of respect, of being impressed by something great and lofty. The subjects might be gods or men, the objects gods, men or things. As yet there is no specific religious sense in σεβ-. But it is typical of the Gk. world that this stem should become a specific expression for a religious attitude. Linguistically the Semitic world has no par. to σέβομαι. The equivalent of הִשְׁתַּחֲוָה is προσκυνεῖν (→ VI, 760, 23 ff.), but in Gk. this remains limited to a single act and does not form the starting-pt. for wider development.[2] A related physical process is trembling, but though fear and trembling are sometimes close to σέβομαι,[3] the instances are exceptions which do not conceal the fact that σέβομαι has really nothing to do with fear and trembling. From the "Woe is me, for I am undone" of Is. 6:5 to the σέβας μ' ἔχει εἰσορόωντα of Homer (→ 169, 21 ff.) is a μετάβασις εἰς ἄλλο γένος; it is the μετάβασις from the OT to the Gk. world.

---

[1] Boisacq, s.v.; Hofmann, s.v.

[2] προσκυνεῖν used gen. for adoration of God is "very rare" in Hellenism, J. Horst, Proskynein (1932), 179.

[3] Aristoph. Nu., 293 f.: καὶ σέβομαι ... οὕτως αὐτὰς (the clouds) τετρεμαίνω καὶ πεφόβημαι, Plat. Phaedr., 254b : ἔδεισέ τε καὶ σεφθεῖσα ἀνέπεσεν ὑπτία, Plat. Leg.,

2. σέβομαι in Classical and Hellenistic Usage.

σέβομαι still means "to shrink from" an offensive action in Plat. Tim., 69d : σεβόμενοι μιαίνειν τὸ θεῖον, cf. Leg., VII, 798d. "Reverent awe" at seeing something
majestic (the face of the dead king) is the sense in Aesch. Pers., 694 f. But then σέβομαι and the rarer act. are used to denote an attitude. Apoll. will be called a σέβων
because of his intercession for Admet., Aesch. Eum., 725; cf. Soph. Ant., 745. In the
Phaedr. Plato describes how the uninitiated on the sight of beauty οὐ σέβεται προσορῶν, "does not behold it with admiring respect"; [4] in contrast is the one who when
he sees a θεοειδὲς πρόσωπον first falls into trembling but then προσορῶν (sc. τὸ
πρόσωπον or its bearer) ὡς θεὸν σέβεται and would even sacrifice to it if he did
not fear to seem mad, Phaedr., 250e-251a. In the main it is not something visible, as
here, which by reason of its greatness, beauty and majesty awakens awe ; σέβεσθαι is
evoked by an inner loftiness represented in things or men. Bagaios saw that they had
"great respect" for the letters and their contents, Hdt., III, 128. The religious element
does not have to be present here, [5] but it is seldom absent. Thus objects of σέβεσθαι
are one's country, Plat. Crito, 51b, a district which is regarded as sacred, Eur. Ba., 566;
Hdt., VII, 197; Plut. Quaest. Nat., 23 (II, 917 f.), the orgies, Aristoph. Thes., 949; Archiloch. Fr., 119 (Diehl³, III, 47), dreams, Aesch. Ag., 274, the good deeds of parents, Plut.
De C. Marcio, 36 (I, 231c), δίκη Plat. Leg., VI, 777d, the τύχη and δαίμων of a man,
Plat. Leg., IX, 877a, his thoughts, Plat. Ep., 7, 344d, or his virtue, Plat. Leg., VIII, 837c,
parents, [6] the dead, and heroes, Plut. Amat., 17 (II, 761d); De Romulo, 27 (I, 35a), also
benefactors, Plut. De Timoleone, 16 (I, 244). The religious element is still there in NT
days : διὸ καὶ τριῶν ὄντων ἃ πεπόνθασιν οἱ πολλοὶ πρὸς τὸ θεῖον, ζήλου καὶ
φόβου καὶ τιμῆς, ζηλοῦν μὲν αὐτοὺς καὶ μακαρίζειν ἐοίκασι κατὰ τὸ ἄφθαρτον
καὶ ἀΐδιον, ἐκπλήσσεσθαι δὲ καὶ δεδιέναι κατὰ τὸ κύριον καὶ δυνατόν, ἀγαπᾶν
δὲ καὶ τιμᾶν καὶ σέβεσθαι κατὰ τὴν δικαιοσύνην, Plut. De Aristide, 6 (I, 322b).
But now there is a much weaker use by which the rich are extolled and highly valued
by most parents. [7]

As regards the content of σέβεσθαι Plut. De Aristide, 6 (I, 322b → lines 22 ff.) is
important with its distinction of σέβεσθαι and δεδιέναι and its relating of ἀγαπᾶν
= "to value highly" and τιμᾶν. [8] In another place (Suav. Viv. Epic., 21 [II, 1101d])
Plut. says that in the untutored masses σέβεσθαι καὶ τιμᾶν in their attitude to God is
mixed up with throbbing of the heart (σφυγμός) and fear (φόβος) which is also
called δεισιδαιμονία; δεδιέναι is quite near in the context. [9]

798b : σέβεται καὶ φοβεῖται πᾶσα ψυχὴ τό τι κινεῖν τῶν τότε καθεστώτων.
 [4] Grammatically like αἰσχύνομαι ποιῶν = "I do with shame."
 [5] Aesch. Pers., 166 : For unguarded treasures one has no respect ἐν τιμῇ σέβειν. Parthe-
nopaios values (σέβειν) his lance more than a god, more than his eye, Aesch. Sept. c. Theb.,
529 f.
 [6] Soph. Oed. Col., 1377: τοὺς φυτεύσαντας σέβειν, Soph. Ai., 666 f.: εἰσόμεσθα μὲν
θεοῖς εἴκειν, μαθησόμεσθα δ᾽ Ἀτρείδας σέβειν.
 [7] τοὺς πλουσίους εὐδαιμονιζόντων καὶ σεβομένων, Plut. Aud. Poet., 14 (II, 36d/e).
 [8] Cf. also Ditt. Syll.³, II, 611, 24 f. (189 B.C.): The Romans will τοὺς θεοὺς σέβεσθαι
καὶ τιμᾶν, Plut. Quaest. Conv., VII, 4, 3 (II, 703a): ἐνίους τὸ κυνῶν γένος ἅπαν σέβεσθαι καὶ τιμᾶν, Lib. Educ., 10 (II, 7e): philosophy teaches ὅτι δεῖ θεοὺς μὲν σέβεσθαι, γονέας δὲ τιμᾶν, where the sense is clearly that philosophy gives no rules for
the way of worshipping the gods but tells us how to honour or esteem them ; this ref. is
also important because it shows that σέβεσθαι is increasingly, though not exclusively,
limited to the attitude to the gods, other words being used for the right attitude and right
conduct to parents. The meaning is again esteem in Dio Chrys. Or., 12, 60 : ταῦτα (τὰ
ἐπουράνια) ... ξύμπαντα ὅ γε νοῦν ἔχων σέβει, θεοὺς ἡγούμενος μακαρίους
μακρόθεν ὁρῶν, since this saying is used as an argument for making statues of the gods.
 [9] Plut. Is. et Os., 18 (II, 358a): crocodiles do not attack those who travel in papyrus
skiffs, they fear (φοβεῖσθαι) or reverence (σέβεσθαι) the goddess ; they fear her power
and punishment and reverence her majesty.

But long ago there had already taken place a shift in usage and σέβεσθαι now denoted an act rather than an attitude, the worship of the gods rather than reverence. One of the oldest assured instances of the sense "to worship" is Xenoph. Hist. Graec., III, 4, 18, where it is reported that Agesilaos and his soldiers dedicated the wreaths won in the gymnasium to Artemis, and it is then said : ὅπου γὰρ ἄνδρες θεοὺς μὲν σέβοιντο, τὰ δὲ πολεμικὰ ἀσκοῖεν ..., πῶς οὐκ εἰκὸς ἐνταῦθα πάντα μεστὰ ἐλπίδων ἀγαθῶν εἶναι. The final expression shows clearly that a visible worship of the gods is in view here. [10] The sense "to worship" is also present in Cornut. Theol. Graec., 16 (p. 25, 22 f.): σέβονται δ' αὐτὸν (Hermes) καὶ ἐν ταῖς παλαίστραις μετὰ τοῦ Ἡρακλέους, where the ref. is obviously to a cultic act in the palaestra. Hence σέβεσθαι with the acc. of a god can then be used for his worshippers : οἱ σεβό-μενοι τὸν Ἄνουβιν, the worshippers of Anubis. [11]

B. σέβομαι in the LXX, Pseudepigrapha, Josephus and Philo.

1. In the LXX σέβομαι is used only once for עֲבֻד, at Is. 66:14, and even there not in all MSS. Elsewhere it is always used for ירא. In comparison with the common rendering of this Heb. stem by φοβεῖσθαι the no. of instances of σέβεσθαι is small (5 : Jos. 4:24; 22:25; Job 1:9; Jon. 1:9; Is. 29:13). σέβεσθαι occurs 13 times with no original, in 7 cases for the worship of pagan gods (including Jos. 24:33b). The best transl. is "to serve" : the god is honoured and worshipped by the doing of his will and command. In Job 1:9 Satan asks : μὴ δωρεὰν σέβεται Ἰὼβ τὸν θεόν; In Is. 66:14 "to serve" God is contrasted with ἀπειθεῖν, and in 2 Macc. 1:3 there is written to the Jews in Egypt : (God) δῴη ὑμῖν καρδίαν πᾶσιν εἰς τὸ σέβεσθαι αὐτὸν καὶ ποιεῖν αὐτοῦ τὰ θελήματα. 3 Macc. 3:4 says of the Jews : σεβόμενοι δὲ τὸν θεὸν ... χωρισμὸν ἐποίουν. To serve the one God is a mark of pious Jews as compared with the Gentiles. In Jon. 1:9 Jonah says of himself : δοῦλος κυρίου ἐγώ εἰμι καὶ τὸν κύριον θεὸν τοῦ οὐρανοῦ ἐγὼ σέβομαι, cf. 4 Macc. 5:24; 8:14.

2. In the pseudepigr. σέβομαι is rare. In Test. XII it occurs only in Jos. 4:6, where Joseph says to Potiphar's wife : οὐχὶ ἐν ἀκαθαρσίᾳ θέλει κύριος τοὺς σεβομένους αὐτόν. On the other hand φοβεῖσθαι is common here with ref. to the relation to God. In Ep. Ar., however, φοβεῖσθαι does not occur at all, though we find φόβος in relation to God in 95, 189, 159. In contrast, σέβεσθαι is used of the right relation to the one God of the Jews in 16, 139, 140. The last ref. is important : Αἰγυπτίων ... ἱερεῖς ... ἀνθρώπους θεοῦ προσονομάζουσιν ἡμᾶς· ὃ τοῖς λοιποῖς οὐ πρόσεστιν, εἰ μή τις σέβεται τὸν κατ' ἀλήθειαν θεόν : The Jews feel they are the only true worshippers of God in the world of their day ; other men worship what is not God, 134. Elsewhere σέβεσθαι is found neither in Ps. Sol. nor the parts of Eth. En. preserved in Gk.; in these φοβεῖσθαι occurs 5 times and εὐλαβεῖσθαι once. In Sib., 3-5 σέβειν occurs with φοβεῖσθαι (θεόν) in 3, 29 and τιμᾶν (εἴδωλα) in 3, 606. This means that in works not composed in Gk. σέβεσθαι is much less prominent than φοβεῖσθαι for the worship of the God of the OT.

---

[10] Cf. Xenoph. Mem., IV, 4, 19, but it is wrong that σέβω or σέβομαι may be found in this sense "to worship" from Pindar, cf. Pr.-Bauer⁵, s.v.; the examples given from Plat. Phaedr., 251a → 170, 6 ff.; Leg., XI, 917b (a forger οὔτε ἀνθρώπους αἰδούμενος οὔτε θεοὺς σεβόμενος) attest only to the sense "to reverence." The Pind. ref. is perhaps Pyth., 6, 23-25, where it is said of Chiron, the teacher of Achilles, that he taught μάλιστα μὲν Κρονίδαν ... θεῶν σέβεσθαι. But since respect for parents follows, it would seem that here σέβεσθαι towards Zeus denotes reverence rather than a particular form of worship.

[11] Plut. Is. et Os., 44 (II, 368 f.); Def. Orac., 45 (II, 434 f.); Ditt. Syll.³, II, 558, 12 (207/6 B.C.), further examples in Pr.-Bauer⁵, s.v. On the other hand, acc. to E. Fraenkel, Aeschylus Agamemnon, III (1950), 761 f. the oldest instance of the sense "to worship" is Archiloch. Fr., 119 : Δήμητρος ἁγνῆς καὶ Κόρης τὴν πανήγυριν σέβων (celebrate); for other examples from tragedy, loc. cit. [H. Kraemer].

3. Apart from the use for "God-fearer" in, e.g., Ant., 14, 110 Joseph. has σέβεσθαι (mostly mid.) for the worship of the God of Israel (Ant., 3, 91; 4, 318; 8, 280; 9, 87) and also of idols. [12] The Gk. nuance "to be reverent" (→ n. 2) is echoed at most in Ant., 4, 318 : τὸ σέβειν τε καὶ τιμᾶν προσήκειν τοῦτον (God) ὑμῖν καὶ τοὺς νόμους. Philo uses σέβειν (mid. only Som., I, 204, elsewhere act.) 8 times both for pagan worship (Spec. Leg., II, 255; Decal., 78) and also for that of the one God the Creator (Virt., 179. 34), with an echo of reverence in Virt., 179 (with ἀσπάζεσθαι) and 34 (with τιμᾶν). This is undoubtedly the meaning in Vit. Mos., II, 198 : τῷ μὴ σέβειν θεὸν ἕπεται τὸ μήτε γονεῖς μήτε πατρίδα μήτ' εὐεργέτας τιμᾶν, ὁ δὲ δὴ πρὸς τῷ μὴ σέβειν καὶ κατηγορεῖν τολμῶν τίνα μοχθηρίας ὑπερβολὴν ἀπολέλοιπε, and Spec. Leg., IV, 33, where ἀλήθεια and πίστις are the objects of σέβειν. The influence of Gk. language and thought is apparent in Philo.

C. σέβομαι in the New Testament.

In the NT σέβομαι (only mid.) is not used of Christians in relation to Christians. Mk. 7:7 and par. quote Is. 29:13. In Ac. 18:13 the Jews accuse Paul before Gallio : παρὰ τὸν νόμον ἀναπείθει οὗτος τοὺς ἀνθρώπους σέβεσθαι τὸν θεόν, and in Ac. 19:27 Demetrius uses the word for the worship of Artemis of Ephesus. In Ac. the word is also used 6 times for the so-called God-fearers, i.e., σεβόμενοι with or without θεόν, → VI, 743, 13 ff. Our present concern is only with the linguistic sense of this. It is used alongside the materially equivalent φοβούμενοι τὸν θεόν, which corresponds to the Heb. ירא יהוה.[13] The change to σέβεσθαι shows how unsuitable the phrase with φοβεῖσθαι sounded to a Greek. σεβόμενοι τὸν θεόν is based on the parallel term for worshippers of pagan deities, → 171, 9 ff. Two things are implicit in it. The first is the claim to worship the only true God, cf. Ep. Ar., 140 → 171, 32 ff. Secondly, σεβόμενος with the accusative of the god denotes worship and not just reverence → 171, 1 ff. If, then, this formula is used for the God-fearers it means that they were not just impressed by, nor did they merely honour, the God of the OT. They also worshipped Him, and they did so in specific acts.

† σεβάζομαι.

1. This word, apparently derived from σέβας, is used esp. as a substitute for the little used tenses of σέβομαι other than the present. Hence it underwent a similar development. It occurs twice in Hom. in the phrase σεβάσσατο γὰρ τό γε θυμῷ (→ 169, 18) and also in the same sense in Anth. Graec., 7, 122 with pass. aor.: Πυθαγόρης τί τόσον κυάμους ἐσεβάσθη, and in Orph. Argonautica, 522 :[1] ἀλλ' ὁπότ' ἂν θεσμοῖς ξεῖνον σεβάσησθε θανόντα.

---

[12] Acc. to Horst, op. cit., 113 Jos. avoids using the same term for the worship of the God of Israel and that of idols. But this is not true of σέβειν, for apart from the ref. in Horst (Ant., 9, 99; 4, 130. 137) this is also used in Ant., 9, 205 in relation to idols : Jeroboam εἴδωλα ... σεβόμενος.

[13] ירא את אל also in Damasc. 10:2 (9:15); 20:19 f. (20:43), though not in the special sense of "god-fearers."

σ ε β ά ζ ο μ α ι. [1] Orph. (Abel), 22.

2. The term does not occur in the LXX but is found in ʼA Hos. 10:5. In Sib. it means "to worship," 5, 405 : οὐ χρυσὸν ... ἐσεβάσθη, with ref. to the gods of Rome in 8, 46 : πάντων ὧν ἐσεβάσθης (subj. Rome). Eus. Praep. Ev., IX, 10, 4 quotes an oracle of Apollo that only the Chaldeans and the Hebrews are αὐτογένεθλον ἄνακτα σεβαζόμενοι θεὸν ἁγνῶς. Aristid. says in Apol., 12, 7 that pagans worshipped (ἐσεβάσθησαν) animals.

3. In the NT it is found only in R. 1:25 : ἐσεβάσθησαν καὶ ἐλάτρευσαν τῇ κτίσει παρὰ τὸν κτίσαντα, where the more general σεβάζεσθαι is given precision by the more specific λατρεύειν (→ IV, 62, 38 ff.), "to worship cultically." From what has been said one may see that σεβάζεσθαι denotes not merely the act of pious reverence [2] but the act or acts of worship : "they worshipped and served the creature instead of the creator," → V, 735, 5 ff.

† σέβασμα.

1. σέβασμα, found from the 1st cent. B.C., means an object of worship or veneration, esp. an idol, e.g., Wis. 14:20; 15:17 and Bel et Draco 27 Θ; in Jos. Ant., 18, 344 : ἐπὶ τῆς οἰκίας ἔχειν σεβάσματα, "to have cultic objects in the house"; Sib., 8, 57 of Hadrian ἅπαντα σεβάσματα λύσει; Dion. Hal., I, 30, 3 : ἐμπειρία τῶν περὶ τὰ θεῖα σεβάσματα λειτουργιῶν, Ps.-Clem. Hom., 10, 21 for idols which the Gentiles say are in themselves only silver and gold but the divine πνεῦμα dwells in them. The term is used very gen. for the obj. of worship in Sib., 3, 550 : οὔνομα παγγενέταο σέβασμ' ἔχε, [1] "regard him as something holy."

2. In the NT the word occurs twice. Ac. 17:23 : ἀναθεωρῶν τὰ σεβάσματα ὑμῶν εὗρον καὶ βωμόν. Here σεβάσματα are not just idols but all objects connected with the cultus, including altars. The altar is not an object of worship but one towards which σέβεσθαι, reverence, is made. Paul is describing it thus, though the continuation shows what he thinks about this "holy place." In 2 Th. 2:4 the ἄνθρωπος τῆς ἀνομίας is characterised as ὁ ἀντικείμενος καὶ ὑπεραιρόμενος ἐπὶ πάντα λεγόμενον θεὸν ἢ σέβασμα. Here, too, σέβασμα cannot be just the idol but it must denote an object of σέβεσθαι. Paul builds on Da. 11:36, but goes beyond the OT with the remarkable λεγόμενον and the adding of σέβασμα. The ἢ is surprising. If Paul has already made his statement very general with the πάντα λεγόμενον θεόν, what can he be mentioning alongside this with an ἢ ? One has only to translate : "above every God or temple," or : "above every God or idol," to see how strange the expression is. If, however, one translates : "above all that is called God or holy" (cf. Sib., 8, 57 → line 20 f.), the meaning is clear : the adversary exalts himself above everything that can be an object of reverent awe. Paul makes his statement as general and comprehensive as possible. We do justice to this if we take the σέβασμα to refer to everything to which

[2] Mi. R., ad loc.

σ έ β α σ μ α. [1] σέβασμ' with A. Kurfess, *Sibyllinische Weissagungen* (1951) as against J. Geffcken, GCS, 8 (1902), who reads σέβας δ'.

σέβεσθαι might be paid, including the orders of family, state and law which for antiquity stood under the protection of the gods and were the object of σέβεσθαι or εὐσεβεῖν. [2]

† Σεβαστός.

1. σεβαστός is the transl. of the Lat. *augustus*, which as an adj. is used of gods and temples, "holy," "sacred." [1] In 27 B.C. the Senate conferred it on the emperor as a title. [2] The meaning of the Lat. title is debated. In an act. sense it calls Augustus the "augmenter" of the kingdom, [3] but it is more probably used in the pass.: "the one who is augmented," "the exalted." [4] At any rate the Lat. terms lifts the emperor above other mortals. The title was conferred by the Senate and in the first cent. A.D. was restricted to the reigning emperor (and in many instances his wife). [5]

2. The rare Gk. σεβαστός denotes something to which religious respect is paid. Thus Numa established a sanctuary of πίστις: οὕτω γοῦν σεβαστόν τι πρᾶγμα καὶ ἀμίαντον ἐνομίσθη τὸ πιστόν, Dion. Hal. Ant. Rom., 2, 75, 3. As a title Σεβαστός is a transl. of Augustus and like it is part of the official style of the emperor. What it meant for Gk. ears is stated by Dio. C., 53, 16, 8 : Αὔγουστος ὡς καὶ πλεῖόν τι ἢ κατὰ ἀνθρώπους ὢν ἐπεκλήθη· πάντα γὰρ τὰ ἐντιμότατα καὶ τὰ ἱερώτατα αὔγουστα προσαγορεύεται· ἐξ οὗπερ καὶ σεβαστὸν αὐτὸν καὶ ἑλληνίζοντές πως, ὥσπερ τινὰ σεπτόν, ἀπὸ τοῦ σεβάζεσθαι προσεῖπον. Philo speaks similarly. [6] Since officially only the dead emperor became *divus* (θεός) by resolve of the Senate,

---

[2] The ancient interpretation that the κατέχων (κατέχον) of v. 6 is for Paul the Roman Empire finds support here, for no matter what we think of individual 1st cent. emperors, Rome was for all the excesses of a Caligula a guardian of law and order ; it protected a σέβασμα.

Σ ε β α σ τ ό ς. T. Mommsen, *Röm. Staatsrecht*, II, 2² (1877), 771-774; C. Cichorius, *Röm. Studien* (1922), 380 f.; F. Muller-Izn, "Augustus," *Mededelingen d. Koninklijke Akad. van Wetenschappen, Afdeeling Letterkunde*, 63, Ser. A, No. 11 (1927), 275-347, with review by A. v. Premerstein, *Philol. Wochenschr.*, 49 (1929), 845-850; S. Reiter, "Augustus ; Σεβαστός," *ibid.*, 50 (1930), 1199 f.; M. A. Koops, "Kaiser Tiberius," *Mnemosyne*, tertia ser., 5 (1937), 34-39; A. v. Premerstein, "Vom Werden d. Prinzipats," *AA Münch.*, NF, 15 (1937), 64, 119, 169; A. Wagenvoort, *Imperium* (1941), 14-19; H. Hommel, *Horaz* (1950), 121-122; H. Erkell, *Augustus, Felicitas, Fortuna* (1952), 9-39, 183-189; M. Bucklisch, *Augustus als Titel u. Name bis zum Ende d. Mittelalters*, Diss. Münster (1957), 5-12, 91-95; F. Taeger, *Charisma*, II (1960), 117-119.
[1] Ovid Fast., I, 609 f.: *sancta vocant augusta patres, augusta vocantur templa sacerdotum rite dicata manu.*
[2] Res gestae divi Augusti (ed. H. Volkmann, Kl. T., 29-30 [1957], 56-59) § 34 : *in consulatu sexto et septimo, bella ubi civilia extinxeram per consensum universorum potitus rerum omnium, rem publicam ex mea potestate in senatus populique Romani arbitrium transtuli. Quo pro merito meo senatus consulto Augustus appellatus sum* (Gk. Σεβαστὸς προσηγορεύθην).
[3] F. Muller-Izn, "Augustus," *Mnemosyne*, NS, 56 (1928): *augusti enim adiectivum eum designat, qui ceteris maius 'augus,' id est arcanam quandam augendi, creandi, alendi vim ostendit a deis oblatam.*
[4] Cichorius ; v. Premerstein, 849; Reiter ; Koops, 39; Wagenvoort, 14; Erkell, 38; Bucklisch, 94 f.; Taeger.
[5] Cichorius.
[6] Leg. Gaj., 143 : ὁ διὰ μέγεθος ἡγεμονίας αὐτοκρατοῦς ὁμοῦ καὶ καλοκαγαθίας πρῶτος ὀνομασθεὶς Σεβαστός ... αὐτὸς γενόμενος ἀρχὴ σεβασμοῦ καὶ τοῖς ἔπειτα.

Σεβαστός has an indefinite character with a sound akin to "majesty." The title plays a part where the living emperor is the object of a cult and of worship. Thus apart from the emperor's day (σεβαστή), we hear of μύσται for the θεοὶ Σεβαστοί, [7] of ὑμνῳδοὶ θεοῦ Σεβαστοῦ, of a σεβαστολόγος or a σεβαστοφάντης. [8] So far as we know the title Σεβαστός did not figure in the trials of Christians ; what was required was to say κύριε Καῖσαρ and to sacrifice or to swear by the genius of Caesar, Mart. Pol., 8, 2; Pass. Sct. Scilit., 2, 5.

3. In the NT the word occurs only in Ac. 25:21, 25 on the lips of Festus. In distinction from the customary Καῖσαρ of the NT, which Festus too uses in v. 12, 21, Σεβαστός has an official ring to it and is very appropriate in the discussion between the Roman procurator and Agrippa II.

In Ac. 27:1 the σπεῖρα Σεβαστή is an expression also found elsewhere for "auxiliary troops." [9]

† εὐσεβής, † εὐσέβεια, † εὐσεβέω.

A. In the Greek World.

1. All three words (least the adj. εὐσεβής), esp. in earlier days, are often provided with more precise definitions to show to whom the εὐσεβεῖν is directed. In this connection the prep. εἰς, περί, πρός or the acc. are used. [1] Even later the habit of giving the obj. of εὐσεβεῖν did not die out. [2] It shows that without further definition εὐσεβής and εὐσέβεια have a broad sense. [3] But even without addition εὐσεβεῖν etc. refer esp. to the relation to the gods, cf. Aesch. Sept. c. Theb., 344, where the destruction of the

---

[7] Ditt. Syll.[3], II, 820, 3-7: μυστήρια καὶ θυσίαι, κύριε, καθ' ἔκαστον ἐνιαυτὸν ἐπιτελοῦνται ἐν Ἐφέσῳ Δήμητρι Καρποφόρῳ καὶ Θεσμοφόρῳ καὶ θεοῖς Σεβαστοῖς ὑπὸ μυστῶν μετὰ πολλῆς ἁγνείας καὶ νομίμων ἐθῶν (83-84 A.D. Ephesus).

[8] Inscr. Perg., II, 374 A, line 4 f.; Deissmann LO, 297, 3. 306-309; Nilsson, II, 353; cf. also W. Foerster, Herr ist Jesus (1924), 102 f.

[9] Haench. Ag., ad loc. with bibl.

ε ὐ σ ε β ή ς, ε ὐ σ έ β ε ι α, ε ὐ σ ε β έ ω. On A.: K. F. Nägelsbach, Die nachhomer. Theol. d. griech. Volksglaubens (1857), 191-227; O. Kern, Die Religion d. Griechen, I (1926), 272-290; U. v. Wilamowitz-Moellendorff, Der Glaube d. Hellenen, I[2] (1955), 15 f., 35 f.; J. C. Bolkestein, ὅσιος en εὐσεβής, Diss. Utrecht (1936); W. J. Terstegen, εὐσεβής en ὅσιος in het grieksch taalgebruik na de vierde eeuw, Diss. Utrecht (1941). On B.: G. Bertram, "Der Begriff 'Religion' in d. LXX," ZDMG, 87 (1934), 1-5; C. H. Dodd, The Bible and the Greeks (1935), 77, 173-175. On C.: H. J. Holtzmann, Lehrbuch d. nt.lichen Theol., II[2] (1911), 306-312; Cr.-Kö., s.v.; F. Tillmann, "Über 'Frömmigkeit' in d. Pastoralbriefen d. Ap. Pls.," Pastor Bonus, 53 (1942), 129-136, 161-165; C. Spicq, St. Paul, Les épîtres pastorales (1947), 125-134; Dib. Past.[3] (1955), Exc. on 1 Tm. 2:2; W. Foerster, "Εὐσέβεια in d. Past.," NTSt, 5 (1959), 213-218; D. Loenen, "Eusebeia en de cardinale deugden," Mededelingen der Koninklijke Akad. van Wetenschappen, Afdeeling Letterkunde, NR, 23, 4 (1960).

[1] Soph. Phil., 1441: εὐσεβεῖν τὰ πρὸς θεούς; Isoc., 1, 13 : εὐσέβει τὰ πρὸς τοὺς θεούς, cf. 3, 2.

[2] Epict. Ench., 31, 1; Diod. S., 19, 7, 3; Dio Chrys. Or., 31, 146; CIG, I, 1446, line 13: Ditt. Syll.[3], Index, s.v. εὐσέβεια.

[3] Antiphon. Or., V, 96 : οὔτε τὸ ὑμέτερον εὐσεβὲς παριείς, said to the judges : "I do not omit εὐσεβές towards you" ; Isoc., 4, 33 : πρὸς τὰ τῶν θεῶν εὐσεβέστατα διακειμένους.

temple in war is called a μιαίνειν εὐσέβειαν. [4] It is plain that in the Hell. and NT period εὐσέβεια without addition expresses in a gen. sense a proper attitude to the gods, "piety." The popular elimination of closer definition is thus the sign of a narrowing of the concept εὐσέβεια, par. to that of σέβομαι, → 171, 1 ff. How this happens is clear when one considers the various obj. of εὐσεβεῖν and εὐσέβεια in older writings. Theogn., 1, 145 f. reads : βούλεο δ' εὐσεβέων ὀλίγοις σὺν χρήμασιν οἰκεῖν ἢ πλουτεῖν ἀδίκως; εὐσεβεῖν here is the opp. of ἀδίκως πλουτεῖν and hence a very gen. concept. To commit perjury is οὐκ εὐσεβεῖν in Plat. Ap., 35c; to assist a dying father is εὐσεβεῖν in Ps.-Plat. Ax., 364c. As children of Agamemnon and Clytaemnestra rather than children of Clytaemnestra and Aegisthus. Electra and Orestes are for Electra εὐσεβεῖς κἀξ εὐσεβῶν βλαστόντες, Soph. El., 589 f.; those whose descent and those whose marriage are not laden with guilt are here called εὐσεβεῖς. When Achilles says of himself in Eur. Iph. Aul., 926 f.: ἐγὼ δ' ἐν ἀνδρὸς εὐσεβεστάτου τραφείς ... ἔμαθον τοὺς τρόπους ἁπλοῦς ἔχειν, the continuation shows that the ref. is to the general conduct of Chiron, not his piety. In all these instances εὐσεβεῖν is directed to a wider sphere than to that of the gods alone.

2. In the light of which usage are we to understand the restricting of εὐσεβεῖν to the religious world ? Apart from the gods and their temples the obj. of εὐσεβεῖν and εὐσέβεια are the dead and their νόμιμα (Eur. Hel., 1277), esp. deceased relatives (Soph. El., 464; Ant., 943), then relatives gen., father, brothers, parents, [5] also the ruler (Soph. Ai., 1350), in NT times the emperor, [6] judges (Antiphon. Or., V, 96), aliens and refugees, [7] the good (Soph. Ant., 731), oaths [8] and law [9] gen. One also finds sympathy with the age of an accused person [10] or a way of life in accordance with philosophy, Plat. Ep., 311d e. Rarer constructions may be left out of account. [11]

This review shows clearly that εὐσεβ- expresses "respect" for the orders of domestic, national and also international life. Proper conduct (εὖ) towards them is σέβεσθαι. This holds them in high esteem and avoids transgressing them. Since all these orders are under the protection of the gods it is understandable that the terms εὐσεβέω, εὐσεβής, εὐσέβεια come to refer increasingly to the gods. The transition may be seen in Isoc., 1, 13 : πρῶτον ... εὐσέβει τὰ πρὸς τοὺς θεοὺς μὴ μόνον θύων, ἀλλὰ καὶ τοῖς ὅρκοις ἐμμένων. The development goes to the pt. where εὐσέβεια as right conduct towards the gods is distinguished from δικαιοσύνη as right conduct towards one's neighbour and σωφροσύνη or ἐγκράτεια as right conduct towards oneself. Thus it is said of Socrates : εὐσεβὴς μὲν οὕτως ὥστε μηδὲν ἄνευ τῆς τῶν θεῶν γνώμης ποιεῖν, δίκαιος δὲ ὥστε βλάπτειν μὲν μηδὲ μικρὸν μηδένα, ὠφελεῖν δὲ τὰ μέγιστα τοὺς χρωμένους αὐτῷ, ἐγκρατὴς δὲ ὥστε μηδέποτε προαιρεῖσθαι τὸ ἥδιον ἀντὶ τοῦ βελτίονος, Xenoph. Mem., IV, 8, 11. [12]

---

[4] Mockingly Menand. Georg., 35, where a field in which plants sacred to Dionysus do esp. well, but others only normally, is called ἀγρὸς εὐσε[βέστερος].

[5] Plat. Resp., X, 615c; Soph. Oed. Tyr., 1431; Ps.-Plat. Ax., 364c; Dio C., 48, 5, 4.

[6] P. Lond., III, 1178, 14 (Claudius); Ditt. Syll.³, II, 814, 2 (Nero); cf. A. Strobel, "Zum Verständnis v. R. 13," ZNW, 47 (1956), 81 (Tiberius); in this case εὐσέβεια consists in sacrifices for the σωτηρία of the emperor, in festivals and in appointed honours.

[7] Eur. Alc., 1148; Aristoph. Ra., 456 ff.; Aesch. Suppl., 336.

[8] Eur. Hipp., 656; Plat. Ap., 35c; Demosth. Or., 9, 16.

[9] Demosth. Or., 19, 22 : εὐσεβῶς ἔχειν, to pardon someone.

[10] Antiphon. Or., III, 2, 11: ἐλεοῦντες ... ἐμοῦ δὲ γεραιοῦ καὶ ἀθλίου τὴν ... κακοπάθειαν ... ἀπολύοντες εὐσεβεῖτε.

[11] Of interest are two expressions in Soph. El., 968, where there is ref. to the εὐσέβεια of the dead father towards his suppliant children, and Antiphon. Or., III, 2, 12 : τὴν ... εὐσέβειαν τούτων τῶν πραχθέντων ... αἰδούμενοι ὁσίως καὶ δικαίως ἀπολύετε ἡμᾶς : the occasion was unusual, a mishap for which the author bore no guilt. εὐσεβής can sometimes mean "honoured," "august," Eur. El., 1272 of an oracle ; Plut. Pomp., 80 (I, 661e): εὕρημα εὐσεβές.

[12] Cf. also Isoc., 3, 2 : τὰ περὶ τοὺς θεοὺς εὐσεβοῦμεν καὶ τὴν δικαιοσύνην ἀσκοῦμεν, Demosth. Or., 9, 16 : τὸ δ' εὐσεβὲς καὶ τὸ δίκαιον ... τίς ἂν ... παραβαίνη (an

3. Plato in his dialogue on piety makes Euthyphron the spokesman for the common view : εὐσεβές τε καὶ ὅσιον is τὸ περὶ τὴν τῶν θεῶν θεραπείαν, Euthyphr., 12e, with the more precise definition : ἐὰν μὲν κεχαρισμένα τις ἐπίστηται τοῖς θεοῖς λέγειν τε καὶ πράττειν εὐχόμενός τε καὶ θύων, ταῦτ' ἔστι τὰ ὅσια, καὶ σῴζει τὰ τοιαῦτα τούς τε ἰδίους οἴκους καὶ τὰ κοινὰ τῶν πόλεων· τὰ δὲ ἐναντία τῶν κεχαρισμένων ἀσεβῆ, ἃ δὴ καὶ ἀνατρέπει ἅπαντα καὶ ἀπόλλυσιν, 14b. Mentioned then as gifts of the gods received by men are τιμή, γέρα, χάρις, 15a. In distinction from Plato's own view that the essence of piety consists in being servants of the gods by doing good, the popular view comes out with increasing clarity in the dialogue as one in which piety is what is done directly towards the gods. Instead of being a reverent attitude towards the gods and the orders protected by them, εὐσέβεια consists in the worship paid to the gods in cultic acts. Since one has to know how the gods are served aright, an element of knowledge enters into piety : ὁ ἄρα τὰ περὶ τοὺς θεοὺς νόμιμα εἰδὼς ὀρθῶς ἂν ὑμῖν εὐσεβὴς ὡρισμένος εἴη, Xenoph. Mem., IV, 6, 4.[13] Ps.-Plat. offers a summary of the various definitions of piety : εὐσέβεια δικαιοσύνη περὶ θεούς· δύναμις θεραπευτικὴ θεῶν ἑκούσιος· περὶ θεῶν τιμῆς ὑπόληψις ὀρθή· ἐπιστήμη τῆς περὶ θεῶν τιμῆς, Def., 412e. Many Hell. inscr. mention εὐσέβεια πρὸς τοὺς θεούς as a standing reason for honouring worthy men. In so far as the context expounds this it means the conscientious and costly practice of cultic acts including expenditure on the furnishing of temples.[14] Later Ael. Aristid. has the def.: τὸ δὲ εὐσεβὲς συνίσταται ἐκ τῆς φυσικῆς παρατηρήσεως τῶς πρὸς τοὺς θεοὺς δικαίων καὶ νομίμων· τὸ δὲ ὅσιον συνίσταται ἐκ τῆς τηρήσεως τῶν δικαίων τῶν πρὸς τὴν πατρίδα ... καὶ τοὺς γονέας καὶ εὐεργέτας καὶ παιδευτάς.[15] In the case of εὐσέβεια and derivates, then, there took place a similar shift as in σέβομαι, → 171, 1 ff.: the honouring of a god became worship of a god. But it should be denoted that εὐσέβεια does not just denote worship as such, i.e., cultic observance. An inner attitude is always expressed in the outward act.[16] Hence ἑκούσιος is not left out of the def. in Ps.-Plat. → lines 15 ff.

4. In the Hell.-Rom. period εὐσέβεια mostly stands for the worship of the gods (including inner involvement), but the broader sense of respect for the orders of life still remains. Thus εὐσέβεια is used for the attitude to relatives· between men and

---

agreement is broken : divine and human law is violated); Diod. S., 1, 92, 5 of the Egyptians examining the life of a dead person : πάλιν ἀνδρὸς γεγονότος τὴν εὐσέβειαν καὶ δικαιοσύνην, ἔτι δὲ τὴν ἐγκράτειαν καὶ τὰς ἄλλας ἀρετὰς αὐτοῦ διεξέρχονται. Epict. Diss., III, 2, 4 : man must heed natural and established relations ὡς εὐσεβῆ, ὡς υἱόν, ὡς ἀδελφόν, ὡς πατέρα, ὡς πολίτην, M. Ant., 5, 33 : θεοὺς μὲν σέβειν ... ἀνθρώπους δὲ εὖ ποιεῖν. In almost all Hell. inscr. for worthy citizens πρὸς (ποτὶ) τοὺς θεούς is added to εὐσέβεια and other terms like εὔνοια are used for the usual ref. to their services to the city which honours them. Ditt. Syll.³, II, 734, 12 ff. (94 B.C.): καθῆκον ... ἐστὶ Δελφοῖς ἀποδέχεσθαί τε καὶ τιμᾶν τοὺς εὐσεβείᾳ καὶ δικαιοσύνᾳ διαφέροντας τῶν ἀνδρῶν.

[13] Cf. Xenoph. Mem., IV, 3, 16 and Plat. Leg., IV, 717a; cf. Diog. L., VII, 119 : εἶναι ... τὴν εὐσέβειαν ἐπιστήμην θεῶν θεραπείας (Zeno); Plut. Aem., 3 (I, 256d): Aemilius Paulus was very conscientious as an augur and κατενόησε τὴν τῶν παλαιῶν περὶ τὸ θεῖον εὐλάβειαν ὥστε ... μαρτυρῆσαι τοῖς φιλοσόφοις, ὅσοι τὴν εὐσέβειαν ὡρίσαντο θεραπείας θεῶν ἐπιστήμην εἶναι.

[14] Cf. Ditt. Syll.³, Index s.v. εὐσέβεια and εὐσεβῶς.

[15] Ael. Arist. De Arte Rhetorica, I, 12, 5, 8 (ed. W. Dindorf [1829], II, 761, lines 2-6).

[16] In Hell. inscr. it is thus customary to add a καλῶς καὶ φιλοτίμως, Ditt. Syll.³, II, 539, n. 14 (216/215 B.C., Delphi): τὰς ... θυσίας ἔθυσε τὰς πατρίους καλῶς καὶ φιλοτίμως; the mere observance of traditional sacrifices is not an adequate sign of εὐσέβεια. Worth noting is the beginning of the burial inscr. of Antiochus of Commagene : ἐγὼ πάντων ἀγαθῶν οὐ μόνον κτῆσιν βεβαιοτάτην, ἀλλὰ καὶ ἀπόλαυσιν ἡδίστην ἀνθρώποις ἐνόμισα τὴν εὐσέβειαν, Ditt. Or., I, 383, 11-14. Cf. also εὐσέβεια as a transl. of dhamma (Sanscrit dharma-), "Buddhist doctrine of salvation" (strictly law) in the Gk.

wives, even for the attitude of slaves to masters and the legions to the emperor, and indeed for the administration of the emperor himself.[17] In the educated there is reserve or criticism in relation to the cultic worship of popular piety, and in connection with this we find a more inward concept of εὐσέβεια in which the element of reverence is the decisive one. Thus Epict. Ench., 31, 1 says: τῆς περὶ τοὺς θεοὺς εὐσεβείας ἴσθι ὅτι τὸ κυριώτατον ἐκεῖνό ἐστιν. ὀρθὰς ὑπολήψεις περὶ αὐτῶν ἔχειν ὡς ὄντων καὶ διοικούντων τὰ ὅλα καλῶς καὶ δικαίως καὶ σαυτὸν εἰς τοῦτο κατατεταχέναι, τὸ πείθεσθαι αὐτοῖς καὶ εἴκειν πᾶσι τοῖς γινομένοις καὶ ἀκολουθεῖν ἑκόντα ὡς ὑπὸ τῆς ἀρίστης γνώμης ἐπιτελουμένοις. If the gods thus order everything justly and well for the pious, he must accept their will in all things and not seek what they do not send; otherwise his piety cannot stand.[18] The true philosopher is the pious man: ὅστις ἐπιμελεῖται τοῦ ὀρέγεσθαι ὡς δεῖ καὶ ἐκκλίνειν (i.e., he who accepts Stoic teaching about what to seek and what not to seek), ἐν τῷ αὐτῷ καὶ εὐσεβείας ἐπιμελεῖται, Ench., 31, 4. When Epict. adds: σπένδειν δὲ καὶ θύειν καὶ ἀπάρχεσθαι κατὰ τὰ πάτρια ἑκάστοτε προσήκει καθαρῶς καὶ μὴ ἐπισεσυρμένως μηδὲ ἀμελῶς μηδέ γε γλισχρῶς μηδὲ ὑπὲρ δύναμιν (31, 5), this shows that for him taking part in the cultus is only a traditional civic duty, not the essence of piety.[19]

Plut. is concerned to differentiate εὐσέβεια from δεισιδαιμονία.[20] The δεισιδαίμων expects evil from the gods: ὁρᾷς δὲ οἷα περὶ τῶν θεῶν οἱ δεισιδαίμονες φρονοῦσιν, ἐμπλήκτους, ἀπίστους, εὐμεταβόλους, τιμωρητικούς, ὠμούς, μικρολύπους ὑπολαμβάνοντες, Superst., 11 (II, 170d/e), but the εὐσεβής knows that the gods are πατρῷοι καὶ γενέθλιοι, σωτῆρες καὶ μειλίχιοι, from whom he seeks wealth, security, harmony, peace and guidance in good words and works, 4 (II, 166d/e). Philosophers and statesmen show τὴν τοῦ θεοῦ σεμνότητα μετὰ χρηστότητος καὶ μεγαλοφροσύνης καὶ εὐμενείας καὶ κηδεμονίας, 6 (II, 167e). Here the element of reverence for what is high and great, contained from the very first in σέβομαι (→ 169, 29 ff.), is again to the fore, and so, too, is the genuinely Gk. feeling that it is in keeping with the majesty and greatness of the θεῖον to be free from human passions and to be only generous and benevolent towards men.

Thus the true content of εὐσέβεια for the educated Greek is reverent and wondering awe at the lofty and pure world of the divine, its worship in the cultus, and respect for the orders sustained by it. It is not being under the unconditional claim of a personal power. Hence εὐσέβεια can be an ἀρετή in the Greek sphere; it is one virtue among others, e.g., σωφροσύνη.[21] We once read: ὅσοι τὸ θεῖον μὴ ἐν παρέργῳ σέβουσιν, οὗτοι καὶ τὰ πρὸς ἀνθρώπους ἄριστοι ἂν εἶεν (Luc. Pro Imaginibus, 17), but this does not mean that piety is radically regarded as the source of all virtues. It belongs with all the other virtues, since the individual ἀρεταί cannot stand in unrelated and unconnected juxtaposition or even opposition to one another. εὐσέβεια can be lauded as a virtue, while its opposite, ἀσέβεια, can be morally condemned.

Asoka inscr. of Kandahar, D. Schlumberger, "Une bilingue gréco-araméenne d'Asoka," *Journal Asiatique*, 247 (1958), 2 [Risch].

[17] Terstegen, 149-151, 154-157.

[18] Diss., I, 27, 14: ἐὰν μὴ ἐν τῷ αὐτῷ ᾖ τὸ εὐσεβὲς καὶ συμφέρον, οὐ δύναται σωθῆναι τὸ εὐσεβές.

[19] Sometimes εὐσέβεια is contrasted with traditional cultic practices: ὅσῳ γὰρ ἂν εὐσεβέστεροι καὶ ὁσιώτεροι γένησθε, τοσούτῳ ἐλάττων ἔσται παρ᾽ ὑμῖν ὁ λιβανωτὸς καὶ τὰ θυμιάματα καὶ τὰ στεφανώματα, καὶ θύσετε ἐλάττους θυσίας καὶ ἀπ᾽ ἐλάττονος δαπάνης, Dio Chrys. Or., 13, 35.

[20] Numa, 22 (I, 75b); Pericl., 6 (I, 154 f.); Fab. Max., 4 (I, 176b); cf. also Adulat., 12 (II, 56e); Superst., *passim*.

[21] CIG, I, 1446: τῆς τε ἄλλης ἀρετῆς εἵνεκα καὶ τῆς εἰς τοὺς θεοὺς εὐσεβείας, cf. Diod. S., I, 92, 5 → n. 12.

B. In Judaism, the LXX, the Pseudepigrapha, Josephus and Philo.

1. In the LXX (apart from 3 and 4 Macc.) εὐσεβεῖν occurs only once in Sus. 63. We find it 4 times in 4 Macc., not at all in Test. XII, Ps. Sol. or Eth. En., once in Sib., 3-5: 4, 187. εὐσεβής is found 8 times in LXX (including Sir.) for צַדִּיק, once for נָדִיב and חָסִיד in Sir. 43:33, twice for טוֹב in Sir. 12:4; 39:27, 10 times with no Heb. original, in Test. XII and Ps. Sol. once each (also as a conjecture but not in the MSS at Ps. Sol. 13:5), and 4 times in Eth. En. at 27:3; 102:4, 6; 103:3, cf. also 3 times in Ep. Ar., 11 in 4 Macc., 10 in Sib., 3-5. εὐσέβεια is used for יִרְאַת יהוה 3 times in the LXX: Is. 11:2 without addition, Is. 33:6 and Prv. 1:7 with πρός [εἰς] τὸν κύριον [θεόν], once in Sir. 49:3 it appears for חֶסֶד and with no original it is used 3 times in 3 Macc. and 47 times in 4 Macc., also 8 times in Ep. Ar., 3 in Test. XII, and 6 in Sib., 3-5. εὐσεβεῖν with acc. 4 Macc. 11:5, εὐσέβεια mostly with no addition but with εἰς τὸν θεόν in 4 Macc. 12:14, with obj. gen. (εὐσέβεια θεοῦ) 16:14, with κατὰ πάντων and πρὸς τὸν θεόν in Ep. Ar., 24 and 42. Antonyms of εὐσεβής in the LXX are πονηροί in Is. 32:7 f., ἀθετοῦντες Is. 24:16, ἀσεβεῖς Prv. 12:12; 13:19; Qoh. 3:16, ἁμαρτωλοί Sir. 11:22; 13:17; 16:13; 33:14; 39:27; Eth. En. 102:6, ἄφρων Sir. 27:11. εὐσεβής is par. to συντηρῶν ἐντολάς in Sir. 37:12, to δίκαιος and ἀληθινός Test. L. 16:2; Eth. En. 102:4; 103:3. An antonym of εὐσέβεια is ἀνομία in Prv. 13:11; par. are σύνεσις in Test. R. 6:4, ἀλήθεια Test. Iss. 7:5, γνῶσις Is. 11:2, σοφία καὶ ἐπιστήμη Is. 33:6, μισοπονηρία 2 Macc. 3:1. But the most common antithesis in Ps. Sol. and Eth. En. is that of δίκαιος and ἁμαρτωλός. The group εὐσεβ- is comparatively rare in works close to Palestinian thought and speech. In the later OT transl. ᾿ΑΣΘ it does not occur at all, and this is no accident, but a conscious repudiation of the Hellenising usage of the LXX and of Hellenism generally.

2. Ep. Ar. is naturally the least imprecise in usage since it was supposed to be written by a Gentile for a Gentile. The question as to the nature of εὐσέβεια is put directly in 210: τί τὸ τῆς εὐσεβείας ἐστὶ κατάστημα; and the answer is: τὸ διαλαμβάνειν, ὅτι πάντα διὰ παντὸς ὁ θεὸς ἐνεργεῖ καὶ γινώσκει καὶ οὐθὲν ἂν λάθοι ἄδικον ποιήσας ἢ κακὸν ἐργασάμενος ἄνθρωπος· ὡς γὰρ θεὸς εὐεργετεῖ τὸν ὅλον κόσμον, οὕτως καὶ σὺ μιμούμενος ἀπρόσκοπος ἂν εἴης. There is no ref. here to the Law. Hence it is no surprise to find the Gk. juxtaposition of εὐσέβεια and δικαιοσύνη (→ 176, 29 ff.) in 131, nor to find εὐσέβεια for the respect and honour paid by the Gentile king to the Jewish God in 42, nor to find the king saying that he seeks in all things τὸ καλῶς ἔχον πρός τε τὸ δίκαιον καὶ τὴν κατὰ πάντων εὐσέβειαν, (24); εὐσέβεια is here the conduct towards men which honours them. Worth noting is 229: τί καλλονῆς ἄξιόν ἐστιν; ... εὐσέβεια· καὶ γὰρ αὕτη καλλονή τίς ἐστι πρωτεύουσα. τὸ δὲ δυνατὸν αὐτῆς ἐστιν ἀγάπη.

If there is no express ref. to the Law in Ep. Ar., this is predominant in 4 Macc. The theme of this work is that αὐτοδέσποτός ἐστιν τῶν παθῶν· ὁ εὐσεβὴς λογισμός (also commonly ὁ τῆς εὐσεβείας λογισμός). How reason and the Law are related is shown in 1:15 ff.: λογισμὸς ... ἐστὶν νοῦς μετὰ ὀρθοῦ λόγου προτιμῶν τὸν σοφίας βίον· σοφία δὴ τοίνυν ἐστὶν γνῶσις θείων καὶ ἀνθρωπίνων πραγμάτων ..., αὕτη δὴ τοίνυν ἐστὶν ἡ τοῦ νόμου παιδεία ... In 1, 32 ff. this is elucidated in practice by various laws: the εὐσεβὴς λογισμός follows the Law: καὶ ἔχθρας ἐπικρατεῖν ὁ λογισμὸς δύναται διὰ τὸν νόμον, 2:14. The Law teaches what εὐσέβεια is. ἡ πάτριος ἡμῶν εὐσέβεια (9:29) or ἡ εὐσέβεια ἡμῶν (9:30): "our kind of worship," almost "our religion," is under discussion in 4 Macc. in relation to the eating of swine's flesh (5:2 ff.). This is ἡ ἐπὶ τῇ εὐσεβείᾳ δόξα which must not be invalidated, 5:18. Thus to honour (σέβειν) the one God is the teaching of the Law in εὐσέβεια, 5:24 f. εὐσέβεια is, then, the totality of the Jewish religion in which gt. and small transgressions of the Law are equal, 5:20 f. εὐσέβεια is to venerate God as one and to worship Him by keeping His Law; the two are the same thing.

Little is to be gleaned from the Sibylline Oracles regarding the use and content of εὐσεβεῖν etc. In 4, 35 f. τρόπος, εὐσεβίη and ἤθεα are par. In 4, 169 f. there is ref.

to εὐσεβίην ἀσκεῖν. Elsewhere we find only gen. ref. to the righteous and the ungodly as the εὐσεβεῖς, δίκαιοι, πιστοί, σοφοί, ἅγιοι, ἄνδρες ἀγαθοί or the ἀσεβεῖς, δυσσεβεῖς, κακοί, ἄνομοι, ἄναγνοι, ἄδικοι, ἀθέμιστοι. In these writings the group εὐσεβ- is used almost always of the relation to God.

3. The situation is different in Josephus. Linguistically εὐσεβεῖν is here used with acc. (obj. God in Ant., 10, 45; Ap., 2, 125; Vit., 113) or with εἰς, Ant., 2, 152. With εὐσεβής or εὐσέβεια we often find πρός or εἰς and obj., also the acc. in Ant., 9, 236, though the simple adj. or noun is enough to denote the relation to God. [22] Mention of the obj. is connected with the fact that εὐσεβής also denotes the relation to men. Mephibosheth uses εὐσέβεια πρὸς σέ for his loyalty to David, Ant., 7, 269. Herod wants to παραδοῦναι his kingdom τῷ διαμείναντι πρὸς αὐτὸν (Herod himself) εὐσεβεστέρῳ, Ant., 16, 92. [23] Jos. is also aware of the distinction between εὐσέβεια and δικαιοσύνη, → 176, 29 ff. Jotham was εὐσεβὴς μὲν πρὸς τὸν θεόν, δίκαιος δὲ τὰ πρὸς ἀνθρώπους Ant., 9, 236. [24] Jos. also uses εὐσεβής and εὐσέβεια for the piety of the Gentiles with ref. to the Athenians, Pythagoras, Xerxes and kings like Croesus. [25] In delimitation from the Gk. world he says not unjustly that Moses οὐ μέρος ἀρετῆς ἐποίησεν τὴν εὐσέβειαν (like the Gks. → 178, 33 ff.), ἀλλὰ ταύτης μέρη τἆλλα, λέγω δὲ τὴν δικαιοσύνην τὴν σωφροσύνην τὴν καρτερίαν τὴν τῶν πολιτῶν πρὸς ἀλλήλους ἐν ἅπασι συμφωνίαν· ἅπασαι γὰρ αἱ πράξεις καὶ διατριβαὶ καὶ λόγοι πάντες ἐπὶ τὴν πρὸς θεὸν ἡμῖν εὐσέβειαν ἀναφέρουσιν, Ap. 2, 170 f.; cf. 181. But since εὐσέβεια is handed down in laws — Ap., 1, 60 : we keep τὸ φυλάττειν τοὺς νόμους καὶ τὴν κατὰ τούτους παραδεδομένην εὐσέβειαν ἔργον ἀναγκαιότατον παντὸς τοῦ βίου — the plur. εὐσέβειαι can be used [26] and piety can be broken down into a series of acts enjoined by the Law. The priests imprisoned in Rome ate only nuts and figs and thereby οὐκ ἐπελάθοντο τῆς εἰς τὸ θεῖον εὐσεβείας, Vit., 14; for the laws ἑωράθησαν δι᾽ αὐτῶν οὐκ ἀσέβειαν μέν, εὐσέβειαν δ᾽ ἀληθεστάτην διδάσκοντες ... ἀδικίας ἐχθροί, δικαιοσύνης ἐπιμελεῖς, ἀργίαν καὶ πολυτέλειαν ἐξορίζοντες, Ap., 2, 291. Naturally it is still insisted that faith in the one God and worship of God in the cultus are the chief part of the Law. The duty of piety is incumbent on the whole people, but esp. the priests, Ap., 2, 188. If Jos. also differs from the Gks. in that they make piety a part of virtue (→ 178, 33 ff.) whereas the Law makes virtue a part of piety (→ lines 16 ff.), he stills pays tribute to the Gk. world by also regarding piety as a virtue, namely, as the cardinal virtue : τὰ πρὸς εὐσέβειαν καὶ τὴν ἄλλην ἄσκησιν ἀρετῆς, Ant., 1, 6, and it is rewarded, 20, 48. Connected with the Gk. influence is the fact that he does not speak of the φόβος θεοῦ. [27]

4. In Philo the εὐσεβ- group occurs some 200 times and ἀσεβ- some 150 times. Definitions with πρός, εἰς etc. are rare, and are used only when the obj. is not God but the emperor (Leg. Gaj., 279 f., 335; Flacc., 103) or parents (Decal., 120) or when the context calls for precision. [28] This shows that the religious content of εὐσεβ- and ἀσεβ- is wholly dominant in Philo. Where the groups refer to the emperor or parents the sense is obviously "to honour," not "to worship." The predominant religious understanding of the terms is also plain in the fact that for Philo εὐσέβεια denotes the relation to God rather than self or neighbour. He associates φρόνησις, καρτερία or σωφροσύνη, δικαιοσύνη and εὐσέβεια as virtues, φρόνησις being the rational con-

---

[22] Cf. Schl. Theol. d. Judt., 96 f.
[23] Ibid., 169.
[24] Cf. also Ant., 8, 121. 280. 300; 12, 43; cf. Schl. Theol. d. Judt., 37.
[25] Ant., 11, 120; Ap., 1, 162; 2, 130 f.
[26] Ant., 18, 127: οὐδὲν ὠφελεῖ πλῆθος ... δίχα τῶν πρὸς τὸ θεῖον εὐσεβειῶν, cf. Schl. Theol. d. Judt., 96 f.
[27] Cf. Schl. Theol. d. Judt., 155.
[28] Mut. Nom., 226 : If you neglect father and mother, ἀσέβει καὶ εἰς τὸ θεῖον.

sideration on wich conduct depends. [29] εὐσέβεια is the ἡγεμονὶς τῶν ἀρετῶν [30] and ἀσέβεια is similarly τὸ μέγιστον κακόν, Congr., 160. εὐσεβ- and ἀσεβ- are a matter of thought as well as action. He who grasps the thoughts contained in the creation story, μακαρίαν καὶ εὐδαίμονα ζωὴν βιώσεται δόγμασιν εὐσεβείας καὶ ὁσιότητος χαραχθείς, Op. Mund., 172. Aristot. said μήποτ' εὐσεβῶς καὶ ὁσίως that the world is eternal and therewith introduced a δεινὴ ἀθεότης, Aet. Mund., 10. It is ἀσέβεια to think of God anthropomorphically. [31] Above all it is a δόγμα κατασκευαστικὸν εὐσεβείας that God is the beginning and end of all things, Plant., 77; cf. Jos., 246, while ὁ λέγων νοῦς, ὅτι ἐγὼ φυτεύσω (namely, the good) ἀσεβεῖ, Leg. All., I, 49. The ἀσεβής believes the νοῦς is αὐτοκράτωρ, Conf. Ling., 125; cf. Sacr. AC, 71; Poster. C., 35, 42, hence those who εἱμαρμένην τε καὶ ἀνάγκην θεοπλαστήσαντες ἀσεβείας πολλῆς κατέπλησαν τὸν ἀνθρώπινον βίον, Migr. Abr., 179. To think God covers wrong is also λέγειν καὶ ἐννοεῖσθαι ἀσεβέστατον, Spec. Leg., II, 11. Action, like thought, is either εὐσεβές or ἀσεβές. τὸ γὰρ ἕνεκα θεοῦ μόνου πάντα πράττειν εὐσεβές, Leg. All., III, 209. The commandments of the Law lead to εὐσέβεια, ἢ πρὸς τὸ ἀγαπᾶν ἢ πρὸς τὸ φοβεῖσθαι τὸν ὄντα, Deus. Imm., 69. Here εὐσέβεια is a θεοῦ θεραπεία. Thus Philo adopts a pagan definition → 177, 1 ff. But he differentiates himself from the common pagan view that sensual gifts might be offered to God; we can bring to God only φιλοδέσποτος γνώμη, Det. Pot. Ins., 56. Naturally literal observance of the Law is for Philo a matter of εὐσέβεια, Ebr., 18, indeed (pagan) ἱερουργίαι γε μὴν καὶ ἡ περὶ τὰς θυσίας ἁγιστεία βλάστημα κάλλιστον, but an evil, namely, δεισιδαιμονία, has grown up here like a shoot, this being the opinion τὸ βουθυτεῖν εὐσέβειαν εἶναι, wherewith wrong can be made good, Plant., 107.

Philo's view of εὐσέβεια lies in the Gk. sphere apart from modifications due to his allegiance to the OT and the Law. Gk. influence (→ 178, 18 ff.) may also be seen in the fact that he can view εὐσέβεια as the correct mean between δεισιδαιμονία and ἀσέβεια, Deus Imm., 163 f. If he says ἀσέβεια rather than ἀθεότης like Plut. (→ 186, 33 ff.), this is connected with the fact that for Philo a true or false view of God is closely connected with moral action. Acc. to him the man who does not turn to the world of the non-sensual, the spiritual, true being, will necessarily turn to that of sensuality and evil. ἀθεότης, ἀσέβεια and ἀδικία are very closely related for Phil. But it again has a Gk. ring (→ 186, 33 ff.) when he says γεννήσει γὰρ ἡ μὲν πρόσθεσις (sc. to piety) δεισιδαιμονίαν, ἡ δ' ἀφαίρεσις ἀσέβειαν, Spec. Leg., IV, 147. Restriction to the religious is the OT legacy in Philo.

C. In the New Testament.

εὐσεβής, always without addition, occurs in Ac. 10:2, 7; 2 Pt. 2:9; twice in the Past. as the adv. εὐσεβῶς. εὐσέβεια, with no defining obj., occurs in Ac. 3:12 and 11 times in the Past., 3 in 2 Pt., but not in the Synpt., Paul or John. εὐσεβέω with acc. is found only in Ac. 17:23; 1 Tm. 5:4.

1. Except in the Past. and 2 Pt. εὐσεβ- is never used in the NT for Christian faith and life. In Ac. 3:12 Peter expressly denies that he healed the lame man ἰδίᾳ δυνάμει ἢ εὐσεβείᾳ. In Ac. 10:2, 7 Cornelius is called εὐσεβὴς καὶ φοβούμενος τὸν θεόν (→ VI, 743, 12 ff.) and one of his soldiers εὐσεβής. In the Areopagus address Paul says to the Athenians, ὃ ... ἀγνοοῦντες εὐσεβεῖτε (Ac. 17:23), the verb fitting in well with the imprecise way in which the religion

---

[29] Cher., 96; Det. Pot. Ins., 73. In the negative Philo puts ἀσέβεια, ἀδικία and ἀκολασία at the end of a longer list of vices, Sacr. AC, 22.
[30] Spec. Leg., IV, 135; Decal., 52: ἀρχὴ ... ἀρίστη ... ἀρετῶν δ' εὐσέβεια, cf. Praem. Poen., 53; Spec. Leg., IV, 147; Abr., 60 etc.
[31] Sacr. AC, 95; Conf. Ling., 134; Leg. All., I, 43; cf. Det. Pot. Ins., 122.

of the Athenians is spoken of at the outset. [32] The reserve of the NT in respect of the group εὐσεβ- is even greater than that of the OT → 179, 2 ff. This is clearly associated with the fact that in Hebrew and in the mother tongue of most of the NT authors there was no direct linguistic equivalent for these Greek terms. This may be seen in a statement like Eph. 5:33 : ἡ δὲ γυνὴ ἵνα φοβῆται τὸν ἄνδρα, which a true Greek would never have made. But there are other reasons as well as the linguistic for the absence of εὐσεβ- from the Gospels and the (older) Pauline Epistles. There is no absolute norm in εὐσεβ-. For Socrates the voice of reason and the laws had unconditional binding force and Xenophon described his conduct as that of a εὐσεβής, → 176, 32 ff.; but the unconditional nature of the commitment does not lie in the word εὐσεβής itself. What evokes εὐσεβεῖν is not a personal entity but a vast order. It is not ὁ θεός but τὸ θεῖον. This makes the group poorly adapted for use in the OT and NT. Furthermore εὐσεβ- lays the emphasis on the conduct of man and evaluates this morally as a virtue, → 178, 33 ff. With moralism the concept of εὐσέβεια also disappears in the NT. Paul speaks, not of the εὐσεβεῖς, but of the ἅγιοι and the ἐκλεκτοί. For him εὐσέβεια is replaced by πίστις and ἀγάπη — concepts which, rightly understood, cannot be qualified morally as virtues.

2. In the Pastorals εὐσέβεια denotes a particular manner of life. εὐσεβής occurs only as the adverb εὐσεβῶς in 2 Tm. 3:12 : πάντες δὲ οἱ θέλοντες ζῆν εὐσεβῶς ἐν Χριστῷ Ἰησοῦ διωχθήσονται, Tt. 2:12 : grace disciplines us ... ἵνα ... σωφρόνως καὶ δικαίως καὶ εὐσεβῶς ζήσωμεν. Here the adverbs refer in true Greek fashion (→ 176, 29 ff.) to the relation of man to self, other men, and God. 1 Tm. 2:2 also has conduct in view : ἵνα ... βίον διάγωμεν ἐν πάσῃ εὐσεβείᾳ καὶ σεμνότητι. Related is the admonition to exercise oneself in εὐσέ- βεια (1 Tm. 4:7), which is contrasted with physical exercise, i.e., a negative asceticism. When v. 8 says that εὐσέβεια holds a promise for this life and for the life to come, the reference is to the positive effect of this mode of life. Similarly Timothy is admonished to pursue εὐσέβεια in 1 Tm. 6:11. This comes after δικαιοσύνη and before πίστις, ἀγάπη, ὑπομονή and πραϋπάθεια. In a similar list in 2 Tm. 2:22 εὐσέβεια is not mentioned. This shows that it is not a central and indispensable concept in the Pastorals. The way of life controlled by εὐσέ- βεια separates the doctrine of false teachers from "sound" doctrine, → II, 162, 9 ff. There can thus be reference to the doctrine corresponding to piety (1 Tm. 6:3) or to a knowledge of the truth in accordance with εὐσέβεια (Tt. 1:1). This manner of life can be called "sound" in contrast with the "sick" teaching of opponents (1 Tm. 6:3). These have something which looks like εὐσέβεια, a μόρφωσις εὐσεβείας, but they deny its power, i.e., its influence in shaping life (2 Tm. 3:5). They regard what they call εὐσέβεια as a source of gain (1 Tm. 6:5 f.). In this connection we find again the thought of 1 Tm. 4:8 that piety is a gain when combined with content. This manner of life described as εὐσέβεια is a mystery which the hymn in 1 Tm. 3:16 intimates : it is rooted in the Christ event. [33]

---

[32] K. Bornhäuser, Studien z. Ag. (1934), 143 thinks the altar to the unknown God was to Yahweh, since Paul would never have used the εὐσεβεῖτε of Ac. 17:23 for idolatry; but he overlooks the fact that εὐσεβεῖν is used only in the Past. and there only in special connections → lines 2 ff.

[33] This interpretation fits in better with the Pastorals as a whole than the equation εὐσέβεια = πίστις = "religion."

εὐσέβεια means "piety," i.e., conduct in relation to God. The piety of the Pastorals is different from that of Judaism and the Greek world. Jewish piety is controlled by the Law → 179, 38 ff. In the Pastorals, however, the Law plays a part only among opponents, 1 Tm. 1:7 ff.; Tt. 1:13 f. There is no trace of a legalistic bondage of εὐσέβεια in the Pastorals. Nor does it consists in cultic acts as in the Greek world (→ 177, 10 ff.), not even in acts of congregational worship. Nor is it a particular, true and worthy idea about deity, though an appeal is made to God the Creator in the repudiation of asceticism. Nor is it a virtue, though it may be pursued like an ideal and it may also be practised, → 181, 26 f. It is not an ideal but a manner of life which can supply the norm for the doctrine. Without definition it is clear what the "sound" doctrine is that corresponds to piety. In the common use of εὐσέβεια etc. in the Pastorals distinction is made from an ecstatic Gnosticising movement in the churches. This movement proclaimed asceticism and regarded creation as evil or bad. In this connection it came to despise all secular orders and standards, to reject authority, to emancipate women and to regard the family with contempt. These things were probably related to the idea that the resurrection was already past, 2 Tm. 2:18. The author of the Pastorals could not allow that this whole approach of his adversaries was εὐσέβεια, a true honouring of God, since God was for him the Creator and Redeemer of all men. But he extends the concept to cover all man's conduct (ἐν πάσῃ εὐσεβείᾳ in 1 Tm. 2:2 = in every type of reverent conduct),[34] and he uses it to denote respect for the divinely created orders which his opponents despise. In the Pastorals, then, εὐσέβεια does not occupy the place which πίστις did in the older Pauline Epistles. It denotes a manner of life. It is the honouring of God the Creator and Redeemer of all men. Born of πίστις, this takes place in everyday life. It is the divine service which remains within the orders of life. These orders, however, are not regarded as absolute in themselves. This may be seen in the statement that those who seek to live εὐσεβῶς in Christ Jesus will be persecuted, 2 Tm. 3:12.

The use of the typically Greek term εὐσέβεια under this threat of error is also connected with the fact that the author always has in view the effect of the walk of Christians on those who are without.[35] While his adversaries, or at least most of them, are not concerned about their influence on non-christians, the author believes that a way of life ἐν εὐσεβείᾳ can elicit a verdict from those who are without by confronting them with piety, with the honouring and serving of God. In the case of this "civil" expression εὐσέβεια the situation is much the same as with the notably imprecise ἀγαθοποιεῖν and ἀγαθοποιΐα of 1 Pt. (→ I, 17, 33 ff.) to which the author attributes such power to win, to repel, and hence to divide.[36] In this sense εὐσέβεια is profitable for everything and has a promise both for this life and for that which is to come (1 Tm. 4:8). In this sense it is a great πορισμός (1 Tm. 6:6), though this does not mean that it is a guarantee against persecution. It is true that in εὐσέβεια there is an echo of the older use of the word to denote reverence for the gods and for the orders protected by

---

[34] Cf. Pr.-Bauer⁵, s.v.; Dib. Past., ad loc.

[35] 1 Tm. 3:7; 6:1; Tt. 2:5, 8, 10; also the ἀνέγκλητος of 1 Tm. 3:10; Tt. 1:6 f. pts. in the same direction.

[36] Cf. W. Brandt, "Wandel als Zeugnis nach dem 1 Pt.," Verbum Dei manet in aeternum, Festg. f. O. Schmitz (1953), 10-25.

them, → 176, 24 ff. The only point is that reverence for the orders is now grounded in the will of the Creator who is also the σωτὴρ πάντων ἀνθρώπων, 1 Tm. 4:10. [37]

3. The word group εὐσεβ- also occurs four times in 2 Pt. The general situation of the false teachers is a very different one here from that in the Pastorals, since libertinism is the problem instead of asceticism. The list of virtues in 1:6 f. does not seem to follow any particular plan. [38] One might try to understand it along the lines of what has been said about the Pastorals. ἐγκράτεια is followed by ὑπομονή as waiting for the *parousia*, this by εὐσέβεια as abiding in the orders, and this by love which also plays a part in similar passages in the Pastorals. In the other references εὐσέβεια is simply the opposite of an ungodly walk. When Lot is delivered from the τῶν ἀθέσμων ἐν ἀσελγείᾳ ἀναστροφῇ (2:7) with their ἄνομα ἔργα (2:8) we go on to read: οἶδεν κύριος εὐσεβεῖς ἐκ πειρασμοῦ ῥύεσθαι (2:9). In 3:11 the plural εὐσέβειαι (alongside the plural ἅγιαι ἀναστροφαί) points to the fact that εὐσέβεια — there is a difference here from the Pastorals — may easily be presented as the sum of individual actions. Coming judgment is the reason for godly deeds. In 1:3 : τὰ πάντα ἡμῖν τῆς θείας δυνάμεως αὐτοῦ τὰ πρὸς ζωὴν καὶ εὐσέβειαν δεδωρημένης — whatever may be our interpretation in detail (→ II, 310, 5 ff.) — εὐσέβεια has the general sense of a pious life, i.e., a life which is morally good.

D. In the Post-Apostolic Fathers.

εὐσεβέω is not used at all in the post-apost. fathers ; εὐσέβεια and εὐσεβής occur only in 1 and 2 Cl.

1. εὐσέβεια occurs in 1 Cl. after πίστις and before φιλοξενία and γνῶσις in the description of the former laudable state of the Corinthian church, 1, 2. The pt. is that the whole conduct of the church was "pious" and "pleasing to God." The letter is written for those who want εὐσεβῶς καὶ δικαίως διευθύνειν par. to ἐνάρετος βίος, 62, 1. In 15, 1 μετ' εὐσεβείας εἰρηνεύειν opp. μεθ' ὑποκρίσεως is to want peace, and in 2, 3 εὐσεβὴς πεποίθησις is the direct opp. of impure confidence. Thus εὐσέβεια and εὐσεβής denote the whole life of the Christian lived with an eye on God. Hence as an act εὐσέβεια, with σύνεσις and works, does not suffice for justification, 32, 4. In 11, 1 it is said of Lot that he was saved διὰ φιλοξενίαν καὶ εὐσέβειαν. In what follows this is linked with hope in God. εὐσέβεια is thus the practice of trust in God. In the prayer for rulers we find the petition that they may exercise their power in peace and πραΰτης εὐσεβῶς, 61, 2. We are reminded of the pagan formula by the saying that those perfected in love from Adam possess the χῶρος εὐσεβῶν, 50, 3. [39]

2. In 2 Cl. ὁ εὐσεβής is a gen. term for the Christian, 19, 4. In 20, 4 τὸ εὐσεβές is the opp. of κερδαλέον. In 19, 1 there is ref. to the young who strive for εὐσέβεια and the goodness of God. Though the material is scanty one may see a developing tendency to use εὐσέβεια as a very gen. term for "piety" and almost "religion."

3. This is very plain in the case of θεοσέβεια (only 1 Tm. 2:10 in the NT) and derivates. 1 Cl. has only θεοσέβεια in a quotation, 17, 3. In 2 Cl., 20, 4 this is the opp. of "making merchandise of the faith." In Mart. Pol., 3, 2 there is ref. to the θεοφιλὲς καὶ θεοσεβὲς γένος τῶν Χριστιανῶν. For Dg., however, θεοσέβεια is simply

---

[37] Cf. Schl. Past., *ad loc.* (122).
[38] Wnd. Kath. Br., *ad loc.*
[39] Cf. Diod. S., I, 96, 5 : τοὺς τῶν εὐσεβῶν λειμῶνας (meadows); Callim. Epigr., 10 (12): ἐν εὐσεβέων (χώρῳ).

"religion": You are τὴν θεοσέβειαν τῶν Χριστιανῶν μαθεῖν, 1, 1, i.e., to get to know, not the godly conduct, but the religion of the Christians, cf. 6, 4 : ἀόρατος δὲ αὐτῶν (Christians) ἡ θεοσέβεια μένει, also 4, 6. In 3, 1 μὴ κατὰ τὰ αὐτὰ Ἰουδαίοις θεοσεβεῖν is stated of Christians, and the question to pagans and Jews is whether their works are θεοσέβεια or μωρία (or ἀφροσύνη), 3, 3; 4, 5.

† ἀσεβής, † ἀσέβεια, † ἀσεβέω.

A. In the Greek World.

1. In the main the linguistic use, range of meaning and content of this group are par. to those of εὐσεβ- etc. Linguistically the older works give the obj. with εἰς, περί, πρός or with acc. [1] As with εὐσεβ- (→ 175, 16 ff.), this shows that there may be different obj. of ἀσεβεῖν, esp. again in the earlier period. Plat. Resp., X, 615c : εἰς ... θεοὺς ἀσεβείας τε καὶ εὐσεβείας καὶ γονέας, Symp., 188c : πᾶσα γὰρ ἀσέβεια φιλεῖ γίγνεσθαι ... καὶ περὶ γονέας καὶ ζῶντας καὶ τετελευτηκότας καὶ περὶ θεούς. Again ἀσεβ- is used esp. for acts against the orders which uphold the state : ὁπόσαι δ' ἐξαπατῶσιν παραβαίνουσί τε τοὺς ὅρκους τοὺς νενομισμένους κερδῶν οὔνεκ' ἐπὶ βλάβῃ, ἢ ψηφίσματα καὶ νόμον ζητοῦσ' ἀντιμεθιστάναι, τἀπόρρητά τε τοῖσιν ἐχθροῖς τοῖς ἡμετέροις λέγουσ' ..., ἀσεβοῦσ' ἀδικοῦσί τε τὴν πόλιν, Aristoph. Thes., 356-367. To deliver up those who seek protection (Hdt., I, 159), not to obey the law (Plat. Leg., IX, 868d), to have a wrong estimation of φρόνησις, ἐπιστήμη and νοῦς (Plat. Phileb., 28a), is ἀσεβεῖν. It is said of a house laden with blood-guiltiness : ὅταν ἀσεβηθῇ, Plat. Leg., IX, 877e. When Plat. wants to prove that the myths record δεινὰ καὶ ἀσεβῆ of heroes, he refers only to violent acts, not to any special offences against the gods, Resp., III, 391c/d. When Dicaiarchus sets up altars for ἀσέβεια and παρανομία (Polyb., 18, 54, 10), he means by ἀσέβεια contempt for those gods who are the guardians of treaties. This is also a common use in Plut. The "silver shields" of Alexander the Gt. are called ἀσεβεῖς καὶ θηριώδεις, Plut. Eumenes, 19 (I, 595a), both because of their way of waging war. The act of Perseus in taking the envoys captive was an ἔργον ἀσεβὲς καὶ δεινόν, Aem., 13 (I, 261d). Agesilaus is supposed to have said that breaking treaties was ἀσεβές in relation to friends but δίκαιον and ἡδύ in relation to enemies, Apophth. Lac., Agesilaos, 11 (II, 209b).

2. With ἀσεβ-, as with εὐσεβ- (→ 176, 24 ff.), a usage may be observed which restricts the group to conduct vis-à-vis the gods and chooses another word for that vis-à-vis laws or neighbours. Xenoph. Cyrop., VIII, 8, 27: φημὶ γὰρ Πέρσας ... καὶ ἀσεβεστέρους περὶ θεοὺς καὶ ἀνοσιωτέρους περὶ συγγενεῖς καὶ ἀδικωτέρους περὶ τοὺς ἄλλους καὶ ἀνανδροτέρους τὰ εἰς τὸν πόλεμον. [2] Xenoph. Ap., 22 is also important : Σωκράτης τὸ μὲν μήτε περὶ θεοὺς ἀσεβῆσαι μήτε περὶ ἀνθρώ-

---

ἀ σ ε β ή ς, ἀ σ έ β ε ι α, ἀ σ ε β έ ω. Cr.-Kö., 989 f.; → I, 154, 18 ff., 156, 21 ff.; C. H. Dodd, The Bible and the Greeks (1937), 76-81, 174 f.

[1] ἀσεβεῖν ἐς τὸν θεόν, Eur. Ba., 490; ἀσεβεῖς περὶ θεούς, Xenoph. Cyrop., 8, 27; ἀσέβεια περὶ θεούς, VIII, 8, 7; acc. Aristoph. Thes., 367: ἀσεβοῦσ' ἀδικοῦσί τε τὴν πόλιν, Plat. Leg., XII, 941a: Ἑρμοῦ καὶ Διὸς ἀγγελίας καὶ ἐπιτάξεις παρὰ νόμον ἀσεβησάντων. Cf. in the NT age Ps.-Luc. Syr. Dea : ἐς θεὸν ἀσεβέοντα, Diod. S., I, 44, 3: ἀσέβεια εἰς τοὺς θεούς, and often in Joseph.
[2] Cf. Xenoph. Cyrop., VIII, 8, 7; Hist. Graec., II, 3, 53 : οὐ μόνον εἰσὶ περὶ ἀνθρώπους ἀδικώτατοι ἀλλὰ καὶ περὶ θεοὺς ἀσεβέστατοι.

πους ἄδικος φανῆναι περὶ παντὸς ἐποιεῖτο, and cf. Plato Prot., 323e : καὶ ἡ ἀδικία καὶ ἡ ἀσέβεια καὶ συλλήβδην πᾶν τὸ ἐναντίον τῆς πολιτικῆς ἀρετῆς, Dio Chrys. Or., 31, 13 : τὰ μὲν περὶ τοὺς θεοὺς γιγνόμενα μὴ δεόντως ἀσεβήματα καλεῖται, τὰ δὲ πρὸς ἀλλήλους τοῖς ἀνθρώποις ἀδικήματα. In Plat. Prot., 323e ἀσέβεια is, with ἀδίκια, subsumed under πᾶν τὸ ἐναντίον τῆς πολιτικῆς ἀρετῆς. Aristot. defines ἀσέβεια as a kind of ἀδικία, specifically ἡ περὶ θεοὺς πλημμέλεια, De Virtutibus et vitiis, 7, p. 1251a, 30 f. In Athenian trials for *asebia* non-belief in the gods in which the *polis* believes is called ἀδικεῖν, Plat. Ap., 24b. In Plat. Leg. all private cults are to be forbidden under the law of *asebia*, VII, 799b; X, 907d-909d, 910e. As long as the ancient *polis* endured *asebia*, the failure to worship the city gods, was a breach of its order. Taking part in the national cult was εὐσέβεια, refusal to do so ἀσέβεια. To the end of antiquity, then, an important part of εὐσέβεια or ἀσέβεια was participation in the national cult or refusal to do this. If because of other national concerns the Roman priest would not fulfil his cultic duties, then quite apart from his inner disposition this was ἀσεβεῖν τοὺς θεούς, Plut. Quaest. Rom., 113 (II, 291c). He who did not believe the myths was thought to be ἀσεβής by those who told them, Luc. Philops., 3. As εὐσέβεια developed from reverence for the gods and the orders protected by them to worship of the gods, so ἀσέβεια developed from a lack of reverence for the gods to neglect of the cultus. Nevertheless, Plat. Leg., X is not concerned only with punctilious observance of the national cultus but also with the warding off of unworthy ideas regarding the gods. Hence he has just before a long disquisition on the existence of the gods, their interest in human affairs, and the fact that they cannot be bribed. He who differs esp. on the last pt. is πάντων τῶν ἀσεβῶν κάκιστος ... καὶ ἀσεβέστατος, Plat. Leg., X, 907b. This concept of ἀσέβεια underwent further development when the Gk. city state lost its basic significance. In popular belief philosophers who denied the existence of the gods were still ἀσεβεῖς, Luc. Tim., 7. But Epic. says : ἀσεβὴς δὲ οὐχ ὁ τοὺς τῶν πολλῶν θεοὺς ἀναιρῶν, ἀλλ' ὁ τὰς τῶν πολλῶν δόξας θεοῖς προσάπτων, Diog. L., X, 123. The argument in Sext. Emp. Pyrrh. Hyp., III, 11 is along the same lines. For Epict. the idea of the ἀσεβής who quarrels with his lot is par. to his view of εὐσέβεια ⟶ 178, 9 ff. He who does not honour the gifts and powers he has received from the gods, e.g., that of speech, is also ἀσεβής, Diss., II, 23, 2.

3. An important result of the development associated with the decline of the city state is the separation of ἀθεότης and ἀσέβεια. In Plut. Superst. εὐσέβεια is the right mean between δεισιδαιμονία and ἀθεότης, but not ἀσέβεια, 14 (II, 171 f.). Plut. makes it plain that ἀθεότης is commonly held to be ἀσέβεια, 10 (II, 69e). But it is no accident that he himself does not speak of ἀσέβεια. ἀθεότης is for him a philosophical opinion which is an error, a lack of feeling for the good which comes from the gods. But this does not make man unhappy and — this may be deduced even though Plut. does not say it — it does not mean that he is without qualification an ἀσεβής. Plat. had already referred to those who do not believe in the gods but to whom there is proper by nature a righteous ἦθος and who love the righteous, and he distinguished these from those who yield to their desires, Leg., X, 908b d. Zeno spoke of two kinds of ἄθεοι : διττὸν δὲ εἶναι τὸν ἄθεον· τόν τ' ἐναντίως τῷ θείῳ λεγόμενον καὶ τὸν ἐξουθενητικὸν τοῦ θείου· ὅπερ οὐκ εἶναι περὶ πάντα φαῦλον, Diog. L., VII, 119. ἀσέβεια is not, then, a negative concept ; it is very positive. In the ancient *polis* there could be no neutrality towards the state cultus. Non-participation meant transgression of the city ordinances. But now one could disbelieve in the gods and not take part in a cultus without transgressing the ordinances. One could be ἄθεος without being ἀσεβής. This is plain in the discussion in Muson., 78, 8-13 which seeks to show that infants are to be reared : ὥσπερ γὰρ ὁ περὶ ξένους ἄδικος εἰς τὸν ξένιον ἁμαρτάνει Δία ..., οὕτως ὅστις εἰς τὸ ἑαυτοῦ γένος ἄδικος (by exposure) εἰς τοὺς πατρῴους ἁμαρτάνει θεούς ... ὁ δέ γε περὶ τοὺς θεοὺς ἁμαρτάνων ἀσεβής. Here ἀσεβής is not just a term for περὶ τοὺς θεοὺς ἁμαρτάνων but goes beyond it, denoting the transgressor in general. Not to have any reverence is not just something negative ; it is genuinely positive.

For the Christian community the difference between ἄθεος and ἀσεβής was very important once the distinction from Judaism was recognised. Christians could not alter the fact that they were regarded as ἄθεοι (→ III, 121, 20 f.), i.e., as people who did not take part in the civic and national cults. But to some degree it was up to themselves whether or not they were also regarded as ἀσεβεῖς, as evil-doers. It is a concern of the Pastorals and 1 Pt. to keep them from ἀσέβεια and to keep them to εὐσέβεια or ἀγαθοποιΐα. With what success may be seen not only from Pliny's letter to Trajan (X, 96, 8) but also from the martyrdom of Polycarp, in which Polycarp is ordered to dissociate himself from the Christians with the cry αἶρε τοὺς ἀθέους. [3] Per flagitia invisos esse (Tac. Ann., 15, 44) the early Christians could not prevent, of course, and 1 Pt. 2:12 tells the Christian churches that the pagans καταλαλοῦσιν ὑμῶν ὡς κακοποιῶν, but this should not be due to any fault of their own, → II, 607, 40 ff.

B. In Greek Judaism.

1. In the LXX ἀσεβέω is used 9 times for פֶּשַׁע, 10 for רָשַׁע, 2 for זוּר, and once each for זִמָּה, מָרָה and תֶּבֶל עָשָׂה. ἀσέβεια occurs 27 times for פֶּשַׁע, 10 for the stem רְשׁע, 11 for חָמָס, 9 for זִמָּה (only Ez.), twice each for חַטָּאת and עָוֹן, and once each for many other words. ἀσεβής is overwhelmingly (144 times) the transl. of the stem רְשׁע, but we also find it 6 times for חָנֵף, 5 for the stem חטא and for כְּסִיל, 3 for זוּר, 2 for רעע, and once each for various other stems, among them פֶּשַׁע, which is not prominent here since no adj. was formed from it. In so far as we have the HT of Sir. ἀσεβ- is there the transl. of רְשׁע 4 times, זָדוֹן 3 times, and some other stems. Only once in 2 Βασ. 22:22 = ψ 17:22 is ἀσεβέω combined with ἀπό (= מִן רָשַׁע); more commonly we find εἰς (with God, the Law only 2 Macc. 4:17), ἔναντι, κατά (τοῦ νόμου Hos. 1:8) or the acc. in Zeph. 3:4. ἀσέβεια is found only once with εἰς in Ob. 10, twice with obj. gen. (γῆς) in Hab. 2:8, 17. With ἀσεβής there is never any more precise indication of obj. This does not mean that only God is the direct object of ἀσεβ-.

A first pt. to notice is that ἀσεβ- never denotes a mere attitude but always action, conduct. Hence ἀσέβεια can often be put in the plur.; [4] at issue are specific acts. If the obj. is indicated only with the verb ἀσεβέω, this is the more surprising in that the group is not used only for cultic or particularly religious acts. A false witness speaks ἀσέβεια, Dt. 19:16; cf. 25:2. ἀσεβής means one who is guilty in the judgment, Ex. 23:7; Dt. 25:1; Is. 5:23. ἀσεβέω means the transgression of judicial directions, Dt. 17:13; cf. 25:2. David protests his loyalty to Saul by saying that he has committed no ἀσέβεια or ἀθέτησις, 1 Βασ. 24:12 (this fits in with the fact that Saul is the Lord's anointed). If notwithstanding no more precise indication is given with ἀσεβής and ἀσέβεια, this is related to the fact that in its use of the group the LXX is unfamiliar with the Gk. distinction (→ 185, 31 ff.) between irreverence towards the gods and unrighteousness towards men. If ἀσέβεια and ἀδικία are used together, they do not refer to two different spheres but are different ways of stating one and the same thing in accordance with Heb. parallelism. [5] In ἀδικία, too, the relation to God is predominant. [6]

---

[3] Mart. Pol., 9, 2; cf. 12, 2 : Polycarp : ὁ τῶν ἡμετέρων θεῶν καθαιρετής, ὁ πολλοὺς διδάσκων μὴ θύειν μηδὲ προσκυνεῖν. Other charges are empty.

[4] ψ 5:11; 64:4; Prv. 28:3; Hos. 12:1; Am. 1 and 2 (8 times); 5:12; Mi. 1:13; 3:8; 7:18; Hab. 2:8, 17; Is. 59:20; Jer. 5:6; Lam. 1:5; Ez. 14:6; 16:58; 18:28, 31; 21:29; 23:27, 48; 3 Macc. 6:10.

[5] Jer. 3:13 : γνῶθι τὴν ἀδικίαν σου, ὅτι εἰς κύριον ... ἠσέβησας, Sir. 15:20 (ἀσεβεῖν par. ἁμαρτάνειν); Job 34:8; 1 Macc. 9:23 ff.; Prv. 28:4; Mi. 6:7; 7:18; Ob. 10; Ez. 21:29; 33:14.

[6] Only in Prv. 11:5 might there be an exception : ἀσέβεια περιπίπτει ἀδικίᾳ, but in what follows ἀσέβεια is caught up in παράνομοι.

A further pt. is that for the LXX ἀσέβεια is not a subjective disposition but an objective fact. Typical is Am. 1, 2, where the crimes of the surrounding nations (mostly in war), the idolatry and despising of the Law in Judah and the social injustices of Israel are all called ἀσέβειαι (plur. = פְּשָׁעִים) in similarly constructed statements. The objective state of affairs which the group ἀσεβ- denotes in the LXX is the violation of the will of God, in whose territory it also occurs. Since the Law regulates all man's conduct, all bad deeds are ἀσέβειαι. Many other expressions can describe the same thing. Da. 9:5 : ἡμάρτομεν, ἠδικήσαμεν, ἠσεβήσαμεν καὶ ἀπέστημεν καὶ παρέβημεν τὰς ἐντολάς σου καὶ τὰ κρίματά σου, [7] and along with ἀσεβής we find words like ἁμαρτωλός, ἄδικος, ἄφρων, ἄνομος, παράνομος etc. Esp. in Prv. — over ¹/₃ the ἀσεβής passages are in Prv. and more than half in the Wisdom lit. — the antithesis which constantly recurs in the parallelism is that of the δίκαιος and the ἀσεβής. The reference is to the whole of life manifested in the sum of acts. This is either orientated to God and the Law or it is contrary to both. Even if one disregards the heaping up of ἀσεβής passages in the Wisdom lit., there is in the LXX a great freedom in the use of ἀσεβ- as contrasted with the reserve in the use of the εὐσεβ- group → 168, 30 ff. Since Hebrew offers no words which structurally suggest transl. by either term the difference in attitude to the two must have its roots in Gk. usage.

For the LXX translators εὐσεβ- was in comparison with φόβος θεοῦ, as may be seen by contrast from Joseph. → 180, 5 ff., 33 f., far too weak and subjective to allow of its common use for correct and obedient conduct in accordance with God's will. But when there is not even this weak and subjective conduct towards God, when one might speak of ἀ-σέβεια, then this word expresses complete contempt for God and His will. Thus to the translators of the LXX ἀσεβ- (as distinct from εὐσεβ-) seemed to be a very apt term for wicked-doers and wickedness. In keeping is the fact that in Greek usage ἀσεβ- can be used for the wicked-doer in the broadest sense → 186, 45 ff. It is also characteristic that ἀθεότης and ἄθεος do not occur in the LXX. [8]

2. In the pseudepigr. ἀσεβ- occurs relatively infrequently in 4 Macc., where it denotes violation of the Law by eating swine's flesh in 6:19 and the conduct of the Syrian king in relation to the martyrs in 9:32; 10:11; 12:11. The group is not found at all in Ps. Sol. and it appears in Eth. En. only at 1:9; 5:6, 7; 13:2; 22:13, and in Ep. Ar. only at 166 (with ref. to informers who are polluted by the stain of their ἀσέβεια). The group is more common in Test. XII, where ἀσέβεια is ar. 'adividual sin in R. 3:14, 15; 4:3; Jos. 5:2; 6:9 (ἀσέβημα in R. 6:3). Elsewhere in Test. XII it is used for the apostasy of the children of Israel in the last times, L. 10:2; 14:1, 2; N. 4:4; A. 7:5; Zeb. 10:3. In Sib., 3-5 the ungodly are sometimes set in antithesis to the righteous, 3, 568; 4, 167. 171; 5, 171, cf. δυσσεβής in 4, 43. 184.

3. Joseph. frequently uses ἀσεβ-, fairly often with πρός or εἰς Ant., 6, 88; 9, 243; 11, 91; Ap., 2, 194; Bell., 3, 369 and 379 (δυσσέβεια); 7, 260. The obj. is usually God, though we also find the people of the Jews or the Gentiles, Bell., 2, 184. 472. 483; 5, 443; the plur. ἀσέβειαι occurs on occasion, Ant., 10, 104 par. παρανομίαι. In Gk. fashion Joseph. sometimes distinguishes between ἀσέβεια and ἀδικία : the sicarii προσυπερβάλλειν ἀλλήλους ἔν τε ταῖς πρὸς θεὸν ἀσεβείαις καὶ ταῖς εἰς τοὺς πλησίον ἀδικίαις ἐφιλονείκησαν, Bell., 7, 260; the Sodomites εἴς τε ἀνθρώπους ἦσαν

---

[7] Cf. Bar. 2:12 : ἡμάρτομεν, ἠσεβήσαμεν, ἠδικήσαμεν, cf. Is. 59:13.
[8] Compared with ἀσεβέω etc. the related δυσσεβέω or δυσσεβής, δυσσέβεια is less common, twice in 1 Ἔσδρ., 7 times in 2 Macc., 2 in 3 Macc.

ὑβρισταὶ καὶ πρὸς τὸ θεῖον ἀσεβεῖς, Ant., 1, 194. This distinction also corresponds to the expression in Ap., 2, 194 to the effect that he who does not follow the decision of the high-priest ὑφέξει δίκην ὡς εἰς τὸν θεὸν αὐτὸν ἀσεβῶν. Not the wicked act but the refusal to obey is described as ἀσέβεια. But the distinction is not a radical one in Joseph., cf. Ant., 10, 104 : Jeremiah to Zedekiah κελεύων τὰς μὲν ἄλλας ἀσεβείας καὶ παρανομίας καταλιπεῖν, προνοεῖν δὲ τοῦ δικαίου. As here the δίκαιον covers all conduct, so ἀσέβειαι and παρανομίαι are par.

4. As concerns Philo three further pts. are to be noted in addition to what was said about εὐσεβ-, → 180, 37 ff.

a. In Philo ἀθεότης can sometimes mean the denial of God's existence, Op. Mund., 170 : Five doctrines result from the creation : πρῶτον μὲν ὅτι ἔστι τὸ θεῖον καὶ ὑπάρχει, διὰ τοὺς ἀθέους, ὧν οἱ μὲν ἐνεδοίασαν ἐπαμφοτερίσαντες περὶ τῆς ὑπάρξεως αὐτοῦ, οἱ δὲ τολμηρότεροι καὶ κατεθρασύναντο φάμενοι μηδ᾽ ὅλως εἶναι. Doubt whether God exists is ἀθεότης. [9] But on the other side τὸ πολύθεον is called an ἄθεον in Fig., 114, and the self-deification of a Caligula is ἀθεωτάτη in Leg. Gaj., 77. In general Philo can often use ἄθεος and ἀσεβής without discernible distinction, Conf. Ling., 114; Det. Pot. Ins., 103 etc. The idea that God repents is an ἀθεότης, worse than the ἁμαρτήματα of the generation of the flood, Deus Imm., 21. The linguistic obliteration of the borders between ἀθεότης and ἀσέβεια is connected with the fact that for Philo denial of God's existence and surrender to the world of the senses and hence to sensuality are indissolubly connected.

b. As Philo ascribes a leading role to εὐσέβεια, so he does also to ἀσέβεια or ἀθεότης : πηγὴ δὲ πάντων ἀδικημάτων ἀθεότης, Decal., 91. [10] On the other hand, however, Philo often suggests that desire is the source of all iniquity and he groups ἀσέβεια with this : ἴσθι οὖν ... ὅτι γενόμενος φιλήδονος πάντ᾽ ἔσει ταῦτα (Sacr. AC, 32), and there then follows a list of vices of over 100 members, among which ἀσεβής comes between ἄτακτος and ἀνίερος, though ἄθεος does not occur. [11] One may say that for Philo immorality leads to irreligion ; ἀδικία is sown and ἀσέβεια reaped, Conf. Ling., 152.

c. In Leg. All., III, 9 the ἀσεβής who flees from God is contrasted with the δίκαιος who stands before Him. From this one may conclude that Philo does not distinguish clearly and radically between ἀσέβεια and ἀδικία. In Conf. Ling., 117 he enumerates the various εἴδη of the one κακία. In so doing he always connects by a μετά members which belong materially together, and thus we find μετὰ παρανομιῶν ἀσέβεια. ἀσέβεια and ἀδικία are closer for Philo than εὐσέβεια and δικαιοσύνη : τὴν δὲ ἄδικον καὶ ἄθεον ψυχὴν φυγαδεύων ἀφ᾽ ἑαυτοῦ ... διέσπειρεν (sc. God) εἰς τὸν ἡδονῶν καὶ ἐπιθυμιῶν καὶ ἀδικημάτων χῶρον, Congr., 57.

C. In the New Testament.

The group ἀσεβ- does not occur at all in Synpt., Ac., the Johannine writings including Rev., Jm. or Hb. There are only 4 instances in the older Pauline Epistles, though the ref. in R. are not unimportant. Here the starting-pt. should not be the quotation in R. 11:26: ἥξει ... ὁ ῥυόμενος, ἀποστρέψει ἀσεβείας ἀπὸ Ἰακώβ (Is. 59:20), for there is no special emphasis on the plur. ἀσέβειαι (which does not fit the context too well), ἀσέβειαι being par. to the ἁμαρτίαι of the following v.

---

[9] Cf. Migr. Abr., 69, where ἡ ἄθεος and ἡ πολύθεος δόξα are opposed to one another ; cf. also Spec. Leg., I, 32, 330, 344.
[10] Cf. Leg. All., III, 13, where there is ref. to the ἄθεος καὶ ἡγεμονὶς τῶν παθῶν δόξα of Pharaoh.
[11] Cf. also Congr., 160 : too gt. licence produces τὸ μέγιστον κακόν, ἀσέβειαν, Conf. Ling., 114 : κακία leads on to ἀσέβεια and ἀθεότης.

1. More important is R. 1:18 : ἀποκαλύπτεται γὰρ ὀργὴ θεοῦ ἀπ' οὐρανοῦ ἐπὶ πᾶσαν ἀσέβειαν καὶ ἀδικίαν ἀνθρώπων (→ I, 156, 21 ff.). A common view is that the reference is to sins against the first and second tables of the Law, offences against God and neighbour. [12] If so, it is natural to conclude, though there is no exegetical support for this, that Paul has irreligion and immorality in view, and that the former is traced back to the latter. [13] Against this, however, is the πᾶσαν, which embraces both terms and binds them closely together. Another counter-argument is that the distinction between sins against God and against men is rare among the Rabbis [14] and is certainly not a Rabbinic distinction. [15] A final point is that in what follows ἀδικία covers both words. The δίκη against which men offend is God's righteousness. [16] Hence ἀσέβεια and ἀδικία in R.1:18 are a hendiadys : "ungodliness and unrighteousness." In R. 4:5 : πιστεύοντι δὲ ἐπὶ τὸν δικαιοῦντα τὸν ἀσεβῆ, the translation "the irreverent" [17] echoes Greek usage. But nearer the mark, and not too far from the Greek either, is the assumption that Paul is here referring in OT fashion to "transgressors." This is strengthened by R. 5:6 : εἴ γε Χριστὸς ὄντων ἡμῶν ἀσθενῶν ἔτι κατὰ καιρὸν ὑπὲρ ἀσεβῶν ἀπέθανεν, for the ἁμαρτωλῶν ὄντων ἡμῶν of v. 8 embraces both ἀσθενεῖς and ἀσεβεῖς.

2. In the Pastorals ἀσεβής occurs once in 1 Tm. 1:9 and ἀσέβεια twice in 2 Tm. 2:16 and Tt. 2:12. 1 Tm. 1:9 has the OT combination of ἀσεβής and ἁμαρτωλός, and the two are materially connected, as are also the preceding ἄνομοι and ἀνυπότακτοι and the ensuing ἀνόσιοι and βέβηλοι. In the βέβηλοι κενοφωνίαι ... ἐπὶ πλεῖον προκόψουσιν ἀσεβείας of 2 Tm. 2:16 the reference is not to teachings as in v. 18b but to their moral and religious consequences. Only in Tt. 2:12 might one ask whether even as the opposite of the εὐσέβεια which the Pastorals demand ἀσέβεια does not denote wilful transgression of the orders, while the "worldly lusts" are the avarice of the adversaries.

3. The other ἀσεβ- passages are all in 1 and 2 Pt. and Jd. 1 Pt. 4:18 quotes Prv. 11:31 and has the common combination of ἀσεβής and ἁμαρτωλός. Jd. 15 (= Eth. En. 1:9) has a quotation from Eth. En. with a fourfold use of the ἀσεβ-group including the expression ἁμαρτωλοὶ ἀσεβεῖς, which is not found elsewhere. In the quotation the genitive in ἔργα ἀσεβείας is a substitute for the adjective, cf. also ἐπιθυμίαι τῶν ἀσεβειῶν in Jd. 18 → n. 15; V, 455, 32 ff. In Jd. and 2 Pt. great sinners of the past, the flood generation and Sodom and Gomorrah, are called ungodly, 2 Pt. 2:5 f., and the false teachers who have arisen in the community are said to be ἀσεβεῖς on account of their life (and teaching ?),

---

[12] Schl. R., ad loc., 49; Mi. R.; Str.-B., ad loc.; but cf. A. Nygren, Der Römerbrief² (1954), ad loc.
[13] Zn. R., ad loc.
[14] Str.-B. on R. 1:18 B.
[15] The other ref. given by Mi. R., ad loc., namely, ψ 72:6; Prv. 11:5 (→ n. 6); Eth. En. 13:2 (περὶ πάντων τῶν ἔργων τῶν ἀσεβειῶν καὶ τῆς ἀδικίας καὶ τῆς ἁμαρτίας) do not prove that the two terms refer respectively to the two tables.
[16] The ref. in vv. 19-23 is to corrupt worship and in v. 24 ff. to sexual and social perversity. But always, even in v. 24 ff., the two are so closely linked that surrender to sin follows corruption in the knowledge of God (v. 25, 28). The changing of the truth of God into a lie in v. 25 is just as much ἀδικία as what results therefrom, and ἀσέβεια embraces θεοστυγεῖς and ὑβριστάς in v. 30.
[17] Brth. R., ad loc.; Mi. R., ad loc., 101, n. 2.

Jd. 4; 2 Pt. 2:6. Both Jd. 18 and 2 Pt. 3:7 pronounce judgment on them and their deeds. Here, then, the group describes great sinners of all ages up to the end as transgressors, ungodly, and sinners.

† σεμνός, † σεμνότης.

A. In the Greek World.

παρὰ τὸ σέβω σεβνὸς καὶ σεμνός, ὁ σεβασμοῦ ἄξιος, ὁ θαυμαστὸς καὶ ἄξιος ἐντροπῆς. καὶ τὰ ἄρρητα δὲ καὶ ἀνεξιχνίαστα σεμνὰ λέγεται, is the old def. in Etym. M., 709, 48 ff. σεμνός, then, denotes anything which evokes σέβεσθαι and σεμνότης is the quality or manner of a σεμνός or σεμνόν. σεμνός, however, does not share in the development of σέβεσθαι and εὐ- and ἀσέβεια, in which the aesthetic element is eliminated from the word.

1. σεμνός is first an attribute of the gods : "lofty," Hom. Hymn. Cer., 1, 486 (par. αἰδοῖος), esp. the Furies in Soph. Ai., 837, in NT days in Cornut. Theol. Graec., 10 and Luc. Bis Accusatus, 4. It is then used of divine things, "august," "sacred," the head of Zeus, Hom. Hymn. ad Minervam, 5, the rites of Ceres, Hymn. Cer., 478, heaven and its order, Dio Chrys. Or., 40, 35, the holiness of the Jewish temple, Philo Leg. Gaj., 198. The nature of the σεμνότης of the gods may be seen from Plut. Superst., 6 (II, 167e): φιλοσόφων δὲ καὶ πολιτικῶν ἀνδρῶν καταφρονοῦσιν (sc. οἱ δεισιδαίμονες) ἀποδεικνύντων τὴν τοῦ θεοῦ σεμνότητα μετὰ χρηστότητος καὶ μεγαλοφροσύνην μετ᾽ εὐνοίας καὶ κηδεμονίας. Plut. would deny emphatically that the δεισιδαίμονες who fear the gods accord them σεμνότης.

2. Used of objects σεμνός first denotes visible majesty and greatness : a royal throne, Hdt., II, 173, 2; βασιλικὴ σεμνότης, Plut. Demetr., 2 (I, 889e) par. ἡρωϊκή τις ἐπιφάνεια, σεμνόταται πομπαί, Ps.-Plat. Alc., II, 148e; Agis ἔτυχε σεμνοτέρας ἢ κατὰ ἄνθρωπον ταφῆς, Xenoph. Hist. Graec., III, 3, 1. Of a town σεμνοτέραν ποιεῖν means to make it more distinguished, Isaeus, V, 45. In relation to clothes σεμνός means "splendid," "magnificent." [1] It is then used of music, Aristot. Rhet., III, 8, p. 1408b, 32 : ὁ ἡρῷος ῥυθμὸς σεμνὸς καὶ λεκτικὸς καὶ ἁρμονίας δεόμενος. [2] In Doric music is πολὺ τὸ σεμνόν, Plut. De Musica, 17 (II, 1136e). But what makes music σεμνοτάτη for Plut. is that the heavenly bodies move in their spheres with music, 44 (II, 1147). Plut. does not call oriental music σεμνός. [3] The use of σεμνός in relation to oratory is similar : ἡ τοῦ ῥήματος σεμνότης, Demosth. Prooemium, 45, 3. Plut., too, speaks of the σεμνότης of Pericles which was regarded by many as δοξοκοπία and τῦφος, Pericl., 5 (I, 154e). In the field of poetry σεμνός is used esp. in relation to tragedy; the actor imitates μάλα σεμνῶς τὸ τοῦ Κέκροπος ... σχῆμα, Luc. Nec., 16; the ἄγαν σεμνόν will then become the τραγικόν, Aristot. Rhet., III, 3, p. 1406b, 7. In Jos. Ant., 1, 24 the obscurity of allegorical presentation constitutes σεμνότης. σεμνός can be used in malam partem for "proud" and "lofty" speech, Soph. Ai., 1107.

σεμνός, σεμνότης. E. Williger, "Hagios," RVV, 19, 1 (1922), 68 f.; G. J. de Vries, "σεμνός and Cognate words in Plato," Mnemosyne, 12 (1945), 151-156.
[1] Aristoph. Pl., 940 : πλοῦτον δὲ κοσμεῖν ἱματίοις σεμνοῖς πρέπει, Xenoph. Cyrop., VI, 1, 6 : σεμνῶς κεκοσμημένος ἐξῆλθε καὶ ἐπὶ θρόνου Μηδικοῦ ἐκαθέζετο.
[2] Cf. Plut. De Musica, 14 (II, 1136b): σεμνὴ οὖν κατὰ πάντα ἡ μουσική, θεῶν εὕρημα οὖσα.
[3] Philo, too, uses σεμνός with ref. to music, Leg. All., I, 14; Vit. Cont., 29.

3. More important, however, are passages which use σεμνός for the inner majesty of things. μητρός τε καὶ πατρὸς ... τιμιώτερόν ἐστιν πατρὶς καὶ σεμνότερον καὶ ἁγιώτερον καὶ ἐν μείζονι μοίρᾳ καὶ παρὰ θεοῖς καὶ παρ' ἀνθρώποις, Plat. Crit., 51a. [4] The virtue of the gods is called σεμνότατον καὶ θειότατον in comparison with their ἀφθαρσία and δύναμις, Plut. Aristides, 6 (I, 322a). Philo speaks of the σεμνότης (dignity, sanctity) of the number seven, Spec. Leg., II, 149; Op. Mund., 111. Philosophising is a σεμνὸν πρᾶγμα, Ps.-Plat. Hipp., I, 288d. This is also the view of Epict. Diss., III, 24, 41 and Dio Chrys. Or., 12, 15, who differentiates between τέχναι and ἐπιστῆμαι σεμνότεραι and ἐλάττονες and reckons μαντική and σοφιστικὴ ἐπιστήμη among the former. [5] οὐθὲν σεμνόν is "nothing special" in Aristot. Eth. Eud., III, 1, p. 1228b, 11. [6] Positively Plut. Col., 20 (II, 1118c): With his ἐδιζησάμην ἐμεωυτόν Heraclitus believed he had reached μέγα τι καὶ σεμνόν. μεγάλαι καὶ σεμναὶ ἀρχαί are "gt. and esteemed preferments," Epict. Diss., IV, 1, 148 f. For Philo (Leg. Gaj., 361) the question as to the reasons for not eating swine's flesh is a μέγιστον καὶ σεμνὸν ἐρώτημα ("important," "serious"). For Philo, too, desires for greater pleasures than gold and silver are σεμνοτέρων ἐπιθυμίαι, Omn. Prob. Lib., 31. [7] Hence tragedy does not fit in with carousing because it is σεμνότερον βοῶσα: the "significant" becomes the "serious." [8]

σεμνός and σεμνότης become more specific in relation to men. Here the words often express an actual position of honour: οἱ μέγιστον δυνάμενοί τε καὶ σεμνότατοι ἐν ταῖς πόλεσιν, Plat. Phaedr., 257d; cf. Euthyd., 303c; Resp., V, 475a-b. For Philo the βασιλέων σεμνότης καὶ τιμή of the priests are their actual position and dignity rather than their eminence, Spec. Leg., I, 142. But mostly σεμνός refers to outward appearance: who is ὅδ' ἄλλος ὁ σεμνὸς ἀνήρ; asks Charon when Cyrus comes, Luc. Char., 9. Pompey tries to express σεμνότης and ὄγκος by the number of his attendants, Plut. Pomp., 23 (I, 630e). Agrippa rejoices in the sight τῆς περὶ τὸν ἀρχιερέα σεμνότητος, Philo Leg. Gaj., 296. In particular, however, σεμνότης denotes a man's visible deportment; it is a matter of the σχῆμα, Ps.-Plat. Def., 413e. The witch of Endor sees Samuel as ἄνδρα σεμνὸν καὶ θεοπρεπῆ, Jos. Ant., 6, 332. Esther comes before the king προσηνὲς καὶ σεμνὸν ἐπικειμένη τὸ κάλλος, Jos. Ant., 11, 234. Pharaoh was struck by Jacob's σεμνότης, Philo Jos., 257; cf. 165 and Flacc., 4. σεμνότης is the mean between two extremes: σεμνότης δὲ μεσότης αὐθαδείας καὶ ἀρεσκείας. [9] Often σεμνότης or seriousness is differentiated from severity: καὶ φαίνεσθαι μὴ χαλεπὸν ἀλλὰ σεμνόν, ἔτι δὲ τοιοῦτον ὥστε μὴ φοβεῖσθαι τοὺς ἐντυγχάνοντας, ἀλλὰ μᾶλλον αἰδεῖσθαι, [10] so that it can be called a μαλακὴ καὶ εὐσχήμων βαρύτης, Aristot. Rhet., II, 17, p. 1391a, 28 f. How close are σεμνός and αὐστηρός may be seen from the fact that the question naturally arises whether Charidemus, being called σεμνός, is not also σκυθρωπότερος, Dio Chrys. Or., 30, 5. οὐκ ἦν αὐστηρὸν οὐδ' ἐπαχθὲς ἄγαν αὐτοῦ τὸ σεμνόν, says Plut. of Nicias in Nicias, 2 (I, 524c) and Muson. Fr., 33 advises: πειρατέον καταπληκτικὸν μᾶλλον τοῖς ὑπηκόοις ἢ φοβερὸν θεωρεῖσθαι· τῷ μὲν γὰρ σεμνότης, τῷ δὲ ἀπήνεια παρακολουθεῖ. Also worth noting is Plut. Cato Maior, 6 (I, 339e): Cato appeared in the cities without a riding animal, with only one δημόσιος, hence without σεμνότης, but ἐν δὲ τούτοις οὕτως εὔκολος καὶ ἀφελὴς τοῖς ὑπὸ χεῖρα φαινόμενος, αὖθις

---

[4] Cf. Luc. Patria, 1: οὐδὲν γλύκιον ... πατρίδος ... ἆρ' οὖν σεμνότερον δέ τι καὶ θειότερον ἄλλο;
[5] Cf. Luc. Somnium, 10, also Nigrinus, 38: ὡς σεμνὰ καὶ θαυμάσια καὶ θεῖά γε ... διελήλυθας.
[6] Cf. Plat. Resp., II, 382b; Plut. Praec. Ger. Reip., 27 (II, 820c): οὐδὲν μέγα πεποίηκεν ἢ σεμνόν, namely, to sail past the Syrtis.
[7] Cf. Jos. Bell., 2, 61: σεμνότερα πράγματα, "more important matters."
[8] Plut. Quaest. Conv., VII, 8, 3 (II, 711e); cf. also Philo Vit. Mos., I, 20; Plant., 167.
[9] Aristot. Eth. Eud., III, 7, p. 1233b, 34 f.
[10] Aristot. Pol., V, 11, p. 1314b, 18 and 20. But σεμνός does not mean morally good, as Williger, 68 f. thinks.

ἀνταπεδίδου τὴν σεμνότητα καὶ τὸ βάρος, ἀπαραίτητος ὢν ἐν τῷ δικαίῳ, cf. Plut. Crass., 7 (I, 546 f.). σεμνότης here is a demeanour which commands respect. Thus Plut. says that the σεμνόν is not easily combined with the ἐπιεικές, Phoc., 2 (I, 742e) and that it is exceptional that it be maintained in the φιλάνθρωπον, C. Gracch., 6 (I, 837e). ¹¹ Clear, too, is Philo's statement in Praem. Poen., 97 that the righteous practice three virtues, σεμνότης, δεινότης, εὐεργεσία: τὸ μὲν γὰρ σεμνὸν αἰδῶ κατασκευάζει, τὸ δὲ δεινὸν φόβον, τὸ δὲ εὐεργετικὸν εὔνοιαν. But Philo links the αὐστηρόν more closely to the σεμνόν, Leg. Gaj., 167: φιλαύστηρος καὶ σεμνὸς βίος, Op. Mund., 164. ¹² Gold and silver etc. do not make a woman respectable (κόσμιος) but ὅσα σεμνότητος, εὐταξίας, αἰδοῦς ἔμφασιν περιτίθησιν, Plut. Praec. Coniug., 26 (II, 141e). The look of a crowd is θεῖον, σεμνόν and μεγαλοπρεπές when it is πρᾷος, καθεστηκώς (quiet) and neither surges with violent and uncontrolled laughter nor is shaken by disorderly tumult, Dio Chrys. Or., 32, 29. In the famous statue of Phidias, Zeus as the protector of cities is marked by σεμνότης and αὐστηρόν, ibid., 12, 77. σεμνός is differentiated from σώφρων, σεμνότης from σωφροσύνη and ἀταραξία, by the fact that the one denotes man's being and conduct in and towards himself, whereas the other has to do with his visible conduct and relation to his neighbour.

σεμνός is that which in the being and conduct of men calls forth σέβεσθαι from others. Its content is orientated to that which in fact produces σέβεσθαι among the Greeks. This might be the majesty of a royal throne, the splendour of dress, the beauty of speech, or the sound of music. Yet not every sound nor all fine speech or adornment is regarded as σεμνός. A thing is σεμνός if the signs of a higher order may be detected in it. In man the orderliness perceived in his attitude and behaviour is felt to be σεμνότης, with an ineffaceable trend towards seriousness and solemnity. Things which the Greeks also loved and valued like the witty answer or easy grace in word and gesture were not regarded as σεμνός. The Greek appreciated them, but did not retreat from them in admiration and respect. If σεμνότης was to be maintained the noble mean of seriousness had not to become a forbidding severity; on the other hand it certainly could not be charming or jesting grace. It is no accident that Eur. Ba., 486: σεμνότητ' ἔχει σκότος, refers, not to the bright clarity of day, but to the solemnity of dark.

B. In the Septuagint and Judaism.

1. σεμνός and σεμνότης occur in the LXX only in Prv. and 2 and 4 Macc., 11 times in all. ¹³ In all the ref. outside 4 Macc. it is possible to take the two words religiously. Wisdom says in Prv. 8:6: σεμνὰ γὰρ ἐρῶ (= נְגִידִים) par. ὀρθά (= מֵישָׁרִים). Since ὀρθά suggests what is right with God, σεμνός must be close to this, e.g., "holy." The same applies in Prv. 15:26, where σεμνός (= עֹנֶג) stands in antithetical parallelism to βδέλυγμα κυρίῳ. In Prv. 6:8a (no HT) the saying that the bee ἐργασίαν ὡς σεμνὴν ποιεῖται may mean that it does its work as something sacred. This not strictly demonstrable understanding of the Prv. ref. is supported by 2 Macc., where the Sabbath is

---

¹¹ Cf. Ditt.-Syll.³, II, 807, 11-16 in an inscr. in honour of T. Claudius Tyrannus, the manumitted physician of Nero, who returned to Magnesia, and who ἀνάλογον πεποίηται τὴν ἐπιδημίαν τῇ περὶ ἑαυτὸν ἐν πᾶσι σεμνότητι, προσενεχθεὶς φιλανθρώπως πᾶσι τοῖς πολείταις ὡς μηδένα ὑφ' αὐτοῦ παρὰ τὴν ἀξίαν τοῦ καθ' ἑαυτὸν μεγέθους ἐπιβεβαρῆσθαι.
¹² Cf. Philo Ebr., 149: πρὸς τὸ σεμνότερον καὶ αὐστηρότερον τὴν δίαιταν ... μεταβαλεῖν, Spec. Leg., II, 19.
¹³ σεμνός also occurs in Ju. 11:35 'Α.

called σεμνοτάτη ἡμέρα in 6:11, where there is ref. to the σεμνοὶ καὶ ἅγιοι νόμοι in 6:28 and God's σεμνὸν καὶ μεγαλοπρεπὲς ὄνομα in 8:15, and to the σεμνότης καὶ ἀσυλία of the universally honoured temple in 3:12. In all these passages "holy" fits the bill and this corresponds to the almost exclusively religious reference of the stem σεβ- in the LXX.

If 4 Macc. does not wholly follow the same lines here, this corresponds to its special position already noted in relation to εὐσέβεια. σεμνός is used of the righteous martyrs : τὸ σεμνὸν γήρως στόμα, 5:36; ὦ μακαρίου γήρως καὶ σεμνῆς πολιᾶς, 7:15. The moon in heaven with the stars is not so σεμνή as the martyrs' mother in 17:5. By the instruction of the Law we learn τὰ θεῖα σεμνῶς καὶ τὰ ἀνθρώπινα συμφερόντως, 1:17. In all these passages "worthy" is hardly an adequate rendering ; "worthy of God" is better. σεμνός does not refer to the quality of the Law as holy ; it is a favourable judgment on man's part.

2. σεμνός and σεμνότης do not occur in Test. XII, Ps. Sol., the Gk. parts of Eth. En., Sib., 3-5. There are instances in Ep. Ar. where the ref. is to the giving of the Law in 5 and 313, the Law, 171, its θεωρία, 31 (cf. 2 Macc.). Very similar is 144, where σεμνῶς ἀνατετάχθαι is said of the giving of the Law allegorically interpreted. But in accordance with the plot of the work σεμνός is also used more generally. Philocrates has πρόσκλισιν πρὸς τὴν σεμνότητα of the Jews in 5, God will give the king τὴν σεμνὴν ἐπίνοιαν in 271, [14] and σεμνός is used of the magnificence of the king's works, as in common Gk. usage (→ 191, 22 ff.), in 56 and 258.

3. In Josephus and Philo, as in passages already adduced → n. 1-3, the use of the two words is par. to that of Gk. authors. Only in Philo may one note a twofold peculiarity. First there is the use of the terms for the law-giver and the Law. As the employment of the comparative or superlative indicates, σεμνός is not here an absolute concept measured by God's holiness. We have a more or less ; by putting the story of creation before that of the giving of the Law Moses has made παγκάλην καὶ σεμνοτάτην ἀρχήν, Op. Mund., 2; the laws are σεμνοὶ ... ἅτε πρὸς τὴν ἄκραν ἀρετὴν ἀλείφοντες, Spec. Leg., IV, 179. The name of God is καὶ αὐτῆς εὐκλεέστερον σεμνότητος, ibid., II, 253; evaluation of σεμνότης is by man. The other pt. is that in Philo σεμνός is a term for the spiritual and suprasensual world as distinct from that of the senses. To rule the body and its desires is σεμνότερον βασιλείας τὸ ἔργον, Sacr. AC, 49; breaking the bonds of the family for the sake of the Law, ἀντιλήμψονται ... σεμνοτέρας καὶ ἱεροπρεπεστέρας συγγενείας, Spec. Leg., I, 317 — the transl. "higher" is appropriate here. Man is a "higher" (σεμνότερον) offering than gold and silver, Decal., 133. It is connected with turning from the world of sense, which plays a gt. role in Philo, that in his works σεμνός and αὐστηρός are usually closer than in Gk. authors, → 192, 36 f. [15]

C. In the New Testament.

1. Only in Phil. 4:8 does σεμνός relate to man's conduct. In ὅσα ... ἀληθῆ, ὅσα σεμνά ..., as the following εἴ τις ... shows, Paul is making a very general statement. [16] He does not define ἀληθῆ, σεμνά, δίκαια etc. In the ἃ καὶ ἐμάθετε ... καὶ εἴδετε ἐν ἐμοί of v. 9 he undoubtedly still has in view what he said in v. 8. For the Greeks Paul in many ways may not have appeared to be an ἀνὴρ σεμνός; on the contrary, he would seem an ἀνὴρ ταπεινός. Hence in v. 8 he does not just accept the validity of the judgment of those outside on what σεμνά

---

[14] One can hardly transl. "pious disposition" with P. Wendland in Kautzsch Apkr. u. Pseudepigr., ad loc.; "serious disposition" is closer to the context → n. 12.
[15] But cf. Vit. Cont., 66.
[16] As against Loh. Phil., ad loc.

is. He assumes, however, that his conduct is true, earnest and just ... to his church and that it might seem so to the Greeks too. He also states it as his goal that the conduct of his churches should make a similar impression on the world around. When in 1 C. 13:5 Paul says of love : οὐκ ἀσχημονεῖ, since σεμνότης is a matter of the σχῆμα, σεμνός is not far away, and when at the end of Phil. 4:9 he speaks of the God of peace, something of the εἰρήνη of 1 C. 14:33a is echoed, → II, 412, 19 ff. [17] In the Philippian passage Paul is deliberately making no restriction so that the eyes of readers will be open to what seems to them to be true, just and σεμνά, to what is serious and noble and worthy of reverence, no matter where it may come from.

2. In the Pastorals σεμνός occurs three times, always among requirements relating to leaders in the churches, deacons in 1 Tm. 3:8, their wives in v. 11, and the aged in Tt. 2:2. If σεμνός is not in the list of duties required of bishops either in 1 Tm. or Tt. this is connected with the fact that in neither epistle do we have a set of circumscribed and clearly differentiated duties. σεμνός in 1 Tm. 3:8 embraces what is put separately in the portrait of the bishop : a σεμνός ἀνήρ is νηφάλιος, σώφρων, κόσμιος, no πάροινος, no πλήκτης, ἐπιεικής, ἄμαχος, ἀφιλάργυρος, 3:2 f. "Serious and worthy" is a suitable rendering for σεμνός in the Pastorals.

3. In 1 Tm. 2:2 σεμνότης is used alongside εὐσέβεια. The one is the piety expressed in respect for the orders, the other is the corresponding "serious and worthy conduct." In 1 Tm. 3:4 : τοῦ ἰδίου οἴκου καλῶς προϊστάμενον, τέκνα ἔχοντα ἐν ὑποταγῇ μετὰ πάσης σεμνότητος, the last three words are not to be taken with προΐστασθαι (→ VI, 702, 10 ff.), which is already defined by καλῶς, but with τέκνα ἔχοντα. The obedience of children is to be won by authority which commands respect. [18] Tt. 2:7 is more difficult. Here παρεχόμενος is to be supplied from what precedes and ἐν τῇ διδασκαλίᾳ ἀφθορίαν, σεμνότητα λόγον ὑγιῆ ἀκατάγνωστον is dependent on this. It is not possible [19] to think in terms of what Titus is to impart to his hearers. The reference is to what he teaches and the way he does it ; σεμνότης relates to the latter. Here too, as in the σεμνός of Phil. 4:8 and the εὐσεβ- passages → 182, 20 ff., it is those outside who are in view, in this case opponents who if they do not find σεμνότης in the Christian community will speak evil of it, and rightly so in the judgment of the author. σεμνότης is the σχῆμα which corresponds to the content of the doctrine, namely, "gravity," "dignity."

D. In the Post-Apostolic Fathers.

In the post-apost. fathers σεμνός and σεμνότης occur only in 1 Cl. and Herm.

1. Acc. to 1 Cl. the Corinthians had previously ordered younger members of the community μέτρια καὶ σεμνὰ νοεῖν and taught wives τὰ κατὰ τὸν οἴκον σεμνῶς οἰκουργεῖν, 1, 3. Here σεμνός is worthy, honourable, measured and disciplined conduct, cf. the NT → line 8 f. This might also be the sense in the only instance of the

---

[17] W. S. van Leeuwen, *Eirene in het NT,* Diss. Utrecht (1940), 201 f. sees here in εἰρήνη subjection to the unity of the community, ἀκαταστασία being revolt, disobedience. But this is hardly in accordance with the context.
[18] Schl. Past., *ad loc.*
[19] As against Schl. Past., *ad loc.*

noun in 41, 1: ἕκαστος ἡμῶν ... ἐν τῷ ἰδίῳ τάγματι εὐαρεστείτω τῷ θεῷ ... μὴ παρεκβαίνων τὸν ὡρισμένον τῆς λειτουργίας αὐτοῦ κανόνα, ἐν σεμνότητι. But already the words have rather a different ring in 1 Cl., cf. σεμνὸν καὶ περιβόητον ... ὄνομα ὑμῶν in 1, 1; σεμνὸν τῆς περιβοήτου φιλαδελφίας ὑμῶν in 47, 5; σεμνὴ τῆς φιλαδελφίας ἡμῶν ἁγνὴ ἀγωγή in 48, 1; εὐκλεὴς καὶ σεμνὸς τῆς παραδόσεως ἡμῶν κανών in 7, 2; ἄμωμος καὶ σεμνὴ καὶ ἁγνὴ συνείδησις in 1, 3. σεμνός is now a specifically Chr. attribute well on the way to taking its place alongside ἅγιος.

2. It follows this way to the end in Herm. Here σεμνός is used of the Spirit in m., 3, 4, κλῆσις in m., 4, 3, 6, ἄγγελος in m., 5, 1, 7. There is also ref. to the σεμνότης τοῦ θεοῦ in v., 3, 5, 1. The works of virtues are ἁγνὰ καὶ σεμνὰ καὶ θεῖα in v., 3, 8, 7, and ἁγνός is again used with σεμνός in v., 3, 5, 1; s., 9, 25, 2. σεμνότης itself is a virtue in m., 6, 2, 3, after δικαιοσύνη and ἁγνεία and before αὐτάρκεια and πᾶν ἔργον δίκαιον καὶ πᾶσα ἀρετὴ ἔνδοξος. It comes after ἁπλότης, ἐπιστήμη, ἀκακία and before ἀγάπη in v., 3, 8, 5. 7 and alongside ἁπλότης and ἀκακία in v., 3, 9, 1. σεμνότης protects against καταλαλιά, for in it is οὐδὲν πρόσκομμα πονηρόν, m., 2, 4, cf. 5, 2, 8. In m., 4, 1, 3 we read: ὅπου γὰρ σεμνότης κατοικεῖ, ἐκεῖ ἀνομία οὐκ ὀφείλει ἀναβαίνειν. To characterise those who walk with a pure heart and have kept the commandments of the Lord the adj. σεμνοὶ καὶ δίκαιοι are sufficient in s., 8, 3, 8. That Herm. has seen all things καλῶς καὶ σεμνῶς in s., 9, 1, 2 also goes beyond simple dignity of conduct. Everything connected with the world of Chr. faith is σεμνός, and σεμνότης is proper to it.

Foerster

---

† σείω, † σεισμός

1. The verb σείω probably goes back to the Indo-Eur. root *tweis-/twis-* etc., Sanskr. *tvis-*, denoting violent movement or disturbance (including lightning). [1] In addition to the gen. sense "to shake," "to move to and fro," e.g., the spear in Hom. Il., 3, 345; 13, 135; door, 9, 583, reins, Soph. El., 713, mane, Anacr., 47 (Diehl[2], I, 4, 176), head, Soph. Ant., 291, and the transf. sense "to disturb," e.g., the heart ἐσείσθη τὴν καρδίαν Philostr. Vit. Soph., II, 1 and 11, state affairs, Pind. Pyth., 4, 272; Soph. Ant., 163, it is used esp. for cosmic disturbances: "to shake the earth." [2] The noun is found from Hdt., e.g., IV, 28 and Soph., e.g., Oed. Col., 95 and usually means "earthquake." Up to a late time this phenomenon was attributed to the angry intervention of Poseidon, e.g., ὅστις νομίζει Ποσειδέωνα τὴν γῆν σείειν, Hdt., VII, 129. The name of Poseidon was explained accordingly: ἴσως δὲ ἀπὸ τοῦ σείειν ὁ σείων ὠνόμασται, Plat. Crat., 403a. He was esp. revered even in inland areas subject to frequent earthquakes. He caused them by moving or by striking with his trident. Even when his name is not explicitly mentioned, e.g., Aristoph. Lys., 1142; Xenoph. Hist. Graec., IV, 7, 4, any ref. to the shaker of the earth is usually to him. [3] Since earthquakes, like other natural

---

σείω, σεισμός. [1] Cf. Walde-Pok., I, 748; Hofmann, 308.
[2] For the most part only in Attic and later writers σείω also means "to accuse falsely," "to denounce" (noun "denunciation"), but this need not be considered here; for examples *v.* Liddell-Scott.
[3] Cf. W. Capelle, Art. "Erdbebenforschung" in Pauly-W., Suppl. 4 (1924), 344-374, esp. 359.

disasters, were usually regarded as unlucky events and manifestations of the anger of deity (→ ὀργή, V, 389, 4 ff.), they were viewed as omens of coming evil, Soph. Oed. Col., 94 f.: σημεῖα δ' ἥξειν τῶνδέ μοι παρηγγύα, ἢ σεισμὸν, ἢ βροντήν τιν', ἢ Διὸς σέλας (lightning), cf. Hdt., VI, 98, e.g., as a warning not to pursue actions or military campaigns already begun, Thuc., III, 89, 1. Acc. to Aristot. Meteor., II, 8, p. 368a, 25 those who give oracles get their prophecies from them. From the time of the pre-Socratics and up to Posidonius there are many attempts to explain earthquakes scientifically. Our knowledge of the various theories rests almost entirely on Aristot. Meteor., II, 7 and 8, p. 364a, 14 ff. and Sen. Quaestiones naturales, VI. [4] They were ascribed by some to congestion of air, cf. esp. Anaxim. A. 21 (Diels, I, 94, 30-34), Anaximand. A, 28 (I, 88, 22-28), Aristot. Meteor., II, 7 and 8, p. 364a, 14 ff. and most ancient physicists. Some explained them in terms of movements of esp. subterranean waters, esp. Democr. A, 97 f. (Diels, II, 107, 8-31) or of volcanic action, so esp. Antiphon B (Diels[9], II, 344, 18 f.). [5] In the Hell. period the growth of manticism led to an attempt to construct a systematic cosmological and theological interpretation of prodigies. Thus we find earthquake books which try to give information on what is presaged by an earthquake that takes place under a particular sign of the zodiac. [6] Efforts were also made to determine what was foretold by dreams of earthquakes. From the religious standpt. it is important that earthquakes are often found in ancient descriptions of theophanies either as warning signs or accompanying phenomena. [7] Nor are these theophanies restricted to Poseidon. They extend also to others, esp. to gods of salvation, cf. the appearance of Apollo in Callim. Hymn. in Apoll., 1 f., [8] or of Aesculapius in Ovid. Metam., 15, 671 f., or of Mars in Statius Thebais, VII, 65. [9] In the so-called Mithras Liturgy, too, theophany is accompanied by an earthquake, 14, 10. This is a sign or accompaniment of the saving *mutatio rerum*. [10] New saving events such as the liberation of Dionysus in Eur. Ba., 585 and the birth of gods or god-men are also accompanied by earthquakes. [11]

2. In the OT the main Hebr. original of σείω is רָעַשׁ (noun רַעַשׁ). רָגַז occurs at Job 9:6; Prv. 30:21; נוּד at Is. 24:20; נוּעַ at Is. 19:1; צָעַן at Is. 33:20; תְּעָה at Is. 28:7; סָעַר at Hab. 3:14. The noun סְעָרָה is transl. σεισμός only at Jer. 23:19, cf. συσσεισμός at 2 K. 2:1, 11, σάλος at Zech. 9:14, καταιγίς at Is. 40:24; 41:16; ψ 106:25, 29; 148:8, λαῖλαψ at Job 38:1 and even νέφος (thunder-cloud) at Job 40:6. A distinctive v. is Prv. 30:21. Here the earth is personified. It shakes because of events which disturb its order. That there are vivid descriptions of earthquakes in the OT is not surprising in view of the prevalence of seismic phenomena in Palestine (the Jordan rift valley), cf. Ps. 18:7; 46:2 f.; 97:4 f. etc. Chronologically only the terrible earthquake under Uzziah

---

[4] Cf. Capelle, 362-373 with specific examples and other physicists (some anon.) not mentioned here.

[5] The Pythagoreans had a remarkable poetic-mythological explanation of the σεισμός as σύνοδος τεθνεώτων, C, 2 (Diels, I, 463, 6 f.). For this idea of the attack on the gates of Hades by the unpurified dead, and their repelling with earthshaking tumult, cf. also Aristot. Meteor., II, 8, p. 368a, 11-35; An. Post., II, 11, p. 94b, 32; Plat. Resp., X, 615e; Plut. Gen. Socr., 22 (II, 591c). On this cf. O. Weinreich, "Gebet u. Wunder," *Genethliakon Wilhelm Schmid, Tüb. Beiträge z. Altertumswissenschaft,* 5 (1929), 169-464, esp. 220.

[6] Catal. Cod. Astr. Graec., III, 48 f.; VII, 167-171; X, 60-65, 132-135, 140-142, 144-148, 203-211; Orph. Fr. (Kern), 285 (283-285).

[7] Cf. E. Pfister, Art. "Epiphanie" in Pauly-W., Suppl. 4 (1924), 319; M. B. Ogle, "The House-Door in Religion and Folklore," *American Journal of Philology,* 32 (1911), 270, n. 2.

[8] Weinreich, *op. cit.,* 229-236.

[9] Ed. A. Klotz (1908).

[10] Cf. in the mantic sphere Plut. De Cicerone, 32 (I, 877b) and Capelle, 361.

[11] Cf. E. Pfister, *op. cit.,* 319 on natural phenomena on the birth of gods and god-men like Alexander and Apollonius. Cf. also the birth of the wonderful child in Verg. Ecl., 4, with express ref. to an earthquake. On Eur. Ba., 585 cf. Weinreich, 282-290.

is noted in Am. 1:1; Zech. 14:5. The more common are theophanic descriptions. Thus when God appears at Sinai in Ex. 19:18 or Horeb in 1 K. 19:11 f. there is a storm which rends the hills and the rocks, an earthquake, a fire, and a gentle wind. [12] In particular the theme occurs in descriptions of the day of Yahweh whose origin is to be found in ancient Israelite and at first not at all eschatological ideas of the holy war to which Yahweh marches out as a warrior to fight and conquer His enemies. [13] Already in the Song of Deborah in Ju. 5:2-31 the idea of the theophany at Sinai changes into that of the warlike march from Edom, though there is here no more detailed description. The joining of the theophany at Sinai to the motif of the holy war is very clear in Ps. 68:7-23. The shaking of heaven and earth is an integral part of both in Ju. 5:4 f.; Ps. 68:8. It is on the basis of this ancient tradition that the intimation of the day of Yahweh develops for the first time in the prophets, Is. 13:1-22; 34:1-17; Ez. 7:1-27; 30:1-9; Jl. 2:1-11; Am. 2:13-16. Heaven and earth are dreadfully shaken and the day brings panic and destruction to enemies and deliverance to Israel. But the idea is also turned against Israel, first in Am. 2:13-16; 5:18-20; 8:9 f., then quite often, e.g., Is. 2:6-21; 7:17-25; Ez. 7:1-27; Zeph. 1:14-18. The dramatic accompanying circumstances help to bring out the meaning of this ultimate theophany, cf. Is. 13:1-22; 24:17-20; Ez. 38:19-22; Nah. 1:2-6; Jl. 3:14-16. [14]

3. In the descriptions of theophany and judgment in later Jewish apoc. the motif of the shaking of heaven and earth recurs, cf. the theophanies in Eth. En. 1:3-9; Ass. Mos. 10:3-7 [15] and the list of annihilating eschatological catastrophes in S. Bar. 70:8 : "And he who saves himself from the war shall die by an earthquake, and he who saves himself from the earthquake shall burn in the fire, and he who saves himself from the fire shall perish of hunger." [16] In 4 Esr. 6:11-17 the seer is prepared for the sounding forth of a mighty voice on which the place where he stands will be shaken. But along with the terrors the last signs also intimate the saving transformation of the world and the new aeon. [17]

4. In the NT the verb σείω is used in a transferred sense (passive) for spiritual disturbance (Mt. 28:4) and also for the almost riotous incitement of a whole city (Mt. 21:10). The compound ἀνασείω (used transitively) also denotes the stirring up of a crowd (Mk. 15:11; Lk. 23:5). The motif of incitement is common in Ac. too, but here σείω and derivates are not employed for it. [18] Though infrequently, σείω is also used for earthquakes or cosmic disturbances, Mt. 27:51; Hb. 12:26, → 199, 4 ff., 27 ff. Rev. 6:13 compares a fig-tree shaken by the storm with the cosmos smitten by eschatological catastrophe ; this comes immediately after the reference to an earthquake in v. 12. The noun σεισμός employed here denotes only cosmic shaking in the NT.

In other apocalyptic texts there are several references to earthquakes. Thus we already find them along with other signs of the end (false prophecy, wars,

---

[12] Cf. Ps. 114:3-8; Is. 64:1 f.; 2 S. 22:8; Ps. 18:7; 68:8; 77:18; 99:1; 104:32 etc.

[13] G. v. Rad, "The Origin of the Concept of the Day of Yahweh," *Journal of Semitic Studies*, 4 (1959), 97-108.

[14] Cf. also on earthquakes accompanying God's judgment Am. 9:1; Is. 29:6; Jer. 8:16; 51:29; Ez. 26:10, 15.

[15] Ass. Mos. 10:4 f.: *et tremebit terra, usque ad fines suas concutietur ... sol non dabit lumen et in tenebris convertent se cornua lunae.*

[16] Descriptions of earthquakes are common along with stellar confusion and darkness and other earthly catastrophes, e.g., Sib., 3, 81 f. For details cf. Volz Esch., 147-163, esp. 155-158.

[17] Cf. Eth. En. 45:4.

[18] κατασείω occurs in Ac. 12:17; 13:16; 19:33; 21:40 and signifies a movement of the hand to ask for silence.

revolutions and famines) in the Synoptic Apocalypse, Mk. 13:8; Mt. 24:7; Lk. 21:11. [19] There are also numerous passages in Rev. in which σεισμοί are mentioned and depicted as terrors of the last time (6:12; 8:5; 11:13, 19; 16:18) in the tradition of later Jewish apocalyptic ideas, → 198, 19 ff. [20] In this connection reference should also be made to Hb. 12:26, which makes a distinctive scribal contrast between the shaking of the earth alone in relation to the first covenant (cf. Ju. 5:4) and the promise of the eschatological shaking of both heaven and earth (Hag. 2:6 LXX) whereby what is created will be done away and what is unshakable (βασιλεία ἀσάλευτος) will abide, Hb. 12:27 f. [21]

This apocalyptic idea of primitive Christianity that the σεισμός is an eschatological tribulation helps to explain a peculiarity in the story of the stilling of the storm in Mt. 8:23-27. Whereas Mk. 4:37 speaks of a great storm of wind λαῖλαψ μεγάλη ἀνέμου (Lk. 8:23 : λαῖλαψ ἀνέμου), Mt. 8:24 refers to a σεισμὸς μέγας ἐν τῇ θαλάσσῃ. The difference can hardly be explained by the idea of a disturbance of the lake by the storm. [22] The expression is rather chosen by the Evangelist as an intentional reminiscence of the apocalyptic significance of the σεισμός in order that the whole story may thus be given a typical and symbolical significance.

Other peculiarities in the Mt. version support this. Thus the two disciple incidents which precede in 8:19-22, and whose slogan ἀκολουθεῖν is taken up again only by Mt. in 8:23, do not seem to belong here naturally. Again certain dramatic touches in Mk., the ship full of water, Jesus asleep on the pillow in the stern, are omitted. Again, the disciples' cry for help is changed into a prayer. Again, the little faith of the disciples is rebuked before the stilling of the wind and the sea. Again, the concluding chorus takes a distinctive form in Mt. 8:27. All these traits help to give to the incident in Mt. the character of a paradigm of discipleship in general. [23]

The earthquakes which accompany the death and the resurrection of Jesus are another peculiarity in Mt. (27:51, 54; 28:2). In these accretions one may undoubtedly discern a motif which is very well-known in Jewish and especially Hellenistic literature, namely, that of depicting τέρατα which accompany the appearance or death of a god or a θεῖος ἀνήρ. [24] These features are considerably

---

[19] In Mk./Mt. these signs are expressly called ἀρχὴ ὠδίνων though distinguished from the end itself (ἀλλ᾽ οὔπω τὸ τέλος, Mk. 13:7; cf. Mt. 24:6). Lk. changes this in 21:9 in acc. with his view of history (ἀλλ᾽ οὐκ εὐθέως τὸ τέλος) and leaves out ἀρχὴ ὠδίνων. Cf. H. Conzelmann, Die Mitte d. Zeit³ (1960), 116-124, esp. 117-119.

[20] Note that earthquakes often come impressively at the end of a story or at a break in the passage.

[21] Cf. E. Käsemann, Das wandernde Gottesvolk² (1957), 29 f.

[22] So Pr.-Bauer⁵, s.v. σεισμός. The passages adduced from Schol. on Plat. Tim., 25c, ed. G. C. Greene (1938), 288; Artemid. Onirocr., II, 38; Diod. S., 26, 8; Max. Tyr., 9, 6a; 11, 7n do not support the idea of a special "sea-quake" (in the scientific sense). We do, of course, hear of the shaking of the sea, e.g., in prophecy, cf. Hag. 2:6 : ἔτι ἅπαξ ἐγὼ σείσω τὸν οὐρανὸν καὶ τὴν γῆν καὶ τὴν θάλασσαν καὶ τὴν ξηράν.

[23] Cf. G. Bornkamm, "Die Sturmstillung im Mt.-Ev.," Überlieferung u. Auslegung im Mt.-Ev., Wissenschaftliche Monographien zum Alten u. Neuen Test., 1 (1960), 48-53; also "Enderwartung u. Kirche im Mt.-Ev.," ibid., 27; H. J. Held, "Mt. als Interpret d. Wundergeschichten," ibid., 191 f. The group σείω/σεισμός is a favourite motif of Mt., cf. G. D. Kilpatrick, The Origins of the Gospel acc. to St. Matthew (1946), 131 f. Only Mt. 24:7 has par. in Mk. and Lk. Not all the ref. have a natural sense. In Mt. 21:10; 28:4 σεισθῆναι is used of the agitation of men, though evoked by the appearance of the Messiah → 198, 28 ff.

[24] Cf. Kl. Mt., ad loc.; Bultmann Trad., 305, n. 3 and Suppl., 42; Capelle, 361.

more in evidence in later apocryphal accounts of the death and resurrection of Jesus. [25] Nevertheless, further explanation is demanded for the events described in Mt. 27:51-53, the earthquake, the cleaving of the rocks, and the resurrection of the bodies of many saints who went into the holy city after the resurrection of Jesus and appeared to many. The point of this element in the story is unquestionably to bring out the eschatological significance of the death of Jesus. By His death the Messianic age is ushered in, and in later Jewish apocalyptic the resurrection of the dead is an integral part of this. Possibly one may also see here the further thought that Jerusalem is the providential site of the resurrection of the people of God. [26] It should also be considered that the relating of Jesus' death and the raising of the saints presupposes the idea of the descent into Hades and the vanquishing of death, which must yield up its captives. At any rate, Christian exegesis took the passage thus. And indeed, even if only in rudimentary and undeveloped form, the thought is present in the incident. [27] In the use of the motif this means that the earthquake here is not just intended generally as a sign of the end but denotes specifically the invasion of the realm of the dead by the divine Victor. Elsewhere a miraculous earthquake takes place when Paul and Silas are in prison at Philippi (Ac. 16:26). Here the foundations of the prison are shaken, the doors burst open and the chains of the prisoners fall off. The earthquake is God's answer to the songs of the two apostles. Similarly, the shaking (σαλευθῆναι) of the place where the community has gathered for prayer is a sign that its prayers are answered in Ac. 4:31. [28]

Bornkamm

| σημεῖον, σημαίνω, σημειόω, |
| ἄσημος, ἐπίσημος, εὔσημος, σύσσημον |

† σημεῖον.

Contents: A.: σημεῖον in the Greek World: I. Linguistic and Etymological Data; II. General Greek Usage: 1. σῆμα in the Early Epic; 2. σῆμα/σημεῖον in Other Greek:

---

[25] Ev. Pt. 6:21 cf. Ev. Naz. Fr. 21 (Hennecke[2], 122 and 97).
[26] Cf. H. Riesenfeld, "The Resurrection in Ez. XXXVII and in the Dura-Europos Paintings," *Uppsala Univ. Årsskrift* (1948, 11), esp. 35-38.
[27] J. Kroll, "Gott u. Hölle. Der Mythos v. Descensuskampfe," *Studien der Bibliothek Warburg*, 20 (1932), 6-10 etc. The contesting of this motif in Mt. 27:51-53 by W. Bieder, *Die Vorstellung v. der Höllenfahrt Christi* (1949), 49-51 is not convincing.
[28] Orig. Cels., II, 34 refers already to ancient par. to Paul's liberation (that of the Bacchantes and Dionysus in Eur. Ba., 445-448, 584-603; v. 498 is explicitly quoted). Cf. also Weinreich, 328-341, esp. 332-336 and 339 f. But the motif is used freely and in a new way by Lk., cf. Haench. Ag.[12] on 16:11-40 (440 f., 442). On Ac. 4:31, too, Haench. refers to par. in Ovid Metam., 15, 669-672; Verg. Aen., 12, 88-92. On the teratological element in the Hell. novel and apocr. Acts cf. R. Söder, *Die apokr. Apostelgeschichten u. d. romanhafte Lit. d. Antike* (1932), 103-112.

σημεῖον. On A.: Thes. Steph., *s.v.*; Pass., *s.v.*; Liddell-Scott, *s.v.*; Pr.-Bauer[5], *s.v.*; P. Stein, ΤΕΡΑΣ, Diss. Marburg (1909); H. Stockinger, *Die Vorzeichen im homer. Epos.*

a. Direct Use ; b. Transferred Use ; c. σημεῖα καὶ τέρατα; III. σημεῖον in Gnosticism.
B.: σημεῖον on Jewish Soil : I. The Greek Old Testament : 1. General Material on the
Pre-Greek Background : The Hebrew Equivalents ; 2. אוֹת in the Old Testament : a. Etymological and Linguistic Data ; b. א(ו)ת in the Lachish Ostraka ; c. The General Use of
אוֹת in the Old Testament ; d. אוֹת as an Object of Sense Perception ; e. אוֹת as a Means
of Confirmation; f. God's Signs and Wonders; g. Symbolical Prophetic Actions; h. Aramaic
את, אתא in Daniel and the Targums ; i. Summary ; 3. σημεῖον in Relation to אוֹת in the
Septuagint : a. σημεῖον for אוֹת in its Formal Character ; b. σημεῖον Interpretatively ;
c. σημεῖα καὶ τέρατα. II. Greek Judaism outside the Bible : 1. Philo ; 2. Josephus ;
3. Apocalyptic. C.: אות/אתא/סימן in Post-Biblical Judaism : I. The Dead Sea Scrolls :
1. Biblical Usage Continued ; 2. A New Sense ? II. אוֹת etc. in Rabbinic Literature : 1. אוֹת
= Mark ; 2. אוֹת = Letter ; III. סימן in Rabbinic Usage : 1. General Considerations ; 2. סימן
= Characteristic, Sign ; 3. Special Rabbinic Use of סימן. D.: σημεῖον in the New Testament : 1. General Data : 1. Statistics ; 2. Parallel Words and Concepts ; 3. Preliminary
Remarks on New Testament Usage ; II. σημεῖον in the Synoptic Gospels and Acts :
1. σημεῖον = Sign, Mark ; 2. The Sign of Jonah ; 3. The σημεῖον Demanded from Jesus ;
4. The Sign of the Son of Man ; 5. σημεῖον ἀντιλεγόμενον (Lk. 2:34) ; 6. σημεῖον in
Acts ; 7. σημεῖα καὶ τέρατα; III. σημεῖον in the Johannine Writings : 1. Features
Common to John and the Synoptists and Acts ; 2. General Aspects of the Distinctive
Johannine Usage ; 3. σημεῖον and ἔργον : a. General ; b. The Sign-Character of Jesus'
ἔργα as His Own ἔργα; c. The σημεῖα of Jesus as God's Revealing Witness to Jesus as
His Son; 4. σημεῖον and πίστις; 5. σημεῖον and λόγος; 6. σημεῖον and δόξα; 7. σημεῖα
of the Risen Lord ? 8. The Distinctiveness and Derivation of John's Special Use of σημεῖον :
a. The Singularity of the Use of σημεῖον in John's Gospel ; b. The Old Testament Background ; c. The Typological Character of Johannine σημεῖα; IV. σημεῖον in the Rest of
the New Testament : 1. Paul : a. General ; b. Specific ; 2. Hebrews. E. σημεῖον in the
Post-Apostolic Fathers.

A. σημεῖον in the Greek World.

I. Linguistic and Etymological Data.

σημεῖον is a development of σῆμα / Doric σᾶμα by way of Ionic σημήϊον / Doric
σᾱμήϊον and related constructs. [1] It occurs only in the form σῆμα in the early epic
and σῆμα / σᾶμα did not disappear later but persisted until well on in the Chr. era. [2]
Esp. in prose, however, σημεῖον came into more general use. It shares with σῆμα /
σᾶμα the sense of "sign," "characteristic," "mark," with its many nuances. Etym.
research has hardly reached any assured results regarding the original sense of the word.
To-day it is usually [3] traced back to Indo-Eur. dhiā-mn, Sanskr. dhyāma [4] "thought." [5]
But this is little if any help.

Ihre Typik u. ihre Bedeutung (1959), On B.: C. A. Keller, *Das Wort OTH als "Offenbarungszeichen Gottes,"* Diss. Basel (1946). On D.: Trench, 218-223; D. Mollat, "Le
semeion johannique," *Bibliotheca Ephemeridum Theologicarum Lovanensium,* 13 (1959),
209-218; J. P. Charlier, "La notion du signe (Sêmeion) dans le IVe évangile," *Revue des
sciences philosophiques et théologiques,* 43 (1959), 434-448.
    [1] Cf. the list in Liddell-Scott, *s.v.*
    [2] Cf. P. Masp., II, 67, 163, 37 (6th cent. A.D.), also σημεῖον *ibid.,* 67, 156, 34; 67, 164, 12,
→ n. 26.
    [3] Cf. Boisacq, 861; Hofmann, 310 f.; Schwyzer, I, 322.
    [4] K. Brugmann, *Grundriss d. vergleichenden Grammatik d. idg. Sprachen,* I² (1897), 275.
    [5] E. Leumann, " 'Suppletivwesen' im Nordarischen," ZvglSpr, 57 (1930), 194; also "Das
nordarische (sakische) Lehrgedicht des Buddhismus," *Abh. f. d. Kunde des Morgenlandes,*
20 (1933-1936), associates with the Gk. σᾶμα the East Iranian *ššāma* "face," "sign."
[But this is phonetically difficult as far as the Greek is concerned, Kirsch.]

II. General Greek Usage.

1. σῆμα in the Early Epic.

a. Since σημεῖον does not occur in the earlier Gk. epic (→ 201, 30 ff.), one must begin with the older but equivalent σῆμα, which is an established part of the vocabulary. The only significant point about this is that one may still see in Homer that the word denotes optical impressions which suggest or make possible certain insights. Thus in Hom. Il., 2, 353 the lightning of Zeus which all see at the beginning of the expedition against Troy is a fateful sign, ἐναίσιμα σήματα, and in 9, 236 f. it is a happy omen making known the favour of the god : Ζεὺς δέ σφι Κρονίδης ἐνδέξια σήματα φαίνων ἀστράπτει. Along with such favourable signs there are others which presage disaster : παραίσια σήματα, Il., 4, 381. In all these instances of σῆμα (always plur.), the fact that the sign brings knowledge is underlined by its use with the act. φαίνω. [6] What we have is a kind of process of revelation, though in a very general sense and with only an anthropological, not a theological reference. δείκνυμι can be chosen as well as φαίνω, Il., 13, 243 f. [7] A no less significant pt. is that at least occasionally epic expressly emphasises the miraculous character of that which gives knowledge by interpreting it as τέρας. [8]

Two passages in Hom. are esp. adapted to confirm this view of σῆμα and to bring it into sharper focus, namely, Il., 23, 326 ff.; Od., 8, 192 ff. In the first case σῆμα is a prominent ξύλον supported both to left and right by white rocks. It serves as a turning-pt. in chariot races. The poet leaves it an open question whether it is originally a monument (σῆμα) to someone long dead (331) or the stele-type kerb-stone of a race-track of former days (332). Two obvious marks of σῆμα, namely, prominence and wide visibility, are to be seen again in the second passage, for here σῆμα, set down as a τέρμα (193), is of such a kind that even a blind man can identify it by touch ; i.e., it is a stick set in the earth. Hence σῆμα is less a sign than an indication or pointer. Intrinsically there is in the word an act. element, and it may be that its later replacement by σημεῖον is connected with the fact that a more abstract term was needed though one which would retain the same idea. Linguistically σημεῖον is related to σῆμα as μνημεῖον is to μνῆμα.

b. A first step on the way to a more general use of σῆμα may be seen when already in Hom. the word is employed for acoustic impressions. An instructive passage in this regard is Hom. Od., 20, 91 ff. [9] Odysseus on his return home receives from Zeus the sign for which he prays. It consists on the one side in a declaration of good omen (φήμη) [10] in the "imprecation" [11] of a maid busy at the mill and on the other in a Διὸς τέρας ἄλλο outside the house, in a clap of heavenly thunder from Olympus. The essential pt. is that the thunder causes the woman to turn to Zeus, for, since there is no cloud in the sky, she can understand it only on the assumption that Zeus wants to give someone a τέρας. Thus her prayer is for the ἄναξ Odysseus a σῆμα, a good omen, which he seeks in view of the day of revenge on the morrow. [12] Apart from the scanning

---

[6] Twelve ref. in Stockinger, 157.

[7] Hence δείκνυμι can also be used abs. in the sense of δείκνυμι σῆμα, e.g., Hom. Od., 3, 173 f., where a τέρας is specifically meant.

[8] Cf. not only Hom. Od., 3, 173 but also the very impressive example in Od., 21, 413 ff.: Ζεὺς δὲ μεγάλ' ἔκτυπε σήματα φαίνων· γήθησέν τ' ἄρ' ἔπειτα πολύτλας δῖος Ὀδυσσεύς, ὅττι ῥά οἱ τέρας ἧκε Κρόνου πάϊς ἀγκυλομήτεω.

[9] Cf. on this Stockinger, 75 f.

[10] "... φῆμαι are utterances which are heard accidentally and relate to what is in the mind of those who hear them even though they have not the least connection with this," Nilsson, I², 166. On φήμη cf. also Stockinger, 144-146.

[11] Stockinger, 137, 146, 155.

[12] Hom. Od., 20, 111: ἥ ῥα μύλην στήσασα ἔπος φάτο, σῆμα ἄνακτι.

of the sky by the girl the whole passage has to do with hearing and what is heard. Yet one may see how strong was the influence of the visible element in σῆμα even here from the fact that twice [13] φαίνω is combined with τέρας, which intrinsically relates to perception by the eye. Related is the fact that in its whole range of usage σῆμα — and later σημεῖον — is orientated to a clear statement or assertion which holds good irrespective of explanations. This clarity distinguishes σῆμα even from → τέρας, close though the use of the two is in so many respects. [14] It is worth noting that we find a similar usage in Hesiod, who in Op., 450 says of the cry of the crane in autumn, which announces the season of ploughing: ἦτ᾽ ἀρότοιό τε σῆμα φέρει, καὶ χείματος ὥρην δεικνύει ὀμβρηροῦ. Here (→ 202, 14 f.) the verb δείκνυμι is also used with σῆμα; this has a fundamental reference to perception with the eye.

c. The basic features of σῆμα as they were worked out later characterise its use in this early period too. Thus in the incident in which Hector challenges the Achaeans and one of their number is chosen to meet him in a duel the poet has Ajax say: γνῶ δὲ κλήρου σῆμα ἰδών ..., Hom. Il., 7, 189. The presupposition here is the preceding information that each hero who takes part in the selection provides his own lot with its own "mark" [15] before all the lots are cast into the helmet of Agamemnon: οἱ δὲ κλῆρον ἐσημήναντο ἕκαστος, Il., 7, 175. [16] The sense of σῆμα here is thus the very general one of "the mark by which someone or something is recognised." With ref. hereto it may thus be radically demanded of a σῆμα that it be very clear μάλ᾽ ἀριφραδές, Hom. Il., 23, 326; σήματ᾽ ἀριφραδέα, Hom. Od., 23, 225; cf. 24, 329, and indeed obvious δέελον, Hom. Il., 10, 466. If this is achieved, the word can be used in many different ways. It can be a sign heralding war σῆμα πολέμοιο, Hes. Scutum, 385. It can also be a monument which by its nature and by certain details denotes the last resting-place of a prominent man, Hom. Il., 7, 84 ff.; cf. 6, 419; Od., 1, 291 etc. It can also be the set finishing-point in a race, Hom. Il., 23, 326, or a mark for individual achievement, 23, 843; Od., 8, 192 and 195. But it can also be a distinguishing mark on the body which serves as identification, Od., 24, 329. Even a writing which both identifies and denounces, thus consigning the one who delivers it to death, can come under the category of σῆμα, Il., 6, 168 ff. [17]

d. By way of summary three things may be said. First, at the central point the early Greek use of σῆμα is quite uniform even where it seems to be divergent. Secondly, the word always has to do with an object or circumstance which makes possible or is designed to make possible a specific perception or insight. [18] Thirdly, it is not from the outset connected with the religious sphere; it acquires a religious nuance only when used in a religious context. [19] Its character is in the last analysis technical and functional; this is not refuted even when its object is a religious

---

[13] Od., 20, 101: ... τέρας ... φανήτω, ibid., 114: τέρας νύ τεῳ τόδε φαίνεις.

[14] Hom. differentiates the terms (→ 202, 15 ff.) quite clearly in the sense that a τέρας may be a σῆμα but does not have to be, though cf. → 206, 37 ff. The equation of the two without comment by Nilsson, I², 166 does not stand up to closer analysis. Stockinger, 153 defines σῆμα as compared with τέρας as "the more neutral term," and he would derive τέρας "from the sphere of manticism and magic" (154).

[15] Cf. ad loc. C. F. v. Nägelsbach, Homerische Theologie³ (1884), 182.

[16] The ref. is only to external marks.

[17] On σήματα λυγρά cf. U. v. Wilamowitz-Moellendorff, Die Ilias u. Hom. (1916), 304, n. 2.

[18] Cf. already → 202, 5 ff. What has been said corresponds fairly well to the def. in Suid., s.v. σημεῖον: σημεῖον· δι᾽ οὗ τὰ ἄδηλα καταλαμβάνεται παρὰ τοῖς Σκεπτικοῖς, ὃ ἀναιροῦσι διὰ συλλογισμῶν.

[19] Hence it is better not to follow Stockinger, 157, who theologises in Hom. the fairly common (→ n. 8) combining of σῆμα with φαίνω and suspects a weakened theophany in the background. Even if this were true, it would need to be expressed more clearly.

or moral truth. Even here it has nothing to do with revelation in the religious sense ; its reference is to disclosure as the indispensable presupposition of all knowledge.

2. σῆμα/σημεῖον in Other Greek.

Now that the nature of σῆμα has been clearly established, the wealth of nuances in the later usage of σῆμα / σημεῖον may be set forth in all its breadth. The two words can be taken together without difficulty, for σημεῖον is always given its meaning by σῆμα. On the other hand, since the core keeps the meaning within specific limits, chronological treatment is unnecessary. Indeed, certain peculiarities in σῆμα may very well be brought out in a general review. In the main σῆμα is less prominent, but it has persisted right on into modern Greek.

a. Direct Use. As "a visual sign by which someone or something is recognised," hence in the original and yet also a very diverse sense, σημεῖον esp., but also σῆμα, is found in the most varied combinations and contexts. It is the "symptom" of an illness or of health in the Gk. physicians, [20] cf. also Diog. L., VIII, 32 : τὰ σημεῖα νόσου καὶ ὑγιείας. As an indication that an animal is present and active it means "scent," σημεῖα δ᾽ οὔτε θηρὸς οὔτε του κυνῶν ἐλθόντος ... ἐξεφαίντο, Soph. Ant., 257 f. [21] Hdt., II, 38 can say that priests in Egypt test (δοκιμάζουσι) the suitability of animals for sacrifice by prescribed "indices" (προκείμενα σημήια) and if the test is passed they furnish the animals with a formal mark (σημαίνω) by their ring (→ lines 31 ff.), a provision being made that if a priest offers an unmarked animal (ἀσήμαντος) he must atone for this with death. Ships are known by their ensigns : σημεῖον ἐν ταῖς ναυσὶν ... ἐνεγέγραπτο, Aristoph. Ra., 933 [22] and, of course, in a fleet the admiral's ship is marked as such τὸ σημήιον ἰδὼν τῆς στρατηγίδος, Hdt., VIII, 92. In the same field σημεῖον is also the standard, esp. that of the king τὸ βασίλειον σημεῖον, Xenoph. An., I, 10, 12. Since standards indicate the position of soldiers, τὰ σημεῖα as a military tt. denotes the camp ἔξω τῶν σημείων, Xenoph. Cyrop., VIII, 3, 19. [23] The diadem is a σημεῖον because it marks a member of the royal house who is privileged to bear it, ibid., 3, 13. The warrior's shield is adorned with his σημεῖον, which also stamps on it the individuality of the owner, Aesch. Sept. c. Theb., 387 and 432; Eur. El., 256 etc.: σῆμα; Hdt., I, 171: σημήια. By way of analogy σημεῖον is also the signet of a ring which both indicates the owner and also serves to ratify his decisions, Aristoph. Eq., 952; cf. Plat. Theaet., 191d: δακτυλίων σημεῖα. σημεῖον is in fact any seal or stamp, BGU, IV, 1064, 18 (2nd cent. A.D.), also the brand on animals, BGU, II, 427, 30 (2nd cent. A.D.), whereby ownership may be recognised. [24] The basic meaning also makes possible and understandable the use of the word for a boundary or a mile-stone, Herodian Hist., II, 13, 9 (an order of Emperor Severus to the army): Members of the legions who took part in the murder of Pertinax, are commanded on penalty of death not to let themselves be captured ἐντὸς ἑκατοστοῦ σημείου ἀπὸ ᾽Ρώμης. Equally possible is the use for the escutcheon of a mummy which serves to identify the corpse (Preisigke Sammelbuch, 4387: Πανισκεῦτος κουρέως σῆμα) or for a heavenly sign or con-

---

Thus it is as well to make a careful distinction in Hom. between mid. φαίνομαι with ref. to the appearing of deities (for material cf. F. Pfister, Art. "Epiphanie" in Pauly-W., Suppl., 4 [1924], 279) and the act. φαίνω with ref. to σήματα.

[20] For examples cf. Liddell-Scott, s.v.

[21] By way of analogy σημεῖον means the "track" left by a man, though less as a confirmation that he was there — this would be ἴχνος — and more as a palpable proof that the report of his absence is correct.

[22] Cf. also Eur. Iph. Aul., 253 ff.; Thuc., VI, 31, 3.

[23] Every ἄρχων has his σημεῖον on his tent in the camp, Xenoph. Cyrop., VIII, 5, 13.

[24] For further examples cf. Preisigke Wört., s.v.

stellation, since the stars give important information about times and places, Eur. Rhes., 528 ff.; Ion, 1156 f.; cf. Arat. Phaen., 10 : αὐτὸς γὰρ τά γε σήματ᾽ ἐν οὐρανῷ ἐστήριξεν etc. [25] So, too, is that for a bodily mark either naturally or as the scar of a wound (→ 203, 27 f.) or through circumcision (Preisigke Sammelbuch, 15, 26 [155/156 A.D.] with ref. to the sons of priests). Another use is for the letter or stenographic symbol, P. Oxy., IV, 724, 3 (2nd cent. A.D.): a slave is given to a teacher of stenography (σημειογράφος) to learn the art (εἰς μάθησιν σημείων). It is particularly instructive that well on in the Chr. age (6th cent.) an illiterate person puts three crosses on a document instead of his name and the scribe who draws it up makes this primitive subscription valid by putting the name of his client (Πέτρου) under the crosses along with the word σῆμα, which in the context can only mean that Petros made the crosses himself and wished them to be understood as his signature, P. Masp., II, 67, 163, 37. [26] In mathematics σημεῖον is the point, Aristot. An. Post., 10, p. 76b, 5 etc. This list of very different meanings could be substantially increased without difficulty. [27]

In all the examples given someone or something is to be recognised and a fact or object perceived with a view to conceptual assimilation and correct classification. [28] The fact that the reference is to correctness and to this alone gives the use of the term an unusual diversity. Also connected with this is the fact that in the course of time, at least in literature, the original σῆμα was almost completely crowded out by σημεῖον.

An exception is the continuing use of σῆμα for "monument" etc., Aristoph. Thes., 886 and 888; Hdt., I, 93 etc.; Plat. Phaedr., 264d; Gorg., 493a with a play on σῶμα / σῆμα cf. Crat., 400b c etc.; Apoll. Rhod., I, 1061 f. etc. Plut. brings out well the special sense which the older term had in the lofty speech of his day as compared with synonyms. He uses it in Oth., 18, 1 (I, 1074e/1075a) along with τάφος and μνῆμα in such a way that σῆμα is the part of the τάφος which singles it out with the ἐπιγραφή, esp. when it is an expensive affair. The passage also shows how σῆμα could be used gen. for the stele → 203, 24 ff., [29] and once again one may see how much even in this later age σῆμα refers to what strikes the eye. [30]

b. Transferred Use. In a broader sense, too, σημεῖον came into more comprehensive use with the characteristic development of early beginnings. Thus in Hdt. it is a summons in the special military sense of a command to depart, VII, 128 : ἀνέδεξε σημήιον καὶ τοῖσι ἄλλοισι ἀνάγεσθαι. This is the more significant in that from the very first in military speech [31] audio-visual elements had been combined in the concept of the signal. More basic, however, is the fact that σημεῖον here becomes a special term for a manifestation of will which impresses itself upon the will of others and shapes their insight. This kind of σημεῖον is fundamentally on the same level as the spoken word, whether the detailed ref. be to enlightenment, instruction, direction, or command.

---

[25] Acc. to tradition a lost work of Theophrast. was entitled περὶ σημείων ὑδάτων καὶ πνευμάτων καὶ χειμώνων καὶ εὐδιῶν.

[26] In par. documents of the same period in P. Masp., II, 67, 156, 34; 67, 164, 12 we find σῆμα, not σημεῖον, → n. 2.

[27] Later popular usage offers many other applications. These are possible because the word has from the very first a formal technical character which makes a very broad use possible, cf. the dict.

[28] In this connection it should not be overlooked that in many of the examples given above (→ 202, 11 ff.) verbs of perceiving are again used with σημεῖον.

[29] For further examples cf. Preisigke Wört., s.v.

[30] There are many instances of σῆμα/σᾶμα, in part synon. with μνῆμα/μνᾶμα, in W. Peek, Griech. Grabgedichte (1960), passim.

[31] In other ways, too, the word plays a role as a military tt. Cf. the dict. and in part what follows.

This is, of course, esp. true when the subject of the σημεῖον is a divine person who in this way wants to tell a man something or to give him necessary information. In such cases the σημεῖον is more embracing than the oracle or dream but it also needs a relevant and competent explanation which will lead to correct understanding. [32] Alexander received such an explanation of an enigmatic event during the siege of Gaza, and it was the more necessary in this case in view of the fact that the σημεῖον had two climaxes. A bird dropped a clod of earth on the king and wounded him, but then perished in the machinery of a siege-engine. The interpretation, which came to pass, was to the effect that the king would be wounded but that he would also be successful in taking the city, Plut. Alex., 25 (I, 679b). Only when one realises how far in such contexts σημεῖον had for antiquity the sense of insight into the mysterious ways of destiny [33] does the term lose on the one side the purely superimposed appearance of emphatically denoting in some circumstances a divine demonstration of religious content. Indeed, this cannot be seriously considered if only because, esp. in later antiquity, even a far-reaching σημεῖον does not have to be divine, as may be shown quite easily from Plut. On the other side this aspect of the use of the term is very closely connected with that which it has in logical deductions and related mental exercises.

Here, whether in philosophy or the appeal to common sense, σημεῖον takes on the meaning argument or proof in the sense of an irrefutable statement or even example in so far as this serves to clarify something and to lead from doubt to certainty. As argument σημεῖον is primarily related to logic and thus it may sometimes need formal refutation, e.g., Plat. Resp., II, 368b : δοκῶ γάρ μοι ἀδύνατος εἶναι — σημεῖον δέ μοι ὅτι ... οὐκ ἀπεδέξασθέ μου. [34] In the sense of example it first serves to illustrate and only then to confirm, e.g., Ael. Arist. Or., 29, 5 : σημεῖον δέ· οὐδεὶς γοῦν οὓς ἀγαπᾷ καὶ οἷς ἀγαθόν τι συμβούλεται, τούτοις κακῶς ἀκούουσιν ἐφήδεται. In the sense of proof a σημεῖον settles and confirms. It is typical that the various shades of usage merge into one another, as in an expression like : ἐγὼ ... τοῦτο ποιοῦμαι σημεῖον ὑπὲρ τῶν γυναικῶν, Plut. Amat., 5 (II, 751c).

In the transferred sense, too, the stress of σημεῖον is still on perception and resolve, and it is so in developed and indispensable form. Even in the distinctive process of what is in the end result a very varied usage the word retains its original, as it were technical character. It continually resists integration into a specifically religious terminology in contexts in which it refers to the actual or supposed direct intervention of divine persons or powers. Even where a σημεῖον serves to mediate religious insights, its reference remains (→ 202, 12 ff.) anthropological and does not become theological. [35]

c. σημεῖα καὶ τέρατα. This phrase, which combines two words characteristically different at root (→ n. 14 and → τέρας), would seem to occur for the first time in Polyb., 3, 112, 18. This says ironically of the population of Rome when threatened by Hannibal after the battle of Cannae : σημείων δὲ καὶ τεράτων πᾶν μὲν ἱερόν,

---

[32] Cf. Plat. Phaedr., 244c d with its distinction of οἰονοϊστική and οἰωνιστικὴ τέχνη.
[33] Thus one of the presuppositions of a σημεῖον in the sense of word is that it be clear and understandable, cf. already Soph. El., 23 f., 885 f. In this connection it should not be overlooked that it is under the same requirement as the word of the philosopher, cf. Plat.
[34] To study σημεῖον in Plat. would take us too far afield. On the usage of Aristot. cf. H. Bonitz, Index Aristotelicus² (1955), s.v. The word plays a special part in Hell. logic. Cf. Philodemus De signis, ed. P. H. and E. A. de Lacy (1941) [Dihle].
[35] The rhetorician and aretalogist Ael. Arist., who claims special interest as a resident of Asia Minor in the 2nd cent. A.D., does not deviate here. He is not acquainted with any specifically religious use of σημεῖον. Setting aside other passages where the use is purely technical, one may see this from Or. Sacr., 2, 73, which refers to a μέγιστον σημεῖον τοῦ θεοῦ τῆς δυνάμεως.

πᾶσα δ᾽ ἦν οἰκία πλήρης. The saying is obviously castigating the fear and naive superstition of the Romans and not emphasising their piety. The tone of Plut. is similar when he says that in the last days before his death Alexander made full surrender to superstition (ἐνέδωκε πρὸς τὰ θεῖα) and became restless and fearful, and thus οὐδὲν ἦν μικρὸν οὕτω τῶν ἀήθων καὶ ἀτόπων ὃ μὴ τέρας ἐποιεῖτο καὶ σημεῖον, ἀλλὰ θυομένων καὶ καθαιρόντων καὶ μαντευόντων μεστὸν ἦν τὸ βασίλειον, Plut. Alex., 75, 1 (I, 706a b). Two related passages in Appian also refer to superstitions. The first describes the mood in the Roman Senate when Caesar had crossed the Rubicon (Bell. Civ., II, 144). The second speaks of the mood in Rome at the height of the conflict between Octavian and Antonius (ibid., IV, 14). In both cases there is ref. to strange events rooted in superstition, e.g., raining blood or stones, sweating idols, lightning striking sanctuaries and statues of the gods, the clash of weapons and neighing of horses for no discernible cause, abnormalities of nature etc. In the first passage all these remarkable phenomena are grouped under τέρατα ... πολλὰ καὶ σημεῖα οὐράνια, in the second they are simply τέρατα καὶ σημεῖα, the ref. of οὐράνια being simply to the fact that some of the things like rain and lightning come down from heaven. One may suspect that in the first ref. the combination of the two terms is not a strict one but is a kind of formula of addition in which two thing that are not the same, τέρας and σημεῖον, are brought together because of their significance for helpless man. In the second passage μάντεις are thought to be needed, and these are brought from Etruria by the Senate. [36] In this connection it should be noted that τέρας and σημεῖον could also be combined as alternatives, as the passage from Plut. shows → 203, 6 f. This is supported by Plut. Sept. Sap. Conv., 3 (II, 149c), where in face of a monster born to a mare (half horse and half man) the demand is made: ἐπισκέψασθαι ... πότερον ἄλλως γέγονεν ἤ τι σημεῖόν ἐστι καὶ τέρας, and the narrator makes a joke of the whole thing by saying that in such a situation Thales could only advise that young grooms should not be used with horses or they should be given wives. Only Ael. Var. Hist., 12, 57 varies from this pattern when in connection with his account of the siege of Gaza by Alexander he speaks of θεοί who sent σημεῖα καὶ τέρατα to intimate the future. Yet superstition is undoubtedly speaking here rather than deeper theological or even religious insight. Fundamentally, then, this odd use does not really go beyond what has been said thus far in this section.

In sum [37] it is thus right to exercise the greatest caution when on Greek soil expressions formed of σημεῖον and τέρας offer themselves for religious interpretation.

III. σημεῖον in Gnosticism.

Difficult though it is to gain a comprehensive picture due to the lack of indexes, there can be no doubt but that σημεῖον does not play any independent role in Gnosticism. So far as may be seen the word is uncommon, it does not seem to bear any specific sense, and above all it is not distinctively religious.

In the so-called Mithras Liturgy σημεῖον does not occur. There are few examples in the Hermetica. In Corp. Herm., III, 2 (Nock-Fest., I, 44, 15) σημεῖον means "constellation" → 204, 41 ff. In Fr., 24 (IV, 56, 9) the sense is "proof," "example" (καὶ

---

[36] Similarly interpretation is indispensable for Epict. when a σημεῖον, which is usually capable of more than one meaning, either is or seems to be present. But Epict. rejects the μάντις as a concession to human cowardice — which is quite consistent from his standpt. — and appeals instead to the inner voice which knows good and evil, cf. Diss., II, 7: πῶς μαντευτέον;

[37] Unfortunately I could not check a ref. in IPE, I², 352, 25 (Chersonesus, 2nd cent. B.C.) adduced in Liddell-Scott, s.v. σημεῖον.

τούτου σημεῖόν ἐστιν ...), and this is also the sense in Fr., 26 (IV, 84, 15 [τῆς παλινδρομίας ἐναργὲς τοῦτο σημεῖον ...]) → 203, 18 ff. A magical prayer to the moon goddess[38] in P. Lond., I, 121 (3rd cent. A.D.) uses σημεῖον in the sense of "form in which the nature of something specific expresses itself." Another text (Scott, IV, 146, 9 f.) says of an angel that he bears his own σημεῖον on his head, i.e., a distinguishing mark[39] which makes individual distinction possible → 204, 29 ff. The use of σημεῖον in all these passages[40] stays within the traditional framework and since the word retains its technical character nothing new is added to our picture of it.

In the Gnostic Mandaean writings רוש(ו)מא "sign" means much the same as σημεῖον in Gk. Gnostic texts. More common than this, in its broad sense as "characteristic," "sign," "mark," it has no specific emphasis and no independent religious content. In particular it does not denote a miracle as such. Derived from רשם "to sign," "to mark," רוש(ו)מא is used to some degree for the uncommon אתא → 217, 30 ff.[41] The term attains its main importance in connection with baptism, which takes place in the "Jordan" → VI, 621, 19 ff.[42] It is called "pure sign" רושומא דאכיא Lidz. Liturg., 49, 5; 51, 9 etc. or "sign of life" רושומא דהייא ibid., 27, 6; 40, 3 etc.[43] In this sphere of sacramental ceremonial the usage is not wholly consistent[44] and it certainly has nothing whatever to do with the solemn marking of the baptismal candidate during the recitation of the formula after immersion.[45] Sometimes the word seems to be synon. with מאצבותא "baptism" to the degree that this carries with it a marking, cf. Lidz. Liturg., 152, 8.[46] In this very fact, however, it ultimately betrays once again its formal character.

B. σημεῖον on Jewish Soil.

I. The Greek Old Testament.

1. General Material on the Pre-Greek Background : The Hebrew Equivalents.

σημεῖον occurs in the Gk. OT some 125 times (including Sir.), 85 times for a Heb. original. The main usage is in the Pent. and the prophets ; the word plays a comparatively minor role in the historical books and the Wisdom literature, including non-canonical books. In a few passages there is no specific original but σημεῖον interprets the HT. This is so in Ez. 9:4, 6, where a certain part of the population of Jerusalem is to be marked on the forehead with a Tau, the last letter of the Heb. alphabet originally written in the form of a cross. Here the name of the letter, which would mean nothing to a Gk. reader, is transl. by σημεῖον, so that the reader can get a picture of something familiar in his own world, → 205, 3 ff. → σφραγίς. The same applies in Jer. 6:1, where מַשְׂאֵת which is transl. σημεῖον, probably means a signalling installation.[47] In some instances σημεῖον is used for Heb. נֵס which means something prominent and therefore easily seen, Nu. 21:8, 9 : a high pole ; Is. 11:12; 13:2; 18:3; Ιερ. 28(51):12, 27:

---

[38] Reitzenstein Poim., 262 f.
[39] Cf. on this A. J. Festugière, La révélation d'Hermès Trismégiste, I² (1950), 257, n. 2.
[40] Corp. Herm., III, 3 (Nock-Fest., I, 45, 14) has σημεῖα ἀγαθῶν, but the text is uncertain (cf. the apparatus).
[41] Cf. E. Segelberg, MASBUTA (1958), 135, n. 5.
[42] Cf. רושמא דיארדנא (Lidz. Liturg., 274, 2 etc.) as a term for baptism.
[43] E. S. Drower, Water into Wine (1956), 161, n. 1.
[44] Cf. Segelberg, op. cit. (→ n. 41), 135-140.
[45] Ibid., 53 f.
[46] Ibid., 54.
[47] Some comm. suggest a high mast, others a signal of fire and smoke. משאת also embraces אות in the Lachish Ostraka, 4 → 209, 22 ff.

a martial banner, sometimes with the horn which is blown to the battle ; Is. 33:23 : a ship's flag etc.,[48] but also a warning signal which cannot be missed, Nu. 26:10.[49] In 2 Ch. 32:24 σημεῖον is also used for מוֹפֵת cf. Ex. 7:9; 11:9 f., which is always connected with a miraculous occurrence and is usually rendered → τέρας in the LXX ; it is not apparent why σημεῖον is selected in these passages.[50] In a good four-fifths of the instances in the canonical OT, however, אוֹת is the original. Since אוֹת for its part, apart from relatively few exceptions, is consistently transl. σημεῖον in the LXX, it is essential to grasp first the meaning of the Heb. word if we are to understand σημεῖον in biblical Gk.

2. אוֹת in the Old Testament.

a. Etymological and Linguistic Data.

The etym. of the word is uncertain. Though it is common in West Semitic, attempts to trace and define the underlying root have thus far been unsuccessful.[51] The fact is that practically no light at all is shed on the historical understanding of the term by connecting it with the Accadian *ittu*, as it customary in many circles. *ittu*[52] can sometimes be an "oracular sign" but it also has other very different meanings. An attempt to make "advice" the main sense and thus to put it in the vocabulary of commerce[53] has been abandoned by its author.[54] On the other side *ittu* has been associated with עֵת rather than אוֹת and the suggestion made that its original sense is "a period of time determined in advance."[55] As yet the Semitic world more generally has not been able to take us much further.

b. א(ו)ת in the Lachish Ostraka.

A non-biblical instance of אוֹת from the OT period is found in Lachish[56] Ostrakon, 4, probably in two passages if,[57] for good reasons, the text of line 10 is transl. as follows : "He has affirmed[58] that we at the signal station (משאת → n. 47) at Lachish pay heed to all the signals (אתת = אותות)[59] which my lord[60] has given ; for a sign (את) was not

---

[48] Cf. the comm., *ad loc.* and → 204, 22 ff.

[49] נֵס has been variously transl. and interpreted. Thus Κύριός μου καταφυγή ("The Lord is my refuge") is a good rendering of the watchword יהוה נִסִּי in Ex. 17:15.

[50] It is clear why in Ju. 20:38 LXX (Cod B) מוֹעֵד "agreement" is rendered σημεῖον: It has to be made clear.

[51] A first suggestion is אוה "to establish," "to mark" (?). Cf. on this the Heb. dict. and bibl. *s.v.*

[52] Cf. *The Assyrian Dictionary*, ed. I. J. Gelb *et al.*, 7 (1960), 304-310 with bibl.

[53] B. Landsberger, *Die Serie* ana ittišu, *Materialien zum Sumerischen Lexikon*, I (1937), 109.

[54] B. Landsberger, "Jahreszeiten im Sumerisch-Akkadischen," *Journal of Near Eastern Studies*, 8 (1949), 294, n. 146.

[55] M. B. Rowton, " 'Tuppu' and the Date of Hammurabi," *Journal of Near Eastern Studies*, 10 (1951), 184-204.

[56] *Lachish, I (Tell ed-Duweir): The Lachish Letters*, by H. Torczyner *et al.* (1938), 75-87; ill. E. Würthwein, *Der Text d. AT* (1952), Ill. 3; text in Heb. K. Galling, *Textbuch z. Gesch. Israels* (1950), 64 f.; cf. also J. Hempel, "Die Ostraka v. Lakiš," ZAW, 56 (1938), 132 f.; K. Elliger, "Die Ostraka v. Lachis," PJB, 34 (1938), 30-58, esp. 44.

[57] Cf. Elliger, *loc. cit.*; also "Zu Text u. Schrift d. Ostraka v. Lachis," ZDPV, 62 (1939), 70-72.

[58] On this transl. cf. Elliger, *op. cit.* (→ n. 56), 54, n. 1; *op. cit.* (→ n. 57), 70-72.

[59] On the orthography cf. Gn. 1:14; Ex. 4:17, 28 etc.

[60] The ref. is to the superior officer of the writer.

seen from Azekah." [61] The ostrakon contains a military report from the penultimate phase in the battle between the troops of Nebuchadnezzar and those of the Judean king Zedekiah in the pause after the temporary withdrawal of the besieging army in the summer of 588 (Jer. 37:5 ff.) [62] and it obviously relates to the organisation or reorganisation of intelligence in the Jewish fortresses whose task it was to guard the routes to the Jewish highlands and Jerusalem against Egyptian invasion from the Philistine plain. This shows that in this ostrakon את is a signal such as can be given by a signalling device, whether by fire or smoke, for the transmission of information. If so, א(ו)ת is here a word which receives its specific content only from the sphere in which it is used. On this ground a recent attempt to show that Lachish Ostrakon, 4 is directed to the prophet Jeremiah, and that the ref. of אתת is to miraculous proofs which are required to endorse a prophet acc. to Dt. 13:2, [63] can only be regarded as mistaken, quite apart from other objections to such an interpretation.

c. The General Use of אות in the Old Testament.

The present HT contains אות 79 times, twice in the same v. at Ex. 4:8 and also Ps. 74:4. [64] About half of all the ref. are in the Pentateuch (39) and another quarter in the major prophets Is., Jer. and Ez. (19). In the narrative books, then, the term is comparatively much less prominent. It will be shown later (→ 219, 5 ff.) that it is illegitimate to draw deductions from this, esp. in a theological respect.

A basic pt. to note is that in a whole series of instances (no less than 18) [65] אות is closely connected with מופת. This is the more remarkable when one also considers that מופת occurs only 36 times in the Heb. OT. In the combination אות usually comes first and the combined expression is in the plur. So far as one can see, it is only relatively late that מופת occurs alone in biblical Hebrew, i.e., in exilic and post-exilic works. [66] We cannot pursue here the question of its meaning → n. 105; 106; → τέρας. It should be pointed out, however, that together אות and מופת are found esp. in Dt.

---

[61] Torczyner, 84 takes נראה as 1st pers. impf. q and את as acc. particle. G. R. Driver (Torczyner, loc. cit.) had suggested נראה be taken as ni and hence את as אֹת, but without winning Torczyner's approval. Hempel, op. cit., U. Cassuto, "Die Ostraka v. Lakisch," MGWJ, 83 (1939), 88, and J. B. Pritchard, Ancient Near Eastern Texts[2] (1955), 322 transl. as Torczyner does. The ref. seems to be to communications, however, and the relevant sentence is perhaps reporting that for reasons which cannot be discussed here (but cf. Elliger, op. cit. [→ n. 56] 54) Azekah — an esp. strong fortified pt. near Lachish acc. to Jer. 34:7 — has dropped out. לא נראה (ni) is OT Hebr., Ju. 19:30; 1 K. 10:12. Translations like "we no longer see the signals of Azekah" (F. M. Cross, "Lachish Letter IV," Bulletin of the American Schools of Oriental Research, 144 [1956], 25) give a false impression of what is actually in the text by assuming that this contains אתת and not the intrinsically broader את.
[62] Elliger, op. cit. (→ n. 56), 30 f.
[63] H. Tur-Sinai (Torczyner), "Lachish Letter IV," JQR, NS, 39 (1948/49), 365-377. Keller (5), in spite of his conviction that אוה derives from the sacral sphere, expressly accepts its secular use in Lachish Ostr., 4.
[64] In Ps. 74:4 many modern comm. either omit the second אתות (e.g., H. Schmidt, Die Ps., Hndbch. AT, I, 15 [1934], ad loc.: dittography; so also Keller, 151, n. 9) or alter the text (H. Gunkel, Die Ps., Hndkomm. AT, 14[4] [1926], ad loc.; F. Nötscher, Die Ps.[4] [1953], ad loc.: beṯôḵō ?). But in view of v. 9 it is best to retain the traditional text (also presupposed in the LXX) with the second אתות.
[65] Ex. 7:3; Dt. 4:34; 6:22; 7:19; 13:2 f.; 26:8; 28:46; 29:2; 34:11; Is. 8:18; 20:3; Jer. 32:20 f.; Ps. 78:43; 105:27; 135:9; Neh. 9:10.
[66] Exceptions Ex. 4:21; Dt. 13:2 f.

(9 times) and that the use in other OT books seems to follow that of Dt. [67] Obviously
this is all important in any attempt to fix the meaning of אוֹת and it must therefore
be kept in mind, esp. as the LXX ᴸormally has σημεῖα καὶ τέρατα for the combination of the two words → 216, 9 ff., cf. → 206, 37 ff.

d. אוֹת as an Object of Sense Perception.

From a whole series of sayings which contain אוֹת it may be gathered with
certainty that what is denoted thereby can be perceived with the senses and is
often meant to be so. As a rule the reference is to visual perception.

In Ps. 86:17 the psalmist prays God for an אוֹת for good that those who hate him
may see it and be ashamed, since God helps and comforts him. In Is. 66:19 there is a
direct connection between the אוֹת given by God and the manifesting of His rule among
the nations, since the former makes the latter plain. In Gn. 9:12 ff. the rainbow is an אוֹת
of the covenant (אוֹת־הַבְּרִית → 214, 12 ff.) between God and the descendants of Noah,
and God says expressly that He will look on this and — like men — be reminded by
it of His covenant with them. Nu. 14:22 and Ps. 74:9 also refer explicitly to the seeing of
אוֹתוֹת. The former speaks of God's wonderful acts done before all eyes in Egypt (cf.
also Nu. 14:11; Dt. 4:34; 7:19; 26:8), while the latter refers not so much to military or
national symbols as to specifically religious symbols which either belonged to the early
equipment of the Jerusalem temple or were perhaps displayed in certain liturgical
practices peculiar to the religion of Yahweh, cf. Ex. 31:13, 17: the Sabbath as אוֹת.
No less conclusive are numerous passages which do not refer formally to seeing but
presuppose that something visible is denoted by the term. Thus circumcision is אוֹת
and is visible, though this does not have to be said particularly, Gn. 17:10 ff. So is the
blood which on the night of the exodus from Egypt the Israelites were to daub on the
posts of their houses to distinguish them, Ex. 12:7 ff. [68] Jer. 10:2 speaks of terror at
אֹתוֹת הַשָּׁמַיִם, i.e., extraordinary heavenly phenomena. This presupposes that the phenomena may be seen, and the same applies when Gn. 1:14 uses אֹתֹת for the lights in
the firmament of heaven which divide day and night. In Is. 19:19 f. an altar (מִזְבֵּחַ)
and a stone monument (מַצֵּבָה) in Egypt are called אוֹת and עֵד for Yahweh inasmuch
as they point to His relation to His chosen people, which is not to be disregarded
→ 213, 32 ff. In Nu. 2:2 each tribe of the people has its אוֹת around which the members
gather and which has to be visible if it is to achieve its purpose ; it is probably a special
emblem. [69] Visibility is plainly presupposed when Aaron's rod (Nu. 17:10) or the plates
on the altar (Nu. 16:38) or the twelve pillars which after the crossing of the Jordan
Joshua set up near the river, and which were later moved to Gilgal (Jos. 4:6 ff.), are
all called אוֹת; this is especially true of the pillars since it is also said of them that
they are to serve as a lasting memorial (לְזִכָּרוֹן ... עַד־עוֹלָם), cf. v. 7 and also vv. 21 ff. [70]
Job 21:29 should also be noted in this connection even though אוֹת serves a specific
purpose here, as strictly it always does → 213, 22 ff. [71]

---

[67] Keller, 60.
[68] Cf. esp. Ex. 12:13 : "... an אוֹת for your protection : when I see the blood ..." The
anthropomorphism on God's lips is irrelevant in this context.
[69] אוֹת is distinguished here from דֶּגֶל which serves also as a standard for each group of
three tribes.
[70] Cf. also אוֹת עוֹלָם in Is. 55:13. This v. raises special problems which cannot be discussed
here, cf. the comm., ad loc.
[71] Cf. F. Stier, Das Buch Ijjob (1954), 305, ad loc.

Compared with seeing, hearing plays only an indirect role in relation to אוֹת.
The word has no direct connection with hearing.

Only once is the verb "to hear" (שָׁמַע) used with אוֹת, and even here it is used in
such a way as indirectly to emphasise the visual character of what is denoted by אוֹת.
In Ex. 4:8 God is considering what to do if the Israelites to whom He sends Moses as
His envoy, and before whom He will demonstrate that Moses is this by אֹתֹת, refuse
to believe or to hear him (לְקֹל הָאֹת הָרִאשׁוֹן), i.e., on the ground of the first אוֹת. Acc. to
the total context of Ex. 3:13 ff. cf. 4:10 ff. this אוֹת and all the further אוֹתֹת which
Moses is to perform are meant to validate him in order that the Israelites may listen to
what he has to say to them on God's commission, and in the last resort, therefore,
may hear him. The hearing awaited here is not a hearing of the אֹתֹת but a hearing
of the words of Moses which are to be accredited by them. With this alone is it in
keeping that Ex. 4:30 f. expressly says that the אֹתֹת are done in the eyes of all the
people and achieve their purpose of kindling confidence in Moses. In the same way
Nu. 14:22 distinguishes between seeing the אֹתֹת of God (→ 201, 15 ff.) and hearing His
voice. There is no instance of *othoth* speaking in the OT. [72] In connection with speech
of any kind their function is on a different level, → 213, 12 ff.

The visual character of the word is probably expressed also in verbs which
relate to the occurring of the אוֹת. These also underline the basic objectivity of
its content. Finally, both are indicated again by the role which the hand often
plays in connection with the אוֹת.

Most instructive are the verses which use שִׂים and שִׁית for the occurring of the אוֹת,
treating it as a monument which is set up. This applies esp. to God's wonders in Egypt
in various contexts, Ex. 10:1 f.; Jer. 32:20; Ps. 78:43; 105:27. It is also found in relation
to a future אוֹת in Is. 66:19. The "mark" of Cain can also be spoken of thus in Gn. 4:15.
Factuality is suggested when the word is combined with עָשָׂה "to make," [73] שָׁלַח "to send"
(Ps. 135:9) and בּוֹא "to come." [74] The first and third of these seem to be ancient. [75]
On the other hand, it must be regarded as a feature characteristic of the view of God
and the world in Dt. that there is almost stereotyped ref. to God's hand in connection
with the wonders in Egypt in Dt. 4:34; 6:21 f.; 7:19; 26:8; 34:11 f.; Jer. 32:20 f. [76] This
undoubtedly catches up an older idea acc. to which God's work with His hand is a basic
element in His self-revelation — with the consequence that the revelation of act is with
the revelation of word, if not before it, a constitutive part of divine revelation generally. [77] Perhaps related to the role of the hand here is the fact that there is frequent ref.
to the giving (נָתַן) of אֹתֹת, Jos. 2:12; Dt. 6:22; Neh. 9:10; once in Jos. 2:12 the ref. is
to a human "sign."

The large range of possible use of אוֹת and the typical verbal combinations in
which it occurs make it as good as certain that in its ultimate nature, as in its
origin, this is a formal concept which receives its narrower sense from the circum-

---

[72] Keller, 57.
[73] Keller, 8 : 8 times in Ex. 4:17; Nu. 14:11, 22; Dt. 11:3; 34:11; Jos. 24:17; Ju. 6:17;
Ps. 86:17.
[74] Keller, 11: 4 times in Dt. 13:3; 1 S. 2:34; 10:7, 9.
[75] Keller, 11.
[76] Underlying this use of hand is the idea of God's work in history, which in turn rests
on particular experiences of God.
[77] On these questions cf. U. Luck, *Hand u. Hand Gottes,* Inaugural Diss., Münster.

stances in which it is employed. Hence the word can denote both things and processes whether in the secular or the sacral sphere. The decisive point in its use is not that the thing it serves to denote has or might have a religious quality but that it is adapted to indicate or to confirm the relevance of certain things or processes, and to promote the corresponding insights. As אוֹת a thing or person is never an autonomous end but a means to an end. The word still stands in need of further investigation from this angle, → lines 12 ff. In its formal character it is suitably rendered by the neutral "sign." Even where the reference is to God's signs in a religious context, the word as such has nothing to do with revelation itself. It is simply an indication, pointing to revelation which is taking place or has already taken place. [78]

e. אוֹת as a Means of Confirmation.

Along with combinations and contexts which give us insight into the nature of אוֹת are others which inform us of the purpose of what is thus designated and thus go beyond what we have been able to describe very generally as indication → 212, 37 ff. [79] Without exception these all make it plain that the אוֹת contains powers which affect the spiritual centre of the one confronted by it and which work for clarification, so that a certainty is established which was not present before. The broadness of the term is seen once again in the fact that this certainty may be either religious or non-religious according to the problem to which the אוֹת relates and to which it is related by the one who gives it.

(a) The best proof of this is in Job 21:29 where אוֹת is quite unquestionably used in a profane sense : those who have gone through the world and know how things are in it have adequate proofs (אֹתֹת) that the doctrine of retribution does not hold water. Acc. to the context the meaning is "that which strikes the eye." The comm. suggest in detail buildings, memorials, inscriptions, [80] victory monuments [81] etc. The context might also point to magnificent tombs. In any case the ref. is to examples whose stories prove [82] that history reflects the triumph of might rather than right, and which thus make possible a significant insight.

(b) In the ancient story of Rahab the harlot (→ III, 1 ff.) and Joshua's spies in Jericho (Jos. 2:1 ff.) אוֹת (v. 12) is combined with a solemn oath to assure Rahab that she and her relatives can count on being saved. This reminds us of Is. 19:19 f., where

---

[78] We thus reject the thesis of Keller acc. to which אוֹת in the OT is originally tantamount to a sign of divine revelation and expressly includes the oracular sign, 144. Keller also thinks (145) that in the course of time the word ceased to be a purely religious one and found a place in secular speech ; this took place fairly early, as shown by the use of אוֹת for "signal" in Lachish Letter 4 (Keller, 5 → 209, 22 ff.). The truth is the exact opposite : אוֹת is basically a formal term which very naturally found its way into religious use. Nor can we accept the view of N. H. Tur-Sinai (H. Torczyner) that אוֹת is "in the Bible ... miraculous testimony," *The Book of Job* (1957), 333. Unfortunately Tur-Sinai's discussion of אוֹת in the Bible and the Lachish inscr. in his Hebrew work הלשון והספר, III (1955), 121-131 was not available.

[79] Cf. on what follows Keller, 56 ff. on the aim and result of *othoth*. Keller's material is used but his conclusions are not adopted.

[80] So A. Weiser, *D. Buch Hiob, AT Deutsch,* 13² (1956), 168 f.

[81] G. Hölscher, *D. Buch Hiob, Hndbch. AT,* 17² (1952), 56 f.

[82] Cf. S. R. Driver-G. B. Gray, *The Book of Job,* ICC² (1950), 189 : "typical illustrations drawn ... from their experience of men and life ..."

אוֹת and עֵד are used together, → 211, 28 ff.; here again the witness has the role of confirming. The confirmatory sign in the Rahab story is not the rope by which the visitors are let down from the window in v. 15 but the crimson-coloured cord amulet of one of them, cf. Gn. 38:18. [83] Whether we may connect this with the blood-colour of Ex. 12:13 [84] must be regarded as uncertain.

(c) To what degree the idea of consolidating powers is present in the understanding of אוֹת may be seen from the fact that when the people passes through the Jordan in Jos. 4:1 ff. the twelve steles are first called אוֹת in v. 6 and then this is explained by לְזִכָּרוֹן in v. 7. אוֹת and זִכָּרוֹן are even used as synon. in Ex. 13:9; Nu. 16:38, 40. Here and in Gn. 9:15 f. and Dt. 7:18 f., where אוֹת is the starting-pt. and fixed point for remembering (זָכַר) certain events, in terms of the root זכר the ref. is to a real "presenting" of the past [85] by means of that denoted by the אוֹת. In Gn. 9:15 the rainbow is the אוֹת and in this quality it reminds God of His covenant with the generation of the flood. In Dt. 7:18 f. the Egypt. אֹתֹת as the basis of recollection are an occasion of confidence for the Israelites in the present. It is worth noting that זִכָּרוֹן and זֵכֶר do not occur at all in Dt., while אוֹת plays an important role here. May one conclude from this that in Dt. אוֹת is deliberately used for these two words and that the reason lies in the significative and demonstrative character which it has by nature? [86]

(d) The "mark" of Cain in Gn. 4:15 [87] points beyond itself to the perception and obligation of others inasmuch as it documents the relation of protection in which Cain stands to God and which has to be respected by other men. Those who see this mark have to realise that they cannot do what they would like to do. Acc. to Gn. 4:15 the mark is in no sense a mark of shame or a brand; it is a sign of protection. Whether it be taken as originally a tribal sign (of the Kenites?) which marks its bearers as worshippers of Yahweh [88] or whether some other explanation is preferred, [89] the whole context undoubtedly forces us to assume that it was a visible sign whose significance was also apparent to others. [90] This makes it improbable that the ancient narrator might have had circumcision in view. [91] The marking must have been in a clearly visible

---

[83] H. Holzinger in Kautzsch, ad loc. M. Noth, Das Buch Josua, Hndbch. AT, I, 7² (1953), 25 on 2:1 ff. thinks the original text was simply ....חסד ואמת ועשיתם rather than חסד ונתתם לי אות אמת....ועשיתם, appealing to the LXX, which does not have a σημεῖον for an אות. On Joseph. → 223, 4 ff. 'A, Σ, Θ read like the Mas.
[84] H. W. Hertzberg, Die Bücher Josua, Richter, Ruth, AT Deutsch, 9 (1953), 21, n. 1 on Jos. 2:1 ff.
[85] Cf. on this P. A. H. de Boer, Gedenken u. Gedächtnis in d. Welt des AT : Die Wurzel zkr, Franz-Delitzsch Vorlesungen 1960 (1961).
[86] In contrast the verb זכר occurs only in Dt. (14 times).
[87] Keller, 69-78.
[88] Basically cf. B. Stade, "Beiträge z. Pentateuchkritik : 1. Das Kainszeichen," ZAW, 14 (1894), 250-318, esp. 299 f. As regards the form of the sign Stade, 301 and many others suggest a cross as a Yahweh sign on the basis of Ez. 9:4 ff. But J. Hempel, Gebet u. Frömmigkeit im AT (1922), 15, with others, argues against any connection between the name of Yahweh and the mark of Cain.
[89] A. Menes, "Die sozialpolitische Analyse der Urgeschichte," ZAW, 43 (1925), 33-62 defines the mark given to Cain as a protective sign but would see in it a kind of divine placet that Cain has gone back from civilisation to a state of nature. But since Menes thinks Yahweh worship begins with the giving of the sign it would be better to speak of a sign of annexation.
[90] This rules out the idea that a mighty revelation of God is given to Cain to confirm God's promise of protection, though this interpretation continues to find supporters.
[91] So H. Zeydner, "Kainszeichen, Keniter u. Beschneidung," ZAW, 18 (1898), 120-125.

place, e.g., the forehead (cf. the זִכָּרוֹן between the eyes in Ex. 13:9) [92] or the hair on the forehead (cf. Lv. 19:27; Jer. 9:25; 25:23; 49:32). Undoubtedly a declaration of the will of Yahweh lies behind the sign. Yet this does not mean that the sign is strictly an objectification of revelation. Though it makes no sense to try to impose a strict either-or, the context unquestionably suggest that the mark of Cain gives information about Cain rather than God. Hence it is better not to attempt combinations such as a "sign of the revelation of protection." [93]

(e) The expression הָיָה לְאוֹת points to a process of perception initiated and set in train by אוֹת. This is not uncommon in later passages [94, 95] and structurally it can be transl. "to serve as a sign" [96] if not precisely "to act as a sign." In all such instances "token" or "sign" is near the mark as a rendering of אוֹת.

(f) Knowledge as the express purpose of אוֹת is unquestionable in passages where what is signified by the verb יָדַע is called the aim or result of אוֹת. [97] Worth noting is the fact that אוֹת does not always have to be used when it is immediately apparent that the ref. is to this for the purpose of perception, e.g., in Jos. 3:10 ff. (... בְּזֹאת תֵּדְעוּן) or 1 S. 6:9 (וְיָדַעְנוּ ... וּרְאִיתֶם ... וְאִם־לֹא). When אוֹת is combined with יָדַע what is denoted has the force of a basis of knowledge no matter whether the object of knowledge is religious or not. Esp. instructive in this regard is Ex. 8:18 f.: God brings a bad plague of flies on all Egypt apart from Goshen, where the children of Israel live, and this is an אוֹת, so that Pharaoh may know with whom he has ultimately to reckon in the person of Moses. This sign is quite unambiguously a mighty declaration of God which speaks for itself. But even here it is better not to speak of revelation [98] because on the one side the "sign" is not given to the children of Israel and on the other it has the effect of hardening Pharaoh, to whom it is supposed to impart or facilitate instruction, v. 28. What is true here is basically true in all passages in which knowledge is the purpose of the sign. Even when the point is to make it known "that I am Yahweh" (Ex. 10:1 f.), the אוֹת used for this purpose derives its distinctive features from the sphere of method rather than content or theology.

(g) At least twice the aim of אוֹת is faith. [99] This is hardly surprising when one considers that in the OT faith is closely related not only to perception but to the knowledge of God. Only the man who knows God can believe in Him. [100] This is finely illustrated in Nu. 14:11: God is surprised that in spite of all His signs among them His people does not believe in Him, i.e., trust (הֶאֱמִין) Him. It has obviously seen in vain and been led to the perception of God in vain. On a second ref. in Ex. 4:8 → 212, 5 ff. It should also be noted once again that אוֹת can be the occasion of and the introduction to recollection, Gn. 9:15 f.; Dt. 7:18 → 214, 6 ff. In the recollection at issue here there is demonstrated the relation to God which the OT calls faith.

---

[92] On the relation of אוֹת to זִכָּרוֹן → 214, 6 ff.

[93] Keller, 75. B. Jacob, *Das erste Buch d. Tora : Genesis* (1934), 146, thinks the mark of Cain is an oracle, but he does not give any cogent arguments for this.

[94] The older expression is הָיָה אוֹת (without לְ) Ex. 8:19; Jos. 4:6.

[95] Gn. 9:13; 17:11; Ex. 13:9, 16; Nu. 16:38; Ez. 20:12, 20.

[96] So C. H. Ratschow, "Werden u. Wirken. Eine Untersuchung des Wortes *hajah*," Beih. ZAW, 70 (1941), 10.

[97] Keller, 58 : Ex. 7:3-5; 8:18 f.; 10:1 f.; 31:13; Dt. 4:34 f.; 11:2 f.; Jer. 44:29; Ez. 14:8; 20:12, 20.

[98] Keller, 58.

[99] Keller, 57.

[100] For this reason faith in the OT comes only on the basis of God's self-revelation. No man knows God of himself ; God must testify to Himself as the One He is if there is to be faith in Him.

According to this review ʾôth is in fact "always a sign in external reality which points to something else." [101] But history has also proved to be its sphere. Itself truly historical, in a given historical situation it is usually directed to eye-witnesses with a view to unleashing historical effects by way of their insight and will. To that degree it finally aims at much more than the mere confirmation which must be its primary goal; it claims or achieves direct influence on personal decisions which will always have historical consequences.

f. God's Signs and Wonders.

When the OT speaks of God's signs and wonders its style takes on what is almost a hymnal character. This is connected with the fact that when the phrase is used [102] the reference is almost always [103] to the leading of the people out of Egypt by Moses and to the special circumstances under which the people stood up to the passage of the Red Sea and in all of which God proved Himself to be the Almighty and showed Israel to be His chosen people. We do not know who first introduced or established the expression אוֹתוֹת וּמוֹפְתִים in this sense. The only sure point is that it is rooted in the Deuteronomic view of history and that what it proclaims is the centre around which the other basic events affecting Israel are grouped in the credo of Dt. 26:5 ff. [104] The author of these events is God, and it may be that the expression which is designed to sum up their character tries to do so in two ways: The extraordinary events at issue here point back to God and they are also of such a kind as to proclaim imminent upheaval [105, 106] cf. esp. 1 K. 13:3, 5; Jl. 2:30 f.; 2 Ch. 32:24. Essential is that the events themselves are dumb and that Israel for its part — this must not be forgotten — is the silent object of what occurs. [107] In the phrase "signs and wonders," then, all the emphasis lies from the very first on the event as such in its quality as a work of God.

The usage in Is. 8:18 is perhaps pre-Deuteronomistic, since the statement seems to be one of the early sayings of Isaiah. [108] Yet here, too, there may be detected in the background ideas in which the certainty of God's work in history is combined with the thought of its revolutionary nature; it is presupposed that Yahweh is the God of Israel and that Israel is God's people. If this is correct, then in a situation similar to that of Israel in Egypt the expression is in a position to embrace the historical data to which the people's assurance of election had long since been orientated. This is how the international situation seems to have been evaluated in Jerusalem at the time of Josiah, for in Dt. religious and political motifs seem to be distinctively combined as in the reforms of Josiah. [109]

---

[101] A. Bertholet, Hesekiel, Hndbch. AT, 13 (1936), 17.
[102] Cf. the list → n. 65.
[103] Exceptions Dt. 13:2 f.; 28:46 (both sing.); Is. 8:18.
[104] G. v. Rad, Theol. d. AT, I (1957), 178.
[105] Whether or how far this is expressed in מוֹפֵת cannot be discussed here (on the etym. → τέρας).
[106] To this degree there is really something apocalyptic about מוֹפֵת, Keller, 61. But one cannot here use the term in the technical sense in which it is used to-day; for one thing it does not specifically or even secondarily denote special heavenly phenomena, G. Fohrer, Die symbolischen Handlungen d. Propheten (1953), 59, n. 1.
[107] v. Rad, loc. cit.
[108] Cf. the comm. on the context of Is. 8:18.
[109] Cf. A. C. Welch, "The Death of Josiah," ZAW, 43 (1925), 255-260; H. W. Robinson, The History of Israel⁷ (1954), 120-123; M. Noth, Gesch. Israels² (1954), 250-253.

Thus the expression "signs and wonders" is not just a principle of Deuteronomic interpretation ; it also stands in need of interpretation. [110] Perhaps connected with this is the surprising way in which the phrase faded into the background in the post-Deuteronomic age. It is essentially replaced by a reference to what it embraces in the usage of Dt. A classical witness to this is the Passover Haggada with its midrash on Dt. 26:5-8 and its miracle litany with the refrain דַּיֵּנוּ, "it would have sufficed for us."

g. Symbolical Prophetic Actions.

Actions claiming to be "signs" occupy a not inconsiderable place in the prophets. [111] Typical of their form as presented in the tradition is that they take place by a divine injunction which demands obedience, and that they are combined with an interpretation. [112] It is significant for their interpretation that eyewitnesses are almost always mentioned or tacitly assumed, [113] and that they have a definite purpose. [114] If they are also symbolical actions it may be seen clearly from the use of אוֹת for them [115] that they are autonomous acts after the manner of divine signs and that they thus have an intrinsic quality of proclamation, so that one must not regard them merely as aids to the delivery of the divine message. [116]

It may be said that these prophetic actions are designed to give force and emphasis to the words [117] only when they are seen in the total context of prophetic proclamation and activity. But in view of their varied nature, their relation to the immediate situation, and the shifting circle of those to whom they are addressed, this is going too far. One need only refer to three accounts of such signs in which they are expressly called אוֹת, namely, Isaiah's giving of a name in Is. 8:1 ff., 18, Isaiah's going naked in Is. 20:3, and Ezekiel's depiction of the siege of Jerusalem with the aid of a tile etc. as in a childish game, Ez. 4:1-3. Though these signs are unmistakably connected externally with the manticism of the ancient Orient, one cannot refer to them as oracular signs. [118] They are signs or symbols, [119] but not magical or mantic actions. Their setting is not an attempt to read the future but the divine commission to extract the future from the present, whether by inspired word or by a symbolical action which speaks for itself. [120]

h. Aramaic אָת, אָתָא in Daniel and the Targums.

אָת, the Aram. equivalent of אוֹת, occurs 3 times in Da. at 3:32 f.; 6:28, and in different ways all three ref. confirm the picture we now have of the biblical אוֹת. Each time we find an expression after the manner of the Deuteronomic אוֹתוֹת וּמוֹפְתִים (→ 216, 14 ff.), though תְּמַהּ, not מוֹפֵת, is the second term. Unfortunately one cannot say whether מוֹפֵת

---

[110] Keller, 110, referring to passages in the Ps., rightly speaks of the formal character of the concept.
[111] Bibl.: G. Fohrer, "Die Gattung der Berichte über symbolische Handlungen der Propheten," ZAW, 64 (1952), 101-120; also op. cit. (→ n. 106); G. v. Rad, Theol. d. AT, II (1960), 108-111; Keller, 94-113.
[112] For details cf. Fohrer, op. cit. (→ n. 111), 101 f.
[113] Ibid., 115 f.
[114] Fohrer (→ n. 106), 64-69.
[115] They can also be called מוֹפֵת Is. 20:3; Ez. 12:6, 11; 24:24, 27, Keller, 58.
[116] Fohrer (→ n. 111), 103, n. 1.
[117] A common view considered and rightly rejected by Fohrer (→ n. 106), 67.
[118] Keller, 103 אוֹת.
[119] Fohrer (→ n. 106), 68.
[120] Cf. on this v. Rad, op. cit., 110 f.

was used by the author of Da., since he does not have it elsewhere. Worth noting is the fact that מוֹפֵת seems to occur in Tg. O. only where it is in the Heb. original. [121] This might suggest that in the tradition it had become a tt. for the wonders in Egypt and hence was not used for other purposes. It may be added that Da. 3:32 f. is speaking of signs and wonders which happened personally to Nebuchadnezzar and which were more astonishing and frightening than miraculous. The same applies to the edict of Darius in 6:28. [122] Thus אָת, אָתָא is also a formal concept in Da. [123]

Among the Targums Tg. O. repeats אוֹתוֹת וּמוֹפְתִים even in Aram. in all the Pent. ref. mentioned in → n. 65. Here then at the very latest c. the middle of the 5th cent. A.D. [124] this phrase was reserved for the wonders in Egypt → 216, 8 ff. It is as well to note this here, even though Tg. O. is Rabbinic, because a very old tradition is perhaps followed at this pt. Tg. Ps., which is much later than Tg. O., [125] has אָתוֹהִי וְתִמְהוֹי for the wonders in Egypt at Ps. 78:43, cf. also 105:27; 135:9; linguistically, then, it follows Da. But Tg. Pro. at Is. 8:18; 20:3 follows the same course as Tg. O. at the Pent. ref. listed in → n. 65. [126] The same is true of Tg. Pro. on Jer. 32:20 f. Thus the picture is not uniform ; two tendencies exist side by side in the receiving and passing on of the text. For this very reason it is worthy of note that the Targums thus far consulted consistently render Heb. אוֹת by Aram. אָת' or אָתָא. [127] For in some respect this means that the formal character of אוֹת, already perceived earlier, is confirmed in the age or linguistic milieu of the Targums.

A special word must be said about the so-called Palest. Pent. Targum. Up to a short time ago this was known only from Geniza fragments, [128] but we now have it all in a MS in the Vatican Library (Neofiti I). [129] It is significant that there is here not a single instance of אוֹתוֹת וּמוֹפְתִים.; Of the two words combined here מוֹפֵת is usually [130] replaced by another but אוֹת is retained. In Dt. 4:34; 7:19; 26:8; 29:2; 34:11 we find פְּרִישָׁא "miraculous deed" in the sense of the extraordinary, once at 34:11 as נִיסֵי פְרִישׁתה for מוֹפְתִים; Dt. 6:22; 13:2 f.; 28:46 have סִימָנָא/סִימָן ("sign," "token," "mark") for this, probably a Gk. loan word → 228, 23 ff. Even more significant is the fact that in almost all the instances in which אוֹת occurs in the Pent. apart from the combination mentioned it is rendered by סִימָן/σημεῖον. [131] Here an unmistakably formal word has replaced אוֹת [132] and the formal character of the latter is thus demonstrated linguistically. This proof is the more significant in that there are many reasons for regarding Tg. Pal. as

---

[121] At Ex. 7:9 Tg. O has אתא for מופת, E. Brederek, "Konkordanz z. Tg. O.," Beih. ZAW, 9 (1906), 10.

[122] On both passages in the LXX → 221, 24 ff.

[123] This is expressed in the fact that the word can be combined with others denoting various nuances of the extraordinary.

[124] Tg. O. derives from Palest. tradition, is probably connected with the school of Akiba, and was edited at the earliest in the 3rd cent. in Babylon. It is very probably a scribal work.

[125] Ed. at least in part before 476 A.D., since it mentions Rome at Ps. 108:5.

[126] J. F. Stenning, The Targum of Is. (1949), 31, 65.

[127] So far as I can see Job 21:29 is the only exception (סִימָן for אוֹת); on סִימָן → 228, 23 ff.

[128] On Tg. Pal. cf. P. Kahle, "Masoreten d. Westens, II," BWANT, IV, 14 (1930), 1*-13*. Cf. 1-65 for all the fr. then known.

[129] P. Kahle has photographs of the MS. On it cf. A. Diez Macho, "Una copia completa del Tg. palestinense al Pentateuco, en la Bibl. Vaticana," Sefarad, 17 (1957), 119-121 (with ill.); P. Kahle, "D. pal. Pent.-Targum u. d. z. Zt. Jesu gesprochene Aram.," ZNW, 49 (1958), 100-116.

[130] Exception Ex. 7:3 : את־אתתי ואת־מופתי for ית נסוי וית פרישתי.

[131] Exceptions Nu. 2:2 (אוֹת = emblem → 211, 31 ff. with n. 69 and → 226, 13 ff.); Ex. 13:9 (סימן at 13:16).

[132] On the use of אוֹת in Heb. in the final years B.C. → 225, 18 ff.

old, [133] and its language is probably close to, if not directly the same as, the Aram. spoken in the time of Jesus. [134]

i. Summary.

When one considers the use of אוֹת in the OT and the adoption, translation or interpretation of the word in the Targums (→ 218, 8 ff.), especially in the ancient Palestinian Pentateuch Targum (→ 218, 21 ff.), there can be little doubt as to the formal character of the word which is rendered σημεῖον in the LXX. Our review also suggests that the term lost much of its original breadth, especially in the post-exilic period → 211, 5 ff. An indication of this may be seen in the fact that it is largely replaced by other words and also in its restriction in the Palestinian Pent. Targum to a fixed expression with a predominantly historical reference, → 218, 23 ff.

3. σημεῖον in Relation to אוֹת in the Septuagint.

a. σημεῖον for אוֹת in its Formal Character.

σημεῖον, which is itself very formal in meaning (→ 205, 15 ff.), which aims at sense impressions with a view to imparting insight or knowledge (→ 206, 29 ff.) and which has from the outset no specific religious reference (→ 203, 34 ff.; 206, 29 ff.), was obviously regarded by the OT translators as the proper rendering of אוֹת, which is also formal and which also aims at conceptual clarification by means of impressions. If in the LXX אוֹת is normally transl. σημεῖον (→ 209, 6 ff.), this is adequate proof how close the two words are by nature. σημεῖον shares fully with אוֹת the distinctive feature that it applies more to the technical side of a process than its result ; the latter is noted also, but only because a specific end, expressly noted or not, is combined with each term in special ways which vary from one case to another → 213, 7 ff.; 217, 7 ff.

Within the limits thus laid down σημεῖον is used in the LXX ⁓ on the basis of the sense of a "sign or mark which identifies something or someone, which thus makes identifiable," and always for אוֹת ⁓ for a scar or the like as a sign of protection in Gn. 4:15 : Cain (→ 214, 19 ff.), or as a term for a relation which cannot be given up in Ex. 13:9, 16; cf. Dt. 6:8; 11:18, or for emblems as religious symbols in ψ 73:4, 9 [135] → 211, 15 ff., or as monuments for recollection and contemplation in Job 21:29 (→ 213, 22 ff.) and Jos. 4:6 (→ 213, 22 ff.), also for circumcision (Gn. 17:11), the Sabbath (Ex. 31:13, 17) and the rainbow (Gn. 9:12 ff.) as signs of God's covenant with His people, the blood of the Passover lamb as a mark to distinguish the houses in which the Israelites live (Ex. 12:13), or for a symbolical action by means of which a prophet draws attention to the menacing future (Ez. 4:3 → 217, 18 ff.). The question τί τὸ σημεῖον in 2 K. 20:8 and the demand δότε ἡμῖν σημεῖον in Ex. 7:9 (but cf. → 220, 15 ff.) are obviously at home in situations in daily life in which for objective or subjective reasons the winning of absolute certainty about someone or something is thought to be inescapable, and the same applies to the positive answer τοῦτό σοι τὸ σημεῖον

---

[133] A. Diez Macho, "En torno a la datación del Targum 'Palestinense,' " *Sefarad*, 20 (1960), 1-16; 2nd cent. A.D. or earlier.

[134] Cf. Kahle, *op. cit.* (→ n. 129).

[135] τὰ σημεῖα ἡμῶν for אוֹתֹתֵינוּ shows that the Gk. transl. did not understand the term in the sense of "(miraculous divine) sign for us (for our comfort)" but took אוֹת here as in v. 4.

etc. in Ex. 3:12; 1 S. 2:34; 10:1; 2 K. 19:29; Is. 37:30; cf. 1 S. 14:10; 'Ιερ. 51:29. Such a sign can thus come from men, though obviously also παρὰ κυρίου, 2 K. 20:9; Is. 38:7. If the ref. is religious it may be a miracle. But it is this, not because it is called σημεῖον, but because in this case God is the author of the σημεῖον, as in other cases with a purely human ref. men are the authors. LXX usage compels us even in instances where σημεῖον is used directly or indirectly for God's action to recognise quite unequivocally the formal character which is proper to the word by nature and which is only strengthened by its Semitic equivalent אוֹת. Under the influence of אוֹת the formal character of σημεῖον does indeed become essentially stricter in Jewish Gk. This limited its use on the one side [136] but increased its interpretative aptness on the other. [137]

b. σημεῖον Interpretatively.

The formal character of σημεῖον may be seen in a series of passages in which אוֹת does not occur but which incline to a sense connected therewith. In all such instances σημεῖον is an aid to precision of thought.

In Ex. 7:9 Moses and Aaron must show the justice of their claim to Pharaoh. The LXX suggests that Pharaoh demands proof by means of σημεῖον ἤ τέρας, whereas the Mas. simply has מוֹפֵת, which corresponds to → τέρας and does not have by nature the power to show and to prove which the context seems to require. The word is used again in the same way in the continuation of the story in Ex. 11:9 f. Another instance with counterplay of מוֹפֵת and σημεῖον is 2 Ch. 32:24. The LXX again interprets the divine wonder of the HT by σημεῖον, and quite pertinently inasmuch as the ref. in the context is not to the miracle as such but to something which is extraordinary and which establishes certainty as a result. In some cases σημεῖον is used for נֵס ("signal," "banner") in order to indicate once again, in a way which pertinently gives greater precision to the thought of the text, that present or absent power is demonstrated in the appearance or non-appearance of a נֵס. Is. 11:12; 13:2; 18:3; 33:23; 'Ιερ. 28:12, 27. [138] Similarly, in Nu. 21:8 f.; 26:10 σημεῖον interprets the נֵס of the original (with אוֹת at 21:8), except that here it contains in a special way the idea of visibility (→ 211, 5 ff.) or of the mediating of a specific insight (→ 213, 12 ff.). In Ez. 9:4, 6 the distinguishing תָּו (→ 208, 29 ff.) is represented by σημεῖον and thus legitimately interpreted for the Gk. reader who does not know the Heb. alphabet and cannot imagine what is meant by a Tau. [139] The same applies in Ez. 39:15, where the word stands for צִיּוּן, which means a marker, probably in the form of an upraised stone, to denote the bones of the dead scattered about. In Ju. 20:38 B σημεῖον is used for מוֹעֵד (A σύνταγή "agreement"); once again it gives greater precision. Finally in Jos. 2:18 σημεῖον is used in the transl. to make it clear why Rahab is to hang out the cord handed to her. In none of these passages has the word independent significance of any kind, let alone religious.

---

[136] The ancient Gk. meanings "gravestone," "marked goal" do not occur at all → 202, 18 ff., 25 ff.

[137] אוֹת, too, can sometimes have an interpretative role. Thus in Nu. 14:22 God's כָּבוֹד may be seen in the signs which He performs. Similarly אוֹת עוֹלָם in Is. 55:13 interprets the greatness of God's שֵׁם.

[138] σημεῖον, however, is not used for נֵס at Is. 30:17 'ΑΘ (Hatch-Redp., 1262 stands in need of correction here). In this v. (LXX σημαία "standard") 'ΑΘ have σύσσημον, always used for נֵס in 'Α, cf. J. Ziegler, "Textkrit. Notizen zu den jüngeren griech. Übersetz. d. Buches Js.," NGG, NF, 1, 4 (1939), 90.

[139] But cf. the transl. in 'ΑΘ (θαυ for תָּו).

This is confirmed by the few passages in which words formed from σημεῖον are used. Thus Σ Dt. 18:10 and Mi. 5:11 render עֹנֵן po'el, [140] which has to do with sooth-saying, by σημειοσκοπεῖσθαι (LXX Mi. 5:11 ἀποφθέγγεσθαι "to proclaim emphatically" or "in ecstasy" → I, 447, 8 ff.). [141] In Αλλ 1 Βασ. 28:3, 9 we find σημειοσκόπος for יִדְּעֹנִי, "one with a spirit of soothsaying," LXX γνώστης. In both cases only the process is in view.

c. σημεῖα καὶ τέρατα.

The Deuteronomic theologoumenon אֹתֹת וּמוֹפְתִים (→ 216, 8 ff.) becomes ση-μεῖα καὶ τέρατα in the LXX. This is always used where the expression occurs in the Mas. text. [142] In additional instances in the Greek Bible, including the Apocrypha, it is almost always connected with recollection of the emancipation of Israel from Egypt. Thus in Greek-speaking Judaism in so far as this stands behind the literature comprised in the LXX the formula σημεῖα καὶ τέρατα, based on the Deuteronomic model, seems to be reserved for God's wonders in the days of Moses.

The ref. in Bar. 2:11 is unquestionably to the divine signs in Egypt. The same may be inferred in Sir. 36:5, for the signs and wonders whose renewal and repetition is sought can only be the Egyptian signs and wonders. [143] Of the two ref. in Wis. Sol. the context of that in 10:16 shows that it can relate only to the signs in Moses' time, though there is ref. here to βασιλεῖς φοβεροί. [144], [145] It is natural to assume, then, that Wis. 8:8 is to be construed similarly, esp. as it is here said of σοφία : σημεῖα καὶ τέρατα προγινώσκει. The thought is possibly that what took place in Egypt is unique thus far, but does not have to remain so, cf. Sir. 36:5 → lines 16 ff.

This possibly casts some light on Δα. Θ 4:2; 6:28 → 217, 31 f. It seems as if the translators detected in both these verses the ancient historical expression. Hence they dropped the whole passage from Da. 3:32 (Mas.) in which Nebuchadnezzar claims it for himself, [146] whereas they could leave it in the second passage in which confession is made by no less a person than Darius that the God of Israel is the Lord of history. It remains to be asked whether the claiming of the phrase by Nebuchadnezzar in the basic text of the book was not regarded by the author as one of the symptoms of the arrogance of the king for which he was brought low.

II. Greek Judaism outside the Bible.

1. Philo.

In a few instances Philo follows LXX usage, e.g., when on the basis of Gn. 4:15 he calls the mark of Cain (→ 214, 19 ff.) a σημεῖον in Praem. Poen., 72; Det. Pot. Ins., 177 f., or when on the basis of Gn. 1:14 he calls the stars σημεῖα in Op. Mund., 55. In the main the word retains for Philo the basic sense acc. to which it denotes things or

---

[140] The root here is of uncertain meaning, cf. Ges.-Buhl, Köhler-Baumg., s.v. עֹנֵן.
[141] 'Α κληδονίζομαι at Mi. 5:11.
[142] Also Neh. 9:10 (B).
[143] HT אֹות and מוֹפֵת, cf. M. Z. Segal, ספר בן סירא השלם (1953), 225, in a collective sense.
[144] Either we have here plur. for sing., cf. J. Fichtner, Weisheit Salomos, Hndbch. AT, II, 6 (1938), 39, ad loc.; Bl.-Debr. § 141, or the author includes with Pharaoh all the other kings with whom the children of Israel had to contend between the exodus and the conquest.
[145] The expression here takes the form τέρατα καὶ σημεῖα.
[146] The first v. is only in Θ. Nor is it in pap. Chester Beatty 967 (1st half of the 3rd cent. A.D.), ed. F. G. Kenyon, The Chester Beatty Biblical Pap., VII, 1 (1937), ad loc. 20.

processes which lead to insight or knowledge by way of perception → 205, 15 ff. Thus [147] laughing (γέλως) is a σημεῖον τῆς χαρᾶς, Praem. Poen., 31. [148] But this concrete use is rare apart from the use in the mathematical sense of "point," Vit. Mos., II, 115; Congr., 146 f.; Op. Mund., 49, 98 etc. — Philo shares this with Gk. mathematics, → 205, 15 ff. Reference to seeing is always in the offing, cf. Abr., 60; Vit. Mos., I, 188; Som., I, 197 (ref. to Gn. 31:12 with ἀναβλέψεις); [149] it may be seen also in the fact that Som., I, 197 speaks of φανέντα σημεῖα and again in the confirmation of a lesson (ἀναδιδαχθῆναι) by three σημεῖα which consist in extraordinary events and which are to be seen and are seen, Vit. Mos. I, 76. [150] This makes it possible for Philo to speak on occasion of σημεῖον as a medical "symptom" along with αἰτία as the cause of sickness and θεραπεία as therapy, Det. Pot. Ins., 43. Predominantly, however, σημεῖον in Philo has reference to mental operations in the sense of "indication," "argument," "proof." σημεῖον δέ [151] is used again and again in deductions to introduce evidence (possibly a text) or to start a proof, e.g., Fug., 204 cf. Gn. 16:11; Congr., 92 cf. Gn. 14:1 ff.; Vit. Mos., II, 18 with ref. to the geographical discrepancy at the giving of the Law. An argument which leads necessarily to a conclusion is a σημεῖον ἐναργές, Vit. Mos., II, 263; cf. Spec. Leg., I, 90. In allegorising, to which Philo's proofs from Scripture often lead, σημεῖον with gen. has much the sense of "points towards," "is to be taken in the sense of ..." e.g., Det. Pot. Ins., 1: The πεδίον of Gn. 4:8 is σημεῖον ἁμίλλης καὶ διαμάχης, i.e., it points in a deeper sense to (imminent) rivalry and strife. Obviously signs can come from God and this in many forms, e.g., the sounding of trumpets at the giving of the Law on Sinai in Spec. Leg., II, 188 f. or the Egypt. signs in Vit. Mos., I, 210 : τὰ κατ' Αἴγυπτον σημεῖα, and they are designed to make perceptible what God wills, cf. the σημεῖον ἀρίδηλον in Vit. Mos., I, 269. Fundamentally all Scripture is for Philo an inexhaustible reservoir of σημεῖα. When he quotes it, then, the ref. is to divine σημεῖα even if he does not say so explicitly.

In this connection it is important to note that for Philo wonders play no very significant role as such. As prayer did not provide him with an occasion of critical contemplation, so wonders were no problem for him. [152] In this he differs completely from the Rabbinate (→ 227, 7 ff.) and also from Jos. (→ 223, 4 ff.). Linguistically this is expressed in the formal character of σημεῖον even when used for divine signs as once [153] in Vit. Mos., I, 210 → lines 22 ff. [154] For Philo σημεῖον is never a wonder in the religious sense.

Hence it is not surprising that he uses σημεῖα καὶ τέρατα very infrequently. In the two instances one may ascribe to him [155] he takes it from the tradition and like this uses it as a comprehensive term for God's signs in Egypt, Vit. Mos., I, 95; Spec. Leg., II, 218 [156] → 216, 8 ff. It is echoed in Philo's own usage when on occasion he calls

---

[147] The following instances are only a selection from the material noted in Leisegang, s.v.
[148] Cf. Aristot. An. Pri., 36, p. 48b, 32 f.
[149] Cf. also Sacr. AC, 80, where it is pointed out that the σημεῖον for a proof and elucidation consists in the re-affirmation of the substance concerned as in the refining of gold : τοῦ ... βεβασανίσθαι καὶ δεδοκιμάσθαι σημεῖον τὸ πεπηγέναι.
[150] The ref. is to the signs of Ex. 4:1 ff.
[151] Best transl.: "This is seen with certainty from what follows."
[152] Cf. I. Heinemann, Philons gr. u. jüd. Bildung (1932), 520.
[153] This is the only instance in Philo.
[154] σημεῖον is an astrological term in Spec. Leg., I, 92; Op. Mund., 58 f. on Gn. 1:14. But Philo limited the influence of the stars to nature. Cf. on this A. Meyer, Vorsehungsglaube u. Schicksalsidee in ihrem Verhältnis bei Philo v. Alex., Diss. Tübingen (1939), 63-67.
[155] A third example in Aet. Mund., 2 : δι' ὀνειράτων ἢ διὰ χρησμῶν ἢ διὰ σημείων ἢ τεράτων, which is distinguished by the differentiating ἢ, is part of the "Hellenic lecture" which Philo probably "preserved in every detail" in Aet. Mund., W. Bousset, Jüd.-chr. Schulbetrieb in Alexandria u. Rom (1915), 136.
[156] God delivered His people in Egypt σημείοις καὶ τέρασι καὶ φάσμασι καὶ τοῖς ἄλλοις ὅσα κατ' ἐκεῖνον τὸν χρόνον ἐθαυματουργεῖτο.

the miracle of the Red Sea crossing a σημεῖον τερατωδέστατον. But this very expression shows how little a σημεῖον as such is for Philo connected with a miracle. When it is, this has to be stated expressly.

2. Josephus.

Like Philo (→ 221, 33 ff.), Jos. took σημεῖον from Holy Scripture for the mark of Cain (→ 221, 35 ff.) in Ant., 1, 59. He did so without adding any explanation: ᾧ γνώριμος ἂν εἴη (loc. cit.). One may gather from this that for Jos., too, what can be called σημεῖον is there to be seen and is adapted and indeed designed to awaken insight or knowledge. In this case the σημεῖον shows that its bearer is not to be touched by wild animals.

The sense is the same when in a description of the principles of Roman military instruction in Bell., 3, 70 ff. Jos. says that the goal of this education is that the undivided attention of the ears should be paid to orders and that of the eyes to σημεῖα, while the hands should concentrate on what they have to do: ὀξεῖαι δ᾽ ἀκοαὶ μὲν παραγγέλμασιν, ὄψεις δὲ σημείοις, ἔργοις δὲ χεῖρες, Bell., 3, 105. Since Jos. normally follows Gk. practice in using σημαία rather than σημεῖον for "standard," [157, 158] one may assume that παράγγελμα is here a military command and σημεῖον an "order by means of a signal which can simply be seen." [159] This is supported by a whole series of passages in which σημεῖον is a pre-arranged "signal" such as is used in connection with surprise arrest (Ant., 12, 404), a tactical manoeuvre (5, 46) or a police action (18, 61, cf. 2, 172). Yet Jos. also uses the word for the sounding of the attack by the trumpet → 73, 32 ff. [160] Blowing the trumpet can also be called a σημεῖον when it proclaims to the hearer that something definite will happen or a goal will be reached when it was not certain before that it would be reached: ... τῷ σαλπικτῇ (trumpeter) σημαίνειν ἐκέλευσαν ... Καῖσαρ δὲ τοῦ σημείου κατακούσας ..., Bell., 6, 68 ff. This shows that a constitutive element in the meaning is the gaining of knowledge by sense perception, even if not in this instance by visual perception. The decisive thing as regards the meaning of the word is the indicated process as such and not the details. It is this formal character which σημεῖον unmistakably has in Jos. too that enables it to be used in the military world for the "watchword" or "password" (Bell., 2, 579; 3, 88) by which it is known that one belongs to the same army. [161] There seems to be a certain plan or system in Jos.' use of the word thus far, for he also has νεῦμα for a sign with the head or eyes in Bell., 2, 498 and σύνθημα for a pre-established sign in Ant., 18, 58; Bell., 2, 326. [162]

In acc. with its formal character σημεῖον can also be used in Jos. for any phenomenon which produces knowledge quite apart from its specific nature. In connection with the fact that for Jos. God directs the history both of nations and of individuals the word necessarily enters the religious sphere when it embraces specific providences. But it

---

[157] As elsewhere in Gk. LXX has σημαία for נֵס at Is. 30:17.

[158] E.g., Bell., 2, 169: τὰς Καίσαρος εἰκόνας, αἳ σημαῖαι καλοῦνται, cf. also 6, 316; 7, 14; Ant., 18, 121. The standard-bearer is σημαιαφόρος in Bell., 6, 68, cf. Polyb., 6, 24, 6.

[159] O. Michel-O. Bauernfeind transl. "standard" in their bilingual ed. of Jos. Bell., I (1959), 331. A. F. Gfrörer, Flavius Jos.' Gesch. d. jüd. Krieges, I (1836), has "sign," H. Clementz, Flavius Jos.' Gesch. d. jüd. Krieges (1900), 318, ad loc. rightly transl. "signal," cf. also J. B. Ott in his transl. (1736): "... the signal ... which is to be given them."

[160] E.g., Bell., 6, 69. Cf. also 3, 86: Trumpet signals tell the Roman soldier (σάλπιγγες προσημαίνουσιν) when it is time to sleep or to go on watch or to awake. These are just as much commands as signals in battle or in training.

[161] Hence in street-fighting by night βοὴ ἀσήμαντος makes it impossible to distinguish friend from foe, Bell., 6, 75.

[162] Thus for Jos. the Roman eagle is a τῆς ἡγεμονίας τεκμήριον but not σημεῖον, Bell., 3, 123.

does not for this reason become a distinctively religious tt. And in particular one cannot say that σημεῖον is a fixed term for miracle in Jos.[163] The only pt. is that by virtue of its formal character the word is able to embrace on the religious plane such data and phenomena as produce certainty or knowledge by means of certain impressions. Some examples will make the situation plain. Thus Jos. tells us that on the very day of the burning of the temple many Jews in Jerusalem, seduced by false prophets, expected to see τὰ σημεῖα τῆς σωτηρίας, i.e., things in which the coming of deliverance and salvation would be intimated, Bell., 6, 285. We are also told that in good time before the death of Tiberius σημεῖόν τι πρόφαντον was given him respecting his successor, i.e., in his situation, a declaration of the will of the gods concerning him, Ant., 18, 211. When Vespasian became emperor, many things he had experienced in his life up to that pt. seemed to be an "intimation" of his new dignity (σημεῖον), including the scene in which the captured Josephus had hailed him as future emperor, Bell., 4, 622 f., cf. 3, 999 ff. and 404. Here the word is never more than a term for the means by which God as the One who reveals Himself in history shows (σημαίνει) what He wills and does.[164]

Jos. thus makes a careful distinction between σημεῖον and τέρας as the extraordinary event behind which higher power is concealed. Thus Herod the Gt. in his struggle for power receives a τέρας in Jericho (Bell., 1, 331 f.) when a house in which he had given a banquet to eminent guests collapsed suddenly just after they had left. He sees in this a sign (σημεῖον) of serious danger just ahead of him and this came the next day when he narrowly escaped death.[165] Similarly, when Isaiah promises Hezekiah recovery, fifteen more yrs. of reign and descendants, acc. to Jos. the king asks of Is. a σημεῖόν τι καὶ τεράστιον ("a confirmatory phenomenon"), Ant., 10, 28 f. cf. 1 K. 20:1 ff. Thus a σημεῖον can be a τέρας in Jos., but it does not have to be.[166] In this respect it is closely related to אוֹת in the Heb. Bible on the one side and σημεῖον in the Gk. Bible on the other → 212, 37 ff.; 219, 14 ff. It is not surprising, then, that with ref. to the imminent destruction of Jerusalem Jos. avoids σημεῖον but calls an act of caprice on the part of the Jews a προοίμιον ἁλώσεως[167] for Jerusalem, Bell., 2, 454.[168]

Jos.' use of σημεῖον is less broad than Philo's. He does not allegorise nor does he adduce mathematical examples → 222, 4 ff., so that he does not need the related vocabulary. Instead he takes examples from military life. Yet in their basic understanding of the term there is no difference between Jos. and Philo. This is to be stressed all the more in that Jos. almost completely avoids σημεῖα καὶ τέρατα, the classical expression for the divine signs at the exodus. In his depiction of the events at the exodus Jos. simply uses (τὰ) σημεῖα for the signs, Ant., 2, 274, 276, 280 etc. The reason is obviously that he does not want them to be seen in the light of apparent or actual magic. He thus protects Moses expressly against the suspicion of τερατουργίαι καὶ μαγεῖαι in Ant., 2, 284 and makes Moses no more than a θεατὴς τεράτων in 4, 43. The Egypt. σημεῖα are God's affair, ἐκ θεοῦ, 2, 327. They rest finally on His πρόνοια καὶ δύναμις, cf. 2, 286. For Jos. they are decisively related to faith; they are meant to kindle this and to deepen it, cf. 2, 274, 276, 283 etc.[169] When God uses the σημεῖον

---

[163] Schl. Jos., 52 and cf. Schl. Theol. d. Jdt., 69.

[164] So correctly Schl. Theol. d. Jdt., 28.

[165] Jos. remains here wholly within the framework of σημεῖον in the LXX. Cf. σημείοις τοῖς ἐκ τοῦ θεοῦ διδαχθεῖσα in his account of Rahab and Joshua's spies in Ant., 5, 12 (→ 213, 30 ff.) and also his story of the σημεῖα Saul received after being anointed by Samuel in Ant., 6, 53 ff. cf. 1 Βασ. 10:1 ff.

[166] Cf. also Bell., 6, 288 ff. and esp. 288 and 295 alongside 295 and 315.

[167] προοίμιον means "prelude."

[168] In Bell., I, 45 a certain battle which is in some respects a symptom is a κληδών "omen."

[169] In the σημεῖον which Hezekiah asked for and received the faith of the king was strengthened acc. to Jos. Ant., 10, 28. Elijah's σημεῖα also differentiate faith from unbelief, cf. 8, 347 with 327, 343 and 350.

He shows thereby that He is the εἷς θεὸς καὶ μέγιστος καὶ ἀληθὴς μόνος, 8, 343. When He works a τέρας, this is not important as such but as a σημεῖον it denotes God's presence and thus points to God. [170] When acc. to Ant., 20, 168 conjurers and deceivers in Jerusalem were already in Nero's day persuading many to go out into the desert where they would show them ἐναργῆ τέρατα καὶ σημεῖα κατὰ τὴν τοῦ θεοῦ πρόνοιαν γινόμενα, the ref. to the time of the exodus is palpable in this formula, cf. 2, 286, [171] and so is Jos.' criticism of false insistence on τέρατα, in which his critical attitude to miracles generally finds expression. The summary mention of σημεῖα καὶ τέρατα preceding the storming of the city and temple in Bell., 1, 28 has merely a descriptive character in the light of the later more detailed account in 6, 288 ff., esp. as the σημεῖα come first and are thus given priority over the τέρατα as Jos. sees it. The problem which arises here is, of course, in the last analysis more a problem of faith than of miracles. At this pt. one may see the gulf which separates Jos. from the Evangelists, close though he may be to them in his fundamental approach to miracles. [172]

3. Apocalyptic.

→ 221, 16 ff.; 232, 24 ff.

C. סִימָן/אָתָא/אוֹת in Post-Biblical Judaism.

I. The Dead Sea Scrolls.

1. Biblical Usage Continued.

Bibl. usage is adopted in the so-called Book of Mysteries in 1 Q 27 Fr. 1 col. 1, 5 (DJD, I, 103) when we read with ref. to what is to come : . . . וְזֶה לָכֶם הָאוֹת כִּי → 213, 13 ff. Here the elements of visibility and confirmation which are obviously native to the word are combined in it after the ancient fashion. [173]

In 1 QH 12:8, in a passage which speaks of the alternation of day and night and the alternation of the seasons, there is ref. to אותות in a way which brings out clearly the designation of the function of the heavenly lights as astronomical אתת which fix the festivals as well as days and years. It is significant that what is linked with the reminiscence is not an astrological concept but the awareness of man in prayer that with his divinely ordained daily prayer at a specific time he is integrated into the great order of creation and brought into immediate proximity to God. In the אותות, the heavenly lights, God in some sense refers the worshipper continually back to Himself as the One who alone makes his worship possible as an ordered worship which orders life. [174] This does not mean, of course, that אות has here the sense of "sign of revelation" as a tt.

---

[170] So Schl. Theol. d. Jdt., 69.
[171] Cf. also Bell., 2, 258-260 (ὡς ἐκεῖ τοῦ θεοῦ δείξαντος αὐτοῖς σημεῖα ἐλευθερίας). The march into the desert will inaugurate the new age of salvation indicated esp. by the slogan ἐλευθερία cf. Ant., 2, 327.
[172] Cf. on this Schl. Theol. d. Jdt., 104 f.; Schl. Jos., 27 f.
[173] On the content of אות cf. O. A. Piper, "The 'Book of Mysteries' (Qumran I 27)," The Journal of Religion, 38 (1958), 95-106, esp. 96 f.
[174] For this reason one should not adduce the passage as an example of the "mysticism of the Qumran sect" as does A. Dupont-Sommer, Die essenischen Schriften vom Toten Meer (1960), 260, n. 1. The worship at issue here has nothing whatever to do with mysticism.

In 1 QS 3:14 it is laid down as the duty of the one who has knowledge (משכיל)
... to instruct and teach all the sons of light [175] לכול מיני רוחותם באותותם למעשיהם
בדורותם ולפקודת נגיעיהם. This whole passage is syntactically extremely difficult. [176] In
spite of many it is best to take the words למעשיהם...נגיעיהם as an elucidation of the
preceding words and esp. באותותם. [177] Then אותות means "all that whereby one knows"
what spirit is at work, and this in such a way that what the בני איש do under this influence is of importance like what comes upon them as a visitation from God. [178] Thus
construed the saying is close to Mt. 7:16 ff. / Lk. 6:43 ff.; Mt. 12:43 ff. / Lk. 11:24 ff.

In the texts thus far published אות is used most commonly in the sense of "standard."
1 QM offers a regular סרך אותות כול העדה in 3:12 ff. with detailed instructions for the
ordering of the האות הגדולה at the head of the whole people as the divine levy in the
battle between light and darkness (3, 12) and also of all the other standards in accordance
with the composition and direction of the host. Here [179] OT usage is sometimes adopted,
cf. Nu. 2:2 → 211, 31 ff. But the Kittim (הכתיאים) also have אותות (1 Q p Hab. 6:1, 4)
and if it can be said of them that they bring them offerings זבח (6:4) this is an argument for identifying the Kittim with the Romans, since a formal cult was connected
with the standards in the Roman armies. [180] In view of this it should be considered
whether this use of אות in the Dead Sea Scrolls, for all its unmistakable ref. to Nu. 2:2,
has not been influenced by the Lat. *signum* as a tt. for military standard.

אות ומולפת seems to be used in the damaged passage 1 QH 15:20. [181] If only מופת
is used in 13:16, a special thought is perhaps linked with אות ומופת here, and we are
probably to see a reminiscence of God's work in Egypt. It is possible that this is really
in the background, cf. v. 19 after v. 18. Yet the connection is fairly general and does
not justify too dogmatic a pronouncement.

2. A New Sense?

A difficult question arises in relation to 1 QS 10:4 : ואות נ with a space, then למפת ת
Does אות here correspond to the Rabb. usage (→ 228, 12 ff.) "letter," so that a mysterious statement is made about the meaning of the sign נ ? [182] Or should the text be

---

[175] The following words from תולדות to איש are better related to what precedes and
not made dependent on להבין וללמד (so P. Wernberg-Møller, *The Manual of Discipline*
[1957], 25 with n. 42; Dupont-Sommer, *op. cit.*, 85), since the sons of light have to
discharge their task in the world around them and the linking of למד with ב is rare (Is.
40:14). In 1 Q Sa. 1:7, as in bPes., 112b, ב לְמֵד seems to be "to teach by means of ..."
[176] Cf. the various transl. and comm.
[177] Wernberg-Møller, *op. cit.*, 67, n. 44 rightly refers to the combination of אות and
מעשה in Dt. 11:3, but his attempt to see a distinction in the use of אות ("sign," "miracle"
there, "characteristic" here) is unconvincing. The transl. always take the three expressions
beginning with ל as par.
[178] How this is to be understood cannot be discussed here.
[179] On details which cannot be pursued here cf. Y. Yadin, *The Scrolls of the War of
the Sons of Light against the Sons of Darkness* (Eng.) (1955), 36-59, also 274-285; Dupont-
Sommer, *op. cit.*, 192-194.
[180] Cf. K. Elliger, *Studien z. Hab.-Komm. vom Toten Meer* (1953), 187 f.; W. Kubitschek,
Art. "Signa" in Pauly-W., 2a (1923), 2342-2345.
[181] Conjectured (with a ref. to 1 QH 13:16) by A. Dupont-Sommer, *Le livre des hymnes
découvert près de la Mer Morte* (1957), 92, n. 9; J. Licht, *The Thanksgiving Scroll* (1957),
198.
[182] Dupont-Sommer, *op. cit.* (→ n. 174), 107, n. 2 detects the influence, which cannot
be assessed in detail, of the kind of numbers speculation seen in the role of 50 for the
Pythagoreans and here brought into connection with the Essene calendar.

regarded as corrupt and the meaning as unintelligible ?[183] Palaeographical considerations favour the view that a word was begun with נ but the writer did not complete it. However things might have been in the original,[184] in the present state of affairs it is not unlikely that אות is meant to be taken here as in Gn. 1:14 (→ 211, 27 ff.), i.e., as "sign."[185] If so, אות remains within the confines of what has proved to be customary usage thus far.[186]

II. אות etc. in Rabbinic Literature.

In the Rabb. אות plays quite a modest role. It retains its formal character as a "mark" and thus comes to denote "sign with whose help something may be recognised or known" on the one side and a "letter" or "character" on the other. The two meanings are grammatically distinct, since the plur. in the first case is אוֹתוֹת while in the second it is usually אוֹתִיּוֹת though → n. 196.

1. אות = Mark.[187]

In Kil., 9, 10 (cf. T. BQ, 11, 12) אות means the imprinted "mark" with whose help weavers and fullers distinguish their goods. Alongside this solitary instance in the Mishnah and Tosefta, אות is in e.g., bBQ, 119, Bar. the stamp such as one can get at a dyer. bBM, 23b lays down that someone who loses a metal object must give a mark (אות) or the weight if he wants to prove he is the real owner.[188] Sometimes there is ref. to the לְאוֹת of Ex. 13:9 in discussion of the tephillin, bMen., 37b, Bar. In an interpretation of 1 K. 20:35 ff. it is said to be of the nature of a prophet to prove himself to be such by giving a sign (יהב אות, bSanh., 89b, though unfortunately the context does not show what is in view). In an old circumcision prayer in bShab., 137b, Bar. circumcision is called אות ברית קודש; this is a liturgical archaism.

Of importance is a tradition in bSanh., 98a/b[189],[190] concerning a conversation between R. Jose bQisma[191] and his disciples which belongs to the period of the war between Bar Cochba and the Romans and in which R. Jose advises loyalty to the latter. Asked when the Son of David or the Messiah will come he first tries to dodge the question by announcing a prodigy ; he must yield to the demand to give a sign (נתן אות)[192] and prove his prophetic authority by a wonder : at his words the water in the cave of Paneas at Caesarea Philippi changes into blood.[193] The vital pt. here is that the original sense of אות (→ 211, 5 ff.) is retained. But it is better not to speak of miracles,

---

[183] So K. G. Kuhn, Konkordanz z. d. Qumrantexten (1960), 139, n. 1.

[184] A. M. Habermann, Megilloth midbar yehuda (1959), 68 would supply [נֶאֱמָן, J. v. d. Ploeg, "Le 'Manuel de Discipline,'" Bibliotheca Orientalis, 8 (1951), 124, n. 100 [נוֹרָא along the lines of Sir. 43:2, 8.

[185] So Wernberg-Møller, op. cit., 142 f., n. 12.

[186] Otherwise we have here the first instance of אות = "letter."

[187] Kassovsky, I, 46a defines אות as רושם וסמן העשוי כדבר להכירו.

[188] נתן אות as tt. is biblical Hbr. → 212, 34 ff.

[189] Par. Tanchuma וישלח, 8 (83b Buber).

[190] On its importance for certain stylistic peculiarities in the Synoptic accounts of miracles cf. A. Schlatter, "Das Wunder in d. Synagoge," BFTh, 16, 5 (1912), 67, n. 3.

[191] Cf. on him Bacher Tannaiten, I², 397-400.

[192] The Hbr. runs בְּקֵּשׁ אות מֵן.

[193] Schlatter, op. cit. (→ n. 190), 67 thinks the miracle was perhaps recounted already in the age of the Mishnah. But it may be asked whether the tradition did not develop so that an original prophecy was changed into a miracle. It should be considered, however, that the prophecy was not fulfilled unless the Son of David was seen in Bar Cochba.

since miracles are performed rather than given. In this respect S. Dt., 83 on 13:2 is also instructive with its distinction between אוֹת and מוֹפֵת, the former being related to heaven and the latter to earth. It is in keeping that for the Midrash a sign alone is not enough to establish faith; in each case the interpretation is also needed, Ex. r., 5, 13 on 4:31. Much the same line is followed by the Haggadic work Leqach tob on Ex. 3:12, [194] which was written only c. 1100 A.D. but contains a good deal of older material, and which distinguishes אוֹת and מוֹפֵת by referring the one to a specific time (still future) and the other to the present moment (לְאַלְתַּר).

The most remarkable thing about the Rabb. use of אוֹת for "sign," "mark," is its paucity. This may be attributed to the fact that the word is broadly replaced by סִימָן (→ lines 23 ff.), though this is not the whole story (→ 235, 31 ff.).

2. אוֹת = Letter.

Not merely in the Mishnah and Tosefta, but in Rabb. literature gen., אוֹת is predominantly used for a single letter of the Hbr. alphabet, e.g., Shab., 7, 2 : כתב שתי אותיות, cf. also 12, 3. 4. 6; T. Shab., 11, 11. 12. 13 etc. As is sometimes stated, this contains 22 characters, Tg. Cant., 1, 4 : עטרין ותרתין אותון. Possibly this usage is connected with the fact that the letters make known the revealed will of God. At any rate the Hbr. characters are regarded sacrally. [195] On occasion special respect is accorded to the letters with which the most holy name of God is written, T. Jad., 2, 12; Sanh., 12, 9. [196]

We simply have transf. usage when אוֹתִיּוֹת can also be used for documents, e.g., bonds, bBB, 75b/76a : אוֹתִיּוֹת are acquired by transfer, i.e., when a promissory note is passed on.

III. סִימָן in Rabbinic Usage.

1. General Considerations.

סִימָן, which in Rabb. usage almost completely replaces אוֹת in the sense of "mark" or "characteristic," [197] is probably [198] at root [199] the Gk. σημεῖον adopted as a loan word. [200] Yet it is worth noting that as a loan word it does not have the full breadth of the Gk. term but seems to have been essentially moulded by אוֹת. This also applies to a typically Rabb. mode of expression which must be dealt with separately → 229, 13 ff.

2. סִימָן = Characteristic, Sign.

This very common word is used, e.g., for the symptoms of someone suspected of a skin ailment which would make unclean, Neg., 3, 3, or for the distinctive features of a place, BM, 2, 7, or for the marks by which a mad (שׁוֹטֶה) dog is known, jJom., 8, 5

---

[194] Ed. S. Buber (1880), 9b.

[195] The original Torah was supposed to have been written by God Himself, cf. Str.-B., IV, 442 under b; cf. also Jos. Ant., 3, 101.

[196] Here in Tannaitic texts the plur. in both cases is (still ?) אוֹתוֹת and not אוֹתִיּוֹת → 227, 10 ff.

[197] The same is true of סִימָנָא in Rabb. Aram.

[198] Cf. K. H. Rengstorf, *Jebamot, Die Mischna*, III, 1 (1929), 202 f.; W. Windfuhr, "Der Terminus סימן bei den Rabb.," OLZ, 29 (1926), 791 f.

[199] This is true in spite of נִסְמָן in Is. 28:25.

[200] On the pronunciation cf. בִּימָה and βῆμα.

(45b, 12 f.); bJom., 83b, [201] or for characteristics which serve to identify a person, Jeb., 16, 3, or for the signs of sexual maturity in a woman, Nid., 5, 8 etc. If someone hurts himself at prayer this is a סִימָן רַע that he may expect something bad, Ber., 5, 5. R. Eli'ezer called rain at Tabernacles a sign of divine displeasure סִימָן קְלָלָה, Taan., 1, 1. [202] The picture presented thus far is generally confirmed when Tg. Pal. (Cod. Neofiti, I) has סימן for הָאוֹת at Ex. 3:12 or when ביקש אות מן (→ 227, 27 f. and n. 192) becomes ביקש סימן in Ex. r., 9, 1 on 7:9. סִימָן thus shares with אוֹת its technically neutral character. This is also true when it is used in astronomy for fixing the calendar, e.g., bAZ, 8a with ref. to Ps. 139:5. When all this is considered one may also include here the use of סִימָנִים for the windpipe and throat of an animal destined to be slaughtered. This is connected with the fact that it serves to show whether the animal is slit correctly and thus slaughtered in accordance with the Law. [203]

3. Special Rabbinic Use of סִימָן.

From the general sense of סִימָן the Rabbinate developed a special academic tt. which is best rendered "cue" and which has a place in the Rabb. system of mnemotechny. [204] The ref. is to words which either enclose a whole complex of arguments, or refer to certain legal cases in a systematic sequence, or are simply acrostically formed catchwords. [205] In so far as the foundations of knowledge are posited in them, the Rabb. use of סִימָן here remains finally within the formal signification which the word shares with the Hebr. אוֹת (→ 219, 5 ff.) and the Gk. σημεῖον (→ 206, 29 ff.). The same holds good when a biblical text is sometimes called סִימָן as a *dictum probans* or *adiuvans,* bAZ, 8a, or when the נ [206] sometimes interpolated into the Mas. text can be called סִימָנִיּוֹת — possibly on the model of the Gk. concern for diacritic signs such as are found in the traditional texts. [207]

D. σημεῖον in the New Testament.

I. General Data.

1. Statistics.

In the NT σημεῖον occurs for certain 73 times, and also in the secondary v. Mt. 16:3. [208] It is used 10 times in Mt., 7 in Mk., 23 in Luke (Lk. 10 and Ac. 13), 24 in John (Jn. 17 and Rev. 6), 8 in Paul and once in Hb. The most common use is in John. In Acts one should note that it is restricted to c. 1-15. It plays a comparatively minor role in Paul and does not occur at all in Gl., Eph., Phil., Col., 1 Th. or Phlm., or in the Past. Nor does it occur in the Catholic Epistles. A surprising pt. is that in Ac. it is predominantly in the plur. and is combined with τέρας in 9 of the 13 instances

---

[201] Gk. veterinarians also speak of σημεῖα in such cases, cf. S. Lieberman, *Hellenism in Jewish Palestine* (1950), 189, n. 68.

[202] Cf. the corresponding expressions סימן יפה in bBer., 34b, סימן ברכה in bTaan., 30b etc.

[203] Cf. on this B. Lauff, *Schechitah u. Bedikah (Schlachtung u. Untersuchung) usw.,* Diss. Tierärztliche Hochschule Berlin (1922), 15 f.

[204] Cf. Windfuhr, *op. cit.,* 792-794.

[205] To pursue this in detail would take us too far afield and would not in any case contribute much to an understanding of σημεῖον in the NT. Hence summary ref. may be made to the sketch in Windfuhr, *op. cit.*

[206] Nu. 10:35-36.

[207] Cf. on this Lieberman, *op. cit.,* 38-43.

[208] Mt. 16:2b-3 do not occur in א B syr^s syr^c Orig Hier. We probably have here an

→ 241, 24 ff. This is the more remarkable in that σημεῖα καὶ τέρατα or τέρατα καὶ σημεῖα does not occur at all in Lk. and is found only once each in Mt., Mk. (Mt. 24:24 = Mk. 13:22 → 241, 7 ff.) and Jn. (4:48 → 244, 13 ff.). Paul has it in typical passages in R. 15:19; 2 C. 12:12; 2 Th. 2:9, and the same applies to Hb. 2:4. Since the expression is linked with firmly established ideas in the OT (→ 216, 8 ff.) it is as well to treat all the passages in which it occurs together → 240, 35 ff.

2. Parallel Words and Concepts.

a. → τέρας, which is common in Gk. and fairly common in the LXX (→ 209, 3 ff.), occurs in the NT only in combination with σημεῖον and only in the pl. σημεῖα καὶ τέρατα or τέρατα καὶ σημεῖα (→ 240, 35 ff.); hence it does not play any independent role alongside σημεῖον.

b. The situation is different in the case of δύναμις, which the expression σημεῖα καὶ τέρατα is extended to include in Ac. 2:22; 2 Th. 2:9; cf. R. 15:19, but which is mostly independent and which in the plur. (δυνάμεις) even becomes a tt. for "miracles" in the NT → II, 301, 26 ff. It should be noted from the outset that in this sense δυνάμεις is most common in Mt. but that it is not found in this sense, or indeed at all, in Jn. If here the verb δύνασθαι is a substitute for much of what is denoted by δύναμις (→ II, 303, 23 ff.), it is still worthy of note that the noun does not occur at all in Jn. and that the verb itself is used only twice at Jn. 3:2; 9:16 with ref. to Jesus' ποιεῖν σημεῖα. One must proceed with caution at this pt. and not try to harmonise John and the Synoptic Gospels too hastily. [209]

c. A final pt. to be considered is that in Jn. → ἔργον is set alongside σημεῖον and that it forms a kind of three-cornered relation with σημεῖον and δύνασθαι. [210] Hence if we are to understand σημεῖον in Jn. a great deal depends on whether or to what degree the relation between σημεῖον and ἔργον in Jn. is successfully defined, → 247, 27 ff.

3. Preliminary Remarks on New Testament Usage.

When one attempts to find angles for arranging the use of σημεῖον in the NT there is seen within it a tension whose explanation is not immediately apparent. On the one side the word is used as the object of a whole group of verbs which emphasise human activity, e.g., ποιεῖν in Jn. 4:54 etc., διδόναι in Mt. 26:48, δεικνύναι in Jn. 2:18, or κατεργάζεσθαι in 2 C. 12:12, or which objectify what is meant by σημεῖον so that one can ask for or demand it, ἐπερωτᾶν, Mt. 16:1; [ἐπι]ζητεῖν (Mt. 12:39) Lk. 11:16; αἰτεῖν, 1 C. 1:22, or see it βλέπειν, Ac. 8:6; ἰδεῖν, Jn. 6:26, or even take up a position towards it, ἀντιλέγειν, Lk. 2:34. On the other side σημεῖον is something which is outside the influence of man. It comes from heaven, Mk. 8:11, or is in heaven, Rev. 12:1 etc., or in the sun, Lk. 21:25, or God is its author, Mt. 12:39 : δοθήσεται, and for this reason it concerns all the more the man whom it is designed to instruct. There are also instances in which the word is somewhere in the middle, e.g., where there is ref. to a σημεῖον τῆς ἰάσεως in Ac. 4:22 or a σημεῖον τοῦ υἱοῦ τοῦ ἀνθρώπου in Mt. 24:30. For here that to which it points, healing or the Son of Man, is outside man's competence but is obviously regarded as something which comes into his sphere of reference by means of the σημεῖον.

---

ancient gloss which acc. to Kl. Mt., ad loc. seems to be freely modelled on Lk. 12:54-56 or which acc. to Zn. Mt., ad loc. might have made its way into the text from Papias.

[209] In → II, 303, 23 ff. the situation in Jn. is not seen in sharp enough focus since the σημεῖα of Jesus are here defined as "unique and incomparable acts" which "express the unique δύναμις of Christ." The portrayal of Christ in Mt. exerts too strong an influence.

[210] This is missed both in → II, 303, 17 ff. s.v. δύναμις and → II, 642, 37 ff. s.v. ἔργον.

If in face of the varied nature of NT usage a basic meaning can be laid down at all, this seems to reside in the fact that in a specific situation which cannot be repeated σημεῖον states or indicates a possibility or intention or the indispensability of a definite human reference. Where σημεῖον occurs there always occurs also in the NT a kind of pointer to the responsibility of the man or men involved in the relevant situation. This offers a wide variety in individual cases, so that one has to say precisely what is concretely at issue in any given instance.

II. σημεῖον in the Synoptic Gospels and Acts.

1. σημεῖον = Sign, Mark.

Lk. 2:12 uses the words καὶ τοῦτο ὑμῖν τὸ [211] σημεῖον, [212] thus adopting an OT expression, [213] as an introduction to the declaration of the angel in which he adduces as a "sign" or "proof" of the truth of his message about the birth of the Messiah the fact that the newborn child has found his first resting-place in a crib. [214] This passage brings out excellently the formal character of σημεῖον, since it is taken expressly from a situation which is unique for all concerned. In this situation it presupposes among those for whom it is meant the perception of certain data (2:15) which for their part serve a purpose of confirmation, 2:16, 20.

The sign which is given to the shepherds lies in the extraordinary situation of the newborn babe, which is in the last resort that of his mother. [215] Within the whole passage Lk. 2:1-20 the σημεῖον given to the shepherds has the significance of setting them in motion so that they for their part can be a sign to Mary, though this does not have to be stated explicitly in the story. [216] In no sense, however, does the crib as a σημεῖον have the task of pointing to the child in it as a "wonder-child," [217] for to do this does not lie in the nature of the σημεῖον as such nor may it be concluded from the way in which the crib is made a sign here.

Mt. (26:48) says that Judas gave a σημεῖον to those ordered to arrest Jesus: ὃν ἂν φιλήσω αὐτός ἐστιν. Here a kiss (→ φίλημα) serves to distinguish the one they were seeking. Once again the elements of sense perception and confirmation are combined in σημεῖον, and once again what is denoted by the

---

[211] There is no art. in B pc. But with most witnesses, as against Nestle, it belongs in the text since the par. in Hb. and the Gk. Bible (→ n. 213) always has the art and this is also the case in, e.g., 1 Q 27:1, I, 5 (וזה לכם האות). The pt. is that in the OT and Jewish view there is always something specific about the sign even when nothing has been said about it before, cf. H. Sahlin, "Der Messias u. d. Gottesvolk," *Acta Seminarii Neotest. Upsaliensis*, 12 (1945), 220.

[212] On the significance of the idea of the sign in the infancy stories in Lk. even where there is no express ref. to it, cf. Sahlin, *op. cit.*, 335-339.

[213] Ex. 3:12; 1 S. 2:34; 14:10; 2 K. 19:29; 20:9; Is. 37:30; 38:7, also 1 Βασ. 10:1 f.: καὶ τοῦτό σοι τὸ σημεῖον ... καὶ εὑρήσεις ...

[214] So, e.g., M. Dibelius, "Jungfrauensohn u. Krippenkind," *Botschaft u. Geschichte,* I (1953), 60.

[215] Cf. on this K. H. Rengstorf, "Die Weihnachtserzählung des Evangelisten Lk.," *Stat crux dum volvitur orbis, Festschr. H. Lilje* (1959), 15-30.

[216] Cf. Rengstorf, *op. cit.*, 26-28. The shepherds should thus be added to Sahlin's list of persons who are themselves signs in the Lucan infancy stories, Sahlin, *op. cit.*, 336 f.

[217] Dibelius, *op. cit.*, 61.

σημεῖον refers to a specific situation and does not go beyond it [218] (→ 206, 29 ff.; on σημεῖον as an agreed sign → 223, 18 ff.). [219] In Mt. 24:3 the disciples ask for the σημεῖον τῆς σῆς παρουσίας καὶ συντελείας τοῦ αἰῶνος. What they have in mind here, as in Mk. 13:4 and Lk. 21:7, [220] is that whereby the imminence of events which are then described in greater detail may be discerned. In Mk. and Lk. the concept and formulation reflect apocalyptic expectation. On the other hand τὸ σημεῖον τῆς παρουσίας in Mt. 24:3 bears no more necessary relation to apocalyptic than the formal par. τὰ σημεῖα τῆς σωτηρίας which Joseph. uses in Bell., 6, 285 to denote the content of what the inhabitants of Jerusalem, deceived by false prophets, still expected on the day of the burning of the temple → 224, 5 ff. Neither in Mt. nor Joseph. is the idea of miracle wholly combined with σημεῖον as such. The word simply denotes something which may be perceived and from which those who observe it may draw assured conclusions, → V, 866, 2 ff.

The nearest formal par. to Mt. 24:3 is in Diodor. S., 3, 66, 3. This refers to τοῦ θεοῦ σημεῖα ... τῆς ἰδίας ... παρουσίας, and here, as in Mt., σημεῖον denotes that which makes something that is very specific, i.e., the appearing of the god, recognisable as such. In the σημεῖα in the sun, moon, and stars in Lk. 21:25 one may see from the par. Mt. 24:29; Mk. 13:24 f. and the underlying apocalyptic passages (Is. 13:10; 34:4) that the reference is to astronomical events which show that the last time is dawning. Here, too, σημεῖον is thus a "sign" with no secondary meaning. If the events are miraculous it is simply because one may see from them that the order of creation is beginning to disintegrate → 70, 9 ff.

It is a common idea in later Jewish apoc. that the beginning of the end will be preceded by cosmic changes which cannot be overlooked and which proclaim what is coming to the wise. In 4 Esr. radical changes in the functions of the sun, moon, and stars (5:4; cf. 7:39) are among the *multitudo signorum quae incipies facere in novissimis, Domine,* 8:63. Here as in many other passages (4:51 f.; 5:1, 13; 6:12, 20; 7:26; 9:1, 6) *signum* corresponds to the Gk. σημεῖον and is clearly distinguished from *mirabile* as a divine miracle in 1:14; 2:48; 7:27 etc. Sib. uses the ancient σῆμα (→ 202, 2 ff.) similarly in 2, 154; 3, 796 and 804. Gr. En. 8:3 has σημειωτικά for the "astrology" of the Eth. text, i.e., "what one must know to handle σημεῖα correctly," but in his excerpts from Gr. En., which he gets from Julius Africanus, the Byzantine chronicler Georgius Syncellus (end of the 8th cent.) has at the corresponding place τὰ σημεῖα τῆς γῆς, τὰ σημεῖα τοῦ ἡλίου, τὰ σημεῖα τῆς σελήνης, in which he undoubtedly follows the ancient usage of apocalyptic, though his authority for his part very probably does not quote Gr. En. directly but by way of the Alexandrian chronicler Panodorus (c. 400 A.D.). [221] For the rest 4 Esr. again follows the ancient use of σημεῖον (→ 220, 11 ff.)

---

[218] Comparison of Mt. 26:48 and Mk. 14:44 also shows that ἔδωκεν in Mt. (corresponding to δεδώκει in Mk.) is to be taken as a pluperf. On διδόναι σημεῖον → 227, 17 ff., on linguistic par. in Jos. → 224, 5 ff. and n. 219.

[219] Cf. Str.-B., I, 995 f.; K. M. Hofmann, Philema hagion (1938), 42 on the kiss of greeting, Lk. 7:45. For a good par. which contains all the elements in the Judas incident, including the σημεῖον, cf. Jos. Ant., 12, 404 : (Demetrius) ἀσπασάμενος τὸν Ἰούδαν μεταξὺ προσομιλῶν δίδωσι τοῖς οἰκείοις τι σημεῖον, ὅπως συλλάβωσι τὸν Ἰούδαν. Cf. Schl. Mt., *ad loc.*

[220] The juxtaposition of the two words raises the question whether Mt. 24:3 elucidates the par. v. Mk. 13:4 (→ V, 865, n. 42 and Bultmann Trad., 71) or whether conversely Mk. here interprets Mt. (Schl. Mk., *ad loc.*), but we need not try to decide this here.

[221] H. Gelzer, *Sextus Iulius Africanus u. d. byzant. Chronographie*, II, 1 (1885), 249-276; Schürer, III⁴, 286.

by putting alongside the *signa* and *somnia* the *interpretationes* which are indispensable to both (14:7 f.).

2. The Sign of Jonah (→ III, 408, 15 ff.).

In Mt. 12:39 f.; 16:4/Lk. 11:29 f. we find a saying of Jesus in which He relates to Himself τὸ σημεῖον 'Ιωνᾶ (Mt. 12:39 + τοῦ προφήτου) from the standpoint of His own work. [222] The saying is obscure not so much by intention [223] as by virtue of its subject. [224] Among the many attempts to explain it (→ III, 408, 17 ff.) the one that has most to commend it is that which takes 'Ιωνᾶ as a genitive of apposition [225] and finds in τὸ σημεῖον 'Ιωνᾶ the sign which Jonah himself is in the singularity of his historical manifestation. [226] This does not answer the question in what sense he is taken to be a sign. According to the context and also the meaning of σημεῖον it seems very probable that the saying characterises Jonah as the one in whom God Himself [227] shows Himself to be present with the prophet and at work through him and his call for repentance. Only to this extent does the saying relate to the authentication of Jonah, and this less in respect of his person than of the cause which he represents. [228]

The referring of the Jonah saying to the prophet in his special historical manifestation is supported on the one side by the Lucan version, which makes Jonah himself the sign and thus does greater justice to the meaning of σημεῖον than either is or seems to be the case in Mt., while on the other side it is also backed up by the view of Jonah in later Judaism. Attention has been drawn to both these factors in → III, 409, 12 ff., though with no ref. to the precise sense of σημεῖον. [229] That attention should be paid to this is suggested by the fact that the Midrash [230] refers to the אותות והנפלאות הגדולות "which the Holy One, blessed be He, did to Jonah (עם יונה)", thus distinguishing אות from נפלאה. [231] How strongly primitive Chr. tradition found the emphasis of the saying

---

[222] The saying, which is usually attributed to Q with (secondary ?) editorial influence on the Matthean version, presents many problems in interpretation. These are increased by the context in which it is set and which is very puzzling since it combines the demand of opponents for a sign with a statement about the Son of Man and His destiny. Cf. Bultmann Trad., 124; A. Vögtle, "Der Spruch vom Jonaszeichen," *Synpt. Studien, Festschr. A. Wikenhauser* (1953), 230-275; W. Grundmann, *Die Gesch. Jesu Christi* (1957), 150, n. 1; W. G. Kümmel, *Verheissung u. Erfüllung*³ (1956), 61.

[223] Caution is necessary here since we do not know what picture of Jonah is presupposed in the hearers.

[224] J. Schniewind, *Das Ev. nach Mt., NT Deutsch*, 2⁹ (1960), ad loc.: "... the saying is a riddle." Cf. H. E. Tödt, *Der Menschensohn in d. synpt. Überlieferung* (1959), 159.

[225] On the various attempts to explain the gen. → III, 408, 17 ff.

[226] This rules out any ref. of σημεῖον to the prophet's preaching of repentance, as in → III, 409, 3 ff., though for different reasons. Cf. → 233, 25 ff.

[227] Cf. the pass. δοθήσεται denoting God in Mt. 12:39; Lk. 11:29.

[228] This obviously carries with it the authenticating of the prophet too, though for a different purpose than that assumed both for the original meaning of the sign and also for its ref. to Jesus in → III, 409, 21 ff.

[229] Schl. Mt., ad loc., 416 (followed by → III, 409, 11 ff.) finds everywhere in σημεῖον, and hence here too, a ref. to "the intervention of the power of God in the course of events," and J. Jeremias (→ III, 409, 3 ff.) on this ground rules out interpretation of the σημεῖον 'Ιωνᾶ in terms of the prophet's preaching of repentance. But both are here going beyond the limits set by investigation of the meaning of σημεῖον. On this cf. what follows.

[230] PREl, 10; Midr. Jon. on 2:11 (A. Jellinek, *Bet ha-Midr.*, I [1938], 99, 22 f.; a degenerate text).

[231] On the formation and meaning of נפלאה (only plur.) "extraordinary miracle" cf. the dict., s.v. פלא.

in the person of Jonah may be seen from the statement in Mt. 12:41/Lk. 11:32 which concludes the series of logia, for it says that a greater than Jonah is present, thus directing attention to the person and in so doing underlining the character of this person as a sign. The implied idea that a person can be God's sign is linked with prophetic figures in the OT, cf. merely Is. 8:18; 20:3; Ez. 12:6 etc. It is also to be found in the NT, where it is again connected with prophetic phenomena. When Mt. 12:39, unlike Lk. 11:29 (→ 233, 9), also calls Jonah a prophet, here already on the basis of OT and Jewish ideas we have a ref. to the way in which he can and must be a sign.

How we interpret the referring of the saying about the sign of Jonah to Jesus, as this is done not only in Mt. 12:40 but also in Mt. 12:41/Lk. 11:32, is naturally dependent on our evaluation of the v. If it is regarded as the Chr. revision of an older Jewish apoc. tradition, [232] then it is a bit of primitive Chr. proclamation which interprets the saying of Jesus in the light of His history, and esp. His death and resurrection, and which thus finds the unity of His Word and history in His Messianic personality. [233] Yet the underlying presupposition is not at all convincing if Lk. 11:30 is also taken into account and it is recognised that the ref. is to the coming Son of Man rather than the Son of Man already present. [234] On the basis of this saying as an authentic threat issued by Jesus [235] it is thus possible to regard the saying in Mt. 12:41/Lk. 11:32 as a genuine testimony of Jesus which uses prophetic categories in self-portrayal [236] but which does not remain tied to them. This is proved by the incomparable authority exercised by Jesus [237] as in the calling of the disciples (→ IV, 444, 7 ff.) or His conduct at the Last Supper ⁓ an authority which ultimately defies categorisation in the primitive Chr. tradition and the Chr. proclamation based upon it. In the present context it is enough to recall certain sayings which express this quite unmistakably, e.g., in addition to Mt. 12:41/Lk. 11:32 the par. Mt. 12:42/Lk. 11:31, [238] the saying in Mt. 12:6 (τοῦ ἱεροῦ μεῖζόν ἐστιν ὧδε) and that in Mt. 11:9/Lk. 7:26 (περισσότερον προφήτου). [239] It should be noted that all these sayings have the comp. in the neuter and thus have something distinctively enigmatic about them.

3. The σημεῖον Demanded from Jesus.

The Jonah saying (→ 233, 3 ff.) is Jesus' answer in Mt. 12:38 ff. and Lk. 11:29 ff. to the demand that He should give a σημεῖον, cf. also Lk. 11:16. There is reference to a similar demand in Mt. 16:1/Mk. 8:11. Finally Lk. in his special material has the story that Herod Antipas hoped to see a σημεῖον from Jesus when Pilate sent Jesus to him as a prisoner because He belonged to Herod's territory and was thus within his jurisdiction (Lk. 23:6), Lk. 23:8. In assessing the significance of this demand or expectation the following points are important. The reference is always to one σημεῖον (sing.) rather than many σημεῖα. Except in Lk. 23:8 the demand arises in scribal circles. [240] The background is formed by

---

[232] Bultmann Trad., 133. Kl. Mt. on 12:40 : "... Mt. in his devotional typology ..."
[233] Cf., e.g., Bultmann Trad., 162 f.; Vögtle, op. cit., 273.
[234] Cf. on this Tödt, op. cit., 49 with n. 53.
[235] Ibid., 48-50 with n. 60 ("... the discriminatory form of authentic sayings of Jesus...").
[236] So rightly Bultmann Trad., 163.
[237] Tödt, 265.
[238] Perhaps it was originally independent and only came into the present context through the interrelating of catchwords (via καὶ ἰδοὺ πλεῖον ... ὧδε).
[239] It should not be ruled out that originally this saying might have had, not the Baptist, but Jesus Himself in view (with a ref. back to Lk. 7:16). This makes it easier to explain the textual difficulties in Lk. and also the relation of Lk. 7:31 ff. to what precedes.
[240] Mk. 8:11: Pharisees ; Mt. 12:38 : scribes and Pharisees ; Mt. 16:1: Pharisees and Sadducees. No more precise definition is given of Jesus' opponents in Lk. 11:29 but His

the miracles of Jesus in which His authority is expressed, Mt. 12:22 ff./Lk. 11:16 ff.; Mt. 15:21 ff./Mk. 7:24 ff. The request or expectation is thus related to the person of Jesus in a particular situation, cf. also Lk. 23:8 with 9:7 ff. The demand for a sign concerns God as the author, Mt. 16:1/Mk. 8:11: σημεῖον ἐκ or ἀπὸ τοῦ οὐρανοῦ cf. Mt. 12:39/Lk. 11:29 : σημεῖον οὐ δοθήσεται → n. 227. To this degree the demand for a sign has to do with the reciprocal relation between Jesus and God on the one hand and on the other hand the relation of those who are interested in a sign to Jesus in the sense of a religious relation (πίστις). When all this is added up, the point of the demand is that Jesus should undertake to show thereby that God, in whose name He works, has unequivocally authorised Him. This authentication will take place when God does something or causes something to happen in relation to Jesus which will prove that any doubt concerning His divine authority is wrong. Hence σημεῖον takes on the significance of a very general framework which, when the demand for it is raised, must be filled in a way which corresponds to the existing situation if the desired goal is to be reached. Once again the formal character of the word (→ 203, 31 ff.) emerges. In keeping is the fact that no material definition of the word is given in the Synoptic Gospels even in connection with the demand for a σημεῖον which is put to Jesus.

In the Synoptic Gospels the current term for the miracles of Jesus is δύναμις, → II, 301, 26 ff.; σημεῖον is never used for them. There are in the tradition reminiscences of the fact that the δυνάμεις of Jesus are not regarded as σημεῖα in the sense of the demand for a sign ; indeed, the miracles give rise to the demand, cf. the whole passage Lk. 11:14 ff. with 11:16. [241] For the non-Jewish contemporaries of Jesus the δυνάμεις are in no way extraordinary, [242] but what they implied affected the biblical world and was regarded by it as sorcery, cf. simply Ac. 8:9 ff.; [243] 19:18 f. The overcoming of demons by Jesus raised for the righteous, who saw themselves constantly threatened by demons, [244] the question who was ultimately at work here, God or merely the prince of the demonic hierarchy, who can sometimes put on a spectacle, cf. Mk. 3:22 and par. Behind the demonological system developed by later Judaism [245] lies a profound fear of the world of demons. [246] The Rabbinate had a definite dread of the אות/σημεῖον (→ 228, 9 ff.) because on the one hand it grounded its authority solely in Scripture and the tradition which helped to a correct understanding thereof, and on the other it found in miracles a symptom of heresy if they took place in the Jewish sphere as human acts. [247] "The sign is at once regarded as indispensable only when a particular divine commission is given to a man and a prophecy ... is to be confirmed," [248] i.e., the sign

---

defence here is included in the controversy with Pharisaism, 11:14-54. Lk. 23:8 presupposes that the king is influenced by scribal circles or by their evaluation of Jesus ; whether this is true cannot be discussed here since we simply have the traditional framework of the relevant portions of the tradition. On the Sadducees cf. Mt. 16:1 → 52, 21 ff. In assessing this passage one should not overlook the fact that Mt. 16:1-4 no longer enables us to say from what context Mt. took it.

[241] Cf. also Mt. 12:22-38, though the pt. is less clear here than in Lk.
[242] → II, 289, 7 ff. on the theurge of antiquity and his δυνάμεις.
[243] Cf. Haench. Ag., ad loc.; E. Haenchen, "Gab es eine vorchr. Gnosis?" ZThK, 49 (1952), 316-349.
[244] Str.-B., IV, 515-521.
[245] Ibid., 509-514.
[246] Cf. Schl. Mt. on 12:23.
[247] Cf. on this Schlatter, op. cit. (→ n. 190), 57 with materials from Tosefta and the Jerusalem Talmud.
[248] Ibid., 69.

applies to the prophet or to one who claims to be such. Any righteous man can ask for a miracle, but when it takes place he is not the author, but God. [249]

In a way which is astonishingly precise, then, the demand for a sign from Jesus corresponds to His appearance as depicted in the Synoptic tradition. It relates to His δυνάμεις, which have all the marks of divine δύναμις but which are done as His own δυνάμεις and not received only in answer to prayer. It also relates to His freedom over against the tradition and His independence in the use of Scripture (e.g., Mk. 12:26 f. and par.) and its exposition (e.g., Mk. 1:21 f.; Mt. 7:29 : ὡς ἐξουσίαν ἔχων). [250] Finally it relates to the question of the rightness or wrongness of His immediacy to God. It does not contest the freedom of Jesus even while demanding that He make answer concerning it. According to the kerygma it is more an assault on God's freedom in so far as it lays upon God its own basic principles concerning what may be and what may not. In the last resort this is what makes of those who demand a sign a γενεὰ πονηρά (Lk. 11:29) or a γενεὰ πονηρὰ καὶ μοιχαλίς (Mt. 12:39) [251] — a society which breaks away from God by emancipating itself from Him in its judgment and acts.

4. The Sign of the Son of Man.

Only Mt. in his version of the Synoptic Apocalypse reports that Jesus, after the sayings about cosmic convulsions just before the end (→ 232, 18 ff.), expressly announces as something specific the appearing (φανήσεται) of the σημεῖον τοῦ υἱοῦ τοῦ ἀνθρώπου, 24:30. In this way the final act in the events of the last time, the parousia of the Son of Man, becomes far more vivid and dramatic than in the other Synoptics. For Mt. divides it as it were into three scenes : the appearance of the sign of the Son of Man, His own unmistakable coming with great power and glory, and the gathering of His elect by His angels, the assembling of the definitive universal community. [252] Unfortunately even though the structure of Mt. 24:30 f. is clear the saying about the sign of the Son of Man is itself mysterious. [253] From the context one may gather only that it is something which is clearly terrifying, since it causes all races on earth to strike up a lament for themselves in their last hopeless distress → III, 850, 22 ff. In other words the sign

---

[249] Ibid., 73-83.

[250] The meaning is that Jesus establishes new halachot without normal authorisation by incorporation in the chain of tradition. Cf. on this D. Daube, The NT and Rabbinic Judaism (1956), 205-216.

[251] → IV, 734, 37 ff., though one needs to distinguish more strongly than here between the two adj. if one is to get the full pt. of their combination. On ἡ γενεὰ αὕτη cf. M. Meinertz, " 'Dieses Geschlecht' im NT," BZ, NF, 1 (1957), 283-289, who refers to the Jewish people as such, not to any particular period.

[252] Mk. has only the last two scenes and on the basis of Mk. 13:24 ff. Lk. restricts himself to the saying about the coming of the Son of Man (Lk. 21:27), so that the whole emphasis in the parousia is concentrated on the coming as such with a gt. stress on the comfort there is in this event for Christendom (21:28). For important observations on this cf. Wellh. Lk. on 21:25. But when Tödt, op. cit., 91-93 suggests that in the Son of Man Lk. sees only the advocate and pledge of the salvation of Christians before God and not the executor of judgment he is undoubtedly going too far, since in the σταθῆναι ἔμπροσθεν τοῦ υἱοῦ τοῦ ἀνθρώπου of Lk. 21:36, which is written with the readers in view, the ἔμπροσθεν plainly contains the idea of the Son of Man as Judge of His people.

[253] Schl. Mt., ad loc.

of the Son of Man is of such a kind that present earthly-human existence reaches its ineluctable end therein. It proclaims this end unconditionally, and this is its true significance.

The combination of the two texts Zech. 12:12, 14 and Da. 7:13 f. with the ref. to the sign of the Son of Man in Mt. 24:30 has been explained in different ways. Since the two texts are also combined in Rev. 1:7 it has been suggested that both passages used a collection of Testimonies. [254, 255] In the main, however, it is supposed that both passages draw on a common tradition [256] and attempts have been made to pin this down, a Jewish original being sought on the one side, [257] a Chr. origin on the other, [258] while account has naturally been taken of the results of modern exegetical work. [259] In all the discussion of this question too little attention has been paid to the fact that the order of the combined OT quotations varies in Mt. 24:30 and Rev. 1:7, for Rev. 1:7 puts the Da. ref. first while Zech. 12:12, 14 comes first in Mt., and furthermore Mt., unlike Rev. and also Jn. 19:37, which also quotes Zech. 12:12, 14, [260] does not include the ref. to "him whom they pierced" in his form of the quotation from Zech. Another pt. is that Mt.'s dependence on tradition for his version of the text cannot be proved. [261] Hence it is probably correct to suppose that Mt. himself arranged the order deliberately. [262] He adduced the ref. from Zech. to show how much the appearing of the sign of the Son of Man already affects the human race in its awareness of itself. This all amounts to the fact that in Mt. 24:30 and the verses which follow the Evangelist is using traditional material to make his own point. This does not, of course, rule out the possibility that he is adopting a fixed phrase in the expression τὸ σημεῖον τοῦ υἱοῦ τοῦ ἀνθρώπου. [263]

The expression τὸ σημεῖον τοῦ υἱοῦ τοῦ ἀνθρώπου proves to be complex in so far as the reference is less to the person of the Son of Man than to His apocalyptic function. [264] In the context Mt. 24:29 ff. is saying that the *parousia* will not come directly but will announce itself first. It may be that in the background is the certainty that the last act of history will begin with a final opportunity for conversion and faith. This is an approach to apocalyptic expectation which fits in well with the picture of the First Evangelist and his basical ethical position. In this light the question how the sign of the Son of Man is to be taken

---

[254] R. Harris, *Testimonies*, I-II (1916-1920).

[255] So, e.g., H. B. Swete, *The Apocalypse of St. John²* (1907), ad loc.

[256] Cf. C. G. Montefiore, *The Synoptic Gospels*, II² (1927) on Mt. 24:30 : "a common source"; Kl. Mt. on 24:30 : "... perhaps using a common source."

[257] R. H. Charles, *A Crit. and Exeg. Comm. on the Revelation of St. John*, ICC I (1920) on 1:7.

[258] W. C. Allen, *A Crit. and Exeg. Comm. on the Gospel acc. to St. Matthew*, ICC³ (1912) on 24:30 finds in the combined quotation "a commonplace of Christian Apocalyptic study."

[259] K. Stendahl, "The School of St. Matthew," Acta Seminarii Neotest. Upsaliensis, 20 (1954), 212-214 considers two possibilities : part of "the church's basic teaching in Christology" or a *verbum Christi* after the manner of 1 Th. 4:15 ff.; he himself favours the latter, 214 and n. 3.

[260] C. H. Dodd, *Acc. to the Scriptures* (1952), 65 thinks we have here a specifically Ephesian or Johannine tradition rather than "something strictly *gemeinchristlich*."

[261] Cf. on this Stendahl, *op. cit.*, 213 f.; Dodd, *op. cit.* for this reason does not discuss the relation between Rev. 1:7 and Mt. 24:30.

[262] Tödt, 74 f. and n. 108.

[263] J. Weiss in *Schr. NT*, I² on Mt. 24:30.

[264] Since the context pts. neither to the cross of Jesus nor to His resurrection and exalta-

concretely is only a secondary one. Nor is it possible to say anything very certain in reply.

In the Palestinian Synagogue the lamentation of Zech. 12:12, 14 is sometimes understood as lamentation for the Messiah, jSukka, 5, 2 (55b, 40): ספדה ... זה הספידו של ...משיח,[265] but this proves only the christological ref. of the passage, which is supported also by Jn. 19:17; Rev. 1:7. An isolated and late Rabb. passage in Pesikt. r., 36 [266] combines an appearing of light with the coming of the Messiah, but one cannot rule out the possibility that this is allegorical. Nor is there either way any ref. to expectation of the Son of Man. In the Church the sign of the Son of Man was quite early found in the cross, Apc. Pt. 1; cf. Ev. Pt. 39; [267] more plainly Epistula Apostolorum 16, where the cross [268] precedes the returning Lord. [269] The context itself does not justify this interpretation → n. 264. It also rules out any identifying of the sign with the Son of Man Himself, [270] as most commentators have rightly seen. [271] On the relation between Did., 16, 6 and Mt. 24:30 → 261, 25 ff.

5. σημεῖον ἀντιλεγόμενον (Lk. 2:34).

In Lk. 2:25 ff. Simeon, depicted here as a prophet, says to the mother of Jesus that this child who is presented in the temple will be a σημεῖον ἀντιλεγόμενον, 2:34. [272] The section 2:21-40 raises a host of problems in the sphere of religious history, the history of the tradition, and the editing of the work. [273] Suffice it to say that even on the critical side the Jewish Chr. character of the whole passage is acknowledged and that in vv. 34-35, even if later additions are conjectured, [274] a part of the original is perceived. [275] It is also recognised that the passage has an OT/Jewish colouring. [276] This is important because it means that there is also agreement on certain linguistic presuppositions in the interpretation of σημεῖον ἀντιλεγόμενον.

Any exposition of the expression must start with the fact that under the comprehensive and basic κεῖται, which points to God as the author, it is parallel to εἰς πτῶσιν καὶ ἀνάστασιν πολλῶν ἐν τῷ 'Ισραήλ. [277] Thus the σημεῖον at issue here, both in its factuality and also its singularity, rests on a direct positing by God. The fact that it is displayed in a man is not unusual in biblical

---

tion there is the less reason not to ascribe Mt. 24:30a to Jesus, for, being so enigmatic, it can hardly be explained as the work of the community or a redactor.

[265] Schl. Mt. on 24:30.

[266] Str.-B., I, 954 f.

[267] Hennecke[3], I, 123.

[268] Ibid., 134. Where the Eth. has "cross" the Coptic text has "sign of the cross" (ⲉⲡⲥⲏⲙⲉ[ⲓ]ⲟⲛ [ⲛ̄ⲡⲧⲥ]ⲧⲁⲩⲣⲟⲥ) cf. C. Schmidt, "Gespräche Jesu mit seinen Jüngern nach d. Auferstehung," TU, 43 (1919), 6* and 56 f.

[269] For further materials on interpretation in the early Church cf. W. Bousset, Der Antichrist in d. Überlieferung des Judt., des NT u. d. alten Kirche (1895), 154-159.

[270] So, e.g., Schniewind, op. cit. (→ n. 224), ad loc.

[271] Cf. → 237, 24 ff. and esp. Zn. Mt., ad loc.; J. Schmid, D. Ev. nach Mt.[4], Regensburger NT (1959), ad loc.

[272] On the presentation of Jesus cf. Str.-B., II, 120-123.

[273] On these cf. the comm. and esp. Bultmann Trad., 326 f., 329-335, and on the linguistic character of the whole passage Sahlin, op. cit. (→ n. 211), 239-242.

[274] εἰς ἀνάστασιν in v. 34 and the saying about the sword which will go through Mary's soul (cf. Sib., 3, 316) in v. 35 i.e., the whole of v. 35a, are sometimes listed among these.

[275] This is then thought to consist of 2:20-28a and 34 with 35b, Bultmann Trad., 326.

[276] Bultmann Trad., 329.

[277] On this meaning of κεῖται cf. Mt. 3:10/Lk. 3:9.

thinking → 231, 23 ff. If a Semitic equivalent is sought [278] it can only be אוֹת. [279] This is supported by what is said in v. 35b about the effect of Him who is called σημεῖον; by Him the thoughts of many hearts will be disclosed. Since this will take place in a twofold way it is better to take ἀντιλέγεσθαι here in the sense of "contradicted" or "contested" rather than "resisted" or "rejected." The bad thing from Simeon's standpoint is that the sign is not regarded as God's sign with all that this implies. Nor does the mother of Jesus escape the discord which He unleashes as the objective sign of God. [280] Since the reference is to the sign which God sets up, according to the attitude taken thereto there is falling (→ VI, 167, 20 ff.) and rising again (→ I, 372, 3 ff.) in Israel (→ VI, 541, 32 ff.). The last point guarantees the Messianic horizon of the term and the filling out of what is here again the formal sign by the definition of Him who is Himself the sign in person, namely, as ἀνὴρ προφήτης δυνατὸς ἐν ἔργῳ καὶ λόγῳ, Lk. 24:19.

6. σημεῖον in Acts.

Apart from the 9 instances in which σημεῖον occurs in the phrase σημεῖα καὶ τέρατα or τέρατα καὶ σημεῖα (→ n. 286), the words occurs 4 times in Ac. Twice in 4:16, 22 it is connected with Peter and his healing in the temple court of the man who had been lame for over 40 years, while the other two ref. in 8:6, 13 relate to Philip, one of the seven, 6:5. In 4:16; 8:6 there is no addition, but in 8:13 we find the phrase σημεῖα καὶ δυνάμεις and finally in 4:22 the healing of the lame man is retrospectively called τὸ σημεῖον τοῦτο [281] τῆς ἰάσεως. The occurrence of σημεῖον is restricted to Ac. 1-12, and the same applies to σημεῖα καὶ τέρατα → 240, 35 ff. This permits us to draw the provisional conclusion that by and large the use of σημεῖον in Ac. is within the same framework as the use in the Synoptics (→ 231, 8 ff.) and that on their native soil (→ 225, 17 ff.).

In combination with 19:11 the distinction between σημεῖα and δυνάμεις in 8:13 is a guarantee that in Ac., too, σημεῖον is not just a "wonder." When 8:6 refers to the doing and seeing of the σημεῖα of Philip and when in 4:16 the members of the Sanhedrin say that a γνωστὸν [282] σημεῖον has occurred through

---

[278] Sahlin, op. cit., 269-272 has attempted a reconstruction of what he supposed to be the basic proto-Lucan text (Hbr.) of the two verses, but in so doing he has demanded too much both of himself and also of the Gk. text. It is no accident that in Schlatter's collections of par. to Lk. (Schl. Lk.) 2:34 f. is left out both in respect of the Pal. Rabb. and also in respect of Joseph. Nor do the Mas. and LXX help us much. Acc. to Schl.'s judgment (Lk., 202 on 1-2) Lk. himself finally decided the form of his Gospel even where on his view he was using the lost Gospel of a Palestinian of the first generation, as in the infancy stories. This gives Lk. its linguistic character and this seems to be very clearly Lucan in 2:24 f.

[279] Sahlin, 271, following L. Brun, Lukas-Evangeliet (1933), 90 and with a ref. to Is. (8:14 f. and 11:10 ff.), suggests נֵס "banner," which LXX sometimes renders σημεῖον → 208, 34 ff. But the idea of a banner which has been set up does not fit the context of Lk. 2:34 f., since the effect of the σημεῖον here is to divide rather than to gather as in Is. 11:10 ff. etc.

[280] Acc. to the context the intervening v. 35a is to be construed thus rather than as an intimation of Mary's destiny to be the mater dolorosa, Schl. Lk., ad loc., 196 (→ VI, 995, 12 ff.). Cf. on this inter al. G. Erdmann, Die Vorgeschichten d. Lk.- u. Mt.-Ev. (1932), 45 f. The saying is not on any account to be interpreted psychologically.

[281] τοῦτο is not in D gig.

[282] γνωστός here means "manifest" and to that degree (v. 16b) "undeniable."

the disciples in the healing of the lame man, there is a further approximation to Synoptic usage (→ 231, 10 ff.); γνωστός underlines the sign character of the healing as a miracle (cf. 4:7: ἐν ποίᾳ δυνάμει ...) all the more impressively in that it may be described as generally known. [283] With this alone is it in keeping that in 4:4 the interpretation of the healing (understood as a σημεῖον) by Peter and John leads to faith. The same is presupposed in 5:12 ff., cf. also 14:3 f. Hence τὸ σημεῖον τῆς ἰάσεως in 4:22 means the healing of the lame man in so far as it is a sign, [284] since it points beyond itself to the One in whose δύναμις and ὄνομα (4:7) it took place primarily as no more than a εὐεργεσία ἀνθρώπου ἀσθενοῦς (4:9). Here then, as elsewhere in Ac., σημεῖον expresses the Christological and kerygmatic reference of the miracle in which Jesus, rejected by His people, not only aims at their hearts by way of the ear in proclamation (2:37) but also shows *ad oculos*, in those commissioned by Him, that He is the living Lord whom God Himself authenticates. To bring this out, we must translate σημεῖον basically by "sign" in Acts also.

Yet in the use of σημεῖον in Ac. there is a new feature as compared with the Synoptics, for now the disciples of Jesus perform σημεῖα in His name whereas in the Gospels we find only one σημεῖον in a given situation, and this only when it is demanded from Him → 234, 29 ff. In the plural use in Ac. with reference to the disciples of Jesus there is reflected the new situation inaugurated by the death, resurrection and ascension of Jesus. In this all the δυνάμεις or τέρατα which take place in His name necessarily become a σημεῖον, a pointer to Him and beyond Him to God as His God (e.g., 2:22 ff.), so that there arises a whole chain of σημεῖα in the sense of a series of indications which cannot be overlooked. These σημεῖα share the lot of the σημεῖον in that they have to be interpreted and in certain circumstances may be interpreted in different ways. Luke was not only aware of this; he also stated it plainly, cf. Ac. 14:3. But this does not affect the nature of the σημεῖον. It affects the nature of faith, which does not live by the miracle but by the Word (cf. 4:16b) to which the miracle is ordered and subordinated as σημεῖον. Thus in the designation of human δυνάμεις as σημεῖα in Ac. there is an element of theologically based self-diffidence. These are no marvels; they are obedient and unselfish acts in the power of Jesus and for His sake. [285]

7. σημεῖα καὶ τέρατα.

This expression occurs in the Synoptists only at Mt. 24:24 = Mk. 13:22. It is not used at all in Lk., but we find it 9 times in Ac. [286] It is seldom used in other books. Paul has it 3 times → 258, 4 ff. Finally there is an instance in Jn. 4:48. The use in Ac. is in essence restricted to c. 1-8, i.e., to that part in which Lk. has undoubtedly edited older and pre-stamped materials. This may well be true also in the two instances

---

[283] On φανερόν cf. φανήσεται in Mt. 24:30.

[284] τῆς ἰάσεως is thus gen. of appos. אוֹת הָרְפוּאָה might correspond in Hbr. (cf. F. Delitzsch, *Hbr. NT*[12] [1937], *ad loc.*). רְפוּאָה is an old Hbr. word (Ex. 30:21) which was much used in the Tannaitic period.

[285] In assessing individual signs in Ac. it should not be forgotten that our criteria are not always the same as those of the first Christians. The reason is, of course, cultural rather than theological.

[286] There are two forms: σημεῖα καὶ τέρατα in 4:30; 5:12; 14:3; 15:12, and τέρατα καὶ σημεῖα in 2:19, 22, 43; 6:8; 7:36.

outside this complex (14:3; 15:12). [287] At any rate one may say that the expression is obviously not specifically Lucan here. It is a patent biblicism (→ 216, 8 ff.) of Palestinian origin. To this degree it is one of the marks of the provenance of the tradition which in whole or in part lies behind Ac. 14:1 ff. and 15:1 ff.

In the use of σημεῖα καὶ τέρατα there are two characteristic differences between the Synoptic Gospels and Acts.

a. In Mt. 24:24 = Mk. 13:22, as in Dt. 13:2, the doing of σημεῖα καὶ τέρατα is projected into the future and incorporated into Messianic expectation, so that it is part of the picture of apocalyptic pseudo-messiahs. All this is in keeping with the current Messianic interpretation of Dt. 18:15, 18. [288] It is presupposed as self-evident, of course, that σημεῖα καὶ τέρατα will accompany the Messiah as the promised prophet. But this is not stated, and the result is that the expression almost seems to belong to the sphere of pseudo-messiahs, though this can hardly be intentional.

There are perhaps two reasons for the obvious reserve in Mt. and Mk. For one thing it is perhaps connected with the fact that according to unanimous tradition Jesus refused to authenticate Himself, or to let Himself be authenticated, by a σημεῖον → 234, 29 ff. For another, we have to consider the view of the Evangelists, and indeed the pre-Easter situation of Jesus, in which He had not yet shown Himself to be ἄρχων καὶ λυτρωτής cf. Ac. 7:35 → 242, 7 ff. Things seem to be rather different in Lk. If, following his sources, he uses the phrase quite often in Ac. but avoids it in the Gospel, this is clearly connected with a typological view of the post-Easter situation which is esp. strong in him → lines 27 ff.; 243, 1 ff. [289]

b. For the author of Ac. the new Mosaic age of eschatological redemption is exhibited in the typical σημεῖα καὶ τέρατα of the present, just as recollection of the redemption from Egypt was bound up with this expression in Judaism, → 216, 8 ff.; 221, 7 ff. The σημεῖα καὶ τέρατα, which now take place afresh as they once did at the exodus with its miraculous accompanying phenomena, are a pledge of the certainty of eschatological occurrence. In this approach the way in which primitive Christianity understood both itself and Scripture typologically finds expression at a central point in a most instructive manner.

---

[287] As regards the context of Ac. 14:3 one may refer to the isolated description of Barnabas and Paul as ἀπόστολοι in v. 4 and the distinctive καταφεύγειν in v. 6. As regards Ac. 15 the relation to Gl. 2:1 ff. is esp. striking. σημεῖα καὶ τέρατα is of a piece with this. But in neither passage do we have "sources" in the ordinary sense. This is ruled out by the fact that typical Lucanisms like, e.g., ὁ λόγος τῆς χάριτος (14:3 cf. Lk. 4:22; Ac. 20:32; on c. 15 cf. Haench. Ag., passim) show that Luke himself is responsible for the form. As regards Ac. 15, the relation to Gl. 2:1 ff. leaves us only with a choice if we are concerned merely with what took place. But the situation has a very different aspect if one considers that the same event can be evaluated very differently when seen and judged by different reporters from different angles, esp. when personal involvement plays a part. Hence Ac. 15 is not specifically concerned about Paul, whereas Paul is writing as a passionate participant in Gl. 2:1 ff.

[288] The most important instance is Jn. 1:21. In Pesikt., 13 (112a) cf. Str.-B., II, 626 f. anti-chr. polemic in interpretation of Dt. 18:18 is combined with a referring of the v. to Jeremiah. Cf. Schl. Mt. on 24:24; Str.-B., II, 479 f.

[289] Lk. in his account of pre-messianic afflictions refers in 21:11 to φόβητρά τε καὶ ἀπ' οὐρανοῦ σημεῖα μεγάλα, cf. the prodigies said to have preceded the destruction of Jerusalem, Schl. Lk., 413, ad loc. The expression seems to be Palestinian, Schl. Lk., 217 on 3:23-38.

An essential point in assessing the situation in Ac. is that among the 9 passages in which the expression occurs (→ n. 286) there are 2 in which it is part of a quotation or allusion : 2:19 = Jl. 2:30; 7:36 = Ex. 7:3. In both of these it is apparent that the author of Ac. was aware that the expression bore a ref. to the time of the exodus. As the class. time of redemption this was regarded as a type of the redemption by Jesus here and now, for in Jesus the promise of a prophet like Moses (Dt. 18:15, 18) had been eschatologically fulfilled (7:37) and Moses himself, including the way he was shamefully treated by his own people (7:35 : ἀρνεῖσθαι, cf. 3:13 f.; 7:27, 39 : ἀπωθεῖν) was seen as a prototype of Jesus → IV, 868, 9 ff.; VI, 845, 16 ff. (7:35 : Moses as ἄρχων καὶ λυτρωτής). [290] In the light of this typological understanding the use of Jl. 2:30 in Ac. 2:19 becomes clear. The eschatological prediction is fulfilled both in the outpouring of the Spirit and its effects and also in certain astronomical events at the death of Jesus as these are also reported in Lk. 23:44 f. For all their differences in other respects Ac. 2:19 and 7:36 are thus at one in their typological interpretation of the expression.

As a whole, then, one may distinguish in Ac. two ways of using kerygmatically the typologically interpreted expression σημεῖα καὶ τέρατα. In the one the typological possibilities are exploited to the full and the three subjects involved are all presented: Moses, Jesus, and those commissioned by Jesus. In the other only Jesus and the apostles are mentioned.

(a) In Peter's address at Pentecost there is added to the τέρατα (מוֹפְתִים) of Jl. 2:30 (→ line 3) etc. [291] a σημεῖα, and this yields the formula τέρατα καὶ σημεῖα (2:19) which is used twice in what follows, first on the lips of Peter with reference to Jesus (2:22), then in the continuation of the story with reference to οἱ ἀπόστολοι (2:43). It may be seen from 2:22 that the phrase is for the author an interpretative key, for he speaks here of δυνάμεις καὶ τέρατα καὶ σημεῖα, thus adopting the description of the miracles of Jesus in Lk. 10:13; 19:37 and integrating it typologically. Things are fundamentally the same in the story of Stephen. The reference here is to the τέρατα καὶ σημεῖα of Moses (→ lines 4 ff.), 7:36; it is naturally assumed that Jesus performs these too. But earlier (6:8) the author has already directed attention to the τέρατα καὶ σημεῖα of the witness, namely, Stephen. Since ultimately it is God Himself who works in the τέρατα καὶ σημεῖα, the ascribing of these to the witnesses of Jesus means that the ἀποδεδεῖχθαι [292] which is said of Jesus in 2:22 applies to them too.

(b) In the second group of passages there is no reference to Moses. Here the spotlight is on the ἀπόστολοι, [293] though in such a way that it moves from Jesus to them. It is His hand which is at work in their σημεῖα καὶ τέρατα (so expressly 4:30; 14:3), and in the last resort it is again God Himself who does the work (15:12; cf. 4:24 ff.; 5:12 ff.). [294] The apostolic σημεῖα καὶ τέρατα seem to be particularly important, for in them is to be found an essential and indispensable part of the divine authentication of the apostles, cf. Paul's τὰ σημεῖα τοῦ ἀποστόλου in 2 C. 12:12. [295]

---

[290] Cf. on this L. Goppelt, *Typos* (1939), 145 f.; Haench. Ag., *ad loc.*
[291] The other ref. need not be discussed here.
[292] Here as often the pass. is used for God's action.
[293] This also applies to 4:30, as 4:33 shows.
[294] Note again the pass. for God's work.
[295] Ref. must also be made to the inauthentic Marcan ending, 16:17 and esp. 16:20. Here only σημεῖα are mentioned, as by Pl. in 2 C. 12:12, but in such a way that one can detect the compound σημεῖα καὶ τέρατα behind them.

It would thus appear that in Ac. "signs and wonders" are mentioned as it were on two different planes, the one that of typological consideration and the other that of apostolic awareness and experience. The remarkable thing is that different forms are used for the different perspectives, τέρατα καὶ σημεῖα for the one and σημεῖα καὶ τέρατα for the other. The former, with all that it implies, is used only in the stories of Stephen and Pentecost; the latter occurs in very different sections but all these seem to be united by a common interest in the apostolate and its nature. Not even formally by choosing a single "signs and wonders" formula did Lk. try to combine the two aspects. Is this because his handling of the material at his disposal is governed by certain principles which for all his freedom in individual formulation are still to be seen again and again in his work? Is it in the last resort the traditional material itself which breaks through at this point? Or are we to assume that there were other reasons? [296]

III. σημεῖον in the Johannine Writings. [297]

1. Features Common to John and the Synoptists and Acts.

a. John knows and uses σημεῖον in the sense of "sign," "pointer," "mark" in such a way as to do justice to the formal character of the word → 206, 29 ff.; 220, 11 ff.

This is shown by the breadth of his usage. σημεῖον can be a "sign" or "portent" with ref. to prodigies in the heavens, Rev. 12:1, 3; 15:1. [298] It can also mean "proof" in self-authentication, Jn. 2:18. Finally, it has the sense of "wonderful acts," esp. on the part of Jesus, but also as performed by powers hostile to God or Christ in Rev. 13:13 f.; 16:14; 19:20 → 255, 25 ff. and → 245, 29 ff.

b. Furthermore the basic thrust of the term is clear in John, for no matter what specific nuances are given by the context the essential reference here again is to visual perception and the assurance this gives, → 204, 12 ff.

The Johannine sign is something one can and basically should see, Jn. 2:23 : θεωρεῖν; 6:2 : ὁρᾶν; 6:14, 30; Rev. 15:1 etc.: ἰδεῖν cf. Lk. 23:8; Rev. 12:1, 3 : ὤφθη. Here then, as in Mt. 16:1 (ἐπιδεικνύειν), a σημεῖον may be said to show itself, Jn. 2:18 : δεικνύειν. But there is also a par. use to that of the Synoptics (→ 231, 10 ff.) and Ac. (→ 239, 15 ff.) in the fact that what is called a σημεῖον in Jn. offers the chance to know something specific, cf. the whole passage Jn. 10:32 ff. [299] In Jn.'s Gospel, of course, the ref. is almost exclusively to the person of Jesus : σημεῖα pose questions about Jesus' appearance in Jn. 6:14; they are a means to reveal His true nature, δόξα, in 2:11; they make it possible to discern in Him the Son of God who has come from the Father and who returns to Him, cf. 14:9 ff.; 16:28; they are a reason for faith in Him, 6:30 etc. Yet all this is just a way of using the word rather than a deviation from its customary sense.

---

[296] The phrase also occurs sometimes in apocr. Acts, σημεῖα καὶ τέρατα in Act. Phil. 144 (Jesus as δεδωκὼς ἡμῖν σημεῖα καὶ τέρατα); Mart. Andreae prius 1 (based on Ac. 2:22) and 3; τέρατα καὶ σημεῖα in Act. Joh. 82 cf. 106. On the use in the post-apost. fathers → 261, 16 ff.

[297] There have been many detailed notes on this but so far no monographs. What follows is thus only a first attempt at systematic presentation.

[298] Apocalyptic usage is naturally present here. On the relation between the use of σημεῖον in Jn. and that in Rev. → 245, 29 ff.

[299] One should not miss this because ἔργον is the slogan here. On the relation between σημεῖον and ἔργον → 247, 25 ff.

c. John is also acquainted with the Synoptic tradition about asking Jesus for a σημεῖον → 234, 29 ff.

Twice Jn. records such a request, once in 2:18 after the cleansing of the temple and with express ref. to this, then in 6:1 ff. after the feeding of the five thousand and thus in connection with a significant σημεῖον (6:30). Unlike the Synoptists John is content simply to speak of a σημεῖον and does not refer to the demand for a σημεῖον ἀπὸ τοῦ οὐρανοῦ → 235, 4 ff. This distinction is based on the portrait of Christ in Jn. More important, however, is the fact that in both the Synoptists and John it is entirely up to Jesus how He will meet the demand. [300] In this we see again the formal character of the word in Jn. too. He is at one with the Synoptists here, though as a constituent part of his kerygmatic vocabulary the word is essentially much more strongly freighted in Jn. than in the Synoptic Gospels or even Ac.

d. For the sake of completeness it should be recalled that the combined expression σημεῖα καὶ τέρατα, which derives from OT and Jewish tradition (→ 216, 8 ff.), occurs once in Jn. at Jn. 4:48. As in the tradition (→ 221, 7 ff.) it probably echoes here too the motif of the Mosaic emancipation and its miracles. But it does not seem to be integrated into the *kerygma* as in Ac. (→ 241, 24 ff.); instead it appears to be used polemically.

The phrase is surprising in view of the fact that in the older Gospels it occurs only in connection with the prophecy of Jesus (→ 241, 7 ff.) and not, as here, in discussions of faith and its basis → 250, 21 ff. Nor is there any contextual relation to the use in Ac. whether from the typological standpt. (→ 241, 24 ff.) or from that of the apostolate (→ 242, 34 ff.). It is thus likely that in Jn. Jesus' rejection of σημεῖα καὶ τέρατα as an appropriate basis for faith is connected with a polemic of the Evangelist against churchly views which either regard σημεῖα καὶ τέρατα as important in principle or at least leave a place for them. For John himself they are obviously superfluous now that Jesus Himself is present — He who in His person is the one and all-sufficient basis of faith.

In gen. the comm. do not go into the expression. Those which do usually treat it as if only σημεῖα were there. [301] We are already helped beyond this by the question whether this is not an attack on a missionary strategy which tries to induce faith by appealing to σημεῖα καὶ τέρατα, and whether it is not also correcting a naive faith in miracles as seen in the Synoptic tradition. Yet the question must be put with greater precision than this. The word is possibly [302] connected with the circle of ideas around the Passover as the feast of remembrance for the exodus and liberation. Jesus opposes in His own people an attitude like that of the wilderness generation in which readiness to believe is made dependent on signs and wonders, [303] signs and wonders being expected from Jesus as from Moses, since Jesus is the promised new prophet like unto

---

[300] This is overlooked by, e.g., P. Gardner-Smith, *St. John and the Synoptic Gospels* (1938), 15.

[301] So also Schl. J., *ad loc.*; A. Schlatter, *Der Glaube im NT*⁴ (1927), 197 f. On what follows cf. Bultmann J. on 4:48.

[302] Bultmann (J., 145, n. 1 on 4:35) rightly rejects the idea of Schl. J. on 4:35 that the journey to Galilee might have taken place in December in view of 4:35. In the outline of the 4th Gospel what is told in c. 3-4 takes place between Passover and Tabernacles in the same year, cf. Jn. 5:1: ἑορτή.

[303] To be sure the son of the βασιλικός whose saving from death is asked of Jesus in Jn. 4:47 f. is not called the eldest or even the only son. Yet this possibility is suggested rather than excluded by the way he is referred to as ὁ υἱός. Hence recollection of the deliverance of the firstborn of Israel in the night of the Egypt. Passover might well underlie the request to Jesus, esp. as Jesus' answer undoubtedly characterises the father as a Jew, Schl. J., *ad loc.*; Bultmann J., *ad loc.*, 152, n. 3.

Moses (→ VI, 845, 16 ff.), cf. esp. Jn. 4:19 and 4:25.[304] Another possibility is that the attack is on an understanding of Christianity in which it is typologically identified with the Israel of Moses' time and signs and wonders are thus regarded as proper to it. It could be that John has in view enthusiastic circles who in their typological thinking are inclined to see in Christianity only the new Israel so that they run the danger of forgetting that they are in principle independent of continual miraculous experiences in virtue of the resurrection of their Lord from the dead. At any rate Jn. 4:48 gives an insight into the nature of Chr. faith and the Chr. community such as is formulated in 20:29b[305] with its independence of any kind of demonstration.

2. General Aspects of the Distinctive Johannine Usage.

a. The distinctiveness of the Johannine use of σημεῖον is that here, both in the Gospel and Rev., the word has taken over the role which δύναμις (→ 230, 12 ff.) plays elsewhere in the NT and especially in the Synoptics,[306] namely, as the exclusive term for certain miraculous events.

What John calls this is the result of a personal action, as is shown by the regular combination of σημεῖον with a word of activity, usually ποιεῖν (so also Rev. 13:13; 16:14; 19:20). Johannine σημεῖα and the person of the one who does them cannot be separated. In some way the σημεῖα also bear the nature of him who is at work in them. Concerning the σημεῖα of Jesus Nicodemus says that no one can do them unless God be with him, Jn. 3:2. In keeping is a saying which emanates from Pharisaic circles after the curing of the blind man on the Sabbath (9:16) and which is to the effect that it is impossible for a sinful man[307] to do τοιαῦτα σημεῖα. The decisive thing is not the quantity of σημεῖα or the greatness of the individual σημεῖον; it is the quality, which depends on the quality of their author. The beast from the abyss, in whom the divine portrays the pseudo-prophet of the pseudo-christ, does σημεῖα μεγάλα in Rev. 13:13. In acc. with his nature they are naturally signs which lead men astray (13:14), so that they fall into idolatry (13:14 ff.). In all this the formal character of σημεῖον is to be seen again quite plainly in both Jn. and Rev.

In John the use of σημεῖον in this way is restricted to Jesus in the Gospel[308] and to ungodly powers in Rev. There is about it something superhuman and distinctly miraculous. In the Gospel there is general reference to the σημεῖα of Jesus (2:23; 3:2; 6:2, 26; 9:16) and sometimes there is summary mention of their great number (11:47; 12:37; 20:30). But a few are specially emphasised. In general

---

[304] Samaritan Messianic expectation (→ 89, 31 ff.) seems to have had the marks of expectation of Moses redivivus acc. to Dt. 18:15, cf. J. Bowman, "Samaritan Studies," *Bulletin of the John Rylands Library*, 40 (1958), 299, n. 5. Within the interpretation given here Jn. 4:44 perhaps leads us closer to 4:46 ff. The saying about the prophet who has no honour in his own country is perhaps taken here by Jn. in the sense that there is something quite inappropriate about calling Jesus a prophet.

[305] Bultmann J., *ad loc.*

[306] Mt. 13:58 has the plur. δυνάμεις corresponding to σημεῖα. The parallel between σημεῖον in Jn. and δύναμις in the Synoptists is supported by a comparison of Jn. 10:41 ('Ιωάννης μὲν σημεῖον ἐποίησεν οὐδέν) and Mk. 6:5 (Jesus οὐκ ἐδύνατο ... ποιῆσαι οὐδεμίαν δύναμιν).

[307] ἄνθρωπος ἁμαρτωλός is a catchword, → I, 328, 1 ff. The question is really that of the legitimacy of Jesus, cf. Bultmann J., *ad loc.*

[308] This is confirmed by Jn. 10:41, where the Baptist, unlike Jesus, performs no σημεῖον. W. Baldensperger, *Der Prolog d. 4. Ev.* (1898), 89, n. 5 was the first to see in Jn. 10:41 an indirect ref. to miracles ascribed to or even told about the Baptist, and he appealed also

they are the kind of miracles expected with the dawn of the Messianic age, cf. the saying in Is. 35:5 (Mt. 11:5/Lk. 7:22).[309] No matter how one computes the number of σημεῖα of Jesus which were particularly important for the Evangelist,[310] those miracles which he records bear Messianic features and are thus in some sense Messianic epiphany-miracles. The miracle at the wedding in Cana of Galilee in Jn. 2:11, the second miracle at Cana (the healing of the son of the βασιλικός) in 4:54, the feeding of the multitude in 6:14 and the raising of Lazarus in 12:18 are all explicitly called σημεῖα. In relation to the σημεῖα mentioned in 9:16 the healing of the man born blind (9:1 ff.) is to the fore, while the healing of the lame man on the Sabbath (5:1 ff.) is adduced more as an example in 6:2.[311] Raising the dead and healings are typical wonders of the Messianic age. The feeding of the multitude and the miracle at Cana fit into this pattern inasmuch as they correspond to the expectation that the Messianic age will put an end to hunger and thirst.

> There is no healing of lepers in Jn., though such healings are even given emphasis in the Synoptics, Mk. 1:41 ff. and par.; Lk. 17:11 ff.; cf. Mt. 11:5/Lk. 7:22; Mt. 10:8. But this is perhaps connected with the fact that so far as may be seen from later Jewish tradition the curing of leprosy was not as such regarded expressly as one of the marks of the Messianic age.[312] Nor does Jn. say anything about exorcisms of demons by Jesus. A survey of the miraculous acts of Jesus which are called σημεῖα in this Gospel suggests that Jn. is less interested in typical Messianic miracles on the part of Jesus than in those which by their greatness raise the question as to the nature of the One who works in them → 249, 23 ff. Thus a fundamental Messianic tendency of the σημεῖα can sometimes be mentioned by John himself, cf., e.g., Jn. 6:15 with 6:1 ff.; 12:13, 18 with 11:1 f. This is in perfect agreement with the aim of the author if the ταῦτα of 20:31 is referring back to the πολλὰ καὶ ἄλλα σημεῖα of 20:30,[313] for in this case the book is presented to the readers as a collection of σημεῖα[314] which is designed to give them assurance that Jesus is the Messiah.[315]

---

to Mt. 14:2 in support. Many comm. have adopted this interpretation, cf. also Bultmann J., ad loc., 300, n. 4. But it is only a conjecture which cannot be substantiated exegetically. It may be added that Jn. 10:41 is not making a judgment but merely stating a fact, and is essentially different from sayings which can be viewed as polemical like Jn. 1:7 f.; 5:35, quite apart from verses in which John has the Baptist himself say that his relation to Jesus is one of inferiority. Cf. also Jn. 3:27.

[309] On this expectation cf. the material in Str.-B., I, 593-596.

[310] Bultmann is certainly justified in protesting (J. on 2:1-12, p. 78, n. 2) against Lohmeyer's attempt ("Über Aufbau u. Gliederung d. 4. Ev.," ZNW, 27 [1928], 12 etc.) at all costs to fix the no. of σημεῖα at seven (2:1 ff.; 4:47 ff.; 5:1 ff.; 6:1 ff.; 6:16 ff.; 9:1 ff.; 11:1 ff.), whether or not one argues the pt. in the same way as Bultmann does. Jn. was interested in certain σημεῖα but not in a certain no., as may be seen from 20:30.

[311] Cf. Bultmann J., ad loc.

[312] The opp. is maintained on the basis of Str.-B., I, 593-596 → IV, 240, 23 ff., but instances are sought in vain unless leprosy is included in the gen. expectation that disease will disappear in the Messianic age. Furthermore it should not be overlooked that lepers, and indeed the dead, are not mentioned in Is. 35:5. On the historical problem of Mt. 11:5, with possible Mandaean influences, cf. R. Reitzenstein, "Das mandäische Buch d. Herrn d. Grösse u. d. Ev.-Überlieferung," SAH, 1919, 12 (1919), 60-63, cf. Lidz. Ginza, XII; Kl. Mt., ad loc.

[313] Strongly emphasised by J. H. Bernard, A Critical and Exegetical Comm. on the Gospel acc. to St. John, ICC, II (1928), ad loc.

[314] M. Dibelius, Die Formgesch. d. Ev.³ (1959), 37, n. 3.

[315] The question whether Jn. took the σημεῖα recorded by him from a special source may be left aside here, since our concern is simply with the meaning of σημεῖον in Jn., cf. A. Faure, "Die at.lichen Zitate im 4. Ev. u. d. Quellenscheidungshypothese," ZNW, 21

b. Another point worth noting in the Johannine use of σημεῖον is that it is restricted to acts of Jesus (→ lines 27 ff.), and this in the broadest sense, since the Evangelist also counts among the σημεῖα the appearance of the Risen Lord to the disciples including Thomas (20:24 ff. cf. 20:30 f.). But he obviously makes no conscious use of a possibility presented by current usage, namely, that of describing a saying which points forward into the future as a σημεῖον. In other words, John never calls a saying of Jesus a σημεῖον. [316]

c. Finally it should not be forgotten that σημεῖον occurs predominantly on the lips of the Evangelist himself (2:11, 23; 4:54; 6:2, 14; 12:18, 37; 20:30) and in sayings which from the standpoint of expounding what follows he ascribes to the Pharisees (9:16; 11:47), to Nicodemus (3:2) or to an anonymous crowd swayed by Jesus (7:31; 10:41). Apart from its use in the expression σημεῖα καὶ τέρατα in 4:48 (→ 244, 13 ff.) Jesus Himself uses the term only once in 6:26, and here in such a way as to suggest that the Evangelist is letting Jesus speak in his own language in order to bring out fully this concept which is so important for his evangelistic goal. [317] In Johannine usage, then, σημεῖον is a key word in theological interpretation, and in this respect there is a fundamental difference from its use not only in the Synoptic Gospels (→ 231, 9 ff.) and Acts (→ 241, 15 ff.) but also in the surrounding world, whether in relation to σημεῖον (→ 204, 4 ff.) or to אוֹת and equivalents (→ 210, 14 ff.).

An instructive example is offered by taking Jn. 7:31 and 5:20 together. What the people say about Jesus in the phrase πλείονα σημεῖα ποιεῖν in 7:31 is expressed by John himself in μείζονα δεικνύναι ἔργα in 5:20. Here σημεῖον is plainly meant to interpret what is at issue in the ἔργα of Jesus.

3. σημεῖον and ἔργον. [318]

a. General.

Most of the 27 ἔργα passages in Jn. are clearly related to the σημεῖα of Jesus (Jn. 5:20, 36; 6:29; 7:3, 21; 9:3 f.; 10:25, 32, 37 f.; 14:10 ff.; 15:24; 17:4). Furthermore they not only establish a close connection between the ἔργα of Jesus as σημεῖα and the work of God effected in the ἔργα (→ II, 639, 41 ff.; 642, 37 ff.; → χείρ). Obviously they also neither can nor will say anything about these ἔργα

(1922), 109 : "book of miracles"; 112 : "miracle source"; Bultmann J. on 2:1-12 and Index, s.v. "σημεῖα-Quelle." For champions of the theory Jn. 20:30 f. is naturally the end of the Johannine miracle-source.

[316] Three times the Joh. Jesus is said to have pointed to the future in an enigmatic way which imposed a need for interpretation, twice with ref. to the manner of His own death (12:33; 18:32) and once with ref. to that of the death ordained for Peter (21:19). But in all these instances σημεῖον is avoided and σημαίνειν is used (→ 264, 24 ff.) to show what Jesus is doing : ἔλεγεν or εἶπεν σημαίνων ποίῳ θανάτῳ ...

[317] To the degree that the comm. discuss this isolated σημεῖον on the lips of Jesus they refer to the typical misunderstanding of the Samaritan woman in 4:15 and thus assume that the saying is ambivalent in John, cf. C. K. Barrett, The Gospel acc. to St. John (1955) on 4:48 and Bultmann J., ad loc. H. Strathmann, Das Ev. nach Jn., NT Deutsch, 4⁸ (1955), ad loc. stresses this even outwardly by writing "Zeichen" in his transl. But in this case would one not expect a sing. σημεῖον in the Gk. as a ref. to the miracle of feeding ? Furthermore the saying does not occur in the story of Jesus and the Samaritan woman.

[318] Cf. on what follows H. H. Huber, Der Begriff d. Offenbarung im Joh.-Ev. (1934), 96-101 on work as a means of revelation ; L. Cerfaux, "Les miracles, signes messianiques de Jésus et oeuvres de Dieu selon l'Év. de St. Jean," Recueil Lucien Cerfaux, II (1954), 41-50:

of Jesus as σημεῖα without thinking at the same time of the ἔργα of God (Jn. 4:34; 5:36; 9:3 f.; 10:32; 14:10; 17:4). This shows us why σημεῖον and ἔργα can be used in such close relation in John, for ἔργον, too, needs more precise definition if it is to be clear. When the Johannine Jesus Himself refers to what John calls σημεῖον He consistently [319] uses the word ἔργον. Like the Evangelist's use of σημεῖον this is a specifically Johannine usage. [320]

b. The Sign-Character of Jesus' ἔργα as His own ἔργα.

(a) The Johannine Jesus never speaks of His works in such a way as to call them His own (τὰ ἔργα μου). Once the Evangelist records that the expression τὰ ἔργα σου [321] was used to Him (7:3), but Jesus at once corrects His brethren by pointing out that in contrast to them the καιρός for His work has not yet come (7:6, 8). His ἔργα, then, are not just within His own competence. Yet they are still His ἔργα. No less than three times He uses the expression τὰ ἔργα ἃ ἐγὼ ποιῶ (5:36; 10:25; 14:12). Though the ἐγώ᾽ used here is a stylistic feature of the revelatory discourses of the Johannine Jesus (→ II, 349, 24 ff.), against this background it has special emphasis in connection with ποιῶ. For each of the sayings stands in a context in which the fellowship of Jesus with God is a full working relationship as well as an essential relationship to God as His Father, Jn. 3:35; 5:20; 8:19; 12:45; 14:9 ff.; 17:1 ff. Acc. to the biblical belief in God the primary revelation of God is in His works. If, then, Jesus is united with God in His operations, then in the works which He does He has a fully responsible share in the divine self-revelation. This finds expression already in the fact that He does not do ἔργα at any time but only when His ὥρα has come, 2:4. He knows this "hour" (e.g., 13:1) because He knows the Father as the Father knows Him (10:15 etc.). In virtue of this fellowship He always knows τί μέλλει ποιεῖν, cf. 6:6. [322] In the sonship expressed in all this, [323] however, the personal distinction between Jesus and God is not removed nor even weakened. He acts as God when He makes the water into wine in 2:1 ff. or feeds the multitude with a minimum of bread and fish in 6:1 ff. or restores a dying boy in 4:47 ff. or calls back to life a dead person who already shows signs of decomposition in 11:1 ff.; indeed, He does more than God would do acc. to the conviction of the Pharisees [324] when on the Sabbath He cures a man who had been lame for decades (5:1 ff.) and also gives sight to a blind man (9:1 ff.). [325] This is

---

H. van der Bussche, *L'Év. de Jean, Études et Problèmes* (1958), 79 f.; Bernard, *op. cit.* (→ n. 313), I, CLXXVI-CLXXXVI : "The Johannine Miracles."

[319] Jn. 6:26 (→ 247, 13 ff.) is an exception.

[320] ἔργα τοῦ χριστοῦ occurs once in the Synoptics at Mt. 11:2. The root of this use of the group ἔργον is probably Semitic. Cf. on this Schl. Mt. on 11:2 and Schl. J. on 8:39, 41. The usage is Chr., cf. Kl. Mt., *ad loc.*

[321] Though the σου of Jn. 7:3 is not in א* DGU Θ syᶜ sah arm, it is to be accepted as genuine, one reason being that it is part of the misunderstanding of the ἔργα of Jesus by His brethren, cf. Bultmann J. on 7:3-5.

[322] Jn. 6:6 is probably a typical parenthetical note on the part of the author.

[323] Cf. on this Schl. Theol. d. Ap., 157-161.

[324] Acc. to the Pharisaic-Rabb. view God as the Giver of the Torah scrupulously keeps its statutes, so Rabban Gamliel II and associates, before 100 A.D.; Ex. r., 30, 9 on 22:1. This includes observing the Sabbath laws → 27, 4 ff. In fact this enshrines a very old tradition when on the basis of Ex. 16:22 ff. it is pointed out in relation to the Sabbath commandment that God blessed and sanctified the Sabbath with the manna, i.e., He rested on the Sabbath by sending down a double portion of manna the evening before, so R. Jishma'el, M. Ex. בחודש 7 (231) on 20:11. Indirectly bSanh., 65b has the same idea when it says the fire of Gehinnom does not burn on the Sabbath, for if the Sabbath is thus respected in Gehinnom one may assume the same is true in heaven.

[325] Both, then, are chronic cases and there is no danger of death → 14, 27 ff. Rabb. interpretation of the Sabbath commandment does not allow help to be given in such instances, cf. Str.-B., I, 623-629; II, 533 f.

why He is accused of making Himself God (10:33), which can only mean that He puts Himself above God and in His place. [326] But this accusation does not affect Him, for He acts, not in self-glory, but within the framework of His sending [326] by the Father, 3:17; 5:36, 38; 6:29, 57; 7:29 etc. The Father, then, is the One who has "given" Him the ἔργα which He does, 5:36; 17:4.

(b) In Jn. Jesus' ἔργα show themselves to be σημεῖα because as His ἔργα they serve God's self-revelation. This corresponds to the fact that God manifests Himself in works as the One He is: the Father of Jesus → lines 23 ff. As ἔργα ἀπὸ τοῦ πατρός these are in every sense ἔργα καλά (10:32), i.e., the kind of works God Himself does, so that one may know who He is. [328] This also brings to light the point at which the specifically Johannine interrelating of σημεῖον and ἔργα is rooted in the usage of the exodus traditions of Israel. Moreover it becomes apparent that the Johannine σημεῖον is not describing the ἔργα of Jesus as miracles [329] but as signs which make a specific insight possible by bringing a certain matter to light. [330] This consists in the fact that Jesus brings a new view of God. Its distinctiveness is that God as Father may be known only in Jesus as Son, 8:19, 54 f.; 14:7; 17:25 f. Hence there is no other way to God than via Jesus, 14:6, 9 ff. But there is another implication. The σημεῖον-character of the ἔργα of Jesus means that in their interpretation, which they need like any other σημεῖον (→ 206, 1 ff.; 217, 7 ff.), no one is competent apart from Jesus Himself. In Jn., then, this too is taken into account in the revelatory discourses which Jesus often gives after His σημεῖα, → 252, 19 ff.

c. The σημεῖα of Jesus as God's Revealing Witness to Jesus as His Son.

No passage in Jn. claims the σημεῖα of Jesus for God so plainly as 12:37b ff., for here, on the basis of Is. 53:1, God's own relation to the phenomenon of Jesus is linked to the σημεῖα. In this way all the work of Jesus is described by the phrase σημεῖα ποιεῖν as though the works were not also accompanied by revelatory discourses in which Jesus, referring to the σημεῖα, speaks of Himself as the Revealer. [331] Regarded as the true characteristic of the total manifestation of Jesus the σημεῖα are attributed to God's arm (Is. 53:1). In this connection it should not be forgotten that in the OT, and especially in the exodus traditions, God's arm (→ I, 639, 27 ff.) is seen in the miraculous demonstrations of divine power which especially promote the election, redemption and preservation of His people (Ex. 6:6 etc.) but which also bring about eschatological salvation (Is. 40:10 etc.). In this light Jn. 12:37b ff. can only mean that on the basis of His σημεῖα Jesus is depicted as the One in whom the fate of all men is decided according

---

[326] On this sense in Rabb. par. cf. Schl. J., ad loc.; Str.-B., II, 542.
[327] On ἀποστέλλειν in Jn. → I, 404, 23 ff., but also R. Bultmann, "D. Bedeutung d. neuerschlossenen mandäischen u. manichäischen Quellen f. d. Verständnis d. Joh.-Ev.," ZNW, 24 (1925), 105-119, and esp. E. Gaugler, "Das Christuszeugnis des Joh.-Ev.," Jesus Christus im Zeugnis d. Hl. Schrift u. d. Kirche (1936), 51-53.
[328] They are thus God's works (→ III, 548, 31 ff.) and to be carefully distinguished as such from the καλὰ ἔργα demanded by Jesus in the Sermon on the Mount (Mt. 5:16; → III, 545, 20 ff.: works of love).
[329] Many comm., though sometimes with qualifications, define Jn.'s σημεῖα thus.
[330] For important insights cf. Bultmann J., 79, n. 1 on 2:1 ff. and esp. 161 on 6:26.
[331] Bultmann J. on 12:37.

to the will of God, [332] not at some point in the future but here and now, [333] i.e., when there is confrontation with Him. The Evangelist underlines this by showing that in relation to Jesus decision and division come about in respect of His ἔργα. These have a divisive and to that degree a revealing power, and herein they are σημεῖα. John can go so far as to have Jesus say that it is due to His ἔργα that His opponents now "have sin," 15:24. [334]

On the one side, then, Jesus' ἔργα are σημεῖα to the degree that they manifest Jesus as the Revealer and thus promote the (self-)revelation of God, → 248, 18 ff. But on the other side they are also σημεῖα because they characterise Jesus as the Son, or, more precisely, as the Son of God His Father. They thus have a theological reference as well as the additional christological reference. By using the word σημεῖον to further the comprehension and comprehensibility of the miraculous deeds of Jesus as an expression of His relation to God John also makes the ἔργα a reflection of His nature. [335]

> This puts a stop to any attempt to relate σημεῖον in John to conscious symbolism whether the starting-pt. be found in the concept of the symbol in Philo and his philosophical tradition or in the symbolical actions of the OT prophets → 217, 7 ff. [336] Caution is demanded in this respect by the mere fact that while any symbolism aims at knowledge John is trying to establish faith, with which he associates and integrates the capacity for knowledge, since this seems to be indispensable to it. [337]

4. σημεῖον and πίστις. [338]

According to Jn. 20:31 the aim of John's depiction of Jesus is faith that Jesus is the Christ, the Son of God. [339] John refers to the σημεῖα of Jesus in such a way as to leave the impression that they are the decisive thing in establishing faith in Jesus as the Messiah (→ 249, 23 ff.) and as though this alone were the content of faith rather than God. Yet for John faith in Jesus is always faith in God as Father (12:44 f.). [340] It is at this very point, then, that in John too the σημεῖα of Jesus unfold their constitutive power for faith. As the ἔργα of Jesus (→ 248, 9 ff.) they are always the confession which God as Father makes of Jesus as His Son (→ lines 7 ff.), while Jesus for His part reveals Himself to be the Revealer of God by proclaiming His name, 17:6, 26. [341] This means that the σημεῖα of Jesus, inasmuch as they establish faith in Him (2:11, 23; 4:53 f.; 11:45), [342] also serve as the basis of faith in God.

---

[332] Cf. Gaugler, op. cit., 40.

[333] Ibid., 51.

[334] Cf. Jn. 3:2b, where the formulation is similar to that in 15:24, but with σημεῖα for ἔργα.

[335] Cf. Cerfaux, op. cit., 47: "On comprend que le Christ seul se serve de la formule (sc. 'oeuvres'); elle est le véhicule qui va lui permettre d'exprimer sa pensée profonde : son unité avec le Père."

[336] C. H. Dodd, The Interpretation of the Fourth Gospel (1953), 133-143; S. H. Hooke, Alpha and Omega (1961), 270-282. J. Leal, "El simbolismo histórico del IV Ev.," Estudios Bibl., 2. época, 19 (1960), 329-348 is no help in solving the problem.

[337] Cf. Schl. Theol. d. Ap., 153-156; Bultmann Theol., 419-421.

[338] → I, 712, 31 ff.; VI, 226, 36 ff.; Schl. Glaube (→ n. 301), 176-221; Dodd, op. cit., 179-186. On the occurrence of the group in Jn. → VI, 222, 20 f.; Schl. Glaube, 595-600.

[339] Schl. Glaube, 176 f.

[340] Cf. also Jn. 14:1 with its singular πιστεύειν εἰς both in relation to Jesus and also to God, "to express the unity of Jesus with God," → VI, 210, n. 269.

[341] Cf. Barrett, op. cit. (→ n. 317), 421 and Bultmann J. on 17:6 ff.

[342] Jn. 12:37b is also important, since here in a note of the Evangelist faith in Jesus is the attitude which it is the point of Jesus' σημεῖα to produce.

The importance of the Evangelist's full concentration of his readers' attention on the σημεῖα of Jesus in Jn. 20:30 f. should not be weakened by seeing here the conclusion of the so-called σημεῖα-source (→ n. 315) which Jn. put in his book in exactly the form in which he found it in the original, by giving this as the reason why he does not expressly mention the ῥήματα here as well as the σημεῖα, and by arguing that fundamentally he ought to have done so, since for him the signs of Jesus are an obvious unity with His revelatory sayings, with the main stress on the latter. [343] One cannot really say that in John the σημεῖα are subordinate to the discourses, [344] for John has accounts of σημεῖα in which there are no discourses, e.g., the two σημεῖα at Cana with which the series opens in 2:1 ff. and 4:47 ff. On the other hand, the discourses serve to interpret the relevant σημεῖα by deriving from them the insight as to who Jesus really is (→ 250, 7 ff.) and how He enforces a decision between faith and unbelief in encounter with Him.

Since they are not linked to succeeding discourses the two Cana stories show particularly well how John depicts the relation between sign and faith, 2:1 ff.; 4:47 ff. In both instances the rise of faith [345] — in the disciples in 2:11, in the βασιλικός and his whole οἰκία in 4:53 — is expressly brought into causal connection with the σημεῖον of Jesus. In the case of the disciples this had already been preceded by a plain confession of the Messiahship of Jesus (1:41, 45, 49), and Jesus Himself in the word πιστεύεις had recognised the faith of Nathanael on the basis of this confession (1:50). [346] Similarly in the case of the βασιλικός the sign of Jesus which awakened faith was preceded by a confident request that Jesus would heal his hopelessly sick son (4:47), and the Evangelist can say that he believed (4:50 : ἐπίστευσεν) the word which Jesus spoke to him in reply. In some sense one may also cite in this connection the confession of faith (9:38) made by the man born blind when he met Jesus after his sight was restored. He obeyed Jesus and with the πηλός (→ VI, 118, 19 ff.) on his eyes went and washed. But this obedient trust is obviously not what John means when he speaks of faith at the end of a σημεῖον-story. This faith is inseparable from the immediate impression of the person of Jesus which is made by the act which reveals His nature. It is thus that there arises the seeing (2:11; 9:37; cf. 1:50) [347] or knowing which rests thereupon (4:53; cf. 11:42 ff.). The significance of the σημεῖα of Jesus goes beyond the immediate hour and those who share in it as spectators. By having Jesus link words of revelation concerning His person with a series of σημεῖα (6:32 ff.; 9:39; 11:25; cf. 5:17), John brings out the fact that the signs have a constant power to establish faith because Jesus always remains the One He is. Since faith also cannot be forced by the σημεῖον, this always develops a critical function alongside its power to establish faith. [348] But while this is limited to

---

[343] Bultmann J. on 20:30 f.

[344] *Ibid.* on 12:37-43.

[345] Note the aorist.

[346] We cannot go into the question whether this is a statement or a question.

[347] μείζω τούτων ὄψῃ in Jn. 1:50 refers to the σημεῖα which are to be recounted later, so also Bultmann J., *ad loc.*

[348] When Wellh. J., *ad loc.* suggests that Jn. 11:25 f. on the lips of Jesus "makes the raising of Lazarus quite superfluous" and "robs the whole story of meaning" this rests on a misunderstanding of what John means by σημεῖον and a failure to see why the σημεῖον is indispensable. In contrast Bultmann J., 301, n. 3, *ad loc.* maintains that one must not overlook the standpt. of the Evangelist himself which is presented here. He finds this on the one side in the two possible attitudes to a σημεῖον expressed here in the difference

the contemporaries of Jesus (12:31), [349] the christological knowledge which the ἔργα of Jesus mediate as σημεῖα is permanent, so that these can become an imperishable part of the divine message (cf. 1 Jn. 1:1 ff. → I, 66, 37 ff. s.v. ἀπαγγέλλω) even in the form of the apostolic βιβλίον (Jn. 20:30; cf. 21:25; 1 Jn. 1:4). Thus the significance which John ascribes to the σημεῖα of Jesus for faith illustrates not merely the uniqueness of his view of Christ but also the interest which he has as an Evangelist in the "historical" Jesus and in the lasting connection of faith with this Jesus.

The miracles of Jesus neither relate to a prophetic claim nor do they arise merely out of compassion in face of specific needs. They are exclusively signs that Jesus is the Christ. [350] Their true basis is that in one person Jesus is both Revealer and Revealed. Hence in Jesus as presented by John the σημεῖα take precedence of the Word so long as He is still ἐν σαρκί (1 Jn. 4:2 cf. Jn. 1:14) [351] and not yet glorified (7:39 etc.). In spite of all arguments to the contrary [352] this is also the point when for John, too, the post-Easter community needs no new σημεῖα. It has the word of the witnesses. To this degree it is superior to the apostles in the way it comes to faith and in its faith, for they could become believers only through divine demonstrations. [353]

5. σημεῖον and λόγος.

If in John the σημεῖα of Jesus point indirectly to the One He really is (→ 249, 23 ff.), in His λόγοι He gives direct information about Himself in answer to the question : σὺ τίς εἶ; (8:25). The wealth of self-predications [354] corresponds to the freedom of Jesus which is the mark of His ἔργα as they are called σημεῖα and thus given the emphasis of revelatory action → 248, 8 ff. σημεῖον and λόγος are mutually related here. If the λόγος interprets the σημεῖον, the σημεῖον authenticates the λόγος, but both in such a way that they find their unity exclusively in the person of Him who has the right to use ἐγώ εἰμι of himself. If the Revealer introduces Himself first as the One who acts (Jn. 2:1 ff.), and if it is an ἔργον/σημεῖον by Him (11:1 ff.) which brings about the decision to seek His death (11:45 ff.), His picture as the Son of God [355] is shaped by that of God Himself, who makes Himself known by His acts [356] and who in the σημεῖα in

---

between Mary and Martha. But in this way justice is also done to the critical function of the σημεῖον without prejudice to the primary christological function as the presupposition of this.

[349] The saying is not part of the context of the Lazarus σημεῖον, cf. 12:9, 37b.

[350] E. Schweizer, EGO EIMI ... (1939), 139.

[351] In John σάρξ means "simply creatureliness in the whole breadth of its possibilities," E. Käsemann, "Aufbau u. Anliegen d. joh. Prologs," *Libertas Christiana, Festschr. F. Delekat* (1957), 93. Cf. also Barrett, *op. cit.* (→ n. 317), on 1:14 : "σάρξ ... represents human nature as distinct from God."

[352] Cf. esp. Bultmann J. on 20:29 f.

[353] Cf. Schl. J. and also Barrett, *op. cit.* on 20:29 ff.

[354] → φῶς Jn. 8:12; → ὕδωρ 4:7 ff.; ἄρτος 6:35 (→ I, 477 f.); ποιμήν 10:11 and v. 9 (→ VI, 494, 16 ff.); θύρα 10:7 ff., v. 9 (→ III, 178, 27 ff.); ἄμπελος 15:1 ff. (→ I, 342 f.); ὁδός 14:6 (→ V, 78, 9 ff.); the Johannine Jesus here uses the formula ἐγώ εἰμι as a recognition formula. On this, which is characterised by a predicative use of ἐγώ, cf. Bultmann J., 167, n. 2; Schweizer, *op. cit.*, 126 f.

[355] This designation dominates the picture of Christ in Jn. from beginning to end, as may be seen from 1:19 ff. with 1:34 and 20:31, but in such a way that it is in full harmony with the name "Christ."

[356] This is also Pauline, cf. R. 1:20.

Egypt has established for His elect people the basis of their relation to Him in faith → 216, 8 ff. But whereas God uses human interpreters who on His commission and with His authority say who God is and what He wills, the Johannine Jesus Himself interprets what He does both with reference to Himself and also with reference to the Father whose relation to Him is manifested in the ἔργα done by Him, cf. Jn. 5:17 and → 249, 23 ff.

6. σημεῖον and δόξα.

In Jn. 2:11 the manifestation of the δόξα of Jesus is linked with His first σημεῖον, the first miracle at Cana → I, 655, 38 ff.; V, 163, 21 ff.[357] It also stands in causal relation to the fact that His disciples came to faith in Him as the Son of God. His δόξα is said to be manifested in the same way at the σημεῖον of the raising of Lazarus in 11:4, 40, though here the reference is expressly to the δόξα τοῦ θεοῦ, in whose manifestion in the σημεῖον of Jesus the Son's δοξασθῆ-ναι δι' αὐτῆς takes place, v. 4. Finally, the σημεῖα of Jesus and the δόξα of God are interrelated in 12:37 ff. with emphasis on the fact that it is the privilege of believers alone to grasp the point at issue. One may thus perceive that in John σημεῖον, δόξα and πίστις (→ n. 338) are very precisely connected with one another. With the σημεῖον faith arises if the δόξα which shines therein is "seen," 1:14.

The relation between σημεῖον and δόξα in John[358] may be defined as follows. In His σημεῖα Jesus in some sense makes Himself transparent[359] and causes His true being, His sonship, to be manifest in its δόξα. This δόξα of His (2:11) is for John the presupposition of Jesus' ἔργα as σημεῖα in which He works creatively like God → 248, 26 ff.; to this extent it is a sign of His unsuspended preexistence (17:5 cf. 1:14) in which His self-awareness is seated (8:58). As concerns what Jesus Himself has chosen (6:70; 13:18; 15:16, 19) or what touches His self-witness in other ways, there is summed up in δόξα the impression made about Him through His σημεῖα (cf. 9:3[360] and 11:4). Actively expressed in His works are omnipotent glory on the part of Jesus and the impression of His personal transcendence or "majesty"[361] on that of the disciples, and both on the premiss of His σημεῖα. This is the basis of the uniqueness of Jesus which John has in view when at the end of his Gospel, with an explicit and comprehensive reference to the σημεῖα, he calls Him ὁ Χριστὸς ὁ υἱὸς τοῦ θεοῦ, 20:31.

The close connection between σημεῖον and δόξα is a further decisive and conclusive argument against any attempt[362] to find symbolism in the use of

---

[357] R. Schnackenburg, *Das erste Wunder Jesu* (1951).

[358] Cf. H. Kittel, "Die Herrlichkeit Gottes," Beih. ZNW, 16 (1934), 241-244, 260 f. and → II, 248, 13 ff.; 249, 6 ff. There is no need to go into the question of the double meaning of δόξα in John.

[359] For this term cf. W. Heitmüller, *Schr. NT* on Jn. 2:11, who by means of it tries to show that the pt. of the Johannine σημεῖον is to bring to light certain higher truths. As he sees it, the truth which shines through in the miracle at Cana is that Jesus transcends and abrogates the Mosaic Law represented by the pots and the water ; for other symbolical interpretations (→ V, 163, 30 ff.) cf. Bau. J., Exc. after 2:12. Heitmüller's term is adopted but in a different connection.

[360] Here we find ἔργα τοῦ θεοῦ with ref. to the coming σημεῖον.

[361] So Schnackenburg, *op. cit.*, 53. Kittel, *op. cit.*, 260 speaks of a distinctive form of the idea of power connected with δόξα in John.

[362] Cf. Dodd, *op. cit.*, 133-143; Hooke, *op. cit.*

σημεῖον in John's Gospel. In John the word is rather a central theological term to the degree that it serves to interpret Jesus not merely christologically but also theologically. Anthropologically, then, it is connected with ethics, not logic, in John. In face of Jesus as Him to whom the σημεῖον is reserved there is decision and division in respect of the will of God, so that sin is manifested as sin, 9:41; cf. 15:24 ff. To that extent the eschatological κρίσις (cf. 12:37 ff.) which Jesus initiates in His person begins to become unmistakable and unavoidable in the σημεῖα of Jesus. [363]

7. σημεῖα of the Risen Lord?

Jn. 20:30 f. mentions πολλὰ καὶ ἄλλα σημεῖα at the end of John's Easter story and of the Gospel as a whole if Jn. 21 is an addition. The question thus arises whether the reference of this expression is to the appearances of the Risen Lord (20) or even to the miracle of the resurrection of Jesus as such. But this is not so. In Jn. the resurrection of Jesus from the dead is no more Jesus' own work than elsewhere in the NT. It is the resurrecting act of God upon Him (cf. 2:22; 21:14). This is in no way altered by the fact that there is one reference to the ἀναστῆναι of Jesus in connection with the Easter event, 20:9. [364] Hence an intentional reference of σημεῖα to the resurrection of Jesus in 20:30 would not be in harmony with the use of the term elsewhere in John. Nor should it be forgotten that the orientation in Jn. 20 is different from that in the preceding part of the Gospel. At issue there is the manifestation of the δόξα of the earthly Jesus by Himself (cf. esp. 2:11 and → 248, 8 ff.). But now interest focuses on the self-witness of the Risen Lord in which He demonstrates His identity with the earthly Jesus, cf. 20:17, 20, 27. All this goes to show that it is better not to refer the σημεῖα of 20:30 to Jesus' resurrection or to His appearances to the disciples. [365]

The same applies with even greater force to the crucifixion. Neither this nor the cross of Jesus as such is ever called a σημεῖον in Jn. [366] Nor is anything else to be expected in view of the character of the word in Jn. Jesus does σημεῖα, but in the crucifixion He does not act; He lets Himself be acted on. Nor in relation to the crucifixion can one speak of the self-revelation elsewhere connected with His σημεῖα. Against this it can hardly be argued that in Jn. the crucifixion is closely related to the glorifying. In the δοξασθῆναι which in Jn. was granted to Jesus on and in the cross (→ II, 249, 17 ff.) it is the Father who works and Jesus is solely and simply the recipient. [367]

---

[363] Thus in Jn., unlike the Synoptics, Jesus' ἔργα/σημεῖα are a central part of His exertions to bring about the conversion of His people, which in Jn. is depicted as a turning from darkness to light.

[364] On the relation between ἐγερθῆναι and ἀναστῆναι in the Easter preaching of primitive Christianity cf. K. H. Rengstorf, Die Auferstehung Jesu⁴ (1960), 27-30.

[365] ἐνώπιον occurs only here in John, as Barrett, op. cit. on 20:30 explicitly maintains. σημεῖα ποιεῖν ἐνώπιον ... is used in Rev. 13:14; 19:20 and there is an Aram par. in jChag., 2, 2 (77d, 57 ff.), Schl. J. on 20:30 f. Wellhausen J., ad loc. says bluntly that ἐνώπιον is not Johannine.

[366] Cf. R. H. Lightfoot, St. John's Gospel (1957), ad loc.: "The crucifixion was to St. John doubtless the greatest sign of all (cf. 12:33; 18:32); but the word 'sign' is not actually applied to it." Hooke, op. cit., 286 makes the unsupported claim that in the light of Jn. 2:19 the whole Johannine passion including the resurrection of Jesus (Jn. 18-20) is the seventh sign.

[367] The pass. δοξασθῆναι pts. to exclusively divine action.

One may conclude, then, that in 20:30 John is simply speaking of the "selection" [368] from the greater number of the σημεῖα of Jesus which he has previously given before the commencement of the passion and resurrection. It would also appear that for the Fourth Evangelist there can be no thought of further σημεῖα from Jesus after His arrest. For John alone says nothing about the various demands that the crucified Jesus should come down from the cross, i.e., free Himself by a miracle, cf. Mk. 15:29 ff. and par., also Lk. 23:8 with σημεῖον. Hence in Jn. 20:30 f. the Evangelist is on the one hand stressing once again and this time comprehensively the matter which is brought to light by the σημεῖα as they are narrated (and interpreted) and which is so powerful that numbers play no decisive part, namely, that Jesus of Nazareth (Jn. 1:45) is the Son of God and as such the Messiah, and therefore whosoever believes in Him does the will of God. Along with this on the other hand there is also a specific christological reference if the passion, cross and resurrection of Jesus have for John no direct connection with His σημεῖα, → 257, 11 ff.

> The separation of the cross and resurrection of Jesus from Jn. 20:30 is supported also by Jn. 21:25, where πολλὰ ἄλλα is repeated (in ἄλλα πολλά) but not σημεῖα. This is esp. significant since the phrase (with ποιεῖν) might well have been regarded by the author as including the narrative in 21:1 ff.

8. The Distinctiveness and Derivation of John's Special Use of σημεῖον.

a. The Singularity of the Use of σημεῖον in John's Gospel.

The use of σημεῖον in the Fourth Gospel with its orientation to the self-manifestation of Jesus in His ἔργα (→ 248, 8 ff.) must be regarded as a peculiarity of the Evangelist or of the tradition which he used. The same applies to the other Johannine writings. Thus in Rev. we twice find the phrase ποιεῖν σημεῖα (13:14; 19:20) which is common in the Gospel. It is here a kind of negative counterpart of the use of the same phrase in the Gospel. It relates to the miracles which the prophet of antichrist does in his capacity as a pseudo-prophet to obscure the truth, to confuse men, and to give a wrong orientation to their inner allegiance. If a formal parallel can hardly be denied here, one must assume dependence on the usage in John's Gospel.

> Hence the par. does not qualify the thesis that John's use of σημεῖον in the sense of "sign" is a distinctive one. ποιεῖν σημεῖον or σημεῖα does, of course, correspond to the Aram. עֲבַד סִימָנָא, jChag., 2, 2 (77d, 57 ff.); jSanh., 13, 9 (23c, 44), [369] but here again the par. is only formal since this has the sense of "to adduce proof for the correctness of something" with the aim of winning confidence (הֵימִן). In the example the ref. is to the taking out and restoring of an eye — a motif obviously based on Ex. 4:6. [370]

b. The Old Testament Background.

> Hell. Gnosticism cannot be considered as a possible background for the Johannine use of σημεῖον, no matter how the relation of the Fourth Gospel to this be defined. [371] The same applies to the Mandaean movement → 208, 9 ff. Very probably ancient

---

[368] Bultmann J. on 20:30 f.
[369] Schl. J. on 20:30 f.; Schlatter, op. cit. (→ n. 190), 69.
[370] Schlatter, op. cit. (→ n. 190), 69, n. 1.
[371] C. H. Dodd, The Bible and the Greeks² (1954), 210-234, discussing the significance

aretalogy must also be ruled out, for if this contains sign-like miracles there is constant use of other terms like ἀρετή [372] and θαῦμα, [373] Lat. *virtus* and *miraculum*. [374] The specifically Johannine use of σημεῖον for, e.g., ἔργον, occurs first in Chr. aretalogies which developed out of the ancient form in connection with the rise of an ecclesiastical cult of saints. [375] But it is here plainly secondary and also very much weaker than in its original, lacking the distinctive colouring of the use in Jn. → 248, 8 ff. As concerns the older period one should not be misled by certain purely formal par. Thus the orator of Asia Minor, Ael. Arist. (129-189 A.D.), refers in Or. Sacr., 2, 73 to a μέγιστον σημεῖον τοῦ θεοῦ τῆς δυνάμεως. [376] But this is not a sign in the sense of Jn.; it is an indication by which the δύναμις of the deity may be confidently known. Hence in this as in other things [377] this author does not break free from the current Gk. use of σημεῖον; in particular he does not even approximate to the Johannine use. [378]

In the LXX (→ 219, 14 ff.) σημεῖον absorbs the Hbr. אוֹת both formally and also in its aptness as an interpretative word. In connection with the view of God in the OT this gives the term the ability to point to the presence of the self-declaration of the one God as the God of Israel. In this sense it is defined by two relations, the one to faith in God, the other to His glory (δόξα), His deity manifested as such. Both these are also marks of the Johannine σημεῖον except that now the ref. is to Jesus. It is so in a highly significant way, since for John Jesus at once unites with God those who unite themselves to Him. To do this in word and deed is His true task as the Revealer who is sent into the world by God, cf. Jn. 17:3 ff. etc. Since in their fulfilment the ἔργα of Jesus are σημεῖα in John, these are theologically of fundamentally the same kind as the classical σημεῖα of the OT, the signs in Egypt in the time of Moses → 216, 10 ff. In other words, from the way in which the author makes the σημεῖα of Jesus serve his kerygmatic goal, which is the knowledge and acknowledgement of Jesus as the Son of God (20:31), one may see that he is a theologian of the divine revelation which is the one theme of the OT. This is the one thing which comes out with clarity from Jn. 1:18 on the one side and sayings of Jesus like 12:45 and 14:9 on the other.

Like that of Jesus (Jn. 2:11 → 253, 8 ff.) the δόξα of God in the OT rests on His works in so far as they manifest His power. No matter how the original sense of כָּבוֹד on the one side or δόξα on the other may be defined, [379] and no matter what may be

---

of Hell. Judaism and the Hermetic lit. for an understanding of Jn., refers to Corp. Herm., III, 2 (→ 207, 43 f.) with σημεῖον, but can relate this only to Gn. 1 ff., esp. 1:14. For Dodd the Fourth Evangelist is certainly no Hellenist in his use of σημεῖον. Though he discerns in John's signs references "in the first instance" to "timeless realities" (*Interpretation* [→ n. 336], 142), in comparison with Philo he can only say that "the Johannine σημεῖον is nearer to the prophetic." → 257, 11 ff.

[372] Cf. Deissmann B, 90-93; O. Weinreich, *Neue Urkunden zur Sarapis-Religion* (1919), *passim*; E. Peterson, ΕΙΣ ΘΕΟΣ (1926), 216-221; R. Herzog, *Die Wunderheilungen v. Epidauros* (1931), 49 f. ἀρετή is close to δύναμις, Peterson, 198, n. 2.

[373] Cf., e.g., Philostr. Vit. Ap., IV, 45 with I, 39. On the chronological question Herzog, 50 f. Aesculapius as θαυματοποιός: Ael. Arist. Or., 39, 14.

[374] Herzog, 51, n. 9. On *miraculum*, e.g., Apul. Met., II, 28, 5; XI, 14, 2; on *virtus* R. Reitzenstein, *Hell. Wundererzählungen* (1906), 9.

[375] E. Lucius, *Die Anfänge d. Heiligenkults in d. chr. Kirche* (1904), 415, n. 5.

[376] The god is the Pergamenian Aesculapius.

[377] σημεῖον is rare in Ael. Arist. and refers not to something done but always to that in a thing which mediates insight or gives information → n. 35. Cf., e.g., Or., 32, 18 (μεγαλοψυχίας σημεῖον); 36, 60 (ἀμφοτέρων σημεῖον); Or. Sacr., 4, 101 (σημεῖα ἐξ ὀνειράτων). This is the more remarkable in that Ael. Arist. often speaks of the ἔργα of a god, e.g., Or., 45 (hymn to Sarapis), 16 ff.

[378] Thus σημεῖα ποιεῖν in Or., 36, 40 is "to advance proofs, examples," → 206, 23 ff.

[379] We should start [H. Schreckenberg] with the Homeric formula ἀπὸ δόξης (Il., 10, 324; Od., 11, 344; ἄλιος or ἀπὸ σκοποῦ are par.). Then δόξα is directed but often unconfirmed "expectation." The theory of M. Leumann, *Homerische Wörter* (1950), 173-178 that as an aor. part. of δοκεῖν δόξα became a fem. by way of παρὰ δόξαν (from

the reasons for the rendering of the one by the other in the LXX (→ II, 248, 42 ff.), there is undoubtedly a close connection between God's signs (אֹתוֹת / σημεῖα) and His כָּבוֹד or δόξα. The most important instance is the passage Nu. 14:10 ff. and esp. v. 22, where δόξα and σημεῖα are very closely related in a saying of God to Moses : [380] πάντες οἱ ἄνδρες οἱ ὁρῶντες τὴν δόξαν μου καὶ τὰ σημεῖα, ἃ ἐποίησα ... One may also refer to the Song of Moses at the Red Sea in Ex. 15:1 ff., which proclaims God's glory on the basis of His mighty acts on the oppressors of Israel. [381] In both cases the ref. is to the signs of God in Egypt. From these (→ 216, 8 ff.; 221, 7 ff.) there can thus be no separating of God's revelation as God in the revelation of His כָּבוֹד or His δόξα.

c. The Typological Character of Johannine σημεῖα.

The Fourth Evangelist did not restrict himself to transferring to Jesus the use of σημεῖον in the Greek Pentateuch and thus making σημεῖον a basic factor in the self-revelation of Jesus. He also gave the term a typological accent within his picture of Christ, and this with emphatic reference to the faith or unbelief of those whom Jesus addresses as Revealer. [382] In this regard [383] two aspects seem to be particularly important to him : the description of Jesus as the "prophet" (Jn. 4:19; 6:14; 7:40; 9:17) on the one side (→ 244, 34 ff.; VI, 845, 16 ff.) and His divine foreordination as the Passover Lamb of eschatological redemption on the other, → V, 900, 19 ff. These are interrelated inasmuch as the age of Moses with the redemption from bondage in Egypt acquires typological force in both. In this framework the σημεῖα of Jesus also take on typological significance. Once the Baptist has proclaimed the imminence of the second and final age of Passover and redemption (cf. Jn. 1:29, 36) they form the prelude to this as the signs in Egypt did to the redemption from bondage to the Egyptians, → 216, 8 ff. At the same time, however, the σημεῖα which Jesus does show that the age of Moses is not just repeated in Him; it is surpassed in Him as He Himself in His person and in what He brings infinitely surpasses Moses, Jn. 1:17. With their typological emphasis, [384] then, the σημεῖα of Jesus in John acquire enhanced christological significance and herein also very considerable theological significance. Against the background of the Mosaic age they make it apparent for all to see that Jesus is in fact more than a new Moses. For Jesus acts as God, and therein He shows Himself to be the Son of God.

Theognis) runs counter to the chronological and material priority of the instances in Hom. and should be rejected (cf. E. Fraenkel's review in Gnomon, 23 [1951], 374).

[380] Cf. Cerfaux, op. cit., 43.

[381] Cf. also v. 11: θαυμαστὸς ἐν δόξαις, ποιῶν τέρατα.

[382] Apart from σημεῖον Jn. distinctively follows the Gk. Pent. by using the verb πιστεύειν for faith (in the one exception in Dt. 32:20 πίστις means "faithfulness").

[383] On the typology of John cf. L. Goppelt, Typos (1939), 215-238; H. Sahlin, "Zur Typologie d. Joh.-Ev.," Uppsala Univ. Årsskrift, 1950, 4 (1950), 8-73. Sahlin finds a thoroughgoing Ex. typology in John but reads more into the texts than they can carry without artificial interpretation. The same applies to the attempt to see in Jn. 6:16-21 a typological adoption of Ex. 14:10 ff. (the crossing of the Red Sea), cf. H. Ludin-Jansen, "Typologien i Joh.-Evangeliet," Norsk Teologisk Tidsskrift, 49 (1948), 144-158; A. Guilding, The Fourth Gospel and Jewish Worship (1960), 66 espouses the same thesis : "The miracle of the walking on the water seems to reflect the crossing of the Reed Sea (Ex. 15)." In → IV, 862, 26 ff., cf. → IV, 872, 11 ff. the Moses-Christ typology in Jn. is correctly restricted in essentials to Jn. 6:14 f., 30 ff.

[384] Goppelt, op. cit., 221, n. 2 is right not to ascribe any typological reference to the individual Johannine σημεῖον. The situation is radically different, however, once one

IV. σημεῖον in the Rest of the New Testament.

1. Paul.

a. General.

In all σημεῖον occurs in Paul only 8 times, and only in 2 Th. apart from R. and 1 and 2 C. → 260, 5 ff. Almost half the instances contain the expression σημεῖα καὶ τέρατα, R. 15:19; 2 C. 12:12; 2 Th. 2:9.

In none of the passages does the usage stray outside the boundaries of the traditional. It simply takes into account the fact that there is now a Christian apostolate. Since the apostle is as the one who sends and authorises him (→ I, 414, 24 ff.; 424, 20 ff.), the problem of the σημεῖον which arises for Jesus is repeated in the case of the apostle → 234, 29 ff. This does not require a new use of σημεῖον; it simply demands that the current use be set in the new situation → 241, 24 ff. In particular there are no links between the specifically Johannine use of the word (→ 243, 13 ff.) and that of Paul.

b. Specific.

In R. 4:11 σημεῖον has purely technical significance in the sense of "sign," "mark." In this respect it makes no odds whether one reads σημεῖον ἔλαβεν περιτομῆς or περιτομήν with AC*pc sy. Either way circumcision is interpreted as → σφραγίς. We thus have legal ideas belonging to the sphere of agreements or legitimation. [385]

> Though the passage is undoubtedly Jewish-Rabb. in conception, there seems to be no Rabb. par. to σημεῖον περιτομῆς. The OT describes circumcision as אֹות בְּרִית or σημεῖον διαθήκης in Gn. 17:11 → 211, 21 ff. But in Rabb. expositions, in which it is clear what is meant, אֹות alone can sometimes be used for circumcision. [386] It is perhaps worth considering, however, whether a similar use is not to be assumed in R. 4:11, so that materially the word is employed here for σημεῖον διαθήκης. If so, one should not read περιτομῆς but περιτομήν understood predicatively and interpreted in terms of σφραγῖδα etc. Cf. in Jub. 15:26, 28 the description of circumcision as "the sign that one belongs to God" and in this sense "the sign of the covenant."

In 2 C. 12:12 σημεῖα τοῦ ἀποστόλου are "visible things which make an apostle discernible as such," not just Paul in his capacity as an apostle. [387] Paul tells us what he has concretely in mind when he goes on to speak of σημεῖα καὶ τέρατα καὶ δυνάμεις. The signs and miracles of the age of redemption which have been done by him "identify" him as an apostle of Christ. [388] 1 C. 1:22 brings us into

---

groups together what John calls σημεῖα. It should not be overlooked, as by Goppelt, that in John σημεῖον and miracle are not precisely the same. Cf. on this ↦ 243, 16 ff.

[385] Cf. the comm., ad loc.

[386] Cf. Str.-B., IV, 32, Exc. "Das Beschneidungsgebot" under e |(אֹות) or f. (σημαντήριον as a loan word).

[387] → I, 433, 19 ff.

[388] It is possible that σημεῖα τοῦ ἀποστόλου, like τὰ ἔργα τοῦ χριστοῦ (Mt. 11:2), had become an established tt. which perhaps played a part in the Corinthian attack on Paul. At any rate Paul refers to them only in a case of urgency and if he does so it is for the sake of the thing rather than his own person (→ I, 440, 30 ff.), cf. Wnd. 2 K., ad loc.

the same context when Paul criticises the Jews because they σημεῖα αἰτοῦσιν. The expression reminds us of the demand put to Jesus that He should authenticate Himself by a sign from heaven (→ 234, 29 ff.) and it is perhaps making the point that this is typical of the Jews. [389] The context leaves us in no doubt but that Paul, like Jesus, rejected the demand that he should prove with signs his claim to stand and speak for God, and that in this he demonstrated his apostleship to be that of Christ. [390] In 1 C. 14:22 Paul calls the gift of tongues (αἱ γλῶσσαι) a σημεῖον for ἄπιστοι and in proof appeals to Is. 28:11 f. His point is that speaking in tongues not only does not open up access into the mysteries of God for the ἄπιστος, but actually bars this. [391] It is a σημεῖον to ἄπιστοι because it shows that they are unbelievers and separated from God. It presents itself in some sort as an argument or ground by which to know their own unbelief. [392] Broader considerations lead too far afield from the text. [393] 2 Th. 3:17 seems to adopt current usage (→ 206, 18 ff.; n. 378) and σημεῖον probably means "proof of authenticity." In this the two factors which are decisive for the meaning of σημεῖον play a role, namely, visibility and resultant assurance for the community. They relate here to the greeting of the author in his own hand (ἀσπασμός), → I, 502, 9 ff.

> The question as to the more precise reasons which might have led Paul to write his own greeting as a σημεῖον [394] need not be discussed here, esp. as it now plays no very decisive part in the debate on the authenticity of the letter but is more related to theological considerations. [395] σημεῖον corresponds here to the occasional σύμβολον (ξύμβολον) which indicates additions to the letters of antiquity in the writers' own hands. [396] It may be that Paul is using the popular speech of his day when he uses σημεῖον instead of σύμβολον. [397]

On the one side Paul uses the expression σημεῖα καὶ τέρατα, which comes from the exodus tradition, in relation to himself in his capacity as an apostle (R. 15:19; 2 C. 12:12), and this from the standpoint of Christ's working through him which shows that he is an accredited envoy, and also in such a way that in both cases δύναμις stands in immediate proximity. In R. 15:19 the σημεῖα καὶ τέρατα seem to make it clear what Paul has in view when he speaks of his apostolic ἔργον, while the foundation of his λόγος is found in the divine πνεῦμα, [398] presupposing that one may dissolve λόγῳ καὶ ἔργῳ thus. [399] In any case Paul is using ἐν δυνάμει πνεύματος to underline the basic significance of

---

[389] Joh. W., 1 K., ad loc.

[390] Schl. K., ad loc.

[391] Schl. K., ad loc.

[392] Ltzm. K., ad loc. suggests the offence taken by the ἄπιστοι "which is then reckoned to them as a fault," but this can hardly be right.

[393] Thus Joh. W. 1 K., ad loc., referring to Lk. 2:34 (→ 238, 15 ff.), speaks of glossolalia as a "means of hardening"; H. D. Wendland, Die Briefe an d. Korinther, NT Deutsch, 7⁷ (1954), ad loc. follows him here.

[394] Cf. the comm., ad loc., esp. Dib. Th., ad loc.

[395] Cf. H. Braun, "Zur nachpaulinischen Herkunft des 2 Th.," ZNW, 44 (1952/3), 152-156 and on this W. Michaelis, Einleitung in d. NT³ (1961), 231.

[396] Cf. the examples in Deissmann B, 212 f.; LO, 132 f., n. 6.

[397] Examples outside the NT are late.

[398] Cf. Mi. R., ad loc.

[399] Perhaps the apocr. Marcan ending (Mk. 16:20) is the best starting-pt. for interpreting this complex expression.

σημεῖα καὶ τέρατα for himself, as is also emphasised by the description as σημεῖα τοῦ ἀποστόλου in 2 C. 12:12 (→ 258, 30 ff.),[400] and also their relation to the age of Christ, which is shown to be such by the operation of the πνεῦμα. In this respect Paul is close to the author of Acts in his use of the phrase → 241, 24 ff. On the other side the *parousia* of antichrist is in 2 Th. 2:9 painted in the colours of the *parousia* of Christ by means of the use of ἐν πάσῃ δυνάμει καὶ σημείοις καὶ τέρασιν with the addition of the distinguishing ψεύδους, as, e.g., in Mt. 24:24; Mk. 13:22 → 241, 24 ff. Whether or not the section 2 Th. 2:1 ff. is by Paul, it is rooted in Jewish apocalyptic tradition at this point, and herein it is closely related to the passages quoted from the Synoptic Gospels. In any case it strengthens the impression that exodus typology has exerted an influence here too.

2. Hebrews.

Hb. 2:4 refers to σημεῖα καὶ τέρατα καὶ ποικίλαι δυνάμεις καὶ πνεύματος ἁγίου μερισμοί as things which God did to accredit the preaching which began with the proclamation of the Lord → VI, 446, 6 ff. The ancient formula, again understood typologically, is here used in expanded form, and obviously on the basis of comprehensive experience,[401] to confirm the superiority of the Gospel over the Torah and also the importance of decision between the two.[402] Here again Ex. 4:1 ff. is the biblical background and Mk. 16:20 is the starting-point of interpretation.[403]

In answer to the question whether these are four equal terms[404] one should reply that σημεῖα καὶ τέρατα is to be taken as a fixed expression. Hence the two words combined here are not to be interpreted separately[405] but as a unity. The usage of the Chr. community is unmistakable here. An important point, as in the picture of Jesus in the Synoptics (→ 240, 35 ff.) and Paul's view of an apostle (→ 258, 30 ff.), is that the reference of the σημεῖα καὶ τέρατα is to the credibility of the preacher.[406] Whether it may be concluded from the text that for the author of Hb. the miraculous powers of the apostolic age have not yet receded[407] is a moot question.[408] All the more, then, should it be noted how emphatically the supporting function of the σημεῖα καὶ τέρατα etc. is anchored in the θέλησις of God.[409] Obviously the author has no religious relation to miracles as such.

---

[400] E. Käsemann, "Die Legitimität des Ap.," ZNW, 41 (1942), 33-71 wrongly plays this down and hence argues that in σημεῖα τοῦ ἀποστόλου Paul is adopting, with ref. only to his sufferings (62 f.), a slogan which his adversaries had tried to apply to themselves in their superiority over him. But 1 C. 2:4 with its ἀπόδειξις πνεύματος καὶ δυνάμεως is enough to show that σημεῖα καὶ τέρατα do not have merely secondary significance for Paul (Käsemann, 63, also Ltzm. K., *ad loc.* App., 213).

[401] Cf. H. Strathmann, *Der Brief an d. Hb., NT Deutsch,* 9 [7] (1954), *ad loc.*

[402] Wnd. Hb., *ad loc.*

[403] Cf. Wnd. Hb., *ad loc.*

[404] Cf. Mi. Hb., *ad loc.*

[405] Mi. Hb., *ad loc.* Rightly on the basis of Ex. 7:3 F. Delitzsch, *Commentar zum Briefe an d. Hb.* (1857), *ad loc.*

[406] Mi. Hb. and Rgg. Hb., *ad loc.*

[407] Rgg. Hb., *ad loc.*

[408] The other members may be left on one side here.

[409] So with Mi. Hb., *ad loc.* against Delitzsch, *ad loc.*, who would relate the words only to the last member of the series.

E. σημεῖον in the Post-Apostolic Fathers.

It is worth noting that σημεῖον does not occur in Herm., Epistle to Diognetus, Mart. Pol., or Ign. Ign. did not adopt John's use of the word, though he follows John in much else. The few instances in other works do not take us beyond ordinary usage. Thus Lot's wife, when she became a pillar of salt, is called σημεῖον [410] ... εἰς τὸ γνωστὸν εἶναι πᾶσιν, ὅτι ..., 1 Cl., 11, 2. In 1 Cl., 12, 7, on the basis of Jos. 2:18, σημεῖον is the mark on the house of Rahab → 213, 30 ff. [411] σημεῖον is a "pointer" when 2 Cl., 15, 4 calls a v. of Scripture (Is. 58:9) a σημεῖον ἐπαγγελίας, and a "proof" when Did., 16, 4 calls the phenomena which announce the Lord's parousia σημεῖα τῆς ἀληθείας in distinction from the σημεῖα καὶ τέρατα of the κοσμο-πλάνος (16, 4) → 245, 24 ff. [412] Of these — 3 in all — express mention is made of the σημεῖον ἐκπετάσεως ἐν οὐρανῷ (→ lines 25 ff.) and the σημεῖον φωνῆς σάλπιγγος, the sign of the sounding of the trumpet, cf. 1 Th. 4:16. In 1 Cl., 25, 1 the myth of the phoenix, if interpreted aright with the author, is a σημεῖον which contains within it the promise of the resurrection of the flesh, cf. 26, 1 ff.

The post-apost. fathers are also traditional in their use of σημεῖα καὶ τέρατα. In 1 Cl., 51, 5 this is used for the signs and wonders in Egypt (→ 221, 7 ff.), in Barn., 4, 14 for all the divine miracles which accompanied the way of Israel and summoned it to faith, in Barn., 5, 8, which adopts a typological understanding of the age of Jesus as the eschatological age of Moses and redemption (→ 242, 20 ff.), for Jesus' own signs and wonders.

The use of σημεῖον in Barn., 12, 5 is outside the common framework at a first glance. Here the serpent which Moses lifted up is typologically referred to Jesus. This is easily explained, however, by the fact that in Nu. 21:8 f. God told Moses to set up the brazen serpent ἐπὶ σημείου → 220, 27 ff. A real difficulty is connected with the expression σημεῖον ἐκπετάσεως ἐν οὐρανῷ in Did., 16, 6 (→ line 12) since it is not clear what ἐκπέτασις means here. Does the opening of heaven mean its ripping apart at the parousia? [413] But if so ἐν οὐρανῷ would not fit very well. Hence it is probably more correct to assume that we have here an intentionally obscure ref. to the fact that on His return the Son of Man will appear with hands stretched out on the cross (ἐκ-πέτασις), [414] esp. as Ev. Pt. already gives evidence of belief in the ascension of the cross and later there are many testimonies to the expectation that Jesus would return on the transfigured cross. [415]

---

[410] Wis. 10:7 uses the interpretative μνημεῖον instead.

[411] The scarlet thread is already seen as a type of the blood of the Lord which achieves redemption. Rahab (→ III, 3, 13 ff.) is neither πόρνη nor hostess (→ VI, 589, 3 ff.) but simply φιλόξενος in 1 Cl., 12, 3.

[412] ἀλήθεια opp. πλάνη here, cf. 2 Th. 2:11; 1 Jn. 4:6.

[413] So Kn. Did. on 16, 6 though not without excluding other possibilities; E. Hennecke in Hennecke², 565; very emphatically H. Lilje, Die Lehre d. zwölf Ap. (1938), ad loc.: "first the sign that heaven opens up ...;" J.-P. Audet, La Didachè (1958), 473: "C'est 'l'ouver-ture dans le ciel,' premier moment de la fin."

[414] Kn. Did., ad loc. Cf. also E. Stommel, "Σημεῖον ἐκπετάσεως (Did. 16, 6)," Röm. Quartalschrift, 48 (1953), 21-42; J. A. Fischer, Review of J.-P. Audet (→ n. 413) in ThLZ, 85 (1960), 525.

[415] Cf. W. Bousset, Der Antichrist (1895), 154-158.

† σημαίνω.

A. σημαίνω on Greek Soil.

σημαίνω, Dor. σαμαίνω, is a normal derivate of σῆμα attested from Hom. →
202, 2 ff. In its basic sense it is shaped by σῆμα, as may still be seen in early Gk.
epic. → 202, 2 ff. Originally its ref. was to optical impressions (→ 202, 5 ff.) except
that these were no longer just there and if necessary open to interpretation, as with
σῆμα, but were now intentionally produced. Furthermore there is expressed in the verb
the desire to sign or characterise something or someone in the sense of establishing
it or relating it to something. Thus we read in Hom. Il., 23, 358 f. that σήμηνε δὲ
τέρματ᾽ Ἀχιλλεὺς τηλόθεν ἐν λείῳ πεδίῳ, and in Od., 12, 25 f. ἕκαστα σημανέω
stands alongside δείξω ὁδόν and thus means that whereby the right way may be
known. ¹ Since sign and command are closely related, σημαίνω abs. in Hom. can
simply mean "to indicate" in the sense "to direct," "to command," "to order," e.g., of
the ἡγεμόνες set over the rowers on a warship (Hom. Il., 16, 172) or Odysseus when
he has the palace cleansed after the slaughter among the suitors, Od., 22, 450. In distinction from κρατέω and ἀνάσσω σημαίνω unmistakably refers to precise and concrete
individual orders in keeping with its derivation from σῆμα, ² Hom. Il., 1, 288 f.; 16, 172. ³
All class. and post-class. usage rests on this foundation. Though there are objections
to attempting systematic classification, ⁴ it might be helpful to distinguish somewhat as
follows : a. "to give a sign" lit., e.g., by a smoke signal καπνῷ πυρός Aesch. Ag., 497,
or on the model of the use in Hom. (→ lines 19 ff.), to give a signal for battle, to re-
inforce an order (Thuc., II, 84, 13), also to give a signal to retreat (V, 10, 3), sometimes
with the use of the σάλπιγξ, Andoc., 1, 45 ⁵ (→ 73, 30 ff.), or as the rider's aid to his
horse, Xenoph. Eq., 7, 10; 9, 4 etc.; b. "to signify," "announce," "declare," also in an
extended or transf. sense, as when it is said of the Delphic Apollo οὔτε λέγει οὔτε
κρύπτει ἀλλὰ σημαίνει (Heracl. Fr., 93 [Diels⁷, I, 172, 6 f.]), i.e., he neither says
openly what is present or imminent nor conceals anything, but "intimates" or "signifies"
it in such a way that interpretation is needed, ⁶ or when it is said of (the need for)
sleep by day (ἡμερήσιοι ὕπνοι) that it "points to" (σημαίνουσι) physical disorder
or some other anomaly (Democr. Fr., 212 [Diels⁷, II, 188, 8 ff.]), or when word and
speech are said to have the power to σημαίνειν, Plat. Crat., 393a etc. Hence comes
τὸ σημαινόμενον for "meaning" of a word, Aristot. Rhet., III, 2, p. 1405b, 8 etc. The
picture presented by the usage as a whole is to this extent uniform and shows that the
verb derived from σῆμα shares its formal character. In keeping is the fact that while
σημαίνω can be used in religious statements none of the presuppositions of strict
religious use are met, nor is any such use found.

B. σημαίνω in Greek Judaism.

1. The breadth of the term may be seen from the fact that on Jewish soil it could be
used in the LXX as a transl. for a whole no. of fairly different Hbr. or Aram. stems.
In this it is, like σημεῖον, a means of interpretation. Thus תָּקַע (בַּ)שׁוֹפָר (→ 78, 17 ff.)
"to blow the trumpet" is sometimes rendered σημαίνειν (τῇ) σάλπιγγι, Jer. 4:5;

σ η μ α ί ν ω. Thes. Steph., Liddell-Scott, Pr.-Bauer⁵, s.v.
¹ On κλῆρον σημαίνεσθαι in Hom. Il., 7, 175 → 203, 15 ff.
² Hence in Hom. the one authorised or in a position to give signs or orders is a ση-
μάντωρ, e.g., a prince in Hom. Il., 4, 431, charioteer in 8, 127, herdsman of oxen or sheep
in 15, 325.
³ Cf. also Hom. Il., 10, 58; 14, 85; Od., 22, 427. In Il., 10, 485 ἀσήμαντος means "without
leader or shepherd."
⁴ In the light of the basic sense the specific meaning can and should usually be read off
from the context.
⁵ Later σημαίνω shares with σῆμα/σημεῖον an acoustic ref.
⁶ Cf. also Xenoph. An., VI, 1, 24 and → 204, 4 ff. on σῆμα/σημεῖον.

6:1; Ex. 33:6, [7] though the reason is not always given. [8] More commonly σημαίνω is used for הֵרִיעַ (→ 78, 21 ff.) — with or without mention of the σάλπιγξ/שׁוֹפָר as the instrument of the "alarm," Nu. 10:9; Ju. 7:21; 2 Ch. 13:12; 2 Εσδρ. 3:11. [9] In any case the "signal" aspect of the blowing is emphasised. σημαίνω is also used for Hbr. הוֹדִיעַ in Ex. 18:20 or Aram. הוֹדַע in Da. 2:15, 23, 30, 45 etc. in various senses ranging from mere "imparting" in Da. 2:15 to "pointing" (the way) in Ex. 18:20 and then "intimating" or "declaring" (by a dream) in Da. 2:45. Thus the LXX follows ordinary Gk. usage and there is no connection with אוֹת/σημεῖον.

2. Philo sometimes distinguishes expressly between "sound" (φωνή) and "meaning" (τὸ σημαινόμενον) as this is rooted in the hidden sense of a word, Congr., 172. This linguistic use of τὸ σημαινόμενον, which he shares with Aristot. (→ 262, 31 f.), plays a solid role in Philo, Som., I, 63, 85, 87; Leg. All., III, 188 etc. [10] The verb σημαίνω means "to signify," "to represent" in Poster. C., 155; "to denote" in Plant., 151 f.; Leg. All., II, 15. In the exposition of Scripture in the deeper sense "to say," "to mean," refers to the hidden signification which is not apparent on the surface, Congr., 155 (on Gn. 16:6 "in thy hands"). [11] Once the laws of Moses (νόμιμα) in their firmness and impregnability (βέβαια, ἀσάλευτα) are called σφραγῖσι φύσεως αὐτῆς σεσημασμένα, i.e., marked by their origin, Vit. Mos., II, 14. In the main the use in Philo stays within the intellectual sphere.

3. Things are very different in Josephus. Here σημαίνω means "to tell," "to notify" in Vit., 206, "to intimate" in Ant., 1, 198, [12] "to make known" in Ant., 6, 50, [13] "to mean," "to signify" in Ap., 1, 82 f., [14] and, since a royal seal can show that a letter is a royal document, it can also mean "to seal" in Ant., 11, 271. Since Jos. also uses the term for divine declarations, [15] it is natural to suppose that he employs it esp. for revelations which intimate God's will in word and work. [16] Even here, [17] however, the use is not specifically religious but is simply a use within religious statements, which is quite possible because the word has more of a technical character. A vital pt. in this respect is that Jos. plainly differentiates between σημαίνω and προφητεύω, Ant., 7, 214: the former may include the latter but does not have to do so.

C. σημαίνω in the New Testament.

Of the 6 passages in the NT 3 are in Jn. (12:33; 18:32; 21:19), one in Rev. (1:1) and 2 in Ac. (11:28; 25:27). Among them the 3 in Jn. occupy a special place and merit special attention.

---

[7] Cf. also Jos. 6:8 LXX.

[8] In Ez. 33:3 σημάνῃ τῷ λαῷ is used for הִזְהִיר אֶת־הָעָם "he warns the people," after an earlier ref. in the HT to blowing the trumpet; the train of thought is the same in v. 6 but the transl. differs. The LXX usually has σαλπίζειν for תקע.

[9] Acc. to Nu. 10:7 הֵרִיעַ seems to be distinguished from תָּקַע by the fact that the former denotes a longer and louder blast, the latter a short and precise blast → 81, 2 ff.

[10] τὸ σημαινόμενον is also used in relation to geometry and logic in Vit. Mos., II, 39.

[11] For other instances of this use of σημαίνω in Philo cf. C. H. Dodd, The Interpretation of the Fourth Gospel (1953), 141 f.

[12] An angel sent (πεμφθείς) to Abraham by God is ὡς σημανῶν περὶ τοῦ παιδός (Isaac).

[13] God makes known (σημαίνει) to Samuel that Saul is chosen as king.

[14] Ap., 1, 82 : τὸ γὰρ υκ καθ᾽ ἱερὰν γλῶσσαν βασιλέα σημαίνει. The ref. is to the meaning of hyk(sos) in Egyptian.

[15] Cf. also esp. Ant., 2, 276 : God σημαίνει to Moses τὴν αὐτοῦ προσηγορίαν (name), also Ant., 10, 238.

[16] So Schl. Jos., 52. Cf. also H. H. Huber, Der Begriff d. Offenbarung im Joh.-Ev. (1934), 78, n. 2 : "σημαίνω is for a him a revelation-term."

[17] The use of σημαίνω in Jos. is like that of σημεῖον → 223, 4 ff.

1. In Ac. 25:27 Festus is speaking about the further handling of Paul's case. He advances the thesis that as the present judge he cannot send Paul to Caesar unless by careful examination he is in a position τὰς κατ' αὐτοῦ αἰτίας σημᾶναι, i.e., "to show" what are the accusations against him. [18]

2. Ac. 11:28 says of Agabus, the primitive Christian prophet in Antioch: ἐσήμαινεν [19] διὰ τοῦ πνεύματος λιμὸν μεγάλην μέλλειν ἔσεσθαι ... The addition διὰ τοῦ πνεύματος confirms that in itself σημαίνω is not for the narrator a tt. for specifically prophetic discourse. It is true that Agabus prophesies, but it is equally true that σημαίνω simply means "to signify ...," and the Spirit is needed in this case because he is foreseeing the future. [20] The situation is the same in Rev. 1:1 with its mention of the ἀποκάλυψις Ἰησοῦ Χριστοῦ, ἣν ἔδωκεν αὐτῷ ὁ θεός, δεῖξαι τοῖς δούλοις αὐτοῦ ἃ δεῖ γενέσθαι ἐν τάχει, καὶ ἐσήμανεν ἀποστείλας διὰ τοῦ ἀγγέλου αὐτοῦ τῷ δούλῳ αὐτοῦ Ἰωάννῃ ... Here ἔδωκεν and ἐσήμανεν are formally parallel. But the subject of the first verb is God and of the second Jesus, since only thus do we have the chain of revelation which is obviously important for the seer of Revelation. [21] Materially, however, δεῖξαι and ἐσήμανεν are naturally parallel. It is by no means easy to say what is the relation between the two in substance. It could be that the second takes up and interprets the sense of the first, that in it the two constitutive elements of σῆμα or σημεῖον, namely, visibility and confirmation, [22] are united, and this with reference to the revelatory visions which underlie the whole book. If this is correct, then here, too, σημαίνω means "to indicate or declare something," [23] and the usage is not specifically religious.

3. Jn. 12:33; 18:32; 21:19 are linked not only by the use of σημαίνω but also by the fact that the use of σημαίνω contains an intimation of Jesus concerning the manner of death, His own in the first two verses and the disciple Peter's in the third: σημαίνων ποίῳ θανάτῳ ἤμελλεν ἀποθνήσκειν or δοξάσει τὸν θεόν. In all three the Evangelist himself is the speaker in a parenthetical note.

The relation between Jn. 12:33 and 18:32 needs no further discussion here, [24] nor does the background of the expression, which consists in the cross of Jesus and His assessment of it. The same applies to the question whether and in what way Jn. 21:19 contains martyrological terminology. [25]

---

[18] Luke's report corresponds exactly to the provisions of Roman penal law. When appeal is made to Caesar the procurator can no longer decide or even pardon; he can only report to the emperor, T. Mommsen, Röm. Strafrecht (1899), 243.

[19] Another reading is ἐσήμανεν (א A etc.).

[20] In the context Haench. Ag.[12], 317, n. 3, ad loc. rejects the view that the term denotes here the intimations of the dispenser of oracles. Cf. on this → 263, 26 f. with Jos. Ant., 7, 214.

[21] So with Had. Apk., ad loc.

[22] The ἃ δεῖ γενέσθαι points already to this aspect.

[23] The observations of Schl. Erl., ad loc., which are based on the view that in Rev. 1:1 the divine simply receives an "indicatory sign" corresponding to the fact that "prophecy is not full knowledge," are neither suggested by the context nor in harmony with the meaning of σημαίνω as we have it here.

[24] Cf. esp. Bultmann J. on the two verses.

[25] On the martyrological use of δοξάζειν cf. Bultmann J., ad loc., 553, n. 3.

In evaluating σημαίνω in all three verses our starting-point must be that for Judaism it is part of the very nature of man not to know the day of his death. [26] Not even Moses, the mediator of the revelation of God, was exempt from this rule, Dt. r., 9 on 31:14. Even more so there is no man, Moses again included, who knows how another man will die unless God Himself tells him. [27] When this is remembered it is clear that in all three passages the Evangelist is deliberately setting Jesus alongside God when he has Him know the manner of His own death and also that of His disciple, thus putting Him far above all other men. In this light the three verses stand materially in close inner relation to Jn. 2:19 ff., and this the more so in that a σημεῖον is in the full sense demanded of Jesus in 2:18. As used by the Fourth Evangelist, then, σημαίνω does not just have its own quality; it points back to the dignity of Jesus which enables Him to "signify" something even where others are not as yet able to see anything.

This renders superfluous all attempts to construe σημαίνω here as a tt. for oracular intimation [28] and hence to interpret it religiously. These attempts are also shattered by the fact that the passages adduced as examples of a corresponding use of the word in antiquity do not in fact prove this use. [29] In his use of the word John does not differ fundamentally from Joseph. → 263, 21 ff. In him, too, its formal character is still quite unmistakable.

D. σημαίνω in the Post-Apostolic Fathers.

In the post-apost. fathers the word occurs only in Barn., 15, 4 — and here only in one part of the textual tradition [30] — in an exposition of Gn. 2:2 relating to the word ἡμέρα : ἡ γὰρ ἡμέρα παρ' αὐτῷ σημαίνει χιλία ἔτη, cf. Ps. 90:4; 2 Pt. 3:8. Formally this is obviously based on the same mode of exegesis as that which Philo employed with his σημαίνει, "this means (in the deeper sense)." Materially there is kinship with the exegetical tradition found also in 2 Pt. 3:8 and indeed in much broader circles. [31]

† σημειόω.

1. A derivate of σημεῖον (→ 201, 30 ff.), Dor. σᾱμειόω from σᾱμεῖον, found from Hippocr. Praenotationes Coacae, II, 20 (Littré, V, 672), [1] but definitely, though modestly, used only in Hell. Gk., σημειόω shares with σημαίνω many meanings like "to denote" (→ 262, 24 ff.) in Polyb., 3, 39, 8, "to seal" (→ 263, 23 f.) in Dion. Hal. Ant. Rom., 4, 47, or "to signal" (→ 262, 20 ff.) in Aen. Tact., 22, 23. [2] In the more common med. the word has a subj. tendency in the sense "to mark for oneself" in Polyb., 21, 28, 9; it also means "to take something as a σημεῖον or τέρας" [3] in Strabo, 9, 2, 11 or, further developed, "to diagnose something (medically) on the basis of symptoms/σημεῖα"

---

[26] Acc. to M. Ex. רעו, 6 (171) on 16:32 (Str.-B., II, 412), no one knows the day of his death.
[27] S. Nu., 114 on 15:34; cf. Schl. J. on 12:33.
[28] Bau. J. on 12:33 on the basis of Bultmann J., ad loc., 331, n. 4.
[29] On Democr. cf. → 262, 29 f., on Jos. → 263, 21 ff.
[30] Cf. the editions.
[31] For examples from Justin, Iren., Hippolyt. etc., and cf. already Jub. 4:30, v. Wnd. Barn., 382.

σ η μ ε ι ό ω. Thes. Steph., Liddell-Scott, Pr.-Bauer⁵, s.v.
[1] Acc. to Pr.-Bauer⁵, s.v.
[2] Acc. to Liddell-Scott, s.v.
[3] I.e., "to grasp something in its character as a sign."

(→ 204, 14 ff.), Gal., 18[2], 851.[4] In documents the word denotes "signing in one's own hand" cf. σημεῖον for the signature. σεσημείωμαι can even mean "I have sealed, stamped" in the sense of "certified" or "approved," etc.[5]

2. The LXX uses the word only in Ps. 4:6 : ἐσημειώθη ἐφ’ ἡμᾶς τὸ φῶς τοῦ προσώπου σου, κύριε. This can only be understood as follows : "The light of thy countenance, O Lord, was (i.e., thou hast) made a σημεῖον to us." In view of what comes just before the point is that in God's turning the worshipper receives a "sign"[6] that in Him good things (τὰ ἀγαθά) are there already for His people.[7] It should be noted that the other Gk. transl. have either (Θ ’A) σημειώσεις τὸ θαυ (’A θαῦμα) or (Σ) σημειῶσαι σημεῖον for הָתְוִיתָ אֶת at Ez. 9:4 → 208, 29 ff.

3. In Philo, who uses only σημειοῦσθαι (med.),[8] the word means "to characterise" in Spec. Leg., IV, 110 : "God distinguishes water-creatures which may be eaten by marking them with two characteristics, wings and scales, σημειωσάμενος,[9] "to show" in Spec. Leg., II, 178 : σεσημειῶσθαι τὴν διαφοράν, "to get proof" in Jos., 235 : μαρτυρίαις σημειωσάμενος, or "to signify" in Spec. Leg., I, 92 : ἐκ τῶν οὐρανίων, good or bad weather, drought, fruitfulness, crop failure etc. noted from observation of σημεῖα in heaven. Joseph. in Ant., 11, 208 tells how Artaxerxes commanded his chroniclers "to note" (σημειώσασθαι) the name of Haman as worthy ; here, then, the notation includes the idea of merit, and the word remains close to its basic sense.

4. 2 Th. 3:14 contains the admonition : If anyone does not heed what we say by letter, τοῦτον σημειοῦσθε μὴ συναναμίγνυσθαι αὐτῷ ἵνα ἐντραπῇ. The meaning of σημειοῦσθαι here is close to that in Josephus (→ lines 17 ff.) but in a transferred sense, the point being that every member of the church who is loyal to the apostle is to note dissenters personally. Though the measure has the character of an act of church discipline it is doubtful whether we are to think in terms of a public identification of those who will not work,[10] for the order does not merely exclude from worship but also forbids daily intercourse.[11] What is forbidden is not so much relationship in everyday things but rather specifically Christian and spiritual relationship,[12] unless the reference is simply to common meals.[13]

5. In 1 Cl., 43, 1, as in Jos. (→ lines 17 ff.), σημειοῦσθαι means "to note"; it is used of Moses with ref. to the ἱεραὶ βίβλοι written down by him.

---

[4] The last passages acc. to Liddell-Scott, s.v.
[5] Cf. Preisigke Fachwörter, 156.
[6] In this context we cannot investigate in detail the relation between the LXX and HT of Ps. 4:6. It seems that in the singular נְסָה־עָלֵינוּ either the transl. caught an echo of נֵס "banner" (often transl. σημεῖον → 220, 23 ff.) (cf. Σ ἐπίσημον ποίησον) or he thought he saw in נסה a ni form of נסס from which comes the hitpo'el of Ps. 60:4; Zech. 9:16 (? cf. the comm., ad loc.). Usually the distinctive נְסָה is equated with נָשָׂא and the v. expounded in terms of Nu. 6:26 (priestly blessing).
[7] At Is. 59:19 ’A has ἐσημειώθη for נֹסְסָה, which can, of course, be pointed differently. Only a brief ref. may be made here to Ps. 60:4 ’A.
[8] Cf. also σημειοῦσθαι with ἐνσφραγίζεσθαι in Det. Pot., 38 and τυποῦν in Plant., 18; Mut. Nom., 135.
[9] Everywhere in Philo, hence also here, a subj. element is noticeably linked with the word.
[10] In the context this is the primary ref.
[11] Dib. Th., ad loc.
[12] Cf. Joh. W. 1 K. on 5:11.
[13] Ltzm. 1 K. on 5:11 and App. p. 174 f.

† ἄσημος.

1. Basically this means "without σῆμα, i.e., without characteristic," and acc. to the ref. it is used of men or things which have nothing to lend distinction. Thus χρυσίον ἄσημον καὶ ἀργύριον in Thuc., II, 13, 4 is "unstamped or unminted" gold and silver, ἄσημα ὅπλα in Eur. Phoen., 1112 are weapons "without emblems" to denote their owners (→ 204, 29 ff.), ἄσημα βοῆς in Soph. Ant., 1209 are "inarticulate" cries, ἄσημοι χρησμοί in Aesch. Proem., 662 are "obscure" oracles, an ἀνὴρ ἄσημος in Eur. Herc. Fur., 849 is an "insignificant" man hardly worth noting, and an ἄσημος πόλις in Strabo, 8, 6, 15 is a city "without significance." In other contexts the meaning can be "without blemish,"[1] and in personal descriptions the sense may be "with no distinguishing mark."[2]

2. The LXX remains within this framework: Gn. 30:42: πρόβατα ἄσημα, "unimportant," "weak" sheep,[3] Job 42:11: τετράδραχμος χρυσοῦς ἄσημος,[4] and 3 Macc. 1:3: ἄσημός τις "some insignificant person."

3. The same is true of Philo, whether he speaks of ἄνδρες ἄσημοι alongside σοφοί in Mut. Nom., 140, of a φωνὴ ἄσημος in Vit. Mos., 2, 164, of a φυλὴ ἄσημος in Vit. Mos., 2, 234, of ἄσημοι in the sense of a "disregarded and insignificant" family in Virt., 222, of an ἄσημος ἀγέλη in Som., I, 255, or simply of ἄσημα "unformed" in Migr. Abr., 79. Joseph. like to use the term with ref. to descent and he calls people "of obscure and doubtful lineage" ἄσημοι, Ant., 16, 301; Bell., 1, 241; 2, 469; Ap., 1, 75. He also follows the usual practice in speaking of unstamped metals, ἄσημον ἀργύριον, Vit., 295 f.

4. As a man of education Luke is using an obviously widespread expression, which is restrained for all the desired emphasis,[5] when in Ac. 21:39 he has Paul call his native Tarsus an οὐκ ἄσημος πόλις and refer to himself as a citizen of it. It may be that this is important to Luke, especially before a Roman χιλίαρχος, since it sets Paul among the cultured men of his age who used this mode of expression, called litotes.[6] The fact is that Luke had a special concern to arouse the interest of educated people in his cause (cf. Ac. 1:1 and Lk. 1:1 ff.); this also finds linguistic expression elsewhere in his works.[7]

† ἐπίσημος.

1. In distinction from → ἄσημος is the person or thing which has a distinguishing or prominent σῆμα or σημεῖον, cf. Eur. Phoen., 1113 f.: ἄναξ ... ἔχων σημεῖον ἐν μέσῳ σάκει. Thus it is used close to ἄσημος to differentiate, e.g., stamped precious metal from unstamped, Hdt., IX, 41, 3. ἀναθήματα οὐκ ἐπίσημα in Hdt., I, 51, 5 are offerings with no label to show who is making them or on what occasion. When

---

ἄ σ η μ ο ς. Cf. the lex., s.v.
[1] Cf. R. Reitzenstein, Zwei religionsgeschichtliche Fragen (1901), 1, n. (ἄσημος "not disfigured" by circumcision).
[2] Examples in Mitteis-Wilcken, 332, n. 1; J. Hasebroek, Das Signalement in d. Pap.-Urkunden (1921), 79, n. 3.
[3] The relation to the HT cannot be discussed here.
[4] The correct theology of the transl. may be deduced from the addition ἄσημος to the HT: Coins with heads or non-Jewish religious symbols were regarded as desecrated money.
[5] Cf. Haench. Ag.[12], 70 (§ 5, 3) and ad loc.
[6] J. Palm, Über Sprache u. Stil d. Diodor v. Sizilien (1955), 153-156.
[7] Haench. Ag.[12], 67 f. (§ 5, 2b).
ἐ π ί σ η μ ο ς. Cf. the lex, s.v.

a sick person is called ἐπίσημος this means that he "visibly carries the symptoms" (→ 204, 14 ff.) of his malady, Hippocr. Morb. Sacr., 8 (Littré, VI, 376). Acc. to the different contexts the word is just as varied in sense as ἄσημος → 267, 1 ff. The main difference, which corresponds to the distinction included in it, is that it can be used both in bonam and also in malam partem, though the latter is comparatively rare, cf. the characterising of Terentius Varro as ἀπὸ γένους ἀσήμου, βίου δὲ διὰ δημοκοπίαν (flattery of the people) καὶ προπέτειαν (insolence) ἐπισήμου (notorious), Plut. Fab. Max., 14 (I, 182a), cf. Eur. Or., 249. In relation to the history of the meaning of σῆμα/σημεῖον it is not without interest that there can sometimes be ref. to a τάφος ἐπισημότατος, Thuc., II, 43, 2 → 203, 24 ff.

2. In the LXX the word is used in bonam partem, cf. ἡμέρα ἐπίσημος for "feast-day" in Est. 5:4; 2 Macc. 15:36, or to denote an "outstanding man" in 3 Macc. 6:1. The expression τόπος ἐπίσημος characterises a place as one which is "generally visible," 1 Macc. 11:37; 14:48. On Gn. 30:42 → 267, 12 ff.

3. Philo almost always uses the term as the anton. of ἄσημος for "recognisable," Migr. Abr., 79, or "distinctive," Rer. Div., 186, or "superior," "powerful," but he once defines τὸ διάσημον as μεγάλως ἐπίσμον, "perfectly plain," Som.., I, 201. Joseph. has ἐπίσημοι ἡμέραι for "feast-days" (cf. LXX) in Ant., 3, 128, and he also uses it for "stamped" precious metal in Ant., 3, 57; 17, 189. In Vit., 7; Bell., 6, 38 ἐπίσημος is used for men of "distinguished" birth and in Ap., 1, 163 for a "significant" historian, but the use in malam partem also occurs in Ant., 5, 233 ("infamous"). ἐπισήμως ἀγωνίζεσθαι in Bell., 6, 92 and 148 means to fight "in an outstanding manner."

4. In the NT ἐπίσημος occurs once each in bonam and in malam partem. In R. 16:7 Paul calls Junius and Andronicus ἐπίσημοι ἐν τοῖς ἀποστόλοις. Apart from the problems posed by the two names and the use of the word ἀπόστολος (→ I, 422, 19 ff.), the expression might mean either that the two are "significant in the circle of apostles" or "highly regarded" among them. [1,2]
In Mt. 27:16 Barabbas is called a δέσμιος ἐπίσημος. Here the adjective is fairly certainly to be understood in malam partem and translated "notorious." This is suggested especially by the par. Mk. 15:7, according to which Barabbas was μετὰ τῶν στασιαστῶν δεδεμένος, οἵτινες ἐν τῇ στάσει φόνον πεποιή-κεισαν. This understanding of the term, which points to kinship of usage between Matthew and Josephus, [3] is at any rate to be preferred to the attempt [4] to understand ἐπίσημος here as a tt. for the leader of a band of Zealots, → IV, 261, 35 ff.

5. In the post-apost. fathers occurrence of the term is restricted to Mart. Pol., 3, 1 (adv.); 14, 1; 19, 1 (adj.), and it is used in bonam partem. In 19, 1 it emphasises the quality of Polycarp as διδάσκαλος, in 14, 1 it catches up the metaphor of the κριὸς ἐπίσημος destined for total immolation, and in 3, 1, in the phrase ἐπισήμως θηριο-μαχεῖν, it seems to reflect incipient martyr terminology, cf. Martyrium Ignatii, 2 (MPG, 5 [1894], 981 C).

---

[1] On the two possibilities cf. Zn. R., ad loc. for the second and Ltzm. R., ad loc.; Schl. R., ad loc.; Mi. R., ad loc., 342, n. 8 for the first. The first is probably to be preferred. If Paul had meant the second he could and should have expressed himself more clearly.

[2] From this not very clear formulation no basic deductions should be made concerning the nature and compass of the primitive Chr. apostolate. The v. has no independent weight in the context.

[3] Cf. the discussion in Schl. Mt., ad loc.

[4] Cf. J. Pickl, Messiaskönig Jesus in der Auffassung seiner Zeitgenossen (1935), 247, but with inadequate support from Jos.

† εὔσημος → II, 770, 6 ff.

† σύσσημον.

1. The attestation of τὸ σύσσημον in literature is relatively late. It appears in the comedian Menand. Pericl., 362[1] and obviously has the same sense as σημεῖον, though with a ref. to the fact that as a "sign" it rests on an agreement or relates to a common tie independent of the individual. Thus the word can be the "signal for battle" in Diod. S., 20, 51, or the "standard" in weights and measures in Strabo, 15, 1, 51, or in the plur. the "insignia" which mark an ἀρχή, Diod. S., 1, 70.

2. In the same way the LXX uses it for מַשְׂאֵת ("signal installation") in Ju. 20:38, 40 B (→ 208, 33 ff.) and נֵס ("banner") in Is. 5:26; 49:22; 62:10, both transl. σημεῖον in other verses. 'A always has σύσσημον (→ 220, n. 138) for נֵס, Is. 11:12; 13:2; 30:17; 33:23; 59:19,[2] and it also uses the term in Ps. 60:4 (LXX σημείωσις); Is. 11:10 (with Σ);[3] it is used by ΣΘ at Is. 33:23 and Σ at Jer. 6:1 (LXX and 'A σημεῖον, HT מַשְׂאֵת). The word is not found in either Philo or Joseph.

3. Mk. 14:44 remains within this usage when it has σύσσημον for "the stipulated sign" of the kiss which Judas gives Jesus to identify Him as the one the officers seek.[4] What Mt. 26:48 simply calls a σημεῖον[5] is thus interpreted as something which Judas had very carefully arranged beforehand.[6]

4. The post-apost. fathers use the word once but only in an OT allusion to Is. 5:26 and with a christological reference: By His resurrection Jesus has eternally set up a σύσσημον for saints and believers, whatever their origin, in the one body of His ἐκκλησία; that is, He has raised a "standard" around which they are to gather, Ign. Sm., 1, 2.

Rengstorf

| σήμερον | → ἡμέρα, II, 943, 21 ff.; νῦν, IV, 1106, 5 ff. |

A. Presuppositions in Greek.

Ion. σήμερον, Dor. σάμερον, Att. τήμερον, the word comes from *κιᾶμερον (*κι- + ἀμέρα).[1] It is attested from Hom. and Pind.: Hom. Il., 7, 29 f.; also 8, 142; Od., 17, 185 f.; Pind. Olymp., 6, 28; Pyth., 4, 1. The ref. of to-day is to the span of

---

σ ύ σ σ η μ ο ν. Cf. the lex., *s.v.*
[1] Cf. also Hedylus in Athen., 8, 345b.
[2] The data in Hatch-Redp., 1323b stand in need of correction.
[3] Cf. BHK, *ad loc.*
[4] Cf. the comm., *ad loc.*
[5] This has sometimes made its way into the text of Mk., cf. Tisch. NT, *ad loc.*
[6] As סִימָנָא σύσσημον is a loan word in the Rabb., Krauss Lehnw., II, 390b. But the few instances are not enough to allow us to draw any conclusions regarding the use in Mk. 14:44.
σ ή μ ε ρ ο ν. [1] Liddell-Scott, Pr.-Bauer[5], *s.v.* On the model of σήμερον/τήμερον is σῆτες (σᾶτες), Att. τῆτες, from κιᾶ-ετες "this year." The same *κι- lies behind the Old High German *hiutu* (from *hiu dagu) "heute" and *hiu jāru* "heuer." Cf. Boisacq, *s.v.*; Schwyzer, I, 319 with n. 2.

human activity embracing a day up to evening ; it is the time at man's disposal, perhaps the last such. Thus we read in Plat. Phaed., 59e : λύουσι γάρ, ἔφη, οἱ ἕνδεκα Σωκράτη καὶ παραγγέλλουσιν ὅπως ἂν τῇδε τῇ ἡμέρᾳ τελευτᾷ. Socrates says in 61c : ἄπειμι δέ, ὡς ἔοικε, τήμερον· κελεύουσι γὰρ 'Αθηναῖοι. This last day is filled by an intensive διασκοπεῖν τε καὶ μυθολογεῖν περὶ τῆς ἀποδημίας τῆς ἐκεῖ, ποίαν τινὰ αὐτὴν οἰόμεθα εἶναι. 61e : τί γὰρ ἄν τις καὶ ποιοῖ ἄλλο ἐν τῷ μέχρι ἡλίου δυσμῶν χρόνῳ; This remained the Gk. usage. For comedy cf. Aristoph. Eq., 68, 1061, 1162 etc.; cf. also Eur. Rhes., 683; Plat. Crito, 43d; Symp., 176e. To-day can obviously be distinguished from or combined with yesterday and to-morrow, e.g., Plat. Symp., 174a: χθὲς γὰρ αὐτὸν διέφυγον ..., ὡμολόγησα δ' εἰς τήμερον παρέσεσθαι, Crat., 396e : τὸ μὲν τήμερον εἶναι ..., αὔριον δέ ...; cf. Epict. Diss., IV, 12, 20 f.; Plut. De cohibenda ira, 11 (II, 459e) εἰ (sc. Alexander) σήμερον ... τέθνηκε, καὶ αὔριον ἔσται καὶ εἰς τρίτην τεθνηκώς. Instead of σήμερον or τήμερον Soph. Oed. Tyr., 1283 says : τῇδε θήμέρᾳ. As already we find in Demosth. Or., 4, 40 μέχρι τῆς τήμερον ἡμέρας etc. there is also found in Hellenism the plerophoric ἐν τῇ σήμερον ἡμέρᾳ with attributive use of the adv., e.g., Ditt. Syll.³, III, 1181, 11 (2nd cent. B.C.); cf. also Plut. Fab. Max., 13, 7 (I, 181e). This means the time of man's activity distinguished to-day as the present.

B. Presuppositions in the OT and Judaism.

1. Acc. to the Jewish understanding of time the day begins in the evening. Naturally cognisance is taken of the span of time up to the evening, but what is primarily expressed in "to-day" is not the time now at man's disposal but the "to-day" of temporally secured or hampered dealings between God and His people. The matter which in the OT is dispersed among some 1800 instances of יוֹם is here set forth in the usage of the LXX (some 286 times). In the LXX σήμερον mostly corresponds to the fixed expression הַיּוֹם, and as σήμερον can transl. the fuller הַיּוֹם הַזֶּה (e.g., Jer. 1:10), conversely the emphatic ἡ σήμερον ἡμέρα is also found, esp. in sacred narrative : ἕως (τῆς) σήμερον (ἡμέρας), Gn. 19:37 f.; 26:33; 35:20 (A) etc.; Jos. 4:9 etc.; Ez. 2:3; 20:29, 31, cf. 24:2. σήμερον can be combined with αὔριον, 4 Βασ. 6:28; Ex. 19:10; Sir. 10:10; 20:15 and distinguished from ἐχθές, 2 Βασ. 15:20; Sir. 38:22; 1 Macc. 9:44. With ἐχθές (or αὔριον) καὶ τρίτην (ἡμέραν) it is often used for an experience which last more than a day, e.g., Ex. 5:7, 14; 19:11; 1 Βασ. 4:7; 2 Βασ. 11:12; without καὶ τρίτην e.g., 1 Βασ. 20:27. Similar expressions are σήμερον τριταῖος in 1 Βασ. 9:20; 30:13, or liturgically ἀπὸ τῆς σήμερον καὶ εἰς τὸν αἰῶνα in Tob. 7:12 (S) cf. 1 Macc. 10:30. Finally "to-day" is distinguished from "a long while" (ἀπ' ἀρχῆς ἡμερῶν σου), Jdt. 8:29; rather differently 12:18.

In the main the time in "to-day" is inaugurated rather than counted. Hence the emphatic ἐγὼ ἐντέλλομαί σοι σήμερον (so often in Dt., comprehensively in 30:15-20). [2] What takes place or obtains "to-day" is from God, whether as command, promise or blessing [3] on the one side, judgment or cursing [4] on the other. Similarly the Israelite knows that, e.g., on the Sabbath, he is bound to "this day." [5] If this is emphasised in relation to secular dealings and encounters, [6] there is often a special reference, [7] strictly to what obtains before God or men

---

[2] Dt. 4:2 etc.; cf. G. v. Rad, Theol. d. AT, I (1957), 80.
[3] Ex. 14:13; 32:29; Dt. 1:10; 6:24; 11:26; 1 Βασ. 10:2.
[4] Dt. 4:25 f.; 8:19; 9:3 ff.; 11:26; Jos. 7:19, 25; 1 Βασ. 15:28.
[5] Gn. 31:43 f.; 40:7; 41:9; Ex. 16:25; Lv. 10:19.
[6] Gn. 30:32; 42:13, 32; 1 Βασ. 4:16; 9:12; 3 Βασ. 1:25.
[7] Gn. 21:26; 30:16; Dt. 31:2; 1 Βασ. 9:19 f.; 2 Βασ. 16:3; 3 Βασ. 1:25.

in a good or a bad sense. [8] "To-day" what is decisive comes about [9] or comes to light. [10] "To-day" is fulfilment, [11] revelation, [12] whether as salvation or disaster. Thus what is said "to-day," if it is the word that is to be said to-day, e.g., an oath or a covenant (→ διαθήκη, II, 106, 16 ff.; 111, 25 ff.), inaugurates that which decides concerning the being or non-being of God's people, its existence. [13] If "to-day" is lost, existence itself is deeply threatened even if not forfeited. [14] Thus "to-day" can be the means [15] as well as the content of revelation. [16] In it God's Word goes forth and also the answer to it, whether it be questioning or prayer (worship). [17] God's Word and what takes place "to-day" can and should be commensurate with one another. This means that all that takes place should be expressed and decided before God and by God. To-day history becomes address, word (ψ 94:7; 2:7). For this reason "to-day" looks back to the past and forward to the present. It thus discloses its truth as the eschatologically accentuated claim to obedience of the Lord of history who teaches His people what they should do, Dt. 4:1. [18] "To-day" is the ever actual time of decision between God and His people, Dt. 26:17-19.

2. Philo can say in Leg. All., III, 25 : ἕως τῆς σήμερον ἡμέρας (Gn. 35:4), τουτέστιν ἀεί· ὁ γὰρ αἰὼν ἅπας τῷ σήμερον παραμετρεῖται, μέτρον γὰρ τοῦ παντὸς χρόνου ὁ ἡμερήσιος κύκλος. But on Dt. 4:4 : (ὑμεῖς δὲ) οἱ προσκείμενοι κυρίῳ τῷ θεῷ ὑμῶν, ζῆτε πάντες ἐν τῇ σήμερον, he says in Fug., 56 f.: τοὺς γὰρ πρόσφυγας καὶ ἱκέτας τοῦ θεοῦ μόνους ζῶντας οἶδε, νεκροὺς δὲ τοὺς ἄλλους· ἐκείνοις δ', ὡς ἔοικε, καὶ ἀφθαρσίαν μαρτυρεῖ διὰ τοῦ προσθεῖναι "ζῆτε ἐν τῇ σήμερον." σήμερον δ' ἐστὶν ὁ ἀπέρατος καὶ ἀδιεξίτητος αἰών· μηνῶν γὰρ καὶ ἐνιαυτῶν καὶ συνόλως χρόνων περίοδοι δόγματα ἀνθρώπων εἰσὶν ἀριθμὸν ἐκτετιμηκότων· τὸ δ' ἀψευδὲς ὄνομα αἰῶνος ἡ σήμερον. ἥλιος γὰρ οὐκ ἀλλαττόμενος ὁ αὐτός ἐστιν ἀεί, ποτὲ μὲν ὑπὲρ γῆς ποτὲ δὲ ὑπὸ γῆν ἰών, παρ' ὃν ἡμέρα καὶ νύξ, τὰ αἰῶνος μέτρα, διεκρίθησαν. Here the ἡμέρα takes precedence over the νύξ as ἥλιος ... σκότους καὶ ... νοῦς, ὁ τῆς ὅλης ψυχῆς ἡγεμών, ὀφθαλμῶν σώματος, Op. Mund., 30. For God called the ἡμέρα οὐχὶ πρώτην, ἀλλὰ μίαν, ἣ λέλεκται διὰ τὴν τοῦ νοητοῦ κόσμου μόνωσιν μοναδικὴν ἔχοντος φύσιν, ibid., 35; cf. Deus Imm., 32. Philo keeps to the OT postulate of unity between God's Word (not just will) and the reality thereby ordained either positively or negatively for man.

3. Like Philo, Joseph. uses σήμερον (and some 7 times τήμερον) almost always in connection with LXX quotations, and only in Ant. apart from Bell., 1, 79. In Ant., 7, 256 cf. 2 Βασ. 19:8 σήμερον means "still to-day" or "even to-day" : ὡς ἐγὼ τήμερον,

---

[8] Dt. 31:26 f.; 32:46; Jos. 14:10 f.; Rt. 2:19; 3:18; 4:9 f., 14; 1 Βασ. 9:27 etc.; also Ju. 9:18; 1 Βασ. 26:21, 23; 2 Βασ. 6:20; 11:12.
[9] Gn. 24:12, 42; Ex. 14:13 f.; Nu. 22:30 f.; Dt. 4:39; 9:1; 1 Βασ. 4:16.
[10] Gn. 50:20; Ex. 14:13; Dt. 9:3; 1 Βασ. 12:5; 24:11 f.; 2 Βασ. 19:6 ff.
[11] Dt. 2:18; 4:36-40; 5:3; 26:3; 1 Βασ. 4:16; 2 Ch. 10:7.
[12] Gn. 22:14; 40:7; 41:41; Ex. 14:13 f.; 19:10 f.; Lv. 9:4; Dt. 11:2 ff.; 26:16-18; 4 Βασ. 2:3, 5; Jdt. 6:2; 3 Macc. 6:13.
[13] Gn. 25:33; 31:43 f., 46; 47:23; Ex. 13:3 f.; 14:13 f.; Dt. 1:39; 4:1 f., 4; 8:18; 9:3 ff.; 11:2 ff.
[14] Gn. 4:14; 25:31 ff.; Dt. 12:8; 31:21; Jos. 22:16 ff.; 1 Βασ. 26:8, 19; Bar. 3:8; Jdt. 7:28; 8:12, 18.
[15] Ex. 2:18; 1 Βασ. 12:5, 17; 14:28 ff. etc.; Is. 38:19; 'Ιερ. 41:15.
[16] 1 Βασ. 12:17 f.; 14:24, 28; 3 Βασ. 18:36; Jdt. 13:11; Is. 37:3.
[17] 1 Βασ. 25:32 ff.; 3 Βασ. 1:48; 5:21; 8:15, 28, 56; 22:5; 1 Ch. 29:5; 2 Ch. 6:19; 18:4; Jdt. 13:17; Prv. 7:14.
[18] Cf. v. Rad, op. cit. (→ n. 2), I, 228-230.

ἂν ἐπιμένης τοῖς ἄρτι πραττομένοις, ἀναπείσας ἀποστῆναί σου τὸν λαόν. In Ant., 6, 305 τήμερον is followed by its opp. ἡ ἐπερχομένη ἡμέρα. 4 times Joseph. uses σήμερον or τήμερον in the sense "until this day," Ant., 7, 366 : ἄχρι τῆς σήμερον ἡμέρας, 8, 55 : ἄχρι τῆς τήμερον without ἡμέρας, 10, 265 : μέχρι τῆς σήμερον ἡμέρας, Ant., 9, 28 without ἡμέρας. Ant., 7, 353, which combines 3 Βασ. 1:30 and 48, is perhaps connected with the Judaean royal ritual formula : [19] καὶ τοῦτο ἔσται τήμερον, cf. 351: εἰ τήμερον ἀποδείξειε τὸν Ἀδονίαν βασιλέα (3 Βασ. 1:13); also 7, 266 : ὅτι σήμερον ἄρχομαι τῆς βασιλείας (2 Βασ. 19:23), 13, 45 : χειροτονοῦμεν δέ σε σήμερον ἀρχιερέα ... 1 Macc. 10:20 runs : καὶ νῦν καθεστάκαμέν σε σήμερον ἀρχιερέα τοῦ ἔθνους σου κτλ. (cf. ψ 2:6). Gn. 41:1 may be adduced here : εἶπεν δὲ Φαραω τῷ Ιωσηφ Ἰδοὺ καθίστημί σε σήμερον ἐπὶ πάσης γῆς Αἰγύπτου. The ritual formula itself occurs in ψ 2:7: κύριος εἶπεν πρός με Υἱός μου εἶ σύ, ἐγὼ σήμερον γεγέννηκά σε (אָמַר אֵלַי בְּנִי אַתָּה אֲנִי הַיּוֹם יְלִדְתִּיךָ). This very close but not on that account physical relation between God and His "son" needs God's Word that it may be acknowledged once and for all and not forgotten (Dt. 32:18) or perverted (Jer. 2:27). As ψ 94:7-11 shows, God's Word is always related to His work, v. 9 : καὶ εἴδοσαν τὰ ἔργα μου, HT גַּם־רָאוּ פָעֳלִי. On the basis of the OT σήμερον took on a new emphasis to the degree that in the term God's revelation sought expression as Israel's history, so that what remained (and not just is) God's will was to be proclaimed "to-day." Naturally a non-theological use of this term for time runs alongside the theological use, though it can, of course, easily shift into the latter.

C. The Usage in the New Testament.

In the NT, too, a non-theological use of σήμερον may be distinguished from the emphatic theological use. But the distinction does not operate when revelation no longer presents historical periods but only a "to-day," i.e., when the address-character of revelation itself is or involves the decisive event.

1. Non-Theological Usage.

a. In Mt. 27:19 Pilate's wife says : ... πολλὰ γὰρ ἔπαθον σήμερον κατ' ὄναρ δι' αὐτόν. This is, of course, a bad omen for the critically decisive day, as v. 24 (Dt. 21:6-8) shows. It is no less significant than the dreams of Joseph or the wise men, Mt. 1:20; 2:12 f., 19. But in the first instance σήμερον means only "this night."

The same applies in the fourth petition of the Lord's Prayer (→ II, 590, 33 ff.) as recorded in Mt. 6:11: τὸν ἄρτον ἡμῶν τὸν ἐπιούσιον δὸς ἡμῖν σήμερον. Lk. 11:3, acc. to D it and other MSS which read σήμερον like Mt., obviously gives added emphasis with τὸ καθ' ἡμέραν. The smoother version in Mt. corresponds to the ancient Jewish style of prayer → n. 17. What is meant in Mt. is the present day. σήμερον agrees with the adj. τὸν ἐπιούσιον (vg supersubstantialem Mt. 6:11; quotidianum Lk. 11:3) in relation to τὸν ἄρτον ἡμῶν (Marcion σου) if ἐπιούσιον is taken to mean crastinus, but this interpretation runs counter to Jewish custom. [20] Since a prayer of this kind is not meant to be disturbed by reflection, ἐπιούσιον must express something that is self-evident. [21] For Jesus and the community, however, the self-evident thing was that God gives them bread. To ask "to-day," then, corresponds best to this sense. Hence σήμερον is not to be understood in the light of ἐπιούσιον but ἐπιούσιον in the light of σήμερον, i.e., as a variant of σήμερον and not apocalyptically.

---

[19] G. v. Rad, "Das judäische Königsritual," ThLZ, 72 (1947), 211-216; also op. cit. (→ n. 2), I, 49, 318; W. Staerk, Soter, II (1938), 218 f.
[20] Except for the Sabbath, Ex. 16:5; cf. Str.-B., I, 420 f., also → II, 595, 6 ff.
[21] E. Lohmeyer, Das Vaterunser (1946), 101, suggests this but does not state it.

As in the prayer those of little faith are to orientate themselves to "to-day" if they are to escape anxiety. For τὸν χόρτον τοῦ ἀγροῦ σήμερον ὄντα καὶ αὔριον εἰς κλίβανον βαλλόμενον ὁ θεὸς οὕτως ἀμφιέννυσιν, Mt. 6:30 par. Lk. 12:28. The peasant shows his knowledge of the weather when he says in the morning: σήμερον χειμών, πυρράζει γὰρ στυγνάζων ὁ οὐρανός, Mt. 16:3. The father in the parable says: τέκνον, ὕπαγε σήμερον ἐργάζου ἐν τῷ ἀμπελῶνι, Mt. 21:28. In Mk. 14:30: ἀμὴν λέγω σοι ὅτι σὺ σήμερον ταύτη τῇ νυκτὶ ..., σήμερον is juxtaposed with ταύτη τῇ νυκτί to the extent that the day begins rather than ends at evening for the Hebrews. Mt. 26:34 leaves out σήμερον, while Lk. 22:34 drops ταύτη τῇ νυκτί and rearranges the verse. [22]

b. Ac. 4:9; 19:40; 20:26; 22:3; 24:21; 26:2, 29; 27:33 all mention σήμερον as the day a speaker is giving his address. If transferred usage is reflected already in Mt. 6:30 par. Lk. 12:28, the intentionally secular saying in Jm. 4:13: σήμερον ἢ αὔριον πορευσόμεθα εἰς τήνδε τὴν πόλιν καὶ ποιήσομεν ἐκεῖ ἐνιαυτὸν κτλ., is to be regarded as typically expressing a foolish mastery over one's own time. [23] On the other hand the biographical apophthegm in Lk. 13:31-33, which taken alone sounds as though it is deliberately non-theological, [24] is to be construed allegorically when set alongside the saying ἰδοὺ ἐκβάλλω δαιμόνια καὶ ἰάσεις ἀποτελῶ σήμερον καὶ αὔριον and seen in the light of the following καὶ τῇ τρίτῃ τελειοῦμαι. In v. 33 the τῇ ἐχομένῃ (ἐρχομένη) perhaps stands in juxtaposition with (σήμερον καὶ) αὔριον, as Ac. 13:44 (?) and 21:26 seem to show. Lk. probably understood v. 33 according to the schema of Ac. 20:15. Only the ὅτι clause in v. 33 gives theological significance to what precedes.

c. A saying apart is that of our Lord from the cross in Lk. 23:43: σήμερον μετ' ἐμοῦ ἔσῃ ἐν τῷ παραδείσῳ (→ V, 770, 27 ff.). Given emphasis by ἀμὴν σοι λέγω, this is a saying of antithesis to the situation of the two victims of crucifixion, the penitent thief and his Lord. It is the saying of one who is leaving the present scene. The present is, of course, lit up by this kind of surrender of the present.

2. Theological Usage.

a. Liturgical style may be seen in the expression in Hb. 13:8: ('Ιησοῦς Χριστὸς) ἐχθὲς καὶ σήμερον ὁ αὐτὸς καὶ εἰς τοὺς αἰῶνας, [25] here applied to Christ. The common LXX phrase ἕως τῆς σήμερον ἡμέρας occurs in R. 11:8 (Dt. 29:4), and in the shorter form ἕως τῆς σήμερον in Mt. 27:8, though the fact that this is a fulfilment of promise is emphasised by the note introduced in v. 9 (Zech. 11:12 f.). In Mt. 28:15 the report that the body of Jesus was stolen is said to circulate μέχρι τῆς σήμερον [ἡμέρας]; the chronological observation shows it to be self-condemned. Another judgment is contained in the saying about Capernaum, which in Mt. 11:23b continues: ὅτι εἰ ἐν Σοδόμοις ἐγενήθησαν αἱ δυνάμεις αἱ γενόμεναι ἐν σοί, ἔμεινεν ἂν μέχρι τῆς σήμερον, cf. v. 24. Paul emphasises the alternative of judgment and fulfilled promise when in 2 C. 3:14

[22] Lk. 24:21 D has τρίτην ἡμέραν σήμερον ἄγει for τρίτην ταύτην ἡμέραν ἄγει without σήμερον. A incorrectly has both.
[23] Dib. Jk. on 4:13.
[24] Bultmann Trad., 35.
[25] D adds ἀμήν.

(→ I, 454, 13 ff.; III, 560, 5 ff.) he says : ἄχρι γὰρ τῆς σήμερον ἡμέρας τὸ αὐτὸ κάλυμμα ... μένει ..., and then again in v. 15 : ἀλλ᾽ ἕως σήμερον ἡνίκα ἂν ἀναγινώσκηται Μωϋσῆς κάλυμμα ἐπὶ τὴν καρδίαν αὐτῶν κεῖται. The stylistically correct expression ἕως σήμερον (LXX) throws light on the positive quotation from Ex. 34:34 which follows : ὅτι (sc. τὸ κάλυμμα) ἐν Χριστῷ καταργεῖται (v. 14). Finally, the aspect of fulfilled promise is again underlined comprehensively [26] by the dominical saying in the synagogue at Nazareth which comes after the reading of the prophetic scripture in Lk. 4:21: (ὅτι) σήμερον πεπλήρωται ἡ γραφὴ αὕτη ἐν τοῖς ὠσὶν ὑμῶν (→ III, 713, 30 ff.). He who would hear Scripture must "to-day" see Jesus, so that in encounter with Him there is definitive division and decision concerning salvation or perdition. Public testimony is borne to this "to-day" by Jesus : εἴδομεν παράδοξα σήμερον, Lk. 5:26. In the infancy story in Lk. 2:11 the angel declares the εὐαγγέλιον : (ὅτι) ἐτέχθη ὑμῖν σήμερον σωτήρ, ὅς ἐστιν Χριστὸς κύριος, ἐν πόλει Δαυίδ. The Christmas story with its wonder transcends and illustrates the royal formula of Judah which is quoted in Lk. 3:22 D in allusion to ψ 2:7 (→ I, 670, 19 ff.): υἱός μου εἶ σύ, ἐγὼ σήμερον γεγέννηκά σε. In the early kerygmatic passage in Ac. 13:33 this quotation from "the second psalm" (D : τῷ πρώτῳ) is related to the Risen Jesus, but here, too, it is regarded as fulfilled prophecy, v. 32 f. The Gospel does not proclaim isolated events ; it proclaims the historical person of Jesus. Jesus in His preaching shows Scripture to be valid. The Gospel does not leave anyone with seeing alone ; above all it demands hearing. He who hears understands that God through Jesus has interwoven all things into His revelation. The word σήμερον may thus be dropped and, e.g., in the Johannine writings replaced by other chronological statements like the more reflective νῦν, cf. also 2 C. 6:2 → IV, 1118, 33 ff.

b. Theologically considered, the classical statements in Hb. confirm that what has been said is a kind of norm for the understanding of the Gospel. [27] Bracketed by the quotation of ψ 2:7 in Hb. 1:5 and 5:5 (→ I, 670, 22 ff.) the enthronement exegesis of Hb. 1-2 is followed in 3 f. by a homily on ψ 94:7-11 which twice repeats the introduction to v. 7 f. (3:15 and 4:7). 3:13 and 4:7 also have a commentary on the catchword σήμερον which introduces the whole passage and which is shown to be christological by ψ 2:7 (Hb. 1:5). Since the fulfilment of the promise is not yet complete (4:1), the ancient λόγος τῆς ἀκοῆς (4:2) is still in force. Thus παρακαλεῖτε ἑαυτοὺς καθ᾽ ἑκάστην ἡμέραν, ἄχρις οὗ τὸ σήμερον καλεῖται, ἵνα μὴ σκληρυνθῇ τις ἐξ ὑμῶν ἀπάτῃ τῆς ἁμαρτίας (3:13 cf. 10:19 ff.). We then read in 4:6 : ἐπεὶ οὖν ἀπολείπεται τινὰς εἰσελθεῖν εἰς αὐτὴν (sc. εἰς τὴν κατάπαυσίν μου, v. 5), καὶ οἱ πρότερον εὐαγγελισθέντες οὐκ εἰσῆλθον δι᾽ ἀπείθειαν (cf. 3:16-17), 7: πάλιν τινὰ ὁρίζει ἡμέραν, σή- μερον, ἐν Δαυὶδ λέγων μετὰ τοσοῦτον χρόνον, καθὼς προείρηται (ψ 94:7 f. follows). He who hears to-day holds fast to the confession of Jesus, the Son of God, as the eternal High-priest, 4:14-16. Terminologically this confession holds open the way which the τελειωθείς (5:9) trod for us. Just as the faith of sons, as obedience in the battle against sin, is to prove itself even to blood (12:4), so this faith, as scriptural exegesis which achieves final illumination, finds in the

---

[26] Cf. H. Conzelmann, *Die Mitte d. Zeit³* (1960), 30-32 etc.
[27] E. Käsemann, *Das wandernde Gottesvolk²* (1957), examines the historical presuppositions of the exegesis which follows ; cf. also Mi. Hb. and C. Spicq, *L'épître aux Hébreux,* II (1953) on the relevant verses.

person of Jesus the enthroned Son of God, since it can unite His heavenly rank with the obedient sacrifice of His unique high-priesthood, 12:1 f. In the confessional language of the Holy Spirit (3:7) the firstborn Son of God, on the basis of the royal promise of dominion fulfilled in His person and work, unites Himself more than regally with us, the sons, "to-day," and thus demonstrates the truth of God's declarations as did once the cloud of witnesses, though now definitively. The true obedience of faith singles out the "to-day" in its new theological vocabulary, and in so doing it supersedes all earlier and outdated biblical exposition.

D. The Post-Apostolic Fathers.

The usage of the post-apost. fathers adds nothing new : σήμερον occurs here some 7 or 8 times, mostly in quotations, e.g., of ψ 2:7. The word carries a full stress in the sacrificial prayer in Mart. Pol., 14, 2.

Fuchs

σήπω → 94, 9 ff.

---

† σής, † σητόβρωτος

1. The noun (gen. pl. Aristoph. Lys., 730 σέων, from Aristot. forms like σητός, σῆτες, σήτων) [1] is attested from Pind., the very rare adj. only from the LXX. Various kinds of small butterflies or moths are denoted by the term. [2] The usual ref. is to moths in clothes, e.g., Aristot. Hist. An., V, 32, p. 557b, 3; Aristoph. Lys., 730. These destructive insects are hard to spot and are thus esp. feared. It was naturally recognised that apart from clothes other goods were exposed to damage in insidious ways. To illustrate the constant threat to human property other destructive creatures were mentioned along

---

σ ή ς, σ η τ ό β ρ ω τ ο ς. O. Keller, *Die antike Tierwelt*, I (1909); II (1920); J. Gossen, Art. "Schmetterlinge" in Pauly-W., 2a (1923), esp. 584 f.; H. Tur-Sinai (Torczyner), *The Book of Job* (1957), esp. 158-161.

[1] Cf. Kühner-Blass, I, 510 f.; Schwyzer, I, 578η. It is probably a Semitic loan word connected with סס (→ 276, 4), H. Lewy, *Die semitischen Fremdwörter im Griech.* (1895), 16 f.; Walde-Pok., I, 702. Acc. to J. Scheftelowitz, "Zur altarmenischen Lautgeschichte," *Beiträge zur Kunde d. idg. Sprachen*, 28 (1904), 289, this Semitic word in turn goes back to an Indo-Eur. root. For other possibilities — relationship with Lat. *tinea* — v. Boisacq, *s.v.* (→ n. 8).

[2] Gossen, 585. σῆτες are a group of → ψυχαί, Aristot. Hist. An., V, 19, p. 551a, 14. Under this name, origin. perhaps used esp. for moths, natural history included all creatures which came out winged from an apparently lifeless larva. But σῆτες are so important that from this stem a general term for all ψυχαί ἢ πτηνὰ ζῷα could be formed, namely, σητοδόκιδες, Hesych., *s.v.* It may be assumed that a more than purely zoological imagination helped to fashion this obscure term, which Liddell-Scott, *s.v.* notes but does not transl. [There is something to be said for the suggestion of H. Hommel that it is connected with δοκίς "meteor," in which case it should be accented σητοδοκίδες.]

with moths, [3] and so too was rust [4] (→ III, 335, 23 ff.). But the moth had to be watched with special care, [5] and in tacit perpetuation of many elements of primitive thinking various mysterious properties were ascribed to this creature. [6]

2. In the OT סָס (→ n. 1) occurs only in Is. 51:8 : וְכַצֶּמֶר יֹאכְלֵם סָס "as wool the moth shall eat them." In the par. half-v. which precedes we read : כַּבֶּגֶד יֹאכְלֵם עָשׁ "as a garment will עָשׁ consume them." עָשׁ is no more different from סָס than בֶּגֶד from צֶמֶר; we are thus to think of another creature (→ 275, 22 f.) but one which is similar to the moth. [7] Is. 50:9 also says that the garment is eaten up by עָשׁ, Job 13:28 by עָשׁ and רָקָב "decay," "fretting" (→ 275, 22 f.; → 96, n. 21). Here, too, one may safely transl. "moth." [8] This destroyer of property is everywhere a symbol of the threat to man himself.

3. The picture presented by the LXX is essentially the same as that of the HT. The moth is primarily a destroyer illustrating feminine malice in Sir. 42:13 and transitoriness in Job 27:18 (→ n. 8). [9] Another illustration of transitoriness (→ 275, 22 f.; line 9) is the ἀράχνη "spider" in Prv. 25:20 (Sir. 19:3 vl.) and a second destroyer is the

---

[3] To stress the durability of gold Pind. Fr., 222 says : κεῖνον οὐ σὴς οὐδὲ κὶς δάπτει, "neither moth nor termite gnaws this away."

[4] ... οἷον ὁ μὲν ἰὸς τὸν σίδηρον, ἂν σκοπῇς, τὸ δ' ἱμάτιον οἱ σῆτες ... Menand. Fr., 538, 4 f. (Koerte).

[5] For practical measures against moths cf. Theophr. Hist. Plant., IX, 11, 11.

[6] Cf. the idea, which can hardly be based on observation, that a garment worn at a funeral is avoided by moths : ... qui sciat vestem a tineis non attingi, qui fuerit in funere, Plin. Hist. Nat., 28, 33.

[7] Since עָשׁ comes from עָשַׁשׁ the word seems to pt. to the frailty and transitoriness of the insect, whereas in the case of סָס (as of other names of animals) onomatopoeia (the buzzing noise) calls for consideration [G. Fohrer]. But this would yield quite a distinction, since the moth is not characterised by a buzzing sound. Acc. to Köhler-Baumg., s.v. both words are to be transl. "moth." Dalman Arbeit, V, 15 f. cf. 7, 212 thinks the סָס is the "caterpillar" and the עָשׁ the "butterfly." Cf. also F. S. Bodenheimer, "Prodromus Faunae Palaestinaè," Mémoires présentés à l'Institut d'Égypte, 33 (1937), 106.

[8] In the 5 instances of עָשׁ without בֶּגֶד the meaning is not so certain. F. Delitzsch, Das Buch Hiob neu übers. u. kurz erklärt (1902), 23, 71 suggests a brittle pipe at Job 4:19; 27:18, but A. Ehrlich, Randglossen zur hbr. Bibel, VI (1918), 195 et al. consider "bird's nest" or "moth's nest" here and in Ps. 39:11 (though → Tur-Sinai, 86, n. 2). In Job 9:9, however, the ref. must be to a star, and "putrefying wound" is possible in Hos. 5:12, cf. Köhler-Baumg., s.v. Here, however, and in Job 13:28 we have the combination with רָקָב (→ 275, 22 f.; line 9) and though the passages are far apart in time it is as well not to transl. differently what had perhaps become a fixed combination, → 96, n. 21. When Job 27:18, speaking of the building of a house which will soon collapse, compares this to the building of a moth's cocoon (וּבָנָה כָעָשׁ בֵּיתוֹ), one may ask whether natural observation alone could produce this image, cf. A. Socin, Art. "Motte," BW, 450 f. Closer to nature is the older transl. (BHK) which reads כָּעַכָּבִישׁ ("like a spider"), G. Hölscher, Das Buch Hiob, Hndbch. AT, 17² (1952), ad loc. But עַכָּבִישׁ occurs elsewhere in the OT only at Is. 59:5 and Job 8:14, so that this simple avoiding of the difficulty is forced, esp. as we cannot say whether the comparison is based on observation. When basic ideas about the עָשׁ (→ n. 6) are taken into consideration, one may weigh the bold alternative to this forced correction suggested by Tur-Sinai, 86, 392-394, namely, that the similarity of name between the harmful עָשׁ and the star עָשׁ in Job 9:9 (or עַיִשׁ in 38:32) is more than accidental. The building of Job 27:18 was the work of a not wholly forgotten rebellious power of the primeval age which was soon thereafter defeated and banished to the tent of heaven. It is obvious, of course, that this hypothesis also raises expository difficulties. In Ps. 39:11 and Job 4:19 the עָשׁ itself is the symbol of transitoriness rather than its house or the material it damages. Experience shows, indeed, that a mortal blow snuffs it out altogether.

[9] So also 1 QH 9:5 : עיני כעש בכבשן "my eye is like a moth in the furnace (?)."

→ σκώληξ. The fact that Prv. 14:30 has σής for רָקָב is not surprising if it is assumed that the combination of עָשׁ and רָקָב was a common one [10] (→ 276, 9; n. 8). Nor is it surprising that in Job 9:9 (and 38:32) only astronomical terms from the Gk. language were considered and that in Job 13:28 the adj. σητόβρωτος is used ("consumed by moths") → 276, 9. As may be expected, σής is the transl. of עָשׁ in Is. 50:9; Job 4:19; 27:18 and of סָס in Is. 51:8. [11]

4. Jesus in Mt. 6:19 f.; Lk. 12:33 demands a resolute turning aside from all obviously perishable treasures, → III, 137, 32 ff. There is nothing which is not threatened by moths, βρῶσις, [12] or theft. But a realistic reference to this threat is only the foil to the promise of genuine treasures which cannot be damaged in this way and to the consequences of this for the heart (Mt. 6:21; Lk. 12:34) → III, 612, 7 ff. The threat in Jm. 5:2, [13] on the other hand, uses a prophetic perfect to insist on the imminent and ineluctable end of earthly wealth, not unrealistically, but with an apocalyptically enhanced (→ n. 6; 8; 10) realism: τὰ

---

[10] More surprising is that the transl. goes its own way in other respects. The HT reads : וּרְקַב עֲצָמוֹת קִנְאָה, "but passion is a fretting in the bones," and this is rendered σής δὲ ὀστέων καρδία αἰσθητική "a heart ruled by sense perception (and not by something higher) brings moths into the bones." This strange statement may be simply due to textual difficulties or problems of translation. In a different way Philo's delight in the allegorical significance of names is adequate to explain what is said about the city of Ramses (Ex. 1:11) in Som., I, 77 (cf. Poster C., 56): ... καὶ ʿΡαμεσσή, τὴν αἴσθησιν, ὑφ' ἧς ὥσπερ σέων [vl. σαιῶν, σητῶν] ἡ ψυχὴ διεσθίεται — ἑρμηνεύεται γὰρ σεισμὸς σητός ..., "and Ramses, sensuality, by which, as by moths, the soul is consumed — it means the 'fretting of moths' ..." (cf. I. Heinemann and M. Adler, Die Werke Philos v. Alex., VI [1938], 189). Since the two statements agree independently in their relating of moths and αἴσθησις (→ I, 187, 32 ff.), it is possible that the superstitious idea of the moth as an unlucky insect (→ n. 6; 8) is spiritualised here : This little creature, though fearsome, can do only material harm ; but he who is ruled by αἴσθησις, his bones (soul) truly fall victim to "moths."
[11] For עָשׁ here LXX does not have a synon. of σής but, with no essential alteration of sense, the "tooth of time" : ἱμάτιον βρωθήσεται ὑπὸ χρόνου. But in Hos. 5:12 — on the text cf. J. Ziegler, "Beiträge zum gr. Dodekapropheton," NGG (1943), 381 — there is a greater alteration (on the basis of 5:14) of what was probably felt to be an unsuitable image : God is not עָשׁ or רָקָב but ταραχή or κέντρον, → III, 665, 29 ff. ταραχή suggests the terror of divine intervention, → VI, 508, n. 44; → 66 f. The verb ταράσσεσθαι is used in the same sense at the end of ψ 38:12 where עָשׁ was previously rendered ἀράχνη "spider," cf. also ψ 38:7b. Sometimes we find σής even where the HT does not speak of moths. On Is. 33:1 cf. J. Ziegler, "Untersuchungen zur Septuaginta d. Buches Isaias," At.liche Abh., 12, 3 (1934), 102 f.; F. Wutz, Systematische Wege von d. Sept. zum Hbr. Urtext (1937), 861; G. Bertram, "Zur Prägung d. bibl. Gottesvorstellung in d. gr. Übers. d. AT, die Wiedergabe von schadad u. schaddaj im Griechischen," Die Welt des Orients, 2 (1954-1959), 504 and 508. "From Is. 33:1d the transl. read כְּנַם "gnat" and בֶּגֶד "garment" and thus got the metaphor of the moth in clothes" [Bertram]. On Job 27:20 vl. cf. the transcriptions to which F. Wutz pts. in his Transcriptionen von d. Septuaginta bis z. Hieronymus (1933), 240 f.; מַיִם might be misread as סָס, and in Job 32:22 יִשָּׂאֵנִי as עָשִׂים or עָשׁ [Bertram]. Cf. also Sir. 19:3 vl. σῆτες καὶ σκώληκες κληρονομήσουσιν αὐτόν → 96, n. 21. Here and in Job 32:22 we find an idea not attested elsewhere in the Gk. world, namely, that man can become a prey to moths. On similar German notions cf. R. Riegler, Art. "Motte" in Handwörterbuch d. deutschen Volkskunde, 1: "Aberglaube," VI (1934/35), 593-595. Σής is again found in deviation from the HT at Mi. 7:4; Prv. 25:20a.
[12] On the basis of Hos. 5:12; Job 13:28 (→ 276, 9; n. 8) "decay" suggests itself as a natural rendering, cf. Pr.-Bauer, ⁵ s.v.
[13] Cf. Theophilus ab Orbiso, "Vae divitibus malis (Jk. 5:1-5)," Verbum Domini, 26 (1948), 77.

ἱμάτια ὑμῶν σητόβρωτα γέγονεν,[14] "your garments are fretted by moths,"
with the implication, one may add, that attempts to protect them are quite useless,
just as gold and silver cannot be protected against rust by their quality as precious
metals (5:3) → III, 335, 26 ff.

> 5. Among the staffs with various defects which Herm. s., 8, 1 uses to illustrate the
> situations of various groups of weak Christians, there are those which are consumed
> (ὡς) ὑπὸ σητός, 8, 1, 6 f.; 4, 5. 8, 6, 4 shows that of all the defects this is the only
> one for which there is no remedy. Since the damage is to wood, κίς would be a better
> term → n. 3; but σής in its gen. sense as a "small creature" expresses the symbolism
> of destruction (→ n. 8; 10) more forcefully. In biblical quotations σής is mentioned in
> 1 Cl., 39, 5 (Job 4:19) and Barn., 6, 2 (Is. 50:9).

Bauernfeind

┌─────────────┐
│ † σικάριος │
└─────────────┘

The term σικάριος, from *sicarius,* "dagger-carrier," "assassin," is found (apart from
Ac. 21:38) esp. in Jos. (→ 279, 3 ff.) and once each in Hipp. (→ 281, 37 ff.) and
Orig. (→ 282, 2 f.), always in the plur. The Rabb., too, speak occasionally of סִיקָרִין/סִיקָרִים
→ 280, 22 ff. The later Jewish and Chr. use of the Lat. loan word presupposes Roman
law.

1. The Sicarii in Roman Law.

From the time of the *lex Cornelia* published under Sulla *sicarius* as a tt. in
Roman law denotes not only the assassin in the narrower sense but also more
generally the violent murderer or inciter to murder;[1] the weapon proves the
intent.[2]

> The *lex Cornelia* applied also against armed robbers (*latrones*) banded in groups.
> Among these, acc. to the Roman view, were guerillas in Italy and esp. the provinces
> who rebelled against the government without declaring war on Rome officially as *hostes*
> or without being considered worthy of a Roman declaration of war.[3] As a punishment

---

[14] In Sib. Fr., 3, 26 the adj. σητόβρωτος is used along with a ref. to spiders → 276, 14;
n. 8; 11.

σ ι κ ά ρ ι ο ς. Pr.-Bauer[5], Liddell-Scott, *s.v.*; Jastrow, Levy, *s.v.* סִיקָרִין; M. Hengel, *Die
Zeloten* (1961); J. Klausner, *Historiah schäl habbayit haschscheniy,* V[4] (1954); R. Meyer,
Der Prophet aus Galiläa (1940), 82-88; O. Michel, "Spätjüd. Prophetentum," *Nt.liche
Studien f. R. Bultmann*[2] (1954), 60-66; Schl. Gesch. Isr., 259-264, 322-327. For further bibl.
→ ζηλωτής II, 884, n. 7 and → λῃστής IV, 257.

[1] Quint. Inst. Orat., 10, 1, 12 : *Per abusionem sicarios etiam omnes vocamus, qui caedem
telo quocumque commiserint.* Cf. T. Mommsen, *Röm. Strafrecht* (1899), 629.
[2] Only the intentional deed came under the *lex Cornelia,* Mommsen, 626.
[3] Pomponius acc. to Justinianus Digesta, 50, 16, 118 (ed. T. Mommsen [1870]): *Hostes
hi sunt, qui nobis aut quibus nos publice bellum decreverimus ; ceteri "latrones" aut "prae-
dones" sunt.*

sicarii or *latrones,* esp. when they were slaves or provincials, were put to death by crucifixion in the imperial period. [4]

2. The Sicarii in Josephus.

Josephus adopts the standpoint of Roman law when he calls the hated freedom-fighters of the first Jewish revolt (→ II, 884, 32 ff.) "robbers" (→ IV, 258, 18 ff.) and "assassins" (σικαρίους). He justifies the term *sicarii* by explaining that they carried daggers under their cloaks with which they stealthily stabbed their opponents in the bustle of pilgrimage feasts. [5]

Sicarii are first said to have appeared under the procuratorship of Felix. They are introduced as a new breed of robbers; their first victim was the then high-priest Jonathan. [6] Later when the Jewish insurgents split up into groups after the victory over Cestius Jos. uses the term *sicarii* for the followers of Menahem who after his assassination retreated into the fortress of Masada, Bell., 4, 399-405, 516; 7, 253, 275, 297, 311. He then uses it for the partisans who escaped to Egypt, 7, 409-419 and finally for the rebellious Jews in Cyrene, 7, 437-446. Yet he does not always keep to this special use. [7, 8] The depiction of the *sicarii* in Jos. is defective and not wholly consistent; hence their peculiar features do not emerge with clarity.

In all probability the *sicarii* were neither an independent party [9] nor the extreme left of the patriots. [10] They were fighting groups banded together by an oath, the guerillas in the Zealot movement. [11] What distinguished them was not doctrine — they shared this with Judas, the founder of the Zealot party [12] — but the courageous nature of their effort, which held life cheap, whether their own or that of others (τολμᾶν, Ant., 20, 165). [13] The weapon of assassination was used esp. when Felix took steps of ruthless severity against the bands in open country, Bell., 2, 253. But it came into force only during the yrs. before the outbreak of the war and it was directed against Jews friendly to the Romans rather than the Romans themselves. The designation *sicarii,* however, derived from the Romans.

---

[4] Paulus Sententiae, V, 23, 1 (ed. P. E. Huschke in Jurisprudentiae Anteiustinianae quae supersunt[5] [1886], 551): ... *humiliores vero aut in crucem tolluntur aut bestiis obiiciuntur.*

[5] Bell., 2, 254 f.; acc. to Ant., 20, 186 the weapon was as big as the Persian *akinake* but was curved and like the Roman *sica.* The curved sword (כידר) mentioned in 1 QM 5:11-14 is too big for assassination.

[6] Bell., 2, 252, 256; acc. to Ant., 20, 185 f. the *sicarii* flourished esp. under Festus; acc. to Ant., 20, 204 Albinus extirpated many of them.

[7] This also applies to the use of "Zealots" which later Jos. mostly reserves for the priestly group which fought in the temple, Bell., 5, 5-105.

[8] Jos. uses interchangeably *sicarii* and bandits, the most common expression for the rebels, Bell., 2, 653; Ant., 20, 185 f., 208-210. In Ant., 20, 163-165 he has ληστάς for definite assassins.

[9] So Jackson-Lake, I, 422 f.; Zahn Ag. on 21:38.

[10] So Klausner, 134, 228-230. On his view the *sicarii,* unlike the religious nationalists (the Zealots), supported a communism adopted from the Essenes, espousing a new order of society and property which was to be brought in by force, and having Simon bar Giora as their leader.

[11] Cf. Bell., 4, 408: συναθροιζόμενοί τε καὶ συνομνύμενοι κατὰ λόχους. Acc. to Ant., 15, 282-291 ten men swore to slay King Herod with hidden daggers.

[12] Cf. Bell., 2, 118 with 7, 418 f. In Bell., 7, 254 Jos. associates the *sicarii* chronologically with Judas. Since their leaders Menahem and Eleazar b. Ari were relatives of this Judas (Bell., 2, 433; 7, 253) their link with him was also dynastic and organisational, Hengel, 50. Finally Judas, like his son Menahem (Bell., 2, 433 f.), forced his followers to carry weapons, Bell., 2, 56; Ant., 17, 251 f.

[13] Jos. Bell., 2, 254-260 contrasts with the *sicarii* the fanatics and deceivers whose "hands were purer"; these popular charismatic leaders feared the use of violence and counted on a divine miracle which would announce symbolically the dawn of the age of salvation.

The reasons which drove the *sicarii* to act were not blind nationalism nor an excessive lust for domination.[14] This common view is due to the polemically distorted account in Jos. The *sicarii* were motivated, not by ungodliness, unrighteousness or fanaticism (Bell., 7, 260 and 437), but by passionate zeal and active self-sacrifice for God's honour and the Torah. The maxim that God alone is to be honoured as Lord was consistently applied. Even Jos. must admit that they accepted suicide or martyrdom rather than the yoke of Roman rule, Bell., 7, 386-401, 410, 418 f. According to their view the majesty of God was infringed not merely by the Romans, who wanted the emperor to be recognised as ruler (7, 418 f.) and who desecrated the land by taxes, coins, statues and the census, but also by Jews friendly to the Romans, who as renegades were regarded as the equivalent of Gentiles (7, 255). Indeed, for the *sicarii* the priests who engaged in a politics of compromise were seducing the people into idolatry, and what Jos. ascribed to a propensity to cruelty (7, 256) really derived from obedience to God's Law, which commanded that apostates and even whole districts which were idolatrous should be rooted out by fire and sword, Dt. 13:7-19. By purgative action of this kind they sought to prepare the way for God's coming and to prevent the land from being smitten with a ban through God's wrath, cf. Mal. 3:24. Stealing and confiscating the goods of the rich (Bell., 4, 402-405, 516; 7, 254; Ant., 20, 185-187), destruction of palaces and burning of archives with promissory notes (Bell., 2, 426-432), cannot be set to the account of greed (7, 256) but were meant to serve the overthrow of the unrighteous mammon and the establishment of the eternal jubilee of freedom and equality.

3. The Sicarii in the Rabbinic Writings.

In the Rabb. writings the name *sicarii* (סִיקְרִים/יִן) is used of the Zealots (קַנָּאִים). It is meant to express the violence in attitude and acts of supporters of the first revolt, who are here sharply condemned. Nevertheless, there is no mention of assassination. Acc. to Maksh, 1, 6 the population of Jerusalem kept fig-cakes concealed in water because of the *sicarii*. Acc. to Eka r. on 4:4 the *sicarii* destroyed the conduit which supplied Jerusalem from Etam.[15] Acc. to Ab RNat., 7 they burned the grain stocks which a rich man of Jerusalem had stored up in the event of siege.[16] Jos. confirms these violent acts : confiscation and destruction of stocks occurred esp. in struggles between the various rebel groups, Bell., 5, 21-26; cf. Tac. Hist., V, 12. Acc. to Qoh. r. on 7:12 the head of the *sicarii* (רֹאשׁ סָקְרִים),[17] Ben Battiach, the son-in-law of R. Jochanan b. Zakkai, was responsible for the burning of the grain. This Zealot, identified by some as Simon bar Giora,[18] is called the "'daddy' of assassins" (אַבָּא סִיקְרָא) in the par. bGit., 56a.

A *sicaricon* law (סִיקְרִקוֹן) is also mentioned in the Rabb. in Bik., 1, 2; Git., 6, 5; S. Dt., 297 on 26:2 etc. It relates to property, esp. landed property, which during and after the first revolt had been expropriated by the Romans. This law has ref. to the Jewish *sicarii* only to the degree that the property confiscated was mostly that of zealous patriots who had fled to the desert.[19]

---

[14] Zeal for the purity of Israel was also a motive in the war against the Romans, but there were many degenerate forms esp. in the last yrs. of the war.

[15] With S. Buber, מדרש איכה רבה (1899) one should read מְסִיקְרִים and מֵעֵיטָם here. Possible this was terrorism against the conduit Pilate had built with temple funds, cf. Bell., 2, 175; Hengel, 51.

[16] Ed. S. Schechter (1887), 20, 2nd version. The קַנָּאִים were responsible acc. to the 1st version.

[17] To be read instead of קֵדְרִין.

[18] Klausner, 230.

[19] Cf. the Exc.: "Das Sikarikongesetz" in Hengel, 52-54; Jastrow, *s.v.* סִיקְרִיקוֹן thinks the word is a corruption of καισαρίκιον.

4. The Sicarii in the New Testament.

a. According to Ac. 21:38 the tribune of the Roman cohort stationed in the Antonia suspected that Paul was the Egyptian who a short time before had incited 4000 *sicarii* to rebellion and led them out into the desert.

Jos. tells of the enterprise of an Egyptian in 2 accounts which differ from one another in details. Acc. to Bell., 2, 261-263 this Egyptian claimed to be a prophet (→ VI, 826 f.), gathered together 30,000 men, and went *via* the desert to the Mt. of Olives, from which pt. he sought to force his way into the city, overpower the Roman garrison, and set himself up as dictator. Not very probable is the account in Ant., 20, 169 that the pseudo-prophet from Egypt preached revolt in Jerusalem itself and led its inhabitants to the Mt. of Olives. But the mention of 400 slain and 200 captured in Ant., 20, 171 sounds more plausible, as is also the ref. to the promise of the Egyptian that at his behest the walls of Jerusalem would fall down and make entry possible, 20, 170. Luke agrees with Jos. in simply speaking of "the Egyptian," in dating his venture under Felix, [20] and in making a link with the wilderness. The numbers in both might have been originally the same as well. [21] Hence there is no doubt that the two have the same event in view; from Ac. 21:38 one might suppose that the people hoped for the return of the Egyptian. [22] Luke, however, follows his own tradition, for acc. to Jos. the march of liberation was not into the desert but from the desert to the Mt. of Olives, which was of eschatological significance in view of verses in the Bible like Ez. 11:23 and esp. Zech. 14:4. Again, the *sicarii* are not mentioned in either of Jos.' accounts. Yet there is ref. to them in the context of both (Bell., 2, 254-257; Ant., 20, 163-165); in Ant., 20, 185-188, just after a description of the *sicarii*, there is ref. to the destruction of a *goes* whose expedition bears some resemblance to that of the Egyptian; and finally Jos. says the unarmed followers of Jonathan, who led the Jews of Cyrene into the desert, were *sicarii*, Bell., 7, 437-446.

It is quite understandable that Luke should use the term *sicarii*, especially on the lips of a Roman officer, for whom, as for the procurators, even unarmed participants in such freedom marches were *sicarii*.

b. It is also worth considering whether the oath of 40 Jews to destroy Paul in Ac. 23:12-15 is not a genuine example of the work of the *sicarii*. The time, method and goal of the plot all support this. It took place under the procuratorship of Felix when the movement was at its height. The participants banded themselves together by a common oath. Their objective was to remove a false teacher and desecrator of the temple who had also been taken under protective custody by the Gentiles.

5. The Sicarii in the Church Fathers.

Hippolyt. mentions the *sicarii* in an account of the Essenes which he took from Jos.; he equates them with the Zealots but erroneously thinks they were a class of Essenes. [23] They are characterised by the dogma of God's sole sovereignty, which they maintained

---

[20] The chronological note πρὸ τούτων τῶν ἡμερῶν is ambiguous, but the context shows it must have been shortly before. On the other hand Felix must have been some time in office (from 52) when Paul was arrested.

[21] Acc. to Jackson-Lake, IV, 277 the very high number in Jos. was perhaps due to misreading Δ = 4(000) as Λ = 30(000).

[22] → VI, 826, 28 ff. That the Jewish people helped to thwart this Messianic undertaking (Bell. 2, 263) is certainly not in accord with the facts. This observation may be traced back to the dogma of the Bellum that the Zealots alone were to blame for every disaster while the people as a whole repudiated the revolt, Hengel, 237.

[23] Ref., IX, 26, 2, cf. Jos. Bell., 2, 119-161. In reality the features here ascribed to the different groups are probably all characteristic of the Zealots, Hengel, 74 f.

even to death, and by sharp hostility to images. Men who speak of God and His laws, but will not accept circumcision, are mentioned as the victims of assassination. [24] Orig. refers to the *sicarii* in a different connection. [25]

Betz

$$\boxed{\dagger\ \Sigma\iota\nu\tilde{\alpha}}$$

A. Σινᾶ in OT and Jewish Tradition.

1. In all sources of the Pent. the tradition of God's revelation at Sinai is linked with that of the exodus of Israel from Egypt. Originally the Sinai story might have been an independent complex which dealt with the giving of God's commandments to His people and which was incorporated secondarily into the context of the wilderness wandering. [1] The Sinai pericope Ex. 19-Nu. 10 has been divided into the older JE section Ex. 19-24; 32-34 and the later P section Ex. 25-31; 35-Nu. 10:10. The former tells of the preparation of the people for the manifestation of God, of the theophany which takes place on the third day, of the proclamation of the will of God, and of the people's commitment to this. [2] There then follow the stories in Ex. 32-34 which depict the sin of the people and the destruction of the tablets of the Law, and which close with a second proclamation of the commandments. On the other hand, the P account is more specifically devoted to the precise instructions given for the making of the tabernacle, the installation of priests, and the order of the cultus. Though there are broad differences between the two accounts they share the basic thought that at Sinai Israel by divine revelation received the ordinances which basically determined its whole life. [3]

It is no longer possible to work back in detail to the historical events behind the extensive Sinai narrative. Even the name of the mount of God has been transmitted in different forms. The older tradition refers to Sinai and this is the name which is mostly found later, [4] but Dt. always has Horeb. [5] Where the mountain [6] was we can no longer

---

[24] Ps. 50:16 was probably given as a reason: "To the wicked God saith: Why dost thou proclaim my statutes and take my covenant in thy mouth?"

[25] Cels., II, 13 (GCS, 2, 142, lines 10-22). He says the Samaritans were thought to be *sicarii* because they clung fast to circumcision. Hadrian compared this to castration, which had been forbidden since Domitian and placed under the penalties of the *lex Cornelia*.
Σ ι ν ᾶ. S. Riva, "Il Sinai egizio e cristiano," *Ricerche Religiose*, 9 (1933), 12-31; P. A. van Stempvoort, *De Allegorie in Gal. 4:21-31 als hermeneutisch Problem* (1953); F. Mussner, "Hagar, Sinai, Jerusalem — zum Text v. Gl. 4:25a," *Theol. Quart.*, 135 (1955), 56-60; W. Schmauch, *Orte d. Offenbarung u. der Offenbarungsort im NT* (1956), 51-54; Pr.-Bauer⁵, *s.v.*

[1] Cf. M. Noth, *Gesch. Israels*⁴ (1959), 120-130; G. v. Rad, *Theol. d. AT*, I (1957), 188-230 (with further bibl.).

[2] One theory is that this section is based, not on historical events, but on a "feast-legend" connected with the ancient feast of the renewal of the covenant, cf. v. Rad, *op. cit.*, 190.

[3] Cf. v. Rad, 190.

[4] J and E: Ex. 19:1 f., 11, 18, 20, 23; 34:2, 4, also 16:1; 24:16; 34:29, 32; P: Ex. 31:18; Lv. 7:38; 25:1; 26:46; 27:34; Nu. 1:1, 19; 3:1, 4, 14; 9:1, 5; also Nu. 10:12; 26:64; 28:6; 33:15 f.; Ju. 5:5; Ps. 68:9; Neh. 9:13.

[5] Dt. 1:2, 6, 19; 4:10, 15; 5:2; 9:8; 18:16; 28:69; also J and E: Ex. 3:1; 17:6; 33:6; also 1 K. 8:9; 19:8; Ps. 106:19; Mal. 3:22. Sinai is mentioned in Dt. only in the blessing of Moses in 33:2. It may be that the occurrence of the name Horeb is secondary in some verses in the Pent. Cf. M. Noth, *Überlieferungsgeschichtliche Studien*, I (1943), 29.

[6] LXX, on the basis of the HT, has Σινα at Ex. 16:1; Ju. 5:5 etc.; τὸ ὄρος τὸ Σινα at

say for certain, though it is most likely that Sinai is to be sought in the south of the Sinaitic Peninsula, which is named after it.[7] We may assume that here the divine epiphany was given to the tribes which with others constituted the circle of the tribes of Israel.[8] In the older tradition the name of Yahweh is more than once mentioned in close connection with Sinai, so that from an early period this was regarded as His mountain, cf. Ju. 5:4 f.; Dt. 33:2; Hab. 3:3. Here He made His name known, Ex. 3:14 (E); 6:2 f. (P), so that the Sinai passage tells the story of the self-revelation of God as well as the impartation of the Law. All Israel confesses this as an experience which is basic to the history of God's people. For later tradition, then, the exodus and Sinai traditions are a unity telling how Yahweh called and led His people and gave it the Law.

2. On the basis of the OT tradition Judaism often speaks of the event at Sinai[9] and in many cases gives an expanded description of it. Moses received his call on Sinai acc. to Jub. 48:2. God strode across all mountains and hills and caused His *sheᵏkhina* to rest on Mt. Sinai, bSota, 5a. Here He declared His ordinances to Moses (Jub. 50:1), and gave him His Law from heaven (Or. Sib., 3, 256).[10] Moses received the command to pass on to the children of Israel as obligatory directions the words of the Torah which God had laid on him on Sinai, 1 Q 22:4 f. (DJD, I, 92). Through the making of the covenant at Sinai God "elected a people for the time of His good-pleasure," 1 Q 34 bis 3, II, 5 (DJD, I, 154).[11] The events which acc. to Jewish tradition transpired at the giving of the Law at Sinai are signs of divine election. There were loud thunderclaps. Lightning flamed. Burning fire fell from heaven and its smoke enveloped everything. The threatening voice of God from the midst of the fire filled all with terror, Philo Decal., 44-49. When the Israelites stood at Sinai, in a miraculous way they were set in paradisial conditions : they were free from all sicknesses and sorrows ;[12] even the angel of death had no power over them.[13] For Israel was to receive the Torah at Sinai as a people of pure members in whom was no blemish. But when in fact they sinned with the golden calf "they returned to their infirmities."[14] Acc. to later Rabb. tradition even the evil impulse was destroyed when Israel stood at Sinai and Moses told them God would give them the Torah.[15] They were to see God, and the radiance which had once been given to Adam in Paradise and then withdrawn after the fall was given them afresh at Sinai, → II, 246, 27 ff. Naturally it was taken away again when they sinned with the golden calf, and the radiance of the *sheᵏkhina* will return permanently only in the Messianic age.[16]

Ex. 19:11, 18, 20, 23; 24:16; (τὸ) ὄρος Σινα at Ex. 19:16; Lv. 7:38; 25:1; 2 Esr. 19:13 etc. ᾽Α Σ Θ use the form Σιναι, which is closer to the sound of the Hbr. word, at Ex. 19:11; ψ 67:9.

[7] Cf. the critical discussion of the various hypotheses in Noth, *op. cit.* (→ n. 1), 121-125.

[8] Noth, 125.

[9] Philo and Jos. mention Sinai only when they follow the OT : Philo Rer. Div. Her., 251 quoting Ex. 19:18 (cf. Χωρήβ only at Som., II, 221 quoting Ex. 17:6); Jos. Ant., 2, 264 f. (instead of Horeb, Ex. 3:1); also Ant., 3, 62, 75 f. (the giving of the Law at Sinai); 8, 349 (for Horeb, 1 K. 19:8); Ap., 2, 25 : Moses came εἰς τὸ μεταξὺ τῆς Αἰγύπτου καὶ τῆς ᾽Αραβίας ὄρος, ὃ καλεῖται Σίναιον. Sir. 48:7 says that Elijah heard reprimands at Sinai and retributive judgments at Horeb. As the parallelism shows, Sinai and Horeb are full equivalents here.

[10] In a Jewish Chr. Moses apocr. of a later time we have a description of the conversation between God and Moses on Sinai, which had been lifted up to heaven, cf. H. Duensing, "Ein Mosesapokryphon," ZNW, 49 (1958), 251-258.

[11] Cf. F. Nötscher, "Zur theol. Terminologie d. Qumrantexte," *Bonner Bibl. Beiträge*, 10 (1956), 174.

[12] M. Ex., 20, 18 (78b); Lv. r., 18 (118a) on 15:1 f.; bAZ, 5a, Bar.; for further examples cf. Str.-B., I, 594-596; III, 232 f.; IV, 945.

[13] M. Ex., 20, 19 (79a); further instances in Str.-B., III, 232 f.

[14] R. Jehuda b. Simon (c. 320 A.D.); Nu. r., 7 on 5:2; cf. Str.-B., I, 595.

[15] Pesikt. r., 41 (174a); cf. Str.-B., IV, 939.

[16] Pesikt., 37a; cf. Str.-B., IV, 940.

The Torah which Moses received with these accompanying phenomena was passed on by him to Joshua, by Joshua to the elders, by them to the prophets, and then to the men of the great synagogue (in the days of Ezra) and to the scribes, Ab., 1, 1. It contains all God's will unfolded not merely in the written Law but also in the orally transmitted tradition. [17] Israel adopted this Law of its God and shaped its life thereby. Originally the Torah was also destined for the Gentiles. Thus acc. to Jewish tradition God's will was declared at Sinai in all languages, and each word from His lips parted into seventy tongues. [18] But the Gentiles refused to obey the imparted Law. In the exposition of the Midrash the name of Sinai is thus explained sometimes as follows: On this mountain the nations of the world made God hated (play on סִינַי/נִשְׂתַּנְּאוּ) and He pronounced sentence on them. [19] Israel alone perceived God's wonders and accepted the Law. Acc. to another view, then, Sinai is the mountains of wonders (נִיסִים) or of the sign (סִימָנָא = σημεῖον), since it came to be a good sign for the Israelites. [20]

Since God's will was declared to His people at Sinai this mountain is for the righteous of Judaism not only the highest and most holy in the area (Philo Spec. Leg., III, 125 cf. Vit. Mos., II. 70: ὄρος ὑψηλότατον καὶ ἱερώτατον τῶν περὶ τὸν τόπον) but also the place of God's presence. [21] Acc. to Jub. 4:26 four places on earth belong to God: the Garden of Eden and the Mountain of the East, Mt. Sinai and Mt. Zion. [22] In Jub. 8:19 the Garden of Eden is the most sacred of sanctuaries and the dwelling of God, while Mt. Sinai is the centre of the wilderness and Mt. Zion is the centre of the navel of the earth. As Sinai was once the site of God's revelation [23] and returning Paradise, so at the end of the days acc. to apoc. God will again come to Mt. Sinai, be manifested with His hosts, and appear in the might of His power from heaven, Eth. En. 1:4. Acc. to this hope Sinai is *the* place of revelation where God once spoke His Word and where He will speak it also in the *eschaton*. This mountain reaches up to heaven and down into the depths to hell. [24] It links heaven and earth. [25] The mountain of God, which is higher than all other mountains (Eth. En. 24:2 f.; 87:3), will be God's throne on the last day; it will bear the tree of life; it will be planted in the holy place by the house of God, the king of eternity, 25:3, 5. [26] In the *eschaton* the mountain of God and the mountain of Paradise will be joined into one. Rabb. tradition also says, then, that in the Messianic age God will bring together Sinai and Tabor and Carmel and build the sanctuary on their summits. [27] If in the history of Israel Sinai and Zion are the places of divine election, at the end of the days God's dominion over His people and the whole world will be visibly displayed to all eyes on the holy mountain of God.

---

[17] Thus scholars who have a good mastery of the Halakah are sometimes called Sinai, bHor., 14a, cf. Str.-B., I, 759.

[18] So already the Bar. from the school of R. Jishma'el (d. c. 135 A.D.), bShab., 88b; other examples in Str.-B., II, 604 f.

[19] Tanch. במדבר (Buber), 7 on Nu. 1:1; Str.-B., III, 571 f. for other instances.

[20] Ex. r., 51 (104a) on 38:21; cf. Str.-B., III, 572.

[21] Cf. Jos. Ant., 2, 265: δόξαν ἔχειν ἐνδιατρίβειν αὐτῷ τὸν θεόν, 3, 76: τὸν θεὸν ἐν αὐτῷ διατρίβειν.

[22] Hence Sinai is God's mountain, → V, 482, 20 ff. and Volz Esch., 415. For historical material on mountains as divine dwellings → ὄρος, V, 475 ff.

[23] Cf. also Eth. En. 89:29, 32 f.

[24] On Jewish ideas respecting the holy rock cf. J. Jeremias, "Golgotha," *Angelos-Beih.*, 1 (1926), 51-58.

[25] Cf. Test. L. 2:3-5 and on this J. T. Milik, "Le Testament de Lévi en Araméen. Fr. de la Grotte 4 de Qumran," *Rev. Bibl.*, 62 (1955), 398-406.

[26] Cf. Jeremias, *op. cit.* (→ n. 24), 52.

[27] R. Ruben (c. 300 A.D.): Pesikt., 144b; cf. Str.-B., IV, 930 f.

B. Σινᾶ in the New Testament.

In the NT Sinai is mentioned twice each in Ac. and Gl.

1. In the sketch of Israel's history in Stephen's speech in Ac. 7, there is an account of the call of Moses on the basis of Ex. 3. But while Ex. 3:1 f. LXX says that Moses ἤγαγεν τὰ πρόβατα ὑπὸ τὴν ἔρημον καὶ ἦλθεν εἰς τὸ ὄρος Χωρηβ and there experienced the encounter with God at the burning bush, Ac. 7:30 reads : ὤφθη αὐτῷ ἐν τῇ ἐρήμῳ τοῦ ὄρους Σινᾶ ἄγγελος ἐν φλογὶ πυρὸς βάτου. [28] When Moses had led the people out of Egypt and through the Red Sea, then on the same Mt. Sinai he received the λόγια ζῶντα (→ IV, 138, 4 ff.), i.e., the Law (→ 283, 11 ff. cf. Dt. 32:47), speaking with the angel (→ IV, 866, n. 209) [29] and acting as mediator between the angel and the people, Ac. 7:38. But Israel persisted in obstinate disobedience against God's will, Ac. 7:39. In the form of the historical preaching of the prophets the dreadful guilt of the disobedient people is then contrasted with the greatness of the divine revelation. With this depiction of the event at Sinai in which the transmission of the living oracles of the Law took place Stephen's speech is very closely related to the historical preaching of Judaism. It is perhaps taken from Jewish tradition and only lightly worked over by the author of Ac. [30]

2. Paul, however, could never have said that λόγια ζῶντα (→ lines 9 ff.) were spoken and given to Israel at Sinai. In the allegory of the two sons of Abraham in Gl. 4:21-31 he links Sinai with the slave Hagar, who conceived and bore her son κατὰ σάρκα and not διὰ τῆς ἐπαγγελίας, v. 23 → VI, 429, 3 ff. The allegorical comparison is : αὗται (the two women Hagar and Sarah) γάρ εἰσιν δύο διαθῆκαι, μία μὲν ἀπὸ ὄρους Σινᾶ, εἰς δουλείαν γεννῶσα, ἥτις ἐστὶν Ἁγάρ, v. 24. The allegorical equation of Hagar with the Sinai διαθήκη (→ II, 130, 29 ff.) is based on a short parenthetical note : τὸ δὲ Ἁγάρ Σινᾶ ὄρος ἐστὶν ἐν τῇ Ἀραβίᾳ, v. 25. This sentence creates such exegetical difficulties, however, that the text is abbreviated even in early MSS and the word Ἁγάρ left out ; in this way a simpler statement is achieved. [31] If this is correct v. 25a is simply a geographical note to the effect that Sinai is in Arabia. But in the context of the whole passage this kind of note hardly yields a satisfying sense. [32]

---

[28] Jos., 2, 264 also says of Moses : ἐπὶ τὸ Σιναῖον καλούμενον ὄρος ἄγει ποίμνια. In answer to the question why God spoke to Moses from the bush the Rabb. said : "To teach that there is no empty place without the shᵉkhina, not even a thorn-bush," Ex. r., 2 (68c). Cf. Str.-B., II, 680.

[29] If God Himself does not speak but transmits His Word through an angel this respectfully safeguards the divine majesty without lessening the significance of the Word spoken. Cf. also Jos. Ant., 15, 136 : ἡμῶν δὲ τὰ κάλλιστα τῶν δογμάτων καὶ τὰ ὁσιώτατα τῶν ἐν τοῖς νόμοις δι' ἀγγέλων παρὰ τοῦ θεοῦ μαθόντων.

[30] Cf. M. Dibelius, "Die Reden d. Ag. u. d. antike Geschichtsschreibung," Aufsätze z. Ag., FRL, 60³ (1957), 145 f.; H. Thyen, "Der Stil d. jüd.-hell. Homilie," FRL, 65 (1955), 19 f.; Haench. Ag. on 7:2-53.

[31] p⁴⁶ ℵ C F G 33 lat Or sah et al. read τὸ δὲ (or γάρ) Σινᾶ ὄρος ἐστὶν ἐν τῇ Ἀραβίᾳ. Cf. Mussner, 56-60, who thinks this is the original reading : "v. 25a is to be regarded as a parenthetical geographical note, but it is necessary if the allegorical line which leads from Hagar via Sinai to present-day Jerusalem is to be possible." In the Old Latin MS d Σινᾶ is left out, so that the sentence runs : "Hagar means mountain in Arabia." But this reading, which Bousset Schr. NT, II, ad loc. prefers, can hardly call for serious consideration in view of its weak support.

[32] Cf. Oe. Gl.², ad loc.: "The clause is quite impossible as a mere geographical note." But v. Mussner's explanation in → n. 31.

One would need to add the further parenthetical thought that the situation of Mt. Sinai — outside the Holy Land in the midst of the subjugated peoples who are the descendants of Hagar [33] — proves that Hagar and Sinai are interconnected. [34] But Paul does not suggest any such train of thought and if need be it can be advanced only with the help of the abbreviated text. The word Ἀγάρ should be retained in v. 25a and one should translate: "But the word Hagar signifies Mt. Sinai in Arabia." This establishes the preceding allegorical equation, [35] which is then extended by the addition of a third member: συστοιχεῖ δὲ τῇ νῦν Ἰερουσαλήμ, δουλεύει γὰρ μετὰ τῶν τέκνων αὐτῆς (v. 25b), so that we have Hagar = Sinai = present-day Jerusalem. [36] These members are held together and inter-related by the fact that slavery is postulated of all of them. The Sinai covenant mediates an enslaving Law which no longer applies in the Jerusalem which is above, in which the children of the free woman live and freedom rules, vv. 26-31. Thus there is a break with Jewish tradition and the Law of Sinai is superseded; for Christ is the end of the Law, R. 10:4. [37]

C. Σινᾶ in the Post-Apostolic Fathers.

In the writings of the post-apost. fathers Sinai is mentioned only in Barn. The name occurs here twice in OT quotations. In a list of testimonies in Barn., 11, 3 Is. 16:1 is quoted in a form which deviates slightly from the LXX: μὴ πέτρα ἔρημός ἐστιν τὸ ὄρος τὸ ἅγιόν μου Σινᾶ; Barn., 14, 1 on the other hand, is attacking the covenant made with Israel and it claims that, while God gave the people the covenant, they were not worthy to receive it because of their sins, → 283, 29 ff. OT quotations are adduced in proof of this thesis, and first the statement in Ex. 24:18: καὶ ἦν Μωϋσῆς νηστεύων ἐν ὄρει Σινᾶ, τοῦ λαβεῖν τὴν διαθήκην κυρίου πρὸς τὸν λαόν, ἡμέρας τεσσεράκοντα καὶ νύκτας τεσσεράκοντα, Barn., 14, 2. [38] But when Moses came down from the mountain and saw the wickedness of the people he threw down the tablets from his hands so that they were smashed. Thus Μωϋσῆς μὲν ἔλαβεν, αὐτοὶ δὲ οὐκ ἐγένοντο ἄξιοι, v. 4. Finally the explicit argument against the Jewish Sabbath begins with the introductory statement that the commandment of rest was among the

---

[33] Cf. Ps. 83:6 f.; 1 Ch. 5:19. Other examples of the Arabian descent of the slave Hagar are assembled in H. J. Schoeps, Aus frühchr. Zeit (1950), 26 f.

[34] Cf. Schlier Gl., ad loc.

[35] To explain this rather obscure argument it has been pted. out that ἐν τῇ Ἀραβίᾳ might mean ἀραβιστί and that the Arab. word ḥadjar ("rock," "stone") suggests Hagar → I, 55 f.; cf. Oe. Gl. and Schlier Gl., ad loc. There is always the possibility that popular etymology lies in the background. Attempts have also been made to solve the puzzle with the help of gematria: ΝΥΝ ΙΕΡΟΥΣΑΛΗΜ (= 1364) — ΑΓΑΡ ΣΙΝΑ (= 1365); cf. Ltzm. Gl., ad loc. But so far no truly satisfying explanation has been found, and one must agree with Schlier Gl., ad loc.: "In my view, then, the sentence is obscure, and hence also the reason and occasion for Paul's linking of Hagar with the Sinai diatheke." The only clear pt. is that v. 25a no longer offers us a plain argument for the allegorical identification of Hagar and Sinai.

[36] Jewish apoc. links Sinai and Zion → 284, 17 ff. But in apoc. the link expresses the holiness of the mountain of God. For Paul, however, Sinai is not the site of God's revelation. The equation of Sinai and present-day Jerusalem shows that the Law enslaves.

[37] Though the name is not given Hb. twice refers to Sinai. In 8:5, on the basis of Ex. 25:40, the command of God to Moses is given: ποιήσεις πάντα κατὰ τὸν τύπον τὸν δειχθέντα σοι ἐν τῷ ὄρει. Hb. 12:18-20 alludes to the fearful accompanying phenomena at the giving of the Law in order to contrast the Then and the Now: προσεληλύθατε Σιὼν ὄρει καὶ πόλει θεοῦ ζῶντος, Ἰερουσαλὴμ ἐπουρανίῳ, v. 22.

[38] Cf. also 1 Cl., 53, 2 and Barn., 4, 7, where Sinai is not mentioned by name but it is said that Moses was 40 days and 40 nights on the mount.

10 words which God spoke to Moses in person on Mt. Sinai, Barn., 15, 1. The Jews, however, interpreted it wrongly, and it has come to its true fulfilment in the eschatological rest which the Chr. community achieves in observance of the Lord's Day.

Lohse

---

† σίναπι

1. τὸ σίναπι, "mustard," is a loan word of obscure origin which was adopted in various forms in Gk.[1] In class. times only τὸ νᾶπυ is found, Hippocr. Morb., III, 15 (Littré, VII, 142); Mul., I, 13 (Littré, VIII, 52); Vict., II, 54 (Littré, VI, 558); Aristoph. Eq., 631; Eubulus (4th cent. B.C.) Fr., 19, 1 (CAF, II, 171); Theophr. Hist. Plant., I, 12, 1; also in later writers, namely, Atticists,[2] e.g., Antyllus (2nd cent. A.D.) in Oribasius Collectiones Medicae, X, 13 (CMG, VI, 1, 2, p. 55-58) 13 times, Ps.-Luc. Asin., 47, cf. occasionally the subsidiary form τὸ νάπειον, Nicand. Alexipharm., 430.[3] But τὸ σίναπι is also found from the later 4th cent. B.C. (→ 288, 2 f.) Anaxippus Fr., 1, 45 (CAF, III, 297); P. Mich., I, 72, 9 (3rd cent. B.C.); P. Tebt., III, 1093, 9 (2nd cent. B.C.); I, 9, 13. 18; 11, 9 (both 119 B.C.); also τὸ σίναπυ in Diocles (4th/3rd cent. B.C.), 120, 3;[4] Zenon-Pap. Cairo,[5] 59608, 31; 59703, 12 (both 3rd cent. B.C.), τὸ σίνηπι in Diocles, 141;[6] Diosc. Mat. Med., II, 154, 1; later τὸ σίνηπυ Nicand. Fr., 70, 16;

σ ί ν α π ι. On 1.: A. Steier, Art. "Senf" in Pauly-W., Suppl., 6 (1935), 812-817; W. Jaeger, *Diokles v. Karystos* (1938), 96-100. On 2.: Str.-B., I, 668 f.; I. Löw, *Die Flora d. Juden*, I (1928), 516-527; Dalman Arbeit, II (1932), 293 f.; H. N. Moldenke-A. L. Moldenke, *Plants of the Bible* (1952), 59-62; K. E. Wilken, *Bibl. Erleben im Hl. Land*, I (1953), 108 f. On 3. a.: A. Schlatter, *Der Glaube im NT*[4] (1927), 105-125; G. Ebeling, "Jesus u. Glaube," ZThK, 55 (1958), 64-110, esp. 90-93. On 3. b.: Comm. and gen. works on the parables, also K. W. Clark, "The Mustard Plant," *Class. Weekly*, 37 (1943/44), 81-83; C. Masson, *Les paraboles de Marc IV* (1945), 45 f.; N. A. Dahl, "The Parables of Growth," *Studia Theol.*, 5 (1951), 132-166, esp. 147 f.; O. Kuss, "Zur Senfkornparabel," *Theol. u. Glaube*, 41 (1951), 40-46; also "Zum Sinngehalt des Doppelgleichnisses vom Senfkorn u. Sauerteig," *Biblica*, 40 (1959), 641-653; C. E. B. Cranfield, "Message of Hope," *Interpretation*, 9 (1955), 150-164, esp. 162 ff.; W. G. Kümmel, *Verheissung u. Erfüllung*, AbhThANT, 6[3] (1956), 122-124; R. Schnackenburg, *Gottes Herrschaft u. Reich* (1959), 98-109, esp. 106 f.; E. Fuchs, "Zur Frage nach dem historischen Jesus," *Gesammelte Aufsätze*, II (1960), 287-291, 341-348; F. Mussner, "1 QH u. das Gleichnis vom Senfkorn," BZ, NF, 4 (1960), 128-130.

[1] The dispensable σι- (νᾶπυ/σίναπι) seems (as in σάρι/σίσαρον, σίλι/σέσελις) to point to borrowing from Egyptian, but there is no such word in Egyptian. Another suggestion is an Austro-Asiatic origin. Cf. Walde-Hofmann[3], II, 142 f., *s.v. nāpus*; II, 541, *s.v. sinapis* [E. Risch]. On the various forms *v.* Jaeger.

[2] Phryn. Ecl., 255 : σίναπι οὐ λεκτέον, νᾶπυ δέ. Cf. Athen., 9, 2 (p. 367a): οὐδεὶς δ' Ἀττικῶν σίναπυ ἔφη (but νᾶπυ); Pliny the Elder (who himself always has *sinapi*) Hist. Nat., 19, 171: *Athenienses napy appellaverunt.*

[3] Cf. also να[π]ίου (gen.) in P. Oxy., XXIV, 2423 recto II, 2 (2nd/3rd cent. A.D.).

[4] Ed. M. Wellmann, *Die Fr. der sikelischen Ärzte Akron, Philistion u. des Diokles v. Karystos* (1901), 167; Jaeger thinks there has been a slip in copying here (for an original σίνηπι), but → 288, 1 f. and n. 8. Cf. also Athen. → n. 2.

[5] Ed. C. C. Edgar, "Zenon Pap., IV," *Catalogue Général des Antiquités Égypt. du Musée du Caire*, 90 (1931), 59 and 133.

[6] Ed. Wellmann, *op. cit.*, 184, 13; Diocles Ep. prophylactica, 2. 3 (ed. Jaeger, 76, 12. 31).

84; ὁ σίνηπυς, Nicand. Alexipharm., 533, ἡ σίναπις Herodotus Medicus (1st/2nd cent. A.D.). [7] Different forms are commonly found in the same author. [8] A later derivate of σίναπι is σιναπίζω, Xenarchus (4th cent. B.C.) Fr., 12, 2 (CAF, II, 472) in the jocular sense "to give a sour look," [9] later found as a medical term "to treat with mustard" (τι "a sore place"), "to put on a mustard-plaster" (→ line 14), Antyllus (→ 287, 10 f.) 9 times; σιναπισμός "mustard-plaster," *ibid.* 5 times; Soranus (2nd cent. A.D.) Gynaecia, III, 28, 6; 44, 5 (CMG, IV, 111, 29; 123, 26). In Theophr. Hist. Plant., VII, 1, 1 f. the mustard is classified among λάχανα (VII, 1, 1: περὶ τοῦ λαχανώδους) and indeed among those which are "cultivated" (ἥμερα in distinction from wild, ἄγρια) and "raised in the garden" (κηπευόμενα). Acc. to Pliny too (Hist. Nat., 20, 236) it is among the cultivated plants (*in sativis*) but needs *nulla cultura, quoniam semen cadens protinus viret* ("sprouts at once"), 19, 170. Not only were the grains valued for their sharp tang [10] but so were the leaves, which were cooked like greens. [11] Mustard was also used in very many ways as a proved curative. [12]

2. In the OT mustard is not mentioned. Yet later Jewish lit. shows that it was well-known in Palestine (Hbr. חַרְדָּל, Aram. חַרְדְּלָא, Arab. *chardal*), → n. 10. Acc. to the Mishnah (in contrast to → line 10) it was not cultivated in gardens but in fields, Kil., 3, 2; cf. 2, 9. [13] It was grown both for the grains (T. Maas., III, 7 [84]) and also the leaves, *loc. cit.*; T. Kil., II, 8 [75]). There is no ref. to medical use. [14] The smallness of the seed was proverbial. In some rules of cleanness the slightest quantity defiles, "even as little as a grain of mustard-seed," Nid., 5, 2; cf. bBer., 31a. Another example is as follows: If someone has vowed to accept the (30 day) Nazirite vow "a basket full" (i.e., as many times as a basket can contain objects), then as the strictest possibility "he should consider the basket full of mustard-seeds — then he is a lifelong Nazirite," Nazir, 1, 5. Even to-day there is an Arab proverb : "No mustard-seed slips from the hands of the miser." [15] Jewish texts do not say that the plant normally grew to a surprising height. As may be seen from the context one is not to take too seriously occasional boasts which are meant to demonstrate the fertility of Palestine and which mention extraordinary mustard-plants, e.g., jPea, 7, 4 (20b, 13 f.): "R. Shim'on b. Chalaphta (c. 190 A.D.) said : I had a mustard-plant in my possession to which I reached up as to the top of a fig-tree." [16] Yet to-day the mustard does in fact grow to a height of 2½-3 metres in the vicinity of Lake Gennesaret. [17]

---

[7] Ed. R. Fuchs, "Aus Themisons Werk über die acuten u. chronischen Krankheiten," *Rhein. Mus.*, NF, 58 (1903), 88 (p. 30 recto 2); identified as Herodotus Medicus by M. Wellmann, "Herodots Werk Περὶ τῶν ὀξέων καὶ χρονίων νοσημάτων," Herm., 40 (1905), 580-604; also "Zu Herodots Schrift Περὶ τῶν ὀξέων καὶ χρονίων νοσημάτων," *ibid.*, 48 (1913), 141-143.

[8] Diocles → 287, 15 f.; Nicand. → 287, 12 and 17 f.; τὸ σίνηπι, Nicand. Theriaca, 878; Antyllus, → 287, 10 f., but τὸ σίνηπι (vl. σίναπι), *ibid.*, X, 13, 18.

[9] Cf. Aristoph. Eq., 631: κἄβλεψε νᾶπυ, καὶ τὰ μέτωπ' ἀνέσπασεν, "and he looked sour and crinkled his forehead."

[10] Nicand. Fr., 70, 16 : σπέρματά τ' ἐνδάκνοντα σινήπυος. Cf. → n. 9. Syr. mustard is sometimes singled out as esp. sharp along with Egyptian, Antyllus in Oribasius Collectiones Medicae, X, 13, 12 (CMG, VI, 1, 2, p. 57, 1 f.).

[11] Plin. Hist. Nat., 19, 171: *cocuntur et folia, sicut reliquorum olerum.*

[12] Cf. already Hippocr. Morb., III, 15 (Littré, VII, 142); Mul., I, 13 (VIII, 52). For directions cf. Plin. Hist. Nat., 20, 236-240 etc.; Diosc. Mat. Med., II, 154; on the preparation and use of a σιναπισμός, Antyllus, *op. cit.* (→ 287, 10 f.).

[13] Mt. 13:31 (ἀγρός) thus reflects the situation in Palestine, Lk. 13:19 (κῆπος) that outside.

[14] But Dalman has found it in modern Palestine.

[15] Acc. to Löw, 522.

[16] With context in Str.-B., I, 656 f. cf. also bKet., 111b (Str.-B., I, 669).

[17] Dalman ; cf. Wilken, who would also have it noted that birds seek out the shade of the big leaves. Mustard-seeds are at any rate used by them as food, Moldenke, 61.

3. In the NT σίναπι occurs only twice in two bits of Synoptic tradition : first in the parable of the grain of mustard-seed in Mk. 4:30-32; Mt. 13:31 f.; Lk. 13:18 f.), then in the saying about faith as a grain of mustard-seed in Mt. 17:20; Lk. 17:6. In both instances the stress is on the smallness of the grain of mustard-seed, which was proverbial in Palestine → 288, 19 ff. In Mk. 4:30 ff. and par. the size of the plant is also depicted in contrast to the smallness of the seed.

To many commentators the depiction of strong growth does not fit the plant. Hence ref. has been made to the so-called mustard-tree (Salvadora Persica L) [18] which is sometimes found in Palestine and is called *chardal* in Arab. There is no evidence, however, that the Aram. חַרְדְּלָא covers both plant and tree and σίναπι certainly cannot do this. Furthermore the tree is not of outstanding size among trees [19] and is thus not very suitable for use in the parable. [20] σίναπι is also expressly reckoned among λάχανα in Mk. 4:30 ff. That the bush finally grows into a δένδρον (Mt. 13:32; Lk. 13:19) is not incorrect. Theophr. Hist. Plant., I, 3, 1-4 in his classification of plants notes that there are transitions, e.g., many λάχανα grow ἐν σχήματι δενδρώδει (3, 4): τῶν τε ... λαχανωδῶν ἔνια ... οἷον δένδρου φύσιν ἔχοντα γίνεται (*loc. cit.*), so that the term δενδρολάχανα occurs, *loc. cit.* [21] This is in every way suitable for the mustard plant, → 288, 31 f. [22] The parable thus remains in the sphere of the actual. [23] More precisely the black mustard is meant (Sinapis nigra L = Brassica nigra). The seeds of this are extremely small if not absolutely the smallest ; 725-760 make up a gramme. [24]

a. The saying about the faith which works miracles is found in three different versions in the Synoptic Gospels : Mk. 11:23 (par. Mt. 21:21); Mt. 17:20; Lk. 17:6.

The context also varies and is secondary ; the logion was originally handed down as an isolated one. [25] The second part refers in Mt. 17:20 to the mountain which is moved, [26] in Mk. 11:23 to the mountain which is cast into the sea, and in Lk. 17:6 to the mulberry tree which is transplanted into the sea. The unusual formulation in Lk. 17:6, which can hardly be called of secondary origin, has perhaps the best claim to be regarded as original. Mt. 17:20 might well be an early assimilation to a current ex-

---

[18] Cf. J. F. Royle, "On the Identification of the Mustard Tree of Scripture," *Journal of the Royal Asiatic Society,* 8 (1846), 113-137; for the Lucan version Loh. Mk. *ad loc.* In opposition cf. Jülicher GlJ, II, 575 f.

[19] Nor are its seeds small. What Loh. Mt., *ad loc.* says is not to the pt., cf. Moldenke, 60.

[20] L. Szimonidesz, "Eine Rekonstruktion d. Senfkorngleichnisses," *Nieuw Theol. Tijdschr.,* 26 (1937), 128-155 thus says — quite arbitrarily — that the ref. is to the Indian fig-tree (Ficus bengalensis), which does not in fact grow to a gt. height ; he finds in this another "basic connection of Jesus with Buddhism," 153.

[21] Cf. Clark.

[22] Acc. to Dalman Arbeit, I, 2 (1928), 369 f. the Arabs use *shadjara* (= tree) for the mustard plant. It should be remembered that most trees in Palestine are not very big.

[23] δένδρον is not, of course, in Mk., nor is it found in the Copt. Gospel of Thomas, → n. 35.

[24] Acc. to Löw, 521.

[25] Though given an introduction in v. 5, Lk. 17:6 is still isolated in the context. Mt. weaves 17:20 into the story of the epileptic boy, cf. the original of this in Mk. 9:14-29. Mk. connects 11:23 with the cursing of the fig-tree (oral tradition had perhaps combined it with v. 24, but v. 25 belongs to a different context).

[26] 1 C. 13:2 also seems to allude to this version : κἂν ἔχω πᾶσαν τὴν πίστιν ὥστε ὄρη μεθιστάναι. Cf. also the independent tradition in the logion in Copt. Gospel of Thomas, 49 (cf. J. Leipoldt, "Ein neues Ev.," ThLZ, 83 [1958], 487; Copt. text in P. Labib, *Coptic Gnostic Pap. in the Coptic Museum at Old Cairo,* I [1956], Plate 89, 24-27): "When two make peace with one another in the same house, they shall say to the mountain : Turn around, and it shall turn around." There is a variant in Logion 103 of the Gospel of Thomas.

pression [27] and also an exaggeration (the tree becomes a mountain). Mk. 11:23 is then a combination of the two. Yet there can be no certainty in the matter. [28] It would seem that the paraphrase of πίστις in Mk. 11:23 : ὃς ἂν ... μὴ διακριθῇ ἐν τῇ καρδίᾳ αὐτοῦ ἀλλὰ πιστεύῃ ὅτι ὃ λαλεῖ γίνεται is fairly obviously a secondary version and interpretation of the much bolder statement in Lk. 17:6 and Mt. 17:20 : ἐὰν ἔχητε (Lk. εἰ ἔχετε) πίστιν ὡς κόκκον σινάπεως.

"Grain of mustard-seed" is used here simply to denote the smallest quantity. [29] A particularly big faith is not needed ; the largest promise applies even to the smallest faith. The question of more or less faith is set aside by the radical question whether there is faith or unbelief. [30] If only there is real faith its quantity is irrelevant. Faith shows itself to be such by not looking to itself but solely to God. If it will only let God work the impossible is possible for it. This justifies materially the pre-Marcan (→ n. 25) linking of the saying in Mk. 11:23 with logia which deal with prayer (v. 24 f.). [31] Mt. 17:20 is also in keeping with the reference to prayer in Mk. 9:29. The faith of which the logion speaks finds its expression in prayer, which entrusts all things to God, → VI, 206, 23 ff.

b. The parable of the grain of mustard-seed, which in the tradition used in Mt. 13:31 f. and Lk. 13:18 f. is paired with that of the leaven, seems to have been originally an isolated parable according to the testimony of Mk. 4:30-32 and the Coptic Gospel of Thomas. [32] The parable has been handed down in different forms. [33] Thus Mk. describes a fact and Lk. a process, [34] while Mt. combines the two. The Gospel of Thomas supports the form in Mk., and like Mk. emphasises the contrast between the smallness of the seed and the size of the plant. [35] This contrast [36] is the decisive feature of the parable. [37] Its concern is not with the

---

[27] Examples in Str.-B., I, 759; cf. also Is. 54:10. 1 C. 13:2 and Gospel of Thomas, 49 and 103 (→ n. 26) might have adopted the proverb in independence of the Synoptic tradition, though there is no ref. to faith moving mountains outside the NT.

[28] The comm. all differ here. Ebeling, 92 thinks Mt. 17:20 is the original version, but if so, how did Lk. 17:6 come into being ?

[29] The interpretation of the expression in Loh. Mt., ad loc. has made its way from the parable of the mustard-seed into the logion.

[30] ὀλιγοπιστία in Mt. 17:20a (only here in the NT) perhaps weakens an original ἀπιστία to spare the disciples. Similarly the hard question to the disciples in Mk. 4:40 : πῶς οὐκ ἔχετε πίστιν; — often emended in the textual tradition of Mk. — is softened to ὀλιγόπιστοι in Mt. 8:26.

[31] Cf. Schlatter, 117 f.

[32] In the Coptic Gospel of Thomas (→ n. 26) the parable of the grain of mustard-seed is Logion 20 while the parable of the leaven is Logion 93.

[33] Cf. Loh. Mt., ad loc.

[34] Is the version used in Lk. perhaps a secondary assimilation to the parable of the leaven ? v. 19a is in exact correspondence with v. 21a.

[35] Gospel of Thomas, Logion 20 (Leipoldt, op. cit. [→ n. 26], 485, Coptic text in Labib, op. cit. [→ n. 26], 84:26-33): "The disciples said to Jesus, Tell us what the kingdom of heaven is like ? He said to them, It is like a grain of mustard-seed. (This is) smaller than all seeds. But when it falls into the earth which a man tills, it sends out a great branch and gives protection to the fowls of heaven." There is no proof that this version is dependent on one or more of the Synoptic Gospels ; it represents an independent tradition, cf. C. H. Hunzinger, "Aussersynoptisches Traditionsgut im Thomas-Ev.," ThLZ, 85 (1960), 843-846. Yet some scholars like L. Cerfaux, "Les paraboles du Royaume dans l'Évangile de Thomas,'" Le Muséon, 70 (1957), 311 f. argue for dependence on Mk.

[36] Even if Lk. does not stress the contrast, the choice of the mustard-seed for use in the parable is a convincing proof that this contrast is in view from the very outset, as against C. H. Dodd, The Parables of the Kingdom² (1936), 190.

[37] Jeremias Gl.⁵ (1958), 127-130; cf. already J. Weiss, Die Predigt Jesu vom Reiche

process of growth, as though the gradual extension of the kingdom of God or the Church were depicted. [38] Smallness and greatness are set in antithetical juxtaposition. Nor is interest focused on the end result of size, as though the overpowering greatness of the future βασιλεία were being described [39] — Jesus' hearers hardly needed to be taught about this. [40] Rather the focus of the parable is obviously on the starting-point, which in its surprising smallness looks so different from what one would expect in view of the end result, but which is still the necessary presupposition and guarantee of the latter, whether in the mustard plant or in the βασιλεία. Behind the parable there clearly lies the claim that the βασιλεία is already present in sign in the contemporary work of Jesus, even though it is now concealed and inconspicuous. The aim of the parable is that this inconspicuous presence should not be an offence but a guarantee of confidence. In the concealment of present demonstrations of God's power lies the promise of an imminent victorious exercise of His dominion. God has already made a beginning; this is the pledge that He will carry through His cause to the end. [41] The parable of the grain of mustard-seed summons to this confidence.

Hunzinger

---

† σινιάζω

This word [1] comes from σινίον (σεννίον, P. Ryl., II, 139, 9) "sieve" and means "to sift" (Vg *cribrare* from *cribrium*). [2] It is found for the first time in Lk. 22:31. Here the main verb ἐξῃτήσατο (→ I, 194, 15 ff.) expresses a demand claimed by σατανᾶς (and

---

Gottes² (1900), 83; also, e.g., Kümmel, Schnackenburg, Fuchs, 342; older bibl. in Kümmel, 123, n. 94.

[38] Kümmel, 119, n. 79; 123, n. 93 mentions defenders of this previously widespread interpretation, which is shattered by the fact that the idea of the βασιλεία as something which develops gradually is in itself wide of the mark → I, 581 ff. For a modern representative cf. Kuss Sinngehalt, 653. "The kingdom of God 'grows,' that is, there is a kind of 'progress' or 'development' to the final stage which is very different from its modest beginning" and "this is also to be seen in the history of the Church." As a particularly vivid example we may also refer to F. Jehle, "Senfkorn u. Sauerteig in d. Hl. Schrift," NkZ, 34 (1923), 713-719, who sees in the collection of parables in Mt. 13 a "sketch of the history of the Church of Jesus Christ" (716) and who deduces from the present parable that "the mustard-seed needs time to develop into a great tree" (717). This is one thing the parable is certainly not saying.

[39] The description of the mighty plant reminds us of Ez. 17:22 f.; 31:2-4; Da. 4:17-19, cf. Dodd, *op. cit.,* 190; cf. also 1 QH 6:14-16 and on this Mussner.

[40] Rightly pted. out by Fuchs, 288 f.; cf. → I, 584, 10 ff.

[41] The same pt. is made in another form in the parables of counting the cost in Lk. 14:28-32 (cf. also the parable of the assailant in the Gospel of Thomas, 95), cf. C. H. Hunzinger, "Unbekannte Gleichnisse Jesu aus dem Thomas-Ev.," *Festschr. J. Jeremias,* Beih. ZNW, 26 (1960), 209-220.

σ ι ν ι ά ζ ω. [1] Cf. Pr.-Bauer, Liddell-Scott, *s.v.;* Bl.-Debr. § 108, 3; Kl. Lk., *ad loc.;* Bultmann Trad., 287 f. and Suppl. (1958), 39; A. Fridrichsen, "Scholia in NT, 1. Lk. 22:31," *Svensk Exegetisk Arsbok,* 12 (1947), 124 f.; W. Foerster, "Lukas 22:31 f.," ZNW, 46 (1955), 129-133; Galling BR, *s.v.* "Sieb."

[2] Fridrichsen, *op. cit.* compares it to λικμάω (→ IV, 280, 11 ff.) Am. 9:9 ('ΑΣ : κοσκινίζω, Sir. 27:4 : ἐν σείσματι κοσκίνου διαμένει κοπρία).

granted to him?) that he may sift Simon and his companions as wheat: (ὑμᾶς) τοῦ σινιάσαι ὡς τὸν σῖτον. This demand is opposed by the prayer of our Lord (cf. v. 33): ἐγὼ δὲ ἐδεήθην περὶ σοῦ ἵνα μὴ ἐκλίπῃ ἡ πίστις σου (v. 32a). In v. 32b a separate theme is introduced: καὶ σύ ποτε ἐπιστρέψας στήρισον τοὺς ἀδελφούς σου. In v. 33 f. contact is made again with the original in Mk. 14:29 f., though another typical Lukan interpolation follows in Lk. 22:35-38. Lk. 22:31 f. justifies de facto the Petrine confession of Mk. 14:29 f.: Simon [3] would not doubt Jesus; Jesus' intercession for him was successful; Satan was beaten as he would be beaten again in the future, Lk. 22:35-38. This means 1. that in v. 32a πίστις is tantamount to confessional fidelity; [4] 2. that in v. 32b not only the Lukan ἐπιστρέψας [5] but the whole clause is an addition of the Evangelist, who rounds off the thought along the lines of vv. 35-38; and 3. that in contrast v. 31 and v. 32a may well go back to older (Palestinian?) tradition. This tradition would not record Peter's denial but rather emphasise his faithfulness. Since Peter later became a figure of controversy in Gl. 2:11-14 the solemn saying to Simon could easily be regarded as a primitive Christian prophecy which in its own way supports the title Cephas. The saying set forth in the name of the exalted Lord presupposes the event in 1 C. 15:5. As a saying of the historical Jesus it could be motivated only by the supposed denial of Peter in the passion story, which it seems to contradict. The clause in v. 32b smooths everything over.

There is no need to discuss whether Lk. 22:31 has in view a (larger) sieve to sift out foreign matter or a fine sieve for the wheat itself, since the *tertium comparationis* is in any case that of sifting or testing which seeks only one thing, in this case πίστις (materially cf. Job 1 f. → 157, 1 ff. From the very outset the saying about sifting wheat is meant to be metaphorical. [6]

Fuchs

Σιών, Ἰερουσαλήμ, Ἰεροσόλυμα, Ἰεροσολυμίτης

Contents: A. Zion-Jerusalem in the Old Testament: I. Occurrence, Etymology and Meaning: 1. Zion and Related Terms; 2. Jerusalem and Related Terms; 3. Rare Terms; 4. The Use of the Names Zion and Jerusalem; II. The Historical Development of the Significance of Zion-Jerusalem: 1. The Pre-Israelite and Early Israelite Period; 2. The

---

[3] The double Simon does not guarantee historicity. That distinction could be made between the name Simon and the title Cephas or Peter may be seen from Jn. 21:15 etc. The "office" of the Risen Lord is clear: R. 8:34; 1 Jn. 2:1. The fact that Peter and Paul disagree in Gl. 2:11-14 shows that the Jesus of history had not come forth as the Messiah, cf. Ac. 2:36.

[4] On πίστις → VI, 174 ff., esp. 208, 11 ff. (2 Tm. 4:7; Rev. 2:13). Confessional fidelity alone does not plumb the depths of faith.

[5] So Bultmann Trad., 288.

[6] Julicher Gl. J., I, 57 rightly says: "What σινιάσαι means in Lk. 22:31 may be pretty well guessed without a dictionary from the accompanying comparison ὡς σῖτον." On the logical problem cf. E. Fuchs, Hermeneutik² (1958), 211-219.

Σ ι ώ ν κ τ λ. For bibl. on the archaeology, topography and history of Jerusalem cf. J. Simons, *Jerusalem in the OT* (1952), 505-507. On A.: H. Vincent, "Les noms de Jérusalem," *Memnon*, 6 (1913), 88-124; A. Causse, "Le mythe de la nouvelle Jérusalem du

A. Zion-Jerusalem in the Old Testament.

I. Occurrence, Etymology and Meaning.

1. Zion and Related Terms.

a. In the OT צִיּוֹן is used 154 times. It is very unevenly distributed. [1] In almost a third of the instances there is no addition or par., esp. in Is., Jer. and Ps. Mostly, however, there is an addition ; in 20 cases this is the geographical and topographical designation הַר, "Mount." We also find the plur. הָרְרֵי "mountains" in Ps. 133:3 (textually uncertain) and the combined הַר בַּת "mountain of the daughter" in Is. 10:32 conj.; 16:1. מְצֻדָה also occurs in 2 S. 5:7; 1 Ch. 11:5 in the sense of "inaccessible place"

Deutéro-Es. à la IIIᵉ Sibylle," RevHPhR, 18 (1938), 377-414; N. Avigad, *Ancient Monuments in the Kidron Valley* (1954) (Hbr.); J. Klausner, *Gesch. d. zweiten Tempels*[4] (1954) (Hbr.); H. Vincent, *Jérusalem de l'AT*, I-III (1954-56); H. Schmid, "Jahwe u. d. Kulttraditionen v. Jerusalem," ZAW, 67 (1955), 168-197; M. Avi-Yonah, *Sepher Jeruschalajim*, I (1956) (Hbr.); A. Parrot, "Der Tempel v. Jerusalem" in *Bibel u. Archäologie*, II (1956), 7-89; "Judah and Jerusalem," *The Twelfth Archaeological Convention* (1956) (Hbr. with English summary); O. Eissfeldt, "Silo u. Jerusalem," Suppl. to VT, 4 (1957), 137-147; M. Noth, "Jerusalem u. d. isr. Tradition" in *Gesammelte Studien z. AT* (1957), 172-187; M. Join-Lambert, *Jérusalem israélite, chrétienne, musulmane* (1957); J. S. Wright, *The Building of the Second Temple* (1958); S. Zimmer, *Zion als Tochter, Frau u. Mutter. Personifikation von Land, Stadt u. Volk in weiblicher Gestalt*, Diss. Munich (1959); A. van Deursen, *Jeruzalem is welgebouwd* (no date). On B.: H. Vincent-F. M. Abel, *Jérusalem*, I (1912), II (1914-26); D. H. McQueen, "The New Jerusalem and Town Planning," Exp., 9, 2 (1924), 220-226; F. Dijkema, "Het hemelsch Jeruzalem," *Nieuw Theol. Tijdschr.*, 15 (1926), 25-43; Str.-B., Index on "Jerusalem"; G. Dalman, *Jerusalem u. sein Gelände* (1930); Volz Esch., 371-376; A. Causse, "De la Jérusalem terrestre à la Jérusalem céleste," RevHPhR, 27 (1942), 12-36; K. L. Schmidt, "Jerusalem als Urbild u. Abbild," *Eranos Jahrbuch*, 18 (1950), 207-248; H. Bietenhard, "Die himmlische Welt im Urchr. u. Spätjudt.," *Untersuchungen z. NT*, 2 (1951), 192-204; T. Maertens, *Jérusalem cité de Dieu* (1954); E. Stauffer, *Jerusalem u. Rom im Zeitalter Jesu Christi* (1957); J. Jeremias, *Jerusalem z. Zt. Jesu*[2] (1958). On C.: A. v. Harnack, *Die Apostelgeschichte* (1908), 72-76; R. Schütz, "Ιερουσαλημ u. Ιεροσολυμα im NT," ZNW, 11 (1910), 169-187; Dalman Orte, 286-402; E. Lohmeyer, "Galiläa u. Jerusalem," FRL, 52 (1936); A. Parrot, "Golgotha u. d. Hl. Grab" in *Bibel u. Archäologie*, II (1956), 91-199; W. Schmauch, *Orte d. Offenbarung u. d. Offenbarungsort im NT* (1956), 81-121; C. Kopp, *D. hl. Stätten der Ev.* (1956), 339-465.

[1] The greatest occurrence is in Is. (47 times), Jer. (17), Jl. (7), Mi. (9), Zech. 1-8 (6), Ps. (38) and Lam. (15). The name is used once or twice in 2 S., 1-2 K., Am., Ob., Zeph., Cant., 1-2 Ch. and not at all in the other books. LXX has Zion for ירושלם at 3 Βασ. 8:1

rather than "fortress." Many other additions relate to the population : בַּת "daughter" 23 times or בְּתוּלַת בַּת "virgin daughter" in 2 K. 19:21; Lam. 2:13,[2] more explicitly יוֹשֶׁבֶת "inhabitants" in Is. 12:6; Jer. 51:35 and בְּנֵי or בְּנוֹת צִיּוֹן "sons or daughters of Zion" in Is. 3:16 f.; 4:4 etc. We also find expressions like "gates of Zion" in Ps. 87:2, "Zion of the Holy One of Israel" in Is. 60:14 and "song of Zion" in Ps. 137:3.

A series of par. terms is associated with Zion and helps to bring out its many different meanings. Only rarely is it equated with the Davidic part of the city by the par. "city of David," 2 S. 5:7; 1 K. 8:1; 1 Ch. 11:5; 2 Ch. 5:2, but "Jerusalem" is very often a par. (more than 40 times) and once "Salem" in Ps. 76:2. Other par. bring out its religious or cultic function. It is the "city of Yahweh" (Is. 60:14) to which one resorts (Jer. 31:6), the "city of our God" in Ps. 48:2, His "holy mountain" in Jl. 2:1; Ps. 48:2 and His "sanctuary" in Ps. 20:2. Materially par. are the apposition "my holy mountain" in Jl. 3:17; Ps. 2:6 and the par. "temple hill" with "Jerusalem" in Mi. 3:12; cf. Jer. 26:18. Finally "Zion" is par. with "Israel" in Is. 46:13; Zeph. 3:14 f.; Ps. 149:2, "Jerusalem" and "Jacob" in Lam. 1:17, "him that turns from iniquity in Jacob" in Is. 59:20 and the "community of the righteous" in Ps. 149:2. The synthetic juxtaposition is also instructive. With Zion we find "Judah" in Jer. 14:19, the "land" in Is. 66:8, the "cities of Judah" in Ps. 69:35; Lam. 5:11 and "daughters of Judah" in Ps. 48:12; 97:8. With "sons of Zion" we find "Judah" and "Ephraim" in Zech. 9:13, with "Mount Zion" the "tribe of Judah" in Ps. 78:68.[3]

b. There is as yet no clear picture of the etym. of the name Zion.[4] It is transmitted as a proper name without art. and undoubtedly comes from pre-Israelite times. Apart from earlier explanations[5] a non-Palestinian origin is often sought, e.g., the Elamite čijām "temple" (from a Sumerian loan word),[6] or the Hurrian šejᵃ "water," "river," hence מְצֻדַת צִיּוֹן "fortress of waters," i.e., the fortress which guaranteed Jerusalem's water supply.[7] But it seems to be more to the point to seek a Palestinian-Semitic root,[8] e.g., צִין "to protect" (= "fortress")[9] or צוה "to set up" with צָוּוֹן as a transitional form[10] and a postulated relation to צִיּוֹן "pillar," so that the name refers to a soaring

---

and קָדְשֶׁךָ at Da. 9:24, as an explanatory addition at 3 Βασ. 3:15; Is. 1:21; 52:1; ψ 72:28; Da. 9:19, erroneously in Is. 9:10; 22:1, 5; 25:5; 32:2; Ιερ. 38(31):21, also in B at Jos. 13:21; 19:26 and S* at Is. 23:4, in other MSS at Is. 23:12, in various MSS as a Gk. slip, B at Jos. 13:19; 2 Ch. 32:30 and S* at 2 Εσδρ. 23:4.

[2] For the divergent sense in LXX → V, 833, 1 ff.

[3] These expressions show that Zion is meant when other terms are used. e.g., politically the "city of David" for Davidic Jerusalem (2 S. 6:10 ff.) or the old part of the city (1 K. 3:1 etc.), esp. in connection with ref. to the royal tombs (1 K. 2:10 etc.). Other terms refer to Zion as the site of the temple or cultus, esp. when "mountain" is used, Ex. 15:17; Is. 25:6 f.; 27:13; 30:29; Ez. 17:22; 20:40; Zech. 8:3; Ps. 3:4; 68:16, also "my sanctuary" in Ez. 24:21 and "city of God" in Ps. 46:4.

[4] Cf. H. Vincent, Jérusalem antique. Topographie (1912), 145 f.; Jérusalem, III, 632; Simons, 61-64.

[5] P. de Lagarde, Onomastica sacra (1870), 39, 43. 198; F. Wutz, "Onomastica sacra," TU, 41 (1914 f.), 81, 96 f., 120, 193 f., 312, 409.

[6] G. Hüsing, "Zur Ophir-Frage," OLZ, 6 (1903), 370; also "Nachträgliches zur Ophir-Frage," OLZ, 7 (1904), 80; also "Semitische Lehnwörter im Elamischen," Beiträge zur Assyriologie, 5 (1906), 410; also "Elamisches," ZDMG, 56 (1902), 791 f.

[7] S. Yeivin, "The Sepulchres of the Kings of the House of David," Journal of Near Eastern Studies, 7 (1948), 41 with a ref. to E. A. Speiser, "Introduction to Hurrian," The Annuals of the American Schools of Oriental Research, 20 (1940-41).

[8] We may rule out derivation from the Bibl.-Aram. צִיּוּן "making known" (of burial places) and also from צִי "wildcat," A. Šanda, Die Bücher d. Könige, I (1911), 212.

[9] J. G. Wetzstein in F. Delitzsch, Commentar über die Gn.⁴ (1872), 578. Cf. P. Haupt, "Critical Notes on Micah," Amer. Journ. of Semitic Languages and Literatures, 26 (1909-10), 219 : protection, protected place.

[10] F. Delitzsch, Comm. über die Ps., I³ (1873), 70.

massif. [11] Arab. par. also lead to the sense "top of an eminence" and then "fort," "citadel." [12] Another suggestion is that the basis is the Syr. * צהה = * ציה "to be barren, dry," hence צָהִיוֹן in the sense of "bare and barren hill." [13] Others have thought it could be explained in terms of צִיָּה "dry territory" or צִיוֹן "waterless land" in the sense of "barren land." [14] But thus far no accepted and illuminating explanation has been found. The most that can be said is that the name is pre-Israelite and that it probably relates to the nature of the terrain for which it is used (on עֹפֶל → n. 15).

c. Originally Zion seems to have been a topographical term for the south-east hill of the later city which was the site of a Canaanite settlement. A similar term is Ophel for the summit of the north-east hill to the north on which Solomon built his residence, cf. Is. 32:14; Mi. 4:8. [15] The settlement on the hill of Zion itself bore from early times the name of "Jerusalem." Under David it came to be known instead as the "city of David," but from Solomon onwards the extended city area is again called "Jerusalem" and "city of David" is used for what is now the old city. On the other hand "Zion" hardly occurs at all as a topographical term or even as a name in the period which follows. Only in the later monarchy does it reappear, and now there has been an extension and shift of meaning. The name is used now for the whole east hill or for the whole city, or else it refers to the north-east hill as the temple hill.

> Zion is once used in a transf. sense. In Am. 6:1 the "careless in Zion" are par. to "those who trust in the mountain of Samaria." To these, even though they belong to the "house of Israel," the whole invective and threat applies. In this case, then, Zion is a technical expression for the situation of the capital; Samaria is the "Zion" of the Northern Kingdom.

2. Jerusalem and Related Terms.

a. As compared with the less common צִיוֹן the name יְרוּשָׁלַם ("Jerusalem") is found 660 times in the OT. It occurs often in some books, [16] less so in others. [17] In many cases we simply find "Jerusalem" without addition or par. It denotes the original Canaanite city in Jos. 10:1 etc., the capital of the kingdom of David and Solomon in 2 S. 5:5-1 K. 11:42 and par. in 1-2 Ch., the capital of the Southern Kingdom of Judah

---

[11] H. Hupfeld, "Die topographische Streitfrage über Jerusalem, namentlich die "Ακρα u. den Lauf der zweiten Mauer d. Jos. vom AT aus beleuchtet," ZDMG, 15 (1861), 224 f.

[12] G. A. Smith, Jerusalem, I (1907), 145.

[13] W. Gesenius, Thesaurus linguae hebraicae et chaldaicae (1835 ff.), s.v.; P. de Lagarde, "Übersicht über die im Aram., Arab. u. Hbr. übliche Bildung der Nomina," AGG, 35, 5 (1889), 198.

[14] G. Dalman, Jerusalem u. sein Gelände (1930), 126.

[15] עֹפֶל is used of the north-east hill in Is. 32:14 and Mi. 4:8 with no art. as a proper name, but with art. in the Chronicler at 2 Ch. 27:3; 33:14; Neh. 3:26 f.; 11:21 in place of Zion, elsewhere used for the temple hill and denoting the Jebusite city only in 1 Ch. 11:5; 2 Ch. 5:2. The name is based on the terrain and means a "swelling" or "hump" on the earth's surface, cf. 2 K. 5:24 and Mesha inscr. 22 (medically in Dt. 28:27; 1 S. 5:6 ff.; 6:4 f.); Simons, 64-67; A. Schwarzenbach, Die geographische Terminologie im Hbr. d. AT (1954), 21.

[16] Cf. 2 S. (30 times), 1-2 K. (90), Is. (49), Jer. (102), Ez. (26), Zech. (39), Ezr. (48), Neh. (38), 1-2 Ch. (151).

[17] Cf. Jos. (9), Ju. (5), 1 S. (1), due to the historical situation; also Jl. (6), Am. (2, setting in the Northern Kingdom), Ob. (2), Mi. (8), Zeph. (4), Mal. (2), Ps. 51-147 (17), Cant. (8), Qoh. (5), Lam. (7), Est. (1), Da. (10). The name does not occur at all in the books not mentioned here or in → n. 16. LXX has some additional instances: for יִשְׂרָאֵל Gn. 36:31 A; Is. 1:24 A etc., בְּנְיָמֵן 2 Ch. 25:5, אֲרִיאֵל Is. 29:7 B and שָׁלוֹם 4 Βασ. 22:20 without

in 1 K. 12:18-2 K. 24:18 and par. in 1-2 Ch., the city chosen by Yahweh (1 K. 11:36 etc.) as the cultic centre (1 K. 12:27 etc.), or in simple chronological notes, Jer. 1:3 etc. "Jerusalem" also occurs with various additions. These relate to the territory of the earlier city state : "environs of Jerusalem" in Jer. 17:26; 32:44, or are simply topographical : "hill" in Is. 10:32; "walls" in Ps. 51:18; "gates" in Jer. 1:15 etc.; "lanes" only in Jer. (5:1 etc.), "places" in Zech. 8:4 and "centre" in Jer. 6:1; Zech. 8:8. Other additions mention the inhabitants : בַּת "daughter" in 2 K. 19:21; Mi. 4:8 etc.; יוֹשֵׁב in Is. 5:3; 8:14 or יוֹשְׁבֵי "inhabitants" esp. in Jer., Ez., 2 Ch.; בְּנֵי "sons" in Jl. 3:6; בְּנוֹת "daughters" only in Cant.; בְּתוּלֹת "virgins" in Lam. 2:10; "prophets" in Jer. 23:14 f. In connection with the fate of the city there is ref. to the "remnant" in Jer. 24:8 and the גָּלֻת "deportees" in Ob. 20.

Other expressions par. to "Jerusalem" are "ridges of the Jebusites" in Jos. 15:8, "city of the Jebusites" in Jos. 18:28; Ju. 19:11 and "Jebus" in Ju. 19:10 f., more commonly "Zion" (in later passages apart from Mi. 3:10, 12), "hill of Zion" (later passages, 2 K. 19:31; Is. 10:12 etc.), "daughter of Zion" (later passages, Is. 52:2; Zeph. 3:14), "inhabitants of Jerusalem" in Jer. 51·35; this parallelism is almost exclusively exilic or post-exilic. Other par. are "gate of my people" in Mi. 1:9, "this people" in Jer. 4:11, "my people" in Is. 65:19, also the "hill of Yahweh Zebaoth" in Zech. 8:3 and the "temple" in Jer. 26:6, 9, 12 [18] — hence the "forecourts of the house of Yahweh" are the "centre of Jerusalem," Ps. 116:19.

There is synthetic juxtaposition in many different forms. Legal or regional relationship may be seen in the expressions quoted → 307, 15 ff. There is more of antithesis in the mention of "Samaria" and "Jerusalem" in Ez. 23; Mi. 1:5. Once each we find "Jerusalem and all its towns" (Jer. 19:15) and "Jerusalem" with the "temple and palace" (Jer. 27:18). There are many kinds of combinations, esp. with ref. to the inhabitants. Only in a few does Jerusalem come first, Is. 5:3; 22:21; Zech. 8:15; 2 Ch. 21:11; usually Judah is first, Jer. 17:20; Zeph. 1:4; 2 Ch. 20:15 etc. Later the two are sometimes associated more closely, Ezr. 4:6; 2 Ch. 20:27. Finally there is ref. to the "house of David and inhabitants of Jerusalem," Zech. 12:10; 13:1. Instructive for an understanding of Jerusalem are the appositions : "holy city" in Is. 52:1; Neh. 11:1, "holy mountain" in Is. 27:13; "throne of Yahweh" in Jer. 3:17; 14:21; 17:12. It is "thy city Jerusalem," "thy holy hill," Da. 9:16. Worth noting is that these are only exilic and later voices. [19]

b. Almost without exception the consonantal form of the name in the HT is ירושלם; it is vocalised as qere perpetuum יְרוּשָׁלַם (for יְרוּשָׁלַיִם) and is thus to be pronounced jerušalajim. [20] Only in 5 later texts enumerated in a Mas. note on Jer. 26:18 do we find the form ירושלים corresponding to the qere reading : Jer. 26:18; Est. 2:6; 1 Ch. 3:5; 2 Ch. 25:1; 32:9. [21] With the usual form this also occurs on Jewish coins of the age

---

HT equivalent, partly due to the more expansive LXX text. On the other hand LXX often replaces it : by Ισραηλ 3 Βασ. 15:4 Orig except Σ; 4 Βασ. 8:26 ΒΑ etc.; Δαυιδ 2 Ch. 28:27; Σιων 3 Βασ. 8:1.

[18] Ez. 21:7 is probably to be read similarly : "Jerusalem" and "its sanctuary" (not "sanctuaries").

[19] Acc. to these expressions and speech-forms Jerusalem is meant when other terms are employed : the simple designation "the city" (common in Ez.), the rather contemptuous "this city" (common with Baruch in Jer. 19:11, 15; 21:1-10 etc.; cf. Ez. 11:2, 6), "city of bloodguiltiness" in Ez. 22:2; 24:6a, "city which sheds blood" in Ez. 22:3, "this great city" in Jer. 22:8, "joyful city" in Is. 22:2; 32:13, "holy city" in Is. 48:2, "city of Yahweh" in Ps. 101:8.

[20] With pause יְרוּשָׁלָ͏ִם (same form without pause in Ps. 79:3; 137:5) with ה locale יְרוּשָׁלֵ͏ְמָה (instead of יְרוּשָׁלַיְמָה in 1 K. 10:2; 2 K. 9:28; Is. 36:2; Ez. 8:3, written יְרוּשָׁלַיְמָה by 27 MSS at 1 K. 10:2).

[21] ירושלם is also read in 1 Ch. 3:5, the full form with ה locale in 2 Ch. 32:9. In the Dead Sea Scrolls ירושלם occurs 3 times in 1 QpHab and ירושלים 5 times in 1 QM.

of Simon (142-135 B.C.) or of the first revolt against Rome (66-70 A.D.).[22] It is occasionally found too in Rabb. lit.[23] The ending -ajim rests neither on the ancient name nor on the demands of the solemn reading of Scripture in divine worship. Rather we may accept the traditional explanation that this is an artificial dual construction designed to express the twofoldness of the city as the upper and lower city or that on the east hill and that on the west. The older and more correct pronunciation is undoubtedly that of the ketib : יְרוּשָׁלֵם. This arises out of the consonants and is confirmed by a ref. in the Aristotelian philosopher Clearchus of Soli to Ιερουσαληημ,[24] by the transcription Ιερουσαλημ in the LXX and NT (on which the Cpt. and Arm. versions are based),[25] and by the Bibl.-Aram. form יְרוּשְׁלֵם (also יְרוּשְׁלֵם).[26]

There is also another form of the name with a long tradition. This perhaps begins with the oldest mention of Jerusalem known thus far, namely, in the Egypt. proscription texts from the beginning of the 2nd millennium[27] (*'wš'mm* = Uršalem or Rušlem-Rušalem).[28] It is plainly present in the Sumerian ideogram form âlDI-ma = Urusilimma in a list of gods (probably 18th cent.),[29] also in the Bab. form Urusalim (U-ru-sa-lim or Uru-sa-lim) in the Amarna letters of the 14th cent.[30] and in the Assyr. form Ursalimmu (Ur-sa-li-im-mu) on the Sennacherib prism from the beginning of the 8th cent.[31] It occurs again in the Syr. Urišlem (Hbr. transcr. אורשלם).[32] The difference between the ketib form and these predominantly Mesopotamian forms is due to the change necessitated by putting into Accadian ; hence these forms are an exact equivalent of ירושלם.

---

[22] M. Lidzbarski, *Hndbch. der nordsemitischen Epigraphik* (1898), 290; G. A. Smith, *op. cit.*, 251.

[23] So e.g., T. Ket., 4; usually ירושלם, e.g., Zebachim, 14, 8; Men., 10, 2 and 5; Ar., 9, 6.

[24] Clearchus (4th/3rd cent.) is quoted in Jos. Ap., 1, 179 f. He adds to the name the Gk. ending η, while Jos. himself uses Ἱεροσόλυμα.

[25] Cf. Vincent noms, 91.

[26] In the OT 26 times : Da. 5:2 f.; 6:11; Ezr. 4:8, 12, 20, 23 f.; 5:1 f., 14-17; 6:3, 5, 9, 12, 18; 7:13-17, 19. Cf. also A. Ungnad, *Aram. Pap. aus Elephantine* (1911), 1, 18.

[27] K. Sethe, *Die Ächtung feindlicher Fürsten, Völker u. Dinge auf altägypt. Tongefässscherben des Mittleren Reiches* (1926); G. Posener, *Princes et pays d'Asie et de Nubie* (1940). In the Sethe texts, which might come from the 20th cent., Jerusalem is mentioned in e 27-28; f 18, and in the Posener texts (19th cent.) in E 45. Cf. also R. Dussaud, "Nouveaux renseignements sur la Palestine et la Syrie vers 2000 avant notre ère," *Syria*, 8 (1928), 216-233; W. F. Albright, "The Egypt. Empire in Asia in the Twenty-First Cent. B.C.," JPOS, 8 (1928), 223-256, also "The Land of Damascus between 1850 and 1750 B.C.," *Bulletin of the Americ. Schools of Oriental Research*, 83 (1941), 30-36; A. Alt, "Herren u. Herrensitze Palästinas im Anfang d. zweiten Jahrtausends v. Chr.," ZDPV, 81 (1941), 21-39; H. Vincent, "Les pays bibl. et l'Égypte à la fin de la XIIᵉ dynastie égypt.," *Rev. Bibl.*, 51 (1942), 187-212. The objections of A. Jirku, "Bemerkungen zu den ägypt. sog. 'Ächtungstexten,'" *Archiv Orientálni*, 20 (1952), 167-169, to the attestation of Jerusalem are not very convincing.

[28] Vincent Jérusalem, III, 612, n. 4.

[29] O. Schröder, *Keilinschriftl. aus Assur verschiedenen Inhalts* (1920), No. 145, 6 (cf. *Cuneiform Texts from Babyl. Tablets in the British Museum*, 24 [1908], 20-46) with the names of various lands and cities for the goddess Ishtar. So acc. to F. M. T. de Liagre Böhl, "Älteste keilinschr. Erwähnungen d. Stadt Jerusalem u. ihrer Göttin ?" *Acta Orientalia*, 1 (1922), 76-80, though H. Schmökel, *Hl. Hochzeit u. Hoheslied* (1956), 98, does not think the ideogram âlDI-ma can possibly be read as Urusilimma.

[30] J. A. Knudtzon, *Die El-Amarna-Tafeln*, II (1908), No. 285-290; cf. K. Galling, *Textbuch z. Gesch. Israels* (1950), 23-29. The letters of the king of the city of Jerusalem may be dated from c. 1360.

[31] H. C. Rawlinson, *The Cuneiform Inscr. of Western Asia*, I (1861): so-called Taylor-Prism; D. D. Luckenbill, "The Annals of Sennacherib," *Oriental Institute Publications*, II (1924): Prism of the Oriental Inst. of Chicago. Vincent noms, 91, n. 4 refers to the variant Ur-sa-li-im-ma found elsewhere.

[32] It was once thought אורשלם also occurred on a Nabatean inscr. (Corpus Inscr. Semiti-

c. The etym. of the name יְרוּשָׁלֵם, regarding which the OT is no help, was up to quite recently a field wide open to all kinds of speculation. [33] Serious modern attempts to explain at least the first part of the name as יְרוּשׁ *possessio* (*pacis*) [34] or יְרוּ (from ירה) *fundatum, fundatio* (*pacis*) [35] have been undermined by the discovery of the Amarna letters with the Bab. form Urusalim, which favours the view that Jerusalem is not a Palestinian or Canaanite name but a Babylonian. [36] Of the possible explanations in terms of a Palestinian-Canaanite background there are many reasons why we cannot accept "city of Salem" (יִרוּשָׁלֵם = אֻרֻשָׁלֵם = [עֻרֻ]וֹ[שַׁ]לֵם) or "light of Salem." [37] The first element in the name is the word יְרוּ* "foundation" ($\sqrt{}$ ירה), which is to be taken neither as a perf. [38] nor a jussive impf. [39] but as a noun st. c. [40] The second element is the name of the god Šlm who obviously played some part in Syria and Palestine. [41] This god is mentioned in the Ugaritic texts 17, 12; 52, 12 f., 107, 8, [42] sometimes with the god Šhr ("morning twilight"), so that he represents "evening twilight" (or more exactly "completion of the day"). [43] Šhr and Šlm, the twin sons of El, are probably as the stars of morning and evening two hypostases or aspects of the (male) morning and evening star 'Attar. [44] The same name Šlm probably underlies the divine name Sal-majāti in the Amarna letters of Abimilki of Tyre. [45] Some have even thought they could see in the Jerusalem Amarna letters a ref. to a temple in Jerusalem dedicated to Šlm. [46]

---

carum, I [1881], 294, No. 320 B and Plate 41), so still Smith, 252 and Schütz, 169, n. 2. But the researches of A. Jaussen-R. Savignac, *Mission archéol. en Arabie : Médâin Sâleh* (1909), 245 and Plate 29, No. 183 have shown that we should read אדר שלם|.

[33] J. Grill, "Beiträge zur hbr. Wort- u. Namenerklärung, 1. Über Entstehung u. Bdtg. des Namens Jerusalem," ZAW, 4 (1884), 134-148; I. Marquart, "שַׁבֹּלֶת = ephraimitisch סַבֹּלֶת = שַׁבֹּלֶת," ZAW, 8 (1888), 152; P. Haupt in T. K. Cheyne, *Isaiah* (1899), Exc. on 19:1; F. Prätorius, "Über einige Arten hbr. Eigennamen," ZDMG, 57 (1903), 782; G. A. Smith, "The Name Jerusalem and Other Names," Exp., VI, 7 (1903), 122-135; E. Nestle, "Zum Namen Jerusalem," ZDPV, 27 (1904), 153-156; J. A. Montgomery, "Paronomasias on the Name Jerusalem," JBL, 49 (1930), 277-282; Vincent noms, 87-124; also Jérusalem III, 611-613.

[34] A. Reland, Palaestina ex monumentis veteribus illustrata (1714).

[35] Gesenius, op. cit.

[36] Haupt esp. (op. cit.) supports this view, cf. Smith, op. cit. (→ n. 12), 258, Vincent noms, 97-99.

[37] Cf. in detail Vincent noms, 99-105.

[38] W. F. Albright, "The Egypt. Empire in Asia in the Twenty-First Cent. B.C.," JPOS, 8 (1928), 248.

[39] W. F. Albright, "Palestine in the Earliest Historical Period," JPOS, 15 (1935), 218, n. 78.

[40] J. Lewy, "Les textes paléo-assyriens et l'AT," RHR, 110 (1943), 61 f.

[41] Cf. KAT, 224, 474-477. A. Jeremias, *Das AT im Lichte d. Alten Orients³* (1916), 291 and 426; H. S. Nyberg, "Studien zum Religionskampf im AT," ARW, 35 (1938), 352-364 adduces other names made up of Šlm from the Phoenician world and also both normal and variant forms in Ugaritic, making wide deductions in relation to the OT. Cf. also S. Yeivin, "The Beginning of the Davidids (Hbr.)," *Zion*, 9 (1944), 53, n. 30. 33 with bibl. But as against Lewy, op. cit., 61 f. Šlm is not identical with אֵל עֶלְיוֹן.

[42] As numbered in Gordon Manual.

[43] Cf. also Lewy ; Nyberg, 352 f. Šhr may be seen in the theophoric name Kšhr'ib'i in the Egypt. proscription texts, cf. Posener, op. cit., 74, while Šlm occurs in the name of the Moabite king Salamanu in the 8th cent. (KAT, 475) and in the name 'apšlm in an ostracon of tell el-chlēfi (Ezeon-Geber) in the 5th/4th cent., N. Glueck, "Ostraca from Elath," *Bulletin of the Americ. Schools of Oriental Research*, 82 (1941), 3-11.

[44] Cf. J. Gray, "The Desert God 'Attr in the Literature and Religion of Canaan," *Journal of Near Eastern Studies*, 8 (1949), 73-83.

[45] Cf. J. A. Knudtzon, op. cit., 1254-1256; C. Lindhagen, *The Servant Motif in the OT* (1950), 8-10.

[46] J. Lewy, "The Šulmān Temple in Jerusalem," JBL, 59 (1940), 519-522 interprets

Furthermore an Assyrian list of gods with the names of the goddess Ishtar in various lands and cities [47] probably contains the statement that the Ishtar of Urusilimma bears the name Šul-ma-ni-t(u). This goddes Sulmitu (or Sulmanitu), who is often mentioned in ideographic form, [48] is obviously the female counterpart of the god Šalmānu or Sulmānu, [49] who in the Cannanite form Šlm occupies a lowly place in the pantheon. [50] No matter whether or not the female deity was also worshipped along with Šlm (and אֵל עֶלְיוֹן as a local form of the Canaanite god El), in naming the settlement a common notion was adopted, namely, that which traces back the origin of a place to the express declaration of the will of a deity or to his presence, and which names the place accordingly. Jerusalem is "the foundation (or city) of Šlm (Šalim, Šalem)." [51]

d. The meaning of Jerusalem remains the same and has always done so. Unlike Zion it did not change but referred from the very first to the whole settlement. It continued to do so when the settlement grew, so that sometimes the name Jerusalem can be explicitly distinguished from the partial designations "Zion" and "city of David," 1 K. 3:1; 8:1; 11:27.

3. Rare Terms.

a. The name שָׁלֵם "Salem" occurs only twice. In Ps. 76:2 it is par. to Zion and obviously means Jerusalem. Echoing the similar sounding adj. it characterises the city as "undamaged," "peaceful." Hence LXX has ἐν εἰρήνῃ. The ref. in the Melchizedek episode in Gn. 14:18 (LXX Σαλημ) is debated. Since there is no closer definition except for the vicinity of the valley שָׁוֵה [52] — "this is the king's vale" — some think the ref. is to some other place rather than Jerusalem. [53] Yet Ps. 76:2, the etym. of Jerusalem and the connecting of Melchizedek with the Davidic dynasty in Ps. 110:4 all support the view that this is Jerusalem, as many witnesses state. [54] In this case Salem is obviously a code-name. The full word is intentionally avoided since it already had a plainly developed theological ref. at the time when the story in Gn. 14 was written.

---

letter 290 in lines 14-17: "The capital of the district of Jerusalem whose name is Bīt Šulmani ... has turned recreant." Bīt Ninib can be taken thus since the god Šalmānu or Sulmānu is obviously a designation of the god Ninurta = Ninib and the equation makes sense. But one may ask whether the ref. is not to a district in the Jerusalem territory rather than to the actual capital of the royal writer.

[47] Schröder, op. cit., No. 145, 6.
[48] Ibid., 42, col. II, 20; 72, 10 and 19; 78, 12.
[49] On this whole question cf. de Liagre Böhl, op. cit.
[50] This form is found in the name of the Assyr. king Salmanassar = Šulmānu-ašaridu, "Sulmānu is the first in rank (among the gods)."
[51] The place-name יְרוּאֵל in 2 Ch. 20:16 (cf. also יְרִיאֵל in 1 Ch. 7:2) is a par.
[52] Acc. to Jos. Ant., 7, 243 f. it was near Jerusalem.
[53] Some follow Hier. Ep., 73, 7 (MPL, 22 [1845] 680) here, who on the basis of Σαλίμ in Jn. 3:23 suggests the insignificant place south of Scythopolis (Besan). Others follow Eus. Onomasticon (GCS, 11, p. 150, 1 ff.), 290, 55 ff. who equates it with Salem east of Shechem. Cf. in detail P. Winter, "'Nazareth' and 'Jerusalem' in Luke chs. I and II," NTSt, 3 (1957), 136-142.
[54] Thus Genesis-Apocryphon in Col. 22, 13 expressly identifies Salem as Jerusalem by the note היא ירושלם. There is no reason to see in this an addition, as P. Winter does in "Note on Salem-Jerusalem," Nov. Test., 2 (1957), 151 f. Similarly the Tg. and Jos. Ant., 1, 180 τὴν μέντοι Σόλυμα ὕστερον ἐκάλεσεν Ἱεροσόλυμα equate the two.

b. Only in Is. 29:1 f., 7 do we find אֲרִיאֵל (LXX Αριηλ). [55] In Ez. 43:15 f. this means "sacrificial hearth" in the sanctuary on which was a fire for burning the offerings. [56] In 2 S. 23:20; 1 Ch. 11:22, however, it means "warrior," "hero" (taken as a proper name in LXX 2 S. and LXX L 1 Ch.). [57] It is a proper name in Ezr. 8:16. Is. obviously had in view "the city where David moved into camp" in 29:1. The "sacrificial hearth" denotes Solomon's part of the city with the palace and temple precincts, and this in turn represents the whole city. [58]

c. Finally the city is called יְבוּס "Jebus" (LXX Ιεβους, also in Jos. 18:28 for הַיְבוּסִי) in Ju. 19:10 f.; 1 Ch. 11:4. It never actually bore this name. The idea that it might have done so is due to the fact that it was inhabited by the Canaanite Jebusites.

4. The Use of the Names Zion and Jerusalem.

It is patent that the use of Zion and Jerusalem is uneven, → n. 1, 16, 17. As compared with Jerusalem Zion is far less prominent in Ez, Mal., Ezr. and Neh. and practically also in 2 S., 1 K. and 1-2 Ch., since in these books Zion is used only 4 times for the actual Canaanite city of the Jebusites. It is also comparatively or extremely rare in 2 K., Jer., Zech. and Cant. On the other hand it is more prominent than Jerusalem in Ps. and Lam.

This state of affairs may be explained by the use of Zion (partially par. to Jerusalem) for various aspects → 307, 13 ff. The most common employment is for the city of the eschatological age of salvation (Is. 1-39, Jer., Dt. Is. and Tt. Is., Joel, Mi. 4 and Zech. 1-9). Quite often, too, it denotes the seat and city of God, esp. in the Ps. and also in some prophetic sayings. Another group with a smaller number of instances is constituted by the use for the royal residence and capital, the symbol of the people or community (esp. Dt. Is., Ps. and Lam.), the cultic site and temple city (esp. Ps. and Lam.). Even less common is the use of Zion for the city of sin and judgment (mainly Jer.), for the court and sacral centre (Ps.), and for mythical aspects. It is seldom used for subsidiary concepts and not at all for the city of theocracy, perhaps because of its strong eschatological thrust.

In pre-exilic prophecy Zion, like Jerusalem, is the royal residence and capital which is also the city of sin and judgment. Other instances in the prophets belong for the most part to exilic and post-exilic eschatology. Dt. Is. uses Zion in part as a symbol of the community. In the Ps. the name denotes esp. the seat and city of God, also the community and the site of the cultus and temple; sometimes, too, court-sacral, mythical and eschatological aspects are indicated. In Lam. Zion is used for the people or community, for the site of the cultus and temple, and rarely for the city of sin and judgment. In contrast the name Jerusalem does not concentrate on specific aspects; it is used fairly evenly for all aspects.

II. The Historical Development of the Significance of Zion-Jerusalem.

Jerusalem does not enjoy significance by virtue of its natural features or situation. These were in fact a hindrance and might well have condemned the city to obscurity

---

[55] Perhaps at Is. 33:7 one should read אֲרִיאֵל or אֲרִיאֵלִים "people of Ariel" for the corrupt אֶרְאֶלָם.

[56] For derivation and other details cf. K. Galling in G. Fohrer-K. Galling, *Ez., Hndbch. AT,* I, 13 (1955), 239 f.

[57] Cf. for details W. Rudolph, *Chronikbücher, Hndbch. AT,* I, 21 (1955), 98 f.

[58] For details of the debate about this cf. Vincent noms, 111-115; Jérusalem, III, 613 f.

rather than development and prominence. [59] Natural features favoured other places in Palestine for the capital rather than Jerusalem, which is not at a central point in the country and which is also hard of access in the mountains of Judah. Indeed, it is not even the natural centre of the narrower territory of Judah. Its rise to the significance it attained was not due to nature but to historical events. This rise took place over many centuries and was not uniform ; there were frequent and long periods of recession.

1. The Pre-Israelite and Early Israelite Period.

In the pre-Israelite age Jerusalem and district, [60] like many other towns, was one of the city states which characterised bronze-age Palestine. It was inhabited — at least later — by the Jebusites [61] and ruled by a city king. Obviously, then, it never played more than a local role and was never the capital of a comprehensive state or of Palestine as a whole. As an independent principality it may be traced from the 19th/18th century to almost the end of the second millennium B.C. with the help of the Egypt. execration texts → n. 27. But archaeological excavations in various parts of the city of the Jebusites or of David [62] show that the beginning of the settlement is to be put earlier. [63] The 6 Amarna letters which the city king Abdi-Hepa [64] sent to Pharaoh c. 1360 (→ n. 30) are concerned about the same things as the other letters and tell little about the specific history of Jerusalem. Another king of Jerusalem mentioned in the OT tradition is Melchizedek, Gn. 14:18; Ps. 110:4. It may be seen from him that the king exercised priestly functions. [65]

Acc. to J the city of Jerusalem was originally in the sphere of interest of the tribe of Benjamin ; P takes the same view in Jos. 15:8; 18:16. More to the pt. than this theoretical allotment is the express statement that the city could not at first be taken, so that the Jebusites lived on as neighbours of the Benjamites (Ju. 1:21) and the men of Judah (Jos. 15:63). Jerusalem was regarded as a foreign city in which no Israelite would spend the night since no compatriots lived there, Ju. 19:11 f. Thus after the conquest Jerusalem was pretty well an independent city state which so sharply divided Judah and related groups in the South from the main body of Israelites settled in the North that apparently they did not submit to the monarchy of Saul but developed separately. The later rise of independent and divided kingdoms in Judah and Israel was mainly due to the existence of Canaanite Jerusalem.

---

[59] On what follows cf. A. Alt, "Jerusalems Aufstieg," ZDMG, 79 (1925), 1-19.

[60] This district was certainly not large ; in the case of many city states it might be no more than the setting. In the case of Jerusalem the natural setting is a sunken plain between the mountain ridges. This is of about 3 km. diameter between the semi-circular crest to the West and the similar chain of the Mt. of Olives to the East.

[61] These usually come last in the lists of Palestinian nations, Gn. 15:21; Ex. 3:8, 17; Dt. 7:1; Jos. 3:10; Ju. 3:5; 1 K. 9:20; 2 Ch. 8:7 etc. They are next to the last in Jos. 11:3, in the middle in Nu. 13:29; Ezr. 9:1; Neh. 9:8. The Hexateuch sources obviously use a current arrangement in the lists. The Jebusites are called descendants of Canaan in Gn. 10:16; 1 Ch. 1:14 and the inhabitants of ancient Jerusalem in Jos. 15:63; Ju. 1:21; acc. to 2 S. 5:6, 8 they lived in the district (אֶרֶץ) as well as the city. The name of the city in Jos. 15:8; 18:16, 28 also shows that they were the inhabitants.

[62] R. Weill, La cité de David, I. Campagne de 1913-1914 (1920); II. Campagne de 1923-1924 (1947); R. A. S. Macalister-J. G. Duncan, "Excavations on the Hill of Ophel, Jerusalem 1923-1925," Palestine Exploration Fund Annual, 4 (1926); J. W. Crowfoot-G. M. Fitzgerald, "Excavations in the Tyropoeon Valley, Jerusalem 1926," ibid., 5 (1929).

[63] Decades ago very early ceramics were found by excavation, cf. H. Vincent, Jérusalem sous terre : les récentes fouilles d'Ophel (1911), 30-32, Plates 7-12.

[64] The city king has the Hittite or Hurrian name ARAD-hepa = Abdi-Hepa or Puti-Hepa. Reminiscence of the city's early Amorite or Hittite history seems to have influenced Ez. 16:3.

[65] E in Jos. 10:1, 3 mentions a city king Adonizedek of Jerusalem, but the elaboration of this in vv. 3, 5, 23 and the list of captured kings, including that of Jerusalem, in 12:10 are ascribed to D. Since the Adonibezek of Ju. 1:6 f. (J) is not called the king his relation

2. The Period of the Davidic Monarchy to Josiah.

a. When David became king of Judah (2 S. 2:4) and then Israel (5:3) he saw the need both to set aside the Canaanite barrier between the two states and also to choose a residence acceptable to both. He solved the double problem by the surprise capture of Jerusalem. The short account of this in 2 S. 5:6-8 is difficult both textually and materially, so that there can be no certainty as to the details. [66] The important thing is, however, that David took the city in a private attack by his mercenaries. The result was that he did not incorporate it into either North or South but made it and its territory his own possession, so that it acquired the new name the "city of David." During the whole period of the Davidic dynasty it remained the possession of the kings and politically occupied a special position alongside both Judah and Israel. To some degree its increasing importance rests on this; the high estimation of the Davidic dynasty in Judah was transferred to the royal city as well. David seems to have made no basic alterations in the conquered city. With the help of Phoenician builders and materials he simply built a new palace for himself and his court and brought a small part of the land to the North into the walled city, 2 S. 5:9-11.

Since David's rule over Jerusalem rested on the right of conquest he simply became the successor of the previous kings of the Canaanite city state. He took over their rights and duties, including the priestly functions rooted in Canaanite tradition, cf. Ps. 110:4. In this connection the cult of אֵל עֶלְיוֹן was fused with the belief in Yahweh. This is supported by the fact that as compared with the names of the sons born to David in Hebron those of the 11 or 12 born in Jerusalem mostly have El rather than Yahweh as the theophorous element [67] and Jedidiah, the "beloved of Yahweh," receives or adopts the name Solomon (שְׁלֹמֹה), which apart from the echoing of שָׁלוֹם is, like Absalom, connected with the divine name Šlm contained in "Jerusalem." An unmistakable indication of what happened is that the Canaanite priestly family of אֵל עֶלְיוֹן, whose head was then Zadok, now became — at first along with Abiathar the priest of Yahweh, but later alone — the officiating priests of Yahweh. [68] Above all, this fusion, in which Yahweh came out the victor, explains how the most important aspects of the El religion of Jerusalem came to be transferred to Yahweh. [69]

Yet these Canaanite influences were very dangerous and might in time have pushed into the background the distinctive character and inheritance of Israel. David worked against this by seeing to it that the sacred ark, which had been located at Shiloh, was brought up to Jerusalem when the defeat of the Philistines made this possible, 2 S. 6. In this way David transferred the holy traditions of the Mosaic period to Jerusalem and with them the national and religious values embodied in Shiloh. We thus have an extension and development of faith in Yahweh as expressed in the name "Zebaoth, Cherubim-Enthroned." [70]

---

to Adonizedek is not clear. The note in Ju. 1:8 that the men of Judah captured and sacked Jerusalem may be based on a misunderstanding of 1:7.

[66] Cf. for details H. J. Stoebe, "Die Einnahme Jerusalems u. der Sinnôr," ZDPV, 73 (1957), 73-99, who discusses the various theories.

[67] Specifically noted by H. S. Nyberg, op. cit., 373 f.

[68] Cf. esp. H. H. Rowley, "Zadok and Nehushtan," JBL, 58 (1939), 113-141; also "Melchizedek and Zadok (Gn. 14 and Ps. 110)," Festschr. A. Bertholet (1950), 461-472.

[69] For details cf. Schmid, 197.

[70] On this cf. O. Eissfeldt, "Jahwe Zebaoth," Miscellanea Acad. Berolinensia, II, 2 (1950), 128-150. The idea of the Cherubim-Enthroned is Canaanite, but Zebaoth is taken in different ways. Eissfeldt, 135-150 thinks it is an abstr. plur. "might," "mighty one." This is perhaps nearest the mark but cf. Eichrodt Theol. AT, I² (1939), 94 f.: "epitome of all heavenly and earthly being"; A. L. Williams, "The Lord of Hosts," JThSt, 38 (1937), 56; W. F. Albright, From the Stone Age to Christianity (1949), 286: the hosts of Israel; V. Maag, "Jahwäs Heerscharen," Schweizerische Theol. Umschau, 20, 3-4 (1950), 27-52: the nature-powers of Canaan disarmed and subjugated to Yahweh.

The significance of Jerusalem is based on the fact that it is elevated to be the residence of the house of David, that it becomes the place of the presence of Yahweh Zebaoth the Cherubim-Enthroned, and that Yahweh belief is expanded by the incorporation of Canaanite ideas. On the other hand, one need not assume that there was any further development of amphictyonic concepts. [71] In this way David initiated a development which came to its conclusion with the building of the temple by Solomon.

    b. Solomon planned and executed a significant enlargment of the Jerusalem comprised under the name the "city of David." In direct extension of the existing city, and with a common wall to embrace the whole area, he built a new part of the city to the North. The enlargment fulfilled a double purpose. It made possible the building of a new residence corresponding to the public requirements of the ruler of a great kingdom. It also relieved the cramped situation in the older city, since there was room for the growing population alongside the public buildings. The public buildings were of very gt. historical significance for Jerusalem. After the manner of the Egypt. New Kingdom the palace and temple were grouped in a single architectural complex. Since Israel had no building tradition of its own this complex, like David's palace, was constructed on Canaanite models with the help of the Phoenicians.

    The building of the temple proved to be very important for Jerusalem in the age which followed. [72] Since palace and temple were in the same city and surrounded by a wall, clear expression was given to the fact that the temple belonged to the ruling dynasty [73] and was a state sanctuary in which the king's offerings were presented and the official national cultus was practised. Thus Yahweh became the state God and Jerusalem was declared to be the supreme and most eminent cultic site. Since the architecture followed the Canaanite pattern, and its erection continued the dominant practice of established local centres, the sanctuary itself also became a holy place which had its own importance as such and which made possible the infiltration of other Canaanite ideas and customs. Thus the ark very quickly lost its former significance, while the temple cultus to a large degree followed the Canaanite model. Radiating out from Jerusalem there was thus a new shift in Yahweh belief. This was now developed esp. along cultic and national lines.

The building of the temple and the moving of the cultus from the city of David to this brought revolutionary change and development as compared with the beginnings under David, and the further historical role of Jerusalem was mainly due to this. The presence of Yahweh, who now as King controlled a house, was

---

[71] A first pt. against this is that in Saul's time there was apparently no concern about the ark, 1 Ch. 13:3. Again, when moved into Solomon's temple it played no further part and no longer contributed to the importance of Jerusalem. The fear of Jeroboam after the disruption that his subjects might continue to go up to the temple at Jerusalem (1 K. 12:26 ff.) is thought to be a Deuteronomic idea which does not prove either recognition of Jerusalem by Israel or a 10th cent. distinction between the political and religious position of the city. Similarly Jer. 41:5 does not presuppose a continuing acknowledgement of the Jerusalem sanctuary but reflects the incorporation of almost all the earlier kingdom of Israel into Judah under Josiah. In virtue of this pilgrims from various places in Mt. Ephraim could in 586 come to what the Deuteronomic reform had established as the one valid temple, and this led to a distinction between the political and religious significance of Jerusalem.

[72] On the building of the temple cf. K. Möhlenbrink, Der Tempel Salomos (1932); C. Watzinger, Denkmäler Palästinas, I (1933), 88-95; BR, 516-518; W. F. Albright, Archaeology and the Religion of Israel (1942), 139-155; G. E. Wright, Bibl. Arch. (1957), 136-145.

[73] Cf. K. Galling, "Königliche u. nichtkönigl. Stifter beim Tempel v. Jerusalem," ZDPV, 68 (1951), 134-142.

transferred to the temple. The dedicatory speech of Solomon (1 K. 8:12 f.) contains the idea of Yahweh's "dwelling" in Jerusalem. He is connected primarily with the temple itself but then with the temple hill (Is. 8:18 : "He who dwells on the hill of Zion").

c. Already under Solomon some of the border territories broke away. After his death even the union between Judah and Israel was snapped and two separate kingdoms arose. Jerusalem underwent a particular crisis, for it lay close to the border of Judah and might have had to be abandoned as the residence of the house of David. But its aura and the policies of the government overcame all difficulties. [74] Both dynasty and people regarded it as natural to stick to Jerusalem. It is unlikely that the city grew much during the later stages of the monarchy. Its general situation was not in keeping with further expansion. Yet work was done on the walls (2 Ch. 26:9; 27:3; 32:5; 33:14) [75] and the names of new districts are mentioned (2 K. 22:14; Zeph. 1:10 f.). [76] In pre-exilic times, however, the broader and higher western hill was not yet brought into the walled city. [77] Esp. important was the improvement of the water supply under Hezekiah, who brought water from the Gihon spring in the vale of Kidron into the city through the Shiloah tunnel and thus made the city capable of withstanding a long siege, 2 K. 20:20; 2 Ch. 32:30. [78] The need for this may be seen from the fact that on the outbreak of the Syr.-Ephraimite war king Ahaz inspected the water-works in person, Is. 7:3. The Jerusalem temple also continued to play the role assigned to it by Solomon. As the sanctuary of the house of David it was naturally the most important holy place in the state of Judah.

Of all the events under the monarchy up to the death of Josiah in 609 only two affected the position of Jerusalem in any vital way. [79] Sennacherib made a vain attempt to bring it under his control in 701. Against all expectation it was saved by his sudden retreat, 2 K. 18 f. cf. Is. 36 f. Though the historical details are none too clear, since many reasons are given or suggested for the retreat, [80] the episode served to enhance considerably the importance of Jerusalem and its temple. The almost invincible Assyrian had been repulsed by it and forced into a retreat which had the nature of a flight. The Isaiah stories and the sayings of the prophet contained in them show that this experience of deliverance led finally to what was almost the dogma of the inviolability and impregnability of Jerusalem, Jer. 7:4.

The second decisive event was the politico-religious reform of Josiah in yrs. when the Assyrian empire was beginning to crumble (after 626). This included not only

---

[74] To overcome the border problem the Davidic kings were always trying to extend the frontier to the North and occupy as much as possible of Benjamin. For a time at least the border was almost a day's journey north of Jerusalem and this was enough to guard against surprise invasion.

[75] Cf. also in 2 Ch. 26:9 the work to repair the damage done to the northern walls by Jehoash of Israel acc. to 2 K. 14:13.

[76] The most important are the new city (whose name shows it to be later) and the mercantile district ; these are often thought to be the same, cf. BR, 303.

[77] As against Simons, 227-281, and Vincent Jérusalem, I, 90-113. Quite wide of the mark is Dalman, op. cit. (→ n. 14), who assumes that at the latest in David's time there was a double city on the west and east hills, and that Solomon put a new wall round both sections.

[78] Cf. on this Simons, 178-188, 222-225; Vincent Jérus., I, 269-279; on the Shiloah inscr. cf. Galling, op. cit. (→ n. 39), 59 (with bibl.).

[79] We may disregard the sacking by Pharaoh Shishak in 1 K. 14:25 f., the breaking down of the northern wall in 2 K. 14:13, and the Syr.-Ephraim. war in 2 K. 16:5, also the abortive attempts to overthrow the Davidic dynasty in 2 K. 11:1; 21:23; Is. 7:6. As against earlier exegetes the invasion by Philistines and Arabians in 2 Ch. 21:16 f. did not affect Jerusalem ; these were perhaps border forays.

[80] Rumours from Assyria, 2 K. 19:7; approach of an Egypt. relief force, 19:8 f.; plague in the Assyr. camp, 19:35.

the purifying of the temple and cultus but above all the overthrowing of all other shrines in the country. There was left only the one sanctuary in Jerusalem which Yahweh had chosen to cause His name to dwell there. This idea of the election of Jerusalem and its temple derives from Deuteronomic theology and is bound up with the concept of "dwelling" and the restriction of the cultus to Jerusalem.[81] By giving the chosen city a special position as the site of the sanctuary, Deuteronomic theology reached a goal not hitherto attained. Jerusalem became the cultic centre and the most important place for all believing Israelites. This was strengthened by the astonishing political successes of Josiah, who was able to annex large areas from the Palestinian portion of the waning Assyrian empire, so that finally he ruled over at least all the earlier parts of Judah and Israel. In this way Jerusalem again became for a short time, as in the days of David and Solomon, the capital of the greater part of Palestine.

3. The Period of the Last Kings of Judah and the Exile.

Babyl. attacks destroyed the state of Judah in two decades. The territory of Judah was integrated into the provinces of Edom and Ashdod. Jerusalem, however, was treated differently.[82] It still stood, but was no more than the chief place of a small territory which was simply a larger city state, an administratively separated appendage of the neighbouring province of Samaria to the North. Against all expectation Jerusalem survived this annihilating blow. The chosen dynasty of David was ended, but the election of Jerusalem by Yahweh as the only cultic centre had in a short time so firmly embedded itself in the belief of Israel that after its destruction even people from the Isr. territories which had been annexed by Josiah went there on pilgrimage to offer sacrifice, Jer. 41:5. It is true that the Babylonians had destroyed the temple as the sacred symbol of national independence. They had also shaken severely the belief in the city's invincibility, → 304, 28 ff. But this was interpreted as Yahweh's judgment on the sin of Judah, and the gradual development of eschatological hope in a future time of salvation made it supportable.

By and large the importance of Jerusalem grew for many groups of deportees during the exile and inspired them with fervent longings (cf. Ps. 137) and bold expectations (Dt. Is. and other exilic prophecies).[83] The eschatologically induced enhancement of the regard for Jerusalem was facilitated by the fact that after the overshadowing of the ark by the temple as the place of the presence of Yahweh the temple building itself could be overshadowed by the sacred site of Jerusalem as the geographically secure and only valid cultic centre, so that the city with its holy hill could develop into a focal point for believing Israelites both in Palestine and also in the Dispersion. In the time which follows not merely the temple but Jerusalem itself and the temple hill become decisively important. As compared with the age of the monarchy relations are reversed. The high regard for Jerusalem no longer rests primarily on its splendour as a royal city (→ 302, 1 ff.), which is then enhanced by its inner significance as the site of the temple. Its repute now rests on its inner significance for faith, which is enhanced by its outward position. There thus takes place a change which makes

---

[81] → IV, 145-168; cf. T. C. Vriezen, *Die Erwählung Israels nach dem AT* (1953), esp. 46 f., but also K. Koch, "Zur Gesch. d. Erwählungsvorstellung in Israel," ZAW, 67 (1955), 205-226.

[82] On what follows cf. A. Alt, "Die Rolle Samarias bei der Entstehung d. Judt.," *Kleine Schriften z. Gesch. d. Volkes Israel,* II (1953), 316-337.

[83] For the position in Palestine cf. E. Janssen, *Juda in der Exilszeit* (1956). But many of the details here are open to criticism, cf. the review by F. Maass in ThLZ, 82 (1957), 685 f.

Jerusalem a religious and spiritual centre rather than predominantly a political centre.

4. The Post-Exilic Period.

a. In the early post-exilic period the religious and spiritual significance of Jerusalem increased even more. [84] It is true that the Persians took over from the Babylonians the provisional arrangements made for Judah. But then the upper classes deported from Jerusalem and Judah returned, the population was restored to its earlier structure apart from the monarchy, and Jerusalem was again invested with cultic authority, so that it regained its religious privileges in relation to the rest of Judah, Samaria and Galilee. This had two consequences. On the one hand, with the complete loss of sovereignty and political autonomy there necessarily developed in and around Jerusalem a community which was essentially a cultic and later a temple community. On the other hand, the restoration of cultic rights led to the building of the second temple in Jerusalem, even if this could be completed only in 515 as a result of the work of the prophets Haggai and Zechariah. This temple, however, was not a royal possession ; it belonged to the people. [85] This was of very gt. significance. The new temple was not merely a focus for the Jerusalem community. It developed increasingly into a religious centre for the growing Judaism of the Dispersion.

b. The separate province of Judah, which was formed gradually and over a long period in time, was finally established by Nehemiah with the support of the Babylonian Dispersion. [86] Nehemiah calls himself the governor appointed by the king "in the land of Judah," Neh. 5:14. The existence of a special governor in Judah alongside that in Samaria is attested for the year 408 by the Elephantine Pap. [87] Connected with these measures was the rebuilding of the city walls in addition to the temple castle, which had already been built in the post-exilic period, Neh. 2:8 cf. 3:1; 7:2. [88] Though the province embraced only a part of the total area of Judah, [89] Jerusalem again achieved the status of a capital, even if of lower rank. In distinction from the pre-exilic period with its predominantly Canaanite population the city was ncw inhabited almost exclusively by Israelites. Begun after the exile, this development too reached its climax under Nehemiah.

The political constitution with its degree of separation was followed by a constitutive social order including the religious separation demanded already by Haggai (2:10-14). This was the work of Ezra. Seeking to create around the temple a divine community under the leadership of the priestly hierarchy, Ezra founded Judaism in the true sense

---

[84] Cf. on what follows esp. A. Alt, op. cit.; W. Rudolph, Esr. u. Neh., Hndbch. AT, I, 20 (1949), XXVI f.; for a different view of the early post-exil. period cf. K. Galling, "Die Exilswende in d. Sicht des Propheten Sacharja," VT, 2 (1952), 18-36; also "Von Naboned zu Darius," ZDPV, 69 (1953), 42-64; 70 (1954), 4-32.

[85] Cf. Galling, op. cit. (→ n. 73).

[86] On the difficult question of the relation between Ezra and Nehemiah, esp. chronologically, cf. the survey by H. H. Rowley, "Nehemiah's Mission and Its Background," Bulletin of the John Rylands Libr., 37 (1954-55), 528-561.

[87] E. Sachau, Aram. Pap. u. Ostraka aus einer jüd. Militärkolonie zu Elephantine (1911), No. 1/2, cf. No. 3 and 4; A. E. Cowley, Aram. Pap. of the Fifth Cent. B.C. (1923), No. 30-33.

[88] This is usually regarded as a precursor of the castle which Hyrcanus built and which was later replaced by Herod's Antonia, but Dalman, op. cit. (→ n. 14) distinguishes between them.

[89] To the province of Judah belonged the area between Bethlehem and the north side of Hebron and the eastern part of the highlands around Kegila, i.e., of the earlier districts Jericho, Beersheba, Beth-Zur, Bethlehem and Kegila. The southern districts of Debir, Hebron and Maon formed the province of Arabia (later Idumaea), the western districts of Ekron, Adullam and Lachish belonged to the province of Ashdod.

and also gave Jerusalem its final consecration. Thus for all the differences the later Chronicler can find the ideal of theocracy realised in the concrete Jewish community. Finally it is also due to the Persian measures taken up to the time of Nehemiah that Jerusalem could in essentials maintain its character under the rule of the Ptolemies (from 301 onwards) and the Seleucids (from 198 onwards). For Judah with Jerusalem was the land of the people, not the king. It was the distinctive dwelling-place of the ἔθνος τῶν ᾽Ιουδαίων which was normally ruled, and represented before the king, not by a royal governor but by the native aristocracy in the form of a *gerousia*. Only Antiochus IV Epiphanes made the rash attempt to turn Jerusalem into a Hell. πόλις. At the very latest in the Hell. age the broader and higher western hill, which had not been inhabited before the exile (→ n. 77), was brought into the city boundaries and defended by an extension of the wall. This is the so-called second wall. [90]

III. Aspects and Meanings of the Terms Zion and Jerusalem. [91]

1. Royal Residence and Capital.

a. Many of the instances of the name Jerusalem, and rather fewer of Zion, relate to the city as a political concept : the Canaanite city state in Jos. 10:1 ff. etc., the capital and residence of David in 2 S. 5:5 ff. etc., the empire of David and Solomon in 2 S. 8:7-1 K. 11:42, then often the capital and royal residence of Judah, 1 K. 12:18-2 K. 24:18 etc. Also to be noted in this connection is the official Persian phrase "Jerusalem in Judah," Ezr. 1:2 f., i.e., the Jerusalem located in Judah. Similarly Nehemiah takes measures to defend the capital of the new province of Judah (Neh. 7:1-3) and to increase its population (7:4-72a).

b. Jerusalem often occurs in longer or shorter political formulations in which the surrounding territory or other territories are also listed. Thus Is. 8:14 refers to Jerusalem, the royal possession, along with Judah and Israel as the "two houses of Israel." In Jer. 17:26; 32:44; 33:13 the state of Judah is described acc. to its geographical [92] and political structure. Apart from the cities of Judah and the land of Benjamin Jerusalem and district (סְבִיבוֹת or סְבִיבִים) is an integral part. Mostly we find the short formulation which mentions the city state of Jerusalem (Jer. 14:19 Zion) [93] and the tribal state of Judah (Is. 3:1, 8; Jer. 2:28 etc.), the two most important parts of the kingdom, the tiny territory of Benjamin being omitted. Acc. to Jer. 19:15 "Jerusalem and all its cities" in Jer. 34:1 refers in the last analysis to the provincial towns of Judah. The influence of this political distinction may still be found in the different relationships of the exilic and post-exilic periods, in which we find "Jerusalem and Judah" or the "cities of Judah" (Zech. 1:12; Ezr. 4:6) or "Zion and the cities of Judah" (Ps. 69:35; Lam. 5:11).

2. Court-Sacral Aspects.

In connection with the significance of Jerusalem as the capital and royal residence there are the beginnings of a court-sacral theology in which the city plays a certain

---

[90] Cf. on this H. Guthe, "Die zweite Mauer Jerusalems u. die Bauten Constantins am heiligen Grabe," ZDPV, 8 (1885), 245-287; H. Vincent, "La deuxième enceinte de Jérus.," *Rev. Bibl.*, 11 (1902), 31-57, also Jérus., I, 90-113; Simons, 282-343.

[91] We are not considering the rare secondary meanings of Zion-Jerus.: 1. geographical in Jer. 22:8 f.; 37:12; Ez. 7:23; 9:9; Zech. 14:4 f.; Ps. 125:2; 133:3; 2. topographical as the city of David and Ophel, eschatological reconstruction in Jer. 31:38-40; Zech. 14:10, details in Jer., Ezr.-Neh., 1-2 Ch.; 3. sociological in Cant. 1:5; 2:7 etc.; 4. historical in Qoh. 1:1 etc.; Est. 2:6; and 5. chronological in Zech. 7:7; Ps. 137:7; Est. 2:6; Da. 1:1; cf. Ez. 40:1.

[92] The geographical structure includes the plains, hills and Negeb. It is put before the political structure in Jer. 33:13.

[93] Similarly Jer. 4:31 differentiates between Zion, which is viewed ironically, and the land, which is thought of with sympathy.

part. Ref. may be made here to the story of the setting up of the first altar to Yahweh in Jerusalem in 2 S. 24, which is a kind of ἱερὸς λόγος about Jerusalem. One may also mention the story of the ark, which tells of its adventures in the war with the Philistines and its later removal to Jerusalem, 1 S. 4-6; 2 S. 6. The uniting of royal and priestly functions derives from the Melchizedek tradition, which court theology related specifically to the Davidic dynasty, Ps. 110:4. Furthermore a vital element in the enthronement of the king was his adoption by Yahweh on Zion, the holy hill of Yahweh, Ps. 2:6. So, too, was his symbolical sacral investiture with the sceptre as investiture with the power conferred by Yahweh, Ps. 110:2. The later or post-Solomonic justification and authentication of the Davidic dynasty as a whole in 2 S. 7:8-16, 18-29 invests the monarchy in Jerusalem with a special consecration. This court-sacral theology finds its ultimate expression during the monarchy in the Deuteronomic statement that the house of David and Jerusalem are divinely elected, 1 K. 11:13, 32. This states and enhances the official view in a new way.[94] Similarly Ps. 132 relates the divine oath to David in v. 11 f. with the choice of Zion as the dwelling-place and resting-place of Yahweh in v. 13 f. Hence the official theology expects gt. material blessings (v. 15), the inner happiness of the community of the righteous (v. 16), and the might and permanence of the monarchy (v. 17). The later Ps. 78 also speaks of the choice of Zion as the cultic centre and of David as the righteous and able ruler (vv. 68-72). Nevertheless, one should not overestimate the importance of this court theology with its combining of Yahweh, monarchy and Jerusalem.

3. Symbol of the People or Community.

a. Sometimes the term Zion-Jerusalem is used in transition from designation of the city to symbolising of its inhabitants. It is the city of the temple and servants of Yahweh, the community (Ps. 79:1 f.), which as Zion exults in Yahweh with the cities of Judah (Ps. 97:8). It can also be personified and as such it may speak (Mi. 7:8-20), suffer (Is. 51:17-23), or be delivered (Is. 46:13), since the divine community is within it (Ps. 147:12). Esp. in the Chronicler, who often speaks expressly of the inhabitants of Jerusalem (e.g., 2 Ch. 32:26, 33), we find not only the influence of the earlier political structuring of the kingdom as Judah and Jerusalem but also a use of the two terms together for the land and the city inhabited by the divine community of Israel. The terms symbolise the dwelling-places of the theocratic community, 1 Ch. 5:41; 2 Ch. 2:6 etc. In all such instances one may observe an approximation to actual equation with the people or community.

b. Along with specific ref. to the inhabitants of Zion-Jerusalem (→ 294, 1 ff.; 296, 6 ff.) we find from Jer. onwards the use of the city as a symbol for the people or community. Thus the "leading away of Jerusalem" in Jer. 1:3 is that of its inhabitants. We find alongside one another "Jerusalem" and "this people" in Jer. 4:11; 8:5, "Judah, Jerusalem and this wicked people" in Jer. 13:9 f., "Judah" and "Zion" in Jer. 14:19, and "Jerusalem" and "the inhabitants of Zion" in Jer. 51:35; the "remnant of Jerusalem" in Jer. 24:8 also refers to specific groups of people. Jer. 4:14 summons Jerusalem to cleanse itself from evil, but obviously refers to the population, cf. 4:3 f. In Ez. 5:5 the hairs used in the symbolic action are said to represent Jerusalem ("this is Jerusalem") but in fact they represent the inhabitants. Similarly in Lam. Zion in part embodies the people as a predominantly political entity, the ref. even being to all Israel in 1:17: Zion - Jacob - Jerusalem. The concept "daughter of Jerusalem" is partly an embodiment of the city and partly an embodiment of the people dwelling in it, 2:1. The true glory of Zion is its young men, 4:2. For Dt. Is. Jerusalem is not just the Palestinian city but also

---

[94] Chronicles, too, speaks of the election of David in 1 Ch. 28:4; 2 Ch. 6:6, of Solomon in 1 Ch. 28:5 f.; 29:1, and of the city of Jerusalem in 2 Ch. 6:6, 34, 38; 12:13; 33:7, though also of the priests and Levites in 2 Ch. 29:11 and of the Jerusalem temple in 2 Ch. 7:16.

a symbol of "my people" (Is. 40:1 f.), i.e., the total community in all places and times, so that they are called after the city (48:2) and Zion can receive the designation "my people," 51:16. The parallelism of "Jerusalem" and "my people" in expectation of the promised last time may also be seen in Is. 65:19-25, while in Is. 59:20 we find together "Zion" and "those that turn from transgression in Jacob." Finally some passages may be adduced from the Ps. in this connection. In Ps. 78:68 "tribe of Judah" and "hill of Zion" are par., in 126:1 the ref. might just as well be to "us" as to "Zion," in 128:5 f. "Zion-Jerusalem" is a symbol for Israel, and in 149:2 the "sons of Zion" are Israel. Hence Jerusalem is exclusively a city of the Jews. No one else has any part, right, or memorial in it, Neh. 2:20; cf. Hag. 2:10-14; this is why the temple must be cleansed, Neh. 13:4-9.

4. Seat and City of God, Cultic Centre and Temple City.

a. One may trace at least in outline (→ 302, 1 ff.) the historical development of the article of faith that Zion-Jerusalem is the true site of the presence of Yahweh. First, the presence of Yahweh Zebaoth, the Cherubim-Enthroned, is brought up to Jerusalem with the symbol of the ark. Perhaps "foot-stool of his feet" in Lam. 2:1 also refers to the ark. After the building of Solomon's temple we find the expression the "dwelling" of Yahweh; this says that first the temple (1 K. 8:12 f.), then the city hill and the city itself is God's seat. [95] An important v. relating to this extension and transferring of the expression "to dwell" is Ps. 43:3, which equates the temple and the holy hill as Yahweh's dwelling. If there is here an obvious interrelation between "to dwell" and "hill," already in the days of Isaiah the term is connected with the hill of Zion (Is. 8:18; Ps. 74:2), and it is later extended to Jerusalem in general, which in its totality is the dwelling-place of Yahweh (Jl. 3:21; Ps. 76:2 etc.). The idea is also combined with Deuteronomic election theology, Ps. 132:13 f. A contrary view may be found in 1 K. 8:27; Is. 66:1 f. Since the temple is a kind of earthly palace corresponding to the heavenly palace of Yahweh, Jerusalem may also be called the city of King Yahweh. Jer. 8:19 and 14:19 represent at least the popular view that the temple is the palace of Yahweh the King and Jerusalem His royal city. Ez. 43:7 unites the monarchy of Yahweh with His presence in the temple. According to Ps. 9:11 He is enthroned on Zion. The two thoughts are combined in the Song of Moses at the Red Sea: Yahweh has prepared in Jerusalem a dwelling, the temple, in order that He may reign there for ever as King, Ex. 15:17 f. The city hill is also included as the hill of His possession and it is said to be the hill of God in view of the fact that Yahweh dwells and reigns there. Deuteronomic theology defines the relation of Yahweh to the holy city more precisely by saying that He causes His name to dwell there; in this way it plainly refers the earlier idea of Yahweh's dwelling in Jerusalem to His presence in revelation → V, 256, 15 ff.; 506, 22 ff. [96] To this Deuteronomic theology adds the idea of election (→ 304, 33 ff.). In Dt.

---

[95] As compared with יָשַׁב "to sit" or "to dwell" שָׁכַן has been taken to mean "to live in tents" in the nomadic sense, so that God "dwells" in heaven but the mystery of His presence on earth is confessed by saying that He "tabernacles" among His people, cf. F. M. Cross Jr., "The Tabernacle," *The Biblical Archaeologist*, 10 (1947), 65-68; G. E. Wright, *Bibl. Arch.* (1957), 144 f. But שָׁכַן comes from the Accad. šakānu "to lay down" = Ugaritic škn "to dwell" and not from a nomadic concept, while יָשַׁב comes from the Ugaritic jtb (jšb) "to sit" → σκηνόω.

[96] On the LXX transl. → VI, 524, 10 ff.

itself this is limited to the cultic site but the Deuteronomic authors of Kings extend it to the city of Jerusalem, 1 K. 11:13, 32, 36; 14:21; 2 K. 21:4, 7. Chronicles also speaks of an election both of the temple itself (2 Ch. 7:16) and also of the city of Jerusalem (2 Ch. 6:6; 12:13; 33:7). Thus the Jerusalem temple, Mt. Zion and Jerusalem are not merely the only legitimate cultic centre; they are also signs of the revelatory presence of God.

b. Crucial for the growing reputation of Jerusalem as the city of God was the steady extension and transferring of the holiness (→ I, 90, 4 ff.) of the *loci* of revelation : from the ark to the temple, then the temple hill, then the whole city. The equation of the temple and the temple hill is already made in Ps. 15:1; 24:3. The temple is parallel to the "hill of Yahweh" or the "holy hill." Since this is called "Zion," Zion is the holy hill of Yahweh, Is. 31:4; Jl. 2:1. Thus the temple and Zion can be parallel. As Ps. 78:68 f. compares the building of the temple with the creation of the world, so according to Ps. 68:16 the hill of God, Zion, is linked with the temple as a symbol of God's revelatory presence. Furthermore the holy hill of Yahweh is set in parallelism with Jerusalem as His city (Is. 45:13) in Da. 9:16 f. Since God loves Zion-Jerusalem, the temple city, more than all other places in Israel and will not allow any other cultic centres, He Himself has founded it on the holy hills as the "city of God"; in this way Ps. 87 draws all the threads together. Hence Jerusalem is ultimately the "city of God" (Ps. 46:4), the "city of our God, of the great King" (Ps. 48:2), the "holy city" (Is. 48:2; 52:1; Neh. 11:1). "To Zion" means "to Yahweh" (Jer. 31:6) and "from Zion" means "from Yahweh" (Ps. 14:7).

c. It is thus a common belief that Yahweh, who dwells in Jerusalem, is God in Zion, Ps. 65:1; 99:2; 135:21.

When Ez. in a vision sees Yahweh burn and abandon the city (9:3a; 10:2, 7, 18 f.; 11:22 f.), he takes for granted God's revelatory presence in help or judgment. The Persian government also uses the official phrase : "This is the God who is in Jerusalem," Ezr. 1:3, cf. His "habitation in Jerusalem" in 7:15. In keeping with Yahweh's revelatory presence in Jerusalem, the seat and city of God, is the fact that theophany is from thence as the new Sinai in Ps. 68:17. Ez. has a vision of Yahweh in Babylon when Yahweh, following the caravan route, approaches from the North, Ez. 1:4. The manifestation of Yahweh is reflected on Zion, the "crown of beauty," Ps. 50:2. [97] Later Yahweh comes from Zion to judgment. The saying of Jer. which depicts Yahweh as a warrior roaring from heaven over His pasture Jerusalem (Jer. 25:30) is applied in Jl. 3:16 to Zion-Jerusalem as the true seat of the revelation of Yahweh, and in Am. 1:2 it is prefixed to the whole book as a motto : From Zion-Jerusalem as the city of God judgment goes forth over Northern Israel (Am. 1:2) and the nations (Jl. 3:16). But Mt. Zion and Jerusalem are also symbols of Yahweh's protection; eternal as they is God's help for those who trust in Him, Ps. 125:1 f. Thus a new blessing can even be coined : "Yahweh bless thee from Zion," Ps. 128:5; 134:3; this confers the powers of the holy places on those who are thus blessed.

d. Micah sees no future for Jerusalem as the cultic centre (3:12). In Baruch's account of the temple oration of Jeremiah (Jer. 7:1-15) the threat is extended from the temple to Jerusalem as the temple city, 26:6-12. Nevertheless, there is

---

[97] On the other hand in the account of the call of Isaiah in Is. 6 the Jerusalem temple can hardly be the site of the theophany but rather the heavenly palace of Yahweh seen in a vision. Cf. on this I. P. Seierstad, *Die Offenbarungserlebnisse der Propheten Am., Js.*

confidence that it will survive. For Zion, first the temple and then more broadly the city of Jerusalem, is the foundation of Yahweh (Is. 14:32; Ps. 125:1; 132:13 f.). The whole eminence with the temple is holy to Him as His possession, Ez. 43:1-9. Though the great post-exilic Diaspora, scattered but growing increasingly in importance, is unable to take part in the temple cultus except by pilgrimage, it not only clings to the indissoluble relation between temple and community and the decisive redemptive significance of membership of the temple community, which even eunuchs and aliens may join (Is. 56:1-8), but also regards the temple as a house of prayer for all nations (→ II, 793, 2 ff.) and the spiritual centre of the whole world, Is. 56:7. There may be distinction between Jerusalem and the temple (Ps. 68:29), for which the metaphors of the tent (Lam. 2:4) or tabernacle (2:6) are used, but in general, because of the equation of Zion and the sanctuary (Ps. 20:2), the whole city is regarded as the temple city (Ps. 48; Ezr. 5:15 ff. etc.), since the temple is situated in the midst of it (Ps. 116:19). If God is seen in Zion (Ps. 84:7), the reference is to the climax which the pilgrim experiences in the cultus. In this context Zion is both the cultic centre and also the cultus itself which is practised there, → I, 519, 22 f.; II, 667, 17 ff.

5. City of Sin and Judgment.

a. In contrast to the positive estimation of Jerusalem is the prophetic criticism in which the city is granted no privileged status but regarded as the city of sin in the midst of a sinful people. Mostly the prophetic denunciation applies equally to Jerusalem and Judah, so that the city as such is not iniquitous as distinct from the land. If Micah attacks and threatens Jerusalem and Samaria in particular this is because those who are truly responsible, and who must bear the chief blame for the sin of the whole people, live in the capital as the centre of national life, Mi. 1:5. The capital plays in relation to the country the representative role which is played in individual localities by the "gate," the place of public life, Mi. 1:9.

As always in prophetic theology the true sin of Jerusalem or its inhabitants consists in apostasy from God and rebellion against Him, Is. 3:8, 16 f.; 22:1-14; 28:14. This sin is dramatically depicted as the infidelity of Jerusalem, which has sunk to the level of a harlot, → VI, 587, 8 ff. The metaphor points to defection from God by the cultic sin and idolatry which prophetic criticism finds in Jerusalem no less than the land of Judah or Israel, Is. 10:11; 65:11; Jer. 1:16; 2:28; 11:13. [98] Equally serious is the ethical and social sin that Micah finds in the building activity of his time, which involves wickedness and blood, Mi. 3:10. [99] Jeremiah recalls that there was an earlier period of love for Yahweh and he compares this to a honeymoon, Jer. 2:2 ff. → I, 32, 35 ff. In his own time, however, he does not think he can find a single upright man in Jerusalem (5:1). The very essence of the city is oppression; it causes iniquity to gush forth like water (6:6 f.). Ezekiel thinks that ethical and social transgressions as well as the religious and cultic sins summarised as idolatry are so serious that he simply calls Jerusalem the "city of blood-guiltiness," Ez. 22:2 f., 19; 24:6. In addition

---

u. Jer. (1946), 65 f.; J. Steinmann, Le prophète Isaïe² (1955), 34-40, but also G. Fohrer, Das Buch Jesaja, I (1960), 22.

[98] On prophetic criticism of the temple → III, 238, 43 ff.

[99] On prophetic criticism of wealth → VI, 324, 6 ff.

there is political sin, i.e., wooing the favour of the great powers (16:23-25; the ref. in vv. 26-29 is to the politics of the last years of Zedekiah), with treaties which involve also religious and cultic commitments. [100]

In view of the prophetic criticism it is understandable that Jer. should constantly refer contemptuously to Jerusalem as "this city" (Jer. 21:1-10 etc.) and that Ezekiel should sometimes do this too (Ez. 11:2, 6). [101] It is also understandable that Ezekiel should stress the pagan descent of Jerusalem from the Amorites and Hittites, that unlike Is. (1:21) he should regard this as setting the tone for the city from the very beginning, and that in contrast to contemporary Deuteronomic theology he should count the city as part of the heathen world, 16:1-3. The people of Jerusalem are worthless by nature, Ez. 15:6. If a company of them is saved from judgment, it is simply in order that the exiles may view them and see in them the justness of the punishment, 14:22. They are more disobedient than all peoples, 5:6, cf. Jer. 2:10 f. on Judah generally. They are worse than Samaria and Sodom, Lam. 4:6; Ez. 16:44-58. In the Deuteronomic spirit the accusation is levelled more against their rejection of the Law, their idolatry (Am. 2:4 f.), or the pagan abomination of marriage with strange women (Mal. 2:11).

b. Because Jerusalem is the city of sin, it will also be the city of judgment. This is the threat of the prophets. The city which David once besieged and took will again be besieged in fulfilment of the divine punishment, Is. 29:1-7. Then the joyful city will be laid waste, 32:13 f. Yahweh will search it closely to bring all the guilty to account, Zeph. 1:12. In Nebuchadnezzar the agent of judgment draws near, Ez. 21:25-27. For this Yahweh gathers the men of Judah as in a furnace, not to sift out the base metal as in Is. 1:21, 25; Jer. 6:27-29, but to destroy them all in the smelting, Ez. 22:19. It thus avails nothing if Jerusalem tries to seduce its enemies like a harlot; there are heard only the death-cries of the judged, Jer. 4:30 f. For the most part the prophets think the judgment entails a war with its horrors (Jer. 6:23) and the resultant deportation of the inhabitants (Ez. 12:1-11). The judgment will be executed without pity, Jer. 15:5. Deliverance is possible, but only if there is the radical conversion and change (Jer. 4:3 f.) which Jerusalem either cannot or will not accept. The accomplished judgment is considered in retrospect in Jer. 42:18; 44:13, also 2 K. 24:13, 20; Lam. 1-5. If it is clear for Jeremiah that God's wrath and fury have been poured out upon Jerusalem (42:18), the disaster seems to be an unexpected and incomprehensible catastrophe in Lam. 1-5, though one also finds the view that the "day of Jerusalem" (Ps. 137:7) had been threatening for a long time as a judgment for sin. As the sin of Jerusalem has no parallel, so, too, its judgment, Da. 9:12.

6. City of the Eschatological Age of Salvation.

a. The hope of a restoration of Jerusalem is almost always an imminent eschatological hope, for during the exile the prophetic message of *either* judgment on the sinful city or possible deliverance through radical conversion was changed

---

[100] Hence Ez. 16:16-21 can go on to extend the metaphor of infidelity to the cultus.
[101] Cf. also Jer. 32:3, 28 f.; 33:4 f. On the cup of wrath → VI, 149, 21 ff. In Ez. 12:10aβ-b the threat is against the princes in Jerusalem and the whole house of Israel there. In 12:19 the threat of 12:17-20 is redirected from the whole land to Jerusalem. Ez. 5:10 f. gives details of the judgment and 5:3-4a presupposes a remnant and a new purifying judgment. In Ez. 24:25 the end of the silence is related to the day of the capture of Jerusalem, while in 33:21 it is related to the news of this. 24:26 reconciles the two by equating the arrival of the messenger with the day of the capture.

into a Before and After in time : first judgment and then salvation. Since the destruction of Judah and Jerusalem was undoubtedly the judgment threatened by the prophets, there could only follow the age of salvation which now that judgment is over will be definitive and eternal and will involve the actualising of God's dominion. Then Zion-Jerusalem will be and will remain the city of this eschatological age of salvation.

> The starting-point of the eschatological understanding is to be found in Lam. 4:22. Judgment on Zion is completed, though as yet no turning or age of salvation is proclaimed, only punishment for the hated Edomites. In Dt. Is., however, the statement that the judgment is over is combined with the comforting of Jerusalem in view of the imminent turning (Is. 40:1 f.), the proclamation of the manifestation of Yahweh (40:3-5), and the summons to Jerusalem to awake (51:17). Then Zech. explicitly contrasts the concluded age of wrath with the approaching convulsion of the times and the promise of a future age of salvation for Judah and Jerusalem (Zech. 8:15), so that it can be asked in complaint when this age will dawn for Jerusalem seeing the 70 yrs. of wrath [102] foretold by Jer. (25:11; 29:10) have passed, Zech. 1:12.

b. Yahweh's pity for Jerusalem implies the dawn of the last time, Zech. 1:12. Yahweh has been the first to declare approaching salvation to Jerusalem (Is. 41:27). It is He who grants the imminent salvation to it (Is. 46:13). For he can no more forget Zion than a woman her child (Is. 49:14 f.). Into the discouraging situation of the moment comes the intimation of the great change, Zeph. 3:16. Indeed, in contrast to earlier prophetic threats the exile now seems to be presented as the great chance for Yahweh to demonstrate His power to Zion and to save and liberate its exiled inhabitants, Mi. 4:10. [103] The approaching eschatological turning after the exile is declared to Jerusalem by the prophet of Is. 60. Jerusalem's future salvation, its light, is at the centre of his thought. It will be achieved when the glory of Yahweh shines forth (v. 1). This will be a repetition of the creation of the world, so that the end of the world corresponds to its beginning, v. 2.

> In the dark world Jerusalem will stand like a castle of light with an irresistible power of attraction, Is. 60:2 f. In spite of appearances to the contrary God is zealous for Zion-Jerusalem. He protects His claim to it with anxious love, Zech. 1:14; 8:2. He will choose it afresh, Zech. 1:17; [104] 2:16. "Yahweh who elects Jerusalem" can even be used as a title, Zech. 3:2. Hag. and Zech. look for the fulfilment of these promises in connection with the building of the second temple. The age of salvation begins with the laying of the new foundation (Hag. 2:19) or the insertion of the last stone into the temple (Zech. 4:6aβ-10a).

There is expected the return of Yahweh to Zion as seen by Ezekiel (43:1-9). The messengers of peace and joy announce His coming (Is. 52:7 ff.; → II, 708, 20 ff.). A plague of locusts suggests it (Jl. 2:1). As at the exodus from Egypt He will come down (Is. 4:5) when He has gained the victory over His heavenly

---

[102] On the different form in the LXX → V, 411, 44 ff.

[103] Mi. 4:10 seems to be only proclaiming the exile, but in fact this is presupposed. For the author the path of suffering leads to glory.

[104] The hope is extended to cover Judah : "My cities shall overflow with prosperity," though cf. T. H. Robinson-F. Horst, *Die Zwölf Kleinen Propheten*, Hndbch. AT, I, 14² (1954), 220 : "Cities are without prosperity in the dispersion" — which demands alteration to עָרִים and a special sense for פוּץ "to scatter," "to be in dispersion," rather than "to overflow."

foes, Is. 24:23. He is then visibly present in Jerusalem, Is. 4:5; 30:20. His hand rests on the mountain, Is. 25:10. The inhabitants of Jerusalem dwell in His sight, Is. 23:18. Yahweh, the rock of Israel, is again on His hill, Is. 30:29. Thus Jerusalem becomes once again and definitively the city of God, the city of Yahweh (Is. 60:14), the holy city (Is. 52:1), the sanctuary (Jl. 3:17). Apart from the thought of election other ancient concepts recur in this connection. Yahweh "dwells" on "Zion" (Zech. 2:14; 8:3; Jl. 3:17). "Zion" is the place of His "name," Is. 18:7.

There Yahweh will inaugurate His royal eschatological rule, Is. 24:23; 52:7; Ob. 21; Mi. 4:7; Zeph. 3:15; Zech. 14:9; Ps. 146:10; 149:2; → I, 568, 16 ff.; V, 861, 43 ff. It is worth noting that this thought of the dominion exercised by Yahweh is usually connected with Jerusalem itself and the names Zion-Jerusalem are mentioned in Messianic prophecies only in that of the entry of the Messianic ruler [105] in Zech. 9:9 f. [106] It is true that Haggai and Zechariah simply assume that the Messiah Zerubbabel (Hag. 2:20-23) or the two Messiahs Zerubbabel and Joshua (Zech. 4:1-6aα, 10b-14; 3:8 f.; 6:9-15) [107] live in Jerusalem, and this may well be so in other cases too. [108] Yet Jerusalem is much too much the city of Yahweh Himself for it to be called the residence merely of the Messiah as His viceroy. The very common non-Messianic eschatology which awaited God's direct rule joined hands with earlier ideas of Jerusalem as God's seat and city to promote the view that the city will be the eschatological residence of God Himself. He will establish there an acceptable regime, Jer. 3:15; [109] → II, 405, 12 ff. He will extend protection and aid by His presence, Is. 4:5 f.; Jl. 3:16 f.; Ps. 46. He wins the victory like a hero, Zeph. 3:17. He protects the city outwardly like a wall of fire and inwardly He is its glory, Zech. 2:9.

c. The eschatological glory of Jerusalem rests wholly and utterly on God's saving work, Is. 62; 66:10-15. The promised reconstruction of the devastated city (Is. 49:16 f.; Zech. 1:16) will be with indescribable magnificence and splendour; it will be built of precious stones like a fairy city, Is. 54:11-17. The old topographical landmarks are used to describe the compass of the new city, Jer. 31:38-40; Ez. 48:30-35; Zech. 14:10. It is mostly portrayed with walls, Is. 60:10; 62:6; Mi. 7:11), which are necessary for defence (Is. 26:1), [110] though the gates will be open day and night because of the many caravans, Is. 60:11. On the other hand Zech. 2:6, 8 f. finds no place for the building of new fortifications, since walls merely limit the rich fulness of blessing and God Himself will

---

105 Pre-exilic acc. to Robinson-Horst, *op. cit.*, 247 f. S. I. Feigin ref. to Accad. par. in his "Babylonian Parallels to the Hebrew Phrase 'Lowly, and riding upon an ass,'" *Studies in Memory of Moses Schorr* (1944), 227-240.

106 Perhaps one might also refer to Zech. 12:9-13:1, though it is not likely that the "house of David" means a Messianic dynasty.

107 The text of Zech. 6:9-15 is corrupt. The original (cf. 6:9, 10b, 11a-bα; 12a, 13, 15aα) deals with the command to crown Zerubbabel, which Zech. is to do as a symbolic action; on the text cf. Robinson-Horst, *op. cit.*, 236; K. Elliger, *Das Buch d. zwölf Kleinen Propheten, II, AT Deutsch*, 25² (1951), 119. For the saying about the high-priest Joshua as the Messiah cf. 3:8 f.

108 With the same duality as Zech., but as an established institution, Jer. in 33:17 f. expects a series of Messianic Davidic kings and an enduring Levitical priesthood. The ref. to the "throne of the house of Israel" suggests that Jerusalem is the site, though the city is not mentioned by name.

109 Jer. 3:14-18 is sometimes regarded as a post-exilic section not by Jer., but cf. W. Rudolph, *Jer., Hndbch. AT*, I, 12² (1958), *ad loc.*

110 J. Lindblom, *Die Js.-Apokalypse* (1938), 85-90 does not think Is. 26:1-14 is eschatological; it refers to a historical situation.

defend Jerusalem. Naturally the rebuilding of the temple is part of the reconstruction, Is. 44:28; Zech. 1:16. Haggai and Zech. press for this in order that the new temple may be a sign of the dawn of the last time. It will be magnificently adorned, Is. 60:13; Hag. 2:7-9. Jerusalem will be inhabited again (Is. 44:26) and for ever (Jl. 3:20) and the land will be blessed with fruitfulness (Is. 4:2; 30:23 ff. cf. Jl. 3:18). Edom pays it tribute, Is. 16:1. Tyre sends its trading profits as a gift, Is. 23:18. The commerce of Egypt and Cush is brought to it, Is. 45:14. The possessions and wealth of all the nations will stream unceasingly into Jerusalem (Is. 60:5-11) as a result of the eschatological revolution, Hag. 2:7 f. Then Zion will be indeed a paradise and the garden of Yahweh, so that the wonderful primal age will return in the last time, Is. 51:3 → V, 767, 4 ff.

Jerusalem will be the eschatological capital (Is. 16:1) and religious centre (Is. 45:14) and it will thus be secure from all enemies (Is. 52:1; Jl. 2:32; 3:17 etc.). On account of its dignity it will receive a new name (Is. 62:2) which, given by Yahweh, will express the rights of Yahweh (→ V, 253, 13 ff.) and the new nature of the city (on the new name → V, 254, 30 ff.; VI, 524, 32 ff.). This is "my delight in her" (Is. 62:4), "sought out," "city which is not forsaken" (Is. 62:12), "throne of Yahweh" (Jer. 3:17 cf. 14:21; 17:12; → III, 162, 30 ff.), "Yahweh our righteousness" (Jer. 33:16), "Yahweh is there" (Ez. 48:35) or "the faithful city" (Zech. 8:3 cf. Is. 1:21, 26),[111] while the temple hill is expressly called the "holy mountain" (Zech. 8:3 and Jl. 3:17). Against the background of prophetic denunciation and threat there is expressed here the expectation of a new and better Jerusalem which can be created only by God's saving and redeeming action. It is the starting-point for the later idea of an upper or heavenly Jerusalem (→ 326, 3 ff.; 336, 28 ff.; 338, 28 ff.), though this does not yet occur in the OT. All the OT passages refer to the earthly city, which is viewed simply as the new and future Jerusalem of the age of eschatological salvation. All kinds of earlier ideas are woven into this understanding.

One may perceive only too human traits in the eschatological expectations for Jerusalem. These show that eschatology is dealing with concrete historical factors and is not abstractly sublimated and spiritualised, → V, 847, n. 33. Within this framework there already begins in Dt. Is. and Hag. the often crassly material depiction of the age of salvation. Whereas Is. 66:13 primarily promises the divine consolation, there is added the thought that Jerusalem will be comforted by its eschatological splendour and glory rather than by God, → V, 790, 3 ff. Acc. to Mi. 4:8 the Zion which in the disaster of 586 had been powerless and shrunken like a little shepherd's tower will itself — not Yahweh — exercise widespread dominion. On the other hand Zech. 12:7 proclaims that Yahweh will help Judah before Jerusalem in order that the people of Jerusalem should not be over-arrogant.

d. Other sayings refer to the inhabitants of the new Jerusalem of the last time. Their existence rests on the forgiveness and grace of God, who blots out the blood-guiltiness of Jerusalem that Ezekiel had censured and washes away the filth of its sin (Is. 4:4), and who is already waiting to bless His people (Is. 30:18 f.). Hence the redeemed will return to Zion, Is. 35:10; 51:11. They are the holy remnant, 2 K. 19:31; Is. 4:3; → IV, 205, 24 ff.; Hag. and Zech. do in fact identify the returned exiles as the remnant. In the post-exilic period there thus arises the hope that the *Diaspora* will return, first that in Babylon (Zech. 6:8, 15a), then that in all parts of the world (Is. 27:13; 62:11 etc.).

---

[111] This faithfulness is properly that of the divine community in the city, so that the term "Jerusalem" again comes close to symbolising the community.

The goal of the return to Jerusalem is the setting up of a true and perpetual covenant relationship (Jer. 50:5) in faithfulness and righteousness which God imparts to His people in order that they may cleave to His fellowship (Zech. 8:8). There is thus the birth of a new people in Zion (Is. 66:8) which is upright and loyal (Is. 26:2) and inviolable (Ob. 17), so that the righteous in Zion-Jerusalem are constantly delivered from all their troubles, Jl. 2:32. Hence the people multiplies (Jer. 3:16; Zech. 2:8; 8:5) and space is restricted (Is. 49:20 f.), esp. as the span of life which had been reduced by sin (cf. Gn. 5; 6:1-4) becomes longer again (Is. 65:20; Zech. 8:4). The ideal of long and abundant life is accompanied by that of heroic strength (Zech. 12:8) and economic prosperity even apart from the wealth of other nations, Is. 62:8 f.; Zech. 2:8. In Jerusalem, then, sheer joy will reign at its new good fortune (Is. 61:3; Jer. 33:11; Zech. 2:14) and thanksgiving and praise will sound forth (Is. 12:4-6; 61:3; Jer. 33:11).

e. Finally, the nations are related in different ways to Zion-Jerusalem as the city of the eschatological age of salvation. There is concrete reference to the Babylonians and Edomites, who were esp. hated because of the disaster they brought on Judah and Jerusalem, and who are threatened with divine vengeance in the day of eschatological reversal, Jer. 51:24; Ob. 17 f., 21; Zech. 1:14 f.; 2:2 etc. Yet one stream of eschatological prophecy expects dire events, → VI, 509, 6 ff. In the last time the Gentiles will wage a campaign against Jerusalem and attack it, though naturally without success, Is. 29:8; Mi. 4:11. For the nations which take the field against Jerusalem will be annihilated before it, Is. 17:12-14; [112] Zech. 12:2-6 etc. Is. 10:12 alludes to this common idea, [113] while Jl. 3:9-12, 13-17 has express descriptions of the approach and assembling of the peoples, upon whom God holds the last judgment from Zion-Jerusalem. [114] The whole earth will be a desert when Jerusalem triumphs, Mi. 7:13. Zeph. 3:14 f., however, does not depict the nations as summoned to final decision before Jerusalem; here there is already present a hostile power which stays in the land and oppresses the people. If in all these prophecies it is Yahweh who finally judges the nations, nationalistic ideas are sometimes present. The prosperity of the people of Jerusalem and vengeance on their foes are commonly associated, cf. Mi. 4:13; Ps. 149:6 ff. Significant esp. in relation to these developments is the other strand in eschatological prophecy which brings the nations into a positive relationship to Jerusalem, cf. Is. 18:7; 45:14. Here God prepares the eschatological banquet for all peoples and takes away the veil or cover from their eyes so that they know Him, Is. 25:6 f.

Thus there is a great pilgrimage to the temple on Zion. Here the nations are taught by Yahweh how to live according to His will, Is. 2:2-4 cf. Mi. 4:1-3. [115] Here they will seek Him and propitiate Him, Zech. 8:22. They assemble with one accord in the temple to convert themselves (Jer. 3:17) and to serve Yahweh (Ps. 102:22). Thus everyone finds his spiritual home in Jerusalem no matter where he was born, Ps. 87:5. By acknowledgment of Yahweh the other peoples become members of the people of God. The mark of membership is confession

---

[112] The apparent dependence of Is. 17:12-14 on Ez. 38 f. makes it difficult to claim this saying for Is.

[113] The "king of Assur" means the legatee of Assyrian power in the time of the author.

[114] The idea of Yahweh's roaring from heaven in Jer. 25:30 is transferred to Zion-Jerusalem in Jl. 3:16. Hence it is neither taken from Am. 1:2 (Robinson-Horst, op. cit. on Jl. 3:16) nor is the ref. to theophany, A. Weiser, Das Buch d. zwölf Kl. Propheten, I, AT Deutsch, 24² (1956), on Jl. 3:16.

[115] This saying, which occurs in two forms with only minor differences, exemplifies the spirit of post-exilic universalist eschatology, so that often it is not ascribed to Is. or Mi., though cf. G. v. Rad, "Die Stadt auf dem Berge," Ev. Theol., 8 (1948-49), 439-447; H. Wildberger, "Die Völkerwallfahrt zum Zion, Jes. II, 1-5," VT, 7 (1957), 62-81.

of the one true God, Zech. 2:15. There is no more war, Is. 2:4 = Mi. 4:3; Ps. 46:9; → VI, 511, 7 ff. Nationalistic ideas have, of course, permeated this universalist eschatology at many points, cf. Is. 25:8; 60:3 f., 10 ff.; Jer. 33:9; Zech. 8:3; 14:16-19.

7. Mythical Aspects.

a. From the early exilic period onwards originally mythical ideas, divested of their strictly mythical character, are used as metaphors and symbols to bring out the significance of Zion-Jerusalem. The most common are that of the highest mountain and that of the water of life and blessing. Thus we often find the idea that Jerusalem lies on the highest mountain, Is. 2:2; Mi. 4:1; Ez. 17:22; 40:2; Zech. 14:10; Ps. 48:3. [116] This is a Mesopotamian motif, for South Babylonian Eridu was regarded as the garden of God and, since the god Ea is enthroned in the cosmic Eridu, it was held to be a copy of the cosmic hill of the gods. [117] But it is also a Canaanite motif, for El lives on a hill of God [118] which has been identified by some as Zaphon (Mons Casius) in North Syria. [119] The two motifs fused to produce the idea of Paradise, or they combined with this, so that Jerusalem, resting on the highest hill or hill of God, is also Paradise, → V, 481, 10 ff.; 482, n. 81; 482, 20 ff.; 505, 5 ff.; 767, 4 ff.

From this or from the temple there flows forth a stream of water of life and blessing, Ez. 47:1-12; Jl. 3:18; Zech. 14:8; Ps. 46:4. In Is. 33:21 this is a river with broad banks. [120] The idea might well be connected with the actual situation in Jerusalem, the reference being to the wells of Gihon and Rogel [121] through which the water of the underground flood comes to the surface. [122] But mythical motifs are again decisive. On the Canaanite hill of God there spring forth "(two) rivers" and "(two) floods," [123] and out of the Garden of Paradise flows the river of blessing or the four cosmic rivers. [124]

---

[116] The rock is not yet given symbolical significance in the OT (→ VI, 96, 9 ff.) on the basis of the fig. language of myth, cf. H. W. Hertzberg, "Der hl. Fels u. das AT," JPOS, 11 (1931), 32-42.

[117] Cf. Jeremias, op. cit. (→ n. 41), 66 f., 77, also the survey in → V, 475-479.

[118] → V, 479, 5 ff. and cf. the Ugaritic texts Gordon Manual, 51, IV, 20 ff.; 137, 13 ff.; 'nt III, 21 ff. M. H. Pope, El in the Ugaritic Texts (1955), thinks there are two stages of belief in El. Acc. to the older El lives on the divine mount, acc. to the later he is banished by the young Baal to the underworld where he lives on an underground mountain near the sources of the subterranean cosmic waters. Apart from the fact that even there one finds an association of mountain and springs, it may be argued that his banishment in one part of the Ugaritic texts does not have to mean that the same applies wherever he is worshipped, esp. in view of the popular part which he plays in what is acc. to Pope his central sanctuary in modern Chirbet Afqa (about halfway between Byblos and Baal-bek).

[119] Cf. O. Eissfeldt, Baal Zaphon, Zeus Kasios u. d. Durchzug d. Israeliten durchs Meer (1932). Hence the hill of Zion in Ps. 48:2 is "the most distant part of the north (Zaphon)"; on the LXX → V, 482, n. 86.

[120] Cf. Is. 66:12, where Yahweh gives eschatological Jerusalem "peace like a river, and the glory of the Gentiles like a flowing stream"; → VI, 596, 29 ff.

[121] Hezekiah brought the water of Gihon through a tunnel to the pool of Shiloah (2 K. 20:20), and in Is. 8:6 f. it is a symbol of Yahweh's rule. Perhaps it had cultic significance in ancient times, cf. 1 K. 1:33, 45. Neh. 2:13 mentions the dragon well (Rogel). Jos. Bell., 5, 410 refers to "Shiloah and all the springs outside the city" but seems to have known only the first. It is unlikely there was another well in the temple precincts, Ep. Ar., 89; Tac. Hist., V, 12. Cf. Simons, 47 f., 157-194.

[122] A. R. Johnson, Sacral Kingship in Ancient Israel (1955), 47-77, thinks harvest or tabernacles was the background of many Ps. The theme is not just Yahweh's kingship in nature and history but expectation of the autumn rains. He links with this allusions to a spring or river on Zion.

[123] Gordon Manual, 51, IV, 21 f.

[124] G. Hölscher, Drei Erdkarten (1949), 35-44.

b. Other mythical images are less common. Jerusalem lies in the midst of the nations (Ez. 5:5), for repopulated Palestine is the navel of the earth (Ez. 38:12). [125] Images from the conflict with chaos are used for the threatening peoples ; the city stands firm and impregnable in this conflict, Ps. 46:1-3, 5; 125:1. The disaster which smites the city is like the fall of a heavenly or paradisial being, perhaps the primal man, Lam. 2:1 cf. Is. 14:12-15; Ez. 28:17, [126] while later the Messiah in Jerusalem is depicted as the great cosmic tree (cf. Ez. 31:1 ff.) in whose shade all peoples will find a place, Ez. 17:22-24.

8. City of Theocracy.

In other broad circles of the post-exilic period eschatological expectation was almost completely obliterated by a cultic-legal attitude. The circle which produced the work of the Chronicler is one of these. [127] The main aim of this work is to prove that Judah alone, and within it the capital Jerusalem, is the seat of theocracy, since here alone the true Davidic dynasty is located and the true cultic centre of Yahweh stands. Theocracy is based on the separation of Israel from the Gentile world, i.e., on the election of Judah and Jerusalem, where David has his throne and Yahweh His temple.

Jerusalem is thus much more central here than in 1-2 K., for, as 2 Ch. 6:6 says by way of foundation, Yahweh has chosen Jerusalem that His name may be there, and David that he may govern Israel. Yahweh is the "God of Jerusalem" (2 Ch. 32:19) who has taken up residence there for ever (1 Ch. 23:25) and made it a holy place for His name (2 Ch. 33:4, 7). He has publicly acknowledged the Jerusalem temple to be the place of revelation and sacrifice by fire sent down from heaven (2 Ch. 7:1 ff.). The temple is the only cultic site (2 Ch. 30:5). It is open to the Gentiles (2 Ch. 6:32 f.), and the — not very numerous — true believers in Yahweh in Northern Israel, which has relapsed into idolatry, may come thither (2 Ch. 11:14, 16; 30:11). In keeping is the fact that symbolically if not historically all Israel took Jerusalem (1 Ch. 11:4) and brought up the ark into it (1 Ch. 15 f.), that there David before the assembled rulers of all Israel named Solomon as the successor chosen by Yahweh (1 Ch. 28:1), and that the city is mentioned again and again as the place where the Israelites subject to the Davidic dynasty (2 Ch. 15:10 etc.) or their elders (2 Ch. 34:29) assemble. The main aim of the cultus is to render praise and thanksgiving that Yahweh has chosen Jerusalem as the city of theocracy.

In thus teaching the post-exilic community that it was the true Israel the Chronicler conferred supreme dignity on Jerusalem. Not in an uncertain end-time but in the present God's rule is actualised in and around it.

9. Summary.

In the cultic, legal and national forms of OT theology and the tense eschatological expectations the special position of Jerusalem became both an expression of the humble obedience of faith under the awaited or established rule of God and also a sign of ungodly obstinacy and frivolous self-assurance. Belief in the

---

[125] In Ju. 9:37 Gaal calls Gerizim the navel of the earth, in Is. 19:24 Israel is the centre of the world. For the later period cf. Eth. En. 26:1 f.; Jub. 8:12, 19; bYoma, 54b; bSanh., 37a. Mohammed also thought Jerusalem was the centre until Mecca and later Baghdad took the position. Mediaeval maps group the countries around Jerusalem and the navel of the earth is shown like a cup in the Church of the Holy Sepulchre. Similar ideas are common : Delphi as ὀμφαλός, Rome as umbilicus orbis, China as central kingdom. Cf. W. H. Roscher, Der Omphalosgedanke bei verschiedenen Völkern, bes. den semitischen (1918).
[126] For details cf. Fohrer Ez. on 28:17; though also J. Dus, "Melek Ṣōr-Melqart ?" Archiv Orientální, 26 (1958), 179-185.
[127] On what follows cf. Rudolph Esr. u. Neh., XXVII-XXX ; also Ch., XVII-XVIII.

impregnability of the holy city because of its special protection by God could be a danger. Only too quickly the certainty of faith changed into religio-political audacity. With the cry : "This is the temple of Yahweh, the temple of Yahweh, the temple of Yahweh !" there was too ready an evasion of the admonition and conditional promise : "Amend your ways and your doings, and I will cause you to dwell in this place" (Jer. 7:3 f.). In contrast the great individual prophets pursued neither cultic-national dogma, theocratic illusion, nor eschatological speculation. For them Jerusalem was in the last resort no different from all the cities of Judah, since what counts is not the place of revelation but the self-revealing God. They viewed the people of Jerusalem as under the same divine demand, threat and promise as all other Israelites or non-Israelites. They did not hesitate to proclaim to the city and its inhabitants the judgment of God by which God would show Himself to be independent of Jerusalem and superior to it. That the history of revelation does not end there was discovered by Ezekiel. His call (Ez. 1:1-3, 15) showed him already that God is not tied to Jerusalem and its temple. He can meet man and be near to him in a foreign land. Revelation and salvation are not indissolubly bound to Zion-Jerusalem. The believer can experience the presence of God anywhere ; earthly relations cannot separate him from God either in space or time.

Fohrer

B. Zion-Jerusalem in Post-Biblical Judaism.

I. Usage.

In Gk. צִיּוֹן is transl. Σειών or Σιών. [128] For יְרוּשָׁלַיִם we find in the Hell. period the two forms Ἰερουσαλήμ and Ἱεροσόλυμα. [129] The former alone occurs in the LXX, the latter being found only in the Apcr., 1 Macc. 10:43; 11:34; [130] 2 Macc. 1:1, 10; 3:6, 9, 37 etc.; 3 Macc. 1:9; 3:16; 4 Macc. 4:3; 18:5. Since in Gk. an echo of ἱερός was heard, [131] Jewish Hell. writers prefer Ἱεροσόλυμα, so always Jos. and Philo Leg. Gaj., 156, 278, 288, 312 f., 315. [132] The name is mostly used without art. With art. we usually find in LXX and Test. XII ἡ Ἰερουσαλήμ. Ἱεροσόλυμα [133] is occasionally taken as a fem. sing. Tob. 14:4 AB, but almost always as a neut. plur., [134] so in Jos., also Philo Leg. Gaj., 278 etc.; Polyb., 16, 39, 4; Strabo, 16, 2. 34. 36. 40; Dio C., 37, 15-17; Ps.-Hecataeus in Jos. Ap., 1, 197; Agatharchides, *ibid.*, 1, 209; Manetho, *ibid.*, 1, 241; Lysimachus, *ibid.*, 1, 311; [135] Timochares in Eus. Praep. Ev., IX, 35; Preis. Zaub., II, 13, 997.

---

[128] On the orthography cf. Bl.-Debr. § 38*; 56, 3.
[129] -α is added to keep the final Semitic consonant, *ibid.* § 38*.
[130] Elsewhere 1 Macc. also has Ἰερουσαλήμ : 1:20, 29, 35, 38, 44; 2:1, 6, 18, 31 etc.
[131] The breathing in Ἱεροσόλυμα echoes ἱερός, Bl.-Debr., 39, 1; 56, 1. Cf. Eus. Praep. Ev., IX, 34, 13 : τὴν πόλιν ἀπὸ τοῦ ἱεροῦ Ἰερουσαλήμ ὀνομασθῆναι, ὑπὸ δὲ τῶν Ἑλλήνων φερωνύμως Ἱεροσόλυμα λέγεσθαι.
[132] Ἰερουσαλήμ only in Philo Som., II, 250, probably because an allegorical explanation is here connected with this form, → 320, 35 ff.
[133] Unique is the magic formula ὁρκίζω (σε) τὸν ἐν τῇ καθαρᾷ Ἱεροσολύμῳ, Preis. Zaub., I, 4, 3069. Cf. also *ibid.*, II, 13, 233 : ἐν τῷ ἱερῷ τῷ ἐν Ἱερωσολύμῳ.
[134] Gen. Ἱεροσολύμων Strabo, 16, 2, 34; dat. τοῖς Ἱεροσολύμοις Preis. Zaub., II, 13, 997; Strabo, 16, 2, 36; Dio C., 37, 17.
[135] Lysimachus (acc. to Jos. Ap., 1, 310 f.) maliciously maintained that the city was originally called Ἱερόσυλα because the Israelites plundered the temples of the inhabitants of the country (τὰ ἱερὰ συλῶντας).

'Ιεροσολυμίτης [136] is coined for the citizens, Sir. 50:27 (29); 4 Macc. 4:22; 18:5; Jos. Ant., 12, 246; Ap., 1, 311 etc.

As compared with that of the OT the use of the name shows no changes in content. Jerusalem is the lofty city to which one goes up, 1 Macc. 13:2; 1 Εσδρ. 8:5 etc. Zion is the mountain on which the holy place stands, e.g.: "And they went up Mt. Zion with joy and rejoicing and offered burnt offerings there," 1 Macc. 5:54, cf. also 4:60; 7:33; 14:26 etc. But sometimes the whole city or its population can be called Zion. Isaiah comforted the sorrowful of Zion, Sir. 48:24. After the destruction of Jerusalem the seer sees the weeping woman Zion bewailing her grief, 4 Esr. 9:38-10:24. Holy city and holy place are an inseparable unity : Zion's misfortune is Jerusalem's sorrow, 4 Esr. 10:20. Often the hill of Zion and the city of Jerusalem are mentioned together in the same sentence : He who honours Zion honours Judah and Jerusalem, 1 Εσδρ. 8:78. The enemies who attack Jerusalem attack Judah and Mt. Zion, 1 Macc. 6:48. Wisdom says it took up dwelling in Israel : "In the holy tent I rendered him (God) priestly service, and so I was established on Zion. In the beloved city he gave me a resting-place, in Jerusalem is my dominion," Sir. 24:10 f. There is invocation of God : "Have mercy on the city of thy sanctuary, Jerusalem, the place where thou dost rest. Fill Zion with blessings of thy promise and thy temple with glory," Sir. 36:12 f. [137] What happens to Zion and Jerusalem affects the whole land. Thus Cyrus ordained that a house should be built for the Most High God in Judah and Jerusalem, 1 Εσδρ. 2:2. Later the Maccabeans rebelled against the abominable things done in Judah and Jerusalem, 1 Macc. 2:6. When victory is won in the final battle there is a summons to common rejoicing : "Zion, rejoice greatly, and break forth in rejoicing, Jerusalem, and be jubilant all ye cities of Judah," 1 QM 12:13.

Jerusalem is the city of God and Zion the dwelling of His glory. [138] As in the OT then (→ 296, 29 ff.) Jerusalem is the "holy city," 1 Macc. 2:7; 2 Macc. 1:12; 3:1; 9:14; 15:14; Tob. 13:10; Sir. 36:12; 49:6; Jos. Ant., 4, 70 and 200; 20, 118; Ap., 1, 282; Philo Som., II, 246, [139] the "most holy city of God," Jos. Bell., 7, 328, the "beloved city," Sir. 24:11. On Jewish coins and in the Talmudic writings it is called עיר הקודש. [140] For all Jews in Palestine and the Dispersion Jerusalem is ἱερόπολις, Philo Leg. Gaj., 225, 281, 288, 299, 346, or μητρόπολις, Philo Flacc., 46; Leg. Gaj., 203, 281, 294, 305, 334. The name points to God's election, יִרְאֶה and שָׁלוֹם being found in it. Thus we read in Jub. 18:10 (cf. Gn. 22:14): "And Abraham called this place : God has seen, so that it is said : God has seen, this is Mt. Zion." The later Midrash has a similar explanation. [141] In Philo Som., II, 250 this etym. explanation is the occasion of an allegorical inter-pretation of the name : Jerusalem means ὅρασις εἰρήνης. It is thus deduced : ὥστε μὴ ζήτει τὴν τοῦ ὄντος πόλιν ἐν κλίμασι γῆς ..., ἀλλ᾽ ἐν ψυχῇ ἀπολέμῳ καὶ ὀξυδορκούσῃ <τέλος> προτεθειμένῃ τὸν [δὲ] θεωρητικὸν καὶ εἰρηναῖον βίον. [142] Another common explanation links Jerusalem with Salem (Gn. 14:18), Jos. Ant., 1, 180; 7, 67; Bell., 6, 438 → 299, 17 ff. With these two names, found together in the Genesis Apocryphon 22:13, [143] there is linked in the Tosefta expectation for Jerusalem's future : Once it was the city Salem, then it was called Jerusalem and fell under God's judgment. The ancient name is again found in Ps. 76:2 : "In Salem also is his tabernacle, and his dwelling place in Zion." This is to be taken as a sign that God has turned to it again

---

[136] 'Ιεροσολυμήτης in 2 Macc. 4:39 vl.
[137] Cf. the exposition of the passage → VI, 525, 16 ff. and n. 56.
[138] Cf. the 14th benediction of the Prayer of Eighteen Benedictions and Sir. 36:12 f. When Sennacherib sent his army against Jerusalem his act violated God's honour : "He stretched forth his hand against Zion and blasphemed God in his pride," Sir. 48:18.
[139] Jos. and Philo do not have ἀγία πόλις but ἱερὰ πόλις cf. → VI, 524, n. 51.
[140] For examples cf. Str.-B., I, 150; Schürer, I, 762.
[141] Midr. Gn. r., 56, 10 (36a) on 22:14. Cf. Str.-B., II, 253; S. Krauss, "Zion and Jerusalem," PEQ, 77 (1945), 15-33; Winter, op. cit., 139 f., n. 1.
[142] Cf. → VI, 529, 9 ff. and Volz Esch., 60.
[143] Salem — that is Jerusalem, → n. 54.

in love and restored its former name. Since the city of Salem/Jerusalem is set on a hill, the Shekinah will return to its midst when it is made into a mountain, for it is written in Gn. 22:14 : "And Abraham called that place 'Yahweh sees,' so that it is still said to-day : on the mountain 'Yahweh appears,' " T. Ber., 1, 15. [144]

II. Jerusalem from the Maccabean Period to Its Destruction by the Romans.

During the time when the Persians, Ptolemies and Seleucids governed Palestine Jerusalem played only a minor part in political affairs. But now all believing Jews recognised it as the one place where Yahweh was to be worshipped. The Chronicler had offered a theological basis for this position of the holy city when he had tried to show that Jerusalem alone is the legitimate seat of theocracy → 318, 8 ff. These ideas were taken up in 3 Esr. and emphasised in a history of the temple from Josiah's reforms to the time of Ezra → 304, 33 ff. [145] It is true that the Davidic monarchy had collapsed ; yet Zion remained. Only in Jerusalem should the Passover be celebrated, 1 Εσδρ. 1:1-20; 7:10-15. Hence the post-exilic community assembled around the holy city and rebuilt it in spite of every obstacle. The sanctuary and the Law proclaimed by Ezra were very closely related, so that for the author of 3 Esr. Ezra becomes the high priest (1 Εσδρ. 9:40, 49), exercising his office in Jerusalem by the reading of the Torah.

The inhabitants of Jerusalem included not only those circles which were loyal to God but also many friends of Hell. culture who wanted to turn Jerusalem into a Hell. city. To attain this goal they set up a gymnasium and tried to introduce pagan customs, 1 Macc. 1:11-15; 2 Macc. 4:9-17. The pioneers in this development were priestly groups, and the Syrian king Antiochus Epiphanes wanted to help it to full success. He built a strong fortress in the city (1 Macc. 1:29-35), forbade the worship of the God of Israel, and gave the temple the name of Olympian Zeus (1 Macc. 1:41-64; 2 Macc. 6:2-5). "Jerusalem was uninhabited as a desert ; none of its children went in or out. The sanctuary was trampled underfoot ; strangers lived in the castle," was the lament of the righteous, 1 Macc. 3:45. These rebelled against the abominable things which were done in Judah and Jerusalem, 1 Macc. 2:6. They regarded these events as God's judgment. God was angry with the city for a short time because of the sins of its inhabitants, 2 Macc. 5:17.

Under Maccabean leadership armed conflict began. [146] Three years after its defilement by the Syrians the temple could be cleansed and reconsecrated, 1 Macc. 4:36 (165/4 B.C.). The host went up Mt. Zion (1 Macc. 4:37) and restored the legitimate cultus, 1 Macc. 4:36-59; 2 Macc. 10:1-9. Zion was fortified (1 Macc. 4:60), for there was still a strong Syr. garrison in the Acra. [147] The castle was taken only in 142/1 B.C. when Simon Maccabeus forced the Syrians to capitulate after a long siege, 1 Macc. 13:49-52. The restored and heavily fortified city (1 Macc. 10:10; 12:35 f.; 13:10) now became the residence of the Hasmoneans who not only appropriated the high-priestly office but united it with the monarchy. This political development, which almost inevitably reopened the door for Hell. customs and practices, was not approved of by many of the righteous. They either became opponents of the Hasmonean dynasty or left Jerusalem. [148]

---

[144] *Ad loc.* cf. E. Lohse-G. Schlichting, *Tosefta Berakot* (1956), 17 f.
[145] Cf. Rudolph, *op. cit.*, IV-XIX.
[146] Cf. also Polyb., 16, 39, 4, which says that οἱ περὶ τὸ ἱερὸν τὸ προσαγορευόμενον Ἱεροσόλυμα κατοικοῦντες rebelled against Antiochus.
[147] The Hell. party was still conspiring with the Syrians, cf. Fr. Q p Na on 2:11 f.: Demetrius, king of Greece (Demetrius III ?) "sought to come to Jerusalem on the advice of those who speak smooth things." Cf. J. M. Allegro, "Further Light on the History of the Qumran Sect," JBL, 75 (1956), 90, 92.
[148] The Qumran community called Jerusalem the city "where the ungodly priest practised abomination and defiled the sanctuary," 1 Q p Hab 12:7-9.

Pompey put an end to the Hasmoneans in 63 B.C. He let Hyrcanus retain the office of high-priest and entered Jerusalem in force, even making forcible entry into the temple.[149] To Jews faithful to the Law this desecration of the most holy place by a Gentile must have seemed to be God's judgment on the holy city (Ps. Sol. 2:1-25), a punishment of the Most High visited on the inhabitants of Jerusalem because of their evil conduct (8:1-34).

From now on the Romans ruled Jerusalem. With the consent and approval of the Romans the Idumaean Herod entered Jerusalem, forcing its gates (37 B.C.). During his long reign Herod did much building, completely changing the face of his capital. On the north-west side of the temple square he made the castle built by the Hasmoneans into a strong fortress and called it Antonia. Four mighty towers were put at the four corners so that the temple precincts could all be seen and supervised.[150] Some yrs. later a second palace was built on a raised site in the west part of the city; this was protected against attacks by strong walls and towers.[151] In 20 B.C. Herod began a significant enlargement of the temple square and created roomy precincts. After the model of Solomon's temple and with careful attention to the provisions of the Torah the whole temple structure was rebuilt and lavishly adorned over a period of several decades.[152] But the king, who ruled with a hard and ruthless hand, was still hated by the Pharisees and the people subject to him.

When in 6 A.D. the Romans transferred government over Judaea to procurators these chose Caesarea as their residence, stationed a garrison in the Antonia, and visited Jerusalem occasionally, esp. to keep a watchful eye on doings in the city during the chief Jewish festivals.[153] The sequence of Roman governors was broken only by King Herod Agrippa in 41-44 A.D. Herod Agrippa wanted to improve the fortifications of Jerusalem by building a new wall, the so-called third wall, northwards from the existing one. But he could not finish this.[154] Because of Roman provocations Jewish hatred increased steadily in the yrs. which followed, and finally disaster came.[155] The revolting Jews at first succeeded in driving the Romans out of the city (66 A.D.) but Jerusalem was finally encompassed by the Roman legions under Vespasian and Titus (70 A.D.).[156] For the inhabitants, whose ranks were swollen by many Passover pilgrims, there was no escape. After months of siege the city was taken and destroyed; the temple, which Titus was able to enter briefly, went up in flames.[157] God had delivered up his most holy city to the fire, Jos. Bell., 7, 328. Acc. to the righteous the enemy soldiers were not the executors of judgment. God Himself sent angels from heaven who, with torches in their hands, stationed themselves at the four corners of the city and set fire to it, S. Bar. 6:1-8:5. God visited Jerusalem for the sins committed in its walls.[158] From now on all pious Jews remembered this day with sorrow, for the

---

[149] For this cf. not only Jos. but also the Roman historians, Tac. Hist., V, 9; Strabo, 16, 2, 40; Dio C., 37, 15-17.

[150] Cf. the description in Jos. Bell., 5, 238-246. On the Antonia cf. Simons, 432-435; Vincent Jérusalem, I, 193-221; Marie Aline de Sion, La forteresse Antonia à Jérusalem et la question du prétoire (1955).

[151] Cf. the description in Jos. Bell., 5, 176-183; Simons, 265-271; Vincent Jérusalem, I, 222-232.

[152] Cf. Jos. Bell., 5, 184-227; Ant., 15, 380-420; on this Simons, 393-432; Vincent Jérusalem, II, 432-470; Parrot, 63-81. On the deviation of the Mishnah from Jos. cf. L. H. Vincent, "Le Temple hérodien d'après la Mišnah," Rev. Bibl., 61 (1954), 5-35.

[153] Cf. E. Lohse, "Die röm. Statthalter in Jerusalem," ZDPV, 74 (1958), 69-78.

[154] Cf. Jos. Ant., 19, 326 f.; Bell., 5, 147.

[155] The righteous feared approaching judgment on the city's sins: R. Zadoq had fasted forty yrs. that Jerusalem might not be destroyed, bGit., 56a (Str.-B., II, 243).

[156] Cf. F. M. Abel, "La topographie du siège de Jérusalem à 70," Rev. Bibl., 56 (1949), 238-258.

[157] On the capture of the city cf. Jos. and Tac. Hist., II, 4 f.; V, 9-13.

[158] The Rabb. give a list of the sins on account of which God judged the city, e.g.,

holy place had gone up in smoke and ashes. [159] But as Zion's grief will be turned into glory by God, [160] so all who mourn the destruction of Jerusalem have the promise that they will also see Jerusalem's future joy. [161] Hence: "Be comforted, Jerusalem, he will comfort thee who names thee by name ... Lift up thine eyes to the east, Jerusalem, and see the joy which comes to thee from God," Bar. 4:30, 36.

III. Jerusalem in the Days of Jesus.

In the days of Jesus and the apostles Jerusalem was a large city with a big population, the upper western city being separated from the lower eastern by the Tyropoeon valley. [162] Contemporary writers exaggerated the number of inhabitants [163] but it must have run to about 25,000. [164] Through Herod's many building projects and the connections of the capital with the rest of the country trade and commerce had undergone considerable development. [165] It was said of the people of Jerusalem that they were reliable in matters of the Torah but not so in business dealings. [166] Questions pertaining to Jewish life in Palestine and the Dispersion were decided by the Sanhedrin, which as the highest Jewish court met in Jerusalem → συνέδριον. Knowledge and study of the Law were promoted by the renowned scribes who had their schools in Jerusalem. [167] Students came from far and wide to sit at their feet and to study Scripture and tradition. [168] To get the correct exposition of Scripture one had to consult the priests and scholars in Jerusalem. [169] There was a whole group of synagogues in the city in which the Law was read and expounded. [170] Devoted care and reverence were accorded the sepulchres of the patriarchs, prophets and saints located on the borders of the city. [171]

On Zion lay the temple in its new splendour. [172] The holy place was surrounded by the broad square, → III, 233, 35 ff. The outer court, which Gentiles might enter, was separated by a barrier from the inner court. Here were warnings to the Gentiles in their own languages Greek and Latin forbidding them to cross the barrier. [173] Death

---

neglect of the Law (cf. Str.-B., II, 253 f. for examples), mutual hate, love of Mammon (*ibid.*, I, 366 and 937 for examples).

[159] On mourning on the day of the destruction of the city cf. the examples in Str.-B., I, 195 f.; II, 243; IV, 79-82, 87-89, 100. With the mourning there are penances (Jos. Bell., 5, 19) in the hope that Jerusalem will arise again even more gloriously if only God, who destroyed it, is propitiated.

[160] Cf. 4 Esr. 9:26-10:59, also S. Bar. 81-85.

[161] bTaan., 30b; cf. Str.-B., IV, 88 f. Cf. also Bar. 4:9-5:9; Jerusalem's lament is followed by its song of comfort and God's consolation and promise for Jerusalem.

[162] On the situation of the city cf. Jeremias, I, 20 f.

[163] Acc. to Ps.-Hecataeus (Jos. Ap., 1, 197) there were supposed to be 120,000 inhabitants. Jos. Bell., 6, 420 says more than a million were killed when the city was captured by the Romans. Tac. Hist., V, 13 also has the high figure of 600,000 during the siege.

[164] Cf. J. Jeremias, "Die Einwohnerzahl Jerusalems z. Zt. Jesu," ZDPV, 63 (1943), 24-31.

[165] On the economic affairs of Jerusalem in the time of Jesus cf. Jeremias, I, *passim*.

[166] bShab., 120a, cf. Str.-B., III, 624.

[167] Apart from Rabb. accounts one may refer to the inscr. on a Jerusalem ossuary which bears the title διδάσκαλος and the name of the deceased, → VI, 963, n. 26 with bibl.

[168] Examples in Jeremias, II B, 111 f.

[169] Cf. the legend in Ep. Ar. that before the transl. of the OT into Gk. could begin a request was made to the high-priest in Jerusalem to send a group of scholars to Alexandria.

[170] Cf. Ac. 6:9; 24:12 and Str.-B., II, 661-665. From the 1st cent. A.D. we have the inscr. of a Jerusalem synagogue built by a certain Theodotus. Cf. Deissmann LO, 378-380; K. Galling, *Textbuch z. Gesch. Israels* (1950), 81; C. K. Barrett, *The NT Background* (1956), 51 f.

[171] Cf. J. Jeremias, *Heiligengräber in Jesu Umwelt* (1959), 51-72, 114, 121 f.

[172] Cf. the account in Ep. Ar., 83-91 with its exaggerated description of the city and temple. The supposed abundance of water is certainly untrue, 89-91.

[173] Cf. Jos. Ant., 15, 417; Bell., 5, 194 and the inscr. found on the east slope of the temple hill, Galling, 80; cf. also → III, 234, 19 ff.

was threatened to any of alien descent who disregarded the prohibition. [174] The way
then led through the court of women, that of the Israelites and the adjoining priests'
court to the altar of burnt offering and the temple. [175] Here the priests, with the high-
priest and chief priests at their head, discharged their office (→ III, 262, 12 ff.; 268, 1 ff.;
270, 27 ff.) [176] and offered daily the prescribed number of sacrifices. [177]

IV. Jerusalem the Sacred Metropolis of the Jews.

Morning, mid-day and evening each Jew prayed towards the holy city. [178] If he
lived in the city he prayed towards the temple. [179] The eyes of all pious Jews in the
land or the *diaspora* were directed thither. Those abroad sent gifts to the temple as
a contribution to the sacrificial cultus. [180] Those who could went up on pilgrimage on
the feast-days "to worship and to offer first-fruits and tithes of the fruits of the earth,"
Tob. 5:14. On the three gt. feasts, esp. the Passover, the number of pilgrims was often
much greater than that of the inhabitants. [181] It was possible to find accommodation
for them all only by extending the city limits so widely as to include Bethphage. [182]
The citizens had to entertain foreign pilgrims for nothing, for Jerusalem is the possession
of all Israel. [183] One of the 10 miracles of God in the sanctuary, i.e., while the temple
still stood, was that no one in Jerusalem ever said to another that there was no room
to put him up for the night. [184]

The goal of pilgrimage was the temple; to all who came to Jerusalem this looked
at a distance like a snow-capped hill, for its radiance was visible from afar. [185] Prayer
in the consecrated place carried with it a special promise : "He who prays in Jerusalem
is as one who prays before the throne of glory ; for there is the gate of heaven and
the open door to the hearing of prayer." [186] If anyone who is laden with guilt ascends
the hill of Zion and offers a sacrifice in the temple, expiation is made and he goes
forth righteous. [187] Thus Jerusalem was the ἱερόπολις (Philo Leg. Gaj., 225, 281 etc.)
or μητρόπολις not merely of Jews in Palestine but of Jews in all lands (*ibid.*, 281 etc.).
It lies in the centre of Judah (Ep. Ar., 83) and is the centre of all Israel [188] and indeed
of the whole earth, Eth. En. 26. Thus the hill of Zion, God's place (Jub. 4:26), is called

---

[174] Tradition tells of culprits who boldly entered the holy place but were then overtaken
by divine punishment, 1 Macc. 6:12 f.; 2 Macc. 9:1-29; Ps. Sol. 2:26-31.
[175] Cf. the careful description in Parrot, 63-81, who assesses the partially conflicting
accounts in Jos. and the Mishnah ; there are sketches, *ibid.*, 70, 77.
[176] On the Jerusalem priests and Levites in Jesus' time cf. Jeremias, II B, 2-87.
[177] Acc. to 1 Εσδρ. 6:30 there was daily sacrifice and prayer for the Persian kings. In
the days of Jesus this daily offering was for the Roman government.
[178] Cf. Da. 6:11; T. Ber., 3, 15 f.; other examples in Str.-B., I, 852 f.; II, 246 f.
[179] Cf. T. Ber., 3, 16; S. Dt., 29 (71b) on 3:26; cf. Str.-B., II, 246 f.
[180] On the temple tax of two drachmas which every Jew had to pay cf. Str.-B., I, 760-
770. Cf. also Philo Leg. Gaj., 156 : The Jews in Rome sent gifts of money to the temple in
Jerusalem.
[181] Cf. Jeremias, I, 89-97. T. Pes., 4, 3 even says 12 million were there at one Passover,
cf. Str.-B., II, 710; IV, 42.
[182] Examples in Jeremias, I, 68-70.
[183] bYoma, 12a; bMeg., 26a; cf. Str.-B., I, 988 f.; II, 144; IV, 41 f.; also Jos. Bell., 4, 136 :
Jerusalem takes in all fellow-Jews without any special arrangements (ἀπαρατηρήτως).
In Bell., 4, 275 the Idumaean Simon calls Jerusalem τὴν ἅπασι τοῖς ἀλλοφύλοις ἀναπεπτα-
μένην εἰς θρησκείαν πόλιν, "the city which is open to all strangers for divine worship."
[184] Ab., 5, 5; cf. Jeremias, I, 69; Str.-B., IV, 42.
[185] Jos. Bell., 5, 223 : τοῖς γε μὴν ἀφικνουμένοις ξένοις πόρρωθεν ὅμοιος ὄρει
χιόνος πλήρει κατεφαίνετο.
[186] Midr. Ps. 91 § 7 (200b); Str.-B., II, 437.
[187] Ex. r., 36 (95c) on 27:20; Str.-B., II, 247.
[188] jChag., 1, 1 (75a, 57 f) says : "And Siloam lay in the middle of the land." Siloam is
pars pro toto for Jerusalem. Cf. Jeremias, I, 58.

the centre of the navel of the earth, Jub. 8:19. [189] Zion-Jerusalem is the mother of all Israelites (4 Esr. 10:7; S. Bar. 3:1-3) [190] who has brought up her children, Bar. 4:8.

Even for the fellowship of the righteous who separated from the ungodly priesthood in Jerusalem and withdrew into the desert, this was still the elect city. It is now the place where "the ungodly priest commits abomination and defiles the sanctuary of God," 1 Q p Hab 12:7-9. But judgment will fall on the ungodly priests of Jerusalem because they have desecrated the holy place, ibid., 9:3-7. [191] To survive in the battle which must be fought in the last days men have gone forth from Jerusalem to the holy war (1 QM 7:4) and the armed sons of light are camped in the steppe of Jerusalem, 1 QM 1:3. When they come home triumphant after the battle and return to the Jerusalem community there will be written on the trumpets of retreat "God has assembled" and on the trumpets of homecoming "God's rejoicing at homecoming full of salvation," 1 QM 3:10 f. → 82, 21 ff. Then there will be the summons to exultation : "Zion, rejoice greatly, and break forth in rejoicing, Jerusalem, and be jubilant all ye cities of Judah," 1 QM 12:13. [192] In the coming age of salvation the temple will be rebuilt in the new Jerusalem acc. to the specifications laid down in Scripture, and the cultus will be set up again in priestly purity. [193]

V. The New Jerusalem.

Each day every pious Jew prays his God to have mercy on His people Israel and His city Jerusalem and Zion the habitation of His glory [194] and to take up His residence again on Zion. [195] The righteous will rejoice when Jerusalem is built. [196] When the last attack of hostile powers is repulsed before Zion, and the sinister warring hosts are destroyed, [197] then God will fulfil the hopes of the pious and build up Jerusalem. Then Jerusalem will be the place of eschatological salvation. The expectations focused on this Jerusalem of the last days are many and varied. [198] On the one hand Jerusalem at the end of the days is the city of David built again with glory and magnificence. On the other the new Jerusalem is thought of as a pre-existent city which is built by God in heaven and which comes down to earth with the dawn of a new world. [199]

---

[189] Cf. also Jos. Bell., 3, 52 : ... τινὲς οὐκ ἀσκόπως ὀμφαλὸν τὸ ἄστυ τῆς χώρας ἐκάλεσαν.

[190] Cf. Tg. Cant., 8, 5; Pesikt. r., 26 (132b); Str.-B., III, 574.

[191] There is also ref. to the desecration of Jerusalem in 4 Q Testimonia, 28-30 : "And they shall commit defilement in the land and gt. shame among the sons ... blood like water on the wall of the daughter of Zion and in the precincts of Jerusalem." Cf. J. M. Allegro, "Further Messianic Ref. in Qumran Literature," JBL, 75 (1956), 186. 1 Q p Mi Fr, 11 on Mi. 1:8 f. (DJD, I, 78) speaks of the "priests of Jerusalem who have led astray." Jerusalem is also mentioned on some small fr. from Cave 1, but the context is missing, DJD, I, 82, 100.

[192] Cf. also 1 QM 12:17; 19:5.

[193] Cf. the Aram. Fr. which describe the new Jerusalem which is the hope of the Qumran community, 1 Q 32 (DJD, I, 134 f.) and M. Baillet, "Fr. aram. de Qumran 2 — Description de la Jérusalem nouvelle," Rev. Bibl., 62 (1955), 223-245.

[194] 14th Ben. of the Shemone E., cf. W. Staerk, "Altjüd. liturgische Gebete," KlT, 58² (1930), 13, 18.

[195] 16th Ben. of the Shemone E., cf. Staerk, op. cit., 14, 18.

[196] Cf. the prayer hᵃbhinenu, Staerk, 20.

[197] Apoc. ideas of a defeat of the Gentile attack on Jerusalem vary in detail. Acc. to 4 Esr. 13:35 the Messiah will appear on the top of Mt. Zion and lead the final battle against the hostile forces ; acc. to S. Bar. 40:1 f. the last enemy regent will be brought to Mt. Zion and put to death there by the Messiah. Cf. also Eth. En. 56; Sib., 3, 663-697; Volz Esch., 149-152, 225.

[198] Cf. the material and discussion in Str.-B., IV, 883-885, 919-931; Volz Esch., 371-376; Causse Nouvelle Jérusalem. On the various metaphors for the new Jerusalem cf. Volz Esch., 412.

[199] The ideas connected with the heavenly Jerusalem also vary. With the expectation

Common to the various eschatological hopes is the fact that the future Jerusalem will be a city of ineffable glory and indescribable majesty.

The clearest ref. to the heavenly Jerusalem which God built before all time is in Apc. Bar. 4:2-6. The city of which God says: "I have graven thee upon the palms of my hands" (Is. 49:16), is not the earthly Jerusalem; it is that prepared in heaven. God built it already when He resolved to create Paradise. Adam could see it before the fall. Abraham and Moses saw its image. "And so it is held in readiness with me, as Paradise also is," v. 6. Acc. to the seer of Apc. Esr., the days will come in which the signs mentioned earlier will be seen, and then the invisible city, heavenly Jerusalem, will appear, 4 Esr. 7:26.[200] At the end of the ages Zion will appear from heaven and be visible to all as a perfectly constructed city, 4 Esr. 13:36. Eth. En. 90:28 f. describes how God dismantled the ancient house (= old Jerusalem):[201] "The pillars were taken down; all the beams and decorations of that house were wrapped up with it. It was taken away and put in a place in the south of the land." But then God brought a new house, bigger than the first, and put it on the site of the first. "All its pillars were new, and its decorations were new and greater than those of the old house which he had pulled down." Here the new Jerusalem is not depicted as a pre-existent city but there is ref. to its origin in the act of God alone. The apoc. idea of the heavenly Jerusalem then passed into Chr. apoc. (Rev. 21 → 337, 26 ff.) but it is nowhere mentioned in Rabb. lit.[202]

Acc. to the dominant view espoused by the Rabb. the new Jerusalem would be built with gt. splendour by God or the Messiah.[203, 204] It would be freed from all the impurity of the Gentiles,[205] and from the holy place healing power would go out into all lands, Jub. 1:28; 4:26. "Jerusalem will be built with sapphires, emeralds and precious stones, its walls and towers and fortifications with pure gold. And the streets of Jerusalem will be paved with beryls and carbuncles and stones from Ophir. And all streets will say: Hallelujah! and offer praise in the words: Praised be God who has exalted (thee) to all eternity," Tob. 13:17 f. The city built of costly materials[206] will be fortified with enormous walls and towers.[207] It will take up much more space than the older city which has fallen into a ruinous state. To be able to encompass the whole people of Israel and the fulness of Gentiles who stream into it, it will at God's command extend so far that there is room for all. The wall will reach to Joppa, says Sib., 5, 251 f. Others think it will extend to Damascus.[208] God Himself will dwell in the city (Sib., 3, 787) and it will bear the name of God; for Yahweh has promised to call it by a new name which only His lips may utter, Is. 62:2.[209] Because He resides in the midst it can also be called the "throne of Yahweh."[210] At God's behest Sinai, Tabor and

---

that it will descend to earth is also found the thought that it is an abode of the blessed in the world above. Thus the seer in Slav. En. 55:2 is caught up into the supreme Jerusalem in heaven. Cf. Volz Esch., 372-375.

[200] Acc. to 4 Esr. 10:27, 54 the new Jerusalem is to be built on a square but with no foundation for a building there. The place of salvation is no longer tied to the site of old Jerusalem. But the Jerusalem of glory replaces the city sunk in grief and sorrow, cf. Str.-B., IV, 812; Volz Esch., 374.

[201] Ad loc. cf. Str.-B., IV, 920; Volz Esch., 373.

[202] It occurs for the first time in the much later Midrashim. For examples cf. Str.-B., III, 796; Bietenhard, 194 f.

[203] Cf. Sib., 5, 414-433; cf. Str.-B., IV, 920.

[204] Sometimes the Rabb. distinguish between Jerusalem above and below, the latter being an image of the original in heaven. Cf. the examples in Str.-B., III, 573. But no Rabb. ever says the heavenly Jerusalem will come down to earth.

[205] Ps. Sol. 17:22, 28; other examples in Str.-B., III, 148, 151 f.

[206] Rabb. examples in Str.-B., II, 586; III, 848, 851 f.; IV, 920 f.

[207] Examples, ibid., III, 850.

[208] S. Dt., 1 (65a) on 1:1; Pesikt., 143a, also ibid., III, 849 f.; IV, 921 f.

[209] bBB, 75b and ibid., III, 797; IV, 922 f.

[210] Gn. r., 49 (31a) on 18:17 and cf. ibid., III, 795.

Carmel come to Zion and on the summit the sanctuary will be built, the temple of the age of salvation.[211] The holy vessels and the ark of the covenant will come back to the holy place and God will be worshipped where He has set His dwelling.[212] The Israelites will come from all quarters and the Gentiles will make pilgrimage to Jerusalem to bring their gifts, Tob. 13:13; Ps. Sol. 17:30 f.; Eth. En. 57; 90:33; 4 Esr. 13:13; S. Bar. 68:5.[213] Then all peoples and kingdoms will gather in Jerusalem, as it is said : "All the nations shall be gathered to Jerusalem because of the name of Yahweh," Jer. 3:17.[214] The new Jerusalem will be the place of the saints who may live in its unending splendour. If the heavenly Jerusalem was once made by God along with Paradise (S. Bar. 4:3), at the end of times Paradise will also return with the new Jerusalem.[215] The Paradise of the end time and new Jerusalem are so close together that they form the one place of salvation : "The saints will rest in Eden and the righteous will rejoice over the new Jerusalem," Test. D. 5.[216] Because such ineffable glory is promised for the age of salvation the glances of all the hopeful righteous are directed upon Jerusalem, Tob. 13:16.

C. Zion-Jerusalem in the New Testament.

I. Occurrence and Usage.

1. Σιών [217] is mentioned only 7 times in the NT. It occurs 5 times in OT quotations : Mt. 21:5 (= Is. 62:11; Zech. 9:9) and Jn. 12:15 (= Is. 40:9; Zech. 9:9) have the population in view when they speak of the daughter of Zion. In R. 9:33 a quotation from Is. 28:16 and 8:14 is adduced in which the accent is on λίθον προσκόμματος. λίθος is also emphasised in 1 Pt. 2:6 (Is. 28:16). To prove the eschatological salvation of Israel from Scripture Paul in R. 11:26 appeals to Is. 59:20; Ps. 14:7: ἥξει ἐκ Σιὼν ὁ ῥυόμενος. Only in Hb. 12:22; Rev. 14:1 is there no quotation.

2. Jerusalem is commonly mentioned in the Gospels and Ac., sometimes in Pl., in Hb. and Rev., but never in the Catholic Ep. Terms for Jerusalem which are taken from Jewish usage are occasionally used for Jerusalem → VI, 530, 28 ff. It is the city on the hill in Mt. 5:14,[218] the ἁγία πόλις [219] in Mt. 4:5; 27:53; Rev. 11:2, the beloved city in Rev. 20:9, the city of the great king in Mt. 5:35. The holy city is also called the heavenly Jerusalem in Rev. 22:19, cf. also Hb. 11:10, 16; 12:22; Rev. 3:12; 21:9-27; 22:14. In most passages Jerusalem is the city itself but sometimes the inhabitants are included, Mt. 2:3; 3:5; 23:37 par. Lk. 13:34; Lk. 2:38; Ac. 21:31; these are called Ἱεροσολυμῖται in Mk. 1:5 and Jn. 7:25.

As in Jewish writings (→ 319, 21 ff.) both Ἰερουσαλήμ and Ἱεροσόλυμα occur. Ἰερουσαλήμ is always the name in Rev. and Hb., in Paul except at Gl. 1:17 f.; 2:1, in Mt. only at 23:37,[220] and partly in Lk. and Ac.,[221] though in Lk. and esp. Ac. we

---

[211] Pesikt., 144b and ibid., IV, 930.

[212] Examples, ibid., IV, 932-934 : "It was self-evident for Jewish thought that the temple should not be missing in the new Jerusalem." Cf. IV, 884, also III, 852.

[213] Cf. Volz Esch., 358; Rabb. examples in Str.-B., III, 853.

[214] R. Shim'on bGamliel (c. 140), AbRNat, 35, cf. Str.-B., III, 853. R. Jochanan (d. 279), however, makes a distinction : "The Jerusalem of this world is not the Jerusalem of the future world. Anyone who wills may go up to the Jerusalem of this world, but only those who are invited to that of the future world." bBB, 75b, cf. Str.-B., III, 22, 148.

[215] Cf. Volz Esch., 412 f.

[216] Further examples in Str.-B., IV, 1151 f.

[217] On the orthography → n. 128 and Bl.-Debr. § 38*; 56, 3.

[218] Cf. v. Rad, op. cit. (→ n. 115), 439-447.

[219] But we do not find ἱερὰ πόλις (→ n. 139), cf. also Schmidt, 230.

[220] The fact that Ἰερουσαλήμ is used here in Mt. may be due to the adoption of an established saying from the tradition. Cf. Schmauch, 83; Pr.-Bauer⁵, s.v.

[221] When the art. is used (cf. Bl.-Debr. § 261, 3) we find ἡ Ἰερουσαλήμ in Ac. 5:28; Gl. 4:25 f.; Rev. 3:12; cf. also ὅλη Ἰερουσαλήμ in Ac. 21:31; v. Bl.-Debr., 275, 2.

sometimes find ‘Ιεροσόλυμα, which is used in the other Gospels and the two Pauline vv. referred to above. [222] It is hard to say why there is the alternation in Luke's writings. [223] It is certainly not because one source uses one name and another the other, [224] for the author and also Paul have both forms. ‘Ιερουσαλήμ is easily predominant in Paul. [225] Since Luke has ‘Ιεροσόλυμα only 4 times in the Gospel at Lk. 2:22; 13:22; 19:28; 23:7, and elsewhere ‘Ιερουσαλήμ, one may conclude that he preferred the form corresponding to the Hb. because biblical usage suggested it. [226] Similarly in the first 7 chapters of Ac., which deal with the beginnings of the primitive community in the holy city, he always uses the older ‘Ιερουσαλήμ except at 1:4. Only from c. 8 onwards do the two forms occur together with no obvious rule governing their alternation. [227]

II. Sayings of Jesus about Jerusalem.

1. Apart from sayings which deal with His approaching sufferings in Jerusalem, the name of the city is mentioned only 3 times in the preaching of Jesus. [228] The parable of the Good Samaritan begins with the statement : ἄνθρωπός τις κατέβαινεν ἀπὸ ‘Ιερουσαλήμ εἰς ‘Ιεριχώ, Lk. 10:30. An accident in Jerusalem led to the saying in Lk. 13:4 : The eighteen upon whom the tower fell in Siloam (→ VI, 955, 19 ff.) and killed them were not more guilty than all other men who live in Jerusalem. [229] This event is rather to be understood as a warning to repent. [230] Jesus forbids all oaths (→ V, 177, 31 ff.), including that εἰς ‘Ιεροσόλυμα [231] (Mt. 5:35); for to swear by the name of Jerusalem, which is the city of the great king, is to swear by God Himself, → V, 180, 15 ff. Hence if Jerusalem is invoked as a witness to frequent and insincere oaths, this is to take the name of God in vain.

2. The two sayings in Lk. 13:33 and Mt. 23:37-39 par. Lk. 13:34 f. deal with the martyrdom of prophets. Jesus says it is impossible that a prophet should perish outside Jerusalem (Lk. 13:33), thus referring to the legends of the prophets de-

---

[222] With art. τὰ ‘Ιεροσόλυμα in Jn. 2:23; 5:2; 10:22; 11:18, but πᾶσα ‘Ιεροσόλυμα in Mt. 2:3, cf. Bl.-Debr., 56, 4.

[223] Cf. Pr.-Bauer⁵, s.v.

[224] Cf. the efforts of older criticism along these lines, P. L. Couchoud and R. Stahl, "Les deux auteurs des Actes des Apôtres," RHR, 97 (1928), 9-17. Winter, op. cit., 141, rightly says : "The reading ἱερουσαλήμ is not proof of a Hebrew or Aramaic source for any section of the Lucan writings."

[225] Since the Pauline verses are easier to survey attempts at explanation usually begin with Paul. Harnack, 73 says : "When Jerusalem is a religious concept (Gl. 4:25, 26) and in solemn speech where Paul is thinking of 'the saints' in Jerusalem (R. 15:25, 26, 31) he says ‘Ιερουσαλήμ, i.e., he chooses the Hbr. name ; elsewhere he writes ‘Ιεροσόλυμα (Gl. 1:17, 18; 2:1)." But R. 15:19; 1 C. 16:3 do not fit into this schema. In criticism cf. Schütz, 177-179. Schmauch, 82-93 tries to distinguish between ‘Ιεροσόλυμα as unholy Jerusalem and ‘Ιερουσαλήμ as the chosen places preserved through every attack.

[226] Schütz's suggestion that the Hbr. form is used on the lips of those who speak Aram. does not stand up to examination. Cf. Haench. Ag. on 1:4.

[227] Cf. Pr.-Bauer⁵, s.v. ‘Ιεροσόλυμα; Harnack, 75 f.; on Schmauch's suggestion → n. 225. Winter, op. cit., 142, n. 1: "No definite norm for the preference of either spelling in particular instances can be detected in the Third Gospel or in the Acts of the Apostles."

[228] On Mt. 22:7 → 330, 34 ff., on Lk. 21:20, 24 → 332, 6 ff.

[229] There is no other account of this accident, cf. Str.-B., II, 197.

[230] On the Jewish view of the link between suffering and guilt, cf. Str.-B., II, 193-197.

[231] There is no Rabb. instance of swearing by Jerusalem ; it is mentioned only in vows of renunciation, cf. Str.-B., I, 333. On the other hand in Hell. magic pap. we find formulae

veloped in post-biblical Judaism, → V, 714, 8 ff.; VI, 834, 29 ff. [232] It seems to have been an iron rule that prophets should suffer and die violent deaths in the holy city. But Jesus is not just quoting a common view. He is preparing to accept the prophet's passion Himself → V, 714, 5 ff.; VI, 841, 21 ff. [233] The decision must be taken in Jerusalem. But Jerusalem [234] slays the prophets and stones those who are sent to it, Mt. 23:37-39; Lk. 13:34 f. [235] The introductory sentence, which emphasises the guilt of Jerusalem, [236] is followed by a lament: ποσάκις ἠθέλησα ἐπισυναγαγεῖν τὰ τέκνα σου, ὃν τρόπον ὄρνις ἐπισυνάγει τὰ νοσσία αὐτῆς ὑπὸ τὰς πτέρυγας, καὶ οὐκ ἠθελήσατε, Mt. 23:37. Jesus can hardly have been saying that He Himself had *often* wanted to gather Jerusalem as a hen gathers her chickens under her wings. [237] A lament raised by wisdom possibly underlies the saying: [238] it has wooed in vain and been rejected. In words which echo Jer. 22:5 doom is then proclaimed: ἰδοὺ ἀφίεται ὑμῖν ὁ οἶκος ὑμῶν (ἔρημος). The threat is followed in v. 39 par. Lk. 13:35 by a concluding sentence which is to be taken as a promise (possibly added by the community): [239] The abandonment of Jerusalem will last up to the hour of the *parousia*. At the *parousia* Jesus will appear and He will be greeted as the Messiah with the joyful cry from Ps. 118:26: εὐλογημένος ὁ ἐρχόμενος ἐν ὀνόματι κυρίου. [240]

3. Jesus was crucified before the gates of Jerusalem. The community which confessed the crucified and risen Lord interpreted and passed on the whole tradition of Jesus' preaching in the light of this event. The sayings in which He intimates to His disciples His imminent death in Jerusalem and His resurrection on the third day (Mk. 8:31 and par.; 9:31 and par.; 10:32-34 and par.) are given their form by the *kerygma* of the community. This is to be seen most clearly in Mk. 10:33 f., where the details of the passion are listed as in the oldest passion narrative. [241] Mk. 8:31 says that Jesus must be rejected and put to death by the elders, chief priests and scribes, and that after three days He will rise again. Matthew expressly mentions the name of the holy city in this connection and emphasises that it must take place thus according to God's decree: δεῖ αὐτὸν εἰς ʽΙεροσόλυμα ἀπελθεῖν καὶ πολλὰ παθεῖν, Mt. 16:21. In the second prophecy of the passion (Mk. 9:31 and par.), which echoes the community's *kerygma* least clearly, the name of Jerusalem is not mentioned. [242]

---

like ὁρκίζω (σε) τὸν ἐν τῇ καθαρᾷ ʽΙεροσολύμῳ, Preis. Zaub., I, 4, 3069 or ἐξώρκισά σε, τέκνον, ἐν ... τῷ ἱερῷ τῷ ἐν ʽΙερωσολύμῳ, ibid., II, 13, 233; cf. also II, 13, 997.

[232] Cf. H. A. Fischel, "Martyr and Prophet," JQR, 37 (1946), 265-280, 363-386; H. J. Schoeps, "Die jüd. Prophetenmorde," *Aus frühchr. Zeit* (1950), 126-143; E. Lohse, "Märtyrer u. Gottesknecht," FRL, 64 (1955), 73.

[233] On the authenticity of Lk. 13:31-33 cf. Bultmann Trad., 35; G. Bornkamm, *Jesus*[3] (1959), 142.

[234] Double address is common, cf. the examples in Str.-B., I, 943.

[235] Lk. 13:34 f. is based on ʽΙερουσαλήμ in v. 33. On the context in Mt. cf. Bultmann Trad., 120 f.; Suppl. (1958), 16; E. Haenchen, "Matthäus 23," ZThK, 48 (1951), 56; W. G. Kümmel, *Verheissung u. Erfüllung*, Abh. ThANT, 6[3] (1956), 73-75.

[236] Mt. 23:37 par. Lk. 13:34 speaks of stoning and putting to death, not crucifying; hence it cannot be called *vaticinium ex eventu*.

[237] This is a good Palestinian metaphor, cf. the examples in Str.-B., I, 943.

[238] Cf. the quotation Lk. 11:49 par. Mt. 23:34 and on this → VI, 835, 7 ff.; M. Dibelius, *Die Formgeschichte d. NT*[3] (1959), 246; Bornkamm, op. cit., 143.

[239] Kümmel, op. cit., 74 f. attributes v. 39 to Jesus and concludes "that Jesus expected a longer period of time between His death and the *parousia*," 75.

[240] On the exegesis of Mt. 23:37-39 cf. esp. Haenchen, op. cit., 55-57.

[241] Mk. 10:33: ʽΙεροσόλυμα, Lk. 18:31: ʽΙερουσαλήμ.

[242] Jerusalem is mentioned in the passion story at Mk. 11:1, 11, 15, 27; Mt. 21:1, 10; Lk.

III. Jerusalem in the Four Gospels.

1. Mark.

Apart from the passion sayings (→ 329, 19 ff.) and the passion story (→ n. 242) Jerusalem is mentioned in only a few passages in Mk. The effect of the preaching of John the Baptist was so great that the inhabitants of the capital came out to him at the Jordan, Mk. 1:5 and par.; cf. also Jn. 1:19. In the summary in 3:8 it is said that men came to Jesus from Jerusalem and all the regions inhabited by Jews, cf. Mt. 4:25. Scribes from Jerusalem accuse Jesus of possessing Beelzebul and driving out demons with the help of the prince of the devils, Mk. 3:22 and par. [243] Pharisees and scribes who journey from Jerusalem, the centre of scribal learning, to Galilee, [244] upbraid Jesus because He and His disciples transgress the laws of cleanness, Mk. 7:1-23 par. Mt. 15:1-20. Jerusalem is the dwelling-place of the enemies who exert themselves to bring Jesus to the cross. They confront Him with pitiless hostility, Mk. 11:18; 14:1-2 and par. [245] But when Jesus died on the cross, the temple curtain was ripped into two pieces, Mk. 15:38 and par. → III, 246, 2 ff.; 629, 33 ff.; IV, 885, 1 ff. God's judgment on the temple and the city begins herewith.

2. Matthew.

In Mt. Jerusalem is mentioned already in the infancy stories. The wise men come to Jerusalem and find out where the new-born King of the Jews is, Mt. 2:1. Herod is startled, and all Jerusalem with him, 2:3. The promised Anointed, the King of the age of salvation, is born in Bethlehem, cf. 21:5. Homage is to be paid to this King of Jerusalem by the Gentiles who come from afar. Jerusalem is the holy city because the temple stands in it, 4:5; cf. 27:53. [246] But as the prophets suffered and died in Jerusalem (23:37), so the Son of Man must go to Jerusalem and be put to death on the cross, 16:21. [247] In Jerusalem Jesus has His decisive debate with the scribes and the leaders of Judaism (23) and He gives instruction to His own concerning the last things (24-25). He dies on the cross as the King of Israel. In the hour of His death not only is the curtain of the temple torn but there is an earthquake, the rocks are shattered (27:51), graves open before the gates of Jerusalem, and the bodies of dead saints are raised, get out of their tombs, go into the holy city and appear to many, 27:52 f. The sanctuary is destroyed, but the risen saints assemble with the Messiah in the holy city to demonstrate the eschatological reversal which has taken place with His crucifixion. [248] Judgment falls on the city which rejected the invitation of the King. He sends forth His

---

19:28. The question of the passion and death of Jesus in Jerusalem cannot be discussed here. On topographical matters cf. esp. the researches of Dalman, Simons, Vincent Jérusalem, Parrot and Kopp.

[243] Pharisees in Mt. 12:24.

[244] "Jerusalem is thus the seat of the hostility to Jesus," Lohmeyer, 32.

[245] "Jerusalem is the city of mortal enmity against Jesus, of sin and death," ibid., 34.

[246] Mk. 1:5 : πᾶσα ἡ 'Ιουδαία χώρα καὶ οἱ 'Ιεροσολυμῖται πάντες, Mt. 3:5 : 'Ιεροσόλυμα καὶ πᾶσα ἡ 'Ιουδαία καὶ πᾶσα ἡ περίχωρος τοῦ 'Ιορδάνου (Jerusalem first).

[247] Jerusalem is not mentioned in Mk. 8:31; ὅτι δεῖ αὐτὸν εἰς 'Ιεροσόλυμα ἀπελθεῖν in Mt. 16:21 expands the Marcan original.

[248] Cf. Schmauch, 92 f.

armies, seizes the murderers, and burns up their city with fire, 22:7.[249] The threat ἰδοὺ ἀφίεται ὑμῖν ὁ οἶκος ὑμῶν (ἔρημος) (23:38) is fulfilled. But the day will come when Jerusalem will greet the returning Lord with the words : εὐλογημένος ὁ ἐρχόμενος ἐν ὀνόματι κυρίου, 23:39.

3. Luke.

The significance of Jerusalem is emphasised much more strongly in Lk. than in the other Synoptics.[250] At the beginning (1:5-25) and the end (24:53) there is reference to events which took place in the temple. The promise given to the ancient people of God is fulfilled in the history of Jesus and His Church. The true Israel assembles in the holy place.[251]

In the temple at Jerusalem the priest Zacharias was promised that a son would be born who was to bear the name John, 1:5-25. The parents of Jesus brought the boy to be presented in the temple, 2:22. They offered the statutory sacrifices, 2:24. In Jerusalem Simeon (2:25-35) and Anna (2:36-38) awaited the παράκλησις τοῦ Ἰσραήλ (2:25), the λύτρωσις Ἰερουσαλήμ (2:38).[252] With His parents Jesus at 12 years of age journeyed to Jerusalem for the Passover (2:41-52) and He engaged in discussion with the scribes in the temple. He is at home here, so that He asks His parents with astonishment : οὐκ ᾔδειτε ὅτι ἐν τοῖς τοῦ πατρός μου δεῖ εἶναί με; 2:49. In the story of the temptation Luke puts at the end the scene in which the devil takes Jesus up on a pinnacle of the temple, 4:9. This is where the last decision is made by which Jesus vanquishes the tempter.[253] During His Galilean ministry Jesus met with people from all over the country. He had debates with the Pharisees and scribes who came ἐκ πάσης κώμης τῆς Γαλιλαίας καὶ Ἰουδαίας καὶ Ἰερουσαλήμ, 5:17. Men turned to Him ἀπὸ πάσης τῆς Ἰουδαίας καὶ Ἰερουσαλήμ καὶ τῆς παραλίου Τύρου καὶ Σιδῶνος, 6:17.

Jerusalem is the site of His passion, 9:31; 13:33; 18:31. He goes there with His disciples, 9:51-19:27.[254] From the very first this journey is under the sign of the passion.[255] His wanderings bring Him to Jerusalem and the cross, 9:51, 53; 13:22; 17:11; 19:11.[256] The entry brings Jesus directly to the temple, 19:28-38, 45. He

---

[249] Not necessarily an allusion to the destruction of Jerusalem (cf. Jeremias Gl., 57) but perhaps a topos of royal sovereignty which was an established part of the tradition, so K. H. Rengstorf, "Die Stadt d. Mörder (Mt. 22:7)," *Judentum — Urchristentum — Kirche, Festschr. f. J. Jeremias,* BZNW, 26 (1960), 104-129.

[250] Cf. esp. H. Conzelmann, *Dile Mitte der Zeit³* (1960), 66-86, 124-127.

[251] Cf. Schmauch, 97 f.

[252] The vl. Ἰσραήλ is only weakly attested (348a r¹ vg^cl).

[253] Thus 4:13 reads: ὁ διάβολος ἀπέστη ἀπ' αὐτοῦ ἄχρι καιροῦ. The devil returns only in the passion story, again at Jerusalem, 22:3. On this cf. Conzelmann, *op. cit.,* 68, n. 3; 73; 146.

[254] On the Lucan journey cf. K. L. Schmidt, *Der Rahmen d. Geschichte Jesu* (1919), 246-273; W. Gasse, "Zum Reisebericht d. Lk.," ZNW, 34 (1935), 293-299; J. Blinzler, "Die literarische Eigenart des sog. Reiseberichtes im Lk.-Ev.," *Synpt. Studien f. A. Wikenhauser* (1953), 20-52; J. Schneider, "Zur Analyse des Lk. Reiseberichtes," *ibid.,* 207-229; E. Lohse, "Missionarisches Handeln Jesu nach dem Ev. d. Lk.," ThZ, 10 (1954), 1-13; Conzelmann, *op. cit.,* 53-66; W. Grundmann, "Fragen der Komposition des lk. Reiseberichtes," ZNW, 50 (1959), 252-270.

[255] Cf. Conzelmann, *op. cit.,* 57: "Jesus' sense of suffering is expressed as a journey."

[256] Lk. 19:11 introduces the parable of the pounds. When Jesus and the disciples are just before Jerusalem, eschatological instruction is given to the disciples : "Luke develops his eschatology in explicit antithesis to the concept of Jerusalem," Conzelmann, *op. cit.,* 67.

seizes this in order that it may be again a house of prayer, 19:45 f. In the temple Jesus goes out and teaches the people daily, 19:47; 20:1; 21:37. Only with the feast of the Passover does He enter the city itself according to Lk. 22:10. Then the πειρασμοί of Jesus begin, 22:28, cf. v. 3. Events move on to His death. Jerusalem does not understand τὰ πρὸς εἰρήνην (19:42); hence it will be destroyed, ἀνθ' ὧν οὐκ ἔγνως τὸν καιρὸν τῆς ἐπισκοπῆς σου (19:44). Jerusalem will be encircled by hostile armies, taken, and trampled underfoot by the Gentiles (21:20, 24). This is why Jesus, on His way to crucifixion, tells the daughters of Jerusalem not to weep for Him but for themselves and their children, 23:28 → III, 725, 7 ff. For Jerusalem has not perceived the hour of its visitation. It has nailed the Messiah to the cross. Hence judgment will fall ineluctably on the city. [257] The Jews are guilty of condemning Jesus. [258] The election will thus be taken from them and given to the community of Jesus. In and around Jerusalem (24:13, 18, 33, 52) the Risen Lord appears to His disciples and commissions them to preach the sufferings and resurrection of Christ — ἀρξάμενοι ἀπὸ 'Ιερουσαλήμ, 24:47. The company of the exalted Lord is in Jerusalem and assembles in the temple, which belongs to them as the place where praise of God is sounded forth : [259] καὶ ἦσαν διὰ παντὸς ἐν τῷ ἱερῷ εὐλογοῦντες τὸν θεόν, 24:53.

4. John.

In Jn. Galilee and Jerusalem alternate as the centres of Jesus' ministry. Jesus often journeys from Galilee to Jerusalem, 2:13; 5:1; 7:10; (11:55;) 12:12. Since the 'Ιουδαῖοι are hostile to Him from the very first, Jerusalem is repeatedly the place where Jesus manifests His glory [260] and must contend with the representatives of the unbelieving cosmos. [261]

> Several places in Jerusalem are mentioned as the sites of acts of Jesus. The cleansing of the temple comes at the beginning because it has programmatic significance for the contest with the 'Ιουδαῖοι, 2:13-22. At the pool of Bethesda in 5:2 [262] Jesus cures a man who had been lame for 38 yrs. The description of the place with its 5 porches (5:2) is in full agreement with archaeological findings. [263] To the north of the temple square by St. Anne's Church a double pool has been discovered which dates from the time of Herod the Gt. This had the form of a trapezoid. Around it 4 porches were built and a fifth was built on a wall running through the middle and some 6.50 metres

---

[257] "The journey, the passion, the guilt of the Jews and (in this light) the fate of the city form a solid complex. It is the work of the Jews that Jerusalem does not fulfil its destiny. The Jews destroy their election by slaying Jesus," Conzelmann, 125.

[258] Acc. to Lk. 23:6-12, Herod, Jesus' sovereign, who is in the city for the feast (23:7), has a hand in condemning Jesus. Pilate, on the other hand, pronounces Him innocent, 23:4, 12-16. He finally yields to the clamour of the Jews and passes sentence on Jesus, 23:18-25, τὸν δὲ 'Ιησοῦν παρέδωκεν τῷ θελήματι αὐτῶν, 23:25.

[259] "The city is the link between the history of Jesus and the existence of the Church," Conzelmann, 124.

[260] Jn. 4:45 refers to many deeds, ὅσα ἐποίησεν ἐν 'Ιεροσολύμοις ἐν τῇ ἑορτῇ.

[261] "Thus Jerusalem is at the heart of the Gospel only because Golgotha is at its heart," Lohmeyer, 41.

[262] κολυμβήθρα is to be taken with Βηθεσδά and πύλη is to be supplied with ἐπὶ τῇ προβατικῇ, cf. Neh. 3:1, 32; 12:39. Βηθεσδά (C 𝕽 Θ pm f q sy) is probably the correct name ; Βηθζαθά in א (L) 33e or Βελζεθά in D (a) was the name of the northern suburb of Jerusalem.

[263] Cf. Dalman Orte, 325-327; J. Jeremias, "Die Wiederentdeckung von Bethesda," FRL, 59 (1949), also Kopp, 364-371.

wide. A second story of healing is located at the pool of Siloam in the south of the city. The spring of Siloam, which was linked to the city by a tunnel in the days of Hezekiah (cf. 2 K. 20:20 → 304, 15 ff.), was the only spring in Jerusalem. The pool mentioned in Jn. 9:7 was probably a reservoir at the end of the tunnel.[264] The Evangelist gives no further details but emphasises the allegorical significance of the name Σιλωάμ = ἀπεσταλμένος in 9:7. Jesus taught in the temple in 7:14. When in Jerusalem for the Feast of the Dedication He was ἐν τῷ ἱερῷ ἐν τῇ στοᾷ τοῦ Σολομῶνος, 10:22 f. One of the porches on the west side of the temple was then called after Solomon because it was thought to have been part of the original structure of Solomon.[265] In Bethany, 15 furlongs from Jerusalem acc. to 11:18, lived Mary and Martha, the sisters of Lazarus. All the notes in the Fourth Gospel concerning the sites in Jerusalem rest on surprisingly good local knowledge.

Jesus entered Jerusalem with His disciples (12:12) and the crowd (cf. 11:55) greeted Him as the βασιλεὺς τοῦ Ἰσραήλ (12:13) with the cry of jubilation from Ps. 118:25 f. But during the final days He was in Jerusalem Jesus did not address the crowd, the Parting Discourses being delivered to the disciples, 13-16. Nor is the name Jerusalem ever again mentioned by the author in connection with the passion story. The Risen Lord appeared to His disciples in Jerusalem (c. 20).[266] The time had now come when the Father would be worshipped neither in Gerizim nor Jerusalem, 4:20 f. → VI, 764, 20 ff.; ἀλλὰ ἔρχεται ὥρα καὶ νῦν ἐστιν ὅτε οἱ ἀληθινοὶ προσκυνηταὶ προσκυνήσουσιν τῷ πατρὶ ἐν πνεύματι καὶ ἀληθείᾳ, 4:23.

IV. The Significance of Jerusalem for Primitive Christianity.

1. The Primitive Community in Jerusalem.

No direct accounts of the beginnings of the Christian community in Jerusalem have been preserved. But Luke's historical work and Paul's letters agree that only a very short time after the appearances of the Risen Lord the apostolic band and first Christians were gathered together in the holy city.[267] On the Day of Pentecost a greater number of disciples had gathered in Jerusalem.[268] By calling itself ἐκκλησία τοῦ θεοῦ or οἱ ἅγιοι this company expressed the fact that it regarded itself as the people of God to whom the promises of the old covenant appertain. But the people of God has its centre in God's chosen city, Jerusalem.[269] Hellenistic Christians who were expelled from Jerusalem carried the glad tidings into the land, Ac. 8:1. The church in Jerusalem, led at first by the apostles and then by James, the Lord's brother, was regarded with honour by all believers and became the headquarters of Christianity as a whole. From the first community messengers were sent to the others, Ac. 8:14; 11:22; Gl. 2:12. Prophets also went

---

[264] Dalman Orte, 327 f.; Str.-B., II, 530-533; Kopp, 371-376.

[265] Jos. Ant., 20, 220 f.; Bell., 5, 185; cf. Str.-B., II, 625 f.; Dalman Orte, 310 f.; Simon, 401 f., 421; Vincent Jérusalem, II, 467-469; Kopp, 344, 349 f.

[266] The name of the city is also not mentioned by Jn. in the Easter story.

[267] The problem of the Galilean traditions will not be discussed here, since we are simply referring to the significance of Jerusalem for the primitive Church.

[268] On questions relating to Pentecost → VI, 50, 9 ff. and G. Kretschmar, "Himmelfahrt u. Pfingsten," ZKG, 65 (1954), 209-253.

[269] Cf. E. Schweizer, "Gemeinde u. Gemeindeordnung im NT," Abh. ThANT, 35 (1959), 30 f.: The settling of the primitive community in Jerusalem shows that "it took itself to be the new Israel, the Israel of the last time."

forth from it, Ac. 11:27; 15:32; 21:10. It was in Jerusalem that Christians gathered to decide on matters of concern to the whole Church, Gl. 2:1-10; Ac. 15:1-35. Missionaries and messengers returned here after accomplishing their tasks, Ac. 11:2; 13:13; 19:21; 21:15. For Jerusalem was the centre of primitive Christianity.

2. Jerusalem in Paul.

The apostle Paul always acknowledged that the Gospel had come forth from Jerusalem, R. 15:19, 26-31. Hence the primitive community had a right to the thanks and love of all Christians. Like the apostles in Jerusalem, Paul knew that he was put in trust with the Gospel (1 C. 15:1-11) beside which there can be no other (Gl. 1:6-9). But Paul had not received his apostolic office from the authorities in Jerusalem. He is an apostle οὐκ ἀπ᾽ ἀνθρώπων οὐδὲ δι᾽ ἀνθρώπου ἀλλὰ διὰ Ἰησοῦ Χριστοῦ καὶ θεοῦ πατρὸς τοῦ ἐγείραντος αὐτὸν ἐκ νεκρῶν (Gl. 1:1). Hence he did not have to have his call confirmed by Jerusalem. To show his independence of the first apostles he emphasises the fact that only three years after his conversion did he go up to Jerusalem and that during his stay of two weeks he saw only Cephas and James, the Lord's brother, Gl. 1:18-20. [270] When he went to Jerusalem a second time 14 years later this was not in answer to a summons by the authorities there but κατὰ ἀποκάλυψιν, Gl. 2:1 f. The leaders of the primitive community recognised Paul's preaching and work, Gl. 2:7-9. They agreed he should 1. share in the missionary task : ἡμεῖς εἰς τὰ ἔθνη, αὐτοὶ δὲ εἰς τὴν περιτομήν (Gl. 2:9) and 2. arrange a collection for the poor, Gl. 2:10. [271] Paul promoted this collection energetically in his churches, 1 C. 16:1-4; 2 C. 8-9; R. 15:25-31. The gifts which he helped to gather in the Gentile Christian churches were brought to Jerusalem, not as an obligatory tax [272] but as an act of generosity by which the Gentiles displayed in practical love their bond of gratitude to the primitive community, R. 15:27 → IV, 282, 18 ff. For Paul, too, Jerusalem was still the centre of Christianity. [273] When he looks back on his apostolic work on projecting his journey to Rome, he describes this as extending ἀπὸ Ἰερουσαλὴμ καὶ κύκλῳ μέχρι τοῦ Ἰλλυρικοῦ, R. 15:19. Though he never worked as a missionary in Jerusalem, he puts it first here. [274] The Gospel is for Ἰουδαίῳ τε πρῶτον καὶ Ἕλληνι, R. 1:16. As Peter is an apostle, no less so is Paul, Gl. 2:8. But the apostles are always linked with Jerusalem, the city of the people of God. Hence Paul says concerning his apostolic work that it went forth ἀπὸ Ἰερουσαλήμ.

---

[270] Acc. to Gl. Paul could hardly have visited Jerusalem very soon after his experiences in Damascus, cf. Ac. 9:26-30.

[271] On Ac. 15:1-35 cf. Gl. 2:1-10. Cf. M. Dibelius, "Das Apostelkonzil," *Aufsätze zur Ag.*, FRL, 60³ (1957), 84-90; Haench. Ag. on Ac. 15.

[272] So K. Holl, "Der Kirchenbegriff d. Pls. in seinem Verhältnis zu dem der Urgemeinde," *Gesammelte Aufsätze*, II (1928), 60 f., but in refutation → IV, 282, 20 ff. (Kittel).

[273] Holl, *op. cit.*, 63.

[274] This does not mean that Paul actually worked in Jerusalem but that Jerusalem remained central in his thinking, Mi. R., ad loc. and n. 1. Cf. also A. S. Geyser, "Un essai d'explication de Rom. XV, 19," NTSt, 6 (1959/60), 156-159 : "Rom. XV, 19 est donc rien que l'attestation que donne S. Paul de l'authenticité de son apostolat ... Rom. XV, 19 représente alors la *formule de l'apostolicité*. Celle-ci à son tour, comprend les *notae apostoli*," 158.

3. Jerusalem in Acts.

The depiction in Ac. is a direct continuation of that in Lk. → 331, 5 ff. Jerusalem links the history of Jesus with the beginning of that of the community, cf. Ac. 10:39; 13:27, 31.[275] The disciples obeyed the command of the Risen Lord to stay in Jerusalem (Lk. 24:49) and to wait there for the descent of the Spirit (Ac. 1:4),[276] cf. Ac. 1:12. They received the commission to be our Lord's witnesses in Jerusalem, in all Judaea and Samaria, and to the uttermost parts of the earth, 1:8 cf. Lk. 24:47. At Pentecost the gift of the Spirit was imparted to them and they proclaimed the message that Jesus, the Crucified and Risen, was the κύριος and χριστός, 2:36. The inhabitants of the city (2:14; 4:16; cf. 1:19) and the strangers living there (5:16; cf. 2:5, 9-11; 8:26 f.) saw their deeds (2:43) and accepted the preaching of the apostles, who filled all Jerusalem with their doctrine, 5:28. It is true that the Jewish rulers in Jerusalem (4:5) tried to take steps against the movement, but they could not prevent it that ὁ λόγος τοῦ θεοῦ ηὔξανεν καὶ ἐπληθύνετο ὁ ἀριθμὸς τῶν μαθητῶν ἐν Ἰερουσαλὴμ σφόδρα, 6:7. The community grew and it met in the temple as the place belonging to the people of God, the true Israel, 2:46; 3:1-3, 8; 5:20 f., 25, 42.[277] When the Christian message spread to Judaea and Samaria, the leadership of the quickly growing Church remained in the hands of the authorities in Jerusalem, 8:14-25; 11:2, 22; 12:25; 13:13.

According to Ac. Paul's career is also closely connected with Jerusalem. Saul was known in Jerusalem for his exemplary Jewish way of life, 26:4. He did the Christians much harm there, 9:13, 21; 22:19 f.; 26:10. Armed with full power by the high-priest he went from Jerusalem to Damascus to arrest Christians there, 9:2; 22:5; 26:12. But he was then called as a chosen vessel (9:15) to fulfil God's plan of salvation → V, 919, 18 ff. According to the outline in Luke this means that he was to be a witness of Jesus from Jerusalem to the ends of the earth up to Rome. Soon after his conversion he came to Jerusalem and was conducted by Barnabas to the apostles and introduced into the community, 9:26-30. In the temple at Jerusalem Paul fell into a trance and received the commission to leave Jerusalem and preach to the Gentiles, 22:17 f.[278] Twice Paul went up to Jerusalem as an envoy of the church at Antioch, 11:27-30; 12:25; 15:2, 4.[279] He concluded the second missionary journey ἀναβὰς καὶ ἀσπασάμενος τὴν ἐκκλησίαν, 18:22. He then set forth again, 18:22 f. In Ephesus he resolved to go as a pilgrim (cf. 24:11) to Jerusalem (19:21) and to be there for the feast of Pentecost, 20:16, 22. He was warned not to go up, 21:4, 12 : τὸν ἄνδρα ... δήσουσιν ἐν Ἰερουσαλὴμ οἱ Ἰουδαῖοι καὶ παραδώσουσιν εἰς χεῖρας ἐθνῶν, 21:11. But Paul was ready to die at Jerusalem, 21:13.[280] When he reached the city (21:15) he was received

---

[275] Cf. Lohmeyer, 92; Conzelmann, 68 and 124 f.

[276] Acc. to Holl, op. cit., 55 Ac. 1:4 originally meant that the disciples were to await the parousia in Jerusalem. But there is nothing in the text to suggest an original ref. to the parousia.

[277] We are told that the community met in the homes of believers (2:2, 46; 12:12) and the temple or the porch of Solomon (3:11; 5:12 ↦ 333, 5 ff.). It was when going to the temple that Peter healed the lame man at the Beautiful Gate of the temple, 3:1-10. On the site of this cf. Haench. Ag., ad loc.

[278] "The call comes into force only as it is confirmed at the place designated in salvation history," G. Klein, "Die zwölf Apostel," FRL, 77 (1961), 155. On the sequence in Gl. → n. 270 f.

[279] On the problems relating to the account in Gl. cf. Haench. Ag. on 11:27-30.

[280] Ibid., on 21:13 : "As once for Jesus, so now for His disciple Jerusalem is the city of

by the leaders of the community, 21:17. Because of an incident which the Jews staged in the temple he was arrested, 21:27-36. In prison the Lord appeared to him : ὡς ... διεμαρτύρω τὰ περὶ ἐμοῦ εἰς 'Ιερουσαλήμ, οὕτω σε δεῖ καὶ εἰς 'Ρώμην μαρτυρῆσαι, 23:11. The way which he must take is thus indicated. His case will not be decided in Jerusalem, 25:1, 3, 7, 9, 15, 20, 24. Because he has appealed to Caesar he is brought to Rome. Having first preached τοῖς ἐν Δαμασκῷ πρῶτόν τε καὶ 'Ιεροσολύμοις, πᾶσάν τε τὴν χώραν τῆς 'Ιουδαίας καὶ τοῖς ἔθνεσιν (26:20), he is now as δέσμιος ἐξ 'Ιεροσολύμων delivered up εἰς τὰς χεῖρας τῶν 'Ρωμαίων (28:17). Thus by his imprisonment Paul builds the bridge from Jerusalem to Rome, obedient to the command to be the Lord's witness to the ends of the earth.

4. Zion-Jerusalem in Revelation.

In a vision John the Divine sees the Lamb on Mt. Zion surrounded by the 144,000 (Rev. 14:1). In c. 13 the severe tribulation which awaits the community is depicted and then this new image answers the question whether the people of God can withstand the attack of satanic forces. Mt. Zion [281] is mentioned as the place of eschatological preservation [282] which shelters the 144,000 who bear the mark of God's possession and the Lamb's.

> Though the name of Jerusalem is not given, Rev. 11 speaks of the city ὅπου καὶ ὁ κύριος αὐτῶν ἐσταυρώθη, 11:8. What is meant, then, is Jerusalem, [283] the theatre of Christ's sufferings and of the death of the eschatological witnesses. The city which kills the κύριος and the μάρτυρες has become the seat of ungodliness, blasphemy and obduracy. It is thus said of it : καλεῖται πνευματικῶς Σόδομα καὶ Αἴγυπτος, 11:8. Hence it has fallen under judgment : τὴν πόλιν τὴν ἀγίαν πατήσουσιν (sc. τὰ ἔθνη) μῆνας τεσσεράκοντα [καὶ] δύο, 11:2. [284] The outer court of the temple is also delivered up, but the temple of God, the altar and worshippers in the sanctuary, i.e., God's people, are to be preserved, 11:1 f.

V. The New Jerusalem.

In NT usage we find the following expressions : ἡ ἄνω 'Ιερουσαλήμ, Gl. 4:26; 'Ιερουσαλὴμ ἐπουράνιος, Hb. 12:22; ἡ καινὴ 'Ιερουσαλήμ, Rev. 3:12; 21:2.

1. Paul.

In the proof from Scripture which Paul adduces in Gl. 4:21-31 the following equations are made. On the one hand the son of the slave is the Sinaitic covenant (= Hagar, → 285, 19 ff.) and ἡ νῦν 'Ιερουσαλήμ, i.e., those who are not free but

---

destiny." "Like Jesus Himself, Paul is not taken unawares by suffering but goes into the darkness with full clarity and sure resolve," Haench. Ag.[12], 535.

[281] It is the place of deliverance acc. to Jl. 2:32. Acc. to 4 Esr. 13:35 the Messiah will come on the top of Mt. Zion in order that Zion may be glorious and judgment may be held on the nations.

[282] We are not told whether it is in heaven or on earth. But since earth is the site of the acts depicted in c. 13 and there is ref. to the heavenly Jerusalem only at the end of the book, this is probably the earthly Zion.

[283] V. 8 makes it impossible to think of Rome and to see in the two witnesses Peter and Paul. The number in v. 13 would also be much too small for Rome. But cf. J. Munck, *Petrus u. Pls. in d. Offenbarung Johannes* (1950); M. E. Boismard, "'L'Apocalypse' ou 'les Apocalypses' de Saint Jean," *Rev. Bibl.*, 56 (1949), 534 f.

[284] In Rev. 11:1-13 the divine probably adopted a Jewish tradition with only slight

stand under the Law. On the other hand the son of the free woman διὰ τῆς ἐπαγγελίας — the second διαθήκη — ἡ δὲ ἄνω 'Ιερουσαλήμ; to this Paul adds the further explanation that the Jerusalem which is above ἐλευθέρα ἐστίν, ἥτις ἐστὶν μήτηρ ἡμῶν, Is. 54:1 serving as Scripture proof for this. Since the Jerusalem which is above is free and the type of all who are not in subjection to the Law, a foundation is laid for the allegorical equation of ὁ δὲ ἐκ τῆς ἐλευθέρας and ἡ δὲ ἄνω 'Ιερουσαλήμ. Paul took the metaphor of the Jerusalem which is above from the apocalyptic tradition, → 325, 18 ff. This is not a higher form of the earthly city but stands in sharp contrast to the Jerusalem which now is. By setting in antithesis to present-day Jerusalem, not the future Jerusalem but that which is above, he makes it plain from his Scripture proof that eschatological salvation is not awaited in an indefinite future but has come already. [285] We who believe in Christ are children of our mother, the Jerusalem which is above, Gl. 4:31.

2. Hebrews.

Hb. contrasts with the Sinaitic διαθήκη the new διαθήκη established in the sacrificial death of Jesus, and says to the community : προσεληλύθατε Σιὼν ὄρει καὶ πόλει θεοῦ ζῶντος, 'Ιερουσαλὴμ ἐπουρανίῳ, Hb. 12:22. [286] The heavenly mount and the heavenly city [287] are here mentioned in direct proximity (→ 326, 3 ff.) as the site of the gathering of thousands of angels and the community of the firstborn. But this place is not just the goal of the pilgrimage of the people of God which has no abiding city on earth, 13:14. The community has already come to Zion, the heavenly Jerusalem. The new Jerusalem is the city in which the new διαθήκη has been made through the blood of Jesus. The way of the people of God leads from this Jerusalem on to the heavenly goal, which will again bear no other name but that of Jerusalem. [288]

3. Revelation.

Acc. to John's Apocalypse the new Jerusalem which the divine can perceive already will come down from heaven to earth at the end of the days. To the overcomer who remains faithful in the battle the promise is given : γράψω ἐπ' αὐτὸν τὸ ὄνομα τοῦ θεοῦ μου καὶ τὸ ὄνομα τῆς πόλεως τοῦ θεοῦ μου, τῆς καινῆς 'Ιερουσαλὴμ ἡ καταβαίνουσα ἐκ τοῦ οὐρανοῦ, Rev. 3:12 → III, 247, 11 ff. He who is called by this name will have citizenship in the heavenly Jerusalem which with the dawn of the new world of God will appear as a bride adorned for her husband (21:2) when the holy city (→ VI, 532, 12 ff.) comes down from God to the earth (21:10). Paradise will return with the new Jerusalem (22:1-5), a never-ending glory which is described with a wealth of images. [289]

---

editorial revision. Cf. E. Lohse, *Die Offenbarung des Johannes*, NT Deutsch, 11 (1960), ad loc.

[285] Cf. Bietenhard, 198.

[286] *Ad loc.* cf. the comm. and also E. Käsemann, *Das wandernde Gottesvolk*, FRL, 55³ (1959), 27-32; → V, 722, 15 ff.; VI, 531, 32 ff.; C. Spicq, "La panégyrie de Hebr. XII, 22," *Studia Theologica*, 6 (1952), 30-38.

[287] The idea is apoc. in origin, though the expression "heavenly Jerusalem" does not occur in Jewish apoc. Cf. Volz Esch., 375.

[288] "The whole Chr. pilgrimage takes place from beginning to end in the presence of the heavenly Jerusalem," Käsemann, *op. cit.*, 31.

[289] The material used here is taken from various traditions and woven into a new unity. For details → VI, 532, 12 ff.

Whereas according to the eschatological hope of Judaism the eschatological Jerusalem will have a temple (→ 327, 1 ff.), there is no temple in the heavenly Jerusalem of the Apocalypse : ὁ γὰρ κύριος ὁ θεὸς ὁ παντοκράτωρ ναὸς αὐτῆς ἐστιν, καὶ τὸ ἀρνίον, Rev. 21:22.

D. Zion-Jerusalem in the Early Church.

1. In the writings of the post-apost. fathers the names Zion and Jerusalem occur only once each. Barn., 6, 2 quotes Is. 28:16 and 1 Cl., 41, 2 mentions Jerusalem in the context of exhortation. Every Christian must please God in his own place and not transgress the rule laid down for his cultic ministry, just as sacrifices are not made to God everywhere but only in Jerusalem.

2. Jerusalem is mentioned more often in the apocr. Gospels. Ev. Pt. [290] and Ev. Hb. [291] always have 'Ιερουσαλήμ. Ev. Eb. says that πᾶσα 'Ιεροσόλυμα came to John the Baptist. [292] Pr. Pt. says the resurrection and ascension of Christ took place πρὸ τοῦ 'Ιεροσόλυμα. [293]

3. The allegorical interpretation already given to the name of Jerusalem in the Hell. Synagogue (→ 320, 35 ff.) was adopted by Chr. theologians and transferred to the Church or believers. [294] Jerusalem "is the Church, for the city of God is the Church, the vision of peace (ὅρασις εἰρήνης)," Orig. Hom. in Jer., 9 on Jer. 11:2. [295] "The city of the great King" — this is "the true Jerusalem or the Church, built up of living stones," ἔνθα ἱεράτευμα ἅγιον, πνευματικαὶ θυσίαι ποοσφέρονται τῷ θεῷ ὑπὸ τῶν πνευματικῶν καὶ τὸν πνευματικὸν νενοηκότων νόμον, Orig. Comm. in Joh., 13, 13 on Jn. 4:19 f. [296] Elsewhere Orig. uses the interpretation of Jerusalem as ὅρασις εἰρήνης with ref. to the soul which "is privileged to see Jerusalem," Hom. in Jer., 13 on Jer. 15:5-7. Once it was the city of the Jebusites, Jebus meaning "trodden down." This old name refers to the soul oppressed by hostile powers. But the transformed soul, having coming into contact with the divine doctrine, is now called Jerusalem, ὅρασις εἰρήνης, loc. cit.

4. The idea of the Jerusalem which is above (→ 326, 3 ff.; 336, 28 ff.) is adopted by Cl. Al. to portray the ideal city whose original is in heaven along the lines of Platonism, Strom., IV, 172, 2 f. To the Gnostic distinction between the upper and the lower worlds corresponds the contrast between Jerusalem above and Jerusalem below ; this is found in various forms in Gnosticism. The Valentinians identified sophia with the Jerusalem which is above, where the angels dwell, Hipp. Ref., VI, 34, 3 f. The Ophites contrasted Jerusalem in the height, which is the mother of all living creatures, with Egypt as τὴν κάτω μῖξιν. The v. in Ps. 82:6 : "Ye are gods, and all of you children of the Most High," refers to those who flee from Egypt and come to the Jerusalem which is above, Hipp. Ref., V, 7, 39. Jerusalem below is distinguished from Jerusalem above. Jer. bewailed it, τὴν κάτω 'Ιερουσαλήμ ... τὴν κάτω γένεσιν τὴν φθαρτήν, Hipp. Ref., V, 8, 37. [297] But Jerusalem above belongs to the incorruptible world of light.

Lohse

---

[290] Ev. Pt. 5:20; 7:25; 9:34.
[291] Ev. Hb. 6; cf. P. Vielhauer in Hennecke³, I, 88 and 95 = Ev. Naz. 3.
[292] Epiph. Haer., 30, 13; cf. Vielhauer, op. cit., 103 = Ev. Eb. 2.
[293] Cl. Al. Strom., VI, 15, 128.
[294] Cf. Schmidt, 215 f., 232-248.
[295] Cf. the allegorical explanation of Jerusalem by Philo → 320, 35 ff.
[296] Cf. also Comm. in Joh., 6, 42 on Jn. 1:28.
[297] Cf. also Act. Joh. 97: John sees the Lord standing in a cave which He fills with radiance. He says to John : τῷ κάτω ὄχλῳ ἐν 'Ιεροσολύμοις σταυροῦμαι. In Mandaean writings the Jerusalem of the Jews is part of the evil aeon, cf. Schlier Gl. on 4:26.

---

† σκάνδαλον, σκανδαλίζω

Contents : A. Derivation and Non-Biblical Usage. B. The Word Group in the Old Testament : I. Hebrew Equivalents ; II. The Word Group in the Septuagint : 1. σκάνδαλον; 2. σκανδαλίζω; III. The Word Group in the Later Translations of the Old Testament : 1. Aquila ; 2. Symmachus ; 3. Theodotion. C. The Word Group in the New Testament : I. Formal and Material Dependence on the Old Testament ; II. The Word Group in the Sayings of Jesus and the Synoptic Records : 1. Adoption and Adaptation of Old Testament Prophecies ; 2. Present σκάνδαλα; 3. Present σκανδαλισμός [1]: a. Falling Away of the Unstable, b. σκανδαλισμός at Jesus, c. Avoidance of Causing the Faith of Disciples to Stumble ; III. The Word Group in Paul : 1. The σκάνδαλον of the Gospel ; 2. The Danger of Falling in the Life of the Community ; 3. The σκάνδαλον of Heresy ; IV. The Word Group in John. D. The Word Group in Patristic Literature.

A. Derivation and Non-Biblical Usage.

1. σκάνδαλον is synon. with σκανδάλη and the genetically later though in lit. earlier attested form σκανδάληθρον. [2] This word occurs in Aristoph. Ach., 687 in the phrase σκανδάληθρ' ἱστὰς ἐπῶν, which Phot. Lex., s.v. ascribes already to Cratinus Fr., 457 (CAF, I, 129). σκανδάλη (fem.) is found only once in Alciphr. Ep., II, 19, σκάνδαλον probably first in a pap. of the early 3rd cent. B.C., Pap. Cairo Zenon, 59, 608, 6 f. [3] The stem σκανδ- is perhaps etym. connected with Lat. scando "to mount" and Sanskr. skandati "he springs," and it means originally "to spring forward and back," "to slam to." [4] The nouns formed from this then denote "the means whereby one closes something," e.g., the stick in a trap, Alciphr. (→ lines 16 ff.): κρεᾴδιον τῆς σκανδάλης ἀπαρτήσας, "after I had secured a piece of meat on the stick." This is probably the basic meaning of σκάνδαλον and σκανδάληθρον [5] too, but

---

σ κ ά ν δ α λ ο ν, σ κ α ν δ α λ ί ζ ω. Liddell-Scott, s.v. σκανδάλη κτλ.; Moult-Mill., s.v. σκανδαλίζω; Cr.-Kö., 994-997; J. Vorstius, De hebraismis Novi Testamenti commentarius (1778), 87-105; A. Carr, "The Use of σκάνδαλον and σκανδαλίζειν in the NT," Exp., 5, 8 (1898), 344-351; also Horae Biblicae (1903), 58-68; Helbing, 127; J. H. Moulton, "Σκάνδαλον," Exp. T., 26 (1914/15), 331 f.; J. Moffatt, "Jesus upon 'Stumbling-blocks,' " ibid., 407-409; W. C. Allen, The Gospel acc. to St. Mark (1915), 199-202; J. Lindblom, "Skandalon. Eine lexikalisch-exegetische Untersuchung," Uppsala Univ. Årsskrift (1921); O. Schmitz, Vom Wesen des Ärgernisses² (1925); G. Stählin, Skandalon. Untersuchungen zur Gesch. eines bibl. Begriffs (1930); K. Schilder, "Over het 'Skandalon,' " Geref. Theol. Tijdschr., 32 (1931), 50-67, 97-130; Joh. W. 1 K. on 1:23; E. Fuchs, "Das entmythologisierte Glaubensärgernis," Zum hermeneutischen Problem in d. Theol. (1959), 230-236.

[1] This abstract word, found neither in LXX nor NT, but occurring in 'A at Is. 3:6 (cf. Stählin, 84-86, also → 343, 28 ff.) and the fathers, is used in what follows as a term for the process of σκανδαλίζεσθαι.

[2] The ancient lexicographers Hesych. and Phot. Lex., s.v. already call σκάνδαλον and σκανδάληθρον synon. On views as to the genetic relation of the two forms cf. Stählin, 11, n. 2; on σκανδάληθρον cf. ibid., 13 f.

[3] Ed. C. C. Edgar in Catalogue Général des Antiquités Egypt. du Musée du Caire, 90 (1931), 58. An overseer of Zenon writes : φρόντιζε οὖν πρὸ πολλοῦ περὶ τῶν σκανδάλων (Edgar's probably correct conjecture for σκανδάνων)· ἔρρωσο.

[4] Cf. Schol. on Aristoph. Ach., 687 (ed. F. Dübner [1883]); Etym. M. and Etym. Gud., s.v.; A. Cramer, Anecdota Graeca e codicibus manuscriptis Bibliothecarum Oxoniensium, II (1835), 410, 412; Stählin, 18 f. with n. 4; Boisacq, s.v.; Hofmann, s.v.

[5] Cf. Schol. on Aristoph. Ach., 687 (→ n. 4); Suid., s.v. σκανδάληθρον, Poll. Onom., s.v.; ῥόπτρον is often ref. to as a synon. Cf. also T. Nicklin, " 'Stumbling-block,' " Exp. T., 26 (1914/15), 479.

then, *pars pro toto,* the trap itself is meant. Before and alongside the bibl. use σκάνδαλον occurs only in popular and special use and is thus rare. [6] σκανδάληθρον is used
metaphorically in Aristoph. Ach., 687 (→ 339, 16 f.): ἐρωτᾷ σκανδάληθρ' ἱστὰς
ἐπῶν, "he sets traps with his questions." [7] There is no intellectual or abstract extension
of the meaning of σκάνδαλον outside the Jewish-Chr. sphere. But the original sense
lives on in the post-chr. period along with some special forms. Thus σκάνδαλον is used
of a kind of acrobat in Chrys. Hom. in Mt., 59 on 18:7 (MPG, 58 [1862], 574): τὰ
σκάνδαλα ἐπὶ τῆς σκηνῆς = οἱ τὰ σώματα διαστρέφοντες. The derivate σκανδαλιστής already occurs in the same sense in an inscr. of the 2nd cent. A.D. [8] This
continuation of popular usage [9] is the more surprising when one realises that the
biblically influenced sense of "offence" "reason for punishment," also came into popular
speech, P. Lond., IV, 1338, 26 f.; 1339, 11 (8th cent.): σκάνδαλον διδόναι, "to lay
onself open to punishment." [10] But even in the 12th cent. Theodorus Prodromus can
invent with the popular sense a new and playful construct formed after the conventions
of lofty poetic speech, Catomyomachia, 31: σκανδαλοπλόκως, "harmfully" from
σκάνδαλον πλέκειν, "to tie a noose." [11]

2. The verb σκανδαλίζω with its gen. denominative suffix -ίζω [12] is in itself a
genuinely Gk. construct, but there are no examples of use independent of the Bible and
the par. σκανδαλόω in 'A (→ 343, 35 ff.) suggests that σκανδαλίζω was not much
used at that time. On the other hand σκανδαλιστής (→ lines 8 ff. with n. 8) presupposes a profane use of σκανδαλίζω in the sense "to set traps" etc.

B. The Word Group in the Old Testament.

I. Hebrew Equivalents.

Fundamental to the further development of the meaning of σκάνδαλον and σκανδαλίζω is the fact that they came into use in the LXX and that they did so as renderings
of two different verbal stems יקשׁ (נקשׁ) and כשׁל and their noun derivates מוקשׁ and
מכשׁול. a. יקשׁ (נקשׁ) originally means "to strike (slam)" and then "to catch in a snare,"
Ps. 124:7, fig. Ps. 38:12. The noun מוקשׁ originally means "stick," "throwing stick"

---

[6] Lindblom, 50 and Helbing, 127 show that σκάνδαλον (and σκανδαλίζω) is not
just a *vox biblica.*
[7] Cf. the similar fig. use of σκάνδαλον, e.g., ψ 139:6 : ἔκρυψαν ὑπερήφανοι παγίδα
μοι ... ἐχόμενα τρίβου σκάνδαλον ἔθεντό μοι.
[8] Ditt. Syll.³, II, 847, 5 (2nd cent. A.D.); here the callings ascribed to the Nonnos
honoured in Delphi, i.e., κοντοπαίκτης ("tight-rope walker") cf. Chrys. Hom. in Hb., 16, 4
on 9:15-18 (MPG, 63 [1862], 127) and καλοβάτης ("walker on stilts"), make it likely
that σκανδαλιστής means "acrobat" (Dittenberger "illusionist"), so W. Kroll, Art. "Σκανδαλιστής" in Pauly-W., 3a (1929), 438; cf. Suppl. Epigr. Graec., 2, 328; H. Pomtow,
"Delphische Neufunde, II : Neue Delph. Inschr.," *Klio,* 15 (1918), 33 and n. 1; Liddell-
Scott, *s.v.* σκανδαλιστής. With the art the word *scandalista* passed into Lat., cf. Ps.-Aug.
De Symbolo, II, 2, 4 (MPL, 40 [1887], 639), probably also (Stählin, 457 and n. 2) Ps.-
Prosper. De Promissionibus et Praedicationibus Dei, 5, 14 (16) (MPL, 51 [1861], 856 A);
cf. Stählin, 322 f., 349, 456 f. On various forms of this cf. H. Blümner, "Fahrendes Volk im
Altertum," SAMünch., 1918, No. 6 (1918), 10, where there is ref. to what Chrys. seems to
mean by σκάνδαλα (→ lines 6 ff.) though without the term, *ibid.,* n. 44, 51.
[9] It is open to question whether the use of *scandalum* for animal seed in a Geoponicum
(cf. Du Cange, Glossarium ad Scriptores mediae et infimae graecitatis [1958], *s.v.*) also
belongs here.
[10] Cf. Stählin, 322, 361.
[11] Theodorus Prodromus Catomyomachia, ed. R. Hercher (1873), cf. Stählin, 348, 360-
362.
[12] A. Debrunner, *Griech. Wortbildungslehre* (1917), 129. Helbing, 127 also states that
σκανδαλίζω is not at all non-Hell. in spirit, though cf. Kl. Mk. on 4:17.

(= "boomerang"?), cf. Am. 3:5; Job 40:24, then "trap," Ps. 64:5; 69:22; 140:6; 141:9. Dominant, however, is the transf. use for "occasion of misfortune," "cause of ruin," e.g., Ex. 10:7; 1 S. 18:21; Job 34:30. b. The other term כֶּשֶׁל leads into a different world of ideas; it means "to slip," "to stumble," e.g., Is. 8:15. מִכְשׁוֹל is thus "an obstacle on the path over which one falls," Lv. 19:14; Is. 57:14; fig. Is. 8:14; Jer. 6:21; Ez. 3:20. Transf. this can also mean "cause of disaster," e.g., Ps. 119:165, opp. שָׁלוֹם 1 S. 25:31: מִכְשׁוֹל־לֵב, then in Ez. 7:19; 14:3 f., 7 cf. 44:12, also 18:30 and Sir. 47:24 [29], often with עָוֹן "occasion of sin" and hence leading to punishment, which is again disaster. [13] c. A third equivalent, [14] found in the OT only in Hbr. Sir but common in the Mishnah and Talmud, [15] is the Aram. loan word תְּקֵל (synon. כֶּשֶׁל) [16] and the derived תְּקָלָה. This is not rendered σκανδαλίζω in the LXX but προσκόπτω (→ VI, 748, 34 ff.) or πλανάω in Sir. 15:12, while תקלה is ξύλον προσκόμματος in Sir. 31:7 (→ VI, 747, 2 ff.). But תקל is probably the word Jesus used when we find σκανδαλίζω in His sayings at Mt. 5:29 f. and par.; 11:6 and par.; 13:21 and par.; 17:27; 18:6 and par.; 24:10; 26:31 and par.

II. The Word Group in the Septuagint.

1. σκάνδαλον. Since the Hbr. מוֹקֵשׁ and מכשׁול in a transf. sense meant "cause of ruin" (→ lines 2, 7 f.) it was quite possible to use the same terms for this in the LXX: πρόσκομμα, σκῶλον and σκάνδαλον. Of these πρόσκομμα and σκῶλον mean "that over which one stumbles," "the obstacle on the path," which corresponds to the basic sense of מכשׁול, while σκάνδαλον corresponds to מוקשׁ. But the assimilation of the two groups was so complete that secondarily (→ VI, 748, 32 f.) מוֹקֵשׁ could even take on the fig. sense of מכשׁול "obstacle," "hindrance" (Sir. 32[35]:20 → πρόσκομμα, VI, 745, 32 ff.) and similarly σκάνδαλον could be used for מכשׁול where it obviously has the sense of stumbling-block" as in Lv. 19:14; 1 S. 25:31. [17] As often in the LXX the similarity in sound between מכשׁול and σκάνδαλον had a hand here, cf. פח - παγίς etc. [18] But the distribution of σκάνδαλον in the LXX is uneven. The translators of the prophets avoid it; thus Ez. uses βάσανος and κόλασις (also similar in sound to מכשׁול) for "torment," "punishment" (for sin, in transl. of עָוֹן מִכְשׁוֹל → lines 6 f. and n. 13). On the other hand, σκάνδαλον as the equivalent of מוקשׁ still has quite clearly the sense of "trap," esp. when used with nets, gins, snares etc. as a metaphor for the devices of the wicked ψ 139:6; 140:9. A trap for men, obviously a military stratagem and perhaps a kind of wolf-pit, is a σκάνδαλον in Jdt. 5:1.

---

[13] מוקשׁ does not occur in the Dead Sea Scrolls but מכשׁול is common, sometimes with עָוֹן, so 1 QS 2:12, 17; 1 QH 4:15; 8:35 ("chains of stumbling"); 9:21, 27; 10:17; 16:15, 22.

[14] For other equivalents cf. Stählin, 44, 88 f. (Job 28:8).

[15] Cf. Levy Wört., s.v.; Dalman Wört., s.v. with other derivates; e.g., Ber., 4, 2, cf. O. Holtzmann, Die Mischna, I, 1 Berakot (1912), p. 61.

[16] In the Tg. תקל (like σκανδαλίζω in the LXX) occurs for כשׁל, e.g., Ps. 31:11; Mal. 2:8, also for נקשׁ, e.g., Dt. 7:25; 12:30; Ps. 9:16, cf. Levy Chald. Wört., s.v.; Str.-B., I, 303, 779. In Sir. it is in parallelism with נקשׁ at 31:7 or מוקשׁת at 32:20.

[17] Cf. also Hier. in Mt. on 15:12 (MPL, 26 [1884], 111): quia crebro teritur in ecclesiasticis scripturis scandalum, breviter dicamus, quid significat. Scolon et scandalon nos offendiculum vel ruinam et impactionem pedis possumus dicere. He then says scandalizare means occasionem ruinae dare. For discussion of an originally close relation between מוקשׁ and מכשׁול as concreta cf. Moulton, 331. Allen, 199 f. tries to show that in LXX and NT σκάνδαλον mostly means "trap" and σκανδαλίζω "to fall into a trap," but his attempt is artificial and unconvincing.

[18] Cf. Stählin, 44-47.

But mostly in the LXX there is little of either figure left and σκάνδαλον simply means "cause of ruin," the figures contributing the three elements of unexpectedness, knavery and violence (→ V, 593, 5 f.), cf. 1 S. 18:21; 1 Macc. 5:4.[19] In this sense σκάνδαλον along with the synon. σκῶλον serves esp. as a distinctive means to express the Deuteronomic view of history acc. to which the sins of the people constantly become reasons for divine punishments, and more than any other the sin of idolatry : οἱ θεοὶ αὐτῶν (sc. the Canaanites) ἔσονται ὑμῖν εἰς σκάνδαλον, Ju. 2:3. The Canaanites themselves ἔσονται ὑμῖν εἰς παγίδας καὶ εἰς σκάνδαλα, Jos 23:13, cf. Ju. 8:27; ψ 105:36; Dt. 7:16 (LXX σκῶλον, Hexapla reading σκάνδαλον). Perhaps the same idea lies behind ψ 68:23 (→ 354, 25 ff.): "Their meal (sc. that of the wicked) will be to them a snare (εἰς παγίδα) and their sacrificial meals[20] a trap (εἰς σκάνδαλον)." Perhaps a syncretistic background led the Psalmist to see in the "table" of the wicked a kind of "table of demons" (cf. 1 C. 10:21), unless this is one of the instances in which hymnal confession is rated above the sacrificial cultus.[21] σκάνδαλον could become a term for images, since these were the occasion and object of very serious sin and punishment in Israel, cf. LXX Hos. 4:17: Ephraim ἔθηκεν ἑαυτῷ σκάνδαλα, also Σ Zeph. 1:3 (→ 344, 5 ff.). This produces the antithetical thought that God is the source of salvation and idols are the cause of destruction. But any other transgression of the Law, being a reason for divine punishment, can be called a σκάνδαλον or "cause of evil," cf. ψ 48:14; 118:165. Again in 1 S. 25:31: καὶ οὐκ ἔσται σοι τοῦτο βδελυγμὸς καὶ σκάνδαλον τῷ κυρίῳ μου, מִכְשׁוֹל־לֵב is originally the "occasion of a penal misfortune which threatens (David's) life," לֵב here in the sense of נֶפֶשׁ and σκάνδαλον (LXX Cod B) the "cause of evil" as a penalty for the βδελυγμός which David would have committed by smiting Nabal.[22]

If σκάνδαλον often meant a ground for divine punishment of sin, it was only a step to the further sense of an "occasion of sinning" on one's own account or "temptation to sin" by others. In later Jewish syncretism and the related antithesis between the righteous and the wicked σκάνδαλον thus came to be used in various ways. There is often contained in it the idea of the evil which sin brings with it (παγίς has the same twofold sense in, e.g., ψ 118:110), cf. ψ 48:14 : αὕτη ἡ ὁδὸς αὐτῶν σκάνδαλον αὐτοῖς, "the apparently successful way of the ungodly is in reality a continual cause of sin and destruction"; Jdt. 12:2 : eating pagan foods would be a sin for Judith ; Sir. 7:6 : θήσεις σκάνδαλον ἐν εὐθύτητί σου, "thou wilt put a load of sin on what is otherwise thine uprightness." In the sense of "temptation" the ref. may be to the traps of the ungodly in ψ 139:6; 140:9. The only instance from Ps. Sol. is clearer, for in 4:23 : ὁ κύριος ... ῥύσεται ἡμᾶς ἀπὸ παντὸς σκανδάλου παρανόμου, the ref. is to every temptation to transgression of the Law emanating here from ἄνθρωποι δόλιοι καὶ ἁμαρτωλοί.

---

[19] For the transition from fig. to transf. use note that σκάνδαλα as "traps" for souls in Wis. 14:11 (with παγίς as net for the feet) is interpreted as φθορὰ ζωῆς in v. 12, cf. v. 21 and the synon. expressions παγίδες τοῦ βίου (→ V, 593, 13) and παγίδες θανάτου (cf. Stählin, 102), ψ 17:6.

[20] For ולשלומים read וְשִׁלֻמֵיהֶם with Tg.; cf. BHK apparatus, ad loc.; Stählin, 65, n. 1. Paul (R. 11:9 → 354, 25 ff. and n. 88) followed a text with ἀνταπόδοσις or ἀνταπόδομα which he put (for emphasis ?) at the end. On this whole question cf. Stählin, 64 f.

[21] Cf. A. Weiser, Die Psalmen, AT Deutsch, 14/15⁵ (1959), ad loc., also Intr. 48.

[22] Cf. Stählin, 36-39, 66-68. The literal rendering σκάνδαλον καρδίας in the Hexapla recension Cod A might seem to involve a change of meaning due to the influence of the later sense "offence of conscience," "scruple," → 355, 32 ff. In fact, however, we simply have external assimilation to the HT, which is hardly less mechanical in A than in 'A → n. 27. In ψ 118:165, too, σκάνδαλον might be taken as the opp. of εἰρήνη in the sense of "disquiet of conscience," but it is open to question whether this is a possible sense in the age of the LXX.

2. σκανδαλίζω. This verb, which in the NT is twice as common (30 times) as the noun σκάνδαλον, is rare in the LXX and occurs only in the later OT books, once at Da. 11:41 vl. and 3 times in Sir. at 9:5; 23:8; 32:15, also once in Ps. Sol. 16:7. Da. 11:41 vl. is the only time σκανδαλίζομαι occurs for כשל;[23] it is here used abs. (πολλαὶ σκανδαλισθήσονται) and is echoed in the NT at Mt. 24:10 [24] → 346, 3 ff. In Sir. the Hbr. original, so far as there is one, is נקש (9:5; 32:15). In all 3 instances we find the instrumental-causal ἐν which NT use esp. at Mt. 11:6 par.; 13:57 par.; 26:31 par., 33 : at Sir. 9:5 "to suffer injury" through fines ; at 23:8 : λοίδορος καὶ ὑπερήφανος σκανδαλισθήσονται ἐν αὐτοῖς, sc. ἐν τοῖς χείλεσιν, "the slanderer and the braggart will catch themselves in their own words, i.e., fall into sin and punishment"; at 32[35]:15: ὁ ὑποκρινόμενος [25] σκανδαλισθήσεται ἐν αὐτῷ, sc. ἐν νόμῳ, "the hypocrite will fall into destruction by the same Law "as that in which the honest searcher of Scripture finds satisfaction and fulfilment. Whereas in the 4 OT ref. the pass. is used as med., Ps. Sol. 16:7 is the first passage prior to the NT to use the act., and this of a woman "who seeks to lead fools astray," γυνὴ πονηρὰ σκανδαλίζουσα ἄφρονα.

III. The Word Group in the Later Translations of the Old Testament.

One of the distinctive features of the history of σκάνδαλον and σκανδαλίζω is that they are not used at all in Hell. Jewish lit., neither in Philo, Jos. nor Ep. Ar., with the sole exception of translations of the Bible and Ps. Sol. As regards the use in the later translators ('ΑΣΘ) the fragmentary state of the tradition permits us to present only an incomplete picture.

1. Aquila. Aquila follows a rigid principle of translation which equates the basic senses of the Hbr. and Gk. equivalents, → 341, 17 ff. Thus σκάνδαλον is used for מכשול (and σκῶλον for מוקש) e.g., Is. 8:14. Here, too, σκάνδαλον usually means "cause of ruin," e.g., Ez. 3:20, this being imposed by God's judgment, Is. 57:14; Jer. 6:21. By the slavishly lit. transl. of the expression מכשול עון in passages like Ez. 7:19 : σκάνδαλον τῶν ἀδικιῶν, 14:3 : σκάνδαλον ἀνομίας, σκάνδαλον perhaps takes on the formal sense of "occasion" of sin or transgression of the Law. The slavish rendering of מכשלה ("ruins") as a derivate of כשל by a derivate of σκανδαλίζω leads to the first use of the verbal noun σκανδαλισμός in Is. 3:6, probably in the sense of the "disaster" which God's wrath brings, just as later σκανδαλισμός is mostly used only in a pass. sense, e.g., Orig. Comm. in Joh., 32, 5 on 13:6 ff.; Hom. in Lc., 17 on 2:35 ff. (GCS, 35, 118). In keeping is that practically the only use 'A makes of the verb is in the pass. σκανδαλίζομαι "to come to hurt," Prv. 4:12; Is. 3:8; 40:30; Da. 11:41; the exception is ψ 63:9. The same applies to the form σκανδαλόω which 'A seems to prefer : act. "to seduce" ἐσκανδαλώσατε πολλοὺς ἐν νόμῳ, Mal. 2:8; pass. "to fall," Is. 8:15 (LXX ἀδυνατήσουσιν); 59:14 : ἐσκανδαλώθη ἐν πλατείᾳ [26] ἀλήθεια; 63:13; ψ 26:2; cf. 30:11: ἐσκανδαλώθη ἐν ἀνομίᾳ μου [ἡ ἰσχύς μου], "the collapse

---

[23] In the same c. LXX replaces it 3 times by προσκόπτω (v. 14, 19, 33), though it is doubtful whether there is a conscious distinction, or at least one can no longer say what this might be. Elsewhere, esp. in the prophetic books, LXX iikes ἀσθενέω for כשל, twice in Jer. 18:15; Mal. 2:8, also for hi הכשיל and thus with trans. construction ; sometimes (Jer. 6:21) ἀσθένεια is also used for מכשול. This rendering, preferred by Σ and Θ (→ 344, 12 f.), seems to rest on the Aram. linguistic sense of the translators → I, 490, 21 ff.

[24] Near this v. there is a good deal of quotation from Da. (v. 15, 21, 30), just as Mt. 26 f. often cites Zech. (26:15, 28, 31; 27:9).

[25] For the uncertain מתלהלה "fool" ? cf. Ges.-Buhl, s.v. להה II ; "mocker" ? cf. R. Smend, Die Weisheit d. Jesus Sirach, II (1906), ad loc.; "hypocrite" ? cf. H. L. Strack, Die Sprüche Jesus', des Sohnes Sirachs (1903), 63 (s.v. להה).

[26] Read thus as in Σ (acc. to Eus.), cf. Field, II, 549, n. 35; Stählin, 124 and n. 6.

of my powers came through my sin," cf. also Ιερ. 8:12; 18:23; 27(50):32; Hos. 14:10, though these are preserved only in the Syrohexapla. [27]

2. Symmachus. Like the LXX Symmachus has σκάνδαλον for both מוֹקֵשׁ and מִכְשׁוֹל and mostly in the sense of "cause of disaster," Prv. 29:6; 22:25; Is. 8:14 (→ 352, 20 ff.; 353, 5 ff.), "death," Prv. 13:14; 14:27. In both cases the opp. is πηγὴ ζωῆς. Important in view of Mt. 13:41 (→ 346, 3 ff.) is the rendering of Zeph. 1:3 : τὰ σκάνδαλα σὺν τοῖς ἀσεβέσι, "idols [28] — cf. the σκάνδαλα of LXX Hos. 4:17 (→ 342, 14 ff.) — with their ungodly worshippers." The τέκνα σκανδάλου of Job 28:8 are probably idolaters too. [29] The verb σκανδαλίζω occurs in Σ only at Mal. 2:8; Is. 8:21.

3. Theodotion. There is nothing independent in the use of σκάνδαλον in Theodotion. He follows either LXX (Ju. 8:27; ψ 68:23) or Σ (Prv. 13:14; 14:27; Is. 8:14; Ez. 14:3 f.). In gen. he uses σκάνδαλον for מוֹקֵשׁ, and seems to stick consistently [30] to ἀσθενέω for כשׁל → I, 490, 19 ff.

C. The Word Group in the New Testament.

I. Formal and Material Dependence on the Old Testament.

Both formally and materially the NT use of σκάνδαλον and σκανδαλίζω is exclusively controlled by the thought and speech of the OT and Judaism. How far the words are from Greek thought may be seen not only from their absence from Greek literature but also from the need which the fathers repeatedly felt to explain the meaning of the NT σκάνδαλον. [31] It is worth noting that the two terms are almost always used by NT authors whose roots are in Judaism. [32]

The words are used in sayings of Jesus at Mt. 13:41; 16:23; 18:7 and par.; 5:29 f. and par.; 11:6 and par.; 13:21 and par.; 17:27; 18:6 and par.; 24:10; 26:31 and par. They occur in Paul at R. 9:33; 11:9; 14:13; 16:17; 1 C. 1:23; Gl. 5:11; R. 14:21 vl.; 1 C. 8:13; 2 C. 11:29. In Jn. we find them at 6:61; 16:1 (cf. also 1 Jn. 2:10; Rev. 2:14) and in Mk. at 6:3 (= Mt. 13:57). [33] A point particularly worth noting is that Mt. alone has all the relevant sayings of Jesus and many of them alone, cf. also 15:12; 13:57 and par. Luke has the group in dominical sayings only at 7:23 ↦ Mt. 11:6; 17:1 f. = Mt. 18:6 f.; neither in the Gospel nor Acts does he use them in his own formulations. (They do not occur either in Past., Hb. or the Cath. Ep.) [34] Luke even avoids sayings which focus on σκανδαλίζειν [35] and which were probably known to him (esp.

---

[27] For details cf. Stählin, 121-127. The purely external translation method of Aquila makes it impossible to draw from him any sure conclusions as to the meaning of the words, cf. P. Katz, "Ein Aquila-Index in Vorbereitung. Prolegomena und Specimina, I," VT, 8 (1958), 272 f.; → V, 584, n. 13.

[28] τὰ σκάνδαλα is probably to be taken thus in view of vv. 4 ff., though cf. Stählin, 90.

[29] Cf. Stählin, 88 f.

[30] Even the one exception in Mal. 2:8 is uncertain ; cf. Stählin, 121, n. 2, 124.

[31] E.g., Orig. Cels., 5, 64; Hom. in Nu. 25:1 (GCS, 30, 233, 10-13, 15); Athanasius Vita Antonii, 23 (MPG, 26 [1887], 877 A); Cyr. Hom. in Lc. 17:1 (MPG, 72 [1864], 828 D-829 C); Bas. De Baptismo, II, 10, 1 (MPG, 31 [1885], 1617 C); also Regulae Brevius Tractatae, 64 (ibid., p. 1125 A → n. 45); Hier. in Mt. 15:12 (MPL, 26 [1884], 111 → n. 17); Cassiodorus Expositio in Ps. 118:165 (MPL, 70 [1865], 896 A, B); cf. Stählin, 297, 356 f., 465 f., 45, n. 2 and 398, n. 1.

[32] In so far as the authors of the 2nd and 4th Gospels were Palestinians.

[33] Cf. also Barn., 4, 3 and 9 from the post-apost. fathers.

[34] 1 Pt. 2:8 is a quotation and the whole ep. is Pauline in colouring → 353, 5 ff.

[35] For other reasons Lk. does not have at all the σκάνδαλον passages peculiar to Mt. (13:41; 16:23).

Mt. 5:29 f. and par.; also 24:10), or else he expresses the same thing in another way, cf. Lk. 8:13 and Mt. 13:21; Lk. 4:28 f. and Mt. 13:57; Lk. 22:31 f. and Mt. 26:31; in other passages, too, Luke has the thing itself but puts it in his own words and even in a very striking way, cf. Lk. 2:34; 20:17 f. (→ n. 79, 61).

Though πτῶσις is used rather than σκάνδαλον (→ VI, 167, 21 ff.) Lk. 2:34 is in fact one of the purest expressions of the central NT concept of the *skandalon* : οὗτος κεῖται εἰς πτῶσιν καὶ ἀνάστασιν πολλῶν ἐν τῷ 'Ισραήλ. As regards the meaning of this prophecy it makes no difference whether the fall is due to stumbling on a stone or not (→ VI, 167, n. 3, but cf. → I, 372, 3 ff.). In any case the ministry of Jesus can have two results, life on the one side and death on the other. This thought, which is developed esp. by Paul, is very strikingly presented here, and this is in keeping with the Jewish Chr. origin of the infancy stories in Lk., just as Paul finds his model in the Jews → 354, 3 ff. Naturally in view of the closeness to Paul one may ask whether the Pauline concept has not had some influence. The appended expression σημεῖον ἀντιλεγόμενον carries the same thought. The person and work of Jesus are a divine sign (cf. Lk. 11:29 f.) which demands faith and finds it in some, but meets with opposition and rejection in many. It is ordained (→ 353, 25 f.) to disclose the inner attitude of all by acceptance or rejection, and in this division into believers and unbelievers to make the final decision concerning salvation or perdition, cf. Lk. 12:51 ff.

Some LXX expressions recur in the same form in the NT but with a new content: σκάνδαλον τίθημι [36] ψ 139:6; Jdt. 5:1; cf. Lv. 19:14 in R. 14:13; 9:33; (εἰς) σκάνδαλόν εἰμί τινι 1 S. 25:31; ψ 48:14 in 1 C. 1:23; [37] σκανδαλίζομαι ἔν τινι Sir. 9:5 etc. in Mt. 11:6; 26:31; R. 14:21 vl. There are also many allusions to the OT, so in Rev. 2:14 to Nu. 25:1 f.; 31:16; Mt. 24:10 to Da. 11:41, yet not always to the LXX form but twice at least to a transl. which seems to have influenced Σ, cf. Mt. 13:41 [38] and Σ Zeph. 1:3 (→ 344, 5 ff.), also R. 9:33; 1 Pt. 2:8 and Σ [39] Is. 8:14. Sometimes there is almost lit. quotation from the LXX : ψ 68:23 in R. 11:9. Except in R. 11:9 the metaphor in σκάνδαλον, if discernible at all, is more that of the stone, → 341, 21 f. This is supported by the following considerations. 1. Instead of παγίς (cf. LXX Jos. 23:13; ψ 68:23; 139:6) πρόσκομμα is the controlling companion-term in R. 9:33; 1 Pt. 2:8; R. 14:13, cf. v. 21 vl.: προσκόπτει ἢ σκανδαλίζεται. 2. The expression πέτρα σκανδάλου from Is. 8:14 takes on fundamental significance. 3. There is an undoubtedly deliberate link between πέτρα (Πέτρος) and σκάνδαλον in Mt. 16:18, 23 → 348, 10 ff.

In the NT as in the OT what is at issue in σκάνδαλον is the relation to God → 342, 3 ff. The σκάνδαλον is an obstacle in coming to faith and a cause of going astray in it. As in the OT it is the cause of both transgression and destruction (→ 342, 28 ff.), for a fall in faith is a fall in the absolute sense. The force of the verb σκανδαλίζω is even stronger than that of the noun σκάνδαλον in the NT. Whereas σκάνδαλον is only an "occasion of falling" which might lead to a fall or not, σκανδαλίζω is the causing of a fall and σκανδαλίζομαι the actual taking place of the fall. [40]

---

[36] Related but new in the NT as compared with the LXX are βάλλω σκάνδαλον in Rev. 2:14 and ποιέω σκάνδαλον in R. 16:17.

[37] Cf. σκάνδαλόν τινός εἰμι in Mt. 16:23 and σκάνδαλόν ἐστιν ἔν τινι in 1 Jn. 2:10, also new as compared with the LXX.

[38] One must take into account here the possibility that τὰ σκάνδαλα καὶ τοὺς ποιοῦντας τὴν ἀνομίαν is the direct rendering into Gk. of a logion preserved in Aram. LXX : ἀσθενήσουσιν οἱ ἀσεβεῖς.

[39] 'Α (cf. Ltzm. Gl.³ Exc. on 4:31) with its εἰς στερεὸν σκανδάλου is further from Pl. than Σ with its (uncertain) εἰς πέτραν σκανδάλου which has a similar ring to R. 9:33 (and 1 Pt. 2:8), cf. Stählin, 82 f., 87 and n. 1. Acc. to Theophylact. and Procop. Σ preferred εἰς πέτραν πτώματος (J. Ziegler [*Isaias* (1939) apparatus, *ad loc.*]), but cf. Hatch-Redp., *s.v.* σκάνδαλον "Is. 8:14 twice"). Cf. → 353, 8 ff. and n. 81.

[40] σκανδαλίζομαι is thus the opp. of the metaphorical aor. ἐπίστευσα and ἀπιστέω

II. The Word Group in the Sayings of Jesus and the Synoptic Records.

1. Adoption and Adaptation of Old Testament Prophecies.

The Logia tradition has Jesus quote twice from OT passages, Zeph. 1:3 in Mt. 13:41 and Da. 11:41 in Mt. 24:10. [41] Both have an eschatological slant: Mt. 24:10 deals with the great eschatological σκανδαλισμός (→ n. 1), while Mt. 13:41 refers to the eschatological destruction of σκάνδαλα. What is an event within history in Da. 11:41, though in the last time (v. 40), becomes in Mt. 24:10 the great tribulation within the Messianic Woes between the ἀρχὴ ὠδίνων (v. 8) and the τέλος (v. 13 f.). It is not related directly to the wars mentioned just before. Rather the powers of apostasy (τὰ σκάνδαλα, Mt. 18:7; 13:41 → n. 46 and cf. Mt. 24:5, 11, 24) along with the great tribulation in its many forms (Mt. 24:21) gain the upper hand (cf. Rev. 13:7 f., 12-17), subduing both faith and love (v. 10b, 12) in the great majority (Mt. 24:5, 11 f.), i.e., in all Christians except the few elect (v. 22, 24, 31; cf. 22:4), and thus depriving them of deliverance (cf. v. 22) in the ἐπισυνάγειν of the angels (v. 31, cf. 40 f. → 347, 2 ff.). In the expression τὰ σκάνδαλα καὶ τοὺς ποιοῦντας τὴν ἀνομίαν in Mt. 13:41 we have an allusion to a revised form of the LXX of Zeph. 1:3 which Symmachus later had before him (→ 344, 5 ff. but cf. → n. 38). Like the prophet the exposition of the parable speaks of the end of the age (v. 40), cf. the old equation of harvest and judgment. The further equation ζιζάνια = υἱοὶ τοῦ πονηροῦ (v. 38) = τὰ σκάνδαλα καὶ οἱ ποιοῦντες τὴν ἀνομίαν (v. 41) [42] makes two things clear: 1. σκάνδαλον here, and only here in the NT, [43] is patently used of persons. [44] The OT ring of the second member (transgressor of the Law) suggests that τὰ σκάνδαλα are those who seduce into breaking the Law. [45] In the NT interpretation they are those who lead into sin and apostasy, cf. 1 Jn. 3:4. 2. As the ζιζάνια are sown by the devil (v. 39, cf. 15:13 → 350, 34 ff.), so the σκάνδαλα are the devil's children [46] (cf. Jn. 8:38, 41, 44; 1 Jn. 3:10) who work against God in the kingdom of the Son of Man (ἐκ Mt. 13:41) and try to cause as many as possible

---

(ἀπειθέω) of the pres. πιστεύω. But this does not mean there is no more hope for the ἐσκανδαλισμένοι, cf. in Herm. v., 4, 1, 3 the prayer for the gift of μετάνοια for the ἐσκανδαλισμένοι, and in m., 8, 10 the admonition: ἐσκανδαλισμένους ἀπὸ τῆς πίστεως μὴ ἀποβάλλεσθαι, "not to let those who have erred in faith fall." Cf. → n. 75.

[41] Both passages are peculiar to Mt. and their authenticity is disputed, 13:41 on the ground that it is in a secondary interpretation and 24:10 on the ground that it is in the Synoptic Apocalypse whose apocalyptic features might be in large part the work of the community.

[42] Cf. Is. 1:4 LXX where σπέρμα πονηρόν and its apposition υἱοὶ ἄνομοι are identical.

[43] Nor is there any instance in the LXX, though it is often said predicatively of men (Jos. 23:13; 1 S. 18:21; 1 Macc. 5:4) that they become σκάνδαλα. In a secondary tradition there is another example of the personal use of σκάνδαλον at Mt. 18:17. Instead of ὥσπερ ὁ ἐθνικὸς καὶ ὁ τελώνης Pist. Soph., 105 f. (GCS, 45³ [1959], 173, 21 f. 36 f.; 174, 3 f.; 175, 17 f.) 4 times has the form ὡς σκάνδαλον καὶ ὡς παραβάτης. This pair is strikingly similar to that in Mt. 13:41 and may be an echo of Zeph. 1:3. Cf. E. Nestle, Philologica Sacra (1896), 58.

[44] By means of πάντα, which is not repeated before τοὺς ποιοῦντας τὴν ἀνομίαν, it is closely related to this expression; αὐτούς (masc. v. 42) also refers to both; cf. Loh. Mt., ad loc., 224 with n. 2.

[45] Kl. Mt., ad loc. cf. the definition of σκανδαλίζω in Bas. Regulae Brevius Tractatae, 64 (MPG, 31 [1857], 1125 A): σκανδαλίζει μέν τις παρανομῶν λόγῳ ἢ ἔργῳ καὶ ἕτερον πρὸς παρανομίαν ἐνάγων ... ἢ κωλύων ποιῆσαι τὸ θέλημα τοῦ θεοῦ.

[46] This is possible (in spite of → VI, 559, 25 ff.). This demonic character of the σκάν-

to fall. [47] Their end will come with that of the devil and his hosts (on v. 42 cf. Rev. 20:10). The counterpart (cf. v. 30) to the gathering out of the σκάνδαλα from the kingdom of the Son of Man is the gathering of the elect from all the kingdoms of the world (Mt. 24:31), both by angels. [48]

2. Present σκάνδαλα.

The very way in which the OT quotations are used shows that not only eschatological tempters are at work to destroy faith and cause apostasy (τὰ σκάνδαλα, Mt. 13:41) but also that the eschatological falling away (σκανδαλί-ζομαι Mt. 24:10) has already begun, for the coming of Him who was to come (Mt. 11:3) has brought with it also the coming of the σκάνδαλα which were to come (18:7), and Jesus' radical demand for faith is accompanied by the radical hampering of faith.

a. Mt. 18:7 (= Lk. 17:1): οὐαὶ τῷ κόσμῳ ἀπὸ τῶν σκανδάλων· ἀνάγκη γὰρ ἐλθεῖν τὰ σκάνδαλα, πλὴν οὐαὶ τῷ ἀνθρώπῳ δι' οὗ τὸ σκάνδαλον ἔρχεται.

In Mt. this saying of Jesus is in a chain of sayings from 17:(24,)27-18:9 whose members are interconnected by the catchwords σκάνδαλον and σκανδαλίζω (17:27; 18:6-9) and which in 18:6 is interwoven with another chain (18:1-14) whose catchword is οἱ μικροί, 18:6, 10, 14 (cf. μείζων in v. 1, παιδίον in vv. 2-5). [49] Mk. too, though he does not use σκάνδαλα, binds the sayings together by the words σκανδα-λίζω in 9:42, 43, 45, 47, πῦρ in v. 43, (44, 46), 48, 49 and ἅλας in v. 49, 50. In Lk., however, the two sayings about the σκανδαλίζειν of the μικροί (→ 351, 22 ff.) and the coming σκάνδαλα, which are independent in Mt. 18:6 f., are recast and fused into a single saying, Lk. 17:1 f.

The three-membered logion in Mt. 18:7 says on the one side that the coming σκάνδαλα are inevitable (v. 7b) but on the other it pronounces woes on those who have a passive [50] (v. 7a) or active (v. 7c) part in their coming. [51] Both woes show how terribly dangerous σκάνδαλα are. At issue are the loss of eternal salvation and eternal perdition. This may be seen also from the saying about the λίθος μυλικός in Mt. 18:6; Lk. 17:2 (→ 351, 26 ff.) and that about the σκανδαλίζειν

δαλα of Mt. 13:41 (cf. the irrational ἐφάνη of v. 26 with its echo of epiphany) is on the one side related to Zeph. 1:3 (→ 344, 5 f.), for from of old idols and demons were connected, in the NT cf. 1 C. 10:20 f.; Rev. 2:13; cf. 9:20 : προσκυνήσουσιν τὰ δαιμόνια καὶ τὰ εἴδωλα, while on the other side it is related to the apocalyptic understanding of ἄνομος and ἀνομία, cf. 2 Th. 2:7 f.; Mt. 24:12, also 2 C. 6:14, where ἀνομία is a correlate of σκότος, Βελιάρ and εἴδωλα, → VI, 750, 23 ff.

[47] Jesus calls Peter a σκάνδαλον in exactly the same sense in Mt. 16:23 → 348, 21 ff.

[48] Cf. G. Stählin, "Christus u. d. Engel" in A. Rosenberg, Begegnung mit Engeln (1956), 61.

[49] Zn. Mt. entitles the whole chapter "Skandala in the Community." Cf. also Moffatt, 407-409.

[50] This woe on the victim is rare (cf. only Mt. 24:19 and par.). The woe is usually on the one responsible, for in general it is an anticipation of damnation at the Last Judgment, cf. Lk. 6:24-26 etc.

[51] Lk. omits the first woe and the word σκάνδαλον in the second, just as Mk. 14:29 leaves out the second σκανδαλισθήσομαι, cf. Mt. 26:33. Among the agrapha (from Ps.-Clem. Hom., 12, 29 in A. Resch, Agrapha, TU, 30, 3 and 4² [1906], 106 f.) there is a beatitude which is a counterpart to esp. Lk.'s form of the logion : τὰ ἀγαθὰ ἐλθεῖν δεῖ, μακάριος δέ, δι' οὗ ἔρχεται. If genuine this would give us a correspondence of μακάριος and οὐαί as in Lk. 6:20-26, but the triteness of the thought betrays its secondary origin.

of the members in Mt. 18:8 f. and par. (→ 351, 31 ff.; IV, 560, 10 ff.). Like the Gospel, σκάνδαλα apply to the world, to all mankind (cf. Mt. 24:14; 28:19). Like the Gospel again (cf. Mk. 13:10 δεῖ), they stand under a divine necessity (ἀνάγκη Mt. 18:7, ἀνένδεκτον Lk. 17:1), and they are integrated into God's plan. [52] The verb ἐλθεῖν shows that in these σκάνδαλα, as in those of Mt. 13:41 (→ 346, 4 ff.), we have originally eschatological entities which are already present along with many other entities which will come according to God's plan → 347, 9 ff. Thus these obstacles to faith are a decisive strand in the web of history, which is composed of decisions either for God or against Him.

b. The present fulfilment of this coming is also the theme of the saying to Peter in Mt. 16:23, much of which is preserved in Mt. alone. [53] The antithesis to v. 18 : σὺ εἶ Πέτρος καὶ ἐπὶ ταύτῃ τῇ πέτρᾳ οἰκοδομήσω μου τὴν ἐκκλησίαν, shows that σκάνδαλον has the figurative sense of "stone." [54] Peter, just called a πέτρα on which the whole building of the ἐκκλησία is to be erected, now becomes a kind of πέτρα σκανδάλου, an obstacle to Jesus Himself on His way of suffering [55] — Peter is the only one to be called this in the whole of the NT. In spite of the basic distinction (→ n. 54) the role of Peter seems often to correspond in striking fashion to that of Jesus Himself. Thus Jesus is the foundation-stone (cf. 1 C. 3:11 etc.); He is the stone of salvation (R. 9:33b; 1 Pt. 2:6); He is also for many the πέτρα σκανδάλου, R. 9:33a; 1 Pt. 2:8, → 352, 20 ff.; cf. esp. Lk. 20:17 f. Again, one sees here, as in Mt. 13:41, a direct relation between σκάνδαλον and Satan (→ 158, 28 ff.), who confronts Jesus in Peter. Peter, who protects the community against the forces of the underworld, himself becomes their tool. Having only just become the recipient of a divine revelation, Peter is already impelled by thoughts which are all too human rather than divine. The σκάνδαλον arises out of the difference between God and man which is expressed here with uncompromising sharpness (cf. Mt. 7:11; 15:19; 12:34). He who thinks and wills in human fashion sets himself in opposition to God and His will and thus becomes an instrument of Satan. The point where decision is made is the cross of Jesus, → 354, 15 ff. Because the way of Jesus to the cross became a σκάνδαλον for Peter, he himself became a σκάνδαλον for Jesus, [56] i.e., a personified temptation to turn aside from God's will.

---

[52] Cf. G. Stählin, "Die Feindschaft gg. Gott u. ihre Stelle in seinem Heilsplan für die Welt" in Die Leibhaftigkeit des Wortes, Festschr. f. A. Köberle (1958), 47-62, esp. 60 f.

[53] Mk. 8:33 has the command ὕπαγε ... σατανᾶ and the reason ὅτι οὐ φρονεῖς κτλ. but not σκάνδαλον εἶ ἐμοῦ. Lk. leaves out the whole dialogue (between 9:22 and 23).

[54] C. F. D. Moule, "Some Reflections on the 'Stone'-Testimonia in Relation to the Name Peter," NTSt, 2 (1955/56), 56-58, also thinks the name Peter is related in various ways to the many-faceted image of the stone in biblical thought.

[55] Possibly the metaphor of the way is echoed also in ὕπαγε ὀπίσω μου, if this means "Get out of my way." In view of the address σατανᾶ this is more likely than "Start following me again" in spite of the ὀπίσω μου ἐλθεῖν which occurs just after (v. 24). As with the ὕπαγε in the similar situation in 4:10 the most natural meaning is "Go away," cf. ἀπῆλθον εἰς τὰ ὀπίσω in Jn. 6:66 (synon. ὑπάγειν in v. 67). Cf. O. Cullmann, Peter [1953], 174, n. 61.

[56] Cf. Bengel, ad loc. (note on the transl.): mundo scandalum est crux ; quae cruci contraria sunt, scandalum erant Christo.

3. Present σκανδαλισμός.

a. Falling Away of the Unstable.

Where the λόγος τῆς βασιλείας is preached, there in consequence of the Gospel afflictions arise which are an anticipation of the woes of the Messiah (→ 346, 5 ff.) and the result is a σκανδαλίζεσθαι (Mt. 13:20 f. and par.; Mk. 4:17), [57] i.e., a going astray from the Word, a falling away from the Gospel (Lk. 8:13 : ἐν καιρῷ πειρασμοῦ ἀφίστανται), as the prelude to the eschatological σκανδαλισμός. As in Mt. 24:10 (→ 346, 12 ff.) the reference is to men who have already accepted the Gospel, and indeed εὐθὺς μετὰ χαρᾶς, Mt. 13:20. But the reasons for falling away may vary. Whereas in Mt. 24:21 f. it is the overwhelming force of tribulation, in Mt. 13 it is an unstable (πρόσκαιρος) and religiously superficial nature which is easily enthused but cools off just as easily, Mt. 13:5, 21. But falling away includes destruction, just as in the OT the σκάνδαλον which is the occasion of apostasy and sin, and the temptation to these, is also the cause of ruin, → 342, 25 ff.

b. σκανδαλισμός at Jesus.

When in the Gospels an ἔν τινι added to σκανδαλίζομαι gives the reason for going astray or falling, the reference in each case is to Jesus, Mt. 26:31, 33; 11:6 par. Lk. 7:23; Mt. 13:57 par. Mk. 6:3, though cf. R. 14:21 vl. → 355, 19 ff. These passages show that σκανδαλίζεσθαι ἐν αὐτῷ can be the opposite of πιστεῦσαι εἰς αὐτόν. As the Synoptic Jesus often announces His passion, He also predicts a severe crisis for His disciples. Mk. 14:27: πάντες σκανδαλισθήσεσθε, "you will all give way, fall away (from me)," extended and elucidated in Mt. 26:31: πάντες ὑμεῖς σκανδαλισθήσεσθε ἐν ἐμοὶ ἐν τῇ νυκτὶ ταύτῃ, "this night you will all have doubts about me, lose your faith in me." It is possible that the πειρασμός of which the disciples become victims is already regarded as part of the eschatological woes, cf. Mk. 14:38 and par., also Mt. 6:13. Their fall corresponds, then, to that of Mt. 24:10 (→ 346, 5 ff.) and 13:21 (→ lines 3 ff.). [58] In relation to His own destiny and also that of the disciples Jesus quotes Zech. 13:7, a saying which prophesies great affliction for a Messianic figure and His followers, though this will ultimately bring salvation. As the flock loses its rallying-point with the death of the shepherd, and is gripped by panic and scatters, so the death of Jesus causes the disciples to fall away from Him; as the loss of the common focus and centre it brings about the disruption of their fellowship, cf. Jn. 16:32. [59] Mk. 14:50 and par. must also be taken in this sense. Peter's denial follows Jesus' quotation of the prophecy from Zech., Mk. 14:29-31 and par. This is provoked by the fact that Peter will not accept the application of this prediction of general apostasy to himself: εἰ καὶ πάντες σκανδαλισθήσονται, ἀλλ' οὐκ ἐγώ, Mk. 14:29. Once again Mt. expands in 26:33 : εἰ πάντες σκανδαλισθήσονται ἐν σοί, ἐγὼ οὐδέποτε σκανδαλισθήσομαι. [60] The incident is in

---

[57] It has been seen for a long time that the distinctions between the three kinds of seed which bear no fruit are fluid. σκανδαλίζεσθαι is used of only one group simply for effect within the three-fold structure of popular story-telling. Fundamentally all the first three groups are the σκανδαλιζόμενοι as compared with the fourth.
[58] Cf. Loh. Mk. on 14:27.
[59] Though cf. Loh. Mt. on 26:31.
[60] On the other hand the pap.-fr. from Fayum (KIT, 83 [1929], 23, 5 ff.; cf. P. Savi,

noteworthy antithesis to Mt. 16:21-23. There Peter will not accept suffering for Jesus, but here he accepts it not only for Jesus but also for himself, Lk. 22:33, cf. Mk. 14:31. There Peter becomes a σκάνδαλον for Jesus, but here he is told that in spite of all his good intentions, in spite of every warning, and in spite of the intercession of Jesus (Lk. 22:32) Peter will fall victim to σκάνδαλον at Jesus,[61] cf. → 348, 30 ff. Another saying which stands under eschatological influence is that to John the Baptist : καὶ μακάριός ἐστιν ὃς ἐὰν μὴ σκανδαλισθῇ ἐν ἐμοί, Mt. 11:6; Lk. 7:23. Every beatitude and every woe (cf. Mt. 18:7) on the lips of Jesus is an eschatological judgment → IV, 367, 33 ff. In this case it is of decisive significance in the Last Judgment whether a man loses confidence in Him or not. The macarism here is closely connected[62] with the depiction (on the basis of Is. 35:5 and 61:1) of salvation that has already come. The present age of salvation is also the age of decision. It offers two possibilities, that of faith and that of unbelief, and both in Jesus ; for the presence and work of Jesus have the power to awaken faith but they can also result in the missing of faith.[63] Since Jesus refers to Himself both the prophetic sayings and also the possibility of σκανδαλισμός, His self-awareness finds remarkable expression in the Gospels. He realises that a σκάνδαλον, a cause of unbelief, attaches to His words and deeds, and that this cannot be avoided ; nevertheless, the aim which He expressly pursues and frequently states is the avoidance of σκανδαλισμός, cf. 17:27; 18:8 f.; Jn. 16:1; also 1 C. 8:13; R. 14:13. The eschatological emphasis of σκανδαλίζεσθαι in Mt. 11:6 and par.; 26:31 and par. rests also on the σκανδαλισμός of the people of Nazareth : καὶ ἐσκανδαλίζοντο ἐν αὐτῷ, Mt. 13:57; Mk. 6:3. This cannot simply mean that they took offence at the irreconcilable contradiction between His origin and His work, which also carried with it an unmistakable claim. It means rather that on this account they refused to believe in Him. In Lk., who gives a broader depiction of the incident but again avoids the word σκανδαλίζομαι (→ 344, 28 ff.; n. 61), the unbelief becomes mortal hatred, Lk. 4:28 f. The (absolute)[64] σκανδαλίζομαι of Mt. 15:12 bears the same sense : the disciples point out to Jesus ὅτι οἱ Φαρισαῖοι ἀκούσαντες τὸν λόγον ἐσκανδαλίσθησαν, → IV, 106, 30 ff. Here, too, σκανδαλίζομαι is more than just "feeling hurt."[65] Naturally this is part of it in view of Jesus' personal attack on them, v. 8 f. But the primary meaning is "deep religious offence" at the preaching of Jesus, and this both causes and includes denial and rejection of Jesus. One may see this from the reply of Jesus. By their σκανδαλίζεσθαι the Pharisees show that they are

---

"Le fr. évangélique du Fajoum," *Rev. Bibl.*, 1 [1892], 326; A. Harnack, "Das Evangeliumfr. von Fajjum," TU, 5, 4 [1889], 489 and 493) offers a shorter (or pre-Marcan ?) text : καὶ εἰ πάντες, οὐκ ἐγώ.

[61] Here as in 8:13 Lk. avoids σκανδαλίζομαι, though he expresses the thing itself in the ἐκλίπῃ ἡ πίστις of v. 32. The most important difference between Lk. and the other Synoptists is that the falling away of the disciples is God's doing (πατάξω) in Mk. and Mt. but Satan's in Lk. (22:31). How primitive Chr. faith can combine the two may be seen from, e.g., Mt. 4:1; 2 C. 12:7-9; 1 C. 5:4 f.

[62] The attempts to reconstruct the text on the basis of connections with Prv. (8:31) in S. Hirsch, "Studien zu Mt. 11:2-26," ThZ, 6 (1950), 247, are not very convincing.

[63] "Mt. 11:2 ff. implies that the same reality which is an incognito and possibility of offence also means responsibility and is thus a basis of faith," P. Althaus, Review of E. Brunner, *Der Mittler*, in ThLZ, 54 (1929), 476; Stählin, 234.

[64] The prepositional expression with ἐν is represented here by ἀκούσαντες τὸν λόγον.

[65] Cf. Loh. Mt., *ad loc.*: "The disciples are advisers of their Master, who do not want to annoy respected leaders" ; cf. just before : "The statement ... shows that the Pharisees had gone away incensed."

a devilish plant which is to be rooted up. [66] The presupposition is that he who is from God will show this, as in Jn. (cf. 10:3 f., 27; 8:47; 1 Jn. 4:6), by hearing and receiving the Word of Jesus. The metaphor of the blind leading the blind carries the same stress as σκανδαλίζομαι, [67] Mt. 15:14. For blindness means unbelief, cf. Mt. 13:13 ff.; Jn. 9:39. As blindness and falling into the ditch are inevitably connected, so are unbelief and destruction, cf. 1 Pt. 2:8 → 353, 13 ff. The occasions of this σκανδαλίζεσθαι are manifold. First there is personal irritation at Jesus' freedom in relation to the Law, which in other places, too, seems to be a main reason for the unbelief of His Jewish adversaries, cf. Mk. 2:23 ff.; 3:1 ff. etc. No less annoying is His sharp distinction between God's ἐντολή and human παράδοσις (Mt. 15:3 ff.) or His complete reversal of the Jewish concept of purity (Mt. 15:11). But offence at His message also becomes offence at Jesus Himself and a turning from Him in unbelief. In Mt. 17:27 Jesus gives as a reason for payment of the temple tax, which in itself was a matter of indifference for Him and His disciples, v. 25 f.: ἵνα ... μὴ σκανδαλίσωμεν αὐτούς. Here σκανδαλίζω means in the first instance the giving of offence or causing of irritation by transgression of the Law, Ex. 30:13. But ineluctably this offence becomes rejection of Jesus in Sadducean circles. The kerygmatic point of the story [68] is the same as that of Paul's warnings to the strong in Rome (R. 14:13) and Corinth (1 C. 8:13). To guard against unbelief in others one must be able to forego one's own freedom and privileges, → 355, 13 ff.

c. Avoidance of Causing the Faith of Disciples to Stumble.

In the logion of the σκανδαλίζειν of the μικροί (→ IV, 650, 31 ff.) in Mk. 9:42, which has come down to us in all three Gospels (cf. Mt. 18:6 and with some formal deviation Lk. 17:2), [69] the point is the avoidance of σκανδαλισμός. This is again an eschatological saying, [70] for the only thing more terrible than being drowned with a mill-stone about one's neck is damnation at the Last Judgment. [71] The punishment fits the offence. σκανδαλίζειν means "to cause loss of faith," i.e., "to rob of eternal salvation." Thus the σκανδαλίζων is himself plunged into eternal perdition. σκανδαλίζω or σκανδαλίζομαι, like πιστεύω, is a present process with an eschatological effect. Finally, the saying about the σκανδαλίζειν of the

---

[66] The metaphor is similar to that in 13:24 ff. (→ 346, 25 ff.) but with the difference that here, in contrast to 13:28 f., there is obviously the possibility of a weeding of what God has planted.

[67] This is a guilty blindness and blinding in the same sense as 23:13b and the proverbial expression πλανῶντες καὶ πλανώμενοι in 2 Tm. 3:13 → VI, 230, 30 f.; 249, 24 f.

[68] Regarded as late by some because of the free attitude to the Jewish cultus, to which (as to the temple) the primitive community of Ac. remained firmly attached except for Stephen and possibly some other "Hellenists."

[69] With Mt. 26:24 the logion is quoted in 1 Cl., 46, 8 : καλὸν ἦν αὐτῷ εἰ οὐκ ἐγεννήθη, ἢ ἕνα τῶν ἐκλεκτῶν μου σκανδαλίσαι· κρεῖττον ἦν αὐτῷ περιτεθῆναι μύλον καὶ καταποντισθῆναι εἰς τὴν θάλασσαν ἢ ἕνα τῶν ἐκλεκτῶν μου διαστρέψαι. Cl. was perhaps using a collection of sayings compiled for catechetical and homiletical purposes, cf. J. A. Fischer, Die Apost. Väter (1956), ad loc. and on 1 Cl., 13, 2.

[70] The threat to those who cause stumbling in faith is a counterpart to the blessing of those whose faith does not stumble in Mt. 11:6 and par.

[71] J. Schniewind, Das Ev. nach Mk., NT Deutsch, I⁹ (1960) on 9:42 : "This would be a mild fate compared with that which threatens the seducer. One is reminded of sayings like 3:28 f.," cf. also Schl. Mk., ad loc. and A. Loisy, Les évangiles synoptiques (1908), II, 77 f. The idea of suicide (cf. C. V. A. Juvencus, Evangeliorum Libri Quattuor, III, 404-406 [CSEL, 24, 96]) is unlikely.

members (Mk. 9:43-48; Mt. 18:8 f.; 5:29 f.; → IV, 560, 8 ff.) stands in the same eschatological light. Mt. follows Mk. in one version of the saying (18:8 f.) but another tradition in the other (5:29 f.). [72] The form in Mk. refers to 3 members (hand, foot and eye), the other to only 2, though even in 18:8 f. Mt. makes the 3 members of Mk. into 2 by grouping together the hand and foot, so that here, as in 5:29 f., we have a double saying. Since Mt. puts the saying in antithesis to the 7th commandment in 5:27-32, it follows that the meaning he presupposes for σκανδαλίζω is "to entice to sin." [73] Sin against the 7th commandment is so important that it brings about βληθῆναι (or ἀπελθεῖν) εἰς γέενναν, obviously because, like unbelief, it separates from God and thereby plunges into perdition. Mk. is saying much the same thing. [74] No price is too high to pay to avoid σκανδαλίζεσθαι. [75] In keeping is the absolute relentlessness of the demand if Jesus intends the command ἀπόκοψον, ἔκκοψον (→ III, 860, 1 ff.), ἔκβαλε, ἔξελε, βάλε ἀπὸ σοῦ, just as literally as He takes the reality of the seducing power of the members. [76]

III. The Word Group in Paul. [77]

Paul, too, speaks of a σκάνδαλον which is unavoidable (Gl. 5:11; 1 C. 1:23; R. 9:33; 11:9; cf. Mt. 18:7 and par.; 24:10; 26:31 and par.) and also of a σκανδαλισμός which must be unconditionally avoided (1 C. 8:13; R. 14:13, 21 vl.; cf. Mt. 5:29 and par.; 11:6 and par.; 17:27; 18:6 and par.).

1. The σκάνδαλον of the Gospel.

In support of his insight that the message about Jesus contains an offence which neither can nor should be avoided, Paul in R. 9:33 (→ IV, 276, 19 ff.; VI, 97, 39 ff.; 754, 22 ff.) adduces as Scripture proof a mixed quotation from Is. 8:14; 28:16. As the Rabbis thought the "stone" of the two passages (→ IV, 272, 22 ff.; 273, 12 ff.) [78] referred to the Messiah, so Paul saw in it a reference to Jesus. By the fusion of the two verses Scripture itself becomes the crown witness for the twofold meaning of the stone, i.e., the twofold operation of Jesus. He who is placed there for faith Himself becomes an "obstacle to faith." Hence He who is appointed for salvation can also be a "cause of perdition," → 348, 18 ff.;

---

[72] Probably Q ; Lk. left the saying out intentionally. It is not very likely that Mt. 18:8 f. par. is a Roman form and 5:29 f. a Palestinian (because of δεξιός, Loh. Mt., ad loc. [128, n. 1]), cf. Loh. Mk. on 9:42 (196, n. 2).

[73] Perhaps this is why he puts the eye before the hand here, cf. v. 28 as compared with 18:8 f. and par. This order would, of course, agree with Rabb. sayings to the effect that all offence comes only from the eyes, cf. Str.-B., I, 302.

[74] From the fact that Mk. has εἰσελθεῖν εἰς τὴν ζωήν (or βασιλείαν τοῦ θεοῦ) as the positive counterpart of ἀπελθεῖν (βληθῆναι) εἰς τὴν γέενναν one may hardly conclude (Loh. Mk. on 9:42; cf. Loh. Mt. on 5:29) that as distinct from Mt. he took the saying to be the promise of a reward for giving up a seducing member.

[75] Here σκανδαλίζω as distinct from σκανδαλίζομαι (→ 345, 37 ff.) does not include the actual destructive effect ; it means "to entice to sin," or it may be taken de conatu "to threaten to plunge into sin and corruption."

[76] εἰ in Mt., like ἐάν in Mk., expresses the reality.

[77] Included here are the only two NT instances of σκάνδαλον outside the three gt. NT blocks in the Synoptists, Paul and John, since they are closely connected with Pauline usage ; we refer to 1 Pt. 2:8 (→ 353, 5 ff.) and Rev. 2:14 (→ 356, 23 ff.).

[78] Cf. bSanh., 38a; Stählin, 190, n. 3. It is open to question whether one may presuppose a pre-Pauline "stone theology" which included as a constitutive element a twofold meaning and operation of the stone as foundation and destruction, → IV, 276, 19 ff.; also Stählin, 196.

345, 36 ff. In the sphere of this possibility of opposing effects inherent in Christ and His Gospel the word σκάνδαλον becomes a tt. in which the main OT meanings — "occasion of guilt" and "cause of destruction" — are fused into a total unity in the NT reconstruction — for in the NT unbelief is the basic sin. [79]

1 Pt. 2:6-8 (→ IV, 276, 37 ff.; VI, 98, 23 ff.; 754, 22 ff.) is very close to R. 9:33 both in thought and also in the use of OT quotations; only the way they are combined is different. [80] Is. 28:16 is adduced in proof in v. 6, and then in v. 7 this is interpreted and elucidated by Ps. 118:22 (→ n. 79) and Is. 8:14. An even more pointed saying concerning the twofold operation of Jesus is thus attained. [81] What is said about the effect on the unbeliever in v. 7b and v. 8 is bracketed by the sayings about the believer in v. 7a and v. 9. In distinction from Paul, who in R. 9 contrasts unbelieving Jews and believing Gentiles, 1 Pt. simply divides all men into believers and unbelievers. Especially impressive here is the way in which everything is combined in a single process by the statement that "Christ is a rock of stumbling." ἀπειθεῖν and σκανδαλίζεσθαι — 1 Pt. uses here the synon. προσκόπτειν — are combined in the same way (v. 8) as πιστεύειν and μὴ καταισχυνθῆναι (= "to be delivered," v. 6). The fall of unbelievers is the result of their sin and this in turn is the result of their taking offence at Christ. In the fact that the unbeliever does not believe in Him Christ shows Himself to be to the unbeliever the πέτρα σκανδάλου, just as the believer, by believing in Him, finds in Christ τιμή (1 Pt. 2:7a) and δικαιοσύνη (R. 9:30). This interrelationship is expressed with particular clarity if one takes the dative τῷ λόγῳ in 1 Pt. 2:8 to be related ἀπὸ κοινοῦ to προσκόπτουσιν and ἀπειθοῦντες. In the λόγος as such there is the possibility of doubt and unbelief and consequently of being confounded. The double possibility of the operation [82] of Christ and the Word about Him is by divine appointment (τίθημι in v. 6, cf. κεῖται in Lk. 2:34 → 345, 5 ff.). This applies not merely to the possible fall of unbelievers but also to their actual fall (ἐτέθησαν v. 8), and quite naturally, of course, to its opposite, faith and salvation. An essential part of faith is the overcoming of the *skandalon*

---

[79] By quoting Zech. 13:7 in Mk. 14:27 and par. (→ 349, 29 ff.) and esp. Ps. 118:22 in Mk. 12:10 and par. the Evangelists try to show that Jesus Himself, not unaware of His character as a *skandalon* (cf. Mk. 6:3 and par.; Mt. 11:6 and par.; 15:12 → 350, 28 ff.), found this predicted already in Scripture. Here, too, the stone represents Jesus; it illustrates His divergent estimation by God and men. Lk. 20:17 f., in distinction from Mk. and Mt. who take the κεφαλὴ γωνίας in a fully positive sense, sees depicted in it the destructive effect on those who do not believe in Jesus (cf. v. 18 with the allusion to Da. 2:34 f. → IV, 272, 32 ff.); on the other hand, his understanding of Ps. 118:22 is similar to that of Mk. and Mt. in Ac. 4:11 f. But 1 Pt. 2:7 f. takes the κεφαλὴ γωνίας like Lk. 20:17 f., namely, as synon. to λίθος προσκόμματος καὶ πέτρα σκανδάλου → n. 82.

[80] Cf. on this H. Vollmer, *Die at.lichen Zitate bei Pls.* (1895), 41; O. Michel, *Pls. u. seine Bibel* (1929), 40-43; Mi. R. on 9:32 f. (220, n. 1); Stählin, 193.

[81] The form of Is. 8:14 behind 1 Pt. 2:8 is obviously the same as in R. 9:33. Acc. to a not very secure tradition (Stählin, 192, n. 2) it is supposed to be that of Σ → n. 39. The basis of NT quotations of the OT has often been observed to be close to the text of Σ, cf. Stählin, 143 and 147. No one can say whether we have here a revision of the LXX or whether this form comes from a florilegium taken over from Judaism. The combining of materially and theologically related passages might just as well derive from oral tradition.

[82] The fact that on the one side the τιμή of 1 Pt. 2:7 catches up the ἔντιμος (v. 6) of Is. 28:16, and on the other the ἀκρογωνιαῖος goes with κεφαλὴ γωνίας, which in v. 8 is expounded as λίθος προσκόμματος καὶ πέτρα σκανδάλου (καί before λίθος means "namely"), already gives to ἀκρογωνιαῖος in v. 6 a dual sense (unlike Eph. 2:20), similar to that of λίθος in Lk. 20:17 f. (→ n. 79).

posed with this appointment of God in Christ. Without the *skandalon* faith in Christ would not be true faith in the NT sense.

For Paul the Jews are the paradigm of this destructive offence at the Gospel, just as they are for John the paradigm of the world's hatred. This is expressed even more radically in 1 C. 1:23 than in R. 9:32 f. (→ 352, 21 ff.): κηρύσσομεν Χριστὸν ἐσταυρωμένον, ᾿Ιουδαίοις μὲν σκάνδαλον, ἔθνεσιν δὲ μωρίαν. Strictly the reference in 1 C. 1:18 ff. is merely to the divine folly of the σταυρός. As a parallel to its μωρία for the Greeks, however, Paul also speaks of the σκάνδαλον for the Jews. The folly of the cross makes Greeks unbelievers and ἀπολλύμενοι, while its "religious offensiveness" does the same for Jews. Both characteristics are an integral part of the Gospel. [83] Fundamentally what is called μωρία is only another form of the σκάνδαλον and *vice versa*. [84] The opposition of the Jews finds expression, as in the days of Jesus (Mk. 8:11 f. and par.), in the demand for signs (→ 345, 14 ff.), [85] i.e., for visible demonstrations of the divine origin and authentication of this offensive message. [86] In the passionate polemical statement in Gl. 5:11 a different aspect of the σκάνδαλον τοῦ σταυροῦ is to the forefront, namely, repudiation of the message of grace and of freedom from the Law. The short saying ἄρα κατήργηται τὸ σκάνδαλον τοῦ σταυροῦ tacitly presupposes the idea that offence is of the very essence of the Gospel. This is not to be abandoned at any cost, nor is it to be softened by treating the cross and circumcision as equally good alternatives. To do this is to weaken the uncompromising demand for faith and to render nugatory the offensive character of the cross, but in so doing to make equally ineffective the saving power of the cross [87] and faith. Thus the Galatian weakening of the scandal of the message is just as dangerous as the Corinthian softening ἐν σοφίᾳ λόγου, 1 C. 1:17; 2:4. In R. 11:9 Paul finds the scandal for the Jews predicted in Ps. 69:22 → 342, 9 ff. [88] Probably Paul selected this quotation primarily for the sake of the word σκάνδαλον, [89] for he obviously catches it up again with πταίω and παράπτωμα in v. 11. Paul is referring to the majority of the Jewish people (cf. v. 4 ff.) who fall victim to the σκάνδαλον and persist in hardness of heart. Yet for them the σκάνδαλον means only πταίειν, not πίπτειν [90] (v. 11), not definitive ἀποβολή (v. 15).

---

[83] Cf. U. Wilckens, *Weisheit u. Torheit. Eine exegetisch-religionsgeschichtliche Untersuchung* (1959), 37; also "Kreuz u. Weisheit," *Kerygma u. Dogma,* 3 (1957), 77-108; cf. also H. Schlier, "Kerygma u. Sophia," *Die Zeit der Kirche* (1956), 206-232; E. Schlink, "Weisheit u. Torheit," *Kerygma u. Dogma,* 1 (1955), 1-22.

[84] On the par. between Jews and Gks. cf. Wilckens, *Weisheit u. Torheit,* 222, also 22 and 39, n. 1.

[85] The same demand characterises Paul's opponents in the community, cf. 2 C. 13:3; 12:12.

[86] On the "weakness" of the revelation in Christ cf. 1 C. 1:25; 2 C. 13:4; Hb. 5:2, and on the "weakness" of its preachers 1 C. 2:3; 4:10; 2 C. 10:10; 12:9 f.; 13:9, cf. Wilckens, *Weisheit u. Torheit,* 217 f.

[87] Perhaps in the Semitic usage of primitive Chr. a mysterious echo of מַשְׂכֵּל "cross" was found in מִכְשׁוֹל "offence."

[88] Paul quotes a form of the LXX, as v. 10 shows (= ψ 68:23). But he changed the text (instead of 3 members 4 by the addition of θήρα from ψ 34:8) and also reinterprets it → 342, 9 ff. and n. 20. It is not clear how τράπεζα is to be taken in Pl., whether of the Passover or the cultus generally. The only clear pt. is that something intrinsically good becomes an "occasion of stumbling."

[89] Cf. Mi. R. on 11:9 (238, n. 4).

[90] As in Lk. 2:34 (→ 345, 5 ff. πτῶσις). If one prefers not to take πίπτω synon. with πταίω (cf. v. 22) or to put full stress on the ἵνα one must maintain that πίπτω is used here in the sense of ἀπόλλυμαι, cf. 1 C. 10:12 with v. 9b, also Rev. 18:2, 3 vl., also Is. 24:20

In itself, however, the scandal of the Gospel is not restricted to Jews or to non-Christians generally. Paul, like Jesus (Mt. 18:6 and par.), finds σκανδαλίζεσθαι in the fellowship of disciples too. 2 C. 11:29 : τίς ἀσθενεῖ, καὶ οὐκ ἀσθενῶ; τίς σκανδαλίζεται, καὶ οὐκ ἐγὼ πυροῦμαι; In distinction from the usage of Theodotion (→ 344, 12 f.) [91] there is here a plain distinction between ἀσθενέω and σκανδαλίζομαι. Both are almost technical expressions in the missionary work and pastoral government of the primitive community. [92] For ἀσθενεῖν, being assaulted in faith, there applies in the apostolic cure of souls the rule of 1 C. 12:26; [93] R. 12:15, συμπαθεῖν τῇ ἀσθενείᾳ (Hb. 4:15). On the other hand, the response of Paul to σκανδαλίζεσθαι, "stumbling in faith," "rejection of the Gospel," is one of heart-felt distress, cf. 3 Macc. 4:2 : στεναγμοῖς πεπυρωμένη καρδία.

2. The Danger of Falling in the Life of the Community. [94]

The second main form of skandalon in Paul is that which arises as a result of differences of conviction in the Pauline churches. In Paul's pastoral handling of the debate between the strong and the weak in Corinth (1 C. 8:1 ff.; 10:23 ff.) and Rome (R. 14:1-15:7) the words σκάνδαλον, σκανδαλίζομαι, πρόσκομμα, προσκόπτω and ἀπρόσκοπος are the crucial catchwords. The main principles of Paul in settling the problem are to be found in R. 14:13 : τοῦτο κρίνατε [95] μᾶλλον, τὸ μὴ τιθέναι πρόσκομμα [96] τῷ ἀδελφῷ ἢ σκάνδαλον, 14:21: καλὸν τὸ μὴ φαγεῖν κρέα μηδὲ πιεῖν οἶνον μηδὲ ἐν ᾧ ὁ ἀδελφός σου προσκόπτει ἢ σκανδαλίζεται ἢ ἀσθενεῖ, [96] and 1 C. 8:13 : εἰ βρῶμα σκανδαλίζει τὸν ἀδελφόν μου, οὐ μὴ φάγω κρέα εἰς τὸν αἰῶνα, ἵνα μὴ τὸν ἀδελφόν μου σκανδαλίσω. In both Rome and Corinth tensions of faith in members of the churches are the cause of σκάνδαλον. [97] The problems are different (→ II, 693, 40 ff.). In Corinth the issue is that of idol meats, while in Rome we find certain encratistic tendencies on the part of the weak (→ IV, 66, 19 ff.). In both cases something of the past has not been overcome ; this is equally true of both Jewish and Gentile Christians. In both churches the collision of divergent views and attitudes causes a σκάνδαλον for the weak, though in manifestly different forms according to the rejection or acceptance by the weak of the freedom of faith practised by the strong. In the one case the σκάνδαλον can lead to division in the community or to the separation of the weak from it. In the other the danger is that the weak will act against conscience and with wavering faith (1 C. 8:10; R. 14:20, 23). [98] To describe the

---

and Ps. Sol. 3:10, which both stress the finality : "He can never rise again"; in Ps. Sol. 3:10 πίπτω is just as abs. and definitive as προσκόπτω in v. 9 → VI, 746, 2. In R. 11:11, too, the προσέκοψαν of R. 9:32 is probably in view as well as v. 9; cf. Mi. R. on 11:11.

[91] Cf. on this Stählin, 112 f.; also R. 14:21 vl. → n. 96.

[92] Also in Mk. 6:3 acc. to M. Dibelius, *Die Formgeschichte d. Evangeliums*³ (1959), 53.

[93] 1 C. 9:22 is formally similar but in the light of 8:9 ff. the pt. is different. Here it is a matter of taking seriously the concerns of the weak (cf. Joh. W. 1 K. on 9:22), there of sympathy with those under assault, cf. Wnd. 2 K. on 11:29.

[94] On this whole section cf. → VI, 753, 9 ff.; Stählin, 255 f. etc.

[95] This expression is within a play on words in which Paul, as often (cf. W. Stählin, *Symbolon* [1958], 90), uses the same word (here κρίνω) in a different sense.

[96] The tradition is not uniform ; πρόσκομμα ἤ is not gen. attested in v. 13 nor ἤ σκανδαλίζεται ἤ ἀσθενεῖ in v. 21. In both cases the longer form is probably the original one.

[97] As there are two forms of σκάνδαλον in the NT, so there are two closely related forms of ἀσθένεια, the weakness of Christ and His messengers (→ n. 86) and that of the weak in the churches.

[98] Cf. Schl. R., *ad loc.*

inner danger to the weak Paul chiefly uses the two synon. word groups [99] προσκόπτω, πρόσκομμα and σκανδαλίζω, σκάνδαλον. In distinction from R. 11:9 the danger denoted here is a final danger of eschatological seriousness: σκανδαλίζεσθαι means ἀπόλλυσθαι (1 C. 8:11). In 1 C. 8 ff. and R. 14 f. one may see most vividly what is included in the multiplicity of σκανδαλίζεσθαι. The strong with his freedom destroys the brother whom Christ has saved (R. 14:15); he wounds the conscience of his brother (1 C. 8:12); [100] he thus overturns the work of God (R. 14:20), i.e., the saving work of Jesus, [101] which includes the οἰκοδομή of the community as well as the individual. [102] The weak, by acting against his conscience and faith and thus falling victim to σκάνδαλον, κατα-κέκριται, "has (already) fallen under the condemnation of the judge" (R. 14:23). Paul shares the faith of the strong (R. 15:1) but as a pastor he takes the side of the weak. His concern for these reminds us of Jesus' care for the little ones → 351, 23 ff.; both seek to guard against σκανδαλισμός.

3. The σκάνδαλον of Heresy.

R. 16:17 deals with false teachers, though the concrete examples in v. 18 do not allow us to say what was the precise nature of the error, → III, 788, 18 ff. Along with the division which false teachers cause in the congregation σκάνδαλα παρὰ τὴν διδαχὴν ποιεῖν probably means "to tempt into falling away from sound doctrine." The expression is thus synon. with ἐξαπατᾶν in v. 18, which carries the thought of the temptation of the deceiver, cf. 2 C. 11:3; 1 Tm. 2:14; 2 Th. 2:10; also R. 7:11. Here too, then, σκάνδαλον is indirectly a work of Satan (cf. v. 20), as in Mt. 13:41; 16:23; also 15:12 ff. A similar use of σκάνδαλον to that in R. 16:17 occurs in Rev. 2:14. The singular expression βάλλω σκάνδαλον (→ n. 36) is reminiscent of the προστίθημι σκάνδαλον in Lv. 19:14. Its transf. sense cor-responds to that of τίθημι, δίδωμι, ποιέω σκάνδαλον: "to entice to sin," i.e., to apostasy from God; this is suggested not only by φαγεῖν εἰδωλόθυτα but also by πορνεῦσαι, which could mean "to commit fornication" as well as "to be unfaithful to God." One can no longer say for certain what is meant in detail. Probably the doctrine of Balaam at Pergamos (→ I, 525, 4 ff.) [103] is closely re-lated to that of the Nicolaitans (cf. v. 15: ὁμοίως) and also to that of Jezebel in Thyatira, v. 20. Common to all of them is that they tempt Christians into both apostasy and immorality, → VI, 594, 16 ff.

IV. The Word Group in John. [104]

The noun σκάνδαλον has a semi-fig. sense in 1 Jn. 2:10: "cause of aberration and falling"; in Jn. 6:61 σκανδαλίζω means "to unsettle in faith"; σκανδαλίζομαι in 16:1 means "to be unsettled in faith." The concept of σκάνδαλον in 1 Jn. 2:10 is close to that of Lv. 19:14 to the degree that in both not seeing, blindness, or darkness is a presupposition of σκάνδαλον, cf. Jn. 11:9 f. → VI, 752, 34 ff.; R. 11:8, 10. The Christian who does not love is in darkness ἕως ἄρτι (v. 9) in spite

---

[99] On the question of the distinction between σκάνδαλον and πρόσκομμα cf. Stählin, 171 f.
[100] Cf. Stählin, 257.
[101] Hence σκανδαλίζειν is a ἁμαρτάνειν εἰς Χριστόν, 1 C. 8:12.
[102] Cf. Zn. R., ad loc.; Mi. R., ad loc.; → V, 141, 25 ff.
[103] Cf. H. Karpp, Art. "Bileam" in RAC, II, 362-373.
[104] For the one instance in Rev. → lines 23 ff.

of v. 8 (φῶς ἤδη φαίνει); he is thus blind (v. 11) and susceptible to σκάνδαλον; indeed, this is in him. [105] The compulsion to go astray (σκάνδαλον), a weapon of the darkness to which the loveless Christian in his lovelessness has given a place within (v. 11), is also a snare from without. Love and faith are closely related here ; for the man who abides in love there is no obstacle on the way of faith. [106]

In Jn. 6:61 Jesus replies to the murmuring of His disciples with the astonished, sad and reproachful question : τοῦτο ὑμᾶς σκανδαλίζει; "Doth this cause you to be offended at me (or in your faith)?" Like γογγύζω (→ I, 734, 14 ff.), σκανδαλίζω is a tt. for the crisis of faith in the band of disciples. In the verdict σκληρὸς λόγος, which is more often pronounced on sayings of Scripture [107] and which applies here to the sacramental statements [108] of Jesus (6:51b-58), expression is given to the disciples' lack of understanding, which is noted by John with particular frequency and emphasis. This lack of understanding causes σκανδαλισμός, and the result in many is that they leave Jesus (v. 66), and in one the betrayal (v. 70 f.). [109] As in the Synoptic Gospels (cf. Mt. 11:6 and par. → 350, 6 ff.; 18:6 f. and par. → 351, 23 ff.; 346, 10 ff.; 17:27 → 351, 13 ff.) Jesus is concerned to avoid σκανδαλισμός. Probably this is the point in 6:62 with its reference to seeing the ascended Son, obviously a work of the πνεῦμα. In sight, which in John is closely related to faith (e.g., 6:40), [110] and by the work of the Spirit, the σκάνδαλον or "temptation to unbelief" is overcome. But the Spirit is already given in the Word of Jesus (v. 63), so that there is in this a ready weapon against σκάνδαλον. This means, however, that Jesus simply opposes assertion to assertion. His Word, which can lead the disciples to stumbling in faith (cf. also v. 64), is the very power of the Spirit which can induce faith, and Peter confirms this counter-assertion of Jesus expressis verbis with his confession, v. 68 f.

The Parting Discourses of Jesus in John (cf. 13:19; 14:27, 29), like His last words in the Synoptists, are designed to protect against defection, e.g., Mt. 24:25; Lk. 22:31. But whereas σκανδαλισμός seems to be inevitable even for the disciples in the Synoptists (cf. Mt. 26:31 ff. and par.), the Johannine Jesus holds out hope that it may be overcome. As in 6:63 His weapon against σκανδαλίζεσθαι is the Word : ταῦτα λελάληκα ὑμῖν ἵνα μὴ σκανδαλισθῆτε (16:1), and what He has in mind here is His prediction of the approaching tribulation and the coming "Comforter," Jn. 15:18-27. Here, as so often, the intimation of suffering is accompanied by a Scripture proof, cf. R. 9:33; 1 Pt. 2:8; also, e.g., Lk. 24:26 f. A primary purpose of the prophecy, which brings to light God's plan, is to prevent σκανδαλισμός, whether it be the hampering of coming to faith or of remaining in faith. [111]

---

[105] This σκάνδαλον saying of Jn. is materially close to what Paul says about ἁμαρτία in R. 7, cf. W. Nauck, Die Tradition u. der Charakter des ersten Johannesbriefes (1957), 39 f., 138, n. 2, who adduces not only ψ 118:165 and Jdt. 5:20 (cf. Stählin, 182) but also 1 QS 12:17 (→ n. 13) and Jub. 1:21 as par.

[106] Cf. Stählin, 183.

[107] Cf. Str.-B., II, 485 on Jn. 6:60.

[108] On the authenticity of 6:51b-58 cf. Bultmann J., ad loc., 161 f., 174-177; E. Lohse, "Wort u. Sakrament im Joh.-Ev.," NTSt, 7 (1960/61), 110-125. But the sacramental statements, like the eschatological, are part of the original of the Fourth Gospel, cf. O. Cullmann, Urchr. u. Gottesdienst² (1950), 38-115.

[109] Here again, therefore, Judas is connected with the σκάνδαλον, and in him (v. 70) the devil, cf. Mt. 18:7 with 26:24; 16:23 with 4:10, also 13:41; 15:12; 1 Jn. 2:10 → 346, 25 ff.

[110] There is, of course, scandal and unbelief in spite of seeing the δόξα, 6:36.

[111] In this important element in the all-pervasive NT complex of prophecy and fulfilment

D. The Word Group in Patristic Literature.

In the age which followed σκάνδαλον and σκανδαλίζω played no part except in patristic works (→ 340, 4 ff.), for the occasional use in Pist. Soph. 33:22 (= ψ 68:23) and 105 f. (→ n. 43) is merely in the sphere of bibl. reminiscence and allusion. Rarely, too, does patristic use have the depth of the NT understanding. In particular there is development and trivialising in two directions. First (1) there is the psychological development, which is partly suggested or anticipated by the NT use, e.g., Mt. 13:57; 15:12 (→ 350, 28 ff.); 17:27 (→ 351, 13 ff.).[112] Then (2) there is the moral development, cf. esp. the interpretation of the *scandalizari* of 2 C. 11:29 as *carnis pati desiderium* in the comm. of Ambrosiaster,[113] which is promoted perhaps by an erroneous understanding of πυροῦμαι along the lines of 1 C. 7:9. Here and in many other instances of the extensive development[114] of the NT use of the group in both the Eastern and the Western Church[115] one may say in fact that what was begun in the spirit was completed in the flesh.[116]

Stählin

† σκεῦος

A. Profane Greek.

The etym. of σκεῦος is uncertain.[1] Par. to the verb σκευάζειν, "to prepare," "see to," "get ready," the noun means a vessel of any material serving a specific purpose : "vessel," "utensil," "container," "equipment" τὸ σύνθετον καὶ πλαστόν, ὃ δὴ σκεῦος ὠνομάκαμεν, Plat. Soph., 219a. It is mostly in the plur.

1. Lit.: a. "Household utensils," "jugs," "drinking-vessels," Aristoph. Thes., 402, of wood, earth, gold or silver, Plut. De Caesare, 48, 7 (I, 730 f.). b. γεωργικὰ σκεύη, "agricultural implements," Aristoph. Pax, 552. c. "Luggage," Aristoph. Ra., 12. d. "Military equipment" : καὶ ὅπλων καὶ τῶν περὶ τὸ σῶμα σκευῶν, "(heavy) weapons and personal equipment," Thuc., VI, 31, 3; τῶν ἵππων σκεύη, Xenoph. Cyrop., IV, 5, 55; τὰ σκεύη, "laden vehicles," V, 3, 40. e. Nautically σκεύη τριηρικά, "gear" for triremes, Demosth. Or., 47, 19; ἐν τοῖς τῆς νεὼς σκεύεσιν, in the "tackling" of the ship, Plat. La., 183e; after the theft of a σίδηρος (anchor? iron hook?) we read in pap. Zenon, 6, 10 (258/7 B.C.):[2] ἄνευ τῶν ἀναγκαίων σκευῶν πλεῖν τὰ πλοῖα.

E. Schwartz, *Aporien im 4. Ev.*, III (1908), 167, n. 1 sees a typical later form of the proof from prophecy.

[112] Cf. Stählin, 279 f.

[113] MPL, 17 (1879), 347; cf. Stählin, 240 for further examples.

[114] Linguistically, too, there are many developments, cf. not only σκανδαλισμός (→ n. 1) and σκανδαλιστής (→ 340, 8 ff. with n. 8) but also ἀσκανδάλιστος ("not seducible"), e.g., Pall. Hist. Laus., 32, and for other examples Stählin, 348 f., σκανδαλώδης, e.g., Epiph. Haer., II, 69, 23; Stählin, 347, and in Lat. not just *scandalista* (→ n. 8) but also *scandalizabilis*, e.g., Opus imperfectum in Matth. Hom., 49 (MPG, 56 [1859], 911), Stählin, 457 f.

[115] Cf. the account in Stählin, 282-470.

[116] Stählin, 469.

σ κ ε ῦ ο ς. Pass., Liddell-Scott, Moult.-Mill., Pr.-Bauer⁵, *s.v.*

[1] Boisacq, *s.v.*; Hofmann, *s.v.*; Pokorny, 950 f.

[2] Preisigke Sammelbuch, III, 89, No. 6712.

f. "Cultic vessels" : ἱερὰ σκεύη, Thuc., II, 13, 4; P. Oxy., V, 840, 14. 21. 29 f. (non-canonical 4th cent. Gospel).

2. Transf.: a. of a man as the tool of others ὑπηρετικὸν σκεῦος, Polyb., 13, 5 and 7; σκεῦος ἀγχίνουν καὶ πολυχρόνιον, "a clever instrument available for a long time," *ibid.*, 15, 25, 1. b. In pre-NT secular Gk. σκεῦος is not used for the body as a vessel of the soul. One should not adduce Plat. Soph., 219a (→ 358, 20 f.) in this connection, though this is often done. In Secundus [3] (2nd cent. A.D.) Sententiae, 7 and M. Ant., III, 3, 6 ἀγγεῖον is used and in the Latins Lucretius De Rerum Natura, III, 440 and 554 f. and Cic. Tusc., I, 22, 52 *vas* is used, the sphere being thus restricted. c. "The reproductive organ," Anth. Graec., 16, 243, 4 (Antistios, 1st cent. A.D.); Ael. Nat. An., 17, 11.

B. Septuagint.

1. σκεῦος covers much the same field as כְּלִי (bibl. Aram. מָאן, Jewish Aram. מֵ(א)נָא) both being used for any vessel serving the most diverse ends. Of about 320 instances of כְּלִי only about 50 are transl. by other words, e.g., ἀγγεῖον (15 times), ἄγγος (4). In 1 and 2 Ch. ὄργανον is used 11 times for a "musical instrument" (6 of these being for כְּלִי (הַ)שִׁיר "melody ?"). The material can be very different : gold in Ex. 35:22, iron or wood in Nu. 35:16, 18; clay in Lv. 11:33; leather in Lv. 13:49, 52 f. Transl. is acc. to purpose : a. "Vessels," "drinking-vessels," [4] Nu. 19:17; Rt. 2:9; 3 Βασ. 10:21; 4 Βασ. 4:3 ff. b. In agriculture τὰ σκεύη τῶν βοῶν, "yoke for oxen," 2 Βασ. 24:22; σκεύη ποιμενικά, "shepherd's gear," Zech. 11:15. c. Of clothes σκεῦος ἀνδρός, "male attire," Dt. 22:5. d. Often of "military equipment," "weapons" [5] : כְּלִי מִלְחָמָה σκεύη πολεμικά, Ju. 18:11, 17 (A); σκεύη ὀχυρώσεως, "fortifications," [6] 1 Macc. 14:10; ὁ αἴρων τὰ σκεύη, "weaponbearers," Ju. 9:54; 1 Βασ. 14:1, 17; τὰ σκεύη, "equipment," 1 Βασ. 31:9; "baggage," 1 Βασ. 10:22; God's armament : σκεύη θανάτου, "deadly missiles," ψ 7:14; ἤνοιξεν κύριος τὸν θησαυρὸν αὐτοῦ καὶ ἐξήνεγκεν τὰ σκεύη ὀργῆς αὐτοῦ, Ιερ. 27:25. e. Ship's gear : ἐκβολὴν ἐποιήσαντο τῶν σκευῶν, Jon. 1:5. f. A good third of the instances refer to the "sacred vessels" of the tabernacle, temple, or altar : πάντα τὰ σκεύη τῆς σκηνῆς, Nu. 3:8; τοῦ θυσιαστηρίου, Ex. 38:23; οἴκου κυρίου 2 Ch. 4:19; ἀπὸ τῶν ἱερῶν σκευῶν τοῦ κυρίου, 1 Εσδρ. 1:39, 43; τὰ σκεύη τὰ λειτουργικά, Nu. 4:12.

2. The distinctive mode of thought of the OT finds expression in the way כְּלִי is used fig. of man. a. Pure comparison with a vessel suggests the fragility, worthlessness and transitoriness of man : ἐγενήθην ὡσεὶ σκεῦος ἀπολωλός, ψ 30:13; ἠτιμώθη Ιεχονιας ὡς σκεῦος, οὗ οὐκ ἔστιν χρεία αὐτοῦ, Ιερ. 22:28, cf. also of Israel, Hos. 8:8; cf. ψ 2:9; Is. 30:14; Lam. 4:2. b. Transf. use can also express the radical superiority of God to man as His instrument. Going beyond its commission, Assyria has no right to vaunt itself against the One who has sent it against Israel, just as the axe and saw may not boast before (LXX without) the one who uses them, Is. 10:15; Is. 54:16 f. c. The metaphor often occurs in connection with the art of the potter. Man esp. is the material which takes shape in the hand of Him who creates and fashions him. Materially this image finds its supreme form in Jer. 18:1-11. Here 'Α and Σ have σκεῦος for the double כְּלִי of 18:4, but LXX has the more vivid ἀγγεῖον. Yet the point is clear. The ref. is to God's freedom to abandon His original project if the people's conduct inclines Him to do so. But this freedom is not caprice. It is related to His

---

[3] Ed. F. W. A. Mullach, Fragmenta Philosophorum Graecorum, I (1860), 513.
[4] Thus כְּלִי is occasionally rendered ποτήριον and κυλίκιον, Est. 1:7.
[5] Jer. 21:4; Ez. 32:27 have ὅπλα, cf. also כְּלִי זַעַם personified ὁπλομάχοι, Is. 13:5.
[6] On ἔργον for כְּלִי → II, 636, 23 ff.

benevolent will to give life rather than to destroy, just as the potter wants well-made and not marred vessels. Israel is thus admonished and required to turn every man from his evil ways in order that God may not fulfil His intention to destroy the people. Later the comparison is used in many different ways, cf. Is. 29:16; 45:9; 64:7. Acc. to Wis. 15:7 f. the potter makes of the same clay vessels for clean and unclean functions. The continuation has the familiar motif of the maker of idols [7] who, himself a piece of clay, fashions his idol out of material that may be used for what is clean or unclean. d. It is uncertain whether כְּלִי in 1 S. 21:6 is used for the "body" or the "reproductive organ." Either way the ref. is to the "instrument" used in sexual intercourse.

C. Later Judaism.

1. As in the AT, so in later Judaism כְּלִים is used for utensils of various materials, e.g., glass, metal, wood, fabric, which are employed for the most varied purposes in home and field, in war and peace, in the secular world and the sacred. In Rabb. lit., instead of giving many detailed ref., one may simply adduce the Mishnah and Tosefta tractate כֵּלִים which deals with the purity of vessels and utensils. Philo and Joseph. use σκεῦος for the "temple vessels": τὴν σκηνὴν καὶ τὰ σκεύη πάντα αὐτῆς, Philo Leg. All., III, 102; τὰ πρὸς τὰς ἱερουργίας σκεύη, Jos. Bell., 6, 389. In the Dead Sea Scrolls one may mention כְּלֵי הַמִּלְחָמָה in 1 QM 8:8, which is based on Ju. 18:11. Elsewhere, too, the Scrolls remain within the confines of the use in the OT and Judaism.

2. כְּלִי is common in a transf. sense. a. The Torah is a costly vessel by which the world was created and which was given to the Israelites, Ab., 3, 14. [8] Acc. to the Mishnah proposition no vessel contains blessing in it like peace, Uqzin, 3, 12. [9] b. When man is called a כְּלִי, the first pt., on the basis of the metaphor of the potter, is that he is created by God and is used as an instrument either by God or the devil. In relation to the peril of the time R. Eleazar b. Azariah extols the glory of the presidency which he is offered in the academy : "(Use) a (precious) murrah-vessel for a day even though it breaks by morning," [10] bBer., 28a. [11] The emperor's daughter mocks at the outward ugliness of R. Jehoshuah b. Chananiah : "glorious wisdom in a repulsive vessel," bTaan., 7a [12] cf. bNed., 50b. R. Eleazar b. Simeon, when he insults a man for being misshapen, is told by him to take up the matter with the Creator : "How ugly is this vessel which thou hast made !" bTaan., 20b. [13] The devil says to the serpent in Paradise : "Be my tool" (i.e., to tempt Adam), Apc. Mos. 16; God curses it : "Because thou hast become a σκεῦος ἀχάριστον, [14, 15] Apc. Mos. 26. Similarly the accursed of Belial are called כְּלֵי חָמָס, "instruments of violence" (cf. Gn. 49:5), 4 Q Test. 25. [16] The idea that man, like a hollow vessel, contains something yields another transf. use. In his totality he is thus the container for the devil or God dwelling within him, or else his body is the vessel which contains the human soul. The former use is rooted in Jewish thought, the latter in Gk. thought, in which the body is a prison of the soul : [17] καὶ ὁ διάβολος

---

[7] Cf. Is. 44:9 ff.; Jer. 10:3 ff.; Wis. 13:10 ff.
[8] bAb., 3, 18   (Str.-B., II, 693).
[9] Str.-B., I, 215.
[10] I.e., it is precious enough to fulfil this office only for a day and then to die.
[11] Str.-B., III, 271 f.
[12] Str.-B., I, 861.
[13] *Ibid.*, 285 f.
[14] Cf. σκεῦος ἄχρηστον in Hos. 8:8 LXX.
[15] Behind the Gk. expression is the Hbr. כְּלִי בְּלִיָּעַל, cf. C. Fuchs on Vit. Ad. in Kautzsch Apokr. u. Pseudepigr., II, 511; L. Ginzberg, *The Legends of the Jews*, V⁵ (1955), 121, n. 117; 123, n. 130.
[16] Text in J. M. Allegro, "Messianic Ref. in Qumran Literature," JBL, 75 (1956), 185.
[17] M. Dibelius does not take this distinction into account in his influential exc. on σκεῦος,

οἰκειοῦται αὐτὸν ὡς ἴδιον σκεῦος, Test. N. 8:6. Death parts man from the earthly body: ..., "when they are separated from this corruptible vessel," 4 Esr. 7:88. The Gk. notion has a firm grip on Philo, though he uses ἀγγεῖον rather than σκεῦος: ὅπερ ἦν τὸ ψυχῆς ἀγγεῖον τὸ σῶμα, Det. Pot. Ins., 170; [sc. νοῦς] περιέχεται ὡς ἐν ἀγγείῳ τῷ σώματι, Migr. Abr., 193.

3. A special problem is posed by the use of כְּלִי for woman. There is no instance of כְּלִי/σκεῦος having the direct sense of woman in the Rabbis.[18] But this does not settle the question whether the use is always parabolic or whether there is not a factual element too. The following observations and considerations should be weighed.

a. In Egypt. Aram. texts and the Targums we find the loan word לְחֵנָה "concubine," which is from the Accad. laḫanatu (1) "harlot," (2) "vessel."[19] One may see here an oriental understanding of sexual intercourse on the part of the male as the using of a container or vessel.

b. bMeg., 12b is of decisive importance: "But when the worldly nations eat and drink they are concerned only with words of wantonness. So it was at the feast of this transgressor. Some said the women of Madai were more beautiful, others said the women of Paras were more beautiful. Then said Ahašveroš. The vessel which I use is neither from Madai nor Paras, but from Kasdim. Do you want to see her? They answered: Of course, but she must be naked."[20] The expression "the vessel which I use" כְּלִי שֶׁאֲנִי מְשַׁמֵּשׁ בּוֹ has a plain sexual sense. The ref. to Est. 1:10 (where the king's heart was merry with wine), the abandon of the guests and the demand that the queen (Vashti) should appear naked all have a bearing here. So, too, does the distinctive double sense of the verb שׁמשׁ. The piel (Aram. pael) means not only "to serve," "to use someone," but is often a tt. for coition.[21] All this leads to the conclusion that "to use a vessel" is one of the euphemisms which the Talmud uses and presupposes in the sexual sphere.

c. Less clear is the answer in which the widow of R. Eleazar b. Simeon rejects marriage with Rabbi (sc. R. Jehuda Hanasi, the first redactor of the Mishnah) as beneath her dignity: "Then Rabbi sent and asked for the hand of his (Eleazar's) wife. She rejected him: How can a vessel which has been used for what is holy be used for what is profane?" bBM, 84b, cf. on this Pesikt. X, 94b etc.[22] The woman is obviously citing a proverb.[23] But it is not impossible that this is occasioned by the catchword "to use a vessel" and that it thus bears a double sense.

d. The image is much more strongly influenced by the reality when in bSanh., 22b R. Samuel b. Uniah says in the name of Rab (d. 247): "Woman is a formless mass[24] and makes a covenant only with him who makes this a ready vessel; for it is said:

Dib. Thess.[3] on 1 Th. 4:4. Hence he expounds later Jewish examples too much in terms of Gk. influence.

[18] Dib. Thess.[3] Exc. σκεῦος on 1 Th. 4:4.
[19] For details cf. W. Baumgartner in Köhler-Baumg., s.v. and Suppl., 203 (with bibl.).
[20] Str.-B., III, 632.
[21] The construction varies: "to use one's couch," bGit., 70a; with suffix "to use someone" (either man, bNed., 14b, or woman, bKet., 71b); often abs., bBek., 8a; Nidda, passim.
[22] Str.-B., III, 632.
[23] bBM, 84b adds a Palestinian proverb expressing the distinction between the householder and the wandering shepherd. For the forbidding of putting to profane use what has been used for sacred things, though without כְּלִי, cf. bSanh., 48b.
[24] גּוֹלֶם: 1. "Unformed mass," as, e.g., Adam before God breathed into him the breath of life; 2. "not yet completed vessel," cf. Levy Wört., s.v.

362   σκεῦος C 3-D 1, 2

For thy husband is thy Creator, the Lord of hosts is his name," cf. Is. 54:5. The decisive words which lie behind the quotation are בֹּעֲלַיִךְ עֹשַׂיִךְ. No matter what may be the construction in the Mas., [25] in the Talmudic text בֹּעֲלַיִךְ is the subj. whose task is to bring the woman to completion in a par. to God's creative work. The verb whose part. is used has a crucial sexual ingredient. Already in the OT בָּעַל (with or without אִשָּׁה) means "to take in marriage" (→ 366, 2 ff.) and in later Judaism it becomes a tt. for engaging in sexual intercourse (→ 366, 14 ff.). The husband becomes the wife's lord and master in marriage primarily by possessing her sexually. Thus the saying that the husband makes the wife a (completed) vessel is again very close to a sexual euphemism.

e. To summarise, one may say that purely formally כְּלִי is used of the woman only in a figurative sense. But the underlying phrases "to use as a vessel," "to make one's vessel," etc. are to be regarded as established euphemisms for sexual intercourse. If so, however, they take us beyond the confines of a mere metaphor. The old terms are ready to be combined with a new content and hence to extend their true sense.

D. The New Testament.

1. In the NT, too, the word is used for the most varied things. a. Any vessel that can be carried: "And would not suffer that any man should carry any vessel (anything) through the temple," [26] Mk. 11:16. Vessels of ivory, costly wood, brass, iron and marble are mentioned in Rev. 18:12. b. Household utensils of all kinds. In the saying about those who overcome in Rev. 2:27 individual Christians are given power to rule over the nations and to destroy them like earthen vessels, Ps. 2:9. At the foot of the cross there is a "jug" with vinegar, Jn. 19:29. In the saying about the light under a vessel Lk. 8:16 uses the vaguer σκεῦος whereas Mk. 4:21 has μόδιος. [27] On the other hand Lk. 11:21 replaces the collective τὰ σκεύη ("goods") of Mk. 3:27 and Mt. 12:29 by τὰ ὑπάρχοντα "possessions." [28] σκεῦός τι ὡς ὀθόνην μεγάλην in Ac. 10:11, 16; 11:5 is a container like a great linen sheet. The meaning in Ac. 27:17: χαλάσαντες τὸ σκεῦος, is uncertain. Prob. the ref. is not so much to taking down the sails as to throwing the draganchor overboard to lessen the speed of the ship → 358, 29 f. [29] c. τὰ σκεύη τῆς λειτουργίας, "the vessels appointed for divine worship," Hb. 9:21.

2. In the Pauline corpus, especially under OT influence, σκεῦος is used as a metaphor or similitude to denote certain aspects of man.

a. To understand the parable of the potter in R. 9:19 ff. note should be taken of the context. [30]

The divine choice between Jacob and Esau (v. 13) or Moses and Pharaoh (v. 17) is not absolute election to individual salvation or perdition. What is at issue is the way in which God leads the old and new covenant people in their mutual relations, cf.

---

[25] Probably "thy Creator" is subj. and "thy husband" predicate.
[26] Loh. Mk., ad loc. and Str.-B., II, 27 suggest that the temple hill was being used as a short cut for goods. But σκεῦος is quite indefinite here.
[27] Materially → λύχνος, IV, 326, 1 ff. and Jeremias Gl.[5], 103 f.
[28] On the saying about binding the strong man and spoiling his house → ἰσχυρός, III, 399, 39 ff.
[29] Bibl. in Pr.-Bauer[5], s.v. and Haench. Ag., ad loc. ἡ σκευὴ τοῦ πλοίου ("ship's tackling"?) in Ac. 27:19 is to be distinguished from τὸ σκεῦος.
[30] For decisive insights cf. K. Barth, K.D., II, 2 (1942), 244-256 (C.D., II, 2 [1957], 222-233), who has had a strong indirect influence on later comm.

11:30 ff. Like v. 14, v. 19 is dealing with the defiant question of the Jews [31] how God can hold the individual accountable for his sin if He Himself "capriciously" assigns to each his role. The retort to this question in v. 20 f. should not be taken as an independent piece detached from the context. It stands in the closest connection with vv. 22 ff., where the teleological link between the vessels of wrath and those of mercy is decisive. V. 24 and its basis in the quotations from Scripture in vv. 25-29 show that from the very outset Paul's concern is with the urgent question of the relation between hardened Israel and the obedient Church. In his reply to and overcoming of the objection of v. 19 Paul makes new use of the parable of the potter with allusion to various OT passages. Protesting man is first forbidden any right to speak by a ref. to Is. 29:16; 45:9. As the clay cannot complain against the potter, so the creature cannot complain against the Creator, v. 20. Then v. 21, echoing Jer. 18:6 and esp. Wis. 15:7, emphasises the right of God to make vessels for different ends from the same lump.

Now it is true that in view of κεραμεύς the reference here is plainly to vessels or vases etc. But the original sense of "implement" or "instrument" is still to the fore with its concept of purpose or service. God as Creator has the indisputable right to use the vessels which He makes for honourable or less honourable functions, v. 21. Yet it is not enough simply to beat down the defiant protest of man (v. 19) by force. The anacoluthon of vv. 22-24 [32] offers a broader and more convincing answer. Hence one should not expect as a conclusion: "No further remonstrance on man's part is possible." [33] Rather the sentence which begins with εἰ δέ is to be understood in analogy to R. 11:12, 15. Further development is to be expected. Thus vv. 22 ff. may be paraphrased as follows: "What if God in fulfilment of His will, [34] to demonstrate His wrath and reveal His power, endured with much patience vessels of wrath appointed for destruction, and did so [35] for the one purpose that He might reveal the riches of His glory, which He works on the vessels of mercy which He prepared beforehand to His glory and to which He has called us not only from among the Jews but also from among the Gentiles, how much the more then should defiant obstinacy turn into humble praise?" [36]

The close final connection between the par. statements in v. 22 and v. 23, and the decisive declaration in v. 22 (ἤνεγκεν ἐν πολλῇ μακροθυμίᾳ) make it quite plain both that God's wrath stands in the service of His mercy and also how it does so (→ V, 426, 17 ff.). Mercy shines forth in a twofold way even over the vessels of wrath (→ IV, 382, 20 ff.); the first statement stands in the service of the second. First God's μακροθυμία is seen in the fact that the vessels appointed to be smashed are not yet destroyed but are kept alive in spite of their opposition to God and are used in the

---

[31] The revolt is from the Jewish side, which finds the doctrine of retribution threatened by the free work of God's grace, cf. E. Gaugler, Der Brief an d. Römer, II (1952), on 9:19.

[32] V. 23 is not to be regarded as a conclusion as against A. Nygren, Der Römerbrief (1954), ad loc. and Bl.-Debr. § 467 App. With Nestle and against Tischendorf the question-mark is to be put only after v. 24, since this is the climax of the question.

[33] Mi. R., ad loc. Cf. Ltzm. R., ad loc.: "So that is his affair, and you can say nothing against it."

[34] θέλων is neither concessive (→ V, 425, n. 315) nor causal (Gaugler, ad loc.; Mi. R. and Ltzm. R., ad loc.; P. Althaus, Der Br. an d. Römer, NT Deutsch, 6⁹ [1959], ad loc.) but modal (Zn. R., ad loc.; Barth, op. cit., 248 (E.T. 225 f.).

[35] καί is left out in B 69 vg Or etc. It does not relate the statements (v. 22 and v. 23) syntactically as though a second purpose of God were mentioned alongside the first (Zn., Ltzm. and Schl. R., ad loc.) but brings out epexegetically what is the purpose of God's μακροθυμία towards the vessels of wrath, Mi. R., ad loc.; Gaugler, op. cit., ad loc.; Barth, op. cit., 248 (E.T. 225 f.).

[36] Cf. Gaugler, op. cit., ad loc.

execution of God's plan, v. 22 cf. v. 17. But this μακροθυμία is grounded in and serves an ever larger purpose. Two deductions *a minore ad maius* are intertwined. First there is an antithetical crescendo. The wrath of God on the first vessels brings out for the first time His mercy on the second. The second crescendo is direct. If God's mercy is at work even on the vessels of wrath, how much the more surely, as mercy, will it lead to fulness of glory!

The expression σκεύη ὀργῆς is formally parallel to the "weapons of wrath" in 'Ιερ. 27(50):25; Is. 13:5 Σ (→ 359, 26 f.; V, 425, 24 ff.), but its meaning is very different. The difficult genitive is to be taken as a genitive of quality. [37] The vessels are those through which God works out His wrath and also those on which He works out His wrath. The reference is to the line which leads from Esau by way of Pharaoh to contemporary disobedient Israel after the flesh. There is in the OT no parallel to the analogously formed σκεύη ἐλέους. As may be seen from the use of ἔλεος in the context of salvation history, [38] the reference here is to the line from Isaac by way of Moses to the contemporary Church. Both terms are used indefinitely, so that there can be no human counting on individual predestination. Indeed, to the vessels of mercy to-day belong Gentiles from the world of Pharaoh and also members of the people of Israel, even though Israel now represents the vessels of wrath in a special sense. This shows plainly that the way of the divine action includes change from the one side to the other. There is a parallel here to the branches which are grafted in contrary to nature (R. 11:23 f.), and the decisive thought in the parable of the potter in Jer. 18 has had some influence, → 359, 42 ff. The point of this is that the people should turn from its wickedness and be made into a new pot. [39] This means that according to the divine if not the human order there is the possibility that the present σκεύη ὀργῆς may be received again into the superabundant divine mercy. This thought is not expressed, of course, but it is clearly the background of the Pauline statements.

b. With the rise of false teachers 2 Tm. 2:20 f. applies the figure of different vessels to the situation in the Church. [40] Features from the building of a house in 1 C. 3:10 ff. are also introduced. [41] The strict thought of R. 9:21 ff. (→ 363, 16 ff.) that God in His free sovereignty uses vessels to honour and vessels to dishonour is less prominent. The evaluation of the vessels is also according to purpose. But combined with this is evaluation by the quality of material too. [42] The whole is used as a summons to self-purification from error. [43]

c. Of thematic significance in the structure of Ac. is the saying of the Risen Lord about Paul's election in Ac. 9:15 : "For he is a chosen [44] vessel unto me (→ VI, 863, n. 6), to bear my name before the Gentiles, and kings, and the children

---

[37] Schl. R., *ad loc.* restricts the sense by taking the gen. as a gen. auctoris.

[38] Paul uses ἔλεος for God's mercy in salvation history, → II, 484, 1 ff.

[39] G. Schrenk, *Die Weissagung über Israel im NT* (1951), 32 f.

[40] Schl. Past., *ad loc.*: "The same division (sc. as between Israel after the flesh and after the spirit) takes place also in Christianity."

[41] The θεμέλιον of 1 C. 3:10 ff. becomes the house ; the gold, silver and wooden materials of 1 C. 3:12 become corresponding vessels under the influence of R. 9:21 ff.

[42] The καί of v. 20b has an explicative sense so that the evaluation by material is the same as that by purpose, so most modern exegetes, though not Wbg. Past., *ad loc.*

[43] ἀπὸ τούτων relates to the heretical activities, but materially, of course, separation from the heretics is also involved.

[44] The hebraicising gen. of quality is used for ἐκλεκτός → IV, 179, 3 ff.

of Israel."⁴⁵ There is material agreement here with Paul's own account of his conversion in Gl. 1:15 f. inasmuch as both emphasise the divine initiative and thus call Paul an instrument in the hand of God or Christ. The relating of election to service and suffering is also in keeping with the statements of the apostle himself (cf. 2 C. 11:23 ff.; 12:9). Along the same lines is the saying that Paul and his colleagues have the treasure of the Gospel only ἐν ὀστρακίνοις σκεύεσιν, 2 C. 4:7. The reference is not to the body bearing the soul but to the whole man bearing the message.⁴⁶ In the first instance ὀστράκινος refers to the lowliness and weakness of Paul through which God's power is at work.⁴⁷ This includes the frailty of the body, which is subject to death, though this thought is expressed only in the statement which follows in v. 11.

3. 1 Th. 4:4 is much debated: εἰδέναι ἕκαστον ὑμῶν τὸ ἑαυτοῦ σκεῦος κτᾶσθαι ἐν ἁγιασμῷ καὶ τιμῇ. From the time of the fathers two different interpretations have been proposed for σκεῦος: body⁴⁸ and wife.⁴⁹ In favour of the former a few parallels may be adduced from the Greek world in which the body is the container of the soul → 359, 5 ff.; 360, 37 ff. In favour of the second one may cite the Jewish euphemism whereby the woman is called a vessel, → 361, 6 ff. A further question is whether the present κτᾶσθαι is to be given the ingressive sense "to gain" or whether it may have the durative sense normally expressed by the perfect, i.e., "to possess." The former does not go at all with the meaning "body," while the latter yields the sense "to have the body in one's power."⁵⁰ If σκεῦος refers to the woman then either the unmarried in Thessalonica are being urged to marry as a remedy against fornication (ingressive sense)⁵¹ or those who are married are being told to hold their own wives in esteem (durative sense).⁵² It is not easy to make a clear-cut decision between the various alternatives. The parallels to σκεῦος do not offer convincing support either one way or the other. The best way is not to examine the two words σκεῦος and κτᾶσθαι individually but to relate the whole expression to the larger linguistic context and to consider the reciprocal interaction between Greek and Hebrew usage.

---

⁴⁵ Cf. Paul's addresses before the Gentiles (Ac. 17:22 ff.), the Jews (13:16 ff.; 22:1 ff.; 28:17 ff.) and Agrippa II (26:1 ff.), also the ref. to the emperor (27:24).

⁴⁶ Ltzm., Schl. K., ad loc. Cf. then esp. Rabb. par. which call man the vessel of the Torah or God's wisdom, → 360, 22 ff.

⁴⁷ Cf. 2 C. 3:5, also 1 C. 1:26 ff.

⁴⁸ Tert. De resurrectione mortuorum, 16, 11 f. (CCh, 2, 940); Chrys. Hom. in 1 Th. 5, ad loc. (MPG, 62 [1862], 424); Thdrt. Interpretatio ad 1 Th., ad loc. (MPG, 82 [1864], 424); Pelagius Expositiones tredecim epistularum Pauli (ed. A. Souter, TSt, IX² [1926], 429, ad loc.); Ambrosiaster Comm. on 1 Th., ad loc. (MPL, 17 [1879], 473); J. Calvin, Comm. on 1 Th., ad loc. (Corp. Ref., 80, 161); H. Grotius, Annotationes in NT (1756), ad loc.; Bengel, Dib. Th.³, Schl. Erl., ad loc.; B. Rigaux, St. Paul, Les Épitres aux Thess. (1956), ad loc.; cf. also Dob. Th. and Rigaux, ad loc. for further details on → n. 48; 49.

⁴⁹ Theod. Mops. Comm. on 1 Th., ad loc. (MPG, 66 [1864], 932); Aug. Contra Julianum Pelagianum, IV, 10 (MPL, 44 [1865], 765); Dob. Th., Wbg. Th., ad loc.; A. Oepke, Die Br. an die Thess., NT Deutsch, 8⁷ (1955), ad loc.; G. Delling, Pls. Stellung zu Frau u. Ehe (1931), 61, n. 36; W. Vogel, "εἰδέναι τὸ ἑαυτοῦ σκεῦος κτᾶσθαι," ThBl, 13 (1934), 83-85 etc.

⁵⁰ Schl. Erl., ad loc.; G. Milligan, St. Paul's Ep. to the Thess. (1908), ad loc.

⁵¹ Dob. Th. and Wbg. Th., ad loc.; E. Lövestam, Aektenskapet i nya Testamentet (1950), 173-176.

⁵² Delling, op. cit. (→ n. 49), 60, n. 23. Vogel, op. cit. (→ n. 49), 84 suggests the husband's wooing of his own wife's favour. Oepke, op. cit. (→ n. 49) follows him in part, but this interpretation is too psychological.

The pt. at which to begin is the OT and Jewish בְּעַל אִשָּׁה. In the OT בעל has two senses : 1. gen. a. (ingressive) "to take in possession" Jer. 3:14; 31:32; b. (durative) "to be lord, owner" Jer. 26:13; 2. special with or without woman as obj. a. (ingressive) "to woo a wife," "to become lord and master in marriage" Dt. 21:13; 24:1 etc.; b. (durative) "to possess a wife," "to be a husband" Dt. 22:22; Is. 54:1. Since in the commencement and continuation of marriage acc. to OT and Jewish law the beginning and continuation of sexual relations is an essential part, בעל ingressively refers not merely to marriage in gen. but specifically to the establishment of sexual intercourse as its basis. This alone clarifies the text of Dt. 21:13; 24:1; Is. 62:5. This is also why at these and other places the LXX, also Σ at Prv. 30:23, transl. בעל by συνοικεῖν, συνοικίζειν, "to live in sexual fellowship, as married people." The durative form of בעל is found esp. in the participial בְּעֻלַת־בַּעַל, "the woman belonging to a man as (bride) wife," transl. by the LXX at Gn. 20:3 by συνῳκηκυῖα ἀνδρί, "the woman who has taken up (and who continues in) sexual relations with a man." Rabb. Judaism detaches בעל from its basic meaning "to be lord" and uses it as a tt. for the consummation of sexual intercourse [53] whether within marriage or outside it. [54] Comments on Dt. 24:1 are consistently to this effect. [55] Thus בְּעַל־אִשָּׁה comes to mean "to take a woman sexually," and in relation to marriage this might be either ingressive or durative.

In the Jewish Hell. sphere there is a parallel shifting of emphasis from the purely ingressive aspect to the durative in the verb κτᾶσθαι. As in class. Gk., e.g., Xenoph. Sym., 2, 10, so in the LXX we find the ingressive κτᾶσθαι γυναῖκα, "to woo or marry a wife," Sir. 36:24; Rt. 4:10. But in the Jewish sphere, under the influence of the similar development of בעל, κτᾶσθαι comes to have a stronger durative sense. This is apparent in Is. 26:13, where the LXX takes בְּעָלוּנוּ, "(sc. alien lords) have ruled over us," as an imperative and transl. it by κτῆσαι ἡμᾶς, which obviously has to be durative : "Be lord over us, reign over us." In bibl. Gk., [56] therefore, the examples of the durative sense of non-perfect forms of κτᾶσθαι take on greater importance : πίστιν κτήσασθαι "to keep faith," Sir. 22:23; ἐν τῇ ὑπομονῇ ὑμῶν κτήσεσθε τὰς ψυχὰς ὑμῶν, "by your patience you will preserve your lives," Lk. 21.19.

The fact that בעל and κτᾶσθαι are thus parallel suggests that Paul, who spoke both Hebrew and Greek, would translate the Hebrew tt. בְּעַל אִשָּׁה ("to possess a woman sexually") by κτᾶσθαι γυναῖκα, thus imparting a durative sense to the Greek phrase. Under the influence of the Jewish euphemism שִׁמֵּשׁ כְּלִי he is led, then, to the new expression σκεῦος κτᾶσθαι, "to use a woman as a vessel (instrument)." In the light of this linguistic development, which would be possible for any bilingual Jew and not just for Paul alone, the most probable interpretation of 1 Th. 4:3 f. is as follows : "For this is the will of God, even your sanctification, that you keep yourselves from fornication, that [57] every one of you know how to hold his own vessel in sanctification and honour (i.e., live with his wife in sanctification and honour), not in passionate lust like the Gentiles who know not God." Materially, then, the phrase εἰδέναι ἕκαστον ὑμῶν τὸ ἑαυτοῦ σκεῦος κτᾶσθαι, which is linked with the warning against fornication, corresponds exactly to 1 C. 7:2 : διὰ δὲ τὰς πορνείας ἕκαστος τὴν ἑαυτοῦ γυναῖκα ἐχέτω. Material

---

[53] Levy Wört., Jastrow, s.v. בָּעַל

[54] Cf. בּוֹעֵל "adulterous lover" in Sota, 5, 1; of Jael and Sisera, bJeb., 103a.

[55] bQid., 4b, 9b. קנה comes to be used for the legal wooing of a wife ; it already has this sense in later OT Hbr., Rt. 4:10, cf. Qid., 1, 1, where a woman may be wooed in three ways (by money, deed, or cohabitation).

[56] In profane Gk. one may cite only the pap. But here, too, the meaning of κτᾶσθαι begins to vacillate between "to woo" and "to possess," cf. Moult.-Mill., s.v.

[57] The related inf. ἀπέχεσθαι and εἰδέναι set forth the content of God's will.

as well as linguistic considerations favour "wife" rather than "body" in interpretation of 1 Th. 4:4. Not even in 2 C. 4:7 (→ 365, 5 ff.) does Paul show any acquaintance with the idea of the body as the container of the soul or the individual ego. One never finds in him an individual ethics centred on the body. On the other hand, the demand for a marriage lived in sanctification is reminiscent of Jewish traditions. According to Wis. 13-14, which is used in R. 1, the Gentiles do not know God and consequently they do not know the meaning of marriage. [58] Hence in 1 Th. 4:3 ff., referring to the knowledge of God now accessible in the Gospel, Paul presents the antithesis between ἁγιασμός and ἀκαθαρσία and puts the following demands : Renounce free and unbridled love (v. 3b); keep your own marriage holy (v. 4), the opposite of the uncontrolled expression of desire (v. 5); and respect your brother's marriage (v. 6 → VI, 639, 30 ff.).

1 Pt. 3:7, which is influenced by 1 Th. 4:4, is thus a correct commentary on Paul when it uses σκεῦος for the wife and interprets בעל/κτᾶσθαι as συνοικεῖν : "Likewise you men, live according to knowledge [59] with your wife as the weaker vessel." συνοικοῦντες and ἀπονέμοντες are two participial imperatives which find a common conclusion in the final clause εἰς τὸ μὴ ἐγκόπτεσθαι τὰς προσευχὰς ὑμῶν. [60] Thus the physical marriage relationship is linked to the ordination of the partners to the future inheritance. In this way it receives its supreme justification and also its ultimate profundity.

E. The Post-Apostolic Fathers.

The post-apost. fathers use σκεῦος in various ways : a. directly of any "utensils," Dg., 2, 2-4; esp. of "hollow vessels," Herm. m., 11, 13; b. transf. Man is a vessel of the "holy" Spirit, who dwells alongside the evil spirit [61] but may be crowded out of the vessel by this, Herm. m., 5, 1, 2, cf. ἀγγεῖον, 5, 2, 5; the body of Christ as a vessel of the Spirit (of God or Christ ?), Barn., 7, 3; the land of Jacob as a vessel of the Spirit (of God), Barn., 11, 9; ἕως ἔτι τὸ καλὸν σκεῦός ἐστιν μεθ᾽ ὑμῶν, "so long as you are still in your bodies," Barn., 21, 8; [62] c. in relation to the parable of the potter the new pt. is made that the potter can refashion vessels only so long as he has not fired them ; a summons is thus made to repentance in the time restricted to the present life, 2 Cl., 8, 2.

Maurer

---

[58] On Gentile ignorance of God's will (1 Th. 4:4 f.) cf. Wis. 13:1; 14:22; 15:2 ff. and R. 1:21, 28; on marital and sexual vices associated with idolatry (1 Th. 4:3, 7 f.) cf. Wis. 14:23 ff. and R. 1:24, 26 f.; on God's retributive intervention (1 Th. 4:6) cf. Wis. 12:23; 14:31; 16:1 and R. 1:24, 26, 28.

[59] κατὰ γνῶσιν is a weak but perhaps intentional reminiscence of the connection between God's will and the order of marriage, cf. 1 Th. 4:4 (εἰδέναι) and v. 5 (μὴ εἰδότα). There is no need to see any ref. to the Jewish and Chr. tradition that the woman is (religiously) weak against the demons and Satan, so A. Fridrichsen, "Scholia in Novum Testamentum," *Svensk Exegetisk Årsbok,* 12 (1947), 145 f.

[60] Punctuation as in Nestle, but cf. B. Reicke, "Die Gnosis d. Männer nach 1 Pt. 3:7," *Nt.liche Studien f. R. Bultmann* (1954), 296-304. Reicke relates ὡς ἀσθενεστέρῳ σκεύει κτλ. to what follows, thus robbing both συνοικοῦντες and σκεῦος of their special sense, the former being given only the meaning "to direct domestic affairs" and the latter the sense of "the weaker being or element."

[61] A Chr. magical prayer, which cannot be dated with precision, refers to a demon-possessed man : ἐξορκίζω σε ἐξελθεῖν ἀπὸ τοῦ σκεύους τούτου καὶ διαλύθητι ἀπὸ τῶν μελῶν αὐτοῦ καὶ μὴ κρυβῇς ἐν μηδενὶ μέλει σώματος αὐτοῦ, F. Pradel, "Griech. u. süditalienische Gebete, Beschwörungen u. Rezepte des Mittelalters," RVV, 3, 3 (1907), 9, 11 f.

[62] On this cf. 4 Esr. 7:88 → 361, 1 f.

σκηνή, σκῆνος, σκήνωμα, σκηνόω,
ἐπισκηνόω, κατασκηνόω,
σκηνοπηγία, σκηνοποιός

† σκηνή.

A. Greek Usage.

The etym. of σκηνή can no longer be fixed with certainty, and the probable root never yields the meaning "tent" in other languages. [1] Nevertheless, the history of the word shows that from the very first and consistently "tent" is the basic sense from which all others derive. As later development in the LXX (→ 369, 14 ff.) emphasises, the meaning "tent" is in no way to be regarded as simply a specialisation of the general sense of "dwelling," "home." Where outside the Bible σκηνή seems to mean "dwelling," "abode," "lodging," "accommodation" etc., as in P. Hibeh, I, 86, 8 (3rd cent. B.C.); Polyb., 12, 9, 4, this is because the original sense has retreated into the background. The word "hut" (Luther Bible: "Hütte") can kindle false associations in so far as this suggests a dilapidated or small and mean-looking house. It might be defended if meant as a small covered dwelling which is sufficient for its purpose and in good order. [2]

σκηνή is first found in the tragedians, not Hom., who has κλισίη instead, e.g., Il., 24, 448. It undoubtedly means "tent" as in a camp in the open, esp. used by herdsmen or soldiers, made of branches, poles or planks, with a roof and sides of matting of straw or rushes, skins, cloth or carpeting, [3] cf. Aesch. Eum., 686; σκηναὶ ναυτικαί, Soph. Ai., 3; Eur. Hec., 1289; σκηνὴ στρατιωτική, Xenoph. Cyrop., IV, 5, 39; βασιλικὴ σκηνή, Diod. S., 17, 76; cf. 17, 36, 4 f.; a "market booth," Theocr., 15, 16. For pitching tents ποιεῖν, Thuc., II, 34, 2, πηγνύναι, Plat. Leg., VII, 817c; for striking tent: κατα-λύειν, Polyb., 6, 40, 2. "Accommodation in a tent" can also be called σκηνή, Xenoph. Cyrop., II, 3, 1; IV, 2, 34 etc. Those who took part in gt. religious feasts and the games camped in tents, e.g., Ditt. Syll.[3], I, 422, 11 (Delphi, 269 B.C.); II, 736, 34 and 38 (Andania, 92 B.C.). Sometimes shrines were set up among them in portable tents, e.g., Eur. Ion, 806; Diod. S., 20, 65. The basic meaning is preserved when the "cover" of a wagon is called σκηνή, Xenoph. Cyrop., VI, 4, 11; Diod. S., 20, 25 or a "cabin" on the deck of a ship, P. Hibeh, I, 38, 7 (3rd cent. B.C.); Poll., 1, 89.

σ κ η ν ή. A. Frickenhaus, Art. "Skene," Pauly-W., 3a (1929), 470-492; E. Lohmeyer, "Die Verklärung Jesu nach dem Mk.-Ev.," ZNW, 21 (1922), 185-215; H. Bornhäuser, Sukka, Giessener Mischna, II, 6 (1935), esp. 126-128; H. Riesenfeld, "Jésus transfiguré," Acta Seminarii Neotestamentici Upsaliensis, 16 (1947), esp. 146-205, c. X: "La Cabane"; A. Alt, "Zelten u. Hütten," Kleine Schr. zur Gesch. des Volkes Israel, III (1959), 233-242; W. Michaelis, "Zelt u. Hütte im bibl. Denken," EvTh, 14 (1954), 29-49.

[1] σκη- (Doric σκᾶ-) might be related to an Indo-Eur. root skai- ski- from which are formed words meaning "shadow" and "light," "radiance" (Eng. "shine"), the basic meaning being "to glow," "shadow (reflection)" (Pokorny, 917 f.). Hence "tent" (Gk. only) as "half-darkness"? [Debrunner] → n. 2.

[2] If the etym. starting-pt. is a "covered place" (Frickenhaus, 470: "shady roof") the primary ref. is not to a place which is shady by nature but to the cover which man constructs for protection against light and heat.

[3] Frickenhaus, 470: "Thus a building without solid walls," to be distinguished from σκιάς "bower" once the Gks. adopted the art of tent-building from the Orient during the Persian wars, 471.

The element of transitoriness in σκηνή is expressed in the saying often ascribed to Democr.: ὁ κόσμος σκηνή, ὁ βίος πάροδος· ἦλθες, εἶδες, ἀπῆλθες (Diels[8], II, 165, 7 f.). Cf. also σκηνή πᾶς ὁ βίος, Anth. Graec., 10, 72 and ἡ σκηνή βίου, Max. Tyr., 7, 10. Underlying this, of course, is the use of σκηνή for the "stage" of a theatre. This is extremely widespread,[4] cf. Aristot. Poet., 24, p. 1459b, 25; Ditt. Syll.[3], I, 330, 28 (306 B.C.); IG, 11, 2, No. 161, n. 115 (3rd cent. B.C.). In the 5th and 4th cent. B.C. this σκηνή was still a tent in the strict sense, a framework of pillars with movable walls. These could be changed and in tragedy consisted of purple hangings, in comedy of pelts. In early Hellenism, when stone came to be used, the σκηνή was the house before which the players acted, while the ὀρχήστρα was reserved for the chorus. Later, when there was a raised podium for acting, this also came to be called the σκηνή.[5] In the theatre, then, σκηνή gradually lost its original character as a tent.

B. The Septuagint.

1. From the NT standpt. the most important part of the early history of σκηνή lies within the LXX. Here σκηνή occurs about 435 times, 65 of these having no Mas. equivalent or occurring in works with no Mas. In 245 of the other 370 instances σκηνή is the transl. of אֹהֶל, in 93 of מִשְׁכָּן, in 25 of סֻכָּה (also סָכּוּת in Am. 5:26 → n. 34), in 6 of חָצֵר (elsewhere = ἔπαυλις), also of סֹךְ (ψ 26:5 [par. אֹהֶל] cf. also ψ 41:5 where סָךְ is misread as סֹךְ → 383, n. 3). אֹהֶל, which is the characteristic Hbr. word for "tent" and occurs 330 times, is also transl. by σκήνωμα (46 times), οἶκος or οἰκία (19 or 4), and 9 other terms (16 times). It is not surprising that the main equation is that of אֹהֶל and σκηνή (or σκήνωμα). Yet the relation to מִשְׁכָּן is also strong, since the 93 instances of σκηνή (and 1 of κατασκήνωσις) are supplemented by 17 instances of σκήνωμα, 8 different words being used in the 8 other occurrences in the Mas. The obvious predominance of σκηνή (and σκήνωμα) for מִשְׁכָּן is surprising and demands explanation (→ 371, 9 ff.) in view of the fact that מִשְׁכָּן means "dwelling" rather than "tent."[6] The picture is even more consistent in relation to סֻכָּה; apart from ὕλη in Job 38:40 (= סֹךְ "thicket"? cf. Jer. 25:38; Ps. 10:9) only σκηνή is used for this (26 times) apart from σκήνωμα (once) and in חַג הַסֻּכּוֹת σκηνοπηγία (5 times instead of the customary ἑορτὴ [τῶν] σκηνῶν). σκηνή also occurs in the other transl., esp. Σ (38 times, 'Α 12 and Θ 19). About two thirds of the examples relate to the tabernacle, and it is here that the decisive shift in the meaning of σκηνή in the LXX began. Hence a brief survey should first be made of the general use.

2. In Israel, too, the use of tents was common in every age. With the help of the σκηνή passages one might almost follow the whole story of Israel. This story begins with the patriarchs in the tents of Abraham (Gn. 12:8; 13:3; 18:1 f., 6, 9 f.), Isaac (26:25)

---

[4] Most of Frickenhaus' art. is devoted to this, 474-492 B: "Die Skene des Theaters." Many derivates were formed from this special sense, e.g., σκηνικός, "belonging to the theatre," σκηνοβατέω, "to come forward in the theatre," σκηνογράφος, "theatre painter." On the fig. "stage of life" etc. cf. also E. Peterson, "ΕΙΣ ΘΕΟΣ," FRL, NF, 24 (1926), 257 f., 260.

[5] In this sense σκηνή is then a loan word in Lat. (scaena, scena) and other languages. Cf. Frickenhaus, 492. On the Lat. scena (scaena by way of Etruscan scaina from Doric σκᾶνᾶ) cf. Walde-Hofmann, II, 485 [Debrunner].

[6] When Lohmeyer, 104, n. 1 writes that מִשְׁכָּן means "dwelling in gen. and tent in particular" this is incorrect, since a tent can be מִשְׁכָּן without this being a tent. It is also hazardous to conclude from the Mandaean use of משכן for the sanctuary that this must come from a tradition which regarded the tabernacle of the wilderness period as the ideal (→ 371, 8 f.), cf. W. Frei, Gesch. u. Idee d. Gnosis, Diss. Bern (1958), 7. How far the code-names Ohola and Oholiba in Ez. 23:4 ff. are related to אֹהֶל is debated (LXX transcribes Οολα, Οολιβα).

and Jacob (31:25). We then find Jethro's tent (Ex. 18:7), those of Korah and his company (Nu. 16:26 f., 30; Dt. 11:6), that of Achan (Jos. 7:21 ff.), that of Heber and Jael (Ju. 4:11, 17 f., 20; 5:24), that of Holofernes (Jdt. 5:22; 6:10; 10:15 etc.) and many others of importance. The wandering nomads live in tents in Gn. 4:20 or 2 Macc. 12:11 f., [7] also herdsmen in Ju. 6:5; Is. 38:12 HT (→ n. 23); ᾿Ιερ. 6:3; 30:24 (HT 49:29), with their flocks, 2 Ch. 14:14 (אֹהֶל).[8] In war the army lives either in the open, cf. 2 S. 11:11 ff. (→ lines 24 ff.) or in tents, Ju. 7:8 B; 2 K. 7:7 f., 10; Jdt. 7:18; Jer. 37:10 HT. At the Feast of Tabernacles (Lv. 23:34; Dt. 16:13; 2 Ch. 8:13; 2 Εσδρ. 3:4; Neh. 8:14-17; 2 Macc. 10:6) living in tents (Lv. 23:42 f.) is meant to recall the wilderness wandering, Dt. 1:27; Wis. 11:2; Hos. 12:10. It is worth noting that in the Mas. סֻכָּה is always used in this connection, though in the desert Israel used אֹהָלִים. The question thus arises whether the LXX, which always has σκηνή, is right to see no distinction between the two.

3. From the OT little can be gleaned concerning the form or construction of tents. [9] There is ref. to σκηνώματα of cedar in Cant. 1:5, and once they are said to be dark in colour — even to-day bedouin tents are black. We read of the "tent-peg" (יָתֵד = πάσσαλος) in Ju. 4:21; cf. Is. 33:20, and more often of the "hanging" or "curtain" יְרִיעָה, sometimes transl. δέρρις and interchangeable with אֹהֶל = σκηνή at Is. 54:2; Jer. 4:20; 10:20, sometimes itself transl. σκηνή, 2 Βασ. 7:2; Hab. 3:7. If אֹהֶל can also be transl. οἶκος or οἰκία (→ 370, 20 f.) and tent and house can be mentioned together, this does not allow us to make any deductions concerning the appearance of tents. [10] On the other hand, one may observe in the OT the difference between pointed tents and matted structures illustrated in depictions from Assyria and Egypt. [11]

It seems as though אֹהֶל is a pointed tent and סֻכָּה a matted structure. This explains why the latter and not the former is used by Uriah to David (2 S. 11:11) even though one would expect tents in a military expedition. The point is that the levies of Israel and Judah, and esp. the ark of the covenant, were lodged in matted structures, while the international mercenary brigade camped in the open, cf. also 3 Βασ. 21:12. Again, when Am. 9:11 speaks of the fall of the סֻכָּה of David one is not to think of a ruined palace and certainly not of a mean and dilapidated house. The ref. is rather to a fine matted structure in which the king lived and held audience when in camp but which has now collapsed. [12] The fact that סֻכּוֹת is also used with ref. to Tabernacles (→ 370,

---

[7] Cf. also the "bedouin highway" in Ju. 8:11, Michaelis, 41 f. In Gn. 25:27 Jacob is a smooth man dwelling in tents (LXX οἰκία) as compared with Esau, the open-air man. It is open to question whether the plur. אֹהָלִים is connected with the fact that the story already has nations in view, so V. Maag, "Jakob-Esau-Edom," ThZ, 13 (1957), 420.

[8] Cf. Gn. 25:16 (חָצֵר) par. טִירָה ἔπαυλις cf. Jdt. 3:3) and the explanation of the place-name סֻכֹּת in Gn. 33:17 (cf. ψ 59:8; 107:8).

[9] Cf. K. Galling, Art. "Zelt," BR, 539 f.; H. Haag, Art. "Zelt," Bibel-Lex. (1956), 1747.

[10] In transf. usage a tent can be called the "house" of the tent-dweller, cf. Nu. 16:27, 32. Where tent and house are par. (Prv. 14:11; Job 5:24 [σκηνή here = נָוֶה cf. Is. 33:20, though נוה is not transl. in Job 18:15]; 8:14 [not HT]), different modes of dwelling are being mentioned and distinction is thus presupposed. Usually they are set in antithesis, cf. 2 S. 7:5 f. (= 1 Ch. 17:4 f.); Sir. 14:24 ff. and ᾿Ιερ. 42(35):7, 10 (of the Rechabites). In clinging to the practice of dwelling in tents the Rechabites are influenced by the "nomadic ideal" of Israel's early days, cf. A. Alt, Art. "Rechabiten," RGG², IV, 1736. It is unlikely that the story of the Tower of Babel reflects Rechabite influence (in the fact that the מִגְדָּל of 11:4 f. is not a temple tower but a fortress tower as in a city (so E. Sellin, "Nachtrag," ZDMG, 91 [1937], 370 f. and O. E. Ravn, "Der Turmbau zu Babel," ibid., 352-370 → VI, 954, n. 8).

[11] Alt, 235-239.

[12] Michaelis, 37 f. David's βασίλειος σκηνή in 4 Macc. 3:8 (→ 368, 22 f.) was also a magnificent matted structure, but not the σκηνή (אֹהֶל) Δαυιδ of Is. 16:5.

8 ff.) shows that these were not imitation tents but booths or huts whose walls and roofs were made of thickly entwined leaves, Lv. 23:40; Neh. 8:15.[13] It is doubtful, of course, whether a distinction can always be made between the tent and the house. When the booth outside the city (Jon. 4:5) and the shed in the vineyard (Is. 1:8) are called סֻכָּה, but an אֹהֶל is set up on the roof in 2 S. 16:22 (cf. Jdt. 8:5), the difference mentioned above seems to be preserved.

4. Yet it is also worth noting that the tabernacle, for all its frequent mention (→ 369, 31 ff.), is never called סֻכָּה, though it seems to have been more like a matted structure than a tent.[14] It is usually called אֹהֶל, also מִשְׁכָּן. The term אֹהֶל remained in continuous use because in the light of the desert wandering, when all Israel lived in tents, it was hard to think of the tabernacle as anything but a tent.[15] If it is also called מִשְׁכָּן (→ 369, 22 ff.) this expresses a rather different view of its character. As אֹהֶל the tabernacle, as may be seen from the very common phrase אֹהֶל מוֹעֵד ("tent of meeting"),[16] is not regarded as a place where God resides but rather as the place where He may be met with from time to time. But the term מִשְׁכָּן seems to presuppose that God dwells in the tabernacle. Later ideas, already orientated to the Jerusalem temple, probably had some influence here.[17]

The LXX uses σκηνή (and σκήνωμα) for both terms. But the correspondence between מִשְׁכָּן (for the tabernacle) and σκηνή is closer than that between אֹהֶל and σκηνή to the degree that only in Nu. 16:27; Is. 22:16 does מִשְׁכָּן = σκηνή not refer to the tabernacle (or the מִשְׁכָּן for the ark in the Jerusalem sanctuary under David, 1 Ch. 16:39).[18] If the statistical pattern is obviously controlled by the fact that the tabernacle is so often called מִשְׁכָּן in the Mas., nevertheless one may speak of a firmly established usage in view of the gt. number of instances (91 all told). The result is that in the programmatic saying of Nathan in 2 S. 7:5 f., in which אֹהֶל and מִשְׁכָּן are used together for the tabernacle in v. 6 Mas. (both in antithesis to the temple as בַּיִת = οἶκος in v. 5), σκηνή is used for מִשְׁכָּן rather than אֹהֶל, κατάλυμα being selected for the latter.

If the rendering of מִשְׁכָּן by σκηνή impressed itself on the translators as the natural one, this was not because σκηνή had of itself the sense of "dwelling." Even outside the Bible this meaning plays too small a part.[19] Rather, it seemed to the translators that σκηνή was the predestined word for מִשְׁכָּן because the two terms contain the same three consonants skn in the same sequence. Similar observations in relation to σκήνωμα

---

[13] On the other hand the booths of Jewish art (e.g., the synagogue of Dura-Europos, Ill. 4 in Riesenfeld) have led some to suppose that the tents of the wilderness period were booths, Michaelis, 38 f.

[14] Alt, 239, n. 1; Michaelis, 38.

[15] In this usage, too, one may see in some sense "a legacy of the people's nomadic past." In the period when Israel had long since been settled Alt, 240 finds this also in the common phrase of dismissal at the end of a campaign: "Every man to his tent" (→ 383, 28 ff.). The Rabb. took "tent" here to be a code-word for "wife," cf. Str.-B., IV, 755.

[16] On the linguistically incorrect but not meaningless transl. by σκηνὴ τοῦ μαρτυρίου → IV, 482, 22 ff.; 485, 40 ff.; Michaelis, 40.

[17] Cf. M. Noth, *Überlieferungsgesch. d. Pent.* (1948), 264-267; A. Kuschke, "Die Lagervorstellung d. priesterlichen Erzählung," ZAW, 63 (1951), 82-84; K. Elliger, "Sinn u. Ursprung d. priesterl. Geschichtserzählung," ZThK, 49 (1952), 132 f. Cf. also L. Rost, "D. Wohnstätte des Zeugnisses," *Festschr. F. Baumgärtel zum 70. Geburtstag* (1959), 158-165.

[18] In Nu. 16:26 f. מִשְׁכָּן comes between 2 instances of אֹהֶל and this is perhaps why it is transl. σκηνή. On the other hand, this transl. was possible only because σκηνή was already an established rendering.

[19] The choice of σκηνή was not facilitated by the fact that σκηνή and οἶκος counted as synon., since this was not so, → n. 10.

(→ 383, 18 ff.), σκηνόω (→ 385, 16 ff.) and esp. κατασκηνόω (→ 388, 5 ff.) confirm the fact that the principle of transl. by similarity of sound, which may be noted elsewhere in the LXX, [20] was normative in the case of מִשְׁכָּן and σκηνή too.

What was the result when מִשְׁכָּן as a term for the tabernacle and more generally came to be translated so consistently by σκηνή (and σκήνωμα)? It is hardly conceivable that the Hbr. word should now take on the sense of "tent" and come to refer to what is passing and transitory. At most one can only expect that in bibl. Gk. σκηνή and the whole group should under LXX influence assume the character of a ref. to what is fixed and constant even though this is opposed to the original sense of "tent." [21]

5. There are few statements which without any specific ref. to the tabernacle or temple [22] speak of Yahweh's dwelling in heaven or on earth in a σκηνή. Usually any such statement is fig. or poetic. Is. 40:22 is a simile : God stretches out heaven like a curtain and spreads it out like a tent to dwell in, ὡς σκηνὴν κατοικεῖν = כָּאֹהֶל לָשֶׁבֶת → V, 514, 4 ff. [23] When 2 S. 22:12 par. ψ 17:12 says that God makes darkness his pavilion (σκηνή, סֻכָּה) round about, the meaning is not that He dwells in a tent but that He dwells in darkness. Nor strictly does Job 36:29 (σκηνή, סֻכָּה) speak of a heavenly tent. [24] In wording ψ 26:5 refers to God's סֻכָּה and אֹהֶל (both σκηνή in the LXX), but here we either have a metaphor for protection (cf. ψ 30:21) or a ref. to the tabernacle or temple, ψ 26:6. Acc. to Ex. 26:30 (מִשְׁכָּן); cf. 25:9, 40; 27:8, the tabernacle is made acc. to a heavenly prototype, but this does not presuppose that God lives in heaven in a kind of tabernacle or tent, but rather that there is a heavenly pattern for the earthly tabernacle. The μίμημα σκηνῆς ἁγίας ἣν προητοίμασας ἀπ' ἀρχῆς of Wis. 9:8 is also to be taken in this sense unless the ref. here is to the tabernacle as the predecessor of the temple. [25]

6. If the idea of God's dwelling in a tent were more common, [26] we should find it in an eschatological variation. But this is hardly so. One may refer only to Jl. 3:21; Zech. 2:14 f.; 8:3, 8 and Ez. 37:27; 43:7, 9; in these cases the HT has מִשְׁכָּן or שָׁכַן and though the LXX uses κατασκήνωσις or κατασκηνόω (→ 387, 31 ff.) it is not trying to push the idea of a tent to the forefront. [27] One should not expect, then, that

---

[20] Examples in Michaelis, 45 f. → 388, n. 4.

[21] Michaelis, 46.

[22] When Tob. 13:11 expresses the wish : καὶ πάλιν ἡ σκηνή σου οἰκοδομηθήσεταί σοι μετὰ χαρᾶς (א; BA slightly different), the ref. is to Jerusalem and thus the temple is called a σκηνή.

[23] Is. 38:12 is also a metaphor ; here Hezekiah, speaking of his sickness, says that a booth (דּוֹר II, confused with דּוֹר I by the LXX and transl. συγγένεια) has gone from him like a shepherd's tent (כְּאֹהֶל רֹעִי, LXX ὥσπερ ὁ καταλύων σκηνὴν πήξας). There is no need to try to see any cultic significance in the shepherd's tent in connection with the king as shepherd (cf. God as Shepherd), Riesenfeld, 175; cf. 79; cf. also → VI, 487, 23 ff.

[24] It is thus doubtful whether, with an appeal to 2 S. 22:12; Job 36:29 f., the tabernacle is modelled on the universe, Lohmeyer, 193, n. 1.

[25] In Sir. 14:23 f. divine wisdom lives in a solid house. In 14:24 f. the man who wants to tarry with it pitches his tent by its walls. Acc. to Sir. 24:8 wisdom has its σκηνή in Israel as a lasting resting-place and dwelling (καταπαύω and κατασκηνόω [cf. Dt. 33:12], both שָׁכַן → 388, 23 ff.).

[26] This cannot have been a developed or widespread idea. It is thus unlikely that it should be accepted as the more important motif behind the story of the tabernacle or the Feast of Tabernacles.

[27] Lohmeyer, 192 says that "the tent of Yahweh" becomes in the OT "a symbol of future redemption and glory" and that "the idea of the tent is thus a part of eschatological expectation." But his examples do not stand up, → lines 25 ff. Again, while Ex. 25:8; 29:44 f.; Lv. 26:11 look to the future they are not eschatologically orientated. Jer. 23:6 is not speaking of God's dwelling.

eschatological salvation will be described as a dwelling in tents. The σκηναὶ δικαίων of ψ 117:15 are not meant eschatologically. In Hos. 12:10 we read : ἔτι κατοικιῶ σε ἐν σκηναῖς καθὼς ἡμέρᾳ ἑορτῆς (כִּימֵי מוֹעֵד), but there it is plain that the motif of the wilderness-time / end-time underlies the idea of an eschatological dwelling in tents. There is no promise that God Himself will tabernacle among His people.[28] In the vision of the future pilgrimage of the nations to Jerusalem in Zech. 14:16 f. "the feast of tabernacles becomes the cosmic feast"[29] (σκηνοπηγία, Zech. 14:16, 18 f.). Neither in the OT nor in the LXX is there any ref. at all to the Messiah dwelling in a tent.[30]

C. Non-Biblical Judaism.

1. Philo mostly uses σκηνή in connection with the OT. Acc. to Poster. C., 98 the κτηνοτρόφοι of Gn. 4:20 dwell in tents. Israel lived in tents at the exodus (Vit. Mos., I, 169) and then in the wilderness (Spec. Leg., II, 250 f.; Vit. Mos., I, 313, 200; II, 213; Spec. Leg., IV, 129). These are like shady dells, Vit. Mos., I, 289. In Vit. Mos., II, 282 Philo has σκηναί at the extirpation of the company of Korah (Nu. 16:32 οἶκοι). In connection with Tabernacles (ἡ τῶν σκηνῶν ἑορτή, Migr. Abr., 202; Fug., 186; Spec. Leg., I, 189) there is ref. to σκηναί in Spec. Leg., II, 41, 204, 206 f.; Flacc., 116. At the LXX feast on the island of Pharos the participants lived in σκηναί acc. to Vit. Mos., II, 42. The tabernacle, called τὸ θεῖον ἐκδιαίτημα in Congr., 116, is either σκηνή μαρτυρίου (Leg. All., II, 54 f. on the basis of Ex. 33:7; Ebr., 127 and 138 f.: Lv. 10:9; cf. Det. Pot. Ins., 160) or ἱερὰ σκηνή (Vit. Mos., II, 141; Mut. Nom., 190; Rer. Div. Her., 112) cf. καθιερωμένη σκηνή in Vit. Mos., I, 317 and ἀδιάλυτος σκηνή in Congr., 89, or else the simple σκηνή is enough when the context makes the ref. clear, Leg. All., III, 102; Mut. Nom., 43; Vit. Mos., II (III), 146 and 153. In connection with the explanatory description of the tabernacle in Vit. Mos., II, 74 ff., 79, 82 f., 89, 90 ff. cf. also Rer. Div. Her., 112 (the tabernacle as σοφίας ἀπεικόνισμα καὶ μίμημα); Leg. All., III, 46 (wisdom as a tent in which the wise man dwells → 389, 1 ff.; interpretation of Ex. 33:7 cf. also Gig., 54); Det. Pot. Ins., 160 (the tabernacle as a symbol of virtue; cf. Ebr., 134 and 139); Leg. All., III, 95 (fittings of the tabernacle as ἔργα τῆς ψυχῆς). Philo also uses σκηνή in the sense of "stage" : σκηνή καὶ μῦθος, Congr., 62; ὥσπερ ἐπὶ σκηνῆς, Deus Imm., 102; Flacc., 20; Leg. Gaj., 111; cf. Agric., 35; ἐπὶ τὴν σκηνήν, Leg. Gaj., 203; Flacc., 95.[31]

2. Josephus, expanding on Ex. 19, refers in Ant., 3, 79 and 82 to the tents in which the people encamped at Sinai, then to Achan's tent in 5, 33 (cf. Jos. 7:1, 21 f.), the tents of the Midianites in 5, 219 and 221 (cf. Ju. 7:13), military tents in 9, 77 and 82; Bell., 3, 79 and 82 etc., and the σκηναί at the Feast of Tabernacles (→ 391, 8 ff.) in Ant., 3, 244 ff.; 11, 157. The tabernacle is explicitly described in Ant., 3, 100, 102-133 or 150. Here, and in Ant., 3, 180 f.; 4, 54; 5, 107, 150; 7, 90; 8, 25 and 101 etc. it is simply σκηνή, but σκηνὴ τοῦ θεοῦ in Ant., 4, 22 and 79; 5, 343; 6, 66; 7, 156 and ἱερὰ σκηνή in 5, 68 → line 20 f. Unlike Philo, Jos. does not use the brief σκηνή only where the context permits ; it is a full-fledged term for *the* tabernacle. This receives God acc. to Ant., 3, 189 and its design is of supreme importance acc. to 3, 180 f. Acc. to 8, 103 the

---

[28] E. Sellin, "Das Zelt Jahwes," At.liche Studien, Festschr. R. Kittel, BWANT, 13 (1913), 168-192 argues (181) that HT עַד is a slip for עָמְדִי but this thesis is not convincing.

[29] Lohmeyer, 193, n. 2.

[30] Riesenfeld (esp. 203 f.) "has not really been able to prove" that in later Judaism or even the OT we find the idea of a tent or tents of the Messiah, W. G. Kümmel, Review in Symbolae Bibl. Upsaljenses, 11 (1948), 53. On c. X of Riesenfeld, where he tries to prove the cultic and eschatological character of the "hut" (with gt. emphasis on חֻפָּה), ibid., 49-56. Cf. also in criticism E. Percy, "Die Botschaft Jesu," Lunds Univ. Årsskrift, NF, 49, 5 (1953), 300-307: Exc. on the Transfiguration.

[31] Philo also uses σκηνικός and σκηνοβατέω (→ n. 4); cf. Leisegang, s.v.

cherubim were so fashioned over the ark as to shelter it as under a σκηνή or dome (θόλος). In Ap., 2, 12 the tabernacle is called the πρώτη σκηνή as compared with Solomon's temple. The young king Joash, who at his coronation (4 Βασ. 11:14) stood ἐπὶ τοῦ στύλου (par. ἐπὶ τῆς στάσεως αὐτοῦ, 2 Ch. 23:13), stood ἐπὶ τῆς σκηνῆς acc. to Ant., 9, 151. The ref. is obviously to a dais or podium. ὥσπερ ἐπὶ σκηνῆς (→ 373, 30 f.) occurs in Ant., 6, 264; 17, 234; Bell., 2, 251; 4, 156.

3. The pseudepigr. are still under OT influence, → 384, n. 5. Jub. 7:7 alludes to Gn. 9:21 etc., 13:15 to Gn. 13:3 (both אֹהֶל, LXX οἶκος in the first and σκηνή in the second). In 7:35 Noah encourages his progeny to build cities. It is not clear whether this is meant as opposition to living in tents or as proof of greater enterprise. 16:21 mentions Tabernacles, cf. 16:30. The customary Jewish expression "feast" is used alone in 32:27-29 with ref. to the eighth and last day. In 1:10 the tabernacle (or perhaps the temple) is called God's tent, cf. 49:18, where the tabernacle is contrasted with the later temple, cf. also 1:29.[32] Eth. En. refers repeatedly to dwellings, dwelling-places etc. (38:2; 39:4; 41:2; 45:1 etc.) but not to tents or booths; Gr. En. has κατοίκησις at 1:3; 15:7 f. and οἶκος at 14:10. S. Bar. 4:5; 6:7 calls the tabernacle the tent. Test. Jud. 25:2 mentions the σκηνή of Benjamin. The simile of a shed in the vineyard occurs in an interpolation in Test. Jos. 19:12 (ὡς ὀπωροφυλάκιον). Acc. to Vit. Ad. 1 Adam and Eve built a hut when expelled from Paradise. Acc. to Vit. Ad. 16 the devil's angels live in dwellings in heaven. Along the lines of the tabernacle Metatron has a tent in Hb. En. 15 B 1, cf. 24:7 f.; 25:7; 29:2, also 17:6.

In Damasc. 3:8 (4:7), on the basis of Nu. 14:2, Israel's murmuring in its tents is illustrated by a quotation from Ps. 106:25, cf. Dt. 1:27. Damasc. 7:14 ff. (9:5 ff.) first quotes Am. 5:26 f. in the reading "from the tents of Damascus" ("beyond Damascus" HT 5:27) and then Am. 9:11 (the סֻכָּה of David = the books of the Law). In the Qumran Manual "tent" does not occur. We find מָעוֹן in 1 QS 8:8; 10:1, 3, בַּיִת in 8:5; 9:6, and זְבוּל in 10:3. In the hymns in 1 QH 12:2 there is ref. to God's holy dwelling and in 12:3 to the place of His tent. This is conventional usage, since the Scrolls cannot be referring to the Jerusalem temple. So far מִשְׁכָּן has not been found in them; on שָׁכֵן → 389, 6 f.[33] Cf. also → 378, 21 ff.

D. The New Testament.

σκηνή occurs 20 times in the NT; 10 of the instances are in Hb. and 8 in the discussion of the one theme in Hb. 8 f. Yet σκηνή is more common than σκῆνος and σκήνωμα, which between them occur only 5 times.

1. σκηνή is used in OT quotations in Ac. 7:43 and 15:16. Since Luke follows the LXX version of Am. 5:25-27 in Ac. 7:42 f., he has τὴν σκηνὴν τοῦ Μόλοχ in v. 43.[34] As in Am. 5:26 LXX, so also in Ac. 7:43 the σκηνή is a cultic tent like the tabernacle, cf. Ac. 7:44 → 375, 5 ff.

Ac. 15:16, quoting Am. 9:11 f. (LXX), refers to the ruined σκηνή of David → 370, 28 ff. For Luke the rise of the Christian community is the restoration of

---

[32] With ref. to the promise of Jub. 1:26 that God will dwell with Israel to all eternity Riesenfeld, 183 notes that in the context this relates to the temple (cf. 1:17), but since it was given in the desert at Sinai one may just as well think in terms of Yahweh's dwelling in His eschatological tent.

[33] On encampments at Qumran cf. A. S. van der Woude, *Die messianischen Vorstellungen der Gemeinde von Qumran* (1957), 236 f. [Bertram].

[34] In the HT סֻכּוּת is a proper name (= סַכּוּת, cf. Haench. Ag.[12], ad loc., 235, n. 3); LXX read סַכָּת.

David's σκηνή which Amos promised and which is now being achieved. [35] If the first part of the prophecy has been fulfilled in Jewish Christians (15:16), these should be convinced that the second part is also being fulfilled (15:17) and that the Gentile mission is thus legitimate.

Even apart from these two quotations [36] the OT is always in view when σκηνή is used, esp. in relation to the tabernacle. Directly after Ac. 7:42 f. v. 44 speaks of the σκηνή τοῦ μαρτυρίου (→ n. 16) of the wilderness period and refers to God's command to Moses (Ex. 25:40) to build it κατὰ τὸν τύπον ὃν ἑωράκει → 372, 19 ff. In 7:45 it is added that the fathers under Joshua took the tabernacle with them into Canaan (on σκήνωμα in Ac. 7:46 → 384, 5 ff.). In Rev. 15:5 what is called the "temple of God in heaven" in 11:19 is described as ὁ ναὸς τῆς σκηνῆς τοῦ μαρτυρίου ἐν τῷ οὐρανῷ → 377, 24 ff.; IV, 502, 32 ff.; 888, 21 ff.

2. The expression σκηνή τοῦ μαρτυρίου is not used in Hb. [37] Hb. simply speaks of the σκηνή and it distinguishes the true (ἀληθινή 8:2) or heavenly (cf. ἐν τοῖς οὐρανοῖς 8:1) σκηνή from the earthly one, the tabernacle. 8:2 says of the heavenly σκηνή that God Himself pitched it : ἣν ἔπηξεν ὁ κύριος. Here a formula from Nu. 24:6 LXX, used of the tents of Jacob (24:5), is changed from the plural to the singular and referred to the heavenly sanctuary. Τὸ ὁ κύριος the author adds : οὐκ ἄνθρωπος, to make plain who alone is the builder of the σκηνή ἀληθινή. Conversely it is said of the earthly tabernacle that God certainly gave the command to erect it but is not Himself to be regarded as its builder. This is Moses : he was to ἐπιτελεῖν τὴν σκηνήν (8:5). Hence the tabernacle is said to be built by human hands (cf. χειροποίητα ἅγια 9:24). The heavenly σκηνή, however, is not χειροποίητος (9:11), which means : τοῦτ᾽ ἔστιν οὐ ταύτης τῆς κτίσεως. In the same passage it can be called μείζων καὶ τελειοτέρα in the same sense.

As regards the relation between the heavenly and the earthly σκηνή (→ V, 540, 13 ff.) one learns from the quotation of Ex. 25:40 in 8:5 that the tabernacle is furnished according to the pattern of the heavenly σκηνή. But whereas the OT statements simply accord the heavenly prototype the task of serving as a model for the earthly copy, with no independent significance of its own, Hb. presupposes that the heavenly σκηνή has its own *raison d'être*. The fact that the heavenly σκηνή pre-dated the tabernacle as its τύπος is used in Hb. as evidence of the high antiquity and indeed the pre-existence of the heavenly σκηνή before all times. [38] It is true that the heavenly σκηνή is not called αἰώνιος or αἰωνία in Hb. [39] Yet it is called ἀληθινή (8:2 → I, 250, 22 ff.) and fundamentally this

---

[35] Acc. to Haench. Ac. on 15:16 Luke is not thinking of "the restoration of the Davidic monarchy" (but "the story of Jesus culminating in the resurrection of Jesus," which is more doubtful).

[36] It is a singular but accidental coincidence that both Am. 5:26 and 9:11 are also quoted in Damasc. → 374, 22 ff. Cf. also Haench. Ag.¹² on 7:42 f., 235, n. 3.

[37] μαρτύριον occurs in Hb. only at 3:5 → IV, 504. 19 ff.

[38] The view is rather different from that in, e.g., Nu. r., 12 on 7:1: "At the time when the Holy One, blessed be He. commanded Israel to set up the tent His words also included a command to the ministering angels that they should set up a tent on high," cf. Str.-B., III, 701 f.; Mi. Hb., 185, n. 1. This includes the thought of correspondence between the two tents, but not of following a model. With the throne of glory the sanctuary is one of the seven things made before the creation of the world, but it is not called a tent, cf. Str.-B., II, 145 etc.

[39] Cf. λύτρωσις αἰωνία in 9:12, αἰώνιος κληρονομία in 9:15, διαθήκη αἰώνιος in 13:20. In these instances, however, αἰώνιος carries more of the thought of eschatological eternity.

can only mean that it is eternal in character. Its eternity is more strongly brought out in Hb. than in Jewish parallels. In the latter it is assumed that the tabernacle corresponds perfectly to the heavenly σκηνή, but the presupposition in Hb. is that the tabernacle can be no more than a "shadowy copy" of the original, cf. 8:5 → II, 33, 20 ff. with n. 2. [40]

In Hb. 9:1 the tabernacle is described as the ἅγιον κοσμικόν or earthly sanctuary, → III, 278, 22 ff.; 897, 21 ff. On the basis of Lv. 8:10 f., 15 a brief account is given of its consecration in Hb. 9:21. Hb. 9:2 ff. deals with its inner appointments. Here (9:2 f.) the sanctuary and the holy of holies are differentiated as the πρώτη and δευτέρα (9:7) σκηνή. The reference of πρώτη/δευτέρα is spatial, so that πρώτη has the rare sense, found only here in the NT (→ VI, 866, 13 ff.), of "front." [41] This distinction between the sanctuary and the holy of holies as the first and second or front and rear σκηνή is not attested anywhere else. [42] Yet it can hardly be called inappropriate, [43] nor can one bring against the author the objection that in 8:5 and 9:21 he refers to the whole tabernacle as the σκηνή in the singular. [44] In 9:8, too, the πρώτη σκηνή is the front part of the tabernacle. Here Hb. finds in the presence of a special sanctuary separate from the holy of holies a proof that the very erection of the earthly tabernacle shows that the way to the true sanctuary (→ V, 75, 30 ff.) had not yet been revealed. [45] Herein lies the significance of the first tabernacle as παραβολή, 9:9. [46]

In 9:11 it would then seem that the heavenly sanctuary is also divided into two parts. To be sure, in 8:2 and 9:8 a single concept seems to embrace the whole of the heavenly sanctuary, namely, τὰ ἅγια → I, 102, 32 ff. But in 9:11 it is striking that Christ εἰσῆλθεν εἰς τὰ ἅγια "through the greater and more perfect tabernacle, not made with hands, that is to say, not of this building," and that He did so by His death (διὰ τοῦ ἰδίου αἵματος 9:12). This greater tabernacle can hardly be the body and humanity of Christ, as the fathers believed (cf. also 10:20 → V, 76 f., n. 124), since οὐ ταύτης τῆς κτίσεως would not be appropriate in this case. [47] Nor may one refer the greater tent to the heavenly regions (cf.

---

[40] It is clear that if the heavenly sanctuary can also be called σκηνή the word σκηνή cannot possibly refer to the corruptibility of the tabernacle nor to the situation of the "wandering" people of God, cf. Mi. Hb., ad loc. It is also evident that for the author the earthly sanctuary is the tabernacle and not the temple (ναός does not occur in Hb.). cf. Rgg. Hb. on 9:8 ff.; O. Moe, "Das irdische u. das himmlische Heiligtum. Zur Auslegung von Hb. 9:4 f.," ThZ, 9 (1953), 23-29.

[41] The usage in Hb. is in no way connected with the πρώτη σκηνή of Jos. Ap., 2, 12 → 374, 2 ff.

[42] Jos. Ant., 3, 122 divides the tabernacle into τρία μέρη and thus speaks of three parts, the holy of holies being the τρίτον μέρος, the rear one. Curtains are already mentioned in the OT, cf. the δεύτερον καταπέτασμα of Hb. 9:3, → III, 630, n. 25; Str.-B., I, 1043 f.; III, 733.

[43] Rgg. Hb. on 9:2 f. thinks the author was trying in this way "to bring out as strongly as possible the distinction and independent significance of the two chambers."

[44] The wording of 9:2 ff. also make is quite plain that when the author speaks of the first and second σκηνή he has in mind the two parts of the tabernacle; the reader cannot possibly confuse this division with the distinction between the heavenly and earthly σκηνή mentioned earlier in 8:2, 5.

[45] Rgg. Hb. on 9:8.

[46] This is true no matter whether ἥτις in 9:9 refers to the whole erection of the tabernacle (by attraction to παραβολή, Wnd. Hb. on 9:9) or specifically to the πρώτη σκηνή of 9:8.

[47] So also Mi. Hb. on 9:11. Cf. also W. Köster, "Platonische Ideenwelt u. Gnosis im Hb.," Scholastik, 31 (1956), 547 on F. J. Schierse, Verheissung u. Heilsvollendung. Zur theol. Grundfrage d. Hb. (1955), 57-59.

the οὐρανοί of 4:14) in distinction from τὰ ἅγια as the true dwelling-place of God.[48] What is meant is rather that the heavenly sanctuary, too, has a front part which is greater and more perfect as compared with the tabernacle but which is still to be distinguished from the true sanctuary, the holy of holies. It does not seem to be presupposed in Hb., and it is certainly not expressly stated, that God is to be thought of as present in this sanctuary or holy of holies. Even 8:1 does not imply that God's throne (→ III, 165, 13 ff.) is directly in the ἀληθινή σκηνή (8:2, though cf. 9:24 and on this → V, 527, 13 ff.; 528, 7 ff.). In Hb. the heavenly sanctuary is not called God's σκηνή (cf. Rev. 21:3).

It is very doubtful whether the author of Hb., but for the preceding exposition in c. 8 f., would have used οἱ τῇ σκηνῇ λατρεύοντες in 13:10 and not preferred οἱ τῷ θυσιαστηρίῳ παρεδρεύοντες (cf. 1 C. 9:13) or the like. He is obviously speaking of the priests of the OT cultus (cf. λατρεύειν in 8:5; 9:9; 10:2 → IV, 63, 1 ff.). But he could hardly have said that they serve the σκηνή if he had not told his readers about the tabernacle in 8:5; 9:2 ff.[49]

σκηνή also occurs in Hb. 11:9, where Abraham is described as ἐν σκηναῖς κατοικήσας. Though παροικέω provides the main motif of the saying (→ V, 851, 23 ff.), the fact that dwelling in tents bears vivid witness to Abraham's alien status is not unimportant. The use of σκηναί in the plural is a reminder that Abraham was always on the march and that he and his descendants had to be constantly pitching their tents in new places, Gn. 12:8; 13:12; cf. 26:25; 33:19; 35:21. Living in an established city (11:10) is the opposite of this life in tents, the sign that believers are pilgrims and strangers,[50] → VI, 531, 32 ff.

3. The author of Rev., who speaks of the heavenly "temple of the tabernacle" in 15:5 (→ 375, 9 ff.), says in 13:6 that the aim of the blasphemies of the beast from the sea was to blaspheme God's name (→ V, 279, 37 ff.) καὶ τὴν σκηνὴν αὐτοῦ. σκηνή here is not to be regarded as an abbreviation of the longer form which was to follow in 15:5; on the contrary, 15:5 is a combination of ναὸς τοῦ θεοῦ in 11:19 and σκηνή in 13:6. As concerns 13:6, it is not without significance that in 7:15 it is already said of God that He who sits on His throne in His heavenly temple and receives there the ministry of martyrs, σκηνώσει ἐπ' αὐτούς. Whereas σκηνόω is combined with σκηνή and not ναός in the corresponding statement in 21:3 (→ 380, 31 ff.), the reference in 7:15 is to the ναός. But the close relation between ναός and σκηνή in Rev. may be seen in other verses too, cf. 15:5 and the connection between the ark and the temple in 11:19.[51] The content of the pertinent sayings shows plainly that the meaning of σκηνόω here must be "to dwell continuously" (→ 381, 5 ff.) and that σκηνή, too, implies a lasting stay. This obviously governed the choice of the word in 13:6. If to τὸ ὄνομα αὐτοῦ καὶ τὴν σκηνὴν αὐτοῦ there is here added τοὺς ἐν τῷ οὐρανῷ σκηνοῦντας, then on the basis of 12:12 : εὐφραίνεσθε, οὐρανοὶ καὶ οἱ ἐν αὐτοῖς

---

[48] Mi. Hb. on 9:11 as against Rgg. Hb., ad loc.

[49] Rgg. Hb. on 13:10, who strongly emphasises that only the earthly sanctuary can be meant in 13:10, rightly notes in the same connection that the σκηνή cannot be God's community, since this is called οἶκος τοῦ θεοῦ in 3:6 but not σκηνή. The same applies throughout the NT : only ubi Christus (not ubi ecclesia), is God's σκηνή, Rev. 21:3 → 380, 31 ff.

[50] Cf. O. Kuss, Der Br. an die Hb., Regensburger NT, 8 (1953), ad loc.

[51] Cf. Loh. Apk., ad loc.; H. Bietenhard, "Die himmlische Welt im Urchr. u. Spätjudt.," Wissenschaftliche Untersuchungen z. NT, 2 (1951), 131 f.

σκηνοῦντες (→ V, 533, 27 ff.) it seems natural to think of the perfected in heaven in the apposition of 13:6 too. [52] Nevertheless, the apposition may also relate to God's ὄνομα and σκηνή, which are then assumed to be in heaven → 386, 2 f. [53]

4. Lk. 16:9 speaks of eschatological σκηναί in the plural : καὶ ἐγὼ ὑμῖν λέγω, ἑαυτοῖς ποιήσατε φίλους ἐκ τοῦ μαμωνᾶ τῆς ἀδικίας, ἵνα ὅταν ἐκλίπῃ δέξωνται ὑμᾶς εἰς τὰς αἰωνίους σκηνάς. The "eternal huts" [54] of this saying are unquestionably to be understood eschatologically no matter whether ὅταν ἐκλίπῃ refers to the collapse of mammon, to dying, or to the end of the world, and no matter whether the angels are the subject of δέξωνται or the favours shown to friends. [55] This is settled by the term αἰώνιος if we are to translate it "eternal" (→ I, 209, 3 f.) and especially if it corresponds to our word "eschatological." [56]

If the σκηναί of Lk. 16:9 were huts or tents in the usual sense, this would be in unbearable contradiction to the idea of duration and eschatological glory bound up with αἰώνιος. [57] We are rather to assume that the word shares in the eschatological character of the saying. One possibility is that dwelling in σκηναί, as in the wilderness days, is an attribute of the eschatological consummation. [58] But the OT hardly prepares the way for this eschatological use of σκηνή (→ 372, 29 ff.) and it is doubtful whether the idea enjoyed any wide circulation in later Judaism. [59] One should rather remember that already in the LXX σκηνή, being used for מִשְׁכָּן (→ 371, 18 ff.), had taken on something of the character of the continuous and lasting → 372, 7 ff. Did Jesus perhaps speak quite simply of "eschatological dwellings" in Aram. ? [60] The idea of God's abiding

---

[52] So Loh. Apk. on 13:6. But σκηνοῦντες can hardly be called a tt. for the perfected (ibid. on 12:12), since the no. of examples is too small.

[53] So Loh. Apk.², 208 in the addenda on 13:6 : ὄνομα and σκηνή are hypostatised and acc. to Aram. usage the verb is in the masc. Michaelis, 48 has reservations about this explanation but these are unnecessary. Open to question is Loh.'s further observation : "There is thus a trinity : θεός-ὄνομα-σκηνή? Is this connected with θεός-λόγος-ἐκκλησία? or θεός-Χριστός-ἐκκλησία?" The order shows that βλασφημῆσαι τὸ ὄνομα κτλ. is amplifying βλασφημίας πρὸς τὸν θεόν; hence ὄνομα and σκηνή are a pair and cannot be taken with God to form a trinity. Cf. also → n. 49.

[54] Luther, Zurich Bible, H. Menge, A. Schlatter etc.

[55] So Jeremias Gl., 35 and n. 7, but cf. W. Michaelis, Die Gleichnisse Jesu³ (1956), 265, n. 163.

[56] Cf. W. Michaelis, Versöhnung des Alls (1950), 47.

[57] Cf. Michaelis, 33 f.

[58] Cf. Jeremias Gl., 35, n. 7.

[59] Jeremias Gl., 35, n. 7 quotes Lohmeyer, 191-193 (but cf. → n. 27), Riesenfeld, 181-183 (but cf. → n. 23, 30, 32) and Bornhäuser, 126-128. The latter also quotes Lohmeyer (127 f.) and can only offer examples from Jos. (Ant., 20, 167 f., 188; Bell., 2, 259, 351; 7, 438 ff.) and the NT (Ac. 21:38; Rev. 12:6) for the conviction that the "ideal time of the future" "must begin with a 'wilderness time.'" Unless there are examples which expressly say this, one cannot assume that this analogy implies living in tents. The fact that "the סֻכָּה of the Feast of Tabernacles" is "a reminiscence of the wilderness age in which God acc. to P dwelt among His people in a tabernacle" (Bornhäuser, 127) cannot supply the missing link in the chain ; though the LXX transl. סֻכָּה by σκηνή (→ 369, 17, 27 ff.), the tabernacle is never called סֻכָּה (→ 371, 7 ff.), cf. also Bornhäuser 28 f. and → n. 63. Jeremias adduces from the NT not only Mk. 9:5 but also Ac. 15:16 and Rev. 7:15; 21:3. The two vv. from Rev. refer only to God's eschatological dwelling in a tent, → 377, 29 ff. Ac. 15:16 is not eschatological in the context (→ 374, 39 ff.) and is also too much influenced by the idea of the σκηνή of David to be able to yield the idea of a general dwelling in tents. This leaves only Mk. 9:5 and par. On the question whether this refers to correspondence between the wilderness time and the last time → 379, 8 ff.

[60] F. Delitzsch, סיפרי הברית החדשה¹² (1937), selects מִשְׁכְּנוֹת עוֹלָם at Lk. 16:9 in his transl.

presence was especially connected with the concept of the shekinah in later Judaism. [61] One may be quite certain that no contemporary of Jesus would take the expression to refer to dwelling in a tent → 372, 5 ff. On the other hand we find all the necessary presuppositions for an influence of the idea of the shekinah on the use of the group σκηνή, σκηνόω etc. in the Greek sphere, → 380, 26 ff.; 381, 8 ff.; 385, 30 ff.; 387, 9 ff. If Lk. 16:9 is an authentic saying of Jesus [62] the logion shows that the idea of dwelling in eschatological σκηναί must have been familiar to Jesus Himself. [63]

On the occasion of the transfiguration and with the appearing of Elijah and Moses Peter says : ῥαββί (Mt. κύριε, Lk. ἐπιστάτα), καλόν ἐστιν ἡμᾶς ὧδε εἶναι, καὶ ποιήσωμεν (Mt. εἰ θέλεις, ποιήσω ὧδε) τρεῖς σκηνάς (Lk. σκηνὰς τρεῖς), σοὶ μίαν καὶ Μωϋσεῖ μίαν καὶ Ἠλίᾳ μίαν, Mk. 9:5. Peter's proposal or offer to build three σκηναί [64] is obviously with a view to a fairly lengthy stay rather than a temporary one. It is also evident that the σκηναί are not for the disciples but for Jesus and His heavenly companions Moses and Elijah, so that they may take up lodging in these σκηναί for a longer time, if not for ever. [65] The whole context, and the singularity of the three figures who are to reside in the σκηναί, suggests that an eschatological or Messianic understanding of this dwelling in σκηναί has to be taken into account here. But it is hard to say what the particular background is.

The three σκηναί can have nothing to do with the tabernacle in spite of Moses' connection with it. For the reference is to Elijah and Jesus as well as Moses. There are to be three σκηναί, and God's presence is not related to any one of them as to the tabernacle. [66] It may be accepted that there are at least formal connections between the Synoptic story of the transfiguration and Moses' ascent of the mount (Ex. 24:9-18) and transfiguration on it (Ex. 34:28-35), → IV, 869, n. 228. Whether these are enough to identify Jesus as the prophet like unto Moses (Dt. 18:15, 18; → IV, 869, 4 ff.) may be left open here. [67] At any rate σκηναί play no part in either Ex. 24 or Ex. 34, and

---

of the NT into Hbr. He also has מִשְׁכָּן at Rev. 13:6; 15:5; 21:3 and Hb. 8:2; 9:2, but סֻכָּה at Mk. 9:5 and par. For μοναί in Jn. 14:2 he uses מְעוֹנוֹת (LXX = κατοικητήριον, οἶκος, τόπος etc.); he might also have used מִשְׁכָּנוֹת. μοναί = "abiding-places" (→ IV, 580, 8) is in any case par. to αἰώνιοι σκηναί in Lk. 16:9.

[61] On שְׁכִינָה cf. Str.-B., II, 314 f.; Bousset-Gressm., 315 and 346; → IV, 580, 30 ff.

[62] This might well be even if the connection with the parable 16:1-7 is secondary. Jeremias Gl.⁵, 35 f. thinks 16:9 is brought into connection with the parable by a catchword (36, n. 1: v. 4 δέξωνταί με εἰς / v. 9 : δέξωνται ὑμᾶς εἰς). G. Bornkamm, *Jesus v. Nazareth*² (1957), 185, n. 39 prefers the link "houses" / "huts." But the σκηναί of 16:9 are even more permanent dwellings than the οἶκοι of v. 4.

[63] Bornhäuser, 127; but he refers to "the idea of dwelling in tabernacles in the Messianic age," which is untenable in the light of → n. 59.

[64] The meaning of the first phrase is not "it is good to be here" (Luther ; 1956 revision, like A.V.: "it is good for us to be here") = "we (you three and we disciples) want to stay and make our home here," but "it is a good thing that we disciples are here. We can take in hand the building of σκηναί."

[65] We are not told where the disciples were to stay when the σκηναί were erected. The wording of Peter's remark rules out the idea that he hoped they would be invited to stay in the σκηναί. Nor does there seem to be any thought of their building other σκηναί for themselves. Presumably they would have had to camp out in the open.

[66] Even if there is a close relation between cloud and tabernacle in the OT (→ IV, 905, 39 ff.), it is somewhat bold (cf. A. Oepke → IV, 908, 30 ff.) to introduce the idea of a cloud as a tent into the transfiguration story (Lohmeyer, 196-199 does not do this), and in any case the fact that there were to be three σκηναί is disregarded on this view.

[67] Cf. S. Schulz, "Die Decke d. Moses," ZNW, 49 (1958), 30, n. 149. Also G. Schille, "Die Topographie d. Mk.-Ev.," ZDPV, 73 (1957), 159, n. 45.

therefore the σκηναί of Mk. 9:5 and par. cannot be claimed as arguments in favour of a Moses-Christ typology.

Are the σκηναί of the transfiguration story in any way connected with the booths of the Feast of Tabernacles? There would probably be on the high mountain of Mk. 9:5 and par. the materials needed to make huts or tents of leaves. [68] But this possibility alone does not establish a connection with the feast. Living in σκηναί or huts might well have been the normal way of staying for a period on an afforested mountain. [69] Since the σκηναί were not to be built for the disciples but for Jesus, Moses and Elijah (cf. also → n. 65) they also cannot be regarded as arguments in favour of the expectation that dwelling in tents or booths will be granted to the people in the last time somewhat along the lines of Hos. 12:10 (→ 373, 2 ff.), for the disciples rather than Jesus, Moses and Elijah correspond to the people in the transfiguration story. Again, Peter's proposal has nothing whatever to do with the idea of God's eschatological dwelling in a σκηνή even if this could be shown for certain to be a contemporary view → 372, 25 ff. For the σκηναί are not to be made for God, and in the story itself the connection between God or God's voice and the cloud contradicts this explanation.

There is even less to be said for a connection with the idea of an eschatological dwelling of the Messiah. It cannot be shown that this was a current notion (→ n. 30), and from within the story itself there also arises the objection that there are to be three σκηναί and not just the σκηνή of the future Messiah. Is it an adequate answer to this objection to say that Moses and Elijah are perhaps mentioned here as precursors of the Messiah? In the strict sense the precursor motif applies only to Elijah (→ II, 931, 16 ff.; 936, 10 ff.). Messianically Moses is a type or countertype of the Messiah, a predecessor rather than a precursor (→ II, 938, 15 f.), while Elijah for his part is not a type. If Moses and Elijah are a pair and obviously have the same function, this can hardly be in terms of the precursor motif. [70] We do better, then, not to try to link the dwelling in σκηναί in the transfiguration story with specific eschatological or Messianic themes but to regard it simply as an expression of God's gracious and abiding presence. This holds good no matter what may be the Aram. original of Peter's saying → 378, 20 f. [71]

5. Neither the transfiguration story (→ 379, 21 ff.) nor Hb. (→ 377, 4 ff.) says anything about God dwelling in a σκηνή. We find this idea, however, in Rev. 21:3: ἰδοὺ ἡ σκηνὴ τοῦ θεοῦ μετὰ τῶν ἀνθρώπων, καὶ σκηνώσει μετ' αὐτῶν, καὶ αὐτοὶ λαοὶ (→ IV, 55, n. 104) αὐτοῦ ἔσονται, καὶ αὐτὸς ὁ θεὸς μετ' αὐτῶν ἔσται. The influence of OT prophecies, especially Zech. 2:14 f.; 8:3, 8; Ez. 37:27 (→ 372, 26 ff.), is unmistakable here. In spite of the reciprocity of individual expressions, neither the OT passages nor Rev. [72] say that men for their part will

---

[68] Even if we have here a visionary happening (→ V, 354, 3 ff.) the ὧδε of Mk. 9:5 and par. shows that Peter's saying is based on the actual situation of the disciples, i.e., the setting depicted in 9:2 and par.

[69] For further though not very cogent arguments in favour of a link with the Feast of Tabernacles cf. H. Baltensweiler, "Die Verklärung Jesu," Abh. ThANT, 33 (1959), 37-61.

[70] Though there is elsewhere (very rare) witness to the coming of two precursors of the Messiah, this does not completely overcome the difficulty → II, 938, 24 ff. For in such cases the two are almost always (→ II, 939, 1 ff.) Enoch and Elijah. It is open to question whether Rev. 11:6 is speaking of Moses and Elijah (→ II, 939, 4 ff.; cf. also → IV, 867, n. 214). That we have in the transfiguration story a diluted form of the idea that both Moses and Elijah have the function of precursors (→ IV, 866, 14 ff.) is unlikely since the undiluted form is only a postulate. The idea that Moses and Elijah come together because both are to be regarded as sufferers (→ II, 939, 10 ff., 16 ff.; IV, 867, 1 ff.) is by no means certain, → V, 911, n. 54. Even if true, it does not explain the dwelling in σκηναί.

[71] It is probable that Peter was speaking of huts, → lines 4 ff. The eschatological thrust of the story derives more from the actual transfiguration than from the saying of the voice from heaven.

[72] Zech. 2:15 LXX (not HT) refers to a κατασκηνοῦν of the ἔθνη, but the idea of a tent is no longer clearly bound up with κατασκηνοῦν → 387, 31 ff.

dwell in tents at that time. There is no idea of a vast heavenly camp with God's tent in the middle. Rev. 21:3 reminds the reader not so much of 15:5 (→ 375, 9 ff.) as of 13:6 (→ 377, 24 ff.) and especially 7:15 (→ 377, 29 ff.). He thus realises at once that this is a vivid metaphor for God's abiding presence.

Compared with the σκηνώσει ἐπ᾿ αὐτούς of 7:15 the σκηνώσει μετ᾿ αὐτῶν of 21:3, and with it the preceding μετὰ τῶν ἀνθρώπων and the ensuing μετ᾿ αὐτῶν (unless we are to read just αὐτῶν),[73] lays strong emphasis on the closer relationship between God and man which is a feature of the new world.[74] Here, too, one cannot help but notice the correspondence to the shekinah concept → 378, 21 ff. As the OT parallels (→ 380, 34 ff.) suggest and Rev. 21:2 confirms, the thought behind the σκηνὴ θεοῦ is that of the new Jerusalem or the new heaven and the new earth generally, 21:1. The christological reference found in the σκηνοῦν of Jn. 1:14 (→ 386, 9 ff.) is quite absent from the promise of Rev. 21:3. Instead it points forward to future eschatological salvation, and this prospect may well be regarded as the climax in the history of σκηνή in the NT.[75]

E. The Post-Apostolic Fathers.

In the post-apost. fathers σκηνή occurs 3 times in 1 Cl. On the basis of Nu. 17 c. 43 is speaking of the tabernacle; it is σκηνὴ τοῦ μαρτυρίου in 43, 2 and 5 and just σκηνή in 43, 3. 56, 13 quotes Job 5:24 → n. 10.[76]

† σκῆνος.

1. σκῆνος (Doric σκᾶνος) is rather later than σκηνή.[1] It means "tent" but is seldom used of real tents: cultic σκ<ήν>η (plur.) on an inscr. from Teos, CIG, II, 3071 (2nd cent. B.C.). The normal use is the transf. one for a body dead or alive, the human body, e.g., Democr. Fr., 37 (Diels⁷, II, 155, 2), 187 (II, 183, 9), 223 (II, 190, 4 and 7), 270 (II, 201, 4), 288 (II, 205, 13); Corp. Herm., 13, 12 (I, 246, 23 Scott), also that of an animal, e.g., Democr. Fr., 57 (Diels⁷, II, 157, 11).[2] This use is so firmly established that one may ask how far there was still any sense of the meaning "tent" or whether the rendering "tent" does not stress this too much, so that it is better simply to transl. by "body" (so always Diels).

2. In the LXX σκῆνος occurs only at Wis. 9:15: φθαρτὸν γὰρ σῶμα βαρύνει ψυχήν, καὶ βρίθει τὸ γεῶδες σκῆνος νοῦν πολυφρόντιδα. As ψυχή and νοῦς are par. here, so are σῶμα and σκῆνος. Hence the dominant non-bibl. meaning "body" is the right one. The author shares this; there is no need to suppose that he had before him any special comparison of the body with a tent.[3] In keeping is the fact that neither in the LXX nor elsewhere is σκηνή ever used as a synon. for "body."

---

[73] Cf. Loh. Apk., ad loc.
[74] Loh. Apk. on 7:15.
[75] Michaelis, 49.
[76] Acc. to Ev. Pt. 33 the Roman soldiers set to watch the tomb of Jesus pitched a tent for their stay. Acc. to Prot. Ev. Jm. 1:4 Joachim, when he went into the desert, lived in a tent there because this was suitable for living in the desert (with no ref. to Israel's wilderness period etc.).

σκῆνος. For bibl. → σκηνή.
[1] The relation between the two forms is not clear. On σκῆ-νος cf. P. Chantraine, La formation des noms en grec ancien (1933), 420 [Debrunner].
[2] Cf. Pass., Liddell-Scott, s.v.; Moult.-Mill., 577.
[3] K. Siegfried in Kautzsch Apkr. u. Pseudepigr., I, 493 transl. "earthly tent" and notes that this is the same image as in Job 4:19. Now it is true that in Job 4:19 men as opposed to the angels in 4:18 are said to live in houses of clay and this refers to the human body,

3. σκῆνος does not seem to occur in Philo or Joseph. Nor do the Rabb. use "tent" for "body." [4]

4. In the NT σκῆνος is found only in 2 C. 5:1, 4. In 5:1 the apostle Paul, who never uses σκηνή, writes : ἐὰν ἡ ἐπίγειος ἡμῶν οἰκία τοῦ σκήνους καταλυθῇ, οἰκοδομὴν ἐκ θεοῦ ἔχομεν, οἰκίαν ἀχειροποίητον αἰώνιον ἐν τοῖς οὐρανοῖς.

Later, after using τὸ οἰκητήριον ἡμῶν τὸ ἐξ οὐρανοῦ in 5:2, Paul takes up the οἰκία τοῦ σκήνους of v. 1 in οἱ ὄντες ἐν τῷ σκήνει in v. 4. At a first glance this might suggest that in οἰκία τοῦ σκήνους the greater emphasis is on σκῆνος. But this is refuted by the fact that in 5:1 f. the word group οἰκία, οἰκοδομή, οἰκητήριον is in the main predominant, and the use of καταλύω is consonant with this in so far as it can be used for pulling down a house (cf. e.g., Mk. 14:58; 15:29 par. and → IV, 338, 5 ff.) as well as striking a tent → 368, 24 f.

If one presupposes that for Paul, too, σκῆνος denotes the body and virtually means this (on σκήνωμα in this sense in 2 Pt. 1:13 f. → 384, 15 ff.), [5] then the combination of σκῆνος and οἰκία is not a violent linking together of opposites. It would be if οἰκία meant a solid house and σκῆνος a flimsy tent. But though οἰκία is a house in the sense of a solid structure, 5:1 shows that the apostle can call not only our future heavenly corporeality but also our present fleeting corporeality an οἰκία, so that this word is neutral as concerns the question of durability or transitoriness. In particular, it is in no sense antithetical to σκῆνος if one may assume that this means "body." [6] Since the solidity and durability of the eschatological mode of existence are denoted not only by ἀχειροποίητος but also by αἰώνιος and finally by ἐν τοῖς οὐρανοῖς (cf. ἐξ οὐρανοῦ in 5:2), and since they are also expressed comprehensively by ἐκ θεοῦ, it is natural to suppose that on the opposite side σκῆνος as well as ἐπίγειος is designed to bring out the corruptibility of the earthly mode of existence. The more strongly, of course, σκῆνος bears the sense of "body" rather than "tent," the more ἐπίγειος alone has the task of characterising the present οἰκία, [7] → V, 146, 33 ff.

If the use of σκῆνος in 2 C. 5:1, 4 is the current one, the apostle's employment of σκῆνος is not the only link with Gnostic views and modes of expression. The equation of tent and body (also house and body → V, 132, 27 f.; 147, 10 ff.) certainly cannot be Jewish, → line 1 f. Hence the observation is correct that Paul's statement shows a certain kinship to Gnosticism, → V, 133, 9 ff.; cf. 147, 6 ff.; 155, 33 ff. [8] Nevertheless, the

---

but the Hbr. is בָּתֵּי־חֹמֶר (LXX οἰκίαι πήλιναι) and hence there is no thought of a tent as in Is. 38:12. Cf. also → V, 132, 24 ff.; 133, n. 11.

[4] Cf. Str.-B., III, 517 on 2 C. 5:1.

[5] Even though the apostle is acc. to Ac. 18:3 a σκηνοποιός by trade (→ 393, 21 ff.) this does not lead to a different interpretation of σκῆνος.

[6] Since the apostle has no occasion to use σκηνή in the extant letters one can only conjecture that he would have used this and not σκῆνος for tent.

[7] The epithets on the two sides are not balanced against one another. ἐπίγειος is the opp. of both ἐν τοῖς οὐρανοῖς and αἰώνιος, and there is no opp. of ἀχειροποίητος. J. Héring, La seconde épître de Saint Paul aux Corinth., Comm. du NT, 8 (1958), ad loc., 47, n. 2 thinks the wording of 5:1 indicates an "opposition entre la tente faite de main d'hommes et la maison céleste" and that it is reminiscent of the language "qu'emploie l'épître aux Hébreux (c. 8 et 9) et Philon, pour contraster le tabernacle juif et le sanctuaire céleste," but this is to introduce alien thoughts. Hb. and Philo do not use σκῆνος, and Paul would never forget that man's earthly body was created by God and not by men's hands, cf. 1 C. 12:18; 15:38, though Héring, ad loc. has the paraphrase "par la génération humaine."

[8] Cf. W. Schmithals, "Die Gnosis in Korinth," FRL, NF, 49 (1956), 225 f.

more strongly one must assume that σκῆνος bears the sense "body" the less σκῆνος itself can be adduced in favour of this view, especially as the corresponding Gnostic statements prefer σκηνή to σκῆνος. [9] That the apostle was influenced by the terminology of the Feast of Tabernacles in his choice of σκῆνος [10] is a conjecture which is quite wide of the mark. [11] Nor does the possibility that he is using ecclesiological terms in 2 C. 5:1 ff. merit serious consideration. [12] Even if σκῆνος means "body" there is no connection with the idea of the community as a body (or house).

5. σκῆνος does not occur in the post-apost. fathers.

† σκήνωμα.

1. σκήνωμα, from σκηνόω (→ 385, 1 ff.), means "tent" or "tent-like dwelling." At first it is mostly plur., Eur. Hec., 616; Ion, 1133; Xenoph. An., II, 2, 17; VII, 4, 16, also of a temple or chapel, Paus., III, 17, 6, late and rare, also sing. of the "body," esp. the dead body of a man or animal, e.g., Stob. Ecl., I, 396, 1; τὸ σκήνωμα τῆς ψυχῆς, Sextus [1] (Pythagorean) Sententiae, 320; Ps.-Callisth., I, 24, 11; Schol. on Nicander Theriaca, [2] 694; Preis. Zaub., II, 19a, 49 f.

2. In the LXX σκήνωμα occurs 80 times (also 3 or 4 in ᾿Α, 4 in Θ and one in Σ). This is only a fifth of the use of σκηνή, with which it is fully synon. For the Hbr. equivalents → 369, 20 ff. [3] It is hard to see why σκηνή was chosen in some places and σκήνωμα in others. In part the vocabulary of the translators played a role : σκήνωμα does not occur at all in Gn.-Lv., in Nu. only at 16:27 (vl. for σκηνή; there is frequent vacillation in the MSS), in Dt. only at 33:18; on the other hand σκήνωμα is more common than σκηνή in Ps. The use of σκήνωμα or σκηνή does not seem to be connected with the sing. and plur. → lines 11 ff. The distribution among various spheres is proportional to that of σκηνή → 369, 34 ff. The tabernacle and temple are comparatively rarely called σκήνωμα, 3 Βασ. 2:28; 8:4; 1 Εσδρ. 1:48; Jdt. 9:8; ψ 14:1; 25:8; 42:3; 60:5; 73:7; 77:60; 83:2; 131:5, 7, also Lam. 2:6 → n. 3. 2 Macc. 10:6 speaks of solemn ceremonies in the σκηνώματα in connection with the dedication of the temple, though the Feast of Tabernacles is ἡ τῶν σκηνῶν ἑορτή, → 369, 29 f. We find established usage when on demobilisation or in the summons to each to go back home (or the corresponding narrative → 371, n. 15) σκήνωμα is used, 1 Βασ. 4:10; 13:2; 2 Βασ. 18:17; 19:9; 20:1, 22; 3 Βασ. 8:66 (par. 2 Ch. 7:10); 12:16 (par. 2 Ch. 10:16), 24 t (B); 4 Βασ. 8:21; 14:12; 2 Ch. 21:9; 25:22. There is ref. to a tent for the sun (LXX ἐν τῷ ἡλίῳ) in ψ 18:5 (cf. σκηνόω in 3 Βασ. 8:12). God's σκήνωμα symbolises His protection in ψ 60:5, cf. σκηνή in ψ 26:5 → 372, 17 ff. Ac. 1:20b, quoting ψ 68:26, has ἐν αὐτῇ (= ἐν τῇ ἐπαύλει, 1:20a) for ἐν τοῖς σκηνώμασιν αὐτῶν.

---

[9] Cf. Wnd. 2 K., 158 (Exc. on 5:1, rightly rejecting the thesis of K. Bornhäuser, Die Gebeine d. Toten [1921], 37-39 that one is to distinguish between tent and tent-poles = flesh and bones) → V, 133, n. 11; 149, n. 8.

[10] Cf. W. D. Davies, Paul and Rabbinic Judaism (1939), 313; T. W. Manson, "ἱλαστήριον," JThSt, 46 (1945), 1-10. Called "plausible" by Héring, op. cit., 47, n. 2.

[11] Even if σκῆνος had the prior sense of "tent" Paul would have had אֹהֶל in mind, not מִשְׁכָּן, Bornhäuser, 126. In any case σκῆνος is never used in relation to Tabernacles.

[12] K. Barth, K.D., IV, 2 (1955), 711 (E.T. [1958], 629): By the οἰκία τοῦ σκήνους we are "comprehensively to understand the community in its present form ... and only then, and included in this, the present physical existence of the individual Christian as he lives in the σῶμα."

σ κ ή ν ω μ α. Bibl. → σκηνή.

[1] Ed. A. Elter (1891 f.); H. Chadwick, The Sentences of Sextus, TSt, NS, 5 (1959).

[2] Ed. O. Schneider (1856).

[3] 3 times without Mas., 8 in works with no Mas. There is confusion with אֹהֶל in ἔθνη

3. Philo does not appear to use σκήνωμα. [4] In Joseph. one may refer to Ant., 11, 187. The συμπόσιον which Artaxerxes gave, and which took place ἐν αὐλῇ οἴκου τοῦ βασιλέως acc. to Est. 1:5, was held in a magnificent σκήνωμα seating thousands. [5]

4. In the NT σκήνωμα occurs only at Ac. 7:46 and 2 Pt. 1:13 f. (→ 383, 34 f.). In Stephen's speech (Ac. 7:46), close to the σκηνή passages in 43 f. (→ 374, 35 ff.; 375, 4 ff.) and in free allusion to ψ 131:5, there is mention of David's resolve εὑρεῖν σκήνωμα τῷ οἴκῳ (vl. θεῷ) 'Ιακώβ. It is added in 7:47: Σολομὼν δὲ οἰκοδόμησεν αὐτῷ οἶκον, cf. 3 Βασ. 6:2; 8:20. Only from what follows may the reader gather that this building of a solid house under Solomon was an aberration as contrasted with the building of a σκήνωμα. Though σκήνωμα can also be used in the LXX for the temple (→ 383, 24 ff.), the wording of ψ 131:5 must have been welcome to the speaker since σκήνωμα was used here, and not least under the influence of the σκηνή passages in 7:43 and especially 7:44, this could evoke the idea of a tent-like dwelling, cf. 2 S. 7:5 ff. [6]

In 2 Pt. 1:13 the author uses the expression: ἐφ' ὅσον εἰμὶ ἐν τούτῳ τῷ σκηνώματι and adds in 1:14: εἰδὼς ὅτι ταχινή ἐστιν ἡ ἀπόθεσις τοῦ σκηνώματός μου. This expression is not attested in the LXX, but the designation of the body as σκήνωμα is not finally alien to the later non-biblical use → 383, 12 f. It also reminds us of σκῆνος in 2 C. 5:1, 4 → 382, 3 ff. Yet one may not assume that the author of 2 Pt. could speak in this way only under the influence of the Pauline statements. [7] Whereas 1 Pt. strongly emphasises the fact that Christians are strangers on earth (→ V, 853, 6 ff.), this is not very prominent in 2 Pt., so that there is in σκήνωμα no special stress on the idea of corruptibility. The word means "body" rather than "tent" or "dwelling," especially as ἀπόθεσις in 1:14 refers more to the putting off of a garment than the pulling down of a house or tent, cf. ἀποτίθεσθαι in R. 13:12; Col. 3:8 etc.

5. The only ref. in the post-apost. fathers is Dg., 6, 8 : ἀθάνατος ἡ ψυχὴ ἐν θνητῷ σκηνώματι κατοικεῖ. Here one should transl. "dwelling" rather than "tent," or even perhaps "body" (cf. Sextus, → 383, 13 f.) in spite of the use of σῶμα in 6, 7, which is perhaps for stylistic variety. But here, unlike 2 Pt. 1:13 f. (→ lines 15 ff.), the thought that Christians are strangers stands in close proximity, cf. v. 8b. [8]

καὶ σκηνώματα == גּוֹיִם וֵאלֹהָיו, 2 Βασ. 7:23, probably also confusion in πάντα τὰ σκηνώ-ματα == כֹּל שֶׁעֲמָהֶם 1 Ch. 5:20 and cf. 2 Ch. 11:14. Whether κατάσχεσις == אֲחֻזָּה here (as usually in the LXX, cf. the order), or whether it is used for מִגְרָשׁ, is open to question; σκήνωμα will correspond either way to the other term. In ψ 107:8 Succoth == σκηναί (vl. σκηνώματα → 370, n. 8). σκήνωμα == שֵׁי in Lam. 2:6; LXX can hardly have read מִשְׁכָּן (cf. BHK) but probably took or read שֵׁי as שֹׂ, → 369, 18 f. מְסֻכְּנוֹת is confused with מִשְׁכְּנוֹת in 3 Βασ. 9:19 A.

[4] It does not occur in Leisegang. Philo Quaest. in Gn. IV 11 has in ... tabernaculo corporis, but acc. to the Vg the Gk. might be σκήνωμα (Vg NT and OT) or σκηνή (Vg OT and NT except for Hb. 11:9) or σκῆνος (Vg 2 C. 4:5; habitatio in 5:1).

[5] Where we do not have the Greek of the pseudepigr. it is impossible to say whether σκήνωμα might have been used instead of σκηνή where there is ref. to tents → 374, 7 ff.

[6] The neutral τόπος in ψ 131:5 (מָקוֹם) is undoubtedly even more apt to protect David against any reproach. The author probably combined εὑρεῖν in ψ 131:5a with σκήνωμα in 131:5b (HT plur.) because of the (to him) important τῷ οἴκῳ 'Ιακώβ — there is no need to decide between οἴκῳ and θεῷ as the original, cf. Haench. Ag., ad loc.

[7] Nor is the choice influenced by Jos. Ant., 4, 177 ff. (cf. Wnd. Pt., ad loc.).

[8] Eus. Hist. Eccl., III, 31, 1 calls the burial of the apostles Paul and Peter the κατάθεσις of their bodies or corpses (σκηνώματα).

† σκηνόω.

1. More common than σκηνόω is the verb σκηνέω, derived from σκηνή.[1] But σκηνόω is also fairly common in non-bibl. works. It means "to live or camp in a tent," Xenoph. An., II, 4, 14; VII, 4, 12; Cyrop., II, 1, 25; P. Greci e Latini, IV, 340, 10 and 13 (257/6 B.C.); cultically σκηνοῦν ... καὶ πανηγυράζειν, Ditt. Syll.[3], I, 344, 3 (Teos, 303 B.C.). Also with ref. to other dwellings, Ditt. Syll.[3], I, 523, 9 (220 B.C.); κατὰ τὰς κώμας, ἐν ταῖς οἰκείαις ἐν τῇ ἀκροπόλει, Xenoph. An., IV, 5, 23; παρὰ τούτοις ἐσκήνωσα, Diogenes Cynicus,[2] Ep., 37, 1 (4th cent. B.C.). Rarely trans. "to pitch a tent," "to inhabit a tent," e.g., τὸν τόπον τὸν νῦν σκηνοῖ, Zenon Pap.,[3] 59, 499, 89 (3rd cent. B.C.).[4]

2. In the LXX the simple σκηνόω is rare as compared with the compound κατασκηνόω → 387, 14 ff., which must be regarded as the true LXX term for "to tabernacle," "to dwell." σκηνόω occurs only 5 times. In Gn. 13:12 (vl. ἐνσκηνόω, found only here) it is used for אָהַל.[5] In the other ref. it corresponds to שָׁכֵן: Ju. 5:17 B (twice; A κατασκηνόω); 8:11 B (→ 370, n. 7; A κατοικέω); 3 Βασ. 8:12 or God's dwelling ἐν γνόφῳ (κατασκηνόω in the par. 2 Ch. 6:1).[6] In 'Α σκηνόω occurs 10 times — a sign of the affinity 'Α must have perceived between שָׁכֵן and σκην-, → 388, n. 5. In Θ it is found 3 times and in Σ twice. Only in 3 of these passages does LXX also have σκηνόω or κατασκηνόω: 3 Βασ. 8:12; ψ 64:5; 138:9. שָׁכַן is always the HT original; סֹכֵן is misread as this by 'Α at Is. 22:15.

3. Philo, who seldom uses κατασκηνόω (→ 389, 1 ff.), does not seem to have σκηνόω at all.[7] Joseph. in Vit., 244 says that in Gabara he ordered that the troops should σκηνοῦν κατὰ τὸ πεδίον, cf. Ant., 3, 293 f.; 17, 217.[8]

4. In the NT σκηνόω occurs in Jn. 1:14 and several times in Rev. In none of these instances does it refer to dwelling in a real tent, though in the NT σκηνή does mostly denote a real tent, even if in part only metaphorically → 374, 31 ff. Rev. 7:15 speaks of God's dwelling among the redeemed; the sense is that of residing permanently, since the context speaks of God's sitting on His throne, not of a divine σκηνή in heaven → 377, 29 ff.; on ἐπ' αὐτούς → 381, 5 ff. On the parallel promise in Rev. 21:3 → 380, 31 ff. This does speak of God's σκηνή, but σκηνή here is a figure of speech for His abiding and gracious presence, and the

---

σ κ η ν ό ω. Bibl. → σκηνή.

[1] Cf. Pass. and Liddell-Scott, s.v. σκηνέω arose from σκηνάω by an incorrect inference from the fut. σκηνήσ-. Cf. E. Fraenkel, Gr. Denominativa (1906), 90, 93 and n. 3 [Debrunner].

[2] Ed. R. Hercher, Epistolographi Graeci (1873), 251.

[3] Ed. C. C. Edgar, Catalogue Gén. des Antiquités Égypt. du Musée du Caire, 58 (1928), 217.

[4] On usage in the pap. cf. also Moult.-Mill., 578, s.v.; Mayser, I, 3², 134 and 141.

[5] אָהַל occurs elsewhere only in Gn. 13:18 where it is transl. ἀποσκηνόω (hapax legomenon, though cf. Ps. Sol. 7:1). Cf. also Is. 13:20 BH.³

[6] Apart from the compounds already mentioned we also find ἐγκατασκηνόω in the LXX at 2 Βασ. 7:10 vl., though → 387, n. 2. ἐπισκηνόω does not occur. Cf. σύσκηνος (twice) or σύσκηνιος (once) for אֲשֶׁר בְּאֹהֶל at Ex. 16:16 or גֵּר בַּיִת at Ex. 3:22.

[7] Acc. to Leisegang.

[8] Apart from κατασκηνόω (→ 389, 4 ff.) Joseph. uses the compounds παρασκηνόω "to camp by" (Ant., 3, 289) and συσκηνόω "to be a tent-companion" (5, 219); cf. συσκηνέω in Bell., 6, 188 (→ n. 6).

passages in 7:15 and 21:3 are connected with the shekinah concept involved here. Rather more remotely this applies also to Rev. 13:6 unless the σκηνοῦν in heaven relates to God's ὄνομα and σκηνή → 377, 38 ff. The meaning in 13:6 obviously cannot be that a tent dwells in a tent. Precisely when σκηνή refers to the heavenly tabernacle or temple (15:5; 11:19 → 377, 24 ff.) σκηνόω means "to be permanently." When the perfected are described as οἱ ἐν αὐτοῖς (sc. ἐν τοῖς οὐρανοῖς) σκηνοῦντες (12:12) one must suppose that the meaning is "to reside permanently" → 378, n. 52. There is no idea of living in tents. [9]

Jn. 1:14 is important: καὶ ὁ λόγος σὰρξ ἐγένετο καὶ ἐσκήνωσεν ἐν ἡμῖν. It undoubtedly suggests that the σκηνοῦν of the incarnate Logos is to be regarded as an expression for the fact that His earthly stay was for Him no more than an episode between His pre-existence and post-existence as the exalted Lord, [10] in which case the translation "he tabernacled among us" is more apt and suitable than "he dwelt among us." [11] Yet it is more correct, especially in relation to Jn. 1:14, to recall what the LXX has in view when it uses σκηνή as the rendering of מִשְׁכָּן (→ 371, 18 ff.) and κατασκηνόω as that of שָׁכַן (→ 387, 20 ff.) — the same cannot be said to come out with the same clarity in respect of σκηνόω itself (→ 385, 11 ff.) — and also to take into account the degree to which the group denotes lasting presence elsewhere in the NT (→ 377, 35 ff.; 380, 26 ff.; 381, 7 ff.; 385, 30 ff.; 387, 7 ff.). In this light it would appear that ἐσκήνωσεν ἐν ἡμῖν in Jn. 1:14 does not refer to the temporary and transitory element in the earthly existence of the Logos but is designed to show that this is the presence of the Eternal in time. [12]

5. σκηνόω does not occur in the post-apost. fathers or the Apologists.

† ἐπισκηνόω.

1. A rare word [1] meaning "to enter, take up residence in a tent or dwelling," e.g., ἐπὶ τὰς οἰκείας, Polyb., 4, 72, 1; ταῖς οἰκείαις, 4, 18, 8. It does not occur in LXX, Philo, [2] or Joseph.

2. The only NT use is at 2 C. 12:9: ἵνα ἐπισκηνώσῃ ἐπ᾽ ἐμὲ ἡ δύναμις τοῦ Χριστοῦ. In terms of etymology and general use one can hardly speak of a

---

[9] As against Bornhäuser, 127: "As compared with κατοικεῖν (οἱ κατοικοῦντες ἐπὶ τῆς γῆς, 3:10 etc.) it denotes (sc. σκηνοῦν: οἱ ἐν τῷ οὐρανῷ σκηνοῦντες, 12:12; 13:6) the special nature of dwelling and life in heaven. The expression is not saying that the heavenly dwelling is flimsy; it is to be associated with the later Jewish view of dwelling in a tabernacle in the Messianic age." The latter pt. is highly questionable → 378, 12 ff.; 380, 7 ff.

[10] Cf. Stauffer Theol., 41; 99; 245, n. 124; 386; Bultmann J., 43 f. on 1:14 and on this Michaelis, 48 f. It is hard to see what is the basis of the observation of E. Pax, "ΕΠΙ-ΦΑΝΕΙΑ," Münchener Theol. Studien, 1, 10 (1956), 215 that "the idea of concealment is reflected in the verb σκηνοῦν" in Jn. 1:14.

[11] Michaelis, 35 f.

[12] Cf. also K. Barth, K.D., IV, 3, 2 (1959), 701 (E.T. [1962], 612).

ἐ π ι σ κ η ν ό ω. [1] Not derived from ἐπίσκηνος or ἐπισκήνιον (cf. Pass. and Liddell-Scott, s.v.) but a compound of σκηνόω → 385, 1 ff.

[2] Acc. to Pr.-Bauer⁵, s.v. Philo has ἐπισκηνόω for ἐπισκιάζω. This comes from the first ed. of E. Preuschen (1910) and is a slip [W. Bauer].

descent of Christ's power. [3] This idea would arise at most only if the δύναμις of the exalted Christ were thought to be resident above. But this presupposition obviously does not lie behind ἐπισκηνόω, which is horizontally orientated rather than vertically. For here ἐπί τινα means "to" rather than "upon." Hence it is better to speak of an entry [4] of the power of Christ, of its taking up residence in the apostle (on ἐπί with acc. → 386, 27).

Since the word is so rare one may ask what caused Paul to use it. There is much to be said for the view that he took the preposition ἐπί, which is construed with σκηνόω in Rev. 7:15 (→ 381, 5 ff.), and combined it with the verb, that he thus started with the idea of gracious presence which is so strongly linked with σκηνόω or the whole group, [5] and that he was trying to say that in his experience Christ's strength came to abide in him precisely in his weaknesses, → II, 316, 38 ff. cf. → I, 491, 29 ff. [6]

3. ἐπισκηνόω occurs neither in the post-apost. fathers nor the Apologists.

† κατασκηνόω.

1. Compound of σκηνόω [1] in the sense "to pitch one's tent or camp," "to enter one's tent," "to camp," e.g., Xenoph. An., II, 2, 16; Cyrop., IV, 5, 39; Diod. S., 13, 96, 2; P. Lond., II, 231, 33 (346 A.D.). The verb is not very common, and the noun κατασκήνωσις is even rarer, "occupation of tent or lodging," e.g., Ditt. Or., I, 229, 57 (Smyrna, 3rd cent. B.C.); Polyb., 11, 26, 5; Diod. S., 17, 95.

2. The frequent use in the LXX is surprising compared with the paucity outside the Bible. The only explanation is the clear correspondence between שָׁכַן and κατασκηνόω. It is true that שָׁכַן, which occurs about 140 times, is rendered directly by κατασκηνόω only 55 times. [2] But σκηνόω is also used 4 times (→ 385, 14 ff.) and if γείτων is not inappropriately used for שָׁכֵן or שָׁכַן some 13 times, these instances lie in the same group and are not to be listed among passages with other terms. Of these there are 67. They are divided among 27 different words, most of which are used for שָׁכַן only 1-3 times. ἀναπαύω occurs 8 times, καταπαύω twice, κατοικέω 17 times, κατοικίζω 3, οἰκέω twice, and οἶκος, οἰκήτωρ and πάροικος once each. Though the transl. of שָׁכַן is thus far from uniform, it is plain that κατασκηνόω predominates. Furthermore the use of ἀναπαύω etc. and κατοικέω etc. shows what is the thrust of κατασκηνόω (along the lines of שָׁכַן). The verb denotes, not a fleeting stay, but longer or permanent residence. As regards κατασκηνόω the picture is even more precise. The word occurs 66 times

---

[3] Wnd. 2 K., 393 ad loc.; cf. 392 : "At the price of his weakness Paul draws down Christ's strength upon him."

[4] Wnd. 2 K., 392, ad loc.

[5] Cf. Schl. K., 669, ad loc.: "In ἐπισκηνῶσαι 'to pitch one's tent, to stay, to be present with someone,' he is using a Palestinian formula which was customary for God's presence among His people and in the temple." Schl. is rightly thinking here of the influence of the shekinah concept. It should merely be added that his transl. of ἐπισκηνόω reflects this explanation ; it is not fully supported by the non-bibl. examples. Cf. Ltzm.-Kümmel K, 212 (Suppl. on 116, line 4; material par. from S. Dt., 6, 5).

[6] → I, 491, 29 ff., on the basis of 2 C. 12:9, finely characterises ἀσθένεια as "the place where the divine δύναμις is revealed on earth."

κ α τ α σ κ η ν ό ω. Bibl. → σκηνή.

[1] More common than κατασκηνάω, e.g., Plat. Resp., X, 614e; Xenoph. An., III, 4, 32. κατασκηνέω is late. Cf. Pass. and Liddell-Scott, s.v.

[2] 2 Βασ. 7:10 has the vl. ἐγκατασκηνόω (hapax legomenon). One should read ἐγκατασκηνώσει (H. B. Swete, The OT in Greek, 1 [1887], ad loc.) and not ἐν κατασκηνώσει (Rahlfs).

including vl. In 5 instances there is no Mas. and in 6 others it is used for 4 other words. In all the other instances it corresponds to שָׁכַן or שָׁכֵן including 3 instances of Aram. שְׁכַן and מִשְׁכַּן. One may thus see that κατασκηνόω is the preferred rendering for שָׁכַן and that to a higher degree than σκηνόω it is the most developed equivalent of שָׁכַן.[3] The transl. is acc. to similarity of sound[4] as in the rendering of מִשְׁכָּן by σκηνή → 371, 31 ff. If it is asked why the compound κατασκηνόω is so much more common than the simple σκηνόω the answer is that the κατα- is designed to lay further stress on the idea of a longer stay, cf. κατοικέω, καταπαύω, etc.[5]

κατασκηνόω is used in Nu. 14:30; 2 Βασ. 7:10 etc. for the gift of land (as a lasting dwelling-place). Cf. also the juxtaposition of שָׁכַן and יָשַׁב in 2 Ch. 6:1 f. (both times κατασκηνόω) and abiding εἰς αἰῶνα αἰῶνος in ψ 36:27, 29; also ψ 67:19; 101:29 etc. Lasting and secure dwelling is at issue in Dt. 33:12, also ψ 15:9; Prv. 1:33. In the first case לָבֶטַח "secure," "unthreatened" is transl. by πεποιθώς, "confident," "full of confidence" (cf. also Σιρ. 4:15), in the second by ἐπ' ἐλπίδι and בֶּטַח in the third by ἀφόβως, cf. Ju. 18:7 B, 10 B, 27 B; Hos. 2:20. Causatively it means "to cause to dwell" in ψ 22:2; Jer. 7:12. The ref. is to God's abiding in Nu. 35:34; 3 Βασ. 6:13; 1 Ch. 23:25; 2 Εσδρ. 7:15; ψ 5:12; 67:17; 73:2; Ez. 43:9; Jl. 3:17, 21; Zech. 2:14 f.; 8:3, 8, and to the dwelling or causing to dwell of the divine name in 2 Εσδρ. 11:9; Jer. 7:12; Ez. 43:7 → V, 330, n. 83, cf. σκήνωμα τοῦ ὀνόματός σου in ψ 73:7, also Ps. Sol. 7:6. In Sir. 24:4 divine wisdom says concerning the time of her pre-existence: ἐγὼ ἐν ὑψηλοῖς κατεσκή-νωσα. As the following statement shows: ὁ θρόνος μου ἐν στύλῳ νεφέλης, κατασκη-νόω is not referring to the transitoriness of this stay in heaven but to permanent abiding, cf. also Job 29:25. If in Sir. 24:8 wisdom is then given the task: ἐν 'Ιακὼβ κατασκήνωσον, this, too, refers to the permanent nature of the connection, being preceded by ὁ κτίσας με κατέπαυσεν τὴν σκηνήν μου, → 372, n. 25.

In Mi. 4:10 the opp. of dwelling in the city is κατασκηνοῦν ἐν πεδίῳ (cf. 7:14) as permanent residence. Da. 4:12 Θ says of wild beasts that they κατεσκήνουν under the gt. tree described just before (LXX ἐσκίαζον = HT 4:9 טְלַל "to seek shade"). It is said of birds, however, that they κατῴκουν in the branches of this tree (LXX ἐνόσσευον). In Da. 4:21 Θ, however, it is said that birds κατεσκήνουν in the branches (LXX τὰ νοσσεύοντα = HT 4:18 שְׁכַן). The context and esp. the parallelism with νοσσεύω shows clearly that, notwithstanding the σκιάζειν of θηρία, κατασκηνόω is not a brief and fleeting halt in the shade of the tree but nesting. Cf. also ψ 103:12 (v. 17: ἐννοσσεύω) and the two verses Ez. 17:23; 31:6, in which ἀναπαύομαι or νοσσεύω is used.

The noun κατασκήνωσις occurs 6 times in the LXX. Its equivalent in Ez. 37:27 is מִשְׁכָּן, the ref. being to God's sanctuary in the midst of reunited Israel. In 1 Ch. 28:2 κατασκήνωσις has the verbal sense of "erection," "building": τὰ εἰς τὴν κατασκή-νωσιν ἐπιτήδεια, "what is necessary for the construction (of the afore-mentioned resting-place for the ark)." Tob. 1:4 and 2 Macc. 14:35 speaks of God's ναὸς τῆς κατασκηνώσεως or σκηνώσεως, and in Wis. 9:8 Jerusalem is called the πόλις of God's κατασκηνώσεως.

3. Philo equates the tabernacle with wisdom in Leg. All., III, 46: ἐν ᾗ κατασκηνοῖ καὶ ἐνοικεῖ ὁ σοφός. Though κατασκηνόω would not have been used had not the ref. been to the σκηνή commanded by God, the meaning is par. to that of ἐνοικέω

---

[3] 'Α has σκηνόω 5 times, Θ 9 times, Σ 12.

[4] One must say similarity of sound; it is a mistake to speak of a kinship of root (Wnd. 2 K., 392 on 12:9). There is obviously no etym. connection between the Hbr. root and Gk. stem.

[5] If 'Α prefers the simple form (→ n. 3; 385, 16 ff.) this is perhaps an attempt to express the correspondence of שָׁכַן and σκην- in the no. of syllables too.

"to stay." [6] Joseph. uses κατασκηνόω in Ant., 9, 34 of Elisha's dwelling in a tent (an embellishment of 4 Βασ. 3:12). In 3, 202 the ref. is to God's dwelling in the tabernacle, in 8, 106 to His presence in Solomon's temple. In the Dead Sea Scrolls the only term found thus far is the noun שָׁכֵן "neighbour" in 4 Q Testimonia 24. [7]

4. In the NT κατασκηνόω is used only under OT influence. Within the quotation of ψ 15:8-11 in Ac. 2:25-28, Ac. 2:26 includes a literal citation of ψ 15:9c: ἔτι δὲ καὶ ἡ σάρξ μου κατασκηνώσει ἐπ᾽ ἐλπίδι. Hope here is not the place where David or Christ will dwell; ἐπ᾽ ἐλπίδι, corresponding to לָבֶטַח (→ 388, 12 f.), means "as may be hoped"; [8] κατασκηνόω, then, is used in the abs.: "to tarry," "to live on" (= not to perish, cf. Ac. 2:27). Luke finds the OT prophecy fulfilled in the resurrection of Jesus, → II, 532, 34 ff. [9]

In the parable of the mustard-seed (→ 290, 17 ff.) Mk. 4:32 says concerning the tree which grows out of it: ποιεῖ κλάδους μεγάλους, ὥστε δύνασθαι ὑπὸ τὴν σκιὰν αὐτοῦ τὰ πετεινὰ τοῦ οὐρανοῦ κατασκηνοῦν (Mt. ὥστε ἐλθεῖν τὰ πετεινὰ τοῦ οὐρανοῦ καὶ κατασκηνοῦν ἐν τοῖς κλάδοις αὐτοῦ; Lk. καὶ τὰ πετεινὰ τοῦ οὐρανοῦ κατεσκήνωσεν ἐν τοῖς κλάδοις αὐτοῦ). The influence of Ez. 17:23; 31:6 (→ 388, 34 f.), even more so Da. 4:12 Θ, and especially Da. 4:21 Θ (→ 388, 26 ff.), is plain, [10] and this proves that what is meant is not temporary alighting but settling with a view to staying, to building nests. [11] Whether one may allegorically equate the birds with the Gentiles is open to question. At any rate the conclusion of the parable plainly expresses an expectation of the kingdom of God as a reign of universal peace. [12]

5. In the post-apost. fathers κατασκηνόω is used trans. for "to cause to dwell" (→ 388, 15 ff.) in the prayer in Did., 10, 2: ὑπὲρ τοῦ ἁγίου ὀνόματός σου, οὗ κατεσκήνωσας ἐν ταῖς καρδίαις ἡμῶν (→ 388, 17 ff.). The ref. is to baptism as the event in which God's name enters the believer. κατασκηνόω also occurs in 1 Cl., 57, 7 in a quotation of Prv. 1:33 (→ 388, 12 ff.). This passage is also adduced in 58, 1: ἵνα κατασκηνώσωμεν πεποιθότες ἐπὶ τὸ ὁσιώτατον τῆς μεγαλωσύνης αὐτοῦ ὄνομα.

---

[6] The transl. of I. Heinemann, *Die Werke Philos v. Alex.*, III (1919), 101: "in which the wise man tabernacles and dwells," is too literal and wrongly suggests that the emphasis is on staying in a tent (as a comparison).

[7] Ed. J. M. Allegro, "Further Messianic Ref. in Qumran Literature," JBL, 55 (1956), 174-187.

[8] Haench. Ag., *ad loc.* transl. "on the basis of hope," an approximation to R. 4:18; 8:20. But cf. Pr.-Bauer[5], *s.v.* ἐλπίς 2a (with ref. to OT usage).

[9] On later Rabb. exegesis of ψ 15:9 cf. Str.-B., II, 618 on Ac. 2:26.

[10] The σκιά reminds us more of the Ez. passages but cf. σκιάζω in Da. 4:12 MT and LXX. It is not surprising the NT versions also show familiarity with Θ.

[11] This is supported by the fact that in the saying of Jesus in Mt. 8:20 par. Lk. 9:58 κατασκηνώσεις obviously means nests or places where birds can stay to nest. Michaelis, 34 and 47; W. G. Kümmel, *Verheissung u. Erfüllung*[3] (1956), 123, n. 92. In 2 C. 6:16 Paul quotes Lv. 26:12 but puts it in the 3rd person and begins with ἐνοικήσω ἐν αὐτοῖς from Ez. 37:27 though in a free form, since this (→ 388, 36 f.) begins: καὶ ἔσται ἡ κατασκήνωσίς μου ἐν αὐτοῖς. Cf. A. Wikenhauser, *Die Christusmystik des Ap. Pls.*[2] (1956), 39 f.

[12] Michaelis, 47.

† σκηνοπηγία.

1. Based on σκηνὴν πηγνύναι (→ 368, 24), the verb σκηνοπηγέω or σκηνοπηγέο-
μαι meaning "to pitch or set up a tent or hut or booth," and the noun σκηνοπηγία
meaning the "erection of a tent etc." (cf. constructs like κλινοπηγία, ναυπηγία),
are extremely rare outside the Gk. Bible and the writings dependent on it.[1] In the
Doric form σκανοπαγέομαι the verb occurs several times in a sacrificial order from
the island of Cos, Ditt. Syll.[3], III, 1000, 1. 3-8. 10-17. 26 (2nd cent. B.C.). Unfortunately
one cannot say for certain whether the ref. is more to tents or huts or whether they
are for the putting up of participants in the feasts or for cultic purposes → 368, 26 ff.[2]
σκηνοπηγέω is also used for putting up καπηλεῖα, "stalls," in Damon Historicus Fr.,
1 (FGrHist, III B, 389, probably Hell.). The noun σκηνοπηγία is used in Aristot.
Hist. An., IX, 7, p. 612b, 22 for the building of nests by swallows.

2. The LXX does not use the verb but has the noun 9 times in Dt. 16:16; 31:10;
1 Εσδρ. 5:50; Zech. 14:16, 18 f.; 1 Macc. 10:21; 2 Macc. 1:9, 18. Always except in 2 Macc.
the ref. is to the Feast of Tabernacles. In 2 Macc. the ref. is to the temple dedication
in 164 B.C. Since this was in analogy to Tabernacles,[3] it, too, is an indirect testimony
to the use in connection with the latter. 2 Macc. 1:9 speaks of ἡμέραι τῆς σκηνοπηγίας, and perhaps 1:18 is to be read in the same way.[4] But elsewhere we find
(ἡ) ἑορτὴ (τῆς) σκηνοπηγίας or ἡ τῆς σκηνοπηγίας ἑορτή (1 Εσδρ. 5:50). Where
there is an original (Dt. and Zech.) it is חַג הַסֻּכּוֹת, also transl. (ἡ) ἑορτὴ (τῶν) σκηνῶν
in Lv. 23:34 etc. With ἑορτή, σκηνοπηγία does not actually mean the feast but the
"erection of tabernacles."
   The use of σκηνοπηγία cannot be due to the Hbr. original, since this is merely
סֻכּוֹת. When Tabernacles is mentioned in Lv. 23:34-36, 39-43; Dt. 16:13 ff. there is no
ref. to the πηγνύναι of σκηναί, common though σκηνὴν πηγνύναι is in the LXX.
Of some 44 instances of πηγνύναι 16 refer to the putting up of σκηναί. For σκηνή
the Mas. is always אֹהֶל and never סֻכָּה. With the latter we find ποιεῖν σκηνήν, Gn.
33:17; 2 Εσδρ. 18:15-17; Jon. 4:5.[5] This shows why Ἀλλ has σκηνοποιΐα for σκηνοπηγία (LXX) at Dt. 31:10[6] but only emphasises the more the fact that πηγνύναι
σκηνάς does not occur with ref. to Tabernacles in the LXX, so that the use of σκηνοπηγία cannot be explained along these lines. Is it connected with the fact that Tabernacles was originally a Feast of Tents? If so, the common πηγνύναι σκηνάς with
ref. to tents would be an important par. But even if there were stronger support than
there is for the thesis that the Feast of Tabernacles developed out of an older Feast
of Tents,[7, 8] one can hardly suppose that the LXX would contain a reminiscence of

σ κ η ν ο π η γ ί α. Deissmann LO, 92 f.; Str.-B., II, 774-812 (Exc. 5: "The Feast of
Tabernacles"); H. Bornhäuser, *Sukka* (1935), esp. 32, 34-39; H. J. Kraus, "Gottesdienst in
Israel. Stud. z. Gesch. d. Laubhüttenfestes," *Beiträge z. Ev. Theol.*, 19 (1954); E. Kutsch,
Art. "Feste u. Feiern, II. In Israel," RGG[3], II, 910-917, esp. 912 f. (916 f. Bibl.).
   [1] On the adj. σκηνοπαγής, attested in Suid., *s.v.* θαλάμη as vl. for κηροπαγής in
Anth. Graec., 6, 239, cf. Liddell-Scott and Pass., *s.v.*
   [2] Deissmann, 93, n. 2 f. but as opposed to Deissmann, Pr.-Bauer[5], *s.v.*, Moult.-Mill., 577
Liddell-Scott dates the inscr. in the 1st cent. B.C.
   [3] Cf. A. Kamphausen in Kautzsch Apkr. u. Pseudepigr., I, 86 f., *ad loc.*
   [4] Kamphausen, *op. cit.*, 87 A c, though cf. the conjecture of O. Fritzsche in Rahlfs on
1:18.
   [5] Cf. also אֹהֶל in Ex. 31:7; 1 Ch. 15:1. Cf. (no Mas.) Gn. 13:4 vl.; Jdt. 8:5.
   [6] Cf. also σκηνοποιεῖν in Σ Is. 13:20; 22:15 (סֹבֵך read as שֵׂבֶך [P. Katz]).
   [7] Kraus, 26-30.
   [8] Kraus, 26 f. thinks the original ref. in Lv. 23:42 f. must have been to tents rather than
booths and that this was an ancient tradition. But v. 42 f. is usually put in the later section

the older character of the festival when this is no longer evident in the HT. [9] Again, the choice of σκηνοπηγία is probably influenced by the non-bibl. use of the group. It should be noted, however, that thus far the noun σκηνοπηγία has not been found for the erection of tents or huts at cultic festivals, though this use is not outside the bounds of possibility. [10]

3. It is not surprising that in writings dependent on the LXX σκηνοπηγία is closely related to Tabernacles. Philo, though he often mentions the feast, does not use the word but says ἡ τῶν σκηνῶν ἑορτή etc. → 373, 14 f. [11] On the other hand Jos. (→ 373, 35 ff. plainly prefers σκηνοπηγία. This is certainly connected with his use of πηγνύναι σκηνάς with ref. to Tabernacles (e.g., Ant., 3, 244 and 247) and also of σκηνοπηγέω in this sense : τῆς ἑορτῆς καθ᾽ ἣν σκηνοπηγοῦσι τῷ θεῷ, Ant., 13, 304. [12] The designation ἡ τῆς σκηνοπηγίας ἑορτή occurs in Ant., 4, 209; 8, 100; 13, 241; Bell., 2, 515. He mostly has the brief ἡ σκηνοπηγία for the feast itself, Ant., 8, 123 (τὴν σκηνοπηγίαν καλουμένην ἑορτήν); 11, 154; 13, 46 and 372; 15, 50. Acc. to Ant., 8, 100 Tabernacles is ἑορτὴ ἁγιωτάτη καὶ μεγίστη, cf. 15, 50. It is worth noting that in an inscr. (13 B.C.) from Berenice in Cyrenaica (CIG, III, 5361, 1 f.) Tabernacles is called σύλλογος τῆς σκηνοπηγίας. [13] If one cannot say that this is the most common [14] of the various terms for the feast, Jos. and this inscr. show that it was widespread and this along with its use in the LXX explains its occurrence in the NT. [15]

4. σκηνοπηγία is used only once in the NT [16] at Jn. 7:2 : ἦν δὲ ἐγγὺς ἡ ἑορτὴ τῶν Ἰουδαίων ἡ σκηνοπηγία. As the use in apposition shows, σκηνοπηγία here has the value of a full title and means Feast of Tabernacles, → lines 13 ff.

Jn. 7:3 ff. tells us what preceded the journey of Jesus to this feast, and then in vv. 14 ff. we learn what went on during the feast after He arrived at Jerusalem. How long the stay was is hard to say, since the details connected with the course and

---

of Lv. 23 and regarded as an attempt to link the harvest festival with the exodus, cf. E. Kutsch, *Das Herbstfest in Israel*, Diss. Mainz (1955) and also ThLZ, 81 (1956), 493-495. In criticism of Kraus, 29 one may ask when the amphictyony celebrated a feast in the wilderness. The ref. in P to the order of the camp can hardly be adduced in support, as in Kraus, 28. Ex. 33:7 ff.; Nu. 11:24 ff. suggest that this is secondary. Acc. to the older tradition the tent of meeting was outside the camp and not its centre, as in P. But in particular the older traditions do not relate the tent and the ark. P does this and also says the tent was in Shiloh, Jos. 18:1; 19:51; 1 S. 2:22. But this is the central link in the whole thesis [E. Kutsch].

[9] Also to be rejected is a combining of the Feast of Tabernacles with a hut in which the king celebrated the ἱερὸς γάμος, G. Widengren, *Sakrales Königtum* (1955), 79. The feast probably took its name from the vineyard huts in which the harvest was celebrated, cf. the diss. of E. Kutsch → n. 8.

[10] Hence one should speak only with caution of "assimilation to rites" already present in the world of the *diaspora*, Bornhäuser, 32. It might be that as a meal could be called the breaking of bread by virtue of the opening act (→ III, 729, 23 ff.), so the erection of the booths at the beginning of the feast led the whole feast to be called σκηνοπηγία, but the conjecture is not supported by any special emphasis anywhere on this erection, → 390, 24 ff.

[11] Philo uses πηγνύναι fairly often (Leisegang, 649 f., s.v.), but not with σκηναί.

[12] Jos. also has σκηνοποιεῖσθαι in the same sense, Bell., 1, 73; 6, 300.

[13] Cf. Schürer, III, 79, n. 20.

[14] Deissmann, 92.

[15] When the Feast of Tabernacles is used in non-Gk. texts there is nothing to support a use of σκηνοπηγία in the Gk. sphere. On the pseudepigr. → 374, 10 ff.; on the Dead Sea Scrolls, cf. Kutsch, 914.

[16] The secondary addition of ἡ σκηνοπηγία in Jn. 5:1 is under the influence of 7:2 and is not connected with a description of Tabernacles as *the* feast in the OT (Kutsch, 912)

practices of Tabernacles [17] are hardly mentioned. The temple visit in 7:14 is set in the middle of the feast; ἤδη δὲ τῆς ἑορτῆς μεσούσης means the 4th day of the 7 or 8 day festival. [18] There is another note of time in 7:37: ἐν δὲ τῇ ἐσχάτῃ ἡμέρᾳ τῇ μεγάλῃ τῆς ἑορτῆς. Though "great day" is found neither for the 7th day nor for the 8th and concluding day, [19] there can be no doubt but that it refers to the 7th day. With the opening day this was a high point in the festival and was celebrated with special pomp; [20] the 8th day fell short of it in significance and was regarded almost as a special feast. [21] The dispensing of water took place only on the 7 days of the feast proper and not on the 8th day; 7:37 f. is obviously alluding to this practice. [22]

How long this 7th day lasts one cannot say. [23] But the expression φῶς τοῦ κόσμου or τῆς ζωῆς in 8:12, notwithstanding par. not connected with Tabernacles like 9:5; 11:9; 12:35, 40, suggests that there is here yet another allusion to the feast, namely, the magnificent illumination of the temple from the onset of darkness to morning. [24] There is thus good reason to suppose that 8:12 (cf. the simple link in πάλιν) was spoken on the same 7th day.

Significant though the connections are between Jn. 7:37 f. (→ VI, 605, 28 ff.); 8:12 and the Feast of Tabernacles (they are weaker in 8:12 than 7:37 f.), in the main we find in c. 7 and c. 8 no more than occasional allusions which in fact are intelligible only to those acquainted with the details of the Jewish feast, → IV, 277, 21 ff. But the Evangelist was not writing exclusively for readers of this kind and therefore it would not appear that the connection with Tabernacles was important for him or that he invented it for his own ends, since in this case he would have had to make it much plainer. This strengthens the impression that it has no particular theological significance and that Tabernacles is for him simply the background to the visit of Jesus to Jerusalem. [25]

On the fact that the story in Mk. 9:2 ff. par. is not connected with motifs from the Feast of Tabernacles cf. ⟶ 380, 3 ff.

---

and NT days (Bornhäuser, 34). Even if c. 5 and c. 6 are left in their present order, 5:1 is probably the Passover, and this is certain if the chapters are transposed (Bultmann J., 179 on 5:1). If in c. 7 ἑορτή alone is used in v. 8, 10 f., 14, 37 this is obviously not connected with the description of Tabernacles as the feast. It is just the ordinary way of referring to a feast already specified above, e.g., Mk. 14:1 f.; Jn. 13:1, 29.

[17] For the time of Jesus cf. esp. Str.-B., II, 774-812 and Bornhäuser, 3-7. On the history of Tabernacles cf. → Bibl., also → n. 8 f.; 372, n. 26; 373, n. 30; 378, n. 59.

[18] Cf. Bultmann J., 218, n. 3 on 7:1 f.; 222, n. 7 on 7:14. The ref. might be to one of the other semi-feast days in the middle of the festival, Bornhäuser, 35.

[19] Acc. to Rabb. usage the "last" day alone is the concluding feast, cf. Str.-B., III, 490 ff.

[20] Bornhäuser, 7.

[21] Str.-B., II, 808.

[22] J. Jeremias, Golgotha (1926), 80-84; Bornhäuser, 35-38; Bultmann J., 228, n. 4 on 7:37; 230, n. 3 on 7:39; → VI, 605, 28 ff.

[23] The next note of time in 10:22 refers to the much later feast of the dedication in winter; 8:2 is secondary.

[24] Bornhäuser, 6, 38, 137-155; Str.-B., II, 805-807; H. Riesenfeld, "Jésu transfiguré," Acta Seminarii Neotest. Upsaliensis, 16 (1947), 278 f. A connection between Jn. 8:12 and Ex. 34:29 is much less apparent, as against H. Sahlin, "Zur Typologie d. Joh.-Ev.," Uppsala Univ. Årsskrift, 1950, 4 (1950), 32 f.

[25] Can this be used to support the historicity of the situation and the authenticity of the relevant sayings of Jesus? This best explains the allusions to Tabernacles, but perhaps it is going too far to say with Bornhäuser, 39 that "here as so often the Fourth Evangelist" shows himself to be "an eye-witness acquainted with what transpired in Jerusalem."

† σκηνοποιός.

1. σκηνοποιός, a rare word outside the Bible and Chr. works influenced by Ac. 18:3, is obviously another term formed by combining σκηνή and ποιέω, like σκηνοποιέω or σκηνοποιέομαι and σκηνοποιΐα, which for their part are on the whole a little more common. The act. σκηνοποιέω occurs in Σ Is. 13:20; 22:15. More common is the med. σκηνοποιέομαι, e.g., Herodian. Hist., VII, 2, 4; Aristot. Meteor., I, 12, p. 348b, 35; Polyb., 14, 1, 7; Diod. S., 3, 27, 4; Ps.-Callisth., II, 9, 8.[1] The noun σκηνοποιΐα, found, e.g., in Aen. Tact., 8, 3; Polyb., 6, 28, 3 and an Amphipolis inscr. (3rd/2nd cent. B.C.),[2] is used by ᾿Αλλ for LXX σκηνοπηγία at Dt. 31:10 → 390, 28 f. As a rule[3] the ref. is to the pitching or erection of a tent, hut, or booth, cf. σκηνὴν ποιεῖν in the same sense, also → 390, 27 f. and n. 5. None of the examples refers to the making of σκηναί[4] though one cannot rule out the possibility that σκηνοποιός is used for the trade of "tent-maker." For one thing this meaning is wholly within the range allowed by the etym. and it is indeed the most natural, since a construct with -ποιός can hardly denote a casual and not a permanent activity.[5] Again, Poll. Onom., 7, 189, in connection with ancient Attic comedy, uses σκηνοποιοί as well as μηχανοποιοί for those whose job it was to get things ready on the stage.[6] Stob. Ecl., I, 463, 7 ff. has another instance of σκηνοποιός[7] which does not exclude the possibility that the word might mean tent-maker in other writings. Since the tents of antiquity were usually made of leather[8] it is likely that the σκηνοποιός is a leather-worker.

2. In the NT σκηνοποιός occurs only in Ac. 18:3 and the reference is to some kind of manual work. We are told that when the apostle Paul came to Corinth he got to know the couple Aquila and Priscilla (18:2), διὰ τὸ ὁμότεχνον εἶναι ἔμενεν παρ' αὐτοῖς καὶ ἠργάζοντο· ἦσαν γὰρ σκηνοποιοὶ τῇ τέχνῃ. Though παρ' αὐτοῖς refers to Aquila and Priscilla, only Paul and Aquila can be the subjects of ἠργάζοντο and especially ἦσαν. Hence one does not have to think in terms of a τέχνη in which the co-operation of the wife was possible or even customary. The context itself does not show us what the τέχνη was. Even when Paul in his letters says that he earned his own keep there is nothing to show that he was referring to hard manual work (1 C. 4:12; 1 Th. 2:9; 2 Th. 3:8; cf. Ac. 20:34).

σ κ η ν ο π ο ι ό ς. Zn. Ag., 632-634; Pr.-Bauer⁵, 1496 (cf. esp. the longer addition as compared with ⁴1373 f.).

[1] For further examples cf. Liddell-Scott, s.v.

[2] *Revue Archéologique*, 3 (1934), 40.

[3] In Dio C., 67, 2 σκηνοποιΐα, on the basis of the use of σκηνή in the theatre (→ 369, 4 ff.), refers to the erection of a theatre.

[4] Pertinently noted by Pr.-Bauer⁵.

[5] Thus soldiers or hunters could hardly be called σκηνοποιοί even though it was part of their way of life to live in tents and to put up tents.

[6] Pr.-Bauer⁵, who disputes the view that σκηνοποιός can denote one who manufactures the parts of a tent or the tent itself, notes under 1. the sense of "maker of things necessary for the theatre." Confusion of σκηνογράφος "theatre-painter" with σκηνορράφος "sewer or maker of tents" produces the strange notion that 18:3 is referring to "landscape-painters," cf. W. M. Ramsay, ExpT, 8 (1896/97), 109 and E. Nestle, *ibid.*, 153 f.

[7] φύσις is here described as πλάστρια or shaper of the ἀγγεῖα prepared for souls after their descent to earth. The adj. σκηνοποιός, which defines πλάστρια, is not connected with σκηνή but with σκῆνος in the sense of "body" (cf. also Corp. Herm., 13, 12 → 381, 25 f.) and denotes nature as the fashioner of bodies. Cf. also C. F. G. Heinrici, *Die Hermes-Mystik u. d. NT* (1918), 108 and n. 3.

[8] Cf. A. Sizoo, *Die antike Welt u. d. NT* (1955), 107 f.

In so far as tents were made of fabric, a coarse cloth woven from goats' hair was often used for them ; this was called *cilicium* by the Romans because it was usually made in Cilicia → 57, 7 ff. and n. 9, 10.[9] Now Paul came from Cilicia (Ac. 9:11; 21:39 etc.) and it has often been assumed that in his youth, perhaps with his father, he learned to weave *cilicium* and was thus a weaver of tent-fabric or carpets.[10] But there is little basis for this hypothesis. For one thing *cilicium* was not used only for tents. For another, most tents were made of leather. Again, Aquila came from Pontus, Ac. 18:2. Furthermore, if it is argued that Paul learned the trade of the σκηνοποιός simply as a Rabbinic scholar, the objection arises that weaving was regarded as a disreputable occupation which a young scholar would hardly adopt.[11] It is thus more probable that Paul and Aquila[12] were "leather-workers" or "saddlers" and that as such they manufactured tents, for which there was considerable use in antiquity.[13] Patristic witnesses sometimes explain the σκηνοποιός of Ac. 18:3 by σκυτοτόμος, "leather-worker."[14] The fact that the apostle could follow the trade of a σκηνοποιός meant that he did not have to depend on the churches for support, cf. especially 1 C. 9. Cf. also → 382, n. 5.

Michaelis

| σκιά, ἀποσκίασμα, ἐπισκιάζω |

† σκιά.

A. Greek Usage.

1. The word σκιά (Ionic σκιή) is found in Gk. lit. from Homer. Like the Sanskr. *chāyā* "shadow," "reflection," "copy," it develops from an Indo-Eur. word of the same sense.[1] Strictly σκιά means "shadow" or "shade,"[2] esp. that offered by trees and rocks :

---

[9] Zn. Ag., 633.

[10] So Str.-B., II, 746 f. with ref. to Ex. 26:7 and esp. the widespread use of coverings of Cilician material in Palestine (655) which led to the adoption of *cilicium* as a Rabb. loan word קִילְקִי. Cf. Luther's "carpet-maker" and Paul as a weaver in A. Deissmann, *Pls.*² (1925), 41.

[11] Strongly emphasised by J. Jeremias, "Zöllner u. Sünder," ZNW, 30 (1931), 293-300, esp. 299; but cf. Haench. Ag., *ad loc.*

[12] Was Jason also an artisan as suggested by Zn. Ag., 634, *ad loc.* ? ὑποδέδεκται in Ac. 17:7 suggests merely that Paul was hospitably entertained by Jason.

[13] It cannot be objected that Aquila would not be a tent-maker when he had workshops in the great cities of Rome, Corinth and Ephesus, cf. Ac. 18:2 f.; 1 C. 16:19 etc. (Pr.-Bauer⁵, *s.v.*), since the manufacture of tents could well be a city job. Pr.-Bauer does not offer his own explanation of σκηνοποιός. It is clear that though Paul and Aquila were of Jewish descent they would not just be making booths for the Feast of Tabernacles. This was a job for the pilgrims. Booths were not kept in stock, and saddlers were not needed in their erection, cf. Sukka, 1, 1 ff.

[14] Cf. Zn. Ag., 633 f., n. 10; E. Nestle, Art. "Pls. d. Apostel," RE³, 15 (1904), 70 f.; also "Pls. als Riemenschneider," ZNW, 11 (1910), 241; F. W. Grosheide, "Παῦλος σκηνοποιός," *Theol. Stud.* (Utrecht), 35 (1917), 241 f. σκηνορράφος (cf. Zn. Ag., 633, n. 10) is sometimes adduced and it should be taken in the same sense, since it certainly does not mean weaver, → n. 6.

σκιά. [1] Cf. Pokorny, 917 f.; Boisacq, 875 f.; Hofmann, *s.v.*; M. Mayrhofer, *Kurzgefasstes etym. Wörterbuch des Altindischen*, I (1956), 407.

[2] Cf. Liddell-Scott, Pr.-Bauer⁵, Pass., Pape, Moult.-Mill., *s.v.*

οὔθ' αἱ τῶν δένδρων οὔθ' αἱ τῶν πετρῶν σκιαί, Xenoph. Cyrop., VIII, 8, 17; πετραίη τε σκιή, Hes. Op., 589; contrasting shadows in painting : τὰ λαμπρὰ τῇ σκιᾷ τρανότερα ποιοῦσι, Plut. De Herodoti Malignitate, 28 (II, 863e), cf. also P. Oxy., VIII, 1088, 43.

2. Much more common in extant lit. is the transf. sense. Used thus σκιά denotes the unreality of an object : τὴν σκιὰν θηρεύειν, Luc. Hermot., 79; εἴδωλον σκιᾶς, Soph. Fr., 598, 6 (TGF, 275); "shadow" as contrasted with reality : τὸ δὲ ὕδωρ τῶν ἀνθέων ἦν κάτοπτρον, ὡς δοκεῖν τὸ ἄλσος εἶναι διπλοῦν, τὸ μὲν τῆς ἀληθείας, τὸ δὲ τῆς σκιᾶς, Achill. Tat., I, 15, 6, cf. Xenoph. Mem., II, 1, 22. Proverbially what is unstable, fleeting, empty : σκιᾶς ὄναρ ἄνθρωπος, Pind. Pyth., 8, 95 f.; ὁρῶ γὰρ ἡμᾶς οὐδὲν ὄντας ἄλλο πλὴν εἴδωλα ... ἢ κούφην σκιάν, Soph. Ai., 125 f.; the vanity of human affairs : τἄλλ' ἐγὼ καπνοῦ σκιᾶς οὐκ ἂν πριαίμην, Soph. Ant., 1170 f.; καπνοὺς ... καὶ σκιάς, Eupolis Fr., 51 (CAF, I, 270); "shade" of a dead person, phantom as an expression of life after death : τοὶ δὲ σκιαὶ ἀΐσσουσιν, Hom. Od., 10, 495; cf. Aesch. Eum., 302; σκιᾷ τινι λόγους ἀνέσπα, Soph. Ai., 301 f.; σποδόν τε καὶ σκιάν, Soph. El., 1159; the worthlessness or vanity of things : αἱ τοῦ δικαίου σκιαί, Plat. Resp., VII, 517d, σκιαὶ καὶ ἐν ὕδασιν εἰκόνες, Plat. Resp., VI, 510e, εὐτυχοῦντα μὲν σκιά τις ἂν τρέψειεν, Aesch. Ag., 1328 f. and the uninvited guest who is brought by one who is invited, Plut. Quaest. Conv., VII, 6, 1 (II, 707a), also Suid., s.v.

B. Shadow in the Old Testament.

1. צֵל is usually literal in the OT. It may refer to the shadow of the sundial in Is. 38:8, of a tree or plant in Ez. 17:23; 31:6, 12, 17; Hos. 4:13; 14:8 (?); Jon. 4:6; Ps. 80:10; Job 40:22; Cant. 2:3, of a cloud in Is. 16:3; 25:4 f., of a roof in Gn. 19:8, of a mountain in Ju. 9:36, of the rock in Is. 32:2, of evening in Jer. 6:4 (Job 7:2), of the hand in Is. 51:16; 49:2. In a transf. sense the metaphor can be used positively, the shadow of Yahweh's wings in Ps. 17:8; 36:7 etc. (protecting and sheltering His people). But it can also be negative when it denotes man's corruptibility and vanity in Ps. 102:11; 109:23; 144:4; Job 8:9; 14:2; Qoh. 6:12; 8:13 etc.

2. צַלְמָוֶת [3] really means "darkness," Am. 5:8; Job 3:5; 12:22; 16:16; 24:17; 28:3; 34:22. In a transf. sense it has an exclusively negative ring ; in contrast to light as a symbol of good fortune and life it means distress in Is. 9:1; Jer. 13:16; Ps. 107:10, danger of death in Jer. 2:6; Ps. 23:4; 44:19, and even the world of the dead in Job 10:21 f.

C. Usage in the Septuagint and Later Judaism.

1. The Septuagint.

σκιά occurs in the LXX some 30 times. It is mostly used for צֵל and for צַלְמָוֶת only twice in the OT at Job 16:16 and Am. 5:8 Cod B A. The fixed combination σκιὰ θανάτου is also commonly used, however, for the Hbr. צַלְמָוֶת, e.g., Job 3:5; ψ 43:20; Is. 9:1 etc. In the LXX, too, the literal sense is often found with ref. to the shadow of the tree or trees in Ju. 9:15 Cod B; Jon. 4:6, or the hut in Jon. 4:5, or the mountains in Ju. 9:36, or the evening in Jer. 6:4 (also Cant. 2:17), or the sundial in 4 Βασ. 20:9, 10, 11; Is. 38:8, more generally the shade for which the slave longs, Job 7:2.

---

[3] The splitting of the long צלמות into צל and מות as a mode of interpretation was called נוטריקון by the Rabb. and was used by the translators (also 'A) [Katz]. In reality the derivation is from צלם II "to become black, dark," while צל comes from צלל III "to become shady, dark" [Fohrer].

In the overwhelming number of instances in which σκιά occurs it has a transferred sense. There are sayings about the shadow of death, about the corruptibility and vanity to which even the righteous man of the OT is exposed, Job 3:5; 28:3; ψ 87:7; 106:10. The desperate man confesses : αἱ ἡμέραι μου ὡσεὶ σκιὰ ἐκλίθησαν, ψ 101:12, also 108:23. More clear-cut is 1 Ch. 29:15 : ὡς σκιὰ αἱ ἡμέραι ἡμῶν ἐπὶ γῆς, man born of woman fades away ὥσπερ σκιά (Job 14:2), his days pass ὡσεὶ σκιά (ψ 143:3). But this σκιὰ θανάτου is not an autonomous event of nature ; God can bring out εἰς φῶς σκιὰν θανάτου, Job 12:22. Even ἐν μέσῳ σκιᾶς θανάτου (ψ 22:4) God is for the Psalmist the saving Lord who leads the redeemed ἐκ σκότους καὶ σκιᾶς θανάτου (ψ 106:14). The birth of the divine child is for those who dwell ἐν χώρᾳ καὶ σκιᾷ θανάτου, Is. 9:1.

The usage is metaphorical when there is reference to the σκιὰ τῶν πτερύγων of God (ψ 56:2), to the glory of Yahweh which will be εἰς σκιὰν ἀπὸ καύματος (Is. 4:6), and to the σκιά which the anointed of the Lord brings on His people, Lam. 4:20. In Ez. 17:23 and 31:6 Israel is set in relation to a tree in whose shade birds will nest and the peoples dwell. σκιά is also used in a positive and possibly a Messianic sense in Is. 32:2 Σ : ὡς σκιὰ πέτρας ἰσχυρᾶς. [4]

2. Philo.

σκιά is used only occasionally in the lit. sense in Philo, e.g., Virt., 118 and 181 or Jos., 146, where it is par. to νύξ. In by far the majority of cases it has a transf. sense. In Rer. Div. Her., 290 it means "shadow of death" as in the LXX (paraphrasing ψ 83:11); in Virt., 18 it is par. to ἴχνος and denotes the shadow or trace of the feminine. But the word acquires its true theological significance in Philo in his well-known "original-copy" speculation, in which he combines Platonic-Alexandrian thought with his OT legacy. To prophets after Moses God will appear only in a vision, i.e., ἐν σκιᾷ, and not ἐναργῶς and ἐν εἴδει as to Moses, Leg. All., III, 103 f. σκιά here is the opp. of εἶδος, Somn., I, 188. In terms of an etym. of Bezaleel Philo expounds his view of shadow-copy (σκιά-εἰκών) and original-prototype (ἀρχέτυπος-παράδειγμα) dualism in Leg. All., III, 96. Acc. to Somn., I, 206 Bezaleel means ἐν σκιᾷ θεοῦ, from which Philo deduces that Bezaleel produces only σκιαί and μιμήματα and not, like Moses, the παραδείγματα and archetypal φύσεις, Plant., 27. Hence Philo can say that God's *logos* is his σκιά and εἰκών and there are men like this Bezaleel who stand in relation to this *logos* as the *logos* to God. The *logos,* though he is only εἰκών and σκιά, becomes the archetype and paradigm of other beings and things. God's works of creation are σκιά, Leg. All., III, 99 f., ἴχνος and αὔρα, Mut. Nom., 181. Their only significance is to spur men to move by way of analogy — the classical cosmological proof of God — from these shadows to God, Leg. All., III, 99 f. In bad men there is neither σκιά nor εἴδωλον of the virtuous idea, Conf. Ling., 69. They do not even have a σκιά ... καλοκἀγαθίας, 71. Human work and action are σκιά and αὔρα and therefore nothing, Deus Imm., 177. Shadows (and the par. φάσματα) are over the world of things, Jos., 140. Thus the soul finally rejects the *logos,* since this with the help of shadows and ῥήματα wants to show it objects and bodies, which is not possible, Rer. Div. Her., 72. For the ὄνομα is related to the πρᾶγμα as the σκιά to the σῶμα, Decal., 82; σκιᾷ μὲν δὴ καὶ μιμήματι ἔοικεν ἑρμηνεία, σώμασι δὲ καὶ ἀρχετύποις αἱ τῶν διερμηνευομένων φύσεις πραγμάτων ... For this reason σκιά is finally related to σῶμα and μίμημα to ἀρχέτυπος as δοκεῖν to εἶναι, Migr. Abr., 12. This speculative dualism is also the reason why fig. exposition distinguishes between the wording of a statement (= the shadow of the body) and the meanings presented by the wording, which are present in truth, Poster. C., 112.

---

[4] Cf. Just. Dial., 113, 6; → πέτρα, VI, 99, 22 ff.

3. Josephus.

Archelaus is accused in Bell., 2, 28 of coming to ask the emperor for the shadow of rule when he had long since grasped the body by making the emperor the lord not of things (= σῶμα) but of names (= σκιά). Distress among the besieged was so great that war broke out when there seemed to be only a shadow of food available, Bell., 6, 194.

4. Dead Sea Scrolls.

In the Scrolls the word occurs only twice.[5] In 1 QH 5:33 those who oppress the worshipper build a fence in the shade (= צלמות), i.e., cause him the severest affliction.[6] The usage in 1 QH 6:15 is undoubtedly transf. This refers to a mythical tree whose top reaches to heaven and whose roots go down to Tehom. This tree gives shade (= צל) to the nations or the earth.[7]

5. The Rabbis.

The figure of the shadow is rare in Rabb. theology. The days of man are not even like the shadow of the flying bird, Gn. r., 96 on 47:29, cf. Midr. Qoh., 1, 2 (4b). It is best to eat simple plants and sit in the shade than to feed on dainties and then be uneasily exposed to prosecution by creditors, bPes., 114a. The lit. use may be found in jAZ, 3, 13 (43b, 50 f) and Ex. r., 34 on 25:10.

D. The New Testament.

1. The Usage in the Synoptic Gospels and Acts.

The literal use of σκιά is found in the Marcan version of the parable of the grain of mustard-seed (Mk. 4:32): the birds of heaven nest under the shade of the great branches of the grown plant (→ 290, 17 ff.; 396, 15 f.; 397, 9 ff.). It also occurs in Ac. 5:15 : The shadow of Peter falls over the sick (→ 400, 7 ff.).

The transferred sense of the shadow of death is found in the NT only in expressions taken from the OT, → 395, 25 ff. Mt. 4:16 uses the prophetic word of Is. 9:1 with reference to the resolve of Jesus to visit Capernaum on the Sea of Galilee in the territory of Zebulon and Naphtali. The Evangelist Matthew (4:13-16, peculiar to Mt.) thinks the prophecy is fulfilled in this visit. For him Jesus is the "great light," the rising of the eschatological Messianic light for those who sit in the land and shadow of death, in this case Galilee of the nations. But the content of the prophecy is so interpreted by Mt. that the expression "shadow of death" now denotes the sphere of perdition which characterises the Gentiles who are separated from the Messiah and Son of God, Jesus. For Mt. the land and shadow of death mean the same as the lostness of the heathen to whom only the Messiah can give eschatological deliverance as the great light which has risen.

The same expression "shadow of death" is used in a very similar way by Luke in the Benedictus, 1:79. If in Mt. 4:16 this combination can be properly interpreted only in the light of the theology of the Evangelist Matthew, in Lk. 1:79

---

[5] K. G. Kuhn, *Konkordanz zu d. Qumrantexten* (1960), s.v.
[6] So H. Bardtke, "Die Loblieder v. Qumran," ThLZ, 81 (1956), 591.
[7] Cf. on this A. Dupont-Sommer, "Le Livre des Hymnes découvert près de la mer Morte (1 QH)," *Semitica*, 7 (1957), 53.

it can be expounded only in the light of the theology of the circles around John, for the Benedictus (1:68 ff.) is part of the greater complex of the NT tradition deriving from the community of the Baptist.[8] John the Baptist would seem to be depicted as the Messiah according to the themes embodied in the canticle. As the Messianic ἀνατολὴ ἐξ ὕψους[9] and the προφήτης ὑψίστου (→ VI, 837, 22 ff.) he is the eschatological light which will give light to those who sit in darkness and the shadow of death. In his communities, to which the canticle preserved by Luke belongs, the prophecy of Isaiah was referred to John. He is the light predicted by Is. which will give light to and enlighten those who, alienated from God, live in darkness and the shadow of death, and are thus delivered up to judgment.

2. Colossians.

In Col. 2:17 the Law is called the shadow of future things ; contrasted with it is the eschatological presence of the body of Christ. The pair σκιά-σῶμα derives from the thought-form of Hellenistic theology (→ 396, 40 ff.) and is used for the typical antithesis between shadow and reality, whose basis is the further form of copy and original, → 396, 22 ff. The parallel between Law and shadow represents theological relativisation. It should not be overlooked that the shadow already points to a reality, namely, that of the body. For as there is no body without a shadow, so there is no shadow without a body.[10] Later Jewish Hellenistic theology, which for its part adopted and adapted the ancient legacy of Plato, prepared the way here for primitive Christian preaching. To this degree the historical genesis is clear. But this σκιά-σῶμα (appearance-reality, copy-original) dualism of later Jewish Hellenistic theology, which lies in a timeless metaphysical dimension, is critically expanded in two ways in Col. 2:17: eschatologically : τῶν μελλόντων, and christologically : σῶμα τοῦ Χριστοῦ. The familiar Pauline thought-forms of promise-fulfilment and old aeon-new aeon, which Paul uses to describe the two realities of *nomos* and Christ, are enriched in Col. 2:17 by the antithesis of appearance-reality, which comes from a different religious milieu.

3. Hebrews.

Very closely related to Col. 2:17 are the σκιά sayings in Hb. In Hb. 8:5 ὑπόδειγμα is parallel to σκιά → II, 33, 14 ff.; III, 278, 28 ff.; V, 540, 19 ff. A point worth noting is that this sense occurs only in the section 8:1-10:18.[11] The opposite is τύπος (a quotation from Ex. 25:40), which in turn means the same as εἰκών.[12] With the help of the Hellenistic philosophical category "heavenly reality-earthly shadow" the Jewish priesthood and its ministry are relativised by the high-priestly office of Jesus. This polemical relativising is expressly supported by the citation of the Mosaic Scripture. The same religio-historical and theological milieu controls the σκιά saying in 10:1. Since the *nomos* contains only a shadow of the heavenly reality, it cannot achieve the perfection on which everything depends → 396, 18 ff.

The word does not occur at all in the post-apost. fathers.

---

[8] Cf. P. H. Vielhauer, "Der Benedictus des Zacharias," ZThK, 49 (1952), 266-272.
[9] On this cf. M. Lambertz, "Sprachliches aus LXX u. NT, I," *Wissenschaftliche Zschr. der Univ. Leipzig* (1952/53), 79-89.
[10] Cf. Loh. Kol., *ad loc.*
[11] Cf. Mi. Hb., *ad loc.*
[12] Cf. Mi. Hb., *ad loc.*

† ἀποσκίασμα.

This word occurs in Hell. works only in post-Chr. texts, e.g., Porphyr. Comm. on Introductio in Claudii Ptolemaei opus de effectibus astrorum. [1] It is not used in the LXX.

In the NT it is a hapax legomenon and occurs in Jm. 1:17. The use is literal. τροπῆς ἀποσκίασμα means the darkness caused on earth by the movements of the constellations. [2]

† ἐπισκιάζω.

1. In profane Gk. the word is found from Hdt. and means lit. "to shade," "to overshadow," "to cast one's shadow," "to cover": τῇ μὲν (τῶν πτερύγων) τὴν ᾿Ασίην, τῇ δὲ τὴν Εὐρώπην ἐπισκιάζειν, Hdt., I, 209; ἐπισκιάζεσθαι τὸν ἥλιον, Geoponica, 5, 29, 3; Aristot. Gen. An., V, 1, p. 780a, 30; Theophr. De Causis Plantarum, II, 18, 3. Transf. it means "to conceal": λαθραῖον ὄμμ᾽ ἐπεσκιασμένη, Soph. Trach., 914; τὰ δεινὰ ἑτέροις ὀνόμασιν, Juncus acc. to Stob. Ecl., IV, 1062, 23 ff. In the Gk. understanding of being and its light-metaphysics "to cast a shadow on something" is always something negative, an obscuring which hampers a true view of the object to be expounded because something is taken from the light (of knowledge) and the thing cannot be known and presented as it is in reality. Thus far, then, no positive use of ἐπισκιάζειν has been found in secular Gk. The only instance outside the sphere of common use is Hdt., I, 209. But this relates to a phenomenon of the ancient oriental or Iranian world whose elements Hdt. has preserved with astonishing fidelity in other places too. To the Persian Cyrus there appears his successor Darius with wings on his shoulders. With one he overshadows Asia, with the other Europe. Here the typically oriental background of the meaning of ἐπισκιάζειν is plain. It obviously presents in visible form the manifestation of political power → lines 27 ff. [1]

2. The term occurs only a few times in the LXX. It is employed positively acc. to oriental usage. "To cast a shadow" is both a proof and a work of power ὕπαρξις πλουσίου ἀνδρὸς πόλις ὀχυρά, ἡ δὲ δόξα αὐτῆς μέγα ἐπισκιάζει, Prv. 18:11. Wealth is for the rich man a strong castle whose splendour casts a far shadow. This effect and emanation of power is even more plainly expressed in Ex. 40:34 f. The cloud overshadows the tent pitched by Moses (ἐπισκιάζειν for Hbr. שכן). The cloud is the mode of divine efficacy and possession. As a manifestation of the divine presence it rests permanently on the tent with its shadow. Hence Moses cannot go into the tent of the covenant. This is further underlined by the par. καλύπτειν and πλησθῆναι. The transf. sense occurs in ψ 90:4 and 139:8. ἐπισκιάζειν here (for סכך) means "to shelter," "to defend" with ref. to God's special protection.

3. Philo uses ἐπισκιάζειν with surprising frequency. The lit. sense is found only occasionally, e.g., Som., II, 102: clothes cover the secrets of man's nature. Both actively and passively the word is also found in a transf. sense. ἐπισκιάζειν is a kind of keyword in the well-known spirit-senses dualism of Philo. Like the sun the spirit overshadows the senses when awake but lets them run abroad when asleep, Leg. All., II, 30. Desires overshadow even the sharpest senses (Jos., 49) and put τὸ λογικόν in the shade

---

ἀ π ο σ κ ί α σ μ α. [1] Ed. Anon. in officina Petriana (1559), 193.
[2] Cf. Dib. Jk., ad loc.
ἐ π ι σ κ ι ά ζ ω. [1] [Kleinknecht].

in those who are irrational (Leg. All., II, 58; cf. Som., II, 196). Indeed, men cast a shadow over eternal ἀρετή (Migr. Abr., 126; also Conf. Ling., 170), over the radiance of truth (Vit. Mos., II, 271), over truth in gen. (Op. Mund., 170) and over God's δόξα (Leg. All., III, 7). ἐπισκιάζειν is also linked with light in Deus Imm., 3, with τὰ καλά in Vit. Mos., II, 27, with the eye of the soul in Migr. Abr., 191, and with dreams in Jos., 106.

4. In the NT the word is comparatively rare. The literal meaning "to over-shadow," "to cast a shadow," occurs in Ac. 5:15. In the background is the popular view of the apostle Peter as the person who heals all sickness. The word is also found in all three Synoptic accounts of the transfiguration (Mk. 9:7 and par.; Mt. 17:5 : νεφέλη φωτεινή). The combination of νεφέλη and ἐπισκιάζειν in this pre-Synoptic tradition corresponds both linguistically and materially to the usage of the LXX. As in Ex. 40:35 (→ 399, 29 ff.) ἐπισκιάζειν denotes the resting of the cloud → IV, 908, 19 ff.; 909, n. 44. As in the Sinai story, so in that of the transfiguration the cloud (→ 399, 29 ff.) is a manifestation of God and it over-shadows those assembled on the high mountain. [2]

The word is used in a special way in Lk. 1:35. Historically the only meaning possible is that of "to overshadow," "to rest," "to cover" as in LXX Ex. 40:35 → 399, 29 ff. ἐπισκιάζειν is thus the opposite of human pro-creation. Never-theless, it must be emphasised that in religious sources the word is never a tt. nor even a euphemism for sexual intercourse. It is true that ἐπισκιάζειν is more concrete than the par. ἐπέρχεσθαι in 1:35, since the latter simply denotes the advent of the Spirit or dunamis while the former denotes His activity. The word thus denotes the fact of divine generation but does not describe the mode. This singular sense can be understood only in the light of the theology of Hellenistic Judaism. Here, on the basis of Greek and Egyptian notions, there may be found the theologoumenon of the generation of the saviour by God to the exclusion of the natural father. This includes rather than excludes the idea of the creative power of God's Spirit to which the OT already bears witness, [3, 4] → II, 300, 20 ff.; VI, 402, 14 ff.

5. The word does not occur in the post-apost. fathers.

Schulz

---

[2] Cf. the comm., ad loc.; Bultmann Trad., Suppl., 36 f.
[3] Cf. E. Lohmeyer, "Die Verklärung Jesu nach d. Mk.," ZNW, 21 (1922), 197 f.; E. Norden, Die Geburt d. Kindes³ (1958), 92-99; M. Dibelius, "Jungfrauensohn u. Krippen-kind," Botschaft u. Gesch., I (1953), 18-22; → πνεῦμα, VI, 402, 1 ff. (and the material given there); Bultmann Trad., Suppl., 44; M. Lambertz "Sprachliches aus LXX u. NT," Wissenschaftliche Zschr. d. Univ. Leipzig (1952/53), 79-87, esp. II; P. Winter, "Some Observations on the Language in the Birth and Infancy Stories of the Third Gospel," NTSt, 1 (1954/55), 111-121.
[4] On the basis of the textually difficult 1 QSa 2:11 ff. (DJD, I, 110) it may be added that the theology of Qumran — "even if not so clearly" — shows acquaintance with a divine generation of the Messiah. Cf. O. Michel and O. Betz, "Von Gott gezeugt," Judt., Urchr., Kirche, Festschr. J. Jeremias (1960), 3-23, esp. 11 f. and 15.

---

† σκιρτάω

A. Greek Usage.

σκιρτάω [1] is used in descriptions of young horses which gallop across the fields. In Plato it denotes the impulsive restlessness of the animal. It is transf. to men, esp. the young who cannot be still for a moment, Plat. Leg., II, 653e, or desires which stir in sleep, Plat. Resp., IX, 571c, or the god-forsaken lawless man, the arrogant or conceited, who leaps about without discipline and confuses everything, Plat. Leg., IV, 716b. In the famous myth of the soul the white horse obeys the reins while the black horse, resisting reins, spurs and whip, runs away and drags the rider violently into the sensual question of aphrodisiac affection, Plat. Phaedr., 254a. Thus the word has a negative ring in Plato and in this respect displays its kinship with the animal. In later witnesses we find a more favourable use. With kindly but biting irony, Dio Chrys. Or., 19, 3 tells how he associates with a herd of cattle which is flourishing and handsome but makes a lot of noise and is inclined to leap about. [2] In the paraphrases on Ps.-Oppian's hunting descriptions Cynegetica (c. 200 A.D.) [3] the word is used of a dog leaping for joy after getting the scent of the hare, cf. the gambolling of new-born lambs in the shepherd idyll of Longus (2nd cent. A.D.): σκιρτήματα ποιμνίων ἀρτιγεννήτων, also the leaping of rams on the mountains, ibid., I, 9, 1. Impulsive movement characterises the expression σκιρτᾶν partly in the sense of joy and partly in that of animal desire. The impulse towards metaphorical use was probably given by Plato.

B. The Usage in Hellenistic Judaism.

1. The word is used in Jl. 1:17 LXX — the HT has a different text — to denote the movement of calves tearing at their stalls in fear. Wis. 17·18 speaks c˙ the invisible course of stamping animals, σκιρτώντων ζῴων δρόμος ἀθεώρητος. Elsewhere we find the more original sense of leaping for joy, e.g., Mal. 4:2 : "You shall leap" for joy "like calves released from their chain," or 'Ιερ. 27:11 (50:11): "you sprang like heifers in the meadows." Cf. also ψ 113:4 : "The mountains skipped like rams and the hills like rams of the flock" (cf. v. 6). The Hbr. equivalents are פּושׁ' in Mal. 4:2; 'Ιερ. 27(50):11: "to stretch oneself," "to rise up, to stamp wantonly," [4] and רקד in ψ 113:4, 6 : "to dash, beat, spring, hop," pi "to dance." [5]

The word is used in a different sense from that hitherto noted at Gn. 25:22 : ἐσκίρτων δὲ τὰ παιδία ἐν αὐτῇ. The HT leaves us in no doubt that the ref. here is not to the

---

σ κ ι ρ τ ά ω. [1] The word is perhaps a development of $\sqrt{sqer}$ "to spring," "to hop," v. Hofmann, Boisacq, Liddell-Scott, s.v.; Schwyzer, I, 352.

[2] Dio Chrys. is speaking of rhetoric and its audience; cf. W. Schmid, Art. "Dion Cocceianus" in Pauly-W., 5 (1905), 848-877, esp. 866.

[3] Euteknios' paraphrase of Oppian's Cynegetica, ed. O. Tueselmann, AGG, NF, 4, 1 (1900), 18, 3 (cf. Cohn, Art. "Euteknios" in Pauly-W., 6 [1909], 1491).

[4] At Hab. 1:8 פּושׁ is transl. ἐξιππάζεσθαι ("to ride forth") in the LXX. The ni in Na. 3:18 has a very different sense and is transl. ἀπαίρειν.

[5] Qoh. 3:4; Is. 13:21; 1 Ch. 15:29 have ὀρχεῖσθαι for רקד, Job 21:11 προσπαίζειν, Na. 3:2 ἀναβράσσειν, Jl. 2:5 ἐξάλλεσθαι, ψ 28:6 λεπτύνειν.

movement of the child in the mother's womb but to the fact that the twins jostled one another ; רצץ hitp "they jostled one another" to be born first. [6] The Rabb. speculated a great deal about this fact that even in the womb the children were already acting with intent or in orientation to their divine destiny. [7] The LXX obviously uses a word which expresses the movement natural in the animal kingdom. In this way, contrary to the true sense of the HT, it refers to the involuntary movement of a child in the womb which is always felt to express joy in living. We do not know whether the LXX was the first work to use the term thus. There is only one other instance in the NT → lines 18 ff. [8]

2. Philo has the word in the parable in Spec. Leg., I, 304. He uses it for an animal which throws off the reins and leaps about freely. Joseph. uses the term metaphorically in Bell., 5, 120 when he tells how the Jews leaped for joy over a successful stratagem in the war against the Romans.

C. σκιρτάω in the New Testament.

In Lk. 6:23 the word is used to denote joy. It has become a pure metaphor and the connection with the original sense no longer plays any part. In the two other instances in Lk. 1:41 and 44 [9] σκιρτάω describes the movements of the child in the womb. In 1:44 these movements express joy, jubilation. This use is not attested in non-biblical Greek. [10] Two motifs control the use in Luke : the natural movement of the child in the womb, and eschatological joy at the coming of Christ. The former is prefigured in Gn. 25:22 (→ 401, 31) the latter in Mal. 4:2 (→ 401, 28), where the comparison gives expression to joy at eschatological salvation. [11]

D. σκιρτάω in the Post-New Testament Period.

In Herm. s., 6, 1, 6 and 2, 3 ff. those who separate themselves from God and give themselves to the world are compared to sheep leaping to and fro on lush pastures. The Platonic colouring of the word has no influence here. OT images are used, but they are given a negative apocalyptic turn. In Dg., 11, 6 the word is a pure metaphor for joy.

Fitzer

---

[6] רצץ q "to break," "ill-treat" occurs in the hitp only here.
[7] Str.-B., II, 100 f.
[8] Field notes σκιρτάω in Σ 2 S. 6:16 and Prv. 7:22, also Hb. on Jer. 2:23; he also notes σκιρτοποιέω Θ in the Quinta on ψ 28:6, 'Α σκιρτόω.
[9] And the dependent Prot. Ev. Jc. 12:2.
[10] There is no lexical support for the view of E. Norden, *Die Geburt des Kindes*[3] (1958), 104 that σκιρτάω is a Jewish Hell. term for the movements of an infant in the womb.
[11] D. Tabachovitz, *Die Septuaginta u. d. NT* (1956), 95 f. Bengel on Lk. 1:41: *Conjuncti motus embryonis et matris spirituales,* and on 1:44 : *neque is saltus salutatorius unicus fidei actus fuit : plenus fuit Spiritus sancti,* "the child was full of the Holy Ghost." Here the spontaneous natural movement and that which is from God are combined in a play on words.

σκληροκαρδία → III, 613, 25 ff.
σκληρός → V, 1028, 12.
σκληρότης → V, 1028, 34.
σκληροτράχηλος → V, 1029, 23.
σκληρύνω → V, 1030, 1.

σκολιός

From the Indo-Eur. root *sqel-* (*qel-*) "to bend" this means "bent," esp. for parts of the body (heel, knee, hip),[1] "crooked," also morally ; it is connected with σκέλος "thigh," perhaps also → σκώληξ "worm" and κυλλός "twisted," "lame." In Lat. we find *scelus* "offence," and in New High German *scheel*. There thus result such further meanings as "winding," "twisted," "tortuous," "slanting" and in a transf. sense "crooked," "dishonest," "false," "artful," "cunning." Cf. Hesych., *s.v.*: σκολιός that is δυσχερής, ἐπικαμπής, ἄνισος, δύσκολος, Suid., *s.v.* uses πανοῦργος in explanation, cf. Tzetzes Schol. on Hes. Op., 7 (c. 1200 A.D.):[2] τὸν ποικίλον τὸ ἦθος διὰ πανουργίαν.

A. σκολιός in Secular Greek.

1. In the lit. sense the word is mostly used of rivers (Hdt., I, 185; Strabo, 12, 8, 15) and roads, also transf. of roads, Pind. Pyth., 2, 85, etc., of the difficult access to knowledge, Vett. Val., VI, 3 (250, 23 Kroll). Eur. Hec., 65 speaks of a crooked staff. The word and derivates are also used of snakes and dragons and their movements (Arat. Phaen., 70), of a confusing labyrinth (Callim. Hymn. in Delum, 311), of ringlets or matted hair σκολιόθριξ (Nonnus Dionys., 15, 137), σκολιοπλόκαμος (*ibid.*, 26, 56, cf. 14, 182), of a medical instrument (Hdt., II, 86), σκολιότης of a Parthian bow etc. (Plut. Crass, 24 [I, 558b]).

2. Already in Hom. the word is used in a transf. sense, Il., 16, 387: σκολιὰς κρίνωσι θέμιστας, cf. Hesiod in various combinations : σκολιῶς ὀνοτάζων, Hes. Op., 258; μύθοισι σκολιοῖς ἐνέπων, 194; σκολιῶν δικῶν, 264, cf. 219. Often it is a matter of straightening what is crooked, ἰθύνει σκολιὸν ... Ζεύς, Hes. Op., 7 and Theogn., 536 (Diehl³, II, 35): οὔποτε δουλείη κεφαλὴ ἰθεῖα πέφυκεν, ἀλλ᾽ αἰεὶ σκολιή, cf. also 1147 (II, 68). There is a fig. use in Plat. Phaedr., 253e, where the three εἴδη of the soul are compared to a pair of horses and the charioteer controlling them ; the good horse is the straight and orderly one, the other is the σκολιός, → 401, 4 ff. The words κρατεραύχην, βραχυτράχηλος, ὕβρεως καὶ ἀλαζονείας ἑταῖρος are used to show what is meant by this crookedness or restiveness. Acc. to Plat. Gorg., 525a health of soul is ruined by an unrighteous ruler ; everything is "spoiled" (σκολιά) by lying and deceit.[3] But acc. to Plat. Theaet., 173a bondage leads to crooked action, cf. also 194b

---

σ κ ο λ ι ό ς. Bibl.: Walde-Pok., II, 598; Pr.-Bauer⁵, 1498; Pape, II, 902; Thes. Steph., VII, 417; Liddell-Scott, *s.v.*

[1] Cf. עָקֵב "heel," עָקֹב "what is humpy, uneven" transf. "deceitful," עָקַב "to cheat."

[2] Ed. T. Gaisford in Poetae Graeci Minores, II (1823), 40.

[3] The continuation shows what concepts underlie the idea of the distortion of the soul : ὑπὸ ἐξουσίας καὶ τρυφῆς καὶ ὕβρεως καὶ ἀκρατίας τῶν πράξεων ἀσυμμετρίας τε καὶ αἰσχρότητος γέμουσαν τὴν ψυχήν.

and Leg., XII, 945b; Resp., II, 365b, where Pind. (= Fr., 213) is quoted in a phrase not found elsewhere : σκολιαὶ ἀπάται. The term is often an attribute of concepts like word, speech and song, e.g., Aristot. Pol., III, 14, p. 1285a, 38; Luc. Bis Accusatus, 16. An ambiguous oracle is called σκολιός in Diod. S., 16, 91. In Plot. Enn., I, 6, 9 the word is on the frontier between lit. and fig. use. As a sculptor works on his piece, so one should work at one's own image : ἀπεύθυνε ὅσα σκολιά ... μὴ παύσῃ τεκταίνων τὸ σὸν ἄγαλμα. σκολιός has not been found thus far in the pap. Hence it does not seem to have been very common in popular Hell. usage. This may explain why it is not too prominent in Chr. works in spite of its emphatic use in OT wisdom. It still lives on in its old sense in modern Gk.

B. σκολιός in the Greek Old Testament.

1. In the OT the distribution of the word in the various books calls for notice. Of 28 instances of σκολιός and related terms in the LXX 14 are in Prv. (σκολιάζειν 3 times) and another 3 in Wis. Of the other 11 Dt. 32:5 and ψ 77:8 are the same ; there are 3 in Job, 3 in Is., 1 in Hos., 1 in Jer. and 1 in Ez. (σκολιότης). There are another 7 in the Hexapla tradition. In 8 of the grand total of 35 (34) instances there is no Hbr. original. Several Hbr. words are used in the others ; the roots עקש (8 times) and הפך (4) are the most prominent. In the other 15 (14) passages 12 different Hbr. words are used. Obviously the content of the group [4] was so precise for the Gk. transl. that where it seemed to correspond to the sense they could use it for difficult and little known Hbr. terms.

2. The lit. sense was a familiar one. Thus Leviathan in Is. 27:1 is a coiling snake. LXX and Σ render this נָחָשׁ עֲקַלָּתוֹן[5] by ὄφις σκολιός. Yet in Gn. 3:1 (LXX φρονιμώτατος, ᾽ΑΣΘ πανοῦργος, [6] -ότερος) the ref. is less to its mode of locomotion than to its nature, as also with the Egypt. snakes of Wis. 16:5, where their entry is not described but the wickedness and malice of their conduct. ψ 124:5 in the HT is contrasting with the good and honest the violence of the wicked, who incline to crookedness LXX has ἐκκλίνοντες εἰς τὰς στραγγαλιάς, ᾽Α διαπλοκάς, Θ διεστραμμένα, while Σ has εἰς τὰς σκολιότητας αὐτῶν. The image of the way, which is perhaps lost already in the HT, [7] is presupposed neither in LXX nor Σ. But often the way is the true image and only where this is used in a transf. sense or interpreted is the term brought into the picture. Thus behind Is. 40:3-5 lies the mythical idea of the divine road and the related Parsee notion of the future levelling of all mountains and hills. The ref. is to uneven rather than crooked ways, and to a made road through difficult country. [8] But the idea of God's road requires allegorical interpretation such as is found in LXX and 1 QS 8:15. Preparation for God is the study of the Torah. ἔσται πάντα τὰ σκολιὰ εἰς εὐθεῖαν in Is. 40:4 is taken in the same way. The word road is of no account. The adj. have broken free and demand an allegorical understanding. O. Sol. 34:1 offers comfort :

---

[4] The content obviously includes arrogance, self-deception, and the deception of others.
[5] עֲקַלָּתוֹן (only Is. 27:1) and עֲקַלְקַל (only Ju. 5:6 and Ps. 25:5) are from the root עקל. In Hab. 1:4 we have the part. pu : "distorted," "perverted." LXX has διεστραμμένος at Ju. 5:6; Hab. 1:4.
[6] Cf. the explanation of the word in Suid. (→ 403, 13) and Tzetzes (→ 403, 13 f.).
[7] Ps. 125:5 might be transl.: "Your distortions seduce you, Yahweh leads forth the wicked" (obj. of both verbs). Cf. Is. 44:20 : "The heart which is misled seduces him."
[8] For this eschatological expectation in Parseeism cf. Plut. Is. et Os., 47 (II, 370a-c): When the earth has become smooth and even there will be a uniform life and only the one state of happy men with a language common to all. Bibl. statements might have been influenced by this. Thus Is. 45:2 has ὄρη ὁμαλιῶ (cf. Σ Is. 40:3 : ὁμαλίσατε). On the mythical road of God cf. H. Gressmann, Der Messias (1929), 185-188 and 165 on Is. 2:2-4, cf. also Rev. 21:10. Rabb. expositors retained this eschatological interpretation and hence a lit. understanding, cf. Dt. r., 4 (201b) on 12:20; Str.-B., II, 154 on Lk. 3:4.

"There is no rough way where there is a simple heart."[9] In Is. 42:16 the ref. is to preparation by God, not for God. It is part of His revelation in creation and is thus meant lit., though the individual words (unknown way, darkness, light, roughness, smoothness) demand spiritual exposition. Is. 57:14 also refers to stumbling-blocks on the way ; here LXX has σκῶλα for מִכְשׁוֹל. The prophets are hampered by their opponents or by the obstinate people. Thus Hos. 9:8 speaks of snares set for the prophet on all his paths. LXX has παγὶς σκολιά in a free rendering of פַּח יָקוֹשׁ. It took יָקוֹשׁ[10] as an adj. and has in view a malicious persecution of the prophet on all his ways.

3. Bibl. wisdom speaks a gt. deal about way and walk in the transf. sense. Prv. esp. fashioned its own moral and religious vocabulary in the LXX transl.[11] The present term finds a specific use in connection with the road. Thus Prv. 2:15 warns against "crooked" paths : αἱ τρίβοι σκολιαὶ (Σ σκαμβαί, Θ στρεβλαί) καὶ καμπύλαι αἱ τροχιαί, Prv. 14:2 Mas. runs : "He who goes crooked ways, despises him (God)." But the LXX speaks of the dishonesty of the σκολιάζων[12] rather than his ungodliness. At Prv. 22:14a (no Mas.) LXX introduces ὁδὸς σκολιά on its own. ἐν ὁδοῖς σκολιαῖς is independent in Prv. 22:5. The one who treads crooked paths in 28:18 is the man of little moral worth.[13] The transf. sense of the word comes out plainly in connection with other nouns. Thus it refers to malicious and slanderous speech in Prv. 4:24. 10:8 LXX reads : "He who slanders thoughtlessly is deceived" : ὁ δὲ ἄστεγος χείλεσιν σκολιάζων ὑποσκελισθήσεται cf. also 23:33 : λαλήσει σκολιά (Σ στρεβλά); Prv. 8:8 : σκολιόν = נִפְתָּל with עִקֵּשׁ = στραγγαλῶδες.[14] For לֵב עִקֵּשׁ in 17:16a LXX has ὁ δὲ σκολιάζων (τοῦ μαθεῖν), in 17:20 σκληροκάρδιος. Similarly 'Α Jer. 17:9 has σκολιὰ καρδία for עָקֹב הַלֵּב. LXX βαθεῖα (vl. βαρεῖα), also 'Α Jer. 13:10 σκολιότης καρδίας for שְׁרִרוּת לֵב. In 'Α, then, the term is plainly negative from a moral and religious standpt. In Ez. 16:5 LXX has σκολιότης ψυχῆς for גֹּעַל נַפְשֵׁךְ (גֹּעַל hapax

---

[9] G. Diettrich, Die Oden Salomos (1911), 116; A. Harnack, Ein jüd.-chr. Psalmbuch aus d. 1. Jhdt. (1910), 65.

[10] יָקוֹשׁ "setter of traps," but to be taken as a verbal form, 3rd sing. masc. q intr. perf., cf. T. H. Robinson, Die zwölf kleinen Propheten, Hndbch. AT, I, 14[2] (1954), ad loc.

[11] G. Bertram, "Die religiöse Umdeutung altoriental. Lebensweisheit in d. griech. Übers. d. AT," ZAW, NF, 13 (1936), 153-167.

[12] σκολιάζων for נָלוֹז. לוֹז in Prv. 2:15 is par. to עִקֵּשׁ, LXX καμπύλος, 'Α θρυλοῦσιν, Θ μυκτηρίζουσιν, and 4:24 : לְזוּת שְׂפָתַיִם par. to פֶּה עִקְּשׁוּת, LXX : ἄδικα χείλη, Prv. 3:21 q LXX : μὴ παραρρυῇς (cf. Hb. 2:1 and the admonition in Hb. 12:12 f.), 3:32 ni part. LXX παράνομος, 4:21 hi LXX : μὴ ἐκλίπωσιν, Σ μὴ παραρρυησάτωσαν, Θ : μὴ χλευασθήτωσαν. Elsewhere נָלוֹז only Is. 30:12 LXX : ὅτι ἐγόγγυσας, and Sir. 34(31):8 LXX ψεῦδος. There is thus no fixed Gk. transl. of לוּז.

[13] At Prv. 28:6 LXX has ψευδής for עִקֵּשׁ דְּרָכַיִם. At Jer. 6:28 LXX has πορευόμενοι σκολιῶς for הֹלְכֵי רָכִיל, at Is. 59:8 Σ has αἱ τρίβοι αὐτῶν ἐσκολιώθησαν αὐτοῖς. When the idea of the two ways is adopted in primitive Christianity, σκολιός is used for the black way, that of death in Did., 5, 1; Poimandres, 29; cf. Barn., 20, 1: ἡ τοῦ μέλανος ὁδός ἐστιν σκολιὰ καὶ κατάρας μεστή.

[14] Orig. Comm. in Mt. Fr. Α 3, 1 ff. uses Prv. 8:8, 9 on Mt. 5:9. Peacemakers are those who find nothing distorted or perverted in the divine revelations but understand them consistently and simply even where they seem to be in contradiction. In his address of thanks to Origen, Gregory Thaumaturgos uses the figure of the pilgrimage which might be hampered by what is σκολιὸν καὶ ὕπουλον καὶ σοφισματῶδες, 14, 171 (ed. P. Koetzschau [1894], 33, 6) cf. 15, 175 (33, 27). In the Lat. fathers the equivalent pravitas and perversitas are used of heretical distortion, Tert. Adv. Prax., 1, 4 (CCh 2, p. 1159); Praescr. Haer., 4, 5; 34, 2; cf. Aug. De catechizandis rudibus, 7 (MPL, 40 [1887], 318): singula perversorum

legomenon "abhorrence"). [15] ἀνὴρ σκολιός is used in Prv. 16:28 to denote the character of a man (for אִישׁ תַּהְפֻּכֹות), and it is perhaps a double transl. in 16:26b (no Mas.), though in the text the word again refers esp. to speech. In Prv. 21:8 the Mas. is as follows : "Winding is the way of the guilt-laden man, but the pure, his work is straight." But LXX adds God as subj. and thus develops the idea of retribution : πρὸς τοὺς σκολιοὺς σκολιὰς ὁδοὺς ἀποστέλλει ὁ θεός. What is said in Wis. 1:3 is presupposed : σκολιοὶ γὰρ λογισμοὶ χωρίζουσιν ἀπὸ θεοῦ. These distorted thoughts and this perverted reason are in contrast with the pious reason which in 4 Macc. 16:4 is lauded as the power which controls the impulses. The end of crooked thoughts is not in doubt. Thus Job 5:13b reads in Σ : βουλὴ δὲ σκολιὰ ταραχθήσεται, LXX : βουλὴν δὲ πολυπλόκων ἐξέστησεν. In the LXX, as in the Mas., God is the subj.; He is also the logical subj. in the pass. of Σ. In Job 4:18 the word is used for a hapax legomenon, LXX : κατὰ δὲ ἀγγέλων αὐτοῦ σκολιόν τι ἐπενόησεν (cf. also 9:7 and the quotation in 1 Cl., 39, 4). In sense this corresponds to Σ : καὶ ἐν ἀγγέλοις αὐτοῦ εὑρήσει ματαιότητα. [16] Finally the term is used in a theologically significant v. at Job 9:20. Mas. here runs : "I am innocent, but he blames me." For this LXX has : ἐάν τε ὦ ἄμεμπτος, σκολιὸς ἀποβήσομαι. Thus the word can be used for the sinner gen., cf. Dt. 32:5 and ψ 77:8. The various expressions in the Mas. (Dt. 32:5 : corrupt and perverted generation, Ps. 78:8 : apostate and rebellious generation) are combined in the LXX with the help of the term. The continuation in ψ 77:8 offers an explanation, κατευθύνειν obviously being in antithesis to the σκολιός. [17]

In the main σκολιός in the Greek OT expresses the nature of the man who does not walk in the straightness and uprightness which God has ordained for him but who in a way which is guilty and worthy of punishment is crooked, cramped, distorted and hence corrupt. [18]

C. σκολιός in the New Testament.

The OT development of σκολιός stands behind the usage of the NT. The word occurs 4 times in the NT in three different ways.

1. A transferred sense naturally suggests itself for the quotation from Is. 40:3-5 in Lk. 3:5. Deliverance from corruption, from σκολιά, is the decisive act

---

genera (Judaeos vel haereticos) ... pravae opiniones ; 8 : perverse et prave opinati (ibid., 319); Vincent of Lerins Commonitorium, 2 (MPL, 50 [1865], 639): veritatem ab haereticae pravitatis falsitate discernere.
[15] Thus σκολιότης becomes a gen. term for sin, Herm. v., 3, 9, 1.
[16] → μάταιος, IV, 519 ff.; G. Bertram, "Hbr. u. griech. Qoh. Ein Beitrag z. Theol. d. hell. Bibel," ZAW, NF, 23 (1952), 26-49.
[17] Philo interprets Dt. 32:4-6 in Sobr., 10, 11; γενεὰ σκολιὰ καὶ διεστραμμένη = τὰ πολλὰ σφαλλόμενοι ἐν ταῖς κατὰ τὸν ὀρθὸν βίον πράξεσιν. Philo does not seem to use σκολιός. Synon. in him are στρεβλός in Poster. C., 28, ἀνώμαλος and τραχύς in Congr., 28, also δύσκολος and πανοῦργος. He has the parable of the charioteer and two horses for the powers of the soul, but in a different way from Plato (→ 403, 29 ff.). In Philo we find courage and desire, and the latter, the feminine principle, is characterised by πανουργίᾳ χαίρουσα, Agric., 73, cf. 83; Leg. All., I, 72.
[18] Cf. Ps. 18:26 (2 S. 22:27): וְעִם עִקֵּשׁ תִּתְפַּתָּל καὶ μετὰ στρεβλοῦ διαστρέψεις (2 S. 22:27: στρεβλωθήσῃ) and cf. Prv. 21:8. God's action is denoted by a different word from that of man, though this is not noted in LXX 2 S. 22:27. ψ 17:27 is quoted in 1 Cl., 46, 3 acc. to LXX. לֵבָב עִקֵּשׁ in ψ 100:4 is transl. καρδία σκαμβή. We also find στρεβλή and διεστραμμένη, cf. Prv. 6:14 תַּהְפֻּכֹות בְּלִבֹּו διεστραμμένη καρδία. But Prv. has other par. expressions too, though Luther always transl. "verkehrt." In Jos., as in Hdt. and Strabo (→ 403, 17), σκολιός is used in relation to the construction of a military road (Bell., 3, 118 :

of God (Ac. 2:40) or the act of Christ.[19] The moral hindrances to Christ's coming are to be set aside. This is the task of the fore-runner and his preaching, though in the sense of the conviction of the primitive Church that the Logos Himself is at work in John the Baptist.[20] A precise distinction between σκολιά "humpy," "crooked," and τραχεῖα "rough," "uneven," is neither necessary nor possible.[21] The word σκολιός still has an ethical nuance.[22] It expresses the ethical and social misconduct which is rooted in ungodliness and unbelief and which will vanish with the coming of the Messiah. The reference is universal. As all will see the salvation, i.e., the Saviour, so the setting aside of σκολιά (πᾶσα φάραγξ, πᾶν ὄρος) will take place in all mankind.

2. Ac. 2:40; Phil. 2:15 adopt the OT expression γενεά σκολιά → 406, 18 ff. Under this judgment of crookedness stands either the Judaism around Jesus, the human race of the time, or that of all times and places. The word is based on Jesus' own preaching (Mk. 9:19; Mt. 17:17; Lk. 9:41)[23] and it castigates the inner contradiction of Jewish or human conduct. According to Ac. 2:13, which speaks of mocking,[24] the statement certainly applies to the Jews.[25] The primary reference is to them in Phil. 2:15 too. In contrast to them and among them as a crooked and perverse people, those addressed are to live as the blameless children of God.[26] But the judgment embraces much more than this. As Christians should bring light into the world, this world of Jews and Gentiles, i.e., the whole human race, needs the light because it is corrupt.[27] All who hear and accept the missionary preaching are to be saved out of this world, cf. Gl. 1:4.[28] Thus the judgment has universal validity. Mankind as a whole is affected by it.[29]

3. In 1 Pt. 2:18 the word is generally thought to be used as a practical ethical concept to denote the bad master as compared with the good and kind. Christian

---

τὰ σκολιὰ τῆς λεωφόρου κατευθύνειν), also in relation to the notable name Jerusalem (Ap., 1, 179 : τὸ δὲ τῆς πόλεως αὐτῶν ὄνομα πάνυ σκολιόν ἐστιν).

[19] Cf. Cramer Cat. on Lk. 3:5 : "All that hinders the development of virtue will be corrected by Christ." Previously one reads : "Make straight the paths of God, who goes His way in righteousness ; iniquity is crooked (σκολιά)." This is an ethical understanding. Human passions and demonic attacks are to be destroyed : "He describes as abysses, mountains and hills the passions and the opposition of demonic powers ... But this has all become smooth, for Christ has vanquished Satan ... By the rough he understands all human corruption, i.e., the life of publicans, harlots, robbers and wizards, who were perverse but then entered the straight way." Mt. 21:31 is adduced in illustration.

[20] Cramer Cat. on Lk. 3:4.

[21] Bengel, ad loc. Acc. to Kl. Lk. on 3:4 one should compare the contrast between high and low in Lk. 18:14. But this does not speak of levelling ; it refers to the transvaluation in the estimation of man.

[22] τραχύς occurs again in the NT only for cliffs in Ac. 27:29, Haench. Ag., ad loc. The word is seldom used in the lit. sense in the LXX.

[23] Dib. Gefbr. on Phil. 2:15.

[24] Aptum Judaeis epitheton, quorum nonnulli perseverabant irridere, Bengel on Ac. 2:40.

[25] Deliverance from this unfaithful generation means deliverance from the judgment which must pass on the current generation of Jews for its rejection of the Messiah. Zn. Ag. on 2:40.

[26] Cf. Dt. 32:5.

[27] Loh. Phil. on 2:15, cf. R. A. Lipsius, Brief an d. Phil., Hand-Comm. z. NT, II, 2² (1892), ad loc.

[28] A missionary expression, Haench. Ag. on 2:40.

[29] Vivunt quidem in terra fideles impiis permisti ... sed interea memineritis Dei adoptione vos separatos esse ab illis, Calvin on Phil. 2:15 (Corp. Ref., 80, 34).

slaves should submit themselves to their masters in the fear of God. [30] Unreserved obedience [31] must be shown even to those who are crooked and perverse. [32] But perhaps the reference is more to the attitude of non-christian masters to Christian slaves than to the individual attitude of various masters to their slaves. The σκολιοί put obstacles and prohibitions in their way, → V, 921, 15 ff. [33] In this case, as in the OT and the NT passages already discussed (→ 406, 29 ff.; 407, 11 ff.). σκολιός is not meant in a general ethical sense but it is used for pagan masters who are enslaved in idolatry and to whom obedience is required out of fear of God. [34]

D. σκολιός in the Early Church.

In the post-apost. fathers the word occurs in 1 Cl., 39, 4 quoting Job 4:18 (→ 406, 12 ff.). In Herm. v., 3, 9, 1 the noun σκολιότης ("perverseness") is used with πονηρία ("wickedness") as a general term for sin. Note should also be taken of Barn., 20, 1, where we find the metaphor of the crooked way of the scoundrel, which does not occur in the NT. This presupposes choice or decision between the crooked path and the straight path. In this secondary form of the image of the two ways (Did., 5) Barn. brought the term into the text. [35] Just. Dial., 50, 3 quotes Is. 40:3-5. There are no other instances in this body of literature.

Bertram

---

[30] B. Weiss, *Das NT, Handausgabe mit kurzen Erläuterungen* (1902), ad loc.; Schl. 1 Pt., ad loc. etc.: fear of men.

[31] Schl. 1 Pt. on 2:18.

[32] Luther takes this to mean "coarse," "ill-tempered," cf. Wbg. Pt., ad loc. δύσκολος, "morose," "disagreeable," "difficult," from the neg. prefix δυσ- and the unexplained -κολος (Frisk, I, 426) occurs in the LXX at Jer. 30:2 (49:8) for אֵיד "corruption," "trouble," in Θ at Ez. 2:6 for סָרָב, "refractory," and in an Αλλ at 4 Βασ. 2:10 for קשׁה hi "to make difficult," also at LXX Job 34:30 δυσκολία for מוקשׁ. In the NT it occurs only in Mk. 10:23, 24 par. for the difficulty the rich have in entering the kingdom of God, so also Herm. s., 9, 20, 2 and 3; cf. s., 9, 23, 3; m., 4, 3, 6; 9, 6, cf. 12, 1, 2; 12, 4, 6; s., 8, 10, 2, also Ign. R., 1, 2; Sm., 4, 1. Calvin comments on σκολιός at 1 Pt. 2:18 as follows (Corp. Ref., 83, 248): *pravos aequis opponit vel humanis: atque hoc verbo saevos et intractabiles designat, vel qui nihil humanitatis et clementiae habent.*

[33] H. v. Soden, *Briefe d. Pt., Hand-Comm. z. NT,* III, 2³ (1899) on 1 Pt. 2:18.

[34] Ltzm. K. on 1 C. 7:21 f.; cf. Wnd. Kath. Br. on 1 Pt. 2:18.

[35] Wnd. Barn., ad loc.

| † σκόλοψ | → III, 819, 12 ff. κολαφίζω.

This is not a very common word [1] but its possibilities of use are clearly defined. Lit. it means "what is pointed," and it is related to σκάλλω "hack." [2]

1. a. It is first attested in the sense "pointed stake" (Suid. *s.v.* σκόλοψ· ξύλον ὀξύ, Hesych., *s.v.* σκόλοπες· ὀξέα ξύλα ὀρθά) used in fortifications to repulse attackers, Hom. Od., 7, 45; Il., 8, 343; 15, 1, cf. 12, 55 f.: here expressly σκολόπεσσιν ὀξέσιν. On one such the head struck off an enemy can be impaled, Hom. Il., 18, 176 f. Stakes surround a wall, Hdt., IX, 97, or are put on the earthworks resulting from digging a defensive ditch, Xenoph. An., V, 2, 5, cf. the specifications for fortifications in Philo Byzant. Mechanica Syntaxis, 84, 47-50. [3] Stakes are also put in concealed pits as a defence against cavalry and naturally it is esp. important that these be pointed, Dio C., 40, 40, 5. Fig. Straton in Anth. Graec., 12, 205, 3 f.: [4] Strong places and palisades are necessary to protect the mature boy (against homosexuals). Gen. σκόλοπες then serve the purpose of enclosure, Artemid. Onirocr., II, 24 (p. 118, 14), cf. also Suid., *s.v.*: Concealed pointed stakes prevent damage to vineyards. An inquisitive person climbed a tree to see into the holy place of a sanctuary of Aesculapius and his eyes were impaled on σκόλοπες, Ditt. Syll.[3], III, 1168, 92. The sense of pointed stake is also decisive in Luc. when he says of the teeth of a mythically gigantic whale that they were as sharp as σκόλοπες, Verae Historiae, I, 30.

b. Killing by means of a σκόλοψ is one of the modes of execution, cf. throwing to wild beasts, Eur. El., 896-898, hurling from cliffs, Iph. Taur., 1429 f., stoning, Eur. Fr., 878 (TGF, 643), crucifying — it is thus distinct from this — Plut. An. Vitiositas ad Infelicitatem Sufficiat, 3 (II, 499d), hanging on trees, Diod. S., 33, 15, 1. Vett. Val., 2, 40 (p. 127, 26 Kroll) mentions σκολοπισμός along with death by fire, snakes and wild beasts, → 410, 3. The one concerned is fastened to the σκόλοψ, πήγνυμι, Eur. El., 898; Iph. Taur., 1430; Plut., II, 499d, or hanged on it, Diod. S., 33, 15, 1. In connection with ἀνασκολοπίζεσθαι Philo speaks of προσηλοῦσθαι, Somn., II, 213; Poster. C., 61 both times in the transf. sense, which very gen. can mean "being fastened." In Luc. Judicium Vocalium, 12 ἀνασκολοπίζειν undoubtedly means putting to death on a T

σ κ ό λ ο ψ. Bibl.: P. Andriessen, "L'impuissance de Paul en face de l'ange de Satan," *Nouvelle Revue Théol.*, 91 (1959), 462-468; C. Bruston, "L'écharde de saint Paul et l'abandon du pécheur à Satan," *Revue de Théol. et des Questions Religieuses*, 21 (1912), 411-418; T. K. Cheyne, Art. "Hanging," EB, II, 1958 f.; H. Clavier, "La santé de l'apôtre Paul," *Studia Paulina in honorem J. de Zwaan* (1953), 66-82; F. Fenner, "Die Krankheit im NT," UNT, 18 (1930), 30-40; H. Fulda, *Das Kreuz u. d. Kreuzigung* (1878), 113-116; P. Joüon, "2 C. 12:7," *Recherches de science religieuse*, 15 (1925), 532; P. H. Menoud, "L'écharde et l'ange satanique (2 C. 12:7)," *Studia Paul. in hon. J. de Zwaan* (1953), 163-171; A. Plummer, *A Crit. and Exeget. Comm. on the Second Epistle of St. Paul to the Cor.* (1925), 348-351; N. G. Smith, "The Thorn that Stayed," *Interpretation*, 13 (1959), 409-416; Wnd. 2 K., 382-388.

[1] It is not found in most of the many printed indexes.
[2] Boisacq, *s.v.* σκάλλω.
[3] Cf., 82, 41; ed. H. Diels-E. Schramm, AAB, 1919, 12 (1920), 27 and 34. Cf. also Eur. Rhes., 116.
[4] There is an allusion in the context to the metaphor of the vineyard.

shaped cross. In connection with ἀνασταυροῦσθαι Prometheus, 1 speaks of outstretched hands. There is no longer any distinction between the two verbs [5] in Luc., cf. Test. L. 4:4. He calls Jesus τὸν ἄνθρωπον τὸν ἐν τῇ Παλαιστίνῃ ἀνασκολοπισθέντα or τὸν ... ἀνεσκολοπισμένον ἐκεῖνον σοφιστήν, Pergr. Mort., 11 and 13. [6] Because → σταυρός and σκόλοψ both mean "pointed stake" in the first instance, the two corresponding verbs can be used interchangeably. ἀνασταυροῦν is the impaling of the head of a dead person on a stake, Hdt., IV, 103; VII, 238; IX, 78; Herodian. Hist., III, 8, 1. But Hesych. still finds this use for ἀνασκολοπίζειν : [7] ὀξύνοντες ξύλον διὰ τῆς ῥάχεως τοῦ νώτου, he uses the comparison with fried fish on a spit (s.v. σκόλοψιν ὡς ὀπτῶσιν) cf. Eur. Rhes., 514, ἀμπείρας ῥάχιν. Sen. Ad Marciam de Consolatione, 20, 3 mentions as various cruces hanging by the feet, the outstretching of the arms on a cross, and thirdly : alii per obscena stipitem egerunt. This is also presupposed in Sen. Ep., 101, 11 f., which speaks of sitting on the acuta crux, [8] cf. Sen. Ep., 14, 5 : cogita ... adactum per medium hominem, qui per os emergeret, stipitem. [9] Impaling of the living body may be meant in Diod. S., 5, 32, 6 : The Gauls τοὺς ... κακούργους ... ἀνασκολοπίζουσι τοῖς θεοῖς and then burn them with other offerings. The one impaled is left as food for the birds, so expressly Eur. El., 897 f.; Rhes., 515. Corpses are also suspended on stakes as a mark of disgrace, Plut. De Cleomene, 38 f. (I, 823b): κρεμαννύναι, ibid., ἀνασταυροῦν (I, 823e); Hdt., III, 125; Jos. Ant., 6, 374, cf. also → III, 917, 14 ff.

2. a. First found in the LXX (→ 411, 14 f.) [10] is the sense of "splinter" or "thorn" stuck, e.g., in the finger, Aesopus Fabulae, 279, 11 [11] or foot, 198, I, 4; Geoponica, 17, 23, 2; [12] Hegesippus in Anth. Graec., 7, 320; [13] Sext. Emp. Pyrrh. Hyp., I, 238; τὸν

---

[5] The clarification in Hdt., who uses the 2 verbs 6 times each (but not the simple form), is too far afield. Cf. J. E. Powell, Lex. to Herodotus (1938), s.v. (→ line 6; 409, 7 f.).

[6] For the Luc. ref. cf. C. Jacobitz, Luc. 4 (1841), Index (on σταυρός he notes expressly al; σταυροῦν does not occur). Except at Prometheus, 1 Luc. seems to use ἀνασταυροῦν only in De Sacrificiis, 6 (Prometheus) and Verae Hist., I, 42 (in a fantastic context ; nailing is meant). ἀνασκολοπίζειν, however, occurs 11 times : of Prometheus riveted to the Caucasus, of whom Luc. does not speak negatively, Prometheus, 2 and 7 (cf. 10) and Jup. Conf., 8; of καλοὶ κἀγαθοὶ ἄνδρες, ibid., 16, of men who did no wrong, Jup. Trag., 19, of the unhappy Polycrates, Charon, 14. Luc. himself is threatened with ἀνασκολοπίζεσθαι in Piscator, 2. Those executed are meant in Luc. Cataplus (Tyrannus), 6. If Luc. Pergr. Mort., 11 and 13 speaks contemptuously of the crucified Jesus, this is by reason of the context, as against Pr.-Bauer[5], 1499. Jos. Bell., 5, 451 speaks of προσηλοῦν in different σχήματι. He does not have ἀνασκολοπίζειν but ἀνασταυροῦν (24 times) or rarely σταυροῦν (Ant., 17, 295); the compound outside Ant., 6, 374 (body hung up without the head) always ref. to the predominantly Persian or Roman mode of execution, also Ant., 2, 73; at the end of terrible torture, 12, 256.

[7] This is the usual verb to denote putting to death with the help of a σκόλοψ. The simple is obviously rare and there is no instance of its use in the sense of the compound. The pass. seems to mean "to be surrounded by palisades," Stadiasmus sive Periplus Maris Magni, 115 (Geographi Graeci Minores ed. C. Müller, I [1882], 470).

[8] Fulda, 115 f. misunderstands the passage ; novissime in 101, 10 means "finally."

[9] The same procedure seems to be originally denoted by ἀνασχινδυλεύειν, Plat. Resp., II, 362a as a particularly horrible form of death. E. Benz, "Der gekreuzigte Gerechte bei Plato, im NT u. in d. alten Kirche," AAMainz, 1950, No. 12 (1950), 1029-1074, transl. "to nail on the cross" (1036), "to crucify" (1061). He does not go into the special sense of the verb. Cf. also Cl. Al. Strom., II, 125, 2, cf. IV, 78, 1: For His name we are persecuted, put to death, ἀνασκινδυλευθησόμεθα. In V, 108, 3 Plat. Resp., II, 362a is quoted. Hesych., s.v. ἀνασκινδυλεύεσθαι· ἀνασκολοπισθῆναι.

[10] Aesop's Fables (→ line 21 f.) are available only in later versions.

[11] Ed. A. Hausrath-H. Haas, I, 2 (1956), 95.

[12] Ed. H. Beckh (1895), 481, 12 f.

[13] Beckby, ad loc. transl. "thorn." Cf. Archimelos in Anth. Graec., 7, 50 : The way of the tragic poet when first entered is χαλεποῦ τρηχυτέρη σκόλοπος (line 4). Beckby, ad loc. transl. "rougher than a thicket of thorns."

πόδαν πονεῖς ἀπὸ σκολάπου, BGU, II, 380, 8 f. Doctors remove it by plasters, Serapion of Alexandria Fr., 150 f.;[14] Oribasius Collectiones Medicae, 9, 25, 1 f. (CMG, VI, 1, 2, p. 28, 29), sodium salt, 9, 34, 3 (CMG, VI, 1, 2, p. 32, 21), ointment, Diosc. Mat. Med., IV, 49, cf. IV, 174; II, 9, 2; II, 27. ἄκανθαι and σκόλοπες thickets of thorn bar access, Artemid. Onirocr., IV, 57 (p. 326, 27). To dream of such signifies hampering — they hold fast the intruder — or cares διὰ τὸ τραχύ, III, 33 (p. 181, 11-18); transf. Sib. Fr., 1, 23-25 : You have left the beaten path and gone astray on to that which leads through thorns and thickets. Spines of a palm as a means of fastening in magic, Preis. Zaub., II, 36, 270. Demons are supposed to put prickles on a woman's temples, ibid., 152. In a trumpet, Quintus Maecius in Anth. Graec., 6, 230.

b. In the LXX σκόλοψ is not used for "stake." In Sir. 43:19 the shapes of winter frost are compared to the points of σκόλοπες. In Hos. 2:8 God tells His disobedient wife Israel that He will block (φράσσειν) the way she has chosen with thickets so that she will return to Him, v. 9. Non-Israelites who oppress the people are compared in Nu. 33:55 LXX to a "splinter" in the eye, and in Ez. 28:24 those who treat it scornfully are compared to the "thorn."[15] One may perhaps connect these two passages with the use of σκόλοψ in the NT[16] even though the ref. here is hardly to oppression by men.[17]

3. The σκόλοψ of which Paul speaks in 2 C. 12:7 is one of the ἀσθένειαι referred to in v. 5, 9b and affecting the whole existence of the man Paul. The nouns in v. 10 refer also to his bodily life. In v. 7 one of the ἀσθένειαι is especially said to afflict Paul's σάρξ.[18] "For"[19] this a σκόλοψ was given to him by God.[20] That the idea of pain is bound up with σκόλοψ in Paul's mind may be seen from what follows. Obviously behind it is the concept that Satan receives from God the power or commission to cause Paul grief through one of his emissaries, though the emphasis is not on the figure of an ἄγγελος; this term is plainly meant in a figurative sense.[21] The ill-treatment (→ III, 819, 12 ff.) which Paul receives is compared to the sharp pain a σκόλοψ can cause someone.

Naturally the two expressions are not wholly adequate as figures, but they are not completely different. It is not possible, however, to take σκόλοψ as a stake to which Paul's flesh is bound because it "must not be stimulated and incite him to pride."[22] Again, the ref. as regards the flesh cannot be to the "selfish desire which arises in man

---

[14] Ed. K. Deichgräber, Die griech. Empirikerschule (1930), 167, 13; 168, 3 f.

[15] Ez. 28:24 : σκόλοψ πικρίας καὶ ἄκανθα ὀδύνης (סִלּוֹן מַמְאִיר וְקוֹץ מַכְאִב) "pricking thorn and painful barb," Gk. in both cases gen. noun for Hbr. part. מַמְאִיר here does not come from מאר "to break open" but from מר, מרר "to be bitter." → VI, 123, 20 and n. 5; 127, 7 ff. [P. Katz].

[16] Plummer, 349 on 2 C. 12:7 thinks it possible that Nu. 33:55 is the source of Paul's phrase. Linguistically closer is a fig. expression in Accad. to which R. Borger (Review), Archiv f. Orientforschung, 18 (1957/58), 417 refers in connection with the LXX and NT : "siḫil širi lit. means 'thorn of the flesh,' which ... denotes vexation."

[17] Some early expositors referred the σκόλοψ of 2 C. 12 to individuals, Plummer, ad loc., 350.

[18] Formally cf. 1 C. 7:28; here, too, τῇ σαρκί is materially dependent on a noun → n. 28.

[19] Is Paul adopting a current phrase ? The "text" in Fenner, 30 : σκόλοψ ἐν σαρκί, is obviously not attested anywhere.

[20] The strong purposiveness of the σκόλοψ (ἵνα ...) favours this view. Cf. Wnd. 2 K., ad loc., 383; Plummer, ad loc., 348. Esp. clear is the intentional replacing of the act statement by the pass. in 1 C. 10:5 (LXX Nu. 14:16 κατέστρωσεν, Paul κατεστρώθησαν).

[21] Formally cf. the image of the messenger in v. 8 (on this → n. 28).

[22] Schl. K., ad loc., 666. The blows — and obviously the stake too — are in his view the accusations of Satan reminding him of his wicked acts in Jerusalem, 667. W. G. Kümmel

under the stimulus of the body."[23] Acc. to the realistic utterances of Hesych., Eur., Sen. (→ 410, 8 ff.) it is also not very likely that what Paul wants to say is that he is like one who is impaled.[24] The connection of σκόλοψ with the ἀσθένειαι in 2 C. 12 makes it most improbable that the barb is that Paul cannot win over the Jews to faith in Christ.[25, 26] Even less satisfying is the interpretation of religious psychology which speaks of depressions after coming down from the heights of ecstasy;[27] in the context there is nothing for this and much against it, esp. v. 8 f.

The material understanding of σάρξ as the physical life,[28] and the lexical interpretation of the σκόλοψ as a "thorn" or "splinter," remains the most likely one. v. 7 suggests that the apostle's "thorn for the flesh" was given in the time of the events mentioned in v. 2,[29] i.e., in that part of his life to which allusion is made in Gl. 1:21. Whether there is specific reference to the result of physical ill-treatment[30] (cf. 2 C. 11:23-25) or to a complaint which Paul contracted at the beginning of his missionary work it is obviously impossible to say.[31] The context does not indicate that his affliction attracts general attention. v. 9a and 10 make it probable that it hampered Paul himself in his work; a prickle or thorn would do this in the natural sphere. For a theological understanding one should not miss the point that the idea of divine instruction plainly stands behind 2 C. 12:7 (→ V, 623, 31 ff.); this is prophylactic here: ἵνα μὴ ὑπεραίρωμαι. The physical disability keeps the apostle from the arrogance which might result from the visions and revelations granted to him, → V, 352, 25 ff.; 357, 15 ff. He was given this insight in the answer of the Lord of the mission to his vehement request to be freed from the hampering thorn, → I, 466, 22 ff. → χάρις, → τελέω.

4. It would seem that σκόλοψ and ἀνασκολοπίζω (→ n. 7) are seldom used in Chr. literature to denote the mode of Jesus' execution.[32] In Orig. Cels. the word mostly

---

in Ltzm. K., ad loc., App., 212 f.: "The view of Schlatter ... is quite impossible," cf. also Menoud, 164. The idea of the gnawing conscience of the persecutor is not new, cf. Bruston, 414.

[23] Schl. K., 666. Bruston, 412 thinks Pl. is saying that his carnal nature, esp. pride, is put to death on the stake; he takes σκόλοψ to be the cross, v. Gl. 5:24; cf. 417 f. But v. 8 f. refutes this. Cf. on the other side Menoud → n. 26.

[24] Wnd. 2 K., 384 considers this idea seriously.

[25] Menoud, 168-170. On the theory of hindrances to Paul's missionary work, ibid., 168, cf. already the Eastern fathers, Clavier, 79, n. 2. Acc. to Andriessen the thorn refers to Jewish persecutions.

[26] Menoud, 168, n. 3 is formally right to call τῇ σαρκί a dat. incommodi, but it is a poor solution to say that σάρξ characterises Paul's desire to convert Israel as very personal and vital (Menoud following C. Masson).

[27] Cf. Clavier, 78-80 for this view.

[28] On this sense of σάρξ cf. Col. 1:24; Gl. 4:13 f.; physical life is at least included in 1 C. 7:28 too → n. 18. A μου after σαρκί (some witnesses, cf. Tisch. NT, ad loc.) is superfluous in view of the preceding μοι. On Satan as one who harms the σάρξ cf. 1 C. 5:5 (cf. 10:10). Naturally Satan's part is less emphasised in 2 C. 12:7 than 1 C. 5:5.

[29] Stressed by Bchm. K., ad loc., 398; cf. Menoud, 164.

[30] Some Gk. fathers thought the ref. was to the persecutions themselves (Plummer, 350), cf. also Severianus of Gabala (Staab, 297, 22 f.). The common theory of migraine (dolorem, ut aiunt, auriculae vel capitis, Tert. Pud., 13 [CSEL, 20, p. 245, 8] cf. Preis. Zaub., II, 36, 152 → 411, 9 f.) is to be rejected since the ref. is to Satan's work, and hence to persecutions, cf. Photius of Constantinople: oppressions of men serving Satan (Staab, 602, 7-9).

[31] On the endless debate about Paul's complaint → III, 819, 15 ff. For a basic and very restrained discussion cf. A. Deissmann, Paulus² (1925), 49.

[32] Neither word occurs in the post-apost. fathers, Apologists, Cl. Al., Orig. Comm. in Mt., Joh., etc.

comes from Cels.,[33] though once Orig. himself uses it when he says that Jesus resolved to endure hanging on the stake (τὸ ἐπὶ σκόλοπος κρεμασθῆναι).[34] ἀνασκολοπίζειν, too, is usually in quotations in Orig. Cels.: of Christ in II, 36, of Chr. martyrs in VIII, 39; VII, 40 (p. 191, 14 f.), though Orig. himself adopts it, e.g., in III, 32 (p. 229, 9) in a gen. note on crucifixion alongside and in the same sense as σταυροῦν. Hipp. has ἀνασκολοπίζεσθαι of Jesus in his account of the teaching of the Marcionite Apelles, Ref., VII, 38, 4. In the same connection Epiph. has σταυροῦσθαι, Haer., 44, 2 and 7. Eus. Hist. Eccl., II, 25, 5 uses ἀγασκολοπισθῆναι to describe the manner of Peter's death. σκόλοψ is also found (c. 450) in the empress Eudoxia for the cross of Jesus, De Sancto Cypriano,[35] I, 47, 77, 191; σκόλοψ θεῖος, II, 413, also σταυρός, I, 63, 171, 212; II, 382, 392, 404, 458. While σκόλοψ and ἀνασκολοπίζειν do occur in Chr. writings, there is hardly an instance of ἀνασταυροῦν.[36] Christ crucified death, Cl. Al. Protr., 114, 4; τῷ ἰκρίῳ προσηλοῦτο ἀνασταυρούμενον, Eus. Theoph. Fr., 3 (p. 13*, 22). Obviously a fixed usage developed quite early in relation to the cross of Jesus ; προσηλοῦν occurs only occasionally, Ps.-Clem. Hom., 11, 20, 4.

Delling

┌─────────────────────────────────┐
│   σκοπός, σκοπέω, │
│   κατασκοπέω, κατάσκοπος │
└─────────────────────────────────┘

† σκοπός.

1. The word [1] is attested from Hom. in two senses : a. it denotes one who directs a watchful glance on something, e.g., as an overseer, Hom. Il., 23, 359; γυναικῶν δμφάων, Od., 22, 396; also a spy *sensu malo*, Od., 22, 156; kings and gods are σκοποί of a *polis,* Pind. Olymp., 1, 54 etc., up above is Zeus the watcher, the refuge of all the afflicted : [2] τὸν ὑψόθεν σκοπὸν ἐπισκόπει, φύλακα πολυπόνων βροτῶν, Aesch. Suppl. 381 ff. The most common use from Hom. Il., 2, 792 is the military one for the guard, spy, or scout, ἀπὸ τειχέων σκοποί, Eur. Tro., 956; σκοποὺς δὲ κἀγὼ καὶ κατοπτῆρας στρατοῦ ἔπεμψα, Aesch. Sept. c. Theb., 36 f. b. σκοπός means the "mark," e.g., of shooting in Hom. Od., 22, 6, which one may hit (τυχεῖν Pind. Nem., 6, 27) or miss (ἁμαρτάνειν, Plat. Theaet., 194a). Thus man has a goal which controls his whole life οὗτος ἔμοιγε δοκεῖ ὁ σκοπὸς εἶναι πρὸς ὃν βλέποντα δεῖ ζῆν, καὶ πάντα εἰς τοῦτο τὰ αὑτοῦ συντείνοντα καὶ τὰ τῆς πόλεως, ὅπως δικαιοσύνη παρέσται καὶ σωφροσύνη τῷ μακαρίῳ μέλλοντι ἔσεσθαι ..., Plat. Gorg., 507d cf. Resp.,

---

[33] Orig. Cels., II, 55, 68 f. The ref. is to two passages in Cels., the second quoted more than once in II, 68 f. In a third passage Cels. has σταυρός, VI, 34 and 36. ἀνασταυροῦν is not attested in Cels., cf. the weaker attestation in Luc. as compared with ἀνασκολοπίζειν → n. 6.

[34] Cels., II, 69 (p. 191, 22 f.).

[35] Ed. A. Ludwich (1897).

[36] Orig. Comm. in Joh., 20, 89 f. on 8:40 with ref. to and in the sense of Job 6:6.

σ κ ο π ό ς. Note : My assistant Dieter Nestle made a substantial contribution to this art. He checked and supplemented the philological material. Bibl.: Liddell-Scott, Pr.-Bauer[5], *s.v.* and the comm. on Phil. 3:14.

[1] On the formation as nomen agentis cf. Schwyzer, I, 459.

[2] For Aesch. cf. J. G. Droysen, ed. W. Nestle[2] (1957), 141.

VII, 519c, also : ἔστι δὲ σκοπὸς τυραννικὸς μὲν τὸ ἡδύ, Aristot. Pol., V, 10, p. 1311a, 4. c. Worth noting also is Polyb., 7, 8, 9 : σκοπὸν προέθηκε κάλλιστον, in which σκοπός may be transl. "model." [3]

2. The word occurs in the two main senses in the LXX too. It is usually the rendering of part. q of צפה and means "scout," "watcher" on the wall, 1 Βασ. 14:16 etc. Like the watcher the prophet watches over the people, Jer. 6:17; Ez. 3:17; 33:2, 6 f. [4] Man sees himself as the mark or target which God has set in His wrath, Job 16:12; Lam. 3:12; cf. Wis. 5:21.

3. The only instance in the NT is at Phil. 3:14 : κατὰ σκοπὸν διώκω [5] εἰς [6] τὸ βραβεῖον τῆς ἄνω κλήσεως τοῦ θεοῦ ἐν Χριστῷ Ἰησοῦ. [7] As in 1 C. 9:24 the background here is one which is common in the diatribe, namely, that of the contest in the arena (on βραβεῖον → I, 638, 17 ff.). The main point is not Christian effort — which is a *sine qua non* — but the fact that the Christian's course has a mark or goal. This is given or proclaimed to him as the λόγος τοῦ σταυροῦ τοῦ Χριστοῦ, and he has to hold to the truth of this proclamation by bearing witness through the obedience of faith that his life is now future : τὰ μὲν ὀπίσω ἐπιλανθανόμενος τοῖς δὲ ἔμπροσθεν ἐπεκτεινόμενος, v. 13. His will unites with God's will in such a way that He pursues God's goal by believing.

4. The theme of the games is also a common one in the post-apost. fathers : ἐπαναδράμωμεν ἐπὶ τὸν ἐξ ἀρχῆς παραδεδομένον ἡμῖν τῆς εἰρήνης σκοπόν, 1 Cl., 19, 2; cf. 2, 4; 6, 2. The term "goal of peace" (explicative gen.) may be explained by the fact that here at the beginning of a new section, as in 2, 2 and 15, 1, the author introduces the key-term of 1 Cl. : εἰρήνη (cf. 63, 2). Cf. also 63, 1: ἐπὶ τὸν προκείμενον ἡμῖν ἐν ἀληθείᾳ σκοπόν. 2 Cl., 19, 1 is interesting : σκοπὸν πᾶσιν τοῖς νέοις θήσομεν, since here σκοπός has the sense of "model" which is not generally mentioned in the lex. [8] → IV, 667, 13 ff. [9]

† σκοπέω.

A. Outside the New Testament.

1. With the corresponding forms we find σκοπέω [1] (from Pindar) in Attic for the traditional pres. and imperf. forms of σκέπτομαι (so Hom.); forms apart from the pres. are found only from the post-class. period. The meaning is "to look at," esp. "to look at

---

[3] Cf. Kn. Cl. on 2 Cl., 19, 1.
[4] σκοπός has a special sense in Hos. 9:10; Na. 3:12 for רָהוּבָּכ "early fig."
[5] κατασκοπῶν acc. to Ti syp mg arm etc.
[6] ἐπὶ א D G al.
[7] So ℌ א pm as against G and D.
[8] Kn. Cl., ad loc.
[9] Acc. to E. Bizer, "Die reformierte Orthodoxie u. der Cartesianismus," ZThK, 55 (1958), 340-347 the word *scopus* has had from the time of the Dutch theologian Christoph Wittich (Leiden, 1682) a special emphasis as a hermeneutical principle in bibl. exegesis. Wittich was a Cartesian and was close to Coccejus.

σ κ ο π έ ω. [1] On the formation as a "deverbative" of σκέπτομαι cf. Schwyzer, I, 720.

critically" as the judge does τὴν δὲ τούτων γάμου χρόνου συμμετρίαν τε καὶ ἀμετρίαν ὁ δικαστὴς σκοπῶν κρινέτω, Plat. Leg., XI, 925a, or the philosopher σκοπεῖσθαι οὖν χρὴ ἀνδρείως τε καὶ εὖ, καὶ μὴ ῥᾳδίως ἀποδέχεσθαι ..., σκεψάμενον δέ, ἐὰν εὕρῃς, μεταδιδόναι καὶ ἐμοί, Plat. Crat., 440d; cf. Phaedr., 270c; 230a etc.; Antiphon Fr., 44 B, col., 2, 15-20 (Diels⁸, II, 353), or the historian ἐκ δὲ τεκμηρίων ὧν ἐπὶ μακρότατον σκοποῦντί μοι πιστεῦσαι ξυμβαίνει, ... νομίζω ..., Thuc., I, 1, 3, but also the one who in the theatre inspects the faces of the spectators with ref. to their callings τῶνδε τοίνυν τῶν θεωμένων σκόπει τὰ πρόσωφ', ἵνα γνῷς τὰς τέχνας, Aristoph. Pax, 543 f. This inspection can also be with a view to ascertaining a propitious time σκοποῦντες καιρόν, Thuc., IV, 23, 2, or avoiding danger σκοπῆτε καὶ τηρῆτε μὴ καὶ προσπέσῃ ὑμῖν ... πρᾶγμα δεινόν, Aristoph. Thes., 580 f., or accomplishing a purpose σκόπει, ὅπως ἂν ἀποθάνοιμεν ἀνδρικώτατα, Aristoph. Eq., 80 f. Finally σκοπεῖν can also mean "to hold something as a model before one's eyes" τὰς Ἀμαζόνας σκόπει, ἃς Μίκων ἔγραψ' ... μαχομένας, Aristoph. Lys., 678 f.

2. σκοπεῖν occurs only twice in the LXX: Εσθ. 8:12g : σκοπεῖν δὲ ἔξεστιν ... ὑμᾶς ἐκζητοῦντας, and 2 Macc. 4:5 : τὸ δὲ σύμφορον κοινῇ ... σκοπῶν, while σκοπεύειν, which is not used in the NT and which means "to have a watchful eye on," occurs 7 times at Ex. 33:8; 1 Βασ. 4:13; Job 39:29; Prv. 5:21; 15:3; Cant. 7:5; Na. 2:2.

B. In the New Testament.

1. With the exception of Lk. 11:35 σκοπεῖν occurs only in Paul. Phil. 3:17 (→ IV, 667, 26 ff.) reminds us of the sense "to consider something critically and then to hold something before one as a model on the basis of the inspection," → lines 1 ff. The apostle gives the admonition: συμμιμηταί μου γίνεσθε, ἀδελφοί, καὶ σκοπεῖτε τοὺς οὕτω περιπατοῦντας καθὼς ἔχετε τύπον ἡμᾶς, because many others lead their lives as enemies of the cross of Christ, being shamefully out to get what is earthly, v. 18 f. Less precise[2] in its usage is the impressive warning in R. 16:17: παρακαλῶ δὲ ὑμᾶς, ἀδελφοί, σκοπεῖν[3] τοὺς τὰς διχοστασίας καὶ τὰ σκάνδαλα παρὰ τὴν διδαχὴν ἣν ὑμεῖς ἐμάθετε[4] ποιοῦντας, καὶ ἐκκλίνετε[5] ἀπ' αὐτῶν. v. 18 draws on Phil. 3:19. The passage is less broad than Phil. 4:9, 11 and reminds us of what may be an editorial gloss[6] at R. 6:17b. Paul's concern may be seen again in the radical expression in 2 C. 4:18: μὴ σκοπούντων ἡμῶν τὰ βλεπόμενα ἀλλὰ τὰ μὴ βλεπόμενα· τὰ γὰρ βλεπόμενα πρόσκαιρα, τὰ δὲ μὴ βλεπόμενα αἰώνια, "we do not look at what presents itself to the eye but (regard) what does not present itself to the eye, since the former perishes with time and only the latter endures for ever," → III, 463, 38 ff.; V, 349, 22 ff. Thus the σκοπῶν will make a critical decision between the eternal and the transitory and keep from what presents itself to the eye because he knows something better. In relation to brothers who are guilty of specific faults we then read : σκοπῶν σεαυτόν, μὴ καὶ σὺ πειρασθῇς, Gl. 6:1. This self-examination

---

[2] Cf. Phil. 3:2 : βλέπετε τοὺς κύνας, Mt. 7:15 : προσέχετε ἀπὸ τῶν ψευδοπροφητῶν; but σκοπεῖν is again non-interchangeable in 2 C. 4:18.

[3] ἀσφαλῶς σκοπεῖτε D G it ; Vg : rogo (cf. ἐρωτῶ D*) autem vos fratres, ut observetis eos, qui ...

[4] add λέγοντας ἢ p⁴⁶ D G it.

[5] ἐκκλίνατε p⁴⁶ A ℵ D G pl.

[6] R. Bultmann, "Glossen im Römerbrief," ThLZ, 72 (1947), 202.

finds a criterion in the admonition in Phil. 2:4 : μὴ τὰ ἑαυτῶν ἕκαστοι σκοποῦν-τες, [7] ἀλλὰ καὶ [8] τὰ ἑτέρων ἕκαστοι. The rule of 2:12 f. applies to τὰ ἑαυτῶν; in Paul only the fear of God can τὸ ἑαυτοῦ σκοπεῖν. [9]

2. Lk. 11:35 [10] has been replaced by Mt. 6:23b in D it. But if Mt. 6:23b seems to be a projection in relation to 6:22, 23a, this is even more true of Lk. 11:35, 36 in relation to 11:34. The one responsible for the pedantic v. 36 seems to have seen in v. 35 a transition (though the οὖν in v. 36 is in juxtaposition to that of v. 35): σκόπει οὖν μὴ τὸ φῶς τὸ ἐν σοὶ σκότος ἐστίν. Vg : vide ergo ne lumen, quod in te est, tenebrae sint. The saying is thus to be taken as an indirect counterquestion, [11] and σκόπει μή as par. to Epictetus' ὅρα μόνον, μὴ Νερωνιανὸν ἔχει χαρακτῆρα, Diss., IV, 5, 18.

Lk. 11:35 runs : "Take heed ; test whether the light in you is darkness." This is an idea which can also be applied morally, → VI, 555, 28 ff. [12] The involved mode of expression in Lk. 11:34-36 should not mislead us as to the fact that the ὀφθαλμός and σκοπεῖν, i.e., the eye and scrutiny in the sphere of the → σῶμα (here the whole man), denote the will, its orientation, and therewith the self-examination appropriate to the will. In keeping is the fact that the glance can convey all that the will intends. [13] What is to be tested, then, is whether one is free from stimulations which cloud the glance. This direction of the glance, which is also indicated in Mk. 7:15 ff. and par., is carried a stage further in Lk. 11:36, as though the wishes could be adjusted according to faith. Thus the originally hermeneutical significance of the dominical saying has been given an ascetic twist.

C. The Post-Apostolic Fathers.

1 Cl., 51, 1 runs : καὶ ἐκεῖνοι δέ, . . ., ὀφείλουσιν τὸ κοινὸν τῆς ἐλπίδος σκοπεῖν. Only the whole church and not just a party can be the bearer of Christian hope ; "these" should remember this and thus understand the letter to be an expression of this hope which includes all ; then they would be ἀρχηγοὶ στάσεως.

† κατασκοπέω.

1. This word, usually mid., does not occur before Eur. Eur. Hel., 1606 f. says of Menelaos : ἔχων ὅπλα, ὅποι νοσοῖεν ξύμμαχοι κατασκοπῶν. In Xenoph. Cyrop.,

---

[7] vl. σκοπεῖτε or σκοπείτω if ἕκαστος is read.

[8] D* G K pc it vg^cl om. Vg : non quae sua sunt singuli considerantes, sed (et) ea quae aliorum.

[9] Cf. Lysias in Plat. Phaedr., 232d.

[10] On what follows cf. W. Brandt, "Der Spruch vom lumen internum," ZNW, 14 (1913), 97-116, 177-201, esp. 179 f.

[11] Bl.-Debr. § 370, 3.

[12] This thought reminds us of the passage from Aristot. Topica, I, 17, p. 108a, 11 quoted in Kl. Mt. on 6:23b : ὡς ὄψις ἐν ὀφθαλμῷ νοῦς ἐν ψυχῇ, also Philo Op. Mund., 53 : ὅπερ γὰρ νοῦς ἐν ψυχῇ, τοῦτ' ὀφθαλμός ἐν σώματι, Epicharmus in Cl. Al. Strom., VII, 4, 27, 5: καθαρὸν ἂν τὸν νοῦν ἔχῃς, ἅπαν τὸ σῶμα καθαρὸς εἶ. Schl. Lk., 518 on 11:35 adduces in relation to σκόπει the expressions ἐσκόπουν τί δεῖ ποιεῖν, Jos. Ant., 6, 8, τὸ δίκαιον σκοπῶν, Ant., 12, 30 and σκοπεῖσθαι κελεύοντες τί πρακτέον ἐστὶν αὐτοῖς, Vit., 313.

[13] Cf. Mt. 20:15 and the Jewish par. in Kl. Mt. on 6:22.

VII, 1, 39 it can also be transl. by "to look around critically" : ἀναβῆναι ἐπὶ τῶν πύργων τινὰ καὶ κατασκέψασθαι εἴ πη καὶ ἄλλο τι μένοι τῶν πολεμίων. More specifically, as a stronger form of the simple, it means "to spy out" : ναῦν δ' ἀποστεῖλαι κατασκεψομένην τὰ τῶν πολεμίων, Plut. Solon, 9, 4 (I, 83b); cf. Thuc., VI, 50, 4.

2. Τὸ κατασκοπεῖν "to spy out" (τὴν πόλιν 2 Βασ. 10:3 = τὴν γῆν 1 Ch. 19:3) LXX prefers the later κατασκοπεύειν which is found in profane Gk. only from the 2nd cent. B.C. There is no difference in meaning. The obj. is almost always τὴν γῆν etc. Gn. 42:30; 1 Macc. 5:38; not Ex. 2:4. It is used esp. of the spies of Jos. 2:1 ff., so also in the quotation in 1 Cl., 12, 2. Cf. also Dt. 1:24; Jos. 6:23; 14:7.

3. In the only instance in the NT (Gl. 2:4) we seem to have [1] a (popular?) use which is based on military usage : that of (unwarranted) spying out which includes an element of suspicion : διὰ δὲ τοὺς παρεισάκτους ψευδαδέλφους, οἵτινες παρεισῆλθον κατασκοπῆσαι τὴν ἐλευθερίαν ἡμῶν ἣν ἔχομεν ἐν Χριστῷ Ἰησοῦ, ἵνα ἡμᾶς καταδουλώσουσιν. Not the so-called leaders of the community (οἱ δοκοῦντες στῦλοι εἶναι, v. 9) but the Judaistic "brethren" demanded a legally definable subjection of Paul, because they had joined the community to put things right, i.e., to bring under subordination to a legalistic belief in God what was to them an intolerable freedom. κατασκοπέω thus carries the nuance of distrust. It expresses a typically bureaucratic tendency which is fundamentally alien and unacceptable to the eschatological Gospel because it is quite incompatible with the χαρά of εἰρήνη, R. 14:17; 5:1-11.

† κατάσκοπος.

1. As the noun of κατασκοπέω, κατάσκοπος occurs from Hdt., I, 100, 2; 112, 1 etc. in place of the simple form and usually in the sense of "spy" : κατάσκοπον ... πολεμίων ... πέμπειν, Eur. Rhes., 125; also τῶν λόγων, Aristoph. Thes., 588 etc. In Thuc., IV, 27, 3 it means "inspector." Later it can also be used metaphorically and man can be called the κατάσκοπος βίου, Secundus Sententiae, 7. [1]

2. In the LXX (10 times) κατάσκοπος is used for part. pi of רגל in the sense of "spy," Gn. 42:9-34 (6 times). Absalom's spies are called this in 2 Βασ. 15:10, while the word has a specifically hostile sense in Sir. 11:30 : καρδία ὑπερηφάνου ... ὡς ὁ κατάσκοπος ἐπιβλέπει πτῶσιν.

3. In the NT κατάσκοπος is used only in Hb. 11:31 in connection with the spies of Jos. 2:1 ff. [2] Some MSS [3] also emend the ἀγγέλους of Jm. 2:25 to κατασκόπους.

Fuchs

κ α τ α σ κ ο π έ ω. [1] The phrase "to spy out our freedom" is difficult. The statement carries the nuance of inquiry with a claim to the right of supervision, which corresponds to ἐπισκέπτομαι (→ II, 599). In view of the play on words in Phil. 3:2 and Gl. 5:12 there is reason to suppose that the κατασκοπῆσαι of the text ironically catches up an ἐπισκοπῆσαι which the (Galatian?) brethren were using.

κ α τ ά σ κ ο π ο ς. [1] Ed. F. W. A. Mullach, Fragmenta Philosophorum Graecorum, I (1860), 513. Cf. also Epict. Diss., III, 22, 24.
[2] Cf. 1 Cl., 12, 2.
[3] C Kmg L 1739 al ff (*exploratores*) syp. hmg.

---

† σκορπίζω, † διασκορπίζω,
σκορπισμός

---

1. σκορπίζω, [1] "to scatter," "disperse," "divide," is Ionic acc. to Phryn. Ecl., 193; it is used by Hecataeus of Miletus, and corresponds to Attic σκεδάννυμι. The note of Phryn. is the only ref. to its use in the early Gk. period. It is fairly common in Hell. lit. The first instance is in Polyb., 1, 47, 4 : The surge and violent flow cause that materials put in to erect a dam are at once torn away and dispersed (παρωθεῖσθαι καὶ διασκορπίζεσθαι). Cf. also Polyb., 27, 2 and 10; then Strabo, IV, 4, 6; Plut. De Timoleonte, 4 (I, 237d); Ps.-Luc. Asin., 32; Ael. Var. Hist., 13, 45; also pap.: P. Lond., I, 131, 421; P. Herm., I, 7, 11 and 18; 28, 14; P. Flor., II, 175, 22; P. Leid., 10, 8, 39; 5, 11 and 19. [2]

2. In the LXX it is used for various Hbr. equivalents : פּוּץ is obviously the most important, but note also פָּזַר (esp. in later Jewish writings) [3] and פָּרַד. The compound διασκορπίζω is more important. [4] For the same Hbr. words LXX also uses the group διασπείρειν (διασπορά) and lays even greater stress on this. The bibl. material thus demands that both Gk. verbs : (δια)σκορπίζω and διασπείρω, be considered.

3. In the OT σκορπίζω occurs for God's judgment on the enemies of the Psalmist, 2 S. 22:15 (ψ 17:15); in the parallelism ἐξίστημι (συνταράσσω) is used. In the same style ψ 143:6 prays for the scattering of enemies (σκορπίζω, συνταράσσω). This is in the Sinai tradition and reflects ideas of the holy war against God's enemies. God intervenes in the earthly battle with thunder and lightning and frightens and chases away the enemy. [5] In Wis. 17:3 there is a description of

---

σ κ ο ρ π ί ζ ω, σ κ ο ρ π ι σ μ ό ς. Bibl.: Pass., s.v. διασκορπίζω and σκορπίζω; Liddell-Scott, s.v.; Hatch-Redp., 310; 1275 f.; Pr.-Bauer, s.v. διασκορπίζω, σκορπίζω, σκορπισμός.

[1] The verb σκορπίζειν is derived from σκορπίος "scorpion," also a military engine for shooting arrows, Hero mechanicus, Belopoeica, 74, 6 (ed. R. Schneider [1907]); Plut. De Marcello, 15 (I, 306e); IG², II, 1627, 333; for other senses of ὁ σκορπίος cf. Liddell-Scott, s.v. It is related to Anglo-Saxon sceorfan "to scrape" and Old High German scirbi "fragment," scarbōn "to cut in pieces." Gk. καρπός, Lat. carpo etc. seem to come from (s)qer(e)p from the Indo-Eur. root (s)qer "to cut," "to cleave." Cf. on this P. Persson, Beiträge z. idg. Wortforschung (1912), 786 and 861; Walde-Pok., II, 581; Hofmann, s.v.; Boisacq, s.v.
[2] Moult.-Mill., s.v. σκορπίζω.
[3] Jastrow, s.v. פּוּר.
[4] Cf. Hatch-Redp., s.v. διασκορπίζω. Acc. to Thackeray, 285 διασκορπίζω with διασπείρω is usually lit. while διασκεδάννυμι is esp. used for "to scatter" in a transf. sense.
[5] The traditional and historical cultic connection with Sinai is seen and rightly emphasised by A. Weiser, Die Psalmen, AT Deutsch, 14⁴ (1955) on 18:15. On the historical understanding cf. W. F. Albright, Archaeology and the Religion of Israel (1953), 117 f.; G. Widengren, "Early Hebrew Myths and their Interpretation" in S. H. Hooke, Myth, Ritual and Kingship (1958), 163. Ref. is made here to connections with Canaanite motifs. The terminology and image exert further influence up to the Dead Sea Scrolls : Enemies

the fate of the transgressor who sins against the holy people — the reference is to Egypt as a type of the opponent of God in primal time. The Egyptians are scattered (ἐσκορπίσθησαν) by fearful wonders and through phantoms are gripped by terror (ἐκταρασσόμενοι). The great word of judgment in Ez. 5:1-17 threatens the besieged inhabitants of Jerusalem with decimation by fire, sword and dispersion. The final third [6] will be scattered to the four winds. Different yet related is the threat in Zech. 13:7-9 : The sword will smite the shepherd of God, the people of His fellowship, and the sheep will be scattered. [7] The metaphor refers to historical events but has apocalyptic traits, and one is perhaps to see a reference to the woes of the Messiah.

4. That Zech. 13:7 points to the future is proved by Damasc. 19:7-9 (9:3 f.), which expressly quotes and paraphrases the OT scripture. When the Messiahs of Aaron and Israel come, the sword will smite sinners and the unfaithful. The paradoxical feature that God will smite the good shepherd, the man of His fellowship, is not expounded. The Damascus community identifies itself with the scattered sheep. The poor of the sheep (עֲנִיֵּי הַצֹּאן) are those who have regard to God (= keep faith with Him). In the day of visitation they will be delivered like those who bear the sign of deliverance on their foreheads, Ez. 9:4. But the hand of God wields the sword against the rest (הַנִּשְׁאָרִים) These are men outside the sect who misuse God's gifts. Acc. to the Dead Sea Manual members of the community are scattered in dwellings abroad, 1 QS 6:2. Similarly the stay in Damascus is regarded as a sojourn in a foreign land, Damasc. 6:5 (8:6).

On the basis of the threats in Dt. which proclaim the dispersion of Israel in case of disobedience (Dt. 4:27 f.; 28:64), later Judaism regards the rise of the dispersion as a divine judgment, → II, 100, 4 ff. Sir. 48:15 emphasises that in spite of the miracles of Elijah and Elisha the people did not repent but sinned further until the land was taken from them and they were scattered throughout the world (διεσκορπίσθησαν ἐν πάσῃ τῇ γῇ). Yet later the dispersion is also the place of God's presence. Cf. Nu. r., 7, 10 on 5:2 : When the Israelites are scattered, the divine presence (= shechinah) is with them. In bPes., 87b we find the thesis of R. Hoshaiah : "The Holy One, blessed be He, did Israel a favour by dispersing them among the nations." Ps. Sol. 17:11-14 (an addition) depicts the wicked deeds of Pompey : He emptied the land of its inhabitants and sent them to the far West. This is an allusion to the disaster of 63 B.C. [8] An older passage (17:16 ff.) is directed against the rule of the Hasmoneans : "The righteous who love assemblies of the saints fled before them like birds fluttering from their nests. They wandered in the wilderness to save their souls from destruction, and it seemed to them worth while to be in exile if life at least was saved. They were scattered abroad over the whole earth by the wicked (ὁ σκορπισμὸς αὐτῶν)." Here, too, the σκορπισμός of the righteous is understood in terms of salvation history. A constantly repeated prayer and promise is that in the future God's judgment will be lifted from the people and the dispersion will end ; Tob. 13:5 says of God : "(He will) gather us (συνάξει) from all the peoples wherever you have been scattered (σκορπισθῆτε). The 10th

---

are as chaff before the wind, 1 QH 7:22 f. On the trumpets to be blown for departure (→ 82, 3 ff.) stands: "Mighty acts of God when He scatters the foe" (לְהָפִיץ אוֹיֵב) 1 QM 3:5, and on those for retreat from the battle : "The gathering of God" (אֹסֶף אֵל) 1 QM 3:10. The Kittim are scattered till assembly is no longer possible (play on words וְכִתִּיִּים יִכָּתוּ) 1 QM 18:2.

[6] LXX τέταρτον as distinct from Mas. v. 2 : διασκορπίσεις, v. 12 B σκορπιῶ and A διασπερῶ, the better text διασκορπιῶ, cf. J. Ziegler, Septuaginta, 16, 1: Ezechiel (1952) on 5:2, 12.

[7] While the chief witnesses read ἐκοπάσατε A has διασκορπισθήσονται. Here there is perhaps assimilation to the Synoptics. The sing. τὸν ποιμένα of many MSS seems to be an assimilation to the Mas.

[8] K. G. Kuhn, Die älteste Textgestalt d. Ps. Sal. (1937), 64 f.

petition of the Sh. E. is to the same effect : "Blessed be thou, Lord, who dost gather the dispersed of His people Israel."

Philo recalls that in isolation and dispersion men can be bitten by the serpent, i.e., lust and passion, and that God sends a cordial from the rock of His wisdom and heals the soul, Leg. All., II, 84 ff. The term ἐσκορπισμένοι refers to those who have left relatives, friends and country, and Philo associates it with the image of the scorpion in Dt. 8:15. Here, too, one finds the motif of the *diaspora*. σκορπίζω in used in a military sense in 1 Macc. 4:4; 10:83; 2 Macc. 14:13; Jos. Ant., 6, 116; 13, 96. It is used of the spreading of a rumour in Jos. Ant., 16, 10 (ἐσκόρπιζον τοὺς τοιούτους λόγους). bBB, 10b mentions a word of advice given by R. Eliezer : "What does one do to get children ? One disperses (יְפַזֵּר) money among the poor."

5. In the Synoptic sayings we find the two-membered, mashal-like dominical word : "He that is not with me is against me ; and he that gathereth not with me scattereth abroad," Mt. 12:30; Lk. 11:23. [9] There is no reason to think that this is not an authentic saying of Jesus, e.g., on the ground that it contradicts Mk. 9:40. [10] Impelled by God's Spirit, it was perhaps directed to undecided and procrastinating hearers, such as the Pharisees of Galilee. He who refuses to follow and acknowledge Jesus disrupts and hinders God's own work. God Himself accomplishes through Him the eschatological gathering of the children of God, Jn. 11:52.

In fact there is a political par. in Cicero Pro Ligario, 11. Here Cic. summons Caesar : *Valeat tua vox illa, quae vicit. Te enim dicere audiebamus nos omnes adversarios putare, nisi qui nobiscum essent, te omnes, qui contra te non essent, tuos.* The followers of Pompey saw opponents in political neutrals, Caesar the political realist saw friends. Expressions of this kind were probably widespread. But the saying of Jesus in Mt. 12:30 and par. is undoubtedly historical and Palestinian. The saying added to Mk. 9:39 in v. 40 perhaps comes from another situation. It is more sober and considered than Mt. 12:30, nor does it refer to Jesus' own mission (μετ' ἐμοῦ) but to the work of a fellowship (καθ' ἡμῶν). [11]

For the antithesis of scattering and gathering cf. also the mashal-like saying of Hillel : "At the time when men gather, scatter, and when they scatter, gather," bBer., 63a; jBer., 9 (14d, 5 f.); T. Ber., 7, 14. It is likely that the underlying Hbr. verbs are כָּנַס pi and פָּזַר pi and that the basic ref. is to Palestinian practices and images connected with the harvest. The original meaning of Hillel's saying can no longer be determined. Jewish tradition took the saying to refer to the scattering and withholding of the Torah according to the receptivity of the people. On the other hand the antithesis of gathering and scattering in S. Dt., 321 on 32:25 (137b) is interpreted as follows : "In time of war gather the foot (do not hold it back) lest thou fall into the power of the enemy ; in time of famine scatter the foot (go many different ways) to buy food." [12]

---

[9] Cf. the older discussion of this in W. Nestle, "Wer nicht mit mir ist, ist wider mich," ZNW, 13 (1912), 84-87; A. Fridrichsen, "Wer nicht mit mir ist, ist wider mich," ZNW, 13 (1912), 273-280; also C. F. Burney, *The Poetry of Our Lord* (1925), 68, 132; Bultmann Trad., 11, 78, 84, 103, 161, 181. Formally cf. the saying of Hillel in Ab., 1, 13 : "He who does not add takes away."

[10] In Lk. 11:23 א* Θ syrs add με. Acc. to Damasc. 13:9 (16:2 f.) the overseer (מְבַקֵּר) has the duty of bringing back all rejected members as a shepherd does his flock.

[11] Schl. Mk. on 9:40 rightly sees that "in contrast to Mt. 12:30 this saying refers not merely to Jesus but to us, to Him and to the community founded by Him."

[12] Cf. Bacher Tannaiten, I² (1903), 6 f. and Str.-B., I, 635.

According to the traditional Synoptic account in Mk. 14:27; Mt. 26:31 Jesus quotes Zechariah 13:7 when going up the Mt. of Olives for the Feast of the Passover. He has in view His approaching passion. The blow from God smites the shepherd and the flock is scattered (διασκορπισθήσονται). The catastrophic character of this eschatological event is worked out in the Johannine parallel in Jn. 16:32. The hour has now come for the dispersal of the band of disciples and it means that Jesus, the Servant of the Lord, is forsaken by men. [13] According to Jn. 11:52 Jesus dies for His people. The Evangelist is adopting here what is obviously an ancient Jewish Christian thesis. But Jesus does not die for His people alone ; His aim is also to gather into one the dispersed children of God. Now it is the OT and Jewish expectation that in the future the dispersed people of God will be gathered again, Is. 43:5 ff.; Ez. 34:12 f.; Ps. Sol. 8:28. John, however, has in view the present gathering of men by the death of Jesus, Jn. 1:12 f.; 10:16: 17:21. The chief point of this second goal is that it vindicates the Gentile mission of Christianity. He who becomes a child of God by faith was already God's possession according to His plan of salvation. The Gnostic idea that the reference is a cosmic and metaphysical one to the redeemer who assembles his scattered light-members, the souls of men, is quite alien to the Evangelist. Scattering in the present epoch is for John a mark of the historical existence of the children of God, as it is for the Damascus sect → 419, 11 ff. [14] In the parable of the Good Shepherd in Jn. 10:11 ff. the contrast between (συν)άγω and σκορπίζω again plays a part. The original image, the polemic and the promise merge in the Palestinian form of address. The Good Shepherd protects and gathers, while the beast of prey scatters the flock, Jn. 10:12. A glance at the prediction of Paul in Ac. 20:29 will show how this part of the symbolism is understood practically in the life of the community.

In accordance with the OT tradition about God's victory over His earthly foe Lk. 1:51 paraphrases the OT text of ψ 88:11; in this connection it should be noted that ἐν τῷ βραχίονι is related to διεσκόρπισας in the original. The hymn of Lk. 1:51-53 has worked over elements connected with the Chasidim and even Zelotism. [15] σκορπίζω is used in a very different sense in 2 C. 9:9, which quotes ψ 111:9 : "He hath dispersed abroad ; he hath given to the poor ; his righteousness remaineth for ever." σκορπίζω bears a special emphasis here. The quotation sounds like a Jewish blessing on the righteous man whose memorial remains for ever. [16]

In the NT διασκορπίζω can take on different nuances according to the context. The juxtaposition of σπείρω and διασκορπίζω in Mt. 25:24, 26 suggests the

---

[13] Loh. Mk. on 14:27 has doubts about the wording of Mk. 14:27 (note in Mt. and Mk. πατάξω for πατάξατε or A πάταξον). Acc. to him Jn. 16:32 is to be preferred to Mk. 14:27: "... a saying of similar content might be the original saying of Jesus underlying this prophecy in Mk."

[14] E. Percy, Untersuchungen über den Ursprung d. joh. Theol. (1939), 216.

[15] Acc. to Kl. Lk., ad loc. only enemies are strictly scattered, the proud being humbled ; there is thus confusion between בָּזַר "to scatter" and בָּצַר "to reduce" (ἐλαττοῦν). Cf. P. Winter, "Magnificat and Benedictus-Maccabaean Psalms ?" Bulletin of the John Rylands Library, 37 (1954), 1-6.

[16] Cf. Wnd. 2 K., ad loc., 278-280. On the poor in Judaism — Paul adopts the vocabulary (righteousness = almsgiving, pauper = beggar) — cf. S. Krauss, Talmudische Archäol., III (1912), 63-66. Chrys. Hom. in 1 K., 20, ad loc. (MPG, 61 [1862], 533) has the paraphrase "dispensing in superabundance" (μετὰ δαψιλείας διδόναι) for σκορπίζω.

metaphor of the scattering of seed. The material used in the two verses suggests a Palestinian setting. If in Mt. 25:24, 26 διασκορπίζω means the same as the preceding σπείρω, we have synonymous parallelism.[17] On the other hand διασκορπίζω here might refer to the winnowing of grain.[18] If so θερίζω refers to the cutting of the grain and συνάγω denotes the gathering into the barn of the grain that has been purged of the chaff (ἀποθήκη). Since συνάγω is often used in this sense in the NT (Mt. 3:12; 6:26; 13:30; Lk. 12:17 f.) there is much to be said in favour of the latter interpretation.

In Lucan usage διασκορπίζω sometimes has the ring of "to waste," "to squander" (Lk. 15:13 : διεσκόρπισεν τὴν οὐσίαν αὐτοῦ, 16:1: ὡς διασκορπίζων τὰ ὑπάρχοντα).[19] Ac. 5:37 echoes the military accounts of the OT (→ 420, 7 f.): The followers of the Galilean Judas were scattered (διεσκορπίσθησαν). The reference is to Judas of Gamala, the well-known Zealot leader (Jos. Ant., 18, 4 ff.), whose end is not recounted in Jos. The account in Acts is thus the more valuable.[20]

6. In the eucharistic prayers in the Didache there is a petition for the future uniting of the scattered Church in the kingdom of God. "For as this bread was scattered (διεσκορπισμένον) on the mountains, and gathered together (συναχθέν), and became one, so let thy Church be gathered together from the ends of the earth into thy kingdom," 9, 4.[21] This prayer, which is part of the Chr. agape, has a Palestinian and Jewish Chr. ring ; its antiquity is guaranteed by the saying of Paul in 1 C. 10:7. There is no analogous metaphor in relation to the wine.[22] The connection with Johannine motifs is unmistakable. Ign., when he portrays his martyrdom, also speaks of the scattering of his bones (Ign. R., 5, 3 : σκορπισμοὶ ὀστέων). What was for the righteous of the OT a sign of extreme affliction and dereliction (ψ 21:15), or the severest punishment of the ungodly (ψ 52:6), is for Ign. the means to make him a partaker of Jesus Christ.

Michel

---

[17] In Is. 28:25 'A uses διασκορπίζω in this sense (LXX σπείρω). Yet 'A might have transl. Hbr. הֵפִיץ lit. by διασκορπίζω without regard to Gk. usage, while LXX with a true feeling for Gk. uses σπείρω.

[18] So Liddell-Scott, *s.v.* διασκορπίζω, C. F. D. Moule, "A Note on Didache 9, 4," JThSt, NS, 6 (1955), 241.

[19] Cf. Catal. Cod. Astr. Graec., II, 162, 7: τὸν πατρικὸν βίον.

[20] Cf. M. Dibelius, "Die Reden d. Ag. u. d. antike Geschichtsschreibung," *Aufsätze zur Ag.,* FRL, 60 (1951), 159 f.; Haench. Ag.[12], *ad loc.,* 211.

[21] Moule, *op. cit.* thinks the image behind Did., 9, 4 is not that of the scattered seed of which the unity of bread finally consists but the gathering up of the fragments left after the feeding of the 5000 (κλάσματα, Jn. 6:12 f.). He argues against the traditional view 1. that κλάσμα is not a good term for a unity, 2. that διασκορπίζω is never used in the sense of σπείρω, and 3, that it is hard to think of grain growing on the mountains. But διασκορπίζω does not have to denote sowing and may simply refer to the scattered nature of the grains swelling on the ears distributed across the field, while συνάγω is used gen. for the combining of these into bread. The use of κλάσμα may be based on eucharistic practice ; other traditions of the prayer have ἄρτος, e.g., Athanasius De Virginitate, 13 (MPG, 28 [1887], 265c); Const. Ap., 7, 25. Cf. on this H. Riesenfeld, "Das Brot von den Bergen," Eranos, Acta Philologica Suecana, 54 (1956), 142-150. The uniting of the grain in the bread is depicted in terms which had long been customary in Jewish descriptions of the gathering of the scattered members of God's people.

[22] We thus have an eschatological interpretation of the bread as in later Jewish Passover writings. Cf. J. Jeremias, *Die Abendmahlsworte Jesu*[3] (1960), 54, n. 3, 110 f.; J. P. Audet, *La Didachè. Instructions des Apôtres* (1958), 175, 189, 207, 463.

σκότος, σκοτία, † σκοτόω,
† σκοτίζω, † σκοτεινός

Contents: A. The Word Group in Classical Greek (and Its Influence): 1. Usage; 2. Meaning; 3. The Group in Philosophy. B. The Word Group in the Old Testament: 1. Ancient Oriental Background; 2. Usage; 3. General Features; 4. Specific Features; 5. Cosmology; 6. Eschatology; 7. Anthropology (Wisdom). C. Judaism: 1. Usage; 2. Dead Sea Scrolls; 3. Rabbinic Writings. D. Hellenism, Gnosticism: 1. General Data; 2. Philo; 3. Corpus Hermeticum; 4. Odes of Solomon; 5. The Mandaeans; 6. The Manichees; 7. Christian Gnosticism. E. The New Testament: I. Synoptic Gospels (with Acts and Revelation): 1. Literal Use; 2. Figurative Use; 3. Transferred Use; II. The Pauline Corpus: 1. Paul; 2. Colossians and Ephesians. III. John. F. The Post-Apostolic Fathers.

σ κ ό τ ο ς κ τ λ. Note: R. Bultmann, who was originally in charge of this art., has placed his rich collection of material at our disposal. Bibl.: Gen.: R. Bultmann, "Die Bdtg. d. neuerschlossenen mandäischen u. manichäischen Quellen f. d. Verständnis des Joh.-Ev.," ZNW, 24 (1925), 100-146; H. Odeberg, The Fourth Gospel (1929), 130-149; E. Percy, Untersuchungen über d. Ursprung d. joh. Theol. (1939), 23-76; S. Aalen, "Die Begriffe 'Licht' u. 'Finsternis' im AT, im Spätjudt. u. im Rabbinismus," Skrifter utgitt av det Norske Videnskaps-Akad. i Oslo, Historisk-filosofisk Klasse, 1951, 1 (1951) (with bibl.); C. H. Dodd, The Interpretation of the Fourth Gospel (1953), 30-41; also The Bible and the Greeks² (1954), 99-144; G. Baumbach, Der Dualismus d. Sektenrolle im Vergleich mit dem Dualismus in d. spätjüd. Apokalypsen u. d. Joh.-Ev., Diss. Berlin (1956). On A.: R. Bultmann, "Zur Geschichte d. Lichtsymbolik im Altertum," Philol., 97 (1948), 1-36. On B.: A. M. Gierlich, "Der Lichtgedanke in d. Psalmen," Freiburger Theol. Stud., 56 (1940). On C.: F. Nötscher, "Zur theol. Terminologie d. Qumran-Texte," Bonner Bibl. Beiträge, 10 (1956), 92-148; H. Braun, "Spätjüd. u. frühchr. Radikalismus, I," Beiträge zur Hist. Theologie, 24 (1957), v. Index s.v. "Dualismus" and σκότος; H. W. Huppenbauer, "Der Mensch zwischen zwei Welten," Abh. ThANT, 34 (1959); O. Betz, "Offenbarung u. Schriftforschung in d. Qumransekte," Wissenschaftliche Untersuchungen z. NT, 6 (1960), 111-114. On D.: 1. G. P. Wetter, "Phos," Skrifter utgifta af Kungliga Humanistiska Vetenskaps-Samfundet i Uppsala, 17, 1 (1915); W. Bousset, Kyrios Christos, FRL, 21² (1921), 172-177; Jonas Gnosis, I, 103 f., 262-283; II, 99-121; F. Cumont, Lux perpetua (1949); further bibl. in K. Prümm, Religionsgeschichtliches Hndbch. f. den Raum der altchr. Umwelt² (1953), Index, s.v. "Licht." 2. J. Pascher, "Βασιλικὴ ὁδός," Studien z. Gesch. u. Kultur des Altertums, 17, 3 f. (1931), passim; E. R. Goodenough, By Light, Light (1935); W. Völker, Fortschritt u. Vollendung bei Philo v. Alex., TU, 49, 1 (1938), 163 f., 178-192, 304-307: H. A. Wolfson, Philo, I and II (1947), passim. 3. A. J. Festugière, La révélation d'Hermès Trismégiste, I-IV (1949-54), passim, esp. IV, 241-257. 5. S. Schulz, Art. "Mandäer" in Evangelisches Kirchen-lex., II (1958), 1226-1228; K. Rudolph, "Die Mandäer, I," FRL, 74 (1960), 118-194. 6. A. Adam, Art. "Manichäismus" in Evangelisches Kirchenlex., II (1958), 1229-1233, and A. Adam, Texte zum Manichäismus, KlT, 175 (1954); G. Widengren, "Mani u. d. Manichäismus," Urban-Bücher, 57 (1961), 33, 48-76, 146-159. On E.: E. Percy, Untersuchungen über den Ursprung d. joh. Theol. (1939), 23-76; H. Bakotin, De notione lucis et tenebrarum in Ev. Joh. (1943); C. H. Dodd, The Interpretation of the Fourth Gospel (1953), 30-41 (Dodd Interpretation); W. Nauck, "Die Tradition u. d. Charakter des 1 Joh.," Wissenschaftliche Untersuchungen z. NT, 3 (1957), 61 f.; on Jn. and Qumran (apart from Nauck): K. Schaedel, Das Joh.-Ev. u. d. Kinder des Lichts, Diss. Vienna (1953); F. M. Braun, "L'arrière-fond judaïque du quatrième évang. et la communauté de l'alliance," Rev. Bibl., 62 (1955), 5-44; W. F. Albright, "Recent Discoveries in Palestine and the Gospel of St. John," The Background of the NT and Its Eschatology (Dodd Festschr.) (1956), 153-171; H. H. Malmede, Die Lichtsymbolik im NT, Diss. Bonn (1959), 431-434, 475-480.

A. The Word Group in Classical Greek (and Its Influence).

1. Usage.

The masc. σκότος [1] "obscurity," "darkness," [2] occurs from Hom. Il., 5, 47; Od., 19, 389; cf. Eur. Hec., 1. [3] As a neut. it is attested from Pind. Fr., 42, 6 (Snell), then Xenoph. An., II, 5, 9; Plat. Resp., VII, 518a. [4] The fem. σκοτία is Hell., Apoll. Rhod., IV, 1698. [5] The verb σκοτόω "to darken" is class. from Soph. Ai., 85; Plat. Resp., VII, 518a and LXX, σκοτίζω in the same sense is Hell., found rarely in Plut. Col., 24 (II, 1120e) and LXX. Both verbs are found in the NT only in the pass. [6] Of the many other derivates only σκοτεινός, first attested in Aesch. Choeph., 286, 661, is found in the NT. [7]

2. Meaning.

The group is used in both a literal and also a transferred sense. But its development is not equivalent to that of → φῶς. In comparison to this it gains independent significance only in a narrowly circumscribed circle of later syncretism. [8] The whole range of meaning may be understood in terms of the basic sense : darkness, not in connection with its optical effect, [9] but experienced as an enveloping sphere and described in its significance for existence, i.e., as a hindrance to movement and action, to foresight, as the sphere of objective peril and subjective anxiety. [10] This sense may be seen in the conferring of an attribute, e.g. στυγερός (Hom. Il., 5, 47; 13, 672; 16, 607). [11] If light is the sphere of true potentiality (→ φῶς), cutting off from light, going into the dark, means death (Hom. Il., 18, 10 f.; Eur. Iph. Aul., 1506 ff.). Death is dark, Eur. Alc., 237. In Hom. σκότος is almost

---

[1] Cf. Gothic skadus, Old High German scato, shadow ; Walde-Pok., II, 600.

[2] Opp. φάος Aesch. Choeph., 319 or φῶς Plat. Resp., VII, 518a → IV, 1123, 13 ff.

[3] The masc. is Attic, E. Fraenkel, "Beiträge z. Griech. Grammatik," Z. vgl. Spr., 43 (1910), 195-202; in the NT only Hb. 12:18 vl.

[4] Then gen. Hell. On the LXX cf. Thackeray, 159.

[5] Pr.-Bauer⁵, s.v. LXX Job 28:3; Mi. 3:6; Is. 16:3; also Is. 25:7 'A and Θ; Is. 59:9 Θ; Gn. 1:5; Ez. 12:7 Σ.

[6] LXX σκοτόω act. Qoh. 10:15 vl.; Sir. 25:17.

[7] σκοτεινός is obviously an analogous construct to φαεινός, and it then leads in turn to φωτεινός, Fraenkel, loc. cit. [Risch]; P. Kretschmer, "Literaturbericht f. d. Jahr 1910, Flexionslehre," Glotta, 4 (1912), 338.

[8] The main history of the group seems to be literary in epic, tragedy, epigram, Anth. Graec. It hardly occurs at all in inscr., pap. (v. Indexes ; Preisigke Wört.) except in some magic pap. where there is Jewish influence, cf. Preis. Zaub., I, 4, 2472; 5, 101 and 464 f. The antithesis of light and dark is naturally a favourite one, Plut. Consolatio ad uxorem, 8 (II, 610e); Col., 24 (II, 1120e). We may have the simple antithesis, Aesch. Choeph., 319; the movement from dark to light is, however, more important, Plat. Resp., VII, 518a (→ n. 45, 162).

[9] Scientific observation is naturally concerned first with the phenomenon of light connected with luminaries, cf. Emped. A 57 (Diels, I, 294, 3-17).

[10] Here the Gk. understanding is the same as that of the OT. One is "in the dark" (lit. and fig.): Aristoph. Pax, 691; Aesch. Choeph., 661 ff.; OT ψ 81:5; 90:6 (→ V, 943, 9 ff.; VI, 571, 4 ff.); one "gropes" in it (ψηλαφᾶν), Plat. Phaed., 99b; OT Dt. 28:29; Is. 59:10; Job 5:14; 12:25. On Corp. Herm., 1, 19 → VI, 240, 27 ff.

[11] This way of seeing the world is obviously different from that of the OT. The distinction is even clearer in relation to → φῶς. There are no attributes in the OT except at Qoh. 11:7 (light); on the Gk. attributes cf. B. Snell, Die Entdeckung des Geistes³ (1955), 263 f. Only in an "unnatural" sense can dark make actions possible : attack by night in Hom. Il., 10; Ju. 7:9 ff.; crime. Evil abhors the light ; men dislike doing evil in it, Eur. Herc. Fur., 1:59 f. OT Job 24:14 ff.; Sir. 23:17 ff.

always the encompassing darkness of death, Hom. Il., 4, 461. [12] Hades is dark as the realm of the dead [13] and the place of punishment: [14] shadowy existence in it is no true life → 428, 29 ff. The underworld already projects into the present life. The Eumenides are the children of Skotos and Gaia, Soph. Oed. Col., 40. [15] The dark can affect man in the form of blindness. [16] For the Greek sight is quite simply the possibility of life and self-orientation in it. [17] This helps us to understand the transition from a literal to a transferred use in the case of both φῶς and σκότος: 1. Darkness as an objective situation is concealment, obscurity, and as a subjective attitude secrecy, deception; [18] 2. it is the obscurity of a thing or a speaker; [19] and 3. it is a lack of knowledge or insight, i.e., error. [20]

3. The Group in Philosophy.

The nexus of seeing, knowing and understanding oneself in the world must be presented under → φῶς, since Greek epistemology starts, not with the confrontation of opposites, but with reflection on the process of illumination, or it views the process under the image of the way from darkness to light. [21] This judgment is not affected in the least by the formation of contrasting pairs in cosmogony (the ἀρχή or ἀρχαί), even if to some degree this does bring the innocuous assertion of contrariety (→ n. 8) into reflection. For σκότος with its non-mythical character is subordinate to other concepts like chaos or Erebos. Again, in Pythagorean lists φῶς/σκότος is only one pair in a series. [22] The word does not attain

---

[12] Cf. Eur. Phoen., 1453: καὶ χαίρετ'· ἤδη γάρ με περιβάλλει σκότος.

[13] In this case Hom. says ζόφος, Il., 15, 191; 21, 56; Od., 11, 57; cf. Aesch. Pers., 839; Eur. Hec., 1: σκότου πύλαι cf. Job 38:17. On the idea of Hades cf. Verg. Aen., VI, 264 ff. Paradoxically (Ajax longing for death in his agony) Soph. Ai., 394 f.: ἰὼ σκότος, ἐμὸν φάος, ἔρεβος ὦ φαεννότατον; Job 10:20 ff.; ἔρεβος in Hom. Il., 16, 327 (cf. 325); Od., 12, 81 etc. Acc. to Jos. Bell., 3, 375 Hades is σκοτεινός, and σκοτεινότερος for the suicide [Rengstorf]. At the latest in the Byzantine period, and probably earlier, σκοτώνω (> σκοτόω) is a current word for "to kill," and it has become the usual verb in this sense in modern Gk. [Dihle].

[14] σκότος καὶ βόρβορος are the lot of the wicked in the Eleusinian mysteries, Ael. Arist., 22, 10 (Keil); Rohde, I, 313, n. 1. Philo Exsecr., 152; Ps. Sol. 14:9.

[15] Cf. Aesch. Eum., 72: The gray children of the night ... σκότον νέμονται Τάρταρόν τε. The underworld intervenes in a very different way in the OT, manifesting itself as affliction, sickness, imprisonment, Job 17:12 f.; Ps. 49:15, 20; 88:12 → 428, 21 ff.

[16] Opp. "eyesight" in Soph. Oed. Tyr., 419 with the paradoxical "to see the dark" etc.; Eur. Phoen., 376 f., 1533 ff.; OT Dt. 28:29; NT Ac. 13:11.

[17] Bultmann Lichtsymbolik, 14 and 16.

[18] (a) Obscure Pind. Olymp., 1, 83; Nem., 7, 12 f.; Plat. Symp., 197a; concealed Xenoph. An., II, 5, 9; private Plat. Leg., VI, 781c; (b) secret Pind. Nem., 4, 40; esp. the adj. σκότιος Hom. Il., 6, 24; hide something Xenoph. Cyrop., IV, 6, 4; deception Soph. El., 1396 f.; Ant., 494.

[19] Aesch. Choeph., 661 ff.; cf. Plat. Critias, 109e: σκοτειναὶ ἀκοαί; Philo Som., II, 3: σκοτίως (opp. τηλαυγῶς) μηνύειν. Of the orator the "obscure" Heracl. (examples Diels, III, Index, s.v. σκοτεινός). In the OT only Prv. 1:6: σκοτεινὸς λόγος for מְלִיצָה, "saying with secret allusions."

[20] Knowledge through αἰσθήσεις is "obscure" compared to γνησίη through διάνοια, Democr. Fr., 11 (Diels⁷, II, 140, 14 ff.).

[21] Parm. Fr., 1 (Diels⁷, I, 228, 17 ff.); W. Jaeger, Paideia, I³ (1947), 240; also Die Theol. d. frühen gr. Denker (1953), 112-123; B. Snell, op. cit. (→ n. 11), 197-200.

[22] Cf. Aristot. Metaph., 1, 5, p. 986a, 22. Acc. to Aristoxenos' Life of Pythagoras, 11 (Diels⁷, I, 102, 5 f.) Pythagoras was a pupil of Zaratas (Zoroaster). W. Kranz (Diels⁷, I, 489) thinks there was an intellectual link, but J. Kerschensteiner, Platon u. der Orient

to high conceptual rank in philosophy. [23] Mention of darkness serves to set off
light ; it has no philosophical content of its own. [24] This may be seen in the whole
development of early nature philosophy by way of Plato's discourses on illumination (Resp., VII, 517 f.; Ep., 7, 341c d) [25] and Aristotle's ontological statement
(An., II, p. 418 ff.) to Stoicism. [26] There is no direct line from this to the light
metaphysics and dualism of later antiquity. [27] But these ideas of later antiquity
may be found in older texts (Pythagoreans, Plato, the Stoic fire → πῦρ VI,
930, 34 ff.). [28]

B. The Word Group in the Old Testament.

1. The Ancient Oriental Background.

Brightness and darkness are very important for life, thought and religion. They
denote salvation and perdition. [29] Nevertheless, there is no developed terminology. Light
is not abstracted from the luminaries. There is ref. to the sun, day and night ; the natural
basis is always clear. Since the sun shines by night in the Egypt. underworld its description as dark is obviously rare, as in the Egypt. Book of the Dead, 175 (AOT, 6 f.).
A special place is occupied by the "potter oracle" on a Gk. pap. of the 3rd cent. A.D.
which refers to the darkening of the sun in a time of crisis, this being followed by an
age of salvation, AOT, 49 ff. [30] In Babylonian cosmogony, however, the underworld is
dark, Gilgamesh epic (AOT, 150-198), the descent of Ishtar (206-212). Cosmology is
dominated by the idea of chaos and primal darkness which has left traces in the OT
→ 429, 18 ff. [31] The effect on the OT consists not merely in the development of the

---

(1945), 142 f., 211 f. (→ φῶς) is sceptical. For a fine survey cf. the mockery of Orphic
cosmogony (on this Jaeger Theol., 69-87) in Aristoph. Av., 690 ff.
[23] Heracl. (cf. later Stoicism) speaks of the "fire," Fr. 67 (Diels⁷, I, 165, 8 ff.): God is
day and night, cf. 62 (164, 9 f.): life and death ; Hippocr. in his De victu, I, 5 (183, 1 f.)
has light and darkness. On Fr., 67 cf. H. Fraenkel, "Heraclitus on God and the Phenomenal
World," Transactions and Proceedings of the American Philological Association (1938),
230-244.
[24] J. Stenzel, "Zur Entwicklung des Geistbegriffs in d. gr. Philosophie," Antike, 1 (1925),
256. A philosophical dualism is not worked out ; the antitheses of Heracl. are relative, cf.
O. Gigon, Untersuchungen zu Heraklit (1935), 20-42; in Parm. Fr., 1 (Diels⁷, I, 228, 17 ff.)
night represents non-being, cf. O. Gigon, Der Ursprung d. gr. Philosophie (1945), 247. The
mythical notion of chaos/primal darkness (Orphism) is not worked out philosophically.
Against this notion cf. Aristot. Metaph., 11, 6, p. 1071b, 26.
[25] J. Stenzel, "Der Begriff der Erleuchtung bei Platon," Die Antike, 2 (1926), 235-257;
P. Friedländer, Platon, I² (1954), 70-89 → φῶς.
[26] Since all being is physical for the Stoa it speaks of "fire" (→ VI, 930, 34 ff.) rather
than "light," which is to be differentiated → n. 23. In its view of the world there is no
place for a dark underworld. The atmosphere is black or dark, Philo Op. Mund., 29; Spec.
Leg., I, 85 etc. On the stay of souls in this cf. Rohde, II, 319 f.
[27] The constitutive factor is missing, namely, the specific linking of cosmology and
soteriology.
[28] A very fine example of the continuation of the class. view is Plut. Lat. Viv., 6 (II,
1129 f.), which contains the whole Gk. understanding in nuce. A later intensifying of the
antithesis has been detected in Plut., i.e., in his cosmological and mythically stylised descriptions, cf. Plut. Gen. Socr., 2 (II, 590 f.); Fac. Lun., 26 (II, 942b-f); esp. Plut. Is. et Os., 46 ff.
(II, 369 f.); 77 (II, 382); cf. E. Delph., 21 (II, 394a-c) → n. 33.
[29] Law of Hammurabi, col. 5, 1 ff. (AOT, 383), 26r, 18-80 (408); H. Frankfort, Kingship
and the Gods (1948), 308.
[30] On the connection with older Egypt. ideas, U. Wilcken, "Zur ägypt. Prophetie," Herm.,
40 (1905), 544-560.
[31] The chief Egypt, example is Akhnaton's hymn to the sun (AOT, 15 ff.); cf. A. Erman,

concept but also in the influence of the world-picture, the ideas of the first and last time, the upper world and the lower world. [32] We have practically no source material at all for ancient Iranian usage. A bright sphere plainly stands in confrontation with a dark sphere but there is no evidence that this antithesis was stated in the terminology of light and darkness or that these concepts parted company with their basis in nature. [33] This is not to dispute an Iranian influence on Judaism. The question is whether it shaped the dualistic usage of Judaism or whether a genuinely Jewish usage was modified by Persian ideas → n. 33. [34]

2. Usage. [35]

The field is dominated by the group חשך, [36] while אפל [37] has the same sense. עֲרָפֶל is closer to the natural phenomenon. [38] עֵיפָה occurs twice in Am. 4:13; Job 10:22. Absolute darkness is צַלְמָוֶת, understood as σκιὰ θανάτου → 428, 23 ff. No special trend may be discerned in the LXX. [39] חשך is consistently transl. by σκοτ-. Sometimes considerations

---

Die Lit. d. Ägypter (1923), 187-196, e.g., 195 : "Thou light which cometh from darkness ! Thou fat for the cattle !" Transf. use a. Egypt, Ptah causes the perjurer to see darkness by day, A. Erman, *Die Religion d. Agypter*[3] (1934), 41; "His (Pharaoh's) heart is straight ; there is no darkness in his breast," H. Kees, "Ägypten" in A. Bertholet, *Religionsgeschichtliches Lesebuch*, 10[2] (1928), 38; b. The Sumerian Job says : "For me the day is dark," S. N. Kramer, "Man and His God," *Wisdom in Israel and in the Ancient Near East*, VT Suppl., 3, Festschr. H. H. Rowley (1955), 170-182.

[32] These ideas are then modified in Israel, and the change finds expression precisely in the detaching of the concepts from the original basis.

[33] H. Lommel, *Die Religion Zarathustras* (1930), 128; O. G. v. Wesendonck, *Das Weltbild d. Iranier* (1933), 212; J. Duchesne-Guillemin, *Zoroastre, Etude critique avec une traduction commentée des Gâthâ* (1948); also *Ormazd et Ahriman. L'aventure dualiste dans l'antiquité* (1953); S. Pétrement, *Le dualisme chez Platon, les gnostiques et les manichéens*, Diss. Paris (1947); H. Humbach, *Die Gathas des Zarathustra*, I, II (1959); W. Hinz, *Zarathustra* (1961). The natural character may be seen in Yasna, 44, 5 : "What artist created the lights (plur.) and the darknesses ?" On the question form cf. Is. 40:12 ff.; Job 38, though it should be noted that the style in the OT is different. The most important ref. is Yasna, 30, 3-5. The difference between Iranian and Jewish terminology may be seen clearly from comparison with a passage influenced by this, i.e., 1 QS 3:17 ff. → 432, n. 65. On Yasna, 30, 3-5 cf. Lommel, 22 f., 163; Hinz, 92-98; H. S. Nyberg, *Die Religionen des Alten Iran* (1938), 102-109. Our oldest instances of the use of light and darkness in Parseeism are late Gk. passages : a. Plut. Is. et Os., 46 (II, 369e); unfortunately it cannot be shown that this ref. comes from the Theopomp. quoted in the context, FGrHist., IId, 365, 20 ff. in Comm. on Theopomp. Fr., 65, ad loc.; T. Hopfner, *Plut. über Is. u. Os.*, II (1941), 201-215; b. Διόδωρος δὲ ὁ Ἐρετριεὺς καὶ Ἀριστόξενος ὁ μουσικός φασι πρὸς Ζαράταν τὸν Χαλδαῖον ἐληλυθέναι Πυθαγόραν· τὸν δὲ ἐκθέσθαι αὐτῷ δύο εἶναι ἀπ' ἀρχῆς τοῖς οὖσιν αἴτια, πατέρα καὶ μητέρα· καὶ πατέρα μὲν φῶς, μητέρα δὲ σκότος, Hipp. Ref., I, 2, 12. The alleged Basilides fr. in Hegemonius Acta Archelai, 67, 4 ff. is quite worthless. On the supposed influence of Zoroaster on Pythag. → n. 22, also J. Bidez-F. Cumont, *Les mages hell.*, I (1938), 33-50. Other texts are Plut. Aetia Romana, 26 (II, 270d e); Porph. Vit. Pyth., 41. The dubious aspect is in the transl. into Gk., which suggests the description of a known dualism in these terms, esp. later, cf. on Plut. → n. 28; cf. also the list of opposing divine predicates in Plut. E. Delph., 21 (II, 394a b).

[34] There is a similar problem in the Gk. world.

[35] Cf. Gierlich, 67-112 for a survey.

[36] חָשַׁך (σκοτόω, σκοτάζω, σκοτίζω), מַחְשָׁך, חֹשֶׁך, חָשֹׁך, חֲשֵׁכָה, חָשַׁך.

[37] אֹפֶל, אֲפֵלָה, אָפֵל.

[38] An important equivalent is γνόφος, with theophany as the material context.

[39] Sometimes there is mistransl., e.g., אֹפֶל "darkness" for עֹפֶל "hill" at 4 Βασ. 5:24 — an example of leaving out the guttural [Katz]. Alterations of sense elsewhere do not affect the term, cf. Ps. 18:11; Job 15:22 ff. There is spiritualising in Mi. 3:6. On Wis. → 431, 1 f.

of sound affect the transl. [40] The whole group is most common in the Wisdom lit. and certain sections of the prophets. Materially, in addition to designation of the darkness of night, there are three main areas of use : a. cosmology (→ 429, 18 ff.), in which elements of the oriental view of the world are revised along the lines of the monotheistic belief in the Creator ; b. eschatology (→ 430, 1 ff.); and c. anthropology (→ 430, 12 ff.). It is only in Judaism that the group takes on true theological significance. [41]

3. General Features.

As in the early Greek world (→ 424, 10 ff.), so also in the OT natural darkness is not viewed theoretically but mentioned as the content of direct experience. The onset of darkness corresponds to the streaming in of light (Ps. 112:4). Darkness envelops (Job 23:17); one finds oneself in it → n. 10. The connection with natural phenomena, also with the regular rhythm of day and night or metereological changes (clouds), is, of course, more strongly asserted than in the Greek world. [42] Darkness as it is experienced can serve to describe the human situation (Jer. 13:16), especially as life is lived in this world, in the sphere of brightness (light = life), or, where there is greater reflection, of the ordered alternation of brightness and darkness → 429, 18 ff. Darkness denotes the whole range of what is harmful, or evil — in the sense of the threat to life, of what is bad for me, as well as in that of moral evil — or fatal. Blindness (→ n. 16) is meant in Dt. 28:29; Is. 42:6 f.; Tob. 5:10 (vl.). In a transferred sense the darkness of the eyes is sorrow (Lam. 5:17; cf. Ps. 6:7; 31:9; 69:3), disaster (Ps. 69:23). Darkness is also an expression for captivity (Ps. 107:10 ff.), evil (Ps. 44:19; Job 19:8; 22:10 f.; 30:26), and wickedness (Ps. 10:7 ff.; 11:2; 74:20; 82:5). The connection between darkness and sorrow is to be found in the root קדר, and that between darkness and death especially in צַלְמָוֶת. Cosmologically the idea of the underworld merges into that of the ocean depths ; both are dark spheres of non-being. The world of the dead is not depicted as it is in Homer. Instead we are told what it means for man and what is the fate of the shadowy beings in it. Most instructive in this regard is Ez. 32:17-32. Similarly Job 10:20-22 declares : As light means happiness and life, so darkness means disaster and death. Hence the realm of the dead is the land of darkness. It is so dominant, and death is so final an end to the life of brightness, that even what might seem to be radiance to shadowy beings is in reality darkness. Death is a complete termination with no return to the light and with not the least spark of life. It is also characterised as the supreme terror, especially as darkness represents something dreadful for the Israelites. [43] The

---

In 2 Βασ. 1:9 the hapax legomenon שְׁבָץ is transl. σκότος δεινόν. Trendelenburg in Schleusner, V, 62 proposes σκοτόδινος (vertigo [P. Katz]).

[40] σκότος-γνόφος. Plerophory Dt. 4:11 (cf. Ex. 10:22): חֹשֶׁךְ עָנָן וַעֲרָפֶל = σκότος γνόφος θύελλα, Jl. 2:2 (cf. Is. 60:2; Zeph. 1:15): יוֹם חֹשֶׁךְ וַאֲפֵלָה יוֹם עָנָן וַעֲרָפֶל (σκότος, γνόφος, νεφέλη, ὁμίχλη).

[41] As against Aalen, 3. It is true that the Law is called light, but there is no real antithesis to this on the negative side.

[42] On this cf. P. Reymond, "L'eau, sa vie et sa signification dans l'AT," VT Suppl., 6 (1958), 13 f. A line may be drawn from this to the description of theophany, esp. by עֲרָפֶל Ex. 20:21; Dt. 4:11 etc. Naturally oriental mythical motifs play a part here and these are not orientated to natural phenomena but to the total scheme of the mythical view of the world.

[43] [Fohrer] On Ps. 44:19 H. Schmidt, Psalmen, Hndbch. AT, I, 15 (1934), ad loc. For the manifestation of sheol in this world in disaster, sickness, cf. G. v. Rad, Theol. d. AT,

psalmist feels that he is already cast into it, Ps. 88:6, 12; Job 17:12 f. The expression has, of course, become a figure of speech and is no longer to be taken mythically in the strict sense.

4. Specific Features.

This formal sense, which finds analogies wherever there is reference to light and darkness, is concretely defined by the OT concept of God and the world. God is the sovereign Lord of both light and darkness. He creates both (Is. 45:7, par. good and evil), sends both (Ps. 105:28), and manifests both (Job 12:22); no darkness can hide from Him (Job 34:22; Is. 29:15). He gives light and also darkens (Am. 5:8 both in a literal and also a transferred sense). He can darken the eyes, but He makes even darkness bright before the eyes of the blind (Is. 42:16 ff.). Statements are thus made which are not even possible in the Greek world, for in spite of its threatening aspect darkness is only a penultimate entity. If God shines forth light (Hab. 3:4) and darkness is not dark with Him (Ps. 139:11 f.), there is nevertheless a contrast. Darkness expresses His hiddenness (1 K. 8:12 = 3 Βασ. 8:53a cf. 2 Ch. 6:1) and thus becomes a motif in theophany, Ps. 18:9 ff.; 2 S. 22:10; Ps. 97:2 ff.; Ex. 24:15 ff. This, too, serves to set forth His sovereignty.

5. Cosmology.

The material is not uniform, as the juxtaposition of Gn. 1 and 2 shows. In the one the pre-existent state is viewed as a primal sea over which primal darkness broods, while in the other it is a primal waste. Obviously the latter idea penetrated into Gn. 1:2, where we find the waste and void alongside the flood. From the very outset, then, darkness is connected with this primal flood. The earth begins with light. The elements in this cosmogony derive from the oriental world around, but they have been significantly reduced in the process of adoption. Even where we may still catch a glimpse of mythical motifs concerning the battle against chaos or the dragon (Ps. 74:13 f.; 89:10; Job 26:12; Is. 27:1), the depiction of chaos is not as such the point of the account. The emphasis is not on the fact that chaos once existed as an independent force but on the fact that it is vanquished by God's might (or mighty Word), cf. Ps. 74:16; 89:11 f. Gn. 1 and Is. 45:7 achieve the supreme clarity of reflection which repels the mythical element. In Gn. 1 light is detached from the cosmic luminaries. [44] This fixes the understanding of darkness. It is not created by God as in Is. 45:7. But again it is not active ; it puts up no resistance. It becomes a constituent part of the cosmos only with the creation of light. [45] The same intention finds expression in Is. 45:7 when it says that God created light and darkness, good and evil. [46] Here for the first time we have a clear formulation of the connection between creation and salvation. [47]

I (1957), 385 f. The link with the idea of chaos (Job 38) expresses the fact that the dark depth is not a fixed place but an out-reaching entity. For the sea cf. O. Eissfeldt, "Gott u. das Meer in der Bibel," *Studia Orientalia J. Pedersen* (1953), 76-84; Reymond, *op. cit.,* 182-198; O. Kaiser, "Die mythische Bdtg. d. Meeres in Ägypten, Ugarit u. Israel," Beih. ZAW, 78 (1959), esp. 112-120, 153-159.

[44] This is reversed again in Judaism → 431, 10 ff.

[45] Light is good but darkness is not evil, Aalen, 12, 14, n. 1. It is integrated into the cosmos in another way in Job 26:10; there is a similar intention in Job 38 (v. 8 f.). The familiar expression "light out of darkness" occurs in the Gk. transl. of Job 37:15 : φῶς ποιήσας ἐκ σκότους, for "as he causes the light of his cloud to gleam"; → n. 162 [Bertram].

[46] Cf. Am. 4:13.

[47] Cf. Jer. 31:35 ff.

6. Eschatology.

In the first instance statements about the beginning and the end are not consciously interrelated. Development begins with Amos and his polemical inversion of the naive expectation of salvation. The day of Yahweh will be darkness and not light (Am. 5:20). By this one may know that it is God's action and see it as a sign. Primarily Am. is here proclaiming historical judgment on Israel and light and darkness are meant figuratively. But in the background is the eastern cosmological notion of the breaking in again of chaos, as may be seen from Am. 8:9. Even this perversion of nature is God's sovereign deed, an active darkening. [48] In Jl. 2:2 darkness has become a description of the "day." [49] Here it is no longer meant figuratively but literally.

7. Anthropology (Wisdom).

Different styles jostle and merge with one another. We find that of prayer [50] and then the typical style of wisdom with individual moral reflection. [51] Here, too, thinking is focused on the positive process of illumination. Figurative and transferred expressions are found alongside one another. [52] Even intellectually God is the One who illumines. Judaism then speaks of the darkening of reason, Test. XII cf. R. 1:21 → 442, 13 f. The OT is familiar with God's active darkening in the usual sense of sending evil, Lam. 3:1 ff. Worth noting is the use of this terminology in the dogma of retribution. [53] Darkness smites the ungodly (Job 15:22 ff.; 20:26) and his light is put out (Job 18:15 ff.; 22:11 ff.); for the counterthesis cf. Job 21:17 f. Instances could easily be multiplied. The wicked man is darkened, but even in darkness the upright man can put his hope in God (Ps.

---

[48] This is so even when it is the breaking in again of chaos, Is. 5:30; 13:10; Jer. 4:23 f. The reduction of the mythical may also be seen in the fact that the disaster is a figure of man's predicament and that a link is made with sin, though Aalen, 21 f. overstates this. On the other hand the cosmic catastrophe cannot be regarded as no more than poetic embroidery, as against J. Lindblom, *Die Js.-Apokalypse Js. 24-27* (1938), 107. The connection with sin and judgment may be seen esp. in Job, cf. 5:14; 12:25 : blinding; 15:22, 23; 18:6, 18; 22:11 etc.: disaster as judgment. In Mi. 6:14 : σκοτάσει ἐν σοί, LXX formulates the thought independently of the Mas. In Ez. 31:15 LXX B has σκοτάζω as a sign of sorrow at the fall of the king of Assyria, cf. also Is. 47:1. In ψ 54:6 LXX has σκότος (darkness of life) for the rare פַּלָּצוּת [Bertram].

[49] Malmede, 476. Eschatological darkening Is. 13:10; Jl. 2:30 f.; 3:15 (Ac. 2:20); Zeph. 1:15; Rev. 6:12, 17; 8:12, cf. also Ez. 34:12 f.: judgment on the people ; Prv. 20:20 : on individuals [Fohrer].

[50] Psalms : Prayer for the making dark of the way of enemies, 35:6.

[51] Naturally this is also found outside the circle of the Wisdom lit. in the narrower sense, e.g., in the prophets, v. J. Fichtner, "Js. unter d. Propheten," ThLZ, 74 (1949), 75-80; J. Lindblom, "Wisdom in the OT Prophets," *VT Suppl.,* 3 (*Festschr. H. H. Rowley*) (1955), 192-204. Its influence in apocalyptic is also plain to see (Da., Eth. En.).

[52] Fig. Prv. 4:18 f.; image of the way Prv. 2:13. Transf. (folly) Ps. 82:5; the standard is naturally knowledge of the commandment. Illumination is instruction and it is achieved in obedience → φῶς.

[53] On the problems relating to this concept cf. K. Koch, "Gibt es ein Vergeltungsdogma im AT ?" ZThK, 52 (1955), 1-42; G. v. Rad, *Theol. d. AT,* I (1957), 382-384 and in criticism H. Gese, *Lehre u. Wirklichkeit in d. alten Weisheit* (1958), 42-50. Our concern is simply with the fact that the idea of retribution (whether advocated or contested — Job) is expressed in these terms. Job 18:5a : "The light of the wicked is put out" is a proverb or current saying, cf. Prv. 13:9; 24:20; in a different form Prv. 4:19; 20:20 [Fohrer].

97:11; 107:14; 112:4). The broadest development of the spiritualisation and transferred use is in Wis. 17:19 f. cf. 18:1-4. [54]

C. Judaism (apart from Philo). [55]

1. Usage.

In usage there is continuity with the OT but also the modification which one associates with the term Judaism, i.e., a strengthening of legal thinking, [56] an enhancing of the transcendence of God, and a change in the picture of the world through adoption of belief in the hereafter and apocalyptic expectation. Darkness is now damnation in the next world, Jub. 5:14; Eth. En. 17:6; Slav. En. 7:1; Ps. Sol. 14:9; Ps.-Philo Antiquitates Biblicae, 16, 3; 51, 1. [57] A spatial view of the world crowds out the temporal view. [58] The primary ref. is no longer to the rhythm of day and night. The cosmic order is now viewed as a static thing connected with the movements of the constellations. [59] The creation story is changed in such a way that the creation of light no longer precedes that of the heavenly lights, Jub. 2; 4:6; Sib., 3, 1 ff. and Fr., 3; Eth. En. 96. [60] Correspondence is seen between the cosmos and man. Through knowledge of the cosmos man understands himself, and a new style of Wisdom lit. mediates this. [61] Naturally much more is said about eschatological darkness, Eth. En. 63:6; 103:8; 108:11 ff.; Sib., 5, 344 ff.; Ass. Mos. 10:5; Ps.-Philo Antiquitates Biblicae, 19, 13 (→ n. 57). But at the end darkness will be destroyed, Eth. En. 58:6; 92:4 f. The metaphor of the way becomes that of the two ways (→ V, 56, 21 ff.). The evangelistic style is a distinctive new element; cosmological instruction leads to a personal appeal. [62]

2. Dead Sea Scrolls.

The Dead Sea Scrolls are plainly in the OT tradition on the one side but are also a distinctive development of this on the other. There has been further detachment from the natural phenomena. [63] The terms have become a means to present

---

[54] Cf. already 17:1 ff. The Mosaic story in Ex. 10:21 ff. is changed into an image of apocalyptic and eschatological character, G. Kuhn, "Beiträge zur Erklärung d. Buches d. Weisheit," ZNW, 28 (1929), 335.

[55] For non-literary sources → φῶς; bibl.: E. R. Goodenough, *Jewish Symbols in the Greco-Roman Period*, I-VIII (1953-1958), Index, s.v. "Light," "Darkness."

[56] The "light" of the Torah → φῶς.

[57] Ed. G. Kisch (1949). On 4 Esr. 14:20 : the world lies in darkness, cf. Aalen, 181: This is not a general judgment on the world as a whole but refers to the position immediately after the destruction of Jerusalem. But cf. also Eth. En. 48:7; 108:11.

[58] Aalen, 69; cf. the static juxtaposition of the upper world of light and this world in Slav. En. 25-27 and on this Aalen, 166. Naturally there are echoes of OT sayings (Test. A. 5:1 ff.) and the temporal element in apocal. expectation compensates for the spatial cosmogony. Light and darkness are constituent parts of the world in Jub. 2:6; 4:6.

[59] Aalen, 159; cf. the break in the parallelism in Sir. 43:1 ff.

[60] In Jub. the element of movement vanishes from the creation narrative; seven things are listed instead, Aalen, 164. For speculative development cf. Ps.-Philo Antiquitates Bibl., 60, 2 : *tenebrae et silentium erat antequam fieret saeculum, et locutum est silentium et apparuerunt tenebrae*. There is modification of the chaos motif in Joseph and Asenath, 12, 10 (ed. P. Batiffol, *Studia Patristica*, I [1889]): lion/devil; darkness/ocean depth. Following the Bible Jos. Ant., 1, 27 puts the creation of light first. LXX had ἀόρατος for תהו, but Jos. has βαθεῖ μὲν κρυπτομένης σκότει (concealment in primal darkness?).

[61] Eth. En. 41, esp. 41:8; wisdom occurs immediately after in 42.

[62] Esp. plain in Joseph and Asenath, 8, 6, cf. 12, 1 f. and 15, 12 (→ n. 60).

[63] Where natural phenomena are described the terms light and darkness recur, 1 QH 1;

a dualism of eschatological decision. [64] Persian ideas have influenced this. [65] But one may ask whether light and darkness have also been borrowed from these as a mode of expression or whether a development is to be assumed within Judaism itself. [66] Series of correspondences may be seen; thus darkness (חושך) corresponds to עול etc. The dualism has a cosmic dimension. Two spheres in which we walk (1 QM 11:10), and which have their own controlling powers, confront one another and determine the being of man. [67] They are to be seen in their representatives, their "spirits" on the one hand and their "generations" on the other. [68] The fact that very strong emphasis is placed on personal decision implies no inner contradiction. The concept of predestination is a genuine structural element in this thinking. Each individual act is qualified in advance by life either in the one sphere or the other. A good work is *a priori* impossible in darkness, 1 QM 15:9. [69] But this very principle is a summons to decision. Alongside the cosmic conceptuality there· is a personal [70] and a social. [71] Whole statements relate to entry into the covenant to which salvation is linked. In retrospect the convert sees that his conversion was the work of God. [72] He perceives that his former lost estate was something both passive and active, 1 QH 5:5 ff. → n. 69. He can now say that "there is no more darkness," 1 QH 18:28 cf. 9:26. From the standpoint of the covenant he views the whole of his new life as a constant movement away from the "children of darkness" in the demanding of hatred for them, 1 QS 1:9 f. The present battle in the world is a foretaste of the eschatological conflict, 1 QM; darkness will be done away, 1 QM 1:8. The two possibilities are definitive : eternal life in eternal light (1 QS 4:7 f.) or eternal perdition in the fire of dark places (1 QS 4:12 f. cf. 2:8; 1 QH 3:29 ff.).

---

1 QM 10; the daily course, 1 QS 10:1 f. cf. 1 QH 12:4 ff. God did not create darkness but תהומות 1 QM 10:12 f.; 1 QH 1:13 f.

[64] It should be noted that the light/darkness duality occurs only in a small portion of the works thus far available, esp. 1 QS 3:13 ff.; 1 QM 13:10 ff.; not 1 Qp Hab. or Damasc.

[65] Persian ideas are plainest in the section on the two spirits in 1 QS 3:13 ff. (→ n. 33); cf. H. Wildberger, "Der Dualismus in d. Qumranschr.," *Asiatische Studien,* 8 (1954), 163-177. It is naturally a temptation to derive the light/darkness usage from this, since it is esp. common in these passages, cf. K. G. Kuhn, "Die Sektenschrift u. die iranische Religion," ZThK, 49 (1952), 296-316. But cf. the arguments against this → n. 33; the genuinely Jewish element is unmistakable, esp. on the positive side (illumination), → φῶς, and, e.g., 1 QH 18:29; 5:32; 1 Q 27 col. 1, 5 f. (DJD, I, 103) (fig.).

[66] Cf. Nötscher, 79-92.

[67] Darkness has its cosmic place 1 QS 3:19 ff. → 152, 13 ff. It exercises power, seducing through its representative Belial and having its "commandments," 1 QM 13:12.

[68] The expressions "lot of darkness," "of Belial" etc. are interchangeable, cf. 1 QS 2:5; 1 QM 1:1; 1:11 → n. 70; H. W. Huppenbauer, "Belial in d. Qumrantexten," ThZ, 15 (1959), 81-89.

[69] For complete perversion cf. 1 QS 3:3 f.: Those who do not enter the covenant regard the way of darkness as that of light, nor are they swept away by fate, but work out their own being : "they yearn for darkness," 1 QM 15:10.

[70] The two spirits 1 QS 3:19 ff. On the other side, from below, men are "sons" of light or darkness 1 QS 1:9 f.; 1 QM. The ethical significance of the terms may be seen in the confrontation between the angel of truth (מלאך אמת) in 1 QS 3:24 and the רוח עולה in 4:9, and in the description of children of darkness as אנשי העול respecting their "lot," בני השחת in Damasc. 6:15 (8:12); 13:14 (16:7). Sphere and person are interchangeable : walking in darkness in 1 QS 11:10 = in the spirit of darkness in 1 QM 4:12 → n. 68. On the structured difference between the two spirits on the one side and the two Rabb. impulses on the other → 153, 8 ff.

[71] Esp. "lot"; the fellowship is more than the sum of its members.

[72] Esp. in the hymns of praise 1 QH 13 ff.

Test. XII belong to the same milieu. [73] Decision is demanded in them, Test. L. 19:1: ἐκλέξασθε ἑαυτοῖς ἢ τὸ φῶς ἢ τὸ σκότος, ἢ τὸν νόμον κυρίου ἢ τὰ ἔργα τοῦ Βελίαρ. Darkness is represented by Beliar → 152, 3 ff., Test. N. 2:7; Jos. 20:2. Beliar in turn has his spirits, Iss. 7:7; D. 1:7; B. 3:3. Finally the eschatological repelling of darkness is presupposed, L. 18:4. But the link with the Wisdom lit. is stronger; the psychological aspects of darkening and illumination (conversion) are more prominent. This may be seen in the fig. use: the expelling of darkness, G. 5:7; B. 5:3, and also in the transf. use: darkness = evil, wrong, L. 19:1 cf. 14:4; B. 4:2 cf. Mt. 6:22 f. It may also be seen in the consistent interweaving with ethical concepts (πλάνη etc.) σκοτίζω τὸν νοῦν, R. 3:8 cf. G. 6:2; D. 2:4; cf. also the use of τυφλόω etc.; conversion in G. 5:7; Jos. 2:4; 8:5; 9:1 f. 19:3a.

3. Rabbinic Writings. [74]

The Jewish development is partly continued and partly broken. [75] The equation of darkness and wickedness is no longer made on cosmological grounds but merely occurs sometimes in exegesis. [76] The word darkness with its derivates is less prominent. The opposite of God's light is not darkness but the absence of light. [77]

D. Hellenism, Gnosticism.

1. General Data.

The specifically new thing in this era can be seen only in the use of → φῶς. As before light is salvation, but the understanding of salvation has changed. Light symbolism becomes a metaphysics of light. Light is the transcendent sphere and it is also a substance. Cosmology and soteriology are interwoven. Illumination is mystical rapture and it is also transformation, divinisation. There is nothing corresponding to this mixture of space and substantiality in the Dead Sea Scrolls. Hence the relation of man to his sphere is understood quite differently in the two areas. Dualistic terminology is restricted to a relatively clearly defined circle. In general darkness is not an active counter-force but what one leaves behind, ἄγνοια. In this respect there is formal agreement with the Gk. view, but the concrete significance has changed in acc. with the understanding of γνῶσις → I, 692, 36 ff. [78] Thus the σκότος group is less prominent where thought is controlled by the mysteries, i.e., by the idea of the epiphany of light (→ IV, 19, 37 ff.), [79] and illumination is sought in mystical ecstasy. [80] The same is true in the sphere of astral

---

[73] Cf. the abs. use "the" darkness in Test. B. 5:3 cf. L. 18:3 f. Here, too, being is expressed in works, N. 2:10 : οὕτως οὐδὲ ἐν σκότει ὄντες δύνασθε ποιεῖν ἔργα φωτός. The cleavage is stressed in N. 2:7, though this is only a metaphor, Nötscher, 114, n. 28. Two spirits, L. 20:1, but clearly psychologised. On the hist. interrelationship of Test. cf. O. Eissfeldt, Einl. in d. AT² (1956), 780-786.
[74] Str.-B., IV, Index, s.v. "Finsternis"; cf. II, 427 f.; Aalen, 258-314.
[75] In innocuous transf. use Midr. Ps., 72, 2 on 27:1; Str.-B., II, 552; the darkness of the place of punishment, Str.-B., IV, 1075-1079.
[76] Aalen, 278-282 tends to overrate the cosmological aspect.
[77] Aalen, 318. Satan is not viewed primarily as a representative of this sphere. An exception is the late Pesikt. r., App. 2 (203a, 31): "The angel-prince of darkness"; Str.-B., III, 616, 820; IV, 1046. Speculation is discouraged in bTamid., 32a : The question whether light or darkness was created first need not be discussed; Odeberg, 144; Aalen, 268. In the sphere of Merkaba speculation (3 En.) there is no longer any ref. to darkness at all.
[78] Cf. Bultmann Lichtsymbolik, 24. Darkness and ἄγνοια Philo Som., I, 114; Ebr., 157 (ἀλογία); Corp. Herm., 7, 2 (→ n. 95); Iambl. Myst., II, 11 → I, 118, 42 ff.
[79] Wetter, 98-101. Cf. Apul. Met., XI, 23 f. Why one does not need to speak of darkness in this milieu may be finely seen from Plut. Is. et Os., 77 (II, 382c d).
[80] Mention of darkness simply serves to expound illumination, Philo Som., I, 218; Iambl.

religion where light is connected with the stars, [81] and also in the related astrology. [82] Darkness takes on independent significance only with the Gnostic revolution in which the light of the heavenly bodies is rejected as "cosmic" and the world of light is completely transcendent and capable of being apprehended only by its own sparks scattered in this world. Here all earthly light becomes σκοτεινὸν φῶς, Corp. Herm., 1, 28.

2. Philo (→ IV, 243, 34 ff.; 550, 8 ff.).

Philo is wholly of the illumination school. He naturally speaks of darkness in cosmology and in expounding the bibl. creation story. [83] Yet he interprets it, not in terms of the antithesis of light and darkness, but in terms of the confrontation between heavenly and earthly or first and second light, Op. Mund., 26 ff. (→ n. 83); Som., I, 75 f. This leads on to a description of the individual process of illumination. [84] To a large degree the cosmology and anthropology adopt Platonic ideas but they are not in any sense a pure or straightforward development of these. In the fusion of the Greek tradition with that of the OT new elements come in. Thus a new product emerges [85] and at many pts. we have a preliminary stage of Gnosticism. [86] The customary transf. use naturally continues. [87]

3. Corpus Hermeticum.

In comparison with φῶς, σκότος is surprisingly rare here. [88] In the few instances there is a distinctively Gnostic element. The basic passage is the artificially "mythical" cosmogony of Poimandres. [89] This follows the tendency to give priority to light over darkness. [90] Later this is surrounded by light in time as well as space. [91] This speculative

---

Myst., III, 6. It is the weak part, *ibid.*, III, 13. The proper opp. is ἀφώτιστος, Wetter, 63.

[81] Bultmann Lichtsymbolik, 26-29; also *Das Urchr. im Rahmen d. antiken Religionen*[2] (1954), 163-173 (with bibl.); F. Cumont, *Die orientalischen Religionen im röm. Heidentum*[4] (1959), esp. 112-123.

[82] Bibl.: Bultmann Urchr., 245, n. 17. What is said applies also to the magic pap. σκότος etc. are rare and occur only where there is Jewish or Chr. influence in formal phrases, cf. Audollent Def. Tab., 242, 13 : τὸν θεὸν τὸν φωτίζοντα καὶ σκοτίζοντα τὸν κόσμον. Preis. Zaub., I, 5, 98 ff.: σὲ καλῶ ... τὸν κτίσαντα νύκτα καὶ ἡμέραν, σὲ τὸν κτίσαντα φῶς καὶ σκότος. How unimportant the concept is in the main may be seen from, e.g., Preis. Zaub., I, 4, 976, 2242.

[83] Op. Mund., 29 : πρῶτον οὖν ὁ ποιῶν ἐποίησεν οὐρανὸν ἀσώματον καὶ γῆν ἀόρατον καὶ ἀέρος ἰδέαν καὶ κενοῦ· ὧν τὸ μὲν ἐπεφήμισε σκότος, ἐπεὶ μέλας ὁ ἀὴρ τῇ φύσει ... 33 : μετὰ δὲ τὴν τοῦ νοητοῦ φωτὸς ἀνάλαμψιν, ὃ πρὸ ἡλίου γέγονεν (but → n. 60), ὑπεχώρει τὸ ἀντίπαλον σκότος (cf. 35).

[84] Jonas Gnosis, I, 105, n. 1.

[85] *Ibid.*, II, 70-99, 114.

[86] Not more ! σκότος is a term of relation in Som., I, 79. But the new element is intimated in Praem. Poen., 36 ff. On Gnosticism in Philo → I, 702, 16 ff.

[87] The transition from fig. to transf. use may be seen already in Spec. Leg., IV, 231: ἰσότης δὲ φῶς ἄσκιον, ἥλιος, εἰ δεῖ τἀληθὲς εἰπεῖν, νοητός, ἐπειδὴ καὶ τοὐναντίον ἀνισότης, ἐν ᾗ τό τε ὑπερέχον καὶ τὸ ὑπερεχόμενον, σκότους ἀρχή τε καὶ πηγή. Transf. Leg. All., III, 7; Ebr., 157 (ἀλογία); Som., I, 114 (cf. 115 ff.); II, 39 : ὁ δὲ φῶς ἀντὶ σκότους μεταδιώκων ἐγρηγόρσεως, Spec. Leg., I, 54 : σκότος αἰρούμενοι πρὸ αὐγοειδεστάτου φωτὸς καὶ τυφλὴν ἀπεργαζόμενοι διάνοιαν ὀξὺ καθορᾶν δυναμένην. In a series of antitheses Gig., 41; Rer. Div. Her., 207 ff.

[88] Corp. Herm., 1, 4. 6. 19. 20. 28; 3, 1; 7, 2; 13, 9. 11; Ascl., 25 and 29b.

[89] 1, 4 f. with exposition following, cf. Dodd Bible, 99-144; Dodd Interpretation, 30-41 seems to me to overrate the influence of Gn. 1 in spite of Corp. Herm., 1, 17 and 3, 1; cf. Gn. 2:7; at any rate the true intention of the passage cannot be explained in the light of this.

[90] In this it differs completely from Gn. 1, though cf. 3, 1: The world-view of the corpus is not consistent.

[91] Dodd Bible, 113 : Darkness "has a kind of inherent property of gravity which makes it tend downwards."

scheme has soteriological significance. Light and darkness are spheres and powers. Knowledge of them is a call to conversion. Man is to understand himself against a cosmological horizon and thereby he is to be brought into the light = life. It has to be perceived that everything that seems to be light in the world is only σκοτεινὸν φῶς compared with the true light. [92] The anthropological thrust of cosmology is thus strongly dualistic, though in itself the cosmology cannot be described thus. [93] Darkness finds actualisation in the σῶμα. [94] The missionary pathos of dualism dominates the 7th tractate. [95] It is in the style of Hell. missionary preaching with the schema of wandering in the body and ascent to salvation, ἐπὶ τὰς τῆς γνώσεως θύρας, ὅπου ἐστὶ τὸ λαμπρὸν φῶς, τὸ καθαρὸν σκότους, [96] cf. the 13th tractate, 13, 9-11. A striking pt. is that in hymns and prayers there is no ref. to darkness, 1, 31 and esp. 13, 18 ff.

4. Odes of Solomon. [97]

Here, too, light does not lie in the sphere of man's natural possibilities. Man is in darkness. [98] This is a place and a situation. The Gnostic idea of the garment of light — at least as an expression — is applied to it. [99]

5. The Mandaeans.

Here dualism is evident even in the mode of expression. [100] We find a bewildering medley of ideas; it is futile to try to reduce them to a common denominator. [101] But the structural elements of this kind of thinking may be discerned. The soteriological point of mythical speculation is always patent. The soul's existence in the world is portrayed as one of lostness, and revelation from beyond through the summons of the envoy or envoys is the way into the world of light. The Gnostic bracketing of the world as the sphere of death and evil is consistently adopted. [102] All earthly light, esp.

---

[92] Corp. Herm., 1, 28; Jonas Gnosis, I, 149.

[93] It is not Iranian in type (on this cf. Jonas Gnosis, I, 255-257, 284-328); cf. Festugière, III, 24. The cosmogony and soteriology are not really congruent.

[94] Corp. Herm., 1, 20 (cf. also ὕλη, e.g., 7, 3); this means materially that we are in πλάνη and ἄγνοια, 1, 28; cf. 1, 19: ὁ δὲ ἀγαπήσας τὸ ἐκ πλάνης ἔρωτος σῶμα, οὗτος μένει ἐν τῷ σκότει πλανώμενος, αἰσθητῶς πάσχων τὰ τοῦ θανάτου. One cannot say that this terminology is "ethical" in thrust; the old virtues are now hypostatised as cosmic δυνάμεις, cf. Corp. Herm., 13, 8 f.

[95] Corp. Herm., 7, 2: πρῶτον δὲ δεῖ σε περιρρήξασθαι ὃν φορεῖς χιτῶνα, τὸ τῆς ἀγνωσίας ὕφασμα, τὸ τῆς κακίας στήριγμα, τὸν τῆς φθορᾶς δεσμὸν, τὸν σκοτεινὸν περίβολον, τὸν ζῶντα θάνατον, τὸν αἰσθητὸν νεκρόν, τὸν περιφόρητον τάφον ... περίβολος is taken by Scott, I, 172, ad loc. to be garment in view of χιτών, cf. 7, 3; O. Sol. 21:3 etc., but Nock-Fest., I, 81 f., ad loc. construes it as prison in view of Plat. Crat., 400c.

[96] The emphasis on the purity of light is widespread, cf. Philo Abr., 205; Ev. Veritatis, 32, 26 ff. (ed. M. Malinine, H. C. Puech, G. Quispel [1958]).

[97] We need not discuss the question of genuinely Chr. elements in these since our concern is with material comparison, not literary interconnections.

[98] The familiar elements of Jewish illumination style are to be seen in O. Sol. 11:19: way from darkness to light; 15:2: dispelling, but the Gnostic transposition is unmistakable in 42:16: descent of the redeemer into Hades. The cosmological tradition may be seen in 31:1.

[99] O. Sol. 21:3: And I put off darkness and put on light.

[100] This takes place wherever the redeemer myth is presented as mythical cosmology. But the liturgies almost always speak of light alone, cf. the 3rd Book of Lidz. Ginza L, 505-596.

[101] Jonas Gnosis, I, 262-283; cf. esp. the 3rd Book of Lidz. Ginza R, 63 ff. The examples are so numerous that we have given only a random selection.

[102] Jonas Gnosis, I, 106-120. The fate of Adam, Lidz. Ginza R, 113, 28 f.

astral, stands in the active service of this evil sphere. [103] We find together the two basic types of Gnostic world-view : primal fall and primal darkness/chaos. [104] On the one side darkness is just there, [105] on the other there is strong emphasis on the fact that light is earlier. [106] On the one side the two are abs. differentiated, [107] on the other the being of the world rests on their admixture, Lidz. Joh., 216, 14 ff.: It lives by the constituent portions of light within it. [108] This is why it seeks so strenuously to keep it. Like light, darkness is a sphere and substance. [109] As such it is an overpowering force which rages and howls (Lidz. Ginza R, 277, 20), which forms destructive plans (Lidz. Ginza L, 529, 17), which seeks to captivate man [110] by binding him to the body, the dark house (Lidz. Ginza L, 514, 19 ff.; Lidz. Liturg., 102), which is a part of the body (Lidz. Ginza L, 468, 20 f.). [111] Even among the Mandaeans it has its personal representatives : Ruha, the mother of darkness (Lidz. Ginza R, 175, 10 ff. cf. 164, 20 ff.); her son, the king of darkness Ur ; [112] the planets (→ n. 103); and finally their children (Lidz. Joh., 240; Lidz. Ginza R, 78, 1 ff.). In accordance with their nature their ultimate fate is destruction. The pt. of the myth is eschatological. The view of man, the world and redemption is non-historical. Judgment is a cosmic process. [113] Even where darkness is spoken of in a transf. sense [114] the strict metaphysical sense is in the background. [115] Ethics is understood against a mythical horizon. [116] Error is absolute ; there are no stages between it and truth. It is deadly and inescapable. Redemption is possible only from above ; it takes place through the "call." [117] Darkness does not understand light, Lidz. Liturg., 131. It fights against it, Lidz. Ginza R, 77 ff. But it falls victim to destruction. Here again the pt. of the myth is to induce decision. [118]

---

[103] The (seven) planets are the futile rebels of darkness, Lidz. Ginza L, 479, 25 ff., the watchers which keep the world, the prison, cf. the description of the way of the soul past the guard-houses in Lidz. Ginza R, 183 ff.; L, 443 ff.

[104] Cf. the 3rd Book of Ginza R, e.g., 70, 30 f., 90; on this Jonas Gnosis, I, 266-277.

[105] Lidz. Joh., 216, 14 ff.: Invasion of the cosmos by pre-cosmic darkness → n. 112.

[106] Lidz. Ginza R, 75 f., though cf. Jonas Gnosis, I, 268.

[107] Lidz. Ginza R, 77, 31 ff.: Water does not mix with pitch and darkness does not belong to light, cf. Lidz. Joh., 160.

[108] Without this the world and the body perish, Lidz. Ginza L, 517.

[109] Percy, 24. The spatial concept may be seen in the expression "gates of darkness," Lidz. Ginza R, 88, 1; 102, 12 etc.

[110] Lidz. Ginza R, 113, 28 ff.; its activity, Jonas Gnosis, I, 114-118.

[111] Lidz. Ginza L, 511, 8 ff. (= Liturg., 159): "Hail to thee, hail to thee, soul that thou hast left the world. Thou hast left corruption and the stinking body in which thou didst dwell, the dwelling of the wicked, the place which is wholly sinner, the world of darkness, hate, jealousy and discord, the dwelling in which the planets live ..."

[112] Lidz. Joh., 55, 82 f. etc. His rise, Lidz. Ginza R, 277, 31 ff.: He is formed from black water through his own evil nature, → n. 105.

[113] The victory over Ur and destruction of the children of darkness, Lidz. Ginza R, 77 ff.; the destruction of the planets, ibid., 203, 11 ff.

[114] Thus in the sense of error, wickedness ; Lidz. Ginza R, 71 and 276, 31 ff.: "Their heart is full of darkness."

[115] Percy, 24; cf. Lidz. Ginza R, 405, 1 ff.: "Darkness oppresses them and they stumble away from the light ... Ruha rests on them and holds them captive in the dwellings of debauchery."

[116] Lidz. Ginza R, 113 f.; Jonas Gnosis, I, 116-118.

[117] Lidz. Ginza R, 150 ff., L, 453 ff.; Jonas Gnosis, I, 120-122.

[118] Bultmann J., 113, n. 1 on 3:18; Lidz. Ginza R, 60, 27 ff.: "Every man who converts, his soul shall never be cut off ... But the wicked, liars, condemn themselves ... they will be destroyed in darkness ...," cf. Lidz. Joh., 244, 20 ff.; 203, 19 ff.: "The wicked are blind and do not see ; I call them to the light but they bury themselves in darkness."

6. The Manichees.

A consistent duality of two principles which are there from the very beginning holds sway in Manicheeism. These are once more portrayed as spheres and substances [119] and they have their representatives. Each sphere consists of five elements. [120] The drama of redemption is a mingling and separating of the two spheres. At the beginning we do not have a fall from above but a revolt from below in which darkness develops its own satanic intelligence. [121] Dualism is a nature system; the metaphysical finds physical expression. The visible light of the sun and moon has a redemptive quality. [122] The equivalence of the two opposing entities is, of course, purely formal. In reality light is superior, if not as substance, at least in inner quality. [123] This may be seen in the fact that darkness has no visible bearers in the cosmos. [124] The superiority finds tangible expression in the work of the emissaries of light. The prospect of the final victory rests on it. This whole cosmic process is now revealed through Mani, the pt. being that he is also part of the process. Hence the process is not just the content of teaching; it is a task for the called. By hearing cosmic decisions, these are taken up into them. [125]

7. Christian Gnosticism.

A great part of the extant writings offers little that is new compared with what has been said above. Transcendent salvation is consistently depicted by light (the world of light). But darkness does not have to be mentioned as its opposite. This is true in the narrative literature which belongs to the illumination type. Phrases with "darkness" are less prominent or remain within the sphere of the commonplace. [126] Naturally the term is even less prominent in the theoretical literature, in the speculative unfolding of cosmology. For here the duality is enclosed within a comprehensive view of the world

---

[119] Historically we have a gnosticising of Persian dualism; this may be seen in the operation of the light/darkness terminology. On Persian Gnosticism cf. C. Colpe, "Die religionsgeschichtliche Schule. Darstellung u. Kritik ihres Bildes vom gnostischen Erlösermythus," FRL, 78 (1961), 177-182.

[120] Darkness itself is regularly one of the 5 elements. There are many examples.

[121] Within this framework there is, of course, a fall too, that of primal man, and precisely this has the defeat of darkness as its final result. Sometimes this fall is regarded as a self-sacrifice by which darkness is outwitted.

[122] The Zodiac circle operates like a great winch (Jonas Gnosis, I, 316) to lift out the particles of light from the world and to transport them back to their own place.

[123] Jonas Gnosis, I, 290. What makes the prince of darkness inferior is that he desires something outside himself; darkness hates itself while light wants only itself, cf. Widengren, 59 f., 72-76.

[124] It can manifest itself only in the night. Another sign of inequality is that the Manichees could never succeed in balancing their antithetical series. They could oppose 5 vices to the 5 virtues (love hate etc.), but in relation to spiritual forces they had to use mere negations (reason/dark reason). On these series cf. W. Lentz, "Mani u. Zarathustra," ZDMG, 82 (1928), 179-206.

[125] Manichean Homilies and MSS in the collection A. Chester Beatty, I (ed. H. Polotsky [1934]), 12; Kephalaia, I (Manichäische Hdschr. der staatlichen Museen Berlin, I ed. C. Schmidt-H. J. Polotsky-A. Böhlig [1940]), 23 and 186; A Manichaean Psalm-Book (Manich. MSS in the Chester-Beatty Collection, II, ed. C. R. C. Allberry [1938]), 56 etc.

[126] E.g., Act. Thom., Joh. Darkness is the place of punishment in Act. Thom. 57 (173, 21); Act. Joh. 36:6 (169, 16 ff.), Satan in Act. Joh. 84 (192, 18 f.), cf. Ptolemy Flora, 7 in Epiph. Haer., 33, 7, 7, where God and the adversary are set in antithesis, the latter being φθορά καὶ σκότος — ὑλικὸς γὰρ οὗτος καὶ πολυσχιδής. The word is also used esp. as a foil for deliverance in conversion, Act. Thom. 28 (145, 13 f.): ἐξέλθετε ἀπὸ τοῦ σκότους, ἵνα τὸ φῶς ὑμᾶς προσδέξηται, cf. Act. Pl. 8:32: ἀπολείπετε τὸ σκότος, λάβετε τὸ φῶς, Act. Thom. 157 (267, 1). Cf., too, Act. Thom. 34 (151, 14 ff.): confession of the redeemed.

even where it has any part at all.[127] Where the Iranian type may be discerned a triadic solution is presented.[128] This conclusion is all the more worth noting in view of the record of Basilides' interest in the Persian religion, where he is supposed to have found the duality of light and darkness → n. 33.[129] Things are exactly the same in the available texts from Nag Hammadi (Chenoboskion),[130] the Ev. Veritatis,[131] the Coptic Gospel of Thomas,[132] and the writings of the Coptic Pap. Berolinensis, 8502,[133] though the Apocryphon of John occupies in some sense a special position among these. Worthy of note is Pist. Soph.[134] Ref. to darkness are many and esp. varied here. It is once again the realm of lostness represented by personal beings, its ἄρχοντες, ἐξουσίαι, δυνάμεις.[135] The cosmic apparatus serves to depict the fate of the soul : fall, lamentation of the fallen, redemption, jubilation. Blundering Pistis Sophia complains : "And I went and found myself in darkness ... And I cried for help and my voice did not break through the darkness ... And when I sought the light they (the archons) gave me darkness, and when I sought strength they gave me matter (ὕλη)," Pist. Soph., 32 (p. 28-30). When saved Pistis Sophia rejoices : "I am delivered out of chaos and redeemed from the bands of darkness," 68 (p. 96). Here we again have a clear statement of the Gnostic understanding of redemption.

E. The New Testament.

σκότος (neuter) is most common. John prefers σκοτία.[136] σκοτίζομαι occurs 5 times, and σκοτόομαι 3 times, both always in the passive. The group has theo-

---

[127] Cf. the two spheres in the diagram of the Ophites, reconstructed in H. Leisegang, Die Gnosis⁴ (1955), Ill. behind p. 176.

[128] Light and darkness and πνεῦμα between, Hipp. Ref., V, 19, 4.

[129] Hegemonius Acta Archelai (GCS, 16), 67, 4 ff.; the passage says nothing about Basilides' own view (as against Dodd Interpretation, 103 f.).

[130] Among them is the well-known Apocryphon of John → n. 133.

[131] Ev. Veritatis (→ n. 96). Cf. the supplementary material in H. M. Schenke, "D. fehlenden Seiten des sog. Ev. d. Wahrheit," ThLZ, 83 (1958), 497-500 (this does not contain the word darkness). H. M. Schenke, Die Herkunft d. sog. Ev. Veritatis (1959) (with bibl.); W. Till, "Die Kairener Seiten d. Ev. d. Wahrheit," Orientalia, 28 (1959), 170-185; survey in W. C. van Unnik, Newly Discovered Gnostic Writings (1960). Ev. Veritatis, 18, 12 ff.: Illumination of those who are in darkness through oblivion; 24, 37 ff., cf. 25, 12 ff.: Darkness dissipates when light comes. On the Gnostic Gospels as a whole cf. H. C. Puech in Hennecke³, 158-166.

[132] Cf. J. Leipoldt, "Ein neues Ev. ?" ThLZ, 83 (1958), 481-493; "dark" does not occur and "light" is rare, influenced by the NT, cf. J. Leipoldt-H. M. Schenke, Koptisch-gnostische Schriften aus d. Papyrus-Codices von Nag-Hamadi (1960), 10-26.

[133] Ed. W. Till, "Die gnostischen Schr. des kpt. Pap. Berolinensis 8502," TU, 60 (1955). a. Gospel acc. to Mary : The mounting soul passes the ἐξουσίαι, the 4th of which has 7 forms, one of the μορφαί being darkness, 16:6 (p. 73); cf. the Apocr. of John 55:4 ff. (p. 151), where darkness is one of the 4 ἐξουσίαι, cf. Till, 28. b .The Apocryphon of John is of the emanation type with demiurges. With other things darkness depicts imprisonment in matter (55:4 ff.) or seduction by the beauty of Paradise. We have here the Gnostic inversion of the OT, cf. Iren., I, 30, 7; Jonas Gnosis, I, 222. Gn. 6:1 ff. is similarly inverted in Apocryphon Joh. 76 f. Darkness follows but cannot attain to the ἐπίνοια of light, 59:11 ff. c. In the third work in the Cod., the Sophia of Jesus Christ, darkness has no significance.

[134] In the two books of Jeû (ed. C. Schmidt-W. Till, GCS, 45² [1954], 257-329) light is completely dominant ; in the 2nd it holds true orgies by which darkness seems to be swallowed up, cf. the "Unknown Ancient Gnostic Work," ibid., 335-367, though this has nothing distinctive to offer. In the 4th book of Pistis Sophia, a Gnostic apoc., outer darkness is the place of punishment, as in books 1-3.

[135] Pist. Soph., 143 (p. 246); v. Index, s.v. "Finsternis," "Äon(en)," "Archonten," "Drache," "Heimarmene," "Sphära."

[136] With no distinction of sense except at Jn. 3:19; 1 Jn. 1:6. Elsewhere the fem. occurs only in the quotation in Mt. 4:16 BD (Is. 9:1: ἐν σκότει).

logical significance only in John (the Gospel and 1 Jn.). It is used literally, figuratively and in a transferred sense.

I. The Synoptics (with Acts and Revelation).

1. Literal Use: a. Of the darkness of the sun at the crucifixion, Mk. 15:33 and par.; this is a miraculous eclipse, a sign. [137] There are many parallels to this. [138]

In the passion story this seems to be one of the secondary traditional (rather than literary) elements. The aim is to stress the saving significance of Jesus' death by ref. to its eschatological and cosmic dimension. [139] Its symbolical meaning is indicated already by the Marcan chronology. Darkness falls between crucifixion and death. The connection with salvation history is brought out by a second and materially related sign, the tearing of the temple curtain. [140] Darkness, however, does not indicate merely the cosmic extension of the passion, its breadth ; it is also a sign of its depth. For it points to what is stated in the verse then quoted. This shows to what length the suffering of Jesus had to go, but it is also shows that this suffering is God's work, and that Jesus understood it thus. For in His dereliction He quoted prophecy. The reader understands that God's plan of salvation is being fulfilled here. [141] The situation is different in Luke. The mood when darkness falls is altered by the preceding ref. to the immediate entry of Jesus into Paradise. Ps. 22:1 is replaced by Ps. 31:5. This final word corresponds to Luke's understanding of the passion as a martyrdom. [142] The discussion concerning Elias is cut out. [143] John does not mention any accompanying signs but only the accompanying acts of men.

b. The use is also literal when σκότος denotes the future place of punishment in Matthew's phrase: τὸ σκότος τὸ ἐξώτερον (Mt. 8:12; 22:13; 25:30) [144] and also Jd. 13 / 2 Pt. 2:17. [145] The power of the underworld (ἐξουσία τοῦ σκότους) rules in the passion of Jesus (Lk. 22:53). [146]

---

[137] The par. material supports this → n. 138. The ref. is to an eclipse of the sun, not just darkness of the atmosphere, as rightly seen by Lk.; it covers the whole earth, as against → I, 677, 15. That this was astronomically impossible at the time of the Passover is no argument to the contrary.

[138] Jewish : Str.-B., I, 1040 ff.; Jos. Ant., 14, 309; 17, 167; Philo De Providentia, II, 50 acc. to Eus. Praep. Ev., 8, 14, 50 : θείαις γὰρ φύσεσιν ἡλίου καὶ σελήνης ἐπακολουθοῦσιν ἐκλείψεις· αἱ δὲ μηνύματά εἰσιν ἢ βασιλέων τελευτῆς ἢ πόλεων φθορᾶς.

[139] K. H. Schelkle, Die Passion Jesu (1949), 187; Mt. lays even greater stress on this (27:45 ff.). Cf. Loh. Mk. ad loc.; Malmede, 485-491.

[140] M. Dibelius, Die Formgeschichte d. Ev.³ (1959), 195 f. Mt. modifies the sense by heaping up eschatological signs. Mk.'s strict chronology is blurred, cf. Mk. 15:25 with Mt. 27:36, also Lk. 23:35.

[141] Dibelius, op. cit., 194 f.

[142] Ibid., 204.

[143] H. Conzelmann, Die Mitte d. Zeit³ (1960), 81, cf. 51.

[144] If the expression is taken strictly the place is on the edge of the world ; but the phrase was a current one and does not run counter to the common view that the place of punishment is beneath, cf. Jos. Ant., 2, 344.

[145] ζόφος τοῦ σκότους, cf. Ael. Arist., 24, 44 (Keil). On Hades in Jos. → n. 13.

[146] On the phrase cf. Col. 1:13 (→ n. 175), though the meaning is not the same. On the role of Satan cf. Lk. 22:3; Jn. 13:2, 27; 14:30. Satan is not the cause (→ 158, 21 ff.). In kerygmatic ref. to the passion he is never mentioned (Pilate is in the Creed, not Satan), cf. Ac. 2:23 etc. He is only a marginal figure. His power is not his own ; it is given to him, Lk. 4:6. Nor should his part in the acts against Jesus be confused with that of the human agents. If he had a hand this does not make them less guilty but simply discloses the real depth of these events.

c. Finally the apocalyptic use of the group is also in the sphere of literal usage, for the darkness with which the end of the world is ushered in is a genuine cosmic darkness. In this connection we may refer first to Mk. 13:24 / Mt. 24:29 → 431, 16 ff. [147] Though Mk. borrows his phrase from the OT there has been a shift of sense along apocalyptic lines. Darkness does not characterise the last day itself; it is a preceding sign in the last and wicked period which intimates the day of salvation. [148] Its character as a sign is expressly emphasised by Mark. [149]

Lk. changes the text of Mk. considerably. The gt. historical crisis of the last time, which is still ahead in Mk., is now replaced by the fall of Jerusalem. This means that he has to guard against deducing the time of the *parousia* from this event. [150] This historicising of the world crisis in Lk. does not mean that final cosmic expectation is itself spiritualised. It is true that Lk. does not have the catchword σκοτίζομαι. But materially the darkening is present in Lk. 21:25 f., and indeed the apocalyptic colouring is even more vivid.

In the opening of the Pentecostal address (Ac. 2:17-21) this picture of the last time is reinforced by a quotation from Jl. 2:28 ff. The translation is not wholly literal. The antitheses are more sharply stressed in Ac. Whereas in Jl. darkness expresses the terrible nature of the day, Luke depicts the day as an epiphany, cf. also Lk. 21:25 ff.

The apocalyptic motif of darkening links the Synoptic Gospels and the Revelation of John. Since this does not display the features of Johannine usage, it should be dealt with here. There are three passages. Rev. 8:12 (σκοτίζομαι): On the sounding of the 4th trumpet (→ 87, 6 ff.) the stars are smitten and lose a third of their radiance. [151] The mathematical note shows that the event is planned. The whole idea is abstract. The depiction is not controlled by observation of natural phenomena, as may be seen at once from the combining of the darkening with the astral-mythical motif of the fall of the stars (8:10 f. → IV, 26, 39 ff.). [152] Rev. 9:2 (σκοτόομαι): The sun is obscured by smoke from the abyss; we have here the idea of the fire of hell, → I, 10, 1 ff.; VI, 938, 3 ff. Rev. 16:10: With the pouring out of the fifth vial the βασιλεία of the beast is darkened; his power is overthrown. [153] The direct result is a final revolt, but this is merely a sign of desperation.

2. Figurative Use. The metaphor of Is. 8:23; 9:1 f. is adopted in Mt. 4:15 f. and Lk. 1:79. [154] The version in Mt. stands between the Hebrew and the LXX. [155]

---

[147] Str.-B., I, 955; Bousset-Gressm., 250 f.; Kl. Mk., ad loc.; cf. Is. 13:10; 34:4.

[148] Malmede, 476.

[149] The chronology is also important for him (μετά κτλ.), cf. v. 26 (καὶ τότε). He wants to distinguish the preceding historical crises from the final act of cosmic shaking and thus prevent any calculation of the time of the *parousia*; H. Conzelmann, "Geschichte u. Eschaton nach Mk. 13," ZNW, 50 (1959), 210-221.

[150] Conzelmann, op. cit., 116-121, 126.

[151] Cf. 8:12; Lk. 21:25 f.; on Rev. 6:12 → IV, 551, 6 ff. The ninth plague of Egypt (Ex. 10:21 ff.) has also had some influence here.

[152] Malmede, 475. Cf. also that the night becomes a third part darker; Loh. Apk. on 8:12 comments as follows: "... as if the temporal significance of day and night corresponded to the spatial significance of sun, moon, and stars (cf. already Am. 8:9)." This is not a naïve view (Bss. Apk. on 8:12) but a specifically apocalyptic equation of temporal and spatial concepts.

[153] Cf. here too Ex. 10:21 ff.; Is. 8:22; Ps. 105:28.

[154] For a similar image in Gk. style cf. Luc. Nigrinus, 4: ὥσπερ ἐκ ζοφεροῦ τινος ἀέρος τοῦ βίου τοῦ πρόσθεν ἐς αἰθρίαν τε καὶ μέγα φῶς ἀναβλέπων.

[155] On the transl. of the OT text cf. K. Stendahl, The School of St. Matthew (1954), 104-106, though he uses Hexapla B for comparison [Katz].

The most important difference is that the Masoretic is in the perfect, but the LXX has changed this into a future, a good rendering of the prophetic perfect. By going back to the perfect Mt. is claiming that the prophecy has been fulfilled. He also makes the text serve an understanding of revelation in which special emphasis is laid on the element of lowliness. Despised Galilee has become the place of eschatological fulfilment. [156]

3. Transferred Use. What is dark is what is hidden in Mt. 10:27 / Lk. 12:3 f. (→ III, 705, 5 ff.; V, 553, 6 ff.). [157] The Synoptic tradition uses this saying to portray the nature of revelation, which in preaching breaks free from its concealed or supernatural origin and becomes public. Mt. introduces a specific historical consideration in which he makes use of the Marcan motif of the Messianic secret. He distinguishes between the epoch of the earthly work of Jesus as the time of concealment and the epoch of the Church as that of proclamation. With this interpretation of the historical Jesus he thus gives the Church its present task in face of every threat. The mode of expression is paradoxical in Mt. 6:22 f. / Lk. 11:34-36. [158] Mt. 6:22 introduces the double saying. [159] In terms of the metaphor ἁπλοῦς (→ I, 386, 22 ff.) means healthy and πονηρός (→ VI, 555, 28 ff.) sick. But Mt. also has in view the evil or envious eye (cf. Mt. 20:15); this influences the metaphor. One may see this from the context, for Mt. has put the saying after a warning against gathering earthly treasures. [160] In keeping is the admonition in v. 23b in the form of a conclusion a minori. Luke makes the saying into an exhortation. The owner is responsible for the state of his eye. [161] Then, of course, he changes the final warning into a promise, → n. 62.

II. The Pauline Corpus.

1. Paul.

The word has no special significance in Paul, who stays within the frame-work of Jewish usage, → 431, 3 ff. Conversion is illumination, a transition from darkness to light. It is seen in analogy to creation in 2 C. 4:6 → n. 62 : [162] God's creative

---

[156] E. Lohmeyer, Galiläa u. Jerusalem (1939), 36-39.

[157] Possibly two originally independent sayings are combined here (the first also occurs in Mk. 4:22/Lk. 8:17; Bultmann Trad., 86 f., 99 f.). Do we originally have a proverbial warning (cf. Qoh. 10:20)? In Lk. the saying becomes a promise to the disciples. It is also a promise in Mt., though here the two epochs in salvation history, that of concealment and that of disclosure, are set in juxtaposition. In the dark = secretly, H. Grimme, "Studien zum hbr. Urmatthäus," BZ, 23 (1935), 244-265, 347-357.

[158] On the expression cf. also Eur. Alc., 385 (σκοτεινὸν ὄμμα). Jeremias Gl., 141 assumes that this is originally a simple experience-saying which Mt. took as an allegory. But it would be better styled a wisdom sentence, since the experience has already been worked up into a wisdom view of life. Bibl.: C. Edlund, Das Auge der Einfalt (1952); E. Sjöberg, "Das Licht in dir," Studia Theol., 5 (1951), 92; H. J. Cadbury, "The Single Eye," HThR, 47 (1954), 69-74; S. Aalen, "The Concept of Light in the Synoptic Gospels" (Norwegian), Svensk Exeget. Årsbok, 22/23 (1957/58), 21-24 → φῶς.

[159] Cf. Kl. Mt., ad loc.

[160] Cf. Jeremias Gl., 141.

[161] Cf. the context — signs which can and therefore must be understood if one is not to be lost ; K. H. Rengstorf, Das Ev. nach Lk., NT Deutsch, 3³ (1958), ad loc.

[162] It is based on Gn. 1:3, but with some influence of ψ 111:4 or Is. 9:1. "Out of" darkness is a current phrase, cf. Wnd. 2 K., ad loc. → IV, 25, 11 ff., examples : Plat. Resp., VII, 518a:

activity is repeated in the work of the apostle. This figurative description of conversion derives from Judaism [163] and was widespread in Christianity, Ac. 26:18; 1 Th. 5:4 f.; Eph. 5:8; 1 Pt. 2:9. [164] Worth noting is the dualistic intensification by mention of the "god of this aeon," v. 4. Darkness characterises paganism as evil both as a sphere and as a state, R. 13:12 → IV, 1125, 37 ff. We have here a typically Pauline, eschatological argument in favour of the demand to set aside the works of darkness, cf. also Eph. 5:11; Gl. 5:19 ff. The expression reminds us of the Dead Sea Scrolls, → n. 73 and → V, 298, 30 ff. [165] The eschatological progression, of course, is depicted in terms of ἡμέρα / νύξ rather than φῶς / σκότος. Naturally these are closely related. [166] Darkness can denote that which is hidden and will be disclosed at the Last Judgment, 1 C. 4:5. [167] This, too, is soundly Jewish (→ n. 167); one may even ask whether Paul is quoting an apocryphon here. [168] The style of R. 1:21 is that of Wisdom literature : darkening of the καρδία is a punishment for the perversion of the knowledge of God [169] as in R. 2:19. [170] In the latter verse a Jewish quotation has again been suspected. [171] Questions have been raised as to the authenticity of 2 C. 6:14 [172] (→ IV, 54, 41 ff.), which deals with the impossibility of κοινωνία ἀνομοίων. [173] The vocabulary of the section is that of Jewish decision-dualism. [174]

2. Colossians and Ephesians. The main line of Pauline thought is developed here (Eph. 4:18 cf. → n. 169) but with a tendency to think in terms of spheres. Darkness has its ἐξουσία, Col. 1:13 → II, 567, 34 ff. [175] The material context is again that of conversion (→ n. 163, 164), as in 1 Pt. 2:9, where σκότος is used in a transferred sense, and Eph. 5:8-11, where ἦτε γάρ ποτε σκότος has a Gnostic ring, as though man were identified with his sphere → 433, 22 ff.; in fact, however this is simply an epigrammatic form of expression. [176] Eph. 6:12 (→ III, 914, 1 ff.)

ἐκ σκότους εἰς φῶς — ἐκ φωτὸς εἰς σκότος, Crat., 418d: ἐκ τοῦ σκότους τὸ φῶς ἐγίγνετο, Philo Spec. Leg., IV, 187: ... ἐκ δὲ σκότους φῶς ἐργασάμενος, 1 QH 9:26 f.: "For thou hast caused a lamp to be lighted out of darkness," cf. also Str.-B., III, 274, 516 → n. 8, 45.

[163] Joseph and Asenath, 8 : καλέσας ἀπὸ τοῦ σκότους εἰς τὸ φῶς. Materially cf. Test. XII (→ 433, 1 ff.); → n. 45.

[164] 1 Cl., 59, 2; 2 Cl., 1, 4 ff.; Barn., 14, 5 f.

[165] This may also be a gen. qual., Prv. 2:13, cf. 1 QS 2:7: works are כחושך.

[166] On the metaphors cf. Dib. Th., ad loc.

[167] Cf. Da. 2:22.

[168] Note the parallelism ; cf. Joh. W. 1 K. and Ltzm. K., ad loc. On the gen. "what is concealed in darkness" cf. R. 2:16; 1 C. 14:25; cf. Bl.-Debr. § 263, 4.

[169] On the expression : Eph. 4:18 (διάνοια); Ltzm. R. Exc. on 1:25.

[170] Cf. Wis. 18:4; Is. 42:6 f.; 49:6.

[171] Ltzm. R., ad loc.; on the Jewish style Str.-B., III, 98-105.

[172] Cf. Wnd. 2 K., ad loc. The authenticity is contested by R. Bultmann, "Exeget. Probleme d. 2 K.," Symbolae Bibl. Uppsalienses, 9 (1947), 14, n. 16; cf. J. A. Fitzmeyer, "Qumran and the Interpolated Paragraph in 2 C. 6:14-7:1," Catholic Bibl. Quarterly, 23 (1961), 271-280.

[173] Cf. Jos. Ant., 4, 228 f. (on the same statute to which the v. alludes, cf. Lv. 19:19; Dt. 22:10); Sir. 13:2, 15 ff.; Philo Ebr., 57; Fug., 14; supposed Philo fr. in Jn. of Damascus Sacra Parallela (MPG, 95 [1864], 1233 C): ἀμήχανον συνυπάρχειν ἀλλήλοις φῶς καὶ σκότος, Lidz. Joh., 160 → n. 107.

[174] More so than elsewhere in Paul (apart from Eph. 6:10 ff. → 442, 19).

[175] In Lk. 22:53 the same expression denotes the underworld, cf. Ac. 26:18, but here the world itself. On the confessional style cf. E. Käsemann, "Eine urchr. Taufliturgie," Exeget. Versuche u. Besinnungen, I (1960), 34-39.

[176] Is this fashioned in analogy to the description of a figure as light in Is. 42:6; 49:6; R. 2:19; Lk. 2:32; Jn. 1:9 etc. ?

is more strongly dualistic. We are again reminded of the Dead Sea Scrolls, →
431, 22 ff. The temporal understanding of R. 13:12 is replaced by a spatial understanding. [177]

III. John.

In John the duality between light and darkness has been raised to the level of
the theological and conceptual. His thinking does not begin, of course, with a given
duality but with the greatness of light and its manifestation. [178] The problem of
historical interrelationship has been reopened with the Dead Sea Scrolls (→
431, 22 ff.), but naturally it has not been solved → φῶς. In both there is decision
between light and darkness. But in John this is related to the concrete manifestation of light. There is no connection between Qumran and the Johannine idea of
"the" true light. [179] Gnostic parallels (→ 434, 17 ff.) maintain their hermeneutical
priority at this point. Not only is there darkness in the world ; the world itself
is darkness (Jn. 8:12; 12:35, 46; 1 Jn. 1:5 f.; 2:8 ff.). It is for this very reason that
no cosmological dualism develops ; it would disrupt the radicalism of thought. In
John, too, darkness is a sphere = power, but it is not, as in Gnosticism, a substance too ; it is the world's proper nature in which this flourishes. [180] Johannine
style may be seen in Jn. 1:5 even if the verse is taken from a source. [181] At a first
glance the saying seems to be figurative, [182] but the second half of the verse shows
that the terms are used literally. Darkness puts up no effective resistance. The
thought that it cannot understand light [183] is modified here along the lines of
historical decision : the world is darkness as it asserts itself as such against the
light. Its nature is due to guilt, not fate. That the situation of decision is not
set up by the nature of the world but by the manifestation of light may be seen
from Jn. 3:19 → VI, 557, 14 ff. [184] The negative decision of the world is declared
by its works. This does not mean that moral wickedness is more original than

---

[177] In exposition note Eph. 2:2 and the gen. cosmology of the epistle. The earth is the
lower surface of the universe with no underworld. Life extends up from it to the ἐπουράνια
and is exposed to the powers which inhabit this realm. Its lowest sphere is the air, the seat
of the ἄρχων τῆς ἐξουσίας τοῦ ἀέρος = διάβολος, cf. Asc. Is. 7:9 ff.; 10:29; 11:23.
Apart from this Eph. has no firmament as a wall between the upper and lower realms.
The pt. is that the upper realm is open, which accords with the idea of the body of Christ.
The baptised can survive the battle against the powers because they have been placed in the
body of Christ and are no longer under the powers but over against them. On the cosmology cf. H. Schlier, Christus u. d. Kirche im Eph. (1930), esp. 5 f., also Schlier Eph., 290-
298 on 6:12 ff.
[178] Even formally the two concepts cannot have developed in analogy to one another.
Only → φῶς carries a gen.
[179] The Dead Sea Scrolls have no view of the world corresponding to John's.
[180] Cf. Bultmann Theol., 362.
[181] In analysis cf. Bultmann J., 1-5; E. Käsemann, "Aufbau u. Anliegen d. joh. Prologs,"
Festschr. F. Delekat (1957), 75-99; R. Schnackenburg, "Logos-Hymnus u. johann. Prolog,"
BZ, NF, 1 (1957), 69-109; S. Schulz, Komposition u. Herkunft d. joh. Reden (1960), 7-69.
[182] Jn. 1:5 might have evolved from a fig. saying, cf. the pres.; Bultmann J., ad loc., 26,
n. 4 thinks the original contained an impf. or Aram. part. The community naturally takes
the pres. to apply to its own present as this is shaped by revelation.
[183] Lidz. Liturg., 131; O. Sol. 42:3 f. καταλαμβάνειν does not mean "to overpower"
(→ IV, 10, 22 ff.). The meaning may be gathered from v. 10 (οὐκ ἔγνω), cf. v. 11. The
word is taken to be ambiguous by C. K. Barrett, The Gospel acc. to St. John (1955), ad loc.;
M. Black, An Aram. Approach to the Gospels and Acts² (1954), 10; W. Nagel, "Die
Finsternis hat's nicht begriffen (Jn. 1:5)," ZNW, 50 (1959), 132-137.
[184] μᾶλλον ἤ naturally has an exclusive sense here. Lidz. Ginza R, 285, 31: "Those who

religious wickedness; in Johannine anthropology the subject and his works are not abstractly divided. Wickedness actualises itself precisely in this decision. It does not consist only in this, but what man is already is brought to light here. [185] The "abiding" of Jn. 12:46 expresses the fact that the decision is now definitive. Closer to figurative use is Jn. 12:35, where there is vacillation between a figurative and literal sense. Revelation has its time. This leads to the summons not to delay lest darkness become definitive, not in itself, but for those addressed. [186] Like 12:35, 8:12 uses the concept of περιπατεῖν (→ V, 945, 12 ff.), which in the realm of darkness is naturally a going astray. [187]

1 Jn. 1:5 f. states the thesis which is discussed in what follows. [188] The meaning is controlled by φῶς. σκότος is not an opposing sphere. It is used in a transferred sense and serves to give emphasis by negation of the opposite. [189] The thrust is ethical, as may be seen from the linking with ἁμαρτία and → ψεῦδος. [190] The ontological thesis is followed by practical application with a polemical attack (ἐὰν εἴπωμεν ... cf. 2:4; 2:9; 4:20) on an enthusiasm which preaches habitual sinlessness. The paradox is advanced that we walk in light but do not claim sinlessness. [191] The basic thought of 1 Jn. 2:8-11 [192] is similar. Being in the light comes to expression in περιπατεῖν. [193] As in the former passage one notes, in contrast to John's Gospel, the ethical concern. [194] The contradiction between the two passages is only apparent; in 1 Jn. 1:6 walking in darkness is a reason for breach of fellowship with God, while here it is a result. [195] The fact that it may be both is worth noting. The horizon is not the world as in the Gospel; it is the Church

---

leave the call of light and love the call of darkness." Philo Spec. Leg., I, 54 : σκότος αἱρού-μενοι πρὸ αὐγοειδεστάτου φωτός. The ref. here is to something very different, the apostasy of the Jews. The usage is fig., not lit.

[185] "He actually decides on the basis of his past, but in such a way that he gives meaning to the past only in this decision" (Bultmann J. on 3:20 f.). This shows that for John judgment is not a cosmic process, as for the Gnostics (Odeberg, 130-149; Bultmann J., ad loc., 113, n. 6), but a historical act. On darkness and its dread of the light cf. Lidz. Joh., 203.

[186] καταλαμβάνειν (→ n. 183) is not to be taken mythically here either; it is a common phrase for the approach of darkness (→ IV, 10, 22 ff., though the v. is taken differently here); cf. 1 Th. 5:4 f.; Philo Jos., 145.

[187] Cf. Corp. Herm., 1, 19 : οὗτος μένει ἐν τῷ σκότει πλανώμενος (→ VI, 238, 1 ff.). Bultmann associates the last three passages in his reconstruction of a "discourse on light" (Bultmann J., 237 and 260; cf. H. Becker, "Die Reden d. Joh.-Ev. u. der Stil d. gnostischen Offenbarungsrede," FRL, 68 (1956), 114-116. Ref. to the light-ritual of Tabernacles (H. Riesenfeld, Jésus transfiguré [1947], 278 f.) cannot explain John's terminology.

[188] Stylistic arguments are hardly adequate to support assignment to a written source, R. Bultmann, "Analyse d. 1 Joh.," Festschr. A. Jülicher (1927), 138-158.

[189] As against Wnd. Kath. Br., ad loc. Stylistically 1 Jn. 4:8; Jn. 4:24; Lucretius De Rerum Natura, I, 4 f., 22 f.; 1 QS 11:11; 1 QM 10:4 f.; 1 QH 1:8; 10:9; Lidz. Joh., 84, 2 ff.; 244, 18 ff.; Lidz. Ginza R, 20, 19 ff.; Nauck, 19-26. On the thesis cf. Philo Som., I, 75. Materially Jm. 1:17; Slav. En. 31:2; Philo Abr., 205.

[190] Nauck, 89-94 thinks the vocabulary is perhaps related to that of baptism, but it is better to connect it with that of conversion, R. 13:12; Philo Abr., 70; Joseph and Asenath, 8 and 15 passim.

[191] H. Braun, "Literar-Analyse u. theol. Schichtung im 1 J.," ZThK, 48 (1951), 262-292.

[192] Bultmann Analyse, 144 f. assigns vv. 9-11 to the source.

[193] The style varies, e.g., conditional clauses and apodictic participles. Nauck, 28-42 sees a possible connection with Jewish sacral law (OT, 1 QS).

[194] ἐν is not to be pressed as though σκοτία were a sphere in the Gnostic manner; this is common Gk. (→ n. 10), cf. Luc. De Calumniis, 1: ἐν σκότῳ γοῦν πλανωμένοις πάντες ἐοίκαμεν, Plut. Carn. Es., II, 1 (II, 997a). There are many OT examples. In the first instance 1 Jn. 2:11 also seems to have natural darkness in view.

[195] Schnackenburg J., ad loc.

in the world. Darkness is disappearing; in view of this one can look forward to the victory of light.

F. The Post-Apostolic Fathers.

The group does not occur in Ign. 1 Cl. has it in the usual transf. manner in 36, 2 : darkening of the διάνοια, cf. 2 Cl., 19, 2. 1 Cl., 38, 3 looks back to our origin : ἐκ ποίου τάφου καὶ σκότους ὁ πλάσας ἡμᾶς καὶ δημιουργήσας εἰσήγαγεν εἰς τὸν κόσμον αὐτοῦ. Barn. uses the word in characterisation of the two ways, 5, 4; 18, 1.[196]

Conzelmann

---

† σκύβαλον

A. The Greek World.

The derivation has not been cleared up. Suid., *s.v.* takes it as κυσίβαλόν τι ὄν, τὸ τοῖς κυσὶ βαλλόμενον = what "is thrown to the dogs," but this is popular etym. σκύβαλον occurs only in later Gk. (earliest instances Leonidas of Tarent. Anth. Graec., 6, 302 and P. Zenon, 59494, 16 [3rd cent. B.C.]) [1] and is rare. Only with hesitation does literature seem to have adopted it from popular speech. Lit. σκύβαλον means 1. "dung," "muck" both as "excrement" cf. Etym. M.: τὸ δι' ἐντέρων ἐκδιδόμενον, cf. περίσσωμα τροφῆς καὶ σκύβαλον, Plut. Is. et Os., 4 (II, 352d): ἐξιᾶσι σκύβαλον καὶ οὖρον, Alex. Aphr. Problemata, 1, 18; also Artemid. Onirocr., 1, 67; 2, 14; Strabo, 14, 1, 37, and also as "fodder or food that has gone bad" χόρτον σαπρὸν καὶ ὅλον λελυμένον ὡς σκύβαλον, P. Fay., 119, 7; 2. "scraps," "leavings" esp. after a meal σκύβαλα χόρτου, P. Greci e Latini, III, 184, 7; ἀποδειπνιδίου γευόμενος σκυβάλου, "what is left" after a meal, Anth. Graec., 6, 302, 6; δεῖπνον ... ἀπὸ σκυβάλων, meal from the "sweepings," *ibid.,* 6, 303, 4; τέφρης ... σκύβαλον, "ashes," *ibid.,* 7, 382, 2; 3. "refuse," θαλάσσης σκύβαλον, "flotsam and jetsam," Achill. Tat., II, 11, 5. In the transf. sense the word is used of persons and things to denote pitiful and horrible remains, a corpse half-eaten by fishes as the remnant of a much-bewailed sea-voyage πολυκλαύτου ναυτιλίης σκύβαλον, Anth. Graec., 7, 267, 2; Thessaly will be the "tragic dregs of war" σκύβαλον πολέμου λυγρόν, Sib., 7, 58. Under Hellenism popular pessimism uses the term for man's corruptibility. On a cup from the silver finds at Boscoreale a skeleton pours a libation on bones lying on the ground. The inscr. εὐσεβοῦ· σκύβαλα and the τοῦτ' ἄνθρωπος on the other side characterise man's remains as refuse. [2] This view [3] is worked out and given a philosophical basis in the radical dualism of later Gnosticism. Here the human body, the material and ungodly

---

[196] Cf. Did., 1, 1 f.: life/death.

σ κ ύ β α λ ο ν. Pape, Pass., Liddell-Scott, Moult.-Mill., Pr.-Bauer⁵, Preisigke Wört., Boisacq⁴, Hofmann, *s.v.*; Walde-Pok., II, 556; Str.-B., III, 622; comm. on Phil. 3:8.

[1] Ed. C. C. Edgar, *Catal. Gén. des Antiquités Égypt. du Musée du Caire,* 85 (1928), 210.

[2] F. Winter, "Der Silberschatz von Boscoreale," *Jbch. d. Kaiserlich-Deutschen Archäol. Instituts,* 11 (1896), 82; A. Michaelis, "Der Silberschatz v. Boscoreale," *Pr. Jbch.,* 85 (1896), 43; cf. Dib. Ph.³, *ad loc.*

[3] In the OT Job 20:7 with ref. to the ungodly, cf. Zeph. 1:17 and 1 K. 14:10 [Bertram].

garment of the soul, is often described by the contemptuous word "filth" or similar terms and concepts. In the Ginza, e.g., it is said of the soul as the "treasure of life" : "They put it in filth (the unclean body) and clothe it in the colour ot flesh," R, 96, 29 f., cf. L, 430, 17 etc. In gen. the word carries with it the thought of what is worthless and useless, also abhorrent and unclean.

Synon. with σκύβαλον is σκυβάλισμα "table crumbs," Ps.-Phocylides, 156. The noun σκυβαλισμός in Polyb., 30, 17, 12, in accord. with its structure, denotes the activity of the verb σκυβαλίζειν, "to treat contemptuously," cf. Dion. Hal. De Oratoribus Veteribus, 1, later σκυβαλεύειν, Schol. on Luc. Nec., 17. There are 2 forms of adj. derivates : σκυβαλικός "scorned," "filthy," ἀργυρίοισι σκυβαλικοῖσι, Timocreon in Plut. Them., 21 (I, 122d) and σκυβαλώδης "waste," Anon. Londinensis, 29, 39. [4]

B. Hellenistic Judaism.

The employment of the word in Hell. Judaism remains within the compass of Gk. usage. In the LXX σκύβαλον occurs only once in a late work and in a transf. sense. Sir. 27:4 uses the image of lumps of manure (κοπρία) remaining in the sieve to illustrate the refuse, i.e., the impurity and wickedness in the mind of man (σκύβαλα ἀνθρώπου). Symmachus has σκύβαλον for בָּל at Ez. 4:12, 15 (LXX βόλβιτον).

Philo and Joseph. use the word only in the lit. sense. In Philo the nondivine parts of an offering are to be given as "refuse" (ὥσπερ σκύβαλα) to the mortal race, Sacr. AC, 109; in the whole offering this is nothing but the remains of food (τροφῆς σκυβάλων) and the skin, ibid., 139. Joseph. tells how the inhabitants of Jerusalem, during the famine when the city was besieged by Titus, had to search sewers and dung for something to eat, Bell., 5, 571.

C. The New Testament.

In the NT σκύβαλον is used only once by Paul at Phil. 3:8. As one who has been led to faith by Jesus Christ he is evaluating all the natural and religious factors (v. 5 f.) which seemed to him to be very important in his former life : ἡγοῦμαι σκύβαλα, "I count them all as dung." [5] The threefold use of ἡγεῖσθαι forms a crescendo. The perfect ἥγημαι (v. 7) relates to conversion ; since this Paul has learned to regard all his former κέρδη as ζημία (→ II, 890, 32 ff.) for Christ's sake. The present ἡγοῦμαι (v. 8a) confirms that this is his judgment now. The second present ἡγοῦμαι (v. 8c) strengthens this [6] by substituting σκύβαλα for ζημία. The intensification lies in the element of resolute turning aside from something worthless and abhorrent, with which one will have nothing more to do. [7] The choice of the vulgar term stresses the force and totality of this renunciation. [8] The divine privileges of Israel (R. 3:1 ff.; 9:4 f.) and the spiritual character of the Law are not herewith denied. [9] But the striving for self-righteous-

---

[4] Ed. H. Diels, Supplementum Aristotelicum, III, 1 (1893), 55.
[5] Cf. G. Ricciotti, Der Ap. Pls. (1950), 154 f.
[6] With Haupt Gefbr., ad loc. against Ew. Ph., ad loc.
[7] Against J. B. Lightfoot Phil.[6] (1881), ad loc., 149, who appeals to κύνας in v. 2 for the sense of "refuse," i.e., scraps from the table ; so also J. H. Michael, The Ep. of Paul to the Phil., MNTC[6] (1954), ad loc.
[8] Cf. P. Bonnard, L'épître de saint Paul aux Phil., Comm. du NT, 10 (1950), ad loc.
[9] Mich. Ph., ad loc. To soften the harsh judgment of Paul, Chrys. Hom. in Phil., ad loc. (MPG, 62 [1862], 265) and Thdrt. Comm. on Phil., ad loc. (MPG, 82 [1864], 580 f.) bring in the relation between wheat and chaff, cf. M. R. Vincent, Phil., ICC[3] (1922), ad loc., 101.

ness by one's own achievement is unmasked as πεποιθέναι ἐν σαρκί (v. 3), as a carnal and worldly enterprise, the complete antithesis of faith. Materially, perhaps, Paul chose σκύβαλα, which in religious Hellenism was used for the dualism of the divine and the secular (→ 445, 28 ff.), to echo the contrast between spirit and flesh, Χριστός (πνεῦμα) and σάρξ, in the passage. [10] To the degree that the Law is used in self-justification, it serves the flesh and is not just worthless but noxious and even abhorrent. The two elements in σκύβαλον, namely, worthlessness and filth, are best expressed by a term like "dung."

The post-apost. fathers do not use the word.

Lang

---

† Σκύθης

1. The Scythians in the Ancient Orient.

The Scythians were Iranian nomads who lived in the South Russian steppes. About 700 B.C. they burst into Asia Minor. They first drove out the related Cimmerians, who lived on the north coast of the Black Sea, and then pressed on through the eastern passes of the Caucasus into the territory of the Medes, Hdt., I, 103 f. Hdt. says that from there they moved on through Palestine to Egypt, where Psammetich I (663-609) staved them off by gifts ; on their return they destroyed the shrine of the fertility goddess in Ascalon, I, 105. For 28 yrs. the Scythians terrorised the Near East (I, 106) but they did not establish any lasting kingdom. According to the Gadd chronicle [1] the Umman-Manda (Manda hordes) made alliance with Nabopolassar and helped to overthrow the Assyrian empire. The alliance of Babylonians, Medes and Scythians took Assur in 614, Nineveh in 612, and Haran in 609.

2. The Scythians in the Old Testament.

The depiction of the Scythians in Hdt. (→ lines 13 ff.) corresponds to that of the invaders in the threats of Jer. and Zeph. towards the end of the 7th cent. B.C. Acc. to Jer. they come from the north, 4:6; 6:22 f.; cf. 1:13. They are swift riders, 4:13, 29. They are like a storm (4:13) or a lion (4:7). They are an ancient people whose language is not understood in Judah, 5:15. Zeph. declares that the day of Yahweh and judgment on Judah and Jerusalem will be brought in by alien hosts, 1:2-18. It is not certain,

---

[10] Cf. Loh. Phil., *ad loc.*

Σ κ ύ θ η ς. Liddell-Scott ; Pr.-Bauer[5], *s.v.*; J. B. Lightfoot, *St. Paul's Ep. to the Col. and to Philemon* (1904), Exc. on Col. 3:11; K. Kretschmer, Art. "Scythae" in Pauly-W., 2a (1923), 923-942, 942-947; G. Beer, Art. "Scythopolis," *ibid.*, 947 f.; F. Hommel, *Ethnologie u. Geographie d. Alten Orients, Hndbch. KIAW*, III, 1, 1 (1926), 29-30, 194-198, 210-214, 485 f.; J. Oehler, Art. "Skythai," Pauly-W., 3a (1929), 692 f.; F. Humborg, Art. "Skythes, 1," *ibid.*, 693 f.; T. Hermann, "Barbar u. Skythe," ThBl, 9 (1930), 106 f.; H. Bengtson, *Griech. Gesch., Hndbch. KIAW* (1950), 88; Loh. Kol. on 3:11; T. T. Rice, *The Scythians* (1957).

[1] C. J. Gadd, *The Fall of Nineveh. The Newly Discovered Babylonian Chronicle No. 21901 in the Brit. Museum* (1923). Cf. K. Galling, *Textbuch z. Gesch. Israels* (1950), 59-63.

however, that these invaders in Jer. and Zeph. are the Scythians.[2] In the list of nations in Gn. 10:3 Gomer and Ashkenaz are mentioned among the sons of Japheth, cf. 1 Ch. 1:6. Gomer represents the Cimmerians while Ashkenaz is perhaps to be read as Ashkuz (ן = ג, Assyr. *aškūza*) and equated with the Scythians.[3] In Jer. 51:27 Ashkenaz is mentioned along with the kingdoms of Minni (Armenia) and Ararat.

3. The Scythians in the Graeco-Roman World.

Acc. to the saga of the Pontian Gks. Hercules visited the Scythians, Hdt., IV, 8-10. Scythes was the son of Hercules and Echidna and came to rule over the people, who were then called Scythians after him. Behind this is the historical fact that through establishing several colonies on the north shore of the Black Sea the Gks. came into close contact with the Scythians. Hes. Fr., 55 mentions the Σκύθας ἱππημολγούς along with the Ethiopians and Ligurians. Athens had police forces called Σκύθαι after their homeland and τοξόται after their equipment, Plat. Prot., 319c; they were also called Πευσίνιοι after their founder, Schol. on Aristoph. Ach., 54.[4] Up to the 4th cent. they maintained order and discharged municipal duties. Between 510 and 480 B.C. Scythes, a vase-painter of Scythian origin, was at work in Athens.[5]

For the Gk. historians the Scythians were a simple and strong people unaffected by the ills of civilisation. Aesch. referred to the εὔνομοι Σκύθαι in Fr., 198 (TGF, 66), while Strabo speaks of their modest way of life, their moderation, and their sharing of goods, 7, 3, 7. Far more common, however, is censure of their crudity, excess and ferocity, so that the verb σκυθίζειν (compound ἐπισκυθίζειν) has a sinister ring. Ref. is made to their practice of scalping fallen enemies and this is called σκυθίζειν, Eur. El., 241; Epigr. Graec., 790, 8. The same verb can mean "to drink immoderately," Hier. Rhodius in Athen., 11, 101. ἐπισκυθίζειν means the pouring out and drinking of unmixed wine, Hdt., VI, 84; Athen., 10, 29. Scythian speech also gave offence. Aristoph. ridicules the speech of a Scythian archer in Thes., 1001 ff. Scythian speech comes to mean what is rough and uncultured and jarring, Plut. Vit. Dec. Orat., 8 (II, 847 f.); Menand. Fr., 612, 13 (Körte). The crudeness of the Scythians in matters of love is censured in Philostr. Ep., 5. For the Gks., then, the Scythians are a vivid example of the barbarian way of life. The adj. Σκυθικός is used in connection with men, localities etc. in Alcaeus Fr., 318;[6] Cratinus Fr., 336 (CAF, I, 111 f.); Zosimus, IV, 20, 3;[7] Luc. Toxaris, 54. In the Graeco-Rom. world the Scythians represented a specific oriental slave-type located around the Black Sea.[8] Cicero, too, refers to them as good examples of barbarians. He pts. out that the inhumanity of his Roman opponents exceeds even that of the Scythians, Cic. Verr., II, 5, 150; Oratio in Pisonem, 8, 17; Nat. Deor., II, 1; III, 4.

---

[2] W. Rudolph, *Jeremia, Hndbch. AT,* I, 12² (1958) on 1:13-16; T. H. Robinson-F. Horst, *Die zwölf kleinen Propheten, Hndbch. AT,* I, 14² (1954), Exc. "Das Skythenproblem," 188-189; S. B. Frost, "Eschatology and Myth," VT, 2 (1952), 76-78.

[3] G. Hölscher, "Drei Erdkarten," SAH, 1944-1948, 3 (1949), 22, n. 9, 45-56, esp. 53, is against this equation; he suggests (53) that the name = Ἀσκάνιοι (Phrygians).

[4] Ed. W. Dindorf (1838). In Hom. Il., 13, 5 Ἱππημολγοί is the name of a people along with the Thracians and Mysians. The ref. is to a Scythian or Tartar tribe, cf. Liddell-Scott, *s.v.*

[5] H. Nachod, Art. "Skythes, 2" in Pauly-W., 3a (1929), 694-696: "The Scythian was one of the most gifted painters of his age; esp. in the new style which had just come in he cleverly adorned vessels with the most daring compositions characterised by a strong note of humour," 694. This stranger from a barbarian land probably owned his own workshop in Athens. The potter Criton is thought to have been his son.

[6] Ed. E. Lobel-D. Page, Poetarum Lesbiorum Fr. (1955).

[7] Ed. L. Mendelssohn (1887), 174, 21.

[8] Scythes is attested as a slave-name. Thus a slave called Scythes was an eye-witness of the assassination of his master Pompey on landing in Egypt, Plut. Pomp., 78 2 (I, 661a).

4. The Scythians in Later Judaism.

The Gk. name of the ancient city of Beth-Shan on the eastern edge of the Plain of Jezreel is Σκυθόπολις, written Σκυθῶν πόλις (obviously the older name) [9] in Polyb., 5, 70; Jdt. 3:10; 2 Macc. 12:29; Ju. 1:27. Acc. to Syncellus, I, 405 [10] the name derives from the invasion when the Scythians overran Palestine and took Beth-Shan. In the Jewish world, too, the ferocity and crudity of the Scythians was known and abhorred. In 2 Macc. 4:47 stress is laid on the injustice of the death sentence passed by Antiochus Epiphanes on the opponents of Menelaus, and it is argued that in reality these men were so innocent that they would have been acquitted even among the Scythians. In 3 Macc. 7:5 the royal letter condemns the tyranny of the enemies of the Jews who slay their victims without investigation and in so doing behave so cruelly that they surpass the Scythians in ferocity — a comparison which reminds us of Cic. → 448, 33 f. Jos. Ap., 2, 269 says of the Scythians that they were bloodthirsty and hardly differed from the beasts. But they adhered passionately to their ancestral customs and condemned to death their own countryman, the wise Anacharsis, because he adopted Gk. practices, cf. Hdt., IV, 76. Philo groups the Scythians with the Parthians and Sarmatians and says they are no less wild than the Germans, Leg. Gaj., 10. For him the Egyptians and the Scythians are two very different representatives of barbarian peoples who, like the Athenians and Spartans in the Gk. sphere, differ very sharply in their laws and hence are not disposed to accept one another's customs, Vit. Mos., II, 19.

5. The Scythians in the New Testament.

Col. 3:10 f. (cf. Gl. 3:27 f.) seems to contain solemn phrases from a primitive baptismal liturgy in which the "putting on of the new man" or the Messiah is described. The emphasis in these phrases is on praise and thanksgiving. In contrast to similar Jewish praises all distinctions between men of the old aeon in respect of nationality, salvation history, or social status are done away in the act of baptism. The mark of the new aeon is the creation of the new man. Along with the different antithetical and supplementary pairs of concepts we find the connected terms βάρβαρος and Σκύθης (→ I, 552, 22 ff.). These have a distinctively non-liturgical ring and it is hard to say whether Σκύθης is simply an outstanding example of a barbarian people or whether βάρβαρος and Σκύθης are meant to differ from one another culturally, geographically and racially. [11] It is possible

---

[9] E. Risch, "Griech. Determinativkomposita," *Idg. Forschung,* 59 (1948), 263.

[10] Georgius Syncellus, ed. W. Dindorf (1829). Cf. Schürer, II, 171; G. Hölscher, *Palästina in d. pers. u. hell. Zeit* (1903), 43-46; A. Rowe, "The Topography and History of Beth-Shan," *Publications of the Palestine Section of the Museum of the Univ. of Pennsylvania,* I (1930), 42.

[11] Bengel on Col. 3:11 already considered two possibilities : a. βάρβαρος-Σκύθης is a contrast like Ἕλλην-Ἰουδαῖος; b. Σκύθης is a stronger form of βάρβαρος. Examples from Graeco-Rom. rhetoric support the idea of a crescendo. The Scythian is *barbaro barbarior* (Bengel, *loc. cit.*) or "the lowest type of barbarian," Lightfoot, 216. But the context of 3:11 supports an antithesis. Bengel thought the list of Greeks, Jews, barbarians and Scythians contained representatives of the nations in the four quarters of West and East, South and North. The barbarians would be esp. the Numidians. In fact the name Scythian in NT days was referred to the nomadic or settled tribes of South-East Europe (Sarmatians); for Strabo the whole of North Asia was the land of the Scythians, 11, 6, 2. Hermann, 106 f. pts. out that in the anon. Periplus maris Erythraei, 2 (ed. C. Müller, Geographi Graeci Minores, I [1855], 258) modern Ethiopia is called the land of the barbarians ; Ptolemy

that the name Σκύθης is mentioned separately because of the peculiar relations at Colossae ; this is more likely than that the apostle is simply following ancient academic usage and rhetorical tradition by associating the two groups. The obvious meaning is that even the offence which a Scythian must give to natural sensibility is overcome by the baptism of the Messiah Jesus.

6. The Scythians in the Apologists.

In the Apologists and later polemical discussion one can still see the influence of the earlier use of the term Σκύθης. Just. refers to the Scythians and Parthians to demonstrate the principle of the new Chr. order. This does not rest on an externally visible privilege such as the circumcision of the flesh, but on the true knowledge of God and His Christ and the keeping of the commandments. Under these conditions even a member of such rude and immoral peoples can become the friend of God, Dial. c. Tryph., 28. The dialogue in Ps.-Luc. Philopatris, 17 seems to rest on a view of this kind when it puts the question whether the deeds of the Scythians are also written in heaven.

Michel

---

† σκυθρωπός

A. Outside the New Testament.

1. σκυθρωπός, made up of σκυθρός "serious," "sad," and οπ-, means "serious- or sad-looking." The adj. and the corresponding verb σκυθρωπάζειν are used to denote various types of men with their psychically controlled physiognomies : the rich man who "looks gloomy," Aristoph. Pl., 756; the "serious" philosopher, Amphis Fr., 13 (CAF, II, 239); Alchibiades "heavy with thought," Ps.-Plat. Alc., II, 138a; the "gloomy" fishseller, Antiph. Fr., 218, 3 (CAF, II, 107); the "angry" member of the people, Xenoph. Cyrop., VI, 2, 21; the "serious" wit, Aeschin. Tim., 1, 83; the officially "solemn" dignitary, Or. in Ctesiphontem, 3, 20; the worker "embittered" even more by the better work of another, P. Zenon, 59481, 30; [1] the man "of measured demeanour" in a visit of condolence, Theoph. Char., 14, 7; the "psychically depressed" and intellectually unfruitful, Plat. Symp., 206d; [2] the avaricious whe puts on a "gloomy look" in order not to have to

---

Geographica, I, 17, 6; IV, 7, 4 calls the east coast of Ethiopia and Somaliland "Barbaria." Hence the barbarians might be the most southerly and the Scythians the most northerly of uncivilised peoples. There is a second antithesis between them ; they represent the black race and the white. Johannes Philoponus in his comm. (in Syr.) on the Categories of Aristot. (Διαιτητής cod. Syr. Vat., 144 f. 17 v b, ed. A. Šanda, Joh. Philoponi Opuscula Monophysitica [1930]) notes that the Scythians were distinguished from the Ethiopians by their white skin as the servant is distinguished from the master and the subject from the ruler. One might also pt. out that in the Cyrus-Cylinder, 13 (AOT, 369) a distinction is drawn between the "black-headed (-haired)" Babylonians and Umman-Manda, the light or blonde Iranians, cf. Hommel, 485, n. 2.

σ κ υ θ ρ ω π ό ς. [1] Ed. C. C. Edgar, *Catal. Gén. des Antiquités Egypt. du Musée du Caire*, 85 (1928), 197-199.
[2] σκυθρωπόν τε καὶ λυπούμενον (σκυθρωπάζον τε is also read for σκυθρωπόν τε), v. *Platon, Oeuvres compl.*, IV, 2, ed. L. Robin⁶ (1958), 61, ad loc. The ref. is possibly not

give, Demosth. Or., 45, 68. Eur. uses the word of Medea with her "dark looks," Med., 271, for the bringer of bad tidings, Hipp., 1152; Phoen., 1333, and for a "cross" old man, Ba., 1252. Hippocr. uses it of a sick person "of sorrowful countenance," Epid., III, 17, 14 (Kühlewein, I, 243, 17). μέλη σκυθρωπότατα is used for the very "melancholy" flute-music at the Pythian games ; this was finally given up because of its doleful character, Paus., X, 7, 5. Himerius uses σκυθρωπός of the river Melas on whose banks he received the news of the death of his son Rufinus, Or., 8, 22.[3] There is a similar link between human and natural sadness in Or., 9, 4; when Bacchus was torn asunder, the wine mourned also (σκυθρωπὸς οἶνος). Ps.-Dion. Hal. uses σκυθρωπότης in Art. Rhet., 11, 8 with ref. to the oratorical excess which causes annoyance.

2. In the OT σκυθρωπός corresponds to a. Hbr. זֹעֵף in Da. 1:10 Θ : "poor appearance of the face," b. Hbr. רַע Gn. 40:7 : "cross faces" τὰ πρόσωπα ὑμῶν σκυθρωπά cf. 2 Εσδρ. Β 12:2 ScL καὶ ἤμην σκυθρωπός. c. There is no Hbr. equivalent in Sir. 25:23, where πρόσωπον σκυθρωπόν is used for the "morose face" of a bad woman. σκυθρω-πάζειν is used 3 times for the Hbr. קָדַר: The oppressor (ψ 34:14 and 41:10) or his own guilt (ψ 37:7) forces the righteous to go "sadly." σκυθρωπάζειν is used for the "down-cast countenance" רוּחַ נְכֵאָה in Prv. 15:13 → VI, 361, 16. In 'Ιερ. 19:8 σκυθρωπάσει corresponds to Hbr. שָׁמֵם in the sense "to shudder," "to start back," as expressed in the features. In ὁ Λίβανος ἐσκυθρώπασεν at Ez. 31:15 Θ the grammatical subj. as opp. to the Mas. is not Yahweh, though He is there in the background as the logical subj.

3. Jos. has the adverbial σκυθρωπότερον at Ant., 2, 19 and σκυθρωπάζειν at 11, 54. The "sorrowing" Nehemiah who refrained from washing himself was κατεσκυθρωπα-κώς in 11, 164.[4]

B. In the New Testament.

The σκυθρωποί of Mt. 6:16 are men who in their fasting want to appear "sad" to men. Jesus calls them hypocrites because in a religious act their serious mien made them appear other than they were[5] and they did not turn in conversion to the Judge who sees what is hidden. Jesus demands cheerful penitence from His disciples because they encounter the Judge who forgives them as Father. The two who went to Emmaus were σκυθρωποί (Lk. 24:17) because their hope that Jesus of Nazareth would show Himself to be the deliverer of Israel had been dis-appointed, 24:21.

Bieder

---

to intellectual creation, cf. W. Gilbert, "Der zweite Teil des Logos der Diotima in Platons Gastmahl," *Philol.,* 68 (1909), 54.
[3] Ed. A. Colonna (1951), 85.
[4] Schl. Mt. on 6:16.
[5] *Loc. cit.*

σκώληξ, σκωληκόβρωτος

† σκώληξ.

A. The Greek World.

σκώληξ is related to the same root as σκέλος; σκωλ- is a development of Indo-Eur. *sqel- "bend," "lean," "crooked," ethically "perverted," esp. parts of the body, "flexible joint."[1] The suffix -ᾱκ- is diminutive and pejorative.[2] The word is found from Hom. and is used chiefly in natural history and comedy. It means 1. "worm" lit., esp. in the earth, "earthworm," ὥστε σκώληξ ἐπὶ γαίῃ κεῖτο ταθείς, Hom. Il., 13, 654; plur. "worms" on trees[3] and plants οἱ σκώληκες (of the mistletoe) μεγάλοι καὶ ἡδίους ἢ οἱ ἐκ τῶν δένδρων τῶν ἄλλων, Theophr. Hist. Plant., III, 12, 6; θηρία δὲ γίνεται ταῖς μὲν ῥαφανίσι ψύλλαι, τῇ δὲ ῥαφάνῳ κάμπαι καὶ σκώληκες, VII, 5, 4; in filth and muck, dirt καὶ σηπομένοις μὲν πᾶσι σκώληξ (γίνεται), VIII, 11, 2; τὰ δ' ἐκ βορβόρου ὡς σκώληκες (γίνεται), Sext. Emp. Pyrrh. Hyp., 1, 41; in animals κάμηλον μυδῶσαν ἤδη καὶ σκώληξι ἐπιβρύουσαν, Alciphr. Ep., I, 20, 3; in graves[4] σκώληκες ὑπὲκ σοροῦ αὐγάζονται, Anth. Graec., 7, 480, 3 cf. 10, 78, 3; fig. wretchedness and obtuseness τί σκώληξ ὢν λέγεις, ὅτι ἄνθρωπος εἶ, Epict. Diss., IV, 1, 142; ἀναίσθητος καὶ ὅλως τοῦ σκώληκος οὐδὲν διαφέρων, Luc. Vit. Auct., 27; transf.: in relation to flatterers οἱ κόλακές εἰσι τῶν ἐχόντων οὐσίας σκώληκες, Anaxilas Fr., 33, 1 (CAF, II, 274). 2. The "larvae of insects," so often Aristot. σκώληξ δ' ἐστὶν ἐξ οὗ ὅλου ὅλον γίγνεται τὸ ζῷον, Hist. An., I, 5, p. 489b, 8 f., cf. Gen. An., II, 1, p. 733a, 1 ff.; Hist. An., V, 19, p. 551b, 1 f., but also[5] ὥσπερ οἱ σκώληκες ἐν τοῖς κυττάροις κινούμενοι, Aristoph. Vesp., 1111; Theophr. Hist. Plant., VIII, 10, 4. 3. Transf. the "thread" which is spun by the distaff τοὺς τρεῖς μόνους σκώληκας ἔτι τούτους μ' ἔασον καταγαγεῖν, Epigenes, 7 (CAF, II, 418). 4. Aeolic for κολόκυμα: the "wave[6] of the sea" κωφὸν ὕδωρ τὸ ἄροιζον ... τοῦτο δὲ Ἀττικοὶ κολόκυμα, Αἰολεῖς δὲ σκώληκα καλοῦσι, Schol. on Hom. Il., II, 14, 16;[7] τὸ παυόμενον θαλάσσιον κῦμα

σ κ ώ λ η ξ. Pape, Pass., Liddell-Scott, Moult.-Mill., Preisigke Wört., Hatch-Redp., Pr.-Bauer[5], s.v.; not in Cr.-Kö.; F. Ast, Lex. Platonicum (1835), v. Arnim. Index, Leisegang, Ditt. Syll.[3], Index, s.v. Thes. Steph., Art. "σκώληξ," VII (1848-54), 476; Schenkel, Art. "Würmer," V, 679; E. Riehm, Art. "Würmer," HW, II, 1797; G. E. Post, Art. "Worm" in Hastings DB, IV (1902), 940; H. Guthe, Art. "Würmer" in BW, 732; Jastrow, s.v. רִמָּה, תּוֹלֵעָה; A. E. Shipley-S. A. Cooke, Art. "Worm" in EB, IV, 5353 f.; J. M. Casanowicz, Art. "Worm" in Jew. Enc., XII, 559 f.; K. Bornhäuser, "Die Gebeine d. Toten," BFTh, 26, 3 (1921); H. Haag, Art. "Wurm," Bibellex. (1951-56), 1728.
    [1] Cf. Boisacq, s.v.; Pokorny, 928; Hofmann, s.v.
    [2] Schwyzer, I, 497.
    [3] The woodworm is ὁ θρίψ (in living wood) or ἡ τερηδών (in dead).
    [4] Cf. Teles (ed. O. Hense [1909]), 31, 3 : κατορυχθέντα ὑπὸ σκωλήκων.
    [5] On ἰὸς σκώληκος aerugo vermicularis cf. τοῦ δὲ λεγομένου σκώληκος ἰοῦ δισσὸν εἶδος ὑπάρχει, Diosc. Mat. Med. V, 79, 6.
    [6] Cf. Galen, De differentia pulsarum, I, 25 (Kühn, 8, 551) on the κυματώδης and σκωληκίζων σφυγμός : τῷ δὲ σκωληκίζοντι σκώληκος ἐοικέναι πορείᾳ καὶ αὐτοῦ τοῦ ζῴου κυματωδῶς κινουμένου.
    [7] Ed. W. Dindorf, IV (1877), 39.

καὶ ἀρχόμενον, Plato Comicus Fr., 25 (CAF, I, 607), cf. Phryn. Praep. Soph., 108, 1 ff.; σκώληξ· τὸ πρὸς τῇ γῇ οἴδημα τῆς θαλάσσης· οἷον τὸ προσαράσσον κῦμα, Phot. Lex., s.v. 5. A kind of "cake" shaped like a worm πυτίας μοι δοκεῖ καλοῦσιν αὐτὰ καὶ σκώληκας (τὰ πέμματα), Alciphr. Fr., 6; Ep., IV, 13, 10. 6. "Heap of threshed grain" ἀπὸ τῆς ἅλω τὸ δινηθὲν καὶ συναχθὲν εἰς λικμητόν, Hesych., s.v.

B. The Old Testament and Later Judaism.

1. The Old Testament.

a. The Hebrew Equivalents.

In the LXX σκώληξ occurs 18 times, 9 in writings only in Gk. The usual Hbr. original is תּוֹלֵעָה, which in 7 of its 8 occurrences is transl. by σκώληξ, Ex. 16:20; Dt. 28:39; Is. 14:11; 66:24; Jon. 4:7; Ps. 22(21):6; Job 25:6. In Is. 41:14 LXX omits it, while Ἀ, Σ and Θ all have σκώληξ Ἰακώβ. שְׁנִי תוֹלַעַת[8] is originally the "shield-louse"[9] whose eggs and bodies are pulverised to make "crimson dye" (תּוֹלַעַת שְׁנִי Lv. 14:4, 6, 49, 51 f.; Nu. 19:6).[10] It is then used for crimson-coloured material, Ex. 25:4; 26:1, 31, 36; 27:16; 35:6, 23, 25, 35; 36:8, 35, 37; 38:18, 23; Nu. 4:8. Crimson is usually third in the colours of the priestly vestments, Ex. 28:5 f., 8, 15, 33; 39:1-3, 5, 24, 29, cf. 1 QM 7:11. Similarly תּוֹלָע in Is. 1:18; Lam. 4:5 means material dyed crimson. Along with the broader term תּוֹלֵעָה, which like σκώληξ means not only the worm but all kinds of insects, רִמָּה in keeping with its basic meaning (from רָמַם "to rot, decay"), is used primarily for "maggots" in decaying matter. This word occurs 7 times in all, and the LXX transl. it 3 times by σαπρία (Job 17:14; 21:26; 25:6), twice by σκώληξ (Ex. 16:24; Job 7:5), and once by σῆψις (Is. 14:11); in Job 24:20 the text is doubtful. The two terms תּוֹלֵעָה and רִמָּה occur together in parallelism in Is. 14:11; Job 25:6 and Is. 41:14, where we should probably read רִמַּת יִשְׂרָאֵל for מְתֵי יִשְׂרָאֵל (LXX ὀλιγοστὸς Ισραηλ; Ἀ τεθνεῶτες Ισραηλ; Σ ἀριθμὸς Ισραηλ; Θ νεκροὶ Ισραηλ). Σ also has σκώληξ in ψ 77:47 for the destructive flood (חֲנָמַל) and in Ez. 32:5 for רָמוּת "rubbish."[11]

b. Meanings.

Sometimes σκώληξ is the worm in the narrower sense.[12] The ref. in Dt. 28:39 is to cochylis ambiguella, the worm which infests grapes.[13] Acc. to Jon. 4:7 God prepared an unspecified[14] worm whose sting caused the gourd which had grown with such miraculous speed to wither. LXX uses the term for the woodworm in Prv. 12:4; 25:20,[15] as opposed to the Hbr. text and Gk. usage. The usual ref. is to "maggots" in rotting foods and decaying bodies, in the manna Ex. 16:20, 24, in corpses, graves and the realm of the dead Job 7:5; Sir. 7:17; 10:11; 19:3; Is. 14:11; 66:24, cf. Jdt. 16:17; 1 Macc. 2:62, in a sore

---

[8] Ἀ transl. this by σκώληκος (τὸ) διάφορον at Ex. 25:4; 28:5; 35:23, 35.
[9] Cf. I. Löw, Die Flora d. Juden, I (1924), 630 f.
[10] K. Galling, Art. "Farbe u. Färberei, 2" in BR, 153.
[11] רִמָּתֶךְ is thus to be read here.
[12] The חֲלִי אֶרֶץ (LXX σύροντες γῆν) of Mi. 7:17 are not earthworms but snakes. Similarly the creeping things (ἑρπετά), which acc. to Wis. 11:15 (LXX) were worshipped by the Egyptians, were probably crocodiles and snakes.
[13] Cf. Löw, op. cit., 101 f.
[14] Haag "snail."
[15] Two anon. transl. have "woodworm" at Hab. 2:11: quasi vermis in ligno loquens (sexta ed.); σκώληξ de ligno loquetur (septima ed.). This is obviously a free rendering of the Hbr. hapax legomenon כָּפִיס "spar in the beams" or "plaster" [G. Bertram].

Job 2:9c (LXX). The eating of a living body by worms is a serious illness in 2 Macc. 9:9. The worm is used metaphorically for the weak, the insignificant and the disfigured in Job 25:6; Ps. 22:6; Is. 41:14.

c. The Worm as a Sign of Eternal Damnation.

The basic passage for this idea is Is. 66:24 : כִּי תוֹלַעְתָּם לֹא תָמוּת, LXX ὁ γὰρ σκώληξ αὐτῶν οὐ τελευτήσει. Verses 23 f. may well be a later addition. Outside the city, in the Vale of Hinnom (→ I, 657, 23 ff.), the corpses of apostate Israelites lie as a spectacle for pious visitors to the temple in the time of salvation. Corruption (the worm) and burning (fire) are mentioned together as the two most common ways of disposing of dead bodies. Three possible interpretations of the worm which never dies call for special consideration. 1. The worm constantly receives fresh food from the bodies of dead apostates brought there. But the author can hardly be assuming that there would for ever be apostates in Jerusalem. [16] 2. The worm does not die until it has completed its work and the bones as well as the flesh of the dead are consumed, so that all hope of restoration to life is extinguished. The expression thus denotes total destruction. [17] 3. The worm describes a process of unending bodily corruption which the soul of the dead person experiences as pain, cf. Is. 50:11: מַעֲצֵבָה place of torment. It is thus a sign of eternal perdition and its pains. [18] The HT of Is. 50:11 tends to favour the third interpretation. At any rate apocalyptic [19] later took the expression to signify eternal suffering. In this way the passage (the fire more than the worm) became a dominant figurative expression for eschatological damnation.

2. The Rabbis.

The Rabb. continue to use both תוֹלָעָה and רִמָּה in the OT sense → 453, 7 ff. Wood in which a worm is found must not come on the altar ; priests not qualified to serve the altar must sort it out, Mid., 2, 6b. Maggots and worms are the lot of man in the tomb, Ab., 3, 1, cf. 4, 4a, With regard to the 12-month judgment of the transgressors of Israel in Gehinnom a tradition which may be traced back to R. Jose (c. 150 A.D.) says that the usual punishment for sinners is annihilation of body and soul but that for very bad heretics, mockers and opponents of the resurrection etc. there will be everlasting torment acc. to Is. 66:24, Seder Olam r., 3, 20-29. [20] R. Jehuda (c. 150 A.D.) also takes Is. 66:24 to refer to endless punishment, which God gives sinners special strength to endure, bSanh., 100b, Bar. [21]

---

[16] Cf. B. Duhm, D. Buch Js., Handkomm. AT, III, 1⁴ (1922), ad loc.

[17] Bornhäuser, 13 f., 23.

[18] P. Volz, Js. II, Komm. AT, 9 (1932), ad loc.

[19] Eth. En. 10:13; 46:6; 67:8 f.; 4 Esr. 7:36; Apc. Abr. 31:4 : Food for hell-fire ... the body filled with worms, cf. Volz Esch., 320-325. The two LXX ref. at Jdt. 16:17 and Sir. 7:17 are both obviously dependent on Is. 66:24, though they do not relate unequivocally to the punishment of hell. In Jdt. 16:17 the nations which rise up against Israel are threatened with God's punishment on the Judgment Day δοῦναι πῦρ καὶ σκώληκας εἰς σάρκας αὐτῶν, καὶ κλαύσονται (better with 583, Lat, Syr. καυθήσονται, cf. P. Katz in J. Ziegler, "Beiträge z. Jeremias-Septuaginta," Mitteilungen d. Septuaginta-Unternehmens, 6 [1958], 32) ἐν αἰσθήσει ἕως αἰῶνος. Sir. 7:17b HT probably meant that "the fate of all men is the worm" (V. Ryssel in Kautzsch Apkr. u. Pseudepigr., ad loc.); LXX reads : ἐκδίκησις ἀσεβοῦς πῦρ καὶ σκώληξ.

[20] Str.-B., II, 19 f.

[21] Ibid., 20; cf. the saying of R. Isaac II (c. 300 A.D.): "The worm in the flesh of the dead is as painful as a needle in the flesh of the living," bBer., 18b, Str.-B., II, 229.

3. Philo and Josephus.

The word does not occur in Philo. Jos. says that manna kept in store for the following day became inedible ὑπὸ σκωλήκων καὶ πικρίας, Ant., 3, 30.

4. The Qumran Community.

The Dead Sea Scrolls follow in the main the usage of the OT → 453, 7 ff. The worm denotes esp. human vanity and corruptibility. The word (תולעת) is normally used in connection with dust for the grave and death : "Those who lie in the dust lift up a standard, and like a worm the dead raise a standard to [eternal life]," 1 QH 6:34; [22] "to raise up the dead, the prey of worms, from the dust to (eternal) fellowship," 1 QH 11:12. [23] This is also how we are to construe 1 QS 11:9 f. (לסוד רמה ... חטאתי) : Death and corruption are the lot of sinful man, cf. line 9 : ולסוד בשר עול. [24] In these works the worm is nowhere clearly mentioned in connection with the suffering of the damned in the eternal fire of hell.

C. The New Testament.

In the NT the word occurs only in Mk. 9: [44, 46,] 48 [25] in a quotation from Is. 66:24, though a present is used instead of the LXX future : ὅπου ὁ σκώληξ αὐτῶν οὐ τελευτᾷ. The quotation goes with γέεννα and is designed to characterise eschatological hell. Since we find in contemporary Judaism both the idea of the annihilation of the damned and also that of their unceasing punishment (→ VI, 937, 39 ff.), both interpretations are possible here, too, according to the wording. Exegetes refer the non-dying of the worm either to full destruction, the definitive loss of life → 454, 14 ff., [26] or to unremitting corruption, eternal torment → 454, 16 f. [27] In view of τὸ πῦρ τὸ ἄσβεστον in v. 43 (→ VI, 945, 36 ff.) the latter interpretation is to be preferred. [28] There is no suggestion that the worm and fire are to be related separately to soul and body [29] along the line of gnawings of conscience and physical pain. In the first instance both terms describe the destruction of corpses and they are then used figuratively for the punishment of hell which affects the whole man.

D. The Post-Apostolic Fathers.

OT ideas predominate here → 453, 27 ff. The worm symbolises man's pettiness in 1 Cl., 16, 15 (the pre-existent Messiah predicts His abasement in ψ 21:7-9 [lit. acc. to the

---

[22] Cf. H. Bardtke, Die Handschriftenfunde am Toten Meer, II (1958), 243.

[23] Bardtke, 250. But cf. A. Dupont-Sommer, "Le Livre des Hymnes découvert près de la mer Morte (1 QH)," Semitica, 7 (1957), 78 : "afin d'élever cette vermine qu'est l'homme de la poussière vers [ton] secret [de vérité]," with ref. to Is. 41:14 for תולעת מתים.

[24] Worm and darkness might also characterise the host of the damned, cf. H. Bardtke, op. cit., I (1953), 108.

[25] The attestation in v. 44, 46 in the Western and Syr. MSS is due to later assimilation to v. 48.

[26] Bornhäuser, 13 f.; Loh. Mk., Hck. Mk., Schl. Mk., ad loc.

[27] Pr.-Bauer⁵, s.v.; Kl. Mk.; J. Schniewind, Das Ev. nach Mk., NT Deutsch, 1⁹ (1960); Wbg. Mk.; E. P. Gould, The Gospel acc. to St. Mark, ICC⁹ (1955), ad loc.

[28] Cf. Apc. Pt. 10:25 : ἐπέκειντο δὲ αὐτοῖς σκώληκες ὥσπερ νεφέλαι σκότους.

[29] Bengel, ad loc.

LXX]) and it is a sign of eternal perdition in 2 Cl., 7, 6; 17, 5 (lit. quotation from Is. 66:24 LXX). A new feature is the ref. to the worm which came forth from the decaying flesh of the phoenix bird in 1 Cl., 25, 3 (cf. Artemid. Onirocr., IV, 47: ἐκ τῆς σποδοῦ σκώληκα λέγουσι γεννᾶσθαι).

---

† σκωληκόβρωτος.

---

1. Outside the New Testament.

Composite verbal adj. (βιβρώσκω), "consumed by worms," "worm-eaten," cf. σκω-ληκοφάγος "consuming worms," Aristot. Hist. An., VIII, 3, p. 592b, 16, σκωληκοτόκος "generating worms," ibid., I, 5, p. 489a, 35; IV, 11, p. 538a. 25 f. Other compounds with -βρωτος are, e.g., λυκόβρωτος, "assailed by wolves," Aristot. Hist. An., VIII, 10, p. 596b, 7 and φθειρόβρωτος "eaten up by lice," Hesych. Milesius, 69 (FHG, IV, 176). Infrequently one also finds ἀσκωληκόβρωτος, "with no damage from worms," P. Gradenwitz, 7, 11 f.[1] (3rd cent. B.C.) and ὁλοσκωληκόβρωτος "totally consumed by worms," P. Osl., II, 26, 14 (1st cent. B.C.). σκωληκόβρωτος is normally used of plants, trees and fruits : μεσπίλη Theophrast. Hist. Plant., III, 12, 6; κάλαμος, ibid., IV, 11, 1; grain : P. Greci e Latini, V, 490, 14 (3rd cent. B.C.); γῆ P. Tebt., III, 701, 74 and 81 (3rd cent. B.C.). The word has not yet been found as a medical tt. for severe illness, though there is ref. to men being eaten up by worms.[2] The persecutor Antiochus Epiphanes was visited by a loathsome and fatal worm-disease ὥστε καὶ ἐκ τοῦ σώματος τοῦ δυσσεβοῦς σκώληκας ἀναζεῖν, καὶ ζῶντος ἐν ὀδύναις καὶ ἀλγηδόσιν τὰς σάρκας αὐτοῦ διαπίπτειν, 2 Macc. 9:9. In relation to the last illness of Herod the Gt. Jos. mentions sores in the entrails and pains in the bowels : τοῦ αἰδοίου σῆψις σκώληκας ἐμποιοῦσα, Ant., 17, 169; cf. Bell., 1, 656. It seems to have been cancer of the bowel.[3] The false prophet Alexander of Abonuteichos (2nd cent. A.D.) came to a terrible end διασαπεὶς τὸν πόδα μέχρι τοῦ βουβῶνος καὶ σκωλήκων ζέσας, Luc. Alex., 59. Death by worms was regarded as a divine punishment for particularly serious offences, Hdt., IV, 205.

2. In the New Testament.

In the NT σκωληκόβρωτος occurs only in Ac. 12:23 in relation to the death of Herod Agrippa I (d. 44 A.D.). As a punishment for his arrogance the angel of the Lord smote him καὶ γενόμενος σκωληκόβρωτος ἐξέψυξεν. The tradition used by Luke was probably influenced by the common motif of eating up by worms as a divine judgment → lines 18 ff.[4]

σκωληκόβρωτος. [1] Ed. G. Plaumann, Griech. Pap. d. Sammlung Gradenwitz, SAH, 15 (1914).
[2] Acc. to Diog. L., 3, 40 Plato was eaten up by lice.
[3] W. Otto, Art. "Herodes" in Pauly-W., Suppl., 2 (1913), 143.
[4] Cf. W. Nestle, "Legenden vom Tod d. Gottesverächter," ARW, 33 (1936), 246-269, esp. 263 f.

The account of the same event in Jos. Ant., 19, 346-350 differs in details. It says that Agrippa was attending a performance in the emperor's honour at Caesarea and was dressed in a magnificent silver robe. When this glistened in the sun flatterers did homage to him as a god. Because he accepted this he was at once smitten by severe pains and died five days later. [5]

Lang

σμύρνα, σμυρνίζω

† σμύρνα.

1. Myrrh comes from the tree commiphora abyssinica of the family of burseraceae (balsam trees). It is found esp. in South Arabia and North Ethiopia. [1] The sap which exudes at the breaks in the younger twigs, and which contains gum, volatile oil and resin, soon dries up. The taste is bitter, but a strong scent is given off, esp. when it is heated. σμύρνα is employed for myrrh in all its uses. When it is made fluid by pressing and heating στακτή is also employed. [2] μύρρα means the same as σμύρνα, Sappho Fr., 44, 30. [3] This is rare in Gk., but passed into Lat. as *murra*. It is obviously borrowed from the Semitic, cf. esp. Hbr. מוֹר, מֹר, from מרר "to be bitter." The origin of σμύρνα, however, is uncertain. [4] In antiquity myrrh was found among the Egyptians, Greeks, and Romans as a perfume, as incense, and as a medicine with many different uses. Acc. to Hdt., II, 86 it was employed by the Egyptians in embalming. [5]

2. In the OT myrrh occurs in Ex. 30:23 as the most important ingredient in holy anointing oil, and in Ps. 45:8 along with other sweet-smelling resins. There is a ref. to its sweet scent in Sir. 24:15. Myrrh is also mentioned several times in Cant., as incense

---

[5] Haench. Ag.[12], 330 f. on 12:23; Bauernf. Ag. on 12:23; A. Wikenhauser, *Die Ag. u. ihr Geschichtswert* (1921), 398-401.

σ μ ύ ρ ν α. Steier, Art. "Myrrha, 2" in Pauly-W., 16 (1935), 1134-1146; K. Galling, Art. "Harze, 3" in BR, 266; R. O. Steuer, "Myrrhe u. Stakte," *Schriften d. Arbeitsgemeinschaft d. Ägyptologen u. Afrikanisten in Wien* (1933).
[1] Botanically cf. Steuer, 9-18; A. Tschirch, *Hndbch. d. Pharmakognosie, s.v.* "Myrrha," esp. III, 2 (1925), 1115-1130; I. Löw, *D. Flora d. Juden*, I, 1 (1926), 305-311.
[2] On the meaning of στακτή cf. Steuer, 25-30 for LXX usage and 31-40 for Egypt. examples. In the NT we find στακτή from στάζω "to drip, trickle," cf. Herm. v., 3, 9, 1; not Barn., 12, 1; but cf. the conjecture of P. L. Couchoud, "Notes de critique verbale sur S. Marc et S. Matthieu," JThSt, 34 (1933), 128 on Mk. 14:3 (Loh. Mk., *ad loc.*).
[3] Ed. E. Lobel-D. Page, Poetarum Lesbiorum Fr. (1955), 36, cf. Liddell-Scott, *s.v.*; Pass. and Preisigke Wört., *s.v.* confuse things by mixing up myrrh and myrtle, → IV, 800, n. 2.
[4] H. Lewy, *Die semitischen Fremdwörter im Gr.* (1895), 42 f.; Steier, 1134 f.; Str.-B., II, 48 f. Is σμύρνα a popular etym. assimilation to the name Σμύρνη, which was an important commercial city in early days [Risch]? Perhaps σμ- is to be explained by μύρον μυρίζω, which can have the initial sound σμ-. At any rate σμύρνα is not to be related etym. to the group μυρ- → IV, 800, n. 2.
[5] Cf. Steier, 1141 f.; T. Reil, *Beiträge z. Kenntnis des Gewerbes im hell. Ägypten* (1913), 146 and bibl. → IV, 800, n. 1.

in 3:6, as a sweet ointment in, e.g., 4:14, and as anointing oil in 5:5, 13. [6] Cf. also σμύρνινον ἔλαιον in Est. 2:12. [7]

3. In the NT σμύρνα occurs in Mt. 2:11; Jn. 19:39. [8] In Mt. 2:11 it is among the gifts brought by the μάγοι and comes after frankincense, [9] so that the reference is perhaps to incense, → IV, 264, 1 ff. and n. 11. In Jn. 19:39, however, it is found alongside ἀλόη : [10] Nicodemus brought a mixture of myrrh and aloes, ὡς λίτρας ἑκατόν, some 100 (Roman) pounds. [11] These sweet-smelling substances, called ἀρώματα in 19:40, were laid in pulverised form between the clothes in which the body of Jesus was wrapped. One can hardly speak of embalming, especially as it is expressly emphasised that Jewish burial rites were followed. [12] Nevertheless, it is plain, as also in the related Mk. 16:1; Lk. 23:56; 24:1, that the body was being protected against rapid decomposition, and a speedy resurrection of Jesus was not expected. This feature is not without importance in relation to our understanding of the resurrection stories.

† σμυρνίζω.

The verb σμυρνίζω [1] occurs in Mk. 15:23 : at the place of crucifixion, and before the account of this in v. 24, the soldiers give Jesus ἐσμυρνισμένον οἶνον· ὃς δὲ οὐκ ἔλαβεν.

The mingling of myrrh with wine is known from other sources in antiquity and in spite of the bitter taste which myrrh has of itself the ref. is to a spiced wine which was a special fancy. [2] This makes it doubtful whether Mk. 15:23 is speaking of a stupefying

---

[6] Perhaps botanically Hbr. מֹר embraces more than myrrh in the true sense. G. Schwein-furth, "Balsam u. Myrrhe," Berichte d. Pharmazeutischen Gesellschaft, 3 (1893), 218-232, esp. 223, argues that מֹר does not mean myrrh but balsam. Cf. Steuer, 25-28. LXX always transl. מֹר by σμύρνα or σμύρνινος (→ line 1 f.) except at Cant. 1:13 : στακτή ('ΑΣ σμύρνα); Prv. 7:17: κρόκος → IV, 800, n. 3.

[7] Jos. has σμύρνα only at Ant., 3, 197 (Ex. 30:23), cf. Schl. Mt. on 2:11. Cf. Eth. En. 29:2; Jub. 16:24 (incense). The word does not occur in Test. XII or Gr. En.

[8] On vl. σμύρναν at Rev. 18:13 → IV, 801, n. 15. The common koine spelling ζμ- (cf. Radermacher, 50) occurs in Mt. 2:11 D. On א cf. Thackeray, 108; Bl.-Debr. § 10.

[9] On incense and myrrh, found together both in and outside the Bible, → IV, 264, n. 8 and 1 Cl., 25, 2, the only instance of σμύρνα in the post-apost. fathers : the phoenix bird makes for itself a coffin of frankincense and myrrh and other aromatic substances. Cf. G. Ryckmans, "De l'or, de l'encens et de la myrrhe," Rev. Bibl., 58 (1951), 372-376.

[10] ἀλόη occurs only here in the NT. Perhaps Jn. 19:39 had some influence when א put ἀλόη for ἀλώθ with σμύρνα in Cant. 4:14 [Katz]. On Prv. 7:17 cf. Schl. J. on 19:39.

[11] The gt. amount is usually thought to be an expression of gt. honour. Cf. Bultmann J., ad loc. But cf. B. Weiss, Joh., Kritisch-exeget. Komm. über d. NT⁹ (1902), ad loc. Cf. P. Gaechter, "Zum Begräbnis Jesu," Zschr. f. katholische Theol., 75 (1953), 222 f.

[12] Embalming is not a Jewish practice, Str.-B., II, 53; J. Benzinger, Art. "Begräbnis bei d. Hebräern," RE³, 2 (1897), 531. The phoenix legend shows that aromatic herbs like myrrh in no way prevent corruption, 1 Cl., 25 → n. 9 [Bertram].

σμυρνίζω. Bibl. → σμύρνα.

[1] Rare outside the bibl., Diosc. Mat. Med., I, 66, 1. Not in the LXX and only trans. in the NT.

[2] Cf. also the wine spiced with anointing oil in Cant. 8:2. The Romans did not think

drink which Jesus refused because He wanted to die fully conscious. [3] Is not the ref. simply to a soldiers' wine which executioners handed to the exhausted on the way to the place of execution ? bSanh., 43a bears witness to a Jewish custom of giving a cup of wine mingled with frankincense to a condemned person. This was usually donated and brought by prominent ladies and the idea was to blunt self-awareness. [4] But this is not an exact par., for the ref. in Mk. 15:33 is to Roman soldiers rather than Jewish ladies and myrrh is mixed in rather than frankincense. Lk. and Jn. have nothing corresponding to Mk. 15:23, while Mt. 27:34 has οἶνον μετὰ χολῆς μεμιγμένον for Mk.'s ἐσμυρνισμένον οἶνον. This alteration is connected to Mk. 15:36 and par. or to Ps. 69:21. In its own way it shows that Mt., too, did not think Mk. 15:23 was referring to a stupefying drink, → V, 289, 18 ff.; 635, n. 30.

Michaelis

---

† Σολομών

Contents : A. King Solomon in Jewish Tradition and Legend : 1. Solomon as Poet and Author ; 2. Solomon's Magnificence and Wealth ; 3. Solomon's Wisdom ; 4. Solomon's Magical Power and Healing Skill. B. King Solomon in the New Testament : 1. Solomon's Temple ; 2. Solomon as the Ancestor of Jesus ; 3. Solomon's Glory and Wisdom.

A. King Solomon in Jewish Tradition and Legend.

Many individual traditions about the reign of Solomon [1] are contained in 1 K. 2:12-11:43. These tell of the king's wealth and splendour and also of his wisdom. [2] A wise heart was given him by Yahweh in answer to his request, and riches and goods of all kinds were also given him, 1 K. 3:5-15, so that he was richer and wiser than all the kings on earth, 10:23. The narrative does not suppress the fact that through his many foreign

---

vinum murratum very intoxicating. It was thus greatly favoured by women. Myrrh was also a way of making wine keep longer, cf. Steier, 1143 f.; A. Schmidt, *Drogen u. Drogenhandel im Altertum* (1924), 31 and 62.

[3] Cf., e.g., Hck. Mk., *ad loc.* Did Jesus really reject the wine because of a pledge of abstinence ? Cf. J. Jeremias, *Die Abendmahlsworte Jesu³* (1960), 204, n. 4.

[4] Str.-B., I, 1037.

Σ ο λ ο μ ώ ν. M. Seligsohn, Art. "Solomon" in Jew. Enc., XI, 436-448; S. Cohen, Art. "Solomon," *The Universal Jew. Encyclopedia,* IX (1948), 636 f.; K. Preisendanz, Art. "Salomo" in Pauly-W., Suppl., 8 (1956), 660-704; Pr.-Bauer⁵, *s.v.*

[1] On the etym. of the name cf. M. Noth, "Die isr. Personennamen im Rahmen d. gemeinsemitischen Namengebung," BWANT, III, 10 (1928), 165; Köhler-Baumg., *s.v.* שְׁלֹמֹה, 981; J. J. Stamm, "Der Name d. Königs Salomo," *Festgabe W. Eichrodt,* ThZ, 16 (1960), 285-297. שְׁלֹמֹה is written in different ways in Gk. Most common is Σαλωμών, gen. -ῶνος or -ῶντος, acc. -ῶντα, 3 Βασ. 1:10, 11, 12, 13, 17, 19, 21 etc., also Σαλωμώ, 1 Ch. 29:28 A*, Σολομών, gen. -ῶντος, acc. -ῶνα, 3 Βασ. 2:12 A ; 4:30 A etc., and Σολωμώ, 'A 4 Βασ. 23:13. Hell. lit. has the following forms : Σαλομών, Σολομών, Σαλαμών, Σαλωμών, Σαλωμώ, Σαλυμῶν, Σολωμῶν, Σωλομόν. Cf. Preisendanz, 660. Jos. and the NT (→ n. 30) have Σολομών.

[2] For historical questions relating to the reign cf. M. Noth, *Gesch. Israels⁴* (1959), 187-198; R. B. Y. Scott, "Solomon and the Beginnings of Wisdom in Israel," *Festschr. H. H. Rowley,* VT Suppl., 3 (1955), 262-279.

wives Solomon was also led into idolatry. Yahweh thus laid on him the punishment that after his death the 10 tribes would secede from the house of David and only Judah would remain faithful, 11:1-13. The Chronicler, however, plays down this aspect and depicts Solomon exclusively as a legally righteous king whose one concern was to build a worthy temple for the God of Israel, 2 Ch. 1:1-9:31.

The depiction of King Solomon in later Judaism rarely sticks to the OT accounts, [3] cf. Jos. Ant., 8, 1-211. In most of the stories told of David's successor a lively imagination has led to a wild growth of legend and saga designed to increase the glory of this wise and indescribably wealthy monarch. Solomon's wisdom was extolled in the OT ; it surpassed that of the Egyptians, 1 K. 4:29 f. "And he spoke 3000 proverbs, and his songs were 1005. But he spake of trees from the cedar tree that is in Lebanon even unto the hyssop that springeth out of the wall : he spake also of beasts, and of fowl, and of creeping things, and of fishes. And there came of all people to hear the wisdom of Solomon, from all kings of the earth, which had heard of his wisdom," 1 K. 4:32 f. Attempts were made in legend and saga to illustrate in broader descriptions what is said here briefly and crisply (cf. also 1 K. 3:16-28; 10:1-10, 13, 24). The incredible richness of Solomon's inspiration as a poet and author was exalted, the magnificence and costliness of his court was depicted, anecdotes were told about his wisdom, and he was made into an expert on nature, a master of demons, and a helper against suffering and sickness. This opened the door, of course, to superstition and to the magical ideas which invaded Judaism from the syncretistic circles of later antiquity, so that many Rabb. were not sparing with sharp criticism which could even be directed against the person of Solomon himself.

1. Solomon as Poet and Author.

Acc. to 1 K. 4:32 Solomon wrote proverbs and songs. He was thus thought to have written many proverbial sayings, canticles and books. Among the canonical works of the OT Ps. 72 and 127, [4] Proverbs, Song of Songs and Ecclesiastes are ascribed to him. Much of the wisdom in Proverbs is said to be his, Prv. 1:1; 10:1; 25:1. In Song of Songs he is often mentioned by name as the bridegroom and the poet of love, 1:1, 5; 3:7, 9, 11; 8:11 f. The author of Qoheleth introduces himself as the son of David, 1:1, king in Jerusalem, cf. 1:12, and gives a sample of the great treasures of wisdom which the old king had assembled. These three books which were adopted into the canon [5] were said to have been written by Solomon with the help of the Holy Spirit acc. to later Rabb. tradition, Cant. r., 1, 1 on 1:1; Qoh. r., 1, 1 on 1:1. The boundary set by the canon did not mean, of course, that other works could not be ascribed to Solomon. Indeed, it was only after the fixing of the canon that the range of his authorship began its true extension. The Psalms of Solomon, written during the 1st cent. B.C., do not refer to him, but they are accepted as his work. The Wisdom of Solomon is pseudepigraphical and Solomon himself speaks in it, 1:1; 6:1-9:18. [6] The praise of wisdom set on his lips is in Gk. and combines Hell. material with the oriental and OT inheritance. From Chr.-Gnostic circles we have the Odes of Solomon, which use older material but were written in the 2nd cent. A.D. The rather later Testament of Solomon combined Jewish elements and syn-

---

[3] Up to the Talmudic age awe prevented the use of Solomon's name, as of that of Abraham, Moses and David, cf. Noth, op. cit. (→ n. 1), 60.

[4] The depiction of the reign of the king of peace in Ps. 72 is attributed to Solomon because of v. 10. The building of the house in Ps. 127 is obviously identified as that of the building of the temple.

[5] As regards Cant. and Qoh. serious objections had to be met before they were admitted into the canon, cf. the discussions in Jad., 3, 5; bMeg., 7a and → III, 984 f.

[6] Since Jewish Wisdom lit. was almost exclusively regarded as the work of Solomon Sir. was sometimes regarded as Solomonic too. Cf. V. Ryssel in Kautzsch Apkr. u. Pseudepigr., I, 232 f.

cretistic influences and has come down in various Chr. versions. [7] Nor can one overlook the many works and magical books which at the end of antiquity and in the Middle Ages speak of Solomon's power over spirits and of his magical skill. [8] These many scientific, astrological and magical works reflect the high esteem for Solomon, not only among the Jews but further afield in the Hell. world, as a king of incomparable wisdom and a magician of divine power. Jos., adopting and enlarging the account in 1 K. 4:29 ff. (→ 460, 10 ff.), says that Solomon wrote 1005 books, odes and songs and spoke 3000 parables and proverbs. "For about every tree, from the hyssop to the cedar, he spoke a parable, also about beasts of burden and all other creatures on earth and in the sea and sky. For he knew each species and passed nothing by without investigating it, but philosophised on everything and showed supreme knowledge of its characteristics," Ant., 8, 44. Jos. then continues : "But God granted it to him to learn also the art of exorcising demons to the profit and healing of men. He composed sayings (ἐπῳδάς) by which sicknesses could be cured and left incantations by which demons could be bound and expelled so that they would never return. And this art of healing is still highly esteemed among us," 8, 45. Already in NT days, then, Solomon was thought to be the author of a very varied literature consisting of songs, proverbs, and healing and magical formulae.

2. Solomon's Magnificence and Wealth.

The magnificence and luxury of the edifices and court of Solomon, which were extolled already in the OT accounts, were more expansively described in Jewish tradition. To build the temple he wrote Hiram of Tyre [9] and the king of Egypt and received from them 160,000 workers and costly materials for the project. [10] With the help of these royal friends and those of his father Solomon built the temple in Jerusalem and adorned it with cedar, gold and precious stones. How glorious the temple and its furnishings were thought to be later may be seen, e.g., from the list of cultic vessels in Jos. Ant., 8, 91-94 : 80,000 wine-pots, 100,000 golden and 200.000 silver goblets, 80,000 golden and twice as many silver bowls in which to present meal at the altar, 60,000 golden and twice as many silver vessels in which to mix meal and oil, 20,000 golden and twice as many silver measures, 20,000 golden incense-boxes, 50,000 other vessels of incense, 1,000 priestly vestments for the high-priests, innumerable costly priestly garments with 10,000 purple girdles, 200,000 trumpets, 200,000 byssus garments for the Levites and 40,000 musical instruments. No wonder that the Queen of Sheba was startled and astonished by this inconceivable magnificence, Jos. Ant., 8, 168 f. With God's help it was possible for this tremendous work of building and equipping the temple to be finished quickly, 8, 130. Miracles took place in its erection, for spirits and demons as well as men had to help so that it could be done rapidly and with due splendour, Ex. r., 52 on 39:32. [11]

Solomon's rule was like that of an emperor, Sib., 3, 167-170. Nothing was spared at his court. The foods served were beyond compare. [12] Each morning each of the 1,000 wives prepared breakfast in the hope the king would come and eat it with her. [13] The OT says Solomon had 700 wives and 300 concubines, and these led him into idolatry, 1 K. 11:3. Jos. also notes (8, 190-198) that the extravagance of Solomon and his foreign

---

[7] Cf. the ed. of C. C. McCown, *The Test. of Solomon*, UNT, 9 (1922), also Preisendanz, 684-690.
[8] Note the survey in Seligsohn, 446-448 and the Hell.-Rom. Solomon lit. in Preisendanz, 684-699.
[9] Cf. also Jos. Ant., 8, 50-54, 55-60.
[10] Acc. to Eupolemus in Eus. Praep. Ev., IX, 30, 8-34, 18.
[11] Test. Sol. says the demons had to help Solomon build the temple. Cf. also → 463, 6 ff. In Semitic legend the building is described with wonder and the story is often told. Cf. G. Salzberger, *Salomos Tempelbau u. Thron in d. semitischen Sagenliteratur* (1912).
[12] BM, 7, 1; T. Taan., 4, 13 (221); cf. Str.-B., I, 438.
[13] Midr. Ps., 50 § 2 (140b); Par. in Str.-B., II, 205 f.

wives inclined his heart to heathen cults. If attempts were made to free him from the charge of worshipping idols himself he was guilty at least of allowing the foreign wives he took to engage in idolatry. [14] But R. Jizchaq believed the ruin of Israel began when he married Pharaoh's daughter. It was then the angel Gabriel came from heaven and set a reed in the sea. This produced a sandbank and on this the city of Rome was built. [15] The criticism which some felt they should bring against Solomon went so far that certain scholars would place him amongst those who have no portion in the world to come. They were won over from this over-severe judgment, however, by a voice from heaven which spoke in Solomon's favour. [16]

3. Solomon's Wisdom.

As concerns Solomon's wisdom the OT accounts and the books ascribed to him (→ 460, 24 ff.) had given so many proofs that it was the common view he was the wisest of all kings. He had expressed his wisdom in many proverbs, 4 Macc. 18:16. As a ruler he took decisions in the power of the Holy Spirit who granted him help and knowledge, [17] so that he was sometimes reckoned among the prophets, bSota, 48b. He could answer all questions put to him. When Hiram of Tyre sent him difficult riddles he could solve them all, Jos. Ant., 8, 143. [18] He was never at a loss for an answer when the Queen of Sheba came to test his wisdom. [19] His knowledge included natural history, control of demons, and cure of illnesses, Jos. Ant., 8, 42-49. It was so comprehensive that anyone who saw him in a dream might hope to become wise, bBer., 57b. Acc. to the Rabb., of course, true wisdom was bound to the Torah. Hence Solomon was often depicted as a great believer in the Torah. [20] Some of the benedictions of daily prayer and rules concerning an erub and handwashing are also ascribed to him, bBer., 48b; bShab., 14b; bErub, 21b. His wisdom was pre-eminently displayed in the study and exposition of the Law. The only one he could not equal was Moses, though he tried to; for it was laid down by the word of Scripture that after the death of Moses there would arise in Israel no prophet like him, Dt. 34:10. [21]

4. Solomon's Magical Power and Healing Skill.

Acc. to 1 K. 4:32 ff. Solomon did not merely write proverbs and songs but his wisdom was so gt. that he spoke of trees, cattle, birds and creeping things. Legend and saga added to this OT account a vivid set of astonishing stories about Solomon's knowledge of the plant and animal kingdoms, his astrological learning and his magical power. [22] The author of Wis. already has the king say of himself that God gave him inerrant

---

[14] bShab., 56b. Other Rabb. tried to excuse Solomon on the ground that he married foreign wives only to try to convert them to the Torah and bring them under the wings of the shekinah, R. Jose, jSanh., 2, 5 (20c, 24 f.). To take away anything offensive from the visit of the Queen of Sheba many argued that the ref. of מלכת שבא was not to a woman. מַלְכַת־שְׁבָא was read and this was taken to mean the kingdom of Sheba, bBB, 15b.

[15] bShab., 56b; bSanh., 21b; jAZ, 1, 2 (39c, 33-36) (here Michael for Gabriel).

[16] bSanh., 104b and further par. in Str.-B., I, 130 f.

[17] bMak., 23b : acc. to R. El'azar the Holy Spirit appeared in Solomon's school-room. When he had to decide which of the two women was the mother of the infant both claimed, a voice sounded from heaven : This is his mother.

[18] Cf. also Jos. Ant., 8, 144-149 and Ap., 1, 111-120, which tells of a battle of riddles between the two kings as they sent the most difficult questions to each other by post.

[19] Midr. Prv. on 1:1 (20b); cf. Str.-B., I, 651 f.

[20] Cf. already the account in the Chronicler that Solomon carefully kept the law of sacrifice, the festal calendar and the Sabbath, 2 Ch. 2:3; 8:13.

[21] bRH, 21b; cf. Str.-B., I, 131.

[22] Cf. McCown, 90-104 and Preisendanz, 660-703.

knowledge of being, so that "I know the system of the cosmos and the force of the elements," Wis. 7:17. The course of the stars, the progress of the years, the nature of animals, the power of spirits, the various plants and the healing properties of roots — all are known to him, 7:18-21. In the days of Jesus the popular opinion was that Solomon was pre-eminently versed in magical sayings and conjurations and that he transmitted these skills to posterity, Jos. Ant., 8, 45. [23] The king was able to exploit this divinely conferred power in the building of the temple, using gt. hosts of demons to complete the work rapidly with the help of their superhuman might. [24] The Rabb. enjoyed describing the story of the building of the temple and constantly embellished it. In a way which is hardly credible Solomon could subdue the demon Shamir and engage him in commissions. [25] Though these stories were told with relish even in Jewish circles, [26] it was realized that traffic with demons is very dangerous and once Solomon almost lost his throne because a demon was able temporarily to take his place. [27] Since the Rabb. could not support the belief in magic they were also critical of Solomon as the magician and the author of magical books. From Qoh. 1:12 — "I the Preacher was king over Israel in Jerusalem" — it was concluded that Solomon's rule underwent steady diminution. First he was king over upper beings (spirits), then only over lower beings (men), later only over Israel, then Jerusalem, finally only his bed and then only his staff, for it is written: "And this was my portion of all my labour," Qoh. 2:10 (bSanh., 20b). In non-Jewish circles, however, the powerful name of Solomon could be used without scruple to work magic with his help, or to make astrological reckonings, or to effect healings. Protective amulets and magic pap. inscribe his name for help and protection. Innumerable writings designed to introduce to mysterious arts were handed down from hoary antiquity as works of the wise king, since he knew the power of spirits and demons as none other, and could force them to do his will. [28] Thus the syncretistic world adopted Solomon and his figure found its way into the legend and saga of many peoples. His wisdom, quasi-divine magical power and magical skills were extolled in both East and West from generation to generation. [29]

B. King Solomon in the New Testament.

1. Solomon's Temple.

King Solomon is only rarely mentioned in the New Testament. [30] In Stephen's speech, which offers a survey of Israel's history from Abraham to the building of the temple, [31] Solomon is called the builder of God's house, Ac. 7:47. After

---

[23] Cf. the accounts in Jos. Ant., 8, 46-49 and Test. Sol. 1:5-7 which tell of Solomon's power over demons. Acc. to Jos. Ant., 8, 44 f. one may assume that even in the 1st cent. magical books supposedly written by him were in circulation. The repudiation in the Mishnah refers to such: "Hezekiah hid the book of remedies and the scribes approved," Pes., 4, 9.

[24] Cf. the descriptions in the various recensions of Test. Sol.

[25] bSota, 48b Bar.; other Rabb. examples in Str.-B., IV, 533 f.

[26] Cf. esp. bGit., 68a; Str.-B., IV, 510-512.

[27] bGit., 68b. The end of Test. Sol. tells how Solomon took a wife from among the Jebusites and fell into idolatry through her. The punishment which overtook him was that he lost his power over demons, his words became empty and he became a butt of mockery to idols and demons, Test. Sol. 26:1-7.

[28] For good examples cf. Preisendanz, 660-703.

[29] Solomon plays an important role in Semitic saga and the Islamic tradition. Cf. G. Salzberger, *Die Salomo-Sage in d. semitischen Lit.* (1907).

[30] In the NT Solomon's name (→ n.1) is always Σολομών, gen. Σολομῶνος or Σολομῶντος apart from Σαλωμών at Ac. 7:47 AC, Σαλωμών at Ac. 7:47 א; Σολομών is acc. at Mt. 1:6 א. Cf. Bl.-Debr. § 55, 2; Pr.-Bauer⁵, *s.v.*

[31] Cf. M. Dibelius, "Aufsätze z. Ag.," FRL, 60³ (1957), 145 f.; H. Thyen, "Der Stil d. jüd.-hell. Homilie," FRL, 65 (1955), 19 f.; Haench. Ag.¹², 238-241 on 7:2-53.

David had prayed that he might provide a home for the God of Israel, his son was allowed to build it. This structure went down in dust and ashes when the Babylonians captured Jerusalem. But it was generally assumed in the days of Jesus and the apostles that a hall on the east side of the temple was part of the original structure built by Solomon and had survived the changes and chances of time. [32] It was thus called the στοὰ Σολομῶνος. Here Jesus came at the Feast of the Dedication (Jn. 10:23) and gave His last public address to the Jews. Here Peter and John preached to the people (Ac. 3:11) who had gathered to gaze with astonishment on the two miracle-workers. Here the primitive community met (Ac. 5:12), showing by its choice of the spot that it kept continuity with the OT people of God and could rightly claim to be the ἐκκλησία τοῦ θεοῦ. The author of Acts does not hesitate to emphasise, however, that God does not dwell in houses made with hands (Ac. 7:48) and he quotes Is. 66:1 f. to this effect. [33] Hence Solomon's temple cannot be regarded as the place of true worship. It represents apostasy, since heaven is God's throne and earth the foot-stool of His feet. How can one try to build Him a house? (Ac. 7:48-50). These words of sharp criticism for Solomon's temple form the transition to the conclusion of Stephen's speech in which the Jews are severely attacked for their hardness of heart.

2. Solomon as the Ancestor of Jesus.

In the genealogy of Matthew the relationship of Jesus and His community to the ancient people of God is expressed by the chain of 3 times 14 links which leads from Abraham by way of David, the kings and the post-exilic generations to Jesus Christ, Son of David and Son of Abraham, Mt. 1:1-17. This series tells us that David begat Solomon of the wife of Uriah (→ III, 1, n. 5 and 3, 32 ff.) and that Solomon begat Rehoboam, 1:6 f. The serious offence of which David was guilty is not concealed. [34] But it was precisely through this union that Israel's God pushed forward the history of His people, making the wife of Uriah the mother of Solomon and the latter the ancestor of Jesus. [35]

3. Solomon's Glory and Wisdom.

In two dominical sayings which Mt. and Lk. took from Q there is mention of Solomon. Jesus tells His disciples not to be anxious about food and drink and clothing, Mt. 6:25-34 par. Lk. 12:22-31. To illustrate the pointlessness of such anxiety Jesus turns to the κρίνα τοῦ ἀγροῦ which grow even though they neither toil nor spin. God gives them raiment which is more glorious than that which Solomon wore in all his splendour, Mt. 6:29 par. Lk. 12:27. [36] But if God so

---

[32] Jos. Ant., 20, 220 f.; Bell., 5, 185; also Ant., 15, 396-401; Bell., 5, 190-192. Rabb. examples in Str.-B., II, 625. Cf. Dalman Orte, 310 f and Jerusalem u. sein Gelände (1930), 116 f.; J. Simons, Jerusalem of the OT (1952), 401 f., 421; L. H. Vincent, Jérusalem de l'AT, II (1956), 467-469; C. Kopp, Die heiligen Stätten der Evangelien (1959), 344, 349 f.

[33] Cf. also 1 K. 8:27; 2 Ch. 6:18.

[34] But cf. the attempts of some Rabb. to lessen David's guilt, Str.-B., I, 28 f.

[35] Lk. 3:31 mentions Nathan rather than Solomon as the next link. It is hard to reconcile the differences between the two records but cf. the attempt of E. Nestle, "Salomo u. Nathan in Mt. 1 und Lk. 3," ZNW, 8 (1907), 72.

[36] κρίνα probably refers gen. to the flowers which adorn the fields of Palestine in spring, cf. Pr.-Bauer⁵, s.v. κρίνον. But if the ref. is to the purple anemone (cf. Dalman Orte,

wonderfully clothes the passing flowers of the field that even the famous attire of King Solomon (→ 461, 18 ff.) [37] is far behind them in glory, how much more will He provide clothing for men too. Hence : μὴ οὖν μεριμνήσητε λέγοντες· τί φάγωμεν; ἤ· τί πίωμεν; ἤ· τί περιβαλώμεθα; (Mt. 6:31 par. Lk. 12:29).

Jesus refers to the wisdom of Solomon in a judgment saying in Mt. 12:42 par. Lk. 11:31. Even the queen of the south, who was only a Gentile, [38] came from a distance (→ 462, 16 ff.) to hear the wisdom of Solomon (cf. 1 K. 10:1-10; 2 Ch. 9:1-9), but this unbelieving generation persists in its impenitence. In the Last Judgment, then, the queen of the south will come forward and accuse the Jews of unbelief. Her complaint will lead to condemnation, for the Jews have not perceived the seriousness of the hour of decision and have refused to accept the preaching of Jesus. "And behold, a greater than Solomon in there," [39] for the eschatological Son of David is incomparably superior to the historical Son of David. [40]

Lohse

σοφία, σοφός, σοφίζω

† σοφία, † σοφός.

Contents : A. From the Early Greek Period to the Philosophical Usage of Later Antiquity : 1. From the Early Greek Period to Socrates ; 2. Socrates, Plato and Aristotle ; 3. The Philosophical Schools of the Hellenistic Period ; 4. The Philosophy of Later Antiquity. B. The Old Testament : I. Terminology ; II. Wisdom as an Ancient Oriental and Israelite-

---

169 f.), the comparison is even more pointed : the purple of the flowers, which have done nothing to fashion their raiment, is far more glorious than all the splendour of King Solomon.

[37] Solomon was πάντων βασιλέων ἐνδοξότατος (Jos. Ant., 8, 190), λευκὴν ἡμφιεσμένος ἐσθῆτα (8, 186).

[38] Cf. the associated story of Jonah and the people of Nineveh (Mt. 12:39 f., 41 par. Lk. 11:29 f., 32), who, though pagans, repented at the preaching of Jonah, whereas this unbelieving generation rejects the preaching of Jesus.

[39] The "refrain" at the end of Mt. 12:41 f. par. Lk. 11:31 f. may have been added by the community, Bultmann Trad., 118.

[40] Solomon is not mentioned in the post-apost. fathers. But in Chr. works from c. 200 A.D. — esp. at the time of transition from antiquity to the Middle Ages, but also later — there are many ref. to sagas and legends about Solomon. These were developed even more in Chr. tradition, and the belief in magic, which was widespread even in Chr. circles, often appealed to the protective or magical power of Solomon. For rich materials on these ideas and their ramifications cf. the comprehensive art. of Preisendanz.

σ ο φ ί α, σ ο φ ό ς. Bibl.: Gen.: Pape, Pass. (Cr.), Liddell-Scott, Cr.-Kö., Pr.-Bauer[5], s.v.; G. Hoennicke, Art. "Weisheit" in RE[3] 21 (1908), 64-73; H. Leisegang, Art. "Sophia," Pauly-W., 3a (1929), 1019-1039; A. R. Gordon, Art. "Wisdom" in ERE, XII, 742-747; U. Wilckens, "Weisheit u. Torheit," *Beiträge z. historischen Theol.*, 26 (1959), cf. the critical review by H. Köster in *Gnomon*, 33 (1961), 590-595. On A. : F. v. Paula-Eisenmann, "Über Begriff u. Bdtg. d. griech. σοφία von den ältesten Zeiten an bis Sokrates," *Programm d. Wilhelmgymnasiums München* (1895); B. Snell, "Die Ausdrücke f. den Begriff des Wissens in d. vorplatonischen Philosophie," PhU, 29 (1924), 1-20; W. Schmid, *Gesch. d. griech. Lit., I-V, Hndbch. KlAW*, VII; W. Nestle, *Platons ausgewählte Schriften, IV, Pro-*

Old Testament Phenomenon : 1. Mesopotamia ; 2. Egypt ; 3. The Rest of the Ancient Orient ; 4. Israel ; III. The "Wisdom" (Sagacity and Knowledge) of Man : 1. Magic and Manticism ; 2. Skill and Ability ; 3. Cleverness, Slyness and Cunning ; 4. Practical Wisdom ; 5. Culture ; 6. Rules of Behaviour ; 7. Ethical Conduct ; 8. Piety ; 9. Academic Wisdom ;

---

*tagoras*⁷ (1931), 1-51; H. Gundert, "Pind. u. sein Dichterberuf," *Frankfurter Studien z. Religion u. Kultur d. Antike,* 10 (1935), 61-76; B. Snell, *Leben u. Meinungen d. Sieben Weisen* (1938); E. Schwartz, *Die Ethik d. Griechen,* ed. W. Richter (1951), 167-170, 250; B. Snell, *Die Entdeckung des Geistes*³ (1955), 403-410, 414 f. On B. : J. Meinhold, *Die Weisheit Israels* (1908); H. Gressmann, *Israels Spruchweisheit im Zshg. d. Weltliteratur* (1925); H. Ranston, *The OT Wisdom Books and Their Teaching* (1930); W. Baumgartner, *Isr. u. altoriental. Weisheit* (1933); J. Fichtner, *Die altoriental. Weisheit u. ihrer isr.-jüd. Ausprägung* (1933); W. Zimmerli, "Zur Struktur d. at.lichen Weisheit," *ZAW,* 51 (1933), 177-204; G. Boström, *Prv. Studien* (1935); A. Drubbel, "Le conflit entre la Sagesse profane et la Sagesse religieuse," *Biblica,* 17 (1936), 45-70, 407-428; H. Duesberg, *Les scribes inspirés,* I-II (1938/39), *passim* ; R. Gordis, "The Social Background of Wisdom Literature," *HUCA,* 18 (1943/44), 77-118; J. C. Rylaarsdam, *Revelation in Jewish Wisdom Literature* (1946); H. Ringgren, *Word and Wisdom* (1947); J. Kázmér, *Wesen u. Entwicklung des Weisheitsbegriffes in d. Weisheitsbüchern d. AT* (1950); O. S. Rankin, *Israel's Wisdom Literature*² (1954); H. Gese, *Lehre u. Wirklichkeit in d. alten Weisheit* (1958); E. G. Bauckmann, "Die Proverbien u. d. Sprüche d. Jesus Sirach," *ZAW,* 72 (1960), 33-63. On C. : J. Grill, *Untersuchungen über d. Entstehung d. 4. Ev.,* I (1902), 149-200; W. Schencke, "Die Chokma (Sophia) in d. jüd. Hypostasenspekulation," *Videnskapsselkapets Skrifter,* II, Historisk-Filosofiske Klasse, 1912, 6 (1913); J. R. Harris, "Athena, Sophia and the Logos," *Bulletin of the John Rylands Library,* 7 (1922), 56 ff.; R. Bultmann, "Der religionsgeschichtliche Hintergrund des Prologs zum Joh.-Ev.," EYXAPIΣTHPION, *Festschr. H. Gunkel,* II (1923), 3-26; Bousset-Gressm., *passim,* esp. 343-346; Moore, I, 263-280; J. Pascher, "BAΣIΛIKH OΔOΣ, Der Königsweg zu Wiedergeburt u. Vergottung bei Philon v. Alex.," *Studien z. Gesch. u. Kultur d. Altertums,* 17, 3 f. (1931); Volz Esch., 218, 222, 393; E. R. Goodenough, *By Light, Light, The Mystic Gospel of Hell. Judaism* (1935), 265-305; W. Staerk, "Die 7 Säulen der Welt u. des Hauses d. Weisheit," *ZNW,* 35 (1936), 232-261; T. Arvedson, *Das Mysterium Christi, Eine Studie z. Mt. 11:25-30* (1937), 77-93; W. L. Knox, "The Divine Wisdom," *JThSt,* 38 (1937), 230-237; W. Völker, *Fortschritt u. Vollendung bei Philon v. Alex.,* TU, 49, 1 (1938), 318-350; W. Staerk, *Die Erlösererwartung in d. östlichen Religionen* (Soter II) (1938), 71-85; C. Spicq, "Le Siracide et la structure littéraire du prologue," *Mémorial Lagrange* (1940), 183-195; P. Dalbert, "D. Theologie d. hell.-jüd. Missionsliteratur unter Ausschluss von Philo u. Jos.," *Theol. Forschungen,* 4 (1954), 77-85 and *passim* ; H. Becker, "Die Reden d. Joh.-Ev. und der Stil d. gnostischen Offenbarungsrede," FRL, 68 (1956), 41-53; G. Ziener, "Die theol. Begriffssprache im Buche d. Weisheit," *Bonner Bibl. Beiträge,* 11 (1956), 109-113; J. Jervell, "Imago Dei. Gn. 1:26 f. im Spätjudt. in d. Gnosis u. in d. paul. Briefen," FRL, 76 (1960), 46-50; D. Rössler, "Gesetz u. Gesch. Untersuchungen z. Theol. d. jüd. Apokalyptik u. d. pharisäischen Orthodoxie," *Wissenschaftliche Monographien z. AT u. NT,* 3 (1960), 43-105; H. Jaeger, "The Patristic Conception of Wisdom in the Light of Biblical and Rabbinical Research" in *Studia Patristica* (ed. F. L. Cross), TU, 79 (1961), 96-106. On D.: R. Reitzenstein, *Zwei religionsgeschichtliche Fragen nach ungedruckten gr. Texten der Strassburger Bibliothek* (1901), esp. 108-112, 129-131; Reitzenstein Poim., esp. 44 f., 233, n. 2; W. Bousset, *Hauptprobleme d. Gnosis,* FRL, 10 (1907), Index, *s.v.*; R. Reitzenstein, "Das mandäische Buch des Herrn d. Grösse," SAH, 1919, 12 (1919), esp. 56-58; K. Müller, "Beiträge zum Verständnis d. valentinianischen Gnosis," NGG (1920), 197-228; Reitzenstein Ir. Erl., esp. 208-213, 240-242; E. Waldschmidt-E. Lentz, "Die Stellung Jesus im Manichäismus," AAB, 1926, 4 (1926), 38-196; W. Foerster, "Von Valentin zu Herakleon, Untersuchungen über d. Quellen u. d. Entwicklung d. valentinianischen Gnosis," Beih. ZNW, 7 (1928); H. Schlier, "Religionsgesch. Untersuchungen zu d. Ignatiusbriefen," Beih. ZNW, 8 (1929); also "Christus u. d. Kirche im Eph.," *Beiträge z. historischen Theol.,* 6 (1930), esp. 60-75; E. Käsemann, "Leib u. Leib Christi." *Beiträge z. hist. Theologie,* 9 (1933), 51-96, 149 f.; G. Bornkamm, "Mythos u. Legende in d. apokr. Thomasakten," *Beiträge z. Geschichte d. Gnosis u. z. Vorgeschichte d. Manichäismus,* FRL, 49 (1933), 82-89, 103-166; E. Käsemann, "Eine urchr. Taufliturgie," *Exeget. Versuche u. Besinnungen,* I (1960), 39-43; E. Haenchen, "Gab es eine vorchr. Gnosis ?" ZThK, 49 (1952), 316-349; G. Quispel, *Gnosis als Weltreligion* (1954), *passim* ; also "Der gnostische Anthropos u. d. jüd. Tradition," *Eranos-Jbch.* 1953 (1954), 195-234; Schlier Eph., 159-166;

10. Eschatological Blessing and Apocalyptic Endowment ; IV. The "Wisdom" (Sagacity and Knowledge) of God : 1. God Possesses Wisdom ; 2. God Attains and Creates Wisdom ; V. The Origin and Source of Sagacity and Knowledge : 1. Tradition of the Fathers ; 2. Personal Experience ; 3. Means and Methods ; 4. The Gift of God ; VI. Value, Result and Criticism of Sagacity and Knowledge : 1. Value and Result ; 2. Criticism. C. Judaism : 1. The Septuagint ; 2. Wisdom in Hellenistic Judaism ; 3. Jewish Apocalyptic ; 4. The Dead Sea Scrolls ; 5. Rabbinic Judaism ; 6. A Wisdom Myth in Judaism. D. Gnosticism : 1. The Odes of Solomon ; 2. The Gnosis of Simon ; 3. Barbelognosis and the Gnostic of Irenaeus ; 4. The Gnostic in Plotinus ; 5. Coptic Gnostic Texts ; 6. The Valentinian ; 7. Manicheeism. E. The New Testament : 1. Traditional Anthropological Use ; 2. The Logia ; 3. Paul ; 4. Deutero-Pauline Writings ; 5. Revelation ; 6. James ; 7. 2 Peter. F. The Post-Apostolic Fathers and Early Apologists : 1. Sophia Christology ; 2. Common Christian Usage.

A. From the Early Greek Period to the Philosophical Usage of Later Antiquity.

From the adjective σοφός, which is first attested from the 6th century and is common from Theognis and Pindar on, there developed quite early the abstract noun σοφία (Ionic σοφίη Hom. Il., 15, 412 [though → n. 4]; Hom. Hymn. Merc., 483 and 511) and the verb σοφίζομαι (ναυτιλίης σεσοφισμένος, Hes. Op., 649), then σοφιστής (from Pind. and Herodot.). [1] An important point is that in contrast to specific epistemological terms like γνώμη (→ I, 717, 10 ff.), γνῶσις (→ I, 689, 13 ff.), σύνεσις, μάθημα, ἐπιστήμη and others, in which we have verbal abstracts, σοφία is derived from an adjective and always denotes a quality, never an activity. This is the reason for the great shift which took place in its meaning. [2] In general σοφία denotes a materially complete and hence unusual knowledge and ability. In the early Greek period any practical skill of this kind counted as wisdom, then during the classical period the range of meaning was strongly restricted to theoretical and intellectual knowledge, and finally in the usage of the philosophical schools of Hellenism and later antiquity the practical element was united again with the theoretical in the ideal picture of the wise man. In formation σοφός belongs to the type of nomina agentis represented by ἀοιδός, though any other connection is most uncertain. [3]

E. Käsemann, "Das wandernde Gottesvolk. Eine Untersuchung zum Hb.," FRL, 37[2] (1957). 45-105. On E. : H. Windisch, "Die göttliche Weisheit d. Juden u. d. paul. Christologie," Nt.liche Studien f. G. Heinrici (1914), 220-234; E. B. Allo, "Sagesse et pneuma dans la première épître aux Corinth.," Rev. Bibl., 43 (1934), 321-346; J. de Finance, "La σοφία chez S. Paul," Recherches des Sciences religieuses, 25 (1935), 385-417; W. L. Knox, Paul and the Church of the Gentiles (1937), 55-81, 113-124; J. Dupont, Gnosis. La connaissance religieuse dans les épîtres de S. Paul (1949), 82-84 and passim ; R. M. Grant, "The Wisdom of the Corinthians" in F. C. Grant, The Joy of Study (1951), 51-55; L. Cerfaux, Le Christ dans la théol. de S. Paul[2], Lectio divina, 6 (1954), 189-208; R. Bultmann, "K. Barth, 'Die Auferstehung d. Toten,'" Glauben u. Verstehen, I[2] (1954), 40-44; A. Feuillet, "Jésus et la sagesse divine d'après les évangiles synoptiques. Le Logion 'Johannique' et l'AT," Rev. Bibl., 62 (1955), 161-196; W. D. Davies, Paul and Rabbinic Judaism (1955), 147-176; E. Norden, Agnostos Theos. Untersuchungen z. Formengeschichte religiöser Rede[4] (1956). 277-308; H. Schlier, "Kerygma u. Sophia," Die Zeit d. Kirche (1956), 206-232; Bultmann Trad., 73-113, 117-121, 171 f.; U. Wilckens, "Kreuz u. Weisheit," Kerygma u. Dogma, 3 (1957), 77-108; G. Bornkamm, "Glaube u. Vernunft bei Pls.," Studien z. Antike u. Urchr. (1959), 119-137; M. Dibelius, Die Formgesch. d. Ev.[3] (1959), 279-284; E. Peterson, "1 K. 1:18 f. u. d. Thematik d. jüd. Busstages," Frühkirche, Judt. u. Gnosis (1959), 43-50.

[1] [E. Risch.]
[2] Cf. on this Snell Ausdrücke, 17 f.
[3] Cf. Schwyzer, I, 459; there is much that is doubtful in Boisacq and Hofmann, s.v. [Risch].

1. From the Early Greek Period to Socrates.

In the early period a man was wise who was fully and pre-eminently experienced and adept in a specific skill, mostly manual. The earliest example is in Hom. Il., 15, 411 f.,[4] which refers to the σοφία of a τέκτων who pursued his craft acc. to the directions of Athene.[5] After Hom. we read in the same sense of the wisdom, i.e., mastery of, e.g., the builder, general, statesman, physician, wagoner, wrestler, goldsmith etc.[6] σοφία here is always combined with τέχνη, ἐπιστήμη, ἔργον etc.[7] Yet the ref. is not just to specific manual skill; it is also to mastery and superiority in a matter.[8] Acc. to Pind. Nem., 7 and 17, e.g., a wise man can predict the weather; acc. to Eur. Ion, 1139 he can calculate the surface of a tent. Always the pt. is: ὁ χρήσιμ' εἰδώς, οὐχ ὁ πόλλ' εἰδὼς σοφός.[9] Hence wisdom is often distinguished from sheer physical force.[10] One is not wise by nature; wisdom comes only by learning.[11] Wisdom has nothing in common with μανία, Gorg. Pal., 25 (Diels, II, 300, 20 ff.). In particular it is distinguished from τύχη, Democr. Fr., 197 (186, 3 ff.). It always stands out; the wise man is different from others.[12] σοφία is a gift of divine grace, Soph. Fr., 226 (TGF, 184), cf. Gorg. Hel., 6 (Diels, II, 290, 3 f.). Various legends tell how it once came down from the gods to men.[13] Originally it was a possession of the gods alone: Athene (Plat. Prot., 231d), Hephaistos and esp. Apollo[14] were the gods of wisdom. The Muses mediate it to the poets.[15] Hence these are reputed to be wise κατ' ἐξοχήν.[16] Pind. realises that he is a σοφὸς ποιητής in whom musical inspiration and the artistic art of constructing verse

---

[4] τέκτονος ..., ὅς ῥά τε πάσης εὖ εἰδῇ σοφίης ὑποθημοσύνῃσιν 'Αθήνης (only instance in Hom.). Acc. to U. v. Wilamowitz-Moellendorff, Ilias u. Hom. (1916), 239 these verses are a later interpolation. This is supported by the fact that the formation σοφίη is singular in Hom., cf. E. Risch, Wortbildung d. homerischen Sprache (1937), 107. Cl. Al. Strom., I, 3, 24 f., who quotes the verse, adduces other examples to show that σοφία here means πᾶσαν τὴν κοσμικὴν εἴτε ἐπιστήμην εἴτε τέχνην. Cf. also Suid., s.v. Σοφία and Poll. Onom., V, 164.
[5] On Athene as goddess of wisdom cf. Leisegang, 1028.
[6] Examples in Snell Ausdrücke 6 f., Leisegang, 1019, Schwartz, 168 and Nestle, 1-3.
[7] Examples in Snell Ausdrücke, 7, n. 6; cf. Schmid, V, 293, n. 12.
[8] Aristot. excellently calls this gen. concept of wisdom ἀρετὴ τέχνης, Eth. Nic., VI, 7, p. 1141a, 12.
[9] Aesch. Fr., 390 (TGF, 113); cf. Heracl. Fr., 40 f. (Diels, I, 160, 3 ff.). τὸ σοφόν is here contrasted with πολυμαθίη as ἐπίστασθαι γνώμην, ὁτέη ἐκυβέρνησε πάντα διὰ πάντων.
[10] E.g., Xenophanes Fr., 2, 12 (Diels, I, 129, 2); also Hdt., III, 127, 2.
[11] Democr. Fr., 59 (Diels, II, 157, 16 f.): οὔτε τέχνη οὔτε σοφίη ἐφικτόν, ἢν μὴ μάθῃ τις. Cf. Heracl. Fr., 129 (Diels, I, 181, 1 f.), who extols the πολυμαθίη of Pythagoras, also Anaxag. Fr., 21b (Diels, II, 43, 20), who lists σοφία with ἐμπειρία, μνήμη and τέχνη.
[12] This helps us to understand the sometimes exaggerated self-awareness of the wise man. Thus Democr. is said to have called himself Σοφία Α 2 (Diels, II, 85, 1), cf. Α 18 (87, 26) and esp. Xenophanes Fr., 2, 11 ff. (I, 129, 1 ff.): οὐκ ἐὼν ἄξιος ὥσπερ ἐγώ.
[13] Acc. to Aesch. Prom., 62 and 944 Prometheus is the sage (σοφιστής) who taught the τέχναι, ibid., 110 f. Cf. the Sophist version of this legend in Plat. Prot., 321c d. Acc. to Pind. Olymp., 7, 72 the sons of Helios received σοφώτατα νοήματα ἐπὶ προτέρων ἀνδρῶν. Ps.-Plat. Min., 319c speaks of Zeus as the wise teacher (σοφιστής) of a παγκάλη τέχνη.
[14] Pind. Pyth., 1, 12; Eur. Iph. Taur., 1238; Xenoph. An., I, 2, 8; Athen., 14, 32 etc.
[15] Cf. Solon Fr., 1, 51 f. (Diehl³, I, 24): ῎Αλλος 'Ολυμπιάδων Μουσέων πάρα δῶρα διδαχθείς, ἱμερτῆς σοφίης μέτρον ἐπιστάμενος. So already Hom. Il., 2, 485: ὑμεῖς γὰρ θεαί ἐστε πάρεστέ τε ἴστε τε πάντα. Esp. common and typical in Pind., cf. Gundert, 61-76. Cf. also → VI, 792, 10 ff.
[16] Cf., e.g., Athen., 14, 32: τὸ δ' ὅλον ἔοικεν ἡ παλαιὰ σοφία τῇ μουσικῇ μάλιστ' εἶναι δεδομένη; also Cic. Tusc., I, 1, 3; Strabo, I, 2, 6; Plat. Phileb., 17c. Thus Homer (Snell Ausdrücke, 10, n. 4) and Simonides (Plat. Resp., I, 331e etc.) etc. are regarded as wise men. Schmid, III, 14, n. 2.

are combined. [17] Thus the poets are precursors of the philosophers. Hesiod's theogony precedes the Ionic cosmogonies and Solon, Xenophanes, Parmenides, Empedocles etc. presented their teaching in poetic form. [18] But this is also the place were σοφία becomes concentrated on theoretical knowledge. After publishing his laws in Athens Solon went on a world tour for the sake of θεωρία and was thus the first to seek "to fulfil the ideal of knowledge of the Homeric Muses." [19] These earliest sages were regarded as wise not merely for their learning but also and especially for their conduct. σοφία is linked to ἀρετή [20] and the wise man is ἀγαθός. [21] In this respect the 6th cent. sages were shining lights even for a later time. Relatively early — attested from Plat. Prot., 343a and constantly thereafter — we find the idea of a college of seven wise men : Thales, Bias, Pittacos, Cleobulos, Solon, Chilon and Periander (for whom other names are also substituted). [22] These are not philosophers but men of outstanding practical wisdom and a much admired power of practical political judgment. Esp. praised is their superior insight into the reality of the world around, their deep and universal knowledge of men, and the soundness and independence of their political counsel. [23] Several legends clustered around them ; these originated in Ionia and the Delphic priesthood influenced their formulation. [24] The most widespread is that of the tripod which came forth from the sea with the inscr. ΤΩΙ ΣΟΦΩΤΑΤΩΙ, was handed round from one to the other, finally dedicated by the seventh (or all of them) to Apollo as the supreme sage, and brought to Delphi. [25] Short proverbs were ascribed to these men which sum up practical wisdom in definitive form. [26] Yet under Ionic leadership a new type of sage was developed from the 6th cent.; the wisdom of this new sage is a resolute application to theoretical inquiry. Here σοφία is fully understood as established knowledge which can be learned (→ n. 11) and the mastery of which is τέχνη, this being treasured as the art of comprehending general laws. We may refer esp. to the gt. Ionic natural philosophers, who investigated the φύσις, γένεσις or ἀρχή of all things. [27] Thus σοφίη is very common in the Ionic of the period, [28] whereas it is hardly found at all in Attic

---

[17] E.g., Isthm., 1, 45 ff.; Olymp., 1, 116; 2, 86; 7, 53; Pyth., 4, 248. Cf. Gundert, 128, n. 225; Schwartz, 168; Snell Ausdrücke, 6 f.; Schmid, I, 595. n. 13.

[18] Snell Ausdrücke, 8 f. On ancient theories as to the priority of poetry over prose cf. R. Hirzel, *Der Dialog,* II (1895), 208, n. 4.

[19] Snell Entdeckung, 404 (cf. Hom. Il., 2, 485 → n. 15).

[20] Cf. Snell Ausdrücke, 12 f.

[21] E.g., Soph. El., 1089; Phil., 119 and esp. Eur. Alc., 602 : ἐν τοῖς ἀγαθοῖσι δέ πάντ' ἔνεστι σοφίας. Cf. Eur. Ba., 395. But morally indifferent expertise is only τὸ σοφόν, far removed from true wisdom, Eur. Fr., 583 (TGF, 544). Schmid, III, 690, n. 9. In the same sense Gorg. Hel., 1 (Diels, II, 288, 2 ff.) says: κόσμος πόλει μὲν εὐανδρία, σώματι δὲ κάλλος, ψυχῆ δὲ σοφία, ... λόγῳ δὲ ἀλήθεια. τὰ δὲ ἐναντία τούτων ἀκοσμία. Cf. Heracl. Fr., 112 (I, 176, 2): σωφρονεῖν ἀρετὴ μεγίστη, καὶ σοφίη ἀληθέα λέγειν καὶ ποιεῖν κατὰ φύσιν. On the whole subject cf. W. Jaeger, "Über Ursprung u. Kreislauf des philosophischen Lebensideals," SAB, 1928, 25 (1928), 390-421.

[22] On the seven sages cf. Schmid, I, 371-374, also Barkowski, Art. "Sieben Weise" in Pauly-W., 2a (1923), 2242-2264; Hirzel, 132-157; U. v. Wilamowitz-Moellendorff, "Zu Plutarchs Gastmahl der Sieben Weisen," *Herm.,* 25 (1890), 196-227; also *Platon,* II (1919), 272; Snell Leben, 60-65.

[23] Cf., e.g., Themist. Or., 31-34.

[24] Schmid, I, 371.

[25] For texts cf. Diels, I, 61-66 and Snell Leben, 107-113.

[26] E.g., γνῶθι σεαυτόν. — μηδὲν ἄγαν. — καιρὸν γνῶθι. — μέτρον ἄριστον etc. Cf. Plat. Prot., 343a-b. The themes are assembled in Barkowski, 2256 f. The first collection of such sayings is in Demetr. Phal. The earliest attested group of sagas is in the novel of Andron of Eph. Τρίπους in fragmentary form (beginning of the 4th cent.), cf. Schmid, I, 373 f. From the later Hell. period we have Plut.'s Feast of the Seven Sages, cf. Wilamowitz, *op. cit.,* also L. Radermacher, "Aristophanes' 'Frösche,'" SA Wien, 198, 4 (1921), 29.

[27] Cf. esp. E. Jaeger, *Die Theol. d. frühen gr. Denker* (1953), e.g., 28-49. Thus the disciples of Heracl. are σοφοί in Phileb., 43a, cf. also Xenoph. Mem., I, 1, 11.

[28] Cf. Hdt.; *v.* J. E. Powell, *A Lexicon to Hdt.* (1938), *s.v.* Cf. also Schmid, II, 574, n. 2.

prose. [29] The Sophists are the first to use it. Basically contesting the knowability and expressibility of being they resolutely and consistently make thought and language an instrument for mastering practical living. For them there is no wisdom in the sense of the older philosophers. [30] Wisdom as the power of clever speech subjects the world to the sophist. [31] Wisdom may thus be taught, and the Sophists worked out a varied programme of instruction. Publicly rejected, [32] they finally went down under the devastating criticism of Socrates, Plat. [33] and Aristot. [34] Only from this time on does σοφιστής, previously used positively as a synon. of σοφός, [35] take on a negative ring and come to be sharply differentiated from σοφός.

2. Socrates, Plato and Aristotle.

Socrates shares with the Sophists the critical insight that thought is not just part of being. What he castigates is not their criticism ; it is their frivolously premature breaking off of criticism in favour of self-grounded wisdom. The penetrating question : τί δή ἐστιν τοῦτο περὶ οὗ αὐτός ·τε ἐπιστήμων ἐστὶν ὁ σοφιστής (Plat. Prot., 312e; Ps.-Plat. Theag., 122e-123), or the question as to the αἴτιον of his σοφία, [36] is one the Sophist cannot answer. By contrast Socrates' wisdom consists in the critical knowledge that any autonomous wisdom is no wisdom at all ; Apollo called him wise because he knew he knew nothing. [37] In this respect he does not abandon the basic definition of σοφία as knowledge (εἰδέναι, ἐπιστήμη). But the knowledge whose absence Socrates perceives in his wisdom is not a τέχνη. Wisdom knows the being of all that is, which is what man is not granted to know. Plato took up this ontological line of questioning and in so doing could

---

σοφίη here is a master-concept for all intellectual ability, crowned in this case in "wise" legislation, cf., e.g., VII, 102, 1: τῇ Ἑλλάδι πενίη μὲν αἰεί κοτε σύντροφός ἐστιν, ἀρετὴ δὲ ἔπακτός ἐστι, ἀπό τε σοφίης κατεργασμένη καὶ νόμου ἰσχυροῦ.

[29] It does not occur in Aeschin. Demosth. has it once. σοφία is not found in Thuc., though once each we find σοφός (III, 37, 4), σοφιστής (III, 38, 7) and σόφισμα (VI, 77, 1). In Attic poetry it is used rarely by Aesch., rather more by Soph., very often by Aristoph. and Eur., cf. Schmid, III, 690, n. 4. But the last three were writing in the Sophist period.

[30] For Heracl. Fr., 108 (Diels, I, 175, 6) σοφόν as the "divine" above the world of experience is πάντων κεχωρισμένον, cf. W. Jaeger, 144 f.; H. Fränkel, Dichtung u. Philosophie d. frühen Griechentums (1951), 495 [Krämer].

[31] Cf., e.g., Anaxarchus Fr., 1 (Diels, II, 240, 1 ff.). Words must be cleverly chosen in relation to people : χρὴ δὲ καιροῦ μέτρα εἰδέναι· σοφίης γὰρ οὗτος ὅρος· οἳ δὲ ἔξω καιροῦ ῥῆσιν ἀείδουσιν, κἢν πεπνυμένην ἀείδωσιν, οὐ τιθέμενοι ἐν σοφίηι· γνώμην αἰτίην ἔχουσι μωρίης. Even more plainly Gorg. Hel., 4 (Diels, II, 289, 9 ff.): Some ask for wealth, others for fame or beauty, but those who ask for wisdom will like them all be determined ὑπ' ἔρωτός τε φιλονίκου φιλοτιμίας τε ἀνικήτου and thus possess all other gifts. Cf. the Sophist in Aristides, 46 (Diels, II, 252).

[32] Cf., e.g., Soph. Fr., 98 (TGF, 151): esp. Eur. Med., 294-301, also Fr., 905 (652): μισῶ σοφιστήν, ὅστις οὐχ αὐτῷ σοφός.

[33] Cf. esp. Plat. Prot., 313c; Hi., I, 281b ff.; Euthyd., 293d; Soph., 233b, 268c-d; Lys., 222e; Symp., 185c and most aggressively Hi., II, 365e ff. (whether liars are σοφοί).

[34] E.g., Aristot. Sophistici elenchi, 1, p. 165a, 21 : ἔστι γὰρ ἡ σοφιστικὴ σοφία φαινομένη, οὖσα δ' οὔ κτλ. Cf. also H. Bonitz, Index Aristotelicus (1955), 689, s.v.

[35] Pind., e.g., calls poets σοφισταί, Isthm., 5, 28; cf. Aesch. Fr., 314 (TGF, 97). On the seven wise men Hdt., I, 29; Isocr., 15, 235 etc., also → n. 13.

[36] Plat. Hi., I, 281c. Cf. also the malicious irony with which Socrates has Hippias say that the seven sages were poorer περὶ τὴν σοφίαν than the modern Sophists in their τέχνη, 281d.

[37] Plat. Ap., 20c-23c. Cf. esp. 20d: δι' οὐδὲν ἀλλ' ἢ διὰ σοφίαν τινὰ τοῦτο τὸ ὄνομα ἔσχηκα. ποίαν δὴ σοφίαν ταύτην; ἥπερ ἐστὶν ἴσως ἀνθρωπίνη σοφία· τῷ ὄντι γὰρ κινδυνεύω ταύτην εἶναι σοφός. But such wisdom consists in : οὗτος ὑμῶν, ὦ ἄνθρωποι, σοφώτατός ἐστιν, ὅστις ὥσπερ Σωκράτης ἔγνωκεν ὅτι οὐδενὸς ἄξιός ἐστι τῇ ἀληθείᾳ

lean in part on Parmenides. σοφία is for him a knowing acceptance of true being, which man cannot control as such, but which — as he maintains in opposition to the Sophists — is not wholly unattainable. The unquestioning nature of Sophist τέχνη is for him narrow-minded, Plat. Symp., 203a. The ignorance of the true sage brings him under the overpowering might of ἔρως which, very different from ἀμαθία, impels him to seek after σοφία: ὥστε ἀναγκαῖον Ἔρωτα φιλόσοφον εἶναι, φιλόσοφον δὲ ὄντα μεταξὺ εἶναι σοφοῦ καὶ ἀμαθοῦς. [38] The content of wisdom is being, the ideas, and especially the ἀγαθόν and καλόν "beyond being." [39] As the idea of the good and the beautiful is not a special thing in the world, but something divine, so wisdom is proper to God alone: [40] θεῶν οὐδεὶς φιλοσοφεῖ οὐδ᾽ ἐπιθυμεῖ σοφὸς γενέσθαι — ἔστι γάρ, Symp., 204a. θαυμαστόν, then, consists in the fact that philosophy is possible. [41] It is possible through the power of ἔρως, which in its function as a mediator between ἀμαθία and σοφία corresponds to the ontological μέθεξις through which the χωρισμός between being and non-being is not removed but sustained in direct relation. It is in this light that one is to understand the position and task of the προεστῶτες and ἄρχοντες in the polis, which Plato would like to see entrusted to those who pursue philosophy, Resp., IV, 428e-429a. The virtue which accrues to them from the four cardinal virtues of σοφία, ἀνδρεία, σωφροσύνη and δικαιοσύνη is thus wisdom, the greatest of all virtues Prot., 330a etc. The definition of σοφία in Ps.-Plat. Def., 414b is finally an excellent summary of Plato's teaching: Σοφία ἐπιστήμη ἀνυπόθετος· ἐπιστήμη τῶν ἀεὶ ὄντων· ἐπιστήμη θεωρητικὴ τῆς τῶν ὄντων αἰτίας. Φιλοσοφία τῆς τῶν ὄντων ἀεὶ ἐπιστήμης ὄρεξις· ἕξις θεωρητικὴ τοῦ ἀληθοῦς, πῶς ἀληθές· ἐπιμέλεια ψυχῆς μετὰ λόγου ὀρθοῦ. [42]

In contrast to Plato Aristotle regards σοφία and φιλοσοφία as identical. This equation is ultimately based on Aristotle's criticism of Plato's doctrine of χωρισμός and μέθεξις. For Aristotle σοφία is an attainable and quite specific knowledge. If there is reference to the wisdom of, e.g., a Phidias or Polyclitus as a particular ἀρετὴ τέχνης (Eth. Nic., VI, 7, p. 1141a, 9 ff.), this is not wrong in itself, for every individual τέχνη, in contrast to mere ἐμπειρία, has something to do with σοφία. The τεχνίτης knows αἰτία. [43] Yet wisdom in the strict sense is the knowledge which perceives and knows πρῶται αἰτίαι καὶ ἀρχαί. [44] Thus σοφία is

---

πρὸς σοφίαν, 23b. Cf. positively in Phaed., 96a the young Socrates wrestling critically with natural philosophy.

[38] Plat. Symp., 204b. Cf. Phaedr., 279a: ἐπὶ μείζω δέ τις αὐτὸν ἄγοι ὁρμὴ θειοτέρα· φύσει γάρ, ὦ φίλε, ἔνεστί τις φιλοσοφία τῇ τοῦ ἀνδρὸς διανοίᾳ; also Resp., V, 475b, 477a, 480a; VI, 484b etc.

[39] On this cf. G. Krüger, Einsicht u. Leidenschaft² (1948), 215-227.

[40] Plat. Phaedr., 278d: τὸ μὲν σοφόν, ὦ Φαῖδρε, καλεῖν ἔμοιγε μέγα εἶναι δοκεῖ καὶ θεῷ μόνῳ πρέπειν· τὸ δὲ ἢ φιλόσοφον ἢ τοιοῦτόν τι μᾶλλόν τε ἂν αὐτῷ καὶ ἁρμόττοι καὶ ἐμμελεστέρως ἔχοι. Cf. Ap., 23a; Symp., 203e-f; Lys., 218a.

[41] Cf. esp. Krüger, op. cit., 155 f.

[42] Cf. Xenocrates Fr., 6 (ed. R. Heinze [1892], 161): σοφία is one special φρόνησις (cf. Plat. Prot., 333b) in which the theoretical is one with the practical. This is explained by the fact that for Plato σοφία is knowledge of the good and the beautiful. On the relation between σοφία and φρόνησις in Plat. Leg. cf. G. Müller, "Studien z. d. platon. Nomoi," Zetemata, 3 (1951), 13-33, 42, 51-56, 74. On the relation between σοφία and δικαιοσύνη cf. Resp., IV, 443e.

[43] Aristot. Metaph., 1, 1, p. 981a, 24-30. Cf. 3, 3, p. 1005b, 1: ἔστι δέ σοφία τις καὶ ἡ φυσική, ἀλλ᾽ οὐ πρώτη, cf. 11, 4, p. 1061b, 32.

[44] Aristot. Metaph., 1, 2, p. 982b, 8 f., cf. 1, 1, p. 981b, 28, also 1, 9, p. 992a, 24 f.: ὅλως δὲ ζητούσης τῆς σοφίας περὶ τῶν φανερῶν τὸ αἴτιον. It considers τὸ ὄν ᾗ, ὄν, 5, 1,

the πρώτη φιλοσοφία,[45] "the most complete form of knowledge,"[46] for he who knows first causes knows all things, since the ἀρχαί underlie all that exists, Metaph., 1, 2, p. 982a, 21 ff. Hence the wise are distinguished from all other men by this knowledge,[47] especially from the Sophists, against whom Aristot. fights just as strongly as Plato : the σοφοί know the τιμιώτατα.[48] Their wisdom is divine knowledge, and it is so as ἐπιστήμη, ἣν ... μάλιστ᾽ ἂν ὁ θεὸς ἔχοι, with the divine as its content : ὅ τε γὰρ θεὸς δοκεῖ τῶν αἰτίων πᾶσιν εἶναι καὶ ἀρχή τις, καὶ τὴν τοιαύτην ἢ μόνος ἢ μάλιστ᾽ ἂν[49] ἔχοι ὁ θεός, Metaph., 1, 2, p. 983a, 5 ff.[50] What differentiates the wise so plainly from other men is their concern not with the human, with what is beneficial to themselves, but with the extraordinary, the astonishing, the demonic, Eth. Nic., VI, 7, p. 1141b, 6 f.; cf. VI, 13, p. 1143b, 15 ff. For Aristot., as distinct from Plato, wisdom is a purely theoretical or dianoetic virtue (Eth. Nic., VI, 3, p. 1139b, 17; cf. Eth. M., I, 35, p. 1197b, 3) and not, like φρόνησις, a practical virtue. It does not merely know what results from origins but considers the truth of the ἀρχαί themselves, Eth. Nic., VI, 7, p. 1141a, 17 f.[51] It is knowledge of the τέλος and the ἀγαθόν, Metaph., 2, 2, p. 996b, 10 ff. It does not itself contribute anything to εὐδαιμονία but is intrinsically ἡδίστη τῶν κατ᾽ ἀρετῶν ἐνεργειῶν and has θαυμασταὶ ἡδοναί within it.[52]

3. The Philosophical Schools of the Hellenistic Period.

The beginning of the Hell. period is characterised essentially by the political decline of the small city states, the rise of Alexander's empire, the resultant kingdoms, and the process of religious and cultural syncretism which suddenly became so widespread in consequence. This new situation on the larger canvas meant a wholly new basic experience for the individual. He was largely detached from the old, developed, native sphere of the *polis* and thus left defenceless in the broader sphere of the cosmos. He was now basically alone.[53] This experience leads to a new approach to life which takes shape in the ideal of the wise man that almost all philosophical schools sought to set up — the image of the whole man who can find his way in the relations of the day and preserve the ancient ideal of εὐδαιμονία in changed surroundings.[54] Thus the philosopher is often the tutor who prepares the sons of the wealthy for life in the broadest

---

p. 1026a, 31, cf. 11, 3, p. 1060b, 31. In Aristot. the philosophical ἔρως of Plat. is found consistently as metaphysical-technical ζητεῖν.

[45] Aristot. Metaph., 1, 1, p. 981b, 28; 1, 2, p. 982b, 9; 2, 2, p. 996b, 9; ἔστι δὲ σοφία τις καὶ ἡ φυσική, ἀλλ᾽ οὐ πρώτη, 3, 3, p. 1005b, 1 f. Aristot. speaks of the πρώτη φιλοσοφία in Metaph., 5, 1, p. 1026a, 24 ff.; 11, 4, p. 1061b, 19, cf. 11, 1, p. 1059a, 18 ff.

[46] Aristot. Eth. Nic., VI, 7, p. 1141a, 17, cf. Metaph., 1, 1, p. 981b. 28; 1, 2, 982; cf. σκέψις as an ἐπιστήμη τοῦ φιλοσόφου, 3, 3, p. 1005a, 21 f., cf. 11, 4, p. 1061b, 25.

[47] One admired the first inventor ὡς σοφὸν καὶ διαφέροντα τῶν ἄλλων, Aristot. Metaph., 1, 1, p. 981b, 13 ff., cf. Eth. Nic., VI, 7, p. 1141b, 6 f.

[48] Aristot. Eth. Nic., VI, 7, p. 1141a, 20b-3 ff., cf. I, 12, p. 1101b, 10 ff.; Metaph., 12, 7, p. 1064a, 28-b14; 6, 1, p. 1026a, 10 ff.

[49] Note the difference from Plat. → n. 40.

[50] For Aristot., however, the πρώτη φιλοσοφία is not θεολογία, which in the strict sense he distinguishes from real philosophy as pre-scientific mythologising, cf. Jaeger, *op. cit.*, (→ n. 27), 13 f. (examples, *ibid.*, n. 15).

[51] Hence σοφία is the basic dianoetic virtue in which ἐπιστήμη and νοῦς find fulfilment, *ibid.*, lines 9-15.

[52] Namely, καθαρότητι καὶ τῷ βεβαίῳ, Eth. Nic., XI, 7, p. 1177a, 22-27, cf. VI, 12, p. 1144a, 3 ff.

[53] On this cf. J. Kaerst, *Gesch. d. Hell.*, II² (1926), 80-84.

[54] On the early history of this idea cf. the material in F. Dirlmeier, *Die Nikomachische Ethik, Aristoteles Werke in deutscher Übers.* (ed. E. Grumach), 6 (1956), 284 f.

sense. [55] We find this ideal picture of the sage first of all in the Megarics, [56] then in the Cynics, and finally esp. in the Stoics and Epicureans. [57]

The Stoic ideal of wisdom exerted a strong influence for centuries. The Stoic school founded by Zeno, developed by Chrysippus and then persisting basically unchanged into the Christian era, is a fundamentally dogmatic system which finds its comprehensive goal in the prototype of the σοφός or σπουδαῖος. The leading concern is to impart to individuals knowledge of the system, which is thought to be in essential harmony with the ontic system of the cosmos, and thus to give them the final shelter which rejection of the metaphysics of Plato and Aristotle had called in question for the Stoics. [58] Hence σοφία is defined as ἐπιστήμη θείων τε καὶ ἀνθρωπείων πραγμάτων, [59] which in the Stoic sense means controlling knowledge of the universe as ἐκ θεῶν καὶ ἀνθρώπων ... σύστημα. [60] Now knowledge is for the Stoic a διάθεσις, i.e., an immutable basic attitude. Hence σοφία as knowledge is the διάθεσις which corresponds to the λόγος that constitutes the unity of the cosmos, [61] so that essentially it is an ethical attitude too. Thus σοφία is regarded as the only basic virtue which essentially combines practice and theory. [62] Wisdom is actualised knowledge, [63] and philosophy is its practical execution. [64] Stoicism, then, can basically explain σοφία only with reference to the conduct of the wise man. The σοφός is the true and necessary subject of Stoic philosophy. The rigour of the image is typical. Only the sage can have ἐπιστήμη; [65] to him alone are all things accessible. [66] Error is ruled out for the sage. [67] He is divine by nature. [68] He does all things well. [69] He alone possesses all virtues and hence he alone is happy: [70] πάσαις μὲν ταῖς κινήσεσι, πάσαις δὲ

---

[55] Schwartz, 169 humorously but incorrectly characterises the ideal as follows: "One might say that the σοφός is not an ideal figure but a mannequin on which ethical ideas are displayed."

[56] Stilbon acc. to Sen. Ep., 9, 1 ff.; Stob. Ecl., III, 738, 7-748, 4. Cf. Schwartz, 145 f., 169.

[57] Diog. L., X. 117 ff., cf. H. Usener, Epicurea (1887), 330-341 with quotations and fr. from other authors. On what is common to the 2 schools cf. Schwartz, 149-170, on Epicurean ethics in detail, 171-191.

[58] Cf. the materially pertinent observation of Simplicius: "What was peculiar to the ideas the Stoics transferred to the sage," O. Rieth, Grundbegriffe stoischer Ethik (1933), 93.

[59] Aetius Placita, I, 2 (v. Arnim, II, 35); Sext. Emp. Math., IX, 13.

[60] Arius Didymus Fr., 29 (v. Arnim, II 528).

[61] It is in this light that we are to understand the basic ethical formula of Zeno which sums up the τέλος of all conduct as ὁμολογουμένως ζῆν. On Stoic τέλος formulae cf. esp. O. Rieth, "Über das τέλος d. Stoiker," Herm., 69 (1934), 13-45, also G. Bornkamm, "ΟΜΟΛΟΓΙΑ," Herm., 71 (1936), 377-393.

[62] Cf., e.g., Cic. Fin., III, 55 and esp. Lucullus, 8. On the divergent teaching of Ariston of Chios cf. Wilckens Weisheit, 254, n. 2.

[63] Or τέχνη τοῦ βιοῦν (ars vivendi), Cic. Lucullus, 8; Fin., III, 4; IV, 19; Tusc., II, 12; Epict. Diss., IV, 1, 63; I, 14, 2; 15, 2 f. etc., cf. M. Pohlenz, "Grundfragen d. stoischen Philosophie," AGG, III, 26 (1940), 62 f. For other examples P. Wendland, Quaestiones Musonianae (1886), 12, n. 2.

[64] Aetius Placita, I, 2 (v. Arnim, II, 35): ἄσκησις ἐπιτηδείου τέχνης.

[65] Sext. Emp. Math., VII, 151.

[66] Diog. L., VII, 83 and esp. 125. Cf. Sext. Emp. Math., VII, 432: μόνος ὁ σοφὸς ἀληθεύει.

[67] Stob. Ecl., II, 111, 10; Diog. L., VII, 122: ἀναμαρτήτους.

[68] ἔχειν γὰρ ἐν ἑαυτοῖς οἱονεὶ θεόν, Diog. L., VII, 119; cf. Cic. De Legibus, 17, 22; Dio Chrys. Or., 1, 42; Epict. Diss., I, 9, 4 f. etc. → n. 60.

[69] Stob. Ecl., II, 111, 10 and the passages assembled in v. Arnim, II, 557-566.

[70] Cic. Fin., III, 26; Philo Quaest. in Gn., IV, 92; Dio Chrys. Or., 69, 4 etc.; v. Arnim, III, 585-588.

ταῖς σχέσεσιν ὁ σπουδαῖος ἐπαινετός, ἔνδον τε καὶ ἔξω κτλ. [71] These Stoic paradoxes, which are probably hyperbolical, can be understood only if one takes into account the fact that all the non-wise are judged equally rigorously as φαῦλοι of whom the harsh alternative is true. [72] It is typical of Stoic teaching that hardly one of the actual heads of the school claimed to be a sage or even a simple philosopher. A further point is that in spite of the strict and absolute antithesis between the two classes of men [73] Stoicism still emphasised the relative distinction between the φαῦλος and the προκόπτων. Its rigour did not result in resignation but was an ultimate concern and also an unconditional goal of Stoic pedagogy, → VI, 706, 26 ff.

In the later Hell.-Roman age we find eminent Stoics as tutors at the imperial court (Seneca), and in the 2nd cent. the empire itself even had a Stoic sage at its head for some yrs. in the person of Marcus Aurelius. On the other hand we also find the peregrinating Stoic-Cynic philosopher. [74]

4. The Philosophy of Later Antiquity.

From the time of Middle Stoicism [75] the various views begin to overlap. In gen. σοφία, often synon. with φρόνησις, is regarded as the chief of the four cardinal virtues, cf. Plut., who sees in it the basic intellectual virtue related to immutable being and pure spirit. [76] In what is called Middle Platonism the eclectic traditionalism typical of the whole of later antiquity enters a characteristically new atmosphere. [77] In these circles a new definition of the τέλος of philosophy as ὁμοίωσις θεῷ κατὰ τὸ δυνατόν was formulated on the basis of Plat. Theaet., 176b. [78] This played a gt. role not only in Neo-

---

[71] Philo Praem. Poen., 113; cf. Stob. Ecl., II, 65, 12 and esp. Cic. Fin., III, 26.

[72] Stob. Ecl., II, 106, 18 f.: τῷ δὲ σπουδαίῳ ὁ φαῦλός ἐστιν ἐναντίος and esp. Plut. Comm. Not., 10 (II, 1062e): πάντας ἐπίσης κακοὺς καὶ ἀδίκους καὶ ἀπίστους καὶ ἄφρονας τοὺς μὴ σοφούς. Zeno already divided men into δύο γένη between whom is no transition whatever, Stob. Ecl., II, 99, 3 ff.; Cic. Fin., IV, 56. Cf. esp. Rieth, op. cit., (→ n. 58), 167.

[73] Omnium insipientiam, iniustitiam, alia vitia similia esse, omniaque peccata esse paria, eosque, qui natura doctrinaque longe ad virtutem processissent, nisi eam plane consecuti essent, summe esse miseros, neque inter eorum vitam et improbissimorum quicquam omnino interesse, Cic. Fin., IV, 21. Cf. the metaphor of the shipwrecked person in Plut. Comm. Not., 10 (II, 1063a b).

[74] Their teaching followed a specific form (διατριβαί), cf. R. Bultmann, "Der Stil d. paul. Predigt u. d. stoisch-kynischen Diatribe," FRL, 13 (1910).

[75] On Poseidonios' theory concerning a broad and steady development of human culture through the promotion of knowledge and morality as the task of the philosopher as sapiens cf. esp. Sen. Ep., 90.

[76] Cf. esp. Plut. De Virtute Morali, 5 (II, 443e-444e): ἔστι γὰρ περὶ τὰ ἀεὶ κατὰ ταὐτὰ καὶ ὡσαύτως ἔχοντα (as distinct from φρόνησις as the basic moral virtue which as βουλευτικὸν καὶ πρακτικὸν relates to πῶς ἔχοντα πρὸς ἡμᾶς). Thus wisdom is ἡ ἀπροσδεὴς τοῦ ἀλόγου καὶ περὶ τὸν εἰλικρινῆ καὶ ἀπαθῆ νοῦν συνισταμένη which with φρόνησις is the δύναμις ᾗ τὸ θειότατον ἐγγίγνεται τῆς ἐπιστήμης καὶ μακαριώτατον. If one detects here the influence of Aristot. and Middle Platonism, in gen. a more Stoic understanding predominates in the usage of Cicero, though cf. the echoes of Middle Platonism in, e.g., Off., I, 153. The Stoic def. of φρόνησις (═ σοφία), which is also described as the first cardinal virtue as in Plat., calls it ἐπιστήμη ἀγαθῶν καὶ κακῶν καὶ οὐδετέρων, cf. as a typical example of the period Alcinous Introd. in Platonem, 29 (ed. C. F. Hermann, Plato, VI [1892], 183, 7, cf. 182, 24).

[77] For a good summary cf. H. Dörrie, "Die Frage nach dem Transzendenten im Mittelplatonismus," Sources de Plotin, Entretiens Tome, V (1960), 193-241.

[78] The first example is in Arius Didymus in Stob. Ecl., II, 49, 17 f. For all the 42 instances cf. K. Praechter in GGA, 168 (1906), 904 and 171 (1909), 542 f.

Platonism but also in later eastern Chr. theology. [79] In it one may see esp. clearly the specifically theological principle of all the Platonism of later antiquity. But here philosophy is understood Platonically as ὄρεξις σοφίας, [80] so that wisdom is the fulfilment of this philosophical approximation to the divine. [81]

Plotinus built on this. For him the goal of philosophy as θεῷ ὁμοιωθῆναι is to be reached in the main *via negationis*, as a flight of the soul from the lower sphere of the physically evil to the heights of the divinely good, Enn., I, 2, 1. This is the upward path of virtue which is first traversed in the four civil virtues but has then to be purified on a higher level. On this level of true philosophy σοφία (or φρόνησις) is the vision of the spirit : ἡ σοφία μὲν καὶ φρόνησις ἐν θεωρίᾳ ὧν νοῦς ἔχει, Enn., I, 2, 6. [82] For the upper intellectual sphere has three stages : the "good" as the one ; νοῦς, which alone shares in the good by vision ; and the soul, which in the purified state is able by nature to live in accordance with the upper spirit, II, 9, 1 and 8. In this vision wisdom relates purely and totally to the νοῦς as to being, [83] but the spirit itself to the one and the good as πρὸς τὸ ἐπέκεινα τοῦ ὄντος, I, 3, 5. Human wisdom, then, shares in it fundamentally through the mediation of the spirit. Thus σοφία or φρόνησις is the most valuable thing in us, I, 3, 5. It perfects the natural virtues, I, 3, 6. In confrontation with the Gnostics, then, Plotin. gave free rein to the whole fervour of his philosophical spirit and made a bitter attack on them because they expressly taught that σοφία is an essence which has fallen down from the upper sphere, II, 9, 10 f. → 511, 14 ff.

As a typical example of this later eclecticism, into which the Neo-Platonic tradition was integrated along with Aristot. and under the influence of Poseidonian and Neo-Pythagorean concepts, one may cite the description of σοφία which goes back to Aristocles Messenius and which is found in John Philoponus (6th cent. A.D.). [84] Here φιλοσοφία is first defined as φιλία σοφίας and this is also derived etym. from σαφής : "σοφία is also called σάφειά τις οὖσα because it makes everything clear. But this clarity is also described as an illuminating (φαές τι) beyond (normal) illumination and light since it brings to light what is hidden. Since the rational and the divine, as Aristot. says in Eth. Nic., X, 7, p. 1177a, 15. b 30, is luminous in its own nature but seems dark to us, and is hard to perceive, because of the darkness of the body laid upon us, he rightly described the knowledge (ἐπιστήμη) which leads us into the light as wisdom," lines 8-17. In what follows we are then told how those who remained after a disastrous flood began to find their way about and first discovered σοφία in a very elementary sense, namely, as εἰς τὰ ἀναγκαῖα τοῦ βίου τὸ λυσιτελές, line 41. Later, however, the τέχναι were invented as higher σοφία and those who practised them were called the wise. Then came the famous seven wise men who created the laws, then the nature philosophers who discovered knowledge of the divine (line 57), and finally Pythagoras, who as the first ἐπὶ μόνης τῆς τῶν ἀϊδίων ἐπιστήμης τὸ τῆς σοφίας θεὶς ὄνομα,

---

[79] Cf. the interesting passage in Bas. Spir. Sct., 1, 2 : πρόκειται ἡμῖν ὁμοιωθῆναι τῷ θεῷ, κατὰ τὸ δυνατὸν ἀνθρώπου φύσει. Ὁμοίωσις δέ, οὐκ ἄνευ γνώσεως· ἡ δὲ γνῶσις, οὐκ ἐκτὸς διδαγμάτων.

[80] So, e.g., Alcinous Introd. in Platonem, 1 (*op. cit.* → n. 76), 152, 4.

[81] The formally Stoic def. of σοφία in Alcinous Introd. in Plat., 1 as ἐπιστήμη θείων τε καὶ ἀνθρωπείων πραγμάτων has here a non-Stoic and specifically later Platonic sense, as may be seen from the immediately appended def. of philosophy as λύσις καὶ περιαγωγὴ ψυχῆς ἀπὸ σώματος, which is understood in the sense of ὁμοίωσις θεῷ, *ibid.*, 28 (181, 16 f.).

[82] Cf. Enn., I, 2, 7 : ἐν ψυχῇ τοίνυν πρὸς νοῦν ἡ ὅρασις σοφία καὶ φρόνησις, ἀρεταὶ αὐτῆς.

[83] The spirit *is* being inasmuch as it *thinks*, for νοεῖν and εἶναι are one and the same, Enn., V, 9, 5, — fundamentally, of course, in such a way that τὸ ὂν τοῦ νοῦ προεπινοεῖν ἀνάγκη, V, 9, 8, cf. 7.

[84] Johannis Philoponi in Nicomachi isagogen Arithmeticam Scholia, ed. R. Hoche, *Gymnasialprogramm Wesel* (1864), printed in H. Heiland, Aristoclis Messenii Reliquiae, Diss. Giessen (1925), 23.

καὶ φιλοσοφίαν τὴν τῆς σοφίας ταύτης φιλίαν ὠνόμασε. τοῦτο γάρ ἐστι τῆς σοφίας τὸ τέλος, ἡ τῶν θείων πραγμάτων γνῶσις, lines 60-63.

Wilckens

B. The Old Testament.

I. Terminology.

Since the LXX normally uses σοφία/σοφός for the Hbr. stem חכם, in essentials this alone need be considered. The verb חכם occurs 26 times (q 18, pi 3, pu 2, hi 1, hitp 2), חָכָם as adj. or noun occurs 135 times, the noun חָכְמָה 147 times and in the plur. חָכְמוֹת 4[85] times. 73 instances are in the historical books (חכם 3, חָכָם 31, חָכְמָה 39), 41 in the prophets (חכם 1, חָכָם 24, חָכְמָה 16), 13 in the Psalms (חכם 4, חָכָם 2, חָכְמָה 7),[86] 180 in the Wisdom lit. proper (חכם 18, חָכָם 76, חָכְמָה 86),[87] and 5 in the other books. Thus about three-fifths of the total may be found in the Wisdom books. It is worth noting that in the historical books the words mostly denote technical or artistic ability (→ 484, 1 ff.) or cleverness and knowledge such as the wisdom of Solomon (→ 484, 24 ff.), more rarely magical craft, practical wisdom, and ethical or religious conduct (→ 486, 14 ff.). In the prophets they denote human ability of various kinds, the wisdom and the magicians of other nations; they are also found in criticism of wisdom and very rarely, and only in prophecy, in the context of eschatology, → 488, 30 ff. In the Wisdom lit. (→ 476, n. 87) the terms may sometimes be used for cleverness and prudence, but as in the Psalms they are employed in the main for rules of behaviour, for ethical or religious conduct. Qoh. stands apart, since it uses the words for the doctrinally clearly etched wisdom of the schools. In the few other instances the ref. is to magic or knowledge.

In the Aram. portions of the OT we also find the noun חַכִּים "wise man," which is used 14 times for men to whom one goes for the interpretation of dreams, and the noun חָכְמָה, which is used in Ezr. 7:25 for the Torah and elsewhere for the gift of interpreting dreams granted to Daniel.

The survey shows that the common translation "wise," "wisdom" is unfortunate and to a large degree inexact. It does justice neither to the broad range of the Hebrew terms nor to their precise meaning. If knowledge is presupposed in detail, this is not so much a deeper knowledge in the theoretical mastery of the questions of life and the universe as a solution of a practical kind on the basis of concrete demands. The reference is to prudent, considered, experienced and competent action to subjugate the world and to master the various problems of life and life itself. When detailed aspects are taken into account חכם means "cleverness and skill for the purpose of practical action." The fact that לֵב is often added[88] makes it plain that this is not a quality but can arise out of a feeling for the right

---

[85] Also in Prv. 14:1 instead of the adj. On חכמות as a plur. cf. for details E. Brønno, *Stud. über hbr. Morphologie u. Vokalismus* (1943), 187 f. This is probably a plur. of extension, intensity and majesty used as a title and denoting comprehensive, pure, authentic and supreme wisdom.

[86] Terms of the stem חכם are as much as possible avoided in Ps. because they became fixed quite early. Materially one group of Ps. is influenced by the Wisdom lit. or even belongs to it.

[87] Job, Prv. and Qoh.

[88] So Ex. 28:3; 31:6; 35:25; 36:1 f., 8; Job 9:4; 37:24; Prv. 10:8; 11:29; 16:21; "understanding" 1 K. 5:9.

thing which is fostered by traditional knowledge, education and personal experience. As it is with man, so it is with the gods and Yahweh, though one cannot say that one idea developed out of the other.

In keeping with this sense of חכם is the fact that the most common par. are derivates of בין "to perceive," "to understand (how to act)": נָבוֹן "perceptive," "skilled," [89] בִּינָה "insight," [90] and תְּבוּנָה "insight," "skill" (of the artisan). [91] Then we find derivates of ידע (→ I, 696, 17 ff.) emphasising either "understanding" [92] or "experience" (Dt. 1:13, 15), but also denoting the "skill" of the artist or magical "art." [93] The ref. is again to practical conduct when the following par. are found with terms derived from חכם: "uprightness," "honesty" Prv. 4:11, "to lead the heart along the right way" Prv. 23:19, and צַדִּיק "righteous," "pious" Dt. 16:19; Prv. 9:9; 23:24; Qoh. 9:1. One notes a similar connection in the antitheses: the "fool" (→ IV, 833, 31 ff.; 916, 30 ff.) is incapable of right action rather than stupid. [94] The corresponding terms relate less to thought and knowledge and more to action. Folly is disorder in a man's life which first finds expression in his conduct and then in imprudence and arrogance. [95]

II. Wisdom as an Ancient Oriental and Israelite-Old Testament Phenomenon.

On the one side the content of חכם is largely defined by a corresponding world of thought common to the ancient Orient, so that the terms, and the OT Wisdom books in which they mostly occur, belong to the circle of a Wisdom literature which in essentials is the same throughout the region. On the other hand the development was stronger in Israel than elsewhere and the international and suprareligious doctrine of wisdom in the true sense was both nationalised and also integrated into faith in Yahweh and adjusted to it.

1. Mesopotamia. In Mesopotamia there is no word corresponding to the Hbr. חכם. [96] Apart from the textually and philologically difficult Sumerian texts [97] Bab. has *nēmequ* "wisdom" and several adj. "wise" (*enqu, mūdû, ḫassu, etpēšu*). But these are

---

[89] Gn. 41:33, 39; Dt. 1:13; 4:6; 1 K. 3:12; Is. 5:21; 29:14; Jer. 4:22; Hos. 14:10; Prv. 1:5; 17:28; 18:15; Qoh. 9:11.

[90] Dt. 4:6; Is. 29:14; Job 28:12, 20; 38:36; 39:17; Prv. 2:3; 7:4; 9:10.

[91] Ex. 36:1; 1 K. 5:9; 7:14; Jer. 10:12; 51:15; Ob. 8; Job 12:12 f.; Prv. 2:2; 3:19; 15:1; 24:3.

[92] Jer. 4:22; Job 34:2; Qoh. 6:8, cf. also מַע "understanding," Prv. 26:16.

[93] 1 K. 7:14; Is. 47:10. דַּעַת "insight," Prv. 5:2; 15:2, 7; 21:11; "knowledge" Qoh. 1:18; "experience" Is. 33:6.

[94] With אֱוִיל "foolish," "stupid" cf. אֱוִלִי "inept," "unserviceable," while אִוֶּלֶת "(impious) folly" with עשׂה means "to act imprudently." כְּסִיל is religiously "bold" and "foolish" in practical matters. לֵץ "babbler," "mocker" (→ IV, 797, 24 ff.), is the man who demonstrates in his words his lack of acquaintance with what is right. נָבָל "vain," "foolish," means "without understanding" in mind or ethical conduct, נְבָלָה with "stupidity" is used euphemistically for serious sin. סָכָל is the one who acts "foolishly" (cf. the noun סִכְלוּת in Qoh.). From פתה I "to be inexperienced, misled," אֶוִ is used for the simple and inexperienced young man who is easily led astray. Cf. also → I, 275, 43 ff.

[95] Cf. W. Caspari, "Über d. bibl. Begriff d. Torheit," NkZ, 39 (1928), 668-695.

[96] W. G. Lambert, *Babylonian Wisdom Literature* (1960), 1.

[97] J. J. A. van Dijk, *La sagesse suméro-accadienne* (1953), 17-21 thought he had found in Sumerian ME the central concept in the sense of an "immanence divine dans la matière morte et vivante, incréée, inchangeable, subsistante, mais impersonnelle," but this seems doubtful in the light of criticism, cf. T. Fish's review in *Journal of Semitic Studies*, 1 (1956), 286-288.

seldom used in the sense of OT Wisdom lit. [98] The ref. of "wisdom" is usually to skill in the cultus and magic, and the wise man is the initiate in these fields. In the text "I will praise the lord of wisdom" [99] the god Marduk is meant and his wisdom consists in skill in the rites of exorcism. The Accadian *hakâmu* "to grasp or understand something" is probably a West Semitic loan word, and, since it is synon. with *lamâdu* "to learn," it was probably adopted as a handy tt. [100]

Though the inclusive term is missing, there is a fairly extensive Mesopotamian lit. corresponding in content to the OT Wisdom books. [101] This is extant mostly in Accad., but much of it goes back to Sumerian traditions. Many collections of proverbs have been preserved in the Sumerian version (e.g., on school tablets), and these are usually grouped by the first characters. [102] Their authors obviously belonged to the same circle as those who created the Sumerian categorisation which made possible a systematic arrangement of the whole world of objects and experience. [103] In its practical use this arrangement is not explained rationally but illustrated by myths and poems which tell of the creation or restoration of order after chaotic relations. For the Sumerians the lists were a systematising supplement to the purely paradigmatic poems. The Babylonians and Assyrians adopted and developed them and there thus arose a whole branch of Wisdom lit. in the form of a cultural wisdom which received its definitive form esp. in the gt. series *ḪAR-ra* (*ḫubullu*) with 24 tables and thousands of entries. As these seek to master the world by means of the order of names, so the collections of proverbs try to grasp the regularity of life in order to be able to gain the mastery over it. Other texts, in the form of wisdom sayings, deal with ethical questions and impart practical counsel for a life which corresponds to the order of things and is thus successful. [104] Or else they tackle the problems which result from this view of life, [105] so that they might be regarded as precursors of the OT Job. [106] Finally one finds here traditional fables, disputes and debates and other wisdom texts which it is at times hard to classify by genre. [107]

2. Egypt. There is a clearer impulse towards development of the concept in Egypt. The norm of conduct which the wisdom doctrines seek to mediate is now described by the term *maat*. [108] This central word is not unequivocal and is hard to translate : usually "truth," better "right," "rightness," "primal order," "cosmic order." No distinction is made between divine and human or heavenly and earthly right and order, since there is

---

[98] Lambert, 99 mentions the wisdom sayings as a possible example, *Counsels of Wisdom*, 24 f.

[99] AOT, 273-281; J. B. Pritchard, *Ancient Near Eastern Texts²* (1955), 434-437.

[100] Cf. Ges.-Buhl, *s.v.* חכם.

[101] AOT, 284-295; Pritchard, 410 f., 425-430, 434-440; Lambert, *op. cit.*

[102] S. N. Kramer, "Sumerian Wisdom Literature. A Preliminary Survey," *Bulletin of the American Schools of Oriental Research*, 122 (1951), 28-31; J. J. A. van Dijk, *op. cit.*, 5-11 (bibl.); Pritchard, 425-427; E. I. Gordon, "The Sumerian Proverb Collections. A Preliminary Survey," *Journal of the American Oriental Society*, 74 (1954), 82-85; also "Sumerian Proverbs: 'Collection Four,'" *ibid.*, 77 (1957), 67-79; also "A New Look at the Wisdom of Sumer and Akkad," *Bibliotheca Orientalis*, 17 (1960), 122-152. Only a small portion has been published thus far, but it demonstrates the similarity to Prv.

[103] Cf. in detail L. Matouš, *Die lexikalischen Tafelserien der Babylonier und Assyrer in d. Berliner Museen*, I (1933); W. v. Soden, "Leistung u. Grenze sumerischer u. bab. Wissenschaft" in *Die Welt als Gesch.*, 2 (1936), 411-464, 509-557; also *Zweisprachigkeit in d. geistigen Kultur Babyloniens* (1960).

[104] Texts in Lambert, *op. cit.*, c. 4-5.

[105] Texts in Lambert, *op. cit.*, c. 2-3 (and perhaps 6).

[106] Cf. with further bibl. J. J. Stamm, *Das Leiden des Unschuldigen in Babylon u. Israel* (1948); A. Kuschke, "Altbabyl. Texte zum Thema: 'Der leidende Gerechte,'" ThLZ, 81 (1956), 69-76; Gese, 51-69. From the standpt. of form criticism, however, the texts are more like Ps. than Job and materially there are basic differences from Job as well as peripheral par.

[107] Cf. Kramer, *op. cit.*; van Dijk, *op. cit.*; Gordon New Look, 122-152.

[108] A. de Buck, "Het religieus karakter der oudste egypt. wijsheid," *Nieuw Theol.*

only one order obtaining equally throughout the world. The goal of wisdom teachings is to level the way for the order (maat) [109] which comes from God by transmission. With an almost total disregard for personal experience, which plays a big role in OT wisdom teaching, the wise teachers regard themselves as the faithful handers on of an objectively true order which has been present and valid for a long time. [110] As knowledge of the nature of this maat is transmitted, it is established and a condition of harmony is thus set up in state and society. Since maat as the right way of life is unchangeable, it applies equally and immutably to all those in the social group which is being addressed. The task of man is to subject himself to it and to see in it the criterion of wise action. The ideal of this man is the man of silence or — to use the term maat — of true silence — the person who is always master of the situation and who exercises self-control because he acts according to maat, restraining himself both outwardly and inwardly and avoiding all excitement. [111] His opposite is the heated person who is subject to his passions and uncontrolled. [112] Results correspond to conduct. If success and inner truth form a unity, it should not be overlooked that in part the basis of rules of behaviour is purely utilitarian. Profit and success beckon the obedient man, loss and damage threaten the transgressor. [113] But in part there is simply added instead: "For this is God's will," or: "This is an abomination to God." The two foundations belong together in Egypt. thought, for he who offends against maat also transgresses the divine will and consequently suffers loss.

Egypt. Wisdom lit. [114] influenced Israel more strongly than the incipient development of the concept. [115] Since maat embraces what are two different spheres in modern thought, cosmic order and the order of human life, two different genres are found in the Wisdom lit.: the serial knowledge of the Onomastica, [116] which is probably influenced by its Sumerian counterpart, [117] and the "teachings" or "instructions" [118] for which a fixed form developed [119] and of which we have seven in full or almost in full, another five in

---

Tijdschrift, 21 (1932), 322-349; H. Frankfort, Ancient Egypt. Religion (1948), passim; H. Brunner, "Die Weisheitslit." in Hndbch. d. Orientalistik, I, 2 (1952), 93-96; R. Anthes, "Die Maat des Echnaton v. Amarna," Suppl. Journal of the American Oriental Society, 14 (1952); Gese, 11-21.

[109] Brunner, op. cit., 93: "As a goddess, Maat is found in the religious system of Heliopolis, where she is the daughter of the sun-god. She came down to men as the right order of all things in primal time. This order was disrupted by the wicked attacks of Seth and his companions, and restored by the victory of Horus. As the embodiment of Horus each new king at his coronation established this right order afresh, and a new state of Maat, i.e., of peace and righteousness, breaks forth."

[110] In keeping is the fact that in Is. 19:11 the advisers of Pharaoh explain their knowledge by the fact that they are students of the sages and kings of the past.

[111] Cf. also G. Lanczkowski, "Reden u. Schweigen im ägypt. Verständnis, vornehmlich des Mittleren Reiches," O. Firchow, "Ägyptologische Studien," Festschr. H. Grapow (1955), 186-196.

[112] Prv. 15:18; 22:24; 29:22 use חֵמָה for a "fiery" man, and Prv. 29:11 says that the fool lets his agitation increase while the wise man calms it.

[113] The full rejection of a utilitarian understanding by Gese, 7-11 goes too far.

[114] A. Erman, Die Lit. d. Ägypter (1923), 86-121, 238-302; R. Anthes, "Lebensregeln u. Lebensweisheit d. alten Ägypter," AO, 32, 2 (1933); AOT, 33-46; Pritchard, 405-410, 412-425, 431-434; F. W. v. Bissing, Altägypt. Lebensweisheit (1955).

[115] Esp. W. O. E. Oesterley, The Wisdom of Egypt and the OT (1927); P. Humbert, Recherches sur les sources égypt. de la litt. sapientiale d'Israël (1929); A. Causse, "Sagesse égypt. et sagesse juive," RevHPhR, 9 (1929), 149-169; S. Morenz, "Die ägypt. Lit. u. d. Umwelt," Hndbch. d. Orientalistik, I, 2 (1952), 194-206 (with bibl.); E. Würthwein, Die Weisheit Ägyptens u. d. AT (1960). K. Galling, Der Prediger, Hndbch. AT, I, 18 (1940), 47-90 pts. esp. to par. with the Egypt. pap. Insinger.

[116] A. H. Gardiner, Ancient Egypt. Onomastica (1947); H. Grapow, "Wörterbücher, Repertorien, Schülerhandschriften," Hndbch. d. Orientalistik, I, 2 (1952), 187-193.

[117] A. Alt, "Die Weisheit Salomos," Kleine Schriften d. Volkes Israel, II (1953), 95-97.

[118] The Egypt. title can denote "education," "instruction," esp. theol. teaching.

[119] Thus the usual title is: "Beginning of the instruction which X wrote for his son (pupil) Y."

fragments, and the titles alone of six or seven others. [120] We also find specific works which are not directly instructional but reflective or polemical, and which are traditionally reckoned in the Wisdom lit.

3. The Rest of the Ancient Orient. No Wisdom lit., or very little, has come down to us from the rest of the ancient Orient. [121] Israel, however, was acquainted with the wisdom not merely of the Babylonians (Jer. 50:35; 51:57; cf. Is. 44:25; 47:10) and the Egypt. (1 K. 4:30; cf. Gn. 41:8; Ex. 7:11), but also of other nations : the Canaanites (Ez. 28:3, 17: the Phoenicians gen.; Ez. 27:8: צמר probably Sumra, north of Tripoli, near Arvad ; Zech. 9:2: Sidon), [122] the Edomites (Jer. 49:7; Ob. 8; Job 2:11), [123] and the people of the East in the district of Safa in northern East-Jordan (1 K. 4:30). [124] Though the wise men mentioned in 1 K. 4:31 — Ethan the Ezrahite, and Heman, and Chalcol, and Darda, the sons of Maho, are presumably Edomites or Canaanites, there are difficulties. [125] In addition to acquaintance and influence the dependence of the Israelite Wisdom teaching on that of the ancient Orient extends into the traditional texts of the OT. In Prv. 22:17-23:11 we have extracts from the Egypt. teaching of Amen-em-ope. [126] Prv. 23:13 f. is borrowed from the teaching of Achiqar. We have the words of Agur the son of Jakeh "the Massaite" [127] in Prv. 30:1-14 and the words of Lemuel the king of Massa in 31:1-9 — both belonging to tribes outside Israel. [128]

4. Israel. In spite of the uniform intellectual background חָכְמָה has many layers of meaning. Both its connection with the ancient Orient and also its distinctiveness may be observed at many stages of historical development.

a. On the basis of experience there has always been a practical acquaintance with the laws of the world and the activities of life. At all cultural stages man has seen it as his task to master his environment and to control his life in it. There has thus been a need to seek order and regularity in the various phenomena and events, to integrate oneself into this and to make use of it. This finds expression esp. in popular proverbs which

---

[120] For details cf. Brunner, 96-110; also B. Gemser, "The Instructions of 'Onchsheshonqy and Biblical Wisdom Lit.," *VT Suppl.,* 7 (1960), 102-128.

[121] In spite of its Syr. and Aram. form the book of Achiqar may go back to an Assyr. original.

[122] Cf. W. F. Albright, "Some Canaanite-Phoenician Sources of Hebr. Wisdom," *VT Suppl.,* 3 (1955), 1-15; also C. L. Feinberg, *Ugaritic Lit. and the Book of Job,* Diss. Baltimore (1945); C. I. K. Story, "The Book of Proverbs and Northwest-Semitic Lit.," JBL, 64 (1945), 319-337; M. J. Dahood, "Canaanite-Phoenic. Influence in Qoh.," *Biblica,* 33 (1952), 30-52, 191-221.

[123] R. H. Pfeiffer, "Edomitic Wisdom," ZAW, 44 (1926), 13-25; also "Wisdom and Vision in the OT," ZAW, 52 (1934), 93-101; also *Introd. to the OT* (1941), 678-683, has gtly. overestimated the influence of Edomitic thought on Israel.

[124] Cf. O. Eissfeldt, "Das AT im Lichte d. safatenischen Inschr.," ZDMG, 104 (1954), 88-118.

[125] Edomites : E. Meyer, *Die Israeliten u. ihre Nachbarstämme* (1906), 350; Canaanites : W. F. Albright, *Archaeology and the Religion of Israel* (1953), 127 f.

[126] Bibl. in B. Gemser, *Sprüche Salomos,* Hndbch. AT, I, 16 (1937), 9; O. Eissfeldt, *Einl. in d. AT*² (1956), 583, n. 1. The opposite view that Amenemope is dependent on Prv. (esp. W. O. E. Oesterley, "The 'Teaching of Amen-em-ope' and the OT," ZAW, 45 [1927], 9-24 etc.; R. O. Kevin, "The Wisdom of Amen-em-apt and its Possible Dependence upon the Hebr. Book of Proverbs," *Journal of the Society of Oriental Research,* 14 [1930], 115-157; O. Drioton, "Sue la Sagesse d'Aménémopé," *Mélanges bibl. André Robert* [1957], 254-280; also "Le Livre des Proverbes et la Sagesse d'Aménémopé," *Sacra Pagina,* I, *Biblioth. Ephemeridum Theologicarum Lovaniensium,* 12 [1959], 229-241) is les próbable. Cf. P. Montet, *L'Égypte et la Bible* (1959), 111-128.

[127] Read הַמַּשָּׂאִי instead of "the oracle."

[128] Gemser, 81 and 83 ref. to par. Minaean-Sabaean names and other details and suggests an Arabian tribe. But W. F. Albright, "The Biblical Tribe of Maśśā and some Congeners," *Stud. Orientalistici G. Levi Della Vida,* I (1956), 1-14, thinks the ref. is to a semi-nomadic

embody knowledge and experience and transmit these to men so that they may draw conclusions from them regarding their conduct, 1 S. 24:14; Prv. 11:2a; 16:18; 18:12. The saying may be quite paradoxical, Prv. 11:24; 20:17; 25:15; 27:7. Thus insights are assembled and set alongside one another, even when they contradict one another, in an attempt to grasp the framework and boundaries of the orders, though without seeking to deduce general principles or to create a system. The gt. significance of such proverbs may be seen from the fact that a second line was often added later to bring out the application to human conduct, Prv. 25:23; 26:20; 27:20; Sir. 13:1.

b. In spite of what were probably earlier contacts with ancient oriental and Egypt. wisdom teaching, in the true sense it was during Solomon's reign that at court and in the developing establishment wisdom became native to Israel, and it was promoted at the school of wisdom which may be presumed to have existed at least in Jerusalem. [129] Hence it is not surprising that there is very common ref. to the wisdom of Solomon (→ 462, 10 ff.), [130] which was that of ruler, judge, and scholar alike. [131] Nor need one be surprised that Prv. at least was ascribed to him as the model of the wise man. [132] The ancient ref. to his wisdom in 1 K. 4:32 f. gives fuller details : [133] "He spake 3000 proverbs, and his songs were 1005. And he spake of trees, from the cedar that is in Lebanon even unto the hyssop that springeth out of the wall ; he spake also of beasts, and of fowl, and of creeping things, and of fishes." If one allows for possible hyperbole and also for the ascription to Solomon (as absolute ruler) of things which applied to his age and reign in general, in form and content one may perceive two types of wisdom teaching : 1. the serial knowledge which arises out of the concern of wisdom for the phenomena of the plant and animal kingdoms, the Jerusalem lists apparently comprising 1005 or 3000 key-words [134] and relating to more than natural data, so that this might be better called cultural rather than nature wisdom ; 2. the practical wisdom which may be inferred from the specified form of proverb (מָשָׁל → V, 747, 18 ff.; 855, 5 ff.) and song [135] and which imparts prudent, moral and in many cases religious rules of conduct. [136] In Israel too, then, one finds the two main branches of ancient oriental wisdom teaching as these are found in Mesopotamia and Egypt (→ 478, 7 ff.; 479, 20 ff.). Between them lies the riddle, which is related to wisdom in 1 K. 10:1 (cf. also Prv. 1:6), also the numbers saying and fable which probably developed out of the riddle. [137]

The situation in the 8th cent. is characterised on the one side by the fact that Isaiah

---

Aramaean tribe in the Syrian desert, the words of Agur and Lemuel being a slightly Hebraicised form of original Aram. texts of the 10th cent. or even earlier.

[129] Cf. K. Galling, Die Krise d. Aufklärung in Israel (1952), 5-10.

[130] 1 K. 2:6, 9; 3:12, 28; 5:9-11, 14, 21, 26; 10:4, 6-8, 23 f.; 11:41; 2 Ch. 1:10, 12; 2:11; 9:3, 5-7, 22 f.

[131] M. Noth, "Die Bewährung v. Salomos 'Göttlicher Weisheit,'" VT Suppl., 3 (1955), 225-237.

[132] Though his authorship of Qoh. seems to be a fiction of the writer's cf. 1:16 and other details. The songs of 1 K. 4:32 seem to be the basis for ascribing Cant. to Solomon.

[133] Cf. Alt, op. cit., though he wrongly relates the proverbs and songs to practical wisdom.

[134] Only occasionally is there further development of the proverbs and songs for special purposes, e.g., in the numbers sayings in Prv. and God's address in Job 38 ff.

[135] The wisdom song or poem can be called מָשָׁל in Ps. 49:4. Comparison of the poems in Job 18:5-21 and 20:4-29 is instructive since one may see that the second, as distinct from the first, is made up of proverbs or groups of proverbs. In 20:4-29 the description is not a connected composition. The sequence of strophes is capricious and the total impression is not uniform. Often independent sayings are adopted without being fused into the whole, v. 10, 16, 24 f.

[136] Cf. in this connection the distinctive salvation sayings (→ IV, 365, 5 ff.) of the Wisdom lit. which in distinction from the בָּרוּךְ of the cultic blessing are introduced by אַשְׁרֵי.

[137] Cf. on this whole subject esp. J. Hempel, Die althebräische Lit. u. ihr hell.-jüd. Nachleben (1930), 44-56; J. Schmidt, Stud. zur Stilistik d. at.lichen Spruchliteratur (1936); A. R. Johnson, "מָשָׁל," VT Suppl., 3 (1955), 162-169.

thinks he must adopt a critical attitude towards the wise men with their apparently clever but in fact ruinous plans and measures. [138] It is plain that he has in view the ruling class, so that as in Solomon's time wisdom is the culture and morality of the official world in the broader sense. In keeping on the other side is the fact that acc. to the authentic-sounding superscription in Prv. 25:1 the whole collection Prv. 25-29 was made by the men of Hezekiah, king of Judah (c. 700 B.C.). In all probability this period was one when wisdom teaching played an important role in public life.

Only toward the end of the 7th cent. does the base seem to have broadened. Jer. 50:35 and 51:57 still ref. simply to the ruling class (in Babylon), but minor leaders are meant in Dt. 1:13, 15 and all who administer justice in 16:19. Jer. 8:8 f. speaks of the wise along-side the priests and the prophets, their task being to give counsel. Again Jer. 10:9 has, after 1 K. 7:14, the earliest use of חכם for manual skill, which is not commonly referred to before the post-exilic period. The constant expansion of the terms is a sign that from the later 7th century and on into the post-exilic age wisdom teaching was ceasing to be the culture and morality of the establishment and becoming an affair of broader circles with no social or sociological restrictions. It was transmitted and taught by a class of wisdom teachers whose typical representatives the author of Job used as models for the friends of Job and one of whom speaks in the author of the discourses of Elihu, 32-37. The pupil of Qoh. also calls the latter a teacher of this kind in 12:9-11, while in 2:14, 16 חכם is used as a tt. for the teaching sage, who is no longer judged so favourably, cf. later Sir. 39:1 f., 8; 51:23.

Underlying this wisdom teaching, which lives on from Solomon's time to a later age, though not without change, is an ideal of the culture and training of the whole man. Although, like proverbial wisdom, this has as its goal a cleverness and ability which can master the world, it is no longer seeking merely to establish the orders and laws of the world or life, but on this basis it is deliberately trying to educate man. Its ideal, like that of Egypt. teaching, is the cool person of Prv. 17:27 as distinct from the fiery man (→ n. 112, 116), the patient man as distinct from the wrathful (Prv. 14:29), [139] the self-possessed man who does not yield to searing passion (Prv. 14:30) but controls his emotions and impulses.

c. In post-exilic Israel with its profound intellectual developments the concept of wis-dom was to a great degree thought out and used theologically among the so-called teachers of wisdom. Wisdom was regarded as a divine summons to man, as a means of revelation, as the great teacher of Israel and the Gentiles, and even as the divine prin-ciple set in the world at creation. All theological thinking thus became more or less wisdom thinking; at any rate, to a hitherto unknown degree, theology was unified and concentrated in the master concept of wisdom. [140] Apart from Prv. 1-9 and Job 28 there are hints of this in the inspired wisdom of Elihu, who by revelation and illumination knows that he possesses it (→ 493, 27 ff.), and also in the speech of God Himself in Job, in which the natural world, as God's creation, is at least initially brought into connection with the revelation made to man.

The incorporation of creation and revelation into this wisdom theology entails the inclusion of spheres which the cleverness and skill of cultural and practical wisdom had left on one side untouched. A comprehensive theological system is thus forged. [141] But in view of its unavoidable overemphases and inadequacies this system was almost bound to give rise to criticism, → 495, 20 ff. [142]

---

[138] Cf. J. Fichtner, "Jesaja unter d. Weisen," ThLZ, 74 (1949), 75-80.

[139] In gen. wrath is regarded as dangerous (→ V, 395, 14 ff.) because it is destructive and has evil effects, Prv. 6:34; 15:1; 16:14; 19:19; 27:4, because it questions God's righteous rule, Job 8:3, and because it undermines fear of God, Job 15:4. The angry man is thus compared to a fool, Prv. 14:17, 29.

[140] G. v. Rad, Theol. d. AT, I (1957), 439.

[141] v. Rad, 449: "It would thus seem that the later wisdom teachers must have had a very comprehensive and indeed encyclopaedic theology."

[142] The criticism was not, of course, because the system threatened to sever contact with

d. In this development a first evident mark of the wisdom of Israel is its nationalising and integration into the life of the people. On the one side this means that it gradually ceases to be a class affair and comes to correspond to the general human factor above all social and sociological boundaries. A sign of this is the adoption of many popular proverbs into collections like Prv. On the other side wisdom even in detail is adjusted to the situation in Palestine. Thus the onomasticon which underlies God's address in Job does not follow the Egypt. pattern but is shaped by the view of things and the details of geography, climate and zoology in Palestine, so that the examples selected correspond to the peculiarities of the Palestinian scene.

Another mark is the analogous religious concentration by which inter-religious wisdom is adjusted and subordinated to faith in Yahweh. This explains the great role played by ethical instruction and ethical or religious behaviour as compared with secular wisdom, and esp. the marked correspondence to the demands of Israel's belief in Yahweh. In particular one may note that not merely is the name of Yahweh often used rather than the general "God" or "Godhead," so that the God of creation and the cosmos is fully equated with Yahweh, but also that the "fear of Yahweh" is regarded as the beginning of wisdom.

The third mark is the comprehensive development of the concept with the help of חכם All the cleverness and skill needed for practical doing or non-doing, even in the most difficult and complicated matters, is expressed by the one stem, cf. also the opposite לֹא חָכָם "unwise" in Dt. 32:6.

III. The "Wisdom" (Sagacity and Knowledge) of Man.

1. Magic and Manticism.

In some instances the use of חכם corresponds to the Mesopotamian mode of expression. The Egypt. חכמים are similar to the magicians מְכַשְּׁפִים, Ex. 7:11. The חכמה of Babylon is its magical art, Is. 47:10, cf. v. 9, 12. The חכמים of Pharaoh are also similar to the priestly soothsayers חַרְטֻמִּים, Gn. 41:8, i.e., men who practise the mantic technique of knowing the future through interpretation of dreams. [143] Hence they are mentioned along with soothsayers [144] and those who seek oracles in Is. 44:25; חכם is a term for the one who pretends to know the background of events and also future events. Even animals — the ibis and cock [145] — have the ability to give advance notice of storms, Job 38:36. Similarly חכמים are later those who understand the times (Est. 1:13), i.e., astrologers who can foretell destiny on the basis of their knowledge of the stars, cf. the friends of Haman whom he asks concerning what will come to pass, Est. 6:13. [146] Thus the חכמים of Babylon are a college of soothsayers, magicians, and interpreters of dreams and signs, whom the king summons for the interpretation of his dreams, cf. Da. 2:27; 4:3.

2. Skill and Ability.

חכם is a man who has mastered something, even if it be only the doing of wickedness, Jer. 4:22. Thus magicians know and use their powerful formulae, Is. 3:3; Ps. 58:5, certain women know and use laments, Jer. 9:16, and priests know and use the Law of Yahweh,

---

Yahweh's work in history (v. Rad, 451) but because of the basic assertions and finally because of the very existence of a system, cf. Job and Qoh.

[143] Possibly Is. 19:12 is also referring to those who interpret the future.

[144] Read בָּרִים for the scribal error "empty chatter."

[145] Cf. on this G. Fohrer, *Das Buch Hiob, Komm. AT,* 16, ad loc.

[146] Neither v. is textually very certain. 1:13 may be referring to legal experts who know the laws (הַדָּתִים), while the ref. in 6:13 may be just to friends (cf. the versions).

which they are able to falsify acc. to their own will, Jer. 8:8 f. The word group is often used for technical or artistic skill. חכם is used of the accomplished artisan or artist (Ex. 36:8; 2 Ch. 2:12 f.) who has the masterly skill and artistic sense for any task (Ex. 31:3; 35:10, 31; 36:4; 1 Ch. 28:21), esp. in the sanctuary (Ex. 31:6; 36:1 f.) or in the making of idols (Is. 40:20). In this category one may include skilful metal-workers (1 Ch. 22:15; 2 Ch. 2:6), i.e., the smith (Ex. 35:35), worker in brass (1 K. 7:14) or goldsmith (Jer. 10:9), also the carpenter, or the weaver and dyer (Ex. 35:35) who can fashion materials of purple (2 Ch. 2:6) and make costly garments (Jer. 10:9) like those of Aaron (Ex. 28:3). חכמה is the skill of women at spinning (Ex. 35:25 f.), the business ability of the merchant (Ez. 28:3 f.), the knowledge of husbandmen concerning the work which has to be done (Is. 28:23-29), and the skill of sailors, which fails only in face of even mightier tempests, Ps. 107:27.

חכם often denotes the art of government. He who is master of this can become king even though he is poor (Qoh. 4:13), and he who is king needs it (2 Ch. 1:10). Part of it is the ability of the conqueror to subjugate peoples (Is. 10:13) or with diplomatic skill to propose a treaty (1 K. 5:7). Part of it is the ability to judge (1 K. 3:28), to separate the guilty from the community (Prv. 20:26), or to make a perspicacious resolve to build a residence (2 Ch. 2:11). The high officials of the king as חכמים are experienced in the art of government (Jer. 50:35; 51:57), whether they discharge specific tasks alone (Gn. 41:33) or impart political counsel (Is. 19:11). Finally every leader, even the most lowly, must have the appropriate ability, Dt. 1:13, 15.

3. Cleverness, Slyness and Cunning.

The ostrich, whose stupidity is proverbial, lacks wisdom (Job 39:15, 17), but other animals, even though small, act sensibly and with a view to self-preservation, so that "washed with all waters" they are exceedingly wise, Prv. 30:24-28. These examples show that חכם can be used for a non-moral cleverness and skill deployed in self-preservation. [147] Such cleverness or cunning is possessed by the woman who sends Joab to David artfully to secure favour for Absalom (2 S. 14:2) and also by the woman who treats with Joab and protects her district from destruction by offering the head of the rebel Sheba, 2 S. 20:16 ff. If this political wisdom serves to ward off a greater evil, the political cunning of the Egyptians hurts the unwanted Israelites by weakening their power through forced labour, Ex. 1:10; this is action in self-interest to the detriment of others. Cunning of this type is even more plain to see in the crafty counsel which Jonadab gave David's son Amnon to pacify his desire for his half-sister Tamar, 2 S. 13:3. David also suggests that Solomon should plot slyly and cunningly to bring about the destruction of Joab and Shimei; as a wise man he will know how to do this, 1 K. 2:6, 9. Similarly in Job 5:13 the cunning in a bad sense are par. to the crafty נִפְתָּלִים with their wily machinations and crooked ways, cf. Dt. 32:5; Ps. 18:26; Prv. 8:8. Again, acc. to the view of Elihu the friends of Job had been grieved to find in Job a חכמה for which they were no match and which only God could overcome, i.e., a cleverness in the bad sense which continually evaded their arguments, Job 32:13.

4. Practical Wisdom.

חכמה is closely related to prudence, knowledge and reflection (Prv. 8:12) and in this sense it is best understood as the practical wisdom which is on top of life in all relations and situations. It is the skill of the helmsman תַּחְבֻּלוֹת (Prv. 1:5; 11:14), a technique

---

[147] Qoh. 2:19 is not unequivocal. The question is whether the heir is clever enough to administer and enjoy the inheritance left to him or whether he has the necessary business ability.

whereby one can make one's way through the perils of life to the desired goal. It knows wealth and poverty, [148] joy and pain, the necessity of work and the effect of friendliness, gifts, and bribes, Prv. 10:15; 12:25; 13:7 f.; 14:10, 13, 20; 15:13, 30; 16:26; 17:8; 18:16; 21:14. It knows the right attitude for the enjoyment of life and for dealings with others. [149] This prudence, taught by the example of the ant (Prv. 6:6), is what truly distinguishes man as his crown, Prv. 14:24. [150] With it a man realises that God rules the world (Dt. 32:29), is aware of all that happens on the earth, and can distinguish good and evil — like the angel of God acc. to the flattering statement of 2 S. 14:17, 20 — or he is at home in all knowledge (Da.1:4) and has understanding in all learning (1:17). Thus the lady at the court of Sisera's mother who tries to explain why Sisera has not yet returned is experienced in the ways of the world (Ju. 5:29), in contrast to the child which in the crisis of birth-pangs cannot find the way out at the right time (Hos. 13:13), or to the Edomites who do not see what Yahweh has in store for them even though disaster already looms (Jer. 49:7), or to the average man who dies unawares without noting in advance or even being conscious that his end has suddenly come, Job 4:21.

5. Culture.

Though man's higher culture is connected with חכמה in 1 K. 4:29 ff. it played a greater role than would be suggested by the OT tradition, which is not very interested in this. At any rate חכם describes the culture of the educated person. It finds primary expression in the onomastica of serial learning which were often used later as the basis of groups of proverbs or poems. These might embrace organic and inorganic nature, cf. Ps. 104; 148; Job 38:4-39:30; Prv. 30:15-33. Or they might relate to the earth and its peoples, cf. Gn. 10; 15:19 f. Or they might list specific types of men, cf. Job 24:5-8, 14-16a; 30:2-8. They are based on genuine observation which considers phenomena in the world from the standpt. of their difference from the observer and their mutual teleological relation. The goal is the practical one of mastering this world. This may be seen most clearly in Job 28 in the — vain — search for the final secret of the world whose possession will mean, not just theoretical knowledge, but practical control. There is, of course, little place for cultural wisdom in the OT writings. One can deduce Israel's attainments in this sphere only from the comparatively few pieces which use the materials of this wisdom, cf. Gn. 1:1-2:4a; Ps. 8:7 f.; 147; Job 28; 36:27-37:13; 37:15-18; 40:15-24; 40:25-41:26; Cant. 2:11-13a; 3:9-10; Qoh. 1:5-7; Δα. 3:52-90. [151]

6. Rules of Conduct.

חכם is often used for "rules of conduct" or "directions" for right conduct. When Elihu seeks to teach Job חכמה in Job 33:33 his aim is to give him rules of conduct and to lead him to do what is right. Acc. to Prv. 2:2 man lends his ear to חכמה when he listens to words and commandments, i.e., rules of conduct. Thus the task of the teacher of wisdom is to teach knowledge, to arrange sayings critically, so that from them will come חכמה as direction for proper behaviour. It is the task of writing fine and true sayings, Qoh. 12:9-11. As he himself possesses knowledge and prudence (Prv. 14:24) and is ready to be instructed (12:15), he imparts his insights to others (15:2, 7). The fool can pass as wise only so long as he remains silent ; once he tries to teach rules of life he betrays himself. Thus the *si tacuisses, philosophus mansisses* finds its counterpart in the OT, Prv. 17:28; Job 13:5. חכם is one who gives counsel עֵצָה as the priest does תּוֹרָה and the

---

[148] For details cf. Fichtner, 15-17.
[149] *Ibid.*, 17-23 for details.
[150] Read עָרְמָה for "riches."
[151] Later Sir. 39:26 ff.; 4 Esr. 7:39-42. Cf. esp. Alt, *op. cit.*; G. v.Rad, "Hiob 28 u. d. alt-

prophet דָּבָר (Jer. 18:18). But he himself listens to this counsel (Prv. 12:15) to which the man who lacks wisdom is referred (Job 26:3). If prudent and instructive words come thus from the heart (Prv. 16:23), and if anyone can give instruction thus (16:21), in distinction from ordinary speech this is not like "deep water" in a cistern which is no use to the thirsty but like a springing well which is of help to all who will drink of it (18:4). Even a wrathful king may be softened, since the proper rules of conduct can be conveyed to him (16:14). In distinction from the fool and the mocker the חכם listens to these rules and pays heed to salutary correction (15:12, 31), calming rather than intensifying his irritation (29:11), not causing a disturbance but pacifying others (29:8), not merely having enough for himself but feeding others by his instruction, i.e., leading them on the way to life (cf. 6:23; 10:17; 15:24 (on the way → V, 52, 25 ff.) and nourishing them with vital strength (3:18; 10:11; 13:14; 16:22 cf. the originally mythical metaphors of the tree of life and the water of life).

7. Ethical Conduct.

Directions and rules lead to the right conduct taught thereby, and this is also called חכם in Prv. 8:33; 19:20; 28:26. This grants understanding, but its practice also presupposes understanding. It is vain to try to achieve right conduct when there is no understanding, 17:16. Thus one must behave properly even in seeking and attaining right conduct. It is a matter of reverence and dedication, so that the mocker cannot reach the goal, 14:6. It is a matter of the inner disposition (16:23) which is not to be surrendered when one has it, 23:23. Seriousness is measured hereby, Qoh. 7:4. Thus one must be on guard against all that which wise ethical conduct would avoid (2:9-11) and which will corrupt it if one yields or falls victim thereto, [152] e.g., wine and strong drink (20:1), tippling and carousing (23:20 f.), bad company (2:12-15) and strange women (2:16-19; 5:1; 7:4 → IV, 731, 15 ff.; VI, 586, 5 ff.), [153] wealth (Ez. 28:16 ff. → VI, 39, 25 ff.; 324, 29 ff.) and unlawful gain (Qoh. 7:7), violent and passionate speech with no substance or truth (Job 15:2), taking the property of others, esp. by shifting landmarks or using false weights and measures, [154] partiality in judgment, giving or receiving of bribes, and false witness. [155] Right conduct is marked by uprightness and honesty (Prv. 4:11; 23:19). It involves the righteous and gentle treatment of the poor, widows and orphans [156] and a right attitude to parents and personal enemies. [157] It is the same as judgment (Ps. 37:30) and hence can distinguish between right and wrong and practise the right, Dt. 16:19; 1 K. 3:12. It consists in a life controlled by following wise rules (Prv. 2:2) or the divine commandments (Dt. 4:6). The divine Law, the Torah, can be regarded as the true source of sound ethical conduct, Ps. 19:7; 119:98. [158]

ägypt. Weisheit," *VT Suppl.,* 3 (1955), 293-301; H. Richter, "Die Naturweisheit des AT im Buche Hiob," ZAW, 70 (1958), 1-20; also R. B. Y. Scott, "Solomon and the Beginnings of Wisdom in Israel," *VT Suppl.,* 3 (1955), 262-279.

[152] → VI, 234, 29 ff.

[153] There are many warnings against illicit love, adultery and fornication, Prv. 5; 6:24, 25-35; 7:5-23. Adultery violates the marriage of another and is a trespass. Later we find religious and ethical motifs, Prv. 5:21-23, cf. adultery as a "heinous deed" (זִמָּה) in Job 31:11. Cf. Fichtner, 27 f.

[154] For details cf. Fichtner, 25-27.

[155] *Ibid.,* 28-30.

[156] *Ibid.,* 30-32.

[157] *Ibid.,* 33 f.

[158] The Law in the strict sense is not mentioned in Prv., Job, or Qoh., *ibid.,* 81-90.

8. Piety.

If חכמה as ethical conduct is often linked with religious ideas, the term can in several instances denote man's piety. As the unwise man offends against God (Dt. 32:6), so the חכם has the inner religious insight that God rules the world (Dt. 32:39). He understands the words of the prophets and the ways and gracious acts of Yahweh (Hos. 14:10; Ps. 107:43). He also perceives his own sin (Ps. 51:6) and the way in which life is circumscribed by God (Ps. 90:12). This type of insight breeds humility (Prv. 11:2; 13:10). But it is also the basis of true faith and trust (Ps. 90:12). [159]

חכמה is often connected with the fear of Yahweh. [160] In detail the two are not the same. According to Prv. 9:10 the fear of Yahweh is the beginning (תְּחִלָּה) of חכמה; according to Prv. 1:7; Ps. 111:10 it is the starting-point (רֵאשִׁית); according to Prv. 15:33 it is the chastisement which leads to חכמה. In Job 28:28, however, חכמה consists in the fear of Yahweh and in Prv. 14:16 the חכם is one who fears God, so that the two concepts are equated. On the other hand, in Prv. 2:6 man understands the fear of Yahweh and acquires the knowledge of God through the חכמה which is given to him, so that the fear of Yahweh here is neither the presupposition of pious knowledge nor is it equated with this; theologically defined חכמה raises the claim that it leads to God. The expression "fear of Yahweh or God," which is a favourite one in wisdom teaching, always denotes piety. It does not mean terror but religious awe which is offered to Yahweh as God or to any god by his devotees. It does not find expression in the cultus, which has a very minor role here. [161] It is the practical religion of what is done or not done day by day, i.e., ethical conduct (→ 486, 14 ff.; VI, 470, 41 ff.). He who practises the fear of Yahweh as practical piety (חכמה) has valuable insight (Ps. 111:10), so that the most important knowledge of life is attained in the sphere of right action rather than in that of the cultus or of thought. Hence Job 37:24 can say that God does not regard the חכמי־לב those who are skilled in wisdom or wise in understanding, but those who bring Him, the Lofty One, reverence. Similarly Prv. 3:7 contrasts wisdom in one's own eyes with the fear of Yahweh.

To the fear of Yahweh corresponds the non-doing of evil, Job 1:1; Prv. 3:7; 14:16. This negative mode of expression does not derive from the model of apodictic law with its categorical prohibitions, nor is the חכם hostile to evil as in prophetic theology. Rather he holds aloof from evil and carefully avoids it. This corresponds to the way of life and piety which is controlled by prudence and the sense of what is profitable, seeking to avoid all offences and to steer clear of all dangers.

---

[159] Cf. A. Weiser, *Die Psalmen,* II, *AT Deutsch,* 15⁵ (1959) on 90:12.

[160] Cf. "fear of God," e.g., Job 1:1. The shorter יִרְאָה occurs only in the speeches of Eliphaz in Job 4:6; 15:4; 22:4, the mere verb ירא only in Prv. 14:16.

[161] On the cultus and prayer, which by contrast plays a gt. role in Wisdom, → II, 797, 20 ff.; III, 239, 10 ff.; Fichtner, 36-46. v. Rad is quite wrong when he argues (*op. cit.,* 431) that the one instructed in wisdom was a member of the cultic community, that his life stood under cultic statutes, and that wisdom was limited to the ordering of life outside the cultus. In Prv. (apart from the later 3:9) 15:8, 29; 20:25; 21:3, 27; 28:9; 30:12 are more or less critical of the cultus, the emphasis is not on cultic action but on the uprightness of the worshipper, and what finally counts is prayer rather than sacrifice, Fichtner, 41 f. For the

In this light one may understand the proverbs which according to an originally Egyptian notion describe God as the One who weighs and tests the heart (Prv. 16:2; 17:3; 21:2; 24:12), which are aware of the pleasure or displeasure He takes in man's good or evil conduct (11:1, 20; 15:8 f., 26; 16:5, 7; 17:15; 20:10, 23; 22:11), and which refer to the limits sets for man's potentialities by God's intervention (16:1, 9; 19:21; 20:24; 21:30 f.). In the last resort this, too, brings it about that man's trust is set in Yahweh, 22:19.

9. Academic Wisdom.

Later, at least, the various aspects (→ 485, 33 ff.) form a great unity. In the later post-exilic age we find a theologically well-rounded body of instruction → 482, 31 ff. The impulse towards this was there from the outset, as may be seen from the ancient notes on Solomon's wisdom (→ 481, 9 ff.) in wich חכמה is almost a tt. already, and is certainly a tt. for comprehensive skill and learning (in distinction from the later period), cf. 1 K. 4:29 ff.; 10:4-8, 23; 11:41. Elihu speaks of the "wise" in Job 34:2, 34 more in the sense of an attitude to life, with a ref. to teachers of wisdom as well as to all those who live acc. to the principles taught. Job in 12:2 pours scorn on the self-assured conceit of his friends, who think they alone are the ones who possess all the wisdom alongside which no other attitude is possible; he suggests contemptuously that wisdom will perish with them, its only representatives. [162] More plainly Job 8:8 says that the content of wisdom is that "sought out" (חֵקֶר) by the fathers and in 11:4 the content of the preceding speech of Job is called "teaching" (לֶקַח). Qoh. esp. finds himself confronted by a closed body of teaching so that in him חכמה and חכם may be transl. academic wisdom and the academic teacher of wisdom (or wise man), e.g., 2:12 f., 14, 16, 21; 8:17. He, too, has learned it, has sought to establish all things by it, and is un-ceasingly concerned to attain the desired goal with its help, namely, the mastering and assuring of life by prudence, 1:13, 16. In fact wisdom has some advantages over folly. It can teach man not to find happiness in mere indulgence (2:3) and also to avoid ob-stacles (2:14). In the main, however, Qoh. is critical of wisdom (→ 495, 25 ff.); he is plainly referring to this wisdom of the schools.

10. Eschatological Blessing and Apocalyptic Endowment.

Twice חכמה is called an eschatological blessing. In Is. 33:6 חכמה and דַּעַת are Zion's riches of salvation and the fear of Yahweh is its treasure. In addition v. 5 refers to the right and righteousness with which Yahweh fills the city. Thus חכמה is used in the sense of the practical piety (→ 487, 1 ff.) which will be the wealth of Jerusalem in the age of eschatological salvation. According to Is. 11:2 the Spirit of Yahweh will fall on the Messianic ruler of the last time as a lasting possession; it is the spirit of חכמה, insight, counsel, knowledge, and the fear of Yahweh, but also of strength. The reference, then, is to the combination of חכמה in various forms with strength, as in Yahweh Himself according to Job 9:4; 12:13. This special and enduring endowment with the Spirit of Yahweh means that the mediated gifts both of wisdom in its various aspects and also of strength surpass the normal human measure, so that the Messianic ruler of the last days can be God's vice-gerent and execute the divine will, with which he knows he is at one. The con-ditions which result in the eschatological reign are depicted in the following verses.

---

rest the natural incorporation of the wise man into the cultic community and its rules is an unproved presupposition.

[162] Cf. the debate between Aeschylus and Euripides in Aristoph. Ra., 868 f.

In Daniel we have the beginning of the fusion of later wisdom theology with apocalyptic. Daniel's חכמה‎ differs from that which is proper to man. It does not merely surpass it (2:30); as a divinely given wisdom it is fundamentally different (5:11, 14). The secrets of the future are known to him by means of it.

IV. The "Wisdom" (Sagacity and Knowledge) of God.

1. God Possesses Wisdom.

חכם‎ is ascribed to God more rarely than to man. 2 S. 14:20 says the angel of God is wise, and Job 15:8 speaks of the wisdom of His entourage. It is comparatively late, however, that God Himself is said to have wisdom. Apparently it took time before the Mesopotamian and Egypt. idea of gods of wisdom in various senses [163] and the Canaanite concept of the wisdom of El [164] could be integrated into the belief in Yahweh. Initially the presupposition that חכמה‎ has its origin in God and is His possession tacitly underlies the description of it as God's gift to man, cf. already the story of Solomon and the Joseph cycle (→ 493, 8 ff.). Is. is more explicit. In debate with the supposedley clever politicians of his age he says in 31:1 f. that God, too, is חכם‎, and from the example of the farmer he shows that according to a given situation God can impart new and different counsel (עֵצָה) to His prophet, 28:23-29. Yet only later is it explicitly stated that חכמה‎ is a possession and faculty of Yahweh, not with ref. to history, [165] but esp. with ref. to God as the Creator who has made all things wisely, i.e., with technical and artistic mastery, Is. 40:13 f., 28; Jer. 10:12; 51:15; Ps. 104:24; Job 26:12; Prv. 3:19 f., who understands how to make the clouds float in the sky even though they are laden with water, Job 37:16; cf. 36:29, and who counts them with a skilful hand so that they may come in due measure and do not bring too much or too little rain, 38:37. God's חכמה‎ is also His mysterious action corresponding to man's ethical conduct according to the principle of retributive justice, 11:6. It is the codification of the principles of righteous human conduct in the law-code of Ezra (Ezr. 7:25) and the declaration of the mysteries of the future (Da. 2:20 f.; 5:11, 14). Since He has no rival with similar skill and ability among the peoples (Jer. 10:7), and since esp. He has the might and power to actualise what He has wisely thought out and skilfully planned (cf. the hymn of praise in Job 12:13 [166] and the bitterly ironical complaint of Job in 9:4), [167] no human understanding can stand against Him, Prv. 21:30. He confounds all the human cleverness which withstands His will, Is. 19:11-15; 29:14; 31:2 f.

2. God Attains and Creates Wisdom.

a. The poet of Job 28 uses חכמה‎ for the principle which holds sway in all the world and in all life. Knowledge of this gives insight into all things and mastery over them. In opposition to the customary admonition to get חכמה‎ (e.g., Prv. 4:5) the idea that man can control it is thus contested. [168] In spite of his Faustian urge

---

[163] For details Fichtner, 117 f.

[164] Gordon Manual Text, 51, IV 41; 51, V 65; 'nt V 38; cf. 126, IV 3.

[165] Cf. also J. Fichtner, "Zum Problem Glaube u. Gesch. in d. isr.-jüd. Weisheitslit.," ThLZ, 76 (1951), 145-150.

[166] Cf. Prv. 8:14 on personified חכמה‎.

[167] Job is not saying that respect is man's proper attitude in face of the absolute right of God (A. Weiser, Das Buch Hiob, AT Deutsch, 13² [1956], ad. loc.) but in justification of His complaint against God he is explaining why man can never be in the right.

[168] It makes no difference whether the song is a later addition put on the lips of Job in a rearrangement of the third round of speeches. Its negative judgment provides a reason

to know what it is that holds the world together at its core, [169] only God has found the way to wisdom, has attained it, sought it out, and used it in the creation of the world. Possession of חכמה, then, is not a theoretical knowledge of the world. It is practical control over it, vv. 25-27. Though חכמה is subject to God, being incorporated into His creative work and equated with the secrets of the divine creation, its original autonomy may still be glimpsed in the poem. It was a heavenly, pre-existent and independent entity side by side with God at a place to which God alone had access. It is not here a personified power of God or an independently evolved entity in the form of a hypostasis. [170] It is a material reality which is sought like other things (mineral wealth) and which has its own location like these. Now there is an element of speculation in this view, but it is also based on mythical notions. [171] In particular a Gnostic myth lies behind it ; this may be seen quite plainly both in this and later texts [172] → 507, 20 ff. The reference to this in Job 28 says that man's search for חכמה, for the secret of the world, has always been a vain one, and that it is subject to God's full disposal.

Other roots have been considered for the idea. Egypt and Babylon both spoke of an eternal divine wisdom which is proper to the gods or embodied by them or by hypostases or personifications. [173] An Iranian-Chaldaean origin has also been suggested, [174] cf. esp. personified piety (ārmaiti in the Avesta) [175] or personified religion and faith (daēnā in the Avesta), [176] or the Semitic goddess of love and heaven (Ishtar, Astarte), [177] or gen. an originally feminine deity which was co-ordinated with and subordinated to God and seen as an essential attribute. [178] There can certainly be no question of Gk. influence. [179]

b. As one of several elements the same myth stands behind the term חכמה in Prv. 1-9, the latest part of the book, in which several older sayings are employed in a new theological setting. [180] The main themes in this collection are an urgent and heart-felt commendation of both wisdom and the fear of God (1:7-9, 20-23;

---

for the addition in this case. The pt. of the poem is to explode once and for all the theology of the friends of Job and to repudiate their attempts to solve the riddle of human suffering. This does, of course, fit in with the supposed speaker (Job), who had first tried to solve his problem on the same premisses as those of his friends. The recommending of the fear of God in v. 28 seems to be a later addition and may be left out of account.

[169] O. Eissfeldt, "Religionshistorie u. Religionspolemik im AT," VT Suppl., 3 (1955), 94.

[170] Cf. esp. Schencke; J. Goettsberger, Die göttliche Weisheit als Persönlichkeit im AT (1919); P. Heinisch, Personifikationen u. Hypostasen im AT u. im Alten Orient (1921); also Die göttliche Weisheit d. AT in religionsgeschichtlicher Beleuchtung (1923); P. van Imschoot, "La Sagesse dans l'AT est-elle une hypostase?" Collationes Gandavenses, 21 (1934), 3-10, 85-94; Ringgren; R. Marcus, "On Biblical Hypostases of Wisdom," HUCA, 23, 1 (1950/51), 157-171.

[171] Baumgartner, 28, with ref. to Achiqar, line 95 (AOT, 458).

[172] Bultmann Hintergrund, 3-26.

[173] Baumgartner, 28.

[174] Reitzenstein Buch des Herrn d. Grösse, 46-58.

[175] Though cf. Bousset-Gressm., 520.

[176] Loc. cit.

[177] Boström, 12-14; W. F. Albright, From the Stone Age to Christianity (1949), 283 f. suggests an older Canaanite goddess of wisdom like the Mesopotamian Siduri Sabitu. But against this one must recall the different meaning of wisdom in Mesopotamia, → 477, 26 ff.

[178] G. Hölscher, Das Buch Hiob, Hndbch. AT, I, 17² (1952), 68.

[179] R. Kittel, Gesch. d. Volkes Israel, III, 2 (1929), 731 f.; E. Sellin, Gesch. d. isr.-jüd. Volkes, II (1932), 181.

[180] The claim of Albright, op. cit. (→ n. 177), 281 f., that Prv. 8-9 is Canaanite in origin is exaggerated. Linguistic echoes are due to the use of mythical ideas and creation statements.

2; 3:1-26; 4; 8; 9) and a warning against the strange woman (5; 6:20-35; 7). The two themes are often interwoven (2:16-19; 7:1-5; 9). חכמה, which in Job 28 is inaccessible to man, now speaks to him as teacher and revealer. This is made possible by the ideas of the Gnostic myth according to which חכמה seeks a dwelling among men, though in the myth it does not find this and returns to heaven; in Sir. 24:8 ff. it finds it in Israel and Jerusalem and in Sir. 24:23 ff. it can be equated with the Torah. In any case what it says to man is quite intelligible.

In Prv. 8:22-31, as in Job 28, חכמה is pre-existent and before all the works of creation. But it has no primal existence alongside God, who has to discover it. It was created first by Him and was then present at the further and true creation, not as a helper, but as a child playing in its father's workshop. [181] As God's favourite child (אָמוֹן v. 30) it played with creation and with man. [182] In distinction from Job 28 it is here a personal entity, created by God and having no part in creation. [183] God does not attain it; He creates it. The difference is due to the influence of a second myth, that of the primal man who was created before all worlds and who thus has a special wisdom of experience. By means of this myth, which is used in another way in Ez. 28:1-10, 11-19 and Job 15:7-8 as well (→ 493, 19 ff.), חכמה is personified. The point of the discussion is that חכמה shows its patent of nobility: [184] the older the nobility the higher it is in rank, and similarly, the older wisdom is, the more normative it is (cf. the argument in Job 15:7 f.). Thus the weight and authority of the address to man are enhanced.

חכמה is also personified in Prv. 1-9. She is a preacher in 1:20, a bride and wife in 4:6-9, a life-companion in 6:22; 7:4, a hostess in 9:1. As other personal metaphors show, these personifications are also figurative, cf. Is. 59:14; Ps. 85:10 f.; Prv. 9:13-18. Thus wisdom is no longer the neutral teaching passed on to man by the words of a sage; it summons man as a person, and it raises its voice like a prophet in the centres of public life in villages (1:20 f.) and at cross-roads (8:2). This pathos of prophetic proclamation is the third element in the current concept of wisdom (→ 493, 27 ff. on Elihu). Wisdom speaks with special authority. It invites and threatens. Like a prophet it sets man before the decision of life and death. [185] For it offers life, true, full and happy life in the OT sense, the life which is real salvation, 3:18, 22; 4:13, 22 f.; 8:35; → II, 845, 33 ff.; 851, 17 ff. In this respect it is the revelation of God's will to man. Hence man must track it down (2:4), find it (3:13), woo it (4:7), accept the invitation which it offers to the feast as beloved (4:6 ff.), sister, or bride (7:4). For in so doing man accepts God's will and does it, so that God is well-pleased with him (8:35). That this applies not merely to Israel but to man generally may best be seen from 8:1-21. In its metaphors and modes of expression all this is again influenced by the mythical concept of חכמה seeking a dwelling and union with man. [186] The fact that this con-

---

[181] Gemser, op. cit., 39.

[182] The later Jewish transl. of אָמוֹן in v. 30 as "master builder" rests on later ideas → n. 291. In the LXX God is made the subj. of v. 31.

[183] The apparently divergent statement in Prv. 3:19 f. is due to the fact that an older proverb is present here which uses חכמה in the technical-artistic sense.

[184] G. Wildeboer, Die Sprüche, Kurzer Hand-Comm. AT, 15 (1897), 27.

[185] On good and evil → III, 478, 22 ff.

[186] In this light it is clear that חכמה is not the rival of Ἀφροδίτη παρακύπτουσα who through strange women entices the Israelites to take part in aphrodisiac cults (as suggested by Boström, 127-147).

cept is adopted soberly and in a way which is not detrimental to faith in Yahweh is based on the fundamental theological understanding, which is marked by incorporation of the prophetic element. [187]

V. The Origin and Source of Sagacity and Knowledge.

1. The Tradition of the Fathers.

In distinction from the teaching tradition of Egypt, tradition is only one source of sagacity and knowledge in the OT. The Egypt. situation is excellently characterised in Is. 19:11 when Pharaoh's advisers say that they are students of the sages and kings of former times to whom many of the teachings may be traced back ; they draw exclusively on the tradition of the fathers. The friends of Job do this too, but for them tradition is not the only source of their counsel. This is in keeping with all instruction in Israel, which lays special emphasis on introduction to the traditions of the fathers. [188] Bildad appeals to the teaching of former generations because these are superior to the experience of an individual or a single generation, Job 8:8-10. Eliphaz appeals to the teaching tradition which lives on into his own generation and is confirmed by it, and which is pure and unperverted because of the absence of aliens from other tribes or countries at the time of its origin, 15:19 f.

2. Personal Experience.

A second source of knowledgeability is the experience a man gathers in the course of life. This is why old men are usually regarded as the repositories of wise experience with an adequate insight into things, Job 12:12; 15:10; 32:7; cf. Ez. 7:26. Along these lines Eliphaz appeals to what he has perceived and discovered, 8:4; 5:3, 27; 15:17, so that he can pass it on in the instruction of others. Job adduces his own very different experience, 21:6. Qoh. in particular either refers to his own perceptions and experiences or depicts them, e.g., 1:13a, 16-17a; 2:1, 3a, 4-8, 12a, 24; 3:10 f., 16; 4:1, 4a, 7. In form-critical analysis this element is one of the factors in many of the statements in Qoh., which are constructed acc. to the schema of gathering experience ⁓ result (a proverb as basis or confirmation). [189]

3. Means and Methods.

The two means to mediate sagacity and knowledge to others, or learn them oneself, on the basis of tradition and experience are instruction and correction (→ II, 473, 25 ff.; V, 604, 30 ff.), cf. Prv. 19:20; 21:11. The ref. may be to simple teaching (Prv. 4:11; 9:9; 13:14; Ps. 105:22) as one has converse with the wise (13:20). It may be loving (31:26), but it may also take the form of correction (9:8), censure (Qoh. 7:5), or the rod (Prv. 29:15). It takes place by means of מָשָׁל (Prv. 1:1, 6) and דָּבָר (1:6; 22:17) and other forms of address, e.g., 1:6. Since the wise man can understand hard sentences and give their interpretation (פֵּשֶׁר) for the learner (Qoh. 8:1) his words have the same function as the ploughman's goad and smite like nails which are driven in (12:11). If

---

[187] On the many contacts with Is. (esp. 40-66), Jer. and Dt. cf. for details A. Robert, "Les attaches littéraires bibl. de Prv. I-IX," *Rev. Bibl.*, 43 (1934), 42-68, 172-204, 374-384; also 44 (1935), 344-365, 502-525.

[188] Cf. Ex. 13:8 ff.; Dt. 4:9; 6:7, 20 ff.; 11:19 ff.; Jos. 4:6 f., 21; Ps. 78:5 ff.; cf. L. Dürr, *Das Erziehungswesen im AT u. im Alten Orient* (1932), 107 f.

[189] Qoh. 1:12-15; 1:16-18; 2:1-11, 12b (threefold sequence); 2:12a, 13-17 (twofold sequence but altered); 3:16 f.; 4:1-3; 4:4-6; 4:7 f.; with double experience 2:24-26; 3:10-15 (in 3:1-15).

this instruction is not enough there is chastisement (Prv. 8:33; 13:1) and the rod (29:15). Knowledge develops with great labour and many blows ; this was perhaps the original pt. of the proverb which is used in a different sense in Qoh. 1:18.

4. The Gift of God.

a. If a man usually acquires sagacity and knowledge from tradition and experience by the way of learning and chastisement, there is also the possibility of extraordinary endowment with the gift of חכמה; this is a divine endowment, even though it takes place only in specific instances. God endowed special men in this way, e.g., Joseph in Gn. 41:16, 38 f., Joshua by the laying on of the hands of Moses in Dt. 34:9, Solomon in 1 K. 3:12, 28; 5:26; 10:24; 2 Ch. 1:12, and Daniel in Da. 1:4, 17, 20; 5:11, 14. One may refer similarly to individual prophetic inspiration in Jer. 9:11 and the experience of nocturnal revelation by Eliphaz in Job 4:12-21, and cf. too artistic ability in Ex. 28:3; 31:3, 6; 35:31; 36:1 f. and skill in husbandry in Is. 28:26. The oldest instances are in the story of Solomon, the Joseph cycle, and Is. 28:26, the others being later, cf. also Ps. 60:7; 94:10; 119:98; Prv. 28:5; Qoh. 2:26. In Job, too, God gives wisdom (11:6; 38:36) or keeps far from it (17:4). The gen. view is espoused here that God gives a measure of חכמה to man but that this cannot compare with His own, so that many things appear wonderful and mysterious to man, 42:3.

b. The situation is different when in accordance with the myth of the primal man (cf. Ez. 28:1-10, 11-19) someone might claim that he was born before the rest of creation and that as the oldest he was thus the wisest man, or that like the primal man he was admitted to the heavenly counsel and thus shared something of the divine חכמה, Job 15:7 f. cf. Jer. 23:18, 22. Only thus can he be superior to the teachings of tradition or the experience of the ancients. These conditions naturally do not apply to Job, so that Eliphaz is using the originally mythical ideas as fig. comparisons to beat down what seems to him to be the presumptuous presentation of Job.

c. In later wisdom teaching we find another view which first comes to the surface in the speeches of Elihu in Job 32-37. The knowledge and teaching which Elihu possesses and wants to impart is described by him as דֵּעַ ("knowledge") in 32:6, 10, 17; 36:3 (fem. plur. דֵּעוֹת 36:4); materially, however, this is the same as חכמה. The rare word denotes either God's own knowledge (37:16; 1 S. 2:3; Ps. 73:11) or that imparted by Him (Is. 28:9; Jer. 3:15) and has been deliberately selected for Elihu's speeches in order to show from the very outset that Elihu is conscious of having God's own knowledge and the knowledge imparted by Him. [190] This is why he says that he has it "from afar," i.e., in view of the par. "creator," from God, 36:3. It has been mediated to him by God's "spirit" and "breath" so that he has not had to garner the experiences of a long life or to learn the tradition of the fathers ; in spite of his youth he is wise because by inspiration he has received divine wisdom as an enduring possession, 32:7-10. The view of Elihu, then, is that חכמה is first God's possession. He then claims that it neither remains hid from man (Job 28) nor is mediated only in specific cases but that it has been granted to him gen. and in toto. What he has received is his "portion" (32:17) of the totality of divine wisdom and this is enough to give a full answer to Job and his friends. This knowledge is sinless (33:3, probably based on Zeph. 3:9) and perfect or — as the plur. form is designed to show — comprehensive and unsurpassable, 36:4. Acc. to the serious and by no means ironical view of the author of the speeches, what Elihu teaches is the final conclusion of divine wisdom. Elihu thus claims for himself the same dignity of supernatural illumination and direct inspiration as the prophet. He stands alongside the

---

[190] In keeping is the fact that Elihu uses the more common דַּעַת only when he says that Job or the sinner does not have wisdom or knowledge, 34:35; 35:16; 36:12.

prophet or in his place, and even surpasses him inasmuch as the inspiratory Spirit fills him wholly and permanently. [191]

Along these lines the figuratively personified חכמה of Prv. 1-9 is the mediator of revelation in the sense that in her proclamation she is like a prophet and can claim supreme authority, revealing God's will to man, offering man life, and regarding acceptance as that of the divine will → 491, 31 ff. Eschatological Messianic חכמה and apocalyptic חכמה (→ 488, 30 ff.) are also viewed as a permanently granted possession.

VI. Value, Result and Criticism of Sagacity and Knowledge.

I. Value and Result.

Instruction in sagacity and knowledge is as profitable to the pupil as a springing well compared to a cistern with deep standing water, Prv. 18:4. The teacher who instructs in rules of life is as valuable to his listeners as a ring and jewel of gold, 25:12. Wisdom is a costly treasure (21:20); indeed, it is more precious than treasure (3:15; 8:11; cf. Job 28:15-18). For חכמה protects and delivers a man (Prv. 2:8, 20) so that he avoids obstacles (Qoh. 2:14, 16), steers clear of trouble (Prv. 14:3), masters every difficulty (Qoh. 8:5), escapes the snares of death (Prv. 13:14) and evades misfortune (28:26). Positively wise conduct profits a man (Prv. 9:12), so that he may expect success (Qoh. 9:11a) and great prosperity (Job 22:25; cf. 5:12; 6:13; 11:6) and reach the goal of his way (Prv. 14:8). He achieves honour (Prv. 3:35) and is blessed (12:18), for חכמה builds up (14:1) and achieves lasting results (24:3). Not mere knowledge, but practically applied sagacity and understanding are strength, 21:22; Qoh. 7:19; 9:15. Sometimes we read of their value for others. In particular the father or teacher rejoices in the one who has become wise (Prv. 10:1; 15:20; 23:15, 24) and he can give an answer to those who scorn him as a poor teacher, Prv. 27:11.

One can hardly overlook the fact that this view of life has a certain utilitarian or eudaemonistic aspect. It is not for nothing that in Job the value of piety is often weighed by wise counsellors (22:2 f.; 35:6-8) and Job is attacked for contesting this (34:9; 35:3) or he himself suggests that only sinners dispute it, 21:15. [192] Conduct not only has its origin in a basic attitude; it also seeks a specific end and result. This is true not least in the חכם as sagacity and knowledge for the purpose of a specific manner of life. The two are inseparably related; prudence and understanding are always directed to a particular result. Yet as compared with pure utilitarianism a distinction is to be made. There is no essential difference or antithesis between the inner worth of a deed in act or conduct as such and its outer result. [193] The two are one and the same when the חכם seeks to know the orders in the world and in life so that he may subjugate the world and master life. Thus Job's friends constantly exhort him to submit to the orders and to integrate himself into them; this is the proper inner attitude which leads to right conduct and guarantees outer success, so that fresh salvation beckons him on. It is true, of course, that God's address says of this cosmic order (עֵצָה) that as a divine order it is unfathomable to man. Hence Qoh. 3:1-15 draws the conclusion that there can be no assurance as to the success of human action.

---

[191] He thus claims he should be heard like a prophet (32:10) and believes that he has better arguments to present than Job's friends in the difficult situation (32:14). He must speak unconditionally as a vessel of the divine Spirit (32:18-20) since the Spirit compels him to speak like a prophet, cf. Jer. 20:9.

[192] Cf. the ethical final clauses → III, 330, 13 ff.

[193] So rightly Gese, 7-41.

The order of the world and of life is never abandoned by God ; it is established and upheld by Him. He is thus pleased with prudent, intelligent or pious integration into it and displeased with attacks upon it. Acc. to His retributive justice He thus grants to the חכם prosperity and success as blessing and salvation, but evil to the fool and evil-doer. Thus the two-sided belief in retribution is a basic pillar of practical wisdom → IV, 711, 7 ff. Acc. to this conviction a good act will always issue in good and a bad act in evil. Wisdom teaching stands or falls with the principle that man's conduct and state correspond. This correspondence is not, of course, mechanical, but goes back to God, who necessarily acts thus in accordance with His righteousness.[194] If the facts seem to be against this, the suffering of the innocent can be explained by saying that he endures the fate of man who is imperfect and inadequate by nature (Job 4:17-21) or that God uses suffering to educate him (5:17; 33:13-24). The prosperity of the wicked is said to be one of appearance only, since in reality he is plagued by many torments, Job 15:20-22. In the case of both there is a glance beyond individual life to retribution visited on children, Ps. 37:25; Job 5:4 f.; 18:19; 20:10; 27:14; Prv. 13:22; 20:7. Finally, this view leads to a developed doctrine of retribution in which every sin bears a specific penalty and a line is drawn from the effect (good fortune or ill) to the cause (piety or sinfulness). This shows plainly the value and result of prudent and instructed conduct in the ethical or religious sense.

2. Criticism.

If earlier criticism of חכמה is directed against pagan soothsaying or the art of interpretation (Gn. 41:8; Is. 44:25), then against the ostensibly clever politicians of Jerusalem (Is. 5:21; 29:14; 31:1-3), at a later date it is focused on the comprehensive and established system of teaching.

Qoh. grants that academic wisdom has a relative value (2:3, 14, 16; 4:13; 10:12), but in the last resort he does not think it brings any real advantage (2:15; 9:11a), since it is no better than equally ineffectual folly (1:16 f.; 6:8). Thus it is useless from the standpt. of possessions, which one must leave behind, so that all one gets from them is trouble, 2:21. It is also valueless in face of death, which smites all men impartially, 2:15 f. (cf. Ps. 49:10), and which, since one can neither anticipate it nor avoid it, forms an impenetrable frontier for the wisdom of the schools. Another frontier is woman (not just the strange woman of Prv.), who ensnares and seduces the wise man, so that he forgets his life-principles and his concern for the shaping of life becomes illusory, if God so wills, 7:26. The fate of the wise does not depend, as their teaching maintains, on their just and pious conduct, but is prepared already in God's hand in a way which cannot be fathomed or known, 8:17; 9:1. The only option, then, is to live actively and enjoy to the full the share of life granted, 9:7-10.[195]

If in spite of this plea for an active enjoyment of life Qoh. does not try to shape life constructively but recommends an acceptance of the portion of life given, and above

---

[194] The roots lie in the original idea that every act creates a sphere which surrounds man for good or ill, so that by its very character a good act has good results, while a bad one is destructive. At most only the relics of this view are to be found in Yahweh religion, as against J. Pedersen, *Israel,* I-II (1926), 336-377; K. H. Fahlgren, *Sedaqa nahestehende u. entgegengesetzte Begriffe im AT* (1932), 4; K. Koch, "Gibt es ein Vergeltungsdogma im AT?" ZThK, 52 (1955), 1-42. The almost magical and mechanical equation of good act and success, bad act and disaster, is here completely subordinate to the personal sway of Yahweh and His retributive righteousness. Cf. the discussion in Gese, 42-50; H. Graf Reventlow, "Sein Blut komme über sein Haupt," VT, 10 (1960), 311-327.

[195] This criticism is itself criticised in Qoh. 12:12-14, where the author sees a danger for the student in the gt. no. of books with their many different opinions. That Qoh. is in view may be seen from the fact that his divergent view is comprehensively interpreted and corrected. Qoh. is now championing an ethics grounded in God's commandment and the concept of final judgement on the hidden deeds of men.

all a marked restraint, the author of Job wrestles with the doctrine of retribution in an attempt to achieve a new structure of life which will lead to true human existence beyond mere living. If this is not to be found in the traditional teaching of Job's friends, which is proved false by Job [196] and rejected as sinful by God (42:7 f.), [197] neither is it to be found in the Promethean-Titanic pretension of Job, who at first tries to snatch his good fortune from God, protesting his blamelessness and opposing God in an attempt to triumph over Him, 31:35-37. Real understanding is gained only from personal encounter with God. Right conduct consists in humble and devoted silence on the basis of rest in God. This is rooted in the experience that the destiny of man rests on the puzzling and inscrutable but purposeful acts of God. It is rooted in the assurance of fellowship with God, which outweighs all else, 40:4 f.; 42:2-3, 5-6. Is. 51:7 f. and Ps. 73:25-28 are to the same effect. Hence man must not glory in his own wisdom but only in the knowledge of Yahweh, i.e., in fellowship with the God who rules the world and men, and in the life which is ordained by Him, Jer. 9:22 f.

Fohrer

C. Judaism.

1. The Septuagint. [198]

In the LXX חָכְמָה is with striking regularity transl. by σοφία and חָכָם by σοφός. [199] The only recurrent synonyms are → φρόνησις / φρόνιμος / φρονεῖν, → σύνεσις / συνετός and ἐπιστήμη. The Hellenising in the transl. is perhaps most evident in the rendering of the verb חָכַם, usually paraphrased as σοφὸς εἶναι or σοφὸς γίγνεσθαι. [200]

---

[196] For the doctrine in the speeches of Job's friends, and his rejection of it, cf. E. Würthwein, *Gott u. Mensch in Dialog u. Gottesreden des Buches Hiob*, Tübingen (1938).

[197] The friends spoke what was not true. This is a mild expression like many others in the prose narrative (1:5, 11, 22; 2:5, 9), but to speak of God in a way which is not seemly is here the worst sin and the most to be feared (1:5, 22; 2:10). On the sin of the tongue → I, 721, 5 ff.

[198] On this cf. G. Bertram, "Die religiöse Umdeutung altorient. Lebensweisheit in d. griech. Übers. d. AT," ZAW, 54 (1936), 133-167; also "Der Begriff d. Erziehung in d. griech. Bibel," *Imago Dei, Festschr. G. Krüger* (1932), 33-51; also "Praeparatio evangelica in d. LXX," VT, 7 (1957), 225-249, esp. 228-230.

[199] σοφία is used 127 times for חָכְמָה (also once for חכם in Prv. 17:28) and only 11 times all told for other words, twice for בִּינָה, 3 times for תְּבוּנָה, twice for דַּעַת, once each for חָכְמָה. מְחָקָק, שֵׂכֶל, מַחֲשֶׁבֶת, מוּסָר is usually transl. σοφία but 8 times φρόνησις (only 3 Βασ.), 3 σύνεσις and 4 ἐπιστήμη (only Ez. 28). σοφός is used 141 times for חָכָם or חָכָם and חָכְמָה (3 times σοφῶς), but only twice for בִּין and once each for חַרְטֹם (Da.) and נָבֹן. חָכָם is mostly transl. σοφός, other words being used only 10 times, namely, φρόνιμος 4 times, σοφιστής, τεχνίτης, πανοῦργος, ἀληθές once each, φίλοι twice (Est.). The verb חָכַם is rendered 24 times by σοφίζειν / σοφίζεσθαι, σοφὸς εἶναι or σοφὸς γίγνεσθαι, and only once by κατασοφίζεσθαι and twice by φρονεῖν. The picture is much the same in the Hexapla tradition. Here σοφίζειν is more prominent. In the Wisdom books חכם and derivates are uniformly transl. by σοφός etc. Only in the historical book and the prophets do we occasionally find φρόνησις, φρόνιμος, συνετός or αἴσθησις [Bertram].

[200] For the pi and hi of חכם the LXX translators coin σοφίζειν, which is not attested earlier, only σοφίζεσθαι, rarely pass., e.g., Hes. Op., 649, mostly mid., e.g., Theogn. Fr., 1, 19 (Diehl³, II, 4) "to write poetry," cf. Schmid, III, 14, n. 2. In the LXX, as elsewhere, we find the act. σοφίζω as a factitive alongside σοφίζομαι (rare in the pass., common in the mid.), along the lines of the Hbr. hi of חכם, Helbing Kasussyntax, 40. For examples cf. P. Katz, "Zur Übersetzungstechnik d. LXX," *Die Welt d. Orients*, 2 (1954 ff.), 271 f. The transl. of Lam. goes furthest in this regard, *v.* P. Katz in J. Ziegler, "Beiträge z. Jeremias-LXX,"

Whereas in Hebrew חָכָם and חָכְמָה are thought of verbally as act, conduct, practical being, in Gk. σοφία and σοφός always have the sense of a quality → 467, 18 ff. In keeping is the fact that Gk. has no verb of the stem σοφ- apart from σοφίζεσθαι (→ 527, 1 ff.), which is clearly dependent on σοφία / σοφός → n. 200. [201]

The two traditions are close only where חָכְמָה, like σοφία in the early Gk. period (→ 468, 1 ff.), denotes technical ability → 484, 1 ff. [202] In content many wisdom sayings also seem to overlap many similar sayings in Gk. and Hell. wisdom, [203] and a person with some Gk. culture in the Hell. period, when he reads of the prudent conduct of the ἀνδρεῖος in the LXX, will recall the corresponding pedagogic instructions for the wise man which were taught in contemporary popular philosophy, → 472, 20 ff.

At every pt., however, one may see how alien the Hbr. חָכְמָה was to the spirit of the Gk. language. The LXX translators were not able to overcome the fundamental difficulty of translation. Thus the direct juxtaposition of φόβος κυρίου and σοφία (→ 487, 10 ff.) is quite strange to the Gk. ear. Again, it is sometimes apparent that in their use of the vocabulary of popular philosophy for basic wisdom concepts the translators did not merely handle this as the one with which they were most familiar but in many cases changed the Hbr. text in accordance with their own intellectual tradition when they put it into Gk. Typical are the following examples from Prv. At Prv. 10:14 the Mas. reads: חֲכָמִים יִצְפְּנוּ־דָעַת. Now LXX always has αἴσθησις for דַּעַת, and this is the transl. her⸳. But since perceptions cannot possibly be the basis of wisdom for the Gks., LXX takes צָפַן in sensu malo and offers the rendering: σοφοὶ κρύψουσιν αἴσθησιν. Cf. also Prv. 18:15: καρδία φρονίμου κτᾶται αἴσθησιν, ὦτα δὲ (!) σοφῶν ζητεῖ ἔννοιαν. The LXX changes the synon. parallelism of the Mas. into antithetical parallelism, contrasting the getting of αἴσθησις with the wise man's search for ἔννοια. If there are other possible explanations in these instances, so that they should not be allowed to count too heavily, there seems to be a deliberate alteration in the examples which follow. Prv. 21:30 Mas. reads: "There is no wisdom nor understanding nor counsel before Yahweh." This obviously makes no sense to the translator and so he writes: οὐκ ἔστιν σοφία, οὐκ ἔστιν ἀνδρεία, οὐκ ἔστιν βουλὴ πρὸς τὸν ἀσεβῆ; hence the saying is to the effect that the ungodly man has no wisdom, while the righteous naturally does. Prv. 10:23 Mas. reads: "It is as sport to a fool to do mischief, but wisdom is for the man of understanding." Now LXX often has φρόνησις for תְּבוּנָה, so that here we find σοφία with φρόνησις. It is a common philosophical doctrine, however, that σοφία as basic knowledge makes possible φρόνησις as the chief cardinal virtue. Hence the transl. writes: ἡ δὲ σοφία ἀνδρὶ τίκτει φρόνησιν. Finally Prv. 13:10 Mas. says: "By pride the vain man causeth contention; but with the well advised is wisdom." LXX renders נוֹעָצִים by ἑαυτῶν ἐπιγνώμονες and thus the Gk. version acquires a sense close to the famous Γνῶθι

Mitteilungen d. LXX-Unternehmens, 6 (1958), 53. It continues a construct found only in Ionic and the koine, Debr. Griech. Wortb. (1917), Index, s. v. "Faktitiva" [Katz].

[201] Fundamentally the same is true of the relation between יָדַע/דַּעַת and γιγνώσκειν / γνῶσις → I, 696, 17 ff.

[202] E.g., Ex. 35:26; Qoh. 10:10; Is. 40:20; Jer. 9:16; also Test. Zeb. 6:1 etc., though surprisingly one often does not find σοφία/σοφός in such cases, e.g., Jer 10:9 τεχνίτης and 3 Βασ. 7:2 τέχνη. For the transl. σοφία is obviously too strongly theological a term. This is why the wise men of Egypt in Ex. 7:11 and those of Babylon in Da. (5 times) are not σοφοί but σοφισταί — a word with a very negative ring from the time of Socrates' criticism of the Sophists → 470, 11 ff. σοφία/σοφός or σύνεσις/συνετός can be used, however, in Ex. 28:3; 31:6; 35:35; 36:1 f., 8 (cf. 1 Ch. 28:21) because the ref. is to work in the sanctuary and the skill is expressly said to be given by God, cf. Ex. 31:3 and 35:31 : πνεῦμα σοφίας.

[203] Cf., e.g., Prv. 24:5 : κρείσσων σοφὸς ἰσχυροῦ καὶ ἀνὴρ φρόνησιν ἔχων γεωργίου μεγάλου, and the saying of Xenophanes → n. 10.

σεαυτόν of the sage Thales in Plat. Prot., 343b, and connected with the idea of the autarchy of the wise man : [204] οἱ δὲ ἑαυτῶν ἐπιγνώμονες σοφοί.

2. Wisdom in Hellenistic Judaism.

a. In gen. Sir. stands wholly within the tradition of the חׇכׅמׇה of Israel. It consists in large part of older proverbial material relating to all spheres of practical — mostly domestic — life and the daily piety of the individual. Everything which contributes to a pious and happy life — propriety and decorum, honesty and prudence in dealings with others, control of speech and language, esp. the avoidance of all evil and the keeping of the commandments in the fear of the Lord [205] — constitutes the wisdom of the sage. But some parts go beyond Prv., Qoh. and Job.

In particular there is here a much clearer and less veiled description than in Prv. (9:1-6; 4:6-9; 7:4) of wisdom as a heavenly person and the student of wisdom as her lover. He now follows her tracks like a spy, peers through her window, listens at her doors, and finally goes to her and enjoys all the delights of union with her (Sir. 14:22-27). [206] In Sir. 4:11 f. wisdom is both mother and bride, cf. also 15:2. The union with her is expressly depicted in Sir. 51:13-30. Worth noting on the one side is the fact that her heavenly and divine nature is essentially enhanced as compared with Prv., with a corresponding radicalising of her hiddenness and inaccessibility on earth, [207] while on the other side it is the grace of a special heavenly revelation to find her and to be able to hear her teaching. [208] Wisdom belongs to God Himself, is created by Him προτέρα πάντων, and is thus ἐξ αἰῶνος (1:4). God alone "saw it and counted it and poured it out on all his works" (1:9). [209] In the song of wisdom in Sir. 24 she speaks expressly of her pre-existence (24:3-7), cf. Prv. 8:22-31. [210]

b. The Wisdom of Solomon, which comes from Jewish Hellenistic circles in Egypt, takes an essential step further in this direction. Here, too, wisdom is a heavenly person with whom the student lives in union. [211] But she also lives in

---

[204] On this whole subject cf. G. Gerleman, "Studies in the LXX, III : Proverbs," *Lunds Univ. Årsskrift*, NF, I, 52, 3 (1956), 17-24.

[205] The well-known principle of Israel's חׇכׅמׇה (→ 487, 10 ff.) that the fear of Yahweh is the beginning of all wisdom (Prv. 1:7; 9:10; cf. 15:33; Job 28:28; Ps. 111:10) is used in the series in Sir. 1 (1:1, 11-13, 14,16, 18, 20) and is also common elsewhere, cf. 18:28; 19:20; 21:11; 27:11; 34:8; 39:1; 40:26, also Ps. Sol. 2:33; 4:9.

[206] Cf. Sir. 6:18-31 and on this Arvedson, 180-201.

[207] Cf., e.g., Sir. 6:22: σοφία γὰρ κατὰ τὸ ὄνομα αὐτῆς ἐστιν καὶ οὐ πολλοῖς ἐστιν φανερά. He who seeks her must stretch forth his hands to the height of heaven, 51:19. Cf. also 1:6 : ῥίζα σοφίας τίνι ἀπεκαλύφθη; and 1:3 : σοφίαν τίς ἐξιχνίασει; (τίς εὑρήσει of a rare and costly possession, Prv. 31:10 cf. 3:13-15).

[208] Sir. 4:18 : ἀποκαλύψει αὐτῷ τὰ κρυπτὰ αὐτῆς, cf. 14:21. What seems to be a yoke and chain for the ordinary man (6:24 f.) is for her pupil εἰς στολὴν δόξης (6:29, 31) and as a στέφανος ἀγαλλιάματος (15:6; 1:11). Where she is, there is δόξα, 14:27, cf. 4:13; 17:13; 24:16 f.

[209] Cf. the κτίσεως ὕμνος in Sir. 42:15-43:33, before the πάτερων ὕμνος in 44:1-50:24, and esp. 42:21. The section on creation in 16:26-17:17 is the knowledge of wisdom in 16:24 f., cf. also the Syr. version of 17:3 in V. Ryssel, Kautzsch Apkr. u. Pseudepigr., 313o.

[210] Note the Lat. addition to Sir. 24:3 : "Firstborn of all creation," and on this Bousset Hauptprobleme, 256, n. 1.

[211] Cf. Wis. 6:14 : πάρεδρον γὰρ εὑρήσει τῶν πυλῶν αὐτοῦ (cf. 6:15 f.). 7:28 : οὐθὲν γὰρ ἀγαπᾷ ὁ θεὸς εἰ μὴ τὸν σοφίᾳ συνοικοῦντα. 8:2 : ταύτην ἐφίλησα καὶ ἐξεζήτησα

union with God. [212] There is here an essential relation of correspondence, for the union of the student with wisdom is in 8:2 f. and 9:10 [213] expressly referred back to that of God with wisdom. This union is the knowledge which wisdom imparts to its student. The content of this knowledge is again, pre-eminently, wisdom herself (6:12-9:18). [214] To know her is to attain to her, indeed, to be of like nature with her : ἀθανασία ἐστὶν ἐν συγγενείᾳ σοφίας (8:17), which is to gain a share in the εὐγένεια which the union with God means for her (8:3). Her union with God is also knowledge. Not only does she have perfect insight into the secrets of all creation (7:18-21; 8:8); she was present at creation and indeed had a hand in it [215] as μύστις ... τῆς τοῦ θεοῦ ἐπιστήμης καὶ αἱρετὶς ἔργων αὐτοῦ (8:4). Thus by making known to her pupil the knowledge of herself wisdom also imparts her own immediacy to God, namely, ἀφθαρσία (cf. 8:17), which ἐγγὺς εἶναι ποιεῖ θεοῦ (6:19). According to Wis. this is the point of the intertwining of the idea of union and the knowledge of wisdom. Union with wisdom is the mystical repetition of the union of God with her as the experience of a special, heavenly knowledge of revelation. The whole address on wisdom in Wis. 6-9 is thus correctly introduced as a mystery logos in 6:22 → IV, 814, 3 ff. [216] The answer to the two questions : τί δέ ἐστιν σοφία; and πῶς ἐγένετο; (6:22) [217] is given in 7:25 f.: the origin and nature of wisdom as mediator of revelation are identical. In her operation she is ἀτμὶς ... τῆς τοῦ θεοῦ δυνάμεως καὶ ἀπόρροια τῆς τοῦ παντοκράτορος δόξης εἰλικρινής, for in her nature she is ἀπαύγασμα ... φωτὸς ἀιδίου καὶ ἔσοπτρον ἀκηλίδωτον τῆς τοῦ θεοῦ ἐνεργείας καὶ εἰκὼν τῆς ἀγαθότητος αὐτοῦ. [218] Here, then, σοφία is an agent of revelation by nature. Hence the knowledge mediated by her has the character of direct revelation. Wisdom cannot be controlled ; she must be prayed for (7:7; 9:1-18), and she comes as

ἐκ νεότητός μου καὶ ἐζήτησα νύμφην ἀγαγέσθαι ἐμαυτῷ καὶ ἐραστὴς ἐγενόμην τοῦ κάλλους αὐτῆς. 8:9 : ἔκρινα τοίνυν ταύτην ἀγαγέσθαι πρὸς συμβίωσιν, cf. 8:16.

[212] Wis. 8:3 f.: εὐγένειαν δοξάζει συμβίωσιν θεοῦ ἔχουσα, καὶ ὁ πάντων δεσπότης ἠγάπησεν αὐτήν. 9:4 : δός μοι τὴν τῶν σῶν θρόνων πάρεδρον σοφίαν.

[213] On ἀπὸ θρόνου δόξης σου in Wis. 9:10 cf. πάρεδρος τῶν σῶν θρόνων in 9:4. On the whole theme cf. 9:4 with 6:14 (πάρεδρος); 8:3 with 8:9, 16 (συμβίωσις); 9:9 with 6:23; 7:28; 8:18; 9:10 (συνοικεῖν etc.); 8:3 with 6:12; 7:10; 8:2, 18 (love).

[214] All the good things given the pupil with the knowledge of wisdom are from her hand, and she is γενέτις τούτων, Wis. 7:11 f.

[215] Wis. 7:21 : πάντων τεχνῖτις, cf. 8:5 and esp. 9:9 : καὶ μετὰ σοῦ ἡ σοφία ἡ εἰδυῖα τὰ ἔργα σου καὶ παροῦσα, ὅτε ἐποίεις τὸν κόσμον κτλ. The idea of wisdom's presence at creation or share in it may be seen already in Prv. 3:19 f.; 8:22-31; Job 28:25-27 (38:36 f.); Ps. 136:5; Jer. 10:12 f. (Is. 10:13 f.); Sir. 1:4-10; 24:3-5, 9; 42:21, and it had prolonged influence, cf. S. Bar. 56:4; Tg. J. II on Gn. 1:1 (combined with Prv. 8:22); Gn. r., 1 (Str.-B., II, 356 f.); Midr. Tanch. on Gn. 1:1; bNed., 32a; Slav. En. 33:4 (cf. 30:8); Ps.-Clem. Recg. 2:12 (cunctorum genetrix); Ps.-Clem. Hom. 16:11 f. Const. Ap., VII, 34, 6; 37, 5 (cf. VII, 36). Cf. Gn. r., on 1:1 of the Torah. Finally בראשׁית is even equated with in filio (for wisdom or the Torah in Chr. authors) cf. the fathers in the Beuron Vetus Latina on Gn. 1:1, Vetus Lat., 2 (ed. B. Fischer [1951-1954]), 3-5, and C. F. Burney, "Christ as the ΑΡΧΗ of Creation," JThSt, 27 (1925/26), 160-177 [Katz].

[216] Goodenough, 268-276. This explains the structure of the address which follows : Wis. 7:1-21 depicts the seeking and finding of wisdom, i.e., the genesis of the knowledge mediated by her; 7:22-8:1 is the central section, the revelation of the nature of wisdom in her relation to God; 8:2-21 then depicts the union with wisdom; 9:1-18 is a prayer for the gift of wisdom; c. 10 finally illustrates the work of wisdom by a series of examples from Israel's history.

[217] Note the typically Hell. nature of the questions. The nature of wisdom will be known from her origin, and this knowledge can come only by revelation on the part of the wisdom sought.

[218] Materially, then, the 4 concepts simply describe what is expressed by the idea of

πνεῦμα σοφίας (7:7) [219] to those who seek her. [220] He who knows her is himself qualified to be a mediator of revelation. [221] "Passing into holy souls from generation to generation, she equips them as friends of God and prophets," 7:27. This work of σοφία is illustrated by a series of individual paradigms in Wis. 10. Always the guiding principle is essentially soteriological. At issue in the work of wisdom is σωτηρία. [222]

c. Philo's teaching about wisdom is similar. A typical feature both of his teaching gen. and also of his use of the word [223] is, of course, that all kinds of intellectual and religious tendencies in the surrounding world flow together headlong in him. But if there is need to try to separate these critically from the standpt. of the history of religion and thought, it is hard to get an understanding of Philo's own distinctive teaching. Thus we find the Stoic def. of σοφία as ἐπιστήμη θείων τε καὶ ἀνθρωπίνων, [224] and esp. the Stoic ideal of the sage, [225] side by side with the Platonic view of wisdom as the desired goal of philosophical ἔρως [226] and the understanding of σοφία as τέχνη τεχνῶν in the Aristotelian sense, Ebr., 88 cf. 86 → 471, 27 ff. Often σοφία, with φρόνησις, is described as a virtue by which man frees himself from everything worldly and physical, and from all desire for this. [227] This motif, "release (ἄφεσις) from all earthly strivings" (Migr. Abr., 32), is a dominant one in Philo. We have here one of his central concerns : Abraham, the prototype of the wise man, receives the command : ἄπελθε ... ἐκ τοῦ περὶ σεαυτὸν γεώδους, τὸ παμμίαρον ... ἐκφυγὼν δεσμωτήριον, τὸ σῶμα, καὶ τὰς ὥσπερ εἰρκτοφύλακας [228] ἡδονὰς καὶ ἐπιθυμίας αὐτοῦ, Migr. Abr., 9. There thus begins his wandering on the "royal way" whose goal is the ἱερὸς λόγος and whose sphere is σοφία (28 cf. 46), [229] which as ἡ τοῦ φιλοδώρου θεοῦ σύνοδος is the source of all the good things prepared for the wise at the end of their journey, 30. [230]

---

union. This is why the idea follows at once in 7:28. On εἰκών cf. on the one side 9:1 f., on the other 2:23. The εἰκών idea here is not developed from Gn. 1:26 but as an independent concept is secondarily combined with this v. So in Philo. On the concept cf. Käsemann Leib Christi, 90 f., also Taufliturgie, 137 f.; F. W. Eltester, *EIKON im NT* (1958), 114-116; Jervell, 23-29.

[219] σοφία is expressly defined as πνεῦμα in Wis. 7:22 f.; the Stoic and magical doctrine of πνεῦμα has had some influence here. Stoic terminology may also be found in 7:24 and 8:1. Cf. σοφία and πνεῦμα as parallels in 9:17 and 1:6.

[220] Wis. 6:13 : φθάνει τοὺς ἐπιθυμοῦντας προγνωσθῆναι.

[221] Cf. Wis. 7:13 f. and already Sir. 24:30-34; 51:23-30.

[222] Cf. esp. Wis. 9:18 : καὶ τῇ σοφίᾳ ἐσώθησαν, which sums up all that precedes and forms a direct transition to c. 10.

[223] σοφία is used by Philo over 200 times, and σοφός some 300 times, also σοφίζεσθαι 5 times in the sense "to be wise," σόφισμα 19 times, also *in sensu malo*, e.g., Gig., 59 and Det. Pot. Ins., 38 synon. with ἀπάτη, but also positively in the sense of rational instruction, e.g., Rer. Div. Her., 302 : οἱ πιθανῶν σοφισμάτων εὑρεταί. σοφιστεία occurs 14 times, σοφιστής 40 and σοφιστικός 13, always negatively as in the criticism of the Sophists, e.g., with ref. to magic.

[224] Congr., 79 with the Poseidonian addition καὶ τῶν τούτων αἰτίων. Cf. the Stoic relating of wisdom as a basic virtue to the three γένη of the Stoic system, Virt., 8; Vit. Mos., 76.

[225] Cf., e.g., Praem. Poen., 113 (→ h. 71). ὁ σοφὸς μόνος ἐλεύθερός τε καὶ ἄρχων, Poster. C., 138; μόνος ὁ σοφὸς ἄρχων καὶ βασιλεύς, Som., II, 244, cf. Migr. Abr., 197; also Mut. Nom., 152 f.; Som., II, 243. The wise man as cosmopolitan, Migr. Abr., 59 f. etc.

[226] Op. Mund., I, 70, cf. 77; Spec. Leg., I, 50; Mut. Nom., 37; Abr., 224, 271.

[227] E.g., Leg. All., I, 103 : σχεδὸν γὰρ σοφίας ἔργον τοῦτ' ἐστίν, ἀλλοτριοῦσθαι πρὸς τὸ σῶμα καὶ τὰς ἐπιθυμίας αὐτοῦ.

[228] Note the closeness to the Gnostic idea of demons as watchers, esp. in Mand. lit.

[229] The same of the λόγος, Migr. Abr., 3 and 28, cf. Fug., 94.

[230] Wisdom is the only thing suited for the human race (οἰκειότατον), so that for it

But the goal is none other than God Himself, He who is, surrounded by His "powers." [231] To reach Him in the γνῶσις and ἐπιστήμη θεοῦ is the goal of the way. σοφία, however, is not just God's sphere. It is also the way and the guide thereto, the τελεία ὁδὸς ἡ πρὸς θεόν. [232] The identity of way, guide and goal pts. to the mystical character of wisdom as the mediator of revelation, a constitutive feature in Wis. (→ 499, 13 ff.) but also in Gnosticism (→ 509, 24 ff). Hence there is in fact a series of texts from which may be deduced a complete wisdom mystery which was obviously known to Philo and which bears close affinity to the Isis mystery as transmitted in Apul. and Plut. [233] Fug., 108-112 describes how the high-priest as the devotee of God his father and wisdom his mother is born again to the λόγος, putting on his radiant garment, which bears the four elements as a symbol of his dominion over the cosmos. Wisdom as his mother is also God's consort by whom He begat the world. [234] In the same way, i.e., on a level with the cosmos, the regeneration of the devotee takes place. Hence this is not supracosmic. [235] In a special consecration, however, the wise man can be led beyond the level of the cosmos to the direct proximity of God. This takes place through union with wisdom, which corresponds mystically to God's union with her. [236] Thus the wise man is like wisdom, entering into the union with God which as knowledge of God is also the vision of God [237] and even divinisation. [238] At this level he is so one with wisdom that he no longer needs her as leader and path. [239] This complex of ideas in Philo is remarkably similar to that in Wis. 6-10, cf. also the formal description of the knowledge of revelation. In Philo, too, the content and the means of knowledge are identical : "By wisdom what is wise is seen ; but unlike light wisdom is not just the instrument of seeing, it also sees itself ..." [240] Heavenly wisdom thus transports into νήφουσα μέθη, Fug.,

---

one should traverse the whole world, eventually attaining to the direct vision of God by it. Migr. Abr., 218.

[231] On this cf. Jonas Gnosis, II, 94 f.

[232] Deus Imm., 142 f. cf. 159 f. In this σοφία has the same function as the λόγος, Migr. Abr., 175 : ἡγούμενος τῆς ὁδοῦ. Cf. Goodenough, 22 f., 161.

[233] Apul. Met., XI; Plut. Is. et Os., 49 ff. (II, 371a ff.). On the wisdom mystery cf. esp. Pascher, 9 f. and his schematic reconstruction, 262-264, though his thesis is contested by Michaelis → V, 63, n. 60; cf. the bibl. in H. Thyen, "Die Probleme d. neueren Philoforschung," ThR, 3 (1955), 233, n. 2. On Plut. cf. also A. Torhoudt, Een onbekend gnostisch systeem in Plutarchus' de Is. et Os. (1942), who pts. to close connections with the later Valentinian system.

[234] Ebr., 30 f. expounding Prv. 8:22.

[235] Fug., 108; Ebr., 30; Abr., 100 ff., though here, as in Fug., 110 the birth is the genesis of virtues in the sage, a sign that ideas of regeneration along the lines of the mysteries were already accepted in Philo, cf. Corp. Herm., 13, 1 f. and of the mystagogue, 1, 29.

[236] Fug., 49-52. Cf. Quaest. in Ex., II, 39-47 (cf. II, 3 and Quaest. in Gn., IV, 97), and esp. Cher., 42-50. In interpretation cf. Pascher, 60-105. On the connection of this complex of ideas with Valentinian and pre-Valentinian redemption systems cf. Wilckens Weisheit u. Torheit, 145-159.

[237] Leg. All., I, 43 : τὴν μετάρσιον καὶ οὐράνιον σοφίαν... καὶ γὰρ ἀρχὴν καὶ εἰκόνα καὶ ὅρασιν θεοῦ. Its image (μίμημα) is ἐπίγειος σοφία. For an exact par. cf. Conf. Ling., 146 f on the λόγος, cf. also Leg. All., I, 65 : ἡ δὲ [σοφία] ἐστὶν ὁ θεοῦ λόγος. σοφία as the source of the λόγος river Som., II, 242, the λόγος as the source of the river of wisdom Fug., 47 and 97. Cf. also Rer. Div. Her., 204; Deus Imm., 155; Leg. All., II, 86.

[238] Quaest. in Ex., II, 40 : Animam sanctam deificari notatur per istam ascensionem, non in aërem vel aethera vel in supremum omnium caelum, sed super omnes caelos. Post autem mundum non est locus, sed Deus. Cf. II, 29 : ... transmutatur in divinum, ita ut fiat deo cognatus vereque divinus. But cf. the correction of this idea in Mut. Nom., 179 ff.

[239] Cf. the corresponding statement about the λόγος in Migr. Abr., 175.

[240] Migr. Abr., 39 f., cf. Spec. Leg., I, 287 f.; III, 6; Congr., 47 f.; Vit. Cont., 68, also statements about αὐτομαθὴς σοφία in Sacr. Acc, 78 f.; Det. Pot. Ins., 30; Poster. C., 78. The process of illumination is depicted in Migr. Abr., 34 f. cf. 79 f.: "God comes to the ascending soul which wants to see him (cf. Wis. 6:13) and makes his own nature known."

166 cf. 137. To this degree it is identical with the divine πνεῦμα. [241] "For God can be grasped only through God and light through light," Praem. Poen., 40.

d. In other Hell. Jewish writings the usage of Aristob. may be compared with that of Wis. and Philo. [242] Acc. to him, too, wisdom is pre-existent, 2, 10. As the light in which one sees all things was created on the Sabbath, so "all light goes forth from wisdom," 2, 1 ff. Without it all men are ignorant and wicked, but when the sevenfold λόγος receives the revelation of wisdom it attains thereby to "knowledge of the truth," 2, 40. Thus divine wisdom alone leads to γνῶσις ἀνθρωπίνων καὶ θείων πραγμάτων, 2, 22 ff. [243] He who follows it like a torch can lead an undisturbed life, 2, 10. Elsewhere σοφία is used either as a gen. term for intellectual superiority [244] or as a comprehensive word for a respectable life. [245]

e. Joseph. occupies a special place, for though he is concerned to put himself and his people in a favourable light to the Hell. Roman world, in distinction from all the other Jews who write in Gk. he thinks and writes at bottom wholly on the basis of the theological tradition of Palestinian Judaism. This may be seen also in his use of σοφία / σοφός. For him, as for the Rabb. (→ 505, 14 ff.), wisdom is the content of the Torah. [246] It thus derives from God and as σοφία θεοῦ is close to the δικαιοσύνη θεοῦ. [247] Of men, therefore, only those can be called wise who are so on the basis of, and by, the wisdom of God. Ezra was this when he undertook κατὰ τὴν τοῦ θεοῦ σοφίαν to set up just judges τοὺς ἐπισταμένους σου (sc. θεοῦ) τὸν νόμον, Ant., 11, 129. But above all the scribes, who know the Torah and can expound it, are "the wise." [248] This wisdom is the source of all human wisdom, to which Jos. ascribes more justification and significance than the Rabb. do to worldly wisdom (→ 507, 15 ff.). Joseph.'s view of man is shaped hereby. The man who knows and keeps God's Law attains to comprehensive culture and virtue in the world and surpasses all non-Jews. [249] The σοφισταί often seem to be far removed from this true wisdom. Joseph. likes to use this term when his own opinion differs from that of the Rabb. scholars of whom he tells us, esp. in relation

---

[241] πνεῦμα σοφίας (cf. Wis. 7:7, 22 f.; 9:17) Gig., 47 cf. Som., II, 12; also cf. Rer. Div. Her., 264 f. with Migr. Abr., 34 f.

[242] Texts in W. N. Stearns, Fr. from Graeco-Jew. Writers (1908), 77-91. Cf. Dalbert, 105, 133.

[243] In Aristob. this Stoic def. of wisdom (→ 473, 10 ff.) is meant in a very non-Stoic sense, but in 4 Macc. 1:15-19 (with the addition καὶ τῶν τούτων αἰτίων as in Philo) it is Stoic in sense. To be sure, this Stoic wisdom is equated with the "culture achieved through the law," but the material context is wholly Stoic: One chooses the "life of wisdom" μετὰ ὀρθοῦ λόγου, and by wisdom one learns "divine things in a worthy way and human things in a helpful way," i.e., by learning as their γένη the 4 cardinal virtues, of which φρόνησις, which controls the impulses, is chief. Cf. 4 Macc. 7:23.

[244] Cf. Eupolemus, 1, 2 (Dalbert, 40 f.), who says Moses is the first sage, who gave the Jews the alphabet and wrote their laws, 1, 4. Cf. also Aristobulus, 3, 16 ff., who suggests that all nations took every intellectual good from Moses, the sage. Similarly Artapanus, 2, 3 can tell of Joseph who surpassed all other men in σύνεσις and φρόνησις, Dalbert, 48.

[245] So Ep. Ar., 207 and 260. For the author God, as Giver of the Law, is trying to keep men pure in body and soul by the gift of the Law, ibid., 139.

[246] σοφία τῶν νόμων Ant., 18, 59 and 82, cf. 20, 264; Bell., 2, 118. When Ant., 4, 319 says: "The laws which he (God) himself brought forth (γεννήσας) and gave us," the word γεννᾶν was probably suggested by the common ref. of Prv. 8:25 to the Torah, cf. Schl. Theol. d. Judt., 69, and on this whole subject ibid., 63 f.

[247] Cf., e.g., Ant. 11, 268 and on this Schl. Jos., 26. On the other hand σοφός is never used as a quality of God in Jos. [Rengstorf].

[248] Ant., 18, 82: ἐξηγεῖσθαι σοφίαν νόμων τῶν Μωυσέως. Cf. 20, 264: σοφία ascribed only to those τοῖς τὰ νόμιμα σαφῶς ἐπισταμένοις (= Halachah) καὶ τὴν τῶν ἱερῶν γραμμάτων δύναμιν ἑρμηνεῦσαι δυναμένοις (= Haggadah). σοφιστής is also used with ref. to the scribes, → n. 250, 251.

[249] Thus the wisdom of Joseph (Ant., 2, 87: σοφία = φρόνησις) and esp. that of

to Zealot aspirations which he rejects. [250] The Zealots are a party and have nothing whatever to do with orthodox Jews. [251] Naturally the orthodox will, if required, give their lives for the Law of God. [252]

3. Jewish Apocalyptic.

Many wisdom passages may be found in Jewish apocalyptic. Thus in the Daniel stories in Da. 1-6 Daniel is portrayed as wise in contrast with the Babylonian σοφισταί. [253, 254] In particular the exhortations of Eth. En. [255] have the structure of wisdom lit. In Prv. 1-9 the content of חָכְמָה is already focused wholly upon the fear of Yahweh, and in ever new general expressions the commands of wisdom refer to the whole relationship with God. Similarly apocal. teaches that the whole of the divine relationship is observing or "keeping" the "Law" and not just "fulfilling" a summary of the commandments as in the Rabb. [256] This Law is often equated with God's wisdom and righteousness as observance of the Law with the wisdom of the wise. An important link is Sir., who clearly prepares the way for this development. [257] This usage soon establishes itself, esp. in apocal. lit., and one may assume that it was widespread in the NT. [258] Particularly characteristic of apocal. is that keeping the Law is the criterion of the *iustificatio iusti* in the Last Judgment: He who was faithful to the Law prior to the judgment will enter into life as the righteous man he showed himself to be. This idea is often depicted as an investing of the righteous with righteousness. Since righteousness and wisdom are identical, the first and basic redemptive gift to the righteous is wisdom, → 488, 30 ff. [259] Hence the righteous are told: "For you Paradise is open, the tree of

---

Solomon is held up as an example (8, 49 : σοφία == σύνεσις), cf. Schl. Theol. d. Judt., 138. Cf. also 20, 264 on the difference between Jewish sages (→ n. 248) and all others.

[250] Cf., e.g., the account (Bell., 1, 648 and 650, cf. Ant., 17, 151 and 155) of two famous rabbis (σοφισταί) who called on the young people to remove by force the golden eagle which Herod, contrary to the Torah, had had put on the gt. gate of the temple. Cf. also Ap., 2, 236 (ἀδόκιμοι σοφισταί), Schl. Theol. d. Judt., 200 f., also W. R. Farmer, *Maccabees, Zealots and Josephus* (1956).

[251] Judas the Galilaean was σοφιστὴς ἰδίας αἱρέσεως οὐδὲν τοῖς ἄλλοις προσεοικώς, Bell., 2, 118.

[252] Cf. esp. Ant., 18, 59 : ἡδονῇ δέξεσθαι τὸν θάνατον ἔλεγεν ἢ τολμήσειν τὴν σοφίαν παραβήσεσθαι τῶν νόμων.

[253] When חַכִּים is used for the wise men of Babylon LXX mostly has σοφισταί, Da. 2:14, 18, 24, 48; 4:18, 37c, Daniel being differentiated from them as a σοφός. Cf. expressly Da. 1:20: σοφωτέρους δεκαπλασίως ὑπὲρ τοὺς σοφιστάς, also 5:12 and 2:48 in Theodotion.

[254] Cf. esp. the ideal of the wise youth in Da. 1:4 with that of the early monarchy in 1 S. 16:18. In Da., of course, wisdom consists chiefly in the gift of interpretation of dreams as a knowledge of μυστήρια βαθέα καὶ σκοτεινά which God reserves for Himself (cf. Da. 2:21 f.) but which He discloses to the wise. From this it is only a small step to the specific apoc. understanding of wisdom as knowledge of the secrets of the divine plan for history which God has revealed to the apocalyptist.

[255] Eth. En. 91:1-11; 92; 94-105. Cf., e.g., 99:10 : "But in those days all they will be blessed who receive and know the words of wisdom, have regard to the ways of the Most High, walk in the way of his righteousness, and do not sin with the ungodly, for they shall be saved."

[256] On the Law in apocal. as distinct from the Rabb. cf. Rössler.

[257] E.g., Sir. 19:20 : "All wisdom is fear of the Lord and all wisdom is doing of the law." Cf. 21:11; 34:8; 1:26; 15:1; 2:16; 6:37; 32:14-17, 24-33:3; 38:34b-39:5; 39:6-11, and esp. the express relating of the song of wisdom in Sir. 24 to the Law : ταῦτα πάντα βίβλος διαθήκης θεοῦ ὑψίστου, νόμον ὃν ἐνετείλατο ἡμῖν Μωυσῆς κτλ., 24:23.

[258] E.g., Eth. En. 98:9; 99:10; 24:3; 32:3-6 (tree of wisdom); 4 Esr. 8:12; 13:54 f.; S. Bar. 38:2; 44:14; 46:4 f.; 48:24 f., 33; 51:3 f., 7; 54:13 f.; 59:7; 61:3-8; 66:2; 70:5; 77:16 f.; Test. L. 13:7 f.; N. 8:10; Mart. Is. 2:3 (also 4 Macc. 1:16 f.). The rightous as "wise" S. Bar. 46:4 f.; 51:3 f.

[259] Cf. Eth. En. 5:8; 91:10; cf. 32:3-6; 48:1; 49:1 (61:11); 90:35; S. Bar, 54:13; 4 Esr. 8:52;

life is planted, the future aeon inaugurated, felicity ordained, the city built, the home-land chosen, good works created, wisdom prepared" etc., 4 Esr. 8:52. [260] These are all gifts of God, for He is the "Lord of glory and the Lord of wisdom," Eth. En. 63:2 f. In His wisdom He has created all things and He sees and knows all things, [261] and so in His wisdom He has given man the Law and the commandments. [262] But in His special revelation He also gives the apocalyptist of His saved community a glimpse of the mysteries of His wisdom, both the order of the universe and the stars [263] and also the course of history as it moves on to its end acc. to His plan. [264] In this knowledge of secrets which is entrusted to him the apocalyptist is the source and the lamp of wisdom in the saved community. [265]

Finally it is also wisdom which manifests the Son of Man as the just and holy One, Eth. En. 48:7. Like חָכְמָה He is pre-existent and kept hidden with God until the last days when He will hold judgment. In Him dwells "the spirit of wisdom," [266] so that close to Him the apocalyptist sees the well of righteousness and around it the "many wells of wisdom," 48:1. "Wisdom is poured forth like water, and glory never ends before him from eternity to eternity. For he is mighty above all the mysteries of righteousness," 49:1. In the similitudes of Eth. En. the judgment of God in its significance for the just is thus personified in the wisdom of the Son of Man. [267]

4. The Dead Sea Scrolls.

In the texts published thus far [268] חָכְמָה occurs 10 times and חָכָם 4. To the degree that a survey is possible the term is shaped by an idea which is typical of the theology of the sect, namely, that of God's embracing plan. By the wisdom of the divine knowledge all things are set in their times and orders. [269] If these statements about God's wisdom are also influenced quite clearly by the language of Ps. and Prv., they stand here in a context of ideas which is closely akin to many apocal. texts : The wisdom of the Creator is also that of Him who planned all events from the very first. "All things arise through his knowledge (דַעַת) and he has directed all that is by his plan (מחשבת)," 1 QS 11:11, cf. 3:13-4:26. In particular He has created two sharply contrasting spirits, 4:15-26, and in the secrets of his prudence and the wisdom of his glory ברזי שכלו ובחכמת כבודו he has prepared or established for the one spirit corruption (עָוֶל) and an (eschatological) end (4:18), while to the elect of the other spirit will be given "true insight into the know-ledge of the Most High and the wisdom of the heavenly sons" as a gift of eschatological

---

Test. L. 18, cf. Rössler, 66, n. 4. With wisdom, other gifts of salvation are glory, life, light, peace, joy etc. These eschatological gifts correspond exactly to wisdom's gifts in Wisdom lit.
[260] These gifts are withheld from the wicked, 4 Esr. 8:55.
[261] Eth. En. 63:2 f.; 84:3; 101:8; S. Bar. 54:13 — in full Wisdom style.
[262] Eth. En. 101:8; 4 Esr. 8:12; cf. also Eth. En. 92:1.
[263] Eth. En. 82:2 f. at the end of the astronomical book, cf. 69:8 f.
[264] Eth. En. 37:1-4 in the intr. to the similitudes (cf. 52:2). Cf. also 4 Esr. 13:53 f.; S. Bar. 28:1; 54:5; 59:7 f.
[265] Already Da. 12:3 (of the righteous gen.). Cf. also Eth. En. 99:10; 100:6; 104:12 (wise and righteous); 4 Esr. 12:36 ff., 42; 14:13, 25, 38-40, 46 f.; S. Bar. 28:1; Slav. En. 48:7, 9.
[266] Eth. En. 49:3 (Is. 11:3). Cf. 51:3; Text. L. 18 (Armen. text; Gk. reads σύνεσις and ἁγιασμός); Ps. Sol. 17:23, 37 (the Messiah). On this cf. H. L. Jansen, Die Henochgestalt (1939), 90 f.
[267] Cf. esp. Eth. En. 51:3 : "In those days the chosen one will sit on my throne and all the secrets of wisdom will come from the thoughts of his mouth, for the Lord of spirits has granted it to him and glorified him." On homage to him cf. 61:7, 11.
[268] We shall be considering material from Cave 1 (1 Q) and Damasc. On what follows cf. esp. F. Nötscher, "Zur theol. Terminologie d. Qumrantexte," Bonner Bibl. Beiträge, 10 (1956), 40-79, also H. Braun, Spät.-jüd.-häretischer u. frühchr. Radikalismus, I (1957), passim, esp. 20, n. 4.
[269] 1 QH 1:20 : ובחכמת דעתכה הכינותה תעורדתם בטרם היותם, and cf. 1:7, 14.

salvation. [270] Thus far the two spirits fight one another and we walk "in wisdom and folly." [271] But then God will defend the cause of those who pray to Him (1 QH 9:23 f.), "for in the mystery of thy wisdom thou hast corrected me (ברז חכמתכה הוכחתה בי) and thou hast hidden thy wisdom to the time of judgment." If there are among men differences in insight, honour, and power, God's power, glory and wisdom are without measure, 9:14-18. Man is forbidden to try to peer into God's secrets, but God grants such knowledge to His elect in a special revelation. [272] The members of the sect alone are the elect : hence they alone are wise (חכמים) and righteous (צדיקים).[273] As in apocal., wisdom as the special knowledge of God's secrets or plan which is mediated by revelation corresponds to the wisdom which is the righteous keeping of the Torah. To teach both is the task of the instructor (משכיל).[274] In the sect there is also a special class of "the wise" (חכמים) who in the eschatological hierarchy come immediately after "the heads of the fathers of the community." [275]

5. Rabbinic Judaism. [276]

The teaching of the early Rabb., too, is closely connected to the wisdom tradition. If in this (cf. esp. Sir. → n. 257) חכמה was largely used for the Torah and Torah scholarship, this meaning of wisdom became very common in the Rabb. tradition. Cf. the motto of Hillel : "... the more Torah, the more life ; the more school, the more wisdom (חכמה) the more counsel, the more understanding (בינה) the more beneficence, the more peace," Ab., 2, 7. [277] If wisdom here is expressly understood as academic knowledge, it is typical of Rabb. usage in this connection that the concept of the wise man (חכם) very gen. became a tt. The wise man is the finished and recognised scribe, the ordained rabbi. Already in Sir. 38:24-39:11 the scribe (סופר = γραμματεύς) is the one who is wise through constant study of the Torah. [278] Similarly, the "wise" and the "scribes" are materially identical in Rabb. usage, [279] though in the main the ancient title סופר is reserved for the

---

[270] להבין ישרים בדעת עליון וחכמת בני־שמים, 1 QS 4:22.

[271] 1 QS 4:24, יתהלכו בחכמה ואולת.

[272] 1 QS 2:3; 4:3-6; 11:5 f.; 1 QH 7:26 f.; 10:4 f.; 1 QM 10:16. Cf. also Damasc. 2:3 (2:2 f.).

[273] Note the parallelism of wisdom and righteousness in 1 QH 1:34 ff. cf. Damasc. 4:3 f. (6:3 ff.) where the "understanding" (נבונים) of Aaron and the "wise" (חכמים) of Israel are those who dig the well of the Torah.

[274] 1 QS 3:13 cf. 9:12, 21; Damasc. 12:20 (15:2). Cf. the parallelism of המשכילים and מצדיקי הרבים in Da. 12:3.

[275] חכמי הדעת; 1 QSa 2:16, cf. 1:28. 1 QS 4:3-6 also ref. to these "wise men." Cf. their function in expounding and teaching the Torah in Damasc. 4:3 f. (6:3), whereas the whole community is undoubtedly addressed in 1 QH 1:24 ff.

[276] On this cf. the material in Levy Wört.², II, 48 f.; Kassovsky² (1957), 680-685; L. Goldschmidt, Subject Concordance to the Babyl. Talmud (1959), 183 f.; Jastrow, I, 432, 462 f., s.v. חכם, חכמה, חוכמא; K. Kohler, Art. "Wisdom" in Jew. Enc., XII, 538; Jüd. Lex., s.v. "Chochma," "Weisheit."

[277] Cf., e.g., bBB, 9b in Str.-B., IV, 554.

[278] He "reflects on the law of the Most High and seeks out the wisdom of the ancients," 39:1. He seeks the Lord, esp. in prayer, 39:5. God "fills him with the spirit of understanding" so that he "makes wise speeches" and "glories in the law of the covenant of the Lord." 39:8. The praise of his wisdom reaches to all peoples and his name is magnified in the congregation, 39:10 f.

[279] חכם and סופר are synon., e.g., bGit., 67a : "Isi ben Jehuda (2nd cent.) listed the qualities of the wise : R. Mëir is a wise man and a writer (חכם וסופר), R. Jehuda is a wise man whenever he will (חכם לכשצרה)," i.e., when he gives a lecture, cf. Levy Wört., s.v. חכם. But the sense is characteristically different when Enoch is called the first to learn "writing and knowledge and wisdom," Jub. 4:17.

older, pre-Chr. rabbis, [280] חכם being in common use for those of the post-Chr. period. [281] The man who claims to be a sage must "know how to answer if he is asked a learned question in any field," bQid., 49b. [282] Thus חכם, with נשיא and אב בית דין, is "from the time of Simeon ben Gamaliel" (1st cent.) one of the academic titles of honour, bHor., 13b. To teach "in the name of the scribes" (בשם החכמים, e.g., jQid., 1, 2, 59a, 24 f.) is thus to claim gen. recognised authority for one's teaching. In this sense there is a common technical and specific use in Rabb. lit. If the view of a single, recognised scribe is against that of the majority, this is called the teaching of the scribes. [283] The term may also be used when an accepted view is adduced without mentioning a particular rabbi. [284] Later the Rabb. used instead of חכמים the new title תלמיד חכם "pupil of the scribes." [285] This not only manifests personal modesty but also seeks to express a certain sense distance from the gt. founders of the Rabb. teaching tradition. [286]

As it is necessary for Israel's salvation that there be scribes within it, [287] so it is a supreme honour and aim to belong to the circle of these authorities. [288] In relation to this R. Simeon bZoma (2nd cent.) in a slogan calls the man who has learned from anyone wise (Ab., 4, 1), and we also read in bNidda, 70b : "What does a man do when he becomes wise ? He (R. Jehoshua b. Chananiah [2nd cent.]) answered him : He spends a lot of time in school and not much in trade. They replied : Many do that and it profits them nothing. Rather, he prays for mercy to Him to whom wisdom belongs, as it is written : 'For the Lord grants wisdom, from his mouth are knowledge and under-

---

[280] Cf. Str.-B., I, 79-82, also W. Bacher, *Tradition u. Tradenten in den Schulen Palästinas u. Babyloniens* (1914), 163. A title worth noting is "father of wisdom" for Moses, *v.* the instances in Jaeger, 97, n. 1.

[281] If חכם means rabbi, חכים is a gen. term for learning (חכימה) as distinct from the wisdom of the ordained scribe. Thus in bBM, 85b-86a the astronomer Samuel is called חכים but not rabbi, and jTaan., 4, 2 (68a, 22 ff.) tells how Rabbi (Jehuda Hannasi) would not call R. Chami bar Chanina (3rd cent.) "rabbi" but only חכים because he once quoted a v. from the Torah incorrectly.

[282] דברי החכמה "academic question," cf. also bNidda, 69b (Str.-B., III, 80), where such questions are distinguished from "haggadic" and "foolish" questions, also those about manner of life, by being devoted to the Halachah.

[283] The two opposing views are then quoted as follows : דברי ר' והחכמים.... or .... ר"
והחכמים אומרים אומר... (Bacher, *op. cit.*, 148, n. 1; cf. the many examples, 145-155). Cf., e.g., bChul., 85a : "Rabbi (the editor of the Mishnah) granted (in the one Halachah) the view of R. Mëir, thus adducing it as the pronouncement of the Chachamim (בלשון חכמים); (in the other) he accepted the view of R. Simon, so that he adduced this as the pronouncement of the Chachamim." In both cases he appended his own view, Levy Wört., II, 48.

[284] Cf. the examples in Bacher, 156-162. Even where a view is simply introduced by אמרו, החכמים is to be supplied as the obvious subj., Bacher, 160.

[285] Cf. the examples in Levy Wört., *s.v.* Earlier תלמיד was used for Rabb. students, e.g., bQid., 49b. Cf. → VI, 962, 19 ff.

[286] Cf. the quotation from the "book of the first man" in bBM, 85b-86a, Str.-B., III, 277.

[287] Cf. bBB, 12a : "From the day the temple was destroyed prophecy was taken from the prophets and given to the wise," with ref. to the deaths of important rabb., cf. bSota, 49b : "With the death of R. Akiba the arms of the teaching of the Law (תורה) disappeared and the sources of wisdom (חכמה) were stopped." From the disaster of 70 A.D. the wise were the only guarantee of Israel's salvation and Israel's assurance of salvation rested on them personally. Cf. also R. Jonathan bEliezer (3rd cent.): "God counts it as though wise disciples who were occupied with the doctrine brought him offerings and incense," bMen., 110a. Thus, as the wise man has taken the place of the prophet, he also discharges the function of the priest.

[288] Cf., e.g., the slogan of R. Jose bJoëzer (one of the earliest pre-Chr. Rabb.) יהי ביתך בית ועד לחכמים "let your house be a place where the wise assemble," Ab., 1, 4.

standing' " (Prv. 2:6). [289] Wisdom (חכמה) is thus the gen. recognised and eternally valid teaching of the "scribes." This is how the Rabb. construe the bibl. statements about חכמה, either taking the sayings as they stand, so that only the context shows that wisdom is understood in the specific Rabb. sense, or else adding a short interpretation to make the sense explicit. Thus Prv. 8:22 is often discussed. Pre-existent wisdom is here construed as the Torah, [290] and in particular what is said about its part in creation [291] and also about its 7 pillars [292] is referred to the Torah, for the scribe who knows the Torah knows God's will by which all things were created. All the good things mentioned in the Wisdom books are described and extolled as gifts of wisdom, and are thus regarded as fruits of the teaching of the Law, e.g., life [293] and dominion. [294] The ref. to the high value of wisdom [295] or to partaking of its feast [296] is construed as a ref. to the incomparable worth of the teaching of the Torah. The sense is the same when R. Abin I (c. 325) calls the Torah the image of the wisdom which is above (חכמה של מעלה) [297] or when bSanh., 104b says : "Blessed be he who chose the children of Abraham and imparted to them of his own wisdom." [298] For through the gift of the Torah to Moses Israel received a treasure of wisdom which cannot be outweighed by all the world's wisdom. [299] Thus a sharp distinction was made between חכמה as the wisdom of the Rabb. scholars and חכמה as the wisdom of the world. But even in worldly wisdom the Jewish scribes always surpassed the wise of this world ; this is the theme of many stories in the Talmud. [300]

6. A Wisdom Myth in Judaism.

From the collection of proverbs in Prv. 1-9 all the texts discussed above derive the more or less clearly expressed idea of wisdom as a divine and heavenly person. This is often regarded as the result of a process of hypostatising — a rather obscure term designed to denote something midway between simple metaphor and

---

[289] Cf. bBer., 55a R. Jochanan bZakkai with allusion to Da. 2:21 : "The Holy One — blessed be he — grants wisdom only to him who already has wisdom," also the benediction in bBer., 58b : "Blessed be he who has imparted of his wisdom to those who fear him(ברוך אשר חלק מחכמתו ליריאיו). The sense seems to be the same when the 4th benediction in the Prayer of 18 Bened., usually חונן הדעת, is called חונן חכמה in bBer., 33a.

[290] Cf. the instances in Str.-B., I, 974 f.; II, 353 f., and esp. S. Dt., 37 (76a) on 11:10 (cf. Moore, I, 266); 309 (134a) on 32:6; 317 (135b) on 32:14; Moore, III, 92, n. 32. The fact that the shekinah is also in view in bibl. ref. to wisdom in the Rabb. tradition (esp. in the Midrashim) is stressed by Jaeger, 94-96, who also pts. (97 f.) to the charismatic nature and homiletical character of Rabb. wisdom.

[291] Cf. Moore, I, 266-269. The Rabb. take אמון in Prv. 8:30 as אומן == "masterbuilder," so Gn. r., 1, cf. Str.-B., II, 356 (with many other examples, e.g., Ab., 3, 14 : The Torah of God is God's instrument in the creation of the world). Another v. on which there is much comment is Prv. 3:19 (Moore, I, 268).

[292] E.g., Lv. r., 11, 3 on 9:1; cf. Moore, I, 265. Cf. Nu. r., 10, 1 on 6:2 : "The words of the Torah are marble pillars because they are the pillars of the world" (Jer. 33:25).

[293] E.g., Lv. r., 25, 1 on 19:23 and Nu. r., 5, 8 on 4:19 (with ref. to Prv. 3:18; 4:22).

[294] E.g., Nu. r., 4, 13 on 4:5; 13, 17 on 7:24 f.; 14, 4 on 7:48; Cant. r. on 1:3 (with ref. to Prv. 8:15 f.).

[295] E.g., Gn. r., 35, 3 on 9:16; Nu. r., 6, 1 on 4:22; 10, 4 on 6:2 (with ref. to Prv. 3:14 f.; 8:11).

[296] E.g., Nu. r., 2, 3 on 2:2; 13, 15 f. on 7:18 (with ref. to Prv. 9:5).

[297] Gn. r., 17, 5 on 2:21 cf. 44, 17 on 15:12 (Str.-B., III, 672).

[298] Cf. already Bar., 4, 4 : "Blessed are we, Israel, for what is well-pleasing to God is known to us."

[299] Cf. e.g., bQid., 49b : "Ten kab (measures) of wisdom came down into the world; the land of Israel received nine and the whole world only one."

[300] Cf., e.g., the contest for greater wisdom between R. Joshua bHananiah (2nd cent,) and

direct personification. This academic judgment, which seeks to enclose the pertinent detailed phenomena in the theory of a general, non-historical and abstract phase of religious development, has been unable to explain the actual texts themselves. On the other hand, detailed investigation of religion in the world surrounding Judaism has produced evidence of many wisdom deities similar to the figure of personal wisdom. To be sure, it has not succeeded in proving any specific connection. [301] But in view of the very non-Israelite features of personal wisdom, especially its union with God and man, justice is best done to the texts if one supposes that the rise of this idea is due to a particular religious influence. What is described theoretically as hypostatising can be better understood as the result of theological reaction in Israel, as the adaptation of alien myths to the specific structure of Israel's faith. In keeping is the observation that later, especially in the Hellenistic sphere of Judaism, the originally alien mythical features are not held so firmly in check and come out more clearly — a process which reaches its culmination in Philo, who, hesitantly and with strong reservations, speaks of the divinisation of man by union with wisdom (→ n. 238); this is not to be regarded as a much later Hellenistic intrusion but as the originally though hitherto more rigorously restrained trend of the ancient oriental influence which had been at work from the time of Prv.

In this connection it is especially worth noting [302] that a common wisdom myth lies behind various Jewish texts. This is most plainly to be seen in the section Eth. En. 42 which has been secondarily incorporated in the astronomical context of the work: "Since wisdom found no place where she could dwell, a place was allotted to her in heaven. When wisdom came to make her dwelling among the children of men and found no dwelling, wisdom returned to her place and took her seat among the angels. When iniquity burst its bounds, she found those who did not seek her, and came down amongst them, (as welcome) as rain in the desert and dew on a thirsty land." [303] There is here an open reference to the futile descent of heavenly wisdom and her resigned ascent. The only trace of Jewish editing is the name of her evil opponent, i.e., wickedness. More strongly integrated into the theology of Jewish apocalyptic are the open allusions to the same myth in Eth. En. 94:5 f. cf. 98:3; 93:8; [304] 4 Esr. 5:9 f.; [305] S. Bar. 48:33-36. [306] But many statements in the wisdom tradition patently have the myth as their background. The preaching of wisdom in Prv. 1:20-33 may easily be fitted into the mythical

---

the wise of the Athenaeum, bBek., 8b-9a : To the initial warning of the emperor : "But they are wise," the rabb. laconically opposes : "We are wiser than they," 8b. Cf. bTamid., 32a-b; bNidda, 69b-70b. But from the days of the Maccabees there was also resolute rejection of Gk. wisdom, and even hostility, e.g., bBQ, 82b (Str.-B., I, 493) : "Cursed be the man who teaches his son Gk. wisdom (חכמה יונית)," cf. bMen., 64b and bSota, 49b. On the attitude to Gk. wisdom as a whole cf. Str.-B., IV, 405-414.

[301] On the various theories concerning the origin of personal wisdom → 490, 16 ff. and cf. also Köster, 595.

[302] Bultmann Hintergrund, 6-23; cf. Albright, op. cit. (→ n. 177), 282 f.

[303] Cf. in Albright, 283 the ref. to an Aram. Achiqar logion : "Wisdom is from the gods, and to the gods is she precious; for ever her kingdom is fixed in heaven, for the lord of the holy ones (i.e., the gods of heaven) hath raised her." AOT, 498, and bibl., 457, n. 54.

[304] The ascent of wisdom is fused here with the rapture of Elijah.

[305] Cf. 4 Esr. 5:1, and the same of "truth" in 14:17.

[306] Cf. S. Bar. 14:8 f.; 75:1-6, also Eth. En. 84:2 ff. On Mt. 23:37-39 par. 34-36 → 515, 16 ff. Cf. also the late testimony in Hbr. En. 3-7 on the removal of the shekinah from the earth, esp. 5:13; 6:3.

situation of wisdom which comes to seek a dwelling and men and which then returns in resignation. Above all, however, the wisdom song in Sir. 24 is to be interpreted against this background. Here we read first of the pre-existence of wisdom (3-6), then of her search for a resting-p.:·· c·. earth (7), and then of God referring her to Israel as an inheritance where she finds a permanent abode (8-12). This time there is no resigned ascent; the author is thinking of the Law (Sir. 24:23 → n. 257). Thus the first part of the myth is adopted in order to magnify the gift of the Law to Israel. [307] A similar witness from a later period is the preaching of wisdom in Bar. 3:9-4:4. Wisdom is hidden and inaccessible in principle, but in contrast it is sent to Israel, to which an urgent summons for repentance is addressed. Here, too, wisdom is construed as the Law, 4:1. One may at least conjecture that the myth finally spoke of the few elect who found access to the wisdom which had everywhere been rejected on earth. [308] Thus the Israelite referring of wisdom to the Law is to be regarded as an adaptation of this final section of the myth. This would explain the absence of the idea from the corresponding Jewish texts, while on the other hand a smooth connection may be made with the other non-Israelite ideas of revelation which against the background of the fundamental hiddenness of wisdom try to show that the knowledge of wisdom may still be imparted to the few elect by union with her. We thus find a single, harmonious complex of ideas which are alien to the faith of Israel, which only with difficulty, and with varying degrees of consistency, could be adjusted to its structure, but which were then taken up and characteristically worked out especially in Gnosticism.

D. Gnosticism.

In almost all Gnostic witnesses of the most diverse nature and origin the figure of Σοφία plays an essential role. Indeed, one must regard the Sophia myth as one of the few structural elements common to Gnosticism and hence constitutive of it. In Gnosticism Σοφία is everywhere of supernatural origin and divine nature. But it has fallen from its first heavenly estate and has to be redeemed out of the world as its prison. In this fate it is also a picture of the Gnostic, who through knowledge of its fall and redemption can himself be set free from his imprisonment in the world and restored to his true divine nature. In Gnosticism, then, wisdom in its prototypical form has the soteriological function of a revealer for the Gnostic in need of redemption. In this respect it has fused in part with the figure of the Gnostic primal man, whose fall and redemption is the theme of one branch of the Gnostic tradition.

1. The Odes of Solomon. Strikingly close to the image of personal חכמה in later Wisdom literature are the statements about "goodness" in O. Sol. 33. [309] Here goodness comes down to negate destruction with all its panoply, 33:1 f. She stands [310] in the

---

[307] Cf. the description of the blessed work of the Law as the "water of life" and "tree of life" in Sir. 24:13-17.

[308] Cf. esp. O. Sol. 33 → 509, 37 ff.

[309] So rightly Arvedson, 171 as against Boström, 27 f.

[310] In the first part of the hymn (1-5) a surprising pt. is that what is obviously the same figure of "goodness" is sometimes feminine (1:5) and sometimes masculine (2-4). Acc. to W. Bauer, Die Oden Salomos (1933), 65, n. b "he" is the redeemer "in whom goodness came down from above," cf. Ep. Apostolorum, 4 ff. (ed. C. Schmidt-J. Wajnberg, TU, 43 [1919],

midst of the world, [311] draws to herself all who will listen (33:3 f.), and preaches redemption to them as a spotless virgin (6-13), cf. Prv. 1:20-33. She seeks to bring them to her, to lead them out of destruction, and to make them wise in the ways of truth, 8. As God's goodness she says to them : "Listen to me and be redeemed," 10. He who puts her on will have incorruptibility in the new world, 12. The ascent of the redeemed to union with truth as their leader is depicted in 38:7, 15, where the mythical image of the ascent has the soteriological significance of a means of knowledge. [312]

2. The Gnosis of Simon. In what is perhaps the oldest form of Simonian Gnosticism [313] Simon proclaims himself to be the "supreme power" which as the father was originally joined in union with female ἔννοια, who then plunged into the depths and was held captive by the demons, but was then liberated and redeemed by the "supreme power" which came down from heaven in Simon. Fallen Ἔννοια is the image of the Gnostics, who receive redeeming γνῶσις through Simon by which they are freed from the power of angelic forces. [314] It is highly probable that this myth has close affinities to O. Sol. 33, 38 and thence to the Jewish wisdom myth. At the same time the two witnesses of O. Sol. on the one side and the ancient Simonian Gnosticism on the other are important links clarifying the connection between the Gnostic and the Jewish wisdom myths.

3. Barbeliognosis and the Gnostic of Irenaeus. This connection may be seen esp. clearly in a part of the so-called Barbelio-Gnostic system handed down in part in Iren. Haer., I, 29. This is an early form of Valentinianism. It tells of the rise of the pleroma and then of the fall of Sophia (= Prunikos). [315] While all the other aeons found a σύζυγος, she sought one uncertainly, stretched downwards, and finally plunged into the depths, where she bore the demiurge, who in turn made powers and forces. Startled, Sophia fled and returned to the heights. This description is closely related to the wisdom myth in Eth. En. 42 (→ 508, 21 ff.). Sophia's search for a syzygy corresponds to the search of heavenly wisdom for a resting-place [316] on earth. It is presupposed in both texts that wisdom's original home is in heaven; her descent is also portrayed in both. The only difference is in the understanding of the principle hostile to wisdom. In Gnosticism a front of demonic powers replaces "unrighteousness."

43-51 → 511, 30 ff.). But one may adduce in comparison the pre-Valentinian systems in Iren. Haer., I, 29 f. where the male redeemer and female wisdom, united in a syzygy, come down to redeem. Cf. Wilckens Weisheit, 136-139.

[311] "And he did not appear as a wicked one," 33:4. Behind this there probably lies the Gnostic idea of a changing of the descending redeemer into the figure of an archon, cf. Wilckens Weisheit, 137, n. 4.

[312] Cf. also O. Sol. 17:22 f.; 41:11-16. On the soteriological significance of the idea of the syzygy cf. 42:18 : "We too may be redeemed with thee, for thou art our redeemer." Cf. also 2:2-8 (on this Iren. Haer., I, 30, 12); 5:15; 17:14 f.; 42:8. Cf. also the Mandaean passage Lidz. Liturg., 38 : "Thou (Manda d'Haije) camest down and didst cause us to dwell at the springs of life. Thou didst pour into us and fill us with thy wisdom, understanding and goodness. Thou didst show us the way on which thou didst come from the house of life. On it we will tread the path of true believing men so that our spirit and soul may dwell in the skina of life and be clothed with splendour and covered with light."

[313] In analysis of the various traditions in Iren. Haer., I, 23; Hipp. Ref., VI, 9-18; Just. Apol., I, 26, 1-3; Dial., 120; Ac. 8:9 f. cf. Haenchen, 316-350, also H. Schlier, "Das Denken d. frühchr. Gnosis" in Nt.liche Stud. f. R. Bultmann² (1957), 67-78.

[314] Simon's disciples honoured him as the "supreme power" and soon fused the redeemer myth with the Samaritan legend of Simon and Helena. The witness of Ac. (8:9 f.) shows that the form of Simon was christianised fairly early. Cf. G. Kretschmar, "Zur religionsgeschichtlichen Einordnung d. Gnosis," Ev. Theol., 13 (1953), 357-360. On Satornilus cf. also Schlier, op. cit. (→ n. 313), 78-81, and on him and Menander Quispel Anthropos, 199 f., who also tries to show that here the first stage of Gnosticism may be understood as a sophia myth with as yet no redeemer, ibid., 202, cf. 233 f.

[315] Iren. Haer., I, 29, 4. She is also called πνεῦμα ἅγιον.

[316] ἀνάπαυσις is also in Gnosticism a common expression for the completion of redemption or the establishment of the aeons and Gnostics.

Closely akin to the Barbeliote system is that of the so-called Gnostics in Iren. Haer., I, 30. Here, too, there is ref. to a fall of Sophia-Prunikos and her incarceration in the world of demonic power. By virtue of her nature as light she can free herself and mount up again to heaven, but portions of the substance of light remain caught, and she works for their redemption in conflict with her son Jaldabaoth and his crew, I, 30, 4 ff. She constitutes the ogdoad above the 7 zones of demons and seeks to impart knowledge of their origin to her people, counteracting the measures taken by Jaldabaoth to bind the rope of light to his sphere. [317] Finally at her request the supreme mother sends Christ as redeemer, and he, hidden in the form of demons, comes down through the 7 zones, unites with his sister Σοφία, [318] and with her becomes the one figure of Jesus Christ (Iren. Haer., I, 30, 12), who conceals his nature on earth, is crucified by the demons, but in virtue of his nature as light ascends up again on high, and draws the fastened rope of light to himself, so that the work of redemption moves on steadily to its completion.

4. The Gnostic in Plotinus. The system fiercely attacked by Plotinus (Enn., II, 9, 10 → 475, 17 ff.) must have been much the same : "They claim that the soul falls and with it a certain 'wisdom' — whether the soul makes it do this, or the cause comes from 'wisdom,' or the two are identical ; other souls fell with them and as 'members of wisdom' (μέλη τῆς σοφίας) have been clothed (ἐνδῦναι) with (human) bodies ; but that on account of which the others fell will not herself come down again, will not, as it were, fall, but will simply lighten the darkness." What is meant here is naturally the deliverance of Σοφία and her redemptive activity in relation to the seed which has fallen further into matter and been banished by the demiurge into bodies, as briefly recounted by Plotinus.

5. Coptic Gnostic Texts. The two systems in Iren. Haer., I, 29 f. are obviously dependent on a form of the Gnostic Sophia myth such as in found in the Coptic Gnostic texts of Cod. Berolinensis, 8502, esp. the Apocryphon of John and the Sophia of Jesus Christ. [319] Here, too, we read of the redemption of Gnostics by Christ in union with the wisdom redeemed by Him. "But this is what she (Sophia) did in the world (κόσμος): she established her posterity." [320] The redeemer is the union of the male σωτήρ and female σοφία. [321] In a later degenerate form we find the same myth in Pistis Sophia, I, 29-II, 82. There is an interesting earlier variant in Ep. Apostolorum. [322] This describes how Christ in His soteriological descent, putting on the wisdom of the Father and the

---

[317] Iren. Haer., I, 30, 9-11. Cf. the closeness to the work of wisdom in Wis. 10 → 500, 3 ff.

[318] Here we find the union motif : et descendentem Christum in hunc mundum induisse primum sororem suam Sophiam et exultasse utrosque refrigerantes super invicem; et hoc esse sponsum et sponsam definiunt, Iren. Haer., I, 30, 12.

[319] Cf. W. Till, TU, 60 (1955). On the literary dependence of Iren. Haer., I, 29 on the Apocr. of Jn. cf. C. Schmidt, "Irenäus u. seine Quelle in adv. Haer., I, 29," Philotesia f. P. Kleinert (1907), 317-336. The Sophia myth does not occur in the Ev. Veritatis from Cod. Jung (ed. M. Malinine, C. H. Puech, G. Quispel [1956]). This simply offers a specifically Gnostic soteriological doctrine of knowledge corresponding to the later Valentinian doctrine of redemption in which the myth debouches. It is thus a mistake to conclude from the absence of the myth here that there was an earlier non-mythical stage of Gnosticism. The term σοφία is rare in Ev. Veritatis (cf. 23:18 f. of that of the Father, cf. 31:16 ff. as a gift of redemption to Gnostics); σοφός occurs only twice (19:21, 26 : those who are truly wise in contrast to those who merely seem to be so).

[320] Apocr. of Jn. 76:2-5 cf. 75:10-13. The revealing work of Sophia is summed up in 53:10-17 : It enlightens all creation on the origin of its blemish and shows it its ascent. In this γνῶσις they become wiser than Jaldabaoth, 71:14 - 72:2 cf. 52:8-11, like wisdom itself, 71:15 f.

[321] Sophia of Jesus Christ 102:15-103:9. Sophia as Father-Mother, Apocr. of Jn. 75:10 ff.; she sends γνῶσις Sophia Jes. Chr. 104:7-106:9. On this whole matter cf. Wilckens Weisheit, 126-131.

[322] Ep. Apostolorum, 4 ff. On the Gnostic character of the passage cf. Wilckens Weisheit, 131 f.; Schmidt, 283 and G. Kretschmar, Stud. z. frühchr. Trinitätstheol. (1956), 49 do not think it is Gnostic.

power (δύναμις) of His might, and thus unrecognised by the demons, traverses the demonic heavens and by His ascent completes the work of redemption to the glorifying of the Father. At this pt. we are close to 1 C. 2.

6. The Valentinian. The most explicit form of the same myth is transmitted in the Valentinian system. [323] This depicts the story of Sophia from the establishment of the heavenly pleroma, her fall, and her final reunion with her σύζυγος. The same process is repeated on the lower level in the destiny of her image, the lesser Sophia (= Achamoth = הַחָכְמָה), who is established again by Christ at the centre, the ogdoad. But her fall, like that of the higher Sophia, initiates a further stage in the catastrophe which in rapid sequence, and in an increasing alienation of the parts of her being separated from her, leads to a process of disastrous deterioration. Hence the world arises at three levels, the pneumatic, psychic and hylic. Men are created by the demiurge and in their souls Sophia scatters her heavenly seed, which grows in them and is the real cause of their redemptive gnosis. At the last Sophia is fetched back from the middle place to the pleroma and restored to her σύζυγος, and the pneumatic seed redeemed by her, Gnostics, may, like her, associate in the nymphon of the angels as their σύζυγοι. Here lesser Sophia is obviously the mythological prototype of the Gnostic, but she is also the one who steadily promotes the redemption of Gnostics by mediating knowledge to them. The presupposition of redemption is likeness of essence between the Gnostic and Sophia (and between Sophia and her higher mother and the other aeons of the pleroma). This is manifested in the steadfast striving of Sophia for the redemption of her seed. The completion of redemption is the full identity of redeeming Sophia with the redeemed. This finds mythological expression in the idea of the syzygy, but it is worked out radically for the first time in the doctrine of redemption which is based on the myth and which has γνῶσις as its theme. [324]

Very closely akin to the Valentinian doctrine of Sophia are the two epicleses in the Acts of Thomas. In 50 (166, 7 ff.) there has been interpolated into a eucharistic epiclesis to Jesus an epiclesis to a female deity, the hidden mother and companion of the male aeon associated with her. [325] Prayer is made to her for the revelation of hidden mysteries. She thus has the function of a revealer and redeemer. [326] The same applies in respect of the second epiclesis in 27 (142, 7 f.), though in the last petition a male deity replaces the mother who is invoked first. This is the third emissary of the Manichees. She is obviously united with him as her syzygos in the same way as the third emissary of Manicheeism is united with the virgin of light. [327] The two together bring redeeming γνῶσις

---

[323] Iren. Haer., I, 1-7 (cf. Epiph. Haer., 31, 9-32); I, 21 : Hipp. Ref., VI, 29-36; Cl. Al. Exc. Theod., 29-68; Epiph. Haer., 30 f. Cf. Müller, 179-228; Foerster, 3-101; Jonas Gnosis, I, 362-375; F. M. M. Sagnard, "La gnose valentinienne et le témoignage de St. Irenée," Études de philosophie médiévale, 36 (1947); G. Quispel, "The Original Doctrine of Valentine," Vigiliae Christianae, 1 (1947), 43-73 (reconstruction of the original text). Wilckens Weisheit, 100-111.

[324] Cf. esp. Iren. Haer., I, 6, 1. The active soteriological function of Sophia as revealer of γνῶσις is expressed particularly clearly in Hipp. Ref., VI, 36, 2 : ἔγνω (sc. the demiurge) διδαχθεὶς ὑπὸ τῆς Σοφίας τὸν Κρείττονα· κατηχήθη γὰρ ὑπ᾽ αὐτῆς καὶ ἐμυήθη καὶ ἐδιδάχθη τὸ μέγα τοῦ Πατρὸς καὶ τῶν αἰώνων μυστήριον. Similarly the content of this revelation in Basilides is σοφία, Hipp. Ref., VII, 26,. It is able to discharge this function because by origin it is the εἰκὼν τοῦ πατρός, Iren. Haer., I, 5, 1. Cf. also the two formulae by which ascending souls ward off the powers, ibid., I, 21, 5 (cf. Epiph. Haer., 36, 3, 1-6), also those of the Marcosians, ibid., I, 13, 6.

[325] In analysis cf. Bornkamm Mythos, 90 f.

[326] Cf. also Act. Phil. 115 (46). Here wisdom is the daughter of the father (line 2) and also the sister (line 6) of the Gnostic, cf. Bornkamm Mythos, 97 f.

[327] Cf. Bornkamm Mythos, 100 f. On the fusing of the Manichaean emissary and Valentinian Sophia cf. also Bousset Gnosis, 74-77. Jesus is also equated with the virgin of light, cf. Reitzenstein Buch d. Herrn, 52 f.; Waldschmidt-Lentz, 38, 64, 97-111 (Fr. H, line 16d, 44d, 75a, 76b), 126 (M, 10).

which is also wisdom.[328] The marriage of Sophia with the Father, in which Gnostics may participate, is hymned in the wisdom song of Act. Thom. 6 f. (109 f.).[329] Once again the marriage is simply a mythological symbol of perfected gnosis.

7. Manicheeism. A direct line again runs from the Act. Thom. to the Manichaean texts in which Jesus often seems to be equated with wisdom. In the Chinese hymn scroll of London wisdom is often a predicate of Jesus.[330] On the one side this is closely connected with the relationship of the Manichaean envoy and Sophia, on the other it is closely connected with the equation of Jesus and the virgin of light, who for her part is again Sophia.[331] Thus Jesus can be invoked directly as the "compassionate mother, wisdom."[332] In the Coptic Manichaean Psalms and Homilies, however, σοφία is for the most part a term for Mani's doctrine of revelation. Thus Mani says : "I have no master and no teacher from whom I might have learned this wisdom ... but when I received it, I received it from God through his angel ... For this whole world had gone astray and fallen into error ; it had fallen away (wickedly) from the wisdom of God, the Lord of all. But I have received it from him and revealed the way of truth in the midst of the cosmos, so that the souls of these many may be saved."[333] A liturgical doxology invokes this as "the true wisdom which instructs souls," also invoking "light in the highest," "mighty strength," and the Father, the Son, and the Holy Ghost. This truth also seems to be identical with the "compassionate mother" who is mentioned in the same series and who "gives her milk for us."[334] We are reminded of the Jewish wisdom myth by a passage in the Homilies :[335] "O wisdom of greatness, O panoply of the apostle of light ! Whither hast thou wandered ... and whence comest thou ? In what place art thou to be found ?" The "wisdom of the living Spirit" builds the new heaven,[336] just as Chokmah is the wisdom of the Creator of the world.

To sum up, one may conclude a. that one and the same wisdom myth may be clearly discerned in all the Gnostic texts which have been adduced and this is always a basic element in the system. Wisdom is a heavenly being who has fallen from the realm of her origin and is redeemed again from her lost estate. She has also become the author of the fall of men and of their redemption. To this extent she is a mythical symbol of the Gnostic, who in knowing the nature and destiny of wisdom must also come to see that he is identical with her. This process of

---

[328] Bornkamm Mythos, 102. Thus, e.g., in Act. Thom. 132 (239 f.) Jesus is equated with Sophia as His δύναμις. Act. Phil. 144 (84, 9-11) says : κύριε 'Ιησοῦ Χριστέ ... ὁ σοφίσας ἡμᾶς ἐν τῇ σοφίᾳ σου καὶ δοὺς ἡμῖν τὴν σὴν σύνεσιν. Cf. also Act. Phil. 77 (30, 17 f.); Act. Thom. 85 f. (200-202). Similarly on πραΰτης.

[329] On this cf. R. Reitzenstein, Hell. Wundererzählungen (1906), 134 and 150. Bornkamm Mythos, 68-81; Schlier Kirche, 56 f.; Käsemann Leib, 74; Wilckens Weisheit, 115-118.

[330] Cf. Waldschmidt-Lentz, 28. 97 ff. (→ n. 327). Cf. the Manichaean blessings : "Through the power of the Father, through the blessing of the Mother, and through the wisdom of the Son." ibid., 126. Jesus is "the great sage of beneficent light" (62), "power" and "wisdom full of life" (105, 64, 68). Cf. also Reitzenstein Buch d. Herrn d. Grösse, 48.

[331] Cf. the Turkish Fr. T II D 176, Waldschmidt-Lentz, 35, also Kephalaia, VII (ed. C. Schmidt [1940] 35).

[332] Waldschmidt-Lentz, 37.

[333] Manich. Homilies, 47, 7-16 (ed. H. J. Polotsky [1934]). Cf. also esp. a passage from the Manich. Psalms, A Manichaean Psalm-Book, II (ed. C. R. C. Allberry [1938]), 86, 23-26: "I have constantly practised (μελετᾶν) in the holy wisdom (σοφία), which has opened the eyes of my soul unto the light of the glory and made me see the things that are hidden and that are visible, the things of the abyss and the things of the height." On σοφία as "doctrine of revelation," even in many cases a written book, cf. Manich. Homilies, 20, 20; 23, 2; 28, 9 f.; 33, 17 and 22; 43, 16 f.; 75, 25; 80, 16.

[334] Manich. Psalm-Book, 190, 17-24.

[335] Manich. Homil., 25, 10.

[336] Manich. Psalm-Book, 144, 21 f.

knowledge is said to correspond to that of her destiny. As wisdom helps man to knowledge, she has the decisive redemptive function.

One may also conclude b. that it is no less clear that this Gnostic wisdom myth is closely akin to the later Jewish wisdom myth. There are at least good grounds for conjecturing a common historical origin for the two conceptions of wisdom. [337] But there is probably a direct connection as well. In its basic structure the Gnostic Sophia myth has its roots in the Jewish myth, and the closely associated Gnostic doctrine of redemption (redemption as union with the wisdom which mediates the knowledge of revelation) has its roots in the corresponding Jewish doctrine of revelation. This finding is of decisive importance for an understanding of the σοφία statements in the NT inasmuch as we have here a historical connection in the light of which the Jewish elements in these statements may be consistently understood in their fusion with the corresponding Gnostic ideas.

E. The New Testament.

1. Traditional Anthropological Usage.

In the OT-Jewish or consciously "biblical" linguistic stratum we find two notes on Jesus as a growing boy in the Lucan infancy stories : Already as a child "he developed and grew strong in ever-increasing wisdom, [338] and the grace of God was on him," Lk. 2:40, cf. 2:52. The description is intentionally modelled on OT descriptions of the growth of, divinely endowed children, cf. 1 S. 2:26. σοφία here epitomises a pious manner of life which shapes the character and which finds expression in early and astonishing knowledge of the Law → 498, 4 ff. [339] Luke portrays Stephen similarly in Ac. 6:3, 10 except that here πνεῦμα is used as well as σοφία, so that his wisdom of speech is shown as a divine gift. Wisdom is manifested here in theologically informed and irresistible utterance, Ac. 6:10. Luke (Lk. 21:15) also interprets the saying in Mk. 13:11 and par. along these lines. [340] Joseph (Ac. 7:10) is also described in this way in his position in relation to Pharaoh. [341]

According to Mk. 6:2 (cf. Mt. 13:54) it is the wisdom of Jesus which along with His mighty acts (δυνάμεις) [342] causes astonishment among the people (ἐξεπλήσσοντο). Neither the wisdom nor the acts can be reconciled with the carpenter's son who was thought to be well known in His own town, Mk. 6:3. The context shows that σοφία refers to Jesus' teaching in the synagogue. This is given to Him by God (δοθεῖσα τούτῳ, cf. the ἐξουσία of Jesus in Mt. 7:29), but

---

[337] So already Bousset Gnosis, 260-273.

[338] The koine group and Θ pl add πνεύματι. Cf. Ac. 6:3, 10.

[339] Note the context Lk. 2:40-52, which is brought under the key-word σοφία by the two comprehensive statements in v. 40, 52 → VI, 713, 8 ff.

[340] Cf. also Lk. 12:11 f., which says that Christians can triumph even when brought to trial through the teaching of the πνεῦμα ἅγιον.

[341] "He gave him grace and wisdom before Pharaoh, king of Egypt." Ac. 7:22 refers to Moses' education in "all the wisdom of the Egyptians," cf. Philo Vit. Mos., I, 23. The wisdom of the Egyptians was proverbial not only in Israel (→ 479, 20 ff.) but also in Greece, esp. in the Hell. age (Plut. → 501, 7 ff.), cf. esp. the material in A. Wiedermann, Herodots zweites Buch mit sachlichen Erläuterungen hsgg. (1890), 453 f.

[342] For σοφία and δύναμις together cf. 1 C. 1:24, also already Is. 11:2 of the Messiah and Job 12:13 of God, cf. Loh. Mk., ad loc., 111, n. 3.

in accordance with current experiences in the Church the Evangelist interprets it as charismatic utterance (cf. 1 C. 12:8; Col. 1:28; 3:16), just as the δυνάμεις are also spiritual. [343] In the traditional image of the Jewish teacher of the Law Jesus is for him the prototype of all Church charismatics.

2. The Logia.

In the Logia source we find two threats against "this generation" (Mt. 23:34-36; Lk. 11:49-51) and against Jerusalem (Mt. 23:37-39; Lk. 13:34 f.), [344] which both in form and also in content are plainly connected with the eschatological σοφία sayings in Jewish apocalyptic and hence also with the apocalyptically adapted wisdom myth → 508, 20 ff. Mt. has preserved the sequence of the logia [345] while Lk. has preserved the introduction to the threat against "this generation" (→ VI, 835, 7 ff.); διὰ τοῦτο καὶ ἡ σοφία τοῦ θεοῦ εἶπεν (Lk. 11:49)). In the Logia source both sayings are thus wisdom sayings on the lips of Jesus. But this means that relatively early it presented the idea that Jesus is the wisdom of God. The first logion refers to the persecution of the "prophets, wise men and scribes" [346] whom wisdom has sent. [347]

The wisdom myth stands even more plainly behind the threat against Jerusalem: As the wisdom which has come down from heaven, which seeks a home (Eth. En. 42 → 508, 22 ff.) and which preaches (Prv. 1:20-33 → 491, 22 ff.), Jesus wanted to gather the inhabitants of Jerusalem around Him, but they "would not," so that judgment now hangs over them. [348] In the judgment rejection of wisdom means destruction for its despisers. [349] Those who now "would not" will be left alone in their ravaged house. From now on they will no longer see Jesus until it is said in the eschatological revelation of the Son of Man: "Blessed is he that cometh in the name of the Lord." But then it will be too late. [350]

---

[343] Cf., e.g., Mt. 7:22; Ac. 6:8; 2 C. 12:12. Note the association of λόγος ἀληθείας and δύναμις θεοῦ in 2 C. 6:7, also λόγος σοφίας in 1 C. 12:8 and ἐνεργήματα δυνάμεων in 12:10, cf. also Ac. 4:33.

[344] On this cf. Bultmann Trad., 119-121, also A. v. Harnack, Sprüche u. Reden Jesu (1907), 119; W. Bousset, Kyrios Christos² (1921), 51, n. 3; Davies, 155 f.; Reitzenstein Buch d. Herrn d. Grösse, 41-59; H. H. Schaeder in R. Reitzenstein-H. H. Schaeder, Stud. zum antiken Synkretismus aus Iran u. Griechenland (1926), 232-236.

[345] So Bultmann Trad., 120 (older bibl. n. 2), though cf. W. G. Kümmel, Verheissung u. Erfüllung³ (1956), 73-75; E. Haenchen, "Matthäus 23," ZThK, 48 (1951), 56 f.

[346] On the identity of σοφοί and γραμματεῖς → 505, 22 ff. On the slaying of the prophets cf. H. J. Schoeps, "Die jüd. Prophetenmorde," Aus frühchr. Zeit (1950), 126-143. It is linked here with the apocal. motif of the rejection of wisdom.

[347] Cf. Wis. 7:27: κατὰ γενεὰς εἰς ψυχὰς ὁσίας μεταβαίνουσα φίλους θεοῦ καὶ προφήτας κατασκευάζει. On this cf. Bultmann Hintergrund, 15-17.

[348] Here, as often in the NT, the idea of judgment has the same structure as the early OT idea of the fateful human act, cf. K. Koch, "Gibt es ein Vergeltungsdogma im AT?" ZThK, 52 (1955), 1-42.

[349] Cf. Prv. 1:24 ff.: "Because I have called, and ye refused . . . I also will laugh at your calamity . . . Then shall they call upon me, but I will not answer; they shall seek me early, but they shall not find me . . ." Cf. also → 491, 24 ff. and 507, 20 ff. for further instances.

[350] This is the point (cf. Mt. 24:37 ff. par. 7:22 f.; 8:11 f.; Lk. 13:25 f.). For Mt. 23:39 as a Chr. addition in Q cf. Haenchen, 57. It is hardly likely that in the wisdom saying wisdom suddenly changes into the figure of the Messiah (Reitzenstein Buch d. Herrn, 43) or is thought to come along with the Messiah (Bultmann Trad., 121). But v. 39 might well be a Chr. interpretation of the idea of judgment in the original logion.

The sense is the same in the Q logion in Mt. 11:16-19 / Lk. 7:31-35. Here this generation is compared to a group of capricious children at play. Both John and Jesus come to it in vain ; they reject both. Yet in the approaching judgment wisdom is justified [351] in virtue of her works (Mt. 11:19) [352] or on the part of all her children (Lk. 7:35). [353] Here, then, John and Jesus, like Jesus and the prophets in Mt. 23:34-36, 37-39 and par., are regarded as the messengers of wisdom. [354]

The double threat from the Logion source in Mt. 12:42 / Lk. 11:31 [355] may be cited in the same connection. On the Day of Judgment the "queen of the south" (cf. 1 K. 10:1-13) will rise up as a witness against "this generation." She "came from the uttermost parts of the earth to hear the wisdom of Solomon ; and, behold, a greater than Solomon is here." The reference is to God's wisdom on the lips of Jesus. Here, too, the rejection of wisdom by "this generation" is presupposed.

Wisdom motifs may also be found in a passage which has not yet been explained historically, [356] namely, Mt. 11:25-30 / Lk. 10:21 f., esp. in the third logion in the group in Mt. 11:28-30 (→ V, 992, 40 ff.), which is not in Lk. [357] The union concept stands behind the metaphor of the yoke → 498, 26 ff. [358] Rest as a gift of wisdom and blessing of revelation is often found in wisdom texts and apocalyptic, also Gnostic, references → 501, 23 ff. [359] Above all, however, the form of the saying corresponds to the preaching

---

[351] δικαιωθῆναι here does not mean "condemned" (as against Schl. Mt., 374 f. on 11:19) but eschatologically "justified". It is the pass. of the factitive or declarative act. δικαιόω = צדק [Katz].

[352] The Western text reading τέκνων has fairly certainly been taken from Lk. 7:35 (→ II, 214, n. 13).

[353] The reading ἔργων (א) comes from Mt. 11:19. πάντων does not occur in D sy etc. and is put back in the koine MSS. The difference in Mt. and Lk. shows that the pt. of the conclusion is that at the end wisdom will be justified in relation to her activity (Mt.) or in the circle of those who have remained true to her in contrast to the mass of despisers, cf. Arvedson, 209 f. M. Dibelius, Die urchr. Überlieferung v. Johannes dem Täufer (1911), 19 takes ἀπό in the sense of "apart from" (מן exclusively, not comparatively, cf. Bl.-Debr. § 247a in the Amer. edit. of P. Katz); in this case the ref. would be to an eschatological rehabilitation of wisdom as distinct from her children, who have denied her.

[354] Cf. again Wis. 7:27 and the further material in Bultmann Hintergrund, 15-19.

[355] In Q it stands alongside the par. saying about the sign of Jonah, Mt. 12:41/Lk. 11:32 and is materially related to the Woes on the Galilean cities, Mt. 11:21-24/Lk. 10:13-15; cf. Bultmann Trad., 118.

[356] Following Norden, 277-308, Dibelius, 281-284 has stressed the Hell. character of the concept of revelation in Mt. 11:25-30. Arvedson (esp. 107 f.) tries to show that the passage is a mystery liturgy for the enthronement of Christ. On the other hand Bultmann Trad., 171 f. finds the Hell. vocabulary of revelation only in v. 27, and thinks v. 25 f. is an original Aram. saying from the primitive Palestinian community. Dupont, 58-62 thinks v. 27 is a Jewish and specifically an apocal. logion. The section is regarded as an authentic saying of Jesus by W. Grundmann, Jesus d. Galiläer u. d. Judt. (1940), 209-223; J. Bieneck, Sohn Gottes als Christusbezeichnung d. Synpt. (1951), 79-82; E. Stauffer, "Agnostos Christos : Joh. XI 24 u. d. Eschatologie d. vierten Ev., "The Background of the NT and Its Eschatology. Festschr. C. H. Dodd (1956), 295 f.; O. Cullmann, Christologie d. NT² (1958), 292-294.

[357] Norden, 277-308 thinks Mt. 11:25-30 is an originally three-membered composition corresponding to the fixed schema of Jewish Hell. revelation sayings. Dibelius, 279-284 agrees, assuming that the three logia were already a unity in the source (280, n. 1), though he believes vv. 28-30 were originally an independent saying. But Bultmann Trad., 171 f. thinks Mt. was the first to associate the three different logia. Nowadays the original autonomy of vv. 28-30 is almost universally accepted.

[358] Cf. Sir. 6:30; 51:17, 26, v. Arvedson, 174-200. Rabb. usage speaks of the "yoke" of the Law, cf. Str.-B., I, 608-610.

[359] Cf. Dibelius, 281, n. 2. Arvedson, 201-209 finds a union motif here.

of wisdom in self-commendation. [360] Here Jesus comes forth like wisdom, summons the "weary and heavy-laden" to Himself, [361] and promises them "rest for their souls." [362] The first logion in v. 25 f. speaks of a special revelation of the Father to the νήπιοι, whereas He has concealed it from the σοφοί and συνετοί → III, 973, 40 ff. Understanding of the saying depends on an original Aramaic, the historical explanation, and an original connection, or not, with v. 27 f. The possibility of an original Aram. form is not to be dismissed forthwith, [363] although in Jewish apocal. lit. there are no instances of a concealment of apocal. revelation from the wise and prudent. It is in fact the wise to whom the revelation is imparted, so that they have knowledge. Sometimes the LXX speaks of a preferring of the νήπιοι, [364, 365] but in these ref. we do not find the contrast with the "wise and prudent" which is basic to Mt. 11:25 f. Materially close is 1 C. 1:19 f., though νήπιος is used *sensu malo* in 1 C. 3:1. In Mt. 11:25 the content of the revelation is simply indicated by ταῦτα and αὐτά, though one may not infer from this that Mt. is simply quoting from some other literary source. [366] It is most probable that v. 27 originally belonged to the logion, this being suggested by the same abs. use of πατήρ and υἱός. If so, the content of revelation is the knowledge of the Son, or of the Father through the Son, and this revealed soteriological knowledge of the Revealer finds many par. both in later Jewish Wisdom lit. and also in Gnosticism. There is also good ground for regarding the whole section, including the third saying in vv. 28-30, as a unity. The Revealer is speaking of revelation itself. This can be controlled neither by those who receive it (νήπιοι) nor by those whom it passes by (σοφοί καὶ συνετοί). The Revealer is Himself the content of what is at first simply called revelation, and He calls His own to Himself. In this regard the passage is strikingly similar to Sir. 51. [367]

3. Paul.

a. The traditional anthropological usage occurs when Paul in relation to his missionary work describes himself as a "wise masterbuilder" who laid the foundation in Corinth (1 C. 3:10), or again when he demands that disputes in the community should be settled by those that are wise instead of in pagan courts (1 C. 6:5), cf. Jos. Ant., 11, 129 (→ 502, 19 f.). But Paul's question: "Is there not a wise man among you?" probably has a special ironic undertone in view of the controversy concerning the wisdom of the Corinthians in 1:18-3:21 → 519, 1 ff.

---

[360] Cf. esp. Prv. 1:20-33; 8:1-36; Sir. 24:19-22; 51:23-30; also O. Sol. 33 and later Corp. Herm., 7, 1 f.; 1, 27. For more Hell. material cf. Dibelius, 283 f., though also Bultmann Trad., 172. The two scholars agree in disputing any historical link between the idea of revelation in Jewish wisdom and that in Gnosticism.

[361] Cf. the equation of the חכמים and נמהרים in 1 QH 1:35.

[362] Bultmann Trad., 172 thinks the saying is a "direct quotation from a Jewish Wisdom writing." Cf. also E. Dinkler, "Jesu Wort vom Kreuztragen," *Nt.liche Stud. f. R. Bultmann zum 70. Geburtstag* (1957), 115-117.

[363] So Bultmann Trad., 172 (bibl. n. 3). Cf. also esp. M. Black, *An Aram. Approach to the Gospels and Acts*[2] (1957), 140 f.: reconstruction of a conjectural Aram. original.

[364] Esp. in some Ps. ψ 18:8; 114:6; 118:130. Wis. 10:21 says of wisdom that it "opens the mouth of the dumb καὶ γλώσσας νηπίων ἔθηκεν τρανάς," cf. also Sir. 3:19 (vl.): πολλοί εἰσιν ὑψηλοὶ καὶ ἐπίδοξοι, ἀλλὰ πραέσιν (ולענוים) ἀποκαλύπτει τὰ μυστήρια αὐτοῦ.

[365] On the other hand there is a similar thought in the Gnostic Ev. Veritatis (→ n. 319) 19:21-21:7: "There came the wise (σοφοί) in their own hearts... They hated him because they were not really wise. After these came the little children, whose is the knowledge of the Father... They knew, they were known, they were glorified, they glorified. In their hearts the living book was revealed..." "They receive this from the Father, they turn back to him...., 21:6 f.

[366] So Bultmann Trad., 172, Dibelius, 280, n. 4 adducing Mk. 11:28 and par., thinks ταῦτα is a matter of style; but in Mk. 11:28 it could easily refer to the miracles of Jesus, as the context shows, whereas there is no such concrete ref. to be seen in Mt. 11:25 f.

[367] Cf. Sir. 51:1-12: ἐξομολογήσομαί σοι, 51:13-22, description of the speaker's know-

b. In R. 11:33-36 [368] Paul concludes his great and, in the context of Romans, decisively important discussion of the history of the divine election (R. 9-11).

In form the section is hymnal. Three terms dominate it : πλοῦτος, σοφία, γνῶσις. All are related in the same way to βάθος, v. 33. They are expounded in reverse order in the three questions which follow in v. 34 f. [369] and which all bear the wisdom stamp : 1. "Who has known the mind of the Lord?" Answer : No one can measure the "knowledge of God," i.e., the secret of His election : ὦ βάθος γνώσεως θεοῦ. [370] But in Wisdom lit. this question is answered in the affirmative in relation to the person of wisdom. Wisdom was in God's immediate presence at the creation of the world (→ n. 215), knows all His secrets and plans, and also knows from eternity what is pleasing to Him. [371] Hence this question leads on at once to the second, which has in view the association with pre-existent wisdom : 2. τίς σύμβουλος αὐτοῦ ἐγένετο; Is. 40:13. [372] The answer which every man must give is : No one. But wisdom answers : ἡνίκα ἡτοίμαζεν τὸν οὐρανόν, συμπαρήμην αὐτῷ κτλ. Prv. 8:27: [373] ὦ βάθος σοφίας. 3. "Who hath first given to him, and it shall be recompensed unto him again?" [374] Answer : No one. Once again wisdom alone shares with her pupils the rich treasures of God which she possesses : [375] ὦ βάθος πλούτου.

Thus Paul, extolling the whole course of election in salvation history, expresses God's plan of salvation in wisdom terms and with wisdom ideas which are typical of Judaism in its description of the form and function of personal wisdom. For apocalyptic Judaism, however, the Law was the historically controllable demonstration of the divine plan of salvation, and keeping the Law was the guarantee of membership of the saved community (→ 503, 16 ff.). In contrast, Paul proclaims Christ as the "end of the law" (R. 10:4) and faith in Him as the only way to participation in salvation — a participation not under our own control (R. 10:9 f.). For Paul the criterion for being caught up in the historical process of election history and for membership of Israel as the saved community is πίστις ἐξ ἀκοῆς, ἡ δὲ ἀκοὴ διὰ ῥήματος Χριστοῦ (R. 10:17). In Paul's sense, then, the concluding wisdom sayings in R. 11:33-36 are to be vitally related, materially, to the function of Christ in salvation history. [376]

---

ledge of revelation; 51:23-30 : the revelation cry ἐγγίσατε πρός με, ἀπαίδευτοι. On this cf. Norden, 277-308; Dibelius, 279-284; Arvedson, 10 f., 82-94.

[368] On this cf. Norden, 240-250, esp. 243, n. 3; G. Harder, Pls. u. das Gebet (1936), 51-55; G. Bornkamm, "Der Lobpreis Gottes (R. 11:33-36)," Das Ende des Gesetzes² (1958), 70-73; Dupont, 91-93, 325.

[369] Cf. Bornkamm, op. cit. (→ n. 368), 72 f.

[370] Ibid., 72. On γνῶσις θεοῦ in the OT sense as the election grounded in the divine plan of history → I, 706, 16 ff., also Dupont, 51-104.

[371] Cf. esp. Wis. 6:15-21; 8:4, 9; 9:9-13, 16 f.

[372] Cf. Job 15:8; 11:7; Jer. 23:18.

[373] For further illustrations of the concept of wisdom as πάρεδρος θεοῦ and of her union with God corresponding to the union of wisdom as σύμβουλος (Wis. 8:9) with her pupils → 498, 25 ff.

[374] On the text, which diverges from the LXX, cf. Ltzm. R., ad loc.

[375] Cf. e.g., Wis. 7:11-14 (v. 13 πλοῦτος σοφίας); cf. Prv. 3:16; 8:18; Wis. 6:14 (vl.); 8:5, 18; Sir. 24:17. Θησαυροὶ σοφίας Prv. 2:4; 3:14; 8:21; Wis. 7:14; Sir. 1:25.

[376] That Paul is acquainted with Christological ideas which equate this function of Christ with that of personal wisdom may be seen from 1 C. 10:1-5. Here Christ is typologically the One who accompanies the people of Israel through the wilderness, and the same is said of wisdom in Wis. 10:17 f. Wis. 11:4 mentions the water from the rock (Ex. 17:6; Nu. 20:7-13), and Philo, too, regards this as the work of σοφία, Leg. All., II, 86 : ἡ γὰρ ἀκρότομος πέτρα ἡ σοφία τοῦ θεοῦ ἐστιν κτλ., also of the λόγος, Det. Pot. Ins., 115 ff.; Leg. All.,

c. There was, then, in primitive Christianity, as the Q logia also show (→ 515, 5 ff.), a σοφία Christology. [377] But it is also apparent in the important passage 1 C. 1 f. that Paul would not accept the particular form of this σοφία Christology which the theological ideas of his Corinthian church had obviously developed. [378] He calls the Corinthian doctrine σοφία λόγου (1:17) or λόγος καὶ σοφία (2:1) and πειθοῖ σοφίας λόγοι (2:4), and incisively contrasts it as such with the λόγος τοῦ σταυροῦ (1:17 f., 22-25; 2:2). This very pointed antithesis shows that in contesting the Corinthian doctrine Paul is attacking, not a particular form, but a specific content in their preaching by which the cross of Christ is made of none effect (1:17). [379] That is to say, Paul in 1 C. 1 f. is fighting a Christology which is diametrically opposed to his *theologia crucis*, which is for him the heart of Christian faith and Christian proclamation. In keeping, however, with the dialogical character which is typical of Paul's theological disputations is the fact that in 1 C. 2:6-16 he himself adopts the vocabulary and ideas of his opponents and is not afraid of the danger of using them in positive form as this is possible in the light of the preceding antithesis in 1:18-2:5. It is thus that we really learn what was understood by σοφία in Corinth. In spiritual and charismatic utterance (cf. 1 C. 12:8), [380] which was restricted in principle to the exclusive circle of the τέλειοι (2:6) and πνευματικοί, [381] there is reference to a wisdom which is "not of this aeon, nor of the archons of this aeon" (2:6), but θεοῦ ἐν μυστηρίῳ (2:7). This wisdom of God is described in 2:7 as a blessing of salvation wholly along the lines of Jewish apocalyptic, → 503, 18 ff. [382] It was previously concealed and has been prepared by God in heaven for our (eschatological) glorification. None of the archons knew it, for if they had "they would not have crucified the Lord of glory" (2:8). Here, then, the wisdom of God is obviously identical with the Lord of glory. In the background stands the widespread Gnostic idea of the descent of the Redeemer through the zones of the archons, His true form being concealed from them and made known only to His own people who

---

III, 162. On this cf. also Rer. Div. Her., 204 (on Ex. 14:20); Deus Imm., 155. On the concept of wisdom (or the λόγος) as a spring of water cf. Som., II, 242; Fug., 47 and 97. Rabb. exposition, Str.-B., III, 405-408.

[377] On this cf. Windisch, 220-234; Knox, 111-115; Cerfaux, 189-208; Schlier Eph., Exc. on 3:10 f. (162, n. 1). On the influence of Sophia Christology in the 2nd and 3rd cent. cf. Kretschmar, 27-61.

[378] On what follows cf. R. Bultmann, "Karl Barth, 'Die Auferstehung der Toten,' " *Glauben u. Verstehen,* I² (1954), 40-44, also Wilckens Weisheit, 5-96, 205-213.

[379] Cf. E. Peterson, "1 K. 1:18 f. und d. Thematik des jüd. Busstages," *Frühkirche, Judt. u. Gnosis* (1959), 44: "It should be noted that the whole section 1:18-31 is not merely contending against a false assertion of the λόγος in rhetorical technique but also against a different view of σοφία . . . It is plain that the problem of the cross and wisdom is much more important for Paul than the problem of the cross and eloquence, which is only marginal to the discussion." But cf. Schlier, *Kerygma u. Sophia,* 206-232; Wilckens Kreuz, 77-108.

[380] On λαλεῖν as a tt. for charismatic utterance cf. Dupont, 222-226.

[381] 1 C. 2:13-15; 3:1 as distinct from the ψυχικοί. On the Gnostic character of these terms cf. Wilckens Weisheit, 87-91; Dupont, 151-155 tries to show, however, that the vocabulary is Jewish.

[382] Almost all exegetes take the σοφία of 2:6 f. to refer to God's plan of salvation. In Jewish apocal., however, it mostly does not mean this; it denotes the most important and comprehensive eschatological blessing, or, in association with this, God's law (→ 503, 12 ff.). Since σοφία in the sense of the plan of salvation is also impossible in the Gk. sphere and is not attested elsewhere in the NT, this interpretation may be ruled out. The only possible derivation is from the apocal. sense. Cf. the idea behind Eph. 3:10 → 523, 25 ff.

are redeemed by Him. [383] We also find this descent especially in connection with the Jewish Gnostic Sophia myth → 508, 20 ff. Very probably the Christological ideas of the Corinthians had been very strongly influenced by an early Gnostic form of the myth which for its part was closely akin to the Jewish Sophia myth → 508, 20 ff. Here, then, σοφία can be an eschatological blessing in the apocalyptic sense and yet it can also be described as the descending Redeemer in specifically Gnostic concepts. The two together serve to explain the Christian faith in the raised and exalted Lord, who as the wisdom of God, as the Revealer and Redeemer, has given redeeming knowledge of Himself to His own as perfect pneumatics. Behind 1 C. 1:21 stand Jewish ideas of the pre-existence of wisdom as the mediator of creation (→ n. 215), invested with which, [384] and thus enabled to know God, the world is created for God. It would seem that in Corinth the revelation of Christ was regarded as present spiritual knowledge (2:10-16) by which those who have received revelation have become spiritual (2:13-16) and wise, so that all things, the world, life, death, present and future, are open to them (3:21 f.), and they already live on the far side of eschatological judgment in the perfection of the new aeon (4:7 f.), free from any judicial authority, empowered rather to pass definitive sentence on all other men (2:15). Against this madness, which was based on a Jewish Gnostic [385] Sophia Christology and which resulted in the formation of sects in Corinth (1:11 f. cf. 3:3 ff., 22), Paul feels impelled to make a passionate protest, for it nullifies the cross of Christ (1:17). Even though the Corinthians laid wordy emphasis on the fact that it was God's wisdom which had made them wise, Paul deflates the catch-word of his opponents by calling it worldly wisdom [386] and he dismisses the spirituality which they claimed as a "carnal" existence. [387] For who God is and what He has done, God Himself has revealed only in the event of the cross, which to the Gnostic self-understanding can seem only folly and weakness (1:23 f.). But "this foolish thing of God is wiser than men, and the weakness of God is stronger than men" (1:25), inasmuch as God has given salvation in the crucified Christ and has resolved to save believers in the folly of the preaching of the cross of Christ, 1:21. God Himself and alone was the One who raised up the weak and crucified Christ, so that He has life ἐκ δυνάμεως θεοῦ, and in the same way "we are weak in him, but we shall live with him by the power of God toward you," 2 C. 13:4. As in relation to the crucifixion there is no identity between Christ and God, so in relation to the believer there is no identity between Christ and him. This means also that there is no Gnostic being wise in Christ, no personal wisdom. [388] The structure of faith is

---

[383] For the rich Gnostic material cf. Ltzm. K., ad loc. and App., 170.

[384] ἐν τῇ σοφίᾳ in 1 C. 1:21 is to be taken in the local sense, so correctly H. Schlier, "Von den Heiden (R. 1:18-32)," Die Zeit d. Kirche (1956), 32; Schlier Kerygma u. Sophia, 210; Bornkamm, 72 f. Wilckens Weisheit, 32 f. discusses the various possible ways of translating ἐν.

[385] Cf. the explicit ref. to the Greeks and Jews in 1 C. 1:23. The Ἕλληνες are Gnostics, not philosophers in the sense of the Greek philosophical tradition, though for Paul the spirit of their teachings, which is alien to him as an apocalyptically minded Christian, seems to be one with the ungodly pagan spirit of "Greek" wisdom. Cf. also R. 1:14, where Paul is a preacher to Greeks and barbarians, σοφοῖς τε καὶ ἀνοήτοις ὀφειλέτης. The formulation here, however, is from the Gk. standpt., not the Jewish as in 1 C.

[386] 1 C. 2:5, cf. also 2 C. 1:12 : ἐν σοφίᾳ σαρκικῇ.

[387] 1 C. 3:1. There could be no sharper condemnation of the Corinthian position in Gnostic terms.

[388] Cf., e.g., Corp. Herm., 13, 6 : δοκοῦντος γάρ μου ὑπὸ σοῦ σοφοῦ γεγονέναι. Cf. also the Gnostics attacked by Plotinus in Enn., II, 9 and 10 → 511, 14 ff.

so shaped by the event of the cross that for believers Christ is the power and wisdom of God (1 C. 1:24) to which they are basically referred, and the implication for Christians is that for them, as Paul says in 1 C. 3:18 f. in pointed debate with the Corinthians, there is Christian wisdom only in their becoming fools, → IV, 846, 14 ff. Accordingly God has not called the wise, i.e., those who reckon themselves to be wise (1 C. 3:18) and who, as spiritual, regard those that are psychic as fools (1 C. 2:14). On the contrary, He has called fools and thus confounded the wise (1 C. 1:26 f.). Similarly He has not chosen the strong but the weak (1 C. 1:27). He has not chosen the highly esteemed but the lowly and despised. And in all this, as in the creation of the universe, He has chosen things which are not to negate things that are (1:28), that no one should be able to boast before God (1:29 cf. 3:21) like the καυχώμενοι in Corinth (1 C. 4:7; 5:6; 2 C. 5:12; 11:12, 18 cf. 10:8, 13-17; 11:30; 12:1-9). Seeing that ἐκ θεοῦ Christians exist in Christ as their wisdom, righteousness, sanctification and redemption, all boasting is excluded (1 C. 1:30 f.), just as all Judaistic boasting on the ground of self-righteousness (R. 10:3) is excluded (R. 3:27). God Himself has declared in Scripture (Is. 29:14 cf. Ps. 33:10) [389] that He "will destroy the wisdom of the wise, and will bring to nothing the understanding of the prudent" (1 C. 1:19). Paul finds this declaration fulfilled in the Christian present: In the kerygma of the crucified Christ God has made the wisdom of the world foolish (1:20), both that of the Greeks who seek after wisdom (1:22) — "Where is the wise?" (1:20) probably refers to the Ἕλληνες [390] — and also that of the Jews who ask for a sign (1:22) — "Where is the scribe?" (1:20) refers to the Jewish rabbis. The last of the three biblically formulated [391] questions in 1:20 includes both Greeks and Jews with their wisdom which is the wisdom of the world: "Who is there of this aeon who can conduct a learned disputation here?" There applies to both Jews and Gentiles, to all men, the dictum of R. 1:22: "Professing themselves to be wise, they became fools." If Paul affirms the Jewish idea that God invested His creation with wisdom, so that all the world may truly know God (1 C. 1:21 cf. R. 1:19 f.), for him all the emphasis is on the fact that "the world in its wisdom did not know God" (1 C. 1:21), that though knowledge of God is open to men through creation [392] men "did not glorify God, and were not grateful to him, but became foolish in their thoughts, their stupid heart was darkened, and professing themselves to be wise, they became fools" (R. 1:20 ff.). [393] But as God has still justified the unrighteous on the ground of faith (R. 3:21-26; 4:5; 5:6-11), so He has resolved "by the

---

[389] Following H. St. J. Thackeray, *The Septuagint and Jewish Worship* (Schweich Lectures, 1920)² (1923), 95 f., Peterson, *op. cit.*, 44-50, alluding to echoes of Bar. 3:9-4:4 (→ 509, 8 ff.), conjectures "that Pl. in 1 C. 1:18 f. is homiletically expounding the text of the (Jewish) day of repentance (Jer. 8:13-9:24) in a way similar to that of the preacher in the Book of Baruch," *ibid.*, 46. Schlier agrees, Eph., 160, Exc. on 3:11 f. But the arguments in favour of this hypothesis are hardly adequate.

[390] Schl. K., *ad loc. et al* find a single ref. to the rabbis in all three questions in 1 C. 1:20. This is possible in respect of σοφός (→ 505, 20 ff.) but is less probable in view of the context (1:22).

[391] Cf. Is. 33:18 f.; 19:11 f. For bibl. on the suggestion of a florilegium behind 1 C. 1:19 f. cf. Wilckens Weisheit, 25, n. 2; 26, n. 1.

[392] Cf., e.g., the characterisation of primal wisdom in Corp. Herm., 3, 1: σοφία εἰς δεῖξιν ἁπάντων ὤν.

[393] On this cf. esp. G. Bornkamm, "Die Offenbarung des Zornes Gottes (R. 1-3)," *Das Ende des Gesetzes*² (1958), 18-26; also "Glaube u. Vernunft bei Pls.," *Stud. zu Antike u. Urchr.* (1959), 119-121.

foolishness of preaching to save them that believe" (1 C. 1:21), and both in virtue of the resurrection of the crucified Christ from the dead. Thus Christ is proclaimed, "not with excellence of speech or of wisdom" (1 C. 2:1), but only "in weakness, and in fear, and in much trembling" (2:3), so that it may be quite plain that the preaching is "in demonstration of the Spirit and of power" and that the faith is "not in the wisdom of men, but in the power of God" (2:4 f.). In this sense Paul can adopt very positively all that the Corinthians say about Christ, the wisdom of God and the πνεῦμα as the power of Christian revelation and Christian life (1 C. 2:6-16) 394 because, rightly interpreted, they present the exclusive basic initiative of God and, rightly understood, they do not exclude but essentially include Christian folly (1 C. 3:18 f.). Finally, there is very closely connected with the grounding of Christian faith in the event of the cross the fact that Paul, in face of the eschatological extremism of the Corinthians, adheres firmly to the temporal distance of the believer in relation to the eschaton. 395

Most exegetes in expounding the whole discussion in 1 C. 1:18-2:5 concentrate on the phrases σοφία λόγου in 1:17, ὑπεροχὴν λόγου ἢ σοφίας in 2:1, and ἐν πειθοῖς σοφίας λόγοις in 2:4. It thus seems that in this section the Chr. preacher is opposing any philosophical or rhetorical presentation of the Gospel acc. to the standards of Gk. philosophy. Against this, however, is the fact that the section 1:18-2:16 is not theological reflection but a polemical discussion closely related to the situation in Corinth, cf. the direct and by no means angular transition in 1:17. σοφία is obviously a catch-word of Paul's opponents. What is meant may be seen from 2:6-16. His opponents are thus Gnostics, not Gk. philosophers. 396 Following the gen. polemical and apologetic tradition of Judaism, Paul thus viewed them as "Greeks" even though, historically, Corinthian gnosis was drawing on concepts from Hellenised Jewish apocalyptic → n. 385. Throughout the section he is arguing against the concrete position held in Corinth. The customary interpretation has to accept a profound inconsistency both in the relation between 1:18-2:5 and 2:6-16 and also in the use of the term σοφία. To be sure, Paul is attacking a specific λόγος of his adversaries. Yet this is not traditional Gk. rhetoric, which without adequate foundation is often associated with Apollos simply because he is called ἀνὴρ λόγιος in Ac. 18:24 and one of the parties in Corinth happened to be linked to his name (1 C. 1:12). On the contrary, what is at issue is Gnostic charismatic utterance, as may be seen from a comparison of 2:1 and 12:8 and esp. from Paul's argument in 2 C., cf. 11:6 and 10:10. The initial discussion in 1 C. belongs to the same context as the later one in 1 Cor. 8-14. A final pt. in this regard is that the attack on σοφία λόγου is not so much on the form of speech as on the content, i.e., on the whole theological position of the Corinthian adversaries, whose wisdom would appear to have been a Gnostically absolutised Pneuma-Christology. At any rate, Paul's verdict that the cross of Christ is made of none effect by the Corinthians' wisdom (1:17) may be understood in its ramifications and breadth only in the light of the polemical argument. On the other hand, Paul does not say in 1 C. that it is impossible in principle to preach the Gospel in the language of Gk. philosophy or that this would be a distortion of the Chr. kerygma. In terms of his own experience he probably could not say this. There is no evidence in the epistles that he was educated in one of the Gk. philosophical schools.

394 Paul's evaluation of the λόγος σοφίας is wholly positive in 1 C. 12:8, cf. also the speaking of mysteries in 14:2 ff. and his praising of the wealth of charismata in the congregation in 1:5, 7.
395 1 C. 4:7 f. is a criticism of the Corinthians. On the basic connection between Chr. existence in the event of the cross and the future character of the eschaton as this is affirmed in faith cf. esp. 2 C. 13:4 (ζήσομεν).
396 Cf. already W. Lütgert, "Freiheitspredigt u. Schwarmgeister in Korinth," BFTh, 12/13 (1908), 103, 108 etc.

4. Deutero - Pauline Writings.

In Col. and Eph. we find a traditional Gentile Chr. use of σοφία. In wisdom terminology Col. 1:9 and Eph. 1:8 describe steady growth in the Christian knowledge of faith as σοφία, σύνεσις πνευματική and φρόνησις. This involves knowledge of the will of God (Col. 1:9) [397] and walking worthy of the Lord (Col. 1:10 cf. 4:5 : ἐν σοφίᾳ περιπατεῖτε πρὸς τοὺς ἔξω, Eph. 5:15 : περιπατεῖτε μὴ ὡς ἄσοφοι ἀλλ᾽ ὡς σοφοί κτλ., R. 16:19 : σοφοὺς εἰς τὸ ἀγαθόν, ἀκεραίους δὲ εἰς τὸ κακόν). Such wisdom and knowledge is given by God's grace (Eph. 1:7 f.) as πνεῦμα σοφίας (Eph. 1:17). [398] In content it is described in Eph. 1:17 f. as ἀποκάλυψις ἐν ἐπιγνώσει αὐτοῦ by which the eyes are enlightened to knowledge of the eschatological blessings enclosed in Christ. Similarly in the Church's preaching according to Col. 1:28 every man must be urgently admonished and taught in all wisdom (cf. Col. 3:16) in order that he may stand perfect in Christ at the Last Judgment. The content of this instruction in wisdom, however, is the revelation of the mystery which from eternity was concealed from all former generations, "the riches of the glory of this mystery among the Gentiles, which is Christ in you, the hope of glory," Col. 1:26 f. Thus Christ — again in a formulation wholly along the lines of wisdom apocalyptic — is "the mystery of God . . . in whom are hid all the treasures of wisdom and knowledge" (Col. 2:3 cf. R. 11:33-36 → 518, 1 ff., esp. n. 375). On the other hand the position of the false teachers at Colossae is rejected as human teaching even though they themselves call it λόγος σοφίας. [399] In Colossae, then, σοφία, like → φιλοσοφία (Col. 2:8), is a positive designation used by the heretics for their doctrine. In Col., as in 1 C. 1 f., it is downgraded as human teaching, but it is propagated by the Colossians as divine wisdom. Finally, Eph. 3:10 is a difficult verse. The passage speaks of the grace given the apostle to "preach among the Gentiles the unsearchable riches of Christ" (3:8), and in so doing to bring to light the divine economy of salvation grounded in the μυστήριον which from eternity [400] was hidden in God, the Creator of all things (3:9), "to the intent that now unto the principalities and powers in heavenly places this might be made known by the church as the πολυποίκιλος σοφία τοῦ θεοῦ" (3:10). In both v. 8 f. and v. 11 f. the context demands that this wisdom of God be understood as the divine plan of salvation which has been fulfilled with the common entry of both Jews and Gentiles into Jesus Christ. Its revelation is by the Church (→ III, 509, 32 ff.; IV, 821, 36 ff.) in which Jews and Gentiles are united but which is depicted here as a heavenly entity made known to the cosmic principalities and powers.

---

[397] In Eph. 1:9, however, θέλημα is the divine plan of salvation, cf. 1:10 : οἰκονομία τοῦ πληρώματος τῶν καιρῶν. In Eph./Col. σοφία itself is not the plan of salvation.

[398] Cf. Wis. 7:7, 15 ff.; 8:9; 9:4, 10.

[399] In interpretation of this difficult v. cf. Dib. Gefbr., ad loc., also G. Bornkamm, "Die Häresie d. Kol.," Das Ende d. Gesetzes² (1958), 151 f.

[400] ἀπὸ τῶν αἰώνων is often taken personally in the sense of the concealment of the mystery from the aeons, who are then equated with the principalities and powers in v. 10, cf. the par. Eph. 2:2. On this cf. Reitzenstein Ir. Erl., 235-237; Schlier Kirche, 53 f.; Schlier Eph., 153, 1; 154, 2 on 3:9 f.; Dib. Gefbr. on Eph. 3:9 f.

Behind this, however, there obviously stands a Christological idea connected with the Sophia Christology described above (→ 519, 1 ff.). As *chokma* in Prv. 8; Sir. 24 etc. was hidden with God before the creation of the world (→ 498, 20 ff.), so was what is here called the πλοῦτος τοῦ Χριστοῦ, the content of the soteriological mystery which in turn is identical with the wisdom of God. [401] Perhaps there also stands behind v. 10 the concept of the Jewish and later Gnostic wisdom myth of the heavenly revelation of ascending wisdom to the powers whose front it penetrated (at first unrecognised) on its descent, → 509, 24 ff. The word πολυποίκιλος is probably best explained along these lines ; it occurs in many Near Eastern, Hellenistic and esp. Gnostic texts, particularly in designation of Isis, the goddess of wisdom. [402]

5. Revelation.

In Rev. 5:12 σοφία is one of the eschatological gifts of salvation which the "Lamb slain" is worthy to receive, cf. also the hymn in 7:12, where wisdom, with other eschatological gifts, is extolled as God's possession. [403] In the related verses 13:18 and 17:9 σοφία has the specific Christian-apocalyptic sense of esoteric knowledge. The number of the second beast which rises up from the earth (13:11), and which tries to make men on the whole earth worship the first beast (13:15) and bear his mark (13:16), is 666 → I, 462, 16 ff. [404] To "count" it, i.e., to gather from it the name of the man in view (13:18), special understanding (νοῦς) is needed. The author believes his readers have both this and also true wisdom (σοφία): ὧδε ἡ σοφία ἐστίν. 17:9 : ὧδε ὁ νοῦς ὁ ἔχων σοφίαν, is to be understood in the same way. This wisdom is displayed to the reader in the exposition of the vision in 17:8-18. In both cases, then, σοφία is the knowledge which is reserved for Christian confessors and which enables them to perceive the true meaning and ramifications of the events which were taking place on earth in their day.

6. James.

In James, too, there is a use of the word in the wisdom tradition. Jm. 1:5 is a single saying linked to what precedes by a catch-word and leading on in vv. 6 ff. to a series of sayings about prayer and faith : [405] "If any of you lack wisdom, let him ask of God, that giveth to all men liberally, and upbraideth not ; and it shall be given him." [406] For James wisdom is a morally upright walk, 3:13, 17 f. It has

---

[401] Cf. also Col. 1:15-20 and on this Käsemann Taufliturgie and Dib. Gefbr. on Col. 1:14 f.

[402] On this cf. the explicit discussion and full material in Schlier Eph., 162-166 on 5:21 ff., bibl., 164, n. 1. The Wisdom-Gnostic idea of the union is also part of the intellectual background of the section Eph. 5:22-32.

[403] Cf. also R. 16:27 as the conclusion of the doxology of 16:25 ff. Here God is praised as the only wise God who has revealed "the mystery which was kept secret since the world began" and made it known "by the scriptures of the prophets" to the obedience of faith of all nations in the Gospel and *kerygma* of Jesus Christ, v. 25 f. We have here primitive Jewish-Chr. tradition, cf. Mi. R., *ad loc.* Cf. the instances of μόνῳ σοφῷ θεῷ given there and also Corp. Herm., 14, 3.

[404] Even Iren. could not say what name was meant by 666 (Haer., V, 30, 1). In explanation cf. on the one side Loh. Apk., *ad loc.* and on the other, with varying solutions, J. Behm, *Die Offenbarung d. Johannes, NT Deutsch,* 11⁶ (1953), *ad loc.*; E. Stauffer, "666," Coni. Neot., 11 (1947), 237-241; O. Cullmann, *Der Staat im NT*² (1956), 57-59 (ET [1956], 80 ff).

[405] Cf. Dib. Jk.⁹, *ad loc.*

[406] For similar exhortation cf. Jewish Wisdom lit., e.g., Prv. 2:3-6; 4:5-9; Wis. 6:12 ff.; 7:7; 8:2-21; 9:1-18.

nothing whatever to do with the so-called wisdom which people were claiming for themselves and against which the author is arguing. The wisdom of his opponents leads to strife, discord and disorder, 3:14, 16. In contrast, true wisdom manifests itself in gentleness (3:13), peaceableness, readiness to come to terms, and orderliness, 3:17 f. The nature of the polemic in 3:15 enables us to see what kind of wisdom he was attacking, for he was obviously exposing it with the help of its own terminology, which is elsewhere quite alien to the epistle : οὐκ ἔστιν αὕτη ἡ σοφία ἄνωθεν κατερχομένη, ἀλλὰ ἐπίγειος, ψυχική, δαιμονιώδης. ⁴⁰⁷ The vocabulary is closely related to that in 1 C. 2. The adversaries speak of a heavenly wisdom which comes down from above, which contrasts with everything earthly, psychic and devilish, and which is thus heavenly, spiritual and divine by nature. The fact that discord and contention occur in relation to this wisdom teaching also corresponds to the situation in Corinth (1 C. 1:11 ἔριδες, cf. 4:6b). For the adversaries of Jm., too, σοφία is obviously a personal revealer. But the author has no access to speculations of this kind. He merely sees the practical moral results and regards it as his task simply to oppose to this Gnostic wisdom teaching an upright moral life.

7. 2 Peter.

In final support of apostolic legitimacy 2 Pt. 3:15 says of Paul that he wrote to the readers "according to the wisdom given unto him." Here, then, σοφία has already begun to be equated with apostolic and church theology.

F. The Post-Apostolic Fathers and Early Apologists.

1. Sophia Christology. There is no further development of primitive Sophia Christology in the first half of the 2nd cent.; only in the second half of the 2nd and in the 3rd cent. does this play a part in the working out of the early Chr. doctrine of the Trinity. ⁴⁰⁸ Yet Prv. 1:23-33 is quoted in 1 Cl., 57, 3-7 in order that these warnings (58, 1) of πανάρετος σοφία (57, 3) may be a summons to obedient perseverance in the flock of Christ, whereas the disobedient in Corinth, who seek higher esteem, are in danger of being ejected from hope in Him. In 1 Cl., 57, 2, then, the saving relation to Christ corresponds to the relation to personal wisdom in Prv. Just. Dial., 61, 1, 3 ff. goes further, for here Prv. 8:21-36 is cited as a testimony to the pre-existence of the Son. ⁴⁰⁹ Just. himself understands this traditional concept in fully Hell. fashion : "As ἀρχή before all creatures God has generated from himself a λογικὴ δύναμις which is called δόξα κυρίου by the Holy Ghost, often υἱός, often angel, often God, often κύριος and λόγος ...," 61, 1. ⁴¹⁰ Athenag. Suppl., 24, 1 has the Trinitarian series Father, Son and Holy Ghost along with the Christological triad νοῦς, λόγος, σοφία.⁴¹¹ With no Christological ref. Just. Dial., 38, 2 speaks of the "great wisdom of the Creator of all

---

⁴⁰⁷ Cf. also Jd. 19 and on this Dupont, 153, who thinks there is literary dependence on Jm. 3:15.

⁴⁰⁸ Cf. on this J. R. Harris, The Origin of the Prologue to St. John's Gospel (1917), 162-170, also Kretschmar, op. cit. (→ n. 322), 27-61.

⁴⁰⁹ It is connected with the personal concept of wisdom that Prv. is often called σοφία in the early Church, e.g., Just. Dial., 129, 3, cf. Melito of Sardis in Eus. Hist. Eccl., IV, 26, 14.

⁴¹⁰ The basis here is Prv. 8:22 rather than Jn. 1 — hence σοφία. Cf. the Christological predicate of sophia in Just. Dial., 100, 4, and Christ is σοφία διὰ Σολομῶνος in 126, 1. But in Just. Apol., 22, 1 the wisdom of Jesus is His piety, or perhaps His "culture" in the Gḫ sense.

⁴¹¹ On Theophilus cf. Kretschmar, 27-33, 36 f. On Sophia ecclesiology, ibid., 54-57.

things and Almighty God." [412] Herm. v., 1, 3, 4 relates the idea of God's wisdom at creation to the formation of the Church.

2. Common Christian Usage. In gen., however, σοφία is an unstructured term used either for morally blameless conduct or for the knowledge of faith (as a synon. of γνῶσις, σύνεσις etc.). [413] Thus Barn., 21, 5, on the basis of Eph. 1:17, calls wisdom the gift of knowing God's statutes — a gift sought from God as Ruler of the world. God dwells within us in His Word of faith, in calling to His promise, in the wisdom of the statutes and in the commandments of doctrine, 16, 9. The wise man shows his wisdom in good works rather than words, 1 Cl., 38, 2. σοφία (and νοῦς) is also the divinely revealed knowledge of the hidden secrets of God which no one knows but the wise and understanding man and the man who loves the Lord, Barn., 6, 10. [414] To be a believer and to be able to utter knowledge one needs to be wise in distinguishing words and pure in works, 1 Cl., 48, 5. This wisdom is often sharply differentiated from general human wisdom. Thus in Pauline terms 1 Cl., 32, 4 says that we are not justified of ourselves, neither by our wisdom, our understanding, our piety, nor our works ... but by faith, cf. Just. Dial., 102, 5. This is not by human wisdom but by the δύναμις θεοῦ, Just. Apol., 60, 11. Quoting Is. 29:14, [415] Just. calls on the Jews to cease misleading themselves and their adherents and to learn from Christians what has been taught by God's grace, Dial., 32, 5 cf. 78, 11; 123, 4. Because of their wickedness God has concealed from them the ability to know "wisdom in the words," i.e., Scripture, 55, 3. Similarly Tatian distinguishes between souls that are persuaded and by wisdom (σοφίᾳ) put on the related πνεῦμα and those that will not be convinced and reject the Servant of God who has suffered, thus showing themselves to be θεομάχοι rather than θεοσεβεῖς, Tat. Or. Graec., 13, 3. He has thus nothing but bitter and savage criticism for the wisdom of the Greeks, [416] not because he is an enemy of philosophical wisdom, but because Christians are its true defenders and the Greeks are its destroyers. [417] The word of truth and wisdom is a brighter and sharper light than that of the sun and shines into the depths of the heart and the understanding, Just. Dial., 121, 2.

[412] Cf. also 1 Cl., 60, 1; Dg., 8, 10.
[413] Cf. esp. the usage of Eph. and Col. → 523, 1 ff. In relation to the use of σοφία in patristic lit. Jaeger, 101-106 distinguishes a primary "homiletical and spiritual" sense, edifying knowledge, from a derived Christologically orientated doctrinal system.
[414] In this sense Pol., 3, 2 speaks of Paul's wisdom, cf. 2 Pt. 3:15 → 525, 18 ff.
[415] Cf. also the quoting of Jer. 9:22 f. in 1 Cl., 13, 1 and the statement based on 1 C. 1:18 ff. in Ign. Eph., 18, 1.
[416] Cf., e.g., Tat. Or. Graec., 1, 3: τούτου χάριν ἀπεταξάμεθα τῇ παρ' ὑμῖν σοφίᾳ κἂν εἰ πάνυ σεμνός τις ἦν ἐν αὐτῇ (as, e.g., Minos as law-giver, 34, 1). In interpretation of this v. cf. esp. M. Elze, "Tatian u. seine Theol.," Forschungen z. Kirchen- u. Dogmengeschichte, 9 (1960), 20 f. Cf. esp. 26, 2: The Gks. have divided the one wisdom whose ἀρχηγός is Moses (31, 1) into several contradictory wisdoms, so that they fight themselves. Just., however, concedes without difficulty that Pythagoras was a man who reflected a great deal about wisdom, Dial., 2, 4, cf. the quotation from Pind. Pyth., 3, 54 ff. in Athenag. Suppl., 29, 1. Just. also seeks to orientate himself by the Gk. concept of philosophy as ἐπιστήμη and σοφία, also εὐδαιμονία, Dial., 3, 4.
[417] On this cf. Tat. Or. Graec., 26, 2 (→ n. 416) and Elze, op. cit., 21-27, 36-40.

† σοφίζω.

1. In the act. σοφίζω with acc. "to make someone wise," first found in the LXX for חכם hi ψ 18:8; 104:22; 118:98, previously rarely pass. (Hes. → 496, n. 200, cf. Diog. L., V, 90, also P. Oxy., XV, 1790, 23) and commonly mid. as a general term for "understanding something," → 496, n. 200.[1] A derivate is σοφιστής, in pre-classical times used positively for a person with knowledge or skill, but then used *sensu malo* in Plato's criticism of the Sophists.[2]

2. In the LXX σοφίζειν is the main transl. of חכם, → 496, n. 199; 1 Βασ. 3:8 is the sole exception (ἐσοφίσατο = וַיִּבֶן). Wisdom dominates its meaning (cf. the description of Solomon's wisdom in 3 Βασ. 5:11 and the ref. in the Wisdom lit., e.g., Prv. 16:17; Sir. 50:28), but the choice of this Gk. word (rather than σοφός) often carries a negative emphasis (e.g., Qoh. 7:16 : μὴ σοφίζου περισσά, also Sir. 7:5; 32:4), cf. σοφιστής, which is used for Pharaoh's wise men in Ex. 7:11 etc., also Da. → 497, n. 202.[3] In the three passages in the Ps. in which we have the act. of σοφίζειν (→ n. 7) the ref. is to being made wise by the Law of God, cf. esp. ψ 18:8 : "The law of the Lord is perfect, converting souls (to God); the testimony of the Lord is sure, σοφίζουσα νήπια." Cf. ψ 118:98 : ὑπὲρ τοὺς ἐχθρούς μου ἐσόφισάς με τὴν ἐντολήν σου.

3. The use of the word in 2 Tm. 3:14 f. is similar to that in the Ps. (→ n. 7): "But continue thou in the things which thou hast learned and hast been assured of, knowing of whom thou hast learned them, and that from a child thou hast known the holy scriptures, τὰ δυνάμενά σε σοφίσαι εἰς σωτηρίαν διὰ πίστεως τῆς ἐν Χριστῷ Ἰησοῦ." Here, then, the term occurs in the context of traditional Jewish usage according to which knowledge of the Law makes men wise. The author adopts this usage and transfers it without a break to Christian instruction in the OT, by knowledge of which a man attains to salvation in Christian faith. Compare the continuation in v. 16 f., where this wisdom is expounded as the morally blameless conduct of the man of God.[4]

The word occurs in the passive in 2 Pt. 1:16. With a derogatory wave of the hand the author is dismissing the errors as "cunningly devised myths" (→ IV, 789, 4 ff.): "οὐ γὰρ σεσοφισμένοις μύθοις ἐξακολουθήσαντες have we made known unto you the power and coming of our Lord Jesus Christ, but we were eyewitnesses of his majesty," i.e., at the transfiguration (v. 17 f.). On these myths cf. 1 Tm. 1:4; 4:7; 2 Tm. 4:4; certain unspecified Gnostic teachings are in view in 2 Pt. 1:16, but the warning is a general one to shun contact with all false doctrines, which can pass on only myths and not the realities of revelation. σεσοφισμένος

σ ο φ ί ζ ω. Liddell-Scott, Pr.-Bauer⁵, *s.v.*; W. Schmid, *Gesch. d. gr. Lit., Hndbch. Kl. AW*, VII, 3 (1940), 14, n. 2.

[1] On the philosophical use in Aristot., who concedes a μυθικῶς σοφίζεσθαι to older "theologians" like Hesiod in Metaph., 2, 4, p. 1000a, 9 and 18, cf. W. Jaeger, *Die Theol. d. frühen gr. Denker* (1953), 19-21.

[2] On this cf. esp. W. Nestle, *Platons ausgewählte Schriften, IV, Protagoras⁷* (1931), 1-42. κατασοφίζεσθαι "to overreach" in Ac. 7:19 (= Ex. 1:10, in LXX elsewhere only Jdt. 5:11; 10:19), a word found only from the 1st cent. B.C. (Diod. S., 17, 116).

[3] On the usage in Philo and Jos. cf. Schl. Theol. d. Judt., 100, n. 2 → 500, n. 223.

[4] On σοφίζειν in this positive sense cf. also Barn., 5, 3; Ign. Sm., 1, 1; Just. Dial., 30, 2; 32, 5. Cf. also Act. Phil., 144 (p. 84) → 513, n. 328.

is thus used *sensu malo* : Christians have nothing in common with the insubstantial pseudo-wisdom of heresies. [5]

Wilckens

σπείρω → 536, 17 ff.

---

† σπένδομαι

---

1. σπένδω in the Graeco-Roman World.

a. The verb σπένδω, [1] a cultic term, means to pour out a portion of drink on the ground or on a cultic site as an offering to the gods. [2] It thus has the same sense as the poetic λείβω, while χέω means the complete pouring out of a liquid. [3] Already in Minoan culture the libation was a constituent part of the ritual of sacrifice, as may be

---

[5] σοφίζω is used in the same negative sense in, e.g., Barn., 9, 4; Just. Apol., 14, 4.

σ π έ ν δ ο μ α ι. Bibl.: Pr.-Bauer, Liddell-Scott, *s.v.*; K. Bernardi, "Das Trankopfer bei Hom.," *Abh. zu d. Programm d. königlichen Gymnasiums zu Leipzig* (1885); J. v. Fritze, *De libatione veterum Graecorum*, Diss. Berlin (1893); D. Feuchtwang, "Das Wasseropfer u. d. damit verbundenen Zeremonien," MGWJ, 54 (1910), 525-535, 713-729; 55 (1911), 43-63; O. Schmitz, *Die Opferanschauung d. späteren Judt. u. d. Opferaussagen d. NT* (1910), 213-237; P. Stengel, *Opferbraüche d. Griechen* (1910), 173-186; also D. Griech. *Kultusaltertümer Hndbch. Kl. AW*, 5, 3 (1920), 103-105; E. Busse, "Der Wein im Kult d. AT," *Freiburger Theol. Stud.*, 29 (1922), 18-70; I. Benzinger, *Hbr. Archäologie*[3] (1927), Index, *s.v.* "Trankopfer"; H. Wenschkewitz, "Die Spiritualisierung d. Kultusbegriffe," *Angelos-Beih.*, 4 (1932), 70-87; F. Blome, *Die Opfermaterie in Babylonien u. Israel*, 1 (1934), *s.v.* "Libationsopfer"; L. Ziehen, Art. "νηφάλια" in Pauly-W., 16 (1935), 2481-2489; K. Hanell, Art. "Trankopfer, Spender, Libationen" in Pauly-W., 6a (1937), 1232-1235; J. Pedersen, *Israel, Its Life and Culture*, III-IV (1940), 334-336, 342 f., 353 f.; L. Köhler, *Theol. d. AT*[3] (1953), 183-189; P. Seidensticker, "Lebendiges Opfer," *NT Abh.*, 20, 1-3 (1954), 225-262; K. Weiss, "Pls., Priester d. chr. Kultgemeinde," ThLZ, 79 (1954), 355-361; O. Betz, "Le ministère cultuel dans la secte de Qumran et dans le christianisme primitif, La secte de Qumran et les origines du christianisme," *Recherches bibl.*, 4 (1959), 162-202.

[1] Root "spend," Hittite *šip(p)and* : "to pour out," "to offer a libation," "to offer an animal sacrifice." Cf. H. E. Sturtevant-E. A. Hahn, *A Comparative Grammar of the Hittite Language*, I (1951), 14 and 30; J. Friedrich, *Hethitisches Wörterbuch, Kurzgefasste kritische Sammlung d. Deutungen hethit. Wörter* (1952), 193; Cf. G. Kronasser, *Vergleichende Laut- u. Formenlehre d. Hethitischen* (1956), 30 on the initial letter, 38 on the a of the stem syllable. Lat. *spondeo* (iterative) : "to pledge solemnly," "to vouch for something." On the whole subject cf. Walde-Pok., II, 665; Hofmann, *s.v.*; Boisacq, *s.v.*; Pokorny, I, 989.

[2] In the gt. Gortyn inscr., GDI, 3, 2 (1905), 4991 ἐπισπένδω is an inheritance term denoting the securing of a specific portion through the father to his daughter who marries before his death, 4, 52 f.; 5, 3; 6, 11 and 13 f., cf. J. Kohler-E. Ziebarth, *Das Stadtrecht v. Gortyn* (1912), 63 f.; E. Schwyzer, *Dialectorum Graecarum exempla epigraphica potiora* (1923), No. 179.

[3] The noun σπονδή thus denotes esp. the libation of wine, though other drinks too, Athen., 12, 510d; Diod. S., 5, 62, 5; Paus., II, 11, 4, but χοή is a tt. for libations to the dead (Hom. Od., 10, 518) and chthonic deities (Aesch. Eum., 107). The χοή is fully poured out. The poetic λοιβή can be used for any drink-offering. In gen. the distinction in the use of the verbs is not so strict as in the use of the nouns.

seen from excavated vessels and the depictions on receptacles used at offerings. [4] In the religious life of Greece libations were on a par with animal sacrifices (Hes. Op., 335-341), and they are found independently as well as in connection with other offerings. When the Gks. of Homer wanted to ask the gods for aid in difficult situations [5] and also in drinking at meals (Hom. Il., 7, 480; Od., 8, 89), they used to pour out a portion of their mixed wine on the earth for the Olympian deities. The offering was not made at all times when they drank (Il., 9, 202 ff.; Od., 1, 147), and prayer was esp. connected with drink offerings, also in the post-Homeric period. [6] The libation supported prayer. Later it seems to have become the custom to pour out a few drops on all occasions. There also seems to have developed a certain regularity in libations to specific deities. Thus it was customary to pour out a few drops for the ἀγαθὸς δαίμων [7] at the end of a meal, Athen., 15, 692 f-693 f. At a symposium acc. to Schol. on Pind. Isthm., 6, 10; Schol. on Plat. Phileb., 66d the first drink offering was to Olympian Zeus and the other Olympians, the second to the heroes and the third to Zeus Soter. Later there were official libations, e.g., when the Athenian fleet sailed for Sicily (Thuc., VI, 32) or when the procession set off for Eleusis (Ditt. Syll.³, II, 885, 29 f.). In meat offerings libations were indispensable. In Homeric times the master of the feast poured out the main offering on the burning flesh, Hom. Il., 1, 462; 11, 775; Od., 3, 459, while acc. to Od., 3, 334, 340 f. all participants took part in a common libation at the end of the sacrifice. Later the libation came between the preliminary offering (κατάρχεσθαι) and prayer, Aristoph. Pax, 433. [8] Participants often poured wine on the burning flesh, 1102 ff. Incense might be offered with the drink offering, Diod. S., 13, 3, 2. Some deities, esp. chthonic and agrarian, [9] accepted no libations, so that we do not find these at the σφάγια. Instead there were poured out to these gods more sober drinks νηφάλια, Aesch. Eum., 107-109, e.g., water for the dead or for chthonic demons, Athen., 9, 410a, milk, Soph. El., 894 f., honey, IG, 12, 5, 2, No. 1027, 4, and perhaps oil, Aesch. Pers., 616 f. Milk and honey were often poured out as a mixture μελίκρατον, Hom. Od., 10, 519; Ditt. Syll.³, III, 1025, 32 ff.; Diod. S., 5, 62, 5. νηφάλια are older than wine libations, just as the chthonic deities were worshipped before the gods of Olympus. Later the idea was that threatening gods might be appeased by milder drinks. In the cult of the dead wine was offered as well as νηφάλια, [10] partly mixed, Plut. De Aristide, 21 (I, 332a), partly unmixed (Eur. El., 511). Only unmixed wine was offered at the solemn swearing of oaths, Hom. Il., 2, 341; 4, 159; Aristoph. Lys., 197. Underground deities were to be stirred up against perjurers rather than appeased.

---

[4] Cf. M. P. Nilsson, *Minoan-Mycenaean Religion* (1927), 104-106, 122-131, 226 f.

[5] In Hom. Il., 16, 227 Achilles pours from a special vessel and prays to Zeus when he sends forth Patroclos to battle with the Myrmidons. In Hom. Il., 24, 283-287 Hecabe brings Priam a cup of wine as a libation for Zeus when he goes with the herald to the Gk. camp.

[6] Hom. Il., 9, 174-184; 23, 194 ff.; Od., 3, 393-395; Plat. Phaed., 117b c. Cf. Stengel Opferbräuche, 54 f.

[7] The ἀγαθὸς δαίμων is probably a noumenon derived from misunderstanding of the saying ἀγαθοῦ δαίμονος. It fixes man's inner destiny, just as his outward fate is subject to τύχη. Later the ἀγαθὸς δαίμων was equated with Dionysus, Diod. S., 4, 3, 4. Cf. J. Fischer, Art. "ἀγαθὸς δαίμων," Pauly-W. Suppl., 3 (1918), 37-59.

[8] The sprinkling of the sacrifice with water before the offering could also be called κατασπένδειν, Plut. Alex., 50 (I, 693d); Def. Orac., 51 (II, 438a); Schol. on Aristoph. (ed. F. Dübner [1883]) on Pax, 960, 968; Ra., 479.

[9] E.g., Hades Eur. Alc., 424; in Athens etc. the Muses, Nymphs, Helios, Selene, and Dionysus, Schol. on Soph. Oed. Col., 100; in Olympia the Despoinai and Nymphs, Paus.. V, 15, 10; esp. the Eumenides, who could be called ἄοινοι θεαί, Soph. Oed. Col., 100. Cf. Stengel Opferbräuche, 180-183. Many deities accepted both wine offerings and νηφάλια, Plut. De tuenda sanitate praecepta, 19 (II, 132e); Dion. Hal. Ant. Rom., 1, 33, 1.

[10] Milk, honey, water, wine and oil are listed in Aesch. Pers., 609-617; wine, milk and honey in Eur. Iph. Taur., 159 ff.

b. From the drink-offering at the swearing of oaths comes the use of the mid. of σπένδω for "to conclude a treaty," "to arrange an armistice." [11] In the difficult passage Eur. Ba., 284 f. σπένδομαι is probably pass. rather than mid.; here Teiresias says to Pentheus, who will not recognise Dionysus as a god, that the god Dionysus is poured out as a libation to the gods so that through him men might have the good things mentioned in 280 ff. [12]

c. In a few instances σπένδω denotes the pouring out of blood, e.g., in the mystery order of Andania, in which blood and wine together are poured out at the swearing in of priests, Ditt. Syll.[3], II, 736, 1 ff., or in the description of an ancient human sacrifice in which the blood of a child offered to Zeus Lycaios is poured out on the altar, Paus., VIII, 2, 3. There are also libations of various kinds in magic. [13]

d. σπένδω is used a few times in a transf. sense, e.g., in the cultic sphere. In Eur. Or., 1239 Orestes and Electra invoke the aid of their murdered father, pouring out tears and lamentations on his grave as libations for the dead. In an Apollo aretalogy of the 2nd cent. A.D. we read that Daulis, the leader of an enemy army which penetrated to Delphi, and seized the Pythia and the sacred vessels, threatened that he would slay the prophet of Apollo when he sought to prevent further transgressions, and pour out his blood as a libation to the god Ares, who delights in slaughter. [14] The religious character of σπένδω is less prominent, however, when the sword of Alcaios is said to have often shed the blood of tyrants (Anth. Graec., 9, 184, 7 f.), or when a poet asks the Muses to lavish clear and melodious sound upon him (9, 364, 1 ff.).

e. The Lat. word for pouring out a drink offering is libare (libatio). In the main Roman libations were similar to the Gk. Wine and more sober drinks were offered both alone and also along with other offerings. Wine and incense are often combined in the Roman cultus : tus ac vinum were the usual sacrificial gifts in the daily domestic cultus,

---

[11] Hdt., III, 144; Xenoph. An., I, 9, 7; Thuc., I, 18, 3. The plur. σπονδαί means "treaty," "armistice." Concluding a treaty involves sacrifice, libation, and handshake. Hom. Il., 4, 158 f. The usual verb for slaughtering the σφάγια, τέμνειν, is used with ὅρκια τέμνειν for "to conclude a treaty" (Il., 3, 94, 256) and can even be combined with σπονδαί, Eur. Hel., 1235 : σπονδὰς τέμωμεν.

[12] Neither the context nor mythology speaks of a treaty Dionysus made with other gods in man's favour. The sophist Prodicos Fr., 5 (Diels[7], II, 317, 3 ff.) explained the rise of belief in the gods by assuming that men first worshipped the things on which life depended (stars, rivers, bread, wine etc.), then at a higher stage of culture they worshipped those who imparted knowledge and customs; hence Demeter and Dionysus were related to the basic elements of nourishment. If Eur. is ref. to this view here, then he has the second stage in view in Ba., 274 ff. and the first in 284 f. (wine ═ Dionysus acc. to Prodicos). But perhaps 284 is not a play on words on the basis of sophist speculations. It possibly presupposes a primitive religious notion which localised Dionysus in some way in the wine, since the power of the mighty nature-god was seen at work in this. The designation Dionysos Botrys might be connected with this, cf. the Philippi inscr. from the Roman period, L. R. Farnell, The Cults of the Greek States, V (1909), 289. A similar concept may well lie behind Eur. Cyc., 519-529. On the passage cf. W. Nestle, Euripides, der Dichter d. griech. Aufklärung (1901), 81 f.; G. Norwood, The Riddle of the Bacchae (1908), 27, 108-125; W. Nestle, Vom Mythos zum Logos (1940), 349-360; E. R. Dodds, Euripides, Bacchae[2] (1960), 105.

[13] Theocr. Idyll., 2, 43; A. Dieterich, Abraxas, Stud. z. Religionsgeschichte d. späteren Altertums (1891), 204, 4; P. Lond., I, 46, 255.

[14] Cf. the ed. of W. Schubart, "Aus einer Apollon-Aretalogie," Herm., 55 (1920), 188-195; G. Manteuffel, De opusculis Graecis Aegypti e pap., ostracis lapidibusque collectis (1930), 28, 95-99. On the content cf. S. Eitrem, "Daulis in Delphoi u. Apollons Strafe, Δράγμα M. P. Nilsson dedicatum," Skrifter utgivna av Svenska Institutet i Rom, Ser. altera, 1 (1939), 170-180. A. M. Denis, "Versé en libation (Phil. 2:17) ═ versé son sang?" Recherches de science relig., 45 (1957), 567-570 thinks the threat of Daulis might mean that in acc. with sacrificial practice at Delphi he would pour out the blood of the priest of Apollo instead of the water usually sprinkled on the animal offering. The true sacrifice dedicated to Ares would

Plaut. Aulularia, 25.[15] Acc. to Tacitus both Seneca[16] and Thrasea[17] said before death that they would bring a drink offering to Jupiter Liberator. For this Seneca used the water of the vapour bath, which after various other attempts finally brought him death as he sprinkled some drops of it on slaves close to him,[18] while Thrasea sprinkled the blood streaming from his opened veins on the earth. The rare name Liberator for Jupiter seems to be based on the Gk. Ζεὺς ἐλευθέριος, Pind. Olymp., 12, 1; Thuc., II, 71, 2. Perhaps the invocation is meant to remind us that death was greeted as a liberator by the Stoics. On the other hand, some have seen here a sarcastic allusion to Nero, who sometimes called himself liberator and issued coins inscribed Jupiter Liberator.[19]

2. σπένδω in the Old Testament.

a. The LXX uses the verb σπένδω for Hbr. נָסַךְ in the sense "to pour out a drink offering."[20] The noun corresponding to σπονδή, נֶסֶךְ in Ex. 29:40; 30:9, נֵסֶךְ in Nu. 15:5 etc. Aram. נִסְכָּא (*נְסַךְ)[21] in Ezr. 7:11, is often used in a fig. etym. as an object of נָסַךְ.[22] On the basis of the related ceremonial נָסַךְ in Is. 30:1 signifies the dedication of a covenant,[23] while in Ps. 2:6 it means the institution of a king. The noun נָסִיךְ, "prince,"

---

then consist in the massacring of the rest of the temple personnel, about which there is, of course, nothing in the text, cf. on this Eitrem, 172, n. 3.

[15] "To pour out drink offerings, to offer incense, and to taste the sacrificial meat," σπένδειν, θύειν and γεύεσθαι τῶν ἱερείων, was required of everyone who wanted to clear himself of suspicion of Christianity in the Decian persecution. Cf. P. Greci e Latini, 5, 453, 5-10; P. Oxy., IV, 658, 7 and 11; BGU, I, 287, 11; C. Wessely, "Les plus anciens monuments du christianisme," Patrologia Orientalis, 4, 2 (1906), 112-124.

[16] Tac. Ann., 15, 64 : postremo stagnum calidae aquae introiit, respergens proximos servorum addita voce libare se liquorem illum Jovi liberatori.

[17] Ibid., 16, 35 : porrectisque utriusque bracchii venis, postquam cruorem effudit, humum super spargens... "libamus" inquit "Jovi liberatori."

[18] In committing suicide Seneca ref. back to Socrates, expressly getting poison, which was taken in Athens by those under popular condemnation, though in Seneca's case it was ineffective. It is not clear, however, whether the sprinkling of the bath-water as a drink offering was an answer to Socrates' question whether he should offer a libation from the cup of poison handed to him, Plat. Phaed., 117b. Acc. to Xenoph. Hist. Graec., II, 3, 56, Theramenes, whose execution Critias had forced through, dashed the remainder of the poison to the ground with the words : "That to the fine Critias." Later Theramenes and Socrates were taken as examples of steadfast dying and often confused. Cf. O. Hense, Teletis reliquiae (1889), 12; Cic. Tusc., I, 40, 96 ff.

[19] Cf. K. Latte, Art. "Liberator," Pauly-W., 13 (1926), 93; cf. also Ditt. Syll.³, II, 814, 41.

[20] Ges.-Buhl.¹⁷, s.v.; Köhler-Baumg., s.v.; F. Zorell, Lex. Hebraicum et Aramaicum Veteris Testamenti (1957), 519 f. נָסַךְ also denotes the pouring out of metal in Is. 40:19 (LXX ποιεῖν) and 44:10 (LXX γλύφειν). Is. uses נָסַךְ in a transf. sense in the judgment saying Is. 29:10 : God has poured out a spirit of deep sleep on Judah so that the people is unable to receive God's direction. But שָׁפַךְ (LXX ἐκχέω) is used for the pouring out of God's Spirit in Jl. 2:28.

[21] In Da. 2:46 the Aram. verb נְסַךְ is used for offering meat offerings and incense. LXX has the free transl. θυσίας καὶ σπονδὰς ποιῆσαι, Θ the lit. μαναα καὶ εὐωδίας... σπεῖσαι. With this extension of usage one may compare the history of the Arab. nasak. It originally meant "to pour out," but was then used for animal sacrifices, probably in indication of the pouring out of the blood, which in every animal sacrifice flowed on the altar as the true gift to the deity. Finally it became a gen. term for a cultic art. Cf. on this W. R. Smith, The Religion of the Semites (1899), 173; J. Wellhausen, Reste arab. Heidentums² (1897), 142.

[22] In this combination the verb may be either in the q (Ex. 30:9) or the hi (Gn. 35:14; Nu. 28:7; 2 K. 16:13; Jer. 7:18; 19:13; 32:29; 44:17, 18, 19, 25; Ez. 20:28; Ps. 16:4). נָסַךְ is used abs. in the ho in Ex. 25:29; 37:16, where ref. is made to the vessels used in libations.

[23] Cf. the Gk. σπονδὰς σπένδεσθαι in Thuc., V, 14, 4 (→ 530, 1 ff.).

is perhaps reminiscent of the ancient privilege of presenting the drink offering. [24] Like the whole sacrificial cultus, [25] the custom of offering a libation in Israel was adopted from the pagan world around, and esp. from the Canaanites. Already in Accadian texts [26] and then in Ugaritic epics there is ref. to libations, and sometimes the same verb is used (nsk). In these passages the original purpose is clear : God needs drink as well as food, Aqhat, II, 6, 29 f.; cf. also II, 2, 18 f., 28. [27] The drink offering plays a particularly important role in fertility cults. [28] In Israel there were libations to other deities during the Monarchy, e.g., along with cakes baked in the Ishtar cult, Jer. 7:18; 32:29. Acc. to Gn. 35:14 Jacob poured a drink offering over the pillar he set up at Bethel, and he poured oil over it. In the pre-exilic period when there was no generally accepted legislation [29] the drink offering usually seems to have been combined with the burnt offerings and meat offerings. [30] In the lists of sacrifices in Lv. 23:37; Nu. 29:36-39 it seems to have been an independent offering, but elsewhere it is, like the meat offering, an appendix to the main offering. [31] Thus the morning and evening sacrifice (Tamid offering) was of a lamb, and there was added a meat offering (oil cakes) and ¼ hin of wine as a drink offering, Ex. 29:38-41; Nu. 28:7-10. The rule for feasts is similar, Lv. 23:12 f., 18; Nu. 28:9 f., 14 f., 24, 31; 29:6, 11 ff. The proportion was ¼ hin per lamb, ⅓ per ram, ½ per bullock, Nu. 28:14, [32] The act consisted of pouring out the wine on (עַל) the altar, God's table, or on the burnt offering, Ex. 30:9; Nu. 28:24. In addition to wine, water was sometimes drawn and poured out before Yahweh, 2 S. 23:16 f.; 1 Ch. 11:18. Oil also played a gt. part (Mi. 6:7: streams of oil). Finally, there is ref. in Ps. 16:4 to a drink offering of blood (נִסְכֵּיהֶם מִדָּם) in connection with an alien cult.

---

[24] Jos. 13:21; Ez. 32:30; Mi. 5:4; Ps. 83:12. In Sir. 16:7 נְסִיכֵי אָדָם are the giants produced by the union of angels and women in Gn. 6:1 ff. The noun נָסִיךְ can mean both "drink offering" in Dt. 32:38 and "molten image" in Da. 11:8. For the cultic tasks of the king cf. 2 K. 16:13-15; Ez. 45:17, also G. Widengren, Sakrales Königtum im AT u. im Judt. (1955), 14-43. נָסִיךְ in the sense "prince" nasiku in Assyr. "prince," "regent," "bedouin sheikh." But derivation from נָסַךְ "to pour out a drink offering" is by no means certain. Cf. P. Jensen, Assyr.-Bab. Mythen u. Epen, Keilschr. Bibliothek, ed. E. Schrader, VI, 1 (1900), 417, who associates nasaku "to cause to fall," "to throw down," "to pour out" (?) with maššaku "offering" (m formation of našaku), nis(š)akku, the term for a priestly class, and masiku "prince," lit. "outpourer," "sacrificer." But there is no sure evidence that nasaku means "to pour." F. Delitzsch, Assyr. Handwörterbuch (1896), 472 takes nasiku to mean "the instituted one," "prince," from nasaku "to posit," "institute," "lay," "do," cf. also Ps. 2:6. C. Bezold, Babyl.-assyr. Glossar (1926), 201 does not give a derivation for nasiku but simply calls it a West Semitic loan word meaning "prince," "regent," "bedouin sheikh," cf. KAT, 650.

[25] Köhler, 171.

[26] How important the drink offering was for true piety may be seen from the fact that acc. to the Bab. work ludlul bēl nēmeqi the ungodly man may be known from his failure to bring drink offerings to the god, 2:12-22, esp. 12 (ed. W. G. Lambert, Babylonian Wisdom Lit. [1960], 38 f.).

[27] Ed. G. R. Driver, Canaanite Myths and Legends (1956), 51 and 55.

[28] Acc. to Baal VI, 2, 19-21; V, 2, 31; V, 4a, 9 f., 24 (Driver, 74 f., 84 f., 88 f.) apples of love were laid in the ground at the command of Baal and a peace offering was poured into "the liver of the earth" (note the combination nsk šlm).

[29] Köhler, 181 and 183.

[30] Acc. to 1 S. 10:3 three men go to Bethel with 3 kids, 3 loaves and a bottle of wine; acc. to 2 K. 16:13, 15 Ahaz of Judah offers burnt offerings, meat offerings and drink offerings on a newly built altar constructed after the pagan pattern.

[31] Acc. to Nu. 10:10 the trumpets were to be blown only on feast days at the burnt and peace offerings (→ 79, 43 ff.), but acc. to Tamid, 3, 1; 7, 3 three blasts at the morning offering separated the drink offering from the preceding ritual (→ 85, 4 ff.). Later, then, the drink offering seems to have taken on more independent significance. Thus it is described in Sir. 50:15-17 as the conclusion and climax of the high-priest's ministry. Cf. A. Büchler, "Zur Gesch. d. Tempelmusik u. d. Tempelpsalmen," ZAW, 20 (1900), 107-114.

[32] 1 hin = 6, 6 litres (BR 367).

b. The verb שָׁפַךְ ("to pour out") as well as נָסַךְ can denote the pouring out of a drink offering (Is. 57:6), though this word is in the main reserved for blood. Here, too, we have ancient Semitic word : Accadian *šapaku* ; cf. Ugaritic *špk* ... *dm Aqhat* (→ n. 27), III, 1, 23 f. שָׁפַךְ relates to the shedding of the blood of sacrificed animals, Ex. 29:12; Lv. 4:7, 18, 25, 30, 34; 17:13; Dt. 12:16, 24, 27; 15:23 etc. Underlying this sacrificial rite is the statement in Lv. 17:11 that blood expiates through the life dwelling in it. The animal's soul, poured out on the altar with its blood, makes expiation (כִּפֶּר == covering) for the one who makes the offering and who would otherwise fall under God's judgment. שָׁפַךְ also denotes the shedding of blood in murder, Gn. 9:6; 37:22; Nu. 35:33; Dt. 21:7; the dying man pours out his soul, Lam. 2:12; Job 30:16. Violent death can be compared to the slaying and offering of a sacrifice, Jer. 11:19; 46:10; Zeph. 1:8; Is. 53:7-10. Worth noting is the statement in Is. 53:12 that the Servant of the Lord "poured out his life into death" (הֶעֱרָה).[33] It denotes the substitutionary sacrifice which is offered with the voluntary surrender of life.

3. σπένδω in Later Palestinian Judaism.

a. In later Judaism the use of נָסַךְ or σπένδω is normatively controlled by understanding of the sacrificial cultus, which varies. Sometimes there is glad acceptance and sometimes cool reserve. In particular there begins in the sects of Palestinian Judaism, then in Hell. circles outside Jerusalem, and finally in the rabbinate, a spiritualising of the cultic legislation of the OT, which was originally taken literally.[34] For Sir. sacrificial worship is a national treasure which he fittingly extols. The drink offering is not mentioned in the list of cultic acts entrusted to Aaron (45:14 ff.), but the concluding libation is very clear in the description of the high-priest Simon (50:15). Though the law of sacrifice does not prescribe this (Ex. 30:9), the high-priest stretches his hand over the sacrificial bowl and pours out the wine on the support of the altar. Acc. to Jos. Ant., 3, 234 drink offerings are poured out around the altar,[35] and the same applies to the blood of the slain beasts, 3, 226. Philo ref. to the same practice, Spec. Leg., I, 205.[36] There are sundry other ref. The drink offering is not mentioned in the account of the dedication of the temple in 1 Macc. 4:52 ff. or in the sacrificial Torah which Levi receives from Isaac in Test. L. 9:6 ff. (though note the offering of the first-fruits of wine in 9:14). But it is expressly emphasised among the offerings in Sib., 3, 576-579.[37] In the Achikar story[38] (Syr. version p. 22, 10) a son is admonished to pour out his wine on the graves of the just rather than drink it in the company of the wicked. The Book of Jubilees tells

---

[33] The rare עֶרָה hi is to be transl. "to pour out" here, Ges.-Buhl, *s.v.* Cf. ἐκένωσεν ἑαυτόν in Phil. 2:7 for הֶעֱרָה נַפְשׁוֹ in Is. 53:12. Paul possibly has in view the sacrifice of life rather than the kenosis of the incarnation, → V, 711, 15 ff.; J. Jeremias, "Zur Gedankenführung in d. paulinischen Briefen," *Stud. Paulina, Festschr. J. de Zwaan* (1953), 154; on this O. Michel, "Zur Exegese v. Phil. 2:5-11," *Festgabe f. K. Heim* (1954), 83-89.

[34] Cf. on this Betz, 163-202.

[35] Later practice seems to have been different. Acc. to Sukka, 4, 9 the wine of the drink offering was not poured out at the foot of the altar but into a bowl on it; this had a pipe leading down, so that the water of the water libation and the wine flowed down together, 49a; jSukka, 4, 7 (54d, 1 ff.); T. Sukka, 3, 14 f.; cf. also Zeb. 6:2 f.; T. Zeb., 7:7; Tamid, 4, 3 and on this Büchler, 110; H. Bornhäuser, *Sukka* (1935), 132 f. Acc. to Jub. 7:5 Noah when offering sacrifice after the first vintage surprisingly threw the wine of the drink offering into the fire, cf. also Jub. 6:3.

[36] Jos. Ant., 3, 234 : σπένδουσι δὲ περὶ τὸν βωμὸν τὸν οἶνον; Ant., 3, 226 : τὸν κύκλον τῷ αἵματι δεύουσι τοῦ βωμοῦ; Philo Spec. Leg., I, 205: τὸ δ' αἷμα κύκλῳ προσχεῖται τῷ βωμῷ, διότι ...

[37] Here λοιβή is used in Gk. for drink offering : οἳ ναὸν μεγάλοιο θεοῦ περικυδανέουσιν λοιβῇ τε κνίσῃ τ' ἠδ' αὖθ' ἱεραῖς ἑκατόμβαις ..., Sib., 3, 575 f.

[38] Ed. F. C. Conybeare, J. R. Harris, *et. al., The Story of Aḥikar²* (1913), 104.

how Abraham offered meat and drink offerings as well as animals and birds, 14:9-19, cf. also 15:1 f. The order established by P and valid at the time was thus traced back to the early period. In the Aram.-Gk. Fr. of Test. L. we find rules for drink offerings as well as burnt offerings and meat offerings, Fr. § 44. In the Dead Sea Scrolls drink offerings are not specifically mentioned. In the speeches of Moses, of which only fr. have been preserved, blood is to be sprinkled on the earth as one of the rites of expiation for the people and the land on the great Day of Atonement, 1 Q 22:4, 2 (DJD, I, 95). In the spiritual baptism of the end-time God will sprinkle the elect with the spirit of truth as with cleansing water and thus free him from all ungodly stains incurred through contacts with untruth, 1 QS 4:21 f. The sacrifice of the sectaries separated from the Jerusalem temple was mostly spiritual; the praise of the lips and a righteous walk in the living sanctuary of the community have the same atoning efficacy as the legal offerings, 1 QS 8:5 f.; 9:3-6, 24-26; 1 QM 2:5. A later principle was that chastisements have as much expiatory force as offerings, or more, M. Ex., 79b on 20:23; S. Dt., 32 (73b) on 6:5. In particular 4 Macc. 1:11; 6:28 f.; 9:24 say that atonement is made for the land by the patience of the just, and that expiation is achieved in suffering.

b. In the rites of the second temple sprinkling of blood played a gt. role. Acc. to P the climax of the Day of Atonement was when the high-priest sprinkled the blood of the victim on the cover of the ark and before the ark itself, Lv. 16:14 f. This was carried through in the second temple on the spot where the ark had stood before the exile, S. Lv., 16, 3; Yoma, 5, 1 ff.; 52b; cf. Str.-B., III, 182 f. [39] At the Passover the lambs were slain by the people, and the blood was drained into bowls and sprinkled by the priests at the base of the altar, Pes., 5, 5-9. [40] Water from Siloam was poured out on the altar on the first seven days of Tabernacles. Water and wine poured down from the altar, Sukka, 4, 9; T. Sukka, 3, 14. A halachah from Moses on Sinai acc. to T. Sukka, 3, 16; jSukka, 4, 1 (54b, 29 ff.), the pouring of water probably derived from an ancient fertility rite, [41] for it was related to the blessing of the rainy season beginning in the autumn, T. Sukka, 3, 18; Zech. 14:17. It was also a type of future salvation, and esp. of the outpouring of the Holy Spirit. [42] The OT idea that the killing of wicked foes is equivalent to an offering (Nu. 25:13) recurs in the Rabb. saying (possibly Zealot) that "everyone who sheds the blood of the ungodly offers a sacrifice," Nu. r., 21, 3 on 25:13; Tanch. Phinehas, 3; cf. Jn. 16:2. [43]

---

[39] Cf. also Yoma, 5, 6: "When he had sprinkled the surface of the altar 7 times he poured out the rest of the blood on the west base of the outer altar. What remained at the outer altar was poured on the ground at the south."

[40] Pes., 5, 6: "The priest closest to the altar sprinkles it as a sprinkling on the base of the altar."

[41] Cf. 1 K. 18:34 f.; Is. 12:3; on the fertility rite cf. bRH, 16a: "Why did the Law command the pouring of water at the Feast of Tabernacles? The Holy One, blessed be He, said: 'Pour me out water at the Feast of Tabernacles that the rain of the year may be blessed for you.'" The Samaritan liturgy directs that the king pray for rain at the Feast of Tabernacles so that Yahweh may open heaven. Cf. on this Widengren, op. cit., 41.

[42] Cf. on this Str.-B., II, 799-807; A. Marmorstein, "The Holy Spirit in Rabbinic Legend," Stud. in Jewish Theol. (1950), 122-144. Cf. the river of blessing in Ez. 47:1 ff. (Zech. 14:8) and the fountain of Zech. 13:1.

[43] In 1 QH 2:31 ff. the worshipper gives thanks that God has redeemed his soul. His foes had planned to destroy him and to shed his blood because of or in the service of God (probably דָמוֹ is to be taken as the obj. of לִשְׁפּוֹךְ: לִשְׁפּוֹךְ דָּמוֹ עַל עֲבוֹדָתֶךָ). The enemies might seem to be the logical subj. of עֲבוֹדָתְכָה. They thought they were doing God service by killing those who were apostate in their eyes. Cf. Jn. 16:2 and the Rabb. passage above (→ lines 29 ff.). In keeping with this interpretation is the fact that the zeal of the petitioner's enemies is stressed in 1 QH 2:31. But in the same hymn the petitioner is undoubtedly the logical subj. of עֲבוֹדָתְכָה in 2:36. Hence this is also more likely in 2:33: Because he serves God his enemies want to shed his blood. In this case the v. is not to be taken cultically.

4. Cultic Traditions in Josephus and Philo.

a. Joseph. ref. to the drink offering as a means of atonement in his description of the healing of the well of Jericho by Elisha, Bell., 4, 462, cf. 2 K. 2:19-22.[44] The prophet threw a vessel full of salt into the bubbling water, stretched out his right hand to heaven, and poured out atoning drink offerings on the earth. The rite, not mentioned in the OT, reminds us of an oriental fertility rite. Jos. also tells of instances in which shed human blood was regarded as a cultic transgression because the sacrifice itself was interrupted by murder. When Pompey stormed the temple the priests went on sacrificing and were slain at their sacred task, Bell., 1, 150 : σπένδοντες δὲ ἀπεσφάττοντο καὶ θυμιῶντες, cf. Ant., 14, 66 f. Acc. to Bell., 2, 30 Archelaos mercilessly slaughtered men in the sanctuary over their sacrifices. There is a similar tradition in Lk. 13:1, which tells us that the blood of the Galileans mingled with their sacrifices.[45]

b. Philo takes spiritually the custom of sprinkling blood in a circle around the altar. The Law demands, with the offering of blood, the life itself, so it is teaching fig. that man should declare his readiness to serve God with word and will and work, Spec. Leg., I, 205, cf. Vit. Mos., II, 150 f. Acc. to Philo true worship consists in the piety of the soul which loves God, Mos., II, 108. When acc. to 1 S. 1:15 Hannah pours out her heart before God, this means that the mind is to be offered wholly to God as a drink offering, Ebr., 152. The ministry of the high-priest in the sanctuary is also taken spiritually. He is a type of the soul which loves God, since he offers the blood of the life-force as a drink offering and consecrates his whole reason to God, the Saviour and Benefactor, Leg. All., II, 56.[46]

5. σπένδομαι in the New Testament.

Twice in the NT σπένδω is used in the passive ; in both instances the reference is to Paul's martyrdom, Phil. 2:17; 2 Tm. 4:6. The sayings are modelled on the passion sayings of later Judaism or the Hellenistic world. What is meant is a historical cultic act which will conclude the life and work of the apostle. The judgment of men which snuffs out the elect of God is transcended by the apostle's own solemn, sacral interpretation of death. The image of the drink offering suggests perhaps a secondary offering alongside the main one → 532, 10 ff. If so, the main offering consists in the faith of the community which the apostle conveys to God. But this interpretation is by no means certain.[47] It should be borne in

---

[44] Jos. Bell., 4, 462 : κἀπὶ γῆς σπονδὰς μειλικτηρίους χεόμενος.

[45] J. Blinzler, "Die Niedermetzelung v. Galiläern durch Pilatus," Nov. Test., 2 (1597/58), 24-49.

[46] Leg. All., II, 56 : εἰσελεύσεται σπεῖσαι τὸ ψυχικὸν αἷμα.

[47] With a ref. to Arrianus De expeditione Alexandri, VI, 19, 5 (ed. F. Dübner-C. Müller [1877]): καὶ σπείσας ἐπὶ τῇ θυσίᾳ τὴν φιάλην ... ἐνέβαλλεν ἐς τὸν πόντον χαριστήρια ("he poured out the bowl over the sacrifice"), Schmitz, 232 with n. 4 construes Phil. 2:17 thus : "Granted that I will also be poured out as a drink offering over (= on the occasion of) the sacrifice and priestly offering of your faith." The term θυσία denotes the faith of the Philippians as their sacrificial gift, while the word λειτουργία shows that this offering is made by Paul. Some, however, think the solemn words θυσία καὶ λειτουργία τῆς πίστεως ὑμῶν are to be taken as nomina actionis with Paul himself as the subj : "If I should rather bleed to death in sacrifice to your faith," Dib. Ph.³, ad loc.; Weiss, 357. Here Paul is the officiant (R. 1:9; 15:16) but also the drink offering which concludes the priestly ministry. Τῆς πίστεως ὑμῶν is in this case an obj. gen. J. B. Lightfoot, Ep. to the Phil. (1903), ad loc. suggests the sacrifice (θυσία) and ministry (λειτουργία) in which the faith of the Philippians exhibits itself (appos. gen.). Thus Paul's drink offering is the accompanying libation.

mind that the priestly ministry of the apostle and the corresponding sacrifice in the offering up of the Gentiles are fundamentally established by R. 1:9; 15:16. In this sense the apostle's priestly ministry is controlled by the concept and reality of the Gospel of God. From this develops the new form of cultic thinking. On the other hand the life of believers is also a sacrifice and sacral ministry according to R. 12:1 (θυσία, λατρεία, → IV, 65, 18 ff.), so that older cultic categories are imported into the secularity of the Christian life. The two possibilities of exegesis are also present in Phil. 2:17 → IV, 227, 21 ff.

In the solemn words of parting in 2 Tm. 4:6-8 (perhaps an older tradition) the same material is used as in Phil. σπένδομαι reminds us of Phil. 2:17, ἡ ἀνάλυσίς μου of Phil. 1:23 (ἀναλύειν). Here, too, the drink offering (σπένδομαι) represents the offering up of life. The apostle sheds his blood as a drink offering is poured out at the foot of the altar → 533, 23 ff. There thus develops in Christianity, too, a vivid passion vocabulary which stresses the dignity and significance of death in cultic thought-forms. [48]

Michel

> † σπέρμα, σπείρω, σπορά,
> † σπόρος, σπόριμος

A. The Word Group in the Greek World.

1. σπέρμα.

The word is found in Gk. lit. from Hom. in the sense of "seed." [1] The underlying verb σπείρω may be seen in New High German "sprühen," Old High German "spriu" and New High German "Spreu." a. It is often used for the seed of plants, Hdt., III, 97; Hes. Op., 446 and 448; Xenoph. Oec., 17, 8 and 10, and the time of sowing, Hes. Op., 781. b. But it is also found for animal seed μυελὸν ... εἰς σπέρμα καὶ γόνον μερίζεσθαι, Tim. Locr., 100b : σπέρματα τῶν ἀκμαζόντων, Xenoph. Mem., IV, 4, 23 (also Plat. Leg., VIII, 839b); σπέρμα παραλαβεῖν, Eur. Or., 553; σπέρματος πλῆσαι, Plut. Lycurgus, 15 (I, 49a); in the sense "offspring" : σπέρμα θνατόν, Pind. Nem., 10, 81. Similarly there is ref. in Gk. lit. to divine seed : φέροισα σπέρμα θεοῦ, Pind. Pyth., 3, 15; σπέρμα φέρειν Ἡρακλέους, Pind. Nem., 10, 17. In a transf. sense there is a twofold development. c. In relation to plant seed we find "core," "original or basic material,"

It is a mistake to link the prepositional ἐπὶ τῇ θυσίᾳ καὶ λειτουργίᾳ with the statement which follows : "I will rejoice at the sacrifice and service of your faith," Ew. Ph., *ad loc.*

[48] Cf. Ignatius' plea that the Roman church will not try to stop him being offered as a drink offering, the altar being ready, Ig. R., 2, 2 : πλέον δέ μοι μὴ παράσχησθε τοῦ σπονδισθῆναι θεῷ, ὡς ἔτι θυσιαστήριον ἕτοιμόν ἐστιν.

σ π έ ρ μ α κ τ λ. [1] Very probably to be found already in Mycenaean texts (σπέρμα and σπέρμο), usually in the sense of "grain" (wheat?) [Risch]. On the etym. cf. Boisacq and Hofmann, *s.v.*

"basis," "element," anything which has in it quickening or creative force σπέρμα πυρὸς σῴζειν, Hom. Od., 5, 490 (the only instance in Hom.); σπέρμα φλογός Pind. Olymp., 7, 48; σπέρματα = στοιχεῖα, Anaxag. Fr., 4 (Diels, II, 34, 5 ff.); σπέρμα ἄφθιτον Λιβύας, Pind. Pyth., 4, 42 f.; ὑπάρχει σπέρμα τῆς στάσεως, Plut. Mar., 10 (I, 410e); σπέρμα τοῦ ὅρκου, Ps.-Long., 16, 3. d. In connection with human seed we have a poetic use for "scion," "descendant," "offspring," "child" : σπέρμα Πελοπιδῶν, Aesch. Choeph., 503; Ἀργεῖαι ... σπέρματ᾽ εὐτέκνου βοός, Aesch. Suppl., 275; τὸ πᾶν σπέρμα τῶν συναιμόνων, σπέρμα παίδων, Soph. Trach., 1147; Eur. Med., 669; Ἰνάχειον σπέρμα, Aesch. Prom., 705; βρότεια σπέρματα, Aesch. Eum., 909; τὰ ἐμαυτοῦ, σπέρματα, Soph. Oed. Col., 600; ἀνθρώπων σπέρματα, Plat. Leg., IX, 853c. Along the same lines we find "tribe," "race," "descent," Soph. Ant., 981 (also Pind. Olymp., 7, 93 and Soph. Oed. Tyr., 1077): τίνος εἶ σπέρματος ... πατρόθεν, Soph. Oed. Col., 214; γένεθλον σπέρμα τ᾽ Ἀργεῖον, Aesch. Suppl., 290.

2. σπείρω.

Among the Gks. this means a. lit. "to sow," "to sow seed," Hes. Op., 389, σῖτον Hdt., IV, 17, 1; στάχυν, Eur. Cyc., 121. It occurs in the abs. as the opp. of θερίζω in Hes. Op., 391. But it can often mean "to sow spiritual seed" αἰσχρῶς μὲν ἔσπειρας, κακῶς δὲ ἐθέρισας, Aristot. Rhet., III, 3, p. 1406b, 10; ἡ ῥητορικὴ καρπὸν ὧν ἔσπειρε θερίζει, Plat. Phaedr., 260d; of corrupt orators θερίζειν καὶ σπείρειν ταῖς γλώσσαις, Aristoph. Av., 1697; of new poetic creations καινοτάταις σπείρειν διανοίαις, Aristoph. Vesp., 1044; "to sow" ideas with the help of the ink-bearing reed, Plat. Phaedr., 276c. b. In the sense "to sow (e.g., a field)" σπείρειν is found from Hes. Op., 463 and Hdt., IX, 122; cf. Xenoph. Ag., 1, 20; Cyrop., VIII, 3, 38; proverbially of vain efforts πόντον σπείρειν, Theogn., 106 (Diehl³, II, 9) and transf. τοὺς ἐν γράμμασι κήπους σπείρειν καὶ γράφειν "to sow and describe literary gardens," Plat. Phaedr., 276d. c. Then σπείρειν means "to scatter, disseminate, disperse" χρυσὸν καὶ ἄργυρον, Hdt., VII, 107; "to break up" ἐκ τευχέων σπείρειν δρόσον, Eur. Andr., 167; of parts of the population : γένη κακῶς ἐσπαρμένα, Plat. Leg., III, 693a; ἐσπάρησαν κατὰ τὴν ἄλλην Ἑλλάδα, Thuc., II, 27, 2; σπεῖρέ νυν ἀγλαΐαν τινὰ νάσῳ, Pind. Nem., 1, 13. d. Finally and esp. it means "to generate," "to beget," Soph. Trach., 33; Eur. Ion, 49 etc.; ἄθυτα παλλακῶν σπέρματα, "illegitimate offspring," Plat. Leg., VIII, 841d; φύσις σπαρεῖσα, Plat. Resp., VI, 492a; ματρὸς ἀγνὰν σπείρας ἄρουραν ... ῥίζαν αἱματόεσσαν, Aesch. Sept. c. Theb., 753; proverbially : εἰς πέτρας τε καὶ λίθους σπείρειν, Plat. Leg., VIII, 838e.

3. σπορά.

Among the Gks. σπορά originally means "sowing," σπερμάτων, Ps.-Plat. Amat., 134e; transf. μαθημάτων εἰς ψυχήν; then "what is sown," "seed," Eur. Andr., 637, also "generation," "birth," Aesch. Prom., 870, also "progeny," "race," Soph. Ai., 1298, and finally "the one begotten," "child," Soph. Trach., 316 : οὔτε ... ἄρσην οὔτε θήλεια σπορά, Eur. Tro., 503, cf. Hec., 659.

4. σπόρος.

In Gk. lit. σπόρος [2] means "sowing," Hdt., VIII, 109; Xenoph. Oec., 7, 20; Plat. Tim., 42d; then fruit, Soph. Phil., 707 and poetically "son," "child," "scion," Lycophron Alexandra, [3] 221, 750, 943.

---

[2] Cf. Schwyzer, I, 458 f., 460.
[3] Ed. E. Scheer² (1958).

5. σπόριμος.

In Gk. lit. this adj. means "sown," "to be sown," "adapted for sowing or to be sown," Xenoph. Hist. Graec., III, 2, 10; Theophr. Hist. Plant., VI, 5, 4. The noun τὰ σπόριμα "fields of grain" occurs in Geoponica, I, 12, 37; [4] Sib., 8, 181.

Schulz

B. σπέρμα and Equivalents in the Old Testament.

1. LXX Data.

a. σπέρμα, "sowing," "seed," "yield," is used 217 times in the LXX, mostly and rightly for זֶרַע. In acc. with the basic sense almost half the ref. are economic or physiological. In the others, as in the original and other Semitic languages, the terms of the group are used metaphorically at a higher level for more or less fundamental, mostly positive and occasionally negative statements about the forms of organic life, e.g., those ref. to family and national life, such as the "seed of Abraham" (Is. 41:8), the "seed of Jacob" (Is. 45:19) and the like. In this function σπέρμα is a term for "what has grown," "what is growing," "what is alive," "new growth," and it denotes the organic and purposeful structure of the national body; all are homogeneous and develop in the fellowship of the energy of growth within them, a significant figure of speech, the more so as the opp. has a part in it too. Late authors use σπέρμα to denote the compact vitality of corruption (Is. 57:3 f.: σπέρμα μοιχῶν καὶ πόρνης, τέκνα ἀπωλείας, σπέρμα ἄνομον (= שֶׁקֶר), and in so doing they recognise that the uncannily productive force of untruthful evil is just as strongly rooted and fruitful as is meaningful life, with no possibility of reconciliation. The development of the concept is thus in different directions. It also comes to cover that which is not is keeping with the basic physiological sense. The transference of meaning follows an inner logic whereby only that which is regarded as generative and germinating can share in this use of σπέρμα. Formally the process corresponds to Gk. metonymy, [5] and was perhaps understood in this way by the translators and readers. The only pt. is that in Hbr. transference of sense is not to be explained in terms of a controlled sense of style, like Gk. metonymy. σπέρμα takes on this quality simply in virtue of a strong dynamic which engenders the larger sense [6] that any reader may perceive without difficulty. Thus in Gn. 3:15 (J) God's speech puts enmity between the "seed" of the serpent and the "seed" of the woman. But this does not have to mean that the physiological sense issues in the idea of the future and the totality of the species. The "seed" of the woman, called "the mother of all or of all living" (πάντων τῶν ζώντων) by the same author in Gn. 3:20, undoubtedly stands for mankind, and it carries an elegiac accent, for hostility to the serpent race implies an enduring threat. The reader sees the sequence of human generations under the image of the "seed of tears" (Ps. 126:5 : σπείροντες ἐν δάκρυσιν), perhaps with hope, perhaps without. This is not an academic form in the area of logic and rhetoric. It is destiny seen and stated in a simple figure of speech. The almost stereotyped instances of σπέρμα for "posterity" in Gn. 7:3; 9:9; 12:7; 13:16 etc. are to be viewed similarly. One sees here a thinking which in logical tendency might already be called secular. At any rate the linguistic unity in describing fructification in man (κοίτη σπέρματος = שִׁכְבַת זֶרַע

---

[4] Ed. E. Beckh (1895).
[5] On this cf. E. König, *Stilistik, Rhetorik, Poetik in Bezug auf d. bibl. Lit.* (1900), 17.
[6] J. Pedersen, *Israel*, I (1926), 167 : "The word is the form of vesture of the contents of the soul, its bodily expression."

Lv. 15:16), beast (Jer. 31:27) and plant (מַזְרִיעַ זֶרַע, Gn. 1:12) yields a profound insight into "nature."

b. The Gk. constructs related in root lag far behind σπέρμα in use. σπόρος occurs only 11 times and this limited use is restricted to the agronomic sphere : Ex. 34:21 for חָרִישׁ "tilling the field," Lv. 26:20 for יְבוּל "increase of the land." It also occurs for זֶרַע, but metonymically perhaps only in Job 21:8 for the "growth" of evil.

c. Even rarer is the exclusively agronomic use of σπορά (2 K. 19:29) [7] and σπόριμος (Gn. 1:29).

d. In contrast the verbs σπείρω (some 59 times) and διασπείρειν (some 67 times) are frequently used with slightly varying nuances for the diaspora of the people (→ II, 99, 11 ff.), cf. Lv. 26:33 : διασπερῶ (M אֱזָרֶה) ὑμᾶς εἰς τὰ ἔθνη; Jer. 15:7; Ez. 12:15 etc. A construct peculiar to LXX is ἐκσπερματίζειν in Nu. 5:28. Whereas the simple σπερματίζειν (Ex. 9:31 = גִּבְעֹל) denotes the forming of the seed of the flax, the compound, following the original, depicts human generation from the agronomic standpt. → n. 17. Act. ἐκσπερματιεῖ σπέρμα : "She (the woman proved innocent in the ordeal) shall conceive seed" for pass. נִזְרְעָה זָרַע "she shall be provided with seed." Elsewhere σπείρειν is used only of plants except for Prv. 11:21: ὁ σπείρων δικαιοσύνην (for זֶרַע צַדִּיקִים) and Prv. 11:24, where the generous man (מְפַזֵּר) is depicted as a sower (οἱ τὰ ἴδια σπείροντες), also Hos. 10:12 : σπείρατε ἑαυτοῖς εἰς δικαιοσύνην, Jer. 4:3 (→ 541, 11 f.); 31:27; 4 Macc. 10:2 (ἔσπειρέν με πατήρ). In view of these data it is surprising that the noun διασπορά (11 times → II, 99, 23 ff.) is never used, as one might expect, for גּוֹלָה or שְׁבִי [8] but is reserved for more emotional words, including זְוָעָה and זַעֲוָה in Dt. 28:25; Jer. 34:17, which both mean "trembling, dread," and thus seek to express the spiritual core of the distress of the deported. The part. σπειρόμενον in Is. 19:7 is a correct [9] equivalent for מִזְרָע "seed-corn" or perhaps "sown land." ἐσπαρμένη in Jer. 30:17 ref. to outcast (נִדָּחָה) Jerusalem. The other originals of σπείρειν (פּוּץ, זרק, זרה hi) are synon. for sowing; they are of no particular interest and are self-explanatory. [10]

2. The Masoretic Data.

Things are much the same in the original text. [11] The root זרע and derivates, esp. the noun זֶרַע, dominate the picture in the various nuances found for σπέρμα. [12] The verb

---

[7] But cf. the Gn. Fr. Δ 3 (P. Strassb., 748), which 3 times in Gn. 26:3, 4 has σπορά, not σπέρμα, for "progeny," v. A. E. Brooke-N. McLean, *The OT in Gk.*, I (1917), Apparatus on Gn. 26:3 f. [Katz].

[8] For these words we find αἰχμαλωσία 37 times for שְׁבִי and 12 for גֹּלָה, ἀποικεσία 6 times for גֹּלָה, ἀποικία 15 times for גֹּלָה, ἀποικισμός twice for גֹּלָה, twice for שְׁבִי, μετοικεσία 4 times for גֹּלָה, παροικιά 2 Esdr. 8 : 35 (גֹּלָה) etc.

[9] So Köhler-Baumgartner, s.v. A statement like "it dries up, withers, and disappears" does not necessarily ref. to the ground. Whether *nġr mdr'* = נֹצֵר מִזְרָע "watcher of the seed" in Ugaritic, who acc. to Gordon Manual Text, 52, 69 ff. gives the young gods access to bread and wine, derives his title from the district or from the fruit grown there, is uncertain. For "sown land" Mas. usually has שְׂדֵה זֶרַע ז', בֵּית ז' or מְקוֹם ז'; 1 S. 8:15 is the only instance of זַרְעֵיכֶם in this sense.

[10] For זֶרַע we also find γένος (e.g., γένος τοῦ βασιλέως, Jer. 41[48]:1; βασιλικὸν γένος Da. 1:3; τὸ γένος Ἰσραήλ Jer. 31 [38]:36 f. and γένος Ἰουδαίων Est. 6:13); γενεά (ἡ γενεὰ ἡ Μηδική Da. 9:1 [Θ σπέρμα] cf. Est. 9:28), and ἔθνος (only Est. 10:3). (ἄμπελος) καρποφόρος is good for זֶרַע אֱמֶת in Jer. 2:21 with its emphasis on the pt. of comparison to the people.

[11] Cf. also the use of the Accad. *zêru*.

[12] It is not clear whether זֶרַע is a special term for a particular operation. לקש in the Gezer

occurs 52 times, including the ni, pu and hi forms, and the noun 188 times. It is of little significance that the use of σπέρμα etc. in the LXX is greater than that of the materially equivalent זֶרַע in the Mas. More or less good reasons for this are to be found in the greater or lesser ability or convenience of the translators, and naturally one could not expect attempts at strict equation.

As derivates of זרע one may mention not only מִזְרָע (already referred to) and Aram. זְרַע (Da. 2:43 : זְרַע אֲנָשָׁא, Θ σπέρμα ἀνθρώπων, LXX correctly εἰς γένεσιν ἀνθρώ- πων) but also the part. זֹרֵעַ in Prv. 11:18 metaphorical זֹרֵעַ צְדָקָה = σπέρμα δι- καίων; alongside par. תְּפֶשׂ מַגָּל in Ιερ. 27(50):16 one finds the metaphorically veiled כָּרְתוּ זוֹרֵעַ מִבָּבֶל = ἐξολεθρεύσατε σπέρμα ἐκ Βαβυλῶνος. Also the hybrid זֵרוּעַ in Is. 61:11 for "vegetables," and more gen. in Da. 1:12 זֵרֹעִים and Da. 1:16 (ן)...זֵרְעֹנִים for "vegetarian diet," Θ : σπέρμα, LXX : τὰ ὄσπρια.

b. Some instances of the questionable use of σπέρμα for other roots are worth noting. Thus we find it for נִין in Gn. 21:23; Is. 14:22 etc. — the basic meaning of this is as obscure as that of the additional and complementary נֶכֶד.[13] We also find it for אַחֲרִית "future" (perhaps more concretely and without eschatological emphasis "new growth") in Nu. 24:20 in a saying about Amalek. Again it is used for בָּשָׂר "flesh" in Is. 58:7b : οἱ οἰκεῖοι τοῦ σπέρματός σου, which can hardly be right. The use for בֵּן "son" (Dt. 25:5 : σπέρμα μὴ ᾖ αὐτῷ) is doubly imprecise when compared with the similar statement about the priest's daughters in LXX Lv. 22:13 : σπέρμα δὲ μὴ ἦν αὐτῇ, which in distinction from the first saying rests on a basic זֶרַע אֵין לָהּ and perhaps means "children," whether sons or daughters. In the Levirate law it is not clear whether the Gk. form is a deliberate and considered extension of meaning in favour of existing daughters, esp. as v. 6 refers to a later "first-born" (τὸ παιδίον, ὅ ἐὰν τέκη), or whether σπέρμα זֶרַע is to be construed as "male child" like 1 S. 1:11 (LXX זֶרַע אֲנָשִׁים = σπέρμα ἀν- δρῶν), where what follows proves this.

c. The LXX (and Vg) transl. שָׂרִיד כִּמְעַט in Is. 1:9 ("hardly escaped") very freely as σπέρμα (semen), though at the very most, and only by logical interrelation, can one see here an allusion to Lot in Gn. 19:17.[14] The wresting is so obvious[15] that it can be explained only on dogmatic grounds, or, more modestly, in terms of a stage in Bible interpretation in which the ideology of the people of God and its future began to be orientated to the impressive slogan זֶרַע הַקֹּדֶשׁ, Ezr. 9:2; Is. 6:13c → 542, 21 ff. 'A, which correctly has λεῖμμα ("remnant") rather than the obscure σπέρμα, either did not know or did not accept these tendencies.

<hr>

farmers' calendar in lines 1 and 2 (AOT, 444) supports this, cf. also Am. 7:1. The relation of זֶרַע to זְרוֹעַ, אֶזְרוֹעַ "poor" is unexplained, cf. also Ugaritic dr' and ḏr' (Gordon Manual, 5, 4), and it is no help to an understanding. The palpable distinction of sound in the Ugar. is reason enough not to interrelate the similar sounding Hbr. roots. Hexapla has ζαρω for זֵרְעוֹ at ψ 88:30, 37.

[13] If the tradition is right at Ps. 72:16 : יָנִין, Q יְנוֹן, also the context 16a, the root might mean "to sprout." The transl. or conjecture at Job. 18:19 is ἐπίγνωστος.

[14] Or is F. Wutz, Die Transkriptionen von d. Septuaginta bis Hieronymus (1933), 76, right when he think the basis of the LXX σπέρμα is a transcription confusing σαρειδ and σαρε and read as זֶרַע or זֹרֵעַ ? It is hard to say whether the fact that שָׂרִיד = σπέρμα is repeated in Dt. 3:3 (cf. also Is. 15:9 פְּלֵיטַת מוֹאָב = τὸ σπέρμα Μωαβ) counts for or against this technical possibility, esp. as the idea that Dt. 3:3 was influenced by Ezr. 9:2 can hardly be supported.

[15] That כִּמְעַט in Is. 1:9, as an adv. measure (C. Brockelmann, Hbr. Syntax [1956], 95), goes with the verbal noun שָׂרִיד and not the next clause, is hardly disputable in view of the formal and material par. in Ps. 94:17 : לוּלֵי יהוה עֶזְרָתָה לִּי כִּמְעַט "unless the Lord had finally

3. The Seed and Related Motifs in Sayings about God's Work.

In the linguistic data presented the rich metonymic use is an instructive and significant example of the constructive force of a simple, readily understandable, physiological word. Transposed into the spiritual mood it shares its clear underlying sense — the biological seed and basis of the development of organisms — with phenomena and associations whose vital force would be more difficult to communicate, and might be overlooked, without this metaphor. The actuality and seminal power of sociological and cultural values and other aspects of life is illustrated by the seed motif with its ref. to pregnant life. Event, essence and act are also viewed from the standpoint of natural semination. The seed aims at the harvest; *in nuce* this is contained in every metonymic statement, and Jeremiah's warning not to sow among thorns (4:3) gives the term a very broad range in relation to gen. conduct. Worth noting is the fact that the distinction between good or true seed זֶרַע אֱמֶת in Jer. 2:21 and less good or poor seed זֶרַע שֶׁקֶר in Is. 57:4 becomes less prominent, while disparaging expressions in the sense of "tribe," e.g., זֶרַע מְרֵעִים Is. 1:4; 14:20; cf. Ps. 37:28, are reserved for angry and scornful speech. As a rule the seed motif expresses salvation and blessing, or positive values, cf. "seed of man" and "seed of beast" in Jer. 31:27, [16] Vegetative force is divine force. This is the insight of nature religion which lives on latently in faith in Yahweh and which finds fruitful expression in the use of the seed motif in the OT writers. [17]

This is instructively worked out in the classical expression of God's part in agriculture in the mashal in Is. 28:23-29. [18] God teaches the farmer; He shows him what is the right thing to do. Sowing (לִזְרֹעַ v. 24) is not just a matter of manual labour with the plough and harrow. What is first demanded is intelligent consideration of needs and possibilities in the use of the land. The right solution comes from God. This profoundly pious train of thought shows us to what degree work on the land depends on God's help. It is not just profane technical work. It follows the direction of God, who, withdrawing the curse on the earth in Gn. 3:17, has appointed seedtime and harvest as a continuing order as long as the world endures, Gn. 8:22.

Yet the religious use of the seed motif is comparatively restrained when one considers the similarly orientated and strongly emotional use of the נטע family ("to plant") or the image of God as His people's gardener who sets cedars, acacias, myrtles and olive-trees on the steppes and cypresses and elms on the plains, as only the Creator can do, Is. 41:19 f. God planted the cedars of Lebanon, the "trees of Yahweh" (Ps. 104:16), the "cedars of God" (Ps. 80:10). His people is the vine which He took out of Egypt and planted with His right hand in the place where its branches may reach to the sea and its roots to the river, Ps. 80:8 ff., 15. Jeremiah loves this metaphor (2:21: God's failure with the goodly vine, cf. 11:17; 18:9 etc.) and even uses it in relation to the ungodly, 12:2. We find it at the end of Amos in 9:15 and in the oracles of Balaam in Nu. 24:6b, and

---

been my help." In both verses there is metrical objection to כמעט, but in both it bears a decisive accent. Otherwise "almost as Sodom" would be out of place in Is.

[16] The name of the city of Jezreel, which undoubtedly ref. from the very outset to the fertility of the area, is in Hos. 1:4 explained with no regard to the promise in the root: "God sows"; it is proclaimed as a symbol of admonition and threat because of the bloodthirsty act of Jehu there. It gets back its ancient ring in 2:24 and this is fully heard in 1 Ch. 4:3, where it is a personal name.

[17] Cf. Ez. 36:9: "You shall be tilled and sown" (נֶעֱבַדְתֶּם וְנִזְרַעְתֶּם) for the elements of fortune and hope in the motif, found also in the Talmudic זַרְעִית "family."

[18] To see God Himself in the sower (O. Procksch, *Jes.*, I, *Komm. AT*, 9, 1 [1930] on 28:23 ff.) is impossible in view of "his God" in v. 26. The passage is independent of its environment.

Is.'s ref. to the garden of Yahweh (Judah) in 5:7. Ps. 94:9 applies it to God's creative work in the human organism.

The metonymy of the seed sayings is almost completely unaffected by this wealth of mythical themes. These sayings are more sober and basic. Man and his doings are more prominent as the subject than God is. It seems almost as though calling God the sower is deliberately avoided. Expressions like "seed of Abraham, Israel, David" belong to the non-mythical human sphere. They stands for what comes forth from the loins, 2 S. 7:12. They simply serve to express the sequence of generations and inclusion in blood-relationship. Only once is there ref. to God's seed, and here the wording is uncertain, so that no firm deductions may be made. Mal. 2:15 asks: "And what does the one seek?" and the next two words: "God's seed," are perhaps the answer. But what do they mean? The preceding and stylistically difficult section is dealing with the urgent problem of a people led astray by mixed marriages and permits the conjecture that God's seed is the national progeny which has its origin in God. The realistic economic idea of right seed (Jer. 2:21) or pure (i.e., unmixed) seed (Lv. 11:37) [19] is applied metonymically to the progeny befitting God's people. But the gen. "God's" puts it almost in the mythical sphere, which is not in keeping with the saying, since here as elsewhere זֶרַע is close to human generation and this is not part of the picture of God, [20] but involuntarily conjures up, not the divine father, but the alien idea of the wife of the gods, which in Elephantine and pre-Moslem Arab lit. is a remnant of the ancient paganism found in Ugaritic. [21] There seems to be a plain connection between Mal. 2:15 and the "holy seed" (זֶרַע הַקֹּדֶשׁ) of Ezr. 9:2, which the people of Israel has adulterated by marriage with the women of the "peoples of the lands," thereby committing sacrilege (מַעַל). The holy seed is regularly used for God's people in the time of Ezra, along the lines of the Deuteronomic development of the ideology of election, cf. Dt. 7:6 (עַם קָדוֹשׁ אַתָּה לַיהוָה). The expression must have been coined in this period. The art. gives the gen. the quality of a fixed fact which is no longer open to discussion. The holy seed is unmistakable, and to use the phrase is to confess this acknowledged fact. When there is no definition (Is. 6:13c (זֶרַע קֹדֶשׁ) a loose subjective image is presented to the reader and seeks his approval. If, then, the text of Is. from Cave I of Qumran has זרע הקדש at 6:13c, it is natural to suppose that the scribe was following a usage current in his group and that Ezr. 9:2 had not been without influence. The wrested LXX text at Is. 1:9: שָׂרִיד כִּמְעַט = σπέρμα → n. 15 is thus to be traced back to the formula in Ezr. 9:2 rather than the secondary Is. 6:13c, which is probably later than Ezr. This v. is particularly important in view of the fact that it is quoted in R. 9:29. The rendering may be arbitrary, but it is also plain to see that it gives the statement not only a new but also a stronger emphasis which was what allowed Paul to quote it in full and in the new sense of the σπέρμα γενέσεως of Wis. 14:6. [22]

Quell

---

[19] Cf. Pedersen, I, 486.

[20] J. Hempel, *Das Ethos d. AT* (1938), 177 f. σπέρμα θεοῦ, which is astonishingly like the mythological-physiological ref. in Pind. Pyth., 3, 15 (→ 536, 29) to a woman's conceiving by Apollo, is worth noting only as an odd linguistic exaggeration.

[21] J. Wellhausen, *Reste arab. Heidentums*[2] (1927), 24; E. Sachau, *Aram. Pap. u. Ostraka aus Elephantine* (1911), Pap. 18 VII 6. Cf. also "daughter of a strange god" in Mal. 2:11. For Ugar. cf. M. Pope, "El in the Ugaritic Texts," VT Suppl., 2 (1955), 39-42.

[22] The seed motif is not as important in the OT as in some fig. expressions in the NT, e.g., the parables of the seed delivered by Jesus → 545, 3 ff.; 546, 4 ff.; 546, 36 ff., or the contrasting of σπορὰ φθαρτή and ἄφθαρτος in 1 Pt. 1:23 → 546, 31 ff. Only in rudimentary fashion is the image used for the work of God's Word and Kingdom, cf. Is. 61:11. The motif of sowing that may or may not thrive is represented by the metaphor of the rain which falls on the earth and makes it fruitful for new sowing, Is. 55:10.

C. Judaism.

1. σπέρμα.

a. Philo.

The term is much favoured by Philo in both the lit. and the transf. sense. Thus he speaks of the seed of living creatures and plants in Leg. All., III, 227; Poster. C., 171; Deus Imm., 87, and esp. of the seed of men in Rer. Div. Her., 34. All living creatures are formed by the movement of seed, Leg. All., II, 37. Seed is the origin of the coming into being of all living creatures, Leg. All., III, 185; Aet. Mund., 94. But it is a mean thing (Leg. All., III, 67), being like slime (loc. cit.). Phusis is over it. It begins with the lowly seed but ends with the developed structure of animal and man, 68.

The transf. use is equally common in Philo. Bodies arise from human seed, souls from divine seed, Vit. Mos., 279. God has made seeds and roots for the gt. plant of the cosmos, Plant., 48. Hence man must be grateful to the generous God who has scattered luminous, radiant, and rational grains of seed in the soul like the stars in heaven, Leg. All., III, 40. In this context we find phrases like "seed of virtue" in Leg. All., III, 68, "of wickedness," 242, of καλοκαγαθία, Migr. Abr., 24 ;"the seed destined for incorruptibility" Ebr., 212; "the seed of the power of thought" Deus Imm., 130, "of peace" Leg. Gaj., 108, "of hope" Praem. Poen., 12, "of felicity" Cher., 49 and "of insight" Poster. C., 135. All these expressions, though typical of Philo and Jewish Hellenism, are rooted in the linguistic tradition of Hell. philosophy. In particular ref. should be made to the Stoic doctrine of the λόγος σπερματικός, i.e., the dividing of the finest substance, the thinking, fire-like world soul, among individual living creatures, esp. men, Zeno Citieus Stoicus Fr., 102 (v. Arnim, I, 28, 26); 108 (I, 32, 17), in whose soul the ἡγεμονικόν is a σπερματικὸς λόγος of this kind. This leads to the very common phrase σπέρματα τῆς ἀρετῆς, since virtue in Hell. ethics is ultimately the unfolding of reason. In Philo's theology, then, the palm goes to these θεῖα σπέρματα, Cher., 46; Ebr., 30; Poster. C., 170 f. This idea of the divine seed may perhaps be ascribed to Philo's contacts with Hell. mystery wisdom.

b. The Qumran Essenes.

זרע is seldom used in the Dead Sea Scrolls. It occurs only once in the lit. sense, the time of "sowing," 1 QS 10:7. Elsewhere the transf. sense rules : "progeny," "descendants." God has upheld His covenant with the "descendants of the fathers" (1 QM 13:7); to those who serve God faithfully "posterity" is promised for ever (1 QH 17:14); the "progeny of the elect of God" will fill the surface of the earth (Damasc. 2:12 [2:9]); the "off-spring of Israel" (i.e., the Qumran Essenes) must live acc. to the legal statutes (Damasc. 12:2 [15:3]). In another sense there is ref. to the "fruits" of the earth which carry within them the blessings of eternity for the children of light, 1 QS 4:7.

c. The Rabbinate.

זֶרַע means "seed," "plant" in jShebi, 2, 7 (34a, 17 ff.), transf. "progeny" : "Eve saw the offspring whose origin is elsewhere. Who was this ? The King Messiah," Gn. r., 23, 5 on 4:25, cf. also 51, 8 on 19:32. There is transf. usage in bShab., 31a, where the tractate has זרעים for "faith," since the sower believes in the divine world-order.

2. σπείρω.

a. Philo is very fond of this word. It is not common in the lit. sense. The sower sows in Leg. All., III, 227, men sow and plant in Op. Mund., 80, cf. also Leg. All., III, 170, and it is man's natural destiny to sow physical seed, Ebr., 271. The transf. use is far more common, "to sow virtue" in Leg. All., III, 180, which is naturally to sow and plant in the soul (I, 80), or to sow unrighteousness, Conf. Ling., 152. It is God alone who sows the ideas of immortal and virginal virtues (Cher., 52) or τὰ καλά (Leg. All., I, 49). Philo says this again and again. God sows understanding and virtue in Leg. All., I, 79, earthly virtue in I, 45, cf. also Conf. Ling., 196; Leg. All., III, 181; Migr. Abr., 142 etc. God alone brings it about that men sow noble deeds, Ebr., 224. He sows and begets εὐδαιμονεῖν in souls, Leg. All., III, 219. Philo's allegorical theology develops the strange combination "psychic husbandry," which in distinction from physical husbandry sows virtues and reaps a happy life as fruit, Agric., 25. Wisdom, the mother of all things, sows learning, culture, knowledge, understanding, and good and praiseworthy acts in the soul, Fug., 52.

b. In Rabb. lit. זָרַע means "to sow," "to scatter seed," jSota, 1, 8 (17a, 63 ff.); Gn. r., 83, 5 on 36:43. In the hi the word means "to void seed," of the male, bBer., 60a. זָרַע means "to sow." bRH, 16a : he should sow betimes ; jPea, 7, 4 (20b, 10): he sowed the field with carrots, also bChul., 93b. For transf. usage cf. jKil., 1, 6 (27a, 59): "Fructifying takes place" (of two different fish).

3. σπορά.

In Philo we find the lit. sense "sowing" of plants, Op. Mund., 41, 59; Virt., 145; also "seed" : the eunuch cannot put forth seed, Som., II, 184; birth of children, Spec. Leg., III, 62, also 113. A fixed expression in Philo is σπορὰ καὶ γένεσις "begetting and birth of children," Spec. Leg., I, 326, also Vit. Mos., 111, 132, 137 etc. Marriage, then, is the sowing and children are the fruit, Spec. Leg., II, 133; III, 179. All else is illegitimate, Vit. Mos., I, 302. But in the main the use in Philo is transf. Leah received the "seed of virtue" from God, Leg. All., III, 180. The number 7 arose without generation, Vit. Mos., II, 210. This Philo can speak of "the holy and divine seed of virtue," Vit. Mos., I, 101 and of "the invisible seed of reasonable teachings," Som., I, 199.

4. σπόρος.

The lit. sense "seed" occurs in Philo Spec. Leg., I, 165; Virt., 90. Furrows are made for sowing, Op. Mund., 115, also Spec. Leg., III, 32. Sowing is the origin of all life, harvest its end, Fug., 171. But the term also carries the sense of human semen, Spec. Leg., I, 216, and Philo can even speak of the holy seed of the high-priest in Spec. Leg., I, 105, cf. also Som., I, 202. In a transf. sense he speaks of the "seed of virtue" which sinks into good ground, Spec. Leg., III, 29. The seed also receives divine seed, Exsecr., 160.

5. σπόριμος does not occur in Philo.

D. The New Testament.

1. σπέρμα.

a. The Synoptists. In its literal sense the word "seed" occurs only in the parabolic tradition : the parable of the wheat and the tares (Mt. 13:24, 27), its interpretation (13:37, 38), and the parable of the grain of mustard-seed (Mt. 13:32 par.). In each case the reference is to the seed of plants which the farmer sows in his field. The Synoptic story of the question of the Sadducees uses the term more than once in the transferred sense of "progeny," "offspring," "child" (Mk. 12:19, 20, 21, 22 and par.). In the Magnificat God is extolled as the eternally faithful God who keeps the promises which He has given to Abraham and his "descendants" (Lk. 1:55). We find the same usage in Ac. 3:25; 7:5, 6 : "seed of Abraham," and 13:23 : "seed of David."

b. The Johannine Tradition. Here the word is found only 5 times all told. The use is always transferred. The Christ promised by the OT will be the "descendant of David" (Jn. 7:42). The Jews are "Abraham's seed" according to their own saying in 8:33 and that of Jesus in 8:37. The sense is the same in Rev. 12:17 : the demon-dragon wages war on the "progeny" of the woman, i.e., Christian martyrs. The meaning is rather different, however, in 1 Jn. 3:9. He who is born of God does not sin, because His seed abides in him. As the examples show, the idea of God's seed does not occur in Pharisaic or Qumran Essene circles but is common in Hellenistic Judaism (→ 543, 11 ff.) and the mystery religions.[23] But the sphere of the Hellenistic mysteries is transcended by 1 Jn. inasmuch as the seed of God here is the Spirit who manifests Himself in His Word → I, 671, 8 ff.[24] Baptism is not primarily in view.

c. Paul. Paul's usage is along the lines indicated thus far. The transferred sense predominates. There is reference to the seed of plants only in 1 C. 15:38 and to the seed in the sower's hand only in 2 C. 9:10. Elsewhere Paul follows the Israelite Jewish tradition and is always referring to the seed of David, Abraham, or Isaac. Statistically it is worth noting that easily the most common reference is to Abraham's "seed" (R. 4:13, 16, 18; 9:7; 11:1; 2 C. 11:22; Gl. 3:29), and this is related typologically to Christ (Gl. 3:16, 19) and hence to the NT community (→ II, 583, 27 ff.; III, 721, 5 ff.). R. 9:8; Gl. 3:29 etc. There is only one reference each in Paul to David's "seed" (R. 1:3) and Isaac's "seed" (R. 9:7).

d. In the Pastorals the term occurs only once in 2 Tm. 2:8 for the "descendants" of David.

e. In Hb. 11:11 we find a sense unusual in the NT, namely, "human seed." In 2:16 the reference is to "Abraham's progeny" and in 11:18 to that of Isaac.

---

[23] Cf. Wnd. Kath. Br., *ad loc.* for examples.
[24] Cf. *ibid., ad loc.*

2. σπείρω.

In the main the use of this word follows that of secular Greek → 537, 14 ff. In the Synoptic Gospels the literal sense predominates : "to sow," "to scatter seed," especially in the parables [25] of the sower (Mt. 13:3 f., 18 f., 20, 22, 23 and par.), the wheat and the tares (Mt. 13:24 [25 : ἐπισπείρω], 27, 37, 39) and the grain of mustard-seed (Mt. 13:31). Cf. also Mt. 25:24, 26 and par. and Mt. 6:26 and par. The word is used a transferred sense for the logos and for events which summon man to decide either to accept (or yield) or to reject, Mk. 4:15; Mt. 13:19. In the Johannine writings the term is found only twice and both times in the literal sense, Jn. 4:36, 37. Paul is rather fond of the word ; with a few exceptions (2 C. 9:10; 1 C. 15:36 f.) it is used only in the transferred sense, e.g., 1 C. 9:11. In 1 C. especially it is a key-word for Paul in his debate with the Gnostic Jewish Christians. In 1 C. 15 alone it occurs 7 times, v. 36, 37, 42, 43, 44. The familiar process whereby the seed dies when it is sown and then is made alive again is applied by the apostle to the resurrection from the dead, → III, 811, 10 ff. : "It is sown a body in corruption, dishonour and weakness," 1 C. 15:42 ff., and in contrast to this, the physical body, stands the spiritual body. In the pregnant context the image of sowing has theological significance for Paul because he believes that by means of it he can decisively meet the γυμνότης eschatology (→ VI, 420, 17 ff.) of his opponents, 1 C. 15:35 f. and 2 C. 5:1 ff. As Paul sees it, the line of thought suggested by sowing can show how far there may be a bodily life in the eschaton in spite of death and raising to life again. For Paul the *tertium comparationis* in this metaphor lies in the fact that continuity of physical existence persists even and precisely through death. In 2 C. 9:6 σπείρω refers to Christian liberality ; for Paul the amount sown, the richness of the gift, is causally connected with the amount of the harvest. In Gl. 6:7 f. sowing and reaping are related to man's decision *vis-à-vis* the *kerugma*. Man can sow either to the flesh or to the spirit. The very different sowing will produce a fundamentally different eschatological harvest. Elsewhere the term occurs only in Jm. 3:18 (→ II, 200, 39 ff.), which speaks of sowing the fruit of righteousness.

3. σπορά.

This word is a hapax legomenon in the NT and occurs only in 1 Pt. 1:23. In a transferred sense it denotes here the living and abiding divine word of baptism by which Christians are born again.

4. σπόρος.

This word is not common in the NT. The literal sense predominates in the Synoptists : earthly, corruptible "seed" which the farmer scatters on the land, Mk. 4:26 f. and par., so also 2 C. 9:10. In Lk. 8:11 this seed is equated with God's Word, and in 2 C. 9:10 it is the seed of liberality, to which Paul is summoning the Corinthians.

---

[25] On these cf. N. A. Dahl, "The Parables of Growth," *Stud. Theol.,* 5 (1951), esp. 152-165.

5. σπόριμος.

The neuter plural occurs in the NT in the sense of "sown fields," "fields of grain," identifying a locality, Mk. 2:23 and par.

E. Post-Apostolic Fathers.

1. σπέρμα.

In 1 Cl., 24, 5 there is lit. ref. to the "seed" of plants on the basis of 1 C. 15:35 ff. and probably also the Synoptic parable of the sower. In the sense of "progeny" the term occurs in 1 Cl., 10, 4-6 in 2 OT quotations from Gn. 13:14 ff. and Gn. 15:5 f. (cf. also 1 Cl., 32, 2; 56, 14 and Barn., 3, 3). The ref. is to God's promise of numerous descendants to Lot and Abraham. In Herm. v., 2, 2, 2 σπέρμα means "progeny" in the sense of "family." 1 Cl., 16, 11 quotes Is. 53:1-12. The seed which lives for a long time is the spiritual offspring. Similarly in Herm. s., 9, 24, 4 the angel of repentance promises "eternal offspring" to the righteous. Acc. to Ign. Eph., 18, 2 Christ was born of the "seed of David" (just David in R., 7, 3) and the Holy Spirit.

2. σπείρω.

This occurs in the lit. sense in 1 Cl., 24, 5 : the sowing of seed, and in, Barn., 9, 5 in an inaccurate quotation from Jer. 4:3 : sowing among thorns. Ign. has it twice in a transferred sense for the sowing of bad teaching, against which he issues a warning in Eph., 9, 1.

3. σπόρος.

This word occurs only once in the lit. sense for the sowing of seed, 1 Cl., 24, 4.

Schulz

† σπλάγχνον, † σπλαγχνίζομαι, † εὔσπλαγχνος, † πολύσπλαγχνος, † ἄσπλαγχνος	→ ἔλεος, II, 477, 1 ff.; → οἰκτίρω, V, 159, 15 ff.

Contents : A. Greek Usage : 1. The Noun ; 2. The Verb ; 3. The Compounds. B. The Word Group in Later Jewish Writings : 1. The Septuagint ; 2. The Testaments of the Twelve Patriarchs ; 3. Philo and Josephus. C. New Testament Usage : 1. σπλαγχνίζομαι in the Synoptic Gospels ; 2. σπλάγχνα in Paul ; 3. The Rest of the New Testament. D. The Word Group in the Post-Apostolic Fathers and Early Christian Writings.

A. Greek Usage.

1. The Noun. In early Gk. lit. the noun[1] occurs almost always in the plur.[2] It originally denotes the "inward parts" of a sacrifice, and specifically the nobler parts as distinct from the ἔντερα, ἔγκατα, i.e., the heart, liver, lungs, and kidneys, which are separated in the sacrifice and consumed by the participants at the beginning of the sacrificial meal. The word can then go on to mean the "sacrifice" itself.[3] From the 5th cent. it is used anthropologically for the "inward parts" of man, so that the resultant ambiguity gives rise to jests : A boy who has eaten too much of the σπλάγχνα and drunk too much wine at the sacrificial feast says to his mother : ὦ μῆτερ, ἐμῶ τὰ σπλάγχνα. ἡ δὲ εἶπεν· οὐχὶ τὰ σά, τέκνον, ἃ δὲ κατέφαγες, Corpus Fabularum Aesopicarum, 47, I.[4] Individual parts like the liver, lungs and spleen can be called σπλάγχνα.[5] Finally the term as an anthropological one is a particularly forceful expression for the lower part of the body, esp. the "womb" ὑπὸ σπλάγχνων ἐλθεῖν, Pind. Olymp., 6, 43[6] and the "loins" as the seat of the power of procreation, τῶν σῶν ... ἐκ σπλάγχνων ἕνα, Soph. Ant., 1066, cf. IG, 14, 1977, 3 f. Derived from this use is the occasional description of "children" as σπλάγχνα : οἱ παῖδες σπλάγχνα λέγονται, Artemid. Onirocr., I, 44 (p. 42, 2 f.).[7] But this is no autonomous sense : it is very closely related to that of "inner parts," as may be seen very clearly from the statement ὁ μὲν

σ π λ ά γ χ ν ο ν κ τ λ.   Pr. Bauer, Liddell-Scott, Moult.-Mill., s.v.; H. Braun, Spätjüd.-häretischer u. frühchr. Radikalismus, II (1958), 126; J. B. Lightfoot, To the Philippians[12] (1896) on 1:8; Loh. Phil. on 1:8.

[1] Orig. plur. of σπλήν "spleen," v. Schwyzer, I, 408, 489, n. 1 cf. Boisacq, 899.

[2] The plur. is not a Semitism, Bl.-Debr. § 108, 3. Agreement with the Hbr. plur. רַחֲמִים is no accident but is materially apt. For the Hbr. equivalents → 550, 5 ff.

[3] Liddell-Scott, Pass., s.v.

[4] Ed. A. Hausrath, I, 1 (1940), 64 f.

[5] Examples in Liddell-Scott, s.v.

[6] Cf. τὸ κοινὸν σπλάγχνον οὗ πεφύκαμεν in Aesch. Sept. c. Theb., 1031; the sing. here stresses descent from one and the same womb.

[7] Cf. the context : ὁ μὲν γὰρ ὄψεται παῖδας ἰδίους, ὁ δὲ κτήματα. καὶ γὰρ οἱ παῖδες σπλάγχνα λέγονται ὡς ἐντόσθια, καὶ ὥσπερ οἴκῳ κτήματα, οὕτω τὰ σπλάγχνα τοῖς λαγόσιν ἐγκεῖται... δεινὸν δὲ πᾶσι τὸ ὑπό τινος κατανοεῖσθαι τὰ σπλάγχνα· πραγμάτων γὰρ πονηρῶν καὶ δικῶν ἐπαγωγὴν σημαίνει καὶ τὰ κρυπτὰ ἐλέγχει, Artemid. Onirocr., I, 44 (p. 42, 2 ff.).

γὰρ ἀετὸς τὸ ἔτος ἐσήμαινεν, ἐν ᾧ ἔμελλεν αὐτῷ ὁ παῖς τεχθῆναι, τὰ δὲ σπλάγχνα τὸν παῖδα, *ibid.*, V, 57 (p. 264, 15 ff.).[8] In an approach to the transf. use the σπλάγχνα are seen as the seat of "impulsive passions" such as "anger" σπλάγχνα θερμῆναι κότῳ Aristoph. Ra., 844; cf. 1006; Eur. Alc., 1009, "anxious desire," σπλάγχνα δέ μου κελαινοῦται, Aesch. Choeph., 413, "love" ἰδών σε ... ἐκύμηνε τὰ σπλάγχν' ἔρωτι καρδίην ἀνοιστρηθείς, Herond. Mim., I, 57, cf. Theocr. Idyll., 7, 99; Dion Hal. Ant. Rom., 11, 35, 4; the word finally comes to mean much the same as "heart" in its transf. sense as the centre of personal "feeling" and "sensibility," cf. esp. the compounds of σπλάγχνα → line 24 ff. In distinction from καρδία (→ III, 608, 9 ff.),[9] which is more the seat of nobler affections like love and hate, courage and fear, joy and sorrow, σπλάγχνα is either more comprehensive or it is often a more blunt, forceful and unequivocal term.[10]

Greek usage, at any rate in the pre-Christian period, does not view the σπλάγχνα as the seat of heart-felt mercy, as in later Jewish and the first Christian writings. There is no developed transferred use, and the word is never employed for mercy itself. This rather rough term seems none too well adapted to express Christian virtue or the divine dealings.[11]

2. The Verb. σπλαγχνεύω is based on the use of σπλάγχνα for the inner parts of a sacrifice and means a. "to eat the inner parts" (at the sacrificial meal), Aristoph. Av., 984; Dio. C., 37, 30; Dorotheus in Athen., 9, 78 (410b), and b. "to use the entrails in divination."[12] In secular Gk. σπλαγχνίζω occurs only once in an inscr. from Kos (4th cent. B.C.) in sense a.[13] No transf. use has been found outside Jewish and early Chr. lit.

3. The Compounds. Of the compounds used in Jewish and early Chr. lit. we occasionally find only ἄσπλαγχνος and εὐσπλαγχνία in pre-Chr. Gk. writings; πολυ(εὐ)-σπλαγχνος has not been found thus far in the class. world. ἄσπλαγχνος means "cowardly," "without strength or savour" (cf. "no guts"): μή τοι φύσιν γ' ἄσπλαγχνος ἐκ κείνου γεγώς, Soph. Ai., 472. εὐσπλαγχνία means "boldness" (or perhaps "magnanimity"): λαβὼν δ' ἄν φημι κάλλιστον Φρυγῶν δῶρον δέχεσθαι τῆς ἐμῆς εὐσπλαγχνίας, Eur. Rhes., 191 f. Like this one, other compounds refer esp. to one's "mettle": cf. μεγαλόσπλαγχνος for the "unbounded pride" of Medea which does not shrink from infanticide, Eur. Med., 109; θρασύσπλαγχνος for "fearless," "bold," Aesch. Prom., 730; Eur. Hipp., 424; κακόσπλαγχνος for "cowardly," "without spirit," Aesch. Sept. c. Theb., 237. But there is the possibility that in post-class. usage a change of meaning took place and mercy replaced courage, for in a fr. of the Stoic Chrysipp. ἄσπλαγχνος is expounded as τὸ μηδὲν ἔχειν ἔνδον συναλγοῦν, Fr., 902 (v. Arnim,

---

[8] On the close relations of individual parts to the various objects of prediction and interpretation *v.* Artemid. Onirocr., I, 44 (p. 41, 27 ff.).

[9] Cf. Liddell-Scott, *s.v.*

[10] The kind of love meant may be seen from the use of the adj. σπλαγχνικός in a conjuration in love magic, P. Osl., I, 1, 144-150: σοὶ δὲ, ᵗΙσι καὶ ῏Οσιρι καὶ χθόνος ... καὶ δαίμονες οἱ ὑπὸ τὸν χθόνον, ἐγίρεσθαι, οἱ ἐκ τοῦ βάθους καὶ ποιήσαται τήν ... ἀγροιπνῖν, ἀεροπετῖσθαι, πινῶσαν, διψῶσαν, ὕπνου μὴ τυγχάνουσαν ἐρᾶσθαι ἐμοῦ ... ἔρωτι σπλαγχνικῷ, ἕως ἂν ἔλθη καὶ τὴν θηλυκὴν ἑαυτῆς φύσειν τῇ ἀρσενικῇ μου κολλήσῃ. Liddell-Scott, *s.v.* transl. "tender" here, but gives no other instances.

[11] BGU, IV, 1139, 16-18 (from a written petition) is difficult and uncertain: ... Διὸ ἀξιοῦμέν [σε] | τὸν πάντων σωτῆρα καὶ ἀντιλήμπτορα ὑπὲρ σπλάγχνου ("for the sake of mercy"?) τὸν ἀγῶνα | ποιούμενοι ... (Moult.-Mill., "for pity's sake").

[12] For examples *v.* Liddell-Scott, *s.v.*

[13] R. Herzog, "Heilige Gesetze v. Kos," AAB, 1928, 6 (1928), 12, Inscr. No. 4: line 12: ... τοὶ ἀεὶ ἡβῶντες ἐπα]ρξάμενοι καὶ τῶν σπλάγχνω[ν

II, 249, 12 ff.). It is true that already Gal. complains that this passage is hard to understand, and in pre-Chr. Gk. lit. there is no other example of this use of the term in compounds.

B. The Word Group in Later Jewish Writings.

1. The Septuagint. The noun and the verb, the former only in the plur., are none too common in the LXX. The noun is mostly restricted to later portions. Hence the Hbr. equivalents are available only in a few instances : Prv. 12:10 : רַחֲמִים; 26:22 : בֶּטֶן; [14] Sir. 30:7 Syr. "heart." [15] In all the other 12 instances either the Hbr. is missing [16] or — and this is the rule — the Gk. is the original.

The verb occurs only in Prv. 17:5 (mid.) and 2 Macc. 6:8 (act.); in neither case is there a Hbr. original. The LXX, then, does not enable us to say what was the OT Hbr. background for the use of σπλάγχνα in Jewish works in Gk. The normal LXX equivalent for רַחֲמִים is not σπλάγχνα but οἰκτιρμοί → V, 160, 8 ff. Similarly for רחם the LXX has οἰκτίρω (in the NT only in an OT quotation at R. 9:15) or ἐλεέω, never σπλαγχνίζομαι. [17] The verb is a sacrificial term in 2 Macc. 6:8 : Antiochus' command ... τὴν αὐτὴν ἀγωγὴν κατὰ τῶν Ἰουδαίων ἄγειν καὶ σπλαγχνίζειν, "to carry out the required sacrifice"; cf. σπλαγχνισμός for the official sacrificial action in 2 Macc. 6:7, 21; 7:42; also σπλαγχνοφάγος in Wis. 12:5. Other ref. have the gen. sense of "entrails." [18]

But sometimes the σπλάγχνα are also the "seat of feeling." One may see the transition to this sense in 2 Macc. 9:5 f.: ἄρτι δὲ αὐτοῦ (sc. Ἀντιόχου) καταλήξαντος τὸν λόγον ἔλαβεν αὐτὸν ἀνήκεστος τῶν σπλάγχνων ἀλγηδὼν ("unbearable sorrow came upon him in his inward parts") καὶ πικραὶ τῶν ἔνδον βάσανοι, πάνυ δικαίως τὸν πολλαῖς καὶ ξενιζούσαις συμφοραῖς ἑτέρων σπλάγχνα ("the hearts of others") βασανίσαντα. In this connection cf. also Prv. 26:22 : "Flattering speech goes down to the inmost parts of the σπλάγχνα"; Sir. 30:7 : "At the slightest cry of the spoilt child the father's σπλάγχνα are moved"; Sir. 33:5, where the σπλάγχνα of the fool are compared to a carriage-wheel. There are at least hints of a more specific use in two verses in Prv.: τὰ δὲ σπλάγχνα τῶν ἀσεβῶν ἀνελεήμονα in 12:10 presupposes that

---

13 : τῶν ἐπὶ τοῦ βωμοῦ] καὶ τοῦ λίθου τοῦ ἐν ταῖς ἐλα[ίαι
14 : ς ἀψάμενοι ὄμνυντι᾽ σπ]λαγχνίζεται πράτιστα μὲ[ν
15 : τὰ ἐπὶ βωμοῦ, εἶτα τὰ] ἐπὶ τοῦ λίθου καὶ τὰ ἀπὸ τοῦ λί
16 : θου ...
Acc. to Herzog the ref. is to a ceremony like the manhood oath at Athens; lines 12 ff. speak of the actual taking of the oath.

[14] Sᶜ reads κοιλία here, obviously a later correction acc. to the HT.
[15] "Heart" in Gk. Sir. is usually ἔγκατα or τὰ ἐντός, R. Smend, *Die Weisheit des Jesus Sirach erklärt* (1906) on Sir. 19:26; 21:4.
[16] Ιερ. 28:13 : ἥκει τὸ πέρας σου ἀληθῶς εἰς τὰ σπλάγχνα σου, is uncertain; either there is a slip in transl. or the Hbr. original was different from ours. The present Mas. (Jer. 51:13) has בָּא קִצֵּךְ אַמַּת בִּצְעֵךְ "Thine end has come, the ell of thy cutting (= the thread of thy life is cut off)," cf. W. Rudolph, *Jer., Hndbch. AT,* I, 122 (1958), ad loc. LXX obviously read בְּמֵעַיִךְ for בִּצְעֵךְ. מֵעִים is an exact Hbr. equivalent of σπλάγχνα.
[17] Only later transl. occasionally have σπλάγχνα for רַחֲמִים; cf. ᾽ΑΣ LXX [75 c 3] at Gn. 43:30 (LXXʳᵉˡˡ ἔντερα); ΣΘ at Is. 63:15 (LXX οἰκτιρμοί vl); ᾽Α at Am. 1:11 (LXX μήτρα). σπλαγχνίζομαι occurs in Σ at 1 Βασ. 23:21 for חמל and in Σ at Ez. 24:21 for מחמל (LXX πονέω in the first v. and φείδομαι, the commonest Gk. word for חמל, in the second).
[18] Ιερ. 28:13; 2 Macc. 9:5; very vivid in the description of the martyrdom of the 7 brothers in 4 Macc. 5:30 : οὐδ᾽ ἂν ἐκκόψειάς μου τὰ ὄμματα καὶ τὰ σπλάγχνα μου τήξειας, cf. 10:8; 11:19; for "corpse": .... οἱ τεθνηκότες ἐν τῷ ᾅδῃ, ὧν ἐλήμφθη τὸ πνεῦμα αὐτῶν ἀπὸ τῶν σπλάγχνων αὐτῶν, Bar. 2:17.

the σπλάγχνα might be regarded as the seat of the positive stirring of pity. [19] The only instance of the mid. σπλαγχνίζομαι in the LXX has the verb for the first time in the sense "to be merciful" at Prv. 17:5 : ὁ δὲ σπλαγχνιζόμενος [20] ἐλεηθήσεται. Elsewhere σπλάγχνα in a transf. sense denotes only "natural feelings." It is "mother love" in 4 Macc. 14:13; εὐσέβεια vanquishes this, 15:1. The brave mother of the seven martyrs will not be guided by this συμπάθεια σπλάγχνων (14:13), ἀλλὰ τὰ σπλάγχνα αὐτῆς ὁ εὐσεβὴς λογισμὸς ἐν αὐτοῖς τοῖς πάθεσιν ἀνδρειώσας ἐπέτεινεν τὴν πρόσκαιρον φιλοτεκνίαν παριδεῖν, 15:23. Hence the laudation ὦ μῆτερ ἔθνους, ἔκδικε τοῦ νόμου καὶ ὑπερασπίστρια τῆς εὐσεβείας καὶ τοῦ διὰ σπλάγχνων ἀγῶνος ἀθλοφόρε, 15:29. Finally Abraham is expressly mentioned as a model in this war of feelings, 14:20; 15:28. In Wis. 10:5, too, Abraham is the righteous man whom σοφία kept unspotted before God and helped him to conquer even ἐπὶ τέκνου σπλάγχνοις ("in face of merely creaturely love for his son").

2. The Testaments of the Twelve Patriarchs. These offer many instances of a use which differs plainly from that of the LXX.

a. σπλάγχνα can be a "portion of man's inward parts as the seat of feelings," par. to καρδία and ἥπατα, Test. S. 2:4; Zeb. 2:4 f.; Jos. 15:3, but also as the "centre of human feeling and sensibility generally," i.e., the whole person in respect of the depth and force of feeling ἐγὼ δὲ ἐκαιόμην τοῖς σπλάγχνοις μου ἀναγγεῖλαι ὅτι πέπραται Ἰωσήφ, "I burned ...," Test. N. 7:4; ὦ τέκνον χρηστόν, ἐνίκησας τὰ σπλάγχνα Ἰακώβ, "thou hast vanquished Jacob in his deep sorrow," B. 3:7. Cf. also Test. Abr. : ἐκινήθησαν δὲ τὰ σπλάγχνα τοῦ Ἀβραὰμ καὶ ἐδάκρυσεν, "Abraham was overcome by grief," 3 A (p. 80, 6 f.); cf. 5 A (82, 20; 83, 2). [21] The ref. is esp. to man's nobler feelings and higher will, ὑπόστασις "conviction" in Test. Zeb. 2:4; συμπάθεια "sympathy" [22] in Test. Zeb. 7:4, cf. S. 2:4. But the σπλάγχνα are above all the seat of "mercy" ἔχετε οὖν ἔλεος ἐν σπλάγχνοις ὑμῶν, Test. Zeb. 5:3 : οὐκ ἐποίησαν ἔλεος ἐν σπλάγχνοις αὐτῶν, 5:4. This leads on to the transf. use found in the expression σπλάγχνα ἐλέους, "loving mercy," Test. Zeb. 7:3; 8:2, 6. [23]

b. Once in Test. Zeb. 4:2 : ἐγὼ δὲ σπλαγχνιζόμενος τὸν Ἰωσὴφ οὐκ ἔφαγον, the verb σπλαγχνίζομαι denotes the mere "emotion," but in all other passages it expresses the guiding inner disposition which leads to mercy : καὶ ὑμεῖς οὖν ... ἀδιακρίτως πάντας σπλαγχνιζόμενοι ἐλεᾶτε, Test. Zeb. 7:2, also 6:4; 7:1; 8:3.

c. In this connection we find for the first time εὔσπλαγχνος and εὐσπλαγχνία for the human virtue and disposition of "pity" : Ἰωσὴφ ... εὔσπλαγχνος καὶ ἐλεήμων ὑπάρχων, Test. S. 4:4 cf. B. 4:1. The exercise of εὐσπλαγχνία πρὸς πάντας is a universal and urgent commandment, Test. Zeb. 5:1 cf. 8:1. The crown of glory is promised for observing it, B. 4:1.

d. This anthropological use in Test. XII simply corresponds to a theological use in the narrower sense. The most important element in the new usage which begins in Test. XII is that the originally rather crude term σπλάγχνα can be applied to God Him-

---

[19] Prv. 12:10 (→ 550, 7) is the only LXX instance of σπλάγχνα for רַחֲמִים. In meaning it is in full correspondence with the Hbr., cf. → ἔλεος, II, 480, 18 ff.

[20] BS ἐπισπλαγχνιζόμενος.

[21] The unsupported assertion of N. Turner, "The 'Testament of Abraham': Problems in Bibl. Gk.," NTSt, 1 (1954/55), 219-223, that the use of σπλάγχνα etc. in Test. Abr. corresponds at all pts. to that of the OT and NT is much too general. In this respect Test. A. is in direct proximity to Test. XII and Herm. (→ 558, 5 ff.); cf. the example from Test. A. → n. 25.

[22] To be distinguished from συμπάθεια σπλάγχνων in 4 Macc. 14:13 → lines 5 ff.

[23] All three passages are in the part of Test. Zeb. transmitted in only one portion of the MSS (b d g in Charles).

self. At the end of the days stands the revelation of the σπλάγχνα of God ἐπ' ἐσχά-
των τῶν ἡμερῶν ὁ θεὸς ἀποστελεῖ τὰ σπλάγχνα αὐτοῦ ἐπὶ τῆς γῆς, Test. Zeb.
8:2. The ἄνθρωπος ποιῶν δικαιοσύνην καὶ ποιῶν ἔλεος (i.e., the Messiah) is called
τὸ σπλάγχνον [24] Κυρίου, Test. N. 4:5 cf. L. 4:4. [25] To the admonition to exercise pity
corresponds the principle ἵνα καὶ ὁ Κύριος εἰς ὑμᾶς σπλαγχνισθεὶς ἐλεήσῃ ὑμᾶς,
Zeb. 8:1 cf. 8:3. ἐλεήμων was already current to denote the divine mercy and now the
word εὔσπλαγχνος is used as well, [26] Zeb. 9:7. It is esp. in relation to God's eschatological acts that σπλάγχνα and εὐσπλαγχνία are used to characterise the divine
nature : ἀλλ' ἐπισυνάξει ὑμᾶς ἐν πίστει διὰ τῆς εὐσπλαγχνίας αὐτοῦ A. 7:7. The
well-known end-time promise καὶ ἀνατελεῖ ὑμῖν τοῖς φοβουμένοις τὸ ὄνομά μου
ἥλιος δικαιοσύνης καὶ ἴασις ἐν ταῖς πτέρυξιν αὐτοῦ (Mal. 3:20) is quoted with a
typical addition : ... καὶ ἴασις καὶ εὐσπλαγχνία ἐν ταῖς πτέρυξιν αὐτοῦ, Test.
Zeb. 9:8. [27]

Though hinted at only in two verses of Prv. in LXX (→ 550, 28 ff.), this usage is
thus the main one in Test. XII. σπλάγχνα is no longer employed for "entrails" in the
gen. sense, and the verb no longer gives evidence of its original connection with sacrifice
(the act. does not occur at all). As a rule "mercy" and "to be merciful" are the best
transl., and σπλάγχνα in this sense is the theme of discussion in Test. Zeb.

Considering the usage of Test. XII as a whole, we find that σπλάγχνα,
σπλαγχνίζομαι and εὔσπλαγχνος have completely replaced the LXX words
οἰκτιρμοί, οἰκτίρω and οἰκτίρμων → V, 160, 8 ff. They are thus a new translation of the Hebrew words רַחֲמִים, רחם, and רַחוּם. The combination of חֶסֶד and רַחֲמִים
(→ II, 479, n. 31), which is a common one in the Hebrew OT, no longer corresponds to ἔλεος and οἰκτιρμοί as in the LXX (e.g., Hos. 2:21), but to ἔλεος and
σπλάγχνα. In particular we are referred back to later Hebrew usage, and hence
to the Dead Sea Scrolls, by the genitive combination σπλάγχνα ἐλέους (Test.
Zeb. 7:3; 8:2, 6), which is a literal rendering of the Hebrew חַסְדֵי רַחֲמִים (1 QS
1:22) or רַחֲמֵי חֶסֶד (1 QS 2:1). [28] The translation of רַחֲמִים by σπλάγχνα, which was
not really introduced in the LXX but in later Jewish writings, and which retains
especially the eschatological element in the Hebrew word (→ II, 481, 9 ff.),
is undoubtedly the direct presupposition of NT usage. It also explains why the
common οἰκτιρμοί etc. of the LXX are so notably rare in the NT (→ V, 161, 6 ff.),
whereas in some early Christian writings σπλάγχνα etc. express very clearly the
sense of the Hebrew רַחֲמִים.

---

[24] This is the only instance in the sing. in Test. XII. This is due to the personifying of
the divine mercy in the figure of the Messiah.

[25] We cannot discuss here the question of Chr. additions to Test. XII. The three last
passages have all been viewed as Chr. interpolations. But this use of σπλάγχνα is not
typically Chr. and finds par. in early Chr. writings only where there might well have been
later Jewish influence, cf. Herm. → 558, 5 ff. In other later Jewish lit. the verb is once used
thus of God in contrast to man : God blames Abraham ὅτι οὐ σπλαγχνίζεται ἐπὶ τοὺς
ἁμαρτωλούς, ἀλλ' ἐγὼ σπλαγχνίζομαι ἐπὶ τοὺς ἁμαρτωλοὺς ὥστε ἐπιστρέψουσιν ...
καὶ σωθήσονται, Test. A. 12 B (p. 116, 31 f.).

[26] Two non-Chr. par. have εὔσπλαγχνος (not in the LXX) as a divine predicate : Prayer
of Man. 7 (Odae, 12, 7): σὺ εἶ κύριος ὕψιστος, εὔσπλαγχνος, μακρόθυμος καὶ
πολυέλεος. P Leid., V, 9, 2 f.: ...κρατῶν τὸν λίθον (the magic stone which represents
deity) τὸν εὔμετρον, τὸν καλοποιόν, τὸν θεῖον, τὸν ἀγνόν, τὸν χρήσιμον, τὸν
φειδωλόν, τὸν εὔσπλαγχνον... The passages are not independent witnesses to this usage
outside the Jewish-Chr. sphere; note the OT name of God in the epiclesis of P. Leid.

[27] The addition καὶ εὐσπλαγχνία finds support in no known form of Mal. 3:20. A new
idea has obviously been imported.

[28] The combining of two synonyms in a st. c. is not common in OT Hbr. but is a feature
in the Dead Sea Scrolls [F. M. Cross Jr.].

3. Philo and Josephus. σπλάγχνα is mostly used in a purely physiological sense in Philo, e.g., in the description of the peace offering λόβος δ᾽ ἥπατος τοῦ κυριωτάτου τῶν σπλάγχνων ἐστὶν ἀπαρχή, Spec. Leg., I, 216, cf. Ebr., 106. σπλάγχνα are also among forbidden means of telling the future, Spec. Leg., I, 62. Stomach, heart, lungs, spleen, liver and kidneys are differentiated as τὰ ἐντὸς μέρη = λεγόμενα σπλάγχνα from the head, breast, trunk and members as τοῦ σώματος τὰ ἐκτὸς μέρη, Op. Mund., 118, cf. Leg. All., I, 12. The σπλάγχνα are the hidden inward parts of the body (Abr., 241) and may thus be used fig. for the kingdom of virtue which only the eye of reason can penetrate : ὁ δὲ τῆς διανοίας ὀφθαλμὸς εἴσω προελθὼν καὶ βαθύνας τὰ ἐν αὐτοῖς σπλάγχνοις ἐγκεκρυμμένα κατεῖδε, Poster. C., 118. In the saying παρελεύσονται καὶ μέχρι σπλάγχνων αἱ τηκεδόνες ἀθυμίας ... ἐμποιοῦσαι σὺν ἐκθλίψει, Exsecr., 151, σπλάγχνα might mean the "inner being" in a transf. sense, but it is more likely that the ref. is a realistic one to physical torments as the consequence of ungodliness. In Leg. Gaj., 368, however, πληγαὶ κατὰ τῶν σπλάγχνων is par. to βάσανοι, κατατάσεις τῆς ὅλης ψυχῆς, so that there can be no doubt but that σπλάγχνα = "inward being," "heart," "soul." The same is true in another passage in Philo which has been wrongly adduced as an instance of the meaning "child": Jacob's lament over what he assumes to be the dead Joseph νυνὶ δ᾽, ὡς λόγος, ἀτιθάσοις καὶ σαρκοβόροις θηρσὶν εὐωχία καὶ θοίνη γέγονας γευσαμένοις καὶ ἑστιαθεῖσι τῶν ἐμῶν σπλάγχνων, who have at the same time eaten "my own heart," i.e., what is near and dear to me, Jos., 25.

There are even fewer approximations to a transf. use in Joseph. than in Philo, though Joseph. often uses the term. Most of the ref. are rather bloodthirsty ones for which the only NT parallel is in the account of the death of Judas in Ac. 1:18, e.g., μέχρι τῶν σπλάγχνων ὑπ᾽ ἀκράτου τῆς λύπης σπαραττομένων, "until his entrails were torn out by constant pain," Bell., 1, 81; cf. 1, 84 (the death of Aristobulus); whipping μέχρι πάντων τὰ σπλάγχνα γυμνῶσαι, Bell., 2, 612, cf. 1, 635. But it is hard to detect any transf. sense even in other cases. Thus when hunger is said to grip the inward parts and the marrow (σπλάγχνα and μυελοί) in Bell., 6, 204, the meaning is obviously literal. In the description of civil war καὶ κατὰ τῶν σπλάγχνων τῶν ἰδίων τὸ ἔθνος στρατολογεῖν the word is used fig., but not in a transf. sense for the inner organism of the nation, Bell., 6, 263.

C. New Testament Usage.

Except at Lk. 1:78 (→ 556, 24 ff.) the noun and adj. do not occur in the Synoptic Gospels. In contrast the use of the verb in the NT is restricted to the Synoptics.

1. σπλαγχνίζομαι in the Synoptic Gospels.

The usage of Test. XII (→ 551, 14 ff.) is continued here. But outside the original parables of Jesus there is no instance of the word being used of men. It is always used to describe the attitude of Jesus and it characterises the divine nature of His acts. This use persists in the one early Christian writing which has the verb apart from the Synoptic Gospels, namely, the Shepherd of Hermas, where the reference is restricted to God alone, → 558, 5 ff. Finally, then, the verb σπλαγχνίζομαι has become solely and simply an attribute of the divine dealings.

a. The verb occupies a central place in three parables of Jesus and here it quite definitely denotes a specific attitude on the part of men. This is to be noted first even though in two of the parables this human attitude is ultimately to be expounded in terms of the coming of the kingdom of God. In the parable of the wicked servant (Mt. 18:23-35) the servant prays μακροθύμησον ἐπ' ἐμοί ... (v. 26) and in answer we read in v. 27: σπλαγχνισθεὶς δὲ ὁ κύριος τοῦ δούλου ἐκείνου ἀπέλυσεν αὐτόν. [29] This gives the term σπλαγχνίζομαι a certain precedence over μακροθυμέω (→ IV, 379, 37 ff.) and ἐλεέω, which are also used in this parable (v. 26, 29, 33). If, with some shift of accent, the juxtaposition of σπλαγχνίζομαι and ὀργίζομαι also underlies the second parable, that of the prodigal son in Lk. 15:11-32, cf. v. 20: εἶδεν αὐτὸν ὁ πατὴρ αὐτοῦ καὶ ἐσπλαγχνίσθη, καὶ δραμών ... with v. 28: ὠργίσθη δὲ (ὁ υἱὸς ὁ πρεσβύτερος) καὶ οὐκ ἤθελεν εἰσελθεῖν. In these parables of Jesus human emotions are described in the strongest of terms in order to bring out the totality of mercy or wrath with which God claims man in His saving acts. [30] In the third passage taken from the oldest stratum of the Synoptic tradition, the illustrative parable of the good Samaritan, σπλαγχνίζομαι is shown to be the basic and decisive attitude in human and hence in Christian acts: Σαμαρίτης δέ τις ὁδεύων ἦλθεν κατ' αὐτὸν καὶ ἰδὼν ἐσπλαγχνίσθη, Lk. 10:33.

b. The Messianic use of the term in the other Synoptic passages is patently different from the usage in these original parables of Jesus. σπλαγχνίζομαι occurs 4 times in Mk. But in what seems to be the oldest stratum of the Marcan tradition it occurs only once, namely, in the account of the feeding of the five thousand in 6:34: καὶ ἐξελθὼν εἶδεν πολὺν ὄχλον, καὶ ἐσπλαγχνίσθη ἐπ' αὐτούς. The word also occurs in the par. story in 8:2, but this can hardly be claimed as an independent instance. The secondary formulation in direct speech (cf. 8:2 and 6:34) does show, however, that σπλαγχνίζομαι must have been an original part of the story of the feeding of the multitude. In Mk. 1:41 and 9:22 the word occurs in healings, but does not seem to have been in the original text. [31] Nevertheless to see in the word a mere embellishment is to miss its true importance in these secondary passages. [32] Jesus is theologically characterised here as the Messiah in whom the divine mercy is present. [33] The only doubt is whether this kind of theological statement is part of the oldest stratum of the tradition. In the relevant par. in Mt. the statements from Mk.'s two accounts (6:34; 8:2) are adopted (Mt. 14:14; 15:32). Mk. 6:34 is used by Mt. a second time in the introduction to the sending forth of the twelve [34] ἰδὼν δὲ τοὺς ὄχλους ἐσπλαγχνίσθη περὶ αὐτῶν ὅτι ἦσαν ... ὡσεὶ πρόβατα (Mt. 9:36). Mt. also takes σπλαγχνισθεὶς (δὲ ὁ Ἰησοῦς) and puts it in the text (from Mk.) of the healing of the (two) blind men (20:34). He thus finds a counterpart to the appeal κύριε ἐλέησον at the beginning of the story, Mt. 20:30 and par. In each case we have, as in Mk., a Messianic characterisation of Jesus rather than the mere depiction of an emotion. All these inter-

---

[29] τοῦ δούλου ἐκείνου goes with ὁ κύριος, not as an obj. gen. with σπλαγχνισθείς. Indication of the object of the feeling in the gen. would be very poor Greek, cf. Bl.-Debr. § 176.

[30] Braun, 126.

[31] Mk. 1:41 D has ὀργισθείς for σπλαγχνισθείς, but this can hardly be original. The par. Mt. 8:3 and Lk. 5:13, which follow Mk. word for word, use neither term. σπλαγχνισθείς occurs in Mk. 9:22 in a passage (vv. 21-24) which is perhaps a secondary interpolation into the story of the healing of the epileptic boy (Mk. 9:14-29); there is no par. for it in Mt. or Lk.

[32] Braun, 162; rightly Kl. Mk. on 6:34 and 8:2.

[33] Cf. Loh. Mk. on 1:41.

[34] Mt. composed the introduction to the charge from Mk. 6:6 and 6:34, cf. Wellh. Mt. on 9:36.

jections are thus part of the tendency of the tradition to describe Jesus increasingly in terms of Messianic attributes. The same applies to the one instance in Lk. apart from the parables already mentioned, i.e., the young man at Nain : ... καὶ ἰδὼν αὐτὴν ὁ κύριος ἐσπλαγχνίσθη, Lk. 7:13. [35]

2. σπλάγχνα in Paul.

Only the noun is found in Paul. As compared with the usage of Test. XII (→ 551, 16 ff.) there is a distinctive but typically Pauline change, σπλάγχνα has not only lost completely the sense of creaturely or natural emotion ; it also shows no traces here of the later Jewish sense of "mercy" → 551, 25 ff. Like other anthropological terms, e.g., καρδία, νοῦς, [36] the word is used in Paul for the whole man, [37] and this especially in so far as he is able as a Christian to give and to experience personal liking and love between man and man. [38] An essential part of the original meaning has been retained to the degree that σπλάγχνα concerns and expresses the total personality at the deepest level. It thus remains a very strong and forceful term which occurs only when Paul is speaking directly and personally, as in 2 Cor. or Philemon, or in a transferred sense in Phil. In 2 C. 6:12 σπλάγχνα is parallel to καρδία : στενοχωρεῖσθε δὲ ἐν τοῖς σπλάγχνοις ὑμῶν, "but you are deeply closed in your capacity to love me, while my heart is wide open to you" (v. 11). 2 C. 7:15 says positively of Titus : τὰ σπλάγχνα αὐτοῦ περισσοτέρως εἰς ὑμᾶς ἐστιν, "he has a deep love for you," the word being parallel here to πνεῦμα "the human spirit," v. 13. Twice in Philemon there is reference to the ἀναπαύειν of the σπλάγχνα (τῶν ἁγίων, v. 7; μου v. 20). The word is again used for the whole person which in the depths of its emotional life has experienced refreshment through consolation and love. The very difficult v. Phlm. 12 is to be taken along the same lines : (Ὀνήσιμον ...) ὃν ἀνέπεμψά σοι, αὐτόν, τοῦτ᾽ ἔστιν τὰ ἐμὰ σπλάγχνα. It is as if Paul, in the runaway slave, came to Philemon in person with his claim to experience love. [39] The frequent use of the word in this short letter shows how personally Paul was involved in the matter.

The two instances of σπλάγχνα in Phil. are disputed and are undoubtedly difficult. εἴ τις [40] σπλάγχνα καὶ οἰκτιρμοί (Phil. 2:1) is to be taken as a summary of the three preceding clauses [41] in which Paul appeals with an oath [42] to the distinctive marks of the life of the Christian community. [43] If elsewhere in

---

[35] Rather oddly Lk. leaves the word out in his version of the feeding of the multitude.

[36] Cf. on this esp. Bultmann Theol., 207-222 (§§ 19, 20).

[37] Hence in almost all the instances one might use the personal noun or pronoun for σπλάγχνα.

[38] Cf. Wnd. 2 K. on 6:12. The sense "love" brings out a special aspect of the OT רַחֲמִים → II, 480, 23 ff.

[39] Transl. of σπλάγχνα by "my son" is rightly rejected by Lightfoot, ad loc., cf. also Dib. Gefbr., ad loc. No more felicitous is "cet objet de ma tendresse," P. J. Verdam, "St. Paul et un serf fugitif," Symbolae van Oven (1946), 214.

[40] The solecism εἴ τις σπλάγχνα καὶ οἰκτιρμοί is not a scribal error and is acceptable if one assumes that ᾽τις has become fixed like τι and εἴ τις is felt to be one word, this being supported by the position of οὖν in the first part of the sentence (εἴ τις οὖν...), Dib. Ph., ad loc.; cf. Bl.-Debr. § 137, 2; 475, 2; Moulton, 89.

[41] So correctly Loh. Phil., ad loc.

[42] ἔι τις means "as sure as there are" (Dib. Ph., ad loc.).

[43] The subj. is not God (Loh. Phil., ad loc.) but the members of the community.

Paul σπλάγχνα means the capacity of man for love or man as one who loves, in this context the word can only mean "love" itself. The word is used in a transferred sense and as a synonym of ἀγάπη, though it is distinct from this inasmuch as it is not a virtue, but love as the mutual experience and gift among Christians. In this sense σπλάγχνα is to be differentiated somewhat from the parallel οἰκτιρμοί. [44] σπλάγχνα καὶ οἰκτιρμοί is thus a pregnant phrase in which "love from the heart" and "personal sympathy" comprehensively describe the essential elements in Christian dealings. A unique expression is the μάρτυς γάρ μου ὁ θεός, ὡς ἐπιποθῶ πάντας ὑμᾶς ἐν σπλάγχνοις Χριστοῦ Ἰησοῦ in Phil. 1:8. [45] The sense here is obviously transferred and σπλάγχνα is thus a pointed term for personal love. But for Paul emotions which might be regarded as personal inclinations are an expression of his being ἐν Χριστῷ, and they have their origin here. Only in the light of this basic relation of the believer to Christ, which is usually called Christ mysticism, [46] can one understand the addition of Χριστοῦ Ἰησοῦ (gen. auctoris) to ἐν σπλάγχνοις. [47] This love and affection which grip and profoundly move the whole man are possible only in Christ. [48]

3. The Rest of the New Testament.

Apart from Ac. 1:18, where σπλάγχνα means "entrails," [49] primitive Christian usage developed either under the influence of Paul or, more commonly, under the direct influence of later Jewish usage. σπλάγχνα οἰκτιρμοῦ is one of several Christian virtues in Col. 3:12 [50] (χρηστότης, ταπεινοφροσύνη, πραΰτης, μακροθυμία). The phrase can hardly have been coined without literary dependence on σπλάγχνα καὶ οἰκτιρμοί in Phil. 2:1 (→ 555, 31 ff.) [51] and it is thus to be translated by "loving mercy" in Pauline fashion. On the other hand διὰ σπλάγχνα ἐλέους θεοῦ ἡμῶν, ἐν οἷς ἐπισκέψεται ἡμᾶς ἀνατολὴ ἐξ ὕψους (Lk. 1:78) reads almost like a quotation from Test. XII → 551, 38 ff. [52] The eschatological character of the term is more strongly felt, and along the lines of the view expressed in Test. XII God's final act of revelation is seen as the outflowing of His heart-felt

---

[44] Hence we do not have a hendiadys, → οἰκτίρω, V, 161, 19 ff., cf. Dib. Ph., ad loc.

[45] In discussion cf. the comm., also O. Schmitz, Die Christusgemeinschaft d. Pls. im Lichte seines Gen.-Gebrauchs (1924), 217-219.

[46] Loh. Phil., ad loc. would restrict the expression to the special relationship of the apostle with Christ in martyrdom.

[47] This was already correctly noted by Bengel, ad loc.: in Paulo non Paulus vivit, sed Jesus Christus; quare Paulus non in Pauli sed Jesu Christi movetur visceribus. Cf. also Dib. Ph., ad loc.

[48] At root, then, the expression is no more remarkable than ἡ ἀγάπη τοῦ Χριστοῦ συνέχει ἡμᾶς, κρίναντας τοῦτο . . . , 2 C. 5:14; cf. R. 5:5. Naturally Paul is not suggesting that this love came to esp. vivid expression with the human manifestation of Jesus.

[49] On the gushing out of the bowels v. the par. in Pr.-Bauer, s.v. Cf. also Haench. Ag. on Ac. 1:18.

[50] Loh. Kol., ad loc. thinks we have in the v. a description of heavenly beings (ἐκλεκτοὶ θεοῦ) rather than a list of virtues. If so Col. 3:12 would be one of the passages which speak of σπλάγχνα as a divine quality. But Loh. is surely mistaken.

[51] At the corresponding pt. Eph. 4:32 has εὔσπλαγχνος, which Col. must have altered under the influence of Phil. 2:1 (cf. ταπεινοφροσύνη in Col. 3:12 and Phil. 2:3). Otherwise σπλάγχνα οἰκτιρμοῦ is par. to σπλάγχνα ἐλέους in Test. XII; Lk. 1:78.

[52] ἐπισκέπτομαι is also directly connected with σπλάγχνα in Test. L. 4:4, cf. the comm., ad loc. for other par. from the OT and later Jewish lit.; cf. also 1 QS 1:22; 2:1 → 552, 25 ff.

mercy. [53, 54] ὅτι πολύσπλαγχνός [55] ἐστιν ὁ κύριος καὶ οἰκτίρμων (Jm. 5:11) also stands in an eschatological context. The saying sounds like an OT quotation and is unquestionably a Greek translation of the common OT יהוה וְחַנּוּן רַחוּם or similar Hebrew formulae. [56] Yet the LXX never uses πολύσπλαγχνος for the relevant Hebrew words. [57] In James, then, we find the same usage, independent of the Greek OT, as in Lk. 1:78 and Test. XII. σπλάγχνα etc. are characteristic terms for God's eschatological mercy. We also find in the NT the hortatory use of the terms corresponding to the theological use. When it is said that we are not to close our σπλάγχνα to a starving brother (1 Jn. 3:17), the reference is not to the bowels as the seat of all possible feelings, as in Greek literature → 549, 3 ff.; it is to the "heart" as the centre of the compassionate action which is commanded. [58] In this connection one might also refer to the hortatory use of εὔσπλαγχνος, which is sometimes mentioned among other Christian virtues, Eph. 4:32; [59] 1 Pt. 3:8. [60] Since we have here various lists, and εὔσπλαγχνος occurs in later lists of a very different kind, [61] it is plain that the use of the term is by no means restricted to a single hortatory tradition.

D. The Word Group in the Post-Apostolic Fathers and Early Christian Writings.

1. Only once is there a plain trace of Pauline usage outside the NT: κατὰ τὰ σπλάγχνα, ἃ ἔχετε ἐν Χριστῷ Ἰησοῦ, Ign. Phld., 10, 1. This passage is undoubtedly based on Phil. 1:8 (→ 556, 8 ff.) and the sense is the Pauline one of "love": "on the ground of the love which you have in Christ Jesus." [62] With no hint of the specific influence of a developed usage σπλάγχνα means the "heart" as the seat of religious conviction in 1 Cl., 2, 1. [63] Dominant elsewhere is the influence of the meaning developed in later Judaism. σπλάγχνα etc. are thus used esp. of God. That the ref., as in Test. XII (→ 551, 38 ff.), is originally to God's mercy in eschatological salvation may be seen from 2 Cl., 1, 7: ἠλέησεν γὰρ ἡμᾶς καὶ σπλαγχνισθεὶς ἔσωσεν. But usually the eschatological element has been toned down or completely lost. 1 Cl., 23, 1 is saying that God "has a heart" (ἔχει σπλάγχνα) and 1 Cl., 14, 3 is recalling His εὐσπλαγχνία and γλυκύτης, though with no special ref. to revelation. σπλάγχνα has become a quality of the kindly Father. [64] Equally non-eschatological is ἀγαπῶντες τὸν ἐπιεικῆ καὶ

---

[53] Kl. Lk., ad loc. "a heart full of pity" is more vivid.

[54] On the distinction from the specifically Chr. view of the saving event cf. Braun, 162.

[55] πολύσπλαγχνος occurs here for the first time, but it can hardly have been coined by the author of Jm. It is common in Herm. with πολυεύσπλαγχνος (read by 1 al at Jm. 5:11); so, too, is the derived noun. Cf. Just. Dial., 55, 3; Cl. Al. Quis Div. Salv., 39, 6 with πολυέλεος; cf. also Dib. Herm. on 1, 3, 2.

[56] Ps. 103:8; 111:4; cf. Ex. 34:6; Jl. 2:13 etc.

[57] The same applies to εὔσπλαγχνος; in the LXX only οἰκτίρμων, ἐλεήμων, πολυέλεος, μακρόθυμος are common.

[58] Cf. πάντοτε σπλάγχνον ἔχοντες ἐπὶ πάντα ἄνθρωπον for those who give alms freely, Herm. s., 9, 24, 2; this is the only instance of the noun in Herm. → 558, 5 ff.

[59] With χρηστός.

[60] With ὁμόφρων, συμπαθής, φιλάδελφος, ταπεινόφρων.

[61] Pol., 5, 2 as a virtue of deacons with ἀφιλάργυρος, ἐγκρατής, ἐπιμελής etc.; Pol., 6, 1 as a virtue of presbyters with ἐλεήμων; 1 Cl., 54, 1 with γενναῖος and πεπληροφορημένος ἀγάπης.

[62] κατά here = διά, also in the preceding κατὰ τὴν προσευχὴν ὑμῶν, v. Bau. Ign., ad loc.

[63] τοὺς λόγους αὐτοῦ (sc. Χριστοῦ) ἐπιμελῶς ἐνεστερνισμένοι ἦτε τοῖς σπλάγχνοις (par. τὰ παθήματα αὐτοῦ πρὸ ὀφθαλμῶν), 1 Cl., 2, 1.

[64] So in 1 Cl., 23, 1 we find οἰκτίρμων, εὐεργετικός, ἤπιως, προσηνῶς with σπλάγχνα

εὔσπλαγχνον πατέρα ἡμῶν in 1 Cl., 29, 1. [65] Generalised, too, is ... παρὰ τοῦ εὐ-
σπλάγχνου καὶ πολυελέου πατρὸς τῶν ὅλων θεοῦ in Just. Dial., 108, 3. [66] Finally,
the hortatory use of εὔσπλαγχνος in Pol., 5, 2; 6, 1; 1 Cl., 54, 1 has no eschatological
emphasis. [67]

2. The eschatological element in the usage of Test. XII (→ 551, 14 ff.) is adopted
again only in Herm. The special position of the group in the theological vocabulary of
this early "revelation" finds external expression already in the consistent restriction of
σπλαγχνίζομαι and the derivates πολύσπλαγχνος, πολυσπλαγχνία, πολυεύσπλαγχνος and πολυευσπλαγχνία [68] to God. [69] God's mercy is both the basis of the prophet's
sense of mission and also the content of his summons to repentance. ὁ κύριος ἐσπλαγχνίσθη καὶ ἔπεμψέ με δοῦναι πᾶσι τὴν μετάνοιαν, s., 8, 11, 1; πολύσπλαγχνος οὖν
ὢν ὁ κύριος ἐσπλαγχνίσθη ἐπὶ τὴν ποίησιν αὐτοῦ καὶ ἔθηκεν τὴν μετάνοιαν
ταύτην, καὶ ἐμοὶ ἡ ἐξουσία τῆς μετανοίας ταύτης ἐδόθη, m., 4, 3, 5. The eschatological character of the usage is shown by the close connection between the proclamation
of God's mercy and the summons to repentance. This last chance of repentance before
the end is provided by the σπλαγχνίζεσθαι or πολυσπλαγχνία of God   the passages already adduced and also s., 7, 4; 8, 6, 1 and 3; 9, 14, 3. Through su_h μετάνοια
there takes place the ἀνακαίνωσις τῶν πνευμάτων, v., 3, 8, 9; cf. 12, 3; s., 8, 6, 3;
9, 14, 3, or the gift of the πνεῦμα, s., 8, 6, 1, πνεῦμα being in both cases an eschatological quality.

Sometimes the usage of Test. XII is quite apparent, cf. ἴασιν δώσει in s., 7, 4 or
ἰάσεται in s., 5, 7, 4, both with σπλαγχνίζομαι or πολύσπλαγχνος. Mal. 3:20 is obviously reflected here in the form it is given in Test. Zeb. 9:8 → 552, 9 ff. As in Test.
Zeb. 8:6 μνησικακία is the opp. of σπλάγχνα ἐλέους → 551, 27 ff.; it is used there
of men, cf. Herm. m., 9, 2 f.: γνώσῃ τὴν πολυσπλαγχνίαν αὐτοῦ ... οὐκ ἔστι γὰρ
ὁ θεὸς ὡς οἱ ἄνθρωποι μνησικακοῦντες, ἀλλ' αὐτὸς ἀμνησίκακός ἐστιν, καὶ
σπλαγχνίζεται ἐπὶ τὴν ποίησιν αὐτοῦ. Thoroughly OT-Jewish and eschatological is
the fact that mercy is not regarded as a constant factor in God's immutable nature but
as a change in His dealings; He repents of His previous acts. [70] Hence God's mercy
can be manifested as His acts of revelation through the prophet: ἀκούσαντες τὴν
ἀποκάλυψιν, ἣν ὑμῖν ὁ κύριος ἀπεκάλυψεν, ὅτι ἐσπλαγχνίσθη ἐφ' ὑμᾶς, v.,
3, 12, 2 and 3. It is this πολυσπλαγχνία which leads the believer through the perils of
the end time, [71] will never abandon him (m., 9, 2), and gives abundantly to those who
pray to God without ceasing, s., 5, 4, 4.

3. σπλάγχνα and εὐσπλαγχνία are used very differently as divine predicates in
the apocr. Act. Thom. and Act. Joh. As the fixed part of an epiclesis we find: ἐλθὲ τὰ
σπλάγχνα τὰ τέλεια, [72] Act. Thom. 50; cf. ἐλθὲ ἡ δύναμις τοῦ ὑψίστου καὶ ἡ

---

as divine qualities. It is worth noting that here and in the passages which follow God is
always πατήρ.
  [65] This is true even though a traditional eschatological saying is appended: ὃς ἐκλογῆς
μέρος ἡμᾶς ἐποίησεν ἑαυτῷ.
  [66] Just. speaks once of God's πολυσπλαγχνία in a similar weaker sense, Dial., 55, 3.
  [67] On the NT par. → 557, 12 ff.
  [68] The verb occurs in v., 3, 12, 3; m., 4, 3, 5; 9, 3; s., 7, 4; 8, 6, 3 and 11, 1; 9, 14, 3, cf. s.,
6, 3, 2. πολύσπλαγχνος, -νία, v., 1, 3, 2; 2, 2, 8; 4, 2, 3; m., 4, 3, 5; 9, 2; s., 5, 4, 4; 8, 6, 1.
πολυεύσπλαγχνος, -νία, s. 5, 4, 4A, 8, 6, 1A.
  [69] Only σπλάγχνον (used once in s., 9, 24, 2; → n. 58) refers to men; ἄσπλαγχνος is
used of the avenging angel in s., 6, 3, 2.
  [70] Note the aor. ἐσπλαγχνίσθη ἐπὶ τὴν ποίησιν αὐτοῦ, cf. m., 4, 3, 5. Up to m., 9, 3 the
verb is always in the aor. Naturally this change in God's dealings is in keeping with His
nature.
  [71] v., 4, 2, 3; these dangers are symbolised by the terrible beast.
  [72] On this v. G. Bornkamm, "Mythos u. Legende in d. apokr. Thomasakten," FRL, 49
(1933), 102; U. Wilckens, Weisheit u. Torheit (1959), 112.

εὐσπλαγχνία ἡ τελεία, 27; also 48. Sophia is invoked as ἡ μήτηρ ἡ εὐσπλαγχνος, 27. But this kind of epiclesis is addressed esp. to Jesus ; hence the Messianic use of the verb by the Synoptics is adopted in a distinctive way. Finally there can be ref. (→ 553, 38 ff.) here to the pity of the apostle as there is to that of Jesus in the Synoptics : ὁ δὲ ᾽Ιωάννης σπλαγχνισθεὶς ... ἐκάλεσε τὰ τέλεια σπλάγχνα καὶ ἀνυπερή-φανα, εἶπε· Κύριε ᾽Ιησοῦ Χριστέ ..., Act. Joh. 24. The fact that this is done in conscious correspondence to the invocation of Jesus as τέλεια σπλάγχνα expresses the oneness of the Gnostic with the divine mercy of Jesus in a way the NT itself could never have done.

Köster

σπορά, σπόριμος, σπόρος → 537, 34 ff.

> † σπουδάζω, † σπουδή,
> † σπουδαῖος

Contents : A. The Word Group in Classical and Hellenistic Greek. B. The Word Group in the Septuagint and Later Judaism : 1. The Septuagint and Hexapla ; 2. Josephus ; 3. Philo. C. The Word Group in the New Testament. D. The Word Group in the Early Church.

A. The Word Group in Classical and Hellenistic Greek.

σπουδή, "haste," "zeal," is attested from Hom. Il., 2, 99. It is a verbal abstr. of σπεύδω "I make haste," also trans. "I urge on." [1] From this come the adj. σπουδαῖος (from Hom. Hymn. Merc., 332; Hdt., VIII, 69) and the verb σπουδάζω, known from the class. age.

1. σπουδάζω means intrans. "to make haste" and is thus closely related to "to be zealous, active, concerned about something." Fuller definition is in the inf. σπουδάζομεν ... μανθάνειν, Eur. Hec., 817, or the part. ἐσπούδαζες διδάσκων, Xenoph. Oec., 9, 1, or a ὅπως clause : ὅπως ... εἰσποιηθῇ αὐτῷ υἱός, Demosth. Or., 43, 12, or a simple dat. τοῦ ἵππου ... ᾧ ἐσπουδάκει, Epict. Diss., I, 11, 27, or a prepositional link with a material or personal obj. ἐφ᾽ οἷς οὐδ᾽ ἂν μαινόμενος σπουδάσειεν, Xenoph. Mem., I, 3, 11; πρὸς φίλον σπουδάσειεν, Plat. Gorg., 510c.

Trans. σπουδάζω means "to push on with something quickly, assiduously, zealously," τὰ τοῦ παιδὸς καλὰ μᾶλλον ἢ τὰ ἑαυτοῦ ἡδέα σπουδάζοντα, Xenoph. Sym., VIII, 17, also pass. τοῖς μάλιστα ἐσπουδασμένοις σίτοις ... χρῆσθαι, Xenoph. Cyrop., IV, 2, 38, of a person δοκεῖ γὰρ σπουδάζεσθαι, Aristot. Rhet., II, 3, p. 1390a, 26, where the opp. καταφρονεῖσθαι shows that σπουδάζω here means "to respect," "to treat respectfully." The external sense of quick movement in the interests of a person or thing has become the inner one of high estimation. Thus σπουδάζω comes to be used for ethical motivation. But the meaning acquires an important nuance in another direction

---

σπουδάζω κτλ. [1] Formed like πομπή from πέμπω, v. Schwyzer, I, 460. Cf. σπεύδω with Lithuanian spáusti "to press" (spáud-), spaudà, spūdeti "to stoop, to exert oneself," v. Boisacq, Hofmann, s.v.; Pokorny, 998 f.

too. As the opp. of παίζω it comes to be used for serious effort, for taking things or people seriously. We find the two verbs together in Dion Hal. De Lysia, 14. Cf. also Aristoph. Pl., 557 : σκώπτειν πειρᾷ καὶ κωμῳδεῖν τοῦ σπουδάζειν ἀμελήσας, "you jest and play the fool and are lacking in seriousness" ; also Xenoph. Mem., I, 3, 8. In the main there is no change in Hellenism. In pap. of the imperial period σπούδασον is often used as the form of urgent petition, P. Oxy., XIX, 2229 (346-350 A.D.) etc. In P. Oxy., XII, 1424 (318 A.D.) the one addressed is asked "to get intensively involved" (in a religious matter): σπούδασον ... τοῦτον ῥύσασθαι τοῦ λειτουργήματος.

2. The oldest instance of σπουδαῖος is in Hom. Hymn. Merc., 332. It is used of people in the sense "speedy," "diligent," θεραπευτικοὶ καὶ σπουδαῖοι, "submissive and eager to serve," of men in political life, Plut. Aem., 2, 5 (I, 256b), then "proficient," esp. in arts and crafts τὰς ... τέχνας ... σπουδαίους, Xenoph. Mem., IV, 2, 2. From this develops the sense of "good" == "concerned for the good," "noble," σπουδαῖοι τῶν Λακεδαιμονίων, Xenoph. Hist. Graec., III, 1, 9, cf. Isoc. Or., 5, 19 : anton. πονηρός, Xenoph. Hist. Graec., II, 3, 19 f. or φαῦλος, Xenoph. Cyrop., II, 2, 24; Aristot. Eth. Nic., II, 4, p. 1105b, 30. It is here more patently a moral term κατὰ τὰς ἀρετὰς ἢ τὰς κακίας λεγόμεθα, namely, σπουδαῖοι and φαῦλοι, cf. ἔοικε γὰρ ... μέτρον ἑκάστῳ ἡ ἀρετὴ καὶ ὁ σπουδαῖος εἶναι, IX, 4, p. 1166a, 12 f. ἀρετή and σπουδαῖος are on the same level. The σπουδαῖος is the worthy man who decides acc. to his ἀρετή, not his οἰκεία ἕξις. With φιλάνθρωπος and δίκαιος σπουδαῖος sums up all that is worthy καθόλου σπουδαῖον ἐν πᾶσι, Diod. S., 1, 51. σπουδαῖος can also be used in the sense "nimble," "alert" of the ὀφρύες, Xenoph. Sym., VIII, 3, then "keen," then "worth striving for," τέλος σπουδαῖον, Aristot. Metaph., 4, 16, p. 1021b, 23 f., as the obj. of the will, Aristot. Eth. Nic., V, 11, p. 1136b, 8, "important," ὡς ταῦθ᾽ ὑμῖν σπουδαιότατ᾽ ἐστί, Demosth. Or., 24, 4, then "good," "productive" of fields σπουδαῖαι νομαί, Hdt., IV, 23, of tragedies σπουδαία-φαύλη, Aristot. Poet., 5, p. 1449b, 17, of a "good" thing χρῆμα σπουδαῖον, Hdt., V, 78, σπουδαῖον πρῆγμα, Theogn. Elegia, I, 70 (Diehl³, II, 7), ibid., 116, 642 (II, 9 and 41), a "good" word which has an effect on the angry, Menand. Fr., 518 (Koerte), of the σπουδαία ἕξις in contrast to the φαύλη, Aristot. Eth. Nic., VII, 9, p. 1151a, 27 f. σπουδαῖος is also used in contrast to γελοῖος in the sense of "serious" (→ 561, 26 ff.), Aristoph. Ra., 390, so tragic poets τῶν δὲ σπουδαίων ... τῶν περὶ τραγῳδίαν ἡμῖν ποιητῶν, Plat. Leg., VII, 817a, also βελτίω τε λέγομεν τὰ σπουδαῖα τῶν γελοίων, Aristot. Eth. Nic., X, 6, p. 1177a, 3, "serious work," σπουδαῖον ἔργον, Xenoph. Hist. Graec., I, 4, 12, "serious" affairs of state τὰ σπουδαιέστερα τῶν πρηγμάτων ὑπερετίθετο ὁ Κανδαύλης, Hdt., I, 8. In popular Hell. speech the most common use is for "goodness," "of a good disposition," so in pap. of the imperial period, P. Ryl., II, 243, 7 (2nd cent. A.D.); P. Oxy., VII, 1064, 6 f.; VI, 929, 3 (2nd/3rd cent. A.D.); P. Lond., II, 413, 5 (346 A.D.).

σπουδαῖος in the moral sense (synon. σοφός, φρόνιμος, ἀγαθός) is common in the Hell. and imperial period, esp. among the Stoics. Xenoph. already uses it for "upright," "good" in the moral sense, Hist. Graec., II, 3, 19, also Isoc. Or., 1, 1, 4. Aristot. esp. uses σπουδαῖος for the "worthy," "morally qualified" man as distinct from the φαῦλος, πονηρός → VI, 548, 9 ff. τὸ δὲ σπουδαῖον εἶναί ἐστι τὸ τὰς ἀρετὰς ἔχειν, Eth. M., I, 1, p. 1181a, 28; cf. Cat., 8, p. 10b, 8; πρᾶξις ... σπουδαία, Cat., 5, p. 4a, 16. σπουδαῖος as an adj. "worthy," Eth. Nic., VI, 7, p. 1141a, 21: πράγματα ... σπουδαιότερα, Rhet., I, 7, p. 1364b, 8. Among the Stoics it is used for the true Stoic. The σπουδαῖος is the one who has a direct share in virtue μετέχοντα τῆς ἀρετῆς, Diog. L., VII, 94. What he does is determined by virtue ποιεῖ ... κατ᾽ ἀρετήν, Stob. Ecl., II, 106, 7. The σπουδαῖοι as a group, seen dualistically, are in contrast to the φαῦλοι, non-Stoics, who have no share in Stoic thought and knowledge.[2] The σπουδαῖος is

---

[2] ἀρέσκει γὰρ τῷ τε Ζήνωνι καὶ τοῖς ἀπ᾽ αὐτοῦ Στωικοῖς φιλοσόφοις δύο γένη τῶν ἀνθρώπων εἶναι τὸ μὲν τῶν σπουδαίων, τὸ δὲ τῶν φαύλων, Stob. Ecl., II, 99, 3 ff.

depicted as a truly moral man.[3] On the same basis of thought the σπουδαῖοι agree together τοὺς σπουδαίους πάντας ὁμονοεῖν ἀλλήλοις διὰ τὸ συμφωνεῖν ἐν τοῖς κατὰ τὸν βίον Stob. Ecl. II, 93, 19. They are engaged only in noble competition with one another τῶν σπουδαίων ἄλλους ἄλλων προτρεπτικωτέρους γίγνεσθαι καὶ πειστικωτέρους ἔτι δὲ καὶ ἀγχινουστέρους, Stob. Ecl. II, 113, 24 ff. They alone have the right social qualities, πολίτας καὶ φίλους καὶ οἰκείους καὶ ἐλευθέρους τοὺς σπουδαίους μόνον, Diog. L., VII, 33, handed down as a saying of Zeno. In spite of his relation to self and his inner independence, the σπουδαῖος is not, it is argued, I-centred, ἀλλὰ μὴν οὐδ' ἐν ἐρημίᾳ, φασί, βιώσεται ὁ σπουδαῖος· κοινωνικὸς γὰρ φύσει καὶ πρακτικός, Diog. L., VII, 123. As the σπουδαῖος is the perfect man, free from emotions, he never makes a mistake or does anything morally wrong, as can be very confidently stated in Stoic lit. ἐν μηδενὶ δὲ τὸν σπουδαῖον ἁμαρτάνειν, Stob. Ecl., II, 109, 7.[4] In relation to objects σπουδαῖος is in this circle of thought "that which is worth striving for," πάντα δὲ τἀγαθὰ ὠφέλιμα εἶναι ... καὶ σπουδαῖα καὶ πρέποντα, Stob. Ecl., II, 69, 11. None of the worthwhile moral values alights on the wicked τῶν σπουδαίων μηδὲν εἰς φαύλους πίπτειν, Stob. Ecl., II, 105, 14.

3. σπουδή reflects the same shift in sense. It means the "haste" with which something must be done, ἐκ σπουδῆς, Ps.-Aristot. De Mirabilibus, 86, p. 837a, 15, the quick building of a wall κατὰ σπουδήν, Thuc., I, 93, 2, a fast military manoeuvre ἦγε τὴν στρατιὴν σπουδῇ, Hdt., IX, 1. σπουδή then means "work" as distinct from σχολή, Theophr. Char., 3, 6, "expenditure of force" etc., "with effort, trouble," e.g., Hom. Il., 13, 687; Od., 3, 297 etc., "zealously, expeditiously," Od., 15, 209; ἀπὸ σπουδῆς "earnestly," Il., 7, 359; ἄτερ σπουδῆς τάνυσεν μέγα τόξον Ὀδυσσεύς, "with no expenditure of force," Od., 21, 409; τοσαύτην δὲ σπουδὴν ἐποιήσατο, Diod. S., 17, 114, cf. Luc. Salt., 1, but already Plat. Symp., 177c. σπουδή can also mean "seriousness" as the opp. of jesting → 560, 34 ff., μετὰ σπουδῆς, ἀλλ' οὐκ ἐν παιδιᾷ Aristot. Eth. Nic., X, 6, p. 1177a, 2 f., cf. σπουδῆς μὲν ... μεστοί, γέλωτος δὲ ἴσως ἐνδεέστεροι, Xenoph. Sym., I, 13; οὐ σπουδῆς ... χάριν, ἀλλὰ παιδιᾶς ἕνεκα, Plat. Polit., 288c (→ παίζω V, 626, 10 ff.). Various prepositional combinations are found: σὺν σπουδῇ, Xenoph. An., I, 8, 4; ἐπὶ μεγάλης σπουδῆς, Plat. Symp., 192c; μετὰ πολλῆς σπουδῆς, Plat. Charm., 175e express the "zeal" or "dedication" with which something is done, with personal obj. τοῦ δήμου περὶ αὐτὸν σπουδῇ, Herodian. Hist., V, 4, 11; also unfavourably πατρίς τε γαῖα σῆς ὑπὸ σπουδῆς δορὶ ἁλοῦσα, Aesch. Sept. c. Theb., 585 or Πενθεὺς πρὸς οἴκους ὅδε διὰ σπουδῆς περᾷ, Eur. Ba., 212. Cf. σπουδὴν ἔχειν, e.g., σπουδὴν δὲ ἔχειν σπονδὰς γενέσθαι, Hdt., VII, 149, 1. In Hell. pap. and inscr. κατὰ σπουδήν means "in haste," e.g., P. Ryl., II, 231, 13 (40 A.D.). But the main sense here too is that of "zeal," "effort," "seriousness," τῶν φίλων σπουδῆς τυχόντος, P. Tebt., II, 314, 9 (2nd cent. A.D.), "dedication," cf. ἐκ π(άσης) ἐνεργίας καὶ σπουδῆς καὶ φιλείας, P. Tebt., II, 616, 2 ff. (2nd. cent. A.D.). Esp. interesting is the inscr.:[5] ἄνδρα ἀγαθὸν γενόμενον καὶ διενέγκαντα πίστει καὶ ἀρετῇ καὶ δικαιοσύνη καὶ εὐσεβείᾳ ... τὴν πλείστην εἰσενηνεγμένον σπουδήν, Ditt. Or., II, 438, 5 ff. (1st cent. B.C.), cf. Ditt. Syll.³, II, 694, 15 (2nd cent. B.C.). This reflects the basic moral sense

---

[3] καὶ τὸν μὲν σπουδαῖον ταῖς περὶ τὸν βίον ἐμπειρίαις χρώμενον ... τὸν σπουδαῖον μέγαν εἶναι καὶ ἁδρὸν καὶ ὑψηλὸν καὶ ἰσχυρὸν ... οὔτε ἀναγκάζεται ὑπό τινος οὔτε ἀναγκάζει τινά, οὔτε κωλύεται οὔτε κωλύει, ... οὔτε δεσπόζει οὔτε δεσπόζεται, οὔτε κακοποιεῖ τινα οὔτ' αὐτὸς κακοποιεῖται, οὔτε κακοῖς περιπίπτει οὔτ' ἐξαπατᾶται οὔτ' ἐξαπατᾷ ἄλλον, οὔτε διαψεύδεται οὔτε ἀγνοεῖ οὔτε λανθάνει ἑαυτὸν οὔτε καθόλου ψεῦδος ὑπολαμβάνει., Stob. Ecl., II, 99, 9 ff. The σπουδαῖοι are often depicted in much the same way as the σοφοί, cf. v. Arnim, IV, s.v. σοφός.

[4] M. Pohlenz, Die Stoa (1948), esp. 111-158; G. Teichmüller, Aristoteles Philosophie d. Kunst erklärt (1869), esp. c. 1 § 2: "Die drei verschiedenen Bdtg. von σπουδαῖος u. ihr Zusammenhang."

[5] Quoted in Deissmann LO, 270, n. 1 and 2.

σπουδή had acquired. σπουδή is thus ranked with χαρά and προθυμία as "cheerful readiness," P. Lond., III, 1178, 23 (194 A.D.). σπουδὴν εἰσφέρειν is another common phrase, σπουδὴν καὶ φιλοτιμίαν εἰσήνεγκαν προθυμίας οὐδὲν ἐλλείποντες, Ditt. Syll.³, II, 656, 12 ff. (166 B.C.), cf. II, 667, 10 (an Athenian decree concerning victors at the Thesean games, 161 B.C.) etc. or προσφερο(μένην σ)πουδήν, P. Tebt., I, 27, 45 f. (113 B.C.) or σπουδὴν ποιεῖσθαι in the most varied combinations, P. Hibeh, I, 71, 9 (245 B.C.); P. Greci e Lat., IV, 340, 6 (257-6 B.C.); σπουδὴν περιτίθεμαι, P. Giess., 79 col. II, 7 (c. 117 A.D.); σπουδὴν εἰσφέρεσθαι, Ditt. Syll.³, II, 694, 15 f. (129 B.C.) In Inscr. Magn., 85, 12 σπουδή denotes "religious dedication" πρὸς τὴν θεὰν ... σπουδή, cf. a Decretum Amphictyonicum of 216/5 B.C. πλείσταν σπουδὰν ποιούμενος τὰς ἐν τὸ δαιμόνιον εὐσεβείας, Ditt. Syll.³, 539 A 15 f.

B. The Word Group in the Septuagint and Later Judaism.

1. The Septuagint and Hexapla.

LXX has σπουδάζω chiefly for forms of בהל in the sense "to hasten," e.g., Qoh. 8:3 "to leave with haste." It thus uses it for חשׁה, a subsidiary form of חושׁ hi "to hasten," at Job 31:5. [6] But it also takes בהל ni to mean the same, and hence uses σπουδάζω, though the real sense is "to be terrified," Job 21:6; 23:15; Is. 21:3, or "to lose courage," Job 4:5. The same applies to the pi and hi of בהל trans. "to terrify," Job 22:10; 23:16. Possibly ἐσπούδασέν με in Job 23:16 may mean: "he is concerned about me," "he visits me," σπουδή is used similarly for בְּעָתָה "terror" at Jer. 8:15, perhaps because בְּעָא Aram. means "to meet unexpectedly," "to confuse," "to startle," but also "to do something quickly." The latter sense must have been decisive. Thus 2 Εσδρ. 4:23 B has ἐπορεύθησαν ἐν σπουδῇ εἰς Ιερουσαλήμ for אֲזַלוּ בִבְהִילוּ לִירוּשְׁלֶם in Ezr. 4.23. σπουδή is also used for רֶגַע "suddenly" in Lam. 4:6, for the pass. part. of נחץ, נָחוּץ in 1 S. 21:9, for מהר pi "to hasten," "press," Ex. 12:33, for חִפָּזוֹן "hastly flight" ἔδεσθε αὐτὸ μετὰ σπουδῆς, Ex. 12:11, ἐν σπουδῇ ἐξήλθετε ἐξ Αἰγύπτου, Dt. 16:3. But even where it is inappropriate בַּבֶּהָלָה (ψ 77:33) is transl. μετὰ σπουδῆς, cf. the ni of בהל in Zeph. 1:18: συντέλειαν καὶ σπουδὴν ποιήσει. In the sense of "haste" Θ uses it even more than LXX, so Da. 2:25; 3:91 (24); 6:20. At Da. 3:9 LXX has σπεύσας ↗ ↗ 'A and Θ ἐν σπουδῇ for Aram. בְּהִתְבְּהָלָה (hitp of בהל "to frighten") in the sense of "haste." In many cases in which LXX has σπουδή with no Hbr. equivalent it means "haste," 1 Macc. 6:63; 1 Εσδρ. 2:25; cf. 2 Εσδρ. 4:23; Wis. 19:2; Sir. 20:18; 21:15. In Θ it is used for "fright" in Da. 11.⁴⁴ cf. 9:27 vl.: ἕως συντελείας καὶ σπουδῆς But it can also mean "force," "zeal," "desire," 2 Macc. 14:43; 3 Macc. 5:24, 27; 1 Εσδρ. 6:9; Wis. 14:17; Sir. Prol. 30; 27:3.

The tendency to transl. forms of בהל and Hbr. equivalents of the same meaning by σπουδάζω or σπουδή occurs also in 'A, Σ and Θ, e.g., Is. 65:23, where all three have εἰς σπουδήν for לַבֶּהָלָה "sudden terror" (LXX εἰς κατάραν). Θ also has σπουδασμός for בַּלָּהוֹת from בַּלָּהָה at Ez. 27:36 and σπουδή for בְּרָגֶּוּ ("trembling," "apprehension") at Ez. 12:18 (LXX μετὰ βασάνου). At Lv. 26:16 'Αλλ have σπουδή for בֶּהָלָה, possibly they read בְּבֶהָלָה. Naturally 'A, Σ and Θ use σπουδάζω for "to hasten," like LXX, Prv. 20:9b LXX: μερὶς ἐπισπουδαζομένη, Prv. 20:21 ΣΘ: κληρονομία σπουδαζομένη "hastily acquired inheritance." Ιερ. 38 (31): 2 Αλλ is unique: πορευομένους ἐν

---

[6] The compound ἐπισπουδάζω also means "to hasten" in LXX, while κατασπουδάζω means "to pursue zealously."

σπουδαῖς Ἰσραήλ, for יְהִרְגִיעוֹ. רֶגַע means "short while" in Jer. 18:7, 9 ἐν σπουδαῖς is to be understood accordingly. Thus רֶגַע "suddenly" can be transl. by σπουδῇ, ἐμεγαλύνθη ἀνομία ... ὥσπερ σπουδῇ, Lam. 4:6. [7]

In the main it is clear that LXX has not taken over the Gk. content of σπουδάζω (→ 559, 29 ff.) or σπουδή (→ 561, 21 ff.), that it uses the group essentially in the sense of "haste," "to hasten, speed," and that by natural extension and assimilation to the stem בהל it has σπουδή ("haste") even where the meaning is "dread." Hence there is a constriction of meaning. One cannot speak of a true equivalent for the group in the OT and later Judaism. The thought of moral exertion along the lines of Hell. philosophy, along with the idea of self-determination and self-perfecting (cf. esp. σπουδαῖος → 560, 12 ff.), is quite alien to Jewish thinking. [8]

2. Josephus.

a. σπουδάζω in Jos. means "to be zealously engaged," "to exert oneself," "to pursue assiduously," "to be concerned," "to show interest," "to intercede for someone," Bell., 1, 431 cf. Ant., 16, 230. The verb occurs in a new sense with God as subj. when it is said of the prophet Elisha: σπουδασθεὶς ὑπὸ τοῦ θεοῦ, Ant., 9, 182. But Jos. can also use σπουδάζω as elsewhere in Gk. for "to be concerned about the deity," περὶ τὴν τοῦ θεοῦ θρησκείαν ἐσπουδακώς, Ant., 1, 222. The sense of "haste" is less prominent, being found at most in an expression like Δαμασκηνοὶ ... τοὺς παρ᾽ ἑαυτοῖς Ἰουδαίους ἀνελεῖν ἐσπούδασαν, Bell., 2, 559, v. also Ant., 15, 119.

b. σπουδαῖος is found in Jos. only in the gen. sense of "zealous," "conscientious," Ant., 9, 5, esp. in the adv. form, also the adv. as superlative or elative διακονήσειν σπουδαίως, Ant., 8, 6; συνίστη σπουδαιότερον, "he received (the embassy) in the best possible way," 16, 85, also "conscientiously" τὴν ὑπὲρ σοῦ καὶ τοῦ ἔθνους ⟨πρεσβείαν⟩ σπουδαίως διέθεντο, 14, 307. One might expect the philosophical sense, but there is no trace of this.

c. For σπουδή Jos. knows the sense the "grace" of God τοσαύτη γὰρ ὁ θεὸς περὶ Μωυσῆν ἐχρήσατο σπουδῇ, Ant., 2, 225; τοσαύτη περὶ αὐτὸν (sc. Ἴσακον) σπουδῇ χρώμενον (sc. τὸν θεόν), 1, 260, cf. 1, 224. One also finds the sense of religious "concern," "piety" τῆς περὶ αὐτὸν (θεὸν) σπουδῆς ἀξίως ὑπὸ τοῦ θεοῦ τετιμημένος (Abraham), 1, 256; πάσῃ δὲ χρησάμενος σπουδῇ καὶ φιλοτιμίᾳ περὶ τὸν θεὸν (Hezekiah), 10, 25; cf. the common Gk. combination → 562, 2 ff.; περὶ τὸ θεῖον (Antiochus), 13, 245. The meaning "goodwill," "thankful, benevolent disposition" is well-developed in Jos.: πάσῃ περὶ αὐτοὺς σπουδῇ χρώμενος, Ant., 2, 197; of "attentiveness" to someone περὶ αὐτόν (Solomon), 8, 182; "interest" περὶ τὸν Ἰωνάθην,

---

[7] Further deviations from LXX rest on other readings, so Is. 33:11, where the HT of Θ must have been different (perhaps a defective תָּשִׂישׂוּ, "you will rejoice"), so that he could transl.: γαστρὶ λήψεσθε σπουδῇ τέξεσθε καλάμην.

[8] σπουδαῖος is not used of men in LXX. The adv. σπουδαίως occurs in Wis. 2:6, "as quickly as possible" or "efficiently." בֵּהַל also occurs in Talmud in the sense "to become confused, frightened, unsettled," so in the well-known saying in jJoma, 6, 3 (43c, 62 f.): למה אתה מבהלינו (temple), "why dost thou unsettle us?" or Pesikt.r., 36 (162a): מתבהלים all peoples "were disquieted," also sudden destruction, disaster or death, jBik., 2, 1 (64d, 5): לשנים מתהₛשל בהלה. In later Jewish lit. σπουδάζω has no specific sense; it means "to hasten," Ep. Ar., 10 and 39; Test. N. 3:1; D. 6:3, or "to be in a hurry," Test. G. 4:3. In a vl. Test. Jud. 1:4 has σπουδαῖος for ὀξύς, possibly for מָהִיר. But there may be here something of the Stoic sense of σπουδαῖος (→ 560, 39 ff.), also Test. L. 13:7, where a vl. adds μετὰ σπουδῆς to σοφίαν κτήσεσθε ἐν φόβῳ κυρίου.

13, 85, v. also 14, 252 and 386; "liking" ἤ τε τοῦ πατρὸς σπουδὴ περὶ αὐτούς, 17, 16, cf. also 18, 292; Bell., 2, 22. σπουδή is thus used with προθυμία in Ant., 4, 105; 7, 220, with φιλοτιμία in Ant., 6, 292; 12, 134; 14, 154; 15, 312, with εὔνοια in Ant., 6, 355, with εὔνοια and χάρις in Ant., 7, 69, with φιλία in Ant., 7, 111, with πίστις in Ant., 14, 192 par. τιμή in 14, 151-155. διὰ σπουδῆς ἔχειν is also to be taken in this sense "to be friendly to someone," "to hold him dear," Ant., 14, 186 and 257: Vit., 98, also Ant., 16, 302. In many cases σπουδή means "zeal," "effort," Ant., 1, 115; 2, 222, 340 etc. In a way typical of Jos.' ideal of education σπουδή means patriotism in Ant., 14, 283 περὶ τὴν πατρίδα σπουδή with εὐσέβεια καὶ δικαιοσύνη, the Hell. ethical ideal of a right relation to God, country and fellow-men. σπουδή can also mean "concern," "dedication," "involvement" ἄνδρες ἑπτὰ οἱ καὶ τὴν ἀρετὴν καὶ τὴν περὶ τὸ δίκαιον σπουδὴν προησκηκότες, Ant., 4, 214, "care" διὰ σπουδῆς ἀνεθρέψαμεν, 4, 261, cf. also 8, 187; 10, 44; 13, 212, also "seriousness," "earnest will," οὗ (Abraham's) τὴν σπουδὴν καὶ τὴν προαίρεσιν μὴ ὑβρίσητε, Ant., 1, 254. In this connection cf. ἦν γὰρ αὐτοῖς σπουδή, "it mattered to them," Bell., 4, 215, cf. Ant., 4, 123; 5, 120; 16, 214. σπουδῆς ἄξιον is "something about which one is concerned, which is important and worthwhile," ἔπραξέ τι σπουδῆς ἄξιον, Ant., 5, 272; εὐπρεπῆ δὲ καὶ καλὸν τά τε ἄλλα σπουδῆς ἄξιον, 6, 167 cf. also 6, 139; 8, 23; 12, 12; 13, 356 and 418. In Ant., 6, 67 one finds ἐν σπουδῇ καὶ λόγῳ, i.e., in "word and deed" or "word" and active "concern." In contrast to moral longing and will σπουδή in Jos. denotes the exertion evoked by emotion, the desire for something, also erotically ἡ δὲ βιαιότερον ἐχρῆτο τῇ σπουδῇ (Potiphar's wife), Ant., 2, 53; also "desire" for death σπουδὴ δὲ τῶν λιμωττόντων ἐπὶ τὸν θάνατον ἦν, Bell., 6, 213. Finally it should be mentioned that σπουδή is used for "haste" in Jos., μετὰ σπουδῆς, Ant., 7, 223; σπουδὴν ἐποιεῖτο (forced march), Ant., 12, 421; σπουδὴν ἔχειν, 14, 440; σπουδὴν ποιεῖσθαι, Bell., 7, 190.

3. Philo.

What is not found in Jos. is all the more common in Philo, namely, the use of σπουδαῖος for the morally "good" as in Stoic circles → 560, 39 ff. (opp. φαῦλος). The σπουδαῖος is the "upright and virtuous man," Leg. All., III, 67 cf. Mut. Nom., 31: πάντως οὖν σπουδαῖος ἐκεῖνός ἐστιν, ᾧ φησιν· ἐγώ εἰμι θεὸς σός. Characteristic here is the way in which the religious saying about election in Gn. 15 is turned into a moral statement. It is because Abraham is a σπουδαῖος that God says to him: "I am thy God." The σπουδαῖος is the "wise man," τοῦ σπουδαίου βίος ἐν ἔργοις, ἐν λόγοις δὲ ὁ τοῦ φαύλου θεωρεῖται, Som., II, 302. The σπουδαῖος is free, as the whole of Omn. Prob. Lib. seeks to show: τὸν δὲ σπουδαῖον οὐκ ἔστιν οὔτ᾽ ἀναγκάσαι οὔτε κωλῦσαι· οὐκ ἄρα δοῦλος ὁ σπουδαῖος, 60. He is thus an occasion of good to others, for God blesses the unworthy for the sake of the worthy, τοῦ θεοῦ τὸν ἀπεριόριστον καὶ ἀπερίγραφον πλοῦτον αὐτοῦ διὰ τοὺς ἀξίους (σπουδαίους) καὶ τοῖς ἀναξίοις δωρουμένου, Sacr. AC, 124. Materially σπουδαῖον is "the good" as opp. to the φαῦλον, Gig., 56. The good comes from God πάντα φέρων σπουδαῖα ὁ θεός, Mut. Nom., 256, more precisely described as ἐνέργειαι καὶ πράξεις, Som., II, 34, cf. Leg. All., I, 74. Thus the use and signification of σπουδή is narrower than in Jos., being restricted in the main to the ethical understanding. Yet the word can have the gen. meaning "effort" in a morally negative sense αἱ τοῦ θνητοῦ βίου σπουδαί, Som., II, 70. The combinations point to this sense: διδασκαλία and προκοπή, Congr., 112; βελτίωσις and τελείωσις, Agric., 166; προθυμία, Sacr. AC, 59. The expression μετὰ σπουδῆς is a common one. The obj. is often denoted by ὑπέρ, Leg. Gaj., 242, or πρός, Som., II, 67. πᾶσα σπουδή means "all diligence" applied to something, Leg. Gaj., 338; Sacr. AC, 68. The expression σπουδῆς ἄξιος (cf. Jos. → lines 16 ff.) is used by Philo for what is morally "worthwhile," "essential," "important." Finally there is a hint of the older sense of "haste" in the phrase μετὰ σπουδῆς, μετὰ σπουδῆς καὶ τάχους, Vit., Mos., II, 144.

C. The Word Group in the New Testament.

1. There are various gradations in the NT use of σπουδάζω. Thus it can mean "to make haste" in formulae familiar from the Greek and especially the Hellenistic world (→ 559, 22 ff.), σπούδασον ἐλθεῖν πρός με (2 Tm. 4:9); σπούδασον πρὸ χειμῶνος ἐλθεῖν (2 Tm. 4:21); σπούδασον ἐλθεῖν πρός με εἰς Νικόπολιν (Tt. 3:12), i.e., in the phrases found in letters of the period. Then in Paul σπουδάζω can mean "zealous effort" as an expression of the life of the community. In Gl. 2:10 the apostle tells us how he himself "sought strenuously" to honour the commitment made at the Apostolic Council, that is, how he was concerned constantly to carry out the order. Again, in 1 Th. 2:17 he assures the Thessalonians how he and his companions have made efforts, though unsuccessfully, to see them again in person, cf. 2 Pt. 1:15.

From this, one might say, simple sense there must be differentiated another which is found only in the later epistles and which shows plain traces of the deeper meaning of σπουδαῖος in philosophical writings. Here σπουδαῖος is used to characterise the total conduct of the Christian in the sense of an actualising of his saved position, a fulfilling of what grace has opened up for him. Naturally the word which imparts grace is not understood here as in Paul's letters. It is instruction on a matter which can be rationally grasped and to which moral action and conduct must be added, whereas in Paul action and conduct come as the word itself is heard, and indeed consist in the fact that what is done in hearing the word and answer to it is right. To the degree that the former understanding of word and teaching spread, later parts of the NT share in the Hellenistic understanding of σπουδάζω → 559, 22 ff. [9] Cf. Eph. 4:3: σπουδάζοντες τηρεῖν τὴν ἑνότητα τοῦ πνεύματος ἐν τῷ συνδέσμῳ τῆς εἰρήνης, the unity of Jews and Gentiles achieved by Christ is to be maintained, and Christians must exert themselves to this end. This special admonition is part of the general theme of exhortation: ἀξίως περιπατῆσαι τῆς κλήσεως, ἧς ἐκλήθητε, 4:1. Cf. also the admonition in 2 Tm. 2:15: σπούδασον σεαυτὸν δόκιμον παραστῆσαι τῷ θεῷ, moral concern to be approved. Hb. 4:11 anticipates the concluding admonitions of the epistle, summoning the readers to strive zealously for the rest which God has prepared (→ 34, 30 ff.), i.e., to act in such a way that as members of the people of God they will not be excluded from this rest. [10] 2 Pt. 1:10 (→ IV, 180, 14 ff.) is related to Eph. 4:1-3. Here, too, the reference is to the κλῆσις which must be secured and confirmed by the conduct of those who are called. σπουδάσατε denotes the total demeanour of the Christian whose daily task is to ratify, activate and practise his calling. The author of 2 Pt. remains within the eschatology which he expressly defends when he issues the further call in 3:14: διό, ἀγαπητοί, ταῦτα προσδοκῶντες σπουδάσατε ἄσπιλοι καὶ ἀμώμητοι αὐτῷ εὑρεθῆναι ἐν εἰρήνῃ. The whole moral seriousness of Christians is to be directed to the end of being found as ἄσπιλοι καὶ ἀμώμητοι.

---

[9] A summary ref. (e.g. Schl. Past., 209, n. 1 on Tt. 3:12) to Gl. 2:10; Eph. 4:3; 1 Th. 2:17 is hardly adequate, for there is a plain distinction between 1 Th. 2:17 on the one side and Eph. 4:3 on the other.

[10] Mi Hb., ad loc.: "In primitive Chr. exhortation (Eph. 4:3; 2 Tm. 2:15; 2 Pt. 1:10; 3:14) σπουδάζω expresses the seriousness and concern we owe to God's Word." Entry into rest demands zeal and effort. It is true that the eschatological character of the admonition is not wholly clear at this pt. But Mi. sees that this is a prevalent form of exhortation.

2. The adjective σπουδαῖος does not bear any Hellenistic or specifically Stoic colouring (→ 560, 39 ff.) and this shows how remote Paul and the NT as a whole are from this usage. 2 C. 8:17 bears witness to the particular "zeal" of Titus in the matter of the collection, and this is a gift of God according to v. 16. The same applies to the unknown brother of v. 22 whose zeal is matched by the confidence he has in the Corinthians. There is an echo of Hellenistic expressions in this stress on zeal → 560, 9 ff. [11] The adverb is often used in the NT to emphasise intensive asking: παρεκάλουν αὐτὸν ('Ιησοῦν) σπουδαίως (Lk. 7:4), or seeking: σπουδαίως ἐζήτησέν με (2 Tm. 1:17), or preparation for a journey: σπουδαίως πρόπεμψον (Tt. 3:13). [12] Paul also uses the adverb in the superlative comparative in Phil. 2:28: σπουδαιοτέρως οὖν ἔπεμψα αὐτὸν ... "as quickly as possible." [13]

3. In the NT σπουδή first means "haste," especially in the phrase used by Jos. (→ 564, 23 ff.): μετὰ σπουδῆς. Thus we read in Mk. 6:25: καὶ εἰσελθοῦσα (εὐθὺς μετὰ σπουδῆς) [14] πρὸς τὸν βασιλέα, and in Lk. 1:39: ἐπορεύθη (Μαριὰμ) εἰς τὴν ὀρεινὴν μετὰ σπουδῆς εἰς πόλιν 'Ιούδα. [15] But then it means "zeal" with reference to various functions in the community. The important thing about what the προϊστάμενος has to do (→ VI, 701, 37 ff.) is that it be done ἐν σπουδῇ, "with true commitment": ὁ προϊστάμενος ἐν σπουδῇ (R. 8:12). This statement carries a reference back to v. 6: ἔχοντες δὲ χαρίσματα κατὰ τὴν χάριν τὴν δοθεῖσαν ἡμῖν διάφορα. R. 12:11 has the general admonition: τῇ σπουδῇ μὴ ὀκνηροί. σπουδή, then, is one of God's spiritual gifts. [16] The dative is one of relation, "in respect of zeal." What is meant is the "holy zeal" which demands full dedication to serving the community. If σπουδή can be used in this connection it is because of the way the concept was deepened in Hellenistic thought → 561, 18 ff. Any attempt to construe σπουδή as "study" or "teaching" is to be resisted. [17] There is too little support for this in Greek (and especially contemporary) usage.

σπουδή also means "zealous concern" for the apostle, the concern to make restitution which results from true repentance, τὸ ... λυπηθῆναι πόσην κατειργάσατο ὑμῖν σπουδήν, 2 C. 7:11. Paul can say that the final aim and point of his sharp letter was to stir up this zeal, ἕνεκεν τοῦ φανερωθῆναι τὴν σπουδὴν ὑμῶν τὴν ὑπὲρ ἡμῶν πρὸς ὑμᾶς ἐνώπιον τοῦ θεοῦ, 7:12. It is obvious that this σπουδή is a fruit of the Spirit which the Spirit brings forth through the apostle and his work in the church. Hence σπουδή denotes a new attitude on the part of the Corinthians. [18] With πίστις, λόγος, γνῶσις, ἡ ἐξ ἡμῶν ἐν ὑμῖν ἀγάπη, Paul also mentions πᾶσα σπουδή as something the Corinthians have in abundance; what he means is the power of action, the zeal to perform, 2 C. 8:7. [19] He does not write κατ᾽

[11] Schl. Lk. on 7:4 ref. to Jos. Ant., 8, 6: διακονήσειν σπουδαίως, and Ant., 14, 307: ὑπὲρ σοῦ καὶ τοῦ ἔθνους σπουδαίως διέθεντο.
[12] Dib. Past., ad loc.: As the ἵνα clause shows, σπουδαίως πρόπεμψον means to look after them well and send them on (cf. 3 Jn. 6).
[13] Loh. Phil., ad loc., 120, n. 3. For σπουδαιοτέρως D* FG read the more correct σπουδαιότερον. The comparative seems to have a superlative sense here, cf. Bl.-Debr. § 244, 1.
[14] Left out by D it.
[15] Schl. Lk., ad loc. ref. to par. in Jos. Ant., 19, 348; Vit., 91. These might easily be multiplied as indicated. The NT follows here the Hell. usage represented by Jos.
[16] Mi. R., ad loc,, esp. 271, n. 5; v. H. Greeven, "Propheten, Lehrer u. Vorsteher bei Pls.," ZNW, 44 (1952), 32.
[17] Mi. R., ad loc., 271, n. 5.
[18] Esp. Schl. K., ad loc.
[19] Schl. K., ad loc.

ἐπιταγήν but, alluding to the mutual zeal which is of the essence of Christianity, he prefers διὰ τῆς ἑτέρων σπουδῆς, 8:8. In the same chapter with its many references to σπουδή he can also speak of the "zeal" of Titus too, i.e., his zeal for work in the Corinthian church. But this σπουδή is again the gift of God for which the apostle gives thanks, 8:16. The expression πᾶσαν σπουδὴν ποιούμενος γράφειν ὑμῖν in Jd. 3 is a common one in Greek for which there are various parallels. [20] In Hb. 6:11 σπουδή refers to the plenitude of the assurance of hope in the sense of the whole epistle, especially c. 11; this is to be preserved by readers to the end, 3:6, 14. What is at issue then is full salvation, Christian felicity, which must be maintained. This "zeal" is once again regarded as a fruit of the Spirit. [21] The αὐτήν (6:11) does not refer to the services previously mentioned; it means that all are to display the same zeal. It is not to be lacking in anyone. It is thus part of being a Christian. Here, then, the concept takes on universal and radical significance as a note of the true Christian who knows what he is and who is not going to lose what he has been given. One is reminded of the σπουδαῖος of the Stoics (→ 560, 39 ff.) except that the theme and object are materially different. σπουδή is used in the same way in 2 Pt. 1:5, though with a bigger stress on the moral character: σπουδὴν πᾶσαν παρεισενέγκαντες. This reminds us of the same expression in an inscription → 561, 40 ff. [22] The zeal which is to be deployed relates to the whole Christian ethos unfolded in the climax which follows in vv. 6-10. This climax bears unmistakable Hellenistic traits. One may thus assume that σπουδή is here used Hellenistically in the sense of the basic orientation of the σπουδαῖος, of the truly worthy, moral man whose mind is set on the good.

D. The Word Group in the Early Church.

This feature seen in later NT writings is found again in the post-apost. fathers.

1. Here again σπουδάζω can mean "to make haste," Ign. Eph., 1, 2; Mart. Pol., 13, 2. or gen. "to strive," Barn., 1, 5; 4, 9; 21, 9. But in most instances it denotes definite striving after true Chr. conduct ἐὰν γὰρ σπουδάσωμεν ἀγαθοποιεῖν, διώξεται ἡμᾶς εἰρήνη, 2 Cl., 10, 2; σπουδάζω τὴν δικαιοσύνην διώκειν, 18, 2; negatively μὴ σπουδάζοντες ἀντιμιμήσασθαι αὐτούς (non-christians), Ign. Eph., 10, 2; cf. Mg., 13, 1; μιμηταὶ δὲ τοῦ κυρίου σπουδάζωμεν εἶναι — τίς πλέον ἀδικηθῇ; τίς ἀποστερηθῇ; Eph. 10, 3. This striving is discipleship in the sense of imitating the moral example of the Lord (cf. 1 Pt. 2:21-23), where for the first time in the NT the example of the suffering Lord is introduced as ethical motivation for the proper conduct of the slave. Ign. goes a step further when he makes correct ecclesiastical conduct a matter of ethical concern, i.e. being a true Christian as a member of the community in submission to the bishop: σπουδάσωμεν οὖν μὴ ἀντιτάσσεσθαι τῷ ἐπισκόπῳ, ἵνα ὦμεν θεῷ ὑποτασσόμενοι, Eph. 5, 3; σπουδάζετε οὖν πυκνότερον συνέρχεσθαι εἰς εὐχαριστίαν θεοῦ καὶ εἰς δόξαν, 13, 1, cf. Phld., 4 with a special emphasis on the unity of the sacrament. Thus ἐν ὁμονοίᾳ θεοῦ σπουδάζετε πάντα πράσσειν (under the example of the bishop

---

[20] Wnd. Kath. Br., ad loc. ref. to Hdt., V, 30; Isoc. Or., 5, 45.
[21] Mi. Hb., ad loc., 155, n. 1.
[22] Wnd. Pt., ad loc. also ref. to a decree of Stratonicea, CIG, II, 2715a, 4: καλῶς δὲ ἔχι πᾶσαν σπουδὴν ἰσφέρεσθαι ἰς τὴν πρὸς (αὐτοὺς εὐσέ)βειαν, also to Deissmann LO, 270, who compares the inscr. from Ditt. Or., II, 438, 9 f. (1st cent. B.C.), where similar virtues to those in 2 Pt. 1:5 are listed, with the conclusion καὶ ... τὴν πλείστ(η)ν εἰσενηνεγμένον σπουδήν, cf. also par. in Jos. Ant. 11, 324; 20, 204 → 564, 7 f.

and elders) means that there is to be an effort to maintain doctrinal purity, Mg., 6, 1. The gen. θεοῦ is to be taken as a subj. gen. — the unanimity which God has brought into being. 23

2. σπουδαῖος is also used in the pregnant sense of "the man who is concerned about knowledge or right conduct," par. ἐνδεής, cf. ἐπεὶ οὕτως ἐνδεὴς εἶ καὶ σπουδαῖος εἰς τὸ γνῶναι πάντα, Herm. v., 3, 1, 2, here then in the form σπουδαῖος εἴς τι. The statement in Ign. Pol., 3, 2: πλέον σπουδαῖος γίνου οὖ εἶ, "be even more zealous than you (already) are," also ref. gen. to the total disposition and conduct of the one addressed.

3. σπουδή, however, is only used adverbially, μετὰ σπουδῆς, "in haste" (Mart. Pol., 8, 3), or in the sense "with zeal" (Dg., 12, 1), or with acc. and inf. to express zealous attention to something. Mart. Pol., 7, 2. The use, then, does not go beyond the confines of that customary in Hellenism.

Harder

---

† στάσις   ← ἀκαταστασία, III, 446, 19 ff. → μάχη, IV, 527, 8 ff.

A. The Word Outside the Bible.

The word is attested outside the Bible [1] from Alcaeus and Solon (c. 600 B.C. → line 29 f.). It has in the main the character of a nomen actionis (→ lines 29 ff.), but can also denote the result of an action. [2] Apart from the not very common trans. use (ἵστημι) for the "appointment" or "installation" of leaders (Polyb., 5, 60, 7), ἀγάλματος (Dio C., 37, 34, 4), it is esp. used intr. (ἵσταμαι) in the following senses.

1. a. "Standing," στάσιν βεβαίαν ἔχειν (Dio C., 40, 23, 3), "standing firm" as opp. to movement, "standing still," "rest," Plat. Soph., 250a, 254d etc.; Philo Op. Mund., 120; Leg. All., II, 99. Firmness and immutability are essential qualities of God, Som., II, 237 and 222; Poster. C., 29, [3] and are to be sought after by the righteous, *ibid.*, 23; Gig., 49 par. μονή "firmness," "steadfastness," Abr., 58; sometimes also "standing" as distinct from sitting, Plat. Leg., IX 855c; Dio C., 55, 18, 4. b. "Position," Hdt., II, 26; IX, 21, also transf. στῆναι στάσιν πολεμίου, "to take the standpoint of an enemy against someone," M. Ant., VI, 41, 2; "situation," "state," Plat. Phaedr., 253d.

2. "Taking a stand," esp. "rebelling" and first a. — the sense in the earliest examples, τῶν ἀνέμων στάσιν for the "uproar of the winds" in Alcaeus Fr., 46a, 1 (Diehl², I, 4, 108); στάσις ἔμφυλος (with πόλεμος) in Solon Fr., 3, 19 (Diehl³, I, 28) — "civil

---

23 Bau Ign., *ad loc.* ref. to Ign. Mg., 6, 2; 15, 1; Phld. Inscr. and 1, 2; 8, 1; Pol., 1, 3.

σ τ ά σ ι ς . [1] On the formation Schwyzer, I, 505, 3; W. Porzig, *Die Namen f. Satzinhalte im Griech. u. im Idg.* (1942), 331; on the function of nouns in -σις v. E. Benveniste, *Noms d'agent et noms d'action* (1948), 75-86 [Risch].
[2] For further details cf. Liddell-Scott, *s.v.* and → n. 6, 7.
[3] The anthropomorphic OT statements about God's standing (στάσις θεία) are applied allegorically by Aristobulus to the "fixity" of the individual parts or species of creation (e.g., sun, moon, animal, man) which do not change into one another, Fr., 2 (Eus. Praep. Ev., VIII, 10, 9-12).

strife"; to extol this is useless, Xenophanes Fr., 1, 23 (Diehl³, I, 65); στάσις ἐμφύλιος ἐς ἑκάτερα κακόν, Democr. Fr., 249 (Diels, II, 195, 3 f.); transf. of the cosmos, there is no στάσις in the divine sphere, Emped. Fr., 27a (Diels, I, 324, 8). Hostility between those who belong together is στάσις, while hostility between enemies is πόλεμος, Plat. Resp., V, 470b; hence hostility between Hellenes is to be called στάσις, 470c d → II, 401, 23 and 28; transf. also of the inner conflict of the soul ἐν τῇ τῆς ψυχῆς στάσει, Resp., IV, 440e. Aristot. Pol., V deals with στάσεις, which lead to constitutional changes along the ancient lines of democracy, oligarchy etc.; the causes are esp. discussed in 1-4. στάσις is here connected with μεταβολή "revolution" on the one side (2, p. 1302a, 16 f., 23) and with the personal dissension of individuals on the other (4, p. 1303b, 28, 31 f.; 1304a, 11 f.); this can also lead to political unrest (1303b, 38; 1304a, 9). στάσεις usually arise out of little things and lead on to big things, 1303b, 17-19. Always there is political confusion as to the question of ἰσότης, 1, p. 1301b, 27-29 → III, 345, 37 ff. στάσεις par. πολιτικαὶ ταραχαί in 2, p. 1302a, 21 f., μάχαι πρὸς ἀλλήλους in IV, 11, p. 1296a, 27 f., στάσιν κινεῖν ("to stir up") in V, 4, p. 1304a, 36 → n. 15 In the speech of Ael. Arist. to the men of Rhodes on harmony the deep rift between ὁμόνοια and στάσις is well brought out, Or., 24, 4, 19-21, 41-44 etc. The ephebe swears μηδὲ στάσιος ἀρξεῖν, Ditt. Syll. ³, I, 527, 60 f. (Dreros, c. 220 B.C.). Par. ταραχή for public confusion and unrest, Philo Som., II, 251; Poster. C., 119; Leg. Gaj., 113 etc., both transf. of the soul, Congr., 176, opp. εὐστάθεια, Leg. Gaj., 113; Flacc., 135, ἐμφύλιος στάσις "civil war", Rer. Div. Her., 246, a mark of ochlocracy, Agric., 45, transf. Ebr., 98, of the conflict of the four emotions and the five senses, Congr., 92. God is the one who makes peace, removing political στάσεις and those between the parts of the universe, Spec. Leg., II, 192. If only the inner strife in man can be settled, political conflicts will cease too, Poster. C., 185, cf. καταπαύσας . . . τὴν ἐν αὐτῷ στάσιν, 183. In Philo's day there was no longer a clear-cut distinction between πόλεμος and στάσις; war disturbs public rest and order, Leg. Gaj., 113, cf. Poster. C., 119. The distinction takes rather different lines in the ep. of Claudius to the Alexandrians whose ταραχή and στάσις against the Jews — because they are so vehement — are rightly to be described as πόλεμος, CP Jud. II, 153, 73 f., cf. Jos. Ant., 20, 184; also with ref, to unrest concerning the Jews CP Jud. II, 444, 30 (c. 117/118 A.D.) cf. διὰ τοὺς τῶν Ἰουδαίων θορύβους, line 25 f. Jos. often uses the word in different connections. It can denote the "confusion" in Syria after Alexander's death, Ap., 1, 194; the inner "confusion" amongst the Jews which is settled by force, Bell., 1, 236; 4, 376; Ant., 14, 22; the actions of the Zealots on the occasion of the census of Quirinius, 18, 8 (with πόλεμοι, 7); the revolt in Jerusalem under Cumanus, even though there was this time no direct use of force, 20, 105, cf. 109, 117; cf. also Bell., 2, 10; the rebellion of the Jews against foreign rulers, 1, 88; Ant., 14, 120; the revolt of the people against Moses, Ant., 4, 59 and 76, or against God's Law, 4, 140; the unrest of Jews and non-Jews in Caesarea, 20, 174; confusion in the house of the Hasmoneans, 14, 491, or Herod, 16, 73 and 189; πόλεμος without, στάσις within, Bell., 5, 98 etc. Acc. to Inscr. Magn., 114, 3 f. and 11 f. (probably Ephesus at the end of the 2nd cent. A.D.) a strike of bakers obviously led to tumultuous scenes on the Agora which involved the people; στάσις, ταραχή, θόρυβος are the terms used. In the interests of the population the proconsul decided to bring the bakers to reason by a διάταγμα rather than by due punishment. He forbade assemblies and demanded obedience to decrees and a resumption of work; appropriate punishment would be meted out to those who resisted by holding meetings or stirring up θόρυβος and [στά]σις. [4]
b. The word is then used gen. for any "disagreement" between groups, Jos. Vit., 143 (→ n. 10) or individuals, between women, Aesch. Pers., 188, "conflicts" between the gods, Jos. Ap., 2, 243, between slaves, Menand. Fr., 784, 3 (Koerte). στάσις is always used in this sense in Artemid. Onirocr.: domestic "strife," I, 31 (p. 32, 20 f.), cf. 27 p. 29, 22). Dice (III, 1, p. 170, 5), fighting cocks (III, 5, p. 171, 13 f.), anything that divides

---

[4] In interpretation cf. W. H. Buckler, "Labour Disputes in the Province of Asia," *Anatolian Studies . . . to W. M. Ramsay* (1923), 30-33, 46 f. and Plate II.

or separates (I, 52, p. 50, 6 f.), will lead to στάσεις, with φιλονεικία etc. (I, 73, p. 65, 24 f.); Philo Spec. Leg., I, 108; λογικαὶ στάσεις are "academic wranglings," Rer. Div. Her., 248.

B. The Septuagint.

In the LXX (all ref. are given) στάσις has the trans. sense of "what is set up," "boundary-stone" in Ju. 9:6 (מַצֵּבָה), "statute" (קְיָם) in Da. 6:8 LXX Θ, 16 Θ, "treaty" in 1 Macc. 7:18. We also find the intr. sense as follows.

1. "Stability" of the sun and moon, Jos. 10:13 (עָמַד, the sentence construction differs in the Hbr.); "place where one stands," Da. 8:17 LXX Θ, or esp. to which one attains, 2 Ch. 23:13 (עַמּוּד); 30:16; 35:10, 15; 2 Εσδρ. 18:7; 19:3; 3 Βασ. 10:15 (par. καθέδρα) and 2 Ch. 9:4. The last passage leads on at once to the transf. sense of "position" Is. 22:19 (par. οἰκονομία); 2 Εσδρ. 23:11. In these 12 passages the word is used for forms of עמד as well as מַעֲמָד and עֹמֶד. 5 In other vv. in which other Hbr. terms are the equivalents it is sometimes harder to say what the transl. had in mind. Cf. "location" in 1 Ch. 28:2 (הֲדֹם "stool"), "place of rest" (strong place) in Dt. 28:65 (מָנוֹחַ); Na. 3:11 (מָעוֹז) regulated "state" in 2 Ch. 24:13 (מַתְכֹּנֶת). With no Hbr. we find "standing" (of the bow of light around God) in Ez. 1:28, "position" (of the heavens) in 2 Εσδρ. 19:6, 6 "situation" in Sir. 33:12, "location" in 3 Macc. 1:23, στάσις ποδός in 1 Macc. 10:72.

2. Personal "discord" occurs only in Prv. 17:14 (רִיב). 7

C. The New Testament.

1. In the NT the word occurs in the sense of "unchanged existence" only in Hb. 9:8 (→ 568, 23 f.) for the σκηνή of the old order, relativised by ἔτι. 8

2. In the Synoptic Gospels the meaning in Mk. 15:7 is "uproar" (with στασιαστής), while the reference in Lk. 23:19, 25 is to an otherwise unknown sequence of events, whether in the form of revolt against the Romans or strife among the Jews themselves (→ 569, 32 f.), which Luke locates (in part at least) in Jerusalem. In Ac. 19:40 it is the "uproar" which threatens political security and thus gives rise to complaint. 9 On the other hand Ac. 15:2 is speaking of lively "conflict" about questions of faith in the Christian community. In Ac. 23:7 a στάσις between the Pharisees and the Sadducees, i.e., a theological clash (v. 8, 29), takes certain violent forms (v. 9 f.). 10 In Ac. 24:5 the expression is perhaps intentionally am-

---

5 In a mechanical transl. at Da. 10:11 Θ too (LXX correctly τόπος, for the ref. is not to someone standing).

6 "Vett. Val., 38, 17 uses στάσις for 'planetary connection,'" P. Katz, Philo's Bible (1950), 148, with a ref. also to the sense mentioned in → n. 7 [Katz].

7 1 Βασ. 13:23; 14:1 Θ: στάσις "unit," "troop" (of the Philistines). For this sense cf. Aesch. Choeph., 114 and 458; Eum., 311. Θ has στάσις (Mas. מַצָּב) in the sense of "post." In other vv. the Hexapla use is like that of the LXX [Bertram]. It is uncertain whether στάσις was a Rabb. loan word, v. Levy Wört., I, 119a.

8 This seems to be the natural sense not just in the narrower context but acc. to the whole scheme of thought in Hb., not "stand" (possible acc. to Pr.-Bauer). Cf שני מעמד "years of existence" in Damasc. 2:9 (2:8).

9 στάσις is not used in the accounts of other disturbances in Ac. 14:4 f. (→ V, 470, 25 ff.); 17:3, though cf. ταράσσω in 17:13.

10 There is a formal reminiscence of Jos. Vit., 143, where the accused by a clever defence is able to win over one part of his accusers and thus causes a στάσις between them.

biguous. The orator appointed by the high-priest says before the procurator that official Judaism throughout the *ecumene* finds Paul a κινοῦντα (→ 569, 15) στάσεις πᾶσιν τοῖς 'Ιουδαίοις. [11] The reference here is to more than theological squabbling. The charge obviously begins by deliberately stressing the εἰρήνη which has been achieved between Judaism and the Roman procurator. [12] This is placed in jeopardy by the accused. If all kinds of "unrest" are caused by him among the Jews, not only in Palestine but beyond, then it is incumbent upon the procurator to intervene at once.

στάσις occurs in the sense of "uproar," "strife," esp. in Ac. (also ταράσσειν), and is often found with ταραχή outside the NT → 569, 14, 18 ff., 43). But στάσις is never used in the NT for conflicts within the Chr. community; for these Pl. has ἀκαταστασία (but cf. Lk. 21:9 → III, 446, 20 ff.) and διχοστασία (→ I, 514, 5 ff.). [13] In Ac. esp. we also find θόρυβος, which first means "noise" in gen., then "uproar," [14] 20:1, cf. 17:5 and Mk. 14:2 par. Only in Ac. 19:29 do we find σύγχυσις, while the corresponding verb "to set in uproar" occurs only in 21:27, 31.

D. The Post-Apostolic Fathers.

Here only 1 Cl. has στάσις (9 times) and στασιάζω (7), the noun with ἔρις (9 times in 1 Cl.; elsewhere only Ign. Eph., 8, 1) in 3, 2; 14, 2; 54, 2, with διχοστασία in 51, 1 (→ I, 514, 5 ff.), in a series ζῆλος (→ II, 882, 9 ff.) καὶ φθόνος, ἔρις καὶ στάσις (→ n. 13) etc. at 3, 2, cf. φθόνος and ἔρις in R. 1:29; Phil. 1:15, ἔρις and ζῆλος in R. 13:13; 1 C. 3:3; 2 C. 12:20 and esp. Gl. 5:20. We thus have a fixed vocabulary which in 1 Cl. is not taken from the NT. In 1 Cl. (as outside the NT) the antonym is ὁμόνοια (13 times) or ὁμονοέω at 62, 2. The author takes στάσις to mean "rebellion" as well as "discord." This may be seen from the ref. to Nu. 16 (the revolt of Korah and his company) in the exhortation regarding the στάσις in Corinth, which the whole ep. is designed to remedy, 1 Cl. 4, 12; 51, 3 f. Both these passages ref. to στασιάζειν against Moses, and the author speaks expressly of στασιάζειν against the presbyters in 47, 6 (cf. 57, 1: ὑποτάγητε τοῖς πρεσβυτέροις), while the required ἡσυχάζειν (aor. part. 63, 1) τῆς ματαίας στάσεως is a bending of the neck and return to obedience, and comparison is made with unrest in πόλεις in 55, 1 etc. The vocabulary is obviously taken from the political sphere as in the call for ὁμόνοια, [15] of which examples are found in the stars and the natural order even down to the smallest creatures (20, 3-11), and esp. in the animals in the ark, 9, 4. Christianity prays for peace and concord [16] for itself and for all men (60, 4), and for rulers too (61, 1). Its restoration in Corinth is the concluding goal of the letter in 65, 1 (with the political term εὐστάθεια as in 61, 1). In the NT the older [17] ὁμόφρων or τὸ αὐτὸ → φρονεῖν corresponds to the group.

Delling

---

[11] τοῖς 'Ιουδαίοις means "among the Jews," Wdt. Ag., *ad loc.*; Jackson-Lake, I, 4, 298; Bau. Ag., *ad loc.*; H. W. Beyer, *Die Ag., NT Deutsch* 5[8] (1957), *ad loc.*, or "against the Jews," Haench. Ag., *ad loc.*; the transl. of Pr. Ag., *ad loc.* leaves both possibilities open: "for the Jews." In the main the depiction of Paul's work in Acts supports the first rendering.

[12] On the actual situation in Palestine under Felix *v.* Schürer, I, 573-577.

[13] Cf. also ἔρις (→ II, 661, 10 f.), which is used with στάσις in Soph. Oed. Col., 1234 and Aristoph. Thes., 788 and which like it can be used of both political and personal affairs.

[14] Examples in Liddell-Scott, *s.v.*

[15] ὁμόνοια is obviously the opp. of. στάσις, cf. H. Kramer, Quid valeat ὁμόνοια in litteris graecis, Diss. Göttingen (1915), 17 f., 26 f. etc.; H. Fuchs, *Aug. u. d. antike Friedensgedanke* (1926), 96-138. For details on ὁμόνοια cf. also B. Keil, Εἰρήνη, *Berichte über die Verhandlungen d. Sächsischen Gesellschaft d. Wissenschaften, Philol.-historische Klasse*, 68, 4 (1916), 39 n. 1; L. Sanders, "L'Hellénisme de S. Clément de Rome et le Paulinisme," *Studia Hellenistica*, II (1943), Index, *s.v.*

[16] Found together in Ditt. Syll.[3], II, 685, 13 (139 B.C.); opp. διάστασις, *ibid.*, line 15 f.

[17] Cf. Kramer, *op cit.* (→ n. 15), 8-13, 28 (the ephebe oath).

σταυρός, σταυρόω, ἀνασταυρόω

σταυρός

Contents: A. The Cross and Crucifixion in the New Testament World: I. The Meaning of the Word; II. The Penalty of Crucifixion. B. σταυρός in the New Testament: I. The Cross of Jesus; II. The Theology of the Cross; III. The Figurative Use of the Word; IV. The Later Use of the Word.

A. The Cross and Crucifixion in the New Testament World.

I. The meaning of the Word.

1. σταυρός[1] is an upright stake.[2] σταυροί· οἱ καταπεπηγότες σκόλοπες, χάρακες καὶ πάντα τὰ ἑστῶτα ξύλα, ἀπὸ τοῦ ἑστάναι, Hesych., IV, 72. This is used for fencing, Hom. Od., 14, 11; Il., 24, 453; Thuc., IV, 90, 2; Xenoph. An., V, 2, 21; Plut. Artaxerxes, 17, 7 (I, 1019e). Posts serve as foundations, Thuc., VII, 25, 5, cf. Philo Agric., 11, where we find the sense of "palisade."

2. The σταυρός is an instrument of torture for serious offences, Plut. Ser. Num. Vind., 9 (II, 554a); Artemid. Onirocr., II, 53 (p. 152, 4 ff.); Diod. S., 2, 18 (→ III, 411, n. 4). In shape we find three basic forms. The cross was a vertical, pointed stake (σκόλοψ, → 409, 4 ff.), or it consisted of an upright with a cross-beam above it (T, crux commissa), or it consisted of two intersecting beams of equal length[3] (†, crux immissa).[4]

σ τ α υ ρ ό ς . Bibl.: I. Gen. H. Fulda, Das Kreuz u. d. Kreuzigung (1878); H. Marucchi, Art. "Croix" in Dict. Bibl., II (1899), 1127-31; H. Hitzig, Art. "crux" in Pauly-W., 4 (1901), 1728-31; V. Schulze, Art. "Kreuz u. Kreuzigung" in RE³, 11, 90-92; H. Leclerq, Art. "Le supplice de la croix" in DACL, III, 2, p. 3045-48; E. G. Hirsch, Art. "Crucifixion" in Jew. Enc., IV, 373 f.; J. Gutmann, Art "Kreuzigung" in EJ, X (1934), 414-17; U. Holzmeister, Crux Domini atque crucifixio (1934); A. Wikenhauser, Art. "Kreuzigung" in Lex. Th. K., VI (1934), 259 f.; J. J. Collins, "The Archaeology of the Crucifixion," The Catholic Bibl. Quarterly, 1 (1939), 154-159; T. Innitzer, Leidens- u. Verklärungsgeschichte Jesu⁴ (1948), 259-268; P. Caligaris, "La crocifissione," Paideia, 7 (1952), 218-222; S. Rosenblatt, "The Crucifixion of Jesus Christ from the Standpoint of Pharisaic Law," JBL, 75 (1956), 315-321; E. Stauffer, Jerusalem u. Rom im Zeitalter Jesu Christi (1957), 123-127; H. Lietzmann, "Der Prozeß Jesu," Kleine Schriften, II (1958), 251-263; also "Bemerkungen zum Prozeß Jesu," ibid., 264-276; W. Grundmann, Die Gesch. Jesu Christi³ (1960), 343-8; J. J. Blinzler, Der Prozeß Jesu³ (1960), 263-271; also Art. "Kreuzigung" in Lex. Th. K.², VI (1961), 621 f.; P. Winter, On the Trial of Jesus (1961), 62-66. II. On the cross in Chr. art: W. Wood Seymour, The Cross in Tradition, History and Art (1898); V. Schultze, Art. "Kreuzes-zeichen" in RE³, 11, 93-96; G. d'Alviella, Art. "Cross" in ERE, IV (1911), 324-329; J. Hempel-R. Günther, Art. "Kreuz" in RGG², III, 1289-93; further bibl. in E. Dinkler, Art. "Kreuz, II" in RGG³, IV, 46 f.

[1] Etym. Ancient Nordic staurr "stake," cf. στυ- in στῦλος "pillar," στύω "rise." Cf. Boisacq, s.v.; Schwyzer, I, 347 and 349; Pokorny, 1008 f. [Risch].

[2] Cf. G. Curtius, Grundzüge d. gr. Etymologie⁵ (1879), 212.

[3] Cf. Hitzig, 1730: "Originally a tree or a post thrust ad hoc into the ground was used (for crucifixion) ... At any rate it has not been shown and is most unlikely that the cross necessarily, always and everywhere had the form familiar to us and described by the fathers. The development of this form, i.e., the adding of the horizontal cross-beam, is probably connected with the punishment of the patibulum in the case of slaves."

[4] LXX does not have the word, and it is rare for cross (as a means of punishment) in Philo, e.g., Flacc., 72, 84.

II. The Penalty of Crucifixion.

1. It seems that the Persians invented or first used this mode of execution. [5] They probably did so in order not to defile the earth, which was consecrated to Ormuzd, by the body of the person executed. [6] Later the cross is used by Alexander the Great, the Diadochoi princes and esp. the Carthaginians, Polyb., 1, 24. From these it came to the Romans, who called the instrument used the *crux*. In Greece this punishment was restricted to slaves, cf. the Amyzon inscr. from Caria, BMI, IV, 2. No. 1036 (2nd/1st cent. B.C.); it was never even considered for free Greeks, Diod. S., 16, 54, 4. [7] Only barbarians crucified free men, Hdt., I, 128; IV, 43 etc. In Rome it was already a mode of executing slaves even in the days of the republic. [8] In the imperial period it was regarded as *servile supplicium* but was also used on aliens who were not Roman citizens. It could not be imposed on citizens, Cic. Verr., II, 5, 62, 162-165. But autocratic governors ignored this. [9] In the Roman provinces the penalty of crucifixion was one of the strongest means of maintaining order and security. Governors imposed this servile punishment esp. on freedom fighters who tried to break away from Roman rule. [10] Jos. mentions innumerable crucifixions — mass executions of rebels — in Judea. [11] The Maccabean king Alexander I, when he had captured the rebellious city of Bethome, had the prisoners brought to Jerusalem and he crucified 800 men (Jews), Jos. Ant., 13, 380.

2. Crucifixion took place as follows. The condemned person carried the *patibulum* (cross-beam) to the place of execution — the stake was already erected. Then on the ground he was bound with outstretched arms to the beam by ropes, or else fixed to it by nails. [12] The beam was then raised with the body and fastened to the upright post. About the middle of the post was a wooden block which supported the suspended body; there was no foot-rest in ancient accounts. [13] The height of the cross varied; it was either rather more than a man's height or even higher when the offender was to be held up for public display at a distance. [14] On the way to execution a tablet was hung around the offender stating the *causa poenae,* and this was affixed to the cross after execution so that all could see.

Crucifixion was regarded as one of the worst forms of execution. Cicero calls it the supreme capital penalty, the most painful, dreadful and ugly. [15] Jos. Bell., 7, 203 agrees.

---

[5] Hdt., I, 128; III, 132 and 159; Thuc., I, 110, 3.

[6] Blinzler Prozess, 262.

[7] For evidence cf. K. Latte, Art. "Todesstrafe" in Pauly-W. Suppl., VII (1940), 1606, also E. Benz, "Der gekreuzigte Gerechte bei Plato, im NT u. in d. Alten Kirche," *AA Mainz* (1950), 1037 f.

[8] Latte, *op. cit.,* 1606 f.

[9] Cf. Blinzler Prozess, 264.

[10] Cf. Benz., *op. cit.,* 1051.

[11] Jos. Ant., 11, 261. 266. 267; 17, 295; 20, 102. 129. 161; Bell., 5, 449-451; for details Blinzler Prozess, 264; Benz, 1051-53; Stauffer, 123-127.

[12] Blinzler Prozess, 266, 279-81. There are not many instances of nailing, cf. J. W. Hewitt, "The Use of Nails in the Crucifixion," HThR, 25 (1932), 29-46.

[13] Blinzler Prozess, 265.

[14] For details, *ibid.,* 266.

[15] Cic. Verr., V, 64, 165: *crudelissimum taeterrimumque supplicium;* V, 66, 169: *servitutis extremum summumque supplicium;* Pro Rabirio, 5, 16: *nomen ipsum crucis absit non modo a corpore civium Romanorum, sed etiam a cogitatione, oculis, auribus.* Tac. Hist., IV, 3, 11: *mors turpissima crucis.* Cf. the description in Winter, 65 f. Cf. also A. Réville, *Jésus de Nazareth,* II (1897), 405 f.; M. Goguel, *The Life of Jesus* (1933), 535 f.; T. Mommsen, *Röm. Strafrecht* (1899), 918, n. 5.

Scourging usually preceded it. The condemned person was exposed to mockery. Sometimes he was stripped and his clothes were divided among the executioners, though this was not the common rule. Crucifixion took place publicly on streets or elevated places. Usually the body was left to rot on the cross. But it could also be handed over for burial. The physical and mental sufferings which this slow death on the cross involved are unimaginable. Crucifixion as a capital penalty was ended only by Constantine the Great.

3. Jewish law did not prescribe crucifixion.[16] Stoned idolaters and blasphemers were to be hanged on a tree, not in execution, but as an additional penalty. It showed that those who had been put to death were accursed by God, Dt. 21:23 (LXX): "Any man who hangs on a tree is accursed by God" → III, 917, 12 ff. This saying was applied by Judaism to those who were crucified.[17]

B. σταυρός in the New Testament.

I. The Cross of Jesus.

The Synoptic Gospels and John have no special theology of the cross. They tell the story of the crucifixion. Yet they do not just give a sober account of the historical event. Their narratives have a kerygmatic and cultic quality.[18] In the background, esp. in Jn., there lies the thought that Jesus dies as the sacrificial lamb of the new covenant.

The events preceding the crucifixion (scourging, mocking and stripping) are along the lines of current custom → lines 1 ff. The fact that the execution took place on a raised site (Golgotha) outside the city has in itself no particular significance → line 3. Only the Fourth Evangelist ascribes theological weight to the lifting up of Jesus on the cross (→ ὑψόω).[19] If the crucifixion itself[20] corresponds to the general picture of this form of execution,[21] there are also some Jewish touches: the stupefying drink, wine mixed with myrrh (Mk. 15:23),[22] and the taking down of the body of Jesus on Friday evening, Jn. 19:31 cf. Dt. 21:22 f.

The cross which the Romans set up to execute Jesus was like any other, consisting of an upright post with cross-beam. It stood alone, at some distance from the crosses of the malefactors crucified with Him. One may gather from Mk. 15:32, 36 that it was rather higher than usual.[23] The accounts show that Jesus was nailed to it, Lk. 24:39;

---

[16] Cf. Sanh., 6, 4; bSanh., 43a; 46a; T. Sanh., 9, 7; Winter, 66: "Crucifixion was not a punitive measure used by Jews or adopted by Jewish judicial institutions at any time in history," as against Stauffer, 123-127. Cf. also A. Büchler, "Die Todesstrafen d. Bibel u. d. jüd.-nachbibl. Zeit," MGWJ, 50 (1906), 703; so already J. Derenbourg, *Essai sur l'histoire et la géographie de la Palestine* (1867), 203, n. 1.

[17] Cf. on this Blinzler Prozess, 264.

[18] Cf. G. Bertram, *Die Leidensgeschichte Jesu u. d. Christuskult* (1922); also Bultmann Trad., 297-308.

[19] Jn. 3:14; 8:28; 12:32-34. Cf. Wellh. J., 113: "The crucifixion was called ὑψωθῆναι in a sense approximating to δοξασθῆναι."

[20] For details cf. Benz, 1044-59; Blinzler Prozess, 263-81; E. Bickermann, "Utilitas crucis," RHR, 112 (1935), 169-241; W. S. van Leeuwen, "Een zin van den kruisdood in de Synpt. Ev. ξύλον en σταυρός," *Nieuwe theol. Stud.*, 24 (1941), 68-81.

[21] Cf. Benz, 1055: "At point after point the story of the crucifixion corresponds to the Roman practice of imposing the shameful form of servile execution on patriots who rose up against the empire."

[22] Cf. on this Blinzler Prozess, 269: "Acc. to Talmudic tradition (bSanh., 43a; Str.-B., I, 1037) high-placed ladies in Jerusalem used to give an intoxicating drink to the condemned before execution in order to make them insensitive to the pain."

[23] Blinzler Prozess, 226.

Jn. 20:25. [24] The question whether the narratives give an exact description is hard to answer. Perhaps some details in the tradition were added under the influence of the proof from prophecy. [25] One cannot conclude, however, that the passion narrative is simply a product of this proof which diverges to a greater or lesser extent from the actual course of events. [26]

II. The Theology of the Cross.

1. Paul was the first to establish a theology of the cross. [27] He is not concerned to depict the historical event of the crucifixion of Jesus but rather to show its saving significance. In Phil. 2:8 he concludes the first strophe of the hymn to Christ with the words that Christ was obedient μέχρι θανάτου, θανάτου δὲ σταυροῦ, → II, 278, 30 ff. The death on the cross was the lowest stage of humiliation but also the completing of obedience. In obedience to God's will He accomplished the work of redemption. [28] In 1 C. 1:17 (→ 518, 18 ff.) Paul refuses to use words of wisdom because these cannot grasp or expound the saving significance of the cross of Christ. Philosophical preaching which puts human wisdom in the place of God's wisdom robs the cross of Christ of its essential content, → III, 587, 25 ff.; 662, 4 ff. [29]

---

[24] Except at Lk. 24:39 the Synoptists do not say that Jesus was nailed to the cross. Cf. Winter, 185, n. 23; also M. Dibelius, *Die Formgesch. d. Ev.*[3] (1959), 189. Ev. Pt. 6:25 says the Jews took the nails out of the hands of the Lord. It is likely enough that the feet were fastened by nails as well as the hands. The later idea of a "three-nail-cross" possibly sprang up for symbolical reasons. For details cf. Blinzler Prozess, 266. On the cause of death cf. H. Mödder, "Die Todesursache bei d. Kreuzigung," *Stimmen d. Zeit*, 144 (1949), 50-59; cf. E. Sons, "Die Todesursache bei d. Kreuzigung," *ibid.*, 146 (1950), 60-64, also "Zur Todesursache bei d. Kreuzigung," *Benediktinische Monatsschrift*, 33 (1957), 101-106. Cf. also the medical bibl., Blinzler Prozess, 276, n. 54.

[25] Cf. on this K. Weidel, "Stud. über den Einfluss des Weissagungsbeweises auf d. evang. Geschichte," ThStKr, 83 (1910), 83-109, 163-195; 85 (1912), 167-286; F. K. Feigel, *Der Einfluss d. Weissagungsbeweises u. anderer Motive auf d. Leidensgesch.* (1910), 27-29; Bertram, *op. cit.*, 74-95. Acc. to Bultmann Trad., 303-305 literary and dogmatic factois influenced the passion story as well as the proof from prophecy. Bertram says (79): "Cultic requirements brought it about that the few known facts were set in the light of prophecy and pious curiosity created a legend where the obscurity of the past could no longer be pierced." Cf. also E. Schick, *Formgeschichte u. Synoptikerexegese* (1940), 226-238.

[26] Cf. esp. Blinzler Prozess, 46-49. Also Dibelius, *op. cit.*, 187-189.

[27] Cf. NT theologies, also E. Riggenbach, *Das Geheimnis d. Kreuzes Christi*[3] (1927); P. Althaus, "Das Kreuz Christi" in *Mysterium Christi* (1931), 237-271; G. Wiencke, *Pls. über Jesu Tod* (1939); K. H. Schelkle, *Die Passion Jesu in d. Verkündigung d. NT* (1949), 51-126; F. W. Dillistone, *Jesus Christ and His Cross* (1953); L. Morris, *The Apostolic Preaching of the Cross* (1955); E. Lohse, "Märtyrer u. Gottesknecht," FRL, 64 (1955), 147-162.

[28] Here the emphasis is less on the saving significance of the death of Jesus (Mich. Ph., *ad loc.*) than on His act of obedience. Cf. E. Schweizer, *Erniedrigung u. Erhöhung bei Jesus u. seinen Nachfolgern*[2] (1962); Loh. Phil., *ad loc.* Cf. also E. Lohmeyer, "Kyrios Jesus. Eine Untersuchung z. Phil. 2:5-11," SAH (1927/28), 4, 72; E. Käsemann, "Krit. Analyse v. Phil. 2:5-11" in *Exeget. Versuche u Besinnung,* I (1960), 51-95; U. Wilckens, *Weisheit u. Torheit* (1959), 25.

[29] Cf. Ltzm. K., *ad loc.:* "By its very nature the preaching of the cross stands in divinely willed antithesis to philosophy; hence a 'philosophical' preaching of Christ is a contradiction in terms." On this cf. H. Schlier, "Über d. Erkenntnis Gottes bei d. Heiden," *Ev. Theol.,* 2 (1935), 10; also "Kerygma u. Sophia" in *Die Zeit d. Kirche*[2] (1958), 206-232. W. Schmithals, "Die Gnosis in Korinth," FRL, 66 (1956), 56-58 argues that in Corinth a Gnostic wisdom teaching had been put in place of the cross, not just that Christ crucified was being preached with esp. *sophia* (58). Wilckens, *op. cit.* (→ n. 28) 20 thinks that there lies behind the σοφία λόγου attacked by Paul a doctrine which related essentially and centrally only to the exalted Christ and the saving significance of baptism, but which contained nothing about the saving significance of the death of Christ; *v.* also U. Wilckens, "Kreuz u. Weisheit," *Kerygma u. Dogma,* 3 (1957), 77-108.

The preaching of Christ crucified cannot be done with the instruments of human wisdom because the λόγος τοῦ σταυροῦ (v. 18) is regarded neither by the world nor by Christian believers as σοφία τοῦ κόσμου. It is regarded as μωρία by the lost (→ IV, 846, 23 ff.) and as the δύναμις θεοῦ by the saved (→ II, 309, 11 ff.). Hence the preaching of the cross is wisdom to the perfect because it is the revelation of God's wisdom, 2:6, 7 (→ IV, 819, 16 ff.) The word of the cross is thus the power and wisdom of God. [30] In Phil. 3:18 Paul calls certain people enemies of the cross of Christ. He is speaking of Christians who do not deny the saving significance of the cross but who spurn the cross of Christ by their manner of life. They do not accept its implications for the shaping of practical life. [31] In Gl. 6:12 Paul argues that Judaisers try to force circumcision on the Galatian Christians in order that they may not suffer persecution for the cross of Christ [32] but win recognition among the Jews → IV, 1068, 32. [33] The persecutions which the apostle himself had to suffer at the hands of the Jews were very closely connected with his preaching of the cross, Gl. 5:11. If he had proclaimed circumcision rather than Christ's cross as the ground and means of salvation there would have been peace between him and Judaism, → 354, 15 ff. But circumcision and the cross are mutually exclusive. [34] In Gl. 6:14 Paul confesses Christ's cross to be the decisive revelation in salvation history. Hence the cross is his only glory; all self-glorying is done away. [35]

2. The cross of Christ is regarded as a means of atonement (→ I, 258, 31 ff.) in Col. 1:20; 2:14 and Eph. 2:16. In Col. 1:20 Paul declares that the reconciling act of Christ is not for man alone but for all things, earthly and heavenly beings alike. [36] The ground of reconciliation is the blood shed by Jesus at the cross. [37] This has all-embracing expiatory power. [38] Col. 2:14 speaks of the significance of

---

[30] Cf. on 1 C. 1:18 Wilckens, op. cit. (→ n. 28), 21-26. Schlier Kerygma, 214: The kerygma is "the proclamation of the events of the death and resurrection of Jesus Christ as these have taken place and continue their work." W. T. Hahn, Das Mitsterben u. Mitauferstehen mit Christus bei Pls. (1937), 61: "The logos of the cross is unthinkable without the message of the resurrection." On ἀπολλύμενοι and σῳζόμενοι v. Wilckens, 23. H. D. Wendland, 1 K., NT Deutsch, 7⁸ (1962), ad loc.: Salvation and perdition "are present facts though not yet definitively consummated. God's future eschatological decision ... has already become a present one." On δύναμις → II, 309, 9 ff.; W. Grundmann, Der Begriff d. Kraft (1932), 85, n. 3. Cf. also E. Fascher, "Dynamis Theou. Eine Studie zur urchr. Frömmigkeit," ZThK, NF, 19 (1938), 82-108; O. Schmitz, "Der Begriff δύναμις bei Pls.," Festg. A. Deissmann (1927), 139-167.

[31] The ref. is not to Christians who renounced their faith in time of persecution (Loh. Phil., ad loc.).

[32] τῷ σταυρῷ in Gl. 6:12 is dat. causae, cf. Bl.-Debr. § 196.

[33] Cf. Schlier Gl. and Oe. Gl., ad loc.

[34] Cf. on this G. Stählin, Skandalon (1930), 210. Cf. also Schlier Gl. ad loc., who takes τὸ σκάνδαλον τοῦ σταυροῦ as a single term: "the scandalous cross."

[35] Cf. Schlier Gl., ad loc.

[36] On the history of the exposition of Col. 1:20 cf. E. Percy, Die Probleme d. Kol.- u. Eph.-Briefe (1946), 87 f.

[37] Loh. Kol., 67 on 1:20 thinks the puzzling expression "the blood of his cross" is based on the sprinkling of the lamb's blood seven times in the holy of holies. But cf. E. Käsemann, "Eine urchr. Tauffliturgie" in Exeget. Versuche u. Besinnungen, I (1960), 34-51, who finds here the adaptation of a pre-Chr. hymn as a baptismal liturgy and thinks "by the blood of his cross" in v. 20 is a Chr. interpolation into the earlier hymn, 37.

[38] Cf. J. Gewiess, Christus u. das Heil nach d. Kol.-Br., Diss. Breslau (1932), 5 and 8. Cf. also C. Masson, L'Épitre de S. Paul aux Col., Comm. du NT, 10 (1950), 129, n. 7.

the cross of Christ for the relation between God and man. [39] Reference is made to the writing which witnesses against man "in virtue of the ordinances," → II, 231, 22 ff. → χειρόγραφον is normally used of a promissory note. Since the ordinances are obviously the statutes of the Mosaic Law, χειρόγραφον is here a writ of accusation based on the Law. As a sign of His pardoning grace God Himself has set this aside by affixing it to the cross. What is God's reconciling act in the cross reaches a special climax in Eph. 2:16. The reference here is to Christ's work of peace-making, → II, 413, 11 ff.; 718, 28 ff. He has removed the hostility between Jew and Gentile by abolishing the Law → IV, 625, 10 ff. He has thus made the two groups into one new man and in His body [40] reconciled them to God by the cross.

3. Hb., which uses σταυρός only once, declares in 12:2 that Jesus took up the cross ἀντὶ τῆς προκειμένης αὐτῷ χαρᾶς. How the saying is to be construed depends on ἀντί. This can mean "instead of": Jesus had a choice between heavenly bliss and the death of the cross, and He chose the cross. But ἀντί can also mean "for the sake of": Jesus took up the cross to win the heavenly joy held out before Him; eternal glory is the reward of His obedience. Both interpretations are possible. But the more natural one is that Jesus renounced the προκειμένη αὐτῷ χαρά to tread the way of obedience and suffering. [41]

III. The Figurative Use of the Word.

Jesus demands of those who would be His disciples that they deny themselves, take up their cross, and follow Him on the way of suffering.

1. The saying about taking up the cross occurs 5 times in the Synoptic Gospels. It is put in different contexts. Mk. 8:34 (par. Mt. 16:24; Lk. 9:23) [42] places it after Peter's confession and the first intimation of the passion. The sayings in Mt. 10:38 and Lk. 14:27, which are from Q, come in a series of statements about the conditions of discipleship. The wording differs in Mt. and Lk., and Q has a negative form as compared with the positive one in Mk. The par. to Mk. 8:34 in Lk. 9:23 takes a distinctive turn, for by adding καθ' ἡμέραν Lk. formulates the saying of Jesus in such a way that taking up the cross seems to be a task which disciples must accept afresh each day. As a secondary variant at Mk. 10:21 we find the words ἄρας τὸν σταυρόν in a number of MSS as one of the conditions which Jesus laid down for the rich young ruler. The relevant verbs are αἴρω in Mk. 8:34; Mt. 16:24; Lk. 9:23, λαμβάνω in Mt. 10:38, and βαστάζω in Lk. 14:27. [43] The original tradition is probably the one in Q. In Mk.

---

[39] Deissmann LO, 282 thinks the formulation in Col. 2:14 is rooted in a rite of annulment unknown to us.

[40] ῞Εν σῶμα in v. 16 is undoubtedly Christ's body on the cross, so Schlier Eph., ad loc.; cf. E. Percy, Der Leib Christi (σῶμα Χριστοῦ) (1942), 29. On Eph. 2:14-18 v. Schlier Eph., 136: "In His death (Christ's) He slew the mortal enmity of the claim of cosmic powers which took palpable form in the Law of the Jews, and hence in His embracing and sustaining body of death He established all men anew, both Jews and Gentiles, as the humanity which is reconciled to God by Him and in Him, and which is united to God by Him and in Him."

[41] For ἀντί "instead of" one might ref. to ἀντί in Hb. 12:16. Cf. also Mi. Hb., ad loc. But cf. Wnd. Hb., ad loc.: ἀντί = "for the sake of."

[42] Cf. Bultmann Trad., 86.

[43] "Profane examples support βαστάζειν τὸν σταυρόν or occasionally φέρειν, but there are no instances of λαμβάνειν or αἴρειν," E. Dinkler, "Jesu Wort vom Kreuztragen," Nt.liche Stud. f. R. Bultmann, Beih. ZNW, 21 (1954), 112, n. 6. σταυρὸν φέρειν, Lk. 23:26.

following is no longer a condition; it has its own glamour and worth. [44] Q is better preserved in Lk. than in Mt. [45]

2. There is no corresponding saying in later Rabb. writings; these refer only to "accepting sufferings (chastisements)." [46] Cross-bearing in the sense of *patibulum ferre* finds no par. in Semitic at all. [47] In essentials the following explanations have been advanced: a. "To take up one's cross" was a profane popular expression [48] which perhaps arose among the Zealots and was then applied to discipleship of Jesus. [49] b. Jesus saw in His approaching death a pattern for the way of His disciples. He thus demanded of the disciples a readiness for suffering and even crucifixion. [50] If the view that Jesus predicted His death on the cross is rejected, one is compelled to see in this form of the saying the work of the community. [51] c. The saying about taking up the cross is to be understood in the light of Mt. 11:29a. The ἄρατε τὸν ζυγόν μου ἐφ᾽ ὑμᾶς of Mt. is the basis of Mk. 8:34 and par. Only after the death of Jesus did the saying about taking on the yoke become: "Let him take up his cross." [52] d. The proper starting-pt. is the carrying of the cross by the condemned man. This suggests a beginning of discipleship which then becomes a lasting state; the disciple of Jesus is a cross-bearer, and he remains this his whole life. [53] e. Bearing the cross is meant as a marking. [54] To understand the saying one must turn to cultic marking in Israel, esp. Ez. 9:4-6, [55] where the sign

---

[44] Dinkler, *op. cit.*, 113. Cf. Bultmann J., 325, n. 6 on 12:26. Bultmann sees in Jn. 12:26 a variant of Mk. 8:34 par. "The Evangelist has shortened the version of the saying before him by leaving out the cross-bearing and lengthened it by καὶ ὅπου κτλ. etc." Cf. also C. K. Barrett, *The Gospel acc. to St. John* (1958), 353.

[45] Dinkler, *op. cit.*, 111.

[46] Str.-B., I, 587. Cf. G. Dalman, *Jesus-Jeschua* (1922), 172 : "There is no model in the Rabb. for the fig. use of the expression."

[47] Dinkler, 114.

[48] Cf. A. Fridrichsen, "Sich selbst verleugnen," Coni. Neot., 2 (1936), 3. Cf. H. v. Campenhausen, *Die Idee d. Martyriums* (1936), 59.

[49] So Schl. Mt. on 10:38.

[50] Cf. J. Schniewind, *Das Ev. nach Mt., NT Deutsch,* 1⁹ (1960) on 10:38: "The way of discipleship demands readiness for the shameful and painful death of a criminal." Cf. also C. F. D. Moule, "The Judgment Theme in the Sacraments," *Festschr. C. H. Dodd* (1956), 475.

[51] So, e.g., Wellh. Mk. on 8:34: A. Harnack, *Sprüche u. Reden Jesu* (1907), 150. Cf. Kl. Mt. on 10:38. Bultmann Trad., 173 is inclined to see in Mk. 10:38 an authentic dominical saying : "Might not σταυρός have been even earlier a traditional metaphor for suffering and sacrifice?" But he conjectures (176) that Lk. 14:27 is perhaps the work of the primitive community, so also Dinkler, 112 and Schweizer, *op. cit.* (→ n. 28), 15 f.

[52] T. Arvedson, *Mysterium Christi* (1937), Preface, IV. Cf. Dinkler, 115-117.

[53] Cf. A. Fridrichsen, "Ordet om 'å baere sit Kors,' " *Gamle spor og nye veier, Festschr. L. Brun (1922)*, 17-34 and E. Percy, *Die Botschaft Jesu* (1953), 171-173. Schl. Mt. on 10:38 had already said that λαμβάνειν τὸν αὐτοῦ σταυρόν makes a primarily ethical claim on the disciples. Crucifixion is set before them because in it "the condemned man in his own action grasps that which will put him to death." Fridrichsen, 30 emphasises that bearing the cross means "venturing a life which is as difficult as the last journey of a condemned man." Percy, 171 f. stresses the fact that the logion refers only to martyrdom; it has in view the lit. following which was part of discipleship during the earthly life of Jesus.

[54] E. Dinkler, "Zur Gesch. d. Kreuzessymbols," ZThK, 48 (1951), 148-172; also *op. cit.* (→ n. 43), 110-129. Cf. E. R. Goodenough, *Jewish Symbols in the Greco-Roman Period,* I (1953), 131 f.; W. Michaelis, "Zeichen, Siegel, Kreuz," ThZ, 12 (1956), 505-525; Schweizer, *op. cit.,* 15, n. 45; Bultmann Trad. Suppl., 25.

[55] On Ez. 9:4-6 v. G. Fohrer, *Ez., Hndbch. AT,* I, 13 (1955), ad loc.: "The sign (on the forehead), as תו shows, has a cross-like form acc. to early Hbr. script (χ or †), and it is a sign of protection granted on the basis of confession of Yahweh. It is obviously connected with the customary marking of possessions (the branding of slaves or cattle); its bearer is marked as being Yahweh's property and standing under His protection." For similar signs of protection and confession (→ 208, 29 ff.; 214, 19 ff.) cf. Gn. 4:15; Is. 44:5; Gl. 6:17; Rev. 7:3-8 ; 9:4 ; 13:16 f. ; 14:1. Cf. also on Ez. 9:4-6 W. Zimmerli, *Ez., Bibl. Komm. AT,* 13 (1960), 226 f.

Tau [56] is a sign of protection and indeed of possession. [57] Adoption of the sign of the cross is thus to be regarded as a seal of possession. Fig. it is marking the forehead with a Tau ; it is confession that one belongs to Jesus. Naturally there is no question here of actual cultic tattooing. After the crucifixion the Tau was related to the historical cross of Jesus. Hence the claim of Jesus which demanded from His followers an eschatological sealing and dedication to God was interpreted as a call to suffering. [58] It is not possible, however, to integrate this explanation into the world of thought of Jesus Himself. f. Interpretation of σταυρός must start with the basic meaning of the word "stake," "palisade" → 572, 13. Since Mk. and Mt. think the carrying of the beam of execution by Simon of Cyrene was an act of mockery — the soldiers treat the condemned Jesus like a general whose palisade (pillory) is carried by an orderly — it may be that in Mk. 8:34 and par. we have a call to follow Jesus as the commander who has prepared a new life for His men behind the bulwark set up by Him. It is still true, of course, that following Jesus always demands dedication of life. [59] The weakness of this explanation is that the Synoptists never use σταυρός in the sense of "palisade."

Closest to the original point of the saying of Jesus is the view that the reference is not merely to martyrdom but that we have a vivid metaphor for self-denial, [60] for saying No to self (→ I, 471, 12 ff.; V, 291, 15 ff.), [61] which in the last analysis might involve the surrender of life itself [62] → 578, 8 ff.

IV. The Later Use of the Word.

1. Among the post-apost. fathers Ign. and Barn. were particularly interested in the cross of Christ. In Ign. Eph., 9, 1 this cross is a mysterious μηχανή which, with the Holy Ghost, raises up Christians as living stones prepared for the heavenly building of the temple of God. [63] The significance of the cross is even more profound in the fig. of the trunk of the cross which puts forth branches, Tr., 11, 2. Living force issues from the cross of Christ. All who belong to Christ are set in the life-giving nexus of the passion and redeeming death of Jesus ; they are the κλάδοι τοῦ σταυροῦ, the branches of the trunk of the cross. Ign. is thinking of orthodox Christians. In Sm., 1, 1 he

---

[56] Bibl.: S. Liebermann, *Greek in Jewish Palestine* (1942), 185-191: X and Θ; E. Stauffer, "Zu den Kreuzeszeichen v. Talpioth," ZNW, 43 (1950/51), 262 ; H. Rahner, "Antenna Crucis, V: Das mystische Tau," *Zschr. f. Kath. Theol.*, 75 (1953), 385-410; J. Sonne, "The X-Sign in the Isaiah-Scroll," VT, 4 (1954), 90-94.

[57] Cf. already R. Eisler, 'Ιησοῦς βασιλεὺς οὐ βασιλεύσας, II (1930), 239 f. who with a ref. to Ez. 9:4, 6 speaks of the cross-sign of the elect, the tribal sign of the Rechabite Kenites who had no land or home, and who suggests a tattooing which was practised in primitive Christianity, which originally pted. to self-denying entry into the state of the humble bearer of the cross, but which was then quickly reinterpreted along traditional lines. Cf. on this Grundmann Mk. on 8:34.

[58] Dinkler, *op. cit.* (→ n. 54), 148-172, who has shown from ossuaries that there was a pre-Chr. Jewish use of the cross in the days of Jesus, thinks the original sense of the saying is best reproduced if one reads the text as follows: ὃς οὐ λαμβάνει τὸ σημεῖον αὐτοῦ καὶ ἔρχεται ὀπίσω μου οὐ δύναται εἶναί μου μαθητής, Dinkler, *op. cit.* (→ n. 43), 127.

[59] So O. Glombitza, "Das Kreuz," Domine, dirige me in verbo tuo, *Festschr. z. 70. Geburtstag v. M. Mitzenheim* (1961), 60-67.

[60] Schweizer, 15.

[61] Grundmann, 249 f.; E. Fascher, "Jesus d. Lehrer," *Sokrates u. Christus* (1959), 144.

[62] W. G. Kümmel, *Verheissung u. Erfüllung*³ (1956), 72 finds a rather unlikely ref. to persecutions which were not to take place in the lifetime of Jesus.

[63] On the religious background of this idea v. H. Schlier, "Religionsgeschichtliche Untersuchungen z.d. Ignatiusbriefen," Beih. ZNW, 8 (1929), 110-124. The metaphor recurs in Iren., Hipp., Method. and Chrys., also Mart. Andreae prius 14 (ed. R. Lipsius-M. Bonnet, Acta Apostolorum Apocr., II [1959]), For details cf. Bau. Ign. on Eph., 9, 1.

writes that Christians are nailed to the cross of the Lord Jesus Christ both in the flesh and in the spirit. He has in view the steadfastness of faith of the Christians in Smyrna. There is no ref., however, to the dying of Christians with Christ effected in baptism. [64] The historical fact of the crucifixion of Jesus plays no gt. role in Ign.; it is mentioned only in Eph., 16, 2 and Tr., 9, 1. [65] σταυρός occurs with the traditional saving facts of the θάνατος and ἀνάστασις in Phld., 8, 2, but Ign. shows no acquaintance with Paul's interpretation [66] even though he quotes 1 C. 1:18 ff. fairly lit. in Eph., 18, 1 and 2. The main concern of Barn. is to prove from Scripture the necessity of the crucifixion of Christ. The wood which figures in relation to the red heifer in Nu. 19:6 is for him ὁ τύπος ὁ τοῦ σταυροῦ, 8, 1. In Gn. 14:14, which mentions the 318 servants of Abraham, the no. 300 (= T) is a ref. to the cross, while 10 and 8 yield the letters IH = Jesus; the 300 is added because the sign of the cross in the letter T represents grace, 9, 8. [67] The ξύλον of Ps. 1:3 also has typical significance for Barn.; it pts. to the cross of Christ, 11, 1 and 8. [68] Polycarp speaks of the μαρτύριον τοῦ σταυροῦ in 7, 1. The cross bears witness to the true corporeality of Christ. He who holds docetic views shows thereby that he is of the devil. In the Gospel of Peter 10:39 the cross is an independent entity. The author describes the moment of the resurrection. The soldiers see three men come out of the grave and two support the one and a cross follows them. [69] A double cross, one earthly and one heavenly, occurs esp. in the Gnostic cross speculations of the apocr. Acts, in which a cross of light stands in contrast with that of Golgotha. This cross, which may be seen only by mystery initiates in a vision, is like the Redeemer or actually is the Redeemer. [70]

2. The use of the word in the pap. is very varied. Most pap. in which it occurs are post-bibl. But they offer little or no evidence of the distinctive NT use. Only in a Chr. prayer from the 4th or 5th cent. (P. Oxy., VII, 1058, 2) does σταυρός mean "cross" = "hardship." The Egypt. graffito in Preisigke Sammelb., 2273 has σταυρός for "sign of the cross." In Byzantine times the sign of the cross is common in letters, e.g., P. Jandanae, II, 16 (5th/6th cent.). [71] Three crosses often serve as marks for the illiterate, e.g., P. Lips., I, 90, 10. Cf. also P. Monacenses, [72] I, 7, 91 (6th cent.); Preisigke Sammelb., 5608; 4818, 4 (Byzantine) → 205, 7 ff. For the cross as a sign of prayer P. Lond., 1917, 6 (330-340 A.D.). [73]

---

[64] Percy, op. cit., 108.
[65] Cf. Schlier, op. cit., 67. The nailing of Jesus to the cross is incidentally mentioned in Ign. Sm., 1, 1. 2.
[66] Schlier, 68.
[67] Cf. Pr.-Bauer, s.v.
[68] The text in Barn., 12, 1: "The Lord said : When a tree bends and rises (again), and when blood drips from the wood," is of doubtful provenance. Wnd. Barn., ad loc. comments : "I think we have here a free conflation of quotations which Barn. found in his testimonies or composed himself."
[69] Hennecke³, I, 123.
[70] Act. Joh. 98-100 ; Mart. Andreae prius 14 ; Act. Pt. 96:43 ; cf. Act. Verc. 37-39 ; also Act. Phil. 138, 141. For details Schlier, 102-110, 122, n. 1; also W. Bousset, "Platons Weltseele u. d. Kreuz Christi," ZNW, 14 (1913), 273-285 ; J. Leipoldt, Von Epidaurus bis Lourdes (1957), 116-134. For the lifegiving and enlightening power of the cross cf. Mart. Andr. prius 16 ; Act. Phil. 133.
[71] Ed. C. Kalbfleisch et. al., II (1913), 57.
[72] Ed. A. Heisenberg and L. Wenger, Byzant. Pap., Veröffentlichungen aus d. Pap.-Sammlung d. Königlichen Hof- u. Staatsbibl. z. München, I (1914).
[73] P. Lond., 1912-1929, ed. H. I. Bell, Jews and Christians in Egypt (1924).

σταυρόω.

A. σταυρόω outside the New Testament.

1. "To put up posts," "to protect by a stockade," Thuc., VI, 100, 1; VII, 25, 7; Artemid. Onirocr., II, 53 (p. 152, 4 ff.); 56 (p. 153, 19 ff.); cf. Diod. S., 24, 1, 2: ξύλοις μεγίστοις καὶ ἀγκύραις τὰ βάθη ἐσταύρωσαν. The expression seems to ref. to a square enclosed by stakes or posts.[1] The transf. sense "to crucify" is rare : Polyb., 1, 86, 4 ; Diod. S., 16, 61; Strabo, 14, 1, 39.

2. In the LXX σταυρόω is used twice for "to hang on the gallows" for תָּלָה at Est. 7:9 and Εσθ. 8:12r; also Lam. 5:13 vl.: νεανίσκοι ἐν ξύλω ἐσταυρώθησαν (ἐν ζύλῳ for cross). Jos. has the word occasionally, e.g., Ant., 2, 77; 17, 295.

B. σταυρόω in the New Testament.

1. The term occurs in the third prediction of the passion by Jesus in Mt. 20:19. In Mt. 23:34, in the condemnation of the scribes and Pharisees, Jesus intimates His own fate by referring to that of the prophets, sages and teachers in Israel → VI, 835, 6 ff. Some were put to death and crucified, some whipped in the synagogues, and others chased from city to city. In Ac. the preaching of the apostles (Peter's sermon in 2:36 and his confession before the Sanhedrin in 4:10) severely reproaches the whole people of Israel for crucifying Jesus → V, 39, 11 ff. In doing this Israel sinned greatly against God.[2]

Ac. 13:28 D has a ref. to the crucifixion: ᾐτοῦντο τὸν Πιλᾶτον τοῦτον μὲν σταυρῶσαι.

In 1 C. 2:8 — this is an isolated statement in Paul — the apostle declares that the rulers of this world, i.e., the ungodly powers which govern this aeon, brought Jesus to the cross.[3] In their shortsighted demonic wisdom they had no insight into the wisdom of God. They thought that they could strengthen their position by delivering Jesus up to the cross. But on the cross their power was broken.[4] In 2 C. 13:4 Paul states that Christ was crucified on the basis of weakness. This means that the Crucified did not dispose of any power of His own.[5] But the

---

σ τ α υ ρ ό ω . Bibl. J. Blinzler, *Der Prozess Jesu*³ (1960), 263-271; U. Wilckens, *Weisheit u. Torheit* (1959). For further lit. → σταυρός.

[1] Cf. Moult.-Mill., *s.v.* Cf. also F. Bilabel, *Griech. Pap., Veröffentlichungen der Badischen Pap.-Sammlung,* II (1923), 49, n. 1 on 30:12: "σταυρουμ[ένου suggests any space marked off by posts."

[2] If one considers the other ref. in Ac. which do not have σταυρόω but speak of Jesus' death it may be seen that the apostles hold the Sanhedrin (5:30 ; 7:52) and the inhabitants of Jerusalem (3:17-19; 13:27-29) responsible for the crucifixion of Jesus. It is worth noting that there is no ref. to the guilt of the Romans. Yet it is also said that the cross was willed by God, since it is part of the divine plan of salvation (2:22 f.; 4:25-28) and acc. to the Scriptures (3:17-19 ; 4:28 ; 13:27); cf. on this Blinzler, 323-329. Cf. also K. L. Schmidt, "Der Todesprozess des Messias Jesus. Die Verantwortung der Juden, Heiden u. Christen f. d. Kreuzigung Jesu," *Judaica,* 1 (1945), 1-40.

[3] So also W. J. P. Boyd, "1 C. II 8," Exp. T., 68 (1956), 158 ; Wilckens, 61 f.; Blinzler, 330 f. The ref. is not to earthly human rulers as J. Isaac, *Jésus et Israel* (1948), 510 and T. Ling, "A Note on 1 C. II 8," Exp. T., 68 (1956), 26 suppose. Cf. also J. Schniewind, "Die Archonten dieses Äons (1 K. 2:6-8)" in *Nachgelassene Reden u. Aufsätze* (1952), 104-109. On the history of exposition cf. Wilckens, 60-71.

[4] There is a similar thought in Col. 2:15.

[5] So also Wilckens, 37 and 49.

power of God was set forth in Him, for God raised Him from the dead. Hence He now lives by the power of God as the exalted Lord, → II, 304, 30 ff.

There is a ref. to the crucifixion of Christ in Rev. at 11:18. Here the divine sees the great city (Jerusalem) in which Christ suffered death → 336, 19 ff. The bodies of the two martyred witnessess now lie in its streets.

2. Statements with the verb are of theological significance only in Paul. In 1 C. 1:23 the apostle says that the true content of his message is Christ crucified (Χριστὸν ἐσταυρωμένον). The Jews demand signs and wonders and the Greeks ask after wisdom → 354, 4 ff. But Christians, who are called to salvation, confess the Crucified as the revelation of God's power and wisdom. To both Jews and Gentiles they thus proclaim the same crucified Christ as the power of salvation. [6] In 1 C. 2:2 Paul declares that he set forth in Corinth no other knowledge than that of Jesus, and of Jesus as the Crucified. [7] The form of preaching is in accord with the content. It involves, not impressive words of wisdom, but, for all its human weakness, a demonstration of spirit and power, vv. 3-4, 13. [8] Discussing the problem of factions in Corinth, Paul will not let himself be hailed as a party chief by one group in the church. Christ alone was crucified for the community, 1 C. 1:13.

3. In Galatians Paul uses the term mostly in a transferred sense. In 3:1 he says to the Galatians who are being bewitched by the Judaisers : κατ᾽ ὀφθαλμοὺς Ἰησοῦς Χριστὸς προεγράφη ἐσταυρωμένος. [9] The Crucified is universally proclaimed as the central content of the Pauline kerygma (→ I, 771, 9 ff.), [10] and this in such a way that what is set before the spiritual eyes of the Galatians is the Crucified Himself and not just the significance of the cross in salvation history. In Gl. 2:19 Paul makes a personal confession. He has nothing more to do with the Law; it has no claim on a dead man ; Χριστῷ → συνεσταύρωμαι, cf. R. 6:6. In Gl. 6:14 Paul boasts of the cross of Christ by which the world is crucified to him and he to the world. As an event in salvation history the cross of Christ is a radical No to the world. [11] For the apostle, who has been given a share in this basic event by baptism, it is thus the place where his link with the world is broken. The perfect ἐσταύρωται expresses the fact that this is an event which has enduring effects. The position of the apostle in relation to the world, and that of the world in relation to him, is fixed once and for all by it. [12] There is a similar saying in Gl. 5:24: οἱ δὲ τοῦ Χριστοῦ Ἰησοῦ τὴν σάρκα ἐσταύρωσαν σὺν τοῖς παθήμασιν καὶ ταῖς

---

[6] Ibid., 38.

[7] The perf. part. pass. is worth nothing, v. A. Deissmann, Pls.² (1925), 153 f.; O. Schmitz, Die Christusgemeinschaft d. Pls. im Lichte seines Genetivgebrauchs (1924), 182 ; J. Schneider, Die Passionsmystik d. Pls. (1929), 25. The perf. part. signifies more than the aor. part. It denotes an event which took place in the past but which still has an effect in the present. The ἐσταυρωμένος is the One who once died on the cross but who is present now in preaching and the cultus. In the Marcionite tradition there is an unequivocal confession of the ἐσταυρωμένος of Paul in Apelles, cf. A. Harnack, Marcion² (1924), 182. In popular speech of the post-class. period the perf. part. pass. increasingly took the place of the pres. part. pass. (cf. modern Gk.) but with no discernible shift of meaning [Dihle].

[8] Cf. Wilckens, 50 f.

[9] As Schlier Gl., ad loc has esp. shown, προγράφω does not means "to write before, earlier," nor "to depict before the eyes" but "to proclaim, placard publicly."

[10] So also Schlier Gl., ad loc.

[11] Cf. Oe., Schlier Gl., ad loc.

[12] Cf. on this A. Schettler, Die paul. Formel "durch Christus" (1907), 37. Cf. also E. Käsemann, "Eine paul. Variation des amor fati," ZThK, 56 (1959), 150.

ἐπιθυμίαις. It is no accident, nor is it without significance, that here Paul states actively what elsewhere he puts in the passive. He is speaking of an act of will on the part of those who belong to Christ. They have renounced fellowship with sin, whose seat in the σάρξ. Is Paul thinking of baptism?[13] This is not very likely. The apostle has in view the free moral decision which believers who belong to Christ by baptism have taken on the basis of baptism, since they are pledged by baptism to walk in a new life, R. 6:4. In baptism they are snatched by God's act from the dominion of sin. Now they for their part say a radical No to sin and thus pass judgment on the whole of their previous life. Hence Gl. 5:24 refers, not to the mystery of baptism, but to an ethical act on the part of Christians.[14]

C. The Word in the Early Church.

In early Chr. writings the word is common in the sense "to crucify." One may refer esp. to the famous Quo vadis passage in Mart. Pt., 6 (p. 88, 6 ff.). As Peter is going out of the gate of Rome he sees the Lord coming in and puts the question: ποῦ ὧδε; to which the answer is given εἰσέρχομαι εἰς τὴν ‘Ρώμην σταυρωθῆναι. Astonished, Peter asks : κύριε, πάλιν σταυροῦσαι ; The answer is : ναί, Πέτρε, πάλιν σταυροῦμαι. Then Peter returns to Rome. In Act. Pl., 7, 39 (p. 54, 39) the Lord says to Paul : Πα[ῦλ]ε, ἄνωθεν μέλλω σταυ[ροῦσθαι]. The point is that He will suffer crucifixion afresh in Rome in the person of the apostle.[15] There is an echo of Paul in Ign. R., 7, 2 : ὁ ἐμὸς ἔρως ἐσταύρωται, "my passionate love (of the world) is crucified." Ign. is saying that love of the world is put to death by fellowship with the Crucified.[16] The basis is quite different in Tr., 9, 1. Here, in answer to the Docetic idea that Jesus suffered only in appearance, Ign. affirms: ἀληθῶς ἐσταυρώθη, "He was truly crucified." In Ign. ἐσταυρώθη is with ἀπέθανεν and ἠγέρθη a constituent part of the Chr. kerygma.[17] It also has an established place in the Christological formulae of Just., e.g., Dial., 85, 2 ; 132, 1; Apol., 61, 13. The verb is common in other Chr. writings too.[18] In Ev. Pt. 2:3 we find the rare verbal form σταυρίσκω.

† ἀνασταυρόω.

This verb means "to fence around," "to enclose," Hdt., III, 125 ; IX, 78 ; it is identical with ἀνασκολοπίζω. Pass.: Thuc., I, 110, 3 ; Plat. Gorg., 473c. In Roman times "to crucify," Polyb., 1, 11, 5 ; 24, 6; Plut. Fab. Max., 6, 5 (I, 177e). In Jos. Bell., 1, 97; 2, 75, 241. 253. 306; 5, 449; Ant., 2, 73; 6, 374 (cf. LXX 1 Βασ. 31:10 κατέπηξαν); 11, 246 ; Vit., 420 it is synon. with the simple form, with no sense of repetition. Philo has ἀνασκολοπίζω (ἄχρι θανάτου) in Poster. C., 61. Plat. Resp., II, 362a uses ἀνα-

---

[13] For an affirmative answer cf. Oe. Gl. and Schlier Gl., ad loc., who states that the event denoted by ἐσταύρωσαν takes place in Christians with baptism. Cf. also R. Schnackenburg, Das Heilsgeschehen bei d. Taufe nach dem Ap. Pls. (1950), 61, though he also considers the possibility the ref. might be to conversion.

[14] Cf. Schnackenburg, op. cit., 61: "σταυρόω is thus taken ethically," so that the thought of crucifixion becomes "an ethical motive."

[15] Cf. C. Schmidt, Πράξεις Παύλου (1936), 128.

[16] Cf. Schneider, op. cit. (→ n. 7), 129 and 135.

[17] Cf. on this H. Schlier, "Religionsgesch. Untersuchungen zu den Ignatiusbriefen," Beih. ZNW, 8 (1929), 69.

[18] Cf. Sophocles Lex., s.v.

σχινδυλεύω "to impale," "to crucify" in the description of the suffering and death of the righteous. [1]

In the NT the word occurs only at Hb. 6:6. The author is arguing that wilful apostasy from faith rules out any fresh repentance. Those guilty of such apostasy are called ἀνασταυροῦντες ἑαυτοῖς τὸν υἱὸν τοῦ θεοῦ. Since ἀνασταυροῦν usually means "to crucify," one should strictly translate : "they personally crucify the Son of God," aligning themselves with those who brought Christ to the cross and thus committing the same sin as these did. But πάλιν ἀνακαινίζειν comes just before and this plainly supports the rendering "to crucify a second time." [2]

For the later use cf. Cl. Al. Prot., XI, 114, 4 : τὸν θάνατον εἰς ζωὴν ἀνεσταύρωσεν, and Martyrium Ignatii Colbertinum, 2: [3] τὸν ἀνασταυροῦντα τὴν ἐμὴν ἁμαρτίαν. The subj. is the σταυρωθείς or ἐσταυρωμένος, who crucifies death (Cl.) or sin (Ign.).

J. Schneider

ἀ ν α σ τ α υ ρ ό ω. Bibl: Lex., *s.v.;* comm. on Hb. 6:6 ; → σταυρός.

[1] Plato speaks of the one who is inwardly righteous being scourged, tortured, put in chains, blinded in both eyes, and finally fixed to the cross, cf. E. Benz, "Der gekreuzigte Gerechte bei Plato, im NT u. in d. alten Kirche," *AA Mainz* (1950), 1031-1043 ; also "Christus u. Sokrates in d. alten Kirche," *ZNW*, 43 (1950/51), 213 f., 223 f. Cf. also E. Fascher, *Sokrates u. Christus* (1959), 91. In the theology of the early Church the description in Plato was regarded as a prophecy of Christ, Acta Apollonii, 40 and 42 (ed. R. Knopf, *Ausgewählte Märtyrerakten*[3] [1929], 34); Cl. Al. Strom., V, 14, 108, 1-2 ; IV, 7, 52, 1-2. Cf. Benz Gerechter, 1059-1074.

[2] Rgg. Hb., *ad loc.* thinks only the context can fix the meaning of the ἀνα- and this favours repetition. But Wnd. Hb., *ad loc.* argues for "to crucify" rather than "to crucify afresh." Cf. also Mi. Hb., *ad loc.*, 149, n. 3.

[3] Ed. O. v. Gebhard, A. Harnack, T. Zahn, Patrum Apostolicorum Opera, II (1876), 303, 1 ff.

† στέγω

A. Linguistic Aspects.

Etym. the verb belongs to the Indo-Eur. stem *(s)teg* "to cover," "to conceal." From this basic sense come the Sanskr. *sthágati* "covered," "hidden," Lat. *tegere* (tectum, *tegulum, teges, tegula, toga*), Gk. στέγος, τέγος, στέγη, τέγη "roof," "house," στεγανός, "covering," "sheltering," "covered," "hidden," στεγνός "covering," "protecting," "covered," "hidden," "compact," "solid," στεκτικός "covering," "sheltering,"[1] words which in their wide range of meaning are all embraced by the Gk. στέγω "I cover," "conceal," "protect," "hold back," "hide," "bear," "endure," "persist."

The word is not very common in lit. It is found in neither Hom. nor Hes. It is used in the pre-Socratics Democr. Fr., 152 (Diels, II, 172, 20 f.) in the sense "to keep."[2] In poetry it occurs in Pind. Pyth., IV, 81. Aristoph. uses it in Vesp., 1295. Aesch., Soph. and Eur. have it 6 times each, Plat. about 12 times and Thuc. 12, Aristot. 3, Theophr. 2. We also find it in Xenoph., Polyb., Diod. S. and Plut. It is equally rare in pap. and inscr. In Philo it occurs in Flacc., 64, in Jos. at Ant., 5, 314; 19, 48, and in the LXX only at Sir. 8:17. It is more common in Anth. Graec.[3]

A surprising pt. is that the simple form, attested only from the 5th cent. B.C., persisted until well on in the post-class. age in prose and common speech. For with στέγω we find καλύπτω, ἕννυμι, ἐρέφω, κρύπτω and compounds, the compounds of στέγω itself, and στεγάζω and compounds.[4] The reason for this astonishing fact lies in the broad range of meaning esp. in the transf. use, which led to frequent use in popular speech.[5] The basis of this broad range is probably that στέγω was from the very first a durative verb probably found at first only in the present stem.[6] In this case the basic meaning would be "to keep covered," cf. Tabula Heracleensis, I, 142 (IG, 14, 645); "to provide a house with a roof," i.e., to keep it covered; Pind. Pyth., IV, 81: ἀμφὶ δὲ παρδαλέᾳ στέγετο, "to cover oneself on all sides" against the rain "with the skin of a panther." The covering is for protection. Thus στέγω takes on the sense "to protect": πύργοι ... πόλιν στέγουσιν, Soph. Oed. Col., 14 f (vl.); cf. Aesch. Sept. c. Theb., 797; the camp "protects" men against the cold, Plat. Resp., III, 415e; a house "protects" men, IG 2², 2498, 23.

The tendency of Gk. towards linguistic ambivalence helps us to see why στέγω can have an outward as well as an inward ref. and mean not only "to protect" but also "to ward off," "to hold back." δόμος ἅλα στέγων is a structure which holds off the salt floods, namely, a ship, Aesch. Suppl., 135; δακρύων τ' ὄμματ' οὐκέτι στέγει, Eur. Iph. Aul., 888.[7] The sense "to hold back" leads to that of "make tight" on a ship, Diod. S., 11, 32; οὐκ ἂν δυναίμην μὴ στέγοντα πιμπλάναι, Eur. Fr., 899 (TGF, 649), cf. Aristot. Probl., 8, 19, p. 889a, 11; "to make something watertight," Theophr. Hist. Plant., V, 4, 5; 7, 4; finally "to be watertight" νῆες ... οὐδὲν στέγουσαι,

---

στέγω. Pass., Liddell-Scott, Pr.-Bauer⁵, *s.v.*; Walde-Pok., II, 620 f.; A. Harnack, "Das hohe Lied d. Ap. Pls. von d. Liebe (1 K. 13) und seine religionsgesch. Bdtg.," SAB, (1911), 132-163; G. H. Whitaker, "Love springs no leak," Exp., VIII, 21 (1921), 126-8.
[1] Walde-Pok.
[2] Kern conjectures στέλλειν (Diels, II Appar., *ad loc.*).
[3] The post-apost. fathers do not have στέγω, but we find the noun στέγος for "roof," 1 Cl., 12, 6.
[4] [Dihle].
[5] [Risch].
[6] [Dihle].
[7] The text is uncertain; cf. Murray, *ad loc.*

"ships which are not watertight," Thuc., II, 94, 3, and "to hold fast," "to hold," Aristot. Meteor., I, 14, p. 352b, 9. The sense "to ward off," "to protect," seems to be the starting-pt. for the further meanings "to endure," "to support," "to bear." A tower which has resisted the assault on a city has endured it, Aesch. Sept. c. Theb., 797. How this can lead to "bear" in the technical sense may be seen from Jos. Ant., 5, 314 : οἶκος δ' ἦν δύο κιόνων στεγόντων αὐτοῦ τὸν ὄροφον, pillars which endure the weight of the roof bear it, cf. Diod. S., 3, 34 where ice stands up to and thus carries a marching army, cf. also Aristot. Fr., 209, p. 1516a, 17, where it is said of the water of the sea that it στέγει τὰ βάρη, also Anth. Graec., 6, 93, 4. The figurative power of the word helps us to understand why even the oldest witnesses use it in a transf. sense. Thus it means "to cover, conceal" an intellectual matter, Eur. Phoen., 1214, "to hide," Soph. Trach., 596, synon. κρύπτεσθαι "to keep secret," Thuc., VI, 72, 5, "to withhold" a judgment, Polyb., 4, 8, 2 and then esp. "to keep silent" : τί χρή με... στέγειν, ἢ τί λέγειν; Soph. Phil., 136, cf. Oed. Tyr., 341; Eur. El., 273 ; Polyb., 8 ; 14, 5 ; Jos. Ant., 19, 48, and the one LXX ref. at Sir. 8:17: λόγον στέγειν "to keep a confidence."

With the silence complex the main transf. use of στέγω is for "to bear," Philo Flacc., 64 ; the stench of an ulcer, Agathias Historicus, IV, 21d [8] or intr. "to hold out," P. Oxy., XIV, 1775, 10 (4th cent. A.D.). A review of the usage thus yields the following results. At the core of its meaning στέγω denotes an activity or state which blocks entry from without or exit from within. [9] It is not inwardly related to any particular subj. or obj. and refers to the hampering of ingress or egress, so that it may be used either of material or intellectual things : "to cover," "to conceal," with a ref. later to the function of that which separates: "to be compact, watertight," "to bear," "to sustain."

B. The Use in Paul.

In the NT στέγω occurs only in Paul at 1 Th. 3:1, 5 and 1 C. 9:12; 13:7. It has no object in 1 Th. 3:1, 5 and means "to endure." Paul, impelled by his missionary task, can no longer bear not to have an influence on the development of the young church in Thessalonica. μηκέτι στέγοντες (3:1) or μηκέτι στέγων (3:5) he sends Timothy to Thessalonica because he cannot come himself. In 1 C. 9, which deals with the rights and manner of life of the apostle, v. 12 is parenthetical. In vv. 1-11 Paul emphasises that he has the same right as other apostles to eat and drink, to take a wife with him, and to live by his missionary labours : ἀλλὰ πάντα στέγομεν ἵνα μή τινα ἐγκοπὴν δῶμεν τῷ εὐαγγελίῳ τοῦ Χριστοῦ. This should not be translated: "We bear or suffer all things," [10] for in the preceding and following verses the reference is not to the sufferings but to the rights and freedom of the apostle. Hence the meaning is : "But we refrain from all this (i.e., from all that pertains to the legitimate private sphere of an apostle) in order that we may not give an offence to the Gospel which belongs to Christ." [11]

The most difficult passage is 1 C. 13:7. This is shown by the many different

---

[8] Ed. L. Dindorf, Historici Graeci Minores, II (1871).
[9] There is clearly a tendency to use the word esp. with ref. to water and fluids.
[10] As against Ltzm. 1 K. and H. D. Wendland, Die Briefe an d. Korinther, NT Deutsch, 7[8] (1962), ad loc.
[11] This seems to be backed by v. 18 f., where, after already focusing the rights of the apostle upon that of support by the church (v. 13 f.), Paul sums up the whole section along these lines.

renderings [12] and by the fact that the African NT in Cyprian's day has for πάντα στέγει *omnia diligit* = πάντα στέργει. [13] Along with the multiplicity of lexical possibilities one has also to consider the varying usage of Paul in 1 Th. 3:1, 5 and 1 C. 9:12. Now it may be taken for certain that στέγω does not mean the same as ὑπομένω, [14] for Paul would not spoil his fine three-membered formula [15] for the sake of a term of the same meaning, especially as πιστεύω, ἐλπίζω, ὑπομένω here agree with the πίστις, ἐλπίς and ἀγάπη of v. 13. The use of other uncommon words in vv. 4-7 [16] also supports the view that Paul has made a careful selection of terms here. Hence one may rule out the senses "to endure," "to tolerate," "to bear" (→ n. 12). There is also no lexical basis for "to excuse." There thus remain the renderings "to cover all things" and "to restrain itself" (→ n. 12). An argument against the latter is that it would demand the med. στέγομαι rather than στέγω. Furthermore, in contrast to the other three members, the action of ἀγάπη would be self-orientated on this view. Another consideration is that this sense does not occur among the examples. To be recommended, then, is the translation "covers all things." This raises no problems in the light of our review of the usage. The idea of covering with the cloak of love accords well with it. It is also supported by 1 C. 9:12. The only question is whether πάντα στέγει might not be construed even more specifically as "to keep silent about all things" (which it might be harmful to others to utter). [17] But materially this differs little from "to cover all things." Hence v. 7, amplifying what is said about faith, hope and endurance by a reference to the covering up of unfavourable things, offers an apt summary of vv. 4-6, which show that the love which is rooted in God's love, and which has already entered this world of death, is the eschatological reality of full self-giving to one's neighbour.

Kasch

---

[12] Cf. Luther Bible : "tolerates all things" ; Menge : "excuses all things" ; Zurich Bible : "endures all things" ; Heinr. 1 K., *ad loc.*: "restrains itself" ; Harnack, 147: "covers all things"; J. Héring, *La première ép. de S. Paul aux Cor., Comm. du NT,* 7 (1949), *ad loc.*: "en toutes circonstances, il est plein de pardon," cf. Whitaker, 126.

[13] H. v. Soden, "Das lat. NT in Afrika zu Zt. Cyprians," TU, 33 (1909), 598.

[14] Harnack, 147; Héring, *op. cit.* (→ n. 12), *ad loc.*

[15] On the triadic formula πίστις, ἐλπίς. ἀγάπη → I, 51, 32 ff. with n. 147.

[16] χρηστεύεται and περπερεύεται (→ VI, 93, 8 ff.) in v. 4 are hapax legomena, while ἀσχημονεῖ and παροξύνεται in v. 5 occur only once elsewhere in the NT. The choice of unusual words is obviously meant to give emphasis to the unusual nature of ἀγάπη.

[17] Whether Paul's contemporaries would understand στέγω in the sense "to keep silent" in so singular an expression is conclusively answered by the uncommon use in Jos., where στέγω undoubtedly means "to bear" in Ant., 5, 314 and "to keep silent" in 19, 48.

στέλλω, διαστέλλω, διαστολή,
ἐπιστέλλω, ἐπιστολή,
καταστέλλω, καταστολή,
συστέλλω, ὑποστέλλω, ὑποστολή

---

† στέλλω.

1. Found from Hom., στέλλω has the basic sense "to put," "to leave," not mechanically but by volitional act in relation to a precisely fixed goal. This yields a fair breadth
of usage. This ranges from the active "to place," "to draw up," subsidiary sense "to
make disposition" for battle ἑτάρους στέλλοντα καὶ ὀτρύνοντα μάχεσθαι, Hom. Il.,
4, 294, or "to put something in (the right) place," cf. sails ἱστία νηὸς ... στεῖλαν,
Hom. Od., 3, 10 f., cf. 16, 353, also abs. Polyb., 6, 44, 6, to "to make ready," e.g., of
ships ἐννέα νῆας στεῖλα, Hom. Od., 14, 248, ἐξ ὀφθαλμῶν μιν ἀποπέμπεται
στείλας πλοῖον Κέρκυραν, Hdt., III, 52, 61,[1] or an army, corps, troop, ἔστελλε
τὴν στρατιήν, Hdt., III, 141, στέλλων στρατιάν, Aesch. Ag., 799 and "to provide
with something," esp. clothes στείλας αὐτοῦ τὴν θυγατέρα ἐσθῆτι δουληίῃ ἐξέπεμπε
ἐπ' ὕδωρ ἔχουσαν ὑδρήιον, Hdt., III, 14, 2,[2] πρεπούσῃ στολῇ δὲ ταύτας ἐσταλμένας
καταβατέον, Plat. Leg., VIII, 833d, στειλάμενοι (med.) ἐσθῆτι Luc. Philops., 32,
and then on to a trans. use with personal subj. "to send" πεντηκόντορον (a ship propelled
by 50 rowers) στείλας, Ps.-Plat. Hipp., 228c or with neuter subj. "to tread" τὴν
ὁδὸν ... εἰς Κόρινθον στέλλειν, Luc. Hermot., 27 and then intr. "to set out," "to go,"
"to journey," "to travel" τὸν δὲ αὐτὸν τοῦτον χρόνον ... ἔστελλε ἐς ἀποικίην in
order to settle somewhere else, Hdt., IV, 147, 1,[3] also med. very gen. "to get ready"
τὰ νῦν δὲ ... βούλομαι στέλλεσθαι πρὸς τὴν κρίσιν, Plat. Phileb., 50e.

In gen. the word is comparatively rare. Aristot. has it as a nautical tt. (→ lines 11 f.,
18 f.) τοῦ ἱστίου μέρος στέλλεσθαι, Mechanica, 7, p. 851b, 7 f.[4] Of the few instances
in Plat. the med. "to get ready" (→ line 22 f.) covers about half.[5] With time the med.
gained in importance. This is related to a more or less conscious concentration of the
subj. on itself which can go to the pt. of self-isolation and self-questioning, cf. Epict.
in the mocking expression καλὴν στέλλεσθαι ταύτην τὴν ἐμπορίαν, Diss., III, 24, 80.
The personal side may also be seen in Plut. in expressions like πρὸς ἀποδημίαν στέλλεσθαι, De Timoleonte, 8 (I, 239b) etc., which have to do with getting ready, e.g., for
separation and departure. The same probably applies to the use of the word in a burial
epigram (2nd/1st cent. B.C.) to a young woman who died suddenly on the feast of
Demeter, Suppl. Epigr. Graec., II, 615: στέλλεο Περσεφόνας ζάλον, χρυσέα
Στρατονίκ[η]. The summons is given to the dead woman: "Prepare thyself[6] for

---

σ τ έ λ λ ω . Pape, Liddell-Scott, Pr.-Bauer⁵, s.v.; Cr.-Kö., 1017 f.
[1] Note the difference between στέλλω and ἀποπέμπω.
[2] Here στέλλω and ἐκπέμπω are plainly distinct.
[3] In distinction ἄγειν εἰς ἀποικίην denotes responsible emigration, e.g., Hdt., V, 124, 2.
[4] H. Bonitz, Index Aristotelicus (1955), s.v. has no other instances.
[5] Examples in F. Astius, Lex. Platonicum (1835-38), s.v.
[6] W. Peek, Griech. Grabgedichte (1960), 203 transl. "avoid" (cf. also Pr.-Bauer, s.v., 2)
but overlooks the fact that acc. to the context Hades has taken Stratonike in the same way
as Persephone his wife, and on the feast of Demeter, thus plainly showing his love for her.
Stratonike is thus the bride/wife of Hades as ruler of the underworld (ἄναξ ἐνέρων, line 2).
This arouses the jealousy of his ancestral consort.

Persephone's jealousy, golden Stratonike." Her fate is thus depicted as a glorification which she must be ready to endure. [7] Polyb., 8, 20, 4 speaks of οὐ δυναμένων ... τὴν ἐκ τῆς συνηθείας καταξίωσιν στέλλεσθαι "to leave aside." [8] Cf. Hippocr. Vet. Med., 5 (CMG, I, 39 vl.) where στέλλεσθαι is used with ἀπέχεσθαι for "to avoid" with ref. to certain foods.

2. The LXX has the word only in the med. There is a Hbr. equivalent in Mal. 2:5 נָחַת (חתת ni). But the basic text raises difficulties [9] and it is by no means certain that in view of the parallelism στέλλομαι is to be taken as analogous to φοβοῦμαι in the Gk. transl. [10] Acc. to the context another interpretation is possible and is probably to be preferred. This takes into account the idea of priestly service, namely, "to place oneself at disposal," "to be available (for ministry)." In Prv. 31:25 it is hardly possible to establish a clear relation between the Gk. transl. τάξιν ἐστείλατο τῇ γλώσσῃ αὐτῆς, and the Mas. text תּוֹרַת־חֶסֶד עַל־לְשׁוֹנָהּ. [11] Wis. 14:1: πλοῦν τις ... στελλόμενος, and 2 Macc. 5:1: τὴν δευτέραν ἔφοδον ... εἰς Αἴγυπτον ἐστείλατο, stay within current Gk. usage when they combine στέλλομαι with an acc. and use it in the sense "to prepare for something" → 588, 30 ff. Wis. 7:14 with its distinctive πρὸς θεὸν ἐστείλαντο φιλίαν (sc. θεοῦ) is probably to be taken in the same way, since receiving the divine → φιλία, even in the wise, always rests finally on God's decision (cf. Jm. 2:23 ; M. Ex. בחודש 6 on 20:6). In 3 Macc. 4:11 στέλλομαι has the sense "to set forth" (→ 588, 20 f.), while 3 Macc. 1:19 (αἱ προσαρτίως ἐσταλμέναι) is referring to married women who have retired to the bridal chamber for the festal reception of the bridegroom (cf. Mt. 25:6). [12] The meaning is much the same when Gn. 8:1 'A has ἐστάλησαν for the withdrawal of the waters of the flood (Hbr. שׁכך, LXX ἐκόπασεν).

3. Jos. uses act. στέλλω mostly for "to send," though the personal aspect is still present in his use, Ant., 1, 278: Jacob by his mother to seek a bride εἰς Μεσοποταμίαν στελλόμενος ..., 18, 19 : The Essenes are εἰς δὲ τὸ ἱερὸν ἀναθήματα στέλλοντες ..., 14, 469 : Sossios is a ὑπ' Ἀντωνίου σταλεὶς σύμμαχος. For moving Jos. also has στέλλειν ἀποικίας as a tt., 1, 110. The med. στέλλεσθαι occurs in Ant., 5, 141. The sense of moving from the original place, which is native to the term, is also found in Jos. He uses it for the moving away and abating of a storm in 9, 213: ὁ χειμὼν ἐστάλη, and also for the allaying of distress in 5, 280: βουλομένη τὴν ἄλογον τἀνδρὸς λύπην σταλῆναι. There is a link with the use in 3 Macc. 1:19 → lines 20 ff.

4. The two NT instances of the word have it in the med., like the LXX → lines 6 ff.

a. In his discussion of congregational discipline Paul admonishes the Thessalonian Christians : στέλλεσθαι ὑμᾶς ἀπὸ παντὸς ἀδελφοῦ ἀτάκτως περιπατοῦντος, 2 Th. 3:6. This admonition, which is given added weight by being issued "in the name of the Lord Jesus Christ" (→ V, 278, 34 f.), is without exact parallel linguistically [13] and is thus to be expounded directly from the context and not by

---

[7] Hades is sometimes depicted in other burial poems as a stealer of brides who snatches to himself beautiful young women or maidens, Peek, 306. The idea is old and widespread.
[8] So, unlike Pr.-Bauer, s.v., 1, W. R. Paton, *Polybius, The Histories,* III (1954), 495.
[9] Cf. BHK and comm. *ad loc.*
[10] Hesych.: στέλλεται· φοβεῖται. Several commentators follow him.
[11] Perhaps v. 25 and v. 26 of the Mas. have been confused.
[12] Cf. the discussion of possible explanations in C. L. W. Grimm, *Kurzgefasstes exeget. Hndbch. zu den Apkr. d. AT,* IV (1857), 231 f. But the referring of ἀπάντησις to the approaching cohabitation is to be rejected.
[13] Mal. 2:5 is no parallel, → lines 6 ff.

reference to Gl. 2:12 (Cephas ὑπέστελλεν καὶ ἀφώριζεν ἑαυτόν) or Hb. 10:38 (→ 598, 31 ff.). [14] It should not be overlooked that the text itself does not suggest either formal excommunication from the church or the suspension of table fellowship, cf. 1 C. 5:11. More important than a more precise material definition of the expression used by Paul [15] is that interest focuses not so much on the individual Christian whose walk is disorderly but rather on the other members of the congregation who might be led into similar courses by contact with him. If a key to interpretation is sought in Paul himself, the first passage to call for consideration is thus 1 C. 14:33 f. The rule which Paul propounds includes a disciplinary measure but is designed especially to make mature Christians willing and able to protect themselves, and to do so by following the apostle. Its purpose is to keep the community pure rather than to purge it from unhealthy elements. This is possible only if in certain circumstances one may "hold aloof" even from a Christian brother.

b. In 2 C. 8:20, in a section which deals with the collection for the poor saints in Jerusalem (8:4), Paul, having enlisted his fellow-workers in this task (8:16 ff.), provides a reason for so doing: στελλόμενοι τοῦτο, μή τις ἡμᾶς μωμήσηται ἐν τῇ ἁδρότητι ταύτῃ τῇ διακονουμένῃ ὑφ' ἡμῶν. The verse undoubtedly faces the possibility that the plenitude of gifts might give rise to the suspicion that Paul would have control of them and might spend them on himself. But if responsibility for the correct disbursement of the collection was committed to his companions, there would be no ground whatever for such ideas. Though this is clear enough, the question as to the exact meaning of στελλόμενοι τοῦτο is more open. Usually the expression is regarded as an expression of the apostle's fear as formulated in the concluding μή clause: "as we steer clear of this, seek to avoid it," [16] or "since we avoid" [17] or "(we are) in fear lest." [18] The implied equation of στέλλομαι with φοβοῦμαι is defended by supposed parallels from antiquity and also by reference to the appended μή, which favours a synonym of φοβοῦμαι. [19] But the parallels adduced, to the degree that they are not to be rejected like Mal. 2:5 (→ 589, 6 ff.), seem rather to suggest [20] that στελλόμενοι τοῦτο μή . . . is expressing the thought: "inasmuch as I see to it, or take steps, lest . . . [21] This understanding accords better with the nature and conduct of the apostle than the usual one, since always, and not just in difficult situations, he was concerned not merely to demonstrate his integrity but also so to act that no suspicion might even arise concerning it.

---

[14] So Dob. Th., ad loc.
[15] For this cf. the comm.
[16] So Pr.-Bauer⁵, s.v. 2 ; Ltzm.K., ad loc.
[17] So Schl. Erl., ad loc., also H. D. Wendland, Die Briefe an d. Korinther, NT Deutsch, 7⁸ (1962), ad loc.
[18] O. Kuss, Die Briefe an d. Römer, Korinther u. Galater, Regensburger NT, VI (1940), ad loc.
[19] So Wnd. 2 K., ad loc.
[20] Cf. esp. the burial epigram, Suppl. Epigr. Graec., II, 615 → 588, 32 ff. Hippocr. Vet. Med., 5 (CMG, I, 39 vl.) certainly uses στέλλομαι for "to avoid," but in the sense of leaving on one side, which can hardly be the meaning in 2 C. 8:20.
[21] Wnd. 2 K., ad loc. thinks this sense is "not impossible," and Cr.-Kö., 101 f. adopts it.

† διαστέλλω.

1. Found in Gk. from Plato this word means act. "to divide," "to differentiate," e.g., ξίφει ... διαστέλλων, Jos. Bell., 5, 62, "to dissect," "to sub-divide," [1] also a logical act, e.g., δίχα, Plat. Polit., 265e, "to define," e.g., τὰ λεγόμενα, Plat. Euthyd., 295d, then "to order," "to give precise instructions or commands," e.g., ἐπιτακτικῶς, Diod. S., 28, 15. In the sense "to order" the word presupposes a power of differentiation in the subj. [2] so that what is ordered is a planned and conscious decision. In the developed senses the med. use is based exclusively on the fact that what is described thereby has its place very specifically in the sphere of the subj., cf. Plat. Resp., VII, 535b : ποῖα (sc. ἤθη) δὴ διαστέλλῃ ; "What (qualities) do you define (in this case as of decisive importance)?" [3]

2. The LXX, which has the verb some 50 times or more, uses it for no less than 22 roots, [4] though all are in different ways concerned with separating, dividing, distinguishing, differentiating etc., or are understood thus in the transl. All the instances show the importance of the subj. The use of the med. is less prominent and is almost [5] completely limited to God. In this case the ref. is always to the precise, irrevocable and definitive directions of God and declarations of His will, cf. esp. Jdt. 11:12: ὅσα διεστείλατο αὐτοῖς ὁ θεὸς τοῖς νόμοις αὐτοῦ μὴ φαγεῖν, also Ez. 3:18-21, but also Ep. Ar., 131.

3. In the NT the main occurrence is in Mk., [6] where we find 5 of the 8 instances.

a. Mk. uses the word only of Jesus. By means of it he shows that certain directions which Jesus gives His disciples are categorical commands, or, more precisely, strict prohibitions in 5:43 ; 7:36 twice ; 9:9 and a definite warning in 8:15. It would seem that not merely the commands but also the warning against the leaven of the Pharisees and the leaven (→ II, 906, 3 ff.) of Herod in connection with the second feeding (8:15) are related to the keeping of the secret of Jesus by His disciples during His lifetime. [7] Hence Mk. seems deliberately to have reserved the word for Jesus. At any rate it enables him to lay great stress on the hidden majesty and power of Jesus in the light of its future manifestation. One can hardly say for certain whether at this point he was consciously following the use of the word for God's revelatory speech in Hellenistic Judaism.

In Mt. 16:20 διεστείλατο (א C 𝕽 Θ pl) and ἐπετίμησεν (B * D e syᶜ) are par. to Mk. 8:30 (the forbidding of the disciples to say that Jesus is the Messiah). Since Mk. has ἐπετίμησεν here (Lk. ἐπιτιμήσας) and since this is the only instance of διαστέλλο-

---

δ ι α σ τ έ λ λ ω. Cf. the dict., esp. Liddell-Scott, Pr.-Bauer⁵, s.v.

[1] Cf. the use in grammar for the dividing punctuation mark.

[2] Cf. the characterising of God as μόνον ἀψευδέσι καὶ ἁπλανεστάτοις κριτηρίοις τὰς κατὰ μικρὸν διαφορὰς διαστέλλοντα in Philo Vit. Mos., II, 237.

[9] There is another good example in Jos. Ant., 4, 197 when he uses the compound προδιαστέλλομαι for "to set forth clearly in advance" with ref. to possible misunderstandings or misrepresentations.

[4] Cf. Hatch-Redp., s.v. Cf. also Lv. 24:12 Αλλ for פרש and Job 38:25 ᾿ΑΘ for פלג [Bertram].

[5] The exceptions are 4 Βασ. 6:10 (addition to LXX on the basis of the Mas. in Origen: καὶ διεστείλατο αὐτῷ, cf. the comm.); Ju. 1:19 (misunderstanding?).

[6] The word is in the med. except at Hb. 12:20 → 592, 18 ff.

[7] Rightly noted by M. Dibelius, Die Formgesch. d. Ev.⁴ (1961), 230. Cf. also Loh. Mk., ad loc.

μαι in Mt. and it is well attested, one need have no doubts as to its authenticity. [8] Nor is it beyond the bounds of possibility that Mt. deliberately used it here, and here alone, in a scene in which only in his Gospel Peter calls Jesus ὁ υἱὸς τοῦ θεοῦ τοῦ ζῶντος, 16:16. If this is so, the word has theological significance in Mt. as it also has in the LXX → 591, 14 ff.

b. In the so-called apostolic decree in Ac. 15:24 we read : ... οἷς οὐ διεστειλά-μεθα. The Christian church at Jerusalem and its leaders are here stating that those Christians who have gone out from Jerusalem and unsettled the (Pauline?) churches in Syria and Asia Minor by certain rigorous demands have not received any real instructions from them but have acted — we read this between the lines — in a purely private capacity. In the context, then, the word is correcting a false impression among those addressed and is also stating that this kind of legalism is just as alien to the original community as is the tendency to advance claims to authority.

In gen. the comm. ignore the word and its meaning here. [9] It seems to have been selected by Lk. deliberately. At any rate the usual rendering "to give a commission" is much too general. The ref. is not to a commission but to strict orders.

c. In Hb. 12:20 τὸ διαστελλόμενον (pass.) is "that which God [10] has strictly commanded (at Sinai)" [11] → lines 5 ff.; 591, 21 ff. [12] This v., too, fits in with the theological use of the word in the NT.

† διαστολή.

1. Derived from διαστέλλω, but unlike this not found in Plat. but for the first time only in Aristot., [1] this comparatively uncommon word follows the verb in its various senses. In medicine it denotes the separation of organs, Aristot. De Audibilibus, p. 800a, 35, or "incision," "indentation," τῆς ῥινός, Plut. Cicero, 1 (I, 861b), or. transf. "separation," "division" (God speaks through Moses to Pharaoh): καὶ δώσω διαστολὴν ἀνὰ μέσον τοῦ ἐμοῦ λαοῦ καὶ ἀνὰ μέσον τοῦ σοῦ λαοῦ, Ex. 8:19 [2] or "exact, precise exposition" Polyb., 16, 14, 2 or "decision," "order," "instruction" P. Tebt., I, 24, 45 (2nd. cent. B.C.) or, in grammar, "punctuation mark to separate" Dion. Thr. Art. Gramm., 629.

2. There is no specific use in the LXX. It has the word for two different ideas, Ex. 8:19 (→ line 25): פְדֻת "liberation," "redemption"; [3] חֻקַּת הַתּוֹרָה = ἡ διαστολὴ τοῦ

---

[8] So, e.g., Kl. Mt., ad loc. Nestle prefers ἐπετίμησεν, but is there not here attempted harmonisation with Mk.?

[9] Cf. Wdt. Ag., ad loc.; Jackson-Lake, I, 3, ad loc.; H. W. Beyer, Die Apostelgesch., NT Deutsch, 5⁹ (1959), ad loc.; Bauernf. Ag., ad loc.; Haench. Ag., ad loc.; C. S. C. Williams, A Comm. on the Acts of the Ap. (1957), ad loc., to name but a few.

[10] Here, too, God stands behind the pass. as author.

[11] Rightly noted and considered by Mi. Hb., ad loc.

[12] 2 Macc. 14:28: τὰ διεσταλμένα (as against Mi. Hb., ad loc.) is not a material par. since the ref. here is to what is agreed between two parties.

δ ι α σ τ ο λ ή . Dict., esp. Liddell-Scott, Pr.-Bauer⁵, s.v.

[1] The ref. of Pr.-Bauer⁵, s.v. to Anaximand. A, 23 as the first instance is erroneous, since this is a doxographical note in later academic speech (v. Diels, I, 87, 23) [Krämer].

[2] Cf. also Philo Vit. Mos., II, 158: διαστολὴ ἁγίων τε καὶ βεβήλων, ἀνθρωπείων τε καὶ θείων.

[3] Cf. BHK and comm.

νόμου, Nu. 19:2; [4] מִבְטָא שְׂפָתַיִם = διαστολή τῶν χειλέων, Nu. 30:7. There is yet another sense in 1 Macc. 8:7 where διαστολή is a piece of land which is to be ceded.

3. Of the three NT passages R. 3:22 and R. 10:12 are closely related. The "distinction between Israel and the Gentiles," which was made when Israel was elected and given the revelation of God's will at Sinai, is abolished by the divine event in Christ, so that the special status of Judaism, which seemed to be unchangeable to the OT community (→ 592, 25 f. and n. 2), is set aside. In the two passages this assertion is made from different angles, namely, on the basis of the fact that Israel is sinful as well as the Gentiles in R. 3:22 (Paul shares this insight with apocalyptic), [5] and on the basis of the fact that the Gentiles too are called to the faith and follow it in R. 10:12. The essential point here is that the abolishing of the διαστολή caused by historical revelation is not viewed as a unifying of mankind but is seen theologically, i.e., as the establishment of the universal reign of God in Christ. [6] 1 C. 14:7 has no theological significance. The figure of a διαστολή of φθόγγοι remains within the sphere of the current acoustic use of διαστολή. [7] This relates here to the various notes and also the varying length of the notes. [8]

ἐπιστέλλω, ἐπιστολή.

1. ἐπιστέλλω is a tt. from Hdt. (e.g., III, 40, 1) for "transmitting a message or direction" either by word of mouth or more esp. in writing. ἐπιστολή is "what is transmitted by the messenger," usually the "letter." The usage is so common that examples are superfluous, esp. as there is nothing distinctive in Jewish Hellenism (the LXX, Philo and Jos.) or Gnostic writings in Gk. [1]

2. In the NT the whole group is very close to διαστέλλομαι in so far as this presupposes an actual or at least a claimed authority → 591, 21 ff. The few instances of the verb (Ac. 15:20; 21:25; Hb. 13:22) bring out very clearly the authoritative and almost official nature of the primitive Christian epistle. It is a generally acknowledged fact to-day that the apostolic letters collected in the NT are marked by this. Connected herewith is the point that for all their formal

---

[4] Liddell-Scott: "command, injunction, order." But Z. Frankel, Über den Einfluss d. palästinischen Exegese auf die alexandrinische Hermeneutik (1851), 334 is surely right when, citing Para., III, 1 f., he says: "A halachic element: this law demands a special separation for the priest." The ref. then is to the distinction ordered by the Law. On the original sense of חֻקַּת הַתּוֹרָה cf. R. Hentschke, "Satzung u. Setzender. Ein Beitrag zur isr. Rechtsterminologie," BWANT, V, 3.

[5] On this cf. Mi. R., ad loc.

[6] "Universal" means that the Jews are not only not excluded as might have happened through their own refusal (cf. R. 3:22) but that they are definitely included through the universal revelation of God's grace in Christ.

[7] In elucidation cf. Epict Diss., III, 6, 8, though διαστολή is not used here. Cf. Joh. W. 1 K., ad loc.

[8] Cf. W. Straub, Die Bildersprache d. Ap. Pls. (1937), 84.

ἐ π ι σ τ έ λ λ ω, ἐ π ι σ τ ο λ ή. Dict., esp. Liddell-Scott, Pr.-Bauer⁵, s.v.

[1] An art. on epistles in the NT such as the importance of the subject might demand is beyond the scope of TDNT. Hence only a few theologically significant passages will be discussed.

similarity to the epistles of antiquity the NT epistles constitute a special genre. [2] As has long since been recognised, their distinctiveness is to be seen not merely in the way in which the authors introduce themselves as deputies of Christ but also in the prefaces, even though these differ and Paul's letters occupy a special place of their own. [3] At any rate the NT epistles, like oral proclamation and the Gospels, seek to say a last and definitive word about the historical situation of the individual, humanity and the world in the light of the Christ event as God's eschatological act. They also try to show that the world cannot escape this. Though both the outer and inner presuppositions of the early Roman imperial era are quite different, they are at one in this with the classical written prophecy of the OT, and it is very likely that their authors, e.g., Paul and the writer of the seven letters of Revelation, which are certainly not letters in the Pauline sense, [4] were fully aware of this. It is certainly quite evident in Paul, e.g., when he quotes Is. 52:7 in R. 10:15 or echoes Is. 61:1 f. in R. 1:1, cf. also Gl. 3:2. Again 2 C. 3:1-3, though it is difficult in many respects, reflects Paul's conviction that all his epistles are ultimately Christ's epistles.

2 C. 3:1-3 is the one place in the NT in which ἐπιστολή is used figuratively. Starting with the fact that his opponents use συστατικαὶ ἐπιστολαί (3:1) [5] and thus give themselves the weight of human authority, Paul stresses the fact that he personally does not need to do anything of this nature in relation to the Corinthian church, since the church itself is in some sense an ἐπιστολή whose true author is Christ, though Paul wrote it as Christ's fellow-labourer (3:3a). [6] With this clear metaphor there is then combined a second which obviously has less to do with the epistle as a scroll than with its contents, 3:2 and 3:3b. The unavoidable tension between the two metaphors leads to an overloading of the few verses with imagery, so that things are very difficult for the expositor, the more so as the second complex branches out again into two thoughts a. you are written in our hearts as a letter and b. your being a letter rests on the work of the Spirit of the living God in your own hearts. [7] Nor is the first complex a wholly simple one, since it carries with it the thought that the Corinthians, as Christ's epistle, are also His epistle, or one of His epistles, to the world. [8] Probably for Paul himself it was the Spirit's work in his work which, having the Corinthian Christians as its fruit, formed a significant centre for the apparently divergent images of this short section. [9] The fact that Paul uses the by no means obvious metaphor of a church as a letter of Christ or

---

[2] Cf. the brief survey by J. Schneider, Art. "Brief" in RAC, 2, 574-6 (with bibl.). A monograph is needed on the primitive Chr. epistle.

[3] E. Lohmeyer, "Briefliche Grussüberschriften" in Probleme paul. Theol. (1955), 7-29 ; G. Friedrich, "Lohmeyers These über das paul. Präskript kritisch beleuchtet," ThLZ, 80 (1955), 342-346.

[4] This is not to say that the letters belong to the category of "heavenly letters" as Schneider (op. cit., 576) supposes.

[5] On the use of letters of commendation cf. the rich material in Wnd. 2 K., ad loc.

[6] The passage incidentally throws light on the technical side of the rise of official letters in antiquity and its significance for the development of Paul's own letters acc. to his own understanding.

[7] A fresh complication here is the recollection of the tables of the Law at Sinai, which were written on stone.

[8] On the composition of the imagery cf. the comm., ad loc. and also W. Straub, Die Bildersprache d. Ap. Pls. (1937), 82 f.

[9] Straub, op. cit., 83 finds in the second "an inextricable confusion in the use of imagery."

of an apostle brings out in a special way his certainty that with Jesus Christ the legitimate apostle has a necessary and inalienable place in the revelation of God in Christ.

† καταστέλλω, † καταστολή.

1. First found in Eur. Ba. in the sense "to put in its right place" (of a strand or lock of hair πλόκαμον), the verb καταστέλλω soon became a tt. for "to put on or to arrange clothes," Aristoph. Thes., 256 ; Plut. Adulat., 28 (II, 69c).[1] The word also means "to restore order," "to pacify," esp. in the case of unrest, revolt, or panic, hence καταστέλλειν θορυβοῦντας ... νέους, Plut. Apophth., 12 (II, 207e), but also with an inward ref. καταστέλλειν τὴν ἐπιθυμίαν, Epict. Diss., III, 19, 5. LXX 2 Macc. 4:31: καταστέλλειν τὰ πράγματα (= τὴν στάσιν), 3 Macc. 6:1:[2] καταστέλλειν πρεσβυτέρους, and Jos. Ant., 20, 174; καταστέλλειν τὴν ταραχήν, 20, 106 : καταστέλλειν τὸν νεωτερισμόν (revolt), Vit., 17: καταστέλλειν τοὺς στασιώδεις, have the verb only in this sense.[3] The contexts of the ref. adduced show that the one who does what is indicated by the verb must have authority. This is not seen in the success of his efforts to attain order or quiet; it is their presupposition. καταστέλλειν is thus used only of an official or someone who commands respect. For children this might be a nurse → 595, 6 f. with n. 1.

So far as may be seen the noun καταστολή appears first in Hippocr. De Decentia, 5, 8 (CMG, I, 27, 5) in the sense "modesty," "propriety." The intr. meaning is thus "appropriate, ordered conduct" and the trans. "action with a view to ordered conduct." In Inscr. Priene, 109, 186 f. (2nd. cent. B.C.) we find it with εὐσχημοσύνη[4] and in Epict. Diss., II, 10, 15 between αἰδώς and ἡμερότης. The further sense of "clothes, clothing" derives from the fact that decorum finds a first visible expression in clothing.[5] LXX Is. 61:3: καταστολὴ δόξης, and Jos. Bell., 2, 126 : καταστολὴ καὶ σχῆμα σώματος again share a common use in this respect.

2. In the NT καταστέλλω occurs only in Ac. 19:35 f.: The secretary of the council at Ephesus can "pacify" the excited crowd which had gathered in the theatre, obviously because of his high office.

We are not told how he did it. The contrast between him and the Jew Alexander, who cannot prevail against the tumult (Ac. 19:33 f.), is much to the pt.; the latter does not have the necessary authority. More important, however, is the fact that in a similar scene later in Ac. 21:27 ff. Luke does not use καταστέλλω for his hero Paul when he brings the people to order but simply has him give a sign with his hand κατέσεισεν. Paul was not a person who could command respect acc. to contemporary standards. He was a witness of Jesus Christ with the authority appropriate to such a witness.

κ α τ α σ τ έ λ λ ω, κ α τ α σ τ ο λ ή. Dict., esp. Liddell-Scott, Pr.-Bauer⁵, s.v.

[1] The passage is a vivid one. When children fall their nurses run to lift them up (ἐγείρειν), clean them (περιπλύνειν) and put their clothes in order again (καταστέλλειν).

[2] In the sense "to calm" 'A uses καταστέλλω at ψ 64:8 (HT שבח hi ; LXX συνταράσσω) [Bertram].

[3] Philo does not appear to use either verb or noun.

[4] Cf. also Ep. Ar., 284 f.

[5] So Pr.-Bauer⁵, s.v.

In 1 Tm. 2:9 the author expects the ladies of the community to adorn themselves ἐν καταστολῇ κοσμίῳ μετὰ αἰδοῦς καὶ σωφροσύνης, → I, 171, 21 ff. It is hard to say whether καταστολή here means "demeanour" as in Epict. (→ 595, 22 f.) [6] or "clothing" as in Is. 61:3 → 595, 24 ff.). [7], [8] Yet if one takes into account a certain parallelism between v. 9 and v. 8 there is more to be said for the first view (→ 595, 19 ff.). Another point in favour of this is that the rules given here for men and women probably apply to divine service. [9]

> The post-apost. fathers have neither verb nor noun, so that they cannot help us to decide. The same applies to the Apologists. Here the simple στολή is used for "garment," though largely in quotations. This has to be taken into account at least in relation to 1 Tm. 2:9.

† συστέλλω.

1. Found from Eur. Tro., 377 this is the opp. of διαστέλλω (→ 591, 1 ff.) and means "to draw or put together," e.g., τὰ ἱστία, Aristoph. Ra., 999, then "to shorten," e.g., τὴν διαιτίαν, Plut. Cato Minor, 4 (I, 761c) and fig. "to humble," so Plat. Lys., 210e with ταπεινόω.

2. LXX has the word both for "to abase" Ju. 8:28 ; 11:33 (כנע); 1 Macc. 5:3 and also for "to confound" 1 Macc. 3:6 ; 2 Macc. 6:12 ; 3 Macc. 5:33 (cf. also ψ 72:21 Σ). In Jos. we find it at Ant., 9, 174 with ταπεινόω for (militarily) "to overwhelm," Ant., 14, 74, or geographically "to press closely," Ant., 16, 248 συστέλλειν αὐτόν "to make oneself little." Philo uses the noun συστολή in Praem. Poen., 47 for "restriction." The pass. ὑποστέλλομαι with ἐρημάζω in Leg. All., III, 35 may mean "to be cast back on oneself."

3. The verb occurs only twice in the NT. Both passages raise certain difficulties.

a. In 1 C. 7:29, in a discussion of marriage and celibacy, Paul says concerning the situation of Christians and the world in view of the imminent end of all things : ὁ καιρὸς συνεσταλμένος ἐστίν. According to current usage [1] this can only mean : "The time (still at our disposal) is compressed, i.e., short." Probably primitive Christianity would see God as author behind the passive. But it is uncertain whether what Paul means is that by the coming of Jesus and the prospect of His

---

[6] So with a good deal of cultural material Dib. Past., ad loc.

[7] So most commentators, ad loc.

[8] In this respect καταστολή is close to the Lat. habitus which at this period (Sen. Rhet. Contr., II, 1, 6 ; Tac. Hist., III, 73, 3) could mean "clothing" as well as "demeanour" [Risch].

[9] Dib. Past., ad loc. It should be noted v. 9c is not speaking expressly of ἱματισμός. καταστολή as "measured conduct" gathers together the many individual rules under a common centre which concentrates upon the essential pt., and thus takes away from the passage any air of casuistry.

συστέλλω. The dict., esp. Liddell-Scott, Pr.-Bauer[5], s.v.

[1] Apollon. Dyscol. De Pronominibus, 11, 19: δίχρονα συνεσταλμένα "syllables of double length which are shortened"; Luc. Icaromenipp., 12 : The γῆ seen from the moon seems ἐς βραχὺ συνεσταλμένη, Diod. S., 4, 20, 1: τοῖς ὄγκοις συνεσταλμένοι, "of stunted stature"; Plut. Apophth. Lac., 3 (II, 216 f.): συνεσταλμένως ζῆ, "he lives a restricted life," i.e., under imposed self-denial.

quick return God has suddenly shortened the time of apocalyptic expectation and thus compelled those who have knowledge to concentrate on the goal. [2] Passages like Gl. 4:4 ; R. 1:2 ff., which stress the fulfilling of time by the Christ event, make this interpretation highly improbable. Possibly Paul has simply adopted a proverbial saying [3] and exploited it in exhortation relating to the imminent expectation of his generation. The saying does not seem to carry any reference to the idea of future tribulations, as some have supposed. [4]

b. Ac. 5:6 records that after the sudden death of Ananias οἱ νεώτεροι συνέστειλαν αὐτὸν καὶ ἐξενέγκαντες ἔθαψαν. Here exegesis has vacillated from ancient times [5] between "to wrap up," "to snatch up" and "to remove." [6] Probably the idea is that the dead man was wrapped in his clothes and taken away in them [7] unless those charged with the burial [8] first covered him with a shroud. [9]

† ὑποστέλλω.

1. Used from Pind. Isthm., II, 40, ὑποστέλλω means act. "to draw aside, away, back," always for a specific purpose, intr. also "to retreat" (many instances, esp. military, in the historians, e.g., Polyb., 6, 40, 14 ; 10, 32, 3 ; Plut. Demetr., 47 [I, 912]), sometimes "to hide" Philo Spec. Leg., I, 5, med. "to withdraw," "to hold back," "to keep to oneself," always with the aim of concealing oneself, with gen. "to keep away from," abstaining from τροφή Aristot. Probl., 1, 46, p. 864b, 36 also from ἀλήθεια Jos. Bell., 1, 387, [1] then "to keep silence," "to conceal," τὰ ἁμαρτήματα τοῦ πατρός, Jos. Bell., 1, 452, with σιωπάω Ap., 1, 52.

2. The few LXX ref. round out the picture. ὑποστέλλομαι in Job. 13:18 means "to hide" (God), cf. also the difficult Hab. 2:4, while the sense in Dt. 1:17; Wis. 6:7 seems to be "to shrink from," and in Hag. 1:10 the par. ἀνέχω establishes the meaning "to hold back." [2] Philo has the word a few times for "to subject, subordinate" ὑπεστάλθαι ἀριθμῷ of bodily excretions Op. Mund., 123 ; intr. λόγῳ ὑποστεῖλαι τῷ γεγωνῷ, Leg. All., III, 41.

3. The verb occurs 4 times in the NT with three different nuances.

a. In his account of what happened in Antioch after the apostolic council

---

[2] Joh. W. 1 K., ad loc.
[3] Cf. Ab., 2, 15 (R. Tarfon): "The day is short" (הַיּוֹם קָצֵר).
[4] Cf. Schl. K., ad loc.
[5] Cf. the short but comprehensive survey in Pr.-Bauer⁵, s.v.
[6] One cannot appeal to Philo Leg. All., III, 35 for this view (Vg : amoverunt), as against Pr.-Bauer, s.v. (→ 596, 21 ff.).
[7] Cf. S. Klein, Tod u. Begräbnis in Palästina z. Zt. d. Tannaiten, Diss. Freiburg i. Br. (1908), 25.
[8] Cf. Semachot, 12 (v. Strack Einleitung, 73).
[9] Klein, op. cit.; Dalman Arbeit, V, 168.

ὑ π ο σ τ έ λ λ ω. Dict., esp. Liddell-Scott and Pr.Bauer⁵, s.v.
[1] ὑποστέλλεσθαι can even be used in antithesis to λέγειν τἀληθές, Jos. Bell., 1, 594, hence οὐχ ὑποστέλλεσθαι means "to say freely," Jos. Bell., 5, 566, cf. Vit., 278 ; Bell., 1, 518. Cf. Philo Sacr. AC, 35 : οὐδὲν ὑποστειλαμένη μετὰ παρρησίας λέξω, also Rer. Div. Her., 42.
[2] LXX usage is not uniform, though in this context we cannot discuss the reasons. A distinctive expression is ἡ ὑποστέλλουσα ἡμέρα as a variant alongside ἡ ἐπιτελοῦσα or ἐπιοῦσα ἡμέρα, 3 Macc. 5:20.

(Gl. 2:11 ff.) Paul writes about Peter's conduct in the matter: ὑπέστελλεν καὶ ἀφώριζεν ἑαυτόν (→VI, 110, 7 ff.). Though a comprehensive charge of hypocrisy is expressly raised in v. 13, in defining the relation between the two verbs in v. 12 one cannot take them as synonyms. Both in time and materially what is denoted by the first precedes what is denoted by the second. The usual construing of ὑποστέλλω as an intr. in the sense "to withdraw" is very largely in keeping with this. But one cannot rule out the possibility that Paul for his part also had in view the sense "to hide." This is supported by the fact that Paul stresses most emphatically the public nature of what he said to Peter on this occasion, v. 14.

> Linguistically there is no objection to taking ἑαυτόν only with the ἀφώριζεν, but materially this greatly restricts the two statements bound together by καί. For the total understanding of Paul's account it is highly significant that ὑποστέλλω is the exact opposite of ὀρθοποδεῖν πρὸς τὴν ἀλήθειαν, v. 14 → n. 1.

b. In Luke's account of Paul's address in Miletus (Ac. 20:18 ff.) the apostle twice uses the verb ὑποστέλλομαι in very similar phrases, and both times by way of negation (v. 20 with οὐδέν as acc. of object, v. 27 in a simple negation by οὐ) with a view to emphasising his integrity as a messenger of the Gospel and teacher of the churches. In the context the use of the term is probably explained by the expectation of ἄνδρες λαλοῦντες διεστραμμένα, v. 30. Paul is no ὑποστειλάμενος because he has given the churches the whole truth and not kept back anything that is συμφέρον. The negative form of the statement should not blind us to the fact that the thrust is most emphatically positive. With the negation the word means here "to say or do something openly and with no reservation."

> In this type of expression Lk. is very close to Jos. [3] The influence of current terminology on the Miletus address in Lk. is brought out by closer examination. In his own words Paul is depicting himself as an honest man acc. to the standards of the age. Within the structure of Ac. his farewell discourse to the presbyters of Asia Minor at Miletus thus has the function of a counterpart to the term σπερμολόγος which the academic philosophers of Athens used to describe him in Ac. 17:18. The verses 20:33 ff. serve esp. to bring out the contrast.

c. Hb. has ὑποστέλλομαι at 10:38 in a quotation (Hab. 2:4). The two parts of the quotation are reversed. The prophetic saying (→ 597, 24 f.) is taken christologically [4] (v. 37) and applied in exhortation. In this interpretation the author relates the ὑποστείληται of the quotation to the δίκαιος, i.e., the believer. For him the direction in the biblical saying is that there can be no ἀποβάλλειν τὴν παρρησίαν (v. 35) expressed in a ὑποστέλλεσθαι, in "concealment," for this is contrary to the commitment of believers to ὁμολογία (cf. 4:14) [5] and will end in hopeless παραρυῆναι (2:1) (→ also ὑποστολή, 599, 1 ff.).

---

[3] Cf. also Vit., 278 : 'Ἰησοῦς ... οὐδὲν ὑποστειλάμενος ἀναφανδὸν εἶπεν.
[4] For details cf. Mi. Hb., ad loc., also F. Delitzsch, Comm. z. Briefe an d. Hebräer (1857), 508.
[5] So correctly Delitzsch, op. cit., 509 f.

† ὑποστολή.

This rare word is sometimes used in Plut. for "abstinence" from certain foods in sickness, De Tuenda Sanitate Praecepta, 14 (II, 129c), while in Asclepiodotus Tactica, 10, 21 [1] means "reserve" and in Jos. "furtiveness," Bell., 2, 277: λάθρα καὶ μεθ᾽ ὑποστολῆς, and "secrecy," Ant., 16, 112 : οὐδεμίαν ὑποστολὴν ποιοῦνται κακοηθείας. It does not occur in either LXX or Philo.

The only NT instance is at Hb. 10:39 with a ref. back to the ὑποστείληται of the quotation from Hab. 2:4 in v. 38. As a constitutive part of the interpretation of this scripture by the author it is to be interpreted within the tension with πίστις, and the best rendering is "lack of steadfastness," "unreliability" (cf. 2:1: μήποτε παραρυῶμεν).

Rengstorf

ὑ π ο σ τ ο λ ή. [1] H. Köchly-W. Rüstow, *Griech. Kriegsschriftsteller*, II, 1 (1855), 180.

---

† στενάζω,   † στεναγμός,   † συστενάζω

A. The Word Group outside the New Testament.

1. στενάζω "to sigh," "to groan" is a development of στένω, from which derive στενάχω, στεναχίζω and στενάζω, στεναγμός, στέναγμα. Hom.: στόνος, στοναχή, στοναχῆσαι. [1] στεναγμός "sigh," collective "sighing" from Pind. Fr., 168, 4. συστενάζω "to sigh, groan with" is very rare, with dat. Eur. Ion, 935: ὡς συστενάζειν γ' οἶδα γενναίως φίλοις, Test. Iss. 7:5; without dat. Nicetas Eugenianus, I, 342. [2] In the tragic poets sighing is esp. at destiny or individual blows of fate, e.g., Eur. Alc., 199; Iph. Taur., 957; Phoen., 1035; Soph. El., 1299. Soph. Oed. Tyr., 30 says of Hades: "Αιδης στεναγμοῖς καὶ γόοις πλουτίζεται.

2. In LXX the group including the compounds ἀνα- and καταστενάζω finds no sure original in the HT. The noun אֲנָחָה is transl. only by στεναγμός. The verb is used in 17 passages for 11 Hbr. words. In 5 the Mas. has a different text, 3 are in Sir., 5 only in Gk. books or books preserved only in Gk. In Ez. 24:17 the noun στεναγμός is used for a 12th Hbr. verb אָנַק ni. אֲנָקָה and אֲנָחָה are transl. only by his group (4 times καταστενάζω, once ἀναστενάζω). In sum LXX has the group 65 times. Human complaint is expressed by it more consistently than in the Mas. [3]

Details include sighing at child-birth in Jer. 4:31, in mortal conflict in Ez. 26:15; Is. 59:10, for the dead in Jdt. 14:16, for personal suffering esp. in Job, Ps. Examples: ἡ χεὶρ αὐτοῦ βαρεῖα γέγονεν ἐπ' ἐμῷ στεναγμῷ, Job 23:2; ἐκοπίασα ἐν τῷ στεναγμῷ μου, λούσω καθ' ἑκάστην νύκτα τὴν κλίνην μου, ψ 6:7; ἐξέλιπεν ἐν ὀδύνῃ ἡ ζωή μου καὶ τὰ ἔτη μου ἐν στεναγμοῖς, ψ 30:11; ὠρυόμην ἀπὸ στεναγμοῦ τῆς καρδίας μου, ψ 37:9. As a prayer to God: εἰσελθάτω ἐνώπιόν σου ὁ στεναγμὸς τῶν πεπεδημένων, ψ 78:11. There is sighing at the people's affliction, at God's judgment in history (Ez., Is., Jer., Lam.), at eschatological events, Is. 24:7; Wis. 5:3, as a sign of penitence, Is. 30:15; Ιερ. 38 (31):19; Mal. 2:13. In particular sighing expresses deep distress of spirit. It leads to prayer, which may be combined with it. Tob 3:1 S: περίλυπος γενόμενος τῇ ψυχῇ καὶ στενάξας ἔκλαυσα καὶ ἠρξάμην προσεύχεσθαι μετὰ στεναγμῶν. God hears the sighing of His people, Ex. 2:24; 6:5. In the future salvation there will be no more sighing ἀπέδρα ὀδύνη καὶ λύπη καὶ στεναγμός, Is. 35:10, cf. 51:11. There is a vivid description of prophetic declaration in Ez. 21:11 f.: "But thou, son of man, sigh! with broken thighs and in bitter grief, sigh! When they ask thee why thou sighest, then answer them: Because of a message of terror." For sighing at the receiving of revelation Is. 21:2: νῦν στενάζω καὶ παρακαλέσω ἐμαυτόν (Mas. different).

3. Philo often has στενάζω with δακρύω and κλαίω, e.g. Migr. Abr., 15, 155; Deus Imm., 138; Exsecr. 170 or στεναγμός with λύπη. Leg. All., III, 211. He often gives an allegorical explanation of Ex. 2:23, e.g., Det. Pot. Ins., 93 and 94; Migr. Abr., 15; Leg. All., III, 211 f. The sighing of the children of Israel under Egyptian bondage is that of the soul. Leg. All., III, 211 f. is very typical. There are some remote echoes of R. 8:26 f. (→ 602, 7 ff.) in Migr. Abr., 155: "The spirit is conscious of its

---

στενάζω κτλ. [1] Cf. German "stöhnen," Sanskr. staniti "thunders, rumbles, roars" etc. Cf. Boisacq, s.v.; Hofmann, s.v.; Pokorny, 1021 [Risch].

[2] Scriptores Erotici Graeci, ed. G. A. Hirschig (1885).

[3] [I am indebted to Bertram in this section.]

impotence and weeps and laments when it does not attain all that it desires," and in Det. Pot. Ins., 93: "But he who is good and gracious does not reject those who pray to him, esp. when sighing under Egyptian labours and sorrows they cry sincerely and simply. For then, says Moses, the words mount up to deity (Ex. 2:23), who hears them and redeems them from the evils which came upon them," cf. also Migr. Abr., 15. On the meaning of conscience for the divinely blessed soul which sighs with respect to the time devoted to sin, Deus Imm., 138 says: "When this divinely inspired being (viz. conscience) ... enters the soul it stirs up thought about all misdeeds and sins, not that the soul should commit them again, but that it should strike up a gt. lament (μέγα στενάξασα καὶ μέγα κλαύσασα), bewail its earlier fall and turn from them, following instead that wherein the interpreter of God, the logos and the prophet, instructs it."

4. Jos. depicts in Bell., 6, 272 a scene from the capture of Jerusalem: συνήχει δὲ ἡ φλὸξ ἐπὶ πλεῖστον ἐκφερομένη τοῖς τῶν πιπτόντων στεναγμοῖς.

5. In ancient magic there is sighing in magical practices, love magic, and the conjuring up of a dream, Preis. Zaub., I, 4, 1406; II, 7, 763; 12, 945.

6. στεναγμός means "sigh of love" in Test. Jos. 7:2 Potiphar's wife says: πόνον καρδίας ἐγὼ ἀλγῶ, καὶ οἱ τοῦ πνεύματος στεναγμοὶ συνέχουσί με, cf. also 7:1: στενάζουσα συντόμως. Joseph resists the "enticements"; καὶ ἐγὼ συνίων τοὺς στεναγμοὺς ἐσιώπων, 9:4; cf. also Sir. 30:20; 36:25 στενάζω expressing sexual craving.

B. The Word Group in the New Testament.

Sighing takes place by reason of a condition of oppression under which man suffers and from which he longs to be free because it is not in accord with his nature, expectations, or hopes.

1. 2 C. 5:2: ἐν τούτῳ [4] στενάζομεν (→ I, 559, 38 ff.; II, 318, 19 ff.). In v. 4 the apostle repeats the statement and explains it as follows: οἱ ὄντες ἐν τῷ σκήνει στενάζομεν βαρούμενοι. Existence in the house of the earthly body is felt to be a severe burden for Christians. It is a sign that they are not yet in the state of perfect redemption. Only in the moment when the mortal is swallowed up by life will the sighing which is a mark of all creatures in this age cease.

2. In R. 8:22-27 the apostle speaks of a triple sighing, that of all creation, that of Christians and that of the Spirit. This sequence is a crescendo. In v. 22 Paul declares that all creation up to this present sighs together [5] and with pain awaits regeneration. [6] The reason for the sighing is that through the fall of Adam creation

---

[4] ἐν τούτῳ in v. 2 is not to be taken adverbially but τῷ σκήνει (v. 1) is to be supplied (→ 381, 20 ff.): In this present state in which we are in the house of the earthly body, cf. Wnd. 2 K., ad loc. The ἐπιποθοῦντες gives the reason for the στενάζομεν. Less likely is the possibility considered in Wnd. 2 K., ad loc. that ἐπιποθοῦντες gives the result: Our sighing sets up a longing which carries with it the removal of the burden and which is directed to the heavenly οἰκητήριον.

[5] συστενάζω means "to sigh together," not "to sigh with." But this is not the common sighing and suffering of creation with the children of God; it is a sighing in which all non-human creation is at one, cf. Mi. R., ad loc.; also Schl. R., ad loc.: "All have a common pain which gives them a common complaint and the same yearning for redemption; these are not individual beings sighing and suffering alone."

[6] On this cf. A. M. Dubarle, "Le gémissement des créatures dans l'ordre divin du cosmos (R. 8:19-22)," RevThPh, 38 (1954), 445-465. Cf. also A. Viard, "Expectatio creaturae (R. 8:19-22)," Rev. Bibl., 59 (1952), 337-354.

is subject to bondage (v. 20). It waits with longing for the day when the glory of the children of God will be manifested. [7] But Christians sigh too, v. 23. To be sure, their situation differs from that of the rest of creation. For they are already a new creation in Christ and as first-fruits of eschatological being they possess the Spirit. Yet their body is still subject to corruption. Because they wait for the redemption of their body, namely, the transforming of their earthly body into the body of glory, they sigh. To the sighing of creation and the children of God there then corresponds the sighing of the Spirit, [8] v. 26 f. Since the reference is not to something which takes place in us, the apostle cannot be thinking of the sighing of Christians in prayer. He is referring rather to times when we are unable to pray, when because of our "weakness" we do not know what we ought to pray for. This means that he cannot have in view speaking in tongues [9] or the inarticulate stammering of ecstatics in worship. [10] What he is saying is rather that the Spirit acts in our place and intercedes for us, performing the function of a Paraclete [11] and helping us in our weakness in prayer. The process which Paul has in view is thus a process in the heavenly and divine sphere. [12] Hence the στεναγμοὶ ἀλάλητοι (v. 26) are not unspoken, wordless sighs but sighs which cannot be grasped in words, like the ἄρρητα ῥήματα of 2 C. 12:4. But God understands the language of the Spirit, "because he intercedes for the saints in a way which corresponds to the will of God," v. 27.

In the Herm. writings and later Jewish apoc. there is a certain par. to Paul's statements in 2 C. 5:2-4 and R. 8:22-27, but one cannot presuppose any direct influence on Paul. Κόρη κόσμου, 33 (Scott, I, 474, 22) says that souls are banished into human bodies. They groan at their distress (ὠδύροντο καὶ ἐστέναζον) because they are enclosed in wretched σκηνώματα (→ 383, 9 ff.) and they beg for redemption. [13] Gr. En. 9:10; 12:6 ref. to the laments of the slain souls of men [14] and to the sighing of heavenly powers under judgment. [15] Note may also be taken of 4 Esr. 9:38-10:24 where the wife Zion bewails the loss of her son and the destruction of men. Finally one may refer to the Naassene hymn in Hipp. Ref., V, 10, 2, which says of the soul: "If it is to-day in the realm of light, to-morrow it is already in misery, sunk deep in sorrow and tears. And wandering in the labyrinth, it seeks the exit in vain." [16]

---

[7] Mi. R., ad loc. rightly conjectures that the image of the woes of the Messiah underlies Paul's statement.

[8] Cf. on this W. Bieder, "Gebetswirklichkeit u. Gebetsmöglichkeit bei Pls. Das Gebet d. Geistes u. d. Beten im Geist," ThZ, 4 (1948), 22-40; J. Schniewind, "Das Seufzen d. Geistes R. 8:26, 27," Nachgelassene Reden u. Aufsätze (1952), 81-103.

[9] Zn. R., ad loc.

[10] Ltzm. R., ad loc.

[11] Paul does not use παράκλητος but he is obviously following a primitive Chr. παράκλητος tradition, Mi. R., ad loc., 174, n. 4. Cf. N. Johansson, Parakletoi (1940), 271-273.

[12] Cf. Mi. R., ad loc. But this is an intercessory-priestly process, not an apocalyptic one, as Mi. supposes.

[13] Cf. Wendland Hell. Kult., 182, n. 4: This is the mood of the Naassene hymn and also of the sighing of the creature in Paul.

[14] "The souls of the dead cry and mourn so that it reaches to the gates of heaven and their sighing has risen up (ἀνέβη ὁ στεναγμὸς αὐτῶν) and cannot escape the sight of the violence done on earth," Gr. En. 9:10.

[15] "The watchers of heaven who have left the holy eternal city and defiled themselves with women will have no peace nor remission of sins." Their children will be slain "and they will bewail the destruction of their children" (ἐπὶ τῇ ἀπωλείᾳ τῶν υἱῶν αὐτῶν στενάξουσιν), Gr. En. 12:6.

[16] Cf. on this whole section Mi. R., on 8:22 ff., 175, n. 3.

According to Hb. 13:17 salutary pastoral results are achieved when the leaders perform their responsible task with joy and not with sighing. Jm. 5:9 charges Christians so to order their mutual relations that they have no cause for sighing against one another. The reference is to inner sighing not to open complaints. [17] In the story of the curing of a deaf mute we read: "And looking up to heaven, he (Jesus) sighed, and saith unto him, Ephphatha, that is, Be opened" (Mk. 7:34). στενάζω here undoubtedly denotes a prayer-sigh.

There is no par. for the expression in the other Synoptists or Jn. But one may adduce Jn. 11:41 f. where Jesus follows a similar pattern of acts even though στενάζω is not used: "Jesus lifted up his eyes, and said ... he cried with a loud voice, Lazarus, come forth." Non-bibl. par. hardly shed light on the process with their equation of the acts of Jesus and ancient magical practices. The explanation has been given that looking up and sighing are part of the technique of healing, and that sighing is a means to effect the cure. [18] But sighing is preparatory in Jesus. It establishes the inner relation with God and represents explicit prayer for the power of healing. The healing action itself is solely and simply through the healing word. It is true that sighing plays a role in ancient magic (→ 601, 14 f.) but the historical par. pt. to a world of ideas quite alien to that of Jesus and the writers of the Gospels.

In Ac. 7:33 f. there is a series of quotations from Ex. V. 34 quotes Ex. 3:7 f. LXX. At his call Moses is given the divine assurance: ἰδὼν εἶδον τὴν κάκωσιν τοῦ λαοῦ μου τοῦ ἐν Αἰγύπτῳ, καὶ τοῦ στεναγμοῦ αὐτοῦ ἤκουσα, καὶ κατέβην ἐξελέσθαι αὐτούς.

C. The Post-Apostolic Period.

στενάζω and στεναγμός are rare in the post-apost. age. Herm. v., 3, 9, 6 contains a warning to the rich. They are so to act that those who suffer want do not sigh, lest their sighing rise up to the Lord. Mart. Pol., 2, 2 says of martyrs that they have achieved such bravery [19] that they do not sigh and groan in martyrdom — an idea also found in later Judaism: ὁ μεγαλόφρων καὶ 'Αβραμιαῖος νεανίας οὐκ ἐστέναξεν, 4 Macc. 9:21. [20] 1 Cl., 15, 6 simply quotes ψ 11:6. On the basis of passages like Rev. 21:4 or Is. 35:10; 51:11 later Chr. burial inscr. express the wish that the dead may be far from ὀδύνη καὶ λύπη καὶ στεναγμός καὶ πᾶν ἁμάρτημα, Preisigke Sammelbuch, I, 4949, 12 (753 A.D.) Similar formulae are common, e.g., I, 5716, 12; IV, 7428, 12; 7429, 8; 7430, 9; cf. III, 6133, 7: μὴ στέναζε πολλάκις.

J. Schneider

[17] Cf. Dib. Jk., *ad loc.*
[18] Kl. Mk., *ad loc.;* M. Dibelius, *Die Formgesch. d. Ev.*[4] (1961), 83 f. with n. 1.
[19] Cf. Pr.-Bauer[5], *s.v.* γενναῖος, "true," "noble" is a typical term for martyrs as in 4 Macc., cf. 1 Cl., 5, 1; Mart. Pol., 3, 1; 2, 1. Cf. H. W. Surkau, *Martyrien in jüd. u. frühchr. Zeit* (1938), 132: "Lauded in Polycarp and his disciples is their γενναιότης, and we have here once again a typical concept of later Jewish martyrs, and one that belongs to the settled vocabulary of Chr. martyrs too," cf. 2 Macc. 6:28, 31; 4 Macc. 6:10; 8:3.
[20] In explanation of Mart. Pol., 2, 2 cf. H. v. Campenhausen, *Die Idee d. Martyriums in d. alten Kirche* (1936), 89, esp. 154, n. 4: "Belief in an actual immunity to pain of a miraculous kind which was granted to martyrs, and which may often have been an actual accompaniment of ecstatic faith, is combined in Mart. Pol., 2, 2 with a magnifying of heroic indifference to pain which claims our admiration." Cf. also Surkau, *op. cit.,* 126-134.

---

† στενός, † στενοχωρία, † ατενοχωρέω

A. Profane Usage.

Attic στενός, Ionic στεινός (στενϝός) mean "narrow," "thin," "paltry," "poor," "wretched." We find τὸ στεῖνος "narrow place" in Hom. Il., 8, 476; 12, 66, "press" in battle 15, 426, "narrow pass" 23, 419 etc. From Thuc. we find the noun στενοχωρία "narrow place," and later the verb στενοχωρέω "to be squeezed, pressed," more commonly "to confine," "to compress." In the lit. sense the word is often used in topographical descriptions, Thuc., VII, 51, 2; 70, 6; Plat. Tim., 25a; Aesch. Pers., 413. In a transf. sense it is found from the Hell. period, medically in Hippocr. Praecepta, 8 (Littré, IX, 262) and in astrological [1] texts, and as a value concept it can denote the paltriness of a question or narrow-mindedness of exposition. [2] Finally it is used for the "straits" or "stresses" of inner or outer problems and difficulties. The exact meaning cannot always be given. Thus in Ps.-Plat. Ep., III, 319c it is not clear whether the ref. is to an external threat to the author on his departure or whether he feared the inner stress of a relation disrupted by his utterance. [3] Sometimes we find θλῖψις, θλίβω with στενοχωρία, στενοχωρέω. Antonyms are πλατύς, εὐρύς εὐρυχωρία, ἄνεσις etc., Aesch. Pers., 875; Hdt., II, 8, 3; VIII, 60, 2; Plat. Leg., V, 737a; Plut. Quaest. Conv. V, 6 (II, 679e-f).

Materially important here are esp. the statements of Hell. philosophy, namely, Stoicism, e.g., Ceb. Tab., [4] a work of morality from the 1st cent. A.D. wrongly ascribed to a Pythagorean of the 4th cent. B.C. Ceb. Tab., 15, 1-3 speaks of a narrow door, a little trodden way and a difficult ascent to true culture, ἀνάβασις στενὴ πάνυ... πρὸς τὴν ἀληθινὴν παιδείαν. [5] The idea that Chr. preaching is a means and way to such paideia finds a basis in the Gk. OT [6] and was adopted quite early in Chr. theology. [7] The obstacles, which are not always clearly perceived, are set forth in a fundamental statement in Epict. which is wholly in the spirit of the autarky of the sage: It is we ourselves who create inner and outer problems for ourselves by nurturing wrong ideas about fortune and misfortune and by building our lives on this false foundation. [8]

στενός κτλ. Pape, Liddell-Scott, s.v.; Walde-Pok., II, 627; Trench, 124 f.; F. Melzer, *Der chr. Wortschatz d. deutschen Sprache. Eine evangelische Darstellung* (1951), 152 f.

[1] F. Boll, *Aus d. Offenb. Johannis* (1914), 135: στενοχωρία is common in astrological texts with θλῖψις, e.g., Catal. Cod. Astr. Graec., VII, 169, 21.

[2] P. Giess., 40, Col II, 7 in an edict of the emperor Caracalla, July 11, 212.

[3] Cf. → n. 2; often also in Artemid. Onirocr., I, 66 (p. 61, 13); 79 (p. 78, 9); II, 3 (p. 88, 8) etc. Luc. Nigrinus, 13.

[4] Cebes figures in Plat. Phaed. *passim* as a pupil of Socrates.

[5] On the motif of the two ways → V, 43, 35 ff. (Hes. Op., 287 ff and the allegory of Prodicus about Hercules at the cross-roads in Xenoph. Mem., II, 1, 21-34) and → V, 72, n. 103, 105. For further material Kn. Did. on 1, 1.

[6] G. Bertram, "Der Begriff d. Erziehung in d. gr. Bibel," *Imago Dei, Festschr. G. Krüger* (1932), 33-51; also "Praeparatio evangelica in d. LXX," VT, 7 (1957), 228-230 → V, 603, 30 ff.

[7] "What we usually style rather vaguely as the Hellenising of the Chr. religion I would understand more concretely as the adoption of Gk. paideia by the Chr. religion and its transforming into the paideia Christi," W. Jaeger, "Paideia Christi," ZNW, 50 (1959), 2.

[8] Epict. Diss., I, 25, 26, 28. "For Epict. there is thus no θλῖψις or στενοχωρία in the bibl. sense," A. Bonhöffer, *Epict. u. d. NT* (1911), 118 f.

B. The Usage in the Greek Old Testament.

1. The word group is not very common in the Gk. OT. It relates to external events which overtake men. Topographically the adj. στενός (mostly צַר) occurs in the OT at Nu. 22:26 "narrow pass"; 4 Βασ. 6:1; Is. 49:20 "lack of space"; Jdt. 4:7 "narrow entry"; Prv. 23:27 "narrow well." The ref. in Zech. 10:11 seems to be to the narrow passage between the waters; the transl. takes it to be the "narrow" sea through which Israel passes. HT presupposes a transf. use of צָרָה.[9] It might be rendered: "And oppression (i.e., the Egypt. oppressors) perished in the sea, and the waves cast it (them) into the sea." The original HT Is. 30:20 undoubtedly means meagre bread and sparse water in the original.[10] In the first instance the transl., too, was meant lit., but it has to be taken fig.: bread which is eaten in affliction or trouble, and water drunk in oppression or anxiety[11] (LXX ἄρτον θλίψεως καὶ ὕδωρ στενόν, ΄ΑΣΘ: στενοχωρίας for לֶחֶם צָר וּמַיִם לָחַץ), denote a life under external pressure or psychologically in inner depression. LXX also sees a ref. to the evil of famine at Job 18:11, but the HT reads differently. At Jer. 30:7 Mas. has "time of anxiety" (עֵת־צָרָה; ΄ΑΣ: χρόνος θλίψεως) and the LXX at Ιερ. 37:7 (χρόνος στενός) is thus to be taken in the sense of "time of oppression." The ref. at 1 Βασ. 13:6 in both LXX and HT is to inner troubles, cf. also 2 Βασ. 24:14; 1 Ch. 21:13; Bar. 3:1; Sus. 22 Θ; 1 Βασ. 28:15 ΄ΑΣ; ψ 30:10 ΄Α; 68:18 ΄Α.

2. The noun στενοχωρία is rare and there is no fixed Hbr. original. We find it in connection with threats of punishment in Is. 8:22 f.; 30:6 (HT the uncommon צוּקָה or מוּצָק), also Dt. 28:53, 55, 57 always with θλῖψις and in a transf. sense like the original. The same two words are often used together eschatologically, cf. Εσθ. 1:1g with other apoc. expressions; they also occur ψ 118:143 Θ (LXX θλῖψις καὶ ἀνάγκη). In 1 Macc. 2:53 the ref. is to the tempting of Joseph,[12] cf. Sus. 22 Θ. Elsewhere the term means "mourning" in Εσθ. 4:17k, the "calamity of war" or "affliction" in 1 Macc. 13:3; 3 Macc. 2:10. Wis 5:3 has στενοχωρία for the anxiety of the ungodly as compared with the justification of the righteous by God, their terror leading to fear and remorse. This describes the eschatological situation.

3. The verb στενοχωρέω occurs 5 times in the LXX and twice in Σ. It relates to external straits or oppression. In Ju. 16:16 B it means "to oppress with words" for the hapax legomenon אלץ (Α παρενοχλέω). παρενοχλέω is used in Ju. 14:17. The Hbr. original varies. It is צרר (from צַר = στενός) in Is. 49:19. The original in 1 Βασ. 22:2 Σ is מָצוֹק (→ line 20 f.) and Is. 29:2 צוּק. At Is. 28:20 the LXX drops the Hbr. image of the too narrow couch and has στενοχωρούμενοι in a transf. sense.

C. The Occurrence of the Word Group in the New Testament.

1. στενός, Mt. 7:13, 14 and Lk. 13:24 (→ V, 70, 17 ff.; VI, 922, 22 ff.).

In the sayings of Jesus we find the figure of the narrow gate or door in Mt. 7:13 f. and Lk. 13:24 → III, 178, 6 ff.[13] Combined with this in Mt. is the metaphor of the two ways and the two gates. The adjective στενός occurs only in this connection

---

[9] Cf. K. Marti in Kautzsch, ad loc.; T. H. Robinson, Die zwölf kleinen Propheten, Hndbch. AT, I, 14² (1954), ad loc. Luther: "sea of anxiety."

[10] Vg: Panem artum et aquam brevem.

[11] In Luther and some other Protestant translations the understanding of the Gk. OT prevails, whereas Jerome's Vg follows the HT literally.

[12] H. Gunkel, Gn., Handkomm. AT³ (1910) on 39:7-20; J. H. Korn, "Πειρασμός. Die Versuchung des Gläubigen in d. griech. Bibel," BWANT, 20 (1937), 63 f.

[13] Lk. 13:24 θύρα, vl. πύλη.

in the NT. It is thus found in an invitation. In Lk. it is the answer to the question about the small number of the saved, and it has a particular urgency here. "Therefore strive" is the introduction, cf. Lk. 16:16. Mt., on the other hand, offers an impressive prophetic admonition [14] by warningly contrasting the broad gate and the broad way with the strait gate and the narrow way. Most men — it is assumed — ignore the admonition and warning, not so much because they are fast bound in the earthly, but rather because they are not ready to accept the new and alien authority of Jesus and to tread the narrow way to which He directs them, passing through the strait gate which in the last analysis He Himself claims to be, Mt. 19:22; Jn. 10:7. How narrow the gate is may be seen from the image of the camel (→ III, 593, 19 ff.) which can pass through the eye of a needle more easily than a rich man through the gate to the kingdom of God, Mk. 10:25; Mt. 19:24; Lk. 18:25. [15] The contrast between a broad gate and a narrow gate raises difficulties for some, but we can easily think in terms of the narrow way and the broad way. The former is for the small company of the elect, the other for the great mass of men. There is no mention of special hazards confronting those who walk on the narrow way. Only when the attributes στενός and τεθλιμμένος are taken in the sense of the OT trouble and anxiety (→ 605, 10 ff.) is what was no doubt an original saying of Jesus, which was strictly eschatological in character and which spoke of entry into God's kingdom [16] on the one side and the kingdom of hell on the other, changed into a twofold ethical saying which speaks of the possibilities of man along the lines of the two-way image so common among both Jews and Greeks (→ V, 43, 35 ff.; 53, 49 ff.; 61, 19 ff.). [17] As concerns the combining of gate and way in Mt. 7:13b, 14, the concept of the gate is sometimes regarded as an interpolation, first in 7:14 to establish a connection with the image of the gate in 13a, then in 13b to complete the parallelism with 14. [18]

2. στενοχωρία, στενοχωρέω in the Pauline Tradition.

In Paul the noun στενοχωρία occurs 4 times and the verb στενοχωρέω 3 times in varied connections. In the first instance the concept is a negative one in Paul. As in the prophetic threats of the OT (→ 605, 19 f.) the noun is used for the

---

[14] Bultmann Trad., 126.

[15] Cl. Al. Quis Div. Salv., 26, 7 was already combining the sayings about the needle's eye and the narrow way: On the confined way the rich man is at a disadvantage as compared with the camel. Cf. Wellh. Mt. on 7:13 f.

[16] Philo Agric., 104 reads "But the paths of reason, reflection and other virtues, if not untrodden, are not easily traversible; for only a small company of men treads them (the company of those) who have devoted themselves to true wisdom and who seek fellowship only with the morally good unencumbered by anything else." Acc. to Poster. C., 154 ff. God changes what at first seems to be a hard way into a highway, cf. Sir. 4:17 and on this Bertram Erziehung (→ n. 6), 41 f. The image is slightly different in Slav. En. 42:10: "Crooked (?) is the way of this vain world, but the way to life is straight." Cf. S. Wibbing, "D. Tugend- u. Lasterkataloge im NT," Beih. ZNW, 25 (1959), 33-42, 61 f. → V, 57, 35 ff.; 63, 11 ff.

[17] Chr. exegesis, following the Jewish Hell. tradition, integrated Mt. 7:13 f. into the paideia Christi, cf. Chrys. Hom. in Mt., 23, 6 on 7:13 f. (MPG, 57 [1862], 315): "He instructs His hearers not to follow the easy-going mass but the hardship of the tiny company."

[18] The present form of the Mt. tradition suggests an expansion or embellishment which expunges the eschatological character of the sayings, though cf. A. Harnack, Sprüche u. Reden Jesu (1907), 49 f., who regards Q as original. Lk. has adapted an extract from Q to his own purpose.

revelation of God's wrath.[19] It is well-nigh impossible to differentiate between θλῖψις and στενοχωρία in R. 2:8 f.[20] The use of the two synonyms together is for increased effect. Where Paul has two nouns like the OT, we should perhaps prefer an adjective and noun: "severe affliction." What smites the sinner is the inner and outer tribulation which robs him of peace, 2:10.[21] The two terms relate to present and future experiences on earth, but they also carry a reference to the Last Judgment → III, 940, 35 ff.[22] According to R. 8:35 Christians in their following of the Lord are by no means exempt from earthly afflictions.[23] They have to bear in full measure what the saints of the OT had to bear again and again. But affliction and distress, and whoever is behind them, cannot separate believers from the God whom they follow (R. 5:3-5) and thereby bring about their dereliction.[24] στενοχωρία and στενοχωρέω also occur in hymnal contexts in 2 C. 4:8 and 6:4.[25] If one may detect here stylistic and material parallels to the Hellenistic diatribe, the real content of the sayings, the passion piety of the apostle orientated to Christ, is without model or parallel. In four expressions, each with two participial concepts, the apostle delineates the affliction and its in no sense definitive effect, expressing the truth that he is oppressed but not crushed.[26] If trouble and affliction are put first here (→ III, 146, 36 ff.), they are best taken as a comprehensive anticipation of the expressions which follow, as in R. 8:35. 2 C. 6:3-10 contains an explicit list of afflictions. Paul's own life and sufferings are set out in this depiction of the servant of God (6:4). In what follows patience (→ IV, 587, 11 ff.) is to be regarded as

---

[19] R. 2:9 describes the eschatological judgment.

[20] With a ref. to 2 C. 4:8 στενοχωρία is usually taken to be stronger than θλῖψις, cf. B. Weiss, *Der Br. an d. Römer, Krit.-exeget. Komm. über d. NT*⁹ (1899), ad loc., who quotes Is. 8:22; Dt. 28:53. H. Grotius, Annotationes in NT, ed. C. E. v. Windheim (1769), ad loc. refers to Is. 30:6 צָרָה וְצוּקָה. Like Thomas Aquinas, Super Epistolas S. Pauli Lectura, ed. R. Cai (1953) on R. 8:35 some distinguish between external affliction and inner anxiety, or, like Bengel on R. 2:9, between present affliction and anxiety about the future: θλῖψις, *afflictio premit*; στενοχωρία *aestuat et urget ... Nam ira Dei eo tendit, ut creatura peccans ... discat odisse se ipsam.* Luther, *Römerbriefvorlesung* (1515/16), WA, 56 (1938), 196, 17 ff., ad loc. combines trouble and anxiety as consequences of wrath and displeasure. The ungodly and even at times the righteous can be betrayed into this hopeless situation. Cf. Calvin on R. 2:9 (Corp. Ref., 77, 35): *ex quatuor quae recensentur duo posteriora quasi effectus esse priorum. Nam qui Deum sibi adversum iratumque sentiunt, extemplo prorsus conteruntur.*

[21] A. Jülicher, *Der Br. an d. Römer, Schr. NT*, II³ (1917), ad loc.: anxiety and torment, the opposite of peace.

[22] Eth. En. 98:10: Day of destruction, of great judgment, of affliction and of great shame for your spirit.

[23] 2 Cl., 20, 1 refers to the earthly affliction which the slaves of God must suffer as compared with the wicked. In Herm. both verb and noun are often combined with the concept of sorrow, v., 4, 3, 4; m., 5, 1, 3; 10, 2, 6.

[24] Calvin on R. 8:35 (Corp. Ref., 77, 165): *Qui enim persuasus est de Divina erga se benevolentia, potis est in gravissimis afflictionibus subsistere.* Bengel, ad loc. notes that Paul does not ask what can separate us but who, for behind the forces and the affliction are enemies.

[25] R. Bultmann, *Der Stil d. paul. Predigt u die kynisch-stoische Diatribe* (1910), 71, 73, 80 f.; R. Höistad, "Eine hell. Par. z. 2 K. 6:3 ff.," Coni. Neot., 9 (1944), 22-27; A. Fridrichsen, "Zum Thema Pls. u. d. Stoa. Eine stoische Stilparallele z. 2 K. 4:8 f.," ibid., 27-31 (also on 2 C. 6:4 f.).

[26] Weiss, op. cit., (→ n. 20), on R. 2:8 f. compares R. 2:8 f. with Is. 8:22. There is no impasse for Paul, no spiritual exhaustion, so Didym. in Staab on 2 C. 4:8. Cf. also Calvin on 2 C. 4:8 (Corp. Ref., 78, 58), Bengel, also Grotius, who transl. back: נלחצים ולא נחלשים "oppressed, but not weakened."

the master concept. Three series of three expressions [27] each then follow, and στενοχωρίαι comes in the first with ἀνάγκαι [28] between θλίψεις and it. 2 C. 12:10 continues the list of tribulations in 11:23 ff. after a reference to the revelations Paul has been given (12:1 ff.) and then to the thorn (→ 412, 8 ff.) in his flesh, 12:7. 2 C. 12:10, under the basic concept of "infirmities," speaks of reproaches, necessities, persecutions, and then distresses; "for Christ's sake" is added with a general reference to all these. Here, then, στενοχωρία is at the heart of the passion piety of Paul. [29]

In 2 C. 6:12, in his personal conflict with the Corinthians, Paul uses the verb στενοχωρέω with reference to both his own attitude and theirs. The charge [30] of narrowness has been brought against him by the church. He rejects such accusations. [31] It is the Corinthians themselves who have created difficulties for Paul and let themselves be driven into opposition to him. Nevertheless, Paul's appeal to the church is from the heart. [32] His mouth is wide open to the Corinthians, and his heart, too, is broad [33] and ready to receive them with all their worries and suspicions, their complaints and accusations. They have no need to fear any narrowness of heart. So the apostle hopes that they can overcome their own narrowness of heart [34] and show themselves to be equally open to him, → IV, 702, 19 ff.

Bertram

---

[27] Bengel, *ad loc.*: *sequuntur ter tria patienda, quibus patientia exercetur pressurae, plagae, labores. Primus ternarius continet genera, secundus species adversorum, tertius spontanea.*
[28] Cf. 1 Th. 3:7; Weiss on R. 2:8 f.
[29] J. Schneider, "Die Passionsmystik d. Pls.," UNT, 15 (1929), 52-61.
[30] Wnd. 2 K., *ad loc.*
[31] Ltzm. K., *ad loc.*
[32] Early exegesis took the passage didactically, pedagogically and paraenetically, so Severian of Gabala, Didym. and Phot. acc. to Staab, 294; 31; 591.
[33] Bengel, *ad loc.*: *sat spatii habet cor nostrum ad vos capiendos.*
[34] Grotius, *op. cit.* (→ n. 20), *ad loc.* קְצַרְתֶּם. The term is used here for inner anxiety as in Epict. → 604, n. 8.

† στερεός, † στερεόω, † στερέωμα

A. Greek Usage.

στερεός, from the root *ster-,* cf. German "starr," "störrisch," with guttural expansion "stark" and labial expansion "sterben," Eng. "starve,"[1] means "stiff," "tight," "rigid," *rigidus,* also "hard," "obstinate," "firm," "true," "healthy," "ripe" (grain),[2] *validus, integer, perfectus,* lit. of bodies, objects and materials, transf. of the inner disposition and its forms of expression. The adj. is fairly common. But outside the Bible the verb στερεόω is rare; it means "to make stiff, strong, firm, hard," and the noun στερέωμα means accordingly "what is made firm or thick," "basis," "foundation," "solid body," "support," e.g., skeleton.[3] Already in Hom. we have ref. to hearts "harder" (στερεωτέρη) than stone, Od., 23, 103. In a transf. sense we find στερεῶς ἀποειπεῖν, Il., 9, 510; ἀρνεῖσθαι, 23, 42, in contrast to flattering words those that are hard Il., 12, 267, serious or mortal sins, Soph. Ant., 1262, hard threats, Aesch. Prom., 173. In antithesis to κενός or κοῖλος and with πλήρης the term is used of the elements, Aristot. Metaph., 1, 4, p. 985b, 7, cf. Phys., I, 5, p. 188a, 22 f. In Aristot. and Plat. there is a mathematical use for solid bodies.[4] There can be nothing solid without earth, says Plat. Tim., 31b, cf. 43c. Acc. to Plat. Phaedr., 246c the soul seeks matter and combines itself with a body. Cosmologically (aether-earth) and anthropologically the group belongs to the negative side of matter.[5]

B. Septuagint Use.

Development in the Bible is influenced by the choice of στερέωμα for רָקִיעַ in the creation story. The concept of the firmament is taken from ancient oriental cosmology. Perhaps the idea is that of the vault of heaven as an embossed bowl[6] or of the heavenly dyke of the zodiac,[7] for the primary meaning of the root רקע is "to stamp firm."[8] στερέωμα is used for רָקִיעַ 9 times in Gn. 1 and 4 times in the vision at the call of Ez. in Ez. 1, also once in the vision in Ez. 10:1 and elsewhere in the hymns in Ps. 19(18):2; 150:1 and Sir. 43:1, 8.[9] στερέωμα thus acquires a new meaning derived from biblical

---

στ ε ρ ε ό ς κτλ. [1] Pokorny, 1022-32; Walde-Pokorny, II, 627-632; Boisacq. Hofmann, *s.v.*

[2] Preisigke Wört., *s.v.*

[3] Skeleton as distinct from bones etc. Aristot. Part. An., II, 9, p. 655a, 22.

[4] H. Bonitz, Index Aristotelicus[2] (1955), *s.v.;* F. Astius, Lex. Platonicum (1956), *s.v.;* Philo's usage is influenced by Gk. philosophy, cf. Leisegang, *s.v.;* K. Staehle, *D. Zahlenmystik bei Philon v. Alex.* (1931), Index, *s.v.* From this western learning has become familiar with the term stereometry and related concepts.

[5] Aristot. Gen. Corr., I, 8, p. 324b, 25-326b, 28 often uses στερεός in his account of the teachings of Emped., Leucipp, and Democr.

[6] In Phoen. מרקע means "embossed bowl"; the Hbr. root רקע "to beat out," "to hammer firm" is explained in terms of this [Fohrer].

[7] A. Jeremias, *Hndbch. d. Altorient. Geisteskultur* (1929), 139.

[8] Acc. to J. Wellhausen, *Prolegomena*[6] (1905), 388, n. 1, רקע in the q means "to hasten." It cannot mean "to spread out" nor (from רקע pi) "to beat thin" (→ n. 6), רָקָע "sheet metal." On Is. 45:12, where στερεόω (usually רקע) is used for נטה, cf. P. Katz, "Two Kindred Corruptions in the Septuagint," VT, 1, (1951), 265.

[9] LXX thus has στερέωμα for the Hbr. everywhere except at Da. 12:3. It also uses

and oriental cosmology. Like the Lat. *firmamentum* it denotes the solid vault of heaven, and its formation or establishment can be expressed by the verb. God has established the vault of heaven in its solidity ψ 32:6: [10] ἐστερεώθησαν for the vaguer עָשָׂה,[11] cf. Hos. 13:4; Is. 45:12; 48:13. God is the revered one of the firmament, Dt. 33:26; [12] cf. Δα. 3:56. The verb στερεόω is also used when God is said to have established fast the earth ψ 74:4; 92:1; [13] 135:6; Is. 42:5; 44:24; [14] cf. also Sir. 42:17, 25. In the par. ψ 17:3 and 2 Βασ. 22:2 (πέτρα) the connection with מְצוּדָה (ὀχύρωμα) "fortress" [15] yields the image of the celestial retreat, the sure refuge with God the Deliverer and Liberator. The transl. of סֶלַע by στερέωμα avoids the misunderstanding of an object-ification of God, as also in ψ 70:3. [16] In Is. 51:1, however, there is an even greater shift; the pass becomes an act., and thus any false ref. of στερεὰ πέτρα to Yahweh, which was surely not intended by the HT, [17] is ruled out. The adj. στερεός does not share in the transcendental development of στερέωμα and στερεόω in the LXX. The use remains within the framework of ordinary Gk. usage with a negative thrust where the ref. is to people. In Ιερ. 37(30):14 it is God who visits His people with "hard chastisement" (παιδεία στερεά), cf. 15:18; Lam. 2:4. As God Himself is constancy and firmness, He confers this both in the good and also in the bad. He confirms the righteous, 1 Βασ. 2:1. [18]

---

it frequently (29 times in all) in free transl. of the HT, mostly for "firmament." Θ has στερέωμα at Da. 12:3 for the radiance of heaven (LXX οὐρανός), while Job 37:18 Θ has it for רָקִיעַ = "firmament." The HT here is תַּרְקִיעַ לִשְׁחָקִים. G. Hölscher, *Das Buch Hi.*, *Hndbch. AT*, I, 17[2] (1952), ad loc. transl. שְׁחָקִים here by "high clouds," A. Jeremias, *Das AT im Lichte d. Alten Orients*[4] (1930), 52 rejects "clouds," but G. Fohrer [in a letter] supports "cloud cover." At Dt. 33:26 LXX has στερέωμα for שְׁחָקִים, 1 QM 10:11 מפרש שחקים; H. Bardtke, *Die Handschriftenfunde am Toten Meer*, II (1958), 225 transl. "who spreads out clouds," but J. Carmignac, *La Règle de la Guerre* (1958), 146-8 has the more correct: "qui a déployé le firmament," and O. Betz *Offenbarung u. Schriftforschung in d. Qumransekte* (1960), 53 seems to prefer this.

[10] Orig. Comm. in Joh., 1, 39 on 1:1, on the basis of Ps. 33:6, expressly emphasises the solid material of the firmament acc. to the plan (*logos*) of God. From Ex. 24:10 Philo finds in the firmament, which is the place of the unmoved and unchanging God, and which stands for the visible world, at least an indirect image of God; the *logos* is the true image.

[11] Here, too, the meaning of the verb στερεόω is controlled by the noun. Thus it can be used for עָשָׂה and for verbs which in themselves presuppose other ideas, e.g., נטה, טפח "to spread out."

[12] Under obvious Jewish influence the God Iao, as ruler of the firmament, is invoked on an ancient cursing tablet, cf. R. Wünsch, *Antike Fluchtafeln*, KIT, 20 (1912), 18, 22.

[13] On Ps. 93:1 cf. H. J. Kraus, *Die Psalmen, Bibl. Komm. AT*, 15 (1960), ad loc. and the catena on R. 9:33 in Staab, 69.

[14] Cf. also ᾿Α Is. 26:4.

[15] A. Jirku, *Altorient. Komm. z. AT* (1923), on ψ 18:15 (᾿Α probably στερεός); LXX also has στερέωμα for סֶלַע at ψ 70:3. Cf. on this G. Bertram, "Der Sprachschatz d. LXX u. der d. hbr. AT," ZAW, 57, (1939), 93-98.

[16] At ψ 27:1; 30:3; 61:8; Is. 30:29; Dt. 32:31 ᾿Α and some other Hexapla transl. have στερεός for צוּר "rock" as a term for God. LXX simply has θεός, ΣΘ often φύλαξ, cf. also ψ 60:3 Σ, perhaps also ᾿ΑΘ R. 9:32 f.; 1 Pt. 2:8 take Is. 8:14 christologically. LXX has πέτρας πτώματι, ᾿Α στερεὸν σκάνδαλον. Is. 50:7: πρόσωπον ὡς στερεὰ πέτρα, is taken christ-ologically with a ref. to the passion in Barn., 5, 14; Just. Apol., 38, 3. The symbol of the hard rock in Is. 50:7 is ref. in Barn., 6, 3 to the fact that "the Lord has powerfully offered His flesh (Himself)" → VI, 98, 30 ff.; 99, 24 ff.

[17] The mythical concept of derivation from a rock, here equated with Abraham, pts. in another direction, cf. B. Duhm, *Das Buch Js., Handkomm. AT*, III, 1[4] (1922), ad loc.

[18] Cf. ᾿Α ψ 26:5; Σ ψ 26:14; 30:25.

Acc. to Hab. 1:12 Mas. Yahweh is the rock who summons a people to correction. [19] LXX read a form of יצר "to form" for צור "rock" and transl. accordingly. [20] The Hexapla transl. also felt the HT use of rock with Yahweh to be a difficulty and evaded it in different ways. The group is also used for "hardening," Da. 8:24, cf. Jer. 5:3; ψ 17:18; Ez. 2:4 (στερεοκάρδιος). ἐστερεώθη in Is. 51:6 is based on textual corruption. [21]

Again in O. Sol. 22:12 (after the destruction of the world "the foundation will be for all thy rock"), the rock, like the way in 22:11, is to be taken as a figure for hypostatised truth [22] and even as a personification of the Messiah. It is the στερεὰ πέτρα which will be the foundation of God's kingdom. O. Sol. 31:9 also alludes to Is. 50:7 and the passion story attested in the OT: "I stood there impregnable like a solid rock" in the waves of persecution. [23] The poet experiences the sureness of this foundation in the Last Judgment, O. Sol. 35:4 f., cf. 24:7, [24] where we are perhaps to presuppose στηρίζω (→ 653, 8 ff.) or βεβαιόω (→ I, 600, 14 ff.).

C. The Jewish Gnostic View of the World.

In the OT only one firmament is presupposed. Philo keeps to this, Op. Mund., 36. But in later Judaism, as in the Bab.-Iranian tradition, there is evidence of the idea of several firmaments. God's throne is not related to these, nor are they identical with the supreme heaven as His seat. In them is the kingdom of Sammael, the prince of this world, and his hosts, Asc. Is. 7:9; 10:28. [25] Unrecognised (cf. Paul in 1 C. 2:8) the Redeemer comes down through the gates of the firmaments past the guards (Pist. Soph., 10) to pass through the eternal gates on His ascent (Ps. 24) [26] and into the intermediate kingdom, where He liberates the prisoners of the archons, Eph. 4:8. [27] Acc. to Pist. Soph., 11 the gates open to Him and the powers and dominions fall down before Jesus as He ascends into heaven, cf. Asc. Is. 11:23. The same or a similar cosmology is presupposed elsewhere, e.g., the Mandaean tradition, Lidz. Ginza R, 198, 7 f.; 231, 5 ff.; Lidz. Joh., 8-9, [28] cf. also the Hermetic tractates [29] or the account of religious strife in Persia. [30] The concept is

---

[19] In 'A the thought of firmness or hardness is transferred to the enemy summoned by Yahweh, also Σ. 1 Q p Hab 5:1 ff. claims the solidity of the rock for the community, which has the Messianic task of judging and correcting all nations and sinners in its own people, so essentially G. Molin, Die Söhne des Lichtes (1952), 13. Bardtke, op. cit., 127 still has the address "O rock" to God. But he finds it also in 5:6 (צור for צר affliction) and thus arrives at the same interpretation.

[20] Cf. G. Bertram, "Der Begriff d. Erziehung in d. griech. Bibel," Imago Dei, Festschr. G. Krüger (1932), 49.

[21] Cf. Katz, op. cit. (→ n. 8), 262-5; Ex. 14:17 Αλλ has στερεόω for חזק pi. In Qumran חזק hi is used for firm adherence to the Law, cf. H. Braun, Spätjüd.-häret. u. frühchr. Radikalismus (1957), 107.

[22] Cf. also O. Sol. 11:3, 5; G. Diettrich, Die Oden Salomos (1911) ref. to the Essenes in connection with 11:5 and Mt. 16:18 in connection with 22:12.

[23] Acc. to A. Harnack, Ein jüd.-chr. Psalmbuch aus d. ersten Jhdt. n. Chr. (1910) this is a self-predication of the Messiah. The text is Chr.

[24] Cf. W. Bauer, D. Oden Salomos, KIT, 64 (1933), ad loc.

[25] J. Kroll, "Gott u. Hölle. Der Mythus vom Descensuskampfe," Stud. d. Bibliothek Warburg, 20 (1932), 60-67.

[26] G. Bertram, "Der religionsgesch. Hintergrund des Begriffs d. 'Erhöhung' in d. LXX," ZAW, 68 (1956), 57-71; also Art. "Erhöhung" in RAC, VI.

[27] Reitzenstein Ir. Erl., 112; Lidz. Liturg,. 78.

[28] Kroll, op. cit., 283-288; cf. Lidz Ginza, R, 354, 6 ff.

[29] C. F. G. Heinrici, Die Hermesmystik u. d. NT (1918), 24 f., 184; Reitzenstein Poim., 46 f., cf. Stob. Ecl., I, 463, 10 ff.

[30] H. Usener, Das Weihnachtsfest (1889), 35; F. J. Dölger, ΙΧΘΥΣ. Der hl. Fisch in d. antiken Religionen u. im Christentum, II (1922), 254.

not clear or precise, but acc. to these ideas the way of the soul, the Gnostic, or the disciple follows that of the Redeemer through the firmaments. In Gk. outside the bibl. sphere στερέωμα is not attested in the sense of firmament, and even *firmamentum* takes on its specific sense only in the Bible [31] and Chr. Latinity, e.g., Aug. De Genesi ad litteram, II, 1.

D. New Testament Usage.

1. στερεός.

In Hb. 5:12, 14 in the metaphor of "solid food" στερεός is used in a very special connection so that there is hardly any relation to usage elsewhere in the Bible. Food is here called "solid," and as the less readily digestible nourishment of adults it is contrasted with the lighter fluid food appropriate to children. [32] These figurative expressions are based on an academic tradition of Hellenistic Judaism [33] which contains elements of the wisdom of Stoic pedagogy. [34] In the Christian community the source of nourishment is basically the same for all ages, namely, revelation. [35] But when Hb. 6:1 (→ VI, 209, 6 ff.) lists the first principles of Christian instruction, there remains as solid food for the perfect a Christian gnosis at the heart of which, as in Paul, are the cross and exaltation to the right hand of God, Hb. 12:2. [36]

As compared with Gnostics who change or develop the Christian hope of the resurrection in a spiritualising sense, 2 Tm. 2:9 refers to the sure foundation stone of faith: ὁ μέντοι στερεὸς θεμέλιος τοῦ θεοῦ ἕστηκεν. God Himself is the firm foundation, and He gives it. θεμέλιος (→ III, 63, 1 ff.) corresponds to the πέτρα (→ VI, 95, 9 ff.) and λίθος (→ IV, 268, 10 ff.) in many OT and NT metaphors. As God is the rock in the OT, so here He is the foundation stone, which is also laid by Him. στερεός as an attribute belongs integrally to Him; it is a term for God in Aquila → n. 16. We thus have all the associations which are bound up with στερεός and στερέωμα in the OT → 609, 20 ff. God is He by whom the world and the believing community stand (ἕστηκεν). [37] He is constant and He makes constant, and He demands true purifying and preparation, v. 20, 21. The orientation

---

[31] Cf. Heinrici, *op. cit.*, 108, n. 1 and on this E. v. Dobschütz, *Nachträge,* 222. One may also presume oriental-Jewish influence in the gt. Paris magic pap., which says of the name of the god invoked that it is διῆκον ἀπὸ τοῦ στερεώματος μέχρις τοῦ βάθους, Preis. Zaub., I, 4, 1210

[32] In Diod. S., 2, 4, 4 f. cheese is solid food as compared with milk. Philo Agric., 9 has ἐκ πυρῶν πέμματα, → γάλα I, 645, 35 ff.; βρῶμα I, 642, 23 ff.; → νήπιος IV, 920, 14 ff.

[33] Materially Philo Congr., 19; Som., II, 9 demands advance from academic instruction of the child in theoretical disciplines to the practical instruction of the adult in virtues. He makes the same distinction between the προκόπτων and the τέλειος as Stoicism. In Agric., 159 the ἀρχόμενος comes first; this is the νήπιος of 9; → προκοπή VI, 709, 25 ff.; W. Völker, *Fortschritt u. Vollendung bei Philon v. Alex.* (1938), 158-198.

[34] Stoic pedagogy often distinguishes between the intellectual and philosophical food of adults on the one side and the playful element in the instruction of children on the other, cf. the comm., also A. Bonhöffer, *Epict. u. d. NT* (1911), 61-63, who quotes Quint. Inst. Orat., II, 4, 5 and Epict Diss., II, 16, 39; III, 24, 9; Clemen, 316 f.

[35] Mi. Hb., *ad loc.*; cf. Calvin on Hb., *ad loc.* (Corp. Ref., 83, 66): sic etiam initio lac e scriptura sugendum est ut eius pane deinde vescamur. Caeterum ita inter lac et firmum cibum discernit, ut sanam doctrinam utroque nomine intelligat.

[36] On Hb. 12:2 cf. G. Bertram, "Die Himmelfahrt Jesu vom Kreuz aus," *Festschr. A. Deissmann* (1927), 213-217.

[37] This ἕστηκεν is in Philo a basic saying about God: Poster. C., 30; Leg. All., II, 83 etc., cf. Leisegang, *s.v.* ἱστάναι; Völker, *op. cit.*, 326.

of the saying about the foundation stone is not in the first instance to the Church [38] or the system of doctrines but to the individual members of the believing community whom God has known. [39] Hence the foundation stone referred to is the constancy and faithfulness with which God calls His community afresh each day, and the individual within it, [40] and holds them fast to Jesus Christ, the Crucified and Risen Lord. In this way He is the firm foundation of faith. [41]

With reference to men the adjective στερεός is used in the admonition in 1 Pt. 5:9 to resist the devil: ᾧ ἀντίστητε στερεοὶ τῇ πίστει. Those addressed are not to hold fast to the faith but steadfast [42] in faith they are to resist the devil. τῇ πίστει can be taken either as a dative of relation (Ac. 16:5; 1 C. 14:20) or as a dative of cause (R. 4:20). πίστις is the chief term, and στερεοί could well be left out without any essential alteration of sense. It simply serves to strengthen the admonition to resist, cf. 2 C. 1:24: τῇ γὰρ πίστει ἑστήκατε. [43] Here as in the other NT references the use of στερεός is positive.

2. στερεόω.

Ac. 3:7 and 3:16 seem to be recounting a quasi-medical process. But στερεόω is not a medical term. It is to be interpreted in the light of the OT → 609, 27 ff. [44] As the term relates to creation in the OT, so the NT healing story proclaims a process of creation or new creation. The feet and ankles of the lame man become firm. According to 3:15 it is the "author of life" in whose name the apostles act. [45]

The saying: ἐστερεοῦτο τῇ πίστει καὶ ἐπερίσσευον τῷ ἀριθμῷ (Ac. 16:5), in this form which is supported by MS E, [46] refers to the internal and external growth of the churches, and, like 2:41 and other verses, it constitutes a concluding formula which in content corresponds to the sayings in 1 Pt. 5:9 and Col. 2:5. The stress on inner strengthening "in faith" is in material agreement with the NT concept of God, but if it were original [47] one would expect it to come second.

---

[38] But cf. H. Grotius, Annotat. in NT, II, 2 (1757), ad loc.: Deus, moliens civitatem illam aeternam, decreta quaedam substravit, velut fundamenta, quae manent inconcussa.

[39] Calvin on 2 Tm., ad loc. (Corp. Ref., 80, 370): nos revocat ad Dei electionem, quam metaphorice appellat fundamentum, firmam et stabilem eius constantiam hoc nomine indicans… proprium Dei est, nosse quinam sint sui.

[40] B. Weiss, Die Br. Pauli an Tm., Krit.-exeget. Komm. über d. NT, 11⁷ (1902), ad loc., rejects the institutional and dogmatic interpretation; God calls persons to the fellowship of faith.

[41] That the ref. is to the foundation of faith and not of the church may be seen from the preceding v. 2:18, in which the danger of turning from the faith is considered. Eph. 2:20; 1 Tm. 3:15 are related sayings, but they establish the distinctiveness of 2 Tm. 2:19.

[42] Calvin on 1 Pt., ad loc. (Corp. Ref., 83, 289) transl.: firmi fide (Vg fortes fide), and comments: in fide satis esse firmitudinis.

[43] The στερεῇ φρενί in Quintus Smyrnaeus Posthomerica, 5, 597; 9, 508 (ed. A. Zimmermann [1891]), a poet of the 4th cent. A.D., is different; in this expression, quoted by Pape and Pr.-Bauer, s.v. στερεός, στερεός is the chief term and φρήν is dispensable.

[44] Grotius, op. cit., ad loc. ref. to Ps. 93:1 כּוּן ni (cj acc. to Ps. 75:4 תכן pi BHK³); F. Delitzsch, הברית החדשה (Hbr. transl. of the NT) (1954), ad loc. usually has חזק. C. C. Torrey, The Composition and Date of Ac. (1916), 14-16 conjectures תקף which is rare in the OT.

[45] Cf. Haench. Ag.¹³, ad loc.

[46] Cf. A. C. Clark, The Acts of the Apostles (1933), ad loc. and 237, who quotes Cod E (Laudianus pars Latina): confirmabantur fidei, follows the Gk. case connection.

[47] Cod D does not have τῇ πίστει, so that στερεόω is directly par. to περισσεύω with the same dat. object τῷ ἀριθμῷ.

3. στερέωμα.

Paul in Col. 2:5 weaves into the introductory admonitions the acknowledgment: "Though absent in the flesh I am with you in the spirit and see that your faith in Christ is orderly and firm." The reference here is to faith more precisely defined by the concepts of orderliness and firmness. [48] The term τάξις reminds us of the metaphor of a military division drawn up in ranks. [49] στερέωμα, which is used for the solidity of a hard, because self-enclosed body, might also suggest a military metaphor in the sense of a castle or bulwark → 610, 7 ff. [50] Paul is speaking of men, of the believing attitude of the community confirmed in a fixed order; [51] Col. 1:23 and 2:7 allude to the same thing in other words. In spite of the preceding and then repeated ὑμῶν, the genitive τῆς πίστεως goes with the two concepts of order and of steadfastness, and gives them their content. [52] The author is presupposing for the Colossian church the situation claimed for the righteous by the Psalmists. [53] They are pressed by enemies, but they can stand fast in the stronghold of their faith and trust. [54] In the NT faith in Christ is the true basis of the steadfastness of the community. The terms τάξις and στερέωμα are only here in the NT connected with the concept of πίστις. They point back to the foundation of faith in Christ, but they threaten to restrict the liberty of faith in Christ to the degree that institutional thinking [55] finds a possible point of contact in them. Col. 2:5, however, has in view the faith which is solidly grounded in Christ [56] and which gives the community the needed strength to stand firm in its conflict in the world.

Bertram

---

[48] Both nouns are obj. of both part., Loh. Kol., *ad loc.* Calvin, *ad loc.* (Corp. Ref., 80, 101): *Fidem a constantia et stabilitate laudat.*

[49] Cf. A. Harnack, *Militia Christi* (1905), 38, 122. The Qumran community calls itself a camp and the order of the camp must be maintained at all costs, e.g., 1 QS 10:25: "the firmly established limit, to keep the faithfulness and right of strength for the righteousness of God"; 4:4: "a sacred enterprise in well-established purpose." סדר is battle order, e.g., 1 QM 3:1; סרך is the fixed monastic-military regimentation of community life; it comes in the titles of many of the works: 1 QM, 1 QS, 1 QSa. Cf. F. Nötscher, *Zur theol. Terminologie d. Qumrantexte* (1956), 53; Carmignac, *op. cit.*, 1, 25, 44; A. S. van der Woude, *Die messian. Vorstellungen d. Gemeinde v. Qumran* (1957), 28 equates סדר and τάξις. סרך might correspond to στερέωμα, but cf. also יסוד which denotes the basic order of creation in Damasc. 4:21 (7:2), or תכון in 1 QS 9:12, which means order and is connected with the root כון or תכן; both are transl. στερεόω in the OT.

[50] Cf. 1 Macc. 9:14; 1 Εσδρ. 8:78.

[51] W. Lueken, *Der Brief an d. Kol.,* Schr. NT, II, *ad loc.*: "The community stands firm like a well-ordered and well-entrenched army."

[52] Cramer Cat., *ad loc.,* cf. Dib. Gefbr., *ad loc.*

[53] Cf., e.g., Ps. 17:7-9; 18:2-5; 37:31-33 etc.

[54] Cf. also 1 QH 2:25: "By this grace I have a solid position ... men of war have camped against me ... ," also O. Sol. 31:9: the metaphor of the rock which stands.

[55] Institutional thinking and some regimentation were necessarily present in the Chr. community from the very first, even if alien to the Gospel of Jesus Himself. Qumran influences might have strengthened these tendencies.

[56] Cf. Oecumenius of Trikka in Staab, 454: True faith has τὸ βέβαιον καὶ τὸ σταθερόν. Bengel, *ad loc.: Fides est firmamentum, cum ipsa firma est.*

---

† στέφανος, † στεφανόω

Contents: A. The Use and Significance of the Crown (Wreath) in the Ancient World: I. Meaning; II. The Nature of the Crown; III. The Use of the Crown: 1. The Cultus; 2. Oracles; 3. Processions and Feasts; 4. As a Sign of Salvation and Protection; 5. The Mysteries; 6. Political Life; 7. The Games; 8. The Army; 9. Private Life: a. As a Sign of Joy and Respect; b. At Weddings; c. At Symposia; 10. The Cult and Honouring of the Dead. B. The Crown and Crowning in the Old Testament: 1. Occurrence; 2. Use of the Crown; 3. Figurative Use. C. The Crown and Crowning in Judaism: 1. Use of the Crown; 2. Figurative Use; 3. The Crown in Apocalyptic; 4. Rabbinic Theology; 5. The Metaphor of the Contestant in Philo. D. The Crown in the New Testament: 1. The Figurative Use in Paul; 2. The Crown of Victory and Life; 3. The Crown as a Symbol of Divine Honour; 4. The Crown of Thorns in the Gospels. E. The Crown and Crowning in the Early Church: 1. The Martyr's Crown; 2. The Crown in Gnosticism; 3. Early Christian Art; 4. The Crown of Thorns in Early Christian Art; 5. The Wedding Crown in the Early Church; 6. The Rejection of the Non-Christian Use of Crowns; 7. The Use of Crowns in the Post-Constantinian Era.

A. The Use and the Significance of the Crown (Wreath) in the Ancient World.

I. Meaning.

στέφανος has from the very first the basic sense of "crown," στεφανόω "to crown." Hom. speaks of crowns which girls have in the round dance in Il., 18, 597: καὶ ῥ' αἱ μὲν καλὰς στεφάνας ἔχον, but there is no other ref. to crowns in his poetry. Yet the crown soon appears in lit. and monuments. Linguistically στέφανος and στεφανόω are connected with the verb στέφω "to enclose, encircle."[1] Hom. Il., 13, 736 reads: πάντη γάρ σε περὶ στέφανος πολέμοιο δέδηε, "the battle is kindled around thee." Pind. Olymp., 8, 32 calls the encircling walls of Troy στέφανος. In Eur. Herc. Fur., 839 the encircling company of beautiful children is called καλλίπαις στέφανος. The verb στεφανόω from στέφανος is used in the same way: Hom. Il., 5, 738 f.: αἰγίδα ... ἣν πέρι μὲν πάντη φόβος ἐστεφάνωται, Od., 10, 195: νῆσον, τὴν πέρι πόντος ἀπείριτος ἐστεφάνωται. Heaven is encircled by stars which embrace it like a crown: ἐν δὲ τὰ τείρεα πάντα, τά τ' οὐρανὸς ἐστεφάνωται, Hom. Il., 18, 485, quoted in Tert. De Corona, 13 (CSEL, 70); cf. Hes. Theog., 382: ἄστρα τε λαμπετόωντα, τά τ' οὐρανὸς ἐστεφάνωται. Zeus sitting with scanning eye high on the top of Gargaros — ἀμφὶ δέ μιν θυόεν νέφος ἐστεφάνωτο, Hom. Il., 15, 153.

The crown derived from the twig which was placed on the head, often open, perhaps doubled, and granting life and fertility to its bearer as a symbol of life. It is thus a sign of life and fruitfulness, and possibly a symbol of light too in virtue of the connection

---

στέφανος κτλ. Bibl.: Liddell-Scott, Pr.-Bauer, s.v. K. Baus, "Der Kranz in Antike u. Christentum," *Theophaneia*, 2 (1940); L. Deubner, "Die Bdtg. d. Kranzes im klass. Altertum," ARW, 30 (1933), 70-104; O. Fiebiger, Art. "Corona" in Pauly-W., 4 (1901), 1636-43; R. Ganszyniec, Art. "Kranz" in Pauly-W., 11 (1922), 1588-1607; J. Klein, "Der Kranz bei d. alten Griechen. Eine religionsgesch. Studie auf Grund d. Denkmäler," *Beigabe z. Jahresbericht d. königlich-humanistischen Gymnasiums zu Günzburg* (1912); J. Köchling, "De coronarum apud antiquos vi atque usu," RVV, 14, 2 (1914); A. de Waal, Art. "Corona," *Realenz. d. chr. Altertümer,* I (1882), 333-6.

[1] Etym. obscure, cf. Boisacq, Hofmann, s.v. Perhaps related to Hittite *istapmi* "I cover, enclose" [Risch].

between life and light. [2] In it the blessing of deity comes on its bearer. It thus acquires a place in the cultus and as a means of blessing can mediate power and illumination, ward off evil, and grant protection. The closed crown is thus used as magic. The more the magico-cultic ref. of the crown slackens, the more it is an expression of festal joy, a sign of honour, but also an expression of sorrow. Thinkers outside the magico-cultic circle find in crowns and crowning a symbol; στέφανοί εἰσιν ἀρετῆς σημεῖον, Demosth. Or., 22, 75. Excellence of every kind is acknowledged by a crown. Plut. Tit., 24 (I, 382 f.) speaks of the στέφανος δικαιοσύνης καὶ χρηστότητος, Dion. Hal. Ant. Rom., 4, 3, 1 of the στέφανος ἀριστείας. When ἀνδρὸς στέφανος παῖδες are mentioned in Hom. Epigrammata, 13, [3] cf. also Eur. Iph. Aul., 192 ff.: κατεῖδον δὲ δύ' Αἴαντε συνέδρω, τὸν Οἰλέως Τελαμῶνός τε γόνον, τὸν Σαλαμῖνος στέφανον, στέφανος has a purely symbolic sense. Aristoph. speaks of στεφανοῦν: τοὺς πρεσβυτέρους ἤθεσι χρηστοῖς στεφανώσας, Nu., 959.

II. The Nature of the Crown.

The use of crowning is attested in Egypt, [4] in ancient Greece, [5] and independently in Rome. [6] The simplest form of the crown is a bent twig or two twigs tied together. Acc. to Plin. Hist. Nat., 22, 3. 6 f. the Roman victor's crown was originally a simple wreath of grass. Flowers and leaves are also used. "Each charming flower, each kindly leaf of green, each kind of grass or tendril" is "sacred to some head," Tert. De Corona, 7 (CSEL. 70). Meadow flowers were borne in honour of Artemis: σοὶ τόνδε πλεκτὸν στέφανον ἐς ἀκηράτου λειμῶνος, ὦ δέσποινα, κοσμήσας φέρω, Eur. Hipp., 73 f. Men put wreaths of roses on their heads ῥόδοις στεφανοῦν, Aristoph. Eq., 966, cf. also Anacr., 76 (Diehl², I, 4, 183). Demeter is crowned with a wreath made of ears of grain, cf. also the Egypt. Isis, Tert. De Corona, 7. Among the Romans the ancient agricultural fraternity of the Arvals wore similar wreaths with white bands at their festivals; this fraternity traced its origin to Romulus who gave them their crowns at their foundation pro religiosissimo insigni, Plin. Hist. Nat., 18, 2. 6. [7] Ivy is the sign of Dionysus and is worn in the Dionysus cult: στεφανοῦν τε κρᾶτα κισσίνοις βλαστήμασιν, Eur. Ba., 177; στεφανοῦσθε κισσῷ, 106. The followers of this god, the god of death and life, also crown themselves with the leaves of oaks ἐπὶ δ' ἔθεντο κισσίνους στεφάνους δρυός τε μίλακός τ' ἀνθεσφόρου, 702 f., [8] for this wreath is esp. significant in the cult of the dead. Acanthus as an ever-green is also used in this cult. The Egypt. Osiris is crowned with

---

[2] On the crown as a symbol of life and fertility cf. Nilsson, I², 127; as a symbol of light, W. Bousset, Hauptprobleme d. Gnosis (1907), 147: "The account in the Chr. Book of Adam, which is related to the presentation in the Syr. Treasure Cave, points to Persian affinities: 'Namrud saw a luminous cloud under heaven from Satan... and he called to one named Santal, a craftsman, and said: Fashion me a gt. crown in the form of this cloud; and he made him a crown, and Namrud took it, and put it on his head, so that people said a cloud came down from heaven upon him.'"

[3] Ed. A. Baumeister, Hom. Hymn. (1915).

[4] For the crown in the cultus and at meals and feasts in Egypt cf. A. Wiedemann, Das alte Ägypten (1920), 97 f., 308; H. Kees, Kulturgesch. d. alten Orients, Hndbch. kl. AW, III, 1 (1933), 67, 94. The goddess Hathor of Denderah is called "the mistress of the weaving of wreaths," A. Erman, Die Religion d. Ägypter (1934), 368, cf. also 364 f., 372.

[5] Vases and terracottas show the early spread of the crown in Greece, also the monuments of early Laconian culture, cf. R. M. Dawkins, The Sanctuary of Artemis Orthia at Sparta (1929), 154, Ill. 109, also Plate 94, 97, 2; 181f., 189 f., 195, and cf. p. 207, 251, 260 f.; F. Poulsen-C. Dugas, "Vases archaïques de Délos," BCH, 35 (1911), 411 Ill. 70; H. Lamer, Griech. Kultur² (1922), 87 Ill. 131.

[6] Cf. Plin. Hist. Nat., 18, 2, 6; 22, 3, 6; the crown has cultic significance and is used to acknowledge military bravery. Baus, 3 f. notes Etruscan connections, cf. esp. Etruscan crowns for the dead.

[7] Cf. W. Henzen, Acta fratrum Arvalium (1874), 24 f.

[8] W. F. Otto, Dionysos, Mythos u. Kultus² (1939) 142 f. etc.

ivy, Tert. De Cor., 7. Neptune and Pan wear wreaths of fig-leaves. Zeus wears a crown of laurel, as does Apollo, who took a crown of laurel berries after defeating the dragon Delphys. Tert. De Cor., 7. Aphrodite is similarly crowned, and soldiers wear the laurel when receiving imperial bounty and at triumphs, Tert. De Cor., 12. With the laurel wreath the olive wreath is in particular the victor's crown. It is also carried at feasts. Petitioners carry it on their hands and heads. Hercules also wears it, Tert. De Cor., 7. 12; cf. Hdt., VIII, 26, 2; Aristoph. Pax, 1044; Plat. Leg., XII, 946b; Aeschin. Or., II, 46. The myrtle, a sign of love, is consecrated to Venus, Tert. De Cor., 12, but it also has a place in the Eleusinian mysteries. 9 The leaves of vines as well as ivy and oak are used in the Dionysus cult. The crown of flowers, leaves and twigs finds a copy in the crown of gold used in respectful and dedicatory offerings, Thuc., IV, 121, 1; Plat. Ion, 530 d; Aristoph. Av., 1274 f.; Xenoph. An., I, 7, 7. Aristot, mentions the replacing of golden crowns by crowns of white paste-board, Oec., 2, p. 1353b, 24-27. Ariadne received from Dionysus the gift of a crown of gold and precious stones, the work of Hephaistos, Tert. De Cor., 7. Golden crowns were worn by magistrates in Rome and Athens, 13. Etruscan crowns were made of precious stones and golden oak-leaves. Similar crowns were used in Rome in connection with processional chariots, 13.

III. The Use of the Crown.

The crown is used in the cultic sphere. Persons and objects participating in or belonging to a cultic action, and thus withdrawn from the secular sphere, are adorned with a crown: the priest and altar, the sacrificer and sacrifice (→ lines 26 ff.), also the seer → 618, 15 ff. From this cultic relation the crown moves into the sphere of banquets (→ 622, 35 ff.), the games (→ 620, 15 ff.), the Roman triumph (→ 621, 25 ff.) and the cult of the dead (→ 623, 31 ff.).

1. The Cultus.

In cultic acts the priest wears a crown, ὁ τῆς ἱερωσύνης στέφανος, Heliodor., VII, 8. In some places, e.g. Panarama, Aphrodisias and Cyrene the ceremony of priestly institution is called παράληψις τοῦ στεφάνου. 10 Concerning priestly dedication in the taurobolium Prud. Peristephanon, 10, 1011 ff. says that the high-priest is put in a deep hole, adorned with a band round his forehead, with bands round the temples, his hair set back under a golden crown. Schol. on Aristoph. Pax, 1044 says of the sacrificing priest: 11 δάφνη ἐστεφανοῦντο εἰς γνώρισμα τῆς τέχνης. In Pergamon the priest, probably of Zeus, had to wear an olive wreath with purple bands, Ditt. Syll.³, III, 1018, 1 ff., cf. also Philostr. Vit. Soph., I, 21, 2; Ditt. Or., II, 470, 21 f.; Lib. Or., 53, 4. Priests also crowned themselves when sacrificing: οἱ μὲν ἐστεφανώσαντο, Thuc., IV, 80, 4, cf. Xenoph. An., VII, 1, 40; Cyrop., III, 3, 34. 12 Those who offered were crowned as well; inscr. order this, e.g.: "when they bring offerings citizens and aliens are all to bear crowns" CIG, II, 3595 (c. 218 B.C.), also III, 4697, 50 (204 B.C.). When Aeneas first trod Roman soil he crowned his brow with a green twig as he prayed to the gods of the land, Verg. Aen., VII, 135 ff. Through the crown the favour of the gods was won. Acc. to Ovid Fast., IV, 865-870 Roman harlots knew that Venus could be won over by a crown. The sacrifices and altars were also crowned, Eur. Iph. Aul., 1080; Pind. Isthm.,

---

9 G. Pringsheim, Archäol. Beiträge z. Geschichte d. eleusinischen Kults, Diss. Bonn (1905) 14.
10 Cf. Ditt. Or., II, 767, 12 ff., also H. Oppermann, "Zeus Panaramos," RVV, 19, 2 (1924), 56 f.
11 Ed. F. Dübner (1883).
12 The practice seems to have met opposition when it came to Greece, probably from the Orient, cf. on this Baus, 10, n. 56.

3, 80. [13] Crowns were even used as offerings, i.e., in the form of wreaths of foliage and flowers, Luc. De Sacrificiis, 2 f., but also in that of gold crowns, Livy, 2, 22, 6: *Latini* ... *coronam auream Jovi donum in Capitolium mittunt,* also 3, 57, 7 etc., [14] IG, 7, 3498, 60; Xenoph. Hist. Graec., III, 4, 18. The crowning of images belongs in this connection, Aesch. Eum., 39, cf. also Aristoph. Pl., 39. This took place when the statue was dedicated to cultic use and it was repeated on feasts of the god or other occasions. It expresses reverence and homage. When Emped. was crowned with wreaths he took it as a mark of divine worship, Emped. Fr., 112, 6 (Diels, I, 355, 1); IG, 7, 4252, 11 ff. also tells of a similar act of veneration and gratitude in 331 B.C.: ἐπειδὴ ὁ θεὸς καλῶς ἐπιμελεῖται τῶν ἀφικνουμένων ᾿Αθηναίων καὶ τῶν ἄλλων εἰς τὸ ἱερὸν ἐφ᾿ ὑγιείᾳ καὶ σωτηρίᾳ πάντων τῶν ἐν τῇ χώρᾳ, στεφανῶσαι τὸν ᾿Αμφιάραον χρυσῷ στεφάνῳ ἀπὸ Χ δραχμῶν καὶ ἀνειπεῖν τὸν κήρυκα τοῦ δήμου, ὅτι στεφανοῖ ὁ δῆμος ὁ ᾿Αθηναίων τὸν ᾿Αμφιάραον χρυσῷ στεφάνῳ. [15]

2. Oracles.

The crown also has cultic significance in relation to oracles. Aesch. mentions μαντεῖα στέφη in Ag., 1265. The crown evokes true dreams. *Laurum si dormientibus ad caput posueris, vera somnia esse visuros,* Fulgentius Mythologiae, I, 14. [16] The χρησμολόγος who proclaims oracular words at the offering wears one, Aristoph. Pax, 1044. The Delphic Pythia is also crowned, Schol. on Aristoph. Pl., 39. [17] Eunapios says of Aidesios, son of the prophet Chrysanthios, the teacher of Eunapios from the Pythagorean circle, that is sufficed him τὸν στέφανον ἐπιθεῖναι τῇ κεφαλῇ καὶ πρὸς τὸν ἥλιον ἀναβλέποντα χρησμοὺς ἐκφέρειν καὶ τούτους ἀψευδεῖς, Vitae Sophistarum, 23, 5, 3. [18] Branchus receives a crown and branch from Apollo and begins to prophesy, Lactantius Placidus Comm. Statii Thebais, VIII, 198: [19] *accepta corona virgaque vaticinari coepit.* When Creon comes back crowned after consulting the oracle he is seen as a messenger of joy, Soph. Oed. Tyr., 82 f. Roman frescoes in Pompeii and Herculaneum depict crowned prophetesses. [20] The poet is close to the seer, and he, too, can be called by the Romans *vates* — an idea also found among the Gks., cf. Eur. Herc. Fur., 676 f.: μὴ ζῴην μετ᾿ ἀμουσίας, αἰεὶ δ᾿ ἐν στεφάνοισιν εἴην. The one who consults the oracle as well as the one who gives it is crowned, so Fabius Pictor in 216 B.C., who is told by the priests of Delphi not to put off the crown until his return to Rome and then to lay it as a votive offering on the altar of Apollo, Liv., 23, 11, 5.

3. Processions and Feasts.

Processions and feasts also lie in the cultic sphere. We find prayer-processions with στεφανοφορίαι in the Roman world, Liv., 27, 37, 13; 40, 37, 3; 43, 13, 8 etc. By Attic custom three-year old children were adorned with wreaths on the second day of the Feast of Flowers. At the autumn feast of the Apaturia these children were enrolled,

---

[13] Further examples in Baus, 23-28.
[14] Cf. the many examples in Baus, 21.
[15] Acc. to Ael. Arist. Or., 47, 45 (Keil), too, the crown expresses recognition and veneration. In a dream he is told by the healing god Aesculapius to eat eggs and vegetables and put on a wreath from the temple of the god. Probably the wreath is also thought to have healing power.
[16] Ed. R. Helm (1898).
[17] Ed. F. Dübner (1883).
[18] Ed. J. Giangrande (1956).
[19] Ed. R. Jahnke (1898), 389.
[20] S. Reinach, *Répertoire des Peintures Grecques et Rom.* (1922), Ill. 29, 3; cf. W. Helbig, *Wandgemälde d. vom Vesuv verschütteten Städte Campaniens* (1868), No. 203, 1391b.

Philostr. Heroic., 12, 2, cf. Schol. on Plat. Tim., 21b. [21] The crowns protect and nurture child life. They have magical power and also express joy. On the New Year Feast in Rome at cock-crow houses were adorned with δάφνης τε κλάδοις καὶ ἑτέροις εἴδεσι στεφάνων, Lib. Progymnasmata, 12, 5, 7. These crowns promised protection and good luck in the new year. At the well-feasts, the Fontanalia, celebrated by bakers and millers, donkeys are crowned and millstones decked with garlands, while ploughing oxen are crowned at the feriae sementivae, Ovid Fast., I, 663; VI, 311 f. [22]

4. As a Sign of Salvation and Protection.

How strongly crowns were felt to be a sign of salvation and protection may be seen from some examples. In Aristoph. Pl., 21 f. the slave Carion, when he comes from the oracle with his master Chremylos, is safe against the blows of the latter because he is crowned: οὐ γάρ με τυπτήσεις στέφανον ἔχοντά γε, but he receives the reply: μὰ Δί', ἀλλ' ἀφελὼν τὸν στέφανον, ἢν λυπῇς τί με. The emperor Tiberius put on a laurel crown during thunder-storms because the laurel was a protection against lightning, Plin. Hist. Nat., 15, 134 f., cf. 2, 146. The entrance to a Roman house in Syria has a laurel wreath under which are two snakes with the inscr. intra feliciter, CIL, 3, 120. When a boy was born in Attica an olive wreath was put at the entrance to the house, Juv., 9, 85 f. The crown is also a means of power and protection in invoking gods and demons in magic, cf. the invocation of Apollo: εὐχόμενος δὲ στέφανον ἔχε δάφνινον τοιοῦτον..., Preis. Zaub., I, 2, 27 f.; each of the leaves of the wreath is inscribed with magic words and the magician goes to rest with wreaths and branches. If he wants to invoke Apollo he must be στεφανωσάμενος σαμψουχίνῳ στεφάνῳ, Preis. Zaub., II, 7, 729. [23]

5. The Mysteries.

As in the public cultus, so, too, in the mysteries the crown has a significant role. An Eleusinian relief shows the coming of Triptolemos to bring agriculture to men; before setting out he is crowned for this. The myrtle branch is borne by the mystagogue in the Eleusinian mysteries. The sacred κίστη is crowned, Plut. Phoc., 28 (I, 754c). In the Isis mysteries the neophytes bear crowns: caput decore corona cinxerat palmae candidae foliis in modum radiorum prosistentibus, sic ad instar Solis exornato me, Apul. Met., XI, 24. Here the crown is a sign of the light of the sun and it brings illumination and apotheosis to the neophyte. In the Sabazios mysteries the mystagogues bear crowns of fennel and paste-board, Demosth., 18, 260. In the dedication mysteries in the grotto of Mithras a crown is handed to the mystagogue; this is set on a sword. They then take it off his head again and say: "Mithras is my crown." He who does this is at once recognised as a soldier of Mithras when he casts down the crown and says that his crown is in his god, Tert. De Cor., 15 (CSEL, 70). Also based on mystery practice is the act of Socrates in Aristoph. Nu., 255 ff. when he crowns Strepsiades to prepare him for initiation into his teaching. When he takes this to be a sacrificial act Socrates answers: οὔκ, ἀλλὰ ταῦτα πάντα τοὺς τελουμένους ἡμεῖς ποιοῦμεν. The Serapis hymn says of the worshipper of the god: ... διὰ τὴν εὐσέβειαν ἐστεφανώθη ὑπὸ τοῦ θεοῦ, IG, 11, 1299, 9 f.

---

[21] Ed. G. C. Greene (1838), 281, cf. L. Deubner, Attische Feste (1956), 114 f.
[22] Cf. also G. Wissowa, Religion u. Kultus d. Römer² (1912), 221, n. 9, also Deubner, op. cit., 74 f. Fig. Plat. Resp., VIII, 560e speaks of a procession of desires: ὕβριν καὶ ἀναρχίαν καὶ ἀσωτίαν καὶ ἀναίδειαν λαμπρὰς μετὰ πολλοῦ χοροῦ κατάγουσιν ἐστεφανωμένας.
[23] Deubner, 90-92, 101 f.; Baus, 32 f.

6. Political Life.

The close connection between cultic and political life throughout antiquity means that the crown and crowning have a place in the latter too. Holders of national offices bear crowns as a sign of their dignity. Demosth. speaks of the ἄρχων ἐστεφανωμένος, Or., 21, 17. In judgment the ἄρχων βασιλεύς wears a myrtle wreath which he puts off when he tries murders, Aristot. Respublica Atheniensium, 57, 4.[24] The nine Attic archons (Aeschin. Tim., 19), members of the Attic Council (Lyc. Or. in Leocratem 122) and even officials of private societies[25] wear crowns. When politicians appear as orators in the Attic popular assembly they put on crowns, Aristoph. Eccl. 122 f., 130 f., 148, cf. also Av., 463; this is a sign of their immunity. The processional relief on the Ara Pacis of Augustus shows the emperor and his family, the priests and state officials crowned for the procession. This monument demonstrates very clearly that the cultic and the political are closely related, and that the origin and meaning of political forms are to be sought in cultic practice.[26]

7. The Games.

The sporting contest shares in this connection between the cultic and the political. As the Patroclus games show (Hom. Il., 23), the origin of these contests is in rites for the dead. Verg. Aen., V, 104-663 follows Hom. when he describes the games Aeneas held in honour of his father Anchises. The sporting contest breaks free from this connection, however, and comes to be held on the gt. festivals in honour of the gods. Like priests, the leaders of the games bear crowns when sacrificing.[27] Tert. confirms the double nature of the games and their differing meanings, De Cor., 13 (CSEL, 70), cf. De Spectaculis, 11 (CCh, 1, 238): et ipsi (agones) sacri vel funebres instituti aut deis nationum aut mortuis fiunt. The god or deceased is honoured when the victor is crowned. Aristot. Eth. Nic., I, 9, p. 1099a, 4: Rhet., 4, p. 1426, 13 f.: ἕνεκα τοῦ στεφανωθῆναι ὑπὸ τῶν πολιτῶν πολλοὺς πόνους καὶ κινδύνους ὑπομένουσιν speaks of the strenuous efforts the contestants make to win the crown. In his address to young people Basil the Gt. also describes the efforts and renunciations, the discipline and practice, which contestants must accept, so that their life before the games is one long preparation for the contest. They suffer and do all this to attain a wreath of olive-leaves or ivy and to be proclaimed victor by the herald, Bas. Ad Adulescentes, 6 (MPG, 31 [1885], 580 B). The herald called the name of the victor, his father, and his town, and handed over the wreath, Schol. on Pind. Olymp., 5, 18.[28] In the Olympic games the olive leaves were cut by a παῖς ἀμφιθαλής with a golden sickle from the most sacred olive-trees and handed over to the victor, Schol. on Pind. Olymp., 3, 60,[29] cf. also Paus., V, 15, 3. The Delphic laurel wreath was fetched from the temple vale by a παῖς ἀμφιθαλής. The victory celebration ºnded in the victor's home, which was also honoured by a wreath, Xenoph. Mem., III. 7, 1. In this rite the victor offered his crown to the deity, Xenoph. Hist. Graec., III, 4, 18. A victor's crown in the games was regarded as supreme earthly fortune.

8. The Army.

Military practice was an essential part of the connection between public life and the cultus. The Spartans crowned themselves when they went out to battle; perhaps this crown is connected with the sacrifice offered before a fight, and the thought of the

[24] Ed. G. Kaibel and U. v. Wilamowitz-Moellendorff (1898); cf. Poll. Onom., VIII, 90.
[25] Cf. F. Poland, Gesch. d. gr. Vereinswesens (1909), 421.
[26] Cf. G. Rodenwaldt, Kunst um Augustus² (1943), 44-49.
[27] Cf. Klein, 58, n. 3.
[28] Ed. A. B. Drachmann (1903); cf. Baus, 145 f.
[29] Ed. Drachmann.

protective side of the crown, with its promise of good luck, may also be present here; Xenoph. says: στεφανωσάμενος ... ἐλάμβανε τὰ ὅπλα, An., IV, 3, 17, cf. also Hist. Graec., IV, 3, 21; Resp. Lac., 13, 8. Plut. De Lycurgo, 22 (I, 53e) tells us that during the sacrifice before battle the Spartan king gave the order that the army should crown itself for the marching song which he then struck up. On an Attic-Corinthian Hydria we have a depiction of Thetis giving Achilles a crown along with the weapons forged by Hephaistos. [30] Philip of Macedonia ordered his soldiers to put on laurel crowns for the battle against the Phocians. The promise of good luck and victory which the crown carries with it may be seen from Xenoph. Hist. Graec., V, 1, 3: When the Spartan admiral Teleutias sets sail the soldiers appear ὁ μὲν ἐστεφάνωσεν, ὁ δὲ ἐταινίωσεν, οἱ δὲ ὑστερήσαντες ὅμως καὶ ἀναγομένου ἔρριπτον εἰς τὴν θάλατταν στεφάνους καὶ ηὔχοντο αὐτῷ πολλὰ καὶ ἀγαθά. He is promised a safe return. [31] In the Roman army the general puts on a crown to purify the host before battle, and perhaps the soldiers do so too. The lustration purges all misdeeds and thus the crown is supposed to influence the outcome, Plut. De Bruto, 39 (I, 1001f.). If the crown is significant before battle, it is esp. a sign of victory and triumph afterwards. The goddess of victory is depicted as coming with a crown of victory in her hand. The Argonauts after victory crowned the ship's tackling. Apoll. Rhod., II, 159 f.: δάφνῃ ἐρέφειν. The crown is for the victor: τοῦδε γὰρ ὁ στέφανος, Soph. Phil., 841, cf. also Ai., 465. When Sulla, sacrificing before battle, saw the form of a laurel wreath in the liver of the victim, he was sure of victory, Plut. De Sulla, 27 (I, 468 f.). In a picture in his villa in Tusculum the same Sulla records that a simple grass wreath was handed to him as the reward of victory, Plin. Hist. Nat., 22, 6, 12. From the 3rd or 4th cent. B.C. we get gold crowns whose leaves are held together by a small figure of Nike; this is in the neighbourhood of Armento. [32] In Rome the general and soldiers bear laurel wreaths as a sign of victory. Tert. De Cor., 12 mentions the laurel wreath of the triumph. By origin this wreath is supposed to have a purifying effect: laureati milites sequebantur currum triumphantis, ut quasi purgati a caede humana intrarent urbem, Festus De Significatione Verborum, 84 (104, 23), [33] cf. Plin. Hist. Nat., 15, 30, 135. Common in Rome was the corona civica of oak leaves given to the deliverer in battle. It is common on burial inscr. from the time of Octavian Augustus. In 27 B.C. it was given to Augustus by the senate; he had it put on the gate of his palace. [34] Another Roman custom whose meaning has been much debated is that of causing prisoners of war sub corona venire, i.e., offering them for sale as slaves with a crown on, cf. Festus, 442 (400, 6 ff. → n. 33). This probably derives from an old Germanic custom of sacrificing prisoners, Strabo, 7, 2, 3. A Pompeian fresco shows Orestes and Pylades as prisoners crowned before Thoas. [35] Acc. to Gellius Noctes Atticae, 6, 4, 4 [36] the expression comes from soldiers surrounding prisoners like a crown, but this seems to be a later rationalisation.

9. Private Life.

Crowns and crowning are used in private life as well as in the cultus and the public sphere. Here, too, there is a cultic connection. But more and more the crown and crowning become a matter of custom, take on significance for joy or sorrow, and break

---

[30] Corpus Vasorum Antiquorum, 1, 4; Musée du Louvre, 3 (1925), Ill. 12, 1; 13.
[31] Ships were often crowned and garlanded when setting sail or returning, cf Deubner, 73 f.
[32] R. Delbrück, "Denkmäler spätantiker Kunst" in Antike Denkmäler, ed. Deutsch. Archäol. Institut, 4, 1 (1927), Plate 43; for Octavian Augustus cf. the Gemma Augustea of the Vienna collection, Rodenwaldt, op. cit., 51.
[33] Ed. W. M. Lindsay (1913).
[34] Baus, 147 f.
[35] In the Casa del Citarista in Pompeii, cf. H. Speier, "Zweifiguren-Gruppen im 5. u. 4. Jhdt. v. Chr." Röm. Mitt., 47 (1932), 71 f. Plate 27, 1.
[36] Ed. C. Hosius, I (1959).

free from the cultus. From the priest and the seer, the contestant and the victor, the crown passes to other groups, e.g., singers, flautists and harpists. [37] In so doing it undergoes increasing secularisation and generalising; enlightenment and the growth of irony, e.g., in comedy, contribute to this. [38]

a. As a Sign of Joy and Respect.

Crowns and crowning denote joy and respect. In Soph. Trach., 178 the joyful messenger is καταστεφής and this shows that his news is good, cf. also Xenoph. Hist. Graec., VI, 4, 19: ἔπεμψαν ... ἄγγελον ἐστεφανωμένον. Aristoph. mocks the common use in nis Knignts. When a dealer in sausages tells the council that since the outbreak of war anchovies have never been so cheap as now, he is crowned as a bringer of good news εἶτ᾽ ἐστεφάνουν μ᾽ εὐαγγέλια, Eq., 647. The goddesses of charm, the Graces, turn from men who have no crowns, Sappho Fr., 81b, 1 ff. [39] Pandora, the first woman acc. to saga, was given a crown by them, Tert. De Cor., 7. How much the crown was a sign of joy may be seen from the fact that Xenoph., crowned for sacrifice, took off the crown when told of the death of his son. But then when a second messenger told him his son died as victor he put it on again, Ael. Var. Hist., 3, 3, cf. Plut. Cons. ad Apoll., 33 (II, 118 f.). In Rome the money-changer Fulvius is imprisoned by official order and held in prison to the end of the Second Punic War because in a difficult stage of the war he looked out on the forum from his office adorned with a wreath of roses, Plin. Hist. Nat., 21, 3, 8.

b. At Weddings.

It is quite natural that there should be crowning at weddings. The Gks. speak of the στέφανος νυμφικός, Chariton, III, 2, 16 [40] or of στέφος γαμήλιον, Colluthus, 28, [41] cf. Bion, 87 f. [42] In the Schol. on Aristoph. Av., 161 (→ n. 11) we read ὅτι οἱ γαμοῦντες στεφανοῦνται. Of the moment when Menelaus and Helena depart after their marriage Stesichorus says: πολλὰ μὴν Κυδώνια μᾶλα ποτερρίπτευν ποτὶ δίφρον ἄνακτι, πολλὰ δὲ μύρσινα φύλλα καὶ ῥοδίνους στεφάνους ἴων τε κορωνίδας οὔλας, Fr., 10 (Diehl², II, 49). Clytaemnestra says to Achilles about Iphigenia: "whom I crowned and led to thee as a bride, I now bring as a sacrifice," Eur. Iph. Aul., 905 f. What is stated here is depicted on the monuments. An amphora shows the bridal pair on a chariot; a female figure approaches the bride and gives her a crown which she carries in her hands. On other depictions the bride herself has the crown in her hands. [43] The guests at the feast wear crowns, Act. Thom., 5 (107, 2 ff.). [44]

c. At Symposia.

Those who take part in banquets and the ensuing symposia are adorned with wreaths, Aristoph. Av., 463, also Plat. Symp., 212e: κιττοῦ τέ τινι στεφάνῳ δασεῖ καὶ ἴων, and Aristot. Fr., 108, p. 1495b, 18 f.: στεφάνοις ἐχρῶντο ἐν τοῖς συμποσίοις. The

---

[37] Baus, 150-153.
[38] There are examples in the comedies of Aristoph., e.g., Eccl., where women secure crowns to speak at the popular assembly in accordance with Attic custom, cf. 131, which says with ref. to a woman about to speak: περίθου δὴ τὸν στέφανον τύχἀγαθῇ.
[39] Ed. A. Lobel-D. Page, Poetarum Lesbiorum Fragmenta (1955).
[40] Ed. W. E. Blake (1938).
[41] Ed. W. Weinberger (1896).
[42] Ed. U. v. Wilamowitz-Moellendorff, Bucolici Graeci (1905), 125.
[43] Corpus Vasorum, op. cit. (→ n. 30), Ill. 65, 1. 4.
[44] Cf. Deubner, 77.

depiction of a family meal in Pompeii shows a woman whose head is circled by roses. [45] The Vatican Museum has a sarcophogus lid with the picture of a meal in which a girl has a wreath in her right hand resting on her head. [46] On the gravestone of Eques singularis T. Aurelius Decimus natione Mysius, found by the Pignattara Gate, a man reclining at table has a wreath in his raised right hand. [47] The origin of this wreath at meals is cultic. "The ancients ascribed the reason for gathering for the symposium to deity, and at it they used the wreaths, hymns and singing proper to the gods," Athen., 5, 19 (192b). Ael. Arist. Or., 45, 27 (Keil) is familiar with a feast in connection with the Serapis cult at which there was a symposium and the god himself was thought to be present and entertained as a guest. In his honour the participants and members of the cult wore crowns. With the crowns they take home τὴν ἀγαθὴν εὐθυμίαν when they have undertaken the epiclesis of the god in antiphonal singing. The crown at feasts derived originally from the preceding offerings. It became an expression of festal joy and took on a profane sense in course of time, cooling the head during the drinking of wine and expressing the joy of feasting and carousing. Plut. Quaest. Conv., III, 1, 3, (II, 647d e); Athen., 15, 17 (675c-e). It represented festal usage, and the bowls and vessels were also adorned with wreaths, as also the walls of the room where the feast was held. [48] The crown was a common and favourite gift as an expression of association and friendship. [49]

10. The Cult and Honouring of the Dead.

Crowns and crowning are found also in the cult and honouring of the dead. The custom of putting wreaths on the dead, biers and gravestones is widespread. A wreath is put on the deceased on the day of burial. We find the first ref. to this in the Alcmaionis Fr., 2: νέκυς δὲ χαμαιστρώτου ἔπι τείνας/εὐρείης στιβάδος, παρέθηκ᾽ αὐτοῖσι θάλειαν/δαῖτα ποτήριά τε, στεφάνους τ᾽ ἐπὶ κρασὶν ἔθηκεν. [50] Acc. to the cultic constitution of the Iobakchos society on a MS from the Roman period found in the Bakcheion at Athens, a wreath up to 5 denarii was to be brought for a dead Iobakchos. [51] Plut. tells how Pericles was overcome by grief when he put the wreath of the dead on his son, Pericl., 36 (I, 172c). Artistic depictions show that it was common in antiquity to crown the dead. [52] Burial stelae were also crowned; endowments were set up for this, and the money for regular adornment with wreaths was called τὸ στεφανωτικόν. [53] A permanent wreath was also carved on the gravestone. [54] The meaning of the crown for the dead is the same as that of the crown for divine images and reminds us of the common view of antiquity that the dead are heroes, Tert. De Corona, 10 (CSEL, 70). The primary point of wreaths on or over graves is probably that they are memorial

---

[45] Cf. F. J. Dölger, ΙΧΘΥΣ. Der hl. Fisch in d. antiken Religionen u. im Christentum, V (1943), 518 f. Ill. 316.

[46] Dölger, V, 409 f.

[47] Cf. F. Matz-F. v. Duhm, Antike Bildwerke in Rom mit Ausschluss d. grösseren Sammlungen, III (1882), 177, No. 3882, cf. also Dölger, V, 426 f. with further examples and 449 f., also III (1922), Plate 62, 1.

[48] Cf. Deubner, 96 f.; Baus, 74-78; on the question of the feast of the gods Baus, 84 f.

[49] Cf. Baus, 34 f. with many examples.

[50] Ed. G. Kinkel, Epicorum Graec. Fr., I (1877); we find the fr. in Athen., 11, 2 (II, 460b).

[51] Cf. E. Maass, Orpheus. Untersuchungen z. griech., rom., altchr. Jenseitsdichtung u. Religion (1895), 31 f.

[52] Cf. C. Watzinger, Griech. Holzsarkophage aus d. Zeit Alexanders d. Grossen (1905), 8, Ill. 15; cf. Dölger, V, 5 f., n. 13. The wreath was later replaced by a crown of precious metal, cf. Baus, 115-117; for vases depicting the dead with crowns cf. W. Zschietzschmann, "Die Darstellung der Prothesis in d. griech. Kunst," Ath. Mitt., 53 (1928), 17-36. Crowns and vessels of oil occur together on the base of a stele in H. Lamer, Griech. Kultur im Bilde[3] (1922), Ill. 137.

[53] Cf. Poland, op. cit. (→ n. 25), 511; B. Laum, Stiftungen in d. gr. u. röm. Antike, I (1914), 83-85.

[54] Cf. W. Altmann, Die Grabaltäre d. röm. Kaiserzeit (1905), 260.

gifts and honour the dead, Plut. De Aristide, 21 (I, 332a). Perhaps the crown for the dead was designed to protect him against harmful demons when passing into the realm of the dead; without it he would be at their mercy. The Alcmaionis Fr. (→ 623, 22 f.), however, seems to pt. in a different direction. The wreath of the dead is connected with the meal of the blessed in Elysium. Plat. hands down from Musaios, who was close to the Orphic circle, the idea that there is prepared for the righteous in Hades a symposium in which they will take part adorned with crowns, Plat. Resp., II, 363c-d, cf. Orph. (Kern) Fr., 4 (p. 83). Aristoph. Fr., 488, 6 (CAF, I, 517) scoffs at this view: "After death we will not be laid out with the adornment of crowns or anointed with sweet-smelling oil as if those who went down into the underworld at once needed a drink." The mysteries promised their adherents that in the hereafter they would tread on glorious meadows free and unencumbered, adorned with crowns and festively enjoying the company of pure and blessed men, Stob. Ecl., IV 1089, 17 ff. Many depictions on the graves of antiquity show a connection between crowning and the feast of the dead. [55]

B. The Crown and Crowning in the Old Testament.

1. Occurrence.

στεφανόω and στέφανος in the LXX and other Gk. transl. of the OT are used for the Hbr. verb עטר, which also has the basic meaning "to surround" and which is related to the Accadian *etru* (probably the "head-band"), and for the derivate עֲטָרָה. The basic sense may be seen in Ps. 5:12, which says of the righteous that "thou dost compass him as with a shield of favour," [56] and in 1 S. 23:26, where the verb has the sense "to encircle," "to surround."

When one steps out of the world of Greece and Rome, of the Near East and Hellenism, into that of the OT, one realises how slight in comparison is the use of "wreath," "crown" and "crowning." [57] Only in the later strata of the OT are the words more common, but then it is mainly in connection with relations outside Israel or in a figurative sense. This shows plainly that while outside Israel the crown and crowning derive from the cultus, Israel itself stands under the second commandment which forbids images and therefore their emblems as well, including the wreath of the gods and their worshippers. Thus the silence of the OT confirms the cultic-magical origin of the use of crowns and is a sign of the distinctiveness of Israel.

2. Use of the Crown.

There are many features which fit in with or depict the common use in the world surrounding Israel.

One of the most ancient passages is 2 S. 12:30 par. 1 Ch. 20:2, which tells of the golden crown of the king of Rabba in the land of the Ammonites. David took this from him

---

[55] Cf. Dölger, IV (1927), Plate 264. In the pictures in the Vibia vault on the Appian Way (non-chr.) Vibia is brought crowned to the feast of the blessed. For a grave in Cilicia cf. R. Herberday and A. Wilhelm, "Reise in Kilikien," *DA Wien*, 24 (1896), 6, Ill. 156; this shows a row of figures bearing crowns, fishes etc., cf. Dölger, V, 474, also 402-9 on the sarcophagus of a child from Syria; cf. also on this F. Cumont, "Un sarcophage d'enfant trouvé à Beyrouth," *Syria*, 10 (1929), Plate 43, 2; on the grave of a married couple from Sardis in Lydia J. Keil and A. v. Premerstein, "Bericht über d. dritte Reise in Lydien ...," *DA Wien*, 57, 1 (1914), 63 f. These wear crowns with bows.

[56] צִנָּה is the big shield which covers the body.

[57] 49 instances of στέφανος have been counted in the LXX, and some others in the later transl.: στεφανόω occurs 7 times.

and put it on his own head. It was set with precious stones. The fact that LXX uses στέφανος rather than διάδημα shows that it did not regard the milkom of Rabba as an independent sovereign but assigned him the role of a vassal. [58] Est. 8:15 tells of the large crown of gold and mantle of purple linen which Mordecai was given. Acc. to 1 Macc. 10:20 Alexander institutes Jonathan as high-priest, gives him the title of "king's friend," [59] sends him the purple robe and crown, and seeks his friendship. In 1 Macc. 13:37 the crown and palm-branch which the high-priest Simon sent to king Demetrius are mentioned and confirmed in a letter of the king to Simon; from now on this token will exempt from homage, 13:39. Alcimus acts similarly in 2 Macc. 14:4. The purple and crown of the ruler are mentioned in Sir. 40:4. A threat of Yahweh is directed against the proud crown of the drunkard Ephraim, the well-sprayed wreath of flowers and his beautiful adornment, [60] which are to be trodden underfoot, Is. 28:1, 3. It is free thinkers who say in Wis. 2:8: "We will crown ourselves with roses before they wither." The crown which the king of Israel wears is a gift from Yahweh, Ps. 21:3. Because of his pride expressed in the building of a rock-tomb, which is not his due, [61] the foreign official Shebna will have his crown of office taken from him. But the servant of God — Eliakim, son of Hilkiah acc. to a redactor — receives the royal crown, Is. 22:18, 21 LXX. Yahweh is Lord of kings and mighty men. He gives the crown and can take it away. Ez. 28:12 speaks of the king of Tyre under the metaphor στέφανος κάλλους. The direction in Zech. 6:11 to prepare for Joshua, son of Josedech, a crown from the gifts of those who have returned from exile, and to put it on him, might have been originally a prophecy relating to Zerubbabel. His crowning by the prophet is a prophetic sign alongside the institution of the Messianic high-priest Joshua (c. 3). The hopes placed in Zerubbabel were not fulfilled, and so, the argument runs, the prophetic act was later referred to the high-priest Joshua. But the crown was kept in the temple as a votive offering in memory of those who gave the gifts, as v. 14 shows. In a later reading (acc. to the LXX) v. 13c is altered along the lines of the priestly monarchy: "And he will be priest on his throne" (for "one will be priest at his right hand"). [62] The v. thus shows that later the high-priest, too, wore a crown. Acc. to Sir. 45:12 this golden crown is part of his turban. The costliness and beauty of this head-gear, which is part of the official regalia [63] of the high-priest, are esp. praised. 1 Macc. 10:20 may also be quoted in this connection. In the cities of Israel Holofernes is received with wreaths and dances and drums to honour him as the representative of Nebuchadnezzar, Jdt. 3:7. After his fall the Israelite women crown themselves with olive-branches. The men follow them in arms, also crowned, and they strike up songs of praise, 15:13. There are no previous instances of wreaths in Israel at similar joyous proclamations. Ep. Jer. 8 refers to the wreaths of pagan images. Acc. to 1 Macc. 1:22 there were crowns in the temple which Antiochus IV Epiphanes took away with the furnishings. They were set up again at the rededication of the temple, 4:57. [64] Crowns

---

[58] Cf. R. Delbrück, "Antiquarisches zu d. Verspottungen Jesu," ZNW, 41 (1942), 125: "Only the king wears the diadem, a white headband bound with a bow at the neck; vassals etc. simply have golden wreaths."

[59] Cf. E. Bammel, "Φίλος τοῦ Καίσαρος," ThLZ, 77 (1952), 205-210.

[60] LXX στέφανος τῆς ὕβρεως cf. the transl. of P. Riessler (1924 f.).

[61] The further point of the cry: "Thou shame for the house of thy lord" in Is. 22:18 HT is not clear.

[62] Cf. K. Elliger, Das Buch d. zwölf kl. Propheten, II, AT Deutsch, 25⁴ (1959) on Zech. 6:9-15.

[63] Cf. G. Widengren, Sakrales Königtum im AT u. im Judt. (1955), esp. 25 f. Cf. also A. E. Cowley, The Samaritan Liturgy, II (1909), 786: The king to the priest: "... peace on thee, the priest of the true God! Peace on thee, clothed in diadem and crown."

[64] It is an open question whether the golden crowns (borders) of 1 Macc. 1:22; 4:57 correspond to the bronze borders which the Babylonians took away as loot acc. to Ιερ. 52:18 (στεφάνη). Ep. Ar., 58-65 describes the table of the shew-bread which Ptolemy gave for the temple in Jerusalem and here a distinction is made between border = στεφάνη and decorative crown = στέφανος [Bertram].

are among the tax obligations of Israel to the Seleucids; remission is referred to in 1 Macc. 10:29; 11:35; 13:39. The wedding crown (→ 622, 22 ff.) is also found in Israel, Cant. 3:11.

3. Figurative Use.

Yahweh crowns the year with His goodness; the harvest is like a wreath awarded for achievement; it is God's blessing, Ps. 65:11. Yahweh crowns man with glory and honour and institutes him, thus crowned, the lord and ruler of the works of His hands — a metaphor for man's special position in God's creation, Ps. 8:5. Among the blessings which God gives man, and which man should never forget in praising God, is crowning with grace and mercy. God's protective care is for man an invisible but effective crown, Ps. 103:4. Thus the Lord can be the crown of His people, an eschatological promise to the remnant of Israel, Is. 28:5. This saying is older than that from the Mithras cult: "Mithras is my crown" → 619, 32 ff. Israel is God's crown which He holds in His hands before the nations, Is. 62:3; this denotes Israel's worth for God. Ez. 16:12, in an enumeration of the things Yahweh has done for Jerusalem, says: "I put a beautiful crown (LXX στέφανον καυχήσεως) upon thy head." Acc. to Lam. 2:15 HT Jerusalem is perfect beauty יֹפִי כְּלִילַת, LXX "crown of beauty" στέφανος δόξης, cf. Ez. 28:12.

The crown denotes man's honour. This is implicit in the instances of fig. use already given. Job 19:9 reads in parallelism: "He has stripped me of my glory, and taken the crown from my head." What Job says of himself Jer. 13:18 says of Israel, and in Lam. 5:16 the Israelites confess with lamentation: "The crown is fallen from our head." Yet what has happened through the fall and banishment of the people is not final. The prophet looks for the eschatological turning-pt. which changes everything. He calls to the ungodly king: "Away with the diadem and off with the crown! This shall not remain. Up with the lowly and down with the lofty!" Ez. 21:26 f.

The fig. use is broader in the Wisdom lit. A virtuous woman is her husband's crown, Prv. 12:4. [65] Grandchildren are the crown of the aged, 17:6. Gray hair is their crown, 16:31. So is rich experience, Sir. 25:6. Children bear fatherly discipline and motherly admonition as a crown on their heads, Prv. 1:9. But wisdom esp. — children receive it through fatherly discipline and motherly admonition — is the power of which it is said: "She shall give to thine head an ornament of grace, a crown of glory shall she deliver to thee," Prv. 4:9 cf. also 14:24. Since the fear of the Lord is the beginning of all wisdom (1:7), the fear of God can also be called "renown and honour and a glad crown of joy," Sir. 1:18, [66] cf. also 6:31. This crown of wisdom is bound by eternal glory; wisdom will find gladness and a crown of joy, and inherit an eternal name, Sir. 15:6 → 622, 6 ff. He who is elected to be leader of the people, for him good administration (εὐκοσμία) procures a crown, Sir. 32(35):2. The righteous will receive the royal crown of glory (τὸ βασίλειον τῆς εὐπρεπείας) and the diadem of beauty (διάδημα τοῦ κάλλους) from the Lord's hand, Wis. 5:16. Wis. 4:2 says of virtue: καὶ ἐν τῷ αἰῶνι στεφανηφοροῦσα πομπεύει τὸν τῶν ἀμιάντων ἄθλων ἀγῶνα νικήσασα. The metaphor of the triumph is used here.

C. The Crown and Crowning in Judaism.

In post-biblical Judaism there are ref. to non-Jewish practice and traces of its infiltration into Judaism, along with development of the biblical statements.

---

[65] עֲטָרָה is a feminine name in 1 Ch. 2:26. Since there is a personal ref. of crowns or wreaths elsewhere (Prv. 17:6), the name of Stephen in Ac. 6:5 may well be understood in the light of the OT, esp. as he was a Hellenistic Jew. In the B.C.-period the name is rare and in the Gk. form it can be understood only as an abbreviation, e.g., of Stephanocles [Bertram].

[66] Its effect is to cause only salvation to bloom; thus the crown is a symbol of power.

1. Use of the Crown.

Jos. mentions the victor's crown → 621, 15 ff. When the young Herod returned to Jerusalem after defeating Antigonus, Hyrcanus and the people handed him crowns as the victor's reward, Ant., 14, 299. Titus gave golden crowns to those who distinguished themselves in the Jewish war, Bell., 7, 14. Jos. differentiates Jewish conduct under the Torah from the life where gold and silver and crowns are the victor's reward, Ap. 2, 217 f. There is also ref. to the victor's crown in the games → 620, 15 ff. To R. Simeon bLaqish (c. 250 A.D.) is ascribed the saying: "The strong overcame the weak and received a crown for his head," Ex. r., 21 (84b) on 14:17. The dead Herod was carried to the grave on a golden bier adorned with many costly stones (→ 623, 20 ff.); he was arrayed in the royal purple; "the deceased was adorned with a diadem with a golden crown jutting forth, and his right hand held the sceptre," Jos. Ant., 17, 197. That the crown was a sign of joy (→ 622, 6 ff.) and freedom may be seen from the practice of Israelite slaves in the year of Jubilee between New Year's Day and the Day of Atonement: they do not go into their houses nor serve their masters any more, but "they ate and drank and were merry and had crowns on their heads," bRH, 8b.

2. Figurative Use.

There is a connection between Wisdom sayings (→ 626, 25 ff.) and the older Jewish martyr theology in 4 Macc. 17:15, which says of the conflict of the Maccabean martyrs: "But the fear of the Lord remained victor and handed a crown to her warriors." In Ep. Ar., 280 the author replies to the king: "Those who hate evil and . . . act justly" are worthy to be instituted as royal governors, "and this is your experience, O king, to whom God has given the crown of righteousness." Righteousness is a gift of God and the adornment and honour of the king, but not an eschatological gift. Test. B. 4:1 ascribes the crown to Joseph as the reward of a good man. The στέφανος δόξης is a halo of light around the head. In the story Joseph and Asenath, 5, 5 Joseph is depicted with a golden crown on his head adorned with 12 selected precious stones which radiate golden beams, cf. the archangel Michael in 14, 3. [67] The description of the appearance of Joseph has a priestly character. In Test. L. 8:9 seven men clothe Levi as high-priest: "the sixth set a crown on my head. The seventh set the diadem of priesthood on my head," cf. Sir. 45:12. [68] The threefold golden crown of the high-priest is mentioned in Jos. Ant., 3, 172, cf. also Philo Vit. Mos., II, 114.

3. The Crown in Apocalyptic.

In Asc. Is., which has a basis in Jewish apoc., the ascending one sees "Enoch and all who were with him divested of the fleshly garment . . . and they were as the angels, . . . but they did not sit on their thrones, nor were the crowns of glory on their heads"; they will receive these only at the *parousia* of the Messiah, 9:9 ff. He also sees "many garments laid down and many thrones and many crowns," and he asks to whom they belong, and learns that they are reserved for believers, 9:24 ff. The book closes with the promise: "And you too shall be in the Holy Spirit that you may receive your robes and the thrones and crowns of glory which are kept in the seventh heaven," 11:40. The same idea is found in the Qumran community: The "sons of truth" will be led to the "crown of glory with the robe of splendour in eternal light," 1 QS 4:7 f., cf. also the textually incomplete passages 1 QSb 4:2 f., 28. Rab says of the righteous in the future age that "they sit there with crowns on their heads and delight in the radiance of the shekinah," bBer.. 17a. For those who are merciful to the poor "God will plait a crown

---

[67] Ed. P. Batiffol, *Studia Patristica,* I (1889). Materially cf. O. Betz, "Geistliche Schönheit, Die Leibhaftigkeit des Wortes," *Festschr. A. Köberle* (1958), 71-83, esp. 76 f.
[68] Cf. on this Widengren, *op. cit.,* 49-53.

in the world to come," bShab., 104a. The fig. usage shows that in many of these examples the crown suggests radiance and glory. The crown is an eschatological reward for victory and an eschatological honour.

4. Rabbinic Theology.

Rabb. theology speaks of three crowns, that of the Torah, the priesthood and the monarchy. That of the priesthood is given to Aaron, that of the monarchy to David, but that of the Torah can be won. "All the strength of those two crowns comes only from the strength of the Torah," S. Nu., 119 (40a) on 18:20, cf. Midr. Qoh., 31a on 7:1. The crowns of the priesthood and the monarchy cannot be had for money, but one reads of the crown of the Torah: "He who will accept toil for the Torah, let him come and take it," AbRNat, 41. R. Jochanan (d. 279 A.D.) gave the tradition another turn, bYoma, 72b. We also find the tradition of the three crowns in Ab., 4, 17 (R. Shimeon): "There are three crowns, the crown of the Torah, the crown of the priesthood, and the crown of the monarchy; but the crown of a good name is higher than these." Along Wisdom lines the metaphor of the crown is taken from the world around and distinctively developed.

For the righteous, for whom this world was created and the coming world comes acc. to S. Bar., the present age is "toil and labour with much effort," but the world to come is a "crown with great glory," S. Bar. 15:7 f. The crown of radiance is a sign of the victory of the righteous who have endured. Midr. Ps., 2 on 21:2 refers to the prohibition of crowns and to the crowning of the Messiah: "One is not to crown oneself with the crown of a king of flesh and blood, but the Holy One gives His crown to the King Messiah, as it is said: Thou settest a crown of pure gold on his head," Ps. 21:3.

5. The Metaphor of the Contestant in Philo.

Philo of Alexandria adopts esp. the metaphor of the contestant → 620, 16 ff. He is critical of the games in the stadium in Agric., 110 ff., esp. 117: "How is it that the same men condemn and mercilessly punish misdeeds in private life but publicly honour them with crowns and proclamations (στεφάνους καὶ κηρύγματα) in theatres and circuses?" He compares the contestant in the stadium to the man who seeks knowledge, who lives his life without falling, and who finally, arriving at the goal, receives the deserved crowns and rewards of victory στεφάνων καὶ ἄθλων ἐπαξίων τεύξεται πρὸς τὸ τέλος ἐλθών. "Or are not these already crowns of renown, to have sought not unsuccessfully the goal of his exertions, but to have come to the extreme boundaries of knowledge which are reached with such difficulty?" Migr. Abr., 133 f. The patriarchs are compared to a contestant like this, e.g., Isaac to a pugilist or wrestler περὶ νίκης καὶ στεφάνων ἀγωνιζομένῳ, Cher., 80, or Jacob who in the contest by doing good works took the birthright from Esau, τὰ βραβεῖα καὶ τὸν στέφανον, Sacr. AC, 17. Issachar also did good works: "the effort is not in vain but will be crowned and rewarded by God," Leg. All., I, 80. Philo demands: "Oppose (to the desire of the senses) the mind which fights the serpent; fight this finest of fights and in the battle against all other dominant lusts of the senses strive to win the beautiful and glorious victor's crown (καλὸν καὶ εὐκλεᾶ στέφανον) which no festal assembly of men can give thee," Leg. All., II, 108. The victor's crown, however, is the vision of God ὁ στέφανός ἐστιν ὅρασις θεοῦ, Praem. Poen., 27, [69] not as an eschatological gift, but as the cognitive process of insight into the divine order of the cosmos which is hidden from the normal eye. This is

---

[69] In Sacr. AC, 53: στεφανῶσαι θεὸν μὴ ἑαυτόν, στεφανόω means "to honour" on the basis of ancient practice; acc. to Philo this στεφανοῦν is to take place εἰ οἷόν τε ἀχρόνως καὶ ἀμελλητί.

granted to the contestant Jacob, "who through unceasing effort and unshakable character laid hold on virtue," 27. [70]

D. The Crown in the New Testament.

στέφανος and στεφανόω occur in the NT 18 times and 3 respectively. [71] The few instances are evenly distributed over the various books. There are none in Luke (Lk. or Ac.), nor in R. and Gl. Four relate to the crown of thorns; in all the others the crown is the eschatological gift of God to believers.

1. The Figurative Use in Paul.

Like Philo (→ 628, 23 ff.) Paul draws on the perishable crown which is given to the victor as an award in the games (→ 620, 16 ff.) and he compares the Christian life to a sporting contest. The point of comparison is the self-controlled abstinence (→ II, 339, 22 ff.) which is practised for the sake of the goal: πᾶς δὲ ὁ ἀγωνιζόμενος πάντα ἐγκρατεύεται, ἐκεῖνοι μὲν οὖν ἵνα φθαρτὸν στέφανον λάβωσιν, ἡμεῖς δὲ ἄφθαρτον (1 C. 9:25). The comparison of the Christian life with a race in the arena is a recurrent one in Paul, cf. not only 1 C. 9:24-26a but also Gl. 2:2; 5:7; Phil. 2:16; 3:12-14; [72] → I, 638, 32 ff. The imperishable crown, which is characterised by the adjective ἄφθαρτος as στέφανος τῆς ζωῆς, is an eschatological gift of God which is granted to the victor in the contest. The metaphor itself is not explained. It is used again with reference to Paul's own life in 2 Tm. 4:8 — a statement whose significance remains unaltered whether or not the Pastorals are regarded as pseudepigraphical. [73] Paul is looking back on his life as death approaches (4:6): "I have fought a good fight, I have finished my course, I have kept the faith" (4:7). There will thus be given to him ὁ τῆς δικαιοσύνης στέφανος, the crown which will bring final justification (cf. 1 C. 4:1-5) "at that day." The crown will be given by the Lord who is ὁ δίκαιος κριτής, [74] and He will give it not only to Paul but to all τοῖς ἠγαπηκόσι τὴν ἐπιφάνειαν αὐτοῦ (v. 8); that is, the presupposition of receiving it is faithfulness to Christ which is grounded in His appearing and which works itself out in love for this — a statement which is close to Jm. 1:12 and Rev. 2:10 → 630, 27 ff. 2 Tm. 2:5 formulates a general rule. Different

---

[70] In this important passage Philo depicts Abraham as the first to come out of error to the truth, receiving confidence in God as a reward. With him are Isaac and Jacob. Isaac, having a favourable natural disposition, attains to virtue by his own listening and learning and instruction, and receives joy as a reward. In contrast is Jacob, the practised warrior, who receives his reward. The comparison closes with the question: "But could one think of anything more wholesome or worthy than confidence in God, joy which lasts throughout life, and the constant vision of him who is?"

[71] Cf. R. Morgenthaler, *Statistik d. nt.lichen Wortschatzes* (1958), s.v. στέφανος, στεφανοῦν.

[72] The passages are close in time if one assumes that Phil. was written during an Ephesian captivity. 1 C. and Gl. were written during Paul's stay in Ephesus, Deissmann 10, 262 f.

[73] If 2 Tm. is regarded as pseudepigraphical, it contains comparatively the most material from Paul's circle. The depiction of the end must have come from information accessible to a trusted disciple of Paul, 1 Cl., 5, 5 and Phil. 1:15-18 both suggest that opposition from within Chr. groups contributed to his condemnation.

[74] Linguistically cf. Ep. Ar., 280: στέφανος δικαιοσύνης. But whereas 2 Tm. is referring to the eschatological process of justification, Ep. Ar. has in view the present state of a just king. A link between the passage is that in both ὁ στέφανος τῆς δικαιοσύνης is understood as God's gift. The linguistic similarity makes it likely that the expression came to the NT authors from the Wisdom lit.

metaphors are used in the passage; vv. 3 and 4 speak of the soldier (→ VI, 641, 15 ff.), v. 5 of the athlete (→ I, 167, 23 ff.) in the arena (ἀθλέω), and v. 6 of the husbandman. It is said of the athlete: ἐὰν δὲ καὶ ἀθλῇ τις, οὐ στεφανοῦται, ἐὰν μὴ νομίμως ἀθλήσῃ. The requirement for attaining the crown of victory is νομίμως (→ IV, 1089, 4 ff.) ἀθλεῖν. What νομίμως is may be seen plainly from Jesus Christ (2 Tm. 2:8) and his apostle (v. 1 f.).

The metaphor of the crown is used by Paul in another way. He calls the community the crown with which he will appear before the Lord, cf. Phil. 4:1: ἀδελφοί μου ἀγαπητοὶ καὶ ἐπιπόθητοι, χαρὰ καὶ στέφανός μου, and 1 Th. 2:19 f., where in a lively style which adopts the rhetorical question as an answer into the question and then repeats the answer directly with an affirmative γάρ, he says: τίς γὰρ ἡμῶν ἐλπὶς ἢ χαρὰ ἢ στέφανος καυχήσεως — ἢ οὐχὶ καὶ ὑμεῖς — ἔμπροσθεν τοῦ κυρίου ἡμῶν Ἰησοῦ ἐν τῇ αὐτοῦ παρουσίᾳ; ὑμεῖς γάρ ἐστε ἡ δόξα ἡμῶν καὶ ἡ χαρά. The passage adopts ideas such as those in Prv. 12:4; 17:6 → 626, 25 ff. It comes in a passage which is important theologically. Paul realises that he and all believers are definitively saved by the Lord. But in the judgment the fruits of his life will be measured and judged, cf. 1 C. 15:10; also 3:11-15; 4:1-5; 5:5; 9:5-18 (→ I, 346, 32 ff.); 2 C. 5:10 etc. Paul does not merely want to be saved personally. He wants a reward and praise for the results of his life because they prove to be enduring. The fact that they endure finds expression in the churches as his crown [75] and joy and hope and glory on the day of the parousia. Worth noting here is the association of crown and joy → 622, 6 ff. — the crown expresses joy — and also that of crown and glory — the crown is its sign and figure, and hope is directed to it. With this crown Paul receives from God his glory and praise, hence the crown of glorying.

2. The Crown of Victory and Life.

In Rev. 2:10 the church of Smyrna, threatened by persecution and suffering, is summoned: γίνου πιστὸς ἄχρι θανάτου, καὶ δώσω σοι τὸν στέφανον τῆς ζωῆς. The saying corresponds in content to the beatitude in Jm. 1:12: μακάριος ἀνὴρ ὃς ὑπομένει πειρασμόν, ὅτι δόκιμος γενόμενος λήμψεται τὸν στέφανον τῆς ζωῆς, ὃν ἐπηγγείλατο τοῖς ἀγαπῶσιν αὐτόν. Also close to it is 2 Tm. 4:8. The inner relation between the three sayings, which promise to those who suffer, and in some circumstances may even suffer martyrdom, the victor's crown from the Lord's hand, points to a common hortatory basis. [76] Jm. 1:12 with its ὃν ἐπηγγείλατο refers to a concrete promise which can be given in a dominical saying. [77] The στέφανος τῆς ζωῆς [78] means that if the crown is the reward of

---

[75] It is expressly called στέφανος καυχήσεως in 1 Th. 2:19, i.e., a crown which procures or denotes renown, Deissmann LO, 315.

[76] For similar hortatory features of primitive Christianity which are found in many passages but with no literary dependence, so that they must go back to a common original, → II, 258, 17 ff.; cf. W. Grundmann, "Die ΝΗΠΙΟΙ in d. urchr. Paränese," NTSt, 5 (1958/59), 188-205. It has been suggested that Rev. 2:10 and Jm. 1:12 may have such an original in a dominical saying. Cf. A. Resch, Agrapha² (1906), 34 f. with a ref. (280) to Act. Phil., 135 (p. 67, 18); cf. also J. Jeremias, Unbekannte Jesusworte³ (1963), 71-73. This thesis finds further support in Logion 58 of the Copt. Gospel of Thomas, which has a saying of the Lord: "Jesus said, Blessed is the man who has suffered. He has found life," ed. A. Guillaumont et al. (1959), 32 f.

[77] The saying ὃν ἐπηγγείλατο has no subj. ὁ κύριος is supplied in P 𝔐 syh and ὁ θεός in a few MSS. The tradition without subj. avoids the name of God.

[78] Cf. Dib. Jk., ad loc.: "not immediately explicable."

victory the content conferred with it is life. Close to this saying stands the metaphor of the tree of life (Rev. 2:7). One might imagine that the crown is plucked from this tree. It is the life which no death can ever snatch away from the one who is crowned therewith. This crown is the promise and gift of the Lord (δώσω Rev. 2:10) for those who love Him [79] and are faithful to Him, Jm. 1:12; 2 Tm. 4:8. Faithfulness is shown in resisting assaults and enduring suffering. Rev. 3:7 ff. bears witness to the church of Philadelphia that it has held fast to the Word and person of the Lord (v. 8b), and in face of impending assault it receives the promise: κἀγώ σε τηρήσω (v. 10), along with the admonition in view of the imminent coming of the Lord: κράτει ὃ ἔχεις, ἵνα μηδεὶς λάβῃ τὸν στέφανόν σου (v. 11). The crown of victory is a promised gift; by holding fast to the Word (3:8, 10) it will hold fast this gift which is promised in Him. The form of expression is shaped by Jewish Wisdom literature → 626, 25 ff.

According to 1 Pt. 5:4 the crown of life is ἀμαράντινος τῆς δόξης στέφανος, that is, it is woven of imperishable leaves whose imperishability consists in their radiant nature. [80] Life and light belong together like darkness and death. The crown of life is a crown of light, and it is thus represented as a halo around the head. 1 Pt. 5:4 is addressed to the leaders of the community. As shepherds of the flock they are to be examples and on the imminent manifestation of the chief Shepherd they will then receive the crown of victory and life → VI, 665, 39 ff. The saying comes between Pauline statements and those grouped around Rev. 2:10.

3. The Crown as a Symbol of Divine Honour.

The divine in Rev. sees in the Spirit 24 elders sitting on 24 thrones, [81] περιβεβλημένους ἐν ἱματίοις λευκοῖς καὶ ἐπὶ τὰς κεφαλὰς αὐτῶν στεφάνους χρυσοῦς (Rev. 4:4), i.e., in radiant form. They are worshipping Him "who liveth for ever and ever," and in homage (→ III, 166, 8 ff.) they cast their crowns before Him, 4:10. [82] The woman in heaven (Rev. 12:1) also appears in radiant splendour: περιβεβλημένη τὸν ἥλιον καὶ ἡ σελήνη ὑποκάτω τῶν ποδῶν αὐτῆς, καὶ ἐπὶ τῆς κεφαλῆς αὐτῆς στέφανος ἀστέρων δώδεκα (→ II, 323, 9 ff.). Against her rises up the great dragon, the symbol of hostile power, seven-headed καὶ ἐπὶ τὰς κεφαλὰς αὐτοῦ ἑπτὰ διαδήματα, 12:3. Like the dragon is the beast which rises up out of the sea (13:1), the image of the power which is authorised and controlled by him and which is called the conqueror in 6:2: καὶ ἐδόθη αὐτῷ στέφανος, καὶ ἐξῆλθεν νικῶν καὶ ἵνα νικήσῃ. The locusts in Rev. 9:7 are described as beings which bear crowns. The image is weaker here, and like everything in the description of the plague of locusts it is a simile: ἐπὶ τὰς κεφαλὰς αὐτῶν ὡς στέφανοι ὅμοιοι χρυσῷ. Finally the Son of Man also appears on a cloud ἔχων ἐπὶ τῆς κεφαλῆς αὐτοῦ στέφανον χρυσοῦν (Rev. 14:14) and He comes as a Rider on a white horse ἐπὶ τὴν κεφαλὴν αὐτοῦ διαδήματα πολλά (19:12), this distinguishing Him as the One who is called βασιλεὺς βασιλέων καὶ κύριος κυρίων, 19:16.

---

[79] To love is also to believe, cf. 2 Tm. 4:7: "I have kept the faith"; this equation is esp. common in Jn.

[80] Cf. Apul. Met., XI, 24: imperishable radiance.

[81] There is much debate as to who the 24 elders are, cf. Bss. Apk. on 4:4.

[82] Cf. Tac Ann., 15, 29, 2: ad quam (sc. effigiem Neronis) progressus Tiridates ... sublatum capiti diadema imagini subiecit.

4. The Crown of Thorns in the Gospels.

The picture of the appearing of the λόγος τοῦ θεοῦ as King of kings and Lord of lords (Rev. 19:11-16) at the end of the NT is a counterpart to the description of the crown of thorns in the Gospels after the condemnation (Mk. 15:17; Mt. 27:29, before Jn. 19:2, 5) whereby Pilate tries to persuade the crowd to agree to the release of Jesus by making Him an object of contempt and pity. The crown was probably made of acanthus, a prickly weed which grows in Palestine, [83] or of Phoenix dactylifera. [84] It was a mocking imitation of the royal crown worn by vassals of Rome and was designed to throw scorn on Jesus. Whether it was also intended to cause pain by scratching and wounding (Cl. Al. Paed., II, 73-75), or was simply a mock crown [85] as would seem to be suggested by all the mock regalia, [86] must be left an open question.

There has been much discussion of the crowning of Jesus with the crown of thorns. [87] One view is that the soldiers decked Jesus out as king of the Saturnalia. [88] Others refer to the Sacae festival [89] or to miming. [90] But in the upshot it seems the incident must be explained in terms of the situation. The Saturnalia, a Roman carnival, took place in December, and the condemnation and execution of Jesus were at a different time. The Sacae festival and esp. the supposed human sacrifice connected with it are hypothetical; the human sacrifice seems to be an embellishment of Dio Chrys. and without it this festival, whose infiltration into the Roman army has to be postulated, bears hardly any relation to the mocking of Jesus. [91] This is rather connected with the condemnation of Jesus for His Messianic claim; he is mocked by the soldiers as the King of the Jews. The crown of thorns is an imitation of the royal emblem. Stage reminiscences such as those recalled in Philo Flacc., 56 might have had some influence. What the Roman soldiers did with the deposed Vitellius is an interesting par., Dio C., 65, 20 f. [92] The soldiers treat him as they do Jesus. The incident is expanded in Ev. Pt. 3:7 ff.: "And they put on him a purple robe and set him on the judgment seat and said, Judge justly, O king of Israel! And one of them brought a crown of thorns and put it on the Lord's head ... and some scourged him and said, With such honour will we honour the Son of God." [93]

---

83 Cf. Delbrück, op. cit., 129, also Pr.-Bauer⁵, s.v. ἄκανθος (with bibl.).
84 H. St. J. Hart, "The Crown of Thorns in John 19:2, 5," JThST, NS, 3 (1952), 66-75: Jesus as divus Jesus radiatus after the manner of the divine emperor.
85 So Delbrück, 129 with a ref. to Tert. De Corona, 9 (CSEL, 70): impietas contumeliosa... et dedecus.
86 Cf. J. Blinzler, Der Prozess Jesu³ (1960), 240-242.
87 Cf. the bibl. → n. 83-86, also P. Wendland, "Jesus als Saturnalienkönig," Herm., 33 (1898), 175-179; W. R. Paton, "Die Kreuzigung Jesu," ZNW, 2 (1901), 339-341; H. Reich, "Der König mit der Dornenkrone," N Jbch Kl Alt, 13 (1904), 705-733; H. Vollmer, Jesus u. d. Sacäenopfer (1905); also "Der König mit d. Dornenkrone," ZNW, 6 (1905), 194-198; K. Lübeck, Die Dornenkrönung Christi (1906); J. Geffcken, "Die Verhöhnung Christi durch d. Kriegsknechte," Herm., 41 (1906), 220-229; H. Vollmer, "Nochmals das Sacäenopfer," ZNW, 8 (1907), 320 f.; K. Kastner, "Christi Dornenkrönung u. Verspottung durch d. röm. Soldateska," BZ, 6 (1908), 378-392; also "Nochmals die Verspottung Christi," BZ, 9 (1911), 56; H. Allroggen, "Die Verspottung Christi," Theol. u. Glaube, 1 (1909), 689-708; H. Zimmern, Zum Streit um d. Christusmythe (1910), 38 f.; T. Birt, Aus dem Leben der Antike³ (1922), 189-202; H. Riesenfeld, Jésus transfiguré (1947), 48-52.
88 Wendland, op. cit. (→ n. 87).
89 Vollmer Jesus (→ n. 87).
90 Reich, op. cit. (→ n. 87).
91 Cf. Vollmer König, 194 f. (Dio Chrys. De regno, 4, 66); also Geffcken, 222-226; Birt, 190 → n. 87.
92 Birt, 199-201 (→ n. 87).
93 Cf. Hennecke³, I, 121.

In the One who is crowned with thorns John sees the Victor over the world (16:33) as the One vanquished by it, who as the Vanquished is Victor over it (19:30; 20:28; cf. 1:49). Hb. 2:9 (quoting Ps. 8:4-6) has the testimony: βλέπομεν ᾿Ιησοῦν διὰ τὸ πάθημα τοῦ θανάτου δόξῃ καὶ τιμῇ ἐστεφανωμένον.

E. The Crown and Crowning in the Early Church.

If the crown and crowning occur in some significant passages in the NT, but comparatively infrequently, they become most important in the early church in a development on the NT basis. At the same time there is a controversy with the Hell. practice of wearing crowns on various occasions, which found both advocates and critics in Christianity. The adoption of the symbol of the crown in early Christianity is based on the NT understanding of it as the crown of victory (→ 630, 27 ff.) which God will give to those who are faithful even to death. [94]

1. The Martyr's Crown.

The martyr esp. bears the crown of victory and life in the early church. In Mart. Pol., 17, 1 the satanic adversary tries at least to destroy the martyr's body when he sees the martyr ἐστεφανωμένον τε τὸν τῆς ἀφθαρσίας στέφανον καὶ βραβεῖον ἀναντίρρητον ἀπενηνεγμένον, cf. also 19, 2. Ignatius as a martyr receives the crown of righteousness, Martyrium sancti Ign. Antiocheni, 5, 1. [95] Cyprian writes to the martyrs and confessors: quosdam iam comperi coronatos, quosdam vero ad coronam victoriae proximos, Ep., 10, 1 (CSEL, 3, 2). Coronari can even mean "to become a martyr," cf. Commodianus Instructiones, II, 20, 3 (CSEL, 15). The martyr Meletios, who was hanged on a fir, sees in prayer "heaven open and his crown which was prepared for him by God the Lord," Martyrium sanctorum Meletii, Joannis, Stephani et aliorum, 25. [96] On early Chr. monuments martyrdom is followed by coronation by Christ or by the hand of God. [97] In the post-Constantinian age the believing daily service of a pious soul was regarded as martyrdom — devotae mentis servitus cotidianum martyrium est. So Hier. writes to Eustochium on the death of her mother, and he consoles her: mater tua longo martyrio coronata est. The martyrdom of shed blood receives a corona de rosis et violis, that of daily service de liliis, Hier. Ep., 108, 31 (CSEL, 55). In Herm. s., 8, 2, 1 crowns of palm branches are used. With them the angel of the Lord crowns the men who have given in staves with shoots and fruit, and they are admitted to the tower seen in the vision. The allegory is interpreted, and it is said of those who are crowned: "All who fought with the devil and defeated him are crowned; these are they who suffered for the Law of God (= the Son of God preached to the ends of the earth, s., 8, 3, 2)," s., 8, 3, 6. There is a plain line from Rev. 2:10 and Jm. 1:12 (→ 630, 27 ff.) to these statements and the testimonies of the martyrs. Indeed, it may be seen already in the martyr theology of Judaism → 627, 18 ff. He who fights victoriously against evil desire and turns to righteousness in the fear of God is addressed: σὺ οὖν νῖκος λαβὼν καὶ στεφανωθείς, and he is to give it the reward of victory, Herm. m., 12, 2, 5, a Chr. version of the offering of the crown to the god in antiquity (→ 620, 38 ff.), cf. also Rev. 4:10 → 631, 23 ff. [98] In the

---

[94] Cf. Baus, 157-230.

[95] Ed. F. X. Funk-F. Diekamp, Patres Apostolici, II² (1913), 332.

[96] Ed. P. Franchi de Cavalieri, Studi e Testi, 65 (1935), 330, 34 ff.; cf. also the examples in Baus, 180-184.

[97] For further examples cf. Baus, 185-190.

[98] The offering of the crown is also attested for the ruler cult in the Hell. period. Acc. to Anabasis Alexandri, VII, 23, 2 (ed. A. G. Roos [1910]) envoys from Greece come to Babylon to honour Alexander the Great as a god by bringing him golden crowns. On a sarcophagus in the Lateran Museum — cf. W. Neuss, Die Kunst d. alten Christen (1926), Ill. 3 — the magi also offer the Christ child a crown in homage. "The act of offering a crown denotes subjection, acknowledgment of the ruler's sovereignty," Baus, 198.

ancient Chr. sermon 2 Cl. sayings from the Past. like 2 Tm. 2:5 (→ 629, 29 ff.) are quoted and the crown of victory is promised to the good fighter, the image of the fighter being taken from the sporting arena, 2 Cl., 7, 1-4.

2. The Crown in Gnosticism.

The crown was highly significant in the symbolical language of Gnosticism. In the Coptic κατά μυστήριον λόγος, 45 ff. Jesus crowns His disciples at the threefold Gnostic baptism, the crowns being plaited from various plants. [99] The symbol of the crown is common in O. Sol. For the Gnostic singer the *Kurios* Himself is a crown, like Mithras in the Mithras mysteries and Yahweh for the holy remnant of Israel in Is. 28:5: "The Lord is a crown on my head from whom I will not separate myself." Par. is the following saying: "Woven for me is the crown of truth; its branches have sprouted on me," for (the *Kurios* is addressed): "Thou are not like a withered up wreath which does not sprout," O. Sol. 1:1-3. [100] The crown of truth which is the *Kurios* Himself brings forth the fruits of salvation, 1:5. The idea recurs in 5:12: "He (the *Kurios*) is as a crown on my head, hence I do not waver." The crown gives stability; it is more than a symbol; it is a power. This is plain in 17:1, 4 f., where the confession: "I am crowned by my God, he is my living crown," is elucidated: "I received the countenance and form of a new being, entered in, and was redeemed. True thought guided me." Here the connection between the two sayings: "The Lord is my crown," and: "The crown of truth was wound round me," is clear. Of it one reads: "An eternal crown is truth... and a costly stone. There were even wars about the crown. But righteousness won it and gave it you (righteousness = *Kurios*), so that the crown places in firm connection with the Lord," 9:8-11a. In a spiritualising of the concept of sacrifice crowning in sacrificial usage is also spiritualised: "Put on the rich grace of the Lord, enter his Paradise, recline at table in his friendliness," 20:7. The crown of sacrifice plucked from the tree of life in Paradise is worn at the sacrificial banquet.

3. Early Christian Art.

In early Chr. art we find many examples which illustrate the literary testimonies. In the apse mosaic of Santa Pudenziana in Rome Christ is enthroned with the book of life before the heavenly Jerusalem, surrounded by the apostles, and two women bring crowns and hold them over the heads of Peter and Paul to crown them. [101] In San Vitale in Ravenna Christ enthroned on the globe hands Saint Vitalis a golden crown inset with precious stones. [102] In the martyr processions in San Apollinare Nuovo in Ravenna the martyrs bear their crowns of victory in their hands in solemn procession and offer them in homage to Christ, who sits between the angels and whose head is encircled by a halo with a cross. [103] On these mosaics, as noted, Christ has a halo or a halo with cross. So does the martyr Laurentius on a mosaic in the tomb of Galla Placidia in Ravenna. [104]

---

[99] Cf. C. Schmidt-W. Till, *Kpt.-gnostische Schriften*, I, GCS, 45³ (1959), 308, 28 f. 309, 39 f.; 312, 32 f. For the Mandaeans cf. K. Rudolph, *Die Mandäer*, II, FRL, NF, 57 (1961), 175-181.

[100] Cf. Hennecke³, I, 437-472; cf. also the ed. of R. Harris, *ad loc.*

[101] Ill. in W. Volbach-M. Hirmer, *Frühchr. Kunst* (1958), Ill. 130. The significance of the two women is uncertain; L. v. Sybel, *Chr. Antike*, II (1909), 329 thinks they are Pudenziana and Praxedis, but J. Kollwitz, "Christus als Lehrer u. d. Gesetzesübergabe an Petrus," *Röm. Quartalschr. f. die Altertumskunde u. Kirchengeschichte*, 44 (1936), 65 etc. thinks two churches are offering their crowns.

[102] Ill. F. W. Deichmann, *Frühchr. Bauten u. Mosaiken v. Ravenna* (1958), esp. Ill. 351 f., 354.

[103] Deichmann, Ill. 100-106, 119-127.

[104] *Ibid.*, Ill. 5 and 7. In the Ravenna mosaics Christ has a halo with cross, the prophets, apostles and martyrs the simple halo. In the apse mosaic of Pudenziana in Rome (→ n. 101) Christ has a simple halo.

4. The Crown of Thorns in Early Christian Art.

On a passion sarcophagus in the Lateran Museum in Rome [105] there is a depiction of Christ's crowning with thorns. A soldier is putting the crown on his head. But it is no crown of thorns; it is the imperial *corona laurea triumphalis*. In depicting Jesus in regal composure and supremacy the artist is trying to express what Cyril of Jerusalem says in a sermon: "They also put on him a purple robe; they did so in mockery, but it was a prophetic act; for he was truly king. Even if they did it in in scorn, they still did it, and this was a symbol of his imperial dignity. Though the crown was of thorns, it was still a crown, and it was woven by the soldiers; for the emperors were acclaimed by soldiers," Cyr. Hom. in Paralyticum, 12 (MPG, 33 [1857], 1145B). In the middle of the sarcophagus there is a big crown around the monogram XP on the cross, beneath which the guards sit; this crown is held up by an eagle. What is expressed is Christ's cross and resurrection, His triumph on the cross: "Through the victorious sign of the cross the Lord triumphed," Martyrium Montani et Lucii, 4, 4. [106] The passion is interpreted as victory over death and hence as the way of triumph. By His suffering the Lord treads the path to glory and faith sees the cross and the glorifying together. [107] The crucified Lord is the glorified Lord whom believers confess with the confession: The Lord is my crown, → 626, 11 f. There are crowns on the gable of the building from which Christ comes bearing His cross and on that of the building in which Pilate washes his hands.

5. The Wedding Crown in the Early Church.

The examples show that on the NT basis elements from the contemporary world have invaded Chr. concepts and depictions. As concerns the basic understanding of the crown as that of victory it is significant that the custom of the wedding crown (→ 622, 22 ff.) came into Christianity in the post-Constantinian period. It was permitted on the ground that the crown is a sign of victory over lusts: "Crowns are put on their heads as a sign that they never yielded and now come to marriage, because they were not overcome by lusts," Hom. in 1 Tm., 9, 2 on 2:11 ff. (MPG, 62 [1862], 546). [108]

6. The Rejection of the Non-Christian Use of Crowns.

In early Christianity Tert. esp. fought against the use of crowns by non-Christians. [109] He did so in his work De corona (CSEL, 70) with uncompromising severity, showing that within Christianity there were advocates of this use. For Tert. the use of crowns is a sin which the Christian must shun, De cor., 2. He calls it unnatural, since flowers have no business on the head, 6. He traces its origin to the pagan cultus, 7. He also pts. out that there is no justification for it in the Bible, 9. Christ wore only the crown of thorns, 14. God alone has the right to crown men. Hence the Christian will not put on a crown himself; he will only take it from God in the eternal consummation, 15. [110] The crown is God's eschatological gift to the believer who has overcome. Cyprian De lapsis, 2 (CSEL, 3) takes the same position as Tert. when in praise of those who have stood fast in persecution he says: *frons cum signo dei pura diaboli coronam ferre non potuit, coronae se Domini reservavit*. Materially Cl. Al. also expresses Christianity's rejection

---

[105] Baus, Plate 16; cf. also K. Wessel, *Der Sieg über den Tod. Die Passion Christi in d. frühchr. Kunst d. Abendlandes* (1956), Ill. 4-8 and p. 7 f. Cf. also H. Leclercq, Art. "Instruments de la Passion, 5: La couronne d'épines," DACL, 7 (1926), 1155-57.
[106] Ed. R. Knopf-G. Krüger, *Ausgewählte Märtyrerakten³* (1929), 75.
[107] For the primitive Chr. basis of the early Chr. view cf. Grundm. Mk., 312 f. → 633, 1 ff.
[108] Baus, 98-111.
[109] Cf. H. Leclercq, Art. "Militarisme, 7: L'enseignement de Tert.," DACL, 11 (1933), 1122-26.
[110] Baus, 37-73.

of the use of the crown in the contemporary world, and gives arguments for this taken both from reason and also from faith's repudiation of idolatry, cf. Paed., II, 72, 2 ff.; 73, 1 ff. He makes extensive use of the comparison of the Chr. life with the contest of antiquity, as Paul and the Hell. synagogue did before him, Quis. Div. Salv., 3, 3-6.

7. The Use of Crowns in the Post-Constantinian Era.

Constantine helped to make the use of crowns esp. important in the Church. The sign in which he was to conquer was that of the cross in the solar disc. His soldiers carried the monogram of Christ on their shields and after the campaign against Licinius the emperor carried with him a standard with the cross, the *labarum*, [111] Eus. Vit. Const., I, 31. In his imperial palace in Constantinople he had a cross set with gems, III, 49. Probably he also set a crown round it like the Christ monograms on the army standards. This was the form which became normative on household vessels, e.g., lamps. [112] It is said that Julian, when sacrificing, saw in the entrails of the offering a cross encircled by a crown σταυρὸν στεφανούμενον, Greg. Naz. Or. contra Julianum, 1, 54. [113] One finds this also on the passion sarcophagus of the Lateran Museum (→ 635, 2 ff.) and with variations in many other places too, e.g., on tablets of ivory in Milan Cathedral, which depict a crowned Lamb, a cross of glory, and Christ taking into his outstretched hands crowns offered to Him by two men. [114] The tomb of a Cilician bishop has a crown with the inscr. φίλτατος ὁ μακάριος πάπας ὁ θεοῦ φίλος, probably alluding to his name Theophilus. [115] In combination the cross, the Christ monogram and the crown came to be of fundamental significance in the symbolism of early Christianity.

Grundmann

στήκω, ἵστημι

στήκω.

The verb στήκω is a Hell. construct. from the stem of the perf. ἕστηκα intr. "to stand" (from ἵστημι → 640, 36 ff.), and it is used alongside this. [1] It is one of several substitutes for ἵστημι or ἵσταμαι which in part were newly coined and in part derive from non-Attic dialects. They owe their origin to the popular post-class. dislike for verbs in -μι. [2] στήκω lives on in the modern Gk. στέκω "to stand."

1. στήκω is rare in the LXX, or at any rate is not gen. attested, so that from a comparison of the texts one may assume that Chr. redactors put it in place of forms of ἵστημι: Ex. 14:13 (A στήκετε with στῆτε in other MSS) [3] in the summons of Moses to the people when they were afraid of the approaching Egyptians: "Fear ye not, stand still, and see the salvation of the Lord, which he will shew to you to day"; this has the

---

111 Cf. A. Alföldi, "Hoc signo victor eris," *Pisculi f. F. J. Dölger* (1939), 1-18.
112 Cf. Dölger (→ n. 45), V, 177.
113 *Ibid.*, 177 and 637 f.
114 *Ibid.*, 554-578, also Delbrück, op. cit. (→ n. 32), 5-8 and Plate 5. 6.
115 Cf. W. M. Ramsay, *Studies in the History and Art of the Eastern Provinces of the Roman Empire* (1906), 23 and Plate 5, also Dölger (→ n. 45), III, 69, 1; V. 623 f.

στήκω. 1 Cf. Bl.-Debr. § 73; Mayser, I, 2, 123; Schwyzer, I, 767; II, 286.
2 Radermacher, 97.
3 With A cf. the derived group, probably a pre-Hexapla assimilation to the HT [Katz].

ring of στήκω in the NT; Ju. 16:26 of the pillars on which the house stands (B στήκει, other texts ἐπεστήρικται); [4] 3 Βασ. 8:11 of the priests who cannot stand in the sanctuary because the cloud of the Lord fills it (B οὐκ ἠδύναντο ... στήκειν, others στῆναι "enter"). [5]

2. In the NT the verb occurs chiefly in Paul. Elsewhere one finds it at Mk. 3:31 of the relatives of Jesus standing outside (ἔξω στήκοντες); Jn. 1:26 in the Baptist's witness to the unknown Jesus: μέσος ὑμῶν στήκει ὃν ὑμεῖς οὐκ οἴδατε, with ἕστηκεν in P66, ℵ as Θ; Rev. 12:4 of the dragon which tries to seize the woman who is clothed with the sun: καὶ ὁ δράκων ἔστηκεν (or ἔστηκεν); Mk. 11:25 with ref. to standing before God in prayer, [6] an example of the practice of standing for prayer in Palestine, cf. Lk. 18:11.

Paul uses the verb mostly in the imperative form στήκετε, so that the question arises whether it is for him the normal imperative for ἕστηκα "stand" as distinct from στῆτε "approach." In 1 C. 16:13: στήκετε ἐν τῇ πίστει, one catches an echo of Ex. 14:13 (→ 636, 32 ff.). In his life a man may either stand or he may have no stability, i.e., he may fall (→ VI, 164, 10 ff.) or be pushed aside or change his position. The standing of the Christian community is given to it in faith. Paul in his admonition is repeating the familiar play on words of Is. 7:9: "If ye will not believe, surely ye shall not be established." In faith man attains to the position which allows him to stand firm. [7] This standing does not result from secular securities such as health, power, property, or connections. It is based on the transcendent God on whose promise faith is fixed. [8] It is here that human existence finds its foundation and establishment. This phenomenon, familiar in the OT from Is. and fundamental to the NT, is a singular one in the history of religion. In the NT the divine promise on which faith is fixed and which gives man his basis is spoken to man in Jesus Christ. Hence Paul can also give the admonition: στήκετε ἐν κυρίῳ, Phil. 4:1. "To stand in faith" (→ lines 12 ff.) is "to stand in the Lord," for faith looks to the Lord and unites with Him. [9] The choice of κύριος shows that the one who stands in Him is determined by Him and receives from Him the standing which is given to him as faith by God's saving work in Jesus Christ; he now has to listen to the Lord and follow Him. στήκετε ἐν κυρίῳ might thus be translated: "Stand in obedience to the Lord." 1 Th. 3:7 f. shows plainly that the comforted life and work of the apostle Paul and his companions depend on this standing in the Lord. The conditional clause ἐάν with indicative, which is rare in the NT, has a hidden hortatory meaning: Continue to stand in obedience to the Lord, for this will give comfort and power to our life and work in many afflictions. Standing in the Lord has sustaining power and also the power to create fellowship. If Christians have their standing in the

---

[4] στήκω does not replace a form of ἵστημι here, but another verb. The text is from the early 4th cent.; εἱστήκει in the catena group dependent on B seems to come from it [Katz].

[5] At Jos. 10:19 ᾽Α Θ have στήκω for עמד, LXX ἵστημι, Σ ἀφίστημι.

[6] Cf. bBer., 6b: "... and standing means no other than prayer(ואין עמידה אלא תפלה), for it is said (Ps. 106:30): Phinehas stood and prayed."

[7] On this cf. G. Ebeling, "Jesus u. Glaube," ZThK, 55 (1958), 70-79.

[8] Ebeling, 75: "Faith does not come on the basis of an existence ensured of enduring, and hence it is not an individual act grounded in existence. Faith is that wherein existence is given its establishment"; it is "the existence which is sure of its foundation and which is thus grounded, which stands," 76.

[9] J. Pascher, Η ΒΑΣΙΛΙΚΗ ΟΔΟΣ, Der Königsweg zu Wiedergeburt u. Vergottung bei Philon v. Alex. (1931), 236-8, thinks that in Phil. 3:8-4:1 "the individual motifs of the mystical way are not unclearly utilised and at the end of the ideal of 'standing fast in the Lord' is proclaimed," just as "standing" is in Philo the end of this way which leads to deification.

Lord, Paul can also expect of them: στήκετε ἐν ἑνὶ πνεύματι, Phil. 1:27; for unity in spirit is given in the Lord, 1 C. 12:4-6; Eph. 4:4-6. Because the Lord gives freedom from the destructive powers of sin, law and death, because faith in the promise of the Word grasps and attains this freedom, the Galatians are admonished: τῇ ἐλευθερίᾳ ἡμᾶς Χριστὸς ἠλευθέρωσεν· στήκετε οὖν καὶ μὴ πάλιν ζυγῷ δουλείας ἐνέχεσθε (Gl. 5:1 → II, 899, 18 ff.). All these connections must be taken into account when we read in 2 Th. 2:15: στήκετε καὶ κρατεῖτε τὰς παραδόσεις ἅς ἐδιδάχθητε, the reference to παραδόσεις suggesting to some a deutero-Pauline formulation. R. 14:4 is uttered in a differently employed circle of ideas (→ 648, 42 ff.) when it says that each servant stands or falls to his own master, i.e., the Lord, not men, will have the last word concerning the standing or falling of His servant, → VI, 165, 6 ff.

The word στήκω seems to be preferred by Paul. It is linked by him with the theological point already noted, namely, that in faith man attains to a standing which is not grounded in the world in which he is set by the Lord and will be upheld by Him, which gives him freedom from the destructive powers of the world, and which aims at fellowship in one spirit. This new verb sometimes took on a more general sense in post-Pauline usage. The Pauline development of στήκω is part of the use and meaning of the very common word ἵστημι → 651, 5 ff.

3. Outside the NT the verb does not occur in writings close to the primitive Chr. age. We find it later in a series of passages in the apocr. Acts, so Act. Andr. et Matth. 32 (p. 114, 12); Joh. 114 (p. 214, 8); Phil. 65 (p. 27, 1. 9); Thom. 78 (p. 193, 5) and 135 (p. 242, 5) etc.; [10] also Corpus Hippiatricorum Graecorum, I, 69. 2. 4; [11] Epigr. Graec., 970; Preis. Zaub., I, 4, 923; II, 36, 273; cf. P. Lips,. 40, II, 4 (4th/5th cent. A.D.): παρὼν καὶ στήγων for στήκων.

ἵστημι.

Contents: A. ἵστημι in Greek-Hellenistic Usage. B. Theological Aspects in the Old Testament. C. Judaism: 1. Sirach; 2. Philo; 3. Qumran. D. ἵστημι in the New Testament: I. Employment corresponding to General Usage; II. Theological Aspects of New Testament Usage.

ἵστημι is one of the verbs which take their sense from the relations in which they stand. It also involves the place where a person is set or stands and the question of what endures in the flux of time with its changes.

A. ἵστημι in Greek-Hellenistic Usage.

1. The verbal forms of ἵστημι are developed from the root aor. ἔστην, [1] on the one hand the duplicated pres. ἵστημι, ἵσταμαι with various senses, on the other the perf. ἔστηκα meaning "to stand." The Sanskr. connection may be seen plainly from ἵ στημι si sto and the stem στα- Lat. stare, Germ. "stehen" (stahn), "stand." On the one side standing is the opp. of sitting (often expressing dignity when someone stands before them, → III, 440, 16 ff.), reclining (→ III, 654, 4 ff.), and falling (→ VI, 161, 1 ff.), in contrast with which getting up is standing; it is also the opp. of movement. Plato emphasises the distinction between movement and standing still when he puts the question of being (τὸ ὄν). τὸ ὄν is not κίνησις καὶ στάσις ..., ἀλλ' ἕτερον δή τι

---

[10] [Bertram].
[11] Ed. E. Oder and C. Hoppe, I (1924).

ἵστημι. [1] [Risch].

τούτων. κατὰ τὴν αὑτοῦ φύσιν ἄρα τὸ ὂν οὔτε ἔστηκεν οὔτε κινεῖται, and he asks: εἰ γάρ τι μὴ κινεῖται, πῶς οὐχ ἔστηκεν; ἢ τὸ μηδαμῶς ἐστός, πῶς οὐκ αὖ κινεῖται; τὸ δὲ ὂν ἡμῖν νῦν ἐκτὸς τούτων ἀμφοτέρων ἀναπέφανται, Soph., 250c d. But he also asks whether ἑστάναι and κινεῖσθαι are possible at the same time, and has to answer this in the affirmative: εἰ γάρ τις λέγοι ἄνθρωπον ἑστηκότα, κινοῦντα δὲ τὰς χεῖράς τε καὶ τὴν κεφαλήν, ὅτι ὁ αὐτὸς ἔστηκέ τε καὶ κινεῖται ἅμα, οὐκ ἂν οἶμαι ἀξιοῖμεν οὕτω λέγειν δεῖν, ἀλλ᾽ ὅτι τὸ μέν τι αὐτοῦ ἔστηκε, τὸ δὲ κινεῖται· οὐχ οὕτω; — οὕτω, Resp., IV, 436c d. Archimedes raised the question of the immovable pt. from which the earth is moved. Pappus Alexandrinus Collectio, VIII (p. 1060, 1-4)[2] says about this: τῆς αὐτῆς δέ ἐστιν θεωρίας τὸ δοθὲν βάρος τῇ δοθείσῃ δυνάμει κινῆσαι· τοῦτο γὰρ ᾽Αρχιμήδους μὲν εὕρημα [λέγεται] μηχανικόν, ἐφ᾽ ᾧ λέγεται εἰρηκέναι· δός μοί (φησι) ποῦ στῶ καὶ κινῶ τὴν γῆν.

2. Formed from the root aor. the pres. ἵστημι, fut. στήσω, aor. ἔστησα, has the basic sense a. "to cause to stand still," "to stop." Narration of events which have befallen is broken off: στήσαντες ἐπὶ τούτων τὴν διήγησιν, Polyb., 3, 2, 6. For the medical use cf. Aristot. Hist. An., VIII, 26, p. 605a, 27 ff. It is said of the dying Socrates: τὰ ὄμματα ἔστησεν, "he held his eyes still," i.e., they grew dim, Plat. Phaed., 118. Plat. Crat., 437a says of ἐπιστήμη: ἔοικε σημαίνοντι ὅτι ἵστησιν ἡμῶν ἐπὶ τοῖς πράγμασι τὴν ψυχήν. b. But these forms can also have the meaning "to set up," "to set upright," "to raise up," "to erect," e.g., Hom. Il., 6, 433: Andromache asks Hector: λαὸν δὲ στῆσον. Soph. Oed. Col., 11: στῆσόν με κἀξίδρυσον, Eur. Suppl., 1229 f.: σύ με ἐς ὀρθὸν ἴστη. Soph. El., 27 says of a horse pricking up its ears: ὀρθὸν οὖς ἵστησιν. Eur. Hipp., 1203 reads: ὀρθὸν δὲ κρᾶτ᾽ ἔστησαν οὖς τ᾽ ... ἵπποι. In Hom. Il., 15, 126 f. Athena takes away the lance and sets it upright: ἔγχος δ᾽ ἔστησε ... χάλκεον. Monuments of victory are set up; Heracles complains in Soph. Trach., 1102: κοὐδεὶς τροπαῖ᾽ ἔστησε τῶν ἐμῶν χερῶν, cf. also Isoc. Or., 4, 150; 5, 148. A monument to the dead (στήλη) is set up, Hom. Il. 17, 435; Dio C., 69, 10, 2: ἱστάναι μνημεῖον Aristoph. Eq., 268. Mixing bowls are set up for a banquet στήσαντο κρητῆρας ἐπιστεφέας οἴνοιο, Hom. Od., 2, 431. This is also done in honour of the gods ἐπουρανίοισι θεοῖς αἰειγενέτῃσι κρητῆρα στήσασθαι, Il., 6, 527 f. Choirs are set up and arranged for feasts; Electra in Soph. El., 280 is concerned that Clytemnestra honour the day of Agamemnon's death: ταύτῃ (ἡμέρᾳ) χοροὺς ἵστησι, cf. also Eur. Alc., 1155; also Hdt. III, 48, 3: ἵστασαν χοροὺς παρθένων τε καὶ ἠιθέων. Anacharsis prays to and praises the mother of the gods for a safe return and sets up offerings καὶ παννυχίδα στήσειν, Hdt., IV, 76, 3. Soldiers, too, are set up and arranged τελευταίους μέντοι στήσω τοὺς ἐπὶ πᾶσι καλουμένους, Xenoph. Cyrop., VI, 3, 25. The voice of God which summons Oedipus to Colonos causes terror among those who hear it, ὥστε πάντας ὀρθίας στῆσαι φόβῳ δείσαντας ἐξαίφνης τρίχας, Soph. Oed. Col., 1624 f. c. From this it is only a step to the sense "to appoint," "to institute," "to make," e.g., τύραννον αὐτόν ... στήσουσιν, Soph. Oed. Tyr., 939 f.; Creon says: ἀλλ᾽ ὃν πόλις στήσειε, τοῦδε χρὴ κλύειν, Soph. Ant., 666. Theseus will not rest, he says to Oedipus, πρὶν ἄν σε τῶν σῶν κύριον στήσω τέκνων, Soph. Oed. Col., 1041. "To set up as king" is common, Dion Hal. Ant. Rom., 1, 61, 2; Dio C., 71, 13, 3. d. In other connections we finds nuances like "to stir up": κονίης μεγάλην ἱστᾶσιν ὀμίχλην, Hom. Il., 13, 336; (μάχην) Γίγαντες ἔστησαν θεοῖς, Eur. Ion, 987 f.; μῆνιν τοσήνδε ... στήσας ἔχεις, Soph. Oed. Tyr., 699; "to cause to rise" νεφέλαι, Hom. Il., 5, 523; cf. Od., 12, 405, of hope, Eur. Iph. Aul., 788; "to lift up," Thoas in Iph. Taur., 1307 asks: τίς ἀμφὶ δῶμα θεᾶς τόδ᾽ ἵστησιν βοήν; e. Finally ἵστημι is used in weighing "to place on the scales," "to cause the scales to come to rest," "to weigh," cf. ἀριθμοῦντες καὶ μετροῦντες καὶ

---

2 Ed. F. Hultsch, III (1878); cf. also Plut. De Marcello, 14 (I, 306a); Simpl. Comm. in Aristot. Phys., II, 4 on II, 5, p. 196a, 24 ff. (ed. H. Diels, Comm. in Aristot. Graeca, 9 [1882], 331, 15 ff.); Johannes Tzetza, Chiliades, 2, 130 (ed. T. Kiessling [1826]) [C. Schneider].

ἱστάντες, Xenoph. Cyrop., VIII, 2 and 21; χρυσοῦ δὲ στήσας 'Οδυσεὺς δέκα πάντα τάλαντα ἦρχ', Hom. Il., 19, 247 f. cf. Il., 24, 232; ἱστᾶσι σταθμῷ πρὸς ἀργύριον τὰς τρίχας, Hdt. II, 65, 4.

3. The mid. ἵσταμαι with fut. στήσομαι and root aor. ἔστην has an intr. sense and means a. "to stand still," "to remain standing," "to come before," Hom. Od., 10, 97 and 148: ἔστην δὲ σκοπιὴν ἐς παιπαλόεσσαν ἀνελθών. Oileus, springing from the chariot, comes to Agamemnon ... ἐξ ἵππων κατεπάλμενος ἀντίος ἔστη, Il., 11, 94; fig. the dream sent by Zeus comes to Agamemnon and stops where his head lies στῆ δ' ἄρ' ὑπὲρ κεφαλῆς, Il., 2, 20. Achilles summons the shade of the dead Patroclus: ἀλλά μοι ἆσσον στῆθι, Il., 23, 97. In Soph. Trach., 1076 Heracles says to Hylios: στῆθι πλησίον πατρός, cf. Xenoph. Cyrop., IV, 1, 1: στὰς εἰς τὸ μέσον. In Xenoph. An., I, 10, 1: οὐκέτι ἵστανται, ἀλλὰ φεύγουσιν, the people do not "stand" with Ariaios against the enemy but flee, cf. IV, 8, 19: οἱ δὲ πολέμιοι, ὡς ἤρξαντο θεῖν, οὐκέτι ἔστησαν, ἀλλὰ φυγῇ ἄλλος ἄλλη ἐτράπετο, and Dion. Hal. Ant. Rom., 9, 28, 2: οἱ μὴ στάντες παρὰ τὰ δεινά, who do not "stand" against dangers. In his fourth Philippic Demosth. Or., 10, 10 says of Philippus: οὐ στήσεται πάντας ἀνθρώπους ἀδικῶν, and he seeks to take from his hearers the fear this οὐ στήσεται τοῦτ' ἄνευ μεγάλου τινὸς κακοῦ, 10, 36. b. The mid. forms also mean "to arise," often with ὀρθός "to stand up." Hom. Od., 18, 241 says of Iros: οὐδ' ὀρθὸς στῆναι δύναται ποσίν. The priest in Soph. Oed. Tyr., 50 says to Oedipus that the men of Thebes have been raised up by him and now fall: στάντες τ' ἐς ὀρθὸν καὶ πεσόντες ὕστερον. Oedipus asks the people of Thebes to rise up and prepare offerings for the faults they have committed: ὑμεῖς μὲν βάθρων ἵστασθε, 142 f., and the priest takes up the words: ὦ παῖδες, ἱστώμεσθα, 147. c. Closely related is the sense "to begin." Thus the first third of the month in the Attic calendar is called μὴν ἱστάμενος, "the beginning or advancing month," in distinction from μὴν μεσῶν and μὴν φθίνων, cf. Hdt., VI. 57, 2; 106, 3. ἵσταμαι occurs with adv. for "to behave" in Polyb., 18, 3, 2: ἀδίκως ἵστασθαι καὶ λίαν ἀγεννῶς, 18, 33, 4: εὐλαβῶς ἵστασθαι. d. The forms of ἵσταμαι are close to and indicate presence in a strong sense. It is said of Philoctet. in Soph. Phil., 174 f. that he suffers every lack ... ἀλύει δ' ἐπὶ παντὶ τῷ χρείας ἱσταμένῳ, and the Schol.[3] comments: ἐπὶ παντὶ ἐν χρείᾳ γινομένῳ ἀπορεῖ. Bribery (Soph. Ant., 298 f.) affects even the souls of upright mortals πρὸς αἰσχρὰ πράγμαθ' ἵστασθαι, so that they undertake shameful things. In Hom. Il., 10, 173 we find the proverb "the matter hangs by a thread," ἐπὶ ξυροῦ ἵσταται ἀκμῆς. Polyb., 21, 9, 3: ἔστη τῇ διανοίᾳ, "he stood firm in his conviction."

4. The perf. and pluperf. forms ἕστηκα εἱστήκειν mean "to stand," so Eur. Suppl., 987: τί ποτ' αἰθερίαν ἕστηκε πέτραν, Hom. Il., 18, 171 f. φύλοπις αἰνὴ ἕστηκε πρὸ νεῶν. The Trojans stand erect, frightened by the appearance of Achilles, ὀρθῶν δ' ἑσταότων ἀγορὴ γένετ' ... Il., 18, 246. The forms can thus come to mean "to be." Creon in Eur. Phoen., 968 says: ἐν ὡραίῳ γὰρ ἕσταμεν βίου, "we stand in the bloom of life," and he also says of the trouble of the people of Thebes through the disclosed sin of Oedipus: ... ἵν' ἕσταμεν χρείας, "because we are in such straits...," Soph. Oed. Tyr., 1442 f. Acc. to Soph. Trach., 1271 τὰ δὲ νῦν ἑστῶτ' are "existing relations" in contrast to τὰ μὲν οὖν μέλλοντ', 1270. Plat. Resp., VIII, 545a speaks of the type of rulers κατὰ τὴν Λακωνικὴν ἑστῶτα πολιτείαν, Polyb., 3, 105, 9 refers to λογισμὸς ἑστώς, a "solidly grounded opinion." Plat. Leg., VII, 802c mentions ἡ ἑστηκυῖα καὶ ἔμφρων ἡλικία, Polyb., 6, 25, 10 ineluctably existing and ordered necessity: χρεία ἑστηκυῖα καὶ τεταγμένη. In P. Tebt., III, 703, 176 f. (late 3rd cent. B.C.) there is ref. to τιμαὶ ἑστηκυῖαι, "firm rewards." Chronologically Hom. Il., 19, 117: ὁ δ' ἕβδομος ἑστήκει μείς, "the seventh month stands," i.e., it has begun and is present.

---

[3] Ed. P. Papageorgius (1888).

5. The fut. and aor. pass. σταθήσομαι, ἐστάθην are relatively late and share the general meaning of the word.

B. Theological Aspects in the Old Testament.

1. Usage. LXX usage corresponds to that of Gk. generally. ἵστημι occurs for 36 different Hbr. verbs, of which only two are common. These are עָמַד (338 times) and קוּם (116 times). נצב and יצב occur 37 times between them, שׁקל (תכל) 17 times, שׂים 6 and the other 29 some 48 times all told.

a. ἵστημι trans. means "to make to stand still," "to stop," "to set up" etc. in Gn. 43:9; 47:2, 7; Lv. 27:11; Nu. 3:6; 27:19, 22; also of cultic signs etc. Gn. 28:18; 31:45, 48; 35:14; Nu. 21:8 f.; Dt. 27:2, 4; Jos. 4:20; 3 Βασ. 7:7 (1 K. 7:21), of a tomb Gn. 35:20; in cultic things cf. also Gn. 12:8; 21:28 f.; 33:19 f.; Ex. 40:2, 17 f.; Nu. 9:15; 1 Ch. 25:1; 2 Ch. 8:14. ἵστημι is used in the sense "to appoint," "to make" in 1 Βασ. 10:19; 3 Βασ. 10:9; 2 Ch. 25:14; 2 Εσδρ. 16:7, and in the sense "to weigh" in 2 Εσδρ.8:33; 3 Βασ. 21:39; 2 Βασ. 14:26; Job 6:2; Is. 46:6. [4]

b. ἵσταμαι intr. in the sense "to stand still," "to come before," also "to stand erect," "to get up," occurs in Gn. 29:35; 30:9; Ex. 14:13; Nu. 9:17; 10:12; Dt. 31:15; 1 Ch. 11:14; 28:2; Jdt. 10:16; Jos. 3:13, 16; 10:12; Jon. 1:15; Dt. 24:11; Nu. 35:12; Ex. 9:13; Nu. 27:2. For "to endure" cf. 1 Βασ. 13:14; 24:21.

c. The perf. and pluperf. forms ἕστηκα, εἱστήκειν "to stand" are used in, e.g., Gn. 24:13, 30, 31; Ex. 3:5; 20:21; 33:8; Dt. 5:5.

d. For the passive forms cf. esp. Job 28:15: οὐ σταθήσεται ἀργύριον ἀντάλλαγμα αὐτῆς (sc. σοφίας) "wisdom is not to be had for money."

2. The LXX uses ἵστημι with the διαθήκη, ὅρκος, and λόγος or ἐντολή of Yahweh. Its sense is always "to set up," "to appoint," "to make valid and inviolable." It makes plain that God's word and work establish a fact which has validity, on which one may rely, and which possesses the character of a divine statute. [5]

There is with διαθήκη (→ II, 106, 10 ff.) and ὅρκος (→ V, 457, 1 ff.) a link which is peculiar to the patriarchal narratives and Jer. στήσω τὴν διαθήκην μου πρὸς σέ in Gn. 6:18 directs Noah into the sheltering ark which saves him from the flood. [6] After the flood the same formula is used in God's promise to Noah and his family (πρὸς ὑμᾶς) that this judgment will not be repeated, Gn. 9:11 f. [7] This promise has lasting validity εἰς γενεὰς αἰωνίους, v. 12. A similar covenant is made with Abraham and his seed, 17:7. If for Abraham this refers materially to issue by Sarah, for Isaac it means: στήσω τὴν διαθήκην μου πρὸς αὐτὸν εἰς διαθήκην αἰώνιον καὶ τῷ σπέρματι αὐτοῦ μετ' αὐτόν, 17:19, cf. v. 21. Moses is reminded of this covenant with the fathers in Ex. 6:4. The covenant with Israel is based on it, Lv. 26:9: καὶ ἐπιβλέψω ἐφ' ὑμᾶς καὶ αὐξανῶ ὑμᾶς καὶ πληθυνῶ ὑμᾶς καὶ στήσω τὴν διαθήκην μου μεθ' ὑμῶν, cf. also v. 11; [8] the content of God's promise is given in vv. 11-13. In the fulfilment of the promise God confirms the covenant made with the fathers, Dt. 8:18. It and not Israel's merit or

---

[4] HT קוּם, only at Gn. 23:17, elsewhere שׁקל; LXX thus follows Gk. usage in these passages.

[5] Cf. J. Éllul, "Die theol. Begründung des Rechtes," Beiträge z. Ev. Theol., 10 (1948), which brings out the significance of the covenant as a basis of law, cf. esp. 37-44.

[6] The forms of ἵστημι are used here for the hi of קוּם. The pt. of the usage may be seen from the linking of the verbs with vows to yield the sense "to be in force." A promise with ἵστημι/קוּם means that it is valid, so that one can rely on it, and that it is binding; on the vow cf. Nu. 30:5 f., 8, 12, 14 f. and Dt. 19:15; two or three witnesses confirm a thing; v. also Rt. 4:7.

[7] Gn. 9:9 has ἀνίστημι with διαθήκη, v. 11 στήσω.

[8] Lv. 26:11 Mas.: "I take my dwelling among you," LXX: "I set my covenant among you."

worthiness is the basis of Yahweh's help, Dt. 9:5. On the foundation of the covenant promise there are certain concrete climaxes in various historical situations, οὗτοι οἱ λόγοι τῆς διαθήκης, οὓς ἐνετείλατο κύριος Μωυσῇ στῆσαι τοῖς υἱοῖς Ισραηλ ἐν γῇ Μωαβ, πλὴν τῆς διαθήκης, ἧς διέθετο αὐτοῖς ἐν Χωρηβ. The covenant set up by Yahweh can be broken by the people when it does not keep the statutes or concrete directions related to the promise. Josiah sets up the covenant anew ἀναστῆσαι τοὺς λόγους τῆς διαθήκης, and the whole people establishes itself on the charter of the covenant: καὶ ἔστη πᾶς ὁ λαὸς ἐν τῇ διαθήκῃ, 4 Βασ. 23:3. The response to the setting up of the covenant by God's reliable promise is its establishment on the part of those to whom the promise applies by its becoming the reality which shapes their lives. Baruch, the scribe of Jeremiah, proclaims to the exiles the re-establishment of the covenant as an eternal covenant: καὶ στήσω αὐτοῖς διαθήκην αἰώνιον, Βαρ. 2:35.

In connection with the covenant and the oath Yahweh's self-commitment is plainly apparent in the ἵστημι used in both cases. Regarding the covenant promised to Abraham we read in a saying to Isaac in Gn. 26:3: στήσω τὸν ὅρκον μου, ὃν ὤμοσα Αβρααμ τῷ πατρί σου. In Jer. 11:5 also the content of the covenant promise (11:4) is called an oath; God makes covenant with Israel as its God: ὅπως στήσω τὸν ὅρκον μου, ὃν ὤμοσα τοῖς πατράσιν ὑμῶν.

Dt. 28:69 and 4 Βασ. 23:3 ref. to the λόγοι τῆς διαθήκης which are established by the promise and thus made valid and inviolable. The dying David speaks of God's commandments and statutes to Solomon, who is to do them ἵνα στήσῃ κύριος τὸν λόγον αὐτοῦ, the ref. being to the promise which David received from God regarding the permanence of his dynasty, 3 Βασ. 2:4. At the building of the temple Yahweh Himself confirms David's admonition and says to Solomon: στήσω τὸν λόγον μου ὃν ἐλάλησα πρὸς Δαυιδ, 3 Βασ. 6:12 vl, cf. also 12:15; Bar. 2:1, 24. In ψ 118:38 the Psalmist prays: στῆσον τῷ δούλῳ σου τὸ λόγιόν σου — the petition is based on his purpose: ὀμώμοκα καὶ ἔστησα τοῦ φυλάξασθαι τὰ κρίματα τῆς δικαιοσύνης σου, v. 106. Man can thus establish and validate God's word and statute by fulfilling them. [9] Concerning Saul God says to Samuel: τοὺς λόγους μου οὐκ ἔστησεν, 1 Βασ. 15:11, [10] while Saul falsely claims: ἔστησα πάντα ὅσα ἐλάλησεν κύριος, v. 13. Josiah carries out his measures of temple reform ἵνα στήσῃ τοὺς λόγους τοῦ νόμου, 4 Βασ. 23:24. Nehemiah seeks to root out from Israel each ὃς οὐ στήσει τὸν λόγον τοῦτον, 2 Εσδρ. 15:13.

The creation and consummation of the world are seen in the light of Israel's encounter with its God in the covenant. God sets up His creation and gives it permanence: ἔστησεν αὐτά (i.e., all that He has made) εἰς τὸν αἰῶνα . . . , ψ 148:6. This is esp. the message of Dt. Is.: God it is ὁ στήσας ὡς καμάραν τὸν οὐρανόν, Is. 40:22. With His hand, says Yahweh, ἔστησα τὸν οὐρανὸν καὶ ἐθεμελίωσα τὴν γῆν, 51:16; note esp. the parallelism of ἔστησα and ἐθεμελίωσα, cf. also Philo Som., II, 237: standing and being established. Similarly Qoh. 1:4 can say: ἡ γῆ εἰς τὸν αἰῶνα ἔστηκεν. Apocal. prophecy, sated with the inconstancy of historical events, expects the eternal kingdom of God: στήσει ὁ θεὸς . . . βασιλείαν . . . εἰς τοὺς αἰῶνας, Da. 2:44.

God's historical action in the covenant, His work of creation and His eschatological action are all grounded in His counsel of which Dt. Is. says: πᾶσά μου ἡ βουλὴ στήσεται, Is. 46:10. Related to this established counsel of God is the statement that He moves for the salvation of His people and will not stand still: ἐν γὰρ τῷ σῴζεσθαί σε οὐ στήσεται οὐδὲ χρονιεῖ, Is. 51:14.

---

[9] ἔστησαν ῥῆμα . . . or τὴν ἐντολήν, Ιερ. 42:14, 16 means "to obey," "to establish a command, to acknowledge it as valid and binding, by following it." Cf. also Da. 6:6, 8.
[10] Other readings have ἐτήρησεν or ἐφύλαξεν alongside ἔστησεν.

3. The covenant is the place where God is with His people and they may come before Him.

a. God is with those to whom He gives the covenant. When the people grumbles at the lack of water Moses is told: ἐγὼ ἕστηκα πρὸ τοῦ σὲ ἐκεῖ ἐπὶ τῆς πέτρας from which he is to smite water, Ex. 17:6. At the commitment to the Law of the covenant Moses and his attendants see on the mount τὸν τόπον, οὗ εἱστήκει ἐκεῖ ὁ θεὸς τοῦ Ἰσραηλ, Ex. 24:10. Ezekiel at the end of his call is summoned to the valley and told: καὶ ἰδοὺ ἐκεῖ δόξα κυρίου εἱστήκει as he has seen it in the vision, Ez. 3:23. The Psalmist sees: ὁ θεὸς ἔστη ἐν συναγωγῇ θεῶν, ἐν μέσῳ δὲ θεοὺς διακρίνει, the ref. being to the judges of the people who have broken the Law, ψ 81:1. God's coming here is to judge, not to save. The angel of God (→ I, 76, 40 ff.) comes as well as God Himself. Tobit finds Raphael (5:4 S), τὸν ἄγγελον ἑστηκότα ἀπέναντι αὐτοῦ, and, not knowing he is an angel, gets him as a companion. 1 Ch. 21:15 f. speaks of the angel of judgment which brings destruction to Jerusalem. David sees him ἑστῶτα ἀνὰ μέσον τῆς γῆς καὶ ἀνὰ μέσον τοῦ οὐρανοῦ, v. 16. [11]

b. More common is the ref. to man's standing before God in the covenant. Abraham comes in intercession for Sodom ἦν ἑστηκὼς ἐναντίον κυρίου, Gn. 18:22, cf. also 19:27. Moses is summoned: στήσῃ μοι ἐκεῖ ἐπ' ἄκρου τοῦ ὄρους, Ex. 34:2, cf. also Dt. 4:10; 5:31. He is the mediator who stands between the Lord and the people, Dt. 5:5, κἀγὼ εἱστήκειν ἀνὰ μέσον κυρίου καὶ ὑμῶν. Elijah, too, is called before God: στήσῃ ἐνώπιον κυρίου ἐν τῷ ὄρει, 3 Βασ. 19:11, cf. v. 13. So is Job: στῆθι νουθετοῦ δύναμιν κυρίου, Job 37:14. With Moses the whole congregation comes before God: ἔστησαν ἔναντι κυρίου, Lv. 9:5 cf. Dt. 29:9; Jos. 24:1; 3 Βασ. 8:14. The sacrificial goats are cultically set before God, Lv. 16:7, 10. The woman suspected of impurity is to be set before God by the priest for judgment, Nu. 5:16, 18, 30. All worship is a coming before God. At the dedication of the temple the priests cannot enter the sanctuary because of the cloud, the symbol of God's presence (2 Ch. 5:14), while Solomon goes to the altar for the dedicatory prayer (2 Ch. 6:12) and then like a priest comes before the congregation and blesses it, 3 Βασ. 8:55. The Levites are appointed τοῦ στῆναι πρωὶ τοῦ αἰνεῖν ἐξομολογεῖσθαι τῷ κυρίῳ καὶ οὕτως τὸ ἑσπέρας, 1 Ch. 23:30, cf. 2 Ch. 5:12. They are chosen by the Lord, στῆναι ἐναντίον αὐτοῦ λειτουργεῖν, 2 Ch. 29:11. All servants of the Lord who are summoned to praise Him are οἱ ἑστῶτες ἐν οἴκῳ κυρίου, ψ 133:1; 134:2. When it is asked who may ascend the temple hill καὶ τίς στήσεται ἐν τόπῳ ἁγίῳ αὐτοῦ; the answer is: he who has clean hands and a pure heart, ψ 23:3 f. This question and answer show that there is a false standing before the Lord; Jer. attacks this: he who does evil cannot rightly come before God in His house, 7:10.

c. Not only the men He has chosen, the congregation of the sanctuary and its ministers, come before God, Yahweh Zebaoth. The heavenly hosts also stand before Him, 2 Ch. 18:18: εἶδον τὸν κύριον καθήμενον ἐπὶ θρόνου αὐτοῦ, καὶ πᾶσα δύναμις τοῦ οὐρανοῦ εἱστήκει ἐκ δεξιῶν αὐτοῦ καὶ ἐξ ἀριστερῶν αὐτοῦ. From these comes a πνεῦμα, καὶ ἔστη ἐνώπιον κυρίου, ready to deceive Ahab, king of Israel, and to become a lying spirit in the prophets surrounding him, 2 Ch. 18:20-22; cf. 3 Βασ. 22:21 f.

4. It is part of God's dealings with man to give him a place. David's song of thanksgiving says that God is ἐπὶ τὰ ὕψη ἱστῶν με, 2 Βασ. 22:34. This is taken up in the Ps.; God is extolled as ἐπὶ τὰ ὑψηλὰ ἱστῶν με, ψ 17:34, also 30:9: ἔστησας ἐν εὐρυχώρῳ τοὺς πόδας μου. God gives man the standing which includes deliverance and freedom. Thus the Psalmist can confess: ὁ γὰρ πούς μου ἔστη ἐν εὐθύτητι, ψ 25:12. There is a singular saying in Qoh. 2:9: The wisdom of the man who gets power and wealth "remains," σοφία μου ἐστάθη μοι.

---

[11] In 1 Ch. 20:1 the census is the work of Satan who comes against Israel: ἔστη διάβολος ἐν τῷ Ἰσραηλ, and tempts David, so that he brings about the intervention of the angel of judgment; in 2 S. 24:1 God Himself in His wrath impels David to hold the census.

C. Judaism.

1. In Judaism one sees the OT line in Sir. Sir. 44:20 f. speaks of the covenant of God with Abraham, the great father of the fulness of nations ἐν ὅρκῳ ἔστησεν αὐτῷ ἐνευλογηθῆναι ἔθνη ἐν σπέρματι αὐτοῦ, a covenant constituted by the sign of circumcision: ἐν σαρκὶ αὐτοῦ ἔστησεν διαθήκην, v. 20. As a teacher of wisdom Sir. admonishes: στῆθι ἐν διαθήκῃ σου, 11:20; he says of the covenant: διαθήκην αἰῶνος ἔστησεν μετ᾿ αὐτῶν, 17:12. Bribery is transient and dangerous, but the lasting character of faithfulness is a principle of wisdom: πίστις εἰς τὸν αἰῶνα στήσεται, 40:12. There is admonition to follow the counsel of the Lord: καὶ βουλὴν καρδίας στῆσον, οὐ γὰρ ἔστιν σοι πιστότερος αὐτῆς, 37:13. The question of what abides is to be seen in these admonitions.

2. This question also lies behind Philo's thought in the sphere of Hell. Jewish theology.

a. Philo begins by recognising the relativity of movement and standing still. This is shaped by a geocentric cosmology, so that he can say that all that is most mobile of the things under heaven seems to stand still (ἑστάναι) when compared with the course of the sun, the moon, and the stars, Poster. C., 19, cf. Conf. Ling., 99 f.: The world seems to stand still and not to move. The senses deceive man, for what stands still seems to move and what moves seems to stand still ἔτι δὲ τὰ ἑστῶτα κινεῖσθαι καὶ τὰ κινούμενα ἑστάναι, Ebr., 183. Thus the sun and moon seem to the eyes to stand still, but they move, Conf. Ling., 100. From all parts of the world the earth is stable (ἑστῶσα παγίως) and it is thus called Ἑστία, Cher., 26. Man himself can be shaken and moved in the stability which he has reached in his opinions. Thus Joseph shakes his brothers when they think they stand fast in their convictions, ἑστάναι παγίως ἐπὶ τῶν ἰδίων οἰομένους δογμάτων, Migr. Abr., 22. The fool who continually changes his views has no stability: ἐπὶ μηδενὸς ἑστάναι παγίως, Poster. C., 24.

b. God alone stands: οὐ γὰρ στήσεται ὁ θεός, ἀλλ᾿ ἀεὶ ἔστηκεν, Poster. C., 30. God is ὁ ἑστώς, Mut. Nom., 87 and 91; Som., I, 246; II, 221; Conf. Ling., 30. God, that is: μόνος ἔστηκα ἐγώ (Ex. 17:6) καὶ τὴν τῶν πάντων φύσιν ἱδρυσάμην, τὴν ἀταξίαν καὶ ἀκοσμίαν εἰς κόσμον καὶ τάξιν ἀγαγὼν καὶ τὸ πᾶν ἐπερείσας, ἵνα στηριχθῇ βεβαίως τῷ κραταιῷ καὶ ὑπάρχῳ μου λόγῳ, Som., I, 241, cf. also Leg. All., II, 83: ἀκλινὴς ἔστηκεν ἀεί. Like God, the boundaries of the good are also firm; they are not set up by men, Poster. C., 91. God can give man a solid standing. As what is moved is impelled with a vertically falling plumb-line, so is the movement of man's existence: κράτει τοῦ ἑστῶτος ἐπέχεταί τε καὶ ἵσταται, Poster. C., 28. Man must τὸ περὶ τοῦ μόνον ἑστάναι τὸν θεὸν ἐν ψυχῇ δόγμα γυμνάζεσθαι καὶ συνασκεῖσθαι πρὸς ἀλειπτικῆς ἐπιστήμης, οὐχ ᾗ τὰ σώματα πιαίνεται, ἀλλ᾿ ὑφ᾿ ἧς διάνοια ἰσχὺν κτᾶται καὶ ῥώμην ἀνανταγώνιστον, Som., I, 250. To acquire stability and to attain a constancy of soul τὸ στῆναι καὶ ἄτρεπτον κτήσασθαι διάνοιαν is to come closer to God's power which is constant, while what is created is by nature corruptible, Cher., 19. If by discipline in love a man brings the mutability proper to the creature to light and to a halt (στῆναι ποιήσας), he unmistakably approaches divine felicity θείας εὐδαιμονίας ἐγγὺς ὤν, 19. The man is righteous who stands before God and does not flee: δίκαιος δὲ ὁ ἑστηκὼς ἐναντίον σου καὶ μὴ φεύγων, Leg. All., III, 9, with a ref. to Gn. 18:22 (cf. Poster. C., 27). On the basis of Dt. 5:28 it is a saying proclaimed to the prophet that constancy and immovable rest are an approximation to God who always stands unmoved, στάσις τε καὶ ἠρεμία ἀκλινὴς ἡ παρὰ τὸν ἀκλινῶς ἑστῶτα ἀεὶ θεόν Gig., 49 cf. also Conf. Ling., 30 f. which speaks of the putting off of doubt and the vacillation of the unstable soul and which calls a firm and steady frame of soul faith. Philo thus gives a religious and philosophical turn to Archimedes' question as to the ποῦ στῶ → 639, 8 ff. For him this στάσις τε καὶ ἠρεμία ἀκλινής is the goal of the royal way which the wise man treads and on which he draws close to God who as the

One that stands immovable gives him stability too.[12] Som., II, 226 says of Abraham, who is called a wise man, that the spirit can stand open and no longer wavers like a pointer on the scales "when he dwells before God, contemplating and contemplated." Standing and being established (cf. Is. 51:16 → 642, 36 ff.) are attained by man (Som., II, 237) "in the proximity of being, of the logos of being, of the wise man, and of the one who makes progress." Acc. to Som., II, 237 this is understood as remaining the same acc. to what is constant and unshakable. It is not an eschatological goal but the goal of the wise man in this life.

3. The questions raised by Philo in relation to ἵστημι have special significance for the Qumran Teacher of Righteousness, though in a different way from Philo. The thanksgivings confess: "Those who measure up to thy demands will stand before thee — יעמודו — for ever / and those who walk on the way of thy heart will endure — יכונו — for ever. / And I, by clinging fast to thee, will raise up and establish myself — ואקומה — against those who scorn me," 1 QH 4:21 f.[13] The first part of this basic passage speaks of man's eternal standing before God, the second of a position which must be maintained against scorners who attack it. To achieve this one must hold fast to God, for, as we read further, "Thou hast strengthened my position — עמדי — by the secret of thy wonder," 4:28. The writer knows that "the way of a man does not stand fast unless it is granted to him by God's Spirit to have a blameless walk...," 4:31 f. God's mercy grants man his standing;[14] the Teacher prays to him in the words of the Psalmist: "Thou art the eternal lamp and dost place my foot in (a broad place)," 7:25. "With the multitude of the proofs of thy mercy I rose up and stood — ואקומה — and my spirit clung fast to the place of standing — במעמד — in face of trouble, and I relied on the proofs of thy grace," 4:36 f. This rising up is also a being raised up: "How can I gather my forces if thou dost not set me up — בלא העמדתני" 10:6. This place of standing is before God; God purifies men from their sins and grants them His mercy "to set them up to all eternity before thee," 7:30 f. The place of the Teacher was once different: "I stood in the realm of wickedness and with the wretched in their fate," 3:24 f.[15] But now "thy righteousness has set me up — העמדתני — for thy covenant, and I relied on thy truth," 7:19 f. With God is his place of standing; his persecutors "did not see that with thee is my place of standing — מעמדי" 2:22. This place is one which the righteous can attain to in life by God's grace — "my standing is through thy grace," 2:25, also 9:18 f. Yet it is also eschatological. The singer says of it: "Thou hast purged the perverted spirit from great guilt that he should set himself in the place of standing — להתיצב במעמד — with the host of the saints, and enter into union with the congregation of the heavenly ones," 3:21 f. Whereas the unrighteous loses his standing and slips and stumbles,[16] the righteous overcomes slipping and stumbling and receives the place of standing which he will keep before God for ever. 1 QM 14:6 says of God "that he gives wavering knees a firm location — מעמד", whereas there is for the heroes and strong men of "all the nations of iniquity no standing-place," 14:7 f. In the holy war one may thus be certain of the outcome: "The standing of the wicked has been ended by God's heroic power," 1 QM 4:3 f. The righteous wins a position not only for himself but for others. The Teacher of

---

[12] Cf. J. Pascher, ΒΑΣΙΛΙΚΗ ΟΔΟΣ. Der Königsweg zu Wiedergeburt u. Vergottung bei Philon v. Alex. (1931), 228-238.

[13] Cf. H. Bardtke, Die Handschriftenfunde am Toten Meer, I (1952), 86-110; II, "Die Sekte v. Qumran" (1958), 215-258; also J. Maier, Die Texte v. Toten Meer, I. II (1960).

[14] Cf. W. Grundmann, "Der Lehrer d. Gerechtigkeit v. Qumran u. die Frage nach der Glaubensgerechtigkeit in d. Theol. d. Ap. Pls.," Revue d. Qumran, 2 (1960), 237-259; S. Schulz, "Zur Rechtfertigung aus Gnaden in Qumran u. bei Pls.," ZThK, 56 (1959), 155-185.

[15] Maier, op. cit., II, 79 ignores the past tenses and transl., "I stand..." on the basis of the eschatological character of the context.

[16] Cf. H. W. Huppenbauer, "Der Mensch zwischen zwei Welten," AbhThANT, 34 (1959), 100, n. 435.

Righteousness says of himself: "I will not waver and thou holdest me upright before wicked fighters ... thou dost establish me as a strong tower and as a steep wall," 1 QH 7:7 f. He is attacked; the foes are out to make "all who rely on thy servant stumble and to take away their power so that they cannot cling to the place of standing," 5:28 f. According to God's will the righteous must "come to the place of standing before thee with the eternal host and the spirits (of holiness)," 11:13. God alone causes all sins to disappear from man's heart "to bring it into covenant with thee and that it may stand before thee in the eternal place to be a light to give light," 18:28 f. The Teacher of Righteousness is himself a helper for those who stumble, helping them to the firm place, cf. 2:7 ff.; 7:20; 14:17 ff. It is clear that standing is gained by entry into the Qumran community. This regards itself as a foundation for Israel, as a sanctuary in Aaron and as a house of truth in Israel, 1 QS 5:5 f.; 8:5, 8 f.; Damasc. 3:19 (5:5). To enter the community is thus to enter into God's covenant, cf. 1 QS 5:7; 6:22; 8:21; 1 QH 11:11; also 1 QS 1:16, 18, 22 etc. To enter into God's covenant is to get standing, cf. the garbled 1 QH 18:28 f. → lines 6 ff. The question of Archimedes, which was still a live one in the Hell. world, is answered here by a ref. to the covenant of God with Israel as this was renewed and understood in the Qumran community. In terms of this basic sense the concept of standing can then be used in relation to military and esp. cultic offices in the community. [17] What is said in 1 QH is confirmed in 1 QS, cf. 11:16: " ... thou dost will that the chosen men should stand before thee for ever." Here, too, it is confessed: "If I fall through my sinful flesh, my justification will endure for ever through God's righteousness — תעמוד" 11:12. Whereas Philo, the philosophical thinker, puts his questions under the influence of Hell. considerations, the Teacher of Righteousness puts them under the testimony of the sacred scriptures of Israel and speaks of the experience of his own election. Philo seeks *gnosis* and standing through it, but the Teacher of Righteousness extols the standing he has attained as a gift of the mercy and grace of God. As in Is. 46:10 there is reference to the solid counsel of God on which His whole action rests, "but thy counsel remains erect — תקום — and the plan of thy heart stands fast for ever — תכון" 1 QH 4:13.

D. ἵστημι in the New Testament.

A statistical survey yields 152 instances of ἵστημι, with ἱστάνω, in the NT. [18] Of these 61 are in Lk. (26 the Gospel, 35 Acts), 16 in Paul (+ στήκω 7), 4 of which are thought by some to be deutero-Pauline, 21 in Mt., 9 (+ στήκω 2) in Mk., 18 (+ στήκω 1) in Jn., 21 in Rev., 2 each in Hb. and Jm., 1 each in 1 Pt. and Jd. Quite naturally narrative passages have the word most; among these is a plain preference in Lk. and Rev., with obvious OT influence on the latter. Most of the instances in Paul have theological import.

I. Employment Corresponding to General Usage.

1. ἵστημι "to set," "to set up," "to cause to come."
a. Of persons: Satan sets Jesus on a pinnacle (πτερύγιον) of the temple: καὶ ἔστησεν αὐτόν ... Mt. 4:5, cf. Lk. 4:9. The temple police set the apostles before the Sanhedrin: ἀγαγόντες δὲ αὐτοὺς ἔστησαν ἐν τῷ συνεδρίῳ, Ac. 5:27, cf. 22:30: Paul is placed before the Jews, Jn. 8:3: the woman taken in adultery στήσαντες αὐτὴν ἐν μέσῳ. Stephen's enemies set up false witnesses against him: ἔστησάν τε μάρτυρας ψευδεῖς, Ac. 6:13. Jesus puts a child in the midst of the disciples: ἔστησεν αὐτὸ ἐν μέσῳ αὐτῶν, Mt. 18:2; Mk. 9:36. The congregation places the chosen seven before the apostles: ἔστησαν ἐνώπιον τῶν ἀποστόλων, Ac. 6:6. The apostles appoint two men, one of whom will take the place of Judas in the circle of the twelve, Ac. 1:23.

---

17 Cf. also J. Maier, *op. cit.*, II, 72 on 1 QH 2:22-25.
18 Based on R. Morgenthaler, *Statistik d. nt.lichen Wortschatzes* (1958), *s.v.*

b. Of objects: "to set up," "to bring into force," e.g., the Law R. 3:31; one's own righteousness, R. 10:3; the will of God with the ending of the law of sacrifice, Hb. 10:9. Setting a price or payment Mt. 26:15 (with allusion to Zech. 11:12: στήσαντες τὸν μισθόν μου ... καὶ ἔστησαν τὸν μισθόν μου τριάκοντα ἀργυροῦς): οἱ δὲ (the members of the Sanhedrin) ἔστησαν αὐτῷ (Judas) τριάκοντα ἀργύρια. Possibly ἵστημι here has the sense of weighing in the scales and not just fixing; [19] it is also possible, on the basis of Mk. 14:11; Lk. 22:5, that the sense is "to promise." [20] Ac. 7:60: μὴ στήσῃς αὐτοῖς ταύτην τὴν ἁμαρτίαν, either "to weigh out," "to weigh on the scales," or: "to recompense," "to charge." In either case the prayer seeks forgiveness for the murderers.

2. ἵσταμαι "to stand," "to stand still," "to approach."

a. Of persons: Jesus stands still for pity when the blind men call to Him: καὶ στὰς ὁ Ἰησοῦς ... with a view to helping them, Mt. 20:32 par. Mk. 10:49; coming down from the mount ἔστη ἐπὶ τόπου πεδινοῦ, Lk. 6:17. The bearers of the bier of the young man of Nain ἔστησαν, Lk. 7:14. The ten lepers ἔστησαν πόρρωθεν, Lk. 17:12. The man with the withered hand is told: ἔγειρε καὶ στῆθι εἰς τὸ μέσον· καὶ ἀναστὰς ἔστη, Lk. 6:8. The woman who sinned much στᾶσα ὀπίσω παρὰ τοὺς πόδας αὐτοῦ, Lk. 7:38. A man comes to Cornelius in shining clothes: ἀνὴρ ἔστη ἐνώπιόν μου ..., Ac. 10:30. Paul is summoned by Jesus before Damascus: στῆθι ἐπὶ τοὺς πόδας σου, Ac. 26:16, cf. the prophet Ezekiel in 2:1. There is also a connection with Ezekiel in Rev. 11:11, which on the basis of Ez. 37:10 says of the two witnesses in the streets of Jerusalem:καὶ ἔστησαν ἐπὶ τοὺς πόδας αὐτῶν. The lame man cured in Ac. 3:8 ἐξαλλόμενος ἔστη leaps up from his crouched position and gets to his feet. One should not offer the rich man a good place in the assembly but say to the poor: σὺ στῆθι ἐκεῖ, Jm. 2:3. On the destruction of great Babylon ναῦται καὶ ὅσοι τὴν θάλασσαν ἐργάζονται ἀπὸ μακρόθεν ἔστησαν, Rev. 18:17.

b. Of objects: The treasurer of Candace of Ethiopia stops his chariot on which he is riding with Philip: ἐκέλευσεν στῆναι τὸ ἅρμα, Ac. 8:38. Lk. 8:44 says of the bloody flux of the woman who touches Jesus' garment: καὶ παραχρῆμα ἔστη ἡ ῥύσις τοῦ αἵματος (Mk. 5:29 ἐξηράνθη); Lk.'s expression has a medical tinge.

3. ἕστηκα, εἱστήκειν "to stand."

a. Jesus εἱστήκει in the bustle and surge of the temple procession, Jn. 7:37; His accusers εἱστήκεισαν before Herod, Lk. 23:10; the guards and spectators stand at the cross, Mt. 27:47; Lk. 23:35, 49, cf. also Jn. 12:29; when the apostles are miraculously freed from prison it is said of them: ἰδοὺ οἱ ἄνδρες, οὓς ἔθεσθε ἐν τῇ φυλακῇ, εἰσὶν ἐν τῷ ἱερῷ ἑστῶτες καὶ διδάσκοντες τὸν λαόν, Ac. 5:25. At the ascension the angel asks: τί ἑστήκατε βλέποντες εἰς τὸν οὐρανόν; Ac. 1:11. The place and manner of standing are either to be deduced from the context or are left indefinite, Mt. 20:6; 26:73; Jn. 1:35; 3:29; 20:14; Ac. 22:25. Ac. 9:7: εἱστήκεισαν ἐνεοί, Rev. 5:6: ἀρνίον ἑστηκὸς ὡς ἐσφαγμένον, Ac. 26:6: ἕστηκα κρινόμενος.

b. The place of standing can be expressed adverbially. The mother and brethren of Jesus: εἱστήκεισαν ἔξω, Mt. 12:46 f., cf. Lk. 8:20; the contemporaries of Jesus who do not find the door to the kingdom of God and to whom it is said: ἄρξησθε ἔξω ἑστάναι, Lk. 13:25; [21] the publican praying in the temple μακρόθεν ἑστώς, Lk. 18:13, cf. also Lk. 23:49; Rev. 18:10, 17; καί τινες τῶν ἐκεῖ ἑστηκότων, Mk. 11:5; εἰσίν τινες τῶν

---

[19] Cf. Pr.-Bauer, s.v. ἵστημι, I, b.
[20] On this cf. G. Bertram, Die Leidensgeschichte u. d. Christuskult (1922), 19.
[21] On the figure of speech cf. W. Grundmann, Die Geschichte Jesu Christi[3] (1961), 196-204.

ὧδε ἑστώτων, Mt. 16:28 or τῶν αὐτοῦ ἑστηκότων, Lk. 9:27, cf. also Mt. 20:6; it is said of the βδέλυγμα τῆς ἐρημώσεως: ἑστηκότα ὅπου οὐ δεῖ, it stands in the forbidden place, Mk. 13:14; Mt. 24:15 shows what is meant by this: ἑστὸς ἐν τόπῳ ἁγίῳ.

c. The place of standing can also be expressed prepositionally: ἑστὼς ἐκ δεξιῶν τοῦ θυσιαστηρίου, Lk. 1:11, cf. also Ac. 7:55 → 650, 9 ff. ἐν with the dat. of place: εἶδεν... ἑστῶτας ἐν τῇ ἀγορᾷ ἀργούς, Mt. 20:3, cf. also 24:15. Jn. 11:56: ἐν τῷ ἱερῷ ἑστηκότες, Rev. 19:17: εἶδον ἕνα ἄγγελον ἑστῶτα ἐν τῷ ἡλίῳ. ἐν with a personal ref.: ἐν αὐτοῖς ἑστώς, Ac. 24:21, cf. εἱστήκει ... μετ᾿ αὐτῶν, Jn. 18:5. Rev. has ἑστάναι ἐνώπιον in various combinations, 7:9; 8:2; 11:4; 12:4; 20:12; apart from 12:4 the ref. is to standing before God or the throne, an expression taken from the OT. ἐπί and gen. are used in Ac. 5:23: τοὺς φύλακας ἑστῶτας ἐπὶ τῶν θυρῶν, cf. 21:40; 24:20; 25:10; Rev. 10:5, 8; also ἐπί and dat. Ac. 7:33 quoting Ex. 3:5; ἐπί and acc. Mt. 13:2: πᾶς ὁ ὄχλος ἐπὶ τὸν αἰγιαλὸν εἱστήκει and esp. Rev. 3:20; 7:1; 14:1; 15:2; with παρά and acc. Lk. 5:1 (ἐπί and acc. Mt. 13:2, cf. also Jn. 6:22: ὁ ὄχλος ὁ ἑστηκὼς πέραν τῆς θαλάσσης); παρά and dat. Jn. 19:25; πρό and gen. of place Ac. 12:14: ἑστάναι τὸν Πέτρον πρὸ τοῦ πυλῶνος. πρός and dat. Jn. 20:11 εἱστήκει πρὸς τῷ μνημείῳ, cf. also 18:16: εἱστήκει πρὸς τῇ θύρᾳ ἔξω. In Ac. 4:14 the members of the Sanhedrin see σὺν αὐτοῖς ἑστῶτα τὸν τεθεραπευμένον, cf. Rev. 7:11: οἱ ἄγγελοι εἱστήκεισαν κύκλῳ τοῦ θρόνου.

4. The Passive Forms σταθήσομαι, ἐστάθην.

The star which led the wise men to Bethlehem is halted ἐστάθη, Mt. 2:9. [22] Jesus announces to the disciples: ἐπὶ ἡγεμόνων καὶ βασιλέων σταθήσεσθε ἕνεκεν ἐμοῦ εἰς μαρτύριον αὐτοῖς, Mk. 13:9, cf. Mt. 10:18 D. [23] He Himself is placed before the Roman governor ἐστάθη, Mt. 27:11. The two who are addressed by Jesus on the way to Emmaus ἐστάθησαν σκυθρωποί, Lk. 24:17. Luke prefers the part. form σταθείς, so 18:40 as compared with Mk. 10:49; Mt. 20:32; also Lk. 18:11 of the Pharisee in his self-confident standing in contrast to the humble μακρόθεν ἑστώς of the publican, v. 13; also 19:8; Ac. 2:14; 17:22; 27:21; then 5:20; 25:18 in the sense "to stand there," "to come forward." In the sense "to be put in force" in connection with Dt. 19:15 cf. Mt. 18:16; 2 C. 13:1, paraphrased Jn. 8:17: "Every matter will be established by the statement of two or three witnesses."

II. Theological Aspects of New Testament Usage.

1. He who can put someone in a particular place demonstrates thereby his authority or actual power. It is said of God: τῷ δὲ δυναμένῳ... ὑμᾶς... στῆσαι κατενώπιον τῆς δόξης αὐτοῦ ἀμώμους ἐν ἀγαλλιάσει (Jd. 24). This describes the goal of believers to which God has the power to lead them. God sets the day and hour of judgment and its execution, and therewith of the consummation of the world, however it may be conceived: ἔστησεν ἡμέραν ἐν ᾗ μέλλει κρίνειν τὴν οἰκουμένην ἐν δικαιοσύνῃ, Ac. 17:31. To this day of judgment, which is the day of wrath, there applies the question: καὶ τίς δύναται σταθῆναι; (Rev. 6:17 on the basis of Mal. 3:2 etc.). Jesus Christ is appointed Judge acc. to Ac. 17:31. As Son of Man He may place before His judgment, Mt. 25:33. He has the power to make man stand: δυνατεῖ γὰρ ὁ κύριος στῆσαι αὐτόν, R. 14:4. Man acquires a solid standing

---

[22] So rightly Kl. Mt., ad loc, as against Zn. Mt., 102 f.; Schl. Mt., ad loc.: "In distinction from ἔστη, ἐστάθη implies that the star is halted"; examples are given from Jos. and the Rabb. which fit in with general usage.

[23] G. D. Kilpatrick, "The Gentile Mission in Mark and Mk. 13:9-11," Studies in the Gospels, ed. D. E. Nineham (1957), 153 takes σταθήσεσθε with εἰς μαρτύριον αὐτοῖς and stresses that they are brought forward as witnesses to testify.

through his Lord. The passage compares Jesus and His people with a master and his servants. In principle the servant can be judged only by his own master, for τῷ ἰδίῳ κυρίῳ στήκει ἢ πίστει (R. 14:4 → 638, 9 ff.). This raises the question whether the confident σταθήσεται δέ means that he will be raised up after falling or that, even though judged by others, he will stand in the judgment of his master, who will not let him fall but will hold him up. [24] Even though a man slips and falls in the discharge of his duties, even though he gets into conflict with others and is accused by them to his master, the latter is well able to make him stand, and he will do so. This Master has authority to forgive, Ac. 7:60. According to Luke Jesus demands that His disciples should bend every effort σταθῆναι ἔμπροσθεν τοῦ υἱοῦ τοῦ ἀνθρώπου, [25] Lk. 21:36 → 236, n. 252. In the NT too, especially in Paul, the question of coming to stand and standing is of great importance. As in the Qumran community (→ 645, 9 ff.) this is eschatologically defined, but in distinction from the community and Philo (→ 644, 26 ff.) it is orientated to the act of God in Jesus Christ. Jesus Himself in His temptation by the devil is set on a pinnacle of the temple. Temptation withstood is for Jesus a victorious liberation from the power of the adversary, Mt. 4:5, 11; Lk. 4:9, 13. [26] The congregational assembly has an authority manifested in the fact that it places the seven before the apostles (Ac. 6:6) and puts forward candidates for the apostolic office (Ac. 1:23). But its opponents can also exercise a provisional, though not definitive, power, Mt. 27:11; Ac. 5:27; 22:30 etc.

2. The apostle Paul speaks of the establishment of the Law, R. 3:31 → IV, 1076, 39 ff. Clarifying the distinction between Law and Gospel, he answers the question whether he would see the Law invalidated by faith and done away (καταργεῖν); he rejects any such idea with the statement: μὴ γένοιτο· ἀλλὰ νόμον ἱστάνομεν, v. 31. The Gospel, which seeks faith, establishes the Law in its function as that which convicts of sin and judicially puts to death, so that the Gospel may then come with its promise of liberating and pardoning deliverance from the Law's condemnation through the righteousness of God. The Jews missed this because in their ignorance of the righteousness which is given by God they tried to set up their own righteousness (R. 10:3), as Paul for his part had also done. The use is somewhat different in Hb. 10:9 in an exposition of Ps. 40:6-8. Here the coming of Jesus means in relation to the sacrificial cultus the invalidating (ἀναιρεῖν) [27] of the first covenant order and the bringing into force of the second eschatological covenant order. This carries with it the sanctifying of man, his ordering to God on the basis of the one sacrifice of Jesus. By God's will the ancient sacrificial order has been suspended and the new one has been set up whereby man lives before God on the basis of the sacrifice of Jesus Crist.

---

[24] Cf. Mi. R., ad loc.: "In primitive Christianity standing and falling are figurative expressions for persevering or failing in the fulfilment of a task or the enduring of temptation." As may be seen from R. 14:4 this includes rather than excludes the thought of judgment, for this determines one's standing or falling.

[25] For σταθῆναι D it sy s c Tert read στήσεσθε, changing the dependence on κατισχύσητε or καταξιωθῆτε (vl.) into co-ordination with it.

[26] On this cf. E. Fascher, "Jesus u. der Satan. Eine Studie z. Auslegung der Versuchungsgesch.," Hallische Monographien, 11 (1949), esp. 31-39. If Mk. 3:27 par. is related to the temptation story (→ III, 399, 39 ff., cf. J. M. Robinson, "Das Geschichtsverständnis d. Mk.-Ev.," AbhThANT, 30 [1956], 29-32) there is confirmation here, cf. also Grundmann, op. cit. (→ n. 21), 60 f. and Grundm. Mk. on 3:27.

[27] Cf. on this Mi. Hb.,ad loc., esp. n. 8 and 9.

3. In connection with Jesus there is reference to a coming forth or standing which is theologically significant. Jesus comes to His people as the Risen Lord. He comes out of His invisible concealment with the Father to them: ἦλθεν ὁ Ἰησοῦς καὶ ἔστη εἰς τὸ μέσον, Jn. 20:19, cf. v. 26; also Lk. 24:36: through His coming to them He becomes and is the centre around which everything is grouped. In Rev. 3:20 the Risen Lord says to the church and its members that He is standing before the door of each one and waiting until it is opened: ἰδοὺ ἕστηκα ἐπὶ τὴν θύραν. Though invisible, He is present in His word and supper, and he who opens will have a part in Him. Stephen in Ac. 7:55 sees Ἰησοῦν ἑστῶτα ἐκ δεξιῶν τοῦ θεοῦ, and he bears witness: ἰδοὺ θεωρῶ ... τὸν υἱὸν τοῦ ἀνθρώπου ἐκ δεξιῶν ἑστῶτα τοῦ θεοῦ, 7:56. This confession builds on Lk. 22:69. What Jesus proclaimed before the Sanhedrin His witness confesses to be fulfilled before the same Sanhedrin, [28] though with a characteristic difference, for whereas Lk. 22:69 (with Ps. 110:1) speaks of "sitting at the right hand of God" the present verse speaks of "standing." This may be an ancient tradition, the basic statement being that Jesus "is" at the right hand of God (R. 8:34); in this case "standing" in Ac. 7:55 f. might mean "being." On the other hand the choice of "standing" could also be a development under the influence of the image of the Son of Man standing before the Judge of the world (Eth. En. 49:2 ff.; also Da. 7:10-13); at a later stage, under the influence of Ps. 110:1, this then came to be formulated as sitting at the right hand of God. The standing of Jesus (called the Son of Man in Ac. 7:56) at God's right hand might be construed as expressing subordination if it means more than "being": He stands reverently before God like the angels. [29] But one might also think in terms of standing to judge or to intercede, whether this be to intercede for Stephen or to judge his adversaries, [30] or indeed to prepare for eschatological judgment. [31] Another possibility is that Jesus rose to welcome Stephen. According to Jn. 14:2 f (→ V, 78, 13 ff.) the disciple in the hour of death is brought home by his Lord, who has prepared a place for him in His Father's house that he might be united with Him. Jesus discharges His

[28] If Ac. 7:56 is related to Lk. 22:69, the two last sayings of Stephen in 7:59 and 7:60 are related to Lk. 23:46 and Lk. 23:34. The disciple is conformed to the image of his Master, R. 8:29 has influenced Luke's account here.

[29] Bauernf. Ag., ad loc. considers this with other possibilities, so also S. Schulz, Untersuchungen zur Menschensohnchristologie im J. (1957), 129, n. 5. Bertram refers to the correctio scriptorum in Gn. 18:22 where the original must have been to the effect that Yahweh remained standing before Abraham, but in order to prevent misunderstanding of this disrespectful statement the text was altered into one of the so-called tiqqun sopherim by Rabb. tradition, and now reads: "But Abraham remained standing before the Lord," cf. H. Gunkel, Genesis (1910), ad loc.; E. Würthwein, Der Text d. AT (1952), 20. Cf. also 4 Βασ. 25:8, where LXX renders עֹמֵד by ἑστὼς ἐνώπιον [Bertram].

[30] So C. F. D. Moule, "From Defendant to Judge," Studiorum NT Societas Bulletin, 3 (1952), 46 f.; Stauffer Theol., 119 and n. 446 on R. 8:34; the examples in n. 446 illustrate coming forward to intercede but not the standing of the intercessor at God's right hand. And where do we read that the adversary stands at God's left hand, as Stauffer, 119 maintains?

[31] Cf. H. P. Owen, "Stephen's Vision in Acts VII 55-56," NTSt, 1 (1954/55), 224-226. Owen advances the thesis that Luke uses 6 terms to describe the path of Jesus from His crucifixion to the parousia: ἔξοδος in Lk. 9:31; εἰσελθεῖν εἰς τὴν δόξαν αὐτοῦ in 24:26; ἀναλαμβάνεσθαι = ascension in Ac. 1:2, 11, 22; καθῆσθαι ἐκ δεξιῶν τοῦ θεοῦ in Lk. 20:42; 22:69; Ac. 2:34; ἑστάναι in Ac. 7:55 f.; ἔρχεσθαι = parousia in Lk. 9:26 etc.; Ac. 1:11 etc. If the first three describe Jesus' transition from earthly to heavenly existence, the last three describe His heavenly existence; standing comes in the middle of the second series; "Stephen's vision is also proleptic. He sees forward to the glory of the parousia," 225.

Messianic office whether His act be judicial or intercessory. [32] The connection of Ac. 6:15: εἶδον τὸ πρόσωπον αὐτοῦ ὡσεὶ πρόσωπον ἀγγέλου, with 7:55 [33] indicates that the vision has for Stephen a transfiguring character, [34] so that the last explanation seems to be very much to the point.

4. The term ἵστημι is also used in the NT to denote that which lasts and is stable, not subject to change or decay. 2 Tm. 2:19 says: ὁ μέντοι στερεὸς θεμέλιος τοῦ θεοῦ ἔστηκεν... The common NT metaphor of the Church as a building (→ V, 136, 28 ff.) is used here. The foundation of this building stands fast and does not quake. In contrast to everything mutable one may rely on it and on the seal which the θεμέλιος bears engraved on it: God has elected (= knows) those who are His. This statement about the community's faith and life, which has a catechetical and comprehensive quality, is shown to be impregnable and indestructible by the use of ἔστηκεν. [35] In contrast Jesus says that the household or city which is divided will not last, and He applies this to the kingdom of Satan, Mt. 12:25 f. Of Satan it is said: ἐν τῇ ἀληθείᾳ οὐκ ἔστηκεν (C 𝕬 al οὐχ ἕστηκεν), Jn. 8:44. Because he is the father of lies he has no standing in the kingdom of truth and will inevitably perish. But the community, built on solid ground, is the pillar and stay of truth, 1 Tm. 3:15. Paul often insists that through Christ, as a member of His body, man gets a position and stands, → 648, 42 ff. What he had in view in the admonition in 1 C. 16:13: στήκετε ἐν τῇ πίστει (→ 637, 12 ff.), is also expressed in forms of ἵστημι. The Gentile Christians in the Roman church, who despised Israel, must learn from Paul that the Israelites are like olive-branches which were cut off because of their unbelief, σὺ δὲ τῇ πίστει ἔστηκας, R. 11:20. Here faith is not in the first instance the place where one stands. It is the means and power by which one stands, → VI, 212, 21 f.; 218, 29 ff. The faith which hears and believes the Word helps us to stand. The statement is hortatory; standing must be maintained and not hazarded. This is everywhere true in the Christian life. In 1 C. 7:36 ff. the Corinthians are told that the Christian is free either to marry or not to marry. The important thing is that a man ἔστηκεν ἐν τῇ καρδίᾳ αὐτοῦ ἑδραῖος, 7:37. Standing in faith gives steadfastness of heart, an inner standing in deciding specific questions, for which Paul gives ἐξουσίαν ... περὶ τοῦ ἰδίου θελήματος, v. 37. There are various possibilities of decision for believers, but they are within the standing which is attained through faith and rooted in grace (cf. 1 C. 15:10; 2 C. 12:9), and which encloses and supports all individual decisions in their freedom. The Corinthians are also told: τῇ γὰρ πίστει ἑστήκατε, 2 C. 1:24. This standing grants joy, and the apostle's ministry is an aid to this joy. The message of joy and victory can also be a means and place of standing as well as faith. The

---

[32] On the different possibilities cf. Haench. Ag., ad loc. The two suggested there, that Jesus rose to welcome Stephen or to execute His Messianic office, are not opposed but constitute a unity if one sees behind the statement a tradition like Jn. 14:2 f. Bauernf. Ag., ad loc. refers to the conclusion of Eleazar's speech in 4 Macc. 5:37: ἁγνόν με οἱ πατέρες εἰσδέξονται. He thinks the feature which deviates from the tradition is a mark of authenticity.

[33] Even linguistically cf. ἀτενίσαντες in 6:15 and ἀτενίσας in 7:55. Perhaps 7:1-54 was inserted into an older account. There seem to be additions in 7:55-8:3 as well, among them the assimilation of Stephen's martyrdom to the passion. Perhaps Ju. 13:6: ὡς ὅρασις ἀγγέλου τοῦ θεοῦ ἐπιφανὴς σφόδρα, influenced Ac. 6:15.

[34] The form of Stephen's martyrdom is thus to be grouped with theological passages like Jn. 14:2 f.; 2 C. 3:18; R. 8:29.

[35] Cf. Schl. Past., ad loc., n. 2: "ἔστηκεν with a strong sense was common in Paul."

Corinthians have received this message from Paul and now they stand in and by it: ἐν ᾧ καὶ ἑστήκατε, 1 C. 15:1. [36] Since the Gospel is the Word of grace, Paul can include himself with all Christians in the confession that Christ has given us access τῇ πίστει εἰς τὴν χάριν ταύτην ἐν ᾗ ἑστήκαμεν, R. 5:2. Here, too, grace is the place where the believer has come to stand, and it is also a means whereby he is kept standing and preserved from falling. Related is 1 Pt. 5:12. The author bears witness: ταύτην εἶναι ἀληθῆ χάριν τοῦ θεοῦ, εἰς ἣν στῆτε. The readers are summoned to stand by the grace which the letter has testified to them, i.e., not to let it go. [37]

Paul admonishes those who stand, pointing to the apostasy and destruction of the wilderness generation of Israel: ὥστε ὁ δοκῶν ἑστάναι βλεπέτω μὴ πέσῃ, 1 C. 10:12. Prayer is an aid to standing and to preservation from falling. Epaphras is πάντοτε ἀγωνιζόμενος ὑπὲρ ὑμῶν ἐν ταῖς προσευχαῖς, ἵνα σταθῆτε τέλειοι, Col. 4:12. The standing of the Colossians is to prove itself to be riper, i.e., firmer, not wavering (→ τέλειος). [38] Prayer for this standing is called a warring because the goal of assaults from Satan is to cause those who stand to fall. Hence the standing in grace which is the Lord's gift must be seized with all the force of our will. A help here is the spiritual armour (→ V, 295, 19 ff.) which is to be put on πρὸς τὸ δύνασθαι ὑμᾶς στῆναι πρὸς τὰς μεθοδείας τοῦ διαβόλου, Eph. 6:11. Withstanding (ἀντιστῆναι v. 13) in this armour makes it possible to stand in the evil day: ἅπαντα κατεργασάμενοι στῆναι. [39] The Christian life in faith is a battle in which a man may fall. To survive and to maintain one's stance the spiritual armour is necessary. Armed with it the believer has and occupies the position which he must maintain: στῆτε οὖν (v. 14), equipped with the weapons which are described in detail → V, 302, 19 ff. [40] The saying about standing thus leads to the metaphor of the *miles christianus* who holds the field with his Lord.

Worth noting is the frequent occurrence of forms of ἵστημι in Ac. 26. Paul stands before the judgment — ἕστηκα κρινόμενος — because of his hope in the promise of the Messiah and the resurrection of the dead which was given to the fathers, v. 6 and v. 8. He, the accused, is also a witness to everyone — ἕστηκα μαρτυρόμενος in a parallel form to v. 6 — bearing testimony to the fulfilment of the promise

---

[36] The ἐν is predominantly instrumental, but the δι᾽ οὗ καὶ σῴζεσθε which follows gives a partially local sense, denoting the power and place rather after the manner of the scientific concept of a field of force.

[37] The reading ἑστήκατε in 𝔄 and P, which replaces and thus softens the imp. or aor. conj., maintains that they are standing to this grace.

[38] Cf. W. Grundmann, "Die ΝΗΠΙΟΙ in d. urchr. Paränese," NTSt, 5 (1958/59), 188-205.

[39] = when you have done all, i.e., put on the spiritual armour described in what follows, so Pr.-Bauer, s.v. κατεργάζομαι 1; also Dib. Gefbr., ad loc., though he also considers the possibility "overcoming all"; the first interpretation is the more likely one.

[40] Even if Eph. be regarded as deutero-Pauline (cf. Grundmann, op cit. [→ n. 38], 194, n. 1), the metaphor and context develop Pauline ideas, cf. 1 Th. 5:8. K. G. Kuhn, "Der Eph. im Lichte d. Qumrantexte," NTSt, 7 (1960/61), 334-6 notes connections between Eph. and the Dead Sea Scrolls. With the spiritual armour these also include the exhortation to stand, which presupposes a rising up from the death and sleep of sins, Eph. 5:14, cf. Kuhn, 343-5. The terminology is to be understood in the light of Qumran rather than Gnosticism and it is to be interpreted as both temporal and eschatological, H. Schlier, *Die Kirche nach d. Brief an d. Eph., Die Zeit d. Kirche*² (1958), 159-185, n. 36, cf. Dib. Gefbr. on Eph. 6:13. The examples adduced from Gnosticism, esp. the important Hipp. Ref., VI, 17, 1 ff., have a speculative character and are not controlled by the event of salvation in its hortatory application as in Qumran and the NT. Gnosticism is on the line from Philo, not that from Qumran and the NT.

in Jesus Christ, v. 22 f. He undertook to withstand [41] (v. 9) this fulfilment. The breaking of this resistance by the appearing of Christ caused him and his companions to fall to the earth — πάντων τε καταπεσόντων ἡμῶν εἰς τὴν γῆν, v. 14. But the manifested Jesus raised him up, caused him to stand like Ezekiel when he had fallen down at God's appearing: ... ἀνάστηθι καὶ στῆθι ἐπὶ τοὺς πόδας σου (v. 16 cf. Ez. 2:1 f.), and enlightened him. [42, 43]

Grundmann

---

† στηρίζω, † ἐπιστηρίζω, † στηριγμός, † ἀστήρικτος

Contents: A. The Word Group in Greek. B. The Word Group in the Old Testament. C. The Word Group in Judaism. D. The Word Group in the New Testament. E. The Word Group in the Post-Apostolic Fathers.

A. The Word Group in Greek.

The verb στηρίζω [1] "to make fast" (only aor. and pluperf. in Hom.) is at first developed only gutturally στηρίξω, ἐστήριξα etc.; the fut. στηρίσω, then στηριῶ, are later dental constructs in the koine, the latter esp. LXX, e.g., Ez. 14:8; Sir. 6:37. In the koine we also find the aor. forms ἐστήρισα with ἐστήριξα: στήρισον ψ 50: 14; Lk. 22:32; Rev. 3:2, ἐστήρισεν, 1 Cl., 33, 3. [2] The noun στῆριγξ "support" is attested from Xenoph. Eq., I, 5; it may be the starting-pt. for the verb or a derivative of it. In any case * στηρος "fast," "upright," lies behind it; it occurs, however, only in Hesych. as στῆρα· τὰ λίθινα πρόθυρα.

1. στηρίζω is found in the main sense "to support," "to fix something so that it stands upright and immovable," λίθον ... στήριξε κατὰ χθονός, Hes. Theog., 497 f., λίθον ... στηριχθῆναι ἐκέλευσαν, Ditt. Or., II, 612, 6 ff. and 769, 8 ff., cf. Callim. Hymn., II, 23, "to support a vine by a stake and an aging man by a stick," ἄμπελος ὡς ἤδη κάμακι στηρίζομαι αὐτῷ σκηπανίῳ, Anth. Graec., 7, 731, "to support oneself with the feet," Hom. Od., 12, 434; Il., 21, 241 f.; Tyrtaeus Fr., 8, 21 f. (Diehl[8], I, 14), of the support of

---

[41] The peculiarity of the third account of Paul's conversion lies in the stronger emphasis on the withstanding of God's work. Apart from the thematic v. 9 this may also be seen in the description of the struggle with the disciples of Jesus (vv. 10-12) and the use of the proverbial Eur. Ba., 795 in v. 14, which compares Paul with Pentheus in his resistance to Dionysus.

[42] Another feature of the third account of Paul's conversion is the close connection between standing and being enlightened, cf. Ac. 26:13, 16-18, 23, and on this Eph. 5:14 and Kuhn, op. cit. (→ n. 40), 344 f., for Qumran → 646, 6 ff.

[43] In the post-apost. fathers forms of ἵστημι are rare except in Herm. and have no theological significance. μὴν ἱστάμενος occurs in Mart. Pol., 21, 1 → 640, 24 ff.

στηρίζω κτλ. [1] The meaning of the group suggests derivation from the root stā-stə with suffix -ro-, thus * stāros == (with a slight deviation of sense) Lithuanian stóras, "thick," "strong," "heavy," Eccles. Slavic starŭ "old," Old Nordic stórr "great," "powerful," cf. Sanskr. sthirá "firm," Pokorny, I, 1008. On other poss. etym. connections v. Boisacq and Hofmann, s.v. [Risch].

[2] Cf. the examples in Liddell-Scott, s.v.; Bl.-Debr. § 71 The guttural development does not prove derivation from a noun in - ι(γ)γ - v. E. Risch, Wortbildung d. homerischen Sprache (1937), 258 f. (though cf. Schwyzer, I, 735).

the body, Aristot. Hist. An., II, 1, p. 499a, 17 f., "to support oneself on something," Philostr. Vit. Ap., V, 35 (194, 21), "to lean against," Soranus Gynaecia, IV, 9, 2 (CMG, IV, 140, 14); of a tree which soars into the sky, Eur. Ba., 1073; of the flame which rages up to heaven, Plut. De Sulla, 6 (I, 454e). Fig. "to confirm," Soranus Gynaecia, IV, 5, 4 (CMG, IV, 135, 2), "to commit oneself to something," Diog. L., II, 136; politically "to pacify, stabilize," Appian. Bell. Civ., I, 98; as a tt. linguistically "to speak out loud," Dion Hal. Compos. Verb., 22 (103, 11). στηρίζω is often used for heavenly phenomena: the rainbow which Zeus puts in the clouds, Hom. Il., 11, 27 f., the securing of earth to heaven by silver pillars, Hes. Theog., 799, light which leans against heaven and rests on earth, Eur. Ba., 1082 f., for the station of the planets, Plut. Quomodo quis suos in virtute sentiat profectus, 3 (II, 76d); Paulus Alexandrinus Schol. on Elementa Apoteles-matica, 92,[3] or gen. for the position of a star in heaven or the fixing of signs in heaven, Arat. Phaen., 10. στηρίζομαι is used for constant shining, opp. ἀκοντίζομαι "to be hurled," of lightning, Ps.-Aristot. Mund., 4, p. 395b, 4. στηρίζω can also mean "to support, maintain oneself," so of the ἄπειρον, Aristot. Phys., III, 5, p. 205b, 2 f. Medical use is surprisingly common in Hell. Gk. As an anatomical expression: οἱ δὲ ὄνυχες (claws, nails) γρυποῦνται τῶν στηριζουσῶν αὐτοὺς ἑκατέρωθεν σαρκῶν ἐκτηκο-μένων, Gal. In Hippocr. Progn. Commentaria, II, 60 (CMG, V, 9, 2, p. 313, 6 f.), in a similar sense I, 13 (CMG, V, 9, 2, p. 227, 18), in diagnosis for an illness or pain "gaining a footing," so already class. Gk. ὁπότε ἐς τὴν καρδίαν στηρίξειεν, "as often as the sickness attacked the stomach," Thuc., II, 49, 3, then more broadly in Hell. Gk. Gal. in Hippocr. Prorrheticum Comm., II, 35 (CMG, V, 9, 2, p. 80, 28); Gal. In Hippocr. De Victu Acutorum Comm., II, 31 (CMG, V, 9, 1, p. 189, 26). In the sense "to strengthen" it is used of medicinal means with bodily strength as the obj. in Gal. In Hippocr. Progn. Comm., I, 8 (V, 9, 2, p. 215, 26) or a person gen., Gal. De Diaeta Hippocr. in Morbis Acutis, 4 (V, 9, 1, p. 375, 12).

2. ἐπιστηρίζω means "to support," Aristot. Probl., 23, 13, p. 933a, 10; med. like στηρίζομαι "to rest on," Luc. Philops., 13; Indoct., 6.

3. στηριγμός "steadfastness" is used of lights in Ps.-Aristot. Mund., 4, p. 395b, 7, opp. ἐξακοντισμός In Hell. Gk. it means standing still as distinct from movement, so of philosophy ἐν δὲ τῷ φιλοσοφεῖν οὐκ ἔστι ... στηριγμός, Plut. Quomodo quis suos in virtute sentiat profectus, 3 (II, 76d). It denotes the fixed point of stars between rising and setting, Ptolemaeus Tetrabiblos, I, 8;[4] with ref. to the planets, Diod. S., 1, 81, 4. In pronouncing words στηριγμός is synon. with ἐγκάθισμα and is used for "sustaining" in connection with long vowels, diphthongs, nasals and liquids, Dion. Hal. Compos. Verb., 20 (91, 13). Finally it is used for "firmness" alongside ἐξέρεισμα, Ps.-Long. Sublim., 40, 4.

4. ἀστήρικτος means "unsupported," without βάκτρον, Anth. Graec., 6, 203, 10 f.; Nonnus Dionys., 2, 226. There also seems to be an extended use in poetry and medicine. It can mean "agile," "not sticking to the ground," ἀστήρικτος ... βαίνω, Nonnus Dionys., 3, 319; 11, 48 and 140; 9, 108 f.; cf. the bold figure of the "lively and irresistibly onrushing river," 13, 317; also 43, 294; the unladen, "tossing" ship," Ps.-Long. Sublim., 2, 2; intellectually the γνώμη, Phot. Bibliotheca, 55.[5] Very gen. ἀστήρικτος can mean "weak," of the νέος, Nonnus Dionys., 15, 255; the trace, 16, 375; the god who has no weapon, 22, 159 f, Finally it is a tt. in medicine esp. in relation to the eye, Gal. In Hippocr. Progn. Comm., III, 39 (CMG, V, 9, 2, p. 365, 20); I, 28 (p. 246, 21 f.); I, 10 (p. 223, 12); Gal. De Comate Secundum Hippocratem, I, 4 (CMG, V, 9, 2, p. 182, 13); Gal. In Hippocr. Progn. Comm., I, 8 (CMG, V, 9, 2, p. 217, 14).

---

[3] Paulus Alexandrinus Elementa Apotelesmatica, ed. A. E. Boer (1958).
[4] Ed. F. E. Robbins (1956).
[5] Ed. R. Henry (1959).

B. The Word Group in the Old Testament.

1. There is a varied use of στηρίζω in the LXX, "to support," e.g., the heavenly ladder in Gn. 28:12; the hands of praying Moses in Ex. 17:12; then "to fix the eyes on something," Am. 9:4; Jer. 24:6, esp. in the phrase στηρίζω τὸ πρόσωπον ἐπί, Jer. 21:10; Ez. 6:2; 13:17; 15:7; 21:2 Hebr. שִׂים פָּנִים, Hebr. unemphatic "to plan something," esp. a journey, LXX emphatic, denoting the divine and prophetic turning to a place or person either to test or to judge. The sense "to support" occurs in Is. 63:5 'ΑΣ: αὐτός (sc. θυμός) ἐστήρισέν με, "to refresh" στήρισον τὴν καρδίαν σου Ju. 19:5, 8; cf. ψ 103:15, "to strengthen" inwardly ψ 50:14; 1 Macc. 14:14.

The same is true of ἐπιστηρίζω. A house "rests" on pillars, Ju. 16:26, 29; fig. "to rest on righteousness": τῇ δικαιοσύνῃ αὐτοῦ ἐπεστηρίσατο, Is. 59:16 'ΑΣ ΑλΛ (LXX ἐστηρίσατο). The Psalmist confesses that he is "grounded in God and has relied on him," ψ 70:6. God's hand or wrath is "directed on someone," ψ 37:3; 87:8. The eyes "fix on someone," ψ 31:8.

στηριγμός does not occur in the LXX.

2. There is no fixed Hbr. original for στηρίζω and compounds or the derived nouns. With שִׂים פָּנִים in the sense of turning to we find נָתַן פָּנִים in the same sense in Ex. 14:8; 15:7. For "to support" the Mas. esp. uses שָׁעַן, wich is transl. ἐπιστηρίζω in Ez. 29:7 Σ; Ju. 16:26; 2 Βασ. 1:6; אָמַן is also the original in Ex. 17:12. סָמַךְ is a common equivalent of στηρίζω. This is also used in the sense "to support" in Is. 59:16; Ps. 3:5; 37:17 etc., intr. "to hurl oneself on as an aggressor," Ez. 24:2; Ps. 88:7. In the ni סָמַךְ means "to rest on," Ju. 16:29; 2 K. 18:21; Is. 36:6; 48:2; Ps. 71:6; 2 Ch. 32:8. The part pass. has the sense "unshakable," Is. 26:3; Ps. 111:8. סָמַךְ takes on a special sense in the expression "to lay one's hand on the offering" in Ex. 29:10; 15:19; Lv. 8:14, 18, 22 etc., or on the head of the sinner, Lv. 24:14, or on the head of an ordinand in consecration, Nu. 8:10; 27:18, 23; Dt. 34:9.

C. The Word Group in Judaism.

From the passages last mentioned סָמַךְ becomes a tt. for ordination in later Judaism, bSanh., 14a; bAZ, 8b, [6] and from it derives סְמִיכָה bSanh., 13b; 14a or סְמִיכוּת jSanh., 1, 2 (19a, 40), סְמִיכוּתָא ibid., 41 in the sense of "ordination." סָמַךְ in the pass. means "to be confident," "certain of a matter," bBM, 16a, "to rely on something," bChag., 20b; bAZ, 71b, and in economic life it can be used as a tt. for "to refer the creditor to someone who will pay on behalf of the debtor," jQid., 3, 4 (64a, 16); jBM, 5, 8 (10c, 40).

Noteworthy in the Dead Sea Scrolls is the common use of סָמַךְ for inward strengthening. It can also mean "calm," "firm," e.g., with ref. to the sound of trumpets (→ 82, 28 f.), קוֹל נוּחַ וְסָמוּךְ 1 QM 8:7; cf. 14. The community is called an impregnable realm גְּבוּל סָמוּךְ 1 QS 10:25. Referring to the inner man we find the common phrase יֵצֶר סָמוּךְ "a firm mind," 1 QS 4:5; 8:3; 1 QH 1:35; 2:9. The opp. here is נִמְהֲרֵי לֵב "those who are perplexed or unthinking in their hearts." סָמַךְ means esp. "to strengthen," "to confirm," "to support," 1 QH 7:6 with obj. נֶפֶשׁ 1 QH 2:7. The means of strengthening is God's power 1 QH 7:6, and in the par. v. we then have the noteworthy וְרוּחַ קוֹדְשְׁכָה הֲנִיפוֹתָה "thou hast caused the spirit of thy holiness to fall on me," 7:6 f. The means of confirming can also be אֱמֶת נָכוֹן "faithfulness of being established," 9:32. This is the point in 8:13: With His power עֹז God has strengthened man. [7]

---

[6] Cf. E. Lohse, *Die Ordination im Spätjudt. u. im NT* (1951), 28-66.

[7] Philo and Jos. have nothing to offer in relation to the group.

D. The Word Group in the New Testament.

1. στηρίζω occurs in the original sense "to fix," "to establish" Lk. 16:26: χάσμα μέγα ἐστήρικται, "an unbridgeable cleft is fixed." Lk. 9:51 (→ VI, 776, 22 ff.) follows LXX usage (→ 655, 2 ff.): αὐτὸς τὸ πρόσωπον ἐστήρισεν, "he had set his face on." Jesus is announcing herewith both His own unalterable purpose and also the divine will not just that He should go to Jerusalem but that He should summon it to decision.

Very common in the NT is the transferred use which is found already in the LXX (→ 655, 2 ff.) and then enjoys more extensive usage in the Dead Sea Scrolls (→ 655, 34 ff.). The verb is found with the personal obj. ὑμᾶς (R. 16:25; 1 Th. 3:2; 2 Th. 3:3 and 1 Pt. 5:10, where ὑμᾶς is to be supplied), with καρδίας (1 Th. 3:13; 2 Th. 2:17; Jm. 5:8), ἀδελφούς (Lk. 22:32), πάντας τοὺς μαθητάς (Ac. 18:23), τὰ λοιπά (Rev. 3:2). The passive form occurs in R. 1:11; 2 Pt. 1:12. The strengthening is by God, the Lord, or the truth (2 Pt. 1:12), but also men (1 Th. 3:2). It may be accomplished, besought, or commanded. It presupposes that the Christians who are to be strengthened are under assault and in danger of becoming uncertain or slothful in their faith or walk. What the στηρίζειν consists in may be seen from parallel terms like παρακαλεῖν (→ V, 796, 19 ff.) (1 Th. 3:2; 2 Th. 2:17). In R. 1:11 στηριχθῆναι is used of the apostle himself and it is explained by συμπαρακληθῆναι: "to experience the comfort of the Gospel." The context of 1 Pt. 5:10 offers καταρτίζω, σθενόω, and θεμελιόω in illustration of στηρίζω.

The effect or aim of strengthening is the impregnability of Christian faith in spite of the troubles which have to be endured → 55, 25 ff.: εἰς τὸ στηρίξαι ὑμᾶς καὶ παρακαλέσαι ὑπὲρ τῆς πίστεως ὑμῶν τὸ μηδένα σαίνεσθαι [8] ἐν ταῖς θλίψεσιν, 1 Th. 3:2 f. The same applies in Ac. 14:22 where the compound ἐπιστηρίζω (→ 657 1 ff.) is used; this reads: ἐμμένειν τῇ πίστει καὶ ὅτι διὰ πολλῶν θλίψεων δεῖ ἡμᾶς εἰσελθεῖν εἰς τὴν βασιλείαν τοῦ θεοῦ. 1 Pt. 5:10 also has in view confirmation in face of the afflictions of persecution which had been mentioned earlier. Lk. 22:32: στήρισον τοὺς ἀδελφούς, which is addressed to Peter, is also referring to strengthening in faith, since just before there is mention of Peter's own faith: ἵνα μὴ ἐκλίπῃ ἡ πίστις σου v. 32. Similarly God is to strengthen the hearts of the Thessalonians so that they may be blameless at the parousia of the Lord, 1 Th. 3:13. 2 Th., on the other hand, has moral confirmation in view: ἐν παντὶ ἔργῳ καὶ λόγῳ ἀγαθῷ (2:17), being kept from evil: φυλάξει ἀπὸ τοῦ πονηροῦ (3:3). [9] At issue in the letter of Rev. is preservation from spiritual death: γίνου γρηγορῶν καὶ στήρισον τὰ λοιπὰ ἃ ἔμελλον ἀποθανεῖν (Rev. 3:2). [10] The reference in 2 Pt. 1:12 is to confirmation in present truth, in Christian doctrine, or in Christianity generally.

In R. 1:11 the means of strengthening is the impartation of a spiritual gift: μεταδῶ χάρισμα ὑμῖν πνευματικόν. This comes with the presence of the apostle in person and cannot be sent on in advance in a letter. The reference is obviously to a well-known expression in primitive Christianity, cf. 2 C. 1:15: ἵνα δευτέραν χάριν σχῆτε, i.e., by the presence of the apostle.

---

[8] Dib. Th., ad loc.; cf. also H. Chadwick, "1 Thess. 3:3: σαίνεσθαι," JThSt, 1, NF (1950), 156-158.

[9] On the question whether πονηροῦ is masc. or neut. cf. Dib. Th., ad loc. and → VI, 561, 19 ff.

[10] Loh. Apk., ad loc. recalls the common Gnostic equation of waking with life and sleeping with death.

2. In content the compound ἐπιστηρίζω, which occurs i. Ac. 14:22 (→ 656, 25 ff.); 15:32, 41, does not add anything new. In Ac. 15:32 it seems to be related to παρακαλέω, like στηρίζω.

3. στηριγμός occurs only once at 2 Pt. 3:17. It denotes "perseverance" in the truth mentioned in 1:12, in orthodox teaching, and in a Christian stand. The context makes it clear what is at issue, for στηριγμός is threatened by a fall into error through ἀθέσμων πλάνη. στηριγμός is thus used in a transf. se se for "perseverance," "steadfastness" in the teaching which has been handed down; the same thing is expressed negatively by the metaphor of going away and not abiding in 2 Jn. 9: πᾶς ὁ προάγων καὶ μὴ μένων ἐν τῇ διδαχῇ → V, 739, 11 ff.

4. Similarly ἀστήρικτος, found only in 2 Pt. 2:14; 3:16, means "unstable" with reference to not keeping to sound doctrine. False teachers beguile unstable souls δελεάζοντες ψυχὰς ἀστηρίκτους, 2 Pt. 2:14. Those who are unstable in doctrine confuse the understanding of difficult passages in Paul's letters ἃ (sc. δυσνόητα) οἱ ἀμαθεῖς καὶ ἀστήρικτοι στεβλοῦσιν, 3:16.

E. The Word Group in the Post-Apostolic Fathers.

In the original sense στηρίζω is used of the establishing and setting up of heaven τῷ γὰρ παμμεγεθεστάτῳ αὐτοῦ κράτει οὐρανοὺς ἐστήρισεν, 1 Cl., 33, 3. It is then used as in the NT (→ 656, 8 ff.), for the spiritual confirming of what is falling or about to fall στηρίζειν ... τὰ πίπτοντα, 2 Cl., 2, 6. 1 Cl., 13, 3 refers to the mutual strengthening of Christians. In Ign. Eph., 12, 1 the community is addressed as "secure," i.e., unthreatened. But Jesus Christ in Ign. Phld. inscr. and God in 1 Cl., 8, 5 are also the subjects of strengthening. The means in 1 Cl., 13, 3 is the commandment of the Lord (the ref. is to dominical sayings ἡ ἐντολή and τὰ παραγγέλματα), while in Ign. Phld. inscr. it is the Spirit of Christ ἐστήριξεν ἐν βεβαιωσύνῃ τῷ ἁγίῳ αὐτοῦ πνεύματι, and in 1 Cl., 8, 5 the almighty will of God τῷ παντοκρατορικῷ βουλήματι αὐτοῦ. Finally the effect of confirmation in 1 Cl., 13, 3 is obedience to the ἁγιοπρεπέσι λόγοις. στηρίζω is used gen. in 1 Cl., 35, 5: "firmly fixed on God." Thus the post-apost. fathers do not develop the use of the group beyond the NT. They simply make the same points rather more eloquently and they take "strengthening" essentially in a moral sense.

Harder

┌─────────────┐
│ † στίγμα   │
└─────────────┘

Contents: A. The Graeco-Roman World. B. The Ancient Orient. C. The Old Testament. D. Later Judaism. E. The New Testament. F. Church History.

στίγμα, [1] from στίζω "to prick," "tattoo," "mark" with a sharp instrument (graver), e.g., Hdt., V, 35, 2 f.; VII, 35, 1; 233, 2; Plut. Pericl., 26 (I, 166d); De Nicia, 29 (I, 542b), καταστίζω Philo Spec. Leg., I, 58, means basically "prick," "point," then the "mark" burned on the body with hot iron, then gen. "distinguishing mark," Poll. Onom., III, 78 f.; cf. ἐγκαύματα, Plat. Tim., 26c; Luc. Tyr., 24.

σ τ ί γ μ α. Bibl.: Liddell-Scott, Pape, Moult.-Mill., Preisigke Wört., Diels, II; Ditt. Syll.³, Hatch-Redp., Pr.-Bauer⁵, s.v. On A, and B.: F. J. Doelger, *Sphragis, Studien zu Gesch. u. Kultur d. Altertums*, V, 3-4 (1911); Ant. Christ., I (1929), 66-78, 88-91, 197-211, 229-235, 291-294; II (1930), 100-116, 268-300; III (1932), 25-61, 204-209, 257-259; H. Lilljebjörn, *Über religiöse Signierung in d. Antike*, Diss. Uppsala (1933); J. Diehl, *Sphragis*, Diss. Giessen (1938), esp. 19 f., 54. On C.: B. Stade, "Das Kainszeichen," ZAW, 14 (1894), 250-318;

A. The Graeco-Roman World.

Branded marks were carried especially by domestic animals, slaves, criminals, and later soldiers.

1. It was customary to burn on cattle the owner's mark to make deception and theft more difficult, Vergil Georg., I, 263; III, 157-161. In this connection Gk. records of sales from Egypt (1st and 2nd cent. A.D.) use the term στίγμα in the same sense as καυτήριον, BGU, II, 469, 3-7, → χαρακτήρ BGU, I, 88, 5-8, or χάραγμα, BGU, II, 453, 4-8; → σφράγις can also be used for the brand, Cl. Al. Exc. Theod., 86, 2. We find the same usage in the religious sphere. The stigmata were usually letters burned on the right thigh of the beast, BGU, I, 153, 15 f. (152 A.D.). [2] In Greece there is ref. to the σαμφόρας, a horse from a Corinthian stud, which was distinguished by the letters Σαν (Σ) branded on the loins, Aristoph. Eq., 602; Nu., 122, 1298.

2. A man who bore the stigma was everywhere regarded as dishonoured in antiquity. It is said of Xerxes that he pricked στίγματα βασιλήια, i.e.. the royal name or sign, on Theban deserters, Hdt., VII, 233, 2; in cases of great embitterment the Gks. imitated this barbarous practice in relation to prisoners of war, Plut. Pericl., 26 (I, 166d); De Nicia, 29 (I, 542b). Plat. provided that robbers of temples, if slaves or aliens, should have their guilt inscribed on their foreheads and hands, Leg., IX, 854d; the stigma brands the malefactor. Caligula even had shameful marks branded on the foreheads of honourable citizens condemned to forced labour in the construction of buildings and roads, Suet. Caes., IV, 27, 3: *deformatos prius stigmatum notis.* Petronius refers to the marking of wrong-doers, Saturae, 103, 2; 105, 11. [3] Constantine in 315 A.D. forbade marking on the face, Cod. Justinianus, IX, 47, 17. [4]

The branding of criminals persisted in some European states like Germany, France and Belgium right up to modern times, [5] but only in the imperial period did it come to be used sometimes on free men. In gen. the stigma denoting an offence was marked only on slaves, whether for running away (Aristoph. Av., 760; Lys., 331; Luc. Tim., 17; Petronius Saturae, 103, 4), [6] or stealing (Juv., 14, 21 ff.), or some other transgression or failing (Diog. L., IV, 7, 46; Petronius Saturae, 69, 1). [7] A slave thus marked was called στιγματίας, Xenoph. Hist. Graec., V, 3, 24; Luc. Tim., 17; cf. Tyr., 24; Varro De Lingua Latina, VII, 107; [8] Plin. Ep., I, 5, 2; Petronius Saturae, 109, 8. [9] He was the publicly branded good-for-nothing of the domestic staff, [10] a butt of contempt in comedy and satire, Aristoph Av., 760 f.; Plaut. Casina, 401; Aulularia, 325; Mart., II, 29, 9 f. The scornful name *litteratus* (Plaut. Casina, 401; Apul. Met., IX, 12) or *trium litterarum homo* (Plaut. Aulularia, 325) shows that the custom was to inscribe letters denoting the

---

S. Krauss, "Klassenabzeichen im Alten Israel," ZDMG, 80 (1926), 1-23, esp. 16-21. On E.: W. Heitmüller, "ΣΦΡΑΓΙΣ." *Nt.liche Stud. f. G. Heinrici* (1914), 40-59; E. Dinkler, "Zur Gesch. d. Kreuzsymbols," ZThK, 48 (1951), 148-172; W. Michaelis, "Zeichen, Siegel, Kreuz," ThZ, 12 (1956), 505-526; E. Dinkler, "Jesu Wort vom Kreuztragen," *Nt.liche Stud. f. R. Bultmann*[2] (1957), 110-129; D. P. Andriessen, "Les Stigmates de Jésus," *Bijdragen,* 23 (1962) 139-154.

[1] Etym. Indo-Eur. root *stig, tig;* Sanskr. *tējatē* "to be sharp"; Gothic *Stik-s,* "prick"; New High German "Stich," "Stichel," "stecken"; Lat. *sting(u)ere, di-sting(u)ere, in-stigāre, v.* Boisacq, Hofmann, *s.v.* (and as loan words *stigma, stigmatias, stigmosus*).
[2] Further examples in Doelger Sphragis, 18-20; Ant. Christ., III, 25; Lilljebjörn, 2.
[3] Ed. K. Müller (1961).
[4] Cod. Justinianus ed. P. Krüger in Corpus Juris Civilis, II (1892).
[5] Stade, 251.
[6] Ed. Müller → n. 3.
[7] Ed. Müller → n. 3.
[8] Ed. G. Goetz and F. Schoell (1910).
[9] Ed. Müller → n. 3.
[10] Cf. the def. in Etym. M., *s.v.:* Στιγματίας. καλοῦσι τοὺς οἰκέτας τοὺς στιζομένους ὡς ἀχρησίμους.

offence. The stigma of the runaway was perhaps F(UG), that of the thief FUR. [11] All kinds of devices were used to try to efface the dishonouring sign, [12] but in gen. the brand was for ever: *Quamdiu vixerit, habebit stigmam,* Petronius Saturae, 45, 9; [13] *inexpiabili litterarum nota,* Valerius Maximus Facta et Dicta Memorabilia, VI, 8, 7, [14] cf. Mart., VI, 64, 24-26. In the later imperial period it seems that the eastern practice of branding each slave in mark of ownership was adopted. [15] In particular the recruit to the Roman army was marked by tattooed signs, Vegetius Epitoma Rei Militaris, I, 8; II, 5; [16] from the passage cited from Ambrosius in → n. 15 it appears that the mark was the abbreviated name of the emperor. Whereas the slave was marked on the forehead the soldier was usually marked on the hand: στίγματα καλοῦσι τὰ ἐπὶ τοῦ προσώπου ἢ ἄλλου τινὸς μέρους τοῦ σώματος ἐπιγραφόμενα, οἷα ἐπὶ τῶν στρατευομένων ἐν ταῖς χερσίν, Aetius Amidenus Libri Medicinales, VIII, 12 (CMG, VIII, 2, p. 417, 24 ff.). [17]

B. The Ancient Orient.

1. The mark was commonly used in the cultures of the ancient East known to us. We find testimony to the marking of cattle as a sign of ownership in ancient Babylonia (Cod. Hammurapi § 265) [18] and ancient Egypt. [19] Slaves, too, bore a mark (*abbuttum*) [20] which denotes their status and also their master. The Cod. Hammurapi § 226 f. [21] orders death for the removal of this mark by a barber. It is also laid down that a concubine who rises up against her mistress should receive the *abbuttum* and be regarded as a slave § 146. [22] Later sons who after the death of their fathers treated their mothers badly, [23] or (adoptive) sons who denied their fathers, [24] were marked as slaves. In a transf. sense the Babyl. Job speaks of the mark and chain of slavery which will be taken from the sufferer on the bank of the divine river, *Die Geschichte eines Leidenden* ... III, 103 f. [25]

2. The use is positive when the mark denotes membership of a specific tribe or cultic deity. The Egypt. bore stigmata of this kind (Sext. Emp. Pyrrh. Hyp., III, 202), the barbarians on the Pontus (Xenoph. An., V, 4, 32; Diod. S., 14, 30, 7), the Dacians and

---

[11] A. Hug, Art. "στιγματίας" in Pauly-W., 3 A (1929), 2520-2522; cf. Petronius Saturae (→ n. 3), 103, 4: *Notum fugitivorum epigramma.*

[12] Pliny the Elder mentions plants, roots, pigeon droppings, Hist. Nat., 25, 13, 173 and 175; 26, 4, 22; 30, 4, 30; Mart. refers to doctors in VI, 64, 26 and beauticians, II, 29, 10. A stele in Epidaurus tells of two miraculous healings of branded persons, Ditt. Syll.³ III, 1168, 48-55, 55-68.

[13] Ed. Müller.

[14] Ed. C. Kempf (1888).

[15] Cf. Ambr. De Obitu Valentiniani Consolatio, 58 (MPL, 16 ([1880], 1437B): *Charactere domini inscribuntur et servuli et nomine imperatoris signantur milites.*

[16] Ed. C. Lang (1885).

[17] On the stigma of the Rom. soldier cf. also Ant. Christ., II, 268-280.

[18] AOT, 405.

[19] Thus the cattle belonging to a specific shrine bore its name and a no. Doelger Sphragis, 21-23. After being tested for cultic suitability sacrifices were sealed by a priest, Hdt., II, 38. In the Euphrates district they were marked with the sign of the cultic goddess, Plut. Lucull., 24 (I, 507e).

[20] The etym. of *abbuttum* is unknown, but since the determinative "bronze" is found with it the mark might have had the appearance of a fetter. It was usually on the hand; on sale the new owner put his mark on the other hand, cf. G. R. Driver-J. C. Miles, *The Babylonian Laws,* I (1955), 306-309, 421-425.

[21] AOT, 403.

[22] AOT, 395.

[23] Middle Babyl. text from Nuzi, E. Chiera, *Excavations at Nuzi,* I (1929), 73, 22 f.

[24] B. Landsberger, *Die Serie ana ittišu, Materialien zum Sumerischen Lex.,* I (1937), 101, 23-28.

[25] AOT, 279.

Sarmatians (Plin. Hist. Nat., 22, 2), and esp. the Thracians (Hdt., V, 6, 2; Dialexeis, II, 13 [Diels, II, 408, 14 f. → n. 29]); Cic. Off., II, 25; Strabo, VII, 5, 4; also the Britons (Tert. Virg. Vel., 10, 2; Herodian. Hist., III, 14, 7), and some Ethiopian tribes (Sext. Emp. Pyrrh. Hyp., I, 148). These marks sometimes had a sacral character; in some cases this is expressly noted. In Ethiopia children were dedicated to Apollo by a mark on the knee-cap (Joh. Lyd. De Mensibus, IV, 53). The Syrians consecrated themselves to the gods Hadad and Atargatis by signs branded on the wrist or neck (Ps.-Luc. Syr. Dea, 59). This is also the point of the "barbaric characters" a slave from Bambyke bore on the right hand (P. Par., 10, 8 c. 150 B.C.). [26] An ivy leaf was branded on the devotee of Dionysus, 3 Macc. 2:29 f.; Plut. Adulat., 12 (II, 56e); cf. 17 (II, 60a); Etym. M., s.v. Γάλλος (= priest of Attis). The devotee of the Great Mother also bore a mark, Prud. Peristephanon, 10, 1076-1090, and a note of Tert. shows that the adherent of Mithras probably did so as well, Praescr. Haer., 40, 4; [27] cf. Greg. Naz. Or., 4, 70. Rev. also gives information on sacral stigmata in paganism, for the worshippers of the beast carry his name or the number of this name as a mark → χάραγμα on the right hand or forehead, 13:16 f.; 14:9-11; 16:2; 19:20; 20:4 → 663, 25 ff. The point of this is esp. clear in Hdt., II, 113, 2: When a man was given the sacred mark he was dedicated to the god and became its servant, but he also came under its protection, so that he should not be molested. [28] This led to a different estimation of stigmata from that of the Gks.; what the latter found contemptible was carried in the East with pride, Hdt., V, 6, 2; Sext. Emp. Pyrhh. Hyp., III, 202; Dialexeis, II, 13. [29]

C. The Old Testament.

LXX uses στίγμα (plur.) only in Cant. 1:11 for נְקֻדּוֹת, which has to be understood here as a little ball or point on a piece of jewelry. στιγμή occurs in Is. 29:5 and 2 Macc. 9:11 in the sense of "moment"; the fuller expression ἐν στιγμῇ χρόνου is found in Lk. 4:5. טוֹטָפֹת in Ex. 13:16 (= remembrance signs on the forehead) is wrongly transl. ἀσάλευτον in LXX (with מוּט). כְּתֹבֶת קַעֲקַע ("etched writing") in Lv. 19:28 is transl. γράμματα στικτά.

Though there is in the OT no concept corresponding precisely to στίγμα, the thing itself is present, for in Israel, too, the custom of expressing close attachment to a man or to God by a mark on the body was not unknown.

1. When a slave wanted to attach himself to his master for ever his ear was pierced by an awl at the door-post in God's presence, Ex. 21:6; Dt. 15:16 f.

2. We find sacral marking in Is. 44:5. Here the prophet proclaims that on the eschatological repentance of the nations one will say: "I am Yahweh's," and another shall write on his hand: "Yahweh's." God makes confession of Jerusalem in a similar dramatic way, for He cares for the city as though He had a model of it graven on His hands and its walls were constantly before Him, Is. 49:16. This helps us to understand why the divinely commanded Feast of the Passover (Ex. 13:9) and Redemption of the Firstborn (13:16) are to be taken so seriously as if they were a sign (אוֹת σημεῖον → 214, 28 f.) on the hands and a mark of remembrance (זִכָּרוֹן v. 9, טוֹטָפֹת v. 16) between the

---

26 So U. Wilcken, "Zu d. syr. Göttern," Festg. f. A. Deissmann (1927), 7-9, though cf. Ant. Christ., II, 298; Lilljebjörn, 2 f.

27 Cf. Ant. Christ., I, 88-91.

28 Hdt., II, 113, 2: ἦν δὲ (near Canchos, Egypt) ... Ἡρακλέος ἱρόν, ἐς τὸ ἢν καταφυγὼν οἰκέτης ὅτευ ὦν ἀνθρώπων ἐπιβάληται στίγματα ἱρά, ἑωυτὸν διδοὺς τῷ θεῷ, οὐκ ἔξεστι τούτου ἅψασθαι.

29 Diels, II, 408, 14 f.: τοῖς δὲ Θραιξὶ κόσμος τὰς κόρας στίζεσθαι· τοῖς δ' ἄλλοις τιμωρία τὰ στίγματα τοῖς ἀδικέοντι (= ἀδικοῦσι).

eyes. [30] Here the brand is only a metaphor and comparison. Real stigmata denoting esp. close relationship to God were perhaps carried by the man who in the battle of Aphek showed King Ahab that he was a prophet by taking away his head-band, 1 K. 20:40 f. [31] The head-plate of the high-priest bears the inscription "Sacred to Yahweh" (Ex. 28:36); this in some sense represents the mark which shows its bearer to be a servant of God. [32] On the other hand Lv. 19:28 says: "Ye shall not make any cuttings in your flesh for the dead, nor print any marks upon you: I am Yahweh." This forbids tattooing and also self-mutilation in mourning for the dead, a religious practice which Israelites did in fact follow up to the exile (Jer. 16:6; 41:5), though it was originally pagan (Jer. 47:5; 48:37) and in the Canaanite cult was esp. connected with the fertility god, cf. 1 K. 18:28. Later, esp. in the post-exilic period, the prohibition was enforced for this reason in the case of priests (cf. Lv. 21:5) and generally (Lv. 19:28; Dt. 14:1 f.). This explains the prohibition of tattooing: Yahweh's exclusive claim, which was clearly felt precisely during the exile, is incompatible with the practices of a cult of the dead or a fertility cult.

3. There can be little doubt but that the mark of Cain was a tattooed sign. God Himself marked Cain (Gn. 4:15). But He did not brand him as a murderer. He marked him as His own possession and set him under His protection, → 214, 19 f. The Taw which an angel sets on the foreheads of the faithful in Ezekiel's vision of judgment also has protective power to deliver them from the sword of the avenging angel, 9:4. This mark, like the letter Taw in ancient Hbr. script, is a cross = chi, [33] → 662, 27 ff.

In the OT, then, the sacral sign is given a new significance. It is legitimate and effective only when man does not mark it on his own body but receives it from God as a sign of protection

D. Later Judaism.

1. Ps. Sol. 2:6 refers to the branding of Jewish prisoners under Pompey. [34] The male slave still had a mark (רִשּׁוּם) put on the body in the Rabb. period so that he would not run away, T. Mak., 4, 15. It is probable that his ear was bored as in Ex. 21:6, T. Sota 2, 9, but for clearer identification he also had to carry a label in the form of a seal (חוֹתָם) of clay or metal or a collar round his neck or upper garment, bShab., 58a; bMen., 43b; bQid., 22b. [35]

2. Acc. to 3 Macc. 2:29 f. Ptolemy IV Philopator tried to force the brand of the Dionysus cult an ivy leaf, on the Jews of Alexandria; the king himself bore the tympanon acc. to Plut. Adulat., 12 (II, 56e). Philo says that some apostate Jews of the dispersion were branded on their bodies and were thus barred for ever from the way of penitence, Spec. Leg., I, 58. His abhorrence of the heathen practice perhaps led him to interpret the mark of Cain as a symbol of the lasting evil of folly, Det. Pot. Ins., 177 f. For Jos. Ant., 1,

---

[30] From these scriptures, with Dt. 6:8; 11:18, derived the wearing of phylacteries on the upper left arm and the forehead; originally these were perhaps regarded as a protection against evil spirits.

[31] So Stade, 313: He had a mark tattooed on the forehead which was previously concealed by the head-band. The scars which the prophet had between the hands (i.e., on the breast) in Zech. 13:6 are perhaps to be understood in the same way.

[32] In many African tribes priests and priestesses are distinguished from the laity by signs or tattooing, J. G. Frazer, The Golden Bough, IV, 1³ (1955), 74 f.

[33] Acc. to Job 31:35 this Taw could be used as a signature. Different protective signs at the exodus are the blood on the door-posts (Ex. 12:7, 13) and the purple thread of the spies which saved Rahab's house from destruction (Jos. 2:12 f., 21).

[34] So Doelger Sphragis, 31; Ant. Christ., I, 291-294 ἐν σφραγῖδι ὁ τράχηλος αὐτῶν, ἐν ἐπισήμῳ ἐν τοῖς ἔθνεσιν, Ps. Sol. 2:6.

[35] Krauss, 19 recalls the story in jTaan., 4, 8 (68d, 48). To test the steadfastness of his soldiers Bar Kosiba ordered them to hack off their little fingers. Krauss thinks that in fact the ref. is to a sign of allegiance on the little finger.

59, however, it is simply a distinguishing sign; Jub. 4; Ps.-Philo, 2, [36] Treasure Cave 5; [37] Vit. Ad., 23 do not refer to it. Sacral tattooing was known to the Jews of Palestine and Babylon, but it was no serious danger for them. Acc. to bMak., 21a the prohibition of tattooing in Lv. 19:28 was transgressed only when there was both tattooing (קַעֲקַע), in contrast to signs or marks which could be erased (cf. jShab., 12, 4 [13d, 12 f]; bShab., 120b) and also the inking in of the engraven letters, while for R. Simon bJuda (end of the 2nd cent.) there was transgression only if the name of God was written, bMak., 21a. T. Mak., 4, 15 discusses the case of Israelites tattooing others, and also the question of intention. The connection of tattooing with idolatry is expressly emphasised here. Ben Stada, identified as Jesus by the Amoraeans, is supposed to have introduced magical arts with engraven signs from Egypt acc. to R. Eliezer (c. 100 A.D.), bShab., 104b; bSanh., 67a. Among Jehoiachin's evil deeds was that he set aside the sign of circumcision and had letters deeply tattooed on himself, Lv.r., 19, 6 on 15:25. It is no accident that the repudiation of circumcision is directly connected with tattooing here, for a royal parable brings the stigma of the Gentiles and the seal of Abraham (circumcision) into comparison. [38] This shows that the successful rejection of syncretistic influences from the time of the Maccabees had increasingly immunised the Jews against the common practice of sacral marking in the world around them. In this time of open confession of the Torah circumcision was regarded as the sign of the covenant-people in contrast to the stigmata of pagan cults. On the other hand in pre-cabbalistic writings heavenly beings and even God Himself appear as bearers of engraven letters or names. In the Midr. Shiur Qoma ascribed to R. Ishmael [39] thirty combinations of letters are mentioned which God carries inscribed on His forehead. Acc. to a saying in the Hechaloth [40] which goes back to R. Aqiba an animal (of the throne chariot) at the heavenly feast has the name Israel engraven on its forehead, while another has Truth during the day and Faithfulness in the evening.

3. Ez. 9:4 (→ 661, 17 ff.) was much noted in later Judaism. Damasc. 19:11-14 (9:11 f.) quotes the saying about the protective mark to those who sigh and grieve as a sign of the protection of the saved community in the terrors of the end-time. [41] Ez. 9:4 also influenced Ps. Sol. 15:6-9. Here it is referred to the present and antithetically amplified: The righteous bear God's saving sign so that famine, sword and death will be far from them; the sign of destruction is on the foreheads of the wicked. Similarly in bShab., 55a there stands in contrast to the saving sign a mark of blood which signifies destruction. [42] Finally the signs of the cross on Jewish ossuaries and tombs of the NT period were probably influenced by Ez. 9:4 and are to be regarded as eschatologically protective marks for those who were faithful to Yahweh, → 663, 26 ff. and n. 46. [43] Rabb. exegesis offers many

---

[36] Ps.-Philo Liber Antiquitatum Biblicarum, ed. G. Kisch (1949).

[37] Ed. C. Bezold, II (1888), cf. Riessler, 949.

[38] Ex.r., 19, 6 on 12:50: "Like a king who arranged a banquet for his friend with the order: He who would not carry his seal should not be admitted. So God has prepared a banquet ... and ordered: Who of you does not bear the seal of Abraham in his flesh shall not taste of it."

[39] J. D. Eisenstein, Ozar Midrashim, I (1915), 561 f.

[40] Quoted in C. Bialik, Sepher Ha'aggada (1960), 402.

[41] As against the Mas. the art. is put before תָו ; the letter Taw is meant. The use of Ez. 9:4 in Damasc. does not prove, however, that this group used a mark, as against the conjecture of J. L. Teicher, "The Christian Interpretation of the Sign X in the Isaiah Scroll," VT, 5 (1955), 197; J. Daniélou, Théol. du Judéo-Christianisme (1958), 385.

[42] The Taw may be taken in two (antithetical) ways. It is he first letter both of תִּחְיֶה "thou shalt live" and also of תָּמוּת "thou shalt die," Michaelis, 514. In the 2nd rec. of the Alphabet of R. Aqiba (A. Jellinek, Beth Ha-Midrasch, III² [1938], 50) we read that God did not create the world through the letter Taw, the first letter of Torah, because Taw is the sign (רשום) of those who sigh and mourn. The Taw of the righteous is in ink, that of the wicked in blood.

[43] So Dinkler Kreuzsymbol, 157-169; for difficulties cf. E. R. Goodenough, Jewish Symbols in the Greco-Roman Period, I (1953), 131 f.

interpretations of the mark of Cain, but it is noteworthy that it is never regarded as a tattooed sign, Gn.r., 22, 27 on 4:15.

E. The New Testament.

In the NT στίγμα occurs only at Gl. 6:17 where the apostle closes his letter with the words: ἐγὼ γὰρ τὰ στίγματα τοῦ ᾽Ιησοῦ ἐν τῷ σώματί μου βαστάζω. The question what Paul meant by the marks of Jesus in his body cannot be answered with any certainty. Nevertheless, the following points may be made. Paul sees in the στίγματα τοῦ ᾽Ιησοῦ protective signs which show that he, the slave of Jesus, is a client of the Lord; hence no one can molest him and go unpunished. [44] The στίγματα τοῦ ᾽Ιησοῦ which Paul bears in his body are the antithesis to the circumcision in your flesh of which his Judaising opponents boast, 6:13. If Judaism compared circumcision as the covenant sign with pagan branding (Ex.r., 19, 6 on 12:43; Lv.r., 19, 6 on 15:25), the apostle in his defence against Judaisers appeals to the στίγματα τοῦ ᾽Ιησοῦ as the new eschatological sign. On this view circumcision and the στίγματα τοῦ ᾽Ιησοῦ are related in the same way as bondage under the Law and freedom in the grace of Christ, Gl. 5:1-5. If one asks as to the nature of the marks, it is most unlikely that Paul had had a shortened name of Jesus tattooed on himself; [45] in this respect he would feel bound by the prohibition of the Torah and Pharisaic teaching. [46] The most convincing explanation is that the reference is to his wounds and scars, → V, 932, n. 16. [47] These are palpable proof that Paul suffers with his Lord (R. 8:17 → V, 925, 8 ff.), that he always bears about in his body the dying of Jesus (2 C. 4:10 → III, 144, 6 ff.; IV, 895, 7 ff.), that with his sufferings he pays in his flesh what is still lacking of the afflictions of Christ (Col. 1:24), and that he will thus be fashioned according to Christ's body of glory (Phil. 3:21).

It is no argument against this interpretation that in Rev. those who are faithful receive a stigma. Ez. 9:4 (→ 208, 29 ff.) is eschatologically expounded when in Rev. 7:2 f.

---

[44] There are good formal par. for this view, cf. Preis. Zaub., II, 14, 13 f. (200-250 A.D.) in which a man says that he carries (βαστάζω) the mummy of Osiris (as an amulet) and warns his opponent against bringing complaints (κόπους παρέχειν). Deissmann B., 270 f. was the first to note this par. Cf. too Hdt., II, 113, 2, where a ward of Heracles who has the sacred stigmata must not be molested. The apostle's warning to the Galatians would make good sense in view of the widespread use of tattooing in Asia Minor.
[45] As against Doelger Sphragis, 51; Dinkler Kreuztragen, 125. Wilcken, op. cit., 7-9 and E. Hirsch, "Zwei Fragen zu Gl. 6," ZNW, 29 (1930), 196 f. draw attention to cultic marking in relation to Gl. 6, but do not draw the same conclusions as Doelger.
[46] The Taw of Ez. 9.4, which might be construed as Christ's initial, also rules out tattooing, since it was engraven by God's angel, not by men. This passage, which was so important in later Judaism, probably influenced Gl. 6:17: As God gives the protective sign to the sighing faithful, so the servant who suffers with his Lord receives the protective stigmata whose power avails even in the Last Judgment. στίγματα τοῦ ᾽Ιησοῦ is both a gen. of relation (the signs of Jesus) and a gen. auct. (the signs Jesus has given His servant).
[47] So Phot., cf. Staab, 610. Also ad loc. Zn. Gl.; Ltzm. Gl.²; Oe. Gl.; Schlier Gl.; H. W. Beyer-P. Althaus, D. kleineren Br. d. Ap. Pls., NT Deutsch, 8⁹ (1962); G. S. Duncan, The Ep. of Paul to the Galatians, MNTC, 8 (1955); E. W. Burton, The Ep. to the Galatians, ICC (1952); J. B. Lightfoot, St. Paul's Ep. to the Galatians (1890), 51 f., 225. A pt. in favour of this view is that in Egypt. pap. οὐλαί (= scars) is a tt. for special marks even though the ref. is often to sacral stigmata, Lilljebjörn, 79-92. One need not agree with Hirsch, op. cit., 196 f. in restricting the στίγματα τοῦ ᾽Ιησοῦ to the bodily suffering which Paul experienced at conversion (blinding, Ac. 9:8 f.; 26:13; cf. Gl. 4:13-16) as a sign of being commandeered by Christ, cf. correctly O. Holtzmann, "Zu Emanuel Hirsch, Zwei Fragen z. Gl. 6," ZNW, 30 (1931), 82 f.

(→ IV, 635, 16 ff.) an angel summons the angels of destruction to postpone the over-throw of the earth until the servants of God are sealed on their foreheads, cf. 9:4 → σφραγίς. Rev. 3:12; 14:1; 22:4 show that the name of God or Christ is the protective sign. One may not conclude from these passages that Christians then carried the name of God or Jesus inscribed on their skin, [48] for the protective writing came from heaven, 3:12, 7:2 f. In contrast to the mark of the beast (→ IV, 635, 19 ff.) it was not inscribed by men, 13:16 f. Here again OT and later Jewish custom is followed.

F. Church History.

1. In Gnosticism there is stress on the fact that the eschatological act of recognition is already accomplished with the saving name. Believers are sealed by the Redeemer, O. Sol. 4:7; 8:15, 21; even prisoners in the underworld received His name as a sign of freedom, 42:20. The believing soul adorned with the seal of truth bears the stigmata of Christ, Cl. Al. Exc. Theod., 86, 2. These statements, which refer to baptism, are fig., though in some Gnostic groups there was a real mark. Thus at the initiation of the Carpocratians the novice was sealed with a hot iron on the lobe of the right ear; this was supposed to represent the final baptism of fire which John the Baptist proclaimed, Heracleon in Cl. Al. Ecl. Proph., 25, 1; Iren. Haer., I, 25, 6. The sign (רוּשְׁמָא) which the Mandaean baptismal candidate received (→ 208, 9 ff.) could also have been a stigma.

2. The fathers often mentioned the stigmata of slaves or soldiers to bring out the meaning of the appropriation of the Christian to his Lord in baptism, Ambr. De Obitu Valentiniani Consolatio, 58 (→ n. 15); Aug. Ep., 185, 23 (CSEL, 57); Chrys. Ad illu-minandos catecheses, II, 5 (MPG, 49 [1862], 240). The *signaculum saeculi* of the Roman soldier was naturally unacceptable to one who bore the *signum Christi*, the name invoked over him in baptism, cf. Acta Sancti Maximiliani Martyris, 2. [49]

3. Later, Christians had the sign of the cross or the name of Christ tattooed on their wrists or arms, Procop. Gaz. Comm. in Isaiam Proph. on 44:1-5 (MPG, 87, 2 [1863], 2680 f.); [50] long before we find the practice of making the sign of the cross with the finger (Tert. De Corona, 3 [CSEL, 69]) or its signing on the forehead (Hier. Comm. in Ezech. on 9:4, MPL, 25 [1884], 88B). It is said of St. Radegund (d. 587) and St. Edith (d. 984) that they had themselves "stigmatised"; H. Seuse had the letters IHS incised on his breast. [51]

4. From the Middle Ages to the modern period men distinguished for profound piety and great spiritual power, or weakened by sickness and abstinence so that their bodies are susceptible, have visibly borne the stigmata of Christ (the nailprints, the wound in the side, and more rarely the marks of the crown of thorns, the scourging, and bearing the cross). The Roman Catholic Church recognises over 300 of these, of whom more than 60 are sanctified or beatified. [52] One of the first was Francis of Assisi upon whom, at Monte Alverno in 1224. Christ Himself is supposed to have branded the stigmata by scorching rays from His wounds. In his life of the saint Bonaventura applies the words of Gl. 6:17: *Iam enim propter stigmata Domini Jesu, quae in corpore tuo portas, nemo tibi debet esse molestus,* 13, 9. [53]

Betz

---

[48] So Bss. Apk. on 7:3.
[49] In Acta Martyrum, ed. T. Ruinart (1859), 341.
[50] This is perhaps how we are to interpret the standing sign of the cross which many of earlier so-called "Scipio heads" bore on the forehead, Ant. Christ., II, 281-296. The cross of these heads denoted a priest of Isis or the Mithras cult, Lilljebjörn, 63.
[51] Doelger Sphragis, 39 f.
[52] A. M. Koeniger, Art. "Stigmatisierte" in RGG, V[2] (1931), 807-812 with bibl.
[53] Bonaventura Legendae Duae, ed. Collegium Sancti Bonaventurae (1923).

στίλβω

The ling. derivation of this word is not known; cf. Irish *sell* "eye," *sellaim* "I see," Celtic root *stil(p)n*.[1] Derivates: στιλβόω, στιλβός = στιλπνός, ἡ στίλβη, ἡ στιλβότης, ἡ στιλβάς, ἡ στίλβωσις, τὸ στίλβωμα. τὸ στίλβωθρον, adv. στιλβόντως, στιλβηδόν.[2]

1. Usage in the Greek Sphere.

In Hom. the original use of the word is with ref. to the shining or gleaming of oil. On Achilles' shield young men are "clothed with well-spun clothes, softly gleaming with oil," Il., 18, 595 f. Similarly it is said of the smooth white stones on which Nestor sits before the high gates of the palace that "they gleam with oil," Od., 3, 408. The term is used of men too; Paris is described as "shining" with beauty and finery, Il., 3, 392. Again the figure of Odysseus, when he is rejuvenated by Athene, is depicted as shining with beauty and grace, Od., 6, 237. From the love couch of Zeus and Hera on the summit of Ida there fall to the earth from golden clouds "shining drops of dew," Il., 14, 351. What shines or gleams is here a characteristic of the beautiful, and when transferred to men we obviously have a gift of the gods. In Plato's scientific observation the word occurs with ref. to ὑδάτων ... εἴδη ... ἔμπυρα, Tim., 59e f, i.e., the multiplicity and changes which occur through the union of fire and fluid. We read of the glitter of gold στίλβοντι καὶ ξανθῷ χρώματι κοινωθέν in Tim., 59b, the gleaming of oil λαμπρὸν καὶ στίλβον in 60a, and the word is used for anything that shines. In considering the rise of colours Plato speaks of tears, the coming together of fire and liquid, and how fire (in the eye) shoots forth like lightning, and the other fire comes in, and is extinguished in the moisture of the eye, colours arising in the mixture; hence comes the impression of μαρμαρυγαί (glistening). But what causes this is called λαμπρὸν καὶ στίλβον, Tim., 68a. When this gleaming factor is missing, red arises from fire and blood. When λαμπρόν is mixed with red and white we have yellow. Plat. uses the term synon. with λαμπρός for what shines, 68a b; cf. Phaed., 110 d. Acc. to Plat. Phaedr., 250d beauty is apprehended by the brightest of the senses, the eye, as στίλβον ἐναργέστατα, "shining in the brightest light."

The word is also used for the glittering and shining of moving water, Aristot. Meteor., II, 9, p. 370a, 18, the shining of the eye, Hist. An., VI, 3, p. 561a, 32, the gleaming of the stars, Cael., II, 8, p. 290a, 18 f. ὁ Στίλβων is also used to denote the planet Mercury, Ps.-Aristot. Mund., 2, p. 392a, 26.

2. Usage in the Old Testament Sphere.

Almost all the instances in the Gk. transl. of the OT have the word for the gleaming reflections of metal, bronze, gold, the sword. There are various Hbr. originals: צהב 2 Εσδρ. 8:27; להב Na. 3:3; קלל Da. 10:6; לטש Ps. 7:12; ברק Ez. 21:15, 20. The ref. in 2 Εσδρ. 8:27 is to bronze (מצהב). A very common use is for the lightning of the forked sword. ῥομφαία ἐσπασμένη εἰς σφάγια ... ἐγείρου ὅπως στίλβῃς, Ez. 21:33. Trans. "he will cause his sword to shine" = "draw," Ps. 7:12. "As the sun shone (ἔστιλβε) on the golden and bronze shields, the mountains were agleam (ἔστιλβε) with them and gave light like torches of fire," 1 Macc. 6:39. In a non-Gk. expression the noun is used in Ez. 21:14 f.: ῥομφαία, ῥομφαία ὀξύνου ... ὅπως γένῃ εἰς στίλβωσιν, "Be

---

στίλβω. [1] Cf. Boisacq, *s.v.*; Hofmann, *s.v.*; Pokorny, I, 1035.
[2] Liddell-Scott, *s.v.*

sharpened, sword, ... that thou mayest glitter," cf. v. 20. Ep. Jer. 23 refers to the gold of an idol which has to be polished to shine. The term can be an embellishment, as may be seen in Ez. 40:3. Here the HT vividly describes the man's appearance כְּמַרְאֵה נְחֹשֶׁת "as the appearance of brass," but the LXX adds ὡσεὶ ὅρασις χαλκοῦ στίλβοντος. Theodotion has the same expression to replace the LXX ὡσεὶ χαλκὸς ἐξαστράπτων at Da. 10:6.

3. The Word in the New Testament.

In the only NT instance in Mk. 9:3 the word is used of the glistening of Jesus' raiment at the transfiguration → IV, 25, n. 30: τὰ ἱμάτια αὐτοῦ ἐγένετο στίλβοντα λευκὰ λίαν. It is worth noting that the parallel account in Mt. 17:2, which is in large measure literally the same as that of Mk., has ἱμάτια ... λευκά here, → IV, 241, 21 ff. Mk. has λευκὰ λίαν in explanation of στίλβοντα and he strengthens the explanation by the relative clause, of which there are various readings in the MSS. Shining white garments are a characteristic of epiphany stories.[3] White is the colour of light and life, of the priest, the victor, and heaven.[4] But only Mk. has the uncommon word; he seems to have interwoven it into his original. The word is not an embellishment as in the LXX → line 2. It is used to denote that which glistens, as in Plato → 665, 20 ff. It is also used in connection with clothing, as in Hom. → 665, 8 f.

Lk. 9:29 has λευκὸς ἐξαστράπτων for the shining of Jesus' garment. This word is used to describe the miraculous in the LXX, Ez. 1:4; Da. 10:6 etc.[5]

4. The Word in the Post-Apostolic Fathers.

Herm. s., 9, 2, 2 also uses the word to express supernatural radiance. The hill or rock of God has just received a new entry, a gate, which shines more than the sun, so that all wonder at its radiance.

Fitzer

στοιχέω, συστοιχέω, στοιχεῖον

† στοιχέω.

1. Outside the New Testament.

The verb means "to be in a στοῖχος,[1] a rank of series," "to belong to a series." Its first use is military στοιχοῦσα (sc. ἡ ἑκατοστύς or δεκάς), "in rank," Xenoph. Cyrop., VI, 3, 34; Eq. Mag., V, 7. The Athenian ephebos swears not to bring shame on his

---

3 Loh. Mk., *ad loc.*
4 Wbg. Mk., *ad loc.;* cf. → IV, 241, 21 ff.
5 [Bertram].

σ τ ο ι χ έ ω . Bibl. → στοιχεῖον.
1 στοῖχος from Hdt. "rank" (also in a military sense, cf. Thuc., IV, 47, 3), from στείχω "to march," "to go in ranks" (from Hom., not related to Germ. "steigen") [Risch]. The military use strictly differentiates στοῖχος for those arranged behind one another from ζυγόν for those beside one another, Poll. Onom., I, 126, also στοιχέω and ζυγέω, Aelianus Tacticus, 7, 2; Asclepiodotus Tacticus, II, 6 (ed. H. Köchly-W. Rüstow, *Griech. Kriegsschriftsteller*, II, 1 [1855]).

weapons, οὐδ' ἐγκαταλείψω τὸν παραστάτην [2] ὅτῳ ἂν στοιχήσω, Lyc., 77, cf. Poll. Onom., VIII, 105. Then we find, e.g., a botanical use (abs.) διὰ τὸ στοιχεῖν τὰ γόνατα, Theophr. Hist. Plant., III, 5, 3 etc.

In a transf. sense it means "to agree." Days and months are not in agreement with the moon (συμφωνέω) nor years with the sun (στοιχέω), Geminus Elementa Astronomiae, 8, 26; [3] "to be in harmony" στοιχεῖν ... τῷ λόγῳ Σωκράτους, Muson., 18b, p. 102, 9 or "to act in harmony" par. ἕπεσθαι, 8, p. 40, 14 f.; βουλόμενοι στοιχεῖν τῇ τῆς συγκλήτου προθέσει, Polyb., 28, 5, 6; στοιχῶν τοῖς προειρημένοις φιλοσόφοις "in agreement with the afore-mentioned philosophers," Sext. Emp. Math., XI, 59; ἐν φιλοσοφίᾳ μὲν τῇ τῶν φιλοσόφων (sc. συνηθείᾳ) στοιχήσομεν (in usage), "in philosophy we will adopt that of the philosophers," I, 233; ταῖς πλείοσι (γνώμαις) στοιχεῖν "to assent to," Dion. Hal. Ant. Rom., 6, 65, 1; also "to come to an agreement," Aesop. Fabulae, 57, II, 8: [4] στοιχηθέντα μισθόν, in I, 5 and III, 11 f. ὡμολογημένον ... or συμφωνηθέντας μισθούς. The sense "to agree" occurs in an established usage in the inscr., typically formulated in Ditt. Or., I, 339, 51: βουλόμενος στοιχεῖν τοῖς ὑφ' ἑαυτοῦ πρασσομένοις. [5] The previous conduct of NN is extolled, and it is then said that in his more recent public action he has "stayed in a series" with what went before, Inscr. Priene, 112, 113 (1st cent. B.C.); cf. Ditt. Or., II, 764, 45; [6] the word is used of the council, Ditt. Syll.[3], II, 685, 18 (139 B.C.); "to remain in agreement" with the conduct of one's ancestors, II, 708, 5 (2nd cent. B.C.); cf. II, 734, 6 (94 B.C.): θέλων δὲ καὶ διὰ τῶν ἔργων (sc. NN has thus far preserved εὐσέβεια to the gods in his public speeches) στοιχεῖν αὐτοσαυτῷ. [7] Similarly Ditt. Or., II, 532, 27: But if I act μὴ στοιχούντως [8] καθὼς ὤμοσα, "not in agreement with my oath..." Of calendar dates II, 458, 52 and 72 f.; of stones forming a flat surface, Ditt. Syll. [3], III, 972, 153. The later period develops this sense "to agree, to be in a series with": οὐδεὶς στοιχήσει ταύτῃ τῇ θέσει σου, "no one will agree with this statement of yours," Schol. on Luc. Musc. Enc., 7; [9] Hesych., s.v. uses only συναινέω in explanation, Suid., s.v. στοιχίζω: στοιχῶ δὲ τὸ συμφωνῶ. Pap. of the Byzantine period have the verb regularly in agreements (not earlier pap.): "I have agreed to something," or "something is in accord with my will, is agreeable to me," e.g., BGU, I, 317, 14: στοιχεῖ μοι πάντα τὰ προγεγραμμένα "it satisfies me"; cf. already Qoh. 11:6: οὐ γινώσκεις ποῖον στοιχήσει, ἢ τοῦτο ἢ τοῦτο (the only LXX example of στοιχέω).

2. In the New Testament.

The interpretation of στοιχέω in the NT as a synonym of περιπατέω and πορεύομαι is undoubtedly ancient [10] and has always found supporters, [11] but if

---

[2] παραστάτης "the man beside," ἐπιστάτης "the man behind," Poll. Onom., I, 127.

[3] Ed. C. Manitius (1898).

[4] Corpus Fabularum Aesopicarum, I, 1 ed. A. Hausrath (1940).

[5] Part of the iterative impf.; v. without ὑφ' ἑαυτοῦ Recueil d'Inscr. Grecques (ed. C. Michel [1900]), 544, 14 (114 B.C.), cf. line 28: γνησίως στοιχῶν ἐν πᾶσιν τῇ ἑαυτοῦ καλοκἀγαθίᾳ.

[6] For the opp. cf. also the rather different and not at all certain text Inscr. Priene, 110, 21 (1st cent. B.C.): Virtues "consonant with" his age (?). Abs. perhaps Ditt. Or., I, 308, 21.

[7] Doric for ἑαυτῷ. For this ethical ideal cf. Polyb., 32, 11, 8: ὁμολογούμενον καὶ σύμφωνον ἑαυτὸν κατασκευάσας κατὰ τὸν βίον. Linguistically cf. οὐδὲ γὰρ σύνστοιχοι ἑαυτῶν (sic) γίνεσθε, "you contradict yourself," BGU, IV, 1205, II, 9 f.

[8] Thus στοιχούντως = ὁμολογουμένως. The opp.: "In contradiction with..."

[6] Ed. H. Rabe (1906), 11, 7.

[10] So Vg at Ac. 21:24; Gl. 5:25. Cf. Thes. Steph., though not at Phil. 3:16. In Vg a difference is obviously sensed in the other passages. For περιπατέω transf. it always has ambulare except at Ac. 21:21, but for στοιχέω sectari at R. 4:12, sequi at Gl. 6:16, permanere at Phil. 3:16.

[11] Cf. the comm., ad loc.: Pr., Wdt., Haench. Ag.; Ltzm. Gl.; Dib. Ph.; Loh. Phil. etc.

it were correct the NT would be alone in this use of στοιχέω. [12] The normal use is presupposed in Paul's employment of the compound (→ 669, 22 ff.) and it is surely not forgotten in the simple form. The sense "to walk" would have to be explained by a shift in meaning from "to be in agreement with someone," "to be in step with," by way of "to follow someone," to "to walk." It should be noted, however, that in the NT as in other writings (apart from the absolute use) στοιχέω is always combined with the dative in marked contrast to verbs which plainly mean "to walk" in the sense of conduct.

Thus περιπατέω in this sense [13] (→ V, 944, 6 ff.) occurs 17 times with ἐν, 5 with κατά, and 17 with an adv. (or "so" to be supplied in Phil. 3:18 and "as" in Eph. 5:15), also once with διά and only 3 times with just the dative; πορεύομαι (→ VI, 575, 13 ff.) 3 times with ἐν, 3 with κατά, 1 with ὀπίσω, and only 2 with dat. [14] In 52 instances [15] in which a man's conduct is denoted by one of these verbs in the NT, the dative alone occurs only 5 times. [16] But στοιχέω, which is never used with ἐν, διά, adverb etc., occurs 3 times with the dative (once with part.). It would thus stand alone in the series of verbs of walking.

In fact the word may at least be construed along the lines of the common usage in all the NT instances. [17] At Ac. 21:24 the καὶ αὐτός, [18] found in Ditt. Syll.3, II, 708, 5, → 667, 20, suggests it: All who are zealous for the Law (v. 20) "will see that you too are in the ranks as one who keeps the law." Phil. 3:16 says: "Nevertheless, whereto we have attained, (let us) remain in one and the selfsame thing." [19] In Gl. 6:16 the concept of measuring (→ III, 598, 17 ff.) leads us to expect a corresponding verb: The apostle's wish or promise applies to those who "agree" [20] with the κανών mentioned in v. 15. The special use of στοιχέω for "to keep step" in R. 4:12 has been shown already in → III, 403, 4 ff. [21] Finally Gl. 5:24 f. is certainly parallel in

---

[12] In my view the efforts of O. Lagercrantz, "Elementum," *Skrifter utgivna av Kunglig Humanistiska Vetenskapssamfundet i Uppsala,* 11, 1 (1911), 103-5, to find it in some pre-Chr. authors are not successful → 666, 30 ff. The supposed par. in Moult.-Mill., *s.v.* are taken out of context → 667, 18 ff.

[13] Only the Epistles among the Johannine writings call for consideration here.

[14] In Test. XII it is combined with ἐν 15 times, with κατά 2, with adv. 1, with ὀπίσω 1, with ἐνώπιον 2, and abs. once. The dat. alone occurs only with περιπατέω and even then only at Iss. 5:8 πορεύομαι sometimes occurs with dat. in LXX even where HT has ב, so in most of the examples in Johannessohn Kasus., 57 f. But ἐν is obviously more common, cf. the many instances from Dt. in Johannessohn. The ref. to J. Rouffiac, *Recherches sur les caractères du grec dans le NT d'après les inscr. de Priène* (1911), 34 in Bl.-Debr. § 198, 5 is quite misleading, sinces the instances of στοιχέω given there are misinterpreted, → 667, 7 f., 12 f., 17 f.

[15] Not counting ἀναστρέφομαι "to stay," then "to behave" (cf. *Inscr. Grecques, op. cit.,* 544, 30 with adv.; so often in Polyb.), not "to walk." This occurs with the mere dat. neither in NT nor LXX (Ez. 22:30; Prv. 20:7).

[16] For LXX → V, 942, 28 ff.; VI, 571, 4 ff. For the few instances of transf. usage in non-bibl. writings → VI, 567, 5 ff.

[17] Cf. Cr.-Kö., *s.v.;* also Pass., Pape, F. Zorell, Novi Test. Lex. Graecum (1931), *s.v.;* Oe. Gl. on 5:25 (all the NT ref.); Pr.-Bauer, *s.v.* etc.

[18] καὶ αὐτὸς στοιχεῖν (abs.) βουλόμενος καὶ τοῖς ἐκείνων ἴχνεσιν ἐπιβαίνειν.

[19] MSS GF presuppose for συστοιχέω the customary meaning outside the NT. As regards the Imperial Text cf. Gl. 6:16.

[20] In context the ref. is not to ethical conduct but to the understanding of the event of salvation. The same applies to R. 4:12.

[21] Cf. Schl. R., *ad loc.:* "To keep to the traces." In Ditt. Syll.3, II, 708, 5 (→ n. 18) τοῖς ... ἴχνεσιν naturally does not go with στοιχεῖν, though in other respects the passage offers a good par. (πατήρ and πρόγονοι).

content to v. 16 (→ V, 944, 17 ff.) in contrasting ἐπιθυμίαι and πνεῦμα. But the statement in v. 25 is formulated differently. If our Christian life is fashioned as a new life in the Spirit, then let us "be in harmony with" the Spirit. [22] A life in contradiction with the Spirit is described in v. 26.

3. The Early Church.

The post-apost. fathers and Apologists do not use the word, but it occurs in Mart. Pol., 22, 1: στοιχοῦντας τῷ κατὰ τὸ εὐαγγέλιον λόγῳ ᾿Ιησοῦ Χριστοῦ. This saying emphasises the importance of agreement with the word specified. In Cl. Al the only instance is Strom., III, 66, 1 on the basis of Gl. 6:16. Ps.-Cl. Hom., 10, 15, 1 f. has it in the sense "to be in agreement" with an example (παράδειγμα in the sense of analogy).

† συστοιχέω.

Like the other compounds ἀντι-, ἰσο- and περι-,[1] this means "to be in a series with"; it gives emphasis to the simple form: "to be σύστοιχος," "to be in the same ranks." In connection with rapid advances and retreats it means that soldiers should stay in the same line or rank συζυγοῦντας καὶ συστοιχοῦντας ("to keep in rank"), Polyb., 10, 23, 7. More common is σύστοιχος, "belonging to a series," so in logical discussions. Tasting and sweetness, seeing and white, are σύστοιχα respectively, they "go together," Aristot. De Sensu et Sensibilibus, 7, p. 447b, 30 f.; σύστοιχος opp. ἀντίστοιχος, Mot. An., 6, p. 707a, 11: συστοιχία, "series of related concepts," ἡ ἑτέρα συστοιχία, "opposing series of concepts," Metaph., 10, 9, p. 1066a, 15, cf. 3, 2, p. 1004b, 27; the Pythagoreans set out antithetical series of concepts with the ten ἀρχαί, 1, 5, p. 986a, 23.[2]

Two antithetical series of concepts are accordingly presupposed in Gl. 4:25.[3] Paul has biblical quotations at the commencement of the two series (the Pentateuch v. 21 [→ IV, 1071, 1 ff.], γέγραπται v. 22) in v. 22 f.: the son of the handmaid — the son of the free woman; κατὰ σάρκα — διὰ τῆς ἐπαγγελίας. The series are continued in the typological interpretation in vv. 24-31: Hagar, the handmaid, is allegorically the order of Sinai as the mount where the Law was given [4] — there is no equivalent for this in the other series — and this leads on to the earthly Jerusalem (Judaism, which clings to descent from Abraham κατὰ σάρκα and to the Torah as the way of salvation) living in the bondage of the Law. In the other series we find the Jerusalem which is above (→ 336, 33 ff.) as the mother of Christians, who, as those that have come into life through the promise after the manner of Isaac, are free, cf. R. 4. Since in v. 24 Paul has already given an interpretation of Hagar, he does not equate her directly with the earthly Jerusalem but simply says that she "belongs to the same series."[5]

---

[22] Schlier Gl., ad loc., who transl.: "So we want to orientate ourselves by the Spirit," cf. Oe. Gl.:[1] "to follow the marching orders of the Spirit," paraphrased accordingly in[2]. Zn. Gl., ad loc. takes the usual sense as a starting-pt., but then suggests the forming of ranks by Christians, which does not agree with the dat.; similarly on Gl. 6:16.

συστοιχέω. Bibl. → στοιχεῖον.
[1] Cf. for each of these Liddell-Scott, s.v.
[2] Cf. Ltzm. Gl. on 4:25.
[3] Cf. already Thes. Steph., s.v. (the best presentation), then F. Zorell, Novi Test. Lex. Graecum (1931), s.v. and Ltzm. Gl., ad loc.
[4] v. 25a is the basis of the equation of the order of Sinai and Hagar. Cf. Schlier Gl. on 4:24; → I, 55, 18 ff.
[5] The transl. "to correspond" abandons the idea of series.

† στοιχεῖον.

A. Outside the New Testament.

Since the most important senses of the word (1-4) occur contemporaneously in lit. and are presumed to be familiar, one cannot follow the semasiological development simply from the sequence of examples. [1] In and of itself στοιχεῖον means "what belongs to a series," as στοῖχος denotes the "series" to which an individual person or thing belongs, → στοιχέω 666, 30 ff. with n. 1.

1. στοιχεῖον means the "length of a shadow" [2] by which time is calculated, from Aristoph. Eccl., 652 (c. 390 B.C.) to Luc. Gallus, 9; Saturnalia, 17 etc. In extant texts [3]

σ τ ο ι χ ε ῖ ο ν. Bibl.: R. G. Bandas, *The Master-Idea of St. Paul's Epistles or the Redemption* (1925), 65-81; P. Bläser, "Das Gesetz bei Pls.," NTAbh, 19, 1/2 (1941), 55-62; F. Boll-W. Gundel, Art. "Sternbilder, Sternglaube u. Sternsymbolik bei Griechen u. Römern," Roscher. VI, 867-1071 (Bibl. [to 1937] 867-9); A. Bouché-Leclerq, *L'astrologie grecque* (1899); W. Bousset, *Hauptprobleme d. Gnosis* (1907), 223-234; M. Brändle, *Kosmische Mächte. Eine exeget.-religionsgeschichtliche Studie zum Begriff stoicheia im Kol. 2:8, 20*, Diss. Enghien (1954); W. Burkert, "Στοιχεῖον," *Philol.*, 103 (1959), 167-197; E. W. Burton, *The Ep. to the Galatians*, ICC, II, 10 (1921), 510-518; G. B. Caird, *Principalities and Powers* (1956), esp. 80-96; W. Capelle, *Die Vorsokratiker* (1958), esp. 183-220; A. W. Cramer, *Stoicheia tou kosmou*, Diss. Leiden (1961); F. Cumont, *Astrology and Religion among the Greeks and Romans* (1912); also *Textes et monuments figurés relatifs aux mystères de Mithra*, I (1899), esp. 93-120; A. Deissmann, Art. "Elements" in EB, II, 1258-1262; M. Dibelius, *Die Geisterwelt im Glauben d. Pls.* (1909), 78-85; 227-230; Dib. Gefbr.[3]. 27-29; H. Diels, *Elementum* (1899); A. Dieterich, *Abraxas* (1891), 52-62; also *ABC-Denkmäler, Kl. Schriften* (1911), 203-228; K. Dieterich, "Hell. Volksreligion u. byzantinisch-neugriech. Volksglaube," *Angelos*, 1 (1925), 2-23, esp. 9-16; F. Dornseiff, "Das Alphabet in Mystik u. Magie," ΣΤΟΙΧΕΙΑ, VII (1922); B. S. Easton, "The Pauline Theology and Hellenism," *Amer. Journal of Theol.*, 21 (1917), 358-382. esp. 358-366; S. Eitrem, "Die vier Elemente in d. Mysterienweihe," *Symb. Osl.*, 4 (1926), 39-59; 5. (1927), 39-59; O. Everling, *Die paul. Angelologie u. Dämonologie* (1888), 65-75; W. Gundel, Art. "Astralreligion, Astrologie, Astronomie," RAC, I, 810-836; J. Huby, "St. Paul Les ép. de la captivité," *Verbum salutis*, VIII (1947), 59-67; W. L. Knox, *St. Paul and the Church of the Gentiles* (1939), esp. 90-110, 146-178; H. Koller, "Stoicheion," *Glotta*, 34 (1955), 161-174; J. Kroll, *Die Lehren d. Hermes Trismegistos* (1914), Index, *s.v.* "Elemente," "Planeten," "Sterne"; G. Kurze, *Der Engels- u. Teufelsglaube d. Ap. Pls.* (1915), 125-137; O. Lagercrantz, "Elementum," *Skrifter utgivna av Kunglig Humanistiska Vetenskapssamfundet i Uppsala*, 11, 1 (1911); A. Lumpe, Art. "Elementum," RAC, IV, 1074-1100; C. F. D. Moule, *The Epistles of Paul the Ap. to the Col. and to Philemon* (1957), 90-92; Nilsson (on astrology), I[2], 841-3; II[2], 268-81; 486-519; E. Percy, "Die Probleme d. Kolosser- u. Epheserbr.," *Skrifter utgivna av Kungl. Human. Vetenskapssamfundet i Lund*, 39 (1946), 156-167; F. Pfister, "Die στοιχεῖα τοῦ κόσμου in d. Br. d. Ap. Pls.," *Philol.* 69 (1910), 411-427; K. Prümm, *Religionsgeschichtliches Hndbch. für den Raum d. altchr. Umwelt* (1943), astrology 404-412, sources 404 f., bibl. 411 f. B. Reicke, "The Law and This World acc. to Paul," JBL, 70 (1951), 259-276; K. Reinhardt, *Kosmos u. Sympathie* (1926), *passim*; E. Riess, Art. "Astrologie," Pauly-W.. 2 (1896), 1802-28; A. Ritschl, *Die chr. Lehre von d. Rechtfertigung*, II[1] (1874), 248 f.; L. E. Scheu, *Die "Weltelemente" beim Ap. Pls.* (Gl. 4:3, 9 und Kol. 2:8, 20), Diss. Washington Cath. Univ. (1933); F. Spitta, *Der zweite Br. d. Petrus u. der Br. d. Judas* (1885), 260-281; W. Vollgraff, "Elementum," *Mnemosyne*, IV, 2 (1949), 89-115. (Only works consulted and found important are listed.)

[1] The attempt by Lagercrantz, 93 f. does not seem to me to be successful, cf. Oe. Gl.[2] on 4:3; Koller, 170. For more recent attempts cf. Koller and Burkert.

[2] Burkert, 188: "From the standpoint of the sun the shadow is always 'in step' with man." Vollgraff, 98 deduces from Plut. De Sollertia Animalium, 29 (II, 980a) the sense "unit of measure," but ἐν ἴσῳ τεταγμένον στοιχείῳ means here "ordered in the same relation" (*pari ratione*, F. Duebner, Plutarchi Scripta Moralia, II [1877], 1199).

[3] Phot., *s.v.* attests the meaning (σκιά) in a comedy of Philemon, but does not give the text. Phot.: στοιχεῖον ἐκάλουν τὴν ναυτῶν σκιὰν ᾗ τὰς ὥρας ἐσκοποῦντο. The conjecture αὐτῶν (Vollgraff, 101; doubled ν) is plausible.

apart from Phot., *s.v.* there is always ref. to the hour of the δεῖπνον, also Eubulus Fr., 119, 7 (CAF, II, 206), cf. Poll. Onom., VI, 44: τῇ σκιᾷ δ' ἐτεκμαίροντο τὸν καιρὸν τῆς ἐπὶ τὸ δεῖπνον ὁδοῦ, ἣν καὶ στοιχεῖον ἐκάλουν. This is still presupposed as customary in the 4th cent. A.D.; [4] Schol. on Luc. Gallus, 9 and Saturnalia, 17 [5] speak of it as outdated, but they see a ref. to man's shadow → n. 3.

2. Linguistically in Plat. and the theoreticians before him [6] στοιχεῖον, as distinct from γράμμα (→ I, 761, 37 ff.), refers to the sound which is in a series with others, "part of a syllable or word," [7] so in the fairly early Crat., 393d, 424b-d, 433a, 434a-b etc. Only occasionally does it mean "basic word" as distinct from words added, 422a-b. In the later Theaet. στοιχεῖον is esp. the original part of a word considered in relation to the syllable as the combination (συλλαβή) of letters, 202e-204a, again not as an isolated element but as one in a series, cf. Polit., 278b-d. The meaning "part of a word" is the chief one in Plat. (but → 673, 6 ff.; 679, 3 ff.), though naturally the ref. can also be to the written letter, Polit., 277e; Resp., III, 402a. Sounds are the final elements ἐξ ὧν σύγκειται ἡ φωνὴ καὶ εἰς ἃ διαιρεῖται ἔσχατα, Aristot. Metaph., 4, 3, p. 1014a, 28 f. In Philo, as in most ancient grammar, the main ref. is to spoken parts of words differentiated as silent and vocal, Rer. Div. Her., 210; Agric., 136; also semi-vocal, Congr., 150. Vowels are the best and have most power, Leg. All., I, 14 cf. Sacr. AC, 74. The δύναμις of letters is discussed in Artemid. Oneirocr., III, 66 (p. 195, 18). Thus the question is asked why A is the first letter, Plut. Quaest. Conv., IX, 2, 2 (II, 737e-738a); esp. instructive is the larger fr. of an ancient grammar P. Osl., II, 13 (2nd cent. A.D.) which deals with the doctrine of letters. [8] The divine *logos* comes between the cosmic elements so that they cannot destroy one another just as the vocal elements in words come between the silent ones, Philo Plant., 10. Abr., 81 also ref. primarily to the sound when it says that in the change of name from Abram to Abraham only one letter is doubled in sound, cf. on Sarah Mut. Nom., 61 and 77; Aet. Mund., 113 ref. to the written letters. Letters [9] also play a role in Egypt. administration; the districts of Alexandria are named after the first 5 letters (Flacc., 55) and the records of the property office are arranged alphabetically, BGU, III, 959, 2 (2nd cent. A.D.). The use of numbers for letters is the basis of the combination of the two in gematria, which was so beloved in antiquity, → I, 461, 29 ff. Thus for Cl. Al. the 10 commandments (10 = I) refer to Jesus, Strom., VI, 145, 7; Paed., III, 89, 1, cf. the harp with 10 strings (Ps. 33:2), Paed., II, 43, 3. The no. of Abraham's servants (Gn. 14:14) pts. to the cross (T = 300) and the name of Jesus (I = 10, H = 8), Strom., VI, 84, 3. [10] Letters understood as sounds are esp. important in the *gnosis* of Marcus, Hipp. Ref., VI, 42, 4-52, 11: [11] The 7 heavens constantly sound forth the 7 vowels; their echo becomes the creator of earthly existence, 48, 2 f. The elements from which this world is made are generated from the sound of a letter which rings forth in the upper world, 43, 2 etc. The sense "letter" often merges into that of "element" here. Finally — apart from the mysteriously powerful combinations of letters in a regular order, Preis. Zaub., II, 17a; 19a; 33 a fever amulet (all pap. 3rd cent. A.D.); 36, 115-133; 39 (both 4th cent. A.D.) etc. — the seven vowels are important in magic in constantly shifting arrangements in the same context, e.g., in pap. of the 3rd-5th cent. A.D., II, 7, 476; 9, 3; 10, 43-49 (all 7

---

[4] H. Diels, *Antike Technik*[3] (1924), 159 f.

[5] Ed. H. Rabe (1906), 90, 7-9; 232, 26-28.

[6] Cf. E. Frank, *Plato u. d. sog. Pythagoreer* (1923), 167-172; M. Pohlenz, "Die Begründung d. abendländischen Sprachlehre durch d. Stoa," *NGG Philologisch-hist. Klasse,* NF, III, 6 (1939), 151-198, esp. 151-154.

[7] Cf. Pos.: ἐν γραμματικῇ στοιχεῖα καλοῦμεν τὰ γράμματα διὰ τὸ στοίχῳ καὶ τάξει τὰς ἐξ αὐτῶν πλέκεσθαι συλλαβάς. Commentariorum in Aratum reliquiae, ed. E. Maass (1898), 91, 12-14.

[8] For further material from antiquity Grammatici Graeci, I, 3, ed. A. Hilgard (1901), 30-47, 182-204, 316-344, 483-508.

[9] For their use in enumeration cf. Dornseiff, 11.

[10] Cf. already Barn., 9, 8 (Wnd. Barn., *ad loc.*) [Schneemelcher].

[11] Cf. H. Leisegang, *Die Gnosis*[4] (1955), 326-342; Dornseiff, 126-133.

vowels in 7 different arrangements); 19a, 17-28; Ostrakon 2 (2nd cent. A.D., the magic words here consist mostly of collections of vowels). [12] This explains the popularity of the name of Yahweh [13] (Ιαω Diod. S., 1, 94, 2) in mag. formulae, Preis. Zaub., II, 7, 750 (3rd cent. A.D.); II, 12, 103 and 463 (100 A.D.); II, 19a, 21 f. (3rd cent A.D.) [14] or on amulets, e.g., in the arrangement Ιαω αω ω, II, 7, 220 (3rd cent. A.D.); further material CIJ, I, 514 and 673 f. (3rd cent. A.D.), 679 and 717.

3. From sound as the original part of a word στοιχεῖον probably came to be transf. to the cosmos [15] in place of ἀρχή → I, 480, 1 ff.

a. In antiquity the doctrine of the 4 elements is traced back to Empedocles, who develops it in his work *On Nature*. [16] He does not use στοιχεῖον for these elements but enumerates them or speaks of them in the neut. plur. ("these"); only occasionally do we find a collective word like "roots," Fr., 6, 1 (Diels, I, 311, 15). In the mythical form of his cosmology Emped. can describe original matter — elsewhere sun, earth, heaven and sea, Fr., 22, 2 (Diels, I, 320, 19), cf. earth, sea, air, ether, Fr., 38, 3 f. (I, 329, 1 f.) — by divine names, Fr., 6 (I, 311, 15 ff.), [17] and he calls love and strife the powers which unite and divide them, Fr., 17, 7 f. (I, 316, 1 f.); 26, 5 f. (I, 323, 3 f.); 20, 2-5 (I, 318, 9 ff.); 21, 7 f. (I, 320, 2 f.). But this is hardly more than a form of expression. The four are eternal and incorruptible, Fr., 17, 30-35 (I, 317, 11 ff.), cf. Fr., 12 (I, 313, 27 f.), 15 (I, 314, 10 ff.). Apart from them there is nothing, and from the constant fluctuation of their admixture proceed all the visible things (δῆλα) that were and are and will be, plants, animals, men, and even the gods, Fr., 21, 9-14 (I, 320, 4 ff.); 23, 6-10 (I, 321, 15 ff.); 26, 1-4 (I, 322, 17 ff.): "For I became at once boy, girl, plant, bird and ... fish," Fr., 117 (I, 359, 1 f.). Thus, properly speaking, there is neither birth nor death but only mixing and the changing of what is mixed, Fr., 8 (I, 312, 7 ff.), cf. 9 (I, 312, 12 ff.). Since man consists of the same four as the rest he can know them; with the earthly material in him he knows the earth, with the water he sees water etc., Fr., 109 (I, 351, 20 ff.). How extensive was the influence of the statements of Emped. — with much

---

[12] On vowel series, esp. in magic, cf. Dornseiff, 35-60. The vowel series also controls chains of artificial syllables in magical words, Dieterich, *ABC-Denkmäler*, 213-215. On the north wall of the pronaos of the temple of the Palmyrenian gods in Dura-Europos the Gk. alphabet is painted on a band under a series of figures, perhaps for apotropaic reasons (F. Cumont, *Fouilles de Doura-Eur.* [1926], 119 f.) or perhaps for mantic reasons (an oracle, cf. Plates 51-53).

[13] Cf. W. W. Graf Baudissin, "Der Ursprung des Gottesnamens 'Ιαω," *Studien z. semitischen Religionsgesch.*, I (1876), 179-254. ΙΑΩ is made up of the middle, first and last vowels, 243.

[14] For exsecration tablets cf. Audollent Def. Tab., Index, *s.v.* Ιαω, p. 465a b; 466b; 469a; 470b.

[15] Cf. M. Pohlenz, *Die Stoa*, I (1947), 37; *v.* also Frank, *op. cit.,* 169 f. Cf. Plat. Theaet., 201e. Aristot. Metaph., 4, 3, p. 1014a, 26-37 also moves on from the smallest parts of speech to those of bodies; he then calls proofs, e.g., in mathematics, πρῶται (basic) ἀποδείξεις.

[16] Cf. W. Jaeger, *Die Theol. d. frühen griech. Denker* (1953), 147-176, esp. 149-161. Capelle, 183-186 and the transl. of the related Fr., 189-204. Eitrem, 5 (1927), 46-54 raises difficulties. Brändle, 226: "In Emped. the elements are ... original, besouled, divine substances and ... are called gods in the strict sense of the word"; he tries to prove this, 135-226. By means of 3 ref. to Emped.'s calling of the elements gods, he seeks (125-134) to show that from the 4th cent. B.C. (Aristot. Gen. Corr., II, 6, p. 333b, 20-22) to the 3rd cent. A.D. (Hipp. Ref, VII, 29, 23) "the description of the *stoicheia* as gods was familiar to both educated and semi-educated," so "that Paul's *stoicheia* ... can also be understood as gods," 134. His initial thesis is "that the question of the origin of the world implicit in cosmogonies was also the question of God, since God was thought of essentially as the origin and source of (all) being," 163.

[17] Acc. to Athenag. Suppl., 22, 1 Zeus is fire, while Hera is air (ἀέρα) acc. to Philo Decal., 54; Vit. Cont., 3. It may be doubted whether these interpretations agree with Emped., cf. W. Kranz, "Emped. und die Atomistik," *Hermes*, 47 (1912), 18-42, esp. 23, n. 1; but cf. Capelle, 193, n. 1.

alteration and popularisation — may be seen again and again right up to the def. of Hesych., *s.v.*: στοιχεῖον· πᾶν τὸ ἄτμητον καὶ ἀμερές, *s.v.* στοιχεῖα: πῦρ, ὕδωρ, γῆ καὶ ἀήρ, ἀφ' ὧν τὰ σώματα, and Suid., *s.v.*: στοιχεῖόν ἐστιν, ἐξ οὗ πρώτου γίνεται τὰ γινόμενα καὶ εἰς ὃ ἔσχατον ἀναλύεται. τὰ δὴ δ' στοιχεῖα εἶναι ὁμοῦ τὴν ἄποιον οὐσίαν, τὴν ὕλην κτλ.

b. Plato [18] does not use στοιχεῖον for the four cosmic elements, Tim., 56b cf. 48b-c, but he has the word in the cosmology of Tim. for an "original constituent" (57c) which is not perceptible, 56b. [19] For the elements he either speaks of the four or the like (32b-c; 49b; 82c) or of the four γένη, 53a; 78a; 82a, cf. Ps.-Plat., (→ n. 59) Epin., 984c. Acc. to Plato the four elements can change into one another: water hardens into earth, melts (τηκόμενον) into air, heated air becomes fire etc.; in this cycle becoming takes place. Tim., 49b-c, cf. 56d-e. etc. Behind the visible is an invisible and formless entity which cannot be called fire, water etc. (51a) but appears in different forms in the four; this is the "nurse of becoming," 52d. Before the ordering of the universe the four separated themselves from this in a provisional state, and only God then gave them their true form, 53a-b. He then created from them the world, which He alone can dissolve, 32b-c. Later Plato mythically describes the fashioning of man from the four, cf. esp. Tim., 73e; 74c; 78b. He logically regards sickness as a result of changes in the right relationship of the four γένη in the body (στάσεις, 82a), which he then discusses in detail. Plato did not invent this use of the doctrine of the basic elements. Its medical importance may be seen from Gal.'s work περὶ τῶν καθ' Ἱπποκράτην στοιχείων [20] and also from its actual use in teaching on health. [21] The ἀρχαί of man, blood and seed, consist of the elements but in different mixtures. The seed has more οὐσία of fire and air, the blood more of the other two elements, Gal. De Sanitate Tuenda, I, 2, 2-4 (CMG, V, 4, 2). Health is the συμμετρία τῶν στοιχείων, I, 5, 12. The doctor's task is to promote the right admixture, VI, 3, 40 f. For Aristot. the four elements were heat and cold (the ποιητικά), dryness and moisture (the παθητικά), Meteor., IV, 1, p. 378b, 10-13. These proceed from undivided ὕλη, Gen. Corr., II, 1, p. 329a, 24-26, and from them come fire, water etc., p. 329a, 33-35, the ἁπλᾶ σώματα, II, 3, p. 330b, 1-32. The properties of the elements are united in these, p. 331a, 3-6. They arise out of one another (II, 4, p. 331a, 7 f.) and change into one another (a, 26-30), so that there is a cycle (p. 331b, 2 f.).

c. The Stoa distinguishes a passive (first matter) and a causal element (the *logos* materially considered), the eternal and imperishable ἀρχαί, from the four στοιχεῖα, the passive elements of earth and water and the active elements of air and fire, Nemesius De Natura Hominis, 5 (MPG, 40 [1863], 625B). [22] These perish in the cosmic conflagration, Diog. L., VII, 134, just as they arose from fire as the first element in the sequence air-water-earth, Chrysipp. in Stob. Ecl., I, 129, 3-23. Through the changing of

---

[18] On the relation of Plato's doctrine of the elements to that of earlier philosophers cf. P. Friedländer, *Platon*, III[2] (1960), 342-345, 615-617. On → lines 17 ff., *ibid.*, 350-353. Cf. also W. Schmid, *Epikurs Kritik d. platon. Elementenlehre* (1936).

[19] Cf. Plat. Theaet., 201e; 202b; Soph., 252b.

[20] Gal. De Elementis ex Hippocratis Sententia, ed. G. Helmreich (1878). From this work we also learn the doctrine of the physician Athenaeus (1st cent. A.D.) (cf. M. Wellmann, "Die pneumatische Schule," PhU, 14 [1895], 133-136), who is obviously influenced by Aristot., though Wellmann misses this.

[21] Cf. also the technical sciences, e.g., Vitruvius De Architectura, VII, 3, 7; II, 5, 2 (ed. F. Krohn [1912]) in an explanation of the process of burning lime (elements = *principia*), cf. E. Jüngst-P. Thielscher, "Vitruv über Baugrube, Baugrund u. Grundbau," *Röm. Mitt.*, 51 (1936), 145-180, esp. 166-169.

[22] Formally the distinction is Aristotelian, but it does not refer to qualities as in Aristot. Acc. to Pos. the demiurge effected through πνεῦμα θεῖον (→ VI, 354, 32 ff.) a first ordering of the previously irregularly wandering στοιχεῖα, *op cit.* (→ n. 7), 90 8-14. Augustine's statements that the Stoics believed that fire, the first of the four elements of which the visible world consists, is alive, is the fashioner of the world and all things, and is God (cf. Aug. Civ. Dei, 8, 5), gives a Chr. tinge to the — average — Stoic view.

the elements [23] the cosmos arises, and from their mixture come plants, animals etc., Diog. L., VII, 142. [24] Later Stoicism takes up the thought of the constant changing of the elements into one another (earth-water-air-ether [25] and *vice versa* from "above" to "below"), Epict. Fr., 8, and it adds a hortatory thought: Death is nothing terrible — it takes man whence he came to friends and relatives, the στοιχεῖα. What was fire in man goes back to fire etc., Epict. Diss., III, 13, 14 f. [26] M. Ant. plays on this thought continually. If the change is not bad for the elements (VI, 17, 1), why should change and dissolving be so for man? κατὰ φύσιν γάρ· οὐδὲν δὲ κακὸν κατὰ φύσιν, II, 17, 4, cf. VIII, 18, 2; IV, 5; M. Ant. can sometimes use for dying ἀναλύεσθαι εἰς τὰ στοιχεῖα, "to dissolve into the elements," IV, 32, 3. Nothings perishes, just as nothing comes from nothing, IV, 4, 3. [27] Everything will return to the cosmic basis (λόγος), X, 7, 5. To reflect constantly on the interchange of the elements and to consider the course of the stars washes away the filth of earthly life, VII, 47, cf. Epict. Fr., 8. For traditional assessments of the world of sense are conventional. In fact only the στοιχεῖα exist, M. Ant., VII, 31, 4 on the basis of Democr. Fr., 125 (Diels, II, 168, 6), where we find ἄτομα. How widespread was the doctrine of the elements, esp. in its application to man, may be seen in the ironical account of a young man who denies his parents φύσει λέγων γεγονέναι τὰ πάντα καὶ τὴν τῶν στοιχείων σύγκρασιν αἰτίαν εἶναι γενέσεως, οὐχὶ τοὺς πατέρας, Alciphr. Ep., II, 38, 2. [28] It may also be seen in the concept that all men are brothers for this reason, Schol. on Luc. Pergr. Mort., 13: [29] κοινὸν ἅπασι τὰ κοσμικὰ στοιχεῖα, ἐξ ὧν καὶ συνιστάμεθα. The difference between slaves and free men is also relativised by it: *Animas servorum et corpora nostra materia constare putat paribusque elementis,* Juv., 14, 16 f. [30] Neo-Pythagoreanism finally unites the animal kingdom to man in a kind of ἀδελφότης through sharing the same elements and the mixture of them, Iambl. Vit. Pyth., 108 cf. 169. [31] Dio Chrys. Or., 40, 35-39 uses the thought of the harmony of the elements

---

23 Cf. Neo-Platonism, Plot. Enn., II, 1, 1.

24 For details A. Schmekel, *Die positive Philosophie in ihrer geschichtl. Entwicklung,* I (1938), 241-255.

25 Fire and ether are often related. They are either equated or ether is viewed as refined fire. In Ps.-Aristot. Mund., 2, p. 392a, 5-9 ether, of which heaven and the stars consist, is plainly distinguished from the four elements; it is ἀκήρατόν τε καὶ θεῖον. The element placed "below," earth, is the centre of the universe. It is enclosed by water, this by air, this by fire, this by ether, 3, p. 393a, 1-3. Cf. Diod. S., 1, 7, 1-7 and the express account in Manilius Astronomica, I, 149-172 (age of Tiberius), ed. J. v. Wageningen (1915). From the passage in Ps.-Aristot. Mund, 3 Brändle deduces the meaning ("quickened and alive," 335) "spheres of the universe" (290 f., 316), which he then sees again in many texts in Stoicism (335 and 345), Philo (309, 318 f., 357-360) and the NT. These are "no other ... than the localising of the original substances in the cosmos," 345.

26 Obviously the whole man dissolves into the elements, including the soul, which consists of πῦρ and πνεῦμα, cf. A. Bonhöffer, *Epict. u. d. Stoa* (1890), 30. Acc. to Plut. man's body is from the earth, his νοῦς from the sun and his soul from the moon, Fac. Lun., 28 (II, 943a), and they go back to these at death, 30 (II, 945a). Hence Plut. calls the moon the στοιχεῖον (element) of souls, ἀναλύονται γὰρ εἰς ταύτην. That such ideas were common may be seen from Gr., VI, 1942, 7-9 (2nd/3rd cent. A.D.): "I once came into being of water and earth and air (πνεύματος) and (now) I lie (here) having given back all to all these in death ... Whence the body came it has again dissolved itself thither ... "

27 On the influence of the saying of Emped. (→ 672, 17 ff.) cf. Ps.-Aristot. Mund., 4, p. 396a, 28-32: The processes in earth, air and sea bring becoming and perishing to the individual but keep the totality imperishable and eternal.

28 Cf. the use of στοιχείωσις in 2 Macc. 7:22, where it denotes the development of man — from the primal materials — before birth (par. γένεσις, v. 23), cf. Lumpe, 1080.

29 Scholia in Lucianum, 217, 28 f.

30 Cf. Diels, 47 for details.

31 Finally στοιχεῖον is used very gen. "the sea is a pitiless element hostile to man," Babrius Mythiambi, 71, 4 in Babrii Fabulae Aesopeae, ed. O. Crusius (1897); cf. Plut. Quaest. Conv., VIII, 8, 2 (II, 729b). Cf. τὰ τῶν στοιχείων πάθη, Jos. Bell., 1, 377; Sib. → 683, 9 ff.; also Aesop Fab., 32 I, 9 and II, 8; Earth, water, air οὔτε τόπος ἄλλος, Corpus Fabularum Aesopicarum, I, 1, ed. A. Hausrath (1940). Cf. Liddell-Scott, *s.v.* for details.

in his call for political unity; without this harmony the elements, which are ἄφθαρτα and θεῖα, would perish. [32] 40, 36 and 38 f. ref. to the order in the course of the stars, though these are clearly distinguished from the στοιχεῖα. What Dio Chrys. says theoretically about the elements here in a traditional form, though for a hortatory purpose, he seeks to put in the form of a myth about the four horses of Zeus [33] in 36, 42-46; these are related to Helios (the swiftest), Hera (the slower air), and Poseidon and Hestia (the motionless). But the doctrine of the elements cannot all be put in this myth. Thus 36, 51 speaks of the changing of the elements, and Dio Chrys. combines the myth with other metaphors and mythical statements. The one that fits in best is that of Zeus as the one who steers the fiery chariot of the starry heaven, 36, 42-44. When Dio Chrys. speaks of a corresponding Persian cult in 36, 41, he is referring to specific facts of religious history. [34] But in the main it seems that his hortatory purpose evokes the myth rather than any religious worship in his own world. [35] Around the birth of Christ we see in allegorising a mixture of the rationalising of myth and religious statements about nature; [36] both Philo and the Apologists obviously play on this. In his interpretation of Homer, Heracl. imports the current doctrine of the elements into poetry. [37] When Hom. Il., 20, 67 f. speaks of the fight between Apollo and Poseidon he has in view the στοιχεῖα of fire and water, Heracl. Hom. All., 7; Zeus and Hera are ether and air (the softest element), 15 on Il., 1, 55; cf. Cic. Nat. Deor., II, 66. Hom. presupposed the doctrine of Anaxag. when he said in Il., 7, 99: You may all become water and earth, Heracl. Hom. All., 22, cf. Sext. Emp. Math., X, 314. Emped. Fr., 6 (→ 672, 14) follows the Homeric allegory, Heracl. Hom. All., 24 etc. The elements are not yet personified here; the old view of the gods is rather demythologised, cf. on Hom. Ps.-Luc. De Astrologia, 22; also 21 and 10-20. [38]

d. In Alexandrian [39] Judaism the concept of brotherhood on the basis of the elements is adopted: Antiochus IV Epiphanes is chided because he torments the Jews who are men as he is ἐκ τῶν αὐτῶν γεγονότας στοιχείων, 4 Macc. 12:13. Philo uses the idea very gen. as a basis of intrahuman relations in ethics, Spec. Leg., I, 294. He takes up the Stoic principle that man shares the same elements of which the world consists, Decal., 31; Op. Mund., 146, cf. Aet. Mund., 29, and that he gives these back to it, Rer. Div. Her., 282 —

---

[32] Cf. Ps.-Aristot. Mund., 5, p. 396b, 1-7, esp. 396b, 34-397a, 5.

[33] This is how we are to understand it; the obscurity of the doctrine of the elements (Zeus as symbol of the fifth element, ether) does not help in interpretation of the myth.

[34] The cult of fire etc. is not as such a cult of the elements. Cumont Textes, 107 f.: The combination of the Persian fire cult with Stoic ideas is first found in Dio Chrys. On the worship of fire, the winds etc. in Persia cf. 93-109 (the oldest Gk. ref. Hdt., I, 131). Acc. to Cumont, 108, however, worship of the elements is connected with Babylon. On Dio Chrys. Or., 36, 39-60 cf. J. Bidez-F. Cumont, Les mages hellénisés, II (1938), 142-153.

[35] "This myth is so fully steeped in Stoic concepts and forms that it is hard to say what is really Iranian in it," Nilsson, II², 676. On Dio Chrys. Or., 36 and 39 ff. ibid., 676-678.

[36] On the religious version of the doctrine of the elements in the 1st cent. A.D. cf. Cornut. Theol. Graec., 28 (p. 53, 12-18): Hestia, it is said mythically, is the first and last because there dissolves in her all that developed out of her; she wears white bands because she is encircled by the lightest element. Here Hestia, as usual, is not the earth but fire.

[37] Cf. Heracl. Hom. All., esp. 22-25, 40 f.

[38] In Fr. P. Heidelberg, 194, II, 1-7 (2nd cent. A.D.) (ed. E. Siegmann, "Literarische griech. Texte d. Heidelberger Papyrussammlung," Veröffentl. aus d. Heidelb. Pap.-Samml., NF, 2 [1956]) there is a polemic against those who speaks of a conflict (μάχη) of the στοιχεῖα and who invent fables (μύθους → IV, 778, 31 ff.) of the revolt of the giants (against the gods) — they probably related the two. Among the Naassenes we sometimes read that the body is made of μάχιμα στοιχεῖα (Hipp. Ref., V, 8, 19) on the basis of Job 40:32.

[39] That earth is the heaviest and lowest element, fire the lightest and highest (with water and air between), and that God made the world of four elements, is also a common thought in Rabb. exegesis. Element here is יֵצַב "what is formed"; Nu. r., 14 (62d) on 7:78 (v. R. Meyer, "Hellenistisches in d. rabb. Anthropologie," BWANT, IV, 22 [1937], 127), cf. Gn. r., 10 (7b), on 2:1 (Str.-B., IV, 410e).

nothing disappears into non-being, every creature returns to its origin, Spec. Leg., I, 266. But he deviates decisively from the Stoic view when he says that man's νοῦς is formed from an imperishable στοιχεῖον, Deus Imm., 46, cf. Rer. Div. Her., 283. In exhortation Philo in his allegorical interpretation of Nu. 19:17 refers to the mean elements of which man is composed; this is a warning against presumption, Spec. Leg., I, 264 f. The idea of the changing of the elements [40] which gives them immortality (Aet. Mund., 109) enables him to explain the miracles of the age of Moses: μεταβαλὼν τὰ στοιχεῖα God brought manna out of the air, Vit. Mos., II, 267; κατὰ τὴν τῶν στοιχείων φύσει μεταβολήν air changed into fire (on Lv. 9:24), Vit. Mos., II, 154. He clings fundamentally to God's sovereignty; of this he says with ref. to the miracles of Moses that God gave Moses a share in it, so that the element obeyed him when he altered its mode of operation, ἀλλάττον ἦν εἶχε δύναμιν, Vit. Mos., I, 156. Miracles of punishment are called τῶν στοιχείων νεωτερισμός, "the tumult of the elements," I, 216; II, 65. Philo expressly rejects the worship of the elements by equation with gods (Demeter, Poseidon etc.), cf. Wis. 13:2; the στοιχεῖα are matter without soul, [41] subject to God, Vit. Cont., 3 f. They are properly connected with religion in the Jewish cultus; the altar of incense is appointed for thanksgiving for the four elements; the materials used in the incense offering (Ex. 30:34 f.) symbolise the elements, Rer. Div. Her., 197 and 226; the curtains before the holy of holies, which are made of four materials, serve the same function: the four elements of which the universe is created are used as a sanctuary for the Father and Governor of the universe; hence the temple is a reflection of the cosmos, Vit. Mos., II, 88; Congr., 117. We also find a cosmological interpretation of the building of the temple in Jos. Bell., 5, 213; Ant., 3, 183, cf. also Cl. Al. Strom., V, 32, 3 for the curtain with a ref. to God's revelation. If Judaism can adopt some of the principles of Gk. cosmology, it emphatically attributes to God the εἰδέναι σύστασιν κόσμου καὶ ἐνέργειαν στοιχείων etc., which He teaches through His σοφία, Wis. 7:17, 21; στοιχεῖον occurs in the LXX only at Wis. 7:17; 19:18; 4 Macc. 12:13. In Corp. Herm., III there is an open attempt, perhaps contemporary with Philo, [42] to combine notions from the Stoic and Platonic doctrine of the elements with the biblical creation story; [43] textual resemblances may be seen esp. 1-3. Primary stress falls on the idea that God is the beginning and end of all cosmic occurrence. By divine power there first existed fine (hence material) pneuma, then arose sacred light, and the elements crystallised (ἐπάγη III, 1), though they were not as yet differentiated. Then the lighter elements rose up, while the heavier ones became a base (ἐθεμελιώθη); heaven appeared in 7 circles, the stars and the upper world with their gods, III, 2. Through his own δύναμις each god brought forth what he was charged to do, [44] animals and plants, and finally they (the gods, plur. as in Gn. 1:26?) caused men to arise, who were to contemplate the encircling course of the heavenly gods and the working of φύσις, III, 3. Men finally go back εἰς ταὐτό from which they arose. Through the gods there will then be brought about the renewal of the passing world, III, 4. If these gods are plainly subject to God, it is they who truly work in the elements. [45]

---

[40] Cf. already Wis. 19:18: δι' ἑαυτῶν γὰρ τὰ στοιχεῖα μεθαρμοζόμενα (on the Egypt. plagues).

[41] Earth and water speak in Philo Spec. Leg., I, 266, but this is only rhetorical personification, as against Scheu, 65 f. etc. Very dubious is the interpretation of Philo in Brändle, 356-370, who tries to find here a basis for Paul's understanding of the στοιχεῖα as cosmic powers, 370.

[42] Acc. to Philo it is Moses' conviction that the stars rule all earthly events in obedience to God; but they are not gods, Spec. Leg., I, 13-20. Philo can call them visible gods in Op. Mund., 27.

[43] Cf. on this C. H. Dodd, The Bible and the Greeks (1935), 210-234.

[44] Acc. to Plat. Tim., 41a-d the stellar deities shared in the creation of living creatures on their mortal side.

[45] In Stob. Ecl., I, 403, 9 — 405, 25 the elements are displeased with man and petition God against him, but this is poetic dramatisation rather than deification (cf. Schlier Gl. [12], 191, n. 3 on 4:3). The earth addresses God as leader of the στοιχεῖα subject to Him in Stob.

e. It is by no means obvious that the elements are understood as beings when religious modes of speech are used. [46] The "Hephaestus" called στοιχεῖον in Orph. Hymn., 66, 4 (→ 683, 12 ff.) is "unwearying fire"; he "inhabits the bodies of mortals" (66, 1 and 9), naturally as the basic element permeating all things → 673, 35 ff. Nektanebo uses the element (→ n. 31) of water in magic, destroying images of enemies in a dish of water. The mariners of the song in Preis. Zaub., II, 29 (3rd cent. A.D.) command the winds and the kingdoms of the sea, but they pray to the Lord of these and call the seas His kingdoms. The hymn to the sun god used in Preis. Zaub., I, 4, 436-441, 1957-1962 (4th cent. A.D.); P. Lond., I, 122, 74-81 (4th cent. A.D.) describes him (in good Stoic fashion) as unwearying fire, the one who generates and dissolves all things, from whom the elements (στοιχεῖα) have come forth which turn the world acc. to his laws. Here the god Helios is personal, [47] but not the elements. On the other hand there are early signs that using religious terms for the elements will dedivinise the world. Thus comedy mocks: When "Epicharmus says the gods are winds, waters, sun, fire and stars," I prefer to think "the only gods useful to us are silver and gold," Menand. Fr., 614, 1-4 (Koerte). An important religious pt. is that the one redeemed by Isis is no longer subject to the power of the elements: Isis is *elementorum omnium domina*, Apul. Met., XI, 5, 1; they must obey her, *tibi ... serviunt elementa*, XI, 25, 3. They are not said to be divine forces. [48]

f. In relation to the NT the ref. to the elements in 2nd cent. Chr. writings are not without importance. Herm. v., 3, 13, 3 is aware that the world is sustained by the four elements. The express repudiation of worship of these basic materials, found already in Aristid. Apol., 3-6, shows how important the doctrine of the elements was at the time. That man, too, cannot be divine is shown by the fact (Aristid. Apol., 7 etc.) that he consists of the four elements as well as soul and spirit, and that he will be destroyed by them — a popular usage (→ n. 31) found only with ref. to fire, water etc. Just. Dial., 62, 2 combines the fact that man consists of the elements with the concept of creation; Gn. 1:26 (plur.) is said, not to the elements, but to the Logos, 62, 1. Tatian attacks the worship of deified elements in an allegorical interpretation of myths, Or. Graec., 21, 3, cf. Aristid. Apol., 7, 4: σέβονται ... τὰ φθαρτὰ στοιχεῖα. Athenag. Suppl., 10, 3 f. rejects the charge of atheism, pointing to the host of angels and ministers whom God has set over the elements acc. to Chr. belief. Christians do not fall down to the weak and beggarly elements (cf. Gl. 4:9), nor do they worship air and matter, 16, 2 f. If the elements were gods, these gods would arise out of matter (Emped. Fr., 6 [Diels, I, 311, 15 ff.]) and acc. to the Stoic doctrine of the cosmic conflagration they would perish with the basic materials, Athenag., 22, 1 and 3. One cannot see God in the elements, their orders and movements,

---

Ecl., I, 404, 18 f.; He calls these "holy children worthy of the great Father" in 405, 14. At the end they again go to and fro in discharge of their office. On the elements in Corp. Herm. cf. also Lumpe, 1083.

[46] They are not really seen personally even when art symbolises them in human form, so air, earth and water on an altar relief of the age of Augustus (Roscher, II, 2151 f.) → n. 45. With regard to the στοιχεῖα as "spheres of the universe." Brändle speaks of a "cosmomorphic idea of God" (346). The Gk. idea of person is certainly not the same as the modern one, but Brändle exaggerates the difference (129 cf. 226) and also regards the στοιχεῖα as active beings even in Philo (356-8, 360, 362, 364 → n. 106). Cramer, 174 f. questions whether the assertion of Jewish and Chr. apologists that pagans worshipped the στοιχεῖα proves the view that the world was given up to elemental spirits. For pagans the elements were probably no more than manifestations or attributes of nature deities.

[47] Elsewhere there is prayer to send a messenger, Preis. Zaub., II, 14, 5, cf. II, 7, 797. It is sometimes stressed in magic pap. that the gods invoked have power over the elements; thus of Hermes: "Thou dost rule the elements, fire, air ..., since thou didst become helmsman of the cosmos," II, 17b, 15f.; of the Lord of the aeons: "By thy power are the elements and all things ... in air and earth" etc., 12, 250 f., cf. K. Keyssner, *Gottesvorstellung u. Lebensauffassung im griech. Hymnus* (1932), 21. There is nothing in the context to suggest a ref. to elemental spirits.

[48] As against M. Dibelius, "Die Isisweihe bei Apul. u. verwandte Initiations-Riten," *Botschaft u. Geschichte*, II (1956), 50 f.

but only through the λόγος; they are nothing without the rule of God's providence and they do not move without the Creator, 22, 6-8. In a lively polemic Cl. Al. Prot., 64 f. attacks the deification of the elements which Cl. alleges that philosophers took from eastern religions. [49] The elements were created by the one God, 65, 4 (on Gl. 4:9), cf. Strom., I, 50, 6; 52, 2-4 (on Col. 2:8), who made their discord harmony, Prot., 5, 1. Yet the idea that the elements are changeable — God changes them, Cl. Al. Ecl. Proph., 18, 2 — and that they will one day perish [50] is in agreement with Chr. teaching, Strom., I, 52, 3; Prot., 78, 4 (on Mt. 24:35 etc.); Strom., V, 104, 5. Cl. is again following pagan ideas when he says in Strom., V, 106, 4 that the journey of the soul after death leads through the four elements, [51] or when in De Providentia Fr., 42 (GCS, 17, 221, 1 f.) he describes death as a dissolution of bodies by the change of elements in death. This is ordained by God, just as the elements, by God's direction, are controlled by those co-ordinated with them (cf. Athenag. Suppl., 10, 4), Strom., VI, 148, 2. That the doctrine of the elements is assumed to be known in popular writing may be seen from its use in Act. Thom. 165: The four soldiers who lead Judas to the place of execution and then put him to death remind him of the four elements from which he came; ἐκ τῶν τεσσάρων στοιχείων ἐγενόμην or ἐκ τεσσάρων εἰμί. Act. Thom. 141 adopts (→ n. 31) popular usage: σὺ κατάπαυσον τὸ στοιχεῖον τοῦτο. For the Marcionite Apelles the body of Christ is not composed of the Stoic elements (→ 673, 32 ff.) but of the Aristotelian elements (→ 673, 25 ff.) as preparatory stages of the basic human materials (which are higher for Apelles, cf. Tert. De Carne Christi [CSEL, 70] 6, 3; 8, 4). In death Christ restored to each element its property, warmness to warmth etc., and thus put off the body of flesh, Epiph. Haer., 44, 2, 8 cf. Hipp. Ref., VII, 38, 3 and 5. For the role of στοιχεῖα in Gnosticism cf. Hipp. Ref., VI, 9, 5; VI, 53, 1; X, 12, 1 with the appropriate contexts. [52]

4. Not just letters and the elements are the "smallest parts which stand in relation with others" and to which that which is composed of them can be traced back. The same applies to notes in music, Bacchius Isagoge, II, 67, [53] points in a line, Iambl. In Nicomachi

---

[49] Cf. Tert. Marc., I, 13, though this shows clearly that the deification remains formal, → 675, 3 ff.; 677, 1 ff.; 680, 10 ff.

[50] The Epicurean Lucretius De Rerum Natura, V, 156-194, 235-379 (ed. J. Martin[4] [1959]) stresses the corruptibility of the elements (primordia; they are mortalia, 248) in support of the view that the world was not created by the gods, but arose out of the movement of atoms, esp. 432-508. Manilius, op. cit. (→ n. 25), I, 485-494 attacks this view on the ground of order. From the ratio obtaining in the universe it follows mundum divino numine verti... nec forte coisse magistra, 483-5. The view that the four elements had no "father" faciuntque deum per quattuor artus and that there is nothing above them, Manilius, I, 137-144 more cautiously accepts as one of the possibilities of the origin of the world (on the eternity of the world, its origin from atoms, from one of the elements etc. 122-146), but I, 485-494 shows plainly that he regards the view sketched in 137-144 as atheistic and does not accept it himself.

[51] Cf. Dibelius, op cit. (→ n. 48), 49-51. On the adoption of such views of the elements in Cl. Al. cf. Strom., II, 31, 3; VII, 34, 1; God is like fire acc. to Dt. 4:24; τὸ πῦρ ἰσχυρότατον τῶν στοιχείων καὶ πάντων κρατοῦν..., τῶν στοιχείων ὑπερέχει, Ecl. Proph., 26, 1 f.

[52] In Ps.-Cl. Hom., too, στοιχεῖα always means the constituent parts of the world in the sense of the 4 elements except at 10, 9, 5, where "heaven... earth and sea and all that therein is" are called στοιχεῖα. But in acc. with the origin of Ps.-Cl. Hom. (v. B. Rehm, Art. "Cl. Romanus, I" in RAC, III, 198; G. Strecker, "Das Judenchristentum in d. Pseudoklementinen," TU, 70 [1958]) the statements are not consistent, quite apart from ref. to views not accepted by the author or editor. The στοιχεῖα, called οὐσίαι in 19, 12, 3, are those of Aristot. (warmth etc.) in 20, 3, 8, but not in 6, 5, 4, where the chief element is fire. Alleg. interpretation of pagan myth leads in 6, 13, 1 to ideas from the doctrine of the elements. Religious evaluation of the "first four" is rejected in 6, 24, 1; 10, 25, 1. On the basis of theodicy it is argued that the evil one arose by admixture of the 4 elements (στοιχεῖα 19, 12, 6), which came forth from God, 19, 12, 3; v. H. J. Schoeps, "Die Dämonologie d. Ps. Clem.," Aus frühchr. Zeit (1950), 39-45. That men consist of 4 μέρη is an accepted idea acc. to 20, 5, 7. Const. Ap., VIII, 12, 10-12 shows that God created water, air, fire, sea and earth for specific purposes, obviously in man's service.

[53] Ed. C. Jan in Musici Scriptores Graeci (1895), 306, 18 ff.

Arithmeticam Introductionem, 80, one in the world of numbers, *ibid.*, 36; Philo Rer. Div. Her., 190,[54] στοιχεῖον thus comes to mean more gen., with no thought of a series, "foundation": στοιχεῖον παιδείας ἐστὶ τὸ ἀφορᾶν πρὸς τὸ θεῖον, Cornut. Theol. Graec., 14 (p. 15, 17 f.); also the "rudimentary," e.g., in the care of infants, Plat. Leg., VII, 790c. "Part of a word" may be mentioned in this connection → 671, 6 ff. If letters are the basis of speech and their knowledge that of instruction, στοιχεῖον can soon come to mean "what is basic or primary," cf. Plat. Theaet., 206a-b, or "the elementary details" in musical education. The plur. is the more common στοιχεῖα πρῶτα καὶ μέγιστα χρηστῆς πολιτείας, Isoc. Or., 2, 16 (the additions show that the use is older than c. 370 B.C.); στοιχεῖα μὲν ταῦτ' ἐστὶ τῆς ὅλης τέχνης (transf. sense), Nicolaus Fr., I, 30 (CAF, III, 384); Euclid wrote about the στοιχεῖα ("first principles") of mathematics.[55] The στοιχεῖα of mathematical and other proofs are called the "first" among many, Aristot. Metaph., 4, 3, p. 1014a, 36-b, 1. Artemid. Oneirocr., I, 2 (p. 4, 25-5, 5) describes as the "basic phenomena" of dreams which predict the future, and which may thus be interpreted, the six στοιχεῖα φύσις, νόμος, ἔθος, τέχνη, ὀνόματα, χρόνος, IV, 2 (esp. p. 203 f.), cf. I, 3 (p. 9 f.). The idea of the four elements plainly influences the statement in Porphyr. Marc., 24 that four "basic realities" (στοιχεῖα) must be established in man's relation to God, πίστις, ἀλήθεια, ἔρως, ἐλπίς.[56]

5. A connection between elements and stars[57] arises from the fact that stars are composed of fire, the chief and finest element (also called ether), so traditionally Emped. etc.; Plut. Plac. Phil., II, 13 (II, 888d-f); Stob. Ecl., I, 201-204. "A star, says Poseidonios, is a divine body, consisting of ether, luminous and fiery," Stob. Ecl., I, 206, 19-21. Acc. to Philo Op. Mund. the stars are made of the finest matter. Acc. to Som., I, 135 each star is supposed (λέγεται) to be the purest νοῦς. In ancient thinking there is no necessary contradiction here, since the intellectual can be thought of only in material form. Acc. to Corp. Herm., X, 18 fire is the body of νοῦς, and acc. to ancient tradition God is for Heracl. the eternal periodic fire. Stob. Ecl., I, 35, 7, for Democr. νοῦς ... ἐν πυρὶ σφαιροειδεῖ, I, 34, 19, for Pos. thinking and fiery *pneuma* moving acc. to its will, I, 34, 26 f., and for the Stoics the purest part of ether, Diog. L., VII, 139. The view that the stars have souls is expressly rejected by the pre-Socratics, e.g., Anaxag. acc. to Plat. Ap., 26d; Plat. ascribes deity to the stars only in the mythical language of the Tim.: θεοὶ θεῶν, 41a; τὸ θεῖον, 40a; θεοί, 40c; the earth, too, is one of these heavenly gods. Plat. speaks of a διανοεῖσθαι of the stars in 40a (and of the processes of thought of the universe in 90c),[58] but only with ref. to the course they take, not in a personal sense.

---

[54] Cf. Aristot. Metaph., 4, 3, p. 1014a, 26 - b, 15 (→ n. 15). On the use in music cf. Koller.
[55] Euclides Elementa, ed. J. Heiberg (1883 ff.).
[56] Cf. the Gospel of Philip, Saying 115 (127, 18-30), cf. H. M. Schenke, ThLZ, 84 (1959), 21: "The world's husbandry is in four ways: one gathers into the barn by water, earth, wind (πνεῦμα), and light. God's husbandry is also fourfold: through faith (πίστις), hope (ἐλπίς), love (ἀγάπη), and knowledge (γνῶσις). Our earth is faith because we have our root in this." Water is hope, wind love, and light knowledge. This Gospel (3rd cent.) and Porphyr. are obviously not dependent on one another.
[57] The naming of the planets as Aphrodite, Zeus, Kronos, Ares and Hermes from Plat. or Aristot. (cf. F. Boll, Art. "Planeten" in Roscher, III, 2525) does not mean equation with them, as the usage shows: "In good Greek we always find ὁ τοῦ Διός and only much later ὁ Ζεύς etc.," *ibid.*, 2525, cf. the examples from Vett. Val., *ibid.*, 2527. In Ps.-Aristot. Mund., 2, p. 392a, 23-28 three planets are assigned to different gods, so that the links were not fixed in the 1st cent. A.D. "Astrology gave the planets the names of the ancient gods but could not take over their worship. For these powers ... were ... threatening, terrible powers" except for the sun god, Nilsson, II², 507 f.
[58] In virtue of the *ratio* governing the courses of the stars these are to be counted as gods, Cic. Nat. Deor., II, 54. Manilius, I, 484 f. deduces from the order of the universe (the immutability of heaven, I, 523) that the universe (or heaven) is a god, but here we have the same usage as among the Gks. → lines 31 ff.; 680, 5 ff.: immutability is a divine trait; a *numen* rules over the order of the cosmos, I, 484, 531 → n. 50; deity may best be seen

They are called visible gods in Tim., 40d (θεοὶ ὁρατοὶ καὶ γεννητοί), and there is
an even fuller statement in Ps.-Plat. [59] Epin., 984d; 985d (cf. the continuation). The
steadfastness of their course (982d) shows that God has given them souls (983b). In a way
which is obviously intentional Aristot. uses only [60] θεῖος for the heavenly bodies, Cael.,
II, 12, p. 292b, 32. [61] That this does not imply deification may be seen from the designation
of the stars as σώματα θεῖα in Ps.-Aristot. Mund., 2, p. 391b, 16; 392a, 30; cf. the wholly
astronomical description of the cosmic movements which are directed by God, 6, p. 399a,
etc. [62] The Stoics differentiate the cosmos, stars and earth from God as the νοῦς which
is "wholly above" in the ether, as the imperishable primal fire, Stob. Ecl., I, 38, 1-3.
The former are evolved and perishable gods, Plut. Stoic. Rep., 38 (II, 1052a). [63] How
widespread was the use of "gods" in this connection may be seen from the statement
handed down in Diog. L., VIII, 27, namely, that for Pythagoreanism the sun, moon and
stars were gods because warmth, which is the author of life, preponderated in them,
cf. 28: "Everything that shares in warmth is alive." Finally the stars are visible gods
for Neo-Platonism too, in distinction from the νοητοὶ θεοί whose image is the cosmos,
Plot. Enn., II, 9, 8; cf. V, 1, 4, and to whom the visible gods are subordinate. More
precisely, the visible gods are bound up with the stars like the radiance round each star,
III, 5, 6. The stars are no more eternal than earthly creatures; they simply last longer,
II, 1, 1. The applying of religious terms to the stars [64] is naturally connected with the
fact that antiquity was inclined in part to think that the stars as well as the sun and
moon influenced earthly events, esp. the weather, growth etc. [65] That this idea was not
connected with worship of the stars is shown by Philo, who radically rejects such worship
as a confusion of creature and Creator, Abr., 69; Migr. Abr., 181, [66] but who is still
convinced that the 7 planets produce growth and ripening on earth, Op. Mund., 113. [67]
He also thinks the Pleiades influence seasonal events: μεγάλων ἀγαθῶν αἴτιαι γίνονται
πᾶσι, ibid., 115. [68] In gen. Philo can say that earthly things depend on heavenly things
acc. to a natural συμπάθεια, 117, cf. Abr., 69; v. Sext. Emp. Math., IX, 79 f.; Moses

in this: sentirentque deum gentes quam maximus esset. I, 37. Perceiving this order is a
divine gift, I, 25-37.
[59] Nilsson, I², 841 f. leaves the question of authorship open. Materially cf. loc. cit.
[60] On the gen. use of θεῖος → III, 122, 1 ff.
[61] Cf. H. Bonitz, Index Aristot.² (1955), s.v. θεῖος and θεός. On this whole matter cf.
G. Mau, Die Religionsphilosophie Kaiser Julians (1907), 41-44; on Aristot. W. Jaeger,
Aristoteles (1923), 144-158, also 369-375.
[62] Cf. Phil. Cher., 23; Agric., 51 on Ps. 23:1.
[63] The Stoics also say that the stars are ζῷα (cf. Plat. → 679, 33 ff.) on the ground of
their ordered movement and power of judgment, Eudorus (c. Christ's birth) in Comment. in
Aratum reliquiae, op cit. (→ n. 7), p. 41, 5-10, cf. the context, Reinhardt, 74-80. That the
description is of little moment is apparent when the Stoics say that men regard the stars as
gods because they fulfil a course (θέοντας v. Plat. Crat., 397d) and the sun and moon
because they make θεωρεῖν possible, Aetius De Placitis Reliquiae, I, 6, 11 (H. Diels,
Doxographi Graeci [1879]).
[64] The idea, ridiculed in Aristoph. Pax, 832 f., that the deceased become stars obviously
has nothing to do with a deifying or personifying of stars, cf. the setting among the stars
of the hair offered up by Berenice c. 244 B.C.; v. U. v. Wilamowitz-Moellendorff, "Die Locke
d. Berenike," Reden u. Vorträge, I⁴ (1925), 197-217.
[65] On various approaches to this and their development cf. E. Pfeiffer, "Studien zum
antiken Sternglauben," ΣΤΟΙΧΕΙΑ, II (1916).
[66] Cf. already Wis. 13:2 f. Like other ancient writers Philo says that the cult of the stars
came from Babylon, so Cumont Astrology, 36-72; Cumont Textes, 109 also derives from
thence the veneration of the stars in Mithraism (109-120). Acc. to Nilsson, II², 275 the
astrological system of the Hell. period "arose in Egypt under the normative influence of
Gk. astronomical science," cf. 268-276.
[67] The ref. is obviously to natural processes in Philo Quaest. in Ex., II, 78 as well.
[68] The astronomer Geminus attacks this idea in the 1st cent. B.C., recognising only the
influence of the sun and moon, Elementa Astronomiae, 17, 1 f. 14-17, ed. C. Manitius (1898),
Reinhardt, 51.

apparently affirmed the συμπάθεια τοῦ παντός, Migr. Abr., 180, → V, 935, n. 3. On the other hand Philo disputes the dependence of human fate on the stars (181), [69] as did later Plot., who devoted a tractate to the theme: εἰ ποιεῖ τὰ ἄστρα, concluding that they indicate but do not cause the acts of men, Enn., II, 3. [70] The starry world takes on special significance in doctrines of redemption which include an ascent of the soul after death (the idea is old; [71] Celsus in Orig. Cels., VI, 21 refers to Plat., cf. Phaedr., 248a in context). This ascent through the courses of the planets — so a symbolical depiction in the Mithras cult [72] — leads from the sphere of Saturn by way of those of Venus, Jupiter, Mercury, Mars and the moon to that of the sun, Orig. Cels., VI, 22. [73]

One must refer to these passages because in later antiquity στοιχεῖον can come to mean "star" or "constellation." [74] Specifically astrological examples leave open the possibility that it reached this sense by way of "sign" (στοιχεῖον = "sign of destiny"). [75] A certain connection between basic materials and stars (as factors influencing man's life) may be seen in Vett. Val., for whom the 4 elements with the planets [76] replace the ancient gods; he adjures his pupil Marcus by them, VII, 5 (p. 293, 25-27). [77] With this belief is combined a fatalism which destroys religion. Prayer and sacrifice are useless, V, 9 (p. 220, 28-30). He calls the elements στοιχεῖα in VII, 5 (p. 293, 27), cf. ἀθάνατα στοιχεῖα in IX, 7 ((p. 343, 33 f.). But in his fairly full astrological discussions he does not use στοιχεῖον for star etc. (2nd cent. A.D.). On the other hand Just. assumes this is familiar: "heavenly body," Apol., II, 5, 2; Dial., 23, 3. Tat. Or. Graec., 9 f first uses it in

---

[69] For the Rabb. and astrology cf. Str.-B., II, 402-5.

[70] That belief in the dependence of human destiny on the course of the stars does not imply their necessary deification is shown by Manilius, who accepts the belief (I, 52-65, 112, 119) but still depicts the universe scientifically (acc. to his age, cf. I, 173-213) and distinguishes it from the deity, on which it is modelled (211-213), → n. 50, 58. The Neo-Pythagorean Apollonius of Tyana is supposed to have written a work περὶ μαντείας ἀστέρων; Philostr. speaks of it at a respectful distance. An Indian gave Apollonius 7 rings related to the 7 planets, and he wore one each on the proper day of the week, Vit. Ap., III, 41.

[71] Cf. Nilsson, II², 490-495. Such ideas are not primarily related to belief in the stars, 494. Cf. the popular idea in Titus' speech in Jos. Bell., 6, 47: The souls of the fallen are taken from the καθαρώτατον στοιχεῖον, the ether, and set in the stars, from whence they appear to their relatives as δαίμονες δ' ἀγαθοὶ καὶ ἥρωες εὐμενεῖς.

[72] "Specifically astrological gods enjoyed no cultus except in the mystery religions, esp. Mithraism," Nilsson, II², 497. On the stellar powers in this cf. ibid., 506.

[73] The familiar names of the planets are used here rather than the Gk. terms. Acc. to the depiction in Orig. this is not Ophitic Gnosticism, cf. Cels., VI, 24 ff. On the ascent of the soul through the stellar world Kroll, 296-308; Nilsson, II², 497; O. Gruppe, Griech. Mythologie, II (1906), 1037, Cf. Cl. Al. → 678, 8 ff.

[74] Dornseiff, 15 thinks this use is connected with the sense "length of a shadow," cf. Scheu, 40: "Designation of a sector, a twelfth of the circle of heaven." Later antiquity also found a connection between letters and the stars. A very common comparison is criticised in Plut. E. Delph., 4 (II, 386a-b): As 7 letters have their own sound (→ 671, 34 ff.), so 7 stars have their own independent movement. Then in the 2nd cent. the Neo-Pythagoreans relate the 7 vowels to the 7 planetary spheres which all have their own sounds, Excerpta ex Nicomacho, 6 (ed. C. Jan, Musici scriptores Graeci [1895], 276, 8-13), Diels, 44. Procl. In Rem. Publ., 38 finally calls the vowels the letters (στοιχεῖα) of the planets, while the consonants (7 and 10) belong to the zodiac. Scheu, 40 conjectures that the sense "letter" led to that of "star," though he gives no reasons. Cramer, 37-44 and 174 agrees that the use for star does not occur before the 2nd cent. A.D.

[75] Bouché-Leclerq, 216 f., n. 3 considers the equation στοιχεῖον = μοῖρα for P. Lond., I, 130, 60 f. (100 A.D.) → 682, 8 ff.

[76] Cf. also Wis. 13:2, though the elements are not here a group as in Philo Decal., 53.

[77] Philo Spec. Leg., II, 5 accepts an oath by the stars, earth, heaven, the cosmos, but because of their immutability, not their divinity — an oath by God is to be avoided, II, 2 and 6. How little an oath by the elements implied their deifying or personifying may be seen from the oath of those who received the book of Ps.-Clem. Hom., Ps.-Clem. Hom. Diamartyria, 2, 1: "I call to witness heaven, earth, water, ἐν οἷς τὰ πάντα περιέχεται, and the air which permeates all these, without which I cannot breathe . . . ," cf. 4, 1.

a polemical context in which he rejects belief in the dependence of man's destiny on the stars. Hipp. Comm. in Danielem, I, 8 (GCS, 1, 1, p. 15, 5) (204 A.D.) calls the sun and moon στοιχεῖα, and Theophil. Autol., II, 15 cf. I, 6 speaks of the course of the στοιχεῖα. The known instances are not before 100 A.D. [78] Later we have Diog. L., VI, 102: [79] τὰ δώδεκα στοιχεῖα "signs of the zodiac," [80] Manetho, IV, 624: ταῦτά τοι οὐρανίων ἄστρων στοιχεῖα τέτυκται, [81] and Preis. Zaub., I, 4, 1303: The Bear is addressed as στοιχεῖον ἄφθαρτον (MS 4th cent. A.D.). C. 190 A.D. Polycrates calls Philip and John στοιχεῖα μεγάλα, "important stars," Euseb. Hist. Eccl., III, 31, 3 = V, 24, 2. A horoscope in P. Lond., I, 120, written after rather than before 100 A.D., is thus far the oldest instance of the astronomical or astrological use of στοιχεῖον, στοιχείῳ Διός, line 60 f. It is not obvious from the texts that the stars were regarded as beings in the NT age. [82] If one consults the account of the Bab. doctrine of the stars in Diod. S., 2, 30 f., there is ref. to the judicial (→ n. 93) or governing office of some stars, and 30, 7 speaks of a superiority over other stars (τούτων κυρίους εἶναι φασι), but the main pt. is that the gods decide events in heaven (30, 1) and that the planets declare the will of the gods: ἑρμηνεύοντες τοῖς ἀνθρώποις τὴν τῶν θεῶν ἔννοιαν, 30, 4. Clearly the gods are above the stars here and distinct from them by nature. If some of the physical and mental processes of man are traced back to the 7 planets (Stob. Ecl., I, 77 f.), the ref. is obviously to the influence of impersonal powers on man. In Plot. there is a clear distinction between heavenly bodies and the related deities → 680, 16 f.

In the astronomical part of Eth. En. 72-82 Uriel is the leader of the heavenly lights in 72:1 etc., and there is ref. to leaders of the stars in 72:3. 82:11-14 sketches a whole hierarchical system in the stellar world. The stars etc. rule in heaven and are leaders for day and night, 75:3. The detailed description of the course of the sun in 72:4-37; 75:4 is technical. The dominion of the heavenly bodies may be seen in their influence on seasonal events in nature (82:16-20), [83] esp. the divisions of the year (82:11), the ref. being to the calendar, which is regulated acc. to Jub. 6:23-37 and is seen to be of religious importance (82:4-7). The teaching which Uriel gives En. does not relate to the independent religious significance of the heavenly bodies or their leader, nor to any personal connection with man, but to their "courses" or "laws," 80:6; 79:1 f., cf. also 33:3 f. The view that the heavenly bodies are gods is a sign of the utter confusion of the end-time, 80:7. It is God who gives the sun its path, 83:11. The disobedience for which some stars are punished in 18:13-16 (cf. 21:3-6) consists quite simply in their failure to come forth in their time, 18:15.

6. The later presence of the idea of stellar spirits [84] may be seen, however, from the use of στοιχεῖον for this and then more gen. for "a spiritual being." Thus στοιχεῖον is

---

[78] Cf. K. Dieterich, 9; further examples 11, n. 3. The passages adduced in Schl. Gl.[12] on 4:10 from Eth. En. 72-82, Jub. and Q do not support the "exacting character of these elemental stellar beings" (Schl. Gl.[12], 193 on 4:3).

[79] Even though Diog L. is here using an important older source (Oe. Gl.[2], 94 on 4:3, Diels, 45: at the latest 1st cent. A.D.), VI, 102 does not mean that this source used στοιχεῖα for the signs of the zodiac. Brändle, 13-35 does not think the ref. is to the zodiac anyway.

[80] The signs of the zodiac, which next to the planets are esp. important in ancient astronomy, are represented from the 4th cent. B.C., Boll-Gundel, 1052 f. Cf. L. Deubner, Attische Feste[2] (1956), 248-254, Plates 34-40: here the signs are significant only for the calendar.

[81] Ed. H. Koechly in Corpus Poetarum Epicorum Graec., VII (1858). On the date of Book VII v. S. Kroll, Art. "Manethon," Pauly-W., 14 (1930), 1104.

[82] Cf. Schlier Gl.[12], 191, n. 3 on 4:3; Gundel, 811 f., whose presentation includes the later period and whose interpretation on p. 820, Sctn. V is open to question.

[83] Cf. also Slav. En. 19:2: The angels set over the stars "make the ordinances and teach the course of the stars and the return of the sun"; in 19:1 their faces shine "more than the rays of the sun." On stellar and elemental spirits in later Judaism cf. Bousset-Gressm., 321-4; Moore, I, 403.

[84] The misleading or wrong interpretations of many passages adduced for this sense, or for "spiritual beings," can hardly be discussed here. One striking example may be given. Acc.

used alongside δαίμων (→ II, 3, 20 ff.) and πνεῦμα (→ VI, 339, 16 ff.) in Test. Sol. [85] 8:1 f.; 18:1 f. 8:4 ref. to stars to which these στοιχεῖα belong, which are described as gods. [86]

B. In the New Testament. [87]

1. In the Pauline corpus στοιχεῖον is used three times in the expression στοιχεῖα τοῦ κόσμου at Gl. 4:3; Col. 2:8, 20, and the meaning is essentially the same at Gl. 4:9. Outside the NT, as one would expect, the combination means primarily the "four elements," so Philo Aet. Mund., 109 for the constantly changing and hence immortal "elements." Popular use may be seen in Sib., 8, 337 f. and cf. 2, 206 f. and 3, 80 f., which give evidence of biblical influence, the elements being emptied of life in eschatological judgment. In Orph. Hymn., 5, 2-4 κόσμου στοιχεῖον ἄριστον ref. to ὑψιφανὴς Αἰθήρ as the "basic material" of which the stars are made; cf. 66, 4-6, where Hephaestus (fire) is lauded as κόσμοιο μέρος, στοιχεῖον ἀμεμφές and equated with ether and the stars, which consist of it → 679, 19 ff. P. Osl., II, 13, Col. III, 7-14 [88] (2nd cent. A.D.) says of the τοῦ σύμπαντος κόσμου στοιχεῖα as the "basic materials" of the world that everything consists (συνεστάναι) of them and will be dissolved (τὴν ἀνάλυσιν ἀναλαμβάνειν) in them. Grammar takes this to be a familiar usage and thus employs it as an analogy for understanding speech. The syllable consists (συνεστάναι) of στοιχεῖα and is broken up into them (ἀναλύεσθαι), ibid., lines 3-6. The grammarian Heliodor. says that letters are called by some στοιχεῖα ... ἐκ μεταφορᾶς τῶν κοσμικῶν στοιχείων (as these by their admixture give rise to our bodies, so ...). [89] Materially κοσμικὰ στοιχεῖα (→ 674, 20 f.) has the same sense in Ps.-Callisth., I, 1, 3; it ref. to the water and earth [90] Nektanebo uses in analogy-magic. The statement in 13, 1 that Alexander's birth has κοσμικῶν στοιχείων σημείωσίν τινα [91] bears an obvious ref. to the accompanying phenomena described in 12, 9, namely, lightning, thunder and earthquake, so that the whole cosmos was moved. It is thus speaking of the "cosmic elements." [92] In Preis. Zaub., II, 39. 18-20 (4th cent. A.D.) there is ref. not only to the 12 στοιχεῖα τοῦ οὐρανοῦ (the signs of the zodiac) but also to the 24 στοιχεῖα τοῦ κόσμου; [93] this is a special usage.

---

to Scheu, 52 στοιχεῖον is used for stellar gods in Simpl. in Aristot. De Caelo Comment., I, 3, 49b (ed. J. Heiberg, Comment. in Aristotelem Graeca, 7 [1894], 107, 15f.). But here στοιχεῖα does not mean stars. It means the elements of which living creatures are begotten and in which they dissolve again acc. to Simpl. The στοιχεῖα are not called gods; the ref. is to the gods set over them, Liddell-Scott, s.v. στοιχειοκράτωρ. Finally, what is the significance for the NT of the usage which Scheu claims for the 6th cent. A.D.?

[85] Acc. to McCown, 108, the editor of Test. Sol., neither passage is prior to the 4th cent. A.D., and the sense under discussion (→ 682, 35 ff.) is not attested before Test. Sol. (Burton, 514; Bandas, 68, 81; Deissmann, 1260 on Test. Sol.: "our main examples").

[86] Later examples in K. Dieterich, 12, n. 4 (the fathers); Sophocles Lex., s.v.

[87] Lagercrantz, 39-55 takes στοιχεῖον in the NT essentially in its (supposed) "original sense," 39: It "is synon. with θεμέλιος or θεμέλιον," 54.

[88] The context supports the reading, κόσμου is unequivocal.

[89] Grammatici Graeci, I, 3 (→ n. 8), 317, 24-26, cf. 324, 35-38; στοιχεῖα κοσμικά is also used for the elements in 197, 6 f.; 329, 5; 356, 3. κοσμικὰ στοιχεῖα occurs in Stob. Ecl., I, 387, 12 for the cosmic elements.

[90] For details cf. Pfister, 416 f.

[91] So Kroll's ed.; for the text cf. Pfister, 420, n. 37.

[92] In the additions to Ps.-Callisth., 12 adduced by Pfister, 420 κοσμικὰ στοιχεῖα again means elements, cf. Pfister, n. 35 f. Kroll does not give these in his ed.

[93] S. Eitrem, P. Osl., I, p.20 ref. to Diod. S., 2, 31, 4 (cf. F. Boll, "Aus d. Offenbarung Johannis," ΣΤΟΙΧΕΙΑ, I [1914], 35 f.). This says of Bab. astrology that it emphasises 24 stars as well as the zodiac. The visible ones have significance for the living, the invisible (called δικαστὰς τῶν ὅλων) for the dead. But the interpretation of Diod. S. here is itself uncertain, Bouché-Leclerq, 43, esp. n. 4. Since the two groups of στυκία in P. Osl., I, 4, 18

If στοιχεῖον in Galatians and Colossians is to be understood in the light of usage outside the NT, the most obvious sense is "element." According to the widespread ideas sketched → 673, 32 ff. a man of NT days would take στοιχεῖα τοῦ κόσμου to refer to the "basic materials" of which everything in the cosmos, including man, is composed. Even in the 2nd century, when the sense "star" began to develop, exegesis still interpreted στοιχεῖον in Gl. and Col., not astrologically, but for the most part [94] cosmologically. Only the context of Gl. or Col. can yield any other sense.

2. Among the στοιχεῖα τοῦ κόσμου in Gl. 4 is on the one side the Torah [95] with its statutes (4:3-5: the ref. is by no means to the cultic provisions alone), and then on the other side the world of false gods whom the recipients once served, 4:8 f. [96] The expression στοιχεῖα τοῦ κόσμου thus draws attention to something common to Jewish and pagan religion → II, 899, 19 ff. In both — this thought is obviously decisive in the context of 4:1-11 — men lived in bondage to the στοιχεῖα. The inclusion of the Torah in the στοιχεῖα makes it improbable that the reference is literally to original materials, [97] and it certainly cannot be to the stars. [98] To speak of spiritual forces [99] is a forced solution which conflicts with the linguistic findings and is hardly in accord with the context. [100] Furthermore there is nothing to show that the term στοιχεῖα, the cosmic elements, the stars, or related spirits etc., played

---

(4th cent. A.D.) are simply mentioned in a conjuration. and stand alone, no deductions can be made from the text as to the point of the 24 στυκία, From Vett. Val., VII, 5 (p. 293, 25-27) (→ 681, 13 f.) one might also infer that originally the ref. was to the 4 elements, the present 24 being related to ideas such as those in Hipp. Ref., VI → 671, 34 ff.

[94] Cl. Al. takes Col. 2:8 to refer to the "rudimentary teaching" of pagan philosophy, Strom., VI, 62, 3. Tert. sees in Gl. 4 a ref. to the "fundamentals" of the Law, Marc., V, 4. There is a survey of patristic exegesis in Scheu, 8-16; cf. Huby, 64 f.

[95] Cf., e.g., Ltzm. Gl. on 4:3; Knox, 104, n. 3. Cramer, 175 even thinks that in Gl. 4:3 the expression refers exclusively to the Law, v. 128.

[96] Thus even as pagans the Galatians stood already under the στοιχεῖα, Ltzm. Gl. on 4:3. Ritschl, 249, n. 27, to maintain a ref. to the angels who gave the Law (249), transl. πάλιν ἐπιστρέφειν in v. 9 by "to be converted a second time," and relates πάλιν ἄνωθεν only to δουλεύειν.

[97] For this cf. W. Schmid, "Die Rede d. Ap. Pls. vor den Philosophen u. Areopagiten in Athen," Philol., 95 (1943), 108, n. 91 (as against Pfister, 425 f.). Kurze, 135 argues for it as follows: "Pagan and even Jewish ceremonial laws relate to material things, to festivals which are fixed by the position of the sun and moon, to abstinence from food and drink, to circumcision ... purifications, washings, the slaying of offerings" etc. But the broader context speaks of the Law in principle, so that one cannot restrict it to the cultic or ceremonial Law. Zn. Gl.³, 197, n. 75 on 4:3-5 ref. gen. to the "material constituents of the world." The idea of the binding of human existence to elements in the environment is naturally present (esp. → 674, 15 ff. with n. 26, 28; → 678, 15 ff.).

[98] Quite arbitrary is the statement of Easton, 364 that "the Law was the work of astral deities." Dibelius Geisterwelt, 85, n. 1; Knox, 108 f., though his interpretation uses various senses and possibilities of transl. It should not be overlooked that belief in the stars, though it had become quite a force among the educated in the Hell. age (Nilsson, II², 486), did not become popular until the beginning of the imperial period (281) → n. 72.

[99] This is not supported even by Gl. 4:2, 8, Burton, 517; Bandas, 80. In opposition to a mythological ref. to personified powers, spirits etc. cf. Cramer, 176, cf. 154-8. The history of the word shows that in Paul the term denotes "an impersonal agent," "the elements of religious-moral habit of 'old man,'" 176. On Gl. 4:2 → V, 150, 17 ff. ; S. Belkin, "The Problem of Paul's Background," JBL, 54 (1935), 41-60, esp. IV: The Terms ἐπίτροπος and οἰκονόμος Used by Paul, 52-55. Stellar spirits are presupposed in 1 C. 15:40.

[100] This is not the place for criticism of the usual obscure ref. to the spirit world (→ IV, 919, 2 ff.), which either explicitly or implicitly follow Everling, Dibelius etc. (though cf. Spitta, who refers to Ritschl). For a survey of the history of interpretation of στοιχεῖα in

any particular role in the Galatian churches.[101] It seems that Paul himself[102] contributed[103] the phrase στοιχεῖα τοῦ κόσμου in both Gl. and Col. It is naturally used in a negative sense, as may be seen from Gl. 4:9. Gl. 4:1-11 is controlled by a series of parallel antitheses: minor-son, slave-heir, bondage-ransom. V. 4 is a conspicuous turning-point. What was before this belonged to the past world and hence to the στοιχεῖα τοῦ κόσμου. These are weak στοιχεῖα (4:9) — here Paul says of the Torah the same as in R. 8:3 → I, 493, 25 ff.; IV, 1075, 3 ff. One may ask whether ἀσθενῆ καὶ πτωχά do not expound the gen. τοῦ κόσμου.[104] At any rate the two negative terms are a comprehensive judgment on all pre-Christian religion. Paul is here using his initial expression — στοιχεῖα τοῦ κόσμου — in a new way.[105] But in so doing he is obviously building on thoughts common to his age. στοιχεῖα τοῦ κόσμου denotes that whereon the existence of this world rests, that which constitutes man's being → n. 97. Paul uses it in a transferred sense for that whereon man's existence rested before Christ even and precisely in pre-Christian religion, that which is weak and impotent, that which enslaves man instead of freeing him.

3. Fundamentally the use of στοιχεῖον in Col. 2 is to be regarded as independent of the use in Gl. 4.[106] In the context of Col. 2:6-3:4 κατὰ τὰ στοιχεῖα τοῦ κόσμου in 2:8 is parallel to κατὰ τὴν παράδοσιν τῶν ἀνθρώπων and in antithesis to κατὰ Χριστόν. The expression is thus a value judgment. According to vv. 12-15 the Χριστός of 2:8 is Christ's saving work in the crucifixion and resurrection, whose significance for Christians is denoted by the σύν in 2:12, 20 and 3:1. 2:20-3:3 is

---

Gl. and Col. cf. Scheu, 2-5, 19-23, 25-36; Brändle, 9-109. For a criticism of elemental spirits in Everling, Brändle, 62-74. Scheu takes στοιχεῖα to refer to evil angelic beings, the rulers of this world, 100 etc. Caird, 47-51 does not discuss how one arrives at the supposed "angelic mediators ... of the law as elemental spirits" (for to say that the Law is demonic in Paul [41, 43] is no argument for this view); both are simply equated with the "powers" in Paul, 82, 86, 93, 95. It is simply affirmed that the στοιχεῖα τοῦ κόσμου seem to have links with the Law on the one side and astrology on the other, VIII. The deliberations of C. Maurer, *Die Gesetzeslehre des Pls.*, Diss. Zürich (1941), 24 f. show what difficulties arise for the interpretation of the στοιχεῖα as stellar spirits when an attempt is made to relate this to the general understanding of the Law in Gl. Yet Maurer clings to this view. For the first time to my knowledge Reicke, 266-8 tries to base upon Paul's understanding of the Law the inclusion of the OT Law (disputed by Maurer) among the elemental spirits of the world, which Reicke equates with the angels of 3:19 (261-3).

[101] G. S. Duncan, *The Ep. of Paul to the Galatians*, MNTC[8] (1955) on 4:9: "a worship of the Elemental spirits." Acc. to Gundel, 825 Paul is attacking an astrological choice of days, but cf. → IV, 641, 22 ff. Acc. to Schlier Gl.[12], 23 Paul regards an "insistence on keeping the calendar" as "worship of the στοιχεῖα τοῦ κόσμου," cf. 20 and on 4:10.

[102] This is supported by the formal par. in the two epistles, though obviously they do not seem to be dealing with the same error.

[103] Cf. Reicke, 261. "The expression ... might well ... come from Paul," H. Hegermann, "Die Vorstellung v. Schöpfungsmittler im hell. Judt. u. Urchr.," TU, 82 (1961), 161.

[104] Bandas, 77: Paul qualifies the στοιχεῖα by τοῦ κόσμου. Cf. Reicke, 264 f. → IV, 1075, 20 ff. Cf. 1 C. 1:27: τὰ ἀσθενῆ τοῦ κόσμου also σοφία τοῦ κόσμου in 1 C. 1:20; 3:19 → III, 885, 26 ff.

[105] The very negative judgment of στοιχεῖα by Paul is not sufficiently brought out when a ref. is seen to the first principles of human religion, W. Gutbrod, "Die paul. Anthropologie," BWANT, IV, 15 (1934), 142; Burton, 518; Bandas, esp. 78; Str.-B., III, 570; cf. Knox → n. 98.

[106] → n. 102. Bandas, 72 f., 76 f. (like Ritschl) finds Essene influence in the Colossian error. The Dead Sea Scrolls show that it is not impossible that there were some connections between this error and the thought represented by Qumran. Brändle, 378-381 only gives some hints as to his interpretation of Col. 2:8, 20. He suggests that the στοιχεῖα are "the spheres of the universe understood as active beings ...," 378 → n. 108.

framed by the ἀπεθάνετε in 2:20 (εἰ, as is actually the case) and 3:3 (γάρ), to which συνηγέρθητε in 3:1 is an antithetical parallel, cf. the antithesis ἐν κόσμῳ 2:20 — ἄνω 3:1 f. This ἐν κόσμῳ obviously takes up the second genitive in ἀπὸ τῶν στοιχείων τοῦ κόσμου → IV, 1067, 29 f.; the genitive is thus be taken qualitatively. The religious ordinances (2:20 → II, 231, 22 ff.) are human traditions (2:8) and they are thus στοιχεῖα τοῦ κόσμου, inadequate bearers of man's being. The negative use of the expression is again no indication that it was a phrase in the Colossian heresy [107] or denoted a special aspect of this. [108] It is used in general rejection of this error, → 30, 17 ff. In Col. 2, then, Paul can use the same expression as in Gl. 4. For the reference is again to religion before and outside Christ, and the same judgment falls on this. At best it is only a shadow of the fulfilment (2:17), and in fact it proves to be a deception when the one who believes in Christ thinks his existence can be supported by its ordinances (2:8) even though the fulness of God's power is at work in Christ alone, 2:9 → VI, 303, 24 ff. By dying with Christ the Christian is indeed set free from this delusion, 2:20 → IV, 1075, 43 ff. [109] Cf. on the one side Gl. 6:14, which refers to the circumcision demanded by the Torah, which is set among the στοιχεῖα τοῦ κόσμου by Gl. 4:3, and on the other side R. 7:6, which says that by dying with Christ the Christian is freed from the grip of the Law. We thus have here a distinctive circle of ideas or a specific usage which links the sayings about the στοιχεῖα in Gl. and Col. with the other Pauline letters. The best translation seems to be: "the elements of the world."

4. In 2 Pt. 3:10, 12 the only possible meaning is obviously "elements" (→ 673, 32 ff.) or "stars" (→ 681, 10 ff.). The former is suggested (→ III, 644, 16 ff.; V, 515, n. 136) by the use of terms found in the widespread doctrine of the elements, e.g., λύεσθαι (Plat. Tim., 56e; 57b) and τήκεσθαι [110] (→ 673, 10 f.) It is supported by the adoption of the Stoic idea of a cosmic conflagration in which the other elements will dissolve into the primal element of fire. [111] The use of "dissolution of the elements" for the destruction of the world, which is adequate in itself, is elucidated in 3:10 by a description of the overthrow of the main parts of the visible world consisting of the highest and lowest elements; for this reason the earth does not need to be mentioned again in 3:12. It is improbable that the οὐρανοί as the vault of heaven are being differentiated from the stars (στοιχεῖα) which belong to it. [112]

---

107 Essentially under the general rubric of the "elements of the world" Loh. Kol., 3-8 and 103-105 attempts an ingenious reconstruction of the Colossian heresy. Cf. also L. Goppelt, *Christentum u. Judt.* (1954), 137-140; G. Bornkamm, "Die Häresie d. Kol. Das Ende des Gesetzes," *Beiträge z. Ev. Theol.,* 16 (1958), 139-156; Dib. Gefbr.³, 38-40. But cf. Percy, 160-167. Acc. to Dibelius, *op cit.* (→ n. 48), 63-67 Col. is directed against Christians who also have themselves initiated into a mystery cult of the elements, 55 f. H. Conzelmann, *Der Br. an d. Kol.,* NT Deutsch, 8⁹ (1962) on 2:8 takes κόσμος to be "the body of the cosmic god, the elements being his members"; "the Christians of Colossae think Christ is the universal god whom one must worship in the elemental powers."

108 Thus the angels are not the στοιχεῖα in 2:18 nor are the powers in 2:10. Nor is σῶμα in 2:19 the cosmos which consists of regions of the universe, as Brändle argues, 306 cf. 379 → n. 25, 106.

109 Lumpe, 1086; Pr.-Bauer, *s.v.*

110 Cf. Is. 34:4 MS B and Lucian: τακήσονται πᾶσαι αἱ δυνάμεις τῶν οὐρανῶν.

111 This is clear even without conjecturing ἐκπυρωθήσεται for εὑρεθήσεται, F. Olivier, "Tutto sarà divorato dal fuoco," *Religio,* 11 (1935), 481-489.

112 Wnd. Kath. Br., *ad loc.*

5. The meaning in Hb. 5:12 is clearly "first principles" (→ 679, 2 ff.) with a slightly derogatory nuance: τὰ στοιχεῖα, "mere rudiments," "ABC" (→ I, 646, 1 ff.; IV, 138, 22 ff.). The idea of first principles is strengthened, or brought to expression, by τῆς ἀρχῆς, cf. the rhetorical amplitude of Isocrates → 679, 8 f.

Delling

---

† στολή

1. In Greek.

στολή Ionic, Aeolic σπόλα, [1] first means in class. Gk. the "equipping" of an army or fleet, Aesch. Pers., 192, 1018; Suppl., 764, then "fitting out" in gen., esp. "dress," "clothes," Soph. Phil., 223 f.: σχῆμα μὲν γὰρ Ἑλλάδος στολῆς ὑπάρχει cf. P. Oxy., IV, 839 (1st cent. B.C.): ἦλθέ μοι γυμνὸς κεκινδυνευκώς. εὐθέως ἠγόρασα αὐτῷ στολήν. To specify an adj. is used, e.g., ἱππική in Aristoph. Eccl., 846, τοξική, Plat. Leg., VIII, 833b, but also Περσική, Xenoph. An., I, 2, 27, Σκυθική, Hdt., IV, 78, 4 f., βαρβαρική, Xenoph. An., IV, 5, 33, also male or female, Eur. Ba., 827 f.: ἐγὼ στελῶ... τίνα στολήν; ἢ θῆλυν; [2] στολή can then mean the "upper garment," esp. that which is long and flowing, Soph. Oed. Col., 1357, 1597 cf. pap., e.g., Preisigke Sammelbuch, III, 6715, 32 (258 B.C.); 6750, 4 (252 B.C.) etc. [3] Priests always wore a special robe, Ditt. Syll.[3], III, 1025, 7 f. (300 B.C.); 1003, 14 (2nd cent. B.C.), also those who entered a shrine; [4] cf. also the robes of hierophants in the mysteries, Lys. Or., 6, 51. [5] Finally στολή can be used (rarely) for the act of dressing, Oribasius medicus (4th cent. A.D.), Synopsis, V, 21, 2. [6]

We no longer know whether a specific garb was important in the Hell. mysteries. Archaeology yields next to nothing on the subject, perhaps because all cultic furnishings were kept strictly secret. While the mystagogue of the Eleusinian mysteries did not wear

---

σ τ ο λ ή. Cf. Thes. Steph., Pape, Pass., Liddell-Scott, Pr.-Bauer, Moult.-Mill., Preisigke Wört., *s.v.*

[1] στέλλω "to make ready," later "to send," cf. στόλος "equipment," "expedition": *v.* Boisacq, Hofmann, *s.v.;* but cf. also Schwyzer, I, 295.

[2] Cf. Dt. 22:5 → n. 16. For Gk. clothes cf. R. Delbrueck, "Antiquarisches zu d. Verspottungen Jesu," ZNW, 41 (1942), 124 f. with bibl.

[3] On the relation of στολή to *stola* cf. G. Leroux, Art. "Stola" in Darembg.-Saglio, IV, 1521 f.

[4] White, i.e., clean unspotted clothing was not limited to priests but was also worn by the laity in some circumstances, cf. Nilsson, I[2], 93.

[5] Cf., e.g., the requirement on an inscr. from a shrine of Artemis in Delos in F. J. Dölger, ΙΧΘΥΣ, II: "Der hl. Fisch in d. antiken Religionen u. im Urchr." (1922), 55, n. 3: (χε)ροῖν καὶ ψυχῇ καθα(ρᾷ, ἔ)χοντας ἐσθῆτα λευ(κὴν ἀνυ)ποδέτους. Cf. also Inscr. Priene, 205 (3rd cent. B.C.) and the other examples in Pr.-Bauer, *s.v.* λευκός. Cf. also Philo Cher., 95: "Clothed in white with spotless garments" the Gentiles go into the temple. Also Act. Joh. 38: λευκοφοροῦντες. Cf. also the vesting with a special robe (*vestis lautiuscula*) on initiation into robber bands, Apul. Met., VII, 9; cf. Ant. Christ., I, 195. For Chr. attire (κοσμίως ἐστολισμένους) cf. Cl. Al. Paed., III, 79, 3. For further details Ant. Christ., V, 66-75 [Bertram]. Cf. also J. Braun, *Die liturgische Gewandung im Okzident u. Orient* (1907); C. M. Kaufmann, *Hndbch. d. chr. Archäologie*[2] (1913), 569-586.

[6] Ed. J. Raeder, CMG, VI, 3 (1926).

or don any special apparel, [7] white was worn in, e.g., the mysteries of Andania. [8] The only source to tell us anything specific about the function and significance of special robes is the account in Apuleius of the initiation of Lucius into the Corinthian Isis mysteries, Apul. Met., XI, 14 ff. [9] Here twelve garments are given to the mystagogue which he has to put on successively to symbolise the mystical progress which Isis enables him to make through the twelve cosmic zones. Finally he is invested with the *olympiaca stola,* a garment of fine linen with the twelve signs of the zodiac. This symbolises mystical identification with the heavenly deity itself, which lifts him up to itself and in so doing causes him to overcome the whole world in his ascent. [10] Though one cannot deduce from this account of Apul. what garment rites there might have been in other mystery cults, here at least one sees quite clearly the structure of a specifically religious idea of clothing which must have been widespread in the primitive Chr. period. Philo is acquainted with it, as may be seen from his allegorising of the high-priestly garb of office, Spec. Leg., I, 84-97; Vit. Mos., II, 117-135; Quaest. in Ex., II, 107-123. [11]

From the standpoint of religious history it is to a large extent in the light of this complex of ideas that we are to understand the Pauline view of baptism as a vesting of Christians (→ II, 514, 38 ff.) with Christ Himself (Gl. 3:27; R. 13:14) or the new man (Eph. 4:24; Col. 3:10) or the spiritual armour of Christian virtues (R. 13:12; 1 Th. 5:8; Eph. 4:24; 6:11, 14; Col. 3:12). [12] In Gnostic texts as well we find a cosmologico-soteriological concept of raiment, especially in connection with the ascent of the soul. [13]

2. In the Septuagint.

In the LXX στολή is used 98 times (also στολισμός 3 times and στόλος 4) for בֶּגֶד (45 times), לְבוּשׁ (6), שִׂמְלָה (5), and other terms. After ἱμάτιον/ἱματισμός (218 and 32 times) it is the most commonly used word in transl. of Hbr. terms for clothing. [14]

---

[7] On this question cf. H. G. Pringsheim, Archäol. Beiträge zur Gesch. d. eleusinischen Kults, Diss. Bonn (1905), 14-16.

[8] It was also laid down that women's clothes should not cost more than 10 drachmas or that of girls more than 1 drachma, cf. C. Lécrivain, Art. "Mysteria" in Darembg.-Saglio, III, 2141. For other sacral regulations regarding the clothing of initiates cf. Nilsson, II², 96.

[9] Cf. on this G. Lafaye, Art. "Isis" in Darembg.-Saglio, III, 582-5; Nilsson, II², 624-639; M. Dibelius, "Die Isisweihe bei Apul. u. verwandte Initiations-Riten," Botschaft u. Gesch., II (1956), 30-79; esp. J. Pascher Η ΒΑΣΙΛΙΚΗ ΟΔΟΣ, Der Königsweg zu Wiedergeburt u. Vergottung bei Philon v. Alex. (1931), 54-57, 78 f.

[10] It seems that the highest degree of initiation was not reached with investiture with the gay robe of Isis, which symbolised the cosmos as a whole. This came when the radiantly white robe of Osiris was put on (cf. on this Plut. Is. et Os., 77 [II, 382c-e]) symbolising the identification of full initiates, i.e., priests, with the sun god, cf. also Philo Som., I, 216-218.

[11] Cf. on this Pascher, op. cit. (→ n. 9), 37-51 and passim.

[12] But cf. Oepke (→ II, 320, 8 ff.). For Jewish apoc. elements → 689, 12 ff. and 691, n. 35. For a systematic survey of this NT raiment concept cf. E. Peterson, "Theol. d. Kleides," Marginalien zur Theol. (1956), 41-55.

[13] On this cf. esp. E. Käsemann, "Leib u. Leib Christi," Beiträge z. hist. Theol., 9 (1933), 87-94 → n. 35. Cf., e.g., O. Sol. 11:10-14: "And I have to leave folly behind, cast down to the earth, and I have put it off and thrown it from me. And the Lord renewed me by his garment, and made me ready by his light ... And the Lord (was) as the sun over the face of the earth. He enlightened my eyes," cf. 21:3-6.

[14] Cf. ἔνδυμα 15 times usually for לְבוּשׁ, ἔνδυσις twice, ἐσθής 4 times, ἔσθησις twice (only 1 Εσδρ. and 2/3 Macc.). χιτών is also used 37 times, with few exceptions always for כְּתֹנֶת, which is once transl. στολή at Is. 22:21. χιτών = tunica is a Semitic loan word = כתונת = Arab. kattān (Engl. "cotton") [Bertram]. For the various articles of clothing cf. Dalman Arbeit, V, 208-220, 228-232, 248-251.

In the LXX, as in class. Greek, στολή first means "clothing" of any kind, especially the "upper garment." But often the idea prevails that the clothing denoted by στολή is not just an outward covering but is something by which a man is essentially stamped in his current status. Joseph changes clothes when he comes before Pharaoh as a prisoner (Gn. 41:14) because the presence of the king does not allow of non-regal clothing. [15] Clothing thus belongs essentially to a specific circle of life which excludes all unseemly garb. This may be seen, for example, from the fact that Pharaoh gives Joseph linen robes (Gn. 41:42), along with the ring and golden chain, to establish his position: "See, I have set thee over all the land of Egypt," v. 41 [16] Sitting on the throne is an official sign of royalty along with the donning of royal garments, 2 Ch. 18:9, cf. Est. 8:15. Clothing, then, shows what a man is; a specific garment is part of a specific position. This idea is obviously so fundamental that it applies to the relation to God as well. Return from idolatry is signalised by a change of raiment, Gn. 35:2, cf. Lv. 6:4; 16:23 f., 32. On the other hand Job 9:31 has the noteworthy statement: "Thou wouldst dip me in refuse that my own clothes would abhor me."

In keeping is the robe of glory (στολή δόξης) in Wisdom teaching. This clothes wisdom, and with it she desires to clothe her pupils too, Sir. 6:29, 31. The garment here expresses heavenly life; the one who wears it has or gets a share in the life of heaven. This can be developed eschatologically in Jewish apocalyptic. The good things which God has prepared in heaven for the elect on the day of their entry into the new aeon are often described as garments in which they will then be clothed, cf. especially En. 62:15 f.: "The righteous and elect will then rise up from earth and cease to look down and they will be invested with the robe of glory. And this shall be their garment, a garment of life with the Lord of spirits: Your raiment will not grow old and your glory will not perish before the Lord of spirits." [17] Fundamentally, however, this use in eschatology simply brings to light the broader and determinative conceptual horizon under which alone one can understand both the practical and also the religious estimation of clothing, namely, the idea that clothing expresses the specific status by which a man's existence is stamped at a given time. All the things which Yahweh has given man, which are about him and which shape his being, are as it were the raiment with which Yahweh clothes him (לבשׁ), e.g., רוּחַ, [18] צְדָקָה or צֶדֶק, [19] הוֹד וְהָדָר [20] etc. [21] Here a whole complex of concepts, alien to modern thinking, may be seen quite plainly in what is said about dress. [22]

---

[15] Cf. also Est. 6:8; 1 Ch. 15:27; 2 Ch. 5:12.

[16] Cf. also Joseph's gift of clothes to his brethren in Gn. 45:22, the putting off of prison clothes by Jehoiachin when he was raised up to eat at the king's table in Jer. 52:33, the exchange of raiment between Ahab and Jehoshaphat before the battle in 3 Βασ. 22:30, also the forbidding of men to wear women's clothes (στολή γυναικεία) in Dt. 22:5. In Jos. 7:21 'A the garment which Achan took in spite of the ban is called a Bab. *stola*. In 4 Βασ. 23:7 Cod L uses στολαί ("robes") for the houses or huts of the *asherah* [Bertram].

[17] Cf. Apc. Abr. 13 and later Slav. En. 22:8 ff.; 56:2; 62:14, 16; 71:16 f. Cf. Bousset-Gressm., 277 f.; Volz Esch., 398 and → IV, 245, 17 ff.

[18] E.g., Ju. 6:34 etc. Cf. P. Volz, *Der Geist Gottes u. die verwandten Erscheinungen im AT u. im anschliessenden Judt.* (1910), 6 f.; L. Köhler, *Theol. d. AT*³ (1953), 97.

[19] E.g., Is. 59:17; Ps. 132:9; Job 29:14 etc. Cf. K. Koch, צדק *im AT*, Diss. Heidelberg (1953).

[20] Ps. 104:1; Job 40:10 etc.

[21] Cf. Ps. 73:6; 32:10; 104:2; Is. 59:17; Ps. 71:13; 109:29; 89:45; Job 19:9 etc. Closely related to the idea of robing is that of girdling or crowning with the blessings of salvation.

[22] Cf. the use of the prep. e.g., in בְּשֵׁם־יְהֹוָה, where the idea of an enveloping and

In this connection one may also refer to the common use of στολή to denote the priestly vestments (over 40 times). The priestly robe is a στολή ἁγία (Ex. 28:2 etc.) which Aaron and his sons put on (Ex. 40:13 etc.) so long as their priesthood lasts and put off when it is ended (Nu. 20:26) [23] or when, e.g., their cultic duty brings them into contact with what is unclean (Lv. 6:4 etc.). The priests themselves and their garments are "sanctified" by sprinkling with the blood of the altar, Ex. 29:21 etc. [24] → VI, 979, 13 ff. Later the priestly vesture can even be described as στολή δόξης, Sir. 45:7; 50:11, cf. also Wis. 18:24 on the robe of the high-priest.

In all this the use of στολή differs characteristically from that of ἱμάτιον/ἱματισμός. Whereas the idea of a garment which marks man's specific status, esp. the priestly robe, is combined with στολή, the group ἱμάτιον/ἱματισμός mostly denotes clothing in gen., and is never used for the sacerdotal vestments. Finally, ἐσθής is also employed in a general sense.

3. In the New Testament.

In the NT στολή denotes only the "upper garment." [25] It stands in contrast to the usual ἱμάτιον where special clothing is to be stressed, though the usage is fluid. In Rev. the two alternate, [26] and Luke, when he wants to speak of specially striking clothing, prefers ἐσθής to στολή. [27]

Fully along the lines of what has been said above (→ 689, 1 ff.) the fine raiment with which the father has the prodigal robed when he comes back home (Lk. 15:22) is a sign of his taking back into the father's house. The fact that it is a πρώτη στολή [28] visibly expresses a point which is twice emphasised in the parable, namely, that the prodigal is honoured as one who was dead and is alive again, Lk. 15:24, 32.

In Mk. 12:38 (Lk. 20:46) Jesus warns against the scribes who go about in the long and flowing robes [29] which mark them as such and who claim for themselves the greetings of the people in the market, places of honour in the synagogue, and the best seats at feasts. The charge is not directed so much against specific excesses of personal vanity or avarice [30] but rather against the general claim of rabbis that in virtue of their teaching, to which they accord the dignity of direct revelation, [31]

---

determining sphere undoubtedly stands in the background, so that זֶ has local as well as instrumental significance. This again sheds light on vv. like R. 13:14 and Gl. 3:27 → 688, 15 ff.

[23] When Moses took the robe of office from Aaron and put it on Eleazar, Aaron died, cf. also Jos. Ant., 3, 151.

[24] Materially cf. K. Koch, "Die Priesterschrift von Ex. 25 bis Lv. 16," FRL, NF, 53 (1959), 19-27.

[25] For clothing gen. we find ἱματισμός or τὰ ἱμάτια, also ἔνδυμα.

[26] Cf. Rev. 6:11; 7:9, 13 with 3:5, 18; 4:4; also 7:14; 22:14 with 19:13.

[27] This is esp. so when Luke speaks of "shining white garments," cf. Lk. 24:4; Ac. 1:10 with Mk. 16:5 (in Lk. 9:20 ἱματισμός is used because it is Jesus' ordinary robe which becomes radiantly white). In this connection we should also ref. to the mocking of Jesus by Herod Antipas περιβαλὼν ἐσθῆτα λαμπράν, Lk. 23:11; cf. Delbrueck, op. cit. (→ n. 2), 135 f., who compares (141) Ac. 12:21: ἐσθὴς βασιλική, and Jos. Ant., 19, 344: στολὴν εὐθὺς ἐξ ἀργύρου πεποιημένην. The white garment was the national robe of the later Jewish kings, ibid., 140-142.

[28] On this sense of πρῶτος cf. Pr.-Bauer, s.v.

[29] On this cf. esp. Str.-B., II, 31-33. Loh. Mk., ad loc. reads στοαῖς with sys (cf. syc on Lk. 20:46). Grundm. Mk., ad loc. thinks both readings are of equal worth.

[30] So esp. Loh. Mk., ad loc. quoting Prv. 3:34.

[31] Cf. materially Mt. 23:2: ἐπὶ τῆς Μωϋσέως καθέδρας ἐκάθισαν. Oral teaching has the same rank in Rabb. theology as the written Torah itself. On this cf. esp. D. Rössler, Gesetz u. Gesch. Wissenschaftliche Monographien z. AT u. NT, 3 (1959), 15-20.

they have a most important function in the saved community and should be given appropriate honour by the people. [32]

The white robe of the angel at the empty tomb (Mk. 16:5: περιβεβλημένον στολὴν λευκήν cf. Mt. 28:3: ἔνδυμα αὐτοῦ λευκὸν ὡς χιών [cf. Da, 7:9 Θ], and Lk. 24:4: ἐν ἐσθῆτι ἀστραπτούσῃ) shows that the one thus manifested is a heavenly being [33] and that his message about the resurrection of Jesus (v. 6) is an eschatological revelation. The same idea underlies the saying in Rev. 6:11 that a στολὴ λευκή is already given the souls of martyrs when they enter into the short season of rest, or the saying about the white-robed host of the redeemed before the eschatological throne of the Lamb (Rev. 7:9 cf. v. 13: περιβεβλημένοι τὰς στολὰς τὰς λευκάς), their robes having taken on the eschatological colour when they washed them "and made them white in the blood of the Lamb" (7:14 cf. 22:14), i.e., when they came out of the great θλῖψις of the last time and entered into the eschatological kingdom of salvation → IV, 249, 16 ff. Here and in the parallel Rev. 3:4 f. one may see clearly that the washing of clothes white does not have an active sense (martyrdom) but a passive sense: To the οὐκ ἐμόλυναν τὰ ἱμάτια αὐτῶν (3:4) corresponds (3:5) the eschatological receiving of the robe of glory περιβαλεῖται ἐν ἱματίοις λευκοῖς (3:5). [34] Similarly entry into the new aeon is consistently represented in apocalyptic literature as the reception of salvation, and in Rev., as often in apocalyptic, [35] it is sometimes described as robing with new garments, cf. also 1 C. 15:53 f.; 2 C. 5:3. Here, too, the garment expresses being and investing expresses the gift of new being.

Wilckens

---

[32] On this v. J. Jeremias, *Jerusalem z. Zeit Jesu*[2] (1958), II B 112-114, 124 f.

[33] Cf. → IV, 245, 17 ff. with bibl. Ev. Pt. 13:55 is based on Mk. 16:5. It is the only instance of the word in primitive Chr. writings outside the NT [Schneemelcher].

[34] Cf. the changing of the clothes of the high-priest Joshua in Zech. 3:1-7.

[35] Cf. → 689, 20 ff.; → IV, 249, 16 ff. For examples of the Gnostic idea of raiment, which is esp. common in Syrian Gnostic texts (O. Sol., Mandaean writings) (→ n. 13), and which is so like the structure of the eschatological understanding in Jewish apoc. that one may speak of historical kinship, cf. Loh. Apk. on 3:4 f.; Bousset-Gressm., 277 f. (both with bibl.).

| στόμα | → πρόσωπον, VI, 768, 6 ff. |

Contents: A. The Use of the Word in Profane Greek. B. Data from Religious History. C. The Old Testament. D. Judaism: 1. The Septuagint; 2. The Targums; 3. Rabbinic Texts; 4. Philo; 5. Qumran. E. The New Testament.

A. The Use of the Word in Profane Greek.

στόμα (Avesta *staman* "mouth" [1]) is found from Hom., e.g., Od., 11, 426 for the human "mouth" and the "maw" or "jaws" of animals, Hes. Scutum Herculis, 146 and 389. It can also mean the "face" or "front" of men, [2] as in phrases like ἐπὶ στόμα, Aesch. Fr., 351 (TGF, 105); Plut. De Artaxerxe, 29 (I, 1026d) and κατὰ (τὸ) στόμα, Plat. Leg., IX, 855d. In Aesch. Choeph., 573 f. κατὰ στόμα and κατ' ὀφθαλμούς are par.; the phrase is used of the organ of speech (→ I, 719, 20 ff.); we find epithets which denote the speaker or what is said rather than the mouth as such, e.g., ἀψευδές in Aesch. Fr., 350, 5 (TGF, 105), σοφόν in Anth. Graec., 7, 4, 1, cf. 7, 6, 3, μισόχρηστον in Philodem. Philos. De Pietate, 1077 I O (p. 93, 25 f.). [3] στόμα denotes the organ of speech in many expressions: στόμα οἴγειν Aesch. Prom., 611, διαίρειν Demosth. Or., 19, 112, λύειν Eur. Hipp., 1060, (συγ)κλείειν Aristoph. Thes., 40, κοιμᾶν Aesch. Ag., 1247 and δάκνειν "to be silent" Aesch. Fr., 397 (TGF, 115); Soph. Trach., 976 f., ἀνὰ στόμα ἔχειν "to be talking about" Eur. El., 80, ἀπὸ στόματος εἰπεῖν Plat. Theaet., 142d, ἐξ ἑνὸς στόματος Plat. Resp., II, 364a etc. [4] The transition to the sense "speech" (→ I, 720, 6 ff.), "word," "order," is fluid, e.g., when the ref. is to the "mouth" of those who are divinely inspired in Aesch. Fr., 350, 5 (TGF, 105): τὸ Φοίβου θεῖον ἀψευδὲς στόμα [5] or to the saying of the seer or the oracle in Soph. Oed. Col., 603: τὸ θεῖον αὐτοὺς ἐξαναγκάζει στόμα. But it is often natural enough, Soph. Oed. Tyr., 426 f.: τοὐμὸν στόμα προπηλάκιζε (the saying of Teiresias), cf. epithets like ἀνόσιον in Soph. Oed. Col., 981, καλόν in Soph. Fr., 844, 2 (TGF, 327), ἐλεινόν in Soph. Oed. Tyr., 671 f. The sense can become the narrower one of speaking or writing "style," Dion. Hal. De Lysia, 12: τὸ Λυσιακὸν ... στόμα.

More broadly στόμα denotes "openings, entries or exits," of all kinds, Hom. Od., 5, 441: ποταμοῖο κατὰ στόμα, 22, 137: στόμα λαύρης of a lane, Soph. Ant., 119: ἑπτάπυλον στόμα (of Thebes), Xenoph. An., IV, 5, 25: τὸ μὲν στόμα (sc. οἰκιῶν) ὥσπερ φρέατος, Aristot. An. Post., II, 11, p. 94b, 15: πρὸς τῷ στόματι τῆς κοιλίας. Again the sense "face," "front" (→ 692, 8) leads to the use of the word gen. for the "front side," Xenoph. An., III, 4, 43; Asclepiodotus Tacticus, II, 5, [6] and perhaps this yields the meaning "extreme limit," Hom. Il., 14, 36: ἠϊόνος στόμα, Eur. Phoen., 1166 f.: εἰς ἄκρον στόμα πύργων, Xenoph. Ag., 11, 15: πρὸς τῷ στόματι τοῦ βίου. But expressions like πτολέμοιο μέγα στόμα in Hom. Il., 10, 8, cf. 19, 313 and ὑσμίνης (of the battle) ... στόμα in 20, 359 quite obviously have their root in the idea of the open

---

στόμα. [1] Walde-Pok., II, 648; Pokorny, I, 1035, Boisacq, *s.v.* Though the sense differs the Hittite *ištaman* "ear" is identical, H. Kronasser, *Vergleichende Laut- u. Formenlehre d. Hethitischen* (1956), 222 (Hofmann, *s.v.* is wrong here) [Risch].

[2] Worth noting is the paucity of this use in Gk. as compared with the Lat. *os* [Dihle].

[3] Ed. T. Gomperz, *Herkulanische Studien,* II (1866).

[4] Cf. Liddell-Scott, *s.v.*, I, 3.

[5] Anth. Graec., 9, 26, 3 lists the στόμα Ἀνύτης among the poetesses called θεόγλωσσοι γυναῖκες.

[6] Ed. C. H. and W. A. Oldfather, The Loeb Class. Library (1948).

jaws of a monster, cf. στόμα μαχαίρας Asclepiodotus Tacticus (→ n. 6), III, 5, στόμα τῆς αἰχμῆς, Philostr. Heroic., 19, 4 (p. 199, 16), cf. also (ξυστά) κατὰ στόμα εἱμένα χαλκῷ "spears clad to the fore with bronze," all based on the thought of a biting or tearing maw, though it may be there is also the thought of the foreside, the foremost thrust, the forward edge, the point of an instrument. [7]

B. Data from Religious History.

In the ancient Orient and Egypt the spirit and life given by the deity, and the life-creating word of the deity, are dominant religious notions. [8] In this connection mention is naturally made of the mouth of the deity from which the breath or word comes. Thus Enuma eliš, IV, 19-26 (AOT, 117) tells of a garment which symbolises the cosmos and which is destroyed and created anew by the mouth of Marduk. [9] In ancient oriental songs to the word of deity [10] we often find expressions like: "As goes forth from thy mouth," "the utterance of thy (his) mouth," "the pure word of thy mouth" etc. [11] A good breath, the life of men and lands, divine blessing — all proceed from the mouth. [12] The same is true of Egypt. texts. What comes forth from the mouth of deity is good, existence, life. The word in and from God's mouth creates life. It effects what it says. [13] Indeed, the gods themselves come forth from the mouth of the primal god, as do the king and all parts of creation. [14] This takes place either as an utterance which works with creative force or as a physical generation in which the mouth is the organ of generation in the narrower sense. [15]

Either way the mouth of God or parts of it (lips, tongue, teeth) are equated with other gods which discharge the described functions of the mouth: Anu and Antum are

---

[7] Cf. Pass., s.v. στόμα, 1 b aa; Liddell-Scott, s.v., III, 1 a b.

[8] Cf. J. Hehn, "Zum Problem des Geistes im Alten Orient u. im AT," ZAW, 43 (1925), 210-225; L. Dürr, "Die Wertung d. göttlichen Wortes im AT u. im antiken Orient," Mitteilungen d. vorderasiatisch-ägypt. Gesellschaft, 42, 1 (1938).

[9] On this whole complex of ideas cf. R. Eisler, Weltenmantel u. Himmelszelt, I (1910), esp. 220-235.

[10] Assembled by Dürr, op. cit.

[11] Cf. Keilinschr. Bibliothek, VI, 2 ed. E. Schrader (1915), 79 and 83; H. Zimmern, Bab. Hymnen u. Gebete, AO, 13, 1 (1911), 9, 21; F. Thureau-Dangin, Rituels Accadiens (1921), 108 and 110.

[12] So M. Jastrow, Die Religion Babyloniens u. Assyriens, II (1912), 53; E. Ebeling, "Quellen zur Kenntnis d. bab. Religion," Mitteilungen d. vorderasiat. Gesellschaft, 23, 1 (1918), 5, 23 f.; 23, 2 (1919), 38, 31.

[13] Thus on a casket from Saft el Henneh we read of King Nektanebo: "The word which is on the place is like that which goes forth from the mouth of Rê" (Dürr, op cit., 32). Cf. also AOT, 14; Hehn, op cit., 217; Reitzenstein Poim., 62; A. H. Gardiner, "Hymns to Amon from a Leiden Pap.," Zschr. f. ägypt. Sprache u. Altertumskunde, 42 (1905), 39; H. Kees, "Göttinger Totenbuchstud.," Zschr. f. ägypt. Sprache u Altertumskunde, 65 (1930), 74; also "Ägypten" in Religionsgeschichtliches Lesebuch, 10, ed. A. Bertholet² (1928), No. 4. The same applies to the king in the Amarna period, cf. J. A. Knudtzon, Die El-Amarnatafeln (1915), 609, 19 f.; 617, 21 ff.

[14] Cf. the hymn to Amon-Rê, AOT, 14 = Kees Ägypten, No. 11: "Thou (Rê) art the one ... from whose mouth the gods came forth," ibid., No. 15b: "But him (the sun-god) whom thy mouth begat ..." ; Dürr, op. cit., 26 (acc. to A. Moret, Mystères Égypt. [1913], 64): "Thou (the king) hast proceeded to heaven in this thy form which came forth from the mouth of Rê"; Kees Ägypten, No. 25: "He (Chnum) has fashioned four-footed things from the breath of his mouth, he has breathed forth flowers and [...] on the meadow."

[15] Cf. the two versions of the generation of Shu and Tefnut in Kees Ägypten, No. 2a and b; also AOT, 2; Kees Ägypten, No. 15b: "Breath comes forth from thy nose (Ptah's), water from thy mouth"; cf. G. Ebers, "Die Körperteile, ihre Bdtg. u. Namen im Altägyptischen," AAMünch., 21 (1898), 153 f.

the lips of Ninurta, [16] Thot is the tongue of Ptah, [17] the "nine (of Ptah) are the teeth and lips in this mouth which named the names of all things." [18] The Memphis monument from which these words are taken is perhaps the most impressive and also the most ancient witness to the creative power of the word linked to the organ of speech, for it extends the idea of the commanding and efficacious word of God to the mouth or tongue of all creatures: "It came to pass that the heart and tongue achieved power over (all) members by teaching that he (Ptah) who (as heart) is in every body and (as tongue) in every mouth of all gods, all men, all cattle, all creeping things (and) all (else) that lives, thinking (as heart) and (as tongue) commanding all things that he will ... And thus it is that all works and crafts are done, the action of the arms, the going of the legs, the movement of all members acc. to this command which is thought by the heart and which comes forth from the tongue and which constitutes the meaning of all things." [19] The organ of creation is thus the mouth "which named all things." [20]

A corresponding negative significance is ascribed to the mouth of the demon in Sumerian and Assyrian-Bab. conjurations. His mouth and spittle are to go forth from the one who is demonised. [21] Sorceries are generated on the tongue of the witch and mischiefs on her lips. [22] A wicked mouth, tongue, lips and spittle smite men. [23] In Egypt the dead man who has reached the land of light rejoices that the breath of the mouth of those who speak against him can no longer reach him. [24] On the other hand a man can pacify the angry heart of one who fumes against him by charming and chewing a knot of straw and then taking it from his mouth and laying it on the breast of the one who is angry. [25]

The significance of the mouth of deity enables us to understand the attested Bab. custom of washing and opening the mouths of newly dedicated images with special rites,[26] a ceremony of purification which priests and penitents also perform on themselves or have performed on them, [27] and which, terminologically at least, seems to live on in the cultic meal of the Mandaeans. [28] In Egypt the mouth of the dead must be cleansed if the ferry-man is to take him over. [29] But the opening of the mouth of the dead who has become Osiris, [30] as in the Osiris myth, [31] is simply to enable him to take food.

---

[16] Cf. Ebeling, op cit., 23, 1 (1918), 48, 16 ff.
[17] Cf. K. Sethe, Dramatische Texte zu altägypt. Mysterienspielen (1928), 50 (cf. 54) = Kees Ägypten, No. 15a.
[18] Sethe, 57 and 59 = Kees Ägypten, No. 15a.
[19] Sethe, 55 = Kees Ägypten, No. 15a. Cf. the stele in H. Kees, Totenglaube u. Jenseitsvorstellung d. alten Ägypter² (1956), 284, on which the deceased expects life from the breath of the mouth of those who pass over if they speak and cause his name to live.
[20] Cf. G. van der Leeuw, Phänomenologie der Religion² (1956), 480.
[21] A. Falkenstein, "Die Haupttypen d. sumerischen Beschwörung," Leipziger semitistische Studien, NF, 1 (1931), 93.
[22] B. Meissner, Babylonien u. Assyrien, II (1925), 228.
[23] Ibid., 235.
[24] Kees Totenglaube, 187.
[25] Meissner, op. cit., 235.
[26] For similar rituals in Egypt cf. H. Bonnet, Reallex. d. ägypt. Religionsgeschichte (1952), 487-490; E. Otto, "Das ägypt. Mundöffnungsritual," Ägypt. Abh., 3 (1960). On the Bab. ritual and its later history cf. H. Zimmern, "Das vermutliche bab. Vorbild d. Pehtā u. Mambuhā d. Mandäer," Oriental. Stud. f. T. Nöldeke, II, ed. C. Bezold (1906), 959-963.
[27] Zimmern, 694. W. Schrank, "Bab. Sühneriten bes. mit. Rücksicht auf Priester u. Büsser," Leipziger semitist. Stud., 3, 1 (1908), 86: "The āšipu (expiating priest) who makes the land healthy am I; ... the āšipu of Eridu whose mouth is washed am I"; 67: "Washing of my mouth, that my hands may be in order, I effect."
[28] Zimmern, 965-7; E. S. Drower, "The Sacramental Bread (Pihtha) of the Mandaeans," ZDMG, 105 (1955), 115-150.
[29] Kees Totenglaube, 99 and 191.
[30] Ibid., 285: "Greetings to thee, Osiris. Look on me, I come, I am Horus, who opens thy mouth with Ptah ... " ; also Ill. 1. Cf. A. Erman, Die Religion d. Ägypter (1934), 267 f.
[31] Erman, op cit., 71.

Of special significance is the idea that the mouth of the priest, inasmuch as the deity uses it, becomes the mouth of the deity itself and has the same efficacy. [32]

C. The Old Testament.

1. In both the lit. and the transf. sense the sphere of the use of פֶּה is essentially the same as that of στόμα (→ 692, 6 ff.), [33] but the transition to the sense of "word," "command," is more unequivocal and consistent in Hbr. than in Gk. The Gk. expressions are found in Hbr. is essentially the same sense. Thus פֶּה אֶל־פֶּה, which is fuller than κατὰ στόμα, means direct encounter, and cf. expressions relating to the mouth as the organ of speech, סכר פֶּה ni, פֶּה אֶחָד "with one voice," also קרא פֶּה "to call with a loud voice," and קפץ,פצה and פתח קרא מִפִּי "to dictate," עַל־פֶּה (פֶּה) שִׂים יָד "to be silent," בהל עַל־פֶּה pi "to speak without thinking" etc. [34] We also find epithets describing the speaker or what is said, cf. פֶּה חָלָק "flattering" in Prv. 26:28 and פִּי תַהְפֻּכוֹת "perversion" in 8.13. In פְּרִי פִי־אִישׁ in Prv. 12:14; 13:2; 18:20 there is ascribed to the mouth that which man achieves by what he says. Whereas for לְפִי־חֶרֶב in Gn. 34:26 etc. the question of symbolical background arises (→ 693, 1 ff.), this is plain when פִּי אַרְיֵה is used for an enemy in Ps. 22:21 and also in the case of פִּי צָר "affliction" in Job 36:16, for, abstract though the use of the image already is in this v., the underlying thought is plainly that of jaws which tear and grind and swallow, and which one cannot escape. The same applies to the maw of Babylon's Bel in Jer. 51:44, from which God promises He will snatch what it has swallowed, and also in the case of the threat to the false shepherds in Ez. 34:10, where God says He will snatch the flock which they have swallowed from their jaws. The simple meaning "opening," "entry," occurs in פִּי־אֲדָמָה at Gn. 4:11 cf. Nu. 16:30 etc. and פִּי־שְׁאוֹל at Is. 5:14; Ps. 141:7 etc. [35] The original content of the term is very weak in the combinations עַל־פִּי, לְפִי, כְּפִי "according to," "after the measure of," "corresponding to," "as," [36] and also in fractional units of measure formed with פֶּה like פִּי־שְׁנַיִם "two thirds." [37] Among uses of פֶּה, which have religious significance the ref. to God's mouth (almost always פִּי יהוה, very seldom פִּי אֱלֹהִים) is of primary importance. In this respect a literal understanding is to be plainly (though not always) differentiated from the transferred sense of "word," "speech."

2. Even when the ref. is to God's mouth in the lit. sense, [38] this is always, with the exception of Ps. 18:8 = 2 S. 22:9 and Job 37:2, God's mouth as the organ of speech. [39] This shows already that we have here no naive anthropomorphic formula. Only in 2 Ch. 35:22; 36:12 does it occur in narrative sections; elsewhere we find it in prophetic, poetic and didactic texts. The use sometimes has its basis in poetic style and may be

---

[32] Schrank, 14: "His (Ea's) pure incantation he has laid in my incantation, his pure mouth he has laid in my mouth, his pure spittle he has laid in my spittle, his pure blessing he has laid in my blessing"; 15 (prayer to Ea): "Lay thy pure mouth in my mouth."

[33] Cf. Ges.-Buhl, s.v., 1, 3-5 and Köhler-Baumg., s.v., 1-6.

[34] Examples in Ges.-Buhl, s.v., 1b; Köhler-Baumg., s.v., 4.

[35] Behind both one may perhaps see mythical ideas, though Eichr. Theol. AT, II[4], 58 f. seems to be right when he finds in פִּי־שְׁאוֹל only a poetic figure of speech, for both the Bible (Is. 38:10; Job 38:17; Mt. 16:18, cf. Eichr. Theol. AT, II[4], 143 f.; G. Beer, "Der bibl. Hades," Theol. Abh., Festg. f. H. J. Holtzmann [1902], 3-29) and the Babylonians (cf. AOT, 185, 206-212; A. Jeremias, "Hölle u. Paradies bei d. Babyloniern," AO, 1, 3[2] [1903], 18-20) speak of שְׁאוֹל only as an underground place with solid gates.

[36] Cf. Ges.-Buhl, s.v. with prefixes 1 and 2; Köhler-Baumg., s.v., 7.

[37] Ges.-Buhl, s.v., 6; Köhler-Baumg., s.v., 8.

[38] Not more than 39 times all told.

[39] Thus the real organs of speech לָשׁוֹן Is. 30:27 and שְׂפָתַיִם Is. 30:27; Ps. 17:3; 89:34; Job 11:5; 23:12 can be used instead of פֶּה.

explained by parallelism, Ps. 33:6; 105:5; Job 23:12. Sometimes again the use of the expression with the divine saying imparted is meant to give a special emphasis, esp. with commands → lines 17 ff. Yet one must also consider whether the formula was not used later to avoid speaking directly of God. [40]

If it is asked what proceeds from God's mouth, the direct creative word so prominent in ancient oriental and Egyptian texts (→ 693, 7 ff.) is surprisingly much less in evidence. Only in Ps. 33:6, in parallelism to דְּבַר יהוה, do we find רוּחַ פִּיו as that by which heaven and its host (the stars) were made, and כָּל־מוֹצָא פִי־יהוה in Dt. 8:3 is the manna created by God's word. [41] Ps. 105:5 and 1 Ch. 16:12 demand recollection of the (פִּיו) מִשְׁפְּטֵי פִיהוּ. According to Lam. 3:38 good and evil as the destiny which overtakes man proceed from the mouth of the Most High. In the first place, however, stands prophetic speech, [42] which characteristically determines the דְּבַר יהוה in the OT (→ IV, 94, 1 ff.) and which is called speech from God's mouth. In the second place are the predominantly later texts which speak of law, teaching, and wisdom which come forth from God's mouth, Ps. 105:5; 119:13, 72, 88; Job 22:22; 23:12; Prv. 2:6.

3. More common is the transf. or better the abstract ref. to the פִּי יהוה, mostly in the expression עַל־פִּי יהוה, which is found 21 times, most frequently in Nu. It normally denotes a command from God's mouth as elucidated by the expansion כַּאֲשֶׁר צִוָּה יהוה in, e.g., Nu. 3:16, 51. Hence expressions like עבר "to transgress" in Nu. 14:41; 22:18 etc. or מרה אֶת־פִּי יהוה "to resist" in Nu. 20:24; Dt. 1:26, 43; 1 S. 12:14 f. etc. are possible. שֵׁבֶט פִּיו in Is. 11:4 also means the word which issues from God's mouth [43] and is at the same time fulfilment.

4. But as among men there can be an exchange whereby one man puts his words in the mouth of another (נתן, שׂים 2 S. 14:3, 19) and this other becomes his mouth, [44] so God uses the mouth of men as His own. This applies primarily to the Word of God which is set in the mouth of the prophets or given to them; [45] in Jer. 15:19 God says to the prophet: כְּפִי תִהְיֶה. The mouth summoned hereto is cleansed or sanctified by the touch of God or the fire of His altar, Is. 6:7; Jer. 1:9. God's Word is in this prophetic mouth (בְּפִי־), 1 K. 17:24; 2 Ch. 36:21 f. It goes forth from this mouth. It will also be in the mouth of succeeding generations, Is. 59:21 cf. Dt. 31:19, 21. [46] The Torah from the mouth of the priest is also God's Word, Mal. 2:7. God can even make Necho's mouth His own, so that Necho speaks words מִפִּי אֱלֹהִים, 2 Ch. 35:22.

---

[40] Cf. what W. Graf Baudissin, "'Gott schauen' in d. at.lichen Religion," ARW, 18 (1915), 198 says about the use of the phrase "God's face": "The use of the word 'face' undoubtedly became later a kind of weakening rather than an emphasising of direct vision. There is often ref. to God's face in OT writings when the author does not wish to name God. His face is a specific side of His being." Cf. also what is said about מֵימְרָא for פִּי יהוה in the Tg. → 697, 25 ff.

[41] The spiritual understanding of this expression, as acc. to Am. 8:11, is palpable for the first time in the LXX transl. → 699, 4 f.

[42] Is. 1:20; 34:16; 40:5; 45:23; 48:3; 55:11; 58:14; 62:2; Jer. 9:11, 19; 15:19; 23:16; Ez. 3:17; 33:7; Hos. 6:5; Mi. 4:4; 2 Ch. 36:12. In 4 of these ref. (Is. 1:20; 40:5; 58:14; Mi. 4:4) we find the formula כִּי פִי יהוה (צְבָאוֹת) דִּבֵּר. K. Marti, Das Dodekapropheton, Kurzer Hand-Comm. AT, 13 (1904) on Mi. 4:4 regards all these as secondary.

[43] LXX τῷ λόγῳ τοῦ στόματος αὐτοῦ.

[44] Cf. Ex. 4:15 f.:.... (sc. Moses) וְשַׂמְתָּ אֶת־הַדְּבָרִים בְּפִיו (sc. Aaron) .... וְהָיָה הוּא יִהְיֶה־לְךָ לְפֶה....

[45] שׂים: Nu. 22:38; 23:5, 12, 16; Is. 51:16; 59:21; נתן: Dt. 18:18; Jer. 1:9; 5:14.

[46] Even the רוּחַ שֶׁקֶר is given by God into the mouth of the prophets in 1 K. 22:22 f.

5. But even in the case of men in whose mouth God does not put any special word with a special commission the mouth is usually the organ through which the relation to God is effected and proved, Dt. 32:1. Each Israelite is commanded: לְמַעַן תִּהְיֶה תּוֹרַת יהוה בְּפִיךָ Ex. 13:9 cf. Jos. 1:8. The prayer of the righteous is that God's word should not depart from his mouth, Ps. 119:43. The words of his prayer are נִדְבוֹת פֶּה v. 108, cf. 141:3. The theme of the praise of God in the mouth of His people is a recurrent one in the Ps., cf. 8:2; 34:1; 40:3; 89:1 etc. Agreement of heart and mouth is here presupposed as the normal case, Dt. 30:14; Ps. 141:2 ff. If the mouth does not speak as the heart thinks or the hand does, the righteous, the prophet, or God Himself raises the gravest complaint and accusation, Is. 29:13; Jer. 12:2; Ez. 33:31; Ps. 50:16; 55:21; 62:4 etc. It is said of those who openly blaspheme: שַׁתּוּ בַשָּׁמַיִם פִּיהֶם, Ps. 73:9. Finally it may be noted that ritual piety pays strict regard to the ritual cleanness of the mouth, Ez. 4:14.

D. Judaism.

1. The Septuagint. For פֶּה the LXX [47] partly has the lit. στόμα [48] and partly ῥῆμα, πρόσταγμα, φωνή, λόγος to express the sense of "speech," "command," in the expressions מרה אֶת־פִּי יהוה and (אֶל־)עָל־(אֶל־)עברby פִּי יהוה → 696, 17 ff. Acc. to the sense κύριον alone can be used for אֶת־פִּי יהוה in Jos. 9:14 and ἐμοὺς λόγους for אִמְרֵי־פִי in Prv. 5:7. The adv. formulae כְּפִי and לְפִי are rendered by κατά, καθότι, ἡνίκα etc., but an expression like כְּפִי נִדְרוֹ in Nu. 6:21 can be transl. more fully by κατὰ δύναμιν τῆς εὐχῆς αὐτοῦ. פִּי־חֶרֶב is φόνος μαχαίρας, פִּי הַנֵּבֶל φωνὴ τῶν ὀργάνων, פֶּה in the sense "opening" περιστόμιον. At Ps. 18:8; 55:21; Prv. 22:6 פִּיו is transl. πρόσωπον, but this is based on the reading פָּנָיו. [49] The confession of σοφία in Sir. 24:3: ἐγὼ ἀπὸ στόματος ὑψίστου ἐξῆλθον, takes on significance in the light of ideas common to the ancient Orient → 693, 7 ff.

2. The Targums. The Targums [50] disregard the different senses of פֶּה and with few exceptions (Ps. 33:6; Lam. 3:38; Job 22:22) have מימרא for it no matter whether the sense is lit. or transf. This means that the choice of the term is primarily for stylistic reasons and the true meaning "saying," "word," is the decisive one. Where this is remote from the Hbr. or even ruled out, other transl. are used like לְפום for לְפִי and פתגמא for פִּי. [51] That the use of מימרא־יהוה for פִּי־יהוה has nothing whatever to do with the idea of a divine hypostasis may be seen esp. from the fact that מימרא is also used for פִי

---

[47] Of the 461 instances of στόμα in the LXX (163 in the historical books, 106 in the prophets, 192 in the writings), 109 (46, 42 and 21) ref. to revelation from the mouth of God, the prophets, or wisdom, and 166 (27, 25 and 114) to positive or negative religious and ethical statements in which the mouth is esp. the organ of human utterance in this field. Striking in Prv. are the gen. combinations: στόμα ἀσεβῶν in 10:6, στόμα δικαίου in 10:31 etc., 18 instances in all, in which the gen. is the logical subj. in Gk.; this corresponds to the st.abs. of the HT and controls the term στόμα. In reality it is not the mouth but the utterance made by it which is good or bad, righteous or wicked. Thus alongside sentences with στόμα in the nomin. we find the casus obliqui or prep. sayings esp. with instrumental ἐν (בְּ); in Sir. these have crowded out the nomin. except at 21:17; 27:23 (twice) [Bertram].

[48] Even פֶּה אֶל־פֶּה is transl. στόμα πρὸς στόμα.

[49] MS variations explain some other instances. Thus dittographic כִּי פִי underlies τὸ γὰρ στόμα κυρίου ἐλάλησεν for כִּי יהוה דִּבֵּר at Is. 24:3; 25:8, while the absence of στόμα in the transl. of Is. 40:5 כִּי פִי יהוה דִּבֵּי is due to haplographic omission.

[50] What follows is based on V. Hamp, Der Begriff "Wort" in d. aram. Bibelübersetzungen (1938).

[51] Ibid., 24, n. 3.

[52] Cf. already Str.-B., II, 305-308.

and עַל־פִּי in relation to men. [53] If פֶּה is also transl. מֵימְרָא when the ref is to Yahweh's mouth in the lit. sense, this agrees with the finding that this transl. is also used for other parts of the body like the eye, face, hand, heart, and also the spirit, soul and voice of God. [54] This means that מֵימְרָא in this case serves to avoid anthropomorphism, though not consistently. [55]

3. Rabbinic Texts. In Rabb. texts no need is felt to interpret the expression "mouth of God." When bBB, 17a, Bar. attributes the death of Aaron and Moses עַל־פִּי יהוה Nu. 33:38 and Dt. 34:5 to a kiss of Yahweh, this is simply in accordance with a Jewish view whereby all the righteous die thus. [56] bChag., 14a speaks uninhibitedly of Yahweh's mouth and says that each word which issues from it becomes an angel. Cant. r., on 4:4 shows that a ⁓ naturally negative ⁓ significance attaches to the mouth of idols; the ref. here is to the evil-smelling mouth of Dagon.

4. Philo. Philo, however, can understand the mouth of Yahweh only as σύμβολον τοῦ λόγου (Leg. All., III, 176) and the ἐνεφύσησεν of Gn. 2:7 LXX only in a transf. sense as endowment with πνεῦμα or the giving of the soul; he decidely rejects a νομίσαι θεὸν στόματος ἢ μυκτήρων ὀργάνοις χρῆσθαι, Leg. All., I, 36. [57]

5. Qumran. [58] As regards the use of פֶּה in the religious sphere the Dead Sea Scrolls follow the OT. It is in keeping with their style and content that we often find ref. to the mouth (tongue, lips) of all men or all the righteous praising God, 1 QH 1:31; 6:14; 11:24; 17:17; 1 QM 14:6 (the individual worshipper, 1 QS 10:14, 23 f.), or the sacrifice of the lips, 1 QS 9:5, 26; 10:6, 8, or to the pure mouth (lips) of the righteous, 1 QS 10:21 f., 24. We also read of the mouth (tongue, teeth, lips) of the wicked enemy of the righteous, 1 QH 2:11, 34; 5:11, 13 f., 24, 27, of lying prophets, 1 QH 4:16, לשׁון גדופים "scornful speeches," 1 QS 4:11 and שׂפה עָרוּל "uncircumcised lips," 1 QH 2:18. Regulations come עַל־פִּי of the priests (1 QS 5:2, 3, 21; 6:19; 9:7; 1 QSa 1:23, 24) and the whole congregation (1 QS 5:22; 6:19, 21; 8:19; 9:2). The mouth and lips of the eschatological נשׂיא of the community are to have power to destroy the wicked, 1 QSb 5:24 f.

E. The New Testament.

So far as one may follow the use of a word which is none too common in the NT, its sphere of meaning is the same here as in the secular realm. The στόμα is the "mouth" of men or the "maw" of animals, while στόμα πρὸς στόμα in 2 Jn. 12; 3 Jn. 14 refers to the give and take of dialogue. Mostly στόμα is the organ of speech, e.g., in the common ἀνοίγω τὸ στόμα, which usually stresses the significance of what is being said, also R. 15:6: ἐν ἑνὶ στόματι → 692, 19. The transf. sense "word," "speech," occurs in Mt. 18:16 and 2 C. 13:1 (≡ Dt. 19:15): ἐπὶ στόματος δύο μαρτύρων..., Lk. 19:22: ἐκ τοῦ στόματός σου κρινῶ σε, 21:15: δώσω ὑμῖν στόμα καὶ σοφίαν. The looser extended use occurs in the expressions στόμα μαχαίρης in Lk. 21:24; Hb. 11:34 (→ 693, 1 ff.) and στόμα τῆς γῆς (→ 695, 21 ff.) in Rev. 12:16.

1. In the temptation story Jesus adopts the OT reference to God's mouth when He quotes Dt. 8:3 (LXX) in answer to the tempter's suggestion that by His Word

[53] Hamp, 141.
[54] Ibid., 26-34.
[55] Ibid., 25, 71-73.
[56] Ibid., 23, n. 3.
[57] In Vit. Mos., II, 213 he describes as παραδοξότατον the idea of a divine φωνὴ ὁρατή (Ex. 20:18).
[58] In this section I am indebted to the Leipzig OT Seminar, II.

He should change the stones of the desert into bread. [59] This saying has, of course, a twofold content. The first is that of the Mas. text, which says that the word proceeding from God's mouth creates manna for the sustenance of life (→ 696, 8 f.), with an emphasis on God's mouth, while the ῥῆμα which is added in the LXX lays the accent on the Word of God which confers eternal life, → II, 851, 23 ff.; VI, 579, 15 ff.

2. In view of the earthly life of Jesus it would be natural for the NT to refer again and again to the mouth of Jesus. Yet the only mention of His mouth in the ordinary human sense is in connection with the drinking of vinegar at the cross in Jn. 19:29. Luke likes to use ἐκ (ἀπὸ) τοῦ στόματος αὐτοῦ in relation to Jesus (4:22; 11:54; 22:71), but this evokes the idea of the majesty of this mouth and the validity and truth of what is spoken by it; λόγοι τῆς χάριτος (→ III, 38, 18 ff.) proceed from it, 4:22. The same applies to the words with which Mt. 5:2 introduces the Sermon on the Mount: ἀνοίξας τὸ στόμα αὐτοῦ ἐδίδασκεν αὐτοὺς λέγων. It is to the mouth of Christ that 1 Pt. 2:22 refers the prophetic witness οὐδὲ εὑρέθη δόλος ἐν τῷ στόματι αὐτοῦ (Is. 53:9), and this is the mouth which according to Mt. 13:34 f. will speak in parables of the kingdom of heaven, Ps. 78:2. In Ac. 22:14 [60] Paul heard from the mouth of the δίκαιος, the Messiah (→ II, 186, 26 ff.; 188, 44 ff.), the voice which elected him to be an apostle to humanity. But here already there speaks the mouth of the Risen Lord who is given the authority of the eschatological Judge in Rev. 1:16; 2:16; 19:15, 21. The sword which goes forth from the mouth is both figuratively and materially related very closely to the שֵׁבֶט פֶּה of the shoot of David in Is. 11:4 → 696, 22 f. The two are related with one another and with the ῥάβδος σιδηρᾶ (ψ 2:9) in Rev. 19:15, → VI, 494, n. 87; 969, 1 ff. What follows in Is. 11:4, namely, that He will scatter the wicked with the breath of His lips, is also applied to Jesus at 2 Th. 2:8 in the words ἀνελεῖ (τὸν ἄνομον, antichrist) τῷ πνεύματι τοῦ στόματος αὐτοῦ. [61] Spewing out of the mouth of Jesus is also an act of judgment, Rev. 3:16.

Among the apoc. figure in whose mouth the authority of eschatological judgment is put we also find the two witnesses (Moses and Elijah?), [62] from whose mouth there goes forth fire which burns up all their enemies (Rev. 11:5), and then again the horses from whose jaws proceed fire, smoke, and brimstone (Rev. 9:17-19). But the destructive power of the ungodly apoc. forces represented by the beasts also lies essentially in their mouths and jaws. The dragon, the serpent, sends forth from his mouth a stream of water to drown the woman, Rev. 12:15. The beast which represents antichrist (13:1-7) has a στόμα λαλοῦν μεγάλα καὶ βλασφημίας (v. 5, cf. his model in Da. 7:7 f.). The trinity of the dragon and the two beasts, antichrist and the false prophet [63] cause three unclean demonic spirits to hop forth from their mouths in the form of frogs, 16:13.

---

[59] Lk. 4:4 quotes only the first and negative part of the OT saying, while the Western texts which amplify the text leave out both here and in Mt. 4:4 the words which are of present interest: ἐκπορευομένῳ διὰ στόματος. In both cases it seems that offence was taken at the apparent anthropomorphism.
[60] Cf. Haench. Ag. on 3:14 with n. and on 22:14.
[61] Cf. Dob. Th., 284, n. 3.
[62] So Loh. Apk., ad loc. For Peter and Paul cf. J. Munck, Pt. u. Pls. in d. Offenbarung Johannis (1950), 56-81; O. Cullmann, Petrus² (1960), 99-101, esp. 100, n. 1.
[63] Cf. Loh. Apk., Exc. on 13:10.

3. The OT idea of God's Word in the mouth of the prophets (→ 696, 24 ff.) is found in the NT as God's speaking διὰ στόματος τῶν προφητῶν (Lk. 1:70; Ac. 3:18) or as the speaking of the Holy Ghost διὰ στόματος Δαυίδ (Ac. 1:16; 4:25). [64] Here, of course, Scripture is always interposed as intermediary → VI, 832, 28 ff. The reference is usually to it either explicitly (Ac. 1:16) or implicitly by quotation. But after the pattern of the OT prophet (Ez. 2:8-3:3) God's Word can also be put in the mouth of the primitive Christian prophet in the dramatic form of swallowing a little book, Rev. 10:8-11. This is apocalyptic prophecy. But as in the case of the prophets God also causes the missionary word, the evangelical message, to go out to the nations διὰ τοῦ στόματος of the apostles, as Luke has Peter himself say in Ac. 15:7. [65] The attack of the enemies of God and the Gospel is also directed against the mouth of the apostle in Ac. 23:2. [66]

4. In the mouth of him to whom the word of faith is proclaimed faith in the κύριος Ἰησοῦς becomes the confession which saves, as Paul says in R. 10:8-10 quoting Dt. 30:14 → VI, 209, 17 ff.; 217, 22 ff. The community as a whole is also to agree ἐν ἑνὶ στόματι in confession, laud and praise, R. 15:16 and in the words of Is. 45:23: πᾶσα γλῶσσα ἐξομολογήσηται, Paul also extends confession to the whole cosmos both in the sense of a praising of the κύριος (Phil. 2:11) and also in the sense of an eschatological confession of guilt (R. 14:11). Hb. 13:15, like Is. 57:19, has καρπὸς χειλέων for the sacrifice of praise and for confession, which are closely related, → V, 202, 27 ff.; 209, 15 ff.; 212, 13 ff.

5. To the high function accorded to the mouth there corresponds in apostolic exhortation the repeated demand to keep the mouth pure from all immoral or unchristian speech and to cause to be heard only that which is serviceable to the Christian life, Eph. 4:29; Col. 3:8; 1 Pt. 3:10 = Ps. 34:13. The abhorrent and unnatural use of the same mouth to praise God and curse man is sharply censured in Jm. 3:10-12. Rev. 14:5, using OT words, says of those who are perfected in heaven that no lie was found in their mouths. In so far as there is reference here to the purity of the mouth, this rests on the purity of what is spoken, and this again on the purity and renewing of the whole man, Col. 3:9 ff. Hence the NT can no longer speak of the ritual cleansing of the mouth (→ 694, 22 ff.; 696, 28 f.; 697, 11 f.). Jesus Himself in His teaching that what defiles a man is not that which passes through the mouth but that which comes from the heart and out of the mouth substitutes a moral concept of purity for the ritual concept. It is similarly said of

---

[64] On the text of 4:25 cf. Haench. Ag., ad loc. with n. In view of 1:16 I think it inadvisable to excise πνεῦμα ἅγιον from the text as a later addition. Cf. also H. W. Moule, "Ὁ τοῦ πατρὸς ἡμῶν κτλ. (Acts 4:25)," Exp. T., 51 (1939-40), 396; C. F. D. Moule, "H. W. Moule on Acts 4:25," Exp. T., 65 (1953), 220 f.

[65] Their preaching is also introduced by ἀνοίγω τὸ στόμα in Ac. 8:35; 10:34; 18:14; cf. ἄνοιξις τοῦ στόματος Eph. 6:19.

[66] This seems to me to be a sufficient reason why the high-priest struck Paul on the mouth. Paul had been speaking the previous day about his call to be the apostle of the Gentiles, and this aroused the hostility of the Jews, Ac. 22:21 f. When he said that he was walking with a clear conscience before God, Ananias was moved to punish him. He obviously regarded Paul's saying as something which could not be answered for before God.

the wicked man that his mouth confirms and reveals his nature → 697, 10 f. To show this Paul in R. 3:13 f. (→ III, 334, 27 ff.) uses the strong statements about this in the Psalms (ψ 5:10; 139:4; 9:28), cf. also Jd. 16. But the man whose mouth speaks otherwise than his heart is also castigated by Jesus (Mk. 7:6 and par.) with the prophetic saying in Is. 29:13 (LXX), and in 1 Jn. 3:18 a warning is given against loving only in tongue and not in deed.

Weiss

---

† στρατεύομαι, † στρατεία,
† στρατιά, † στράτευμα,
† στρατιώτης, † συστρατιώτης,
† στρατηγός, † στρατόπεδον,
† στρατολογέω

→ πανοπλία, V, 295, 19 ff.
→ πόλεμος, VI, 502, 21 ff.

Contents: A. The Word Group in Greek. B. The Word Group in the Old Testament. C. The Word Group in Judaism: 1. Josephus; 2. Philo; 3. Qumran. D. The Word Group in the New Testament: 1. The Apocalyptic Reference; 2. The Ordinary Reference; 3. Lucan Narrative; 4. Paul; 5. The Pastorals; 6. The Catholic Epistles; 7. A. Comparison. E. The Word Group in the Post-Apostolic Fathers.

A. The Word Group in Greek.

στρατός seems to be originally a part. (verbal adj.) of the root ster-[1] "to spread," hence first "spread out camp," then "army." Hom. uses the word 64 times in this sense, and 3 times the derived verb (ἀμφ-)εστρατόωντο "they lay in the field," Il., 11, 713. The meaning "army" became the norm.[2] In accounts of the deeds of individual heroes

---

στρατεύομαι κτλ. Bibl.: F. E. Adcock, *The Greek and Macedonian Art of War* (1957); E. Auerbach, J. Gutmann, Art. "Kriegswesen" in EJ, 10 (1934), 422-434; R. Bainton, "The Early Church and War," HThR, 39 (1946), 189-220; H. Bengtson, "Die Strategie in d. hell. Zeit. Ein Beitrag z. antiken Staatsrecht, I-III," *Münchner Beiträge z. Papyrusforschung u. antiken Rechtsgesch.*, 26 (1937); 32 (1944); 36 (1952); E. Bilabel, Art. "Strategos" in Pauly-W., 4a (1932), 183-252; C. D. Buck. "Words for Battle, War, Army and Soldier," *Class. Philol.*, 14 (1919), 1-19; G. Busolt, *Griech. Staatskunde*, I, 2³, Hndbch. Kl. AW, IV, 1, 1 (1926), esp. 1121-1131. G. T. Griffith, *The Mercenaries of the Hellenistic World* (1935); A. v. Harnack, *Militia Christi* (1905); S. Kraus, Art. "Heerwesen d. Juden," Jüd. Lex., II (1928), 1498-1501; E. and F. Lammert, Art. "Kriegskunst, griech.," Pauly-W., 11 (1922), 1827-1859; F. Lammert, Art. "Kriegskunst, röm." in Pauly-W. Suppl., 4 (1924), 1060-1101; M. Launey, *Recherches sur les armées hellén.*, I (1949); II (1950); W. Schwahn, Art. "Strategos" in Pauly-W. Suppl., 6 (1935), 1071-1158; H. Trümpy, *Kriegerische Fachausdrücke im griech. Epos,* Diss. Basel (1950).
1 Walde-Pok., II, 638; Boisacq, *s.v.*; Pokorny, 1030; Hofmann, *s.v.*; cf. στόρνυμι, στρώννυμι, στρωννύω.
2 In Aesch. Eum., 683 στρατός is synon. with λεώς (Attic for λαός), 681 and it means, not the army as mostly in Hom. Il., but the whole people → IV, 31, 12 ff. στρατός has the same sense when Orestes takes an oath of peace χώρα τῆδε καὶ τῷ σῷ στρατῷ, "to this land and thy people," Aesch. Eum., 762 or when Pind. Pyth., II, 87 distinguishes the σοφοί and τύραννοι from the λάβρος στρατός "the unruly mob." We are not to think here of a special non-military development of the concept of the spread out camp. It is rather presupposed that the men capable of bearing arms are the natural protectors and the only obvious representatives of the whole.

of the earlier period, the stem στρατο- found only limited use. [3] But when the ref. was to the achievements of larger groups it was employed more often and led to several derivates and constructs.

1. The oldest derivate (from Aesch., Hdt.) is στρατεύω act. "I am in the στρατός," mid. (mostly intr.) "I undertake a campaign," "do military service" (also as a profession). [4] But the act. and mid. are not always strictly differentiated: στρατεύειν ἐπὶ τοὺς Πέρσας, Hdt., I, 77, 3; Ἀσσύριοι δὲ στρατευόμενοι, VII, 63. Both can take an acc. obj.: οὐδεὶς στρατεύσας ἄδικα σῶς ἦλθεν πάλιν, Eur. Fr., 353 (TGF, 466); τὸν ἱερὸν καλούμενον πόλεμον ἐστράτευσαν (→ VI, 503, n. 3), Thuc., I, 112, 5; οἶσθ' ἦν στρατείαν ἐστράτευσ' ὀλεθρίαν, Eur. Suppl., 116. With the mid. we often find στρατείας, cf. τὰς στρατείας στρατευόμενος, Isaeus Or., X, 25, cf. Ditt. Syll.[3], I, 346, 55 f. A use which is not strictly military is possible; higher beings say: ἑνὸς δ' ἐπ' ἀνδρὸς δώματα στρατεύομεν, Eur. Herc. Fur., 825 (conjecture). From Eur. we find the compound ἐπιστρατεύω, Ba., 784 → 705, 15 f.

2. From στρατεύω comes the noun στρατεία (from Aesch., Hdt.). It denotes the essential activity of him who is in the στρατός, "campaign": ἀπὸ στρατείας ἄνδρα σώσαντος θεοῦ, "the man who by divine protection comes back from the campaign," Aesch. Ag., 603, or "military service": πολεμικοὶ ἀθληταί must be a match for the many vicissitudes ἐν ταῖς στρατείαις, Plat. Resp., III, 404a. It then means "military discipline" ὅσα πρὸς διαφθορὰν τῆς ἀκριβοῦς στρατείας εὕροντο, "which was invented to corrupt strict military discipline," Dio C., 78, 36. In the section Epict. Diss., III, 24, 31-37, which has many military comparisons, it can be said of human life: στρατεία τίς ἐστιν ὁ βίος ἑκάστου, 24, 34.

3. The collective στρατιά (from Pind., Aesch.) is synon. with "army": Ἀθηναῖοι γὰρ ... πολλῇ στρατιᾷ ὥρμηνται καὶ ναυτικῇ καὶ πεζῇ, Thuc., VI, 33, 2, also VII, 15, 1. It can also denote a non-military (Pind. Pyth., XI, 50) or superterrestrial "host": τῷ δὲ ἔπεται στρατιὰ θεῶν τε καὶ δαιμόνων, Plat. Phaedr., 246e. It is often used in the sense of στρατεία "campaign," πολλοῖς δ' ἑτέροις ἀπὸ τῶν ὤμων ἐν ταῖς στρατιαῖς ἔρριπται τὸ σκιάδειον, Aristoph. Thes., 827 ff., or (rarely, and never in inscr.) στρατεία can be used in the sense of στρατιά: ὃς ἐς (vl. γᾶν) Τροίαν χιλιόναυν ἦλυθ' ἔχων στρατίαν, Eur. Rhes., 261 ff. In prose this is probably to be explained in many cases by the influence of itacism, while metrical reasons explain it in poetry. Only by extreme conjectures can one avoid the sense "campaign" for the oxytone στρατιά. [5]

4. στράτευμα (from Aesch., Hdt.) is mostly used for "army division": ὁρῶ δὲ φῦλα τρία τριῶν στρατευμάτων, [6] Eur. Suppl., 653; τὰ κλεινὰ ποῦ 'στί μοι στρατεύματα; Eur. Hel., 453; τῆς τε στρατιᾶς παμπληθοῦς συνειλεγμένης, ὅτε δὴ ἀντίπαλα καὶ ἰσόρροπα ᾠήθη εἶναι τὰ ἑαυτοῦ στρατεύματα τῷ πλήθει τῶν βαρβάρων, Herodian. Hist., VI, 5, 1. Xenoph. Hist. Graec., IV, 4, 19 distinguishes τὸ πολιτικὸν στράτευμα from the σύμμαχοι. The simple τὸ πολιτικόν is used for this in V, 3, 25 → 703, 28 and 34. "Division" is not an exact equivalent and in some passages there seems to be no distinction between στράτευμα and στρατός or στρατιά, e.g., στράτευμα μὲν (vl.) Παλλάδος κριθήσεται, Eur. Suppl., 601, cf. Eur. Cyc., 283. Larger groupings are usually meant, but one cannot speak of a minimum strength below which there can be no talk of στράτευμα.

---

[3] Cf. Trümpy, 180.
[4] Schwyzer, II, 232.
[5] M. Scheller, Die Oxytonierung d. griech. Subst. auf -ιᾱ, Diss. Zürich (1951), 84 f.
[6] vl. συστρατευμάτων is secondary.

5. The individual on military service could be called στρατευόμενος, an ἐκ κατα-λόγου στρατευόμενος, Xenoph. Mem., III, 4, 1 is "in military service from the prescribed age." For the position into which one came when enlisted acc. to the κατάλογος or enrolment list there then came into use the noun στρατιώτης [7] from the same stem but more strictly as a term denoting a profession; this is found from Hdt., e.g., IV, 134, 3, and it is a tt. there. [8] Since the fem. adj. στρατιῶτις "warlike" is found already in Aesch. Ag., 46, the noun can hardly be new in the age of Hdt. [9] Alongside the deeds and responsible decisions of the whole στρατός, however, those of the individual στρατιώτης are not so prominent as those of the individual fighters in the different conditions of Homer's day, Hom. Il. This does not mean, however, that στρατιώτης is used in a somewhat disparaging sense. The bearer of the designation was "only" a στρατιώτης in the same sense as his superior was "only" a στρατηγός → 704, 16 ff. Some of the respect for the μαχηταί and αἰχμηταί [10] of earlier times was transferred to the στρατιῶται. They took the στρατιωτικὸς ὅρκος (→ VI, 504, 22 f.) [11] for which there are no modern analogies. Within the population they thus constituted a pledged society whose ethos was respected, [12] and which could be trusted, as it was to good effect by Philip II of Macedonia and Alexander. Yet in spite of their success recruitment could not be restricted as a rule to native peasants and citizens; indeed, this was already the exception in the time of these kings. For already from the end of the Peloponnesian War it had been shown more and more that long-service professional soldiers were in gen. superior to citizen soldiers. But these professionals were mostly mercenaries (μισθοφόροι); [13] they were also called στρατιῶται from the 4th cent. on. [14] This brought new and and in part adverse associations to the word. One may see this, e.g., when Aristot. discusses a question which arises in every age, namely, what motive apart from fear of punishment will cause men to stand to the death in an apparently hopeless situation. He declares: ... οἱ στρατιῶται δὲ δειλοὶ γίνονται, ὅταν ὑπερτείνῃ ὁ κίνδυνος καὶ λείπωνται τοῖς πλήθεσι καὶ ταῖς παρασκευαῖς· πρῶτοι γὰρ φεύγουσι, τὰ δὲ πολιτικὰ μένοντα ἀποθνήσκει, Aristot. Eth. Nic., III, 11, p. 1116b, 15 ff. He thus finds the motive he seeks only in the citizen army which has its domestic and religious roots in the πόλις and which is driven to fight quite unequivocally by a desire to protect the motherland. This army prefers θάνατος to αἰσχρόν, ibid., 1116b, 15 ff. Aristot. is thinking here in terms of the πόλις and does not take into account the change already wrought by the professional soldiers of territorial states, but his terminology is influenced by this, for he uses τὰ πολιτικά for the citizen army and στρατιῶται only for the μισθοφόροι who on his view are in the last resort unreliable. When the avarice and luxury-loving of μισθοφόροι are criticised, they can be called στρατιῶται without any reservation: μισθοφόρων ἁρπαξιβίων σκηνὴ στρατιωτῶν, "a feast which is

---

[7] Cf. Schwyzer, I, 500; G. Redard, Les noms grecs en -της, -τις (1949), 9.

[8] Trümpy, 180.

[9] Later we sometimes find the noun with part.: τοῖς στρατιώταις τοῖς παρὰ τεῖ πόλει στρατευομ[ένοις], Ditt. Syll.[3], I, 485, 21.

[10] Trümpy, 129 and 176.

[11] τῶν γὰρ τριῶν ταγμάτων ἔτι κύριος ἦν τοῖς στρατιωτικοῖς ὅρκοις κατειργο-μένων, καὶ οὐδεὶς ἀπολείπεσθαι τῶν σημείων ἠξίου· τοσοῦτον ἴσχυσεν ὁ τῶν ὅρκων ἐν ἑκάστῳ φόβος, Dion. Hal. Ant. Rom., 6, 45, 1; 6, 23, 2.

[12] The rejection of suicide in Platonic and Pythagorean circles is influenced by the soldierly ethos. The φρουρά in which men find themselves (Plat. Phaed., 62b) is a military post not to be left without orders: vetat Pythagoras iniussu imperatoris, id est dei, de praesidio et statione vitae decedere, Cic. De senectute, 73, cf. Epict Diss., I, 9, 24; III, 24, 99 etc. Cf. R. Hirzel, "Der Selbstmord," ARW, 11 (1908), 75-104, 243-284, 417-476, esp. 422 f., 262 f., 273, n. 3, and 466.

[13] The ἄμισθοι mentioned in the oath of Eumenes I in Ditt. Or., I, 266, 56 are στρατιῶται πολιτικοί as distinct from mercenaries, cf. Bengtson, II, 204, esp. n. 2.

[14] Liddell-Scott, s.v., I, 2.

arranged by mercenary στρατιῶται who live by booty," Archestratos Fr., 61, 4. [15] One may thus see that στρατιῶται were not entirely popular among the people. [16] But professional soldiers would not have come to stay if their unpopularity and the rather anachronistic judgment of Aristot. had been true symptoms of the morale of the στρατιῶται of antiquity. Long-serving "soldiers of fortune" (στρατεύεσθαι ... μισθοῦ, Xenoph. Mem., III, 4, 1) were found to be quite satisfactory. They rated well as πολεμικοί, Xenoph. Cyrop., III, 2, 7. Their discipline and the fearless fulfilment of their military duties, esp. in the Roman army, found acknowledgment in popular philosophy → n. 12. That the name στρατιώτης, in keeping with its derivation, [17] remained a good one may be seen from the compound συστρατιώτης (from Xenoph.) "comrade in arms." Only those who had been through experiences of battle together greeted one another thus, Xenoph. Hist. Graec., II, 4, 20, cf. Plat. Resp., VIII, 556c. The word takes on something of the nuance of φίλος, Aristot. Eth. Nic., VIII, 11, p. 1159b, 27 ff. Acc. to Suet. Divus Julius, 67 Caesar used the honour his troops with the address commilitones (συστρατιῶται, Polyaen. Strat., VIII, 23, 22).

6. στρατηγός (from Archiloch., Aesch., Hdt.) is the "military leader," though later the usage goes much beyond this original and persistent sense. This may be connected with the fact that military leaders were often entrusted with the oversight of civil affairs (→ n. 2) and possibly with the fact that military designations were often transferred to civil offices. But a more basic pt. is that in the great days of Athens the στρατηγός, though formally subject to the ἄρχων, had very high political importance, and the official vocabulary of Hell. governments was much influenced by Athens. Hence στρατηγός became one of the main terms for leading provincial [18] or municipal officials, BGU, III, 729, 1 (3.X. 144 A.D.); it was also the transl. of consul [19] or praetor, Ditt. Syll.[3], II, 601, 1. Military leaders and directors of the royal hunt could both be called by the same title στρατηγός: στρατηγοὶ πολέμων καὶ κυνηγησίων, Ps.-Aristot. Mund., 6, p. 398a, 24 f. [20] στρατηγέω (from Hdt.) "I am στρατηγός," can thus relate to a high military (Hdt., V, 28; Andoc., I, 147) or civil office (BGU, VI, 1297, 4 [248/7 B.C.]), including that of consul (Polyb., 2, 21, 7) or praetor (Plut. Anton., [6, I, 918e]). Where the noun στρατηγία (from Hdt.) is used in a military sense it means "leading the army" in gen. (Plat. Resp., VII, 527d) or "strategy" in part. (Xenoph. Mem., III, 1, 5, 6), also "tactics" (Xenoph. Cyrop., I, 6, 12), then the "office of general" (Eur. Andr., 678, 704) and sometimes "generalship," Diod. S., 17, 23. In the civil sphere it is used for the office of a high official [21] or his sphere of office, Strabo, 12, 1, 4. στρατήγημα (from Ion of Chios) means lit. "act of a general"; it is used for "generalship" in Xenoph. Mem., III, 5, 22; transf. τὸ στρατήγημα τῶν λόγων, Ps.-Dion. Hal. Art. Rhet., IX, 8.

7. στρατόπεδον (from Aesch., Hdt.) is as such the site of the στρατός, the "camp": στρατὸς στρατόπεδον λιπών, Aesch. Sept. c. Theb., 79. But it can also be used for the army itself (Hdt., IX, 53, 1) or a part of it, e.g., a legion: ἔστι δὲ παρὰ 'Ρωμαίοις

---

[15] Ed. P. Brandt in Corpusculum Poesis Epicae Graecae Ludibundae, I (1888).
[16] On the life of soldiers cf. M. Rostovtzeff, Gesellschafts- u. Wirtschaftsgesch. d. hell. Welt, III (1956), 1097 f., n. 16 - n. 20.
[17] The derivation should be noted when the word is transl. "soldier" (Germ. Soldat) which now means more than its lowly but forgotten derivation from Söldner = "mercenary" implies. Thus far no simple term has been found to denote the higher allegiance which differentiates the two.
[18] Publ. de la Société Royale Égypt. de Papyrologie, ed. O. Guéraud, I (1931), 1, 12.
[19] στρατηγὸς ὕπατος Polyb., 1, 52, 5; στρατηγός alone, 6, 15, 7 f., later usually ὕπατος alone.
[20] Bibl. v. Pr.-Bauer[5], s.v.
[21] Publ. (→ n. 18), I, 63, 10.

τὰ πάντα τέτταρα στρατόπεδα ῾Ρωμαϊκὰ χωρὶς τῶν συμμάχων, Polyb., 1, 16, 2 etc. cf. BGU, II, 362, 13, 17 (215 A.D.). [22] From it comes στρατοπεδεύω (mid. from Hdt.) "I pitch a camp" (Xenoph. An., VII, 6, 24) or gen. "I take up a position" (Hdt., VII, 124 of a fleet). The verb leads to the noun στρατοπεδεία "camp," "camp-site," Xenoph. Hist. Graec., IV, 1, 24. στρατοπεδάρχης is a "camp commandant" or gen. a military "commander," Dion. Hal. Ant. Rom., 10, 36. [23]

8. στρατολογέω "I enlist for military service" is found from the 1st cent. B.C.: στρατολογήσαντες ... τοὺς ὅπλα φέρειν δυναμένους, Dion. Hal. Ant. Rom., 11, 24. The word is used in the same sense in the pass., e.g., Plut. De Caesare, 35 (I, 724 f.).

B. The Word Group in the Old Testament. [24]

In view of the common use of the group we should expect its frequent occurrence in the translation of a book like the OT which deals so much with wars and warriors. But the findings correspond to our expectations only to a limited degree.

1. The simple στρατεύω occurs only 3 times in transl. of a Hbr. word: Is. 29:7 for צָבָא; Ju. 19:8 and 2 S. 15:28 for מָחַה hitp. The compound ἐπιστρατεύω occurs 4 times: Is. 29:7 f.; 31:4; Zech. 14:12 for צָבָא and ἐκστρατεύω for יָצָא at Prv. 30:27. The simple is also found in its lit. sense at 1 Εσδρ. 4:6; 2 Macc. 9:23, and in a transf. sense for martyrdom at 4 Macc. 9:24: ἱερὰν καὶ εὐγενῆ στρατείαν στρατεύσασθε περὶ τῆς εὐσεβείας. ἐπιστρατεύω occurs in the lit. sense at 2 Macc. 12:27; 3 Macc. 5:43. ᾽Α and Σ at Ex. 38:8 and ᾽Α at Nu. 8:24 have στρατεύω for service in the tabernacle as a rendering of צָבָא.

2. στρατιά or στρατεία [25] is used 22 times for צָבָא. Since this means "military service" as well as "army" (Nu. 31:36; Dt. 24:5 → 702, 18) and can also be used fig. for the afflictions of the "conflict" of life (Is. 40:2; Job 7:1; 10:17; 14:14; Da. 10:1 → 702, 22 f.), there is naturally an analogy between the Gk. and Hbr. terms. But both the verb צָבָא (Nu. 4:23; 8:24; 1 S. 2:22) and the noun (Nu. 4:3, 23, 30, 35) can also be used for cultic service. In this, and in the connection of צָבָא with the name of God [26] יְהוָה צְבָאוֹת (→ II, 292, 26 ff.) one may see the special sanctity which always was attached to the term, and not just when there was ref. to a supernatural צָבָא in the good (Jos. 5:14; 1 K. 22:19; 2 Ch. 18:18; Is. 34:4; 40:26 etc.) or the bad sense (Dt. 4:19; 17:3; Jer. 19:13 cf. Ιερ. 7:18); in contrast pre-Chr. Gk. lit. speaks only rarely of a "holy" [27] division of the army. In a people who always retained some awareness of the holy war (→ VI, 507, 34 ff.) צָבָא could thus denote the military representatives of the totality only to the degree that the

---

22 The first and second senses occur shortly after one another in Hdt., IX, 53, 1. 4.
23 Bibl. Pr.-Bauer⁵, s.v. In Ac. 28:16 στρατοπέδαρχος or στρατοπεδάρχης is secondary.
24 Cf. on this P. Katz, "The Text of 2 Macc. Reconsidered," ZNW, 51 (1960), 10-30. The emendations there proposed on good grounds for the group (23-28) are taken into account in what follows. Thus στραγγεύω is perhaps to be read for στρατεύω in Ju. 19:8; 2 S. 15:28, and στρατοπεδεύω in 2 Macc. 15:17, though cf. στρατεύω for στρατοπεδεύω at Ex. 14:10; Dt. 1:40; 2 Macc. 9:23. στραγγεύω is probably the original at Gn. 12:9 for στρατοπεδεύω, also στρατιά for στρατηγία at 1 K. 2:35 and στρατήγημα for στράτευμα at Jdt. 11:8.
25 Mostly στρατιά. On the hard problem of distinguishing the two (→ 702, 27 ff.) cf. P. Katz, Philo's Bible (1950), 149. στρατεία is certain in LXX 4 Macc. 9:24 (→ line 18 f.), also ᾽Α Is. 40:2; Job 7:1; 10:17 etc.
26 Cf. on this the express discussion in Katz, op. cit., 146-149.
27 ... καὶ ἱερᾶς συγκλήτου καὶ δήμου τοῦ ῾Ρωμαίων καὶ ἱερῶν στρατευμάτων, Ditt. Syll.³, II, 880, 6 f.

totality was the people of the one God. Hence the correspondence between צָבָא and στρατιά is very limited. It is understandable why צָבָא is transl. 5 times as often by δύναμις (→ II, 290, 32 ff.) as by στρατιά.

3. στρατόπεδον is used in Ιερ. 41(34):1 for חַיִל "military might." It is not a transl. at Ιερ. 48:12; 2 Macc. 8:12; 9:9; 3 Macc. 6:17; 4 Macc. 3:13. In the last 2 instances it means "camp," in the others "army." στρατοπεδεύω occurs 7 times as a transl.: Ex. 13:20; 14:2 for חנה; Gn. 12:9; Ex. 14:10; Dt. 1:40 for נסע; Nu. 24:2 for שכן. The verb occurs without Hbr. equivalent at Prv. 4:15; 2 Macc. 15:17 (vl.); 4 Macc. 3:8; 18:5 vl. Finally the noun στρατοπεδεία is used for מָלוֹן ("night quarters") at Jos. 4:3, and it also occurs in 2 Macc. 13:14.

4. The most common word of the group in the LXX is that which is furthest from the military sphere in non-bibl. lit. (→ 704, 22 ff.): στρατηγός. סָגָן "governor," "head," is transl. by this at Ιερ. 28:23, 28, 57; Ez. 23:6, 12, 23; Neh. 2:16 etc., also Aram. סְגַן at Da. 3:2, 3, then מֶלֶךְ at Job 15:24 and שַׂר at 1 S. 29:3 f.; 1 Ch. 11:6; Da. 10:20. The LXX στρατηγός, when used for the Hbr. term, is thus a civil leader. When there is ref. to a military leader the various ranks are mentioned: πεντηκόνταρχος, 2 K. 1:9; Is. 3:3; ἑκατόνταρχος and χιλίαρχος, 1 S. 22:7; also ἄρχων Ju. 7:25; 2 S. 18:5; 24:2; 1 K. 15:20; 2 K. 4:13 etc. When στρατηγός was used it was often combined with the prefix ἀρχι- to give ἀρχιστράτηγος, which is not found prior to the LXX, Gn. 21:22 etc. στρατηγός never occurs alone for שַׂר צָבָא or שַׂר־הַצָּבָא. In keeping is the fact that στρατός in 2 Macc. 8:35; 4 Macc. 3:8 etc., along with derivates like στράτευμα (1 Macc. 9:34; 2 Macc. 5:24; 8:21; 12:38; 13:13; 4 Macc. 5:1), στρατηγέω in 2 Macc. 10:32; 14:31, στρατήγημα in Jdt. 11:8; 2 Macc. 14:29, and the adj. στρατιῶτις in 4 Macc. 16:14, occur almost exclusively in the Books of Maccabees, i.e., in texts not influenced by a Hbr. original.

5. Worth noting is that even the important noun στρατιώτης occurs in transl. (for חָלָל) only once at 2 S. 23:8 and here only as vl. for what is certainly the more original τραυματίας. It then occurs only in 2 Macc. 5:12; 14:39; 3 Macc. 3:12; 4 Macc. 17:23. The ref. in 4 Macc. 3:7, 12 is to Jewish soldiers. The LXX would actually have given rise to a false impression if it had used στρατιώτης for the warrior of ancient Israel, אִישׁ מִלְחָמָה ,אִישׁ־הַמִּלְחָמָה, גִּבּוֹר etc. For this we often find μαχητής and πολεμιστής, i.e., terms which were the most important and central ones for the fighter in non-bibl. Gk. until Hdt. made στρατιώτης a tt. → 703, 5 f. [28]

The translators did not intentionally slight the group but when they had the Hebrew before them they saw the difference between it and OT ideas and were thus able to make only comparatively sparing use of it. This difficulty did not exist when they were not under the control of a Hebrew text. It is significant that of the instances of the group more than a third are in the Books of Maccabees. There the authors could write as they were accustomed to speak.

C. The Word Group in Judaism.

1. Josephus. The same applies to Ep. Ar., [29] Philo, and Joseph. as to Maccabees. In the case of Jos. his readers and circumstances meant that there could be no objection

---

[28] Trümpy, 180.
[29] στράτευμα Ep. Ar., 37; στρατηγός, 280; στρατόπεδον, 20.

to the group. He uses all the terms which occur in the NT in their lit. sense,[30] also ἀρχιστράτηγος for Abner in Ant., 6, 235 → 706, 18 ff.

2. Philo. In Philo the patriarch Judah is ἀρχιστράτηγος in Congr., 125. Philo also uses other words of the group lit., στρατός in Poster. C., 119; στρατιά "military service" in Virt., 28; στρατηγός Vit. Mos., I, 313; στρατηγικός Agric., 87 (Moses knew τακτικὰ καὶ στρατηγικά, first lit., then transf.); στρατήγημα "cunning" (not really military) Spec. Leg., IV, 51; Virt., 37; Pream. Poen., 25; στρατόπεδον Agric., 11. It is perhaps significant that though he has στρατιωτικὸς κατάλογος (→ 703, 2 ff.) for military enrolment in Virt., 23 and 31 the word στρατιώτης itself is not used. He could hardly be kept back from using it by the idea of the warrior of earlier days, → 706, 28 ff. What restrained him was the thought of the contemporary Roman legionary. To his way of thinking this was a figure which should not be connected with the lofty subjects under discussion; it should not be talked about.[31]

Philo uses the military expressions of the group more commonly in a transf. sense in theological or psychological statements. He calls God τὸν ἄρχοντα τῆς μεγαλοπόλεως, τὸν στρατάρχην τῆς ἀηττήτου στρατιᾶς, "the leader of the invincible host," Decal., 53, cf. Virt., 77. In connection with the civil war of desires (→ VI, 512, 29 ff.) he declares that no one still on this campaign can be a priest τὴν ἀνθρωπίνην καὶ θνητὴν στρατευόμενος στρατείαν, Ebr., 75 f.; but Moses can be called στρατευσάμενος γὰρ στρατείαν τὴν ὑπὲρ ἀρετῆς, Leg. All., III, 14. The holy concepts of reason οἱ ἱεροὶ λόγοι take him as ἡγεμών and στρατηγός, Sacr. AC, 130. στρατιά is always the heavenly host of the stars, Op. Mund., 113; Spec. Leg., I, 267; III, 187; Praem. Poen., 41. With ref. to the planets Decal., 104 also speaks of the τάξις τοῦ θείου στρατοπέδου; in Ebr., 143 the universe in gen. is θεῖον στρατόπεδον. Yet στρατεύεσθαι is also used of the human σῶμα which is far from the divine σκηνή (Det. Pot. Ins., 160) or the μετὰ σώματος βίος (Ebr., 99 f.), war (→ 702, 21 ff.) and its tumult (πολέμου φωναί, Ebr., 104) being the normal state (φυσικώτατα Ebr., 99) with no trace of εἰρήνη (→ VI, 513, 4 ff.) (μετουσίαν εἰρήνης οὐκ ἔχοντα, Leg. All., III, 46, cf. Gig., 54; Ebr., 124).

3. Qumran. Whether the military structure of the Qumran communities, apart from the bibl. basis and Roman influence (1 QM), was also determined by the Gk. ethos expressed in the word group, it is hard to say. If one were to imagine a Gk. transl. of the Scrolls it would be equally possible to envisage both a common use of words derived from στρατο- and also their complete absence.[32]

---

[30] The Jewish soldiers under his command are στρατιῶται for Jos. at Bell., 2, 578, 620, 634 etc. He notes incidentally in 2, 583 that he can rely on μισθοφόροι (→ 704, 5 ff.) more than his own people. The נַעַר (LXX παιδάριον) who accompanies Gideon into the enemy camp in Ju. 7:10 f. is also a στρατιώτης in Ant., 5, 218. στρατολογέω is sometimes used in a surprisingly broad sense. In Bell., 5, 395 Jos. uses the verb to show that the Romans were brought to Palestine by the Jews themselves, while it expresses the securing of God as an ally in 5, 380. Also worth noting is the fact that στρατεία is used in distinction between real military action and police action (with πόλεμος) τὴν μὲν στρατείαν οὐ στρατείαν ἔλεγεν, ἀλλ' ἐπὶ δικαίαν τῶν ἰδίων ἀπαίτησιν χρημάτων, Ant., 16, 343.

[31] Krauss Lehnw., I, 214 pts. out that in Judaism στρατηγός as a loan word (אסטרטיגוס) is also used for the ordinary soldier. This shows "that for the Jew a simple Roman soldier might be as terrible as the highest officer." στρατιά(אסטרטיא) and στρατιώτης (אסטרטיוס) also occur as loan words, cf. Krauss, II, 83 f., 97 f., 380, 413.

[32] στρατηγός, στρατόπεδον and στρατοπεδεύω would be the most likely. For the military expressions found in the Scrolls → V, 298, 25 ff.

D. The Word Group in the New Testament.

1. The Apocalyptic Reference.

According to Mk. 13:7; Mt. 24:6, cf. Lk. 21:9 the communities of the NT period had to reckon with πόλεμοι and ἀκοαὶ πολέμων before the end of the present aeon. If they were the victims of military operations such as that of the στρατόπεδα of Titus besieging Jerusalem, they saw therein a necessary action which Jesus Himself had foretold (Lk. 21:20) and which demanded of them a readiness for extreme suffering but not in any sense for active participation on either side. The divine in Rev. 9:15 saw the demonic στρατεύματα appointed to destroy a third part of the race, and in another vision in 19:19b he saw the heavenly στράτευμα (19:14 plur.) of the Rider on the white horse (v. 13), the λόγος τοῦ θεοῦ (→ III, 339, 7 ff.), the βασιλεὺς βασιλέων καὶ κύριος κυρίων, v. 16. In the same vision the seer also saw the earthly στρατεύματα which under the command of the kings of the earth came out to fight the βασιλεὺς βασιλέων and His στράτευμα (v. 19a). What he does not see is the positive counterpart one might have expected, namely, another earthly στράτευμα which, impelled by faith, allies itself with the heavenly host and hurries to the aid of the βασιλεὺς βασιλέων, cf. Ju. 5:23. For primitive Christianity the idea that this King needed the help of earthly στρατεύματα, or even wanted it, would have been more than *sancta simplicitas;* it is not found at all in its visions of the future. [33] It does occur in relation to the biblical past. Heroes of the holy wars of every age (Hb. 11:33 f) belong to the cloud of witnesses of Hb. 12:1. Nevertheless, the ἀγών (→ I, 138, 19 ff.) of this v., which the witnesses encourage us to endure victoriously, is no στρατεία. The witnesses offer an example of πίστις, not of warlike achievement, → VI, 514, 22 ff.

2. The Ordinary Reference.

Roman στρατεύματα formed an important factor in the life of the churches. Christians came into contact with soldiers and their officers, and they had to take up a position in relation to them. Unlike contemporary Jews, they did not have to see in them potential enemies in a future struggle. But it was clear to them that contemporary military practice was dominated by pagan (or Zealot-Jewish) thinking. Where that could lead, and would necessarily lead, might be seen from Ps. 2:2 (cf. Ac. 4:25-28) quite apart from Rev. 19:19. No Gentile could accept responsibility for the serious offence of refusing obedience before the enemy just because in this case the enemy was the God of the Jews and His Anointed. For Christians, however, this insight was accompanied by the further insight that there was resistance to the true God in all circles and not merely among soldiers (Rev. 13:16 f.). These soldiers could hardly see in their status anything other than a particularly brave and disciplined profession. Christians, who knew they owed unconditional obedience to

---

[33] The reader is naturally aware that the believer to his dying day in this world is engaged in battle with hostile transcendent forces. The weapons in this war may be compared with earthly weapons (→ V, 300, 28 ff.) and as in earthly wars he fights alongside others of like mind. But the bond which unites those who fight on this front is so different from that of a στράτευμα that the NT never uses words of the group for the fight of believers against Satanic power. Where the words are used with no express mention of the enemy, one is not then to supply the idea of Satanic opposition.

God, could observe and value as such the unconditional obedience a soldier rendered to his superior even though the bond might finally be an evil one, Mt. 8:5-13; Lk. 7:1-10. Thus the obedience of the στρατιώτης to a hecatontarch threw light on the authority of Jesus, Mt. 8:9; Lk. 7:8. In the passion story, of course, the στρατιῶται who are under orders to carry out the crucifixion arbitrarily make sport of Jesus, Mk. 15:16 ff.; Mt. 27:27 ff.; Lk. 23:36 f.; Jn. 19:2 ff. But what would seem to be the very earliest tradition (Mk. 15:39; Mt. 27:54; Lk. 23:47) also tells of the centurion who confessed Jesus after His death. If στρατιῶται are expressly mentioned in relation to the dividing of the clothes (Jn. 19:23 f.) and the thrust in the side (Jn. 19:32, 34), one can hardly deduce from this that their guilt is particularly emphasised thereby. On the other hand it is on theological grounds that Mt. in 28:12 tells of the way in which the military watch on the tomb of Jesus was ready to take a bribe.

3. Lucan Narrative.

Concerning the usage of Lucan narrative it may be noted that only here in the NT do we find the words στρατηγός (→ 704, 22 ff.), στρατόπεδον (→ 704, 39 ff.) and στρατιά. The last term is employed only for super-terrestrial hosts (→ 707, 21 ff.). The στρατιὰ τοῦ οὐρανοῦ is mentioned in Ac. 7:42 to call to remembrance, on the basis of Jer. 19:13 and Jer. 7:18 LXX, the idolatry of the past which has not yet been finally eliminated. The στρατιὰ οὐράνιος (vl. οὐρανοῦ) of Lk. 2:13, however, praises the one God at the nativity. Lk. 3:14 mentions στρατευόμενοι among John's audience without saying whether they were Gentile or Jewish troops. In Ac. 27:42 the στρατιῶται want to kill Paul and the other prisoners lest they escape, though only a short time before (27:31 f.) they had readily followed Paul's advice. But it is another member of the army, a centurion, who shows favour to Paul and restrains them. This was the man who earlier (v. 11) had overruled Paul when he did not really know him. The στρατιῶται mentioned elsewhere in Ac. (12:4, 6, 18; 21:32, 35; 23:23, 31; 28:16) always behave with correctness. In Ac. 12:19 it would seem that the freeing of Peter cost his military guards their lives even though they carried out their orders, but the author does not stop to tell us about this tragedy. The chiliarch Claudius Lysias decides overhastily to examine Paul by scourging after his speech (Ac. 22:24), but earlier (21:40) and then again when he has seen his mistake (22:27) he is friendly and affable towards him (23:10, 17-30). The considerable size [34] of the στράτευμα (v. 27) which in Ac. 23:23 guards Paul on the way from Jerusalem to Antipatris and Caesarea at the chiliarch's command shows how seriously a Roman chiliarch [35] could take Paul's case. Finally

---

[34] Cf. Haench. Ag., ad loc. The other στρατεύματα mentioned in Lucan narrative are obviously much smaller. Ac. 23:10 refers to a division of the watch in the castle Antonia and Lk. 23:11 to a modest military detail which Herod took with him for his stay in Jerusalem. The fact that the same term can be used for companies of very different size is common in all ages. Naturally one cannot say what is the size of the στρατεύματα of the king in the parable of Jesus in Mt. 22:7.
[35] Lk. never speaks of a στρατηγός of similar understanding, but he does not use this term in a military sense → 706, 14 ff. The στρατηγὸς τοῦ ἱεροῦ of Ac. 4:1; 5:24, 26 is the head of the temple police, cf. Haench. Ag. on 4:1. His highest subordinates bear the same title in Lk. 22:4, 52. The στρατηγοί in Philippi in Ac. 16:20, 22, 35, 36, 38 are the chief officials, Haench. Ag. on 16:20. Christians often seem to have had more to fear and less to hope for from the caprice of civil authorities than from disciplined troops.

the pious centurion Cornelius (Ac. 10 f.) stands at a decisive point in Luke's depiction of the story of the Christian mission; we also read of a στρατιώτης εὐσεβής in his company, 10:7. One may well ask whether in the period spanned by Acts στρατιῶται were not often ruthless in their dealings with Christians. Luke seems to prefer to mention them in situations in which they act according to his own understanding. He obviously believes in general that members of the army are no less open to the Gospel than other pagans. On the other hand, one should not overlook a certain reservation in Luke. He never expresses the hope that a Christian will behave like a soldier and it certainly never occurs to him to describe a Christian in a transferred sense as the στρατιώτης or στρατευόμενος of his κύριος, or to have the apostle Paul use expressions of this kind. As he sees it, this would be to lessen the distance there still is between the normal legionary and members of the primitive Christian congregations. In Paul's speeches in Acts Luke avoids the group altogether.

4. Paul.

Paul's own epistles (including Philemon) offer a rather different picture. In 1 C. 9:7 στρατεύομαι in the literal sense serves as a formal parallel to the apostle's work. Without reservation Paul mentions the στρατευόμενος or legionary here along with representatives of civilian professions, the vine-dresser and the shepherd. He is put first because it is obvious in his case that he does not pay his own wages. Paul goes much beyond this somewhat peripheral figure of speech in 2 C. 10:2 ff., where he uses words of the group to answer the charge that his περιπατεῖν is κατὰ σάρκα. In his rejoinder he does not just correct the κατὰ σάρκα (→ 130, 25 ff.). He also intensifies the περιπατεῖν into a στρατεύεσθαι against enemies. The verbs show that the possibility of καθαίρεσις of the foe, which is essential to real στρατεία, is not considered, → III, 412, 32 ff. On the basis of Prv. 21:22 Paul has in mind a siege. The λογισμοί (→ IV, 287, 13 ff.), and each → ὕψωμα which rises up against the knowledge of God, fall to καθαίρεσις and the νοήματα (→ IV, 961, 11 ff.) to captivity. Man himself however (v. 8) does not come under καθαίρεσις but under punishment (v. 6 → II, 444, 1 ff.) in which Christ's πραΰτῆς (→ VI, 650, 1 ff.) and ἐπιείκεια (→ II, 589, 37 ff.) are undoubtedly just as normative as in exhortation (v. 1). It should be noted that Paul does not use στρατεία in any other polemical section, so that 2 C. 10:1-6, striking though it is, is an exception from the standpoint of vocabulary. Epaphroditus is called συστρατιώτης in Phil. 2:25 and Archippus in Phlm. 2. The context shows that the former is especially singled out by being called this rather than συνεργός, and things seem to be the same in the case of Archippus too. It is unlikely that either took part in the στρατεία mentioned in 2 C. 10:3-6; στρατιώτης is rather to be taken in a general sense. Since Paul never uses the group for the Church's work except in 2 C. 10:1-6, the use of στρατιώτης in Phil. 2:25; Phlm. 2 may rightly be called unusual. The conjecture that it bears a technical sense [36] is helpful, but it is impossible to find any trace of a development leading to technical usage in primitive Christianity. Paul seems rather to take the term without modification from a different sphere in which

---

[36] Loh. Phil. and Phlm., *ad loc.*

there was no religious dedication in the Christian sense. [37] Leaving out of account the general comparison in 1 C. 9:7, one gets the impression that the word group is not really at home in the vocabulary of Paul's letters to the churches.

5. The Pastorals.

In the Past. the transferred use of the group for the conduct of Christians seems to have become a current one; otherwise it could hardly have been used in exhortation. From the two relevant passages 1 Tm. 1:18 f. and 2 Tm. 2:3-7 one gathers that the Christian occupying a responsible position in congregational life needed to be admonished and encouraged concerning the στρατεύεσθαι committed to him, but did not need to be told (1 Tm. 1:18 f.), or only to a limited extent (2 Tm. 2:3), in what way work in the Church is a στρατεύεσθαι. [38] The formal starting-point in 1 Tm. 1:18 f. is an understanding of human life in general, and hence also that of the Christian, as a στρατεία → 702, 2 f. Only in relation to Christians, however, may one speak of the καλὴ (→ III, 549, 38 ff.) στρατεία controlled by πίστις and ἀγαθὴ συνείδησις. In waging it Timothy is to be an example to Christians under his care. 2 Tm. 2:3-7 is less general: "Endure hardness, as a good soldier of Jesus Christ. No man that warreth entangleth himself with the affairs of this life; that he may please him who hath chosen him to be a soldier." The introductory imperative συγκακοπάθησον, which is taken up again from 2 Tm. 1:8 (→ V, 937, 25 ff.), seems to offer the occasion for the choice of the word στρατιώτης → 708, 7 f. The three comparisons in vv. 4-6, which remind us of 1 C. 9:7 (→ 710, 16 ff.), point in the same direction. The common idea now is not the reward but self-denying concentration. The στρατευόμενος again comes first, not merely because of the link with v. 3, but because his self-denial is especially striking, as is also his subordination to the will of a superior (στρατολογήσας). That the positive measures which the στρατιώτης of Christ Jesus must take in hardship and self-denial are not without problems in spite of the spiritual preparation may be seen from v. 7. Wrong decisions can be taken if the → σύνεσις does not produce the result which is always to be hoped for from the Lord Himself. Complete freedom is expressed in the way in which the more obvious professional term στρατιώτης [39] (v. 3) is used along

---

[37] Paul does not borrow directly from the usage of Roman troops and their commanders → 704, 9 ff. If one is to seek a possible sphere of influence it is more likely to be found in his own pre-Chr. period, Gl. 1:13 f. It is not improbable that Hell. enthusiasts for Jewish traditions sometimes took words from Gk. military usage and in defiance of foreign troops applied them to themselves. Paul as one of the chief among them might sometimes have spurred on and honoured one of his less advanced contemporaries by calling him συστρα-τιώτης, and then retained this "zealot" term in his vocabulary later. The phrase ζηλῶ γὰρ ὑμᾶς θεοῦ ζήλῳ in 2 C. 11:2, which is part of the section 2 C. 10-13, might well be regarded as a legacy of Paul's past as a Pharisee, if not a strict Zealot, cf. M. Hengel, Die Zeloten (1961), 184. On this view 2 C. 10:3-6 as well as Phil. 2:25; Phlm. 2 can be traced back to the influence of this period. As on this one occasion he uses the group in association with the πραΰτης and ἐπιείκεια τοῦ Χριστοῦ (2 C. 10:1), so once he might often have spoken of his campaign against Christians in the same way, though without πραΰτης and ἐπιείκεια.

[38] The cultic use of צבא (→ 705, 20 f.) hardly calls for serious consideration.

[39] The summons to prove oneself as a στρατιώτης reminds us of Vett. Val., V, 9 (p. 220, 25 ff.), where there is a similar summons to become στρατιῶται τῆς εἱμαρμένης in an astrological context. The fact that the one addressed in 2 Tm. 2:3 holds a responsible position reminds us of the term miles for the third grade in the hierarchy of Mithraism. But the connection seems to consist only in the common use of military terms. Cf. F. Cumont, Die orientalischen Religionen im röm. Heidentum⁴ (1959), XII and 207, n. 7.

with the more general participle στρατευόμενος (v. 4). Thus the one who executes the commission of Jesus bears in a figurative sense the same designation as those who carried out his crucifixion did in a literal sense. Yet the difference between their στρατεία and that meant here is so plain that no contemporary reader could take the common *nomen* as an *omen* for a new era *post Christum* in which the imperative συγκακοπάθησον ὡς... στρατιώτης might apply in a literal sense.

6. The Catholic Epistles.

The fact that στρατεύεσθαι generally involves destruction of life is not entirely eliminated even in figurative usage. Thus the weaker στρατεύομαι of Paul is no longer to be found in the Catholic Epistles. In both the relevant passages the word is used for the endangering of men by the inner foe, by ἐπιθυμίαι (→ III, 168, 12 ff., n. 5) and ἡδοναί (→ II, 919, 9 ff.). In contrast to more innocuous thoughts concerning the well-known phenomenon [40] of this inner enmity, 1 Pt. 2:11, even if only in the subsidiary clause, shows that we have here a mortal threat, a campaign of extirpation, directed against the → ψυχή itself. If a man cannot withstand this στρατεύεσθαι (→ 707, 17 ff.), his ἀναστροφή ("manner of life" → 717, 13 f.) cannot have such an effect upon the ἔθνη (v. 12) among whom he lives as a disliked stranger that he sets them on the way to conversion and to praise of the true God. Jm. 4:1 f. does not speak of the ψυχή or of the effect on pagans; it refers rather to the consequences for the community life of the actual recipients of the epistle. Where στρατεύεσθαι is allowed to develop within, brotherly disagreement becomes a στρατεύεσθαι in which the one seeks to defend himself against the other and to disparage or hurt him. There can even arise μάχεσθαι (→ IV, 528, 2 ff.) and πολεμεῖν (→ VI, 515, 15 f.). At any rate the author has in view the common thought that outward strife arises out of inward conflict → VI, 505, 46 ff.

7. A Comparison.

Since the epistles contain no accounts of the relation of Christians to contemporary soldiers it is possible only to a limited degree to compare what they say with statements in narrative literature. A negative point, however, may still be made. If soldiers had been for Christians terrible people (→ n. 31) who were to be avoided as much as possible and whose very profession was not even to be mentioned (→ 706, 29 ff.; 707, 11 ff.) the use of the group in Paul would make no sense. Christians remained as uninhibited as their special situation (→ 711, 29 ff.) permitted from the very outset. There is thus an agreement which is not to be underrated between the epistles and narrative, including Lucan narrative.

E. The Word Group in the Post-Apostolic Fathers.

In the post-NT period words of the group are none too common at first. στρατιά is meant lit. in 1 Cl., 51, 5 and στρατιωτικὸν τάγμα in Ign. R., 5, 1. στρατευσώμεθα occurs in a transf. sense at the beginning of the section 1 Cl., 37, where it is stressed that the προστάγματα of Jesus Christ are ἄμωμα. The reader himself must decide whether 37, 3 also applies to the ordinances of the earthly βασιλεύς and the ἡγούμενοι. The

---

[40] Cf. Plat. Phaed., 83b and Philo → 707, 24 ff.

tertium comparationis, punctilious obedience, is valid even if one decides in the negative. The Christian obeys the Lord as στρατευόμενοι obey the βασιλεύς, and he obeys ecclesiastical authorities as they obey their ἡγούμενοι, χιλίαρχοι, etc., 37, 3. It need hardly be noted that the second member in this comparison is new in relation to the NT. Ign. Pol., 6, 2 echoes 2 Tm. 2:4: "Seek to please him to whom your military service is rendered and from whom you also receive your pay; let none of you be found a deserter." Here the definitely Roman tt. δεσέρτωρ is used but στρατιώτης is avoided. στρατιώτης θεοῦ (not found in the NT) occurs in Mart. Pl., 4, 6, εἰς Χριστόν στρατευόμενοι Mart. Pt., 7, ἐκείνῳ στρατευόμεθα τῷ βασιλεῖ, Mart. Pl., 2.

Bauernfeind

στρέφω, ἀναστρέφω,
ἀναστροφή, καταστρέφω,
καταστροφή, διαστρέφω,
ἀποστρέφω, ἐπιστρέφω,
ἐπιστροφή, μεταστρέφω

στρέφω.

1. στρέφω is found from the earliest period in Gk. alongside τρέπω, which it gradually replaced.[1] It means esp. "to twist," then "to turn," "bend," "steer," later in act. intr. esp. in Attic. The pass. is also used for the mid. or reflexive. Many senses thus develop; in Plat. Resp., VII, 518c-519b, after the parable of the cave, education is called a turning (par. περιάγω) of the soul to the brightest being, the good.[2] In a transf. sense the word relates to the moral walk and inner turnings, Soph. Trach., 1134.[3]

2. In the LXX στρέφω occurs 37 times with a Hbr. original, 22 times for הפך, e.g., 1 S. 10:6 of the changing of Saul into another man, more often of the changing of cursing into blessing ψ 29:12; 113:8; 2 Εσδρ. 23:2; Est. 9:22 etc. Lam. 1:10 and Da. 10:16 Θ refer to inner conversion through suffering or fear. In 5 instances the original is סבב; 3 Βασ. 18:37 forms a starting-point for the concept of conversion (cf. the vl. ἐπέστρεψας):

στρέφω. Bibl.: Cr.-Kö., Liddell-Scott. Moult.-Mill., Pape, Pr.-Bauer, s.v.; E. K. Dietrich, *Die Umkehr (Bekehrung u. Busse) im AT u. im Judt. bei besonderer Berücksichtigung d. nt.lichen Zeit* (1936); E. L. Dietrich, "שוב שבות. Die endzeitliche Wiederherstellung bei d. Propheten," Beih. ZAW, 40 (1925); J. Fichtner, K. H. Rengstorf, G. Friedrich, Art. "Bekehrung" in RGG³, I, 976-980; W. L. Holladay, *The Root Šûbh in the OT* (1958); A. D. Nock, Art. "Bekehrung" in RAC, II, 105-118; also *Conversion. The Old and the New in Religion from Alexander the Gt. to Augustine of Hippo* (1933); H. H. Schrey, Art. "Bekehrung" in *Evangel. Kirchenlex.*, I, 359-363; R. Seeberg, Art. "Bekehrung" in RE³, 2, 541-545; H. W. Wolff, "Das Kerygma d. deuteronomischen Geschichtswerks," ZAW, NF, 32 (1961), 171-186; P. Aubin, *Le problème de la "conversion." Étude sur un terme commun a l'Hellénisme et au Christianisme des trois premiers siècles* (1963).

[1] The connection with the Indo-Europ. *ster-* with labial expansion *strep-*, *strebh-* etc., Germ. "starr," "straff," is very dubious ("to twist" as "to draw together sharply"?); it is better to assume a special root *streb-*, *strebh-* "to twist," "to wind," v. Walde-Pok., II, 632; Pokorny, I, 1025.

[2] Nock Conversion, 179 f.; W. Jaeger, *Paideia. Die Formung d. griech. Menschen*, III (1947), 379, n. 19: "If one asks concerning the origin of the Chr. concept of conversion Plat. must be called its author. The transition of the term to the Chr. experience of faith took place on the soil of ancient Chr. Platonism."

[3] When a magical formula is uttered there is need to attend, to concentrate, Preis. Zaub., II, 13, 249: λέγε στρεφόμενος.

God will "turn back" the hearts of His people to Himself. [4] In gen. the uncertainty of any fixed usage of the verb may be seen in the Gk. transl.

3. Joseph. has in Ant., 6, 153 the statement that God does not "change" His mind as in philosophical and OT dicta (Nu. 23:19; 1 S. 15:29), though cf. the OT view of God attested in Jer. 26:13; 42:10; Ex. 32:12, 14 etc. Philo has the noun [5] στροφή for cosmic processes, Spec. Leg., I, 91 and for changes in human destiny, Jos., 136.

4. In the NT στραφείς occurs as a formula especially in Luke in introducing dominical sayings, e.g., 7:9, cf. also Mt. 9:22; 16:23; Jn. 20:14, 16. [6] Mt. has the word three times in dominical sayings at 5:39; 7:6; 18:3. Ac. 7:39 follows Nu. 14:3: the turning to Egypt is inward. Ac. 7:42 can be taken either trans. or better intr. God turned aside from Israel and delivered up the people to the worship of stars and therewith to stellar powers. In Ac. 13:46 Paul and Barnabas in their preaching turn fundamentally from the Jews to the Gentiles. In Rev. 11:6 the verb is used for the changing of water into blood, cf. Ex. 7:17, 19. [7]

5. In the post-apost. fathers and Apologists there is an occasional use, Did., 11, 2; 16, 3. Just. Apol., 59, 1 has it for the changing of formless matter. Athenag. Suppl., 22, 6 speaks of the change to matter. [8]

† ἀναστρέφω, † ἀναστροφή, † καταστρέφω, † καταστροφή.

1. The compound ἀναστρέφω also has a wide range of meaning in Gk. and is found from Hom. It means "to convert" (also destructively), "to bring back," intr. "to come back," "to gather," Hom. Il., 23, 436; Soph. Phil., 449; Eur. Hipp., 1228; Hdt., I, 80, 5; Thuc., IV, 43, 4; cf. the cosmos, Plat. Polit., 272e; "to stay," "to be occupied with," "to behave," Hom. Od., 13, 326; Eur. Hipp., 1176; Tro., 993; Plat. Resp., VIII, 558a; Leg., IX, 865e; Xenoph. An., II, 5, 14; "to act," "to walk," Aristot. Eth. Nic., II, 1, p. 1103b, 20; "to walk" as children, Epict. Diss., III, 15, 5. [1] The connection of both verb and noun with walking and walk is common in the Hell. world. In an inscr. honouring a gymnasiarch of Pergamon it is said that he walked well and worthily... [2] The noun was much used in the *koine* and Polyb. took it from this, 1, 9, 7; 4, 82, 1; 9, 21, 5; 25, 1, 10.

---

[4] The root שוב does not seem to occur as an original of the simple form. For the passages Zeph. 3:20; Ιερ. 41(34):15 adduced in Hatch-Redp. the editors (Septuaginta Gottingensis, 15, ed. J. Ziegler [1957]) rightly preferred ἐπιστρέφω and for the hi in Is. 38:8 ἀποστρέφω.
[5] Neither the simple form nor compounds are listed in Leisegang's Index. On the minor role of the group in Philo → 725, 18 ff.
[6] On the tension between ἐστράφη in v. 14 and στραφεῖσα in v. 16 cf. E. Schwartz, "Osterbetrachtungen," ZNW, 7 (1906), 30, n. 1; M. Black, *An Aram. Approach to the Gospels and Acts*[2] (1954), 189 f., who on the basis of the Syr. tradition suggests a word for "to know"; P. Katz, Review of Black, *Gnomon,* 27 (1955), 89. Katz rejects Black's proposal and modifies that of Schwartz. Acc. to Bultmann Jn., *ad loc.* there is no real problem.
[7] Cf. ψ 77:44; 104:29, where μεταστρέφω (→ 729, 20 ff.) is used.
[8] J. Geffcken, *Zwei Griech. Apologeten* (1907), 206 f. attributes the obscurity of Athenag. to the poor use of a source.

ἀ ν α σ τ ρ έ φ ω κ τ λ. Bibl. → στρέφω.
[1] Children are an example of changing and fickle desires which are not seemly in adults, cf. Mt. 11:16, 17; A. Bonhöffer, *Epikt u. d. NT* (1911), 336.
[2] Deissman LO, 264 f.

2. The most common original for the compound in the OT is שׁוּב. [3] The use is varied: "to convert," "to come home," "to come back." Acc. to Ez. 39:25 God will "change" the destiny of Jacob. Return to life is forbidden the dead, 2 Βασ. 12:23; Job 10:21; Prv. 2:19; Sir. 40:11; Wis. 2:5; 16:14 (trans.). Some men fall under God's curse and humbling: "he hurls them from their place," Sir. 33:12. Sometimes הלך hitp is transl. ἀναστρέφω, 3 Βασ. 6:12; Prv. 20:7; Zech. 3:7; Gn. 5:22 Σ; ψ 34:14 Σ; 1 Βασ. 12:2 Αλλ. The noun ἀναστροφή occurs only without Hbr. equivalent, Tob. 4:14; 2 Macc. 5:8 (vl.); 6:23. [4]

3. In the NT ἀναστρέφω does not occur in the Synoptists. [5] In Ac. 5:22 it means "to return." In Jn. 2:15 it is a variant for ἀνατρέπω for the overturning of the tables of the money-changers (Mt. 21:12; Mk. 11:15 καταστρέφω). [6] In the quotation of Am. 9:11 in Ac. 15:16 ἀναστρέψω καὶ ἀνοικοδομήσω [7] is a double translation of

---

[3] The verb occurs some 1040 times in the Mas. The Gk. translators usually have a compound of στρέφω but use more than 90 Gk. words for it, and some 50 Hbr. words as well as שׁוּב serve as the original of the Gk. group, including נבט "to look," which is transl. ἐπιστρέφω; this should not be changed to ἐπιβλέπω. [Katz] שׁוּב means "to return" to the starting-point; other senses developed out of this. Thus the ref. in Ju. 11:8; 2 S. 19:11 (hi); 1 K. 17:27 is to personal contact. The word can mean "return" from exile, "conversion," Jer. 31:18 etc. The name Shearjashub "the remnant that returns" can be taken as either as a threat or a promise. שׁוּב שְׁבוּת means "to restore." In spite of the shortening of the vowel of the stem syllable שְׁבוּת is to be derived from שׁוּב. Only in a few later passages is it derived from שׁבה. and the phrase means "to turn captivity," E. L. Dietrich, "שׁוּב שְׁבוּת. Die endzeitliche Wiederherstellung bei d. Propheten," Beih. ZAW, 40 (1925), 27 f.; W. L. Holladay, The Root Šûbh in the OT (1958), 110-114; E. Baumann, "שׁוּב שְׁבוּת. Eine exeget. Untersuchung," ZAW, 47 (1929), 17-44. We often read of the return of men in death to the dust, the earth, or sheol, Ps. 9:18; 104:29; Job 1:21; 34:15; Qoh. 3:20. In terms of Gn. 3:19 Ps. 90:3b is to be taken in synthetic parallelism to 3a (hi "to turn back to the dust," cf. Job 10:9; 30:23). LXX, however, introduces the idea that humbling is the prerequisite of conversion, cf. Vg. Only in Qoh. 12:7 is there ref. to the return of the spirit to God; the return of the soul to the body is exceptional and a miracle, 1 K. 17:21, 22; cf. 2 S. 12:23. Religiously the word can mean apostasy as well as conversion. Acc. to Holladay 164 passages, some 15%, have the covenantal use, 116-157. The 8th cent. prophets already speak of turning back to God in the sense of conversion. The Deuteronomic tradition, including Jer. and esp. Ez., speaks of turning from evil, cf. H. W. Wolff, "Das Kerygma d. deuteronomischen Geschichtswerks," ZAW, NF, 32 (1961), esp. 177-186. In the Pent. and earlier prophets we find negative formulations: "to turn from God" etc. The verb is a feature of Jer.'s message. It expresses the changing relation between God and Israel. Jer.'s usage influences the later tradition.

[4] We also find this ethical usage in Jos. Ant., 19, 72 etc.; Ep. Ar., 252, cf. 169 συναναστροφή.

[5] The compound and simple are variants at Mt. 17:22. But the reading συστρεφομένων is to be preferred. συστρέφω means "to gather," "to band together," "to conspire." In the Gk. OT it is used esp. for קשׁר, but here it is simply a gen. introductory note: "during their wandering in Galilee" (= ἀναστρεφομένων CᴂD). It can hardly mean "to band together" and perhaps the possibility of this misunderstanding led to the corrections, cf. Zn. Mt., ad loc.

[6] καταστρέφω, καταστροφή have a negative sense. In the LXX they are used esp. for God's destructive work. The model is the overthrow of Sodom and Gomorrah, cf. 2 Pt. 2:6; 1 Cl., 7, 7; 27, 4; 57, 4 (Prv. 1:27). 2 Tm. 2:14 warns against the harmful effects of verbal strife, cf. Herm.m., 5, 2, 1; 1 Cl., 6, 4. The perf. part. pass. is used in Ac. 15:16 in the quotation from Am. 9:11 f. with ref. to the destruction accomplished, LXX τὰ κατεσκαμμένα.

[7] God will turn the overthrow of the house of David and build up its lowliness. The saying is to be taken Messianically, cf. 15:17.

אׇקִים. According to Luke's understanding God promises that He will return and in the resurrection of Jesus establish and fulfil the promise given to David. In the NT Epistles the verb and noun are often used with reference to moral conduct. In 2 C. 1:12 Paul speaks of his conduct in the church. In Eph. 2:3 the life of the Jews (cf. Gl. 1:13) is characterised as a "walking" with those who will not obey. In Eph. 4:22 Paul admonishes his readers to put off the old man with his "walk" in deceitful lusts. [8] According to 1 Pt. 1:18 members of the community are redeemed from the vain "walk" inherited from the fathers. 2 Pt. 2:7, 18 refers to the "walk" in pagan lusts. 1 Tm. 3:15 is speaking of responsible office-bearers in the community, which as God's house and as the pillar (→ 736, 6 ff.) and ground of truth demands a special kind of conduct. Thus the "walk" is a gift of Christians along with possession of the word, love, faith, and holiness, 1 Tm. 4:12. According to 1 Pt. 1:17; 3:2 [9] the "walk" of Christians is shaped by fear of God; according to 3:1 this can have an effect without words simply through good deeds, cf. 2:12; Jm. 3:13. [10] According to 1 Pt. 1:15 the holiness demanded by God embraces the whole walk including the conflict of suffering which is essential for the Christian community according to Hb. 10:33; 13:7. As Hb. 13:18 says, both the author and those to whom he writes must prove themselves in such sufferings. In 2 Pt. 3:11 the demand for a holy walk is given an explicit eschatological orientation, → VI, 726, 19 ff.

4. In the post-apost. fathers ἀναστρέφομαι is the only common compound of στρέφω. It is used as a dep. [11] for moral walk, negatively Ign. Mg., 9, 1; Herm.m., 11, 12; cf. also Just. Apol., 53, 3, and often positively, but usually with an adv., Herm.s., 5, 6, 6: in strong and manly fashion; s., 9, 27, 2; 1 Cl., 21, 8: in holiness, 63, 3; blamelessly, 2 Cl., 5, 6: in holiness and righteousness. Did., 3, 9; Barn., 19, 6 exhort to converse with the humble and righteous. The promise of a "walk" with God in Just. Apol., 10, 2 (ἀναστροφή) corresponds to the story of Enoch in Gn. 5:22, 24 acc. to Σ (ἀνεστρέφετο), which transl. the Mas. literally.

† διαστρέφω.

1. This verb, first found from Aesch. Suppl., 1017, means in Gk. "to twist," "to dislocate," "to confuse." It is used in a transf. sense in, e.g., Aristot. Eth. Nic., II, 9, p. 1109b, 6; VI, 5, p. 1140b, 14. The past. part. pass. which Aristot. has in Poet., 5, p. 1449a, 36 (πρόσωπον αἰσχρόν τι καὶ διεστραμμένον) also occurs in Epict., III, 6, 8: οἱ μὴ παντάπασιν διεστραμμένοι τῶν ἀνθρώπων. Aristot. Eth. Nic., VI, 13, p. 1144a, 34 ff. has the basic statement that deficiency in inner attitude leads to confusion and illusion regarding the starting-point of action. In Hell. and esp. Stoic ethics διαστροφή is a tt. for the moral corruption of the empirical man. The nature of man, which is originally good and oriented to the good, is "twisted" (διαστρέφεται) by bad teaching and example and by environmental influences of all kinds, cf., e.g., Diog. L., VII, 89; Gal. Hippocratis et Platonis placita, V, 462, p. 440, 6 ff. [1]

---

[8] ἀναστροφή "conduct," cf. Dib. Gefbr., ad loc.
[9] 1 Pt. 3:2: ἁγνή, 3:16: ἀγαθὴ ἐν Χριστῷ, 1:15: ἅγιοι.
[10] Cf. Jm. 1:25; 2:17 → II, 651, 11 ff.
[11] The only act. form is in Just. Dial., 56, 17 quoting Gen. 18:14 "to return."

δ ι α σ τ ρ έ φ ω . Bibl. → στρέφω.
[1] Ed. J. Müller, I (1874), cf. also v. Arnim, Index, s.v. διαστροφή and διάνοια, e.g., Chrysipp. Fr., 228-236 (v. Arnim, III, 53, 5 ff.) [Dihle].

2. The compound occurs 36 times in the OT with no fixed original. It is used 6 times for הפך, 24 times for very different words, and 6 times with no Mas. equivalent. The nature and conduct of man are corrupt and "twisted," Dt. 32:5 (→ 406, 17 ff.); Sus. 56; ψ 100:4 Αλλ. A warning against crooked ways is given in Prv. 8:13; 11:20, where LXX goes its own way, though cf. Ju. 5:6; Prv. 10:9; Is. 59:8. Moses and Aaron and also Elijah (cf. Ex. 5:4 and 3 Βασ. 18:17, 18) are accused of confusing the people, cf. false prophets or idols in Ez. 14:5 A, also Nu. 15:39; 32:7; Ez. 13:18, 22; 16:34. The Law (Ex. 23:6) and the prophets (Mi. 3:9) warn against the perversion of right, cf. Hab. 1:4 and also Prv. 4:27a LXX.² In some other passages, with different Hbr. originals, the transl. vacillate between διεστραμμένος, σκολιός and similar expressions, ψ 124:5; Prv. 2:15; 6:14; 8:8; 16:30. A sceptical or radically critical theological attitude may be seen in Qoh. 7:13: "Who can make ordinances when God has smitten him with confusion?" HT: "Who can make that straight, which he hath made crooked?" cf. also 1:15. Wisdom, which leads the righteous through trials, temptations and sufferings, must first "confuse" them, Sir. 4:17, HT "alienate" → V, 609, 23 ff.³

3. NT usage is controlled by the OT.⁴ Thus in Mt. 17:17 and par. the charge of lack of faith which is brought against the disciples because they are unable to heal is supplemented by a reference to the crookedness of the human mind which turns so eagerly to what is evil, Gn. 8:21, cf. 6:5. The judgment is passed on those present, but Matthew and Luke are perhaps seeking to extend it to the unbelieving, non-Christian world of men generally. At Phil. 2:15 the use of the OT quotation from Dt. 32:5 about the crooked and perverse generation is to be explained along similar lines, → 407, 17 ff.

When Jesus is brought before the Roman procurator He is not accused of breaking the Sabbath, desecrating the temple, blaspheming God, or other religious transgressions according to the Jewish Law. The charges levelled against Him are political: He "perverts" the people (Lk. 23:2), i.e., woos them away from the Roman government.⁵ In the three instances of the compound in Ac. 13:8, 10; 20:30 the use is again trans. Along OT lines (→ lines 5 ff.) the Christian community in God's name brings against those who are outside the serious accusation that they corrupt men, that they cause them to fall away from God. Thus Paul tells Elymas (13:10) that he does not cease to "pervert" the straight ways of God, acting in a manner which is directly opposite to Is. 40:4. In the passive expression in Ac. 20:30 the same charge is brought against false prophets in the same term as that used in the OT at Ez. 14:5, cf. Prv. 16:30, namely, that they speak crooked things. The reference is to apostasy from faith.

---

² Cf. Aristot. Rhet., I, 1, p. 1354a, 24: The judge must not let himself be confused by passions, and Pol., III, 16, p. 1287a, 31: Desire and anger distort.

³ Cf. G. Bertram, "Zur Prägung d. bibl. Gottesvorstellung in d. griech. Übers. d. AT: Die Wiedergabe v. schadad u. schaddaj im Griech.," Welt d. Orients, 2 (1959), 502-513; also 'ΙΚΑΝΟΣ in d. griech. Übers. d. AT als Wiedergabe v. schaddaj," ZAW, 70 (1958), 20-31.

⁴ Hell.-Stoic influence is exerted at most only via the Gk. OT.

⁵ Lk. 23:14: ἀποστρέφοντα, raises the same charge of falling away from the emperor, also 23:5: ἀνασείει. At 23:2 Marcion has the addition: "And he causes women and children to fall away." The addition made its way into the Church's tradition and is found in some Western MSS at 23:5, cf. A. Harnack, Marcion (1921), 57 and 229 f.; Zn. Lk., 694 f. on 23:1 ff. Cf. also the Apocryphon Joh. 19 f.: "Through deceit he has led you astray... turned you aside from the traditions of your fathers," cf. W. C. Till in W. C. van Unnik, Ev. aus dem Nilsand (1960), 186.

4. In the early Church the verb is used trans. as in the NT at 1 Cl., 46, 9 (cf. 46, 8 σκανδαλίσαι from Mt. 26:24 par., which is obviously being interpreted); 47, 5. The same applies to 46, 3 quoting ψ 17:27. We find the simile of the potter in 2 Cl., 8, 2: As a potter can fashion again from the same clay a vessel which has gone wrong διαστραφῇ (dep.) or has been broken, so long as it is not yet fired, so we can repent so long as we are on earth. In Just. Dial., 101, 3 we find the expression "to twist" (the lips) for contempt [6] in a paraphrase of ψ 21:8: ἐλάλησαν ἐν χείλεσιν.

† ἀποστρέφω.

1. In Profane Greek.

The verb ἀποστρέφω is found from Hom. and is fairly common. In the main it kept the negative character given it by the prep. It means trans. and intr. "to turn aside, away from," "to turn back," Hom. Il., 15, 62; 22, 197; Hdt., IV, 52, 4; VIII, 87, 4; Thuc., IV, 97, 2; Soph. Oed. Col., 1272; cf. Oed. Tyr., 1154: to tie the hands behind the back; Plat. Soph., 239d: εἰς τοὐναντίον ἀποστρέψει τοὺς λόγους, "to turn" words into the opposite, cf. Resp., VII, 515e (with πρός); Ps.-Aristot. Rhet. Al., 37, p. 1442b, 6 (with εἰς); in an inscr. of thanks to Hadrian in Ephesus 129 A.D. "to avert" (harm), Ditt. Syll.³, II, 839, 14; on an amulet invoking the Lord Zebaoth, 3rd-4th cent. A.D., BGU, III, 955, 1; in the mid. the sense "reject," "repudiate" with the acc. is found in a prayer to Serapis. Preis. Zaub., II, 13, 619: "Reject me not," cf. already Eur. Suppl., 159; Polyb., 9, 39, 6; 3 Macc. 3:23; 4 Macc. 5:9.

2. In the Old Testament.

The verb ἀποστρέφω occurs some 500 times in the O.T. It is mostly (310 times) used for שׁוּב. In 64 cases there is no HT, whether in individual verses or in books extant only in Gk. The other instances are divided between 27 Hbr. words of which only the following 6 are common: סתר "to hide" 29 times, סבב "to surround" 20 times, פנה "to turn" 12 times, סוּג, שׂוּג "to turn from" 8, שׁבת hi "to set aside" 7 (mistaken for שׁוּב?), סוּר "to give way" 6. In another 11 cases the LXX diverges from the HT and the remaining 33 instances or so are divided among 21 Hbr. words.

Most of the instances are of no theological importance. They are in the main spatial, relating to movements of return, going home, turning, also restitution or payment. Passages which speak of the return from exile to Palestine and Jerusalem have some significance with ref. to salvation history, Gn. 28:15; 48:21; 2 Ch. 6:25; Zeph. 2:7; Is. 35:10; 51:11; Ιερ. 22:27; 37(30):3; ψ 52:7B; 84:2. In contrast turning to Egypt is from the very first a gesture of apostasy and turning aside from God, Nu. 14:3, cf. 14:43; Dt. 17:16. But being taken back to Egypt can also be a punishment which God threatens to mete out on Israel, Dt. 28:68; Hos. 8:13. Strictly this means apostasy to other gods, Nu. 32:15; Dt. 31:18B; Jos. 22:16, 18, 29; 23:12; Ju. 2:19; 8:33A; 3 Βασ. 9:6; 4 Βασ. 17:13, [1] cf. 21:3A: "he fell away" (Mas.

---

[6] Cf. ἐκστρέφω Apol., 38, 8. ἐκστρέφω occurs in the NT only at Tt. 3:11: a sectarian who will not be corrected is "rejected" (cf. Dt. 32:20: γενεὰ ἐξεστραμμένη) and judges himself with his sin, v. Dib. Past., ad loc.; cf. also Herm.s., 8, 6, 5: ἐκστρέφοντες τοὺς δούλους τοῦ θεοῦ.

ἀ π ο σ τ ρ έ φ ω . Bibl. στρέφω.
[1] Cf. H. W. Wolff, "Das Kerygma des deuteronom. Geschichtswerks," ZAW, NF, 32 (1961), esp. 178 on 4 Βασ. 17:13.

שוב‎ = again); 2 Ch. 7:19; 29:6. God's turning aside[2] corresponds to the falling away of the people, Dt. 31:17, 18; 32:20; cf. also 23:15; 2 Ch. 7:20 "to cast out" the temple (HT שלך‎.[3] Any movement of renewal begins with the demand "to turn aside" from sins (3 Βασ. 8:35; 2 Ch. 7:14) and to be converted (Jon. 3:8, 10; Zech. 1:4; Is. 30:15; Jer. 18:11; 23:14; 25:5). Prayer is also made to God that He will not "turn away," followed by the appropriate promise or rejection, 2 Ch. 6:42B; 2 Εσδρ. 11:11 S; ψ 9:32; 12:2; 21:25; 73:11, 21; Mi. 3:4; Is. 54:8; 57:17; 59:2; 64:6; Sir. 18:24; Tob. 3:6; 4:7. God must not let us "turn away" (Mas. נטש‎ "cast off"), 3 Βασ. 8:57; He is asked "to turn aside" from our sins, ψ 50:11, cf. also Is. 54:10 Σ. The promise (or denial) of salvation corresponds to the actual situation: alien peoples are to be "turned aside," "driven off" (HT נכנע‎ hi "humbled") in Dt. 9:3, all sickness in Ex. 23:25, evil desires in Sir. 23:5. In many verses God's wrath "turns" or "does not turn" towards; man cannot avert it, Nu. 25:4; Dt. 13:18; 4 Βασ. 23:26; 2 Ch. 12:12; 29:10; 30:8; 35:19ᶜ; Jon. 3:9 (with μετανοήσει); Is. 5:25; 9:11 etc.; 12:1; Jer. 2:35; 4:8; 18:20; 23:20; Job 9:13; ψ 77:38; 84:4, 5; 105:23; Prv. 24:18,[4] cf. 1 Βασ. 15:29; Jer. 4:28 (not Gn. 6:7 Σ). God "turns" back every man's deeds on himself, Ju. 9:56A; 3 Βασ. 2:32, 33. The compound thus becomes almost a tt., though this does not exclude its use in the private or political sphere, e.g., 4 Βασ. 18:14, 24.

In spite of the frequent use in sayings about God's wrath the verb is also used for the change or conversion of man and can mean conversion. This is esp. so in Jer.,[5] Ιερ. 3:10 (vl.); 23:22; 37(30):21, cf. Ez. 3:19; 13:22; 14:6; 18:21. In many cases the figure of turning on the way is used in the sense of inner turning or conversion, Ιερ. 33(26):3; 38(31):21; Ez. 3:18, cf. Job 33:17. ἀποστρέφω can sometimes denote both apostasy and conversion in direct proximity, e.g., Ez. 18:21, 24. The promise of salvation is found esp. in Ez. in I-predication, 23:27, 34, 48; 29:14; 34:16 (vl.); 39:25, 27, 29.

3. In Philo and Josephus.

a. The verb occurs in Philo too. It is typical of him that he rejects as anthropopathisms the many OT sayings which speak of God turning from man, Sacr. AC, 96. Apart from this he remains wholly within the confines of OT usage, cf. Conf. Ling., 129; Migr. Abr., 219; Omn. Prob. Lib.. 61. But the two latter statements, and esp. the formulation in Conf. Ling., 131: "For if the spirit comes back (ἐπιστρέψῃ) to him, that within him which deviates (from God) and turns aside (ἀποστρεφόμενον) will dissolve again,"[6] seem to correspond to Hell. modes of thought.

b. Josephus warns against "turning into its opposite" by transgression a providence which is favourable to man, Ant., 7, 385, cf. Bell., 5, 559; 2, 391; Ant., 6, 148; 8, 245. The sense "to cast off" is found in Bell., 2, 539; Ant., 5, 98; 20, 166. Jos. Bell., 2, 120 says of the Essenes that they "reject" joy as iniquity.[7]

---

[2] God Himself "inverts" (שבת‎ hi) mirth and feasts, new moons and sabbaths, and all festivals, Hos. 2:11; cf. Na. 2:3: God "overthrows" (שוב‎) arrogance.

[3] Am. 1:3, 6 etc. are to be taken negatively in accord. with the HT and the context: I will not "restore ... " ("change" the fate). The Gk. reader might read it in exactly the opposite way: I will not "reject" him, cf. Zech. 10:6 זנח‎ "repel," v. Bl.-Debr. § 308 and Helbing Kasussyntax.

[4] Elsewhere in Prv. always in connection with practical wisdom.

[5] For the HT cf. W. L. Holladay, op cit., 138-142: The root šûbh as an expression of the positive or negative covenant relation in Jer. and the exilic and post-exilic prophets.

[6] Cf. L. Cohn - I. Heinemann, Die Werke Philos v. Alex., V (1929), ad loc.

[7] Cf. 4 Macc. 1:33. Sib., 8, 356 follows the OT → line 1 f.

4. In the New Testament.

In Mt. 26:52 Jesus orders the disciple who has drawn the sword to put it back in its sheath. The expression is Semitic. [8] Mt. 5:42 refers to lending without interest (Ex. 22:25; Lv. 25:37; Dt. 23:20); this is not to be refused. [9] The present text, which is perhaps not the original, hardly seems to presuppose more than moral compulsion or the pressure of someone in trouble (Sir. 4:4). The demand of Jesus is a model which stands in antithesis to the OT concept of retribution. [10] Lk. 23:14 seems to be a secondary echo of 23:2, → 718, 24 ff. The observation of Pilate with its ἀποστρέφω "to pervert" [11] presupposes the Herod incident. The compound also occurs in Marcion's text at 23:2 → 718, n. 5. Ac. 3:26 describes the appearance of the Servant of God. The saying in wholly OT in conception. God's envoy brings conversion as a gift of God's grace. The decisive imperative in the preaching of God's kingdom by both the community of the Baptist and also that of Jesus can be resisted in obduracy. But when it is followed, it is not viewed as a requirement difficult for man to meet but as a divine renewal. If turning from sins is called the content of blessing, the compound obviously does not have a negative thrust but is used positively for conversion. [12] In R. 11:26 Paul quotes Is. 59:20 LXX in confirmation of this view of the Deliverer → VI, 1003, 3 ff. The Deliverer shall turn away ungodliness, primarily from the people of the old covenant.

Mas. has the following text: "There comes for Zion [13] the Deliverer and for those who convert from sins [14] in Jacob." With slight deviations 'ΑΣΘ all follow this. LXX and Paul attest the older and better text: "The Deliverer will come out of (cf. Ps. 14:7) Zion; he will turn away ungodlinesses from Jacob." Acc. to this view the Redeemer brings about liberation from sins, whereas acc. to the Mas. form He appears for those who have already achieved conversion. For Paul the eschatological deliverance of all Israel is based

---

[8] Cf. Ιερ. 35:3 and the transl. of Mt. 26:52 into Hbr. by F. Delitzsch, הברית החדשה [13] (1954).

[9] Str.-B., I, 348-353.

[10] But cf. in the OT Dt.15:7, 9; Prv. 28:27; Sir. 4:4, 5; 29:9; Tob. 4:7. In all these vv. LXX has ἀποστρέφω, though this perhaps came in secondarily for ἀποστέρξεις at Dt. 15:7A. Cf. also Lidz. Ginza R., 40, 37 ff.: "If anyone 'turns' to you with a request and you have to give, do not withold it from him."

[11] Cf. Jos. Bell., 1, 614; Ant., 12, 396.

[12] Cf. 3 Βασ. 8:35 and the passages from Jer. and Ez. → 720, 19 f. What is produced by fear in Job 33:16, 17 is a blessing in Is. 27:8, 9.

[13] 1 QIs a Is. 59:20 (ed. Burrows, I) has אל ציון for לציון ("to Zion"), but the אל might be due to dittography of א.

[14] שבי פשע is common in the Dead Sea Scrolls, cf. Damasc. 2:5 (2:4); 20:17 (9:41); 1 QS 10:20; 1 QH 2:9; 6.6; 14:24, and with שבי ישראל it is almost a term for this community of penitents. Cf. also ברית תשובה in Damasc. 19:16 (9:15) but also שבי ברית "renegades" from the covenant in 1 QH 14:21 f. In 1 QS 3:1 we find משיב חיו "who brought his life to con-version." This is either God as in the OT, E. K. Dietrich, Die Umkehr (Bekehrung u. Busse) im AT u. im Judt. bei bes. Berücksichtigung d. nt.lichen Zeit (1936), 122-127, or a member of the community (cf. Jm. 5:19 f.). We read of conversion from wickedness in 1 QS 5:14 and return to the covenant, the law, the truth in 5:8, 23; 6:15, cf. 1 QS 1:16; 3:3; 5:1; 7:2, 19. תשובה which means "return to the dust" in 1 QH 12:26 (cf. 10:4, also 11:20; 1 QH Fr. 2:11), first became a religious tt. in the Qumran community. The Rabb. then adopted it. It may also be seen in the Baptist community, Jesus, and the Chr. community. Cf. A. M. Habermann, Megilloth Midbar Yehuda (1959), Concordance, s.v. שוב, 156 f. Cf. also H. Braun, "'Um-kehr' in spätjüd.-häret. u. frühchr. Sicht," ZThK, 50 (1953), 243-258.

upon liberation from sins as the decisive act of redemption. The quotation from Is. 27:9 which follows confirms this: God will take away sins from Israel; this is the content of His covenant. ἀποστρέφω and ἀφαιρέω are terms in a synthetic and even, as far as the verbs are concerned, synonymous parallelism constructed either by Paul himself or by a collection of Messianic testimonies from Is. 59:20 and 27:9 along with Ps. 14:7 and Jer. 31:33 f. [15]

The sayings in 2 Tm. 4:4 "They shall turn away their ears from the truth," and Tt. 1:14: "Men that turn away from the truth," differ in grammatical construction but not in logical content. Truth in both verses is the Gospel → I, 244, 34 ff. In 2 Tm. 1:15 the author finds himself "repudiated" [16] — the use is the same as in Tt. 1:14 — by all those in Asia. Christ suffers the same repudiation and rejection in Hb. 12:25 as Paul does in 2 Tm. 1:15. The bearer of revelation who has come from heaven it not to be resisted as the earthly Moses was, the OT antitype of Christ, cf. Hb. 3:1-8. Here the compound gives added force to the synon. παραιτέομαι (→ I, 195, 1 ff.) which is used already in 12:19. Rejection of Christ is denoted by the sharper ἀποστρέφομαι, cf. 12:26 = Hag. 2:6. [17]

5. In Early Christianity.

The compound is fairly common in the post-apost. fathers and Apologists. But there are hardly any new expressions. The verb occurs mainly in OT quotations. In his citing of Is. 5:25 in Dial., 133, 5 Just. deviates from both Mas. and LXX. [18] In these God is the subj. — "his wrath did not turn aside, and his hand is stretched out still," but in Just. the apostate Israelites are the subj. — "they did not turn (convert), and their attitude remained proud." The theocentric OT saying is thus replaced by an anthropocentric interpretation [19] and the concept of conversion, which developed only in the post-exilic age, is introduced. [20] The sense is "to be converted" in 2 Cl., 15, 1. Barn., 20, 2 refers to rejection of the needy; this marks the way of the wicked in an express list of vices, cf. Did., 4, 8. Acc. to Apc. Pt. 8:23 those who have "perverted" righteousness will be tormented in the bottomless pit.

† ἐπιστρέφω, † ἐπιστροφή.

1. In Profane Greek.

This compound and the related noun also have many meanings in profane Gk. To some degree these are the same as in the case of the simple form and other compounds, but obviously with a stronger positive thrust. The verb is both trans. and intr. and means "to convert," "to change" (someone), in Hom. only Il., 3, 370; Hdt., II, 103, 2; VII, 141, 4; Soph. Trach., 566, "to turn to," ibid., 1182, "to turn against," Eur. Andr., 1031. Day and night "wander" over the earth, Hes. Theog., 753; the gods "walk" in heaven, Plat. Phaedr., 247a. In a transf. sense the meaning is "to turn one's attention to," "to take up a matter," "to pay regard to," "to note," "to be intent on," Soph. Phil., 599. The noun "attention"

---

[15] Ltzm. R., ad loc.
[16] Cf. Dib. Past., ad loc.
[17] For the author the prophetic saying is God's Word through Christ, cf. Mi. Hb., ad loc.
[18] Cf. Septuaginta Gottingensis, 14, ed. J. Ziegler (1939), ad loc.
[19] G. Bertram, "Vom Wesen d. Septuaginta-Frömmigkeit," Welt d. Orients, 2 (1956), 274-284.
[20] Cf. Nock Conversion, 179 f., 296. Nock quotes inter al. the philosopher Sallust., 14, 28, 2.

ἐ π ι σ τ ρ έ φ ω, ἐ π ι σ τ ρ ο φ ή → Bibl. στρέφω.

occurs in Aristot. Oec., II, p. 1351b, 31, cf. Fr., 192, p. 1512b, 5. As a tt. in ontology and psychology the noun denotes return to the ground of being or to oneself, Plot. Enn., V, 1, 1; 2, 1; VI, 7, 16. [1] The spirit goes forth from its own disposition and "returns" to itself, V, 3, 6; he who "turns to" himself "turns" to the origin, VI, 9, 2. The "turning of conceptual activity" ἐπιστροφὴ τῆς διανοίας, cf. I, 4, 10 f.; V, 3, 2 is the preliminary theoretical stage of a later act of will. The original cosmic force could both stay with itself and go forth from itself, cf. VI, 6, 3; 7, 8; 8, 16; 9, 7. The spirit "turns" to the one. Theologically this is the One to whom earth and heaven "turn," who is and abides, and in whom all things that truly are find unity, VI, 5, 12. We have here the threefold step of the development and reintegration of being: μονή, πρόοδος, ἐπιστροφή, cf. Damascius De principiis, 72. [2] Plot. is also followed by Procl. Inst. Theol., 31, cf. 15. "To bring about a change of mind, repentance," is the meaning in Plut. Cato Minor, 14 (I, 765b), cf. Alcibiades, 16 (I, 199c); Luc. Quomodo Hist. Conscribenda sit, 5; "to turn and move towards" the good (περισπάω), Plut. Aud. Poet., 4 (II, 21c). Epict. is not a converted man but one who makes progress προκόπτων (Diss., I, 4, 1) to the degree that he is not a wise man in the abs. sense. He advances steadily on the path of culture, or thinks he does or can do, I, 4, 18-21 (→ VI, 706, 10 ff.). He rejects conversion and repentance (→ IV, 976, 1 ff.). Hence the expression in II, 20, 22: ἵν' οἱ πολῖται ἡμῶν ἐπιστραφέντες τιμῶσι τὸ θεῖον, is related to bibl. usage only externally at the very most. The same is true of the opponent of Christianity Porphyr., who demands in Marc., 24 that conversion to God be accepted as the only salvation. Iambl. Myst., I, 13 also uses the word in a similar sense. [3] But one is not to deduce Chr. influence from this.

2. In the Old Testament.

This compound occurs 579 times in the LXX, 408 times for שׁוּב, 30 for סבב, 24 for פנה, 11 for הפך and another 27 for 17 Hbr. verbs. [4] Mostly, then, there is agreement with the HT. But the compounds are easily interchangeable in the LXX and for the most part it is hard to prove that ἐπι- is original as compared with ἀπο-, other compounds, or the simple form. This compound, too, can have antithetical senses in both the lit. and also the transf. use. It can mean "turning to or from," "turning away" or "returning," or religiously "apostasy" or "conversion." Thus the Hbr. original is decisive in fixing the meaning. In many texts and MSS at least the LXX perhaps tries to differentiate by using different compounds.

In narrative the verb denotes movements, turnings, changes of place. Sometimes it can mean "give back" (4 Βασ. 16:6; 2 Εσδρ.15:11) or "repay" (Ju. 9:56, 57; 2 Βασ. 16:8, 12; 3 Βασ. 2:32, 33; 2 Εσδρ. 13:36; "to turn to someone," "to bring to someone's side" (1 Ch. 10:14; 12:24 vl.). The compound can also refer to the march of events and the rotation of the years (3 Βασ. 21:22; 2 Ch. 36:10), also the impermanence of life (ψ 103:29; Qoh. 3:20; 12:7; Sir. 40:1; 1 Macc. 2:63). When the ref. is to movement in relation to Egypt or Babylon the religion of the way [5] can fill the term with symbolical force either as turning

---

[1] Cf. W. Theiler, "Porphyr. u. Aug.," *Schriften d. Königsberger Gelehrten Gesellschaft, Geisteswissenschaftliche Klasse,* 10, 1 (1933), 45-53; O. Becker, *Plot. u. d. Problem d. geistigen Aneignung* (1940) [Dihle].

[2] Ed. C. A. Ruelle (1889).

[3] In the mystery cults of later antiquity we have initiation rather than conversion, cf. Nock Conversion, esp. 138-155; this work deals mainly with the phenomena rather than the history of the concept.

[4] Acc. to Hatch-Redp., cf. also Holladay, *op cit.,* 20-41 for a review of the Gk. verbs used for šûbh, 20 f.

[5] E. Lehmann, *Stället och vägen* (1917), contrasts with cultic religion, which is tied to a site, the prophetic piety of the pilgrim and stranger on earth; cf. G. Rosen - G. Bertram, *Juden u. Phönizier. Das antike Judt. als Missionsreligion u. d. Entstehung d. jüd. Diaspora* (1929), 45-48, 140-143.

to or from. Thus the bringing back of the people from captivity in Babylon is an act of divine grace to which there corresponds the "turning" of the people to God and its "conversion" from sins, 3 Βασ. 8:33-35, 47, 48, cf. 2 Ch. 6:24, 26; 30:9 vl.; Tob. 14:5. The desire to "return" to Egypt shows how stiff-necked the people is (2 Εσδρ. 19:17) and corresponds to the "turning" to evil, 19:28.

In the hagiographa and prophetic writings there is built up on this foundation the vocabulary of conversion in the Gk. Bible. This is related to historical events and uses the same term for apostasy and conversion. At Is. 6:10 the Hbr. text hardly contains the idea of "conversion." For וָשָׁב[6] one should read וְשָׁב, and as an iterative auxiliary verb this should be transl. "again": that the people should heal itself again[7] is excluded by God when He gives the prophet this commission. But the LXX cannot view all this as a hardening which God Himself intends (His "strange" work acc. to Is. 28:21 → II, 640, 38 ff.). For the translator the inability to perceive revelation is rather a punishment for hardness of heart[8] and stiff-necked deafness (βαρέως ἤκουσαν) to the proclamation of God's message. Thus acc. to the LXX the Israelites will neither see nor hear, neither believe nor be converted; if they would God would heal them.[9] If the LXX takes the final indicative statement as a promise, this positive understanding yields ἐπιστρέψουσιν in a reading of א etc. and it is confirmed by the Rabb. understanding of the v. in Is.[10]

Acc. to Jer. 2:27 the apostate people turns its back on Yahweh, cf. Bar. 2:33 (vl.). If Ps. 78:41 Mas. ref. to the repetition[11] of temptations, the Gk. compound denotes the falling away which comes through divine temptation. Acc. to Jer. 11:10 the Israelites "turn" to the wicked acts of their fathers and for this reason shall no more return to their land. But through all human apostasy God's call and His demand for repentance remain, and in spite of all hypocrisy (Jer. 3:10) and obduracy (5:3; 8:5; 9:5) God will bring back His people to the destined land even though further refusal "to be converted" carries with it the threat of destruction, Jer. 12:15, 17. It often seems, then, that conversion is the condition of return; nevertheless, this rests solely on God's grace, ψ 52:7; 84:2 (vl.); 125:1, 4. The prayer of the righteous is orientated exclusively to the possibility that God might "turn again" to His people, ψ 89:13, cf. 6:5; 13:7; 125:4. This explains the simple request: "Convert us" (ψ 79:4, 8, 15, 20) at least in the LXX; the HT has national restoration in view. In Ps. 19:7 again the LXX has in mind an alteration of the state of the soul under the influence of the Law and this has to be called "conversion," whereas the Mas. seems to presuppose restoration in the sense of reviving. The same applies in Ps. 23:3; 85:4, where the compound is used for שׁוּב trans. Ιερ. 38(31):18 in the Mas. reads: "Cause me to turn, that I may turn," but the LXX has the more developed: "Convert me, that I may be converted," cf. Lam. 5:21 and also 1:16, but not 1:11, 19. This gives a basic sense to many passages which speak of the turning of the people in admonition or warning, in positive or negative statements. They break free from the historical situation of the prophetic address and take on a gen. character. "Turning" from idols to Yahweh and "returning" from exile become "conversion." What is partly national piety becomes

---

[6] This as a continuation of יָבִין would have to mean "that it convert (repent)," cf. Holladay, 79.

[7] Cf. B. Duhm, Das Buch Js., Handkomm. AT, 9⁴ (1922), ad loc.; H. Guthe in Kautzsch, ad loc.; cf. Köhler-Baumg., s.v. רפא.

[8] Perf. for imp.: הִשְׁמִין for הַשְׁמֵן, cf. J. Ziegler, Untersuchungen zur LXX des Buches Isaias (1934), 108 f. On hardening acc. to Is. 6:9 f. → V, 554, 29 ff.

[9] But cf. the reading attested in Theodoret, cf. Septuaginta Gottingensis, 14, ed. J. Ziegler (1939) on Is. 6:10.

[10] Str.-B., I, 662 f. on Mt. 13:14 f.; Jeremias Gl.⁶, 13.

[11] In the Gk. OT πάλιν is common for שׁוּב, usually with a verb, cf. Holladay, 66-72. We find it with ἐπιστρέψας for the double שׁוּב of Ps. 71:20. P. Aubin, Le problème de la "conversion" ... (→ στρέφω, Bibl.), 34-36 speaks of Yahweh and Israel turning to one another. This is the most important distinctive feature in the OT view of conversion.

admonition and summons to individuals. This individual piety is the presupposition of universalism. Naturally Israel is still primarily in view in calls like that in Jer. 3:22, [12] cf. 3:14. The promise of 15:19 also applies to it. But already in 18:8 the ref. is fundamentally to any people and not just to the chosen people even though the demand for turning (ἀπο-) is addressed to the men of Judah and Jerusalem in 18:11, and eschatological expectation presupposes "conversion" as a Messianic act ἀπο- with ἐπιστρέφω Ιερ. 37(30):21. Only here does the LXX take גּגֵשׁ, which Mas. has for the ruler's approach to God's throne, in the sense of "to convert," cf. שֵׁב שְׁבוּת in Jer. 30:18 for eschatological restoration. The universalist implications of "conversion" may be seen most clearly in ψ 21:28. [13]

3. In Judaism.

a. ἐπιστρέφω is less prominent in the apocr. and pseudepigr. It occurs occasionally in Test. XII. Part of being a good man acc. to Test. B. 4:1 is to warn and convert the scoffer, cf. also Iss. 6:3; D. 5:9, 11; 6:4; N. 4:3; J. 3:10; B. 5:1. Plain in these works and also in Σ and Philo and Joseph. is the supplanting of ἐπιστρέφω by μετανοέω, cf. Test. G. 5:8; Zeb. 9:7 α β; Zeb. 9:7, 8; Iss. 6:3, 4 with its play on words "to be converted" — "to return."

b. Philo interprets Moses' "turning" to God as θαρρεῖν, εὐτολμία, παρρησία, φιλία. This is the attitude of the wise, Rer. Div. Her., 21. But the "turning" of Lot's wife in Gn. 19:26 (no στραφεῖσα in LXX) or that of Pharaoh in Ex. 7:23 is a turning aside from knowledge, Fug., 121 and 124. Similarly Philo sees in the promise of "turning to" God in Dt. 4:30 an admonition to true knowledge of God, Fug., 142. "Returning home" in Dt. 20:5 ff. (A ἐπιστρέφω, Philo with B ἀποστρέφω) is reinterpreted in Agric., 148, 157-160. The group is here replaced by the specifically Philonic or Stoic (→ n. 3, 15) concepts of the beginner on the first stage of repentance, [14] the one who makes progress, and the perfect man. [15] In Jos., 87 the compound is equated with "to improve"; the prison was made a place of improvement (σωφρονιστήριον) by Joseph. [16] In Som., II, 174 the compound again describes the energetic turning of mankind to righteousness with the elimination of sins. Reminiscent of Hell. or philosophical modes of thought is the idea of a returning of the spirit to itself in Conf. Ling., 131, cf. Migr. Abr., 195. This presupposes that all turning or apostasy from God will be overcome as set forth by Philo in an allegorical explanation of the names Penuel and Gideon (Ju. 8:9), Conf. Ling., 129 f.

---

[12] Jer. 3:22 HT: "Turn, apostate sons, I heal your apostasies" (W. Rudolph, Jeremia, Hndbch. AT, I, 12² [1958], ad loc.): שׁוּבוּ בָּנִים שׁוֹבָבִים אֶרְפָּה מְשׁוּבֹתֵיכֶם. LXX might be transl. "Be converted, sons, who turn, and I will heal your trespasses": ἐπιστράφητε, υἱοὶ ἐπιστρέφοντες, καὶ ἰάσομαι τὰ συντρίμματα ὑμῶν. This presupposes either the root שׁבר = συντρίβω or the root שׁבת, which is more easily confused with שׁוּב.

[13] Cf. Rudolph, op. cit., ad loc. and E. L. Dietrich, "שׁוּב שׁבות. Die endzeitliche Wiederherstellung bei d. Propheten," Beih. ZAW, 40 (1925), 15 f.; E. Baumann, "שׁוב שבות. Eine exeget. Untersuchung," ZAW, 47 (1929), 30.

[14] In Virt., 175-186 μετάνοια (→ IV, 993, 1 ff.) stands only among goods of the second rank. μεταβολή is synon. in Praem. Poen., 163 and 164. In Virt., 181 we find the noteworthy formulation αὐτομολεῖν ἀμεταστρεπτὶ πρὸς ἀρετήν, which strictly excludes the OT gift and requirement of conversion.

[15] Cf. W. Völker, Fortschritt u. Vollendung bei Philo v. Alex. (1938), 107; Aubin, op cit., 29, 56 f.

[16] Cf. E. K. Dietrich, Die Umkehr ... (→ στρέφω Bibl.), 290, 301.

c. In Jos. ἐπιστρέφω occurs only occasionally in a religious or ethical sense. Thus in the story of Josiah in Ant., 10, 53 (4 Βασ. 23:25) the compound is used as a synon. of σωφρονίζω (10, 50) for conversion. [17]

4. In the New Testament.

In the NT ἐπιστρέφω occurs 39 times and the noun ἐπιστροφή once. Half the instances are in Luke's writings. Again about a half have a spatial reference and denote physical movement → 723, 33 ff.; so Mt. 10:13; 12:44; 24:18; Mk. 13:16; Lk. 2:20, 39 (vl. for ὑπέστρεψαν); [18] 8:55 (cf. 3 Βασ. 17:21); 17:31.

a. In Jn. 21:20 ἐπιστραφείς [19] stands in some contrast to the demand for discipleship addressed to Peter. According to this account Peter replied to the summons to discipleship by turning to something else. In Ac. 9:40 the movement is spatial as in the similar OT story in 4 Βασ. 4:35. In Ac. 15:36 the Greek reader could hardly understand the introductory ἐπιστρέψαντες as a mere Hebraism for שוב = πάλιν. The author, too, is trying to say that the apostles have their gaze on the churches and look after them. [20] The common sound of the two verbs thus takes on material significance; Paul is introducing a new part of his missionarv work. Ac. 16:18 describes a physical movement; Paul turns round and turns to the girl. But the alternative in D [21] suggests that ἐπιστρέψας was felt to be parallel to διαπονηθείς. Hence one would have to translate D as follows: "Paul turned his attention to the demon (not his person to the girl possessed by it), made this his business, and said..."

b. In the other 23 passages the compound is used in a transferred sense. Luke 17:4 links outward and inward turning: "If he (thy brother) trespass against thee seven times in a day, and seven times in a day turn again to thee, saying, I repent: thou shalt forgive him." Here ἐπιστρέφω and μετανοέω are closely related. The turning to the injured party is a making of contact, a renewing of personal relation; to this is added the necessary change in inner attitude. In 2 Pt. 2:21 ἐπιστρέφω or the better attested ὑποστρέφω is used in the sense of a falling away from the holy commandment which has been handed down. This is worse for men than never having learned to know the right way at all. When they do it they are like dogs (→ III, 1103, 25 ff.) "returning" (2:22: ἐπιστρέψας) [22] to their vomit. Basically the reference here is to falling back into the old servitude of sinful lusts, and so it is also in Gl. 4:9. The Galatian churches threaten to fall back into astrological superstitions and the related moral dangers.

---

[17] Perhaps this is also the case in Bell., 5, 377 (v. Dietrich, 309) unless the ref. is to a turning back to and recollection of God's mighty act in history. In Ant., 2, 293, however, ἐπιστροφὴν ποιεῖσθαι means "to pay attention." Cf. Dietrich, 224-226 and 233-238.

[18] ὑποστρέφω occurs 38 times in the NT mostly in relation to journeys (Lk. 22 times, Ac. 11, Mt. 8:13 and Mk. 14:40 textually uncertain, Gl. 1:17, Hb. 7:1). The usage is different only at Ac. 13:34 ("to turn again" to corruption) and 2 Pt. 2:21 (𝔊 al ἐπιστρέψαι; א A al ἀνακάμψαι, "to fall away," "to turn again from" the holy commandment).

[19] Cf. Mt. 9:22; Mk. 5:30; 8:33. In Rev. 1:12 the context — the voice behind the divine — shows that the verb must mean "to turn round."

[20] Haench. Ac., ad loc.

[21] Cf. A. C. Clark, The Acts of the Apostles. A Critical Edition (1933), ad loc.

[22] Cf. Prv. 26:11 where the simile is used to describe the attitude of the fool: ἀναστρέψας ἐπὶ τὴν ἑαυτοῦ ἁμαρτίαν. Cf. also Wnd. Kath. Br., ad loc.

c. In 4 passages in the NT Is. 6:9, 10 is quoted (Mk. 4:12; Mt. 13:15; Jn. 12:40; Ac. 28:27). In Mk. and Mt. the quotation is designed to explain why Jesus speaks to the people in parables, and to provide an OT basis for this. According to Mt. hardening is not the purpose of Jesus. It is the reason why the people will not be converted. Mk., however, seems to champion the so-called hardening theory. The people must not be converted. The question is whether the introductory μήποτε has here the same negative sense as it obviously has in the LXX or whether it should not be translated: "unless they be converted" [23] (→ V, 554, 29 ff.). In Jn. 12:40 God is the One who brings about hardening and the rejection of conversion (στραφῶσιν). Jesus, however, will accomplish salvation. [24] This will end the hardening which God brought about and truly manifest for the first time the glory of Jesus. In the fourth reference in Ac. 28:27 the quotation is used in a wholly negative sense. Because of the guilty obduracy of the Jews the preaching of the Gospel is turned to the Gentiles. Acts closes with this.

d. In the revelation to Zacharias concerning the precursor John (Lk. 1:16 f.) there is reference in a fully OT sense (→ 724, 1 ff.) to the leading back (conversion) of many sons of Israel to the Lord their God. At the same time a sign of the age of salvation is given; the disruption of the people will be ended with the turning of the fathers to the sons in love, cf. Mal. 3:24. [25] The compound is never used elsewhere for conversion in the Gospel tradition. Indeed, it is not used at all in the oldest stratum of dominical sayings. Only in Lk. 22:32 (→ 291, 20 ff.) in the material peculiar to Lk. do we find it in a saying to Peter. By reason of the intercession of Jesus Peter's faith will not wholly fail (ἐκλείπω) when he falls. He can turn back to Jesus, or rather the Risen Lord will lead him back by His revelation, so that he can then strengthen the brethren by preaching the resurrection. The connection with Peter's denial might have been made later by adding ἐπιστρέψας. [26] The verb is not used here as a tt. for Peter's conversion. It is used intransitively for the change which is prepared by this saying of Jesus and brought about by the revelation of the Risen Lord.

The verb is employed transitively in the direction to the community in Jm. 5:19 f. This refers to the bringing back of the erring member by the Christian brother. He who accomplishes this restoration has saved a soul from spiritual death and by his act made good his own sins (or those of the other?). [27] In this sense ἐπιστρέφω has a place in primitive Christian exhortation. Twice in Acts, in the requirement of 3:19 and the story of 26:18-20, ἐπιστρέφω and μετανοέω occur together. The two verbs are not simple synonyms. The demand in Peter's sermon runs: "Change your mind, and turn your attention to the fact that your sins are blotted out." [28] Very

---

[23] Jeremias Gl.⁶, 13; C. E. B. Cranfield, *The Gospel acc. to St. Mark, Cambridge Greek Testament Comm.* (1959), *ad loc.*; C. F. D. Moule, *An Idiom Book of NT Greek²* (1959), 143 and 207.
[24] Bultmann J. on 12:40.
[25] Cf. Ιερ. 29(47):3: Fathers are not concerned about their children; the primary reference is to foreigners, but the saying symbolises human disorder and sin which will be ended only in the eschatological age, cf. also Sir. 48:10.
[26] Bultmann Trad., 287 f.
[27] Cf. Wnd. Jk., *ad loc.*; Dib. Jk., *ad loc.*
[28] Haench. Ag., *ad loc.* takes the verb to refer to turning to God and conversion for the forgiveness of sins.

different is the use of the two verbs in Paul's apology to King Agrippa. In 26:18 Paul is quoting the commission given him by Jesus. The apostle is to open the eyes of the blind that they may "turn away" from darkness and the power of Satan and "turn to" the light and God. The twofold content of the Christian concept of conversion is clearly expressed here. It relates to both Jews and Gentiles, though one is to think especially of the latter. [29] Ac. 14:15 speaks of "turning aside" from vain idols (p 45 has the fuller ἀποστῆναι ἀπό). In 26:20 Paul tells how he carried out his commission: he preached μετανοεῖν καὶ ἐπιστρέφειν ἐπὶ τὸν θεὸν ἄξια τῆς μετανοίας ἔργα πράσσοντας. Here repentance precedes turning to God, and both are confirmed by corresponding works. Conversion is thus a change in which the main concern is turning to God.

According to Ac. 9:35 all the inhabitants of Lydda in the Plain of Sharon who had been converted [30] and who thus belonged to the community of Jesus saw the man who had been healed. The verse is not referring to conversion after seeing the man. [31] The converted are believers who are strengthened by the miracle. [32] In Ac. 11:21 "to believe" and "to be converted" supplement one another in the story of the church at Antioch. In Ac. 15:3 Paul and Barnabas tell the Jewish Christian churches of Palestine about the "conversion" (ἐπιστροφή) of the Gentiles when they are on the way from Antioch to Jerusalem. In Peter's speech in 15:7 "to believe" is used in the sense "to be converted," and in 15:19 James speaks of the Gentiles being "converted" to God. In 1 Th. 1:9 Paul reminds the church of its beginnings, how the members were "converted" to God from idols, cf. Ac. 14:15. Elsewhere Paul has the compound only at 2 C. 3:16 in the sense "conversion." But Paul imported this sense into the OT quotation. In the relevant passage Ex. 34:34 the reference is to the spatial going in of Moses to the Lord. [33] Paul allegorises the passage. The people rather than Moses is the subject. All the obscurity of the OT Law is brightened for them when they are "converted" to the Lord. Paul takes this sense from the Exodus narrative, [34] which certainly had need of some such exposition or interpretation in the Judaism of his time.

Finally we must mention 1 Pt. 2:25. The OT form of expression, which is based on the metaphor of the shepherd, refers to the bringing of lost sheep to Christ, the Shepherd and Guardian of their souls. God Himself leads men to Him. After the manner of OT and Jewish piety the passive expression avoids any direct statement about God or mention of His name.

5. In Early Christianity.

In early Christianity as in the NT there is no hard and fast use of the verb. Thus in Barn., 4, 8 and Herm. s., 8, 7, 5 it denotes "falling away" into idolatry as in the OT → 724, 19 ff. On the other hand apostasy and error are the occasion of repeated admonitions to the community to "turn" again to the Lord, to the right way, Pol., 7, 2; 1 Cl., 18, 13, cf.

---

29 Cf. Haench. Ag. on 26:17.
30 So C. Weizsäcker, *Das NT übersetzt*[10] (1912), *ad loc.*
31 Though cf. Luther and most modern commentators.
32 Chrys. acc. to the catena trad., cf. Cramer Cat., III, 166 on Ac. 9:35.
33 Only in 3 Βασ. 22:17 is בוא transl. by this compound. If the verb is taken spatially, it seems that Moses could take off the veil from his face only when he returned to the presence of God on the mount. We Christians always live in the presence of the Spirit of Christ and therefore do not need to turn or to put the veil on or off [Moule].
34 Cf. Wnd. 2 K. on 3:16.

ψ 50:15. [35] God Himself is besought in prayer to "bring back" those who go astray, 1 Cl., 59, 4; for always He has given an opportunity of repentance to those who "turn to" Him, 1 Cl., 7, 5. In this sense 1 Cl. 8, 3 looks like a Chr. paraphrase of Is. 1:18; it is not taken from an apocryphon like other OT verses. [36] Herm. v., 1, 3, 1 and s., 9, 26, 2 speak of sinners in the house of the Lord and the congregation which the prophet is to "convert" and which have the chance of conversion acc. to the revelation given to the prophet. Acc. to Herm. m., 6, 1, 5 conversion leads to the right way which is also the easy one. [37] There is also an admonition to conversion in m., 9, 2; 12, 4, 6; 6, 2. "The Lord is near to those who convert," we read in v., 2, 3, 4 (quoting an apocr. apc.). [38] The words of faith and love spoken by the community have the power of "conversion" and hope (εἰς ἐπιστροφὴν καὶ ἐλπίδα), Barn., 11, 8. Conversion and hope go together like repentance and faith. Conversion and repentance are not a once-for-all event; they control the Christian life, cf. 2 Cl., 15, 1 (ἀποστρέψαι); 16, 1; 17, 2; 19, 2.

The compound is not very common in the Apologists. The use has no new features as compared with that of the Bible.

In the Gospel of Truth from the findings at Nag Hammadi the salvation which comes from above (35) is described as a discovery of him who has come to him who will return. This returning is called repentance. There is then ref. (36) to the receiving of bringing back (through Christ) and the related anointing which is the sympathy of the Father. [39]

† μεταστρέφω.

This verb, which is not very common, means "to turn," "to change." Plat. Resp., VII, 518d speaks of the turning or changing of the soul from becoming to true being, cf. μεταστροφή, VII, 525c, 532b → 714, n. 2.

In the OT the verb is mostly used for הפך. Almost always God is the subj. and He is the logical subj. in the pass. He "changes" His own heart, the heart and plan of men, Ex. 14:5; 1 Βασ. 10:9; 1 Εσδρ. 7:15 (cf. 2 Εσδρ. 6:22: ἐπιστρέφω); ψ 104:25; 3 Macc. 5:8. He turns things into their opposite ψ 65:6; Jl. 2:31; Dt. 23:6; Am. 8:10 etc. In 3 Βασ. 12:15 and 2 Ch. 10:15 the noun μεταστροφή is used for נְסִבָּה, סִבָּה from the root סבב in the sense of a historical turning by God's disposition.

In the NT μεταστρέφω occurs only twice. Ac. 2:20 quotes Jl. 2:31. In Gl. 1:7 Paul maintains that the aim of his opponents is the turning of the Gospel into its opposite. [1]

Bertram

---

[35] Within an existing congregation it is the presbyters (Pol., 6, 1) who are to bring back those who go astray, cf. Herm. m., 8, 10.

[36] Cf. Kn. Cl., ad loc.

[37] Cf. Dib. Herm., ad loc.

[38] The Book of Eldad and Modad, which is known only by name.

[39] Cf. H. M. Schenke in W. C. van Unnik, *Ev. aus dem Nilsand* (1960), 182.

μ ε τ α σ τ ρ έ φ ω . Bibl. → στρέφω.

[1] μεταστρέφω also occurs a third time in Jm. 4:9, where μεταστραφήτω is to be preferred to the reading μετατραπήτω.

```
† στρουθίον
```

1. στρουθίον,[1] found from Anaxandrides Comicus Fr., 7 (FAC, II, 48), is the most common Gk. diminutive [2] of the bird's name στρουθός [3] which is found from Hom. As the latter often does, it means "sparrow" (Lat. *passer*). [4] The poets, [5] probably following popular usage, do not think it important to make an exact distinction between sparrows and other little birds. Nor were the particular characteristics of sparrows of any greater interest in scholarship [6] or art. [7] These birds did play a role in economic life, however, for they were a threat to crops [8] and their flesh was also regarded as good [9] food well worth the price. [10]

σ τ ρ ο υ θ ί ο ν. Bibl.: A. Steier, Art. "Sperling" in Pauly-W., 3a (1929), 1628-1632; Schl. Mt. on 10:29-31; F. S. Bodenheimer, *Animal and Man in Bible Lands* (1960), 56.

[1] στρουθάριον and στρουθίς are less common.
[2] On the formation of diminutives cf. Schwyzer, I, 470 f.
[3] On στρουθός cf. Liddell-Scott, *s.v.* Is there a connection with the onomatopoeic root *strou* (Gk. τρίζω "to twitter")? The etym. is still uncertain, cf. Lat. *turdus* "thrush," Boisacq, Hofmann, *s.v.*, also Walde-Hofmann, II, 718; A. Ernout and A. Meillet, *Dict. étym. de la langue latine*, II[4] (1960), *s.v. sturnus* and *turdus*.
[4] Aristot. Hist. An., V, 2, p. 539b, 33; IX, 7, p. 613a, 29 ff.: στρουθίον, II, 17, p. 509a, 9; VIII, 3, p. 592b, 17; IX, 49, p. 633b, 4: στρουθός. The two words are not synon. inasmuch as στρουθός is used for larger birds. Thus with μεγάλη it means esp. the "ostrich," Aristoph. Av., 875; αἱ μεγάλαι, Xenoph. An., I, 5, 2 etc., without the addition Aristoph. Ach., 1105, later (first in Diod. S., 2, 50, 3) στρουθοκάμηλος (Lat. *struthocamelus*). Cf. E. Risch, "Gr. Deminutivkomposita," *Idg. Forschung*, 59 (1944), 57.
[5] The sacrificial motherly love of weak and helpless στρουθοί is already extolled in Hom. Il., 2, 311-318 μήτηρ δ' ἀμφεποτᾶτο ὀδυρομένη φίλα τέκνα, 315, and what is often the gt. love of men for these little creatures (*passer*, the sparrow of Lesbia) in Catullus Carmina, 2.3 (ed. W. Eisenhut [1958]). But precisely in the case of these two best-known sparrows of ancient poetry the zoological exactitude of the name is open to question (Steier, 1629 f.; J. Kroymann in W. Kroll, C. Valerius Catullus[3] [1959], 295). Cf. perhaps the loose use of the Germ. "Fink," Eng. "finch."
[6] Thus Aristot., *op cit.* (→ n. 4) does not differentiate between individual kinds of sparrows; what he says about the love life of these creatures in Hist. An., V, 2, p. 539b, 33 was common knowledge and applied to the sparrow as the bird of Aphrodite. For details cf. Athen., 9, 46 (391e f), Steier, 1630 f. On the observations of Aristot., Steier, 1629. We first find a distinction between *passer domesticus* (στρουθός ὁ ἥμερος) and *passer montanus* (στρουθὸς ὁ ἄγριος) in Alexander of Myndos. Athen., *loc. cit.*
[7] Except in the erotic field (→ n. 6) the sparrow is seldom portrayed.
[8] Cf. Aristoph. Av., 578 f.; Diod. S., 3, 30, 3. Plin. Hist. Nat., 18, 17, 158. 160 mentions preventive measures
[9] Cf. Athen., 2, 71 (65e); Gal. Comm. in Hippocr. de victu acutorum, IV, 96 (CMG, V, 9, 1, p. 347, 6 f.); on this E. Blümner, *Der Maximaltarif des Diocletian* (1893), 78, n. 2; Plin. Hist. Nat., 30, 15, 141 in an erotic connection. Though sparrows are seldom mentioned as food, the favourable judgment in Anthimus De observatione ciborum, 30 (ed. V. Rose [1877]) probably represents earlier opinion too. The ἰξευτής "snarer of birds" Am. 3:5; 8:1 f.; Ιερ. 5:26 Ἀ΄Σ; Prv. 6:5 Σ seems to have attached gt. importance to the catching of sparrows, though στρουθοπιαστής occurs only later in Aetius Amidenus = Aetius Medicus Libri Medicinales, II, 234 (CMG, VIII, 1, p. 235, 16) and Hesych., *s.v.* ἰξευτής.
[10] The Edict. Diocletiani de pretiis rerum venalium, CIL, 3, 1926-1953 sets the price of στρουθοί (undoubtedly sparrows here) in 1932, No. 4, 35 (to be supplemented by 23285[8], No. 4, 37) as at the most 16 copper denarii for 10 (only a matter of a few pence). Sparrows were the cheapest of all birds, cf. Deissmann LO, 234 f. In the saying of Aesop in Pr.-Bauer, *s.v.*: ... στρουθία πολλοῦ πωλεῖται, Vita Aesopi Cod G, 26 (ed. B. E. Perry [1952]) the ref. is, of course, to the price paid for speaking or at least singing (?) στρουθία, so that it is not certain that the price paid for sparrows as food was higher in Aesop's day than in that of Diocletian. On the transmission of the saying cf. Perry, 44, 3; 85, 29; 281, No. 107; 288, No. (107). What is meant may best be seen from 85, 29: εἰ πετεινὸν λαλεῖ, πολύτιμον εὑρίσκεται.

2. Whereas στρουθίον undoubtedly has the narrower sense "sparrow" (→ n. 4) and we simply have extensions of the basic meaning, the only possible equivalent in the OT', namely צִפּוֹר, [11] merely denotes "birds" in gen. or an individual bird, but nowhere [12] is there anything to suggest a sparrow. At most one might think of vv. where LXX has στρουθίον for צִפּוֹר, ψ 10:1; 83:4 ('A στρουθός); 101:8; 103:17; 123:7; Qoh. 12:4; Lam. 3:52. [13] In several of these (ψ 10:1; 101:8; 123:7; Lam. 3:52) στρουθίον as a helpless bird in danger (→ n. 5) symbolises afflicted man; in Lam. 4:3, where the same applies perhaps in the LXX, στρουθίον is used for יָעֵן. [14] In Prv. 26:2 (→ n. 11) στρουθοί as distinct from ὄρνεα are perhaps small birds, but elsewhere in LXX στρουθός is differentiated from στρουθίον and used for bigger creatures; where בַּת הַיַּעֲנָה (sing. Lv. 11:16; Dt. 14:15; plur. Is. 34:13; 43:20; Job 30:29) is transl. thus it means "ostrich." [15] In Jer. 10:22; Ιερ. 30:28 (49:33) στρουθός is used for תַּן "jackal."

3. A pool which was important to Titus during the siege of Jerusalem and which lay near the castle Antonia was called Στρουθίου acc. to Jos. Bell., 5, 467. One can only conjecture as to the derivation of the name. [16]

4. In the NT στρουθίον occurs only at the beginning and end of the independent section handed down in Mt. 10:29-31 and Lk. 12:6 f. The basic thought here is a cheering (Mt. 10:31a; Lk. 12:7b) deduction a minore ad maius, from the στρουθία to the men addressed: οὐχὶ δύο (πέντε, Lk. 12:6) στρουθία ἀσσαρίου πωλεῖται (πωλοῦνται ἀσσαρίων δύο, Lk. 12:6); πολλῶν [17] στρουθίων διαφέρετε (ὑμεῖς, Mt. 10:31b). The Rabbis after Christ, and perhaps also before, appeal similarly to the comparatively little worth of the bird which supports this conclusion in view of the fact that it still comes within the Creator's providence: "A bird (צִפּוֹר) does not

---

[11] צִפּוֹר comes from צָפַר "to twitter" → n. 3. דְּרוֹר in Ps. 84:3; Prv. 26:2 is the "swallow" acc. to Jewish comm., cf. Köhler-Baumg., s.v.; though this is uncertain there is nothing to be said for "sparrow." עָגוּר in Is. 38:14; Jer. 8:7, cf. J. Ziegler, Jeremias, Septuag. Gottingensis, 15 (1957), 130 f., means a singing bird, "thrush," cf. L. Köhler, "Hbr. Vokabeln, I," ZAW, 54 (1936), 288 f.
[12] Including 1 QH 4:9 and bChul., 65a.
[13] In other transl. also Is. 31:5 Σ; Lv. 14:4 Αλλ.
[14] Cf. BHK, ad loc. At Job 40:29b צִפּוֹר in v. 29a perhaps contributed to the choice of στρουθίον. On Jer. 8:7 → n. 11. Tob. 2:10 offers no data on which to base greater precision, Vg and Luther "swallow."
[15] Only the other Gk. transl. use στρουθοκάμηλος.
[16] Cf. G. Dalman, Jerusalem u. sein Gelände (1930), 114; G. Ricciotti, La guerra giudaica, III² (1949), 204; L. H. Vincent, Jérusalem de l'AT, I (1954), 300; J. M. Allegro, The Treasure of the Copper Scroll (1960), 83. Jos. Bell., ed. O. Michel and O. Bauernfeind, II, 1 (1963), 249 f., Exc. 10; 260, n. 190. Important MSS of the Jos. text read τοῦ θείου for στρουθίου or τοῦ στρουθίου.
[17] 83 it read πολλῷ in Mt., 241 pc a in Lk. The gen. plur. πολλῶν might have arisen from a basic πολλῷ through vowel assimilation to the following gen. plur. στρουθίων or through a fairly common scribal error (ων for ωι) [Katz]. The fact that the many sparrows in the conclusion seem in a sense to correspond to the earlier few would so favour the extension of the secondary reading that the primary one would remain in only a few witnesses. The view which is to modern taste is that originally a qualitative distinction was intended, and perhaps some early workers hit on this too and thus made a significant emendation from πολλῶν to πολλῷ; in this case the inappropriate πολλῷ would have come in with the transition to Greek and would be primary in the Gk. text. Cf. Wellh. Mt. on 10:28 ff.; H. Grimme, "Studien zum Hbr. Urmatthäus," BZ, 23 (1935/36), esp. 260-262.

perish without heaven, how much less a man," jShebi, 9, 1 (38d, 27 f.). [18] The uniqueness of the NT passage is that the starting-point is not found in the general threat of the bird (→ 731, 6 f.) but in the actual situation of its being sold. This also draws attention to the small value of the sparrow as an object of human trade. [19] In contrast to the uncontested human evaluation is the unrestricted care of the Father even for the tiniest creature. But man's judgment is by no means a mere illustration of the creaturely weakness of the sparrow. Though the impressive opening statement makes it unnecessary to labour the point, this judgment is of significance for the whole content of the section. The life of those addressed might be considered by men just as paltry as that of sparrows. The fear for which there is no real basis (Mt. 10:31a; Lk. 12:7b) in view of the incontestable πολλῷ (→ n. 17) διαφέρετε (Mt. 10:31b; Lk. 12:7c) does not apply merely to the general afflictions of creaturely life such as accidents and illnesses. It applies to what might be planned and done by inimically disposed men who are superior in strength. What is meant is not just any danger but the danger of martyrdom. [20] The simple and manifest promise does not contain anything alien to Jewish faith. It might well have been fashioned in the pre-Christian period. But it has been handed down only in the sayings material employed by Mt. and there is no reason to assume that it is in fact older than this collection. Nor are there any traces of the post-Easter experiences of the Christian community which might suggest a later origin or reconstruction. In all probability, then, the saying belongs to the context in which the Evangelists have set it.

Bauernfeind

---

† στῦλος

A. The Pillar in Antiquity.

στῦλος [1] means "pillar" as a basic architectural feature. [2] As such the pillar is found

---

[18] For other ref. cf. Str.-B., I, 583, cf. also Schl. Mt. on 10:29.

[19] Undoubtedly the best bargain among birds for sale was picked on as a particularly good example. Already this was the sparrow, as later at a somewhat higher price level → n. 10. There are par. for a slight reduction in the purchase of 5 (2 farthings in Lk.) as compared with 2 (1 farthing in Mt.). In any case the difference between the two texts is trivial, cf. Deissmann LO, 234. On contemporary prices, cf. also Str.-B., I, 290-294, esp. 291.

[20] Cf. Wellh. Mt. on 10:28 ff. Yet no detailed comparison seems to be intended. The sparrow which is up for sale has already lost its freedom and faces certain death. The fate of helpless animals is noted with some sympathy → n. 5; → 731, 6 f.; Deissmann LO, 235.

σ τ ῦ λ ο ς. Bibl.: Pape, Pass., Liddell-Scott, Pr.-Bauer, Moult.-Mill., *s.v.*; C. Fensterbusch-G. Türk, Art. "στῦλος" in Pauly-W., 4a (1932), 428-434; G. Boström, *Proverbiastudien. Die Weisheit u. d. fremde Weib in Sprüche 1-9* (1935), esp. 3-14; W. Staerk, "Die Sieben Säulen d. Welt u. des Hauses d. Weisheit," ZNW, 35 (1936), 232-261; C. K. Barrett, "Paul and the 'Pillar' Apostles," *Studia Paulina in honorem J. de Zwaan* (1953), 1-19.

[1] On the etym. Boisacq, Hofmann, *s.v.*; Pokorny, 1008 f.

[2] Cf., e.g., Hdt., II, 169, 19 f.: παστὰς λιθίνη μεγάλη καὶ ἠσκημένη στύλοισι, Eur. Iph. Taur., 50 f.: μόνος δ'ἐλείφθη στῦλος ... δόμων πατρῴων (vl.), also BGU, VII, 1713, 4 (2nd/3rd cent. A.D.): στύλων μονολίθων. In the same sense στῦλος can also denote the "main pole of a tent," e.g., P. Zenon, III, 353, 9 (3rd cent. B.C., ed. C. C. Edgar, *Catalogue Général des Antiquités Égypt. du Musée du Caire*, 85 [1928]). The strict word for "pillar" from Hom. is ὁ or ἡ κίων. In comparison στῦλος is rarer: in Hdt., II, 169, 5, an Epidaurus inscr. IG, 4², 102, 66 (4th cent. B.C.), as a fem.; sometimes in tragedy; also various examples from the Hell. and Roman period (also derivates).

not merely in class. and Hell. times [3] throughout the Mediterranean world but also long before in the cultural sphere of Crete-Mycenae (Troy VI, Tiryns, Mycenae), [4] in the Syrian and Palestinian world, in ancient Babylonia of the 2nd millennium, and esp. in the Old Kingdom in Egypt (3rd millennium). It either acts as a support or carrier or else it stands free with a tripod or statue (votive offering). The various steles in the Near East stand free but were regarded sometimes as pedestals of the gods. [5] In view of its carrying or supporting function στῦλος can very occasionally be used in a transf. sense for proved or trustworthy men, cf. Eur. Iph. Taur., 57: στῦλοι γὰρ οἴκων εἰσὶ παῖδες ἄρσενες. [6]

B. The Word in the Old Testament.

With few exceptions [7] στῦλος in the LXX is always used for Hbr. עַמּוּד (101 times). Only in Ex. 26 is קֶרֶשׁ (which hardly appears elsewhere in the HT) rendered στῦλος (24 times). [8] στῦλος in the LXX is primarily architectural, cf. esp. Ju. 16:25 ff. [9] The στῦλοι of the tabernacle have a supporting function acc. to Ex. 26:15-25 etc. LXX. But the pillars of Solomon's temple as expressly described in 1 K. 7:2 ff.; 2 K. 25:13 ff. do not serve this purpose. [10] The pillar of cloud or fire in Ex. 13:21 f. etc. [11] is a sign of God's directing presence. [12] When Jeremiah at his call is named an "iron pillar"(עַמּוּד בַּרְזֶל) in 1:18 — not in the LXX but cf. 'Α Θ: καὶ εἰς στῦλον σιδηροῦν — the par. "brass wall" shows that the ref is not so much to a supporting pillar but rather to a prominent sign. [13] The king's platform, which he mounts on certain official occasions, is called στῦλος in 2 K. 11:14, cf. 23:3.

The word στῦλος has cosmological significance in some hymnal passages in the OT. In the context of concepts of divine epiphany there is ref. to God's shaking the "foundations" of earth [14] (Job. 9:6, cf. 38:6 vl.) or heaven (Job. 26:11) as He established them at the first (ψ 74:4). The primary thought here is that the earth is a house which God has built. This was a common idea in the whole of the Near East. It lived on in oriental Gnosticism and in this historical connection it could be applied to the Church in primitive

---

[3] In the Eastern Roman Empire of the Hell. period the Ionic pillar predominated, cf. Fensterbusch-Türk, 431.

[4] It probably spread from here to Etruria.

[5] Cf. the (isolated) saving in Cl. Al. Strom., I, 163, 4: στῦλος Θηβαίοισι Διώνυσος πολυγηθής, v. the bibl. in Fensterbusch-Türk, 433.

[6] Cf. already Aesch. Ag., 896 ff.: λέγοιμ' ἂν ἄνδρα τόνδε ... ὑψηλῆς στέγης στῦλον ποδήρη, μονογενὲς τέκνον πατρί.

[7] Once for אֶדֶן (Job 38:6 Cod AV), once each for כֹּתֶרֶת, מַצֵּבָה and עֹמֶד.

[8] This notable exception leads D. W. Gooding, *The Account of the Tabernacle. Transl. and Textual Problems of the Greek Exodus* (1959), 20 f. to the theory that a technically unskilled (76 f.) translator deviated from the tt. in a way not found elsewhere. But cf. K. Koch, "Die Priesterschr. v. Ex. 25 - Lv. 16," FRL, 71 (1959), 15, n. 1, who thinks קֶרֶשׁ meant "supporting post" rather than "board," so that the translator equated it with עַמּוּד.

[9] In Ju. 16:25 ff. we find in B the word κίων, which occurs in Hom. but in the LXX only 3 times here and in 3 Βασ. 15:15. Cosmic-mythical motifs perhaps lie behind the story of the tearing down of the pillars in Dagon's temple [Bertram].

[10] Cf. K. Galling, Art "Säule," BR, 452 f., cf. 518.

[11] Cf. also Ex. 14:19, 24; 19:9; Nu. 14:14; Neh. 9:12, 19; Wis. 18:3.

[12] The theme of the pillar of cloud over the tabernacle is the rather different one of a sign of God's cultic presence, cf. Nu. 12:5; Dt. 31:15; ψ 98:7.

[13] [Bertram].

[14] στῦλος, θεμέλιον and στερέωμα are used synon. in these texts, cf. 1 Tm. 3:15 → 736, 6 ff.

Christianity → line 23 f. [15] The same thought occurs in Sir. 24:4 with ref. to the role of wisdom as mediator of creation: ἐγὼ ἐν ὑψηλοῖς κατεσκήνωσα, καὶ ὁ θρόνος μου ἐν στύλῳ νεφέλης. Prv. 9:1 speaks of the building of the house of wisdom itself: ἡ σοφία ᾠκοδόμησεν ἑαυτῇ οἶκον καὶ ὑπήρεισεν στύλους ἑπτά. [16] Behind wisdom here there stands in diluted but recognisable form the wise Ishtar of Babylonia. The seven pillars of her house are the seven planets which encircle the disk of the earth and are the controlling powers of the world. Wisdom was their creator in primal ages. [17]

C. Rabbinic Statements.

The transf. use of עַמּוּד is rare in the Rabb. [18] R. Johanan bZakkai is addressed as "light of Israel, right pillar, [19] strong hammer," bBer., 28b, cf. the par. tradition in Ab RNat, 25 (7a). [20] In Ex. r., 2 (69a) on 3:3 Abraham is called the "pillar" of the world (עַמּוּדוֹ שֶׁל עוֹלָם), God has put Moses in his place. R. Eleazar bShammua says the same about the righteous [21] in bChag., 12b. In those two passages the Rabbi is the pillar as the teacher of the Torah and hence the mediator of revelation, [22] so that there is some analogy to Gl. 2:9. But in bKet., 104a the righteous generally are called pillars, and cf. esp. Tg.J. I on Gn. 46:28, [23] where the mighty men of Egypt are regarded as "pillars," a purely metaphorical use.

D. The Word in the New Testament.

Of the 4 instances in the NT 3 are more or less clearly related to the mythical conception → 733, 22 ff. The fact that James, the Lord's brother, Cephas and John, as the main leaders of the church of Jerusalem at the apostolic council, are held to be pillars acc. to Gl. 2:9, implies rather more than simple metaphorical usage. [24] Presupposed here is the idea of a heavenly building — the Church as

---

[15] On this cf. P. Vielhauer, ΟΙΚΟΔΟΜΗ. Das Bild vom Bau in d. chr. Lit. vom NT bis Cl. Al., Diss. Heidelberg (1939).

[16] On this cf. esp. Boström, 3-14; Staerk, 234-246; but also Barrett, 7 f.

[17] This cosmogonic wisdom myth (→ 489, 33 ff.; 498, 3 ff.) may also be found in Platonised form in Philo (for examples Staerk, 236, also U. Wilckens, "Weisheit u. Torheit," Beiträge z. hist. Theol., 26 [1959], 147-157), but esp. clearly in the Mandaeans, for whom the Jews of Jerusalem are the house of the wicked Ruha and Qudša and their seven sons, the seven pillars which Manda dHaije hews down (Staerk, 236, 238 f.). The concept then has a strong influence on the Ps.-Clem. writings, esp. Hom., 18, 14: ἐκείνους μὲν μὴ ἐγνωκέναι ἑπτὰ στύλους ὑπάρξαντας κόσμῳ καὶ δικαιοτάτῳ θεῷ εὐαρεστῆσαι δυναμένους, cf. Staerk, 232-235.

[18] Cf. Levy Wört., III, s.v.

[19] An allusion to the right side of the temple (יָכִין), 1 K. 7:21.

[20] Cf. Str.-B., I, 208 f.

[21] Cf. R. Mach, Der Zaddik in Talmud u. Midrasch (1957), 142. Cf. the material par. in Gn. r., 14 (10c) on 2:7 and Yalkut Shim'oni, I, 766 (1944), 530b, 40 ff.

[22] Cf. the position of the teacher of wisdom as the mediator of revelation; the commonly attested number 7 here corresponds to the 7 pillars of the house of wisdom in Prv. 9:1, Staerk, 240-246. Vielhauer takes this ref to be a pure figure of speech, op. cit., 20.

[23] Str.-B., III, 537.

[24] So Ltzm. Gl., ad loc. referring to Wettstein, II, ad loc.; F. Sieffert, Der Brief an d. Galater, Krit.-exeget. Komm. über d. NT⁹ (1899), ad loc. For metaphorical use cf. Vita Aesopi Cod G, 106 (ed. B. E. Perry [1952]): Aesop as κίων ("pillar") τῆς βασιλείας, cf. also Rabb. usage (→ lines 9 ff.), though Barrett, 5 f. rightly rules this out in the case of Gl. 2:9.

God's temple (cf. 1 C. 3:10 ff., 16 ff.; Eph. 2:21; Rev. 3:12) [25] — which the three who are mentioned bear up as basic pillars. This is their esteem and claim, [26] which Paul does not contest, though δοκοῦντες is given a slightly ironical note by the abundant use of the term (G. 2:2, 6, 9 cf. Phil. 3:4) [27] and it expresses a certain reserve in relation to the δοκεῖν, i.e., the claim of the three at Jerusalem. [28] Even the very agreement itself (v. 9 f.) [29] shows that their claim to be "pillars" of the Church was in fact restricted to the Jewish Christian community. Furthermore Paul at the very least regarded the position of the pillars as being on one and same level as his own apostolate to the Gentiles. [30] If those in Jerusalem for their part saw in the consent to raise a collection the acknowledgment by Gentile Christians of the precedence of Jerusalem both in salvation history and also in sacral law, Paul in arranging the collection throughout the Gentile congregations undoubtedly interpreted it quite unambiguously as a display of love by Gentile Christians for their Jewish counterparts which was designed to express the equally valid membership of both Jews and Gentiles in the one Church. The same thought surely stands behind the saying to Peter in Mt. 16:18: The rock on which the Church is to be built holds up the house or temple of the ἐκκλησία and thus has the same function as is denoted by στῦλος in Gl. 2. This thought — sometimes with reference to individuals — may also be found in the Dead Sea Scrolls. [31]

Rev. 3:12 is based on the same mythical idea of the heavenly temple of God (→ IV, 888, 32 ff.) which is held up by pillars: "The νικῶν (→ IV, 944, 39 ff.) — i.e., according to the context the one who endures through the last tribulation (cf. v. 8, 10 f.) — will I make a pillar in the temple of my God" — a pillar which cannot be removed (like the candlestick earlier in 2:5) [32] and on which the name of

---

[25] Barrett, 12-16 derives the title of the three Jerusalem leaders from this Jewish and primitive Chr. eschatological concept (→ IV, 886, n. 24 and 887, 18 ff.). Cf. esp. the Dead Sea Scrolls: the community as foundation, edifice, or temple, 1 QS 5:5 f.; 8:5 f., 8; 9:6; 11:8; 1 QH 6:26-29; 7:9 etc., also the terminology in the order of 1 QSa 1:12 ("in the 25th year he may take a place among the סוֹד of the holy community"), cf. H. N. Richardson, "Some Notes on 1 QSa," JBL, 76 (1957), 111, also E. Schweizer, "Gemeinde u. Gemeindeordnung im NT," AbhThANT, 35² (1959), 184, n. 774. For Gnostic par. cf. H. Schlier, "Religionsgeschichtliche Untersuchungen z. d. Ignatiusbriefen," Beih. ZNW, 8 (1929), 120 f.; also "Christus u. d. Kirche im Epheserbr.," Beiträge z. hist. Theol., 6 (1930), 49-60; Schlier Eph. on 2:21; Vielhauer, op. cit., 34-55 and → V, 119, 6 ff.

[26] So rightly Staerk, 246; Schlier Gl., ad loc.; Oe. Gl., ad loc.

[27] Oe. Gl., ad loc. and H. Greeven, "Propheten, Lehrer, Vorsteher bei Pls.," ZNW, 44 (1952/53), 41, n. 100. R. Annand, "A Note on the Three Pillars," Exp. T., 67 (1955), 178, is surely off the track when he suggest that Paul is merely engaging in a witticism in Gl. 2:9.

[28] E.g., Barrett, 2-4, cf. 16 f.

[29] E. Dinkler, "Die Petrus-Rom-Frage," ThR, 25 (1959), 198 suggests we have the actual wording of the agreement in Gl. 2:7 f; cf. also G. Klein, "Gl. 2:6-9 und d. Gesch. der Jerusalemer Urgemeinde," ZThK, 57 (1960), 275-295, who also concludes from the discrepancy between Gl. 2:7 f. and 2:9 that after the apostolic council there was a change in the leadership of the church at Jerusalem, Peter becoming one of the στῦλοι instead of the authoritative apostle in Jerusalem, 295.

[30] Cf. later with ref. to the apostles and prophets Eph. 2:20, also 1 Cl., 5, 2 (Peter and Paul as apostles) οἱ μέγιστοι καὶ δικαιότατοι στῦλοι.

[31] Cf. the examples → n. 25, 35 and esp. O. Betz, "Felsenmann u. Felsengemeinde," ZNW, 48 (1957), esp. 53, 59 f., 63-65.

[32] Loh. Apk., on 3:12.

the city of God, the New Jerusalem, my new name, will be inscribed. The apocalyptic idea that eschatological deliverance is an irreversible integration into the kingdom of God's salvation is here conjoined with the thought of fitting a pillar into the heavenly building, [33] and this combination expresses the central theologoumenon of Revelation, namely, that of the heavenly citizenship of tested Christians.

Finally we read in 1 Tm. 3:15: "That thou mayest know how one ought to behave in the house of God, which is the church of the living God, the pillar and ground of the truth." Here the idea of the heavenly building is less prominent; the author closes the two sections of his church order (3:1 ff., 8 ff.) with this statement. Since he adds a liturgical homology in v. 16, this is enough to yield a cultic understanding of the ecclesiological building-terminology in v. 16. The οἶκος θεοῦ is the worshipping community → II, 364, 20 ff.; V, 127, 15 ff. [34] It is the house of God in the sense of God's temple (cf. Eph. 2:19-22), and as such it is the στῦλος καὶ ἑδραίωμα (→ n. 14) τῆς ἀληθείας. [35]

Describing the angel Rev. 10:1 says: καὶ οἱ πόδες αὐτοῦ ὡς στῦλοι πυρός. Like the other detailed features in the description this reproduces a familiar element in OT theophanies, [36] → n. 11.

Wilckens

† συγγενής, † συγγένεια.

1. The Word Group in Greek.

a. The adj. συγγενής, [1] formed from σύν and γένος and found from Pind., Aesch. and Eur., refers to one who has the same γένος. It thus means "of common origin," "related," → IV, 737, 25 f. [2] It ref. esp. (also as noun, mostly plur. Pind. Pyth., IV, 133) to one of the same race or family [3] including membership of a larger union, the tribe or

---

[33] In relation to this cf. the similitude of the tower in Herm. v., 3, 2-9, which speaks of the fitting of tested Christians as stones into the heavenly tower which is being built (cf. s., 9, 3-16) and on the other side e.g., Lidz. Joh., 136 (p. 133, 11 f.): "Woe to Elizar, the great house, the pillar which supports the temple." On the apoc. notion that the eschatological kingdom of salvation is the New Jerusalem and the renewed temple cf. Volz Esch., 371-378; Bousset-Gressm., 285; Schlier Gl. on 4:26.

[34] So Dib. Past., ad loc. Cf. Eph. 2:19-22; Hb. 3:6; 1 Pt. 4:17.

[35] On ἑδραίωμα τῆς ἀληθείας cf. 1 QS 5:5 f.: "... that they may establish a foundation of truth (מוסד אמת) for Israel, for the community of the everlasting covenant, to atone for all who dedicate themselves to the sanctuary in Aaron and to the house of truth in Israel ... "; also 8:9 and 9:3 f. and esp. 1 QH 6:24 ff.: "But I will be as one who enters a fortified and strong city, a high wall, until one escapes, and to an eternal foundation of thy truth (cf. 7:9), my God. For thou wilt set a group (of men) on a rock and a support (כפים) according to a line which measures correctly, and a sounding-lead of (truth) to (build) tested stones for a strong wall ... " (cf. Betz, op. cit., 55 f.). Cf. Is. 28:16 f and → n. 25.

[36] Cf. Ex. 13:21 f. and Loh. Apk., ad loc.

συγγενής, συγγένεια. W. Michaelis, "Die 'Gefreundeten' d. Ap. Pls.," *Der Kirchenfreund,* 67 (1933), 310-313, 328-334.

[1] On the fem. form συγγενίς (NT at Lk.1:36) cf. Bl.-Debr. § 59, 3 with App. (oldest example Εὐμενίδες [Risch]); Deissmann LO, 370; Moult.-Mill., s.v. On the dat. συγγενεῦσιν for συγγενέσιν 1 Macc. 10:89 vl.; Mk. 6:4; Lk. 2:44 cf. Bl.-Debr. § 47, 4 with App.; Mayser², I, 2 (1938), 57.

[2] The sense of "born with," "native," attested in Pass. and Liddell-Scott, s.v., esp. from Pind., refers either to a quality which is "born with someone" or to one which "had its birth or origin (so γένος from Hom.) with someone" [Debrunner].

[3] Also used as a constitutional tt. Cf. the difference between συγγενεῖς and γεννῆται in Athens, G. Busolt, *Griech. Staatskunde, Handbuch kl. AW,* IV, 1, 1³ (1926), 957.

people, Thuc., I, 95, 1. It can then have the broader sense of "related in disposition and manner," "compatible," cf. Thuc., V, 108, "similar," Aristoph. Eq., 1280, "corresponding," Aristot. Gen. An., V, 8, p. 788b, 9. In a way which is analogous to the use of honorary titles in the oriental and Hell. world — συγγενής can also be used for political or sacral relations — the citizens of Magnesia are called συγγενεῖς ὄντες Μακεδόνων in Ditt. Syll.[3], II, 561, 3 f. (207/6 B.C.) and the inhabitants of Ilium praise the consul Marcus Agrippa (cf. Jos. Ant., 14, 487 etc.) as τὸν συγγενέα καὶ πάτρωνα τῆς πόλεως καὶ εὐεργέτην, op. cit., II, 776, 1 ff. (14/13 B.C.). Cf. also the combination of συγγενής and φίλος: συγγενὴς ὢν καὶ φίλος ὁ δῆμος τοῦ Ῥωμαίων δήμου, II, 591, 18 f. (196 B.C.); cf. II, 559, 29 f. and 52 (207/6 B.C.); on the other hand συγγενεῖς has its usual sense when it comes after φίλοι and ἐχθροί in Praecepta Delphica, ibid., III, 1268, I, 15-17. συγγενής is a Persian court title acc. to Xenoph. Cyrop., I, 4, 27; II, 2, 31 cf. Diod. S., 16, 50, 7; 17, 59, 2. Many witnesses in inscr. and pap. show that συγγενὴς τοῦ βασιλέως etc. is also a Ptolemaic title. [4]

b. The noun συγγένεια, found from Eur., means "relationship" in all the senses applicable to συγγενής. It thus refers to the relationship which exists between men and peoples by descent, e.g., Plat. Resp., VI, 491c, or by agreement and compatibility of disposition, e.g., Aristot. Hist. An., V, 1, p. 539a, 21. [5] συγγένεια also has, from Eur., the concrete sense of "relatives," e.g., Plat. Leg., I, 627c, though it is rarely used of an individual in this sense, Eur. Or., 1233. More broadly συγγένεια is a catchword for the analogy between God and man, the world of ideas and that of the senses, the course of the stars and human destiny. It is used thus both in philosophy and also in popular belief. Since these ideas — and the adj. συγγενής is important here as well — had no influence on the NT, as least in connection with this word group (→ III, 122, n. 6; IV, 557, 4 f.; 661, 27), [6] we may simply give a few examples. [7] In the Protagoras myth in Plat. Prot., 322a one reads: ἐπειδὴ δὲ ὁ ἄνθρωπος θείας μετέσχε μοίρας, πρῶτον μὲν διὰ τὴν τοῦ θεοῦ συγγένειαν ζῴων μόνον θεοὺς ἐνόμισεν, καὶ ἐπεχείρει βωμούς τε ἱδρύεσθαι καὶ ἀγάλματα θεῶν, cf. Leg., X, 899d. The human soul in Resp., X, 611e is called συγγενὴς οὖσα τῷ τε θείῳ καὶ ἀθανάτῳ καὶ τῷ ἀεὶ ὄντι, and for this reason it is immortal cf. Tim., 90a; Phaed., 79d, 80b, 84b. Ps.-Plat. Ep., VII, 344a speaks in class. form of the necessary relation of man to the object which is to be known: τὸν μὴ συγγενῆ τοῦ πράγματος οὔτ' ἂν εὐμάθεια ποιήσειέν ποτε οὔτε μνήμη... τε καὶ τῶν ἄλλων ὅσα καλὰ μὴ προσφυεῖς εἰσιν καὶ συγγενεῖς. The group is significant later esp. in Epict., cf. merely Diss., I, 9.

2. The Septuagint.

In the LXX we find both συγγενής and συγγένεια, but there are few connections between the two.

a. συγγένεια occurs in 44 places (including vl.), of which only 4 are in the Apocr. In the other 40 it corresponds 19 times to Mas. מִשְׁפָּחָה, which is elsewhere transl. (apart from some infrequent renderings) by δῆμος (some 150 times), φυλή (40) and πατριά (25, twice πατρίς). In addition the expression (לְ)תֹלְדֹת is transl. 14 times (between Nu. 1:20 and 1:42 in every second v., also Ex. 6:16, 19) by κατὰ συγγενείας αὐτῶν,

---

[4] Cf. Ditt. Or., Index, s.v., also I, 99, n. 1; 104, n. 2; Preisigke Wört., III, s.v.; Deissmann B, 158; M. L. Strack, "Gr. Titel im Ptolemäerreich," Rhein. Mus., NF, 55 (1900), esp. 168-190; Mitteis-Wilcken, I, 1, 7. Many variations of the title may be noted. συγγενής often denotes the highest grade in the court cursus honorum. "King's relative" was already a title in ancient Egypt, Strack, 173; cf. later "king's cousin" in Italy and England.
[5] On ἥρως συγγενείας in the burial inscr. Ditt. Syll.[3], III, 1245, 4 f. (3rd cent. A.D.) cf. Rohde, I, 254, n. 1; II, 205, n. 5.
[6] Cf. F. Cumont, After Life in Roman Paganism (1932), 96 and 111.
[7] [Kleinknecht].

cf. also Nu. 3:15 without Mas.; elsewhere for תּוֹלֵדֹת the transl. γένεσις is mostly plur. συγγένεια also corresponds once each to מוֹלֶדֶת, טַף, דּוֹד and נִין, all rare words for which there is no other special equivalent in the LXX, or only at the most ἀποσκευή for טַף.[8] In all these instances συγγένεια has the concrete sense of "relations" = "relatives," cf. also Tob. 1:22 א. On the other hand ἐν συγγενείᾳ σοφίας in Wis. 8:17 means relationship to wisdom, cf. συναναστροφή and συμβίωσις in 8:16 and cf. also 2 Macc. 5:9; 4 Macc. 10:3.

b. The use of συγγενής is quite different. Of the 22 instances (also 2 in Sus. Θ), 16 are in the Apocr. and 11 of these in 1-3 Macc. In 4 of the 6 other examples the Hbr. original is plain: דּוֹדָה, Lv. 18:14; 20:20; דּוֹד 20:20 B *; מִשְׁפָּחָה 25:45. In Ez. 22:6, however, the Mas. has זְרוֹעַ "poor man"; LXX obviously read זֶרַע "seed" and used συγγενεῖς for this. In Sir. 41:22 the original in the HT is רֵעַ, though the context indicates that this means "trusted friend" rather than "kinsman." At 2 Βασ. 3:39 one may at most conjecture an original רֵעַ; Mas. has רַךְ, and the Mas. and LXX part company in this v.[9] In the LXX version: συγγενὴς καὶ καθεσταμένος ὑπὸ βασιλέως, it is clear that συγγενής is a court title for the king's "relative." רֵעַ is also a court title in 1 Ch. 27:33, as is רֵעֶה in 2 S. 15:37; 16:16; 1 K. 4:5.[10] συγγενής is also used as a title elsewhere in the LXX. In Tob. 3:15 א; 6:11; Sus. Θ 30, 63, also 2 Macc. 5:6; 8:1; 12:39; 15:18; 3 Macc. 5:49 συγγενής still means "relative," but mostly in the narrower family sense (the ref. in 2 Macc. 5:6 is to the πολῖται of Jerusalem); in all the other instances, however, it is a Persian or Ptolemaic title. In the contest of pages in 1 Εσδρ. 3:1-4, 63 the winner hopes to be called συγγενὴς Δαρείου (3:7),[11] and in 4:42 the king says to the winner: ἐχόμενός μου καθήσῃ καὶ συγγενής μου κληθήσῃ, cf. 1 Macc. 10:89 (→ n. 1); 11:31; 2 Macc. 11:1, 35; 3 Macc. 5:39, 44. Since συγγενής belongs for the most part to the Apocr. it is not surprising that the other transl. have few instances of the term (Σ Gn. 15:2; Αλλ Lv. 25:25); in contrast there are many examples of συγγένεια in ΑΣΘ.

3. Judaism.

a. Philo has συγγένεια over 80 times,[12] mostly in the concrete sense of "relations" = "relatives," often under OT influence, cf. Gn. 12:1 in Abr., 31 and 62, also allegorically interpreted in Migr. Abr., 2, 7. 10; Rer. Div. Her., 69; cf. also the exposition of the legal definitions of relationship in Spec. Leg., IV, 159. Philo has here a very lofty idea of what is constitutive of the συγγένεια of an ἔθνος; to the true ὁμόφυλος καὶ συγγενής belong πολιτεία μία καὶ νόμος ὁ αὐτὸς καὶ εἷς θεός, IV, 159. Hence the righteous man will regard μόνην ἀνδρῶν ἀγαθῶν ὁσιότητα as φιλία and συγγένεια, Vit. Mos., II, 171, cf. Spec. Leg., III, 126: φίλον καὶ συγγένειαν ἐν τὸ θεοφιλὲς εἶναι νομίζοντες. Stronger than relationship πρὸς αἵματος is ἡ πρὸς δικαιοσύνην καὶ πᾶσαν ἀρετὴν ὁμολογία, 155. That all men are related to one another (cf. also Virt., 140) is shown to be important in the treatment of enemies and slaves, Vit. Mos., I, 314; Spec. Leg., II, 82.

---

[8] ἀποσκευή, "luggage," "utensils," here obviously "baggage train" [Bertram].

[9] Cf. P. Katz, "Das Problem des Urtextes d. Septuaginta," ThZ, 5 (1949), 12 f. and the paraphrase in Jos. Ant., 7, 43: ὡς συγγενῆ καὶ φίλον, ἀλλ᾽ οὐχ ὡς ἐχθρόν ... [Katz].

[10] LXX has πρῶτος φίλος at 1 Ch. 27:33, elsewhere ἑταῖρος. ἑταῖρος is not attested as a Ptolemaic title — though it is Macedonian — and hence it is not a good transl. πρῶτος φίλος (cf. also 1 Macc. 10:65; 11:27; 2 Macc. 8:9) is common along with φίλος in LXX, and is a Ptolemaic title esp. in Macc. Cf. also Strack, 188 f.; H. Donner, "Der 'Freund d. Königs'," ZAW, 73 (1961), 269-277.

[11] Cf. 1 Εσδρ. 3:6 f. for details, fine clothes etc., δεύτερος καθιεῖται Δαρείου.

[12] Acc. to Leisegang, s.v.

The strong influence of OT anthropology, which Philo cannot escape, prevents him from adopting without reservation philosophical notions of a συγγένεια between man and God (→ 737, 20 ff.). Only in so far as he is νοῦς does man have τὴν πρὸς τὸν αὐτοῦ (God's) λόγου συγγένειαν, ἀφ' οὗ καθάπερ ἀρχετύπου γέγονεν ὁ ἀνθρώπινος νοῦς, Exsecr., 164. λογικὴ συγγένεια with God is the best of the gifts conferred on him. Op. Mund., 77. For the rest the truth holds good: οὐ ῥᾴδιον πιστεῦσαι διὰ τὴν πρὸς τὸ θνητὸν ᾧ συνεζεύγμεθα συγγένειαν, Rer. Div. Her., 92.

The use of συγγενής (over 160 times in Philo) presents a similar picture. In the sense of "related," "belonging," "corresponding," it is employed in the most varied connections: to the relation between γεῶδες σῶμα and αἰσθήσεις in Det. Pot. Ins., 109, between αἴσθησις and διάνοια in Migr. Abr., 3, between ἀχαριστία and ὑπεροψία in Virt., 165, between ὄψις and ψυχή in Spec. Leg., III, 192. Of man it is said that through the ψυχή he is συγγενέστατος τῷ καθαρωτάτῳ τῆς οὐσίας οὐρανῷ, and even τῷ τοῦ κόσμου πατρί, Decal., 134; cf. Spec. Leg., IV, 14: ἀγχίσπορος ὢν θεοῦ καὶ συγγενὴς κατὰ τὴν πρὸς λόγον κοινωνίαν. Intrinsically, however, only God is συγγενής, οἰκεῖος and φίλος to Himself, Leg. All., III, 205. The noun "relative" occurs in the sing. only at Spec. Leg., I, 160; IV, 159, elsewhere in the plur., e.g., Abr., 245; Vit. Mos., II, 225 f.; transf. ἀρετῆς συγγενεῖς, Som., I, 86. It is common in the expression συγγενεῖς καὶ φίλοι, Vit. Mos., I, 305, 307, 322; II, 171; Spec. Leg., III, 85, 90; IV, 141. Acc. to Spec. Leg., III, 155 φίλοι are a smaller circle within συγγενεῖς, though cf. Vit. Cont., 12; Spec. Leg., II, 126. The adj. συγγενικός is common.

b. There is little worth noting in Joseph. συγγένεια is not common, and is rare in the concrete sense of "relatives," Ant., 2, 165; 6, 247; it usually means "relationship," 1, 142, 165, 211 etc. The ref. is to membership of the Jewish people, or sometimes to relationship with neighbouring peoples, e.g., Bell., 4, 311. We even find the idea of the common relationship of all men, Ant., 2, 94. We also find in Bell., 7, 349 the saying that in sleep ψυχαί, when freed from the disturbing connection with the σῶμα, enjoy relationship with God θεῷ δ' ὁμιλοῦσαι κατὰ συγγένειαν.[13] Nowhere else in Joseph. does either συγγένεια or συγγενής refer to the relation between man and God. συγγενής is very common, and since Joseph. (esp. in Ant.) has to narrate a good deal of family history it is mostly used with ref. to "relatives" in the narrower sense, i.e., immediate members of the family, Ant., 1, 176, 179, 252, 296 f., 316, 343 etc. It can also denote membership of the same tribe, e.g., 7, 260 and cf. 277. Then it can mean membership of the Ἑβραίων γένος in gen., 5, 267 f.; 6, 74 and 82; 14, 396; Bell., 7, 262 and 364. It is often found with φίλος, Ant., 6, 59, 317; 7, 43 and 164; 8, 367; 16, 156 and 381; 18, 23 and 99; Vit., 419; Bell., 3, 436 (opp. ξένος), or οἰκεῖος, Ant., 16, 288. In Bell., 1, 460, 538, 571, 620 one may ask whether συγγενεῖς καὶ φίλοι is not a court title. συγγενής is undoubtedly a title in Ant., 11, 25 (= 1 Εσδρ. 4:42 → 738, 22 f.); 13, 102 (= 1 Macc. 10:89 → 738, 23) and 354, also 17, 235; synon. φίλος as a court title, 7, 270.

c. In Ep. Ar., 241 an answer is given to the question of ὠφέλεια συγγενείας. If the misfortune of relatives is felt as one's own, then show τὸ συγγενὲς ὅσον ἰσχῦόν ἐστιν. In Intr. 7 the author describes as follows his brother Philocrates, to whom he dedicates the work: οὐ μόνον κατὰ τὸ συγγενὲς ἀδελφῷ καθεστῶτι τὸν τρόπον, ἀλλὰ καὶ τῇ πρὸς τὸ καλὸν ὁρμῇ τὸν αὐτὸν ὄντα ἡμῖν. In 147 συγγενικός means "related" with ref. to different kinds of birds. The court title συγγενής does not occur in Ep. Ar.[14]

The word does not occur in Enoch, and the only ref. in Test. XII is in Zeb. 8:6: Resenting wrong only acts divisively καὶ πᾶσαν συγγένειαν διασκορπίζει.

---

13 Cf. Schl. Theol. d. Judt., 18.
14 But cf. φίλος, 45. Cf. P. Wendland in Kautzsch Apkr. u. Pseudepigr., II, 9, ad loc. At Ep. Ar., 185 Wendland, 20 unnecessarily conjectures ὁμονοοῦσι for ὁμογενέσι.

4. The New Testament.

The idea of a relation between man and God, which was alien to the OT and later Judaism (→ III, 114, 27 ff.), in respect of which even Philo had reservations (→ 739, 1 ff.), but which was common in the surrounding world (→ 737, 20 ff.), appears plainly only at one point in the NT, namely, in the quotation from Arat. Phaen., 5 in the Areopagus address in Ac. 17:28: τοῦ γὰρ καὶ γένος ἐσμέν (→ III, 118, n. 377). What the OT and NT say about man's divine likeness is on a different level → II, 390, 10 ff.; 396, 14 ff.; [15] the same applies to the parallel between Christ and Christians. [16] The group συγγενής, συγγένεια certainly has no connections of this type in the NT.

συγγένεια is used in the concrete sense of "relations" = "relatives" in Lk. 1:61, Ac. 7:3 (= Gn. 12:1), and 7:14 in an independently formulated summary of Gn. 45:9 ff., cf. Jos. Ant., 2, 165. In the infancy stories in Lk. we also find συγγενής in 1:58; 2:44 and συγγενίς in 1:36 → n. 1. [17] Reflected here is a high regard for relationship and neighbourliness such as one finds in a village. [18] In 2:44, when the parents of Jesus are looking for Him after He stayed behind in the temple, they ask συγγενεῖς and then γνωστοί, → I, 718, 41 ff. [19] In the saying in 4:24 Luke mentions only the πατρίς of the prophet (so too Jn. 4:44), whereas Mk. 6:4 par. Mt. 13:57 mentions his οἰκία as well, and Mk. 6:4 (→ n. 1) also puts his συγγενεῖς between the two → V, 132, 1 ff. [20] In the parable about the right kind of guests in the material peculiar to Lk. (14:12), one is not to ask φίλοι nor ἀδελφοί nor συγγενεῖς nor rich neighbours. Here φίλοι and συγγενεῖς are not to be taken together → 737, 8 f.; 739, 18 ff., 34 ff. συγγενεῖς and γείτονες (cf. περίοικοι 1:58) are closer. Lk. 21:16 goes further than Mk. 13:12 par. Mt. 10:21 by mentioning συγγενεῖς καὶ φίλοι (i.e., other relatives and friends) as well as parents and brethren; [21] perhaps this twofold statement refers to close acquaintances and friends. This also seems to be the meaning in Ac. 10:24. When the Roman centurion Cornelius summoned τοὺς συγγενεῖς αὐτοῦ καὶ τοὺς ἀναγκαίους φίλους to receive Peter,

---

[15] This is to be maintained, since otherwise a connection between εἰκών and the Hell. συγγένεια teaching might be seen. Cf. A. Willms, *Eikon. Eine begriffsgeschichtliche Untersuchung zum Platonismus*. 1. Teil: "Philon v. Alex." (1935), 33, 62.

[16] It is another question whether or how far, where Gnosticism might have influenced the NT, a part is played by συγγένεια or even identity between Redeemer and redeemed.

[17] The context shows that συγγενίς cannot mean merely that Elisabeth was a Jewess like the mother of Jesus. It either means that both belonged to the tribe of Levi (cf. 1:5 → 739, 32 f.) or that they were even more closely related (cf. the normal use of συγγενής). On the Levitical descent of Mary → IV, 238, 7 ff., but also H. Sahlin, "Der Messias u. d. Gottesvolk. Stud. z. protoluk. Theol.," *Acta Seminarii Neotest. Upsaliensis*, 12 (1945), 136 f.

[18] On the relation between συγγενεῖς and περίοικοι in Lk. 1:58 *v*. Michaelis, 330. The household tables of the NT do not include relatives, friends, and neighbours. For the rest of antiquity cf. K. Weidinger, "Die Haustafeln," UNT, 14 (1928), 34-39, 41.

[19] In the version of Lk. 2:44 in Ev. Thom. Graece A 19:2 (Evangelia Apocrypha, ed. C. v. Tischendorf[2] [1876], 156) only συγγενεῖς and not γνωστοί are mentioned. This shows that the author took them to be more or less synon., συγγενεῖς being close friends.

[20] Cf. P. Oxy., I, 5 (→ V, 132, n. 6) and Copt. Thomas-Ev., Logion, 31 in Hennecke[3], 69.

[21] Cf. the Rabb. par. in Schl. Lk., *ad loc.*

it is unlikely that he had many relatives in Caesarea. [22] "Related" is undoubtedly the meaning in Jn. 18:26. [23]

In Paul συγγενής occurs only in Romans. The meaning is perfectly clear in 9:3: ὑπὲρ τῶν ἀδελφῶν μου τῶν συγγενῶν μου κατὰ σάρκα. The whole context shows that the reference is to Jews with whom the apostle shares his γένος (cf. 2 C. 11:22; Gl. 1:13 f.; Phil. 3:5). The addition κατὰ σάρκα supports this, [24] but it also shows that συγγενής is apparently not precise enough without this, just as ὁ Χριστός in 9:5 [25] or ᾿Ισραήλ in 1 C. 10:18 would hardly be possible without the corresponding addition. It may thus be seen that the word συγγενής, like ἀδελφός (→ n. 24), had now a primary Christian orientation for Paul. If one views R. 16:7, 11, 21 in this light, the question arises whether the Christians whom Paul calls his συγγενεῖς without an addition like κατὰ σάρκα are to be regarded as Jewish Christians.

Since there are also Jewish Christians in the list who are not called συγγενεῖς, namely, Aquila and Prisca in v. 3, Mary in v. 6, and possibly Rufus and his mother in v. 13, it is hard to see in συγγενεῖς in 16:7, 11, 21 a ref. to Jewish nationality as in 9:3. [26] The possibility that the συγγενεῖς of R. 16 are kinsfolk of the apostle in the narrower sense of relatives may be ruled out, since it is most improbable that there would have been six members of Paul's immediate family among those mentioned in R. 16. Membership of the tribe of Benjamin runs into the same objection. [27] Nor is it likely that the ref. is to Jews or non-Jews of Tarsus or Cilicia [28] (on 16:21 → 742, 18 ff.). 9:3 suggests rather that for Paul as a Christian συγγενής had long since been filled out with Chr. content and would thus refer to Jews only with the express addition κατὰ σάρκα. But what is its Chr. content? One may conclude from the phrase ᾿Ισραὴλ κατὰ σάρκα in 1 C. 10:18 that Paul viewed Christians as the true Israel → III, 387, 24 ff. Hence συγγενεῖς κατὰ

---

[22] The ref. cannot be to the family of Cornelius (10:2) since this would not have to be summoned specially. Against the view that the συγγενεῖς are fellow-Romans cf. Michaelis, 330.

[23] Schl. J., ad loc. suggests "compatriot." "Slaves were not Jews" → V, 558, n. 4. Bultmann J., 501, n. 6 rightly objects: "But were the ὑπηρέται slaves and not men of the Levitical temple police?" συγγενής in Jn. 18:26 and γνωστός in 18:15, are often compared: γνωστός does not mean "related" but merely "acquainted." Cf. → I, 719, 1 f.; Bultmann J. on 18:15, Bau. J. on 18:15. On the other hand LXX has γνώριμος for מוֹדָע at Rt. 2:1 and מֹדַעַת at 3:2 and both Hbr. words denote acquaintance in the sense of relative, cf. Ges.-Buhl, s.v. and M. Haller, Rt., Hndbch. AT, I, 18 (1940) on 3:2: "Here it is plain that מוֹדַעַת has taken on the full sense of relatives." This is why Jos. uses συγγενής in his version of Rt. in Ant., 5, 323.

[24] The art. before συγγενῶν shows that the word is a noun. Materially and perhaps also grammatically κατὰ σάρκα goes with τῶν ἀδελφῶν μου too. Only here in his ep. does Paul call the Jews his brethren (→ I, 145, 22 ff.); elsewhere ἀδελφός is a tt. in his Chr. vocabulary.

[25] The order makes it most unlikely that τὸ κατὰ σάρκα goes with ἐξ ὧν [Moule].

[26] So Zn. R., 607 f. on 16:7; Zahn Einl., I, 275, 297, n. 22; Ltzm. R. on 16:7; Schl. R., 400, 404; O. Michel, "Opferbereitschaft f. Israel," In Memoriam E. Lohmeyer (1951), 99.

[27] Intrinsically συγγενής might mean fellow-tribesman in this sense → n. 17. But this is not the sense in 9:3. 11:1 (cf. Phil. 3:5) would lead us in this case to expect φυλέτης or ὁμόφυλος in 9:3 (cf. Jos. Ant., 3, 14; 6, 82). Paul has συμφυλέτης in 1 Th. 2:14, but in a broader sense. M. J. Lagrange, Saint Paul, Ép. aux Romains, Études Bibl., 6 (1950), ad loc., grants that συγγενής cannot mean relative or compatriot in R. 16. He thus suggests a wider kinship ("une sorte de clan") corresponding to oriental ideas of relationship. But 9:3 is against this, nor does it meet the objection of the larger number (6 persons).

[28] J. C. Laurent, Nt.liche Stud. (1866), 33 suggests "natives of Cilicia or Tarsus." Cf. J. S. Semler, Paraphrasis epistolae ad Romanos (1769), 302. Zn. Gl., 58, n. 64 on 1:13 rightly rejects the curious relating of the γένος of Gl. 1:13 to Tarsus by T. Mommsen, "Die Rechtsverhältnisse d. Ap. Pls.," ZNW, 2 (1901), 85, n. 6. W. v. Loewenich, Pls.[2] (1949), 22 thinks the συγγενεῖς of 16:7, 11 belonged to the Jewish association in Tarsus.

σάρκα in R. 9:3 suggests that the viewed Christians as his present συγγενεῖς, his true συγγενεῖς, his συγγενεῖς κατὰ πνεῦμα. The saying of Jesus about His real kinsfolk in Mk. 3:34 f. par. could be regarded as a preparation and par. for this understanding, and one might also recall the transferring of the term λαός to the Chr. community → IV, 54, 6 ff. Against this view, however, is the fact that the μου in R. 16:7, 11, 21 indicates a personal relation between Paul and these six Christians which can hardly be explained by saying that συγγενής simply defines them as fellow-Christians. 29

It is best, then, to see in συγγενής a personal relationship. As an expression of esteem (→ 737, 3 ff.) — in the general sense and not along the lines of courtly style (→ 738, 21 ff.) — it has the sense of "close companion," "intimate," "friend." If this is so, then συγγενής μου is very much like the ἀγαπητός μου of R. 16:5, 8 f. and is one of the many predicates in συν- which the apostle used in R. 16 and elsewhere to single out Christians who were close to him. Since Paul does not call any fellow-worker φίλος, one may suspect that in his vocabulary συγγενής takes the place of φίλος. 30

This is confirmed by the fact that there is no evidence that those addressed in this way were all Jewish Christians. Neither in the case of Herodion in 16:11 nor Andronicus and Junias in 16:7 do the names force us to conclude that these are Jewish Christians. 31 As concerns the συγγενεῖς of 16:21, one cannot rule out the possibility that Jason, if he was the same as the Jason mentioned in Ac. 17:5-9, 32 was a Gentile Christian, 33 and this is fairly certain in the case of Sosipater if he was the man mentioned among the companions from the Pauline churches in Ac. 20:4. As regards Lucius, it is linguistically quite possible that this was Luke. 34 The main argument against this is that Luke was a Gentile Christian acc. to Col. 4:14 (cf. v. 11) whereas the Lucius of R. 16:21 is called a συγγενής. 35 But if συγγενής in R. 16 does not denote a native Jew, this objection falls to the ground, and there is nothing to prevent the equation of Lucius and Luke. 36

συγγενής is thus an instructive example of the way in which a word which must have had a Jewish content for Paul in his pre-Christian period was then totally transferred into the Christian sphere.

5. The Post-Apostolic Fathers.

In the post-apost. fathers one finds only συγγένεια at 1 Cl., 10, 2 f. (v. 3 = Gn. 12:1; v. 2 the intr. thereto). τὸ συγγενικὸν ἔργον in Ign. Eph., 1, 1 means conduct "becoming" the community.

Michaelis

συγγνώμη → I, 716, 25 ff.
συγκαθίζω → 787, 28 f.
συγκακοπαθέω → V, 936, 18 ff.
συγκαλέω → III, 496, 17 ff.

---

29 Where ἀδελφός is used for individual Christians it is usually without pron., R. 16:23; 1 C. 1:1; 16:12; 2 C. 1:1 etc. The only exceptions are 2 C. 2:13 and Phil. 2:25, cf. Mich. Ph., ad loc., though here ἀδελφός means more than fellow-Christians and denotes a personal relation.
30 Cf. F. Normann, *Die von d. Wurzel* φιλ *gebildeten Wörter u. die Vorstellung der Liebe im Griech.*, Diss. Münster (1959), 159 (156-164 App.: "Das NT").
31 Michaelis, 331 f.
32 Cf. W. Michaelis, "Die Gefangenschaft d. Pls. in Ephesus u. d. Itinerar des Timotheus," *Nt.liche Forschungen*, I, 3 (1925), 90-92.
33 As against Zn. Ag., 589, n. 27 on 17:5, cf. Bauernf. Ag., ad loc.
34 Cf. Deissmann LO, 372-377 (App. 4: "Lukios-Lukas").
35 Cf. Schl. R., ad loc.
36 Michaelis, 333 f.

---

† συγκαλύπτω

1. This word is common neither in class. nor Hell. Gk. It originally means "to conceal fully" σὺν δὲ νεφέεσσι κάλυψεν γαῖαν ὁμοῦ καὶ πόντον, Hom. Od., 5, 293 f.[1] In later use there is hardly any distinction between καλύπτω (→ III, 556, 24 ff.) and συγκαλύπτω.[2] It means act. "to cover," "conceal," of men, Plut. De Numa, 10 (I, 67c), the human body, Plat. Resp., V, 452d, the head, BGU, VIII, 1816, 19 (60/59 B.C.); also intellectual matters like the truth, Olympiodorus Alchemista, 1,[3] a word, Aesch. Prom., 523, finally things, e.g., τὴν σκηνήν, Chariton De Chaerea et Callirhoe, V, 2, 9.[4] χρόνῳ τι συγκαλύψαι, Eur. Phoen., 872 means "to cause something to be forgotten with time." Mid. the meaning is "to conceal oneself," Xenoph. Cyrop., VIII, 7, 28; Plut. De Demosthene, 29 (I, 859e); Alex., 69 (I, 703d) and with κεφαλή "to conceal one's head," IG, 4², 126, 6; "to hide," Jos. Ant., 9, 209.

2. In the LXX[5] the use is much the same as in Gk. lit.: "to cover a man," Ju. 4:18; "to conceal shame," Gn. 9:23; Sir. 26:8; "to conceal faults," Prv. 26:26 S *; "to conceal" one's soul, ψ 68:11 vl.;[6] finally 3 times mid. "to disguise oneself," 1 S. 28:8; 1 K. 22:30; 2 Ch. 18:29.

3. In the NT the word occurs only in the proverbial saying of Jesus in Lk. 12:2 (→ V, 553, 8 ff.): οὐδὲν δὲ συγκεκαλυμμένον ἐστὶν ὃ οὐκ ἀποκαλυφθήσεται, καὶ κρυπτὸν ὃ οὐ γνωσθήσεται, which corresponds in content to Mt. 10:26.[7, 8] The contexts show that the meaning of the two is the same. What is being said is that the disciples need not be afraid since the hitherto hidden wickedness of opponents (Mt.) or hypocrisy of the Pharisees (Lk.) will be so manifest that enemies can destroy only the disciples' bodies and not their souls.[9] The only difference between the passages is that the saying in Mt. is more closely integrated into the context and is thus more specific than that in Lk., which is more loosely connected with the context, and which evokes, and is meant to evoke, apocalyptic associations with a general unveiling of the reality of this aeon in God's sight (cf. Lk. 12:3 ff.). Nevertheless, it is hardly possible to connect the differing nuances of the saying with the Lucan συγ-.[10] Here too, then, συγκαλύπτω is to be understood as "to conceal" as in ascertained usage → lines 2 ff.

Kasch

συγκαλύπτω. → III, 556, 21 ff.; Pape, Pass., Liddell-Scott, Pr.-Bauer, *s.v.*

[1] Here the prep. is separated from the verb, hence tmesis.

[2] Except where καλύπτω is closely related to death and burial, → III 556, 26 ff.; 557, 11 ff. This is not found in the case of συγκαλύπτω. Combinations with συν- "together" often give verbs a perf. sense in Gk., Schwyzer, II, 268 and 488.

[3] *Collection des anciens alchimistes grecs,* ed. M. Berthelot, II (1888), 70.

[4] Ed. W. E. Blake (1938).

[5] There is no fixed original in the HT; 9 times כסה pi, 4, כסה; 3, different Hbr. verbs, a different version 2, no equivalent 3 [Bertram].

[6] Septuaginta Gottingensis, 10, Psalmi cum Odis, ed. A. Rahlfs (1931), ad loc.

[7] The only differences in Mt. as compared to Lk. are γάρ for δέ and no συν- though cf. the critical apparatus in Nestle on Lk. 12:2.

[8] Lk. 8:17 and Mk. 4:22 belong together and agree with Lk. 12:2; Mt. 10:26 differs materially for all the similarity of form, since what is hidden in the first passages is Jesus' message about God's kingdom, as against W. Grundmann, *Das Ev. nach Lk., Theol. Handkomm. z. NT,* 3² (1961) on 12:2.

[9] Mt. 10:28: φοβεῖσθε δὲ μᾶλλον τὸν δυνάμενον καὶ ψυχὴν καὶ σῶμα ἀπολέσαι ἐν γεέννῃ. Lk. 12:5: φοβήθητε τὸν μετὰ τὸ ἀποκτεῖναι ἔχοντα ἐξουσίαν ἐμβαλεῖν εἰς τὴν γέενναν.

[10] Schl. Lk. on 5:25: "συγκαλύπτω is just a little more Greek than καλύπτω."

---

† συγκλείω

1. συγκλείω (older Attic ξυγκλήω) can have various senses in Gk. In Gk. and Hell. writers it means a. "to close up together," Eur. Ba., 1300: of the body whose members are "integrated"; cf. Plat. Tim., 76a; Critias, 117e; Isoc. Or., 12, 24; 15, 68. In a military sense it is used of soldiers marching in closed ranks, Xenoph. Cyrop., VII, 1, 33; Thuc., IV, 35, 1; V, 72, 1. It means b. "to close," e.g., the eyes, mouth, Eur. Hipp., 498; Ion, 241; Hec., 430; Xenoph. Mem., I, 4, 6. A further sense is c. "to enclose," "encircle," "surround," Hdt., VII, 41, 2; cf. Thuc., VIII, 67, 2: the assembly which is crowded on to the narrow terrain of Colonos. Of fish in a net, Aristot. Hist. An., IV, 8, p. 533b, 26; cf. Ael. Arist., 32 (Dindorf, I, 606). In a geographical description mountains encircle a lake, Hdt., VII, 129, 1. Militarily soldiers are enclosed by fortifications, Polyb., 1, 7, 10; 1, 8, 2; 1, 17, 8; 1, 49, 8; 3, 117, 11. Then we have d. "to throw into prison," "to shut or lock up," Polyb., 38, 18, 2; Plut. De Dione, 30 (I, 971c). Sense e. is "to envelop." In the polemic against worshipping idols it is said that it is unworthy to envelop the gods in matter (Plut. Def. Orac., 29 [II, 426b]) or to enclose them in temples (Aristid. Apol., 3, 2). Sense f. is "to drive someone into a corner," "to bring into distress or danger," "to enforce work or offerings," "to compel," Polyb., 3, 63, 3; Diod. S., 12, 34, 5; 19, 19, 8. The subject of the compelling may be the critical situation οἱ καιροί, Polyb., 2, 60, 4, or circumstances, τὰ πράγματα ibid., 11, 20, 7. But it is usually Tyche which brings historical personages into these situations and makes action necessary, ibid., 3, 63, 3; 11, 2, 10. Tyche acts as the arbitrer in war by laying down the conditions of historical conflict, 1, 58, 1. συγκλείω is also used of time which "presses," 18, 7, 3; 18, 9, 2. It can also mean "to run out," "to come to an end," Diod. S., 10, 4, 6; GDI, 3087, 19. A further sense g. is "to form a circle," Philostr. Imagines, 6 (II, 400). We also find the noun σύγκλεισις, Thuc., V, 71, 1 (ξύγκλησις); Arrianus Anabasis, I, 4, 3;[1] Theophr. De Odoribus, 36; P. Lond., II, 237, 21 (4th cent. A.D.); it is used esp. of the military line of battle. We also find σύγκλεισμα for "closure," "moulding," "enclosure," 4 Βασ. 16:17 and συγκλεισμός "closure," Hos. 13:8; "siege," 1 Cl., 55, 4 and 5: ἐν συγκλεισμῷ οὔσης τῆς πόλεως. In agreements συγκλεισμός means the "end" of periods of time, e.g., P. Oxy., II, 275, 20 (66 A.D.); III, 483, 17 (108 A.D.); 506, 14 (143 A.D.).

2. In the LXX συγκλείω is used for various Hbr. words, e.g., עָצַר in Gn. 16:2; 20:18 the "closing" of the womb; סָגַר in Ex. 14:3: the desert "surrounds" the Israelites; Jos. 6:1: Jericho is an "enclosed" and fortified city; cf. also Is. 45:1; 2 Macc. 12:7. In 3 Βασ. 6:20 the Holy of Holies is "overlaid" with pure gold (χρυσίῳ συγκεκλεισμένῳ).[2] For הִסְגִּיר συγκλείω means "to deliver up," "to surrender." It is par. to παραδίδωμι in ψ 77:48, 50 and 1 Βασ. 23:12 (Θ παραδώσουσιν, another version συγκλείσουσιν).[3] The city of refuge protects the manslayer from being "delivered up" to the avenger of blood in Jos. 20:5 A. Prisoners of war are "delivered up" to other foes by the victors, Am. 1:6, 9; Ob. 14. The Psalmist thanks God that He has not "delivered" him up to his enemies, ψ 30:9. But God can "deliver up" His own people to the sword, ψ 77:62. He "delivered up" the cattle of the Egypt. to death, ψ 77:50. He can also give the hosts of the Gentiles

---

συγκλείω. Cf. Pass., Liddell-Scott, Pr.-Bauer, s.v.; Levy Wört., Jastrow, s.v. סגר, עצר, צור.

[1] Ed. A. G. Roos (1907).
[2] The expression goes back to Hbr. זָהָב סָגוּר which is modelled on the Accadian hurāsu sagru. Cf. on this C. Bezold-A. Götze, Bab.-assyr. Glossar (1926), 127 and 210.
[3] Cf. Field, 528.

into the hand of Israel, 1 Macc. 3:18; 4:31. συγκλείω is used for פצח pi in Mi. 3:3 A: They have "included" the bones. The other MSS have συνέθλασαν, which is closer to the HT. [4] The Hbr. is צור when it is said of the Chaldeans that they have "invested" the city, Jer. 21:4, 9. συγκλείω also means "to surround" in the military sense in 1 Macc. 5:5; 6:49; 15:25. In 1 Macc. 6:18 the Acra garrison "enclosed" Israel around the sanctuary, cf. Jos. Ant., 12, 362. συγκλείω is used here either in a weaker sense for "to hem in," "to harass," "to cause difficulties," or as a periphrasis for "to slay," "to hew down." [5]

3. סגר hi is employed in the Dead Sea Scrolls in the same way as in the OT. a. God "delivered" Goliath into the hand of David, i.e., his power, 1 QM 11:1 f. In the gt. war of the end-time God will "deliver up" enemies of all lands to the poor, 1 QM 11:13. "To give up to the sword" הִסְגִּיר לְחֶרֶב occurs in Damasc. 1:17 (1:12); 3:10 f. (4:9); 8:1 (9:10) fig. for God's judgment. הִסְגִּיר here resembles מסר in 19:10 (9:10 B). b. But God can also protect the righteous from judgment by "closing" the jaws of lions, 1 QH 5:9 f., 14, cf. Da. 6:23. The ref. here is to avenging angels which visit the earth in the last days. [6] The gates of hell will finally be "closed" for ever over all the creatures of iniquity, 1 QH 3:18; cf. Rev. 20:3. c. סגר q or hi has a legal sense in Damasc. 13:6 f. (15:8); 15:14 f. (19:12). [7] A man who violates the commandments of the Torah will be "closed in" by the sentence of the overseer, i.e., punished and separated from fully accredited members of the sect. In Damasc. 6:12-14 (8:11 f.), on the basis of Mal. 1:10, there is a warning against those who might kindle God's altar in vain in the spiritual sanctuary; one must be as "closers of the door" against them, i.e., not receive them into the sect. This legal use reminds us of the power of the keys in Mt. 16:19; Jn. 20:23. d. סגר has a technical sense in 1 QM 5:7, 9; the ref. is to the "closure" which keeps the lance point in the shaft. e. In ancient mythical contexts we find the idea of a "prison" as the divinely appointed place of punishment for fallen angels and powers, Eth. En. 18:14; cf. the description in 21:2, 7 ff. and the "binding" or "chaining" of these forces, loc. cit. This binding may be for a long (but limited) time or for ever. The prison is not just a spatial one; it signifies a kind of deposing of the powers from their sphere of dominion. Attention has been drawn to the Iranian origin of these notions and to their broad historical dissemination. They are certainly to be seen in Rev. 20:1-3 and the Mandaean writings. [8]

4. The verbs mentioned in relation to the OT also figure in later Judaism. From עצר comes the name of the feast ἀσαρθά in Jos. Ant., 3, 252 (Aram. עֲצַרְתָּא), strictly the concluding feast of the Pesach, bPes., 42b; bShab., 147b. עצר can be used transf. for "to rule," עוֹצֵר is the "ruler" who rules over those who remain in the city and have not gone out to war, bAZ, 71a. With ref. to the wife it is said: "Thou shalt be the one ruled by me," bQid., 6a. In Gn. r., 41 on 12:17 we also find the noun עִיצּוּר "closing," "restraining." and in 52 on 20:17 f. עֲצִירָה "closing," "stopping." סְגַר Aram. סְגַר "to close in" in Da. 6:23 is often referred to the leper who is shut up, Meg., 1, 7. In T. Neg., 6, 1; bSanh., 71a there is ref. to the ruins of the house "infected" with leprosy. סגר also has corresponding nouns: סְגִירָה "enclosing" in Nu. r., 13 on 7:41 f. and סוּגַר "iron collar," "chain" in bShab., 51b; jShab., 5, 4 (7c, 21). צור also Aram. "to compress," "wrap round," bBQ, 49b can take on the sense "to form," "shape," "paint," strictly "to impress with the instrument," [9] bShab., 75b; 103b; Gn. r., 7 on 1:20. God forms man from water, bSanh., 91a. Hence the noun

---

[4] Cf. J. Ziegler, Duodocim Prophetae, Septuaginta Gottingensis, 13 (1943), 42, who views the variants as synon.
[5] Cf. H. Bevenot, Die beiden Makkabäerbücher (1931), 90.
[6] J. Licht, The Thanksgiving Scroll (1957), 99 f.
[7] Cf. C. Rabin, The Zadokite Documents[2] (1958), 75.
[8] Loh. Apk. on 20.1-3.
[9] So Levy Wört., IV, 180. But it is probable that we have here different roots, cf. Ges.-Buhl, 678 f.; Köhler-Baumg., 799.

צוּרָה means "form." Anyone who paints a figure on a vessel on the Sabbath may be punished for working, bShab., 75b; 103b; cf. Gn. r., 7 on 1:20.

5. In the NT we read in the story of Peter's catch of fish in Lk. 5:6: "And when they had this done, they inclosed in their nets (συνέκλεισαν) a great multitude of fishes." The figurative expression is along the lines of general usage, → 744, 9 f. In Paul's thesis in Gl. 3:22 f. he says of Scripture, which is endowed with divine authority, that it shuts up all, i.e., all men, under the dominion of sin in order that the inheritance of the promise might be given to believers on the basis of faith in Jesus Christ → IV, 1074, 31 ff. To support this thesis confession is made that before faith came we were held in custody under the Law, shut up to the revelation of God. The theme of being shut up, which is repeated in the passage, is strengthened by the new and related theme of custody (ἐφρουρούμεθα). This Pauline thesis is to be taken historically. It is thus connected with his apocalyptic doctrine of the aeons and is teleologically orientated to his understanding of salvation. In God's plan of salvation one thing takes place in order that something else may result. The first reference is to Scripture, which in its judgment brings to light the shutting up of man. Then there is reference to the Law, which actually accomplishes this. [10] How important this concept of shutting up is for Paul may be seen from the parallel R. 11:32: God has shut up all men, both Jews and Gentiles, under disobedience, i.e., shown them to be disobedient and thus placed them under the same verdict, in order that He may have mercy on all. The teleological thrust takes on eschatological significance here.

The Pauline expression in R. 11:32 is related to LXX usage, which has συγκλείω and παραδίδωμι for Hbr. הִסְגִּיר → 744, 34 f. One may also remember how Polyb. speaks of the delivering up of some men to historical situations by Tyche, → 744, 19 ff. In Gl. 3:22 f., however, Paul seems quite plainly to have the figure of the prison before him. One might thus think of the shutting up of the dead in *sheol*. As the dead are in the prison of the underworld awaiting the resurrection and judgment, so men are for Paul shut up in the prison of sin. The Law plays the role of the jailer. One cannot tell from Gl. 3:22 f. whether Paul was acquainted with the Gnostic view that the earthly world is a prison in which souls are shut up until the redeemer rescues them by a descent → lines 42 ff. One should not forget the element of polemical distortion in the argument of Gl. 3:23 that the Law does not bring about a holy and blessed enclosing but a shutting up which renders man helpless and captive like imprisonment. ἐφρουρούμεθα can, of course, have the more positive sense of protective custody. [11] If this is the pt. in Gl. 3:22 then συγκλείω is to be taken in the sense of R. 11:32: Scripture shows that men are given up to sin, and for this reason God has through the Law put them in custody to protect them against self-destruction and against the influence of wicked powers until faith is revealed. This understanding gives the Law a limited but positive function and makes Gl. 3:23 par. to 3:24. In 3:23 the Law is depicted as a protector, as the protective prison or warder, while in 3:24 it is the παιδαγωγός who accompanies the immature boy → V, 620, 18 ff.

6. In the dualistic Gnostic view of the world the earth is the domain of the forces of evil. The underworld thus loses independent significance, since the present world takes on its essential features. [12] The Gnostic finds in this a prison in which souls are shut up

---

[10] Schlier Gl. on 3:22 f. What is said about the historical character of revelation (on v. 23) is important. Cf. D. Rössler, *Gesetz u. Geschichte* (1960), 55-70.

[11] Oe. Gl. on 3:22 f.

[12] J. Kroll, "Gott u. d. Hölle. Der Mythus vom Descensuskampf," *Studien d. Bibliothek Warburg*, 20 (1932), 34 f.

until the redeemer comes down to free them. Thus the coming of the redeemer to the world is depicted as a *descensus ad inferos:* "And I opened the gates which were closed, and I broke the iron bars ... and nothing stayed closed before me because I had become he who opens all things. And I went through to all my own who were shut up to free them, that I should not leave any bound or binding," O. Sol. 17:8-11. There is a similar depiction in the Manichaean Ps. of Heracleides. [13] The figure of the bolt also plays a role in Gnosticism in descriptions of the creation of the human body. In the Apocryphon of Jn. 55:3-13 we read that the whole group of archons (ἀρχοντική) put man in the power of the material world and the sphere of mortality by creating for him a coarsely sensual body: "This is the shackle, the grave of the πλάσμα of the body which is put on man as the shackle of matter (ὕλη)." [14] To Horus' question how male and female souls arose Isis answers: When moisture and cold predominated in the putting together of the four elements, the soul enclosed (συγκλειομένη) in the mass was fluid and voluptuous, i.e., female, Stob. Ecl., I, 410, 13. The idea of enclosing is common in Mandaean works. "Speech was difficult in the mouth of Dew, and he enclosed himself in his own container," Lidz. Ginza R, 85, 5 f. etc. "When I saw it, I surrounded it with a ring, which (was made fast?) on the heart of heaven. I created and made a wall for him, an iron wall, and enclosed his whole dwelling with this. Over the wall with which I surrounded him I set guards, guards who would take note of his camp," *ibid.,* 87, 13-21. "Then Josamin beat against his skina. I covered his radiance, and man for man they threw a chain about him," Lidz. Joh., 2-3. [15]

Michel

συγκληρονόμος → III, 767, 33 ff.
συγκοινωνέω → III, 797, 15 ff.
συγκοινωνός → III, 797, 15 ff.
συγκρίνω → III, 953, 14 ff.
συζάω → 787, 4 ff.

συζητέω, συζήτησις, συζητητής

1. The verb means a. "to examine with, together," from Plat., e.g. Crat., 384c; Men., 90b; b. "to dispute," P. Oxy., III, 532, 17; c. "to strive," P. Oxy., XIV, 1673, 20 ff. (2nd cent. A.D.): συνεζήτησα πολλὰ καὶ κατέπλεξα, "I had much strife and confusion."

2. In the NT the verb occurs a. in the sense "to discuss" (Mk. 1:27 [abs.]; Mk. 9:10; Lk. 24:15) and b. "to dispute" (Mk. 8:11; 9:14, 16; 12:28; Lk. 22:23; Ac. 6:9; 9:29).

---

[13] C. R. C. Allbery, *A Manichaean Psalm-Book,* II (1938), 196, 15 ff.
[14] W. Till, *Die gnostischen Schriften d. Pap. Berolinensis* 8502 (1955), 151. On the idea of the human body as a "fetter" cf. H. Jonas, *Gnosis u. spätantiker Geist, I: Die mythologische Gnosis* (1934), 105 f.: The link between the fate of alienation and being taken captive.
[15] Acc. to Lidz. Joh., 30, n. 2 פּארקסא means "chain," then "bar." The question of a possible connection with Bab. *parsigu,* "band of material, wool," is also discussed here.

3. In the post-apost. fathers one finds the meaning a. "to discuss" in Barn., 4, 10, b. "to dispute" in Ign. Sm., 7, 1 and c. "to ponder" in Herm. s., 6, 1, 1. συζητέω is common in Just., so Dial., 64, 2 alongside πυνθάνομαι with ref. to the disputes of the Pharisees with Jesus, Dial., 102, 5; cf. 107, 1: the meaning is also "to dispute" in 120, 5, cf. 93, 5.

† συζήτησις.

1. The noun means "common investigation," "dispute," "quarrel." It occurs only in later lit. Philo has it occasionally, Det. Pot. Ins., 1; Leg. All., III, 131; Op. Mund., 54 vl. "dispute." It has the same sense in Epic. Fr., 74. [1] Cic. adopted it in the Gk. form in Fam., 16, 21, 4: *non est enim seiunctus locus a* φιλολογίᾳ *et cotidiana* συζητήσει (philosophical "disputation"). On the use for "debate," "strife of words," "academic examination" → II, 893, 25 ff., 39 ff.

2. συζήτησις occurs in the NT at Ac. 15:2, 7; 28:29, but only in the textus receptus; it means "dispute," "quarrel," "strife."

† συζητητής.

This word means strictly "one who investigates or disputes with." Thus far it has not been found in non-bibl. Gk.

The only NT instance is at 1 C. 1:20. [1] In v. 18 Paul extols the "folly" of the preaching of the cross by which the wisdom of this world is invalidated. The short ironical questions: ποῦ σοφός; ποῦ γραμματεύς; ποῦ συζητητής τοῦ αἰῶνος τούτου; [2] refer to representatives of Greek and Jewish wisdom and emphasise better than longer presentations could do the triumphant superiority of the apostolic preachers of the Gospel to the teachers of this world's wisdom. [3]

J. Schneider

| † σύζυγος |

1. σύζυγος, originally adj. then noun, is not common. Lit. it denotes "spanned together in a common yoke," but this sense is not found. It leads, however, to the ref. of σύζυγος to two who are bound together, cf. συζεύγνυμι "to span together in the yoke," σύζευξις for "marriage" in Plat., συζυγία "couple" etc., [1] σύζυγος, the (one) "companion," Eur.

συζήτησις. [1] C. Bailey, *Epicurus* (1926), 116.

συζητητής. [1] This v. is quoted in Ign. Eph., 18, 1.

[2] The words of Paul echo Is. 19:11 and 33:18. In Is. 33:18 the questions ποῦ εἰσιν οἱ γραμματικοί; ποῦ εἰσιν οἱ συμβουλεύοντες; express the triumph of Yahweh and His people over secular powers. They relate originally to officials of the Assyr. king. On συζητητής Bchm. 1 K. on 1:20a rightly remarks: "But the conclusion (of Paul's saying) with its συζητητής borrows only distantly from the συμβουλεύοντες of the LXX."

[3] Acc. to Schl. K., 84 all three terms (σοφός, γραμματεύς and συζητητής) relate to Judaism. Against this U. Wilckens, *Weisheit u Torheit* (1959), 28 rightly argues that one may see from v. 22 that in v. 20a Paul uses two other terms in development of σοφός, the one (γραμματεύς) denoting Jewish theology and the other (συζητητής) Gk. philosophy. In his polemic, then, Paul has in view a wisdom "which, though found in different forms in Jews and Greeks, is proper to the whole world, to all men."

σύζυγος. [1] ζεῦγος "pair" is common in LXX for צֶמֶד, also outside the Bible, v. Pr.-Bauer, *s.v.* Cf. συνέζευξεν of husband and wife, Mk. 10:9 par.

Iph. Taur., 250, cf. Aristoph. Pl., 945, also an inscr. from Cos: νεικήσας καὶ ἀποκτείνας τὸν σύζυγον ἀπέθανεν, [2] cf. too CIG, III, 4175; the scribblings of pairs of friends Ἀλλέας σύζυγοι φίλοι Δαμᾶς (4 lines), Inscr. Magn., 321, 1-4, σ]ύζυγοι Βαίβιος Κάλλιπος (3 lines), 328, 1-3; esp. ἡ σύζυγος "spouse," Eur. Alc., 314; God gives her, Test. R. 4:1; cf. Lat. coniux, though ἡ σύζυγος is rare in this sense, σύμβιος being very common in the pap., also inscr., e.g., CIJ, I, 300; σύζυγος "by pairs," Aesch. Choeph., 599; many fish do not live in shoals but by pairs, σύζυγα par. συνδυάζεται, Aristot. Hist. An., IX, 2, p. 610b, 8; in a rather broader sense ἀδελφὰ τούτοις καὶ σύζυγα denoting agreement, Plut. Lib. Educ., 14 (II, 10d). Though not found as such, the word is possible as a proper name, cf. the not very common Σύνδρομος, Ditt. Syll.[3], III, 1143, 3, Σύμμαχος, Diod. S., 12, 72, 3; Paus., VI, 1, 3 etc., and the rare Σύμφωνος, GDI, 2738, 19 etc. [3]

2. σύζυγος does not occur in the LXX. [4] In Ἀ cf. Ez. 23:21: ἐν τῷ ποιῆσαι Αἴγυπτον συζύγους μου, "in that you coupled yourself with the Egyptians."

3. The only NT instance of the term is in Phil. 4:3. In itself it could be a proper name here. Of similar names we have only incidental examples (→ lines 10 ff.) and Σύζυγος might still be found. But γνήσιε in Phil. 4:3 is against this. [5, 6] Nor is "spouse" (→ lines 4 f.) likely, though Cl. Al. Strom., III, 53, 1 took this to be the meaning here. For one thing, it is improbable that Paul was married (1 C. 7:7; 9:5) during his apostolate. Again, γνήσιος does not fit in with this, since if used with "spouse" it would mean "lawful" (→ I, 727, 15 f.). [7] The combination of γνήσιε "tested" [8] (→ I, 727, 22) with σύζυγε "the other of two" (→ 748, 26 ff.) [9] suggests that the one addressed had a specific relationship with Paul which might have been

---

[2] R. Herzog, Koische Forschungen u. Funde (1899), No. 133; be suggests gladiators, cf. the burial inscr. "Put to sleep by fists of the σύνζυγος, I lie here," Epigr. Graec., No. 318, 3, also "whom all σύνζυγοι in the stadium feared," all the partners in the contest, JHS, 34 (1914), 19, lines 7-10.

[3] Σύζυγος belongs to compounds which are "from the very outset appellatives that by virtue of their content seem to be well adapted to serve as proper names," cf. the names → lines 10 ff., F. Bechtel, Die histor. Personennamen d. Griech. (1917), VIII f. There are also combinations with -ζυγος, 185 f.

[4] The synon. συζυγής is found in the sense of "husband" in 3 Macc. 4:8. Philo Poster. C., 60 and 61; Det. Pot. Ins., 15 takes the name Hebron to mean συζυγή and thus suggests חברas a possible Hbr. original, cf. συζεύγνυμι in LXX Ez. 1:11 [Bertram].

[5] The idea that γνήσιος means that Σύζυγος ("the one who yokes together") has proved a true bearer of his name by mediating between the two mentioned in v. 2 is quite untenable, as against Haupt Gefbr. on Phil. 4:2; cf. Ew. Ph., ad loc.; W. C. v. Manen, Art. "Synzygus," EB, IV, 4844, who thinks the use of the symbolical name strengthens the case against the authenticity of Phil.; cf. the art. "Euodia," EB, II, 1427.

[6] γνήσιε cannot be used as a polite form of address; it can only mean "genuine," "true," in this context [Dihle].

[7] Grammatically one would also expect the fem. γνησία on this view, e.g., 1 Cl., 62, 2; adj. gen. are used with 3 endings in the koine, Bl.-Debr. § 59, 1 f.

[8] Cf. φίλων δεῖ γνησίων ἢ διαπύρων ἐχθρῶν, Plut. De Capienda Ex Inimicis Utilitate, 6 (II, 89b); cf. BGU, I, 86, 19 (155 A.D.). Decisive here, too, is the sense "lawful," "true," i.e., one who bears the description aptly. Cf. γνησίως προνοήσαντα, "caring for aright," Inscr. Magn., 188, 9 f.

[9] "Paired companion," "worthy (→ n. 8) companion," Dib. Ph. ad loc. C. Schmidt-W. Till, Kpt.-gnostische Schr., I[3] (1959) transl. σύζυγος in Pist. Soph. (→ 750, 17 ff.) regularly as "(paired) partner."

limited in time and space but which was in some sense unique while it lasted; this explains why the name is not given. [10]

The accounts of Paul's work in Ac. often presuppose a partnership of two, Ac. 13:2, 43; 14:14 etc. (→ lines 10 ff.), though this is not emphasised. [11] The expression γνήσιε σύζυγε occurs only here in Paul; other terms he uses for fellow-workers are συναιχμάλωτος (→ I, 196, 37 ff.), σύνδουλος, → συνεργός, συστρατιώτης → 710, 34 ff. Other personal attributes of individually mentioned Christians with ref. to work are δόκιμος ἐν Χριστῷ in R. 16:10, ἀγαπητός (μου [ἐν κυρίῳ]) in R. 16:5, 8, 12. If a particular worker is sought, Ac. suggests Silas. [12] He is one of the ἡγούμενοι of Jerusalem in 15:22. He is first linked with Judas Barsabbas in v. 22, 27, 32, then with Paul in v. 40, also 16:19, 25, 29. Timothy is not mentioned until Ac. 16:1, then with Silas after Paul leaves them together in 17:14. Yet Timothy is a preacher in 2 C. 1:19 and in 1 Th. 1:1; 2 Th. 1:1 he is mentioned with Silas as a fellow-writer, and later alone in 2 C. 1:1; Phil. 1:1; Phlm. 1; Col. 1:1. [13] The metaphor of the common yoke is used in another way by Paul in 2 C. 6:14 → II, 901, 36 ff.

In post-NT usage the sense "belonging to a pair" is determinative. In Gnosticism (→ VI, 301, 20 ff.; n. 26) there is ref. to the σύζυγος of Pistis Sophia, Pist. Soph. (→ n. 9), 29 (p. 26, 16); 31 (p. 28, 4); 39 (p. 39, 35); 50 (p. 58, 37), whose help she expects, 32 (p. 30, 23); 41 (p. 44, 9); 48 (p. 55, 10); σύζυγος also occurs in 93 (p. 138, 8). The σύζυγος of heaven is earth, Hipp. Ref., VI, 13, that of the Father is Sige, VI, 29, 3 f.; Sophia will bring forth without the σύζυγος, VI, 30, 7; cf. 31, 4 — the sense of "consort" is obviously determinative here. In ecclesiastical usage the term also pts. to relationship by pairs even in the transf. sense. The Holy Ghost is σύζυγος (adj.) of the "sun of righteousness" (Mal. 4:2), Eus. Praep. Ev., 7, 15, 15 and 16, 1; doing follows willing as σύζυγον (cf. Phil. 2:13), Orig. Comm. in Joh., 20, 23 on 8:44 (GCS, 10, 357) etc. Lit. with ref. to the listing of the disciples in pairs in Mt. 10:2 f. Eus. notes that Mt. puts himself after his σύζυγος Thomas, Dem. Ev., III, 5, 84 f.

Delling

συζωοποιέω → 787, 11 f.

---

[10] The partner is in Philippi, so that the recipients of the letter know who is meant. Sometimes Paul does not give the names of fellow-workers in other ref., 2 C. 8:18, 22; 12:18, but the reasons are different here. It is not very likely (Ltzm. K. on 2 C. 8:18) that in the 2 cases in 2 C. 8 the names were struck out later for bad conduct while Paul's praise of the brother was left in.

[11] Phil. 4:3 is taken in the sense of the custom mentioned in → I, 417, 31 ff.; n. 68 by J. Jeremias, "Paarweise Sendung im NT," NT Essays, Stud. in Memory of T. W. Manson, ed. A. J. B. Higgins (1959) 136-143.

[12] Cf. Jeremias, op. cit., 140. So already Bengel, ad loc.: συνεργούς, cooperarios, habuit multos; συζύγους, compares, non multos, primum Barnabam, deinde Silam (vg has compar hat). Acc. to G. Friedrich, Der Br. an d. Phil., NT Deutsch, 8⁹ (1962), ad loc., who divides Phil into two letters, 95 (1:1-3:1a; 4:10-23 and 3:1b-4:9), the ref. is possibly to Timothy.

[13] Opinions differ as to whether בַּר זוּג (זוּגָא, loan word) might stand behind Paul's σύζυγος, cf. Jeremias, op. cit., 136-138; Schl. Mt., 325 f.; examples Krauss Lehnw., 240 f.

```
┌─────────────────────────────┐
│  συκῆ, σῦκον, ὄλυνθος,       │
│  συκάμινος, συκομορέα,       │
│  συκοφαντέω                 │
└─────────────────────────────┘
```

† συκῆ, † σῦκον, † ὄλυνθος.

1. Linguistic Factors.

a. ἡ συκῆ [1] is the "fig-tree," Ficus carica L, Hbr. תְּאֵנָה. Its fruit is usually τὸ σῦκον, [2] "fig," esp. "late fig" → 753, 6 ff., Hbr. תְּאֵנָה. We also find in the LXX the specialised ὁ πρόδρομος, [3] ὁ σκοπός, [4] τὸ σῦκον τὸ πρόϊμον, [5] and perhaps τὰ πρωτόγονα, [6]

σ υ κ ῆ κ τ λ. I. Benzinger, Art. "Fruchtbäume in Palästina," RE³, 6 (1899), 300-306, esp. 303 f.; Olck, Art. "Feige" in Pauly-W., 6 (1909), 2100-2151; F. Goldmann, La Figue en Palest. à l'époque de la Mišna (1911); S. Klein, "Weinstock, Feigenbaum u. Sykomore in Paläst.," Festschr. A. Schwarz (1917), 389-402, esp. 396-399; Str.-B., I, 856-858; Dalman Arbeit, I, 2 (1928), 378-381, 556-564; I. Löw, Die Flora d. Juden, I (1928), 224-254; BR, 85; L. Bauer, "Die Verfluchung d. Feigenbaumes," Der Bote aus Zion, 76 (1961), 15 f.

[1] Contraction of Ionic συκέη, in other dialects συκέα and συκία. But συκῆ is found already in Hom. Od., 24, 246, also συκέαι as 2 syllables 7, 116; 11, 590; συκέας (vl. συκᾶς), 24, 341. LXX always has συκῆ. συκῆ comes from σῦκον (→ n. 2) as, e.g., μηλέα "apple-tree" from μῆλον, "apple" [Risch].

[2] Attested from Hom. Od., 7, 121; Boeotian τῦκον. The etym. is obscure, cf. Walde-Hofmann, I, 492, s.v. ficus, Gk. σῦκον, Lat. ficus, Arm. t'uz "independent borrowing from a Mediterranean... or Asia Minor language," also Hofmann and Boisacq, s.v. σῦκον.

[3] In LXX only Is. 28:4: πρόδρομος σύκου, HT בִּכּוּרָה, undoubtedly ref. to sweet-smelling (i.e., ripe) early figs. Σ (and 'ΑΘ?) also has πρόδρομος for the same Hbr. word at Hos. 9:10. The term is current elsewhere too, cf. Theophr. De causis plantarum, V, 1, 5 ff.; cf. Plin. Hist. Nat., 16, 113: ficus et praecoces habet quas Athenis prodromos vocant; but the usage is not uniform, cf. Olck, 2105-2111.

[4] Hos. 9:10: σκοπὸν ἐν συκῆ πρόϊμον for Hbr. כְּבִכּוּרָה בִתְאֵנָה בְרֵאשִׁיתָהּ; Nah. 3:12: συκαῖ σκοποὺς ἔχουσαι for Hbr. תְּאֵנִים עִם־בִּכּוּרִים. In both vv. many MSS have more common words instead, cf. J. Ziegler, Duodecim prophetae, Septuaginta Gottingensis, 13 (1943), 48, 95 and ad loc. This use is not found elsewhere apart from the fathers on these OT vv., though in the main σκοπός is either completely misunderstood, e.g., Theod. Mops. Comm. in Nah., 3, 12 (MPG, 66 [1844], 421B) or has already been replaced in the OT by another term. It is usually ignored in the lit., even in, e.g., Pape, Pass., Liddell-Scott, Olck, though cf. → 415, n. 4. Perhaps it is popular local use which transf. σκοπός "scout" to the early fig which ventures out so soon, at first even before the leaves. It is explained in terms of σκοπός "goal" by a comm. which draws on older sources, namely, that of Theophylact. of Achrida (11th cent.) on Hos. 9:10: σκοπὸν δὲ ὀνομάζει τὸ πρώϊμον σῦκον, ὃ πάντες ἀποσκοποῦσιν, ὡς πρῶτον φανέν, MPG, 126 (1864), 728 C.

[5] Jer. 24:2 τὰ σῦκα τὰ πρόϊμα for Hbr. תְּאֵנֵי הַבַּכֻּרוֹת. The adj. πρόϊμος is also used for the early fig in Hos. 9:10 → n. 4. Θ even has it as a noun for בִּכּוּרָה at Is. 28:4 → n. 3.

[6] Mi. 7:1, though in the LXX, which deviates from the Hbr., it is doubtful whether τὰ πρωτόγονα refers to the fruits of the fig-tree, and even the בִּכּוּרָה of the HT, though elsewhere it always means "early fig" (→ n. 8), can only with difficulty be given this sense here. On the usual view (e.g., A. Weiser, Das Buch d. zwölf kleinen Proph., AT Deutsch, 24³ [1959], ad loc.: "There is no grape to eat, no early fig for which my soul longs") the parallelism of grape and early fig is very odd, since early figs are not to be expected in autumn after the fruit crop; in this exceptional case, then, בִּכּוּרָה must ref. to late figs. Yet one might also transl.: "There is no longer any grape to eat — my soul longs for an early fig," i.e., the fruit trees are so fully stripped that one begins to long for the appearance of early figs, the first fruits of the new season. Cf. also Is. 28:4 'Α: ὡς πρωτογένημα.

for the "(ripe) early fig," while ὁ ὄλυνθος means the "(unripe) late fig." [7] In the HT בִּכּוּרָה is the "early fig" [8] and פַּגָּה the "unripe late fig". [9] Sometimes LXX has ὁ συκών "fig-garden," "fig-orchard" for the collective Hbr. תְּאֵנָה or תְּאֵנִים. [10] ἡ παλάθη (ἐκ) σύκων (Hbr. דְּבֶלֶת תְּאֵנִים)[11] or simply παλάθη (דְּבֵלָה)[12] is a cake of pressed figs, which could also be used as a "plaster" in healing. [13]

b. συκῆ is common in the NT (12 times in the Synoptists; Jn. 1:48, 50; Jm. 3:12; Rev. 6:13). We also find σῦκον (3 times in the Synoptists; Jm. 3:12) and once only ὄλυνθος (Rev. 6:13).

2. The Fig-Tree in Palestine.

a. In Antiquity. There is literary testimony to the fig-tree in Palestine as early as the middle of the 3rd millennium B.C. [14] In the OT it is one of the most important fruit-trees in the country. In the parable of Jotham in Ju. 9:7-15 the olive, the fig and the vine have first claim to royal dignity among all trees. [15] It is linked esp. with the vine. [16] A proverbial sign of peace and security is that everyone may sit under [17] or eat of [18] his vine or his fig-tree. The everyday phenomenon of the fig-tree leads it to be used fig. in the most varied ways, Is. 28:4; Jer. 8:13; 24:1-10; 29:17; Hos. 9:10; Mi. 7:1; Nah. 3:12; Prv. 27:18. Already in Paradise a fig is presupposed as the only tree mentioned by name, since in Gn. 3:7 Adam and Eve made for themselves aprons of fig-leaves. [19]

---

[7] Cant. 2:13 for Hbr. פַּגָּה, where in the description of spring the budding fruits of the fig-tree are par. to the blossoming of the vines. The ref. is obviously to the later figs which ripen in autumn with the wine. On the manifold profane use (from Hes. Fr., 160, 1) of ὄλυνθος and ὄλονθος cf. Olck, 2105-2111. Etym. the word is plainly pre-Gk. like other words and place-names in -νθος [Risch].

[8] Is. 28:4 → n. 3; Hos. 9:10 → n. 4; Mi. 7:1 → n. 6; plur. בַּכֻּרוֹת Jer. 24:2 → n. 5, also בִּכּוּרִים Nah. 3:12 → n. 4.

[9] Cant. 2:13 → n. 7. The word is common in Rabb. lit. Whether the place-name Βηθφαγή in Mk. 11:1 par. = Rabb. בֵּית פַּגֵּי (also written בית פאגי) derives from it is debatable, cf. Klein, 396, n. 2; Dalman Orte, 271; C. Kopp, Die hl. Stätten d. Ev. (1959), 324, n. 68.

[10] Jer. 5:17; Am. 4:9 (in both with ἀμπελών and ἐλαιών).

[11] 2 K. 20:7; Is. 38:21.

[12] 1 S. 25:18; 30:12; 1 Ch. 12:41; also LXX 4 Βασ. 4:42 for Hbr. כַּרְמֶל; Jdt. 10:5. דְּבֵלָה always means "fig-cake" (mostly with צִמּוּקִים "dried grapes"), but παλάθη as such can be used for any "fruit-cake," e.g., Hdt., IV, 23, 3 of a tree called ποντικός.

[13] 2 K. 20:7; Is. 38:21. On the medical use cf. the wealth of material in Olck, 2138-2142.

[14] Egypt. burial inscr. from Uni c. 2375/50 B.C., line 24 f., AOT, 81; Ancient Near Eastern Texts, ed. J. B. Pritchard[2] (1955), 228.

[15] Cf. the same three in Am. 4:9; Hab. 3:17; LXX Jer. 5:17 (only vine and fig HT); cf. also Jer. 40:10; with the pomegranate Hos. 2:14 and other trees Jl. 1:12, cf. also Nu. 13:23; 20:5.

[16] Is. 34:4; Jer. 5:17; 8:13; Hos. 2:14; 9:10; Jl. 1:7; 2:22; Ps. 105:33; Cant. 2:13; ref. → n. 17, 18; inscr. → n. 14.

[17] 1 K 5:5 ("peace" v. 4, "security" v. 5); Mi. 4:4 (no war, v. 3; "none afraid," v. 4); cf. Zech. 3:10.

[18] 2 K. 18:31 par. Is. 36:16.

[19] The unusual size of fig-leaves played a part in this choice, but so, too, did mythical motifs acc. to Olck, 2146; A. Jeremias, Das AT im Lichte des Alten Orients[4] (1930), 89 f.; E. R. Goodenough, Jewish Symbols in the Greco-Roman Period, VIII (1958), 140 f.; V. Buchheit, "Feigensymbolik im antiken Epigramm," Rhein. Mus., 103 (1960), 200-229. In later Jewish tradition our first parents were sometimes said to have eaten the fruit of the fig-tree, Vit. Ad., 20 f.; bSanh., 70b (R. Nehemiah c. 150 A.D.); from the 5th cent. we also find this idea in Chr. works; cf. on this H. G. Leder, "Arbor Scientiae," ZNW, 52 (1961), 156-189.

b. To-day. To-day, too, the fig-tree is common in Palestine. As in bibl. times [20] figs and vines are often cultivated together. Like the vine, but unlike the olive and the many other evergreens native to Palestine, [21] the fig-tree casts its leaves in autumn and blooms again in spring (at the end of March). The big leaves offer a shady cover in summer, but due to the lack of smaller branches the effect is one of startling bareness in winter. The fruits [22] are distinguished as early figs and late figs. The early ones begin to form in March and are ripe at the end of May. As the first crop of the year they are much appreciated, cf. Is. 28:4. But the late figs are the main crop. These develop on the new shoots. They ripen in late summer and are gathered, not all at once, [23] but from the middle of August to well on in October.

3. In the NT the fig-tree is mentioned in many connections as a familiar part of the scene.

a. The fig-tree is of no particular significance in the account of the meeting of Jesus and Nathanael in Jn. 1:48, 50. This might well have taken place in any other setting. The text offers no indication that the judgment of Jesus in v. 47 rests on what Nathanael was doing under the fig-tree, [24] for we do not know what he was doing there and therefore cannot make any deductions from it. [25] It seems rather that the miraculous knowledge of Nathanael's inner being which Jesus displays in v. 47 is confirmed by something which the latter could check, namely, a demonstration of the fact that Jesus knew something very ordinary and external. This proof wins Nathanael over to faith. The supernatural knowledge of Jesus, which plays quite an important role in Jn., [26] has the same function in the conversation with the Samaritan woman in Jn. 4 (17-19, 39).

b. The metaphor in Mt. 7:16b par. Lk. 6:44b [27] (→ IV, 1062, 21 ff.) uses OT or

---

[20] Cf. esp. Lk. 13:6, also the passages → n. 17; Plin. Hist. Nat., 17, 89, 200; it is not advised, however, by Theophr. De causis plantarum, III, 10, 6.

[21] Dalman Arbeit, I, 1 (1928), 257-261.

[22] Dalman, 556-564.

[23] Thus Midr. Qoh., 5, 11 (28a) tells of a man who looked for ripe figs on his tree every morning, cf. Str.-B., I, 858; for other Rabb. examples, cf. Str.-B., II, 26 f.

[24] Cf. esp. Zn. J., ad loc.

[25] There is no basis for the common view that Nathanael was sitting under the fig-tree to study Scripture (a supposed practice of the scribes), cf. J. Lightfoot, Horae Hebraicae et Talmudicae, I (1654), ad loc.; Str.-B., II, 371; E. Hirsch, Das vierte Ev. (1936), 116; E. C. Hoskyns-F. N. Davey, The Fourth Gospel (1947), ad loc.; W. F. Howard, The Interpreter's Bible, VIII (1952), ad loc.; with reservations Bultmann J., 73, n. 8; C. K. Barrett, The Gospel acc. to St. John (1955), ad loc.; cf. also J. Jeremias "Die Berufung d. Nathanael," Angelos, 3 (1930), 2-5. In an anecdote in Midr. Qoh., 5, 11 (28a) which is linked with the names of various rabbis, incl. R. Aqiba (d. 135 A.D.) we read that a scribe once sat with his pupils under a fig-tree and then moved away again lest they be suspected of wanting to steal the figs. This hardly supports the view that studying under a fig-tree was a widespread custom. At most we have only an isolated instance. The few other texts in Str.-B., II, 371 refer to other trees.

[26] Cf. the examples in Bau. J., ad loc.

[27] Cf. also Logion 46 of Copt. Gospel of Thomas (J. Leipoldt, "Ein neues Ev.?" ThLZ, 83 [1958], 481-496, esp. 487; in the Copt. text p. 88, 31-89, 6): Jesus spake, One does not gather grapes of thorns or pluck figs from thistles. These yield no fruit. [And a goo]d man brings good things out of his treasure ... etc." The Gospel of Thomas is obviously following its own tradition here, cf. C. H. Hunzinger, "Aussersynoptisches Traditionsgut im Thomas-Ev."

Palestinian colours in combining grapes and figs [28] and in the contrasting [29] combination of thorns and thistles. [30], [31]

Originally this was perhaps an independent part of the tradition [32] which could be interpreted in different ways. In its present context, which it was probably given in the tradition underlying both the Sermon on the Mount and the Sermon on the Plain, [33] it serves as an illustration of the generally preserved saying about the bad tree which cannot bring forth good fruit. [34] But the use to which it is put is not uniform. In Lk. it ref. first (6:45 cf. Mt. 12:34) to the speech which shows what a man is, but then in 6:46 ff., in unresolved tension to this and in express disparagement of speech, it ref. to acts, which alone are decisive. In Mt. the saying ref. to acts (7:21, but cf. 12:34), and yet it is aimed esp. at false prophets (7:15, firmly linked with the present saying by v. 16a and v. 20) who are to be judged acc. to their fruits (→ VI, 856, 14 ff.), i.e., not their words, which may deceive, but their performance of God's will, 7:21 ff. [35] The ref. to speech seems to be the original one. But Lk. was not the first to forge the link between Lk. 6:43 f. and 6:45, This is shown by Logion 46 of the Gospel of Thomas (though this is still debated → n. 27) and also by Mt. 12:33-35. [36] One may thus suppose that the combination had already been achieved in the composition which underlies both the Sermon on the Mount and the Sermon on the Plain. The absence of a v. corresponding to Lk. 6:45 in Mt. 7 may be traced back to a change which Mt. himself made in the original. [37]

ThLZ, 85 (1960), 843-846. In the combination of this comparison with the saying about the good and evil treasure and the abundance of the heart the text corresponds to Lk. 6:44b, 45. In the formulation of the saying, however, the Gospel of Thomas partly corresponds to Lk. against Mt. (the form with two verbs) and partly *vice versa* (the order grapes/figs, not figs/grapes; thistles plur. is also closer to Mt. τρίβολοι than Lk. βάτος).

[28] Examples → n. 16.

[29] On this contrast cf. Is. 5:2, 4 (the vineyard which yields ἀκάνθας rather than σταφυλήν); Ju. 9:7-15.

[30] Gn. 3:18 (quoted Hb. 6:8); Hos. 10:8: ἄκανθαι καὶ τρίβολοι.

[31] This fig. material is also used in Stoic lit., cf. the examples in Kl. Mt., *ad loc* (in fact closer to Jm. 3:12 than the Synoptic metaphor), also esp. Sen. De Ira, II, 10, 6: *quid, si miretur spineta sentesque* (thorn bushes) *non utili aliqua fruge compleri?*

[32] Cf. the different arrangement of Mt. 7:16-20 and Lk. 6:43-45 and its complete omission from Mt. 12:33-35 → n. 33.

[33] In Logion 46 of the Gospel of Thomas (→ n. 27) the metaphor is not combined with the saying about the tree and its fruits, though this saying is probably present in Logion 44 in another form, and there may have been a connection between Logion 44 and Logion 46 in the basic tradition → n. 41.

[34] It is worth noting, however, that the metaphor does not illustrate the par. saying about the good tree which does not bring forth bad fruit. Interest focuses on the reverse case, so that some would ascribe the pedantic parallelism of Lk. 6:43 par. Mt. 7:18 (carried further than Lk. in Mt. 7:17) to a secondary generalising trend.

[35] On the patent opposition to antinomian tendencies here cf. G. Barth, "Das Gesetzesverständnis d. Evangelischen Mt." in G. Bornkamm-G. Barth-H. J. Held, *Überlieferung u. Auslegung im Mt.-Ev.* (1960), 68 f.; E. Käsemann, "Die Anfänge chr. Theol.," ZThK, 57 (1960), 162-185, esp. 163 f.

[36] The comparison does not occur at all here (though → n. 40), but the closely related saying about the tree and its fruits is linked, as in Lk. 6:43-45, with the sayings about the good and evil treasure and the abundance of the heart. If the context is different, this simply emphasises the age of the combination which is our primary concern here.

[37] The reason for this change is clear; it is demanded by the subordination of the passage to Mt. 7:15 → lines 10 ff. Mt. also altered the text by reconstructing v. 16a. (cf. Lk. 6:44a) and adding v. 17 (→ n. 34), 19 (taken word for word from Mt. 3:10), 20 (= v. 16a). By omitting Lk. 6:45 Mt. could also avoid too great an overlap with Mt. 12:33-35.

If we go on to ask about the point of the saying, in Lk. 6:43-45 and also in the basic form it has the character of a general rule and belongs to the sphere of proverbial wisdom. The exclusively negative comparison (→ n. 34) which was originally put in the form of a question, [38] carries with it, however, a sharper note, and might have been directed polemically and critically against opponents [39] whose evil disposition was brought to light in their words. The tradition in Mt. 12:33-35 is in fact set in a debate between Jesus and His adversaries, [40] and the context in the Gospel of Thomas points in the same direction. [41] Such a setting might well be more pertinent for the comparison, though one cannot ascribe any specific place to it in the work of Jesus.

c. Jm. 3:12 seems to be reminiscent of Mt. 7:16b and par., but the point of the metaphor is quite different here. It is connected with the warning against sins of the tongue, 3:1-12. The passage gives three illustrations to show how unnatural it is to use the tongue in two ways, both for blessing and for cursing (3:9 f). This is just as absurd as sweet and bitter water flowing from the same source (3:11), as a particular tree bringing forth the fruits of a different tree (v. 12a), or as a brackish spring providing sweet water (v. 12b).

The aptness of the metaphor has been questioned both formally and materially. Formally the point in v. 9 f. and in the first comparison in v. 11 is that a thing cannot bring forth two antithetical things A and B, while the point in the last two comparisons is that A cannot bring forth B. Materially the theme itself (v. 9 f.) and the first and third comparisons (v. 11, 12b) involve genuine antitheses. But in the second metaphor in v. 12a we simply have the juxtaposition of two things which are equally useful and good in themselves (the fig-tree/olives; the vine/figs). If the author had known Mt. 7:16b and par. one might have expected him to use the true antithesis of thistles/figs found there. Jm., however, seems to be following the academic tradition of Stoicism where there are closely related formulations. [42]

d. The parable of the unfruitful fig-tree in Lk. 13:6-9 (→ III, 859, 6 ff.), in material peculiar to Lk., presents no difficulties from the metaphorical standpoint, [43]

---

[38] Now only in Mt. 7:16b; cf. Bultmann Trad., 78.

[39] It is directed against opponents in a new way in Mt. 7:15-20.

[40] The fact that the comparison is not used in Mt. 12:33-35 is perhaps because Mt. found 12:33-35 and 7:16-18 in different traditions and wanted to steer clear of overlapping by stressing different aspects, cf. also → n. 37. In the pre-Mt. form Mt. 12:33-35 would thus include the metaphor.

[41] The saying about blasphemy against the Holy Ghost, which comes just before Mt. 12:33-35 in v. 31 f., is also just before the tradition (Logion 46) in the Gospel of Thomas (Logion 45), and in Logion 44 the saying about the tree and its fruits is a polemic against "the Jews." In view of the considerable differences the Gospel of Thomas can hardly be dependent on Mt. One may ask, however, whether there was an original connection in the basic tradition.

[42] Cf. the examples in Dib. Jk. on 3:12, esp. Sen. Ep., 87, 25: *non nascitur itaque ex malo bonum non magis quam ficus ex olea;* Plut. Tranq. An., 13 (II, 927): νῦν δὲ τὴν ἄμπελον σῦκα φέρειν οὐκ ἀξιοῦμεν οὐδὲ τὴν ἐλαίαν βότρυς.

[43] On the fig-tree in the vineyard → 753, 1 f. Acc. to Dalman, 380 the fig-tree used to bear regularly every year, so that there was little hope after three years without fruit. There is no suggestion that the tree had never borne fruit (so Jeremias Gl. [6], 170); this was rather an older tree which had once been fruitful.

and its thrust is also plain. [44] As a final period of grace is given to this fig-tree, so Jesus' summons to repentance goes forth in the short period of grace before God's judgment; it is the last hour. [45]

e. The cursing of the barren fig-tree occurs in Mk. 11:12-14, 20-22 par. Mt. 21:18-20, cf. v. 21. [46] One theory is that Mk. was the first to link this with the entry into Jerusalem and the cleansing of the temple, there being no original connection with these events. [47] If this is so, it is superfluous to ask whether Jesus could expect to find edible fruits on the tree in spring-time at the Passover. [48] The story itself seems to presuppose that it is the time of figs, since only then is there cause to be disappointed at their absence. [49] The miracle, which stands alone as a miracle of judgment in the Synoptic tradition, [50] and which from the very first was viewed as a symbolical cursing of unfruitful Israel (→ VI, 20, 5 ff.; 843, 11 ff.), is viewed by some as a secondary reconstruction of the parable of the barren fig-tree in

---

[44] There is a similar parable in the Achikar narrative, though not in the Aram. original (fragmentarily preserved in a MS of the 5th cent. B.C.), but only in various versions in Syr. (8, 35), Arab. (8, 30) and Arm. (8, 25), cf. R. H. Charles, *The Apocr. and Pseudepigr. of the OT*, II (1913), 775. But here the request of the unfruitful tree (a palm in Syr. and Arm.) to be given another chance is rejected as pointless. Hence the parable offers only a pitiless "Too late" and justifies punishment, whereas the pt. in Lk. 13:6-9 is precisely that there is still space for conversion, cf. Jeremias Gl.⁶, 170.

[45] One should not allegorise the details of the parable, cf. Zn. Lk. on 13:6-9: The vineyard is Israel, the fig-tree Jerusalem, the gardener Jesus, three years the time from John's coming. The phrase "this year also" simply ref. to the rhythm of nature and not to the length of the period of repentance or of Jesus' ministry etc. Even to speak of the "suspension of God's will" or the "suspension of the resolve already taken to punish" (Jeremias Gl.⁶, 170) is a kind of allegorising. The details are simply designed to bring out the urgency of the situation.

[46] Mk. puts the cleansing of the temple between the saying and its fulfilment, which also take place on two different days. Mt. restores the unity of the event; the curse takes effect at once παραχρῆμα, Mt. 21:19, cf. Bultmann Trad., 232 f.

[47] Mt. rearranges the story so that the entry is followed at once by the cleansing (so also Lk., though Lk. omits cursing of the fig-tree). The cleansing and the question of authority also belong together, as may be seen also in Jn. 2:14-22; cf. too the ταῦτα of Mk. 11:28 and Kl. Mk., *ad loc.*

[48] Ref. is usually made either to unripe early figs (→ 753, 6 ff.) which orientals ate acc. to Dalman, 379-381 and Bauer, 15 f., or to late figs of the previous year which had not ripened in the autumn and had thus remained on the tree during winter (Str.-B., I, 857; firmly opposed by Bauer, 15). The note in Jos. Bell., 3, 519 that grapes and figs were harvested for 10 months by Lake Genneseret would not apply in Jerusalem. Furthermore Mk. 11:13 says expressly that there were no figs at this (Passover) season: ὁ γὰρ καιρὸς οὐκ ἦν σύκων, cf. Rabb. testimonies, Str.-B., II, 26. The fresh attempt of T. W. Manson, "The Cleansing of the Temple," *Bulletin of the John Rylands Library*, 33 (1951), 271-282; J. v. Goudoever, *Biblical Calendars* (1959), 261-265; C. W. F. Smith, "No time for Figs," *JBL*, 79 (1960), 315-327 to show that Tabernacles rather than the Passover is the background of the whole complex Mk. 11:1-12:12 (or Mk. 11-13) would certainly provide a suitable time for the story of the fig-tree but it is less satisfactory in regard to the historical situation of either Mk. or the pre-Marcan tradition.

[49] Mk. 11:13: ὁ γὰρ καιρὸς οὐκ ἦν σύκων, seems to be an added note which puts the story during the Passover though in so doing it increases the material difficulties. Acc. to Dalman, 380 f. what Mk. is saying is that Jesus could expect unripe fruits (since it was not the time of figs); in the time of figs the tree might have been plucked and hence have no figs, though → 753, 9 f.

[50] J. Schniewind, *Das Ev. nach Mk., NT Deutsch,* 1⁹ (1960), on 11:11 ff.: "The only miracle which does not extend aid to others." (At most one might compare only Mk. 6:45-52 and par.).

Lk. 13:6-9,[51] or some similar parable,[52] in the form of a dramatic incident.[53] Another theory is that it came into being as an aetiological legend explaining a prominent withered fig-tree.[54] Yet another hypothesis is that misunderstanding of a saying with a very different point formed the basis for the development of a tradition [55] which we now have at a late and corrupt stage.

f. The parable of the sprouting fig-tree by which one knows that summer is at hand (Mk. 13:28 f. par. Mt. 24:32 f.; Lk. 21:29-31) [56] stands at the end of the Synoptic Apocalypse and is related to the signs of the end, i.e., the future signs of an event which is to be expected in the even more distant future. This might suggest a later stage of Christian apocalyptic and a certain tension with sayings like Lk. 17:20. If like Lk. 12:54-56 its original reference is to present signs, to the signs of the βασιλεία given in Jesus' works rather than to apocalyptic events, to signs which thus guarantee the speedy [57] coming of the βασιλεία,[58] the saying becomes one of the clearest testimonies to immediate and urgent expectation of Jesus.

g. Rev. 6:13 compares the plunging of the stars from heaven at the opening of the last seal to the ὄλυνθοι [59] which the storm shakes off from the fig-tree; a basis is to be sought in Is. 34:4b LXX. [60]

---

[51] In view of the relation to this Lk. would then omit the story even though he follows Mk. in the context.

[52] Hos. 9:10, 16; Mi. 7:1 (Bultmann Trad., 246; Kl. Mk., ad loc.) are not so close. A. de Q. Robin, "The Cursing of the Fig Tree in Mark XI. A Hypothesis," NTSt, 8 (1961/62), 276-281, thinks Mi. 7:1 is the starting-pt., though in the sense that Jesus based His undoubtedly historical action on this.

[53] Cf. Kl. Mk., ad loc.; Schniewind, op. cit. (→ n. 50); V. Taylor, The Gospel acc. to St. Mark (1952), ad loc.; G. Bornkamm, Jesus v. Nazareth⁴, ⁵ (1960), 189, n. 24.

[54] Cf. E. Schwartz, "Der verfluchte Feigenbaum," ZNW, 5 (1904), 80-84; also Schniewind, op. cit.; Loh. Mk., ad loc.; Taylor, op. cit., ad loc.

[55] Acc. to H. W. Bartsch, "Die 'Verfluchung' d. Feigenbaums," ZNW, 53 (1962), 256-260, the saying is not optatively a curse; it is a future apoc. declaration that the last event, fulfilled in the passion, will come in the near future before the next figs ripen. Cf. also Manson, op cit. (→ n. 48), 279 f.

[56] The addition in Lk. 21:29: καὶ πάντα τὰ δένδρα, is incontestable materially but seems not to catch the pt. that the characteristic appearance of the fig made it very apt for this saying, → 753, 5; Jeremias Gl.⁶, 25, 119 f.

[57] ἐγγύς Mk. 13:28, 29 par., Lk. 21:31: ἐγγύς ἐστιν ἡ βασιλεία τοῦ θεοῦ.

[58] Cf. esp. W. G. Kümmel, Verheissung u. Erfüllung³ (1956), 14-16.

[59] Acc. to → 752, 1 we are to think of unripe late figs, perhaps with Dalman Arbeit, I, 1 (1928), 100, n. 2 the very latest which fail to ripen before the end of summer and thus fall victim to the storms of autumn.

[60] Is. 34:4b LXX: πάντα τὰ ἄστρα πεσεῖται ... ὡς πίπτει φύλλα ἀπὸ συκῆς. Is. 34:4a is used in Rev. 6:14a.

† συκάμινος. † συκομορέα.

1. One must distinguish two other trees attested in Palestine in NT days but only distantly related to the fig: a. the "sycamore fig" (Ficus sycomorus L, Hbr. שִׁקְמָה plur. שִׁקְמִים, often mentioned in the OT and still common in Palestine, strong-growing, planted esp. for building wood, cf. 1 K. 10:27; Is. 9:9, the fruits, which resemble the fig but are of less value, being slit to help them mature, Am. 7:14; Theophr. Hist. Plant., IV, 2, 1 ff., and b. the "mulberry," Morus nigra L, which does not occur in the OT but is ref. to for the first time in 1 Macc. 6:24, תות in the Rabb., always for the black mulberry, from whose berries a juice used as a dye is taken (1 Macc. 6:34); the white mulberry (Morus alba L), noted for its use in the silk-worm industry, was introduced into the Mediterranean world in the Middle Ages.

The use in Gk. is complicated. ἡ (sometimes ὁ) συκάμινος [1] can denote both trees, though primarily the mulberry (Theophr. Hist. Plant., I, 6, 1), the sycamore fig being mostly ἡ συκάμινος ἡ Αἰγυπτία, ibid., I, 1, 7 etc. The mulberry is also ἡ μορέα, Nicand. Alexipharm., 69 and its fruit τὸ μόρον, from Aesch. Fr., 264. Only later does the sycamore fig have its own term ἡ συκόμορος, Cels. Med., V, 18, 7, its fruit τὸ συκόμορον, Strabo, 17, 2, 4. It is usually medical writers who make this distinction; συκάμινος remains ambiguous. [2]

LXX correctly calls the fruit of the mulberry τὸ μόρον in 1 Macc. 6:34. But the sycamore fig is inaccurately called ἡ συκάμινος (6 times) and its fruit τὸ συκάμινον, Am. 7:14, also Θ; 'Α and Σ emend to συκόμορος, so too at ψ 77:47, and with Θ Is. 9:10 (9).

2. In the NT these names appear only twice in Lk. ἡ συκομορέα in Lk. 19:4 can denote only the sycamore fig, but ἡ συκάμινος in 17:6 (→ 289, 21 ff.) is ambiguous. The fact that Lk. seems to make a distinction between the two [3] favours the view that he follows more precise usage and is referring to the mulberry. But in the light of LXX usage (→ line 19 f.) and contemporary examples (→ n. 2) he might just as well be speaking of the sycamore fig, which was especially firm and deeply rooted, [4] and which the saying might originally have had in view. [5]

συκάμινος κτλ. I. Benzinger, Art. "Fruchtbäume in Palästina," RE³, 6 (1899), 300-306, esp. 304; S. Klein, "Weinstock, Feigenbaum u. Sykomore in Palästina," Festschr. A. Schwarz (1917), 389-402, esp. 399 f.; Dalman Arbeit, I, 1 (1928), 61-63; I. Löw, Die Flora d. Juden, I (1928), 266-280; A. Steier, Art. "Maulbeerbaum," Pauly-W., 14 (1930), 2331-2338; BR, 86 f.

[1] Borrowed from the Semitic (Hbr. שִׁקְמָה), and assimilated to συκῆ, Boisacq, s.v.; Steier, 2333.

[2] Diosc. Mat. Med., I, 127 equates συκάμινον and συκόμορον, and both trees are συκάμινος in Diod S., 1, 34, 8.

[3] The use of different terms in Lk. 17:6; 19:4 might be due to the use of different sources, cf. T. W. Manson, The Sayings of Jesus (1949), 140 f.

[4] Rabb. examples, Str.-B., II, 234. It is often said of the sycamore fig and the carob that their roots reached down to the depths (Gn. r., 13 on 2:5 f.) and their strong root-systems led to the practical rule that they should be kept at least 50 ells from cisterns (25 ells were enough for other trees), BB, 2, 11.

[5] Acc. to jMQ, 3, 1 (81c, 58 ff.) a carob uprooted itself at the behest of R. Eliezer (c. 90 A.D.) to prove, not his faith, but the correctness of his halachic teaching, cf. the text in Str.-B., IV, 313 f.

† συκοφαντέω.

The derivation of the group from συκοφάντης is etym. clear (σῦκον + φαίνω) but materially obscure. [1] In the oldest instance (Aristoph.) the sense is that of "denunciation" with an obviously negative nuance, i.e., calumnious accusation, e.g., Aristoph. Av., 1410-1468. There then developed the gen. sense συκοφαντέω τινά "to cheat someone" (P. Tebt., I, 43, 26 [2nd cent. B.C.]: συκοφαντηθῶμεν διασεσεισμένοι) or συκοφαντέω τί τινος or παρά τινος, "to extort something from someone," e.g., Lys., 26, 24. This developed sense is also found in the LXX, where the group συκοφαντέω 8 times, συκοφάντης 2, συκοφαντία 5) almost [2] always stands for the root פשׁק and means "oppression."

Similarly in the NT συκοφαντέω no longer has the original concrete sense "to denounce" but means more generally "to oppress" (Lk. 3:14) or "to extort something" (Lk. 19:8).

Hunzinger

---

† συλλαμβάνω

1. Like the simple form (→ IV, 5, 17 ff.) this word denotes first an action: [1] a. "to bring together" with acc., transf. συλλαβεῖν εἰς ἕν, Plat. Theaet., 147d; "to gather" a herd, Philo Agric., 33; mid-pass. "to assemble," Philo Deus Imm., 83; συνειλημμένος "united" often in Aristot. Metaph., 7 with ref. to form and matter, e.g., 10, p. 1035a, 25; 15, p. 1039b, 21 f.; "to enclose" men in cities 1 Macc. 5:26 f.; then "to seize," "to take prisoner," "to arrest," Lys., Xenoph.; in the pap. "to snatch" slaves, συνέλαβον τὸν σημαινόμενον δοῦλον, P. Oxy., II, 283, 12 (45 A.D.). Transf. "to acquire," a language, Hdt., II, 49, 1; IV, 114, 1; "to grasp intellectually," oracles, Hdt., I, 91, 4 f.; III, 64, 5: τοῦτο ... ἱκανῶς συνειλήφαμεν, Plat. Polit., 278c etc. b. Abs., or with acc., of "conception" (a woman or female animal, Lat. *concipere*), so often in Aristot., e.g., Gen. An., I, 19, p. 727b, 8 ff.; Hist. An., VII, 2, p. 582b, 14 ff.; also later. Transf. in Ps.-Long. Sublim., 14, 3 of ideas and formulations which are conceived but not executed, so that they come into the world as imperfect and blind abortions; the are called συλλαμβανόμενα ὑπὸ τῆς ... ψυχῆς in a comparison suggested by fem. ψυχή. The intellectual use of the group is older, ἃ ψυχῇ προσήκει καὶ κυῆσαι καὶ τεκεῖν, Plat. Symp., 209a, ἃ πάλαι ἐκύει, τίκτει καὶ γεννᾷ, 209c etc. c. With dat. "lend a hand, help" someone (→ I, 375, 8 ff.), from Aesch. Choeph., 812; συλλαμβανόντων θεῶν, "with the help of the gods," Plat. Ep., 7, 327c, cf. Leg., X, 905c; sing. Jos. Ant., 4, 198 (mid.); plur. P. Oxy., VI, 935, 3 (3rd cent. A.D.), cf. lines 8-10: "for our πάτριοι θεοί always help us"; also mid. "to take up the cause of someone," Soph. Phil., 282 κάμνοντι, and often later.

συκοφαντέω. E. Nestle, "Sykophantia im bibl. Griech.," ZNW, 4 (1903), 271 f.; K. Latte, Art. "Συκοφάντης" in Pauly-W., 4 A (1932), 1028-1031.

[1] Acc. to the most ancient and widespread explanation συκοφάντης is origin. one who denounces someone for illegally exporting figs from Athens, cf. already Istros (3rd cent. B.C.) in Athen., 3, 6 (74e). But there is no record of any law against this, Latte, 1029. For other attempts to explain the word cf. Latte, 1029 f.; Liddell-Scott, Boisacq, Hofmann, *s.v.*

[2] Exceptions: Gn. 43:18 (for נגל hitp "to fall upon"); Lv. 19:11 (שׁקר pi "to deceive"); Am. 2:8 (where LXX perhaps read עֲנוּשִׁים as עשׁקים). In the later Gk. transl. the equation συκοφαντέω κτλ./פשׁק is consistent.

συλλαμβάνω. [1] For senses not discussed here cf. Liddell-Scott, *s.v.*

2. In the LXX the word occurs a. 23 times for q and 8 for ni of תפש (esp. in 1, 3 and 4 Βασ.) in the sense "to get hold of someone," "to seize or surprise someone," Nu. 5:13; "to catch in a trap" of animals, Ez. 19:4, 8, in a net 12:13 cf. ψ 9:23; "to capture" cities, 4 Βασ. 14:7; 16:9; 18:13; Is. 36:1 Α; Ιερ. 31:41; cf. Ιερ. 30:10 (49:16); also 10 times for q and 9 for ni of לכד "to catch," often of animals, e.g., Ju. 15:4, "to take" of towns, 4 Βασ. 18:10; for קמץ "to seize" only Job 22:16; for לקח twice; "to arrest" in Ιερ. 43:26 and "to take" a neighbour for the Passover, Ex. 12:4. In works with no HT we find only the sense "to seize," "to grasp," → 759, 20 f.; n. 4. The word also occurs b. 24 times for הרה "to become or be pregnant," esp. in Gn. (examples → n. 6, 17); transf. Ps. 7:14 → n. 8; for polel "to be born" in ψ 50:7. Another use is c. mid. "to help" in Gn. 30:8, 2 not in the Hexapla. 'Α has συλλαμβάνω for "to capture" etc. quite often, also "to conceive" (so also Σ and Θ).

3. The following senses occur in the NT.

a. "To take" in a net, 3 Lk. 5:9; "to seize, arrest" someone. Jesus in Gethsemane, Mk. 14:48 = Mt. 26:55 (synon. κρατέω); Lk. 22:54; Jn. 18:12 (... καὶ ἔδησαν); Ac. 1:16; Peter Ac. 12:3; 4 "to take," Paul in the temple precincts, Ac. 23:27; 26:21 med. NT has συμπαραλαμβάνω for "to take with one" at Gl. 2:1; Ac. 12:25; 15:37 f.

b. The verb is used with ref. to the pregnancy (→ V, 835, 12 ff.) of Elisabeth (Lk. 1:24, 36) and Mary (Lk. 1:31). συλλήμψῃ ἐν γαστρὶ καὶ τέξῃ υἱόν, καὶ καλέσεις τὸ ὄνομα αὐτοῦ... (Lk. 1:31) is a fixed 5 phrase in the biblical and Jewish world. 6

Behind the metaphorical mode of expression in Jm. 1:15a there lies a specific biblical tradition. Though הרה is translated by συλλαμβάνω (→ line 8), this does not strictly refer to the act of conceiving but rather to the state of pregnancy. 7 At issue, then, are plans which men have and which they desire to execute. 8 In Jm. 1:15 (→ I, 314, 35 ff.; III, 171, 22 ff.; esp. VI, 29, 16 ff.) 9 vv. 13-15 are connected with vv. 16-18 by the thought that only good comes from God, for by His Word He gives new life (ἀπεκύησεν, v. 18) in a sovereign act, in contrast to the

---

2 Not in Hatch-Redp., where the v. is noted under συμβάλλειν and συναντιλαμβάνεσθαι (→ I, 375, 29 f.). Α reads συνεβάλετο; -βαλ and -λαβ are commonly interchanged in LXX [Katz].

3 Cf. Eur. Or., 1346: οὐχὶ συλλήψεσθ' ἄγραν; Philo Agric., 24.

4 Cf. 1 Macc. 14:3: συνέλαβεν αὐτὸν ..., καὶ ἔθετο αὐτὸν ἐν φυλακῇ.

5 Hence it is not certain that Is. 7:14 influenced Lk. 1:31. Mt. 1:23 quotes Is. 7:14 (acc. to LXX; 'Α has pres. συλλαμβάνει καὶ τίκτει υἱόν, so also Σ; Tg. Pro. on Is. 7:14: מעדיא ותליד "is pregnant and will bear").

6 Test. L. 11:2 συλλαβοῦσα ἔτεκεν υἱόν, καὶ ἐκάλεσα τὸ ὄνομα αὐτοῦ ... cf. Gn. 4:25; 19:36 f.; 21:2 f.; 29:32-35 etc. (also on the basis of Gn. 30:8 ff. — a shorter narrative padded out with chronological notes — Demetrius in Eus. Praep. Ev., 9, 21, 3 f.); ἐν γαστρί with συλλαμβάνειν already in Hippocr. Mul., I, 75 (Littré, VIII, 162) etc.; Pr.-Bauer, s.v., also Is. 7:14 'Α; Gn. 25:21 R λαβεῖν ἐν γαστρί for the simple HT verb, Ex. 2:2; 1 Ch. 7:23 etc., cf. Aristot. Hist. An., IX, 50, p. 632a, 28; ἐν τῇ κοιλίᾳ Lk. 2:21 (κοιλία for the womb: → III, 786, 22 ff.; cf. Test. N. 1:7). Theologically → V, 834, 16 ff.

7 For the lit. use cf. already 1 Βασ. 4:19: συνειληφυῖα τοῦ τεκεῖν.

8 הרה עמל "to go around pregnant with evil" occurs in Is. 59:4, LXX κύουσιν πόνον (the only other LXX use of κύω is at 59:13 transf.; the corresponding term does not occur here in 1 QIs; ἀποκυέω occurs only at 4 Macc. 15:17 with ref. to "perfect righteousness," [obviously transf.] of the mother of the 7 martyred sons), Ps. 7:14 LXX συνέλαβεν πόνον,

process depicted in v. 14 f. [10] which ends with death. ἐπιθυμία plainly refers to the concrete [11] desire [12] which seeks to carry man off and entice him. [13] The image of ἐπιθυμία as a harlot is unlikely in v. 14. [14] Man's own desire- (unlike Philo → n. 14) urges him to the concrete act which destroys him. In v. 14 f. James is trying to make it clear that sin is never caused by God's πειράζειν but is always man's own act → II, 921, 14 ff. [15] If the concrete desire which arises in man is one with his own will, it becomes pregnant, that which is in it quickens, and it brings it forth (τίκτει) [16] in the act of sin.

The same metaphor is found in Philo. In Cher., 57 it is αἴσθησις which the νοῦς approaches, συλλαβοῦσα ἐγκύμων τε γίνεται καὶ εὐθὺς ὠδίνει καὶ τίκτει, but it brings forth, not the deed as in Jm., but the worst evil of the soul, delusion. [17] In Test. XII

---

and Job 15:35 LXX ἐν γαστρὶ δὲ λήμψεται ὀδύνας, 'Α συνέλαβε (πόνον). In Is. 59:4 יֶלֶד אָוֶן follows ("to bear trouble"), so too Job 15:35; the two are separate clauses in Ps. 7:14. For the rest the three vv. run quite differently. Is. 33:11 makes a different point: "You go about pregnant with withered grass ('Α συλλήψεσθε αἰθάλην), you bear straw," i.e., what you plan is futile and will be to your own hurt, cf. Ps. 7:4 etc. Conceiving and bearing are common images for planning and executing in personal life; this should not be overlooked in relation to Test. XII and Jm. On the transf. of gynaecological expressions to men cf. Dib. Jk., Suppl. 13.

[9] Cf. W. Nauck, "Die Tradition u. der Charakter des 1 J.," *Wissenschaftliche Untersuchungen z. NT*, 3 (1957), 90-93, esp. on Jm. 1:18.

[10] On chain sayings in the NT cf. Dib. Jk. on 1:15.

[11] On תַּאֲוָה in Judaism → III, 170, 15 ff.

[12] Cf. Nu. 11:4 and the rebukes in ψ 105:14 and 1 C. 10:6.

[13] δελεάζω (strictly "to lure") cannot mean more. In Jos. it is sometimes used for being drawn away from the Jerusalem temple and its worship, Ant., 8, 225. Closer to Jm. 1:14 is Philo Agric., 103: to be "enticed" by ἡδονή and brought into its net (εἵλκυσται).

[14] Philo uses this for ἡδονή in Op. Mund., 166, but in him this comes first from without and tries to overcome the νοῦς, thus enslaving man. Here and in → lines 12 ff. one finds in Philo the tensions between pagan philosophy, which views man in and for himself, and bibl. and Jewish piety, which sees him before God.

[15] This is also the concern in Sir. 15:11-20. In relation to the opening (μὴ εἴπῃς — μηδείς ... λεγέτω) and certain basic concepts it seems not improbable that the author of Jm. starts from Sir. 15 even though he develops things differently. In Sir. 15, too, there is stress on the fact that God does not cause evil but man is responsible for his own acts whereby he chooses life or death, v. 17a; on ζωή cf. Jm. 1:12. That God gives man into the hands of his יֵצֶר (Sir. 15:14b cf. the context) is perhaps hinted at in Jm. 1:14 if this is a neutral concept in Sir. 15:14 as in the canonical OT. But the meaning of יֵצֶר = διαβούλιον in Sir. 15 is contested, cf. F. C. Porter, "The Yeçer Hara," *Bibl. and Semitic Stud.* (1902), 91-156, on Sir. *v.* 136-146, on Sir. 15:14, 138 f.; cf. Sir. 27:6; 21:11a; 17:31. In Test. XII διαβούλιον is often neutral, cf. on Jm. 1:14 esp. Test. R. 4:9: οὐκ ἐδέξατο τὸ διαβούλιον τῆς ψυχῆς αὐτοῦ ἐπιθυμίαν πονηράν. The διαβούλιον can be good, B. 6:4; the διαβούλιον "of the good man is not in the hand of the spirit of temptation Beliar," 6:1; God tests the διαβούλιον of man, Test. Jos. 2:6.

[16] For the fixed combination συλλαβοῦσα τίκτει cf. chronicle style in the OT and Judaism → 760, 19 f. with n. 6.

[17] Cf. Philo Cher., 46: Virtue conceives divine seed by God and bears to one of its human lovers, in an allegor. exposition of Gn. 29:31 f. (cf. Cher., 47); also Leg. All., III, 181, which ref. to deeds as what is planted by God in the womb; also Fug., 167: The soul conceives and bears "Isaac" (αὐτομαθής), the purest disposition, in a single act (Gn. 21:2: συλλαβοῦσα ἔτεκεν); Sacr. AC, 4: Rebekah = patience has conceived the conflicting φύσεις of good and evil. The passage is somewhat reminiscent of the later Rabb. idea of the two impulses, → II, 917, 41 ff.; III, 170, 15 ff.

it is διάνοια that conceives, cf. the mythologically formulated saying Test. B. 7:2: συλλαμβάνει ἡ διάνοια [18] διὰ τοῦ Βελιάρ. [19] If Beliar is the power of evil understood as the enemy of God, sin is obviously traced back here to its fructifying power which can call to life possibilities latent in man. The close connection between διάνοια and act is plain in Test. R. 5:6: the angels of Gn. 6 ἐγένοντο (καὶ) ἐν ἐπιθυμίᾳ αὐτῶν (human women), καὶ συνέλαβον τῇ διανοίᾳ τὴν πρᾶξιν. Acc. to the context διάνοια here is desire on the way to the act. [20]

In Jm. 1:15 as distinct from Test. B. 7:2 (→ 761, 11 ff.) is not the power of evil which helps desire to bring forth fruit in action. It is man himself who lets himself be seized and enticed by it. The desire and the deed are both his own. When accomplished the deed is, of course, autonomous, and it brings as its fruit death (v. 15b). This is an intentionally paradoxical metaphor. In all other cases birth brings life, but sin "bears" death. Behind this, and perhaps behind v. 14a, stands Gn. 3. [21] But Jm. 1:15b is especially close to Paul, R. 5:12; 6:21, 23 (→ V, 592, 18 ff.); 8:2. Yet the relation between sin and desire is not the same in R. 7:7 as it is in Jm. 1:14a, since ἁμαρτία is viewed by Paul as an independent force, where here as elsewhere Jm. is referring to the individual act of sin. Nevertheless, Paul is also of the opinion that desire leads the will of man to sin, cf. R. 7.

c. The mid. sense "to help" is found in Lk. 5:7. If the summons of Phil. 4:3 is closely related to v. 2 (ναί...), then the unnamed person in this v. (→ 749, 22 ff.) is asked to "help" the two women pastorally to Christian concord.

4. In the post-NT writings of primitive Christianity συλλαμβάνω is used in the same way. Thus in 1 Cl., 12, 2 we find both act. and pass. for "to seize," "to arrest," cf. Mart. Pol., 5, 2; 7, 2; 9, 1; 21. The mid. is used in the same sense in Mart. Pol., 6, 1. συλλαμβάνω "to stand by," "to help," occurs in 2 Cl., 17, 2. [22]

Delling

συλλυπέομαι → IV, 323, 27 ff.
συμβασιλεύω → I, 591, 1 ff.; → 787, 25 ff.

---

[18] διάνοια in Test. XII does not ref. only to man's "mind" or inner disposition (work, word, thought, Test. G. 6:1; Jos. 10:4) but also directly to his acts. It is the place of desire (Test. R. 5:7); it is led into error by sin (4:6), by feminine adornment (5:5). It is deceived by this (5:5); it is dominated by envy (Test. S. 3:2) and brought to ἔκστασις by it (4:8). It is harried by the evil spirit (3:5), darkened by the spirit of anger (Test. D. 2:4), and dazzled by youthful desire (Test. Jud. 11:1, cf. 14:2). It can denote man himself. The good διάνοια does not have two tongues, one of blessing and one of cursing etc., Test. B. 6:5. In all it (he) does, speaks and sees, he knows that the Lord has regard to his ψυχή (6:6) and purifies his διάνοια (6:7).
[19] On the context cf. R. H. Charles on Test. B. 7.
[20] Cf. also Test. R. 3:12: Incited to sin, the διάνοια does not let man rest until he has done it.
[21] So also Philo when he calls death the penalty of ἡδονή, Agric., 100, cf. 99. On Rabb. Judaism v. Str.-B., III, 227-229.
[22] [Section 4. is by Schneemelcher].

† συμβιβάζω

A. The Word outside the Bible.

In non-bibl. Gk. συμβιβάζω [1] means strictly "to cause to stride together" (causative of βιβάω/βαίνω). 1. "To bring together," "to bring about an agreement," Ditt. Syll.[3], I, 75, 24 (428/7 B.C.); "to reconcile by mediation," Hdt. (only) I, 74, 3; Thuc. (only) II, 29, 6; Dio C., (συμβιβάζομαι "to be reconciled"), 45, 8, 2; Plat. (only) Prot., 337e. 2. Intellectually, esp. in philosophical usage, [2] "to compare" (analytically), "to infer," Plat. (only) Hi,, II, 369d; Resp., VI, 504a: ὁ λόγος, reason, συμβιβάζει (acc. with inf.), Ocellus Lucanus, 40, [3] "to draw conclusions," often in Aristot., e.g., Topica, VIII, 11, p. 161b, 37 f.; De Sophisticis Elenchis, 28, p. 181a, 22; then "to show" (with ὡς) that all who are gifted with virtue are of noble birth, Ps.-Aristot. Rhet. Al., 36, p. 1441a, 6 etc. Hence finally "to expound, set forth," Philodem. Philos. Volumina Rhet., I, 57, 19; 174, 3 abs.; 172, 24; [4] cf. Ocellus Lucanus, 40 (→ n. 9). The word is not common. It does not occur in the indexes (on Philo → n. 6) to the orators, poets etc., or in the post-apost. fathers; in the Apologists only Just. Dial., 50, 5 quoting Is. 40:13 f.; in Cl. Al. only Strom., I, 161, 3.

B. The Septuagint.

In the LXX — all ref. given including → line 15 and n. 23 — the word occurs only in a special sense connected with that mentioned → lines 7 ff. It is always used for Hbr. verbs in the hi (5 times ירה, 3 ידע, once בין; never without HT) and means "to teach" someone (something), "to instruct" (in something). If in non-bibl. usage in relation to the mind the verb origin. denotes a concern for logical deduction, or the way of intellectual conviction, in the LXX it refers exclusively to authoritative direction. The distinction is formally confirmed by the syntactical structure: Philodem. Philos. Volumina Rhet., I, 57, 19 (→ n. 4) has the dat. of person, LXX the acc. of person, also of thing, Ex. 18:16; Lv. 10:11 etc. [5] Teachers are God in Ex. 4:12, [6] 15, His angel in Ju. 13:8 B; cf. Da. 9:22 Θ, [7]

σ υ μ β ι β ά ζ ω . Bibl. A. F. G. Rudolph, Ocellus Lucanus, De Rerum Natura (1801), 277-9; on Col. and Eph. Dib. Gefbr. on Col. 2:19; from the bibl. under πληρόω → VI, 286 esp. E. Percy, "Der Leib Christi (Σῶμα Χριστοῦ) in d. paul. Homologumena u. Antilegomena," *Lunds Univ. Årsskrift*, NF, I, 38, 1 (1942), 48-50; also "Die Probleme d. Kol.- u. Epheserbr.," *Skrifter utgivna av Kungl. Humanistiska Vetenskapssamfundet i Lund*, 39 (1946), 324-7, 328-384, 413-6, 427. Cf. also → IV, 597, 8 ff.

[1] Of the many compounds of βιβάζω we also find in the NT those in ἀνά, ἐν, ἐπί, (κατά vl.), πρό, mostly in a lit. sense. All occur in LXX as well, and also constructions with διά and παρά.

[2] Lat. *cogere (co-agere)*. Outside the Bible the authoritative aspect is stronger in the case of διδάσκω, → II, 135, 7 ff.

[3] Ed. R. Harder, NPhU, 1 (1926).

[4] If the reading is correct, ed. S. Sudhaus, I (1892).

[5] With verbs of teaching we also find the double acc. in the NT, *v.* Bl.-Debr. § 155, 1; on the dat. with "to show" *v.* § 187, 3.

[6] Philo Rer. Div. Her., 25 not only quotes this but puts the verb on the lips of Moses. In Ebr., 37, however, where Ex. 18:16 is quoted. Philo has ἀναδιδάσκω instead in elucidation.

[7] συμβιβάσαι σε σύνεσιν, LXX ὑποδείξαί σοι διάνοιαν. Cf. also Is. 55:4 Θ: συμβιβάζοντα for עד, LXX μαρτύριον, 'ΑΣ μάρτυρα with ref. to the authoritative character. At Prv. 6:13 'Α and Αλλ have συμβιβάζει for מֹרֶה of the teaching of the ἄφρων. In both cases the verb is abs. with no ref. to the object of instruction [Bertram].

Moses in Ex. 18:16, Aaron, i.e., the priesthood in Lv. 10:11, fathers in Israel in Dt. 4:9. These have all to declare God's will; only in ψ 31:8 does a righteous man speak of himself to others. Among the objects of instruction are special divine orders in Ex. 4; Ju. 13:8, the commandments in Ex. 18; Lv. 10, the Sinai revelation in Dt. 4:9 f. The affinity to διδάσκω in the LXX is obvious, → II, 137, 2 ff. συμβιβάζω is never used for למד → II, 136, 30, but διδάσκω is used for the verbs listed → 763, 20, esp. the first two.

C. The New Testament.

1. In the NT the word means "to hold together," "to unite," in Col. 2:2, 19; Eph. 4:16. According to Col. 2:19 [8] and Eph. 4:16 the body is held together by the head. In the context the accent is on the fact that the community's life comes from Christ and is mediated to the members by the ἁφαί. [9] Unity is given to the community herein. The man who in arbitrary and self-seeking piety takes up the worship of angels does not cleave to this conjunction with the head, Col. 2:19 → III, 157, 21 ff.; VI, 134, 12 ff. Probably this is the sense in Col. 2:2 also. [10] In the context Paul is emphasising that his apostolic conflict (1:28 f.) is also for churches unknown to him with the aim [11] that through his exhortation their unity in love (cf. Eph. 4:16: εἰς οἰκοδομὴν ἑαυτοῦ ἐν ἀγάπῃ) and their knowledge of faith might be increased → VI, 311, 10 ff. Elsewhere, too, the unity of the community in love and the fulness of the knowledge of salvation in Christ are inseparable.

2. a. In Ac. the word follows Greek usage (→ 763, 7 ff.), of which we are also reminded by the use of ὅτι. The meaning is "to prove conclusively" in Ac. 9:22 with reference to the scriptural proof of the Messiahship of Jesus by Paul, who throws the Jews in Damascus into complete confusion. [12] In the Jewish mission this proof has the character of a compelling demonstration; it presupposes, of course, a belief in the authority of Scripture and in the continuity of God's saving work. The significance of the proof from Scripture (→ I, 752, 19 ff.; 759, 2 ff.) in the Jewish mission may be seen in passages which use related terms, e.g., Ac. 17:2 f., [13] also

---

[8] Col. 2:19 is not to be related to the cosmos, cf. Percy Leib, 49, n. 89; Percy Probleme 382-384, as against Dib. Gefbr. on Col. 2:19.

[9] ἁφή (cf. ἅπτομαι) means "contact," then "place of contact," cf. Liddell-Scott, s.v. Anatomical exactitude is obviously not to be expected here.

[10] So most exegetes. Dib. Gefbr. argues for "to teach," ad loc. C. Spicq, Agapé dans le NT, II (1959), 202 transl. "étant instruits dans la charité," and comments: "συμβιβασθέντες apparait ainsi comme un terme technique de la didascalie, parallèle à παρακληθῶσιν," 204 [Moule].

[11] συμβιβασθέντες is to be taken as final like the preceding ἵνα clause and the ensuing expressions εἰς κτλ, though cf. Loh. Kol., ad loc.

[12] In the sense of causing a lively disturbance, so always συγχέω etc. in Ac. (the only NT book to use the group), cf. the crowd in Ephesus in the Demetrius riot in 19:29, 32, also the crowd at Paul's arrest in Jerusalem in 21:27, 31: the only instance where there is no serious uproar is at 2:6.

[13] On διανοίγων cf. materially Lk. 24:32; the word obviously has a different ring in Lucan usage, cf. Lk. 24:31, 45, also Ac. 16:14; elsewhere lit. The transf. usage in Lk. and Ac. seems to derive from LXX (cf. the negative findings from other fields in the lex.). The verb occurs with ὀφθαλμούς (Lk. 24:31) 7 times in LXX; with σύνεσιν (Lk. 24:45 νοῦν) in Hos. 2:17 (cf. Θ), with καρδίαν (Ac. 16:14) in 2 Macc. 1:4. παρατίθεμαι (Ac. 17:3) has from Plat. to Plut. (etc.) this sense of "convincing demonstration" (but not LXX, not even at Dt. 4:4). Cf. → II, 665, n. 12.

18:28, where we find διακατελέγχομαι "to confound completely,"[14] and also ἐπιδείκνυμι "to show convincingly."[15, 16]

A ὅραμα διὰ νυκτός is the basis of proof in Ac. 16:10 → IV, 1118, 31 ff.; V, 372, 6 ff. The vision itself is fairly perspicuous for the missionary. What is concluded, then, is not so much that βοήθησον means εὐαγγελίσασθαι but rather that the manifestation is a divine order → III, 502, 1 ff.[17] Hence the vision does not render the decision of those who are called superfluous; it shows that this decision is an act of obedience,[18] cf. Gl. 2:2.

b. The LXX meaning "to instruct" (→ 763, 18 ff.) occurs in Ac. 19:33. For the expression ἐκ τοῦ ὄχλου[19] is to be viewed as a Semitism.[20] The opposite in v. 32 is οἱ πλείους; these "did not know ..., but (some) of the crowd" were able "to inform"[21] Alexander — whom the Jews put forward when the impression grew that the τάραχος (v. 23) had arisen about Judaism (v. 34) — that the issue was really the ὁδός (v. 23). 1 C. 2:16 is based on Is. 40:13: τίς ἔγνω νοῦν κυρίου, καὶ τίς αὐτοῦ σύμβουλος ἐγένετο, ὃς συμβιβᾷ[22] αὐτόν;[23] By abbreviating Is. 40:13 (R. 11:34 leaves out the third member) 1 C. 2 sharpens the statement: Who has known the mind of the Lord that[24] he may instruct Him? The man who would teach God[25] must first have penetrated and known His νοῦς.[26] In the situation before Christ this saying was especially adapted to bring out the gulf between man and God. Its use in 1 C. 2, however, manifests the radical distinction[27] in the situation after Christ. Christians have received from God the νοῦς[28] of Christ. They have the Spirit of God who searches out even the deep things of God, v. 10 f. → II, 657,

---

14 On the sociative dat. cf. Bl.-Debr. § 193, 4.

15 So in Plat. etc.; in this way only here in the NT.

16 The language of Ac. shows clearly that thinking processes are involved in preaching and its acceptance, cf. also ἔπειθεν in Ac. 18:4 → VI, 1, 37 ff. How the author views the actual process of proof from Scripture may be seen from the sermons in Ac., cf. J. Gewiess, *Die urapostolische Heilsverkündigung nach d. Reden d. Ag.* (1939), 14-30; J. Dupont, "L'utilisation apologétique de l'AT," *Ephemerides Theologicae Lovanienses,* 29 (1953), 289-327.

17 The text reminds us of Ex. 3:18; 5:3: ὁ θεὸς ... προσκέκληται ἡμᾶς. The LXX has primarily in view the sense "to call to oneself," cf. LXX usage elsewhere. For the author of Ac. at least the idea of a task is implied in the verb.

18 Comparison with Ac. 10:3 ff., 17, 19 (and 11:5-12) is esp. instructive.

19 "Used as a substantive governing a plural verb" (C. K. Barrett, *The Gospel acc. to St. John* [1955] on Jn. 7:40) instead of a partitive gen.

20 Further examples in Schl. J. on 1:24; Pr.-Bauer, *s.v.* ἐκ 4a γ, also on LXX; Bl.-Debr. § 164, 2; rare in class. Gk.; Mayser, II, 2, 352: uncommon in the pap. adduced, more often with ἀπό, 351; common with ἐκ or ἀπό in LXX, Johannessohn Kasus, 18 f.; K. Huber, *Untersuchungen über d. Sprachcharakter des griech. Leviticus* (1916), 69 f. only in relation to Lv.

21 Cf. Wdt. Ag. and Haench. Ag., *ad loc.*

22 Just. Dial., 50, 5: συμβιβάσει, vl. in LXX. Do these follow 1 C., or did Paul find this form?

23 Is. 40:14 is to be read: ἢ πρὸς τίνα συνεβουλεύσατο (God), καὶ συνεβίβασεν (the τίς) αὐτόν (God).

24 Rel. pronoun with fut. ind. "in such sort that," Bl.-Debr. § 379.

25 The context shows that κύριος = God.

26 So first Is. 40:14 LXX (HT יַבֶּן‎).

27 One could speak of a proof from Scripture only *e contrario.*

28 The choice of word (for πνεῦμα) comes from Is. 40:13. Cf. also → II, 820, 23 ff.; IV, 959, 21 ff.

13 ff. What may be known (or not) in both Is. 40:13 and 1 C. 2:16 is the mystery of the work of God; [29] in 1 C. 2:6-16 it is the mystery of His work through the salvation event in Christ.

Delling

συμμαθητής → IV, 460, 8 ff.	συμπληρόω → VI, 308, 19 ff.
συμμαρτυρέω → IV, 508, 38 ff.	συμπνίγω → VI, 455, 8 ff.
συμμέτοχος → II, 830, 16 ff.	συμπρεσβύτερος → VI, 651, 4 ff.
συμμιμητής → IV, 659, 9 ff.	συμφέρω → φέρω.
συμμορφίζω → 787, 23 ff.	σύμφορος → φέρω.
σύμμορφος → 787, 20 ff.	σύμφυτος → 786, 25 ff.
συμμορφόω → 787, n. 99.	συμφωνέω → φωνή.
συμπαθέω → V, 935, 6 ff.	συμφώνησις → φωνή.
συμπαθής → V, 935, 6 ff.	συμφωνία → φωνή.
συμπάσχω → V, 925, 1 ff.; → 787, 13 f.	σύμφωνος → φωνή.

σύν - μετά with the Genitive, † συναποθνήσκω,
† συσταυρόω, † συνθάπτω, † σύμφυτος,
† συνεγείρω, † συζάω, † συζωοποιέω,
† συμπάσχω, † συνδοξάζω, † συγκληρονόμος, † σύμμορφος, † συμμορφίζω,
† συμβασιλεύω, † συγκαθίζω

Contents: A. On the Use of σύν and of μετά with the Genitive: 1. In Classical Greek and the Koine; 2. In the Septuagint; 3. In the New Testament; 4. In the Post-Apostolic Fathers. B. The Range of Meaning of σύν and μετά: I. σύν; II. μετά with the Genitive.

---

[29] Thus 4 Esr. 4:10 f.; 5:40 (Str.-B., III, 295) stresses the inscrutability of God's rule.

σ ύ ν κ τ λ . Bibl.: Pape, Pass., Liddell-Scott, *s.v.*; Mayser, II, 291-294, 398-401, 440-444; Kühner-Blass-Gerth, II, 1, 446 f., 505-507; Schwyzer, II, 481-491. On A. and B.: T. Mommsen, *Entwicklung einiger Gesetze über den Gebrauch d. griech. Präp.* (1874); also μετά, σύν u. ἅμα bei d. griech. Epikern (1874); also *Beiträge zur Lehre von d. griech. Präp.* (1895); Johannessohn Präp. On C.: W. C. van Unnik, "Dominus Vobiscum: The Background of a Liturgical Formula," *NT Essays, Studies in Memory of T. W. Manson,* ed. A. J. B. Higgins (1959), 270-305. On D. and E.: E. Lohmeyer, "Σὺν Χριστῷ," *Festg. f. A. Deissmann* (1926), 218-257; J. Schneider, *Die Passionsmystik d. Ap. Pls.* (1929), 31-74; G. Staffelbach, *Die Vereinigung mit Christus als Prinzip d. Moral bei Pls.,* Diss. Fribourg (Switzerland) (1932), 64-98; W. T. Hahn, *Das Mitsterben u. Mitauferstehen mit Christus bei Pls.* (1937); R. Schnackenburg, *Das Heilsgeschehen bei der Taufe nach d. Ap. Pls.* (1950), 25-77; J. Dupont, Σὺν Χριστῷ. *L'union avec le Christ suivant Saint Paul* (1952); G. Otto, *Die mit σύν verbundenen Formulierungen im paul. Schrifttum,* Diss. Berlin (1952); O. Kuss, *Der Römerbr.* (1957/59), Exc. "Mit Christus," 319-381; G. Wagner, "Das religionsgeschichtliche Problem v. Römer 6:1-11," *AbhThANT,* 39 (1962); E. Larsson, "Christus als Vorbild," *Acta Seminarii Neotest. Upsaliensis* (1962).

C. σύν and μετά in Statements about the Being Together of God and Man: I. In the Greek World; II. In the Bible: 1. God's Promise; 2. The Answer of Faith to the Promise; 3. Attestation by Others; 4. The Statement: We with God; III. The Shepherd of Hermas. D. σὺν Χριστῷ in Paul. E. Compounds in συν- which Develop the σὺν Χριστῷ: 1. The Meaning of the Verbs; 2. Eschatological Statements in Paul; 3. Colossians and Ephesians; 4. The Primitive Christian Hymn in 2 Tm. 2:11 f. F. σύν and μετά in Christ-Sayings in the NT apart from the Pauline σὺν Χριστῷ.

The theological emphasis in the NT use of the preposition σύν is to be found in the Pauline formula σὺν Χριστῷ. Whereas the Greek translations of the OT have μετά with the genitive for the theologically important statement: "The Lord is with thee (or you)," and in an amended form this is adopted in the NT too (including Paul), Paul prefers σύν with the dative, which has no theological significance in the LXX, when he is speaking about the being of Christians "with" Christ. The choice of σύν by Paul [1] may well be based on the widespread Greek and Hellenistic expression σὺν θεῷ, σὺν θεοῖς. What Paul means by σὺν Χριστῷ is worked out in a series of verbs and adjectives in συν-. Greek has similar compounds, but in part those used by Paul in his statements are newly coined on the basis of σὺν Χριστῷ. σὺν Χριστῷ man is set in a context of events expressed in the relevant verbs and adjectives. This process finds both its commencement and its consummation in an act σὺν Χριστῷ. σὺν Χριστῷ denotes the being of man as a believer; it is a being "with Christ." The verbs and adjectives in συν- make it apparent that man σὺν Χριστῷ is caught up in the Christ event. His life, commenced and consummated σὺν Χριστῷ, is lived ἐν Χριστῷ or ἐν κυρίῳ → II, 537, 13 ff. [2] This opens the door to an understanding of the Pauline formula and its influence in the NT writings. To achieve this one must ask concerning the meaning and scope of σύν and compare it with μετά and the genitive.

A. On the Use of σύν and of μετά with the Genitive.

1. In Classical Greek and the Koine. The relation between the prepositions σύν with the dat. and μετά with the gen. fluctuated more than once during the course of the centuries. There is a basic difference in sense. μετά, related to German "mit," [3] means "in the midst," "between," "among" (persons) and is first found (Hom.) with the dat., more rarely the gen., [4] also the acc. in answer to the question "whither?" == "into the midst," "towards." [5] σύν (also ξύν), [6] "whose etym. is obscure," [7] means "together"

---

1 Lohmeyer can hardly be right when he states (229) that it is "impossible to believe the formula was creatively coined by Paul," cf. also 248; → n. 79.

2 Cf. on this F. Neugebauer, *In Christus. Eine Untersuchung zum Paul. Glaubensverständnis* (1961).

3 On the linguistic relation cf. Schwyzer, II, 481 and n. 3. Old Icelandic meþ, Illyric *met,* Gothic miþ. Old High German *mit (i)* etc. For important insights in what follows I am indebted to E. Risch and A. Dihle.

4 Only a few times in Hom., Il., 24, 400; Od., 11, 449; 16, 140.

5 Cf. Schwyzer, II, 482.

6 ξύν is esp. common in ancient Attic usage, cf. Schwyzer, II, 487, n. 2. In the inscr. it occurs after 403 only in compounds and after 378 only in the formula γνώμην ξυμβάλλεσθαι. The same applies to authors of the same period. In inscr. only σύν is found on those from the Cretan, Locrian and Delphic spheres. The Lesbian poets and later Lesbian and Thessalonian inscr. gen. have σύν. But only ξύν (written *ku-su*) occurs in the Mycenaean world, which is clear evidence of the antiquity of the Attic ξύν. The Atticists of the imperial period re-adopted ξύν.

7 Cf. Schwyzer, II, 487, n. 7, also M. S. Ruipérez, "Etimologia de ξύν, σύν," *Emérita,* 15 (1947), 61-70.

and expresses togetherness or coming together (from the very first with a sociative dat.). In Hom. σύν (with dat.) is easily the most common word for "with," while μετά has the older sense of "in the midst." But there are in Hom. some special senses, including μετά with the gen. = σύν. This takes on the sense "in co-operation with" and tends to supplant σύν in the age which follows. It is possible that this usage was already common in the ordinary speech of Hom.'s day, since the epics were written in what was already to some degree a stylised language. In the older dialects, including the literarily important Ionic and Aeolic, σύν was again the normal word for "with." These dialects underlay poetic usage right up to later antiquity, whereas μετά with the gen. is far more common than σύν among philosophers, historians, and orators. [8] With the inscr. these represent pure Attic. One finds here a distribution of meanings which is alien as compared with Ionic, poetic, and post-class. usage. σύν means "with" in the sense of a close fellowship, of assistance and support, while μετά with the gen. expresses accompaniment by persons, things, or circumstances. Xenoph. stands out in Attic prose on account of his preference for σύν. In view of the course of his life he may be regarded as an author who did not write pure Attic.

The *koine* eliminates the Attic distinction between σύν and μετά "with." Hence the use of σύν is again more common. In the Ptolemaic pap., which are significant for the background of LXX usage, σύν clearly predominates in every aspect. Perhaps Ionic influence was normative here. [9] From the 1st cent. B.C. literary prose and pedagogy come under the dominant influence of Atticism, though full adherence is not achieved in respect of the prep. σύν and μετά, but both occur together. With the gradual disappearance of the dat., which was so firmly attached to σύν, this prep. dwindles more and more in the post-Chr. age. Modern Gk. knows only με(τα). In the *koine* we often find compound verbs, nouns and adjectives in συν- where class. Gk. has the simple form. There are many such instances in the Gk. pap. [10]

2. In the Septuagint. The LXX usually has μετά with the gen. This is much more common than σύν, which becomes more frequent only in the later works. This is worth noting against the background of the Ptolemaic pap. with their preference for σύν. The prep. are used with no palpable distinction in meaning. [11] A surprising pt. is that compounds in συν- are often employed with μετά and the gen., e.g., Gn. 14:24; 18:16, 23; Ex. 33:16; Nu. 22:35. The interchanging of μετά and σύν has stylistic significance; certain shifts of accent may be discerned at some pts. [12] In the LXX σύν is often used like καί [13] and can represent the Hbr. copula ן whereas μετά does not share this function;

---

[8] Mommsen Beiträge, 3-7 counts 181 instances of σύν and 5 of μετά with gen. in Hom., 67 and 8 respectively in Aesch., but 400 of μετά with gen. and 77 of σύν in Thuc., 586 and 37 in Plat., 346 and 12 in Demosth., 65 each in Hdt. Soph. has 91 of σύν and 23 of μετά and gen., so that there is a rise of μετά among the poets. This is even more noticeable in Eur. (197 σύν and 101 μετά). In the comic poets μετά and gen. predominates. This is probably connected with their use of everyday language rather than that of solemn poetry. Aristoph. has 85 μετά and 22 σύν.

[9] Mayser, II, 398-401, 440-444.

[10] *Ibid.*, II, 291-294.

[11] Cf. Johannessohn Präpos., 202-212.

[12] There is a definite stylistic alternation in Bar. 5:9: . . . μετ' εὐφροσύνης . . . σὺν ἐλεημοσύνῃ καὶ δικαιοσύνῃ τῇ παρ' αὐτοῦ. 2 Macc. 5:27: σὺν τοῖς μετ' αὐτοῦ; cf. 13:15: μετά = "with," σύν "together with"; Ez. 12:19: . . . μετ' ἐνδείας . . . καὶ . . . μετὰ ἀφανισμοῦ, double μετά for ב, but then σύν: ὅπως ἀφανισθῇ ἡ γῆ σὺν πληρώματι αὐτῆς, translating מן ('Α ἀπό). HT: "The land will be wasted of its fulness . . . " LXX: "The earth with its fulness . . . "

[13] Johannessohn Präpos., 202; cf. Jos. 6:24; 1 Ch. 16:32.

it is the rendering of עִם and אֵת.[14] Another pt. to be noted is the increasing use of σύν in the later writings; this is probably connected with the plainly increasing influence of Atticism in literary prose from the 1st cent. The Macc. offer examples. Here σύν is employed mostly for personal relations, cf. σύν and μετά in 3 Macc. 3:25: ... τοὺς ἐννεμομένους σὺν γυναιξὶ καὶ τέκνοις μετὰ ὕβρεων καὶ σκυλμῶν ἀποστεῖλαι πρὸς ἡμᾶς, and the interchangeability of the two in later textual variants of the older writings of the LXX.[15]

3. In the New Testament. NT usage corresponds to that of the *koine* at an average level of culture. There are vulgarisms like σύν with the gen. which are due to the weakening of a feeling for the dative.

μετά with the gen. is more common than σύν (364 instances compared to 127 of σύν with the dat.).[16] The μετά passages are mostly in the historical books and are fairly evenly distributed.[17] Worth noting are 40 instances in Rev. and 14 in Hb., since σύν does not occur at all in either book.[18] σύν is more common in Lk. and Paul. More than half the NT instances of σύν are in Lk., and with few exceptions Paul has the rest.[19] If compounds in συν- are counted as well, the position of σύν is stronger still.[20] This is even more significant in view of the fact that of all NT compounds those in συν- are the most common.[21] Mt., Mk., Jn., Rev. and Hb. are close to the LXX in their use of

---

[14] Johannessohn, 211. σύν with dat. occurs only occasionally for the nota acc. אֵת, e.g., Ex. 7:4. This is more often (esp. Qoh.) taken as a prep. and transl. by σύν with acc. 'A, which controls the transl. of Qoh., exerts an influence here. Cf. Est. 4:7 σὺν πᾶν = σύμπαν; 6:10; 1 Βασ. 2:22 etc., *v.* Rahlfs *ad loc.* This σύν is impossible Gk. and attempts at smoothing over by combining with a πᾶν or adding πᾶς = σύμπας (Qoh. 1:14; 3:11; 4:2 etc.) change the sense, → V, 892, 3 ff., cf. G. Bertram, "Hbr. u. Griech. Qoh.," ZAW, 64 (1952), 43 [Bertram].

[15] Cf. Ju. 7:4 A: οὗτος πορεύσεται μετὰ σοῦ, αὐτὸς πορεύσεται μετὰ σοῦ, B: οὗτος πορεύσεται σὺν σοί, αὐτὸς πορεύσεται σὺν σοί. But the negative version which occurs in parallelism in God's saying to Gideon has μετὰ σοῦ in both A and B. Cf. also Ju. 16:13 A: μετὰ τοῦ διάσματος, B: σὺν τῷ διάσματι. The B text is from the early 4th cent. A.D. As may be seen from the negative par. in Ju. 7:4 the alteration was not consistent. In some Βασ. passages similar alterations derive from the Origen recension or other sources, 4 Βασ. 15:19: μετ' αὐτοῦ — σὺν αὐτῷ, 3 Βασ. 6:12 ... στήσω τὸν λόγον μου supplemented by σὺν σοί, cf. also 3 Βασ. 8:5; 13:19; also 1 Macc. 9:60: τοὺς μετ' αὐτοῦ — τοὺς σὺν αὐτῷ, and cf. A. Rahlfs, *Septuaginta-Stud.,* III (1911), 214. In later OT transl. σύν is more common, e.g., Gn. 5:22, 24 in 'A: HT: "He walked with God," LXX: "He pleased God" (state or quality for action), 'A adds an awkward σὺν θεῷ in partial assimilation to the HT. Da. 9:26 LXX: μετὰ τοῦ χριστοῦ, Θ: ... σὺν τῷ ἡγουμένῳ τῷ ἐρχομένῳ. μετά and σύν are plainly interchangeable and the use of σύν increases. But this is an academic matter and not a living development in usage.

[16] Cf. R. Morgenthaler, *Statistik d. nt.lichen Wortschatzes* (1958), 120, 145, 160.

[17] Mt. 60 times, Mk. 44, Lk. 54, Jn. 40, Ac. 36.

[18] The Johannine Epistles have μετά 9 times, σύν none; 1 Pt. has μετά once, 2 Pt. σύν once, Jm. σύν once, but not μετά.

[19] Morgenthaler, *op. cit.* counts 127 σύν ref., of which 75 are in Luke, 23 in Lk. and 52 in Ac. There are 37 instances in Paul compared with μετά 69 times. In Mt. we find 4 instances, in Mk. 6 and in Jn. 3.

[20] Cf. H. Schürmann, *Der Passahmahlbericht Lk. 22 (7-14) 15-18* (1952), 95. The author notes that of 94 different NT compounds in συν- Lk. uses 78 (which is a surprisingly high no. in the NT), while 46 are only in Lk. (cf. Morgenthaler, *op. cit.,* 143-146), 14 only in Paul and Lk., and 29 just as common in Lk. as in the rest of the NT.

[21] Cf. Morgenthaler, 160, Section c.

σύν and μετά → 768, 27 ff. [22] Lk., however, is influenced by the writing of the Roman period in his greater use of σύν; Macc. are closest to him in the LXX. The data relating to Lk. are similar to what we find in Xenoph. (→ 768, 14 ff.) in Attic lit. Possibly he was influenced by Paul. Paul uses μετά more than σύν (69 times to 37, though cf. 59 compound verbs in συν-), but he gives σύν a theological importance μετά never has through the formula σὺν Χριστῷ. Paul's use of μετά is traditional; the word has the same theological content in his works as in the LXX and the rest of the NT. [23]

4. In the Post-Apostolic Fathers. Here there are two groups. Did., Barn., 1 and 2 Cl. and Herm. use only μετά in relation to both persons and things; only at 1 Cl., 65, 1 do we find σύν in a personal relation, and this is followed at once by μετὰ χαρᾶς; Barn., 4, 2 has μετὰ ἁμαρτωλῶν καὶ πονηρῶν συντρέχειν. On the other hand Ign., Pol. and Mart. Pol. use μετά mostly in relation to things but σύν is now more common, though only in relation to persons. Ign. also has a series of compounds in συν-, nouns and adj. as well as verbs. Herm. has a similar series.

B. The Range of Meaning of σύν and μετά.

I. σύν.

The basic meaning of the preposition σύν with the sociative dative [24] is "with," and the term has a personal character. It denotes the totality of persons who are together, or who come together, or who accompany one another, or who work together, sharing a common task or a common destiny, aiding and supporting one another. It can also denote sharing things or their possession, which brings into a connection with the owner. [25]

1. Being, acting together. a. Hom. Il., 3, 206: σὺν ἀρηϊφίλῳ Μενελάῳ, 6, 372 f.: ξὺν παιδὶ καὶ ἀμφιπόλῳ ἐϋπέπλῳ πύργῳ ἐφεστήκει, Od., 9, 286: ἐγὼ σὺν τοῖσδε, Xenoph. An., I, 2, 15: Μένων καὶ οἱ σὺν αὐτῷ, cf. also II, 6, 14: καὶ τῇ σὺν ἐμοὶ στρατιᾷ, II, 5, 25 and III, 2, 11: ἐλθόντων μὲν γὰρ Περσῶν καὶ τῶν σὺν αὐτοῖς. b. LXX, cf. Ex. 10:9; Ju. 3:27; 1 Βασ. 7:9; 1 Macc. 3:14; 15:13; 3 Macc. 3:25. The Psalmist in ψ 33:4 demands: μεγαλύνατε τὸν κύριον σὺν ἐμοί. All the dwellers on earth share a common destiny: ἡ γῆ ... σὺν πᾶσιν τοῖς κατοικοῦσιν αὐτήν, Hos. 4:3; cf. Mi. 7:13; also Am. 6:8 of the inhabitants of a city. In the history books (LXX) we find the formula σὺν δυνάμει αὐτῶν, i.e., the whole people apportioned and arranged in divisions, Ex. 6:26; 12:51; Nu. 1:3, 45; also the order of the camp, Nu. 2:3, 9, 10, 16, 18, 24, 25, 32.

---

[22] Even if there are in the NT some rare extensions of meaning (possibly Semitisms), e.g., Mk. 15:28, we do not find the popular instrumental use of μετά. σύν, which enjoyed much less vitality at the time, does not undergo any expansion of meaning at all.

[23] The numbers given in → n. 17-21 and the text vary a little acc. to textual variants, but this does not alter the basic results, cf. the minor differences between Morgenthaler and Schürmann.

[24] σύν with gen. cf. Liddell-Scott, s.v.; Inscr. antiquae orae septentrionalis Ponti Euxini, ed. B. Latyschew, II (1890), σὺν ἡρώων, 383, 5; σὺν γυναικός, 301, 2. Adv. "at the same time," "together," Hom. Il., 23, 879; Od., 10, 42; Aesch. Ag., 586; Soph. Ant., 85, LXX: Qoh. 7:15; 2 Εσδρ. 4:7; Ju. 20:44, 46 also have an adv. sense "altogether valiant men."

[25] Cf. the def. in Dupont, 17 f.: "... c'est d'abord lorsqu'elle se trouve en sa compagnie, en sa société, lorsqu'elle est d'auprès d'elle, lorsqu'elle l'accompagne; ... Cette idée de société ou d'accompagnement entraîne assez facilement l'idée d'assistance, de coopération ... "

c. In the NT, too, σύν is used in this way: Mk. 2:26; 4:10; 8:34; 9:4; Lk. 1:56; 2:5, 13; [26] 8:38, [27] 45, [28] 51; 22:14, 56; 24:33; Jn. 12:2; 18:1. [29]

2. To be, to act together with the goal of supporting and helping one another, e.g., in war Soph. Phil., 920, cf. Xenoph. An., VII, 3, 10: στρατεύεσθαι σὺν ἐμοί, also 1 Macc. 10:24 ... ὅπως ὦσιν σὺν ἐμοὶ εἰς βοήθειαν. This is the basis of the idea of taking the side of someone, so Xenoph. Hist. Graec., III, 1, 18: ὅτι ... βούλοιντο σὺν τοῖς "Ελλησι μᾶλλον ἢ σὺν τῷ βαρβάρῳ εἶναι, IG, 1, [2] 63, 17: ξὺν τῇ βουλῇ, also Ac. 14:4: οἱ μὲν ἦσαν σὺν τοῖς Ἰουδαίοις, οἱ δὲ σὺν ἀποστόλοις.

3. The word σύν is also used with ref. to the things which a man uses, with which he is equipped, or with ref. to the accompanying circumstances of an event or action. The personal structure of the prep. is so strong that the things mentioned almost seem to be personified. Hom. Il., 5, 219: σὺν ἵπποισιν καὶ ὄχεσφιν, cf. 2, 187; 3, 29; 15, 541; 20, 493; also Soph. Phil., 1335; Eur. Herc. Fur., 1383. Ex. 15:19: σὺν ἅρμασιν καὶ ἀναβάταις Pharaoh is drowned in the Red Sea; cf. 2 Βασ. 6:3 f.; 2 Macc. 5:26; NT: Lk. 5:19; Mt. 25:27; Lk. 19:23. Intellectual qualities and spiritual passions proper to a man are expressed by σύν, Hom. Od., 24, 193: Penelope, a woman σὺν μεγάλη ἀρετῇ, Soph. Ant., 135 f.: μαινομένᾳ ξὺν ὁρμᾷ βακχεύων, Soph. Ai., 932: οὐλίῳ σὺν πάθει, Pind. Pyth., 1, 61 f. says: πόλιν ... θεοδμάτῳ σὺν ἐλευθερίᾳ Ὑλλίδος στάθμας Ἱέρων ἐν νόμοις ἔκτισσε. Accompanying circumstances and connections, and the results connected with events, are also denoted by σύν, e.g., Hom. Il., 17, 57: ἄνεμος σὺν λαίλαπι πολλῇ, also 4, 161 ff.: The fall of Troy is a great settling of accounts involving women and children σύν τε μεγάλῳ ἀπέτεισαν, σὺν σφῆσιν κεφαλῇσι γυναιξί τε καὶ τεκέεσσιν, cf. also Soph. Ant., 172; Plat. Gorg., 513a. LXX: Ex. 12:9; Lv. 4:11; 1 Βασ. 14:32-34; 2 Macc. 7:7. In this kind of context σύν can have adv. significance, so σὺν νόμῳ == "acc. to the law," Plat. Leg., XI, 924a; Xenoph. Cyrop., I, 3, 17; cf. VIII, 2, 23: κτᾶσθαι ... σὺν τῷ δικαίῳ καὶ χρῆσθαι ... σὺν τῷ καλῷ ...; An., II, 6, 18; Soph. Phil., 1223.

II. μετά with the Genitive.

1. As a prep. [30] with the gen. [31] μετά means basically "among," "in the midst." a. Hom. Od., 10, 320; 16, 140; Aesch. Ag., 1007; Eur. Phoen., 1006. This means that the next sense of "to be or act in fellowship with..." usually takes a plur. (one is always

---

[26] Cf. on this Pr.-Bauer, *s.v.* σύν.

[27] A peculiarity of Lk. is to insert σύν even where it is not in the Synoptic par., cf. 9:32; 20:1.

[28] But not in all texts; καὶ οἱ σὺν αὐτῷ is attested by the Hesych. group of texts, by D Θ Tat.

[29] In this and the following sections cf. the lex. and grammars, esp. Schwyzer, for further examples.

[30] μετά is used adv. "amongst" in Hom. Il., 15, 67; 2, 446 f., 477; 18, 515; for the adv. sense connected with the prep. and acc. ("after") "afterwards" cf. Hom. Il., 23, 133; Od., 15, 400; 21, 231.

[31] Cf. Kühner-Blass-Gerth, II, 1, 505: "The combination with the gen. is a later one (it occurs only 5 times in Hom.), and yet it not only gradually supplanted the dat., to which it was very close in sense from the very outset (μετὰ Τρωσί 'among the Trojans,' cf. § 426, 1 — μετὰ Τρώων 'in the sphere of the Trojans' cf. § 419, 2) but it also took over the functions of σύν 'with' and thus essentially narrowed the territory of this prep." For examples of the dat. cf. Hom. Il., 11, 64; 13, 668; 15, 118; 16, 15; Od., 2, 148; also Eur. Hec., 355; cf. also on this Mommsen Beiträge, 39-51.

among many) in contrast to the more common sing. with σύν. [32] Cf. II., 13, 700; Soph. Phil., 1103, 1312 f.; Eur. Hec., 209 f.; Plat. Resp., II, 359e; Prot. 315b; Xenoph. An., V, 4, 34. b. μετά with gen. is very common in the LXX, often with the sing. like σύν, e.g., Gn. 3:6, 12; 7:7, a being together which can include animals, 6:18-20; 8:1, cf. also Gn. 12:4, 20; 13:1, 5; 20:16; 23:4; 24:3, 5, 8 etc.; 27:44; 29:14, 19; 42:4 f.; 43:16, 32; Ex. 12:4; 18:12, also sleeping together Gn. 19:32-35; 26:8, 10, also sleeping in a common grave, Gn. 47:30; 49:29, and the union of the living and the dead, Ex. 13:19. The prayers in the Ps. speak of the fellowship of the righteous, renounce fellowship with the wicked, and view the lot which Yahweh assigns as determined by the fellowship in which men stand, ψ 25:4, 5, 9; 27:3; 68:29; 105:5, 6. c. The NT shares LXX usage, Mt. 2:3, 11; 4:21; 20:20; also Mt. 5:25, 41; 9:15; 12:3 f. par. Mk. 2:25; [33] Mt. 15:30; 27:54; Mk. 1:36; 5:40; Jn. 3:26; 11:31, 54; Gl. 2:1, 12; 2 C. 8:18; Phil. 4:3; 2 Tm. 4:11; Tt. 3:15; Hb. 13:23.

2. μετά can also mean "to stand by" someone, "to assist, help" him, "to take his side" → 771, 3 ff. a. Thuc., III, 56, 4; VII, 57, 9; Xenoph. Cyrop., II, 4, 7; Aristoph. Ach., 661. b. LXX Is. 28:15: Hades and death are allies of the rulers of the people of Jerusalem. c. NT: Mt. 20:2; [34] 1 C. 7:12, 13. [35]

3. The means by which help is rendered and the accompanying acts and circumstances are also expressed by μετά in the sense "by means of," "connected with," "with." a. Plat. Phileb., 37e: πολλάκις οὐ μετὰ δόξης ὀρθῆς, ἀλλὰ μετὰ ψεύδους, Phaed., 66b: ἐκφέρειν ἡμᾶς μετὰ τοῦ λόγου ἐν τῇ σκέψει, Xenoph. An., II, 6, 18: μετὰ ἀδικίας. b. LXX Gn. 31:27: μετ' εὐφροσύνης καὶ μετὰ μουσικῶν, τυμπάνων καὶ κιθάρας, cf. Ex. 15:20; ψ 68:31; 80:3; Is. 5:12; 29:6; 38:20; eschatological redemption is not by means of money οὐ μετὰ ἀργυρίου, Is. 52:3, but by Yahweh's love to His people μετὰ ἐλέους μεγάλου, Is. 54:7, μεθ' ἵππων καὶ ἁρμάτων the people is gathered together in the eschatological age, 66, 20. c. The NT has many similar combinations, Mt. 26:55; Jn. 18:3; Mt. 27:34; 14:7; Mk. 9:24 (DΘ 𝔐 Lat.); 10:30; Lk. 17:15; Hb. 5:7; 7:21; μετὰ φόβου καὶ τρόμου, 2 C. 7:15; Eph. 6:5; Phil. 2:12. [36] All these formulae and sayings show that in spite of its basic personal meaning μετά is commonly associated with things in bibl. usage too, whereas σύν retains its strongly personal character and is much less commonly combined with things.

4. Often the combining of μετά and gen. with things can be rendered either adj. or adv. a. Soph. Ant., 115: πολλῶν μεθ' ὅπλων strongly armed, [37] cf. Eur. Or., 573; Iph. Aul., 65 and 544; Thuc., VII, 57, 9 also often in Plat. Theaet., 173a: μετὰ τοῦ δικαίου καὶ ἀληθοῦς, cf. Resp., I, 330e; Polit., 295e; Phaed., 69b. In Ap., 34c Socrates ref. to those who beseech the judges μετὰ πολλῶν δακρύων; he will not do this even if as a result they give their verdict μετ' ὀργῆς. b. LXX often has similar expressions, Gn. 15:15; 26:29, 31; 44:17; 45:2; Ex. 1:14; 11:8; 12:11; 14:25; 32:12; Is. 10:33; 15:3 etc. c. NT: Mt. 13:20; 28:8; Mk. 3:5; 4:16; 6:25; Lk. 1:39; 8:13; 10:17; 14:9; 24:52; Ac. 2:29;

---

[32] Cf. Kühner-Blass-Gerth, II, 1, 507: "As a rule with the plur. or with the sing. of collective names of persons or things thought of in personal terms, of the parts or members of living creatures."

[33] At Mt. 12:3, 4 par. Mk. 2:25, 26 both Mt. and Mk. have μετά in the first v. but Mk. reads σύν and Mt. μετά in the second.

[34] Here, and cf. Gl. 2:12, we thus have a NT example of the combining of verbs in σύν- with μετά as in the LXX → 768, 30 f.

[35] Sometimes in the bibl. books we also find the form ποιέω μετά "to do to...," cf. Bl.-Debr. § 206, 3; § 227. Examples Gn. 21:23; 24:12; ψ 17:26 f.; 85:17; 108:21; 118:65; 125:2, 3; Lk. 1:58, 72; 10:37.

[36] In the combinations in Eph. 6:23; Phil. 1:4; 1 Tm. 1:14; 4:14 μετά means "together with."

[37] σύν and μετά are used together in the same sense in poetic alternation: πολλῶν μεθ' ὅπλων ξύν θ' ἱπποκόμοις κορύθεσσιν, Soph. Ant., 115 f.

4:29, 31; [38] 5:26; 14:23; 15:33; 17:11; 20:19; 24:3, 7; 25:23; 27:10; 28:31; Eph. 4:2; 6:7; Phil. 2:29; 4:6; Col. 1:11; 1 Th. 1:6; 2 Th. 3:12; 1 Tm. 2:9, 15; 3:4; 4:3 f.; 6:6; Hb. 4:16; 10:22, 34; 12:28; 13:17. The many instances shows how strongly μετά with the gen. is related to things.

C. σύν and μετά in Statements about the Being Together of God and Man.

I. In the Greek World.

σὺν θεῷ or σὺν θεοῖς is a constantly recurring phrase among the Greeks. It is found in all epochs of Greek literature. In the form "with God" it has passed into modern languages. [39] It denotes the conviction that man's life, word, counsel and acts stand under the good-pleasure and helpful co-operation of the deity. [40] The hoped for good-pleasure of the deity is thus a spur to resolute action and confident activity in the sphere of earthly life. [41]

1. σὺν θεῷ expresses the favour of the hour, happy circumstances, benevolence to man from the hidden ground of his being. These appear in the form of deities or God. [42] They are combined with the thought that fortune is fickle and favourable circumstances can change, hence Soph. Ai., 383: ξύν τῷ θεῷ πᾶς καὶ γελᾷ κὠδύρεται, "when deity withdraws, fortune changes." Menelaus vanquishes Paris with the aid of supporting Athene: ἐνίκησεν σὺν 'Αθήνῃ, Hom. Il., 3, 439; Tydeus, the father of Diomedes, has done mighty deeds with Athene: σὺν σοί, δῖα θεά, ὅτε οἱ πρόφρασσα παρέστης, Hom. Il., 10, 290. In a difficult situation recollection of the past assistance of the gods helps a man to endure, so Diomedes to Agamemnon σὺν γὰρ θεῷ εἰλήλουθμεν, Il., 9, 49, Achilles to Aeneas σὺν 'Αθήνῃ καὶ Διὶ πατρί, 20, 192, also 24, 430; Od., 8, 493; 13, 391; the whole of the passage 13, 381-391 shows that this divine help is experienced as a disclosure of the dangers and as the help which delivers through them, so that σὺν σοί is the final and decisive word. Homer's poetry has clear ideas, then, concerning the aid of the gods. When Odysseus' son Telemachus looks around for helpers, his father makes it clear to him that the strong protectors whose throne is in the clouds will not hold aloof but will come down to give direct aid, Od., 16, 258-269. Gk. tragedy speaks similarly of the help of the gods, so Aesch. Choeph., 147 f.; Soph. Oed. Tyr., 145 f.; Ai., 765, 779, 950. The examples from Soph. Ai. show that the arrogance of men who want to fight and win without divine aid, in their own strength, will be shattered. The same conviction concerning the aid of the gods may be seen in Xenoph. An., III, 2, 11; Cyrop., V, 4, 22. Pind. in his odes gives solemn expression to his belief in divine assistance, Olymp., 8, 12-14: ἄλλα δ' ἐπ' ἄλλον ἔβαν ἀγαθῶν, πολλαὶ δ' ὁδοὶ σὺν θεοῖς εὐπραγίας, Nem., 8, 17: σὺν θεῷ γάρ τοι φυτευθεὶς ὄλβος ἀνθρώποισι παρμονώτερος.

---

[38] We have here one of the guiding thoughts in Ac. The ref. is to the public proclamation of the message of Jesus Christ in spite of all attempts to silence or suppress it. This is plain from the emphatic position at the beginning and end in Ac. 28:31.

[39] Lohmeyer rightly says (229): "Our common phrase 'with God' is not based on a distinctive thought of the OT or NT but is a legacy of the religious spirit of antiquity."

[40] Cf. Lohmeyer, 228 f.: "An expression of the help which the gods can give men in their acts and journeys"; Dupont, 19: "Avec Dieu, c'est à dire, par la volonté de Dieu, avec son aide et son concours."

[41] Cf. Lohmeyer, 228: "This 'with God' impels to action, and thus action-words are especially combined with it."

[42] Dupont, 19, n. 5 rightly draws attention to the imprecision of the term "God." Materially cf. W. F. Otto, Die Götter Griechenlands⁴ (1956), 127-166; also Theophaneia, Der Geist d. altgriech. Religion (1956), 41-47; cf. Aesch. Suppl., 88: ξὺν τύχᾳ; also Choeph., 138 with σὺν θεοῖς, Ag., 913, 961.

2. Divine support not only assures succour from without but also has an inner effect on man. Nestor hopes that with divine help (σὺν δαίμονι) the good words of Patroclus will touch the heart of angry Achilles, Hom. Il., 11, 792; 15, 403; cf. also Eur. Med., 625: σὺν θεῷ δ' εἰρήσεται, Hdt., I, 86: σὺν θεῷ εἰρημένον, a formula which refers to the divine inspiration of human speech. The formula σὺν θεῷ εἰπεῖν occurs repeatedly in Plat. and gives added emphasis, e.g., Theaet., 151b: γνοὺς ὅτι οὐδὲν ἐμοῦ δέονται, πάνυ εὐμενῶς προμνῶμαι καί, σὺν θεῷ εἰπεῖν, πάνυ ἱκανῶς τοπάζω οἷς ἂν συγγενόμενοι ὄναιντο, also Prot., 317b; Leg., IX, 858b. To denote the aid of the gods Plat. uses μετὰ θεοῦ or μετὰ θεῶν; this occurs 7 times in Leg. and in Alchibiades, I, 105e, also σὺν θεῷ in Menex., 245e. [43] Plat. Soph., 265c contains a basic discussion of the question of the co-operation of the gods, and in relation to the genesis of living creatures it poses the important question: τὴν φύσιν αὐτὰ γεννᾶν ἀπό τινος αἰτίας αὐτομάτης καὶ ἄνευ διανοίας φυούσης, ἢ μετὰ λόγου τε καὶ ἐπιστήμης θείας ἀπὸ θεοῦ γιγνομένης;

3. Found in poetry and prose, the expression σὺν θεῷ also passed into popular usage. This is plain in Aristoph. Pl., 114 f., where we find again the phrase of Eur. Med., 625 (→ line 3 f.): οἶμαι γάρ, οἶμαι — ξὺν θεῷ δ' εἰρήσεται — ταύτης ἀπαλλάξειν σε τῆς ὀφθαλμίας, cf. also Theogn., 1117 f.: Πλοῦτε, θεῶν κάλλιστε καὶ ἱμεροέστατε πάντων, σὺν σοὶ καὶ κακὸς ὢν γίνεται ἐσθλὸς ἀνήρ. In a Gk. pap. of the age of Ptolemy we read: σὺν τοῖς θεοῖς καὶ τῇ σῇ τύχῃ ἐκ τοῦ θανάτου σέσωσμαι, P. Par., 12, 17, and there are many instances of σὺν θεῷ, σὺν θεοῖς, σὺν τῇ ἀγαθῇ τύχῃ, σὺν τῇ τῶν θεῶν εὐμενείᾳ. [44] A magic pap. reads: ἐγώ εἰμι Ἑρμῆς, λαμβάνω σε σὺν ἀγαθῇ Τύχῃ καὶ ἀγαθῷ Δαίμονι. [45] On an Attic devotion tablet (3rd cent. B.C.) we read: I will bind them σὺν θ' Ἑκάτῃ χθονίᾳ καὶ Ἐρινύσιν, [46] and cf. a metrical oracle from Asia Minor: σὺν Ζηνὶ (μεγίστῳ) τεύξῃ ... [47] One sees here quite plainly how σὺν θεῷ found a place in the language of popular piety and even magic.

II. In the Bible.

1. God's Promise.

The Bible has the divine promise: I am with thee, I am with you. In the LXX this is always rendered by μετά with the genitive, and the NT follows suit. In distinction from the Greek σὺν θεῷ, which is uttered by man when he experiences the support of the deity, the biblical statement is a declaration of God Himself by which He binds Himself to man. For this reason faith corresponds to it. This is not a credulity which expects an enterprise to turn out favourably. Faith relies on the declaration and promise of God. The God who makes this promise is not the fortune or benevolence manifested in earthly relationship. It is the divine I speaking and demanding an answer. God's promise that He will be with men applies to earthly life and beyond. It determines human action and makes the recipients strong and courageous to accept difficult and even hopeless undertakings. It tells them to wait patiently for God to work and endure confidently in spite of all appearances.

---

[43] Cf. Mommsen Beiträge, 375 f.; J. v. Loewenclau, "Der platonische Menexenos," *Tübinger Beiträge z. Altertums-Wissenschaft*, 41 (1961), 104.

[44] Cf. Mayser, II, 2 (1933/34), 400.

[45] Deissmann LO, 217.

[46] *Ibid.*, 257, n. 4.

[47] *Loc. cit.*, cf. F. Heinevetter, *Würfel- u. Buchstabenorakel*, Diss. Breslau (1912), 6.

a. Many OT men received God's promise that He would be with them.

This is especially so in the historical books of the OT, and particularly in Gn., Jos., S., Ch., and the prophet Jer., less so Ps. and the other prophets. Examples are to be found in all strata of the Pent. The statement is thus a by no means incidental element in the theological interpretation of the patriarchal age with its brightness and vigour. The divine promise does not belong to that tendency in OT piety and worship in which the individual is absorbed into the people as whole. It is first a promise to the individual and only later to the covenant people in its totality, as in Dt. and Dt. Is. [48] In the Pentateuchal records Abraham is the first to receive this promise as God's self-committal to him: καὶ ἐγὼ ἰδοὺ ἡ διαθήκη μου μετὰ σοῦ, Gn. 17:4. [49] It is then given to Isaac, 26:3, cf. also v. 24, then to Jacob, 28:15, where it means that God is with Jacob in the sense of protection, guidance and support, [50] cf. also 31:3, 13; 32:24-29; 35:13-15; 46:4. We then find Moses in Ex. 3:12, [51] Joshua in Jos. 1:5, 9, Gideon in Ju. 6:12 through the angel of the Lord in the form: κύριος μετὰ σοῦ, δυνατὸς τῇ ἰσχύι. Gideon construes the promise as election disclosed in the fact that God speaks with him ὅτι σὺ λαλεῖς μετ' ἐμοῦ, Ju. 6:16 f. David receives the promise through the prophet Nathan in 2 Βασ. 7:9, cf. 1 Ch. 17:8: καὶ ἤμην μετὰ σοῦ ἐν πᾶσιν οἷς ἐπορεύου, also ψ 88:25: καὶ ἡ ἀλήθειά μου καὶ τὸ ἔλεός μου μετ' αὐτοῦ. For Jeroboam it is linked with a series of conditions relating to the keeping of God's commandments, 3 Βασ. 11:38. It is unconditional at the call of Jeremiah, Jer. 1:8, 17, 19; 15:20. It is thus given to men who are chosen for special tasks and it means that God will assist them in their discharge. Esp. in the story of Gideon it is manifest that the promise does not necessarily embrace the whole of the life of the men concerned. Yet in the case of David and Jer. it embraces at least gt. portions of their lives. [52] The Psalmist is also given the promise, e.g., in ψ 90:15: God's promise to the man who calls upon him as a hearing of the prayer μετ' αὐτοῦ εἰμι ἐν θλίψει καὶ ἐξελοῦμαι καὶ δοξάσω αὐτόν, cf. also Tob. 12:12 f.: the angel of the Lord says to him σὺν σοὶ ἤμην.

God's promise is also given to the whole people. In Am. 5:14 it is conditional on the doing of good and not evil, ὅπως ζήσητε, καὶ ἔσται οὕτως μεθ' ὑμῶν κύριος ὁ θεὸς ὁ παντοκράτωρ. The people thus runs the risk of forfeiting the promise through sin. In Dt. 20:1, 4 — κύριος ὁ θεὸς ὑμῶν ὁ προπορευόμενος μεθ' ὑμῶν συνεκπολεμῆσαι ὑμῖν τοὺς ἐχθροὺς ὑμῶν διασῶσαι ὑμᾶς — the people is given the promise against a much superior enemy, so that it can have a strong heart, steadfastness, and fearlessness. [53] Jos. 7:12 demands purification if Yahweh is to remain with this people. Cf. Ιερ. 26:28: A promise to the people when under threat of destruction which is similar to that given to Jer. himself in Ιερ. 49:11. After the exile the people, when preparing to return to the Holy Land, receives the solemn promise of God through the prophet: μὴ φοβοῦ, μετὰ σοῦ γάρ εἰμι· μὴ πλανῶ, ἐγὼ γάρ εἰμι ὁ θεός σου ὁ ἐνισχύσας σε καὶ ἐβοήθησά σοι καὶ ἠσφαλισάμην σε τῇ δεξιᾷ τῇ δικαίᾳ μου, Is. 41:10; cf. also 43:1, 2, 5; the promise of Is. 58:11: καὶ ἔσται ὁ θεός σου μετὰ σοῦ διὰ παντός, is a word of comfort, while mercy is demanded at the same time from the people.

---

[48] Cf. van Unnik, 284 f.

[49] The passage is ascribed to P and on this view does not belong to the story as such but has been brought into it.

[50] Cf. the various pts. in interpretation in van Unnik, 276 f.

[51] Cf. on this A. Alt, "Der Gott d. Väter," BWANT, 48 (1929), 14-26.

[52] van Unnik, 282 would regard the expression not "as a permanent fact, but as a dynamic experience that acts in special cases which can be sharply discerned." Typical of the promise is "the dynamic conception, this not permanent, but suddenly appearing presence," though this does not rule out the possibility that the promise of special help applies to long stretches of time and not just to individual moments.

[53] The summons not to fear is often linked with the promise; God's confirmed assistance takes away fear.

b. In the NT Mary in Lk. is the first to receive the promise of God from the angel in a way which reminds us of the call of Gideon (Ju. 6:12, 16 f.): χαῖρε κεχαριτωμένη, ὁ κύριος μετὰ σοῦ, Lk. 1:28. This salutation also tells Mary of her election by God's grace: μὴ φοβοῦ, Μαριάμ· εὗρες γὰρ χάριν παρὰ τῷ θεῷ, v. 30. [54] In Ac. 18:9 f. Paul, confronted by dangerous circumstances in Corinth, hears the Lord say to him in a vision: μὴ φοβοῦ, ἀλλὰ λάλει καὶ μὴ σιωπήσῃς, διότι ἐγώ εἰμι μετὰ σοῦ καὶ οὐδεὶς ἐπιθήσεταί σοι τοῦ κακῶσαί σε... The Lord Jesus Christ gives Paul the OT divine promise as His own. This is of basic significance, as may be seen especially in Mt.

When Mt. refers to Jesus for the first time he applies Is. 7:14 to Him. Jesus is Immanuel, and Mt. translates the name μεθ᾽ ἡμῶν ὁ θεός, 1:23. In Him God's promise is a personal reality in history. [55] He is the expression, sign, and actualisation of the covenant of God with men, taking away their sins, Mt. 1:21; 26:28. When this has been done the Risen Lord in Mt. 28:18 can say to the messengers who are to proclaim His accession to the whole world: καὶ ἰδοὺ ἐγὼ μεθ᾽ ὑμῶν εἰμι πάσας τὰς ἡμέρας ἕως τῆς συντελείας τοῦ αἰῶνος, Mt. 28:20. He assures them of His assistance in fulfilling the task laid upon them. [56] Between the beginning in Mt. 1 and the end in Mt. 28, however, there stands Mt. 18:20, which promises the Lord's presence to those who gather in His name and pray: the ἐν μέσῳ αὐτῶν corresponds materially to a μεθ᾽ ὑμῶν. [57] What is said fundamentally at the beginning of the Gospel is thus extended both to the community and also to the messengers. He who is "God with us" shows in His promises that He is this right on to the consummation of the age.

This fact is intrinsic to the Johannine understanding of Christ. Jn. presents the Son in His unity with the Father, 10:30. His words and acts are those of the Father, 5:19-21; 12:44-50 etc. [58] But Jesus says of Himself that this unity is His fellowship with the Father: καὶ ὁ πέμψας με μετ᾽ ἐμοῦ ἐστιν· οὐκ ἀφῆκέν με μόνον, ὅτι ἐγὼ τὰ ἀρεστὰ αὐτῷ ποιῶ πάντοτε, 8:29. This is repeated when His rejection by the Jews leads to His death: καὶ οὐκ εἰμὶ μόνος, ὅτι ὁ πατὴρ μετ᾽ ἐμοῦ ἐστιν, 16:32. This is the basis of the salvation of the disciples, 16:33. He gives them assistance in the Spirit of truth ἵνα ᾖ μεθ᾽ ὑμῶν εἰς τὸν αἰῶνα, 14:16. In Rev. the divine contemplates the σκηνὴ τοῦ θεοῦ μετὰ τῶν ἀνθρώπων in which it will be fulfilled that καὶ σκηνώσει μετ᾽ αὐτῶν... καὶ αὐτὸς ὁ θεὸς μετ᾽ αὐτῶν ἔσται, Rev. 21:3. That which determines the history of God's people is fulfilled in the eschatological consummation.

---

[54] Mary is viewed by Luke as a believer. Her faith is based on this promise, cf. W. Grundmann, *Das Ev. nach Lk.*, Theol. Handkomm. z. NT, 3 (1961), 97 f.

[55] van Unnik repeatedly draws attention to the fact that the promise of God is linked with the outpouring of the Spirit on the one to whom it is made, so that the aid is received in the gift of the Spirit. Jesus is conceived of Mary by the Spirit and as the One conceived by the Spirit He is Immanuel, Mt. 1:20-23. Cf. van Unnik, 287 f.

[56] Cf. W. Trilling, *Das wahre Israel* (1959), 26-28.

[57] Cf. van Unnik, 288, also "in our midst" and "with us" together in 1 QM 12:7-9.

[58] Hence His speaking with men corresponds to God's speaking with them (Jn. 4:27; 9:37; 14:30; Rev. 1:12; 4:1; for the angel cf. Rev. 10:8; 17:1; 21:9, 15).

2. The Answer of Faith to the Promise.

a. In the OT this answer is given by Jacob in prayer and oath, Gn. 28:20, [59] cf. also 31:5; 35:3. From the conflicts of his prophetic destiny Jer. confesses: κύριος μετ' ἐμοῦ καθὼς μαχητὴς ἰσχύων, 20:11. The Psalmist in ψ 22:4 makes a plain confession of God's promise when he passes through the dark valley: οὐ φοβηθήσομαι κακά, ὅτι σὺ μετ' ἐμοῦ εἶ. [60]

With these confessions of individuals stand those of the people as in the solemn saying in ψ 45:8, 12: κύριος τῶν δυνάμεων μεθ' ἡμῶν. Moses speaks for all when he says that he will advance only if God goes with His people, Ex. 33:15 f.; 34:9. He warns the people against acting on their own, Nu. 14:42. Looking back, Dt. confesses that God went with His people, 1:30, 42; cf. 2:7: ἰδοὺ τεσσαράκοντα ἔτη κύριος ὁ θεός σου μετὰ σοῦ. In his parting words Moses assures the people of the divine promise which is the basis of their history, 31:6, 8; cf. 32:12: κύριος μόνος ἦγεν αὐτούς, καὶ οὐκ ἦν μετ' αὐτῶν θεὸς ἀλλότριος, and cf. too the confession of Phinehas the priest: σήμερον ἐγνώκαμεν ὅτι μεθ' ἡμῶν κύριος, Jos. 22:31. David also confesses before the leaders of Israel: οὐχὶ κύριος μεθ' ὑμῶν; 1 Ch. 22:18, and Solomon in 3 Βασ. 8:27, at the dedication of the temple, bears witness to the miracle that God dwells among men (μετὰ ἀνθρώπων, v. 27), praying: γένοιτο κύριος ὁ θεὸς ἡμῶν μεθ' ἡμῶν καθὼς ἦν μετὰ τῶν πατέρων ἡμῶν, v. 57. In the history of the wars of Israel and Judah recounted in 2 Ch. we repeatedly find a confession of God's promise and the confidence that God is not with a host, 2 Ch. 13:12; 15:2; 20:17; 25:7; 32:8. The prophecies of Is. against hostile nations contain the conviction which appeals to God's promise: Immanuel, God is with us, Is. 8:8, 10. Jer. reminds God of His covenant with Israel, Jer. 14:21. There is a testimony from the Maccabaean period in 3 Macc. 6:15, while 1 QM 12:8 has the confession: "The Holy One, the Lord and King of glory is with us," cf. also 19:1. [61] The promise of divine help and support which is given to individuals and which is demonstrated by their fulfilment of the historical tasks laid upon them is not given to them merely on their own behalf. In them it accrues to the people to which they are sent, so that retrospectively and prospectively there can be reference to God's being with His people.

b. The NT as well has the answer of faith in confession of God's promise. We find it in Stephen's speech as a confession of the patriarchal history of the OT; Joseph (Ac. 7:9 f.) experiences God's help and deliverance and is also furnished with grace and wisdom. We also find it in Paul's basic confession of the grace of God which grants and establishes his new life: καὶ ἡ χάρις αὐτοῦ ἡ εἰς ἐμὲ οὐ κενὴ ἐγενήθη, ἀλλὰ περισσότερον αὐτῶν πάντων ἐκοπίασα, οὐκ ἐγὼ δέ, ἀλλὰ ἡ χάρις τοῦ θεοῦ σὺν ἐμοί, 1 C. 15:10. The choice of σύν here shows that God Himself turns to man in Jesus Christ and binds Himself to him in new life and work; this is χάρις.

This personal confession is the basis of the NT apostolic greeting which is found at the end of Paul's epistles and which is shown to be a practice of the community by the fact that it occurs in other epistles too. It reminds us of Solomon's blessing

---

[59] The story shows again how the originally personal link between the God of the fathers and those who worship Him becomes a local link with the place of revelation.

[60] In 2 Ch. 35:21 Pharaoh Necho appeals to the confessional formula of Israel: "God is with me," when he sends envoys urging Josiah not to fight against him.

[61] A bibl. formula is adopted here. Jos.; however, expresses God's help in other ways at the relevant pts. in his history. So, too, does Philo, cf. van Unnik, 280 f. and 300, n. 35 for examples. The clarity of the divine promise is obscured by generalisations in Ant., 15, 138: "Someone might object τὸ μὲν ὅσιον καὶ δίκαιον μεθ' ἡμῶν, but they sought to be stronger and more. First, however, it is unworthy of you to say: μεθ' ὧν γὰρ τὸ δίκαιόν ἐστι, μετ' ἐκείνων ὁ θεός. But when God is present, a multitude and might are present."

at the dedication of the temple → 777, 16 ff. We find it in various forms, so that it has not yet become a fixed formula in apostolic times. μετά with the genitive is always used. We find in the simple form: "The Lord be with you all," 2 Th. 3:16; cf. also Ign. Pol., 6, 2. To Timothy in 2 Tm. 4:22 it runs: "The Lord be with thy spirit," then to all: "Grace be with you." The form in R. 15:33 is: "The God of peace be with you all," also Phil. 4:9; in 2 C. 13:11: "The God of love and peace be with you." [62] In place of God we find His gift, especially His grace. This means that God Himself is present in His gift; in His gift He gives Himself. The simplest form runs: "Grace be with you (all)," [63] Eph. 6:24; Col. 4:18; 1 Tm. 6:21; 2 Tm. 4:22; Tt. 3:15; Hb. 13:25; Mart. Pol., 22, 2. We then have the longer form: "The grace of our Lord Jesus Christ be with you," R. 16:20; 1 C. 16:23; [64] Gl. 6:18; Phil. 4:23; 1 Th. 5:28; 2 Th. 3:18; Tt. 3:15; Phlm. 25; Rev. 22:21; also 1 Cl., 65, 2. [65] Finally there is the triadic form in 2 C. 13:13: "The grace of our Lord Jesus Christ and the love of God and the communion of the Holy Ghost be with you all." Mostly we find "with you (all)," but occasionally "with your (or thy) spirit," Gl. 6:18; Phil. 4:23; 2 Tm. 4:22; Phlm. 25. In Eph. 6:24 we read: "with all who love our Lord Jesus Christ in his incorruptibility." [66] In 2 Jn. 3 we find the introductory petition: "Grace, mercy, and peace be with you from God the Father and from Jesus Christ, the Son of the Father, in truth and love." This is close to 1 Jn. 4:17, which says that God's love μεθ' ἡμῶν is perfected in confidence at the day of judgment. From these sayings there developed in the first or second century A.D. the liturgical formula in which the minister at divine worship greets the congregation: "The Lord be with you," and the congregation answers: "And with thy spirit." This rests on the awareness that the Lord is present with His gifts in the congregation assembled for worship and also on the insight that He equips leading men in the congregation to declare His word and will to it with due authority. It is to be seen against the background of the fact that the gift of the Spirit, in which the Lord Himself is present, is given to the community. [67]

3. Attestation by Others.

Sometimes the narrator bears witness to the acceptance of God's promise by saying that God was with a man. We are also told that men meet someone who is under God's promise, note this, and confirm it. God's promise may thus be seen by others apart from the one with whom God is.

---

[62] Here we have the preceding admonitions: "Rejoice, arm yourselves, be admonished, be like-minded, be at peace." The promise is then given: "And the God of love and peace be with you." Fulfilling God's will in the congregation brings with it the fulness of divine succour.

[63] How strongly God's presence is thought to be there in His gift may perhaps be seen in the fact that the introductory salutations which speak of the grace and peace proceeding from the Father and the Lord Jesus Christ convey this gift with a ὑμῖν, whereas the μεθ' ὑμῶν in the closing blessings is controlled by "The Lord is with you."

[64] Here Paul, expressing his personal relation and presence with the church in spirit (cf. 1 C. 5:3 f.), adds: "My love is with you all in Christ Jesus."

[65] 1 Cl., 65, 2 adds: "And with all who in every place are called by God and through him..."

[66] Barn., 21, 9 has the conclusion: "The Lord of glory and all grace be with your spirit."

[67] Cf. van Unnik, 293-8; 293: "The term defines the dynamic activity of God's Spirit given to particular chosen individuals or the people of God, enabling them to do a work of God in word or deed by protecting, assisting and blessing them; this presence of the Spirit manifests itself in the individual and to the outside world."

a. In the OT the narrators say that God is with Ishmael (Gn. 21:20), Joseph (39:2, 3, 21, 23), Joshua (Jos. 6:27), the tribe of Judah (Ju. 1:19), the judges generally (2:18), Samuel (1 Βασ. 3:19), David (18:14, 28; 2 Βασ. 5:10; 1 Ch. 11:9), Solomon (2 Ch. 1:1), other kings (2 Ch. 15:9; 17:3; 4 Βασ. 18:7). As the judgment of others it is said to Abraham' by Abimelech and his captain Phichol (Gn. 21:22), also to Isaac (26:28 f.), to the sons of Jacob by their father (48:21), to Eliezer by Abraham (24:40), to Moses by Jethro (Ex. 18:19), [68] of Israel by Balaam (Nu. 23:21), to Joshua by the Israelites as a blessing (Jos. 1:17), to Saul by Samuel (1 Βασ. 10:7), to Saul about David by a servant (16:18), to David by Saul (17:37) and Jonathan (20:13), also Nathan (2 Βασ. 7:3, cf. 1 Ch. 17:2; 2 Βασ. 14:17), to Solomon by David (1 Ch. 22:11, 18; 28:20, cf. to Solomon on the lips of Jehoiada 3 Βασ. 1:37), and finally to Israel in the saying of the Persian king Cyrus in 2 Ch. 36:23; this winds up the story of Ch., in which this judgment is particularly common, and it is picked up again in 1 Εσδρ. 2:3 (and 2 Εσδρ. 1:3) as the basis of the new start made by the post-exilic community. This statement, which was so significant for OT historical writing at this period, acquires its point from a promise of Yahweh in the mouth of the post-exilic prophet Zechariah in which we read that ten men of all Gentile languages will cling to the skirts of a Jew and say to him: πορευσόμεθα μετὰ σοῦ, διότι ἀκηκόαμεν ὅτι ὁ θεὸς μεθ' ὑμῶν ἐστιν, Zech. 8:23.

b. The NT narrators adopt this mode of narrative and evaluation, e.g., in relation to John the Baptist (Lk. 1:66) and the men of the apostolic age (Ac. 11:21; 14:27: God's aid enables the apostles to do miracles, so also 15:4). Especially important are the two judgments on Jesus: that of Peter in the house of the centurion Cornelius (Ac. 10:38) on the basis of the saving work of Jesus, and similarly that of Nicodemus to Jesus (Jn. 3:2); [69] with these one must also compare the self-confession of Jesus with its reference to the sign of the crucifixion and resurrection in Jn. 8:29; 16:32 → 776, 24 ff.

4. The Statement: We with God.

In contrast to the promise of God and its acceptance by faith, which play an essential role throughout the OT and NT, the reverse statement: We with God, is seldom used.

The two forms occur together in 2 Ch. 15:2: κύριος μεθ' ὑμῶν, ἐν τῷ εἶναι ὑμᾶς μετ' αὐτοῦ, where εἶναι ὑμᾶς μετ' αὐτοῦ is plainly a condition of κύριος μεθ' ὑμῶν. God's promise implies His support and help. He will be found by those who seek Him, as 2 Ch. 15:2 says in context. Hence εἶναι ὑμᾶς μετ' αὐτοῦ means the yearning which seeks God and the faithfulness to Him which fears apostasy. One often finds this in the Ps. too. ψ 77:8 ref. to the generation whose spirit is unfaithful to God, οὐκ ἐπιστώθη μετὰ τοῦ θεοῦ. v. 37 says the same: ἡ δὲ καρδία αὐτῶν οὐκ εὐθεῖα μετ' αὐτοῦ, οὐδὲ ἐπιστώθησαν ἐν τῇ διαθήκῃ αὐτοῦ. 3 Βασ. 11:4 is to be understood in the light of this: οὐκ ἦν ἡ καρδία αὐτοῦ (Solomon) τελεία μετὰ κυρίου θεοῦ αὐτοῦ καθὼς ἡ καρδία Δαυιδ τοῦ πατρὸς αὐτοῦ, cf. 15:3 of King Abijam, but also v. 14 of Asa: ἡ καρδία (of Asa) ἦν τελεία μετὰ κυρίου πάσας τὰς ἡμέρας αὐτοῦ. The catechetical-type demand of Mi. 6:8 is to be construed similarly, LXX: ποιεῖν κρίμα καὶ ἀγαπᾶν

---

[68] In the last three instances the address has the form of a blessing. It is based on awareness of God's promise and its effectual power.

[69] This is an interesting example of the connection between the Lucan and the Johannine tradition and theology, cf. Grundmann, op. cit., 17-22; P. Parker, "Luke and the Fourth Evangelist," NTSt, 9 (1962/63), 317-336.

ἔλεον καὶ ἕτοιμον εἶναι τοῦ πορεύεσθαι μετὰ κυρίου θεοῦ σου. [70] Mal. 2:6 says of Levi, ancestor of the Levites: ἐπορεύθη μετ' ἐμοῦ, after Yahweh said in v. 5: ἡ διαθήκη μου ἦν μετ' αὐτοῦ τῆς ζωῆς καὶ εἰρήνης. 'A assimilates the LXX in Gn. 5:22, 24 εὐηρέστησεν Ενωχ τῷ θεῷ by σὺν θεῷ (→ n. 15) to the HT אֶת־הָאֱלֹהִים חֲנוֹךְ וַיִּתְהַלֵּךְ, which is saying God catches away Enoch as a response to Enoch's faithfulness in his walk with God. Here it is plain that the fellowship between God and man which God establishes in His promise and by which He engages man to faithfulness extends beyond the earthly sphere. In ψ 72:23 the Psalmist, faced by the surging of the wicked and under oppression, makes the confession: καὶ ἐγὼ διὰ παντὸς μετὰ σοῦ, and he hopes for God's support and guidance, and for translation to God's glory: καὶ μετὰ δόξης προσελάβου με, v. 24. The same hope is expressed in ψ 15:11: [71] πληρώσεις με εὐφροσύνης μετὰ τοῦ προσώπου σου. The earthly fellowship between God and man continues in an eternal fellowship into which man is caught up. This is a statement peculiar to the OT. [72]

A series of statements in the Ps. which in the Hebrew refer to cultic fellowship between God and man seem to have a further reference in the LXX to the fellowship of eternal life with God, so ψ 139:14: καὶ κατοικήσουσιν εὐθεῖς σὺν τῷ προσώπῳ σου (σύν is especially noteworthy here), also 20:7: δώσεις αὐτῷ (the king) εὐλογίαν εἰς αἰῶνα αἰῶνος· εὐφρανεῖς αὐτὸν ἐν χαρᾷ μετὰ τοῦ προσώπου σου. At ψ 138:18 the LXX offers a free rendering in which interpretation depends on ἐξηγέρθην: ἐξηγέρθην καὶ ἔτι εἰμὶ μετὰ σοῦ. The meaning seems to be: "I will be awakened to fellowship with God." This is not just cultic fellowship in life on earth; it goes beyond that. [73] We are thus brought to the very verge of the NT σὺν Χριστῷ.

III. The Shepherd of Hermas.

There is a special modification of the promise in Herm. It is influenced by ideas of angels and spirits such as those found in Qumran. The shepherd, the angel of repentance, promises Hermas his support as moral strength in the battle against bad temper (m., 5, 1, 7) and also against the devil and his enticements (12, 4, 7; 6, 1 f.). This promise applies to Hermas and to all who turn from their wrong path. Since the aid of the angel of repentance is the power which strengthens faith, he can say: ἡ δύναμις τοῦ κυρίου μετ' αὐτῶν ἐστιν, 5, 2, 1. The angel of righteousness is also a support; he awakens good impulses in man from within by coming into the heart. When this takes place, γίνωσκε, ὅτι ὁ ἄγγελος τῆς δικαιοσύνης μετὰ σοῦ ἐστι, m., 6, 2, 3. The succour of the angel of

---

[70] Cf. the pertinent note of Dupont, 29 f.: "Chez les Grecs, les hommes sont protégés par Dieu lorsqu'ils sont avec lui; chez les Juifs, lorsque Dieu est avec eux. Dans la Bible 'être avec Dieu' se situe avant tout sur le plan de la conduite," cf. also 31 f.

[71] Cf. A. Weiser, Die Psalmen, AT Deutsch, 14/15⁵ (1959), ad loc. Weiser calls "living fellowship with God" the basis of all the Ps. When it is present "death loses the fearful significance which it has for . . . man." Weiser speaks of "fellowship with God after death," of "the consummation of salvation whose future form is as yet concealed from the poet."

[72] Cf. G. Haufe, "Entrückung u. eschatologische Funktion im Spätjudt.," Zschr. f. Religions- u. Geistesgeschichte, 13 (1961), 105-113.

[73] But cf. in context Dt. 5:31: Yahweh to Moses: σὺ δὲ αὐτοῦ στῆθι μετ' ἐμοῦ, cf. Ex. 33:21 and Ac. 7:38. 1 Βασ. 2:26 says of the growing Samuel: . . . μετὰ κυρίου καὶ μετὰ ἀνθρώπων. Sir. 44:20 extols Abraham: καὶ ἐγένετο ἐν διαθήκῃ μετ' αὐτοῦ. If 1 Βασ. 2:26 has a more formal character, Dt. 5:31 and Sir. 44:20 express the special position of Abraham and Moses; for them to be "with God" is the privilege of direct access.

repentance is related to the ministry with which Hermas is charged *vis-à-vis* others. For this he is given the promise: ἐγὼ γὰρ μετὰ σοῦ ἔσομαι καὶ ἀναγκάσω αὐτοὺς πεισθῆναί σοι, m., 12, 3, 3. Hermas answers with the confession: κύριε, νῦν ἐνεδυναμώθην ἐν πᾶσι τοῖς δικαιώμασι τοῦ κυρίου, ὅτι σὺ μετ' ἐμοῦ εἶ, m., 12, 6, 4. Both s., 5, 3, 4 and s., 7, 6 show in typical dialogue that this assistance of the angel of repentance takes place when he speaks with Hermas, cf. s., 6, 3, 2; 9, 11, 1; 5, 4, 5.

God's promise is also developed in another way with μετά in s., 9. The ref. here is to the spiritual building of the Church in the similitude of the tower. The ten virgins who watch the building are holy spirits (s., 9, 13, 2) which form the garment of the Son of God that penitents must put on. They want to stay by Hermas (11, 3) and play with him (11, 4) and he dwells with them and stays by them (11, 3. 6. 7); he plays with them and is merry with them (11, 5. 8). He also prays with them without ceasing (11, 7). This all denotes the fashioning of man after the likeness of the Son of God as in the case of Paul's σὺν Χριστῷ.

D. σὺν Χριστῷ in Paul.

1. Paul's σὺν Χριστῷ is linguistically comparable with the Greek expressions σὺν θεῷ and σὺν θεοῖς → 773, 5 ff. The difference is that it is not orientated to active life on earth. Its primary reference is to eschatological being with Christ as eternal, non-terrestrial being. [74] The use of the preposition σύν suggests that the phrase has in view personal fellowship in the sense of coming to and being with → 778, 1 ff.; 770, 16 ff.

a. A starting-pt. may be sought in the expression which LXX has in many Ps. when an originally cultic fellowship with God is interpreted as eternal fellowship → 780, 15 ff. This LXX expression is perhaps influenced by Greek-Hell. ideas both in popular piety and also in philosophical thought in which we find ref. to communion with the gods after death, cf. Socrates in Plat. Ap., 40c-41c, where death is described as a journey in meadows where men live with the great figures of the past. In Phaed. death is a journey which leads men to the gods, 63c; 80d; 85a. There are many examples of such thoughts. [75] On a funerary inscr. from Mysia (2nd cent. A.D.) we read: ἐς δὲ θεοὺς ἀνέλυσα καὶ ἀθανάτοισι μέτειμι· ὅσσους γὰρ φιλέουσι θεοὶ θνήσκουσιν [ἄωροι], Epigr. Graec., 340, 7 f. An Alexandrian graffito from the imperial age contains the statement: εὔχομαι κἀγὼ ἐν τάχυ σὺν σοὶ εἶναι, [76] this being linguistically close to Paul's phrase, though the reunion is with a dead person, not a god. Epict. Diss., I, 9, 16 speaks of man's release from the post where God has set him and says: ὅταν ἐκεῖνος σημήνῃ καὶ ἀπολύσῃ ὑμᾶς ταύτης τῆς ὑπηρεσίας, τοτ' ἀπελεύσεσθε πρὸς αὐτόν, cf. Plat. Phaed., 62b-c.

b. Later Judaism also speaks of eternal fellowship with God. Presupposing Jewish notions, the parable of Dives and Lazarus refers to the fellowship of the beggar with Abraham in Paradise, Lk. 16:22. Eth. En. 62:13 f., in a description of the eternal world, says: "...the Lord of spirits will dwell over them, and they will feast with the Son of Man, and they will lie down and rise up in eternity." 105:2 contains the divine promise: "I and my son will be united with them for ever on the paths of righteousness." [77] S. Lv., 111b says: God will walk with the righteous in the Garden of Eden in the coming

---

[74] Cf. Lohmeyer, 229: "Here death and eschatology constitute being with Christ; there the harrying presence of ever-changing life."

[75] Cf. Dupont, 166-169, 181 f.

[76] Deissmann LO, 257, n. 4.

[77] This statement is possibly a Chr. addition to Eth. En.; it transposes into the eschatological future the OT promise accepted into the NT, cf. Rev. 21:3.

age. Both these sayings are connected with the OT promise "I will be with you" (→ 774, 26 ff.) and they do not lead on directly to the Pauline formula σὺν Χριστῷ Ps. 16, however, shows that fellowship between God and man vanquishes death, and this is probably the theological basis of Paul's statements.

c. The use of the prep. σύν in Paul indicates that its sense is always "together with," cf. R. 16:14, 15; 1 C. 11:32; 16:4, 19; 2 C. 1:21; 9:4; Gl. 1:2; 2:3; Phil. 4:21; Eph. 3:18; Col. 4:9. Sometimes σύν replaces a καί, the sense being still "together with," 1 C. 1:2; 2 C. 1:1; Phil. 1:1. Three instances call for special notice. Col. 2:5: εἰ γὰρ καὶ τῇ σαρκὶ ἄπειμι, ἀλλὰ τῷ πνεύματι σὺν ὑμῖν εἰμι, deals with a fellowship in spirit which can exist even when there is absence in the body, cf. 1 C. 5:4: συναχθέντων ὑμῶν καὶ τοῦ ἐμοῦ πνεύματος σὺν τῇ δυνάμει τοῦ κυρίου ἡμῶν Ἰησοῦ. In Phil. 2:22 Paul ref. to his fellowship with Timothy in a way which also expresses the inner nature of the relation and Timothy's subordination to Paul: ὡς πατρὶ τέκνον σὺν ἐμοὶ ἐδούλευσεν εἰς τὸ εὐαγγέλιον. Gl. 3:9 says of the nations: οἱ ἐκ πίστεως εὐλογοῦνται σὺν τῷ πιστῷ Ἀβραάμ. Abraham is the carrier of the promise for Israel and the Gentiles. The promised seed integrates those who receive Him in faith into the bearer of the promise. This passage leads on directly to the Pauline σὺν Χριστῷ. [78]

Paul did not take over the formula σὺν Χριστῷ from anyone else. He coined it, being attracted by its simplicity. [79]

2. The phrase σὺν Χριστῷ occurs in Paul 12 times. We find it first in three passages in 1 Thess. (4:13 - 5:11). Paul makes a twofold statement: God through Jesus Christ awakens the dead from their sleep of death (v. 16b) and sets them with the living in the train of Christ when He is manifested at the *parousia*, v. 14. [80]

---

[78] The Abraham-Christ relation is expressly established in Gl. 3:13-29, so that there is also a connection between σὺν τῷ πιστῷ Ἀβραάμ and σὺν Χριστῷ.

[79] Lohmeyer (→ n. 1) thinks the formula σὺν Χριστῷ was already a fixed one; he traces it back to a presupposed Son-of-Man Christology common to Paul and John, cf. 237 and 247. But this does not prove that the formula was taken over from elsewhere. P. Bonnet, "Mourir et vivre avec Jésus-Christ selon Saint Paul," Rev. HPhR, 36 (1956), 101-112 suggests a formula taken from the Hell. liturgies of mystery cults, since there is no basis for it in the LXX or the Rabb. writings. But no exact proof is offered. The debate concerning the influence of the mystery religions on R. 6:1-11 still continues, cf. Wagner who does not think any such influence can be proved from the mystery traditions at present available, a view with which G. Delling's review in ThLZ, 88 (1963), 271-3 largely concurs. Kuss thinks Paul coined "with Christ" as well as "in Christ" and "by Christ," and though he cautiously suggests that mystery thinking prepared the way for the idea of the participation of believers in the fate of the bringer of salvation in the cultic act, nevertheless he explains the formula "with Christ" by the Christ event, which is the "entelechy," "the effectual centre of the life process, by which other and at first alien elements are assimilated, so that they now belong to the new unity of life, 'Jesus Christ'," 373. Larsson, 80 thinks the formula arises out of discipleship, so that for him too the Christ event is the origin. Baptism is for him an "act of discipleship," "a reply to the Christ event," "which is not dependent on Paul's relation to the discipleship sayings in the Gospel tradition." Cf. also A. Schulz, "Nachfolge u. Nachahmen," Stud. z. ANT, 6 (1962), 180-186. That the formula cannot be an adopted one is shown by Dupont in his discussion 100-110, where he examines and delimits the formulae adopted by Paul and shows that σὺν Χριστῷ is not demonstrably one of these. He rightly speaks of "une traduction spontanée de l'espérance chrétienne qui voit son object réalisé et rendu concret dans la personne du Christ ressuscité," 190. The fact that we do not have a fixed formula may be seen from the use of σὺν Χριστῷ, σὺν Ἰησοῦ, σὺν αὐτῷ alongside one another.

[80] Paul uses apoc. ideas and images, Dupont, 47-73, cf. Dupont's thesis, based on E. Peterson, "Die Einholung d. Kyrios," ZSTh, 7 (1929/30), 682-702, that Paul's language is drawn from the Hell. form of the royal entry. In our view the origin of Paul's view is to be sought in Jewish apoc., though touches were perhaps added from actual Hell. practices. There is no need to make an absolute choice between the two.

σὺν αὐτῷ (v. 14) means here that "together with Him" they share in His life and glory and victory, → III, 804, 34 ff.[81] The *parousia* is the reuniting of the living and the dead — ἡμεῖς οἱ ζῶντες οἱ περιλειπόμενοι ἅμα σὺν αὐτοῖς, v. 17. Together they are caught up to meet the returning Lord in the air,[82] and then they will be eternally together with the Lord: καὶ οὕτως πάντοτε σὺν κυρίῳ ἐσόμεθα, v. 17. Primarily this again means participation in His life and glory and victory, and it can embrace fellowship with Him,[83] cf. also the formulation in 2 Th. 2:1: ... ὑπὲρ τῆς παρουσίας τοῦ κυρίου ἡμῶν 'Ιησοῦ Χριστοῦ καὶ ἡμῶν ἐπισυναγωγῆς ἐπ' αὐτόν. In 1 Th. 5:10 any discrimination against those already deceased is expressly ruled out again and eternal life is defined as living together with Christ (ἅμα σὺν αὐτῷ ζήσωμεν). This v. takes us further than the others, since "with Christ" is grounded in "Christ for us," this being particularly expressed in the ἵνα. As the Risen Lord the Christ who died for men has dominion over them and a claim upon them, so that salvation is fulfilled in fellowship with Him.

3. In addition to the sayings in 1 and 2 Thess. σὺν Χριστῷ is found in Paul in Phil. 1:23; 2 C. 4:14; 13:4,[84] also R. 6:8; 8:32. Closest to the formulation in 1 Th. is that in 2 C. 4:14. Paul expresses the hope that He who has raised up Jesus Christ καὶ ἡμᾶς σὺν 'Ιησοῦ ἐγερεῖ. He thus speaks out of the conviction that fellowship has been set up between Christ and His community, this being grounded in the death of Christ for us (1 Th. 5:10). Paul hopes that he will be united with the community in fellowship with Christ: καὶ παραστήσει (ἡμᾶς) σὺν ὑμῖν, 2 C. 4:14. Phil. 1:23 (→ V, 771, 28 ff.) takes us a step further. Here Paul is speaking about his coming to Christ through his own death. With this he will attain to Christ's fellowship and to "being with Him." Instead of hoping that he will survive until the *parousia* and thus be changed at that time (1 Th. 4:15-17; 1 C.15:51 f.), so that

---

[81] C. F. D. Moule [in a letter] suggests "that in 1 Th. 4:14 σὺν αὐτῷ may be (God will bring from the dead those who die in Christ) as (he brought) Jesus (from the dead)." He ref. to Jeremias Gl.⁶, 157 on Lk. 11:7: "And the children are as I am (μετ' ἐμοῦ) in bed," also Hb. 11:9: ... ἐν σκηναῖς κατοικήσας μετὰ 'Ισαὰκ καὶ 'Ιακώβ. In these two vv., however, we have μετά, which is used more than σύν in this more gen. sense.

[82] Dib. Th., *ad loc.* takes the view that the derivation of the ideas of *parousia* and encounter from Hell. custom forces us to the belief that the snatching away on the clouds to meet the coming Lord in the air is to bring him back to earth. With Lohmeyer, 224, however, one should take the passage to refer, not to the fetching of the Lord to earth, but to the translation of His people to Him who brings them into the eternal mansions in heaven. In this respect Paul seems to have taken up a basic eschatological idea of Jesus, cf. W. Grundmann, *Gesch. Jesu Christi*³ (1961), 208-211. The exposition of Dib. is influenced by the exaggerated importance he attaches to the world of Hell. imagery.

[83] Dupont, 80-113 argues that in this passage σὺν Χριστῷ means participation in Christ's state of glory rather than the "enjoyment of His presence and fellowship," "une association des chrétiens à la 'vie' glorieuse du Ressuscité et à son règne plutôt qu'une simple communauté de vie," 84. Kuss, too, thinks that apocal. ideas control the ref. in 1 Th. and he considers the possibility that "the image of the train of the eschatological ruler may govern the concept," 321.

[84] For relating Phil. to imprisonment in Ephesus rather than Rome cf. W. Michaelis, *Die Gefangenschaft d. Pls. u. das Itinerar d. Timotheus* (1925); also *Die Datierung d. Phil.* (1933). But this imprisonment took place at the end of the stay in Ephesus, so that on this view Phil. must have been written between 1 C. and 2 C. J. Pongrácz, *Pál apostel Efezusban uiszövetsegi tanulmany Papa* (1931), 151 thinks there is a connection between words in συν-, which are more numerous in Paul after his residence in Ephesus, and the guilds and societies of Gk. cities as we know them from Ephesian inscr.

there is no need to reflect on the state between death and the *parousia,* [85] Paul now takes account of the possibility of his own death; his hope is that through it he will make the transition to "being with Christ." [86] What is stated succinctly here is developed in 2 C. 4:7-5:10. [87] Whereas in previous statements "with Christ" referred to the community in all its members, Paul's hope in Phil. 1:23 is that of his personal "being with Christ." The expression thus comes to denote the personal fellowship between Christ and the apostle, cf. also Gl. 2:20; Phil. 3:8: τοῦ κυρίου μου, 4:13: τῷ ἐνδυναμοῦντί με.

2 C. 13:4 is controlled by the parallelism between the way of Christ and that of the community. The crucifixion of Jesus Christ took place ἐξ ἀσθενείας, but He lives ἐκ δυνάμεως θεοῦ. Having said this, Paul adds an explanatory "for we also..." The parallel to Christ is that we are weak ἀσθενοῦμεν ἐν αὐτῷ — a series of not unimportant texts [88] have σὺν αὐτῷ here too — and Paul then adds: ἀλλὰ ζήσομεν σὺν αὐτῷ ἐκ δυνάμεως θεοῦ εἰς ὑμᾶς. If the textually uncertain εἰς ὑμᾶς "toward you" [89] is original, the ζήσομεν does not refer to the eschatological future but to the historical future of Paul's visit to Corinth, and the meaning is the desired δοκιμή of v. 3. Paul is speaking, then, about the apostle's life with Christ in his apostolic ministry; this is undoubtedly eschatological, but it is also real and efficacious in history, cf. 2 C. 4:7 ff. No matter what the appearance of the apostle, whether he seem to be weak or tried and tested, he is σὺν Χριστῷ in his apostolic office. The decisive point is that σὺν Χριστῷ as an expression of hope is grounded in the parallelism which exists between the way of Christ and that of the apostle or the community.

This parallelism, which has been called a fellowship of destiny, [90] is further

---

[85] In this connection it is worth noting that in Paul the idea of death as sleep occurs only in 1 Th. and 1 C. (1 Th. 4:13-15; 5:10; 1 C. 7:39; 11:30; 15:6, 18, 20, 51), and not again after this. The question of the death of those dead with Christ begins to be discussed in Phil. and 2 C., then R., but "to fall asleep" is not used now. Instead one finds in e.g., Phil. 1:23 ἀναλῦσαι and σὺν Χριστῷ εἶναι. The latter is used in 1 Th. 4:14, 17; 5:10 to denote the state after the *parousia.* Acc. to 2 C. 5:4-9 dying does not deprive believers of their being with Christ; it makes it closer rather than more distant. This is missed by O. Cullmann, *Unsterblichkeit d. Seele oder Auferstehung d. Toten* (1962), cf. also → n. 86.

[86] W. Grundmann, "Überlieferung u. Eigenaussage im eschatologischen Denken d. Ap. Pls.," NTSt, 8 (1961), 12-26. The reason for the change noted → 783, 22 ff. seems to us to lie in the circumstance which led Paul to write 2 C. 1:3-11. On the problems presented by Phil. 1:23 cf. esp. Dib. Ph., Exc. on 1:23; Dib. is surely right as compared with Mich. Ph., Exc. on 1:23, "Tod, Zwischenzustand, Auferstehung." Dibelius is critical of Lohmeyer's interpretation in terms of martyr theology, Loh. Phil., 57-64, cf. also O. Cullmann, *Christus u. d. Zeit*[3] (1962), 212-215 (*Christ and Time* [1951], 238-240). Kuss, too, thinks that in 2 C. and R. Paul is speaking of "an inner relation of believers and the baptised to Jesus Christ" and that he has in view "the eschatological fellowship of life 'with' Christ which results from baptism," 323.

[87] Among the religious and historical presuppositions of this discussion are Hell. philosophical ideas which on the basis of the antithesis of mortal body and immortal soul are developed into the eschatological contrast of old man and the new creation in Christ which begins in the inner man, cf. Dupont, 116-151, 158-165, 173-181. These are very helpful in clarifying the question of death prior to the *parousia.* Paul, however, does not ground his decisive statement in them but in fellowship with Christ.

[88] א A G it syP.

[89] Not found in B D[3] r arm.

[90] Cf. on this expression G. Matern, *Exegese v. R. 6,* Diss. Königsberg (1933), 11: "For him, then, a fellowship of destiny is the point of the relation to the death of Jesus," cf. also 12 etc.

developed in R. → 787, 31 ff. Here the compounds which elucidate the parallelism are more important than the phrase σὺν Χριστῷ, → 786, 5 ff.; → III, 806, 7 ff. R. 6:8 sets forth the basis of σὺν Χριστῷ in ἀπεθάνομεν σὺν Χριστῷ. This dying with Christ is grounded in His substitutionary death for us and it takes effect as appropriation in the renunciation of sin, R. 6:13 f.; 7:6; 8:13. Posited with it is life with Christ. R. 6:8 links dying with Christ indissolubly to Christ's death by putting the latter in a conditional clause and then stating the former as a deduction from it. In R. 5:12-21 the basis of the σὺν Χριστῷ in the substitutionary event of the death and resurrection of Christ which establishes the parallelism as seen from the standpoint that Christ is the second Adam. The working out of the parallelism culminates in R. 8:32. Here we have in direct relation the offering of Christ by God for us ὑπὲρ ἡμῶν πάντων παρέδωκεν αὐτόν and the gift of the universe to us: πῶς οὐχὶ καὶ σὺν αὐτῷ τὰ πάντα ἡμῖν χαρίσεται. The offering "for us all" is the basis of the "with Him." In fellowship with Him the Christian shares in the victory, dominion, and glory of Christ. "With Him" the universe is the Christian's. [91]

4. To these eight sayings one should add four in Col. Though Paul's authorship is disputed, these belong to the same line of Pauline thought as that which begins with Phil. and 2 C. [92] Col. 2:13 (→ 792, 22 ff.) tells us that in baptism men who were dead in their sins are made alive with Christ by the remission granted to them (συνεζωοποίησεν ὑμᾶς σὺν αὐτῷ). In the next v. (14) this event is based on the substitutionary death of Christ. It is true that Col. 2:13 does not refer to dying with Christ as R. 6:8 does. It refers rather to being dead without Christ. Nevertheless, Col. 2:20 does speak of a dying with Christ (ἀπεθάνετε σὺν Χριστῷ) so that the difference makes no great odds. The decisive point is that being dead without Christ denotes the state of being under the dominion of demonic and astral powers from which Christians die with Christ. The mode of expression is thus influenced by the special attack here on the Colossian error. In the two sayings in 2:13, 20 the σὺν Χριστῷ denotes the new existence of Christians. This gives us the clue to the basic statement in Col. 3:3: ἀπεθάνετε γάρ, καὶ ἡ ζωὴ ὑμῶν κέκρυπται σὺν τῷ Χριστῷ ἐν τῷ θεῷ. The new existence of the Christian is his life with Christ. Like Christ's life, this is hidden in God, → II, 866, 10 ff. This life is a Christ-life — Christ is called ἡ ζωὴ ἡμῶν (3:4, cf. Phil. 1:21; Gl. 2:20). What Christians wait for is the manifestation of Christ, i.e., His emergence from concealment, and their own manifestation with Him (καὶ ὑμεῖς σὺν αὐτῷ φανερωθήσεσθε), which takes place ἐν δόξῃ, Col. 3:4. In these passages in Col. σὺν Χριστῷ denotes the present, hidden,

---

[91] τὰ πάντα == "the universe." Christian participation in Christ's royal dominion is based on Mt. 5:3 par. Lk. 6:20. On the Pauline presentation cf. W. Grundmann, "Die Übermacht d. Gnade. Eine Studie z. Theol. d. Pls.," Nov. Test., 2 (1957), 50-72. If "everything" is preferred (→ V, 888, 36 ff.), it amounts to much the same thing concretely.

[92] If Col. is authentic we should be inclined to date it during the imprisonment in Caesarea. The personal notes in Col. 4:7-17 fit this period best. Michaelis Gefangenschaft (→ n. 84) argues for Ephesus, but in relation to these notes (and those in Phlm.) he has to resort to hypotheses which entangle him in difficulties precisely in relation to his own starting-pt. in the itinerary and which force him to say that Col. is one of the oldest of Paul's epistles. As regards the first of these sayings (2:13) one has to consider the possibility that it falls in an extract from a hymn which commences with συνεζωοποίησεν — not ὑμᾶς, which is an assimilation to the situation in the letter — and which continues to v. 15, cf. Loh. Kol., 101 f., 114-121. On the material differences between Col. or Eph. and the main epistles cf. Kuss, 326 f.

eschatological being of Christians. This is where the special emphasis falls in Col. and Eph. What is still to come, and what Christians are waiting for, is no longer called the resurrection of the dead; it is the manifestation of the hidden life, → IV, 815, 5 ff.

E. Compounds in συν- which Develop the σὺν Χριστῷ.

1. The Meaning of the Verbs.

σὺν Χριστῷ enshrines the content of the Christian hope of eternal being with Christ, 1 Th. 4:14, 17; 5:10; Phil. 1:23; 2 C. 4:14; R. 8:32; Col. 3:4. It is grounded in Christ's death for us and embraces the whole existence of the Christian, R. 6:8; Col. 2:13, 20; 2 C. 13:4; Col. 3:3. [93] The process entailed hereby is expressed by Paul in a series of compounds in συν-, 14 in all.

a. συναποθνήσκω, "to die together with someone" [94] (→ III, 7, 28 ff.), occurs in Gk usage from an earlier time, is found in LXX at Sir. 19:10, in Philo Spec. Leg., I, 108, in Hell. authors at, e.g., Polyaen. Strat., VIII, 39, in the NT at Mk. 14:31 (Mt. 26:35 σὺν σοὶ ἀποθανεῖν); it is used to express the close relation between the apostle and his church: ... ἐν ταῖς καρδίαις ἡμῶν ἐστε εἰς τὸ συναποθανεῖν καὶ συζῆν, 2 C. 7:3, [95] cf. 2 Tm. 2:11, → 793, 20 ff.

b. συσταυρόω, "to crucify with, together," pass. "to be crucified with," occurs only in the NT, Mt. 27:44; Mk. 15:32; Jn. 19:32 (Mt. 27:38 and Mk. 15:27 σταυροῦνται σὺν αὐτῷ); R. 6:6; Gl. 2:19 → 791, 12 ff.

c. συνθάπτω, "to bury with, together, at the same time," so Soph. Ai., 1378; Aesch. Sept. c. Theb., 1027; Eur. Phoen., 1658; Alc., 149; Hdt., V, 5; Thuc., I, 8, 1, also inscr., e.g., IG, 14, 943 (Ostia). Transf. Lyc., 50: συνετάφη τοῖς τούτων σώμασιν ἡ Ἑλλήνων ἐλευθερία. Only transf. in the NT, R. 6:4; Col. 2:12 → 790, 14 ff.; 792, 22 ff.

d. σύμφυτος, [96] verbal adj., from συμφύομαι "to grow together," not συμφυτεύω "to plant together." The basic meaning is "native," e.g., of virtue, Pind. Isthm., 3, 14; Eur. Andr., 954; Jos. Ap., 1, 42; 3 Macc. 3:22; memory, Philo Op. Mund., 18; "bound up, related with," e.g., Aristot. Hist. An., V, 32, p. 557b, 18; Topica, VII, 6, p. 145b, 3 and 13; "grown up together with," e.g., Plot. Enn., III, 6, 8: the qualities have grown up with matter; Plat. Phaedr., 246a: various efforts have grown up together; Dio Chrys. Or., 11 (12) 28 of the men of primal days in their relation to the deity: οὐ μακρὰν οὐδ' ἔξω τοῦ θείου ... ἀλλὰ ἐν αὐτῷ μέσῳ πεφυκότες μᾶλλον δὲ συμπεφυκότες ἐκείνῳ. σύμφυτος is more common in Philo, so Vit. Mos., I, 198; Abr., 160; Rer. Div. Her., 272. The word has a broad range and can mean "belonging together," "united with"; in the NT only R. 6:5 → 790, 16 ff.

e. συνεγείρω, "to assist someone in getting up," Ex. 23:5; 4 Macc. 2:14; Ps.-Phoky-

---

93 Paul uses combinations with ἐν Χριστῷ or ἐν κυρίῳ to express present existence or salvation. Cf. on this → II, 537, 12 ff. and Neugebauer (→ n. 2), 148 f.
94 Cf. F. Olivier, "Συναποθνήσκω," RevThPh, NS, 17 (1929), 103-133.
95 In Nicolaus Damascenus Fr., 80 (FGr Hist, II, n. 379) one finds the same antithesis συναποθνήσκω — συζάω as in 2 C. 7:3 → 787, 9 ff.
96 Cf. on this O. Kuss, Zu R. 6:5a, Auslegung u. Verkündigung, I (1963), 154-156; also Mi. R. on 6:5, n. 4.

lides, 140, [97] "to cause someone to rise up or wake up with another," e.g., Plut. Cons. ad Apoll., 30 (II, 117c): τὰς λύπας καὶ τοὺς θρήνους συνεγείρειν, LXX Is. 14:9, NT Eph. 2:6; Col. 2:12; 3:1 → 792, 22 ff.; also Ign. Pol., 6, 1.

f. συζάω, "to live together with someone," e.g., Demosth. Or., 1, 14; 19, 69; common in Aristot. Eth. Nic., IV, 12, p. 1126b, 11; VIII, 3, p. 1156a, 27; VIII, 6, p. 1157b, 7; IX, 9, p. 1170b, 11; Pol. III, 6, p. 1278b, 21; III, 9, p. 1280b, 38; also Plat. Polit., 302b; of living with a wife, Herm. m., 4, 1, 4 f. and 9; with Gentiles Herm. s., 8, 9, 1 and 3; used with συναποθνήσκω, Athen., 6, 54 (249b) of the guards of kings: τούτους οἱ βασιλεῖς ἔχουσι συζῶντας καὶ συναποθνῄσκοντας. In the NT of Paul's relation to the Corinthians in 2 C. 7:3 → 786, 15 ff.; also the relation to Christ in R. 6:8; 2 Tm. 2:11 → 793, 20 ff.

g. συζωοποιέω (→ II, 875, n. 5) only NT "to make alive together with," Eph. 2:5; Col. 2:13 → 792, 22 ff.

h. συμπάσχω, "to suffer with" (→ V, 925, 1 ff.). NT 1 C. 12:26; R. 8:17 → 792, 8 ff.; cf. Pol., 9, 2; Ign. R., 6, 3; Ign. Sm., 4, 2; Pol., 6, 1.

i. συνδοξάζω, "to glorify with" (→ II, 253, 11 ff.); [98] NT R. 8:17 → 792, 8 ff.; cf. Ign. Sm., 11, 3.

j. συγκληρονόμος, "co-heir" (→ III, 768, 18 ff.); NT Eph. 3:6: The Gentiles are συγκληρονόμα καὶ σύσσωμα καὶ συμμέτοχα τῆς ἐπαγγελίας ἐν Χριστῷ Ἰησοῦ, also R. 8:17 → 792, 8 ff.; Hb. 11:9; 1 Pt. 3:7; post-apost. fathers Herm. s., 5, 2, 7 f. and 11.

k. σύμμορφος, "having the same form as," in the pre-Chr. period Nicand. Theriaca, 321, later Ps.-Luc. Amores, 39, cf. Heracl. Hom. All., 77 of Agamemnon: σύμμορφος τρισὶ θεοῖς; NT R. 8:29; Phil. 3:21 → lines 34 ff.

l. συμμορφίζω, "to confer the same form," [99] only NT at Phil. 3:10 → 788, 17 ff.; → V, 932, 10 ff.

m. συμβασιλεύω (→ I, 591, 1 ff.), "to rule together, with," outside the NT, e.g., Polyb., 30, 2, 4; Plut. Lycurgus, 5 (I, 42d) etc.; 1 Εσδρ. 8:26A; NT 1 C. 4:8; 2 Tm. 2:12 → 793, 20 ff.; also Pol., 5, 2.

n. συγκαθίζω trans. "to set someone with someone," only NT Eph. 2:6; intr. "to set oneself with others," LXX Gn. 15:11; Ex. 18:13; 1 Εσδρ. 9:6; NT Lk. 22:55.

2. Eschatological Statements in Paul.

It is in keeping with the predominantly eschatological-future use of σὺν Χριστῷ that the course of events has this as its goal. This is grounded in God's decision and leads by way of calling and justification to glorification, R. 8:29 f.

a. As expounded in R. 6:8 this is summed up in the statement in R. 8:29: οὓς προέγνω, καὶ προώρισεν συμμόρφους τῆς εἰκόνος τοῦ υἱοῦ αὐτοῦ, εἰς τὸ εἶναι αὐτὸν πρωτότοκον ἐν πολλοῖς ἀδελφοῖς. As in the classical expression σύμμορ-

---

[97] Ed. T. Bergk, Poetae elegiaci et iambographi, II (1915).
[98] In Aristot. Pol., V, 9, p. 1310a, 15: νόμων καὶ συνδεδοξασμένων ὑπὸ πάντων, συνδοξάζω means "to agree, resolve together"; in the NT it is governed by δόξα = "glory," not "opinion."
[99] συμμορφόω has the same meaning outside the NT, cf. the Lex.

φος is used here with the genitive. [100] Basic in interpretation is the term εἰκὼν τοῦ θεοῦ, which is controlled by Gn. 1:26 f. and is to be understood in the light of 2 C. 4:4, 6 → II, 395, 25 ff. Christ is God's image. Believers are caught up in the Christ event and become copies of God's Son. The term πρωτότοκος ensures His uniqueness and superiority, for they are fashioned after Him. The words in συν- point everywhere to fashioning in accordance with the Christ event. The context in which the saying occurs speaks of the new eschatological creation in which Christ is God's image and which reaches its goal when believers are made conformable to the likeness of Christ, cf. Col. 3:9 f.; Eph. 4:24. This fashioning is the redemption of the body and glorification. It is thus the end of the process which begins with calling and justification. [101] United with Christ, man acquires a share in what Christ is and is thus made like Him, [102] so that God's purpose as Creator attains its goal.

That this includes a transformation of the being of man may be seen from Phil. 3:21. σύμμορφον refers here to the body and it corresponds to → μετασχηματίσει. Christ will change the body, i.e., man in his whole existence, → IV, 759, 2 ff. Man is subject to death (R. 7:24), is without δόξα (R. 3:23), and is thus far from Christ in his earthly existence, 2 C. 5:6-8. [103] By the transformation man acquires in his corporeality the same form as that of Christ's glorious body. This is again based on the union of those who hope with Christ, Phil. 3:10. It is made possible by His power (κατὰ τὴν ἐνέργειαν...). By this transformation the believer is made conformable to the image of the Son, R. 8:29; → II, 396, 26 ff.; VI, 877, 3 ff. The statement corresponds to what is said in R. 8:23, 29. [104] Hence it does not have significance merely for the martyr. [105] The transformation itself is based on συμμορφιζόμενος τῷ θανάτῳ αὐτοῦ, Phil. 3:10. [106] In view of the present participle

---

[100] Cf. Bl.-Debr. § 182, 1; 194, 2; also on the whole passage and context J. Jervell, "Imago dei, Gn. 1:26 f. im Spätjudt., in d. Gnosis u. in d. paul. Briefen," FRL, NF, 58 (1960), 271-284. Jervell takes σύμμορφοι as a noun and transl. "copies of the image of his son," 276. Cf. also Larsson, 293-307.

[101] Jervell, op. cit., 272 pts. out that what Paul says here — introduced by οἴδαμεν δέ in R. 8:28 — is the content of the hope of the whole community: being made like Christ.

[102] Cf. on this J. Kürzinger, "συμμόρφους τῆς εἰκόνος τοῦ υἱοῦ αὐτοῦ...," BZ, NF, 2 (1958), 294-9. Ltzm. R. on 8:29 follows F. Dölger, ΙΧΘΥΣ. Das Fischsymbol in frühchr. Zeit, I (1910), 82 in pointing to the prayer for the dedication of water in the Euchologion of Serapion, 19, 3, Didascalia, II, 182, 3 (ed. F. X. Funk [1906]): μόρφωσον πάντας τοὺς ἀναγεννωμένους τὴν θείαν καὶ ἄρρητόν σου μορφήν.

[103] This is expressed by the qualifying gen. σῶμα τῆς → ταπεινώσεως (a Hebraism), cf. also 1 C. 15:42-44 and Loh. Phil. on 3:21.

[104] On R. 8:23 cf. also 8:9-11. Loh. Phil, on 3:10 f. says "being made conformable" does not denote transformation from one form to another but being fashioned from the formless to the formed: "life is the dark amorphous stuff from which something new is fashioned by death and resurrection." But this is a philosophical statement which is alien to Paul's belief in creation. Paul's belief leads him to speak of change or transformation, cf. Phil. 3:21; 1 C. 15:49 ff. H. W. Schmidt, Der Brief d. Paulus an d. Römer, Theol. Handkomm. z. NT, 6 (1963), ref. to the primal history of Christ's substitution which means that "every man has salvation only by participation in Christ's history and by the merging of his existence into that of Christ," 106. On 8:20 cf. ibid., 151 f., where ref. is finely made to the close connection between Christology and soteriology and this is taken to be the pt. of Paul's theology.

[105] Loh. Phil.

[106] Mich. Ph., ad loc. (→ V, 931, 19 ff.) finds in 3:10 a chiastic construction in which "his sufferings" and "his death" are equated. "The sufferings include the death, and the death embraces the sufferings." But the chiastic construction is not convincing to us. Materially, however, Mich. agrees with Dib. Ph., ad loc., and both reject Lohmeyer's exposition in terms

συμμορφιζόμενος it is not possible to refer this to baptism. With R. 8:17 — συμπάσχομεν — one is thus to think in terms of Christ's sufferings even to the point of martyrdom, which is endured in prospect of resurrection from the dead: εἴ πως καταντήσω εἰς τὴν ἐξανάστασιν τὴν ἐκ νεκρῶν (Phil. 3:11). [107] The line of thought brings us to the same conclusion as 2 C. 4:14 f. Changing into the same form as the exalted and glorified Christ is based on union [108] with the form of the earthly appearance of the suffering and dying Lord, and it again expresses a fellowship of destiny with Him, → n. 90.

b. Baptism is of decisive significance here. R. 6:1 ff. and 5:12-21 are related not merely in the warding off of misunderstanding, 5:20, 21; 6:1. Paul has contrasted Christ as the second Adam with the first Adam, → I, 141, 27 ff. [109] Each of these represents mankind as a whole and is thus a corporate person. [110] What this corporate person does or undergoes, it does and undergoes not merely for itself but for all the other men it represents. This is the basis of Paul's recurrent Χριστὸς ὑπὲρ ἡμῶν (R. 5:6, 8, 10), which makes possible the ἡμεῖς σὺν Χριστῷ. The union of the individual with the corporate person of Adam is effected by the nexus of begetting and birth, while the union with Christ is brought about by baptism. [111]

---

of martyrdom. Yet Lohmeyer is probably right when he notes that the possibility of martyrdom had noticeably caused Paul to rethink in Phil. and 2 C. the question of death and of life with Christ; the only thing is that his statements must not be restricted to martyrdom, → n. 86.

[107] On ἐξανάστασις ἐκ νεκρῶν, which is rare in Paul, cf. Loh. Phil. on 3:10 f. Loh. sees a ref. not to "the general resurrection of the dead at the last day" but to "a special resurrection from the dead before that day"; he thus relates the saying directly to Phil. 1:23. The idea of two resurrections, that of Christians and that of all men for judgment, is found in the apoc. thinking of primitive Christianity, cf. Rev. 20.

[108] In this passage Paul is saying that the pt. is to know Christ. This γνῶναι αὐτόν includes union, since the γινώσκειν involves entrusting oneself to the one who elects. The context makes it plain that the knowledge is orientated to the exalted Lord. Participation in Him is possible only by participation in His sufferings, Phil. 3:10.

[109] Cf. on this E. Schweizer, "Die Kirche als Leib Christi in d. paul. Homologumena," ThLZ, 86 (1961), esp. 164, 165, 169 f.

[110] Cf. H. W. Robinson, "The Hebrew Conception of Corporate Personality," Werden u. Wesen d. AT, Beih. ZAW, 66 (1936), 49-66; J. Scharbert, "Solidarität in Segen u. Fluch im AT u. in seiner Umwelt," Bonner bibl. Beiträge, 14 (1958), 11-21, cf. 19: "By his acts man creates a sphere which constantly surrounds him for good or evil ... The sphere of activity does not surround an individual but a man who stands in a society. It effects this society by 'infection.'" Cf. also R. Schnackenburg, "Todes- u. Lebensgemeinschaft mit Christus ‑ Stud. z. R. 6:1-11," Münchner Theol. Zschr., 6 (1955), 32-53, esp. 44-47. "There is thus a corporative vicariousness and representation which makes it possible to transfer statements from the one to the many and the many to the one, but in such a way that the true historical precedence of the progenitor is preserved," 45, cf. the discussion of the concept of the father of the tribe by Schweizer, op. cit. (→ n. 109). Schmidt, op. cit. (→ n. 104) calls this the history of Christ's substitution, which he takes figuratively and which has sacramental efficacy, 105 f. Cf. also J. de Fraine, Adam u. seine Nachkommen. Der Begriff d. korporativen Persönlichkeit in d. Heiligen Schrift (1962).

[111] We thus find the origin of the σὺν Χριστῷ and its development in the fact that Paul regards Christ as the second Adam. For a discussion of these questions cf. Kuss, 329-344. Attempts to explain συν- compounds by sacrifice-mysticism (cf. E. Druwe, "Medebegraven en -verrezen met Christus. Rom. VI, 3-11" in Odo Casel, Bijdragen der Nederlandse Jezuïeten, 10 [1949], 201-224) or by the Passover rite (cf. W. D. Davies, Paul and Rabb. Judaism [1948], 102 f.) are unsuccessful. For the development in primitive Christianity cf. G. Braumann, "Vorpaulinische chr. Taufverkündigung bei Paulus," BWANT, V, 2 (1962), esp. 15-18 and 50-56; also → n. 79.

Whereas the crucifixion of Jesus points beyond itself to the men for whom it takes place, baptism leads us back to this beginning and unites "us" with the "Christ for us." [112] For Paul baptism is acknowledgment of the proclaimed dominion of Jesus Christ which He gained in the cross and resurrection. The personal link between Christ and those He represents is an act of substitution. The Christ who died for men has won them to Himself by blotting out their sins and reconciling them to God. He takes them up into His death. In baptism they are appropriated to Him, and this in such a way that they are united to His death which He died for sin (R. 6:10: τῇ ἁμαρτίᾳ ἀπέθανεν, dat. incommodi) and which is their reconciliation with God (R. 5:10, 11; 6:3). [113] This lays them under obligation to renounce sin in their life. Thus they are united with Christ and are also dead to sin, 6:2: ἀπεθάνομεν τῇ ἁμαρτίᾳ, 6:8: ἀπεθάνομεν σὺν Χριστῷ, 6:10: τῇ ἁμαρτίᾳ ἀπέθανεν. Paul expounds this in R. 6:1 ff.

The first statement which develops the theme (v. 4: οὖν) reads: συνετάφημεν αὐτῷ... εἰς τὸν θάνατον, with a ref. to διὰ τοῦ βαπτίσματος, v. 3. This burial implies real death. [114] The second statement, which establishes the first, runs (v. 5): "We have become those who have grown together τῷ ὁμοιώματι τοῦ θανάτου αὐτοῦ, → V, 192, 6 ff. [115] This is given precision by the continuation, which calls for

---

[112] This meaning gains weight if one can accept the interpretation of the cultic process offered by H. J. Kraus, Gottesdienst in Israel (1954), 127 f., who suggests that the aim of the cultus is not to present the original situation of meeting with God but to incorporate into it. In the light of his understanding of mystery religion O. Casel, Das chr. Kultmysterium³ (1948) defines the mystery as "a cultic action in which a reality of salvation is present under the rite; when the cultic community performs this rite, it participates in the act of salvation and thus attains to salvation," 102. For Casel's disciple, V. Warnach, "Taufe u. Christusgeschehen nach R. 6," Archiv f. Liturgiewissenschaft, 3 (1954), 284-366, the difference between incorporation into the original situation and re-presentation in the cultus is not absolute, since the latter can bring about the former. Paul himself does not say how he would bridge the gap in time between the past event of the death of Jesus and the present union of believers with this event. For him it is overcome by the Risen Christ through the gift of the Holy Spirit, since in the Spirit the Risen and Exalted Lord is present and active in His community. Hahn uses Kierkegaard's concept of contemporaneity for this.
[113] Cf. E. Stommel, "Das Abbild seines Todes (R. 6:5) u. der Taufritus," Röm. Quartalschrift, 50 (1955), 1-21, esp. 3-6.
[114] Cf. E. Stommel, " 'Begraben mit Christus' (R. 6:4) u. der Taufritus," Röm. Quartalschrift, 49 (1954), 1-20, esp. 6-8 and 9-11. Stommel shows that only burial definitively divides the dead from the living (cf. also 1 C. 15:3 f.). This is in keeping with the line of thought in R. 6:1 ff., which from the outset aims at the real death of the baptised from sin, so v. 2, 10, 11.
[115] Cf. on this the enquiry of Warnach, op. cit., 284-366; also "Die Tauflehre d. Röm. in d. neueren theol. Lit.," Archiv. f. Liturgiewissenschatf, 5 (1956), 274-322, where there is a full argument for the concept of the cult-symbol. For Warnach thinks ὁμοίωμα τοῦ θανάτου αὐτοῦ is a cult-symbol which is to hand in baptism, and in which the death of Jesus is sacramentally present, cf. his final definition in the second work, 322. Yet though one can grow together with the death of Jesus through the cult-symbol in which it is present, one cannot grow together with the symbol itself. Paul is speaking of a constant state of growth (perfect) which goes on after the cultic act. Cf. also F. Mussner, " 'Zusammengewachsen durch die Ähnlichkeit mit seinem Tode.' Der Gedankengang v. R. 6:1-6," Trierer Theol. Zschr., 63 (1954), 257-265. Cf. also the works mentioned → n. 113, 114, 116. Mussner transl. "grown together through similarity with his death" and thinks (259 f.) Christ is included in the "we." Larsson understands ὁμοίωμα in terms of the dialectic of likeness and difference. "The likeness is that death in baptism is a real death like the death of Christ... The difference is that the death of Christ is a bloody death on the cross, death in the strict physical sense, whereas that of Christians is an effective sacramental copy of this death," 59, cf. also 61.

a recognition (τοῦτο γινώσκοντες). The form of the death of Jesus [116] is the cross, which Paul views as the curse on sin, Gl. 3:13. Paul himself is dead to sin through the Law, which brings sin to light and puts it under sentence of death. He says comprehensively: I am crucified with Christ, Gl. 2:19. That is to say, the curse of the Law has been fulfilled for him on Christ, and with Christ Paul is dead to the curse of the Law, to the Law, and therewith also to sin, 8-10. [117] The statement that "we have grown together with the likeness of his death" means, then, that "our old man has been crucified with him," 6:6. The decisive point in baptism, in which this growing together takes place, is not the rite but the "homology", i.e., the acclamation which is the response to the proclamation κύριος Ἰησοῦς, and which is thus a self-appropriation to Christ. [118]

In R. 6:1-11 there is everywhere a certain finality about crucifixion with Christ. This is negatively expressed by the "dead to sin." The goal of this crucifixion is that the human body which is ruled by sin, i.e., man under sin, should be destroyed, that it should no longer serve sin, v. 6. This demands a total self-commitment, R. 6:12-23. The finality is positively expressed by "alive to God in Jesus Christ." This is summed up in the statement: εἰ δὲ ἀπεθάνομεν σὺν Χριστῷ, πιστεύομεν ὅτι καὶ συζήσομεν αὐτῷ, 6:8, cf. Gl. 2:19, 20. The result of baptism is thus the renewal of life as an outworking of the new life that is no longer ruled by sin. συζήσομεν αὐτῷ does not refer only to the consummation of eternal being with Christ, Phil. 3:21; 2 C. 4:14. As a logical future it also embraces the present outworking in a life for God, cf. 2 C. 4:7 - 5:21. This explains the clause in v.5: "If we have grown

---

[116] So G. Bornkamm, "Taufe u. neues Leben bei Pls.," *Das Ende d. Gesetzes*³ (1961), 34-50, cf. 42, n. 18: "In Paul the meaning in all five passages is 'like form' "; cf. Schnackenburg, *op. cit.*, 35-39, who with Dib. Ph. on 2:6 f. takes ὁμοίωμα to have the sense of "form" (attested in the LXX) without the character of an image, → V, 191, 12 ff.

[117] For the linking of baptism and crucifixion in Paul cf. 1 C. 1:13. E. Klaar, "Die Taufe nach paul. Verständnis," *Theol. Ex.*, 93 (1961), 9 takes συνεσταυρώθη to be an "echo of dominical sayings" like Mt. 10:38 f., cf. on this Larsson, 77-80. Hence R. 6:5 has in view the "concrete, ongoing process of taking up the cross, the self-denying conflict against one's own ego." Klaar calls his non-sacramental interpretation of R. 6:1-11 "voluntaristic," 11. σὺν Χριστῷ is worked out, not in a sacramental event, but in the resolute and obedient acceptance, against the sinful self, of the proclamation of the cross and the resurrection. In his study, which stands in sharp contrast to the works ref. to in → n. 111-115, Klaar finds a starting-pt. in Paul's aor. as compared with the incorrect Lat. perf., which leads to the sacramentalist misunderstanding. Obedience is awakened by the Holy Spirit working through the Word, and baptism is the initiatory act which man decides on when he accepts the proclamation. This study demands serious consideration, but its one-sided voluntaristic interpretation needs to be balanced by a recognition of what is done to man and what sets him in motion. The whole eschatological context of the σὺν Χριστῷ is obscured in Klaar. That Paul's intention is to establish the new life which is liberated from sin is clear enough in the passage, for the sacramental statements in 6:2-10 are enclosed by 6:1 and 6:11-14. The question of v.1 is taken up again in v. 15 and the answer is given in 6:16-7:6. Kuss, 325 rightly notes that "an unceasing dying follows the basic sacramental death." The actualisation in life is a following of the way of Jesus in ethos and suffering, → n. 118.

[118] Stommel, *op. cit.*, is right when he rejects the significance of the rite for an understanding of baptism. His failure is not to do justice to the factor of homology. Worth noting in this connection is W. Joest, "Paulus u. das Lutherische Simul Justus et Peccator," *Kerygma u. Dogma*, 1 (1955), 270-321. Joest raises the question of Paul's doctrine of justification and he reaches the conclusion that "imputed or forensically ascribed justification is an effective living power," so that the believer who is set in Christ goes on in Him to perfection, 276. In this regard Joest says that when the believer is said to be with Christ new life is perfected in Him, 279. The "with Christ" rests on the fact that God has spoken it. This takes place in baptism.

together in the likeness of his death, we shall also be part of the resurrection," this being understood as a power which rules the life for God and fashions it according to the glorious body of Jesus Christ. [119]

c. Paul takes up again in R. 8 his sayings about being with Christ. The man who is controlled by God's Spirit (8:1-13) is set by the Spirit in sonship and shares with Christ the name and status of son, 8:14-17; πρωτότοκος ἐν πολλοῖς ἀδελφοῖς, 8:29. [120] Common sonship, which is God's gift through Christ, is necessarily followed by common inheritance in the common kingdom, cf. R. 8:32; 5:17 → n. 91. Being heirs with Christ is linked to being fashioned like Him: "And if children, then heirs; heirs of God, and joint-heirs with Christ; if so be that we suffer with Him, that we may be also glorified together," R. 8:17. To be a joint-heir and to be glorified together, i.e., to receive the δόξα which man does not have and by which Christ was raised up (3:23; 6:4), are two aspects of the same process; they are future, eschatological, cf. 1 C. 15:43. They are linked to suffering with Christ, which is part of the earthly form of a life lived for God and which is thus endured in the power of being raised with Christ, 2 C. 4:7-14. As suffering and glory, death and resurrection, are woven together in Christ, so they are for those who are with Him. Thus "with Christ" embraces the whole of Christian existence.

3. Colossians and Ephesians.

The points already developed (→ 787, 31 ff.) are taken up again with typical shifts of accent in Col. and Eph.

a. In Col. (2:12 ff.) a formula which reflects R. 6:4 defines baptism [121] as a being buried with Christ, to which there corresponds being raised with him. This takes place in Him (ἐν ᾧ) [122] by faith in the activity of God as this is manifest in the resurrection of Christ. Those who are dead outside Christ are made alive again with Him — συνεζωοποίησεν ὑμᾶς σὺν αὐτῷ — through the gift of remission of sins, Col. 2:13 f. If here being raised again with Christ is plainly related to the existence which is grounded in baptism and infused with life by the message, it takes on a new aspect by reason of the fact that it entails liberation from cosmic powers and astral and demonic forces. [123] The dying of the baptised with Christ

---

[119] Here the question arises whether one should supplement the καὶ τῆς ἀναστάσεως ἐσόμεθα of v. 5b by τῷ ὁμοιώματι σύμφυτοι from 5a. We do not think this is necessary since it might restrict the all-embracing power of the resurrection. Schmidt, op. cit., 7 makes the emphatic point that the new life is given in the Holy Ghost and he calls the Holy Ghost "the redemptive divine power of transformation in the earthly sphere."

[120] Cf. Schl. Erl. on R. 8:14: "Now that we see fully how inwardly and totally Christ has united Himself with us, how seriously and powerfully He raises us up into His likeness, how He gives us a share in all that He has, so that He gives us His Spirit and dwells within us, we may indeed say: Thou art the Son of God and through Thee we too have become the sons and children of God." Christ shares His sonship with His people.

[121] The ἐν in ἐν τῷ βαπτίσματι is to be taken instrumentally, cf. R. 6:4: διὰ τοῦ βαπτίσματος εἰς τὸν θάνατον.

[122] The ἐν ᾧ can be related to βάπτισμα, in which case it has instrumental significance in so far as being buried and being raised take place simultaneously through baptism. But ἐν ᾧ can also be related to Christ as in v. 11 and thus stand for ἐν Χριστῷ. The latter is more probable.

[123] Cf. on this G. Bornkamm, "Die Häresie d. Kol.," Das Ende d. Gesetzes³ (1961), 139-156.

removes them from the dominion of the elemental spirits of the cosmos: ἀπεθάνετε σὺν Χριστῷ ἀπὸ τῶν στοιχείων τοῦ κόσμου, [124] Col. 2:20 → 686, 5 ff. Hence the resurrection life with Christ is already a victorious life in the earthly existence of believers. It is said of this life that it is hid with Christ in God → 785, 30 ff. It will also be manifested with Him, since He Himself is this life, Col. 3:3 f. Here man is not a sleeper in terms of earthly death. Since he shares the resurrection life with Christ, [125] his earthly death is a transition to the life which is hid with Christ in God and which in changed form comes forth visibly from the hiddenness of God at the *parousia*. [126]

b. In a hymnal passage in Eph. 2:1 ff. confession is made ὁ δὲ θεὸς ... ὄντας ἡμᾶς νεκροὺς τοῖς παραπτώμασιν συνεζωοποίησεν τῷ Χριστῷ, this being described as salvation through grace, [127] καὶ συνήγειρεν καὶ συνεκάθισεν ἐν τοῖς ἐπουρανίοις ἐν Χριστῷ Ἰησοῦ (2:4-6). [128] The statement refers to an event in process of completion [129] and thus testifies to the triumphant character of the resurrection life in the sense of a realised eschatology. "With Christ" determines present existence. The believer was dead without Christ in sins, but has been wakened and raised up from death in Him, and with Him he is already set among heavenly creatures, viz. angelic powers, cf. Phil. 3:20. No other statement anticipates the future to the degree that this one does.

4. The Primitive Christian Hymn in 2 Tm. 2:11 f.

Pauline sayings are taken up again in a primitive Christian hymn in 2 Tm. 2:11 f. → V, 216, 26 ff. This is introduced by πιστὸς ὁ λόγος. It builds on the hope that the elect will attain to the salvation given in Jesus Christ with eternal glory, v. 10. It contains two lines:

> "If we be dead with him, we shall also live with him,
> If we endure, we shall also reign with him." [130]

The dying with Him took place in baptism and is worked out in resistance to sin.

---

[124] Cf. Col. 2:14: The elemental spirits are marched in the triumph of Christ, who has gained the victory over them. Kuss, 323 rightly perceives that the significance of the whole event is that "the ensuing participation of believers in the saving way of Jesus Christ from suffering to glory ... leads to conformity to the nature of the glorified Jesus Christ," cf. also 326: "The way of the bringer of salvation ... is also the way of the one who believes on Him to salvation." Larsson, as his title shows, sees in Christ an example, but in the soteriological rather than the ethical and pedagogic sense. Kuss, 321 also draws attention to this when he says that with Christ rests on through Christ, that "as He, so we" rests on "because He, so we."

[125] Note should be taken of the aor. συνηγέρθητε in Col. 3:1. The passage shows that historical actualisation of the resurrection life results from seeking things above and turning from things of earth, v. 2.

[126] Cf. → IV, 815, 5 ff. It is plain that apoc. ideas are adopted here, yet they are altered, for the ref. is not to the disclosure of saving gifts and events already concealed in heaven, but to the manifestation of believers in their life with Christ which is hid in God.

[127] Esp. v. 4: "God, who is rich in mercy, for his great love wherewith he loved us."

[128] The continuation in v. 7 (introduced by ἵνα) unveils the divine purpose of showing to future aeons the superabundant riches of God's grace as this is manifested in His kindness to us displayed in Jesus Christ.

[129] If the hymn has a Hbr. original the verbal forms rendered by the aor. are to be taken as future in the sense of a future eschatology. The aor. form re-interprets them as a process worked out in faith.

[130] Cf. P. Gerhardt's hymn in *Evangelisches Kirchengesangbuch*, 86, 8.

The living and reigning with Him are still future, cf. R. 8:17. Hence the realised
eschatology of, e.g., Eph. (→ 793, 10 ff.) is modified in 2 Tim. 2:18. [131] As a hymn of
the community this verse is important evidence of a simplified understanding of
basic Pauline sayings. In form it is older than what we find in Eph. and Col. (→ 785,
16 ff.; 792, 19 ff.) and it shows how widespread was the influence of Paul's development of the σὺν Χριστῷ.

> That Polycarp knew the hymn may be seen from Pol., 5, 2: "If we walk worthy of
> Him, καὶ συμβασιλεύσομεν αὐτῷ." Pol., 9, 2 recalls the martyrs, among them Ign.,
> and the apostles, esp. Paul, and also witnesses from his own church, and says of them that
> they are at their appropriate place with the Lord (παρὰ τῷ κυρίῳ), ᾧ καὶ συνέπαθον.
> Ign. says about himself: εἰς τὸ συμπαθεῖν αὐτῷ πάντα ὑπομένω, αὐτοῦ με ἐνδυνα-
> μοῦντος τοῦ τελείου ἀνθρώπου γενομένου, Sm., 4, 2. συμπάσχω has here the sense
> of being a martyr with Christ, and this means being with the Lord. The Pauline ref. is no
> longer very clear, but its underlying intention is taken up. Christ the second Adam has
> become perfect man (cf. Hb. 5:8 f.) and with Christ man attains to perfect humanity,
> Eph. 4:13.

F. σύν and μετά in Christ-Sayings in the New Testament apart from the Pauline σὺν Χριστῷ.

1. σύν and μετά are used to describe discipleship. They stand against a background which makes it plain that the NT views man as decisively determined by
his being with others. [132] In the parable of the two sons in Lk. 15:11-32 it is the
wish of the elder brother ἵνα μετὰ τῶν φίλων μου εὐφρανθῶ (v. 29), i.e., at a
banquet, while we read of the younger: οὗτος ὁ καταφαγών σου τὸν βίον μετὰ
πορνῶν (v. 30); but the father reminds his older son: σὺ πάντοτε μετ᾽ ἐμοῦ εἶ,
v. 31. Fellowship with the father is the greatest thing of all; it includes a share in
all his goods and possessions. Not to see this is the fault of the elder brother, and
it is this that makes him so hard. Jesus calls the twelve ἵνα ὦσιν μετ᾽ αὐτοῦ (Mk.
3:14) right up to His hour of suffering (Mt. 26:38, 40), also that they should learn
from His and share in His work. Simon Peter at his denial is accused of being a
disciple in the words that he was with Jesus (Mt. 26:69, 71; Mk. 14:67; Lk. 22:59;
Jn. 18:26, all μετά; cf. Lk. 22:56; οὗτος σὺν αὐτῷ ἦν). He had sworn that he was
ready to suffer and die with Jesus, Mt. 26:35; Lk. 22:33. Jesus addresses His disciples
as those who "have continued with me in my temptations," Lk. 22:28, cf. also 8:1.
The disciples are with Jesus on His journeys (Lk. 22:14). The Gadarene demoniac
asks that he may go with Him (Mk. 5:18; Lk. 8:38). [133] Looking back Jesus reminds
the disciples of His words ἔτι ὢν σὺν ὑμῖν (Lk. 24:44). In Ac. 4:13 the members of
the Sanhedrin see in Peter and John ὅτι σὺν τῷ ᾽Ιησοῦ ἦσαν. [134] The fellowship which

---

131 We find this realised eschatology in Jn. too, though it is still future there as well.
132 Lk. prefers σύν, the other NT writings usually have μετά.
133 Mk. 5:18: ἵνα μετ᾽ αὐτοῦ ᾖ (cf. Lk. 8:38: εἶναι σὺν αὐτῷ).
134 This statement stands against the background of the rich use of σύν for the fellowship
the disciples have with one another, cf. Ac. 1:14, 22; 2:14; 3:4, 8; 4:14; 11:12; 14:20, 28; 15:22,
25; 16:3; 18:8; 20:36; 21:5, 16, 18, 24, 26, 29; 27:2 all σύν (1:26; 9:19, 28, 39; 15:35; 20:18
μετά). This use is to be distinguished from the use of σύν for general relationships in Ac.:
4:27; 5:1, 17, 21, 26; 8:31; 10:2, 20, 23; 13:7; 14:13; 16:32; 19:38; 22:9; 24:24; 26:13; 28:16.
In this connection one may also ref. to 2 Tm. 1:8 (→ V, 937, 25 ff.): συγκακοπάθησον τῷ
εὐαγγελίῳ, Paul being here the one with whom Timothy is to suffer for the Gospel. The
choice of συγκακοπαθέω ("to suffer evil with") is worth noting, cf. also 2 Tm. 2:3. This
word occurs outside the NT in Schol. Eur. Hec., 203, ed. W. Dindorf (1863).

Jesus grants the disciples with Himself is His gift to them. It extends beyond earthly life. To the thief who turns to Him Jesus says: ἀμήν σοι λέγω, σήμερον μετ' ἐμοῦ ἔσῃ ἐν τῷ παραδείσῳ (Lk. 23:43). Jesus takes him with Him as his escort into Paradise and gives him a share in the joy opened up and the life given, [135] cf. also Mt. 25:10.

μετά bears a particular nuance in Jn. Discipleship is fellowship with Jesus on the way (6:3, cf. Mk. 14:18; 6:66). In the hour of parting Jesus speaks of His being with the disciples (14:9; 16:4; 13:33, cf. also 7:33 for the time of His stay among the Jews). The disciples for their part respond to His being with them by their being with Him, so Thomas in his readiness to die with Jesus, 11:16. Jesus finds in their being with Him the basis of their witness for Him, 15:27. Their fellowship with Him points beyond itself, for it is the express will of Jesus [136] vis-à-vis the Father ἵνα ὅπου εἰμὶ ἐγὼ κἀκεῖνοι ὦσιν μετ' ἐμοῦ, 17:24, cf. also 14:3. It is against this background that the answer to Peter at the foot-washing (13:8) takes on significance: ἐὰν μὴ νίψω σε, οὐκ ἔχεις μέρος μετ' ἐμοῦ [137] (→ II, 831, 22 ff.). Purification by Jesus is the presupposition of fellowship with Him in the Father's house. [138]

1 Jn. takes up this question and speaks of κοινωνία (→ III, 798, 10 ff., 807, 39 ff.) "with the Father, and with his Son Jesus Christ," 1:3. When the word of life is proclaimed by the witnesses "you have fellowship with us." The preaching of the witnesses establishes fellowship with them, and herein it also establishes fellowship with Jesus Christ, and through Him with the Father. This binds the community in light and makes possible mutual fellowship, [139] 1:6, 7. The man who breaks this being together has not been governed by this fellowship, 2:19.

2. When Paul speaks of the fellowship of Christians with one another or with men as distinct from their fellowship with Christ he uses μετά, R. 12:15, 18; 1 C. 16:11, 12. He forbids members of the congregation to go to law against one another (1 C. 6:6 f.). He finds no fellowship between believers and unbelievers, between the temple of God and idols, 2 C. 6:15 f. In mixed marriages the partners must decide concerning their being together, 1 C. 7:12 f.

3. Some statements in Rev. are close to the Pauline σὺν Χριστῷ, though μετά is used; cf. the letters to Sardis (3:4) [140] and Laodicea (3:21, cf. R. 8:17; 2 Tm. 2:11 f.), also the reference to the 144,000 who are sealed (14:1); they are οἱ μετ' αὐτοῦ κλητοὶ καὶ ἐκλεκτοὶ καὶ πιστοί (17:14), who will share the Lamb's victory over His enemies and reign with Christ in the millennium, 20:4, 6. This is the reward

---

135 Cf. on this Lohmeyer, 232 and 248, also Dupont, 92 f. though Dupont does not consider the sense of leading and escorting. It is hardly adequate to limit the "with me" to sharing in the joys of Paradise as Dupont does, 93.

136 It is the meat of Jesus to do the will of Him that sent Him (Jn. 4:34), and only here in Jn. does He say: I will.

137 Cf. the important historical examples in Dupont, 90; also W. Grundmann, "Zur Rede Jesu vom Vater im Joh.-Ev.," ZNW, 52 (1961), 213-230.

138 Here we find the same connection as there is in Paul between "Christ for us" and "we with Christ."

139 Note that here fellowship with one another, and with Christ and His Father, is again linked with purifying by Jesus, 1 Jn. 1:7b.

140 Where Paul uses δόξα we have here the image of the white raiment; where Paul speaks of his being with Christ we have here a walk with the living Lord as His people's guide and escort. They are worthy who stand fast and do not let themselves be overcome.

which Christ gives His people and which comes to them with Him at the *parousia,* 22:12. [141]

4. σύν and μετά are particularly important in connection with meals, for the meal creates fellowship, Lk. 15:29 f.; 7:36. Jesus eats with publicans and sinners; His adversaries take offence at this, Mt. 9:10 f.; Mk. 2:16; Lk. 15:2. Judas' betrayal is especially shameful as a breach of table fellowship, Mk. 14:18, 20; Lk. 22:21. Jesus had a particular desire for this fellowship (Lk. 22:15) and He looks forward to its restoration and fulfilment in the Father's kingdom, Mt. 26:29, cf. also 8:11; 25:10. The Emmaus disciples ask their unknown guest to have fellowship at table, Lk. 24:29 f. [142] The community regarded the Lord's Supper as fellowship with the Risen Lord and observed it in expectation of the coming meal in the kingdom of God. This is perfectly plain in the hymn appended to the letter to Laodicea in Rev. 3:20. [143] This is an eschatological saying which is now fulfilled for the community in the Lord's Supper and which is addressed to the individual member (ἐάν τις ἀκούσῃ ... εἰσελεύσομαι πρὸς αὐτόν) with a view to taking him up into reciprocal fellowship with Jesus and maintaining him in it: δειπνήσω μετ᾽ αὐτοῦ καὶ αὐτὸς μετ᾽ ἐμοῦ, → II, 34, 20 ff.

5. μετά is also significant in sayings about the *parousia* and judgment. They have an OT basis in verses like Dt. 33:2 combined with Ex. 19:10 ff. and Zech. 14:5. In the NT μετά is brought into relation to the coming of the Son of Man in Mk. 8:38; Mt. 16:27; Mk. 13:26 par. Mt. 24:30 f.; 25:31; 2 Th. 1:7; 1 Th. 3:13; Mk. 14:62; Rev. 1:7. This coming is described as the master's reckoning with his servants. Mt. 18:23; 25:19. At this judgment various groups come forward together, Mt. 12:41 f. par. Lk. 11:31 f. Of the dead who die ἐν κυρίῳ it is said: τὰ γὰρ ἔργα αὐτῶν ἀκολουθεῖ μετ᾽ αὐτῶν (Rev. 14:13), a counterpart to Wis. 14:10: "What is done will be punished σὺν τῷ δράσαντι." A man's fruits go with him into eternal life. While the *parousia* sayings make it plain that Christ comes accompanied by His court, [144] the judgment sayings show that men are gathered together at the judgment, that their acts are united and present with them, and that they will be measured by one another. [145]

6. A verse apart is Mk. 1:13, which says of Jesus, proclaimed as God's Son, that He was "tempted of Satan; and was with the wild beasts (μετὰ τῶν θηρίων); and the angels ministered unto him." It is plain from this statement, which is to be seen

---

[141] In Herm. s., 9, 24, 4 the descendants of innocent and simple believers are promised: κατοικήσει μετὰ τοῦ υἱοῦ τοῦ θεοῦ. In 2 Cl., 4, 5 an apocr. saying of Jesus, the threat is made against the μετ᾽ ἐμοῦ συνηγμένοι ἐν τῷ κόλπῳ μου that they will be put out if they do not keep Jesus' commands.

[142] Cf. W. Grundmann, "Fragen d. Komposition des lk. 'Reiseberichtes,'" ZNW, 50 (1959), 252-270, esp. 252-254; also Grundmann, *op. cit.* (→ n. 54), *ad loc.*

[143] Cf. Loh. Apk., *ad loc.* On table fellowship with the deity in antiquity cf. S. Rehrl, *Das Problem d. Demut in der profan-griech. Lit. im Vergleich zu LXX u. NT* (1961), 80 f., where ref. is made to Plut. Suav. Viv. Epic., 21 (II, 1102): "It is not the amount of wine and meat that makes us merry at feasts but glad hope and belief in the presence of the god who is gracious and who accepts with satisfaction what is offered."

[144] It is an open question whether the holy ones of Zech. 14:5 and 1 Th. 3:13 are angelic powers or already perfected saints.

[145] 2 Cl., 19, 4 promises to the righteous man in his suffering that, awakened to life up above μετὰ τῶν πατέρων, he will rejoice in eternal felicity.

against the background of Test. N. 8, that the wild beasts could not have anything against Him, → I, 141, 17 ff., III, 134, 16 ff. [146]

7. The passage Mk. 8:27 - 9:29 develops what is stated in the σύν sayings in R. 8:17b, [147] while the σὺν Χριστῷ may be discerned in Ac. in the parallelism between the death of Christ and that of Stephen (Lk. 22:69; 23:34a, 46 — Ac. 7:56, 59, 60), cf. also the sufferings of Christ and those of Paul → 792, 8 ff. [148] At the end of the story of Stephen it is apparent that Christ fetches into His kingdom those who are made like Him in death and passion → 650, 9 ff.

In the NT use of σύν and μετά one sees plainly [149] that salvation is effected in the participation in Christ's destiny (→ 782, 20 ff.; 789, 9 ff.) by which we are made in His image (→ 787, 34 ff.) and in the being with Him in which God binds Himself to man.

Grundmann

---

[146] Cf. Grundm. Mk., *ad loc.*

[147] Grundm. Mk., *ad loc.*, also K. Weiss, "Ekklesiologie, Tradition u. Gesch. in d. Jünger-unterweisung Mk. 8:27-10:52," H. Ristow and K. Matthiae, *Der historische Jesus u. der kerygmatische Christus* (1960), 414-438.

[148] Cf. the ref. in R. Morgenthaler, *Die lk. Geschichtsschreibung als Zeugnis,* I (1948), 182 f.

[149] Theological illumination of the NT message and its understanding is closely related to the use of certain prep., apart from σύν and μετά esp. ἐν, εἰς, διά, ὑπέρ, περί, ἀντί and παρά, and their mutual interrelations.

συναγωγή, † ἐπισυναγωγή,
† ἀρχισυνάγωγος,
† ἀποσυνάγωγος

συναγωγή.

Contents: A. συναγωγή in Profane Greek: 1. The General Meaning; 2. The Meaning of συναγωγή in Relation to Societies. B. συναγωγή in the Septuagint: 1. Occurrence; 2. ἐκκλησία and συναγωγή; 3. Gathering; 4. Assembly; 5. The Whole Congregation; 6. The Individual Congregation; 7. The House of Meeting. C. συναγωγή in Judaism: I. Usage: 1. Greek-Speaking Judaism; 2. Aramaic and Hebrew Equivalents among the Rabbis; 3. The Usage in Qumran. II. The Jewish Synagogue: 1. Origin; 2. Spread; 3. Founding; 4. Architecture: a. Situation; b. Direction; c. Style; 5. Furnishings; 6. Purpose and Significance: a. Teaching the Law; b. Relation to the Temple; c. Place of Prayer; d. School; e. Council House and Place of Assembly; f. Hospice; g. *Aedes sacrae*. D. συναγωγή in the New Testament: I. συναγωγή as Assembly; II. συναγωγή as Community; III. The Synagogue in the New Testament: 1. Relation to Jewish Statements; 2. The Attitude of Jesus to the Synagogue; 3. The Importance of the Synagogue for the Primitive Christian Mission as Depicted in Acts; IV. Ac. 6:9 and Jm. 2:2. E. συναγωγή in the Early Church.

σ υ ν α γ ω γ ή . Bibl.: General: N. A. Dahl, "Das Volk Gottes. Eine Untersuchung zum Kirchenbewusstsein d. Urchr.," *Skrifter utgitt av Det Norske Videnskaps-Akademi i Oslo*, II, *Historisk-Filosofisk Kl.*, 2 (1941), esp. 61-76; H. Kosmala, "Hebräer-Essener-Christen. Stud. z. Vorgeschichte d. frühchr. Verkündigung," *Stud. Post-Biblica*, I (1959), Index, *s.v.*; S. Krauss, *Synagogale Altertümer* (1922); also Art. "Synagoge" in Pauly-W., 4a (1932), 1286-1316; L. Rost, "Die Vorstufen v. Kirche u. Synagoge," BWANT, IV, 24 (1938); C. Vitringa, *De synagoga vetere libri tres*² (1726). On A.: M. San Nicolò, "Ägypt. Vereinswesen z. Zt. d. Ptolemäer u. Römer," II, 1, *Münchner Beiträge z. Papyrusforschung*, 2 (1915), 41-53; F. Poland, *Gesch. d. griech. Vereinswesens* (1909), Index, *s.v.*; also Art. "Συναγωγή" in Pauly-W., 4a (1932), 1284-1286; E. Ziebarth, *Das griech. Vereinswesen* (1896), Index, *s.v.* C.-D.: W. Bacher, Art. "Synagogue" Jew. Enc.,11 (1905), 619-643; Hastings DB, IV (1902), 636-643; J. Buxtorf, *Synagoga Judaica* (1604); E. L. Ehrlich, "Kultsymbolik im AT u. im nachbibl. Judt.," *Symbolik d. Religionen*, III (1959), 86-96; I. Elbogen, "D. jüd. Gottesdienst in seiner geschichtlichen Entwicklung," *Schriften hrsgg. v. d. Gesellschaft z. Förderung d. Wissenschaft d. Judt.*³ (1931), Index, *s.v.*; F. V. Filson, "Temple, Synagogue, and Church," *The Bibl. Archaeologist*, 7 (1944), 77-88; M. Friedländer, *Synagoge u Kirche in ihren Anfängen* (1908), Index, *s.v.*; K. Galling, Art. "Synagoge" in BR, 505-510; also Art. "Synagoge" in RGG³, VI, 557-9; also "Archäol. Jahresbericht, IV: Die Synagogen," ZDPV, 50 (1927), 310-315; also "Erwägungen z. antiken Synagoge," ZDPV, 72 (1956), 163-178; E. R. Goodenough, *Jewish Symbols in the Greco-Roman Period*, I-III, *Bollingen Ser.*, 37 (1953); A. W. Groenman, "De Oorsprong d. joodsche Synagoge," *Nieuw Theol. Tijdschr.*, 8 (1919), 43-87, 137-188; J. Guillet, "Synagogue et prédication apost.," *Parole et Mission*, 1 (1958), 10-30; A. S. Hiram, *Die architektonische Entwicklung d. antiken Synagogen u. altchr. Kirchen im Heiligen Lande* (1960); J. Jocz, *The Jewish People and Jesus Christ. A Study in the Controversy between Church and Synagogue* (1954), Index, *s.v.*; J. Juster, *Les Juifs dans l'empire Romain*, I, II (1914), esp. I, 456-472; H. Kohl-C. Watzinger, "Antike Synagogen in Galiläa," *Wissenschaftl. Veröffentlichungen d. Deutschen Orient-Gesellschaft*, 29 (1916); C. H. Kraeling, *The Synagogue with Contributions by C. C. Torrey, C. B. Welles and B. Geiger, The Excavations at Dura-Europos conducted by the Yale Univ. and the French Acad. of Inscr. and Letters. Final Report*, VIII, Part 1, ed. A. B. Bellinger, F. E. Brown, A. Perkins and C. B. Welles (1956); also "The Earliest Synagogue Architecture," *Bulletin of the Amer. Schools of Orient. Research*, 54 (1934), 18-20; S. Krauss, "Die galiläischen Synagogenruinen," *Gesellschaft f. Palästina-Forschung*, 3. *Veröffentlichung* (1917); also "Die galil. Synagogenruinen u. d. Halakha," MGWJ, 65 (1921), 211-220; H. J. Leon, *The Jews of Ancient Rome*

A. συναγωγή in Profane Greek.

1. The General Meaning.

In profane Gk. the word occurs from Thuc., II, 18, 3 (Attic ξυναγωγή). As a verbal noun it is mostly used trans. and act. like συνάγω and unlike several other derivates [1] of the simple ἄγω. The basic sense is "to lead, bring together," "to gather," "gathering," "union." [2] a. Of persons: διὰ τὴν ἄδικόν τε καὶ ἄτεχνον συναγωγὴν ἀνδρὸς καὶ γυναικός, ᾗ δὲ προαγωγία ὄνομα, Plat. Theaet., 150a; συναγωγὴ τῶν ὄχλων, Polyb., 4, 7, 6, cf. plur. συναγωγαὶ ὄχλου, Ditt. Or., I, 383, 151 (1st cent. B.C.). b. Of things: συναγωγὴ χρημάτων, Polyb., 27, 13, 2; Democr. Fr., 222 (Diels, II, 190); cf. Ditt. Syll.³, I, 410, 13 f. (3rd cent. B.C.); συναγωγὴ ξύλων, P. Mich., II, 84, 15 (3rd cent. B.C.); often for collecting or a collection of books, letters or laws συναγωγὴ καὶ ἀναγραφὴ τῶν νόμων, Dion. Hal. Ant. Rom., 2, 27, 3; Σωκ[ρα]τικῶν ἐπιστο[λ(ῶν)] συναγωγαί, Mitteis-Wilcken, I, 2, 155, 1 f. (from a catalogue of books in Memphis, 3rd cent. B.C.), cf. Plut. De musica, 3 (II, 1131 f.); 5 (II, 1132e); Mearum epistularum nulla est συναγωγή, Cic. Att., 9, 13, 3; 16, 5, 5. The word is often used for the bringing in of the harvest and fruits συναγωγὴ τοῦ σίτου, P. Zenon, 59433, 5 (3rd cent. B.C.), [3] cf. Preisigke Sammelbuch, IV, 7285, 14 (3rd cent. B.C.); Polyb., 1, 17, 9; συναγωγὴ τῶν σιτικῶν καρπῶν, Diod. S., V, 21, 5; cf. Ditt. Or., I, 56, 37 (3rd cent. B.C.); Preisigke Sammelb., III, 1, 6742; 7 etc. (3rd cent. B.C.); οἴνου συναγωγή, Poll. Onom., I, 226. Occasionally συναγωγή can mean the mustering of the army, συναγωγὰς καὶ ἐκτάσεις στρατιᾶς, Plat. Resp., VII, 526d, the drawing together of sail, Preisigke Sammelb., III, 1, 6715, 6 etc. (3rd cent. B.C.). Fig. the knitting of the face (Isoc. Or., 9, 44), the brows (Hippocr. Κῳακαὶ Προγνώσεις, II, 7, 210, Littré, V, 630), the eyes, Aristot. Probl., 4, 2, p. 876b, 10; summing up in Platonic dialectic (= σύνοψις, cf. Plat. Resp., VII, 537c), opp. διαίρεσις, Plat. Phaedr., 266b; in logic the conclusion, deduction, demonstration, Aristot. Rhet., II, 23, p. 1400b, 26; III, 9, p. 1410a, 22; Sext. Emp. Pyrrh. Hyp., II, 135, 143, 170.

(1960), 135-166; O. Linton, *Das Problem d. Urkirche in d. neueren Forschung* (1932), 138-146; L. Löw, "Der synagogale Ritus," *Gesammelte Schriften*, IV (1898), 1-71; H. G. May, "Synagogues in Palestine," *The Bibl. Archaeologist*, 7 (1944), 1-20; B. Meistermann, *Capharnaum et Bethsaïde, suivi d'une étude sur l'âge de la Synagogue de Tell Hum* (1921); A. Menes, "Tempel u. Synagoge," ZAW, 50 (1932), 268-276; Comte du Mesnil du Buisson, "Les deux synagogues successives à Doura-Europos," *Rev. Bibl.*, 45 (1936), 72-90; J. Morgenstern, "The Temple and the Synagogue to 70 CE," *An Amer. Synagogue for Today and Tomorrow* (1954), 10-25; G. Orfali, *Capharnaüm et ses ruines* (1922); J. Parkes, *The Conflict of the Church and the Synagogue* (1934); L. Rost, "Archäol. Bemerkungen zu einer St. d. Jk. (Jk. 2:2 f.)," PJB, 29 (1933), 53-66; M. H. Scharlemann, "The Theol. of Synagogue Architecture," *Concordia Theol. Monthly,* 30 (1959), 902-914; K. L. Schmidt, "Die Kirche d. Urchr. Eine lexikograph. u. bibl.-theol. Stud.," *Festg. f. A. Deissmann* (1926), 259-319; Schürer, II, 497-544; B. Schwank, "Qualis erat forma synagogarum Novi Test.," *Verbum Domini*, 33 (1955), 267-279; S. D. Schwartzmann, "How Well Did the Synoptic Evangelists Know the Synagogue?" HUCA, 24 (1952/53), 115-132; M. Simon, "Verus Israel. Étude sur les relations entre Chrétiens et Juifs dans l'empire Romain, 135-425," *Bibliothèque des Écoles d'Athènes et de Rome*, 166 (1948), 19-162; H. L. Strack, Art. "Synagogue" in RE³, 19, 223-226; Str.-B., IV, 115-152 and Index, *s.v.*; E. L. Sukenik, *The Ancient Synagogue of Beth-Alpha* (1932); also *Ancient Synagogues in Palestine and Greece* (1934); also *The Ancient Synagogue of El-Hammeh* (1935); also "The Present State of Ancient Synagogue Studies," *Bulletin of the L. M. Rabinowitz Fund for the Exploration of Ancient Synagogues*, 1 (1949), 7-23; C. Watzinger, *Denkmäler Palästinas. Eine Einführung in d. Archäol. d. Hl. Landes*, II (1935), 107-116; C. Wendel, *Der Thoraschrein im Altertum, Hallische Monographien* (1950). On E.: A. Harnack, Patrum Apostolorum Opera, III (1877), 115-119 on Herm., 11, 9.

[1] On ἀγωγή and προσαγωγή → I, 128, 15 ff., 133, 27 ff.; Cr.-Kö., 68-70.
[2] Cf. Liddell-Scott, Preisigke Wört., Moult.-Mill. and Pass., *s.v.*
[3] Ed. C. C. Edgar, *Catalogue général des antiquités égypt. du Musée du Caire*, 85 (1928).

2. The Meaning of συναγωγή in Relation to Societies.

In view of the gt. importance of συνάγω in Gk. societies it is not surprising that the verbal noun is also common in this sphere, esp. in many inscr., [4] rarely in relation to the founding or naming of a society, [5] more commonly in the sense of the gathering or periodic meeting, esp. in the Doric isles, Asia Minor and Egypt, e.g., the well-known Testament of Epicteta from Thera in Crete (between 210 and 195 B.C.) ὥστε γίνεσθαι τὰν συναγωγὰν ἐπ' ἀμέρας τρεῖς ἐν τῷ Μουσείῳ, IG, 12, 3, No. 330, 118 f., cf. also line 22, 115, 127 f., 131 f. The society itself, which meets to worship heroes, is called τὸ κοινὸν τοῦ ἀνδρείου τῶν συγγενῶν and has 25 members; women and children are admitted to the συναγωγή (also σύνοδος, σύλλογος). From there we also have the inscr. which mentions a συναγωγή of the κοινὸν τοῦ Ἀνθισ[τῆ]ρος, IG, 12, 3, No. 329, 15 f. We find [σ]υνλόγους καὶ συναγωγάς in the draft of statutes for a cultic guild of Zeus Hypsistos οἱ ἐκ τῆς τοῦ Διὸς Ὑψίστου συνόδου (between 69 and 57 B.C.? from Philadelphia in Fayyum?), Preisigke Sammelb., V, 7835, 12. [6] The use is similar in a clan society of Diomedes in Cos in Asia Minor, Ditt. Syll.[3], III, 1106, 93 f. (c. 300 B.C.), which meets to worship Heracles and the hero who founded the family, though sacrifices are also made to Aphrodite and the Μοῖραι. All members of the family take part in the συναγωγή. Use of the τέμενος for other purposes is explicitly forbidden. Another example is found among the Neoi of Cyzicus, Ditt. Or., II, 748, 15 (3rd cent. B.C.). On a Ptolemaic decree in honour of the πολίτευμα of the Idumeans in Memphis we find the expression ἐπὶ συναγωγῆς τῆς γενηθείσης ἐν τῶι ἄνω Ἀπολλ[ω]νιείωι, Ditt. Or., II, 737, 1 f. (2nd cent. B.C.). [7] In BGU, IV, 1137, 1 ff. (6 B.C.) συναγωγή is used with ref. to the imperial cult and denotes a gathering of the Alexandrian σύνοδος Σεβαστὴ τοῦ θεοῦ Αὐτοκράτορος Καίσαρος which took place ἐν τῷ Παρατόμωι. As on the two previous inscr., the place of meeting is mentioned on one in honour of the board of a guild, ἐπὶ τῆς γενηθείσης συναγωγῆς ἐν τῶι Ἀριστίωνος Κλεοπατρείωι, Preisigke Sammelb., V, 8267, 3 (5 B.C.) from Kôm Truga in the Nile delta, cf. also the resolution from Kôm Tukala, ibid., IV, 7457, 2 f.; also the resolution (104 B.C.) of a union which calls itself: κοινόν (sc. ἐκ τοῦ γυμνασίου), [8] where we find the phrase ἐπὶ τῆς γενηθείσης συναγωγῆς, ibid., V, 8031, 16. Whether συναγωγή has this sense among the thiasites of Nicaea in Bithynia too is contested. The ref. is to a Cybele inscr. acc. to which the priestesses of Cybele and Apollo are to be crowned ἐν τῆι τοῦ Διὸς συναγωγῆι, ibid., I, 4981, 6 (2nd cent. B.C.). If συναγωγή is used metonymically here for the place or site of assembly [9] this is an exception in the non-Jewish and non-Chr. sphere, though it is not impossible (cf. ἀγορά, ἐκκλησία, προσευχή → II, 808, 10 ff.). συναγωγή is also used for a pagan cultic gathering in Ps.-Philo, Eus. Praep. Ev., 1, 10, 52 (GCS, 43, 1 [1954], 53): Ζωροάστρης δὲ ὁ μάγος ἐν τῇ Ἱερᾷ Συναγωγῇ τῶν Περσικῶν φησι. On the burial inscr. in Cos which King Antiochus I of Commagene set up for himself (1st cent. B.C.) συναγωγαί, πανηγύρεις "festal gatherings" and θυσίαι are mentioned together in annual celebration of his birthday and accession, Ditt. Or., I, 383, 94 f. In gen. συναγωγή is used predominantly for the festive assembly or meeting, whether cultic or not; this is esp. so outside Egypt. συναγωγή is close here to συνα-

---

[4] Cf. Poland Vereinswesen, 155 f., 247 f.; Poland Synagoge, 1284-6; Ziebarth, 7, 144; San Nicolò, 41-53; Schürer, II, 505, n. 12 and 506, n. 13.

[5] BCH, 14 (1890), 625, No. 27 (συναγωγὴ τῆς γερουσίας from Tabai), cf. Poland Vereinswesen, 272, n. * and 248, n. *; Poland Synagoge, 1284.

[6] Cf. on this C. Roberts, T. C. Skeat and A. D. Nock, "The Guild of Zeus Hypsistos," HThR, 29 (1936), 39-88; U. Wilcken, "Urkunden-Referat," APF, 12 (1937), 219-221.

[7] Cf. M. L. Strack, "Inschr. aus ptolemäischer Zeit," APF, 3 (1906), 128-130.

[8] Cf. H. Kortenbeutel, "ΓΥΜΝΑΣΙΟΝ u. ΒΟΥΛΗ," APF, 12 (1937), 44-53.

[9] So Pr.-Bauer s.v. and J. Leipoldt in Haas, 9/11 (1926), No. 154 and p. XIX. Preisigke Wört., s.v. and Dib. Jk. on 2:2, however, take συναγωγή to be a society here (M. Perdrizet, "Reliefs Mysiens," BCH, 23 [1899], 595: confrérie), Poland Vereinswesen, 248; Poland Synagoge, 1285 f. festive gathering, also Schürer, II, 505, n. 12.

γώγιον "picnic," "feast," cf. Athen., 8, 68 (365c). In Diog. L., II, 129 it is used (par. ἑορτή) for a feast in the court of Nicocreon.[10] Acc. to the statutes of the guild of Zeus Hypsistos (→ 800, 11 ff.) the ἡγούμενος was to arrange a πόσις for the members monthly ἐν τῶι τοῦ Διὸς ἱερῶι ἐν αἷς ἐν ἀνδ[ρῶνι] κοινῶι σπένδοντες εὐχέσθωισαν, Preisigke Sammelb., V, 7835, 8 f. and cf. the regulations for the feast of the κοινόν in the Testament of Epicteta: The συναγωγή includes the banquet δεῖπνον, drinking, crowns, perfumes μύρον, sacrifices. The same applies to the societies of Anthister, Diomedon, and the Neoi.[11] Cf. also Cl. Al. Paed., II, 4, 4: ταῖς μὲν γὰρ ἐπὶ τῇ εὐφροσύνῃ συναγωγαῖς ἐγκαταλέγοιμεν ⟨ἂν⟩ καὶ αὐτοὶ δειπνάριά τε καὶ ἄριστα καὶ δοχὰς εἰκότως ἂν καλοῖμεν τὴν συνήλυσιν ταύτην.

In distinction from ἐκκλησία, the popular assembly of enfranchised free citizens (→ III, 513, 18 ff.), συναγωγή is not a constitutional term. It is seldom used for a national assembly, cf. with ref. to the council of Andania ἐν τᾶι πρώται συννόμωι συναγωγᾶι τῶν συνέδρων, Ditt. Syll.[3], II, 736, 48 f. (92 B.C.), the Lycian Koinon, Ditt. Or., II, 556, 3 (1st cent. B.C.?) and on a psephism an Attic συναγωγὴ τῶν λογιστῶν (συναγογὲς τō λλογιστōν), Ditt. Syll.[3], I, 91, 9 (c. 420 B.C.). One has to remember, of course, that national gatherings had a religious character, and even if in many cases it was only a formality they opened with prayer and sacrifice.[12]

Though συναγωγή is not a common guild-term, there are instances of its use for guilds themselves. A transition to this may be seen in the decree of the κοινὸν τῶν Ἀτταλιστῶν, CIG, II, 3069, 11 f. (2nd cent. B.C.) in Teos, where συναγωγή and αἵρεσις are par.[13] An inscr. on a marble altar between Rodosto and Eregli near ancient Perinthus calls a barbers' union συν[α]γωγή τῶν κουρ[έ]ω[ν][14] (1st cent. B.C.). On a marble altar in Perinthus we also find συναγω[γ]ὴ [κ]ωποπωλῶν for a rowers' union,[15] and Poll. Onom., IX, 143 mentions a συναγωγὴ ναυτῶν.

One may thus conclude that συναγωγή does not have a purely secular character[16] and that, unlike ἐκκλησία, it is not a political term, though conversely ἐκκλησία plays no part in guild life → III, 513, n. 25. In profane Greek we also do not find, or only exceptionally, the intrinsically possible metonymy meeting = place or house of meeting.

---

[10] Cf. Athen., 5, 19 (192b): πᾶσα δὲ συμποσίου συναγωγὴ παρὰ τοῖς ἀρχαίοις τὴν αἰτίαν εἰς θεὸν ἀνέφερε, and 8, 64 (362e): ἔρανοι δέ εἰσιν αἱ ἀπὸ τῶν συμβαλλομένων συναγωγαί, ἀπὸ τοῦ συνερᾶν καὶ συμφέρειν ἕκαστον. But συναγωγαί is a conjecture based on Eustath. Thessal. Comm. in Il., 1119, 22; the cod. have εἰσαγωγαί here, also Eustath. Thessal. Comm. in Od., 1702, 6 [Krämer]. Cf. also Ditt. Syll.[3], II, 734, 10 (94 B.C. Delphi) and Ditt. Or., II, 748, 15 (3rd. cent. B.C.).

[11] Cf. Poland Vereinswesen, 247 f., 330. 332; Poland Synagoge, 1284 f.; Ziebarth, 144. San Nicolò, 42 f. warns, however, against ref. συναγωγή only to religious and social gatherings as distinct from official meetings of members, or generally against opposing festive gatherings to business meetings. Poland Synagoge, 1285, shows that συναγωγή was used in Egypt for any gathering.

[12] Cf. the bibl. → III, 514, n. 28, also C. G. Brandis, Art. "Ἐκκλησία," Pauly-W., 5 (1905), 2173; O. Linton, Art. "Ekklesia," RAC, IV, 906 with ref. to ἐκκλησία.

[13] Schürer, II, 506, n. 13. Poland Synagoge, 1284 takes συναγωγή to ref. here to the founding and naming of a guild, but for Dib. Jk. on 2:2 and O. Michel, "Das Zeugnis d. NT von d. Gemeinde," FRL, NF, 39 (1941), 12, n. 7 it is a union or society. Poland Synagoge, 1286 notes that συναγωγή was used for a union only among artisans and at a later time.

[14] Archäol.-epigraphische Mitteilungen aus Österreich-Ungarn, 19 (1896), 67, 5 f.

[15] Jahreshefte d. Österreichischen Archäol. Instituts in Wien, 23 (1926), Beiblatt, 172.

[16] The term is not, then, as unburdened and colourless as Rost Vorstufen, 127 f. makes it out to be in order to isolate it from ordinary cultic guilds.

B. συναγωγή in the Septuagint.

1. Occurrence. συναγωγή occurs over 200 times in the LXX, mostly for עֵדָה (some 130 times) and קָהָל (some 35 times). [17] Only 20 times are other Hbr. words transl. by it, and in these it is the equivalent of 16 Hbr. words. עֵדָה is the P term for the national, legal and cultic community of Israel gathered around the אֹהֶל מוֹעֵד. It is the preferred term in Ex. and Lv. and the only word in Nu., but it does not occur in Dt. After and outside P we find it 24 times (only 3 in the prophets), the meaning being essentially the same. [18] קָהָל is used esp. in Dt., Ezr., Neh. and Ch. and means "notice" of, "summons," "coming together" to an assembly for cultic celebration, judgment, or war: with few exceptions the ref. is to all male citizens (עַם). [19] קָהָל and עֵדָה are used with no essential distinction in meaning. [20]

2. ἐκκλησία and συναγωγή. The same applies to the use of ἐκκλησία and συναγωγή (cf. Prv. 5:14: ἐν μέσῳ ἐκκλησίας καὶ συναγωγῆς), esp. as συναγωγή can be used for both Hbr. words. [21] There are no obvious inner reasons why קָהָל should sometimes be rendered ἐκκλησία and other times συναγωγή. In individual books the one term may be used fairly consistently, e.g., συναγωγή in Ex.-Nu. The difference in translation is to be traced back in the main to the difference in translators. But this explanation does not wholly suffice, as may be seen from ψ 39:10 f., where in direct proximity קָהָל רָב is rendered ἐκκλησία μεγάλη the one time and συναγωγή πολλή the other. [22] That קָהָל is mostly transl. συναγωγή in the Pent. may be due to the fact that the translators found in the legal parts of the OT the magna carta of their own synagogal communities and tried to express by this rendering their special link with the "synagogue" of the age that received the Law. [23] Whereas קָהָל could be transl. equally

---

[17] קָהָל is transl. twice as often by ἐκκλησία, yet this is never used for עֵדָה, but almost solely for קָהָל. G. Gloege, "Reich Gottes u. Kirche im NT," Nt.liche Forschungen, II, 4 (1929), 206 stands in need of correction when he says that LXX almost always has ἐκκλησία for קָהָל and only occasionally συναγωγή.

[18] Rost Vorstufen, 32-87.

[19] Ibid., 7-32.

[20] Cf. the passages where both are used, Ex. 16:1 ff.; Nu. 10:1 ff.; 14:1 ff.; 16:1 ff.; 17:6 ff.; 20:1 ff. etc. Dahl, 44, 285, n. 66 rightly stresses against Rost Vorstufen that the distinction is not to be pressed and can be effaced altogether. Cf. also Schmidt, 263; → III, 528, 45 ff.; Linton, 145; Schürer, II, 504 f., n. 11; Krauss Altertümer, 13, H. W. Hertzberg, "Werdende Kirche im AT," Theol. Ex., NF, 20 (1950), 19 thinks the two terms are largely correlative and mean the same in practice. Gloege, op. cit., 208 f. argues that עֵדָה is a sociological term, קָהָל a theocentric one (the saved people gathered before God), but this is quite untenable.

[21] Cf. both in Nu. 16:3; also 10:3 and 7; 17:10 and 12; 20:1, 2, 8, 11 and 4, 6, 10, 12; Ex. 16:1, 2 and 3; Lv. 4:13, 15 and 14, 21. Gloege's view (op. cit., 207) that "LXX draws a sharper line of division between the two terms than HT" is completely without foundation. Cf. → n. 209.

[22] Rost Vorstufen, 114 thinks the translator differentiates here between the legal gathering (ἐκκλησία) and the cultic (συναγωγή), but this is not wholly convincing since ἐκκλησία has a clear cultic ref. in the Ps. (ψ 21:23, 26, v. 26 ἐκκλησία μεγάλη, ψ 34:18: ἐκκλησία πολλή) and only once is συναγωγή used in the Ps. for the worshipping community, ψ 110:1.

[23] Rost Vorstufen, 126 f., 129; Dahl, 66, 68. It may be doubted whether the translators preferred συναγωγή because they wanted to present their communities as religious communities with no political claims (Rost Vorstufen, 128 f., 133). For they were not afraid of using ἐκκλησία for קָהָל even where there might be misunderstanding. Similarly stories which make the συναγωγή responsible for justice and war would surely cause confusion, → 804, 23 ff.

by ἐκκλησία or συναγωγή, עֵדָה was always rendered συναγωγή except in a few instances in which we find Ισραηλ (Nu. 4:34), υἱοὶ Ισραηλ (Nu. 3:7), ἐπισύστασις (Nu. 17:5), συστροφή (Ju. 14:8A), παρεμβολή (Nu. 17:11) etc.

3. Gathering. In detail the following points call for notice. The term is not a tt. even in Lv. Esp. when it is not the equivalent of קָהָל or עֵדָה it has the senses familiar to us from profane Gk. → 799, 2 ff. Thus it means the "collecting" of revenues ἐκοπίασεν πλούσιος ἐν συναγωγῇ χρημάτων, Sir. 31:3, or the "bringing in" of the harvest ἑορτὴ συναγωγῆς, Ex. 34:22, cf. 23:16, and esp. the "assembling" of all kinds of things, men, objects, animals: a pile of stones συναγωγὴ λίθων par. ἐν μέσῳ χαλίκων, Job 8:17, water συναγωγὴ ὕδατος, Lv. 11:36 alongside πηγαί and λάκκος (cf. Is. 19:6; 37:25), a crowd of people συναγωγὴ ὄχλου πολλοῦ (Da. 11:10),[24] a number of young men συναγωγὴ νεανίσκων (Jer. 6:11); a group of νεανίσκοι at the dance: συναγωγὴ παιζόντων (Ιερ. 38[31]:4, cf. v. 13), hosts of peoples συναγωγαὶ ἐθνῶν (Zeph. 3:8). But συναγωγή can have the same meaning when עֵדָה is the original. Here the Gk. word takes on the sense of עֵדָה, "assembly," "host." It is used for a swarm of bees in Ju. 14:8B, συναγωγὴ μελισσῶν, for a herd of bulls in ψ 67:31 συναγωγὴ τῶν ταύρων, in a bad sense for a company of wicked men in ψ 21:17 συναγωγὴ πονηρευομένων, for a gang of violent men in ψ 85:14 συναγωγὴ κραταιῶν,[25] for a host of peoples in ψ 7:8 συναγωγὴ λαῶν. συναγωγή can also take over this purely secular sense from קָהָל, esp. in Ez., where συναγωγή is used 9 times for it and ὄχλος 5 times, cf. also Prv. 21:16: συναγωγὴ γιγάντων; a συναγωγὴ μεγάλη in Ιερ. 51 (44):15 or a συναγωγὴ πολλή in Ez. 38:4 is simply a gt. no., e.g. of women, or horses and riders. In Ez. 26:7 συναγωγὴ ἐθνῶν πολλῶν is used with ἵπποι καὶ ἄρματα καὶ ἱππεῖς to denote the Bab. army, cf. also Da. 11:10-13. Ασσουρ καὶ πᾶσα ἡ συναγωγὴ αὐτοῦ in Ez. 32:22 ref. to the whole people of Assyria (buried in sheol) and its army, cf. Tyre in Ez. 27:27, 34 and Gog in 38:7, also συναγωγὴ μεγάλη par. δύναμις πολλή in 38:15. In this connection συναγωγή is often used in the plur., cf. the surprisingly consistent συναγωγαὶ ἐθνῶν Gn. 28:3; 35:11; 48:4, cf. also Ιερ. 27(50):9.[26]

4. Assembly. A difference from profane Gk. is that the sense "assembly" is comparatively rare. 1 Macc. 14:28 mentions a συναγωγὴ μεγάλη ἱερέων καὶ λαοῦ καὶ ἀρχόντων ἔθνους καὶ τῶν πρεσβυτέρων τῆς χώρας, and we find συναγωγὴ τοῦ λαοῦ in Ιερ. 33(26):17 for a popular assembly or crowd, and a συναγωγὴ τῆς πόλεως in Sus. 28 → 805, 31 ff. Elsewhere συνάγω, Nu. 1:18, 8:9 etc., συνάγομαι, Nu. 10:13; 1 Macc. 2:42, ἐπισυνάγομαι, 1 Macc. 7:12, ἐκκλησιάζω, Lv. 8:3; Nu. 20:8, ἐξεκκλησιάζω, Lv. 8:4; Nu. 20:10 etc., ἐξεκκλησιάζομαι, Jos. 18:1; Ju. 20:1, συναθροίζω, Ex. 35:1, συναθροίζομαι, Nu. 16:11 are all commonly combined with συναγωγή, but in the overwhelming majority of instances in which one might ask whether the meaning is assembly this nuance is certainly present but the accent is put more strongly on the fact that this is a community gathered for common action and not on the fact that the community is in assembly. The two often coincide, so that no strict differentiation can

---

[24] In all 4 instances of συναγωγή in Da. 11:10-13 Θ has ὄχλος.

[25] O. Plöger, "Theokratie u. Eschatologie," Wissenschaftliche Monographien zum AT u. NT, 2 (1959), 49 thinks the HT of Ps. 1:5; 22:16; 86:14 expresses the "manifold distinctions in the post-exilic community" and "its division into conventicles," cf. also Rost Vorstufen, 86, who finds here and in Ps. 68:31; Job 15:34 the party divisiveness of later Judaism, but against this cf. H. J. Kraus, Psalmen, I, Bibl. Komm. AT, 15 (1960) on עֵדָה in Ps. 1:5. It is surprising that where συναγωγή would seem to be closest (Ps. 1:5) LXX has ἐν βουλῇ; this is possibly due to the fact that LXX did not read עֵדָה, but עֵצָה, the usual equivalent of βουλή.

[26] It is quite possible that in Gn. 28:3; 35:11; 48:4 the transl. have in view congregations of proselytes, Dahl, 66; Rost Vorstufen, 117. Perhaps they see a danger in these at Zeph. 3:8: τὸ κρίμα μου εἰς συναγωγὰς ἐθνῶν, Rost Vorstufen, 125.

be made. Yet the aspect of assembling may be less prominent or indeed absent altogether, cf. the various expressions denoting the officers of the συναγωγή, οἱ ἄρχοντες τῆς συναγωγῆς in Ex. 16:22; 34:31 etc., οἱ πρεσβύτεροι τῆς συναγωγῆς in Lv. 4:15; Ju. 21:16, ἀρχηγοὶ συναγωγῆς in Nu. 16:2.

5. The Whole Congregation. συναγωγή means above all the whole congregation of Israel. [27] Par. are terms like λαός in Ex. 17:1 f.; Nu. 14:1 etc., πᾶς Ἰσραηλ in Nu. 16:33 f.; Jos. 22:17 f., οἱ υἱοὶ Ἰσραηλ in Nu. 8:20; 14:27, πάντες οἱ υἱοὶ Ἰσραηλ in Nu. 14:10. Common also are the many more precise descriptions, πᾶσα συναγωγή in Lv. 9:5; 16:33 etc., πᾶσα συναγωγὴ Ἰσραηλ in Lv. 4:13; 22:18 etc., συναγωγὴ Ἰσραηλ in Ex. 12:19; Nu. 16:9. The most popular are πᾶσα ἡ συναγωγή in Lv. 8:3; 10:3, 6 etc. and πᾶσα συναγωγὴ υἱῶν Ἰσραηλ in Ex. 12:3, 47; 16:1 f. etc. This also shows that συναγωγή does not represent a religious entity (→ III, 359, 16 ff.) but the whole people of Israel, cf. Ex. 16:1 ff.; Nu. 14:1 ff. In content the ref. is usually to the congregation assembled for cultic or legal purposes. In most cases the συναγωγή is the cultic community, whether keeping the Passover ἐν τοῖς οἴκοις (Ex. 12:6 f., 46 f.), taking up the ark into the temple (3 Βασ. 8:5 O; 2 Ch. 5:6), or — and this is the rule — engaging in sacrifice and other sacral acts before the sacred tabernacle ἔναντι κυρίου, Lv. 9:5; cf. 8:3 f.; Nu. 8:9 etc. In the συναγωγή (par. cultic ἐγγίζοντες κυρίῳ) God will glorify Himself ἐν τοῖς ἐγγίζουσίν μοι ἁγιασθήσομαι καὶ ἐν πάσῃ τῇ συναγωγῇ δοξασθήσομαι, Lv. 10:3. His δόξα appears here, Lv. 9:5 f.; Nu. 14:10. In Ps. the only ref. to the συναγωγή assembled for worship is in ψ 110:1: ἐξομολογήσομαί σοι, κύριε ... ἐν βουλῇ εὐθείων καὶ συναγωγῇ.

As the national community the συναγωγή has legal functions too. The homicide must answer before the forum of the community ἔναντι τῆς συναγωγῆς εἰς κρίσιν, Jos. 20:9, cf. v. 6. Nu. 35:12, 24 f. also ref. to the κρίνειν of the συναγωγή, cf. Ιερ. 33(26):17. The whole community must stone the blasphemer and the desecrator of the Sabbath, Lv. 24:14, 16; Nu. 15:36. Jeroboam is summoned εἰς τὴν συναγωγήν and made king over Israel, 3 Βασ. 12:20. The συναγωγή is also in charge of military matters. It is distinguished from the πολεμισταί in Nu. 31:27, but it despatches soldiers acc. to Ju. 21:10. The community grumbles in Jos. 9:18 because μάχεσθαι is forbidden, and in Nu. 26:2 πᾶσα συναγωγὴ υἱῶν Ἰσραηλ is used for the men able to bear arms, cf. also Nu. 20:4. One might also ref. to 1 Macc. 3:44: ἠθροίσθη ἡ συναγωγὴ τοῦ εἶναι ἑτοίμους εἰς πόλεμον...

Though the transl. of the LXX might often have identified the OT συναγωγή with their own synagogal congregations, they did not whittle down the strong historical character of the OT συναγωγή. The constitutive events of Israel's history are bound up with the term συναγωγή (ἐκκλησία is not used at all in Ex.-Nu.). Moses and Aaron speak to the συναγωγή: Ἑσπέρας γνώσεσθε ὅτι κύριος ἐξήγαγεν ὑμᾶς ἐκ γῆς Αἰγύπτου, Ex. 16:6. The συναγωγή is the wandering desert community, Ex. 16:1. Ἀνακαλεῖν τὴν συναγωγὴν καὶ ἐξαίρειν τὰς παρεμβολάς belong together, Nu. 10:2. Moving ἀπαίρειν characterises the συναγωγή, Nu. 20:22. Its march is through the wilderness, Ex. 16:1; Nu. 14:35; 20:1. This leads to murmuring, Ex. 16:1 f; Nu. 20:4. Hence it is not an ideal community; it can be called πονηρά, Nu. 14:27, 35. It experiences God's πληγή, Nu. 31:16; Jos. 22:17. But it is also the community which knows God's wonders, Ex. 16:4 ff.; Nu. 20:11. The conquest is promised to it, Nu. 14:7 f. With

---

[27] Women and children are included. L. Rost → III, 529, n. 90 thinks the קָהָל included women and children after the exile but the validity of συναγωγή "was linked with the presence and participation of men alone." But this applies only to the Rabb. συναγωγή = כְּנֶסֶת, not the LXX συναγωγή = עֵדָה, cf. Kosmala, 63. Cf., e.g., Ex. 35:20 with v. 22, 29. συναγωγή is also used for קָהָל and this is the whole community including women acc. to Rost, cf. Rost Vorstufen, 10, 16. 24 f. on Nu. 16:33 and Ιερ. 51(44):15.

passages which call the whole congregation πονηρά there are also those which distinguish the true συναγωγή from a rebellious συναγωγή, Nu. 16:24. The constantly quoted example of such a συναγωγή ἡ ἐπισυστᾶσα (Nu. 27:3) is the συναγωγή Κορε, Nu. 16:1 ff.; cf. 14:27, 35; 26:9; Sir. 45:18, or Αβιρων, ψ 105:17. In relation to this the συναγωγή is told: ἀναχωρήσατε, Nu. 16:24; cf. 26:9 f. and ἀποσχίσθητε or ἐκχωρήσατε ἐκ μέσου τῆς συναγωγῆς ταύτης, Nu. 16:21; 17:10. The true community is that of Yahweh. At God's behest Moses tells it: ἅγιοι ἔσεσθε, Lv. 19:2; cf. Nu. 16:3: πᾶσα ἡ συναγωγὴ πάντες ἅγιοι. It is the συναγωγὴ κυρίου יהוה עֲדַת, Nu. 27:17; 31:16; Jos. 22:16 f., יהוה קְהַל, Nu. 16:3; 20:4. This yields the saying in ψ 73:2 with its theological import: μνήσθητι τῆς συναγωγῆς σου, ἧς ἐκτήσω ἀπ' ἀρχῆς. Finally in Is. 56:8 συναγωγή is used for the saved eschatological community which is gathered from the dispersion: εἶπεν κύριος ὁ συνάγων τοὺς διεσπαρμένους Ισραηλ, ὅτι συνάξω ἐπ' αὐτὸν συναγωγήν, and acc. to Ez. 37:10 the dead of the house of Israel who are brought to life again by God's Spirit constitute a συναγωγὴ πολλὴ σφόδρα. Ιερ. 38(31):4, 13 is also eschatological, and cf. Zech. 9:12 and Ps. Sol. 17:43 f. An important pt. for the time which follows is that the συναγωγή is regarded as the recipient of the Decalogue or the Law. It assembles to hear the Sabbath commandment in Ex. 35:1. In Dt. 5:22 the Decalogue is followed immediately by the statement: τὰ ῥήματα ταῦτα ἐλάλησεν κύριος πρὸς πᾶσαν συναγωγὴν ὑμῶν ἐν τῷ ὄρει. In the blessing of Moses in Dt. 33:4 the νόμος, ὃν ἐνετείλατο ἡμῖν Μωυσῆς is defined as κληρονομία συναγωγαῖς Ιακωβ (plur.!), cf. Sir. 24:23; also Nu. 15:15: νόμος εἷς ἔσται ὑμῖν (sc. the συναγωγή) καὶ τοῖς προσηλύτοις... νόμος αἰώνιος εἰς γενεὰς ὑμῶν. Keeping God's demands is constitutive for the συναγωγή in all ages. [28]

6. The Individual Congregation. In the OT apocr. esp. there is a splitting up of the total community and a shifting of συναγωγή to the local congregation, Sir. 4:7; Sus. 41, 52, 60. Judaism as a whole is then described in the plur. as the συναγωγαὶ Ισραηλ, Ps. Sol. 10:7 or συναγωγαὶ ὁσίων, 17:16. The συναγωγὴ Ασιδαίων in 1 Macc. 2:42 or συναγωγὴ γραμματέων in 1 Macc. 7:12 is even an *ecclesiola in ecclesia,* [29] and ψ 15:4 probably refers to conflicting synagogues which challenge each other's validity, [30] cf. also the συναγωγὴ ἁμαρτωλῶν in Sir. 16:6 or ἀνόμων in Sir. 21:9.

7. The House of Meeting. It may be noted in conclusion that in LXX with exception of Sus. 28 (unless ἐλθόντες ἐπὶ τὴν συναγωγὴν τῆς πόλεως refers to the assembly → 803, 32 f.) [31] συναγωγή is never used for the house of assembly. [32] To be sure, there are spatial implications in the ref. → 803, 8 ff., esp. the rendering of מָקוֹם in Gn. 1:9 and מִקְוֵה in Lv. 11:36, but never is the synagogue as a building in view. How little LXX took συναγωγή in this sense may be seen from the fact that where a spatial understanding is possible even עֵדָה, which is almost always rendered συναγωγή, is transl. by παρεμβολή instead, Nu. 17:11.

---

[28] It is worth noting, however, that in Ezr. and Neh., esp. Neh. 8, ἐκκλησία is used at the reading of the Law, not συναγωγή.

[29] Cf. Dahl, 67 ("closed congregation of the righteous"); Michel, *op. cit.* (→ n. 13), 10; → III, 526, 4 ff.; but cf. Rost Vorstufen, 135 f.

[30] Rost Vorstufen, 125 ref. to συναγωγὴ Ιουδα in 3 Βασ. 12:21 and thinks the transl. is reading back the Samaritan schism into the age of the disruption.

[31] Acc. to Nu. 5:2 A (συναγωγή, other MSS παρεμβολή) lepers are not allowed in synagogues, or one part of them [Bertram] → n. 211. On the reading συναγωγάς in ψ 73:8 → n. 70.

[32] Surprisingly Preisker ZG, 263, n. 2 says it is, but this is due to a misunderstanding of I. Elbogen, Art. "Synagoge," RGG², V, 947.

C. συναγωγή in Judaism.

I. Usage.

1. Greek-Speaking Judaism.

a. In the first instance Gk.-speaking Judaism continues LXX usage. Here too, though rarely, συναγωγή is still found in the profane sense, e.g., Jos. Ant., 15, 346: συναγωγαὶ ὑδάτων with προπαρασκευαὶ σιτίων. Extremely rare is the sense of "gathering," cf. perhaps a badly preserved pap. of the 1st cent. B.C. whose Jewish character is dubious: [33] ἐπὶ τῆς γ[ε]νηθείσης συναγωγῆς ἐν τῆι προσευχῆι, CPJud, 138, 1 and probably also Jos. Ant., 19, 305: συναγωγὴν Ἰουδαίων κωλύοντες εἶναι (→ 808, 4 f.), though → ἀρχισυνάγωγος, n. 15.

Much more numerous are instances of συναγωγή for the Jewish community. We again find here the shift already noted in the apocr. (→ 805, 24 ff.) as compared with stock LXX usage (→ 802, 1 ff.). The συναγωγή is the individual synagogal congregation rather than the total community (→ 804, 5 ff.). This may be seen esp. in the many synagogue inscr. and Jewish burial inscr. from Rome. [34] There is often a clear distinction between συναγωγή == congregation and the building, for which other terms are used. Thus in inscr. from Panticapaion (the Crimea) συναγωγή τῶν Ἰουδαίων is "the Jewish congregation," [35] CIJ, I, 683, 19 and I, 684, 22 f., while the building is called προσευχή, I, 683, 6 f., 13 f. and 684, 6 and 20. In an inscr. from Stobi (Macedonia) συναγωγή is distinguished from ὁ ἅγιος τόπος, CIJ, I, 694, 5 or 10 f., in an inscr. from Gerasa συναγωγή and ἁγι(ω)[τάτῳ] τόπῳ, II, 867, in another from Phocaea συναγωγή and ὁ οἶκος, II, 738, 6 or 2. συναγωγή can also be used abs., so an inscr. from Aegina, CIJ, I, 723, from Acmonia, II, 766, 11, from Gerasa, II, 867, from Lower Egypt, II, 1447. Very often a closer definition is given, so τῶν Ἰουδαίων in the inscr. from Pantikapaion → line 17 f., Nicomedia, CIJ, 799, and Phocaea → line 21 f.; also P. Oxy., IX, 1205, 7 → n. 174. But more often the closer definition consists of the name of a person, place etc., cf. esp. the Roman burial inscr., [36] which agree in putting the name of the relevant synagogue in the gen. Some of the 13 synagogues thus far known are named after famous people: συναγωγή Αὐγουστησίων, CIJ, I, 301, 368, 416, 496; συναγωγή Ἀγριππησίων, I, 425, 503, [συνα]γωγή [Ἡ]ροδίων, I, 173, [37] συναγωγή Βολυμνησίων, I, 343, 417, others after the city districts of Rome: Σιβουρησίων (no συναγωγή), I, 18, 67, 380 etc., συναγωγή Καμπησίων, I, 88, 319, 433, some after the homes of the first members: συναγωγή Τριπολειτῶν, I, 390, Σεκηνῶν (no συναγωγή, Scina in Africa?), I, 7, συναγ(ωγή) Ἄρκ[ης Λι]βάνου, I, 501, [38] some after their occupa-

---

[33] Cf. V. A. Tcherikover-A. Fuks, CPJud, I (1957), 252 f.

[34] Rost Vorstufen, 152, n. 2 thinks συναγωγή in the Roman inscr. refers to the buildings, but there is no basis for this view.

[35] Krauss Altertümer, 112, n. 4 can adduce no examples in favour of the sense "synagogue board" and he is even more mistaken in questioning whether συναγωγή can have the sense of "congregation."

[36] Cf. on this N. Müller, "Die jüd. Katakombe am Monteverde zu Rom," Schriften hrsgg. von d. Gesellschaft zur Förderung der Wissenschaft d. Judt. (1912), 106-121; H. W. Beyer-H. Lietzmann, "Jüd. Denkmäler, I. Die jüd. Katakombe der Villa Torlonia in Rom," Stud. z. spätantiken Kunstgeschichte, 4 (1930), 28-41; Krauss Altertümer, 247-257; Juster, I, 415; Schürer, III, 81-5; J. B. Frey, CIJ, I, LXX-LXXXI; also "Les communautés juives à Rome aux premiers temps de l'Église," Recherches de Science Religieuse, 20 (1930), 269-297 and 21 (1931), 129-168; also "Le Judaisme à Rome aux premiers temps de l'Église," Biblica, 12 (1931), 129-156; S. Collon, "Remarques sur les quartiers juifs de la Rome antique," Mélanges d'Archéologie et d'Histoire de l'École française de Rome, 57 (1940), 72-94; Leon, 46-74, 135-166.

[37] But cf. Leon, 159-162 for another suggestion.

[38] For alternatives to the last two names cf. Leon, 150 f., 163 f.

tion, I, 384, 537 etc.: συναγωγή Καλκαρησίων = calcarienses, "lime-burners," [39] and some after their symbol: συναγωγή 'Ελαίας, I, 509 or 'Ελέας, I, 281. [40] The synagogue of the Vernaculi [41] was for native Roman Jews, while the συναγωγή 'Εβρέων [42] was the congregation which had special links with Palestine by language and derivation. Thus far no more precise definition has been found with the titles μήτηρ or πατήρ συναγωγῆς, CIJ, I, 93 and 166 (both from Rome). In a Stobi inscr. we have a prepositional attribute rather than the gen. ὁ πατὴρ τῆς ἐν Στόβοις συναγωγῆς, CIJ, I, 694, 4 f.

b. Unlike the LXX (→ 805, 31 ff.) NT Judaism uses συναγωγή esp. in the local cultic sense for the "house of meeting," "the synagogue." [43] How and when this metonymy developed we cannot say for certain. It must have been between the LXX and primitive Christianity and in the Dispersion rather than Palestine. [44] The literary attestation is slender. Philo has only one instance εἰς ἱεροὺς ἀφικνούμενοι τόπους, οἳ καλοῦνται συναγωγαί, Omn. Prob. Lib., 81. There are 4 examples in Jos.: Bell., 2, 285, 289 (→ 827, 11ff.); 7, 44; Ant., 19, 300. There is ampler witness on inscr., but dating is highly uncertain in this area. On inscr. the use is often abs. with ref. in each case to the synagogue in or on which the inscr. is placed, so the inscr. from Tafas in Syria, CIJ, II, 861, Aegina, I, 722, Jerusalem, II, 1404, 4 (in all 3 cases with οἰκοδομέω) and Mantinaea in Arcadia, I, 720. Elsewhere a definition is given, on an inscr. from Corinth 'Εβρ[έων], CIJ, I, 718, on others from Side in Pamphylia, II, 781 and Gerasa, II, 867 ἁγιωτάτη (→ n. 157), in Deliler in Lydia ἡ ἁγιοτ[άτη σ]υναγωγὴ τῶν 'Εβραίων, II, 754, 1-3, in Ornithopolis 'Ορνιθοκόμης, II, 878. The senses "congregation" and "synagogue building" cannot always be sharply differentiated, [45] esp. as each congregation had its own building and both bore the same name. Τὸ συναγωγὴ 'Εβρέων in Rome ("congregation") corresponds συναγωγὴ 'Εβραίων in Deliler, II, 754 and Corinth, I, 718 ("synagogue"). In many

[39] A topographical sense is also possible, Frey, CIJ, I, LXXV f.: Calcaria in the neighbourhood of the Circus Flaminius, but cf. Leon, 144. For the above sense cf. Schürer, III, 84; Krauss Altertümer, 256 with a ref. to other Jewish guilds.

[40] Cf. Schürer, III, 83 f. Krauss Altertümer, 230, 255 f. and Frey, I, LXXVII f. prefer a local ref. here too: Elaia in Mysia. Acc. to Schürer, II, 524 the synagogue of Sepphoris mentioned in jBer., 3 (6a, 71) called itself כנישתא דגופנה דציפורין after the emblem of the vine, but cf. Krauss Altert., 210, n. 2 (Synagogue of the Gophnians after the town of Gophna), cf. Levy Wört., I, 352: synagogue on a vineyard; for other possibilities and bibl. Leon, 145-147. Acc. to the daring thesis of W. L. Knox, St. Paul and the Church of Jerusalem (1925), 258, n. 17 the συναγωγὴ 'Ελαίας was the first site of the Roman mission and underlay the metaphor in R. 11:17 ff. Paul is reminding his readers "that though they are at the moment the true synagogue of the Olive, yet the old branches of the cultivated tree, i.e., the Jewish members of the synagogue of the Olive, are really their superiors and are not to be despised."

[41] Συναγωγὴ Βερνακλησίων etc. CIJ, I, 318, 383, 398, 494; cf. Schürer, III, 83; Krauss Altert., 253; Frey, I, LXXVII; Leon, 154-157.

[42] CIJ, I, 510, cf. also 291, 317, 535, cf. Schürer, III, 83; Krauss Altert., 256 f.; Frey, I, LXXVI f. → III, 368, 31 ff.; Müller, op. cit., 109-111; Jackson-Lake, I, 5, 62-65; Knox, op. cit., 277, n. 34; Wnd. 2 K. on 11:22; Dib. Ph. on 3:5; for other suggestions cf. Leon, 148 f., K. Galling, "Die jüd. Katakomben in Rom als ein Beitrag zur jüd. Konfessionskunde," ThStKr, 103 (1931), 354 takes 'Εβραῖος in the sense of 'Ιουδαῖος as the name of the oldest Jewish congregation in Rome, cf. also J. Munck, "Pls. u. d. Heilsgeschichte," Acta Jutlandica, 26, 1 (1954), 212.

[43] The term passed as a loan word into Coptic, Latin, then English, French, German etc.

[44] Krauss Altert., 10, 15; Dahl, 65; but Schürer, II, 518 thinks it was only in the post-Chr. period that the word passed into the usage of the Dispersion. Ac., however, hardly follows Palestinian usage as he supposes.

[45] Cf. [ἐκ τῆς πρ]ο[σ]όδου τῆς συναγ(ωγῆς) ἐμουσώθη, CIJ, I, 723 from Aegina, where the revenues relate to the congregation, ἐμουσώθη to the building.

cases the ref. may be to both. Sometimes the senses may succeed one another: ἡ συναγωγή ("congregation") ἐτείμησεν ... διά τε τὴν ἐνάρετον αὐτῶν [βί]ωσιν καὶ τὴν π[ρ]ὸς τὴν συναγωγὴν ("synagogue building," to whose restoration and furnishing there was ref. earlier) [46] εὔνοιάν τε καὶ σπουδήν, CIJ, II, 766, 11-14 from Acmonia. [47] In Jos. Ant., 19, 305 the two senses "assembly" and "synagogue" obviously part company: συναγωγὴν Ἰουδαίων κωλύοντες εἶναι διὰ τὸ μεταθεῖναι ἐν αὐτῇ (sc. the συναγωγή as "synagogue") τὸν Καίσαρος ἀνδριάντα.

Other Gk. words for the building are προσευχή, [48] προσευκτήριον, Philo Vit. Mos., II, 216: εὐχεῖον, CPJud, 432, 60; σαββατεῖον, Jos. Ant., 16, 164 (→ n. 144); ὁ ἅγιος τόπος, [49] τὸ ἱερόν, [50] ὁ οἶκος, CIJ, II, 738, 2 (from Phocaea); 766, 1 (Acmonia), συναγώγιον, [51] διδασκαλεῖον, Philo Vit. Mos., II, 216; Spec. Leg., II, 62.

2. Aramaic and Hebrew Equivalents among the Rabbis.

The Rabb. equivalent of συναγωγή is not עדה or קהל[52] but Aram. כנשתא[53] or Hbr. כנסת. Both these denote "gathering," e.g., Ab., 4, 11; in Meg., 1, 1 f. כניסה[54] or "con-

---

[46] In line 1 the building is οἶκος. In line 12 L. Robert, "Inscr. Grecques de Sidè en Pamphylie," *Revue de Philologie*, 84 (1958), 41, n. 1 reads δ[ι]άθ[ε]σιν for [βί]ωσιν.

[47] Cf. also the Theodotus inscr. in CIJ, II, 1404 (→ n. 85) if ἐθεμελ[ίω]σαν in line 8 f. is the founding of the congregation rather than the laying of the foundation stone, for in this case συναγωγή is the building and ἥν denotes the congregation, so H. Lietzmann, "Notizen," ZNW, 20 (1921), 171. But θεμελιόω can ref. only to the laying of the foundation stone, cf. Frey, CIJ, II, 334.

[48] Cf. the bibl. → II, 808, n. 9, also Vitringa, 118-130 etc.; Krauss Altert., 16 f.; Krauss Synagoge, 1287 f.; for a non-Jewish example cf. Juv. Satirae, I, 3, 296: *in qua te quaero proseucha*. For Jewish instances → 811, 13 ff.

[49] CIJ, II, 966, 3 (between Jaffa and Gaza); I, 694, 10 f. (Stobi); perhaps also II, 1437 (Alexandria), so Robert, *op. cit.*, 43, n. 4. The superlative is also common, → n. 157. Cf. also the Philo quotation Omn. Prob. Lib., 81 (→ 807, 13 f.) and T. W. Manson, "St. Paul in Ephesus (3). The Corinthian Correspondence," *Bulletin of the John Rylands Library Manchester*, 26 (1941/42), 119 f.

[50] Jos. Bell., 7, 45 of the Antioch synagogue, just before called συναγωγή, cf. also 4, 408; Philo Leg. Gaj., 188, 194, 198, 232, 238, 265 of the synagogue in Alexandria; perhaps also CIJ, II, 758 (Limyra in Asia Minor), so Krauss Altert., 235, but not Frey, II, 22 f.

[51] Philo Som., II, 127 and Leg. Gaj., 311 (Liddell-Scott, *s.v.*; Rost Vorstufen, 147 f.; Moore, III, 88; Frey, I, p. 372); possibly the word means "congregation" here too (Schürer, II, 518, n. 62; Krauss Synagoge, 1287; cf. CIJ, I, 508 from Rome πατὴρ συναγωγίων) or else "meeting" (Dahl, 67). Cf. also P. Katz, "Das Problem d. Urtextes d. LXX," ThZ, 5 (1949), 6, who, disregarding CIJ, I, 508, reads συναγωγεῖον in his effort to steer clear of συναγώγιον == "picnic": "Philo in his flowery way was denoting the place of worship by the suffix -εῖον, which is elsewhere attached to names of the gods." To read συναγωγεῖον in the Jewish inscr. too is contrary to the meaning συναγώγιον == "congregation," though strict differentiation is hardly possible, since ει was then pronounced as a long ῑ and was often written ι [Risch].

[52] עדה and קהל are rare in the Rabb. The former is used only gen. for small societies, Str.-B., I, 733 f.; III, 613; Rost Vorstufen, 141-5; Dahl, 63, 67, 70; Kosmala, 64 f., 72, n. 27; → III, 524, 20.

[53] Almost without exception the Targum has כנשתא for עדה; it occurs in 15 of 112 passages with קהל transl. into Aram. Rost Vorstufen, 98-104.

[54] Cf. Ab., 1, 1a. 2: אנשי כנסת הגדולה. On the Great Synagogue cf. H. L. Strack, Art. "Synagoge, die grosse," RE³, 19, 221-3; K. Marti-G. Beer, *Die Mischna, IV Seder, 9. Traktat* (1927), 3-5 on Ab., 1, 1; Schürer, II, 418; Krauss Altert., 5 f.; S. Zeitlin, "The Origin of the Synagogue," *Proceedings of the Amer. Academy for Jewish Research*, 2 (1930/31), 79-81; E. A. Finkelstein, *The Pharisees and the Men of the Great Synagogue* (1950).

gregation," Yoma, 7, 1; Mak., 3, 12; Bek., 5, 5; Zabim, I, 3, 2,[55] and only seldom "synagogue" as a building, Er., 10, 10; jSanh., 8, 2 (20a, 43); Aram. in Gn. r., 6 on 1:17; CIJ, II, 1195, 6: כנישתא and II, 858, 1 and 3: כנישתה.[56] For the building one usually finds Aram. בית כנשתא or Hbr. בית הכנסת; but כנשתא or כנסת can also be used too, and the two expressions with בית can also be used for the congregation.[57] These merge into one another. Only rarely do we find בית תפלה (Is. 56:7) or בית צלו, corresponding to προσευχή,[58] a simple הבית [59] for ὁ οἶκος, and אתרה קדישה [60] or the simple מקום [61] for (ἅγιος) τόπος.

3. The Usage in Qumran.

Neither כנסת nor בית הכנסת occurs in the Dead Sea Scrolls, but עדה is prominent again.[62] The Damascus "community of the new covenant" and the Qumran sect think of themselves as the eschatological עדת ישראל באחרית הימים (1 QSa 1:1), as עדת הקודש (1:12 f.), and עדת אל (1 QM 4:9) as compared with the עדת בליעל (1 QH 2:22), עדת בוגדים, (Damasc. 1:12 [1:8]) and עדת שו (1 QH 7:34). עדה, of course, has here a narrower ref. It no longer embraces the whole community of Israel (→ 804, 5 ff.) but denotes a congregation which is simply a chosen remnant of the people;[63] the idea of the remnant is strongly attested in the Qumran texts.[64] One cannot be sure how the sect described its place of assembly. Whether the singular בית השתחות ("house of prostration") in Damasc. 11:22 (14:3) means the temple, a synagogue, or a sanctuary in Damascus, is

---

[55] כנסת ישראל is common, bBer., 32b; bShab., 88b; צבור is normally used for both the local congregation and the entire community, examples Str.-B., I, 733-6; Dalman Wört., s.v.; Rost Vorstufen, 143, n. 3; Schmidt, 275; → III, 524, 20 ff.

[56] Krauss Altert., 7 (conceding an exception in Er., 10, 10 and correcting jSanh., 8, 2 [20a, 43] and jNazir, 7, 1 [56a, 33]) and esp. Krauss Synagoge, 1287 disputes metonymy in Hbr. and Aram. and tries to disqualify the above examples. But Rost Vorstufen, 144, n. 1 thinks כנסת is always used in the Mishnah in the sense of בית הכנסת though the passages he cites from Yoma, 7, 1 etc. (→ line 1) almost all prove that כנסת has the sense of congregation; cf. Dahl, 66, 292, n. 142, who also considers Ab., 1, 1 f. → n. 54. Levy Wört., II, 354 f. has examples of place of meeting for כניסה too, e.g., Ab., 3, 10.

[57] Examples in Str.-B., IV, 115, 142.

[58] Examples ibid., II, 742; I, 852 f.; also IV, 115.

[59] So in Nabratein, cf. N. Avigad, "The Lintel Inscr. from Nabratein," Bulletin of the L. M. Rabinowitz Fund for the Exploration of Ancient Synagogues, 3 (1960), 52 f.; cf. also Aram. הדין ביתה in Dura-Europos, CIJ, II, 828a b, cf. Kraeling The Synagogue, 263.

[60] CIJ, II, 1199; 1203, 3 f., 7; 1204, 4 (all three from Noarah).

[61] CIJ, II, 973 ('Alma) and 974 (Kefr Bir'im), cf. Ltzm. K. on 1 C. 1:2; E. Burrows, "Note on the Hebrew Inscr. of 'Alma," Biblica, 3 (1922), 456; Str.-B., III, 321 and the Aram. synagogue inscr., from 'Alma יהי שלום על המקום הזה ועל כל מקמות עמו ישראל. Cf. R. Hestrin, "A New Aram. Inscr. from 'Alma," Bull. of the L. M. Rabinowitz Fund for the Exploration of Ancient Synag., 3 (1960), 65 f.

[62] I count some 70 instances in the concordance to the ed. by A. M. Haberman, Megilloth Midbar Yehuda (1959), 71 f. Cf. K. G. Kuhn, Konkordanz zu d. Qumrantexten (1960), 156 f.

[63] Kosmala, 65.

[64] Ibid., 67, 73 f., n. 35 and 36; H. Bardtke, Die Handschriftenfunde am Toten Meer (1958), 130 f. Cf. also J. Jeremias, "Der Gedanke d. 'Heiligen Restes' im Spätjudt. u. in d. Verkündigung Jesu," ZNW, 42 (1949), 184-194, on Damascus 189 f.

debated. [65] The same applies to בית התורה in 20:10, 13 (9:35, 38), which can be taken symbolically or with ref. to the cultic centre of the sect. [66] Members probably used the gen. בית מועד "house of assembly" for their meeting-place, 1 QM 3:4. [67]

II. The Jewish Synagogue.

1. Origin.

The origin, date, and historical development of the synagogue are wrapped in obscurity. In view of the lack of sources and records no certainty is possible. The many attempts at dating can achieve only approximate results and there are considerable differences, [68] Many even believe a pre-exilic origin is likely. [69] But much discussed texts like Ps. 74:8 [70] and Jer. 39:8 [71] do not prove any precise date. Unless no answer is given, [72] it is best to follow the majority in putting the rise of synagogue under Ezra or during the exile. [73] Isolation from Jerusalem and the temple undoubtedly favoured the development of

---

[65] Cf. W. Staerk, "Die jüd. Gemeinde d. Neuen Bundes in Damaskus," BFTh, 27, 3 (1922), 73; L. Ginzberg, "Eine unbekannte jüd. Sekte," MGWJ, 56 (1912), 446 f. Krauss Altert., 23 f., 87; G. Hölscher, "Zur Frage nach Alter u. Herkunft d. sog. Damask.," ZNW, 28 (1929), 33 f.; Kosmala, 353 f.

[66] Cf. Staerk, op. cit., 87; Ginzberg, op. cit., 688: "centre of the sect in Damascus"; F. Nötscher, "Zur theol. Terminologie d. Qumran-Texte," Bonner Bibl. Beiträge, 10 (1956), 164 finds in the "house of the Law" a par. to the fig. בית המשפט 1 QpHab 8:2 and 10:3. Like [בית אשמ[תם in 4:11 "house of the Law" denotes "groups or fellowships rather than places."

[67] Kosmala, Exc. C: "Das essenische Versammlungshaus," 351-363, and Exc. E: "Das Versammlungshaus u. die Stiftshütte," 378-386. "If no great store is set by the literal transl. of bejt mo'ed into Gk. one may render it quite naturally by συναγωγή," 353. This sheds added light on the fact that Philo in his only instance of συναγωγή is referring to the meeting-place of the Essenes → 807, 13 f.

[68] On investigation up to 1922 cf. Krauss Altert., 52-66 (a selection).

[69] Löw; J. Morgenstern, "The Origin of the Synagogue," Studi Orientalistici in Onore di G. Levi della Vida, II Pubblicazioni dell'Istituto per l'Oriente, 52 (1956), 192-201; cf. also the older authors quoted in S. M. Zarb, De Synagogarum Origine," Angelicum, 5 (1928), 263-8. On the question of a pre-exilic origin cf. E. Janssen, "Juda in d. Exilszeit," FRL, NF, 51 (1956), 105-115.

[70] Whether the places of worship mentioned here (מוֹעֲדֵי־אֵל) are synagogues, as commonly assumed (Strack, 224; Galling BR, 506; Schürer, II, 499 f.; Str.-B., IV, 115; Moore, I, 285 f and III, 92 f.; R. Kittel, Die Ps., Komm. AT, 13² [1914]. ad loc.; C. Guignebert, The Jewish World in the Time of Jesus [1959], 73 f.; L. Finkelstein, "The Origin of the Synagogue," Proceedings of the Amer. Acad. for Jewish Research, 1 [1928/30], 49), is contested, as is also the dating of the Ps. and of the destruction (Bab. or Syr.?) which it records, cf. G. B. Winer, Art. "Synagogen," RW, II, 548; Krauss Altert., 49-51; Galling Erwägungen; 164 f.; Groenman, 47, 60 f.; Bousset-Gressm., 172; Zarb, 265-7; H. J. Kraus, op. cit. (→ n. 25), ad loc. LXX has ἑορταὶ τοῦ θεοῦ, 'A and Σ (Cod B, 264) συναγωγαί.

[71] The dubious interpretation of בֵּית הָעָם as synagogue or as an early form of synagogue is esp. contested by Löw, passim; Löw thinks the synagogue had a political origin, cf. also Zeitlin, op. cit. (→ n. 54), 78. "The origin of the בית הכנסת, synagogue, was not religious, but secular." But cf. M. Rosenmann, Der Ursprung d. Synagoge u. ihre allmähliche Entwicklung (1907), 14, Krauss Altert., 54-56, and esp. F. Landsberger, "The House of the People," HUCA, 22 (1949), 149-155: "A religious manifestation from its beginning," 155. The Rabb. later forbade as a mortal sin the use of בית עמא for the synagogue, bShab., 32a. The Mandaeans seem to have called the Jewish synagogue the "house of the people," Lidz. Joh., II, 75 f.

[72] So K. Kohler, The Origins of the Synagogue and the Church (1929), 6.

[73] Bacher Jew. Enc., II, 619; Schürer, II, 500 f.; Str.-B., IV, 115.

gatherings and buildings for worship in the exile, [74] so that the exiles might well have brought the synagogue back with them from Babylon to Palestine. [75] It is even more probable, however, that the true birthday of the synagogue was in the time after the return and after the binding of the people to the Law which Ezra brought back with him, 445 B.C. [76] Only after the promulgation of the Law by Ezra as the exclusive norm of national life could the synagogue become what it became, for "if there is no Torah there are no synagogues or houses of instruction," Lv. r., 11 on 9:1. [77] The Rabb. could hardly imagine a time without synagogues and ascribed their origin to Moses or even to the age of the patriarchs. [78] This does at least show that the synagogue was a familiar institution with a long tradition, and that very gt. importance was attached to it. Of the same belief as Rabb. Judaism are Jos. in Ap., 173-5 and Philo in Vit. Mos., II, 211, cf. Eus. Praep. Ev., 8, 7, 12 f. [79]

The oldest testimony to a Dispersion synagogue (προσευχή) on an inscr. is to be dated under Ptolemy III Euergetes (247-221 B.C.) and it comes from Schedia in Egypt, CIJ, II, 1440. [80] We also have some pap. from the same period, from Fayyum CPJud, 129 (218 B.C.) and Arsinoe-Crocodilopolis CPJud, 134 (2nd cent. B.C.). [81] Jos. ref. to a synagogue in Antioch under Antiochus Epiphanes, Bell., 7, 44; the treasures plundered from the temple were given to this. Pre-Chr. En. 46:8 and 53:6 have often been adduced, but these can no longer be accepted as bearing witness to the synagogue. [82] Ruins found

---

[74] Cf. Strack, 224; Elbogen, 446; Filson, 78; Moore, I, 283; Menes, 268-276; Galling Erwägungen, 165-8; Finkelstein, 49-59; Zarb, 268 f., 272. On Ez. 8:1; 14:1, 4; 33:31 and other passages cf. Krauss Altert., 47; Rosenmann, 14; J. Bright, A History of Israel (1960), 422 f. On Jos. 22:9-34; Ez. 11:14-16 (on Ez. 11:16 f. → n. 151); 33:23 f.; 20:39 f.; Ps. 40:6-8; 51·16-19; 69:30 f. as evidence of a non-sacrificial cultus in the exilic period cf. Menes, 270-4; J. Parkes, The Foundation of Judaism and Christianity (1960), 12-17. But these are separate questions.
[75] J. Wellhausen, Isr. u. jüd. Gesch.⁹ (1958), 184 f.; RW, II, 548.
[76] Bacher Hastings DB, IV, 636; Watzinger, 107; Groenman, 47-9; Guignebert, 74: "The first steps were taken during the Exile... it was in Palestine during the Persian period that the institution really took definite form"; cf. also Galling Erwägungen, 167 f. on Neh. 8:4-6 (3) and 7-8: "Ezra's reading of the Law is depicted as synagogue worship... If the scene could be shifted from before the Water Gate (outside the temple) into an enclosed place with a roof over it one would have a synagogue." Not unrelated to this is the question whether the synagogue originated in the Dispersion (Friedländer, 53-78; Bousset-Gressm., 172; Krauss Synagoge, 1290-1293, cf. also Moore, I, 287 f.; Kraeling The Synagogue, 33) or in Palestine (Elbogen, 447; Rosenmann, 17 f.; Zarb, 272; F. C. Grant, Ancient Judaism and the NT [1959], 38), cf. Galling Erwägungen, 168.
[77] Among the paintings of Dura-Europos, in a favoured place above the wallniche for the Torah and over the raised place for reading it, there is a depiction of Ezra with an open scroll of the Torah in his hands, proclaiming the Law to the people, Kraeling Synagogue, Ill. 77.
[78] Examples in Str.-B., II, 740; IV, 116 and Krauss Altert., 32 f., 35-52. Acc. to Vit. Ad., 30 there was a house of prayer even in the days of Adam and Eve.
[79] Cf. on this Vitringa, 282 f.; Krauss Altert., 34 f.
[80] Cf. T. Reinach, "Sur la date de la colonie juive d'Alexandrie," REJ, 45 (1902), 161-4; Schürer, II, 499 f. and III, 41; Krauss Altert., 263 and Synagoge, 1306; Frey, CIJ, II, p. 366 f. There are other pre-Chr. witnesses from Xenephyris, CIJ, II, 1441 (2nd cent. B.C.), Nitria, II, 1442 (2nd cent.), Athribis, II, 1443 and 1444 (2nd cent.), Lower Egypt, II, 1449 (2nd or 3rd cent.), and Alexandria, II, 1432 (1st cent.); bibl. Frey, CIJ, II. On CIJ, II, 1449 → n. 175, 176.
[81] Bibl. in CPJud, I, p. 239 and 247; Schürer, II, 499 f., n. 4 c, e. Cf. also the pap. in CPJud, 138 mentioned → 806, 5 ff.
[82] Cf. E. Sjöberg, "Der Menschensohn im äth. Henochbuch," Skrifter utgivna av Kunglig Humanistiska Vetenskapssamfundet, 41 (1946), 107, n. 28 and Galling Erwägungen, 164; C. P. van Andel, "De Structuur van de Henoch-Traditie en het NT," Studia Theol. Rheno-Traiectina, 2 (1955), 31, n. 84, though cf. G. Beer in Kautzsch Apkr. u. Pseudepigr., II, 266 and Str.-B., IV, 115 f.

in Delos probably go back to the 1st cent. B.C. [83] The inscr. on a synagogue door from Corinth might well come from the NT period; it runs [Συνα]γωγή 'Εβρ[αίων], CIJ, I, 718. [84] The oldest inscr. from Palestine dates only from the same age. This is the well-known Theodotus inscr. found in the old city of Jerusalem on Zion's hill (Ophel) in 1913/14, CIJ, II, 1404. [85] On synagogue ruins in Palestine, which are all later, → 816, 9 ff.

2. Spread.

There were synagogues in Palestine as well as the Dispersion. In view of this world-wide spread of Judaism the very large no. of synagogues known to us from the Graeco-Roman world should occasion no surprise. Every country was filled with Jews, Sib., 3, 271, and Jos. quotes Strabo to the effect that it is not easy to find a place which does not shelter this people, Ant., 14, 115. [86] Since Jews and synagogues go together, one might easily say the same thing about the spread of the synagogue. Wherever Jews settled in any numbers there would also be a synagogue. At this pt. the literary sources are very strongly supported and supplemented by archaeological findings from the whole of the ancient world. [87] Some 150 places are now known to have had synagogues, in Galilee and Syria, Babylonia and Mesopotamia, Asia Minor and Greece, Italy and Gaul, Spain, North Africa and Egypt. Even in Panticapaion in the Crimea there was a synagogue in the 1st cent. A.D., CIJ, I, 683 f. Acc. to Philo there was μυρία κατὰ πᾶσαν πόλιν διδασκαλεῖα, Spec. Leg., II, 62 (cf. Vit. Mos., II, 216: κατὰ πόλεις προσευκτήρια), and acc. to bSanh., 17b, Bar. no scholar should live in a city where there was no synagogue. In NT times every significant Jewish community in Palestine and the Dispersion had a synagogue and larger cities had more than one. Swollen figures say that when the temple was destroyed by Titus there were 480 (jMeg., 3, 1 [73d, 28]),

---

[83] So A. Plassart, "La synagoque juive de Délos," *Mélanges Holleaux* (1913), 212; Juster, I, 499. Filson, 78 dates it back to the late 2nd cent. B.C. Cf. also Goodenough, II, 71-75 in defence of the fact that the synagogue and inscr. are Jewish; for a different view Sukenik Present State, 21 f.

[84] Cf. Deissmann LO, 12, n. 8 (with facsimile); 100-200 A.D. is given there as H. v. Gärtringen's suggested date; cf. also Krauss Altert., 242 f.; Juster, 188, n. 2; Jackson-Lake, I, 5, 64.

[85] Θεόδοτος Ούεττηνοῦ, ἱερεὺς καὶ
ἀρχισυνάγωγος, υἱὸς ἀρχισυν[αγώ-]
γ[ο]υ, υἱωνὸς ἀρχισυν[α]γώγου, ᾠκο-
δόμησε τὴν συναγωγ[ὴ]ν εἰς ἀν[άγ]νω-
σ[ιν] νόμου καὶ εἰς [δ]ιδαχ[ὴ]ν ἐντολῶν καὶ
τὸν ξενῶνα κα[ὶ τὰ] δώματα καὶ τὰ χρη-
σ[τ]ήρια τῶν ὑδάτων εἰς κατάλυμα τοῖ-
ς [χ]ρήζουσιν ἀπὸ τῆς ξέ[ν]ης, ἣν ἐθεμε-
λ[ίω]σαν οἱ πατέρες [α]ὐτοῦ καὶ οἱ πρε-
σ[β]ύτεροι καὶ Σιμων[ί]δης.
For the date of the inscr. (mostly put before 70 A.D.) cf. the bibl. in Deissmann LO, 378 f.; Kittel Probleme, 35, n. 4; CIJ, II, p. 332 f., also the facsimile and transl. in Deissmann, and esp. L. H. Vincent, "Découverte de la Synagogue des Affranchis à Jérusalem," Rev. Bibl., 30 (1921), 247-277.

[86] Apart from the bibl. → II, 101, n. 10 cf. A. Stuiber, Art. "Diaspora," RAC, III, 972-982 with bibl.

[87] Cf. Juster, I, 179-209; Krauss Altert., 199-267; Krauss Synagoge, 1293-1308; H. Leclercq, Art. "Judaisme," DACL, 8, 67-90; Str.-B., IV, 116-8; Sukenik Ancient Synagogues, 37-45; S. J. Saller, "A Catalogue of the Ancient Synag. of the Holy Land," *Studi Bibl. Franciscani Liber Annuus*, IV, 1953/54 (1954), 219-246.

or 460 (jKet., 13, 1 [35c, 54]), or 394 (bKet., 105a) synagogues in Jerusalem, [88] and a similarly large no. is given for Bethar, bGit., 58a. Tiberias had 13 acc. to bBer., 8ä and 30b, [89] and Alexandria πολλαί ... καθ' ἕκαστον τμῆμα τῆς πόλεως, Philo Leg. Gaj., 132. An inscr. from Side in Pamphylia mentions a first synagogue, thus distinguishing it from others. Ruins in Galilee also show that there might be several synagogues in a single town, e.g. two each in Nabratein, Kefr-Bir'im, Giscala. It is obvious that this gt. spread of synagogues meant a strong decentralisation of Judaism. [90]

3. Founding.

The founding and support of synagogues was a task for the congregation which in Palestine was identical with the local population. In the Mishnah the synagogue is listed with the ark and the Holy Scriptures as something that belongs to the city, along with baths and streets, Ned., 5, 5, cf. ἀρχισυνάγωγος → 845, 6 ff. Synagogues were built from common funds either through taxes or gifts and endowments. Acc. to Tosefta any Jew might be forced to contribute to the erection of a synagogue, T BM, 11, 23 (396). Acc. to Jos. Bell., 7, 45 the Jews of Antioch adorned and beautified their synagogue with munificent gifts καὶ τῇ κατασκευῇ καὶ τῇ πολυτελείᾳ τῶν ἀναθημάτων τὸ ἱερὸν ἐξελάμπρυναν. T BQ, 11, 3 (370) mentions scrolls of the Torah donated to the synagogue, while bAr., 6b ref. to lights and lamps. Gentiles also gave gifts to synagogues, T.Meg., 3, 3. 5 (224); bAr., 6a; jMeg., 3, 2 (74a, 25), though there is no record of Gentiles building synagogues except in Lk. 7:5. [91] Inscr. with details are almost all later. An inscr. from Aegina says that the synagogue there was adorned with mosaics from its revenues [ἐκ τῆς πρ]ο[σ]όδου τῆς συναγ(ωγῆς), CIJ, I, 723. But most inscr. ref. to the fairly frequent donations. The names of the donors are preserved for posterity on inscr. in the parts endowed. Thus there is an inscr. on the pillar at Capernaum Ἡρῴδης Μο[νί]μου καὶ 'Ιοῦστος υἱὸς ἅμα τοῖς τέκνοις ἔκτισαν τὸν κίονα, CIJ, II, 983. CIJ has many similar Gk. and Aram. inscr. mentioning contributions of money, materials, pillars, thresholds, mosaics etc. [92] Esp. instructive are several inscr. from Apamea in Syria in CIJ, II, 806-818 which tell of the donating of 35, 50, 75, 100, 140 or 150 feet of mosaic, almost always with the addition ὑπὲρ σωτηρίας πάντων τῶν ἰδίων or αὐτῆς καὶ τῶν τέκνων αὐτῆς ἐποίησεν (also with εὐξαμένη "according to a vow"). [93] Larger endowments

---

[88] Acc. to K. F. Keil, *Hbr. Archäol.*² (1875), 166 the no. is "perhaps just taken cabbalistically from the word מלאתי Is. 1:21," cf. RW, II, 548, n. 6. Epiphanius De mensuris et ponderibus, 14 (MPG, 43 [1864], 262 A) says there were 7 synagogues in Jerusalem in the time of Constantine, cf. the "pilgrim of Bordeaux" P. Geyer, Itinera Hierosolymitana saeculi IV-VIII, CSEL, 39 (1898), 22; Dalman Orte, 289. Krauss Altert., 12, n. 4 thinks, however, these were Chr. churches. Cf. further Str.-B., II, 662; Dalman Orte, 295; Krauss Altert., 200 f.; J. Jeremias, *Jerusalem z. Zt. Jesu*, I² (1958), 75.

[89] Str.-B., II, 662 and IV, 117 erroneously quote this as b Meg., 30b.

[90] → 823, 6 ff.; Dahl, 65; Filson, 77.

[91] Cf. Krauss Altert., 306-316; more gen. B. Laum, *Stiftungen in d. griech. u. röm. Antike*, I, II (1914); cf. too M. Kaser, *Das röm. Privatrecht, Hndbch. AW*, III, 3, 1 (1955), 265, n. 48.

[92] Cf. CIJ, II, 982 (Capernaum), II, 971 (Thella), II, 1195 עמודה "pillar"; II, 1195 (Beit Yibrin) עמודא "pillar"; II, 974 (Kefr-Bir'im) שקוף "door-post," "lintel"; II, 987 (Cana) [טבל]ה tabula; II, 981 (Chorazin) דרגות or דרגיה "steps" or "seats," and סטוה = στοά "row of pillars"; II; 1197 (Noarah) מרישת "basin"; II, 754 (Deliler) μασκαύλης "wash-tub"? (→ n. 135); II, 1203 (Noarah) דהב and וכ]סף "gold" and "silver"; II, 856-9 (El-Hammeh) דינרין denarius or parts of this; II, 1203, 1204 (Noarah) מתחזקין or חול[ל]קהון "contribution."

[93] Cf. also CIJ, II, 964, 965 (Ascalon) and 1438 (Alexandria), also the Caesarea inscr. where we find ὑπὲρ σωτ[η]ρίας, M. Avi-Yonah, "The Synagogue of Caesarea, Preliminary Report," *Bull. of the L. M. Rabinowitz Fund for the Exploration of Ancient Synagogues*, 3 (1960), 44.

were not uncommon. An inscr. from Phocaea lauds a certain Tation: τὸν οἶκον καὶ τὸν περίβολον τοῦ ὑπαίθρου (unroofed pillared court) κατασκευάσασα ἐκ τῶ[ν ἰδ]ίων ἐχαρίσατο τ[οῖς ᾽Ιο]υδαίοις, CIJ, II, 738. Another from Stobi says that the πατὴρ τῆς συναγωγῆς acc. to a vow built out of his own resources τοὺς μὲν οἴκους τῷ ἁγίῳ τόπῳ καὶ τὸ τρίκλεινον σὺν τῷ τετραστόῳ (an atrium surrounded on all four sides by rows of pillars), CIJ, I, 694.⁹⁴

4. Architecture.

a. There were obviously no binding rules governing the site and architecture of synagogues. In view of the deficiency of literary sources special regard must be paid here to archaeological discoveries. The only Rabb. rule about the site in T.Meg., 4, 23 (227) says that synagogues must be built on the highest point in a city בגובה של עיר,⁹⁵ but this enjoyed only theoretical validity, as may be seen both from other Rabb. sayings and also from the ruins preserved, esp. outside Palestine — those in Galilee are usually on hills or prominent places. Acc. to bQid., 73b synagogues might be outside a town,⁹⁶ and there are odd instances of synagogues built on the sacred tombs of kings, martyrs, and prophets.⁹⁷ The synagogue at Philippi was before the gates of the city (Ac. 16:13), while that at Corinth was just beside another house (Ac. 18:7), and that at Caesarea was beside the land of a Gentile owner who hemmed it in so that there was only narrow and awkward access to the synagogue, Jos. Bell., 2, 285 f. As may be seen from ἔξω τῆς πύλης παρὰ ποταμὸν ὁ δ ἐνομίζομεν προσευχὴν εἶναι in Ac. 16:13 and an Egypt. pap. from Arsinoe-Crocodilopolis, CPJud, 134, 17. 29 (2nd cent. B.C.),⁹⁸ and as several other inscr. and excavations in and outside Palestine also bear witness,⁹⁹ synagogues might also be put up sometimes besides waters or cisterns → II, 808, 13 ff.; VI, 602,

---

⁹⁴ Cf. also CIJ, II, 744 (Teos); 766 (Acmonia); 829 (Dura-Europos) and the larger parts of synagogues → n. 116, CIJ, I, 720; II, 738, 1441, 1444.

⁹⁵ Cf. bShab., 11a, also Krauss Altert., 286-9; Str.-B., IV, 119, 121; Kohl-Watzinger, 138; Scharlemann, 904 f.

⁹⁶ Cf. Epiph. Haer., 80, 1, 5 (GCS, 37, 485); οὐ μόνον γὰρ ἐν μέσῳ τῶν πόλεων συναγωγὴ ἦν τῶν ᾽Ιουδαίων ἀλλὰ καὶ ἔξω προσευχαῖς ηὔχοντο ὥσπερ τόπον τινὰ ἀφορίζοντες, Chrys. Arm. Cat., p. 291 (quoted Pr. Ag. on 16:13); cf. Chrys. Hom. in Ac., 35 on 16:13 (MPG, 60 [1862], 252), also Str.-B., IV, 119, 121; Elbogen, 449; Krauss Altert., 273 f.; on synagogues in the fields Vitringa, 215-217; Krauss Altert., 273-281.

⁹⁷ J. Jeremias, Heiligengräber in Jesu Umwelt (1958), 22 f., 60, 124 f.; cf. also Vitringa, 219-221; Elbogen, 482 and Winer, op. cit. (→ n. 70), 549, n. 3.

⁹⁸ The pap. mentions a synagogue by a canal, cf. Krauss Altert., 265, 282; CPJud, I, p. 247 f.

⁹⁹ E.g., Delos, Aegina, Miletus, Caesarea, Hammam-Lif; at Capernaum, too, the synagogue was by the lake; Delos had a cistern as well, Goodenough, II, 71 and III, Ill. 875. We have a synagogue with ritual bath (a room with cistern) from near Sepphoris (Dalman Orte, 119), one with 2 cisterns from Yafa (E. L. Sukenik, "The Ancient Synag. at Yafa near Nazareth," Bull. of the L. M. Rabinowitz Fund for the Explor. of Ancient Synagogues, 2 [1951], 15). Cisterns with ducts from the roof have been excavated (1938/39) at Beth-Shearim, Goodenough, I, 208. The synagogue excavated at Khirbet Maʿon (Nirim) in 1957 was also by a cistern, cf. "Chronique Archéol.," Rev. Bibl., 65 (1958), 421 f.; S. Levy, "The Ancient Synag. of Maʿon (Nirim) A. Excavation Report," Bull. of the L. M. Rabinowitz Fund..., 3 (1960), 9; A. S. Hiram, "The Ancient Synag. of Maʿon (Nirim) C. Reconstruction," I, ibid., 19. The κρήνη of a synagogue in Sardis is mentioned in CIJ, II, 751, a κρήνη σὺν τῷ μεσαύλῳ in Side, cf. Robert, op. cit. (→ n. 46), 36, 43-46. The fact that synagogues needed a good deal of water may be seen from a pap. which mentions considerable use of it, CPJud, 432 (113 A.D.); on the place of origin of this pap. (Arsinoe or Hermopolis) cf. Robert, 43, n. 3. → n. 135.

39 ff,[100] possibly to facilitate the washing of hands before prayer or other lustrations, [101] possibly on account of the ritual uncleanness of a Gentile country, [102] possibly because of ancient cosmogonic notions. [103] There is, however, no rule about this.

b. There are no definite regulations about the way a synagogue should face. Acc. to T. Meg., 4, 22 (227) the entrance should be to the East after the model of the tabernacle or temple, Nu. 3:38 or Ez. 44:1-3. [104] Existing ruins show, however, that facing Jerusalem fixed the orientation. Synagogues in Galilee faced South (the entrance to the South), those in East Jordan (e.g., ed-Dikkeh and Umm-el-Kanâtir) and Mesopotamia (Dura-Europos) faced West, Chirbet-Semmâka, which was west of Jerusalem, and those in Greece and Spain faced East, while the synagogue of Eshtemoʿa south of Jerusalem faced North. [105] This orientation to Jerusalem corresponds to the direction of prayer attested in 1 K. 8:38, 44, 48; 2 Ch. 6:34, 38; Da. 6:11 and then demanded in Judaism: "Those abroad turn their faces to the land of Israel and pray... Those in Israel turn their faces to Jerusalem... Those in Jerusalem turn their faces to the sanctuary...", S. Dt., 29 on 3:26. [106] bBer., 31a, 34b (though not with ref. to synagogues) expressly demands that windows and doors be opened towards Jerusalem; this is based on Da. 6:11, cf. also Tob. 3:11. Since the congregation turned towards the "holy thing," i.e., the ark with the Torah, as well as Jerusalem (T. Meg., 4, 21 [227]), it would seem that the shrine with the Torah stood by the entrance or in the main entrance itself during worship, [107]

---

[100] Cf. Vitringa, 217 f.; Elbogen, 448 f.; Krauss Altert., 281-6 (more cautiously Krauss Synagoge, 1288); Sukenik Ancient Synagogues, 49 f.; Schürer, II, 519; Plassart, op. cit. (→ n. 83), 210; Str.-B., II, 742; IV, 119 (not, indeed, in Rabb. writings); Juster, I, 459, n. 1; but cf. Löw, 24-26; Kohl-Watzinger, 138. The much quoted ref. in Jos. Ant., 14, 258: τὰς προσευχὰς ποιεῖσθαι πρὸς τῇ θαλάσσῃ, cannot be accepted since, like Ep. Ar., 305, it may be speaking of prayer, cf. similarly Tert. De ieiunio, 16, 6 (CCh, 2, 1275): per omne litus quocumque in aperto aliquando iam precem ad caelum mittunt, and Nat., I, 13, 4 (1, 32): orationes litorales.

[101] Schürer, II, 519; Str.-B., II, 742; IV, 119.

[102] Sukenik Ancient Synag., 50, n. 1.

[103] Krauss Synagoge, 1288. Krauss Altert., 290-7 finds expressed in the siting by water or on heights or in the open the same principle as in ancient nature worship: synagogues are to stand on "virgin earth." It is unlikely, however, that this type of nature piety would be found in Judaism.

[104] Cf. also Jos. Ant., 8, 64: τέτραπτο δὲ πρὸς τὴν ἀνατολήν.

[105] Cf. Kohl-Watzinger, 139; Sukenik Beth-Alpha, 50, Ancient Synag., 50 f., 83 and Present State, 16; Rost Bemerkungen, 59 f., with bibl. The 1948/49 excavation of the synagogue of the Samaritans in Salbit between Jerusalem and Lydda (probably 4th cent. A.D.) shows that this faced Gerizim to the North-East rather than Jerusalem, cf. E. L. Sukenik, "The Samaritan Synag. at Salbit, Preliminary Report," Bull. of the L. M. Rabinowitz Fund..., 1 (1949), 29. Epiph. Haer., 80, 1, 5 (GCS, 37, 485) ref. to Samaritan synagogues.

[106] Cf. Str.-B., II, 246 f.; IV, 120. Cf. also Ber., 4. 5-6; T. Ber., 3, 14-16 (7); 1 Εσδρ. 4:58. Other Rabb. examples Str.-B., II, 247. Cf. Sukenik Ancient Synagogues, 51 f.; Dalman Orte, 155; Krauss Altert., 331-3; E. Peterson, "Die geschichtliche Bdtg. d. jüd. Gebetsrichtung," ThZ, 3 (1947), 1-15.

[107] Cf. Schürer, II, 530, n. 103; Kohl-Watzinger, 139; Watzinger, 110; Rost Bemerkungen, 57 f., 60, 62-6; Galling Jahresbericht, 311 f. and Erwägungen, 176; Goodenough, I, 209; Wendel, 19 f.; May, 5; H. Rosenau, "A Note on Synagogue Orientation," JPOS, 16 (1936), 33-6; Ehrlich, 91; on different grounds F. Landsberger, "The Sacred Direction in Synagogue and Church," HUCA, 28 (1957), 183-5. But cf. Orfali, 9; Elbogen, 460; Str.-B., IV, 120 f. Wendel, 33, n. 70 rightly objects against Str.-B. that the thesis that location of the ark at the main entrance was impossible fails to take into account either discoveries or the earlier mobility of the ark. Sukenik Present State, 18 f. no longer thinks the stone fragments in Capernaum were part of a Torah shrine but parts of an "elaborate central window in the facade of the synagogue." Krauss Altert., 328, 331, 333 and Synagoge, 1310 contests any specific orientation.

and archaeological discoveries support this.[108] The person attending had thus to turn round after entering so as to have the Torah before him. Later, however, a fixed place was found for the ark in a niche or apse on the side facing the entrance, e.g., Beth-Alpha, Gadara, Gerasa etc., and then this side rather than the entrance faced Jerusalem,[109] but the worshipper still looked toward both the ark of the Torah and Jerusalem.

c. Ancient Rabb. sources give us detailed information on the architecture of the synagogue at Alexandria: a double pillared walk with bema in the middle.[110] But this synagogue, called μεγίστη καὶ περισημοτάτη by Philo in Leg. Gaj., 134, cannot be regarded as typical. The ruins found in many places in Palestine, esp. Galilee, give plain evidence of the contemporary style, but the relation to patterns of the age of the Antonines makes it clear that they can be dated at the earliest only in the late 2nd and early 3rd cent.[111] Nothing is known about the architecture of synagogues in NT days and conclusions from the later age must be drawn only with gt. caution, though it has been conjectured that the Galilean type was not wholly new and can hardly have arisen without some continuity.[112] The Galilean synagogues of an older period (3rd-4th cent.)[113] are comparatively uniform and are distinct in style from the Byzantine period (5th-6th cent.)[114] Their distinctive mark is that they have three naves made by rows of pillars;

---

[108] So Capernaum and Chorazin, cf. Sukenik Beth-Alpha, 34, n. 2, Ancient Synag., 18, 52 f. Rost Bemerkungen, 57 f. ref. not merely to the smaller remains but also to the fact that in Chorazin Moses' seat (→ n. 134) was on the side of entry and that in Capernaum the last seat on the upper row to the west side on the side of entry was singled out by an arm-rest.
[109] Cf. Landsberger, op. cit., 185; Goodenough, I, 210, 225 f.; Wendel, 19 (examples n. 72-9). This shows how the Tosefta passage quoted above, which puts the entrance on the east side, fits in with the gen. discernible principle of orientation. Prayer was offered to the West, which suggests a Bab. relation, cf. Kohl-Watzinger, 139; Bacher Hastings DB, IV, 639; Rost Bemerkungen, 61, n. 2. If, however, the earlier type is presupposed the synagogue would have to be located west of Jerusalem, cf. Galling Jahresbericht, 311 f.; Krauss Altert., 323-5.
[110] T. Sukka, 4, 6 (198), cf. Str.-B., III, 457; IV, 118, 122; Moore, III, 91 f. On דיפלסטון = διπλόστοον Krauss Altert., 261-3; Jeremias, op. cit. (→ n. 88), II, 248, n. 141. There are few literary ref. to the architecture of other synagogues. On Dt. r., 7 on 28:1 (an inner and outer door, hence an ante-room) cf. Str.-B., II, 246; IV, 122; Krauss Altert., 359 f.; on Lv. r., 22 on 17:3 (the middle door of a Tiberias synagogue, hence two other entries with this between) cf. Str.-B., IV, 118 f.; פתחא אחרינא "side-doors" are mentioned in bSota, 39b. On the problem of three doors, Rost Bemerkungen, 61-5.
[111] Cf. Kohl-Watzinger, 204 etc.; Watzinger, 110, 113 f.; Sukenik Ancient Synagogues, 68 f.; G. E. Wright, Bibl. Archäol. (1958), 240; cf. Krauss Altert., 361: the time "when Galilee surged ahead through the work of the Tannaites"; for an earlier date Schürer, II, 520; "the oldest from the 2nd cent. and perhaps even the 1st cent. A.D."; Str.-B., IV, 119: "which belong in part to the 1st and 2nd cent. A.D." But this is impossible even in the case of Tell-Hum (Capernaum). H. Rosenau, "Die paläst. Synagogen u. ihr Einfluss auf d. Kunst d. Abendlandes," ThBl, 13 (1934), 289 puts this as early as the time of Christ's birth and Orfali, 74-86 and Meistermann, 163-291 identify the ruins as those of the synagogue mentioned in Lk. 7:5. But Kohl-Watzinger have shown that the type including Capernaum is surprisingly uniform in gen. forms and essential features and can be put in a restricted period at the end of the 2nd and beginning of the 3rd cent., 147, 173, 204; Watzinger, 112, n. 3; Dalman Orte, 150-7. Many think there is an older stratum going back to the time of Jesus, cf. C. Kopp, Die hl. Stätten d. Ev. (1959), 216; Wright, 240 thinks this cannot be ruled out; but cf. Kohl-Watzinger, 183 ("no demonstrable traces of older buildings") and Sukenik in Kopp, 216, n. 5. Acc. to bMeg., 26b a synagogue was not to be torn down nor its tiles and timbers used for synagogue building before a new one was put up, cf. jMeg., 3, 1 (73d, 20 ff.).
[112] Cf. Str.-B., IV, 119; Schürer, II, 520; Rost Bemerkungen, 59.
[113] E.g., Capernaum, Chorazin, Kefr-Bir'im, Beth She'arim.
[114] E.g., Beth-Alpha, Hammath, Naara, Gerasa.

the broad middle one has the main entrance and the narrow side naves have smaller doors. Over these on the narrow side are galleries with access from outside, probably for women. [115] There is a gable and big window on the front and (or) smaller windows on the entrance side and long sides. Stone seats in one, two or three ranks run along the side walls and sometimes the back. The floor is flagged with stone, and there is also a front terrace and ante-room or porch with a pillared access. [116] We find rich architectural adornment and ornamental or figurative emblems and symbols. Both as a whole and in detail the siting and style betray clearly the influence of ancient monuments (the basilica style of Greece and Rome). [117]

Dura-Europos on the Euphrates (c. 245 A.D.) and Hammam-Lif in Tunisia (3rd cent. A.D.) do not have the same basilica form but are of a simpler type, and the synagogues of Delos, Aegina and Priene are (at least originally) halls or houses. [118] This type might well be older, [119] esp. as Graeco-Rom. influence could hardly be at work in the immediate

---

[115] From the gallery at Capernaum it has been deduced there were galleries in other synagogues too. The separation of the sexes, which is based on the separating of the עֶזְרַת הַנָּשִׁים ("court of women") from the עֶזְרַת יִשְׂרָאֵל, Mid., 2, 5; Jos. Bell., 5, 198. 227; Ant., 15, 418 f. (cf. also Zech. 12:12-14) is also reported in Philo Vit. Cont., 32: διπλοῦς ἐστι περίβολος, ὁ μὲν εἰς ἀνδρῶνα, ὁ δὲ εἰς γυναικωνῖτιν ἀποκριθείς, and Jos. Ant., 16, 164: ἔκ τε σαββατείου ἔκ τε ἀνδρῶνος (on the women's gallery גיסוטרא = ἐξώστρα in the temple, cf. Mid., 2, 6). Cf. also Schürer, II, 520, n. 65; Kohl-Watzinger, 140; Juster, I, 458; Krauss Altert., 356 f.; Elbogen, 466 f.; Goodenough, I, 226, 228; II, 74; Kraeling The Synagogue, 23, 32; Jeremias, op cit. (→ n. 88), II, 247 f. → n. 122.

[116] Parts of such buildings are also known from inscr.: an uncovered pillared court from Phocaea περίβολος τοῦ ὑπαίθρου, CIJ, II, 738; a porch or vestibule from Xenephyris πυλών, II, 1441; a covered fore-court? from Athribis ἐξέδρα, II, 1444 acc. to Kohl-Watzinger, 145, ἐξέδρα here is "a place with stone seats which opens on to the court of the synagogue"; a fore-temple from Mantinea πρόναος, CIJ, I, 720; a porticus from Hammam-Lif, CIJ, 8, 12457b. Cf. also the gifts → n. 92.

[117] Cf. the par. from pagan architecture in Kohl-Watzinger, 147-183 and Watzinger, 108, 110 f.: "the architectural type is from the Hell. period and in basic form may be traced back to the ancient house of assembly, the basilical hall"; for the individual features there are par. in Syr. buildings of the imperial period; cf. Elbogen, 462; Galling Jahresbericht, 311; Goodenough, I, 183. bSanh., 61b and 62a b presuppose that synagogues and pagan temples could be easily interchanged. Adoption of architectural terms also shows the kinship to building of the imperial period. Cf. בסילקי = βασιλική and on this Krauss Altert., 261 f., 334 and Krauss Lehnw., II, 210 f.; Goodenough, II, 85.

[118] Cf. Sukenik Ancient Synagogues, 37 ff.; Goodenough, II, 71, 75, 77; Wendel, 20 f. The newly discovered synagogue in Ostia (3rd cent. A.D.) is a reconstructed peristyle house, H. L. Hempel, "Synagogenfund in Ostia Antica," ZAW, 74 (1962), 72.

[119] Cf. on this Kraeling The Synagogue, 32 f. and Architecture, 18-20; Kohl-Watzinger, 183; Sukenik Ancient Synagogues, 46; BR, 506. Schwank, 269-278 tries to find in Palaestina tempore Christi duo diversi synagogarum typi architectonici, the συναγωγή = house synagogue and the προσευχή = basilica. But this differentiation is an unprovable hypothesis. It is said of συναγωγαί which Schwank, 279 reckons with the humilibus domibus populi, as well as of προσευχαί, that even if only in the post-Chr. period they had mosaics, CIJ, I, 723; II, 781, capitals, II, 781, and a fore-temple, I, 720, and Jos. Bell., 7, 44 says already of the Antioch συναγωγή: οἱ δὲ μετ' αὐτὸν (sc. Antiochus Epiphanes) τὴν βασιλείαν παραλαβόντες τῶν ἀναθημάτων ὅσα χαλκᾶ πεποίητο πάντα τοῖς ἐπ' Ἀντιοχείας Ἰουδαίοις ἀπέδοσαν εἰς τὴν συναγωγὴν αὐτῶν ἀναθέντες, and the sentence quoted → 813, 15 ff. follows. Haench. Ag.10 on 16:13 thinks indeed that the προσευχή of Ac. was an "insignificant building," also A. Loisy, Les Actes d. Apôtres (1920), 633; this is mistaken, however, in view of the description of the προσευχή as μέγιστον οἴκημα καὶ πολὺν ὄχλον ἐπιδέξασθαι δυνάμενον in Jos. Vit., 277. S. M. Zarb, "De Judaeorum ΠΡΟΣΕΥΧΗ in Ac. 16:13, 16," Angelicum, 5 (1928), 91-108 thinks the προσευχή was an aedificium subdiale, 101, cf. Knox, op. cit. (→ n. 40), 250, n. 18; "not a building" but "an open meeting place." Yet the two terms do not denote architectural distinction; they are synon., Vitringa,

post-exilic period. The absence of Rabb. regulations means, of course, that one cannot rule out the co-existence of different types, and the archaeological evidence confirms this. The older synagogue of Dura-Europos, which developed out of a private house, [120] probably represents the most ancient type thus far attainable. [121] If only the basilica form has been found in Palestine — perhaps synagogues of an older type were destroyed in 66-70 and 131-135 A.D. or were built of less durable materials such as sun-dried brick and wood — the simpler form was perhaps originally the normal one there too. This is supported by the fact that acc. to NT statements the women obviously did not sit in special galleries (Mk. 6:3 and par.; Lk. 13:10 ff.; Ac. 16:13); this seems to have been characteristic of the simpler form. [122, 123] Another important pt. is that these synagogues mostly form an extended complex with other rooms. Hammam-Lif had 15 rooms, cf. also Dura-Europos, Miletus, Aegina, Caesarea and in Galilee Beth-Alpha, Naara, Beth-She'arim, El-Hammeh, [124] cf. also from the NT period the Theodotus inscr. → n. 85.

119-130, 227-232. The older προσευχή (→ n. 78-80) seems to have been preferred in the *diaspora* and then to have become much less prominent later. Cf. Schürer, II, 522 f.; Krauss Altert., 282 f. (in debate with older research which saw many distinctions between the two terms); Krauss Synagoge, 1288; Groenman, 65 f.

[120] Cf. the Stobi inscr. (1st/2nd cent. A.D.) which shows that the founders of the synagogue, basilical in type, reserved the right of ownership and the use of the upper storey as a private dwelling τὴν δὲ ἐξουσίαν τῶν ὑπερώων πάντων πᾶσαν καὶ τὴν (δ)εσποτείαν ἔχειν ἐμέ... καὶ τοὺς κληρονόμους τοὺς ἐμοὺς διὰ παντὸς βίου, CIJ, I, 694, 16-24. "Thus the whole building is in the strictest sense what primitive Christianity calls a κατ' οἶκον ἐκκλησία," H. Lietzmann, "Notizen," ZNW, 32 (1933), 94.

[121] The older form of the Dura-Europos synagogue, like the later form, was a hall facing West (Jerusalem) with a niche for the ark and stone benches on all sides, but no pillars or gallery; the main entrance was opposite the niche for the Torah to the East. Here a fore-court was placed before the main room. Acc. to Kraeling The Synagogue, 33, who calls it a "house-synagogue," the older of the two was "the most primitive type of synagogue structure that we can ever expect to find," cf. also L. H. Vincent, Review of Kraeling, *Rev. Bibl.*, 65 (1958), 108. Goodenough, I, 226 f. thinks the basilica type developed in Palestine while the broad house type was esp. common in the Orient, but he leaves open the question of the priority of either type. Galling Erwägungen, 163 also refrains deliberately from postulating an original type, though he thinks the Galilean type of the earlier period was a special form, since the Dura-Europos synagogue and the Jerusalem niche-stone which he dates prior to 70 A.D. seem to show that even the oldest synagogues have a niche, and this gives us a direct line to the later apsidal synagogues, 173 f.

[122] Acc. to Kraeling The Synagogue, 23 the Dura-Europos synag. was attended by both men and women, but the women entered through special doors and sat on benches reserved for them. In the older synagogue, however, Kraeling, 31 f. thinks the women took part in worship from an adjoining room, though cf. Kraeling Architecture, 19: "Apparently it was first created before the necessity of making special provision for women was felt." The Nabratein synagogue, which was later than, e.g., that at Capernaum, also has no gallery, but a separate place for women at ground level, cf. Kohl-Watzinger, 106. Acc. to bQid., 81a Raba put dried reeds to separate the seats for men and women. Goodenough, I, 204, 228 thinks women were excluded from Nabratein and Dura: "they stood outside, in an open court or in the open air, or worshiped... through the worship of their men, and ordinarily they did not themselves go to the synagogues at all," 226.

[123] If Lk. 7:5 is to be relied on (→ 813, 19 f.) we have an instance of a synagogue being built by a single man. Usually parts of synagogues are donated. This probably shows that the synagogue of Lk. 7:5 was a smaller one than those built by many donors, Schwank, 271.

[124] In the light of this one might with Philo (→ n. 67) call the Qumran settlement or the main room surrounded by others — *aulam omnium maximam, quae locus conventus (refectorium, oratorium?) fuisse videtur*, E. Vogt, "Effossiones Hirbet Qumran 1953," *Biblica*, 35 (1954), 548; cf. R. de Vaux, "Fouilles de Khirbet Qumrân," *Rev. Bibl.*, 63 (1956), 542 — a synagogue, though in many ways "monastery" would be more apt. In room B there is at any rate bema-type elevation and the orientation to Jerusalem, cf. Bardtke, *op. cit.* (→ n. 64), 53 f.; Schwank, 273.

5. Furnishings.

Since the synagogue lived by and for the Torah (→ 821, 4 ff.) the most important articles in all synagogues were the Holy Scriptures, esp. the Pentateuch and Prophets (→ I, 99, 17 ff.), and the transportable wooden ark for the Torah (הקדש) ארון or תיבה Aram. ארונא or תיבותא). [125] The Torah scroll was sacred above all other items, Meg., 3, 1. If danger threatened, the scrolls of the Law were to be brought to safety as quickly as possible, Jos. Bell., 2, 291. This was permissible even on the Sabbath, Shab., 16, 1. When a soldier once tore a scroll of the Law and tossed it into the fire the Jews were as much upset as if the whole country were in flames, Jos. Bell., 2, 229 f. Scrolls which could no longer be used were not burned or otherwise destroyed — as sacred scriptures they were not to be violated by the hand of man — but were hidden in the so-called Geniza גניזה of the synagogue, [126] How important the ark of the Torah was later may be seen from the fact that acc. to R. Hona nine people and the ark of the Law are needed for synagogue worship, bBer., 47b, cf. also the statement in Gn. r., 55 on 22:2 that from the ark goes forth light for the world. The ark was placed behind a curtain and at worship it was brought out from a side room, or else it was fixed, and the covered scrolls were taken from it for public reading. [127]

For reading and other liturgical functions (the blessing) there was also a rostrum or podium βῆμα בימה, [128] also ἄμβων, CIJ, II, 781 (Side), and on this a reading desk

---

[125] Rabb. examples in Str.-B., IV, 126-139; Schürer, II, 524 f.; the scrolls and ark are also favourite objects in synagogue art, → II, 385, 14 ff. W. G. Kümmel, "Die älteste religiöse Kunst d. Juden," *Judaica,* 2 (1946), 22-26 rightly pts. out, however, that the Law played a dominant role in all early Jewish art.

[126] Esp. well-known is the Ezra synagogue at Fostat near Cairo, cf. I. Elbogen, Art. "Genisa," Jüd. Lex., II (1928), 1014 f.; K. Schubert, Art. "Geniza," Lex. Th. K.², IV, 675 with bibl.; P. E. Kahle, *The Cairo Geniza* (1962), 1. In Beth-Alpha and Ma'on the geniza was under the βῆμα (→ n. 128), under which the ground was hollowed out, Hiram, *op. cit.,* 20. Cf. also K. G. Kuhn, "Giljonim u. sifre minim," *Judt., Urchr., Kirche, Festschr. f. J. Jeremias,* Beih. ZNW, 26 (1960), 29.

[127] Examples in Str.-B., IV, 137 f.; Krauss Altert., 376-381; Wendel, 20, 24 f. etc. As contemporary mosaics, paintings, reliefs, ossuaries and vases show, the ark is usually a cupboard with 2 doors and a pointed or arched three-cornered gable roof, though there was also a flat ark without a gable. Tube-like cornered cistae and round capsae or chests might have been used instead or together with the ark. Cf. → II, 385, n. 28; Kohl-Watzinger, 142; Krauss Altert., 364-376; Elbogen, 469-472; K. H. Rengstorf, "Zu d. Fresken in d. jüd. Katakombe d. Villa Torlonia in Rom," ZNW, 31 (1932), 34-51; E. G. Budde, *Armarium u. κιβωτός, Ein beitrag z. Gesch. d. alten Mobiliars* (1940); Galling Erwägungen, 169-172; Kraeling The Synagogue, 256 f.; Goodenough, I, 93-6, 190 f., 219, 229 etc.; Wendel, 9 f., 16 f., 22-5.

[128] Sota, 7, 8a; jMeg., 3, 1 (73d, 53); bSukka, 51b. Cf. Jos. Ant., 4, 209 and 2 Εσδρ. 18:4: καὶ ἔστη Εσδρας ὁ γραμματεὺς ἐπὶ βήματος ξυλίνου... v. 5: καὶ ἤνοιξεν Εσδρας τὸ βιβλίον... v. 8: καὶ ἀνέγνωσαν ἐν βιβλίῳ νόμου τοῦ θεοῦ, καὶ ἐδίδασκεν Εσδρας καὶ διέστελλεν ἐν ἐπιστήμῃ κυρίου. From Syracuse we have a βῆμα with inscr., CIJ, I, 653. The ref. here to a marble inscription shows that in the Byzantine period the bema, which was originally made of wood (Schürer, II, 525 thinks it is presupposed even in the time of Jesus), could also be made of stone, Kohl-Watzinger, 143 f. Cf. also Vitringa, 182-190; Str.-B., IV, 139; Elbogen, 473 f.; Sukenik Beth-Alpha, 53 f.; Wendel, 17-22; A. M. Schneider, Art. "Bema," RAC, II, 129 f. Krauss Altert., 385 f. identifies the βῆμα esp. as the place where the leaders had their seats, cf. 392, 394 f., but his arguments are not convincing, though he follows Hck. and Grundm. Mk. on 12:39. The seats of leaders were directly before the platform, cf. G. Dalman, *Jesus-Jeschua* (1922), 39. Acc. to Kohl-Watzinger, 143 they were arranged in a semi-circle behind or in front of the ark. In Elche (Spain), acc. to the inscr. on the floor-mosaic, the πρεσβύτεροι sat in such a way that the ark was in front of them to the side, Kohl-Watzinger, 141, while acc. to T. Meg., 4, 22 (227) they sat with their faces to the congregation and their backs to the sanctuary. Cf. also Kraeling The Synagogue, 256 on

(ἀναλογεῖον כורסיא or אנלגין) facing the congregation. [129] Other articles in the synagogue were lamps and lights. [130] trumpets (→ 83, 9 ff.), [131] and seats. [132] The latter include the seats of honour πρωτοκαθεδρίαι mentioned in the NT (→ VI, 870, 12 ff.) at Mk. 12:39; Mt. 23:6; Lk. 11:43 and 20:46, [133] also the καθέδρα Μωϋσέως, Mt. 23:2. [134] There were also arrangements for washing → 814, 22 ff. [135] Excavations have afforded us a wealth of information about paintings and ornamentation in the synagogue, [136] and

the bema at Dura (256): "merely providing standing room for one person and a reading desk." On the findings at Capernaum, Hammath, Beth-Alpha, Beth She°arim, cf. Sukenik Ancient Synagogues, 143 f.; Goodenough, I, 208, 242; Kohl-Watzinger, 141, 143 f.; BR, 510.

[129] bMeg., 26b; jMeg., 3, 1 (73d, 54). Cf. the examples in Str.-B., IV, 139; Krauss Altert., 386 f.

[130] Rabb. examples Str.-B., IV, 140. In the Hammath synagogue at Tiberias a seven-branched lamp was found in 1921, Sukenik Ancient Synagogues, 55; Goodenough, I, 216, cf. III, Fig. 562; earlier, cf. Kohl-Watzinger, 191 f.; Goodenough, III, Fig. 476, 570-584, 629, 646 etc. From Side in Pamphylia we have a ref. to two such candelabra on an inscr., δύο ἑπταμύχους, CIJ, II, 781. Cf. also → IV, 23, n. 26; E. R. Goodenough, "The Menorah among the Jews of the Roman World," HUCA, 23, Part II (1950/51), 449-492; W. Eltester, "Der siebenarmige Leuchter u. d. Titusbogen," Judt. Urchr. Kirche, Festschr. f. J. Jeremias, Beih. ZNW, 26 (1960), 63-7. Acc. to Rengstorf, op. cit., 52-8 and Eltester, 64 the synagogue lamps symbolise the illuminating power of the Law. For other possible interpretations cf. Goodenough, 458-461 and Eltester, 65.

[131] These were used, e.g., to announce the Sabbath from the synagogue roof, cf. Str.-B., IV, 140-142; Kosmala, 354-361.

[132] Since the stone benches along the walls did not provide enough seating mats and rugs were spread on the floor, bBB, 8b. Cf. Str.-B., IV, 142; Elbogen, 475 f.

[133] Cf. T. Meg., 4, 21 (227); 71 golden seats are mentioned in connection with the synagogue at Alexandria, T. Sukka, 4, 6 (198), cf. Str.-B., IV, 122. On T. Meg., 4, 22 (227) → n. 128. Cf. also the ref. in the Phocaea inscr. to the privilege of a προεδρία in the synagogue, CIJ, II, 738.

[134] Cf. קתדרא דמשה Pesikt., 7a; Ass. Mos., 12, 2 and the bibl. → IV, 864, n. 196; also Watzinger, 108; Krauss Altert., 386; Sukenik Ancient Synagogues, 13, 57-61; Goodenough, I, 182, 197 f., 215, 229; II, 74 (with ref.); Rost Bemerkungen, 58 f.; Kraeling The Synagogue, 17; Scharlemann, 910. It is worth noting that the presence of καθέδραι Μωϋσέως is denied by M. Ginsburger, "La 'chaire de Moïse,' " REJ, 90 (1931), 161-165 and Schwartzmann, 118, n. 12. Earlier Mt. 23:2 was often taken symbolically, e.g., C. G. Montefiore, The Synoptic Gospels, I (1909), 725 f. For I. Renov, "The Seat of Moses," Israel Exploration Journal, 5 (1955), 262-267 and C. Roth, "The 'Chair of Moses' and Its Survivals," Palestine Explor. Quarterly, 81 (1949), 100-111 → n. 143.

[135] In the Beth-Shean synag. (Scythopolis) a wooden vessel or bucket גורנה γοῦρνα is mentioned for washing, jMeg., 3, 4 (74a, 57), in Noarah a basin מרישת, CIJ, II, 1197, in Deliler a vessel? μασκαύλης, II, 754, cf. Krauss Altert., 231, 313 f.; Kohl-Watzinger, 144; Goodenough, I, 182. On the basin in the older synagogue at Dura cf. Kraeling The Synagogue, 27 f., esp. n. 125, 128, on that in the later synag., 13 and Goodenough, I, 227. Fragments of stone basins which might have been used for washing the hands have been found immediately in front of the synagogue in ed-Dschīsch, Kohl-Watzinger, 144 and 111, Ill. 217. On χρησο[τ]ήρια τῶν ὑδάτων in the Theodotus inscr., CIJ, II, 1404, 6 f. cf. Vincent, op. cit. (→ n. 85), 254 f. → also n. 99.

[136] Esp. famous are the mosaics and murals at Dura-Europos. From the vast bibl. the most important studies (to 1935 → II, 383, 14 ff.) are G. Wodtke, "Malereien d. Synagoge in Dura u. ihre Par. in d. chr. Kunst," ZNW, 34 (1935), 51-62; M. Aubert, "Le peintre de la synag. de Doura," Gazette d. beaux arts, 80 (1938), 1-24; M. Rostovtzeff, Dura-Europos and Its Art (1938); Comte du Mesnil du Buisson, 75-90; also Les peintures de la synag. de Doura-Europos (1939); I. Sonne, "The Paintings of the Dura Synagogue," HUCA, 20 (1947), 255-362; A. Grabar, "Les fresques de la synag. de Dura-Europos," Comptes rendus de l'Académie des Inscr. et Belles-Lettres (1941), 77-90; also "Le thème religieux des fresques de la synagogue de Doura," RHR, 123 (1941), 143-192; 124 (1942), 1-35; also "Images bibl. d'Apamée et fresques de la synagogue de Doura," Cahiers archéol., 5 (1951), 9-14; O. Eiss-feldt, "Die Wandbilder d. Synagoge v. Dura-Europos," Forschungen u. Fortschritte, 31

very surprisingly have shown that in the Chr. era figurative depictions occurred even in synagogues in Palestine on mosaics and murals, [137] → II, 384, 23 ff.

6. Purpose and Significance.

a. Teaching the Law. The meaning and purpose of the synagogue derive from the central importance the Torah and Halachah came to have in Judaism. Without the Law there would have been no synagogues. [138] The extraordinarily high evaluation of legal piety forced the synagogues into the service of the teaching and propagation of the Law. In seeking to make the Jewish community acquainted with the Law the synagogues of the Dispersion do not differ from those in the mother country, nor do those of NT days differ from the synagogues of other periods. The synagogue is undoubtedly many other things, but it is primarily the place of the Torah, which is to be read and taught, heard and learned here. The Theodotus inscr. expressly states the purpose of the synagogue built by Theodotus ῳκοδόμησε τὴν συναγωγ[ὴ]ν εἰς ἀν[άγ]νωσ[ιν] νόμου καὶ εἰς [δ]ιδαχ[ὴ]ν ἐντολῶν, CIJ, II, 1404, 3-5. The witness of Jos. is to the same effect: ἑκάστης ἑβδομάδος... ἐπὶ τὴν ἀκρόασιν ἐκέλευσε (sc. ὁ νομοθέτης) τοῦ νόμου συλλέγεσθαι καὶ τοῦτον ἀκριβῶς ἐκμανθάνειν, Jos. Ap., 2, 175. Philo states similarly the aim of synagogue meetings σὺν αἰδοῖ καὶ κόσμῳ τῶν νόμων ἀκροᾶσθαι, Eus. Praep. Ev., 8, 7, 12 or ἐν τοῖς συναγωγίοις... τὰς ἱερὰς βίβλους ἀναγινώσκειν, Philo Som., II, 127. Acc. to the Rabb. Moses himself ordained that there should be reading from the Torah to instruct Israelites in the Law's demands, jMeg., 2, 1 (75a, 19); bMeg., 32a. [139] Ac. 15:21 may be quoted in the same connection: Μωϋσῆς γὰρ ἐκ γενεῶν ἀρχαίων κατὰ πόλιν τοὺς κηρύσσοντας αὐτὸν ἔχει ἐν ταῖς συναγωγαῖς κατὰ πᾶν σάββατον ἀναγινωσκόμενος. Synagogue instruction in the Law includes exposition

---

(1957), 241-9; R. Wischnitzer, The Messianic Theme in the Paintings of the Dura Synagogue (1948); H. L. Hempel, "Zum Problem d. Anfänge d. AT-Illustration," ZAW, 69 (1957), 121-9; Simon, 34-46; Wendel, 8-16; Ehrlich, 91-94; Kraeling The Synagogue (bibl. here, also in O. Eissfeldt, Art. "Dura-Europos," RAC, IV, 367-370), cf. also the reviews of H. Lietzmann, ThLZ, 65 (1940), 113-7; H. Stern, ThLZ, 83 (1958), 249-254 and M. Noth, ZDPV, 75 (1959), 164-181; Goodenough, I, 238-264 (on Hammath, Beth-Alpha etc.); B. Kanael, Die Kunst d. antiken Synagoge (1961).

[137] We find depictions of men, animals, plants and cultic articles (ark, menora, shofar, lulab, ethrog), astral, magical, apotropaic and (esp. in mosaics) bibl. themes, Noah in the ark, the offering of Isaac, crossing the Red Sea, the stories of Elijah and David, the visions of Ezekiel, Daniel in the lions' den etc. Many Rabb. witnesses show that the OT command (Ex. 20:4 f.; Lv. 26:1; cf. also Jos. Ap., 2, 75; Ant., 17, 150 f.) could be evaded and depiction, though not iconolatry, allowed, T AZ 5, 2 (468); bAZ, 42b etc. Cf. J. B. Frey, "La question des images chez les Juifs à la lumière des récentes découvertes," Biblica, 15 (1934), 265-300; Kümmel, op. cit. (→ n. 125), 1-56; R. Meyer, "Die Figurendarstellung in d. Kunst d. späthell. Judt.," Judaica, 5 (1949), 1-40; A. Baumstark, Art. "Bild (jüd.)," RAC, II, 287-302 (bibl. 300-302); Ehrlich, 86-8; E. R. Goodenough, "The Rabbis and Jewish Art in the Greco-Roman Period," HUCA, 32 (1961), 269-279.

[138] Cf. Lv. r., 11 on 9:1 → 811, 6 f.

[139] Cf. Str.-B., IV, 154 f., 171 f.; cf. also Jos. Ap., 2, 175; Ezr. 7:25 and on this Galling Erwägungen, 167 f.

and preaching as well as reading: [140] εἰς ἀναγινώσκει τοὺς ἱεροὺς νόμους αὐτοῖς καὶ καθ᾽ ἕκαστον ἐξηγεῖται, whereupon those who attend the synagogues may return home "enriched in the knowledge of the sacred laws," Eus. Praep. Ev., 8, 7, 13, [141] cf. also Philo Som., II, 127. But since the παράδοσις was no less important than the Torah in the Rabbinate, [142] the synagogue had also to transmit customs and usages, rulings and traditions. [143] μάθησις τῶν ἡμετέρων ἐθῶν καὶ νόμου belong together, Jos. Ant., 16, 43. The goal and centre of the synagogue and its gatherings [144] are thus the passing on, the unfolding and the applying of the νόμος and παράδοσις with a view to practical obedience to the Law.

b. Relation to the Temple. In NT days the temple and the synagogue stood alongside one another, nor was there any thought of antithesis or rivalry. This may be seen from the fact that prior to the destruction of the temple there was a synagogue on the temple hill, [145] and Theodotus, who lived in Jerusalem before 70 A.D., was both ἱερεύς and ἀρχισυνάγωγος, CIJ, II, 1404, 1 f. The founding of synagogues shows that the Rabbis saw in the synagogue an equivalent of the temple, and in the *diaspora* and after the

---

[140] Cf. Ac. 13:15; Rabb. examples Str.-B., IV, 171-188; Krauss Altert., 167-182. With the reading, transl. and exposition of the Law the synagogue service included recitation of the shema, prayer and blessing, Schürer, II, 526-536; Str.-B., IV, 153-188; Elbogen, 14-231; Dalman, *op. cit.* (→ n. 128), 35-41; P. P. Levertoff, "Synagogue Worship in the First Century," *Liturgy and Worship*, ed. W. K. L. Clarke (1932), 60-77; C. W. Dugmore, *The Influence of the Synagogue upon the Divine Office* (1945), 11-25; E. Werner, *The Sacred Bridge, The Interdependence of Liturgy and Music in Synagogue and Church during the First Millennium* (1959); W. Wiefel, *Der Synagogengottesdienst im nt.lichen Zeitalter u. seine Einwirkung auf den entstehenden chr. Gottesdienst*, Diss. Leipzig (1959); further bibl. in F. C. Grant, "Modern Study of the Jewish Liturgy," ZAW, 65 (1953), 74-7.

[141] Cf. Philo's account of the Essene synagogues: The Essenes met on the 7th day in the holy places called synagogues, sat down in order, and listened with due reverence: εἶθ᾽ εἷς μέν τις τὰς βίβλους ἀναγινώσκει λαβών, ἕτερος δὲ τῶν ἐμπειροτάτων ὅσα μὴ γνώριμα παρελθὼν ἀναδιδάσκει, Omn. Prob., 81 f.; cf. 1 QS 6:7 f.

[142] Cf. Mk. 7:1 ff.; Ab., 1, 1; 3, 14; Sanh., 11, 2 f. and v. Weber, 100-105; Str.-B., I, 693 f.; Moore, I, 251-262.

[143] The καθέδρα Μωϋσέως (Mt. 23:2) is a symbol of the authority vested in teachers of the Torah in the synagogue; they sat on this as successors of Moses. Cf. Renov, *op. cit.* (→ n. 134), also "Proceedings," JBL, 70 (1951), VI, But cf. Roth, *op. cit.* (→ n. 134), who thinks the καθέδρα was the place where the sacred scrolls were kept during worship; in Palestine this became "a mere symbol" when the ark was introduced; later this was forgotten and "ultimately it was regarded as the vacant seat reserved for the prophet Elijah," 110. In criticism cf. Goodenough, I, 197, n. 145, who also replies to R. Krautheimer's conjecture that the seat remained empty and "that in its emptiness it recalled the presence of God, the Shekinah."

[144] Meg., 1, 3; bBer., 6a, 7b etc. Since these were mostly on the Sabbath, Jos. Ant., 16, 164 calls the synagogue the σαββατεῖον ("sabbath-house"). One should not view this σαββατεῖον as an improper construct in the list of temple names in -ειον or -ιειον after the names of deities because the unknown author of the imperial decree might have thought of Σαβάζιος [Katz], cf. Katz, "Das Problem d. Urtextes d. LXX," ThZ, 5 (1949), 5 f., n. 6. An inscr. from Thyatira ref. to a σαμβατεῖον, CIJ, II, 752, 2. Cf. also H. C. Youthie, "Sambathis," HThR, 37 (1944), 213-6, who in 216, n. 35 distinguishes between Σαμβαθεῖον temple of Sambathis (Sambethe, Sabbe) and Σαββατεῖον "sabbath-house," "synagogue" (?), with bibl. Elbogen, 445 ref. to Syr. בית שבתא. Cf. also Krauss Altert., 25 f.; Schürer, II, 518, n. 61.

[145] Cf. Yoma, 7, 1; Sota, 7, 7 f.; T. Sukka, 4, 5 (198), also Vitringa, 38 f.; Str.-B., II, 150; Dalman Orte, 317; Krauss Altert., 60-72, 201 f., 335-7. Vitringa, 39 has *in Synagoga Templi* for ἐν τῷ ἱερῷ at Mt. 26:55.

destruction of the temple it was a full substitute. [146] In particular the adoption of the seven-branched candelabra and orientation to the temple (→ 815, 4 ff.) express the abiding significance of the temple. Imitation was demanded by the destruction of the temple. Conduct required in the synagogue corresponds at many pts. to the relevant rulings about the temple, [147] and the same applies to the respective liturgical practices. [148] Thus prayer was offered at the time of the offering of sacrifice in the temple, [149] and there was also prayer in the synagogue for the restoration of the temple, Sh. E., 14, 16 or 14, 17, [150] just as the laws and statutes concerning temple worship and the sacrificial cultus were read, transl. and expounded in the synagogue. The synagogues were sanctuaries in miniature מקדש מעט , bMeg., 29a, Ez. 11:16. In the Tg. on this v. Yahweh says: "I gave them synagogues which take second place (תנין literally a second) after my sanctuary." [151]

This implies no depreciation of synagogues, rather the reverse. [152] Philo asked already whether there was any more important institution than this: ἆρά σοι δοκεῖ ταῦτα ἀργούντων εἶναι καὶ οὐ παντὸς σπουδάσματος μᾶλλον ἀναγκαῖα αὐτοῖς; Eus. Praep. Ev., 8, 7, 14. Priestly worship with altar and offerings was replaced by a ministry of the word influenced by prophetic traditions. The synagogues also liberated Judaism from geographical bondage to one place and filled the many gaps caused by cultic centralisation. In particular the synagogue was a lay institution, or more precisely one which was essentially dominated by Pharisaism. [153] The presence of priests was not mandatory, not even for worship, cf. Meg., 4, 3. [154] With few exceptions the Scriptures might be read by anyone; even women and children seem not to have been excluded. [155]

---

[146] The synagogue ark corresponds to the ark of the covenant (the name ארון is the same), the curtain before it to the temple curtain, and perhaps there are two degrees of holiness ("holy place" and "holy of holies"), Str.-B., IV, 123-142, esp. 123, 125; Krauss Altert., 337 etc.; Dahl, 70. But lack of sources prior to the destruction of the temple makes it difficult to discuss the relation between synagogue and temple, Filson, 84.

[147] Cf. Str.-B., IV, 125.

[148] Cf. Dahl, 69 f.; Str.-B., IV, 153-188; Elbogen, passim (cf. index s.v. "Tempel: Reste aus d. Liturgie").

[149] bBer., 26a. bBar.; jBer., 4, 1 (7b, 3); cf. Str.-B., II, 696-702.

[150] Cf. Dahl, 64 f., 69, 89; eschatological hope, however, was connected almost exclusively with the temple and the gathering of the dispersed to Zion, cf. Volz Esch., 371, 376-8 etc. (though cf. → n. 152). In Babylonia the transplanting of synagogues to Israel was expected, bMeg., 29a. For other eschatological hopes relating to synagogues cf. Weber, 377 f.; → 827, 21 ff.

[151] Cf. Str.-B., IV, 116, 125; Krauss Altert., 93; Moore, III, 91; Filson, 84; Simon, 27 f. On Ez. 11:16 f. Menes, 272, 274. Galling Erwägungen, 165 f. → n. 74.

[152] R. T. Herford, Die Pharisäer (1928), 110 f. rightly finds it surprising that with all the synagogues in Jerusalem one should also be put up in the temple and he thinks this was done "to stress emphatically religious viewpoints which the temple, historically, was not adapted to represent." Acc. to L. Baeck, "Die Pharisäer," Pls., die Pharisäer u. d. NT (1961), 55 f. the juxtaposition of temple and synagogue was bound to lead sooner or later to opposition and to pose the question where the true religious home of the people was. In view of the gt. importance of the Law and learning among the Pharisees the answer of the Tannaitic tradition could only be that "true worship is not sacrifice, i.e., not what the temple gives, but what the synagogue offers, prayer and the exposition of Scripture." In later romanticism the temple in ruins became more influential than the temple still standing: "It gradually becomes a symbol of the past and hence very quickly a dream of the future too," 84 f. Cf. 55-85 and Simon, 27.

[153] Cf. J. Z. Lauterbach, "The Pharisees and Their Teachings," HUCA, 6 (1929), 79, 126 f.; Moore, I, 286 f.; Herford, op. cit., 99-118; Filson, 77, 84 f.; Jeremias, op. cit. (→ n. 88), II, 120; Baeck, op. cit. (→ n. 152), 57-59, 79-84.

[154] Cf. Str.-B., IV, 153; Damasc. 13:2 (15:5) explicitly requires the presence of a priest among ten present, similarly 1 QS 6:3 f.

[155] Examples Str.-B., IV, 156 f., 166 f.; Jeremias, op. cit., II, 248; Elbogen, 170. If a priest was present he alone was to give the benediction, cf. Str.-B., IV, 238 f. for examples.

Prayer in the synagogue was no less valuable than sacrifice in the temple. R. Pineᵉchas (c. 360) said in the name of R. Hosha'ya (c. 225): He who prays in the synagogue is as one who offers a pure mincha, jBer., 4, 1 (8d, 61 f.). [156] The synagogue was τὸ ἱερόν (→ n. 50) and ὁ ἅγιος τόπος (→ n. 49). Synagogues were often called "most holy" ἁγιωτάτη. [157] Even when the building was destroyed the place where a synagogue had stood was a holy place קדשתן אף כשהן שוממין, Meg., 3, 3. [158] God is present in the synagogue as well as the temple. "So long as the Israelites stay in synagogues and houses of instruction God causes his shekinah to stay among them," said R. Yudan (c. 350) in the name of R. Yiçchaq (c. 300), Pesikt., 193a; indeed, the latter is reputed to have said: "As the gazelle springs on the mountains and leaps from one tree to another, so God springs from this synagogue to that synagogue and from this house of instruction to that house of instruction. Why? To bless Israel," Pesikt., 48b. R. Yirmeᵉya (c. 320) said in the name of R. Abbahu (c. 300) that God is to be sought and found in the synagogues and houses of instruction, jBer., 5 (8d, 63 f.). [159]

c. Place of Prayer. This shows why the synagogue is also the preferred place of prayer, → II, 800, 41 ff. [160] Acc. to Jos. Ap., 1, 209 the Jews pray in the synagogues μέχρι τῆς ἑσπέρας. R. Abba bChiyya (c. 320) and R. Chiyya bAbba (c. 280) said in the name of R. Jochanan (d. 279) that man is to pray in the place ordained for prayer, i.e., the synagogue, jBer., 4 (8b, 31 f.), cf. bBer., 8a. The man who has a synagogue in his town and does not pray in it is called a bad neighbour (Jer. 12:14), R. Simon bLakkish (d. c. 275), bBer., 8a. Acc. to Midr. Ps. 4 on 4:5 (23b) Bar. R. Eli'ezer bYa'aqob, II (c. 150) said: "God says to Israel: I have said to thee; when thou prayest, pray in the synagogue of the city." [161] Indeed, acc. to R. Abba Binjamin a man's prayer is answered only in the synagogue, bBer., 6a. Along similar lines Philo, Jos. and many inscr. call the synagogue προσευχή and (if only rarely) προσευκτήριον and εὐχεῖον → 808, 8 f.

d. School. The central position of the Law, to which we have ref. above, meant that synagoues were also places of teaching and instruction; for μανθανέτωσαν δὲ καὶ οἱ παῖδες πρῶτον τοὺς νόμους, Jos. Ant., 4, 211. Along with the parental instruction which from earliest childhood [162] gave children a knowledge of the Law [163] and encouraged them to follow it, they early attended the elementary school בית הספר which taught them to read it and a school devoted to the study of the Mishnah בית המדרש. We find such in Jerusalem before the destruction of the temple, jMeg., 3, 1 (73d, 29 f.). [164] Other passages show that in synagogues there were rooms for educational purposes or that the synagogues themselves were schools. [165]

---

[156] Cf. Str.-B., I, 399; IV, 124.

[157] Inscr. from Deliler, CIJ, II, 754; Side, 781; Gerasa, 867. Also from Hyllarima (Caria) in BCH, 58 (1934), 379, No. 44, cf. Robert, op. cit., 41, n. 6 and 43, n. 4. Cf. also → n. 49, 60 and Jos. Bell., 4, 408 and 7, 45; jMeg., 3, 1 (73d, 51 ff.). Cf. Krauss Altert., 413-433, 436.

[158] Rabb. of the older period think a synagogue may be sold except as baths, tannery, or wash-house, Meg., 3, 2. R. Jᵉhuda (c. 150) even said the purchaser of a synagogue might make of it anything he wanted, Meg., 3, 2. Cf. further Str.-B., II, 663 f.

[159] Examples Str.-B., IV, 124.　　　　　　　　　[160] Str.-B., I, 396-401; IV, 124.

[161] Str.-B., I, 399 (parallels); Krauss Altert., 275.

[162] ἐκ πρώτης ἡλικίας ... παιδευθέντες, Philo Leg. Gaj., 210; Jos. Ap., 2, 178.

[163] Philo Leg. Gaj., 115; Jos. Ant., 4, 211; Ap., 1, 60 and 2, 204. The mother of Joshua, son of Chananiah, took her son in the cradle to the synagogue so that his ears might be fixed on the words of the Torah, jJeb., 1, 6 (3a, 61 f.). Acc. to Rab (d. 247) women earn merit if they have their sons learn Scripture in the synagogue, bBer., 17a.

[164] Cf. Str.-B., II, 150, 662; IV, 121.

[165] On Jewish education cf. Vitringa, 134-144; Schürer, II, 491-497; S. Krauss, Talmudische Archäol., III (1912), 199-239; E. Ebner, Elementary Education in Ancient Israel during the Tannaitic Period (10-220 CE) (1956).

In some cases the synagogues and schools are the same (bBQ, 60b, Bar.; jMQ, 3, 1 [81d, 37 f.]; bChag., 15b) [166] while in others they are distinguished. The two are mentioned together in Ter., 11, 10 and Pes., 4, 4 בבתי כנסיות ובבתי מדרשות, [167] and they seem to have been next door to each other in bBer., 64a. Acc. to bMeg., 26b, 27a the school-house was more holy than the synagogue, since the latter might be changed into the former but not vice versa. Philo calls synagogues the places where virtues are taught: τὰ γὰρ κατὰ πόλεις προσευκτήρια τί ἕτερόν ἐστιν ἢ διδασκαλεῖα φρονήσεως καὶ ἀνδρείας καὶ σωφροσύνης καὶ δικαιοσύνης εὐσεβείας τε καὶ ὁσιότητος καὶ συμπάσης ἀρετῆς, Vit. Mos., II (III), 216, cf. Spec. Leg., II, 62. But the synagogue was not just the school. It was also the place where the rabbi studied, [168] cf. R. Jehoshua' bLevi בתי כנסיות ובתי מדרשות לחכמים ולתלמידיהם jMeg., 3, 4 (74a, 53). Abaye (†338/39) said: "At first I studied at home and prayed in the synagogue. But when I heard what David said: Yahweh, I love the place of thine house Ps. 26:8, I studied in the synagogue, bMeg., 29a; [169] bSota, 22a. Even the man who reads Scripture and studies the Mishnah but does not associate with scholars is regarded as an empty man and a man of the 'am ha-ares. Acc. to Hier. Ep., 36, 1 (CSEL, 54, 268) there was also a library in the synagogue.

e. Council House and Place of Assembly. Synagogues, though only so long as they had not received a sacral character through the permanent erection of the ark, could also serve as places of assembly for communal discussions and meetings. Acc. to bKet., 5a one goes to the synagogue to set public affairs in order. [170] Public mourning for the dead took place there, T. Meg., 3, 7 (224 f.) and bMeg, 28b, Bar. [171] Announcements about articles found and thefts were made there, bBM, 28b; Lv. r., 6 on 5:1; Ar., 6, 1. The poor were fed and sheltered there, bPes., 101a. Public decisions and announcements regarding voluntary almsgiving were also made in the synagogue, [172] so too regarding judicial investigations and proceedings, bJeb., 65b., e.g., the divorce plea of a childless woman, Jos. Vit., 294-302 an ἐξέτασις; [173] oaths were also sworn there, Shebu., 4, 10, and whippings administered → 831, 9 ff. Inscr. from Panticapaion show that the Jews there executed sacral manumission of slaves in the synagogues ἀφείημι ἐπὶ τῆς [προ]σευχῆς θρεπτόν μου Ἡρακλᾶν ἐλεύθερον καθάπαξ κατὰ εὐχή[ν] μου ἀνεπίλεπτον καὶ

---

[166] Cf. Str.-B., I, 144; IV, 121 f.; → n. 163, 164; Krauss Altert., 181, 191 f., 363, 430; Ebner, op. cit., 64 f.

[167] Cf. Schürer, II, 386, n. 50.

[168] Grant is mistaken when he writes (op. cit. [→ n. 76], 39): "The synagogue was really an institute for advanced religious study; it was not the school for children... but... for adult study of the Torah."

[169] Cf. Str.-B., IV, 123 f.

[170] Jos. Vit., 277 and cf. esp. Krauss Altert., 4, 182-198, 341-4; Bacher Hastings DB, IV, 642 f.; Schürer, II, 526. The gt. basilica at Alexandria was not primarily a synagogue but a market-hall used for communal purposes as well as worship, Str.-B., IV, 118; Krauss Altert., 261-3; Goodenough, II, 86. It should be noted, however, that the national political element in the synagogue declined with the cultic and sacral, Dahl, 68.

[171] On mourning in Judaism → III, 841, 40 ff.; Str.-B., IV, 582-590.

[172] Cf. Str.-B., I, 388; P. Fiebig, "Jesu Bergpredigt," FRL, NF, 20 (1924), 99 f.; Krauss Altert., 191.

[173] Cf. also the saying of Pilate in the Nicodemus-Ev. Acta Pilati, 4, 3; λάβετε αὐτὸν ὑμεῖς καὶ ἀπαγάγετε εἰς τὴν συναγωγὴν ὑμῶν, καὶ κατὰ τὸν νόμον ὑμῶν κρίνατε αὐτόν. This also has the Jews discuss in the synagogue what death Joseph of Arimathea shall die, 12, 2; cf. 16, 5.

ἀπα[ρ]ενόχλητον, CIJ, I, 683 (80 A.D.), cf. 684.[174] Ptolemaeus Euergetes[175] granted a Jewish synagogue the right of asylum τὴν προσευχὴν ἄσυλον, CIJ, II, 1449,[176] and this was obviously renewed by Queen Zenobia of Palmyra and her son (c. 270 A.D.).[177]

f. Hospice. Synagogues were also used as hospices for Jews from abroad, esp. at Jerusalem during the gt. feasts. The Theodotus inscr. mentions the building of synagogue, hospice or house of strangers ξενῶν, chambers δώματα[178] and plumbing or baths χρησ[τ]ήρια τῶν ὑδάτων for strangers seeking shelter (= pilgrims, εἰς κατάλυμα τοῖς [χ]ρῄζουσιν ἀπὸ τῆς ξέ[ν]ης) all together, CIJ, II, 1404, 6-8; from this one may deduce that the synagogue and hospice were in a single complex. bPes., 101a also says that foreign guests were lodged and fed in the synagogue.[179] Rabbis esp. found rooms and slept in synagogues, jMeg., 3, 5 (74a, 65).[180]

g. Aedes sacrae. As many inscr. show, several synagogues were dedicated to secular rulers e.g., to Ptolemy kings and queens in Egypt[181] or to Septimius Severus and his sons in Galilean Kasyun.[182] Rulers were also honoured by ψηφίσματα, decrees of homage, Philo Flacc., 97, 103. Acc. to Philo Leg. Gaj., 133 shields, wreaths, pillars and

---

174 Cf. Schürer, III, 23 f., 93 f.; Juster, I, 460; II, 82; Krauss Altert., 239 f.; H. Leclercq, Art. "Judaisme," DACL, 8, 247-250; Deissmann LO, 273 f.; J. B. Frey, CIJ, I, p. 495 f. (with bibl.); F. Bömer, "Untersuchungen über d. Religion d. Sklaven in Griechenland u. Rom, II: D. sog. sakrale Freilassung in Griechenland u. die (δοῦλοι) ἱεροί," AAMainz (1960/61), 101-106. Cf. also P. Oxy., IX, 1205, 7: ἀριθμη[θέντων ἡμῖν ὑπὲρ τῆς ἐλευθερώσεως καὶ ἀπολύσ]εως παρὰ τῆς συνα[γ]ωγῆς τῶν Ἰουδαίων.
175 U. Wilcken, Review, Berliner Philol. Wochenschr., 16 (1896), 1493; M. L. Strack, "Inschr. aus ptolemäischer Zeit," APF, 2 (1903), 541 f. and Schürer, II, 499 f. opt. for Ptolemy III. Euergetes I (246-221 B.C.), others for Ptolemy VII. Euergetes II (145-116). Cf. J. B. Frey, CIJ, II, p. 376.
176 Cf. Schürer, II, 499, n. 4b and III, 41; Krauss Altert., 226 f.; 264 f., 418; Juster, I, 460, n. 4; gen. F. v. Woess, "Das Asylwesen Ägyptens in d. Ptolemäerzeit u. d. spätere Entwicklung," Münchener Beiträge z. Papyrusforschung u. antiken Rechtsgesch., 5 (1923), 9-11; L. Wenger, Art. "Asylrecht," RAC, I, 836-844 (and bibl.).
177 T. Mommsen, Additamenta secunda ad corporis vol. III, Ephemeris Epigraphica, 4 (1881), 25 f.; Woess, op. cit., 10.
178 On δώματα cf. H. Lietzmann, "Notizen," ZNW, 20 (1921), 172; Vincent, op. cit. (→ n. 85), 253 f.; S. Klein, "Das Fremdenhaus d. Synagoge," MGWJ, 76 (1932), 548.
179 Since this is forbidden in T. Meg., 3, 7 (224) the oldest Talmud commentators already assume that side-rooms are meant, Klein, op. cit., 548. Cf. also jBer., 4 (7c, 49) פונדק = πανδοχεῖον. For other Rabb. examples Krauss Altert., 192, 362. In Dura-Europos, too, there was a "guest-house for transient fellow-Jews," Kraeling The Synagogue, 10 f., 32. Probably the guest-house built by R. Eliezer דאורחותא בית דה דה, which an Er-Rama inscr. mentions (CIJ, II, 979), was combined with a synagogue, cf. J. Ben-Zevi, "A Third Cent. Aram. Inscr.," JPOS, 13 (1933), 94-6; Goodenough, I, 213; J. B. Frey, CIJ, II, p. 163; Klein, op. cit., 554-6. On Hammam-Lif cf. Goodenough, II, 90, Capernaum, I, 182, El-Hammeh Sukenik El-Hammeh, 77. Cf. also Gregory the Gt. Ep., 9, 55 (MPL, 77 [1896], 993 C): synagogae ipsae cum his hospitiis quae sub ipsis sunt, vel earum parietibus cohaerent, atque hortis ibi conjunctis, and on this Vincent, 252 f., cf. Vitringa, 225 f.; Klein, 545-557, 603 f.; also "Neues zum Fremdenhaus d. Synagoge," MGWJ, 77 (1933), 81-4.
180 Cf. Str.-B., IV, 144.
181 Cf. the Alexandria inscr., CIJ, II, 1432, 1433, also Nitria, 1442, Athribis, 1443. Cf. as an example the Schedia inscr. (246-221 B.C.): [Ὑ]πὲρ βασιλέως Πτολεμαίου καὶ βασιλίσσης Βερνίκης ἀδελφῆς καὶ γυναικὸς καὶ τῶν τέκνων, τὴν προσευχὴν οἱ Ἰουδα(ῖ)οι, CIJ, II, 1440. Parts of synagogues were also dedicated to the Ptolemies, e.g. the πυλών at Xenephyris (CIJ, II, 1441), the ἐξέδρα at Athribis (II, 1444).
182 CIJ, II, 972 (197 A.D.); the Jewish character of the inscr. is uncertain; cf. J. B. Frey, CIJ, II, pp. 157-9 (with bibl.).

inscr. were also put in synagogues in honour of the emperors.[183] Another form of veneration was to name synagogues after rulers or donors, → 806, 28 ff. Acc. to Philo the Jews give thanks to the imperial house precisely through their synagogues, Flacc., 48; τοῖς πανταχόθι τῆς οἰκουμένης 'Ιουδαίοις ὁρμητήρια τῆς εἰς τὸν Σεβαστὸν οἶκον ὁσιότητός εἰσιν αἱ προσευχαὶ ἐπιδήλως, Flacc., 49. The obvious aim of these acts of veneration and dedication is to express loyalty to rulers and to give thanks for political protection. In NT days synagogues had in the world-empire of Rome privileges corresponding to the *aedes sacrae*.[184]

On the other hand the relation of the native population to the Jews of the Dispersion was not always free of tension, and this naturally affected the attitude to synagogues. Non-Jews did not always respect these as desired. In Caesarea mockery of the Jewish sanctuary went to the pt. of scorning the laws and polluting the sites, Jos. Bell., 2, 289. This instance reported by Jos. was in the tense atmosphere shortly before the Jewish war, and most prudent Jews sought protection from the authorities (Bell., 2, 290), which presupposes a successful outcome. Yet this was no isolated occurrence, as may be seen esp. from the anti-Jewish riots in Alexandria under Flaccus, 38 A.D. Here the nationalistic Alexandrians tried to provoke the Jews by putting statues of the emperor in the synagogues in order that they might then defame the Jews as hostile to the emperor; the result was a regular pogrom in the course of which the synagogues were plundered and desecrated, burned and destroyed.[185] On the other hand there are no other instances of the polluting of synagogues in pagan antiquity, → 839, 14 ff.

The relation of the Jew to his synagogue was one of pride, veneration, and commitment. R. Nechunya bHaqana (*c.* 70) thanks God that He has given him a part among those who sit in the school-house and the synagogue, jBer., 4 (7d, 26 ff.).[186] The pious Jew goes daily to the synagogue; if he misses a day God asks after him, R. Yiçchaq (*c.* 300), bBer., 6b. He who goes to the synagogue early in the morning and late in the evening is assured of a long life, R. Jochanan and R. Joshua bLevi, bBer., 8a, cf. 47b and bSanh., 111b. God rewards steps made to the synagogue, bBM, 107a. He causes him who goes to return laden with blessings, Dt. r., 7 on 28:1 → 824, 19 f. He who attends synagogues and houses of instruction in this world will also enter into them in the next, R. Joshua bLevi, *loc. cit.*[187] With the daily visit synagogues are esp. attended on the Sabbath (σαββατεῖον → n. 144) and feastdays.[188] How closely synagogues and the Jewish community are linked may be seen from the fact that both may be denoted by the same word συναγωγή and its equivalents, → 806, 11 ff. Historically it is unmistakable that there has hardly been a more important or momentous factor for the Jewish community than the rise of the synagogue alongside

---

[183] Cf. Krauss Altert., 161-4.

[184] Cf. Jos. Ant., 19, 300-311 and 16, 162-165; Philo Leg. Gaj., 311; also Krauss Altert., 413-423; Juster, I, 459-472; Schürer, III, 107-121. On the question whether Jewish synagogues (congregations) were *collegia licita* cf. S. L. Guterman, *Religious Toleration and Persecution in Ancient Rome* (1951), 130-156.

[185] Philo Flacc., 41, 53; Leg. Gaj., 132, 134, 138, 188, 238, 245. Cf. A. Bludau, *Juden u. Judenverfolgungen im alten Alexandria* (1906); U. Wilcken, "Zum alexandrinischen Antisemitismus," ASG, 27 (1909), 784-839; H. I. Bell, *Juden u. Griechen im röm. Alexandreia,* Beih. zum AO, 9 (1927), 14-21. On ancient anti-semitism in gen. cf. Juster, I, 44-48; J. Leipoldt, *Antisemitismus in d. alten Welt* (1933); also Art. "Antisemitismus," RAC, I, 469-476; I. Heinemann, Art. "Antisemitismus," Pauly-W. Suppl., 5 (1931), 3-43; Simon, 239-274; W. Holsten, Art. "Antisemitismus," RGG, I³, 456-459.

[186] Cf. Str.-B., II, 240 with par. and Krauss Altert., 427-433.

[187] In a synagogue inscr. from Umm el-ʿamed in Galilee (*c.* 3rd cent. A.D.) we find the expression תרא דמרי שומיא "door of the Lord of heaven"; this is a ref. to the whole synagogue acc. to I Sonne and N. Avigad, "Synagogue Inscr. An Aram. Inscr. from the Synagogue at Umm-el-ʿamed in Galilee," *Bulletin of the L. M. Rabinowitz Fund for the Exploration of Ancient Synagogues,* 3 (1960), 62-64.

[188] Cf. Sukka, 3, 13 (Tabernacles); RH, 4, 7 (New Year); Taan., 1, 2 (Passover).

the temple. The fact that Judaism could withstand the disaster of 70 virtually without a break is undoubtedly to be credited in the main to the synagogue. [189]

D. συναγωγή in the New Testament.

I. συναγωγή as Assembly.

συναγωγή in the sense of assembly is extremely rare in the NT too. We find it in Ac. 13:43 for an assembly of Jews to which the god-fearing proselytes [190] mentioned there also had access. [191] According to many exegetes συναγωγή is also a Christian assembly in Jm. 2:2 → III, 518, 10 ff.; VII, 837, 24 ff.

II. συναγωγή as Congregation.

In Ac. 9:2 the συναγωγαί are the congregations of the Jewish *diaspora* in Damascus. [192] According to Luke these lie under the jurisdictional power of Jerusalem. Embracing ἄνδρας τε καὶ γυναῖκας, they are the sphere in which the first Christians appear, v. 19 f. [193] Ac. 18:26; 19:8 f.; 22:19 (→ n. 231); 26:11 also presuppose that in the first instance the Christians constituted themselves within the synagogue, and were not yet independent of the Jewish synagogue congregations. [194] On Ac. 6:9 → 837, 1 ff.

Rev. 2:9 and 3:9 refer to Jews who calls themselves this but in reality are not → III, 382, 6 ff. These pseudo-Jews are described as συναγωγὴ τοῦ σατανᾶ. One need not decide whether the reference is to all unbelieving Jews [195] or only to those in Smyrna and Philadelphia who are responsible for persecuting Christians → 161, 11 ff. [196] More important is the question whether the concept συναγωγή bears a negative accent here. In the case of Ἰουδαῖοι one may flatly deny this → III, 382, 6 ff. Christians are true Jews. [197] Similarly the attack does not seem to be on the συναγωγή qua συναγωγή but on the satanic congregation stigmatised as συναγωγὴ τοῦ σατανᾶ, so that Christians are the synagogue of God → III, 382, 7 f. It is more likely, however, that the antithesis would be between the synagogue of Satan and the *ecclesia*, not the synagogue, of God.

---

[189] Cf. Bousset-Gressm., 118, 175; Moore, I, 285; W. Bacher, Art. "Synagogue," Jew. Enc., XI, 623.

[190] Cf. on this strange combination of σεβόμενοι and προσήλυτοι → VI, 743, 4 ff.

[191] Whether the pagan population mentioned in v. 44 σχεδὸν πᾶσα ἡ πόλις also had access to a gathering for worship — A. Bertholet, *Die Stellung d. Israeliten u. der Juden zu den Fremden* (1896), 296 thinks it fairly certain on the basis of Jos. Ant., 19, 300 f. and Ovid Ars Amatoria, I, 75 — is of no more interest to Luke than the question whether a synagogue would have been big enough to accommodate this kind of mass meeting, cf. Haench. Ag., *ad loc*

[192] Acc. to Jos. Bell., 2, 559-561 and 7, 368 Damascus had a large Jewish community.

[193] "They were a community within Judaism, not external to it," Jackson-Lake, I, 4, 53.

[194] On the difficult questions which arise here cf. Haench. Ag. on 19:9. Unfortunately Paul's letters do not contain enough information on whether Paul tried to keep the Chr. churches within the synagogue, cf. Bultmann J., 428, n. 4. That conversion did not immediately mean a radical break with the synagogue may be seen not only from Ac. (→ 835, 9 ff.) but also from 2 C. 11:24 f. etc. Cf. also Knox, *op. cit.* (→ n. 40), 84, n. 7 etc.

[195] Cr.-Kö., 71.

[196] This is supported by the lack of art., though this can be taken as a Semitism, cf. Bl.-Debr. § 259. The ἐν in 3:9 for a partitive gen. (cf. Bl.-Debr. § 164) suggests rather a totality.

[197] Cf. Bss. Apk. and Loh. Apk., *ad loc.*

The dualism which we find here between the συναγωγή τοῦ σατανᾶ and the συναγωγή or ἐκκλησία τοῦ θεοῦ can hardly have its origin in the OT in this sharp form, though we often find συναγωγή κυρίου or ἐκκλησία κυρίου and tension between various συναγωγαί in the LXX and Judaism. [198]

One may ask why primitive Christianity chose to call itself ἐκκλησία and avoided συναγωγή. [199] The question is the more incisive in that Israel had given συναγωγή the same "holy history" as ἐκκλησία. [200] Indeed, whereas the LXX has used ἐκκλησία only for קָהָל, συναγωγή included the signification of עֵדָה as well, and it is hardly possible to find any essential distinction between the terms in the LXX. [201] Furthermore, there are instances of other later Jewish titles and designations being adopted into the ecclesiological vocabulary of the NT. One might reply that συναγωγή was a much more common self-designation in Judaism than the far less prominent ἐκκλησία, so that for the sake of distinction the latter would be a better term for the Christian community. [202] It might also be pointed out that συναγωγή had largely lost the universal character which still marked it in the LXX (→ 804, 5 ff.) and was primarily used for the local congregation (→ 806, 11 ff.), whereas ἐκκλησία could be used for both the local congregation and also the entire community, → III, 503, 18 ff. [203] Again, in NT days συναγωγή had become so restricted in meaning that its first ref. was to the building, as may be seen from the usage of Jos., Philo and primitive Christianity → 807, 9 ff. [204] Above all, however, the synagogue was very closely bound up with the νόμος and παράδοσις → 821, 4 ff. This alone makes it easy to see why συναγωγή could not be used in self-designation by a community to which the central position of the Law expressed in the name συναγωγή had become suspect because it knew that it was constituted, not by Moses and observance of the Law, but by the eschatological Christ event. [205] Since συναγωγή was also a guild term, its avoidance is perhaps to be associated also with the consistent avoidance by primitive Christianity of ἔρανος, κοινόν, θίασος, σύνοδος, σύλλογος and other terms used in cultic and mystery societies. Obviously in Gentile Chr. circles the OT legacy behind the term could no more counterbalance a possible misunderstanding of the Chr. community along the lines of these cultic fellowships of antiquity than it could counter a nomistic understanding of the community in Jewish Chr. circles. That Jesus Himself founded a συναγωγή of His own, or that His disciples

---

[198] But cf. as a striking par. the antithesis between the community of Belial עֲדַת בְּלִיַּעַל in 1 QH 2:22 and the community of God עֲדַת אֵל in 1 QM 4:9.

[199] The strong aversion to συναγωγή for the Chr. community may be seen from the emendation of LXX in Ac. 20:28. Ps. 74:2 has עֵדָה, LXX συναγωγή. Yet though עֵדָה is always transl. συναγωγή and never ἐκκλησία in LXX, Ac. 20:28 uses ἐκκλησία because the ref. is to the Chr. community → III, 504, 34 ff.; Stauffer Theol., 276, n. 498. Cf. the Lat. for the συναγωγή of Jm. 2:2 (conventus) and Herm. m., 11 (ecclesia, turba, concilium, coetus). It is of interest that though ἐκκλησία is not used in Ex.-Nu. the wilderness community is ἐκκλησία in Ac. 7:38.

[200] Schmidt, 266 on ἐκκλησία → III, 518, 7 ff.

[201] The choice of ἐκκλησία is not based on LXX usage. It did not commend itself, e.g., because it often has laudatory predicates in LXX, Ltzm. K. on 1 C. 1:1 ref. to 3 Βασ. 8:55 f.; ψ 21:23; 106:32; Jl. 2:16; Schmidt, 273. One may adduce similar statements for συναγωγή, cf. Jl. 2:16 with Lv. 19:2 and ψ 21:23 with ψ 110:1. Both words can be qualified by κυρίου, so that belonging to Yahweh is no reason for preferring ἐκκλησία to συναγωγή, as against Gloege, op. cit. (→ n. 17), 207. Cf. also W. Schrage, "'Ekklesia' und 'Synagoge,' Zum Ursprung d. urchr. Kirchenbegriffs," ZThK, 60 (1963), 180-186. Cf. also → n. 27, 209.

[202] Cf. Schmidt, 272.

[203] But cf. Rev. 2:9; 3:9, also the use of ἀποσυνάγωγος → 848, 1 ff. and Schrage, op. cit., 189-194.

[204] Cf. Rost Vorstufen, 156; Kosmala, 67.

[205] Cf. Schrage, 195-209.

thought of themselves as a sect of this type within Judaism, [206] must be regarded as highly improbable [207] → III, 529, n. 90.

III. The Synagogue in the New Testament.

In the overwhelming majority of instances συναγωγή in the NT means the Jewish building. At most one could only ask whether sometimes the gathering or congregation might not be implied too. [208]

The word occurs in this sense 8 times in Mk., 9 in Mt., 15 in Lk., 2 in Jn., and 16 in Ac. Predominant here is the usage, not of the LXX (→ 802, 19 ff.) but of Judaism (→ 806, 1 ff.). This has determined the Christian use of the term. [209] The narrower sense had obviously become so prominent that it hardly permitted any reference back to the LXX.

1. Relation to Jewish Statements.

a. In the first instance the NT statements simply confirm the above picture of the Jewish synagogue. The gt. spread of synagogues both in Palestine and also in the Dispersion is evident. It is a plain fact for Luke that there are synagogues κατὰ πόλιν, Ac. 15:21. The NT bears witness to a synagogue in Capernaum (Mk. 1:21 etc.), Nazareth (Mk. 6:2 etc.), Pisidian Antioch (Ac. 13:14), Iconium (14:1), Thessalonica (17:1), Berea (17:10), Athens (17:17), Corinth (18:4, 7), Ephesus (18:19 etc.), Philippi (16:13 προσευχή → n. 48), several synagogues in Galilee (Mk. 1:39; Mt. 9:35 etc.; Judaea Lk. 4:44), Jerusalem (Ac. 6:9; 24:12), Damascus (Ac. 9:2, 20) and Salamis (13:5). Also in keeping with Jewish statements is Luke's note that the synagogue was an ancient institution ἐκ γενεῶν ἀρχαίων (Ac. 15:21). All four Evangelists also ref. to teaching and preaching in the synagogue → 821, 10 ff. Of details which are par. to Jewish sources one may mention the following: Mt. ref. to prayer and almsgiving in the synagogue, 6:5, 2; Lk. speaks of the reading of Scripture (Lk. 4:16 ff. the prophet Isaiah; Ac. 13:15 the Law and the Prophets) and of an ensuing λέγειν (Ac. 4:21) or λόγος παρακλήσεως (Ac. 13:15) which the leader (→ 846, 5 ff.) might invite strangers to give, Ac. 13:15.

A pt. worth noting is that προσευχή is used for synagogue only at Ac. 16:13 in one of the so-called We-passages (16:10-17), while συναγωγή does not occur either here or in other We-passages. No other terms are used for the synagogue (→ n. 48-51) in the NT.

b. Additional to Jewish statements are the points that a Gentile might build a synagogue (Lk. 7:5) and that there were in the synagogues πρωτοκαθεδρίαι and a καθέδρα τοῦ Μωϋσέως (→ 820, 2 ff.). It is also noted that healings took place in synagogues, → 833, 15 ff. [210] It is very hard to say whether this locating of healings by the Synoptists is an amplifying of what we know about synagogues from Jewish sources or whether it stands

---

[206] So Schmidt, 278-280; → III, 525, 24 ff.; Zn. Mt. on 16:18; Jocz, 164; Michel, op. cit., 11.
[207] W. G. Kümmel, "Kirchenbegriff u. Geschichtsbewusstsein in d. Urgemeinde u. bei Jesus," Symbolae Bibl. Upsalienses, 1 (1943), 23 f. and n. 76; A. Oepke, Das neue Gottesvolk (1950), 167 f.; K. G. Goetz, "Petrus," UNT, 13 (1927), 24 f.; L. Goppelt, "Christentum u. Judt. im 1. u. 2. Jhdt.," BFTh, 2, 55 (1954), 37 f.; Jeremias, op. cit. (→ n. 64), 191-194.
[208] Cf. Cr.-Kö., 71 and → n. 230.
[209] It is misleading to say that συναγωγή "plays no role worth mentioning outside the LXX and dependent writings" (Rost Vorstufen, 2), since the NT is not dependent on the LXX in its use of the term, as Rost himself states. There are in the NT no LXX quotations containing συναγωγή. It is worth noting that the first such LXX quotation in early Christianity (ψ 21:17) has a bad sense, cf. Barn., 5, 13; 6, 6; Just. Dial., 104, 1; 98, 4; Const. Ap., V, 14, 12. Cf. also → n. 206.
[210] Mk. 1:23-27 (Lk. 4:33-36); Mk. 1:39 (Mt. 4:23); Mk. 3:1-5 (Mt. 12:9-13; Lk. 6:6-10); Mt. 9:35; Lk. 13:10-17.

in contradiction to this. None of the miracles said to be performed by rabbis took place in a synagogue. [211] Yet it is not suggested that healing in the synagogue was contrary to synagogue practice as healing on the Sabbath was. [212] Thus the offence taken by the synagogue ruler in Lk. 13:14 is because the healing took place on the Sabbath, not because it took place in the synagogue. The same is true of the παρατηρεῖν in Mk. 3:2.

In distinction from Jewish statements we also read of judgments and punishments in the synagogue. In particular scourging took place there. The relevant NT passages speak of δέρειν (Mk. 13:9; Ac. 22:19), μαστιγοῦν (Mt. 10:17; 23:34), παραδιδόναι (Lk. 21:12), τιμωρεῖν (Ac. 26:11, cf. also Lk. 12:11) in synagogues. Acc. to Sanh., 14, 12 and Mak., 3, 12 scourging was administered by the synagogue servants חזן הכנסת (the court servants acc. to T. Git., 4, 6 [328]), but there are no Rabb. ref. to its being given in the synagogue itself. [213] One might adduce jBik., 1, 5 (64a, 29) which says that delinquents had to bend over seats; this suggests the synagogue benches. [214] The silence of the Rabb. can hardly be regarded as a cogent argument against the historical probability of the weighty statements in the NT persecution logia and records. In the main we learn little about this institution which was so central in Jewish life. [215] Only from afar can one glimpse in the NT stories the very gt. importance of the synagogue for Judaism.

2. The Attitude of Jesus to the Synagogue.

a. According to the unanimous accounts of the Gospels Jesus often chose synagogues as the place for His preaching and teaching. There is no reason to doubt the historical reliability of this testimony. [216]

---

[211] Cf. Schwartzmann, 125: "healing is never associated with the synagogue." The story mentioned by Str.-B., I, 558 and Bultmann Trad., 258, n. 1 does not take place in the synagogue. But the sick could attend synagogues, cf. the special compartments for lepers, Neg., 13, 12; cf. Str.-B., IV, 140, 754.

[212] Hence one is not to question together synagogue healing and Sabbath healing, as against Schwartzmann, 125, 130. To be sure, there are no Rabb. par., but this is not surprising in the Sabbath healings, since there is deliberate opposition here to what was customary in Judaism, → 21, 13 ff. Just because the Evangelists seem to link synagogue and Sabbath so closely — of 8 ref. to the synagogue in Mk. 5 have to do with the Sabbath, and 7 of 15 in Lk. — it is possible that the locating of Sabbath healings in the synagogue was a later addition. Nevertheless, there is no reason to dispute the gen. possibility of synagogue healings. Lk. 13:10 (→ 832, 4 ff.) shows that the link between healing and the synagogue was already present in the stratum of tradition available to the Evangelists.

[213] Cf. → IV, 516, 3 ff.; Str.-B., I, 577; Krauss Altert., 186 f.; Schwartzmann, 125. Schwartzmann thus goes on to say in n. 55 "that these passages (sc. Mt. 10:17 etc.) refer to acts of a later period." Whether we have vaticinia ex eventu in the Synoptic accounts cannot be decided from Jewish sources, esp. as there in next to nothing about scourging in the synagogue in these.

[214] Krauss Altert., 186 f. Cf. → IV, 516, 28 f. Cf. also some accounts from the early Church. Acc. to Epiph. Haer., 30, 11, 5 a Jewish convert to Christianity was whipped by the Jews in their synagogue and then thrown in the water ἀπάγουσι μὲν εἰς τὴν συναγωγὴν καὶ μαστίζουσι τοῦτον κατὰ τὸν νόμον. Apollinaris of Hierapolis also ref. to μαστιγωθῆναι in synagogues, Eus. Hist. Eccl., V, 16,12.

[215] For this reason Schwartzmann concedes to the Synoptists "only superficial knowledge of the synagogue," 117, cf. 127-129.

[216] Jesus' appearance in the synagogue is "systematised" acc. to H. Conzelmann, Die Mitte d. Zeit, Beiträge z. Historischen Theol., 17³ (1960), 177; Jesus is depicted as a regular attender at the synagogue κατὰ τὸ εἰωθὸς αὐτῷ, Lk. 4:16. Some think this refers to attendance

The historical worth of the ref. to synagogues is not reduced in any way by attempts to show that synagogue situations and topographical notes are part of the redactional material in the Gospels. Synagogues occur not merely in the framework but in the actual stories and they are here a fundamental part of the tradition. Thus Lk. 13:10: ἐν μιᾷ τῶν συναγωγῶν, cannot be regarded as an editorial addition of the Evangelist. It must have grown up with the pericope in the tradition available to Lk. For the note seems to conflict with the idea of a journey through Samaria. [217] Sometimes the names of places in which there were synagogues might have been added later, since only Capernaum and Nazareth are mentioned, and it was natural to record the work of Jesus in the synagogues of His native town and the main centre of His mission. [218] Some think they see clear traces of a later identification. [219] It is worth noting, however, that acc. to Mk. and Mt. Jesus attends only Galilean synagogues. Lk. 4:44 mentions preaching in the synagogues of Judaea, substituting this for the τὴν Γαλιλαίαν of Mk. 1:39. [220] This shows, however, that geographical indications were only loosely associated with the mention of synagogues. In any case we have a general account in Lk. 4:44, not an individual synagogue incident. That the ref. to synagogues might come into such summaries secondarily may be seen from Mt. 9:35 and Lk. 4:15. It might be argued that even where a synagogue is mentioned to link individual incidents geographically this is no part of the original tradition. [221] Jesus' practice of attending synagogues and ministering in them is not in any way challenged, however, by this thesis.

It is true that one should not construe too narrowly the commitment to the synagogue of Him who knew that He was sent to sinners and who enjoyed table fellowship with them, Mk. 2:15 ff.; Mt. 11:19; Lk. 15:2; 19:1 ff. The authoritative ἐγὼ δὲ λέγω ὑμῖν, which does not appeal to the letter of the Torah or tradition, is quite inconceivable within the framework of the synagogue and its worship, cf. also Lk. 4:16 ff. Jesus did not just expound the OT Scriptures in the synagogue. He also proclaimed here the message of the βασιλεία of God, cf. Mt. 4:23; 9:35. At its religious centre — which in Galilee was the synagogue — Jesus confronted the people with His preaching. He also declared His exousia here according to Mk. 1:22.

---

from youth up, cf. for the importance of the synagogue to Jesus prior to His public ministry Dalman, op. cit., 33 f., 40; Moore, I, 288 f.; J. Klausner, Jesus v. Nazareth³ (1952), 319 f.; cf. the address "Rabbi" and → VI, 964, 7 ff. Others see a ref. to His regular attendance as a teacher, cf. B. Weiss, Die Ev. d. Mk. u. Lk., Kritisch-exeget. Komm. über d. NT (1901) on Lk. 4:16; K. L. Schmidt, Der Rahmen d. Gesch. Jesu (1919), 39. Lk. has the impf. ἐδίδασκεν in 4:15, also the plur. ἐν ταῖς συναγωγαῖς (cf. the conjugatio periphrastica in 4:44; 13:10). Cf. also πάλιν in Mk. 3:1 and πάντοτε in Jn. 18:20.

[217] Cf. Bultmann Trad., 388.

[218] Schmidt, op. cit. (→ n. 216), 40 thinks the incident of Lk. 4:16 ff. was located in Nazareth later, also M. Dibelius, Die Formgesch. d. Ev.⁴ (1961), 108, n. 1, but not Bultmann Trad., 31, n. 2; Conzelmann, op. cit., 27; Kl. Lk., ad loc. On the other hand, Schmidt, 50 f. accepts Capernaum in Mk. 1:21 ff. (but not Bultmann Trad., 60, 257, who sees here an editorial addition), and Nazareth in Mk. 6:1 ff., 154-7.

[219] Thus in Mk. 3:1 καὶ εἰσῆλθεν πάλιν εἰς συναγωγήν one is not originally to see a specific synagogue, though Mt. and Lk. and all Mk. witnesses but B and א have added the art.

[220] Schmidt, 60 f. argues for the authenticity of the reading in D, Γ, Δ, Koine, it, vg, syᵖ, arm, eth, and goth at Lk. 4:44, but par. influence is palpable. Cf. Conzelmann, op. cit., 34 f. (with bibl.).

[221] Thus ἐκ τῆς συναγωγῆς ἐξελθόντες in Mk. 1:29 would appear to be added as a transition and introduction to the incident which follows, cf. Bultmann Trad., 364; Loh. Mk., ad loc., but not Hck., Grundm. Mk., ad loc. W. Marxsen, "Der Evangelist Mk.," FRL, NF, 49² (1959), 37 also suggests that Mk. put in an introduction to the healing of 1:23, which has no location, to give it a setting in the synagogue.

There is ref. to Jesus' διδάσκειν in synagogues 3 times each in Mk., Mt., Lk. and twice in Jn., and to His κηρύσσειν once each in Mk. and Lk. and twice in Mt. How strongly the διδάσκειν esp. was linked to the synagogue may be seen in the fact that Mt. and Lk. can introduce διδάσκειν where Mk. ref. to a synagogue, cf. Mt. 4:23; Lk. 6:6. Mt. also expands the summary in Mk. 6:6: περιῆγεν τὰς κώμας κύκλῳ διδάσκων, to read: περιῆγεν ὁ 'Ιησοῦς τὰς πόλεις πάσας καὶ τὰς κώμας διδάσκων ἐν ταῖς συναγωγαῖς αὐτῶν καὶ κηρύσσων κτλ., Mt. 9:35. 222 Lk. at 4:15 even has ἐδίδασκεν ἐν ταῖς συναγωγαῖς αὐτῶν for the κηρύσσων τὸ εὐαγγέλιον κτλ. of Mk. 1:14 f. In Lk., then, Jesus' public ministry does not begin with the proclamation of the coming of God's kingdom but with His teaching in the synagogues of Galilee. 223 Even Mk. himself seems to have introduced into a basic miracle story which was located in the Capernaum synagogue (1:21-28) a ref. to the διδάσκειν of Jesus and the astonishment of the people at His διδαχὴ καινή (v. 22, 27), since these statements are not really to the point. 224

Quite naturally the healing ministry of Jesus (→ 830, 34 ff.) is less closely connected with the synagogue than His preaching ministry. Yet according to Mark and Luke the first miracle of healing takes place in a synagogue, as does also the only Sabbath healing in Mark and Matthew. 225 We do not have θεραπεύειν and δαιμόνια ἐκβάλλειν merely in summaries (Mk. 1:39; Mt. 4:23; 9:35); there are also explicit accounts of the various healings (Mk. 1:23 ff. and par.; Mk. 3:1 ff. and par.; Lk. 13:10 ff.). The synagogue is the site of the first battle between demonic powers and the ἅγιος τοῦ θεοῦ — this confession occurs only here in the synagogue sphere according to the Synoptists, Mk. 1:24; Lk. 4:34. It is also the site of Jesus' victory over these powers.

b. Alongside the majority of instances in which Jesus fits into the synagogue quite naturally there are only a few where one may detect alienation from what is done in the synagogues especially by the synagogal authorities. Closer analysis shows that it is not the institution itself which is the target of criticism and attack; it is the misuse of the institution by the scribes and Pharisees. 226 Thus Mk. 12:39 and par. do not criticise the synagogues; they censure the ambition and desire for recognition of the scribes, 227 who are out for the seats of honour (→ VI, 870, 13 ff.) in the synagogues. In the Sermon on the Mount Jesus is not warning against prayer in the synagogue, nor is He warning against prayer in the temple in Lk. 18:10 ff. His attack is on the hypocrisy and sham holiness of those who love ἐν ταῖς συναγωγαῖς καὶ ἐν ταῖς γωνίαις τῶν πλατειῶν ἑστῶτες προσεύχεσθαι, ὅπως φανῶσιν τοῖς ἀνθρώποις, Mt. 6:5. 228 The same is true of almsgiving, Mt. 6:2 → 86, 14 ff.

---

222 The combination of διδάσκω and κηρύσσω is typical of Mt. (4:23; 9:35; 11:1).
223 Cf. Conzelmann, op. cit., 24 f.; E. Lohse, "Lk. als Theologe d. Heilsgeschichte," Ev. Theol., 14 (1954), 256-275, esp. 267.
224 Cf. Bultmann Trad., 223 f.; → 21, n. 162.
225 Mt., of course, records a disputation at the only synagogue healing, cf. H. J. Held, "Mt. als Interpret d. Wundergeschichten," Wissenschaftliche Monographien z. AT u. NT, 1 (1960), 224 and 232.
226 Jesus' attitude to the temple differs here. To be sure, He criticises abuses here too, but sometimes His criticism goes further, → III, 242, 10 ff.
227 Lk. 11:43 has Φαρισαῖοι for the γραμματεῖς of Mk. 12:39; Lk. 20:46; Mt. has both, 23:6, cf. v. 2.
228 Nevertheless Jesus tells us to pray in secret in v. 6; the ταμιεῖον is the proper place of prayer.

c. In view of the nearness and continuing attachment to the synagogue it is perhaps surprising that a few passages do have a clear polemical thrust against the institution itself, Mk. 13:9; Mt. 10:17; 23:34; Lk. 12:11; 21:12. We undoubtedly have here a later stage of development in relations with the synagogue. Synagogues become the centres of persecution of the community. Hence this group of sayings deals with the contacts of the Christian Church with the synagogue rather than those of Jesus Himself. The reason for the condemnation and punishment of Christians, however, is their discipleship and confession of Christ. Mk. has the following prediction of Jesus [229] in the eschatological address: παραδώσουσιν ὑμᾶς εἰς συνέδρια καὶ εἰς συναγωγὰς δαρήσεσθε, Mk. 13:9. Mt. puts the relevant saying in the charge to the disciples, 10:17. For Mk. the συναγωγαί [230] are parallel to the local συνέδρια, → 841, 17 ff. Lk. 21:12 has φυλακαί [231] instead, and in Lk. 12:11 the Gentile ἀρχαὶ καὶ ἐξουσίαι are parallel to συναγωγαί. Mt. has the sharpest alienation from the synagogue in the Woes on the Pharisees when he calls the synagogues συναγωγαὶ ὑμῶν [232] and in so doing brings out clearly the break between the Synagogue and the Church. Not by chance he now mentions other forms of persecution as well as scourging (→ 831, 7 ff.; IV, 516, 3 ff.), namely, that Christians are put to death and crucified, Mt. 23:34. Confession of Christ (Mk. 13:9; Mt. 10:18; Lk. 21:12) brings Christians before the synagogal courts so that synagogues are not only the place of punishment but also the place of inspired ἀπολογεῖσθαι (Lk. 12:11; 21:14; cf. Mk. 13:11; Mt. 10:19) and μαρτύριον (Mk. 13:9; Mt. 10:18; Lk. 21:13). [233]

Though the persecution motif does not occur in connection with συναγωγή in John, the synagogue seems to be regarded with some reserve. This is shown by the use of ἀποσυνάγωγος (→ 849, 14 ff.) and the sharply reduced prominence of

---

[229] G. R. Beasley-Murray, Jesus and the Future (1956), 193 regards Mk. 13:9 and Mt. 23:34 as precautionary warnings of the historical Jesus → IV, 516, 4 f.; Hck. Mk., ad loc., though acc. to Hck. it is Mk. who puts them in an eschatological context. Loh. Mk., ad loc. thinks there is a reflection here of the fate of Christans in the diaspora congregations, where the synagogal authorities decide against them, similarly Grundm. Mk. ad loc.; cf. Bultmann Trad., 119 f.; J. Schniewind, Das Ev. nach Mk., NT Deutsch, 19 (1960), ad loc. sees a Palestinian background, so too → IV, 516, 5 f.

[230] Wellh. Mk. and Mt. transl. "judicial assemblies," and "courts," at Lk. 21:12. But cf. Schwartzmann, 117, n. 7. The local element may be less prominent in Lk. 12:11: ἐπὶ τὰς συναγωγάς. Cf. Hck. Lk., ad loc.; Kl. Lk., ad loc.; Schwartzmann, 120, n. 21.

[231] Cf. Ac. 22:19: φυλακίζων καὶ δέρων κατὰ τὰς συναγωγάς, though the συναγωγαί here might be the Jewish congregations.

[232] It is striking how often Mt. adds an αὐτῶν to the synagogues mentioned by Mk., Mt. 12:9 (Mk. 3:1); 13:54 (6:2); 10:17 (13:9). In the last instance this does not apply to the par. συνέδρια. It is of interest that Mt. has αὐτῶν even in relation to the Nazareth synagogue, though in the same v. Nazareth itself is τὴν πατρίδα αὐτοῦ, Mt. 13:54, cf. also 4:23 and 9:35. This is no accident; it clearly denotes separation from "their" synagogues. The synagogue has rejected the Rabbi κατ᾽ ἐξοχήν and thus shown its obduracy. G. D. Kilpatrick, The Origins of the Gospel acc. to St. Matthew² (1950), 110 f. thinks that even where the pronouns occur in Mk. and Lk. they are assimilations to Mt., so that for him αὐτῶν is really an addition characteristic of Mt. alone. There is weight in his observation that with few exceptions the pronoun bears no relation to the context: "it has not a varying contextual significance, but a uniform one ... We may then detect in the phrase 'their synagogues' a result of the Birkath ha-Minim, the exclusion of Christian Jews from Rabbinical synagogues."

[233] In interpretation of εἰς μαρτύριον αὐτοῖς in Mt. and Mk. and ἀποβήσεται ὑμῖν εἰς μαρτύριον in Lk. → IV, 508, 28 ff., and W. Marxsen, op. cit. (→ n. 221), 118-120; Grundm. Mk., ad loc.; G. D. Kilpatrick, "The Gentile Mission in Mark and Mark 13:9-11," Stud. in the Gospels, Essays in Memory of R. H. Lightfoot, ed. D. E. Nineham (1957), 145-158.

συναγωγή. Jn. 6:59 has no polemical edge, but this might not be true in 18:20, where synagogue and temple are more precisely defined as places ὅπου πάντες οἱ ᾽Ιουδαῖοι συνέρχονται. It is true that Jn. mentions the synagogue here only to bring out the public character (→ V, 879, 46 ff.) of the preaching of Jesus (παρρησίᾳ... ἐν κρυπτῷ ἐλάλησα οὐδέν). Nevertheless, the strangeness and remoteness (→ III, 377, 24 ff.) suggested by οἱ ᾽Ιουδαῖοι seems to spill over into the synagogue too. This was natural in view of the ἀποσυναγώγους γενέσθαι of Christians.

3. The Importance of the Synagogue for the Primitive Christian Mission as Depicted in Acts.

According to the depiction in Ac. synagogues were one of the most important factors in the history of primitive Christian missions. [234] Even Paul, the apostle to the Gentiles, began his missionary work in synagogues. With the exception of Ac. 18:26, which speaks of a παρρησιάζεσθαι of Apollos in the synagogue of Ephesus, all the passages in Ac. which refer to synagogues deal with the work of Paul, and never, e.g., with that of Peter. Two refer to Paul's persecution of Christians (Ac. 22:19; 26:11) and all the others to his missionary work. Paul is the typical missionary, even in synagogues. His first κηρύσσειν after conversion is not in Arabia (cf. Gl. 1:16 f.) but on several occasions (imperfect) in the synagogues of Damascus (Ac. 9:19 f.). In Ac. as in Lk. 4:16 we find the expression κατὰ τὸ εἰωθός (Ac. 17:2) in connection with attendance at synagogues. It is hardly open to question historically that the synagogues provided Paul with excellent bases for his missionary work (→ 21, 17 ff.; 26, 25 ff.) and that he often enough began his proclamation in them, cf. R. 1:16; 10:14 ff.; 1 C. 9:20 f.; 2 C. 11:24 f. etc. By way of them and the proselytes and God-fearers who gathered in them Paul found a very suitable approach to the Gentiles. [235]

Lk. seems to have made almost a schema [236] and theory of this connection with the synagogues, since almost always he has Paul take up the Gentile mission after being barred from the synagogues, cf. 13:45 f.; 18:6; 19:9; 28:25. The suspicious regularity with which this occurs attracted attention long ago. [237] The theological basis of the schema is given in Ac. 13:46. [238] Here Luke states the continuity and connection in salvation history between the Church on the one side and Israel and its institutions on the other. Yet the

---

[234] Cf. Harnack Miss., 5: "The network of synagogues laid down in advance the lines and centres of Chr. propaganda. The mission ... found in them already an appointed field."

[235] We are often told that Ἕλληνες too were reached in the synagogues (Ac. 14:1; 18:4; cf. 17:12), and elsewhere there is ref. to προσήλυτοι, σεβόμενοι and φοβούμενοι as those who attended the synagogue, Ac. 17:4; 13:16, 43.

[236] With differences in detail one finds the following elements in the schema; contact with the synagogue, success of preaching there, envy of the Jews, persecution and expulsion, Ac. 9:20 ff.; 13:44 ff.; 14:1 ff.; cf. also 14:19 ff.; 17:1 ff. An interesting pt. in this connection is that Luke mentions synagogue preaching only in the diaspora and says nothing about this link in relation to the Jewish mission in the stricter sense (Ac. 8:4; cf. v. 5 and 40; 9:32, 43; 11:19).

[237] Cf. F. Overbeck, Kurze Erklärung d. Ag., revised and expanded by W. M. L. de Wette⁴ (1870), 208; C. Weizsäcker, Das Apost. Zeitalter d. chr. Kirche³ (1902), 93.

[238] Haench. Ag., ad loc. rightly sees in the events at Antioch "a kind of abbreviation of Paul's missionary history"; what happened there has for Luke a representative significance for all that came later.

synagogue mission is for him only the first thing (πρῶτον). The new epoch in salvation history takes us beyond this. [239] By their hardness the Jews themselves drive Paul out of the synagogue to the Gentiles. [240] Now for Paul himself there was undoubtedly a prius of the Jews in salvation history. But it may be doubted whether eo ipso this involved for him a specific missionary technique. [241] Even Luke does not explicitly say that he preached only in places where there was a synagogue, not even where there is mention of a Jewish population as in Derbe and Lystra, Ac. 14:6 ff.; 16:1, 3; cf. also 14:25. [242]

It seem that sooner or later the Christian community everywhere became independent and separated itself from the Jewish congregations and their places of assembly. In Ephesus the ending of synagogal fellowship — not in this case by the Jews but by Paul, who "separated the disciples," Ac. 19:9 — came after only three months, while it would appear to have been even earlier in Corinth, though in neither case did it involve interruption of the mission, Ac. 18:5 f., cf. 11; 19:8-10.

For Paul's work in the synagogue Lk. prefers other terms than those used in the Gospel. In place of κηρύσσω and διδάσκω he has παρρησιάζομαι in Ac. 13:46; 18:26; 19:8; cf. also 9:27; 14:3, and διαλέγομαι in 17:2, 17; 18:4, 19; 19:8; 24:12; neither word is used in the Gospel. It is possible that Luke wished to make a distinction between the synagogue preaching of Jesus and that of Paul. [243] One may also see what elements Luke regarded as important and necessary in Chr. preaching in the synagogues: free, open, and bold speech even in face of a hostile public (→ V, 882, 14 ff., esp. 23 f.), and disputation. [244] Paul's address in the synagogue at Pisidian Antioch (Ac. 13:16-41) is an example of synagogue preaching as Luke understands it. The proof from Scripture is used here, and it seems to have played an important role elsewhere in the synagogue, cf. 9:22; 17:2 f., 11; 18:28. The basic point at issue is simply that Jesus is the Christ, the Son of of God, 9:20; 18:5. The only possible response to this is either πιστεῦσαι = to become a Christian, 14:1, or ἀπειθεῖν, 14:2; 19:9, σκληρύνεσθαι, 19:9, βλασφημεῖν, 13:45; 18:6 = to deny the Messiahship of Jesus. Luke does not suggest that the real reason for the separation between Paul's community and the Jewish synagogue is that Paul preaches freedom from the Law.

---

[239] Cf. Conzelmann, op. cit. (→ n. 216), 25, 176 f.: the connection with the synagogue is a "postulate of salvation history," but it also means "the detaching of the Jews from salvation history," 135. Cf. also Haench. Ag. on 22:1-21. Goppelt, op. cit. (→ n. 207), 87 rightly states that the synagogue "is not just a tactical point of contact, nor merely a historical stage of transition, but a starting-point in salvation history." He accepts this as Pauline.

[240] M. Dibelius, "Die Reden d. Ag. u. d. antike Geschichtsschreibung," Aufsätze zur Ag., ed. H. Greeven, FRL, NF, 42⁴ (1961), 129; Munck, op. cit., 240.

[241] R. Liechtenhan, "Pls. als Judenmissionar," Judaica, 2 (1946), 56-70 is of this opinion.

[242] Krauss Altert., 235 concludes from the preaching in Perga and Attalia — only Perga acc. to Ac. 14:25, since εὐαγγελιζόμενοι αὐτούς in D 614 pc syh is surely an addition — that there must have been synagogues there even though this is not expressly stated, cf. also Paphos in Ac. 13:6 (239). Logically, then, one would have to say the same of Lystra and Derbe in 14:6 and of other places too. But if one assumes that there were synagogues wherever Jews are mentioned it is plain that Luke is not consistent, that he was always referring to synagogue preaching, and that this must have been closer to the historical truth. Yet synagogues were not the only site of Paul's preaching before his breach with them, as may be seen from the fact that Luke obviously connects synagogue preaching with the Sabbath (Ac. 13:14; 17:2; 18:4; 18:19 D → n. 212) but also speaks of daily preaching (17:17; 19:9), cf. also in the case of Athens ἐν τῇ ἀγορᾷ, 17:17.

[243] Conzelmann, op. cit., 209 f. adduces other examples to show that Luke "consciously ascribes different characteristics to the age of Jesus and the age of the Church."

[244] But cf. → II, 94, 46 ff.; yet v. Ac. 9:22, 29; 17:17 f. Even here διαλέγομαι can hardly have any other sense than "to speak of philosophical, religious themes in the form of a dialogue (discussion, disputation)" [Risch].

IV. Ac. 6:9 and Jm. 2:2.

There has been long-standing debate as to whether the reference in Ac. 6:9 is to a congregation or a building. Since Rabbinic literature tells of a Tannaite buying the "synagogue of the Alexandrians" [245] and putting it to private use, it has often been assumed that Ac. 6:9 is also speaking of a building. [246] But since the synagogue of the Alexandrians belongs to a congregation and we know from inscr. that Jewish συναγωγαί = "congregations" were named after their native places (→ 806, 32 ff.), the sense of congregation is equally possible. Ac. 6:9 itself favours this. [247] Luke is not saying that the ἀναστῆναι breaks out in the buildings but that the conflict is caused by members of the Jewish Hellenistic synagogues, → IV, 265, 2 ff. Another point of dispute is whether the reference is to one synagogue or several. Since the synagogue of the Alexandrians is also that "of those of Tarsus" in the par. to jMeg., 3, 1 (73d, 34 f.), namely, bMeg., 26b, and the same synagogue can bear either the one name or the other, [248] the question has been raised whether there was only one synagogue for all Jews of the Dispersion in Jerusalem, [249] or at least whether only one synagogue was meant in Ac. 6:9. [250] Ac. 24:12, however, refers to several synagogues in Jerusalem, and we know from other sources that the Jews organised synagogue congregations along territorial or social lines. [251] The name, too, is overlong, so that it is best to assume that more than one synagogue is at issue in Ac. 6:9. Whether we are to think in terms of two or of five synagogues is uncertain. On linguistical grounds (the double τῶν) the vote usually goes in favour of two. [252]

Since ὑμῶν refers to the Christians here addressed, Jm. 2:2 offers the only NT example to show that συναγωγή could also be used in the Christian sense. The only debatable point is whether the word refers to the place of meeting [253] or the meeting; [254] one thing that can be ruled out is that συναγωγή here means the Christ-

---

[245] בית הכנסת של אלבסנדרים שהיו בירושלם, T. Meg., 3, 6 (224); cf. jMeg., 3, 1 (73d, 34 f.).

[246] So Jeremias, op. cit. (→ n. 88), I, 75 and most comm.

[247] Str.-B., II, 661 and 664; Wdt. Ag., Zn. Ag., ad loc.

[248] Cf. Dalman Orte, 295, n. 8; Krauss Altert., 200 f.; Str.-B., II, 663; Jeremias, op. cit., I, 75 f.

[249] J. Bergmann, Jüd. Apologetik im nt.lichen Zeitalter (1908), 9, n. 1; cf. also Pr.-Ag., ad loc.; Str.-B., II, 664.

[250] Pr. Ag., ad loc.; Jeremias, op. cit. (→ n. 88), I, 75.

[251] The Bab. Jews in Sepphoris, Tiberias and Jaffa had their own synagogue, also the Roman Jews in Machoza on the Tigris (Str.-B., II, 661 f.) and the Cappadocian Jews in Sepphoris and Jaffa (Krauss Altert., 237), cf. also Groenman, 155 f. In Alexandria, however, the organisation was by societies, Str.-B., II, 664; Krauss Altert., 201, 263. In Hierapolis, Phrygia, we read of a Jewish guild of purple-dyers and carpet weavers τῶν πορφυροβά-φων ... τῶν καιροδαπισ[τ]ῶν, CIJ, II, 777.

[252] For two: Overbeck, op. cit., ad loc.; Wdt., Zn. and Haench. Ag., ad loc.; → IV, 265, 6 ff.; Jackson-Lake, I, 4, 66. For five: Vitringa, 253; B. Weiss, Das NT, III² (1902), ad loc.; Schürer, II, 502 f., n. 7. On the much debated question whether the συναγωγή of the Theodotus inscr., CIJ, II, 1404 is the same as the synagogue of the Libertines in Ac. 6:9 cf. the bibl. → IV, 265, n. 3, also J. B. Frey, CIJ, II, p. 334; Jackson-Lake, I, 4, 67 f.; Jeremias, op. cit. (→ n. 88), I, 76; Haench. Ag., ad loc.; H. J. Cadbury, The Book of Acts in History (1955), 88.

[253] So J. E. Belser, Die Epistel d. hl. Jk. (1909), 96-8; J. B. Mayor, The Ep. of St. James (1892), ad loc.; esp. Rost Bemerkungen, 53-66.

[254] Dib. Jk.; Hck. Jk.; Meinertz Kath. Br.; J. H. Ropes, The Ep. of St. James, ICC (1954); J. Marty, L'épître de Jacques (1936) (all ad loc.); Moore, III, 89.

ian community itself, cf. 5:14. [255] In the first instance εἰσέρχομαι εἰς συναγωγὴν ὑμῶν suggests a building, cf. Mk. 1:21; Lk. 4:16; Ac. 18:19; 19:8. The reference to seating and the allocation of places points in the same direction. [256] But "meeting" and "place of meeting" merge into one another here too. [257] Furthermore, the sense "assembly" is incomparably more frequent in the post-apostolic fathers (→ 840, 29 ff.) and the Vulgate already took it in this sense (conventus).

E. συναγωγή in the Early Church.

1. The profane senses persisted in the early Church. 1 Cl., 20, 6 uses συναγωγαί for the places which at creation were formed by the gathering together of the infinite sea. Cl. Al. Strom., VI, 2, 1 speaks of learned collections of books συναγωγὰς φιλομαθεῖς, cf. ἐν τῇ τῶν θαυμασίων συναγωγῇ ἐν Πέλλῃ, Prot., III, 42, 4 and → 801, 7 f. Orig. Comm. in Joh., 13, 46 on 4:36 uses συναγωγή in the secular sense, συναγωγὴ τοῦ καρποῦ.

2. In most instances, however, συναγωγή is used in the early Church to denote the Jewish synagogue (the building), and almost without exception in more or less sharp polemic against it. The synagogues are above all the places where Jews curse Christians. Just. Dial., 16, 4: καταρώμενοι ἐν ταῖς συναγωγαῖς ὑμῶν τοὺς πιστεύοντας ἐπὶ τὸν Χριστόν, cf. 96, 2; 137, 2. Epiph. Haer., 29, 2 mentions cursing thrice daily: τρὶς τῆς ἡμέρας ὅτε εὐχὰς ἐπιτελοῦσιν ἑαυτοῖς ἐν ταῖς συναγωγαῖς ἐπαρῶνται αὐτοῖς καὶ ἀναθεματίζουσι, τρὶς τῆς ἡμέρας φάσκοντες ὅτι Ἐπικατάρασαι ὁ θεὸς τοὺς Ναζωραίους. Hier. often tells us that the Jews blaspheme the name of Christ thrice daily in the synagogues, Comm. in Is., 2, 81 on 5:19 (MPL., 24 [1845], 86 A); 13, 565 on 47:7 (24 [1845], 467 C); he also ref. to the cursing of Christ day and night, 14, 604 on 52:4 (ibid. 498 B). It is hardly surprising then, that he calls synagogues synagogae satanae in Comm. in Jer., 4, 7 on 18:17 (CSEL, 59, 228) and judges that God turns His back on them, not His face towards them. Orig. Hom. in Jer., 19, 12 on 20:1-7 (GCS Orig., 3, 168) says that in the synagogues Jesus was scourged by the Jews with a cursing mouth: εἴσελθε εἰς τὰς τῶν Ἰουδαίων συναγωγάς, καὶ ἴδε τὸν Ἰησοῦν ὑπ' αὐτῶν τῇ γλώσσῃ τῆς βλασφημίας μαστιγούμενον. Acc. to Tert. the rejection of Christ by the Jews has consequences for the synagogues too: Because the Jews rejected Christ, the fons aquae vitae, lacus contritos coeperunt habere, id est synagogas, in dispersione scilicet gentium, in quibus iam spiritus sanctus non immoratur, Adv. Iudaeos, 13, 15 (CCh, 2, 1387 f.). The Chr. view of the synagogue is also affected by the role of synagogues in the persecution of Christians. For Tert. they are fontes persecutionum, Scorpiace, 10, 10 (CCh, 2, 1089). The συναγωγὴ Ἰουδαίων is the συναγωγὴ χριστοκτόνων, Const. Ap., II, 61, 1.

It is remarkable that for all this Christians have to be warned so urgently against attending synagogues. If Christians attend pagan idol worship, the synagogues of the Jews, or heretical conventicles, they will have to answer at the Day of Judgment, or they are even now excommunicated and anathematised, Const. Ap., II, 61, 1 f.; VIII, 47, 65 and

---

[255] Cf. Schmidt, 271; Kümmel, op. cit. (→ n. 207), 23; but → III, 518, 10 ff.

[256] It may be doubted whether Jm. 2:2 f. enables us to make any conclusions as to the type of synagogues in the 1st cent., so Rost Bemerkungen, 53-66. ὧδε and ἐκεῖ are too heavily loaded, H. Greeven in the Suppl. to Dib. Jk., ad loc. But above all the Galilean type which Rost presupposes has not been found in the 1st cent. Rost, 59 thinks the words show that the seats occupied a certain position in relation to the entrance and at the same time indicate the distance of the two types of seats from the leader or speaker, so that one may deduce that the entrance side and the cultic centre were the same. Acc. to Galling Erwägungen, 176 the type presupposed by Rost was only a "special form," → n. 121.

[257] → 807, 22 ff. and Wnd. Jk., ad loc.

71; εἰς μιαρὸν ἐθνῶν and εἰς συναγωγὴν 'Ιουδαίων ἢ αἱρετικῶν εἰσελθεῖν, II, 61, 1 f. are mentioned together. [258] Chrys. Adv. Iudaeos, I, 5 (MPG, 48 [1862], 850) does not see how there can be Christians who say: τὴν συναγωγὴν σεμνὸν εἶναι τόπον. The synagogue is par. to an οἶκος δαιμόνων and it is called σπήλαιον τῶν λῃστῶν, Const. Ap., II, 61, 1-2. Chrys. goes to extremes in this regard. For him synagogues are not just robber caves but μᾶλλον δὲ καὶ πανδοχείου παντὸς ἀτιμότερον τὸ τῆς συναγωγῆς χωρίον ἐστίν. Οὐ γὰρ λῃστῶν οὐδὲ καπήλων ἁπλῶς, ἀλλὰ δαιμόνων ἐστὶ καταγώγιον, Adv. Iudaeos, I, 4 (MPG, 48 [1862], 848 f.). There is no difference between the synagogue and the theatre, indeed ἔνθα δὲ πόρνη ἔστηκεν, πορνεῖόν ἐστιν ὁ τόπος... σπήλαιον λῃστῶν, καὶ καταγώγιον θηρίων, I, 3 (ibid., 847), cf. the comparison with a καπηλεῖον, I, 5. Hence Christians are summoned: φεύγετε, indeed, δέον καταφρονεῖν καὶ βδελύττεσθαι καὶ ἀποπηδᾶν; μισεῖν is used, I, 5 (ibid., 850).

It is not surprising that such preaching had concrete results. As compared with the rare destructions of synagogues in pagan antiquity (→ 827, 9 ff.) we find far more acts of this kind in the early Church. [259] Examples of destruction (usually by fire) range from Magona on Minorca [260] to Rome, [261] from Alexandria [262] to Callinicum on the Euphrates. [263] Repeatedly Theodosius had to deal with Chr. attacks on synagogues, but Christians increasingly influenced imperial legislation against the Jews, until the rebuilding or repair of synagogues was forbidden. [264] The forcible conversion of synagogues into churches was also no rarity. [265]

---

[258] It is astonishing how many ref. there are to synagogues = societies of pagans and heretics, cf. Const. Ap., II, 60-62; Iren. Haer., IV, 18, 4.

[259] On this cf. Simon, 239-274; Krauss Altert., 226, 228 f., 419-422; Juster, I, 461-472; Parkes, 187 f., 204 f., 207 f., 231, 235 f., 238, 244, 263-6; F. Murawski, Die Juden bei d. Kirchenvätern u. Scholastikern (1925), passim.

[260] Cf. Severus Majoricensis, Ep. de Iudaeis (MPL, 20 [1845], 731-746).

[261] Ambr. Ep., 40, 23 (MPL, 16 [1880], 1156 C).

[262] Socrates Hist. Eccl., VII, 13 (MPG, 67 [1859], 760). Synagogues were also destroyed in Palestine, Illyricum, Syria, Ravenna, Daphne and Amida.

[263] This synagogue was set alight by Christians at the prompting of the bishop. Ambr. Ep., 40 (MPL, 16 [1880], 1148-1160) protests expressly against its rebuilding even though the emperor had demanded restoration and the punishment of the guilty parties. Ambrose would rather become a martyr than allow the synagogue to be rebuilt, for this would be apostasy (40, 6-9), the triumphus Iudaeis de Ecclesia Dei and tropaeum de Christi populo (40, 20). The synagogue is for him perfidiae locus, impietatis domus, amentiae receptaculum, quod Deus damnavit ipse (40, 14). Cf. F. Barth, "Ambr. u. d. Synag. zu Callinicum," Theol. Zschr. aus d. Schweiz, 6 (1889), 65-86; H. v. Campenhausen, "Ambr. v. Mailand als Kirchenpolitiker," Arbeiten z. Kirchengesch., 12 (1929), 231-4, 274 f.; Parkes, 166-168; F. H. Dudden, The Life and Times of St. Ambrose, II (1935), 371-379.

[264] Juster, I, 469-472; Simon, 267 f., 269; Parkes, 235-8, 250.

[265] Cf. Antioch, Edessa, Constantinople, Palermo, Cagliari, Daphne, Tipasa and Dertona, Juster, I, 464, n. 3 and 466, n. 3; Kohl-Watzinger, 183; Krauss Altert., 226, 229; Simon, 265, Parkes, 187, 213 f., 236, 238, 303. John of Ephesus boasts he turned seven synagogues into churches, Parkes, 263. Gregory the Gt., Ep., 9, 55 (MPL, 77 [1896], 993 C) thinks it impossible to return a synagogue in Palermo which had already been consecrated as a church but orders compensation. An archaeol. example is the church erected over a synagogue at Gerasa, cf. J. W. Crowfoot and R. W. Hamilton, "The Discovery of a Synag. at Jerash," PEFQ, 61 (1929), 211-219; A. Barrois, "Découverte d'une synag. à Djérasch," Rev. Bibl., 39 (1930), 257-265. In Act. Andr. et Matth., 14 the Jews even in Jesus' time are told by a sphinx τὰ ἱερὰ καταργήσουσιν τὰς συναγωγὰς ὑμῶν, ὡς καὶ γενέσθαι ἐκκλησίας τοῦ μονογενοῦς υἱοῦ αὐτοῦ. Cf. also the consecration rite for synag. converted into churches, Oratio et Preces in Dedicatione loci illius ubi prius fuit synagoga, Liber Sacramentorum Romanae Ecclesiae, cf. Parkes, 401.

3. A new usage in the early Church is that increasingly συναγωγή denotes Judaism as a whole, mostly in antithesis to the Chr. Church. Thus Just. Dial., 134, 3 allegorically relates Jacob's two wives to Judaism and the Church: Λεία μὲν ὁ λαὸς ὑμῶν καὶ ἡ συναγωγή, ʿΡαχὴλ δὲ ἡ ἐκκλησία ἡμῶν, cf. also 53, 4. Later there is an increasingly technical distinction between Synagogue and Church, Commodianus Instructiones, 39, 1-4 (CSEL, 15, 51) and Carmen Apologeticum, 253 (CSEL, 15, 131). This does not have to be polemical, cf. Orig. Hom. in Cant. on 2:3 (GCS Orig., 8, 45): *Salvator noster sororis eius filius est, id est synagogae,* cf. also Gregory the Gt., Moralium Liber in Hiob, II, 36, 59: [266] *Redemptoris mater iuxta carnem Synagoga.* Orig. Comm. in Thr. Fr., 18 on 4:22 (GCS Orig., 3, 242) can even call the ἐκκλησία θυγάτηρ τῆς πάλαι συναγωγῆς. Tert. Ad Uxorem, I, 2, 2 (CCh, 1 374) admits there are fig. connections between Synagogue and Church: *sed licet figuratum in synagogam et ecclesiam intercesserit.*

On the other hand the διαφορὰ ἐκκλησίας καὶ συναγωγῆς is equally plain, Orig. Orat., 20, 1, cf. Ambr. Comm. in Lk. on 6:52 (CCh, 14, 192): *fretum magnum,* and usually συναγωγή = Judaism is to be taken negatively δεδεμένη γὰρ ταῖς ἁμαρτίαις ἦν ἡ τότε συναγωγή, Orig. Comm. in Mt. 16, 15 on 21:5 (GCS Orig., 10, 523 f.). Cl. Al. Strom., I, 96, 2 stresses that συναγωγή is not ὁμωνύμως to ἐκκλησία. Hier. Comm. in Jer., 5, 2 on 24:1 ff. (CSEL, 59, 296) has the series *lex et evangelium, synagoga et ecclesia, Iudaeorum populus et Christianorum, gehenna et regnum caelorum.* He can even call the *synagoga* (Judaism) *fornicaria,* Comm. in Hos., I, 1 on 1:2 (MPL, 25 [1884], 823 B); cf. also Apollinaris of Laodicea, Comm. in Mt. on 16:1-4 and 21:18 f. [267] But there is reflection on the two titles. Well-known is Augustine's explanation that *ecclesia* is the Chr. term and *synagoga* the Jewish because the former denotes the calling together of men and the latter the rounding up of cattle, Enarrationes in Ps. 81:1 (CCh, 39 [1956], 1136).

4. The more surprising it is, then, that συναγωγή is used not only for the assemblies, congregations, and synagogues of the Jews but also for the liturgical meetings and meeting-places of Christians; indeed, συναγωγή can serve as a self-designation instead of ἐκκλησία. For gatherings for worship it is common in the post-apost. fathers. Thus Ign. Pol., 4, 2 admonishes that Chr. gatherings should be as frequent as possible πυκνότερον συναγωγαὶ γινέσθωσαν. In Ign. Tr., 3 (ed. maior) συναγωγή is in a list of synon.: χωρὶς πρεσβυτέρων ἐκκλησία ἐκλεκτὴ οὐκ ἔστιν, οὐ συνάθροισμα ἅγιον οὐ συναγωγὴ ὁσίων. Herm. m., 11, 9, 13, 14 has συναγωγή ἀνδρῶν δικαίων for the meeting for worship. The same sense occurs in Dionyius of Alex., Eus. Hist. Eccl., VII, 9, 2: τῆς συναγωγῆς μετασχεῖν, cf. also VII, 11, 11. 12. 17. Just Dial., 63, 5 has συναγωγή "gathering" and ἐκκλησία "congregation" beside one another: μιᾷ συναγωγῇ καὶ μιᾷ ἐκκλησίᾳ, cf. also 124, 1. Cl. Al. Strom., VI, 34, 3 has συναγωγή τῆς ἐκκλησίας for the meeting of the congregation, cf. also Paed., III, 80, 3, and Eus. Hist. Eccl., IX, 1, 8 has together ἐκκλησίας συγκροτουμένας, συνόδους παμπληθεῖς, συναγωγὰς ἐπιτελουμένας (AM, most MSS ἀγωγάς), συναγωγή being the gathering for worship, perhaps also Act. Verc., 9; cf. also Cl. Al. Exc. Theod., 13, 4: ὅπερ ἐστὶν ἡ ἐκκλησία, ἄρτος οὐράνιος, συναγωγὴ εὐλογημένη. On occasion συναγωγή can also be the building. Incontestably the most interesting example is that the Marcionites could call their buildings for worship συναγωγαί, cf. the inscr. (318/19) found in Deir Ali (Lebaba) south-east of Damascus: Συναγωγὴ Μαρκιωνιστῶν κώμ(ης) Λεβάβων τοῦ κ(υρίο)υ καὶ σ(ωτῆ)ρ(ος) Ἰη(σοῦ) Χριστοῦ..., Ditt. Or., II, 608. [268] Acc. to

---

266 Ed. R. Gillet and A. de Gaudemaris, *Sources Chrétiennes,* 32 (1952), 224.
267 Ed. J. Reuss, "Mt.-Komm. aus d. griech. Kirche," TU, 61 (1957), 26 and 36.
268 Cf. A. v. Harnack, "Zur Gesch. d. marcionitischen Kirchen," *Zschr. f. wissenschaftliche Theol.,* 19 (1876), 102-109; also "Die älteste griech. Kircheninschr.," SAB (1915), 746-766, esp. 754-756; also *Marcion*[2] (1924), 158, 341*-344*; Harnack Miss., 659.

Epiph. Haer., 30, 18, 2 (GCS, 25), Jewish Chr. call the place of meeting συναγωγή: συναγωγὴν δὲ καλοῦσι τὴν ἑαυτῶν ἐκκλησίαν καὶ οὐχὶ ἐκκλησίαν. [269] Again in the later Act. Phil., 50 συναγωγή is used quite freely for the place of Chr. assembly: συναγωγὴ χριστιανῶν, and in 88 there is ref. to an οἰκοδομεῖν συναγωγὴν καὶ ἐπισκοπεῖον ἐπὶ τῷ ὀνόματι τοῦ Χριστοῦ, cf. also Commodianus Instructio, I, 24, 11 (CSEL, 15, 31).

Finally συναγωγή is not uncommon as a self-designation of Christians. It probably meant this already in the Epiph. ref. → 840, 44 ff. Elsewhere, too, συναγωγή denoted the Chr. community, and this not merely in Jewish Christian circles, or where there seems to be a contact with Judaism or Palestine. The Gentile editor of Test. XII calls Gentile Chr. churches συναγωγαὶ (or συναγωγὴ) τῶν ἐθνῶν in Test. B. 11. For Iren. Haer., IV, 31, 1 f. the *duae synagogae* are the Church and the true Judaism of the old covenant. Cl. Al. Strom., VII, 53, 3 calls the Chr. community συναγωγή when he speaks of Paul's missionary methods among the Jews. Orig. Hom. in Jer., 18, 5 on 18:1-16 (GCS, Orig., 3, 157) can use συναγωγή for ἐκκλησία, and Const. Ap., II, 43 ff. uses interchangeably ἡ τοῦ κυρίου συναγωγή and ἡ τοῦ κυρίου ἐκκλησία, cf. also III, 6, 5: τὸ κοινὸν τῆς συναγωγῆς. Indeed, ἀποσυνάγωγος, which in the NT is used unambiguously for excommunication from Judaism (→ 848, 1 ff.), can be used for excommunication from the Chr. Church, and this in direct proximity to ἐκκλησία: παρὰ δὲ ἀποσυναγώγων μὴ λαμβάνετε, πρὶν ἂν τῆς ἐκκλησίας εἶναι μέλη καταξιωθῶσιν, Const. Ap., IV, 8, 3, cf. II, 43, 1; III, 8, 3. Theophil. Autol., II, 14 also interprets συναγωγή by ἐκκλησία when he says that to a storm-battered world God gave like islands in the sea συναγωγὰς λεγομένας δὲ ἐκκλησίας ἁγίας. [270]

† ἐπισυναγωγή.

1. This is a very rare word in secular Gk. On a stele from the island Syme off the Carian coast, in a resolution honouring a worthy citizen, we find the expression τᾶς δὲ ἐπισυναγωγᾶς τοῦ διαφόρου γινομένας πολυχρονίου, "since, however, the collecting of the disputed charges took a long time," [1] IG, 12, 3, Suppl. 1270, 11 f. (1st cent. B.C.). The noun, then, denotes the act of ἐπισυνάγειν with little distinction from συναγωγή. Other profane examples of the post-chr. period occur in the geographer

---

[269] Whether συναγωγή on the Tafas inscr., CIJ, II, 861 is "A Monument of Jewish Christianity in East Jordan?" (the title of A. Alt's essay in PJB, 25 [1929], 89-95) is uncertain; cf. J. B. Frey, CIJ, II, p. 100. So, too, is the suggested reading (H. Lucas) of a Syr. inscr. from 'Edjaz (above the arcade of a large church): "There was intercession (?) by the apostles, prophets and martyrs for the church and congregation ὑπὲρ τ[ῆς συναγ]ωγῆς καὶ τοῦ λαοῦ, cf. M. v. Oppenheim and H. Lucas, "Inschr. aus Syrien, Mesopotamien u. Kleinasien," *Byzantinische Zschr.*, 14 (1905), 53, No. 82. On the note of Hier. Ep., 112, 13 about the Nazarenes *per totas orientis synagogas*, cf. Harnack Miss., 634, n. 1. In the 5th cent. Coptic monastic settlements were called ΣΥΝΑΓΩΓΗ, cf. J. Leipoldt, "Schenute v. Atripe u. d. Entstehung d. nation. ägypt. Christentums," TU, 25, 1 (1903), 96 f.

[270] It should not go unmentioned that in the Sinai Syr. and Pal. Syr. Evangeliarium Hierosolymitanum K'nuštā is used for the Chr. ἐκκλησία as well as the Jewish synagogue; cf. Schürer, II, 504, n. 11; → III, 525, 10 ff.; Schmidt, 276 f.; Rost Vorstufen, 152.

ἐ π ι σ υ ν α γ ω γ ή . Bibl. Cr.-Kö., *s.v.* Deissmann LO, 81; H. Kosmala, "Hebräer-Essener-Christen, Stud. z. Vorgeschichte d. früh-chr. Verkündigung," *Studia Post-Biblica*, I (1959), 347-350; of the comm. esp. Rgg. Hb. on 10:25.

[1] Cf. H. v. Gaertringen in Deissmann LO, 81, n. 3; fascimile, *ibid.*, 82, Ill. 10.

Ptolemaeus, Tetrabiblos, 44; [2] Syntaxis Mathematica, 2, 7, [3] in the sense of summing up. ἐπισυναγωγή also occurs in the title of the 3rd book of Artemid. Onirocr. for the result of an act: τοῦτο τὸ βιβλίον ἐπισυναγωγή ἐστι τῶν παραλειπομένων ἐν τοῖς προτέροις δύο βιβλίοις (Cod L).

2. The usage of the LXX is decisive in shaping the NT concept, for it is here that ἐπισυναγωγή acquires the eschatological note proper to it in the NT. The noun itself occurs only once; it denotes the eschatological gathering and restoration of Israel from dispersion ἄγνωστος ὁ τόπος ἔσται, ἕως ἂν συναγάγῃ ὁ θεὸς ἐπισυναγωγὴν τοῦ λαοῦ καὶ ἵλεως γένηται· καὶ τότε... ὀφθήσεται ἡ δόξα τοῦ κυρίου..., 2 Macc. 2:7 f. The anchoring of the term in the vocabulary of eschatology and its special nuance in relation to the hope of a gathering of the scattered may be seen commonly and clearly in the verb ἐπισυνάγω. [4] This eschatological focus of the verb persists in the NT, as may be seen esp. in the eschatological address of Jesus: ἐπισυνάξει τοὺς ἐκλεκτοὺς αὐτοῦ ἐκ τῶν τεσσάρων ἀνέμων ἀπ' ἄκρου γῆς ἕως ἄκρου οὐρανοῦ, Mk. 13:27; cf. Mt. 24:31. [5]

3. ἐπισυναγωγή occurs twice in the NT. In both instances the context confirms the eschatological orientation → lines 5 ff. In 2 Th. 2:1 ἐπισυναγωγή and παρουσία are closely related (common article), and both introduce the eschatological teaching which follows: Ἐρωτῶμεν δὲ ὑμᾶς, ἀδελφοί, ὑπὲρ τῆς παρουσίας τοῦ κυρίου [ἡμῶν] Ἰησοῦ Χριστοῦ καὶ ἡμῶν ἐπισυναγωγῆς ἐπ' αὐτόν. The object of the ἐπί is expressly stated: the Kurios. It is to Him [6] that the ἐπισυναγωγή of Christians will take place at the Lord's return. This is not active assembling; it is a being assembled and united (cf. ἁρπαγησόμεθα, 1 Th. 4:17).

The sense of ἐπισυναγωγή is harder to fix in Hb. 10:25: μὴ ἐγκαταλείποντες τὴν ἐπισυναγωγὴν ἑαυτῶν. It is most natural to think of the congregation gathered for worship. ἐγκαταλείπω "to leave in the lurch" agrees with this, and so does the singular ἐπισυναγωγή. In the case of liturgical meetings one would expect the plural, [7] though it is hard to differentiate between the assembled congregation and congregational assembling; either way ἐπισυναγωγή has a cultic character. [8] The

---

[2] Ed. F. E. Robbins (1956).

[3] Ed. J. Heiberg (1898), 133. Cf. Liddell-Scott and Thes. Steph., s.v. (with ref. to Procl. and Porphyr.).

[4] Cf. 2 Macc. 1:27: ἐπισυνάγαγε τὴν διασπορὰν ἡμῶν, also ψ 105:47; cf. τὰς διασπορὰς τοῦ Ισραηλ ἐπισυνάξει ψ 146:2; Zech. 13:2 (related here to ἔθνη); Is. 52:12; 2 Macc. 2:18; Ps. Sol. 11:2 f.; 17:26. There is a similar statement about the συναγωγή in Is. 56:8 → 805, 10 ff. Materially cf. Schürer, II, 626 f.; Volz Esch.. 344-348; Bousset-Gressm., 236-8; O. Michel, "Das Zeugnis d. NT von der Gemeinde," FRL, NF, 39 (1941), 19-22.

[5] Cf. also Mt. 23:37; Lk. 13:34; 17:37; Did., 9, 4; 10, 5. קהל and אסף are also eschatologically orientated in the Qumran sect and are used for the assembly or assembling of the eschatological community, Kosmala, 348 f.

[6] ἐπί in the sense of the more common πρός arises through the compound with ἐπί and does not have the subsidiary sense of "up to," Dob. Th.; Wbg. Th.; J. A. Frame, The Ep. of St. Paul to the Thess., ICC (1953), ad loc., though cf. W. Bornemann, Die Thessalonicherbr., Krit.-exeg. Komm. über d. NT, 10⁵, ⁶ (1894), ad loc.

[7] Cf. Rgg. Hb., ad loc.

[8] Cr.-Kö., s.v. thinks, however, that the preceding and ensuing antithesis κατανοῶμεν ἀλλήλους εἰς παροξυσμὸν ἀγάπης καὶ καλῶν ἔργων... ἀλλὰ παρακαλοῦντες suggests conduct which embraces the whole life of the fellowship rather than a single expression of it. Yet love and good works are not the opposite of ἐγκαταλείπειν but κατανοεῖν ἀλλήλους εἰς παροξυσμὸν ἀγάπης... and παρακαλεῖν, both of which lie within the worship of the congregation.

καθὼς ἔθος τισίν which follows rules out the sense of "congregation" for ἐπισυναγωγή, for the conduct which has become a habit in some members of the
congregation (τινές) cannot be a falling away from the community, [9] even though
in the last resort staying away from the congregation which has gathered for worship does mean leaving it in the lurch. [10] In view of the "approaching day" the
mutual strengthening and admonishing which takes place in the liturgical gathering
is all the more necessary: καὶ τοσούτῳ μᾶλλον ὅσῳ βλέπετε ἐγγίζουσαν τὴν
ἡμέραν.

The historical occasion and background of Hb. 10:25 is obscure. It has been suggested
that Christians were attending Jewish synagogues [11] or taking part in mystery cults [12]
or gravitating to other Christian house-churches in the same place, [13] or that the
ἐγκαταλείπειν of the ἐπισυναγωγή was connected with individualism and pride,
persecution, fear of suffering, a flagging zeal, [14] or that the allusion is not to the
peculiarities of an individual congregation. [15]

---

[9] Cf. Cr.-Kö., s.v. and Rgg. Hb., ad loc.

[10] Cf. J. Héring, L'épître aux Hébreux, Comm. du NT, 12 (1954), ad loc.

[11] So esp. older exegesis. W. Manson, The Ep. to the Hebrews (1957), 69 considers the
following possibility: "A group of Jewish Christians derived from, or possibly still continuing
to exist within, a Jewish synagogue at Rome was under stress of one kind or another...
giving up its Christian meetings," so that ἐπισυναγωγή takes on here the sense of "epi-
synagogue" or "Christian appendage to the Jewish synagogue." C. Spicq, L'épître aux Héb.,
Études Bibl., 2 (1953), ad loc.: "Certains convertis... se rendraient au Temple, à la Synagogue,
retrouvant leurs anciens correligionnaires." But there is as little support for these conjectures
as for all other hypotheses which read out of Hb. a danger of relapse into Judaism, cf. E.
Käsemann, "Das wandernde Gottesvolk," FRL, NF, 37² (1957), 10.

[12] Thus J. Moffatt, A Crit. and Exeg. Comm. on the Ep. to the Hebrews, ICC (1952),
ad loc. thinks the warning is directed to people "who combined Christianity with a number
of mystery-cults, patronizing them in turn, or who withdrew from Christian fellowship,
feeling that they had exhausted the Christian faith and that it required to be supplemented
by some other cult." Mi. Hb., ad loc. also thinks it possible there was falling away to other
religious fellowships, but cf. Wnd. Hb., ad loc.

[13] Zahn Einl., II, 144. But here too big a burden of proof is put on the reflexive ἑαυτῶν,
which is not emphatic, cf. Rgg. Hb., ad loc. The continuation is also against this, Wnd. Hb.,
ad loc.

[14] Cf. Moffatt, op. cit., Spicq, op. cit. and Wnd. Hb., ad loc.

[15] Acc. to M. Dibelius, "Der himmlische Kultus nach dem Hb.," Botschaft u. Gesch.,
Gesammelte Aufsätze, II (1956), 161 the ref. in Hb. 10:25 is to "typical manifestations of a
Christianity which has lost its first enthusiasm," so that there is no point in discussing the
reasons for poor attendance. For similar admonitions to attend and warnings against slackness
cf. Ab., 2, 4 and bBer., 8a, Str.-B., III, 743; 1 QS 7:9, 10 f.; Philo Migr. Abr., 90-92; Jos. Ant.,
4, 203 f.; Herm. v., 3, 6, 2; 1 Cl., 46, 2; Barn., 4, 10; Did., 16, 2 (in an eschatological context);
for other examples Wnd. Hb., ad loc.

† ἀρχισυνάγωγος.

1. We find an ἀρχισυνάγωγος [1] in pagan cults and guilds, with no essential distinction from συναγωγός and συναγωγεύς, [2] compounds in ἀρχι- being common in the cultic unions of Greece. [3] Eus. Hist. Eccl., VII, 10, 4 speaks of an ἀρχισυνάγωγος of Egypt. magicians. Jewish synagogue rulers, Samaritans and Chr. presbyters are all lumped together in Ep. Hadriani; they are called astrologers, haruspices, and quacks, Script. Hist. Aug., Vita Saturnini, 8, 2. Similarly in Lampridius Vita Alexandri Severi, 6 Alex. Severus is mockingly called a Syrus archisynagogus. The main occurrence in relation to guilds is on inscr., though we find it only in Macedonia-Thracia and Egypt. A votive inscr. from Olynthos mentions an ἀρχισυνάγωγος at the head of a κολλήγιον: Αἰλιανὸς Νείκων ὁ ἀρχισυνάγωγος θεοῦ Ἥρωος καὶ τὸ κολλήγιον Βειβίῳ Ἀντωνίῳ ἀνέστησεν τὸν βωμόν, CIG, II, 2007 f.; the most interesting pt. here is that the ἀρχισυνάγωγος is an official of the god. Another inscr. from Thessalonica, which contains a decree of the worshippers of Heracles for a guild-member, shows that the society of συνήθ[εις] τοῦ Ἡρακλέος is directed by an ἀρχισυναγωγῶν (part.); after him are three γραμματεύοντες and an epimeletes, BCH, 8 (1884), 463 (155 A.D.). An inscr. of Perinthus in Thracia [4] ref. to an ἀρχισυνάγωγος for a workers' union called a συναγωγή → 801, 20 ff.; this is the only instance of συναγωγή for the society which the ἀρχισυνάγωγος heads: τὸν βω[μ]ὸν τῇ συναγω[γ]ῇ τῶν κουρέω[ν π]ερὶ ἀρχισυνάγ[ωγ]ον. Γ. Ἰούλιον [Ο]ὐάλεντα δῶ[ρ]ον ἀποκατέστη[σα]ν. [5] In the votive inscr. of a military union we find together ἀρχισυνά]γωγος καὶ ἀρχιερεύς for the one person; the ensuing ref. to [...θε]ῶν Φιλοπατόρων shows that this is in the sphere of profane Gk., Preisigke Sammelbuch, 623 (80-69 B. C. Fayyum). From Egypt we also have a resolution (Alexandria) which mentions several ἀρχισυνάγωγοι, τῶν ἀρχισυναγώ[γων, ibid., 8787, 3

ἀ ρ χ ι σ υ ν ά γ ω γ ο ς. Bibl.: Deissmann LO, 378-380; I. Elbogen, "Der jüd. Gottesdienst in seiner geschichtl. Entwicklung," Schriften hsgg. v. d. Gesellschaft zur Förderung d. Wissenschaft des Judt.[3] (1931), 483-5; J. B. Frey, CIJ, I (1936), XCVII-XCIX; J. Juster, Les Juifs dans l'empire Romain, I (1914), 450-453; S. Krauss, Synagogale Altertümer (1922), 114-121; H. J. Leon, The Jews of Ancient Rome (1960), 171-3; B. Lifshitz, "Fonctions et titres honorifiques dans les communautés juives," Rev. Bibl., 67 (1960), 58-64; F. Poland, Gesch. d. griech. Vereinswesens (1909), 355-7; also Art. "συναγωγεύς" in Pauly-W., 4a (1932), 1316-1322; M. San Nicolò, "Ägypt. Vereinswesen z. Zt. d. Ptolemäer u. Römer, II, 1," Münchener Beiträge z. Papyrusforschung, 2 (1915), 8, n. 3 and 61, 63; Schürer, II, 509-513 and III, 88; also Die Gemeindeverfassung d. Juden in Rom in d. Kaiserzeit (1879), 25-28; Str.-B., IV, 145-7; C. Vitringa, De synagoga vetere libri tres² (1726), 580-592; S. M. Zarb, "De membris Synagogae," Angelicum, 5 (1928), 407-423, esp. 411-415; E. Ziebarth, Das griech. Vereinswesen (1896), 55 f., 65, 149.
[1] On Gk. titles in ἀρχι-, which were very popular esp. in the Hell. and Roman period, cf. E. Risch, "Griech. Determinativkomposita," Indogerman. Forschungen, 59 (1949), 281-3. On the verbal compounds in the NT cf. Bl.-Debr. § 118, 2.
[2] συναγωγός occurs esp. in cultic guilds on the Black Sea; the title συναγωγεύς is attested in Delos, Elaeusa, Tomi. Examples Poland Vereinswesen and Ziebarth, Index, s.v.; Poland συναγωγεύς, passim; Schürer, II, 512 f., n. 38. We also find the part ἀρχισυναγωγῶν → line 15 f.
[3] Cf. ἀρχερανιστής, ἀρχιθιασίτης, ἀρχιμύστης, ἀρχιβουκόλος, Ziebarth, Index, s.v. For other examples Preisigke Wört., III, 370 f.
[4] Archäol.-epigraph. Mitteilungen aus Österreich-Ungarn, 19 (1896), 67.
[5] The Chios inscr. mentioned in Schürer, II, 512, n. 38 (CIG, II, 2 2221c), in which there is thought to be ref. to 5 ἀρχισυνάγωγοι as officials of a cultic guild, is often quoted. But the reading of [...]ναγωγοι as ἀρχισυνάγωγοι, Schürer, Ziebarth, 65; J. Oehler, Art. "ἀρχισυνάγωγος" in Pauly-W., Suppl., 1 (1903), 123; also Zum griech. Vereinswesen (1905), 13, is cogently contested by Poland Vereinswesen, 356 and συναγωγεύς 1316-1318 on grounds of lack of space and of grammar. Poland suggests [οἱ συ]ναγωγοί so too G. Dunst, "Χακά," APF, 16 (1958), 173. But the resultant conclusion that we no longer have the many ἀρχισυνάγωγοι typical of Judaism (Dunst, loc. cit., cf. Poland συναγωγεύς, 1316 f.) does not affect the Alexandrian inscr. → 844, 23 f.

(3-4 A.D.). [6] The function of the ἀρχισυνάγωγος in a society was obviously that of the president (often he was also the founder) who convened and led the συναγωγή "(festal) assembly." [7]

2. Whether the title of the Jewish synagogue president was taken from the sphere of the Gk. guild or the latter borrowed from Judaism one can hardly say. [8] At any rate it took on gter. importance in the synagogue than in the guild. The rights of synagogue ownership and administration were vested in the congregation. Since in a Jewish population this was identical with the civil community civil and synagogal government was one and the same. In such purely Jewish communities synagogue affairs were in the hands of a board of seven. Where the population was mixed and the cultic congregation was organised independently, or there were several congregations in the same place, we find a board of three. [9] The true officers of the synagogue are to be distinguished from these: the servant mentioned in Lk. 4:20 (→ ὑπηρέτης חזן הכנסת, Aram. חזנא דכנשתא) [10] and the president, the ἀρχισυνάγωγος ראש הכנסת.

There is abundant testimony to ἀρχισυνάγωγοι in literature and inscr. from all parts of the Roman world. [11] Synagogue presidents were highly regarded. In inscr. they are called τιμι(ώ)τατοι (Apamea in Syria, CIJ, II, 803, 1), ἀξιολογώτατος (Teos, II, 744) and λαμπ(ρότατος) (Sepphoris, II, 991). [12] It was a gt. privilege to wed the daughter of a president of the synagogue, Bar. bPes., 49b. He ranked above the alms treasurer. [13] He was often a member of the community or synagogue board (cf. the inscr. CIJ, I, 265, 282, 553 → n. 26, where ἄρχων and ἀρχισυνάγωγος are used of one and the same person) even though the offices were differentiated; in an inscr. from Apamea we read of three πρεσβύτεροι and three ἀρχισυνάγωγοι who are distinguished from one another, CIJ, II, 803. [14] Priests (CIJ, II, 1404, 1 f. Jerusalem: ἱερεὺς καὶ ἀ[ρ]χι-

---

[6] The question which Poland Vereinswesen, 356 does not clearly decide and W. Ruge, Art. "Teos," Pauly-W., 5a (1934), 559 leaves open, namely, whether the ἀρχισυνάγωγος of the Teos inscr., CIJ, II, 744 is the head of a society or the president of a Jewish synagogue, is answered in favour of the latter by L. Robert, Hellenica Recueil d'Épigraphie, de Numismatique et d'Antiquités Grecques, I (1940), 27 f.; cf. Juster, 190; Krauss, 232; J. B. Frey, CIJ, II, p. 12.

[7] Poland Vereinswesen, 357 and συναγωγεύς, 1318-1321; San Nicolò, 8, n. 3; 61.

[8] Cf. Schürer, II, 512, n. 38.

[9] Ibid., 501-4; Str.-B., II, 661 f.; IV, 142 and 145; Elbogen, 482 f. 485; Zarb, 407-411; → VI, 660, 39 ff.

[10] Str.-B., IV, 147-9; Krauss, 121-131; Elbogen, 485-7; H. Bornhäuser, Sukka, Die Mischna, II Seder, 6. Tractat (1935), 110 f.

[11] Cf. CIJ, I, Index, s.v.; Rabb. in Str.-B., IV, 145-7. K. G. Goetz, "Ist der מבקר der Genizafr. wirklich das Vorbild d. chr. Episkopats," ZNW, 30 (1931), 92 thinks it possible that the Damascus מבקר is simply a linguistically and geographically different term for ἀρχισυνάγωγος or ראש הכנסת.

[12] Cf. also the Beth-She'arim inscr., where a Beyrouth ἀρχισυνάγωγος is called λαμπρότατος, Lifshitz, 58-60, and CIJ, II, 766, 11-14 Acmonia: ἡ συναγωγὴ ἐτείμησεν ὅπλῳ ἐπιχρύσῳ διά τε τὴν ἐνάρετον αὐτῶν (sc. ἀρχισυναγώγων) [βί]ωσιν καὶ τὴν π[ρ]ὸς τὴν συναγωγὴν εὔνοιαν τε καὶ σπουδήν.

[13] Cf. Str.-B., IV, 145 f.

[14] Cf. also the distinguishing of the two titles in Acta Pilati, 1, 6, ed. C. v. Tischendorf, Evangelia apocr. (1896), 221 and Epiph. Haer., 30, 11, 4; 30, 18, 2 (GCS, 25). It cannot be proved that πρεσβύτερος denotes the office of the president of the synagogue in the Theodotus inscr., CIJ, II, 1404 (H. Lietzmann, "Notizen," ZNW, 20 [1921], 173 and G. Bornkamm → VI, 661, n. 55), for it is most unlikely that the πρεσβύτεροι of CIJ, 1404, 9 f. are identical with the ἀρχισυνάγωγοι of line 2 f.; cf. also → n. 26. For the place of πρεσβύτεροι in synagogues cf. CIJ, I, 663; II, 735, 829, 1227; also L. Robert, "Inscr. Grecques de Sidè en Pamphylie," Revue de Philologie, 84 (1958), 41 f.

συνάγωγος, also I, 504 Rome) and Rabb. (cf. II, 1414 Jerusalem: ʿΡαββὶ Σαμου[ηλ] ἀρχ(ι)σ[υνάγωγος Φ]ρύγιος...) could hold the office; the synagogue of Dura-Europos was built בקישׁישׁותה דישׁמואל כהנה, "under the presbyterate of the priest Samuel," II, 828a b.

One of the tasks of the president of the synagogue was to conduct worship and to apportion functions in it, [15] i.e., to choose those who would recite the prayer and shᵉma and read and expound the portions of Scripture. [16] He was also responsible for erecting and maintaining the building, as one may see esp. from inscr. Acc. to CIJ, II, 1404 the ἀρχισυνάγωγος Theodotus built the synagogue. An Aegina inscr. says: Θεόδωρος ἀρχισυν[άγωγος φ]ροντίσας ἔτη τέσσερα [φθαρεῖσαν?] ἐκ θεμελίων τὴν συναγ-[ωγὴν] οἰκοδόμησα, I, 722. Other inscr. mention parts of synagogues, e.g., II, 803 Apamea: ἀρχισυνάγωγος ᾿Αντιοχέων ἐποίησεν τὴν ἴσοδον τοῦ ψηφίου. In a Teos inscr. it is expressly said that the building was financed by the president of the synagogue: ἀρχισυνάγω[γος] ... ἐκ θεμελίων ἐκ τῶν ἰ[δίων], II, 744. An inscr. from Acmonia in Phrygia says that two ἀρχισυνάγωγοι, father and son, paid for repairs to the walls and roof, for strengthening the doors, and for complete redecoration, II, 766. [17] An inscr. from Caesarea in Palestine says of the ἀρχισυνάγωγος, also called φροντιστής: ἐποίησε τὴν ψηφοθεσίαν τοῦ τρικλίνου τῷ ἰδίῳ. [18]

The ἀρχισυνάγωγος, like the ἄρχων (cf. ὁ δὶς ἄρχων τῆς συναγωγῆς Καλκαρή-σις, CIJ, I, 384 etc. from Rome, τρίς in I, 494 from Rome), was perhaps elected for a term (one year?), and could be re-elected. [19] If we find ὁ διὰ βίου ἀρχισυνάγωγος in some inscr. (CIJ, II, 744 and 766, Teos and Acmania), the ref. is perhaps to an honorary ἀρχισυνάγωγος. [20] Often the office remained for generations in the same family: CIJ, II, 1404 Jerusalem mentions grandfather, father and son, I, 584 Venosa and II, 766 Acmonia ref. to father and son. Each synagogue had only one ἀρχισυνάγωγος. [21] The plur. in bPes., 49a; bGit., 59b and Mk. 5:22 denotes the category. [22] CIJ, II, 803 Apamea and Ac. 13:15 are against this; they ref. to several synagogue presidents in the same synagogue at the same time. It has thus been asked whether members of the board were

---

[15] Hence ἀρχισυνάγωγος does not come from συναγωγή = congregation but from συναγωγή = assembly. The ἀρχισυνάγωγος was primarily the "président de réunion," but one cannot go on to say "il se contente de présider les assemblées religieuses," cf. Frey, XCVII; → II, 91, 5 f. Others make the function of the ἀρχισυνάγωγος too close to that of the Rabb. or degrade him to a mere patron with no learning or "spiritual quality," cf. Leon, 171, n. 2.

[16] Cf. Str.-B., IV, 146.

[17] Cf. on Frey's text in CIJ, II, p. 28 the critical note of Robert, 41, n. 1, who suggests painting the walls and roof rather than repairs.

[18] Cf. Lifshitz, 60; M. Avi-Yonah, "The Synag. of Caesarea," Bull. of the L. M. Rabinowitz Fund for the Exploration of Ancient Synagogues, 3 (1960), 47.

[19] Acc. to Juster, 452 the ἀρχισυνάγωγος was nominated by the patriarch, but cf. J. B. Frey, "Les communautés juives à Rome aux premiers temps de l'Église," Recherches de Science Religieuse, 21 (1931), 154; Frey, XCVIII; Leon, 172, n. 2.

[20] In inscr. from Smyrna CIJ, II, 741 and Myndos II, 756, the title is used of Jewish women called Rufina and Theopempta, and it is used of a three-year old child in an inscr. from Venosa in Apulia, I, 587. Cf. S. Reinach, "Inscr. grecqe de Smyrne, La Juive Rufina," Rev. d. Études Juives, 7 (1883), 161-6; Schürer, II, 512, n. 37; E. R. Goodenough, Jewish Symbols in the Greco-Roman Period, II (1953), 80. Of the two explanations (an honorary title and the wife of a synagogue president, Frey, CIJ, II, p. 11, 20) the former is to be preferred for No. 741, 756, cf. Juster, I, 453; Reinach, 165 f., but not Krauss, 118. There can certainly be no question of a woman actually discharging the function of an ἀρχισυνάγωγος.

[21] The verdict of Grundm. Mk. on 5:22 that "a synagogue congregation mostly had several presidents" rest on a confusion between presidents of the synagogue and members of the synagogue board.

[22] Cf. Str.-B., IV, 146 f.; Krauss, 117; cf. Schürer, II, 512: "one of the class of synagogue presidents." Following B. Weiss, Das Markusev. u. seine synpt. Par. (1872), 184 on 5:22, Zn. Ag. on 13:15 thinks one president was customary at least in Palestine.

not also called ἀρχισυνάγωγοι, [23] or whether the ἀρχισυνάγωγοι might have discharged their office successively, [24] but in view of the paucity of sources these are mere conjectures.

3. In the NT ἀρχισυνάγωγος occurs only in Mark (Mk. 5:22, 35, 36, 38) and Luke (Lk. 8:49; 13:14; Ac. 13:15; 18:8, 17). In Lk. the synagogue "ruler" is also the ἄρχων τῆς συναγωγῆς, cf. Lk. 8:41 and 8:49. [25] On the other hand Codex D Ac. 14:2 rightly distinguishes between the ἀρχισυνάγωγοι τῶν Ἰουδαίων and the ἄρχοντες τῆς συναγωγῆς, for Jewish inscriptions always differentiate the two offices, recognising both their vesting in one person [26] and also their distribution among more than one. [27] Named "rulers" of the synagogue in the NT are Jairus in Mk. 5:22, Crispus at Corinth in Ac. 18:8, cf. also 1 C. 1:14, and Sosthenes in Ac. 18:17 (usually thought to be identical with "brother" Sosthenes in 1 C. 1:1). The NT accounts agree with Jewish records (→ 846, 5 ff.) that the "ruler" of the synagogue is responsible for the order and progress of worship. In Lk. 13:14 the ἀρχισυνάγωγος protests against healing on the Sabbath in the synagogue. In Ac. 13:15 the synagogue "rulers" ask Paul and Barnabas for a λόγος παρακλήσεως πρὸς τὸν λαόν after the reading. Ac. 14:2 (D) makes the "ruler" of the synagogue responsible for the persecution in Iconium along with the ἄρχοντες τῆς συναγωγῆς. [28]

4. There are only isolated ref. in the early Church. In Mart. Pt. et Pl. 10 the ἀρχισυνάγωγοι τῶν Ἰουδαίων καὶ ⟨οἱ⟩ τῶν Ἑλλήνων ἱερεῖς resist the successful preaching of Peter and Paul in Rome. Acc. to Just. Dial., 137, 2 the Jewish synagogue rulers taught the Jews to mock Christ after the prayer. Acc. to Epiph. Haer., 30, 18, 2 (GCS, 25) Jewish Christians also had synagogue rulers πρεσβυτέρους γὰρ οὗτοι ἔχουσι καὶ ἀρχισυναγώγους.

---

[23] Str.-B., IV, 147 on Ac. 13:15.
[24] Frey, CIJ, II, p. 56 on No. 803: "probablement avaient-ils rempli cette fonction successivement."
[25] Mt. 9:18, 23 simply has ἄρχων.
[26] Cf. CIJ, I, 265: Stafulo arconti et archisynagogo ... and I, 282: Ἰσαὰκ [ἀρχισυν]άγωγος [καὶ ἄρχων?] συναγωγῆ[ς ... (both from Rome); I, 553 (Capua): Alfius Iuda, arcon, arcosynagogus ... Cf. also I, 504 (Rome), Hence it is incontestable that the same man could be both, and one does not have to postulate linguistic and material confusion in Lk. 8:41, 49, but cf. Krauss, 117. Yet it would seem from the interchangeability in Lk. 8:41, 49 and the replacement of ἀρχισυνάγωγος in Mt. that Lk. and Mt. did take the terms to be synon. and that Lk. is not just ref. to an accumulation of offices, cf. Schürer, II, 511.
[27] CIJ, II, 766 (Acmonia) mentions two ἀρχισυνάγωγοι and an ἄρχων together.
[28] W. L. Knox, St. Paul and the Church of Jerusalem (1925), 86 f., n. 17 says that Chr. ἀρχισυνάγωγοι in the Palestinian and Pauline churches were "responsible for presiding at the common meal," but this is pure fantasy.

† ἀποσυνάγωγος.

This word [1] occurs in the NT only in John, nor are there any examples prior to or outside the Christian use.

1. Since it is always asked to what degree of Jewish discipline ἀποσυνάγωγος is related, a brief account of Jewish practice must be given first. Up to recently it was thought that שמתא denoted the third degree of excommunication, but in fact it is identical with the second נדוי; the two words are synon. [2] Even the distinction between the first and second grades is doubtful in the NT period. [3] The most common lower degree נדוי was a thirty day suspension from the congregation, though it might be extended. [4] It was imposed for many reasons, e.g., pronouncing the divine name (bNed., 7b), dishonouring or opposing teachers of the Torah (bMQ, 16a b; bNed., 50b; Ed., 5, 6), bearing witness against Jews before non-Jewish courts (bBQ), 113b), or esp. spurning the Torah and Halachah (bMQ 16a b). [5] Any Jew was permitted (and sometimes required) to pronounce sentence of exclusion, even a girl (bMQ, 17a; jMQ, 3, 1 [81d, 37 f.]). The proper authority, however, was the court בית דין. נדוי limited dealings with others and made them more difficult. One had not to eat or drink with the suspended person and one had

---

ἀ π ο σ υ ν ά γ ω γ ο ς. Bibl.: a. On Jewish excommunication: S. Bialoblocki, Art. "Cherem," EJ, V, 411-422; R. Bohren, *Das Problem d. Kirchenzucht im NT* (1952), 16-29; M. J. Döller, "Der Bann im AT u. im späteren Judt.," *Zschr. f. kathol. Theol.* 37 (1913), 1-24; W. Doskocil, "Der Bann in d. Urkirche," *Münchener Theol. Stud.,* III, 11 (1958), 10-20; K. Hofmann, Art. "Anathema," RAC, I, 427-430; C. H. Hunzinger, *Die jüd. Bannpraxis im nt.lichen Zeitalter,* Diss. Göttingen (1954); J. Juster, *Les Juifs dans l'Empire Romain,* II (1914), 159-161; E. Kohlmeyer, "Charisma oder Recht? Vom Wesen d. ältesten Kirchenrechts," *Zschr. d. Savigny-Stiftung f. Rechtsgeschichte, Kanonistische Abteilung,* 38, 69 (1952), 4 f.; Schürer, II, 507-9; Str.-B., IV, 293-333. b. On the Birkath ha-Minim: I. Elbogen, "Der jüd. Gottesdienst in seiner geschichtl. Entwicklung," *Schr. hsgg. v. d. Gesellschaft zur Förderung d. Wissenschaft d. Judt.³* (1931), 36-39, 51, 252 f. M. Goldstein, *Jesus in the Jewish Tradition* (1950), 45-51 (bibl. 278, n. 54 and 248-265); F. C. Grant, "Modern Study of the Jewish Liturgy," ZAW, 65 (1953), 64-66; R. T. Herford. *Christianity in Talmud and Midrash* (1903); also "The Problem of Minim Further Considered," *Jewish Stud. in Memory of G. A. Kohut* (1935), 359-369; Hunzinger, 68-70; J. Jocz, *The Jewish People and Jesus Christ* (1949), 51-57, 174-190; K. G. Kuhn, "Achtzehngebet u. Vaterunser u. der Reim," *Wissenschaftliche Untersuchungen zum NT,* 1 (1950), 18-20; J. Parkes, *The Foundations of Judaism and Christianity* (1960), 225 f.; Schürer, II, 543 f.; M. Simon, *Verus Israel. Étude sur les relations entre Chrétiens et Juifs dans l'Empire Romain 135-425. Bibliothèque des Écoles d'Athènes et de Rome,* 166 (1948), 214-238; H. L. Strack, "Jesus, die Häretiker u. d. Christen," *Schr. d. Institutum Judaicum,* 37 (1910); Str.-B., I, 406 f.; IV, 208-220, 237; C. C. Torrey, "The Aram. Period of the Nascent Christian Church," ZNW, 44 (1952/53), 212-214, c. On ἀποσυνάγωγος in Jn. cf. the bibl. under a. and b. and the comm., also K. L. Carroll, "The Fourth Gospel and the Exclusion of Christians from the Synagogues," *Bull. of the John Rylands Library,* 40 (1957/58), 19-32.

[1] On the composition of the word cf. R. Strömberg, "Greek Prefix Studies," *Göteborgs Högskolas Årsskrift,* 53, 3 (1946), 28-31 and the examples there, ἄποικος, ἀπόδημος, "away from home," "abroad."

[2] Schürer, II, 507; Cr.-Kö., *s.v.;* Hunzinger, 5; acc. to Str.-B., IV, 294 f. נדוי is the Palestinian and שמתא the Babylonian term for the lesser expulsion. Further bibl. in Bohren, 24, n. 32. H. Zucker, *Stud. z. jüd. Selbstverwaltung im Altertum* (1936), 188 defends a threefold excommunication.

[3] Cf. Cr.-Kö., *s.v.;* Schürer, II, 507 f. ("possible"); Hunzinger, 5-7, not Str.-B., IV, 294 f., 297-329, who thinks there is proof of two degrees in ancient synagogue practice.

[4] נדוי "separation" from נדה "to detach, separate, exclude"; שמתא from שמד has the same sense, Str.-B., IV, 296.

[5] Other Rabb. examples and reasons in Str.-B., IV, 297-318.

to keep 4 cubits away, bMQ, 16a. The person under suspension had to observe special rites like a mourner; he had not to shave (MQ, 3, 1; bMQ, 15a) nor to wear sandals (T. Taan., 1, 6 [215]; jMQ, 3, 5 [82d, 30 f.]); he had to cover his head (bTaan., 14b, Bar.) and use a special entrance to the temple (Mid., 2, 2). But this shows he was not barred from the temple; he might also teach and be taught, bMQ, 15a. [6] Rules about lifting or loosing the ban vary. [7]

The sharper second degree חרם meant unlimited exclusion from the congregation with avoidance of all contact, including economic and educational, bMQ, 16a. It was imposed by a court, not individuals, and was merely an ultimate sanction when a second נדוי proved unsuccessful, i.e., after 60 days, bMQ, 16a. But this excommunication, too, could be lifted. [8] As a domestic discipline excommunication was designed to amend, convert, or win back the person concerned, not to ban him permanently from the synagogue as in the case of apostates משומדים and heretics מינים.

Neither of the two degrees of exclusion corresponds to ἀποσυνάγωγος, for this means complete excommunication from the synagogue. This shows us at once what is the sense of συναγωγή in the term ἀποσυνάγωγος. The Johannine statements refer neither to a mere prohibition of entry into a συναγωγή (= building → 807, 9 ff.) nor to the barring of participation in a συναγωγή (= assembly → 804, 12 ff.) nor to exclusion from the συναγωγή (= local synagogue community → 806, 11 ff.) but to exclusion from the national and religious fellowship of the Jews, συναγωγή denoting here the entire community (→ 829, n. 203). This alone corresponds to the claim of the Johannine Christ and to the radical nature of the decision at issue (→ 852, 11 ff.). [9] Hence we are to think in terms, not of the discipline of excommunication, but of the cursing of heretics (birkath ha-minim). For only here is there radical cleavage and even hostility.

Acc. to a saying of R. Tarphon (c. 100) heretics are worse than Gentiles and idolaters. The latter deny God without knowing Him, the former know Him but deny Him all the same. T. Shab., 13, 5 (129). "One should not sell to them nor buy from them; one should have no dealings with them; one should not teach their sons a trade; one should not be healed by them whether in respect of property (slaves and cattle) or of person," T. Chul., 2, 21 (503). [10] It is even forbidden to help heretics and apostates in danger; one should not pull them out of the pit but thrust them into it, T. BM, 2, 33 (375). [11] They were excluded from the saving benefits of Israel and condemned to eternal perdition. "Heretics and apostates and traitors and free-thinkers and deniers of the Torah and those who leave the ways of the community and those who contest the resurrection of the dead ... hell is barred behind them and they are judged in it for all generations (for ever)," T. Sanh., 13, 5 (434). [12]

---

[6] For more on the consequences, Str.-B., IV, 304-9. We learn something about the ceremonial only from Babylonia, bMQ, 16a, cf. Str.-B., IV, 302 f.

[7] Str.-B., IV, 320-327.

[8] *Ibid.,* 328, 330, though cf. Schürer, II, 507.

[9] Cf. Cr.-Kö., *s.v.*

[10] Cf. Str.-B., IV, 332; O. Michel, "Polemik u. Scheidung," *Judaica,* 15 (1959), 211 f. transl. the last line: "neither in matters of property nor in bodily injury," Strack, 59* "neither in caring for the health of property ... nor in caring for the health of person." Cf. also bShab., 116a; bSanh., 38b.

[11] Str.-B., IV, 332 f. and Strack, 25 = 56*; also the ref. there, bAZ, 26a b.

[12] Cf. Str.-B., III, 230 and Strack, 26 = 57 f *.

The much-debated question whether minim are Christians [13] or non-Chr., Jewish-Gnostic heretics [14] cannot be decided either way, [15] since arguments can be advanced and examples adduced for both Christians [16] and non-Christians [17] and in many cases an exact distinction is impossible. The ref. is certainly to heretics ("there are minim among the Gentile nations," bChul., 13b) and primarily it is to Jewish Christians. [18] In the oldest Palestinian version of the 12th benediction of the Prayer of Eighteen Benedictions, now known to us through the findings in the Cairo Geniza, Nazarenes הנצרים and minim are mentioned together: "May the Nazarenes (הנצרים = Christians) and heretics (המינים) perish in a moment, be blotted out of the book of life, and not be written with the just." [19] The introduction of this benediction into the Shᵉmone 'Esre and therewith into the liturgy by R. Gamaliel II c. 90 A.D. carried with it a definitive breach between the Chr. Church and Judaism. [20] From then on cursing the Nazarenes became an integral part of synagogue worship and the daily prayer of every Jew. Precisely in this benediction very gt. care was taken to see that the cursing of the minim was done correctly and without abbreviation. Attending the synagogue and taking part in its worship thus became impossible for Christians. Complete separation resulted. In future confession of Jesus Christ meant excommunication and expulsion from Judaism. The Johannine statements belong to this period.

---

[13] For Jewish Christians cf. Herford Christianity, 365-381; Carroll, 20; Jocz, 52 f., 56, 178-181: "first Jewish Christians, then also Gentile Christians," 180; A. Schlatter, Die Kirche Israels vom Jahre 70-130 (1898), 7 f. For Gentile Christians → I, 182, n. 8; H. Hirschberg, "Allusions to the Apostle Paul in the Talmud," JBL, 62 (1943), 73-87; also "Once Again — The Minim," JBL, 67 (1948), 305-318; also "Paulus im Midrasch," Zschr. f. Religions- u. Geistesgesch., 12 (1960), 253 f.: "Disciples of Paul, or better deutero-Pauline propaganda, whether of Jewish or Gentile derivation."

[14] M. Friedländer, Der vorchr. jüd. Gnosticismus (1898), 71-4; also Die religiösen Bewegungen innerhalb d. Judt. im Zeitalter Jesu Christi (1905), 191 f., 206 f., 215-234 etc.; A. Marmorstein, "The Background of the Haggadah," HUCA, 6 (1929), 183; F. C. Grant, The Earliest Gospel (1943), 92 f.; also "Modern Study of the Jewish Liturgy," ZAW, 65 (1953), 65 f.; G. Scholem, Die jüd. Mystik in ihren Hauptströmungen (1957), 393, n. 24: The ref. is to a heretical Gnosticism dualistic and antinomian in character, not to Jewish Christians; Goldstein, 48-50 stresses the relation between Jewish and Chr. Gnostics and thinks both are in view.

[15] Cf. I. Levy, "Le mot 'minim,'" REJ, 38 (1899), 206; Elbogen, 36: "all heresies" (Sadducees, Samaritans, Christians, Gnostics); Schürer, II, 544 and n. 162; J. Bergmann, Jüd. Apologetik im nt.lichen Zeitalter (1908), 7 f.; Str.-B., IV, 330: "Heretics of all kinds including Jewish Christians, the common feature being a rejection to some degree of the Rabbinism dominant in Judaism"; → I, 181, 41 ff.; Simon, 215 f., 218; Hunzinger, 68. Acc. to A. Büchler, "Die Erlösung Elišaʿ b Abujahs aus dem Höllenfeuer," MGWJ, 76 (1932), 412-456. מינים were originally Jewish heretics, but non-Jewish sectaries were also called this in the 2nd and 3rd cent. K. G. Kuhn, "Giljonim u. sifre minim," Judt., Urchr., Kirche, Festschr. f. J. Jeremias, Beih. zu ZNW, 26 (1960), also thinks minim in the older Rabb. texts were always Jews (37) but in the later texts (from 180-200 A.D. on) the ref. was "no longer to heretics within Judaism but to those of other beliefs outside, mostly Christians," 39.

[16] Cf. Simon, 219-238.

[17] Strack, 22-25 = 50*-56*.

[18] Ibid., 47*; Simon, 218, 236; Elbogen, 36; Jocz, 178 f.; Torrey, 212, n. 20; Herford Minim, 362; Goldstein, 46, 49 (bibl.); K. G. Kuhn, op. cit., 36 f.

[19] Cf. Str.-B., IV, 212 f. and Strack, 66 f.* (HT, 31); Schlatter, op. cit., 17.

[20] Cf. the ref. quoted → 838, 16 ff. from Just., Epiph., and Jerome, also bBer., 28b; cf. Str.-B., IV, 218 f., 331; I, 406 f.; Elbogen, 36-8, 252 f.; Kuhn, 20; Simon, 235; Torrey, 214; Jocz, 56; Hunzinger, 69 f.; Grant, 64-6; H. Bietenhard, "Kirche u. Synagoge in den ersten Jhdt.," ThZ, 4 (1948), 176 f.; E. K. Winter, "Das Ende d. Jerusalemitischen Mutterkirche," Judaica, 9 (1953), 12 f.; Michel, op. cit., 211 f.; G. D. Kilpatrick, The Origins of the Gospel acc. to St. Matthew² (1950), 109-115; L. Goppelt, "Christentum u. Judt. im 1. u. 2. Jhdt.," BFTh, II, 55, (1954), 154 f.; Carroll, 21-23.

Since birkath ha-minim is known only after the destruction of the temple, we seem to have in these passages an anticipation of later relations in the life-time of the incarnate Jesus. But John wrote in the 1st century, and therefore the separation of Church and Synagogue presupposed by him reflects the period at the end of this century. [21]

In view of the relation between the Dead Sea Scrolls and the Johannine writings [22] we may briefly survey the many detailed rules about punishment and exclusion in 1 QS 6:24-7:25, [23] cf. also Jos. Bell., 2, 143. With a reduction of rations (1 QS 6:25) we find esp. a temporary exclusion from the community, particularly from the communal meals. [24] There was also irrevocable excommunication, e.g., for calumniation of the "many," 1 QS 7:16 f., or intentional non-observance or transgression of the Torah, 8:16 f., 22 f., or apostasy in times of persecution, 7:1 f., or murmuring against the basis of the community, 7:17. Death was ordained for the improper pronouncing of a curse with mention of the name of God, 6:27. [25] An important pt. in relation to the content of ἀποσυνάγωγος is that only 7:17 seems to suggest a contradiction in faith or an academic fault. [26] All the other penalties relate to conduct, the keeping or transgressing of the Torah, or the order of discipline. There is no ref. to sectaries or heretics or another confession which has to be excluded from the sect. [27]

---

[21] Cf. Str.-B., IV, 331; W. Michaelis, Das NT, I (1934), 357 f.; Goppelt, op. cit., 253; Hunzinger, 68 f., 71; Carroll, 19 f., 31 suggests the beginning of the 2nd cent. Bultmann J. on 16:22 thinks the chronological background is the time when the Chr. community was forced to leave the synagogue (between Paul and Just.). The ref. to possible martyrdom suggests the post-Pauline period when Judaism was no longer content with physical chastisement (2 C. 11:24) and exclusion but saw in the independent existence of the Chr. community a rival which it sought to render impotent by charges before pagan courts.

[22] Cf. K. G. Kuhn, "Die in Palästina gefundenen hbr. Texte u. d. NT," ZThK, 47 (1950), 192-211; W. F. Albright, "Recent Discoveries in Palestine and the Gospel of St. John," The Background of the NT and Its Eschatology, In Honour of C. H. Dodd, ed. W. D. Davies and D. Daube (1956), 153-171; G. Baumbach, "Qumran u. d. Joh.-Ev.," Aufsätze u. Vorträge z. Theol. u. Religionswissenschaft, 6 (1958), 7, n. 5 bibl.; R. E. Brown, "The Qumran Scrolls and the Johannine Gospel and Epistles," The Scrolls and the NT, ed. K. Stendahl (1957), 183-207; F. M. Cross, The Ancient Library of Qumran and Modern Biblical Studies (1958), 153-162, bibl. 153, n. 12; M. Burrows, More Light on the Dead Sea Scrolls (1958), 106-113; R. Mayer-J. Reuss, Die Qumranfunde u. d. Bibel (1959), 114-119.

[23] Cf. H. Bardtke, Die Handschriftenfunde am Toten Meer² (1953), 118-120; Doskocil, 21-24; H. Braun, "Spätjüd.-häret. u. frühchr. Radikalismus," I, Beiträge z. historischen Theol., 24 (1957), 19, n. 2; F. Nötscher, "Zur theol. Terminologie d. Qumran-Texte," Bonner Bibl. Beiträge, 10 (1956), 182; J. van der Ploeg, Funde in der Wüste Juda (1959), 171 f.; P. Wernberg-Møller, The Manual of Discipline, Stud. on the Texts of the Desert of Judah, I (1957), 110-122 (with par. from Damascus).

[24] One cannot say how far the exclusion entails a forbidding of participation in worship, cf. Bardtke, op. cit., 119.

[25] On the presupposed supplementing of the text, cf. Bardtke, 97, n. 3; A. Dupont-Sommer, Die essenischen Schriften vom Toten Meer (1960), 96, n. 2 and Jos. Bell., 2, 145: σέβας δὲ μέγα παρ' αὐτοῖς (sc. the Essenes) μετὰ τὸν θεὸν τοὔνομα τοῦ νομοθέτου, κἂν βλασφημήσῃ τις εἰς τοῦτον, κολάζεται θανάτῳ.

[26] Bardtke, 99 transl. יסוד היחד by "basic teachings of the community," Wernberg-Møller, op. cit., 32 "congregation of the community," T. H. Gaster, The Scriptures of the Dead Sea Sect (1957), 63 "the whole basis of the community," A. Dupont-Sommer, Les Écrits Esséniens découverts près de la Mer Morte (1959), 105 "l'institution de la communauté," op. cit. (→ n. 25), 99 "the institution of the community," G. Vermès, Les manuscrits du désert de Juda² (1954), 148 "l'autorité de la communauté," and van der Ploeg, op. cit., 171 "continually wicked conduct in opposition to the spirit of the rule."

[27] מין in the sense of heretic does not occur in the texts thus far edited.

2. ἀποσυνάγωγος occurs in the NT at Jn. 9:22; 12:42; 16:2. In Jn. 9:22 the
caution of the parents of the man born blind before the Jewish authorities [28] is
motivated by their fear of the Jews, → III, 379, 4 ff.: ἤδη γὰρ συνετέθειντο οἱ
ʼΙουδαῖοι ἵνα ἐάν τις αὐτὸν ὁμολογήσῃ χριστόν, ἀποσυνάγωγος γένηται.
That this is no empty threat is proved by the fact that the man himself was expelled
(v. 34, [29] cf. v. 35) because of his indirect confession (v. 33; cf. vv. 35-39). Jn. 12:42
also connects ἀποσυναγώγους γενέσθαι with ὁμολογεῖν. The confession which
is a necessary part of true faith, but which is not given for fear of the Pharisees [30]
and of expulsion from the community, bears witness that these leaders love the
δόξα τῶν ἀνθρώπων more than the δόξα τοῦ θεοῦ, v. 43, cf. 5:44. While both
passages are set in the life-time of Jesus, the type of exclusion presupposed could
only have taken place after 70 → 850, 9 ff. Jn. 16:2, however, is a prediction of
Jesus which the disciples are to remember in the hour of trial (v. 4): ἀποσυναγώγους
ποιήσουσιν ὑμᾶς. ἀποσυναγώγους ποιεῖν is a sign of the world's hatred and
enmity; the oppression will be even to death, v. 2. Plain in all three references is the
fact that an unbridgeable gulf has now opened up between Church and Synagogue,
so that exclusion on the part of the latter is total. To think in terms of the lesser
synagogue ban [31] (→ 848, 4 ff.) —is a trivialising; this is no mere excommunication
but total expulsion (→ 849, 14 ff.), a result of the birkath ha-minim. [32]

Schrage

συναθλέω   → I, 167, 27 ff.
συναιχμάλωτος   → I, 196, 37 ff.
συνακολουθέω   → I, 216, 7 ff.
συνανάκειμαι   → III, 654, 14 ff.

┌────────────────────────────┐
│   † συναναμείγνυμι   │
└────────────────────────────┘

1. Like the simple μείγνυμι and the compounds ἀναμείγνυμι and συμμείγνυμι,
the double compound [1] συναναμείγνυμι [2] still retains the original concrete sense "to mix

---

[28] Here, as in Jn. 1:19; 5:15; 7:13 etc. οἱ ʼΙουδαῖοι means the Jewish authorities, cf. Bultmann J. on 1:19 and 9:18, though it should also be kept in mind that "the Jews" represent the
unbelieving world, Bultmann J., 59 and Theol.⁴, 357.
[29] ἐκβάλλω here is either ambiguous, Bau. J., ad loc.; → I, 528, 20 ff. and n. 6; Bohren,
18, or it denotes exclusion from the synagogue, Bultmann J., 255, n. 5; E. Käsemann, "Ketzer
u. Zeuge," *Exegetische Versuche u. Besinnungen,* I (1960), 170.
[30] "The Pharisees" often (cf. 7:45, 47 f.; 11:47, 57) seem to be a kind of "judicial court,"
Bultmann J. on 1:19, n. 5; 12:42 f., n. 5 and Theol.⁴, 357.
[31] So Döller, 13 f.; Bialoblocki, 413; Zn. J. on 9:22; Schl. J. on 9:22 and 16:2; Bultmann J.
on 9:22, n. 10; Bohren, 17 f., 26; Doskocil, 41; W. Beilner, *Christus u. d. Pharisäer* (1959),
162.
[32] Cf. Str.-B., IV, 331; Kuhn, 20, n. 1; Kilpatrick, *op. cit.,* 109 f.; Kohlmeyer, 5; Hunzinger,
71.

συναναμείγνυμι. [1] Double compounds are found in Gk, from early times; they
were greatly favoured in the Hell. period, cf. Schwyzer, II, 428.
[2] Found from the 4th cent. Most MSS and current ed. of the NT have -μίγνυμι, but the
correct orthography acc. to inscr. and pap. is -μείγνυμι, ἔμειξα etc. on the one side (-μίγνυμι
is thus an itacism) or μίσγω on the other. Cf. Schwyzer, I, 697 with n. 5; Mayser, I, 1, 91;
v. also Liddell-Scott, s.v. μείγνυμι [Risch].

together." Ps.-Hippocr. uses it thus in a prescription for mixing various ingredients. [3] Theophr. also uses it concretely of different weeds which usually spring up and intermingle with various kinds of grain. [4] The word is also used with ref. to non-material but real things. Philodem. Philos. [5] wants to hold divine beings aloof from any "admixture" with the life of the forces of decay or disintegration lest their incorruptibility be threatened. Acc. to Luc. [6] fear and hope flutter around the heads of men, but ἄνοια remains below and mingles with them. Athenaeus uses the word for the relation of characters in a dialogue. [7]

From the very outset, however, the pass. συναναμείγνυμαι, like the simple and the compounds mentioned → 852, 25, esp. συμμείγνυμαι, can also be used for various kinds of "human intermingling." Clearchus, [8] a pupil of Aristotle, says that in Cyprus the rulers had spies who mixed among the people to pick up their moods and rumours. Plut. Philop., 21 (I, 368d) [9] uses συναναμείγνυμαι to describe how the old men, women and children intermingle with the homecoming army which sorrowfully proclaims the death of Philopoimen. Yet it may be that the meaning here is just "to meet," as in Jos. Ant., 20, 164; [10] συμμείγνυμι has this sense too in Macc. [11] and the pap. [12]

2. Of particular importance as regards the history of the meaning of the word in the Bible is the fact that συναναμείγνυμαι, partly under the influence of the sense of sexual union which is found for μείγνυμαι and συμμείγνυμαι [13] from the time of Homer, denotes "intermingling with other nations" in which the purity of the saved people is forfeited, Hos. 7:8 LXX and probably the addition to the HT at

---

[3] De natura muliebri, 97, 15 (Littré, VII, 414): ὀπὸν σκαμμωνίης καὶ στέαρ, ἐν μάζῃ, ξυναναμ(ε)ίξας (vl. συμμίξας), οἴνῳ δεύσας, ἐν ὀθονίῳ προστίθει. This Hippocratic work is "a worthless abstract of περὶ γυναικείων written by a man of little experience," H. Gossen, Art. "Hippokrates," Pauly-W., 8 (1913), 1829, 61 f.; it can hardly have been written before 380, ibid., 1830.

[4] Hist. Plant., VIII, 8, 3: σχεδὸν δὲ καθ᾽ ἕκαστόν ἐστι τὸ συνεκτρεφόμενον καὶ συναναμ(ε)ιγνύμενον εἴτε διὰ τὰς χώρας... εἴτε δι᾽ ἄλλην τινὰ αἰτίαν. The adj. συνανάμιγος in P. Oxy., IV, 718, 16. 19. 27 (2nd cent. A.D.) denotes location in private lands, Preisigke Wört., s.v.

[5] Philodem. Philos. De Deis, III, 9, 37-40, ed. H. Diels, AAB, 4 (1916/17), 29: ... μακρὰν δεῖν ἀπέχειν (sc. τὰ θεῖα σώματα) τῶν παρ᾽ ἡμᾶς τὰ γεννητικὰ καὶ διαλυτικὰ παρεχόντων, ἵνα μὴ τούτοις συναναμ(ε)ιγνύμενα πρὸς τὴν ἀφθαρσίαν ἐμποδίζηται, cf. Diels, ibid., 6 (1916/17), 32.

[6] Luc. Charon seu Contemplantes, 15: τούτων δὲ ἡ ἄνοια μὲν κάτω ξυναναμέμ(ε)ικται αὐτοῖς... ὁ φόβος δὲ καὶ αἱ ἐλπίδες ὑπεράνω πετόμενοι...

[7] Athen., 5, 3 (187b, 177a b; this rearrangement is almost universally accepted from Casaubonus): ὧν ὁ μὲν Πλάτων τὸν μὲν Ἐρυξίμαχον ἰατρόν, τὸν δὲ Ἀριστοφάνη ποιητήν, ἄλλον δ᾽ ἀπ᾽ ἄλλης προαιρέσεως σπουδάζοντας εἰσήγαγεν, Ξενοφῶν δὲ καί τινας ἰδιώτας συνανέμ(ε)ιξε.

[8] Clearch. of Soloi, Fr. 19: ὧν οἱ μὲν Γεργῖνοι συναναμ(ε)ιγνύμενοι τοῖς κατὰ τὴν πόλιν ἔν τε τοῖς ἐργαστηρίοις καὶ ταῖς ἀγοραῖς ὠτακουστοῦσι κατασκόπων ἔχοντες τάξιν ed. F. Wehrli, Die Schule des Aristot., 3 (1948), 14, 19-21.

[9] ὡς οὖν συνανεμείχθησαν αὐτοῖς (the army) οἱ πρεσβύτεροι μετὰ γυναικῶν καὶ παίδων, ὀλοφυρμὸς ἤδη διὰ παντὸς ἐχώρει τοῦ στρατεύματος...

[10] ... καὶ συναναμιγέντες (sc. the hired assassins) τῷ Ἰωνάθῃ κτείνουσιν αὐτόν. With stronger emphasis on intermingling, 20, 165: συναναμ(ε)ιγνύμενοι (sc. the robbers) τοῖς πλήθεσιν (sc. the pilgrims) ἀνῄρουν μέν τινας ἑαυτῶν ἐχθρούς...

[11] Act. intr. 2 Macc. 3:7; 13:3. In the form συμμίσγω 1 Macc. 11:22; 2 Macc. 14:14. Mostly military encounter.

[12] Cf. Preisigke Wört., s.v. συμμίγνυμι and συμμίσγω; Moult.-Mill., s.v. συναναμίγνυμι. Here, too, always act. intr.

[13] But cf. A. Wilhelm, "Σύμμειξις," Anzeiger d. Akadem. d. Wissenschaften in Wien, philosophisch-histor. Klasse, 74 (1938), 39-57.

Ez. 20:18 LXX. [14] συνανάμειξις is also employed in this sense. [15] But the verb can also be used for intercourse in a more general sense in the LXX. [16]

The only instance of συναναμείγνυμαι in Philo [17] corresponds to the LXX and denotes the intermingling with other peoples which undermines the special position of Israel.

3. In the NT συναναμείγνυμαι occurs only in Paul's letters at 1 C. 5:9, 11; 2 Th. 3:14. [18] In all three instances it denotes (undesired) dealings with men who have placed their membership of the community in question by their conduct, πόρνοι in Corinth, ἄτακτοι in Thessalonica. The point here, as in the OT (→ 853, 17 ff.), is unquestionably that of keeping God's people pure, though not by avoiding all contact with strangers, but by removing evil from the community, 1 C. 5:13. The direct proximity of the metaphor of the leaven (1 C. 5:6-8) keeps in view the thought of cultic pollution. As 2 Th. 3:14 f. shows, the primary purpose of the separation is that of summoning to conversion. The excommunicated person is still viewed as a brother, not as an enemy (→ III, 753, n. 84). If the disciplinary measure does not prove successful, it might result in complete amputation. In 1 C. 5:13 Paul is plainly thinking of the incestuous person whom he has delivered up to Satan.

A first question in relation to the word συναναμείγνυμαι is whether it "became a tt. for unrestricted dealings in the community." [19] It was certainly not taken thus in Corinth, where it was referred to dealings with those outside, 1 C. 5:10. Paul has first to set these straight. Nor does the word have the mark of a tt.: specialised use with no reference to a narrowing of sense. Rather the NT uses the term in exactly the same way as the LXX (→ 853, 15 ff.), Philo (→ lines 3 ff.), and Plutarch

---

[14] HT ref. only to pollution by idols, LXX reads: ἐν τοῖς ἐπιτηδεύμασιν αὐτῶν μὴ συναναμίσγεσθε (B; -μίγνυσθε rel) καὶ μὴ μιαίνεσθε. Here ἐπιτηδεύματα ("practice") is used for HT גִּלּוּלִים as in Ez. 6:9; 14:6; 20:7, 8, 39; 1 K. 15:12. Though LXX has εἴδωλον 13 times and βδέλυγμα once for גִּלּוּלִים in Ez., elsewhere in Ez. it always has euphemisms like ἐνθύμημα (15 times), διάνοια (once) and διανόημα (twice). Behind this spiritualising of idols, however, Ez. 20:18 has a reminder of temple prostitution: μὴ συναναμίσγεσθε. συμμίσγομαι also occurs in Ep. Ar., 142 for the fatal intermingling of Israel with other nations. Cf. also from the 5th cent. B.C. μειξέλλην, μειξοβάρβαρος etc., and on these E. Risch, "Determinativ-Kompos.," Idg. Forsch., 59 (1944), 48 f.

[15] Da. 11:23 Θ: ἀπὸ τῶν συναναμείξεων (HT הִתְחַבְּרוּת) πρὸς αὐτὸν ποιήσει δόλον "from the time of the fraternising of certain Jews with Antiochus (LXX δήμου συνταγέντος μετ' αὐτοῦ) he practises deceit." Cf. the mistranslation at 2 K. 14:14 = 2 Ch. 25:24: καὶ ἔλαβεν τὸ χρυσίον καὶ τὸ ἀργύριον καὶ πάντα τὰ σκεύη τὰ εὑρεθέντα ἐν οἴκῳ κυρίου καὶ ἐν θησαυροῖς οἴκου τοῦ βασιλέως καὶ τοὺς υἱοὺς τῶν συμμίξεων... of alien cults who demonstrate (for the LXX) Amaziah's guilt and bring about his downfall. בְּנֵי הַתַּעֲרֻבוֹת ("hostages") are related to עֵרֶב ("admixture") and hence to bastards or servants.

[16] Prv. 20:19 Θ (not LXX): ἀποκαλύπτων μυστήριον πορεύεται δόλῳ, καὶ ἀπατῶντι χείλη αὐτοῦ μὴ συναναμίσγου (HT לֹא תִתְעָרָב).

[17] Vit. Mos., I, 278: ...ὃς (sc. λαός) μόνος κατοικήσει... μὴ συναναμ(ε)ιγνύμενος ἄλλοις εἰς τὴν τῶν πατρίων ἐκδιαίτησιν (abandoning of customs inherited from the fathers). Compounds in συν- alone do not occur at all in Philo.

[18] In 2 Th. 3:14 textual criticism cannot distinguish between συναναμείγνυσθε and -σθαι, since later the two sound the same. The context — no καί — permits either an inf. or imp. The καί attested by א D*G pl latt sy establishes an imp. and removes the asyndeton. But there would be no pt. in other witnesses eliminating it, hence it is plainly secondary.

[19] Schl. K. on 1 C. 5:9. In 2 Th. 3:6, however, the same prohibition is expressed by στέλλεσθαι ὑμᾶς.

(→ 853, 12 ff.). It should also be noted that συναναμείγνυμαι occurs only in prohibition; συνεσθίω is the positive word for unrestricted intercourse in the community, Gl. 2:12; Ac. 11:3; cf. Lk. 15:2. In 1 C. 5:11 μηδὲ συνεσθίειν serves to give precision to the μὴ συναναμείγνυσθαι of v. 9. Since both private and cultic table fellowship [20] is included in intercourse as the broader term, μηδέ cannot be construed as the adding of something more. The translation "not even" would also be suitable only if we had here a surprisingly penetrating application even to the peripheral adiaphora of intercourse. Private table fellowship, however, could not be regarded as peripheral, let alone the Lord's Supper. As things stand, τῷ τοιούτῳ μηδὲ συνεσθίειν is to be translated epexegetically to μὴ συναναμείγνυσθαι: With such a one you ought not to celebrate the Lord's Supper. This is the first and most important implication. 2 Th. 3:14 with its τοῦτον σημειοῦσθε shows that this does not exhaust the breaking off of fellowship. No matter what this "noting" involves (→ 266, 20 ff.) it serves to restrain members of the community from dealings with the person concerned. [21] Mere exclusion from the sacrament of the bread would not have required "noting". On the other hand, the separation does not rule out νουθετεῖν. Breaking off intercourse is for the purpose of converting and saving the endangered brother. [22]

Greeven

συναντιλαμβάνομαι → I, 376, 4 ff.
συναποθνήσκω   → 785, 12 ff.; III, 7, 28 ff.

---

† συναρμολογέω

1. The compound συναρμολογέω "to fit together" occurs in the NT only twice in Eph., then in the Chr. writings dependent on this. The simple form may be found in the epigrammatist Philippos (1st cent. A.D.): ἡρμολόγησε τάφον "he has erected a tomb," Anth. Graec., 7, 554, 2. The word has a similar architectural sense in P. Ryl., II, 233, 6 (2nd cent. A.D.). In Sext. Emp. Math., V, 78 (2nd cent. A.D.) the use is metaphorical. Like the par. [1] τριμματολογέω "to polish," ψηφολογέω "to work in mosaics" etc. ἁρμολογέω denotes building work: "to fit together," "to join," esp. stones. [2]

---

[20] In view of the role of the Lord's Supper in the life of the primitive churches this must be meant or at least implied in μηδὲ συνεσθίειν. There is nothing to support the view that after exclusion from the cultic meal "refusal of fellowship is now carried to its conclusion," (Schl. K. on 1 C. 5:11, cf. Joh. W. 1 K., ad loc.) and private table fellowship has to be given up too. This would demand a special ref., e.g., the addition μηδὲ ἐν οἴκῳ (cf. 1 C. 11:34).

[21] 1 QS 8:23 offers a contemporary illustration of συναναμείγνυσθαι: " ... and none of the saints should have anything to do with his (sc. the transgressor's) property or his counsel in any matter." Cf. B. Rigaux, *St. Paul. Les épîtres aux Thessal.* (1956) on 2 Th. 3:14. Cf. Did., 15, 3: ... καὶ παντὶ ἀστοχοῦντι κατὰ τοῦ ἑτέρου μηδεὶς λαλείτω μηδὲ παρ' ὑμῶν ἀκουέτω, ἕως οὗ μετανοήσῃ.

[22] The word does not occur in the first Chr. lit. outside the NT. On the other hand it is used in Gnosticism (Cl. Al. Exc. Theod., 40, 4) to denote the fact that the nature of empirical man is a mixture of spiritual, psychic and hylic elements [Dihle].

σ υ ν α ρ μ ο λ ο γ έ ω . Pass., Liddell-Scott, Moult.-Mill., Pr.-Bauer, s.v.

[1] Cf. on this J. A. Robinson, *St. Paul's Ep. to the Eph.* (1903), 260-263, Exc. on συναρμολογέω.

[2] ἁρμός "joint," is attested in building, later metal-work, from the 5th cent. B.C.

2. In Eph. the two metaphors of building and bodily growth merge into one another. [3] Thus Eph. 2:21 refers to the growth of the temple and 4:16 to the building of the body. The preposition συν-, which is a distinctive feature throughout Eph., refers in both instances to both the inner relationship of the community and also the relationship between the community and Christ. [4] In 2:20 f. Christ is both the One in whom the whole building is embedded and also the corner-stone which holds it all together (ἀκρογωνιαῖος, → I, 792, 5 ff.), "in whom the whole building [5] being fitted together grows into a holy temple in the Lord." According to 4:15 f. (→ IV, 566, 12 ff.) the κεφαλή (→ III, 680, 11 ff.; IV, 597, 8 ff.) which governs all things and dispenses life is the source of the body and its growth. The context (vv. 7-10, 11-16) shows that the participles συναρμολογούμενον and συμβιβαζόμενον [6] are designed to emphasise strongly the interplay of the different ministries and tasks within the body: "from whom the whole body — as one which is fitted and held together by each link which serves to support it — corresponding to the activity appropriate to each part achieves growth of the body to the building up of itself in love."

Maurer

σύνδεσμος

A. The Usage in Classical and Later Secular Greek.

σύνδεσμος [1] means the "middle thing" (τὸ μέσον) by which two or more things are joined together. It is thus the "link," "joint," "means of binding" (esp. mortar), "bond," "chain" (→ line 25 f.) or "loop," "that which is bound or held together," "bundle" (Herodian Hist., IV, 12, 6), grammatically "conjunction," → 857, 28 ff. The word is very common and is often used as a synon. of δεσμός.

The compound does not occur in Hom. The simple form means "chain" in Od., 8, 317-360, cf. the fettering of Odysseus when the sirens sing in 12, 54-200. It is also used for

---

[3] P. Vielhauer, Oikodome. Das Bild vom Bau in d. chr. Lit. vom NT bis Cl. Al. (1939), 128 f., 140-143. Historically we are to seek the reasons for the merging of the body and the building in the fusion of the two themes in Gnosticism, while materially they are to be sought in the nature of the living community.

[4] Formally the part ref. to οἰκοδομή or σῶμα, but materially they are also governed by ἐν ᾧ and ἐξ οὗ.

[5] Though there is no art. πᾶσα οἰκοδομή probably means the whole building here, cf. Dib. Gefbr., ad loc.

[6] The first part. in the par. Col. 2:19 (ἐπιχορηγούμενον) is replaced by συναρμολογούμενον in Eph. 4:16, but then, strengthened by the subst. ἐπιχορηγία, it is adopted again, thus bringing out more plainly the reciprocity of ministry.

σ ύ ν δ ε σ μ ο ς. [1] σύνδεσμος belongs to the verb δέω "to bind" (→ II, 60, 1 ff.) cf. δεσμός, δέσμιος (→ II, 43, 2 ff.) from δεjω √de͡ Sanskr. dyáti "binds," di-tá "bound" = δετός, dáman "bond" cf. (ὑπό-)δημα. For details Frisk, 374 f.; Schwyzer, I, 676, 493. From the same stem cf. in the NT δέσμη "bundle" Mt. 13:30, δεσμεύω "to bind burdens" Mt. 23:4, "to chain" Lk. 8:29 (textus receptus δεσμέω), "to arrest" Ac. 22:4, δεσμοφύλαξ "jailor" Ac. 16:23, 27, 36, δεσμωτήριον "prison" Mt. 11:2; Ac. 5:21, 23; 16:26, δεσμώτης "prisoner" Ac. 27:1, 42, διάδημα "headband," "diadem" as a sign of royalty Rev. 12:3; 13:1; 19:12, ὑπόδημα "sandal" Mt. 3:11 etc. συνδέω occurs in the NT only at Hb. 13:3 with δέσμιος in the form συνδεδεμένοι "remember the prisoners as fellow-prisoners," v. Pr.-Bauer, s.v.

the "cable" which holds the ship (13,100) or the "halter" which ties the horse to the stall, Il., 6, 507. Eur. has the heteroclite plur. σύνδεσμα for the "fastening" of the loops on the doeskins of the Bacchae, Ba., 696 f. Phaidra complains about the complete slackness of members λέλυμαι μελέων σύνδεσμα, Hipp., 199 f. It is said of the headband whose dreadful magic sets fire to the one who wears it: ἀλλ' ἀραρότως σύνδεσμα χρυσὸς εἶχε, Med., 1193. The word is also found in Thuc., II, 75, 5.

It acquires a philosophical sense in Plato. The coming into being of the world through God is described in Tim., 31a-c. God made the body of the universe when He began to put it together, first of fire and earth. But it is impossible to join two things without a third. Only a mediating "bond" can make a union between them δεσμὸν γὰρ ἐν μέσῳ δεῖ τινα ἀμφοῖν συναγωγὸν γίγνεσθαι, 31c. Of all unions, however, that is the most beautiful which makes into one both itself and also the two objects joined. Proportion (ἀναλογία) accomplishes this. In the first instance, then, Plato uses the image of the δεσμός or σύνδεσμος. He has in view something far-reaching, that which overcomes dualism of all kinds. Joining, mediating, union presupposes duality and achieves unity. Plato applies this thoughts to the elements and to the physiology of the body. In Ps.-Plat. Epin., 984b c, in the doctrine of the gods, the stars and demons, σύνδεσμος is "that which holds together," the "coherence" of beings which are powerfully made of air and a little of other elements as living creatures. Here and there we find other aspects. Plat. Leg., XI, 921c uses the term for the unity of state or the political union, cf. Resp., VII, 520a. Light is the "band of heaven" in Resp., X, 616c. The ideas of the good and the beautiful, which are formed by laws and are the basis of the state, are the "more divine bond" of the parts of virtue which by nature are dissimilar and strive against one another, Polit., 310a. The Platonic doctrine of σύνδεσμος was later adopted in cosmological and anthropological thinking as the harmonious linking of opposites. [2]

Aristot. uses the word metaphorically when he calls children the "bond" between father and mother and claims that what is common holds together, Eth. Nic., IX, 14, p. 1162a, 27. As a connection it establishes unity, Rhet., III, 12, p. 1413b, 32; thus the Iliad is a unity συνδέσμῳ εἷς, Poet., 20, p. 1457a, 29 f. In Rhet. the word is often used for a connecting word in a rather broader sense than the grammatical "conjunction." "The parts of the whole mode of expression are as follows: the letter, the syllable, the connecting word (σύνδεσμος), the main word...," Poet., 20, p. 1456b, 21; μέν, ἤτοι, δή are adduced as examples, p. 1457a, 4; cf. also Rhet., III, 5, p. 1407a, 20-30; III, 6, p. 1407b, 37 f.

Physiologically the word means "sinew" or "muscle." Gal. In Hippocratis de Articulis Librum, IV, 40 (18, 734) observes that it makes no odds whether one uses σύνδεσμος or νεῦρον συνδετικόν, cf. Gal. De Motu Musculorum, I, 1 (4, 369). Soranus Gynaeciorum, IV, 5, 1 (CMG, IV [1927], 134, 11 f.) (2nd cent. A.D.) speaks of difficulties in birth; the bones have not grown into firm harmony in women as in men, but a σύνδεσμος ἰσχυρὸς ταῦτα πρὸς ἄλληλα συνδεῖ.

---

[2] Acc. to W. Jaeger, Nemesios v. Emesa. Quellenforschungen zum Neuplatonismus u. seinen Anfängen bei Pos. (1914), 101 f. thinks that Pos. "thought through consistently" the Platonic doctrine of σύνδεσμος, "connected it with Heraclitus' doctrine of the harmony of the antithetical, and in his comm. on the Tim. added the doctrine of media to that of the reconciliation of opposites." Jaeger finds the views of Plot. behind those of Nemesius. "Nature has made man with his double psycho-physical nature half animal and half God, on the border of the divine, as a chain and bond to link together the separated halves of the sphere of sense and the world of spirit. He is thus a duality to achieve the eternal unity of nature and spirit." The terms (σύνδεσμος, vinculum) occur in cosmological lit. only after Pos. ἐναρμόνιος δεσμός — σύνδεσμος is no less common — is a final harmony of opposites in divine unity. "Pos. amplified Aristot.'s doctrine of stages not only by the δεσμός teaching of Tim. but also by the microcosm theory of Democritus, and he thus became the true father of this view in the Middle Ages," 135. K. Reinhardt, Art. "Poseidonios," Pauly-W., 22 (1953), 558-826, esp. 607, cf. 624 opposes the deriving of the σύνδεσμος teaching of Nemesius from Pos.: "The main differences relate to 1. the sundesmos of Nemesios in connection with the telos doctrine...," cf. also 773-778, esp. 778.

B. The Usage in the Jewish-Greek Sphere.

1. The term bears no specific, esp. philosophical nuance in the LXX. It occurs 10 times and is the transl. of many Hbr. words. It means "connection" in Da. 5:12 Θ (קְטַר "bond"), cf. the description of a situation of terror in 5:6 Θ: "The binding of the loins is loosed, the knees tremble," where σύνδεσμος is used for קְטַר "joints." We find the same connection with the basic sense in 3 Βασ. 6:10 (ἔνδεσμοι for יָצוּעַ "outhouse"), and cf. the close interrelation of the scales in the description of Leviathan in Job 41:7: ὥσπερ σμιρίτης λίθος, Hbr. סָגוּר from סגר "to attach oneself." In Is. 58:9 and Lv. 26:13 σύνδεσμος and δεσμός are used for מוֹטָה "yoke" and in Is. 58:6 for חַרְצֻבּוֹת "firmly fixed bonds." On 3 occasions the word is used for קֶשֶׁר (from קשר "to bind") in the sense of "union," but also *malo sensu* "conspiracy," 4 Βασ. 11:14; 12:21; Jer. 11:9. The use of σύνδεσμος for קָדֵשׁ "cultic prostitute" in 3 Βασ. 14:24 is hard to understand; [3] elsewhere קְדֵשָׁה is πόρνη Dt. 23:18; Gn. 38:21 or τελετή 3 Βασ. 15:12 (here in the sense of dedication) or the transcription καδησιμ 4 Βασ. 23:7.

2. In Ep. Ar., 85 σύνδεσμος is used for an architectural feature in the temple gate, cf. Hab. 2:11 Σ: σύνδεσμος οἰκοδομῆς ξύλινος for כָּפִיס "part." The simple form in 265 denotes "the indissoluble bond of benevolence" as a special quality in the ruler. [4]

3. Philo uses the word, strengthened by an adj., in the expression τῷ συμπλεκτικῷ συνδέσμῳ in speculation about the four parts of the incense offering in Ex. 30:34, which he takes to be symbols of the four elements of water, earth, fire and air. The lighter elements of fire and air are bound μετὰ συμπλοκῆς. Here the word neither has a symbolical sense nor is it controlled by Platonic usage. The simple form, however, is often used in a cosmological and anthropological context, Rer. Div. Her., 246; Op. Mund., 131; Migr. Abr., 220. [5] σύνδεσμος also occurs as a grammatical literary term alongside ὄνομα and ῥῆμα, Agric., 136; Congr., 149.

C. The Usage in the New Testament.

The general sense of "bond" occurs metaphorically in Ac. 8:23. Peter's saying to Simon Magus: "I see you have become bitter gall and the embodiment of iniquity" (→ I, 156, 31 ff.) is Semitic in spirit. Ordinary words are employed as a curse. [6] In Col. 2:19 σύνδεσμος alongside "sinew" is a philosophical expression: "band" in the sense of tendon or muscle; the word occurs in the context of statements about the σῶμα Χριστοῦ. [7] The other two instances in the NT are stylistically and

---

[3] Perhaps the translator has the jesting of Hermes in view, Hom. Od., 8, 317 ff.

[4] [Bertram].

[5] "Man as the bond (δεσμός) or on the frontier (ἐν μεθορίοις) between the heavenly and the earthly is already a favourite thought in Philo, e.g., Op. Mund., 46," Reinhardt, *op. cit.* (→ n. 2), 773.

[6] הָיָה לְ "to become something" is the underlying expression. Haench. Ag. on 8:23 writes "εἰς again replaces ἐν; D has even altered the text accordingly," cf. Bauernf. Ag., *ad loc.* Haench. Ag. on 8:20 draws attention to Da. 2:5 Θ. Nestle ref. to Is. 58:6. Haench. Ag. on 8:23 is certainly right when he says: "There can be no question of an actual quotation here." Instead of Is. 58:6 one is rather to think of an expression like סוֹד הָעֶרְוָה in 1 QH 1:22 "epitome of shame" — the righteous man's humble confession of his sinfulness, cf. on this J. Maier, *Die Texte vom Toten Meer*, I (1960), 73, also II, 66.

[7] Cf. Loh. Kol. on 2:19, n. 4; Μέγα λεξικὸν τῆς Ἑλληνικῆς γλώσσης, ed. Γ Ἀναγνωστόπουλος (1933 ff.), *s.v.* gives as the second sense: σύνδεσμοι are ἶνες καὶ τένοντες "muscles and sinews" by which the joints and members of the body are linked, cf. Gal. and Soranus → 857, 34 ff.

materially related. The δέσμιος ἐν κυρίῳ of Eph. 4:3-6 (→ II, 43, 2 ff.) summons
the community to a walk worthy of its calling by God; they are to keep the unity
of the Spirit (ἑνότης τοῦ πνεύματος) through the "bond of peace." Similarly Col.
3:14 summons to "love, which is the bond of perfectness, [8] and let the peace of God
rule in your hearts." In both passages there is a formal similarity to the Platonic use
of the word (→ 857, 15 f.). A duality is brought to unity and overcome by the
σύνδεσμος. Here, however, we have a soteriological rather than a cosmological
sphere, or, more precisely, the community in the world.

The basic outlook of Gnosticism is also dualistic and methods are worked out to overcome dualism. Thus far it has not been possible to prove that there is a connection between
philosophical sundesmos teaching and Gnosticism and then between Gnosticism and the
use of the term in Eph. and Col. [9] At any rate, the use in Eph. and Col. does not have
the systematic quality or the philosophical depth which it took on in Plato (→ 857, 7 f.)
and the later sundesmos teaching → n. 2. In Plato and the later comm. of Pos. on the
Timaeus (→ n. 2) we find mediation in general, so that the overcoming of duality or of
the antithetical in σύνδεσμος is affirmed in principle, and the concept thus plays a
significant role in the cosmological and anthropological realm. In Col. and Eph., however,
the mediation is defined as peace, and in the experience of faith within the real community
unity is found in the one God, the one Spirit, the one faith.

D. The Usage in the Post-Apostolic Fathers.

The word occurs only twice in the post-apost. fathers at Barn., 3, 3-5 (quoting Is. 58:6-
10a LXX) and Ign. Tr., 3, 1. In connection with orders in the community and their
spiritual significance Ign. issues an admonition to esteem the presbyters ὡς συνέδριον
θεοῦ καὶ ὡς σύνδεσμον ἀποστόλων, "as the council of God and the band of the
apostles."

Fitzer

συνδοξάζω   → II, 253, 11 ff.
σύνδουλος   → II, 261, 1 ff.
συνεγείρω   → 786, 36 ff.

---

[8] The reading ἑνότης for τελειότης in D * G it is an assimilation to the concept of unity
which plays an important part in the system of thought found in Col. and Eph., cf. Eph.
4:3, 13.
[9] Dib. Gefbr. on Col. 3:14 ref. to Simpl. in Epict., 30: The Pythagoreans called φιλία the
σύνδεσμος πασῶν τῶν ἀρετῶν. Love or friendship is here the quintessence or epitome of
all virtues, cf. Plat. Polit., 310a: θειότερος σύνδεσμος with ref. to virtue → 857, 21 ff. Dib.
also notes that we perhaps have the philosophical concept here, and he ref. to Jaeger's
chapter on "Sundesmos" → n. 2. Even if, with Reinhardt, op. cit. (→ n. 2), we cannot seek
the transmission and transforming of σύνδεσμος in Pos., the material analogy has to be
considered, and one must enquire into the tradition underlying the view in Col., esp. in the
Jewish-Hell. sphere. R. Reitzenstein, "Die Formel Glaube, Liebe, Hoffnung bei Paulus,"
NGG, philosophisch-histor. Kl. (1916), 393 is hardly justified in his criticism of Dib.:
"Any idea that the author of Col. used a philosophical source is naturally to be ruled out.
But a popular religious parallel such as that in the Hermetic tractate might have influenced
him. To me personally this analysis is the final proof that the epistle is not by Paul." Sources
certainly cannot be discerned. The philosophical elements are filtered even in those views
against which the author of Col. is writing. The Judaism of the Dispersion did not just accept
alien views: it subjected them to a process of filtering, cf. H. J. Schoeps, Paulus (1959), 11.

---

† συνέδριον

Contents: A. συνέδριον in Classical and Hellenistic Greek: 1. συνέδριον in Profane Greek; 2. συνέδριον in Jewish-Hellenistic Literature. B. The Jewish Sanhedrin in the Hellenistic-Roman Period: 1. The History of the Sanhedrin in Jerusalem; 2. The Composition of the Sanhedrin in Jerusalem; 3. The Powers of the Sanhedrin in Jerusalem; 4. Jewish Sanhedrins outside Jerusalem. C. συνέδριον in the New Testament: 1. συνέδριον in the Gospels: a. In Sayings of Jesus; b. Jesus Before the Sanhedrin in Jerusalem; 2. συνέδριον in Acts. D. συνέδριον in the Post-Apostolic Fathers.

συνέδριον. W. Bacher, Art. "Sanhedrin" in Hastings DB, IV (1902), 397-402; A. Büchler, "Das Synedrion in Jerusalem u. d. grosse Beth-Din in der Quaderkammer d. jerusalemischen Tempels," 9. Jahresbericht d. isr.-theol. Lehranstalt in Wien (1902), 1-252; J. Z. Lauterbach, Art. "Sanhedrin" in Jew. Enc., XI (1905), 41-4; H. L. Strack, Art. "Synedrium" in RE³, 19 (1907), 226-9; Schürer, II, 237-267 (older bibl.); H. L. Strack, Sanhedrin-Makkoth (1910); G. Hoelscher, Sanhedrin-Makkot (1910); J. Juster, Les Juifs dans l'empire Romain (1914); M. Wolff, "De Samenstelling en het Karakter van het Groote συνέδριον te Jeruzalem voor het jaar 70 n. Chr.," ThT, 9 (1917), 299-320; H. Danby, "The Bearing of the Rabbinical Code on the Jewish Trial Narratives in the Gospels," JThSt, 21 (1919/20), 51-77; Str.-B., Index "Synedrium"; Moore, III, 32-4; H. Lietzmann, Der Prozess Jesu u. Bemerkungen zum Prozess Jesu (1931 f.), Kleine Schr., II (1959), 251-276; M. Dibelius, Das historische Problem d. Leidensgeschichte (1931), Botschaft u. Gesch., I (1953), 248-257; F. Büchsel, "Die Blutgerichtsbarkeit d. Synedriums," ZNW, 30 (1931), 202-210; M. Goguel, "A propos du procès de Jésus," ZNW, 31 (1932), 289-301; P. Fiebig, "Der Prozess Jesu," ThStKr, 104 (1932), 213-228; E. Springer, "Der Prozess Jesu," Preuss. Jahrb., 229 (1932) 135-150; S. Krauss, Sanhedrin-Makkot (1933); F. Büchsel, "Noch einmal: Zur Blutgerichtsbarkeit d. Synedriums," ZNW, 33 (1934) 84-7; E. Bickermann, "Utilitas Crucis," RHR, 112 (1935), 169-241; J. Lengle, "Zum Prozess Jesu," Herm., 70 (1935), 312-321; H. J. Ebeling, "Zur Frage nach d. Kompetenz des Synedrions," ZNW, 35 (1936), 290-5; H. Zucker, Stud. z. jüd. Selbstverwaltung im Altertum (1936), 92-125; U. Holzmeister, "Zur Frage d. Blutgerichtsbarkeit d. Synedriums," Biblica, 19 (1938), 43-59, 151-174; E. Bickermann, "עַל הסנהדרין," Zion, 4 (1938), 356-366; T. G. Bunch, Behold the Man! A Review of the Trials and Crucifixion of Jesus. The Bibl. Record in the Light of Hebrew and Roman Law (1940); P. Benoit, Jésus devant le Sanhédrin (1943), Exégèse et Théol., I (1961), 290-311; K. L. Schmidt, "Der Todesprozess d. Messias Jesus," Judaica, 1 (1945/46), 1-40; S. Zeitlin, "The Political Synedrion and the Religious Sanhedrin," JQR, 36 (1945/6), 109-140; S. B. Hoenig, "Synedrion in the Attic Orators, the Ptolemaic Pap. and Its Adoption by Joseph., the Gospels and the Tannaim," JQR, 37 (1946/7), 179-187; S. Zeitlin, "Synedrion in Gk. Literature, the Gospels and the Institution of the Sanhedrin," JQR, 37 (1946/7), 189-198; also Who Crucified Jesus?² (1947); M. Goguel, "Le procès de Jésus," Foi et Vie, 47 (1949), 395-403; J. Jeremias, "Zur Geschichtlichkeit d. Verhörs Jesu vor d. Hohen Rat," ZNW, 43 (1950/51), 145-150; S. B. Hoenig, The Great Sanhedrin (1953); G. D. Kilpatrick, The Trial of Jesus (1953); J. Cantinat, "Jésus devant le Sanhedrin," Nouvelle Revue Théol., 75 (1953), 300-308; S. Rosenblatt, "The Crucifixion of Jesus from the Standpoint of Pharisaic Law," JBL, 75 (1956), 315-321; T. A. Burkill, "The Competence of the Sanhedrin," Vigiliae Christianae, 10 (1956), 80-96; E. Stauffer, Jerusalem u. Rom (1957), 67-73; J. Jeremias, Jerusalem z. Zt. Jesu² (1958), Index, s.v. "Synedrium"; T. A. Burkill, "The Trial of Jesus," Vigil. Christ., 12 (1958), 1-18; P. J. Verdam, Sanhedrin en Gabbatha (1959); J. B. Tyson, "The Lukan Version of the Trial of Jesus," Nov. Test., 3 (1959), 249-258; P. Winter, "Marginal Notes on the Trial of Jesus," ZNW, 50 (1959), 14-33, 221-251; also "On the Trial of Jesus," Forschungen z. Wissenschaft d. Judentums, 1 (1961); J. Blinzler, Der Prozess Jesu³ (1960); E. Lohse, "Der Prozess Jesu Christi," Ecclesia u. Res Publica, Festschr. K. D. Schmidt (1961), 24-39; H. Mantel, Studies in the History of the Sanhedrin (1961); J. S. Kennard Jr., "The Jewish Provincial Assembly," ZNW, 53 (1962), 25-51.

A. συνέδριον in Classical and Hellenistic Greek.

1. συνέδριον in Profane Greek.

The word συνέδριον [1] is abundantly attested from Hdt. and means first the "place of those who sit together" (σύνεδροι), then their "session," "council," "governing body": στὰς ἐπὶ τὸ συνέδριον, Hdt., VIII, 79, 2; Themistocles λαθὼν ἐξέρχεται ἐκ τοῦ συνεδρίου, VIII, 75, 1; συνέδριον κατασκευάσωμεν, Plat. Prot., 317d; ἐπειδὰν δ'εἰς συνέδρια συνέλθωσιν, Isoc. Or., 3, 19; συνεκάθηντο ἐν τῷ συνεδρίῳ, Xenoph. Hist. Graec., II, 4, 23; [τ]ὰς δὲ συνόδους γίνεσθαι τοῦ συνεδρίου, IG, 4, 68, 70 (4th cent. B.C.); μεταπεμφθέντων εἰς κοινὸν συνέδριον τῶν κατὰ κώμην δεκανῶν τῶν φ[υ]λακιτῶν, P. Tebt., I, 27, 31 (2nd cent. B.C.); μέχρι τοῦ εἰς κοινὸν συνέδριον ἐλθεῖν, *ibid.,* III, 798, 26 (2nd cent. B.C.). Allies come together for common consultation: μετὰ κοινοῦ συνεδρίου τῶν Ἑλλήνων, Aeschin. Tim., 3, 58; συνέρχονται δὲ ἐξ ἑκάστης πόλεως εἰς κοινὸν συνέδριον, Strabo, 14, 3, 3; also Aeschin. Tim., 2, 70; 3, 89; IG, 12, 1259, 4 (4th cent. B.C.) The Roman Senate is συνέδριον in Polyb., 1, 11, 1, cf. also συνέδριον τῶν Καρχηδονίων, 1, 31, 8; τῇ βουλῇ τῇ ἐξ Ἀρείου πάγου, τῷ ἀκριβεστάτῳ συνεδρίῳ τῶν ἐν τῇ πόλει, Aeschin. Tim., 1, 92. The meaning is often "court": ἔμπροσθεν τοῦ συνεδρίου, Demosth. Or., 58, 8: ὅπως ἐν [τῷ συν]εδρίῳ ἐπιπλη[χθῇ] (sc. the thief), P. Tebt., III, 784, 6 (2nd cent. B.C.); ἐν συνεδρίῳ, Lys., 9, 6; cf. 9, 9. 10. But the word συνέδριον did not become a tt. in the Greek-Hell. world. It can still be used for the "place of assembly" in the later Hell. period: τὸ χαλκοῦν μέτρον ἐν τῷ συνεδρείῳ, "the standard bronze measure in the hall of assembly," P. Oxy., IV, 717, 8. 11 (1st cent. B.C.); cf. also Ditt. Syll.[3], I, 243 D 47; 249 Col. II, 77; 252, 71; BGU, II, 540, 25.

2. συνέδριον in Jewish-Hellenistic Literature.

a. The word συνέδριον "assembly" occurs in the LXX: ὅταν γὰρ καθίσῃ ἐν συνεδρίῳ (דִין,), Prv. 22:10b; οὐκ ἐκάθισα μετὰ συνεδρίου ματαιότητος (עָם מְתֵי שָׁוְא) ψ 25:4; ἀνὴρ δίγλωσσος ἀποκαλύπτει βουλὰς ἐν συνεδρίῳ (סוֹד), Prv. 11:13; cf. also 15:22; οὐκ ἐκάθισα ἐν συνεδρίῳ (סוֹד) αὐτῶν παιζόντων, Ιερ. 15:17; εὔγνωστος ἐν συνεδρίοις (שַׁעַר), Prv. 26:26; no Hbr. Prv. 22:10a; 24:8; 27:22; 31:23; also 2 Macc. 14:5; 4 Macc. 17:17 (A). There is no fixed original in the HT, nor is there any Jewish συνέδριον as a governing body in the LXX.

b. Philo uses συνέδριον sometimes: ἐπειδὰν μέντοι πρὸς τὸ τῶν φίλων ἔλθῃ συνέδριον, Som., I, 193; συνέδριον καὶ δικαστήριον, Praem. Poen., 28; often transf. as a place of rest for the ψυχή or νοῦς: συγκαλέσας ὡς ἐν συνεδρίῳ τοὺς τῆς ψυχῆς ἅπαντας λογισμούς, Leg. Gaj., 213; εἰς τὸ ψυχῆς συνέδριον, Conf. Ling., 86; ἐν τῷ ἑαυτῆς (sc. ψυχῆς) συνεδρίῳ καὶ βουλευτηρίῳ, Vit. Cont., 27; cf. also Omn. Prob. Lib., 11; καθίσας οὖν ὁ νοῦς ἐν τῷ ἑαυτοῦ συνεδρίῳ, Ebr., 165.

c. συνέδριον also occurs in Joseph. for "assembly," "council"; Demetrius συνέδριον ἐποιήσατο ἐν τῷ παρὰ τὴν ᾗόνα κατεσκευασμένῳ οἴκῳ, Ant., 12, 103 (par. Ep. Ar., 301); Καίσαρός τε συνέδριον φίλων τε τῶν αὐτοῦ καὶ Ῥωμαίων τῶν πρώτων συνάγοντος, 17, 301; συνέδριον μὲν ὁ βασιλεὺς ἀθροίζει τῶν συγγενῶν καὶ φίλων, Bell., 1, 620. The word is often used for "court": παράγειν εἰς τὸ συνέδριον "to bring to court," Ant., 16, 361; cf. 15, 358; 16, 357, 360; 17, 46; Bell., 1, 571 and 640. A "college" [2] or "governing body" is a συνέδριον: Gabinius πέντε συνέδρια καταστήσας εἰς ἴσας

---

[1] Cf. Liddell-Scott, *s.v.*

[2] Cf. also the inscr. CIJ, II, 777: someone leaves τῷ συνε[δρίῳ τῶν] καιροδαπισ[τ]ῶν "the college of carpet weavers" a sum to adorn his grave at the feasts of Unleavened Bread and Pentecost. Cf. CIJ, II, 779: γερουσία.

μοίρας διένειμε τὸ ἔθνος, Ant., 14, 91. [3] Jos. tells us he appointed τῶν φίλων συνέδριον in Tiberias, Vit., 368. [4] In particular, however, the συνέδριον is the "supreme Jewish authority" in Jerusalem: τῷ συνεδρίῳ Ἱεροσολυμιτῶν, Vit., 62, cf. also Ant., 14, 163-184; 15, 173; 20, 200.

B. The Jewish Sanhedrin in the Hellenistic-Roman Period.

1. The History of the Sanhedrin in Jerusalem.

The post-exilic community grouped around the temple and the Law was governed by priests and elders. Ezr. and Neh. often mention the שָׂרִים or זְקֵנִים, [5] the חוֹרִים and סְגָנִים, [6] who were at the head of the Jerusalem community. The priestly nobility and the heads of the leading clans and families constituted themselves an aristocratic senate. It is true that the γερουσία of Jerusalem is first mentioned in a decree of the Syr. king Antiochus III (223-187 B.C.). [7] But there can be no doubt the governing body in Jerusalem had come into being earlier → VI, 658, 44 ff. Since Hell. cities mostly had a democratic constitution, but the Jerusalem senate — as its name γερουσία shows — was aristocratic, its origin must go back to Persian times. Priests and elders, [8] under the presidency of the high-priest, were its members. When the Hasmoneans took the office of both king and high-priest, the rights of the Gerousia were seriously curtailed. There is mention of it in Macc. at 2 Macc. 1:10; [9] 4:44; 11:27; [10] 14:37 (the age of Judas), 1 Macc. 12:6; [11] cf. also 11:23; 12:35 (age of Jonathan), and 1 Macc. 13:36; 14:20, [12] 28 [13] (age of Simon). [14] Under Queen Alexandra (76-67 B.C.) the Jerusalem council [15] underwent a momentous change. The queen made peace with the Pharisees, who had rejected and opposed the ruling house, Jos. Ant., 13, 408 f. Previously the Gerousia had been made up only of priests and elders, but now Pharisaic scribes were given a place in it.

The word συνέδριον is first used for the Jerusalem council in a decree by which the Roman governor in Syria, Gabinius (57-55 B.C.) introduced a new order of relations in Palestine and divided the land into 5 συνέδρια, Jos. Ant., 14, 91; Bell., 1, 170. A few yrs. later, however, Caesar abrogated these arrangements and the high-priest and the Jerusalem council again began to govern Jews throughout the country. From the time of Herod onwards συνέδριον is often used in the sources for the senate in the Holy City. [16] The Sanhedrin dared to call Herod to account for the capital sentences he carried out in Galilee, Jos. Ant., 14, 163-184. He took a bloody revenge: ὁ γὰρ Ἡρώδης τὴν βασιλείαν παραλαβὼν πάντας ἀπέκτεινεν τοὺς ἐν τῷ συνεδρίῳ, 14, 175. Acc. to 15, 6, after

---

[3] In the par. Bell., 1, 170 we read: διεῖλεν δὲ πᾶν τὸ ἔθνος εἰς πέντε συνόδους.

[4] Cf. Vit., 236: The friends of John of Gischala συνέδριον τῶν φίλων καθίσαντες.

[5] Cf. Ezr. 5:5, 9; 6:7 f., 14; 10:8.

[6] Cf. Neh. 2:16; 4:8, 13; 5:7; 7:5.

[7] Jos. Ant., 12, 138; Antiochus writes that the city of Jerusalem had opened its gates to him καὶ μετὰ τῆς γερουσίας ἀπαντησάντων.

[8] In Antiochus' decree there is ref. to ἡ γερουσία καὶ οἱ ἱερεῖς and the temple personnel, Jos. Ant., 12, 142.

[9] οἱ ἐν Ἱεροσολύμοις καὶ οἱ ἐν τῇ Ἰουδαίᾳ καὶ ἡ γερουσία.

[10] τῇ γερουσίᾳ τῶν Ἰουδαίων, cf. also 1 Macc. 7:33, which ref. to the priests and the πρεσβύτεροι τοῦ λαοῦ as the leaders of the Jews.

[11] Ἰωναθαν ἀρχιερεὺς καὶ ἡ γερουσία τοῦ ἔθνους καὶ οἱ ἱερεῖς καὶ ὁ λοιπὸς δῆμος τῶν Ἰουδαίων.

[12] Σίμωνι ἱερεῖ μεγάλῳ καὶ τοῖς πρεσβυτέροις καὶ τοῖς ἱερεῦσιν καὶ τῷ λοιπῷ δήμῳ τῶν Ἰουδαίων.

[13] ἐπὶ συναγωγῆς μεγάλης ἱερέων καὶ λαοῦ καὶ ἀρχόντων ἔθνους καὶ τῶν πρεσβυτέρων τῆς χώρας.

[14] Cf. also Jdt. 4:8: Ιωακιμ ὁ ἱερεὺς ὁ μέγας καὶ ἡ γερουσία παντὸς δήμου Ισραηλ, cf. 11:14; 15:8.

[15] Cf. Jos. Ant., 13, 428: τῶν Ἰουδαίων οἱ πρεσβύτεροι.

[16] συνέδριον is a loan word (סַנְהֶדְרִין) in Hbr. and Aram.

taking Jerusalem, he had 45 of the chief supporters of Antigonus put to death, so that probably not all the members of the Sanhedrin were slain. Yet it had been decided quite plainly who was now master in the country. The Sanhedrin was packed with people who would not dare speak out against the king. They were ready to sit in judgment on the aged Hyrcanus, 15, 173. When Judaea was then taken over by the Roman procurator, the Sanhedrin was able once again to influence affairs in a modest way. Shortly before the commencement of the Jewish War it condemned James, the Lord's brother, to death under the presidency of the high-priest Ananus, 20, 200. But it then became entangled in the disorders of the revolt (Jos. Vit., 62) and it came to an end with the destruction of Jerusalem. [17] A new Sanhedrin constituted itself in Jabne after 70 A.D.; this was no longer made up of priests and elders, but only of rabbis. It could no longer exercise political functions; its consultations were devoted to exposition of the Torah and the Halachah derived therefrom. [18]

2. The Composition of the Sanhedrin in Jerusalem.

The Sanhedrin probably consisted of 71 members. It is true that we find this no. first only in the Mishnah (Sanh., 1, 6), but it must have applied prior to 70 A.D. as well. Acc. to Nu. 11:16 Moses gathered around him a group of 70 elders, and we read of 70 men for various other Jewish bodies. The Jewish colony in Batanaea was led by 70 chief men, Jos. Bell., 2, 482; Vit., 56. At the beginning of the Jewish War Joseph. himself appointed a council of 70 men in Galilee, Bell., 2, 570; cf. also Vit., 79. The Zealots nominated a court of 70 judges in Jerusalem, Bell., 4, 336. There was supposed to have been a council of 71 elders in Alexandria, T. Sukka, 4, 6 (198). [19] Hence the great Sanhedrin was probably an assembly of 70 or 71 councillors too. [20]

At the head of the body, which convened in the βουλή of Jos. Bell., 5, 144 or the βουλευτήριον of 6, 354, [21] stood the high-priest. [22] He was the leader of the Jewish

---

[17] Büchler Synedrion attempts a different portrayal. Prior to 70 A.D. he distinguishes between a political body (βουλή), a mostly priestly college (συνέδριον) which dealt with transgressions in the temple, and the great Sanhedrin which controlled the religious life of the Jews. Along these lines he hoped to give due weight not only to statements in Jos. and the NT but also to those of Rabb. lit., which depict the Sanhedrin as an assembly of scribes. His thesis has been accepted and developed by many Jewish scholars. Acc. to Wolff there was a little συνέδριον presided over by the high-priest in addition to the gt. Sanhedrin composed of scribes (γερουσία). This was the court which condemned Jesus. Zeitlin Who Crucified Jesus? thinks the political and not the religious Sanhedrin was responsible for the trial of Jesus, and Hoenig Sanhedrin, 12 has tried to prove again the existence of three different bodies: a political, which was composed acc. to the current external power structure, a priestly, and then a scribal, which was the Sanhedrin in the strict sense: "The Great Sanhedrin was a religious body devoted to the interpretation of the biblical and traditional law, the Halakah." On the basis of these theses Mantel (254) states "that the Synedrion of the Gospels is not identical with the Sanhedrin in the Hall of Gazit. The one was a political, the other a religious body." The point of these conjectures is to lend credibility to the Rabb. statements. Schürer's criticism of Büchler applies equally to those who follow him: "It is enough to have adduced these bizarre theories," II, 247, n. 26.

[18] The Mishnah tractate Sanh. describes the Sanhedrin in Jabne, not that in Jerusalem. Hence one cannot assume that the rules of Sanh. apply forthwith to the period before 70 A.D.

[19] Cf. also the 70 (72) translators of the Bible into Gk., Ep. Ar., 46-50; the 70 (72) disciples of Jesus, Lk. 10:1. Cf. B. M. Metzger, "Seventy or Seventy-two Disciples?" NTSt, 5 (1958/59), 299-306.

[20] 70 members and the high-priest as president.

[21] In the Mishnah the place of assembly is sometimes לִשְׁכַּת הַגָּזִית Sanh., 11, 2; Mid., 5, 4 etc. One cannot say for certain whether this is identical with Joseph.'s βουλή (Schürer), cf. Schürer, II, 263-5; Dalman Orte, 350; also Jerusalem u. sein Gelände (1930), 193 f.; Str.-B., I, 998 f.; Jackson-Lake, V, 477 f.; C. Kopp, Die hl. Stätten d. Ev. (1959), 351 f.; Winter Trial, 20-30; Blinzler, 116-120.

[22] Cf. Jos. Ant., 20, 251: τὴν δὲ προστασίαν τοῦ ἔθνους οἱ ἀρχιερεῖς ἐπεπίστευντο.

people; he alone could preside in the Sanhedrin. Around him were the ἀρχιερεῖς, the priestly aristocracy, Sadducean in sympathy (→ 43, 15 ff.; III, 270, 27 ff.). By virtue of their office the chief priests in the temple had a seat and voice in the Sanhedrin and they formed a solid faction. [23] The elders were a second group, → VI, 659, 4 ff. It is true that originally all members of the γερουσία were called elders. Gradually, however, this term acquired a more restricted sense, so that only leaders of the influential lay families in Jerusalem were called πρεσβύτεροι. [24] Without exception these patricians, too, were Sadducean in persuasion → 43, 15 ff. The Pharisees managed to get into the High Council in the days of Queen Alexandra → 862, 20 ff. From then on the power and influence of the γραμματεῖς [25] (→ I, 740, 14 ff.) grew steadily in the Sanhedrin. In the Roman period the ἀρχιερεῖς were still first in rank, but in fact decisions could not be taken or executed without the agreement of the Pharisaic scribes. [26]

When the Sanhedrin groups are mentioned in Joseph. or the NT the ἀρχιερεῖς almost always come first, for they were first in dignity. Thus Joseph. has the following designations: οἵ τε ἀρχιερεῖς καὶ δυνατοὶ τό τε γνωριμώτατον τῆς πόλεως, Bell., 2, 301; οἱ δυνατοὶ σὺν τοῖς ἀρχιερεῦσιν, 2, 316; τούς τε ἀρχιερεῖς σὺν τοῖς γνωρίμοις, 2, 318; τούς τε ἀρχιερεῖς καὶ τὴν βουλήν, 2, 331; οἵ τε ἀρχιερέων ἅμα τοῖς δυνατοῖς καὶ ἡ βουλή, 2, 336; τῶν τε ἀρχιερέων καὶ τῶν γνωρίμων, 2, 410; συνελθόντες γοῦν οἱ δυνατοὶ τοῖς ἀρχιερεῦσιν εἰς ταὐτὸ καὶ τοῖς τῶν Φαρισαίων γνωρίμοις, 2, 411; οἱ δυνατοὶ σὺν τοῖς ἀρχιερεῦσιν, 2, 422; τῶν δυνατῶν καὶ τῶν ἀρχιερέων, 2, 428. The ἀρχιερεῖς may also be called quite simply οἱ τῶν Ἱεροσολύμων ἄρχοντες, 2, 333, cf. also 2. 405, 407 and 627.

In the NT, too, ἀρχιερεῖς is almost always first. We find the following formulae: ἀρχιερεῖς, γραμματεῖς, πρεσβύτεροι, Mk. 11:27; 14:43; Mt. 27:41; ἀρχιερεῖς, πρεσβύτεροι, γραμματεῖς, Mk. 14:53; 15:1. Often two groups are mentioned: ἀρχιερεῖς, γραμματεῖς, Mk. 10:33; 11:18; 14:1; 15:31; Mt. 2:4; 20:18; 21:15; Lk. 19:47; 22:2 (,66); 23:10; ἀρχιερεῖς, πρεσβύτεροι (τοῦ λαοῦ), Mt. 21:23; 26:3, 47; 27:1, 3, 12, 20; 28:11 f.; [27] Ac. 4:23; 23:14; 25:15; ἀρχιερεῖς, Φαρισαῖοι, Mt. 21:45; 27:62; Jn. 7:32, 45; 11:47, 57; 18:3. Sometimes the ἀρχιερεῖς are representatives of the whole body: οἱ ἀρχιερεῖς καὶ ὅλον τὸ συνέδριον, Mk. 14:55 par. Mt. 26:59; cf. also Ac. 22:30; [28] ἀρχιερεῖς alone is also used in Mk. 14:10 par. Mt. 26:14; Lk. 22:4; Mk. 15:3, 10, 11; Jn. 12:10. Very rarely ἀρχιερεῖς is second: πρεσβύτεροι, ἀρχιερεῖς, γραμματεῖς, Mk. 8:31 par. Mt. 16:21; Lk. 9:22; τὸ πρεσβυτέριον τοῦ λαοῦ, ἀρχιερεῖς τε καὶ γραμματεῖς, Lk. 22:66. Only in a very few ref. is there no mention of the ἀρχιερεῖς: οἱ γραμματεῖς καὶ οἱ πρεσβύτεροι, Mt. 26:57; ἄρχοντες, πρεσβύτεροι, γραμματεῖς, Ac. 4:5; ἄρχοντες τοῦ λαοῦ καὶ πρεσβύτεροι, Ac. 4:8; πρεσβύτεροι γραμματεῖς, Ac. 6:12. [29]

This is confirmed by the NT but contradicted by Rabb. tradition, acc. to which two scribes occupied the position of the president (נָשִׂיא) and his deputy (אַב בֵּית דִּין)Chag., 2, 2. This is an attempt to trace back the tradition of the Jabne Sanhedrin to an earlier period and it can hardly claim to be historical. Hence conjectures that there was an exclusively scribal Sanhedrin in the period prior to 70 A.D. are pointless. Cf. → n. 17 and Schürer, II, 254-258.

[23] Cf. Jeremias Jerusalem, II B, 2-87, esp. 38.

[24] Cf. Jeremias Jerusalem, II B, 88-100, esp. 89-93 with many examples.

[25] Ibid., 101-114, esp. 105 f.

[26] Cf. Jos. Ant., 18, 17. The Mishnah requirement (Qid., 4, 5) that all members be of pure Israelite descent must have applied to the Sanhedrin prior to 70 A.D. as well. Cf. Jeremias Jerus., II B, 169.

[27] It is noteworthy that Mt. often omits γραμματεῖς, → VI, 659, n. 46. Since the concept of the scribe found an entry into Mt.'s Church (13:52; 23:34) it was not used so much for the Jewish authorities. Cf. R. Hummel, "Die Auseinandersetzung zwischen Kirche u. Judt. im Mt.," Beiträge z. evangelischen Theol., ed. E. Wolf, 33 (1963), 17 f.

[28] Cf. also Ac. 25:2: οἱ ἀρχιερεῖς καὶ οἱ πρῶτοι τῶν Ἰουδαίων.

[29] Lk. is often less precise → VI, 659, n. 46. Cf. also Lk. 7:3; 22:52; 23:4, 13; 24:20; Ac. 22:30; 25:2.

3. The Powers of the Sanhedrin.

As the supreme Jewish court the Jerusalem Sanhedrin governed secular and religious matters affecting the Jewish population. It had the right to try capital cases and execute the sentence. This is why it summoned Herod to account when he ordered executions in Galilee without consulting the Jerusalem court at all, Jos. Ant., 14, 163-184. When Herod became king, he could not be high-priest or preside in the Sanhedrin because he was not of priestly descent. He packed the Sanhedrin with supporters and let it carry on. But in fact he dispensed royal justice without bothering in the least about the priesthood or the High Council, Ant., 14, 167; 15, 273 f.; 16, 1-5. [30] The power of the Sanhedrin remained *de iure* but *de facto* the ruler alone exercised the *ius gladii.* [31]

The situation changed after 6 A.D. when a Roman governor was appointed for Judaea and took the place of the Jewish ruler. The official sphere of the Sanhedrin was limited to Judaea and the governing power μέχρι τοῦ κτείνειν [32] lay with the procurator. The latter, whose seat was at Caesarea rather than Jerusalem, allowed the Sanhedrin to control matters relating to the native populace. [33] But how wide were the powers of the Sanhedrin in the Roman period, and what rights did the procurator reserve to himself? Undoubtedly the Sanhedrin could decide all matters relating to the cultic community and it could punish offences against the Torah so long as these did not involve the death penalty. It was even conceded the right to punish with death a pagan — even a Roman — who went across the temple barrier and entered the sacred precincts. [34] But one should not deduce from the granting of this special privilege that under the rule of the procurators the Jewish court maintained the right to impose and execute a capital sentence. [35] This is contradicted by Jn. 18:31, acc. to which the death sentence lay in the hands of the procurator alone and not with the Jews.

Nevertheless, some executions were carried out on the orders of the Jewish court between 6 and 70 A.D. [36] (1) The daughter of a priest who had committed fornication was burned to death, Sanh., 7, 2. This was probably during the short reign of Agrippa I (41-44 A.D.) in which the Jews had again their own independent state. [37] (2) The death of James (Ac. 12:2) undoubtedly took place at this time. (3) When Porcius Festus had

---

[30] He simply had the high-priest Hyrcanus discussed by the Sanhedrin and himself passed the death sentence, Ant., 15, 173.

[31] The same applies to Herod's successors. Herod Antipas had John executed without asking the Sanhedrin. Jos. Ant., 18, 116-119; Mk. 6:17-29 par. Herod Agrippa condemned James the son of Zebedee to death, Ac. 12:2. Cf. J. Blinzler, "Rechtsgeschichtliches zur Hinrichtung d. Zebedaiden Jakobus," *Nov. Test.*, 5 (1962), 207-213. The tetrarch Philip on his travels always had a throne set up so that he could act as judge throughout his territory, Ant., 18, 107.

[32] For the appointment cf. Jos. Bell., 2, 117.

[33] It was common Roman practice to accept native law in the provinces but to vest supreme judicial power in the procurator. Cf. L. Mitteis, *Reichsrecht u. Volksrecht in d. östlichen Provinzen d. röm. Kaiserreiches* (1891), 90-110; T. Mommsen, *Röm. Staatsrecht,* III, 1⁴ (1953), 744-9; Bickermann Utilitas Crucis, 172-4; A. N. Sherwin-White, *Roman Society and Roman Law in the NT* (1963), *passim,* esp. 1-47.

[34] For the prohibition cf. Deissmann LO, 62 f.; K. Galling, *Textbuch z. Gesch. Israels* (1950), 80; C. K. Barrett, *The NT Background* (1956), 50; cf. Jos. Bell., 5, 194; 6, 125 f.; Ant., 15, 417; → 323, 22 ff.; I, 762, 10 ff.; III, 234, 19 ff.; E. Bickermann, "The Warning Inscr. of Herod's Temple," JQR, 37 (1946/47), 387-405.

[35] So Juster, II, 133-142 and esp. Lietzmann Prozess Jesu, 258-260; also Burkill Competence, 96: "If in certain circumstances the Jewish authorities could put a Roman citizen to death . . . surely they would be formally empowered to pass and execute a capital sentence on any ordinary Jewish citizen who was found guilty of a religious offence for which the law of Moses required the infliction of the death penalty." Cf. Winter Trial, 74.

[36] There is lively discussion of these cases in the debate following Lietzmann's Prozess. Against Lietzmann cf. esp. Büchsel, and *v.* also Holzmeister; Jeremias Verhör; Blinzler, 163-174.

[37] Jeremias Verhör, 146.

died and his successor had not yet been nominated the high-priest Ananus seized the chance to have James, the Lord's brother, condemned by the Sanhedrin and stoned, Jos. Ant., 20, 200. Because of this arbitrary deed — ὡς οὐκ ἐξὸν ἦν Ἀνάνῳ χωρὶς τῆς ἐκείνου γνώμης καθίσαι συνέδριον, Ant., 20, 202 — Ananus was later called to account and deprived of his office, 20, 203. (4) Stephen, whose martyrdom is recounted in Ac. 7:54-8:2, was obviously not condemned by due process but was the victim of an enraged mob. If the Romans did not stop lynch law or grant free protection to the Jews, their consent was by no means the rule. [38] The Jews did not cease to claim that the power of the sword was theirs by divine right. But during the whole period they were under Roman procurators its free exercise was checked. The Talmudic tradition is recalling this situation when it says that for 40 yrs. before the destruction of the temple the power of life and death was taken from the Jews. [39] The round no. 40 here is not to be taken lit., for the ref. is obviously to the beginning of the Roman procuratorship in Judaea. Only when this was violently brought to an end at the beginning of the Jewish revolt could the Jewish court impose and execute the death penalty in the autumn of 66 A.D. [40] The Zealots made gruesome use of this right during their reign of terror in Jerusalem. During the whole period of the rule of Roman procurators over Judaea, however, the right of imposing a capital penalty was taken from the Sanhedrin, as it had been in practice under Herod. [41] Hence the saying of the Jews to the procurator Pilate in Jn. 18:31 is in keeping with the legal situation at the time: ἡμῖν οὐκ ἔξεστιν ἀποκτεῖναι οὐδένα.

4. Jewish Sanhedrins outside Jerusalem.

Outside the Holy City little courts were set up after the pattern of the great Sanhedrin. These were allowed by the Roman authorities to exercise their own Jewish jurisdiction in Palestine and the *diaspora*, Mak., 1, 10. The institution of these lesser sanhedrins was traced back to the command in the Torah. [42] The Mishnah ordains [43] that in towns of at least 120 adult male Israelites there is to be a sanhedrin of 23 members, Sanh., 1, 6. [44] The term συνέδριον/סַנְהֶדְרִין is attested for these lesser courts. In the case of capital crimes the Mishnah lays down that all 23 persons must pass sentence. In respect of these courts, too, the Jews clung to their claim that the *ius gladii* belonged to them even though the right of the sword was exercised only by the Roman authorities. [45] But acc. to the Jewish view the death penalty ought to be imposed as infrequently as possible. A sanhedrin which passed it once in 7 yrs. was regarded as a "destructive" one, Mak. 1, 10. R. Tarfon and R. Aqiba even said that if they had a seat in the Sanhedrin no one would have been put to death by it, Mak., 1, 10. Court was held twice a week, on Monday and Thursday, Ket., 1, 1. It was never in any circumstances to convene on a Sabbath or feast-day, Sanh., 4, 1; Beza (Yom tob), 5, 2.

The Essene fellowship also exercised its own jurisdiction, passing severe sentences for transgressions of the Law and even imposing the death penalty for blasphemy against Moses, Jos. Bell., 2, 145. Sentence was passed in the presence of at least 100 members of

---

[38] Cf. E. Lohse, "Die röm. Statthalter in Jerusalem," ZDPV, 74 (1958), 77 f.

[39] jSanh., 1, 1 (18a, 36 f.); 7, 2 (24b, 43); also bSanh., 41a Bar.; bAZ, 8b Bar.; cf. Str.-B., I, 1026 f.

[40] Cf. the note in the list of fasts that on the 22nd 'Elul the putting to death of malefactors was begun again, text in G. Dalman, *Aram. Dialektproben*[2] (1927), 2; cf. Jeremias Verhör, 149 f.; Blinzler, 169.

[41] Jeremias Verhör, 148 f. thinks that the story in Jn. 7:53-8:11 also presupposes the Jews did not have the *ius gladii*; but this is uncertain, cf. Burkill Competence, 85-88.

[42] Cf. T. Sanh., 3, 10 (420): Scripture proof from Nu. 35:29.

[43] Cf. Str.-B., I, 257-259, 575 f.

[44] Cf. also T. Sanh., 7, 1 (425); T. Chag., 2, 9 (235); Str.-B., II, 816 f.

[45] Obviously the Roman authorities sometimes allowed Jewish courts to execute the death sentence, cf. Orig. Ep. ad Africanum, 14 (MPG, 11 [1857], 84 A). But in such cases the Romans ignored the fact that the Jews were exceeding their powers, cf. Schürer, II, 247 f.

the order. The Dead Sea Scrolls have an express penal code, 1 QS 6:24-7:25. Jurisdiction lay with the עצת היחד and was exercised by a panel of 12 men and 3 priests, 1 QS 8:1. [46] This had to see to it that the sacred law of God was upheld.

C. συνέδριον in the New Testament.

1. συνέδριον in the Gospels.

a. In Sayings of Jesus.

Jesus warns His disciples in advance that they are to expect persecutions: παραδώσουσιν γὰρ ὑμᾶς εἰς συνέδρια, καὶ ἐν ταῖς συναγωγαῖς αὐτῶν μαστιγώσουσιν ὑμᾶς, Mt. 10:17 par. Mk. 13:9. The sanhedrins here are the local Jewish courts before which Christians will be brought. They will be sentenced to scourging in them. This means that the disciples have not yet broken definitively with the Jewish community; they are still subject to the Jewish authorities in Palestine and the *diaspora*. [47] Whereas it was said to them of old time that murder deserved the death penalty, Jesus sets the evil word spoken to one's brother under the judgment, Mt. 5:21 f.: ὃς δ' ἂν εἴπῃ τῷ ἀδελφῷ αὐτοῦ ῥακά, ἔνοχος ἔσται τῷ συνεδρίῳ → II, 828, 30 ff.; VI, 975, 6 ff. [48] Since συνέδριον is in the singular here, the reference is to the supreme court in the Holy City. [49] The statement, which is crisply formulated in ancient legal style, is thus to the effect that an angry word is just as bad as the deed of murder condemned by the Sanhedrin. [50]

b. Jesus Before the Sanhedrin in Jerusalem.

The Jerusalem Sanhedrin was firmly resolved to arrest and kill Jesus as soon as it had a favourable opportunity to apprehend Him inconspicuously, Mk. 14:1 f. and par.; cf. also Mk. 11:18 and par.

Jn. tells us that owing to the impression left by the raising of Lazarus the ἀρχιερεῖς and Φαρισαῖοι called a session of the Sanhedrin, 11:47. At this meeting the high-priest Caiaphas said it was better for one man to die for the people than for all the people to perish, 11:50. Now this story is patently Johannine, [51] yet it shares with the Synoptic records the fact that the Sanhedrin met for the express purpose of liquidating Jesus, cf. Mk. 14:1 and par.

---

[46] Cf. on this Damasc. 10:4-6 (11:1 f.): acc. to this the college of judges is to consist of 10 men — 4 priests and 6 Israelites, cf. P. Wernberg-Møller, *The Manual of Discipline* (1957), 122 f.

[47] There were συνέδρια not only in Palestine but also in the *diaspora*, e.g., Syria and Asia Minor. The Lucan par. in 12:11 and 21:12 have only synagogues, not sanhedrins. Lk. avoided συνέδρια "since a Gentile Christian could not associate the term with any relevant concrete idea. On the other hand the Gentile Christian community was well acquainted with the institution of the Jewish synagogue," cf. A. Strobel, "Zum Verständnis von Rm. 13," ZNW, 47 (1956), 73.

[48] Since exegesis of the saying has been explicitly dealt with, our present concern is simply to define the word συνέδριον.

[49] But cf. M. Weise, "Mt. 5:21 f. — ein Zeugnis sakraler Rechtssprechung in d. Urgemeinde," ZNW, 49 (1958), 119: "συνέδριον does not mean the supreme religious court in Jerusalem which expiates capital crimes but the 'council of the community' (עצת היחד) which has the authority to execute divine jurisdiction."

[50] The saying formulates sacred divine law. Whether or not the Sanhedrin was in any position at the time to pass and inflict the death sentence (→ 865, 1 ff.) is in no way reflected.

[51] Cf. Bultmann J. on 11:45-54, esp. 313, n. 2.

According to the accounts of Mark and Matthew Jesus after His arrest was brought before the high-priest, who late on the eve of the Passover hastily summoned the ἀρχιερεῖς, πρεσβύτεροι and γραμματεῖς, Mk. 14:53 par. Mt. 26:57. οἱ δὲ ἀρχιερεῖς καὶ ὅλον τὸ συνέδριον ἐζήτουν κατὰ τοῦ 'Ιησοῦ μαρτύριον εἰς τὸ θανατῶσαι αὐτόν, καὶ οὐχ ηὕρισκον, Mk. 14:55 par. Mt. 26:59. Since the false witnesses against Jesus did not help them to achieve the desired goal, the high-priest stood up and put the decisive question: σὺ εἶ ὁ χριστὸς ὁ υἱὸς τοῦ εὐλογητοῦ; Mk. 14:61 and par. When Jesus answered in the affirmative and underlined His answer by quoting Da. 7:13 and Ps. 110:1, the high-priest demanded that the members of the Sanhedrin should pass sentence in view of the patent βλασφημία, → I, 623, 28 ff. [52] οἱ δὲ πάντες κατέκριναν αὐτὸν ἔνοχον εἶναι θανάτου, Mk. 14:64 par. Mt. 26:66. At the end of the prosecution of Jesus the Sanhedrin thus reached a unanimous verdict and condemned Him to death.

In respect of this account in the Synoptics it should be noted first that several rules of the Halachah are broken in the trial of Jesus before the Sanhedrin. [53] (1) Capital trials were only to be held by day acc. to Sanh., 4, 1, but here the Sanhedrin met at night to judge Jesus. (2) No legal procedings were to take place on the Sabbath or feast-days, [54] but here the trial of Jesus before the Sanhedrin took place on the eve of the Passover. (3) Sanh., 4, 1 lays down that sentence of death was never to be passed on the day of the trial itself but only on the following day, but here the Sanhedrin condemned Jesus at once to death. (4) Acc. to Sanh., 7, 5 the blasphemy which is to be punished by death is pronouncing the divine name, but here Jesus did not pronounce the name of God. (5) The trial was obviously held in the house of the high-priest, not in the regular hall of assembly of the Sanhedrin. [55] Since no other source speaks of sessions of the Sanhedrin being held in the high-priest's house, the proceedings described by the Evangelists deviate at this pt., too, from Jewish legal practice. [56]

It should also be noted, however, that the Pharisaic Rabb. Halachah later codified in the Mishnah cannot have been normative for the Sanhedrin in the period prior to 70 A.D. This still acted acc. to the legal understanding of the Sadducees. [57] The Pharisees always represented a milder exposition of the statutes lest any should be condemned unlawfully. [58] Pharisaic views governed the version of the laws in the Mishnah and it

---

[52] βλασφημία means "blasphemy" and should not be given the weaker sense of "offensive utterance," so Bickermann Utilitas Crucis, 176-179, who also takes the κατέκριναν of v. 64 to be a verdict of guilty, not a condemnation, 180-184. But Mk. 10:33 says unequivocally κατακρινοῦσιν αὐτὸν θανάτῳ, cf. Winter Trial, 25 f.; Blinzler, 108, n. 36; P. Lamarche, "Le blasphème de Jésus devant le sanhédrin," Recherches de Science Religieuse, 50 (1962), 74-85. The conjecture of Kennard, 48-51 that βλασφημία means Jesus "was charged with offences 'against Caesar'" (49) is wide of the mark. On this view Jesus was handed over to the procurator for the crimen laesae maiestatis and was condemned by him.
[53] Cf. the surveys in Blinzler, 138 f.; Lohse, 32 f.
[54] Sanh., 4, 1; Beza (Yom tob), 5, 2. Other examples in Str.-B., II, 815 f.
[55] It was impossible to meet at evening in the Qader Hall, the regular meeting-place acc. to Sanh., 11, 2, since the gates of the temple hill were closed by night, cf. Str.-B., I, 997-1001.
[56] Winter Trial, 20.
[57] Blinzler, 146 f., 154-163. On the question of the validity of the penal law of the Mishnah in the time of Jesus, Blinzler, "Das Synedrium v. Jerusalem u. d. Strafprozessordnung d. Mischna," ZNW, 52 (1961), 54-65.
[58] The rule that sentence of death should be pronounced only on the second day may well be due to milder Pharisaic practice, Sanh., 4, 1. Possibly the Rabb. were also the first to restrict the content of blasphemy quite narrowly to the pronouncing of the divine name, Sanh., 7, 5. It is also possible that the rule that capital trials should be held only by day (Sanh., 4, 1) was established by the Rabb. to prevent miscarriages of justice.

cannot be assumed that these obtained in the days of Jesus. [59] The only pt. is that the strict prohibition of legal practice on the Sabbath and feast-days does not just go back to the Rabb. but corresponds to the older Halachah, which was very precisely administered, → 9, 7 ff. [60] There can be no doubt that in the days of Jesus judicial proceedings were strictly forbidden on the Sabbaths, on feast-days, and on the related days of preparation. [61] The Synoptic account of the trial of Jesus before the Sanhedrin [62] seems to be quite incompatible with the rule demanded by the Law. [63]

Evaluation of the account in Mk. and Mt. must begin with the unassailable historical fact that Jesus was not stoned but crucified; in other words He was judged acc. to Roman law. [64] Pilate did not confirm a Jewish sentence and allow it to be carried out. On the basis of a complaint made by the Jews he himself condemned Jesus and had Him executed. The Sanhedrin would hardly have dared to pass sentence of death at a time when the procurator was present in the Holy City, since supreme legal judicial power lay with him alone.

The story in Mk. 14:55-65 is not a simple unity [65] and could have been influenced by the Scripture proof [66] and the Chr. confession. [67] For the high-priest's question whether Jesus was the Christ, the Son of the Most High (Mk. 14:61), is hardly conceivable on

---

[59] Blinzler, 163 concludes that "everything which has been found irregular about the trial of Jesus in the light of the Mishnah is in full harmony with current law, which was Sadducean and which did not know or acknowledge the Pharisaic-humanitarian peculiarities of the Mishnah, which had no basis in the OT." This conclusion is rather too broad. For one thing we know very little about the details of Sadducean law. For another Sadducean law must have been strongly against legal proceedings on the Sabbath or feast-days, → lines 1 ff.

[60] Cf. also → 12, n. 84; Str.-B., II, 815-822, esp. 819: "It has frequently been brought to our attention that in the days of Jesus the rules about Sabbath healing were more rigorous than in the time from which the regulations of the Mishnah come." J. Blinzler, "Die Strafe für Ehebruch in d. Bibel u. Halacha," NTSt, 4 (1957/58), 32-47 has shown that in Judaism adultery was punished by stoning but that in the course of the 1st cent. the milder punishment of throttling was substituted for the ancient practice. In this matter, too, the Rabb. represented the less rigorous exposition of the Halachah.

[61] Cf. Str.-B., II, 820: "There can be no doubt the principle: 'One is not to judge on feast-days,' was recognised Halachah in the days of Jesus too."

[62] Str.-B., II, 821 f. offers the explanation that "extraordinary circumstances demanded extraordinary measures; hence one has to reckon with the possibility that Jesus was condemned on a feast-day," 822. This is not wholly convincing. Cf. Blinzler, 144-6.

[63] Sanh., 11, 4 and T. Sanh., 11, 7 (432) state that a dissenting scholar, an inciter to idolatry, a false prophet and false witnesses are not to be executed at once "but one is to bring them to the Sanhedrin in Jerusalem and keep them in custody until the feast and carry out the sentence on the feast, for it is said: 'And the whole people shall hear it that it may fear and not practise arrogance' (Dt. 17:13)," cf. Str.-B., II, 824. These words of R. Aqiba are purely theoretical, however, and they say only that in certain cases sentences may be carried out on feast-days, Str.-B., II, 824 f.; even Aqiba does not say the Sanhedrin may convene for a capital trial on a feast-day. But cf. J. Jeremias, Die Abendmahlsworte Jesu³ (1960), 72 f.

[64] Cf. Lietzmann Prozess Jesu, 260; G. Bornkamm, Jesus v. Nazareth⁵ (1960), 150 f.; O. Cullmann, Der Staat im NT² (1961), 29 (E. T. [1956], 24 ff., esp. 42).

[65] Mk. 14:58 might well be using a genuine saying of Jesus. But in v. 59 the useless hearing of witnesses is suddenly broken off. We have a turn in v. 60 and the Messianic question is now the decisive pt. In analysis of the account cf. Bultmann Trad., 290-292; M. Dibelius, Die Formgeschichte d. Ev.⁴ (1961), 192 f.; "This is not, then, a single story but an interweaving of several motifs," cf. also 214 f.

[66] For the false witnesses of vv. 55-59 cf. Ps. 27:12; the silence of Jesus in v. 60 f. Is. 53:7; the answer to the high-priest's question in v. 62 Da. 7:13 and Ps. 110:1; the mocking and mistreatment of Jesus in v. 65 Is. 50:6.

[67] It has often been pointed out that the community had no eye-witnesses for the Sanhedrin hearing. In view of the πάντες of Mk. 14:64 one can hardly adduce Nicodemus or Joseph of Arimathea, as against Loh. Mk. on 14:65.

the lips of a Jew. [68] Another problem is why the affirmative answer should rank as blasphemy. [69] But this is readily explicable in the light of the situation of the Chr. community in confrontation with the Synagogue. For in fact the confession of Jesus' Messiahship was the point of bitter controversy between Jews and Christians [70] and the reason why the disciples of Jesus were persecuted by the Jews. In describing the trial of Jesus before the Sanhedrin the community emphasised the part of the Jewish authorities in the execution of Jesus and showed plainly that the difference between Church and Synagogue was over the question whether Jesus is the Son of God or not.

The historical course of events was perhaps that the Sanhedrin, whose Sadducean and Pharisaic members were united in hostility to Jesus, had Jesus arrested, held a brief hearing, [71] and then handed Him over to the procurator to be executed as a political revolutionary, Mk. 15:1 and par. In this case the Jewish court and the Roman governor found they could work together in eliminating Jesus of Nazareth. [72]

Luke's account is essentially tauter than Mk.'s. It says nothing about a Sanhedrin trial but simply that Jesus was arrested at night and that a meeting of the Sanhedrin took place early in the morning, 22:66. [73] When Jesus publicly confessed He was the Messiah the fact of His statement is recorded but no verdict is passed, 22:71. Jesus is taken to Pilate so that he may judge this inciter of the people, 23:2. It does not appear that this sequence of events in Lk.'s record comes from a special Lucan source; [74] it is an abbreviation of the Marcan narrative. [75]

Acc. to Jn. Jesus after His arrest was taken first to the house of Annas, the father-in-law of the ruling high-priest Caiaphas, and was interrogated by him, Jn. 18:12-23. We are not told whether members of the Sanhedrin were present at this hearing. Jn. says nothing about a trial or a sentence passed by the Sanhedrin on Jesus. The decisive proceedings are before Pilate, who under pressure from the Jews condemns Jesus to crucifixion, 18:28-19:16.

2. συνέδριον in Acts.

συνέδριον is often mentioned in Ac. as the court before which the apostles must answer. If it is true enough that the Sanhedrin persecuted Christians, [76] it is also true that the author of Ac. has fashioned his accounts with some freedom. [77] The

---

[68] The two titles mean the same but Son of God is a Chr., not a Jewish, title for the Messiah, cf. Dalman WJ, I, 219-224; W. G. Kümmel, "Das Gleichnis v. d. bösen Weingärtnern," *Aux sources de la tradition chétienne, Festschr. f. M. Goguel* (1950), 130; Jeremias Gl.6 71, n. 1; Lohse, 36 f.

[69] Jewish tradition never says a Messianic pretender was regarded as a blasphemer.

[70] Cf. Jn. 10:36: ὑμεῖς λέγετε ὅτι βλασφημεῖς, ὅτι εἶπον· υἱὸς τοῦ θεοῦ εἰμι, cf. also 5:17 f.; 10:33.

[71] Perhaps Jesus' attitude to the temple (the cleansing) played some part in this. Kilpatrick, 10-13 suggests this was the real βλασφημία with which the Sanhedrin charged Jesus. But this is going too far, for it should be noted that some do not think the saying in Mk. 14:58 is necessarily tied to its present context, cf. Dibelius, *op. cit.*, 215.

[72] Cf. the passion prophecies: Mk. 8:31 and par. runs: καὶ ἀποδοκιμασθῆναι ὑπὸ τῶν πρεσβυτέρων καὶ τῶν ἀρχιερέων και τῶν γραμματέων καὶ ἀποκτανθῆναι, but Mk. 10:33 and par. refers to the death sentence which the Sanhedrin will pass: ὁ υἱὸς τοῦ ἀνθρώπου παραδοθήσεται τοῖς ἀρχιερεῦσιν καὶ τοῖς γραμματεῦσιν, καὶ κατακρινοῦσιν αὐτὸν θανάτῳ καὶ παραδώσουσιν αὐτὸν τοῖς ἔθνεσιν.

[73] Lk. 22:26: καὶ ἀπήγαγον αὐτὸν εἰς τὸ συνέδριον αὐτῶν. συνέδριον here means the place of assembly. Cf. Pr.-Bauer, *s.v.*

[74] As against Winter Trial, 27 f.; cf. Lohse, 26 f.

[75] Cf. Tyson, 249-258; Blinzler, 120-122.

[76] Cf. the persecution of the ἐκκλησία by Paul and the execution of James, the Lord's brother, Jos. Ant., 20, 200.

[77] For analysis of the stories which follow cf. Haench. Ag., *ad loc.*

Sadducees are here the part of the Jerusalem administration which is hostile to Christians (4:1; 5:17; 23:6), while the Pharisees speak out in their favour (5:34-39; 22:30-23:10). In the various hearings which are reported successively there is an unmistakable crescendo. When Peter and John are first brought before the Sanhedrin (4:5-7) [78] they are dismissed with a serious warning (4:5-22). [79] In the second trial the advocacy of Gamaliel (5:34-39) is needed to allow them to be let go with only a beating and another warning to be silent (5:17-42). [80] But then the trial of Stephen, in which the saying about the temple plays a part (6:14), cf. Mk. 14:58 and par.), ends with a general riot and the stoning of the accused (6:8-8:1). When Paul was arrested in Jerusalem, the chiliarch wanted more information about the accusation the Jews brought against him and had a meeting of the Sanhedrin called, 22:30. [81] When Paul stood before the High Council (23:1) he quickly summed up the situation and raised discord among the Sadducees and Pharisees by saying: περὶ ἐλπίδος καὶ ἀναστάσεως νεκρῶν κρίνομαι, 23:6. The Pharisees supported him while the Sadducees opposed him → 53, 37 ff. Paul himself, however, was led away by the Roman officer, 23:10. [82] To protect him against a planned attack of the Jews, who wanted to bring him before the Sanhedrin again and slay him (23:15, 20), the chiliarch then sent Paul with an accompanying letter (23:26-30) to the procurator at Caesarea in order that the latter might decide the case of this Roman citizen accused by the Jews. Paul thus escaped the fate of being condemned by the Sanhedrin like Stephen.

D. συνέδριον in the Post-Apostolic Fathers.

The word συνέδριον occurs only in Ign., who uses it 3 times for "council" in his epistles. In the church the bishop should preside εἰς τόπον θεοῦ and the presbyters εἰς τόπον συνεδρίου τῶν ἀποστόλων, Mg., 6, 1. [83] The church should respect the presbyters ὡς συνέδριον θεοῦ καὶ ὡς σύνδεσμον ἀποστόλων, Tr., 3, 1. The Lord forgives all who repent ἐὰν μετανοήσωσιν εἰς ἑνότητα θεοῦ καὶ συνέδριον τοῦ ἐπισκόπου, Phld., 8, 1.

Lohse

συνείδησις → σύνοιδα.
συνεπιμαρτυρέω → IV, 510, 1 ff.

---

† συνεργός, † συνεργέω

A. The Word Group in Greek.

συνεργός, "fellow-worker," "helper," occurs from Pind. Olymp., 8, 32; Thuc., III, 63, 4, and the derived συνεργέω "to work with," "to help," "to help to something" [1] is

---

[78] On the members of the Sanhedrin in Ac. 4:5-6 cf. Jeremias Jerusalem, II B, 58.
[79] In Ac. 4:15 συνέδριον means "place of assembly."
[80] In Ac. 5:21 συνέδριον and γερουσία are used alongside one another with no difference in meaning. On the construction of the sentence cf. Haench. Ag., *ad loc.*
[81] This raises questions of historicity, since the chiliarch would hardly have the right to attend sessions of the Sanhedrin.
[82] There is further ref. to the hearing before the Sanhedrin in Ac. 24:20 f.
[83] Cf. city constitutions in Asia Minor; we read of a συνέδριον τῶν πρεσβυτέρων at Philadelphia, CIG, II, 3417; cf. Bau. Ign. on Mg., 6, 1. For an understanding of the use of συνέδριον in Ign. this par. is closer than that adduced by Weise, *op. cit.,* 119 f. from the Dead Sea Scrolls, in which the ref. is to a council of the community.

σ υ ν ε ρ γ ό ς κ τ λ . [1] Pape, Liddell-Scott, *s.v.*

found from Eur. Hel., 1427; Xenoph. Mem., II, 6, 21. The more common συνεργάζομαι does not occur in the NT. The ref. is to a work or achievement which is more or less equally divided among fellow-workers or which may be essentially ascribed to the helper, esp. in the case of assisting spiritual powers or divine helpers. Acc. to Plat. Symp., 212b Eros "helps" (συνεργός) man to possession of the divinely beautiful. Plat. Charm., 173d notes that if prudence does not look out unreason "plays a part" in human actions. The verb occurs in Aristot. Eth. Nic., III, 11, p. 1116b, 31: The brave stand up for a worthy end; their indignation [2] "helps" them in this. That reason "co-operates" in acts is a gen. principle handed down in Muson. Fr., 5 (p. 21, 22 f.): συνεργεῖ μὲν γὰρ καὶ τῇ πράξει ὁ λόγος. The word is used in a similar sense in Polyb., 32, 11, 14 and Plut. Amat., 23 (II, 769d). [3] Plot. Enn., III, 4, 6 speaks of the "aid" of the δαίμων in men of excellence and IV, 5, 1 of the "co-operation" of bodies in seeing. In pagan and Chr. pap. there is often ref. to the "co-operation" or "help" of deity: τὸν συνεργοῦντα Ἀπόλλωνα, Preis. Zaub., II, 13, 103 f. (346 A.D.), also P. Amh., II, 152, 4 (5/6th cent. A.D.); cf. also μετὰ τῆς τοῦ θεοῦ συνεργείας, P. Lond., IV, 1349, 35 (710 A.D.). [4] Ps.-Plat. Def., 414a has the saying: χρόνος ἀγαθοῦ τινος συνεργός.

B. The Word Group in Judaism.

1. The verb and noun occur only 4 times in the LXX. In 3 καιρός (→ III, 455, 1 ff.) 1 Macc. 12:1; 2 Macc. 14:5 or νύκτες 2 Macc. 8:7 is the subj. as "helper" in good or evil, cf. Philo Sacr. AC, 65: χρόνος. Once συνεργέω occurs for עבד at 1 Εσδρ. 7:2, a development of the thought in Ezr. 6:13 HT (cf. 2 Εσδρ. 6:13 LXX). [5] Is. 38:12 Θ reads: ἡ ζωή μου ἀπὸ συνεργῶν αὐτῆς ἐξέτεινεν, "he has cut off my life from its nexus (basis)." The HT has here a tt. from weaving and perhaps the rendering by συνεργός originally had in view the fabric as a product of the weaver's work. [6]

2. The words are frequently used in Philo to describe physical and psychic processes. Recollection is a helper in Mut. Nom., 84 and we read of the "co-operation" of reason in Praem. Poen., 43. The term is often used disparagingly in the moral sphere. Sin assures us of companions who "act with" us. This is how Philo understands the plur. demand in Gn. 11:4, Conf. Ling., 110. [7] The worst and truly irremediable evil is the co-operation of all parts of the soul in sin, Conf. Ling., 22. There is no human helper on the way to virtue, Fug., 21 on Gn. 31:27. In opposing idolatry Philo calls all plastic arts συνεργοὶ τῆς ἀπάτης, "deceitful helpers." They definitely "help" to seduce men through idolatry, Spec. Leg., I, 29. The human mind cannot fathom the "working together" of mysterious powers in the constitution of the world. Op. Mund., 61. Only God can truly impart knowledge of God; there is here no "co-operation of men," Praem. Poen., 45. A basic principle in God's work as Creator and Sustainer of the world is that He needed no "helper," Op. Mund., 72; Deus Imm., 87, cf. Som., I, 158. But the situation is different in the exposition of Gn. 1:26 in Op. Mund., 75 and Fug., 68. From the plur. "Let us create man" Philo infers that God used other subordinate beings as "helpers" in the creation of man. God Himself is directly the Creator only of man's spirit with its orientation to the good. The corruptible physical part of man with all its vices is to be ascribed only to subordinate divine forces. [8] In this respect Philo is dangerously close to a dualistic outlook. Similarly

---

[2] The true thumos directed to a noble end, cf. F. Dirlmeier, *Nikomachische Ethik, Erste Gesamtausgabe d. Aristot. in deutscher Übers.,* VI (1956), 343 f.

[3] Cf. also Epict. Diss., I, 9, 26; the adj. συνεργητικός occurs in an ethical context in II, 22, 20 τὸ συνεργητικόν, IV, 4, 18.

[4] Moult.-Mill., Preisigke, *s.v.*

[5] On the basis of a double translation, cf. W. Rudolph, *Jeremia, Hndbch. AT,* I, 20 (1949), ad loc.

[6] P. Oxy., VII, 1069, 8. 12 (3rd cent. A.D.); VIII, 1159, 15. 20 (3rd cent. A.D.); Preisigke Wört., *s.v.*

[7] Cf. Test. R. 3:6; D. 1:7; G. 4:7 (positive and negative use together here).

[8] Cf. L. Cohn, *Die Werke Philos v. Alex. in deutscher Übers.,* I (1909), 58, n. 1.

in Gn. 11:7 the plur. at the confusion of tongues is referred to "co-operating" powers, Cong. Ling., 168, 171. As these once had a helpful and salutary part in creation, so they now work penally on God's commission, cf. Vit. Mos., I, 110. It is thus evident that Philo used the term in many ways. But he seems to avoid it in relation to theological synergism, 9 the co-operation of grace and work. Yet he is still to be regarded as a champion of synergism.

3. In Jos. we find the formula θεοῦ συνεργοῦντος, "with God's help," Ant., 8, 130; Bell., 2, 201, cf. Ant., 7, 91; Bell., 6, 38. 39; with σύμμαχος in Ant., 1, 268, βοηθός in Bell., 4, 616. We also find abstract subj.: ἔρως, 1, 436; ἡ περὶ λόγους ἰσχύς, 1, 453. There is theol. synergism in Ant., 8, 394, which says Yahweh was gracious and "helpful" to him (Jehoshaphat) because he was just and pious: εἶχεν εὐμενές τε καὶ συνεργὸν τὸ θεῖον δίκαιος ὢν καὶ εὐσεβής.

4. There is a materially similar saying in Test. XII. We read in Is. 3:7 f.: God "helped" my simplicity; for I gave the good of the land to the poor and oppressed. 10 Abstract subj. of συνεργέω are ἀδικία in R. 3:6, μῖσος in G. 4:5, 7, ἀγάπη in G. 4:7, cf. also D. 1:7.

5. In the OT one finds hardly any linguistic originals for the group. 11 Nor is there any plain equivalent in the Dead Sea Scrolls. But there is clear synergism in the exposition of Hab. 2:4 in 1 QpHab. 8:1-3. It says here that the righteous lives only by his faithfulness. The interpretation ref. the saying to all who in the house of Judah fulfil the Law and whom God will save from the place of judgment because of their troubles (sufferings) and their loyalty to the Teacher of Righteousness. 12 Elsewhere too in the Scrolls the message of grace is only for the converted 13 of Israel to the degree that they keep clear of sin and pollution by scrupulous observance of the Law and the ordinances of the Qumran community, thus co-operating in their salvation. God's work in creation and salvation is indicated negatively in the Qumran texts: He is the One without whom nothing takes place מבלעדיכה ליא תתם דרך ובלי רעונכה לוא יעשה כול 1 QS 11:17; cf. 1 QH 1:21; 10:9.14 Acc. to 1 QM 1:14 the power of God strengthens the hearts of the sons of light, or acc. to another reading and exposition of the very dubious text He hardens the hearts of the sons of darkness, thus working either for good or evil. 15 Insofar as עזר might be the original of συνεργέω (→ n. 11) one could also ref. to statements about the angelic powers which are depicted as the helpers of the Qumran community, 16 cf. 1 QM 12:7, 13:10, 13, 14; 17:6; 17 1 QH 3:24, 25; 18 perhaps also 1 QM 4:13 (cf. 2 Macc. 8:23) and 1:16.

---

9 W. Völker, Fortschritt u. Vollendung bei Philo v. Alex. (1938) 115-126, with bibl.

10 F. Schnapp in Kautzsch Apkr. u. Pseudepigr., ad loc.

11 עזר "to help" is possible, cf. R. H. Charles, The Gk. Versions of the Testaments of the Twelve Patriarchs (1960), on Test. D. 1:7. This word and derivates occur 126 times in the OT; LXX has βοηθέω and cognates about 100 times, also ἀντιλαμβάνομαι or σῴζω, taking "to help" in the sense "to save." The predominant ref. in the OT is to God's help (65 times). Human help is the theme in a political or military context. It is usually the help sought by the weaker from the stronger (often in vain). The helper of Gn. 2:20, cf. v. 23, is an equal, not an inferior. It is plain from all this that only in a very restricted sense is עזר to be regarded as the OT basis of συνεργέω.

12 H. Bardtke, Die Handschriftenfunde am Toten Meer (1953), 128; F. Horst, Die zwölf kleinen Propheten, Hndbch. AT, I, 14² (1954), 170.

13 F. Nötscher, Zur theol. Terminologie d. Qumran-Texte (1956), 64. Cf. ἐπιστρέφω → 722, 30 ff.

14 Cf. S. Holm-Nielsen, Hodayot. Psalms from Qumran (1960), 24, n. 39; 171 f.

15 J. Carmignac, La Règle de la Guerre des Fils de Lumière contre les Fils de Ténèbres (1958), 20 f.

16 Angels as watchers in the OT Is. 62:6; Da. 4:10, 14; cf. S. Grill, "Synon. Engelnamen im AT," ThZ, 18 (1962), 244 → φυλακή.

17 Carmignac, op. cit. on the passages mentioned.

18 Holm-Nielsen, op. cit. on the passages mentioned.

C. The Word Group in the New Testament.

The noun συνεργός occurs 13 times in the NT, always plur., 12 times in Paul, once in 3 Jn. 8. The verb συνεργέω occurs 5 times, 3 in Paul, once in Jm. 2:22 and once in Mk. 16:20.

1. Paul uses συνεργός in various connections for his pupils and companions, R. 16:21; 2 C. 8:23; Phil. 2:25; 4:3; Phlm. 1, 24. R. 16:3, 9 adds "in Christ"; this describes the sphere of common labour. One is not to see in all this unconditional equality with the apostle. [19] Paul never yielded to anyone the singularity of his position. [20] But he honoured his companions by using this and similar terms, [21] thereby consolidating their authority in the churches. Of a special nature are those statements in which Paul includes himself among others as a συνεργός, cf. (→ III, 1097, 37 ff.) συνεργοὶ τῆς χαρᾶς ὑμῶν in 2 C. 1:24 [22] and συνεργοὶ εἰς τὴν βασιλείαν τοῦ θεοῦ in Col. 4:11, [23] though only the relative clause which follows here makes the connection with Paul. The participial sayings in 1 C. 16:16 and 2 C. 6:1 (→ VI, 682, 23 ff.) [24] may also be mentioned at this point. The categories here are not sociological; Paul is not just honouring his companions. What we have is rather a theological statement: Paul and the rest are in the same service; they are all God's "helpers" and "handymen" (1 C. 3:9) and they are thus "workers" in the kingdom of God. [25] συνεργοί in 1 C. 3:9 (→ I, 442, 14 ff.) corresponds to διάκονοι in 3:5. [26] In this connection one should also refer to 1 Th. 3:2, where in many MSS διάκονος occurs as a synonym of συνεργός which has been left out due to misunderstanding or related by the genitive ἡμῶν to the apostle's assistants. [27]

In 1 C. 16:16 συνεργέω is used alongside κοπιάω (→ III, 829, 36 ff.) for the labour of those who dedicate themselves to ministering to the community. Here the Hebrew equivalents would be עָבַד (cf. 1 Εσδρ. 7:2 where it is the original of

---

[19] F. Delitzsch, הברית החדשה (1954), transl. συνεργός by חבר.at R. 16:3, 9, 21. This root is often the basis of synon. of συνεργός in the Gk. OT, e.g., Is. 1:23; Mal. 2:14; Prv. 28:24; Sir. 6:10; 41:19; 42:3 for κοινωνός; Cant. 1:7; 8:13 for ἑταῖρος; Da. 2:17 for συνεταῖρος; Da. 2:13, 17, 18 Θ; Sir. 7:12; 36:7 for φίλος. Chaber is not the derogatory Rabb. term for a student who could not make ordination, nor does it denote a member of the chaber league; it is used very gen. for a fellow or companion in relation to a given society, cf. Str.-B., III, 318; II, 635.

[20] G. Bertram, "Paulus Christophoros," Stromata, Festgabe d. Akademisch-Theol. Vereins zu Giessen (1930), 27-38.

[21] E.g., συστρατιώτης (→ 710, 32 ff.) Phil. 2:25, κοινωνός (→ III, 807, 19 ff.) 2 C. 8:23, or σύζυγος (→ 749, 15 ff.) Phil. 4:3, which all have the virtually synon. meaning "comrade," "fellow," "companion."

[22] The reading χάριτος for χαρᾶς shows that the ref. cannot be to work together with members of the congregation at Corinth, cf. 2 C. 6:1.

[23] Loh. Kol., ad loc. thinks Paul intentionally avoids a personal relation "work with me" for a material relation "work together for God's kingdom," cf. also Bchm. 2 K. on 8:23.

[24] "And we work together at this" Ltzm. K., ad loc.; perhaps one should supply θεῷ: the work is in God's service, i.e., in the ministry of reconciliation, 2 C. 5:18.

[25] Luther transl. "assistant," only at 1 C. 3:9 "co-worker." For corresponding Jewish ideas cf. J. Bergmann, Jüd. Apologetik im nt.lichen Zeitalter (1908), 112.

[26] This work carries a reward, as 3:8 shows; cf. Mt. 10:10; Lk. 10:7; 1 Tm. 5:18; Jm. 5:4.

[27] Thus συνεργοί in Paul corresponds to ἐργάται or δοῦλοι in the Synoptic parables of the kingdom of God, Mt. 20:1, 2, 8; Lk. 13:27; Mt. 13:27; 18:23; 21:34 etc. Paul uses ἐργάται partly in a negative sense 2 C. 11:13; Phil. 3:2 and partly in a positive sense 1 Tm. 5:18; 2 Tm. 2:15.

συνεργέω) and עמל. [28] This perhaps corresponds to the use of עבד and יגע together in Is. 43:24, [29] where the reference is to God's own work: He Himself bears the burden and care of human sins and iniquities. Paul's self-designation as δοῦλος is to be understood in the light of these OT presuppositions. As a parallel to this συνεργοὶ θεοῦ means "God's workers" in 1 C. 3:9. By using these terms Paul raises a theological claim for himself and his helpers. Their assistance in proclaiming the Gospel means that they share with the apostle the burden of the ministry of reconciliation. Along the lines of Is. 43:24 they thus share in God's own work with its toil and labour. Hence they are God's servants and workers. As such they can claim the obedience of the community. Nevertheless they are not lords of the community in the human sense; they are helpers of its joy, 2 C. 1:24.

In itself the saying in R. 8:28 [30] is quite plain, but τοῖς ἀγαπῶσιν τὸν θεόν might give rise to the suspicion of synergistic theology. [31] In accordance with Pauline thought one would expect to read: τούτοις, οὓς ὁ θεὸς ἀγαπᾷ. But Paul is speaking of those who love God. For such God is the supreme good according to the Hellenistic view. If they have Him, they cannot suffer any hurt which they feel as such. Along these lines the πάντα συνεργεῖ εἰς ἀγαθόν of R. 8:28 might seem to be expressing an optimistic Stoic philosophy of life and view of the world. Judaism undoubtedly took over such ideas from the world around and integrated them into its belief in creation. [32] This kind of religio-historical understanding of Paul's statement would have an even stronger basis if one could point to expressions from Hellenistic mystery piety in the vicinity of R. 8:28. [33] But throughout R. 8 and elsewhere in Paul's works the dominant concept is the biblical one of election, and it is this that must govern exposition of the present v. [34] In R. 8:29 it is God who has called, foreseen and predestined. Hence it follows that the love which man has for God is the gift and reflection of God's love. In the statement which follows, then, God must be supplied as the subject of συνεργεῖ. [35] Many ancient MSS (p⁴⁶ AB etc.) did in fact supply this subject. [36] πάντα thus became an accusative object. God is a helper for good in all things; He turns all for good for the righteous. [37]

---

[28] עמל denotes the care and toil of work. The root and derivates occur 74 times in the OT, 35 being in Qoh., cf. G. Bertram, "Hbr. u. griech. Qoh.," ZAW, NF, 23 (1952), 36-39.

[29] Cf. Bertram, op. cit., 36, n. 3.

[30] Cf. E. C. Blackman, "A Further Note on R. VIII 28," Exp. T., 50 (1938/39), 378 f.; F. Ceuppens, Quaestiones selectae ex epistulis S. Pauli (1951); J. P. Wilson, "Romans VIII 28. Text and Interpretation," Exp. T., 60 (1948/49), 110 f.

[31] Cf. Plat. Resp., X, 612e for something of the same: τῷ δὲ θεοφιλεῖ οὐχ ὁμολογήσομεν, ὅσα γε ἀπὸ θεῶν γίγνεται, πάντα γίγνεσθαι ὡς οἷόν τε ἄριστα;

[32] Examples: "For the cosmos (with its forces) battles for the righteous," Wis. 16:17; "Creation (with the raging of its forces) does not cease to do good to those who trust thee," 16:24 (cf. J. Fichtner, Weisheit Salomos, Hndbch. AT, II, 6 [1938], ad loc.): "Good is done for the good from the very first," Sir. 39:25; the gifts of creation are "all for the good of the righteous," 39:27. We find the same ideas in syncretistic traditions: "All (is) good for such a man (the righteous), even though it is bad for others," Corp. Herm., IX, 4, cf. Clemen, 337 f. on R. 8:28.

[33] Cf. J. Weiss, "Die Bdtg. d. Pls. f. den modernen Christen," ZNW, 19 (1919/20), 134 f.; Reitzenstein Hell. Myst., 115; A. Bonhöffer, Epiktet u. d. NT (1911), 319.

[34] Mi. R. on 8:28.

[35] Zn. R. on 8:28, n. 38.

[36] Cf. Pr.-Bauer, s.v. συνεργέω, Nestle and the comm., ad loc.

[37] Cf. Gennadius in Staab, 383: πάντα αὐτοῖς τὰ περὶ αὐτοὺς συμβαίνοντα γίνεσθαι παρασκευάζει πρὸς ἀγαθόν, also Theod. Mops., ibid., 141 f. For Jewish par. Str.-B., III, 255 f. e.g., R. Akiba acc. to bBer., 60b: "Man customarily says, All that He, the All-merciful, does, He does for good." Cf. also Mi. R. on 8:29.

2. The debated saying Jm. 2:22 [38] is perhaps to be explained as a rebuttal of misunderstandings of Pauline statements. The author is arguing for justification by works as seen in the example of Abraham. But he has to deal with Gn. 15:6, and he thus comes to the conclusion that faith works together with works → I, 452, 24 ff. [39] It is first knowable and visible in works, and in them it thus comes to fulfilment.

3. Outside the Pauline sphere συνεργός occurs only in 3 Jn. 8. We read here: συνεργοὶ γινώμεθα τῇ ἀληθείᾳ, [40] with the textual variant ἐκκλησίᾳ. By receiving itinerant Gentile missionaries members of the community work together for the propagation of the true message or for the Church. The dative is thus a dative of interest. It relates to the partnership of members of the community in their common ministry.

4. In the inauthentic Marcan ending at Mk. 16:20 [41] we find the familiar form of the absolute genitive in a comprehensive saying which refers back to v. 17, 18: τοῦ κυρίου συνεργοῦντος. With this we find a second absolute genitive which tells us in what the Lord's "working together" consists: He confirms the word, i.e., the apostles' message about Christ and their preaching, with signs following (→ III, 714, 4 ff.), thus bearing witness to Himself as the Risen Lord who has taken His seat of dominion at the right hand of God, Mk. 16:19. By means of this common formula the Marcan ending is thus declaring its belief in the Lord's present work. It attests to the fact that word and sign belong together, as also presupposed in Hb. 2:4 → 260, 14 ff. [42]

D. The Word Group in Early Christianity.

In Herm. s., 5, 6, 6, [43] in the allegory of Christ's person, the σάρξ is depicted as the handmaiden of the spirit which in sanctification and probity of walk has not stained it but rather laboured with it and (if the text is in order) [44] co-operated in the whole work of redemption. In Act. Thom. 24 (p. 139) God's grace works together with the painful (suffering) labour of the apostle who built the heavenly dwelling. In Just. Dial., 142, 2 we find a double gen. abs.: ἐπιτρέποντος τοῦ θεοῦ καὶ συνεργοῦντος, "with God's permission and co-operation." In Apol., 9, 4 the verb relates to co-operation in the sphere of idolatry, which is fatal for man.

Bertram

συνέρχομαι → II, 684, 26 ff.
σύνεσις   → 889, 1 ff.
συνετός   → 889, 26 ff.

---

[38] Cf. the debate in Hck. Jk. and Dib. Jk., *ad loc.*

[39] Dead works are works which are not from God; dead faith is faith which does not manifest itself. The concepts and their attributes are on different levels, cf. G. Eichholz, "Jakobus u. Pls.," *Theol. Ex.*, NF, 39 (1953), 23-51, who stress the difference on the one side and the unity on the other: "Since Paul's concern is for the true obedience of man he focuses everything on faith, and since James' concern is for total obedience he presses uncompromisingly for works," 40. The same conclusion is reached by the author in his "Pls. u. Jakobus," *Theol. Ex.*, NF, 88 (1961), 44 f.

[40] Wnd. Kath. Br., *ad loc.* cites Ps.-Clem. Hom., 17, 19.

[41] Cf. Hck. Mk., *ad loc.*, who transl. συνεργέω "promotes." The disciples' successes "are in a higher sense deeds of Christ who as the Risen Lord promotes their work."

[42] Cf. Loh. Mk., *ad loc.*

[43] Dib. Herm., *ad loc.*

[44] Dib. Herm., *ad loc.* rightly pts. out that the sentence is overloaded. If with him one follows the Lat., συνεργέω drops out.

$$\boxed{\dagger \; \text{συνέχω}, \; \dagger \; \text{συνοχή}}$$

† συνέχω.

1. συνέχω in Greek Usage.

The basic sense of συνέχω from Hom. is "to hold something together," [1] so that it does not fall apart but hangs together. The verb is used in the act., mid. and pass. in this sense. [2] Among derived and special uses the following are particularly significant.

a. "To hold together" so that something is maintained in good order: πᾶσα ἕξις καὶ δύναμις ὑπὸ τῶν καταλλήλων ἔργων συνέχεται καὶ αὔξεται, namely, going by the practice of going etc., Epict. Diss., II, 18, 1. [3] Esp. "law which upholds the state in unity": ἡ τὰ πάντα πολιτεύματα συνέχουσα εἰς ἓν δίκη, Plat. Leg., XII, 945d. [4] συνέχω is very commonly used of the relation of God to the cosmos; the deity holds the whole world together: οἵ (sc. the eternal gods) καὶ τήνδε τὴν τῶν ὅλων τάξιν συνέχουσιν ἀτριβῆ, Xenoph. Cyrop., VIII, 7, 22; cf. Mem., IV, 3, 13. Here συνέχω is a fixed term in formulating a fundamental concept of Gk. cosmology. How fixed it is may be seen already from Plato. Socrates opposes the natural philosophers who think they have found an Atlas who "holds together" all things (ἅπαντα συνέχοντα) better than this Atlas of ours, yet they think ὡς ἀληθῶς τὸ ἀγαθὸν καὶ δέον συνδεῖν καὶ συνέχειν οὐδέν, Plat. Phaed., 99c. It is virtues which hold the world together: φασὶ δ' οἱ σοφοὶ... καὶ οὐρανὸν καὶ γῆν καὶ θεοὺς καὶ ἀνθρώπους τὴν κοινωνίαν συνέχειν καὶ φιλίαν, Gorg., 507e-508a. In Stoicism συνέχω occurs with διήκω or διοικέω in describing the functions of the world soul: ὥσπερ δὲ ἡμεῖς ὑπὸ ψυχῆς διοικούμεθα, οὕτω καὶ ὁ κόσμος ψυχὴν ἔχει τὴν συνέχουσαν αὐτόν, Cornut. Theol. Graec., 2. [5] In Neo-Platonism divine beings of a certain rank are called συνοχεῖς. [6] This developed philosophical usage continues in the religious terminology of Hellenism. Dependence on philosophical

---

σ υ ν έ χ ω . Bibl.: Liddell-Scott, Moult.-Mill., s.v.; Wettstein on Mt. 4:24; Loh. Phil. on 1:23; E. Kutsch, "Die Wurzel עצר im Hbr.," VT, 2 (1952), 57-69.

[1] The sense "to have several things together" is formed only later: Ἀριστόδημος... δύο σχολὰς συνεῖχε, πρωὶ μὲν τὴν ῥητορικήν, δείλης δὲ τὴν γραμματικὴν σχολήν, Strabo, 14, 1, 48; cf. BGU, II, 577, 17 (3rd cent. A.D.). Very late and linguistically out of place is the use of συνέχω for ἀπέχω σύν τινι, "to hold something together with someone," P. Tebt., I, 242, 25. 27 (2nd cent. A.D.), cf. Preisigke Wört., s.v.; Moult.-Mill., s.v.

[2] E.g.: ὅθι ζωστῆρος ὀχῆες χρύσειοι σύνεχον, "where the golden clasps held the girdle together," Hom. Il., 4, 132 f.; ὁ δὲ καρπὸς... κἂν μὴ πλυθῇ... συνέχεται, Theophr. Hist. Plant., III, 15, 4; τὰ ἐμπί[π]τοντα συνέχηται [μέ]χρι τῆς εἰς Ἀλεξάνδρειαν ἀποστο[λ]ῆς, "those who fall into thy hands should be held (fast) until they are sent to Alexandria," P. Tebt., III, 1, 703, 220-222 (3rd cent. A.D.) (on the meaning and transl. of the neut. τὰ ἐμπίπτοντα, v. the editor's note, III, 1, p. 100).

[3] This explains the sentence in a petition: ἐρωτῶ σε ταχύτερον συσχεῖν τ[ὸ] πρᾶγμα "to arrange the matter as quickly as possible," P. Tebt., II, 410, 11-12 (1st cent. A.D.).

[4] Cf. of the Jewish Law: ταῦτα καὶ πολλὰ τούτοις ὅμοια τὴν πρὸς ἀλλήλους ἡμῶν συνέχει κοινωνίαν, Jos. Ap., 2, 208.

[5] Many instances in J. B. C. d'Anssee de Villoison and F. G. Osann, Cornutus de natura deorum (1844), 230-232, 413-415; also v. Arnim, II, 144-147; cf. F. Cumont, Les religions orient.⁴ (1929), 227, n. 57.

[6] Procl. Comment. in Platonis Parmenidem, 494 (ed. G. Stallbaum [1840], 184); Damascius Philosophus (5th-6th cent. A.D.), De Principiis, 96 (ed. C. E. Ruelle [1899]); M. Psellus, Hypotyposis, 4 f. in G. [W.] Kroll, De Oraculis Chaldaicis, Breslauer Philolog. Abhandlungen, 7, 1 1894, 73 f., cf. 19 Also quoted as the teaching of Pythagoras. Plat. and the Stoics is the fact that the cosmos is imperishable through the πρόνοια καὶ συνοχὴ θεοῦ Plut. De Placitis Epitome, II, 4, 2, Doxographi Graeci, ed. H. Diels² (1929), 331.

usage here is beyond question. [7] In cosmological speculations it is said of the first movement which brings forth universal nature (φύσις τοῦ παντός) acc. to its δύναμις, in plain dependence on Stoicism: διήκει διὰ τοῦ σύμπαντος κόσμου καὶ ἐντὸς συνέχει, Stob. Ecl., I, 289, 23 f.; elsewhere ἀνάγκη [8] (= εἱμαρμένη), [9] which is clearly distinguished from πρόνοια, is described as ἡ συνέχουσα καὶ περιέχουσα (sc. τὸν ὅλον κόσμον), ibid., I, 79, 24; cf. "Ερωτά τε καὶ 'Ανάγκην... ἐν τοῖς πρῶτα ἐγέννησεν, ὅπως αὐτῷ τὰ πάντα συνέχοιεν, Ael. Arist. Or., 43, 16. [10] The same terminology is to be found in the divine predications of Hellenism: μητέρι τῇ πάντων 'Ρείῃ... τε γενέθλῳ "Αττει θ⟨εῷ⟩ ὑψίστῳ καὶ συ[νέχο]ντι τὸ πᾶν, IG, 14, 1018, 1 f. (4th cent. A.D.): ἐπικαλοῦμαί σε, ἀέναε καὶ ἀγένητε, τὸν ὄντα ἕνα, μόνον τῶ[ν] πάντων συνέχοντα τὴν ὅλη[ν] κτίσιν, Preis. Zaub., II, 13, 841-843.

b. "To enclose," "lock up," e.g., of the skin which "encloses" the bones and flesh, Plat. Phaed., 98d; of a military force shut up behind protecting walls συνεῖχε τοῦ τείχους ἐντός, Plut. De Camillo, 23, 5 (I, 141a); cf. Polyb., 10, 39, 1; once of holding one's breath: συνέχοντας ὡς ἐπὶ τὸ πολὺ τὸ πνεῦμα, Strabo, 13, 4, 14. [11] In the Hell. period one finds the sense "to take or hold captive," esp. in the pap., [12] e.g. προσαπήγαγέν με εἰς φυλακὴν καὶ συνέσχεν ἐφ' ἡμέρας δ', P. Magd., 42, 7; οὗτος δὲ ἀπήγαγέν με εἰς ἀῶθι δεσμωτήριον, εἶπεν τῷ δεσμοφύ[λακι] δι' ἣν αἰτίαν συνέσχημαι, P. Lille, 7, 15. [13] This is also the meaning in the complaint of a woman against her husband who has run away: διὸ ἀξιῶ συντάξαι καταστῆσαι αὐτὸν ἐπὶ σὲ ὅπως ἐπαναγκασθῇ συνεχόμενος ἀποδοῦναί μοι τὴν [φ]ερνὴν σὺν ἡμιολίᾳ, "that he may be forced by imprisonment to pay me back one and a half the amount of the dowry," P. Oxy., II, 281, 23-28 (20-50 A.D.). [14] The expression εἶναι αὐτὸν ἀγώγιμον καὶ συνέχεσθαι μέχρι τοῦ ἐκτῖσαι κτλ. is a technical formula for imprisonment for debt in the pap. [15]

c. "To oppress," "overpower," "rule." This sense develops out of b. "to enclose," "hem in" in the transf. sense, and it may have either a physical or spiritual ref., cf. of poor sleep λυπεῖ καὶ συνέχει... καὶ σφίγγει (lit. "to tie together") τὸ σῶμα, Gal.; [16] to forbid knowledge of good and evil... μόνον ἔοικε συνέχειν τὸν νοῦν τὸν ἀνθρώπινον, Jul. Gal., I, 94 A. In this sense we usually find the pass. [17] with the reason (always given) in the dat. [18] The seriousness of the situation, esp. emphasised by συνέχω, is a constraint which seems to exclude any escape or alternative, whether the ref. be to a theoretical problem — πάσῃ συνεσχόμεθα ἀπορίᾳ, Plat. Soph., 250d — or to a desperate situation,

---

[7] It is doubtful whether like Cumont, op. cit. one can speak of a usage in the mysteries. Cumont's instance from Agorius Praetextatus in Zosimus Historia Nova, IV, 3, 3 (ed. L. Mendelsohn [1887]), where it is said of Eleusis τὰ συνέχοντα τὸ ἀνθρώπειον γένος ἁγιώτατα μυστήρια, is only part of a widespread Hell. use.
[8] Cf. the parallelism of πρόνοια and συνοχή → n. 6.
[9] Nock-Fest, III, p. LXXXI f.
[10] Cf. J. Amann, "Die Zeusrede d. Ael. Arist.," Tübinger Beiträge z. Altertumswissenschaft, 12 (1931), 76-79.
[11] Normally ἐπέχω is used for this as for stopping the ears (Ac. 7:57) → II, 816, n. 1; cf. Liddell-Scott, s.v. ἐπέχω.
[12] This use is not limited to the pap., cf. τὰ αἰχμάλωτα συνείχετο, Luc. Toxaris, 39.
[13] Further examples in Moult.-Mill. and Preisigke Wört,, s.v. There is a first ref. to this use in Deissmann B., 158.
[14] This passage is wrongly quoted under Phil. 1:23 (→ 883, 27 ff.) as an example of the abs. use of συνέχομαι, "to be oppressed," Moult.-Mill., s.v.
[15] Preisigke Wört., s.v.
[16] Gal. in Hippocratis de natura hominis Comm., III, 13 (CMG, V, 9, 1).
[17] The only example of the mid. "control oneself" is perhaps ἀλλὰ πείθετ[α]ι τὸ παραχρῆμα συνοχεθῆναι "he was persuaded to control himself" (cf. the editor's transl.), P. Tebt., III, 768, 17 f. (2nd cent. A.D.).
[18] Never in class. Gk. and only occasionally in Hell. Gk. is a prep. used for this, cf. [δ]ιὰ τὸ ἀσθενῆ με εἶναι τῇ ὁράσει καὶ ὑπὸ γήρους συνεχόμεν[ον], P. Oslo, III, 124, 11-13 (1st cent. A.D.); on the LXX → 881, 13 ff. and Test. XII → 882, 6 ff.

of a youngster πατρὶ συνείχετο ... ὀργὴν χαλεπῷ, Hdt., III, 131, 1; in a citizens' petition: καὶ τὴν μέλλουσαν δουληίην ὑπομεῖναι ἥτις ἔσται, μᾶλλον ἢ τῇ παρεούσῃ συνέχεσθαι, Hdt., VI, 12, 3; σπάνει βίου συνεχόμενος, "constrained by lack of the means of sustenance," Plut. Fluv., 7, 1 (II, 1153 f.). Worth noting is the use of the part. συνεχόμενος and συσχεθείς in the sense of "afflicted," "overpowered" with ref. to something that might cause death, esp. illnesses: εἰ μέν τις μεγάλοις καὶ ἀνιάτοις νοσήμασιν κατὰ τὸ σῶμα συνεχόμενος μὴ ἀπεπνίγη, Plat. Gorg., 512a; τινὰ ἰδεῖν τοιούτῳ συνεχόμενον πάθει, namely, scurvy, [19] leprosy and elephantiasis, Artemid. Onirocr., III, 47 (p. 187); πυρετῷ συσχεθεὶς οὐκ ἀπέστη τῶν στρατειῶν, ἕως οὗ ... ἀπέθανεν, Jos. Ant., 13, 398; [20] ἀγρυπνίαις συνεχόμενος, "driven by insomnia to despair," Ditt. Syll.[3], III, 1169, 51; "swept away" by violent emotions: Ismenos smitten by Apollo's bow, plunges into the river ἀλγηδόνι συνεχόμενος, Plut. Fluv., 2, 1 (II, 1150d); cf. Stymphelus ἀθυμίᾳ συσχεθείς, ibid., 19, 1 (II, 1162b); cf. 17, 3 (II, 1160c). On the other hand the philosopher Chrysippos supposedly died of a fit when he had given his ass unmixed wine to drink γέλωτι συσχεθέντα, Diog. L, VII, 185. "Being governed" by passions and impulses can also be expressed by συνεχόμενος, so of Commodus: ἀλλεπαλλήλοις καὶ διαφόροις συνεχόμενος ἡδοναῖς, αἷς δὴ καταλαβούσῃ ὥρᾳ καὶ ἄκων ἐδούλευεν, Herodian. Hist., I, 17, 9; ὀδυρμῷ συνείχοντο, Ael. Var. Hist., 14, 22; οἴκτῳ καὶ ἔρωτι συσχεθείς, Conon. Fr., 40, 3. [21] Of special interest in interpreting Phil. 1:23 (→ 883, 27 ff.) is a passage which speaks of double rule: οἱ μὲν ἰδιῶται δισσαῖς συνέχονται περιστάσεσιν ("distress"), ὑπό τε τῶν παθῶν αὐτῶν καὶ οὐχ ἧττον ὑπὸ τοῦ τὰς περιστάσεις ("situation") ταύτας κακὰς εἶναι φύσει δοκεῖν, Sext. Emp. Pyrrh. Hyp., I, 30.

2. συνέχω in the Septuagint.

a. The verb occurs 48 times in the LXX. In the main the use corresponds to the Gk. senses "to hold together," "to enclose," "to oppress," though with typical deviations due in part to the underlying Hbr. A Hbr. original is to hand in 31 instances, and 16 different Hbr. verbs are rendered by the term. Only one of these is frequently transl. συνέχω. In 17 instances there is no Hbr. equivalent; in 9 of these we have free or incorrect transl., while in the other 8 there is no Hbr. text.

b. The only word frequently rendered by συνέχω is עצר [22] (12 times). This root is the only significant equivalent in the OT, and συνέχω is the only Gk. word used more than occasionally for it. [23] But apart from Dt. 11:17 and 2 Εσδρ. 16:10 (Neh. 6:10) all the instances are in 1-4 Βασ. and 1-2 Chr. Again it is only in these OT works that derivates of עצר and similar roots are transl. by συνέχω: מַעְצוֹר "restraint," "obstacle" in 1 S. 14:6; [24] צוּר "to enclose" in 1 S. 23:8; [25] צָרַר "to bind together" in 2 S. 20:3. Outside

---

[19] ψώρα cf. τοὺς ὀφθαλμοὺς ἐν ψώρᾳ συνεχομένους, Philodem. Philos. Fr., 14 (ed. S. Sudhaus Philodemi Volumina Rhet., II [1896], 142 f.).
[20] Once the ref. seems to be only to light fever (πυραίτια), P. Oxy., VI, 896, 33 f. (316 A.D.), though 2 doctors are sent. But this account has come down only in mutilated form.
[21] FGrHist., I, 205, 11 f.
[22] Cf. Ges.-Buhl and esp. Kutsch.
[23] More than 20 Gk. words are used for עצר in the LXX, but apart from συνέχω none occurs more than 3 times and most of them only once.
[24] This word occurs only here in the OT. The LXX obviously did not understand the related מַעְצָר "restraint," "control" in Prv. 25:28.
[25] Cf. Dt. 20:19; in both instances צוּר means "to invest" in a siege, but LXX has συνέχω only at 1 S. 23:8, περικαθίζω being used at Dt. 20:19.

these books only the later translators used συνέχω for עצר elsewhere, e.g., Gn. 16:2; Is. 66:9; Jer. 20:9; 39(46):15; cf. also 1 Βασ. 21:6.

In rendering עצר etc. by συνέχω the LXX obviously uses the term always in the sense "to enclose." But this does not recapture the rich nuances of the Hbr. [26] Only when the latter is still not too far from the basic sense of "restrain" does the Gk. συνέχω get fairly close to the meaning, cf. the "holding back" of heaven so that there is no more rain, Dt. 11:17; 3 Βασ. 8:35; 2 Ch. 6:26; 7:13; [27] also of pestilence, 2 Βασ. 24:21, 25; and cf. the transl. of the derivate מעצור οὐκ ἔστιν τῷ κυρίῳ συνεχόμενον ("it is not barred to the Lord") σῴζειν ἐν πολλοῖς ἢ ἐν ὀλίγοις, 1 Βασ. 14:6. But the LXX is already off the mark in 1 Ch. 12:1: ἔτι συνεχομένου ἀπὸ προσώπου Σαουλ, the pt. of the HT being that David was shut off from dealings with Saul. 2 Εσδρ. 16:10 (Neh. 6:10) reads: καὶ ἐγὼ εἰσῆλθον εἰς οἶκον Σεμεϊ... καὶ αὐτὸς συνεχόμενος καὶ εἶπεν..., but the rendering συνεχόμενος is open to question here, just as the meaning of the basic עצר is contested. [28] It is best to take the HT to mean that he was under constraint since he had to tell the governor about a plot on his life. [29] In this case the LXX might well be using συνεχόμενος correctly in the sense of "constrained," though nowhere else in Gk. is the word used thus without indication of the reason; [30] hence the use shows us that in the translation Gk. of the LXX there is further departure from the original meaning than anywhere else, even to the pt. of omitting altogether the giving of the reason. There is undoubtedly misunderstanding of the HT at 1 Βασ. 21:8: καὶ ἐκεῖ (sc. in the sanctuary) ἦν ἐν τῶν παιδαρίων (servants) τοῦ Σαουλ... συνεχόμενος νεεσαρ [31] ἐνώπιον κυρίου. The Gk. transl. is saying that Saul's servant was detained in the temple but the meaning of HT נעצר is "to celebrate." [32] Finally συνεχόμενος is used for עצור in the archaic and up to quite recently disputed expression עצור ועזוב, which occurs 5 times in the OT at Dt. 32:36; 1 K. 14:10; 21:21; 2 K. 9:8; 14:26 and is 3 times rendered συνεχόμενος καὶ ἐγκαταλελειμμένος at 3 Βασ. 20:21; 4 Βασ. 9:8; 14:26. [33] This Gk. transl. "shut up and left" misses the most likely original sense of the HT "minors and adults." [34]

In none of the passages mentioned is there any question of a special sense under the influence of the basic Hbr. עצר. Even less may one detect any influence of the Hbr. on the Gk. word when in acc. with its original Gk. meaning this is used in the LXX for a whole series of Hbr. words.

c. The sense "to hold together" is quite rare: Ex. 26:3; 28:7; 36:11 (39:4 Mas.) for Hbr. חֹבְרֹת, 3 Βασ. 6:10 for אחז, 6:15 no Hbr., also Job 41:9. [35] In this connection it is simply worth noting that we find the Gk. cosmological use in Wis. 1:7: the Spirit of the Lord fills the circle of the earth καὶ τὸ συνέχον τὰ πάντα γνῶσιν ἔχει φωνῆς.

---

26 Cf. Köhler-Baumg., Ges.-Buhl, s.v. and the main senses in Kutsch, 57.

27 συνέχω is used in the same sense for כלא at Gn. 8:2.

28 On variour expository possibilities v. esp. W. Rudolph, Esra u. Neh. samt 3. Esra, Hndbch. AT, I, 20 (1949), ad loc. and Kutsch, 59 f.

29 Cf. Kutsch, 60.

30 On Lk. 12:50 → 884, 4 ff.

31 So acc. to L, which has the most accurate transcription of the Hbr. נעצר. B has νεεσσαραν through dittography of the following ἐν-ώπιον, while an ε has dropped out of A through haplography: νεσσαραν.

32 Cf. Kutsch, 67 and 65 f.

33 In Dt. 32:36 (again outside S., K., and Ch.) we have ἐν ἐπαγωγῇ καὶ παρειμένους for this. At 1 K. 14:10 (= 3 Βασ. 12:24m) the expression does not occur in LXX; it was added only by Orig. with ※ (ἐπεχόμενος καὶ ἐγκαταλελειμμένος, 3 Βασ. 14:10).

34 So acc. to Kutsch, 60-65, who also gives earlier explanations of this ancient legal formula.

35 For לכד here in the hitp. "to join together"; there is only one other instance in the hitp at Job. 38:30 "when ... the surface joins the flow" (G. Hölscher, Das Buch Hiob², Hndbch.

d. συνέχω is also used for other Hbr. equivalents in the sense "to enclose." 8 words are rendered thus either once or twice: אטר "to shut" Ps. 69:15; [36] אלם "to be dumb," "to close one's mouth" Ez. 33:22; חבק "to embrace" Prv. 5:20; כול "to hold" Jer. 2:13; [37] כלא "to hold back" Gn. 8:2; [38] לכד ni "to be taken captive" Job 36:8; [39] מנע "to hold back" Prv. 11:26; קפץ "to close" Is. 52:15; Ps. 77:9; cf. also צרר "to bind together" in 2 S. 20:3 and צור "to invest" in 1 S. 23:8. Closest to Hell. usage is "to shut up" in the sense "to take or hold captive," 2 Βασ. 20:3 (cf. 1 Macc.13:15); [40] 1 Βασ. 23:8; 2 Macc. 9:2. [41] Along these lines συνέχω also means "to shut" in a way which is quite in keeping with Gk. usage but coloured by the Hbr. original, e.g., of water in a cistern in Jer. 2:13; the mouth in Is. 52:15; Ez. 33:22; the mouth of a well in ψ 68:16; withholding grain in Prv. 11:26; [42] transf. "shutting up words in the heart" in Job. 38:2; of God "shutting up his mercy" in ψ 76:10. [43]

e. "To oppress," "overpower" is a sense which συνέχω bears only in Job and Wis. and once each in Jer. and 4 Macc. There are no Hbr. equivalents. Even where there is a Hbr. text the transl. is so free that συνέχω does not correspond to any specific term. In the pass. the usage is usually good Gk. with the agent of oppression in the dat. (→ 878, 29 f.); once in Jer. 23:9 we find a prepositional phrase, but this is not a Hebraism; [44] once in Job 7:11 no reason is given → lines 21 ff. The word is used positively for "being claimed" by affairs, Wis. 17:19 (20). Elsewhere it always denotes "inner oppression," whether by God Job 31:23; [45] Jer. 23:9, [46] or by spiritual pangs, 4 Macc. 15:32; Job 2:9d; [47] 3:24; [48] 10:1; [49] Wis. 17:10 (11). The only instance where there is no dat. of cause is ἀνοίξω πικρίαν ψυχῆς μου συνεχόμενος, Job 7:11. This is an abs. use, and it cannot be attributed to the Hbr. [50] One can only conclude that in the transl. Gk. of the LXX an abs. use of the pass. may occur, or the giving of the cause by a prepositional phrase. There is no discernible reason in the original Hbr. why this should be so.

AT, I, 17 [1952], ad loc.), i.e., freezes into ice. LXX has πρόσωπον δὲ ἀβύσσου τίς ἔπηξεν;
[36] The only instance in the OT.
[37] LXX read כלא here → n. 38.
[38] Cf. 'A at Jer. 32(39):2; → n. 27, 37.
[39] For the hitp of לכד → n. 35.
[40] συνέχω has the same sense in Ιερ. 39:2 'A (for כלא → n. 37, 38) and 46:15 'A (for עצר; LXX has φυλάσσω at 39:2).
[41] καὶ ἔδωκαν τὸν τοῖχόν μου ὡς συνεχόμενον ἐμοῦ καὶ αὐτῶν in Ez. 43:8 is a very free rendering of the HT; συνέχω is to be taken here in the neutral sense of "to enclose."
[42] The closing of the womb in Σ Gn. 16:2; Is. 66:9 (HT עצר; LXX συγκλείω or στεῖραν ποιέω).
[43] Mi. 7:18, however, is to be taken differently: οὐ συνέσχεν ... ὀργὴν ..., ὅτι θελητὴς ἐλέους ἐστίν. If this is not a mistranslation of אפו . . . לא־החזיק the meaning is: "He does not keep to his anger." In any case this use of συνέχω in transl. of חזק hi is very rare.
[44] συνεχόμενος ἀπὸ οἴνου is here the transl. of עברו יין
[45] Free transl. of the HT.
[46] On the transl. → n. 44.
[47] No HT for Job 2:9a-d.
[48] In total deviation from the HT.
[49] For אדברה במר נפשי but cf. Job 7:11 (→ n. 50) where συνεχόμενος is added to a similar expression; in neither case is there any basis in the original. πικρία in Job 10:1 is a correct indication of the cause of oppression in the dat., but in 7:11 πικρίαν is the acc. obj. of ἀνοίξω and there is thus no dat. of cause.
[50] In the HT אשיחה במר נפשי there is no support for συνεχόμενος → n. 49.

3. συνέχω in Later Jewish Literature.

a. In the Test. XII, as in Job, συνέχω is used almost exclusively in the sense "to oppress" etc. [51] The only pt. of interest is that the act., rare elsewhere, is here as common as the pass.: ἡ συνείδησίς μου συνέχει με, Test. R. 4:3;[52] οἱ τοῦ πνεύματος στεναγμοὶ συνέχουσί με, Test. Jos. 7:2; (πορνεία) συνέχει αὐτὸν ἐν πόνοις καὶ μόχθοις, Test. Jud. 18:4.[53] In the pass. the cause of oppression is never in the dat. but a prepos. phrase is always used: συνείχετο [54] ἀπὸ τῆς λύπης, Test. Jos. 8:5; ἐν τοῖς μιασμοῖς, Test. B. 8:3; ἐν λιμῷ, Test. Jos. 1:5. It is impossible to say how far this rests on the influence of a Semitic original. In sense the use of συνέχω is good Gk. in Test. XII. But the fact that the common dat. of cause (→ 878, 29 f.) is consistently replaced here by prepos. phrases can be explained only as a phenomenon of translation Greek.

b. In Philo [55] the verb is common, always in the sense "to hold together." The gen. use is rare, cf. ὑπὸ μιᾶς ὁλκοῦ δυνάμεως συνεχόμενοι of iron rings "held together" in a chain by a magnet, Op. Mund., 141; salt which "holds the body together," so that it does not decay, Spec. Leg., I, 289. We are already on the way to a technical philosophical use when the task of philosophy is said to be among other things that of investigating τὰς αἰτίας δι' ἃς ἐγένετο (sc. the individual parts of the world) καὶ δυνάμεις αἷς συνέχεται, Spec. Leg., III, 190. In this connection συνέχω is very common and it plays an important part in Philo's own thought. Philo himself shows it is taken over from the vocabulary of Gk. philosophy when he sometimes ref. to specific theories of Gk. cosmology concerning that which holds the world together both in detail and as a whole: the mountains are not destroyed by rain τῆς συνεχούσης αὐτὰ δυνάμεως (namely fire), Aet. Mund., 137; cf. λυθέντος γὰρ δεσμοῦ τοῦ συνέχοντος, loc. cit.; also Op. Mund., 131 on the moisture by which the earth is held together and prevented from crumbling. Among the conflicting theories of the world Philo also adduces the one acc. to which the universe does not perish διὰ τὸ κραταιοτέρῳ δεσμῷ, τῇ τοῦ πεποιηκότος βουλήσει, συνέχεσθαι, Rer. Div. Her., 246; cf. ἡ συνέχουσα φύσις, Aet. Mund., 37; also 75. Yet Philo's own opinion, taken from Stoic philosophy (→ 877, 20 ff.), is integrated into the Jewish belief in creation: ὁ δὲ ποιητὴς τῶν ὅλων, ὁ τοῦ κόσμου πατήρ, γῆν καὶ οὐρανὸν ὕδωρ τε καὶ ἀέρα καὶ ὅσα ἐκ τούτων ἑκάστου συνέχων καὶ διακρατῶν, Vit. Mos., II, 238; cf. Abr., 74; Sacr. AC, 40; Rer. Div. Her., 23. A variant of this Philonic view is the stress on the fact that this holding together of the world is by means of invisible forces (Migr. Abr., 181) or the logos (Fug., 112). Even here dependence on Stoic usage is plain, cf. esp. τοῦ συνέχοντος (sc. λόγου) καὶ διοικοῦντος τὰ σύμπαντα τὸ λογεῖον, Vit. Mos., II, 133. This introduction of philosophical usage into Jewish theology had at first no influence on primitive Chr. use. Only much later was there a similar penetration into Christianity. [56]

4. συνέχω in the New Testament.

In the NT the verb is more common only in Lk. and Ac. (together 9 times). It is very rare elsewhere (once in Mt., twice in Pl.). The basic sense "to hold together" (→ 877, 7 ff.) is not found in the NT; it occurs again only in the post-apost. fathers → 885, 7 ff.

---

[51] The only exception is in Test. Jos. 14:3: τί συνέχεις τὸν αἰχμάλωτον ... ἐν δεσμοῖς, "to hold captive."
[52] Cf. Wis. 17:10 → 881, 21.
[53] Cf. Job 2:9d → 881, 22.
[54] Only MS α uses the word, cf. R. H. Charles, ad loc.
[55] The few instances from Joseph. have already been dealt with under Gk. usage, → n. 4; → 879, 9 ff.
[56] Dg., 6, 7 → 885, 12 ff.

a. Variants of the sense "to enclose," "to close" are common in Luke's works. In a phrase not found elsewhere in Gk. (→ n. 11) we read in Ac. 7:57: συνέσχον τὰ ὦτα αὐτῶν, the members of the Sanhedrin stopped their ears so they would not have to hear the blasphemy of Stephen. [57] οἱ ἄνδρες οἱ συνέχοντες αὐτόν in Lk. 22:63 has the sense "to hold prisoner" which is also attested in the pap. → 878, 15 ff. In Lk. 8:45: οἱ ὄχλοι συνέχουσίν σε, and 19:43: οἱ ἐχθροί σου ... συνέξουσίν σε πάντοθεν, the primary meaning is simply "to surround" but with a plain undertone of "hemming in," esp. in 8:45 where it is used for the συνθλίβω of Mk. 5:31 and alongside ἀποθλίβω. Elsewhere, too, Luke sometimes puts συνέχω for other words in his source, → lines 13 ff., 21 ff.

b. In the sense "to oppress," "to rule" the verb is mostly in the passive in the NT, as in Gk. literature, and in good Gk. fashion the indication of cause is usually in the dative → 879, 4 f. The sway of diseases is often described thus → 878, 29 ff. In this way, as in Gk. usage, the severity of the sickness is clearly stressed: πενθερὰ τοῦ Σίμωνος ἦν συνεχομένη πυρετῷ μεγάλῳ, Lk. 4:38. Here, in contrast to Mk. 1:30: κατέκειτο πυρέσσουσα, the heightened emphasis in Luke is achieved not merely by the addition of μεγάλῳ but already by the use of the word συνέχω itself; for Lucan usage cf. also Ac. 28:8. In Mt., too, the word is once used in this way in a phrase which deviates from the source: ποικίλαις νόσοις καὶ βασάνοις συνεχομένους, Mt. 4:24. [58]

The verb occurs in a transferred sense at Lk. 8:37: φόβῳ μεγάλῳ συνείχοντο "they were gripped by great fear." This is again a sentence which Lk. has added independently to the Marcan original in Mk. 5:17. συνείχετο τῷ λόγῳ [59] ὁ Παῦλος in Ac. 18:5 means that after the coming of the brethren from Macedonia [60] Paul "could devote himself completely to, or let himself be totally claimed by, the task of preaching," → IV, 115, n. 190. [61] "To be claimed, totally controlled" is also the meaning of the verb in two passages in Paul's letters: 2 C. 5:14 and Phil. 1:23. It is the love of Christ which "completely dominates" Paul [62] (2 C. 5:14) so that on the basis of Christ's death the only natural decision for him, as for all other believers, is no longer to live for self but to live for Christ. This is how Paul defends his conduct before the Corinthians here; Christ's love claims him in such a way that in relation to others he can no longer exist for himself — in contrast to his opponents, who boast to the Corinthians that they are religious and spiritual, that they are

---

[57] Perhaps an ancient custom, cf. Haench. Ag., ad loc.

[58] Hence there is no need to see the hand of Luke the physician in such formulae; cf. also Τίμων δὲ συνείχετο πυρετῷ πολλῷ, Act. Barn., 15.

[59] ℵ pm syhmg read πνεύματι to show that the oppression is by a supernatural force, but this is not the original point. The text deviates even more to avoid the unusual though good Gk. expression; cf. Haench. Ag., ad loc.; Jackson-Lake, I, 3, 172. On this passage v. also E. Henschel, "Zu Ag. 18:5," Theol. Viat., II (1950), 213-5. Henschel tries to take συνέχομαι as a mid. here "to hold oneself in bounds" and transl. "Paul limited himself to his teaching and missionary work," 215. He admits, however, that he has not so far been able to find any examples of this mid. sense, 214.

[60] "Probably Timothy had brought a gift of money which enabled Paul to give up earning his way by manual work," Haench. Ag., ad loc.

[61] Cf. Jackson-Lake, I, 4, 224; also Haench. Ag., ad loc., n. 2.

[62] As in the preceding 2 C. 5:12 f. the plural ἡ γὰρ ἀγάπη τοῦ Χριστοῦ συνέχει ἡμᾶς is to be referred to Paul himself (perhaps along with his co-workers?), cf. Bl.-Debr. § 280; C. F. D. Moule, An Idiom Book of NT Greek² (1959), 118 f. → II, 356, 1 ff. with bibl.

something in themselves. [63] In the passive formulation in Phil. 1:23: συνέχομαι δὲ ἐκ τῶν δύο, the agent of control is indicated by a prepositional phrase. [64] This does not alter the sense: [65] "I am governed by two things," and am thus divided. [66]

Lk. 12:50: καὶ πῶς συνέχομαι ἕως ὅτου τελεσθῇ, causes the greatest difficulties in interpretation. The derivation and meaning of the double saying in Lk. 12:49 f. are not immediately apparent and have given rise to considerable debate. [67] The passive use of συνέχω in a transferred sense with no indication of cause would be quite unique and very hard to explain. The only parallel to this absolute use of the passive is συνεχόμενος in the LXX as a rendering of the Hebrew עָצוּר (→ 880, 10 ff.) "to hold back" or in a transferred sense "to be oppressed" Neh. 6:10 = 2 Εσδρ. 16:10). But this was not an established use in the LXX; only the exigencies of translation caused the solecism. The customary translation of πῶς συνέχομαι: "how troubled I am" [68] or "how pressed I am," [69] is hardly justified by the LXX use. [70] Yet even though the latter contributes nothing to the meaning of συνέχομαι in the absolute, the absolute use as such may still be regarded as under LXX influence. Only the context can decide the specific meaning in this verse. It is naturally correct that the baptism with which Jesus is to be baptised is His death. [71] But does this have to mean that συνέχομαι denotes fear of death? It is surely better to see parallelism [72] with the preceding saying about fire (Lk. 12:49: καὶ τί θέλω εἰ ἤδη ἀνήφθη), [73] which undoubtedly yields a positive translation: "How I am totally governed by this." Like the τί θέλω of the saying in v. 49, which rests on an Aramaic foundation, [74] the exclamatory πῶς in 12:50, in keeping with Hellenistic usage,

---

[63] The transl. "takes us captive" (→ I, 49, 33) is thus impossible in the context. Paul is not pointing out that all strife is ended by virtue of the fact that all are included together in the love of Christ, that they are one on the basis of His all-inclusive death, G. S. Hendry, "2 Cor. 5:14," Exp. T., 59 (1948), 82. The fact that Christ died for all, and that all are thus dead, means more in the context than that no one, even Paul as an apostle, can escape this. In exposition cf. Ltzm. K., ad loc.

[64] More correct would be συνέχομαι τοῖς δυσί, ἐκ τοῦ . . ., cf. Sext. Emp. Pyrrh. Hyp., I, 30 (→ 879, 19 ff.). On prepos. phrases for the dat. in Hell. lit. → n. 18, in Test. XII → 882, 4 ff.; cf. also Bl.-Debr. § 187, Intr.

[65] The use is not abs., and it is wrong to cite P. Oxy., II, 281, 25 (→ 878, 19 ff.) as a par.

[66] Loh. Phil., ad loc. is quite wide of the mark when he suggests "to be bound." The use here has nothing whatever to do with Paul's being a prisoner.

[67] Cf. the comm., ad loc., also esp. Bultmann Trad., 165 f. and Suppl.[2] (1962), 25 f.

[68] Kl. Mk., ad loc.; cf. Luther; Menge.

[69] Pr.-Bauer, s.v.; this at least avoids taking πῶς συνέχομαι as an expression of emotion on Jesus' part. The only basis for the transl. of K. H. Rengstorf, Das Ev. nach Lk., NT Deutsch, 3[9] (1962), ad loc. "How I am held fast to it," is the same LXX usage. Nor is it plain what "to hold fast" means here.

[70] Pr.-Bauer can adduce only one instance of συνεχόμενος without dat. ("tormented") in Leontius of Neapolis, Leben d. hl. Joh. d. Barmherzigen, Erzbischofs v. Alexandrien, 16 (ed. H. Gelzer [1893]), but this is from the 7th cent. A.D.

[71] Cf. O. Cullmann, Christologie d. NT[3] (1963), 66. In fact the only par. in which Jesus speaks of His being baptised (Mk. 10:38) is to the same effect; but → n. 77; on the whole subject → I, 538, 28 ff.

[72] Wellh. Lk., ad loc. is dubious about the parallelism, since v. 49 ref. to a "general work which Jesus longs to do" and v. 50 to "a passing personal experience." The latter would at most be true only if v. 50 were the reminiscence of a personal saying of Jesus, but on this → n. 77. Certainly the community did not view Jesus' death as a passing personal experience.

[73] It makes no difference at this pt. whether the two sayings were originally linked or whether 12:50 was added by Lk. Bultmann Trad., 165 f. tries to expound the two as a unity in terms of Gnostic myth, but runs into serious difficulties.

[74] Cf. M. Black, An Aramaic Approach to the Gospels and Acts[2] (1954), 87-89.

expresses a strong wish. [75] This is a further sign that only Luke himself, who almost alone in the NT uses συνέχω, [76] can have formulated the expression. As Luke understands it, the saying thus expresses the direction of Jesus' path to a martyr's death. [77] Like the fire (→ VI, 944, 7 ff.) which Jesus has come to kindle (12:49), Jesus' death is the beginning of the age of the Church (12:50).

5. συνέχω in the Post-Apostolic Fathers.

In the sense "to hold together," which does not occur in the NT, συνέχω is used 3 times in the post-apost. fathers in typically Gk. formulations: the inscrutable judgments of the underworld are "upheld" by the same ordinances (τοῖς αὐτοῖς συνέχεται προστάγμασιν) as those by which the cosmos is also ruled, 1 Cl., 20, 5. The influence of the philosophical cosmological vocabulary of Hellenism on this expression is plain to see; [78] indeed, the whole of 1 Cl., 20 is governed by the same Hell. terminology. [79] In Dg., 6, 7 the function of maintaining the order of the cosmos, which is assigned in Gk. philosophy (and esp. Philo) to the Godhead or the *logos,* is transferred to Christ: As the soul is enclosed in the body, [80] but yet holds it together (συνέχει), so Christians are held (κατέχονται) in the cosmos as in a prison, "but they hold the world together" (αὐτοὶ δὲ συνέχουσι τὸν κόσμον). [81]

Like Paul (→ 883, 26 ff.), Ign. uses the word once in the sense "to constrain," "to rule": συμπαθείτω μοι, εἰδὼς τὰ συνέχοντά με, R., 6, 3. Ign. asks that nothing be put in his path to martyrdom, but that there should be understanding [82] of "what totally dominates him," namely, the urge for martyrdom. [83] In the post-apost. fathers one also finds the adv. συνεχῶς ("unceasingly," "continually") at Barn., 21, 8; this does not occur in the NT.

---

[75] On the exclamatory πῶς (for ὡς) cf. πῶς . . . ἀκοῦσαι βούλομαι, Corp. Herm., I, 3; *v.* also Nock-Fest., I, 10, n. 6; Bl.-Debr. § 436; Moule, *op. cit.,* 207.

[76] Neither Mk. nor the Q source in Mt. has this word. Where Lk. uses it, it is in his own formulations. Perhaps one might say that Lk. formulates "biblically" here.

[77] It seems to me that the saying about the baptism of death in Mk. 10:38 is a *vaticinium ex eventu* and that it is thus a formulation of the community. Lk. omitted it in his reproduction of Mk. 10 in Lk. 18 but used it as the basis of 12:50 instead.

[78] → 8 ˙, 20 ff. Philo also took συνέχω from the vocabulary of philosophy → 882, 15 ff.

[79] Cf. on this Kn. Cl. on 1 Cl., 20, 1; W. Jäger, "Echo eines unerkantten Tragiker-Fr. in Clemens' Brief an d. Kor.," *Rhein. Mus.,* NF, 102 (1959), 330-340.

[80] On this idea cf. H. I. Marrou, "A Diognète," *Sources Chrétiennes,* 33 (1951), 66.

[81] Cf. Marrou, *op. cit.,* 144-149; for the further development of the idea 149-176.

[82] συμπαθέω here certainly does not mean "to have sympathy" but either has the sense of συμπάσχω in R. 8:17; Ign. Pol., 6, 1 (→ V, 926, 12 f.) or it means "to understand" (→ V, 936, 14 ff.) Bau. Ign., *ad loc.*

[83] The transl. "what oppresses me" in Bau. Ign., *ad loc.* runs into the difficulty that neither συνέχω without indication of cause nor the context in Ign. justifies this understanding.

† συνοχή.

1. Greek Usage.

The noun συνοχή corresponds to the verb συνέχω in its various senses. It thus means "holding together," "oppression," "prison." [1] For the first cf. the use with ref. to clothes, Apoll. Rhod., I, 744, also Epict. Diss., IV, 11, 12. [2] For the second the "press of battle," Apoll. Rhod., I, 160; οἱ ἐν συνοχῇ ὄντες are the poor, slaves, prisoners etc., Artemid. Oneirocr., II, 3 (p. 88). The third sense is rare, P. Lond., II, 354, 24 (10 B.C.). In the second sense the word bears a special nuance in the usage of ancient astrology. It denotes here the misfortune indicated by unfavourable constellations, thus an eclipse of the sun in the second decade of the ram: βασιλέων συνοχὴν καὶ πολλὴν ἀδημονίαν, Catal. Cod. Astr. Graec., VIII, 1, p. 267, 5; [3] earthquakes in the sign of the lion: ἐν ἐκείνῳ τῷ τόπῳ γενήσονται καὶ συνοχαὶ θλίψεως· καὶ νόσος ἔσται τοῖς ἀνθρώποις, ibid., V, 4, p. 163, 2-3; cf. also οὐκ ἀπολυθήσῃ τῆς συνοχῆς, Astrampsychus Oraculorum decades, CIII, 42, 8; [4] καλῶς ἀπολυθήσῃ τῆς συνοχῆς, ibid., 48, 9 f.; εἰς συνοχὰς ἥξουσι σιδηρήεντά τε δεσμά, Manetho Astrologus Apotelesmaticorum, I[V], 313. [5] συνοχή thus comes to mean "anxiety," "despair," quite clearly in the following passages on the basis of astrological pronouncements concerning those born under the sign of Capricorn: ἔσται ὀλιγόψυχος ... ἀπὸ συνοχῆς πνεύματος κίνδυνον σχῇ, Catal. Cod. Astr. Graec., XII, p. 189, 15 f.

2. The Greek Old Testament.

In the LXX the word occurs only in Ju. 2:3; Job 30:3; 38:28 (Cod. A and V); Jer. 52:5; Mi. 4:14. In the first 3 instances the Hbr. original is not clear. In the last 2 συνοχή is used for מָצוֹר "affliction," [6] usually περιοχή in LXX. [7] In the later transl. συνοχή also occurs for עָצַר at ψ 106:39; Prv. 30:16, מֵצִיק at ψ 118:143; cf. ψ 24:17, קְפָדָה at Ez. 7:25. These are Hbr. words for affliction. Once we also find the meaning "prison" here; instead of εἰς οἰκίαν τῆς φυλακῆς at Ιερ. 44:15 Σ has εἰς οἶκον συνοχῆς for לְבֵית הַכֶּלֶא, Jer. 37:15. Of significance is the role συνοχή "affliction" took on in the usage of the Ps. in later translations, cf. αἱ θλίψεις τῆς καρδίας μου ἐπλατύνθησαν ἐκ τῶν συνοχῶν μου, ψ 24:17 Ἀ (LXX ἐκ τῶν ἀναγκῶν); θλιμμὸς καὶ συνοχὴ εὗρόν με, ψ 118:143 Ἀ (LXX θλῖψις καὶ ἀνάγκε εὕροσάν με); ἀπὸ συνοχῆς κακῆς καὶ ταλαιπωρίας, ψ 106:39 Σ (LXX ἀπὸ θλίψεως κακῶν καὶ ὀδύνης). συνοχή thus became a substitute for θλῖψις or a par. to this or synon. words in the sense "oppression," "trouble." [8]

3. In the New Testament.

συνοχή occurs twice in the NT. ἐκ γὰρ πολλῆς θλίψεως καὶ συνοχῆς καρδίας ἔγραψα ὑμῖν in 2 C. 2:4 corresponds entirely to the usage of the Ps. in later versions

---

συνοχή. [1] Cf. Liddell-Scott, s.v.
[2] Cf. the philosophical use already mentioned s.v. συνέχω, → 877, 20 ff.; n. 6.
[3] Cf. σημαίνει in connection with an eclipse in the first decade, also σημεῖον in Lk. 21:25 → 232, 15 ff.
[4] Ed. R. Hercher (1863), 24, 26.
[5] Ed. A. Koechly (1858), 97.
[6] → 879, 31 ff.: συνέχω for עצר, צוּר and צרר.
[7] 4 Βασ. 19:24; 24:10; 25:2; 2 Ch. 32:10 etc.
[8] In Test. XII and Philo we do not find the noun συνοχή at all, but it occurs once in Ep. Ar. (61), cf. also Jos. Ant., 8, 65.

→ 886, 23 ff. Paul is referring to the tribulation and affliction which he suffered through hostility at Corinth. He uses the same terms as those used by the OT Psalmist when speaking of the distress which God's enemies caused him.

The background is quite different at Lk. 21:25: καὶ ἔσονται σημεῖα ἐν ἡλίῳ καὶ σελήνῃ καὶ ἄστροις, καὶ ἐπὶ τῆς γῆς συνοχὴ ἐθνῶν ἐν ἀπορίᾳ ἤχους θαλάσσης. The first half of this sentence is a free adaptation of Mk. 13:24 f., but from καὶ ἐπὶ τῆς γῆς on it is wholly by the pen of Luke, for whom ψ 64:8 served in part as a model. [9] Yet only the reference to the raging of the sea comes from the Ps.; there is no support in the usage of the Greek OT for the employment of συνοχή to denote the "anxious fears of mankind at the raging of the elements." [10, 11] It should also be noted that, in distinction from Mk. 13:24 f., Lk. 21:25a does not speak of a stellar disaster as part of the general cosmic catastrophe at the end of apocalyptic confusion, but rather of stellar signs (→ 232, 18 ff.) [12] evoking "unease and anxiety" among men: [13] συνοχή ... ἐν ἀπορίᾳ. This is to be seen as parallel to ἀποψυχόντων ... ἀπὸ φόβου in Lk. 21:26. [14] According to Luke, then, the *parousia* is preceded, not by an apocalyptic collapse of the cosmic order, but by astrological constellations which bode disaster and which thus make men mortally afraid. This is not, of course, a reason why Christians should be afraid, for they know that these signs indicate the closeness of their redemption, Lk. 21:28.

4. συνοχή occurs only once in the post-apost. fathers: ἐν συνοχῇ δὲ γενόμενος, Did., 1, 5, in a free rendering of Mt. 5:25 f. for εἰς φυλακὴν βληθήσῃ. Here, then, συνοχή means "prison," a meaning current at the time. [15]

Köster

συνθάπτω   → 786, 21 ff.

---

[9] ψ 64:8: ὁ συνταράσσων τὸ κύτος τῆς θαλάσσης, ἤχους κυμάτων αὐτῆς. ταραχθή-σονται τὰ ἔθνη (cf. ψ 64:9: ἀπὸ τῶν σημείων).

[10] Kl. Lk., *ad loc.*

[11] In later transl. of the Ps. συνοχή simply denotes personal oppression by enemies → 886, 27 ff.

[12] Here in Lk. as in the astrological texts cited (→ 886, 7 ff.) σημεῖον ref. to stellar constellations.

[13] In distinction from Mk., Lk. 21:26 distinctly says οἰκουμένη. This word is taken from contemporary Gk. usage and denotes the world of men in contrast to the uninhabited cosmos, → V, 157, 4 ff.

[14] There are par. to Lk. 21:26 in profane Gk., but not in LXX or Jewish apocalyptic, cf. Kl. Lk., *ad loc.*

[15] On the corresponding meaning of συνοχή in the pap. → 886, 8 f.; 886, 15 ff. But LXX does not use the word in this sense, although cf. Ιερ. 44:15 Σ → 886, 25 ff.

---

† συνίημι, † σύνεσις,
† συνετός, † ἀσύνετος

A. The Word Group in Profane Greek.

1. The verb συνίημι or ξυνίημι[1] means primarily "to bring together," e.g., to battle, Hom. Il., 1, 8 etc., mid. "to come together," "to come to an agreement," e.g., Hom. Il., 13, 381; this sense not in the NT. Trans. the verb means "to perceive," Hom. Od., 1, 271, primarily by hearing, "to accept something by hearing" and to follow it, e.g., an ἔπος, Od., 6, 289.[2] It is usually construed with gen. of the person or thing heard: γλώσσης ἀνθρωπίνης, Plut. Sept. Sap. Conv., 4 (II, 150e) and acc. of the content, Il., 2, 182.[3] More broadly it means "to note" οὐ ξυνεὶς δόλον Ἕλληνος ἀνδρὸς οὐδὲ τὸν θεῶν φθόνον, Aesch. Pers., 361 f.; and gen. "to understand," e.g., a language, Hdt., IV, 114, 2; Thuc., I, 3, 4; Xenoph. An., VII, 6, 9; Cyrop., I, 6, 2, or a thing: τὸ γεγονὸς τοῦτο, Hdt., III, 63, 4; τὰ ναυτικά, Xenoph. Hist. Graec., I, 6, 4; cf. also Soph. Ant., 403; Plat. Parm., 128a. If the group first denotes an activity, in the pre-Socratics already it comes to be used more and more for a faculty, i.e., intelligence, understanding, Heracl. Fr., 51 (Diels, I, 162). In Alcmaion Fr., 1a (Diels, I, 215, 1 ff.), i.e., the earliest accessible stratum of Pythagoreanism, ξυνιέναι is a specifically human faculty, other beings having only αἰσθάνεσθαι.[4] The same applies to the noun, Democr. Fr., 77 (Diels, II, 160); 181 (II, 181 f.); 183 (II, 182). The Sophists had a hand in developing the meaning; their intellectualism is reflected in this as in other groups.[5] But this was obviously viewed with some distrust in Athens, cf. the meagre findings in Plato.[6] Neither verb nor noun achieved the status of a philosophical term.[7]

συνίημι κτλ. Bibl. Boisacq, s.v.; Levy Wört., Levy Chald. Wört., Jastrow, s.v. ידע, שׁכל, בין and derivates; J. Botterweck, "'Gott erkennen' im Sprachgebrauch d. AT," Bonner Bibl. Beiträge, 2 (1951); H. Braun, "Spät.-jüd.-häretischer u. frühchr. Radikalismus, I," Beiträge z. Hist. Theol., 24 I (1957), esp. 20 f.; W. Nestle, "Thukydides u. d. Sophistik," NJbch. Kl. Alt., 17 (1914), 653 f.; also Vom Mythos z. Logos (1940), 257, 471, 496, 517; F. Nötscher, "Zur theol. Terminologie d. Qumrantexte," Bonner Bibl. Beiträge, 10 (1956), 52-79; B. Snell, "Die Ausdrücke f. den Begriff des Wissens in der vorplatonischen Philosophie," PhU, 29 (1924), 16-20, 40-59.

[1] Snell, 18.

[2] Ibid., 40-53 on the obj. up to Pindar.

[3] Kühner-Blass-Gerth, II, 1, 357-359; the gen. is the rule when verbs of hearing mean "to note something," 359, n. 6; cf. Schwyzer, II, 107.

[4] On the other hand Democr. A, 135 (Diels, II, 119, 26 ff.) expressly identifies ξύνεσις and αἴσθησις [Dihle].

[5] Nestle Thukydides, 653 f.

[6] Snell, 57. In authentic works the noun occurs 11 times. 5 are in the "etymologies" of Crat: 411a (2), 412a c, 437b. (On Crat. cf. J. Abramczyk, Zum Problem d. Sprachphilosophie in Platons "Kratylos," Diss. [1928]; K. Buchner, Platons Kratylus u. d. moderne Sprachphilosophie [1936]). The other instances are Soph., 228d; Polit., 259c; Phileb., 19d; Phaedr., 232c; Menex., 237d; Resp., II, 376b. Plat. is aware of the Sophistical origin of the concept, cf. Euthyd., 278a: Prodicos taught differentiation between μανθάνειν and συνιέναι. Aristoph. Ra., 893 scoffs at Eur. for following the Sophists and worshipping new gods, among them (in a series of related concepts) Ξύνεσις.

[7] The role of the group is not to be compared to that of groups of similar sense like νοέω/νοῦς etc.; γινώσκω/γνῶσις, for its themes are less ontological and more hermeneutical, and hence more remote for the Greek. It was not handled epistemologically in philosophy, Snell, 51 f. If one asks about the phenomenon of insight in Plat., one must look at νοέω/νοῦς, cf. G. Krüger, Einsicht u. Leidenschaft[2] (1948), pass. (v. Index).

2. The noun σύνεσις means lit. "union," e.g., of two rivers, Hom. Od., 10, 515, 8 transf. rapid "comprehension," Thuc., III, 82, 7 in the famous description of the perversion of basic concepts. Hesych., 2540 declares: σύνεσις· νόησις.

In the peripatetic Agatharchides σύνεσις is obviously an ethnographic term; it denotes the native practical intelligence of a primeval people. 9 In the class. age there are only the beginnings of a def. in Aristot. σύνεσις is a φυσικὴ δύναμις: ὡς γὰρ ἐν ἀνθρώπῳ τέχνη καὶ σοφία καὶ σύνεσις, οὕτως ἐνίοις τῶν ζῴων ἐστί τις ἑτέρα τοιαύτη φυσικὴ δύναμις, Hist. An., VIII, 1, p. 588a, 29-31. Eth. Nic. goes further. The starting-point is the division of virtues into dianoetic and ethical. The former are σοφία, σύνεσις, φρόνησις, I, 13, p. 1103a, 3-7. Book 6 is devoted to them. σύνεσις is below φρόνησις. It has the same object but in contrast to φρόνησις judges rather than commands. It leads only to a δόξα, for it has to do neither with the unmoved which always is nor with that which becomes, but only with what can be the object of doubt and reflection, VI, 11, p. 1143a, 6-18. It is also under φρόνησις in Chrysipp., who integrates it into the Stoic system of the cardinal virtues and their subsidiaries: ἕπονται δὲ τῇ μὲν φρονήσει εὐβουλία καὶ σύνεσις· τῇ δὲ σωφροσύνῃ εὐταξία καὶ κοσμιότης· τῇ δὲ δικαιοσύνῃ ἰσότης καὶ εὐγνωμοσύνη· τῇ δὲ ἀνδρείᾳ ἀπαραλλαξία καὶ εὐτονία, Chrysipp. Fr. Moralia, 295 (v. Arnim, III, 73, 5-7). The term did not undergo any further development in later Gk. 10

A survey of the usage shows that the word was used gen. for the formal side of perceiving, esp. hearing, and thus for understanding, which is closely connected to learning (→ n. 6), 11 for the "ability to judge." It was often associated with similar terms. 12 Antonyms are ἀξυνεσία, Thuc., III, 42, 3, ἀπαιδευσία, Thuc., III, 42, 1, ἄγνοια, Plat. Resp., II, 376b; Aristot. An., I, 5, p. 410b, 2. σύνεσις is a virtue of the hero and ruler. 13 The group finally takes on the sense of "self-awareness." 14

3. The adj. συνετός (similarly ἀσύνετος) means act. "understanding," e.g., Zeus and Apollo are ξυνετοί καὶ τὰ βροτῶν εἰδότες, Soph. Oed. Tyr., 497 f., pass. "understand-able," e.g., λόγος συνετός, Ps.-Aristot. Rhet. Al., 1, p. 1420b, 12. Like the verb and noun it needs closer definition, e.g., παιδείας ἀσύνετος, Dio Chrys. Or., 2, 75; cf. Sir.

---

8 Hence the transf. meaning in Plot. Enn., VI, 5, 10: χωρὶς ἕκαστος εἰς τὸ φρονεῖν ἀσθενής, συμβάλλων δὲ εἰς ἓν πᾶς ἐν τῇ συνόδῳ καὶ τῇ ὡς ἀληθῶς συνέσει τὸ φρονεῖν ἐγέννησε καὶ εὗρε.

9 Agatharchides in Photius Bibliotheca, 1360 R (ed. J. Bekker [1825]), p. 454a, 35-455b, 2 [Dihle].

10 The noun does not occur in Epict., the adj. συνετός is found at Diss., I, 28, 20 and 21; cf. II, 13, 21. σύνεσις is chiefly the quality of a hero in Plut.

11 Obj. τὰ λεγόμενα, Plat. Prot., 325c; τὰ γεγραμμένα, 325e; τί τὸ λεγόμενόν ἐστιν, Aristot. An. Post., I, 1, p. 71a, 13. On understanding and learning (→ n. 6) cf. Aristot. Eth. Nic., VI, 11, p. 1143a, 1-24. "To know a thing well," Jos. Ant., 2, 76; "expertise," Aristot. Pol., VIII, 7, p. 1342b, 8 f. Synon. ἐπιστήμη in medical writers, Snell, 55.

12 With σοφία Aristot. Eth. Nic., I, 13, p. 1103a, 3-7, a combination we shall find in the OT, Judaism and NT; with παιδεία, Ditt. Or., I, 323, 7; λόγος, Plut. Bruta Animalia Ratione Uti, 10 (II, 992c); φρόνησις, Plat. Crat., 411a; Philo Sobr., 3; ἐπιστήμη, Plat. Crat., 437b. We often have whole series, Aristoph. Ra., 957; Plat. Crat., 411 f. cf. Philo Gig., 27; Plat. Phileb., 19d → n. 13.

13 With ἀρετή, Thuc., IV, 81, 2; cf. esp. Plut., e.g., with τόλμα, De Alcibiade, 21, 4 (I, 202a) etc.; πίστις, De Marcello, 9, 4 (I, 302 f.); φρόνησις, Philo Leg. Gaj., 33. The term also turns up in the lists of virtues in Poll. Onom., IV, 10; Philo Leg. All., III, 205; Vit. Mos., I, 154 etc.; Plut. Amat., 23 (II, 769b); Athenag. Suppl., 1, 15; 7, 52. In contrast the reproach of folly always has a moral tinge in Gk. The Homeric heroes make mistakes through ἀφραδίη [Dihle].

14 οὐδὲ συνῆκα ἡδὺς γυναικὶ διὰ σὲ γεγενημένος, Luc.. Dialogi Deorum, 2, 1. The noun can thus approximate to συνείδησις, Eur. Or., 396 in Plut. Tranq. An., 19 (II, 476 f.); v. also Polyb., 18, 43, 13.

15:7; Test. L. 7:2. The charge of lack of understanding may have a moral tinge, Jos. Bell., 6, 170; Ant., 1, 117. The object is described in a passage which is of special interest in view of its kinship to Ac. 17:27: [15] (of men) ἅτε γὰρ οὐ μακρὰν οὐδ' ἔξω τοῦ θείου διῳκισμένοι καθ' αὐτούς, ἀλλ' ἐν αὐτῷ μέσῳ πεφυκότες, μᾶλλον δὲ συμπεφυκότες ἐκείνῳ καὶ προσεχόμενοι πάντα τρόπον, οὐκ ἐδύναντο μέχρι πλείονος ἀξύνετοι μένειν, i.e., in face of the witness to the divine in nature, in man, Dio Chrys. Or., 12, 28.

B. The Word Group in the Old Testament.

The group is very common in the LXX, esp., of course, in the Wisdom lit. [16] The material peculiarities of the Gk. as compared to the Hbr. are of little account. [17] since the Gk. and Hbr. terms for understanding converge. This is related to the fact that the Gk. group did not attain philosophical dignity → 888, 20 ff. Equivalents are בּין and derivates, שׂכל and derivates, also ידע etc. [18] בּין hi and שׂכל hi, like συνίημι, mean "to perceive," "to note," esp. by hearing (1 K. 3:9; 2 S. 12:19; Ps. 5:1), "to understand" Is. 40:21; Mi. 4:12. In the OT, too, both verb and noun occur along with synonyms. [19]

A difference from Greek thought is that in the OT insight is not a faculty native to man as such. It is the gift of God, 1 K. 3:9; Da. 2:21. One prays God for it, Ps. 119:34. Primarily it is proper to Him. [20] He can withdraw it, Is. 29:14. Dominant here, as throughout OT thought, is practical judgment rather than a theoretical understanding of the world, 2 Ch. 1:10 LXX. 1 Βασ. 2:10 tells us what it means "to understand and know" God. The organ of insight is the heart (Is. 6:9 f.), while the objects are Yahweh's works (Ps. 28:5; Job 36:29), the fear of Yahweh (Prv. 2:5), right and righteousness (Prv. 2:9), the totality of His work and will (Ps. 111:10), or, Hellenistically, wisdom (Wis. 3:9). Prv. 2:1 ff. offers a compendium.

Though insight is a gift, one has to seek it. Lack of understanding is a fault and is punished — a basic thought in the Wisdom lit., Prv. 2:1 ff. etc., cf. R. 1:21 f. The special feature of the Wisdom lit. is its working out of the ideal of the man of understanding. [21] This includes, of course, the fact that he knows to whom he owes wisdom. [22] A certain development may be observed. In more ancient wisdom the

---

[15] E. Norden, *Agnostos Theos* (1913), 18 f.; M. Pohlenz, "Pls. u. d. Stoa," ZNW, 42 (1949), 92 f.; B. Gärtner, "The Areopagus Speech and Natural Revelation," *Acta Seminarii Neotestamentici Upsaliensis*, 21 (1955), 109-112.

[16] Note a shift in favour of the noun from Ps. to Sir. With the forms of συνίημι one finds those of the newer συνιέω, also in the NT → 892, 17 ff. Apart from constructs found in the NT one finds συνετίζω and the barbarous hapax legomenon συνετίζομαι, Jer. 10:8 ᾽Α; συνετέω in ψ 118:158, however, is a misreading for συνθετέω.

[17] Prv. shows peculiarities of transl. Cf. G. Bertram, "Vom Wesen d. Septuaginta-Frömmigkeit," *Welt d. Orients*, 2 (1956), 274-284, esp. 277 f.

[18] Köhler-Baumg., *s.v.* We may ignore the profane sense of שׂכל hi "to enjoy success." Here, too, ᾽Α follows his principle of the consistent transl. of a Hbr. word by a Gk. word; בּינה == σύνεσις, שׂכל == ἐπιστήμη etc.; for Is. 52:13 he coins the verb ἐπιστημονίζω; cf. on this H. Hegermann, "Js. 53 in Hexapla, Targum u. Peschitto," BFTh, II, 56 (1954), 28 f.

[19] Is. 11:2; 43:10; 44:18; Jer. 9:23; Job 12:13; Prv. 2:1 ff.; 4:5, 7; LXX Sir. 1:19; Bar. 3:20 f.

[20] G. v. Rad, *Theol. d. AT*, I (1958), 440-451.

[21] Cf. the use of the adj. in Sir. ἀσύνετος does not occur in Prv. LXX, though one finds it in ᾽Α at 1:22 (LXX ἀσεβεῖς); 30:2 and Θ at 17:12.

[22] There is no understanding against Yahweh, v. Rad, *op. cit.*, 437 f.; H. Gese, *Lehre u. Wirklichkeit in d. alten Weisheit* (1958), 49 f.

appeal to understanding is motivated by a reference to God's will, but in later writings it is motivated by a more specific reference to the Law. [23] A full identification of wisdom with the Torah is achieved in Sirach. [24]

C. The Word Group in Judaism.

1. The Qumran Texts.

Here, too, בִּין, [25] שֵׂכֶל (and יָדַע) are in practice synon., [26] as their association shows; [27] as regards the nouns שֵׂכֶל and בִּינָה are more common than חָכְמָה (and דַּעַת). [28] Understanding is the prerequisite for acceptance into the sect. The candidate is examined on entry "concerning the measure of his understanding and acts (in the Torah)," 1 QS 5:21 ff. [29] But as in the OT understanding is not native to man. All insight comes from the "God of perceptions," 1 QS 3:15 f.; cf. 4:22; 1 QH 1:8 ff.; 10:1 ff.; 12:33 ff. etc. [30] He can enlighten hearts, 1 QS 2:3 and He can also conceal the source of understanding, 1 QH 5:26. He for His part knows men (1 QH 7:26) and pays heed to their works (Damasc. 1:10 [1:7]) which He knows before they exist (2:7 f. [2:6 f.]). Life depends on knowledge, 1 QS 2:3. This is yielded by its object, the "deeds," "wonders" of God, the "mysteries." [31] The primarily formal descriptions acquire a concrete sense from the specific self-understanding of the sect. This views itself as the group of elect in the endtime. It experiences its election in its coming to know God's acts in history, Damasc. 1:1 f. (1:1 f.), in its insight into the basis of election, into predestination, 1 QS 3:13 ff., in its grasping of the sequence of eschatological events, 1 QS 4:18 ff. The condition of salvation is the understanding of God's judgments, 1 QS 4:15. Hence an essential theme is the Law in the radicalised understanding of the sect, 1 QS 1:12; 3:1; 8:9 etc.; 1 QSa 1:5. The sect's whole rule is a carrying out of this interpretation. "Mysteries" are disclosed in the sect. [32] Thus the question of the imparting of understanding is brought into the process of

---

[23] Eichr. Theol. AT, III, 61; v. Rad op. cit., 440 f. rightly states that the wisdom of experience (older style) knows it is given by Yahweh. "Nevertheless, it must be stressed here that this wisdom of experience is in general far from regarding itself as the fruit of a special divine revelation. It was rather a matter of reason and common sense, and hence it was not in any sense attributed to inspiration."

[24] v. Rad, op. cit., 442 f.

[25] On the construction of בִּין with בְּ v. C. Rabin, The Zadokite Documents² (1958), 34, n. 1 on Damasc. 8:12 (9:21); cf. Test. R. 3:8. On the rise of the causal sense of the hi of שׂכל cf. Nötscher, 57, n. 102, cf. 1 QS 9:18, 20 etc.; similarly בִּין hi 1 QS 4:22; Damasc. 13:15 ff. (15:7 ff.). But this use is not very strong in Damasc., Braun, 94, n. 8.

[26] Nötscher, 56 thinks שׂכל contains more strongly than בִּין the element of theoretical knowledge presupposed for entry (1 QS 5:25) and for taking up an office (1 QSa 1:17). But at most the only truth in this distinction is that the aspect of perception by sight is stronger in בִּין and much more so than in the Gk. συνίημι, Damasc. 2:14 (3:1). On the other hand בִּין is par. to שׁמע in Damasc. 1:1 (1:1), cf. also 6:2 f. (8:3 f.). The 2 words are fully synon. in 13:5 ff. (15:7 ff.).

[27] So 1 QS 4:22, where the nature of understanding is quite plain, also the list of ways of the Spirit in 4:3; S. Wibbing, "Die Tugend- u. Lasterkataloge im NT," Beih. zur ZNW, 25 (1959), 46 f.

[28] Cf. O. Betz, "Offenbarung u. Schriftforschung in d. Qumransekte," Wissenschaftliche Untersuchungen z. NT, 6 (1960), 138-140.

[29] We have here a fixed expression, 1 QS 6:18; 1 QH 1:31; Damasc. 13:11 (16:4).

[30] S. Schulz, "Zur Rechtfertigung aus Gnaden in Qumran u. bei Pls.," ZThK, 56 (1959), 156-171.

[31] "I knew this through understanding, for thou hast opened my ear to wonderful mysteries," 1 QH 1:21 (→ n. 36); cf. 1 QS 9:18; 11:2 ff.; 1 QH 10:4 f.; 11:4, 10.

[32] For the contents cf. 1 QS 3:13 ff.; 11:2 ff.; 1 QH 1.

knowledge. On the one side the concept of the Spirit has a part here, → VI, 389, 29 ff. [33] On the other side the Teacher of Righteousness is constitutive as a mediator. To him "God makes known all the mysteries of the words of his servants the prophets," 1 QpHab 7:4 f. [34] His teaching is handed down in the sect, teachers being qualified for this, 1 QS 3:13. From this exposition it is clear that knowledge is not theoretical consideration. [35] It is conscious of itself when it sees itself as a gift and recognises man's vanity; there is here a complete unity of ignorance and sin, knowledge and obedience to the Law. [36] Experience of the gift impels to thanksgiving as the appropriate form of practising understanding, 1 QH 7:26 f.; 11:4. [37]

In Test. XII relationship to the Dead Sea Scrolls is particularly evident in Test. L. But whereas in the Scrolls there is firm attachment to the group as the only place where understanding is a reality, we find here a weaker type of edifying wisdom with the motifs of Qumran piety. [38]

2. The Rabbinic Writings.

Here we find the familiar words and meanings but perhaps with some shift to perception and reason. [39] There is still a combining of synonyms, Ab., 3, 17; Chag., 2, 1. [40]

D. The Word Group in the New Testament.

1. Forms of the Verb.

With the inherited forms of -ίημι we also find, as in the pap. and LXX, new constructs acc. to the conjugation in -ω: συνίω (also ἀφ-). [41] The MS tradition often vacillates. -ίημι is abs. certain only in Ac. 7:25, but other ref. are practically so, Mt. 13:19: συνιέντος, 13:23: συνιείς, Lk. 24:45: συνιέναι. -ίω is abs. certain in R. 3:11: συνίων (quoting LXX), but cf. Mt. 13:13: συνίουσιν, -ιοῦσιν? or vl. συνῶσιν? In 2 C. 10:12 the form in -ίημι:

---

[33] He is the Spirit of truth, 1 QS 4:21 f. → n. 36.

[34] The group's knowledge is related to Scripture, as the many biblical MSS show. There is thus a connection between the earlier revelation to the prophets and the present disclosure of the meaning of prophecy to the Teacher of Righteousness and the group. On the understanding of Scripture, cf. Betz, op. cit. (→ n. 28).

[35] We find this too, i.e., cosmological reflection, though not in the style of Gk. thought but along the lines of the OT, 1 QH 1; 1 QM 10.

[36] On the unity of knowledge and self-knowledge 1 QH 15:12 ff., on that of understanding and walk cf. esp. the double list in 1 QS 4:2 ff.; 5:24; 1 QSa 1:28. The structural element of self-knowledge is in the I form of the Ps.: "But I as one who has understanding have known thee, my God, through the Spirit whom thou hast given me," 1 QH 12:11 f.

[37] The Ps. are not just an expression of thanks for knowledge, nor an exposition of its content, but as songs of thanksgiving they are also its fulfilment.

[38] Some ref.: the verb Test. N. 3:1 with God's will as obj. The noun Test. R. 6:4, cf. L. 2:3: πνεῦμα συνέσεως, 18:7: πνεῦμα συνέσεως καὶ ἁγιασμοῦ, 4:5; 8:2; 13:2; Test. Jud. 20:1 f. ref. to 2 spirits τὸ τῆς ἀληθείας καὶ τὸ τῆς πλάνης. Καὶ μέσον ἐστὶ συνειδήσεως (Rec. A); Καὶ μέσον ἐστὶ τὸ τῆς συνέσεως τοῦ νοός, οὗ ἐὰν θέλῃ, κλῖναι (Rec. B).

[39] The element of seeing is now fully developed in שׂכל, contemplating the stars in bBer., 10a, the rainbow in bSanh., 92a etc., cf. the dict. for usage in Bab. Aram. and Jewish Palestinian Aram. The causal sense of the hi of בין is also developed → n. 25.

[40] Schl. Mt. on 11:25 makes too much of the nuances → n. 44. In fact it is hard to distinguish sharply between the three main groups which call for consideration: ידע, בין, שׂכל or שׂכל, ידע. ידע and דַּעַת relate esp. to knowing, cf. the ref. → 891, 4 ff. and Ned., 40a. בִּינָה is more understanding or prudence and שׂכל has the further nuance of contemplating → n. 39.

[41] Cf. Mayser[2], I, 2, 124 (examples of ἀφίημι and προίημι rather than συνίημι).

συνιᾶσιν, has been handed down without deviation, but not the word itself → 895, 16 ff. Elsewhere the forms are equivocal, e.g., συνίετε Mk. 8:17, 21 etc. [42]

2. The Theological Significance of the Word Group.

The word group did not become theologically significant, nor does it occur at all in the Johannine writings including Rev. The OT Jewish tradition (→ 890, 7 ff.) dominates its meaning, cf. the occurrence of the group in OT quotations, Mt. 13:15; Ac. 28:26 f.; R. 3:11. The first 2 of these are from Is. 6:9 f. This passage is obviously an established part of the OT material used in apologetics, cf. also Jn. 12:40 → IV, 950, 16 ff. There is in the NT no consolidation of use as in the Dead Sea Scrolls → 891, 5 ff. At most one might detect a certain trend in Mt. → 894, 9 ff. [43]

3. The Synoptists.

a. In Q (Mt. 11:25 par. Lk. 10:21) [44] συνετός is par to σοφός → 516, 13 ff. — anton. νήπιος [45] — in the saying about the Revealer. This saying expresses the concept of the contingent and paradoxical nature of revelation. [46] In Mk. 7:14 the verb denotes understanding of what is heard with no further theological reflection. [47] Mk. 12:30, 33 quotes the sh^ema in a four-membered version: καρδία - ψυχή - διάνοια - ἰσχύς, followed by a three-membered: καρδία - σύνεσις - ἰσχύς. One

---

[42] Cf. Pr.-Bauer, s.v.; Bl.-Debr. § 94, 2; on aor. συνήκαμεν or -ατε in Mt. 13:51 cf. Bl.-Debr. § 95, 1.

[43] G. Barth, "Das Gesetzesverständnis d. Evangelisten Mt., Überlieferung u. Auslegung im Mt.-Ev." Wissenschaftliche Monographien zum AT u. NT, 1³ (1963), 99-104. But σύνεσις is not taken from Mk. 12:33.

[44] Mt. 11:25-27 par. Lk. 10:21 f. is not orig. a unity acc. to Bultmann Trad., 171 f. v. 25 has a Semitic character, cf. Sir. 51:1 ff.; Str.-B., I, 606 f.; Jewish material in Schl. Mt. on 11:25. Schlatter judicially notes: "Not knowledge as such, but the knowledge which shapes acts, is the mark of the wise man." But on the basis of an occasional Rabb. saying (→ n. 40) he makes too fine a distinction: "With σοφός = חכם the movement begins in man; he grasps the thought in terms of which he acts. With συνετός = נבון the movement passes from the obj. to the subj." 382. In reality the two terms are synon. If one takes v. 25 alone, ταῦτα seems to lose its reference. Hence many exegetes ask whether this pron. was originally plain in a literary context we can no longer reconstruct, cf. Bultmann Trad., ad loc. But ταῦτα does not need such a context, since the mode of expression betrays liturgical influence and the meaning is clear in the liturgical act. One might add from 1 C. 2:9: "What no eye has seen . . . , all that God has prepared for them that love him." There are no true material par. in the Qumran texts. One may ref. only to 1 QpHab 12:4: Members are the "simple of Judah, doers of the Law," Braun, 60, n. 11 and 1 QH 2:9: "And I will be . . . for the healing of all who convert from sin, for cleverness to the simple." On the whole theme Norden, op. cit., 277-308; M. Dibelius, Die Formgesch. d. Ev.⁴ (1961), 279-284; T. Arvedson, Das Mysterium Christi (1937); E. Percy, Die Botschaft Jesu (1953), 259-271; W. D. Davies, " 'Knowledge' in the Dead Sea Scrolls and Mt. 11:25-30," HThR, 46 (1953), 113-139; H. Mertens, L'hymne de jubilation chez les Synoptiques, Mt. 11:25-30; Lc. 10:21-22 (1953); L. Cerfaux, "Les sources scripturaires de Mt. XI 25-30," Ephemerides Theol. Lovanienses, 31 (1955), 331-342; W. Grundmann, "Die νήπιοι in d. urchr. Paränese," NTSt, 5 (1959), 188-205; → IV, 920, 32 ff.

[45] Regarding νήπιος it should be noted that the antithesis συνετός/νήπιος has a special nuance in the koine inasmuch as νήπιος occurs in prose only in the sense "childlike" (→ IV, 914, 28 ff.); νήπιος "foolish" belongs to the vocabulary of epic poetry → IV, 916, 32 ff. [Dihle].

[46] Naturally thanks are not given because "these things" are reserved for a portion of mankind but because they are revealed to those who humanly speaking could not have expected it.

[47] Cf. Wis. 6:1. The word is often linked with ἀκούω in Herm., e.g., s., 9, 12, 1.

gets the impression of a Hellenistic tinting, [48] though the word has no autonomous meaning. The most important passages are those which come within the orbit of the "Messianic secret," Mk. 6:52; 8:17, 21. [49]

b. The theory about parables [50] (Mk. 4:12 and par.) belongs to the same circle of motifs. From the literary standpoint this is placed in the Marcan editorial material. [51] The catchword συνίημι comes from the free rendering of Is. 6:9 f. [52] One must insist that the failure to understand is God's purpose. [53] Lk. abbreviates sharply, 8:9 f. This corresponds to his changing of the Messianic secret into a passion secret, as may be noted in Lk. 18:34. [54] Mt. greatly extended the passage about the purpose of speaking in parables, 13:10-15. He added the saying from Mk. 4:25 and after the shortened summary of Is. 6:9 f. repeated the passage according to the wording of the LXX. [55] Thus the catchword συνίημι achieves great prominence, especially as Mt. also added it to Mk.'s version in v. 19 and v. 23 → 160, 11 ff. [56] If in Mk. the question relates to the general point of speaking in parables (τὰς παραβολάς, v. 10), [57] Mt. has the disciples ask Jesus why He speaks to the people in parables. [58] The ἵνα of Mk. is replaced by ὅτι. [59] In place of God's purpose one finds a psychological reason, a reference to the nature of man. This is in keeping with the general style of Mt. [60] The disciples' lack of understanding,

---

[48] G. Bornkamm, "Das Doppelgebot d. Liebe," Nt.liche Stud. f. R. Bultmann, Beih. z. ZNW, 21 (1954), 85-93 (also on the relation to Mt. 22:34 ff.); J. Jeremias, "Die Muttersprache des Evangelisten Mt.," ZNW, 50 (1959), 270-274.

[49] As against H. J. Ebeling, "Das Messiasgeheimnis u. d. Botschaft d. Markus-Evangelisten," Beih. z. ZNW, 19 (1939), 147-171, who disputes a connection between the disciples' lack of understanding and the Messianic secret.

[50] So in spite of W. Marxsen, "Redaktionsgeschichtliche Erklärung der sog. Parabeltheorie d. Mk.," ZThK, 52 (1955), 255-271, cf. also Jeremias Gl.[6], 9-14.

[51] Marxsen, op. cit., 255-263; Bultmann Trad., 351, n. 1 and Suppl.[2] (1962), 52 against Jeremias Gl.[6], 9-14. The related Mk. 7:18 does not in itself contain the Marcan theory but simply relates to an actual parable, cf. Mk. 4:10-12; Marxsen, op. cit., 259 f.

[52] On the relation of the Marcan version to LXX and Tg. cf. Jeremias Gl.[6], 11 f.

[53] The same applies to Ac. 28:26 f. and Jn. 12:40, where the passage is quoted as in Mt. → lines 9 ff., though Jn. has νοέω for συνίημι. But cf. Jeremias Gl.[6], 13 f., who like T. W. Manson, The Teaching of Jesus (1931), 76-81 appeals to the rendering in the Tg. for the view that μήποτε means "unless." Against this is the ἵνα, from which one cannot eliminate the final sense, cf. Haench. Ag., ad loc.; D. Daube, The NT and Rabbinic Judaism (1956), 149. Jn.'s introduction to the quotation establishes the final sense, as does also the changing of the imp. into the inf., Bultmann J., 347, n. 2.

[54] H. Conzelmann, Die Mitte d. Zeit[4] (1962), 67, 184 f. There are no other special features in Lk. σύνεσις occurs again in Lk. 2:47, cf. Jos. Ant., 2, 230; Vit., 8. Mk. 6:52; 7:18; 8:17, 21 are in the "gt. lacuna," v. Conzelmann, 45-48. On the quotation in Ac. 28:26 → n. 53. The other ref. are Lk. 2:50; 10:21 (Q); 24:45; Ac. 7:25; 13:7.

[55] But an interpolation is suspected, cf. K. Stendahl, "The School of St. Matthew," Acta Seminarii Neotest. Upsaliensis, 20 (1954), 131. The introductory formula is singular, and the quotations in Mt. do not elsewhere follow the LXX. The agreement with Ac. 28:26 f. is striking. Yet in support of authenticity one might ref. to the extent of the use of συνίημι. This could be explained, however, in the light of the Mk. text, cf. Mt. 13:51.

[56] γινώσκω in 13:11, ἐπιγινώσκω 17:12 and νοέω 15:17; 16:9, 11 are synon.

[57] One may detect the older stratum, cf. the sing. in v. 13.

[58] Barth, op. cit., 100. The disciples do not need an explanation, cf. v. 16 f. Barth ref. to the elimination of Mk. 4:34 by Mt. In relation to Mt. 13:36 cf. v. 51.

[59] On Mt.'s reconstruction of Mk. cf. W. Trilling, "Das wahre Israel, Stud. z. Theol. d. Mt.-Ev.," Erfurter Theol. Stud., 7 (1959), 59 f.

[60] Cf. the healing of the lame man, H. Greeven, "Die Heilung d. Gelähmten nach Mt.," Wort u. Dienst, NF, 4 (1955), 65-78.

which in Mk. can be overcome only by the resurrection, is not so basic here; it is only momentary, cf. 13:34 with 13:51. Mt. alters what Mk. has to say about it accordingly. [61] He did not just fail to understand Mk.; he replaced Mk.'s interpretation with a new one. [62] But this psychologising trend does not change the fact that understanding is a divine gift and hardening a divine ineluctability, → IV, 818, 1 ff. [63]

4. Paul.

In the Pauline homologoumena the group is used a few times in OT quotations or allusions. [64] There are also three independent instances. The noun occurs in 1 C. 1:19, though here the dominant word is σοφία. [65] As in the OT the organ of understanding is the heart, R. 1:21; cf. Col. 2:2. [66] Understanding and conduct are an indissoluble unity. To be without understanding is not just a partial deficiency which might be overcome; it is total darkening, and as such the work of God, who can darken → 442, 13 ff. [67] ἀσύνετος καρδία is practically synon. with ἀδόκιμος νοῦς, R. 1:28. The term occurs once again in the list of vices in R. 1:31. [68]

There remains the disputed passage 2 C. 10:12 f. We have this in two versions. The shorter Western, which omits συνίημι, is often preferred. But the witnesses overwhelmingly support the longer text, [69] and the shorter is most readily explained as a secondary smoothing. [70] The pt. of the passage naturally does not depend on the word συνίημι.

---

[61] Barth, op. cit., 102.

[62] οὐ γὰρ συνῆκαν ἐπὶ τοῖς ἄρτοις (Mk. 6:52) was dropped from Mt. 14:33 because the true nature of Jesus was not hidden from the disciples acc. to Mt., Barth, op. cit., 105 f. In place of hardening is the little faith which merges into worship, an act of understanding. In Mt. 16:9 Mk. 8:17 becomes the temporary failure to understand an enigmatic saying, Barth, 106 f.; Mk. 8:21 is adopted in Mt. 16:11, but leads to final understanding. Mk. 7:18 is related to the parable theory in Mt. 15:10 and adopted with this.

[63] Barth, op. cit., 103, n. 1.

[64] R. 4:11 (ψ 13:2 or 52:3); R. 10:19 (Dt. 32:21); R. 15:21 (Is. 52:15). On the use of the OT in Paul cf. H. Vollmer, Die at.lichen Zitate bei Pls (1895); O. Michel, Pls u. seine Bibel (1929); E. E. Ellis, Paul's Use of the OT (1957).

[65] The passage is an almost word for word quotation from Is. 29:14 LXX; materially cf. also Bar. 3:14, 23. E. Peterson, Frühkirche, Judenchristentum, Gnosis (1959), 43-50 has some interesting though untenable views on the relation to Bar. 3:9 ff. The correspondence between σύνεσις and σοφία and the whole train of thought show that σοφία is not a hypostasis here, as against U. Wilckens, "Weisheit u. Torheit," Beiträge z. Hist. Theol., 26 (1959), 205-213 → 519, 16 ff.; 522, 6 ff.

[66] Cf. ψ 75:6: ἀσύνετοι τῇ καρδίᾳ for אַבִּירֵי לֵב "arrogant," Σ ὑπερήφανοι, the guilt of this attitude being implied [Bertram].

[67] → σκοτός; cf. 1 Cl., 36, 2 and on this J. Jervell, "Imago Dei," FRL, 76 (1960), 185.

[68] With parechesis ἀσύνετος — ἀσύνθετος, cf. P. Masp., 67097, D 84 f. (6th cent. A.D.). On σύνεσις in lists of virtues → n. 13; A. Vögtle, "Die Tugend- u. Lasterkataloge im NT," NTAbh, 14, 4. 5 (1936), 231.

[69] p46 also has it. What Nestle says about Vg is mistaken. Vg has the shorter version but acquaintance with the longer may be seen at the beginning of v. 13: nos autem . . .

[70] W. G. Kümmel in Ltzm. K., 208 f.: he rightly pts. out that αὐτοί at the beginning of the sentence ref. to a new subj., not Paul but his opponents; E. B. Allo, Seconde Ép. aux Cor.² (1956), ad loc. For the Western text Wnd. 2 K., ad loc.; E. Käsemann, Die Legitimität d. Ap. (1956), 44; R. Bultmann, "Exeget. Probleme d. 2 K.," Symbolae Bibl. Upsalienses, 9 (1947), 21 f.

2. The Pauline Antilegomena.

The use here, too, is the normal one. [71] The organ of σύνεσις is the heart, Col. 2:2. The object is God's will, Eph. 5:17. σύνεσις is the gift of the Kurios, 2 Tm. 2:7; cf. 1 Ch. 22:12. The new element is the combination with "mystery" (→ IV, 820, 32 ff.) as the object of understanding. In the first instance this is defined christologically (Col. 2:2), but then it is incorporated into the distinctive ecclesiology of Eph. (3:4). [72]

E. The Word Group in the Ancient Church.

The same trends continue in the post-apost. fathers. 1 Cl. uses the noun in a Stoicising development of the belief in creation, 33, 3 [73] and also in a formally Pauline restatement of the doctrine of justification: οὐ δι' ἑαυτῶν δικαιούμεθα οὐδὲ διὰ τῆς ἡμετέρας σοφίας ἢ συνέσεως ἢ εὐσεβείας ἢ ἔργων, 32, 4. Herm. heaps up the term. [74] In him σύνεσις is personified, but it is still metaphorical. There is true hypostatising only in developed Gnosticism. [75] Synesis is not a typical word, however, like Logos, Sophia, Epinoia etc. [76] It may be mentioned that Just. [77] and Cl. Al. often use the group. [78]

Conzelmann

---

† συνίστημι, † συνιστάνω

---

1. συνίστημι, compound of ἵστημι, means orig. "to put together." συνίστημι offers the only correctly constructed athematic present forms in NT usage. [1] The use, attested

---

[71] With σοφία Col. 1:9 (replaced by φρόνησις in Eph. 1:8).
[72] One may recall the connection between understanding and mystery in the Dead Sea Scrolls, Nötscher, *passim;* Davies, *op. cit.;* J. Coppens, "Le 'mystère' dans la théol. paul. et ses parallèles Qumrâniens," *Littérature et théol. paul., Recherches Bibl.,* 5 (1960), 142-165. But there is no model for the christological ref. nor the fixed form of the μυστήριον passages in Pl.
[73] Kn. Cl., ad loc.; Herm. v., 1, 3, 4.
[74] But with no broad distribution. Of interest are the series in v., 1, 3, 4; 3, 8, 2-8 (Dib. Herm., ad loc.) and s., 9, 15, 2 (interpretation of the allegory of the tower; Synesis is one of the 12 virgins). Cf. also the modified list of virtues in Barn., 2, 2 f. (Wnd. Barn., ad loc.), also Cl. Al. Strom., II, 6, 31, 2; Barn., 21, 5.
[75] For the Valentinians v. Epiph. Haer., 31, 2, 10, where with other terms ordered in syzygies we find νοῦς, πίστις, ἐλπίς, ἀγάπη, σύνεσις, σοφία. In the aeon speculations in the Apocr. Joh. we find together χάρις, σύνεσις, αἴσθησις, φρόνησις. Later Synesis is one of the three aeons at the third light, Apocr. Joh. 33:5-34:1 in W. C. Till, "Die gnost. Schr. d. kpt. Pap. Berolinensis 8502," TU, 60 (1955), 107-9. Cf. also C. Schmidt, "Gespräche Jesu mit seinen Jüngern nach d. Auferstehung," TU, 43 (1919), 140 f.
[76] The findings in the Hermetic writings are negative.
[77] In Just. Dial. esp. of understanding the Scriptures, 110, 2 etc., which is grace, 58, 1.
[78] Some characteristic examples are Cl. Al. Strom., II, 4, 17, 3 f.; II, 16, 76, 2 f.; VI, 7, 62, 4 f.; VI, 11, 93, 1.

συνίστημι κτλ. Bibl.: Pape, Liddell-Scott, Pr.-Bauer, Hatch-Redp., *s.v.;* J. Bartsch, Review of L. Wenger, "Die Stellvertretung im Rechte d. Pap.," APF, 4 (1907), 499 f.; W. Mundle, "Zur Auslegung v. Gl. 2:17, 18," ZNW, 23 (1924), 152 f.; U. Wilcken, "Zu den κάτοχοι des Serapeums," APF, 6 (1913-20), 187 f.; R. A. Ward, "Aristotelian Terms in the NT," *Baptist Quarterly,* 11 (1945), 398-403.
[1] Bl.-Debr. § 93; Radermacher, 100, cf. also the interrelations of συνίστημι-συνιστάνω-συνιστάω, 97.

from Hom. to later Hellenism, is most varied. The following five senses are important for the NT. Intr. a. "to be composed, to consist of something": ἐξ ὀλιγίστων συνεστὸς τῶν αὐτῶν μερῶν, Plat. Tim., 56b; cf. 54c; ἡ μὲν πόλις ἐκ πλειόνων ἢ μυρίων οἰκιῶν συνέστηκε, Xenoph. Mem., III, 6, 14; ἐξ ὧν ὁ κόσμος συνέστηκε, Aristot. Eth. Nic., VI, 7, p. 1141b, 1 f. b. Perf. "to exist," "to be": ἡ πολιτεία συνέστηκε μίμησις τοῦ καλλίστου καὶ ἀρίστου βίου, Plat. Leg., VII, 817b; δεῖν πάντα λόγον ὥσπερ ζῷον συνεστάναι, Plat. Phaedr., 264c; τὸ γὰρ ζῆν διὰ τῆς τροφῆς συνεστάναι, Ep. Ar., 154; μεγάλη συνέστη καὶ θαυμαστὴ δύναμις βασιλέων, Plat. Tim., 25a; cf. 45c; 54a; with a religious ref.: ἀρχαῖος μὲν οὖν τις λόγος καὶ πάτριός ἐστι πᾶσιν ἀνθρώποις ὡς ἐκ θεοῦ πάντα καὶ διὰ θεοῦ ἡμῖν συνέστηκεν, Ps.-Arist., Mund., 6, p. 397b, 13-15; cf. Plat. Resp., VII, 530a; Tim., 61a; σὺ πάντων ὑγρῶν καὶ ξηρῶν καὶ ψ[υχ]ρῶν (supply mistress) ἐξ ὧν ἅπαντα συνέστηκεν, P. Oxy., XI, 1380, 184 f. (2nd cent. A.D.); cf. Philo Rer. Div. Her., 58; ἐξ οὗ τὰ πάντα συνέστηκεν, Preis. Zaub., I, 4, 1768 f. c. "To associate," "to band together," perf. "to stand together," "to stand": εἶπε Δαυιδ πρὸς τοὺς ἄνδρας τοὺς συνεστηκότας μετ᾽ αὐτοῦ, 1 Βασ. 17:26 A; συνέστησαν ἐπὶ Μωυσῆν καὶ Ααρων, Nu. 16:3 B; cf. Ex. 32:1; καὶ ἐπὶ πᾶν συνεστηκὸς ὕδωρ, Ex. 7:19; cf. Lv. 15:3. d. "To commend": ἰατρῷ συστῆσαι περὶ τῆς ἀσθενείας, Plat. Charm., 155b; cf. Polyb., 31, 20, 9; Zenon Pap., I, 59002 (3rd cent. B.C.); [2] P. Hamb., II, 27, 3 (3rd cent. B.C.); P. Hibeh, I, 66, 3 (3rd cent. B.C.); P. Mich., III, 210, 4 (2nd/3rd cent. A.D.) etc.; Epict. Diss. III, 23, 22; 1 Macc. 12:43; 2 Macc. 4:24; 9:25; Jos. Ant., 16, 85. e. "To display," "to prove (to be)": εὔνοιαν συνίστανε, Polyb., 4, 5, 6; διασυνίστησιν αὐτὸν προφήτην, Philo Rer. Div. Her., 258; Jos. Ant., 7, 49.

2. The intr. perf. occurs in Lk. 9:32; 2 Pt. 3:5 and Col. 1:17. In the Lucan account of the transfiguration of Jesus (9:28-36) it means "to stand together." Peter, James and John εἶδαν τὴν δόξαν αὐτοῦ (Jesus) καὶ τοὺς δύο ἄνδρας τοὺς συνεστῶτας αὐτῷ, v. 32. There is thus no theological reference. 2 Pt. 3:5 and Col. 1:17 use it in the sense "to exist." In 2 Pt. 3:5 (→ V, 514, n. 128) we read ὅτι οὐρανοὶ ἦσαν ἔκπαλαι καὶ γῆ ἐξ ὕδατος καὶ δι᾽ ὕδατος συνεστῶσα τῷ τοῦ θεοῦ λόγῳ. The cosmology underlying the v. [3] obviously regards water as a means of creation and a primal element; it thus teaches that the earth is composed of water. [4] In the context of Col. 1:17 the word occurs in an important theological statement. The saying αὐτός ἐστιν (sc. Christ) πρὸ πάντων καὶ τὰ πάντα ἐν αὐτῷ συνέστηκεν, "he is before all things and all things have their existence in him" forms the climax and conclusion of a train of thought which bases the saving significance of Christ on His cosmic significance, → V, 894, 37 ff.; VI, 687, 33 ff. [5]

Paul uses the trans. συνίστημι primarily in the good classical sense "to commend." Thus he commends "Phoebe our sister" to the Roman church, R. 16:1. He asks in 2 C. 3:1 (→ 594, 17 ff.): ἀρχόμεθα πάλιν ἑαυτοὺς συνιστάνειν, ἢ μὴ χρῄζομεν ὥς τινες συστατικῶν ἐπιστολῶν πρὸς ὑμᾶς ἢ ἐξ ὑμῶν; and answers that this is not necessary because the Corinthian church is the apostle's letter of commendation, v. 2 f. His commendation before God to the conscience of any man is the public proclamation of the truth (2 C. 4:2), which is for the church that attains to the truth through this proclamation a ground of thanksgiving, ἀφορμὴ καυχήματος

---

[2] Ed. C. C. Edgar, "Zenon Pap.," Catal. gén. des antiquités égypt. du Musée du Caire, 79 (1925).

[3] Wnd. Kath. Br., ad loc.

[4] Gn. 1:2, 6 ff.; Ps. 23:2; cf. Slav. En. 47:4: "The Lord has ... established the earth on the waters." On the whole idea cf. Ps.-Clem. Hom., 11, 24; Herm. v. 1, 3, 4.

[5] On the concept of Christ as world-soul and world-creator v. the exc. in Dib. Gefbr. on Col. 1:17.

(2 C. 5:12) about the apostle's work. In this understanding of self-commendation and being commended one may see something of the self-awareness of the apostle who spends himself as a δοῦλος of Christ and who is thus without personal concern, and without any need of personal concern, for the establishment of his reputation, → III, 651, 3 ff. This is why he refuses to compare himself with those who commend themselves, 2 C. 10:12; for not ὁ ἑαυτὸν συνιστάνων ἐκεῖνός ἐστιν δόκιμος ἀλλὰ ὃν ὁ κύριος συνίστησιν, 2 C. 10:18. Because Paul is conscious that he has done more than all of them as a δοῦλος of Christ, he says to the Corinthian community: ἐγὼ γὰρ ὤφειλον ὑφ᾿ ὑμῶν συνίστασθαι, 2 C. 12:11.

A second meaning of the trans. συνίστημι is the rare one "to set forth," "to present." In Paul this is related to the former sense to the degree that the basis of genuine commendation is for him the achievement which is publicly evident, cf. 2 C. 3:1 ff. In this sense he can say in R. 3:5 that our unrighteousness θεοῦ δικαιοσύνην συνίστησιν. In the same way God's love demonstrates and commends itself to us. For συνίστησιν τὴν ἑαυτοῦ ἀγάπην εἰς ἡμᾶς ὁ θεὸς ὅτι ἔτι ἁμαρτωλῶν ὄντων ἡμῶν Χριστὸς ὑπὲρ ἡμῶν ἀπέθανεν, R. 5:8. It is thus God's loving action which displays His righteousness and love precisely in our unrighteousness and wretchedness. What the term denotes here is thus close to φανερόω and might be rendered "to bring to light." The aspect of revelation in history is not present, however, in 2 C. 6:4, where Paul refers to himself, in Gl. 2:18, where he refers to the Christian, [6] or in 2 C. 7:11, where he refers to the Corinthian church. Thus in 2 C. 6:4: ἀλλ᾿ ἐν παντὶ συνιστάνοντες ἑαυτοὺς ὡς θεοῦ διάκονοι, the word means "to prove" or "to show," so also 2 C. 7:11. Materially, however, this proof is again based on patent facts, as may be seen with special clarity in Gl. 2:18 with its reference to the Law: εἰ γὰρ ἃ κατέλυσα ταῦτα πάλιν οἰκοδομῶ, παραβάτην ἐμαυτὸν συνιστάνω, → V, 741, 19 ff. [7]

Once again it may be seen, then, that for Paul it is acts which are determinative in the judgment of God, the apostle, and men generally. But this fact, which decisively controls the anthropology of the apostle, makes of God's saving act in Christ a sheer miracle which governs Paul's whole understanding of the Gospel.

Kasch

---

† σύνοιδα, † συνείδησις

Contents: A. Secular Greek: 1: σύνοιδα ἐμαυτῷ; 2. συνειδός, συνείδησις, σύνεσις; 3. The Problem of Conscience. B. Latin. C. The Old Testament: I. The Hebrew Text; II. The Septuagint. D. Judaism: 1. The Rabbis and the Dead Sea Scrolls; 2. The Pseudepigrapha; 3. Josephus; 4. Philo: a. Usage; b. The Task of Conscience; c. The Theological

---

[6] Cf. Mundle; Ltzm. Gl. and Schlier Gl. on 2:18.
[7] Zn. Gl., *ad loc.*

σ ύ ν ο ι δ α κ τ λ. Bibl.: In gen. Pass., Liddell-Scott, Pr.-Bauer, *s.v.* Still basic is M. Kähler, *Das Gewissen,* I (1878); also Art. "Gewissen" in RE³, 6, 646-654; F. Tillmann, "*Zur Geschichte d. Begriffs 'Gewissen' bis zu d. paul. Briefen," Festschr. f. S. Merkle* (1922), 336-347; H. Osborne, "Συνείδησις," JThSt, 32 (1931), 167-179; also "Συνείδησις and σύνεσις," Class. Rev., 45 (1931), 8-10; G. Rudberg, "Ur Samvetets Historia," *Festschr. f. J. A. Eklund* (1933), 165-188; J. Dupont, "Syneidesis aux origines de la notion chrétienne

Context; d. The Question of the Guiding Function of Conscience; e. The Historical Position of Philo. E. The New Testament: 1. General; 2. Paul; 3. Post-Pauline Writings. F. The Post-Apostolic Fathers.

A. Secular Greek.

1. σύνοιδα ἐμαυτῷ.

a. The proper place to start is the non-reflexive σύνοιδα τινί τι or τι or τινός τι or περί τινος: "to have knowledge of something with" another person on the basis of eye-witness.

The one who has this knowledge may be a witness either for the prosecution or the defence: ἢ [sc. Δίκη] σιγῶσα σύνοιδε τὰ γιγνόμενα πρό τ᾽ ἐόντα, Solon Elegiae, 3, 15; [1] σύνοιδέ μοι Κύπρις, Eur. El., 43; or he may share the guilt as well: πλῆθος δ

---

de conscience morale," *Stud. Hellenistica,* 5 (1948), 119-153; also *Gnosis* (1949), 266-282; E. Wolf, "Vom Problem d. Gewissens in reformatorischer Sicht," *Peregrinatio* (1954), 81-112; also Art. "Gewissen" in RGG³, II, 1550-1557; Dib. Past. Exc. on 1 Tm. 1:5; C. A. Pierce, "Conscience in the NT," *Stud. in Bibl. Theol.,* 15 (1955) (Pierce also placed at the author's disposal an amplified MS of his book); O. Kuss, *Der Römerbrief* (1957), 76-82, Exc. "Gewissen"; J. Stelzenberger, "Syneidesis in the Pauline Writings," *The Westminster Theol. Journ.,* 24 (1962), 173-186. On A.: B. Snell, *Die Ausdrücke f. d. Begriff des Wissens in der vorplaton. Philosophie* (1924); F. Zucker, *Syneidesis — Conscientia* (1928), cf. on this Snell's Review in *Gnomon,* 6 (1930), 21-31; G. Jung, "Συνείδησις, Conscientia, Bewusstsein," *Archiv f. d. gesamte Psychologie,* 89 (1934), 525-540; M. Pohlenz, *Die Stoa,* I (1948), 317, 377; II (1949), 158, 183 f.; E. de Places, "En marge du ThW: conscience et personne dans l'antiquité grecque," *Biblica,* 30 (1949), 501-509; O. Seel, "Zur Vorgeschichte d. Gewissensbegriffes im altgriech. Denken," *Festschr. f. F. Dornseiff* (1953), 291-319; P. Rabbow *Seelenführung, Methoden der Exerzitien in der Antike* (1954); H. R. Schwyzer, "Bewusst u. unbewusst bei Plot.," *Les sources de Plotin, Fondation Hardt,* V (1957), 343-378; H. Jaeger, "L'examen de conscience dans les religions non-chrét. et avant le christianisme," *Numen,* 6 (1959), 175-233. On C. and D.: J. S. Boughton, "Conscience and the Logos in Philo," *The Lutheran Church Quart.,* 4 (1931), 121-123; W. Völker, *Fortschritt u. Vollendung bei Philo v. Alex.,* TU, 49, 1 (1938), 95-105; E. Bréhier, *Les idées philosophiques et religieuses de Philon d'Alex.*³ (1950), 295-310; R. J. Z. Werblowsky, "Das Gewissen in jüd. Sicht," *Das Gewissen, Stud. aus dem C. G. Jung-Institut Zürich,* 7 (1958), 89-117; O. J. F. Seitz, "Two Spirits in Man: An Essay in Bibl. Exegesis," *NTSt,* 6 (1959/60), 82-95. On E.: R. Steinmetz, *Das Gewissen bei Pls.* (1911); H. Böhlig, "Das Gewissen bei Pls. u. Sen.," *ThStKr,* 87 (1914), 1-24; C. H. Dodd, "Conscience in the NT," *Mansfield College Magazine,* 9 (1916), 150-154; T. Schneider, "Der paul. Begriff d. Gewissens (Syneidesis)," *Bonner Zschr. f. Theol. u. Seelsorge,* 6 (1929), 192-211; also "Die Quellen d. paul. Gewissensbegriffes," *ibid.,* 7 (1930), 97-112; H. v. Soden, *Sakrament u. Ethik bei Pls.* (1931), *Urchr. u. Gesch.,* I (1951), 239-275; W. Gutbrod, "Die paul. Anthropologie," BWANT, IV, 15 (1934), 55-68 etc.; C. Spicq, "La conscience dans le NT," *Rev. Bibl.,* 47 (1938), 50-80; also *St. Paul, Épitres Past.* (1947), 29-38 Exc. "La bonne conscience et la foi"; M. Pohlenz, "Pls. u. d. Stoa," ZNW, 42 (1949), 69-104; B. Reicke, "Syneidesis in R. 2:15," *ThZ,* 12 (1956), 157-161; Bultmann Theol., 217-221; G. Bornkamm, "Gesetz u. Natur," *Stud. z. Antike u. Urchr.* (1959), 111-118; C. Maurer, "Grund u. Grenze ap. Freiheit," *Antwort, Barth Festschr.* (1956), 630-641; "Glaubensbindung u. Gewissensfreiheit im NT," *ThZ,* 17 (1961), 107-117; J. N. Sevenster, "Paul and Seneca," *Nov. Test. Suppl.,* 4 (1961), 84-102; M. Coune, "Le problème des idolothythes et l'éducation de la Syneidêsis," *Recherches de Science Religieuse,* 51 (1963), 497-534 (extract from the unpublished diss. Η ΣΥΝΕΙΔΗΣΙΣ, *L'enrichissement de la notion de conscience dans le NT,* Louvain, 1962).

[1] Diehl³, I, 28.

ξυνῄδει "the knowing (i.e., conspiring) crowd," Thuc., IV, 68, 4 or he may be the knowledgeable expert in contrast to the ignorant people: βουλήσεται οὖν μᾶλλον ὑπὸ τοῦ συνειδότος αὐτῷ ὅτι ἄξιός ἐστι τιμῆς τιμᾶσθαι, "he (the one honoured) desires to receive honour from those who know with him that he is worthy of honour," Aristot. Eth. M., I, 26, p. 1192a, 25 f.

b. The reflexive expression σύνοιδα ἐμαυτῷ combines in one the person who knows and the person who shares the knowledge. There are thus two different egos in the one subject. In the first instance this process of reflection has no moral significance and emphasises the taking cognisance of accomplished acts or states: σύνοιδα ἐμαυτῷ ποιήσας, "I know, am aware, am clear about what I have done."

> The 1st person plur. is a certain transitional stage to the reflexive when it involves a rhetorical appeal to the given knowledge of several persons: ὡς σύνισμέν γε ἡμῖν αὐτοῖς κηλουμένοις ὑπ' αὐτῆς, "we are aware that we have received a delightful stimulus from it (sc. art)," [2] Plat. Resp., X, 607c. But one may detect something of the same in the sing. When the orator tries to establish probability he must appeal to things familiar to the listeners from their own knowledge: ἕκαστος γὰρ τῶν ἀκουόντων σύνοιδεν αὐτὸς αὐτῷ περὶ τούτων ... ἔχοντι τοιαύτας ἐπιθυμίας, Ps.-Aristot. Rhet. Al., 8, p. 1428a, 29-31.

c. The verb is given a fresh accent in the philosophy that commences with Socrates. Here there is evaluation, and since this is negative it takes the form of condemnation. The judgment is a rational process, but what is judged is a perception, not an act. When a man reflects about himself, however, he is conscious of his own ignorance, and hence of a conflict of knowledge. [3]

> When the accusation is brought against Socrates that by his questioning method he makes citizens seem to be ignoramuses, he defends himself by pointing out how this has come about. Socrates himself was faced by the contradiction that the Delphic oracle had called him the wisest of men and yet he was aware of his own complete ignorance: τί ποτε λέγει ὁ θεός ... ; ἐγὼ γὰρ δὴ οὔτε μέγα οὔτε σμικρὸν σύνοιδα ἐμαυτῷ σοφὸς ὤν· τί οὖν ποτε λέγει φάσκων ἐμὲ σοφώτατον εἶναι; Plat. Ap., 21b. Awareness of this discrepancy was the reason he investigated his own situation, and thus examined himself, by comparison with others. This fortunately led to the birth of Socratic philosophy. Since the issue in this self-knowledge is a deficiency of knowledge rather than a moral lack (ἀμαθία cf. Phaedr., 235c.) it is best to transl. "for I realise that I ... " The same intellectual trend clearly prevails in the famous address to Socrates in which Alchibiades acknowledges how helpless he is in face of the words of his teacher: καὶ ἔτι γε νῦν σύνοιδ' ἐμαυτῷ ὅτι εἰ ἐθέλοιμι παρέχειν τὰ ὦτα, οὐκ ἂν καρτερήσαιμι ἀλλὰ ταὐτὰ ἂν πάσχοιμι, Symp., 216a; σύνοιδα γὰρ ἐμαυτῷ ἀντιλέγειν μὲν οὐ δυναμένῳ ... "I am aware that I can put up no resistance," 216b.

d. When reflection extends to one's own deeds assessed in connection with human responsibility conscience arises in the moral sense.

> The rational character of the knowing process is maintained here. The moral approach is related only to the matter assessed. This may be seen in the oldest instance for reflexive

---

[2] Pierce, 134 f. wrongly puts this passage in the moral group.
[3] Pierce, 21 f. speaks in this connection of a technical and ethically indifferent philosophical use. But in overlooking the intellectual conflict in the ego he seriously underestimates the significance of this group in the history of conscience.

verbs, though the context is not clear: ἔγω δ' ἔμ' αὕτᾳ τοῦτο σύνοιδα, Sappho Fr., 37, 11 f. [4] Hdt., V, 91, 2 is to be taken in the same way: συγγινώσκομεν αὐτοῖσι ἡμῖν οὐ ποιήσασι ὀρθῶς, "we realise that we have done it wrongly." [5] Clear examples of moral values are found only from the 4th cent. In the moral use of the verb, and indeed the nouns, the following groups may be distinguished: [6] 1. In most cases the judgment of the act or attitude is negative. It may be expressly so, as indicated by an added part.: σύνοιδα ἐμαυτῷ ἀδικήσας or ἀδικήσαντι, or by a nominal obj.: σύνοιδα ἐμαυτῷ κακόν (the normal use in a bad sense). The hopeless state of a bad conscience is more precisely set forth psychologically when the matricide Orestes, asked what sickness has seized and destroyed him, replies: ἡ σύνεσις, ὅτι σύνοιδα δειν' εἰργασμένος, [7] Eur. Or., 396. Socrates says of those who bore false witness against him: ἀνάγκη ἐστὶν πολλὴν ἑαυτοῖς συνειδέναι ἀσέβειαν καὶ ἀδικίαν, Xenoph. Ap., 24. Demosth. Or., 18, 263 accuses an opponent of leading the life of a coward and always expecting shattering blows ἐφ' οἷς σαυτῷ συνῄδεις ἀδικοῦντι. Ironically ξυνειδέναι τί μοι δοκεῖς σαυτῷ καλόν, Aristoph. Eq., 184. 2. The matter assessed is not indicated, or is noted only neutrally, but is condemned unequivocally by the context (the abs. use in a bad sense): μηδέποτε μηδὲν αἰσχρὸν ποιήσας ἔλπιζε λήσειν· καὶ γὰρ ἂν τοὺς ἄλλους λάθῃς, σεαυτῷ συνειδήσεις, Isoc. Or., 1, 16. At this pt. one may also ref. to the difficult Soph. Fr. if the unknown context contains no obj.: ἦ δεινὸν ἄρ' ἦν, ἡνίκ' ἄν τις ἐσθλὸς ὢν αὑτῷ συνειδῇ, "how dreadful it would be if one who is noble were conscious of one (something bad)," [8] Soph. Fr., 845 (TGF, 327). 3. Not so common is the negation of a bad conscience (negative use in a bad sense): "I am aware of no evil." Conscience is not positive here; it is free from concrete accusations: τῷ δὲ μηδὲν ἑαυτῷ ἄδικον συνειδότι ἡδεῖα ἐλπὶς ἀεὶ πάρεστι, Plat. Resp., I, 331a. 4. To be distinguished from an empty conscience is one which is positively good in a moral sense: "I am conscious of a good thing," "I am aware of having done good." The three examples given [9] are so placed, however, that one can hardly speak of a morally good conscience. Cyrus fires his officers with confidence: ἀλλ' ἐπείπερ σύνισμεν ἡμῖν αὐτοῖς ἀπὸ παίδων ἀρξάμενοι ἀσκηταὶ ὄντες τῶν καλῶν κἀγαθῶν ἔργων, ἴωμεν ἐπὶ τοὺς πολεμίους, Xenoph. Cyrop., I, 5, 11. Acc. to the context the good and excellent works are simply training in handling weapons, which the enemy lacks. In a letter wrongly ascribed to Demosth. we read: εἰς ἣν [sc. πατρίδα] τοσαύτην εὔνοιαν ἐμαυτῷ σύνοιδα, ὅσης παρ' ὑμῶν εὔχομαι τυχεῖν, Demosth. Ep., II, 20. Here, too, we simply have an assertion rather than a positive moral evaluation: "I have in my self-consciousness (I feel) as great a love for my native place as I hope to find on your part." The passage thus belongs under b. [10] → 900, 6 ff. In these circumstances it is unlikely that the Soph. Fr. (→ lines 18 ff.) is an example of the positive moral use in a good sense.

e. Only a survey can be given of the reflexive formula σύνοιδα ἐμαυτῷ. This occurs from the 7th cent. to the post-Chr. era. It comes to be linked with the phenomenon of the moral conscience in the 5th cent. and becomes relatively common in the comedian

---

[4] Ed. E. Lobel and D. Page, Carminum Sapphicorum Fr., Poetarum Lesbiorum Fr. (1955), 23.

[5] Snell, 27.

[6] We are following Pierce, 22-29. There is a full list of examples from pagan Gk. and an unfortunately incomplete list of those from Hell. Judaism, 132-147.

[7] The reflexive is omitted on metrical grounds.

[8] Other remoter possibilities: 1. (reading αὐτῷ for αὑτῷ) "how dreadful it would be if one who is noble were a witness for him (another man)"; 2. "what a great thing it would be if one were aware of being noble" (→ lines 36 ff.). Pierce, 23 f., n. 6 thinks the interpretation given above (→ line 20 f.) comes from Stob. Ecl., III, 602, 10 ff., while Soph. is ref. to the self-awareness of a noble man (for details v. MS, 29-34). But the positive moral use of σύνοιδα ἐμαυτῷ in a good sense would be strange so early.

[9] Pierce, 132 f., No. 6-8.

[10] Pierce, 23 f., n. 6 (b) admits this is a border-line case.

Aristoph. (→ 901, 14 f.), the historian Xenoph. (→ 901, 11 f., 27 ff.) and in a special sense Plat. (→ 900, 24 ff.; 901, 21 ff.). The closeness of Aristoph. and Xenoph. to the people, also Demosth. in the 4th cent., suggests that what we have here is not an invention of lit. or art but the adoption of a current expression.

It is another question what the formula is meant to express. For Gk. thought self-awareness is above all a rational process. But since reflection is often upset by conflicts in which one's own acts are condemned, the verbal expression usually denotes a morally bad conscience.

In conclusion a negative statement must be made. Neither in a philosophical nor a moral sense has conscience a great deal to do with the deity.

There are only 3 possible instances. In Plat. Ap., 21b Socrates sees that the Delphic oracle has put him in the dilemma of different views of himself → 901, 24 ff. But strictly the oracle plays only a catalytic role by simply affirming that there is no man wiser than Socrates and thereby sharpening the existing problem. Socrates is on the point of leaving the gods behind and finding himself by his own perceptual faculty. The same applies to the 2 other passages in Xenoph. Thus Cyrus receives from his father the assurance that the gods will certainly hear him ὅτι συνειδέναι σαυτῷ δοκεῖς οὐπώποτ' ἀμελήσας αὐτῶν, Xenoph. Cyrop., I, 6, 4. The ref. is not to a clear conscience before the gods, and even less to illumination by them, but very simply to the hope of the king on the basis of his own conduct. Acc. to Xenoph. An., II, 5, 7 the breaker of oaths cannot escape the wrath of the vigilant gods, so that anyone who is conscious of having failed to keep an oath is not to be regarded as fortunate; once again, however, the attitude of the gods is simply a fact to be noted, and conscience is not in any sense a special mode or source of revelation.

2. συνειδός, συνείδησις, σύνεσις.

a. From the 5th to the 3rd cent. B.C. the nouns τὸ συνειδός and ἡ συνείδησις occur only sporadically, and with no consistent meaning. We may ref. first to 2 passages whose authenticity is hotly disputed. In the so-called Hippocrates letter Artaxerxes asks the doctor to free his army from the distress of an epidemic ἀγαθῇ συνειδήσει "with good professional skill," Hippocr. Ep., 1 (Littré, IX, p. 312). But this letter is possibly post-Chr. [11] Then the Stoic Chrysipp. ascribes the instinct of self-preservation to all creatures, not just men: πρῶτον οἰκεῖον λέγων εἶναι παντὶ ζῴῳ τὴν αὐτοῦ σύστασιν καὶ τὴν ταύτης συνείδησιν, "saying that the first property of every creature is its essential constitution and awareness of this," Diog. L., VII, 85. But one should probably read συναίσθησιν for συνείδησιν here. [12] The oldest example of συνείδησις is from the 5th cent. B.C.: ἔνιοι θνητῆς φύσεως διάλυσιν οὐκ εἰδότες ἄνθρωποι, συνειδήσει δὲ τῆς ἐν τῷ βίῳ κακοπραγμοσύνης, τὸν τῆς βιοτῆς χρόνον ἐν ταραχαῖς καὶ φόβοις ταλαιπωρέουσιν, ψεύδεα περὶ τοῦ μετὰ τὴν τελευτὴν μυθοπλαστέοντες χρόνου, Democr. Fr., 297 (Diels, II, 206, 19 ff.) The gen. view is that here συνείδησις means moral awareness of one's own bad deeds. [13] But κακοπραγμοσύνη can also be taken in a non-moral sense, esp. as there is no possessive pronoun ἑαυτῶν. Hence συνείδησις is simply knowledge or experience of the distressing situation of life: [14] "Some people who

---

[11] Schwyzer, 353.

[12] Pohlenz Stoa, II, 65; also "Grundfragen d. stoischen Philosophie," AGG, III, 26 (1940), 7; also Stoa u. Stoiker (1950), 110 f.

[13] Pierce, 34, n. 1 thinks the meaning is the same here as if we had συνειδότες αὐτοῖς τήν...

[14] The verb form would be συνειδότες τὴν ἐν τῷ βίῳ κακοπραγμοσύνην (no reflexive); Schwyzer, 353 transl.: "Know the unhappiness in life."

are not aware of the dissolution of mortal nature but know the misery of life, and pass their time wretchedly in unrest and anxiety, inventing lying myths about the hereafter." In the Menander-monostichon, 654, cf. 597[15] it is hard to say what the meaning of συνείδησις is: βροτοῖς ἅπασιν ἡ συνείδησις θεός. One can hardly adopt the common view that conscience is here said to come from God or to be divine. θεός is rather to be taken predicatively. Is this perhaps a scoffing verse about someone who incorrigibly knows better and who has come to grief? If so one should transl.: "For all mortals their own knowledge (self-awareness) is their god."

The neut. part συνειδός is first used as a noun in Demosth. He does not propose to go into certain things because he assumes ὁμοίως παρ᾽ ὑμῶν ἑκάστῳ συνειδὸς ὑπάρχειν μοι, Or., 18, 110. Here συνειδός is the act. faculty of memory which the hearers have in common with the speaker: "that with each of you as with me there is knowledge (of these things)." There is no hint of a moral use in this case. But twice Demosth. uses the inf. τὸ (ἑαυτῷ) συνειδέναι as a noun in this sense: ὅτι τἀληθὲς ἰσχυρὸν καὶ τοὐναντίον ἀσθενὲς τὸ συνειδέναι πεπρακόσιν αὐτοῖς τὰ πράγματα, Or., 19, 208; ἐπελαμβάνετο γὰρ αὐτῆς [sc. διανοίας] τὸ συνειδέναι, 19, 210. Here for the first time there is an attempt to fashion a noun for the bad conscience. συνειδός and συνείδησις will follow only later. But comparatively early σύνεσις (from συνίημι) is used to indicate a bad conscience. In the v. from Eur. relating to the mad Orestes (→ 901, 8 ff.) the word undoubtedly means "knowledge," "understanding." But the special character of the obj. suggests that here already we think in terms of the special sense of "(bad) conscience." The Menander Fr. is even plainer: ὁ συνιστορῶν αὑτῷ τι, κἂν ᾖ θρασύτατος, ἡ σύνεσις αὐτὸν δειλότατον εἶναι ποιεῖ, 522 (Körte). συνιστορῶν αὑτῷ corresponds to συνειδὼς ἑαυτῷ, so that σύνεσις means a morally bad conscience even though elsewhere in Menand. it means no more than "knowledge," "understanding." In the 2nd cent. Polyb. once compares the σύνεσις to a terrible witness and accuser, thus showing acquaintance with the developed idea of conscience: οὐδεὶς γὰρ οὕτως οὔτε μάρτυς ἐστὶ φοβερὸς οὔτε κατήγορος δεινὸς ὡς ἡ σύνεσις ἡ κατοικοῦσ᾽ ἐν ταῖς ἑκάστων ψυχαῖς, Polyb., 18, 43, 13.[16]

b. From the 1st cent. B.C. the nouns συνειδός and συνείδησις are used for "conscience" quite often in pagan Gk. as well in the Hell.-Jewish (→ 909, 17 ff.; 910, 33 ff.; 911, 26 ff.) and the Roman sphere (→ 907, 11 ff.). συνείδησις occurs esp. in the historians: ἐτάραττε δ᾽ αὐτὸν ἡ συνείδησις, ὅτι... δεινὰ δεδρακὼς ἦν αὐτούς, Dion. Hal. Ant. Rom., 8, 1, 3, also Diod. S., 4, 65, 7 and Philodem. Philos. Fr., 11, 5 f.[17] The ref. is always to the moral conscience in a bad sense. Twice a good conscience (→ 901, 24 ff.) would seem to be mentioned in profane passages in pre-Chr. Hell. But it is unquestionable that post-Chr. sayings are here attributed to the ancient philosophers. Periander is supposed to have said: ἀγαθὴ συνείδησις... ἐστὶν ἐλευθερία, Bias: ὀρθὴ συνείδησις... ἐστὶ τῶν κατὰ βίον ἀφόβων, Stob. Ecl., III, 24, 11 f. Similarly the Epictet. Fr., 97, in view of its echoing of Philonic material (→ 912, 10 ff.), is to be situated in post-Chr. Jewish Hell.: παῖδας μὲν ὄντας ἡμᾶς οἱ γονεῖς παιδαγωγῷ παρέδοσαν, ἐπιβλέποντι πανταχοῦ πρὸς τὸ μὴ βλάπτεσθαι· ἄνδρας δὲ γενομένους ὁ θεὸς παραδίδωσι τῇ ἐμφύτῳ συνειδήσει φυλάττειν· ταύτης οὖν τῆς φυλακῆς μηδαμῶς καταφρονητέον, ἐπεὶ καὶ τῷ θεῷ ἀπάρεστοι, καὶ τῷ ἰδίῳ συνειδότι ἐχθροὶ ἐσόμεθα.[18] The first unequivocal instance of καθαρὰ συνείδησις in paganism is in Egypt, P. Osl., II, 17, 10 (136 A.D.). It ref. to a conscience clear of concrete charges.

The most numerous instances of συνειδός are in Plut., who had contact with the intellectual world of Rome. On the basis of the well-known passage in Eur. Or., 396 (→ 901, 8 ff.) he gives a vivid description of the bad conscience which shares our

---

15 FAC, III, 2 (1961), 956, cf. 950.
16 Acc. to context and content this may be a later addition.
17 Ed. S. Sudhaus, Philodemi Volumina Rhetorica, II (1896), 140.
18 Ed. F. Dübner, Theophrasti Characteres (1842), 25.

knowledge and thus uncomfortably reminds us of our sins and evokes the torments of hell, Plut. Tranq. An., 18 f. (II, 476a-477a). Conscience is like a wound in the flesh. It makes reproaches which burn more than any external fire, for it is the rational man who finds fault with himself. In conversion the bad conscience is repulsed and set aside; the soul ponders πῶς ἂν ἐκβᾶσα τῆς μνήμης τῶν ἀδικημάτων καὶ τὸ συνειδὸς ἐξ αὐτῆς ἐκβαλοῦσα καὶ καθαρὰ γενομένη βίον ἄλλον ἐξ ἀρχῆς βιώσειεν, Plut. Ser. Num. Vind., 21 (II, 556a). ἅμα τῷ συνειδότι τοῦ ἐνδεοῦς δακνόμενος, καὶ δι᾽ ἐλπίδα καὶ πόθον χαίρων, "the man who is advancing on the way to virtue is the man who is also gnawed by conscience, which reminds him of his defects, and yet who also rejoices by reason of hope and desire (sc. for approximation to his model)," Plut. Quomodo quis suos in virtute sentiat profectus, 14 (II, 84d). It is true that in context the thought of conscience warning against fresh misdeeds is not far off. Yet the only task of conscience is still that of reminding us of the corrupt past. In the one instance of συνειδός in Epict. the meaning is "consciousness," "self-consciousness." The consciousness gives the Cynic the protection weapons give to rulers: τὸ συνειδὸς τὴν ἐξουσίαν ταύτην παραδίδωσιν, Epict. Diss., III, 22, 94.

c. By way of summary it may be said that from the 5th to the 3rd century B.C. there is a varied use which is only feeling its way towards a noun to express the moral conscience in the bad sense. Only in the 1st century B.C. do the two nouns συνειδός and συνείδησις outstrip σύνεσις and come into common use. The two can hardly be distinguished in content, though συνείδησις is more often used for self-consciousness in a non-moral sense. [19] The continuation of the non-moral use is a reminder that the two terms were connected only secondarily with the phenomenon of the moral conscience. [20]

3. The Problem of Conscience.

a. In conscience two egos are in juxtaposition and opposition in one and the same person (→ 900, 6 ff.), knowing and evaluating the same facts but from different standpoints. These two egos are controlled by different immanent or transcendent orders. [21] The one order, in virtue of its quality of truth, goodness, and beauty etc., is affirmed and is to be affirmed; it contains within itself an imperative, an "ought." The other is a factual but negated force which destroys the good order by falsehood, evil, and disorder etc. The ethical elements of tension within the one person result from the different natures and operations of the orders. But the conflict begins only when there is acquaintance with disorder. This is why the predominant factor is evaluation of the past (→ 901, 5 ff.; 903, 47 ff.). Moral conscience is not primarily concerned with preparation for approaching decisions (conscientia antecedens) but with assessing and condemning acts already committed (conscientia consequens). Hence the normal case is the bad conscience; the good conscience is an exception. Since conscience is concerned with man's reflection about himself, the accents may

19 συνείδησις ἀλγημάτων, "shared knowledge of griefs on the basis of one's own experience," Soranus De Gynaeciis, I, 4, 3 (CMG, IV, 5); but εἰσφέρειν συνείδησιν "to convey a report," P. Oxy., I, 123, 13 (3rd/4th cent. A.D.).

20 Most modern languages transl. συνείδησις etc. by "conscience" but we have to realise that the moral components, which decisively shape the modern concept, arose only secondarily in the history of the Gk. term.

21 The difficulty in defining conscience is primarily connected with an understanding of the controlling orders, cf. the various views of conscience, Jewish, Roman Catholic, Protestant, psycho-analytical, in "Das Gewissen," Stud. aus dem C. G. Jung-Institut Zürich, 7 (1958).

be placed at two different points. In the one case self-reflection is about being, so that the problem of conscience is especially one of knowledge. In the other it is reflection about action, so that the moral conscience is to the fore. The two strands are found together in the history of the group σύνοιδα κτλ. and they are materially related. It is thus as well to keep the whole phenomenon in view, though the ethical side will demand special attention, this alone being "conscience" in the narrower sense.

b. The sense of moral conscience is reflected in early Greece in notions of the Furies and penitential figures in the underworld, but above all in the distance between man and some of his own deeds as this is found for the first time in the *presbeia* of Hom. Il., 9, 115 ff. [22] A decisive breakthrough is made in the 5th century Enlightenment when the order of the world and the gods crumbles and man becomes the measure of all things. Here σύνοιδα ἐμαυτῷ in the moral sense is adopted from popular speech. Euripides, the rationalist among the tragic poets, depicts the torments of conscience into which man plunges himself by his own deeds → 901, 8 ff.

c. Socratic reflection (→ 900, 19 ff.) understands the human conflict from the standpoint of knowledge. Hence time plays no part and even the line of the irreversibility of events contracts into points. What matters is not later but present awareness of one's own ignorance. But since lack of knowledge can be dialectically removed, knowledge of the contradiction opens the way to victory over it. This takes place on the assumption that man has a share in the divine *logos* which underlies and represents all order. In contrast the Socratic δαιμόνιον (Plat. Ap., 31c d; 40a b etc.) is fully orientated to action. But this cannot be equated with conscience. As a divine voice, which cannot be explained rationally, it delivers impartial judgments on Socrates' acts. But its admonitions relate only to approaching decisions, not to those that belong to the past. [23]

d. The Stoic sets himself the task of avoiding and repelling anything that does not correspond to the divine φύσις proper to him. The true sage lives in agreement with this nature of his and hence he has no conscience in the morally bad sense, just as shame and remorse are also alien to him. When he does something for the sake of conscience it is only to avoid a bad conscience. Nevertheless, a special contribution was made to the later development of the idea of conscience by the Stoic-syncretistic doctrine of the ἐπίτροπος, the divinely appointed overseer of the individual, the reason which makes possible moral and intellectual decisions. When Epict. once adopts συνειδός for this (→ 904, 13 ff.) he makes possible the later extension of conscience to the sphere of positive guidance in advance. But this does not take place in profane Greek prior to the Christian era.

---

[22] Homer's heroes give no evidence of profound reflection about themselves. They ascribe responsibility for their offences to individual parts of themselves like θυμός, φρένες, Hom. Il., 9, 109 f., 119 f., Snell, 29 f. Instructive here is the gradual interiorising of the concept αἰδώς. In Il. νέμεσις is anger at others' misdeeds and αἰδώς is fear of this anger; it is thus social, 13, 122; 15, 561 f. Only gradually does αἰδώς become fear of oneself, cf. Democr., who says that one must have αἰδώς in respect of self (not others), Fr., 84, 244, 264 (Diels, II, 161, 194, 199) [Dihle].

[23] Epict. understands the δαιμόνιον rationally when he relates it to human reason, Diss., I, 14, 12; III, 22, 52, cf. A. Bonhöffer, *Epiktet u. die Stoa* (1890), 83.

e. Significant in analysing the processes of consciousness are the lessons in meditation which in Hellenistic philosophy are meant to promote the progress and development of the individual → VI, 706, 10 ff. In these a widely used formula of nightly self-examination which goes back to the Pythagoreans [24] played an important role: "Thou shalt not take sleep to thy gentle eyes until thou hast considered each of the day's acts: Where did I fail? What was a right act? What was left undone? Begin with the first, go through them, and finally when thou hast done wrong rebuke thyself and when thou hast done good rejoice," cf. Sen. De ira, III, 6. [25] Here the moral conscience with its subsequent assessment enters the sphere of the practical and theoretical deliberations which were to be so fruitful among the Romans (→ 907, 26 ff.) and in Philo (→ 911, 36 ff.). [26] συνειδός and συνείδησις, however, have not yet been found in the Pythagoreans. Seneca (→ 907, 12 ff.) avoids the term *conscientia* at least where he relates himself to the Neo-Pythagorean Sextius, De Ira, III, 36. Perhaps he himself forged the link between Pythagorean self-criticism and this term.

f. Gnosticism offers a radical solution to the conflict of conscience. It is true that instances are very sparse. [27] But the basic dualistic solution involves a full separation between the two egos. The true I of the Gnostic is identical with the divine world of light, while the other I belongs to the chaotic world and is thus to be abandoned. In the final analysis, then, there is no bad conscience for the Gnostic. Naturally this opens the door not merely to asceticism but also to libertinism.

g. Summing up one may say that the history of the word group σύνοιδα κτλ. and the history of the problem of conscience in the Greek world outside the Bible both display a multicoloured and by no means uniform picture. Apart from details there are two main points on the scale of meaning. Both chronologically and materially the starting-point is in the rational understanding [28] (→ 900, 6 ff.) of polarity in the human person and consequently in the consciousness itself. But then there comes to be combined with the verb and the nouns, which come into increasing use from the 1st century B.C. (→ 900, 39 ff.; 903, 30 ff.), the special concept of the moral conscience [29] (→ 904, 17 ff.), particularly at first the bad conscience, compared to which the good conscience is an exception (→ 904, 38 ff.). The idea of conscience

---

[24] Rabbow, 180-188; Bornkamm, 113 f.; Jaeger, 191-203.
[25] Cf. Rabbow, 180.
[26] Pohlenz Stoa, I, 317.
[27] A. Adam, "Die Psalmen d. Thomas u. d. Perlenlied als Zeugnisse vorchr. Gnosis," BZNW, 24 (1959), 11 and 44-46 deduces from the Coptic text of Thomas Ps. 5:24: "My conscience develops into a reason," the Syr. *tīrtā, praecordia,* φρένες. Acc. to Adam the expansion of *tīrtā* to conscience is closely connected with the influence of Gk. philosophy, esp. on the concept of the nous. But is should be remembered that already in OT anthropology the heart and reins occupy the place of the nous in Gk. thought. A testimony to relationship with the OT is the expression *tīrtā tābtā,* "good character," right consciousness," in the letter of the Stoic Mara ben Serapion (ed. W. Cureton, Spicilegium Syriacum [1855], 43, 5; 70, 6), cf. Adam, 45, n. 35.
[28] The rational character of the Gk. συνείδησις concept is emphasised esp. by Dihle (in a letter). It is also clearly asserted in, e.g., Spicq, 50-80.
[29] Concentration on the problem of the moral conscience is methodologically fruitful but carries within it the danger of one-sidedness, as in Pierce, 40-53.

in the narrower moral sense is one that the simple man readily apprehends even though more precise analysis is possible only in connection with a broader anthropology, and so the concept comes into ever closer relation to popular usage. [30] On the other hand, the idea of conscience may be taken so generally that it includes the question of self-consciousness. It is thus possible to speak with relative accuracy of the contribution made to the development of the post-Christian concept of conscience by philosophical work from Socrates (→ 900, 19 ff.; 905, 16 ff.) to the Pythagoreans (→ 906, 1 ff.) and the Stoics (→ 905, 27 ff.). [31] Nevertheless, it is going too far to say that philosophically or religiously the pre-Christian Greek world came anywhere near a developed, let alone a uniform concept of conscience.

B. Latin.

The words *conscius, conscientia* [32] find extended use predominantly, though not exclusively, in Cic. and esp. Sen. The idea of knowing together with other men is sustained much more strongly and consistently than in Greek, whether in the sense of a confidence or of guilty conspiracy. In relation to one's own person self-consciousness or self-awareness is to the fore, so that we often find an obj. gen.: *conscientia virtutis et vitiorum*, "awareness of virtues and vices." The moral aspect is only secondary. Here consciousness becomes conscience. The characteristic Latin transition may be seen in the phrase *animi conscientia*, "consciousness of the spirit," "conscience," Caesar Bellum Civile, III, 60, 2 etc. On the basis of consciousness as the faculty of remembering, *conscientia* means once again the conscience which looks back. But in the ethically robust structure of the Roman officer and lawyer, who knows that his duties are clearly defined and can be discharged, there easily arises the sense of duty done. More strongly, then, than in Gk. *conscientia* takes on the neutral [33] or even the positive sense *bona, praeclara, optima conscientia*, Tac. De Vita Julii Agricolae, 1, 2; Quint. Inst. Orat., VI, 1, 33; cf. *nil conscire sibi*, Horat. Ep., I, 1, 61.

This self-consciousness is the friendly or troublesome witness. Hence *testis* is used, cf. the Stoic ἐπίτροπος: *conscientia mille testes,* Quint. Inst. Orat., V, 11, 41. Nevertheless the accusing or judicial element is much less prominent than that of the applauding or dissatisfied spectator. Everything that takes place without boasting and *sine populo teste* is to be esp. praised; for *nullum theatrum conscientia maius est,* Cic. Tusc., II, 26, 63 and 64. Conscience is the observer even when the public is excluded: *o te miserum, si contemnis hunc testem,* Sen. Ep. Morales, V, 43, 4; *sacer intra nos spiritus sedet, malorum bonorumque nostrorum observator et custos,* IV, 41, 1. Here as much less radically in Philo (→ 912, 31 ff.) the Stoic watcher is combined with conscience. This does not mean that the concept is radically altered, for the ref. is still to the conscience which follows after or is at the most concurrent. Nevertheless, the ground is prepared for the changing of conscience into a norm.

---

[30] Kähler, 191.

[31] As against Pierce, 13-21.

[32] A. Ernout and A. Meillet, *Dict. étym. de la langue Latine*[4] (1959), s.v. *scio;* Spelthahn, ThLL, IV, s.v. *conscientia.* On conscience in Sen. cf. Sevenster, 84-92.

[33] *Magna vis est conscientiae, judices, et magna in utramque partem, ut neque timeant qui nihil commiserint, et poenam semper ante oculos versari putent qui peccarint,* Cic. Mil., 23, 61.

C. The Old Testament.

I. The Hebrew Text.

1. It is an astonishing fact that the OT did not develop any word for conscience. This is connected with its specific anthropology. [34] Man is basically governed by his relation to the God of revelation, Yahweh. As the divine covenant is the all-controlling sphere for the people, so the individual is encircled by this God. The best witness to this is Ps. 139. If it is asked where this knowledge of self comes from, the reply is to be sought, not in a reference to man, but in a reference to the God who speaks and who reveals Himself in His Word. This Word of His, which gives man self-understanding and makes possible responsible action, is very close to man in his heart and mouth, Dt. 30:14. Hence there is knowledge of good and evil only in remembering and keeping God's statutes, cf. Ps. 16:7 f.; [35] 40:8; 119:11 etc. Negation of God as the presupposition of one's own existence is the mark of the fool who hereby deceives himself, Ps. 10:4 ff,; 14:1; 53:1. In the OT the reflection of the I about itself is thus obedient listening to God. Even in contradiction, then, the I is a single person confronting the God who speaks. Conscience is hearing in the sense of willing adherence. The voice of God and one's own voice agree, not in the sense of rational autonomy, but in that of the harmony of the I with God's will. This is why the OT did not develop any term for conscience.

2. Now the OT is also aware of the inner discord in man.

Jacob's sons are ashamed of what they have done to Joseph, Gn. 42:21; David's heart smites him, 1 S.24:5; 2 S. 24:10; his heart staggers and stumbles because he has shed blood without cause, 1 S. 25:31; cf. 1 K. 8:38. [36] When this bad conscience is examined more closely, however, it is at once connected with God's attitude to the deed done and thus set on the plane of judgment and forgiveness. Cain's restlessness is not just the result or expression of a bad conscience. It is an outworking of God's curse, Gn. 4:11 f. The flight of Adam and Eve is a flight from God Himself, Gn. 3:7 f.

This means that God's Word rather than one's own word is the decisive one in man's controversy with his past. There are two consequences. On the one side self-accusation is radicalised, since it can see transgressions better from the concrete directions of the Torah. Muffled disquiet becomes the clear voice of the accuser. On the other side the accusation of man against himself is relativised, since it is not this but the living God who has the decisive word. Confession of sin thus leads from self-tormenting isolation to liberating forgiveness and the stilling of self-accusation, cf. Ps. 32:3 f. with 5 ff. For the later development of the idea of conscience it is of gt. importance that the OT speaks of a purifying and renewing of the heart of man. Decisive here is the prayer of Ps. 51:10; "Create in me a clean heart, O God, and renew a right spirit within me." In the background are the promises of the new covenant in Jer. 31:31 ff., cf. Ez. 36:26 etc. In Ps. 51 the promise for the people becomes a prayer for individual remission and new creation. [37]

---

34 Werblowsky, 94: "The question of the Jewish view of conscience, since we cannot tackle it directly, reduces itself, or broadens out into, the Jewish view of man in general. How does he know? and 'with' whom?" On OT anthropology → ψυχή.

35 Acc. to Werblowsky, 100 f. the reins which admonish us by night correspond to the voice of God, so that their admonition could later come to mean the bite of conscience. It should be noted, however, that the OT avoids equating God's voice with anything within.

36 Sir. 1:28 does not belong here: ἐν καρδίᾳ δισσῇ, "with divided (i.e., hypocritical) heart."

37 Note the verb ברא, which denotes God's creative activity, Ps. 51:10.

At the same time the concept of cleanness becomes personal rather than cultic. לֵב טָהוֹר in Ps. 51:10; Prv. 22:11 is thus added to the many expressions in לֵב → III, 607, 34 ff. This and similar expressions like רוּחַ נָכוֹן in Ps. 51:10 and תָּר־לֵבָב "of a clean heart" in Ps. 24:4; 73:1 prepare the way for a new concept of the clear or good conscience → 918, 40 ff.

II. The Septuagint.

1. The reflexive verb σύνοιδα ἐμαυτῷ occurs once in the LXX, συνείδησις 3 times, συνειδός not at all. In these passages there is a palpable alteration of the Hbr. line of thought by the Hell. concept. οὐ γὰρ σύνοιδα ἐμαυτῷ ἄτοπα πράξας [38] in Job 27:6 is a free rendering of לֹא־יֶחֱרַף לְבָבִי מִיָּמָי "my heart reproaches none of my days." Here for the first time the OT לֵבָב is replaced by moral "conscience" in the Gk. sense → 906, 27 ff. καί γε ἐν συνειδήσει σου βασιλέα μὴ καταράσῃ in Qoh. 10:20 is a mistranslation; in context the Hbr. מַדָּע should probably be transl. "thou shalt not curse the king on thy couch." [39] The translator, however, took it to mean "understanding," "thought," and used συνείδησις. The variant συνείδησις at Sir. 42:18 Cod א is a mere strengthening of εἴδησις "knowledge," "understanding": "The Most High has all knowledge."

The unequivocally morally bad conscience (→ 904, 17 ff.) occurs in Wis. 17:10: δειλὸν γὰρ ἰδίῳ πονηρία μάρτυρι καταδικαζομένη, ἀεὶ δὲ προσείληφεν τὰ χαλεπὰ συνεχομένη τῇ συνειδήσει, "for the wickedness condemned by its own witness is cowardly, and driven into a pass by conscience it always does what is worst." [40] Here for the first time in the encounter between the OT heritage and the Hellenistic heritage, the moral conscience is garbed in concepts from the legal sphere and takes on the function of the prosecutor and judge in one person. In the circle of Hellenistic Egyptian Judaism the son of Sirach had already uttered similar thoughts even earlier, though with no reference to the Hebrew לֵב: μακάριος οὗ οὐ κατέγνω ἡ ψυχὴ αὐτοῦ, Sir. 14:2. A century later and again in Egyptian Judaism Philo of Alexandria would set forth the function of the Law as prosecutor and judge → 911, 36 ff.

2. A second point is important for further development. In the Hellenistic stratum of OT literature the attributes of לֵב constantly increase.

The Hbr. words for a clean heart (יָשָׁר, טָהוֹר, תָּם etc. → III, 607, 34 ff.) are at first rendered by various Gk. adj.: εὐθύς in Ps. 11:2; 32:11 etc., ὅσιος 1 K. 9:4; Prv. 22:11, ὀρθός Prv. 15:14, τέλειος 1 K. 8:61; 11:4 etc., πλήρης 2 K. 20:3; 2 Ch. 15:17 etc., ἀληθινός Is. 38:3. The formula ἀγαθὴ καρδία holds a special place, since the Hbr. equivalent טוֹב־לֵב always has the very different sense "of a merry heart," "good things," Dt. 28:47; Ju. 16:25; 18:20; 19:22; Qoh. 9:7; Sir. 30:25. The slavishly lit. rendering ἀγαθὴ καρδία or διάνοια occurs for this, though only with restraint, Qoh. 9:7; Sir. 30:25; Dt. 28:47. The passages in Ju. use the more suitable verb ἀγαθύνομαι "to rejoice." LXX also has ἀγαθὴ καρδία for ethical and religious perfection, e.g., for לֵבָב שָׁלֵם at 1 Ch. 29:19.

---

[38] On the double negative cf. Pierce, 55.

[39] The proposed vocalisation בְּמַדָּעֲךָ "in thy relationship" and the conjecture בְּמַצָּעֲךָ "on thy couch" cf. Is. 28:20 are both superfluous.

[40] Zurich Bible; the text is uncertain.

This provides the presupposition for a development which leads to a concept hitherto unknown in the Greek world, that of the good conscience, which also includes the *conscientia praecurrens*. This result is the more logical in view of the fact that the idea of a pure heart has a bigger role in the LXX than the Mas. καθαρά καρδία etc. occur not only in passages where the Hbr. suggests them (Ps. 24:4; 51:10) but also for תָּם־לֵבָב (Gn. 20:5 f.), and περικαθαριεῖ τὴν καρδίαν is used for the circumcision of the heart by God, Dt. 30:6. [41]

D. Judaism.

1. The Rabbis and the Dead Sea Scrolls.

Like the OT the Rabb. and the Dead Sea Scrolls have no word for conscience. There is ref. to a good or a bad heart to denote the source of acts or indeed the nature of man. [42] One might also mention the doctrine of the good and evil impulse on the basis of Gn. 6:5; 8:21. [43] Here one sees the conflict of man under the control of different metaphysical orders. But beyond the antitheses man's unity is maintained; he can make one or the other impulse his king. In keeping is the fact that cosmological dualism is not radically taught in the Dead Sea Scrolls. It is overcome by the common Creator God, 1 QS 3:13 ff.

2. The Pseudepigrapha.

The pseudepigr. confirm the LXX line but contribute no new insights. Test. R. 4:3 has συνείδησις in the forensic sense: συνείδησίς μου συνέχει με, cf. Wis. 17:10 → 909, 17 ff. Similar statements are made about the καρδία: "The Spirit of truth bears witness to all things and accuses all, and the sinner is consumed by his own heart and cannot lift his face to the judge," Test. Jud. 20:5; "The righteous and humble man abhors doing evil, not because he is accused by others, but by his own heart," G. 5:3. Positive attributes also occur: "in purity of heart," N. 3:1; "out of a good heart," S. 4:7.

3. Josephus.

Jos. often has διάνοια for Hbr. לֵב. He sees man more under the aspect of thought than of will. [44] This is the starting-pt. for his understanding of the word group συνείδησις κτλ.
The verb has an intellectual thrust. This is shown by the choice of words in the story of the fall: καὶ συνίεσάν τε αὐτῶν ἤδη γεγυμνωμένων, Ant., 1, 44; συνειδὼς αὐτῷ τὴν ἀδικίαν, 1, 45; even διὰ τὸ συγγινώσκειν ἑαυτῷ παραβάντι τὴν τοῦ θεοῦ πρόσταξιν, 1, 46. With the morally negative abs. use in 2, 31 one often finds also the morally positive use. Moses says to the people: ὅτι πολλὰ ἐμαυτῷ καμόντι περὶ σωτηρίας τῆς ὑμετέρας σύνοιδα, 3, 190; cf. 15, 190; Vit., 361. Jos. also uses τὸ συνειδός as vox media. Conscience is the witness whom, with God, one must fear, Ant., 4, 286. Reuben warns his brothers that if they slay their brother conscience will be their enemy and none can escape it, whether it be good or bad, 2, 25. Jos. often adds an

---

[41] Cf. also Job 11:13: εἰ γὰρ σὺ καθαρὰν ἔθου τὴν καρδίαν σου, if the transl. read with the Mas. הֲכִינוֹתָ "thou dost prepare," not הֲזִכּוֹתָ "thou dost cleanse."
[42] Acc. to R. Eleazar the best or worst way a man can choose is a good or bad heart, Ab., 2, 12 f.
[43] Bousset-Gressm., 402-405; Str.-B., III, 92-96; IV, 466-483 Exc. "The Good and Bad Impulse"; Werblowsky, 104-110; Seitz, 82-95.
[44] Schl. Theol. d. Judt., 21.

attribute: πονηρός, 1, 47, also in continuation of what one finds already in the OT (→ 909, 36 ff., 910, 5 ff.) ἀγαθός in Bell., 2, 582 and καθαρός in Bell., 1, 453. ἐκ (ὑπό, ἀπό) συνειδότος has either a good or a bad sense: "out of a bad conscience" Ant., 16, 102, "out of a good conscience" 2, 52; 13, 316.

Jos. also uses συνείδησις, but it is open to question whether this means "conscience" and not just "consciousness," "knowledge of something," "mind." [45] The Zealots are hard to beat in battle συνειδήσει τῶν εἰργασμένων "because of their knowledge of past deeds" which leave them no option but desperate fighting, Bell., 4, 193. When the other Jews meet them ἔσονται τῇ συνειδήσει ταπεινότεροι "they are inferior in self-consciousness (i.e., morale)," 4, 189, cf. 186-188. The emperor, seeing the confusion of Herod's sons, noted that their silence μὴ κατὰ συνείδησιν ἀτοπωτέραν, was due to inexperience, "not a corrupt mind," Ant., 16, 103, cf. the different ἐκ τοῦ συνειδότος "out of a bad conscience," 16, 102. Herod reviled his brother: καὶ σοὶ μὲν ἡ συνείδησις αὕτη συζήσειεν, ἐγὼ δὲ ... "this (sordid) mind may dwell in thee, but I ...," 16, 212.

It is theologically significant that conscience is called a third witness for resurrection after death along with the Torah and God: ἀλλ᾿ αὐτὸς ἕκαστος αὐτῷ τὸ συνειδὸς ἔχων μαρτυροῦν πεπίστευκεν, τοῦ μὲν νομοθέτου προφητεύσαντος, τοῦ δὲ θεοῦ τὴν πίστιν ἰσχυρὰν παρεσχηκότος, ὅτι ... "but each believes, also having conscience, which bears him witness after the law-giver on the one side has given the promise and God on the other has granted strong faith that ...," Ap., 2, 218. Thus conscience is implicated in the problem of the relation between natural and revealed knowledge of God, which was a concern of Hell. Judaism. [46]

4. Philo.

Philo, in whose thought OT and Hellenistic streams converge, is the first to think through theologically a doctrine of consience.

a. Usage.

In a moral sense the verb can be vox media: ὅταν ἠδικηκότι μὲν ἑαυτῷ μηδὲν συνειδῇ, πάντα δ᾿ ὑπὲρ τοῦ κεκτημένου καὶ λέγοντι καὶ πράττοντι, Rer. Div. Her., 6. In all three passages in which συνείδησις occurs it is combined with gen. ἀδικημάτων or ἁμαρτημάτων and is to be transl. as an action noun: "knowledge of one's own unjust acts," Virt., 124; Spec. Leg., II, 49; Det. Pot. Ins., 146. Conscience is συνειδός. Since Philo hardly uses καρδία in the OT sense, [47] συνειδός takes its place, esp. in the phrase ἐκ (ἀπό) καθαροῦ συνειδότος, Praem. Poen., 84; Spec. Leg., I, 203. Philo does not speak of a "bad, evil, unclean conscience." But except in the formula mentioned it is always bad: ἕνεκα τοῦ συνειδότος, Leg. Gaj., 39 (morally bad abs. use → 901, 15 ff.).

b. The Task of Conscience.

The task of conscience is ἐλέγχειν. This comprises the whole process from accusation by the advocate to admonition, threat of punishment and condemnation by the judge.

The common formula ὑπὸ (διά, πρός) τοῦ συνειδότος ἐλεγχόμενος etc. reflects this breadth of meaning: ἐλέγχειν takes place before the inner forum of man, Spec. Leg., I, 235; IV, 6; Jos., 262. Conscience is the only impartial accuser and infallible judge. It cannot be deceived by pretences, Fug., 118; Virt., 206. Its effect is κεντεῖν, "to stab, jab,

---

[45] Schl. Theol. d. Judt., 139 f. relates all the passages which follows to conscience.
[46] *Ibid.*, 15 f., 22.
[47] Leisegang, *s.v.*

torment," Conf., Ling., 121, δουλοῦν, Omn. Prob. Lib., 149, τιτρώσκειν τε καὶ διώκειν, Deus Imm., 100. Philo offers a variegated depiction of the torments of conscience in the person of the foe of the Jews Flaccus (Flacc., 180) and from the standpt. of conscience's work cf. Decal., 87: "When it (the elenchus native to the soul) is once awakened, it comes forth as an accuser, indicts, charges, and shames; on the other hand it also instructs as a judge, giving correction, advising conversion (διδάσκει, νουθετεῖ, παραινεῖ μεταβάλλεσθαι), and when it persuades it is pleased and propitiated, but when it cannot do this it fights implacably, leaving no rest day or night, but inflicting incurable cuts and wounds until it has destroyed the life which is wretched and accursed." [48]

c. The Theological Context.

The theological context of these statements should be noted. As has been seen, conscience belongs to the teaching about fighting sin. [49] It is a spur used by God to induce man's conversion. In the framework of this it leads to self-knowledge and the confession of sin, Praem. Poen., 163 f., cf. Deus Imm., 126. It warns against further transgression ὑπὲρ τοῦ μηκέθ' ὁμοίως ὀλισθεῖν, Op. Mund., 128.

There is a connected exposition of this usus elenchticus in Det. Pot. Ins., 145 f. In education it is better to be beaten than to be expelled by the teacher. "Thus when we are persuaded by the consciousness of our unrighteous acts (οἱ συνειδήσει τῶν οἰκείων ἀδικημάτων ἐλεγχόμενοι) we should beseech God to punish us rather than abandon us. For if He abandons us He makes us no longer His own, the people of the gracious God, but servants of the merciless world. But when He punishes us, since He is kind, clement and gentle, He will make good our offences by sending into our souls the correcting elenchus, His own logos, through whom, having shamed and censured them for their sins, He will save them." The penal function of the elenchus = logos is positive; lack of it would mean the complete abandonment of man by God. This function is also limited, for man's salvation is accomplished by God Himself and not by conscience. It is no accident, but due to the OT legacy with its gracious God, that Philo succeeds in ascribing a positive meaning to the negative task of the prosecutor. The many sayings about God's action should be noted for this reason: ἔλεος, ἵλεως, ἐπιεικῶς, πρᾴως, χρηστὸς ὤν, ἐπανορθώσεται, ἰάσεται.

d. The Question of the Guiding Function of Conscience.

Twice Philo seems to speak of the positive function of conscience as a guide. In the exposition of Gn. 37:15 in Det. Pot. Ins., 23 f. the man who shows Joseph the way is identical with the true Anthropos, the λογικὴ διάνοια, which indwells the soul of man as ruler and king but which also as judge holds the tongue in check by the reins of conscience. This elenchus warns the erring soul about falling into vices and calls it back therefrom. The second passage is yet another allegorical exposition of Gn. 37:15 in Fug., 130 f. [50] Here the elenchus, the true man, is afraid the soul might go astray and leads it to the right track. In both cases, however, Philo's thought is imprecise. He equates similar entities [51] without making any clear distinction between them. The νοῦς in Poster. C., 59; Quaest. in Ex., II, 13 and the θεῖος λόγος in Deus Imm., 134 f. are equated with the elenchus as well as conscience. But these have a real guiding function in moral decisions. In virtue of the parallel equations advance directions may thus be ascribed to conscience too, but this goes beyond the general drift of Philo's doctrine of conscience.

---

[48] Cf. L. Cohn, Die Werke Philos v. Alex. in deutscher Übers., I, (1909), 390.
[49] Völker, 97.
[50] Völker, 100 f.
[51] For the various Philonic versions of the concept Anthropos, including conscience, cf. H. Leisegang, Der Heilige Geist, I (1919), 78, n. 5.

e. The Historical Position of Philo.

To integrate Philo into the history of the term is no easy task. He is connected with popular ideas of his age in the use of the word συνειδός. In his keen analysis of the processes of conscience he owes a good deal to the Neo-Pythagoreans (→ 906, 1 ff.), who had a centre in Alexandria as well as Rome. As concerns Stoic philosophy (→ 905, 27 ff.), which greatly influenced Philo, the link is the idea of the divine νοῦς/λόγος which is implanted in the soul and which now includes conscience: ψυχῇ συμπεφυκὼς καὶ συνοικῶν ἔλεγχος Decal., 87; ἐνιδρυμένος τῇ ψυχῇ, Op. Mund., 128; cf. Det. Pot. Ins., 23. The new thing in Philo, however, is that conscience is now presented as independent and spontaneous compared to ratio. The decisive contribution in the shaping of Philo's doctrine of conscience does not come from the Gk. world but from the OT, though he introduces a wholly new vocabulary as compared with this.

The first thing to bind him to the OT and to distinguish him from the Gk. environment is the use of the words ἐλέγχω, ἔλεγχος in a special sense. The combining of the functions of accusing and judging corresponds exactly to the OT group יכח (→ II, 473, 25 ff.), [52] which occupies an important place in the OT, esp. in proverbial wisdom. ἐλέγχω occurs 64 times in the LXX, 38 of these in Job, Prv., Wis., Sir. ἔλεγχος is used 31 times for תּוֹכַחַת, all but 4 of these being in the same books. ἐλέγχειν, like παιδεύειν, διδάσκειν, ἐπιστρέφειν, νουθετεῖν, is the task of God or of divine wisdom, cf. Sir. 18:13; Wis. 1:6-8; 12:2 etc. In the Gk. world ἐλέγχω means "to shame," "to censure," "to oppose" (in a dispute), "to subject to an examination" etc. The judicial activity of admonishing and condemning, which is essential to the OT, is lacking. The second thing to connect Philo with the OT-Jewish strand is the juridical function of conscience. Polyb. (→ 903, 26 ff.) does once call conscience μάρτυς and κατήγωρ. But no judicial function is expressly allotted to it. This connection is not made until Dio. Chrys. Or., 37, 35 c. 100 A.D., and even here only in incidental comparison. [53] Similarly the Lat. concept of the testis is different from Philo's view, for the testis is the spectator rather than the legal witness → 907, 26 ff. In Philo, however, the juridical aspect is very strongly emphasised, for behind it stands the person of God as Accuser and Judge. This leads us on to the third point which links Philo to the OT: the religious basis of the doctrine of conscience. [54] Conscience is an instrument in God's hand to bring men to conversion → 912, 10 ff. It is true that the Stoic idea of indwelling conscience in Sen. has strong religious traits → 907, 31 ff. But only the differentiation between conscience and the God at work through it, which Philo maintains on an OT basis (→ 908, 28 ff.), makes it possible both to view the accusatory task of conscience more stringently and also to set it in a positive context.

It is not certain that Philo was the first to enunciate such a profound understanding of conscience. For one thing, he was an encyclopedist rather than a great original thinker. For another, the development of Alexandrian Judaism is wrapped in so much obscurity that we cannot say what precursors he might have had. One need have no hesitation, however, in adopting the thesis that the source of Philo's doctrine of conscience is the confluence of two types of moral life and thought, that represented by Hellenism on the one side and that represented by the OT on the other. [55]

---

[52] Kähler, 184 f. correctly indicates the connection but underrates the full material correspondence between ἔλεγχος and תּוֹכַחַת.

[53] Pierce, 45-53 marshalls examples of the tormenting function of conscience, but for express judicial measures he can ref. only to Philo, 48 f.

[54] Völker, 104; Bréhier, 295-310.

[55] Kähler, 172 f.

E. The New Testament.

1. General.

The word σύνοιδα occurs only twice. In one instance it denotes the guilty knowledge of a second person συνειδυίης τῆς γυναικός, Ac. 5:2. In the other it is used with the reflexive pronoun, 1 C. 4:4 → 916, 19 ff. συνειδός does not occur; instead συνείδησις is used 31 times. The distribution in the various works leads us at once to an important conclusion. In view of the OT tradition one would not expect it in the original text of the Gospels. It occurs only once in the story of the woman taken in adultery, and this reminds us of the judicial office in the Philonic sense (→ 911, 36 ff.): ὑπὸ τῆς συνειδήσεως ἐλεγχόμενοι, Jn. 8:9. The other instances may be divided into 2 groups: Pauline and post-Pauline. There are 14 instances in the former and 16 in the latter. One may thus assume that it was Paul who first established the word in the Chr. Church. In the second group there are 6 examples in the Past., 5 in Hb., 3 in 1 Pt. and 2 in Ac. But here the dominant sense is one not found at all in Pl., i.e., that of the good, clear, or bad conscience. There is thus a distinction in use.

2. Paul.

a. No less than 8 of the 14 passages in Paul are concentrated on the issue of idol meats, 1 C. 8:7-13; 10:25-30. This suggests that a current slogan of the community was adopted and reapplied. [56] What Paul himself understands by συνείδησις has to be gleaned from the context, since he does not offer any definitions. At all events he means something more comprehensive than a subsequent bad conscience (→ 906, 27 ff.), [57] for though συνείδησις may be stained it does not have to be, not even when it is weak, 1 C. 8:7. What is presupposed is that it may be assailed, not that it has been. One may seriously ask whether an imprecise view of conscience does not serve prematurely to conceal the problem. [58] In the context (→ II, 693, 40 ff.) the reference is to a γνῶσις which embraces in a totality the perception of a distinction between the facts, the acknowledgment and choice of divinely willed obligations, and self-evaluation. Hence συνείδησις means a "percipient and active self-awareness" [59] which is threatened at its heart by the disjunction of acknowledgment and perception, willing and knowing, judgment and action. But Paul does not venture on either theological systematisation or psychological analysis. Thus συνείδησις is not to be defined as a power of religious and moral evaluation or the like which can be detached from man. [60] It is man himself aware of himself in perception and acknowledgment, in willing and acting. [61] Hence the expressions adopted in 1 C. 8 may be used either of συνείδησις or of man as such: ἀσθενής/ἀσθενῶν (vv. 9-12); [62] οἰκοδομέω (v. 10), τύπτω (v. 12), μολύνω (v. 7). [63] The attitude to one's συνεί-

---

[56] Pierce, 64 f.

[57] As against Pierce, 76 f.

[58] Stelzenberger, 68, 70.

[59] v. Soden, 242, n. 3 limits συνείδησις to "direct self-awareness . . . in the sense of bad co-knowledge" with no element of the will. Schl. K., 260 says: "Paul is now speaking . . . of the judgment which takes shape in man's self-consciousness and which prescribes his conduct." Coune, 509, 527 f. and others think συνείδησις is primarily religious conviction, relating it to וְצַ֣ת אֱלִיהִים, 530 f.

[60] So, e.g., Stelzenberger, 68, 70: "power of religious and moral judgment."

[61] Bultmann Theol.⁴, 217.

[62] Cf. μηδὲ ἡ ψυχή σου ἀσθενείτω, Is. 7:4.

[63] Cf. οἰκοδομεῖν ἑαυτόν or ἕτερον 1 C. 14:4, 17, μολύνω τὴν ψυχήν Sir. 21:28; Test. A. 4:4.

δησις is the attitude to oneself, and the attitude to the neighbour's συνείδησις is the attitude to the neighbour himself. When he deals with the strong and the weak in R. Paul can thus use πίστις (→ VI, 218, 38 ff.) instead of συνείδησις, 14:1 f.

Paul's decisive statements that in the community of Jesus Christ man is in encounter with the one true but gracious God imposes a restriction on συνείδησις [64] which is at one and the same time both a liberation and a commitment. The liberation is especially for the weak, about whom Paul as one of the strong speaks to the strong, 8:4, 7-13. Members of the congregation who are weak because they are used to idols [65] have not yet won through to the liberating acknowledgment of the truth [66] that they themselves are known and acknowledged by the one true God beside whom there are no other gods but only created things, v. 3, 7. They are thus threatened at the very heart of their being when as the weak they try to achieve the insight of the strong, v. 7, 10 f. But because Christ died precisely for the weak (v. 11) the strong should know and acknowledge a weak self-awareness better than the weak themselves can do, v. 13. For the self-awareness which condemns itself there is thus set up a liberating boundary from without. But even more, in the final settlement of disputed questions [67] (10:25-27) the weak are told to refrain from an ἀνακρίνειν διὰ τὴν συνείδησιν, i.e., an examination which might lead to exorbitant demands on themselves. On the basis of the quotation from Ps. 24:1 v. 26 then takes up again the thought of 8:3 f., 6 that the whole of creation belongs to God and not to idols. [68] Hence the weak should take the Gospel promise of their acknowledgment by God more seriously than their own knowledge. That is to say, they must let their own συνείδησις be limited and liberated by this.

For the strong the true perception of the freedom established in Christ carries with it a demand that they should accept the weak, 8:12 f. The detailed result of this commitment may be seen in the extreme case in which the weak cannot overcome their scruples or carry out the injunction laid on them, 10:28-30. [69] In this case the strong should refrain from the offered dish διὰ τὴν συνείδησιν, i.e., in order not to burden the self-consciousness of the weak, 28, 29a. This does not imply that the strong might be hurt by the reproaches of the weak, for their freedom is not subject to the judgment of others, v. 29a b. [70] What it does imply is that the strong, in the freedom they have on the basis of grace, should not lead the weaker brethren astray, wounding their συνείδησις and thus bringing themselves into ill repute, v. 29a, 30.

The formula διὰ τὴν συνείδησιν also occurs in R. 13:5: οὐ μόνον διὰ τὴν ὀργὴν ἀλλὰ καὶ διὰ τὴν συνείδησιν. There are three possible lines of exposition. One should submit to the state 1. to avoid the bad conscience which might otherwise

---

[64] This restriction is clearly worked out in Sevenster, 92-102.

[65] At 1 C. 8:7 one should read συνηθείᾳ with 𝔥 pc. συνειδήσει has been imported from the context and presupposes the moral conscience.

[66] Paul intentionally speaks of a weak rather than an erring συνείδησις.

[67] For all the attempts to distinguish different sources 1 C. 8-10 is to be taken as a unity, cf. Maurer Grund, 630-641.

[68] Joh. W. 1 K., ad loc.

[69] The μηνύσας is hardly the host, so, e.g., Bultmann Theol.[4], 220, nor a provocative pagan, e.g., Ltzm. 1 K., ad loc., but a Chr. guest (→ III, 253, 5 ff.), cf. Joh. W. 1 K., ad loc.; Stelzenberger, 73. One cannot leave this an open question, Schl. K., 304. The pagan Chr. still imprisoned in his own former habits says ἱερόθυτον; the reading εἰδωλόθυτον is secondary.

[70] Kähler, 256-258; Bultmann Theol.[4], 220. v. 29 is not, as Ltzm. 1 K., ad loc. thinks, the argument of an incensed strong Chr. defending his own position.

ensue, [71] 2. out of duty, conviction, or other moral considerations suggested by conscience, [72] or 3. because of the final links which are seen between the state and God's will. [73] A comparison with 1 C. 10:25, 27 f. is adduced is favour of 1., but this is only partly convincing, since in R. Paul is not dealing with troubled people but with those who are critical of the state. Furthermore positive obedience to authority is demanded as compared with refraining from action in 1 C. 10. This obedience is not to be under external pressure. It is to take place in unity between the act and awareness of it. This will not be in face of an immanent authority, but in face of God, the Lord of the state. In the light of v. 6 this involves agreement with God's will. Hence the third possibility is to be preferred. συνείδησις is responsible awareness that the ultimate foundations both of one's own being and also of the state are in God. Members of the community are to have neither a higher nor a lower estimation of the state than as a specific servant of God. The first commentary on the passage in 1 Pt. 2:19, with its strange διὰ συνείδησιν θεοῦ, [74] "for the sake of co-knowledge with God," "for the sake of consciousness of God," bears the same meaning.

b. The other instances in Paul presuppose the Hellenistic-Jewish concept of conscience as ἔλεγχος (→ 909, 17 ff.; 911, 36 ff.) but set this in new connections and hence give it a new point. This may be seen indirectly in the only verse in which Paul has the verb: οὐδὲν γὰρ ἐμαυτῷ σύνοιδα, "I am aware of nothing (bad)," 1 C. 4:4. The context makes is apparent that Paul does not have to fear any human judgment, not even his own, but that the divine verdict alone is normative for him. Self-judging man is seen within the divine judgment which decides concerning him. But since God's judgment accepts man in the justification of the sinner, and consequently liberates him, Paul can make positive statements about conscience which are not to be found in the world around. The self-consciousness based on God can be sure of itself in a good and positive sense. Thus Paul can glory in the witness of his conscience which confirms that he has walked in holiness and integrity, 2 C. 1:12. Materially 1 Jn. 3:19-22 (→ VI, 3, 1 ff.) corresponds to this view of conscience. Here God knows the accusation of the heart and thereby silences the ἔλεγχος. Since this self-confidence is not a subjective opinion but is grounded in God's judgment, with which one's own concurs, it is taken into account that in virtue of this connection man is open to evaluation by the consciences of others (→ VI, 724, 19 ff.) (2 C. 5:11) and that he will thus be accepted positively (2 C. 4:2). Thus, even though the verdict of conscience is positive, as Paul says in un-paralleled fashion, it is not an autonomous verdict, but one which is based on God's Word. When conscience bears witness to the great sorrow of the apostle (R. 9:1), this voice takes on the significance of an oath only when it is not merely governed but also confirmed by the Holy Spirit: συμμαρτυρούσης μοι τῆς συνειδήσεώς μου ἐν πνεύματι ἁγίῳ.

In R. 2:15 Paul is speaking of Gentiles who without knowing the Torah will display its works at the Last Judgment and in this way shame the Jews. The

---

[71] Pierce, 71; Schl. R., ad loc.
[72] Ltzm. R., Mi. R., ad loc.; M. Dibelius, "Rom u. d. Chr. im 1. Jhdt.," Botschaft u. Gesch., Gesamm. Aufsätze, II (1956), 183; Gutbrod, 60-62; Stelzenberger, 55 f.
[73] K. Barth, K. D., II, 2² (1946), 807 (C. D., II, 2 [1957], 722); C. E. B. Cranfield, "Some Observations on R. 13:1-7," NTSt, (1959/60), 246 f.; Bultmann Theol.⁴, 219.
[74] This reading is to be retained. All the witnesses which add ἀγαθήν betray acquaintance with an original gen. θεοῦ.

conscience of the Gentiles, expressed by accusing and excusing thoughts, [75] will thus bear a witness which accompanies the Last Judgment. [76] The existence of this conscience, which is already present and which extends into the future, is thus for Paul, as for later Judaism and especially Philo (→ 912, 10 ff.), an indication of the responsibility of man. Like later Judaism and Philo Paul has in view only the conscience which follows in the sense of the ἔλεγχος, not the conscience which goes in advance and guides. [77] He introduces it only in R. 2, not in R. 1 with its nailing of the Gentiles to their knowledge of God. There is a decisive distinction from Judaism, however, in his statement that this voice does not merely accuse and condemn but also, without prejudice to God's judgment, [78] defends and acquits. For Paul sees man in the light of the accomplished Christ event and he thus reckons with the possibility of unexpected surprises on the coming day of judgment.

Why is it that in Paul the role of conscience as an accusing and convicting elenchus is so much weaker than in later Judaism? The solution is not to be found in the stronger Hellenistic or Rabbinic background of the apostle. It is connected with the new thing which Paul has to tell with his Gospel of Jesus Christ. The accusing voice of conscience is overcome because the incomparably sharper accuser, the revealed Law of God which does not merely accuse but also slays (R. 7:7 ff.), is done away and set aside by the pardoning voice of the God who makes new in Christ.

c. To sum up, one may say that Paul takes συνείδησις with a comprehensive breadth and variety not found in any of his predecessors. For him it is no longer just the popular bad conscience or the Hellenistic-Jewish ἔλεγχος. It has now become the central self-consciousness of knowing and acting man. With few exceptions it had never been anything like this before in literature. Combining the Greek view of man as especially a thinking being (→ 900, 6 ff.) with the Hebrew tradition which stresses the primacy of the Word (→ 908, 14 ff.), Paul raises the whole problem of act, being, and knowledge in anthropology — a step of momentous significance for the centuries which followed. Yet Paul did not present any uniform doctrine of συνείδησις. The concept is simply one of various attempts to understand man, cf. Paul's use of καρδία (→ III, 611, 30 ff.), πνεῦμα (→ VI, 434, 31 ff.), and → ψυχή. Furthermore different streams of tradition flow together in it without intermingling. The whole complex is encircled and held together, however, by the new thing which Paul connects with the idea of conscience. He declares that man is acknowledged by the one true but gracious God in Jesus Christ. This enables him not merely to see more sharply the conflicts of inwardly divided man but also to set them under the promise of healing.

---

[75] The accusation and defence are not in a society but within the individual, Kuss, 69 etc. Reicke, 157-162 suggests "feeling for accusing or excusing thoughts" (obj. gen.), but this is neither linguistically nor materially convincing.

[76] v. 16 is not to be excised as a gloss, as proposed by R. Bultmann, "Glossen im R.," ThLZ, 72 (1947), 200 f. and Bornkamm, 117. On this cf. R. Walker, "Die Heiden u. das Gericht," Ev. Theol., 20 (1960), 311-314.

[77] With Kähler, 302 against Pierce, 85; Stelzenberger, 81; Schl. R. on 2:15. Kuss, 69, 79 sees it as the function of conscience to precede in R. 2:15a and to follow in 15b, cf. also Bultmann Theol.⁴, 217 f.

[78] Bornkamm, 116: "Since in Paul the inner court of man and the divine judgment are not co-extensive, the idea of conscience is for him a purely human idea."

3. Post-Pauline Writings.

In so far as the post-Pauline writings speaks of conscience they almost always characterise it by special attributes like ἀγαθή (Ac. 23:1; 1 Tm. 1:5, 19; 1 Pt. 3:16, 21), καθαρά (1 Tm. 3:9; 2 Tm. 1:3), καλή (Hb. 13:18), ἀπρόσκοπος (Ac. 24:16) or even πονηρά (Hb. 10:22).

a. The Pastorals belong firmly to this tradition. Calling on the Lord ἐκ καθαρᾶς καρδίας (2 Tm. 2:22) is the same as worship ἐν καθαρᾷ συνειδήσει (2 Tm. 1:3). In the formal speech of the Pastorals the pure conscience (→ III, 425, 29 ff.) is the total standing of the Christian. This is particularly plain when the difference between the life of the Christian and that of the heretic is formulated in compendious confessions. The goal of preaching is ἀγάπη ἐκ καθαρᾶς καρδίας καὶ συνειδήσεως ἀγαθῆς καὶ πίστεως ἀνυποκρίτου; from these things false teachers have fallen away, 1 Tm. 1:5 f. Timothy is to fight the good fight ἔχων πίστιν καὶ ἀγαθὴν συνείδησιν, which some have cast aside and made shipwreck in the faith, 1:19. Polluting the νοῦς and συνείδησις corresponds to the discrepancy between saying one knows God and denying this in fact by one's works, Tt. 1:15 f. In these three passages and in others there is a striking connection between conscience and faith: ἔχοντες τὸ μυστήριον τῆς πίστεως ἐν καθαρᾷ συνειδήσει, 1 Tm. 3:9. The brand on the conscience corresponds to apostasy from the faith, 4:1 f. The good conscience is more than an empty and blameless conscience. It is also more than the pure and simple heart of the OT righteous. In all probability the author has in view the renewal of man by the new creation in faith, which embraces the whole life of the Christian. At this point, then, the Pastorals are not the product of Christian respectability; [79] they are a deliberate echo of the Pauline message of justification out of which they grew. [80]

b. Hebrews refers to the purifying of the conscience which takes place in baptism. This applies already to 10:2, where συνείδησις is combined with the obj. gen. ἁμαρτιῶν: "knowledge of sins." In contrast to purely ritual cleansing perfecting κατὰ συνείδησιν is a τελείωσις of the whole man, 9:9. This decisive purifying and total renewing of man from dead works to service of the living God is the Christ event, 9:13 f., cf. R. 6:11 ff. Only after 10:22 is the purifying of the bad conscience (→ VI, 556, 37 ff.) more precisely connected with the washing of the body (→ IV, 304, 18 ff.; VI, 983, 12 ff.). Turning from a bad to a good conscience is limited neither to the moral nor to the cultic sphere. It embraces the whole man in his relation to God. Hence it is possible that συνείδησις καλή (13:18) is again a formula for the Christian life, to which the authors appeal in their request for the prayers of the recipients. [81]

c. In 1 Pt. συνείδησις ἀγαθή again seem to be a formula for the Christian life, 3:16. This is suggested by the baptismal formula in 3:21, which defines baptism as συνειδήσεως ἀγαθῆς ἐπερώτημα, "the request to God for a good conscience" (→ II, 688, 11 ff.). Possibly we have here a current baptismal formula with the

---

[79] Dib. Past. Exc. on 1 Tm. 1:5.
[80] Spicq Epîtres Past., 37: "Avoir une ἀγαθὴ συνείδησις est le propre de l'homme rené dans le Christ."
[81] The participle clause, which is to be taken modally (not causally), is thus to be construed as an elucidation: "wherein we seek to walk aright in all things."

petition καρδίαν καθαρὰν κτίσον ἐν ἐμοί, ὁ θεός (ψ 50:12) in the background, → 908, 34 ff.

d. We have to realise what is displayed in this stratum of the NT to which early catholicism is so often credited. Something absent altogether from the surrounding Greek world and exceptional in Hellenistic Judaism is now proclaimed as the norm of life. This is the good and clear conscience as the healing of inwardly divided man and therewith a new existence by the act of God in Christ.

F. The Post-Apostolic Fathers.

συνείδησις is common and is distributed evenly among the various authors. It is almost always defined by an attribute, but in contrast to the NT has a strongly moralising thrust connected with the popularisation of NT concepts. The woman is to do all ἐν ἀμώμῳ καὶ σεμνῇ καὶ ἀγνῇ συνειδήσει, 1 Cl., 1, 3 cf. Pol., 5, 3. One can and should serve God ἐν ἀγαθῇ συνειδήσει ὑπάρχων, 1 Cl., 41, 1 or ἐν καθαρᾷ συνειδήσει, 45, 7. Ign. reminds us of the battle against heresy in the Past. He who does not stand by the bishop and presbyters οὐ καθαρός ἐστιν τῇ συνειδήσει, Ign. Tr., 7, 2, or he is not εὐσυνείδητος, Mg., 4. Ign. can use this adj. of himself since he has not harmed anyone, Phld., 6, 3. Prayer out of a good conscience saves from death, 2 Cl., 16, 4. One should not come to prayer with a πονηρὰ συνείδησις, Did., 4, 14; Barn., 19, 12. A bad conscience does not go well with the Spirit of truth, Herm. m., 3, 4. The good conscience has become a habit in the formula μετ᾽ ἐλέους καὶ συνειδήσεως, "with mercy and conscientiousness," 1 Cl., 2, 4, cf. 34, 7.

Maurer

συνοικοδομέω	→ V, 148, 14 ff.
συνοχή	→ 886, 1 ff.
συντέλεια	→ τέλος.
συντελέω	→ τέλος.

---

† συντρίβω, † σύντριμμα

Contents: A. The Word Group in the Greek World: 1. Derivation of the Term; 2. Meaning of συντρίβω and Cognates: a. Strict Use; b. Looser Use. B. The Word Group in the Old Testament: 1. Hebrew Originals: a. The Root שבר, b. Other Roots; c. Other Renderings of שבר; 2. Septuagint Sayings Important in Relation to the New Testament. C. The Word Group in the New Testament: 1. Old Testament Quotations and Expressions; 2. Other Passages.

A. The Word Group in the Greek World.

1. Derivation of the Term.

The etym. is obscure.[1] The noun τρίβος, from τρίβω, means a traversed, "well-trodden way," then "intercourse," "circulation" etc. συντριβής and συνδιατρίβω also belong to the sphere of commerce [2] → 921, 17 ff.; n. 12.

συντρίβω, σύντριμμα. Bibl.: Liddell-Scott, Moult.-Mill., Pr.-Bauer, s.v.
[1] Cf. Boisacq, 985; Hofmann, 374.
[2] Walde-Pok., I, 728, 872; F. Kluge, *Etym. Wörterbuch d. deutschen Sprache* (1957), s.v. "treiben." With a ref. to Hesych. Liddell-Scott transl. συντριβής by "living together."

2. Meaning of συντρίβω and Cognates.

a. Strict Use. συντρίβω, attested from the 5th cent. B.C., is made up of σύν and τρίβω. It thus means by composition "to rub together" and in this sense it is used for kindling which is heated and catches fire by friction, Luc. Verae hist., I, 32. Another positive use is when the verb is used for "to grind," "to rub," "to crush," Plut. Def. Orac., 47 (II, 436b), e.g., ointments, medications, or means of magic, CIG, III, 2, 5980, 15 ff. (2nd cent. A.D.). [3] Then the word means "to break," "to smash," "to destroy." It is used for breaking bones [4] or smashing the limbs, skulls, [5] or entire bodies of men or animals, e.g., in battle, Xenoph. An., IV, 7, 4; Eur. Cyc., 705; Lys., 3, 8; 3, 18. Spears are broken in or after the battle, Xenoph. Hist. Graec., III, 4, 14; Diod. S., 15, 86, 2. A fighting force is smashed or destroyed, Diod. S., 12, 28, 2. The verbal noun σύντριμμα occurs in the sense of "breaking," "destruction" from Aristot. De Audibilibus, p. 802a, 34.

b. Looser Use. It is a sign of weakness when something breaks or is crushed and twisted and finally perishes altogether, κλᾶται μὲν γὰρ καὶ συντρίβεται καὶ κάμπτεται καὶ ὅλως φθείρεται, Aristot. Metaph., 4, 12, p. 1019a, 28. This applies in the social and political as well as the psychological sphere. Fear humiliates and wears down a man, Plut. Superst., 2 (II, 165b). In detail trouble, anxiety, or remorse [6] may be meant, Polyb., 6, 58, 13, or shattered hope, Diod. S., 4, 66, 4; 16, 59, 3. In Demades [7] Fr., 12 (4th cent. B.C.) we read that the misfortune of the dead has destroyed the hope of the living.

B. The Word Group in the Old Testament.

1. Hebrew Originals.

a. The Root שבר.

In its basic sense "to break" the root שָׁבַר [8] occurs 145 times altogether in the OT, 35 times in the historical books, 41 in the hagiographical, and 69 in the 4 prophetic books of the Hbr. Canon. The word denotes the breaking of objects, Lv. 6:21; 11:33; 15:12, the smashing of ships, Ez. 27:26; cf. Test. N. 6:5, the crushing of bodies, 1 K. 13:26; cf. Test. Jud. 2:4, and the destruction of enemies, Is. 14:25. In a transf. sense it can be used for "broken" pride, Lv. 26:19, also courage, hope, and broken hearts, Ps. 69:20; 147:3. From the root we have the noun שֶׁבֶר, which occurs 41 times in both the lit. and the transf. sense.

LXX συντρίβω corresponds 134 times to MT שבר, also twice to Hbr. Sir. The few exceptions may be left out of account. The idea of breaking up is common to both words. But the Hbr. root means "to break in pieces," whereas the basic meaning of the Gk. is "to crush" (→ lines 5, 13 f.), so that non-destructive meanings are possible. Yet there is no doubt that when συντρίβω is used for שבר in the Bible it denotes processes of destruction even to radical obliteration, Ez. 26:2; 30:8. The same applies to the nouns συντριβή, σύντριμμα, συντριμμός, normally used for שֶׁבֶר and מִשְׁבָּר.

---

[3] Deissmann LO, 108; other examples of the simple form in Preis. Zaub., I, 1, 249 f.; I, 2, 36 and 38 f.; I, 3, 427 and 455; II, 7, 184 f. and 337; cf. II, 13, 27.

[4] Cf. Preis. Zaub., II, 13, 246 (a conjuration).

[5] The obj. can also be in the gen.

[6] In Hell. philosophy (first attested in the Epicureans) συντριβή is contritio, a tt. in psychagogy and penitential practice, which, based on recognition of a fault, is a necessary presupposition of προκοπή, or moral progress. Cf. W. Schmid, "Contritio u. ultima linea rerum in neuen epikureischen Texten," Rhein. Mus., 100 (1957), 302-327 [Dihle].

[7] Ed. J. Bekker, Oratores Attici III (1823), 489.

[8] Köhler-Baumg., Lisow-Rost, s.v.

b. Other Roots.

In spite of the apparent uniformity of rendering more than 30 other roots are used in addition to שבר, [9] mostly only once each. Manifold though these are, they hardly extend the range of meaning of the Gk. verb. In some cases roots which are broadly related in meaning are transl. by συντρίβω, e.g., דכא "to dash in pieces" in Is. 53:5 'A; [10] Is. 57:15 LXX, חתת "to break" in Ιερ. 31(48):20; the noun מְחִתָּה "terror," "destruction," occurs 11 times in the HT, always transl. συντριβή in the 5 instances in Prv.; כשל "to stumble" in Da. 11:34; Neh. 4:4; Ez. 33:12 'A, שמם ni "to be violently depopulated" Ez. 6:4, שמר ni "to be extirpated" Ez. 32:12, נפץ "to dash in pieces" Ps. 2:9 etc. Is. 46:1 ref. to the overthrow of the Babyl. gods. The verb קרס "to bow," which occurs only in Is. 46:1, 2, obviously seemed to be too weak to the translator. He thus used συντρίβω, which seemed to be in keeping with the ref. to idols. There is a similar sharpening in Ju. 4:23 Θ, where συντρίβω is used for כנע "to humble." The root חול (חיל), which means basically "to be in labour," "to shake," occurs 45 times in HT and is transl. by συντρίβω once at Jl. 2:6. The nations do not merely shake; they are shattered. In Is. 13:6 συντριβή is used for שד from the root שדד. [11] In Neh. 2:13, 15 we have the root שבר "to test." This is transl. συντρίβω in 2 Εσδρ. 12:13, 15; this is obviously due to confusion with שבר. But here the LXX reader could hardly take συντρίβω in the usual negative sense; he would have to assume some such sense as "to be concerned about." [12]

c. Other Renderings of שבר.

Only occasionally is שבר transl. by other Gk. words. Confusion with שרב lies behind ἀποδώσεται in Da. 8:25 LXX (Θ συντρίψει). ἀπολλύω in Is. 14:25, διαλύω in Jon. 1:4 vl., ἐρημόω in Is. 24:10 and θλίβω in Lv. 26:26 are to be regarded as synon. λεπτύνω in 2 Ch. 23:17 ("to make thin") might be taken in the sense "to crush," "to grind." The ref. here is to the destruction of altars and idols.

2. Septuagint Sayings Important in Relation to the New Testament.

Acc. to Ex. 12:10 LXX; 12:46; Nu. 9:12 not a leg of the Passover lamb is to be broken. [13] Acc. to Ps. 34:20 the righteous man is under the Lord's protection; He keeps him so that none of his bones is broken. The cultic regulation has nothing whatever to do with the teaching of the Ps. A connection is made only by the NT passion narrative → 933, 15 f.

Eschatological sayings in the OT proclaim the destruction of weapons and war. The breaking of bows, swords and other weapons signifies the inauguration of the kingdom of peace ψ 45:10; 75:3 f., also 36:15; Ιερ. 25:15 (49:35). Hos. 1:5 relates the breaking of the bow of Israel to the events of 733 B.C. when the plain of Jezreel became part of an

---

[9] Hatch-Redp. needs to be amplified; he lists only 25 roots. שבר in particular is left out.

[10] K. F. Euler, Die Verkündigung vom leidenden Gottesknecht aus Js. 53 in d. griech. Bibel (1934), 29-32.

[11] HT seems to try to explain the divine name Shadday by popular etym. from the root shadad. Cf. G. Bertram, "Zur Prägung d. bibl. Gottesvorstellung in d. griech. Übers. d. AT. Die Wiedergabe von schadad u schaddaj im Griech.," Die Welt d. Orients, II (1959), 502-513.

[12] First spatially: "to prowl around the wall," then "to be concerned about the wall."

[13] G. A. Barton, "A Bone of Him Shall not be Broken," JBL, 49 (1930), 13-19 traces back the Passover ritual to original cannibal customs. Jub. 49:13: "You shall not break any bone that none of the bones of the children of Israel may be broken," seems to connect Ex. 12:46 etc. and Ps. 34:20 along the lines of an apotropaic rite. Qumran seems to confirm the practice archaeologically. The bones of animals as the remnants of feasts have been found there in numerous jars in which they were collected and kept. Cf. A. Scheiber, " 'Ihr sollt kein Bein dran zerbrechen,' " VT, 13 (1963), 95-97; H. Bardtke, "Qumran u. seine Funde," ThR, NF, 29 (1963), 278.

Assyrian province. But in LXX it is to be understood in the light of 2:20. The breaking of all the apparatus of war is here an intimation of the universal kingdom of peace of the age of salvation. πόλεμον συντρίψω in Hos. 2:20 is linguistically very difficult, [14] since in the OT Yahweh is called a man of war, as in Ex. 15:3 and Is. 42:13. [15] When LXX Ex. 15:3 writes κύριος συντρίβων πολέμους (Αλλ: ἀνὴρ πολέμου) and LXX Is. 42:13 κύριος ὁ θεὸς τῶν δυνάμεων ἐξελεύσεται καὶ συντρίψει πόλεμον (Σ: ὡς ἀνὴρ πολεμιστής), then independently of the Hbr. original the LXX has to be taken in the sense of the destruction of war and its weapons. In Gn. 49:24, in Jacob's blessing, it is Joseph who almost as a Messianic hero breaks the bow; LXX reads ותשבר for the ותשב of the corrupt HT. In Mi. 2:8 LXX goes its own way and expresses hope for the destruction of war. The adoption of the divine name of Ex. 15:3 in Jdt. 9:7; 16:2 ref. again to God as the One who wipes out war. [16]

At ψ 68:21 'ΑΣ correctly transl. ὀνειδισμὸς συνέτριψεν (Σ: κατέαξε) τὴν καρδίαν μου. The righteous see themselves as those who are of a broken heart. They know (in the sense of R. 5:3; 8:28) that the Lord is near them ψ 33:19. He accepts a broken spirit as a sacrifice and He does not despise a broken heart ψ 50:19, cf. Δα. 3:39. God heals broken hearts and binds up their wounds (συντρίμματα) ψ 146:3. [17] This is the task of the One sent by God in Is. 61:1. Is. 57:15 declares that God gives life to broken hearts. Here LXX combines part. ni of דכא and the adj. דכּא in the one word συντετριμμένοι (τὴν καρδίαν). Part ni of דכא[18] occurs only here and acc. to Sir.11:5 it seems to mean "oppressed." But LXX understood it in the light of the pi and transl. it thus only in this passage. 'A was the first to render part. pu at Is. 53:5 by συντετριμμένος (ἀπὸ τῶν ἁμαρτιῶν ἡμῶν). Involuntarily — for he has in view a priestly figure offering sacrifice, not the victim — he thereby makes συντετριμμένος a feature of the man of sorrows, the suffering Messiah. As 'A sees it, the ref. is not to martyrdom but to the depression of the priest at the injustice around him.

συντετριμμένος and ταπεινός are already synon. in the OT. At Is. 66:2 four words are used for עָנִי in the different transl. LXX has ταπεινός, 'Α πραΰς, Σ πτωχός, Θ συντετριμμένος, cf. 3 Macc. 2:20. Here συντετριμμένος is used as a self-designation by the penitential community at prayer. 1 QS 8:3 must be taken in the same way: They exercise faithfulness in the land with a steady mind and broken spirit רוח נשברה, cf. 11:1. In the early Chr. tradition ψ 50:19 is quoted in 1 Cl., 18, 17; 52, 4; Barn., 2, 10. There is allusion to Is. 61:1 in Barn., 14, 9. But nowhere is there any special stress on the terms.

---

[14] In Polyb., 2, 63, 4 τρίβω πόλεμον means "to carry on, prolong the war"; it is not a par. to the LXX.

[15] As the God of war Yahweh is called Zebaoth, which is not to be related only to the hosts of Israel, as Ju. 5:20 f. shows. Cf. Eichr. Theol. AT, I, 120 f. and Index, s.v. "Krieg," "Kriegsgott."

[16] Philo Rer. Div. Her., 206 interprets συντρίβω πόλεμον by καθαιρέω and calls Moses the herald of the message of peace of Him who has resolved to end wars, of the God whose constant concern is for peace. Cf. also Virt., 47-49, where Dt. 28:7 is taken to imply a life of peace or of easy and miraculous victory. In Praem. Poen., 93-95 Philo also quotes Lv. 26:6 and he then continues: War will collapse and perish: αὐτὸς καταρρυήσεται καὶ συντριβήσεται πρὸς ἑαυτόν. Ibid., 124 he quotes Lv. 26:13 and ref. to the spirit which up to recently was subject to many lusts and desires and the urge of countless vices, "but God has rubbed away (συνέτριψεν) the sufferings of his servants and brought them to freedom," cf. L. Cohn, Die Werke Philos v. Alex., II (1910), 413.

[17] But Is. 65:14 συντριβὴ πνεύματος might be taken in the sense of "remorse" and "contrition," cf. also Ez. 6:9 'ΑΘ.

[18] דכא occurs in the HT once in the ni, 11 times in the pi, 4 the pu and 2 the hitp. In 1 QH 5:17: "They torment (crush) me (my soul) all the time," the term expresses passion piety, cf. Ps. 44:22; R. 8:36.

C. The Word Group in the New Testament.

1. Old Testament Quotations and Expressions.

The text Mt. 12:20: κάλαμον συντετριμμένον οὐ κατεάξει, [19] is a free formulation which Matthew himself did not coin but which is to be traced back to the adoption by the Christian community of the OT use of συντετριμμένος along the lines of Jewish passion piety, → 922, 14 f. [20] The One to whom the text refers will not come to the apostate people or the tiny remnant with chiding and chastisement like the great prophets of the OT from Amos to Jeremiah. He will gather publicans and sinners around Him. There is thus fulfilled the picture of the Servant of the Lord of Dt. Is., for whom the wretched and oppressed are the recipients of the promises and consolations of God's revelation. [21]

In Lk. 4:18 there is reason to think the saying from Is. 61:1: ἰάσασθαι τοὺς συντετριμμένους τῇ καρδίᾳ, was not part of the original. But it was given practical significance by 𝕶 and is also attested in Iren. Haer., III, 9, 3 et al. [22] The fundamental question is whether Jesus applied the LXX text to Himself in a deliberately changed form faithfully reproduced by Lk. or whether one should not assume that the Evangelist, or the community behind him, saw in the text a pertinent description of the work of Jesus, an OT promise which He fulfilled even down to details. This promise is for men who are broken in heart, inwardly. They are characterised as the humble, but not the maltreated. They are smitten to the quick by the knowledge of their sin and their guilt before God. The Gospel is designed for them. [23]

The crurifragium occurs only in Jn. (19:36). Since the high Sabbath is at hand the Jews ask Pilate to have the legs of the crucified broken and to let their bodies be disposed of, 19:31, 32. [24] The crurifragium is meant to hasten death and it thus carries with it a shortening of the agony.

That it was customary seems to be presupposed in Lact. Inst., IV, 26, 32 f. at the beginning of the 4th cent. A.D. Ev. Pt. 4:14 says is was omitted in the case of one of the malefactors to increase his punishment and this too might suggest that it was the common rule. Acc. to Jn. 19:33 Jesus was already dead and hence the procedure was not necessary in His case. The silence of the Synoptists is thought by some to throw doubt on the authenticity of the account. Acc. to Jn. it is a fulfilment of Ps. 34:20 or Ex. 12:46 → 921, 26 f. In Lact. (→ line 26) another point is made: everything was so arranged *ne laesum ac diminutum corpus ad resurgendum inhabile redderetur.* [25] The form of the quotation is decisively affected by ψ 33:21; this provides the συντριβήσεται. [26] The v. from the Ps. shows that Jesus died as a righteous man, cf. Lk. 23:47. [27] The cultic under-

---

[19] Cf. Just. Dial., 123, 8.

[20] In exposition cf. B. Weiss, *Krit.-exeget. Hndbch. über d. Ev. d. Mt.*⁷ (1890), ad loc.; he sees in the broken reed a metaphor for those "in whom only a weak remnant of good remains and who would thus be easily crushed if treated strictly." Jesus' saving work is for them, cf. Zn. Mt., ad loc.

[21] B. Duhm, *Das Buch Js., Handkomm. AT*, 3, 1⁴ (1922), ad loc.

[22] Cf. Nestle, ad loc. Bengel, ad loc. thinks this text is original. M. Luther, *Das NT* (Revised Text, 1956) omits the phrase.

[23] Cf. H. Grotius, Annotationes in NT, I (1769), ad loc.: *fracti animo, non qui poenitudine peccatorum tanguntur, sed versantes in summis rerum angustiis, ut et Ps. 147:3.*

[24] So Bultmann J., ad loc.

[25] Bengel, ad loc.: *Johannes Psalmum necnon Mosen respicit. Ossa Jesu Christi non sunt perpessa comminuitionem, necnon caro corruptionem: dirissimum suppliciorum, crux: et tamen quodvis aliud corpori mox resuscitando minus aptum fuisset.*

[26] Bau. J., ad loc.

[27] Cf. also the fulfilment of Ps. 69:21 and 22:18 and on this G. Bertram, *Die Leidensgeschichte Jesu u. d. Christuskult* (1922), 79-83, 85 f., 90; Bultmann J., ad loc., n. 5 and 8.

standing of the omission of the crurifragium is based on the referring of the type of the Passover lamb to Christ, cf. Paul in 1 C. 5:7. In Jn. Jesus dies at the hour when the Jews slew the Passover lamb. [28] His death corresponds directly to that of the lamb. Hence there is special significance in the omission of the crurifragium. In spite of the custom and the request of the Jews which might have seemed to impose it, it did not happen to Jesus, and hence the law of the Passover lamb was kept in relation to Him. [29]

The quotation from Is. 59:7 in R. 3:16 is a feature in the description of man's sinful nature with the aid of OT testimonies. In these σύντριμμα (destruction) and misery are both sin and punishment. Men create for themselves the evil in which they destroy one another. [30] The future in R. 16:20: The God of peace will shortly bruise Satan under your feet, seems to combine two ideas: the imminent eschatological shattering of Satan by God, [31] and the rapid victory of believers over the powers of darkness as God lets them tread Satan under their feet. In the case of the latter the optative (infinite or conjunctive), which is commonly attested, [32] is more apt than the future. The image of smashing or trampling Satan is based on Gn. 3:15. [33] Ps. 91:13 is the basis of the idea that the righteous will tread underfoot dangerous beasts and the demonic powers embodied by them. [34]

In R. 16:20 the false teachers of v. 17 are regarded as servants of Satan and the representatives of demonic forces, cf. 2 C. 11:15; Eph. 6:12. [35] Paul is promising the community the help of God in fighting these and rapid victory (συντρίψει) over them, [36] and in so doing he uses mythical or eschatological-apocalyptic terminology, cf. Mal. 4:3. According to Rev. 2:27 the exalted Christ gives His authority over the heathen to him who overcomes and keeps His works to the end. The exercise of this dominion is described in the words of Ps. 2:9 → VI, 494, n. 87. [37] Ruling with

---

[28] The arraignment before Pilate was at midday on the 14th Nisan, the day of preparation for the Passover, Str.-B., II, 836, 840; Bultmann J. on 19:37: Jesus died as the true Passover lamb of Ex. 12:46 while the lambs were being slain: "The end of the Jewish cult or the futility of its further observance is thus maintained," *loc. cit.*

[29] Acc. to A. Loisy, *Le Quatrième Év.* (1903), 885-894 the episode of the crurifragium is unhistorical and is not an organic part of the account. It is taken by Jn. from the Passover ritual. Wellh. J. cuts out esp. the spear incident; v. 36 should come directly after v. 33. Jn.'s main pt. is thus brought out, namely, that Jesus is the real Passover lamb.

[30] Cf. Luther's *Vorlesung über den R. 1515/1516 Scholia, ad loc.,* Weimar ed., 57 (1939). 156; Thomas Aquinas, *Comm. on R., ad loc.,* transl. and ed. H. Fahsel (1927), 117.

[31] Cf. the chaos conflict in the OT. Acc. to Job 38:11 Yahweh broke the pride of the sea; ψ 73:13 echoes the theme of the conquering of the mythical monster of the depths, cf. J. Kroll, *Gott u. Hölle, Der Mythus vom Descensuskampfe* (1932), 315-321; O. Kaiser, *Die mythische Bdtg. d. Meeres in Ägypten, Ugarit u. Israel²* (1962), 140-152.

[32] Cf. Tisch. NT, II, *ad loc.*

[33] Cf. G. v. Rad, *Das erste Buch Mose, AT Deutsch,* 2 (1958), *ad loc.*

[34] Cf. Test. S. 6:6: Then the spirits of error will be delivered up to trampling εἰς κατα-πάτησιν (→ V, 941, 42 ff.) and men will rule over wicked spirits; Test. L. 18:12; Ass. Mos. 10; 1; Jub. 23:29. In Is. 11:8 the battle ends and the kingdom of peace is ushered in with the treading down of the hostile forces. For the Chr. community Jesus Himself is the dragon-slayer, cf. the miniature in the so-called Stuttgart Psalter (10th cent.), H. Preuss, *Das Bild Christi im Wandel d. Zeiten³* (1932), 36, Ill. 19. Cf. Test. A. 7:3.

[35] A. Harnack, *Militia Christi* (1905) 27-43 *passim*; Ant. Christ., III (1932), 187.

[36] B. Weiss, *Der Br. d. Pls. an d. Römer, Krit.-exeget. Komm. über d. NT⁹* (1899), Ltzm. R., *ad loc.*

[37] Cf. Loh. Apk., *ad loc.* Σ has συντρίβω in both halves of Ps. 2:9, while LXX has ποιμαίνω for רעה the first time. The negative sense of this verb (*v.* Loh. Apk., *ad loc.*), i.e., the exploiting and mastering of the flock, is in accord with the context. Cf. also Ps. Sol. 17:24: God will exercise dominion with an iron rod to destroy sins. The text uses Ps. 2:9 but independently of the LXX, being more akin to Σ. The royal ritual of Egypt has the image

an iron rod means that everything of clay is broken. [38] Da. 7:27 and 2:34 f. also refer to the rule of believers under which the heathen are destroyed. [39]

2. Other Passages.

Only in Mk. 14:3 does the story of the anointing [40] have the detailed reference to the breaking [41] of the vessel. In Mk. 4:5 the unclean spirit gives the sick man the power τὰς πέδας συντετρῖφθαι, "to break the fetters," cf. Lk. 8:29: διαρρήσσων τὰ δεσμά. In the story of the epileptic boy (Lk. 9:39) συντρίβω is again used in the description of the sickness. The attacks last a long time and when the unclean spirit finally leaves the boy his forces are completely exhausted. [42] In both instances one sees the destructive work of the demonic powers which Jesus is able to vanquish. [43]

Bertram

συνυποκρίνομαι	→ ὑποκρίνομαι	συστέλλω	→ 596, 12 ff.
σύσσημον	→ 269, 2 ff.	συστενάζω	→ 600, 1 ff.
σύσσωμος	→ σῶμα.	συστοιχέω	→ 669, 1 ff.
συσταυρόω	→ 786, 18 ff.	συστρατιώτης	→ 701, 8 ff.

σφάζω, σφαγή

† σφάζω.

Contents: A. Greek Usage Not Under Biblical Influence: 1. Ritual Slaying: a. Meat Offerings whose Flesh Is Eaten but which are Made to the Olympian Gods; b. σφάγια, 2. Profane Slaying: a. Slaying of an Animal; b. Slaying of a Man. B. Septuagint Usage: 1. Ritual Slaying: a. Animal Sacrifices; b. Human Sacrifices; 2. Profane Slaying: a. Animals;

---

of smashing clay vessels for subjugated peoples (or peoples to be subjugated), cf. H. J. Kraus, *Psalmen, I, Bibl. Komm. AT*, 15, 1 (1960), ad loc. Cf. also W. Jost, ΠΟΙΜΗΝ. *Das Bild vom Hirten in d. bibl. Überlieferung u. seine christologische Bdtg.* (1939), esp. 26 f.

[38] Cramer Cat., VIII, ad loc. already takes the ὡς to signify ἵνα.

[39] Loh. Apk., *ad loc.*: In opposition to the error of a peaceful encounter with the pagan world the divine entertains the proud hope of subjugating all unbelievers (ἔθνη), cf. also B. Weiss, *Die Apk., Das NT, Handausgabe*, 11² (1902), ad loc.

[40] Bultmann Trad., 283, 299. Bertram, op. cit. (→ n. 27), 16-18.

[41] Cf. the vl. in D: θραύσασα. Materially cf. D. G. Lindner, "Zur Salbung Jesu in Bethanien," ZNW, 4 (1903), 179-181: Acc. to Jn. 12:7 Mary was to keep the broken container to put by the body of Jesus at His burial.

[42] J. Weiss, *Die Ev. d. Mk. u. Lk.* (1892) and B. Weiss, *Die Ev. d. Mk. u. Lk., Krit.-exeget. Komm. über d. NT⁹* (1901), ad loc.

[43] In the post-apost. fathers συντρίβω occurs only in OT quotations or expressions → 922, 31 ff.; so also the Apologists. συντριβή, which does not occur in the NT, is used in Barn., 6, 2 in the sense of σύντριμμα for destruction by Christ.

σ φ ά ζ ω, σ φ α γ ή. Bibl.: On A.: Boisacq, Hofmann, Liddell-Scott, L. Meyer, *Hndbch. d. griech. Etym.*, IV (1902), Pape, Pass., Prellwitz Etym. Wört., Thes. Steph.³, VIII, s.v.; S. Eitrem, "Opferritus u. Voropfer d. Griechen u. Römer," *Skrifter utgit av Videnskapsselskapet i Kristiania, 2. Historisk-Filos. Klasse* (1914); also "Mantis u. σφάγια," *Symb. Osl.*, 18 (1938), 9-30; R. Hirzel, "Der Selbstmord," ARW, 11 (1908), 75-104, 243-284, 417-476; P. E. Legrand, Art. "Sacrificium," Darembg.-Saglio, IV, 956-973; K. Meuli, "Griech. Opferbräuche," *Phyllobolia f. P. von d. Mühll*, ed. O. Gigon, K. Meuli et al. (1946), 185-288; Nilsson, I², 132-150; F. Pfister, *Die Religion d. Griechen u. Römer* (1930), 117-120, 180-186; Rohde, Index, s.v. "Opfer"; F. Rüsche, "Blut, Leben u. Seele. Eine Vorarbeit z. Religions-

b. Men. C. Philo and Josephus: 1. Philo; 2. Josephus. D. Rabbinic Writings; E. The New Testament.

A. Greek Usage Not Under Biblical Influence.

σφάζω means "to slay an animal," [1] "to slaughter," or with ref. to men "to kill," "to murder," "to slay," always with some sense of a fig. or transf. use. The word belongs to the stem σφαγ-, cf. φάσγανον "knife," "sword." Other etym. connections have not yet been proved for certain. [2] As regards morphology later Attic σφάττω Xenoph. Cyrop., III, 1, 25; Plat. Gorg., 468c; Aristot. Eth. Nic., V, 15, p. 1138a, 10; Plut. Laud. s. Inv., 22

gesch. d. Opfers," *Stud. z. Gesch. u. Kultur d. Altertums,* Suppl. Vol., 5 (1930), Index, *s.v.* "Opfer"; P. Stengel, *Die griech. Kultusaltertümer, Hndbch. AW,* 5, 3³ (1920), 95-155; also *Opferbräuche d. Griechen* (1910); R. K. Yerkes, *Sacrifice in Greek and Roman Religions and in Early Judaism, The Hale Lectures* (1952); L. Ziehen, Art. "Opfer," Pauly-W., 18, 1 (1942), 579-627; also Art. σφάγια, Pauly-W., 3a (1929), 1669-1679. On B.: Ges.-Buhl., Köhler-Baumg., *s.v.* טבח and שׁחט; A. Bea, "Kinderopfer f. Moloch oder f. Jahwe," *Biblica,* 18 (1937), 95-107; I. Benzinger, *Hbr. Archäologie³* (1927), 358-378; J. Blinzler, "Eine Bemerkung zum Geschichtsrahmen d. Johannesev.," *Biblica,* 36 (1955), 28-32; S. I. Curtiss, *Ursemitische Religion im Volksleben d. heutigen Orients* (1903), 194-276; E. Dhorme, "Le dieu Baal et le dieu Moloch dans la tradition bibl.," *Anatolian Stud.,* VI (1956), 57-61; K. Dronkert, *De Molochdienst in het OT* (1953); R. Dussaud, *Les origines Cananéennes du sacrifice Israélite* (1921), 71-85, 99-104, 109-111, 117-129, 163-173; Eichr. Theol. AT, I, 83-105; O. Eissfeldt, "Molk als Opferbegriff im Punischen u. Hbr. u. das Ende des Gottes Moloch," *Beiträge z. Religionsgeschichte des Altertums,* 3 (1935), 46-65; K. Galling, *Der Altar in den Kulturen d. alten Orients* (1925), 14-16, 36-38, 56-58; A. George, "Le sacrifice d'Abraham," *Études de critique et d'histoire religieuses* (1948), 99-110; G. B. Gray, *Sacrifice in the OT, Its Theory and Practice* (1925); J. Gray, *The Legacy of Canaan,* Suppl. to VT, 5 (1957), 140-152; J. Hänel, "Das Recht des Opferschlachtens in d. chronistischen Lit.," *ZAW,* 14 (1937), 46-67; J. Hoftijzer, "Eine Notiz zum punischen Kinderopfer," *VT,* 8 (1958), 288-292; W. Kornfeld, "Der Moloch. Eine Untersuchung zur Theorie O. Eissfeldts," *WZKM,* 51, 4 (1952), 287-313; H. J. Kraus, *Gottesdienst in Israel²* (1962), 134-148; E. Mader, *Die Menschenopfer d. alten Hebräer* (1909); L. Moraldi, "Espiazione sacrificiale e riti espiatori," *Analecta Bibl.,* 5 (1956), Index, *s.v.* "sacrificio"; F. Nötscher, *Bibl. Altertumskunde* (1940), 320-332; W. Nowack, *Lehrbuch d. hbr. Archäologie,* II (1894), 203-259; W. O. E. Oesterley, *Sacrifice in Ancient Israel* (1937); R. Rendtorff, "Die Gesetze in d. Priesterschr.," FRL, 62 (1954); P. Volz, *Die bibl. Altertümer²* (1925), 116-143. On D.: Levy Wört., Jastrow, E. Ben Jehuda, Thesaurus totius Hebraitatis et veteris et recentioris, 4 (no year) and 14 (1952), *s.v.* טבח and שׁחט; J. J. Berman, Art. "Ritual Slaughtering," *The Universal Jewish Enc.,* 9 (1948), 562-565; J. H. Greenstone, Art. "Shehitah," Jew. Enc., XI (1905), 253-6; B. Lauff, *Schehitah u. Bedikah,* Diss. Tierärztliche Hochschule Berlin (1922); Schulchan-Arukh, II, ed. J. v. Pavly (1888), Jore Dea, 1-28. On E.: Moult.-Mill. and Pr.-Bauer, *s.v.;* C. K. Barrett, "The Lamb of God," NTSt, 1 (1955), 210-218; M. E. Boismard, "Le Christ-Agneau. Rédempteur des hommes," *Lumière et Vie,* 7 (1958), 91-104; C. H. Dodd, *The Interpretation of the Fourth Gospel* (1953), 230-238; E. Lohse, "Märtyrer u. Gottesknecht. Untersuchungen z. urchr. Verkündigung vom Sühnetod Jesu Christi," FRL, NF, 46 (1955), 18-23, 32-37, 44-46, 64-110, 138-146, 191-210; S. Lyonnet, "De notione emptionis seu acquisitionis," *Verbum Domini,* 36, 5 (1958), 257-269; H. Wenschkewitz, "Die Spiritualisierung der Kultusbegriffe Tempel, Priester u. Opfer," *Angelos,* 4 (1932), 70-230.

[1] Usually by stabbing or slitting the throat. The description of a sacrifice in Hom. Od., 3, 447-460 shows that σφάζω denotes neither knocking down (449 f.) nor dividing (456) the animal, but just opening the artery (454); once it is done, the blood spurts out (455). The compound ἐπισφάζω is found with αἷμα as a direct obj., Eur. El., 92. We also find pass. phrases like αἷμα ἐπεσφαγμένον in Aristot. De Coloribus, 5, p. 796a, 15 or προσφάζεται αἷμα in Eur. Hel., 1255. In this connection it should be noted that anatomically σφαγή can mean the throat. Later, of course, the sense σφάττω is weaker: ταὐτόν ἐστιν ἀναιρεῖν, φονεύειν, κτείνειν... σφάττειν, ἀποσφάττειν, Poll. Onom., VI, 193.

[2] Cf. Boisacq, Hofmann, *s.v.* The latter ref. to Arm. *spananem* "I slay."

(II, 547e); Poll. Onom., VI, 193; Ditt. Syll.³, III, 1024, 36; ³ aor. pass. ἐσφάγην Aesch. Eum., 305; less commonly ἐσφάχθην, Eur. Iph. Taur., 177. No matter what the pt. of the sacrifice, an animal offered up was gen. slain. In animal sacrifices the blood is esp. important, so that there is a concern to have it flow out as completely as possible. The blood must also drain off even when the flesh is put to profane use. In antiquity the carotid artery of sacrificial or slaughtered animals was slit. The word is thus found both at ritual slaying and in ordinary slaughtering.

1. Ritual Slaying.

a. Meat Offerings whose Flesh is Eaten but which are Made to the Olympian Gods. ⁴

The slaying of sacrificial beasts takes place after prayer. ⁵ In gen. the pater familias makes the offering when it is in the family, but the priest or his deputy when it is a public sacrifice in the temple. Acc. to the summary account in Luc. De Sacrificiis, 12 the θύοντες seem to slaughter the animals themselves. This was the custom in simple circumstances. But when the beasts were large and special skill or strength was needed an expert slaughterer took charge. ⁶ It seems to be a sign of the high social rank of the sacrificer if he himself does not do the actual slaying. ⁷ When a private individual makes his own offering at a popular temple because the priests and their assistants are overworked, he hires a μάγειρος who understands slaughtering to do the actual killing. ⁸ It is expected that the animal will signify consent to being sacrificed by inclining the head, Aristoph. Pax, 960 and Schol.; Plut. Quaest. Conv., VIII, 3 (II, 729 f.). When an ox is sacrificed it is struck on the neck from behind and killed with a pole-axe, Hom. Il., 17, 520 ff.; Od., 3, 449. Then the front part of the animal is raised so as to bend the neck back, Hom. Il., 2, 422; Od., 3, 453. In this way the neck is raised above the altar or sacrificial bowl (σφαγεῖον) and the blood which gushes out will not be lost. The true slaughtering (σφάζω) now commences. The animal's throat is slit with a knife (σφαγίς, μάχαιρα, ξίφος) ⁹ and the blood pours out. The cutting is usually called σφάζειν. In the case of the ox the raising of the front part (αὐερύω) and the cutting of the throat (σφάζω) come only after the animal has been killed by the axe, Hom. Od., 3, 450. The felling with the axe is omitted in the case of other animals. The great boar has to be stupefied, Hom.

---

³ σφάζω is a iota pres. (σφαγ-j-ω). In analogy to pres. forms like φράττω aor. ἔφραξα (φρακ-) a pres. σφάττω was formed for aor. ἔσφαξα. Cf. K. Brugmann-B. Delbrück, *Grundriss d. vergleichenden Grammatik d. indogerm. Sprachen,* I, 2² (1897), 631, n. 1b; Schwyzer, I² (1953), 715.

⁴ On the various Gk. sacrifices cf. Ziehen σφάγια, 579-597; Stengel Opferbräuche, 92; Meuli, 185-288; Nilsson, I², 132-157.

⁵ On the ritual cf. Stengel Kultusaltertümer, 108-115; Meuli, 211-282; Nilsson, I², 142-151. Meuli thinks the connection with the Olympian deities arose only later, 215. On a broad basis of cultural comparison he argues for a surprising kinship between the Gk. ritual and the slaughtering and sacrificial practices of Asiatic shepherd peoples, which for their part go back to even older customs. He thus reaches "the conviction that the Olympian sacrifice was nothing other than ritual slaughtering" (223) embodying very old hunting practices. This explains esp. the choice of the parts offered to the Olympians, which are in essence the parts hunters did not use but which were left to the slain animal for its "regeneration."

⁶ Athen., 14, 77 f. (659d-f); K. Latte, Art. μάγειρος, Pauly-W., 14 (1930), 393-395.

⁷ In Hom. Il., 1, 447-468 the priest Chryses offers the hecatomb given by the Gks. He pronounces the prayer, burns the parts for the deity, and pours out the wine, while Odysseus and his men slay and cut up the animals. Cf. the similar scene in Od., 3, 429 ff.

⁸ Plat. Euthyd., 301c describes the work of the μάγειρος. Cf. also G. Plaumann, Art. "Hiereis," Pauly-W., 8 (1913), 1422.

⁹ σφαγίς Eur. El., 811; μάχαιρα Aristoph. Pax, 1018; ξίφος Plut. Parallela Graeca et Romana, 35 (II, 314c); cf. S. Reinach, Art. "Culter," Darembg.-Saglio, I, 2, 1584 f.

Od., 14, 425. In the case of smaller animals there is no ref. to this. Their heads are held back and their throats cut, Hom. Il., 1, 459. Other ways of doing it are attested from ill. [10]

b. σφάγια.

To be distinguished from meat and festal offerings are σφάγια [11] whose flesh is not eaten θυσίαι ἄγευστοι, Plut. De tuenda sanitate praecepta, 5 (II, 124c) but is set aside (Eur. El., 513 f.) [12] because the sacrifice either removes a curse as an expiation (Polyb., 4, 21, 8 f.; Plut. Quaest. Rom., 68 [II, 280b c]) or has analogous power as an oath sacrifice (Hom. Il., 3, 300; Aristoph. Lys., 204; Plut. De Pyrrho, 6 [I, 386c]) or because the recipient of the offering claims the whole animal: σφάγιον as an offering to heroes, Plut. De Solone, 9 (I, 83a), to the dead, Eur. El., 514; Hel., 1564, to chthonic powers, Aesch. Eum., 1005 ff.; Xenoph. An., IV, 5, 4. for mantic purposes before dangerous enterprises, Thuc., VI, 69, 2; Hdt., VI, 112, 1; Eur. Phoen., 174; Xenoph. An., I, 8, 15. In σφάγια, however, the true and original sacrifice seems to have been the blood. [13] They are not offered by priests but by seers (μάντεις), Eur. Phoen., 1255; cf. Xenoph. Hist. Graec., III, 4, 23, by officials, Plut. De Aristide, 21 (I, 332b), or at offerings for the dead by relatives, Eur. El., 92. They are not offered on altars but where the forces to which they are made exercise their power. [14] Since shedding the blood is the main pt. of σφάγια the neck of the slain animal is pressed from below so that the blood flows to the head. The body does not need to touch the earth but may be raised on high, Hom. Il., 19, 251. It is important that the head point down so that the blood will flow to where the special numen reigns. The animal is not drugged before σφάζειν, not even oxen, which are seldom used for this. [15] When the head is pressed down (καταστρέφω), the sacrificer slits the neck deeply so as almost to sever the head from the body. The tt. for this is ἐντέμνω, Thuc., V, 11, 1, though other terms are also used; [16] σφάζω in Hom. Od., 10, 532; 11, 45; Xenoph. An., II, 2, 9; Demosth. Or., 23, 68; Plut. De Aristide, 21 (I, 332b) and σφαγιάζω (from σφάγιον) in Xenoph. Hist. Graec., IV, 6, 10; Arrian. Anabasis, I, 5, 7; [17] Plut. Thes., 32 (I, 15e) may be used for ἐντέμνω. The position of the neck of σφάγια explains the expression σφάζω εἴς τι, i.e., the blood is to flow in a specific direction, Xenoph. An., II, 2, 9; Ditt. Syll.[3], III, 1024, 35 f. In exceptionally dangerous crises when the very existence of the state was threatened men were offered as σφάγια in Greece and Rome, as we learn from both legend and history. Thus Themistocles before the battle of Salamis, acting on the advice of the seer Euphrantides, offered 3 Persian prisoners to Dionysos Omestes. [18] σφάζω can also be used for this ritual slaying of men, Aesch. Ag., 1433; Eur. Iph. Taur., 8; Dio C., 43, 24, 3 f.

---

[10] Stengel Opferbräuche, 117, Ill. 1 and 2. Heracles, who tames the stag, and Nike, who slays a bull on a terracotta, lever the right knee on the animal and press it to the ground. Nike is ready to cut the throat. Cf. Haas Lfg., 15 Leipoldt (1930), Ill. 11 and 12. Cf. also Mithra, who strikes on the right side of the neck or body. Cf. Leipoldt, Ill. 11-17, other ill. in M. J. Vermaseren, Corpus inscr. et monumentorum religionis Mithraicae, I (1956), Index, p. 338, s.v. "Mithras as a bullkiller."

[11] Stengel Opferbräuche, 92-104 and Kultusaltertümer, 124-149; Eitrem Mantis, 9-30; Nilsson, I[2], 132 f., 139-142.

[12] Cf. Stengel Opferbr., 95; Ziehen σφάγια, 1674-6. Later men dared to eat of some σφάγια, e.g., Paus., V, 24, 10; cf. Ziehen σφάγια, 1657 f.

[13] Cf. Stengel Opferbr., 104; Ziehen σφάγια, 1679.

[14] Offerings for the dead were made over the grave of the deceased, Eur. El., 92, oath offerings where the agreement was reached, Xenoph. An., II, 2, 9, σφάγια before battle in front of the ranks as near as possible to the enemy, Plut. Thes., 32 (I, 15e).

[15] Stengel Opferbr., 122-124.

[16] τέμνω Hom. Il., 3, 252; ἀποδειροτομέω Od., 11, 35.

[17] Ed. K. Abicht (1871).

[18] Plut. De Aristide, 9 (I, 323 f.); cf. Pelop., 21 (I, 288f-289b); Them., 13 (I, 118f-119a). Cf. F. Schwenn, "Das Menschenopfer bei d. Griechen u. Römern," RVV, 15, 3 (1915), 75 f.

2. Profane Slaying.

a. Slaying of an Animal.

In gen. one may say that in antiquity all slaughtering of animals was connected with sacrifice; the blood and fat were always regarded as the property of the god. Simple ceremonies were not left out at domestic slaughtering and parts of the beasts were always burned for the gods at public sacrifices of feasting, thanksgiving, or intercession. Yet the Gks. of Homer's day did not link all slaying with an offering, cf. Hom. Il., 24, 621-7; Od., 1, 92; 4, 320; 23, 305. They sacrificed to the gods only when they had petitions or feared their wrath. [19] One can thus find a profane use of σφάζω. The method was the same as with meat offerings [20] → 927, 16 ff. σφάζω is also used for the way a wolf falls on its prey and kills it, Eur. Hec., 91; Aristot. Hist. An., IX, 6, p. 612b, 2.

b. Slaying of a Man.

From Hdt. σφάζω is also used for the profane slaying of a man. It is a vivid and grisly expression for murder. Various nuances may be caught: gruesomeness, Eur. Andr., 315; undeserved fate, Eur. Suppl, 813; criminality, Dio C., 73, 6, 4: [21] murder of kin, Aesch. Choeph., 904; massacre after taking a city, Hdt., VIII, 127. Passionate slaying can be denoted by ἀποσφάττω, Plat. Euthyphr., 4c. σφάττω and ἀποσφάττω also occur in descriptions of civil wars and their atrocities in Plut. Mar., 42 (I, 430d); De Sulla, 31 (I, 472a-e); De Cicerone, 48 (I, 885e); Dio C., 40, 48, 1, also suicide, Xenoph. Cyrop., III, 1, 25; VII, 3, 14 f.; Plut. Pelop., 20 (I, 288 f.). [22] Slaughtering men is often mentioned in lists of vices, Aeschin. Tim., 191; Plut. Mar., 44 (I, 432a); Luc. Calumniae non temere esse credendum, 19; cf. also Aristid. Apol., 13, 5. σφάζω seems to be used in a weaker or hyperbolic sense in P. Oxy., II, 259, 33 (23 A.D.): βλέπε με πῶς με ἡ μήτηρ ἡμῶν [ἔ]σφαξε χάριν τοῦ χειρογράφου.

B. Septuagint Usage.

In LXX σφάζω occurs some 84 times. [23] With few exceptions [24] it is used for the

---

19 In Hom. Od., 9, 45 f. Odysseus' men prepare a meal after plundering the Ciconian town Ismaros, with no mention of sacrifice. But in Od., 12, 356 ff. the same men, at the prompting of Eurylochus, slaughter the oxen of the sun-god, and this is expressly depicted as a sacrifice. Fear of the wrath of the god is the motive. Cf. Stengel Opferbr., 61-65.

20 As opposed to Stengel Opferbr., 61-5, Meuli, 212, n. 1 thinks it is only due to the brevity of depiction or the shifting interest of the narrator that in Hom. Il., 23, 30 ff. and Od., 9, 45 f. we are not told the slaughtered animals were sacrifices. As he sees it all slaughtering was sacrificial in Hom.'s time too. This evaluation of the Homeric sources by Meuli is to be seen in connection with his explanation of the origin of Gk. meat offerings.

21 The Gk. thinks the slaughtering of men at altars is esp. heinous, Eur. Andr., 260; Hec., 24; Isoc. Or., 6, 67 f.

22 Aristot. condemns suicide on the ground that it is evasion of responsibilities to the πόλις, Eth. Nic., V, 15, p. 1138a, 9 f.; cf. Hirzel, 252, 259, n. 1. Σφαττομένη, the title of a comedy in Athen., 6, 43 (243e), might mean a woman who commits suicide, cf. Hirzel, 100, n. 3.

23 39 of these 84 are in Lv., 9 in Ez., 8 in 1 S. and 5 in Ex. The word is rare, or not used at all, in the other books.

24 At Nu. 11:32 B reads ἔσφαξαν ἑαυτοῖς ψυγμούς for Hbr. שָׁטוֹחַ לָהֶם שָׁטוֹחַ וַיִּשְׁטְחוּ. At 1 S. 15:33 σφάζω is used for hapax legomenon שָׁסַף, at Is. 22:13 for הרג, at Jer. 19:7 for בקק, at Lv. 17:5; Ez. 34:3 for זבח, (elsewhere transl. θύω). 4 times LXX supplies σφάζω from the context, Lv. 4:29; 17:4; 1 S. 1:25; Ez. 21:15. σφάζω also occurs in 1 Macc. 1:2; 2:24; 2 Macc. 5:14.

Hbr. verbs טבח [25] and שחט. [26] *ṭbḥ* in Accad., Ugaritic and Ethiop. usage means "to sever the neck," "to slaughter," in Arab. "to cook," and in OT "to slay and cut up" an animal for eating. It is hardly a tt. in sacrificial ritual but rather a profane expression. [27] It is used 6 times of men in the sense "to slaughter," "to murder."

In contrast *šḥṭ* Accad. "to take off," "to flay," Arab. "to slaughter," is a cultic term often used in sacrificial ritual (33 times in Lv.). Gn. 37:31 is an exception. שחט means "to kill an animal so that its blood gushes out." In the ritual it comes between laying one's hand on the head and the sprinkling of blood, 2 Ch. 29:24. It corresponds to the non-biblical use of σφάζω → 927, 22 ff.; 928, 22 ff. How the animal was slain so that the blood would flow out the OT does not say. [28] But one may assume that in earlier times it was done in much the same way as by the Rabb., i.e., by slitting the throat. The OT does not precisely define the position of the animal, or its neck or head. [29] שחט is used 4 times for the cultic slaying of men, Gn. 22:10; Is. 57:5; Ez. 16:21; 23:39. It is also used 11 times for the ordinary killing of men, Nu. 14:16; Ju. 12:6; 1 K. 18:40; 2 K. 10:7, 14; 25:7; Jer. 39:6; 41:7; 52:10.

1. Ritual Slaying.

a. Animal Sacrifices.

We find the simplest form of bloody offering in 1 S. 14:32-34, where the soldiers of Saul slaughter and devour the captured cattle. But this is a transgression against God because they just let the blood flow to the ground and eat the flesh before it has completely drained off. Saul, however, has a stone rolled up on which ritual slaughtering may be performed correctly. The animals are brought to this so that the blood will flow directly on to it when their throats are cut. Something of the same was done at sacrifices (זְבָחִים) offered on festal occasions, Ex. 3:18; 1 S. 25:2 ff. Only at such times did the Israelites eat meat in the pre-Deuteronomic period. The slaughtering became a sacrifice inasmuch as the

---

[25] טבח occurs 11 times in the Mas. In 8 of these it is transl. in LXX by derivates of the stem σφαγ- (Gn. 43:16; Ex. 21:37; Dt. 28:31; Ps. 37:14; Prv. 9:2; Ez. 21:15 σφάζω, Jer. 25 [Ιερ. 32]:34; 51[Ιερ. 28]:40 σφαγή). In 1 S. 25:11 and Jer. 11:19 LXX has θύω, and in Lam. 2:21 μαγειρεύω. On טבח cf. Ges.-Buhl, Köhler-Baum., F. Zorell, Lex. hebraicum et aram. Veteris Testamenti (1960), s.v.

[26] שחט occurs 79 times in OT for "to slay," "to kill." In 65 instances, including all those in Lv., LXX has σφάζω. In 19 instances it has θύω (8 of these in 2 Ch.). The expression שָׁחַט הַפֶּסַח is transl. θύω τὸ φάσεκ(χ) in 2 Ch. 30:15; 35:1, 6, 11; cf. also 2 Ch. 30:17: שְׁחִיטַת הַפְּסָחִים == τὸ θύειν τὸ φάσεκ. On שחט cf. Ges.-Buhl, Köhler-Baumg., F. Zorell, op. cit., s.v.

[27] Yet in 1 S. 25:11 טבח is used in the description of Nabal's shearing, which was certainly a sacrificial feast. Cf. A. Wendel, Das Opfer in d. isr. Religion (1927), 92. In 1 S. 9:23 f. a slaughterer or cook (noun טַבָּח) prepares the meat. The root *ṭbḥ* is used cultically in Ugaritic, Gordon Manual, II, 124, 12; II 'nt X, 4, 30 (p. 190). In II, 62, 18-28 there are grave-offerings to the god Baal for vivifying, cf. Kraus, 136. Yet the ref. seems to be to profane slaughtering when in Gordon Manual, 127, 17-20 Keret asks his wife Mšt-hry to slaughter a lamb for him so that he may eat (*ṭbḥ* imr wilhm). C. Virolleaud, "Le roi Kéret et son fils," Syria, 23 (1942-3), 9 thinks *ṭbḥ* has here the more gen. sense "to prepare" ("accommoder").

[28] Cf. the difficulty the Rabb. had in finding Scripture proofs for their method of slaying, Chul., 27a b.

[29] The Egypt. bound the ox, put it on its back, and cut its artery with a segment-shaped flint knife, cf. H. Kees, "Ägypten," Kulturgesch. d. Alten Orients, Hndbch. AW, III, 1, 3, 1 (1933), 69-71. To this days bedouins slaughter sheep and goats by cutting their throats as their heads and necks lie across an altar-stone, cf. Curtiss, 272, n. 2.

blood and the fat and some parts of the animal were set aside for God; fat and esp. blood were taboo, Lv. 3:16; 7:23-27; 17:10-14; 19:26. Atoning power was ascribed to the blood as a result, Lv. 17:11, and it was esp. precious in the sacrifice. The blood had to flow out, and this was achieved by severing the animal's neck. We thus find σφάζω (= שׁחט) in descriptions of sacrifices and esp. in the rituals, cf. Hannah's offering at Shiloh when Samuel was born, 1 S. 1:24 ff., Ez.'s sketch of the duties of the Levites, 44:11, and the rituals in P.

In the case of pre-Dt. offerings (זְבָחִים), which were not brought to the temple, the head of the house usually did the slaying, Ex. 12:6, cf. 1 Βασ. 1:25. Prominent people like Absalom (2 S. 13:23 ff.) or rich men like Nabal (1 S. 25:11) did not do the actual killing themselves. Probably the cook (טַבָּח) mentioned in 1 S. 9:23 f. slaughtered the offering as well as dressing the meat. In public places of sacrifice or sanctuaries there were cultic personnel who understood slaughtering and did it when required, 1 S. 1:25 HT. Even in temple sacrifices as described in Lv. 1:3, 4 the one who brings the offering does the slaying rather than the cultic personnel; the Israelite in Lv. 1:5, the prince in 4:24, the high-priest in 4:4. But this does not apply in the rites for cleansing from leprosy. The leper cannot sacrifice the beast since he is unclean until the rite is over. So a servant (Lv. 14:5) or the priest (Lv. 14:13 HT) does the slaughtering for him. In the plan in Ez. one of the tasks the prophet lays on the disadvantaged Levites is that of slaughtering the burnt offerings and sacrifices brought by the Israelites. These no longer do it themselves as in Lv. 1:3, 4. The LXX seems to have amended the Lv. text acc. to later custom, for instead of the sing. of the HT it puts the plur. so that the ref. is to the cultic personnel (the Levites), cf. Lv. 1:5, 11; 3:13; 4:15, 24, 29, 33. In 2 Ch. 35:5 f., 11; Ezr. 6:20 there appears to have been an attempt to delegate the slaying of the Passover lamb to the Levites, but this met with no lasting success. To the time of the second temple slaying the Passover lamb was a matter for the Israelites, Philo Decal., 159; Vit. Mos., II, 224; Spec. Leg., II, 145; Pes., 5, 6.

Slaughtering was as near as possible to the place where the blood of the animal was to flow. In early times the beast was slaughtered over the altar so that the blood would flow directly on to this, 1 S. 14:32, 34; [30] cf. also Gn. 22:9 f.; 1 K. 13:2; 2 K. 23:20. Things are different when there is no blood ritual. In Ju. 6:19-21 Gideon slaughters and prepares the kid in the house, not at the rock where it is offered. [31] After the centralisation of the cult slaughtering was at the central sanctuary (Lv. 17:3 f.), and acc. to the ritual it was to be at the entrance to the tabernacle (Lv. 1:5; 3:2 etc.), i.e., before the altar of burnt offering in the forecourt of the sanctuary, Ex. 40:6, 29. Lv. 1:11 says that sheep for the burnt offering are to be slain on the north side of the altar. Animals not offered to God but used in purification are to be slain outside the camp so as not to defile the congregation. Acc. to Lv. 14:8 a leper may enter the camp only when cleansed.

b. Human Sacrifices.

(a) For Yahweh: In Gn. 22:10 Abraham stretches out his hand to slay his son with a knife. Acc. to 1 S. 15:33 Samuel slays the Amalekite king Agag whom Saul had spared when fulfilling the ban. This was at the shrine in Gilgal. (b) For heathen gods: Acc. to Ez. 16:17-21 "adulterous" Jerusalem is accused of slaughtering her children to the idols she has made. There are similar charges in Ez. 23:39; Is. 57:5.

---

[30] Acc. to Galling, 56 the ref. in 1 S. 14:32, 34 is to a masseba, not an altar. The blood, the only offering, flows directly on the seat of deity.
[31] On this cf. R. Kittel, "Stud. z. hbr. Archäologie u. Religionsgeschichte," BWANT, 1 (1908), 97-103; Galling, 57 f. Slaughtering does not seem to be a cultic act here. Gideon's gift (מִנְחָה = θυσία) embraces both flesh and also a meal offering, which are offered together at the place of theophany. Cf. on this Kraus, 135, 137.

2. Profane Slaying.

a. Animals.

Before the cultic reforms of Josiah slaughtering was usually connected with communal sacrifice. Later we find two different legal systems. Lv. 17:3-9 forbids any slaughtering outside the cultic sanctuary, but Dt. 12 allows profane slaughtering outside the sanctuary, in Dt. 12:20-25 when the person concerned lives too far away, in Dt. 12:15 f. without restriction. Eating blood is consistently forbidden. σφάζω (שׁחט) rather than θύω (זבח) is used in Dt. 12. But one also finds a profane use of σφάζω. The cattle thief in Ex. 21:37 and the enemy who steals and slaughters cattle in Dt. 28:31 would not observe any ceremony, nor would Joseph's brethren when they slew a kid to daub Joseph's coat with its blood, Gn. 37:31, cf. also Nu. 11:22.

b. Man.

As in non-bibl. Gk. (→ 929, 13 ff.) σφάζω can also mean in the LXX "violently and pitilessly to slaughter a man." Thus God's enemies are slaughtered, as in the Elijah story in 1 K. 18:40. The righteous are also butchered by God's enemies. The wisdom poem ψ 36:14 describes how the ungodly bend their bows to slay the righteous. Finally σφάζω can be used for a massacre in war or civil strife. In Ju. 12:6 Jephthah's men hew down the Ephraimites at the fords of Jordan. Acc. to 2 Macc. 5:12-14 Antiochus after his Egyptian campaign in 169 B.C. let loose his fury in Jerusalem: ἐκέλευσεν... κόπτειν... καὶ... κατασφάζειν.

C. Philo and Josephus.

1. Philo.

Philo makes comparatively sparing use of the verb σφάζω. It occurs in the description of sacrificial ritual in Spec. Leg., I, 212, though καταθύω is more common here, I, 199 and 212; II, 35, [32] or σφαγιάζω, I, 231 and 268. [33] The ref. may be to cultic or profane slaying when Philo says in Aet. Mund., 20 that animals may die for inner reasons (e.g., sickness) or for outer reasons (e.g., slaughtering). [34] As concerns the profane slaying of a man Philo uses σφάζω for murder in Spec. Leg., III, 91 and esp. fratricide, Leg. Gaj., 87: τὸν μὲν ἀδελφὸν... ὠμῶς ἀπέσφαξας, cf. also Leg. Gaj., 92: ὁ σφαγεὺς... τῶν ἀδελφῶν. He uses ἐπικατασφάζω for the suicide of the Xanthians, who did not submit to Caesar's assassin Brutus but slew themselves, Omn. Prob. Lib., 119. [35]

2. Josephus.

Whereas Jos. uses both σφάττω and σφάζω alongside one another in Ant., 3, 237, for the compound in ἀπο- he seems to know only the form ἀποσφάττω. When describing

---

[32] In keeping with the LXX (Lv. 1:5) Philo assumes the burnt offering of the Israelite is slain by a priest. Cf. on this L. Cohn, Die Werke Philos v. Alex. in deutscher Übers., 2. Teil: "Über die Einzelgesetze" (1910), 67, n. 1.

[33] Philo uses σφαγιάζω esp. for the cultic slaying of children, both in the pagan sphere (Abr., 179, 185, 196 f.) and also in connection with the sacrifice of Isaac (Abr., 169, 188, 201).

[34] In Aet. Mund., 20 Philo contrasts correct slaying (σφάττω) with unclean killing by choking θάνατον οὐ καθαρὸν δι' ἀγχόνης. In Jewish slaying he distinguishes between that which is for cultic purposes and that which is for supplying meat, Spec. Leg., I, 147; Virt., 126 and 134. In the piece preserved in Eus. Praep. Ev., 8, 14, 32 the ref. might be to pagan slaughtering.

[35] Philo's account, of course, is full of echoes of the cultus, cf. also the words of the gerousia of the Jews to the legate Petronius in Leg. Gaj., 233-5. In Leg. Gaj., 233 we find the expression παρέχειν ἐν ἑτοίμῳ τὰς σφαγάς, "willingly to offer the throat."

the sacrificial system of the OT he often uses σφάζω in the sense found in non-bibl. Gk. and the LXX: "to slay a sacrifice by cutting its throat," Ant., 3, 226, 237, 242, cf. also 3, 206. [36] With notable frequency Jos. uses σφάζω and ἀποσφάττω for the grisly and mostly illegal slaying of men. [37] This feature is in keeping both with his material and also with the style of his narration. The word occurs first in military descriptions. The ref. in Bell., 2, 71 is to the destruction of a Roman detachment by the shepherd Athronges. Acc. to Bell., 2, 454 the rebels break sworn treaties and hew down the defenceless soldiers of Metilius. ἀποσφάττω is also used frequently for the massacring of civilians, Bell., 2, 305; 4, 80. We have acts of revenge or spontaneous outbreaks of ancient anti-Jewish feeling when we read of the butchering of the Jewish population in Hell. cities, which was quite common at the beginning of the Jewish war, Bell., 2, 468, 547, 561; 7, 362 and 368. Finally σφάζω and ἀποσφάττω are often used in descriptions of political disorder and strife, Ant., 6, 262; 9, 138 and 142; 10, 38 f. This is particularly so in the account of the Jewish conflicts which led up to the disaster of 70 A.D., Bell., 2, 240 and 256; 4, 145 and 318. Among the Jews as among the Greeks it was esp. abhorrent that men should be cut down in the temple alongside the sacrifices, Bell., 2, 30; Ant., 17, 237 and 239. The *sicarii* were bold enough to slaughter men in the temple and were convinced that they were not guilty of any impiety in so doing, Ant., 20, 165.

D. Rabbinic Writings.

1. In the Rabb. טבח means "to slay" with no ritual ref. We find it in expositions of the penalties for rustling in Ex. 21:37: "And he who butchers (הַטּוֹבֵחַ) and sells what another has stolen does not make fourfold or fivefold amends," BQ, 7, 1b. The continuation in 7, 2b adduces instances in which amends must be made: "He who steals and slaughters (וְטָבַח) for healing or for the dogs..." In these statutes it is presupposed that טבח means profane slaying. Further on in the same statement we read that "he who slays (הַשּׁוֹחֵט) and it is seen to be unserviceable, or he who slays (הַשּׁוֹחֵט) what is profane in the temple..." שחט is used here because ritual slaughtering is meant.

2. The verb שחט and the noun שְׁחִיטָה in 2 Ch. 30:17 are the official Rabb. words for correct slaughtering acc. to the Halachic injunction, whether this be the slaughtering of sacrifice שְׁחִיטַת קָדָשִׁים BM, 109b or profane slaughtering שְׁחִיטַת חֻלִּין (Gaonim, Rashi, Alfasi). The main feature of Rabb. slaying is that the animal's gullet or windpipe is slit in a single stroke with a knife with no nicking. In slaughtering it is forbidden to pause, to press the knife, to stick the knife in the neck, to turn the knife aside from the place of slaying, or to detach the windpipe or gullet, Chul., 9a. Basically every Israelite is qualified to slay, Chul., 1, 1; the only exceptions are deaf mutes, the weak-minded, and minors. [38] In a transf. sense שחט is used in the proverbial expression: "A slaughtered ox is before thee," Nidda, 15a. The point is that a relevant legal argument can be presented. [39]

---

[36] Jos. can use θύω as well as σφάζω for the slaying of sacrifice. "Once they are slain, the altar is sprinkled with their blood" θύσαντες δὲ ταῦτα φοινίσσουσι μὲν αἵματι τὸν βωμόν, Ant., 3, 228. The quotation from Manetho in Ap., 1, 249 seems to distinguish between the θύτης and the σφαγεύς.

[37] The adv. ὠμῶς denotes the sharpness of the term σφάζω when used in relation to men, Bell., 2, 30 and 454, cf. also Ant., 6, 262.

[38] The Gemara, however, lays down that meat is acceptable only when the animal is slaughtered by someone who knows the rules of slaughtering (הלכות שחיטה). R. Jehuda ref. to 3 things a scholar must learn: to write, to slaughter, and to circumcise, Chul., 9a. Samaritan slaughtering was acknowledged to be correct by the Rabb., Chul., 3b. On the slaying of the Passover lamb by the Samaritans cf. J. Jeremias, *Die Passafeier d. Samaritaner* (1932), 86-88.

[39] Cf. L. Goldschmidt, *Der bab. Talmud*, IV (1925), 507, n. 19 and IX (1935), 748, n. 79.

E. The New Testament.

In the NT σφάζω occurs only in the Johannine writings, once in 1 Jn. and 8 times in Rev. [40]

a. In 1 Jn. 3:12 σφάζω is a strong term for Cain's fratricide analogous to the ancient use for the murder of brothers or relatives. Since Cain (→ I, 7, 26 ff.) comes from the sphere of the wicked one (→ VI, 559, 6 ff.) fratricide and lack of love are to be rejected as wicked conduct. [41]

b. In Rev. 5:6, 9, 12; 13:8 Jesus Christ is called "the slaughtered Lamb" in an established liturgical reference, → I, 341, 23 ff. [42] The Johannine tradition probably has in view the Passover lamb which bears the mark of slaughtering on its neck. The ὡς corresponds to the Hebrew כ and goes with the veiled and visionary language. The slain Lamb is the basic christological theme in John's Apocalypse. In figurative paradox it denotes the extreme character of the offering and the lasting effect of the Lamb's death on the community and the world. Victory and vesting with power accrue as fruits of this death. Rev. 5:9 expressly refers to the blood of the Lamb which was slain; it is here a ransom for the community → I, 125, 37 ff. In Rev. 13:3 the beast which rises up out of the sea is set in conscious contrast to this christological image. One of its heads has been given a mortal blow, but it has healed over, → III, 134, 30 ff.

Historically one might suggest that this mortal wound (ἡ πληγὴ τοῦ θανάτου) refers to the assassination of Caesar or Nero. The latter is more likely, since Nero was expected to return, Sib., 4, 119-122, 137-139; 5, 143-149, 361-370. Lat. historians are also acquainted with the belief that Nero was still alive and would come back to exact vengeance, Suet. Caes., VI, 57; Tac. Hist., II, 8. In fact several pseudo-Neros one after the other kept Asia Minor and Greece in a turmoil. Less likely is a ref. to the dangerous illness of Caligula, from which he was able to recover, Suet. Caes., IV, 14; Dio C., 59, 8; Philo Leg. Gaj., 14-21. This hardly does justice to the element of violence in the imagery. [43] But one might also accept an explanation in terms of tradition, namely, that the beast is a primal monster which was not completely vanquished but retains his power to the end of the days (cf. Job 40:19 and the Rabb. tradition). [44]

In Rev. 6:9, in the image (fifth seal) of the martyrs (→ IV, 501, 24 ff.) under the heavenly altar, we read that they were slain on account of God's Word and

---

[40] There are no forms of the pres. stem σφάζω in the NT. The compound in κατα- occurs in Lk. 19:27: When the king has taken dominion in his kingdom he has the enemies who tried to oppose his accession bound and slaughtered before his eyes (κατασφάξατε αὐτοὺς ἔμπροσθέν μου) acc. to oriental practice. Ac. 7:42 adopts the rebuke of Am. 5:25, which seems to presuppose that neither sacrifices nor vegetable offerings were made in the wilderness period זְבָחִים וּמִנְחָה = σφάγια καὶ θυσίαι. θύω τὸ πάσχα is used for slaying the Passover lamb in the NT acc. to the usage in 2 Ch. → III, 181, 17 ff. θύω largely supplanted σφάζω, cf. W. Schulze, "Gotica," Kl. Schriften (1933), 545 with n. 2, 3.

[41] Slaughtering is a metaphorical and very strong expression for fratricide (→ 932, 28 f.) in P. Osl., I, 1, 5 (4th cent. A.D.); cf. Schnackbg. J.² (1963) on I, 3:12.

[42] When Paul calls Christ our Passover in 1 C. 5:7 he offers very early testimony to the comparison of Jesus with the Passover lamb. In itself crucifixion as distinct from execution by the sword does not bear any close relation to slaughtering, so that theological interpretation rather than the historical event gives rise to the image of the slaughtered Lamb.

[43] On Rev. 13:3 cf. R. H. Charles, The Rev. of St. John, I (1920), 349-351; Bss. Apk., 361-363, 374-379, 411-413.

[44] Loh. Apk. on 13:3; cf. there the ref. to the "sword" and the "sword wound" in Rabb. tradition, BB, 75a; Pesikt., 188b.

the witness they had. The death of the martyrs is compared to the slaughtering of sacrifices (σφάζω). As the blood of sacrificial beasts flowed out at the foot of the altar of burnt offering in Jerusalem, so the blood of the martyrs flowed out at the foot of the heavenly altar. Since blood is the seat of the soul, their souls are under the altar. [45] The ancient biblical mode of speech according to which the martyrs are slaughtered innocently has influenced Rev. in other places too. In Rev. 18:24 the sentence of the strong angel on Babylon as a type of the demonic city ends with a reference to the murder of the prophets, the saints, and all who were slain on earth. The metaphor of slaughtering may be related more generally to war and murder → 929, 13 ff. Thus the second horseman (→ VI, 952, 30 ff.) in Rev. 6:4 represents the older tradition that war and unrest will come, so that men slay one another, ἵνα ἀλλήλους σφάξουσιν. A sign of this apocalyptic power is the mighty sword to which the older tradition referred already. [46]

† σφαγή.

1. ἡ σφαγή is "slaughtering" (ritual or profane) by cutting or slashing the throat. [1] ἕστηκεν ἤδη μῆλα πρὸς σφαγὰς πάρος, Aesch. Ag., 1057 ref. to the sacrifice in which Cassandra is to take part in the house of Agamemnon, βοῦν ἂν ἐπὶ σφαγὴν ἤγομεν, Luc. Demosthenis Encomium, 40 to the ox led to the slaughter (a simile here), ἔλαφον, οὗ κατα σφαγάς..., Soph. El., 568 to the slaying of a deer in the chase. σφαγή often ref. to the violent slaying of a man. In Eur. Hec., 522 Talthybius tells Hecabe how her daughter Polyxena was slain as an offering for the dead at the grave of Achilles (ἐπὶ σφαγάς), cf. also Eur. Hec., 41, 221, 564-7, 571. [2] Acc. to Aesch. Eum., 187 Apollo directs the Eumenides out of his temple and sends them... where there is patricide σφαγαί τε σπέρματος or a child is slain in its mother's womb... [3] Plat. Resp., X, 610b speaks of the soul which will perish neither of fever nor sickness nor murder ὑπὸ σφαγῆς, nor even when the whole body is chopped into the smallest possible pieces. αὐτόχειρι δὲ σφαγῇ in Eur. Or., 947 ref. to Orestes' suicide. Acc. to Demosth. Or., 19, 260 Philip of Macedonia perpetrated a massacre in Elis, τὰς ἐν Ἤλιδι σφαγὰς πεποίηκε. We find similar expressions in later Gk. lit. quite often with ref. to this type of military action, e.g., Plut. De Marcello, 31 (I, 316d); De Lysandro, 13 (I, 440d); Tib. Gracch., 44 (I, 845a); De Bruto, 27 (I, 996e); Appian. Bell. Civ., II, 24. The ref. is often to the hewing down of men in civil war or party strife. σφαγή may indicate very concretely the bodily result of σφάττειν: κἀκφυσιῶν ὀξεῖαν αἵματος σφαγήν, "breathing out a jet of fresh blood," Aesch. Ag., 1389, cf. ἀπὸ σφαγὴν ἐρῶν, "vomiting out the flesh of the slain," ibid., 1599. Hence σφαγή can also denote the "wound," "slit": καθάρμοσον σφαγάς, "close the wound," Eur. El., 1228; ὁ μὲν χοῖρος ἐσφάγη... σφαγὴν βραχεῖαν, the swine "receives a short slit," Athen., 9, 26 (381a). Anatomically σφαγή means the "throat," the place between the collar-bones where sacrifices are usually slain. Aristot. Hist. An., I, 14, p. 493b, 7 defines this place exactly: κοινὸν δὲ μέρος αὐχένος καὶ στήθους σφαγή, "the common part of the neck and the breast" is called σφαγή. We also find this sense in the plur.: μήποτε τεκούσης ἐς σφαγὰς ὦσαι ξίφος, "not to thrust the sword into the mother's throat," Eur. Or., 291.

2. In the LXX σφαγή occurs 23 times. Apart from paraphrases and additions to the HT for reasons of style at Job 10:16; 27:14; Jer. 15:3 and the transl. of the rare words בַּיּ

---

45 Lohse, 196 f.
46 Cf. Eth. En. 90:19; 91:12; here the sword is given to the righteous as apocalyptic authority.

σ φ α γ ή . 1 Cf. Pr.-Bauer, Pass., Liddell-Scott, s.v.
2 On this cf. Rohde, I, 222; Nilsson, I², 178 f.
3 Cf. Ant. Christ., IV (1934), 16-20.

at Job 21:10 and קֶטֶל at Ob. 10 it is used for הֲרֵגָה in Jer. 12:3; 19:6; Zech. 11:4, 7 and טִבְחָה in Ps. 44:22 or טֶבַח in Is. 34:2, 6; 53:7; 65:12; Ιερ. 27(50):27; 31(48):15; Ez. 21:20; Prv. 7:22. [4] The Hbr. nouns do not differ essentially in content. We are reminded of gen. Hell. usage by 2 Macc. 5:6, 13; 12:16, where σφαγή means a "massacre" in war. In later transl. the word occurs in other OT passages too: 'Α at Jer. 7:32; 11:19; in Σ at Is. 30:25; Jer. 7:32; 11:19; Ps. 42:10; in Θ at Jer. 12:3. In the biblical works the only sense of σφαγή is "slaying," "slaughtering"; the anatomical sense does not occur. It is realised that the primary ref. is to animals, but in metaphor and simile the word is also used of men.

In this connection the image of the "sheep for the slaughter" plays a special role. A popular lament runs: "We are counted as sheep for the slaughter," Ps. 44:22. In the shepherd allegory God gives the commission: "Feed the flock of slaughter," Zech. 11:4; cf. the answer which follows: "And I fed the flock of slaughter" (11:7). The reference here is to the separating of some sheep for slaughter from others which are kept for their wool. [5] It is a perversion of the idea of election when Israel is treated like sheep for slaughter. If the prophet himself is to feed these sheep by God's commission (11:4, 7), this statement is polemically directed against the owners and sellers who pitilessly hand over the people or its members. If the original text laid special emphasis on the symbolic action of the prophet, the accent in the later revision (v. 6) falls on the eschatological delivering up of men to alien "shepherds," cf. Eth. En. 89 f. [6] Yet one cannot wholly rule out the interpretation that the sheep for slaughter will be brought to market, whereas the others will be used for the temple, i.e., for cultic purposes. [7]

The concept of the lamb which is led to the slaughter can have various nuances. In Jer. 11:19 ('ΑΣ εἰς σφαγήν) it denotes the unsuspecting nature of the prophet complaining about the attacks of his enemies in Anathoth. In Is. 53:7 the thought is that the Servant of the Lord does not resist or complain. But the prophet can also pray for the destruction of the ungodly: "Take them off like sheep for the slaughter, and separate them for the day of slaughter," Jer. 12:3. [8] The LXX shortens this: ἅγνισον αὐτοὺς εἰς ἡμέραν σφαγῆς αὐτῶν, Θ keeps closer to the Mas. This gives us the expression "the day of slaughter." It took on apoc. significance. [9] Is. 30:25 Σ and Tg., ad loc. speak of the day of gt. killing when "the great" (Mas. "towers") fall.

---

[4] In Jer. 25(32):34 and 51(28):40 the final inf. לְטַבֹּחַ is transl. by εἰς σφαγήν. σφαγή does not occur in the Torah or the historical books (apart from 1 and 2 Macc.). It is never used for a word from the root שׁחט. In the LXX, then, the noun σφαγή as distinct from the verb σφάζω has no esp. close relation to the cultic sphere, though sometimes we catch an echo of cultic themes, Is. 34:6; 53:7.

[5] H. Gunkel, Die Ps. (1926), 186. From ancient times the Babylonians distinguished between sheep for food and sheep for wool.

[6] On the text of Zech. 11:4-16 cf. K. Elliger, Das Buch d. zwölf kl. Proph., II, AT Deutsch 25⁴ (1959), ad loc.

[7] S. Feigin, "Some Notes on Zech. 11:4-17," JBL, 44 (1925), 204.

[8] 1 QH 15:17 presupposes Jer. 12:3 with its prayer: "But the ungodly hast thou created for the time of thy wrath, from the mother's womb hast thou separated them for the day of slaughter."

[9] Eth. En. 16:1 ref. to the "days of the massacring, destruction and death of the giants" (Gn. 6:1-4) when their spirits left the carnal body to wreak destruction, cf. also Eth. En. 10:12. An apocal. threat from the Enoch quotation in Georgius Syncellus, 26d (ed. W. Dindorf [1829], 46 f.) speaks of the wrath of God which will not leave the descendants of the men (the flood generation) "until the time of the slaughter of your sons" μέχρι καιροῦ σφαγῆς τῶν υἱῶν ὑμῶν. Here the last judgment is obviously depicted under the image of slaughter. The ref. in Ps. Sol. 8:1 is to battle cries and the sound of trumpets blowing slaughter and destruction φωνὴν σάλπιγγος ἠχούσης σφαγὴν καὶ ὄλεθρον. A historical event is un-

3. Philo in a comparison can say of a certain man that food and drink were given him "as to cattle fattening for the slaughter" καθάπερ τοῖς θρέμμασιν ἐπὶ σφαγήν, Flacc., 178. Cultically one finds σφαγή in Abr., 176, where God averts the sacrifice of Isaac. The slaying of enemies in war corresponds to the law νόμιμοι αἱ κατ' ἐχθρῶν σφαγαί, and yet after the campaign against the Midianites Moses has the soldiers of Phinehas make expiation because these were related to the Israelites, Vit. Mos., I, 309, 314. In a list of vices in Spec. Leg., II, 13 murder and bodily injury are called τραύματα καὶ σφαγαί.

The use of the noun σφαγή in Jos. corresponds very largely to that of the verb σφάζω (→ 932, 33 ff.), though as in the LXX (→ 936, n. 4) it is not used so often in the cultic sphere. The ref. in Ant., 1, 225 and 232 is to the sacrifice of Isaac, who consents to his father's decision and goes to the altar. Mostly σφαγή is the savage killing of men, cf. God's decree after the flood σφαγῆς ἀνθρωπίνης ἀπέχεσθαι and the statute for the punishment of murderers, Ant., 1, 102. The ref. in Bell., 2, 473 is to the slaying of individuals in battle, while political murders are σφαγή in Ant., 7, 39; 9, 95; 19, 121. Finally σφαγή is also used for the suicide of the *sicarii* in Masada, Bell., 7, 389, 399. σφαγή means "throat" in Bell., 7, 395 (cf. 7, 397).

4. The Targum on Is. 53 takes the statements about the Servant of the Lord Messianically. It should be noted, however, that the image of the lamb led to the slaughter is referred to the Gentiles delivered up to the judgment of the Messiah: "He will deliver up the strong of the peoples like a lamb to the slaughter." [10] Ps. 44:22 plays a gt. role, esp. in a martyrological sense, in many traditions, though these are later than Paul. The oldest text seems to be M. Ex., 15, 2 (44a): "R. Akiba said: ...Lo, the peoples of the world ask the Israelites: What is thy friend before another friend that thou dost so charge us, Cant. 5:9? that thou dost die forthwith for him and art forthwith slain for him, as it is said: hence thy maidens love thee, Cant. 1:3 ..., and it is also written: For thy sake we are killed all the day long, Ps. 44:22." Sometimes, as in Git., 57b, the same text Ps. 44:22 is referred to circumcision or the demonstration which scribes give of the rules of slaughter on their own bodies; a more important pt. in the same passage is that the verse is applied to the mother with the 7 sons in 2 Macc. 7. Midr. Lam. 1:16 applies the verse to men and women who were put to shame in the Vespasian persecution, cf. also Git., 57b. Midr. Cant., 1, 3; 2, 7; 8, 6 ref. to the martyrs of Hadrian's time. Midr. Cant., 8, 6 speaks of the love that is stronger than death. Acc. to S. Dt., 323 on 6:5 the love for God which is intensified on the basis of the shᵉma (Dt. 6:5) applies even when God takes away life; there is an explicit and established connection with Ps. 44:22. [11] The Mishnah presupposes that there may be 4 modes of execution, among them "beheading" הֶרֶג, Sanh., 7, 1. In JKet., 2, 10 (26d, 36) this penalty is called הֲרִיגָה.

5. R. 8:36 quotes ψ 43:23 to describe the situation of the community under the assault of external enemies. The paradoxical fact that the community as the circle of the elect is delivered up to enemies is just as much at home in the self-understanding of the NT as in that of later Judaism. The unique factor, however, is the certainty that God's love for man persists in this too. According to Ac. 8:32 the eunuch is reading Is. 53:7 f. The quotation refers first to the absence of resistance or complaint and as in the OT uses the image of the beast for the slaughter. But

---

doubtedly meant; this is usually taken to be the storming of Jerusalem by Pompey in 63 B.C. Cf. on this O. Eissfeldt, *Einl. in das AT³* (1964), 829. Acc. to Sib., 5, 379 eternal peace will be preceded by a dreadful time of cosmic disasters and destruction in war and "butchery in the darkness of night" καὶ ἐπὶ σφαγῇσιν ὀμίχλη.
[10] Cf. on this H. Hegermann, "Js. 53 in Hexapla, Tg. u. Peschitta," BFTh, II, 56 (1954), 82.
[11] Cf. Str.-B., III, 258-260.

then it moves on to the lifting of judgment and to exaltation. [12] In Jm. 5:5 we have a reproach and a threat against the rich in apocalyptic style: "You have fed your hearts on the day of slaughter." [13] What is meant is either that they have fed on or for the day when the poor will be slaughtered or that they have fed on the day of judgment which has already dawned or is imminent (→ 936, 26 ff.) and on which the rich themselves will be slaughtered. In the former case ἡμέρα σφαγῆς is a day of judgment or disaster which is already past, [14] while in the latter it is the immediately approaching eschatological judgment on Israel and the nations of the world and corresponds to the "day of wrath" in R. 2:5. [15]

6. 1 Cl., 16, 1 ff. quotes the whole of Is. 53:1-12 to show by way of exhortation that Christ's ταπεινοφρονεῖν is an example for the Chr. community. As the author of faith Christ comes before the prophetic witnesses in 17, 1-18, 17. Barn., 5, 2 quotes Is. 53:5, 7 with ref. to the salvation given in Jesus Christ by sprinkling with His blood. The image of the lamb for the slaughter is subordinate. Barn., 8, 1-7 goes beyond the NT by allegorising Nu. 19: The heifer which is offered up is Jesus Himself, while those who sacrifice it are identical with those who led Him to the slaughter.

Michel

---

[12] Whether περιοχὴ τῆς γραφῆς (Rabb. עִנְיָן) means here an individual Scripture or an OT pericope cannot be said for certain. Luke's interest in Jewish pericope arrangement means that the latter is a real possibility. Cf. Str.-B., II, 687 f.; Haench. Ag. on 8:32.

[13] B א* P 33 vg boh have ἐν ἡμέρᾳ σφαγῆς (A ἡμέραις), the others ὡς ἐν ἡμέρᾳ σφαγῆς. Dib. Jk., ad loc. thinks the latter is a softening. For OT material cf. S. Grill, "Der Schlachttag Jahwes," BZ, 2 (1957), 278-283.

[14] Cf. Eth. En. 100:7. In this case there is the sharp contrast of the poor being slaughtered and the rich feeding. Wnd. Jk., ad loc. speaks of a dreadful day when the rich are spared or their arbitrary rule triumphs, cf. Dib. Jk., ad loc.

[15] In this case one would expect εἰς or ἐπί, but cf. R. 2:5. For this view one can appeal to a rich OT and apoc. tradition which has in view the eschatological day of judgment for sinners, cf. Is. 34:5-8; Jer. 46:10; 50:26 f.; Ez. 39:17; Zeph. 1:7; 1 QH 15:17; Eth. En. 94:9; 98:10; 99:6. Jm. uses the apoc. image sarcastically: The rich have fattened themselves to be' slaughtered on the day of divine slaughter. Cf. F. Spitta, *Zur Gesch. u. Lit. d. Urchr.*, II (1896), 134 f.; J. H. Ropes, *A Crit. and Exeget. Comm. on the Ep. of St. James* (1916), ad loc.; Hck. Jk., ad loc.; J. Chaine, *Ép. de Saint Jacques, Ét. Bibl.* (1927), ad loc.; Meinertz Kath. Br., ad loc.; J. Michl, *Die kath. Br.* (1953), ad loc. J. Marty, *L'Ép. de Jacques* (1935), ad loc. also thinks this interpretation possible. Schl. Jk. on 5:5 ref. to the practice of feasting well when a domestic animal was slaughtered. With this is bound up the idea of the eschatological day of slaughter, which for Jm. will mean primarily the destruction of Jerusalem and the end of the Jewish people. A. Feuillet, "Le sens du mot parousie dans l'Ev. de Mt.," *The Background of the NT and Its Eschatology, Festschr. f. C. H. Dodd* (1956), 272-278, finds in the threatened day of slaughter a ref. to the historical disaster which overtook the Jewish people in 70 A.D. Jm. took this to be an eschatological judgment on Israel which was executed by Jesus, who is Lord in Jm. 5:7, and which is to be distinguished from the final judgment on the nations.

---

† σφραγίς, † σφραγίζω,
† κατασφραγίζω

Contents: A. Seal in the Non-Biblical World: 1. The Composition of Seals; 2. The Legal Significance of Seals; 3. The Religious Meaning; 4. The Metaphorical Use of the Word. B. Seal in the Old Testament: 1. The Meaning of the Word; 2. The Composition of Seals; 3. The Use and Significance of Seals. C. Seal in Judaism. D. Seal in the New Testament: 1. The Word Group in the New Testament apart from Revelation: a. Seal and Seals in the Literal Sense; b. Seal and Seals in the Transferred Sense; 2. The Word Group in Revelation: a. Sealing; b. The Book with Seven Seals; c. The Sealed. E. Seal in the Post-Apostolic Age.

The linguistic origin is unknown. [1] The noun ἡ σφραγίς (Ionic σφρηγίς) "seal" is found from Theogn., 19 (Diehl, II³, 4), the verb σφραγίζω "to seal" in Aesch. Eum., 828. [2]

A. Seal in the Non-Biblical World.

Using seals is an ancient custom in antiquity. They serve to identify things with a sign, figure, letter, or words, or a combination of these. A technical element is presupposed, namely, the making of an instrument by means of which the desired mark can be impressed or copied once or often on a suitable surface, thus producing the stamp or seal. Like σφραγίς and sigillum (from signum) "seal" has two meanings. It can denote the instrument, the signet or ring (δακτύλιον, anulus). It can also denote the impression made by this.

1. Composition of Seals.

Roll seals or seal cylinders are the oldest form. These spread all over the Orient and discoveries attest to their use in Babylon from c. 3000. [3] The height of the cylinder varies from some 10 mm to 20 cm, [4] while the roll was usually 2 to 4 cm. Figures and signs were cut into the sheath of the cylinder; they were usually taken from the mythological or

---

σ φ ρ α γ ί ς κ τ λ . Bibl.: J. Diehl, *Sphragis. Eine semasiologische Nachlese*, Diss. Giessen (1938); F. Dölger, *Sphragis* (1911); *Hazor I. An Account of the First Season of Excavations*, 1955, ed. Y. Yadin *et al.* (1958); *Hazor II. An Account of the Second Season of Excavations*, 1956, ed. Y. Yadin *et al.* (1960); W. Heitmüller, σφραγίς, *Festschr. f. G. Heinrici* (1914), 40-59; A. Reifenberg, "Hebr. Seals and Stamps, IV," *Israel Exploration Journ.*, 4 (1954), 139-142; L. Wenger, Art. "signum" in Pauly-W., 2a (1923), 2361-2448; also *Die Quellen d. röm. Rechts* (1953), 45-49; D. J. Wiseman, *Cylinder Seals of Western Asia* (1958).
[1] Boisacq, Hofmann, *s.v.* Borrowing from a foreign language is likely on material grounds, cf. seal from Lat. *sigillum* (cf. Schwyzer, I, 465). Thes. Steph., *s.v.* pts. to the linguistic connection with φράττω (φρακjω) "to fence in," but the quantitative difference in stem syllables is against this [Risch]. In Da. 8:26; 12:4, 9 (ἐμ)φράττω and σφραγίζω are used synon. in LXX and Θ in the sense "to close." At 2 C. 11:10 some MSS have σφραγήσεται or σφραγίσεται for φραγήσεται, Tisch. NT, *ad loc.*
[2] Liddell-Scott, Pr.-Bauer, Μέγα λέξικον τῆς Ἑλληνικῆς γλώσσης, VIII (1952), *s.v.* Common words developed from σφραγίς are σφράγισμα, σφραγιστήρ, -ιον, σφραγιστής, ἀσφράγιστος; there are compounds of the verb in ἀπο-, ἐπι-, κατα-, προ-, συνεπι-.
[3] A. Moortgat, *Vorderasiatische Rollsiegel* (1940); H. Frankfort, *Cylinder Seals* (1939); F. Delitzsch, *Handel u. Wandel in Altbabylonien* (1910), 19, Ill. 18; AOB, Ill. 475; Wiseman.
[4] AOB, 90; Ill. 314 a 20 cm long lapis-lazuli roll cylinder from Babylon with an image of Marduk c. 850 B.C.; cf. 93; Ill. 326.

cultic sphere. [5] The seal was made by rolling the cylinder on damp clay. There was a further development in Egypt during the 18th dynasty (1500-1300 B.C.). The cylinder was now replaced by the scarab or seal ring with scarab. [6] Scarabs as seals and amulets were exported from the land of their origin to all the countries of the Near East. [7] With roll seals and scarabs we also find knob, cone and cube seals with primitive figures mostly from the animal world. [8] Signatures on will pap. show that the seals of the signatory witnesses had figures of the gods and heroes and other signs, P. Oxy., III, 489 (117 A.D.); 490 (124 A.D.); 491 (126 A.D.). [9] Cl. Al. Paed., III, 59, 2 ref. to Chr. seals with the dove, the fish, the ship etc. and contrasts these with the gods, the sword, the bow, or the picture of the beloved etc. on pagan seals. He rejects the latter as incompatible with Chr. faith and ethics. What this Chr. moralist of the end of the 2nd cent. presented as the custom of his day probably applied to the whole Hell. period, and that not merely in Egypt. But many ancient seals simply have the name of the owner or a sign particularly significant to him.

The material on which the seal was rolled or impressed was usually damp loam or clay. This was then dried off in the air or baked in an oven. We thus have many clay tablets with seals impressed, or vessels on which the handles esp. bear the seal of the potter or the owner. [10] When a document was sealed some clay was put on it and the seal could then be impressed on this. [11] We do not have any examples of wax seals from antiquity. [12] Scrolls, books and letters were sealed by sealing the tie which held them together. [13]

2. The Legal Significance of Seals.

The seal served as a legal protection and guarantee in many ways, esp. in relation to property. [14] All objects suitable for sealing could be marked as the property of the owner in this way. Sealing was part of everyday life in Babylon, cf. esp. Hdt., I, 195, 2: "Every Babylonian carried his handmade stick and also a seal." [15] Anything in the house could be set under a seal ἐπὶ σφραγίδων, chests, jugs (usually sealed on the handle), [16] and of course wills, P. Oxy., I, 106, 12 (135 A.D.), cf. BGU, I, 98, 15 f. (211 A.D.) An intellectual possession could also be safeguarded by a seal, i.e., by inserting a section with the author's name. [17] Sealing to mark ownership probably goes back to a much

---

[5] E.g., Delitzsch, op. cit., Ill. 27; → n. 43-47. Wiseman, 100 a seal with the image of Darius I hunting, and an inscr. in 3 languages.

[6] A. Erman, Ägypten u. ägypt. Leben im Altertum (1885), 313.

[7] BR, 23 f.; cf. Hazor I, Plate CXLIX, 22 a scarab in blue faience 12 mm broad, 18 mm long and 8 mm deep, cf. also J. Spiegel, Das Werden d. ägypt. Hochkultur (1953), 209 f., also Ant. Christ., II (1930), 239. On securing scarabs in rings v. AOB, 170; Ill. 613; here we also have examples of small roll seals on rings.

[8] AOB, 163; Ill. 575 and 576.

[9] Dölger, 5.

[10] H. Biesantz, Kretisch-Mykenische Siegelbilder (1954), 3 and Hazor II, 60 and Plate LXXXIX, 5; CII, 23; CLXII, 5.

[11] Only few such seals are extant, cf. H. Wilcken, "Papyrusurkunden," APF, 4 (1905), 529 on P. Lond., III, 15, 1206 (clay seal on the free margin of the pap., v. Plates 8 and 9); BGU, II, 463 (148 A.D.); BGU, III, 764 (2nd cent. A.D.).

[12] Wenger signum, 2386.

[13] T. Birt, Die Buchrolle in der Kunst (1907), 9, 241-4; O. Roller, Das Formular d. paul. Briefe (1933), 45, 394, n. 205; so already Hdt., III, 128, 2 f. cf. Jer. 32:10 f.

[14] Liddell-Scott, s.v.; Dölger, 18; Ant. Christ., I (1929), 299; Wenger signum, 2361.

[15] O. Rossbach, Art. "Gemmen," Pauly-W., 7 (1912), 1053.

[16] Cf. Hazor II, 60; Cl. Al. Paed., III, 11, 57 and → n. 10.

[17] This was called sphragis, Ant. Christ., I (1929), 299 ref. to Theogn., 19-26 (Diehl, II³, 4), though O. Immisch, "Die Sphragis d. Theogn.," Rhein. Mus., NF, 82 (1933), 298-304 objects that seal here is concrete rather than metaphorical; the author put his seal by the text; F. J. Dölger replies in Ant. Christ., V (1936), 288 f.

older custom, namely, the marking of objects, animals and men, esp. slaves, [18] by notching, slitting, or branding, [19] → 658, 2 ff.; 659, 25 ff.

Misuse of seals was also possible in antiquity. A statute like that of Solon in Diog. L., I, 57 was directed against this. It lays down that a "maker of seals" δακτυλιογλύφος was not to retain the "impression" σφραγίς of a signet-ring δακτύλιος which he had sold. [20] Aristoph. makes use of the theme of the fraudulent making of other people's seals in Thes., 425. [21] The seal belonged to its owner alone; no one else had the right to it. Tac. Ann., 16, 19, 3 bears witness to the practice of breaking one's seal just before death to prevent fraudulent use. [22] The seal also serves as proof of identity. [23] It is put with a signature or in place of it in letters, agreements and private or public instructions. [24] Another way in which it protects property is by sealing the contents of a container, purse, vessel, sack, bale, or packet. [25] Houses and graves can be sealed. [26] The seal is a guarantee against violation. The same applies to texts, hymns, and records. [27] Original documents are sealed, whereas copies usually are not. In early Ptolemaic taxation law (259/58) one finds the provision that both a sealed and also an unsealed and publicly kept document of the same contents should be prepared τὸ δὲ ἕτερον ἀσφράγιστον. [28] The clay tablets of the Cretan archives were also sealed. [29] Wills and testamentary dispositions were sealed both by the testator and also by the witnesses. [30] In P. Oxy., III, 494 (156 A.D.) the testator signs καὶ ἔστιν μου ἡ σφραγὶς Θώνιος. [31] Acc. to Roman law 6 witnesses had to sign and the will could be opened only when each of the 6 broke his own seal. [32] In South Babylonia the beneficiaries also signed or sealed at the dividing of the inheritance. [33] Finally the seal also serves a purpose of accreditation. [34] The standardising of weights may be mentioned in this connection. σφραγίζω means here "to furnish with the correct signs." [35] To ensure the identity of a transferred prisoner he was sealed, i.e., his fetters were given a seal. [36]

---

[18] Erman, op. cit. (→ n. 6), 86; cf. σφραγίζω in BGU, I, 15 (2nd cent. A.D.), 87 (2nd cent. A.D.), 197 (1st cent. A.D.), 250 (2nd cent. A.D.), 356 (3rd cent. A.D.).

[19] Wenger signum, 2362. Laters stamps were also used, cf. Erman, 589. Marks impressed by brands were themselves called σφραγίς, Ant. Christ., III (1932), 31; cf. Verg. Georg., III, 157-161; military signing is another example, Ant. Christ., II (1930), 281-296.

[20] Wenger signum, 2380; Wenger Quellen, 137, n. 18.

[21] Wenger signum, 2380.

[22] [Dihle], cf. Biesantz, op. cit., 4: "The seal was closely related to the personality of the owner. It was laid in the grave with him."

[23] Wenger signum, 2390.

[24] Ibid., 2431; Roller, 612, n. 557: "Sealing played an important role in documents in Bab. and the Near East."

[25] BGU, I, 98 (3rd cent. A.D.), 248 (2nd cent. A.D.), 249 (2nd cent. A.D.); H. Erman, "Die Siegelung d. Papyrusurkunden," APF, 1 (1901), 68; Wenger signum, 2375; P. Oxy., VI, 929, 13 f. (3rd/4th cent. A.D.); Tell Amarna Letters (J. A. Knudtzon [1915]), 7, 68; 20, 49 the sealing of shipments of gold and other valuables; O. Roller, op. cit., 614, n. 563.

[26] Biesantz, op. cit., 3.

[27] Ant. Christ., I (1929), 300 ref. to Sumerian hymns with the no. of lines at the end as a seal of authenticity and accuracy.

[28] Wenger signum, 2362; Roller, 396, n. 208 ref. to Cic. Att., 12, 18, 2 and a pap. letter of the Ammonite sheikh Tubias to Apollonius, the finance minister of Ptolemy Philadelphus, 257/256 B.C., cf. Deissmann LO, 128, facsimile, 407 f.

[29] Biesantz, 3.

[30] Wenger Quellen, 48.

[31] Wenger signum, 2403.

[32] Erman, op. cit. (→ n. 25), 72; cf. Suet. Caes., VI, 17; Roller, 397, n. 208.

[33] Wenger signum, 2431.

[34] Ibid., 2393; σφραγίζω "to accredit" already in 3rd cent. pap. [Risch], cf. Roller, 395, n. 206; 498, n. 337.

[35] Wenger signum, 2366.

[36] Ant. Christ., I (1929), 292 f.

In the oriental and Hell. world the seal had a public as well as a private function. [37] It was used in administration and government, in politics and law. All authorities had seals of office and state (δημοσία σφραγίς), esp. kings. Since it is part of the covering function of the seal to ensure secrecy, [38] special care was taken to secure the seal of state (ὁ ἐπιστάτης) τηρεῖ ... καὶ τὴν δημοσίαν σφραγῖδα, Ps.-Aristot. De Republica Atheniensium, 44, 1, [39] cf. also ἔχουσί τε ἐπὶ τῇ δημοσίᾳ σφραγῖδι τὸν ἕσπερον ἀστέρα ἐγκεχαραγμένον, Strabo, 9, 3, 1. [40] The king's seal expresses royal authorisation. He who has the king's ring is entrusted with his power and represents him. Joseph has Pharaoh's ring, [41] and at the installation of a certain Hwy (Haia) as governor of Nubia c. 1400 B.C. the giving of the ring signifies the transfer of office. [42] In the legal power of holding a seal there is expressed in both private and public life an element of rule; one can make decisions, one has control over things, animals and people. The holder of the seal is the holder of power and has his place in a duly constituted order. Might and right come together in the seal. This is another point of contact with the religious sphere.

3. The Religious Meaning.

From early days and throughout the cultures of antiquity in all times and places seals and signet-rings bear the images of gods or signs of the god. These link the holder and user of the seal with the deity. Many roll seals from Babylon (→ 939, 21 ff.) have scenes from divine history and the cultic sphere as well as figures of the gods. On an Accad. seal cylinder of c. 2700 B.C. the god stands on a chariot and directs a winged lion. [43] Or a god is enthroned on a cushion and a mythical creature, the upper half man and the lower bird, is brought before him by another god. [44] On the so-called fall cylinder from c. 2500 B.C. the god sits on a throne to the right and a female form is to the left, with a sacred tree between them. Behind the left figure the wavy line of an upright snake completes the image. [45] An Accad. roll seal from c. 2500 portrays Etana's ascension. [46] Scarabs (→ 940, 2 ff.) also have figures of standing or enthroned gods and divine emblems or names. [47] This raises the whole question of image and object in the religious sphere. [48] Another question is how far we have in the roll seals with their mythical figures a first technique of duplication for the making of religious statements through images. We have countless seals, but antiquity yields few reproductions or impressions. [48]

When religious thought and practice have a magical emphasis, seals and seal stones and rings take on divine or magical significance → 660, 17 ff. The deity protects, and the same power is ascribed to the image. Note should be taken of the lucky significance of the scarab. Harpocrates, the Gk. version of Horus the Child, who fights wicked Seth, becomes a protective deity. His image is common on seal rings. A heliotrope with his figure has the inscr.: Μέγας Ὧρος Ἀπόλλων Ἁρποκράτ(ης) εὐίλατος (be gracious) τῷ

---

[37] Preisigke Fachwörter, 166; Wenger signum, 2362; but cf. Dölger, 16; Erman, op. cit. (→ n. 25), n. 74.
[38] Wenger signum, 2393; clausa iam et obsignata epistula, writes M. Fronto, Epistulae ad M. Caesarem, III, 4 (ed. J. van der Hout [1954]); cf. Roller, 500, n. 339.
[39] Ed. H. Oppermann (1961).
[40] Further examples in Dölger, 8 f. and Wenger Quellen, 147 f.
[41] Gn. 41:41-43; cf. Dölger, 7; Wenger signum, 2390; AOB, 60; Ill. 189.
[42] Erman, 74.
[43] AOB, 77; Ill. 250.
[44] AOB, 167; Ill. 602.
[45] AOB, Ill. 603. "Thus far no explanation of the image has been established," AOB, 168. Cf. Hazor II, Plate CLXII, 1 and 2.
[46] AOB, Ill. 600; cf. Delitzsch, op. cit. (→ n. 3), Ill. 28, a 4 cm high roll seal with a better execution of the same theme.
[47] AOB, 165; Ill. 584; 166; Ill. 590 and 592.
[48] AOB, 166; Ill. 597. On the question of image and reality cf. H. Schrade, Der verborgene Gott (1949), esp. 13-23 and 128-130.

φοροῦντι, CIG, IV, 7045. With his finger on his lips Harpocrates is also the god of silence, a fine emblem for the seal, which is meant to shut off or conceal something. [49] As the scarab becomes the lucky amulet, [50] so seals have magical significance esp. where the divine figures and signs are no longer understood and hold out promise of a link with mysterious powers. [51]

There is a combination of the cultic and the legal when the word is used for the marking of sacrifices declared suitable by the priest. The priest puts a strip of papyrus round the horns of the beast, puts sealing clay on it, and sets the impress of his signet-ring on this. [52] New constructs are also a sign of this combination of the cultic and the legal. The one commissioned to seal sacrifices in the temple state is the ἱερομοσχοσφραγιστής, Greek Pap., [53] II, 64. The lists kept of animals are βιβλία μοσχοσφραγιστικά, Cl. Al. Strom., VI, 3, 36, 2. The μοσχοσφραγιστής must send the sacrificing priest a written authentication of the cleanness of the beast. For sealing σφραγισμός a stamp duty or tax had later to be paid to the state, BGU, II, 536 (213 A.D.). [54] The seal is a guarantee of inviolability in the cultic sphere too. The chapel with a statue of the god is secured by a clay seal. When the chapel is cultically opened for worship of the god the seal is broken during prayers explaining the action, and it is put on again later. [55] In the mysteries, esp. the Dionysus cult, the seal has again a part to play. Worshippers of Dionysus had the sign of the god, the ivy leaf κισσόφυλλον, burned on them: χαράσσεσθαι καὶ διὰ πυρὸς εἰς τὸ σῶμα, 3 Macc. 2:29. This signing was called σφραγίζειν. It is part of a whole sphere of religious marking practised e.g., in ecstatic forms in the cults of Cybele, Attis, and Mithras, [56] → 659, 25 ff.

4. The Metaphorical Use of the Word.

Signs are familiar and everyday things. They can thus be used as comparisons for purposes of illustration. Plat. Theaet., 192a compares the impressions which memory receives with those made by a signet-ring. Aristot. De Audibilibus, p. 801b, 4 says that voices are clear only when sounds are well articulated, just as seals on rings are so only when they are sharp and well-defined. The lyricist Timotheus of Miletus (c. 400 B.C.), The Persians, Col. VI, 160 [57] ref. to the seal of the mouth, and in Orph. Hymn., 34, 26 cf. 64, 2 it is said of the seal, with ref. to the creator of the world (δημιουργός), that it is stamped on all creation. [58]

B. Seal in the Old Testament.

1. The meaning of the Word.

a. The Hbr. equivalent of σφραγίς is חֹתָם, which occurs 13 times. Once חָח is transl. σφραγίς, Ex. 35:22. It is hard to see why, for the meaning is bracelet as a feminine ornament along with נֶזֶם "earrings" and טַבַּעַת δακτύλιοι "rings" or "signet-rings." The basic meaning of חָח is "hook" and it can be used of the pointed hook or ring put through

---

[49] Dölger, 6.
[50] BR, 23.
[51] BR, 27 Ill. 10-12; Wiseman.
[52] Dölger, 22.
[53] Ed. B. P. Grenfell and A. S. Hunt (1903); cf. also Ant. Christ., II (1932), 35, n. 9 and Plut. Is. et Os., 31 (II, 363b): τὸν δὲ μέλλοντα θύεσθαι βοῦν οἱ σφραγισταὶ λεγόμενοι τῶν ἱερέων κατεσημαίνοντο.
[54] Cf. Ant. Christ., III (1932), 35 f.
[55] Erman, op. cit. (→ n. 25), 371.
[56] Dölger, 42 f.; Heitmüller, 47.
[57] Ed. U. v. Wilamowitz-Möllendorff (1903), 24.
[58] [Dihle].

the nose or jaw of animals or prisoners. LXX has ἄγκιστρον ("hook") at 4 Βασ. 19:28, φιμός ("muzzle," "gag") at Is. 37:29, κημός ("muzzle") at Ez. 19:4, 9. חֹתֶמֶת is used only at Gn. 38:25 in the sense "seal," LXX δακτύλιος. The commonest original on this is טַבַּעַת "seal," "signet-ring," from טבע "to impress in a soft, plastic material," "to seal." But only in 10 of 44 passages is the meaning "signet-ring," and 6 of these are in Est. Worthy of note also is Da. 6:18 LXX and Θ, δακτύλιος for עִזְקָא.

b. The main equivalent of σφραγίζω and κατασφραγίζω is חתם, for act., mid. and pass.; cf. the q forms in Job 14:17; Is. 8:16; Dt. 32:34; in the ni "were sealed" only Est. 3:12. [59] and 8:8; in the pi "hold sealed" only Job 24:16; in the hi "to close" Lv. 15:3 (LXX συνέστηκεν). At Da. 8:26 Θ we find σφραγίζω for סתם "to stop up," "to hold secret," while Da. 9:24 Θ uses it for תמם hi, properly "to get ready," "to finish."

2. The Composition of Seals.

The semasiological and statistical data indicate already that seals and the use of seals are not original in the OT world. The roll seal (→ 939, 21 ff.) comes to Israel from Babylon. The figures are partly Bab. and partly Egypt. [60] The scarab comes from Egypt → 940, 1 ff. We find mythical figures, animals, fabulous winged creatures, men and hieroglyphics along with ancient Hebraic characters. [61] Egypt. and Syr. motifs occur on older seals of the 9th and 8th cent. The inscribing of seals comes only later. [62] We find simple names without figures. [63] With scarabs we have scarab forms, also studs which can be engraved on both sides. [64] A conic seal of black basalt, found in Tell Ta'anak (c. 1000 B.C.), has two stylised gazelles on a tree; cube seals have also been found. [65] Well over a hundred pre-exilic seals have been found in excavations at Megiddo, Gezer, Tell Ta'anak, Hazor etc.

"Seal graving" γλύμμα σφραγῖδος is part of the craft of stone-cutting ἔργον λιθουργικῆς τέχνης — מַעֲשֵׂה חָרַשׁ אֶבֶן פִּתּוּחֵי חֹתָם Ez. 28:11. The stone-cutter חָרַשׁ אֶבֶן λιθουργέω receives his skill from God, Ex. 35:33, 35 Things are different later. In the list of crafts which demand attention day and night and do not leave time to become wise the son of Sirach mentions the stone-cutters οἱ γλύφοντες γλύμματα σφραγίδων, Sir. 38:27.

3. The Use and Significance of Seals.

a. Royal seals have not been found thus far in Israel, but we have the seal of a king's son, Gealiah of Bet Sur, perhaps a son of Josiah at the end of the 7th cent. [66] There are a few ministerial seals with the names of the kings Uzziahu and Jeroboam II, or without mention of the king's name, e.g., that of Jaazaniahu c. 600 B.C. (Mizpah), cf. 2 K. 25:23; with the name we find עֶבֶד הַמֶּלֶךְ "king's minister." [67] Use of the royal seal is mentioned in 1 K. 21:8: Jezebel sends letters in Ahab's name and seals them with his seal. The bolt on the temple door is sealed with the royal seal, which would bear the king's name, and the

---

[59] Est. 3:12 LXX offers a free rendering of the HT.
[60] AOB, 164; Ill. 577; cf. Hazor II, 33 and Plates LXXVI, 11 and CLXII, 1 and 2.
[61] AOB Ill. 581-589.
[62] BR, 481-490.
[63] BR, 485 f. Ill. 19-25.
[64] Cf. a sapphire blue carnelian of the 8th-6th cent. 2.4 times 1.6 cm in size with Shebeniahu and various figures on both sides, AOB, 165; Ill. 588.
[65] AOB, 163; Ill. 575 and 576.
[66] BR, 489 and Ill. 23. On stamps of ownership or delivery lamelekh cf. also J. B. Pritchard, *Hebrew Inscr. and Stamps from Gibeon* (1959), 18-23.
[67] BR, 487 and Ill. 15 with the oldest depiction of a fighting cock.

seal of the priest of Bel, Bel and the Dragon 14 LXX; the stone over the lions' den is also sealed with the seal of the king and his nobles. This denotes common responsibility for the security of the enclosure, for each of those who seal must be present when the seal is opened and confirm that it has not been tampered with, Da. 6:18. [68] He who has the king's ring can use his power. Joseph has Pharaoh's ring and represents him, so that all must bow to him as to the monarch, Gn. 41:42. We find the same motif in Est.3:10: the king takes the ring from his hand and gives it to Haman σφραγίσαι κατὰ τῶν γεγραμμένων κατὰ τῶν Ἰουδαίων "to seal" the measures against the Jews. When Esther and Mordecai later gain power this is said to be sealing with his ring, for no one may oppose what is written at the king's command and sealed with his seal, Est. 8:8-10; these orders are sent out by couriers.

b. The seal makes a document legally valid. Bills of sale are agreed and sealed before witnesses τὸ βιβλίον τῆς κτήσεως τὸ ἐσφραγισμένον, Ιερ. 39(32):10 f., 25, 44; here we are also told that an unsealed copy was prepared and kept in a clay vessel. [69] The marriage contract was also sealed, e.g., by the parents Raguel and Edna for Tobias and Sara in Tob. 7:14. The magna carta of the people was drawn up, inscribed and sealed by the leaders of the people and the priests and Levites — διατιθέμεθα πίστιν καὶ γράφομεν καὶ ἐπισφραγίζουσιν πάντες ἄρχοντες ἡμῶν, Λευῖται, ἱερεῖς — 24 priests, 17 Levites, and 44 leading men are mentioned by name as signatories, 2 Εσδρ. 20:1 or Neh. 10:1. The seal was also meant to protect a document against inappropriate or premature disclosure. It prevented people from reading a work. Is. 29:11: All these words will be like the words of a sealed book, and if it is said to him, You are a man who can read, read this, he will say, I cannot read it: "it is sealed." In the story of the pages in 1 Εσδρ. 3:8 we read that each inscribes his own saying and seals it and lays it under the king's pillow. The seal does not merely close; it is also a safeguard against violation. The king has the temple revenues seized and sealed for repairs, 4 Βασ. 22:4. Purses are sealed τὰ θυλάκια ἐν ταῖς σφραγῖσιν, Tob. 9:5; cf. the use of this practice as a metaphor in Job 14:17.

c. σφραγίζω can also mean to engrave stone or metal in the LXX. The breastplate of the high-priest τὸ λογεῖον τῶν κρίσεων — חֹשֶׁן מִשְׁפָּט in Ex. 28:15 is adorned with twelve different precious stones set in gold and each having the name of one of the 12 tribes cut in it, Ex. 28:21. These are γλυφαὶ σφραγίδων פִּתּוּחֵי חֹתָם. The 12 names are ἐγγεγραμμένα εἰς σφραγῖδας, Ex. 36:21 (39:14). The golden plate on the high-priest's mitre also has an engraving on it → 661, 44 ff., though the LXX has in view a chased rather than engraved inscr. when it transl. ἐκτύπωμα σφραγῖδος, Ex. 28:36. The inscr. reads: Ἁγίασμα κυρίου קֹדֶשׁ לַיהוה "sanctuary of Yahweh." The high-priest's girdle has two emeralds as clasps and these are also engraved with the 12 names of the tribes. The transl. is thinking of carving again when he renders the v. λίθους... γεγλυμμένους καὶ ἐκκεκολαμμένους ἐκκόλαμμα σφραγῖδος, Ex. 36:13 (39:6). These engraved gems and gold plates are no more seals than are women's ornaments, though σφραγῖδες can be used for golden earrings and rings or golden hair-nets and bracelets (or amulets); in this case HT has חֹח "ring," "bracelet," fibula, and the transl. had an engraved ornament in mind, Ex. 35:22.

d. The fact that the contents of a sealed vessel or purse were inaccessible gave σφραγίζω the further sense "to close": to close the lips with an effective seal Sir. 22:27; the wise man gives the prudent counsel: Do not be upset by a wife who keeps house badly, in this case a seal is good (i.e., it is best to keep it all under lock and key), Sir. 42:6. A document is closed and sealed so that it cannot be read easily → 941, 12 ff. σφραγίζω can then

---

[68] [Bertram].
[69] Cf. the preservation of the Dead Sea Scrolls and the Nag-Hammadi codices.

mean "to conceal." Is. 8:16 LXX censures those who seal the Law, i.e., hide it so that no one can learn it. Daniel is to keep secret what he has seen, 8:26. For יהח םהס LXX has πεφραγμένον τὸ ὅραμα, Θ σφράγισον τὴν ὅρασιν. In 12:4, 9 καλύπτω, σφραγίζω and ἐμφράττω are used synon.

e. The seal thus yields a complex nexus of relations. Mixed in it are the motifs of power and authorisation, of legal validity and reliability, of the inviolate, closed and secret, of the costly and valuable. It is no wonder that in the OT the term is transf. from the everyday sphere and used to illustrate other relations. Like a seal with a glowing red stone on a gold ornament is the harmonious sound of music at a banquet, Sir. 32(35):5 f. [70] Mercy is like a signet-ring, 17:22. The seal is used in the imagery of love and faith (→ 660, 34 ff.; 661, 6 ff.) to denote close relationship and high worth, e.g.: "Lay me like a seal on thy heart, like a seal on thine arm," Cant. 8:6. The threat of disaster is uttered by Jeremiah as a saying of Yahweh Himself regarding Jeconiah, son of Jehoiakim, king of Judah, even though he were "the signet upon my right hand," Jer. 22:24. On the other hand, in 520 Haggai calls Zerubbabel the elect of God, God's servant, and he is said to be "made as a signet," Hag. 2:23, cf. Sir. 49:11.

C. Seal in Judaism.

1. The metaphorical use is developed even more broadly and deeply by Philo. σφραγίς, σφραγίζω, ἐπι- (ἐν-) σφραγίζω becomes fig. terms in the vocabulary of religious philosophy. Philo is acquainted with the everyday use of a seal, e.g., as a signature at the end of a letter, Leg. Gaj., 330. In the main, however, he uses σφραγίς metaphorically. He continually develops new aspects of the comparison. "By impression the tiny seal can reproduce copies of very large things, and similarly in a tiny representation in even more tiny letters are revealed the ineffable beauties of the creation of the world written in the laws," Op. Mund., 6. The relation of small and great, and revelation or disclosure are the elements in the use of the image. The fact that the seal makes innumerable copies but itself remains unaltered is often used by Philo as an illustration of the powers around God who give form to the formless and shape to the indistinct without losing anything of their own eternal essence, Spec. Leg., I, 47. But the seal then becomes a simile for the original or idea acc. to which the bodily and that which may be apprehended by the senses are fashioned. The apprehensible world is a μίμημα θείας εἰκόνος, "a copy of the imago Dei, the image of God." Obviously, then, ἡ ἀρχέτυπος σφραγίς is the original seal — the world of knowledge — the very Word of God, Op. Mund., 25. The incorporeal which is the theme of knowledge brings other bodies into being but itself remains incorporeal. It is the ideas, measures, types, seals, Op. Mund., 34. After quoting Gn. 2:4 f. Philo concludes: ἆρ' οὐκ ἐμφανῶς τὰς ἀσωμάτους καὶ νοητὰς ἰδέας παρίστησιν, ἃς τῶν αἰσθητῶν ἀποτελεσμάτων σφραγῖδας εἶναι συμβέβηκε; the incorporeal ideas of knowledge are in some sense seals for inwardly apprehended reality, Op. Mund., 129. There is an obvious difference between this metaphorical use of the seal and that in Plat. Theaet., 192a (→ 943, 25 f.). No passage can be adduced in which Plat. uses the seal as a comparison in his doctrine of the ideas. [71] What Plat. says about memory with his metaphor of the seal is more like what Philo says about potentialities and actualisation. "For as all seal impressions are potentially there in the wax, but in actuality only those which have really been made, so in the soul, which is like wax, all impressions are there in possibility but not in actuality; the reality impressed on it holds sway until effaced by one which is more effective and makes a greater impression," Leg. All., I, 100. Some-

---

[70] For examples of a profane fig. use cf. Diehl, 19-21 [Bertram].

[71] Dölger, 65 f. tries to deduce from Philo's use of the seal in connection with the ideas an origination of the comparison in Plato. This is not really possible since Philo makes extensive use of the image whereas the word is almost accidental and not at all important in Plato. In fact Dölger can adduce only a saying of the Alex. Stoic Ar. Did. Fr., 1 (447) in which σφραγίς is used to characterise Plato's doctrine of the ideas.

times σφραγίζω means "to keep under lock and key" in Philo, Leg. All., III, 106. σφραγίζω and ἐπισφραγίζω can also mean "to determine" by one's own power, so of the unbridled in Spec. Leg., II, 19, of God and His promises in Praem. Poen., 108, or of God who accepts the free choice by the whole people of their ruler or office-bearer by adding His own seal, God who is guarantor of all public things, Spec. Leg., IV, 157. As there is an element of rule in this use of the word, so it can have the nuances "to correspond to a system," "to obey a system." Perhaps there is an echo of the original sense at this pt. Philo has a weakness for the system of numbers and their profound meaning in creation; thus he says that Moses "always paid heed to the doctrine of numbers: ... of numbers after one, ten is the most perfect and sacred, and Moses sealed this with his 10 clean animals," Spec. Leg., IV, 105. The Law "adds to" the seven days of Tabernacles an eighth ἐπισφραγίζεται. To this is appended a systematic treatment of the ogdoad which is the first cubic number and which forms as such the transition from the incorporeal or spiritual to the corporeal, Spec. Leg., II, 211. There is also in Philo a weaker use of σφραγίζω for "to confirm" with no ref. to a seal or sealing, Jos., 212; Spec. Leg., II, 14 and 227.

2. The main role of the seal in Jos. is where it seems important to him in telling the OT stories. Joseph is authorised to use Pharaoh's seal, Ant., 2, 90. The lions' den of Daniel is sealed by the king σῳζομένην τὴν σφραγῖδα εὑρών (10, 258 f.), and Esther receives Artaxerxes' seal and authority (11, 271). The seal protects and gives the protection of the law by closing. Thus when Augustus deposed Archelaus in 6 A.D. the high-priestly vestments were kept in a walled up room in the castle Antonia and were placed under the seal of the priests and keepers of the chamber, 18, 93 f. Jos. tells us that a miracle of healing was performed before Vespasian and his officers by a certain Eleazar, who used a ring enclosing a root recommended by Solomon, 8, 42.[72]

3. Finally, it is important for the history of the word in the Jewish sphere that circumcision is often called a seal → 662, 13 ff.; VI, 80, 33 ff. In the circumcision prayer in jBer., 9, 3 (14a, 49 f.) we read: "Blessed be he who has sanctified his beloved from the mother's womb, who has given a law for his family and as a sign has impressed on his progeny the seal of the holy covenant."[73] In PRE1, 10 Jonah, when brought by the fish to Leviathan, showed him the seal of Abraham, and Leviathan looked away and fled two days' journey from Jonah.[74] Ex. r., 19 (81c) speaks of the "seal חוֹתָם of Abraham in your flesh."[75] Tg. Cant., 3, 8 reads: "Each of them had the 'seal' of circumcision חֲתִימַת מִילָה in his flesh, as it was impressed on the flesh of Abraham ..."[76] It is plain that the word seal is used metaphorically in this connection. The idea of the seal offers many themes in interpretation of circumcision: that of the sign — it is the אוֹת בְּרִית σημεῖον διαθήκης

---

[72] Cf. the fact that many amulets are inscribed σφραγὶς Σολομῶνος, "seal of Solomon." For these cf. G. Schlumberger, "Amulettes byzantins anciens destinés à combattre les maléfices et maladies," Revue d'Étud. Grecques, 5 (1892), 84, 13. Perhaps such seals bore the tetragrammaton (Dölger, 63-5 with material), cf. the suggestion in the Rabb. tradition that Solomon's miraculous seal bears the divine name, bGit., 68a. Important here is the fact that among the Arabs the pentagrammaton and hexagrammaton are called Solomon's seal, cf. also the Mandaeans, E. L. Ehrlich, Kultsymbolik im AT u. im nachbibl. Judt. (1959), 129; M. Lidzbarski, Ephemeris, I (1900-1902), 105. On magical ideas cf. Dölger, 63-5, also Prayer of Man. 3 in O. F. Fritzsche, Libri Apocr. Veteris Test. graece (1871), 92 and V. Ryssel on the Pray. of Man. 3 in Kautzsch Apkr. u. Pseudepigr., I, 168, also the Alexandrian phylacterion (A. S. Dorigny, "Phylactère Alexandrine contre les Epistachis," Rev. d. Ét. Grecques, 4 [1891], 287-296) and the discussion of the meaning of the star of David in Ehrlich, n. 345.
[73] G. Anrich, Das antike Mysterienwesen (1894), 122, n. 2.
[74] Str.-B., I, 644 f.
[75] Ibid., IV, 32 f., with further material.
[76] Ibid., IV, 33; on God's seal cf. Beth Hammidrasch, V, 162, 1, ed. A. Jellinek² (1938), where R. Akiba claims: "God loves only circumcision, for it is the seal of God" (Str.-B., III, 120); cf. also Ehrlich, op. cit. (→ n. 72), 109.

in Gn. 17:11; that of identity of designation; it also points to membership, it is a sign of ownership, and finally the idea of power and protection also plays a part: Leviathan flees, while he who bears the seal is without fear. There is no doubt that behind this fig. use of the word there lies the older idea of providing something with a distinguishing sign or mark, a brand or notch, to denote possession, → 214, 19 ff.; 660, 32 ff. [77]

D. Seal in the New Testament.

σφραγίς with σφραγίζω and κατασφραγίζω occurs 32 times in the NT, 22 of the instances being in Rev.

1. The Word Group in the New Testament apart from Revelation.

a. Seal and Seals in the Literal Sense.

Only in few instances is σφραγίζω used in the direct sense for sealing. The stone at Jesus' tomb is sealed against unlawful opening by the high-priests and Pharisees, Mt. 27:66. The section vv. 62-66 is peculiar to Mt. and is designed to support the resurrection. [78] σφραγίσαντες τὸν λίθον μετὰ τῆς κουστωδίας is a very general depiction. We are not told whose or what seal was used. One can hardly think in terms of the sealing of graves as attested, e.g., in Crete → n. 10. The idea is simply to make the tomb secure, just as Daniel's den of lions was sealed to prevent his coming out of it → 945, 1 ff. In R. 15:28 the collection is handed over under seal as it were, though this certainly does not mean that Paul and the witnesses actually seal the bag as in Tob. 9:5 (→ 945, 27 ff.); at any rate we are not told this in 2 C. 8:20 f. where Paul might have found occasion to mention legal safeguards. His concern is that there should be trustworthiness in the gathering and especially the delivering of the collection. The choice of the word σφραγίζομαι is thus a mark of this trustworthiness in transmission. [79]

b. Seal and Seals in the Transferred Sense.

In 2 Tm. 2:19 σφραγίς is used in the sense of "inscription." The reference is not to the concrete process, for there was no actual impression nor could a seal leave any such on a foundation stone, a hard rock. If the foundation stone with the inscription is itself the seal, it cannot have been sealed by it. Here, then, σφραγίς is used metaphorically. Perhaps the idea of trustworthiness played some part here too, the reference being to God's word of promise and admonition. [80] In 1 C. 9:2

---

[77] Cf. the mark of Cain (→ 661, 15 ff.), the Yahweh mark of the prophets in 1 K. 20:35-43 HT (→ 661, 1 ff.), the נ sign of Ez. 9 (→ 662, 27 ff.), also Dt. 6:8; Jos. 4:6; Is. 49:16; Lv. 19:28; Dt. 14:1; Lv. 21:5; Jer. 16:6; cf. B. Stade, "Beiträge zur Pentateuchkritik: Das Kainszeichen," ZAW, 14 (1894), 250-318; E. Dinkler, "Zur Gesch. d. Kreuzsymbols," ZThK, 48 (1951), 148-172; W. Michaelis, "Zeichen, Siegel, Kreuz," ThZ, 12 (1956), 505-525.

[78] Bultmann Trad., 297 calls it "an apologetically motivated legend."

[79] Deissmann NB, 65 f.; L. Radermacher, "σφραγίζεσθαι: R. 15:28," ZNW, 32 (1933), 87-89 finds two senses. Sealing denotes "the end of the collection and also the authentication of the contents by the seal of a trustworthy man. In this way sealing is an important and significant act," 88. Yet this is not a provincialism but rather an abbreviated mode of expression whose meaning is clear. Pr.-Bauer, s.v.; cf. Ant. Christ., IV (1934), 280: "In my view the idea of a sealing in this expression had become greatly attenuated in popular usage. Cf. Lat. subscribere meaning the same as dare and concedere, 'to give,' 'to grant'."

[80] The context reminds us of Lk. 13:27: οὐκ οἶδα πόθεν ἐστέ· ἀπόστητε ἀπ' ἐμοῦ πάντες ἐργάται ἀδικίας [C. F. D. Moule] cf. ψ 6:9. Dib. Past² on Tm. 2:19 considers a derivation from primitive Chr. poetry and a certain mystical understanding. But this puts the explanation in the realm of uncertainty, and so H. Conzelmann in Dib. Past³, ad loc. rejects the mystical ref. in favour of the concept of the Church and election.

the Corinthians are the seals of Paul's apostolate. As a seal confirms that someone is the holder of an office (→ 942, 7 ff.), so the actuality of the Corinthian Church as a church founded by and belonging to him serves as his seal and validation. [81]

The sense in Jn. 3:33 is "to confirm." The figure of speech is even weaker here, as sometimes in Philo, → 947, 14 ff. In the context the idea of the authority or validity of the witness plays a part. He who receives the witness of Him that comes from heaven confirms God's truth as it were with the authority of the possessor of a seal. [82] That the element of confirming has a role in the use of σφραγίζω in the Fourth Gospel may be seen also in Jn. 6:27. In His sovereign action God has appointed the Son of Man to be the food of eternal life for men, and He has confirmed this with His seal. [83] Some aspects of the concrete use of the seal are adopted, but in essentials the word is just a figure to denote that is reliable.

On the same plane of usage are expressions in Paul's epistles in which circumcision on the one side (→ 947, 26 ff.) and endowment with the Spirit on the other are linked to the image of the seal. The sign of circumcision σημεῖον περιτομῆς is a sealing (→ 662, 12 ff.; VI, 80, 33 ff.), i.e., a ratifying of the righteousness of faith to which Abraham attained even when uncircumcised, R. 4:11. It is clear that circumcision itself is not regarded here as a σφραγίς, a mark of belonging to God. It is rather a confirmation of the bringing back into fellowship with God which has come about in some other way. As used by Paul, then, σφραγίς takes from circumcision its sacramentalist character in favour of God's justifying act. [84] Circumcision does not replace justification; it follows and confirms it. This seal does denote membership, yet not simply of the people as God's people, but of the justified people. In R. 4:11 σφραγίς is more figurative than terminological. [85] In 2 C. 1:22, in a passage in which Paul refers again to the certainty or reliability of the promise and to its establishment, Paul says: "God has sealed us for himself and given us the pledge of the Spirit in our hearts." In sealing believers — the apostle and the church in Corinth — God has made them His own inviolable possession; the pledge of this is the Spirit of God in the heart, cf. R. 5:5. There is a variation on 2 C. 1:22 in Eph. 1:13 f. and 4:30. The Holy Spirit as the pledge of the inheritance is now the seal with which the believer is marked, appointed and kept for the redemption. It shows that he is God's possession to the day of redemption. In all these passages various aspects of the concept of sealing help to fix the metaphorical use in the sphere of faith. There is no direct reference to baptism or circumcision in any of the three even though χρίσας ἡμᾶς θεός in 2 C. 1:21 might be explained in terms of baptism,

---

[81] Joh. W. 1 K., *ad loc.* sees an even more concrete ref. The Corinthians are for Paul a seal on his credentials. But the word has a more general fig. quality such as one finds in Philo. Individual traits have to be read into the text.

[82] Bultmann J., *ad loc.* But one is again reminded of Philo's usage. The Lord is the owner of the seal; he who has the sign both belongs to Him and is also commissioned by Him.

[83] Bultmann J., 166 f., n. 10 assigns the word to a redactor. σφραγίζω does not mean "to authenticate" as in 3:33 but "to dedicate," "to consecrate," cf. Pr.-Bauer, *s.v.* "to endow with heavenly power"; on dedication cf. Ant. Christ., I (1929), 2. The real problem of Jn. 6:27 is not the word σφραγίζω but the relation of God — Son of Man — food.

[84] Ehrlich, *op. cit.* (→ n. 72), 109 restricts the sacramentalist character of circumcision to proselytes.

[85] Anrich, *op. cit.* (→ n. 73), 120 and Dölger, 53 see in R. 4:11 a ref. to the contemporary description of circumcision as a seal and they thus believe that Paul is adopting a terminological expression. But since we have no other examples of the description of circumcision as a seal at this early period, and since Paul's use can be readily explained as a metaphor, no dependence need be assumed, so also Heitmüller, 44 f.

→ I, 603, 20 ff. [86] The decisive thing for Paul is that it is God who is at work not only in justifying but also in sealing. One may thus conclude that the idea of marking as a possession determines the use of the term; the one who belongs to God is marked in the same way as the slave or the soldier, → 948, 3 ff.; n. 77. [87]

2. The Word Group in Revelation.

a. Sealing.

Rev. makes frequent and distinctive use of the word seal in the framework of apocalyptic images. The divine is not to "seal" the words of the prophecy, Rev. 22:10. This means that he is not to keep them secret or conceal them. σφραγίζω occurs in 20:3 in the sense of inviolable sealing as in Mt. 27:66; the angel from heaven, who binds the devil and casts him into the abyss, closes and seals the abyss for a thousand years — as the record is closed and sealed. On the other hand σφραγίζω is also used in a much weaker sense: "to close," "to conceal," not to reveal, 10:4. Elsewhere what is written is sealed against misuse and unauthorised knowledge (→ 941, 12 ff.), but here the combination of "seal" and "do not write" shows how much the concrete idea has faded into the background.

b. The Book with Seven Seals.

A group of "seal" references makes mention of the "sealed book," the book with seven seals, → I, 618, 24 ff. It is a double document. [88] The seven seals remind us of Roman law with its six *testes* for a will along with the *testator*, → 941, 19 ff. The metaphor is not carried through consistently but serves as a literary device in apocalyptic presentation. The opening of the seven seals successively carries events forward, whereas all the seals must be broken or loosened at once in the case of a deed. On the only occasion on which the compound κατασφραγίζω is used in the NT at 5:1 it denotes the sealing of this heavenly document. Only the Lamb has the right and power to undo this seal, 5:1, 2, 5, 9. One seal is broken after the other, 6:1, 3, 5, 7, 9, 12; 8:1. Each enclosed the apocalyptic event which then took place. The idea of a document sealed with seven seals is not developed further. Legally the distinction of seals depends on those who possess them. There is no mention of this here. The number of seals is significant only because of the difference in the contents, which for its part determines the course of eschatological events. [89]

---

[86] Cf. Staab, 280 f.: Severian of Gabala explains 2 C. 1:22 in terms of the fact that "shepherds mark their flocks with a seal to distinguish their own sheep from those of others." Schlier[3] Eph. on 1:13 takes σφραγίζεσθαι to ref. to the laying on of hands for the impartation of the Holy Spirit. Severian similarly describes the sealing of Eph. 1:13 as ... ὁμοίωσις πρὸς χριστὸν διὰ τῆς τοῦ πνεύματος μεταλήψεως, Staab, 306.

[87] καθάπερ γὰρ στρατιώταις σφραγίς, οὕτω καὶ τοῖς πιστοῖς τὸ πνεῦμα ἐπιτίθεται Chrys. Hom. in 2 C. 3:7 (MPG, 61 [1862], 418). Wnd. 2 K. on 1:22 thinks it likely the notion is borrowed from the mysteries. But legal ideas of the pledge and seal are a more natural source. The only point is that such concepts are blunted, cf. on this G. W. H. Lampe, *The Seal of the Spirit* (1951), 3-18.

[88] On the form of sealing cf. Birt, *op. cit.* (→ n. 13), 243 f.; W. Sattler, "Das Buch mit sieben Siegeln," ZNW, 20 (1921), 231-240 and ZNW, 21 (1922), 43-53; K. Staritz, "Zu Offenbarung Johannes 5:1," ZNW, 30 (1931), 157-170; O. Roller, "Das Buch mit sieben Siegeln," ZNW, 36 (1937), 98-113.

[89] Loh. Apk. on 5:1: The choice of the no. seven is not based on Roman law; the number is a religious symbol.

c. The Sealed.

The last group of "seal" statements in Rev. refers to those who are sealed by God and for God. The second angel has "the seal of the living God," 7:2 and 9:4. He restrains the four angels of destruction until "we have sealed the servants of our God on their foreheads," 7:3. From each of the 12 tribes 12,000 are sealed, 7:4-8. [90] From the standpoint of the divine this sealing is a marking of all the members of the people, of the people in its entirety, as belonging to God, as God's possession. Hence this seal keeps them through the terrible events of the end time. In Ez. 9:4 (→ 208, 29 ff.; 578, 16 ff.) this sign is not a fixed and special divine sign, but it becomes this in effect. Rev. 7:2 and 9:4 certainly have a specific sign in view, → 663, 26 ff. Either it is the tetragrammaton or it is ✕, which in the standing form or the more recumbent ✕ was like the ancient Hebrew letter ת. [91] Membership of God's people or fellowship is denoted by the seal of God. Those who bear it belong to God; they are His property. The ancient custom of providing something with a sign of ownership (→ 651, 9 ff.), which becomes an aspect of the σφραγίς, is again normative here. By specific technical development the sign became a seal and then the seal again became a sign, taking on material significance theologically, serving both as a literary image and also as a mode of speech among believers. Signs are indications and need interpretation. In the language of revelation image and reality become a distinctive unity. The reality can take shape only in the metaphor, the transferred use, the figure, the non-literal. It can be expressed only in the impression of a seal. [92] In these basic questions the metaphorical use of the word seal in the NT is also implicated.

E. Seal in the Post-Apostolic Age.

1. In the post-apost. fathers seal is rare, and it is used only once in the lit. sense. In 1 Cl., 43 the author makes use of the story in Nu. 17:16 ff. Moses sealed the 12 staffs of the 12 heads of the tribes with their rings. The keys of the tent of meeting were similarly sealed. The next day the seals were tested and publicly shown to be unmolested in order to give clear legal proof of the miracle of the staff which budded. In 2 Cl., 7, 6 the word seal is to be interpreted in the light of 8, 6: "Keep the flesh and the seal inviolate." It is also said of baptism that it should be kept pure and unsmirched in 6, 9, so that one is tempted to equate seal and baptism. Yet the antithesis of flesh and seal in 8, 6 suggests rather that the author takes the seal to represent the Holy Spirit. [93] In Barn., 9, 6 circumcision is regarded as the seal, i.e., the secret sign pointing to Christ. The statement that

---

[90] A B C P 6. 14. 29 et al. have ἐσφραγισμένοι only twice, in v. 5 and v. 8, but in some MSS the word is repeated for each tribe.

[91] Cf. Loh. Apk. on 7:2 and → n. 101.

[92] Loh. Apk., Exc.: "Die Sprache d. Apk.," 197-9; F. K. Schumann, "Gedanken Luthers z. Frage d. Entmythologisierung," Festschr. f. R. Bultmann (1949), 208-222; E. Schweizer, Ego eimi (1939), 35 f., 44; cf. Schrade, op. cit. (→ n. 48), 23: "For what is real must be able to become a figure; only by the fact that it becomes a figure does it bear witness to its reality"; cf. also what is said about the Son of Man, 281 f.

[93] Dölger, 72 f. thinks the use of τηρέω τὸ βάπτισμα and τηρέω τὴν σφραγῖδα as full equivalents supports his thesis that baptism was very early called a σφραγίς: "proof enough that βάπτισμα and σφραγίς are identical." But though baptism and the Holy Spirit are related, one should distinguish between the seal of the Spirit and the seal of baptism, cf. Schlier[3] Eph. on 1:13.

the people was circumcised εἰς σφραγῖδα is undoubtedly adopting a current Jewish notion (→ 947, 26 ff.), but the author understands it quite differently. Seal here is a secret sign which requires christological interpretation. [94]

The most significant "seal" sayings are in Pastor Hermae. s., 8, 2, 3 f.; 6, 3 and esp. 9, 16, 3-7 and 17, 4 ref. to those who have received the "seal of the Son of God." We are told plainly that "the seal is the water" ἡ σφραγὶς οὖν τὸ ὕδωρ ἐστίν, they go down into the water as dead men and rise up out of it alive κἀκείνοις οὖν ἐκηρύχθη ἡ σφραγὶς αὕτη, 16, 4. In these passages baptism is for the first time clearly and un-ambiguously called a σφραγίς. Naturally the use is metaphorical and attenuated. Water is not a sign in the way circumcision can be said to be, → 947, 36. The usage diverges from the concrete fact. How little specific the use is may be seen from the expression σφραγὶς τοῦ κηρύγματος in 16, 5. Preaching and baptism are the things that sign and Christians are signed and marked by them. But this is an invisible *signum*. The eschatolog-ical motif of concealment, mystery and disclosure undoubtedly plays a part in this develop-ment of the usage, though in Herm. it is not directly evident in connection with the seal of baptism. If Herm. is the first unequivocally to call baptism a seal, witnesses increase toward the end of the 2nd cent. There is already an established usage in Iren., Cl. Al. and Tert. [95] Its genesis is obscure. Whether Herm. adopts a fixed tradition, whether Paul's saying in R. 4:11, or the saying about the Spirit in 2 C. 1:22 along with Eph. 1:13 f.; 4:30, or expressions from the mysteries, or Rabb. usage respecting circumcision serve as models, it is as yet impossible to decide, esp. as it is plain that the word is used in Herm. with ref. to both baptism and preaching. [96]

2. The seal plays an important role in Gnostic writings. We shall select from the abundant material and motifs only a few instances which show the breadth of the "seal" concept in Chr. and esp. non-Chr. Gnosticism. NT usage had no influence worth noting here.

a. As in Herm., so in the apocr. Acts baptism is called a σφραγίς. Thecla asks for the seal in Christ ἡ ἐν Χριστῷ σφραγίς. Paul answers: "Have patience and you will receive the water," Act. Pl. et Thecl. 25. In Act. Thom. there is constant ref. to the seal. King Gundafor and his brother Gad ask the apostle if they might have the seal, for God knows His sheep by the seal. The eucharist is associated with this seal. The baptismal sealing follows in a series of acts. Chr. instruction and anointing follow the prayer and promise; the anointing is also called a seal. [97] It brings only partial revelations, for the real thing has not yet happened, the ἐπισφράγισμα τῆς σφραγῖδος. There then follows a prayer from a Chr.-Gnostic liturgy for the coming and presence of the power of the Most High, the merciful mother, the sacred power of the Spirit, and for sealing in the name of the Father and of the Son and of the Holy Ghost. Baptism obviously follows; this is the real sealing. The eucharist is then celebrated, Act. Thom. 26 f. There is a similar sealing in the name of the Father and of the Son and the Holy Ghost in 49; in the eucharist those who have received the seal get the bread with the sign of the cross

---

[94] Anrich, *op. cit.*, 46; Dölger, 53 construe εἰς σφραγῖδα as confirming belonging to God and thus see a terminological use of σφραγίς. But cf. Heitmüller, 44 f. One cannot supply anything (e.g., "of the people of God") after εἰς σφραγῖδα in Barn. The meaning is yielded by the context. Speculation on the no. 318, which pts. to Jesus and the cross acc. to the author, causes Barn. to see in circumcision a secret sign whose secret is known to the Chr. theologian.
[95] Dölger, 80.
[96] The discussions in Anrich, 120 f.; G. Wobbermin, *Religionsgesch. Studien* (1896), 144 f.; Dölger, *passim;* Heitmüller, 40-59 all suffer from a failure to differentiate the individual aspects of the complex "seal" concept, and to isolate the metaphorical use and the magical element.
[97] There is a sealing with oil in the Mandaeans too, but cf. K. Rudolf, *Die Mandäer,* II (1961), 173 f.

impressed on it.[98] In 131 f. sealing is unmistakably water baptism, which is preceded by a baptismal sermon.[99]

b. The idea of the seal is put to a different use in Od. Sol. The abyss is sealed with the Lord's seal in 24:7 cf. Rev. 20:3 (→ 950, 9 f.). God knows His own, He has elected them before they came to be, and has sealed their faces, 8:15; the ref. is perhaps to marking with God's name, cf. 8:21. God's creatures are marked by His seal, 4:7 — the same idea as in Rev. → 951, 1 ff. God's plan of salvation is compared to a heavenly letter; men rush to it, but start back, for it is sealed and they have no power to break the seal; the seal is stronger than they, 23:5-9.[100] The theme of the sealing of the heavenly letter also occurs in the pearl song in Act. Thom. 111. These 2nd and 3rd cent. Gnostic texts are obviously adopting the Jewish and Chr. motif of the marking of those who belong to God. Hence baptism has a place in this sphere, as circumcision did in Judaism. But in Gnosticism the seal is more than this. It is the mysterious means by which the Gnostic is protected as he traverses the various zones and aeons. "Tell the mystery, and seal yourself with this seal; this is his name" (mysterious groups of letters from the seal), 2nd Book of Jeû 50.[101] In the Naassene hymn Jesus prays for the soul, this visited being: "For his salvation, Father, send me, that I may go down with the seals in my hands, traverse all the aeons, open all mysteries, disclose all divine beings to him, and proclaim to him the secret of the holy way — I call it gnosis."[102]

c. The "seal" concept is also used a good deal in Mandaean works. Lidz. Ginza L, III, 108 (p. 552 f.) reads: "It is a well-sealed letter which goes out from the world; a letter written with Kushta and sealed with the signet ring the Great." The letter is closed by thongs and these are sealed, cf. Liturg., I, 73 (p. 111) and I, 74 (p. 118). Sealing (hatamtā) is part of a baptismal ritual; it protects against demons and evil powers: "In your name, Silmai and Nidbai, with the power of Hibil, Šitil and Anōš, bind, seal and keep these souls which go down into the Jordan and are baptised, with the signet ring of Jōzataq Mandā d'Haijē, the physician for whose power no one is a match," Liturg., I, 13 (p. 20).[103] Baptism is in the name of...; the mention of the name in Mandaean baptism has an apotropaic character and also establishes a direct connection with the idea of the seal. The seal has a name and it puts what is sealed under the legal protection of the one who seals by making it his property. It is obvious that the magical element plays a part here. The seal differentiates, marking off the one from the other. It is thus a means of distinguishing both for initiates in the mysteries and also for any group of an esoteric character. Thus in Manicheanism this idea serves to differentiate the circle of the elect. There are here three seals, the signaculum oris, Aug. De moribus Ecclesiae Catholicae et de moribus Manichaeorum, II, 10, 19 and 13, 27-30 (MPL, 32 [1877], 1353 and 1356-8), the signaculum manuum, ibid., II, 10, 19 and 17, 54-64 (MPL, 32, 1368-72) and the signaculum sinus, II, 10, 19 and 18, 65-73 (MPL, 32, 1372 f.).[104] In the spheres which are under Gnostic influence the elements which esp. determine the use of the "seal" concept are those of belonging, protection, the sign of another power and another world, secrecy, and mystery.

Fitzer

---

[98] Ant. Christ., I (1929), 2-12 on stamps on cultic cakes and seals on sacrificial vessels.
[99] Dölger, 96.
[100] H. Gressmann, "Ode Sal. 23," SAB (1921), 616-624.
[101] GCS, 13, 315-321 cf. Dölger, 160 and Ant. Christ., I (1929), 76.
[102] Dölger, 161; transl. by A. Harnack in Hennecke[2], 436.
[103] Rudolf, op. cit., II 155-174, esp. 168 and 198-201.
[104] Cf. Chant. de la Saussaye, II, 273.

σχῆμα, μετασχηματίζω

† σχῆμα.

A. The Usage outside the New Testament.

1. General. The word is attested from Aesch., Thuc.; it is also found in inscr. and pap. [1] It is related to ἔχω (fut. σχήσω) "to hold." σχῆμα always denotes the outward form or structure perceptible to the senses and never the inward principle of order accessible only to thought. [2] That it always ref. to what may be known from without may be seen from the many derivates like εὐσχήμων (→ II, 770, 31 ff.), ἀσχήμων, σχηματίζω, σχηματισμός etc., which all have to do with outward decency in human conduct. Because of this distinctive ref. to what may be known outwardly the word can easily take on the special sense of "clothing," an element in outward appearance.

2. Specific. σχῆμα means esp. a. "bearing," *habitus*, esp. "carriage," Eur. Med., 1072; Plat. Ion, 536c, [3] then the deportment by which a man manifests his mood, action, place in life, or nature, Xenoph. Ap., 27; Symp., IX, 5, the whole manner of being or expression, Soph. Ant., 1169, conduct, demeanour, esp. a "fine, proud bearing," Luc. Dial. Mortuorum, 10, 8, but also a "humble bearing" Luc. Somnium, 13, [4] "splendour," "state," Plat. Leg., III, 685c; Alciphr. Ep., IV, 7, 1. b. "Form," outward and usually imposing or noble "appearance," Eur. Ion, 238, 240, "look," Soph. Phil., 223; in the plur. esp. "features," "looks," "gestures," Eur. Ion, 992; Hec., 619; Alc., 911; Aristot. Part. An., I, 1, p. 640b, 33 f. One should consult here esp. the def. of "figure" in Plat. Men., 75b-76a. [5] Trans. the word means a dance figure or "position" in dancing, Xenoph. Symp., II, 15, but esp. "form of state," "constitution" of a πόλις or πολιτεία, Thuc., VI, 89, 6; Aristot. Eth. Nic., VIII, 12, p. 1160b, 25, also the distinctiveness of a person or object, Xenoph. Cyrop., VII, 1, 49. The ref. may occasionally be to a military formation, "order of battle," Xenoph. An., I, 10, 10. c. "Form or manner of life," Eur. Med., 1039, also the role someone plays, Plat. Leg., XI, 918e, cf. Ps.-Plat. Alc., I, 135d. d. "Clothing," "garment," "garb," "dress," [6] Aristoph. Ach., 64 etc.; Xenoph. Cyrop., V, 1, 5; cf. Plut. Alex. Fort. Virt., I, 8 (II, 330): Persian court dress put on by Alexander the Gt. [7] e. Transf. "form," "figure," tt. in

---

σ χ ῆ μ α . [1] Cf. Moult-Mill., *s.v.*

[2] σχῆμα is perhaps to be listed with the many abstracts in -μα which were coined in the 5th cent. B.C. in connection with developing learning and philosophy and which often become vogue-words. Only thus can one explain its very common use in tragedy. The shift in sense is best seen in Aristotelian usage. In his vocabulary Aristot. combines the qualities of conceptual strictness and a deliberate closeness in choice of words to current usage [Dihle].

[3] On σχῆμα in Plat. *v.* F. Astius, Lex. Platonicum (1956), *s.v.*

[4] The two ref. in Luc. are important in view of Phil. 2:7. Luc. Somnium, 13 contrasts with the σχῆμα εὐπρεπές the σχῆμα δουλοπρεπές, "slavish bearing or appearance," and in Luc. Dial. Mortuorum, 10, 8 the false philosopher must give up his σχῆμα or assumed "demeanour" to embark on Charon's skiff.

[5] In the dialogue with Menon Socrates says of virtue that even though there are many and varied virtues they have one and the same form. The following def. of form is then given. 1. It is that which always and in all circumstances accompanies colour; 2. it is the boundary of the body. χρώματα καὶ σχήματα "colours and forms" occurs in, e.g., Plat. Resp., X, 601a.

[6] In the post-NT period σχῆμα means esp. "garb," "monastic habit" [Dihle]. Cf. P. Meyer, *Die Haupturkunden f. d. Gesch. d. Athosklöster* (1894), 299, Index, *s.v.* "σχῆμα (das mönchische)"; F. Loofs, *Symbolik*, I (1902), 168; G. Graf, Art. "Schima (σχῆμα)" in LexThK, IX (1937), 251 f. on a special form of monastic habit in the eastern churches, with bibl.

[7] Cf. on this A. Ehrhardt, "Ein antikes Herrscherideal. Phil. 2:5-11," *Ev. Theol.*, NF, 3 (1948/49), 101-110. Haupt Gefbr., 73 ref. to the passage in Plut.

rhetoric, grammar, geometry, astronomy and astrology: fig. of speech Herodianus Rhetor. De figuris, 594; [8] Dion. Hal. ep. ad Pompeium, 5, 4; cf. Cic. Brutus, 37, 141; Aristot. Poet., 19, p. 1456b, 9; Rhet., III, 8, p. 1408b, 21. The word plays a particular part in philosophy, esp. in Aristot.: [9] "sketch," "schedule" for a proceeding, Aristot. Metaph., 6, 3, p. 1029a, 4; Eth. Nic., V, 8, p. 1133b, 1 etc., in logic esp. "forms of syllogisms," Aristot. An. Pri., I, 4, p. 26b, 26-31, [10] mathematical or geometrical "figure," Aristot. An., II, 3, p. 414b, 20-30. Astronomy uses σχῆμα for a "constellation," e.g., phase of the moon, Ptolemaeus Tetrabiblos, I, 7, 21; [11] Vett. Val., II, 34 (p. 106, 28) etc. Astrology also uses the word, e.g., with μοῖρα in a horoscope, [12] P. Lond., I, 130, 21 (1st-2nd cent.). f. Very gen., in a weaker sense, it means "state," "condition," "manner," e.g., Plat. Leg., IV, 718b. g. It can sometimes mean "semblance," "pretext," Ps.-Plat. Epin., 989c; Theophrast. Hist. Plant., III, 12, 7.

3. In LXX the only instance is at Is. 3:17, which ref. to the proud "bearing" of the leading but degenerate women of Jerusalem whose emptiness God will unmask and lay bare. [13]

4. Philo makes rich use of the many senses of the term. In him, too, the primary thought is that of what may be known from without. a. With the help of the senses man can perceive and know objects, their forms and figures, Op. Mund., 120; Cher., 117; cf. Som., I, 27. σχήματα and χρώματα often come together (forms and colours), Cher., 117; Leg. All., III, 15; Sacr. AC, 46; Det. Pot. Ins., 101 and 173; Ebr., 46 etc. The senses are messengers of the spirit which mediate forms and colours to it, Som., I, 27. Philo speaks of the differentiation of things by forms and outlines σχήμασιν καὶ περιγραφαῖς, Conf. Ling., 87, also of the manifoldness of forms and colours, Abr., 148, then of the colours and forms of bodies, Spec. Leg., I, 90. b. The word also means "figure" (Op. Mund., 120), artistic figure, Conf. Ling., 89; Vit. Mos., 128, cf. Spec. Leg., I, 29, where it denotes the figures produced by sculpture and painting, the forms of beauty impressed on material things (Fug., 26), or the form of the moon (Op. Mund., 101). c. Philo can also use the word for the mathematical or geometrical figure, Op. Mund., 50, 97, 98; Plant., 121; Conf. Ling., 87, e.g., the circle as the most perfect figure, Spec. Leg., I, 205. d. "Form of speech," Poster. C., 110. e. Man's "outward bearing," Sacr. AC, 28, his inner "disposition," Rer. Div. Her., 245. f. "Attitude of life," Migr. Abr., 147, "conduct," Spec. Leg., I, 102. g. The word can also be used for the outward "posture and look" in Jos., 72, the dignity, e.g., of a prophet in Spec. Leg., I, 315, the social "position," e.g., of slaves, Spec. Leg., II, 82, the poor, ibid., 106, the social "status" of simple citizens, ibid., 208. h. Finally the term can express the distinctive character of a thing: "At the time of the Passover every house takes on the character and solemnity of a sanctuary," Spec. Leg., II, 148.

5. Joseph., too, makes varied use of the word. Hezekiah exchanges his royal robe for sackcloth and adopts the "attitude" of humility σχῆμα ταπεινόν, Ant., 10, 11, cf.

---

[8] Ed. L. Spengel, Rhetores Graeci, III (1856), 94.

[9] Cf. R. Eisler, Wörterb. d. philosophischen Begriffe, II⁴ (1929), 751, 769 f.; cf. H. Maier, Die Syllogistik d. Aristot., II, 1 (1900), 71, n. 1 and 72-136 on syllogistic forms. Cf. Aristotelis Organon Graece, ed. T. Waitz, I (1844), 384 f.

[10] Other examples, H. Bonitz, Index Aristotelicus² (1955), s.v. Aristot. has 3 forms σχήματα τοῦ συλλογισμοῦ: an apodictic, dialectic and eristic.

[11] Ed. F. E. Robbins (1956).

[12] Cf. Moult-Mill., 619.

[13] The text of Is. 3:17 LXX is corrupt. σχῆμα occurs here for פֹּת . The transl. can make little of the v. Acc. to Schleusner, V, 244 ἄσχημον and αἰσχύνην have been proposed as conjectures. פָּאֵר (cf. Ges.-Buhl, 666) is reflected in the later transl.: κόμην αὐτῶν ἀσχημονήσει Is. 3:17 ᾿Α, τὰ κατὰ πρόσωπον αὐτῶν ἀποκαλύψει Θ; πρόσοψιν Σ, which is just as gen. as σχῆμα [Katz].

βασιλικόν σχῆμα "raiment" in 8, 412; πένθιμον σχῆμα, "look," 4, 257; 7, 182; σχῆμα ἰδιωτικόν, "clothing," 8, 266. The word can be in confrontation with δόξα and περιουσία, Ant., 5, 115. It is said of the Essenes that their "dress and bodily demeanour" καταστολὴ καὶ σχῆμα σώματος, were like those of children, Bell., 2, 126. The temple forecourt was ἐν τετραγώνου σχήματι, "in the form of a quadrilateral," Ant., 8, 96, and Abraham took his wife with him ἐν ἀδελφῆς σχήματι, 1, 207. The phrase σχῆμα τῆς δουλείας occurs in 2, 42; 3, 282. σχῆμα also means the form of a word with τελευτή "ending," a tt. in grammar, 1, 129. In Bell., 7, 267 πολιτικὸν σχῆμα is the opp. of τελεωτάτη ἀνομία, which here means complete freeing from every divine ordinance.

6. The word occurs occasionally in Test. XII: Zeb. 3:7; 9:8; R. 5:1, 2, 4; Jud. 12:3. In Ep. Ar., 105 it means the "size" of the city of Jerusalem.

7. It occurs as a loan word אַסְכְּמָא or אַסְכְּמָא [14] in the Rabb., [15] though not the Mishnah. It is common as a loan word in Syr. (eskēma). [16]

B. The Usage in the New Testament.

In the NT the word is found only at Phil. 2:7 and 1 C. 7:31. Phil. 2:7 is part of the Christ hymn which depicts the self-humiliation of the Son of God. σχήματι εὑρεθείς ὡς ἄνθρωπος does not merely express the reality of His humanity. There is special stress on the fact that throughout His life, even to the death on the cross, Jesus was in the humanity demonstrated by His earthly form. [17] The εὑρεθείς expresses the truth that this fact could be seen by anybody, [18] σχῆμα does not merely indicate the coming of Jesus, [19] or His physical constitution, or the natural determination of His earthly life, or the shape of His moral character. [20] It denotes the "mode of manifestation." [21] The reference is to His whole nature and manner as man. [22] In this respect the outward "bearing" He assumes corresponds to His inner being → n. 4. In 1 C. 7:31 Paul is demanding that we possess material things as though we did not possess them. He bases this on the principle παράγει γὰρ τὸ σχῆμα τοῦ κόσμου τούτου, [23] which is best translated: "This world in its distinctive manifestation (or form) is (already) in process of perishing." [24]

---

[14] Cf. Levy Chald. Wört., s.v.; Dalman Wört., s.v.

[15] E.g., Tg. Prv. 7:10 in the sense of "demeanour," "conduct": בְּאַסְכְּמָא דְזָנָיְתָא "in wanton conduct."

[16] C. Brockelmann, Lex. Syriacum² (1928), 35.

[17] Cf. Mich. Ph., ad loc., who pts. out that γενόμενος ref. more to the incarnation and εὑρεθείς more to the humanity.

[18] Cf. E. Käsemann, "Krit. Analyse v. Phil. 2:5-11," Exeget. Versuche u. Besinnungen, I² (1960), 75.

[19] Dib. Ph., ad loc.

[20] Loh. Phil., ad loc.

[21] Cf. also Käsemann, op. cit., 75 f.; E. Schweizer, Erniedrigung u. Erhöhung bei Jesus u. seinen Nachfolgern² (1962), 94 f.; Pr.-Bauer, s.v.

[22] Cf. Dib. Ph., ad loc., who thinks σχῆμα relates to everything human in Christ apart from His form.

[23] Formal par. to σχῆμα τοῦ κόσμου τούτου are τὸ σχῆμα τοῦ κόσμου ("adornment," "clothing") in Eur. Ba., 832, τὸ σχῆμα τοῦ κόσμου τοῦδε in Philostr. Vit. Ap., VIII, 7 (I, 312, 9) and σχῆμα κόσμου in Preis. Zaub., I, 4, 1139.

[24] Cf. Pr.-Bauer, s.v.

† μετασχηματίζω.

A. The Usage in the Greek World and Judaism.

1. The verb means "to transform," "to alter," "to change the outward appearance of a person or thing," [1] Plat. Leg., X, 903e; 906c; Aristot. Cael., 3, 1, p. 298b, 31 f.; Gen. An., II, 7, p. 747a, 15; De Sensu et Sensibilibus, 6, p. 446b, 8; Plut. Ages., 14, 4 (I, 603); Def. Orac., 30 (I, 426e); Sext. Emp. Math., X, 335; Diod. S., 2, 57, 4, [2] cf. also Iambl. Myst., III, 28; Test. R. 5:6. For later examples cf. Preisigke Sammelb., 5174, 10 (512 A.D.); 5175, 12 (513 A.D.); Byzant. Pap., 13, 46 [3] (594 A.D.). The word is also used in astronomy to denote the changing of the constellations. [4]

2. In LXX the compound occurs only at 4 Macc. 9:22, where it ref. to the transforming of the martyrs into incorruptibility at death. The ref. in 1 Βασ. 28:8 Σ is to the disguising of Saul.

3. Philo has the verb 3 times at Aet. Mund., 79; Leg. Gaj., 80 and 346; it means "to change into a new form." [5] Joseph. Ant., 7, 257 is worth noting. This says that David altered his outward appearance or clothing, cf. 8, 267 with ref. to the disguising of the wife of Jeroboam. Joseph has the simple σχηματίζω in Ant., 8, 79 in the sense "to form" and in Ant., 8, 267 in the sense "to transform," "to bring into another form."

B. The Usage in the New Testament.

The word occurs only in Paul in Phil. and 1 and 2 Cor. In Phil. 3:21 the apostle is expressing the certainty that the coming Lord will transfigure the bodies of Christians. Believers already have the Spirit as the earnest of eschatological consummation and are in possession of heavenly citizenship, but they still live in the flesh. At Christ's *parousia*, however, their bodies will also share in the divine mode of being. Then, as already in the case of Christ (2:8), δόξα will follow ταπείνωσις. The body of glory will replace the body of humiliation which Christians now bear. [6] The One who effects this is Christ, who through the power dwelling in Him will fashion their σῶμα according to the σῶμα τῆς δόξης αὐτοῦ. In 2 C. 11:13-15 the mid. μετασχηματίζομαι is used three times. First (v. 14) Paul declares that the Judaising agitators, who are in truth lying apostles (→ I, 445, 18 ff.), transform themselves into apostles of Christ. [7] Then (v. 14) Paul says that their conduct is not surprising, since Satan himself takes the form of an angel of light and conceals his

---

μ ε τ α σ χ η μ α τ ί ζ ω . [1] The word is vox media. It is not positive or negative in itself, but as in the case of ἐλπίζω, which might mean "to hope," "to fear" or "to expect" acc. to what precedes, this depends on the material context; the meaning of the verb is always the same in Gk. [Dihle].

[2] Cf. V. Gardthausen, *Griech. Paläographie,* II² (1913), 41 and 263.

[3] Ed. A. Heisenberg and L. Wenger (1914).

[4] Examples in Liddell-Scott, *s.v.*

[5] Cf. Som., II, 45, where σχηματίζω is used, but it is said of God that at creation He gave form to what was formless by the *logos.*

[6] But cf. Loh. Phil. on 3:21, who claims that the ref. here is not to "the consummation of the community in the eschatological age," but to "that of the martyr in death." The text, however, does not mention this. Paul is saying something which applies to all Christians.

[7] On the changing of Satan into another form v. Test. Jobi (ed. J. A. Robinson, TSt, V [1897], 104-137) 6:4: ὁ σατανᾶς μετασχηματισθεὶς εἰς ἐπαίτην (beggar); 17:2: εἰς βασιλέα τῶν Περσῶν; 23:1: εἰς πράτην. μετασχηματίζομαι εἴς τι also occurs in Diod. S., 3, 57, 5; 4 Macc. 9:22. There is a good par. in Test. R. 5:6, which says that guardian angels disguised themselves in human form μετεσχηματίζοντο εἰς ἄνδρα and thus deceived earthly women.

true being behind the outward appearance. [8] Third (v. 15) the apostle goes on to draw the deduction from the first two statements. If Satan acts like this, one can readily see why his instruments also appear in the garb of servants of righteousness. In characterising his opponents thus, Paul takes up again the saying of v. 13, but gives it a new turn. The expression διάκονοι δικαιοσύνης is the title of the genuine apostle. In 1 C. 4:6 the verb refers to the form of presentation which Paul has given in the preceding section. The statement ταῦτα δέ, ἀδελφοί, μετεσχημάτισα εἰς ἐμαυτὸν καὶ ᾽Απολλῶν is to be taken in a literary, stylistic sense; there is no real transformation. The explanation that μετασχηματίζω means "to say something with the help of a figure of speech" [9] can hardly be right, then, since there is no figure of speech in the context. Paul ought really to be speaking about the church or parties in Corinth. Instead of censuring them or saying positively how they should behave towards one another, he shows what the true attitude of Christians should be from the example of himself and Apollos. If there are no antitheses between the apostle and Apollos, the church has no right to form a party for the one against the other. [10] μετασχηματίζω thus means "to express something in another than the expected or customary form." What is really meant is in fact subjected to a process of intellectual transformation.

C. The Early Church.

In Herm. v., 5, 1 σχῆμα means "garb" (shepherd garb). Apart from this neither noun nor verb is used in early Chr. literature apart from the NT. For the use in Gnostic terminology one may ref., e.g., to Cl. Al. Exc. Theod., 11, 2; 14, 1; 15, 2.

J. Schneider

---

[8] Paul is using here an apocr. mythical idea. There is nothing about Satan appearing as an angel of light in the OT, but we do find the concept in Vit. Ad. 9 and Apc. Mos. 17, the former with ref. to a second temptation of Eve by Satan and the latter as an interpolation in the bibl. story of the fall of Eve, cf. for details Wnd. 2 K. on 11:14.

[9] So Pr.-Bauer, *s.v.;* cf. Liddell-Scott, *s.v.:* "transfer as in a figure," also F. H. Colson, "μετεσχημάτισα 1 Cor. IV 6," JThSt, 16 (1916), 379-384, esp. 380 and 384: μετεσχημάτισα "transferred in a figure." Cf. Philostr. Vit. Soph., 2, 17 (II, 100, 27); 2, 25, 1 (II, 110, 6); Ps.-Demetr., 287, 292-4.

[10] Cf. Joh. W. 1 K., *ad loc.* Ltzm. K., *ad loc.* transl.: "I have put these statements in such a form as to speak specifically of Apollos and myself; I have used myself and Apollos as an illustration." One must remember, however, that the use of μετασχηματίζω for "to illustrate". etc. is a catachresis and does not correspond to the strict sense. There are also no par. [Dihle]. It is possible that Paul has the metaphors of 3:6-8 in view, but this is by no means certain.

σχίζω, σχίσμα

† σχίζω.

1. Profane Greek.

σχίζω from the root *sk(h)id-* "to split" [1] is almost always used lit.

a. "To split," "to rend": ἔσχισε δώδεκα μοίρας "he divided into twelve parts," Hom. Hymn. Merc., 128; σχίζουσι κάρα φονίῳ πελέκει, "to cleave" the head with the axe, Soph. El., 99; εἰς δύο μέρη, Polyb., 2, 16, 11; ξύλα σχίζω, Xenoph. Cyrop., V, 3, 49; cf. An., I, 5, 12; κεραυνῷ χθόνα, Pind. Nem., 9, 24 f.; λίθος σχισθείς, P. Tebt., II, 273, 43. 52 (2nd/3rd cent. B.C.); ἔσχισε νῆα θάλασσα "the sea broke the ship in pieces," Anth. Graec., 9, 40, 3 (Zosimos); but cf. ἔσχισε Λήμνιον ὕδωρ "he (Xerxes) crossed the water of the Lemnus," P. Oxy., XV, 1795 Col. II, 25 (1st cent. A.D.); of the ploughman: σχίζε νῶτον γᾶς, he "split" the back of the earth, Pind. Pyth., 4, 228; σχίζεται γάλα, milk "separates," Diosc. Mat. Med., II, 70, 3 f.; οἱ ἀποθανόντες ἐσχισμένοις ἐνειλοῦνται ῥάκεσιν, the dead are wrapped in torn rags, Artemid. Oneirocr., I, 13 (p. 18).

b. More weakly "to separate," "to divide"; ὁ γὰρ δὴ Νεῖλος ... μέσην Αἴγυπτον σχίζων, "the Nile divides Egypt through the middle," Hdt., II, 17, 3; σχίζεται τὸ τοῦ Νείλου ῥεῦμα, "the course of the Nile branches," Plat. Tim., 21e; σχιζομένης τῆς ὁδοῦ, Hdt., VII, 31; ἡ στρατιὴ αὐτῶν ἐσχίζετο, "the army divided up," VIII, 34; of boughs branching from the trunk, Theophr. Hist. Plant., I, 1, 9; of parts of the body: τὸ δ᾽ ἐμπρόσθιον τοῦ ποδὸς τὸ μὲν ἐσχισμένον δάκτυλοι πέντε, "the divided forepart of the foot (forms) the five toes," Aristot. Hist. An., I, 15, p. 494a, 12 f.; also the distinguishing of concepts in paideia: δοκεῖ τοίνυν μοι καὶ τοῦτο ἔτι πῃ σχίζεσθαι, "this too seems to me to be capable of sub-division in some way," Plat. Soph., 229d.

c. Rarely metaph. for the difference of views: καί σφεων ἐσχίζοντο αἱ γνῶμαι, "their views (the Greeks') were divided," Hdt., VII, 219, 2; ἐνταῦθα μέντοι ἐσχίσθησαν, Xenoph. Symp., IV, 59; τοῦ πλήθους σχιζομένου κατὰ τὴν αἵρεσιν, "when the crowd was divided into parties," Diod. S., 12, 66, 2.

2. The Septuagint.

a. σχίζω occurs 11 times. It is mostly used for בקע, which is mainly transl. ῥήγνυμι and compounds. There is no obvious explanation of the relation between σχίζω and ῥήγνυμι. In Is. 36:22 37:1 σχίζω is used for קרע with ref. to the rending of garments at the blasphemy of Rabshakeh, but the usual term in this expression is ῥήγνυμι. [2] The other transl. occasionally have σχίζω where LXX uses ῥήγνυμι for בקע, e.g., ψ 77:15 'A; Is. 59:5 'A (twice); Ez. 13:13 ('ΑΣ).

b. As the Hebrew originals show, the strong meaning predominates: "to tear apart," "to split," "to rend"; cleaving wood in Gn. 22:3; 1 Βασ. 6:14; Qoh. 10:9; a bird cleaving the air, Wis. 5:11; a play on σχῖνος "gum-tree": ὁ ἄγγελος τοῦ κυρίου σχίσει σου τὴν ψυχὴν σήμερον, [3] Sus. 55. The opened fissure may be seen when the enemy yields before the hero Eleazar in 1 Macc. 6:45: καὶ ἐσχίζοντο ἀπ᾽ αὐτοῦ ἔνθα καὶ ἔνθα. In

---

σ χ ί ζ ω . [1] On the etym. cf. Boisacq, Hofmann, *s.v.*; Pokorny, 919 f.
[2] Cf. the play on words in 1 K. 11:30 f. where Ahijah proclaims the division of Israel by the tearing of his cloak.
[3] Cf. Θ: σχίσει σε μέσον.

the context of God's acts of deliverance for His people the water of the Reed Sea divides, Ex. 14:21. The theme of water from the cleft rock plays a role in the proclaimed liberation from Babylon: σχισθήσεται πέτρα, καὶ ῥυήσεται ὕδωρ, Is. 48:21. In the saving war against the nations in the last time the Mt. of Olives will divide under the feet of Yahweh, Zech. 14:4. The verbal adj. also occurs τὸ λίνον τὸ σχιστόν, "carded flax," Is. 19:9.

c. Some compounds may be noted: ἀνασχίζω for ripping open the pregnant, Am. 1:13, or opening a fish Tob. 6:4, 5 א. διασχίζω, which is hard to transl., e.g., Wis. 18:23: ἀνέκοψε τὴν ὀργὴν καὶ διέσχισεν τὴν πρὸς τοὺς ζῶντας ὁδόν, "(Aaron) arrested wrath and cut off (for it) the way to the living." [4] ψ 34:15 is obscure: μάστιγες... διεσχίσθησαν καὶ οὐ κατενύγησαν. One should probably transl.: "Scourges (or wounds, blows?) were unleashed (or broken, sc. on me?) and did not rest (?)." κατασχίζω is used of tearing the books of the Law in 1 Macc. 1:56.

d. It may be stated that σχίζω is not used for division of opinion in a group. But one might note ἀποσχίζομαι "to separate oneself," sc. from the ungodly part of the people, Nu. 16:21 (בדל ni); v. 26 (סור q).

3. Later Judaism.

a. In Palestinian Judaism the verbs קרע and בקע have no theological significance beyond that of the LXX in association with σχίζω. Materially however, there is development of the OT verb חלק "to divide," "to distribute." In the Rabb. חלק also means "to differentiate," esp. of Scripture. The ni can then mean "to differentiate oneself," "to differ," "to be of a different opinion." [5] This expresses the same content as σχίζω in profane Gk. (→ 959, 25 ff.). נֶחְלַק עַל becomes a tt. for reports of debates and halachic discussions. The ref. may be to differences in expounding and applying legal statutes, to the divisions between the schools of Hillel and Shammai, (bBB, 158a), to disputes concerning the exposition of the Law (bMak., 23b, Gemara) and judicial practice (Ket., 13, 1). But the q has a further and sharper sense: "He who attacks הַחוֹלֵק עַל... the school of his teachers causes the shekinah to depart from Israel," bBer., 27b, cf. bSanh., 110a.

b. Philo seldom uses σχίζω and always in the weaker sense "to divide," "to distribute." The heavenly sphere is divided into the seven planetary circles, Cher., 23; the *logos* develops into the four virtues, Som., II, 243; the soul divides into its seven parts, Op. Mund., 117; Agric., 30. In Joseph. the verb again has its ancient harsher ring: Ahijah rends his mantle as God will rend the kingdom of Solomon, Ant., 8, 207; Theudas promises he will arrest the river (Jordan), 20, 97.

4. The New Testament.

In the NT σχίζω occurs 9 times in the Gospels and twice in Ac. In the first group the ref. is always to the tearing or splitting of things. Ac., however, uses the term only in the sense of dividing a community intellectually.

a. "No man also seweth a piece of new cloth on an old garment; [6] else the piece

---

[4] Cf. J. Fischer, *Echter-Bibel*, IV (1959), 769.
[5] Levy Wört., Jastrow, *s.v.*; Bacher Term., I, 60 f. The Dead Sea Scrolls have the verb in, e.g., 1 QpHab 6:6; 1 QM 2:13 f., but not in the special Rabb. sense.
[6] Ev. Thom. Logion 47 refashions as follows: "One does not sew an old cloth on a new garment, otherwise a tear will develop," ed. A. Guillaumont, H. C. Puech *et al.* (1959), cf. E. Haenchen, *Die Botschaft d. Thomasev.* (1961), 51.

that is put on teareth (something) [7] from this — the old from the new — and the rent (σχίσμα) is made worse," Mk. 2:21. The radically new thing which has come with Jesus demands its own form of life. [8] Mt. 9:16 uses the noun σχίσμα in the same way as Mk. does, simply trying to make the text run more smoothly, but apart from the verbal construction Lk. 5:36 alters the train of thought: "No man cutteth (σχίσας) a piece from a new garment and putteth it upon an old. Otherwise he [9] will both rend (σχίσει) the new and also the piece taken out of the new will not agree with the old." The Lucan version of the parable gives evidence of a stronger breach between the newly established community and ancient Israel; there is an evident concern to preserve the new cloth → V, 718, 19 ff. Luke has hit the point of the parable, namely, the incompatibility of the old and the new. [10]

b. The rending of the temple veil at the death of Jesus (Mk. 15:38 and par.) has found different interpretations in the light of the context. One cannot say whether the outer or the inner curtain is meant → III, 629, 1 ff. It is very probable, however, that the reference is to the curtain before the Holy of holies, → III, 629, 34 ff. [11] Mt. 27:51 ff. and Lk. 23:45 list the event generally among the miraculous eschatological signs which accompany the death of Jesus, [12] Mk. 15:38, however, regards the incident as an intimation of the end of the temple and hence also of the ancient cultus of Israel. [13] This happening in the Jewish temple and the confession of the pagan centurion are thus complementary. [14] The rent in the veil of the temple proclaims the negative side, the imminent end of OT worship, while the confession of the officer opens up the way of the Gospel to the Gentiles. [15]

There is perhaps a third interpretation in Hb. The tearing of the veil of the temple indicates the new access to the Holy of holies, i.e., to God, which has been effected by the death of Jesus, Hb. 6:19 f.; 9:8; 10:19 f. → III, 630, 10 ff. This is a new theme as compared with the Gospels, since the presentation in Mk. esp. shows great horror at the profanation of the God concealed in the sanctuary. [16]

---

[7] As in Pr.-Bauer, s.v.; Jeremias Gl.[6], 25; Schl. Mt., ad loc.; M. J. Lagrange, Ev. selon Saint Marc (1947), ad loc. etc. αἴρει is to be taken trans. and τι is to be supplied as object. On the difficulty of the sentence cf. Loh. Mk., ad loc. In the Suppl. (ed. G. Sass [1953]) Loh. rejects his own conjecture ἀλλ' αἴρει (= λαμβάνει sc. the one who sews) τὸ πλήρωμα (= ἐπίβλημα) ἀπὸ [ἱματίου] παλαιοῦ ... and takes αἴρει to mean that "the patch comes away from the garment." But this is hardly possible, since an intr. use of αἴρω is not attested. Nor is there much to commend the suggestion of Bultmann Trad., 79; V. Taylor, The Gospel acc. to St. Mark (1955), ad loc. et al. that τὸ καινὸν τοῦ παλαιοῦ, which is in apposition (parallelism), should be eliminated.
[8] Note the par. between σχίσμα and ῥήξει v. 21 f.
[9] The one who sews is to be regarded as the subj. of σχίσει, not τὸ ἐπίβλημα.
[10] But cf. Jeremias Gl.[6], 25, who thinks the point in Mk. is the making of the rent worse, so that one can accuse Luke of missing the decisive issue.
[11] Cf. on this Taylor, op. cit. (→ n. 7), ad loc.; Str.-B., I, 1045, though cf. Loh. Mk., Lagrange, op. cit. (→ n. 7), ad loc.
[12] Cf. the cleaving of the rock as God's eschatological act, Is. 48:21 (→ 960, 2 f.); Test. L. 4:1.
[13] Loh. Mk., Lagrange, op. cit., Grundm. Mk., ad loc.
[14] M. Dibelius, Die Formgesch. d. Ev.[4] (1961), 196.
[15] For the turning from God's old work to His new work in the death of Jesus cf. Loh. Mk. on 15:38; J. Calvin, Comm. in Harmoniam Evangelicam on Mt. 27:51, Corp. Ref., 73 (1891), 782 f.; J. Schniewind, Das Ev. nach Mt., NT Deutsch, 2[10] (1962) on 27:51, though the clear distinction between Mk. 15:38 and 15:39 is nowhere so plain as in Dibelius op. cit., 196.
[16] As against G. Lindeskog, "The Veil of the Temple," Coni. Neot., 11 (1947), 132-137.

c. Heaven torn open (→ V, 529, 33 ff.) at the baptism of Jesus (Mk. 1:10) is a motif in eschatological revelations which God gives at turning-points in the history of His people, Ez. 1:1; 3 Macc. 6:18; Ac. 7:56; 10:11; Rev. 4:1; 19:11; Herm. v., 1, 1, 4. The Marcan text stands particularly related to Is. 64:1; "Oh that thou wouldest rend the heavens, that thou wouldest come down." This may be seen already in the purely linguistic fact that Mark's σχίζω is an independent rendering of the Hebrew קרע, whereas Mt. 3:16 and Lk. 3:21 are assimilated to the LXX, which uses ἀνοίγω. [17] Jesus is the Bringer of acts of God which have not been perceived from all eternity and which no eye has yet seen nor ear heard, Is. 64:4 f. [18]

d. The soldiers do not divide the robe of Jesus but cast lots for it (Jn. 19:24), cf. Ps. 22:18. One should not attach allegorical interpretations to this incident. [19] The statement that Peter's net did not break in spite of the 153 fishes (Jn. 21:11) seems to be made in a deliberate antithesis, probably to Lk. 5:6.

e. Only Luke speaks of the rending of intellectual or spiritual unity (→ 959, 25 ff.; 960, 20 ff.): ἐσχίσθη τὸ πλῆθος, Ac. 14:4; 23:7. In both instances the reference is to the division which is caused between Paul and his opponents by the apostle's preaching of the Gospel.

5. The Early Church.

a. The apocryphon in the Ev. Thom. (Logion 77) [20] reads acc. to the text in P. Oxy., I, 1 recto 3-9 (2nd/3rd cent. A.D.): καὶ [ὅ]που ε[ἷς] ἐστιν μόνος, [λέ]γω· ἐγώ εἰμι μετ' αὐτ[οῦ]· ἔγει[ρ]ον τὸν λίθον κἀκεῖ εὑρήσεις με· σχίσον τὸ ξύλον κἀγὼ ἐκεῖ εἰμι → IV, 269, 23 ff. [21] The redactor of Ev. Thom. rearranges the lines about lifting the stone and cleaving the wood [22] in such a way that the saying suggests pan-Christism. But in P. Oxy, I, 1 the linguistic data and the echoing of Mt. 18:20 in the preceding lines show that Jesus will be present not only with the two or three who gather in His name but also with lonely manual workers. [23] It may be, then, that this stands in antithesis to the pessimistic saying about the dangers of working with stone and wood in Qoh. 10:9.

---

[17] D latt georg assimilate the Marcan text to the later par. The context of Is. 63:7-19 contains the further motifs of God's voice, the acknowledgment of sons (v. 8) and the promise of the Spirit (v. 11, 14). These themes and the opening of heaven also occur in Test. XII in connection with the hope of God's eschatological intervention, cf. the prospect of the rise of the star out of Jacob in Test. Jud. 24 or the raising of the new and eternal priest in L. 18. These promises form the background of the baptism of Jesus.

[18] The later idea found esp. in Mandaean Gnosticism that the redeemer makes a breach in the obstacle between the unredeemed world and the heavenly world does not occur in Mk., cf. H. Schlier, "Christus u. d. Kirche im Eph.," Beiträge z. histor. Theol., 6 (1930), 18-26.

[19] For these cf. Bultmann J. on 19:24, n. 10.

[20] There can be little doubt as to the relation of P. Oxy., I, 1 (2nd/3rd cent. A.D.) to Ev. Thom., cf. Hennecke[3], 61 f., 66 f. and O. Hofius, "Das kpt. Thomasev. u. die Oxyrhynchus-pap., 1, 654 und 655," Ev. Theol., 20 (1960), 21-41, 182-192. On the text and transl. of Ev. Thom. → n. 6.

[21] J. Jeremias, Unbekannte Jesusworte[3] (1963) 100-104; also "Oxyrhynchos-Pap., 1" in Hennecke[3], 68 f.

[22] K. H. Kuhn, "Some Observations on the Coptic Gospel acc. to Thomas," Le Muséon, 73 (1960), 317 f. cf. Haenchen, op. cit. (→ n. 6), 65.

[23] Cf. the infancy story in Thomas 10, where the child Jesus says to the wood-cutter whom He has healed: "Stand up, cleave the wood, and think of me," C. v. Tischendorf, Evangelia apocrypha (1876), 150 f., 174; Hennecke[3], 296.

b. For Ign. separation from the community and its bishop is parallel to Gnostic denial of the sufferings of the incarnate Lord, Ign. Phld., 3, 3: εἴ τις σχίζοντι ἀκολουθεῖ, βασιλείαν θεοῦ οὐ κληρονομεῖ· εἴ τις ἐν ἀλλοτρίᾳ γνώμῃ περιπατεῖ, οὗτος τῷ πάθει οὐ συγκατατίθεται.

† σχίσμα.

1. Profane Greek.

σχίσμα "what is split," "rift," "rent," is rare in secular Gk. It occurs in connection with division in parts of the body or the parts of plants: καὶ ἔστιν τι καὶ διὰ μέσου τῶν σχισμάτων "there is something between the clefts (sc. of the camel's hump)," Aristot. Hist. An., II, 1, p. 499a, 27; τὰ σχίσματα, "the slits" of the maple-leaf aim at a single point, Theophr. Hist. Plant., III, 11, 1.[1] In the law of a cultic society devoted to Zeus Hypsistos the formation of cliques, the inciting of divisions and separation from the fraternity are grouped together and punished in the same way as stealing from or deceiving members καὶ μ[η]ι[δ]ενὶ αὐτῶν ἐξέστω συνταγματαρχήσειν[2] μηιδὲ σχί⟨σ⟩ματα συνίστασ[θαι] μηιδ᾽ ἀπ[ο]χωρήισε[ιν ἐκ] τῆς τοῦ ἡγ[ου]μένου φράτρας εἰς ἑτέραν φράτραν, Preisigke Sammelbuch, V, 7835, 13 ff. (1st cent. B.C.).

2. The Septuagint.

τὸ σχίσμα does not occur but we find ἡ σχισμή: σχισμαὶ ὀρέων "the abysses of the mountains" in Jon. 2:6 and αἱ σχισμαὶ τῶν πετρῶν "the clefts of the rock" in Is. 2:19, 21.

3. Later Judaism.

As with the verb חלק (→ 960, 18 ff.) we will consider here only the special Rabb. sense of מַחֲלוֹקֶת. There is a clear difference from מִין, which became the tt. for the heretic who denies a basic truth of Judaism, → I, 181, 41 ff. In addition to the OT sense "share" (of land) in Jos. 11:23 and "division" (of officials) in 1 Ch. 23:6 etc. מַחֲלוֹקֶת takes on the new sense of "partisanship," "difference of opinion," "controversy." As Ab., 5, 17 shows, the word can be used indifferently: There is controversy for heaven's sake, as between Hillel and Shammai, and there is controversy not for heaven's sake, like that of Korah and his company. Yet the use is almost exclusively in a bad sense. The reasons for controversy in Israel are the people's defective knowledge of the Law (bMeg., 3a) and pride, but esp. inadequate intercourse between pupils and their teachers, bSota, 47b. The topic of debate may be general (bBB, 147a) but usually concerns the exposition and application of the Law by the Rabb. Dissent may extend to formal trivialities like the form of a blessing (bBer., 37a) or it may include the opposition of legal scholars to the chief judicial court, i.e., primary questions of competence, bSanh., 88b; T. Sanh., 7, 1.[3] Thus מַחֲלוֹקֶת does not question the basic decision of the Jewish faith but as personal dogmatism and insubordination it threatens the inner coherence of the people. Joseph. does not use σχίσμα, but he has ἡ σχίζα, "rubble," Ant., 1, 228; 8, 341.

σ χ ί σ μ α . [1] There is some textual obscurity here.

[2] We are to read συνταγματαρχήσειν. συνταγματαρχέω, a military term, is also attested in the negative sense "to be a ringleader," Philo Jos., 176. We are thus to transl.: "No one shall be permitted to make himself the leader of a party or to be the leader of a party or to cause divisions" [Dihle]. The first editors of the late Ptolemaic rule, C. H. Roberts, T. C. Skeat, A. D. Nock, "The Guild of Zeus Hypsistos," HThR, 29 (1936), 39 f. read συντευματαρχήισειν, but this does not make good sense. U. Wilcken, "Urkunden-Referat," APF, 12 (1937), 220 substitutes an unattested συνπ⟨ν⟩ευματαρχήσειν, "to conspire."

[3] Str.-B., II, 816-818 restricts the passages mentioned and par. passages to doctrinal decisions to the exclusion of jurisdictional matters.

4. The New Testament.

a. On Mk. 2:21 and par. → 961, 1 ff.

b. According to Jn. the appearance of Jesus caused a division among His listeners. This arose in the evaluation of His origin (7:43 → V, 588, 22 ff.), His deeds (9:16 → 28, 22 ff.) and His words (10:29 → IV, 361, 20 ff.).

c. The σχίσματα in Corinth are not quite clear, since it is hard to decide how many groups Paul is dealing with. [4] The important point, however, is that it is not firmly formulated doctrinal differences and programmes that separated the various schools. [5] As may be seen from 1 C. 1-4, especially 1:12, the basis and mark of these cleavages is attachment to individual leaders who are played off the one against the other in authority. [6] This makes common thought and utterance difficult (1:10) and especially jeopardises the common meal (11:18). Yet σχίσμα as personal rivalry and αἵρεσις as fundamental error (→ I, 182, 25 ff.) — a distinction which Paul would know from Jewish thought (→ 963, 20 ff.) — are not sharply differentiated along the lines of later ecclesiastical use. [7] The overcoming of schisms rests on the divinely willed anchoring of individuals in the body of Christ, which includes mutual subjection and earnest care for the weak, 1 C. 12:12 ff. The singular σχίσμα [8] of 1 C. 12:25 means in the first instance the rift between members in the human body, but Paul leaps beyond the image and is thinking of divisions between the members of the body of Christ.

5. The Post-Apostolic Fathers.

In the various writings of the post-apost. fathers σχίσματα ("schisms") are grouped with debates, rivalries and similar divisions in 1 Cl., 2, 6; 46, 5. 9; 54, 2; Herm. s., 8, 9, 4. Their opposite is love, which knows no σχίσματα, 1 Cl., 49, 5. The admonition to avoid schisms is accompanied by that to make peace between those who strive, Did., 4, 3; Barn., 19, 12. The use of ἡ σχισμή in Herm. is along the same lines; clefts in the mountain symbolise contentious men, s., 9, 1, 7; 23, 1-3; splits on branches represent contentious calumniators, men who are ambitious and jealous, s., 8, 1, 9 f. 14; 7, 2. 4; 10, 1; cracks in stones point to those who cause discord, s., 9, 6, 4; v., 3, 6, 3. In s., 9, 8, 3 and 8, 5, 1 [9] σχισμαί and σχίσματα are used indiscriminately for cracks in stones and splits in branches.

Maurer

---

[4] Ltzm. K., Schl. K. on 1 C. 1:12; J. Héring, *La première ép. de Saint Paul aux Corinth.* (1949), 17 f.; P. A. van Stempvoort, *Eenheid en Schisma in de Gemeente van Korinthe volgens 1 Korinth.*, Academisch Proefschr. (1950), 165-174; Zahn Einl., I, 207 and 215 think there were four "parties." Joh. W. 1 K., XXX-XXXIX; W. Michaelis, *Einl. in das NT³* (1961), 172 cut out ἐγὼ δὲ Χριστοῦ at 1 C. 1:12 and thus get three groups. F. C. Baur and R. Bultmann, followed by W. Schmithals, "Die Gnosis in Korinth," FRL, NT, 48 (1956), 34-37, think there was only one party, which was a pneumatic-Gnostic group.

[5] J. Munck, "Pls. u. d. Heilsgeschichte," *Acta Jutlandica, Aarsskrift for Aarhus Univ.*, 26, 1 (1954), 127, 160 f. speaks only of quarrels, not parties.

[6] Cf. U. Wilckens, "Weisheit u. Torheit. Eine exeget.-religionsgeschichtliche Untersuchung z. 1 K. 1 u. 2," *Beiträge z. hist. Theol.*, 26 (1959), 16 f.

[7] M. Meinertz, "Σχίσμα u. αἵρεσις im NT," BZ, NF, 1 (1957), 114-118.

[8] Read σχίσμα with p⁴⁶ 𝔥 K *pm* lat sy, not plur. σχίσματα with אﬡ D* G al.

[9] Whittaker, *ad loc.* rightly prefers the reading of the Michigan pap. (σχίσματα) to that of the Athos MS (σχισμάς).

σῴζω, σωτηρία, σωτήρ, σωτήριος

From adj. * σαϝος, σάος "safe" [1] contracted to σῶς (Homer. Attic, σῶος Ionic and koine), [2] we have the factitive verb σαόω, σαώσω, ἐσάωσα, "to make safe, sound," 1. "to deliver from a direct threat," 2. "to bring safe and sound out of a difficult situation." Apart from the pres. we find the contracted forms σώσω, ἔσωσα (for * ἐσάωσα) etc. The isolated pres. σαόω was replaced by * σωίζω, σῴζω, [3] first Hom. Od., 5, 490 and Hes. Op., 376 vl. [4] After Hom. we find the nomen agentis σωτήρ (Pind., Hdt.) and the derived σωτηρία and σωτήριος. [5] Since the verb σῴζω and the noun σωτηρία are largely par. in meaning and use, whereas σωτήρ and σωτήριος present special problems, the latter will be treated only after the first two even though this does not follow the historical development.

† σῴζω, † σωτηρία.

Contents: A. σῴζω and σωτηρία in the Greek World: 1. Saving; 2. Keeping; 3. Benefitting; 4. Preserving the Inner Being; 5. σῴζω and σωτηρία in Religious Usage. B. σῴζω and σωτηρία in the Old Testament: 1. Statistics and Hebrew Equivalents: a. Statistics of Use and Translation in the Septuagint; b. Statistics of Use and Translation of Hebrew Equivalents; c. Relation of the Septuagint and Hebrew Text; 2. The Stem יש׳ in the Old

---

1 σῴζω κτλ. [1] Cf. the Cypriot name Σαϝοκλέϝης. σάος probably from * twawos, Indo-Eur. root * tewə, "to swell," v. Boisacq, Hofmann, s.v. σάος; Pokorny, 1080.
[2] Cf. M. Leumann, "σάος u. σῶς," Kleine Schriften (1959), 266-272.
[3] For the sake of uniformity, sometimes in spite of the editions, the pres. and pass. perf. of σῴζω are always written with iota subscr.
[4] Leumann, op. cit., 270.
[5] [Lines 2-7 are by Risch].

σῴζω, σωτηρία. Bibl. Gen. Meyer Ursprung, III, 390-7; Harnack Miss., I, 129-150; J. B. Colon, "La conception du salut d'après les év. synopt.," Revue d. sciences religieuses, 9 (1929), 472-507; 10 (1930), 1-38; 189-217, 370-415; 11 (1931), 27-70, 193-223, 382-412; J. T. Ross, The Conception of σωτηρία in the NT (1947); F. C. Grant, Roman Hellenism and the NT (1962), 27, 154 f. On A.: H. Haerens, "Soter et Soteria," Stud. Hellen., 5 (1948), 57-68; Nilsson, II², 689; On C.: O. Holtzmann, "Zwei Stellen zum Gottesbegriff d. Philo," ZNW, 13 (1912), 270 f.; Bousset-Gressm., 202-301; Moore, I, 500-506; II, 311-322; Volz Esch., 359-407; Str.-B., I, 67-70; On D.: W. Sanday and A. C. Headlam, The Ep. to the Romans, ICC (1902) on 1:16; W. Wagner, "Über σῴζω u. seine Derivate im NT," ZNW, 6 (1905), 205-235; Zn. R. on 1:16b; H. J. Holtzmann, Lehrb. d. nt.lichen Theol., I (1911), 299 f.; II (1911), 298-300; Joh. W. 1 K. on 1:18; Cr.-Kö., s.v. σῴζω; H. Weinel, Bibl. Theol. d. NT⁴ (1928), 219-222, 322 f.; W. Grundmann, "Der Begriff d. Kraft," BWANT, IV, 8 (1932), 83 f.; M. Goguel, "Les fondements de l'assurance du salut chez l'apôtre Paul," RevHPhR, 17 (1937), 105-144; P. S. Minear, "And great shall be your Reward," Yale Stud. in Religion, 12 (1941), passim; J. R. Branton, "Paul and Salvation," Crozer Quart., 24 (1947), 228-240; M. Meinertz, Theol. d. NT, II (1950), 89-114; M. Barth, Die Taufe ein Sakrament? (1951), 502-4; P. Feine, Theol. d. NT⁸ (1951), 223 f.; J. C. Fenton, "Destruction and Salvation in the Gospel acc. to St. Mark," JThSt, 3 (1952), 56-8; Mi. R. on 1:16; R. M. Wilson, "Soteria," Scott. Journ. of Theol., 6 (1953), 406-416; M. Goguel, "Le caractère, à la fois actuel et futur, du salut dans la théol. paulinienne," Festschr. f. C. H. Dodd (1956), 322-341; W. C. van Unnik, "L'usage de σῴζειν 'sauver' et de ses dérivés dans les Év. synopt.," La formation des Év. (1957), 178-194; U. Wilckens, "Weisheit u. Torheit," Beiträge z. hist. Theol., 26 (1959), 22 f.; W. C. van Unnik, "The Book of Acts, the Confirmation of the Gospel," Nov. Test., 4 (1960), 50-53; G. Braumann, "Vorpaul. chr. Taufverkündigung bei Pls.," BWANT, 82 (1962), 32-37.

Testament: a. Meaning; b. Deliverance, Help, Salvation through Men; c. Limits of Human Deliverance; d. Deliverance, Help, Salvation through God; 3. The Stems פלט and מלט in the Old Testament: a. Nouns of the Stem פלט; b. The Verb מלט. C. σῴζω and σωτηρία in Later Judaism: 1. The Old Testament Apocrypha; 2. The Dead Sea Scrolls; 3. Ethiopic Enoch; 4. The Testaments of the Twelve Patriarchs; 5. The Psalms of Solomon and 4 Esdras; 6. Josephus; 7. Rabbinic Works and Hebrew Enoch; 8. Philo. D. σῴζω and σωτηρία in the New Testament: I. σῴζω and σωτηρία for the Saving of Physical Life. II. σῴζω and σωτηρία in Their Theological Sense: 1. In the Synoptic Gospels; 2. In Paul; 3. In Ephesians and Colossians; 4. In the Pastorals; 5. In Hebrews, the Catholic Epistles and Acts; 6. In the Johannine Writings. E. σῴζω and σωτηρία in the Post-Apostolic Fathers. F. σῴζω and σωτηρία in Gnosticism. G. New Testament σωτηρία in Its Relation to Later Judaism, the Greek World, and Gnosticism.

A. σῴζω and σωτηρία in the Greek World.

1. Saving.

σῴζω and σωτηρία mean first "to save" and "salvation" in the sense of an acutely dynamic act in which gods or men snatch others [1] by force from serious peril. In this use, found from Hom. to the latest period, σῴζω corresponds to Hbr. ישׁע (→ 973, 21 ff.). Among the dangers war Hom. Il., 15, 290 f.; Plat. Symp., 220d; Ael. Arist. Or., 45, 13 (Keil) and sea-voyages Hom. Od., 5, 130; Luc. Dial. Deorum, 26, 2 always play a special part. Things are similar with σωτηρία: ἐπήκουον αὐτῶν καθάπερ ναυαγίαν τινὰ καὶ σωτηρίαν παράλογον διηγουμένων, Luc. De Mercede Conductis, 1. Like ישׁע (→ 978, 10 ff.) σῴζω also denotes "deliverance" from judicial condemnation, Xenoph. Hist. Graec., V, 4, 26; Andoc. De Mysteriis, 31. The sense "to save from an illness," hence "to cure," occurs, e.g., of a physician: πολλούς τε σώσαντος ἐγ μεγάλων ἀρρωστιῶν, Ditt. Syll.[3], II, 620, 13 f.; cf. ἐσώθη, ibid., 1173, 9 (in a collection of stories of healings by Aesculapius) or a medicine: φάρμακον σῷζον, Plut. Adulat., 11 (II, 55c). Unlike ישׁע (→ 973, 28 f.), however, the personal or dynamic element is not necessarily bound up with σῴζω or σωτηρία. The subj. of the saving act does not have to be one who confronts and is even superior to the person saved, as with ישׁע(→ 973, 24 ff.). σῴζομαι can often mean "to save oneself" (Hbr. פלט or מלט), Ps.-Luc. Asin., 34. Feet, knees and horses save heroes from the battle, Hom. Il., 21, 611; 17, 452; 5, 224. Night saves the army from destruction, Hom. Il., 8, 500; 9, 78; 14, 259. A good ship saves from perishing and good counsel can save the ships and people of the Achaeans, Hom. Il., 9, 424; 10, 44. Plut. Sept. Sap. Conv., 19 (II, 163a) speaks of σωτηρία κόρης ὑπὸ δελφῖνος ἐκ θαλάττης. The obj. of salvation may be the body of Hector (Hom. Il., 24, 35) or Patroclus (17, 692, cf. 15, 247), a castle, city, ships, Il., 13, 96; 17, 144; cf. Plut. Sept. Sap. Conv., 18 (II, 161c): σωτηρίας αὐτοῦ καὶ τῆς νεώς. The dynamic element of snatching from immediate danger does not have to be present either in the Gk. word. In relation to the gen. perils of battle and sailing σῴζω may have more of the sense "to keep" or "to protect." Thus Telemachus asks which of the Achaeans will be kept, will come back, Hom. Od., 3, 185. Calchas asks Achilles to protect him from the expected anger of Agamemnon, Il., 1, 83. Telemachus advises Μέδοντα σαώσομεν, Od., 22, 357. σωθῆναι may even be used for a happy homecoming, Il., 9, 393; Epict. Diss., II, 17, 37 f.; Luc. Dial. Meretricii, 9, 1; hence σωτηρία can also mean "safe return," Plut. Lacaenarum Apophthegmata, 11 (II, 241e).

---

[1] Acc. to Gk. mythology gods may also be the obj. of deliverance, Hom. Il., 18, 395 and 405; Cornut. Theol. Graec., 27 (51, 1 f.); Luc. Salt., 8.

2. Keeping.

The element of danger is even less prominent when it is said of the king that he may "keep alive" or slay, Plut. Them., 28 (I, 125 f.). Hence σῴζω comes to mean "to pardon," σωτηρία "pardon," Plut. Cat. Minor, 66 (I, 792a); 72 (I, 794c). The law keeps or protects envoys (even from enemies), Dio Chrys. Or., 75, 9. In Plat. Crat., 400c the body acc. to Orphic teaching is the περίβολον of the soul, ἵνα σῴζηται (sc. ἡ ψυχή). When the Nile did not rise Ptolemy II and the queen levied many taxes ἕνεκα τῆς τῶν ἀνθρώπων σωτηρίας, to keep men from want and perishing, Ditt. Or., I, 56, 17. The pass. σῴζομαι means "to remain in good condition." Thus Dio Chrys. Or., 6, 28 asks: πῶς ἂν ἐσώθησαν οἱ πρῶτοι ἄνθρωποι γενόμενοι, μήτε πυρὸς ὄντος μήτε οἰκιῶν μήτε ἐσθῆτος μήτε ἄλλης τροφῆς ἢ τῆς αὐτομάτου; the mid., too, can mean "to keep oneself": σῴζου τοῖς Ἕλλησιν, Luc. Pergr. Mort., 33. In relation to lifeless obj. we find the following: σπέρμα πυρὸς σῴζων, "to keep a spark of the fire from going out," Hom. Od., 5, 490, 2 a shield which will not "be lost," Plut. Lacaenarum Apoph-thegmata, 17 (II, 241 f.), lost money which will be "got back," Ditt. Syll., I³, 55, 10, the "keeping" of wine, Plut. Quaest. Conv., V, 3, 1 (II, 676b), of goods, Aud. Poet., 8 (II, 27d), even one's beard, Epict. Diss., I, 16, 14. σῴζω is also used with abstracts. Epict. Diss., I, 28, 21 uses τὸ αἰδῆμον καὶ πιστὸν σῴζειν as the opp. of διαφθείρειν, and the verb is also used in relation to the maintaining or loss of προκοπή, IV, 1, 120; 7, 30; Ench., 51, 2; σωτηρία μνήμης is the "preserving of the memory," Plut. De Demosthene, 2 (I, 846d).

3. Benefitting.

In all the above examples there is still the element of keeping from a threat, but this can disappear altogether and σῴζω and σωτηρία can have a purely positive content. σῴζομαι can mean not only "to be cured" but "to be or stay in good health"; δεῖν ἀεὶ θεραπευομένους βιοῦν τοὺς σῴζεσθαι μέλλοντας "he who wants to be and remain in good health must live as though he always needed a cure," Muson. Fr. minora, 36 (p. 123 f.). 3 It is said of an instructor of ephebes: διετήρησεν πάντας (the ephebes) ὑγιαίνοντας καὶ σῳζομένους, Ditt. Syll.³, II, 717, 89 (100/99 B.C.). Dio Chrys. Or., 32, 15 speaks of the water in Alexandria: τὸ μὲν σῷζον καὶ τρέφον καὶ γόνιμον, and cf. the resolution: διατετέληκεν καὶ πόλεις καὶ ἰδιώτας σῴζων, "to benefit," Ditt. Syll.³, II, 761, n. 11 (48/47 B.C.). Along these lines the noun can mean "well-being," e.g., in the amphictyonic oath: If I break the oath, so [... κακίστῳ ὀλέθρῳ τὴν] σωτηρίαν μοι [ἀφέλωσι]ν, μήτε τέκνων μήτε σπορῶν μήτε καρπ[ῶν μή]τε οὐσίας κατόνασθαι ἐάσωσ(ιν) ἐμέ (sc. the gods), Ditt. Syll.³, II, 826, col. II, 14 f. (117 B.C.). In the annual feast of Zeus σωσίπολις in Magnesia the ἱεροκῆρυξ prays (Ditt. Syll.³, II, 589, 26-31) for the σωτηρία of the city, country, citizens, wives, children and other residents, for peace, for wealth, for the growth of the grain and other fruits and cattle. Thus we find σωτηρία with εὐδαιμονία, Ditt. Or., I, 2, 40 f. In letters there is enquiry as to the σωτηρία ("well-being") of those addressed.4 We often find vows for the σωτηρία of the Rom. emperors. The positive content of σωτηρία may be seen in the direction to mourners in Plut. Cons. ad Apoll., 32 (II, 118b) that they should spend the time of their mourning τῆς τοῦ σώματος ἐπιμελείας φροντίσαντες καὶ τῆς τῶν συμβιούντων ἡμῖν σωτηρίας. The formula of self-execration τὴν ἐμὴν σωτηρίαν in Epict. Diss., III, 23, 11 means "by my health." The task of the ruler in the Hell.-Rom. period is to care for the σωτηρία ("well-being") of his subjects: εἰ μὲν γὰρ εὐγνώμων

---

2 This is the only place where Hom. has σῴζω for σαόω.
3 Cf. ἑτέρων... τῶν ὑφ᾽ αὐτοῦ σωθέντων, Dio Chrys. Or., 57, 5; φάρμακον σῷζον, Plut. Adulat., 11 (II, 55c). The many coins with Salus Augusti ref. to the emperor's health, cf. P. L. Strack, Untersuchungen z. röm. Reichsprägung d. 2. Jhdt., I (1931), 49 f., 171-173.
4 Deissmann LO, 148, n. 11; BGU, II, 423.

καὶ φιλάνθρωπος καὶ νόμιμος ὢν ἐπὶ σωτηρίᾳ καὶ τῷ συμφέροντι τῶν ἀρχομένων ἐπιμελεῖται, ... τότε χαίρων μάλιστα ..., ὅταν ὁρᾷ καλῶς πράττοντας τοὺς ἀρχομένους, δυνάμει τε μέγιστός ἐστι καὶ βασιλεὺς ἀληθῶς, Dio Chrys. Or., 3, 39. The ruler is ὁ τὰ πάντα σῴζων, Dio Chrys. Or., 62, 4, cf. Ep. Ar., 240, 281, 292. We often find σῴζω with εὐεργετέω, Muson., 8 (p. 32, 10 f.): δεῖ μὲν γὰρ δήπου δύνασθαι τὸν βασιλέα σῴζειν ἀνθρώπους καὶ εὐεργετεῖν. [5]

4. Preserving the Inner Being.

A special nuance is when σῴζω and σωτηρία refer not to the outer condition but to the inner being or nature of men or things. Dio Chrys. Or., 3, 59 considers how a tyrant σωθήσεται, and his point is not, or not just, how he can stay alive but esp. how he can remain a tyrant. A city (Or., 75, 10) cannot last if the laws are destroyed, the pt. again being that in these circumstances the πόλις ceases to be a πόλις → IV, 1031, 6 ff. In this connection Plat. has the thought that it is the task of the ἄρχων to σῴζειν the state, i.e., not just to preserve it from outer destruction but also to maintain it as a constitutionally ordered state, Leg., XII, 962a-b. In philosophical and religious trains of thought esp. σῴζω and σωτηρία often ref. to the inner "health" of man, e.g., in the saying ascribed to Diogenes τῷ μέλλοντι σῴζεσθαι δεῖ φίλους ἀγαθοὺς ἢ διαπύρους ἐχθροὺς ὑπάρχειν, Plut. Adulat., 36 (II, 74c), cf. Quomodo quis suos in virtute sentiat profectus, 11 (II, 82a-b). [6] The Epicurean Diogenes Oenoadensis Fr., 2, col. 5, 12 - 6, 2 says of himself in his gt. inscr.: ἠθέλησα τῇ στοᾷ ταύτῃ καταχρησάμενος [ἐ]ν κοινῷ τὰ τῆς σωτηρίας προθε[ῖναι] φάρμακα, [7] and for Democr. Fr., 43 (Diels, II, 155, 13 f.) μεταμέλεια ἐπ᾽ αἰσχροῖσιν is ἔργμασι βίου σωτηρίη. The idea that philosophy can preserve a man in his humanity is very pregnantly put in Epict. Diss., IV, 1, 165, which says paradoxically of Socrates: ἀποθνήσκων σῴζεται, οὐ φεύγων. He illustrates this by the example of a good actor who by retiring at the right time σῴζεται, i.e., retains his fame. Socrates did not seek to preserve his σωμάτιον but ἐκεῖνο, ὃ τῷ δικαίῳ μὲν αὔξεται καὶ σῴζεται, τῷ δ᾽ἀδίκῳ μειοῦται καὶ ἀπόλλυται, Diss., IV, 1, 163. What is thus kept or lost is humanity itself: ἂν σῴζηται τοῦτο καὶ περιτετειχισμένον μένῃ καὶ μὴ διαφθείρηται τὸ αἰδῆμον μηδὲ τὸ πιστὸν μηδὲ τὸ συνετόν, τότε σῴζεται καὶ αὐτός, I, 28, 21. The heading of I, 2 runs: πῶς ἄν τίς σῴζοι τὸ κατὰ πρόσωπον ἐν παντί, the pt. being that he keep his character rather than "his face," that true humanity be not lost. When a man acts like an animal the "man" is destroyed, II, 9, 3, cf. I, 28, 22 ff.

5. σῴζω and σωτηρία in Religious Usage.

In the religious sphere σῴζω and σωτηρία are found with all the breadth of usage depicted thus far. Salvation from all the perils of life is expected from the gods, → 1004, 25 ff. An important question in philosophy is how the all can be maintained in its rationally achieved state. Plat. Symp., 208a had said that everything moral will be preserved not by its own enduring but by constantly new things replacing it. [8] Acc. to Plat. Leg., X,

---

[5] The salus (σωτηρία) Augusta on imperial coins is identical with the salus publica and ref. to the imperially guaranteed well-being of the state, cf. Strack, op. cit., 49 f., 171-173.

[6] Cf. τὴν δὲ ἑτέραν ἐπιμέλειαν ἔργον εἶναί φημι τῶν δυναμένων διὰ πειθοῦς καὶ λόγου ψυχὰς πραΰνειν καὶ μαλάττειν. οὗτοι δὲ σωτῆρές εἰσι καὶ φύλακες τῶν οἵων τε σῴζεσθαι, πρὶν ἐλθεῖν εἰς τέλος τὴν πονηρίαν εἴργοντες καὶ κατέχοντες, Dio Chrys. Or., 32, 18. Cf. Ael. Arist. Or., 45, 18 (Keil) which says that Sarapis τὴν μὲν δὴ ψυχὴν ... σοφίᾳ καθαίρων ... σῴζει.

[7] Ed. J. William (1907).

[8] Cf. the Pythagorean Philolaos in Stob. Ecl., I, 173, 16-18; the same thought also occurs in Corp. Herm., 12, 14 f. and Plot. Enn., III, 2, 2.

903b a young man who does not believe that God cares about the world must be convinced that τῷ τοῦ παντὸς ἐπιμελουμένῳ (God) πρὸς τὴν σωτηρίαν καὶ ἀρετὴν τοῦ ὅλου πάντ' ἐστὶ συντεταγμένα. For Cornut. Theol. Graec., 2 (3, 9) Zeus is the one through whom γίνεται καὶ σῴζεται πάντα. [9] Dio Chrys. Or., 12, 29 speaks of Zeus τοῦ σπείραντος καὶ φυτεύσαντος καὶ σῴζοντος καὶ τρέφοντος, cf. also Plut. Comm. Not., 31 (II, 1075b). M. Ant., 10, 1, 3 speaks to his soul to persuade himself that everything will be good that the gods give ἐπὶ σωτηρίᾳ τοῦ τελείου ζῴου, τοῦ ἀγαθοῦ καὶ δικαίου καὶ καλοῦ καὶ γεννῶντος πάντα καὶ συνέχοντος, i.e., of the cosmos. [10] When in the Hell.-Rom. period faith in the divinely sustained harmony of the cosmos loses its force under the pressure of a belief in fate, the σῴζειν of the gods comes to include their power to save and keep from inscrutable destiny. Apul. Met. is an example, though there is no equivalent of σῴζω in Book XI; instead salus is used for σωτηρία for the freeing of Lucius from his animal form and hence from the power of capricious fate → 1005, 33 ff. [11] Philosophy's demand that one should preserve oneself as a rational being is no longer enough; σωθῆναι is sought as the demand for a life which survives death. That which saves may be a mystical experience sensed as grace, as in Corp. Herm., 13, 1: μηδένα δύνασθαι σωθῆναι πρὸ τῆς παλιγγενεσίας. Thus σωθῆναι and σωτηρία approximate to ζωή: τὸ πᾶν τὸ ἐν ἡμῖν, σῷζε ζωή, φώτιζε φῶς, 13, 19. [12]

In the sphere dominated by Gnosticism it is *gnosis* which saves. Man cannot achieve this by his own reason. It is imparted to him by revelation or by a mediator, ὅπως τὸ γένος τῆς ἀνθρωπότητος διὰ σοῦ ὑπὸ θεοῦ σωθῇ, Corp. Herm., 1, 26; ἐγὼ... καθοδηγὸς ἐγενόμην τοῦ γένους, τοὺς λόγους διδάσκων, πῶς καὶ τίνι τρόπῳ σωθήσονται, 1, 29. [13] The content of σωθῆναι is not the self-assertion of humanity as the being of a rational creature (→ 968, 15 ff.) but the salvation of man from the power of death. The soul is saved, Corp. Herm., 7, 1. The passivity of σωθῆναι is that of one who is referred to divine revelation concerning essential man. The presupposition and at the same time the fulfilment of this receiving of revelation is a looking with the eyes of the heart and a shaking off of drunkenness. Only thus does the soul reach the havens of σωτηρία, 7, 1 f. In the mystery religions the devotees participate through the mystery in the salvation of a mythical divine being from death. The god is the θεὸς σεσῳσμένος, as in the verse: θαρρεῖτε μύσται τοῦ θεοῦ σεσῳσμένου. ἔσται γὰρ ἡμῖν ἐκ πόνων σωτηρία, Firm. Mat. Err. Prof. Rel., 22, 1. The passivity of σωθῆναι is that of one who lets a sacramental act be performed on him. The content of salvation is the attainment of a blissful life beyond death. Thus in Apul. Met., XI, 21 the *inferum claustra* and the *salutis tutela* which are in the hands of Isis are found close together; consecration itself is celebrated *ad instar voluntariae mortis et precariae salutis*.

A special form of σωθῆναι is that which acc. to Orig. Celsus reports of Syrian prophets: a prophet, God or God's Son, says: ἤδη... ὁ κόσμος ἀπόλλυται... ἐγὼ δὲ σῶσαι θέλω... τοὺς δέ μοι πεισθέντας αἰωνίους φυλάξω, Orig. Cels., VII, 9. This is salvation from eternal punishment through the worship of an envoy of God and through faith in him.

Foerster

---

[9] Cf. Ael. Arist. Or., 42, 4 (Keil) of Aesculapius.

[10] Cornut. Theol. Graec., 1 (2, 19 f.): the ancients regarded the gods as αἰτίους... τῆς σωτηρίας τῶν ὅλων, cf. 26 (48, 16 f.) and Numenius in Eus. Praep. Ev., 11, 18, 21: ἥ τε τάξις τοῦ κόσμου καὶ ἡ μονὴ ἡ ἀΐδιος καὶ ἡ σωτηρία ἀναχεῖται εἰς τὰ ὅλα.

[11] On Isis as σώτειρα and the Metamorph. gen. cf. Ant. Christ., VI (1950), 266 f.

[12] Cf. Reitzenstein Hell. Myst., 349.

[13] Cf. οἱ δὲ μετὰ τοῦ ἀγαθοῦ οὐσιωδῶς ὑπὸ τοῦ θεοῦ σῳζόμενοι, Corp. Herm., 9, 5 and *numine salvati tuo gaudemus*, Ascl., 41 (354, 7 f.).

B. σῴζω and σωτηρία in the Old Testament.

1. Statistics and Hebrew Equivalents.

a. Statistics of Use and Translation in the Septuagint.

σῴζω "to keep," "to save," is in about three fifths of its occurrences in the canonical books of the Hebr. OT the rendering of the verb ישע, 143 times for the hi "to save," "to free," "to help," "to come to the help of," esp. in Ju.; 1-2 S.; 1-2 K.; 1 Ch.; Ps.; Hos.; Hab.; Zeph.; Zech.; Is. 30 ff.; Jer. 1-26, also 16 times for ni "to receive, experience aid." Once each it is used for the derived nouns יֵשַׁע Hab. 3:13, יְשׁוּעָה Ps. 80:2 and מוֹשָׁעוֹת Ps. 68:20 "experiences of help." In another fifth of the instances it is the transl. of the stems פלט and מלט. σῴζω is used 4 times for פָּלִיט in Is. 45:20; Jer. 42:17; 44:14, 28 and once for פָּלִיט "one who has escaped" in Is. 66:19, 5 times for פְּלֵיטָה "what has escaped," "escaping," "deliverance" in Gn. 32:9; Is. 10:20; 37:32; Neh. 1:2; 2 Ch. 20:24, also for מִפְלָט "place of refuge" in Ps. 55:8 [14] and then for מלט, 37 times ni "to find safety," "to escape," [15] 11 times pi "to save," "to save oneself," and once the rare hi "to save." In the final fifth the word is used for various terms elsewhere transl. differently, in 24 instances for נצל, which is mostly rendered ῥύομαι (→ VI, 999, 21 ff.) and ἐξαιρέω. [16]

ἀνασῴζω "to save again," "to save for oneself," is used for פלט q at Ez. 7:16, but most commonly for nouns derived from this verb: 10 times for פָּלִיט, 3 for פָּלִיט Jer. 44:14; 50:28; 51:50 and 6 for פְּלֵיטָה 2 K. 19:31; Jer. 50:29; Ez. 14:22; Jl. 2:3; 2:32; 2 Ch. 30:6. On the other hand it is used for מלט pi only at Jer. 51:6, for ni twice at Jer. 46:6; Zech. 2:11, and for ישע hi twice. [17]

διασῴζω "successfully to save," is also used only rarely for ישע, 2 times ni Nu. 10:9; Jer. 8:20, 3 hi Dt. 20:4; Hos. 13:10; Zech. 8:13. More often it stands for stem פלט: 2 times for פלט pi Mi. 6:14; Job. 21:10, once hi Mi. 6:14, twice פָּלִיט Ju. 12:4 f., once פָּלִיט Nu. 21:29, 5 times פְּלֵיטָה Ju. 21:17; 2 K. 19:30; Da. 11:42; Ezr. 9:14 f., then esp. for the verb מלט 20 times ni "to achieve safety," "to escape," and 4 times pi "to save," "to save oneself." It is also used 7 times for פָּלִיט, which is par. to and means the same as שָׂרִיד, and just once each for שרד חיה pi and עשת hitp. [18]

---

[14] The only rendering of פלט pi by σῴζω in Ps. 56:7 is based on a corrupt Hbr. text in which the verb has to be altered.

[15] As inner Gk. variants we find in 1 Βασ. 30:17 διασῴζω and περισῴζω, which occurs only here.

[16] We find the following inner Gk. variants of σῴζω: ἀνασῴζω, Ιερ. 31:19; Ob. 21, διασῴζω, Gn. 19:20; Jos. 10:40; 1 S. 30:17; 2 K. 19:37; Ιερ. 48:15; Ez. 17:15; also Da. 11:41 Θ, ἀποσῴζω, Ιερ. 41:3, σωτήρ, Ju. 12:3. Conversely we find a simple σῴζω for ἀνασῴζω at Ιερ. 51:14; Zech. 8:7, for διασῴζω, 1 S. 19:18, for ὠθέω Ιερ. 41:11, for τίθημι 2 Ch. 33:7. σῴζω is replaced by a very different verb in 1 S. 23:2; Is. 38:6; 46:2; 59:1; Ιερ. 2:27; 11:12; 45:18; Ez. 33:12; 36:29; Zech. 12:7; ψ 17:28; 33:7; 106:13; also Da. 3:95 and 6:21 Θ. There are various differences between HT and LXX. σῴζω yields an emendation at 1 S. 14:47 (ישע ni for וַיַּרְשִׁיעַ) and Prv. 19:7 (מלט ni for הֵמָּה) while it is supplementary at 1 S. 10:1 and 1 K. 13:31. We have misreading and mistransl. at Is. 15:7; Mi. 6:9; Job 27:8; Lam. 2:13. Finally LXX has σῴζω in surplus texts at 2 S. 14:4; Is. 12:2; Prv. 10:25; Est. 4:17b; 10:3 f.; Da. 6:23, 28.

[17] Acc. to LXX variants and versions Ob. 21 should probably be altered to ישע ni, while variants at Zech. 8:7 have a simple σῴζω.

[18] Simple σῴζω is a variant at 1 Βασ. 19:18, other verbs at 19:10 and 20:29. HT is altered by LXX at Job 36:12, διασῴζω probably for the misreading ישמעו Without original we find διασῴζω at Gn. 35:3; Jos. 6:26.

σωτηρία "salvation," "preservation," "protection," "well-being," occurs mostly (81 times) for stem י‍ש‍ע: 5 times יֵשַׁע hi 2 S. 22:3; 2 K. 13:5; Is. 38:20; 47:15; 63:8, 12 times יֵשַׁע (after → σωτήρ a second third of the instances), 38 times יְשׁוּעָה and 26 תְּשׁוּעָה "deliverance," "help," "salvation." The word occurs only 6 times for פְּלֵיטָה 2 S. 15:14; Jer. 25:35; Ob. 17; Ezr. 9:8, 13; 2 Ch. 12:7 and even less for other words: 3 times שָׁלוֹם Gn. 26:31; 28:21; 44:17, twice תּוּשִׁיָּה Prv. 2:7; Job 30:22 (where there is an error in the Mas.), once each שֶׁלֶו Job 20:20 (Mas. corrupt) and מָנוֹס Job 11:20 (LXX rearranged). [19] There is often an additional σωτηρία with no original in the HT: Ιερ. 37:6; ψ 117:28; Job 2:9a; Est. 4:17d; 8:12u. [20]

Isolated terms are σωτήρισμα in 2 Εσδρ. 9:8 B[1], σωτηρίαγμα for στήριγμα in B[3], ἀνασωσμός for פְּלֵיטָה in Gn. 45:7 ʼA and διασωσμός for מַפְלָט in Ps. 55:8 ʼAΘ.

b. Statistics of Use and Translation of Hebrew Equivalents.

As σῴζω and derivates occur mostly for stem י‍ש‍ע (except for the transl. of שָׁלֵם by σωτήριον → 1022, 7 ff.), so י‍ש‍ע and derived nouns are with relatively few exceptions transl. by σῴζω etc.: the verb י‍ש‍ע hi 121 times as compared with 22 other renderings (7 ῥύομαι → VI, 999, 27), [21] ni 16 times as compared with 3, יֵשַׁע 33 times as compared with 3, יְשׁוּעָה 78 times with no deviations, תְּשׁוּעָה 31 times as compared with 3 others and מוֹשָׁעוֹת once. Whereas the verb י‍ש‍ע is with 13 exceptions transl. by the corresponding Gk. verbs and the nouns by σωτηρία and σωτήριον, יֵשַׁע is 12 times transl. σωτήρ "saviour" (→ 1013, 9 ff.). [22]

In contrast, for stem פלט LXX more often uses ἀνα- or διασῴζω, though this is mostly with the derived nouns, since the verb is usually transl. differently. As distinct from renderings of the nouns of י‍ש‍ע, these derivates are mostly transl. by verbal forms; פְּלֵיטָה alone is also rendered 6 times by σωτηρία. Thus σῴζω etc. are used only 5 times for פלט, which is transl. in other ways 22 times, mostly by ῥύομαι (→ VI, 999, 26), then ἐξαιρέω, though this occurs 16 times for פָּלִיט (3 times differently), 5 for פְּלֵיט, 22 for פְּלֵיטָה (6 differently) and once for מַפְלָט. [23]

---

[19] LXX variants are σωτήρ in 2 Βασ. 22:47; Is. 25:9; 1 Ch. 16:35 and σωτήριον ψ 11:6. At Da. 11:42 Θ we find σωτηρία instead of διασῴζω for Hbr. פְּלֵיטָה.

[20] On σωτηρία in Is. cf. L. H. Brockington, "The Greek Translator of Isaiah and His Interest in ΔΟΞΑ," VT, 1 (1951), 30.

[21] Note the forms יְהוֹשִׁיעַ in 1 S. 17:47; Ps. 116:6 with retained ה in the impf. (Ges.-K., 53q) and וַיּוֹשִׁיעָן in Ex. 2:17 with connecting a before the suffix in the impf.

[22] יש‍ע is used in a series of proper names sometimes made up of יֵשַׁע and יהוה (יְשַׁעְיָהוּ) or אֵל (אֱלִישַׁע). When it does not replace these by others, LXX transl. the names acc. to sound and irrespective of sense, i.e., without using σῴζω. For the sake of completeness one should with יש‍ע ref. to שׁ‍ו‍ע pi "to call for help" and nouns שׁוּעַ and שַׁוְעָה "call for help," also the name יְהוֹשׁוּעַ or יֵשׁוּעַ Ιησοῦς (→ III, 284, 1 ff.).

[23] The importance of the term may be seen from the many names formed with its help (for LXX renderings → n. 22). The names occur elsewhere in the ancient East and are not peculiar to Israel, cf. M. Lidzbarski, Hndbch. d. nordsemitischen Epigraphik, I (1898), 209; K. Tallqvist, Assyrian Personal Names (1914), 179, 179a; Z. S. Harris, A Grammar of the Phoenician Language (1936), 137; E. Littmann, Nabataean Inscr. from Egypt, II (1954), 235.

In distinction from the nouns derived from פלט, the verb מָלַט[24] is mostly transl. by σῴζω (49 times) and διασῴζω (20); ἀνασῴζω is less prominent (3). These verbs are used for מלט ni 55 times (only 6 differently), pi 16 times (11 ῥύομαι → VI, 999, 28 f. and ἐξαιρέω), and once hi (once differently).[25]

c. Relation of the Septuagint and Hebrew Text.

No basic shift of meaning takes place when σῴζω etc. are used for the stems פלט, ישׁע and מלט. One may see this from the fact that σῴζω etc. are also used for various other Hbr. terms which correspond in sense to the stems mentioned.[26] Yet the LXX rendering of the Mas. is often fairly free and may import a specific sense.[27] This may entail a change in meaning as compared with Mas. In Is. 10:22 the remnant which converts becomes the remnant which is saved. In Zeph. 3:17 the statement that God is a גִּבּוֹר מוֹשִׁיעַ is weakened: He is now δυνατὸς σώσει σε. In Job 20:24 the use of σῴζω for ברח "to flee" changes the sense, also the use for ראה "to look at" in Est. 8:6. There is more drastic alteration of the Mas. in Prv. 10:5, where LXX speaks of destiny rather than the conduct of the prudent, cf. also the eschatological reconstruction[28] of Prv. 10:25, where LXX says of the wise man, who is compared to an enduring foundation in Mas., that he who can avoid (the storm) will be saved for ever, also of Prv. 11:31, where Mas. "If the righteous is recompensed on earth, how much more the wicked and the sinner," becomes in LXX: "If the righteous man is scarcely saved, where will the wicked and the sinner be?" There is also considerable alteration in Ιερ. 38:22, where the obscure and corrupt Mas. "Yahweh does a new thing in the land: the woman protects (encircles, woos) the man," becomes: "The Lord accomplished salvation for a new planting, in which salvation men will walk."[29]

---

[24] Cf. Arab. mlt. or mrt (cf. מרט) "to be smooth, without hair" (cf. C. Landberg, Datina [1909-1913], 1113 on the derived Southern Arab. "to slip away") or Arab. mld ˈcf. מרץ) "to be slippery," "to slip away."

[25] This occurrence in Is. 31:5 in the sense "to save" is open to question, since 1 QIs (ed. M. Burrows, *The Dead Sea Scrolls of St. Mark's Monastery*, I [1950]) has והפליט instead. It is true that 1 QIs 66:7 has מלט hi like the Mas. (also attested outside the Mas.), but as in 1 QH 3:9 the meaning is "to bring forth," LXX ἐξέφυγεν καὶ ἔτεκεν. מלט hitp occurs only in Job 41:11 "to make off" (sparks of fire leap up).

[26] The verbs are used 5 times for עזר "to help" and once for שׂגב pu "to be protected," which are par. in meaning to ישׁע; 14 times for שָׂרִיד "one who has escaped" and once for שׂרד "to escape," which are esp. par. פלט; 6 times for various forms of חיה "to live," "to let live," "to save life" and twice for Aram. שֵׁיזֵב(Hbr. עזב) "to deliver," in closer par. to מלט; finally 24 times for נצל hi which is usually transl. ῥύομαι (→ VI, 999, 21 ff.) but often stands for פלט and מלט. Once each ידע "to pay regard" (to the needs of a man) and עשׁת hitp "to be mindful of" are the originals; acc. to ancient ideas noting and remembering were followed by aid. Since the Hbr. terms can denote not only help and salvation but also their results and effects one can understand why σωτηρία is used 3 times for בְּשָׁלוֹם "in peace," "safe and sound."

[27] LXX transl. thus פדה "to redeem" Is. 1:27; Job 33:28, חסה "to find refuge" Is. 14:32, and סור "to escape" (the underworld) Prv. 15:24. Job 21:20 Mas. "to drink the anger of Shaddai" becomes LXX "not to be saved," and Est. 4:11: "that there is only one law, that someone put him to death," becomes: "that there is no deliverance for him."

[28] Cf. G. Bertram, "Die religiöse Umdeutung altoriental. Lebensweisheit in d. griech. Übers. d. AT," ZAW, 54 (1936), 166.

[29] C. Schedl, " 'Femina circumdabit virum' oder 'via salutis,' " *Zschr. f. kathol. Theol.*, 83 (1961), 431-442 largely follows the LXX in his reconstruction of the text.

In Job 35:14 the LXX transl. with σῴζω deviates altogether from HT, but the latter should not be changed accordingly. All these, however, are isolated instances and do not affect the gen. use of the Gk. terms.

There is, however, a slight basic shift in respect of nouns derived from פלט, which are transl. by σῴζω etc. except for 6 instances of פְּלֵיטָה. "Refugees," "those who escape," become "those who are saved," "that which has escaped" becomes "that which is saved." On the one side this emphasises the passive aspect by drawing attention to the help imparted, while on the other it suggests that they have not just survived or escaped but have been intentionally rescued; cf. the par. theologically shaped terms for the "remnant" in Is. 10:20; 37:32. [30] Of the 6 renderings of פְּלֵיטָה by σωτηρία 5 are to the point, since the Hbr. means "escape," "deliverance" in 2 S. 15:14; Jer. 25:35; Ob. 17; Ezr. 9:13; 2 Ch. 12:7. But though it bears the same sense in Jl. 2:3; 2:32 verbal forms are used. On the other hand σωτηρία is used in 2 Εσδρ. 9:8, though a verbal form would be better since פְּלֵיטָה means "what has escaped" here. [31] There is no obvious reason for the variation.

2. The Stem ישׁע in the Old Testament.

a. Meaning.

The verb ישׁע (cf. Arab. *wasi'a*) means orig. "to be roomy, broad," [32] esp. as opp. to oppression, which is properly "narrowness" צר, cf. צרר "to choke," "to envelop," "to enwrap," hence "to be hemmed in, constricted, oppressed" → I, 345, 38 ff.; III, 140, 11 ff. As oppression is viewed as a kind of spatial hemming in or imprisonment, so rescue from it is a moving out into the open. [33] Thus ישׁע hi means "to make it spacious" for one who is constricted and ישׁע ni that space is given to him. Since this takes place through the saving intervention of a third party in favour of the oppressed and in opposition to his oppressor, we get the sense "to come to the rescue" and "to experience rescue." Deliverance is imparted to the weak or oppressed in virtue of a relation of protection or dependence in which he stands to someone stronger or mightier who saves him out of his affliction. The thought is neither that of self-help nor of co-operation with the oppressed. The help is such that the oppressed would be lost without it. The stem ישׁע in most cases points to personal relations. Deliverance, help and salvation come in favour of persons in situations which are often brought about by the hostile intent of other persons; they do so through the intervention of persons, and only seldom through technical means or their interposition, Is. 26:1; 60:18.

Of the derived nouns יֵשַׁע is formed from the monosyllabic short-vowelled stem after the manner of segolata, יְשׁוּעָה as a fem. after the manner of nouns with a long vowel in the second syllable, [34] and תְּשׁוּעָה after the manner of taqtūl or taqtul constructs as the common

---

[30] שְׁאֵרִית is transl. κατάλειμμα in 4 Βασ. 19:31, ἐγκατάλειμμα in 2 Εσδρ. 9:14, while פליטה is ἀνασῴζω in 4 Βασ. 19:31 and διασῴζω in 2 Εσδρ. 9:14.

[31] Θ also has the noun at Da. 11:42, where LXX more correctly has a verbal form of διασῴζω.

[32] This word occurs on the Moabite Mesha inscr., line 3 f. in the ancient South Arab. names *'ljt'* and *jt''l*, cf. K. Conti-Rossini, *Chrestomathia Arabica Meridionalis Epigraphica* (1931), and as Aram. ויושע in 4 QPsDa (ed. J. T. Milik, " 'Prière de Nabonide' et autres écrits d'un cycle de Daniel," *Rev. Bibl.*, 63 [1956], 413).

[33] C. Barth, *Die Errettung vom Tode in den individuellen Klage- u. Dankliedern d. AT* (1947), 127.

[34] In Jon. 2:10; Ps. 3:2; 80:2 we find the form יְשׁוּעָתָה with no shifting of accent.

middle Hebrew forms of stems mediae ו, [35] while מוֹשָׁעוֹת is the fem. plur. part of יָשַׁע hi. Like many other terms the nouns comprehend a totality which includes not only deliverance or help but also the ensuing state of salvation, though it is impossible to differentiate the ante and post, the cause and effect, since the act and the intended cause cannot be separated, → II, 195, 24 ff.; III, 929, 25 ff.

b. Deliverance, Help, Salvation through Men.

A man without power or strength needs deliverance (Job 26:2). He is in danger of succumbing in conflict with an adversary. This controversy may be legal or military. If help does not come, the children of the fool who has died suddenly may be thrust out of their inheritance (Job 5:4). Or the threatened city may fall unconditionally to the enemy (1 S. 11:3). If one is entangled in such a controversy (רִיב) or brought to such a pass (צָרָה), as the weaker party it is as well to utter a cry for help (זְעַק) at injustice and violence (חָמָס), Ju. 10:12 ff.; 12:2 f.; 2 S. 22:3; Hab. 1:2; Ps. 107:13, 19; 2 Ch. 20:9. Someone stronger than the oppressor should be summoned to the rescue with the cry הוֹשִׁיעָה, 2 S. 14:4; 2 K. 6:26. He should be asked to secure justice (שָׁפַט Hos. 13:10; דִּין Ps. 54:1) or to put forth his power (עֹז Ps. 21:1) to protect the oppressed (Is. 37:35) or to increase his strength (Zech. 10:6; Ps. 86:16). The meaning of stem יָשַׁע may be seen clearly from these passages. Usually a self-evident presupposition of the request for help is the acknowledgment of the lordship and dominion of the one invoked. But a relation of dependence may be established by the request for rescue, as may be seen from the message of Ahaz to Tiglath-pileser: "I am thy servant and thy son; come up, and save me . . . , " 2 K. 16:7. Ahaz annexes his request to his subjection as a vassal under the Assyrian king.

The deliverance sought may be through war. Hos. 1:7 makes it plain that it is usually expected through bows and swords, horses and riders, i.e., military intervention. The judges are charismatic leaders who bring military help against the enemies of Israel, Ju. 2:16, 18; 3:9, 15, 31 etc. Saul does the same against the Ammonites (1 S. 11:9) and the Philistines (9:16, cf. 14:45; 23:5). Two divisions of the army fighting against different enemies promise to come to each other's help if needed, 2 S. 10:11. A third state will give help to one of two warring states, 2 S. 10:19. Sometimes there is the vain looking for a nation that does not save (Lam. 4:17) because the nation from which help is sought is not really a stronger third party. If this condition is met, the intervention of the deliverer brings the desired effect: תְּשׁוּעָה victory, Ju. 15:18; 2 S. 19:3.

Deliverance may also come through the resolving of a legal difficulty. Job, confident in God, looks forward to victory in his litigation, Job 13:16. It is said of Tola the judge in Ju. 10:1 that he should deliver Israel, while elsewhere the expression used is שָׁפַט, "to judge," "to secure the rights." But יָשַׁע and שָׁפַט are not co-extensive, since the ref. of the former is not to securing justice but to a work of liberation from legal oppression. Thus the personal intervention of the king is sought when legal statutes strictly demand condemnation (2 S. 14:4) or cannot be applied in the tangle of relations (2 K. 6:26). Hence saving intervention can be an alternative to litigation, Ju. 6:31.

Human acts of deliverance are expected from military heroes, judges, and Nazirites (Ju. 13:5), cf. David and Jonathan. This kind of hero can intervene powerfully and effectively, cf. Jer. 14:9. Deliverance is also sought from the protecting power; this is for vassals the positive aspect of suzerainty, cf. 2 K. 16:7, Hos. 14:4. Above all, giving help and dispensing justice is one of the tasks of the king (cf. 2 S. 14:4; 2 K. 6:26) which is regarded as laid on him by God and whose discharge secures a happy and prosperous life for the people (Ps. 72:2 f., 12). Hence Hos. can ask: "Where is thy king that he may

---

[35] Cf. C. Brockelmann, *Grundriss d. vergleichenden Grammatik d. semitischen Sprachen*, I (1908), 383; G. Beer and R. Meyer, *Hbr. Grammatik*, I (1952), 108. We also find the form תְּשֻׁעָה.

save thee, and all thine officials that they may establish justice for thee?" Hos. 13:10. [36]
If saving is one of the basic tasks of the king, it is understandable that attempts should
be made to elect a man as king who would act as Gideon did (Ju. 8:22) or of whom one
might expect on the basis of an oracle of Yahweh what was expected of David (2 S. 3:18).

c. Limits of Human Deliverance.

With strong emphasis the OT indicates the limits of all salvation not validated
by Yahweh. It is obvious that idols of wood and stone cannot rescue from calamity
or bring salvation, Is. 45:20b; 46:7; Jer. 2:27 f.; 3:23; 11:12; Hos. 14:4b. Nor can
astrologers, Is. 47:13. Not an angel, who serves chiefly as a messenger, but God
Himself saved Israel out of Egypt, Is. 63:8 f. Israel did not conquer the land in its
own strength; God won the victories, Ps. 44:3 f. In order that the people should not
be able to claim that it delivered itself, only 300 men may fight against the Midianites,
Ju. 7:2, 7. Hence help and victory in battle are not due merely to military power,
Hos. 1:7; 14:4; Ps. 33:16 f. They are not to be expected from men or princes, Ps.
146:3. They are to be sought in quiet waiting for God's intervention and confidence
in this, Is. 30:15; Hos. 14:4b. It is thus a serious sin according to 1 S. 10:18 f. that
Israel should reject its true King Yahweh, who has saved it (מוֹשִׁיעַ LXX σωτήρ)
from distress and affliction, and demand in His place a king from its own ranks; for
in so doing it finally wants to save itself instead of being saved. If a man helps himself by his own hand, as the weaker or legally inferior party compared with his
adversary he must resort to illegitimate measures in order to survive, thus incurring
blood-guiltiness, 1 S. 25:26, 31, 33. Only God, who has all might and right, can give
help and achieve victory and deliverance without running this risk, Ps. 98:1-3. Man
could do it only if he were as God, Job. 40:9, 14. Man's intervention to help and save
(along the lines of the stem יֵשׁע) can take place legitimately only if God works in
them and through them. [37]

> Thus it is said of the judges (→ IV, 158 n. 70; V, 406, n. 179) that Yahweh raised them
> up (Ju. 2:16; 3:9, 15) or gave them (Neh. 9:27) and they delivered Israel; or that He was
> with the judges and saved Israel Himself (Ju. 2:18) or saved them through the hand of
> the judges (Ju. 6:36 f.). In adoption and adaptation of the same thought it is also said
> that Yahweh sent or will send a deliverer to help (2 K. 13:5; Is. 19:20). Always it is God
> who saves by many or by few (1 S. 14:6 cf. also Ju. 13:5, 1 S. 9:16; 2 S. 3:18). One may
> thus see why it is that before the battle against the Midianites Gideon is reluctant to come
> forward as helper and saviour. His family is weak and powerless, and he is ready to
> accept the task only when the desired sign assures him that Yahweh will be with him,
> Ju. 6:14 ff.

d. Deliverance, Help, Salvation through God.

As He saves and helps through men, God also does so Himself and directly as
the One who has all might and right, so that He is best equipped to intervene,
providing for and protecting the weak against their oppressors in the day of
trouble, → VI, 460, 30 ff. If saving is a main task of the hero or king, this is

---

[36] Read אַיֵּה for "I will be," וְכָל־שָׂרֶיךָ for "in all thy cities," and יִשְׁפְּטֶךָ for "and thy judges."
[37] And even then they do not become mediators → IV, 610, 18 ff.

connected with the idea of God's heroic strength (Ps. 80:2) and also with the concept that Yahweh is the King (Is. 33:22; Ps. 44:3 f. → I, 568, 16 ff.) who, after waging war against the powers of chaos at creation, is constantly achieving similar victories (Ps. 74:12 ff.). [38] Thus, as the petitioner comes to his king, so the intercessor comes to God with the cry: הוֹשִׁיעָה, "save," "help." [39]

Israel can look back to such experiences of help in divine victories over its foes. It can thus be called עַם נוֹשַׁע בַּיהוה, "a people victorious through Yahweh," Dt. 33:29. From the deliverance from Egypt onwards (Ex. 15:2; Ps. 74:12; 106:10, 21) God has continually saved it from other peoples and helped it (1 S. 11:13; 14:23, 39; 2 S. 8:6, 14 etc.). The presence of the ark, which guarantees God's presence, holds out hope of victory (1 S. 4:3), though vainly so if God does not will to save because Israel has forsaken Him and gone after other gods which cannot save, Ju. 10:12-14. If, however, Israel is faithful, God's help against the enemy is promised in battle, Nu. 10:9; Dt. 20:4; [40] Hab. 3:13. This help is true each morning (cf. Is. 33:2) as it was on the night of the Passover and at the Red Sea, and it may be known as God's intervention since in those days no man undertook military action by night. [41] Yahweh may thus be hailed as the Hero who brings victory (Zeph. 3:17) or He may be invoked in a popular lament as Israel's Deliverer in time of need, Jer. 14:8.

In the Ps. esp. the stem ישׁע is used for the invoked or experienced help of Yahweh against public or personal enemies; Yahweh is asked to save from those who attack or accuse the intercessor, often using for this purpose his illness, which is interpreted as a retributive divine punishment. In the Ps. the stem is employed almost 80 times in this way for the help of Yahweh against the adversaries of the petitioner, cf. also 1 S. 2:1; Jer. 15:20; 17:14. In many cases the ref. is to a personal opponent at law who harasses and accuses the intercessor and seeks to destroy him, so that help is wanted in a difficult and apparently hopeless legal situation. God can help in war and achieve victory. He can also help against injustice and violence (2 S. 22:3) and save from prison (Ps. 107:13 ff.). "He shall stand at the right hand of the poor, to save his life from his judges," Ps. 109:31. [42] There is deliverance from the perils of sickness, imprisonment, or hostility, whether these come alone or accompany or are the effect of other oppressions. In each case the dangers mean a weakening of strength and they are thus a foretaste of the dead which overpowers the oppressed. Hence deliverance is salvation from death. Trust in this salvation and help of God from all the tribulations and terrors to which man is subject and which, as the many expressions show, always and everywhere oppress him, is an essential element in the believer's self-understanding.

With no reference to specific afflictions or foes the OT also speaks of the general and comprehensive deliverance, help and salvation which God imparts. It is true that Israel resists the saving and helping God to whom it owes its existence (Dt.

---

[38] In opposition to the assertion of E. Beaucamp, "Le Psaume 21 (20.) Psaume messianique," *Richesses et déficiences des anciens Psautiers latins* (1959), 41 f. יְשׁוּעָה is not conferred as saving power; it denotes either the single act of deliverance and salvation or the state of salvation which God establishes thereby.

[39] Ps. 12:1; 20:9; 28:9; 60:5; 86:16; 108:6; with suffix of 1st pers. sing. Ps. 3:7; 6:4; 7:1; 22:21; 31:16; 54:1; 59:2; 69:1; 71:2; 109:26; 119:94; with suffix of 1st pers. plur. Ps. 106:47; with strengthening נָא Ps. 118:25.

[40] The priestly oration in Dt. 20:3 f. would seem not to rest on actual practice but to be a literary fiction, esp. if vv. 2-4 are a later priestly interpolation.

[41] Cf. J. Ziegler, "Die Hilfe Gottes 'am Morgen,'" *At.liche Stud. Festschr. f. F. Nötscher* (1950), 281-288.

[42] Read מִשְׁפָּטָיו for "the judges" (of his soul).

32:15) and who preserved it in the wilderness (Ps. 78:22). It thus falls under His judgment, Is. 17:10. Yet the individual can hope for God's help on the basis of his membership of the people of Yahweh, Ps. 106:4. As God turned everything to good for David and the king (2 S. 23:5; Ps. 18:50), so a later desire for the priests is that they will be clothed with salvation, Ps. 132:16; 2 Ch. 6:41. [43] The point is that, as individuals are robed in the garment of salvation (Is. 61:10), so the filthy raiment which symbolises sin is replaced by raiment which symbolises remission of sins and the blessing of salvation, cf. Zech. 3:4 f. The one thus blessed can raise the cup of salvation as a symbol of God's saving grace (cf. Ps. 16:5) or of thanksgiving (as in the rite of the drink offering), Ps. 116:13.

> To grant the general help and salvation which constituted Job's prosperity (Job 30:15) is the task of God's rule and action on earth, Ps. 18:27; 67:2; Job 22:29. This is not, of course, the portion of the arrogant transgressor but of the humble man who knows that he is little before God, who is pure and simple (Ps. 24:5), who calls upon God with a broken spirit and contrite heart (Ps. 34:6, 18), who takes heed to his ways (Ps. 50:23), who is weak and spiritually poor (Ps. 116:6), who follows God's will (Ps. 119:155, 166, 174), who fears and loves God (Ps. 145:19 f.), and who waits silently for His intervention (Lam. 3:26). Then the righteous can praise Him as the help of his countenance and his God, Ps. 42:5, 11; 43:5.

Though God usually denies His help to the sinner, יָשַׁע can sometimes be used for salvation from judgment. In this case the stem follows its use in legal contexts, 2 S. 14:4 (→ 974, 41ff.) and expresses the fact that the condemnation is just and judgment is really demanded. יָשַׁע thus denotes God's saving work in spite of a condemnation which is legally free from reproach. Thus, like a shepherd assisting his flock, God helps the weak of the population who are oppressed by the authorities even though the oppressed are no less laden with sin than the oppressors, Ez. 34:22. He will free Israel from all its sins and as a mightier third party help it against the superior foe, Ez. 36:29. He will create it anew and redeem it, Ez. 36:24-28. On the other hand, the prerequisite for salvation from judgment may be: "O Jerusalem, wash thine heart from wickedness, that thou mayest be saved," Jer. 4:14.

In this light one can see why יָשַׁע is also used in eschatological theology as a term for the deliverance, help, and salvation of the last time. The Babylonian exiles are to be liberated like prisoners as in the military use of יָשַׁע (Is. 49:8 f.), and in this way they will be delivered for salvation (Is. 45:17). Only Yahweh can do this; beside Him there is no saviour (Is. 43:11; 45:21), and from Egypt onwards, according to the later interpolation Hos. 13:4, He has shown Himself to be Israel's God and Redeemer. But when the eschatological age of salvation dawns, this is to be called the time of true redemption. Since גָּאַל becomes the tt. for this from Dt. Is. on, it is not surprising that יָשַׁע is sometimes one of the parallel terms for the deliverance and salvation of the last time (Is. 43:1-3; 60:16; 63:9), [44] though this did not affect

---

[43] 2 Ch. 6:41-42a is an almost lit. quotation from Ps. 132:8 f. But while Ps. 132:9 has צֶדֶק for salvation (and v. 16 יֵשַׁע), 2 Ch. 6:41 has תְּשׁוּעָה; this shows the two terms are interchangeable.

[44] On the other hand גָּאַל is par. to יָשַׁע in Ps. 72:13 f.; 106:10 in the legal sense " to ransom."

the development of the concept, → IV, 328, 6 ff. On the contrary, in its duality of before and after, cause and effect, the stem ישׁע denotes both the unmerited deliverance which leads to salvation and also the salvation made possible thereby; the same applies to צְדָקָה, with which it may be parallel, Is. 46:13; 51:6, 8 → II, 195, 31 ff. The deliverance which makes salvation possible is preservation from the eschatological onset of the peoples (Zech. 12:7). Above all, however, it is the gathering and bringing home of the dispersed from the whole world (Is. 43:5-7; Jer. 31:7; 46:27; Zeph. 3:19; Zech. 8:7; Ps. 106:47). Thus God by His intervening to help (Is. 59:1; Zech. 8:13) brings in the eschatological age (Is. 46:13; 51:6, 8) unless renewed sinning restrains Him (Is. 59:11). Then the community of the end-time can draw from the wells of salvation which flow forth from Jerusalem (Is. 12:3) and all the world can come to share in this salvation (Is. 45:22; 49:6). In this connection the Messianic ruler, who governs as God's representative on earth, will save and help Israel, as is the function of the king, so that it may dwell in safety (Jer. 23:6), and the Messiah himself will be delivered by God through God's triumph over the wild eschatological attack of the nations (Zech. 9:9).

3. The Stems פלט and מלט in the Old Testament.

a. Nouns of the Stem פלט.

While the verb פלט q means "to get away," pi and hi "to bring to safety," "to deliver," [45] פָּלִיט and פָּלֵיט, [46] which occurs only in the plur., denote both the one who is escaping, the "fugitive," [47] and also the one who has escaped and is in safety, the "refugee." [48] פְּלֵיטָה [49] denotes both "escaping," deliverance" [50] and also esp. "what has escaped" as the result and consequence of escaping. [51] As with nouns of the stem ישׁע (→ 974, 1 ff.) the same term is used with no distinction of temporal sequence for both before and after, both cause and effect.

In the main the words denote escape from mortal danger. [52] An exception is Ju. 12:4, where the Ephraimites accuse the Gileadites of being fugitive West Israelites (who have perhaps run away to escape current obligations). One might also note the relation to capture in Gn. 14:13 and to the subjection of a land by its conquerors in Da. 11:42. Elsewhere, however, the reference is always to escaping the danger of violent death except in passages of a religious character. One flees from a superior enemy in order not to be killed, Nu. 21:29; 2 S. 15:14; Jer. 50:28. One seeks to get away after a lost battle, Ju. 12:5; 21:17. The fugitive who came to Ezekiel in Ez. 33:21 was able to escape when Jerusalem

---

[45] Cf. Accad. balāṭu "to live" (Barth, op. cit., 28-32; W. v. Soden, Akkad. Handwörterb., 2 [1959], 98 f.); Canaan. plṭ "to deliver" (Gordon Manual, 312); Amarna Letter, 185, 25. 33 (ed. S. A. B. Mercer, The Tell-el-Amarna Tablets, II [1939]) paliṭmi "has escaped," "is spared"; Arab. flt "to escape"; Aram. "to flee."

[46] Acc. to J. Barth, Nominalbildung in d. semitischen Sprachen² (1894), 112 פָּלִיט is formed from * paliṭ. but acc. to J. Olshausen, Lehrb. d. hbr. Sprache (1861), 180; P. de Lagarde, Übersicht über d. im Aram. übliche Bildung der Nomina (1889), 85 it is a diminutive.

[47] Hence par. נָס "fugitive," Jer. 50:28; Am. 9:1.

[48] Hence par. שָׂרִיד "refugee," Jer. 42:17; 44:14; Ob. 14; Lam. 2:22.

[49] The form פְּלֵטָה occurs in Ex. 10:5; Jer. 50:29; Ez. 14:22; 1 Ch. 4:43.

[50] 2 S. 15:14; Jer. 25:35; Jl. 2:3; 2:32; Ob. 17; Ezr. 9:13; 2 Ch. 12:7.

[51] Gn. 32:9; Ju. 21:17; 2 K. 19:30 f. (par. Is. 37:31 f.); Is. 10:20; Jer. 50:29; Ez. 14:22; Da. 11:42; Ezr. 9:8, 14 f.; Neh. 1:2; 2 Ch. 20:24.

[52] Cf. the Accad. examples in Barth, op. cit. (→ n. 33), 62. Cf. the German "Pleite"; פָּלִיט is the one who has survived a crash.

was captured by the Babylonians, or perhaps he fled for fear of reprisals after the assassination of Gedaliah; one cannot be sure which. Wily Jacob, menaced as he thought by Esau, tried to escape by dividing his possessions, so that at least one of the camps could avoid the slaughter which he feared, Gn. 32:9. Finally, however, it rests on God's intervention whether Israel will be saved from Pharaoh Shishak (2 Ch. 12:7), whether a remnant will escape and remain from the Assyrian emergency (2 K. 19:30 f.), or whether allied foes will destroy one another, so that no one escapes the battle (2 Ch. 20:24).

On the other hand, the prophets proclaim God's punishment on sinful Israel as a mortal danger which none can escape. Amos is the first to see and hear this: "No fugitive נָס of them shall flee, no refugee פָּלִיט of them shall escape," Am. 9:1. Even though some of the people of Jerusalem might be delivered from the battle and siege, says Ez. 7:16, they will wander about as helpless refugees in the mountains, while Jer. 42:17 threatens those who were determined to flee into Egypt that none of them should escape the sword, famine, and pestilence, cf. 44:14. There will be no escaping on the day of Yahweh, Jl. 2:3 — neither for Jerusalem (Lam. 2:22) nor for the nations overtaken by the divine judgment (Jer. 25:35; 50:29). It is true, of course, that some Israelites in the North did escape the Assyrians, 2 Ch. 30:6. It is also true that the Jews who lived in exile escaped the sword of Babylon (Jer. 51:50) and that some might therefore be expected to survive in Egypt (44:28). [53] But in the controversy with the deportees this expectation was given a radically different interpretation. If a saved company still lived on in Jerusalem in spite of all the plagues, it was only as an object lesson to the exiles, who might see from these sinners that there was good reason for judgment on the city, Ez. 14:12-23.

All this notwithstanding, פָּלִיט and פְּלֵיטָה can still be used as tt. for those who have escaped the divine punishment as a mortal threat, Is. 4:2; 10:20; Ez. 6:8 f.; Jl. 2:32; Ob. 17; Ezr. 9:8; 13 ff.; Neh. 1:2. In this connection the "and I will leave" at the beginning of Ez. 6:8 is designed to stress the fact that it rests on God's will and work if some are spared the sword of judgment. If these who escape are almost an eschatological quantity, this is undoubtedly true of those of the (Gentile) nations who escape, who survive the world-shattering events which begin with the victories of Cyrus and which form the commencement of the events of the endtime, who turn to the one God and who thus let themselves be saved in the eschatological salvation, Is. 45:20-22. Is. 66:19 uses the same term for the converted non-Israelites who escape the Last Judgment, who have access to the temple, and who are sent out by Yahweh as missionaries into the whole world.

b. The Verb מלט.

The meaning of מלט ni "to escape," "to find safety" (from mortal peril), and pi "to let escape," "to save," "to save oneself," is brought out by the par. in Jeremiah's saying to the Cushites who had saved his life, namely, that they would not fall by the sword but their life would be a prey to them, Jer. 39:18. It is also illustrated by the expression "no one escaped" (Ju. 3:29; 1 S. 30:17), which denotes complete victory over the enemy; cf. the corresponding requirement of Elijah in 1 K. 18:40 and the association with a verb for flight (esp. ברח, נוס), in which מלט as the result of flight from a mortal threat intimates that it has been successful and that the fugitive has found safety, 1 S. 19:10, 12, 17 f.; 22:1; 2 S. 1:3 f.; 1 K. 20:20; Jer. 48:6; 51:6; cf. 48:19. [54]

---

[53] This promise, not thought to be by Jer., has caused an explanatory addition to be added at the end of the contrary statement in v. 14 (also not thought to be by Jer.).

[54] In the reverse order only 1 S. 22:20: Abiathar escaped מלט the massacre and fled to David.

מלט thus, like the nouns from פלט, ref. mainly to escape from threatening death. One escapes before calamity strikes, Gn. 19:17-22.[55] Or one gets away from it, so that one can tell about it, Job 1:15 ff. David has to protect his life constantly against the ambushes of Saul, 1 S. 19:11; 23:13; 27:1. Murderers have to escape capture by those who pursue them, Ju. 3:26; 2 K. 19:37; Jer. 41:15.[56] But it is not always a matter of life and death. Is. tells those who live on the coastal plains of Palestine that they cannot escape invasion by the Assyrians, Is. 20:6.[57] Job presupposes that one can save someone out of the enemy's power by money, Job 6:23. מלט also denotes escape from punishment, so that one is spared or delivered, Ez. 17:15; Jer. 48:8; Mal. 3:15; cf. Prv. 11:21; 19:5. Again, it is escape from custody, so that one slips away through a gate, 2 S. 4:6. Or it is escape from court service, so that one can get away and see relatives, 1 S. 20:29.[58] Finally there is the general deliverance of the needy from affliction, Job 29:12.[59]

Along these lines the fathers of Israel who trusted in God were not put to shame but saved, Ps. 22:5. Similarly the innocent man who can present clean and unsoiled hands as a sign of his righteousness will be saved by God, Job 22:30. On the other hand, trust in the strength of a horse (Ps. 33:17) does not make escape possible, nor does reliance on the might of another nation (Is. 20:6), nor trust in riches (Job 20:20; Qoh. 8:8)[60] nor in one's own understanding (Prv. 28:26). But whereas Prv. 28:26 says that a man who follows prudent rules of life will escape misfortune, Qoh. 9:15 shows the uselessness of this wisdom by the example of the wise man who could have saved the city but was disregarded because his wisdom came in unattractive form and not in representative fashion. As God saves the innocent, He destroys transgressors. There is no escaping the divine judgment on a guilty life, whether for worshippers of Baal (1 K. 19:17), or all Israel (Am. 2:14 f.; 9:1), or the king (Jer. 32:4 etc.), or the Babylonian manufacturers of idols (Is. 46:2). Only when God spares the condemned in order to usher in the eschatological age of salvation can prisoners again escape the oppressor thanks to His liberating act, Is. 49:24 f.[61] In the last time those who call on the name of Yahweh will be saved (Jl. 2:32), or those who are written in the book of life (Da. 12:1).

Fohrer

C. σῴζω and σωτηρία in Later Judaism.

The unity of the many special meanings of the group σῴζω is to be found in the idea of the preserving or restoring of the integrity of a person or thing or state or functional nexus, however constituted. Thus persons, things and circumstances may all be subjects

---

[55] מלט ni is used 5 times here in a play on the name of Lot, who can escape.

[56] מלט also means "to save (life)" in 2 S. 19:6; 1 K. 1:12; Jer. 51:45; Ps. 41:2; 89:48; 107:20; 116:4, though LXX does not use σῴζω in these verses.

[57] Cf. 2 S. 19:10: to save from the power of the Philistines (LXX ἐξαιρέω).

[58] Cf. 2 K. 23:18: to let the bones escape destruction, i.e., leave them alone (LXX ῥύομαι); Qoh. 7:26: Not the wise man as such but he who pleases God escapes the (strange) woman (LXX ἐξαιρέω).

[59] In this sense מלט is par. to נצל hi, cf. Ps. 72:12, used in Job 29:12.

[60] In Qoh. 8:8 read עֹשֶׁר instead of "wickedness."

[61] In Is. 49:24, 25 עָרִיץ should be read for צַדִּיק.

of the process. [62] In contrast, the Hbr. יָשַׁע, also מִלַּט and פָּלַט, always have a personal ref. whether in respect of subj. or obj. → 973, 24 ff. Where there is no such ref. other words are used, e.g., שָׁמַר, which a Semite not too well acquainted with Gk. thought and the Gk. language would be more likely to transl. by → φυλάσσω or → τηρέω than σῴζω. In what follows, then, note should be taken of the way in which the use of σῴζω etc. in later Judaism and the NT is influenced by the Greek word σῴζω.

1. The Old Testament Apocrypha.

In parts of the OT for which there is no Hbr. the word group σῴζω gen. refers to the deliverance of men by men or by God and His instruments. Only rarely is there no personal ref. in the subj. or obj.: Wis. 14:5: a raft in the sea saves (διασῴζω); Ep. Jer. 58: a door in the house can διασῴζειν "protect" more than idols; 4 Macc. 2:14: a neut. obj. The saving of men by other men is not very common: Eleazar sacrifices himself before the battle τοῦ σῶσαι τὸν λαὸν αὐτοῦ, 1 Macc. 6:44; Judas Maccabaeus was δυνατὸς σῴζων τὸν Ἰσραηλ, 9:21. The commandment of the (Gentile) king saved the Jews, 3 Macc. 7:20. More often the mid. or pass. is used for saving oneself, mostly by flight, 1 Macc. 2:44; 9:9; 10:83; 11:48. There are compounds with δια- and ἀνα- in 1 Macc. 6:53; 2 Macc. 11:12; Ep. Jer. 54. Whether one can save life by transgressing the Law is the theme of 4 Macc.: 5:6; 6:15, 27; 10:1, 13; 15:27. The answer is that this would be a παράνομος, a πρόσκαιρος σωτηρία, 9:4; 15:2, 8, 27; cf. 2 Macc. 7:25. The Jews released Timotheus for the salvation of their imprisoned brothers, 12:25. The Syrians or Holofernes say to Judith: σέσωκας τὴν ψυχήν σου, Jdt. 10:15, and ἥκεις εἰς σωτηρίαν 11:3. Heliodor. was robbed of all hope, all σωτηρία "assistance," 2 Macc. 3:29, 32. ὁ σῳζόμενος is the ungodly man who has saved himself but still perishes, Sir. 36:8, cf. 2 Macc. 3:38: διασωθῆναι "to escape with one's life." In each case there is an acute threat to life (up to Ep. Jer. 58).

In by far the majority of instances the ref. is to the deliverance of the righteous by God: from an unjust sentence Sus. 60 Θ, 62 LXX and Θ; from the threat of a demon, Tob. 6:18; [63] from the fiery furnace, Da. 3:88 LXX and Θ, where ἐξείλατο, ἐρρύσατο and ἐλυτρώσατο are par. to ἔσωσεν, cf. 3:95 LXX (Θ ἐξείλατο); with ref. to the child Moses, Wis. 18:5; in the crossing of the Red Sea, 1 Macc. 4:9; on the occasion of the brazen serpent, Wis. 16:7 (v. 11 διεσῴζοντο); elsewhere in OT history, Tob. 14:10 B A (twice); Sir. 46:8 διασῴζω; in the trials of the Maccabean war of independence, 1 Macc. 9:46 διασῴζω; 2 Macc. 1:11; 2:17. The hope of the righteous is ἐπὶ τὸν σῴζοντα αὐτούς, Sir. 34:13; for God σῴζει ἐν καιρῷ θλίψεως, 2:11; cf. 51:8 and 34:12 διεσώθην. God can save in war by many or by few, 1 Macc. 3:18; He is ὁ λυτρούμενος καὶ σῴζων τὸν Ἰσραηλ, 1 Macc. 4:11; διασῴζω 2 Macc. 1:25; 8:27; 4 Macc. 4:14; 17:22. The personal ref. is in some sense less prominent when salvation is ascribed to wisdom, and yet this is God's wisdom, Wis. 9:18. Wisdom saved the human race at the flood, 10:4 (B διέσωσεν). There is even less of a personal ref. at Sir. 3:1: ἐμοῦ τοῦ πατρὸς ἀκούσατε, τέκνα, καὶ οὕτως ποιήσατε, ἵνα σωθῆτε, where the author behind the pass. is in the remote background and the transl. "that it may go well with you" is in keeping with Gk. par.

In all these connections we naturally find the noun σωτηρία as well: ἡ παρ' αὐτοῦ (God) σωτηρία, Jdt. 8:17; cf. Bar. 4:22, 24, 29; σωτηρία μὲν δικαίων, ἐχθρῶν δὲ ἀπώλεια, Wis. 18:7, was expected by the Israelites on the night of the Passover; (Joshua) μέγας ἐπὶ σωτηρίᾳ ἐκλεκτῶν αὐτοῦ, Sir. 46:1; cf. 1 Macc. 5:62; 2 Macc. 11:6; 3 Macc. 6:13, 33; 7:16, 22; Wis. 16:6 (the brazen serpent as σύμβολον σωτηρίας). God is in mind as the author of salvation: καὶ εὐοδώθη σωτηρία ἐν χειρὶ αὐτοῦ (of Judas), 1 Macc. 3:6, though σωτηρία has here a more gen. ring; what is in view is the disappearance of

---

62 [These 4 lines are by Dihle].
63 B A σῴζω twice, א in one case has the noun σωτηρία instead.

the wicked from Judah, cf. 1 Macc. 4:25, where the sense of "victory," as in the OT (→ 974, 35), is suggested by the expression καὶ ἐγενήθη σωτηρία μεγάλη τῷ Ισραηλ ἐν τῇ ἡμέρᾳ ἐκείνῃ.

Though less strongly in the Wisdom lit., the decisive pt. in σῴζω and σωτηρία is not what deliverance consists of but the fact that it comes from God. Heathen gods οὔτε σῴζουσιν ἑαυτοὺς ἐκ πολέμου οὔτε ἐκ κακῶν, Ep. Jer. 49. [64] It is thus no basic shift when with the rise of the hope of the resurrection σωτηρία is no longer expected in this life. The background of the emphasis that the martyrs of 4 Macc. despised transient σωτηρία in time is eternal σωτηρία: τὴν εὐσέβειαν μᾶλλον ἠγάπησεν τὴν σῴζουσαν εἰς αἰωνίαν ζωὴν κατὰ θεόν, 4 Macc. 15:3. The same applies in Wis. 5:2: ἐκστήσονται ἐπὶ τῷ παραδόξῳ τῆς σωτηρίας of the ungodly in relation to the righteous man in his gt. παρρησία. σωτηρία means that the righteous will one day be taken or saved out of the afflictions and persecutions of earthly life. In some passages the group has an eschatological ring: οἱ σῳζόμενοι in Tob. 14:7 א are those who are saved for the last times, cf. 14:4 א: in Media there will be more σωτηρία than in Assyria and Babylonia; cf. also Bar. 4:24 (opp. of αἰχμαλωσία in Babylon) and v. 29 (alongside αἰώνιος εὐφροσύνη).

In some passages σῴζω and σωτηρία have more of a Gk. flavour than the Semitic equivalents: πλῆθος δὲ σοφῶν σωτηρία κόσμου, Wis. 6:24; οὐκ ἐπὶ σωτηρίᾳ τῆς πατρίδος, 2 Macc. 13:3. [65]

2. The Dead Sea Scrolls.

Apart from Damasc. 7:14, 21 (9:4, 10), where מלט means "saving oneself by flight," and 4:18 (6:12), where the same is true of נצל and sinful ישׁע, "to help oneself by one's own hand," the verbs translated σῴζω in LXX (נצל, מלט, פלט, פדה and ישׁע) ref. only to God's help or to the impossibility of help by any other. God's deliverance and help are seen first in events in the history of Israel: ביד מלכינו הושעתנו פעמים רבות, thou hast often "helped" us by our kings, 1 QM 11:3; בהושׁיע ישׂראל את הראשונה, when Israel was "saved" for the first time, Damasc. 5:19 (7:19); priests and Levites praise אל ישׁועות the God of "acts of deliverance," 1 QS 1:18 f. In 1 QM 18:7 we read: "Thou hast opened the gates of ישׁועותmany times." In the conflict of the children of light and those of darkness victories follow from God's ישׁועות. After the return from a victorious field the banners are to have ישׁועות אל on them, 1 QM 4:13. In the same situation the song is to be sung: "Blessed be thou, God of Israel, that hast maintained grace with the covenant and testimonies of help to the people of his redemption ישׁועה לעם פדותו, 1 QM 14:4 f. God is always with Israel להושׁיע אתכמה, "to grant you (Israel) the victory," 1 QM 10:4 f. ישׁע is regularly used in this connection.

The groups ישׁע, פלט, פדה and נצל are particularly found in relation to the outer and inner individual conflicts of the righteous both present and future. Outwardly thou hast brought the soul of the poor to safety פלט 1 QH 5:18, or redeemed פדה the soul of the poor from the fellowship of those who sought deception, 1 QH 2:32. Cf. the similar use of נצל in 2:31; 5:13. Physical threats to the intercessor and the doubt whether God will hear him cannot be separated; "Thou redeemest my soul from the hand of the oppressor," 2:35. "Thy law was concealed for a short while, to the time when thy help ישׁעכה was manifested to me," 5:11 f. Hence generally: "Thou hast kept the souls of thy redemption

---

[64] The same thought with διασῴζω "to save oneself" from robbers, or rust, Ep. Jer. 10, 57.
[65] In variants in Tob. א we sometimes find σῴζω and σωτηρία where it does not occur in A and B: ποιεῖν ἔλεος καὶ σωτηρίαν, 8:4, 17; with no par. ὅπως γένηται αὐτοῖς σωτηρία 8:5 אא (normal usage). But there is Gk. influence in the greeting ὑγιαίνων ἔλθοις καὶ σῳζόμενος, "prosperous and well," 5:17; Sir. 3:1.

פדותכה," 1 QM 14:10; this pts. already to eschatological redemption. The manifestations of God's loving-kindness are what helps, 1 QH 2:23 (ישׁע hi), cf. 9:33, where God's שׁלום is what delivers (פלט). "When affliction looms, I will praise him and rejoice at his salvation "פריתה ישׁועה1 QS 10:17, cf. 1 QH 11:23. Since it is God's help and God does not change, present and future merge for the poet. "I extol thee that thou hast redeemed פדיתה my soul from the pit and hast caused me to rise up from the sheol of perdition to the heights of eternity," 1 QH 3:19 f. On the other hand there is prayer: "Redeem פדה [the soul of thy servant] but may the wicked vanish away," 1 QH 17:20 f. [66] In relation to the eschatological age of final tribulations we read: "The covenant of God is sure for them, to save them נצל from all the snares of the pit," Damasc. 14:2 (11:12), but there is no מציל for the ungodly, 1 QM 14:11, cf. 1 Q 27 (DJD, I, 103), col. I, 4 (מלט). The gods of the heathen will not save them נצל on the day of judgment, 1 QpHab 12:13 f. In relation to the end-time it is said that God has created the righteous "to open every affliction of his soul to eternal deliverance" לישׁועת עולם 1 QH 15:16.

In relation to the last time, however, the individual rather than the divine community seems to be in the main the obj. of help. ישׁע in Damasc. 20:20 (9:43), ישׁועה in 20:35 (9:54); 1 QM 1:5; 13:13 and נצל [מבית המשׁפט] in 1 QpHab 8:2 are the terms for God's definitive salvation. Those who see and experience this are the פליטה, the "saved," Damasc. 2:11 (2:9), whereas it is constantly said of the wicked: אין שׁארית ופליטה למו, "there is for them no rest and no escape," Damasc. 2:6 f. (2:5); cf. 1 QM 1:6; 1 QS 4:14. A common word is פדות "redemption," e.g., "the people of God's redemption" in 1 QM 1:12; 14:5, similarly גורל פדותו "lot of his redemption," 1 QM 17:6 or אב'וני פדותכה"the poor of thy redemption," 1 QM 11:9. This is an eternal redemption (1 QM 1:12; 18:11) in which God's lot is established, 1 QM 15:1. The opp. is the destruction of all the peoples of iniquity, 1 QM 15:2. The expression צופים לישׁועתך , those who look for "thy salvation" (1 QH Fr 18:5), is also be taken eschatologically. Here ישׁועה means positively "salvation," as also in 1 QH 15:15, where it is par. to שׁלום (cf. 1 QM 13:13), 1 QH 12:3, where it occurs with ברכה (?), and Damasc. 20:20 (9:43) where it stands alongside צדקה.

In the Dead Sea Scrolls ישׁע and derivates are always used without indication of the need from which there is deliverance. The stress is on the positive fact that this is God's intervening to help. With other terms one often finds more precise details, or these are provided by the context. We learn that deliverance is from external oppression by the wicked and from the inner temptation which this entails: liberation from sin and guilt is denoted neither by ישׁע nor by פלט, מלט, nor פדה. Thus God's assistance in Israel's past in grouped with His help in the history of the Qumran community, His aid in the expected final battle with Belial and his hosts, and His succour in the end-time. If we catch glimpses of the coming age of salvation, e.g., life with the angels, a return of the paradisal age, the Qumran writings thus far published are very restrained in their depiction of this time. We do not find the concepts of world judgment or σωτηρία in the hereafter. Though the rise of the Essene order itself has eschatological significance, and כפר is used in this connection, ישׁע does not occur here. [67]

---

[66] As supplemented by H. Bardtke, "Der gegenwärtige Stand d. Erforschung der in Palästina neu gefundenen hbr. Hdschr.: Die Loblieder von Qumran, IV," ThLZ, 82 (1957), 346.
[67] Cf. J. V. Chamberlain, "Toward a Qumran Soteriology," Nov. Test., 3 (1959), 305-313.

3. Ethiopic Enoch.

In the parts of Eth. En. preserved in Gk. [68] σῴζω is used of the rescue of the three children of Noah from the flood in 106:16 and σωτηρία very gen. in the despairing speech of the righteous μηκέτι εἰδέναι σωτηρίαν in 103:10, where it means earthly "prosperity" acc. to the context, so that we are to transl. "and experience nothing good." [69] Elsewhere, however, the pass. ἐσώθην and the noun σωτηρία are always eschatological, e.g., σωθήσονται δίκαιοι in 1:1, cf. 99:10. The ungodly mock the righteous: ἀναστήτωσαν καὶ σωθήτωσαν "attain salvation" (this salvation is expected after death), 102:7. For the most part, however, it is said of the wicked that there is no σωτηρία or ἐλπὶς σωτηρίας for them, 5:6; 98:10, 14; 99:1; 102:1. The meaning may be seen from par. expressions, [70] and it is plain in the many antithetical sayings about the righteous: ἔσται αὐτοῖς (the ἀμίαντοι) λύσις ἁμαρτιῶν καὶ πᾶν ἔλεος καὶ εἰρήνη καὶ ἐπιείκεια, ἔσται αὐτοῖς σωτηρία, φῶς ἀγαθόν, καὶ αὐτοὶ κληρονομήσουσιν τὴν γῆν, καὶ πᾶσιν ὑμῖν τοῖς ἁμαρτωλοῖς οὐχ ὑπάρξει σωτηρία, 5:6. The broader context shows even more clearly that σωτηρία is the comprehensive final salvation of God, freedom from sin and the fulfilment of the promises of the OT; φῶς, χάρις and εἰρήνη are all found close to σωτηρία. In the similitudes of Eth. En. "to deliver" occurs once for the saving of the righteous from sinners, 48:7, [71] cf. 62:13. Of those who repent at the end of the days it is said: "They will achieve no honour before the Lord of spirits, but will be saved by his name," 50:3. To be freed from the persecutions of the wicked in a life after death, to be saved and to get salvation in the gt. world judgment, this is the content of σωτηρία, while its opposite is eternal perdition. To be righteous and to repent are the ways to σωτηρία, to eternal salvation.

4. The Testaments of the Twelve Patriarchs.

In Test. XII σῴζω and derivates occur in two different circles of thought. The one relates to the righteous individual and his temporal and eternal salvation, the other to the people Israel, sometimes the Gentiles too, and the events of the end-time. In the first circle various terms are used to express the fact that man is not alone in his war with Beliar and his spirits, but finds help, R. 3:9; Jos. 10:3. Yet σῴζω is used only once: ηὐξάμην τῷ κυρίῳ, ὅπως σωθῶ, i.e., in face of man's wickedness, L. 2:4. σωτηρία, however, is more common: τὸ δὲ πνεῦμα τῆς ἀγάπης ἐν μακροθυμίᾳ συνεργεῖ τῷ νόμῳ τοῦ θεοῦ εἰς σωτηρίαν τῶν ἀνθρώπων, G. 4:7; ἡ γὰρ κατὰ θεὸν ἀληθὴς μετάνοια... ὁδηγεῖ τὸ διαβούλιον πρὸς σωτηρίαν G. 5:7; κολλήθητε τῇ δικαιοσύνῃ τοῦ θεοῦ, καὶ ἔσται τὸ γένος ὑμῶν εἰς σωτηρίαν ἕως τοῦ αἰῶνος, D. 6:10. Many vv. show that σωτηρία includes eternal salvation and is not just immanent, A. 5:2; cf. 6:6, where we find eternal life, and B. 4:1, which ref. to the future crowns of glory. The opp. of σωτηρία in R. 5:5 is κόλασις αἰώνιος, cf. L. 4:1; G. 7:5; Zeb. 10:3, which speaks of the everlasting fire which the Lord will bring on the wicked.

If here by prayer and piety the individual with God's help and co-operation achieves temporal and eternal salvation, in the other circle of thought it is God alone who brings

---

[68] The Gk. text of the last cc. of Eth. En.: C. Bonner, "The Last Chapters of Enoch in Greek," *Studies and Documents,* 8 (1937), 32-106.
[69] The Eth. text is different acc. to G. Beer in Kautzsch Apkr. u. Pseudepigr.
[70] E.g.: "To be delivered up to the gt. curse," 97:10; "to be cast into the fiery furnace," 98:3, "to be put in the hands of the righteous and slain," 98:12, "to find a grave," 98:13, "swift destruction" 98:16, "to be swallowed up in the earth," 99:2, "to perish," 99:3.
[71] בֵּאֵל acc. to Beer, *op. cit.* (→ n. 69), *ad loc.*

salvation out of Levi and Judah for the people of Israel and sometimes for the Gentiles too. [72] Tell this to your children ὅπως τιμήσωσιν 'Ιούδα καὶ Λευὶ ὅτι ἐξ αὐτῶν ἀνατελεῖ ὑμῖν κύριος σωτηρίαν [73] τῷ 'Ισραήλ, G. 8:1; cf. Arm. text of Jos. 19:11. [74] Acc. to D. 5:10 τὸ σωτήριον κυρίου will proceed from the stem of (Judah and) Levi. In L. 20:10 Levi is promised περὶ λυτρώσεως τοῦ 'Ισραὴλ κηρύξεις. The continuation extends this beyond Israel, v. 11: καὶ διὰ σοῦ καὶ τοῦ 'Ιούδα ὀφθήσεται κύριος τοῖς ἀνθρώποις, σῴζων ἐν ἑαυτῷ πᾶν γένος ἀνθρώπων, cf. Nu. 8:2-3, where the admonition to remain united to Levi and Judah is based hereupon διὰ γὰρ τοῦ 'Ιούδα ἀνατελεῖ ἡ σωτηρία τῷ 'Ισραήλ, but the continuation runs διὰ τοῦ σκήπτρου αὐτοῦ ὀφθήσεται ὁ θεὸς [κατοικῶν ἐν ἀνθρώποις] ἐπὶ τῆς γῆς τοῦ σῶσαι τὸ γένος τοῦ 'Ισραήλ, καὶ ἐπισυνάξει δικαίους ἐκ τῶν ἐθνῶν. In S. 7:1 f. τὸ σωτήριον τοῦ θεοῦ is again expected from Levi and Judah, for the Lord will raise up a high-priest from Levi and a king from Judah οὗτος σώσει [πάντα τὰ ἔθνη καὶ] τὸ γένος τοῦ 'Ισραήλ. The coming of the σωτήριον τοῦ 'Ισραήλ brings rest for Jacob and all peoples, Jud. 22:2. A. 7:3 also speaks of a σῴζειν of Israel and all nations, but B. 10:5 has the σωτήριον αὐτοῦ, i.e., κυρίου manifested for all peoples. [75]

5. The Psalms of Solomon and 4 Esdras.

a. In Ps. Sol. we find a similar usage to that of Test. XII. σῴζω means God's intervention in the life of the righteous, with a strong emphasis on the idea of chastisement: ἔνυξέν με ὡς κέντρον ἵππου ἐπὶ τὴν γρηγόρησιν αὐτοῦ, ὁ σωτὴρ καὶ ἀντιλήπτωρ μου ἐν παντὶ καιρῷ ἔσωσέν με. ἐξομολογήσομαί σοι, ὁ θεός, ὅτι ἀντελάβου μου εἰς σωτηρίαν, 16:4 f.; ὁ βραχίων κυρίου ἔσωσεν ἡμᾶς... ἀπὸ... θανάτου ἁμαρτωλῶν, 13:2 (cf. v. 7); εἰς βοήθειαν ἤλπισα τοῦ θεοῦ Ιακωβ καὶ ἐσώθην, 15:1. The verb occurs in 6:1, the noun in 3:5; 15:6. [76] There is no trace of a special relation of σωτηρία to judgment in the hereafter. σωτηρία is not used to denote salvation for the people Israel in the two Messianic Ps. 17 and 18, but we find it in 10:8: τοῦ κυρίου ἡ σωτηρία ἐπὶ οἶκον 'Ισραὴλ εἰς εὐφροσύνην αἰώνιον, and 12:6: τοῦ κυρίου ἡ σωτηρία ἐπὶ 'Ισραὴλ παῖδα αὐτοῦ εἰς τὸν αἰῶνα. [77]

b. 4 Esr. speaks of God's intervening help with ref. to Israel's history in 14:29, then with ref. to preservation in and from earthly afflictions esp. in the last time, 14:34; 13:23;

---

[72] The MS tradition vacillates here, and the literary authenticity is even more uncertain. In what follows we adduce passages which are very probably close to the basic text. Words which Charles bracketed as Chr. interpolations are also bracketed here. Cf. A. S. van der Woude, "Die messianischen Vorstellungen d. Gemeinde v. Qumrân," Stud. Semitica Neerlandica, 3 (1957), 190-216; M. Philonenko, "Les interpolations chr. des Test. d. douze patriarches et les manuscrits de Qumrân," Cahiers de la RevHPhR, 35 (1960); M. de Jonge, "Chr. Influence in the Test. of the Twelve Patriarchs," Nov. Test., 4 (1960), 182-235.

[73] The MSS also offer σωτηρία, σωτῆρα, σωτήρ.

[74] As another tradition Charles offers for the last 4 words: ὑμῖν [ὁ ἀμνὸς τοῦ θεοῦ, ὁ αἴρων τὴν ἁμαρτίαν τοῦ κόσμου] σῴζων [πάντα τὰ ἔθνη καὶ] τὸν 'Ισραήλ.

[75] The liberation of Israel from the dominion of the Gentiles plays too small a role to constitute an essential part of the σωτηρία of Israel. But there is ref. to a resurrection of the dead, e.g., Jud. 25:4, and esp. the end of Beliar, S. 6:6; L. 18:12; Jud. 25:3; Zeb. 9:8 (MS bdg); D. 5:11; N. 8:4; A. 7:3. The positive content sometimes includes an age of gen. peace, S. 6:4; L. 18:4; Jud. 22:2; N. 8:4, also God's dwelling among men in Jerusalem, D. 5:13; B. 9:2, and the restoration of Paradise, S. 6:4 f.; L. 18:10. It is hard to say how far the Gentiles were included in the pre-Chr. form of Test. XII. πάντες οἱ λαοὶ δοξάσουσι τὸν κύριον εἰς αἰῶνας in Jud. 25:5 sounds Jewish and is probably older than expressions which speak of the salvation of all peoples or of the peoples and Israel (the peoples first).

[76] Related is the use of ῥύομαι in 4:23; 12:1; 13:4.

[77] σῴζω for the saving of natural life twice in 17:17.

9:7. But *liberare* (פרד) is normally used in this connection (7:27, 96; 12:34; 13:29), or *derelinqui* "to be left" (6:26; 9:8; 13:24, 26). 5:45 and 14:35 speak of the liberating or quickening of creation at the end of the world. But *salvari* is very common. It ref. to the destiny of man at the Last Judgment. The meaning is clear from the one *salus* ref. in 7:66. This says of the dead: *nec enim sciunt cruciamentum nec salutem* (salvation, felicity) *post mortem repromissam sibi*. If the continuation runs: *Nobis autem quid prodest, quoniam salvati salvabimur, sed tormento tormentabimur* (v. 67), it would seem that *salvari* ref. to the raising of the dead for judgment. But *salvari* is not used elsewhere in this neutral sense. It is the opp. of *perire* in 7:60; 9:15 and results in seeing God's salvation (6:25), which consists in the end of evil, a changing of the human heart etc., 6:26-28. Close by we find *iocunditas* and *requies*, 7:36, 38. *Salvari* also has positive content in 8:3: *multi quidem creati sunt, pauci autem salvabuntur;* 9:13: *inquire quomodo iusti salvabuntur. Salvari* involves a legal decision but this is taken acc. to works, 8:39; hence it is not in the strict sense a being saved, [78] but a being preserved (in life). A form of the Hbr. חיה or Aram. חיא is perhaps the basis. Comparison with the seed also leads to this version of *salvari: non ... omnia, quae seminata sunt, salvabuntur* ("will be preserved") ... *sic qui in saeculo seminati sunt, non omnes salvabuntur*, 8:41. Fig. *servari* can be used instead, 9:22. [79]

6. Josephus.

Jos. [80] mostly uses σῴζω and compounds, also σωτηρία, for "salvation" whether of life from death, a city from capture, or the state, or temple, from destruction. σῴζειν ἑαυτόν means "to save oneself" by flight in Ant., 10, 137; οἱ σῳζόμενοι are those who have saved their lives by running, Bell., 5, 550. We find ῥύομαι with σῴζομαι in Bell., 6, 119 f. Another common meaning of σῴζω is "to bless," σωτηρία "blessing"; [81] both terms are also used with ref. to recovery, Bell., 1, 580, 657 f.; Ant., 1, 211. Some expressions go further, showing the influence of the range of meaning in the Gk. Thus σῴζω is used for the preserving of the wood of the ark in Ant., 1, 95, of preservation from a new flood in 1, 97. σεσῳσμένων τῶν πραγμάτων in Bell., 4, 657 means "after relations were restored, normalised." On the entry of Vespasian the soldiers wanted τὸν μόνον δὲ σῴζειν αὐτοὺς καὶ κοσμεῖν δυνάμενον ἀπολαβεῖν "to receive him who alone could restore and exalt their reputation," Bell., 7, 67; the Romans "protect" and "uphold" the sacred laws, Bell., 5, 406. ἀποσῴζω can also denote upholding the name in Ant., 2, 6, the mind in 6, 59, and patriarchal conduct in 12, 10, cf. Ap., 1, 32. When the siege instruments caught fire, the Romans abandoned their σωτηρία, Bell., 5, 480. σωτηρία has a strictly positive sense in Bell., 1, 295, where ἐπ' ἀγαθῷ τοῦ δήμου and ἐπὶ σωτηρίᾳ τῆς πόλεως are par. ἡ τῶν ἀρχομένων σωτηρία in Bell., 7, 65 is the welfare of the subjects.

When God is the subj. the ref. is to the salvation of the people Israel and its individual members from the manifold dangers of outward life. Moses prays: βραβεύων ὁμόνοιαν καὶ εἰρήνην σῷζε τὴν πληθύν (the people) ... ἀπαθῆ τηρῶν αὐτήν, Ant., 4, 50; σῴζω has here as its content "preserving from adversities." Balak says gen. of Israel: πρόνοια γάρ ἐστιν αὐτῶν τῷ θεῷ σῴζειν ἀπὸ παντὸς κακοῦ, Ant., 4, 128. On account of drought the people flees to the temple σωθῆναι δεόμενος with the request for help or deliverance, Ant., 8, 115. With the noun: Jacob gave up hope of salvation

---

[78] So clearly S. Bar. 51:7: Those who are saved (from eternal torment) by their actions. Only in 4 Esr. 14:34 do we read: *post mortem misericordiam consequemini*.

[79] *Salvare* in the sense of divine election in 9:21; *peperci eis vix valde et salvavi mihi acinum de botro*. This might correspond to Hbr. יְשׁוֹ: The berry Israel is chosen from all berries and hence saved. The earthly salvation of Israel S. Bar. 68:3.

[80] Cf. the Jos. concordance of K. H. Rengstorf; complete for ἀνα-, ἀπο-, διασώζω, only Bell. for σῴζω, σωτηρία, σωτήρ and σωτήριος.

[81] Bell., 3, 334, 345, 358 etc.; Ant., 18, 358: σωτηρίᾳ τῆς ψυχῆς εὐεργετούμενον, he who has shown a favour by sparing life.

before his meeting with Esau, 1, 327. Moses says to the people: All that God has promised the people through Moses πρὸς σωτηρίαν καὶ τὴν ἀπαλλαγὴν τῆς δουλείας has come upon it from God, 2, 331. In the story of the manna it is said: ἐν αὐτῷ (God) γὰρ εἶναι τὴν σωτηρίαν αὐτοῦ (the people), 3, 23. God saved (διέσωσεν) Izates and his children from hopeless situations, thereby showing that the reward of piety is not lost by those who trust in Him, 20, 48. Behind the claim of a Zealot prophet on the day before the storming of the temple in 70 A.D. ὡς ὁ θεὸς ἐπὶ τὸ ἱερὸν ἀναβῆναι κελεύει δεξομένους τὰ σημεῖα τῆς σωτηρίας (Bell., 6, 285) [82] there stands in all probability eschatological σωτηρία. Whether Jos. wanted to suggest this special sense of the term, however, is very doubtful. σῴζω and σωτηρία are not theologically freighted terms in his writings.

7. Rabbinic Works and Hebrew Enoch.

a. In Rabb. works ישׁע is less common than נצל for salvation by man. In the debate whether a man should give his own life for that of another נצל is always used except in quoting or alluding to Dt. 22:27, bSanh., 73a; jSanh., 8, 9 (26c, 27). Only in the pre-NT anecdote of the son of Sim'on bShetach does תשׁועה mean "something beneficial," jSanh., 6, 5 (23b, 57). Elsewhere ישׁע and ישׁעה are used alongside גאל and גאלה for God's saving intervention. In perils the Israelite should say in a short prayer הושׁע י"י עמך, Ber., 4, 4. God is named in the benedictions after the morning shᵉma: ישׁענו לדור ודור and later גואלנו. [83] On Ex. 15:2: ויהי לי לישׁועה M. Ex. Hashira (Beshallach), 3 says: ישׁועה אתא לכל באי העולם אבל לי ביותר. ד"א ⟨היה לי ויהיה לי⟩ היה לי לשׁעבר ויהיה לי לעתיד לבא [84] "Thou art a help to all the dwellers on earth, but esp. to me. Another explanation is: 'He will be a help to me,' i.e., he was this to me in the past and will be this to me in the future." [85] Help is God's coming into the life of the righteous to give succour in daily afflictions.

To be noted esp. in the use of ישׁע and גאל with ref. to Israel's redemption from Egypt, since this often leads on to a consideration of eschatological redemption, of which the events of the exodus and the wilderness wandering are a type. [86] Both verbs occur in bSota, 11b; ישׁע in bMeg., 14a; תשׁועה in Ex. r., 18, 9 on 12:41; [87] גאל alone in Pes., 10, 5 f.; גאולה in jJoma, 3, 2 (40b, 36); M. Ex. Parasha Bo, 14 on 12:42, [88] cf. also PREl, 29, [89] ישׁועה can mean eschatological redemption with no addition: צפית לישׁועה thou hast hoped for redemption, bShab., 31a, cf. Tanch. אחרי מות, 166b; [90] bBer., 56b; cf. bMQ, 5a: ישׁועתו שׁל הקדושׁ and Midr. Qoh., 3, 9. [91] גאל and גאולה are also used quite often for Israel's redemption: גאולתן שׁל ישׁראל, jJoma, 3, 2 (40b, 36). As the use of the exodus as a type shows, liberation from the bondage of the kingdoms is an aspect of eschatological redemption too, Tg. Is. 10:27 and 52:13 ff. [92] In this sense it can be said that there is no difference

---

[82] Cf. Bell., 5, 459: σωθήσεσθαι ... τοῦτον (the temple) ὑπὸ τοῦ κατοικοῦντος ... τὸ γὰρ τέλος εἶναι τοῦ θεοῦ. Ant., 14, 470 has ῥύομαι in a similar connection.
[83] W. Stärk, Altjüd. liturgische Gebete² (1930), 6 f.
[84] Ed. H. S. Horovitz and I. A. Rabin, 126, 17 f.
[85] Cf. Winter and Wünsche, ad loc.
[86] J. Jeremias, Die Abendmahlsworte Jesu³ (1960), 197-9.
[87] On the name of Joshua it is said in bSota, 34b: God save thee יושׁיעך from the counsel of the spies.
[88] Ed. H. S. Horovitz and I. A. Rabin, 52, 9-11.
[89] Str.-B., IV, 40.
[90] Ibid., II, 139.
[91] Ibid., 141.
[92] Ibid., I, 69.

between this world and the days of the Messiah as (the ending) of bondage to (heathen) governments, bShab., 63a; bPes., 68a, cf. M. Ex. Parasha Hashira (Beshallach), 1 on Ex. 15:1.

b. The usage of Hbr. En. is related to that of the Rabb. Apart from the phrase "to free one's arm" as an act (always God), יֵשַׁע, יְשׁוּעָה and תְּשׁוּעָה occur only with ref. to the liberation of Israel from subjection to the nations; 48:1 יוֹם הַיְשׁוּעָה, 48:5 תְּשׁוּעָה גְדוֹלָה לְיִשְׂרָאֵל. In 44:10 God asks: How can I לְהוֹשִׁיעַן מִבֵּין אוּמוֹת הָעוֹלָם them, the Israelites? Cf. נצל and יֵשַׁע in 48:8 and גָאַל in 48:10.

8. Philo.

As concerns the range of the group σῴζω Philo is in the Gk. sphere, → 966, 26 f. The verb means "to save a man from danger," mid. and pass. "to save oneself," "to be saved," and the noun σωτηρία means "deliverance" from danger in war, at sea etc. σῴζω also means "to preserve," often with impersonal obj., e.g., monuments in Op. Mund., 145, character in Spec. Leg., I, 59, ταυτότης of movements, Decal., 104, sympathy, Spec. Leg., IV, 202; σῴζεσθαι is even used of ἡδονή "to persist," Leg. All., III, 189; Migr. Abr., 162. σῴζω is often used of the work of the physician, Decal., 12; Jos., 76, or the effect of means of healing, Deus Imm., 66; σῴζομαι can also mean "getting well," Sacr. AC, 123. The noun means the preservation of the state, Deus Imm., 17, cf. also σωτηρία καὶ βελτίωσις (improvement) τῶν ἀνθρωπίνων πραγμάτων, Spec. Leg., I, 197. Health is σωτηρίας αἰτία in Ebr., 140; cf. Agric., 98; σωτηρία here is "well-being," as in ἄνοσος σωτηρία, Spec. Leg., I, 224. Thus διαμονή and σωτηρία can go together, Spec. Leg., II, 195; III, 36; Ebr., 13 (— 967, 6 ff.). As in Gk. usage (→ 967, 45 f.) city officials and army officers are said to have a care for the σωτηρία of those under them, Jos., 63; Vit. Mos., I, 317. [93] Gk. in use and content (→ 968, 37 ff.) is the employment of σωτηρία in a cosmological context: παθήματα ἀέρος γεγόνασιν ἐπὶ σωτηρίᾳ τῶν μετὰ σελήνην τρεπομένου, Spec. Leg., I, 210.

As regards the religious use it should be noted first that for Philo God can save from the dangers and distresses of physical life. This is best seen in Leg. Gaj., 196, where the Jewish envoys including Philo finally say in a hopeless situation: τὰ μὲν οὖν ἐξ ἀνθρώπων ἅπαντα καὶ ἔρρει καὶ ἐρρέτω· μενέτω δὲ ἐν ταῖς ψυχαῖς ἀκαθαίρετος ἡ ἐπὶ τὸν σωτῆρα θεὸν ἐλπίς, ὃς πολλάκις ἐξ ἀμηχάνων καὶ ἀπόρων περιέσωσε τὸ ἔθνος, cf. Virt., 47-49; Vit. Cont., 86. God is σωτήρ in this sense, Sacr. AC, 70 f.; Abr., 176; Jos., 195; Vit. Cont., 87. He is this also as the One who preserves mankind, Abr., 137 (God σωτὴρ καὶ φιλάνθρωπος); Spec. Leg., I, 252, or the cosmos, Spec. Leg., II, 198. [94]

In Philo the emphasis in the use of σῴζω and derivates is on the relation between God and the spiritual: τοῦ μὲν γὰρ αἰσθητοῦ κόσμου δεσπότης καὶ εὐεργέτης ἀνείρηται (God) διὰ τοῦ κύριος καὶ θεός, τοῦ δὲ νοητοῦ ἀγαθοῦ σωτὴρ καὶ εὐεργέτης αὐτὸ μόνον, οὐχὶ δεσπότης ἢ κύριος· φίλον γὰρ τὸ σοφὸν θεῷ μᾶλλον ἢ δοῦλον, Sobr., 55. If Philo can often say that φρόνησις (Ebr., 140) or σωφροσύνη (Virt., 14; Leg. All., II, 105) or the logos, reason (Deus Imm., 129; Som., I, 112; Leg. All., III, 128 and 137) saves the soul, brings it σωτηρία, the true σωτήρ is God, who is called this as τῆς σωτηρίας αἴτιος, Spec. Leg., I, 252. Philo has stated this fundamentally in Mut. Nom., 56, where αἴσθησις, λόγος and βασιλεὺς νοῦς are impotent to do their work without God the σωτήρ. One cannot escape the power of παρανομία ἄνευ τοῦ... ἐπελπίσαι τὴν παρὰ τοῦ μόνου σωτῆρος θεοῦ βοήθειαν, Rer. Div. Her., 60. Acc. to Philo we

---

[93] Cf. Ep. Ar., 240, 281, 292.
[94] Cf. πάντων σωτηρίως ὑπὸ θεοῦ κυβερνωμένων, Jos., 149; also Praem. Poen., 34; cf. Decal., 53: τὸν κυβερνήτην, ὃς οἰκονομεῖ σωτηρίως ἀεὶ τὰ σύμπαντα, also 60, 155; Ebr., 199; Conf. Ling., 98; Abr., 70; Spec. Leg., I, 209.

will return εἰς Αἴγυπτον... τὸν ἀσελγοῦς καὶ ἀκολάστου βίου ὑπόδρομον (place of refuge), εἰ μὴ θᾶττον ὁ σωτὴρ οἶκτον (pity) λαβὼν... ξύλον γλυκαῖον (making sweet) (Ex. 15:25) εἰς τὴν ψυχὴν ἐνέβαλε φιλοπονίαν... ἐργασάμενος, Poster. C., 156. But man is not purely passive or presuppositionless in this. In a longer exposition in Migr. Abr., 122-125 Philo maintains that a small remnant of virtue (122), the bit of good, does not allow despair of παντελὴς σωτηρία. διότι οἶμαι ὁ σωτὴρ θεὸς τὸ πανακέστατον φάρμακον (panacea), τὴν ἵλεω δύναμιν, ... προτείνας ... χρῆσθαι πρὸς τὴν τῶν καμνόντων σωτηρίαν ἐπιτρέπει, 124. He who breaks free from the passions τὴν σωτηρίαν περιμένει τοῦ δεσπότου, Leg. All., II, 104, cf. 101. God gives the soul an ἀφορμὴ εἰς σωτηρίαν παντελῆ, namely, the command Gn. 12:1-3, Migr. Abr., 2: ὁ γὰρ τοῦ θεοῦ λόγος... τοῖς μὲν ἀρετῆς συγγενέσι καὶ πρὸς αὐτὴν ἀποκλίνουσιν ἀρήγει καὶ βοηθεῖ, ὡς καταφυγὴν καὶ σωτηρίαν αὐτοῖς πορίζειν παντελῆ, Som., I, 86. But also of a νοῦς which has long been going astray ἐλεῶν ὁ σωτὴρ ἐξ ἀνοδίας εἰς ὁδὸν εὐπετῶς ἂν ἀγάγοι if it is resolved on fleeing from the bad, as God can also lead man where He wishes by a call (i.e., gather the *diaspora*), Praem. Poen., 117. Not time, but only the omnipotent God can μεταβάλλειν πρὸς εὐκοσμίαν a soul accustomed to license, Spec. Leg., I, 282. If God is often called ὁ σωτήρ in Philo, it is not just because He upholds an order but also and esp. because He is the Deliverer and Helper in the assaults of passions which threaten the soul. God is active for Philo. The helping arms of divine powers are stretched out to spiritual men who want to be free of the bonds of sensuality. If Philo's allegorising entails an importing of alien Gk. thoughts into the text of the Torah, his use of the σῴζω group, esp. σωτηρία, shows that Gk. thinking was not able to destroy entirely the influence of the OT. [95] For Philo the content of σωτηρία is not that man maintains his own humanity but that in Platonic fashion he acquires a share of the divine forces by subduing the passions. The ref. to God's help permits him to speak of a παντελὴς σωτηρία which God grants: God is βοηθός to the contemplative soul ὡς χαρίσασθαι παντελῆ σωτηρίαν αὐτῇ, Ebr., 111; cf. Som., I, 86; Migr. Abr., 2 and 124; Ebr., 72. He thus adopts Gk. ideas from the golden age and the saying in Is. 11:6 ff. in such a way as to emphasise that no mortal can end the hostility between the wolf and the lamb and between all the beasts and man, ὁ δ' ἀγένητος μόνος καθαιρεῖ, ὅταν κρίνῃ τινὰς σωτηρίας ἀξίους Praem. Poen., 87.

D. σῴζω and σωτηρία in the New Testament.

I. σῴζω and σωτηρία for the Saving of Physical Life.

Apart from religious usage σῴζω and σωτηρία occur in the NT only in relation to an acute danger to physical life. The meaning "preservation" or "maintaining" of the natural constitution of a person or thing is not found. The verb and noun denote the saving of the shipwrecked crew and passengers in the account of Paul's shipwreck in Ac. 27:20, 31, 34. σῴζω has the same sense in the story of the stilling of the storm (Mt. 8:25) and that of Peter walking on the water (Mt. 14:30), both times only in Mt. The related διασῴζω occurs in Ac. 27:43 f.; 28:1, 4. [96] σῴζω means to save and succour in mortal stress in the mocking of Jesus on the cross (Mk. 15:30 and par.; Lk. 23:39; Mk. 15:31 and par.; Mt. 27:49), also Hb. 5:7: ἱκετηρίας πρὸς τὸν δυνάμενον σῴζειν αὐτὸν ἐκ θανάτου... προσενέγκας, and Jn. 12:27: πάτερ, σῶσόν με ἐκ τῆς ὥρας ταύτης, if this is meant as a par. to Gethsemane. [97] Hb. 11:7

---

[95] Cf. on this J. N. Sevenster, *Het verlossingsbegrip bij Philo*, Diss. Leiden (1936), 99 f.
[96] διασῴζω "to bring safely," Ac. 23:24.
[97] So Zn. J., Bau. J. and Bultmann J., *ad loc.*; E. Hirsch, *Das 4. Ev.* (1936), 313; R. H. Strachan, *The Fourth Gospel*[3] (1946), 256, who take σῶσόν με as a question dependent on καὶ τί εἴπω. J. H. Bernard, *Gospel acc. to St. John*, I, ICC (1928) on 3:17 also sees here "the idea of rescue from physical death."

refers to the deliverance of the righteous of the old covenant: Νῶε... κατεσκεύασεν κιβωτὸν εἰς σωτηρίαν τοῦ οἴκου αὐτοῦ, cf. 1 Pt. 3:20 (διεσώθησαν); the ref. in Ac. 7:25 and Jd. 5 is to the redemption of Israel out of Egypt.

σῴζω is often used with reference to the healing of the sick, though always in the Synoptists (→ lines 12 ff.) apart from Ac. 4:9, where this verb — followed up in v. 10 by ὑγιής — is perhaps chosen because of σωτηρία in v. 12, Ac. 14:9: ἰδὼν ὅτι ἔχει πίστιν τοῦ σωθῆναι, Jn. 11:12, where the saying of the disciples about Lazarus: εἰ κεκοίμηται, σωθήσεται, is perhaps deliberately ambiguous, [98] and Jm. 5:15.

II. σῴζω and σωτηρία in Their Theological Sense.

1. In the Synoptic Gospels.

a. In stories of healing by Jesus σῴζω [99] occurs 16 times and διασῴζω twice, Mt. 14:36; Lk. 7:3. Since Mk. 3:4 and par.: ἔξεστιν τοῖς σάββασιν... ψυχὴν σῶσαι ἢ ἀποκτεῖναι, is probably [100] based on an Aram. יחא and the twofold meaning of this ("to make alive" and "to make healthy") is echoed, this passage can be mentioned only with qualifications. Half the remaining passages have the phrase ἡ πίστις σου σέσωκέν σε, Mk. 5:34 and par.; Mk. 10:52 and par.; Lk. 7:50; 17:19. The other passages are Mk. 5:23, 28 and par.; Lk. 8:50; the summary in Mk. 6:56; Lk. 8:36. In the healings of Jesus σῴζω never refers to a single member of the body but always to the whole man, and it is especially significant in view of the important phrase "thy faith hath saved thee." The choice of the word leaves room for the view that the healing power of Jesus and the saving power of faith go beyond physical life. This is particularly clear in the fact that ἡ πίστις σου σέσωκέν σε, which perhaps finds its original locus in the story of the woman with a bloody flux, is also said to the woman who is a great sinner in Lk. 7:50 even though there has been no preceding cure in this case → 997, 8 f. Another pointer in the same direction is the fact that Mt. 8:25 puts a σῶσον before ἀπολλύμεθα as compared with the Marcan version. [101]

b. As concerns more strictly religious usage, σῴζω or σωτηρία occurs in the Benedictus (Lk. 1:68 ff.) three times, in v. 69: (ὁ θεός...) ἤγειρεν κέρας σωτηρίας ἡμῖν "a mighty salvation," which is then more closely defined in vv. 71 ff. as σωτηρία ἐξ ἐχθρῶν ἡμῶν... τοῦ δοῦναι ἡμῖν ἀφόβως ἐκ χειρὸς ἐχθρῶν ῥυσθέντας [102] λατρεύειν αὐτῷ ἐν ὁσιότητι. This remains within the bounds of OT usage except that we do not find the joy at the destruction of enemies which is common in later

---

[98] Bultmann J., ad loc. speaks of a gross misunderstanding; cf. Bau. J., ad loc.: "the usual misunderstanding." For ambiguity in Jn. cf. O. Cullmann, "Der joh. Gebrauch doppeldeutiger Ausdrücke," ThZ, 4 (1948), 360-372.

[99] Cf. θεραπεύω 33 times and ἰάομαι 15 times.

[100] Wellh. Mk., Kl. Mk., ad loc.

[101] G. Bornkamm finds here one of the points where Mt. alters the Marcan account of the stilling of the storm, G. Bornkamm, G. Barth and H. J. Held, Überlieferung u. Auslegung im Mt.² (1961), 51. That one should not press things too far in this direction may be seen from Jm. 5:15, where remission of sins is mentioned along with the σῴζειν of believing prayer and ἰαθῆτε is used for σωθῆτε in v. 16. Cf. also G. Delling, "Das Verständnis d. Wunder im NT," ZSTh, 24 (1955), 276 f.

[102] ῥύομαι (→ VI, 1002, 30 ff.) is often paired with σῴζω.

Judaism. The second part of the canticle contains an address to the later Baptist: He will go before the Lord to prepare His way and to give "experience of salvation" (→ I, 706, 35 ff.; 697, 6 ff.) to His people through the remission of their sins, 1:77.[103] A new feature may be seen here which goes beyond contemporary Judaism, for in the latter the remission of sins is not a central theme of the Messianic salvation or deliverance. A parallel in the infancy story in Mt., which is different in other respects from that of Lk., is the explanation of the name Jesus: αὐτὸς γὰρ σώσει τὸν λαὸν αὐτοῦ ἀπὸ τῶν ἁμαρτιῶν αὐτῶν, Mt. 1:21.[104]

Elsewhere in the core of the Synoptic tradition σῴζω and σωτηρία are very much in the background. The group occurs only four times in Mk. Two of these instances are in the Synoptic Apocalypse; in Q the group is not used at all. Mk. 8:35 and par. speak of the saving and losing (→ I, 394, 35 ff.) of life.[105] Even if the saving and finding of life denotes eschatological salvation, σῴζω τὴν ψυχήν is not an established linguistic term for this. The situation is rather different in Mk. 10:26 and par., where the startled disciples ask καὶ τίς δύναται σωθῆναι; σωθῆναι here takes up the preceding εἰς τὴν βασιλείαν τοῦ θεοῦ εἰσελθεῖν. This shows what groups of expressions stand alongside σῴζω, namely, "to enter into the kingdom of God," "to enter into life," "to inherit it." It also shows how rare σῴζομαι is.[106] If there are par. for this use of σωθῆναι in Eth. En. and 4 Esr. (→ 984, 6 ff.; 986, 3 ff.), it is not typical of the oldest tradition of dominical sayings, for if we assume a basic Jewish original[107] the only two passages in which it occurs on the lips of Jesus: ὁ δὲ ὑπομείνας εἰς τέλος, οὗτος σωθήσεται (Mk. 13:13 and par., cf. Mt. 10:22) and: καὶ εἰ μὴ ἐκολόβωσεν κύριος τὰς ἡμέρας, οὐκ ἂν ἐσώθη πᾶσα σάρξ (Mk. 13:20 and par.), both refer to deliverance out of the Messianic woes and into the (intermediate) Messianic kingdom. In the present version the Evangelists take the sayings to refer to eschatological salvation in the comprehensive sense.[108]

In Lk.'s Gospel σῴζω or σωτηρία occurs five times with no Synoptic parallels. In the interpretation of the parable of the sower ἵνα μὴ πιστεύσαντες σωθῶσιν (8:12) is Luke's own formulation. Elsewhere we have either material peculiar to Lk. or a special source. Lk. 13:23: εἰ ὀλίγοι οἱ σῳζόμενοι; shows in the answer the connection between σῴζομαι and entry into the kingdom of God which we have noted already in Mk. 10:26 → 991, 16 ff. Lk. 19:10: ἦλθεν γὰρ ὁ υἱὸς τοῦ ἀνθρώπου ζητῆσαι καὶ σῶσαι τὸ ἀπολωλός, offers an expression which is related to "finding" in Lk. 15:4-6, 8 f., 24, 32.[109] To be lost means death; to be saved means life in the comprehensive sense: but saving and finding takes place in the present. This is expressly stated in Lk. 19:9: σήμερον σωτηρία τῷ οἴκῳ τούτῳ ἐγένετο. The content of σωτηρία here, however, is hard to define with any precision, since the

---

103 Cf. Schl. Lk., ad loc.
104 Cf. Loh. Mt., ad loc.
105 There is variation in the Q par.: Mt. 10:39 twice has εὑρίσκω, which he also uses for Mk.'s σώσει at 16:25; Lk. 17:33 has περιποιήσασθαι or ζῳογονήσει. The latter suggests an Aram. יחא, Hbr. הִצִּיל; cf. Schl. Mt. on 16:25 and van Unnik, 182.
106 Cf. also φυγεῖν ἀπὸ τῆς μελλούσης ὀργῆς (only Mt. 3:7 and par.) or ἀπὸ τῆς κρίσεως τῆς γεέννης (Mt. 23:33), which is less prominent than "not to enter into the kingdom of God."
107 Cf. Ps. Sol. 17:44; 18:6, 9; 4 Esr. 9:7; 13:23; 14:34.
108 Cf. the use of Jl. 2:32 in Ac. 2:21 and R. 10:13.
109 There is doubt whether Lk. 9:56a and Mt. 18:11 are original.

original context of verses 7-10 is uncertain. [110] According to the present context it is decided by σῶσαι in the verse which follows. On Lk. 7:50 → 997, 8 ff.

In the Synoptists, then, σωτηρία is a future event denoting entry into the (future) kingdom of God, and yet it is also a present event in the sayings about that which was lost and is found.

2. In Paul.

In Paul σῴζω and σωτηρία are obviously limited quite intentionally to the relation between man and God. When Paul is referring to other dangers from which he asks God for deliverance, and receives this from him, he uses ῥύομαι, → VI, 1002, 38 ff. Even apart from this there are other differences in his use of σῴζω and σωτηρία. The object of salvation is not the ψυχή; it is either the whole man or his πνεῦμα (1 C. 5:5). Again, forgiveness of sins, reconciliation and justification are differentiated, though not sundered, from σωθῆναι. In R. 5:9 f. δικαιωθῆναι and καταλλαγῆναι are notably distinguished from the future σωθήσεσθαι by the νῦν and the aor. part. Primarily, then, σωτηρία is for Paul a future, eschatological term, cf. 1 C. 5:5: ἵνα τὸ πνεῦμα σωθῇ [111] ἐν τῇ ἡμέρᾳ τοῦ κυρίου, 1 C. 3:15: αὐτὸς δὲ σωθήσεται, οὕτως δὲ ὡς διὰ πυρός. Particularly plain is ἐγγύτερον ἡμῶν ἡ σωτηρία ἢ ὅτε ἐπιστεύσαμεν in R. 13:11, cf. Phil. 1:28; 2:12; 2 Th. 2:13; [112] 1 Th. 5:8 f. Since σῴζω and σωτηρία refer to the Last Judgment in these passages, both words can be used as comprehensive terms for salvation. Cf. R. 9-11, which deal with the deliverance and salvation of Israel and the Gentiles (11:11, 26; 10:9, 13), and also 2 Th. 2:10 and 2 C. 7:10, where the antonym θάνατος brings out plainly the comprehensive sense of σωτηρία. [113]

The goal of Paul's missionary endeavours is also denoted by σῴζω and σωτηρία: ἡ δέησις πρὸς τὸν θεὸν ὑπὲρ αὐτῶν εἰς σωτηρίαν, R. 10:1, ζητῶν... τὸ τῶν πολλῶν (σύμφορον), ἵνα σωθῶσιν, 1 C. 10:33. The apostle can thus speak of an active saving of men by other men: εἴ πως... σώσω τινὰς ἐξ αὐτῶν, R. 11:14; τοῖς πᾶσιν γέγονα πάντα, ἵνα πάντως τινὰς σώσω, 1 C. 9:22; τί γὰρ οἶδας, γύναι, εἰ τὸν ἄνδρα σώσεις; ἢ τί οἶδας, ἄνερ, εἰ τὴν γυναῖκα σώσεις; 1 C. 7:16, cf. λαλῆσαι ἵνα σωθῶσιν, 1 Th. 2:16. In such contexts only κερδαίνω, which is used in the same sense in Mt. 18:15 and 1 Pt. 3:1, is found alongside σῴζω, 1 C. 9:19-22. The common opposite of both terms is ἀπόλλυμι (ἀπόλλυμαι), cf. 1 C. 8:11 and Mt. 18:14. As a comprehensive expression οἱ σῳζόμενοι is also to be understood in the light of the antonym οἱ ἀπολλύμενοι, 1 C. 1:18; 2 C. 2:15; [114] the present expresses the fact that the way to σωτηρία or ἀπώλεια is not yet closed. This

---

110 Bultmann Trad., 33 f.

111 Whether the transl. should be "will be saved" or "can be saved" is something we cannot decide here.

112 Nestle prefers the reading ἀπαρχήν with B G 33 all f vg syh bo.

113 In view of the thetic and generalised formulation as compared with v. 8 f. one can hardly agree with Braumann, 33 that older material is used. The transition from a specific case to a general statement is typically Pauline.

114 This is a set expression elsewhere in the NT only at Lk. 13:23; Ac. 2:47 and in the post-apost. fathers only Mart. Pol., 17, 2. Note that neither οἱ ἀπολυτρούμενοι, -τρωθέντες, οἱ δικαιούμενοι, -ωθέντες, nor οἱ καταλλασσόμενοι, -αγέντες is a tt. for believers in Paul or the rest of the NT.

confirms yet again the fact that σῴζομαι and σωτηρία, in contrast to justification, reconciliation and redemption, refer to future, eschatological salvation. [115]

The content of the coming σωτηρία is developed by Paul along two lines. On the one hand it is salvation from approaching wrath, R. 5:9; 1 C. 3:15; 5:5; 1 Th. 5:9, cf. 1 Th. 1:10. This deliverance, as one should here render σωτηρία, takes place on the day of the Lord's judgment, 2 C. 5:10. But Paul in R. 5:9 f. could hardly have differentiated this awaited σωτηρία from accomplished δικαιωθῆναι or καταλλαγῆναι if σωτηρία had not had for him another and positive content as well. As δικαιωθῆναι and σωθήσεσθαι are distinguished in R. 5, so God's δικαιοῦν is distinguished from His δοξάζειν in R. 8:30 (→ II, 217, 17 ff.; 867, 20 ff.). This passage indicates that endowment with the divine δόξα is the positive content of σωτηρία. The context in which τῇ γὰρ ἐλπίδι ἐσώθημεν (R. 8:24) stands shows that this ἐσώθημεν in hope has ἀπολύτρωσις τοῦ σώματος ἡμῶν as its content. This is supported by the only instance of σωτήρ (→ 1016, 3 f.) in the older Pauline material: σωτῆρα ἀπεκδεχόμεθα κύριον Ἰησοῦν Χριστόν, ὃς μετασχηματίσει τὸ σῶμα τῆς ταπεινώσεως ἡμῶν ("the body of our humiliation") σύμμορφον τῷ σώματι τῆς δόξης αὐτοῦ, Phil. 3:20 f. [116] The same content of salvation lies behind the σωθησόμεθα ἐν τῇ ζωῇ αὐτοῦ of R. 5:10. If lack of the δόξα τοῦ θεοῦ (R. 3:23) is a comprehensive expression for the situation of unredeemed man, being conformed to the image of His Son (R. 8:29) is the positive content of eschatological salvation, [117] cf. 2 Th. 2:14. It should be noted, however, that in Paul this material filling out of eschatological σωτηρία is not described with the same linguistic exclusiveness as present justification. In Gl. 5:5 Paul can call δικαιοσύνη (→ II, 207, 31 ff.) the awaited eschatological blessing of salvation; [118] he can also use δικαιοσύνη and σωτηρία as parallels, → II, 207, 37 ff.: καρδίᾳ γὰρ πιστεύεται εἰς δικαιοσύνην, στόματι δὲ ὁμολογεῖται εἰς σωτηρίαν, R. 10:10. [119] σωτηρία has a rather more general ring in 2 C. 1:6: εἴτε δὲ θλιβόμεθα, ὑπὲρ τῆς ὑμῶν παρακλήσεως καὶ σωτηρίας. [120] Paul is aware that the faith of the Corinthians, and with it their eschatological salvation, will be in danger if he avoids θλίψεις, though, with παράκλησις, ὑπὲρ τῆς σωτηρίας may just have the general sense of "in your best interests," [121] cf. Phil. 1:19. [122] The expression: (τὸ εὐαγγέλιον), δι' οὗ καὶ σῴζεσθε (1 C. 15:2) shows that in Paul σωτηρία extends into the present

[115] As par. Paul uses the Synoptic "inheriting the kingdom of God," 1 C. 6:9; 15:50; Gl. 5:21, or "being made worthy of the kingdom of God," 2 Th. 1:5, or ζωὴ [αἰώνιος], opp. ὀργὴ καὶ θυμός, R. 2:7 f., θάνατος, R. 6:21-23, φθορά Gl. 6:8, cf. 2:16; R. 6:22 f.; 8:6.

[116] The singularity of σωτήρ in Pl. is hardly enough to establish the view of Bultmann Theol.⁴, 81 f. that Phil. 3:20 is referring to a common Christian belief.

[117] Cf. from the Johannine writings 1 Jn. 3:2.

[118] Oe. Gl., ad loc.; Bultmann Theol.⁴, 274; cf. also δικαίωσις ζωῆς, R. 5:18.

[119] Bultmann Theol.⁴, 313 suggests formulated baptismal confession; Braumann, 35 conjectures "that εἰς σωτηρίαν (v. 10) is a firmly developed expression to be understood in the light of baptism." Neither view is quite certain, since Paul's formulation is influenced by Dt. 30:14 (v. 8).

[120] The Hesych. text (Nestle) is probably original, cf. Wnd. 2 C., ad loc.

[121] It is not only too narrow, but incorrect, to ref. σωτηρία here only to "deliverance from every affliction," as Wnd. 2 K., ad loc. does. ῥύεσθαι in v. 10 cannot support this interpretation. The specifically eschatological-soteriological reference which Windisch rejects is in the background. Schl. K., and Kümmel in Ltzm. K., 197 both speak of eternal salvation.

[122] G. Friedrich, Der Br. an d. Philipper, NT Deutsch, 8⁹ (1962), ad loc. suggests "eternal deliverance, salvation," cf. Loh. Phil., ad loc. Mich. Ph., ad loc. does not take this expression so narrowly. As εἰς ἀγαθόν in R. 8:28 includes eschatological salvation without mentioning it, so σωτηρία does here.

too [123] → II, 732, 16 ff. This is very plain in 2 C. 6:2 ἰδοὺ νῦν ἡμέρα σωτηρίας, which makes use of Is. 49:8. [124] In R. 8:24 the eschatological content of σωτηρία is evident (→ II, 218, 8 ff.), but in the aor. ἐσώθημεν Paul may be looking back to the σωτηρία which has fundamentally come to pass with reception of the Gospel.

3. In Ephesians and Colossians.

There is some shift of Pauline usage in Eph. and Col. [125] In Eph. σωτηρία occurs only in 1:13: ὑμεῖς, ἀκούσαντες τὸν λόγον τῆς ἀληθείας, τὸ εὐαγγέλιον τῆς σωτηρίας ὑμῶν..., and σῴζω only in 2:5: χάριτί ἐστε σεσωσμένοι, and 2:8: τῇ γὰρ χάριτί ἐστε σεσωσμένοι διὰ πίστεως. Though the translation in the first reference is "the message of your salvation" or "the gospel which has saved you," [126] one cannot say with any certainty how σωτηρία is to be taken in detail. The other two passages are the only two in the NT to use the perfect σεσωσμένοι. In 2:5 the word is used in a kind of parenthesis and it supplements the statements that precede and follow. The phrase about exceeding riches (2:7) suggests what will one day be manifested as the consummation. [127] But then in 2:5-7 an accomplished salvation is distinguished from its consummation in the coming aeons, and the perfect σεσωσμένοι gives evidence of a different use of σῴζω, though with no basic distinction of content from that discussed thus far. σεσωσμένοι occurs where R. 5:1 has δικαιωθέντες. [128] The usage of Eph. and Col. differs at other points too. [129]

4. In the Pastoral Epistles.

The Past. go a step further. The expression in 2 Tm. 4:18 ὁ κύριος ... σώσει εἰς τὴν βασιλείαν αὐτοῦ τὴν ἐπουράνιον ("save into...") is already new, for elsewhere entry into the coming kingdom of God is σωτηρία itself. There is a similar distinction between the coming σωτηρία and the gift of δόξα in 2 Tm. 2:10: ἵνα καὶ αὐτοὶ σωτηρίας τύχωσιν τῆς ἐν Χριστῷ Ἰησοῦ μετὰ δόξης αἰωνίου. In two instances the order is surprising: ὃς πάντας ἀνθρώπους θέλει σωθῆναι καὶ εἰς ἐπίγνωσιν ἀληθείας ἐλθεῖν, 1 Tm. 2:4; τοῦ σώσαντος ἡμᾶς καὶ καλέσαντος

---

[123] Joh. Weiss 1 K., ad loc. sees here a timeless present of dogma, but one cannot speak of dogma in this connection.

[124] Kümmel in Ltzm. K., 205 says the νῦν denotes "the eschatological now which began with the sending of Christ."

[125] Phil. stands apart among the prison epistles.

[126] So Schlier Eph.[3] on 1:13.

[127] Cf. the context of the similar πλοῦτος τῆς δόξης τῆς κληρονομίας αὐτοῦ in 1:18, which plainly ref. to the consummation. The widespread view that God's grace to the community is displayed to "coming aeons" (H. Conzelmann. Der Br. an d. Eph., NT Deutsch, 8[9] [1962] on 2:7) or "admiring, coming archons" (Dib. Gefbr. on Eph. 2:7) or "the world as it rises over the horizon of history from the hand of the Creator" (Schlier Eph.[3] on 2:7) as personal forces, finds a present statement in v. 7, or one which ref. to the immanent course of history.

[128] But note that elsewhere in similar contexts Paul uses a perf. by way of rejection: 1 C. 4:4: δεδικαίωμαι and Phil. 3:12: τετελείωμαι.

[129] E.g., ἀπολύτρωσις, which is mentioned with remission of sins in Eph. 1:7; Col. 1:14 and is present, denoting the coming eschatological salvation in spite of Eph. 1:14; 4:30. κληρονομία, too, is used in a similar sense in Eph. 1:14, 18; Col. 3:24; there is no par. for this in the older epistles, not even Gl. 3:18. Cf. also Col. 1:13.

κλήσει ἁγίᾳ, 2 Tm. 1:9. [130] If one cannot say for certain in either passage what the precise content of σῴζω is, the word can hardly have the eschatological content of the earlier Pauline letters → 992, 11 ff. In Tt. 3:5 κατὰ τὸ αὐτοῦ ἔλεος ἔσωσεν ἡμᾶς διὰ λουτροῦ παλιγγενεσίας καὶ ἀνακαινώσεως πνεύματος ἁγίου, present σωτηρία is connected with baptism and renewal and the δικαιωθέντες of v. 7 catches up the ἔσωσεν. Reference to final eschatological redemption is not wholly absent from the Past.; it cannot be ruled out at 1 Tm. 1:15: Χριστὸς Ἰησοῦς ἦλθεν... ἁμαρτωλοὺς σῶσαι, nor at 1 Tm. 2:15: σωθήσεται διὰ τῆς τεκνογονίας. [131] An eschatological reference is also included at 2 Tm. 3:15 (ἱερὰ γράμματα) τὰ δυνάμενά σε σοφίσαι εἰς σωτηρίαν, and again at 1 Tm. 4:16: τοῦτο γὰρ ποιῶν καὶ σεαυτὸν σώσεις καὶ τοὺς ἀκούοντάς σου. [132]

5. In Hebrews, the Catholic Epistles and Acts.

a. 1 Pt. uses an astonishing variety of expressions for the coming salvation of the end-time. [133] σωτηρία is one of these. The readers are kept by faith εἰς σωτηρίαν ἑτοίμην ἀποκαλυφθῆναι ἐν καιρῷ ἐσχάτῳ (1:5). As the τέλος of their faith they will achieve the σωτηρία ψυχῶν (1:9). [134] They are to grow εἰς σωτηρίαν (2:2). As in Paul, the finished ἐλυτρώθητε (1:18) is distinguished from this coming salvation. The parallels to this σωτηρία show that its content is not deliverance in judgment but the gift of coming δόξα. The prophets enquired into this σωτηρία, 1:10. The verb σῴζω occurs only twice, at 4:18 in a quotation from Prv. 11:31 LXX (→ 972, 17 ff.) [135] and then in the much debated phrase in 3:21: ὃ καὶ ὑμᾶς ἀντίτυπον νῦν σῴζει βάπτισμα ... δι' ἀναστάσεως Ἰησοῦ Χριστοῦ. [136] Since the flood was for Judaism a parallel to the destruction of the world, baptism here carries a reference

---

130 The comm. avoid the problem of the order of the verbs in various ways. Schl. Past. on 1 Tm. 2:4 calls the second inf. a supporting statement, cf. also J. Jeremias, *Die Briefe an Tm. u. Tt., NT Deutsch,* 9⁸ (1963), ad loc. Schl. Past. on 2 Tm. 1:9 says: "Salvation is imparted to us by the fact that God has called us." "To come to a knowledge of the truth" is "a formula for Christianity in the Past," Dib. Past. on 1 Tm. 2:4. In 2 Tm. 1:9 "the lengthening out of a statement about the objective process into a further statement about present manifestation" is characteristic, *ibid.* on 2 Tm. 1:9; cf. also Wbg. Past. and Jeremias, ad loc. Wbg. Past. on 1 Tm. 2:4 ref. the σωθῆναι to the salvation effected by the first acceptance of the word of salvation.

131 Eschatological salvation from the divine wrath is suggested by the previously mentioned παράβασις, Dib. Past., *ad loc.,* so also Schl. Past., *ad loc.* It is in keeping with the contempt for the natural orders which permeates the Past. that διὰ τῆς τεκνογονίας does not ref. to Mary — so Wbg. Past., *ad loc.* and W. Lock, *The Past. Epistles,* ICC (1952), *ad loc.* — but to the fulfilment of maternal duties by Chr. wives.

132 The coming salvation is denoted expressly, however, by other expressions: ζωὴ αἰώνιος, 1 Tm. 1:16; 6:12; Tt. 3:7; ἡ ὄντως ζωή, 1 Tm. 6:19; ζωὴ καὶ ἀφθαρσία, 2 Tm. 1:10; εὑρίσκω ἔλεος, 2 Tm. 1:18; συζάω and συμβασιλεύω, 2 Tm. 2:11 f.; ὁ τῆς δικαιοσύνης στέφανος, 2 Tm. 4:8; κληρονόμοι γενηθῶμεν, Tt. 3:7.

133 1:3: ἐλπὶς ζῶσα, 1:4: κληρονομία ἄφθαρτος, 2:9: τὸ θαυμαστὸν αὐτοῦ (God's) φῶς, 3:7: (συγκληρονόμοι) χάριτος ζωῆς, 3:9: εὐλογίαν κληρονομεῖν, 3:18: προσαγαγεῖν τῷ θεῷ, 4:13: ἀποκάλυψις τῆς δόξης αὐτοῦ (θεοῦ), similarly 5:1; also 5:10: ἡ αἰώνιος αὐτοῦ δόξα, 5:4: ὁ ἀμαράντινος τῆς δόξης στέφανος.

134 This expression may presuppose acquaintance with Mk. 8:35 and par. → 991, 11 ff. In this regard note that 1 Pt. claims to be of Jewish provenance; cf. the similar observation in respect of Jm. → n. 141.

135 The word finds a par. in Mk. 13:13b, 20 and is to be seen in the light of this.

136 The omitted words, which are designed to protect baptism from misunderstanding, should not obscure the connection of the four last words of the v. with its commencement.

to the Last Judgment. The form used is σῴζει, not ἔσωσεν. In view of the imminent expectation of 1 Pt. this present encloses both present and future; these stand under the νῦν of the last time.

b. In Hb., as in 1 Pt., attention is focused on the coming salvation. This is thought to be discernibly close, 10:25. [137] Thus σωτηρία denotes coming salvation. The angels are sent διὰ τοὺς μέλλοντας κληρονομεῖν σωτηρίαν (1:14) and ἐκ δευτέρου χωρὶς ἁμαρτίας ὀφθήσεται (ὁ Χριστὸς) τοῖς αὐτὸν ἀπεκδεχομένοις εἰς σωτηρίαν (9:28). In 2:10 Christ is called ἀρχηγὸς τῆς σωτηρίας αὐτῶν. In content this σωτηρία is defined by δόξα, as in Paul → 993, 10 ff. But it is typical of Hb. that the coming σωτηρία is viewed as already present. It is true that 5:9: αἴτιος σωτηρίας αἰωνίου, suggests a salvation which is yet to come, but this is hardly true of 7:25: ὅθεν καὶ σῴζειν εἰς τὸ παντελὲς δύναται τοὺς προσερχομένους δι' αὐτοῦ τῷ θεῷ, πάντοτε ζῶν εἰς τὸ ἐντυγχάνειν ὑπὲρ αὐτῶν. Whether εἰς τὸ παντελὲς means "wholly" or "for ever" [138] is not so important as that προσέρχεσθαι takes place, and should take place, again and again (10:22); the same applies to ἐντυγχάνειν. The terminological expansion of the word σωτηρία is even plainer in 2:3: πῶς ἡμεῖς ἐκφευξόμεθα τηλικαύτης ἀμελήσαντες σωτηρίας, ἥτις ἀρχὴν λαβοῦσα λαλεῖσθαι διὰ τοῦ κυρίου ὑπὸ τῶν ἀκουσάντων εἰς ἡμᾶς ἐβεβαιώθη. Salvation itself is proclaimed by Jesus. It is not just that the message of salvation is validly brought to the readers; [139] salvation takes place with the λαλεῖσθαι. It is, however, a τηλικαύτη σωτηρία, since the salvation now proclaimed and effected is also the salvation which will one day be consummated, i.e., δόξα. The τὰ κρείσσονα καὶ ἐχόμενα σωτηρίας of Hb. 6:9 is phrased with deliberate caution. σωτηρία is the opposite of κατάρα in the preceding verse and is thus a term for coming salvation. But σωτηρία also refers to the state of the readers which can lead to this salvation. [140]

A difference from Paul (→ 992, 8 ff.) is that σῴζω and σωτηρία are used for deliverance from physical death in Hb. 5:7 and 11:7.

c. James uses only the verb σῴζω, and except at 5:5, where it means "to make well" (→ 990, 8 f.) it always denotes deliverance at the Last Judgment, εἷς ἐστιν νομοθέτης καὶ κριτής, ὁ δυνάμενος σῶσαι καὶ ἀπολέσαι, 4:12; cf. 5:20. Other passages are to be taken accordingly, 2:14: μὴ δύναται ἡ πίστις σῶσαι αὐτόν; 1:21: δέξασθε τὸν ἔμφυτον λόγον τὸν δυνάμενον σῶσαι τὰς ψυχὰς ὑμῶν. Here and in 5:20 Jm. possibly gives evidence of contact with older usage. [141]

d. In Acts σῴζω and σωτηρία occur 19 times. In the quotation from Jl. in 2:21 σωθήσεται refers to the "great and glorious day of the Lord," i.e., the Last Judgment, which is also at issue in 2:40: σώθητε ἀπὸ τῆς γενεᾶς τῆς σκολιᾶς ταύτης. The formulation of Pharisaic Christians in 15:1: ἐὰν μὴ περιτμηθῆτε... οὐ δύνασθε σωθῆναι and πιστεύομεν σωθῆναι in v. 11 also point to a salvation which has yet

---

[137] Again many expressions are used for this coming salvation: the better resurrection, 11:35, the future city, 13:14, inheritance of the promise, 6:17, the hope which lies before us, 6:18, also — in distinction from Paul — λύτρωσις, 9:12.

[138] Cf. Pr.-Bauer, s.v. (with bibl.).

[139] As against Rgg. Hb., ad loc., who in n. 85 thinks the expression is an abbreviation for ἀρχὴν τοῦ λαλεῖσθαι λαβοῦσα ἐν τῷ λαλεῖσθαι διὰ τοῦ κύριου.

[140] So Rgg. Hb., ad loc.

[141] To save the soul or life occurs only in the Synoptics (→ 991, 11 ff.). Note that acc. to 1:1 Jm. is of Jewish provenance (cf. 1 Pt. → n. 134).

to come. Elsewhere, however, σῴζω and σωτηρία are general terms for Christian salvation, 4:12; 11:14; 13:26; [142] 16:17, 30 f.; the quotation in 13:47, cf. on this R. 11:11. Again and again in Ac. the content of σωτηρία is the forgiveness of sins, 3:19, 26; 5:31; 10:43; 13:38; 22:16; 26:18. It is to be attained in the present, 22:16. Yet it is a mistake to think that σωτηρία is understood only as something present in Ac. [143] In conclusion one should take note of 2:47: οἱ σῳζόμενοι, and the Lucan formulation in the parable of the sower in Lk. 8:12: ἵνα μὴ πιστεύσαντες σωθῶσιν, cf. also the use of ἡ πίστις σου σέσωκέν σε (Lk. 7:50), which is in material peculiar to Lk. [144] Since σωτηρία embraces both present and future in Ac., there is no deliberation on its present or future character.

e. In Jude σῴζω and σωτηρία occur twice (apart from 5: the deliverance out of Egypt → 990, 2 f.): γράφειν ὑμῖν περὶ τῆς κοινῆς ἡμῶν σωτηρίας (v. 3) and σῴζετε ἐκ πυρὸς ἁρπάζοντες (v. 23). [145] Since this short letter with its many terrible examples from the OT is constantly referring to the Last Judgment, σωτηρία means deliverance in this (→ VI, 946, 8 ff.). Yet, as v. 23 shows, the basis is laid for this in the present.

f. The only instance in 2 Pt. is 3:15: τὴν τοῦ κυρίου ἡμῶν μακροθυμίαν σωτηρίαν ἡγεῖσθε. This is to the effect that the readers should use the time still available before the Last Judgment for their salvation by striving to be found blameless and undefiled.

6. In the Johannine Writings.

a. Jn. has σωτηρία only in the puzzling saying: ἡ σωτηρία ἐκ τῶν ᾽Ιουδαίων ἐστίν, 4:22. This might be understood in terms of R. 11, though this is unlikely in the context of Jn., → III, 377, 14 ff.; 589, 19 ff. [146] Apart from the striking use in 12:27 (→ 989, 43 f.) and 11:12 (→ 990, 7 ff.) the verb occurs only four times in 3:17; 5:34; 10:9; 12:47. [147] σωθῆναι is natural when the opposite κρίνειν is present, 3:17; 12:47. It should not be translated "to be saved" but "to attain or give salvation, life," in accordance with the parallels, which are always positive. The object of saving is the cosmos in 3:17; 12:47, the Jews in 5:34, the disciples in 10:9. The theological distinctiveness of John's Gospel does not come to expression in σῴζω or σωτηρία.

b. In Rev. we find only the noun σωτηρία. In all three verses (7:10; 12:10; 19:1) it is God's σωτηρία, it is with Him, it has become His cause. This is noteworthy,

---

[142] The connection between σωτηρία and God's people evident in the infancy stories in Mt. and Lk. (→ 990, 29 ff.) is perhaps also present in Ac., e.g., 13:26, where σωτηρία (in the first instance) is related to the people Israel (esp. v. 23) and stands in close proximity to the remission of sins (v. 38). One might see traces of a similar connection in 4:12 and 2:40, though these links with the situation of the primitive community are much disputed, cf. Wilckens, 187-193.

[143] Wilckens, 184; cf. rather 10:42; 17:31; 24:15 and 14:22; 26:23 etc.

[144] van Unnik, 190 f.

[145] The whole passage is textually insecure, cf. Kn. Pt. and Wnd. Kath. Br., ad loc.

[146] So the comm. Bernard's view (op. cit. → n. 97, ad loc.) that the ref. is to the descent of the Messiah from the tribe of Judah is hardly possible in Jn.

[147] In place of it we find phrases like "to have everlasting life" (3:15, 16, 36 etc.), "to see life" (3:36), "to see the kingdom of God" (3:3), and many metaphors.

for elsewhere in the NT and post-apostolic fathers, when a genitive is used at all, it is always an objective genitive. In all the passages σωτηρία has the familiar OT nuance (→ 976, 7, 16) of "victory," [148] and in all there is confession in hymnal style that σωτηρία belongs to God and has become His, 12:10. In 7:10 the "overcomers" with their ἡ σωτηρία τῷ θεῷ ἡμῶν... καὶ τῷ ἀρνίῳ confess that their victory is God's. In 12:10 there is proclaimed in heaven that after the fall of the accuser the victory, the power and the kingdom have become God's. The same applies in 19:1 after the fall of Babylon.

E. σῴζω and σωτηρία in the Post-Apostolic Fathers.

The only common compound is διασῴζω, used only for the salvation of physical life. [149] The simple form occurs 10 times in 1 Cl., [150] once (16, 16) in a quotation from Ps. 22. It occurs 3 times in Ign., only once in Did. and Pol. (1, 3 quoting Eph. 2:5, 8), 3 times in Mart. Pol., 2 in Dg., and often in 2 Cl. and Herm. The noun σωτηρία occurs 3 times in 1 Cl. and another 2 in quotations, [151] only once in Ign., 3 times in Barn. (including an OT quotation at 14, 8), 4 in Mart. Pol., 4 each in 2 Cl. and Herm., not at all in Did., Pol., Dg.

In 1 Cl. σῴζω is also used for "well-being," "preservation." All the members of the body work together εἰς τὸ σῴζεσθαι ὅλον τὸ σῶμα, 1 Cl., 37, 5, and so too in 38:1: σῳζέσθω οὖν ἡμῶν ὅλον τὸ σῶμα ἐν Χριστῷ Ἰησοῦ, cf. Pol., 11, 4. The final greeting in Barn., 21, 9 has σῴζεσθε in the sense of "fare you well." [152] Probably 1 Cl., 2, 4: εἰς τὸ σῴζεσθαι... τὸν ἀριθμὸν τῶν ἐκλεκτῶν αὐτοῦ also ref. to keeping up the number rather than their deliverance in the Last Judgment. [153] In the gt. prayer of 1 Cl., 59, 4 τοὺς ἐν θλίψει ἡμῶν σῶσον ("keep" and "save") the context and Jewish and Chr. liturgical tradition again support a ref. to physical life. [154] Barn., 5, 10 also has the preservation of earthly life in view. This is true again in the citing of OT stories in 1 Cl., 7, 6 f.; 11, 1; 12, 1; Barn., 12, 3 and 7. But the past history of Israel is a type of the destiny of the Chr. community, and the deliverance of the earthly life of the former righteous from danger and destruction prefigures the salvation of Christians from eternal ruin.

The use of the two words σῴζω and σωτηρία in the theological sense of "salvation" varies a good deal. It is least common in 1 Cl., where σῴζω, apart from an OT quotation, occurs only in 21, 8 and 58, 2, and σωτηρία, apart from quotations, occurs only in 7, 4 and 45, 1. It is most common in 2 Cl. ψυχή is the obj. only in Barn., 19, 10 and Herm. s., 6, 1, 1, ἡ ζωὴ ὑμῶν in Herm. v., 3, 3, 5, and everywhere else man in gen. The subj. is Christ in 1 Cl., 7, 4; 58, 2; Ign. Sm., 2, 1; Mart. Pol., 17, 2; 2 Cl., 1, 4 etc., in addition man's conduct in 1 Cl., 21, 8, [155] so too in the phrase τὰ ἀνήκοντα εἰς σωτηρίαν in 1 Cl., 45, 1; Barn., 17, 1, cf. 4, 1; Herm. v., 2, 3, 2. In Herm. esp. there is ref. to things which can "save" man, cf. m., 10, 1, 2 f.; 2, 1 and 4; s., 6, 5, 7 (λύπη and τρυφαί etc.), and Herm. s., 6, 1, 1: the ἐντολαί are καλαὶ καὶ δυναταὶ καὶ ἱλαραὶ καὶ ἔνδοξοι

---

148 R. H. Charles, *The Rev. of St. John*, I, ICC (1920) on 7:10; 12:10, but cf. Loh. Apk., on 7:10.

149 Mart. Pol., 8, 2; 1 Cl., 9, 4; 12, 5 and 6 (both quotations).

150 At 1 Cl., 59, 3 καὶ σῴζοντα should be cut out on strophic grounds (Bihlmeyer-Schneemelcher and J. A. Fischer, *Die Apost. Väter* [1958], ad loc.; cf. also Kn. Cl., ad loc.).

151 At 1 Cl., 15, 6 one should read ἐν σωτηρίῳ for ἐν σωτηρίᾳ in deviation from LXX (Bihlmeyer-Schneemelcher and Fischer).

152 The real blessing then follows: ὁ κύριος τῆς δόξης... μετὰ τοῦ πνεύματος ὑμῶν.

153 Both Kn. Cl. and Fischer, ad loc. transl. "to save." If the no. is kept up all will be saved, but the term "the number" suggests that the true sense of σῴζεσθαι is "to keep up," cf. Ign. Sm., 11, 2; Pol., 11, 4.

154 Cf. Kn. Cl., ad loc. for examples.

155 σῴζων can have here the broad sense of "salutary" as in 1 Tm. 4:8.

καὶ δυνάμεναι σῶσαι ψυχὴν ἀνθρώπου. Nowhere in the post-apost. fathers are we told precisely from what there is salvation, though the Last Judgment is commonly in view. [156] This means that there is less stress on the aspect of "deliverance." One may see this also from the many parallels, esp. ζωή: ἀκριβεύεσθαι οὖν ὀφείλομεν, ἀδελφοί, περὶ τῆς σωτηρίας ἡμῶν, ἵνα μὴ ὁ πονηρὸς παρείσδυσιν πλάνης ποιήσας ἐν ἡμῖν ἐκσφενδονήσῃ ἡμᾶς ἀπὸ τῆς ζωῆς ἡμῶν, Barn. 2, 10, cf. 1 Cl., 48, 2; Barn., 1, 4 and 6; 6, 17; 8, 5; 11, 11; Ign. Eph., 18, 1; 2 Cl., 19, 1; Herm. m., 3, 3. Consideration of Christ's sufferings does not unconditionally suggest σῴζω, Barn., 7, 2. Most common in Ign. is θεοῦ (ἐπι)τυχεῖν (Eph., 10, 1) or ἐν κλήρῳ (e.g., Ἐφεσίων) εὑρεθῆναι (11, 2, cf. Tr., 12, 3), and accompanying terms are ἀθανασία and ἀφθαρσία.

How far σῴζω and σωτηρία ref. to the coming salvation of the consummation and how far to the present is not always clear. The one aor. ἐσώθησαν in relation to the OT prophets in Ign. Phld., 5, 2 does not prove much as concerns Ign. For the coming salvation he hopes to attain through martyrdom he uses θεοῦ (ἐπι)τυχεῖν and he has many other expressions for present salvation in Eph., 11, 1; Mg., 8, 1; Eph., 12, 1. Barn. combines σῴζω with thoughts of the future: ἐλπίζων σωθῆναι, 1, 3; ὁ ποθῶν σωθῆναι, 16, 10 cf. 2, 10. [157] Only for 2 Cl. is σωθῆναι a present fact: ἀπολλυμένους ἡμᾶς ἔσωσεν, 1, 4, also 1, 7; 2, 7; 3, 3; 9, 2; cf. 8, 2. But this does not rule out a coming salvation: μὴ μόνον οὖν αὐτὸν καλῶμεν κύριον· οὐ γὰρ τοῦτο σώσει ἡμᾶς, 4, 1; here it should be noted that the allusion to Mt. 7:21 which follows replaces the NT "entry into the kingdom of heaven" by σωθήσεται. The phrase ἵνα εἰς τέλος σωθῶμεν in 19, 3 also refers to the coming final redemption. [158] In Herm. we find ἡ ζωὴ ὑμῶν διὰ ὕδατος ἐσώθη καὶ σωθήσεται, v., 3, 3, 5, also μετενόησαν καὶ ἐσώθησαν, s., 8, 6, 1; 9, 26, 8. Baptism brings the remission of sins, but even those who are built up into the tower again by fresh repentance can be removed once more, s., 8, 7, 5. In Herm., then, the ref. to the final consummation predominates in σῴζω and the noun (found only in the expression ἔχειν σωτηρίαν). Par. to σωθῆναι are expressions like ζῆν τῷ θεῷ in m., 2, 6 etc. "to be written in the books (of the living etc.)" in s., 2, 9; 5, 3, 2; 9, 24, 4, "to receive the promises" in v., 2, 2, 6 etc. In Herm. σωθῆναι is best transl. by "to be saved."

F. σῴζω and σωτηρία in Gnosticism.

1. The basic view of Gnosticism is that in this world of passions and astrologically understood forces of destiny a portion of wholly transcendent divine being is stupefied and trapped with no hope of liberating itself from this position. Only an intervention, a "call" from the divine world, can free the imprisoned divine portions from the ungodly world. This provides the starting-point for the use of words of deliverance. It does so in three circles of thought: The divine is snatched away from the power of destiny, it is liberated from the sway of the passions, and it is awakened out of stupefaction. Nevertheless σῴζω occurs only seldom. Terms like ἐλευθερόω, ἀπαλλάσσω, ῥύομαι, μετατίθημι, φεύγω etc. are used for the liberation from the powers of destiny. σῴζω with

---

[156] σῴζω is most closely related to the Last Judgment in Barn., 19, 10: μνησθήσῃ ἡμέραν κρίσεως νυκτὸς καὶ ἡμέρας, καὶ ἐκζητήσεις ... τὰ πρόσωπα τῶν ἁγίων, ἢ διὰ λόγου κοπιῶν καὶ πορευόμενος εἰς τὸ παρακαλέσαι καὶ μελετῶν εἰς τὸ σῶσαι ψυχὴν τῷ λόγῳ. Cf. on the other hand the avoidance of σωθῆναι in 1 Cl., 28, 1 and τόν σε λυτρωσάμενον ἐκ θανάτου in Barn., 19, 2.

[157] Cf. Barn., 6, 17, where οὕτως οὖν καὶ ἡμεῖς τῇ πίστει τῆς ἐπαγγελίας καὶ τῷ λόγῳ ζωοποιούμενοι is present, but acc. to what follows the main clause ζήσομεν κατακυριεύοντες τῆς γῆς expresses the future consummation.

[158] Not to be translated with Kn. Cl., ad loc. "to be saved for the end" but either "at the end, finally" or "entirely, totally" (as Jn. 13:1).

details occurs only [159] in Cl. Al. Exc. Theod., 73, 1: "to keep" from the stars; Ev. Phil. [160] 9 (101, 2 and 12 f.): "to save" from imprisonment by robbers; Nature of Archons, [161] 141, 2. 11 f. "to deliver" from the hands of the lawless, and Cl. Al. Exc. Theod., 84: ἀνασῴζεσθαι from the jaws of lions. σῴζομαι is hardly used for liberation from the passions. [162] There is deliverance from drunkenness and stupefaction only in Apocr. Joh., [163] 69, 10-12 (→ 1001, 11 ff.). σῴζω and σωτηρία normally occur without further information on what the deliverance is from; in Gnosticism they are gen. and positive concepts denoting salvation and achieving salvation. Thus it is said of Simon Magus: *quapropter et ipsum venisse, uti eam (Helenam) assumeret primam et liberaret eam a vinculis, hominibus autem salutem praestaret per suam agnitionem ... secundum enim ipsius gratiam salvari homines,* Iren. Haer., I, 23, 3. In the account of Carpocrates in Iren. Haer., I, 25, 4 we read: ὅταν δὲ μηδὲν λείπῃ (sc. in sins committed), τότε ἐλευθερωθεῖσαν ἀπαλλαγῆναι (sc. the soul) πρὸς ... τὸν ... θεόν, καὶ οὕτως σωθήσεσθαι πάσας τὰς ψυχάς. In the NT expositions of the Naassene Sermon regeneration is the presupposition of salvation: οὐ δύναται οὖν, φησί, σωθῆναι ὁ τέλειος ἄνθρωπος, ἐὰν μὴ ἀναγεννηθῇ διὰ ταύτης εἰσελθὼν τῆς πύλης, Hipp. Ref., V, 8, 21.

2. σῴζω and σωτηρία are more common in Valentinianism. The description of Gnostics as (φύσει) σῳζόμενοι seems to be peculiar to this branch of Gnosticism, [164] without φύσει Heracleon, cf. Cl. Al. Strom., IV, 11, 71, 3 and 72, 4; Exc. Theod., 63, 2; Iren. Haer., I, 3, 5 (quotation), also Corp. Herm., 11, 5; with φύσει Cl. Al. Exc. Theod., 56, 3. The verb and noun play here a greater part gen., esp. in describing the blessed final state of both pneumatics and psychics. The Johannine "ripe for harvest" is for Heracleon an image of being ripe πρὸς σωτηρίαν, Orig. Comm. in Joh., 13, 44 on 4:36, and it is applied to psychics too, who are found ἔξω τοῦ πληρώματος ... ἐν σωτηρίᾳ in 10, 33 on 2:15. Cl. Al. Exc. Theod., 61, 8 says of the pneumatic that it ὑπὲρ ἐκεῖνα (i.e., the psychic) σῴζεται. This ὑπέρ denotes a higher degree of felicity. Exc. Theod., 58, 1 ascribes to Jesus the same ἀνασῴζειν regarding both the pneumatic and the psychic: ὁ μέγας ἀγωνιστὴς Ἰησοῦς Χριστός, ἐν ἑαυτῷ δυνάμει τὴν ἐκκλησίαν ἀναλαβών, τὸ ἐκλεκτὸν καὶ τὸ κλητὸν (the pneumatic and the psychic) ... ἀνέσωσεν καὶ ἀνήνεγκεν ἅπερ ἀνέλαβεν, καὶ δι' αὐτῶν τὰ τούτοις ὁμοούσια. [165] But a distinction is made between the two classes of men not only in their final state — the pleroma or ogdoad — but also in the way in which they attain salvation: σοφίας μὲν γὰρ τὸ πνευματικὸν δεῖται, μεγέθους δὲ τὸ ψυχικόν, Cl. Al. Exc. Theod., 61, 2. In relation to the psychics there is σῴζω in a stricter sense: the pneumatic must be "fashioned," but

---

[159] Cf. W. Völker, *Quellen z. Gesch. d. chr. Gnosis* (1932); Corp. Herm., 1 and 7; Act. Thom.; also Gnostic writings of the Copt. Pap. Berolinensis, 8502, ed. W. Till, TU, 60 (1955); *Coptic Gnostic Pap. in the Coptic Museum at Old Cairo,* I, ed. P. Labib (1956); Ev. Veritatis, ed. and transl. P. Malinine, H. C. Puech, G. Quispel (1956); Ev. Thom., ed. A. Guillaumont, H. C. Puech, G. Quispel *et al.* (1959). The Copt. works are cited acc. to p. and line of the Coptic Text, Ev. Phil. acc. to the enumeration of H. M. Schenke, "Das Ev. nach Phil.: Ein Ev. d. Valentinianer aus dem Funde v. Nag Hamadi," ThLZ, 84 (1959), 5-26 and J. Leipoldt and H. M. Schenke, "Kpt.-gnost. Schr. aus den Pap.-Codices v. Nag-Hamadi," *Theol. Forschung,* 20 (1960). 38-65. Quotations from Lidz. Joh. and Ginza are acc. to p. and line in Lidzbarski.

[160] Ed. Labib, *op. cit.,* Plate 99, 29-134, 19; transl. Schenke, *op. cit.*

[161] Ed. Labib, Plate 134, 20-145, 23; transl. H. M. Schenke, "Das Wesen d. Archonten. Eine gnost. Originalschr. aus dem Funde v. Nag-Hamadi," ThLZ, 83 (1958), 661-670.

[162] Rather evil spirits are "expelled" or "ejected" or "blown" from the soul, they "flow out," "remove themselves," "are consumed," the "root of evil is torn out" etc.

[163] Ed. Labib, 47-80, 9, ed. and transl. Till, *op. cit.,* 33-51, 79-145.

[164] Cf. Al. Strom., V, 1, 3, 3 distinguishes the Valentinian φύσει σῳζόμενος from the φύσει πιστὸν καὶ ἐκλεκτὸν εἶναι of Basilides, though cf. IV, 12, 89, 4.

[165] Cf. Iren. Haer., I, 6, 1: ὅπως αὐτὸ (i.e., the psychic) σώσῃ (sc. the σωτήρ).

the psychic needs a μετάθεσις ... ἐκ δουλείας εἰς ἐλευθερίαν (57), it is raised again (61, 7).

3. In the Gnostic Coptica there are two terms for σῴζω or σωτηρία: ΝΟΥ2Μ̄ and ΟΥΧΑΪ [166] The former occurs with an indication of what there is deliverance from, the power of robbers in Ev. Phil. 9 (101, 2), the hands of the archons, Nature of Archons, 141, 2, the hands of the lawless, 141, 12. The latter has more of the positive sense of salvation. For the difference between them cf. esp. Apocr. Joh. 69, 10-13: "until they are saved from the inability to know (ΝΟΥ2Μ̄), attain to knowledge (and) are thus perfected and saved (ΟΥΧΑΪΤΕ)." In the same work then (65, 5 f.) ΟΥΧΑΪ (with no indication from what) and τέλειος occur together, and in 67, 3 the same word is caught up from 66, 17 with "to live," while in 70, 6-8 the par. is "not to enter into further flesh any more." [167] This terminology shows a striking kinship to that in the Gk. sources, where various words of liberation are used for snatching from the power of cosmic forces, but σῴζω is rare, relating only to the final state. Hence ΟΥΧΑΪ goes back to σῴζω, ΝΟΥ2Μ̄ to, e.g., ἐλευθερόω or ἀπαλλάσσω.

4. In Act. Thom. the dynamic element which σῴζω can have is esp. emphasised. In Act. Thom. this is connected on the one hand with an unmistakable ecclesiastical tendency also expressed in non-Gnostic terms like remission of sins, atonement and judge (God), while on the other it is connected with a powerful sacramental impulse acc. to which the sacrament itself saves. Judas Thomas tells the king's son he has the power to say to the king, his father, that he should "give life to" or "bless" (σῶσαι) those whom he wills, but he himself cannot save (σῶσαι) his soul from death and judgment, while the apostle finds refuge with "the living God, the σωτήρ of kings and potentates, who is the judge of all," Act. Thom. 139. All sacraments (baptism, unction and the eucharist) relate to σωτηρία; in baptism the δύναμις τῆς σωτηρίας comes and resides in the water, 52. The oil of anointing proclaims (εὐαγγελίζομαι) to men their σωτηρία and shows them light in the darkness, while the anointing itself is for the remission of sins, the warding off of the adversary and the σωτηρία of their souls, 157. The eucharist is preceded by the prayer: ... γένηται οὖν ἡμῖν τὸ σῶμά σου σωτηρία καὶ τὸ αἷμά σου εἰς ἄφεσιν ἁμαρτιῶν, with the ending: ἀναβιώσαντες ζήσωμεν καὶ στῶμεν πρὸ σοῦ ἐν κρίσει δικαίᾳ, 158. The eucharist itself is accompanied by the words: γενέσθω ὑμῖν ἡ εὐχαριστία αὕτη εἰς σωτηρίαν καὶ χαρὰν καὶ ὑγίειαν τῶν ψυχῶν ὑμῶν, 158. σωτηρία here has the positive sense of "salvation." The many miracles performed by Jesus' "twin" Judas Thomas are reflections of the might of Jesus which conquers and saves that of the "powers."

5. In the colourful Mandaean literature redemption words play a big part. The most common is פרק "to redeem," "to liberate," פירקא "redemption," "liberation," "redeemer," פורקאנא "redemption," "liberation." פארוקא and מפארקאנא are other terms for "deliverer," "redeemer." We also find words for healing, benefit, salvation. [168] It hardly seems possible to correlate the various words with σῴζω, ἐλευθερόω, λυτρόω and the corresponding nouns. Lidz. Joh., 67, 10-14 is an example: "When they (the wicked) unleash great sickness on thee, who will be thy physician? When the wicked chain thee in their castle, who will be thy liberator? When they set nets for thee on thy way, who will be thy redeemer? Who will be thy redeemer, who will be thy deliverer?" In 69, 3-6 it is not a "deliverer" who comes, but "the messenger, the helper"; he destroyed their guardhouses and breached their fortress and gives consolation: "A man whose name is written

---

[166] ⲤⲰⲦⲈ, which is common in Ev. Phil.: 9 (101, 2 f.); 47 (110, 14); 76 (117, 26); 81 (119, 2 f.) = Gk. ἀπολυτρόω, cf. 125 (133, 29) to redeem prisoners, though there is allusion to Mt. 1:21 in its use in 47 (110, 14). The word also occurs in Ev. Veritatis, 24, 6.

[167] The noun ⲞⲨⲬⲈⲈⲒ in Ev. Veritatis 20:8; 31:18; 35:1 corresponds to Gk. σωτηρία, but the precise content is uncertain.

[168] [Rudolph].

in the house of the great life will not be bound in the dwelling of sinners," 69, 23-25. The special feature of the Mandaean works in this context, however, does not lie in these ideas, for which there are par. in other Gnostic works, but in the fact that individual death and the end of the world bring redemption here. A common expression is "to the day of judgment, to the hour, the hours of redemption," Lidz. Ginza R., 16, 30 f.; 35, 12; 40, 31 f.; 60, 38 f. etc. The connection between death and redemption is esp. plain in the gt. passage on Adam's death in Lidz. Ginza L, 430, 12-18, where the "house of the gt. life" sends a messenger to Adam "to redeem him and to fetch him out of the body, out of this world, out of the stocks... to redeem him and fetch him out of the dirty, stinking, perishing, corruptible body, the rending lion."

G. New Testament σωτηρία in Its Relation to Later Judaism, the Greek World, and Gnosticism.

NT σωτηρία does not refer to earthly relationships. Its content is not, as in the Greek understanding, well-being, health of body and soul. Nor is it the earthly liberation of the people of God from the heathen yoke, as in Judaism. It does not relate to any circumstances as such. It denotes neither healing in a religious sense, [169] nor life, [170] nor liberation from satanic or demonic power. [171] It has to do solely with man's relationship to God. Hence salvation is accomplished neither by man's self-mastery through autonomous reason (as in Greek philosophy, → 968, 15 ff.), nor by perfect contrition, i.e., the absolute acceptance of the heteronomously understood Torah (as in Pharisaism, → 986, 12 ff.). No man can effect salvation for himself. In this respect Gnosticism (→ 999, 31 ff.) and the mystery religions (→ 969, 9 ff.) agree with the judgment of the NT. But the reasons are different. The argument in Gnosticism is that the divine in man cannot mingle with matter (→ 999, 36 ff.), whereas the thesis of the NT is that man's relation to God has been irreparably shattered by sin (→ I, 295, 9 ff.). In both Gnosticism and the NT a "call" brings salvation. But in the former this call awakens the sleeping and bemused divine self in man to self-comprehension, separating it from the powers of matter and fate (→ 999, 37 ff.); in the mystery religions a magical sacramental act mediates and guarantees life after death by reproducing the story of a mythical God (→ 969, 29 ff.). In the NT, however, only the event of the historical coming, suffering and resurrection of Jesus of Nazareth brings salvation from God's wrath by the forgiveness of sins (→ 993, 3 ff.). The universal character of the subjection to wrath, the impossibility of escaping by obedience to the Torah, and the necessity of the remission of sins distinguish NT σωτηρία from that found in Judaism, the Greek world, and Gnosticism. NT salvation is offered and comes to man in the word of the cross (1 C. 1:21), in the Gospel of σωτηρία (Eph. 1:13); this Gospel as preached is δύναμις θεοῦ εἰς σωτηρίαν (R. 1:16; cf. Hb. 2:3 f.). Hence it may be said that the preacher of the Gospel saves others (→ 992, 24 ff.).

Salvation, the removing of sin as guilt, is accomplished with no help from man. Yet man is not just passive in relation to this message. He can accept it or reject it. This is the point in Phil. 2:12 f., where the readers are summoned in an expression unique in the NT to "accomplish" their σωτηρία, though only because it is God who

---

[169] So Harnack, 129-150.
[170] Wagner consistently regards this as the content of σῴζω, σωτηρία and σωτήρ in the NT. His view is not wrong in itself, but not precise enough.
[171] So Holtzmann, I, 299 f.

effects the will and fulfilment. Baptism, then, is not a sacrament which works magically like consecration in the mystery religions; it is the seal of faith.

In Pharisaic Judaism salvation is future. For Qumran God has been fashioning in the history of the order the salvation which appears through the Messianic war and the destruction of Belial as an enhanced continuation of the present (→ 983, 34 ff.). In Gnosticism present and future are differentiated (→ 1000, 6 ff.); basically the Gnostics have salvation already, they are "the saved," but only the consummation brings entry into the pleroma. This is total separation from this world and from that in it which still clings to the divine core of being as an alien component. In the NT, too, salvation is both present and future (→ 992, 3 ff.; 993, 21 ff.). But the emphasis in both σῴζω and σωτηρία is on the future. With the saving event of the cross and resurrection of Christ the new aeon has dawned; Christ the first-fruits has already entered into being in δόξα. Through faith and baptism His people have been drawn into His death and resurrection, but their life is still hid with Christ in God, Col. 3:3. Hence expectant hope is fixed on the day of σωτηρία when all things will be made manifest before God and the body of humiliation will be fashioned according to the glorious body of the Risen Lord. Then the last enemy with all his powers will be destroyed, 1 C. 15:24-26. The creature will also be set free from the bondage of futility, R. 8:19-22. The expectation of Greek longing for the golden age and Jewish hope of the earthly appearing of the Messiah will only then become a reality in a new creation.

Yet the term σωτηρία is still restricted to man and his relation to God. Negatively its content is deliverance from the wrath to come, → 993, 4 ff. Positively it is the attainment of δόξα, → 993, 6 ff. Either way this content is fixed by the preaching, suffering and resurrection of Jesus. Both aspects appear in varying proportion in primitive Christian writings. But the positive side, which is especially prominent in Paul, is often weakened into a general concept of salvation, life, or blessedness, → 997, 1 ff.; 997, 17 ff.; 999, 29.

† σωτήρ.

Contents: A. σωτήρ in the Greek World: 1. Range of Meaning; 2. Gods as σωτῆρες; 3. Men as σωτῆρες: a. σωτήρ as Helper, Saver of Life, Physician; b. Philosophers as σωτῆρες; c. Statesmen as σωτῆρες; d. σωτήρ in the Hellenistic Ruler Cult; e. σωτήρ in Emperor Worship; f. σωτήρ and the Golden Age. B. σωτήρ in the Old Testament.

σ ω τ ή ρ . In gen.: P. Wendland, "Soter," ZNW, 5 (1904), 335-353; H. Lietzmann, Der Weltheiland (1909), Kleine Schr., I (1958), 25-62; F. Dölger, "Ichthys. Das Fischsymbol in frühchr. Zeit, I," Röm. Quartalschr., Suppl. 17, 1 (1910), 406-422; W. Bousset, Kyrios Christos² (1921), 240-245; Deissmann LO, 262, 311 f.; E. Norden, Die Geburt des Kindes (1924), 51-8; P. Feine, Der Ap. Pls. (1927), 437-517; H. Linssen, "θεὸς σωτήρ," Jbch. f. Liturgiewissenschaft, 8 (1928), 1-75; F. Büchsel, Joh. u. d. hell. Synkretismus (1928), 44-6; J. H. Bernard, Gospel acc. to St. John, I, ICC (1928) on 4:42; W. Staerk, Soter, I (1933), II ("Die Erlösererwartung in d. östlichen Religionen") (1938); H. Windisch, "Zur Christologie d. Past.," ZNW, 34 (1935), 213-238; Dib. Past. on 2 Tm. 1:10; K. Prümm, "Herrscherkult u. NT," Biblica, 9 (1928), 3-25, 129-142, 289-301; V. Taylor, The Names of Jesus (1953), 107-109; O. Cullmann, Die Christologie d. NT³ (1963), 244-252. A.: O. Höfer, Art. "Soteira," Roscher, IV, 1236-1247; also Art. "Soter," ibid., 1247-1272; W. Otto, "Soter," Hermes, 45 (1910), 448-460; F. Blumenthal, "Der ägyptische Kaiserkult," APF, 5 (1913), 317-345; G. P. Wetter, Der Sohn Gottes (1916), 36-42; Meyer Ursprung, III, 390-7; J. Kaerst, Gesch. d. Hell., II² (1926), 309-319; J. Mühl, Die antike Menschheitsidee (1928), 52-54, 79-82; F. Dornseiff, Art. "σωτήρ," Pauly-W., 3a (1929), 1211-1221; G. Herzog-Hauser, "Die Evangelien-

C. σωτήρ in Later Judaism. D. σωτήρ in the New Testament: 1. The Occurrence of σωτήρ in the New Testament; 2. σωτήρ in the New Testament apart from the Pastoral Epistles and 2 Peter; 3. σωτήρ in the Pastoral Epistles and 2 Peter. E. σωτήρ in the Post-Apostolic Fathers. F. σωτήρ in Gnosticism. G. The Primitive Christian Use of σωτήρ.

A. σωτήρ in the Greek World.

1. Range of Meaning.

σωτήρ is a nomen agentis formed from the stem σω- with the syllable -τήρ. Basically, then, it embraces the whole scale of meaning of σῴζω and σωτηρία. Only rarely, however, is there ref. to an impersonal σωτήρ, e.g., the river which rescued pursued from pursuers by rising suddenly, Hdt., VIII, 138, 1, though even here its worship shows that it was regarded as a personal divine entity. The situation is somewhat different in the question of the chorus to Medea: τίνα προξενίαν (vl.) ἢ δόμον ἢ χθόνα σωτῆρα κακῶν ἐξευρήσεις; Eur. Med., 359 ff. [1] Apart from isolated ref. of this kind, [2] however, only gods or men are called σωτῆρες. As regards the obj. of the action of σωτῆρες there is again a palpable distinction from the verb and the noun σωτηρία. There is hardly any σωτήρ par. to the "preservation (σωτηρία) of goods," → 967, 16 f. Among non-personal obj. of the work of σωτῆρες are ships (along with sailors) (→ line 27), but elsewhere only the patriarchal hearth in Aesch. Choeph., 264, the *polis* in Aristoph. Eq., 149, the house in Aristoph. Nu., 1161, Hellas (n. 12), the fatherland (→ 1006, 18 f.), then the world order (→ 1005, 32 ff.) — all things indissolubly bound up with man's existence. On the whole, then, σωτήρ is limited to the human sphere. Basically anyone saved or kept is dependent on the one who saves, even though only for a moment. This dependence may not be prominent in σῴζω or σωτηρία (→ 966, 28 ff.), but understandably it can and does have special strength in σωτήρ with its limitation to the human sphere.

2. Gods as σωτῆρες.

The gods on whose rule and intervention men are dependent are σωτῆρες. They save from individual dangers in life. In the oldest instance of σωτήρ Poseidon is σωτήρ νηῶν, Hom. Hymn. ad Neptunum, 22, 5. Of Leda it is also said: σωτῆρας τέκε παῖδας ἐπιχθονίων ἀνθρώπων ὠκυπόρων τε νεῶν, Hymn. ad Castores, 33, 6 f. The Dioscori

---

stimmung bei Vergil," *Studia Philologica,* 4 (1929), 25-38; F. Sauter, "Der röm. Kaiserkult bei Martial u. Statius," *Tübinger Beiträge z. Altertumswissenschaft,* 21 (1934), 4-16, 19-24; L. Bieler, θεῖος ἀνήρ, I (1935), 120-122; W. Schubart, "Das hell. Königsideal nach Inschr. u. Pap.," APF, 12 (1937), 13, 21; H. Haerens, "Soter et soteria," *Stud. Hellenistica,* 5 (1948), 57-68; Nilsson, II², 183-185, 388-391; A. D. Nock, "Soter and Euergetes," *The Joy of Study,* Festschr. f. F. C. Grant (1951), 126-148; K. H. Rengstorf, "Die Anfänge d. Auseinandersetzung zwischen Christusglaube u. Asklepiusfrömmigkeit," *Schr. d. Gesellschaft z. Förderung d. Westfälischen Landesuniversität zu Münster,* 30 (1953), 8-19; L. Cerfaux and J. Tondriau, *Le culte des souverains* (1957); F. Taeger, *Charisma,* I (1957), II (1960), *passim.* C.: Bousset-Gressm., 225 f., 260, 362, n. 2; Str.-B., I, 67-70. D.: W. Wagner, "Über σῴζω u. seine Derivate im NT," ZNW, 6 (1905), 219-225; Cr.-Kö., *s.v.* σῴζω; Harnack Miss., I, 129-150; H. Weinel, *Bibl. Theol. d. NT*⁴ (1928), 219; H. J. Cadbury, "The Titles of Jesus in Acts," Jackson-Lake, I, 5, 370 f.; A. D. Nock, "Early Gentile Christianity and Its Hellenistic Background," *Essays on the Trinity and the Incarnation,* ed. A. E. J. Rawlinson (1928), 87-96; M. Meinertz, *Theol. d. NT,* II (1950), 105; Bultmann Theol.⁴, 81 f.; M. Barth, *Die Taufe ein Sakrament?* (1951), 502-520; L. Koehler, "Christus im AT u. NT," ThZ, 9 (1953), 242 f.; U. Wilckens, *Die Missionsreden d. Ag.* (1961), 175 f.

[1] Whether σωτήρ is noun or adj. in Aesch. Ag., 897: σωτὴρ ναὸς πρότονος, is uncertain, cf. Pind. Fr., 159 (Snell).

[2] It may be noted that ships were also named σώτειρα, Höfer Soteira, 1247.

are also σωτῆρες to the very latest period, [3] and so are many Gk. gods, esp. of course Zeus. [4] In danger Agesilaos sacrifices τοῖς ἀποτροπαίοις καὶ τοῖς σωτῆρσι, Xenoph. Hist. Graec., III, 3, 4; the freeing of the Gks. before the battle of Cunaxa was Ζεὺς σωτὴρ καὶ νίκη, Xenoph. An., I, 8, 16. The saving of Delphi from the Gauls was due to Zeus σωτήρ and the Pythian Apollo, Ditt. Syll.[3], I, 408, 6 f. The third cup at banquets was dedicated to Zeus; he was thus the τρίτος (mentioned third) σωτήρ, [5] Aesch. Suppl., 27. Orestes' thanks after pardon were offered to Athene, Apollo, and the πάντα κραίνων τρίτος σωτήρ, i.e., Zeus, Aesch. Eum., 754-760. Esp. mentioned in the Hell. period as helpers in particular dangers are Aesculapius, the healer of ailments and as such ὁ σωτὴρ Ἀσκληπιός or sometimes simply ὁ σωτήρ, [6] and Hercules. [7] Thus Cl. Al. says of the pagans of his day: τὸν γὰρ εὐεργετοῦντα μὴ συνιέντες θεὸν ἀνέπλασάν τινας σωτῆρας Διοσκούρους καὶ Ἡρακλέα ἀλεξίκακον καὶ Ἀσκληπιὸν ἰατρόν, Prot., II, 26, 8. Then Isis and Sarapis are with special frequency called "deliverers": Σάραπις καὶ Ἶσις καὶ Ἄνουβις καὶ Ἁρποκράτης αὐτοί τε καὶ τὰ ἀγάλματα αὐτῶν καὶ τὰ μυστήρια ταραχὰς καὶ κινδύνους καὶ ἀπειλὰς καὶ περιστάσεις σημαίνουσιν, ἐξ ὧν καὶ παρὰ προσδοκίαν σῴζουσιν· ἀεὶ γὰρ σωτῆρες εἶναι νενομισμένοι εἰσὶν οἱ θεοὶ τῶν εἰς πᾶν ἀφιγμένων, Artemid. Oneirocr., II, 39 (p. 145). In this connection these gods do not come into consideration as mystery deities.

Many Gk. gods, and esp. Zeus, are σωτῆρες not just as helpers in distress but as "protectors" and "preservers" of the polis and its citizens. In this σωτήρ includes a common use of the verb σῴζω and its noun σωτηρία (→ 968, 4 ff.). Thus in Pind. Olymp., 5, 17 Zeus is addressed in a prayer for the blossoming of the city and long life for the Olympic victor. In Aesch. Suppl., 26 f. Ζεὺς σωτὴρ τρίτος and οἰκοφύλαξ ὁσίων ἀνδρῶν are par. The prayer to Zeus in Philadelphia in Asia Minor runs: [Ζεῦ]. σωτή[ρ], τὴν ἀφή[γησιν ταύτην ἱλέως καὶ εὐμεν]ῶς προσδέχου καὶ [... πάρεχ]ε ἀγαθὰς ἀμοιβάς, [ὑγίειαν, σωτηρίαν, εἰρήνην, ἀσφάλεια]ν ἐπὶ γῆς καὶ ἐπὶ θα[λάσσης], Ditt. Syll.[3], III, 985, 60-62. Acc. to Dio Chrys. Or., 12, 74 Phidias depicted in Zeus τὸν βίου καὶ ζωῆς καὶ ξυμπάντων δοτῆρα τῶν ἀγαθῶν, κοινὸν ἀνθρώπων καὶ πατέρα καὶ σωτῆρα καὶ φύλακα. Cornut. Theol. Graec., 9 (9, 14-20) enumerates σωτήρ as the first of the many names of Zeus, and regarding the list he notes that Zeus διατέτακεν εἰς πᾶσαν δύναμιν καὶ σχέσιν καὶ πάντων αἴτιος καὶ ἐπόπτης ἐστίν. In his role as σωτήρ, i.e., upholder of the order of the world and all life within it, Zeus is then accompanied in Hell. by other gods, and in late antiquity by the sun. [8] Though there are no direct instances it may thus be assumed quite confidently that the mystery deities were also called σωτῆρες. [9] σώτειρα undoubtedly stands behind the frequent sospitatrix of Apul. Met., XI, 9, 1; 15, 4; 25, 1. [10] Mithras is twice called salutaris, which pts. in the same direction. [11]

---

[3] Luc. Alex., 4. Paus., II, 1, 9 says of the Dioscori: σωτῆρες καὶ οὗτοι νεῶν καὶ ἀνθρώπων εἰσὶν ναυτιλλομένων, cf. IG, 12, 3, 422: βωμὸν ἔτευξε Διοσκούροις Σωτῆρσι θεοῖσιν.

[4] For gods named σωτήρ cf. Höfer, 1247-1272; Herzog-Hauser, 1211-1221.

[5] Cf. on this Höfer, 1263 f.

[6] Examples in Rengstorf, 11 and Doelger Ant. Christ., VI (1950), 257-266, esp. 260, n. 117. For Bithynian coins cf. C. Bosch, Die kleinasiatischen Münzen d. röm. Kaiserzeit, II, 1, 1 (1935), 106.

[7] J. Fink, "Herakles als Held u. Heiland," Antike u. Abendland, 9 (1960), 73-87.

[8] Ael. Arist. Or., 42, 4 (Keil) says of Aesculapius: οὗτός ἐσθ᾽ ὁ τὸ πᾶν ἄγων καὶ νέμων σωτὴρ τῶν ὅλων καὶ φύλαξ τῶν ἀθανάτων... σῴζων τά τε ὄντα ἀεὶ καὶ τὰ γιγνόμενα, cf. also of Sarapis: he is σωτὴρ αὐτὸς καὶ ψυχοπομπός, ἄγων εἰς φῶς καὶ πάλιν δεχόμενος, πανταχῇ πάντας περιέχων, 45, 25 (Keil). For the sun as the gt. σωτήρ cf. Corp. Herm., 16, 12: σωτὴρ δὲ καὶ τροφεύς ἐστι παντὸς γένους ὁ ἥλιος.

[9] The fact that Isis is often called σώτειρα does not mean she is called this as a mystery goddess.

[10] For the usage in Apul. cf. Haerens.

[11] F. Cumont, Die Mysterien des Mithra[3] (1923), 161, n. 1.

3. Men as σωτῆρες.

a. σωτήρ as Helper, Saver of Life, Physician.

As regards the use of σωτήρ for men two inter-related aspects call for notice. The first is the basic superiority of the one who saves over the one saved, the referring of the latter to the former, while the second is the absence of any sharp distinction between the divine and the human world in the Gk. sphere. This is plain in one of the oldest passages in which σωτήρ appears. In the concluding scene of Aesch. Suppl. Danaos addresses the suppliants: ὦ παῖδες, Ἀργείοισιν εὔχεσθαι χρεών, θύειν τε λείβειν θ᾽ ὡς θεοῖς Ὀλυμπίοις σπονδάς, ἐπεὶ σωτῆρες οὐ διχορρόπως, 980-982. The citizens of the town of Argos saved the suppliants and honours and sacrifices are thus due to them as to the gods of Olympus. In all ages it was possible for the Gks. to honour the σωτήρ in this way. But they did not have to. When the seer Teiresias is addressed: πόλιν μέν, εἰ καὶ μὴ βλέπεις, φρονεῖς δ᾽ ὅμως οἷα νόσῳ σύνεστιν· ἧς σὲ προστάτην σωτῆρά τ᾽, ὦναξ, μοῦνον ἐξευρίσκομεν (Soph. Oed. Tyr., 302-304), supreme honour is paid him but no sacrifice is made. Nor is there any such feature in Hdt. when in a long passage he explains why the Athenians were in his view the σωτῆρες τῆς Ἑλλάδος, VII, 139, 5, nor when Xenoph. speaks of the deliberation of some who wanted to restore εὐνομία in Corinth and who reflected: εἰ μὲν δύναιντο καταπρᾶξαι ταῦτα, σωτῆρας γενέσθαι τῆς πατρίδος, εἰ δὲ μὴ δύναιντο, ... ἀξιεπαινοτάτης τελευτῆς τυχεῖν, Xenoph. Hist. Graec., IV, 4, 6, [12] cf. V, 4, 26, where Cleonymos asks Archidamos σωτῆρα αὐτῷ τοῦ πατρὸς γενέσθαι, namely, by protecting him from judicial condemnation. In Plato, too, σωτήρ in the political sphere suggests only the deliverer and preserver when leaders are called σωτῆρες and ἐπίκουροι by the people in Plato's ideal state, Resp., V, 463b. Diotima calls the spiritual children of Lycurgus σωτῆρες τῆς Λακεδαίμονος καὶ ὡς ἔπος εἰπεῖν τῆς Ἑλλάδος, Symp., 209d. Possibly σωτήρ has a further nuance in Plato when he says that a port engaged in trade μεγάλου τινὸς ἔδει σωτῆρος ... καὶ νομοθετῶν θείων τινῶν that it should not fall into evil ways, Leg., IV, 704d. [13]

In the Roman imperial period σωτήρ is also common in the sense of "saver of life." Unfortunate Timon complains to Zeus that his former friends avoid him τὸν οὐ πρὸ πολλοῦ σωτῆρα καὶ εὐεργέτην αὐτῶν γεγενημένον, Luc. Tim., 5. Two important ref. (→ 1011, 6 ff.) should also be mentioned here. Tacitus says of a certain Milichus who saved Nero from a conspiracy that he conservatoris sibi nomen, Graeco eius rei vocabulo, adsumpsit, Ann., 15, 71, 3. The Gk. word is undoubtedly σωτήρ in the sense of "saver of life." In Herodian. Hist., III, 12, 2 an imprisoned and accused chiliarch is brought before Alexander Severus and says: ἥκω σοι, ὦ δέσποτα, ὡς μὲν ὁ πέμψας οἴεται, φονεὺς καὶ δήμιος, ὡς δ᾽ αὐτὸς εὔχομαί τε καὶ βούλομαι, σωτήρ τε καὶ εὐεργέτης. [14] When σωτήρ is used of a physician it does not always bear the technical sense of doctor. When a doctor himself is ill with all around him and another doctor comes,

---

[12] Cf. Isoc. Areop., 84: ἐγὼ μὲν οὖν ἡγούμενος, ἣν μιμησώμεθα τοὺς προγόνους, καὶ τῶν κακῶν ἡμᾶς τούτων ἀπαλλαγήσεσθαι καὶ σωτῆρας οὐ μόνον τῆς πόλεως, ἀλλὰ καὶ τῶν Ἑλλήνων ἁπάντων γενήσεσθαι, τήν σε πρόσοδον ἐποιησάμην καὶ τοὺς λόγους εἴρηκα τούτους.

[13] Taeger, I, 144, n. 120: Plato's σωτήρ and εὐεργέτης lack "later charismatic traits." Xenoph. Ag., 11, 13 is often quoted: ἐκεῖνον οἱ μὲν συγγενεῖς φιλοκηδεμόνα ἐκάλουν, οἱ δὲ χρώμενοι ἀπροφάσιστον, οἱ δὲ ὑπουργήσαντές τι μνήμονα, οἱ δ᾽ ἀδικούμενοι ἐπίκουρον, οἵ γε μὴν συγκινδυνεύοντες μετὰ θεοὺς σωτῆρα, but again only human features are ascribed to Agesilaos. But cf. Taeger, I, 120: Agesilaos stands out from the common run of men, but in the careful observance of ancient limits he is much behind the gods.

[14] Cf. also VIII, 3, 4, where Crispinus admonishes the citizens of the besieged city to remain loyal to the treaty with the Roman senate and people on the ground they will then be distinguished as σωτῆρες καὶ πρόμαχοι Ἰταλίας πάσης, an honour, but with no question of deification.

κοτέειν ("to be envious") μέλλει καὶ ἐχθρὸν ("rival") ἡγεῖσθαι τὸν αὐτοῦ σωτῆρα καὶ τῶν φιλτάτων, Dio Chrys. Or., 77, 9.[15] σωτήρ is used in address to a doctor in, e.g., Ps.-Luc. Ocyp., 78.

b. Philosophers as σωτῆρες.

"Saviour" is also the content of σωτήρ as applied to philosophers, e.g., Epicurus,[16] where the meaning is confirmed by the common use of ἐλευθερωτής, ἐλευθερία, liberare[17] in relation to him and his philosophy.[18] Dio Chrys. Or., 32, 18 says gen. of philosophers: τὴν δὲ ἑτέραν ἐπιμέλειαν (concern for the healing of hurts of soul) ἔργον εἶναί φημι τῶν δυναμένων διὰ πειθοῦς καὶ λόγου ψυχὰς πραΰνειν καὶ μαλάττειν. οὗτοι δὲ σωτῆρές εἰσι καὶ φύλακες τῶν οἴων τε σῴζεσθαι, πρὶν ἐλθεῖν εἰς τέλος τὴν πονηρίαν εἴργοντες καὶ κατέχοντες.[19] Ibid., 32, 50 tells us the Alexandrians called those who risked their lives in the arena σωτήρ and θεός. There is no path from the proper sense "deliverer" and "benefactor" to this degenerate use. We have here the ultimate reduction of a lofty usage taken from the political sphere.

c. Statesmen as σωτῆρες.

With ref. to terms for politicians and rulers Plut. De Coriolano, 11 (I, 218d-e) says: ῞Ελληνες ἐτίθεντο πράξεως μὲν ἐπώνυμον τὸν Σωτῆρα καὶ τὸν Καλλίνικον, ἰδέας δὲ τὸν Φύσκωνα καὶ τὸν Γρυπόν, ἀρετῆς δὲ τὸν Εὐεργέτην καὶ τὸν Φιλάδελφον, εὐτυχίας δὲ τὸν Εὐδαίμονα. If this is not a precise def. one may see from the passage that this Greek of the 2nd cent. A.D. catches in σωτήρ a ref. to an accomplished act, while in εὐεργέτης, so often associated with it, he finds praise of the disposition. One may at least ask whether σωτήρ in gen., apart from the truncated use mentioned → lines 12 ff., does not always bear a ref. to some real action.[20] The applying of σωτήρ in later authors to Gelon (480 B.C.) Diod. S., 11, 26, 6, to Dionysius of Syracuse (356 B.C.) ibid., 16, 20, 6, cf. Plut. De Dione, 46 (I, 978b), and even camillus, Plut. De Camillo, 10 (I, 134c) can be quoted with certainty only in support of the usage of the authors concerned.[21] But we are on more solid ground with Brasidas in 422 B.C., for Thuc., V, 11, 1[22] says of him that after his death the people of Amphipolis honoured him with annual games and sacrifices νομίσαντες τὸν μὲν Βρασίδαν σωτῆρά τε σφῶν γεγενῆσθαι. The fact that he saved the city is the basis, not the content, of divinisation. Equally sure historically is the fact that Philip of Macedon was honoured by the Thessalonians as φίλος, εὐερ-

---

15 In Luc. Abdicatus, 5 the son who has healed his father is called σωτὴρ καὶ εὐεργέτης, cf. 13. The meaning is more "helper," "saviour" than "doctor." Taeger, II, 517, n. 108: σωτήρ and εὐεργέτης have no charismatic implication in Luc.
16 W. Crönert, "Neues über Epikur," Rhein. Mus., 56 (1901), 625.
17 Luc. Alex., 61, cf. 47; Cic. Tusc., I, 21, 48 (cf. Wendland, 364); Fin., I, 5, 14; cf. Lucretius De rerum natura (ed. J. Martin⁴ [1959]), V, 3-12.
18 Probably Plotina's letter to the Epicureans in Athens has Epicurus in view with its ὑπὲρ τῆς καθηγεμονίας τοῦ σωτῆρος, Ditt. Syll.³, II, 834, 20.
19 Cf. Dio Chrys. Or., 32, 3: παιδεία καὶ λόγος, ὧν οἱ τυχόντες εἰκότως ἄνδρες ἀγαθοὶ γίγνονται καὶ σωτῆρες τῶν πόλεων. In the same sense Heracles is called the σωτήρ of the earth and men, not because he kept off wild animals, but because he punished wild and wicked men and broke the power of tyrants, cf. Dio Chrys. Or., 1, 84. Cf. the typical passage 48, 10: οὐχ ὑμεῖς ἐστε οἱ πολλάκις ἐπαινοῦντες ἡμᾶς δι' ὅλης τῆς ἡμέρας, τοὺς μὲν ἀριστεῖς λέγοντες, τοὺς δὲ Ὀλυμπίους, τοὺς δὲ σωτῆρας, τοὺς δὲ τροφέας.
20 Taeger, I, 329 limits this to the Early and High Hellen. periods, when σωτήρ "always had an actual ref."
21 Wendland, 337, n. 4; Taeger, II, 35.
22 Wendland, 337; Taeger, I, 161; Cerfaux, 460.

γέτης and σωτήρ, Demosth. Or., 18, 43, though it is hard to say with certainty how far religious ideas were linked with these titles. [23] Apart from the ruler cult of the Diadochi this line may be traced up to the time of the Roman penetration: Lysandridas of Megalopolis advised Cleomenes, king of Sparta, to spare the city and thus to become the σωτήρ of a gt. people, Plut. De Cleomene, 24 (I, 816c); in this case there can be no thought of divine or heroic veneration. A statue was erected to Aratus as σωτήρ because he gave εὐνομία to his country, Plut. De Arato, 14 (I, 1033d). In this, and in the fact that the citizens and their wives and children called him πατὴρ κοινὸς καὶ σωτήρ, 42 (I, 1047a), there is no deification. But after his death he was buried as οἰκιστὴς καὶ σωτὴρ τῆς πόλεως in a special spot and annual offerings were made to him, one being on the day he freed the city from tyranny. This was called σωτήρια and was celebrated by the priest of Zeus σωτήρ, I, 1051e-1052a. [24] How close was divinisation may be seen from the votive offering of the town Lathyia in Thessaly, which calls one Sosander εὐεργέτης, or, as one gt. in counsel and conduct, σωτήρ, κτίστης and ἄλλος Ζεύς, IG, 11, 2, 599.

When the Mediterranean world became acquainted with the power of Rome in its generals and ambassadors, σωτήρ predications increased. Three points call for notice in this respect: a. the predicate σωτήρ is always occasioned by specific deeds of the one thus honoured, b. it does not *ipso facto* imply elevation to the status of hero or god, and c. it is not limited to the one ultimately responsible for the act, e.g., Pompey, but may be given also and simultaneously to his legate, cf. the marble slab of Mytilene which is dedicated at the same time to Pompey, τῷ εὐεργέτᾳ καὶ σωτῆρι καὶ κτιστᾷ, his freedman Theophanes, to favour whom Pompey gave the city its freedom, τῷ σωτῆρι καὶ εὐεργέτᾳ καὶ κτιστᾷ δευτέρῳ τᾶς πατρίδος, and Potamon, τῷ εὐεργέτᾳ καὶ σωτῆρος καὶ κτιστᾷ τᾶς πόλιος, Ditt. Syll.[3], II, 752-754. [25] Titus Quinctius Flamininus was the first Roman to get this honour, 196 B.C. When after defeating the Macedonians he declared the freedom of Greece during the Isthmian games, he was called ὁ σωτὴρ τῆς Ἑλλάδος καὶ πρόμαχος by the enthusiastic crowd, Plut. De Tito Flaminino, 10 (I, 375a). When shortly after he protected the Chalcidians from war, public buildings were consecrated to him and Heracles or to him and Apollo, and up to Plut.'s day he had a priest, offerings were made to him, and a paean was sung, whose ending has been preserved: ... μέλπετε κοῦραι Ζῆνα μέγαν Ῥώμαν τε Τίτον θ᾽ ἅμα Ῥωμαίων τε πίστιν· ἰήιε Παιάν, ὦ Τίτε σῶτηρ, ibid., 16 (I, 378c). The ref. to specific events is often expressed by the addition of a gen. to σωτήρ; thus the people of the Gytheans honoured Titus Flamininus τὸν αὐτοῦ σωτῆρα, Ditt. Syll.[3], II, 592. [26] Again σωτήρ does not imply elevation as hero or god. When the Minturnians repented of the resolve to slay Marius, they should have done it because their βούλευμα ἄνομον καὶ ἀχάριστον was ἐπ᾽ ἀνδρὶ σωτῆρι τῆς Ἰταλίας, Plut. Mar., 39 (I, 428c). In the triumph restored exiles called Sulla σωτὴρ καὶ πατήρ because through him they had come back to their own land and to their wives and children, Plut. De Sulla, 34 (I, 473c). [27] Here again there is no direct divinisation, and certainly not, as the circumstances show, in the case of Cato minor, whom the senators of Utica called κηδεμὼν καὶ σωτήρ before his death, Plut. Cato minor, 64 (I, 790e) and thus gave a solemn burial to the εὐεργέτης καὶ σωτὴρ καὶ μόνος ἐλεύθερος καὶ μόνος ἀήττητος, 71 (I, 794b). σωτήρ has here more the sense of preserver and protector than saviour. This broader sense is also present in Cicero's famous saying:

---

[23] Wendland, 338 suggests they were.
[24] Philopoimen also gets τιμαὶ ἰσόθεοι and a feast called σωτήρια, Ditt. Syll.[3], II, 624, 4 and 16. Wendland, 340.
[25] Wendland, 341.
[26] Cf. of Metellus: ὁ δῆμος ... τὸν ἑαυτοῦ σωτῆρα καὶ εὐεργέτην, Ditt. Syll.[3], II, 757 (Pergamum): Pompey τὸν εὐεργέτην καὶ σωτῆρα τῆς πόλεως (after defeating the pirates?), Ditt. Syll.[3], II, 749 B (67 B.C.), Manlius, who rescued Rome from the Gauls, was called *servator patriae*, Liv., 6, 17, 5; the Gks. called Mithridates *deum, patrem, conservatorem Asiae*, after the killing of the Italians, Cic. Pro Flacco, 60.
[27] Here again Plut.'s formulation is not historically certain, Wendland, 337, n. 4.

eum (sc. Verrem) non solum patronum illius insulae, sed etiam sotera inscriptum vidi Syracusis. Hoc quantum est? Ita magnum, ut Latine uno verbo exprimi non possit. Is est nimirum soter, qui salutem dedit, Cic. Verr., II, 2, 63, 154. In the saying: *Quae est melior igitur in hominum genere natura quam eorum, qui se natos ad homines iuvandos, tutandos, conservandos arbitrantur?* Cic. Tusc., I, 14, 32, the three Latin terms might also be transl. by the one Gk. verb σῴζω. [28] How close to deity the κτίστης or σωτήρ of a city or state was in Graeco-Rom. antiquity may be seen from Cic. Rep., I, 7, 12: *neque enim est ulla res, in qua propius ad deorum numen virtus accedat humana, quam civitates aut condere novas aut conservare iam conditas.*

Between these σωτήρ predications and the ruler cult proper stands the veneration which Demetrius Poliorcetes and his father Antigonus received in Athens. Though this was not a national cult it extended beyond the city of Athens itself. After Demetrius won his naval victory and proclaimed freedom to Athens the two were honoured as θεοὶ σωτῆρες and were given a priest. [29]

d. σωτήρ in the Hellenistic Ruler Cult.

In the Hell. ruler cult the official designation of rulers as σωτῆρες is to be distinguished from cases where grateful subjects styled them thus. Acc. to Paus., I, 8, 6 the people of Rhodes called Ptolemy I σωτήρ because of the help he gave when they were besieged by Demetrius Poliorcetes; cf. also the Nesiotes' inscr. (280 B.C.) where the people say they were the first to pay divine honours to the σωτήρ Ptolemy καὶ διὰ τὰς κοινὰς εὐεργεσίας καὶ διὰ τὰς ἰδίους ὠφελείας Ditt. Syll.[3], I, 390, 2730. [30] Here we do not yet have an official ruler cult. This developed under the Ptolemies and Seleucids with σωτήρ or θεὸς σωτήρ (the Ptolemies) as a constituent part of the royal style. It should be noted that in both cases σωτήρ is only one among other names. This is important since in Hell. philosophy (→ 967, 45 ff.) σῴζω is the special task of the ruler and this concept was perhaps combined with the ancient Egypt. ideas that Pharaoh as God's son cares for the welfare of the land like the gods and that a time of blessing begins with him. [31] In the Canopus inscr. (Ptolemy III [239/238 B.C.]) ἀνασῴζω, διασῴζω and σωτηρία ref. to the king's acts, Ditt. Or., I, 56, 11. 17. 18, and the Rosetta inscr. not only says of Ptolemy V κατὰ πολλὰ εὐεργέτηκεν τά θ' ἱερὰ καὶ τοὺς ἐν αὐτοῖς ὄντας καὶ τοὺς ὑπὸ τὴν ἑαυτοῦ βασιλείαν τασσομένους ἅπαντας, ὑπάρχων θεὸς ἐκ θεοῦ καὶ θεᾶς ὥσπερ ˬ Ὧρος ὁ τῆς Ἴσιος καὶ Ὀσίριος υἱός, Ditt. Or., I, 90, 9 f. but also draws a par. between his work and that of the gods, though the title σωτήρ does not occur on either inscr. If this was a developed expression for the ruler corresponding to the ideal worked out by philosophy one would expect it to have become a standing name for all the Diadochi. But this is not so, even though the rulers gave themselves their titles. [32] There are in fact only isolated echoes of these ideas, e.g., when Theocr. Idyll., 17, 125 calls the deceased Ptolemy I and his wife πάντεσσιν ἐπιχθονίοισιν ἀρωγοί, [33] or when

---

[28] A. Oxé, "Σωτήρ bei d. Römern," *Wiener Stud.,* 48 (1930), 38-61.

[29] Delos erected an altar for the θεοὶ σωτῆρες, Cerfaux, 174; on similar cases *ibid.,* 173-187.

[30] It is doubtful whether the styling of Ptolemy as σωτήρ is linked to the services mentioned in the inscr. (liberation of cities, enforcing of ancestral laws, tax relief), Kaerst, II, 315; Cerfaux, 201.

[31] Staerk, II, 231 f., 243-246.

[32] οἱ δὲ Εὐεργέτας, οἱ δὲ Καλλινίκους, οἱ δὲ Σωτῆρας, οἱ δὲ Μεγάλους ἀνηγόρευσαν ἑαυτούς, Plut. Alex. Fort. Virt., II, 5 (II, 338c). Note also that in the Samaritan letter to Antiochus IV the king is addressed: βασιλεῖ Ἀντιόχῳ θεῷ ἐπιφανεῖ, Jos. Ant., 12, 258, but the petition begins: ἀξιοῦμεν οὖν σε τὸν εὐεργέτην καὶ σωτῆρα προστάξαι..., 12, 261.

[33] The scansion demands ἀρωγοί for σωτῆρες here.

three brothers revere the θεοὶ σωτῆρες Ptolemy II and Berenice as σωθέντες. [34] The fact that in Egypt not only the Ptolemies but also their officials (with few exceptions) were called σωτήρ [35] shows highly the title was esteemed in Egypt. The breadth of the meaning of σωτήρ outside the official ruler cult may be seen from the note of Phylarchos that Athenians from Lemnos etc. called the third cup at feasts not Zeus σωτήρ but Seleucos σωτήρ because he had liberated Athens from Lysimachos, Athen., 6, 66 (255a).

e. σωτήρ in Emperor Worship. [36]

The Roman imperial period, intimated already by Pompey, brings a gt. increase in instances of σωτήρ and also an extension in content, since we now read of the σωτήρ τῆς οἰκουμένης or τοῦ κόσμου, [37] and the idea of the golden age crops up along with σωτήρ predications. This raises the question whether σωτήρ takes on a new content, namely, that of the world saviour in the sense of the one who brings in the golden age.

Certain facts should be noted first. σωτήρ was not and did not become part of the imperial style, as among the Diadochi. If it had been a tt. for the world saviour who brings in the golden age one would have expected it to be officially adopted at least by Caligula, Nero, and Domitian. [38] In the Gk. myth of the golden age which the Romans adopted the figure of a human ruler has indeed no place; at most Hes. Op., 109-119; Horat. Epodi, 16, 41-66; Tib., I, 3, 35-48; Ovid Metam., 1, 89-112; Amores, III, 8, 35-44; Vergil Georg., I, 125-128; Arat. Phaen., 108-114; Emped. Fr., 128 (Diels, I, 363); Juv., 13, 38-40 speak only of Saturn. In the two prophecies of the coming new age in Plut. De Sulla, 7 (I, 456a) and Servius Comm. in Vergilii Bucolica, 9, 46 [39] no person is mentioned. Similarly the predicate σωτήρ would not fit the expected boy of the famous 4th Eclogue of Vergil, for he does not save the world from the iron age, and he comes with the new *saeculum* as its ruler, not its bringer.

When a kind of golden age seemed to come under and with Augustus, there was still no established link with σωτήρ, neither in the well-known verses of Vergil Aen., VI, 791-807, nor in Horat. Carm., IV, 5, 17-40; IV, 2, 37-40. Sen. Apokolokynthosis, 4, 1 and even more fulsomely Calpurnius Siculus Bucolica, [40] I, 36-88; IV, 97-146 extol the *saeculum* extravagantly under Nero, as do Statius Silvae, [41] I, 6, 39-50 and Mart., 5, 19, 1-6; 8, 56 (55), 1 f. under Domitian, but again there is no expression which seems to imply σωτήρ. Even if one might explain this by saying that Lat. had not yet coined a word for σωτήρ as the bringer of a new age, *salus* is also missing in this connection. But this is understandable, for the golden age, which was described in mythical terms, had not actually come. [42] There is a whole set of examples to show that σωτήρ was not reserved

---

[34] O. Rubensohn, "Neue Inschr. aus Ägypten," APF, 5 (1913), 156 f.

[35] Schubart, 21.

[36] For inscr. relating to Caesar, Antonius and Augustus cf. L. R. Taylor, *The Divinity of the Roman Emperor* (1931), 267-283.

[37] The former of Caesar, IG, 12, 5, 1, 557. The latter is found only from Hadrian, but the idea is older.

[38] The fact that the φυλή (not δῆμος) name σωσικόσμιος occurs in Egypt in Nero's time and is probably to be traced to his initiative does not mean that σωτήρ τοῦ κόσμου was an official title of Nero, cf. W. Schubart, "Alexandrinische Urkunden aus d. Zeit d. Augustus," APF, 5 (1913), 94-99 and U. Wilcken, "Kaiser Nero u. d. alexandr. Phylen," *ibid.*, 182-184; also Deissmann LO, 311 f.

[39] Ed. H. Hagen (1902).

[40] Ed. C. Giarratano (1943).

[41] Ed. A. Klotz (1911).

[42] Cf. also the judgment of M. Rostovtzeff, *Gesch. d. alten Welt*, II (1942), 289: "But the dominant mood, esp. among the upper classes, was one of profound pessimism. No one felt the new age was heaven on earth.

exclusively for the emperor (e.g., Augustus) and that it did not necessarily imply the divinity of its bearer or the concept of a world ruler. The priest of Augustus and Roma, C. Julius Xenon of Thyatira, was honoured as σωτήρ, εὐεργέτης, κτίστης and πατήρ of his native town after his death. [43] There was no sense of competing with the imperial title σωτήρ. Milichos, who saved Nero's life, could hardly have styled himself by the Gk. equivalent of *conservator* (→ 1006, 31 ff.) if σωτήρ had been a tt. for the status of Nero as world saviour, nor could the chiliarch have called himself σωτήρ and εὐεργέτης before Emperor Alexander Severus (→ 1006, 34 ff.). One might have expected that, as in Egypt, σωτήρ would be reserved for the emperor, at least under Nero and Domitian, but this was not so. [44]

σωτήρ is esp. common in relation to Hadrian. [45] This is connected with his extensive travels in which he showed favours to many cities and private individuals. Yet the numerous inscr. of thanks do not always extol him as σωτήρ τοῦ κόσμου, as one might suppose, but also as the σωτήρ of a city or even an individual, cf. the inscr. of Publius Claudius Demostratus Caelianus ὑπὲρ ἑαυτοῦ καὶ τῶν τέκνων τὸν ἴδιον εὐεργέτην καὶ σωτῆρα. [46] The objection that the emperor's world-saviourhood expresses itself in his being the saviour of a city or individual loses its force when Hadrian is called only the saviour of the city concerned, e.g., CIA, III, 473: ἡ πόλις ἡ Αἰγεινητῶν τὸν ἑατῆς σωτῆρα καὶ εὐεργέτην. The many dedications to Hadrian the σωτήρ and οἰκιστής (IG, 4, 1406) or κτίστης show that predication as σωτήρ refers to specific acts of the emperor for specific towns which he visited. If he is very often styled σωτήρ τῆς οἰκουμένης or τοῦ κόσμου, these are only generalisations of specific instances; they are not general titles. As Plut. rightly observes, σωτήρ applies to specific πράξεις, [47] → 1007, 16 ff. In the (few) cases in which a reason is given, it is always a single act. So already under the Seleucids: In Ilium a statue of Antiochus I Soter was to be set up in the temple of Athene with the inscr.: ὁ δῆμος ὁ ['Ιλιέων βασιλέα Ἀντί]οχον... εὐσεβείας ἕνεκεν τῆς εἰς τὸ ἱερό[ν, εὐεργέτην καὶ σω]τῆρα γεγονότα τοῦ δήμου, Ditt. Or., I, 219, 36-38. [48] Appian. Bell. Civ., II, 106 notes in relation to the fact that oak-garlands were put on some of Caesar's statues after his victory over Pompey: ὡς σωτῆρι τῆς πατρίδος, ᾧ πάλαι τοὺς ὑπερασπίσαντας ἐγέραιρον οἱ περισωθέντες, cf. for Augustus: Ἵππαρχος... ἐκ τῶν ἰδίων διὰ τὴν πρὸς τὸν Σεβαστὸν καὶ εὐεργέτην καὶ σωτῆρα ἑαυτοῦ εὐσέβηαν. [49] Finally it may be noted that the emperor is very seldom called σωτήρ or *conservator* or *salvator* on coins. [50] In emperor worship, then,

---

[43] Nock, 138.

[44] Examples in Nock, cf. esp. the statistical survey, 142 f.

[45] Material in W. Weber, *Untersuchungen z. Gesch. d. Kaisers Hadrian* (1907), *passim*.

[46] *Ibid.*, 217.

[47] M. Scramuzza, "Claudius Soter Euergetes," *Harvard Stud. in Classical Philology*, 51 (1940), 261-266 pts. to the close connection between Claudius' care for the provinces and cities of the empire on the one side and his extraordinary veneration as σωτήρ (τῆς οἰκουμένης) and εὐεργέτης on the other.

[48] Kaerst, II, 317, n. 1 with other examples; cf. Taeger, I, 252-254.

[49] Inscr. Graecae ad res Romanas pertinentes, IV (ed. G. Lafaye [1908], 201); cf. aiso Weber, 220: "As he (the emperor) is called σωτήρ to characterise his helpful activity in face of economic and intellectual ills, so he is κτίστης, the restorer of the ancient Greek world"; *ibid.*, 182 f. on an ancient inscr. from Epidauros, where it is correctly pted. out that the honorary titles σωτήρ and οἰκιστής have real meaning only when Hadrian has done something for the city; cf. Ditt. Syll.[3], II, 839, 7-9: ἡ βουλὴ καὶ ὁ δῆμος ὁ Ἐφεσίων τὸν ἴδιον κτίστην καὶ σωτῆρα διὰ τὰς ἀνυπερβλήτους δωρεάς.

[50] Only Nicopolis in Epirus has a coin Τραϊανὸς σωτὴρ πόλεως, B. V. Head, *Historia Nummorum*[2] (1911), 321.

σωτήρ is a form of the Gk. σωτήρ extended by the range of Roman rule. It is not closely connected with oriental notions of the first and last time etc. [51]

f. σωτήρ and the Golden Age.

Ideas of the golden age, which sprang up again in the Roman imperial period, could easily be connected with the term σωτήρ, and almost had to be. If σωτήρ meant benefactor in the final inscriptions quoted (→ 1011, 11 ff.), it could also enclose a greater content. To the Roman empire, which embraced the known world, Augustus had brought order as well as peace, and with this the validity of law. [52] As regards the meaning of σωτήρ in the witnesses which also recall the golden age, the well-known Calendar inscr. of Priene says that providence brought the Σεβαστός as it had sent to us and our descendants the σωτήρ who ended war and ordered all things, Ditt. Or., II, 458, 33-36. Even plainer is the inscr. of Halicarnassus, [53] according to which the immortal nature of the all brought the emperor into our lives Δία δὲ πατρῷον καὶ σωτῆρα τοῦ κοινοῦ τῶν ἀνθρώπων γένους, with the elucidation: εἰρηνεύουσι μὲν γὰρ γῆ καὶ θάλαττα, πόλεις δὲ ἀνθοῦσιν εὐνομίᾳ ὁμονοίᾳ τε καὶ εὐετηρίᾳ, ἀκμή τε καὶ φορὰ παντός ἐστιν ἀγαθοῦ, ἐλπίδων μὲν χρηστῶν πρὸς τὸ μέλλον, εὐθυμίας δὲ εἰς τὸ παρὸν τῶν ἀνθρώπων ἐνεπεπλησμένων, ἀγῶσιν κἀ[ναθή]μασιν θυσίαις τε καὶ ὕμνοις..., peace, and hence security of husbandry and commerce, good laws and hence the checking of crime, joy and hope for life and connected therewith religion: all this Augustus' regime has brought. Therefore the emperor is σωτήρ in so far as this title does not have a specific application. Political relations in the broadest sense were changed and improved by the σωτήρ Augustus to establish the rule of discipline and custom, and respect for law and the gods. These things were fundamentally upheld by the emperor. This brought back to mind the golden age, causing men to look beyond the emperor to providence or the gods.

Foerster

B. σωτήρ in the Old Testament.

LXX always has σωτήρ for the stem ישע, [54] though contrary to expectations only 7 times for part. hi מוֹשִׁיעַ, elsewhere for יֶשַׁע and יְשׁוּעָה. Only rarely, then, do we find both σωτήρ and מוֹשִׁיעַ, Ju. 3:9, 15; 12:3 B; 1 S. 10:19; Is. 45:15, 21; Neh. 9:27 (2 Εσδρ. 19:27). σωτήρ is a tt. for the judges at most only in Ju. 3:9, 15, though it should be recalled that LXX in Ju. 2:16 and Neh. 9:27, deviating from HT though agreeing with this at Ju. 2:18, lays stress on the fact that after the institution of the judges it was God rather than the

---

[51] Cf. Staerk, II, 231: "One should not expect that this idea (namely, that 'the epiphany of the divine king ... is a turning-point, a new beginning of the historical process') would always find expression in a way which is formally fixed and which exhausts the content of the term soter."

[52] Augustus as *servator mundi*, Prop., IV, 6, 37.

[53] *The Collection of Ancient Gk. Inscr. in the Brit. Museum*, IV, 1, 906, 6-13, ed. G. Hirschfeld (1893).

[54] Only in post-Chr. Judaism does גּוֹאֵל serve to denote the Messiah in the function of מוֹשִׁיעַ: as the destroyer of Gentile world powers and the liberator of Israel from bondage; cf. Str.-B., I, 68 f.

judges themselves who delivered Israel; hence the judges are not regarded as bringers of salvation. Similarly LXX seems to avoid σωτήρ for the kings, cf. 4 Βασ. 13:5. In other passages, along the lines of stem ישע, the ref. is to men and esp. to Yahweh as "helper" and "deliverer" from earthly troubles. The transl. of part. hi מוֹשִׁיעַ is very irregular in the LXX. Apart from the 7 instances of σωτήρ we find σῴζων 9 times (perhaps to emphasise God's work), other verbal forms of σῴζω twice, the impersonal σωτηρία 4 times (perhaps to stress the help brought by the deliverer), and finally βοηθέω 4 times and ῥύομαι once.

It is thus plain that σωτήρ is not a tt. in the LXX. The fact that it is used 12 times (a third of all occurrences) for יֵשַׁע "deliverance," "liberation," "help," "salvation," (7 times in Ps., 4 in the Prophets) and then 4 times for יְשׁוּעָה "help," "salvation," at Dt. 32:15; Is. 12:2; Ps. 62:2, 6, is no argument to the contrary. [55] For these are personal renderings of Hbr. expressions in which God is called the "help" or "salvation" of men, cf. also Is. 17:10; Ps. 25:5; 27:1, 9; 65:5; 79:9. Furthermore the translation is not consistent. יְשׁוּעָה is transl. σωτήρ in Ps. 62:2, 6, but for no compelling reason σωτήριον is used instead in v. 1. Again, in Hab. 3:13 יֵשַׁע is both σωτηρία and σῴζω even though the two halves of the v. are par., and then σωτήρ is the transl. of the same word in 3:18.

One may thus see that σωτήρ is not used as a term for the Messiah in the Greek OT. There is approximation to this in two passages. In Zech. 9:9 it is the Messiah who according to the Hebrew text is delivered by God, while in the LXX it is a king who "saves" (σῴζων), so that one may detect the later Jewish idea of the Messiah as the one who brings salvation. Then at Is. 49:6 the Hebrew text speaks of God's salvation, but in the LXX the Servant of the Lord seems to be understood as a Messianic figure who shall be to salvation (εἰς σωτηρίαν) for the whole world. [56] Along the same lines the NT christological expression σωτήρ finds a philological equivalent in the OT מוֹשִׁיעַ, but with hardly a suggestion that Jesus was called σωτήρ on this basis. [57]

Fohrer

C. σωτήρ in Later Judaism.

1. The noun σωτήρ occurs in the Apocr. only with ref. to God as the One who keeps Israel past and present from many dangers; in the case of the brazen serpent God was the πάντων σωτήρ, the author of deliverance, Wis. 16:7. Before battle the σωτήρ of Israel was invoked and He saved David from Goliath and saved Israel through Jonathan, 1 Macc. 4:30. In 3 Macc. 6:29, 32; 7:16 God is the σωτήρ of the Egypt. Jews from destruction. In Bar. 4:22 Baruch hopes for the speedy σωτηρία of the exiles by their αἰώνιος σωτήρ. [58] In Sir. 51:1 the NT equivalent of θεὸν τὸν σωτῆρά μου is אלהי ישעי

---

55 LXX variants are σῴζων at Ju. 12:3, σωτηρία at 1 Ch. 16:35; 2 Εσδρ. 19:27; but then σωτήρ at Is. 25:9; Prv. 29:25.

56 As against G. Bertram, "Praeparatio evangelica in d. Septuaginta," VT, 7 (1957), 242 f., the LXX did not interpret Is. 62:11 Messianically but read in the original, not יֵשַׁע, but the more likely מוֹשִׁיעַ. The situation is probably different in 1 QIs (Burrows I), since many textual deviations from the Mas. here are open to explanation as Messianic interpretations; cf. J. V. Chamberlain, "The Functions of God as Messianic Titles in the Complete Qumran Isaiah Scroll," VT, 5 (1955), 366-372.

57 The HT and LXX fully support this conclusion of L. Köhler, "Christus im AT u. im NT," ThZ, 9 (1953), 242 f.

58 There is no Hbr. equivalent for the adj. αἰώνιος, but the context of 3 Macc. 7:16 and Bar. 4:22 shows dependence on אֵל עוֹלָם, which LXX Gn. 21:33 transl. by θεὸς αἰώνιος, → I, 208, 17 ff.

(= Ps. 18:46). The ref. is to deliverance from all kinds of dangers and oppression by adversaries.

2. In the Dead Sea Scrolls, [59] Eth. En. [60] and Jub. there is nothing equivalent to a Gk. σωτήρ. The same applies to 4 Esr., S. Bar. and Slav. En. σωτήρ is more common in Test. XII, but only the statement of Joseph is beyond suspicion: ἐν ἀσθενείᾳ ἤμην, καὶ ὁ Κύριος ἐπεσκέψατό με· ἐν φυλακῇ ἤμην, καὶ ὁ σωτὴρ ἐχαρίτωσέ με, Test. Jos. 1:16. The ref. to the σωτὴρ τοῦ κόσμου or τῶν ἐθνῶν are no part of the Jewish original of Test. XII → 985, n. 72. In Ps. Sol. σωτήρ is always used of God in so far as He takes up the righteous and keeps them from stumbling: κύριε σωτὴρ ἡμῶν, οὐ σαλευθησό- μεθα ἔτι τὸν αἰῶνα χρόνον, 8:33, cf. 3:6 and 16:4 f. → 985, 18 f. God is also σωτήρ as the Helper of Israel who raises up the King-Messiah, 17:3. The latter is not himself called σωτήρ.

3. Josephus does not use σωτήρ of God. [61] The word is common for human deliverers. David calls Jonathan σωτὴρ αὐτοῦ τῆς ψυχῆς, Ant., 6, 240. Herod says of Antipater before Varus that he has presented him to the emperor ὡς σωτῆρα τοῦ πατρός, i.e., the one who saved his father from the wiles of the sons of Mariamne, Bell., 1, 625. Jos. says of himself that the Galilaeans called him εὐεργέτης καὶ σωτὴρ τῆς χώρας αὐτῶν, Vit., 244, cf. 259. Of the people of Tarichaea he tells how they hailed Vespasian as σωτὴρ καὶ εὐεργέτης, Bell., 3, 459; this emperor was received in Rome as ὁ εὐεργέτης καὶ σωτὴρ καὶ μόνος ἄξιος ἡγεμὼν τῆς Ῥώμης, Bell., 7, 71. The ref. is always to specific deeds through which the one thus styled saved a land and its inhabitants from destruction or misfortune. Jos. follows a Gk. pattern here.

4. In the Rabb. the Messiah (→ χριστός) is once called מושיע את ישראל in Tanch. B ויהי 12e (on the basis of Is. 11:1). Elsewhere God is גואל, or the Messiah as He discharges His commission to free Israel from bondage to Gentile nations. In this connection גואל can be a Messianic designation, though the examples are late. [62] There is no evidence that "Redeemer" or "Saviour" was a current Messianic title in the NT period.

5. In Sib. the inaugurator of the golden age is not called σωτήρ; even in 2, 27 f.: τότε δ᾽ αὖτε μέγας θεὸς αἰθέρι ναίων ἀνδρῶν εὐσεβέων σωτὴρ κατὰ πάντα γένηται, the σωτήρ, which is used of God, ref. primarily to the salvation of the righteous from the world of iniquity, though what follows speaks of the age of salvation. The poet is obviously not acquainted with σωτήρ or σωτὴρ τοῦ κόσμου as a title for the inaugurator or king of the golden age. Elsewhere God is σωτήρ as the One who delivers from the pangs of hell (the verb here is ῥύομαι), 2, 344 f. The word is linked to ἀθάνατος in 1, 152, 167 and 3, 24 f.; what is meant is the Benefactor who sustains all things, 3, 33 and will keep them at the judgment since He is χρηστός, 1, 159. βασιλεὺς θεός is added to σωτήρ at 1, 73; here again the meaning is Benefactor and Preserver.

---

[59] But cf. the Messianic interpretation of some Is. passages acc. to the view of the Qumran community; functions of deity can lead to the personification or hypostatising of these functions. Their independence of Yahweh is shown by the suffix of the 3rd person of the possessive pronoun in the attributes which follow, so that these are personified, whereas the 1st person of the possessive pronoun in the corresponding HT ascribes the attributes to Yahweh as speaker. Thus in Is. 51:5 ישׁעי is taken personally as saviour by the ref. to "his" arm, whereas Mas. speaks of "my" (Yahweh's) arm alongside "my" help. ישׁעי can also mean "saviour," "helper" elsewhere, e.g., Ps. 27:1: "Yahweh my light and my helper." Cf. Chamberlain, op. cit., 366-372 [Bertram].

[60] Once in the similitudes of Eth. En. an original גּאֵל is conjectured, → 984, 17 f.

[61] Schl. Lk. on 1:47.

[62] Str.-B., I, 68-70.

6. Philo calls God σωτήρ as the Saviour of His people, the Preserver of mankind, and the Upholder of the cosmos → 988, 27 ff. But in Philo God is esp. σωτήρ as the Redeemer and Helper of the soul who assists it in the battle against threatening passions, → 988, 35 ff.

D. σωτήρ in the New Testament.

1. The Occurrence of σωτήρ in the New Testament.

On the basis of OT expressions the word is used of God in Lk. 1:47: ἠγαλλίασεν τὸ πνεῦμά μου ἐπὶ τῷ θεῷ τῷ σωτῆρί μου, cf. Jd. 25 in the final doxology and 6 times in the Pastoral Epistles. Apart from these ref. to God σωτήρ is used once in Lk. 2:11 (again in the infancy stories); in Ac. 5:31 and 13:23; in Phil. 3:20 and Eph. 5:23; in Jn. 4:42 and 1 Jn. 4:14 both times in the phrase ὁ σωτὴρ τοῦ κόσμου; 4 times in the Past.; 5 times in 2 Pt. Since σωτήρ is much less common in the post-apost. fathers than in the Past., in which it is employed at the same time both for God and for Christ, one may ask whether there is not some special reason for the usage in the Past. In view of the frequent use and the significance of σῴζω and σωτηρία as central concepts of NT faith the use of σωτήρ thus confronts us with the task of explaining (1) the restraint in its use in primitive Christianity, and (2) the usage of the Past.

2. σωτήρ in the New Testament apart from the Pastoral Epistles and 2 Peter.

a It is noteworthy that the angel's call in Lk. 2:10 f.: μὴ φοβεῖσθε· ἰδοὺ γὰρ εὐαγγελίζομαι ὑμῖν χαρὰν μεγάλην, ἥτις ἔσται παντὶ τῷ λαῷ, ὅτι ἐτέχθη ὑμῖν σήμερον σωτήρ, ὅς ἐστιν χριστὸς κύριος, ἐν πόλει Δαυίδ, [63] is addressed through the shepherds to the whole people, i.e., the Jewish people, not to all peoples, and that the σωτήρ is referred to without article: "a helper." No doubt historical parallels suggest themselves both for the announcement of the birth of a redeemer and also for the great joy (the shepherds are more difficult). No doubt the idea of the world saviour is suggested thereby. Nevertheless, Luke's source does nothing to awaken these associations. The field of vision is restricted to Israel, and a deliverer is promised like one of the ancient judges. The connection with Lk. 1:69-75 is palpable. Possibly the indefinite σωτήρ is the very reason why Luke added the explanatory and expansive relative clause.

The two passages in Ac. at 5:31: τοῦτον ὁ θεὸς ἀρχηγὸν καὶ σωτῆρα ὕψωσεν τῇ δεξιᾷ αὐτοῦ τοῦ δοῦναι μετάνοιαν τῷ Ἰσραὴλ καὶ ἄφεσιν ἁμαρτιῶν, and 13:23: τούτου ὁ θεὸς ἀπὸ τοῦ σπέρματος (David's) κατ' ἐπαγγελίαν ἤγαγεν τῷ Ἰσραὴλ σωτῆρα Ἰησοῦν, are directed to Jews and God-fearers. The meaning of σωτήρ is also elucidated by the fact that in other speeches in the first part of Acts we find ἀρχηγὸς τῆς ζωῆς (3:15) and ἄρχων καὶ λυτρωτής (7:35). [64] The parallelism of σωτήρ and λυτρωτής and the audiences of the speeches indicate that the reference is to Jewish Messianic hopes but that the content of the redemp-

---

[63] The words ὅς ἐστιν χριστὸς κύριος may well be an explanatory gloss added by Luke. If they are cut out one gets two lines of Hbr.: בִּשַּׂרְתִּי לָכֶם שִׂמְחָה גְדוֹלָה לְכָל־הָעָם / נוֹלַד לָכֶם הַיּוֹם מוֹשִׁיעַ בְּעִיר דָּוִד.

[64] Haench. Ag. on 5:31, though cf. W. Grundmann, "Das Problem d. hellen. Judt.," ZNW, 38 (1939), 63-71, who thinks ἀρχηγός and σωτήρ in Ac. are Hell. and derive from Heracles worship.

tion is the forgiveness of sins, not liberation from the Romans. In content σωτήρ is parallel here to the use of σῴζω and σωτηρία in Luke → 991, 27 ff.; 997, 2 ff.

b. In the older Pauline Epistles σωτήρ occurs only twice. Phil. 3:20 has been discussed already → 993, 14 ff. [65] Eph. 5:23 is difficult: ἀνήρ ἐστιν κεφαλὴ τῆς γυναικὸς ὡς καὶ ὁ Χριστὸς κεφαλὴ τῆς ἐκκλησίας, αὐτὸς σωτὴρ τοῦ σώματος. The αὐτός shows that the author is not expounding κεφαλὴ τοῦ σώματος but wants to make a new point. The κεφαλή quality (→ III, 680, 11 ff.) does not include the σωτήρ quality. Again, the αὐτός seems to indicate that the parallels between the man-wife relation and the Christ-Church relation end here. [66] Yet the statement αὐτὸς σωτὴρ τοῦ σώματος is so developed in v. 25 that with an οὕτως (v. 28) the conduct of husbands in relation to their wives is described in some sense as a parallel to that of Christ in relation to the Church; v. 28: ὡς τὰ ἑαυτῶν σώματα, echoes the αὐτὸς σωτὴρ τοῦ σώματος, and v. 29 further develops the parallel. Vv. 25-27 are thus to be regarded as an elucidation of the σωτὴρ τοῦ σώματος. Christ is σωτήρ, then, in the sense that by His sacrificing of Himself in death He has purified the Church in baptism in order that at the consummation — ἵνα παραστήσῃ refers to this [67] — He may display it for Himself in δόξα (cf. ἔνδοξον). As in Eph. generally the future eschatological aspects are not absent here, but the action of the σωτήρ has a present reference. [68]

c. In John the story of the Samaritan woman closes with the statement of her countrymen: αὐτοὶ γὰρ ἀκηκόαμεν, καὶ οἴδαμεν ὅτι οὗτός ἐστιν ἀληθῶς ὁ σωτὴρ τοῦ κόσμου, Jn. 4:42. The Samaritans, whom the Jews regarded as Gentiles, represent the whole world here. The same phrase occurs at an emphatic point in 1 Jn. 4:14: καὶ ἡμεῖς τεθεάμεθα καὶ μαρτυροῦμεν ὅτι ὁ πατὴρ ἀπέσταλκεν τὸν υἱὸν σωτῆρα τοῦ κόσμου. It is methodologically illegitimate to take κόσμος here in a different sense from that which is bears elsewhere in John → III, 892, 6 ff. especially as σῴζω is combined with κόσμος in Jn. 3:17 too. The meaning of σωτὴρ τοῦ κόσμου is unequivocally defined hereby.

3. σωτήρ in the Pastoral Epistles and 2 Peter.

a. Of the 10 instances of σωτήρ in the Past. 6 are in Tt. (1:3, 4; 2:10, 13; 3:4, 6), one in 2 Tm. (1:10) and 3 in 1 Tm. (1:1; 2:3; 4:10). Only once (1 Tm. 4:10) is σωτήρ used predicatively. Elsewhere it is a title with ἡμῶν. It is used 6 times of God and 4 of Christ. The meaning and significance of the term are connected with the particular thrust of the Past.

---

[65] E. Lohmeyer, Christuskult u. Kaiserkult (1919), 27 f. thinks there is antithesis to the emperor as σωτήρ, but he drops this view in Loh. Phil., ad loc. and Dib. Ph.³, ad loc. also rejects it; cf. Dib. Past. Exc. σωτήρ on 2 Tm. 1:10, No. 1.

[66] So Ew., Dib. Gefbr., ad loc. and C. Masson, L'Épître de Saint Paul aux Éph., Commentaire du NT, 11 (1953), ad loc.; but cf. Wagner, 220 f.

[67] So with → IV, 1105, 1 ff. (Jeremias) against Schlier Eph.³ on 5:27 and Masson, op. cit., ad loc.

[68] For an express discussion of Eph. 5:23 ff. cf. Schlier Eph.³, 253-280; cf. also J. T. Ross, The Conception of σωτηρία in the NT (1947), 250.

Opponents are advancing the thesis that salvation is not for all men. In later Gnosticism this is a deduction from the doctrine of the natures. All the six instances in which God is called our σωτήρ are fairly recognisably related to this teaching. This is plain in 1 Tm. 2:3 f., where prayer for all men, especially for those in authority, is called καλὸν καὶ ἀπόδεκτον ἐνώπιον τοῦ σωτῆρος ἡμῶν θεοῦ, ὃς πάντας ἀνθρώπους θέλει σωθῆναι. It is no less clear in 1 Tm. 4:10: ἠλπίκαμεν ἐπὶ θεῷ ζῶντι, ὅς ἐστιν σωτὴρ πάντων ἀνθρώπων, μάλιστα πιστῶν, and Tt. 2:10 f., where the admonition to a way of life which will adorn the doctrine of our Saviour, God, is supported by the explanation: ἐπεφάνη γὰρ ἡ χάρις τοῦ θεοῦ σωτήριος πᾶσιν ἀνθρώποις. Similarly the author's solemn self-designation as ἀπόστολος Χριστοῦ Ἰησοῦ κατ' ἐπιταγὴν θεοῦ σωτῆρος ἡμῶν (1 Tm. 1:1), and cf. Tt. 1:3: ἐν κηρύγματι ὃ ἐπιστεύθην ἐγὼ κατ' ἐπιταγὴν τοῦ σωτῆρος ἡμῶν θεοῦ, is obviously designed to stress from the very first against opponents the universality of the offer of salvation. The same "all men" occurs in Tt. 2:11, and it is also in view in the preceding verse: ἵνα τὴν διδασκαλίαν τὴν τοῦ σωτῆρος ἡμῶν θεοῦ κοσμῶσιν ἐν πᾶσιν. One may conclude from this that σωτήρ as applied to God is not just an OT mode of expression and it is certainly not an attenuated term with no specific content. Furthermore the ἡμῶν in θεὸς ὁ σωτὴρ ἡμῶν cannot be meant exclusively as though God were "our" Saviour alone and not the Saviour of all men; the σωτήρ means that God is the Saviour whom we know and in whom we believe. Applied thus to God σωτήρ means more than just the Benefactor or Sustainer of earthly life. It is true that χρηστότης and φιλανθρωπία (Tt. 3:4) point in this direction in the light of their use in the ruler cult. Nevertheless, the allusion to baptism in Tt. 3:5 and the continuation καὶ εἰς ἐπίγνωσιν ἀληθείας ἐλθεῖν (1 Tm. 2:4) make the theological content of σωτήρ perfectly clear.

Only in respect of 1 Tm. 4:10 does any question arise. In v. 8 εὐσέβεια has a promise both for this life and also for the life to come. Hence one might ask whether σωτήρ in v. 10 does not have the broader sense of "benefactor," God being the Benefactor and Preserver of all men in this life and of believers in the life to come. [69] Now the false teachers forced the author of the Past. to place a high value on the natural orders of life. Hence this view cannot be completely set aside. All the same it is better not to take this v. apart from 1 Tm. 2:3 f. God is called σωτήρ... μάλιστα πιστῶν because believers have received salvation, and He will be σωτήρ for the rest only when they do so too. Restriction of σωτηρία to a mere few is thus avoided here also.

Apart from Tt. 1:4 all the passages in which ὁ σωτὴρ ἡμῶν applies to Christ offer an elucidation in the immediate context which explains the use of σωτήρ. Grace has now appeared διὰ τῆς ἐπιφανείας τοῦ σωτῆρος ἡμῶν Χριστοῦ Ἰησοῦ, καταργήσαντος μὲν τὸν θάνατον φωτίσαντος δὲ ζωὴν καὶ ἀφθαρσίαν διὰ τοῦ εὐαγγελίου (2 Tm. 1:10). Then there is reference to the expectation of the blessed hope and ἐπιφάνειαν τῆς δόξης τοῦ μεγάλου θεοῦ καὶ σωτῆρος ἡμῶν Χριστοῦ Ἰησοῦ, ὃς ἔδωκεν ἑαυτὸν ὑπὲρ ἡμῶν ἵνα λυτρώσηται ἡμᾶς ἀπὸ πάσης ἀνομίας

---

[69] So Wagner, 221 f. One can hardly agree with Schl. Past. and J. Jeremias, *Die Briefe an Tm. u. Tt.*, NT Deutsch, 9⁸ (1963), *ad loc.*, who think the ref. is to the millennium.

(Tt. 2:13). [70] Finally we read of the Holy Ghost whom God has richly poured out upon us διὰ Ἰησοῦ Χριστοῦ τοῦ σωτῆρος ἡμῶν, ἵνα δικαιωθέντες τῇ ἐκείνου χάριτι κληρονόμοι γενηθῶμεν κατ' ἐλπίδα ζωῆς αἰωνίου (Tt. 3:6 f.). Here, as in R. 5:9 f., accomplished δικαιοσύνη is distinguished from the κληρονόμους γενέσθαι of eternal life which is still awaited in hope, but σωτήρ applies to both, just as expectation of δόξα is nearby in Tt. 2:13, but the task of the σωτήρ is directly explained to be liberation from all lawlessness. In 2 Tm. 1:10 σωτήρ even refers to the historical Lord. Only Tt. 1:4: χάρις καὶ εἰρήνη ἀπὸ θεοῦ πατρὸς καὶ Χριστοῦ Ἰησοῦ τοῦ σωτῆρος ἡμῶν, does not provide any immediate reference for σωτήρ in the context. Apart from this v. the use of σωτήρ in the Past., whether with reference to God or with reference to Christ, is always either suggested or made plain by the context. Only in Tt. 2:13 and 3:6 f. do we have in outline in the expression ὁ σωτὴρ ἡμῶν Ἰησοῦς Χριστός a clear delimitation from some opposing thesis; the counterposition is plain to see in 2 Tm. 2:18.

b. In 2 Peter σωτήρ is used only of Jesus and it is relatively common, 1:1, 11; 2:20; 3:2, 18. The contexts, however, provide no clear basis for its choice. The three titles of Jesus, θεός, κύριος, and σωτήρ alternate for no obvious reason, as may be seen from the expression ἐν ἐπιγνώσει: ἐν ἐπιγνώσει τοῦ θεοῦ καὶ Ἰησοῦ τοῦ κυρίου ἡμῶν (1:2); ἐν ἐπιγνώσει τοῦ κυρίου καὶ σωτῆρος Ἰησοῦ Χριστοῦ (2:20); ἐν ... γνώσει τοῦ κυρίου ἡμῶν καὶ σωτῆρος Ἰησοῦ Χριστοῦ (3:18); cf. also ἐν δικαιοσύνῃ τοῦ θεοῦ ἡμῶν καὶ σωτῆρος Ἰησοῦ Χριστοῦ (1:1). It would seem that σωτήρ was a common title for Christ in the days of 2 Pt. An unmistakable liking for solemn and resounding statements contributed to the frequent use of σωτήρ predication in this letter.

E. σωτήρ in the Post-Apostolic Fathers.

If the use of σωτήρ for Christ seemed to have established itself in the period between Past and 2 Pt., the statistics for the post-apost. fathers are all the more surprising. It does not occur at all in Did., Barn. and Herm. It is used only once in relation to God, with an OT and later Jewish colouring, in 1 Cl. (59, 3). It ref. to Christ only once each in Pol., Mart. Pol., Dg. and 2 Cl., and 4 times in Ign. In most of the instances the word is felt to be full of material content: the dead Polycarp εὐλογεῖ τὸν κύριον ἡμῶν Ἰησοῦν Χριστόν, τὸν σωτῆρα τῶν ψυχῶν ἡμῶν καὶ κυβερνήτην τῶν σωμάτων ἡμῶν καὶ ποιμένα τῆς κατὰ τὴν οἰκουμένην καθολικῆς ἐκκλησίας, Mart. Pol., 19, 2; νῦν δὲ τὸν σωτῆρα δείξας (God) δυνατὸν σῴζειν καὶ τὰ ἀδύνατα, Dg., 9, 6; in the concluding doxology of 2 Cl. we read: τῷ μόνῳ θεῷ ... τῷ ἐξαποστείλαντι ἡμῖν τὸν σωτῆρα καὶ ἀρχηγὸν τῆς ἀφθαρσίας, δι' οὗ καὶ ἐφανέρωσεν ἡμῖν τὴν ἀλήθειαν καὶ τὴν ἐπουράνιον ζωήν, 2 Cl., 20, 5. In 2 of the Ign. ref., again, there is obvious acquaintance with the content of σωτήρ: ἐξαίρετον δέ τι ἔχει τὸ εὐαγγέλιον, τὴν παρουσίαν τοῦ σωτῆρος, κυρίου ἡμῶν Ἰησοῦ Χριστοῦ, τὸ πάθος αὐτοῦ καὶ τὴν ἀνάστασιν, Ign. Phld., 9, 2, where σωτήρ is not used as a title, and Sm., 7, 1: The false

---

[70] The transl. "of the great God, our Saviour Jesus Christ" is championed by Wbg. Past. and W. Lock, The Pastoral Epistles, ICC (1952), ad loc. → IV, 538, 21 ff.; 540, 13 ff. Dib. Past. is indefinite. Schl. Past. and Jeremias, op. cit. (→ n. 69), ad loc. reject it. In 2 Pt. 1:1 this transl. of τοῦ θεοῦ ἡμῶν καὶ σωτῆρος Ἰησοῦ Χριστοῦ is confirmed by the par. τοῦ κυρίου ἡμῶν καὶ σωτῆρος Ἰησοῦ Χριστοῦ in 1:11, but the different position of ἡμῶν in the one case and the adj. μέγας in the other should be noted. Hence Christ does not seem to be called the great God here.

teachers do not confess: τὴν εὐχαριστίαν σάρκα εἶναι τοῦ σωτῆρος ἡμῶν ᾿Ιησοῦ Χριστοῦ τὴν ὑπὲρ τῶν ἁμαρτιῶν ἡμῶν παθοῦσαν. In the other Ign. passages, Eph., 1, 1; Mg. (prologue) and Pol. (prologue) there is no evident reason for the use of the title σωτήρ.

It is clear, then, that while σωτήρ is a title for Jesus it usually has a specific content and is not particularly common. At any rate, ὁ σωτήρ is never used as a current unequivocal designation in the way that ὁ κύριος is. Nowhere does there seem to be any point of contact with σωτήρ as part of the style of imperial Rome, not even by way of antithesis.

F. σωτήρ in Gnosticism.

1. Apart from Chr. influence σωτήρ does not seem to appear in the Gnostic sources. It is not in Corp. Herm., nor the original of the Naassene Sermon, nor is Simon Magus called saviour in what we read of him in patristic accounts. Of the heads of the Gnostic schools only Menander called himself σωτήρ, Eus. Hist. Eccl., III, 26, 1. It is worth noting that the Mandaean writings once ref. to "Jesus the Saviour" מאהיאנא ישו , Lidz. Ginza R., 29, 19; the use here of the Aram.-Syr. stem חיא, not elsewhere employed thus, seems to offer a close par. to Gk. σωτήρ. But this claim of Jesus is rejected in the context, as in *ibid.,* 50, 35, though a different stem is used here. Apart from this, equivalents of σωτήρ play no particular role in the Mandaean lit. In answer to the scornful question of the planetary powers who would be physician, liberator, redeemer, deliverer (→ 1001, 43 ff.), "came the great helper, the messenger, whom life sent," Lidz., Joh. 69, 4 f. Alongside the not very common "redeemer" or "liberator"[71] one often finds "helper" נאצבא.[72] It is said of Mande dHaije: "He is a support for me in the world and a helper in the place of light," Lidz. Joh., 129, 10 f. This term is esp. common in the Ginza.

2. In Chr. Gnosticism the concept is plain to see in the Coptic sources, since the Gk. σωτήρ is adopted. If in Chr. Gnosticism one sometimes finds other saviours, like the ἐπίνοια of light in Apocr. Joh.[73] or Eleleth in The Nature of the Archons,[74] nevertheless Jesus is the decisive Saviour. On the basis of the NT, titles like Χριστός, κύριος, σωτήρ, λόγος, Son of Man and Son of God are used with the name Jesus; in this regard it should be noted that σωτήρ was a familiar title in the Church at the time when the gt. Gnostic systems took shape. "The Son" is mostly used in Ev. Veritatis;[75] σωτήρ occurs only at 16, 38. The two chief names in Sophia Jesu Christi are Christ and σωτήρ. The disciples usually address their Master as σωτήρ, and sometimes the answer comes as "the σωτήρ says" or, mostly, "the perfect σωτήρ says."[76] In Apocr. Joh. σωτήρ occurs twice at 20, 8; 77, 5; elsewhere Χριστός is used. What is meant is that He who gives John the revelation is a figure of the heavenly world. Things are much the same in the Gospel of Philip;[77] here σωτήρ occurs only in Saying 55 (112, 3);[78] elsewhere one finds "Jesus" or almost as frequently "the Lord."

---

[71] The only other instances in Joh. are 186, 10; 223, 9. 17; 226, 22 f.

[72] On the meaning cf. Lidz. Joh., 60, n. 6.

[73] Ed. and transl. W. Till, "Die gnostischen Schr. d. kpt. Pap. Berolinensis 8502," TU, 60 (1955), 33-51, 78-193.

[74] Ed. P. Labib, *Coptic Gnostic Pap. in the Coptic Museum at Old Cairo,* I (1956), 134, 20-145, 23, cf. H. M. Schenke, "Das Wesen d. Archonten," ThLZ, 83 (1958), 661-670.

[75] Ed. and transl. M. Malinine, H. C. Puech and G. Quispel (1956).

[76] "The blessed σωτήρ," 126, 17 f.; "the holy one," 98, 14.

[77] Ed. Labib, *op. cit.,* cf. H. M. Schenke, "Das Ev. nach Philippus. Ein Ev. d. Valentinianer aus d. Funde von Nag-Hamadi," ThLZ, 84 (1959), 5-26.

[78] σωτήρ cannot be descried on the photographic reproduction.

3. In the Gk. sources and records σωτήρ occurs 3 times in the Naassene Sermon, Hipp. Ref., V, 8, 11. 27 introducing a NT quotation, once in the same way ὁ Ἰησοῦς, V, 8, 7, and once on the basis of Eph. 5:14 ὁ Χριστός, V, 7, 33. σωτήρ does not occur in the Gnosis of Baruch nor in the account of Carpocrates in Iren. Haer., I, 25. But it may be found 4 times in Basilides acc. to the accounts in Iren. and Hipp., probably from the source. [79]

4. In Act. Thom. ὁ σωτήρ is common as well as ὁ Χριστός or ὁ Ἰησοῦς, though it seldom occurs in narrative, [80] being found mostly in prayers and preaching, usually with a dependent gen.: πάντων σωτήρ, 48 (164, 12); σωτὴρ Ἰησοῦς πάσης ἀνθρωπότητος, 136 (243, 2 f.); ὁ σωτὴρ βασιλέων καὶ ἀρχόντων, ὅς ἐστιν πάντων κριτής, 139 (246, 19 f.); ὁ σωτὴρ πάσης κτίσεως, ὁ τὸν κόσμον ζωοποιῶν καὶ τὰς ψυχὰς ἐνδυναμῶν, 10 (114, 9 f.); ὁ σωτὴρ ἡμῶν, 39 (157, 3); 155 (264, 5); 161 (272, 21); ὁ σωτὴρ τῶν ψυχῶν, 42 (159, 17); similarly 141 (248, 5); 143 (249, 23); 149 (258, 6).

5. Except in Act. Thom. σωτήρ carries no particular stress in the Gnostic systems mentioned thus far. But the position is different in Valentinianism. Iren. Haer., I, 1, 3 notes that this preferred to call Jesus σωτήρ rather than κύριος. If he is not quite accurate in this, there are only few exceptions. Equally surprising is the fact that the name Jesus is also less prominent in this branch of Gnosticism. This is probably connected with the pt. that Jesus was a very complicated entity. The one who really acts in Him is the figure brought forth by all the aeons as their common "fruit" and called Ἰησοῦς, Χριστός, Λόγος, τὰ πάντα or Παράκλητος, Iren. Haer., I, 2, 6; 3, 1; 4, 5, though His true name, which appears again and again in the records, is σωτήρ. Only in this form of Gnosticism, then, does σωτήρ have an established place. If other Chr. Gnostics use many titles for the Redeemer, and if linguistically possible par. like ἐλευθερωτής, λυτρωτής, βοηθός are notably rare, as they are also in the Church, it is plain that in the main Gnosticism followed Christian terminology and did not produce any of its own. [81] In keeping is the fact that the personal element in σωτήρ (→ 1004, 8 ff.) is less prominent in Gnosticism; the Redeemer is the bearer of a redeeming summons. [82] When the activity of the Redeemer goes beyond the bringing of the call we are usually in the vicinity of a magically understood sacrament, as may be seen from Act. Thom. At this pt. Gnosticism becomes part and parcel of the mystery religions.

G. The Primitive Christian Use of σωτήρ.

Throughout primitive Christianity σῴζω and σωτηρία are important terms denoting salvation or deliverance. Both come from Jesus Himself. Hence it is fundamentally no surprise that σωτήρ is used as a name for Jesus. Its content is determined by σῴζω and σωτηρία. It might have been expected that in view of the frequency with which σῴζω and σωτηρία occur primitive Christianity would have made a similar common use of σωτήρ irrespective of the prior use of the word. But this is far from being the case. Except in the Past (→ 1016, 29 ff.) and 2 Pt. (→ 1018, 15 ff.) one can only say that there is a restraint in the use of σωτήρ which is to be explained by the fact that in the Jewish sphere σωτήρ could easily be linked with the expectation of a liberator from national bondage (→ 987, 25 ff.),

---

[79] Iren. Haer., I, 24, 5: *salvator;* Hipp. Ref., VII, 20, 1; 25, 5; 27, 5. In Hipp. Ref., VII, 27, 8 σωτήρ is the father's own term.

[80] Act. Thom. 1 f. (100, 9; 102, 5); ref. to a dominical saying, 28 (144, 17); also ἤρχοντο εἰς τὸ καταφύγιον τοῦ σωτῆρος, 27 (143, 13 f.).

[81] The Mandaean works are the only exception.

[82] W. Foerster, "Das Wesen d. Gnosis," *Die Welt als Geschichte,* 15 (1955), 111-113.

while in the pagan world it suggested the idea of an earthly benefactor, especially in the figure of the emperor, → 1011, 11 ff. Hence the word might kindle hopes and ideas which the Gospel could not promise to fulfil. Naturally this might also happen with σώζω and σωτηρία, but here the total complex of statements could more easily ward off wrong ideas than in the case of the title σωτήρ. The chief title for Jesus in primitive Christianity is thus κύριος rather than σωτήρ → III, 1088, 26 ff.

The surprising restraint in using σωτήρ for Jesus continues in the post-apostolic fathers, though to a lesser degree. One certainly cannot trace an unbroken crescendo in the use of the terms beginning with the older Pauline letters and moving by way of the Past. to the post-apostolic fathers. Chronologically the Past. stand apart in their usage. In them the ideas connected with the phrase "God our σωτήρ" are just as plain, however, as is the polemical edge of the phrase in answer to the false teachers. When the title is applied to Jesus the related ideas are no less plain, but one can only guess at its polemical thrust → 1018, 12 ff. If the restraint one finds elsewhere in the NT and primitive Christianity is thrown off here, it is clear that this is not due to any relation, whether positive [83] or antithetical, to the ruler cult. [84] The facts can be understood only in the context of the general linguistic distinctiveness of the Past., which is connected with the aim of the epistles to protect the churches again Gnostic fanaticism and which is peculiar to the author and his own brand of theology. Since Gnosticism was a revolutionary reaction against the Greek view of the world, [85] it is no accident that the man who fought it used Greek terms. σωτήρ fits in at this point. [86] Not the title as such, but the content of the σωτηρία which He brought, raises up Jesus as σωτήρ into the divine sphere.

† σωτήριος.

1. In Gk. σωτήριος has all the range of the verb σώζω. Helen is with the Dioscuri ναυτίλοις σωτήριος, Eur. Or., 1637. The brave in war is τοῖς ξύμπασι σωτήριος, Thuc., VII, 64, 2. With bitter irony Dionysos says to Pentheus: πομπὸς δ' εἰμ' ἐγὼ σωτήριος, Eur. Ba., 965; with obj. gen.: τάχ ἂν γενοίμεθ' αὐτοῦ (Ajax) σὺν θεῷ σωτήριοι, Soph. Ai., 778 f. Of animals the horse is σωτηριώτατος τῷ ἀναβάτῃ ἐν τοῖς πολεμικοῖς, Xenoph. Eq., 3, 12. The rays of the sun are called σωτήριοι, Aesch. Suppl., 213; the ἤθη of prudent archons are σωτήρια for the city, Plat. Polit., 311a; water is σωτήριον ("life-sustaining") for fish, Heracl. Fr., 61 (Diels, I, 164, 7). An ἐλπὶς σπέρματος σωτηρίου is a hope for posterity to maintain the race, Aesch. Choeph., 236. The sustaining of the universe: ὁ νοῦς is σωτήριος τῶν ὄντων, Corp. Herm., 2, 12. From the philosopher one hears quae dicuntur utilia ac salubria sunt et errorum atque vitiorum medicinas ferunt, Muson. Fr., 49; politically the Σεβαστεῖον in Alexandria is ἐλπὶς καὶ ἀναγομένοις καὶ καταπλέουσι σωτήριος, gives hope of a fair voyage, Philo Leg. Gaj., 151; religiously τοῦτο μόνον σωτήριον ἀνθρώπῳ ἐστίν, ἡ γνῶσις τοῦ θεοῦ, Corp. Herm., 10, 15. So, too, the adv. σωτηρίως: Τὸ act πολιτικῶς καὶ σωτηρίως means in a way which is politically clever and beneficial to the state, Plut.

---

83 This is the most common view, cf. B. Wendland Hell. Kult., 221 f.; W. Bousset, Kyrios Christos² (1921), 245.

84 C. F. D. Moule, "The Influence of Circumstances on the Use of Christological Terms," JThSt, 10 (1959), 262 f.

85 Jonas Gnosis, I, 214-251.

86 Dib. Past. Exc. on 2 Tm. 1:10 under No. 6 reaches a similar conclusion, rejecting a "single derivation of the Chr. title Soter" and drawing attention to the manifold Hell. use of the term.

Lucull., 5 (I, 495a). σωτηρίως ἔχοντες are sick people who may hope to be cured, Plut. Quaest. Nat., 26, 3 (II, 918d).

The noun τὰ σωτήρια means "thankoffering," with θύω, Xenoph. An., III, 2, 9; with ἄγω "to celebrate a feast of thanksgiving," Luc. Hermot., 86. As a noun the adj. in the sing. normally denotes "means of deliverance": ἐπινοεῖν τι σωτήριον, Luc. Jup. Trag., 18.

Foerster

2. The LXX uses σωτήριον "what is beneficial," "deliverance," for the stem ישע on the one side, once ישע hi at Is. 63:1, 8 times ישע, 36 times ישועה, and 5 תשועה. In this usage it is practically the equivalent of σωτηρία and the two may be interchangeable, cf. Ps. 42:5; 43:5 with 42:11 and Ps. 119:41, 81, 123, 166, 174 with 119:155. σωτήριον also occurs in Gn. 41:16 for שלום, [1] Is. 33:20 for מועד "festive time," 38:11 for one of the two יה, usually taken to be an abbreviation of ישועה, 40:5 in place of יחדו as a par. of כבוד, 60:6 for תהלת "fame" in acc. with the parallelism in v. 18. [2]

On the other side in 72 of 86 instances σωτήριον denotes the offering שלם or שלמים (except at Am. 5:22 always plur.) Ex. 20 — Ju. 21; Ez. 43-46; Am. 5:22; 1-2 Ch., also in the list of sacrificial gifts Lv. 17:4; Jos. 22:29. [3] LXX took this mostly to be a sacrifice of salvation, a sacrifice which brings salvation. On the other hand the transl. in 1 S. — 2 K. uses εἰρηνικός in various ways in the sense of "peace-offering"; this was obviously the work of other hands. In both cases LXX defines the sacrifice materially by its conjectured goal and work, partly under the influence of the occasional emphasis on its joyous character, Dt. 27:7; the Hbr. word, however, is more likely to bear a formal ref. It is true that the offering denoted by שלם or שלמים, [4] by reason of the many meanings of the stem שלם, is often understood in acc. with the LXX as a "salvation-offering" σωτήριον [5] or "peace-offering" [6] or sometimes in other ways. [7] More to the point, however, is derivation from שלם pi in the admittedly rare sense "to complete," i.e., "concluding sacrifice." [8]

Thus the concluding sacrifice always comes last in lists of offerings, 2 K. 16:13; P Nu. 15:8; 29:39; Jos. 22:27. It seems originally to have marked the end of a feast made up of burnt offerings, Ex. 20:24; Ju. 20:26; 21:4; 1 S. 13:9; 2 S. 6:17 f.; 24:25; 1 K. 8:64, for the related sacrificial meal (cf. Dt. 27:7) established close fellowship among those who made the offering and between them and God. [9] This rite was also part of the זבח and offered a fairly early basis for the union of the two forms of offering; in 49 out of

---

σ ω τ ή ρ ι ο ς . [1] Joseph's promise that God (and not he) will answer Pharaoh שלום implies that without God no saving answer can be given.

[2] Is. 63:1; Jon. 2:10; 1 Ch. 16:23 have the variant σωτηρία.

[3] Variants are σωτηρία at Nu. 6:14, θυσιαστήριον at Dt. 27:7, τελεῖαι Ju. 20:26; adj. σωτήριος Am. 5:22.

[4] Cf. also Phoenician שלם as a kind of offering, M. Lidzbarski, *Hndbch. d. nordsemitischen Epigraphik*, I (1898), 376 and Southern Arab. משלם, F. Hommel, "Die südarab. Altertümer des Wiener Hofmuseums," *Aufsätze u. Abhandlungen arabistisch-semitologischen Inhalts* (1892), 138 and 182.

[5] E.g., G. Hölscher, *Gesch. d. isr. u. jüd. Religion* (1922), 77; F. Nötscher, *Bibl. Altertumskunde* (1940), 323.

[6] E.g., B. Baentsch, *Ex., Lv., Handkomm. AT*, I, 2 (1903) on Ex. 20:24; E. Meyer, *Die Israeliten u. ihre Nachbarstämme* (1906), 554; G. E. Wright, *Bibl. Arch.* (1957), 111; E. L. Ehrlich, *Kultsymbolik im AT u. im nachbibl. Judt.* (1959), 41 (with question-marks).

[7] C. v. Orelli, Art. "Opferkultus d. AT," RE³, 14 (1904), 392 f.: "Gemeinschaftsopfer"; A. Wendel, *Das Opfer in d. altisr. Religion* (1927), 96: "Verbrüderungsopfer als eine Form d. Gemeinschaftsopfers"; but cf. G. B. Gray, *Sacrifice in the OT* (1925), 7; H. Haag, "Dankopfer," *Bibellex.* (1951), 311.

[8] Köhler-Baumg., *s.v.*

[9] For the later P ritual cf. Lv. and on this R. Rendtorff, "Die Gesetze in d. Priesterschrift," FRL, 62 (1954), 5-23.

86 instances שְׁלָמִים is combined with זֶבַח. שְׁלָמִים is at first put with זְבָחִים by way of explanation Ex. 24:5; 1 S. 11:15, and thus means "sacrifices which are concluding offerings." Corresponding to the Deuteronomic view is שְׁלָמִים זבח in Dt. 27:7; Jos. 8:31, "to slay concluding offerings (as sacrifices)." P esp. then has closer links in the gen. which make the "sacrifice" less prominent: זֶבַח שְׁלָמִים "a sacrifice consisting of concluding offerings" Lv. 3:1 etc., or זִבְחֵי שְׁלָמִים, "sacrifices consisting of concluding offerings" Ex. 29:28 etc. Finally in lists of various kinds of offerings שְׁלָמִים replaces the absent זֶבַח, Lv. 9:22; Nu. 29:39; Ez. 45:15 etc. It is plain that the sacrifice constantly lost in significance and was first neutralised, then replaced, by the ritually similar concluding offering. [10]

Fohrer

3. In Judaism, as in the OT → 1022, 14 ff., τὸ σωτήριον is used for the "salvation-offering," Sir. 35:1; 47:2 (50:15?); 1 Macc. 4:56; σωτήρια ἄγω "to celebrate a feast of victory," 3 Macc. 6:30; κώθωνα σωτήριον συστησάμενοι, "to establish a feast of deliverance," 3 Macc. 6:31; cf. ἐποίησαν πότον σωτήριον, 7:18. σωτήριος as adj. means "bringing salvation": σωτήριος εὐπείθεια is the obedience which saves (earthly) life, 4 Macc. 12:6, cf. 15:26. The noun τὸ σωτήριον occurs only once with obj. gen.: ἰδοὺ Σιων ἡ πόλις τὸ σωτήριον ἡμῶν, "that which saves us," Is. 33:20; elsewhere with θεοῦ or κυρίου as subj. gen. Is. 38:11; 40:5; 60:6; Sir. 39:18, cf. 4 Macc. 11:7 (A and other MSS ἐλπίδα εἶχες παρὰ θεῷ σωτηρίου).

In the pseudepigr., apart from "salvation-offering" in Test. L. 9:7, σωτήριον is used only for God's "salvation." It will come from Levi and Judah, S. 7:1; D. 5:10 (belonging to the original). This also applies in B. 9:2: ἕως ὁ ὕψιστος ἀποστείλῃ τὸ σωτήριον αὐτοῦ ἐν ἐπισκοπῇ μονογενοῦς προφήτου. Jud. 22:2 is not clear: ἐν ἀλλοφύλοις συντελεσθήσεται ἡ βασιλεία μου, ἕως τοῦ ἐλθεῖν τὸ σωτήριον τοῦ Ἰσραήλ, ἕως τῆς παρουσίας θεοῦ τῆς δικαιοσύνης, τοῦ ἡσυχάσαι τὸν Ἰακὼβ ἐν εἰρήνῃ καὶ πάντα τὰ ἔθνη, cf. B. 10:5: ἕως ὅτου ἀποκαλύψει Κύριος τὸ σωτήριον αὐτοῦ πᾶσι τοῖς ἔθνεσιν, where the last words at least are an interpolation. 4 Esr. speaks of the *salutare* of God, meaning the final salvation in a new world at 6:25, but salvation on this earth, it would seem, at 9:8. OT and later Jewish ref. show that τὸ σωτήριον does not denote "means of deliverance" as in Gk. (→ 1022, 4 f.) but "salvation" itself. [11] In Joseph. σωτήριος occurs as adj.; τὸ σωτήριον τοῦ θεοῦ does not seem to be used, and it is absent from Philo too.

4. In the NT the adjective σωτήριος occurs independently only at Tt. 2:11: ἐπεφάνη γὰρ ἡ χάρις τοῦ θεοῦ σωτήριος πᾶσιν ἀνθρώποις ("bringing salvation"). Elsewhere τὸ σωτήριον is always used in quotations or at any rate in close allusion to the LXX. Lk. 2:30: εἶδον οἱ ὀφθαλμοί μου τὸ σωτήριόν σου, is based on Is. 40:5, a passage which Luke, going beyond Mark, quotes in 3:6 and which is also echoed in Ac. 28:28. [12] Eph. 6:17: τὴν περικεφαλαίαν τοῦ σωτηρίου δέξασθε, follows Is. 59:17, the OT reference being to the "helmet of victory," i.e., God. The link with the OT makes understanding of the expression in Ephesians difficult. Perhaps, as in OT expressions, one should think in term of God's salvation. But possibly the LXX led to the choice of τοῦ σωτηρίου instead of τῆς σωτηρίας. If

---

[10] L. Köhler, *Theol. d. AT³* (1953), 178 f.

[11] As against J. T. Ross, *The Conception of σωτηρία in the NT* (1947), 9, who always takes τὸ σωτήριον as a nomen instrumenti.

[12] τὸ σωτήριον can hardly be "means of deliverance" here, as Ross thinks, *op. cit.*, 29 and 34 f.; on this view Ross is forced in a very artificial way to ref. τοῖς ἔθνεσιν ἀπεστάλη τοῦτο τὸ σωτήριον τοῦ θεοῦ in Ac. 28:28 to Paul and his message, 138 f.

so, this is one of the passages in Eph. in which σωτηρία is already present (→ 994, 12 ff.) and the distinction from the parallel in 1 Th. 5:8: ἐνδυσάμενοι ... περικεφαλαίαν ἐλπίδα σωτηρίας, marks it as peculiar to Eph. [13] → V, 315, 1 ff.

5. In the post-apost. fathers τὸ σωτήριον (θεοῦ etc.) occurs in quotations at 1 Cl., 15, 6; 18, 12; 35, 12. Only in 1 Cl., 36, 1 does it catch up τὸ σωτήριον τοῦ θεοῦ from the preceding quotation and relate it to τὸ σωτήριον ἡμῶν 'Ιησοῦς Χριστός. Thus τὸ σωτήριον takes its sense from the LXX and is used only under LXX influence.

Foerster

---

† σῶμα, † σωματικός, † σύσσωμος

Contents: A. The Greek World: 1. The Period up to Plato; 2. From Plato to Aristotle; 3. The Later Fourth and the Third Centuries; 4. The Period from c. 100 B.C. to 100 A.D.;

---

[13] Ross, 256 transl. here too "the helmet as a means of salvation" and sees an abbreviated rendering of the expression in 1 Th. 5:8: Hope of σωτηρία is a means of defence.

σ ῶ μ α κ τ λ . Cr.-Kö., Liddell-Scott, Pass., Pr.-Bauer, Thes. Steph., *s.v.* C. K. Barrett, *From First Adam to Last* (1962), 73-76, 96 f.; P. Benoit, "Corps, tête et plérôme dans les épîtres de la captivité," *Rev. Bibl.*, 63 (1956), 5-44; E. Best, *One Body in Christ* (1955); Bultmann Theol.[4], 189-199; C. Colpe, "Zur Leib-Christi-Vorstellung im Eph.," *Judt.-Urchr.-Kirche, Festschr. f. J. Jeremias*, Beih. z. ZNW, 26 (1960), 172-187; C. T. Craig, "Soma Christou," *The Joy of Study*, ed. S. E. Johnson (1951), 73-85; M. E. Dahl, *The Resurrection of the Body. A Study of 1 C. 15* (1962); F. W. Dillistone, "How is the Church Christ's Body?" *Theology Today*, 2 (1945/46), 56-68; D. Dimitriakos, Μέγα λεξικὸν τῆς Ἑλληνικῆς γλώσσης, VIII (1950), *s.v.*; C. M. Edsman, "The Body and Eternal Life," *Mélanges J. Pedersen*, II (1946), 34-104; A. J. Festugière, *La révélation d'Hermès Trismégiste*, I-IV (1944-54), esp. II, 75-520; A. Feuillet, "L'Église plérôme du Christ d'après Eph. 1:23," *Nouvelle Rev. Théol.*, 78 (1956), 449-472, 593-610; R. M. Grant, "The Resurrection of the Body," *Journal of Religion*, 28 (1948), 120-130, 188-208; K. Grobel, "σῶμα as 'Self, Person' in the Septuagint," *Nt.liche Stud. f. R. Bultmann*, Beih. z. ZNW, 21 (1954), 52-59; H. Hegermann, "Die Vorstellung vom Schöpfungsmittler im hell. Judt. u. Urchr.," *TU*, 82 (1961), 138-157; R. Hirzel, "Die Person," *SA Münch.*, 10 (1914), 5-7; E. Käsemann, *Leib u. Leib Christi* (1933); also "Anliegen u. Eigenart d. paul. Abendmahlslehre," *Exeget. Versuche u. Besinnungen*, I (1960), 11-34; also "Das Interpretationsproblem d. Eph.," *ThLZ*, 86 (1961), 1-8; C. Kearns, "The Church, the Body of Christ acc. to St. Paul," *Irish Ecclesiastical Record*, 90 (1958), 1-11, 145-157; 91 (1959), 1-15, 313-327; W. L. Knox, "Parallels to the NT Use uf σῶμα," *JThSt*, 39 (1938), 243-246; H. Koller, "σῶμα bei Homer," *Glotta*, 37 (1958), 278-281; J. J. Meuzelaar, *Der Leib d. Messias. Eine exeget. Studie über den Gedanken vom Leib Christi in den Paulusbriefen* (1961); F. Mussner, *Christus, das All u. d. Kirche* (1955), 118-174; A. Oepke, *Das neue Gottesvolk* (1950), 219-236; also "Leib Christi oder Volk Gottes bei Pls.," *ThLZ*, 79 (1954), 363-368; D. R. G. Owen, *Body and Soul* (1956); E. Percy, *Der Leib Christi in den paul. Homologumena u. Antilegomena* (1942); I. J. du Plessis, *Christus als Hoofd van Kerk en Kosmos* (1962); M. Pohlenz, *Die Stoa*, I (1948); II (1949); J. Reuss, "Die Kirche als 'Leib Christi' u. d. Herkunft dieser Vorstellung beim Ap. Pls.," *BZ, NF*, 2 (1958), 103-127; J. A. T. Robinson, *The Body* (1952); H. M. Schenke, *Der Gott "Mensch" in der Gnosis* (1962), 1-3, 16-33, 155 f.; H. Schlier, Art. "Corpus Christi," *RAC*, III (1957), 437-453; Schlier Eph.[3], 90-96, Exc. τὸ σῶμα τοῦ Χριστοῦ; E. Schweizer, "Die Kirche als Leib Christi in d. paul. Homologumena," *Neotestamentica* (1963), 272-292; also "Die Kirche als Leib Christi in d. paul. Antilegomena," *ibid.* (1963), 293-316; O. F. J. Seitz, *One Body and One Spirit* (1960); B. Snell, "Die Auffassung des Menschen bei Hom.," *Die Entdeckung d. Geistes*[3] (1955), 21-25; T. Soiron, *Die Kirche als Leib Christi* (1951); W. D. Stacey, *The Pauline View of Man in Relation to Its Judaic and Hellenistic Background* (1956), 181-193; L. S. Thornton, *The Common Life in the Body of Christ* (1942); also "The Body of Christ" in *The Apostolic Ministry*, ed. K. E. Kirk (1946), 53-111; A. Wikenhauser, *Die Kirche als d. mystische Leib des Christus nach Pls.*[2] (1940).

5. The Post-New Testament Period. B. The Old Testament: 1. Hebrew Equivalents to the Septuagint σῶμα; 2. The Translation of Hebrew Equivalents in the Septuagint; 3. Septuagint Works with a Hebrew Original; 4. Works not in the Hebrew Canon; 5. Summary. C. Judaism: 1. Apocrypha and Pseudepigrapha; 2. Philo: a. The Human and Animal Body; b. The Body as Part of Man along with Soul, Spirit etc.; c. The One Totality of Soul, Cosmos and People; d. The Inorganic Body; e. Summary; 3. Josephus; 4. The Rabbinic View. D. The New Testament: I. Books apart from Paul; II. Paul: 1. σῶμα apart from the Concept of the Body of Christ: a. Generally Accepted Epistles; b. Colossians and Ephesians; 2. The Body of Christ: a. Generally Accepted Epistles; b. Colossians; c. Ephesians; d. σύσσωμος; e. Differences from Paul; III. Survey of the Historical Development of the Concept. E. The Post-New Testament Period: 1. Post-Apostolic Fathers; 2. Apologists; 3. Gnosticism: a. σῶμα alongside ψυχή, πνεῦμα; b. σῶμα in the Sense of the Body Embracing the Redeemed; c. Summary.

A. The Greek World.

1. The Period up to Plato.

The basic meaning of σῶμα is still contested. [1] It crops up for the first time in Hom. for a dead [2] "human or animal body." Whereas man experiences himself as a living body primarily in the functioning of his members, [3] σῶμα is the body on which he stumbles, a thing in the external world. Only Hom. Il., 3, 23 is debatable. [4] The context supports the idea of an encounter with a living wild beast, not a carcass. [5] But what follows speaks only of the devouring of the animal, and the joy of the lion is the sole pt. of comparison. [6] Use for a living body is attested for certain only from Hes. on. [7]

The word comes into clearer focus in the 5th cent. In Hdt., II, 66, 4 it means "trunk" as distinct from head, [8] but also the whole "body." [9] The latter sense is found in the

---

[1] Usually associated with root tewǝ-, tuō- "to swell up," "to become firm," Boisacq, Hofmann, s.v., but cf. J. Wackernagel, "Miscellen z. griech. Grammatik," ZvglSpr., 30 (1890), 298: "Decaying" (σήπομαι); Koller, 280 f.: "Object of damage, robbery" (σίνομαι), phonetically dubious. The Indo-Eur. word for body, found in Lat. corpus, Sanskr. krp-, Avestan kehrp- (H. Lommel, Die Religion Zarathustras [1930], 173), dropped out of Gk. [Risch].

[2] Aristarch. (K. Lehrs, De Aristarchi studiis Homericis [1865], 86, cf. 160), s.v. σῶμα; also Stob. Ecl., I, 293, 5.

[3] Since δέμας is used only in the acc. of relation in the sense "in form" and χρώς means only the surface of the body, there is no comprehensive term for the living body in Hom., Snell, 21-25 (→ 99, 30 ff.), though Hirzel, 5 f. pts. to Il., 1, 3 f.; 23, 65 f. On the connection between body and soul in Hom. R. B. Onians, The Origin of European Thought about the Body, the Mind, the Soul, the World, Time and Fate (1954), 48, 59-61. The belly is in some sense an autonomous entity before the σῶμα, ibid., 88 (→ 1030, 30 ff.).

[4] Fully discussed by Koller, 278-281; cf. Il., 18, 161; Hirzel, 6 and H. Fraenkel, Die homerischen Gleichnisse (1921), 65 f.; F. Krafft, "Vergleichende Untersuchungen zu Hom. u. Hes.," Hypomnemata, 6 (1963).

[5] So Ps.-Hes. Scutum, 426 (ed. C. F. Russo [1950]).

[6] Comparison with joy at a discovered carcass is possible since the enemy confronting Menelaos has been virtually dispatched.

[7] Hes. Op., 540: Hair standing on end on the body, → 102, n. 33.

[8] κεφαλή, alongside πρόσωπον, Hdt., III, 110; IV, 75, 3.

[9] I, 32, 8: As no land is self-sufficient, neither is any man's σῶμα.

tragedians. The impersonal aspect still exerts an influence in Aesch. σῶμα is the warrior dedicated to death — the god of war deals with human bodies, Ag., 438 [10] — or the object of erotic desire, Prom., 859 → 1027, 9 ff. An extreme example of this is Eur. Pr., 775, 2 (TGF, 606) (→ 1028, 19 ff.) where the body sold as a dowry makes man a slave of the marriage bed. Elsewhere, however, the word embraces the whole person, Eur. Andr., 315; Tro., 201; Hec., 301. [11] It can even be used instead of the reflexive pronoun. [12] It distinguishes man himself as a person from his ὄνομα (Hel., 587) or πρᾶγμα. [13] The same is true in Soph. Oed. Col., 1568. [14] But sheer corporeality can be emphasised as when it is said of satyrs that they are mere "bodies." [15] In Pind. Pyth., 8, 81 f. the character of the body as object is plain to see: The athlete falls on four bodies; a tender body is found among the flowers, Olymp., 6, 56; Hermes leads the body into Hades, 9, 34. [16] If the εἴδωλον is regarded, in distinction from the σῶμα, as that which survives after death (Pind. Fr., 131b, 1 ff.), σῶμα in its limitation is the physical existence which ends with death. [17] In Andoc., II, 18 and Thuc., I, 85, 1; VI, 9, 2 (→ n. 65) we again find the body associated with things or goods. If the parallelism of these things, and hence the nature of the σῶμα as object, is to the fore in Thuc., in Attic law ὕβρις is used only for the violation of life and limb and is thus differentiated from all other injuries. [18]

More important is the fact that one finds body along with soul in the Pre-Socratics → 102, 13 ff. [19] Hom. knows the view that at death man is abandoned by the vital force, the breath-soul, [20] and thus becomes σῶμα, "a corpse." This leads to disparagement of the body. Without the soul, i.e., life, it is worse than dung and should be cast aside with no solemn burial, Heracl. Fr., 96 (Diels, I, 172, 14). [21] This takes on a sharper edge when something that survives is contrasted with it. In Eur. Fr., 839 (TGF, 633), 1013 (683) it is still not clear what is meant by this. But physical existence is felt to be an affliction, even something alien. The lot of the σῶμα has fallen to man, Fr., 403, 3 (TGF, 484); the body is his fetter, Fr., 697 (581). These notions are clarified with the coming of the doctrine of transmigration, Xenophanes Fr., 7 (Diels, I, 131, 1-4). [22] Now the mortal body complements the immortal soul. This view carries with it a religious judgment in the Orphics. The σῶμα is the σῆμα (tomb) of the soul: [23] mortal, it is differentiated from the immortal soul, Orph. Fr. (Kern), 228d (244). In contrast the idea of Democr. that when breathing stops the atom of the soul leaves the body [24] is simply a scientific

---

[10] Cf. πολέμια σώματα in Gorg. Fr., 11, 16 (Diels, II, 293, 9 f.).

[11] Cf. Hirzel, 9 f.

[12] Eur. Or., 1075 discusses whether Pylades should kill himself or give back the σῶμα to his father; on this use cf. Lehrs, op. cit., 160.

[13] πρᾶγμα is the more common opp., cf. F. Solmsen, "ΟΝΟΜΑ and ΠΡΑΓΜΑ in Euripides' Helen," Class. Rev., 48 (1934), 119-121 → 1030, 17 ff.; n. 38.

[14] σῶμα means the actual "person"; men will more quickly hear of their δρώμενα than see them (the σώματα), Soph. El., 1333; cf. later Philemon. Fr., 148 (CAF, II, 523).

[15] Cf. P. Oxy., IX, 1174, Col. 6, 8. 12 (2nd cent. B.C.): Soph. in a satyr play.

[16] As the ψυχαί in Hom. On the concept of Hades cf. W. Jaeger, Die Theol. d. frühen griech. Denker (1953), 102 f.

[17] This is at first self-evident. For Hom. corporeal life is the true one, that after death is only shadowy. Yet something is contrasted with σῶμα as surviving. Cf. In Thuc., II, 43, 2 praise and renown with σώματα which are sacrificed.

[18] J. H. Lipsius, Das Attische Recht u. Rechtsverfahren, II, 1 (1908), 420-451 → n. 228.

[19] Paucity of sources does not permit us to follow the development of the two complementary terms. Probably σῶμα in contrast to ψυχή came to denote the living body, Snell, 35 f. [Dihle]. K. Freeman, God, Man and State (1952), 73-75 stresses the importance of the Pythagoreans.

[20] Cf. Onians, 59-61; Jaeger, 100 f.

[21] But cf. Fr., 67a (Diels, I, 166, 9 ff.).

[22] On this cf. Snell, 36, n. 1; on Egypt. teaching cf. Hdt., II, 123, 2.

[23] Chronology is difficult, since the texts are later, cf. Philolaus Fr., 14 (Diels, I, 413, 15); also Orph. Fr. (Kern), 8 (84 f.). On the Pythagorean origin of this view cf. K. Freeman, The Pre-Socratic Philosophers[2] (1949), 231 → 1028, 32 f.

[24] Rohde, II, 190 f., n. 3.

interpretation of the ancient notion of the breath-soul leaving the body, which in some sense prepares the way for the later notion of the corporeality of the soul. [25] But this also leads to emphasis on the relation of body and soul in the living man. When Emped. Fr., 148-150 (Diels, I, 370, 15-18) calls the body that which envelops the (blood-) soul, this is a purely neutral statement. But Heraclitus' thesis that the body as the moist element quenches the fire of the soul is a judgment, cf. Fr., 36 (Diels, I, 159, 8-10); 77 (168, 11-15). [26] To the poet Epimenides is ascribed the experience of ecstasy as alienation of the soul from the body, [27] and this is important, though whether it really can be traced back to him is doubtful. For Gorg. Fr., 11, 4 (Diels, II, 289, 11), not Aesch. (→ 1026, 2 f.), the body is the origin of erotic desires. What medicine is for the body the word is for the soul, Gorg. Fr., 11, 14 (Diels, II, 292, 12-15). Thus at least half a century before Plato the body was viewed as the part of man which stands in contrast with the soul (e.g., that which is open to the word) as another part → 1030, 27 ff. Before Plato we already find νοῦς in Theogn., I, 650 (Diehl³, II, 41), φρένες in Hdt., III, 33; 134, 3, and γνώμη in Andoc., II, 24 as correlative terms, and these may be complementary [28] or antithetical, as the free νοῦς is to the body of the slave, Soph. Fr., 854 (TGF, 329). [29]

When the ref. is to art the idea of external form is linked with σῶμα. Already in the 6th cent. this can be par. to ἰδέα, [30] and a century later to σχῆμα. [31] In the second passage the attribute of the single whole is also conjoined. Here, then, σῶμα is the body encountering the eye as a whole defined by its form. It is in philosophy, however, that the chief development takes place. The earliest instance quoted literally is from the 5th cent. and it ref. to the elements as the five σώματα [32] of which four are within the sphere, Philolaus Fr., 12 (Diels, I, 412, 16). [33] In a philosophical eclectic of the time air is an eternal immortal σῶμα (→ 1030, 1 f.), Diogenes of Apollonia Fr., 7 (Diels, II, 66, 1). How far back the Pythagorean differentiation of μαθηματικά, αἰσθητά, φυσικά σώματα (cf. Aristot. Metaph., 1, 8, p. 990a, 15 f.; Cael., III, 1, p. 300a, 17; Diog. L., VIII, 25) and of the assessability of bodies by numbers and basic forms (Aristot. Metaph., 12, 8, p. 1083b, 11-13; 1, 8, p. 990a, 14-22; Cael., III, 1, p. 300a, 16 f.) really goes is uncertain. Much clearer is Democritus' atomic teaching in the 2nd half of the 5th cent. This distinguishes the σῶμα [34] (δέν) from empty space (μηδέν), Democr. Fr., 156 (Diels, II, 174, 18 f.) [35] and develops the idea of the smallest possible σῶμα → 1032, 1 f. [36] At the same period Melissus Fr., 9 (Diels, I, 275, 11-13) declares that real being has no σῶμα, while Gorg. Fr., 11, 8 (Diels, II, 290, 17) says of the word that in spite of its very small and insignificant σῶμα it does the greatest things. He defines σῶμα as that which is characterised by breadth, length and depth, Fr., 3, 73 (Diels, II, 281, 6 f) [37]

---

[25] Cf. the interpretation of Theophr. De Sensu et Sensibilibus, 11, 58, → 1032, 18 ff.; 1033, 12 ff.

[26] Fr., 4 (Diels, I, 151, 8-10), which speaks of the joys of the body, is extant only in Lat.

[27] Acc. to Suid., 2470 (Adler, II, 370); on Anaxim. cf. Jaeger, op. cit., 100 f. → n. 328.

[28] Epicharmus Fr., 26 (Diels, I, 202, 15): If the νοῦς is pure, the whole body is pure.

[29] Democr. Fr., 171 (Diels, II, 179, 1-3) says fortune alone decides in the sphere of the soul.

[30] Xenophanes Fr., 15, 4 (Diels, I, 133, 3): If animals could draw and mould they would fashion animal shapes and bodies as gods.

[31] Gorg. Fr., 11, 18 (Diels, II, 294, 2): Painters make a single σῶμα καὶ σχῆμα out of many bodies and colours.

[32] E. Sachs, Die fünf platonischen Körper (1917), 1-7 shows that these are not the five Platonic bodies, which are first found in Plato's friend Theaetetus.

[33] In interpretation Sachs, op. cit., 44 f. The fifth body seems to be the cube-shaped surface, not the aether, → 1032, 3 ff.

[34] Gal. De Elementis ex Hippocrate, I, 2 (Kühn, 1, 418, 5-7) uses the expression "atom" and "little bodies."

[35] This is already traced back to Leucippus by the Doxographi, cf. Aristot. Metaph., 1, 4, p. 985b, 4-10.

[36] Democr. Fr., 141 (Diels, II, 170, 3 f.).

[37] Cf. Jaeger, op. cit., 101.

and which must always be at a specific place (→ 1031, 23 f.), so that being is to be understood in terms of τόπος, "in which" something is, and σῶμα, which is "in it," Fr., 3, 70 (Diels, II, 280, 23).

2. From Plato to Aristotle.

The meaning attested thus far takes on new features in Plato. Naturally σῶμα still means first the body, esp. man's. This is the object of the physician's care as a plant is of the husbandman, Theaet., 167b. But the inorganic materials used by artists are also σώματα. [38] If fire, earth, water and air are called visible bodies, the elements as substances stand opposed to the invisible soul, Tim., 46d. [39] If the gods make fire a σῶμα to embody it for the eye, this denotes its subtantiality. [40] Plato also uses the word for the person, e.g., Leg., X, 908a. The body, then, is not just a thing on which one stumbles. It is a single whole which is self-contained and can be considered as such. The body has thus become an object of contemplation, which it never was earlier. It can now be seen as a totality in respect of its form, or it can be distinguished from the soul which for the first time constitutes the living man. This appears first in Plato when he compares speech as an integrated whole with a body that has a head and members, Phaedr., 264c. Indeed, Plato can even say that unified composition is what characterises a σῶμα. [41] The aspect of form is readopted here. The body is the visible part of man so that σχῆμα is an essential attribute. [42] In this sense it is an obj. of erotic desire, distinguished from the character and living relations or from the soul of the beloved, Phaedr., 232e; Symp., 181b → 1026, 2 f.; n. 67. He does not say, however, that it is the whole of the person. Only the soul along with the integrated body is the totality one calls a living being and associates with the attribute of mortality, Phaedr., 246c. In the works of the middle period, then, the body is in essence defined negatively. The soul, which is contrasted with it, controls and guides it, Phaed., 79e; 80a; 94b-e; [43] it is still ruled by its ἡδοναί and παθήματα, Resp., I, 328d; Theaet., 186c, by hunger and thirst and similar sensory qualities, Resp., II, 380e. Hence it needs the skill of the doctor and gymnastic instructor to remain healthy and beautiful, Symp., 186c; Gorg., 452a b; Euthyd., 279a b. Desire for the physical leads the soul down; the body — eye, ear, or some other sense — conducts it to the earthly and changeable, Phaed., 65b c; 79c; 81b-e; Phaedr., 248a-e; Gorg., 523d. If the soul is invisible, divine and immortal, the body is visible, human and mortal, Phaed., 79b; 80a b. It is merely a dwelling for the pre-existent soul. [44] Thus the σῶμα is felt to be the σῆμα of the soul (→ 1026, 29 f.), [45] an evil in which man is trapped like an oyster in its shell, Phaedr., 250c; Phaed., 66b, and which is thus to be despised and avoided as much as possible, 46a b; 65c d. [46] If for Hom. the εἴδωλον was the disembodied shade (→ II, 376, 9 ff.) and for Pind. it was the image which survives man (→ 1026, 12 ff.), Plat. regards the body of the dead as a mere appearance, the soul being the true and immortal part, Leg., XII, 959b → 103, 4 ff. [47] The popular notion that death is the end

---

[38] Polit., 288d: Gold and silver but also hides of ἔμψυχα σώματα. Soph., 265c distinguishes ἄψυχα σώματα from ζῷα θνητὰ καὶ φυτά. Resp., V., 476a has σώματα and πράξεις together → 1026, 6 ff.; 1035, 20 ff.
[39] Tim., 53c: βάθος is typical for this: εἶδος → 1031, 13 f.
[40] Tim., 45b.
[41] Phileb., 29b: εἰς ἓν συγκεῖσθαι → 1034, 28 ff.
[42] Phaed., 66a; 79a b; Crat., 423a; Resp., IV, 425b; VII, 530b → n. 30, 31, 110.
[43] Käsemann Leib, 26-29.
[44] Phaedr., 245-250, Cf. Ps.-Plat. Epin., 980e; 991d → 1026, 24 ff.; 1042, 22 ff.
[45] Gorg., 493a; Crat., 400b c as "sign" for the soul or "tomb;" the sense "prison" (σῴζομαι) goes back to the Orphics → 1040, 32 f.
[46] On this whole matter cf. Festugière, II, 101 f. and → 104, 22 ff.
[47] Cf. Gorg., 523c; 524 f: Bad souls can be hidden by beautiful, noble and rich bodies.

of body and soul is untenable, Phaed., 85e-88b; 91d. [48] Death is the liberation of the soul, which parts from the body and therewith alone becomes pure, 64c; 67a; Gorg., 524b, [49] since the body is a mixture of all kinds of things. [50] In the later works, however, this view changes into that of the body moved by the soul. [51] Though not created by God, it is created by God's sons. [52] Health of body and prudence of soul, sickness of body and wickedness of soul, may be seen as in some sense par., Resp., III, 404e; X, 609c. Indeed, the sensually perceptible beauty of the world can be a spur to ascent to the idea, Tim., 29a; Resp., VIII, 591d; Symp., 211c. Hence the soul is seated in man's head (→ III, 674, 20 ff.) and draws the whole man from the earth up to the related heaven, so that the whole body is held upright from the head. [53]

An essential pt. is that σῶμα is now explicitly and frequently related to the cosmos. Long before Plato the idea of kinship between the human body and the cosmos came to expression. [54] That the cosmos is a living unity, [55] an organic creature, [56] is also asserted. [57] Shortly before Plato Democritus formulated his famous principle in Fr., 34 (Diels, II, 153, 8, 12 f.) that man is a microcosm. [58] If in looser statements the cosmos is depicted after the pattern of man, in philosophical thought man is understood in terms of the cosmos. [59] Such ideas are esp. influential in the later Plato. In Tim., 30b; 39e (→ 1032, 4 ff.) the cosmos is understood as an ensouled and rationally controlled being, → III, 871, 14 ff., so that there is ref. to the σῶμα τοῦ παντός or τοῦ κόσμου, 31b; 32a c; Phileb., 30a, which is a perfect cube-shaped σῶμα made up of many perfect σώματα, Tim., 32d; 34b; 63a; 44d. The duality of guiding reason and obedient body may also be seen in the cosmos, which like the human body is made up of the four

---

[48] Cf. Ap., 40c and Freeman, *op. cit.* (→ n. 19), 102.

[49] Cf. Gorg., 523e and Crat., 403b (only the naked soul can be set right); on the whole question Festugière, II, 92-94.

[50] Cf. the concept of κρᾶσις, Tim., 43a; 74c-e: Bones which contain much or little soul-stuff are sparsely or richly decked by flesh; Leg., X, 889b c (of the world body) etc. → 99, 25 ff.; 1031, 6 f.

[51] E. Haenchen, "Aufbau u. Theol. des Poimandres," ZThK, 53 (1956), 189, n. 1; cf. Festugière, II, 102 f. 144 f.; Käsemann Leib, 28 f.

[52] Tim., 42e, 43a, cf. Festugière, II, 111.

[53] Tim., 90a b; cf. H. Leisegang, *Der Hl. Geist*, I, 1 (1919), 105. Xenoph. Mem., I, 4, 11 also stresses man's upright walk as peculiar to him. The head is a cube-shaped σῶμα and the most divine feature of man → 1041, 29 ff. The σῶμα is given as a servant, Plat. Tim., 44d → n. 106.

[54] F. Hommel, "Mikrokosmos," DLZ, 65 (1944), 30: πνεῦμα is cosmically wind, anthropologically breath, πόλος the vault of heaven and the skull, ἄτλας the bearer of heaven and the upper cervical vertebra, οὐρανός heaven and the arch of the palate, κόρη also the pupil and αἰών man's vital force, cf. W. Kranz, "Kosmos," *Archiv f. Begriffsgeschichte*, II, 1 (1955), 25.

[55] Heracl. Fr., 30 (Diels, I, 157, 11-158, 3); Anaxim. Fr., 2 (Diels, I, 95, 17-19). Cf. Philemon, Fr., 91 (CAF, II, 105); Eur. Tro., 885 f.

[56] Cf. J. Dupont, *Gnosis* (1949), 336-340, 431-446. This view is supposed to go back to Thales acc. to Diog. L., I, 27; Schol. Platonica in rem publicam, I, 600a (ed. G. C. Greene [1938], 272); cf. Diog. L., VIII, 25 → n. 95.

[57] Uncertain is Hecataios of Abdera Fr., 7 (Diels, II, 242, 37-243, 5): τὸ ἄπαν σῶμα τῆς τῶν ὅλων φύσεως, of which the 5 elements are μέρη, → 1039, 21 ff.

[58] Cf. W. Kranz, "Kosmos u. Mensch in d. Vorstellung d. frühen Griechentums," NGG, NF, 2 (1938), 161; also op. cit. (→ n. 54), 49 f. On Anaxim. and his predecessors cf. Jaeger, *op. cit.* (→ n. 16), 95 f. Is the origin of the notion Chaldean? Cf. J. Moreau, *L'idée d'univers dans la pensée antique* (1953), 10 f.

[59] Kranz, *op. cit.*, 133; *op. cit.* (→ n. 54), 17, 20-22; Hommel, *op. cit.*, 30; cf. the common idea that the elements of the human body are taken from the cosmos, Xenoph. Mem., I, 4, 8; Plat. Phileb., 29a-e, where the cosmos is expressly said to be first; cf. also Plat. Menex., 237e; 238a.

elements, Tim., 47c-48b. [60] The cosmos is the body [61] or εἰκών of God uniformly ruled and controlled by the divine soul; [62] it is God made visible (→ 1037, 7 ff.), μονογενής (→ III, 871, 19 ff.). [63] Finally it should also be pointed out that the state is compared to a man, Resp., VIII, 556e; 567c; Gorg., 464b. [64]

The picture is much the same in Xenophon and his contemporaries. Here, too, σῶμα often denotes "person," though usually considered as an object at one's disposal. [65] It can be used for the reflexive pronoun, [66] and can also be a mere object of tactical considerations, Aen. Tact., 1, 1; 2, 1; 32, 8; 40, 4. In erotic language σῶμα is in the first instance the object of desire and the means of fellowship, Xenoph. Resp. Lac., 2, 13. [67] Here, too, the body is associated with the soul, [68] the soul being clearly the leading side partaking of the divine. [69] As the human soul governs the body, so the universe is controlled and ruled by God's reason. [70] Possibly Xenoph. already uses the word for plants. [71] The body-soul relation was applied to the state by his contemporary Isoc.: the constitution is the soul of the state and plays the part of the thinking spirit in the body, Isoc. Or., 7, 14; 12, 138. In this representative of the educated citizen, however, it is plain that in death only fame survives body and soul, 5, 134; 6, 109.

In Aeschin. in the middle of the 4th cent. one finds, with the normal use, [72] the sense of person. As the whole this is contrasted with the name, Aeschin. Tim., 193 → 1026, 7; 1040, 8 f. Civil law decides concerning each individual σῶμα, Tim., 77. Free departure is granted to σώματα, Fals. Leg., 39, 309. σώματα and χρήματα are found alongside each other, Demosth. Or., 9, 121, 40; 18, 247, 66 (→ n. 65; 1039, 3). As distinct from slaves, over 30 free σώματα perish, 34, 910, 10 → 1035, 15 ff. There is always an echo of the body as object, esp. in enumeration. [73] Comedy typifies the understanding of body and soul. The old idea of the body abandoned by the breath-soul in death lingers on in Plato Comicus Fr., 68 (CAF, I, 619); Alexis Fr., 158 (CAF, II, 355). But the ascent of the soul on the death of the body also occurs in Plato Comicus Fr., 68 (CAF, I, 619), the body being always subject to τύχη. [74] Isoc. too (→ lines 13 ff.) is aware that in the nature of man, which is made up of body and soul, the soul is the superior and more valuable part and has the leading role, while the body serves it. [75] Alexis Fr., 70 (CAF, II, 320) demands a spiritual marriage bond which goes beyond ἡδονή after the σῶμα. In Menander, the good body which has a bad soul is compared to a ship with a poor helms-

---

[60] Cf. Leg., X, 898d e: Body and soul of the sun.

[61] Tim., 36d e; Phileb., 30a-d → 1027, 23 ff. and n. 55; W. Theiler, Zur Gesch. d. teleologischen Naturbetrachtung bis auf Aristot., Diss. Basel (1924), 19 f.; Festugière, II, 106-113, 158; A. E. Taylor, A Comm. on Plato's Tim. (1928), 80-82.

[62] As the centre of the cosmos it permeates and surrounds it, Tim., 34b; Festugière, II, 257.

[63] Tim., 92c; cf. Leg., IV, 715c → 1037, 18 ff.; Orph. Fr. (Kern), 21 (90).

[64] Käsemann Leib, 29.

[65] With χρήματα (and πόλεις) Xenoph. An., I, 9, 12; Cyrop., VII, 5, 73; Demosth. Or., 9, 40; 18, 66 → 1026, 14 ff.; 1030, 20 f. The obj.-character is not always stressed, e.g., Dinarch., 1, 38 (younger contemporary of Xenoph.). Cf. Hirzel, 14, n. 5.

[66] So Isoc. Or., 6, 46: τὸ σῶμα διασῴζειν, "to save his bodily existence."

[67] Oec., 10, 4 f.: The spouse is τοῦ σώματος κοινωνός, the couple τῶν σωμάτων κοινωνήσοντες → 1026, 2 ff.; 1039, 5 f.

[68] Weakness of body and unreason of soul are obstacles to man, Xenoph. Mem., II, 1, 31.

[69] Xenoph. Mem., I, 4, 9; IV, 3, 14; Symp., 8, 23, 28-30, cf. the νοῦς, Mem., I, 4, 17 and the soul, Isoc. Or., 15, 180.

[70] Mem., I, 4, 9. 17; cf. Festugière, II, 80-86.

[71] Compared to the human body (→ 1043, 17) Symp., 2, 25 (other readings συμπόσια).

[72] Aeschin. Or., III, 87, 645: health of σῶμα, 82, 636: hand buried apart from the body.

[73] κατὰ σῶμα "person" Aeschin. Or., III, 5, 406, cf. κεφαλή for "person," Onians, op. cit., 98-100.

[74] Anaxandrides Fr., 4 (CAF, II, 137); Philemon Fr., 10 (CAF, II, 481); 95 (II, 508); Apollodor. Fr., 15 (CAF, III, 293).

[75] Isoc. Or., 15, 180 f.: Gymnastics develops the body, philosophy the soul.

man. [76] In the concept of the body one also finds the element of totality, e.g., when Alexis Fr., 212 (CAF, II, 374) speaks of the belly which one might remove from the body without hurt → 1063, 12 f. Finally one may ask whether σῶμα does not already have the sense of "substance." [77]

In Aristot. σῶμα is, of course, primarily the human body, whether with a head [78] or as the trunk contrasted with the head, Probl., 2, 6, p. 867a, 4 f. It is composed of different things, and mixture characterises it. [79] Naturally body and soul are mentioned together. [80] In contrast to Plato, however, the body is primary and is viewed as existing before the soul, Pol., VII, 15, p. 1334b, 20 f. But this does not mean that it is superior; the soul is the more eminent part, Gen. An., II, 1, p. 731b, 28 f. Restraint from bodily desires is to be commended; desire is good, but it is not the supreme good. [81] Since the body is defined by matter and form, [82] the soul must be viewed as its τέλος, the οὗ ἕνεκα which first makes it a specific something. The soul is thus the entelechy which cannot be separated from the body, its εἶδος, An., II, 1 f., p. 412a, 19 ff.; p. 413a, 1-6; p. 414a, 12-22. An essential pt. for the further development in Stoicism is that Aristot. contests the view that the soul is a body consisting of the finest particles, [83] and that his disciple already takes Democritus' principle about the κρᾶσις (→ 1033, 16 f.; 1034, 2 ff.) in such a way as to regard the soul as σῶμα. [84] Sometimes the physical body can be viewed as matter, [85] for σῶμα itself, apart from soul, is by nature "substance," Part. An., II, 8, p. 653b, 21 ff. [86] It can thus embrace corporeality, the substance of individual parts of the body, [87] and presumably the transf. use which calls logical argument the σῶμα of the credibility of a speech is to be understood in this light. [88] It is true of bodies, whether with or without souls, that every αἰσθητὸν σῶμα can in principle be touched, An., III, 12, p. 434b, 12, and is at a place, [89] and two cannot be in the same place at once. [90] Thus all bodies are limited (→ 1040, 7 ff.) and nothing exists outside the θεῖον σῶμα of heaven. [91] Every sensually perceptible body has an active or passive capacity or both, and therefore it cannot possibly be unlimited, Cael., I, 7, p. 275b, 5 f.; cf. III, 8, p. 307b, 20 → 1033, 24 f. It is three-dimensional, Topica, VI, 5, p. 142b, 24 f.; Metaph., 4, 13, p. 1020a, 14 → n. 37, 113. Mathematical bodies are a secondary abstraction. Metaph.

---

[76] Menand. Fr., 1100 (CAF, III, 267).

[77] Eubulus Fr., 151 (CAF, II, 214) and Chaeremon Fr., 17, 2 (TGF, 787) record the description of water as the σῶμα of the river. Is this to be taken metaphorically or analogously to → 1028, 8 f? → 1039, 17 ff.

[78] Rhet., III, 14, p. 1415b, 8; as the metaphor for a speech which should be a totality and have a beginning, not a separate preface.

[79] Ζῷον σῶμα ἔμψυχόν ἐστι, Gen. An., II, 4, p. 738b, 19; σύνθετον, Part. An., II, 1, p. 646a, 17. Cf. An., III, 13, p. 435a, 11 → n. 155. κρᾶσις τοῦ σώματος is typical for amphibians, Hist. An., VIII, 2, p. 589b, 23 → n. 50 and 111.

[80] H. Bonitz, Index Aristotelicus (1870), 744b, 24 - 745a, 4; Käsemann Leib, 34-38.

[81] σωματικαὶ ἡδοναί, Eth. Nic., II, 2, p. 1104b, 5 f. etc.

[82] An., II, 1, p. 412a, 6-9 → 1028, 8 f.

[83] An., I, 5, p. 409a, 32: σῶμά τι λεπτομερές → 1026, 30 ff.; 1032, 19 ff.

[84] Theophr. De Sensu et Sensibilibus, 11, 58. Aristot. himself says the power of the soul shares in another more divine σῶμα, the so-called elements, Gen. An., II, 3, p. 736b, 30 f.

[85] Ὑποκείμενον καὶ ὕλη, An., II, 1, p. 412a, 19-28. σῶμα is certainly not form as distinct from matter σάρξ, cf. J. Barr, The Semantics of Bibl. Language (1961), 37, n. 1.

[86] Cf. the survey of the Pre-Socratics who regard the soul as ἀσώματον or ἀσωματώτατον, An., I, 2, p. 405a, 6 - 405b, 12. Probl., 13, 13, p. 933a, 10-13 is plainest: Sea-water is σωματοειδέστερον than river-water, hence one can swim in it more easily.

[87] The σῶμα of the kidneys is compared to the hollow κοῖλον, Hist. An., III, 4, p. 514b, 32 f.; cf. the ἴδιον σῶμα of the eye, Gen. An., II, 6, p. 744a, 5.

[88] Rhet., I, 1, p. 1354a, 15. Should one transl. "basis," "main point," or is this a slip for ῥῶμα = ῥώμη?

[89] ἐν τόπῳ Cael., I, 7, p. 275b, 7 → 1027, 34 ff.; 1033, 21 f.; 1040, 15 f.

[90] An., II, 7, p. 418b, 17.

[91] Cael., I, 7, p. 275b, 6-9 etc. Θεῖα σώματα also Cael., II, 12, p. 292b, 32 → n. 152.

1, 8, p. 990a, 16 f. Aristot., too, uses σῶμα for the "elements." [92] Thus the term is used
for the primary indivisible bodies in his review of Democr. [93] His fifth element, aether,
Cic. Tusc., I, 26, 65, [94] is given its influential def. as τὸ πέμπτον σῶμα τὸ κυκλοφορη-
τικόν by one of his disciples, Theophr. Fr., 35 → 1042, 10 f. Aristot. still has the concept
of the universe as an ensouled being controlled by divine reason, An., I, 5, p. 411a, 7-14. [95]
Finally it is of interest that he also transfers the image of the body to the state, which
proves that as a totality this is more original than the individual, just as the totality of
man is more original than the individual member, which being dead bears only the name
of hand or foot, Pol., I, 2, p. 1253a, 18-29; V, 3, p. 1302b, 35, cf. ὥσπερ ἕνα ἄνθρωπον,
III, 11, p. 1281b, 5.

3. The Later Fourth and the Third Centuries.

As regards non-philosophical usage in the later 4th cent. Lyc. shows how commonly
σῶμα now means "person." It is the physically present person of the traitor as distinct
from his image, Lyc., 117, [96] or the mortal remains. [97] σῶμα can also be used instead of
the reflexive pronoun, with a special stress on corporeality or on the σῶμα as object. [98]
Epic. occasionally has the traditional differentiation of body and soul, Men., 127, 10-12;
128, 14, 19 f. (Usener, 62). He, too, regards the soul as more important (→ 104, 6 ff.)
and can sometimes "spit at the lusts of the body." [99] But in stricter formulations he uses
σάρξ for σῶμα → 103, 32 ff. For he took over from Democr. a materialism which explains
all movements of the soul mechanically, so that in the strict sense Epic. can distinguish
the soul from the flesh but not from the body. [100] To the horror of his contemporaries and
successors he concludes from this that the body and its movements are sacred; [101] this
led to a long history of misunderstanding and polemics, → 104, 16 ff. In contrast the
popular eclectic Bion in the 3rd cent. declares that the ego is to be completely separated
from the σωμάτιον, from which one departs as from a house at death. [102]
In older Stoicism the relation of body and soul is a special topic of discussion. Aristot.
had already viewed the *pneuma* as a bodily substance the soul uses to sustain and guide

---

[92] E.g., Metaph., 4, 8, p. 1017b, 10; 7, 1, p. 1042a, 8 f.; cf. Gen. Corr., II, 3, p. 330b, 8: The
ἁπλᾶ σώματα are the στοιχεῖα, cf. also Meteor., I, p. 338a, 22 f.: τὰ στοιχεῖα τὰ
σωματικά, I, 2, p. 339a, 11: μία ἀρχὴ τῶν σωμάτων.
[93] An., I, 2, p. 405a, 10; cf. Cael., II, 4, p. 287a, 3: πρῶτον σῶμα, Phys., VIII, 9, p. 265b,
29: ἄτομα σώματα → 673, 25 ff.
[94] Cic. Academicorum posteriorum ad M. Varronem, I, 7, 26: *quinta natura, quintum genus*
→ n. 33. Cf. αἰθέριον σῶμα, Plut. Plac. Phil., I, 7 (II, 881 f.); Stob. Ecl., I, 37, 18 → 680,
3 ff.
[95] The chief effect of Aristotle's principles is to produce an understanding of nature as
the quality which controls the world and first makes matter into a cosmic body, U. Wilckens,
Weisheit u. Torheit (1959), 234-7 (→ 1029, 17 ff.; 1035, 7 ff.; 1038, 9 ff.; 1038, 14 ff.; 1039,
20 ff.; 1039, 29 ff.; 1041, 23 ff.).
[96] As Lyc., 115 and 119 show, one cannot take τῆς ἀδικίας τὸ σῶμα in the sense of the
Lat. *corpus delicti* but the gen. must be construed with ὅμηρον.
[97] αὐτὸ τὸ σῶμα τὸ προδεδωκὸς τὴν πόλιν, Lyc., 115.
[98] παρασχεῖν τὸ σῶμα τάξαι τοῖς στρατηγοῖς "to present oneself for inspection," Lyc.,
57 cf. 77, 147 etc.; cf. Hirzel, 8, n. 5.
[99] Fr., 181 (Usener, 156). In itself ἦδος of the σωμάτιον is quite justifiable but because of
the consequences one must "spit" at many ἡδοναί, cf. Fr., 5, Col. 2, ed. C. Diano (1946), 27:
ἐξ ὄγκων σωματικῶν (if the ref. is really to the soul), cf. his disciple Diogenes Oenoanden-
sis (2nd cent. B.C.) Fr., 39, Col. 2-4, ed. J. Williams (1907), and the purely neutral Fr., 36,
Col. 1, 10 f.; 2, 4-8; Fr., 38, Col. 2 f.; Fr., 39, Col. 1.
[100] Epic. Ad Herodotum epistula, 63 f. (Usener, 19 f.).
[101] Fr., 130 (Usener, 141); 414 (Usener, 281).
[102] In Teles Reliquiae, 2, ed. O. Hense (1909), 15, 12-14. Teles himself is ref. to health and
sickness of body and soul, 3, Hense, 22, 2.

the body. [103] Hence it was no longer easy to maintain a clear-cut distinction between matter and form. [104] In the Stoic doctrine of the *pneuma* which permeates all things with different degrees of force, [105] this is adopted and changed. Naturally the soul is still the guiding principle. It is thus located in the heart by Zeno and probably in the head by Cleanthes → 1036, 22 f.; n. 53. [106] One may also note a certain disparagement of the body, Cleanthes Fr., 537 (v. Arnim, I, 122). More important is the fact that already in Zeno Fr., 99 (v. Arnim, I, 27) the body is not characterised by its weight, i.e. by its substance acc. to popular understanding, as air and fire show, but by its activity and suffering; only the bodily can act and suffer. [107] Thus the soul, like God, [108] is to be thought of corporeally, as warm air. [109] This is demonstrated by his pupil: Children are like their parents not only κατὰ τὸ σῶμα [110] but also κατὰ τὴν ψυχήν, which includes passions, customs, habits of mind. But since only the corporeal can be like or unlike, the soul must be viewed as σῶμα. Cleanthes Fr., 518 (v. Arnim, I, 117), cf. Alex. Aphr. An., II, 146r (I, 117, 9-11), tries to prove the same pt. by showing that the soul suffers with the body and *vice versa*. The principle that two bodies cannot be in the same place is naturally challenged hereby, Chrysippus Fr., 468 (v. Arnim, II, 152) → 1031, 25 f. To Zeno the problem seemed to be solved by his doctrine of mixture in which one body may fully permeate another → 1034, 2 f.; n. 50, 79. [111] This made possible for him the idea of a creative *logos* fashioning the cosmos. [112]

This is worked out in Chrysipp. and his followers. First, the older view is adopted that every body is three-dimensional, is limited, and is in a specific place. [113] Though Stoic teaching was later taken to be that σῶμα simply means "matter" and is thus identical with ὕλη, [114] it is only the special quality which makes matter a body [115] which can act as well as suffer. [116] A much repeated statement is that everything active, [117] and therefore everything causal, [118] is corporeal. A new proof of the corporeality of the soul is the viewing of death as the separation of body and soul, since only the bodily can part from

---

103 Pohlenz, I, 73 f. → n. 100.

104 Cf. Plot. Enn., VI, 1, 26 (Volkmann), similarly Alex. Aphr. An., 126r (I, 17, 15-17).

105 Pohlenz, I, 83; II, 49: In inorganic bodies as ἕξις, in plants as φύσις, in animals as ψυχή, in men as λόγος or νοῦς, cf. Zeno Fr., 158 (v. Arnim, I, 42); cf. Fr., 368 (II, 124); 458 (II, 149). This causes the various σχέσεις *(habitus)*, higher beings sharing in those of lower [Dihle].

106 Pohlenz, I, 87; II, 51.

107 Zeno Fr., 90 (v. Arnim, I, 25); 98 (I, 27); 146 (I, 40); Pohlenz, I, 64. This is connected with the fact that only the infinite is "empty," i.e., ἐρημία σώματος. The cosmos is everywhere full of σώματα, Fr., 95 (I, 26); cf. Chrysipp. Fr., 522-5 (II, 167 f.); Käsemann Leib, 41 f.

108 As σῶμα τὸ καθαρώτατον (the fire as ἀρχή of the all, cf. Pohlenz, I, 71); Zeno Fr., 153 f. (v. Arnim, I, 41).

109 Zeno Fr., 135 (v. Arnim, I, 38). L. Stein, *Die Psychologie der Stoa* (1886), 110-112. Acc. to Nemesius De natura hominis, 2, 30, 36 f. (MPG, 40 [1863], 540 B) even the soul is three-dimensional.

110 Hence in the sense of visible form, → 1028, 18 f.; 1035, 20 f.

111 Zeno Fr., 102 (v. Arnim, I, 28); Pohlenz, I, 72 f.; II, 41 f. → 1031, 7.

112 Under oriental influence? cf. Pohlenz, I, 68 f. On the earlier history, Festugière, II, 76 f.

113 Chrysippus Fr., 503 (v. Arnim, II, 163); cf. Fr., 357-9 (II, 123); Fr., 381 (II, 127); Fr, 315 (II, 114); Fr., 501, (II, 162); Fr., 603 (II, 185); Pohlenz, I, 65; II, 37 (→ 1031, 25 ff.; 1040, 7 f.; 1042, 8 f.; n. 89.

114 Cf. the testimonies on the Stoics assembled in v. Arnim, Fr., 305 (II, 111); Fr., 309 (II, 112): ἄποιον σῶμα, 315 (II, 114); Fr., 359 (II, 123); Fr., 394 (II, 130); Fr., 533 (II, 170); → VI, 392, n. 347.

115 Cf. Plot. Enn., VI, 1, 26 (Volkmann); Alex. Aphr. An., I, 126r (I, 19, 3-5).

116 ὕλη is ἄποιον σῶμα, Fr., 320 (v. Arnim, II, 115), cf. Pohlenz, I, 66; II, 38.

117 E.g., Diog. L., VII, 56; cf. Sext. Emp. Math., VIII, 263; Pohlenz, I, 64.

118 A Stoic view acc. to the witnesses in Aetius Amidenus De placitis reliquiae, I, 11, 5 (Doxographi Graeci, ed. H. Diels [1879], 310) and Sext. Emp. Math., IX, 211.

the bodily, Chrysipp. Fr., 790 (v. Arnim, II, 219); Fr., 791 (II, 219); cf. Alex. Aphr. An., II, 146r (I, 117, 1 f., 9-11, 21-23, 28 f., 30-118, 2). The doctrine of the mixture of bodies is developed, v. Arnim Fr., 463-481 (II, 151-158) (→ 1033, 16 f.; n. 155) and iron which is wholly penetrated by glowing fire is adduced in illustration, Chrysipp. Fr., 473 (v. Arnim, II, 155) and Alex. Aphr. De mixtione, 12, 608 f. (II, 226, 34-227, 17). The relation of body and soul is not analogous, then, to that of vessel and contents nor of things attached to one another; it is understood as full permeation, Alex. Aphr. An., II, 145v (I, 115, 32-116, 1). [119] Thus the soul penetrates the whole body and mediates sense impressions to it (→ 1028, 8 f.), Chrysipp. Fr., 885 (v. Arnim, II, 238); in this regard the analogy between the constitution of the body and that of the soul is carried through rather pedantically. [120] Among other things psychic sicknesses are offered in proof of this permeation, Fr., 471 (v. Arnim, III, 120). Zeno, following Aristot., defined sound as expelled air, i.e., as σῶμα, [121] but Chrysipp. goes further and calls conduct itself σῶμα, also day and night, [122] virtue and vice, cf. Plut. Comm. Not., 45 (II, 1084a-c); Superst., 1 (II, 165a), in short, all qualities. [123] If the soul is σῶμα and σῶμα is so divisible that all its parts are again σῶμα, it follows that αἴσθησις as part of the soul is σῶμα, cf. Alex. Aphr. An., I, 126r (I, 18, 27-19, 1). Nevertheless, as in normal usage, σῶμα can also be the body as distinct from the soul, Chrysipp. Fr., 471 (v. Arnim, III, 120); cf. Sext. Emp. Math., IX, 46. Indeed, one must even speak of a sharp line drawn between the two, [124] not, of course, in such a way as to destroy the monism, but in such sort that the dominion of the *logos* over the body has to be maintained unconditionally. In an age when it was no longer possible to think of spirit apart from the material, Stoicism is able in this way to set a new direction which avoids the conclusions of Epicurus [125] and preserves the ancient principle of the superiority of the soul to the body, Stob. Ecl., II, 80, 22. But this was not enough to guard against misunderstandings and materialism is often charged against the Stoics, the main criticism being that God Himself is thought of as corporeal. [126] Naturally Plato's view is handed down as well → n. 245.

An important pt. is that the idea of totality in σῶμα is taken up in the concept of the σῶμα ἐκ διεστώτων. [127] Distinction is made between σώματα ἡνωμένα καὶ συμφυᾶ, e.g., living creatures (n. 79), σώματα ἐκ συναπτομένων, e.g., a house or ship, [128] and σώματα ἐκ διεστώτων, e.g., a crew or army, Plut. Praec. Coniug., 34 (II, 142e). The people and senate are also examples of the third group, Sen. Ad Lucilium Epist. Morales

---

[119] Cf. Alex. Aphr. In Aristot. topicorum libros octo comment., 93, Comment. in Aristot. Graeca, 2, 2 (ed. M. Wallies [1891], 173, 9-11).

[120] Pohlenz, I, 148; II, 80 f.

[121] *Ibid.*, I, 39 f.; II, 22 f.

[122] Fr., 665 (v. Arnim, II, 197); Pohlenz, I, 70; II, 40 f.

[123] Plut. Comm. Not., 50 (II, 1085e); Simpl. In Aristot. physicorum libros quattuor priores comment., IV, 1, 123v, Comment. in Aristot Graeca, 9 (ed. H. Diels [1882], 530, 11-14); Pohlenz, I, 65 f.; II, 38.

[124] Chrysipp. Fr., 752 (v. Arnim, III, 186, 42-187, 9); the body means nothing and no more belongs to us than fingernails or hair, hence burial should be as simple as possible.

[125] Pohlenz, I, 165 f.

[126] Olympiodorus in Platonis Phaedonem comment., I, 6, 2 (ed. W. Norvin [1913], 35, 3-5); the opponent even deduces that God, too, has ὕλη, Plot. Enn., II, 4, 1: ἄποιον σῶμα. Pohlenz, II, 41. But cf. Chrysipp. Fr., 1049 (v. Arnim, II, 309); God is corruptible, but σῶμα πνευματικὸν καὶ αἰθερῶδες, Orig. Comm. in Joh., 13, 21 on 4:24; Alex. Aphr. De mixtione, 11, 606 (II, 225, 3-10); He is σῶμα, but of different ὕλη, Plot. Enn., VI, 1, 26 (Volkmann); → n. 534 f.

[127] Cf. L. Schnorr v. Carolsfeld, *Gesch. der juristischen Person*, I (1933), 177-9, 183-5; Käsemann Leib, 43-7: The categories of matter and form no longer dominate the discussion but the question of the power which unites the manifold. How ancient the distinction is, is contested, cf. K. Reinhardt, *Kosmos u. Sympathie* (1926), 34-7.

[128] Plut. Praec. Coniug., 34 (II, 142 f.); Achilles Isagoga excerpta, 14, Commentariorum in Aratum reliquiae, ed. E. Maass (1898), 41, 27; Sext. Emp. Math., IX, 78; Sen. Ad Lucilium Ep. Morales, 17, 102, 6, ed. A. Beltrami (1949); cf. Pomponius in Schnorr, *op. cit.*, 177.

(→ n. 128), 17, 102, 6, or choir, army and crowd. [129] Later a distinction is made between the σῶμα made up of a limited no. of individuals and that made up of an unlimited no. [130] Much more important, however, is the fact that the ἐκκλησία as such can be σῶμα: "Often a single body consists of many separate bodies like an assembly and an army and a chorus from which, however, life and thought and instruction comes to each individual." [131] The cosmos is also a constituted σῶμα of this kind, though strictly it belongs to the first group. [132] In Stoicism, too, it is a living entity. [133] As such it is a perfect σῶμα [134] whose unity is everywhere given special emphasis. [135] It is not only created by God [136] but also governed by Him as the world-soul, → III, 75, 1 ff. [137] It is the dwelling of gods and men, σύστημα and πόλις. [138] Indeed, the cosmos is God, → III, 876, 40 ff. [139]

In Middle Stoicism Pos. on the one side stresses the teleology of the body as an organ of the *logos* [140] while Panaitios on the other, though only occasionally and in opposition to his true insight, ref. to the useless corruptible flesh which is adapted only to partake of food. [141] In the non-philosophical and non-religious usage of the 2nd cent. σῶμα, either with or without further def., means the "slave" [142] or is just a numerical term. [143] Worth nothing is the use of σωματοποιέω for the organised uniting of a people and of σωματοειδής for the unity of history. [144] We see here the influence of the concept of united totality implicit in σῶμα, → 1039, 1 ff. The same applies when an astronomer speaks of the whole body of a constellation, → n. 110; [145] the visible form esp. is decisive here. The grammarian distinguishes between the concrete and the abstract use of a word to the degree that it denotes σῶμα or πρᾶγμα. [146] The Orphic-Platonic view of the body as the tomb of the soul finds philosophico-religious expression in a pretentious guide-

---

129 Sext. Emp. Math., IX, 78. Later examples in Schnorr, 177-9.
130 Achilles Isagoga excerpta, 14 (41, 28 - 42, 1); e.g., choir and crowd.
131 Chrysipp. Fr., 367 (v. Arnim, II, 124).
132 Sext. Emp. Math., IX, 78-89 → 1043, 14 ff.
133 Eus. Praep. Ev., 15, 15, 1; cf. also v. Arnim. Fr., 634-8 (II, 192), → n. 95.
134 Chrysipp. Fr., 550 (v. Arnim, II, 173); cf. πᾶν σῶμα perishing in fire, Simpl., *op. cit.*, III, 5, 111r (480, 30).
135 Zeno Fr., 97 (v. Arnim, I, 27); also Aetius Amidenus De placitis reliquiae (→ n. 118), 1, 51 (291): σωματικόν, Gal. De cuiusque animi peccatorum dignotione atque medela, 7 (Kühn, 5, 101): in antithesis to Epic.; Alex. Aphr. Fat., 22, 70 (II, 191, 30 f.); Sext. Emp. Math., VII, 432; Diog. L., VII, 140 (Pos.: cube-shaped; → 1029, 20 f.); Ἕνωσις and συμπάθεια unite it, Alex. Aphr. De mixtione, 12, 609 (II, 227, 8); it is thus ἡνωμένον σῶμα, Sext. Emp. Math., IX, 78. Cf. Festugière, II, 75-520; S. Hanson, *The Unity of the Church in the NT* (1946), 46-57.
136 Philo Aet. Mund., 8: οἱ δὲ Στωικοὶ κόσμον μὲν ἕνα, γενέσεως δ' αὐτοῦ θεὸν αἴτιον.
137 Cleanthes Hymn to Zeus, Fr., 537 (v. Arnim, I, 121, 33 - 123, 5), analysed by Festugière, II, 310-325; also Alex. Aphr. De mixtione, 12, 609 (II, 227, 9f.).
138 Eus. Praep. Ev., 15, 15, 3 f.; cf. already Zeno Fr., 262 (v. Arnim, I, 60, 38 - 61, 12).
139 Philodem. Philos De pietate, Fr., 11, 26-28, ed. T. Gomperz, Herkulanische Stud., II (1866); Eus. Praep. Ev., 15, 15, 6; Diog. L., VII, 139; cf. Philodem. De pietate, Fr., 14, 31 - 15, 4.
140 Pohlenz, I, 196; II, 99 f.; K. Reinhardt, *Pos.* (1921), 384-392.
141 Sen. Ep., 92, 10; Pohlenz, I, 236, 322.
142 Polyb., 2, 6, 6 differentiates σώματα δουλικά and ἐλεύθερα, cf. 1, 85, 1; just σώματα 18, 35, 6, cf. P. Lille, I, 25, 35 (3rd cent. B.C.); often in manumissions, e.g., GDI, II, 2154, 6 f. (2nd cent. B.C.): σῶμα γυναικεῖον, cf. P. Petr., II, 4, 9, 4 (3rd cent. B.C.) → 1030, 22; 1042, 2 f.
143 P. Lille, I, 25, 17 (3rd cent. B.C.); P. Rev., Col. 50, 9; Mitteis-Wilcken, I, 55, 7; 198, 6 (all three 3rd cent. B.C.); cf. P. Petr., III, 59b, 2; 107a, 9 etc.
144 Polyb., 2, 45, 6 (→ n. 193); 1, 3, 4 (→ n. 195, 197); for rhetoric cf. Ps.-Arist. Rhet. Al., 37, p. 1442b, 31 f. → 1043, 22 f.
145 Hipparchus in Arati et Eudoxi Phaenomena comm., II, 2, 46, ed. C. Manitius (1894).
146 Dion. Thr. Art. Gramm., 12 (24, 3) → 1026, 6 ff.; n. 38.

book. [147] In natural science Hero Alexandrinus declares under Stoic influence that there is no ἐλάχιστον σῶμα (→ n. 93) since each body is infinitely divisible. [148] The individual σῶμα is thought of as a compressed molecule which then extends again. [149] The word means "corporeality," "substance," when the same author shows by physical experiment that fire and air are σῶμα, [150] but also says the same of the harmonious mixture of sounds. [151]

4. The Period from c. 100 B.C. to 100 A.D.

In Later Stoicism σῶμα is naturally used for the human body, the head being the most important member, Cornut. Theol. Graec., 20 (35, 13); Heracl. Hom. All., 19 (29, 3 f.); also the divine body of heaven. [152] The element of totality in the term is even stronger here. The body and its parts μέρη are found together in Epict. Diss., I, 22, 10. The classical Stoic distinction between σώματα which consist of independent bodies and σώματα which consist of those that are integrated is still found → 1034, 28 ff. Thus σωμάτιον is now a tt. for a work which is a literary unity, esp. Hom. Il. and Od., Heracl. Hom. All., 60 (81, 6 f.), 76 (101, 19). Even in Lat. σῶμα is a loan word for a literary collection, Cic. Att., II, 1, 3. That the idea of the human body is always present may be seen from the allegorising of the rending and restoration of Dionysus which interprets the myth as a description of the grape-harvest and the flowing of the wine into one σῶμα. [153] Naturally the inter-relatedness of body and soul still has a role, [154] esp. the full mutual interpenetration [155] shown by their common suffering. [156] Current views are assembled in Cic. [157] The estimation of this relation is esp. important for the attitude to death. [158] The λογικόν of the soul occupies the top of the head (→ 1033, 4 f.; 1041, 29 f.) like an acropolis, Heracl. Hom. All., 17 (26, 14 f.). One may cheerfully leave the body at death, 34 (50, 5-7), for it cannot get to heaven [159] and is only a contemptible burden, penalty, fetter and dark abode of the soul, Sen. Ep., 65, 16 f. 22. For Epict., too, death is just separation from the σῶμα or σωμάτιον, Diss., III, 10, 14 f.; 22, 33. Hence the death of the body is not to be feared, only that of the soul, I, 5, 4. In earthly life man is bound to the body, I, 1, 9. 14; 9, 14 (→ 1026, 25 f.); it is alien to us (IV, 1, 66. 130), a corpse (I, 19, 9; III, 10, 15; 22, 41), a beast of burden (IV, 1, 79), the product of filth. [160] Man is thus to be understood as ψυχάριον bearing its corpse with it, Fr., 26. Hence the body is to be tended and washed, though Socrates seldom did this, thereby attesting that it must always be a secondary thing, IV, 11, 17-19; Fr., 23; cf. Ench., 41. But the body

---

[147] Polemon Declamationes, II, 10, 12, ed. H. Hinck (1873); → 1026, 29 f.
[148] Hero Alexandrinus Definitiones, 135, 2, ed. W. Schmidt, H. Schöne, J. L. Heiberg (1899-1914), IV, 96, 13 f. → 1034, 15 ff.
[149] Hero Alex. Pneumatica (→ n. 148), I, 147 (I, 8, 5), 149 (I, 16, 2), 150 (I, 22, 11).
[150] Ibid., I, 146 (I, 4, 5; 6, 4 f.). Water cannot get into a vessel filled with air.
[151] Hero Alex. Def. (→ n. 148), 138, 3 (IV, 162, 24).
[152] Ps.-Aristot. Mund., 2, p. 391b, 16; 392a, 30: θεῖα σώματα → 679, 19 ff.; 1031, 26 ff.
[153] Cornut. Theol. Graec., 30 (62, 15): ἓν σῶμα par. εἰς ταὐτό → n. 196.
[154] In both one may be strong or sick, ibid., 31 (63, 3), cf. 30 (58, 8). λόγος is correlative instead of ψυχή in 16 (26, 3).
[155] Hierocles Stoicus (1st/2nd cent. A.D.), Col., 4, 39 f., ed. H. v. Arnim (1906): Man is ζῷον σύνθετον, 4, 45 f.: Even in its smallest part the body is a mixture, (→ n. 79; 1034, 5 ff.).
[156] Ibid., Col., 4, 10-19.
[157] Cic. Tusc., I, 9, 18 - 11, 22; Festugière, II, 354 f.
[158] Ibid., I, 9, 18; cf. L. Gernet, "L'anthropologie dans la religion grecque," in Anthropologie religieuse, ed. C. J. Bleeker (1955), 52.
[159] Ps.-Aristot. Mund., 1, p. 391a, 8 f. Cf. the examples in Festugière, II, 460, n. 3.
[160] Diss., I, 1, 11; IV, 1, 100; 11, 27; → 111, 19 ff., though here the spirit is on the same level.

bears witness to the wisdom of providence even to the beard which distinguishes man from woman, Diss., I, 16, 9-14. [161]

Statements about the cosmos can be understood only if one realises that its contemplation now had a deep religious character. If Plat. and Aristot. already summoned men to see the eternal divine laws in contemplation of the starry heaven, [162] and Early Stoicism viewed the cosmos as governed by God (→ 1035, 7 ff.), this now developed into a religion of the cosmos. This finds its most impressive expression in the Orphic Fr. The question how early the cosmos was directly called the body of God [163] is hard to answer. It had long since been felt to be an ensouled entity → 1029, 18 ff.; n. 56). Its divinity was established (→ n. 55) and even its identity with God (→ 1030, 2 f.; 1035, 9 ff.) was asserted. In Aesch. Fr., 70 (TGF, 24) [164] Zeus is called aether, earth, heaven and anything else there may be, and the interpretation of the individual parts of the cosmos as members of the body might well be ancient. [165] As man envelops the soul, so does the cosmos Zeus. [166] The idea that Zeus is the air which pervades or the aether which controls all things is also to be seen, perhaps, in many figures of speech. [167] Certainly in Nero's time there is attestation that aether is regarded as the director and thinking substance of the cosmos par. to the head in the body, and also as the chief of the gods, → III, 674, 19 ff. This idea goes back to Pos. [168] One may assume that in the time when the NT was written the Orphic Fr. (Kern), 21a (91) [169] was already stating that Zeus is the head and centre who conceals all things in himself and then causes them to issue forth from him. Fr., 168 goes further and says that all things are in the gt. body of Zeus, and in later statements, though these are not before c. 400 A.D. and some cannot be dated, [170] the sun, moon and stars are regarded as members of Pan (= the universe) or Hephaestus, the god who governs all houses, cities and peoples, [171] and the parts of the cosmos are equated with the members of the body, → III, 676, 24 ff. [172] Already in the Augustan era one finds the god Aion, who "in virtue of the divine nature always remains the same and κατὰ τὰ αὐτά is the one cosmos as it was and is and will be." [173] Undoubtedly, then, in NT days there is identification of the cosmos and God, and undoubtedly too the cosmos is regarded

---

[161] ἐπὶ τοῖς σωματικοῖς ἥδεσθαι τὴν κατὰ ψυχὴν ἡδονήν, III, 7, 9 (of the Epicureans).

[162] Festugière, II, 132-152, 247-259; Aristot. De philosophia Fr., 12a, ed. W. D. Ross (1955), 80.

[163] So Epiph. Haer. Anacephalaeosis tomi primi, 7, 1 (GCS, 25, 165 f.) of the Stoics: σῶμα δὲ αὐτοῦ τὸ πᾶν, the stars being the eyes, along with the identification of the cosmos and God and the statement that God is the understanding and soul of the universe. But this is Epiph.'s own formulation → 1083, 5 ff.

[164] The authenticity is open to question, but it is attested in the 1st cent. B.C.

[165] So Kranz, op. cit. (→ n. 58), 149-159; also op. cit. (→ n. 54), 17 f. on the basis of parodies. He suspects Persian influences on early Gk. thought. Acc. to Diod. S., 1, 11, 6 the 5 elements are the μέρη of the σῶμα τοῦ κόσμου.

[166] Insight of Diog. Babylonicus, acc. to Philodem. Philos. (→ n. 139) De pietate Fr., 15, 14-21.

[167] A. B. Cook, Zeus, I (1915), 33-62; cf. II (1925), 386.

[168] Leisegang, op. cit. (→ n. 53), 102 f.

[169] Attested Ps.-Aristot. Mund., 7, p.401a, 28 - b, 7; → n. 63 and Aristobulus (2nd cent. B.C.) in Eus. Praep. Ev., 13, 12, 4-8.

[170] Orph. Fr. (Kern), 168 (201 f.); first attested Porphyr. and Procl.; cf. Kern, p. 202-7.

[171] Orph. Hymn. (Quandt), 11, 3; 66, 6-9 (p. 44 * hardly before the 2nd cent. A.D.).

[172] Cf. on this R. Reitzenstein and H. H. Schaeder, Stud. zum antiken Synkretismus, I (1926), 69-103; on the idea of God's cosmic body esp. 80 f., Indian par. 85-90, esp. No. 7, 13, 15 f., 18 f., 38. Stob. Ecl., I, 411, 6-16; 412, 5-14 presents the earth as a body with many μέλη, cf. Reinhardt, op. cit. (→ n. 140), 382-4.

[173] Ditt. Syll.³, III, 1125, 10 f. (cf. Festugière, IV, 180-182): "He has neither beginning, middle, nor end" → n. 63.

as the body which is directed by the supreme God as world-soul or head. [174] That the cosmos is a living body is central for Pos., [175] and the author of Ps.-Aristot. Mund. is his pupil. A clear influence at this pt. is the Stoic emphasis on creative operation in the cosmos. [176] The one God, who has many names, is identical with the universe, fate, necessity, 7, p. 401a, 12-27; 401b, 8-14, 23 f. (ref. to Orph. Fr. [Kern], 21 [90]; → n. 63; 1029, 13 f.). The parallelism of cosmos and state is also clear in 5, p. 396a, 33-b, 2; 400b, 7-12; the twofold sense of κόσμος as world and (divine) order" has an effect here. [177] In the 1st cent. B.C. Cic. collects current views about God in Nat. Deor., I, 10, 25-15, 4. [178] Naturally the cosmos is regarded here as a living entity controlled by divine reason, → 1035, 7 f.; → II, 287, 30 ff. Indeed, God can be thought of as simple rather than composite, consisting of all the fixed stars as scattered members, i.e., as the cosmic body, I, 13, 34 f. For Sen. the world body has water and wind flowing through it as blood and breath flow through the human body. [179] What the soul is in man God is in the cosmos, and what the body is in the former matter is in the latter, Sen. Ep., 65, 24. The cosmos is God, and is so as the totality of which we are fellows and members. [180] We are members of a large body, the one, which includes both the divine and the human. [181] Here then, in Lat., one finds direct statements to the effect that each man is the member of a gt. body embracing all things, both men and gods, the body being also identified with God. More restrained are the sayings of Epict., who simply underlines the unity of the cosmos, Diss., III, 24, 10 f. Man is just part of a whole, of a *polis* consisting of gods and men, and only secondarily of the *polis* in the narrower sense, which is a small reflection of the gt. *polis*, II, 2, 25 f.; 10, 3. [182]

We see combined here what were at first the two distinct views of the living body of the cosmos and the living body of the state as integrated totalities comparable to the human body. Well-known in the second area is the widespread fable of Menenius Agrippa (→ IV, 556, 13 ff.; 562, 33 ff.). [183] Behind it stands the common comparison of the political society to a body. In Greek one finds the statement that the *polis* is composed of many parts and this makes it like the human body, Dion. Hal. Ant. Rom., 6, 86, 1 f. (→ 1039, 10 ff.). Only *corpus* is used as a direct term for the state. [184] Sen. is plainer. As members of the body must be one among themselves, so must men as citizens of the world, Sen. De ira, II, 31, 7. If this is a metaphor, he also calls the state a *corpus* in De clementia, I, 12, 2, and in particular he says directly that the state is the body of the emperor, who is

---

[174] On Philo → 1054, 16 f. Hence one should not follow Dupont, *op. cit.* (→ n. 56), 443 in weakening the statement by saying that κεφαλή means only principle or origin, → 1037 16 f. The motif of the cosmic god as a body holding the cosmos together and that of the world soul performing the same function are both incipiently present in Plato. Cf. Hegermann, 95.

[175] K. Reinhardt, Art. "Pos." in Pauly-W., 22, 1 (1953), 655 and on this H. Hommel, "Platonisches bei Lk.," ZNW, 48 (1957), 194, n. 3.

[176] The effect of the trumpet signal in the camp is compared to that of the Creator in the cosmos and the soul in human life, Ps.-Aristot. Mund., 6, p. 399a, 30 - b, 22.

[177] Cf. 2, p. 391b, 9-12 with Chrysipp. Fr., 527 (v. Arnim, II, 168).

[178] Festugière, II, 356 f.; for Cic., 370-459. Cf. the identification of God and world in the survey of Epic. in Nat. Deor., I, 20, 52; the world as God's temple, De legibus, II, 11, 26.

[179] Sen. Naturales Quaestiones, VI, 14, 1: *hoc totum terrarum omnium corpus.* Cf. already Verg. Aen., VI, 727: *Spiritus ... meus ... magno se corpore miscet.*

[180] *Totum hoc, quo continemur, et unum et deus: et socii sumus eius et membra,* Sen. Ep., 92, 30.

[181] *Membra sumus corporis magni, ibid.,* 95, 92.

[182] Cf. the two testimonies in v. Arnim, Fr., 333-339 (III, 81-3), but esp. Cic. Fin., III, 19, 64 and De legibus, I, 7, 23.

[183] Cf. Corpus Fabularum Aesopicarum, 132 (ed. A. Hausrath, I, 1 [1940]); → 1041, 19 f.; cf. Wikenhauser, 136-143.

[184] Cic. in Marcum Antonium oratio Philippica, 8, 5, 15 f.; Verg. Aen., XI, 313; Liv., 26, 16, 19; 34, 9, 3; Ovid Tristia, II, 231 f.

the soul or head of the state. [185] The parallels show that he still has some sense of a simile, but the point has been reached where the metaphorical statements are so natural that the state can be called directly the body of the ruler. [186]

Even outside the range of Stoic influence it is, of course, generally held that man is made up of body and soul. [187] In true marriage the souls of the partners are united too. [188] Where trichotomy is espoused (→ VI, 395, 9 ff.) [189] and the soul is taken bodily as in Epic., *animus* and *anima* are a unity *vis-à-vis* the body, Lucretius De rerum natura (→ n. 189), III, 161 f., 421-424. Indeed, even the Epicurean hesitates to ascribe corporeality to the gods. [190] Where σῶμα means "person," it is usually as a thing, an object for sale or destruction, a ransom, a possession, part of the mass. [191] There is also a clear sense of the unity of the σῶμα. Thus the tactician speaks of the destruction of the whole body of a city, while the historian calls the people the body of a town. [192] Forming a body of supporters is called σωματοποιεῖν, [193] and the writer must compose one body by putting together the things that come to him. [194] When one reduces plurality to unity, one comes closer to the appearance of a body, i.e., the organic. [195] The concept of body and head is present when Alexandria, the second largest city in the world, is said to have the gt. realm of Egypt as its body or, better, appendage, Dio Chrys. Or., 32, 36. Strabo, 17, 2 is nearer the idea of "substance," "mass," when he speaks of the main mass of the Nile flowing straight → n. 77. The same idea is present when, despite all demythologising, [196] Dionysus is introduced as a real personal god. [197] The cosmos is similarly described as a gt. house in contrast to the small individual *polis*, Dio Chrys. Or., 12, 33 f. [198] The doctrine of the total body as universal nature which is made up of the 5 elements as its parts μέρη, so that the body of the cosmos is like the head, hands, feet and other parts μέρη of man, is an Egyptian one, → n. 57. [199]

At the turn of the 1st and 2nd cent. stands Plutarch. As a contemporary of the later NT authors and a collector of various traditions he is esp. interesting. For him σῶμα is the human body [200] or just the trunk as distinct from the head. [201] Then it is the

---

[185] *Tu animus rei publicae tuae es, illa corpus tuum,* Sen. De clementia, I, 5, 1; the spirit of the emperor should spread *per omne imperii corpus... A capite bona valetudo: inde omnia vegeta sunt,* II, 2, 1. Cf. Curtius Rufus Historiae Alexandri Magni Macedoniensis, X, 9, 1-4, ed. T. Stangl (1902); → n. 222, 260.

[186] Cf. Wikenhauser, 130-143, 146 f.; Knox, 243-6; Dupont, *op. cit.* (→ n. 56), 440-6.

[187] Onasander Strategicus (1st cent. A.D.), 1, 84 f.; 9, 326, ed. E. Korzensky and R. Vari (1935); φρόνημα or γνώμη, 14, 595, 33, 918 may be correlative; cf. also Dion. Hal. Ant. Rom., 8, 51, 1.

[188] Ditt. Syll.³, II, 783, 33 f. (1st cent. B.C.); → 1040, 26 f.

[189] Lucretius De rerum natura, III, 212 f., 796 f., ed. C. Bailey (1947).

[190] Philodem. Philos. De pietate fr., 121, 5-12 (→ n. 139); Cic. Nat. Deor., I, 18, 49: they are only *quasi corpus* and have only *quasi sanguinem.*

[191] Onasander (→ n. 187), 35, 975. 988; Dion. Hal. Ant. Rom., 4, 69, 2; Diod. S., 1, 79, 3; 13, 14, 5.

[192] Onasander, 41, 1154; Lib. Or., 1, 210; Dion. Hal. Ant. Rom., 3, 11, 5.

[193] Diod. S., 11, 86, 4 (→ 1035, 17 f.); 18, 10, 2, however, says orators give form to popular demands.

[194] Ps.-Long., 10, 1: καθάπερ ἕν τι σῶμα ποιεῖν.

[195] *Ibid.,* 24, 1 σωματοειδέστερον, → 1035, 18 f.; n. 86.

[196] Acc. to Diod. S., 3, 62, 2 f. The reuniting of the members is the return of strength to the vine after cutting → 1036, 16 ff.

[197] σωματοειδής, Strabo, 63, 1 → n. 195. Cf. σῶμα σοφίης Hippocr. Ep., 10 (Littré, IX, 324, 1).

[198] Cf. also σύστημα ἐξ οὐρανοῦ καὶ γῆς καὶ τῶν μεταξὺ φύσεων and οἰκητήριον θεῶν, Achilles (3rd cent. A.D.?), Isagoga Excerpta, 5, *op. cit.* (→ n. 128), 35, 30 ff. → 1038, 3 f.

[199] Diod. S., 1, 11, 6 (→ n. 96), cf. also Philo → 1054, 16 ff.

[200] The land is the σῶμα of Isis, the Nile the outflow of Osiris, Plut. Is. et Os., 38 (II, 366a).

[201] De Bruto, 43 (I, 1004e); De Artaxerxe, 13, 2 (I, 1017c); Galb., 4 (I, 1054e).

"person," esp. corporeally, [202] an obj. of desire erotically, Quaest. Conv., V, 7, 5 (II, 682c-d). σώματα are with property and friends what is common to married couples. [203] σώματα and χρήματα perish. [204] The σῶμα can even be man's ego, Sept. Sap. Conv., 15 (II, 159a). [205] The 4 primal elements are also σώματα, Comm. Not., 49 (II, 1085c). On the basis of Plat. Tim. mathematical bodies are discussed and it is shown that no sensually perceptible σῶμα is perfectly round, only the element of the soul and reason, Quaest. Plat., 5 (II, 1004c). In Plut. the body is three-dimensional and limited. [206] In debate with Arist. (→ 1031, 22 ff.) τοπικόν is the spatial and abstract while σωματικόν is the corporeal and real, Def. Orac., 26 (II, 424e). σῶμα is the substantial when it is asked whether the sperm is σῶμα; some only call its ὕλη thus, while others also use the term for its effective force, since this is πνευματική. [207] The corporeality of the pneuma naturally underlies this conclusion. In anti-Stoic polemic σῶμα is almost par. to ὕλη when Plut. charges the Stoics with making God σῶμα νοερόν and imprisoning Him in the σωματικόν, i.e., ὕλη. [208] He also accuses them of regarding day and night, virtues, vices, and qualities as σώματα and ζῷα, [209] so that the def. of σῶμα as what is in a specific place is jeopardised. The usage is the same when he ref. to the non-corporeal οὐσία of the Platonic idea, Plac. Phil., I, 10 (II, 882d). [210] Plut. himself regards air as the σῶμα of light, i.e., the material in which it can embody itself. [211] Thus σῶμα can also be positive as the visible embodiment of the idea. [212] Naturally body and soul appear together here again as the parts which define man. [213] Thus the later Plato can be quoted with approval: The body cannot move without the soul nor vice versa, so that the body, working with the soul, is also to be estimated positively, Plut. De tuenda sanitate praecepta, 27 (II, 137e). If Plut. can also speak of the evil desires of the soul which dash against the body and have poor prospects in conflict with it, [214] essentially he follows the early Plato (→ 1028, 25 f.) against Epic. (→ 103, 21 ff.) in speaking of the evil lusts of the body [215] and the basic freedom of the soul. [216] For this reason one should love souls rather than bodies, → 1030, 29 f.; 1039, 5 f.), Instituta Laconica, 7 (II, 237b c). A man should rule over his wife, not like an owner over his property, but like the soul over the body, for which it cares without being enslaved to its desires, Praec. Coniug., 33 (II, 142e). The body is the mill of the soul in which the slaves do penal work, Sept. Sap. Conv., 16 (II,

---

[202] τηλικαῦτα σώματα of athletes, Plut. Apophthegmata Alexandri, 8 (II, 180a).
[203] Praec. Coniug., 34 (II, 143a); cf. 20 (II, 140e): Nature mixes couples in the child διὰ τῶν σωμάτων.
[204] Cons. ad Apoll., 15 (II, 110e); the giant σώματα of prisoners are listed among the booty, Plut. De Marcello, 8 (I, 301 f.); on the destruction of the city free egress is granted to σώματα, Plut. De Sertorio, 18 (I, 577e-f).
[205] This is, of course, the view of the fictitious author and rests on the express argument that every man is σὺν σώματι.
[206] Plac. Phil., I, 12 (II, 882 f.); → 1033, 20 ff.; 1040, 14 f.
[207] Ibid., V, 3 f. (II, 905a b); → 1033, 24 f.
[208] Comm. Not., 48 (II, 1085b c): οὐκ ἔστιν ἀσώματος οὐδ' ἄϋλος, on the other side νοῦς εν ὕλῃ, Def. Orac., 29 (II, 426b).
[209] Comm. Not., 45 (II, 1084a-d); 50 (II, 1085e); Superst., 1 (II, 165a).
[210] Cf. I, 9 (II, 882d): Plato and Aristot. understand ὕλη as σῶμα, not ἄμορφος.
[211] De primo frigido, 17 (II, 952 f); cf. for sound Quaest. Conv., VIII, 3, 4 (II, 722b).
[212] Among the Egypt. the sun is σῶμα τῆς τἀγαθοῦ δυνάμεως ὡς ὁρατὸν οὐσίας νοητῆς, Is. et Os., 51 (II, 372a). F. W. Eltester, Eikon im NT (1958), 108 shows how the schema of paradigm and eikon is compared to that of soul and body.
[213] Cons. ad Apoll., 1 (II, 102a); 3 (II, 102e); 36 (II, 121e); Apophth. Lac., 13 (II, 227e) etc.; διάνοια as correlative Plut. De Arato, 47 (I, 1049b); De tuenda sanitate praecepta, 21 (II, 134a); ψυχή, 16 (II, 130c).
[214] De tuenda sanit. praec., 7 (II, 125b c); 24 (II, 135e); 25 (II, 136b c).
[215] Cons. ad Apoll., 13 (II, 108a); Suav. Viv. Epic., 4 (II, 1088e-1089d).
[216] The enemy is lord over the body but not necessarily the soul, Plut. De Eumene, 21 (I, 596a).

159d). The popular view, considered by Socrates, that death is the end of body and soul (Cons. ad Apoll., 12 [II, 107d]), is thus untenable. It is the separation of the two, 36 (II, 121d-e), the redemption by which the soul becomes for the first time pure and free, 13 (II, 108c-d); 25 (II, 114d). At apparent death the power of thought leaves the body like a pilot falling from the ship and it swoops up to the firmament, though leaving the rest of the soul like an anchor in the body. [217] The most interesting passage is Gen. Socr., 22 (II, 591d e), which expressly affirms that the νοῦς is a δαίμων outside the σῶμα, and that whereas some souls are totally immersed in the body others are only partially so, → 1087, 16 ff.; cf. 1047, 19 ff. We also find the idea of totality with σῶμα. From the divided Peloponnese the Archaeans wanted to create ἓν σῶμα καὶ μίαν δύναμιν (→ 1043, 21 ff.), Plut. Philop., 8 (I, 360c). The σῶμα, i.e., the totality of harmony, indeed, the whole σῶμα of music, i.e.. its structure, consists of unequal parts μέρη sounding forth together, De musica, 23 (II, 1139c). [218] The Stoic distinction between bodies made up of integrated parts like a house or ship, and those made up of separate parts like an army or camp, cf. also the ἐκκλησία → 1035, 3 ff., is also known to Plut., Praec. Coniug., 34 (II, 142e f). The cosmos is a most sacred temple [219] ruled by God, who possesses thinking power and reason, Def. Orac., 29 (II, 425 f., 426a). Ref. is made to Stoic statements about the body of the cosmos being perfect in spite of the imperfection of its part. [220] Plut. also compares the state (→ 1044, 5 ff.) to the members of a body, De Solone, 18, (I, 88c), cf. esp. the fable (→ 1038, 25 f.) in De Coriolano, 6 (I, 216b c). It is said of Caesar that he is clothed with the power of the army ὡς σῶμα, [221] and Galba is called upon to take over the leadership and to offer himself to the Gauls as to a strong body seeking a head, [222] → 1036, 12 ff.; 1039, 10 ff.

5. The Post-New Testament Period.

σῶμα denotes the human body as the body to be cared for, e.g., in the usual salutation at the end of a private letter, [223] or the body which is defiled by unnatural lust, Poll. Onom., VI, 127, or the body which is sacrificed in battle, Lib. Declamationes, 24, 23; cf. Lidz. Ginza R., 18, 20 f.; 36, 27-29, or as a corpse, the most ancient sense → 1025, 19 ff. [224] The head can be distinguished from the σῶμα as trunk [225] or it can be regarded as the body's acropolis (→ 1036, 22 f.; III, 674, 25 ff.), so that the whole body hangs on the head and neck, Artemid. Onirocr., I, 34 (35, 22 ff.); → n. 53. If the generative member is called τὸ παιδοποιὸν σῶμα in Ael. Nat. An., 17, 42, the idea is that of a total, self-enclosed body, but the σῶμα of the heart is put between σάρξ and νεῦρον [226] and thus carries the thought of (muscular) "substance." The same applies to the description of

---

217 Ser. Num. Vind., 23 f. (II, 563e f; 564c); → 674, n. 26.
218 Aristot. Fr., 25 (→ n. 162), p. 92 uses μέλη, but σῶμα may go back to Plut., cf. Plut. De musica, 34 (II, 1143e-f).
219 Tranq. An., 20 (II, 477c) and on this Festugière, II, 233-8.
220 Stoic. Rep., 44 (II, 1054e f). σῶμα ἐκ διεστώτων is the cosmos if one postulates various worlds all directed by God, Def. Orac., 29 (II, 426a).
221 Pomp., 51 (I, 646b); should one transl. "as with"... or "as a body"?
222 Galb., 4 (I, 1054e). On the concept of the head → 1036, 22; 1037, 16; n. 53, 185; → III, 673 f.
223 ἐπιμελοῦ δὲ τοῦ σώματος, P. Par., 32, 30 f. (162 B.C.); P. Lond., I, 42, 32 (163 B.C.).
224 With the addition νενεκρωμένον, IG, 3, 2, 1355, without it Dio C., III, 13, 4 etc.; Alciphr. Ep., I, 10, 4.
225 Ps.-Eratosthenes Catasterismi, I, 3, Mythographi Graeci, III, 1, ed. A. Olivieri (1897), 4, 9 f.; I, 25 (32, 5): constellations; Palaephatus De incredibilibus Mythographi Graeci, III, 2, ed. F. Nesta (1902), 271; 4, 276; 20, 285 (τὸ δ' ἄλλο σῶμα); 24, 287; 38, 301 (fabulous creatures).
226 Alex. Aphr. An., I, 141r (I, 98, 12 f.). It is the seat of the ἡγεμονικόν (→ 1036, 20 f.), loc. cit. (I, 98, 7 f.).

ulcers or tumours as σώματα, Aret., I, 8, 1; VII, 13, 4. Physically water, snow and hail can be called three different σώματα, i.e., "embodiments," Stob. Ecl., I, 245, 3. σῶμα denotes "person," [227] esp. as obj., [228] e.g., soldier in Phryn. Ecl., 355 (→ n. 10), slave, [229] female slave. [230] σῶμα πολιτικόν is the townsman as distinct from the worker on the soil, Gal. De compositione medicamentorum secundum locos, III, 2 (Kühn, 12, 674, 5). It is expressly noted in Apollon. Dyscol. Synt., 86a (67, 28) that σῶμα may be used for a reflexive pronoun, esp. when there is a strong obj. character. [231] For the body generally cf. Sext. Emp. He attacks the three-dimensional def. [232] His presupposition is that of the touchability of an active or passive σῶμα [233] and the understanding of the non-corporeal as the στέρησις σώματος, Pyrrh. Hyp., III, 50 (→ 1040, 7 ff.; n. 107). Heavenly bodies are made up of the fifth circular σῶμα of Okellos and Aristot. [234] The understanding of time as σῶμα is traced back to Heracl., whereas the Stoics regard it as non-corporeal acc. to him, Math., X, 215-218, 231 f., cf. VII, 39. Specially attacked, of course, was the Stoic doctrine of the corporeality of the gods. [235] For Alex. Aphr. An., II, 147r (I, 122, 17-25) the qualities, too, were to be taken neither as σῶμα nor οὐσία. In An., II, 142v-143r (I, 103, 22-104, 18) the author rejects Aristot.'s view of the soul as the entelechy of the body on the ground that this does not apply to technical or general physical bodies but only to organic bodies, and the soul is naturally to be regarded as non-corporeal. [236] The same is affirmed in An., II, 145r (I, 113, 26-34) in opposition to the Stoic concept of the ἄποιον σῶμα, → n. 114, 126.

There are many testimonies to man's being made up of body and soul. [237] Neo-Platonically and Stoically the soul is described as the higher part. [238] The body is

---

[227] Epigr. Graec., 164, 2: The grave contains only the empty οὔνομα σώματος → 1030, 18 f.

[228] E.g., a pledge in Anon. Excerpta Vaticana, 3, Mythographi Graeci, III, 2 (→ n. 225), p. 99 or booty, Ditt. Syll.³, I, 521, 5-26. Punishment εἰς σῶμα is distinguished from εἰς χρήματα, Poll. Onom., VIII, 22 (→ n. 18, cf. n. 262); cf. Appian. Bell. Civ., III, 39, 157; II, 106, 442.

[229] Phryn. Ecl., 355 ref. to this as incorrect for δοῦλα σώματα, cf. Poll. Onom., III, 77 f.

[230] Cf. anon. Periplus of the Erythraeum Mare, ed. B. Fabricius (1883), 31: σώματα θηλυκά (→ n. 142).

[231] Appian. Rom. Hist. (11) Συριακή 41: to yield "oneself" to the officers; (12) Μιθριδατεῖος 27: life and limb on an attack → n. 17.

[232] Sext. Emp. Math., III, 83; IX, 367. Even the adding of substantiality (Math., X, 12) was inadequate, Pyrrh. Hyp., III, 39 f.; cf. στερεόν, Math., VII, 100; similarly Alex. Aphr. An., II, 148r (I, 125, 15); cf. also Stob. Ecl., I, 140, 14; 143, 24 → 1033, 20 ff.

[233] Sext. Emp. Math., IX, 258 → 1031, 23.

[234] Ibid., X, 316; cf. Stob. Ecl., I, 141, 24; Iambl. Myst., V, 4; acc. to Alex. Aphr. Quaestiones, I, 1 (II, 3, 11-13) it is ensouled → 1032, 3.

[235] Sophonias in libros Aristot. de anima paraphrasis, I, 5, Comment. in Aristot. Graeca, 23, 1, ed. M. Hayduck (1883), 36, 12 on Aristot. An., I, 5 p. 411a, 7; Diog. L., V, 1, 32; Cl. Al. Strom., I, 10, 51, 1; V, 13, 89, 2.

[236] Nemesius De natura hominis, 2, 32, 82 - 34, 23 (MPG, 40 [1863], 545A-549A) discusses the corresponding Stoic statements.

[237] Claudius Ptolemaeus (2nd. cent. A.D.) De iudicandi facultate et animi principatu, 7, 1, ed. F. Lammert, III, 2 (1952), defines the body as made up of bones, flesh and similar sensual materials, while the soul is moving force; the one is ὑλικώτερον and ἀνενέργητον, the other κινητικόν, 13, 3; to hazard body and soul, i.e., existence, Dio C., I, 5, 13. The body envelops the soul like a robe, Artemid. Onirocr., IV, 30 (221, 10 f.); Ael. Nat. An., 11, 39; it possesses the soul, Alex. Aphr. An., I, 123r (I, 2, 20). The body reflects the impulses of the soul, Sext. Emp. Pyrrh. Hyp., I, 85; II, 101.

[238] M. Ant., XI, 19, 2 (Pohlenz, I, 341-353, on trichotomy esp. 342 f.). After Epicurus σάρξ increasingly replaces σῶμα → 104, 17 ff.

disparaged. [239] When added it defiles the pure, unalloyed, divine soul, Stob. Ecl., I, 50, 3-5. It is its fetter, I, 293, 5 → 1026, 25 f.; 1028, 23 ff. It is a mere sack, Diog. L., IX, 10, 59. The Orphic-Platonic formula σῶμα-σῆμα (→ 1028, 32 ff.) is taken up repeatedly, [240] and Chr. apologists adopt the doctrine of the pre-existence of the soul, Athenag. Suppl., 36, 1-3. Even in the enslaved body the soul is free, Xenoph. Ephes., II, 4, 4. The image of the snake slipping out of its skin pts. to death in which the soul leaves the body, [241] for in death the soul rises up to the aether, the body goes to the earth, Epigr. Graec., 261, 6-16 → 103, 7 f., 18 ff. Death becomes a journey, the body a worthless corpse, Ps.-Socrates Ep., 14, 7 and 10. [242] The question what is meant by the dissolution of the alloyed body causes some difficulty. [243] Its decay shows that it still has power to suffer as distinct from the immortal σῶμα which, unalloyed, consists of its own ὕλη and is act. rather than pass. [244] A widespread belief is that the soul can leave the body in dreams, ecstasy, trance or delirium, and then return to it. [245] Without sense-impressions on the pure soul we would live ἐν σώματι, untouched by the life of the σῶμα. [246] The Stoic distinctions between organic bodies, composed bodies and independent bodies are still current, though they become blurred in popular usage. [247] So long as it holds together the phalanx forms a σῶμα, Polyaen. Excerpta, 18, 4. Something is missing from the total body of the vine when the individual branches exude sap, Cassianus Bassius De re rustica ecl., 5, 38, 1. [248] The postcript and marginal notes of a work, also the preface as head, are distinguished from its σῶμα in Luc. Quomodo historia conscribenda, 23. [249] Ref. is also made to the σῶμα τῆς λέξεως. [250] ἓν σῶμα is the united whole intellectually too, [251] and σωματοποιέω is used for εἰς ἓν συνάγειν, Artemid. Onirocr., IV prooemium, 198, 6 f. To the Stoic group of unified σώματα belongs the cosmos, as the sympathy of all things shows, Sext. Emp. Math. IX, 78-80; it is naturally limited as a living creature (V, 44 → 1035, 4 ff.), [252]

---

[239] M. Ant., VI, 28; X, 36, 6; cf. E. Schweizer, "Die hell. Komponente im nt.lichen σάρξ-Begriff," Neotestamentica (1963), 30-37.

[240] Anecdota Graeca, ed. J. A. Cramer, I (1835), 386, 19-21. Stob. Ecl., I, 293, 5 interprets Homer's usage in this way. On the renaissance of this view in the 1st cent. B.C./1st cent. A.D. cf. Festugière, III, 27-32.

[241] Artemid. Onirocr., V, 40 (261, 19-21). Indian influence: Arianus Expeditio Alexandri, ed. A. G. Roos (1907-1928), VII, 3, 4-6.

[242] Ed. L. Köhler (1928), 574.

[243] Artemid. Onirocr., I, 47 (44, 12 f.); cf. V, 39 (261, 16 f.); Timaeus Locrus De anima mundi et natura, 14, 103a (ed. J. J. de Gelder [1836]).

[244] So Stob. Ecl., I, 286, 8-15 of the Hermetics; cf. 285, 25-27; on the forming of the body powers come down from divine bodies into mortal bodies.

[245] Clearchus (Platonising disciple of Aristot. in the 3rd cent. B.C.) Fr., 7 f., ed. F. Wehrli, Die Schule d. Aristot. (1948); Apollonius Paradoxographus (2nd cent. B.C.?), Historiae mirabiles, 3, Rerum naturalium scriptores Graeci minores, I, ed. O. Keller (1877); Artemid. Onirocr., V, 43 (262, 7-9); Luc. Musc. Enc., 7; Max. Tyr., 38, 3c-f; 10, 2 f.; Plin. Hist. Nat., 7, 52, 173-9.

[246] Cf. the Neo-Platonist Porphyr. Abst., I, 38 → 1050, 18.

[247] Artemid Onirocr., IV, 30 (220, 25 - 221, 11); in dreams clothing, house, fort and ship ref. to the body, which is always an example of ἡνωμένα καὶ συμφυᾶ, whereas house and ship are traditionally in the group of ἐκ συναπτομένων, → 1034, 29 ff.; cf. Schnorr, op. cit. (→ n. 127), 177-9.

[248] Ed. H. Beckh (1895).

[249] P. Fay., 34, 20 (161 A.D.); P. Lond., III, 1132b, 11 (142 A.D.); P. Oxy., III, 494, 30 (156 A.D.); BGU, I, 187, 12 (2nd cent. A.D.); Thdrt. Eranistes seu Polymorphus (MPG, 83 [1860], 29 B).

[250] The totality or substance of a speech which is not to be corrupted, Longinus De arte rhet., ed. O. Prickard (1947), 560 → n. 144.

[251] Hephaestio (2nd cent. A.D.?), Μετρικὴ εἰσαγωγή, 1 (ed. M. Consbruch [1906], 59, 3 f.): συστηματικὰ δὲ ὅσα ὑπὸ πλειόνων μέτρων εἰς ἓν σῶμα παραληφθέντων καταμετρεῖται ἢ συμπληροῦται, cf. Artemid. Onirocr., III,, 66 (196, 7-9).

[252] On Chrysippus and Pos., 13 cf. Diog. L., VII, 1, 142, cf. 1, 138 and 143; 1, 147; cf. Tert. Apol., 11, 5.

but is uniformly ruled by divine reason. 253 The ingenerate and indestructible body of the cosmos is ordered acc. to its own nature and soul, Alex. Aphr. Quaest., II, 19 (II, 63, 18-20). These thoughts occur in hymnal form in M. Ant. 254 Man is not just a part but a member of the whole. 255 Identification of the cosmos with God is so widespread 256 that it even makes its way into the Gk. Bible, Sir. 43:27. But the image of the body is also used of the state, 257 esp. in the still influential fable → 1038, 25 f. 258 A subject land is the σῶμα τῆς βασιλείας (→ 1038, 26 ff.) acc. to Themist. Or., 8. 117b-c. 259 There is perhaps a Gk. example of the idea of the state as the body of the ruler in this period. 260 On the other hand there is no proof of an earlier use of σῶμα as a corporate body 261 with the gen. of the name of the people. 262 It is found only much later, 263 and σωμάτιον for association is later still. 264

Schweizer

B. The Old Testament.

This art. offers only linguistic data. For matters of bibl. theology cf. the main concepts of OT anthropology רוּחַ, נֶפֶשׁ, לֵב, etc. in the art. → ψυχή.

1. Hebrew Equivalents to the Septuagint σῶμα.

a. בָּשָׂר cf. σάρξ (→ 105, 19 ff.; 108, 10 ff.). b. שְׁאֵר cf. σάρξ (→ 107, 26 ff.; 108, 15 ff.).

---

253 Ps.-Plat. Epin., 980 ff. (heaven, 977a); cf. Lact. Inst., I, 3, 21; De ira dei, 11, 5; Epiph. Haer., 5, 1, 1.

254 M. Ant., IV, 23, 2: ὦ φύσις, ἐκ σοῦ πάντα, ἐν σοὶ πάντα, εἰς σὲ πάντα, cf. VII, 9, 2: one substance, one reason, one law . . . one truth; also XII, 30, 1-4.

255 M. Ant., VII, 13, 1: οἷόν ἐστιν ἐν ἡνωμένοις τὰ μέλη τοῦ σώματος, . . . μέλος εἰμὶ τοῦ ἐκ τῶν λογικῶν συστήματος cf. μέρος VIII, 34, 2. Cf. also V, 8, 4: the cosmos is composed of all these bodies as τοιοῦτον σῶμα; VII, 19, 1: all bodies are bound up with the universe like our μέρη.

256 Ael. Arist. Or., 45, 21. 24 (Keil); Sext. Emp. Math., IX, 95; CIL, 10, 1, 3800: equated with Isis. Cf. the influence on Athenag. Suppl., 63 f., who sees God as constituted of body and soul and views the aether as His σῶμα, while the soul which causes movement is His reason.

257 Cf. M. Ant., VIII, 34, 1-5: Anti-social man is like a limb cut off from the body.

258 J. Zonares, Epitome historiarum, 7, 14, ed. L. Dindorf, II (1869), 128, 21 - 130, 4.

259 Ed. W. Dindorf (1961).

260 Heliodor. Aeth., 10, 4 (Colonna, 317 f.) acc. to the interpretation of A. Fridrichsen, "Sprachliches u. Stylistisches zu NT," *Kungl. Humanistiska Vetenskaps-Samfundet, Uppsala Årsbok* (1943), 34-36. Also K. Kerényi, *Die griech.-orient. Romanliteratur* (1927), 51 follows this interpretation and ref. to Corp. Herm., 24, 11. 13, i.e., Stob. Ecl., I, 411, 6-16; 414, 5-14, where the earth is the body and the lands are the μέλη; cf. also Reinhardt, op. cit. (→ n. 140), 382-4. Curtius Rufus (→ n. 185), X, 9, 1-4 (cf. Mussner, 155 f.) has the same idea. But μέλος ὑμῶν τοῦ σώματος is not to be taken as par. to μέρος τῆς βασιλείας; it describes the parent-daughter relation.

261 T. W. Manson, "A Par. to a NT Use of σῶμα," JThSt, 37 (1936), 385; Suppl. Epigr. Graec., 9 (1938), 8, 58: τῷ τῶν Ἑλλήνων σώματι.

262 Acc. to A. Wilhelm, DLZ, 65 (1944), 31 the ref. is probably to liturgies τῷ σώματι, rather than τοῖς χρήμασιν (→ n. 228). τῷ τῶν Ἑλλήνων is then to be taken with ἐμ μέρει and the omission of a second τῷ assumed.

263 Eus. Hist Eccl., X, 5, 10-12: τὸ σῶμα τῶν Χριστιανῶν, Lib. Or., 13, 42: τὸ τῆς οἰκουμένης σῶμα, on *corpus* cf. E. Seckel, *Heumanns Handlex. zu den Quellen d. röm. Rechts*, 9 (1907), s.v.; cf. A. Ehrhardt, "Das Corpus Christi u. d. Korporationen im spät.-röm. Recht," *Zschr. d. Savigny-Stiftung f. Rechtsgeschichte, Romanistische Abteilung*, 70 (1953), 299-347.

264 F. Poland, *Gesch. d. griech. Vereinswesens* (1909), 155; for σῶμα cf. Dimitrakos, s.v.

c. גְּוִיָּה man's body, Gn. 47:18; Neh. 9:37; body of the cherubim, Ez. 1:11, 23; the angel, Da. 10:6; corpse, 1 S. 31:10, 12 Na. 3:3; Ps. 110:6; animal, Ju. 14:8, 9. d. Aram. גְּשֵׁם "body" of man, Da. 4:30 etc.; animal, Da. 7:11. e. גַּו "back," 1 K. 14:9; Ez. 23:35; Neh. 9:26; גֵּו "back," Is. 38:17; Prv. 10:13 etc.; גֵּוָה "back," Job 20:25. f. נְבֵלָה "carcass" of man, Dt. 21:23; Is. 5:25 etc.; unclean or dead animal, Lv. 5:2; Dt. 14:8 etc. Transf. נִבְלַת הָעָב Jer. 7:33; נִבְלַת שִׁקּוּצֵיהֶם "carcasses" of their gods, i.e., dead idols, Jer. 16:18, cf. פֶּגֶר Lv. 26:30. g. פֶּגֶר 265 human "corpses," passim; פְּגָרִים מֵתִים "corpses," 2 K. 19:35; Is. 37:36; "carcass" of an animal, Gn. 15:11; פִּגְרֵי גִלּוּלֵיכֶם your "dead idols," Lv. 26:30, cf. נְבֵלָה Jer. 16:18. h. גּוּפָה "corpse," 1 Ch. 10:12.

2. The Translation of Hebrew Equivalents in the Septuagint.

a. בָּשָׂר v. σάρξ (→ 108, 10 ff.). b. שְׁאֵר v. σάρξ (→ 108, 15 ff.). c. גְּוִיָּה: σῶμα (11 times). 266 cf. Ju. 14:9: στόμα Cod A, ἕξις Cod B; Ps. 110:6: πτῶμα. 267 d. Aram. גְּשֵׁם: σῶμα (7 times). 266 e. גַּו: σῶμα (3 times). 268 גֵּו: νῶτος Is. 50:6; τὰ μέσα Is. 51:23 (A τὰ μετάφρενα); ὀπίσω μου for אַחֲרֵי גֵוֶךָ Is. 38:17 → n. 279. גֵּוָה σῶμα Job 20:25. f. נְבֵלָה σῶμα (9 times); νεκρός (4 times); θνησιμαῖον (31 times); νεκριμαῖον 1 K. 13:30. g. פֶּגֶר κῶλον (7 times); σῶμα (3); νεκρός (3); φόνος Ez. 43:7, 9; πτῶμα Ez. 6:5 A; πτῶσις Na. 3:3; πεπτωκώς Am. 8:3. 269 h. גּוּפָה σῶμα 1 Ch. 10:12.

Baumgärtel

3. Septuagint Works with a Hebrew Original.

There is, then, no consistent Hbr. equivalent for σῶμα. In transl. of בָּשָׂר it replaces σάρξ about one out of seven times. This is esp. so when what is in view is neither man's transitoriness nor his flesh as distinct from his bones but bodily man in his totality. Almost always the suffering body is meant. Thus σῶμα denotes man as a total phenomenon in Da. 1:15, 270 or man as the victim of illness in Job 7:5, 271 or man enveloped by a sack in 3 Βασ. 20:27. 272 σῶμα is also a pure object in relation to shaving in Nu. 8:7 or washing in Lv. 14:9; 15:11, 13, 16; 16:4, 24, 26; 17:16; Nu. 19:7 f. 273 Man as a totality is always in view. One can make ritual cuttings on the σῶμα (Lv. 19:28) as on the σάρξ (Lv. 21:5), with either the whole body or the muscular parts in mind. The sexual organ is probably in view in Lv. 6:3 (16:4 χρώς) and certainly so in Lv. 15:2 f., 19, → 1041, 31 f.; it is the male organ, not the female. There is perhaps reflected in this usage an awareness that man takes part esp. in sexual functions as a totality, → 1063, 9 ff.

When σῶμα is used for other Hbr. terms it can mean "corpse," → lines 4 ff. 274 Man is understood as a pure obj. when σῶμα denotes "slave" or man as something to be

---

265 2 Ch. 20:25 read בְּגָדִים for פְּגָרִים (LXX σκῦλα).

266 Including Da. Θ and Sir.

267 Na. 3:3: τοῖς ἔθνεσιν αὐτῆς for לְגוֹיָה presupposes a reading with גּוֹי.

268 Including 1 K. 14:9 A.

269 Is. 14:19: for פֶּגֶר LXX reads בֶּגֶר and transl. ἱμάτιον.

270 The Gk. understanding of σῶμα as form (→ 1027, 17 ff.) has had an influence here.

271 At 4 Βασ. 5:10, 14, however, the ref. is to the healing of the σάρξ, i.e., the leprous muscular parts of the body.

272 Just the body is meant here, σάρξ in 4 Βασ. 6:30.

273 The expression is technical and occurs with no Hbr. equivalent at Lv. 15:27; Dt. 23:12.

274 Gn. 15:11 animal sacrifices.

assessed for sale. [275] σῶμα is also often used when the ref. is to the sickness or corruption [276] or healing (Prv. 3:8: שָׁאֵר?) or resurrection [277] of the body. The obj. character is particularly strong when we have dying, being burnt (Da. 7:11; [278] Δα. 3:94 [27]), wounding (Job 20:25 גֵּו), offering up (→ 1041, 28; Δα. 3:95 [28]), or, in madness, exposure to the dew of heaven, Da. 5:21 Θ. The expression (ἀπο)-ρίπτω ὀπίσω σώματος is a formula for "to reject," 3 Βασ. 14:9 A; Ez. 23:35 גֵּו. [279] σῶμα in the sing. can be used here for many, 2 Εσδρ. 19:26: σῶμα αὐτῶν.

LXX often deviates from HT in Job. At 6:4 σῶμα is almost a personal pronoun, the ref. being to a sick person; neither formally nor materially is αἷμα a par. At 33:24 the ref. is the healing of a sick body. At 40:32 (cf. 41:7 A), in a passage obscure in both Hbr. and Gk., σῶμα is the body of the crocodile. 33:17 is difficult: "God keeps man's body from falling," the idea apparently being that man is exposed to temptation. Some verses suggest that anthropological dualism has been read into the HT. The body is made of clay, 13:12. In the textually corrupt 18:15 A is perhaps interpreting the tent as the earthly body. In sickness the soul is parted from the body, 7:15 A, and in the joy of διάνοια the heart leaves the (sick?) body, 36:28b. [280] Finally in Prv. 25:20 (through a slip, cf. Θ?) the σῶμα is the seat of passion which troubles the heart.

4. Works not in the Hebrew Canon.

a. It is no new development when σῶμα is used for a healthy or sick body in Sir. 30:14-16; 2 Macc. 9:9; [281] 4 Macc. 3:18; 6:7; 18:3, a cured body in Sir. 51:2, a body voluntarily given up to pain in 4 Macc. 18:3, or burned by fire in 4 Macc. 14:10, or marked by a brand in 3 Macc. 2:29, [282] or even a corpse in Sir. 38:16; 48:13; 1 Macc. 11:4; 2 Macc. 9:29; 12:39. Nor is there any essential difference from → 1045, 32 f. when σῶμα just means "head" as a numerical unit in 2 Macc. 8:11; [283] 12:26. Along with the description of the torments of the body there is a ref. to violating or torturing individual members in 2 Macc. 7:7; 9:7; 4 Macc. 10:20. Naturally the statement that a good name survives the body in Sir. 41:11; 44:14; cf. Wis. 2:3 f. [284] does not contain any dualism. The body is further disparaged in verses in which σῶμα is a woman's body as the object of licentious passion (Sir. 7:24; 4 Macc. 17:1) or in which it is the place where passion burns, Sir. 23:17; 47:19.

---

[275] Gn. 36:6 for נֶפֶשׁ with other persons, Gn. 34:29 as part of the possessions (Hbr. only חַיִל), Gn. 47:18 for גְּוִיָּה (only body and land can be offered as the purchase price). 2 Εσδρ. 19:37 speaks of dominion over bodies and cattle; similarly Gn. 47:12, where κατὰ σῶμα means "man for man" (cf. Gk. κατ' ἄνδρα, P. Lond., II, 259, 73), i.e., according to the no. of souls.

[276] Prv. 11:17 for שְׁאֵר, Prv. 5:11 the same, Na. 3:3 for גְּוִיָּה — a penalty for licentiousness. For the personal pronoun Job. 6:4, for בַּח "strength" Job. 3:17 → n. 280.

[277] Job 19:26 A and the editor of S; the others, in keeping with עוֹר, transl. δέρμα, but the text is corrupt.

[278] Aram. גֶּשֶׁם in all the Da.-passages mentioned here.

[279] In Is. 38:17 the HT that God has cast behind him all Hezekiah's sins is altered to ὀπίσω μου since the idea of God's back or body is no longer possible. Is σῶμα left out for this reason in spite of the new ref. to Hezekiah, or is it left out because this is not guilty rejection as in other instances?

[280] Does κατάκοποι τῷ σώματι in 3:17 mean loosed from the body and ref. to the state after death (notwithstanding the HT)? The dat. is an argument against this.

[281] Worms rise up from the σῶμα and the σάρξ falls off in pieces.

[282] Perhaps σῶμα is selected here because man as a whole is therewith set under the dominion of Dionysus.

[283] Slaves of whom 90 head are sold for a talent.

[284] Here, then, ὄνομα is not the shadow as opp. to σῶμα the reality, → 1026, 7 f.

b. This leads to some typical passages in which a correlative term for the soul or spirit is used alongside the body. [285] This may be envisaged in such a way that only σῶμα and ψυχή together constitute the whole man, so that in the last resort we have a third entity over against both, or alternatively in such a way that the ψυχή is differentiated from the σῶμα as the true I. The first line of thought may be seen esp. in 2 Macc. σῶμα and ψυχή necessarily correspond to one another. With both Judas is the champion of all the rest, 2 Macc. 15:30. The righteous hazard both and offer up both in martyrdom, 2 Macc. 7:37; 14:38. Affliction of soul finds expression in the appearance and trembling of the body, 2 Macc. 3:16 f. Wis. 8:20 can also say that an unstained body corresponds to a pure soul, and Wis. 2:2-4 says that in death not only is the body reduced to dust but the λόγος ceases, the πνεῦμα blows away like air, and even the ὄνομα itself does not live on. πνεῦμα and σῶμα are oppressed acc. to 4 Macc. 11:11. In the same works, however, σῶμα can also be that which experiences pain, that which is corruptible, whereas the ψυχή voluntarily accepts all this, 2 Macc. 6:30. The persecutor can attack only the body, not the soul, 4 Macc. 10:4. Hence one may sacrifice bodies willingly, for souls are God's true gift, 4 Mac. 13:13. Wis. 9:15 can even adopt the saying about the perishable body which encumbers the soul, Plat. Phaed., 81c.

c. Finally σῶμα and ψυχή are in parallelism in Wis. 1:4, so that strictly each term denotes the whole man. They are probably complementary, however, in 8:20. It is significant that σοφία is distinct from both as the true heavenly component which comes from without into the man who consists of body and soul or even is body and soul, → 1041, 6 ff.; 1050, 20 f. This applies even more strongly when λογισμός plays this role in 4 Macc. 1:20, 26-29. Here body and soul are the site of different passions, of pleasure and pain. [286] Often σῶμα stands alone as the opp. of λόγος Wis. 18:22, or λογισμός 4 Macc. 1:35; [287] 3:18; 6:7; 7:13 f. [288] When the ref. is to bodily pains, there is a shift inasmuch as body no longer denotes the totality of the man who experiences the pain but only the part which does not affect his λογισμός and must be overcome by it, 4 Macc. 3:18; 6:7; 10:19 f.

5. Summary.

For the translators of the LXX and the authors of the original Greek works σῶμα offered a Greek concept which had not yet been developed in Hebrew. They used it with some hesitation. It took over especially the functions of בָּשָׂר (→ 108, 10 ff.). Thus σῶμα was barely used except in so far as it impinges on the sphere of thought denoted by בָּשָׂר. For this reason we do not find the Greek use for inorganic bodies (→ 1028, 7 f.) nor for reality as distinct from mere words, visions etc. (→ 1040, 7 ff.), nor do we find the understanding of σῶμα as a self-enclosed organism, as the microcosm or macrocosm (→ 1032, 4 ff.), [289] nor in particular do we find the specific use for the totality of a city, people, speech etc. (→ 1034, 28 ff.).

It is in this light that the term is to be differentiated from σάρξ. For one thing it does not have intrinsically the character of creatureliness or corruptibility or

---

[285] 12 times ψυχή, 2 πνεῦμα, once each καρδία and λόγος, 4 times λογισμός, once σοφία, twice ὄνομα → n. 284.

[286] There are both σωματικαί and ψυχικαὶ ἐπιθυμίαι, 4 Macc. 1:32. The λογισμός does not rule over its own ἐπιθυμίαι but over σωματικὰ πάθη, 3:1. The adj. occurs in the LXX only at these two places.

[287] The σώφρων νοῦς is par. to this.

[288] With σῶμα we find σάρκες and νεῦρα as parts.

[289] Though there is a liking for the word when man as a whole is denoted.

even sin. [290] Angels, too, have a σῶμα (→ 1045, 1 f.), but no σάρξ. Hence σῶμα does not denote the earthly sphere as distinct from the heavenly → 109, 9 ff. Nor does it denote man as standing before God and understood in relation to Him. The Greek sense also displays its influence in the fact that σῶμα cannot be used collectively like σάρξ, → 109, 22 ff., 26 ff. On the other hand σῶμα can become a numerical unit, → 1030, 21 f. A further point is that σῶμα never denotes the substance of flesh as distinct from bones, hair, tendons and the like, → 109, 4 ff., 25 ff. It is a term for man as a totality, → 109, 5. Kinship with what is meant by בָּשָׂר may be seen in the fact that σῶμα almost always has the sense of "corporeality," and obviously this is always the case where man understands himself as a whole. Man is conscious of his corporeality in pain, sickness, and healing (→ 1046, 19 f.), [291] in death and resurrection, also in sexuality (→ 1045, 30 f.), which is more strongly linked with σῶμα that it is with σάρξ, → 108, 20 ff. In all these experiences man is aware of himself as a totality. [292] Hence they are almost always regarded as a being delivered up to... This applies even to verses in which σῶμα means a dead body (→ 1045, 32) or a body which others control, so that it sinks to the level of a mere object, → 1045, 32 f. Although σῶμα is not used corporately or generally but individually, this is not individuality in the Greek sense, → 1030, 17 ff. Thus the understanding of man as בָּשָׂר exerts a clear influence. In Prv. 11:17, for example, one might put a reflexive in place of σῶμα, or a personal pronoun in Sir. 51:2; Job 6:4; 19:26 A; 33:17; Da. 3:95; 4 Macc. 17:1. If σῶμα can occasionally mean person (→ 1026, 5 ff.), it does not mean personality. Worth noting is the fact that σῶμα does not occur in connection with sacrifice. [293] Nor does σῶμα ever denote active man. [294] It is used for man in confrontation with others, whether God or his fellow-men or other possible forces. There is no sense of his standing at a distance from himself or regarding his corporeality as something which can finally be parted from him. The setting in which he understands himself is provided by God and the world, not by his self-enclosed personality. Only in books conceived in Greek are there indications that σῶμα against its Greek background offers the possibility of expressing anthropological dualism, → 109, 3 ff., 28 ff.; 116, 31 ff. The implication of בָּשָׂר that man does not view himself only corporeally leads to the idea of various parts. Thus one finds the members alongside the body. But for the most part, under OT influence, soul and body are taken together here as a description of corruptible man. Both may be set over against that which is strictly given by God, i.e., wisdom, or reason, → 1046, 19 ff. Anthropological dualism arises, however, only when soul is set in juxtaposition to body or when reason plays the same role. Then the body may be seen at a certain remove. One may abandon it to pain or death, for the true I is the soul or reason which survives death. In certain circumstances this may be the basis of hope in the resurrection, → 118, 21 ff.

---

[290] To express this nuance σαρκός is added to σῶμα (→ 109, 30 f.), cf. 4 Qp Na. 2:6 and on this J. Maier, "Weitere Stücke zum Nahumkommentar aus d. Höhle 4 von Qumran," *Judaica,* 18 (1962), 229 and n. 82.

[291] Illness and healing esp. are felt to be somatic. σωματοποιέω (→ 1039, 12 f.; n. 597) means "to heal" in Ez. 34:4.

[292] Typically Hbr. is the understanding of woman as man's ἰδία σάρξ (→ 109, 27). This formula is not yet rendered by σῶμα in the LXX (→ 1079, 16 ff.).

[293] Once in Gn. 15:11 dead sacrifices are called σώματα. The word is seldom used for the body of animals anyway.

[294] The main impulses in this direction are in a sexual context, but passion and intercourse are regarded more passively than actively.

C. Judaism.

1. Apocrypha and Pseudepigrapha.

Since ancient Semitic had no special word for "body" (→ 116, 31 ff.), examples may be expected for the most part in works extant in Gk. or Lat., and these are late, some of them even belonging to the Chr. era.

a. σῶμα is not used for inorganic bodies or plants → 1028, 7 f.; 1030, 12 f. It always denotes a human or animal body. It is used esp. for a corpse, Ps. Sol. 2:27; Test. B. 12:3; Apc. Mos. 40; Apc. Eliae, II, 1, 4 (35, cf. also 149); Lat. Ps.-Philo Antiquitates Biblicae, [295] 6, 14; Ass. Mos. 11:8; Vit. Ad. 46; S. Bar. 63:8. σῶμα can also be a numerical unit or may characterise man as a mere obj. or possession, Ep. Ar., 20, 22, 24. The ref. is to an animal body only in the late Apc. Abr. 31:7, also once the slain bodies of sacrifices, 13:3. This is the only connection of the term with sacrifice, → 119, 10 f. [296] When a living human body is meant, it is primarily distinguished as that which suffers pain and is smitten by sickness, Eth. En. 67:8; Vit. Ad. 31 and 34; [297] Test. Job [298] 20 (115, 12 f., 22); 25 (119, 5 f.); 26 (119, 8 f.); 31 (122, 14); 47 (134, 20. 24 - 135, 1). The body is also an obj. of care, Ep. Ar., 303, [299] or of self-chosen mortification and subjection to torments, Eth. En. 108: 7 f., or of God's eternal punishment for the lasciviousness of the flesh, Eth. En. 67:8 f. [300] Anxiety may be seen in its trembling, Test. S. 4:8 f.; Apc. Eliae, II, 8, 15-17 (49, cf. 151); Joseph and Asenath, 23. [301] Its beauty can be extolled, Eth. En. 106:2. As a human body it is exposed to temptation, and it is thus kept by God or delivered up to the devil, Apc. Abr. 13:11. More strongly than in the case of σάρξ (→ 119, 14 ff.) σῶμα is again linked to the sexual function → 1048, 12 f. By reason of ἡδονή it is excited to πορνεία, Test. Jud. 14:3. [302] One commits adultery with it, but one can also guard it as the sanctuary of the Holy Spirit. [303] Angels defiled their bodies with the daughters of men (Eth. En. 69:5) and evil spirits went forth from the bodies of the giants born in consequence, 15:9 → 120, 6 ff. The child issues forth from the body. [304]

Possibly the Gk. idea of the organism (→ 1028, 12 ff.) stands behind the distinction between the body and the head (Apc. Abr. 18:6) as that which moves it (Apc. Shadrach [305] 11 [134, 14]) or the members (4 Esr. 8:8 *corpus*; Apc. Mos. 8; Apc. Eliae 8:3). [306] On the other hand the association of body and blood, which does not occur in Greek, is found only on Chr. soil, 5 Esr. 1:32 *(corpus, sanguis)*. The body made up of members is mentioned along with the even more wonderful spirit in Ep. Ar., 155 f. cf. 151 as a proof of

---

[295] Ed. G. Kisch (1949); towards the end of the 1st cent. A.D., cf. M. Philonenko, "Une paraphrase du cantique d'Anne," RevHPhR, 42 (1962), 158.

[296] Eupolemos Fr., 4, 17, *Fragments from Graeco-Jewish Writers,* ed. W. N. Stearns (1908), 37, cf. Eus. Praep. Ev., 9, 33, 1, ref. only to the flesh of sacrifices which is eaten (κρεωφαγία).

[297] The archangel Michael is set over him, Vit. Ad. 41.

[298] Ed. M. R. James, *Apocrypha Anecdota,* TSt, 5, 1 (1897).

[299] 1 Εσδρ. 3:4 if the σωματοφύλακες are valets and not body-guards (so Jos. Ant., 6, 130 etc.).

[300] It is not wholly clear whether the ref. may not be to the burning of the body in a Turkish bath.

[301] Ed. P. Batiffol, *Studia Patristica,* I (1889), 75, 17 f.; cf. 10, 6 (51, 16).

[302] The confusion of the νοῦς is par.

[303] *Extracts from the Test. of Isaac,* Folio 15 (146, 11) and 14 (144, 14-17), ed. W. E. Barnes, TSt, II, 2 (1892). This is a later Jewish work of the 9th/10th cent. A.D. with a tradition reaching back to the 2nd cent. A.D.

[304] σπλάγχνη Ezekiel Tragicus Fr., 2, 7 (Stearns, op. cit. [→ n. 296], 109), cf. Eus. Praep. Ev., 9, 28, 3b; κοιλία Test. Abr. Cod A 10 (114, 17); Ps.-Phocylides Sententiae, 184 (Diehl, II³, 105); *uterus,* Vit. Ad., 18; also Jub. 25:19; 35:22.

[305] Ed. M. R. James, *Apocrypha Anecdota,* TSt, III, 3 (1893).

[306] Rabb. ref. for body and members v. Str.-B., III, 446-9 (→ III, 676, 9 ff.; IV, 559, 9 ff.).

God. The idea of the human body as a microcosm exerts so strong an influence in Apc. Shadrach 11 (134, 9 ff.) that it is extolled in cosmic terms. The head as heavenly director is as bright as the sun and reaches up to heaven, while the brain is a microcosm and the eyes are like stars. Application to the empire is found only as a comparison in 4 Esr. 11:23, 45; 12:3 *(corpus)*, but it is evident how common this already is. The eagle with its wicked body will vanish, and regents are various heads on the body.

b. More important is the relation of body and soul. These belong together, Test. S. 4:8 f.; A. 4:4; Sol. 1:4; Apc. Elias Hbr. 22:6 - 23:3 (cf. 66:4-11 and 22, n. 11); Apc. Esr. 64; cf. Lat. Ps.-Philo (→ n. 295), 16, 3; 43, 7 *(corpus* and *anima)*. The Jew is holy in both, Ep. Ar., 139. Both are ruled by courage (Test. S. 2:5) or rage (D. 3:2). [307] Where the OT has an influence, the body comes to judgment [308] and resurrection. → 118, 26 ff.; 120, 32 ff. In the special section Eth. En. 71:11 the patriarch is depicted as having gone up to heaven with both body and spirit. Both threaten to perish at God's glance, though cf. → 120, 19 f. Acc. to the fantastic expectations of Apc. Abr. 31:4 the damned will burn in hell with bodies full of worms and they will also fly unceasingly through the air. But death is increasingly viewed as the separation of body and soul. [309] This is plainly stated in Test. Abr. In death man (Test. Abr. Cod B [108, 25; 109, 6]) or the soul (8 [113, 5 f.]; 9 [114, 5 f.]) leaves the body. [310] The earthly body is too broad for the narrow gate, 9 (113, 17). The righteous will be taken up into heaven, but his body will remain on earth, 7 (112, 2). Before death, however, Abraham at his own wish was taken up still σωματι-κῶς, 7 (112, 7 f.) or ἐν σώματι, 8 (112, 15 f. 18) into heaven. [311] The soul goes to heaven, the body to the earth, Apc. Esr. 60. Spirit is used instead of soul in Ps.-Phocylides (→ n. 304), 103-8 (99 f.); Apc. Mos. 32. For the trinity of body, soul and spirit in an ascending hierarchy cf. Apc. Abr. 6:3 (→ 1047, 19 ff.; 1052, 18 ff.). In a trance the soul leaves the body and then returns, Paral. Jerem. 9:11-13 (→ 1043, 12 ff.). [312] The tyrant can take no more than the skin of the body, Asc. Is. 5:10 Lat. In purifying rites the body is cleansed, not the soul, Ps.-Phocylides, 228 (108). Angels are non-corporeal, pure spirits, comparable to forces, Apc. Abr. 19:6; Test. Abr. Cod A 3 (79, 29), 11 (89, 21); Slav. En. 20:1. The idea that the body is a garment with which one is clothed occurs in S. Bar. 49:3; Slav. En. 22:8; Apc. Eliae, II, 13, 4 f. (57); Apc. Abr. 13:15; 5 Esr. 2:45. [313] With the new body one begins a new mode of being, becoming incorruptible and understanding angelic speech.

c. There are only late instances of a corporate use of σῶμα. [314] Test. Abr. Cod B 8 (113, 3-6) says of Adam the πρῶτος ἄνθρωπος that he views each soul ἐξερχομένην ἐκ τοῦ σώματος, ἐπειδὴ ἐξ αὐτοῦ εἰσὶν πάντες. In Cod A 11 (89, 21-33), however, it is said that he contemplates the cosmos because all things originate from it, with no use of

---

[307] Heart and body go together in Test. Zeb. 2:5. Acc. to Test. N. 2:2 the Creator assimilates πνεῦμα and σῶμα to one another.

[308] Cf. Apc. Shadrach (→ n. 305), 11 (134, 36); → 1084, 20; n. 553.

[309] Theodotus Fr., 4, 7 (Stearns, *op. cit.,* 104), cf. Eus. Praep. Ev., 9, 22, 11 (δέμας); Lat. Ps.-Philo, 44, 10, cf. 43, 7: God is *iudex inter animam et carnem*, 3, 10.

[310] It is expressly said that this means more than the world, since the body is in a very different way his own ego.

[311] Cf. *Extracts from the Test. of Isaac*, Folio 11 (140, 5), 12 (141, 36), 16 (147, 25 f.). White as snow, Isaac's soul is taken from his body, 17 (150, 22-25).

[312] Similarly PREl, 31.

[313] On religious par. cf. G. Wagner, *Das religionsgeschichtliche Problem v. R. 6:1-11* (1962), 122 (→ 1055, 5 ff.; 1091, 12 f.; n. 331, 381, 597, 602).

[314] There are no older sources than those in B. Murmelstein, "Adam, Ein Beitrag zur Messiaslehre," WZKM, 35 (1928), 263 [Scholem]. L. Ginzberg, *The Legends of the Jews,* V (1925), 75 thinks these speculations are Chr. Cf. R. P. Shedd, *Man in Community* (1958), 3-89, for Rabb. examples esp. 45-48; on the doctrine of the pre-existence of the soul cf. further → 1028, 31 f.; cf. also → 116, n. 151; VI, 379, 12 ff.

σῶμα. Rabb. ideas of the אדם (Adam's) from which all souls derive (→ 116, n. 151) are only later → VI, 379, 35 ff. The same is true of Adam's gigantic body which fills the cosmos and is made up of the elements of the cosmos and the four directions of the wind.[315] From the present works one may ref. only to Slav. En. 25:1-3, where Idoil conceals a gt. stone in his body, bursts apart and releases it, so that all creatures may stream forth therefrom. Acc. to Slav. En. 30:8 the parts of Adam's body are formed of cosmic elements, his flesh (or body) of the earth, his soul of God's spirit and the wind. The expectation that Christ assumes Adam's body and resurrects all bodies therewith (Vit. Ad. 42) or takes it up to heaven at the resurrection, thus making Adam God as he had wanted (Test. Ad. 3:1-11), betrays Chr. influence.[316]

2. Philo.

a. The Human and Animal Body.

σῶμα often denotes the body of an animal, Op. Mund., 66, 86; Spec. Leg., I, 166, 232,[317] 291; III, 47, but it is usually that of man,[318] with or without an added νεκρόν, also an animal carcass (Vit. Mos., I, 105, 100) or human corpse, Spec. Leg., I, 113; II, 16; III, 205; Leg. Gaj., 131; Vit. Mos., I, 39; II, 172, 255; Jos., 25; Abr., 258. σώματα can be shaved òr cut, Spec. Leg., I, 3-11. The totality of the human σῶμα may be stressed, though Philo usually does this expressly by using κοινωνία, e.g., σύμπασα ἡ τοῦ σώματος κοινωνία or the like, Decal., 71, 150; Abr., 74; Spec. Leg., III, 28; IV, 83; Flacc., 190; Jos., 160; Leg. Gaj., 238. He can sometimes speak of the μέρη καὶ μέλη of the σῶμα, Deus Imm., 52, which are created for the harmonious fellowship of the whole body, Op. Mund., 138. But σῶμα in this sense is usually a figure of speech for the cosmos or a society. The term is employed traditionally for sexual union in Abr., 100 f.; Congr., 12; Som., I, 200; Decal., 124. But is always evident that Philo does not find the essential thing in this. Physical union is given by ἡδονή, union of the λογισμοί and ἀρεταί by σοφία. The decisive union is the non-corporeal one between νοῦς or ψυχή and ἀρετή. In adultery the harming of the woman's soul is worse than that of the body. Hence the priest, who must have a pure marriage, should keep both σῶμα καὶ ψυχήν from the harlot, Spec. Leg., I, 102 → 1053, 32 f.

b. The Body as Part of Man along with Soul, Spirit etc.

The usage is not uniform → 121, 26 ff. Philo can grant the body a relative importance. Man consists of body and soul → 1050, 5 ff. Only the two together make him man, Leg. All., III, 62; Cher., 128; Det. Pot. Ins., 19; Agric., 46 and 152; cf. Abr., 96 etc. Both must

---

[315] Cf. Hb. En. 43:3 and comm. thereon, 134 f.; Sib., 3, 24-26; Str.-B., IV, 888, 946. The best collection of ref. is in J. Jervell, *Imago Dei* (1960), 96-107; cf. G. Scholem, "Die Vorstellung vom Golem in ihren tellurischen u. magischen Beziehungen," *Eranos-Jbch.*, 22 (1953), 239-241; G. Quispel, "Der gnostische Anthropos u. d. jüd. Tradition," *Eranos-Jbch.*, 22 (1953), 224-232; W. D. Davies, *Paul and Rabbinic Judaism* (1948). 44-57; Schweizer Homologumena, 163-168.

[316] Though the term is not used, the whole race is viewed as such in Jub. 22:13. In Test. S. 6:2 the patriarch expects his bones and flesh to live on in his race. Cf. the city in Jos. and Asenath (→ n. 301) 15 (61, 9-13), 16 (64, 19 f.), 19 (69, 12 and 18); for Philo → 1055, 9 ff. and cf. also Schweizer Antilegomena, 164 f.

[317] Both times with ref. to sacrifices, though this is by chance. σῶμα is simply the whole as distinct from the parts. Among these one finds blood in Spec. Leg., I, 231, though not near σῶμα; in IV, 122 f. the burying of the non-slaughtered σῶμα with the substance of the soul, the blood, is censured; I, 62 lists entrails, blood and dead bodies in a polemic against soothsaying. J. Jeremias, *Die Abendmahlsworte Jesu*[3] (1916), 213, n. 8 ref. to this passage.

[318] Cf. H. Schmidt, *Die Anthropologie Philons v. Alex.,* Diss. Leipzig (1933), 31-34.

be pure, Spec. Leg., I, 102; II, 6. The Sabbath is necessary for both, II, 260. Fasting is
also good for both, Sobr., 2. Man should be strong in both, Virt., 27. Health of both soul
and body is important, Spec. Leg., I, 222; Virt., 13. There are πάθη of soul as well as
body, Ebr., 171. Indeed, the inclination towards the bad fashioned by subordinate powers
(plur. in Gn. 1:26) is located, not in the body, but in the λογικὴ ψυχή (→ 122, 10 ff.).
Conf. Ling., 179 → 1040, 23 f. [319] One should love κατὰ σῶμα καὶ ψυχήν, Vit. Cont.,
61; Virt., 103, and one will be punished similarly, Virt., 182. The body is the house (Det.
Pot. Ins., 33; Migr. Abr., 93), the holy temple (Op. Mund. 137), and the brother of the soul
(Ebr., 70). Act. and pass. (→ 1033, 24 ff.) it co-operates with διάνοια, Migr. Abr., 219.
Both take part in seeing and hearing (→ 1053, 9 ff.), Sacr. AC, 73. The wise man still
lives in the body, Quaest. in Gn. 2, 25, 45. Hence the glory of the first man, and also his
degeneration from generation to generation, is to be related to both soul and body, Op.
Mund., 136, 140 f., 145; Quaest. in Gn., 1, 21, 32. [320] To be sure, even the animal soul is
more important than the body, → 1026, 18 ff. Like salt, it keeps it from decay, Spec. Leg.,
I, 289. [321] Thus even fish, which have no souls, must have something approaching souls,
Op. Mund., 66. The soul can also remain young when the body ages, Fug., 146.

Philo can say these things because he learns from the OT that God transcends both body
and soul → 122, 16 ff. There thus arises a kind of trichotomy. At birth the body and
its members come into being out of moisture, the soul out of spirit (→ 100, 27 ff.), while
acc. to the view of many the divine invisible λογισμός comes from without, Op. Mund.,
67. The same pt. is made in other terms in Leg. All., I, 32 f. [322] Here the νοῦς is identified
with the earthly (→ χοϊκός) man and as φιλοσώματος belongs to the side of the body.
Only the inbreathed θεῖον πνεῦμα makes it νοερά and a truly living → ψυχή. [323] Finally
one should compare passages in which σῶμα is a unity with αἴσθησις and λόγος, [324]
usually in contrast with the νοῦς, Leg. All., I, 103 f.; Det. Pot. Ins., 159; Migr. Abr., 2,
192, 195, 219; Rer. Div. Her., 119; Som., I, 25 and 33. [325] The divine transcendence of
the OT is preserved here in the Platonic idea of a divine element coming from without. At
the same time the OT estimation of the body and the view of the soul as part of it can
be linked with this, since the spirit which comes from without potentially contains in it
already the functions of the animal soul. [326] We are to understand along the same lines
the ref. to divine providence which first awakens the dead lump of clay to life, Rer. Div.
Her., 58. [327] Thus the soul serves the body. When Moses purified both body and soul by
forty days of fasting heavenly nourishment was wafted to his διάνοια and it sustained
the body through the soul, Vit. Mos., II, 68 f. The eyes of the soul, however, are much
more valuable than those of the body (Rer. Div. Her., 89) and the intoxication of the soul
is far above that of the body, Leg. All., III, 124.

---

[319] E. Haenchen, "Das Buch Baruch," ZThK, 50 (1953), 126, n. 1.

[320] Cf. E. Bréhier, Les idées philosophiques et religieuses de Philon d'Alex. (1950), 122 f.
The positive estimation of the body ruled by νοῦς is stressed also by E. R. Goodenough, By
Light, Light (1935), 134, 149, 179, 207; also An Introduction to Philo Judaeus (1940), 201 f.;
H. A. Wolfson, Philo, I (1947), 424-6. For this thought in the Rabb. cf. Jervell, op. cit. (→
n. 315), 96-107.

[321] Gk.: → 102, 21 ff., cf. also Cic. Nat. Deor., II, 64, 160; Rabb.: R. Meyer, Hellenistisches
in d. rabb. Anthropologie (1937), 25 f.

[322] Cf. Bréhier, op. cit., 122-4; H. Willms, Eikon (1935), 64 and 82 f.; Goodenough Light,
385. Acc. to Leisegang, op. cit. (→ n. 53), 102 trichotomy arose out of purely Gk. speculations
→ 1041, 6 ff.

[323] Leisegang, op. cit., 85-102, cf. Rer. Div. Her., 52.

[324] Also the soul, Leg. All., I, 104; Migr. Abr., 137; Som., I, 128.

[325] In Spec. Leg., I, 211 the νοῦς is between λόγος and αἴσθησις along with σῶμα and
ψυχή. But no specific order is followed.

[326] Pohlenz, I, 374 f.; on the Platonic side of the idea of the spirit coming from without
cf. W. Völker, Fortschritt u. Vollendung bei Philo v. Alex. (1938), 159-161.

[327] Hegermann, 18; cf. → 1053, 34 ff.

If here the νοῦς or divine πνεῦμα is distinguished from the man consisting of body and soul in a way akin to the OT, so that at best only relatively greater worth can be ascribed to the soul, Philo concludes that it is only as νοῦς, which is by nature non-corporeal (Som., I, 30), that man is God's image, while the body is not like God at all, Op. Mund., 67 and 69. If body and soul together form the πόλις which is around each of us (Sacr. AC, 126), the man who lives only by body and soul is not true man, Gig., 33. Thus πόλις can ref. only to the body and is to be seen as a prison, since true man is not to be found in the union of body and soul but in pure νοῦς, Ebr., 101. This leads to Philo's theory of inspiration → 1055, 27 ff. Because the νοῦς is non-corporeal it can know solid bodies only as αἴσθησις leads them to it, Cher., 60 f., 64; Op. Mund., 166; Leg. All., II, 71; III, 57, 64, cf. 50. But when the ref. is to non-corporeal things, it follows that only the man who withdraws from body to νοῦς is capable of vision, Abr., 236, cf. Vit. Mos., II, 288. [328]

All this may be said, however, in terms of the traditional Platonic juxtaposition of body and soul. Plant., 14, cf. Som., I, 135-141 presents the idea of the heavenly θίασος of non-corporeal souls which are partly enclosed in mortal bodies and partly live as heroes or angels which, being of pneumatic substance, appear in bodily form only for man's sake, Abr., 118; Quaest. in Gn., 1, 92. Thus the soul comes down from heaven into the body as into an alien land (Som., I, 181) and it is caught up in it as in a swelling river (I, 147; Gig., 13). Though it is the soul of the body, the soul is ἀσώματος (Det. Pot. Ins., 159), created before the body (Migr. Abr., 200 [329] → 1028, 31 f.), and deriving from divine seed, whereas the body is from human seed (Vit. Mos., I, 279). Thus the body offers the soul the possibility of choice. The ἡδοναί relate to the σῶμα as they do to σάρξ (→ 122, 1 f.), cf. Gig., 33, 60; Agric., 22; Migr. Abr., 18; Som., II, 13; Vit. Cont., 68; cf. Quaest. in Gn., 2, 66. The same applies to πάθη, Congr., 59; Rer. Div. Her., 268; Som., II, 255. Like God Himself, the true man, the first of those created in Gn. 1 and 2, is ἀσώματος and is identical with the divine image, the name of God, the logos, Quaest. in Gn., 2, 56; Conf. Ling., 62-64, 146. [330] Thus the man of the second γένεσις, who is represented by Moses, is also non-corporeal, and is to be distinguished from the man made out of the earth with a body, Quaest. in Ex., 2, 46. Noah corresponds to him as the author of a second humanity, Quaest. in Gn., 2, 56. The soul has to decide, then, whether it will ally itself with the body or turn to virtue, Poster. C., 60. Only in the first case does it call the σῶμα its brother, ibid., 61. If, however, it turns to virtue it makes the true marriage which does not consist in union of bodies, Som., I, 200. Virt., 203 is pertinent in this connection. It says that acc. to Gn. 2:7 God breathed the soul into the first earth-born man, who was fashioned into a body-like statue, → 1086, 12 f. This can leave the body again and purify itself, Migr. Abr., 2. For it the body is δερμάτινος [331] ὄγκος Leg. All., III, 69 (→ 103, 4 f.; 122, 12 f.), a prison and tomb Rer. Div. Her., 85; Som., I, 139; Migr. Abr., 9; Det. Pot. Ins., 158; Leg. All., I, 108; Spec. Leg., IV, 188. [332] Hence the ascetic lives only for the soul, not for the body, Vit. Mos., I, 29; cf. Deus Imm., 55; Gig., 14. It is, of course, bound to the dead σῶμα, and hence from the time of earthly life it has

---

[328] In prophetic ecstasy the wise man leaves the body as a foreign land or fetter; his divine spirit is abroad, Rer. Div. Her., 82-85. On the distinction from Plato cf. Wilckens, op. cit. (→ n. 95), 144 f. and → 1043, 12 ff.

[329] E. F. Sutcliffe, Providence and Suffering in the Old and New Testament (1954), 152-8.

[330] Cf. Eltester, op. cit. (→ n. 212), 39; Willms, op. cit. (→ n. 322), 75 f., 80 f.; Völker, op. cit., 346, n. 1; Leisegang, op. cit. (→ n. 53), 78, n. 5. But cf. Leg. All., II, 96.

[331] This is based on Gn. 3:21. Acc. to Philo the coats of skin are the body with which non-corporeal man was later clothed by God, cf. Quaest. in Gn., 1, 53; Orig. Cels., IV, 40 (GCS, 2, 213, 26 ff.), cf. Hom. in Gn., 1, 13 (29, 15, 7 ff.); → n. 572. Others read אור instead of עור and speak of garments of light, e.g., R. Harris, The Odes and Psalms of Solomon (1911), 67-70; cf. Käsemann Leib, 53-56.

[332] Cf. σωματικαὶ ἀνάγκαι in Quaest. in Gn., 2, 45.

been a corpse-bearer, Leg. All., I, 108; III, 69 f., 74; Gig., 15 → 1036, 28 f.; cf. 1026, 20 ff.; 1040, 29 f.; 1042, 18 ff.

Death brings cleavage, for the body is mortal and corruptible, Spec. Leg., II, 230. Hence man is mortal κατὰ τὸ σῶμα but immortal κατὰ τὴν διάνοιαν, Op. Mund., 135; Virt., 9. [333] In death the soul leaves the body, Plant., 147; Abr., 258; Som., I, 31. [334] Made of earth (Leg. All., III, 161; Spec. Leg., I, 264; Som., I, 210; Op. Mund., 135), the body becomes earth again (Migr. Abr., 3). After death then, in παλιγγενεσία, man is no longer related to σώματα but to ἀσώματα, Cher., 114. From the duality of body and soul there is return to unity, Vit. Mos., 288. Already in this life, therefore, the wise man views the body as a foreign land and as death, Conf. Ling., 81; Leg. All., III, 72. His soul, which loves God, abandons the body, Leg. All., II, 55.

c. The One Totality of Soul, Cosmos and People.

(a) Like the head of a united body, διάνοια is the head of the soul, Som., I, 128. [335] When all is right with the soul, it is also right with its house, the body, Quaest. in Gn., 2, 11.

(b) One often finds the Gk. view of the cosmos as an ensouled body. [336] The cosmos is the greatest σῶμα which contains all other σώματα in itself as its own μέρη, Plant., 7. Here, as in Aet. Mund., 102 with its statement that ἅπαν τὸ σῶμα will be dissolved in fire (→ n. 134), the stress is all on the totality of the cosmos with no necessary implication that it has a soul. But acc. to Migr. Abr., 220 the cosmos is τελεώτατος ἄνθρωπος [337] → 1029, 20 f. Like man, the cosmos consists of σῶμα and ψυχὴ λογική, Rer. Div. Her., 155. God dwells in heaven and heaven in the cosmos as the νοῦς dwells in the ψυχή and the ψυχή in the σῶμα, Abr., 272. [338] The unity of heaven is like that of the members of the body, Quaest in Ex., 2, 74. The τοῦ σώματος ἅπασα κοινωνία (→ 1051, 17 ff.), which obeys the νοῦς, is a proof that the cosmos too, whose μέρη are things, has a king over it, Abr., 74. The par. between the body directed by the soul and the cosmos ruled by the world soul is thus a self-evident presupposition. Fug., 108-113 speaks expressly of the logos whose father is God and whose mother is sophia and which puts on the cosmos as a garment, holding all its parts together as the soul does with the body. [339] Heaven (Som., I, 144) or the logos (Quaest. in Ex., 2, 117) can be depicted as the head of the cosmos. [340] But the situation is different in Aet. Mund., 50 f. Here the σῶμα τοῦ κόσμου is the σωματοειδές, i.e., materiality or corporeal appearance, which the cosmos can lose without ceasing to be the cosmos, → III, 877, 31 ff. Hence one must distinguish the non-corporeal and wholly God-like νοητὸς κόσμος from the corporeal cosmos. Only this is in God's thoughts as the plan is in those of the architect, so that the divine logos is the place τόπος

---

[333] In this sense σῶμα can be a full par. of σάρξ, e.g., Som., II, 232.

[334] Goodenough Light, 176.

[335] On this cf. Colpe, 181, n. 26.

[336] Cf. Festugière, II, 521-585.

[337] Here, too, there is stress on the unity which holds the μέρη together. Cf. also μέγας ἄνθρωπος, Rer. Div. Her., 155; τελειότατον ζῷον, Spec. Leg., I, 210 f.

[338] Acc. to Som., I, 33 f. heaven is in the cosmos alongside air, earth and water as νοῦς (→ III, 674, 26 f.) is in man alongside body, emotion and the faculty of speech; cf. Lv. r., 4, 7 f. and Str.-B., II, 437 f. The cosmos is the son of God and wisdom, Philo Ebr., 30 f.

[339] On the unity of the cosmos par. to that of the body, cf. also Spec. Leg., I, 208 and Dupont, op. cit. (→ n. 56), 435 f.; Völker, op. cit., 161, also the examples assembled in Dib. Gefbr. on Col. 1:16.

[340] All things are set under the logos as members under the body. Thus the body of the cosmos, which has no soul, needs guiding reason, Hegermann, 58 f. The first passage mixes the metaphors of root and foundation for the earth. It is possible there has been Chr. redaction, however, in Quaest. Ex., 2, 117. Colpe, 180, n. 22; Hegermann, 58 f. A related passage is Ps.-Philo De deo, 9 (ed. M. C. E. Richter, VII [1830], 409-414).

(→ n. 89) of the ἐκ τῶν ἰδεῶν κόσμος, Op. Mund., 16-20, cf. 24. [341] Now God and His *logos*, not man, is really τόπος, because He encompasses all things in Himself and is not Himself encompassed by anything, Som., I, 62-64. [342] One thus finds the concept of the body of the cosmos and the all-encompassing God or *logos*, also that of the world soul which permeates the body and therefore holds it together, but not that of the primal man from parts of whom the cosmos is fashioned. Similarly, in spite of the isolated Conf. Ling., 146, only *logos* speculations stand behind the high-priest who bears the cosmic robe (Som., II, 188 f.; Fug., 108-112) → III, 272, 34 ff.; IV, 89, 18 ff. [343]

(c) Finally the body is a figure of speech for the people in whom all the parts, like those of a body, are brought into a κοινωνία, Spec. Leg., III, 131. Thus the one man over a city, the one city over a district, the people which rules over other peoples, is like the head of a body, which derives its life wholly from the forces to be found in and over the head, Praem. Poen., 114, 125. [344]

d. The Inorganic Body.

Last of all Philo can also use σῶμα for the inorganic body, which is characterised by the fact that it is three-dimensional, Op. Mund., 36, 49, 102; Som., I, 26. Heaven is the fifth κυκλοφορικὸν ("moving in a circle") σῶμα, Som., I, 21 (→ 1031, 28 ff.). [345] The question whether τὸ αἴτιον is corporeal or not is also considered in Leg. All., III, 206 (→ 1033, 24 f.). The Aristotelian principle that the δεξόμενον must be before the σῶμα is repeated and leads to the designation of chaos as a place, Aet. Mund., 17 f. Concrete σώματα are accompanied by their non-corporeal shadows; this is applied to the relation of word and thing signified or name and thing denoted, Conf. Ling., 190; Decal., 82; Rer. Div. Her., 72; cf. Poster. C., 112 → 1026, 6 f. On the other hand σῶμα is the mere wording of laws; what counts, as with a living creature, is their ψυχή, i.e., the ἀόρατος νοῦς, Vit. Cont., 78. In antithesis to the body is the incorporeal idea (Vit. Mos., II, 74) whose εἰκών is then σῶμα like the impress of a seal, whereas the concave engraver is not, Ebr., 133. [346] The first of these ref. is esp. interesting because it makes possible for Philo a theory of prophecy. Bodies not yet present are already there in space as ideas and can thus be seen by the prophets → 1054, 34 ff. The incorporeal place of these incorporeal ideas is God the Father of all things and Husband of *sophia*, Cher., 49; cf. Som., I, 127; Fug., 75, where τόπος is "that which is not filled by a σῶμα." In all these passages, then, the concreteness of the body which occupies space is emphasised.

e. Summary.

We obviously have here a very different σῶμα concept from that of the LXX → 1045, 19 ff. It is strongly influenced by the Greek understanding of the term →

---

[341] How the doctrines of the ideas taught by Middle Platonism occur in Philo and are later adopted by the Rabb. is shown by L. Wächter, "Der Einfluss platonischen Denkens auf rabb. Schöpfungsspekulationen," *Zschr. f. Religions- u. Geistesgeschichte*, 14 (1962), 36-56.

[342] *Fragments of Philo Judaeus*, ed. R. Harris (1886), p. 73b, cf. John of Damascus, Parallela Rupefucaldina, 47 (MPG, 96 [1891], 478); cf. Migr. Abr., 4-7; Aet. Mund., 112.

[343] As against E. Brandenburger, *Adam u. Christus* (1962), 152 f., cf. Hegermann, 47-67, esp. 54 f. Even the statement about man's cosmic dimension in Det. Pot. Ins., 84 f. is simply describing his significance by reason of the heavenly origin of νοῦς or λόγος.

[344] This is pointed out by N. A. Dahl, *Das Volk Gottes* (1941), 114 f. Israel is in some sense the head of the world body, cf. Vit. Mos., II, 30.

[345] Acc. to Abr., 272, however, heaven is in the cosmos, and acc. to Rer. Div. Her., 228 it is not encompassed by any other σῶμα.

[346] So too, the first heavenly man is at the same time the idea "man" of which earthly man is only a copy.

1025, 17 ff. This may be seen already in the fact that σῶμα can denote an inorganic body (→ 1031, 22 ff.) in contrast to something incorporeal, whether it be mere appearance or the idea which in the last resort alone has real being. Both these are wholly alien to the Jew, since the idea of non-corporeal being is almost completely inconceivable to him, or at least it has something of the horrendous about it. Furthermore, much more strongly than in Judaism the human body is viewed as that proper to the individual. The circle in which σῶμα is considered is not the world or the space before God's judgment throne; it is the individual, to whom, of course, the divine part belongs. Thus the body is characterised on the one side by its completeness, its single totality, while on the other side it is characterised by its partnership with the soul or reason. Along the first line of thought it is an image for the harmonious soul, the macrocosm, the people. Along the second there is the possibility of differentiating form and content, but also the understanding of the body as corporeality. Thus the body becomes a house or prison for the only essential content, the soul. This is further developed in a notion which was later worked out and exploited systematically in Gnosticism (→ 1088, 5 ff.), namely, that body and soul together comprise earthly man, and over against them is a third, fully transcendent and divine element which, though it certainly dwells in man, is no longer a human faculty or possibility.

3. Josephus.

The human body is strong or weak, Ant., 17, 333. It is fragile and exposed to mistreatment, Ap., 1, 234, 253, 256, 273, 281; 2, 8, 232, 289. Normal care for it embraces washing and feeding, Ant., 8, 357. Ap., 2, 229 ref. to the bodily exercises of the Spartans. σῶμα is very often "corpse," Bell., 6, 2, 276; Ant., 18, 236. It is also "slave," Ant., 12, 156. σῶμα as the whole body is distinguished from σάρξ as the muscular part, Bell., 3, 274, cf. Ant., 6, 71. When in Bell., 7, 265 the masculine relative pronoun ref. to ἐλεύθερα σώματα the sense "person" is already well developed. [347] The unity and totality of the σῶμα are to be seen in the inflaming [348] of a member which is cured or which affects other members and causes the whole body to suffer, Bell., 1, 507; 2, 264; 4, 406; also when the people is compared to a gt. body in Bell., 5, 27, or the phalanx to a single body in 3, 270 or Jerusalem as the capital of the country to the head of the body in 3, 54. ἕν σῶμα is often used with no particle of comparison. The alienated parties become a single body in Bell., 5, 279. David added the castle to the upper town and made a single body, Ant., 7, 66. The whole army is a κόσμος in peace and a single body in battle, Bell., 3, 104. [349] τὸ τῆς Ἀσίας σῶμα for the politically organised province of Asia in a decree of Mark Antony (Ant., 14, 312) is perhaps a Latinism. σῶμα means "substance" only in distinction from σκιά, Bell., 2, 28. In Bell., 1, 15, however, τὸ σῶμα τῆς ἱστορίας is the form of historical writing as the total view. But Ant., 3, 140 distinguishes the σῶμα of a table from the legs.

Far more characteristic is the relation of body and soul in Jos. These can be the dearest friends, Bell., 3, 362. This is why suicide is so heinous and from suicides, who have severed the soul from the body, the right hand is justly cut off, 3, 378. Herod had a body suited to his soul and showed strength of both soul and body, 1, 429 f., cf. also 2, 136. In soldiers

---

[347] Cf. also Ant., 7, 110; Bell., 4, 192. Bodies are delivered up in Bell., 6, 350 (→ n. 231). Without the head the trunk is only τὸ ἄλλο σῶμα, Ant., 6, 187.

[348] Always φλεγμαίνω, cf. Hipp. Ref., V, 9, 2.

[349] For the Rabb. in this regard cf. Dahl, op. cit. (→ n. 344), 226 f. But for Jos. the unity of the cosmos is represented in a temple, Ap., 2, 193, cf. Philo Spec. Leg., I, 66 f. Yet cf. Bell., 6, 359.

both body and soul are hardened, 3, 102. Yet a heroic soul may dwell in a weak body so that the σωματική ἕξις does not have too gt. an effect, 6, 55. If the soul is already purified by righteousness (→ VI, 413, n. 527) the body is also sanctified by baptism, Ant., 18, 117. On the other hand the Essenes argue that the body and its ὕλη are corruptible, that immortal souls are as it were by magic bound in it as in a prison, and that these leave it again after death, Bell., 2, 154 f. Indeed, Jos. himself speaks of the soul as the particle of God, the divine deposit in the body which leaves it in death and then from heaven enters a new body, Bell., 3, 372 and 374 (→ VI, 392, n. 346). Bell., 2, 163 says that the Pharisees held a similar view. [350] In the gt. speech of Eleazar on the immortality of the soul in Bell., 7, 341-388 the body is the mortal part with which there is no real union for the divine part, i.e., the soul, 344. This, which is as invisible as God Himself, can still do a gt. deal even when chained to the body, since it makes the body its instrument, 345-348. But one should seek to loose the soul from the body as the Indians do when they deliver up their bodies to the cleansing flame, 352-355. Sleep, in which the soul returns to God, is already a model of this, 349. The Roman prefers the immortality granted to those who fall in battle over dying in bed, which means that the soul is condemned to the grave with the body, Bell., 6, 46, cf. 1, 650. Ant., 1, 60 says of Cain that he simply sought ἡδονή for his σῶμα instead of repenting. [351] There is thus a strong tendency to see in the body no more than the abode of the soul which alone is the true ego, Bell., 1, 84; Ap., 203. [352]

4. The Rabbinic View.

For Rabb. ideas on body, flesh, person etc. → 114, 22 ff.

D. The New Testament.

When one turns from the Greek and Jewish sphere to the NT it is notable that σῶμα is never used for the inorganic body (→ 1031, 22 ff. → I, 504, 3 ff.) and that the word has true content only in Paul, including Col. and Eph. [353] Even when one counts all the instances in the Synoptic Gospels there are still only 51 as compared with 91 in Paul's Epistles. When the technical use for corpse or slave is omitted, the ratio is 91 to 33 in Paul's favour.

I. Books apart from Paul.

1. σῶμα has the traditional sense (→ 1025, 19 f. etc.; 1045, 32 etc.) of "corpse." It is used for the body of Jesus in Mk. 15:43 and par.; Mt. 27:59; Lk. 23:55; 24:3, 23; Jn. 19:31, 38, 40; 20:12), that of Moses in Jd. 9, that of an animal in Lk. 17:37; Hb. 13:11. Mk. 14:18 and par. should also be mentioned in this connection, since the body of Jesus is expressly said to be anointed for burial. A dead σῶμα can be raised again, Mt. 27:52; Ac. 9:40. [354] This is also so in the one instance in the Johan-

---

350 Wicked souls, however, falls under eternal punishment. K. Schubert, *Die Religion d. nachbiblischen Judt.* (1955), 72 suggests the cosmic גוף (→ 116, n. 151) but this is most unlikely in view of the par., so that this is either a special Pharisaic doctrine or Jos. is in error.

351 Thus used like the reflexive pronoun, but in connection with bodily pleasure. Cf. ὕβρις or ὥρα τοῦ σώματος for fornication in Ant., 4, 245, 134. τὰ κρυπτὰ τοῦ σώματος are the lower body, Bell., 5, 385.

352 Cf. Ant., 2, 191; Bell., 5, 525. Rabb. par in Meyer, *op. cit.* (→ n. 321), 30.

353 In Paul σῶμα often replaces the "spirit" of the Dead Sea Scrolls, cf. W. D. Davies, "Paul and the Dead Sea Scrolls: Flesh and Spirit," *The Scrolls and the NT*, ed. K. Stendahl (1957), 278, n. 40.

354 This is naturally assumed by Jesus too. Hence Mt. and Lk. have σῶμα for the πτῶμα of Mk. 15:(43?), 45.

nine writings in which σῶμα does not mean corpse or slave (as it does in Rev. 18:13). In Jn. 2:21 the enigmatic saying about the temple 355 is related to the dead and resurrected body of Jesus, → 1064, 27 f.

2. The fact that the body experiences sickness and healing (Mk. 5:29), 356 or that it needs food and clothing (Jm. 2:16), is also in keeping with common usage. The formula for washing the body in Hb. 10:22 is technical → 1045, 25 f.

3. More strongly Greek rather than Hebraic are passages in which the body is the whole as compared with the individual members, Mt. 5:29 f. (→ IV, 559, 32 ff.); 6:22 f. 357 and par.; Jm. 3:2 f., 6. 358 Yet along the lines of OT thinking (→ 1048, 6 ff.) the body is regarded as that in which a man has his true life and proves himself and will one day come to heaven or hell. The body is the true I from which a single member can be severed for the salvation of the whole, 359 though it can also influence or reveal the whole. Man is understood in the same way even when body and soul or living force (→ 1051, 31 ff.; 1056, 40 ff.; 1084, 14 ff.) are complementary, Mt. 6:25 and par. 360 Both together are cast into hell, Mt. 10:28. 361 Rather different, however, is the saying that persecutors can kill the body but not the soul, Mt. 10:28 and par. Here already one finds a type of thought in which a man can stand at a distance from his body, → 1028, 23 ff. 362

4. A special note is sounded in Hb. 10:5, 10; (13:11); 1 Pt. 2:24. Now it is true that the reference is to the body of Jesus which dies and rises again or to the bodies of animals which are burnt without the camp. This is wholly in keeping with the usage according to which man is called σῶμα in his experience of death and resurrection → 1046, 2 f.; 1048, 12. The emphasis, however, is on the fact that Jesus consciously offered up His body in sacrifice. 363 This is a new use for which there are scarcely any parallels, → 1046, 4; n. 317, 347. In texts with a strong Hellenistic tinge one can, of course, find a surrender of the body because what counts is the immortal soul. But in these the body is something alien, inauthentic, and unimportant → 1047, 7, 15 f.; 1057, 13 f. What is said here, however, is that the service through which salvation comes is rendered precisely with the body. Elsewhere σῶμα is practically never used in the vocabulary of sacrifice → 1049, 11 f.; n. 293.

---

355 It caused difficulties for the community elsewhere too, and was softened in various ways, Mk. 14:58; 15:29; Mt. 26:61; 27:40; cf. Ac. 6:13 → n. 415.
356 So also Hb. 13:3. So long as man is ἐν σώματι, sickness is possible at any time → n. 362.
357 Cf. E. Sjöberg, "Das Licht in dir," Stud. Theol., 5 (1952), 89-105.
358 Jm. 3:3: horses.
359 The ideal, then, is not at all the complete self-enclosed body. It is the body which lives in God's service and hence waives its totality rather than God. On the idea of the seat of sin in the members → 1064, 21 ff.
360 The parallelism is so strong that ψυχή denotes the vital force (cf. πνεῦμα in Jm. 2:26) sustained by eating and drinking → 1026, 19 f.; 1084, 21 f.
361 Lk. 12:5 avoids this statement → n. 553.
362 The formulation in Hb. 13:3 (→ n. 356) acc. to which man is in the body is close to this thought → 1043, 13 f.; 1060, 26 f. Yet it is not just the Platonic distinction of body and soul, cf. J. N. Sevenster, "Die Anthropologie d. NT," op. cit. (→ n. 158), 172-5. Both terms embrace the whole man though seen from different standpoints, Dahl. 125. Here, too, man is ensouled body and not just incarnate soul, Owen, 182. At any rate the body is not viewed negatively, even though the soul survives it in death. On the influence of the v. → n. 553.
363 In ψ 39:7 σῶμα seems to be a wrong reading for ὠτία, since there is a preceding ο. But cf. F. Wutz, Die Ps. textkrit. untersucht (1925), 101 f. [Bertram] on the fairly late attestation of ὠτία [Katz]. Hb. 10:10 is the first to interpret it as a sacrificed body, → line 29 f.

Possibly the liturgy of the Lord's Supper helped to shape the usage. In it the first explanatory saying is: "This is my body" (Mk. 14:22 and par.). [364] The direct interrelating of σῶμα and αἷμα rather than σάρξ and αἷμα (→ 109, 28 ff.) is just as much without parallel (→ 1046, 9; 1049, 29 ff.) as is the designation of the sacrifice as σῶμα. [365] This would seem to show that the account in 1 C. 11:24 f. is the older (→ III, 731, 20 ff.). [366] Here the two interpretative sayings are not parallel; indeed, they are separated from one another by the whole meal, v. 25a. [367] Since neither σῶμα, σάρξ (Jn. 6:51 ff.), nor an Aramaic equivalent seems to be typical in sacrificial language, it is likely enough that the original reference of the saying was primarily to the I or person of Jesus (→ III, 736, 5 ff.). This would be possible both in respect of the closest related Aramaic term גּוּפָא (→ 116, 24 ff.) [368] and also in the case of the Greek σῶμα (→ 1026, 5 f. etc.). Not the least reason why σῶμα was chosen in translation might well have been that it often denotes the man who suffers death (→ 1058, 21 ff.) and that it offers a linguistic basis for the idea of offering up the body. In this case the original point of the saying is that in the Lord's Supper Jesus gives Himself to the community as the One who is going to His death, because, as the second saying adds, the covenant of God with His people is concluded by His death (His blood). If the sayings were not originally parallel, then it is doubly clear than the undeniable real presence of Jesus is not to be construed in the category of the presence of a substance → 1067, 19 f. [369] Later the two sayings were assimilated. In the process σῶμα in the vocabulary of the community, as may be seen already in Mk., became increasingly the body which was given for it, the sacrificed body, → 1067, 20 ff. [370] But originally σῶμα, like αἷμα, denoted the whole person of Jesus, σῶμα as the I in its totality, αἷμα as the I in the act of dying, [371] → III, 739, 16 ff. [372]

5. σωματικός, which is rare in the Jewish world (→ 1050, 18 f.; n. 286), occurs only in Lk. 3:22 (→ VI, 406, 27 ff.) and 1 Tm. 4:8 (→ I, 775, 41 ff.); in both cases it emphasises corporeality.

---

[364] "This is my body (given) for you," 1 C. 11:24; Lk. 22:19.

[365] E. Lohse, *Märtyrer u. Gottesknecht* (1955), 125 f. also stresses the fact that σῶμα and αἷμα are combined thus only in eucharistic usage and that there is no sacrificial basis, but the reference is to the atoning death of the Servant of the Lord. It is true, of course, that σῶμα is not found for this either.

[366] This does not apply to all the details but only to the structure of the explanatory sayings. In support cf. E. Schweizer, Art. "Abendmahl im NT," RGG³, I, 12-14; for a different view Jeremias, *op. cit.*, 181-195.

[367] What applies to the Last Supper applies also to the first celebrations by the Church.

[368] So already G. Dalman, *Jesus-Jeschua* (1922), 132, but cf. Jeremias, *op. cit.* 191-194.

[369] W. Kreck, "Die reformierte Abendmahlslehre angesichts der heutigen exegetischen Situation," EvTh, 14 (1954), 193-211.

[370] Perhaps indeed this is why σῶμα is chosen in Hb. 13:11 rather than σάρξ (cf. 2:14).

[371] αἷμα esp. denotes the person, not statically, but dynamically in the act of dying.

[372] D. O. Via, "The Church as the Body of Christ in the Gospel of Matthew," *Scottish Journal of Theology*, 11 (1958), 271-286 deals with the passages in which the Church is the Messianic community with whom Christ identifies Himself and in which He is present and continues His ministry, → n. 447. We shall not discuss these here since they are not related to σῶμα.

II. Paul.

1. σῶμα apart from the Concept of the Body of Christ.

a. Generally Accepted Epistles.

(a) Being outside the Body.

An immediate point to call for notice is that the almost technical use of σῶμα for "corpse" [373] or "slave" does not occur. Nor is σῶμα a complementary term to ψυχή or the like except in the traditional (→ 1050, 21 ff.) saying 1 Th. 5:23 (→ III, 767, 5 ff.; VI, 435, 9 ff.). In particular one does not find the Hellenistic view (→ 1053, 39 ff.) in which the soul alone constitutes the true human ego, whereas the body is indifferent or an obstacle. In this respect Paul thinks more consciously along OT lines than the sayings source → 1058, 15 ff. To be sure, Paul can adopt the idea that man is able to make a heavenly ascent outside the body, 2 C. 12:1-3. But it should be noted (1) that he would not think this worth telling about unless forced to do so by his opponents, and (2) that it is a matter of complete indifference whether he was in the body or not, → 1043, 12 ff.

(b) The Resurrection of the Body: The Texts.

In 1 C. 15:35-44 Paul insists that the future life is a bodily one, → 125, n. 215; VI, 420, 4 ff. [374] This is so self-evident that for him the question: "How do the dead rise?" cannot be detached from the further question: "With what body do they come?" [375] 1 C. 15:38 is the only verse in which σῶμα comes close to meaning "form" (→ 1035, 19 f.) [376] in this debate with the opposing view. But even here Paul does not presuppose as modern man would do that the substance of the developing plant is already present in the seed so that there is only a change of form (→ n. 385). As the change to σάρξ shows, he has in view the whole corporeality, the only point being that here this is especially visible in its form. [377]

The disputed passage 2 C. 5:1-10 is more explicit. In v. 6, 8, 10 Paul adopts a manner of speech which understands being ἐν τῷ σώματι (→ 1043, 13 f.) as earthly life, and death as ἐκδημεῖν ἐκ τοῦ σώματος (→ II, 63, 34 ff.). σῶμα, then denotes specifically the earthly body. [378] But here again (1) it is affirmed that we are tested and proved either in it or by it. [379] But then (2) there is no stress at all on the traditional formula about being absent from the body, since Paul's concern is

---

[373] There is reference, of course, to the crucified body of Jesus (→ 1067, 4 ff.), but this is important, not as a corpse, but in the act of self-sacrifice.

[374] In Judaism (→ 1046, 2; 1050, 8 ff.) angels are bodily (→ 1048, 11), but not of flesh → 120, 6 ff. Hence the spiritual body of 1 C. 15:44 (→ VI, 421, 14 ff.) is not just the future body as in later Gnostic exposition of the passage → 1086, 15 ff. The polemic of v. 46 is against speculations like those of → 1053, 26 f.

[375] Acc. to J. Jeremias, "Flesh and Blood Cannot Inherit the Kingdom of God," NTSt, 2 (1955/56), 155, vv. 36-49 are answering the first question and vv. 50-55 the second, but → 128, 27 ff.

[376] Bultmann Theol.⁴, 193 f. and Stacey, 185 shows that we cannot make this our starting-point.

[377] The same applies to δόξα in v. 41 → VI, 421, 3 ff.

[378] Kümmel in Ltzm. K., ad loc. E. E. Ellis, Paul and His Recent Interpreters (1961), 46.

[379] It makes no odds whether the διά is taken temporally or instrumentally (cf. Bl.-Debr., 223, 1 and 2), Ltzm. K., ad loc.

simply that we be at home with the Lord. Only in comparison with this is being in the body a being abroad. At any rate, nakedness is not worth seeking as such in Paul's view (→ II, 319, 40 ff.); indeed, one may suspect that in this notion he simply has in view the completely absurd idea of his adversaries. [380] For him heavenly being is again life in a new "building" or "house" (→ V, 132, 20 ff.), though this is not earthly but comes from God. [381] Both building and house are parallel terms for body and they are probably selected in order to suggest the different nature of the heavenly body. At any rate, Paul's concern is that heavenly being is to be understood as being in a house, not as incorporeality. In the θαρρεῖν (→ III, 27, 17 ff.) future being in the Lord is already present in hope and makes life in the earthly σῶμα both relevant and confident, v. 10. [382] Phil. 3:21 declares that our body will put off its lowliness [383] and be made like Jesus' body of glory. Here σῶμα is not just the external form but the bearer of lowliness or glory; it is thus man's earthly or heavenly being. The body itself is transformed; it is not, then, the abiding or permanent element, the form which is simply filled with a new content. What remains is simply the "we" → VI, 421, 11 ff. Finally it is apparent that a primary concern of Paul is that the believer should be united with Christ even to the point of his corporeality, → 1063, 30 f.

R. 8:11 goes furthest: God will raise up your mortal bodies → VI, 422, 1 ff. But in the context 1 C. 6:14 also refers unmistakably to the body even though Paul says only that "we" shall be raised up, → 1064, 26 ff.; VI, 421, 20 ff. Finally the context of R. 6:12 and the parallel in 8:11 show that the saying about the mortal body in which sin shall not reign means that this, too, will have a share in the resurrection, so that now already it is to be viewed as standing fundamentally in this new life → 1064, 15 ff. Similarly the ἀπολύτρωσις τοῦ σώματος in R. 8:23 is not redemption from the body or from a bodily existence generally but redemption of the body, → IV, 352, 26 ff. It is evident that for Paul the earthly life stands under sin and death and is severely burdened thereby. Yet man cannot detach himself from it. Paul always understands sin and death as man's sin and man's death. They are not merely the result of a corporeality which is tragic destiny but from which man may always

---

[380] One should thus transl. v. 3 with R. Bultmann, "Exeget. Probleme d. 2 K.," *Symbolae Bibl. Upsalienses,* 9 (1947), 3-12: "Presupposing at least that we shall then be found clothed (cf. W. Schmithals, *Die Gnosis in Korinth* [1956], 227 f.) and not naked (as some ridiculous people obviously expect)." There is no discussion of the time of death or transformation, whether before or at the *parousia.* A. Feuillet, "La demeure céleste et la destinée des chrétiens (II C. V, 1-10)," *Recherches de science relig.,* 44 (1956), 381-6 transl.: "If, as is certain, we, once clothed, shall no longer have to pass through nakedness" and ref. the passage, with 1 C. 15:47-54, to the *parousia.* For bibl. *ibid.,* 165-192; cf. also R. F. Hettlinger, "2 C. 5:1-10," *Scottish Journ. of Theol.,* 10 (1957), 174-194, who himself suggests an intermediate state which is a clothing upon but not the final consummation.

[381] That the ref. is to a collective, namely, the whole Messianic host (Ellis, *op. cit.,* 40-43; Robinson, 75 f.; Feuillet, *op. cit.,* 377 f.) is most unlikely in view of the par. for οἰκία (→ V, 132, 24 ff.), σκῆνος (→ 382, 3 ff.), quite apart from the lack of any examples, whereas the terms named are common images for the body, W. L. Knox, *St. Paul and the Church of the Gentiles* (1939), 136 f.; Stacey, 190; → I, 774, 10 ff. Against a view along the lines of → I, 774, 25 ff.; II, 318, 23 ff. cf. Feuillet, 382; Hettlinger, 180-4. The same applies to Ellis, 43-45, who interprets nakedness as a life in guilt apart from the body of Christ. Who would think of this without a comm.? On the other hand putting of earthly clothes and putting on garments of glory are current expressions for death and resurrection → 1050, 27 f.

[382] The formulation in v. 6, 8, which is strange at a first glance, means that knowledge of present being in alienation and future being at home brings consolation.

[383] So acc. to the usage of the LXX and NT and not, e.g., "body of humiliation" as though what was originally heavenly had been abased to corporeality, cf. Loh. Phil., *ad loc.*

break free. Precisely for this reason Paul also realises that God will raise up and transform this body and that consequently this body must already be seen here and now as a body which is being raised up. This is what makes all life in the body so responsible.

(c) The Resurrection of the Body: The Theological Concern.

In 1 C. 15:35-44 life after death is for Paul dependent on the resurrection of the body, since non-bodily life is quite inconceivable for him. But if the body cannot be separated from the I of man, this is a guarantee that the resurrection is wholly God's act. There is no inner part of man in which heavenly life is already man's possession so that he is no longer referred to God's creative act. [384] Paul's opponents no doubt regarded the eternal life already present under the earthly body as God's gift. [385] Yet for them the coming glory was already secured. It was no longer in the hands of God, to whose gracious faithfulness man was constantly referred. It was a possession of sacramentally transformed man himself. This is even more heavily underscored in 2 C. 5:1-10. 5:10 says that there is resurrection only through judgment and that the body, far from being a burdensome envelope for the divine soul, is the very place where man is tested and in terms of which he will be questioned in the judgment. [386] The latter applies especially in R. 6:12; 8:11; 1 C. 6:14. Here awareness of the resurrection of the body determines man's seriousness and responsibility in relation to the body in which he lives on earth and encounters God or his fellows, → 1064, 15 ff.; I, 651, n. 21. Finally in Phil. 3:21 the term σῶμα allows Paul to define as strongly as possible our association with Christ, → 1072, 14 ff. Only in this light can one understand why Paul can see the resurrection simply as a blessing of salvation, for it is viewed aright only as participation in the resurrection of Christ (→ 1084, 1 f.), 1 C. 15:12-23. In spite of R. 2:5 f. Paul is not thinking here of a resurrection to death or perdition, only to a judgment which condemns or praises the works of those raised up to life, 1 C. 3:12-15. [387]

(d) The Body in Sex Life.

As in Judaism (→ 1045, 28 ff., cf. 1049, 21 ff.; 1051, 23 ff.) σῶμα is also the organ

---

[384] It is essential for Paul that God and man remain distinct even in the resurrection. They do not merge into one another. But this is hardly emphasised by the choice of σῶμα. H. Clavier, "Brèves remarques sur la notion de σῶμα πνευματικόν," *The Background of the NT and Its Eschatology, Festschr. f. C. H. Dodd,* ed. W. D. Davies and D. Daube (1956), 361 sees demarcation both from ideas of a shadowy existence and also from those of apocalyptic materialism, cf. also L. Cerfaux, "La Résurrection du Christ dans la vie et la doctrine de saint Paul," *Lumière et Vie,* I, 3 (1952), 81 f.; K. Stalder, *Das Werk des Geistes in d. Heiligung bei Pls.* (1962), 60, n. 31; only Christ is πνεῦμα ζῳοποιοῦν, never Christians.

[385] The idea of a process of growth of the resurrection body (Robinson, 81; Stacey, 188) comes close to this; for another view cf. Ellis, *op. cit.,* 39. That 1 C. 15:36 f. is not to be understood thus is shown by H. Riesenfeld, "Das Bildwort vom Weizenkorn bei Pls.," *Stud. zum NT u. zur Patristik,* TU, 77 (1961), 44-47. Hence one cannot simply compare the spiritual body as ἔσω ἄνθρωπος with the kernel and the psychic body with the husk, cf. Clavier, *op. cit.,* 352 f.

[386] The strong emphasis on the earthly body as the place of testing facilitates adoption of the traditional formula, which simply regards earthly life as life in the body; cf. also Bultmann Trad.⁴, 202 f.

[387] E. Jüngel, *Pls. u. Jesus* (1962), 66-69.

of generation (R. 4:19), the body in which is sexual desire, which engages in the act of sex whether as male or female (1 C. 7:4) and which may be defiled thereby (R. 1:24; [388] 1 C. 7:34). In sex the body belongs to another, → IV, 564, 38 ff. It becomes one with the other in κολλᾶσθαι, 1 C. 6:16; cf. Eph. 5:28. But the body is also given up to the act itself, so that in fornication it is "possessed" by fornication, 1 C. 6:13. The Greek can also speak of the σῶμα in relation to the act of sex, → 1040, 1 ff. etc. But it is understood here as something which the married couple holds in common like their house or fields. Against a Hebraic background σάρξ would seem to be more natural for this. If σῶμα is chosen, it is because of the sense that in sexual intercourse, as in the experience of illness and healing, death and resurrection, man takes part as a totality, → 1048, 11 ff. [389] This is brought to conscious expression by Paul. Eating and drinking affect only the belly, → III, 788, 5 ff. But fornication (→ VI, 593, 30 ff.) is quite different; it rules the body, → 1030, 30 f. Thus, while eating and drinking are often associated with sex in the Hellenistic tradition, [390] Paul can state plainly in 1 C. 6:18 that only the latter really affects the body, → 1070, 12 ff.; I, 651, n. 21; VI, 419, 11 ff.

(e) The Controversy with the Corinthian Spiritualisers.

As compared with 18 instances in the other generally accepted letters of Paul σῶμα occurs 56 times in 1 and 2 C. In Th. one finds only the traditional formula (→ VI, 435, 9 ff.), in Gl. one example, in Phil. three, then in R., which was written in Corinth, 13 times. This alone makes it clear that σῶμα takes on its main importance in the controversy with Paul's opponents in Corinth.

In Corinth Paul came up against a piety in which the chief concern was the spirit, the transformed or liberated inwardness of man, → VI, 416, 1 ff. In contrast Paul speaks of the body. For him this is in the first instance sheer corporeality and as a close equivalent of σάρξ it can denote the concrete presence of the apostle (1 C. 5:3; 2 C. 10:10) or bodily undefiledness as distinct from that of the spirit (1 C. 7:34; 2 C. 7:1). It is the body which blows hurt and on which scars (→ 663, 4 ff.) may still be seen, Gl. 6:17. The last reference shows what Paul really has on his mind. The wounds he bears in his body are the wounds of Jesus. His membership in Jesus, which will be bodily in the consummation (→ 1061, 8 ff.), may be seen already here and now in his body. For Paul, then, it is essential that his faith be worked out not merely in a purely intellectual or emotional sphere but in the whole of his bodily life, to which, of course, thought and feeling also belong. He thus bears about the dying of Jesus (→ III, 20, 15 ff.; 144, 6 ff.) in his body because the life of Jesus will never manifest itself anywhere else but there, 2 C. 4:10. This is because the greatness of God's glory shines only in earthen vessels (→ 365, 5 ff.) which do not destroy God's splendour by their own (2 C. 4:7) and because only Paul's suffering

---

[388] With ἀτιμία in v.26 we are also to construe v. 24 sexually (→ 1041, 26 f.), cf. Mi. R., ad loc.; O. Kuss, Der Römerbr. (1957-1959), ad loc.

[389] In the OT order marriage has a very different basis from that of the Gk. world. There are linguistic reasons for this. The Jew consciously avoids בְּשַׂר when he chooses σῶμα, whereas for the Gk. σῶμα no longer denotes man's totality but the mere body as distinct from the far more important soul, → 1053, 37 ff.

[390] As pleasures of the lower part of the body, Cic. Or. in Pisonem, 66; cf. → 103, 33 ff.; 122, 8 ff.; for further examples Schweizer, op. cit. (→ n. 239), 33-44.

makes the power of his message clear and credible to the community. [391] Thus Paul's dying means life for the community, v. 12. This is the life which begins in the apostle's body and which also means his own true life. [392] So strongly is the corporeality of his suffering emphasised here that σάρξ can be used as an alternative, v. 11. [393] It is in the body which is scourged, which is imprisoned, which is subject to hunger and cold, and which is constantly threatened with death, that this life with Christ is brought into effect for the community. Hence the apostle buffets his body and brings it into subjection in order to set it in the service of Christ, 1 C. 9:27. His message is quite inseparable from this setting in service of the body. Similarly in 1 C. 13:3 the sacrifice of the body is represented as an extreme form of service.

(f) Indicative and Imperative.

σῶμα occurs in R. at the very point where indicative statements yield to imperatives, R. 12:1. [394] Bodies are the place where the life described in the chapters that follow is worked out. [395] It is in this that λογικὴ λατρεία (→ IV, 65, 20 ff.; 142, 29 ff.) takes place; [396] this is the cultus [397] of the community. But one finds the same terminology in R. 6:12 ff. too. σῶμα also occurs in the transitional vv. 11-14, in which indicative and imperative forms are mixed from the very first statement, which presents the implications of the Gospel of God's grace for the question at issue, that of sinning → 1061, 20 ff. If the reflexive pronoun is used for σῶμα (→ 1026, 6 etc.) in v. 13, 16, this shows that σῶμα describes man as a whole, not a part which may be detached from the true I. When τὰ μέλη is used instead in v. 13, 19, this makes it apparent that σῶμα is man as he is subject to temptation and wickedness, [398] → 135, n. 284; 150, n. 401. In Phil. 1:20 it is again a matter of course for Paul that Christ will be magnified in his (Paul's) body, whether by his death or by his remaining alive.

Especially clear-cut is the line of thought in 1 C. 6:12-20 → VI, 593, 37 ff. It is emphatically stated here that man praises God in his body, v. 20. [399] His body is the temple (→ 1058, 1 f.) of the Holy Ghost, v. 19. [400] Evident here is the fact that with

---

[391] The point, then, is not the authentication of the hero of faith or of the philosopher who withdraws into inwardness, cf. 2 C. 1:3-11: Only he who has received consolation can console, and only in suffering is fellowship and faith genuine. Cf. H. Braun, "Exeget. Randglossen zum 1 K.," *Gesammelte Stud. z. NT und seiner Umwelt* (1962), 187-191. This is why the life of Jesus may be seen in the apostle's σῶμα rather than his νοῦς.

[392] But cf. Ltzm. K. on 2 C. 4:10, who here already ref. life to the resurrection. But this is mentioned only in v. 14, where neither σῶμα nor σάρξ is repeated Wnd. 2 K., *ad loc.* suggests the inner strength which overcomes suffering, but the above interpretation finds support in v. 12, also 1:5-7. So, too, Heinr. 2 K., *ad loc.*

[393] Cf. Bultmann Theol.[4], 200 f. § 17, 3.

[394] τῷ θεῷ goes with παραστῆσαι. The verb is Hellenistic (Mi. R., *ad loc.*); its use is sacrificial (→ V, 841, 12 ff.; Pr.-Bauer, *s.v.*) or military, → IV, 561, n. 58.

[395] The exhortation begins in 12:1.

[396] E. Gaugler, *Der Brief an die Römer,* II (1952), *ad loc.*

[397] The cultic vocabulary of this passage has been emphasised by C. K. Barrett, *A Comm. on the Epistle to the Romans* (1957).

[398] Cf. E. Schweizer, "Die Sünde in den Gliedern," *Festschr. f. O. Michel* (1963), 437-9.

[399] Naturally the meaning is not: in the body of Christ, i.e., the community, cf. Shedd, *op. cit.* (→ n. 314), 175. *Koine* MSS alter by adding "and in your spirit."

[400] That Paul is not thinking individualistically may be seen from 1 C. 3:16, where the whole community is this temple.

this use of σῶμα Paul is also stressing the relationship of ownership (→ 1035, 15 ff.; 1045, 33 f.) to which man commits his body. In R. 12:1 God is again the One at whose disposal believers place their bodies as a sacrifice so that they are no longer their own, → III, 185, 6 ff. [401] In R. 6:13 God and sin are opposing masters (→ I, 313, 6 ff; IV, 561, 23 ff.) to whom man may commit his body or members or himself as a slave (v. 16), and their activity is called κυριεύειν, v. 14. According to 1 C. 6:19 the body comes from God and hence belongs to Him. But a reminder of God's creative work is hardly enough; the decisive thing is that God has bought back this body as His own possession. It thus belongs to the κύριος, v. 13. The underlying thought that the κύριος has given Himself for man is so strong that the final statement can be reversed: the κύριος belongs to the body. This makes sense, of course, only when one realises that the association between Christ and the believer is regarded as just as close and physical as that between the two partners in the sex act, so that Paul can regard the body of the believer as a member of Christ, just as in sex a man become the member of a harlot (6:15 f.) because in it he is one body with her, [402] → 1063, 3 ff.; IV, 564, 29 ff. R. 6:12 ff. states expressly that the σῶμα once belonged to sin and by nature would still belong to it, and 1 C. 6:20 says that it does not do so only because it has been redeemed, → I, 125, 22 ff. Paul can thus speak of the σῶμα τῆς ἁμαρτίας (R. 6:6) [403] or the σῶμα τοῦ θανάτου (R. 7:24). In one place then (R. 8:13) σῶμα can have the exceptional sense of that which is sinful in itself (→ VI, 643, 45 ff.), for which only σάρξ is used elsewhere, → 132, n. 267. R. 8:10 is also to be put in this group. Without God's Spirit [404] the σῶμα is dead. But the decisive point now is not yearning for the liberation of the divine soul from the body of death, but the setting of this body in service and its dedication to God. [405]

The common rendering of Paul's σῶμα by "person," "personality" [406] or even "individuality" [407] is thus justifiable to the degree that the word always denotes

---

401 Stressed by F. J. Leenhardt, L'Épitre de St. Paul aux Romains (1957), ad loc.

402 Cf. E. Käsemann, "Zum Thema der urchr. Apokalyptik," ZThK, 59 (1962), 281 f., esp. on 1 C. 6:13, on κολλάομαι → III, 822, 22 ff. The fact that there is ἓν πνεῦμα in the case of Christ does not stress the point that this is a completely different sphere, W. Goossens, L'église corps du Christ d'après S. Paul (1949), 19.

403 This is certainly not to be taken collectively as though, e.g., an aeon of sin were in view, cf. 6:12, as against E. Fuchs, Die Freiheit des Glaubens (1949), 31 f. Only by closer definition is σῶμα sinful or subject to death, Dahl, 126.

404 Bengel, ad loc. stresses already that this and not the soul is the antithesis, though → 1054, 3 ff. There is a specific survey of all proposed interpretations in Kuss, op. cit., ad loc. Cf. W. G. Kümmel, "πάρεσις u. ἔνδειξις: Ein Beitrag zum Verständnis d. paul. Rechtfertigungslehre," ZThK, 49 (1952), 164, n. 4: σῶμα is man's earthly body apart from the pneumatic reality of Christ; acc. to A. Nygren, Der Römerbr.³ (1959), ad loc. σῶμα is the order in which death reigns and the believer has still to endure battle. διά then, denotes the reason. The imprecise transl. "by" is not really necessary, cf. Bl.-Debr. § 222. δικαιοσύνη means being justified as the cause of a new life, cf. Bultmann Theol.⁴, 275 f. § 9, 1, not the righteous act of the Christian, cf. M. Dibelius, "Vier Worte d. R." Symbolae Bibl. Upsalienses, 3 (1944), 12. There is no ref. to the death suffered in baptism, Chrys in J. Huby, "La vie dans l'esprit," Recherches de science religieuse, 30 (1940), 13; similarly Kuss, op. cit., 503, for in this case one would have to supply "on account of the setting aside of sin," and that is not said. Nor is it said that the body is destined for death, Huby, 14. The formulation is not precise, but it is not hopelessly obscure, cf. Knox, op. cit., 99, n. 5.

405 Quite different is Corp. Herm., 13, 14 (→ 1089, 6 ff.), where redemption is found in man's recognition of his own deity rather than his lostness without God, cf. G. Bornkamm, "Sünde, Gesetz u. Tod, Exeget. Studie z. R. 7," Das Ende des Gesetzes⁴ (1963), 66.

406 Joh. W. 1 K., Exc. on 6:13; J. Moffatt, I Cor. (1938), 72; Soiron, 56.

407 C. H. Dodd, The Epistle of Paul to the Romans (1932), 90.

the whole man and not just a part. [408] Yet it does not quite catch Paul's own understanding, since the accent is on the self-enclosed nature of man. In fact σῶμα means man in his confrontation with God or sin or fellow-man. σῶμα is the place where faith lives and where man surrenders to God's lordship. It is thus the sphere in which man serves. [409] Paul has no interest whatsoever in appearance, abilities, or character, but only in the work of the body, in what takes places with it. The I, then, cannot be divided up into an inwardness of soul, affection, or understanding on the one side and an outwardness of the body in which one draws or neglects the consequences therefrom on the other. [410] Hence the imperative which accompanies the indicative is neither a relapse into legalism nor the realistic correction of a heaven-storming and quite unrealistic idealism. [411] It maintains the totality of the σῶμα in which feeling, thought, experience and action can no longer be sundered.

b. Colossians and Ephesians.

In Col. the use of σῶμα for the body of Christ is already so predominant that the σῶμα τῆς σαρκός (1:22; 2:11) is expressly demarcated from it → 136, 19 ff. There are only two other instances. In 2:23 (→ 136, 9 f.) σῶμα means the body neutrally in the physical sense; asceticism bears hard on this. [412] In 2:17 τὸ σῶμα τοῦ Χριστοῦ is contrasted with the shadow (→ 398, 13 ff.) represented by the cultic laws. Thus σῶμα undoubtedly denotes the reality in the sense of → 1039, 17 f.; 1040, 8 f.; 1055, 20 ff. [413] All the Eph. ref. are dealt with → 1077, 17 ff.

---

[408] Cf. J. Pedersen, *Israel*, I³ (1954), 170 f.: "The body is a perfectly valid manifestation of the soul; indeed the body is the soul in its outward form." Schl. R. on 6:6: "Nothing takes place apart from the body, for man does not live apart from the body," → n. 310.

[409] Hereby the σῶμα becomes the possibility of communication, Käsemann Anliegen, 32 f. There is nothing of this in the history of the term, but service in the body is always rendered to one's fellows and σῶμα is thus the place where this service, and therefore communication, occurs. Stalder, *op. cit.* (→ n. 384), 59, n. 30 emphasises solidarity with all sin and demonism, in short with the history of the world.

[410] Käsemann Anliegen, 29 and 32. Bultmann Theol.⁴, 196 thinks that σῶμα denotes man in so far as he has a relation to himself. But this def. is inadequate and leads to the Gk. view of man as a self-enclosed individual, → 1029, 14 ff.; 1048, 26 ff. Jüngel, *op. cit.* (→ n. 387), 57 can even call σῶμα an instrument of activity, cf. 63 f. In contrast F. Neugebauer, *In Christus* (1961), 53 f. rightly emphasises that σῶμα is the person in respect of what it is and what takes place therewith, and this is such a way that man does what takes place therewith, cf. esp. his criticism of Bultmann, 52, n. 45.

[411] With G. Bornkamm, "Taufe u. neues Leben," *op. cit.* (→ n. 405), 35 against H. Weinel *Bibl. Theol.⁴* (1928), 257 and H. J. Holtzmann, *Nt.liche Theol.*, II² (1911), 164.

[412] B. Reicke, "Zum sprachlichen Verständnis v. Kol. 2:23," *Stud. Theol.*, 6 (1953), 47-51 ref. to Luc. Anacharsis, 24 and understands τιμή as "respect to."

[413] Possibly the gen. for the logically more correct nomin. (a copyist?) was introduced because of a current formula. Or else the author understands it as possessive: But the reality (→ 1055, 23 f.; 1056, 36) belongs to Christ. A slip is possible, since τοῦ is textually uncertain. One can hardly agree with Loh. Phil., *ad loc.* that it is an abbreviation: "The body (= the reality), however, is the body of Christ," at any rate not in such a way that the future cosmos, already present proleptically in Christ's body, is contrasted with the present cosmos. C. F. D. Moule, *The Ep. of Paul the Ap. to the Col. and to Philemon* (1957) *ad loc.* thinks there is an echo of the concepts of church and sacrifice along with reality. Related is Hb. 10:1, where the πράγματα are the opp. (→ n. 13), not σῶμα. The figure is rare in the Rabb. and body is never the antithesis, cf. Str.-B., III, 628 f.

2. The Body of Christ.

a. Generally Accepted Epistles.

(a) The Body Given for Us.

When Paul emphasises so strongly the fact that the body is to be dedicated to service and is thus the place where faith takes place in encounter with others, this is probably influenced in part by the development of the eucharistic liturgy (→ 1059, 1 ff.) in which σῶμα as a parallel of αἷμα is increasingly understood as the body of Jesus offered up for men on the cross. This is how τὸ σῶμα τοῦ Χριστοῦ is to be taken in R. 7:4, [414] the only verse in these epistles in which this concept occurs in set form outside the eucharistic passages. [415] This is confirmed by Col. 1:22 (cf. Eph. 2:13f. 16?), where σῶμα is the crucified body, though nearby in 1:18, 24 it means the community, → 1075, 23 ff. [416]

(b) The Eucharistic Texts.

The term is to be understood in the same sense in the eucharistic texts, → 1059, 1 ff. [417] In the explanatory saying concerning the bread (1 C. 11:24) either Paul or the community before him adds to σῶμα the interpretation τὸ ὑπὲρ ὑμῶν. The stress, then, is not on the substance, corporeality, but on the act denoted thereby → III, 736, 25 ff.; 739, 16 ff. As the saying about the blood of Jesus is a figurative robe for the idea of self-sacrifice (→ I, 175, 16 ff.), so the body of Jesus is not important as substance but as the body which is offered up for the community, indeed, as the act which reconciles the community. σῶμα is almost a nomen actionis and therefore, even though it denotes the crucified body of Jesus, it bears a significance quite different from that in the passages quoted → 1057, 30 f. For this reason the crucified body of Jesus, like His blood, is present in the community when it celebrates the Lord's Supper. [418] This presence of the body of Christ which was

---

414 With Mi. R., Kuss, op. cit., ad loc.; Best, 52 f. Gl. 2:19 f. esp. supports this: He who is crucified with Christ is dead to the Law, cf. also Gl. 4:4 f.; for acc. to Gl. 3:13 the curse of the Law reached its climax at the cross. R. 8:8 f. also rests on 8:3 f. (→ 133, 24 ff.; VI, 429, n. 642), as does 7:5 (→ 134, 26 ff.) on 7:4. A. Schweitzer, Die Mystik d. Ap. Pls. (1930), 186, n. 1 relates it to the community into which believers are incorporated, cf. Meuzelaar, 57 f. But "through the community" is impossible in this context. For other champions of these interpretations cf. E. Schweizer, Gemeinde u. Gemeindeordnung im NT (1959), 83, n. 357.

415 W. Hahn, Gottesdienst u. Opfer Christi (1951), 51-73 finds the origin of the body of Christ concept in the Lord's saying about the destruction and rebuilding of the temple (→ 1058, 1 f.), but cf. Kearns, 90, 5; the eucharistic sayings were decisive in relation to its development. Kearns, too, stresses R. 7:4. Cf. also the emphasis on the crucified body of Jesus in K. Barth, K. D., IV, 1 (1953), 740 f. (C. D., IV, 1 [1956], 662 ff.).

416 T. W. Manson, "The NT Basis of the Doctrine of the Church," Journal of Ecclesiastical History, 1 (1950), 7 develops this idea, pointing out that the physical body of the earthly Jesus was the place where God's love met man's need.

417 E. K. Lee, Unity in Israel and Unity in Christ, Stud. in Eph. (1956), 49 interprets wholly in the light of the eucharist, though he recognises some preliminary stages, 43-48. Meuzelaar breaks new ground. He ref. to the eucharist in 27-29, but in 41-46 finds in the problem of (table-)fellowship between Jew and Gentile the setting of the sayings about Christ's body.

418 Cf. T. Boman, Das hbr. Denken im Vergleich mit d. griech.³ (1959), 118-126 and the correction of some exaggerations in R. Bultmann's review in Gnomon, 27 (1955), 556 f.; Barr, op. cit. (→ n. 85), 46-85, but cf. T. Boman's review of Barr in ThLZ, 87 (1962), 262-265.

sacrificed on the cross for the community can be seen in two ways. It is present in the blessing which issues therefrom to liberate the community and to unite it with Christ, 1 C. 10:16. [419] It is also present in the claim to lordship which issues therefrom, 1 C. 11:27, 29. [420] One may incur guilt in respect of the present body and blood of the Lord. The guilt consists in the failure of the community to wait for those who come late and in its celebration of the sacrament with no practical bodily brotherliness, → II, 695, 1 ff. [421] The phrase τὸ σῶμα καὶ τὸ αἶμα τοῦ κυρίου is thus chosen because it echoes the interpretative sayings, but it is to be taken in exactly the same sense as 1 C. 8:12: He who sins against the brother for whom Christ died sins against Christ, v. 11. The body and blood of the Lord, then, are the act of the Lord sacrificing Himself for the brother. [422] The same applies to v. 29, where σῶμα is a brief term for the reconciling sacrifice of Christ which in the Lord's Supper is proffered to the participant. [423] In all these passages, then, τὸ σῶμα τοῦ Χριστοῦ is the body which was offered up for the community on the cross. But, as in the case of αἶμα, this includes the whole act of sacrifice, so that σῶμα is not just something past; it is present in the community in its blessing and claim. [424] Hence one cannot divide the crucified body and the exalted body. [425] The latter is the crucified body in its ongoing operation; [426] it is the place of the Church.

(c) The Community as the Body of Christ: The Figurative Sayings.

The community does not merely live in this place, in the body of Christ; it, too,

---

[419] It seems to me to be quite impossible that in the tradition which Paul had before him σῶμα should have denoted the community, as suggested by H. Lessig, Die Abendmahlsprobleme im Lichte d. nt.lichen Forschung seit 1900, Diss. Bonn (1953), 358-361, 367-369 (→ 1070, 2 ff.).

[420] A. Andersen, "Das Abendmahl in den zwei ersten Jhdt. n. Chr.," ZNW, 3 (1902), 115-122 wants to take σῶμα as always a term for the community and αἶμα as a ref. to the new covenant, but this is artificial. C. F. D. Moule, "The Judgment Theme in the Sacraments," Festschr. f. C. H. Dodd, 473 f. thinks Paul meant by σῶμα the crucified body and the community.

[421] On this esp. G. Bornkamm, "Herrenmahl u. Kirche bei Pls.," Stud. zu Antike u. Urchr. (1959), 142-146, 166 f. On the debate with others cf. Schweizer, op. cit., 11.

[422] So also Lessig, op. cit., 361-366, who pts. out that θάνατος in v. 26 corresponds to σῶμα καὶ αἶμα. But cf. D. M. Stanley, "Christ's Resurrection in Pauline Soteriology," Analecta Bibl., 13 (1961), 116, who combines 10:3 f., 21; 11:27; 15:44-46 and thus thinks only of the Risen Lord.

[423] ἀναξίως, of course, is not repeated, but is caught up by the condition μὴ διακρίνων τὸ σῶμα which controls the whole sentence. Hence one cannot follow Käsemann Anliegen, 26 f. when he speaks of a judgment fulfilled in each Lord's Supper, notwithstanding the material arguments for this. In opp. to the transl. of A. Ehrhardt, "Sakrament u. Leiden," Ev. Theol., 7 (1947 f.), 100: "As he makes no exception for his person (σῶμα)" cf. Braun, op. cit., 195 f. and Lessig, 272.

[424] For a discussion cf. N. Clark, An Approach to the Theology of the Sacraments (1956), 81 f.

[425] So also Bornkamm, op. cit. (→ n. 421), 164.

[426] Possibly Paul was presenting this under the concept of a spiritual body (→ 1071, 6 ff.), but since there are only cosmic examples of such a notion in NT days it seems more probable to me that this was a secondary development after Paul (→ 1093, 16 ff.). Since the Risen One is undoubtedly the Lord who guides the community (→ 1072, 1 ff.) and is invoked by it, one cannot regard the exalted body as something objectively different from the crucified body (→ 1073, 2 ff.) as suggested by, e.g., C. Davis, "The Resurrection of the Body," Clergy Review, 43 (1958), 148 f., who deduces from this the not yet manifested resurrection of the community.

is body. [427] This formulation is to be found only in 1 C. 12:27, and even there it is imprecise: [428] ὑμεῖς δέ ἐστε σῶμα Χριστοῦ, → IV, 596, 22 f. [429] This statement is the conclusion of an exhortation in which σῶμα is used unequivocally in the sense of the parallels adduced → 1034, 28 ff. [430, 431] The picture of the body which cannot be just an eye without being a monster incapable of life is a warning against all feelings of inferiority (vv. 14-20), while the picture of the body in which the head also needs the feet is a warning against all sense of superiority (vv. 21-25). The head here is simply one of the members with no special status. [432] The summons to unity in the community is here shaped by the idea that the body is a single totality consisting of many members. Similarly the metaphor of R. 12:4 is found at the beginning of an exhortation. But this passage represents an advance. In R. 12:5, as in 1 C. 10:17; 12:13, Paul does not merely say that the community is like a body; he says that it is a body. This does not go beyond widespread Greek usage, → 1041, 9 ff. etc. The new point is that in R. 12:5 it is this in Christ. [433] In the first instance this simply means that always in Paul the imperative is grounded in the indicative, exhortation in the fact of salvation. [434] The community is in Christ. That is to say, it is incorporated into the history determined by Him. [435] It is a unity from the very first. In distinction from all Stoic parallels, then, Paul is calling the community to live out in actuality, bodily, what it already is by Christ and in Him. Here, then, ἐν σῶμα might be understood as just a term for the unity of mind and life which, in an advance on the Greek understanding, is then said to be grounded in the fact of Christ. Undoubtedly current Greek expressions played on essential part in the choice of the term. This is also shown by the fact that in this letter it is only in exhortation that Paul speaks of the community as the body of Christ.

---

[427] Craig, 75 states that Christ is body in three ways, as crucified Lord, as the Lord present in the Supper, and as the community. The whole question, with historical material, is fully discussed in Schweizer Homologumena, 161-174. For Roman Catholic research cf. B. M. Ahern, "The Christian's Union with the Body of Christ in Cor., Gal. and Rom.," *The Catholic Bibl. Quarterly*, 23 (1961), 199-201.

[428] Stressed by L. Cerfaux, *La théologie de l'église suivant St. Paul* (1948), 211; Meuzelaar, 40; cf. Bl.-Debr. § 273.

[429] T. Zapelana, "Vos estis Corpus Christ (1 C. 12:27)," *Verbum Domini*, 37 (1959), 78-95 emphasises that what has been said thus far is inadequate in explanation since one might also say that the individual incorporated into the crucified body of Christ is Christ's body.

[430] Stressed already in Percy, 45 and 48. As against Dillistone, 62 this cannot be denied, though one may add that it falls short of what is typically Pauline.

[431] On distinctions from the Stoic view and discussion of the point → IV, 562, 31 ff.; Reuss, 113 f.; Stacey, 193; G. Friedrich, "Christus, Einheit u. Norm d. Christen," *Kerygma u. Dogma*, 9 (1963), 255 f.

[432] Which one might expect if the derivation was from Gnostic par. → III, 676, 20 ff.; cf. → 1056, 31; n. 344, 616, 618, 625. On v. 23 → n. 351.

[433] G. Martelet, "Le mystère du corps et l'Esprit dans le Christ ressuscité et dans l'Eglise," *Verbum Caro*, 12 (1958), 39 emphasises that this is primary compared with the formula "body of Christ."

[434] Cf. also Bornkamm, *op. cit.* (→ n. 421), 162 f. on 1 C. 10:16 f.

[435] Cf. Neugebauer, *op. cit.* (→ n. 410), 39-44, 148 f.; also "Das paul. 'in Christo'," NTSt, 4 (1957/58), 124-138.

(d) The Community as the Body of Christ: The Stricter Sayings.

From the traditional liturgical formula [436] about the bread as fellowship with the body of Christ (1 C. 10:16) the deduction is made that since it is one bread the many are one body, seeing they all partake of the one bread. For Paul it may be taken for granted that the fellowship which comes together at the Supper, and in which the many become one, is also fellowship with Christ, → III, 805, 8 ff. v. 17 does not interrupt the chain of thought, for, as Paul sees it, there is no direct individual fellowship of man with Christ, only that of the community or of the individual member within the community. Paul carefully avoids speaking of fellowship with God or Christ to rule out misunderstanding along the lines of individual mysticism. [437] The same may be said in respect of 1 C. 6:15. Here it is presupposed that the σώματα of the community are the μέλη Χριστοῦ, → IV, 564, 29 ff. [438] To be sure, the reference here is to the individual, for union with a harlot has to be an individual act. When the individual cleaves to the Lord, he is ἓν πνεῦμα (→ VI, 421, 21 ff.) with Him. But it is only here that Paul speaks thus. In v. 15b he refers to the members of the body and in v. 17 he avoids what might seem to be the obvious ἓν σῶμα. The body of Christ is the community, never the individual. But in the community man is represented as united with Christ is such bodily fashion that all other sins are more readily conceivable than fornication, which accomplishes bodily union with someone else and therefore cannot take place within the body of Christ, the two being mutually exclusive. [439] Finally the statements in 1 C. 12:12 f. presuppose a similar unity. If at a pinch one might translate v. 13: "We are baptised into a united whole," the community, [440] or: "We were baptised in order that a united whole might arise," [441] or even: "We were all baptised into the one Christ who died for us" (→ VI, 418, n. 562), [442] the surprising conclusion of the comparison in v. 12: "so Christ," makes sense only if it is self-evident that the one body of the

---

[436] So Käsemann Anliegen, 12. This explains the reversal of the sayings, for Paul can attach his commentary only to the bread saying. Lessig, op. cit., 369 regards v. 16, 17a as pre-Pauline. But it is most unlikely that σῶμα in 10:16 in the strictest parallelism to αἷμα means the community and not the crucified body. Lessig's main argument is that v. 17 interrupts the line of thought, but on this → lines 6 ff. For the same reasons Schmithals, op. cit. (→ n. 380), 210, n. 3 regards v. 16b, 17 (also Did., 9, 4) as Gnostic, though he does not give any instances → 1090, 23 ff. Naturally one cannot adopt the A. V. transl.: "For we... are one bread," cf. Shedd, op. cit. (→ n. 314), 160, n. 151; Goossens, op. cit. (→ n. 402), 21 f.
[437] The sacrifice is made to God and we partake of the Lord's cup and table.
[438] Cf. Manson, op. cit. (→ n. 261), 385. Meuzelaar, 147 f. stresses that only the members of the physical body are members of Christ, not the metaphorical members, i.e., individual Christians; but this does not fit v. 15a too well.
[439] For Paul this does not apply to marriage, though perhaps 1 C. 7:1, 5, 7 f., 14, 32-34 are to be understood against this background → 1079, 11 f. C. F. D. Moule, An Idiom Book of NT Greek² (1960), 196 f. considers a dialogue between Paul's adversaries in v. 18a and Paul himself in v. 18b, but one can hardly accept this, since σῶμα in the sense of his adversaries cannot mean true personality.
[440] So Mussner, 125-131; — VI, 418, 5 ff. Soiron, 70 f. also inclines to this exposition, though with reservations.
[441] Ltzm. K., ad loc. against Kümmel, loc. cit. Cf. Meuzelaar, 87, 89.
[442] Without the addition Χριστοῦ this would make no sense, esp. as there is no ref. to the crucified body elsewhere. ἓν too suggests that the body is the community. Yet is is correct that the two senses cannot be sharply differentiated. The only pt. is that to refer baptism to Christ alone does not yield an adequate understanding of the phrase.

community is no other than the body of Christ Himself. [443] v. 27 is to the same effect, and this certainly cannot be regarded merely as an imprecise way of putting a pure comparison. [444] Hence v. 13 is to be understood along the same lines. [445] The body of Christ is the given fact and not just a product of fellowship → III, 512, 10 ff. [446] Gl. 3:26-29, with v. 16, may also be understood only in the light of this idea, though σῶμα is not used there. In fact Paul has in view a kind of all-embracing body of Christ → VI, 418, 1 ff.; 421, 20 ff. The only question is in what sense this is to be understood. [447] In Jn. 15:1 Christ the vine replaces the vine Israel, which was taken cosmically in Judaism. [448] Independently both of Paul and also of any Gnostic myth this is saying precisely what Paul means by the body of Christ → I, 342, 1 ff. The way had been prepared by many different forces for Paul's adoption of this particular expression. The crucified and risen body of Christ was for Paul a present place where the community was set → 1068, 16 ff. [449] It became a unity thereby, in Greek ἓν σῶμα → 1069, 11 ff. It is thus the one body which has its life in the body of Christ. Yet the final step is hardly conceivable apart from some guiding religious model. Since Gnosticism (→ 1090, 23 f.) prior to Mani is not acquainted with σῶμα in this sense, and since one finds in it only later hints [450] of what is meant, usually in cosmic contexts (→ 1090, 24 ff.), the model is to be sought elsewhere.

---

[443] Percy, 4-6, 16, not Schlier; cf. J. Havet, "Christ collectif ou Christ individuel en I C. XII, 12?" *Analecta Lovaniensia Bibl. et Orientalia*, II, 4 (1948), 1-24, who surveys the exegesis 6-12 and considers parallels 12-21. He himself interprets par. to ἔχει: Thus Christ also has many members. Meuzelaar, 39 takes the same view as → IV, 564, 19 ff. The right pt. here is that one must stress the dynamic character of Christ's body. But the ἐστίν of v. 12a (→ IV, 564, 11 ff.) should not be overlooked. Friedrich, *op. cit.* (→ n. 431), 241 pts. also to 1 C. 1:13, which shows the idea was familiar to the Corinthians.

[444] So Havet, *op. cit.* and the ref. he adduces.

[445] Baptism (and the Lord's Supper? →VI, 418, n. 563) integrates man into this one body of Christ.

[446] With E. Käsemann, "Christus, das All u. d. Kirche," ThLZ, 81 (1956), 590 as against Mussner.

[447] Moule, *op. cit.* (→ n. 413), 6 f. ref. to Ac. 9:4 f.; 22:7 f.; 26:14 f.; Jn. 2:21; Hb. 10:5, 10 but also to sayings of Jesus like Mt. 10:40; 25:40; Lk. 10:16; Jn. 13:20. So also Dillistone, 63; Thornton Body, 55-62; Barth, K. D., IV, 3, 867 (C. D., IV, 3, 757); Kearns, 90, 3-7. M. J. Congar, *Esquisses du Mystère de l'Eglise* (1941), 41 seeks to explain the concept only in the light of the OT idea of the unity of the Messiah with His people. Meuzelaar, 169 recalls metaphorical passages like → 1038, 25 ff.; n. 185, cf. also his ref. to the OT, 11-16. M. Black, "The Eschatology of the Similitudes of Enoch," JThSt, 3 (1952), 8 ref. to the unity of the head and people of the elect in Eth. En. 71, Mi. Hb. on 11:12, n. 3 to the unity of the one with the many in OT thought. J. Bonsirven in a review of J. Klausner, *Jesus v. Nazareth, Biblica*, 35 (1954), 106 uses the idea of the shekinah in explanation of the body of Christ, while Shedd, *op. cit.* (→ n. 314), 163-5 and the authorities he adduces use the image of the bride of Christ. Cf. the survey in du Plessis, 132 f.; Schweizer Homologumena, 272, also *op. cit.* (→ n. 414), 82, n. 353.

[448] Ps.-Philo (→ n. 295), 12, 8 f. along with the image of the building or temple of God (cf. in the NT 1 C. 3:9; Col. 2:7 → 1079, 1 ff.) and in connection with the question whether God might not be able to plant a new vine in place of the ruined one. The Qumran community also views itself as a cosmic planting and building, 1 QH 6:15 f. Cf. further F. Mussner, "Beiträge aus Qumran zum Verständnis d. Eph.," *Nt.liche Aufsätze f. J. Schmid* (1963), 191; cf. Asc. Is. 4:3. Giant stature as a symbol of cosmic significance occurs also in Philo Det. Pot. Ins., 84 f.; cf. J. Daniélou, *Théol. du Judéo-Christianisme* (1958), 303.

[449] Incorporation into Christ's crucified body is stressed esp. by Percy, 25-28; cf. also Thornton Common Life, 298.

[450] On the distinctions from Gnosticism cf. Best, 85-87.

(e) The Unity of Patriarch and People as a Religious Model.

Paul sees in Christ the eschatological Adam (→ I, 141, 27 ff.), the εἷς ἄνθρωπος, [451] whose acts and destiny shape a whole mankind belonging to Him. [452] R. 5:12-21; [453] 1 C. 15:21 f., 45. [454] These two sections are in the two letters which alone speak of Christ's body. Later Judaism has the idea that Adam shapes the destiny of the race, indeed, that this is none other than Adam. [455] Eschatological expectations are even more important. 1. The original divine glory of Adam is granted again to the people of the end-time. 2. The *sophia* of which Adam had a share comes as revealer and reminds man of his divine origin. 3. A second patriarch comes as the end of a damned race and the beginning of a saved race → 1053, 30 ff. [456] Jacob, a plain par. to Adam, will bring about cosmic renewal in his tribe (→ n. 316), Jub. 2:23; 19:24-27. Possibly it was in connection with such expectations that a preliminary draft of Jn. stated that in Jesus as Son of Man the new Jacob-Israel had come, and in him the true vine of Israel → 1071, 8 ff. [457] Christ as the eschatological Adam is a universalistic variation on this. Now the body of Christ, which includes all the members, replaces the vine which includes all the grapes. [458] Once again it is apparent that Paul has no interest in a physical or metaphysical substance which unites Redeemer and redeemed but only in the fact that God's deed in Christ is determinative for believers. This rather than consubstantiality bridges time → VI, 421, 20 ff. [459] The spatial concept of the body of Christ (→ 1071, 6 f.) proclaims in a form conditioned by the age the truth

[451] Cf. Philo Praem. Poen., 23; Conf. Ling., 41, 147 and Ac. 17:26; Hb. 2:11; 11:12, also R. 9:10; 2 C. 5:14; Eph. 2:15; cf. further M. D. Hooker, "Adam in R. 1," NTSt, 6 (1959/60), 297-306.
[452] For the idea of the patriarch, esp. Adam, cf. Percy, 40-44; also Percy, *Die Probleme d. Kolosser- u. Epheserbr.* (1946), 108 f., 127; Thornton Body, 70-76; Best, 34-43; Barrett, 6-21; Brandenburger, op. cit. (→ n. 343), 139-153; also Reuss, 115 f. A. Richardson, *An Introduction to the Theology of the NT* (1958), 136-140, 255 contests the theory that Jesus' title as Son of Man has corporative significance, but he finds the idea of the body of Christ already implicit in it.
[453] Cf. Brandenburger, op. cit. (→ n. 343), 158-266. Nygren, op. cit. (→ n. 404), 172 ref. to the connection of this passage with the idea of growth with Christ in R. 6.
[454] This passage is also stressed by S. F. B. Bedale, "The Theology of the Church," *Stud. in Eph.*, ed. F. L. Cross (1956), 72 f.: 1 C. 15:27 is taken up again in Eph. 1:22. Schlier Eph.3, 19 f. agrees but thinks the idea of primal man begins to exert an influence only in Col. and Eph. and differs from what we find in R. and 1 C. Adam appears rather than Abraham because the concept is applied universalistically to all mankind. How close the idea of the patriarch is in this version may be seen from G. 3:16, 26-29 → 1071, 5 f.
[455] Examples in Schweizer Homologumena, 274-7. Cf. Shedd, op. cit. (→ n. 314), 158: As humanity can be called Adam, so the Church can be called Christ. As the first man includes both male and female, Philo Op. Mund., 76; Leg. All., II, 13; for the Rabb. cf. Jervell, op cit. (n. 315), 107 f., so does the community, Gl. 3:28. Cf. further → 1050, 31 ff.
[456] Examples in Schweizer Homologumena, 279-283. On the angelic form and *logos* character of Jacob-Israel cf. Daniélou, op. cit. (→ n. 448), 180-185. In Eth. En. 90:37 f., cf. 85:3 the Messiah again seems to be the second Adam.
[457] Schweizer Homol., 283-5, cf. also E. Schweizer, "The Son of Man," JBL, 79 (1960), 124-9; on Jn. 1:51 esp. N. A. Dahl, "The Johannine Church and History," *Current Issues in NT Interpretation*, ed. W. Klassen and G. F. Snyder (1962), 136 f.
[458] Bedale, op. cit., 66 also pts. to the par. of the vine.
[459] 2 C. 4:14 can say that God raises up (aor.) Jesus and will raise us up (fut.) with Him. R. Bultmann, "Gnosis," JThSt, 3 (1952), 12 ref. to Phil. 3:9 f., where Paul is already conformed to the death of Jesus and will be found in Him at the resurrection. Col. 3:4 takes it as self-evident that the community will be manifested with Jesus at the *parousia*.

that all the community's life is shaped by the historical act of God in Jesus. [460] Similarly Hb. 7:4-10 says that all future Levitical generations were already there in Abraham's loins. Strictly, then, one cannot separate the crucified body of Jesus, the body of the Risen Lord, and the body of Christ which is the community, → n. 426. One can only see the same body from different angles. [461] The crucified body in its ongoing work is the body of the Risen Lord, and integrated into this body the community is the body of Christ.

(f) Associations of σῶμα.

The choice of the special term σῶμα is probably due to the relations indicated → 1068, 19 ff. [462] It acquired its theological significance from the trains of thought ref. to → 1072, 1 ff. But it also has some associations which are important for Paul. For one thing it is adapted to represent the true bodily union of the community with Christ. [463] But bodily is not the same as physical. [464] In soteriological sections Paul never speaks of the body of Christ, only in hortatory passages → 1069, 23 f. He does not choose the new term, then, to denote a fellowship with Christ which is more real than justification, which is mediated by the sacrament, and which is to be understood in purely religious terms. [465] He uses it rather to emphasise that this unity manifests itself in the body, i.e., in common life with other members of the community, in dealings with the brethren, and in sexual intercourse, that it covers all these things. [466] Faith in the reconciliation achieved by God's saving act in Christ does not have to be secured later, then, by a higher physical union which can be experienced or accepted only as a mystery. This carries within it the second association. For Paul σῶμα is primarily the corporeality in which man lives in

---

[460] Neugebauer, op. cit. (→ n. 435), 137 f.; also "Die hermeneutischen Voraussetzungen R. Bultmanns in ihrem Verhältnis z. paul. Theol.," Kerygma u. Dogma, 5 (1959), 294 f. The transition from temporal thinking to spatial (W. G. Kümmel, Review of F. Neugebauer, In Christus, Zschr. f. Religions- u. Geistesgesch., 14 [1962], 380 adduces R. 8:1; 16:11; Phil. 1:1; 1 C. 1:13; 15:22; Gl. 3:28) is everywhere apparent, Schweizer Homologumena, 285, n. 51; → 1055, 28 f.; VI, 817, 12 ff.

[461] Just as the Hebrew sees man anthropologically from various angles.

[462] The choice was helped by the fact that body is largely par. to building, which had long since been used for God's people → n. 448. As against what is said → V, 147, 10 ff. it may be stated that מבנה is common in 1 QH, e.g., 7:4; 13:14-16, other examples Y. Yadin, "A Note on DSS IV 20," JBL, 74 (1955), 41; S. Schulz, "Zur Rechtfertigung aus Gnaden in Qumran u. bei Pls.," ZThK, 56 (1959), 160 f.

[463] Strongly emphasised in Käsemann Anliegen, 29.

[464] Against a biological misinterpretation which can lead only to totalitarianism in church or state cf. Dillistone, 59 f., 65 f., also Shedd, op. cit., 157.

[465] Soirons, 57 f., cf. 82-6, 176 f., 183 f. says that the ref. is to a physical-spiritual rather than a physical-material unity, but this is hardly adequate. It is not clear whether the physical body of Christ is for Cerfaux, op. cit., 213 f. the crucified body or the physical unity between the community and the exalted Lord. When Benoit, 13-15, cf. Kearns, 90, 148-151, stresses the physical-sacramental realism, he rightly rejects a purely Stoic understanding, but it must be noted that R. 7:4; 12:3 ff.; 1 C. 6:13 ff.; 12:1 ff. do not ref. to the sacrament. Real communion is established by the Word as well as by baptism or the Lord's Supper and is not physical, as in Gnosticism, but historical, as in the OT. One must avoid the fallacy that this is less real than physical realism, Benoit, 18, cf. E. Käsemann, Nt.licher Sammelbericht, II, VF, 1960/62 (1963), 81 f. Meuzelaar, 171 shows that this physical understanding represents the Gnostic rather than the Pauline interpretation.

[466] The "with Jesus" of 2 C. 4:14 (→ n. 459) is also a σὺν ὑμῖν. In 2 C. 7:3 the "mystical" formula of dying and living together is related to the apostle and the community. Hence Paul cannot imagine individual survival after death but even in 2 C. 4:14 is thinking of the parousia when the whole community will appear with Christ, cf. Col. 3:4. This double union with Christ and one's brother is emphasised by T. F. Torrance, "What is the Church?" Ecumenical Review, 11 (1958), 6-21.

this world. [467] It is thus the chance to meet others → 1064, 12 ff. For Paul, then, the body of Christ is in the first instance the body given for others. When he speaks of the community as the body of Christ there lives on in the term σῶμα an understanding which is not found elsewhere in Paul but which is attested in the Gk. par. (→ 1028, 11 ff.), namely, that of the body as a self-contained organism. Thus 1 C. 12:14-27 and R. 12:3-8 deal mainly with the relation of the members to one another. In the last resort, however, Paul does not sunder service within the community from service outside it. Thus σῶμα might also include for him the thought that in the community as His body Christ is the One who offers up Himself to seek the world and to serve it. If this cannot be demonstrated materially from these letters in the direct use of the expression σῶμα Χριστοῦ, the thought is behind the phrase → 1076, 2 f.

(g) The Body of Christ and the People of God.

In the light of what has been said this concept of the Church is to be differentiated from that of the Church as the people of God → IV, 54, 6 ff. [468] The derivation from the Adam-Christ idea shows that the two concepts are at root one. To say "the people of God" is to think primarily in terms of salvation history. The formula "body of Christ" substitutes a spatial category for a temporal one. This is no way affects the fact that here again the community is seen as living wholly by God's act in Jesus Christ and as set in a new divine history. But stress is not laid on the way which leads from that saving act on into the present and the future. What is emphasised is the present character of this saving act of God, the always present union of the Church with the Risen Lord. [469] Not tradition and office, but the unity with Christ granted to the total community is underlined. Every member of the body is basically equal in ministry. In the concept of the people of God, however, the root is in the OT people and the whole historical development up to the modern Church or the *parousia* is essential. Both terms are characteristic of Paul, but that of the people of God was more gen. widespread. The two are not wholly co-extensive in Paul, and neither is conceivable without the other. [470]

b.   Colossians (→ 1066, 14 ff.; III, 509, 20 ff.).

(a) The Cosmic Understanding of the Body of Christ.

This occurs only in a v. which the author borrowed from a Chr. hymn originally consisting of 1:15a, 16a. d, 17-18b (without c), 19 and 20a. [471] This hymn answers the

---

[467] Clark, *op. cit.* (→ n. 424), 78 f. and T. A. Lacey, *The One Body and the One Spirit* (1925), 59 f. emphasise that "body of Christ" does not describe the divine aspect of the Church but the fact that it represents the human body of Christ.

[468] On this Oepke Gottes Volk, 219-226; Oepke Leib Christi, 363-8; H. v. Campenhausen, *Kirchliches Amt u. geistliche Vollmacht*[2] (1963), 60; Käsemann, *op. cit.* (→ n. 402), 275 f.

[469] The concept of Christ existing as the community is heavily stressed by D. Bonhoeffer, *Akt u. Sein*[2] (1956), 89-91 Cerfaux, *op. cit.* (→ n. 428), 249, who along the lines of Corp. Herm., 14, 7 (→ n. 618) understands the community as a dynamic emanation of the Risen Lord, though one can hardly base this on such an isolated and singular use. Cf. against this whole line Barth K. D., IV, 1, 741 f.; IV, 3, 868 (C. D., IV, 1, 662 f.; IV, 3, 758), who sharply rejects the idea that the community is an extension of the incarnation, cf. also IV, 3, 834 f. (C. D., IV, 3, 729 f.) and M. Barth, *The Broken Wall* (1959), 118-122: The wife of Eph. 5:22-33 is not an extension of the husband. Cf. Best, 98-101; Via, *op. cit.* (→ n. 372), 271 f.

[470] Cf. specifically Schweizer, *op. cit.* (→ n. 414) § 7.

[471] For detailed analysis and bibl. Schweizer Antilegomena, 293-301. The formal parallelism between the strophes dealing with creation and redemption is supported by the material fact that in the interposed notes one finds another theology, that of the author → 1075, 21 ff. Moule, *op. cit.* (→ n. 413), 61 believes the whole hymn is Paul's with echoes of Hellen. wisdom literature. In this case, however, one would expect traditional statements in the lines mentioned above.

questions of Hellenists for whom the mastering of the cosmos was an urgent concern. In the cosmos which had escaped their power and understanding they saw themselves subject to evil forces. Earth is separated from heaven, [472] → VI, 392, 28 ff. 2:8, 16-18 give evidence of the attempts at Colossae to meet this cosmic anxiety and to safeguard against cosmic threats. [473] In the group which fashioned the hymn there took place something that was almost inevitable in the light of Gk. usage (→ 1032, 4 ff.), namely, the cosmic interpretation of what Paul says about Christ's body. [474] Originally the universe or cosmos is the σῶμα whose κεφαλή (→ 1076, 16 f.) is Christ. Then the author of Col. reinterprets the body of Christ in Pauline style as the community or Church → 1076, 2 ff. In the borrowed hymn the first strophe (1:15a, 16a and d) and the middle strophe (1:17, 18a) are in the style of wisdom lit. [475] but with the decisive difference that He, i.e., Christ, replaces *sophia*. But the final strophe (1:18b [without c], 19, 20a) carries the new Chr. statement that Christ has reunited heaven and earth by His ascension. [476] It is only in these spatio-physical categories [477] that the Hellenist, without adopting Jewish presuppositions, can keep the content of σῶμα Χριστοῦ and yet prevent it from slipping into the loose sense of a collective held together by Christ as a whole city is held together by common interests or the whole Platonic school is held together by reverence for its master. [478] Eph. too (→ 1078, 10 ff.) shows traces of an earlier stage behind the present statements when Christ was interpreted cosmically. [479]

(b) The Correction in Colossians.

In 1:22 σῶμα τῆς σαρκὸς αὐτοῦ is unequivocally the crucified body of Jesus → 1066, 14 ff.; n. 290. As in the interpolated comment in v. 20b the historical fact of this self-sacrifice is thus the basis of ἀποκαταλλάξαι, → I, 258, 31 ff. [480] The author realises in good Pauline fashion that the spatial structure of the concept "body of Christ" (→ 1068, 17 ff.; 1071, 6 ff.) must not be developed beyond incorporation

---

[472] Cf. E. Schweizer, "Das hell. Weltbild als Produkt der Weltangst," *op. cit.* (→ n. 239), 15-27, 39-50; also *Erniedrigung u. Erhöhung bei Jesus u. seinen Nachfolgern²* (1962), 145-155.
[473] On angel worship cf. Percy, *op. cit.* (→ n. 452), 168 f. and F. O. Francis, "Humility and Angelic Worship in Col. 2:18," *Stud. Theol.*, 16 (1963), 126-130, who takes θρησκεία τῶν ἀγγέλων to be an obj. gen.
[474] One finds the same in Eph. → lines 17 ff. But cosmic reinterpretation does not have to be Gnostic. Reconciliation of the material world with heaven is the precise opp. of the Gnostic hope. No position is taken up *vis-à-vis* the pre-existence or heavenly origin of souls or the identity of Redeemer and redeemed, cf. E. Percy, "Zu den Problemen d. Kolosser- u. Epheserbr.," ZNW, 43 (1950/51), 186, 194. On πλήρωμα (→ VI, 303, 20 ff.) cf. Moule, *op. cit.* (→ n. 413), 164-9; Feuillet, 459-461.
[475] Examples Feuillet, 462-472; Schweizer Antilegomena, 294-6. This is noted by both Cerfaux, *op. cit.* (→ n. 428), 237 f. and Moule, *op. cit.*, 59. On the eschatological εἰς αὐτόν → n. 254.
[476] Cf. D. E. H. Whiteley, "Christology," *Studies, op. cit.* (→ n. 454), 54 f., who ref. to Eph. 1:20 f. and Jer. 23:7 f.; R. Schnackenburg, *Gottes Herrschaft u. Reich²* (1961), 218 f.; Schweizer Antilegomena, 297.
[477] Knox, *op. cit.* (→ n. 381), 159-166.
[478] Cerfaux, *op. cit.*, 254 und 259 rejects this understanding.
[479] The many exeget. difficulties in 2:14-17 are best solved if one assumes that there are still echoes of original cosmic statements about the reconciliation of heaven and earth. 1:10 (cf. Lee, *op. cit.* [→ n. 417], 44) and 4:13 make sense against the same background; 1:20 f. shows that the exaltation was originally understood as a cosmic event → lines 12 ff. Cf. Schweizer Antilegomena, 301-4.
[480] The term comes from the hymn, the only other instances being Col. 1:22 and the dependent Eph. 2:16. v. 22 is thus commentary on the hymn. The idea of reconciliation is rooted in the group which composed the hymn and it shows it to be still non-Gnostic, i.e., Christian.

into the history which is controlled by the crucifixion. This entails a further correction. The body of Christ is understood ecclesiologically, not cosmically (→ 1078, 6 ff.). It embraces the Church rather than the universe. This interpretation is established already by the addition of v. 18a. [481] But then the body of Christ is expressly defined in v. 24: [482] "namely, the church." Similarly in 3:15 the one body is the Church. [483] The cosmic concern is given its due in a full-scale reinterpretation → 1032, 4 ff. [484] According to the commentary in 1:23 the reconciliation of the cosmos comes about as the Gospel is preached to all creation under heaven; that is, cosmic permeation takes place in the Gentile mission. The statement about the growth of the body is rooted in this understanding. As the Gospel takes its course through the world (1:6) there takes place the eschatological event in which the long concealed secret is unveiled (1:26 f.). [485] This is how 2:19 is to be understood too. The growth of the whole body is the growth of the Church. [486] throughout the world. [487] This is the eschatological event (τὰ μέλλοντα) for which everything that came before was only shadow (v. 16f.). There takes place here the growth of God which cannot be promoted by any worship of angels, v. 18. [488] Finally, the new relation of body and head is defined along the same lines → 1069, 6 ff. The understanding of the head as the controlling organ of the body is natural in the light of → 1037, 15 ff.; 1054, 29 ff. The author himself takes the word in the sense of

---

[481] Cerfaux, op. cit., 250 f.; Meuzelaar, 122 f. omit the comma and see a par. to σῶμα τῆς πόλεως, → 1039, 10 f. But it is most unlikely that this usage which is not found elsewhere in the NT should be possible without a ref. to Christ's body. Loh. Kol., ad loc. does not differentiate between hymn and redaction and therefore for him Church and cosmos are one as a mysterious metaphysical quantity where the believer lives in fellowship with the angels. Hence Christ no longer reigns in the obedience of His community and faith becomes belief and sacramental participation, cf. on 3:12-14. Cf. Käsemann Interpretationsproblem, 4-6.

[482] In interpretation → 136, 5 ff.; VI, 307, 11 ff. Bibl. in Soiron, 111 f.; Feuillet, 452 f.; G. H. P. Thompson, "Eph. 3:13 and 2 Tim. 2:10 in the Light of Col. 1:24," Exp. T., 71 (1959/60), 187-189; Kearns (1959), 7-9.

[483] Benoit, 19 f. suggests the crucified body here. On 2:17 → 1066, 17 ff. σῶμα never means the universe outside the hymn, as Benoit rightly notes, 29.

[484] With Cerfaux, op. cit. (→ n. 428), 227 f. one should perhaps distinguish more sharply than → IV, 820, 30 ff. between the cosmic concern of the Colossians and the new interpretation of Col. and Eph.

[485] As against Dib. Gefbr. Exc. on Eph. 4:16 there is here no essential difference from Eph. The "eschatological-mystical Christ mystery" of Col. 2:3; 4:3 is simply the message of Christ the Reconciler of the Gentiles, 1:26 f. Cf. F. Hahn, Das Verständnis d. Mission im NT (1963), 126-134.

[486] As against Dib. Gefbr., ad loc., who sees here the cosmic body, cf. already Percy, 49, n. 89.

[487] For the earlier history of this missionary concept cf. Schweizer Antilegomena, 306-8; for its influence → 1083, 12 ff.; 1087, 14 ff.; for the reinterpretation of cosmic sayings as historical sayings → n. 339, 349; V, 978, 16 ff. Only in the above sense is C. H. Dodd right when he says in The Meaning of Paul for Today (1920), 105 that what Christ has done for us has affected the whole structure of the universe. Manson, op. cit. (→ n. 416), 7 f. is clear: The extension of the body of Christ is the host of disciples in whose physical-bodily service the love of God which seeks men in the physical body of Jesus continues its work. Certainly the phrase "body of Christ" cannot be explained in terms of the idea that Christ also gives His body for the world in the community, Best, 110 f. Materially, however, Col. and Eph. are close to this when they draw deductions from Paul's initial statements. Cf. E. Käsemann, "Pls. und d. Frühkatholizismus," ZThK, 60 (1963), 81.

[488] It is possible there is polemical demarcation here → 1075, 3 ff.: powers of growth come from Christ, not the στοιχεῖα, Mussner, 142 f.

the LXX (III, 675, 1 ff.), Philo (→ 1055, 9 ff. and 1 C. 11:3.[489] In distinction from the original hymn Christ is head for him in the sense of dominion over all forces and powers, which were disarmed at the cross and led in a triumphal procession, 2:10; 14 f.[490] As this Lord He is also Head (→ III, 680, 11 ff.) over the Church, 1:18; 2:19. In opposition to an emotional-enthusiastic understanding of the body of Christ which regards the whole universe as already reconciled physically in Christ, the Pauline view is upheld that talk about the body of Christ is a summons to obedience and to service for the new Lord. Christ is thus Head over the world, but only the Church is His body, and the whole power of growth flows from Him to it. With the fact that the Church is all that it is only in Him, no less sober stress must also be placed, of course, on the distinction of Christ from the Church as the head to which the body must cleave, 2:19.[491] Finally, in further distinction from the hymn, it is God rather than the universe whose fulness dwells in Christ (2:9).[492] Here, then, σωματικῶς means the corporeality in which God encounters man in the world in which he lives.[493] It means the full humanity of Jesus, not a humanity which is a mere cloak for deity.[494]

c. Ephesians.

(a) As in Col. (→ 1075, 21 ff.) the crucifixion of Jesus is the decisive saving event. 2:14 (→ 137, 6 ff.) speaks of this. In 2:16 σῶμα par. Col. 1:22 probably denotes the

---

[489] For this sense of κεφαλή cf. esp. Bedale, op. cit. (→ n. 454), 69 f.; also "The Meaning of κεφαλή in the Pauline Epistles," JThSt, 5 (1954), 211-215; Meuzelaar, 117-123, 164-8 with a ref. to Dt. 28:13; Eth. En. 103:11; Jub. 1:16; Ab., 4, 15. Cf. also → n. 625.

[490] Shedd, op. cit. (→ n. 314), 171 attempts harmonisation. Benoit, 24-28 sees in this thought the reason for introducing the image of the head without any link with the main idea. This is possible, though a cosmic understanding of the head at some earlier stage of Col. and Eph. seems more likely.

[491] V. Taylor, The Names of Jesus (1953), 101 f.; Stanley, op. cit. (→ n. 422), 206; Du Plessis, 136, 139 f. As against Dib. Gefbr. Exc. on Eph. 4:16 Col. does not differ from Eph. here. Only in the original hymn, not in the reinterpretation or the rest of the epistle, is the body of Christ the universe. 2:10 obviously derives from the statements of the Colossians about Christ as the head of the cosmos, but is in obvious tension with their understanding; acc. to them He is Head of a reconciled universe, while acc. to 2:10, 15 (cf. 1 C. 15:25) He is Head of a defeated and subjected universe. The idea of the dominion of Christ and the obedience of the Church is certainly included in 2:19, but the accent is on the power which flows into the Church from its Head. That the body here is not merely the trunk (cf. Goossens, op. cit., 44 f.) is understandable linguistically in the light of → 1037, 15 ff.

[492] One can take πᾶν τὸ πλήρωμα as subj. in 1:19 or supply God as implied subj. in view of the next statement in which πάντα is the obj. of reconciliation, → II, 741, 32 ff.; VI, 303, 4 ff. This is, of course, very difficult, esp. as one must conjecture κατοικίσαι. It fits the hymn better to take πλήρωμα as subj. and to understand it somewhat in the sense of the divine world soul which fulfils all things. The author then interprets it along the lines of → VI, 303, 4 ff., cf. 2:9.

[493] For discussion of various possible interpretations v. Moule, op. cit. (→ n. 413), 92f. The ref. is not to the body of the Risen Lord, as against Cerfaux, op. cit., 245. We have here neither anti-docetic polemic nor rebuttal of doubts as to Christ's deity on the basis of His earthly body, so Knox, op. cit. (→ n. 381), 168, n. 3. One can say the world is already comprehended in Him (Benoit, 38 f.) only if one does not differentiate the theology of the Colossians from that of the author. For Gk. par. cf. M. J. Lagrange, "Les origines du dogme paulinien de la divinité du Christ," Rev. Bibl., 45 (1936), 27.

[494] On this Barth K. D., IV, 2, 94-7 (C. D., IV, 2, 86-8) and esp. there the emphasis on the historical character of the relation between God and man in Jesus Christ (in contrast to the traditional understanding of the doctrine of the two natures).

crucified body of Jesus. [495] It is typical, however, that the letter has ἐν ἑνὶ σώματι which is a full par. of εἷς καινὸς ἄνθρωπος (v. 15). [496] The two senses cannot be separated from one another. [497] The man who is united with another by the crucified body is united with him in the body of Christ, i.e., the community. It is only a question of where the accent falls, → 1073, 3 ff.

(b) Similarly (→ 1076, 2 ff.) σῶμα does not mean the cosmos in Eph., but the Church. The aliens and enemies of Col. 1:21, who are specifically the Gentiles (→ III, 387, 11 ff.), are united with Israel in the Church, 2:12-16. The reference is again to the Church in 1:23; 4:4, 12, 15 f.; [498] 5:23, 30.

(c) The cosmic dimension (→ 1076, 6 ff.) is not forgotten. As in Jewish parallels (→ 1071, 8) the Church as the body of Christ is in 1:23 the fulness of Him that fills all in all → III, 681, 18 ff.; IV, 623, 2 ff.; VI, 292, 6 ff.; 302, 14 ff. Since v. 21 plainly refers to subjected man, for in v. 22 Christ is given to the Church as Head over all things, [499] πάντα ἐν πᾶσιν is in the first instance to be taken cosmically. The Church is the body of Him that fills the universe. [500] Even more strongly than in Col. it is stressed that all growth through the preaching of the Gospel [501] can merely bring to manifestation that which already is. 2:17, like Col. 1:23, speaks of the march of the Gospel through the Gentile world in the context of a statement about reconciliation which here in Eph. develops expressly the theme of the Gentiles reconciled with Israel. [502] The Church now can even be the bearer of the message to demonic powers, 3:10. It is in this ministry to the world, even the demonic world, that the

---

[495] Percy, op. cit. (→ n. 452), 281; also op. cit. (→ n. 474), 191-3. In discussion cf. Schlier Eph.³, ad loc. The addition "through the cross" and the repetition of ἐν αὐτῷ (the cross? the body?) support this interpretation. Mussner, op. cit. (→ n. 448)), 197, n. 80; Meuzelaar, 51-7; W. Lock, The Ep. to the Eph. (1929), 32 ref. to the Church.

[496] Best, 152-4 takes this merely as a ref. to Jews and Gentiles becoming Christians. But cf. Mussner, op. cit., 99 f., cf. Käsemann, op. cit. (→ n. 446), 588. It is possible the one new man was adopted as a common hortatory symbol.

[497] With Dib. Gefbr., ad loc.

[498] The ref. is to the cosmos if with Schlier Eph.³, ad loc. one takes αὐξάνω trans. (not elsewhere in the NT). But this is most unlikely alongside ἓν σῶμα in 4:4 f. and σῶμα = community in 4:16a, cf. Schnackenburg, op. cit. (→ n. 476), 215 f.

[499] I.e., all that God has laid at His feet acc. to Ps. 8:6.

[500] Cf. 4:10. So → VI, 291, 37 ff.; Dib. Gefbr., ad loc.; du Plessis, 136; cf. also Schlier Eph.³, ad loc. The passage is ambiguous, since τὸ πλήρωμα may relate to the Church or to Christ and the verb may be act. or pass., cf. the discussion in Moule, op. cit., 167 f. The many-sided πληρόω or πλήρωμα (→ VI, 286, 17 ff.) is not at all then a tt. as in Gnosticism. Soiron, 144 emphasises the use of the present: Already filling the Church, Christ increasingly fills the universe. Feuillet, 456-9 suggests: The fulness of Him who is completely filled (by God). M. Barth, op. cit. (→ n. 469), 72 notes the relation: Acc. to Col. 2:9 God completely fills Christ, and here Christ fills the Church. What is not said is that Christ comes to fulness only in the Church, Craig, 80.

[501] The growth in 4:12, 16 cf. 3:1-11, esp. 10, is not qualitative, as against Best, 157-9. The Church lives in salvation history during the period of fulfilling, but its mission is in the work of the apostles and the intercession of the community for this. The extensive growth of Col. 1:6 is also interpreted intensively in Col. 1:10.

[502] Possibly the original home of ἐλθών is a view in which the ascending Christ accomplished this filling of all things, cf. 4:10. In 1 Tm. 3:16 the triumphant procession of the Risen Lord through heaven is linked to His triumphant procession through the nations in the cosmos with the preaching of the Gospel.

Church is Christ's body. [503] Herein the growth of the body takes place, 2:21 f.; 4:12, 16; par. Col. 2:19. This is also the growth of the temple (→ IV, 275, 12 ff.; 887, 18 ff.) or the building (→ V, 145, 17 ff.) as God's dwelling-place. [504] Thus the originally pantheistic statement about the permeation of the universe is completely reconstructed along the lines of a penetration which seizes control. [505]

(d) In Eph., too, Christ as Head is contrasted with the Church. As in Col. (→ 1076, 16 ff.) the distinction between the universe and the Church is maintained at this pt. He is over the universe as the Ruler to whom everything is subject, Eph. 1:21-23. He is Head of the Church as the One who grants its growth and on whom it is dependent for its life, 4:16 (→ IV, 566, 12 ff.); 5:23. [506]

(e) The presentation in 5:23-32, however, is new, [507] → 137, 3 ff.; III, 509, 25 ff. Behind the section stands the widespread idea of the ἱερὸς γάμος. But once Christ was seen as the eschatological Adam, this new interpretation of Gn. 2:24 (→ I, 656, 9 ff.) was extremely close [508] quite apart from any developed syzygy concepts → 137, n. 293; IV, 566, 26 ff. Nor is Christ's confrontation as Lord forgotten.

The saying that the woman is man's body (5:28) corresponds to the Jewish formula (→ 109, 27; 119, 16) except that analogously to the passages mentioned (→ 1037, 5 f.; 1040, 2 f.; 1048, 12 f.; 1049, 21 ff.) σῶμα is used for the Hebrew בָּשָׂר (σάρξ). [509] The description of the community as Christ's body, which had already been developed long since, is thus parallel to the idea of woman as man's body. The parallel images of the heavenly city or the heavenly building might well have helped to fashion the concept, → I, 657, 4 ff. [510] What is more important, however, is that 1 C. 6:12-20 had already viewed the corporeality of the relation of Christ and the community as analogous to the sex relation, → 1065, 11 ff.; IV, 566, 5 ff. The statement that members of the community are Christ's members is only indirectly contained in 1 C. 6:15; Eph. 5:30. Eph. 5:32 expressly describes Gn. 2:24, understood thus, as a mystery. [511] The author finds in Gn. 2:24 not merely the command which underlies his exhortation to married couples but also the saving fact on which it is based, the

---

[503] Cf. H. Odeberg, *The View of the Universe in the Ep. to the Eph.* (1934), 13, who also states that ἐν τοῖς ἐπουρανίοις can include the earth, 9; on this cf. Meuzelaar, 102-6.

[504] Both concepts are par. to body, → 1052, 7 f.; n. 448. Cf. J. C. Fenton, "The NT Designation of the True Church as God's Temple," *The American Ecclesiastical Review,* 140 (1959), 103-117; J. Pfammatter, *Die Kirche als Bau* (1960), 35-46.

[505] Behind it, then, we no longer have the cosmic unity of Greece but Jewish subjection, which includes service and obedience, Käsemann, *op. cit.* (→ n. 446), 587, cf. Knox, *op. cit.* (→ n. 381), 187; → n. 487.

[506] 5:23 shows that κεφαλή is taken along the lines of 1 C. 11:3 (Craig, 79) which does not include physical unity, cf. Shedd, *op. cit.* (→ n. 314), 162. The careful formulation in 1:22 distinguishes Christ's relation to the world from His relation to the Church. He is Head of the universe in the Church's favour.

[507] On this cf. Best, 169-183, where other views are also discussed.

[508] Cf. God as the husband of *sophia* → 1054, 28; 1055, 29. Bibl. and historical par. in Schlier Eph.[3] 264-275; F. M. M. Sagnard, *La gnose valentinienne et le témoignage de S. Irenée,* Diss. Paris (1947), 599. Cf. Daniélou, *op. cit.* (→ n. 448), 122, 326-337.

[509] But → n. 292. The body of Christ, however, is never σάρξ → 137, 4 ff.

[510] Cerfaux, *op. cit.* (→ n. 428), 263.

[511] Cf. 1 QpHab 7:4, not in the sense of Ascl., 21, cf. Knox, *op. cit.,* 200, n. 5; → 1085, 15 f.; → IV, 823, 12 ff.

christologically understood indicative the ethical imperative can only follow.[512] The noteworthy saying that Christ is σωτήρ (→ 1016, 3 ff.) τοῦ σώματος (5:23)[513] rests on the fact that as compared with man as the head of woman there is need to show more precisely that in the case of Christ as Head of the Church we do not merely have a superordination which may be explained by the order of creation or by custom but also a relation in which all life comes to the body from the Head, → 1076, 16 ff.

d. σύσσωμος.

This word is attested only in Christian writings.[514] It is so unusual that in Eph. 3:6 it is surely designed to express an emphatic relation to the σῶμα τοῦ Χριστοῦ.[515] It thus catches up 2:16 → 1077, 19 ff.

e. Distinctions from Paul.

Distinctions from Paul's view of the body of Christ in the generally accepted letters are rooted in the new intellectual situation. Christ had to be proclaimed as the answer to the problem which now faced the community, that of the cosmos which had slipped away from man. In these epistles the over-facile solution is avoided that creation-mediation in the form of a doctrine of wisdom or the ascension of Christ guarantees physically that the cosmos is in His hands. In terms of this new problem it is evident that the local community with its questions of mutual service is no longer in the forefront (→ 1069, 4 ff.) but rather the universal Church (→ 1076, 6 ff.). Hence Christ is no longer just the total body (→ 1070, 1 ff.), which might suggest the misunderstanding of a purely physical-metaphysical unity. He is the Head of the body (→ 1076, 16 ff.) which stands over against Him no matter how much it is also one with Him.[516] This carries with it the possibility of an interpretation of the body of Christ which was on the margin in the earlier epistles, since it was essential for the σῶμα concept there, but which is now brought to full development. The body of Christ is precisely the Church in which Christ moves out into the world. The preaching of the Gospel by the Church is the answer to cosmic anxiety → 1074, 30 ff. In this Christ permeates the cosmos. This is the eschatological event of which Paul is the universally visible sign and in which the mystery of God, concealed for aeons, is disclosed, and God's plan of salvation is fulfilled.

---

[512] Syzygy notions (Schlier Eph.³, 268-275) have in Gnosticism the role of explaining how the divided material world arises out of the one immaterial God. There does not seem to me to be any evidence of controversy with this type of cosmogony. Cf. R. A. Batey, "Jewish Gnosticism and the 'Hieros Gamos' of Eph. V 21-33," NT'St, 10 (1963/64), 121-127, who ref. to Justin's Book of Baruch.

[513] There seems to be no reason to think in terms of the pre-existent Church as in Schlier Eph.³, ad loc.

[514] Acc. to Dimitrakos, s.v. the only other instance is in Anastasius Sinaites (670 A.D.). Cf. συνσώματος "fellow-slave," Suppl. Epigr. Graec., 6, 721. E. Preuschen, "σύνσωμος Eph. 3:6," ZNW, 1 (1900), 85 f. would construe it along these lines.

[515] So also Schlier Eph.³, ad loc. Meuzelaar, 65 f. sees in Israel the σῶμα (→ 1055, 9 ff.; 1056, 30 f.) with which the Gentiles are united; cf. Philo Virt., 103.

[516] Cf. O. Cullmann, Die Christologie d. NT³ (1963), 236 f.

III. Survey of the Historical Development of the Concept.

Linguistically a most interesting development comes to a head in Eph. and Col.

Hebrew has no special term for body → 1045, 20 ff. This is perhaps connected with the fact that in OT thought the distinction between matter and form is never emphasised. Thus man does not regard himself as a being which out of his own matter shapes himself as the most perfect possible individual. Man is not the artist who fashions the clay; God is the One who can dash it in pieces. Nor does man view himself primarily as an individual distinct from others so that his character as a microcosm is what essentially controls him. Finally there is no distinction of the body from the true I, as though man is what he is apart from the fleshly body. [517] OT man is flesh, i.e., basically creature. This cannot be altered by anything he does. His work is important only as obedience, i.e., in its orientation to God, not to self-perfecting. For precisely this reason his relation to God and the fellow-creatures with which he shares his being as flesh is far more important than his relation to himself. But for this very reason he accepts his own being as flesh, since it is the place where he meets God and his fellow-man.

The Greek-speaking Jew has to choose between σάρξ and σῶμα. The Gk. view of the body as distinct from the flesh, but also from the soul or spirit, penetrates everywhere in Hell. Judaism.

Paul emphatically adopts the current term σῶμα and by means of it gives new force to the OT legacy. The σῶμα is the divinely given creatureliness which subjects man to God → 1060, 8 ff. It is the place where man meets God and his fellow-men (→ 1066, 2 ff.). It is in the σῶμα, not in a spiritual or intellectual ego, that he truly lives, believes, and serves, → 1064, 13 ff. The great distinction from Stoic preaching lies in the fact that for Paul man can never be understood as a self-contained individual who can be considered in himself. He is always man related to God and his fellow-men, authentic only in this relation to them. In what he says about the community as the body of Christ (→ 1068, 19 ff.) Paul adopts amongst other things a Greek mode of speach which views the body as a self-contained microcosm, → 1029, 14 ff. In the first instance, then, he finds in the body of Christ the community which is also self-contained (→ 1074, 2 ff.), though in him the accent is on mutual service (→ 1069, 8 ff.) and this shatters the self-containment of the individual. If this service is still seen within the community, nevertheless at this point, too, the OT concept comes through strongly. In Col. and Eph., however, the community is no longer a self-contained entity. As the body of Christ it grows in the world. It penetrates it, and in it Christ Himself penetrates the cosmos, → 1076, 7 ff.; 1078, 14 ff. Thus the σῶμα concept is reconstructed, [518] and it is put in the service of Him who gave His body for the world, and who in His body, the Church, is still seeking the world.

E. The Post-New Testament Period.

1. Post-Apostolic Fathers.

a. In anthropological statements σῶμα means "corpse" in Ign. R., 4, 2; Mart. Pol., 17, 1 f. "living body" which is weak or ill in Herm. v., 3, 11, 4; Papias Fr., 3, 2 or which

---

[517] Robinson, 13-16.
[518] Cf. the brilliant if exaggerated thesis of T. W. Manson, *The Servant-Messiah* (1953), 98 that the Church is not the mystical body but the working body of Christ; cf. E. Schweizer, "The Church as the Missionary Body of Christ," *op. cit.* (→ n. 239), 317-329.

suffers martyrdom, Mart. Pol., 15, 2; 16, 1, or which perishes, Herm. v., 3, 9, 3. The body is seen as a whole alongside the various members, Ign. R., 5, 3, but with no special emphasis on this. In Ign. R., 4, 2 martyrdom is complete only when the body disappears altogether in the jaws of the beasts. The dead body is a kind of remnant of continued personal earthly existence; it is part of man's totality. Hence to be without body is demonic and a divine penalty, Ign. Sm., 2, 1; 3, 2 → 146, 15 f.; 148, 25. When it is said of women martyrs that they are weak in body and receive a heavenly reward (1 Cl., 6, 2) this is tantamount to saying that the constitution of the body is not the decisive thing. In 2 Cl., 12, 3 σῶμα is used primarily to describe pure individuality when μία ψυχὴ ἐν δυσὶ σώμασι is lauded. But the continuation bears clear evidence of encratic influence. A saying in the Gospel of the Egyptians [519] is taken to mean that sexual differences must disappear. The further statement that the outward is to be as the inward is referred to body and soul, but in distinction from Paul (→ 1063, 17 ff.; 1084, 16 ff.) and in opposition to the actual wording of the quotation it is in the soul rather than the body that good works will be manifest. In 2 Cl., 5, 4, as in Just. Apol., 19, 7 a conflation of Lk. 12:4 f.; Mt. 10:28 is quoted, cf. Act. Pl. 1:4. In both passages there is an appeal not to fear death but to fear Him who can condemn both body and soul to hell → 1085, 20 f. But in the first clause the mortal body is not distinguished from the soul as in Mt. 10:28 → 1058, 15 ff. In Mart. Pol., 19, 2 the soul is the obj. of Christ's saving work while the body simply stands under His guidance and direction. Slowly, then, a view is gaining ground that the soul alone is to be saved. But there is as yet no negative evaluation of the body. [520] Stoic and Platonic ideas are used in Dg., 6, 1-8. The soul permeates the whole body and its members, v. 2 → 1034, 2 ff. It is an invisible entity caught in the visible body, v. 4 and 7 → 1053, 37 ff. But the true concern of the author is to depict Christians as the soul of the cosmos. They are in the cosmos but not of it. They invisibly hold the cosmos together. [521] Obvious here is the influence of the ancient par. between the human body and the cosmos → 1029, 12 ff.; n. 95. But theologically the ideas of Col. and Eph. are fruitful. In the Church which is growing in the world there takes place the penetration of the cosmos by Christ.

b. Christologically only the quotation of 1 Pt. 2:24 in Pol., 8, 1 ref. to the crucified body of Jesus → 145, 7 ff. Ign. Sm., 3, 2 (→ line 6) presupposes the bodily resurrection of Jesus. The idea of the Church as Christ's body has an influence, but it is not exploited theologically. In 1 Cl., 37, 5 the body is simply a metaphor for the working together of the various members, [522] of which the last useful are εἰς τὸ σῴζεσθαι ὅλον τὸ σῶμα. This is taken up again in 38, 1 in application to individual churches: σῳζέσθω οὖν ἡμῶν ὅλον τὸ σῶμα ἐν Χριστῷ ᾿Ιησοῦ, i.e., as each subjects itself to the other. This can still be taken in a purely Gk. way (→ 1034, 28 ff.) even though ἐν Χριστῷ ᾿Ιησοῦ probably goes with the verb. [523] That the author meant it thus may be seen from his adducing of the par. of the unity of an army → n. 542. 46, 7 goes further, but here too the statements of R. and 1 C. exert an influence when the individual members are seen as μέλη τοῦ Χριστοῦ (1 C. 6:15 → 1070, 11 ff.) and μέλη ἀλλήλων (R. 12:5); the community is thus τὸ σῶμα τὸ ἴδιον against which one cannot rebel. We find the same usage in Pol., 11, 4: Those who go astray are to be summoned back as *membra, ut omnium vestrum corpus salvetis.* Cf. also Ign. Sm., 11, 2, which says that τὸ ἴδιον σωματεῖον, i.e., the community

---

[519] Hennecke[3], I, 111, cf. 215. Not to be confused with the Gospel of the Egyptians discovered more recently at Nag Hamadi, cf. Hennecke[3], I, 109.

[520] σωματικός is negatively evaluated in some MSS Did., 1, 4 → 147, 5 f.

[521] For this sense cf. the cosmic use of συνέχω in Pr.-Bauer, *s.v.;* said of God's πνεῦμα, Athenag. Suppl., 6, 3.

[522] The purely fig. section 1 C. 12:14 ff. has obviously had some influence, Kn. Cl., *ad loc.* The head is one of the members with the feet, 1 C. 12:21.

[523] For the combination of 1 C. 12:17 with the unity of the world body cf. also Ambr. De Officiis ministrorum, III, 3, 17-19.

decimated by persecution, [524] will be restored. The choice of σωματεῖον is influenced by the common use of this for the tortured body of the martyr. [525] But the natural way in which in all these passages the local church is "our, your, their body" and individual Christians are "members (of Christ)" (→ line 23 f.) shows how strongly a formal use had already been developed. Nevertheless the characteristic phrase "the body of Christ" is almost completely absent, and the few instances are linguistically close to → 1034, 28 ff. Materially one sees in this how natural it was for 1 Cl., Ign. and Pol. that believers are not just individuals, that they have their common body in the congregation, that here and no longer in themselves they find their true life. Ign. Sm., 1, 2 represents a theological advance. To be sure, one can still interpret ἐν ἑνὶ σώματι τῆς ἐκκλησίας αὐτοῦ as in the previous passages. But the union of Jews and Gentiles is seen as the decisive sign set up by the resurrection of Christ, so that one should perhaps relate αὐτοῦ (of Christ) to σῶμα. At any rate one may see here the theology which finds cosmic unification effected in the resurrection of Jesus and then worked out in the reconciliation of the nations → 1076, 7 ff. Finally 2 Cl., 14, 2-4 [526] calls the living Church the σῶμα Χριστοῦ, Christ being the male aspect and the Church the female. This pneumatic Church [527] appears in the flesh of Christ. It forms the σάρξ, while Christ is the πνεῦμα → 145, n. 354; 1091, 13 ff. It is plain that Gn. 1:27 is interpreted with ref. to Christ and the Church (→ 1086, 10 ff.), which was natural enough once Christ was understood as Adam. [528] Probably such speculations were directly stimulated by Eph. 5:23-32 → 1079, 11 ff. Though σῶμα is not used, the thing itself undergoes noteworthy development in Ign. The καινὸς ἄνθρωπος (Eph. 2:15) Ἰησοῦς Χριστός is the goal of God's plan of salvation, Ign. Eph., 20, 1, [529] Believers are the members of Christ (4, 2 → 1082, 39) the Head (→ 1076, 16 ff.), Ign. Tr., 11, 2 [530] → 1091, 24 f.; 1092, 12 ff.

2. Apologists.

a. σῶμα is the animal "body" in Just. Dial., 31, 3; Athenag. Suppl., 20, 4, also carcass, Aristid. Apol., 5, 3. The human body is ref. to esp. in connection with weakness, sickness, or wounding, Just. Dial., 69, 7; Tat. Or. Graec., 2, 2; 3, 1; 16, 3; 32, 3. Man lives ἐν σώματι, Just. Apol., 19, 1 → 1043, 13 f. Ritual washings affect only the σάρξ and the σῶμα, Just. Dial., 14, 1 → 1057, 4; the second term seems to be added only because of established usage, → 1045, 26. If there is ref. to the uncircumcision of the body it is because there is a similar uncircumcision of the heart (→ 129, 28 ff.), Just. Dial., 29, 3. The sexual defilement of the body is mentioned along the lines of → 1046, 27 ff.; 1049, 21 ff. in Athenag. Suppl., 32, 3; 34, 1. The earth is a repository for corpses, Aristid. Apol., 4, 3. But bodies will be resurrected, [531] Athenag. Suppl., 36, 1 f.; Tat. Or. Graec., 6, 1,

---

[524] So J. A. Kleist, *The Epistles of St. Clement of Rome and St. Ignatius of Antioch* (1946), 94.
[525] So Bau Ign., *ad loc.*; cf. Mart. Pol., 17, 1; Eus. Hist. Eccl., V, 1, 23 f.
[526] On this Schlier Eph.[3], 268.
[527] Cf. the patriarch representing heavenly Israel → n. 316.
[528] Papias Fr., 6 also relates the creation story to Christ and the Church.
[529] Cf. the τέλειος ἄνθρωπος (Eph. 4:13) in Ign. Sm., 4, 2 and Schlier Corpus, 450, but also → 1054, 20 f.
[530] On the influence of the schema of head and body in the recapitulation doctrine of Iren. and in Aug. cf. Schlier Corpus, 451 f. The idea of the restoration of Adam is plainly adopted by Iren. (→ 1072, 5 ff.) and in Haer., III, 23, 7; V, 18, 2; 20, 2 κεφαλή has the sense of "Lord over . . . " In the important III, 19, 3 it is the tribal head and the tribe is the rest of the body → n. 618, 625. Here, too, in V, 17, 4 the cosmic Christ embraces both Jews and Gentiles, → 1078, 7 ff. In IV, 33, 7 the universal Church is the greater and more glorious body of Christ. Cf. God as *corpus lucidum et immensum* in Aug. Confessiones, 4, 16; cf. 5, 10; 7, 1; this goes back to → 1034, 25 f.
[531] On the Apologists and the doctrine of the resurrection of the body → 148, 19 ff. and Grant, 188-198. Grant shows why body is replaced by flesh, 125-130.

and this in such a way that a man gets back his own body, Just. Apol., 18, 6. The bodies of all men will have a part in the resurrection, *ibid.*, 52, 3. This shows that the resurrection is no longer tied so tightly to that of Jesus Christ → 1062, 22 ff. [532] This is esp. true when it is said that Plato knew of it already, Athenag. Suppl., 36, 2 f. [533] With the body one finds the skin in 24, and the σχῆμα in 20, 4 → 1027, 18 f. Just. Dial., 62, 3 combats the view that inferior angelic powers created the body rather than God, → 1052, 3 ff. If this opposes disparagement of the body, Athenag. Suppl., 36, 2 f. accepts the Platonic doctrine (→ 1028, 22 ff.) that ἀσώματα and νοητά are before σώματα and αἰσθητά. If heaven and the world share in σῶμα, this limits their share in the divine, 16, 3. Here, then, σῶμα means pure corporeality and can be par. to οὐσία in the sense of Aristot., Athenag. Suppl., 16, 2. Athenag. thus disputes the idea that the gods are σῶμα, [534] 20, 1-4; 22, 3. [535] For Tat. Or. Graec., 25, 2 as well God is obviously not σῶμα but ἀσώματος (→ 148, 22 ff.); on the other hand demons possess bodies (→ 148, 24 ff.) though they can be seen only by believers, 15, 3. [536] Division into σῶμα and ψυχή is already common. It is true that only the two together constitute man. Athenag. Suppl., 1, 4 interprets the twofold expression simply as body and life → 1058, 13 ff. There is also ref. to the irrational passions of the soul which the body follows, 36, 1 [537] → 1052, 3 ff. Just. App., 10, 1 stresses that Christ became body, logos and soul. The body is pure when the soul is free from wrong, Just. Dial., 14, 2 → 1057, 2 f. It thus forms the manifestation of the soul → 1039, 18; 1082, 11 ff. Both together come into judgment, Just. Apol., 8, 4 → 1050, 8 f.; 1082, 14 ff. The soul is the living force without which the body cannot exist, just as it cannot exist without the ζωτικὸν πνεῦμα, Dial., 6, 2. That animals can know God because they have a soul is rejected; their particular σῶμα prevents this, and the doctrine of transmigration (→ 1026, 25 ff.; 1090, 3 ff.) and of the imprisoning of the soul in animal bodies is mistaken, 4, 4-7. [538] Tat. Or. Graec., 13, 1 takes a different view. He still believes the soul dissolves with the body (→ n. 533), but it does not die in believers as it does in unbelievers; it is saved by the divine πνεῦμα and will rise again with the σῶμα which is its form of manifestation, 15, 1 f. → 148, 19 ff. Hence in 16, 1, though this is not in exact agreement with what has been said, he can speak of the immortal soul which is hampered by the parts of the body. [539]

Christologically σῶμα is far less common than σάρξ → 148, 2 ff. In the eucharistic sayings it is par. to αἷμα [540] in Just. Apol., 66, 3, σωματοποιήσασθαι in Dial., 70, 4 is

---

[532] Even Rev. 20 uses "resurrection" only in v. 5 f., though this strictly presupposes that there is a kind of resurrection of unbelievers in v. 12.

[533] Hipp. Ref., IX, 10, 6 even finds the resurrection of the flesh in Heracl. Fr., 63 (Diels, I, 164, 11). διαλυθῆναι (e.g., also Just. Apol., 19, 4; Tat. Or. Graec., 13, 1; Stob. Ecl.. I, 291, 5; → n. 597, 606; cf. Corp. Herm., 1, 24 and → 1043, 9 f.) and συστῆναι are tt.

[534] In 6, 3 f. it is ref. to as a thesis of Aristot. (→1031, 27 ff.; n. 126) that αἰθέριον is the σῶμα of God (so only Athenag.), while the λόγος which causes movement is the ψυχή, so that God is a ζῷον σύνθετον, → 1085, 2; 1035, 5 ff.; n. 618.

[535] The formulations here derive from philosophical usage → 1031, 10 ff. The passage shows the influence, not of Gnostic ideas, but of the Stoic concept of the material world (the εἴδη of the ὕλη) as the body of God.

[536] Cf. Cl. Al. Exc. Theod., 14, 1 - 15, 1, which also views angels and souls (→ 1091, 23 ff.) as σώματα in the sense of 1 C. 15:49; cf. 27, 1-3.

[537] *Ibid.*, 36, 1 non-Christians say the soul perishes with the body.

[538] Cf. Dial., 5, 2, where the opponent says souls came into being in and for themselves, not along with bodies.

[539] Cf. σωμασκία "exercise of the body" in 23, 1, also apocr. 3 C. 27. 32 → 147, 24 ff. and n. 374, cf. P. Bodmer, 10 (ed. M. Testuz [1959], 40), where 1 C. 15:37 is rendered by ἐγείρειν τὸ σῶμα τὸ βληθέν and the link with σῶμα, ὀστά and πνεῦμα of Christ guarantees the resurrection of the flesh.

[540] It is later said that by the formula or gesture of consecration the bread becomes Christ's body, cf. Ant. Christ., I (1929), 31 and 36.

a tt. for the incarnation. [541] Finally the σῶμα composed of different μέλη serves as a metaphor for the unity of the Church, Dial., 42, 3, [542] the cosmos in Tat. Or. Graec., 12, 2, or God in Athenag. Suppl., 8, 1 → n. 534. This shows that neither the concept of the body of Christ nor Gnostic ideas of the body of the Redeemer had any influence. The statement is purely metaphorical. [543]

c. Only in Just. Dial., 5, 2 is σῶμα an inorganic body, namely, the cosmos which is a σῶμα στερεόν and σύνθετον → 1035, 6 ff.

3. Gnosticism.

a. σῶμα alongside ψυχή, πνεῦμα.

Paul's insight that the body is the place where faith lives does not occur at all here. There are strata where the body is neutral and is not be judged negatively. [544] Thus in Corp. Herm., 10, 10 [545] the νοῦς, even though perception itself is incorporeal, uses the body as an instrument of knowledge → 1034, 8 f.; 1053, 8 f., since νοητά and ὑλικά penetrate into the body. [546] Acc. to Ev. Phil., [547] Saying 22 (104, 25 f.) the soul lives in the despised body and is more worthy, the body being defiled by sexual union, a reflection of the mystery of marriage, Saying 60 (112, 34-113, 1). [548] But the body of Christ's resurrection is perfect, 72 (116, 33), [549] and the Lord's Supper also purifies the body of the holy man, 108 (125, 3). [550] The resurrection teaching is closer to Paul than that of the official Church; there is resurrection in the flesh, but there is also change → 149, 15 f. [551] On the other hand the Valentinian Heracleon (Fr., 10) [552] states that body and soul

---

[541] Cf. Test. S. 6:7: ὁ θεὸς σῶμα λαβών; this is Chr., as against M. Philonenko, "Les interpolations chr. des Testaments des douze patriarches et les manuscrits de Qoumrân," RevHPhR, 39 (1959), 17. Cf. → n. 560, 612. Elsewhere the incarnation is linked to σάρξ, → 145, 12 ff.; 148, 1 ff. with n. 378.

[542] Fully par. to the Stoic understanding of the δῆμος or ἐκκλησία as a united whole → 1034, 31 ff. In Just. Dial., 39, 4 we find the image of the capture of the cosmos by the exalted Lord par. Eph. 4:8, but without the figure of the body.

[543] Caution in explaining NT vv. from the lit. of the 2nd cent. A.D. is urged by J. de Zwaan, "Some Remarks on the 'Church-idea' in the Second Century," Aux sources de la tradition chr., Festschr. f. M. Goguel (1950), 274 f. On the further history cf. A. Resch, "Agrapha," TU, NF, 15 (1906), 175; Tert. Marc., V, 19 (644); Virg. Vel., 2; De Monogamia, 13; Cl. Al. Strom., VII, 87, 3-88, 2; Orig. Comm. in Joh., 10, 36 (235-8) on 2:18 f.; Aug. Enarratio in Ps. 68, Sermo, 1, 11 (MPL, 36 [1861], 850); Eus. Theol. eccles., 3, 12 (MPG, 24 [1857], 1021 B); Thdrt. De Providentia, 5 (MPG, 83 [1864], 629); H. de Lubac, "Corpus Mysticum," Recherches de science religieuse, 29 (1939), 257-260.

[544] Act. Thom. 30, 67 ref. to the soul in the body, but presupposing that it leaves it.

[545] But → n. 600.

[546] 10:12 is neutral: Emptying of the veins and arteries is the death of the body, also 10:20. Cf. 2:14: all creatures apart from God are body and soul.

[547] Ed. P. Labib, Coptic Gnostic Pap. in the Coptic Mus. at Old Cairo, I (1956), 99, 29-134, 19; transl. H. M. Schenke, "Das Ev. nach Phil.," ThLZ, 84 (1959), 5-26.

[548] True marriage is thus spiritual. But this does not shed light on earthly marriage as in Eph. 5:22-33.

[549] Saying 82 (119, 8) is possibly ref. to the earthly body of Jesus.

[550] Par. in B. Gärtner, The Theology of the Gospel of Thomas (1961), 164 → 1057, 2 f. When 101 (123, 21) says living water is σῶμα one is reminded of → n. 77. But what follows speaks of the putting on of the living man, so it should be asked whether living water does not represent the new man who is put on like a σῶμα, → n. 381.

[551] Cf. R. McWilson, The Gospel of Philip (1962), 87-89 on Ev. Phil. Saying 23 (104, 26-34).

[552] Found in Orig. Comm. in Joh., 13, 60 (291, 34 ff.) on 4:46 ff.

come into hell acc. to Mt. 10:28, so that neither is immortal.[553] In the Ev. Veritatis[554] 23:31 and 26:8 speak of the body of Jesus which was begotten of the word of love.[555] Elsewhere there is ref. to the torn rags that Jesus put off when He put on immortality, 20:30-34, cf. 33:15-23.[556] In the Gospel of Thomas[557] the body for whose sake the spirit came into being is perhaps that of Jesus, Saying 29 (86, 33), cf. 28 (86, 22) → 149, n. 386.[558] Acc. to 56 (90, 31) and 80 (95, 13 f.) the world is a corpse (πτῶμα = σῶμα) and the world is not worthy of those who view it thus. There seems to be polemic against the bodily resurrection of Jesus in 71 (93, 34 f.).[559] On the body of Jesus among the Valentinians → 1091, 18 ff.[560] The Apocr. Joh.[561] takes a middle view. Acc. to 24:16 f. the spirit is not σωματικός, but it is also not without the σῶμα. In 48-55 we find the recurrent Gnostic description of the creation of Adam.[562] His body is adorned (50:5) and fashioned "suitably from(?) the host of angels," 50:12. It is, of course, only the inbreathed πνεῦμα of Gn. 2:7 which enables him to move,[563] 51:15-20 par. 52:20-53:4. He carries the souls of the seven powers in himself.[564] A second version speaks of the structure of matter, darkness, desire and anti-spirit as the chain and grave of the body, 55:3-11[565] → n. 572. In the newly found Nature of the Archons[566] the σῶμα formed by the archons is fashioned acc. to their own σῶμα and the image of God, 135, 26-33. This construct is psychic on the basis of Gn. 2:7a[567] but it cannot be set up by the archons. Only by a new intervention of the πνεῦμα does it become a living soul (Gn. 2:7b) 136:3-16 but → n. 374. This is

---

[553] This v. caused considerable discussion → 1058, 15; 1082, 14 f.; n. 582.

[554] Ed. and transl. M. Malinine, H. C. Puech, G. Quispel (1956), and Suppl. (1961).

[555] So also K. Grobel, *The Gospel of Truth* (1960), on 23:8 f.; σάρξ is avoided in 31:5 (→ 148, 39 ff.) because it suggests what God has rejected.

[556] Possibly the weak obstacles of 33:22 f. are earthly bodies, H. M. Schenke, *Die Herkunft d. sog. Ev. Veritatis* (1959), 49, n. 5a.

[557] Ed. and transl. A. Guillaumont, H. C. Puech, G. Quispel, W. Till, and Y. Abd al Masih (1959), cf. J. Leipoldt, "Ein neues Ev.?" ThLZ, 83 (1958), 481-496.

[558] Gärtner, *op. cit.* (→ n. 550), 194 f. takes this anthropologically: Such an idea is then dismissed as absurd. But anthropologically dependence on the body is bad in Saying 87 (96, 5): "Unhappy is the body which depends on a body" — perhaps a ref. to sex; what follows however: "and unhappy is the soul which depends on both," seems to presuppose that man has two bodies → n. 571, 582; also → 149, 18 ff.

[559] Gärtner, *op. cit.*, 172-4; cf. also 183-6 on Saying 35 (87, 20 ff.); 199 on the pre-existence of the soul, Saying 19 (84, 17 ff.).

[560] There are neutral ref. to the putting on of the body (→ n. 561) in Act. Thom. 143 and Mart. Andreae prius, 12 (ed. R. A. Lipsius and M. Bonnet, Acta Apost. Apocr. II, 1 [1959], 53, 16), but → 1090, 14 ff. The eucharistic body of Christ is viewed positively in Act. Thom. 49, 121, 158. Possibly the liturgical cry of the Marcosites in Iren. Haer., I, 21, 3: ἐν σώματι ἐβασίλευσας, also ref. to the earthly Jesus. ἡ τοῦ σώματος κοινωνία in 13:3 denotes sexual union with no special evaluation → 1040, 2 f.

[561] Gnostic works of the Coptic Pap. Berolinensis 8502 (ed. C. Till, TU, 60 [1955], 33-51, 78-193). Literary criticism in H. M. Schenke, "Nag-Hammadi Stud., I," Zschr. f. Religionsu. Geistesgesch., 14 (1962), 57-63.

[562] K. Rudolph, "Ein Grundtyp gnostischer Urmensch-Adam-Spekulation," Zschr. f. Religions- u. Geistesgesch., 9 (1957), 1-20; J. Doresse, *Les livres secrets des gnostiques d'Egypte* (1958), 217-225. On Cl. Al. Exc. Theod., 50-67 → n. 572, 582-585. On this passage Schenke, 35 f.; Brandenburger, *op. cit.*, 89-92; Gärtner, *op. cit.*, 188 f. On its background → 1053, 34 ff.

[563] This constantly recurring feature shows that the πνεῦμα is originally the breath of life of Gn. 2:7 changed under the influence of the development depicted → 1093, 10 ff.

[564] Cf. Corp. Herm., 1, 16.

[565] Brandenburger, 91 f.; cf. the formula "whole body" in 50:5, 12, cf. also 49:18.

[566] Ed. Labib, *op. cit.* (→ n. 547), 134, 20-145, 23, H. M. Schenke, "Das Wesen d. Archonten," ThLZ, 83 (1958), 661-670.

[567] Cf. the Coptic Gnostic work (no title) ed. Labib, 147, 33 f., transl. H. M. Schenke, "Vom Ursprung d. Welt. Eine titellose Abh. aus dem Funde von Nag-Hamadi," ThLZ, 84 (1959), 243-256.

developed in the Naassene Sermon in Hipp. Ref., V, 7, 2-9. [568] Adam's creation is depicted in the usual way, but he is an image of the perfect man above, Adamas, *ibid.*, V, 7, 6-8. These ideas are not unambiguous. On the one hand the true bi-sexual man [569] lives in every man, [570] only by error represented as τρισώματος, V, 8, 4. [571] Something of the higher primal man is set in the χοϊκόν, [572] the construct of λήθη, V, 7, 30 and 36. [573] On the other hand, because of this forgetting, the pneumatic man, [574] who is proper to the primal man and ὁμοούσιος with him in all things, arises only with regeneration [575] or ascension, [576] V, 8, 10 and 17 f. Only this can save the perfect man who is fashioned from above, V, 8, 21. [577] In this myth true man is completely separated from σῶμα. [578] The lower creation is mortal, that which is begotten from above is immortal. [579] It is deliverance from the streams, from the moist substance of generation and birth, and from fire, the desire for generation and birth; for the body is the grave of real man, V, 8, 16 and 22. [580] It is made of quarrelsome στοιχεῖα and is thus the place of constant battle, V, 8, 19. The son born of a virgin (Is. 7:14), however, is a blessed aeon, V, 8, 45. [581] In the redaction one finds the figure of the reconciliation of the nations as the establishment of cosmic peace (→ n. 487), an echo of Eph. 2:17 except that the opposites are ὑλικοί or χοϊκοί and πνευματικοί or τέλειοι rather than the Gentiles and Israel, V, 8, 22. We find something similar in the Valentinians. From hylic and devilish matter the demiurge creates bodies for souls. Acc. to Gn. 2:7, however, the inner psychic man lives in this hylic σῶμα. This earthly body is simply a dwelling for the soul and demons, but also for the λόγοι that come from above. The inner man is not somatic, [582] Hipp. Ref., VI, 34, 4-7. Unlike men created after the pattern of Adam, Jesus is the new man whose physical form is created

---

[568] Cf. Schenke, 57-60; Brandenburger, 83-89; H. Schlier, *Der Mensch im Gnostizismus*, op. cit., 60-76; P. Pokorny, "σῶμα Χριστοῦ im Eph.", *Ev. Theol.*, 20 (1960), 460-2, though his par. to Eph. are doubtful or derive from gen. Hell. motifs. For literary crit. cf. R. Reitzenstein and H. H. Schaeder, *Stud. zum antiken Synkretismus aus Iran u. Griechenland* (1926), 161-173.

[569] Cf. Festugière, III, 43-51; → 1088, 12 f.; n. 455.

[570] Cf. ἄνθρωπος ἐν ἀνθρώπῳ in Cl. Al. Exc. Theod., 51, 1 → n. 582.

[571] The redactor pts. to the threefold nature of the universe, Hipp. Ref., V, 8, 1-4 → n. 572. Cf. the δίσωμος and hence δίγνωμος Edem in the Book of Baruch, *ibid.*; V, 26, 1 f.

[572] On this cf. Cl. Al. Exc. Theod., 55, 1, where Adam, having been clothed with 3 incorporeal forms, is clothed with a 4th, the earthly, the garments of skin (→ n. 331); cf. C. H. Dodd, *The Bible and the Greeks* (1954), 191-4.

[573] Hipp. Ref., V, 8, 14 says the εἶδος which comes from above, from Adamas, is not perceived by any in the χοϊκὸν πλάσμα. The Chr. editor sees a ref. to Christ, V, 7, 33. Cf. further Thomas-Ps. 13:16, ed. C. R. C. Allberry, *A Manichaean Psalm-Book*, II (1938), 218, 25 f.: The treasure of the living is entrusted to bodies.

[574] Cf. the ἔσω ἄνθρωπος πνευματικὸς ἐν τῷ ψυχικῷ of the Basilidians, Hipp. Ref., VII, 27, 6 → n. 582.

[575] Cf. already Philo → 1053, 28 ff.

[576] The flowing down of the pneumatics from Adamas corresponds to this, V, 8, 41.

[577] Reitzenstein, op. cit. (→ n. 568), 169 conjectures a μή before τέλειος, but against this cf. Schenke, 58. Cf. Hipp. Ref., V, 8, 22. 24. 37.

[578] Elsewhere the perfect man can also be σῶμα, cf. Doresse, op. cit., 241; → n. 570; II, 37, 19.

[579] The redactor equates the σῶμα with Egypt, marked off by the Jordan, which was first made passable by Jesus (= Joshua), *ibid.*, V, 7, 41 → 1089, 19.

[580] The redaction even expounds Mt. 7:6 as an admonition against sexual intercourse, the work of swine and dogs, 7, 33. Jn. 5:28 is taken to ref. to the raising of regenerate pneumatics from earthly bodies, 8, 23.

[581] Redaction: neither psychic nor somatic.

[582] Acc. to Cl. Al. Exc. Theod., 51, 2 (→ n. 570) there is a psychic body which is simply the hylic soul encircling the divine soul → n. 574. It is the body of the elect soul in which the male seed, the discharge of the angelic element, was laid, 2, 1. Mt. 10:28 is saying that only this body will be cast into hell, → n. 553.

by the demiurge but whose essence is fashioned by Sophia, [583] VI, 35, 4 [584] → 1091, 12 ff. Acc. to Iren. Haer., I, 5, 6 there also dwells unknown in the ὑλικὸν σῶμα the κύημα (fruit) of the mother. [585] The soul is from the demiurge, the body from the earth and the flesh from ὕλη, but the pneumatic man is from the mother, Achamoth or Sophia, from whose sorrow at her abandonment [586] all σωματικὰ στοιχεῖα arose, 4, 2. [587] This leads to the familiar trichotomy of the pneumatic (the φύσει σῳζόμενον), the middle psychic, and the hylic which is dedicated to destruction, 6, 1; cf. Cl. Al. Exc. Theod., 56, 3 [588] → VI, 395, 9 ff. This cannot receive salvation. [589] In Cl. Al. Exc. Theod., 67, 1 Paul's σάρξ is interpreted as σῶμα; Paul already lives in some sense outside the body; this provides access for wicked forces, 73, 1. Along this line baptism alters only the soul, not the body, 77, 2. [590] But in this connection cf. also Corp. Herm., 1. [591] Here, too, the νοῦς which lives in man but is also outside (1, 6) is male-female, 1, 9 (→ 1087, 3 f.). It makes man in its image and like itself, 1, 12. It unites with divine-like φύσις, 1, 14. This then creates σώματα after the image of the Ἄνθρωπος, [592] receiving the πνεῦμα from the aether. Thus man is a dual being, ψυχή and νοῦς, 1, 17, [593] mortal in virtue of his σῶμα, immortal in virtue of the οὐσιώδης ἄνθρωπος, [594] subject to heimarmene, a slave within harmony, though deriving from above it, 1, 15. From darkness is moisture and from this the σῶμα, which lives in the αἰσθητὸς κόσμος, 1, 20 → 435, 6 f. Hence one must slay the senses and the works of the body [595] even before the body is delivered up to its own death, 1, 22. [596, 597] If this hylic body is dissolved (→ n. 533), the body itself is changed

---

[583] Ibid., 53, 2. 5. Festugière, II, 547-551; IV, 220-224.

[584] The Italic branch, Heracleon and Ptolemy, speaks of a ψυχικόν, the oriental of a πνευματικὸν σῶμα of Jesus, VI, 35, 6 f. → 1090, 12 ff.

[585] The par. Cl. Al. Exc. Theod., 53, 2 calls it the σπέρμα πνευματικόν sown in the soul of Adam.

[586] The alien character of the soul may be seen also in the Naassene Sermon in Hipp. Ref., V, 10, 2 and Pist. Soph., 32, 32-5.

[587] Cf. the account of the creation of σώματα from ἀσώματα, 4, 5; 5, 2; 46, 1 f.

[588] Cf. the 3 classes Cl. Al. Exc. Theod., 54; 56, 3 f. → VI, 395, 11 ff. For the earlier history → 1041, 6 ff.; 1052, 17 ff. but → n. 611.

[589] Cf. Iren. Haer., I, 21, 4: For some Valentinians redemption is neither somatic (φθαρτὸν γὰρ τὸ σῶμα) nor psychic but pneumatic and being ἀσώματον it should not be mediated by somatic practices like baptism or the sacral bridal chamber.

[590] But → 1084, 18 f. In Cl. Al. Exc. Theod., 85, 3 body and soul denote the whole man. On the psychic body → n. 582. Cf. also Act. Verc. 8, 339r: The original man is chained with a corporeal fetter (par. concupiscentia) by the devil. In Orig. Comm. in Joh., 1, 17 (21, 13-15) on 1:1 the dragon symbolises ὕλη καὶ σῶμα.

[591] Schenke, 44-8: Brandenburger, op. cit. (→ n. 343), 93-5; cf. Haenchen, op. cit. (→ n. 51), 149-191; Pokorny (→ n. 568), 462 f.; cf. Corp. Herm., 13; Festugière, III, 200-210.

[592] One may still glimpse here the Jewish background acc. to which the body is God's image, cf. Schenke, 48, so Iren. Haer., V, 6, 1 and esp. the Audians, who even deduce from this God's corporeality, Epiph. Haer., 70, 2, 4 f. For details cf. Schenke, 135-8.

[593] Another tradition is interpolated in 1, 16 f., cf. Haenchen, op. cit., 175 f.

[594] Cf. Ascl., 7 f.; cf. → 1054, 3 f.

[595] In keeping is the idea that the sleep of the body, i.e., the suppression of the senses (Haenchen, op. cit., 186) is the waking of the soul and leads to θεόπνους (→ VI, 454, 5 ff.) γενέσθαι, 1, 30 → n. 600.

[596] Only the body is subject to death, cf. Haenchen, op. cit., 179, n. 1.

[597] Cf. τοῦ σώματος ἐξιέναι, 10, 16. Only in the earthly body which is subject to suffering are νοῦς, ψυχή and πνεῦμα united in such a way that the one is a cover for the other, 10, 16 f. But if the νοῦς leaves this, it puts on its fiery robe, 10, 16. 18. Acc. to 9, 7 the σώματα of living creatures consist of ὕλη, cf. 8, 3, where all material bodies are girt around by immortality (heaven?). On the meaning of σωματοποιέω in 7, 8 → n. 291, cf. Sagnard, op. cit. (→ n. 508), 243 f. with par. Acc. to Stob. Ecl., I, 291, 3-13 the demiurge is ἐν σώματι and hence he creates διάλυτα (→ n. 533) and θνητὰ σώματα, while there are also immortal σώματα made of incorporeal οὐσία, Acc. to Corp. Herm.; 2, 4. 6 it is from the stars that forces come down into mortal bodies, cf. 3, 21; 4, 5; in 2, 6 f. there is adjustment to Aristotelian teaching (→ n. 534): Time, place and movement are for the sake of the body, and forces cannot exist without bodies, though the soul can.

(→ 1085, 19 f.) and its senses return to their origin, 1, 24. In keeping is the doctrine of regeneration in which a man leaves himself, passes into an ἀθάνατον σῶμα [598] and becomes ἐν νῷ, [599] because the eyes of the body (→ line 19) cannot see God, 13, 3 → 1052, 34 f.; 1053, 8 ff. [600] Only the incorporeal is true, 13, 6. [601] The inner man is shut up in the prison of the body, 13, 7; [602] once the bodily senses cease, therefore, deity is born, 13, 7. How strongly here σῶμα is the corporeal and not just the human body may be seen in 13, 13, acc. to which regeneration is ceasing to think in the category of the three-dimensional σῶμα. The new σῶμα consists of forces and is quite different from the αἰσθητὸν τῆς φύσεως σῶμα, 13, 14. If the new transcendent thing is here called τόπος, [603] Corp. Herm., 2, 2-6; cf. 2, 8 f. 12 describes God as ἀσώματος τόπος (→ 1055, 29 f.) in which the world finds itself as the greatest σῶμα which has within it all σώματα, e.g., air, 2, 11 → 1054, 16 f. [604] The body is viewed quite negatively by the Manichaeans, → 153, 3 ff. Made by sin and furnished with senses Kephalaia, 56 (p. 141) [605] it is the seat of sin, 56 (p. 143, 22 f.) and is disrupted by demons, so that the elect leaves it, 9 (p. 41, 15 f.). [606] Yet he receives a new body clothed in robes of light, 75 (p. 181, 11. 16 f.); 88 (p. 220, 6 f.). [607] In Act Phil., 144 there is prayer for the transfiguring of the μορφή of the body into angelic glory. In the newly discovered writings the body is the prison and tomb of the soul → 1053, 37 ff. [608] It is the essence of desires, the lust for carnal union, symbolised by the Jordan → n. 579. Thus only the ears of the heart, not those of the body (→ 1089,

---

[598] There is a σῶμα ἐκ δυνάμεων συνεστός in 13, 14; on this Festugière, III, 153-8. This is again the individual body, whose substance is described. The use is not collective. Cf. the fiery body which the dead person receives, 10, 16 → n. 597.

[599] This hardly means more than Rev. 4:2. One cannot find here the idea of the νοῦς as a σῶμα which envelopes pneumatics, cf. Pokorny, op. cit. (→ n. 568), 463, n. 21.

[600] Corp. Herm., 1, 30; 7, 2. Similarly 10, 5 f. (→ IV, 757, 17 ff.) describes how man leaves the body in sleep. So long as the soul is in the body it cannot be divinised, 10, 6. It is hindered by bodily πάθη, serves the body, and carries it like a burden, 10, 8. Hence the soul of a child, which has only a small body, is purer, 10, 15. The relation of body and soul is quantitative, 10, 11. For a traditional positive evaluation → 1085, 11 ff.

[601] Cf. Stob. Ecl., I, 275, 18: Nothing true is in the body, everything is without falsehood in the incorporeal.

[602] Acc. to Corp. Herm., 7, 1 the soul is shut up in the body. This is a chain, a living death, a visible corpse, a robber, 7, 2 (→ 1053, 37 ff.), a clinging garment, 7. 3. Par. in H. Lewy, Sobria Ebrietas (1929), 87; A. Adam, "Die Ps. d. Thomas u. das Perlenlied als Zeugnisse vorchr. Gnosis," Beih. z. ZNW, 24 (1959), 66.

[603] Also the σῶμα τέλειον, Preis. Zaub., I, 4, 495 (→ II, 37, 33 f.). On this Brandenburger, op. cit., 79, n. 1; 81, n. 4; 146 f.; E. Peterson, "Die Befreiung Adams aus d. ἀνάγκη," Frühkirche, Judt. u. Gnosis (1959), 110.

[604] The doctrine of the cosmos as God's Son (→ 1030, 1 f.; n. 338) occurs in Corp. Herm., 9, 8; 10, 14.

[605] Kephalaia, Manich. Hdschr. d. staatlichen Museen Berlin, ed. I. Ibscher, I (1940).

[606] On the earthly body cf. also 32 (p. 85, 27), 90 (p. 227, 20), cf. 83 (p. 200, 10-12) and E. Waldschmidt and W. Lentz, "Die Stellung Jesu im Manichäismus," AAB, 1926, 4 (1926), 47, 25-45; 100, 19a-102, 30d; 112, II, 1a-113, II, 5b; → 150, 5 ff., 16 ff. Acc. to Titus Bostrensis Adv. Manichaeos, I, 13. 23 (MPG, 18 [1857], 1085. 1100) Mani regards the body as wicked, as ὕλη, but the soul as good. In the Manich. Homilies, MSS of the A. Chester Beatty Collection (ed. H. J. Polotsky [1934]), 11, 6; 44, 19 f. the body of Jesus seems to be neutral, however, even though it is dissolved (→ n. 533), 54, 17. The body of man is abandoned, 5, 18; 75, 13 f., but destruction seems to await spirits too, 7. 14 f. For a negative evaluation cf. also M. Boyce, The Manich. Hymn-Cycles in Parthian, London Oriental Series, 3 (1954), Huwidagman, 4a 7 f.; 7, 22; Angad Rošnan, 1, 3; 7, 7; 8, 5.

[607] Cf. Boyce, op. cit. Huwidagman, 1, 23. 32; 5c 1; 6c 4. 11 f.; Angad Rošnan, 3c 13; 6, 9; 8, 4.

[608] Doresse, op. cit. (→ n. 562), 234. Cf. the metaphor of the oyster and its shell (→ 1028, 3 f.) which keeps recurring, Doresse, 209.

3 f.), can truly hear. 609 The forces of the body are the works of perverted demon. 610 Thus the soul separates itself from the body of darkness and leaves it in ecstasy. 611

The idea of transmigration is a common one → 1026, 26 ff. Here the body is a prison. as in the Carpocratians, Iren. Haer., I, 25, 4; Hipp. Ref., VII, 32, 4, in Basilides, 612 and in the Corp. Herm., 2, 17. 613 We also read of the incarnation of Helena, who wanders from body to body, Iren. Haer., I, 23, 2. Here the body is simply the place where the non-corporeal may be seen. Her partner Simon, in descending, simply accommodated himself to the beings of this sphere without becoming like them; hence he only seemed to suffer in Judaea, I, 23, 3. Similarly Jesus at His crucifixion left the body of the Edem, the psychic and earthly man, 614 Hipp. Ref., V, 26, 31 f. In Basilides Christ is the incorporeal *virtus* and *nous* of the Father; hence the man who preaches His crucifixion is still enslaved to body-creating forces, Iren. Haer., I, 24, 4. Acc. to Hipp. Ref., VII, 27, 10, however, the disciples of Basilides divide up Christ: His σωματικὸν μέρος suffered but each of the other parts reached its own sphere. 615 For the Valentinians, too, the incarnation and death of Jesus were a difficult problem which they tried to solve by conjecturing a psychic body (→ n. 584), Cl. Al. Exc. Theod., 59, 3-60, 1; 61, 6 f. 616 Act. Phil., 141 speaks of the ὁμοιότης σώματος which the ἀσώματος Redeemer bore to redeem the σώματα τῆς ἁμαρτίας. Formulations like Act. Joh. 103 go furthest; this says that Jesus became man without the body, cf. also Kephalaia (→ n. 605), 1 (p. 12, 21-24), which ref. to Christ's coming in the πνευματικόν and in the σῶμα, yet also without the σῶμα. Ev. Phil. offers a different solution → 1085, 16 ff.

b. σῶμα in the Sense of the Body Embracing the Redeemed.

In this sense σῶμα occurs for certain before Mani (→ 1092, 25 ff.; 1093, 28 ff.) only in Pauline works, → 1082, 31 ff.; 1084, 32 ff. 617 Corp. Herm., 4, 1 f. is to be regarded as

---

609 Doresse, *op. cit.*, 238. Cf. also Ptolem. Brief an die Flora, 3, 11-13, ed. A. Harnack, KIT, 9² (1912); What must be circumcised is not the somatic foreskin but that of the heart (→ 129, 28 ff.); pneumatic fasting rather than somatic is required. Cf. also Act. Thom. 53 and 143; Jesus is really seen not with carnal eyes (those of the σῶμα) but with the eyes of the soul (i.e., in faith).

610 Doresse, 244.

611 *Ibid.*, 170, 172: Reason remains behind in the body (but → 1043, 12 ff.). Cf. Ps. Clem. Hom., 2, 26, 1-4: By magic Simon separates the soul of a child from the body and uses it to make a man by the compressing of air.

612 Orig. in Ep. ad Romanos, 5, 1 (MPG, 14 [1857], 549). In both the last passages μετενσωμάτωσις → n. 541. Cf. further W. Foerster, "Das System d. Basilides," NTSt, 9 (1962/63), 247.

613 Cf. also Kephalaia (→ n. 605), 91 (p. 228, 6-23).

614 Here ψυχή and πνεῦμα are contrasted; the former is earthly. In fact the Gnostic protest was not just against the material, cf. Haenchen, *op. cit.*, 143; but → 1093, 10 ff.

615 When the Valentinian Fr. of Heracleon (Orig. Comm. in Joh., 6, 60 [168, 28 ff.] on 1:29) distinguishes the body of Jesus from being in the body, does it have something similar in view? Cf. Cl. Al. Exc. Theod., 47, 2: The demiurge brings forth the psychic Christ.

616 Cf. the body of light in the anon. older Gnostic work, ed. C. Schmidt and W. Till, *Kpt.-Gnost. Schriften*, GCS, 45 (1954), 347, 5 ff. and in the Manichaeans, Waldschmidt and Lentz, *op. cit.* (→ n. 606), 47, 16-20; 113, III, 5a-b; 115, 5-13; 116, 14-19, also the bodies of law, *ibid.*, 98, 10b and n. 10; 107, 55a-59d and n. 5; 109, 71a-d (also found in Buddhism, Chant. de la Saussaye, II, 125). In the anon. Gnostic work Jesus is Head (→ n. 625) of all immortal bodies, 9 (347, 11 f.) and for His sake resurrection is granted to bodies. Cf. the bodiless members from which man arose, 2 (337, 27 f.) and the bodiless spirits to whom prayer is made, 20 (361, 22).

617 H. Schlier, *Christus u. d. Kirche im Eph.* (1930), 43; Schlier Eph.³, 94.

dependent on the ref. → 1037, 7 ff. when it understands the world [618] as the body of God. → 1089, 9 ff. is also purely cosmic. The correspondence of microcosm and macrocosm occurs in Kephalaia, 60 (p. 151, 9); 70 (p. 169, 24-26; 170, 17). The ancient Gnostic work (→ n. 616), 17 (358, 36 ff.) offers only an apparent par.: "Thou hast borne and created them (sc. the hidden worlds) in thine ἀσώματον σῶμα; for thou hast begotten man in thine αὐτοφυὴς νοῦς and διάνοια and perfect thought." The incorporeal body is in fact the νοῦς which conceives creation, exactly as in → 1054, 33 ff. [619] Possibly later Jewish ref. to the body of Adam (→ 1051, 1 ff.) are a fusion of the idea of the tribal head and speculations on the micro-macrocosm, unless they are meant to rival Chr. statements which had become strongly syncretistic → 1054, 26 ff.; 1075, 5 ff.

Though σῶμα is not used, the discussions in Cl. Al. Exc. Theod. (→ 1087, 17 ff.) are close to what is meant by the σῶμα Χριστοῦ. [620] Here the Redeemer when He comes down assumes pneumatic seed as His σαρκίον [621] and then returns it to the Father after His death, 1, 1 f.; 59, 1; 62, 3. [622] With this pneumatic element which is "in Him" He also saves the Church which is ὁμοούσιος therewith, 58, 1; for Jesus, Church and Sophia are mixed together to form a unity, 17, 1. [623] One can thus say that the visible element in Jesus is Sophia or the Church of the upper σπέρματα or their angels, 26, 1; 35, 1. The hardest text is 42, 2 ff. It is plain that on the cross Jesus carries the σπέρματα on His shoulders into the pleroma, but the saying ἦρεν οὖν τὸ σῶμα τοῦ Ἰησοῦ, ὅπερ ὁμοούσιον ἦν τῇ ἐκκλησίᾳ is obscure. One might simply relate it to the incarnation: Christ bore the earthly body of Jesus in order to be like the community. [624] This idea agrees well with the myth as a whole. But this body is obviously identical with what is elsewhere called σαρκίον. Hence the likeness is not just external. Christ is really enveloped by the seeds or angels to whom the elect on earth correspond and with whom they are to be united "as members with members in unity," 22, 3. The question is then whether ἦρεν is to be related to the incarnation or the resurrection, i.e., whether the ref. is to the assuming and bearing of the earthly body or the lifting up of the pneumatic body into the pleroma. The context and the choice of verb favour the second view. [625] But this is a completely

---

[618] Or God's creative activity as in 14, 7? → 1033, 6 ff. But cf. 2, 2: The cosmos is the supreme body, 11, 19: Heaven is the ἔσχατον σῶμα, cf. Stob. Ecl., I, 194, 7-10 → n. 603. In Corp. Herm., 8, 3 τὸ πᾶν σῶμα is the cosmos as in → 1054, 19. If in Basilides acc. to Hipp. Ref., VII, 23, 3 the μέγας ἄρχων is the κεφαλή (→ n. 625) τοῦ κόσμου, acc. to → 1076, 17 ff. all that is said is that this is the power which fashions and guides it. If his greater son is in Aristot. fashion his soul or entelechy, VII, 24, 1 (→ n. 534), the σῶμα permeated by the son is the ineffable God (VII, 24, 2) who as Head of the cosmos Himself is the cosmos → 1038, 14 ff.; 1044, 4 f.

[619] When the older Gnostic work (→ n. 616), 16 (357, 17. 24) says that "in him are all bodies" it simply means all the elements of the world are in the first-born son (as was said also of Adam in this period → 1050, 31 ff.).

[620] Cf. Sagnard, op. cit., 547-561, esp. 559 f., also 387-415. 501 f.

[621] The body is often called a robe → n. 313.

[622] In the last passage, however, the pneumatic element resides in the bones of Jesus, so that the idea of the robe or body is not strictly applied.

[623] Stoic tt. (→ 1034, 2 ff.), cf. F. M. M. Sagnard, Extraits de Théodote (1948), 216; G. Verbeke, L'évolution de la doctrine du Pneuma du stoicisme à S. Augustin (1945), 64-66. σώματα thus denotes the three bodies, which are thoroughly intermingled without losing their separate qualities.

[624] So R. P. Casey, "The Excerpta ex Theodoto of Cl. of Alex.," Studies and Documents, I (1934), 19 f. 22. 136.

[625] Acc. to 42, 2 Christ is κεφαλή while Jesus (or the cross? cf. Daniélou, op. cit. [→ n. 448], 296) represents the shoulders of the σπέρμα. The head is clearly related to the body, though in its own way → 1041, 29 ff.; III, 678, 7 ff. In Kephalaia (→ n. 605), 64 (p. 157 f.) as in Mandaean works (→ III, 678, 27 ff.) Adam is the head of the race or of all creation → n. 530, 616, 618. Meuzelaar, 167 thus understands the ref. as a combination of Christ as Head of the race of pneumatics and the NT body of Jesus in a metaphorical sense.

isolated use of σῶμα in place of the more common σαρκίον, which does not contain the idea of the embracing organism but only that of the externally visible garment. The Redeemer does not embrace the Church. He puts on the corresponding angels as His garment → 1083, 15 ff. Thus the whole work rests on the law of the communication of the heavenly σπέρματα or angels with the pneumatics on earth → VI, 394, 2 ff. In the background are statements about heavenly angels which decide for the nations or individuals assigned to them. [626] There is also the view of the *sophia* which the Revealer brings to those who have forgotten that something of the divine *sophia* is also given to them → 1072, 7 ff. Strictly the redeemed are thus μέρη of the angels, not the Redeemer. [627]

On the borders of Gnosticism is Pantaenus, the Stoic who became a Christian, Cl. Al. Ecl. Proph., 56, 1-4. Like others he reads σῶμα for σκήνωμα in ψ 18:5 and he ref. this to the Church of believers, obviously in the churchly NT sense. In the first instance he himself takes ἓν σῶμα in Stoic fashion simply as ἑνότης, but then (on the basis of 1 C. 12:14 ff.?) he interprets the various members as the different positions. That the entire Church acc. to ψ 18:5 dwells in the sun corresponds to an ancient view. [628] The Ophites, Valentians and Sethians have a different view of Christ receiving and being enriched by departed souls, while Yaldabaoth is concerned until the consummation is reached with the full assembling of the cable of the spirit of light, Iren. Haer., I, 30, 14. Here the image of the growth of the body of Christ in the earthly Church (→ 1078, 15 ff.) is transferred to the heavenly sphere; the rivalry of Church and Synagogue also plays a part. Materially related is the "perfect man" in Hegemonius Acta Archelai, 8, 7, [629] the pillar of light full of souls which are purified. But here again it is just that the thought of the Redeemer providing access for souls to heaven is vividly depicted in a common metaphor. [630] Pist. Soph., 98, 241 f.; 100, 252-101, 254; [631] Od. Sol. 17:15, [632] perhaps also Act. Joh. 100 may be echoes of Chr. statements. [633] What is meant by τὸ πᾶν τοῦ κατελθόντος ... μέλος in Act. Joh. 100 is not really clear, perhaps "each member of the descended Redeemer." There is expressed here the widespread concept of the eschatological gathering of the scattered members of God's people, possibly fused with Hellen. myths. [634] The same is true of Kephalaia (→ n. 605), 84 (p. 204, 5-8. 13-16); 88 (p. 220, 6-8); 90 (p. 227, 19-24). The Church here lies in the σάρξ of humanity in the sense of → 1082, 21 ff.; 150, 3 ff.,

---

626 Cf. Philo Op. Mund., 117; Da. 10:13, 20 f.; Asc. Is. 7:10; Schlier Eph.[3], 130 f.; G. Quispel, "La conception de l'homme dans la gnose valentinienne," *Eranos-Jbch.*, 15 (1947), 263.

627 They are baptised for them (Cl. Al. Exc. Theod., 22, 1) and are thus substitutes rather than consubstantial or even identical → VI, 394, n. 366. The σῶμα of the κύριος in the non-Valentinian Excerptum, 27 (Casey, *op. cit.*, 9 f.) is to be taken purely individually as in → n. 582. As the earthly body is a body for the soul (27, 1), so the soul is a body for the power (27, 3), i.e., for the Lord who becomes man θεοφόρος (27, 6). Cf. Hegermann, 57, n. 2.

628 Plut. Fac. Lun., 30 (II, 945c); but cf. Schweizer, *op. cit.* (→ n. 472), 153, n. 592. On this whole question v. Casey, *op. cit.*, 12 f.

629 Ed. C. H. Beeson, GCS, 16 (1906).

630 Descending souls had long been seen in the dust of the sun's rays, and later ascending souls; cf. F. Cumont, *Astrology and Religion among the Greeks and Romans* (1912), 188. Identification of the universe with an ἄνθρωπος may be seen in Hipp. Ref., VII, 12, 1 f. → 1029, 12 ff.; 1032, 4 ff.

631 Perhaps Graeco-Roman ideas of the cosmos as a divine body had some influence here.

632 In 3, 2, however, the ref. is to the body of the bridegroom.

633 So also Pokorny, *op. cit.*, 459. It is gen. accepted that mixed Platonic, Stoic and Jewish ideas quite unconnected with the other thoughts have often been adopted as an alien element in Gnostic works. Are the isolated reminiscences of Paul, which are found only in Chr. Gnosis, to be judged differently and regarded as pre-Chr.?

634 Cf. Zech. 2:10; Mk. 13:27; Did., 9, 4; many par. in V. Taylor, *The Gospel acc. to St. Mark* (1952) on 13:27, cf. Oepke Gottesvolk, 226. Perhaps the Osiris myth (T. Hopfner, *Plut. über Is. u. Osiris,* I [1940], 17, cf. 9) or Dionysus myth (Cornut. Theol. Graec., 30 [62, 15]) had some influence → 1036, 16 ff.; so G. Quispel, Review of C. Schmidt, *Kpt.-gnost. Schr.,* ThLZ, 81 (1956), 686; cf. also Waldschmidt-Lentz, *op. cit.* (→ n. 606), 106, 52a-d → VI, 487, 12; 488, 6 ff.; 489, 12 f.; 492, 20 ff.

cf. → 1089, 13 ff. In Epiph. Haer., 26, 13, 2 f. a similar statement is made about the individual soul rather than the Redeemer. [635] Then in Kephalaia, 38 (p. 89-102) the idea of the cosmos as macroanthropos is linked with Chr. and ultimately Iranian ideas, 89, 23. If some Gnostics speak of a gigantic invisible Christ whose size is known exactly, [636] the ref. is simply to His universal saving significance → 1049, 33 ff.; 1051, 2 ff.; 1071, 8 f. and n. 343.

c. Summary.

Definitive assessment is hardly possible until the new finds are published. In so far as the body is regarded as a prison or tomb or alien country for the soul, we simply have the influence of the Orphic-Platonic view → 1053, 37 ff. That the body is left at death or in ecstasy is also Hell. → 1043, 12 ff. It is clear, however, that along the lines of later Jewish development (→ VI, 390, 22 ff.; 391, 30 ff.; 396, 2 ff. and esp. → 1052, 17 ff.) Gnosticism increasingly views body and soul together as the human-earthly aspect, [637] over against which is a divine deposit → n. 588. As already in early impulses in Jewish Wisdom lit. (→ 1072, 7 ff.) this is consubstantial with heavenly *sophia*, which returns to the earth in the Revealer. More than this, namely, the equation of the Primal Man — Redeemer with the redeemed, is not to be found even in the Iranian-Manichaean texts. [638] Above all, however, one must divide the various clusters of motifs. The figure of wisdom as mediator between God and the world, which is influenced by the Elephantine pap. and Isis concepts (→ 489, 33 ff.; 498, 3 ff.), is equated in Hell. Judaism with the *logos* understood in terms of OT and Stoic roots [639] and combined with the idea of the universal God who represents, permeates and controls the cosmic body. This is central in Philo (→ 1054, 27 ff.) and Col. 1:15-20 (→ 1075, 9 ff.) but at most it is connected only very loosely with the concept of the first man. [640] Along a second line non-Jewish accounts of a divine first man, which were used in Ez. 28:12 ff., lead in later Judaism and syncretism to a theology which attempts to put everything in terms of anthropology. [641] Then in early Gnosticism, on the basis of speculations about Gn. 1:27 and 2:7, this produces the statement that the supreme God, as the model on which man was created, is "man." Prior to Manichaeism, however, this is never linked with the Iranian myth of the Primal Man and the dismembering and redeeming of his body. [642] On the one side, then, the derivation of man from the supreme God as his model is extremely important. On the other side, under Platonic influence (→ 1028, 28 ff.) and along the lines of contemporary movements, temporal ideas are transformed into spatial (→ 1072, 14 ff.) and the model becomes the eternal idea "man." In both versions real man is far above the concrete man trapped in matter or in the earthly generally, in the body-soul. The man of regeneration is like him

---

[635] συνέλεξα τὰ μέλη τὰ διεσκορπισμένα cf. Hennecke[3], I, 195. Is man dissipating himself here in lusts and vices along the lines of Col. 3:5, cf. Test. R. 3 (→ 135, n. 284)? On an individual understanding cf. also → n. 603.

[636] Cf. Epiph. Haer., 30, 17, 6 f.; 29, 4, 1; Hipp. Ref., IX, 13, 2. Christ is presented as δύναμις. The Holy Spirit stands alongside Him as a female entity of the same size.

[637] For the growing together of body and soul cf. Festugière, III, 7, n. 3.

[638] C. Colpe, "Die gnostische Gestalt d. erlösten Erlösers," *Der Islam*, 32 (1957), 208-210; Colpe, 172-187; also *Die religionsgeschichtliche Schule*, I (1961), 171-193, esp. 175, 179 f., 185 f. For older research cf. the survey in G. Widengren, *Stand u. Aufgabe d. iranischen Religionsgeschichte* (1955).

[639] Schweizer, *op. cit.* (→ n. 472), 99 f. and n. 650; cf. H. Donner, "Die religionsgeschichtlichen Ursprünge v. Prv. 8," *Zschr. f. ägypt. Sprache u. Altertumskunde*, 82 (1958), 8-18.

[640] Hegermann, 201 f.

[641] Schweizer Homologumena, 274-283; cf. also Hipp. Ref., V, 8, 38 in the Naassene Sermon: The beginning of perfection is the knowledge of man, while the knowledge of God is completed perfection. Cf. Slav. En. 44:1: He who despises the face of man despises the face of the Lord.

[642] Schenke, 69-71, 108 f.; C. Colpe, Art. "Manichäismus," RGG[3], IV, 720 f.

→ 1053, 28 ff.; I, 673, 1 ff. [643] The rise of evil, which is Gk. fashion is explained by cosmogony as a fall of the spiritual into matter, which is repeated individually in the fall of the soul into the body, has to be reinterpreted in Jewish fashion by anthropogony as a fall into sin and death. The two lines intersect. The bibl. account of the creation of man is united with non-bibl. cosmogonies and becomes the myth of the fall of the divine man, though the divine deposit remains embodied in him as the vital force remains in the bibl. Adam. [644] In Hell. style his fall is no longer disobedience; it is a forgetting of the divine element in him. Thus the Revealer is regarded as the One who by bringing this story to light reminds man of his divine part and thus opens the way to redemption. The very isolated ref. to an idea analogous to the body of Christ are found only in Chr. Gnosticism except in so far as they are purely cosmic or simply describe unity. Possible Pauline formulations have an effect here in much weakened form as attempts are made to express the thought that in the Redeemer there comes to man the same divine wisdom as that of which he bears a particle within him. In the Valentinians, of course, the Chr. doctrine of grace also has a strong influence, i.e., the insight that the Redeemer is not just the Revealer but that He really accomplishes the salvation of the redeemed, their access to the Father, → VI, 394, n. 368.

Schweizer

---

† σωρεύω, † ἐπισωρεύω

A. The Word Group in the Greek World.

1. σωρεύω occurs in Gk. lit. only from Aristot., though through σώρευμα it may also be presupposed at Xenoph. Cyrop., VII, 1, 32. It is comparatively rare. The verb does not occur at all in inscr. or pap. It derives from the noun ὁ σωρός, which is found from Hes. Op., 778, is common in the pap., and means "heap". [1] The verb is thus an action verb for building up a heap. The basic meaning is "to pile," "to pile on," "to heap up." The basic ὁ σωρός is used esp. for piles of grain, Theocr. Idyll., 7, 155; σωρὸς σίτου, Hdt., I, 22, 1; Xenoph. Hist. Graec., IV, 4, 12, gen. "multitude," plenitude" χρημάτων, κακῶν, ἀγαθῶν, Aristoph. Pl., 269, 270, 804. The verb is used in 2 ways: a. "to heap on," one thing on another trans. with simple acc. obj. πολλοὺς τῶν πολεμίων νεκροὺς σωρεύσας, Diod. S., 12, 62, 5; σωρεύων πανταχόθεν τὸν πλοῦτον, 1, 62, 5, cf. 5, 46, 5; with acc. obj. and prepos. expression: ἅπαντες γάρ, ὅταν ὑπάρχῃ τι, πρὸς τοῦτο σωρεύειν εἰώθασιν, Aristot. Rhet., II, 15, p. 1390b, 17f.; σωρεύσας δὲ ἐπὶ τοῦ κοσκίνου (sieve) τὰ τεθλιμμένα, Diosc. Mat. Med., IV, 150; ἄλλον ἐπ' ἄλλῳ σωρεύειν ἀεὶ πλοῦτον, Luc. Epigrammata, 12, 5 f. In the pass.: τὸ σωρευόμενον

---

[643] Festugière, IV, 211-218; Nilsson, II² (1961), 687-693.

[644] Already in later Judaism we once find free will or the divine deposit → VI, 390, 22 ff.; 391, 30 ff.

σωρεύω κτλ. Bibl.: Pape, Pass., Liddell-Scott, v. Arnim, Index, Hatch-Redp., Moult.-Mill., Pr.-Bauer, s.v. On C.: J. R. Linder, "R. 12:20," ThStKr, 35 (1862), 568 f.; E. v. Dobschütz, Review of F. Ll. Griffith's *Stories of the High Priests of Memphis* (1900) in ThLZ, 26 (1901), 283 f.; A. Wright, "'Coals of Fire upon his Head,'" *Interpreter*, 16 (1920), 159; E. J. Roberts, "'Coals of Fire upon his Head,'" *Interpreter*, 16 (1920), 239; A. T. Fryer, "'Coals of Fire,'" Exp. T., 36 (1925), 478; Str.-B., III, 301-3; S. Bartstra, "Kolen Vuurs hoopen op iemands Hoofd," *Nieuw Theologisch Tijdschr.*, 23 (1934), 61-8; S. Morenz, "Feurige Kohlen auf dem Haupt," ThLZ, 78 (1953), 187-192; Mi. R.¹², 311, n. 1.

[1] σωρός etym. from * tu͞o-rós (cf. σῶμα from * tu͞o-mn̥?), root * teu, tu͞o 'to swell," cf. Boisacq, Hofmann, s.v.

μέγεθος sc. τῶν στοιχείων, Aristot. Gen. Corr., I, 8, p. 325b, 22; διὰ τοῦ πλήθους τῆς σωρευομένης γῆς, Polyb., 16, 11, 4; and with prepos. expression: χοῦ τε τῆς γῆς μετρίως ἐς αὐτὰ σωρευθέντος, Herodian. Hist., VIII, 4, 4, b. "To heap up," "fill up" (a place) with something τοὺς αἰγιαλοὺς ... σεσωρευμένους ἀναμὶξ πάντων τῶν προειρημένων (sc. νεκρῶν), Polyb., 16, 8, 9; λιβάνῳ ... τοὺς βωμοὺς ἐσώρευσε, Herodian. Hist., IV, 8, 9; στέμμασι σωρεύσας αὐχένας, Anth. Graec., 7, 233 (Apollonidas). There is in profane Gk. no instance of a personal use in the transf. sense.

2. The compound ἐπισωρεύω "to heap on to" is found from the 1st/2nd cent. A.D. It is used for the excessive heaping up of business ἓν ἐξ ἑνὸς ἐπισεσώρευκεν, Epict. Diss., I, 10, 5, overloading with difficulties μὴ ἐπισώρευε τὰς ... ἀμηχανίας Plut. De vitando aere alieno, 6 (II, 830a), with acc. of thing and dat. of pers. τὰ πολλῷ χρόνῳ (καὶ) καμάτῳ ἐπισωρεύοντα τοῖς ἀνθρώποις τὴν παρὰ τούτων ἐνέργειαν, Vett. Val., IX, 1 (332, 24), with acc. and dat. of obj. of the adding of further examples to those already given, Athen., 3, 97 (123e).

B. The Word Group in Hellenistic Judaism.

1. In the LXX one finds the verb σωρεύω only at Prv. 25:22; Jdt. 15:11. As in secular Gk. the main word ὁ σωρός is much more common (9 times). This is used for the Hbr. noun גַּל "heap of stones," Jos. 7:26; 8:29; 2 Βασ. 18:17, or עֲרֵמָה "pile of fruit," 2 Ch. 31:6-9, or גָּדִישׁ "burial mound," Job 21:32 vl. [2] The verb occurs in Prv. 25:22: ἄνθρακας πυρὸς σωρεύσεις (Lat. prunas congregabis) ἐπὶ τὴν κεφαλὴν αὐτοῦ for Hb. חתה "to heap up (coals of fire)," for which other Gk. words (αἴρω Is. 30:14; ἀποδέω Prv. 6:27) are used elsewhere. [3] The constr. ἐπί with acc. corresponds to the πρός or εἰς with acc. attested in Gk. → 1094, 32; 1095, 5. The metaphor of fiery coals גֶּחָלִים or אֵשׁ גַּחֲלֵי (Tg. גּוּמְרֵי דְּנוּרָא) as distinct from פֶּחָם black coals denotes "judgment," 2 S. 22:9, 13; Ps. 18:8, 12; 140:11 or a painful and consuming process, Prv. 6:28; Job 41:13. But in Prv. 25:22 the context demands a meaning in bonam partem. The figure of speech means that the wise man will repay evil to his enemy by good. The idea of heaping coals of fire on the head of another [4] occurs only here in the OT. [5] Behind it there probably lies the symbolic act of

---

[2] In 4 Macc. 9:20 ὁ σωρὸς τῆς ἀνθρακιᾶς has no Hbr. equivalent. In other transl. σωρός occurs another 12 times, Hatch-Redp., s.v.

[3] In Ex. 15:8 LXX reads διέστη τὸ ὕδωρ for נֵעֶרְמוּ מַיִם "the waters dammed up," while Ἀ, Σ and Θ have ἐσωρεύθη τὸ ὕδωρ (Ἀλλ: ἐθημωνιάσθη).

[4] Cf. the Assyr. punishment: "Bitumen is to be poured on her head (the harlot's)," Altassyr. Gesetze, 96 (AOT, 418). In 6 Esr. 2:54 (= 4 Esr. 16:54) burning coals on the head of an impenitent sinner are a symbol of unfailing divine judgment, cf. v. 68 f.

[5] The Rabb. mostly use the expression in quotations of Prv. 25:21 f. For "Yahweh will repay it thee" they read with the Targum "Yahweh will hand him over to thee" or "Yahweh will make him thy friend," Midr. Prv., 21 (49b) on 25:22. They thus take the saying about fiery coals in a missionary sense for the convincing and winning over of enemies by friendly conduct, cf. D. Daube, The NT and Rabbinic Judaism (1956), 338 f., 343. The expression also has a positive sense when the one who hates is seen as the evil impulse, as is often the case, e.g., S. Dt., 45 on 11:18. Eating and drinking with the bread and water of the Torah hold the evil impulse in rein "and Yahweh will give thee peace" AbRNat, 16 (6a) or "Yahweh will reconcile it with thee" bSukka, 52a. When the expression is used apart from Prv. 25:22 the fire mostly signifies judgment → VI, 936, 19 ff. One sees this from the parable of R. Berechiah (c. 340 A.D.) about the baker standing by the oven door: "His enemy came, he took coals of fire from it and heaped them on his head (וְחָתָה גֶחָלִים וְנָתַן עַל רֹאשׁוֹ). His friend came, he took out warm bread and gave it him." The exposition which follows shows plainly that the coals of fire are meant here as a punishment: "The coals of fire and the bread, both came from the (same) oven; similarly God caused fire to fall (from heaven) on the Sodomites and manna to fall from heaven on the Israelites, v. Ex. 16:4," Tanch. בשלח 20 (Buber, 33b), cf. Str.-B., III, 302 f. Prv. 25:22 is not quoted in the Dead Sea Scrolls.

conversion mentioned in the demotic story of Seton Chaemwese whereby a guilty person carries glowing coals of wood (on a bed of ashes) in a brazier on his head → VI, 945, 2 ff. and n. 86. [6] Egyptian influence is also suggested by the fact that "the north wind brings rain" in Prv. 25:23a fits Egypt rather than Palestine. In Jdt. 15:11 we find the common secular constr. (→ 1094, 32 f.) σωρεύω τι ἐπί τινος: Judith packed the loot from Holofernes' tent on her chariot.

The compound ἐπισωρεύω does not occur in the LXX. Σ has it in Job 14:17 for the "storing up" of sin (HT טָפַל "to daub or plaster over"; LXX ἐπισημαίνω) and Cant. 2:4, where he obviously read וְרִגְרוּ, for covering over with love (HT וְדִגְלוֹ עָלַי אַהֲבָה; [7] LXX τάξατε ἐπ' ἐμὲ ἀγάπην).

2. The group does not occur in Philo. [8] Joseph. uses σωρεύω lit. for the heaping up of bones on the king's table, Ant., 12, 211 and pass. for heaped up corpses νεκροὶ ... ἐσωρεύοντο in Bell. 4, 380; νεκροὺς σεσωρευμένους, Bell., 6, 431.

C. The Word Group in the New Testament.

1. The simple σωρεύω occurs in the NT only twice in Epistles. The basic ὁ σωρός is never used. Paul in R. 12:20 quotes Prv. 25:21 f. (→ 1095, 20 ff.); there is a slight deviation in v. 21, [9] but v. 22 is quoted lit. from the LXX. The ἀλλά clause in R. 12:20 sets in contrast to a negative refraining from vengeance the positive demand to overcome evil with good, v. 21. The structure makes it plain that the metaphor of heaping coals of fire on an adversary's head refers to the vanquishing of his hostility by acts of love → 1095, n. 5 and VI, 945, 2 ff. In 2 Tm. 3:6 the pass. σωρεύομαι "to be filled to overflowing with something" (→ 1095, 5 ff.) is used in a transf. sense of persons. The false teachers creep into houses and ensnare esp. γυναικάρια [10] σεσωρευμένα ἁμαρτίαις, dubious women "laden with sins" [11] and driven by all kinds of desires.

2. The compound ἐπισωρεύω occurs only once in the NT at 2 Tm. 4:3 in a transf. sense with acc. of person. In the imminent time of apostasy self-satisfied men will "collect teachers in masses" according to their own wishes. The element of heaping together ironically stresses the superficiality of their desire for knowledge. [12]

D. The Post-Apostolic Fathers.

In the post-apost. fathers we find only the compound ἐπισωρεύω, which is used once with a material dat. obj. in Barn., 4, 6. Here the readers are warned not to increase their sins by accepting the doctrine that God's covenant embraces both Jews and Christians. Here the verb means "to add new sins in great number to those already there."

---

[6] Chaemwese must bring back the magic book of Noferkaptah which had been stolen from the tomb, with a forked staff in his hand and a brazier of coals of fire on his head, Morenz, 189, cf. E. Brunner-Traut, Altägypt. Märchen (1963), 171-192, esp. 185.

[7] From דָּגֵל "flag" or better דִּגֵל "to hold the standard high."

[8] We simply find in Eus. Praep. Ev., 8, 14, 62 a passage from Philo De Providentia: ἐν γὰρ μυχοῖς σεσώρευται φορυτός καὶ σκυβάλων πλῆθος.

[9] Rahlfs reads τρέφε and conjectures that R. 12:20 has influenced the reading ψώμιζε in Cod B.

[10] The diminutive has a contemptuous ring here, cf. Bl.-Debr., 111, 3.

[11] "The result of their previous life," Schl. Past., ad loc.

[12] The prep. ἐπι- is not meant to express the relation to proponents of sound doctrine (cf. Wbg. Past., ad loc.) but is simply a strengthening, cf. B. Weiss, Die Briefe Pauli an Tm. u. Tt., Kritisch-exeget. Komm. über d. NT, 11⁷ (1902), ad loc.; Schwyzer, II, 466.

> † σώφρων, † σωφρονέω,
> † σωφρονίζω, † σωφρονισμός,
>   † σωφροσύνη

---

† σώφρων, † σωφρονέω, † σωφροσύνη.

Contents: A. The Word Group in Greek: 1. Etymology, Occurrence and Meaning; 2. σωφροσύνη in the Greek Hellenistic World. B. The Word Group in the Septuagint and Hellenistic Judaism. C. The Word Group in the New Testament and the Post-Apostolic Fathers. D. The Early Church.

A. The Word Group in Greek.

1. Etymology, Occurrence and Meaning.

σώφρων, contracted from Hom. σαόφρων (so also later in poets, cf. IG, II/III² 3, 1 [1935], 3632, 11; 3753), means first "of sound (σάος, σῶς, σῶος)¹ mind" (φρένες), Hom. Od., 23, 13. 30 has the abstract σαοφροσύνη = σωφροσύνη ² and from the 5th cent. B.C. we find the verb σωφρονέω, Aesch. Prom., 982; Pers., 829; Hdt., III, 35, 2. Etym. is no gt. help and can easily lead to misunderstanding of the group. It should be noted that transl. of this group which is so characteristic of Gk. thought is almost impossible. Lexicographically one can only describe its meaning by certain catchwords. It denotes a. "the rational" in the sense of what is intellectually sound (opp. μανία), Xenoph. Mem., I, 1, 16; Plat. Prot., 323b; Phaedr., 244a; Plat. Resp., I, 331c. ³ It then denotes b. "rational" without illusion, Thuc., I, 80, 2; III, 43, 5. It can also mean c. "rational" in the sense of purposeful, Thuc., VI, 6, 2. Another sense is d. "discretion" in the sense of moderation and self-control, Thrasymachus Fr., 1 (Diels, II, 323, 7); Plat. Resp., IV, 430e; Plat. Phaed., 68c; Plat. Symp., 196c; Diog. L., III, 91; cf. 4 Macc. 1:3. Again, it may mean e. "discretion" as prudent reserve, Thuc., I, 32, 4. Another sense is f. "modesty" and decorum, Eur. Iph. Aul., 1159; Plat. Leg., VI, 784e; Dio Chrys. Or., 15, 4; Stob. Ecl., IV, 588, 17 - 593, 11. ⁴ Then there is g. "discretion" as discipline and

---

σ ώ φ ρ ω ν κ τ λ . Bibl.: Liddell-Scott, Pass., Pr.-Bauer, Preisigke Wört., Thes. Steph., s.v.: F. Dirlmeier, "Apollon. Gott u. Erzieher d. hell. Adels," ARW, 36 (1939), 279-285: The oldest accounts of σωφροσύνη in the Iliad as proclaimed by Apollos himself; also Aristot.'s Nik. Ethik (1956), 347-350; R. Hirzel, "Über den Unterschied d. δικαιοσύνη u. d. σωφροσύνη in der platonischen Republik," Herm., 8 (1874), 379-411; O. Knuth, Quaestiones de notione τῆς σωφροσύνης platonica criticae (1874); A. Kollmann, Sophrosyne, Diss. Vienna (1939), extract in Wiener Stud., 59 (1941), 12-34; K. F. Nägelsbach, Nachhom. Theologie (1857), 227-318; E. Schwartz, Ethik d. Griechen, ed. W. Richter (1951), 54-6, 231; G. Türk, Art. "Sophrosyne," Pauly-W., 3a (1929), 1106 f.; T. G. Tuckey, Plato's Charmides (1951), 18-95; A. Vögtle, "Die Tugend- u. Lasterkataloge im NT," NTAbh, 16, 4-5 (1936), Index, s.v.; G. J. de Vries, "σωφροσύνη en grec class.," Mnemosyne, 11 (1943), 81-101; E. Weitlich, Quae fuerit vocis sophrosyne vis atque natura apud antiquos Graecos ad Platonem, Diss. Göttingen (1922).
¹ On σάος, σῶς cf. M. Leumann, "Μνήμης χάριν," Kl. Schriften (1959), 266-272.
² U. Wyss, Die Wörter auf -σύνη in ihrer histor. Entwicklung, Diss. Zurich (1954), 20 f. Acc. to Wyss poetic terms like σωφροσύνη passed by way of elegy into the vocabulary of the Sophists and then into prose gen., 60 f.
³ On the oxymoron Μανία σώφρων cf. H. Lewy, "Sobria Ebrietas," Beih. z. ZNW, 9 (1929), 52.
⁴ Cf. the funerary inscr. for women, J. Pargoire, "Inscr. d'Héraclée du Pont," BCH, 22 (1898), 496; G. Cousin, "Inscr. de Termessos de Pisidie," BCH, 23 (1899), 301; G. Mendel, "Inscr. de Bithynie," BCH, 25 (1901), 88; cf. also Vögtle, 91 f.; G. Delling, "Paulus' Stellung zu Frau u. Ehe," BWANT, NF, 5 (1929), 18. Acc. to Stob. Ecl., IV, 454, 15 f. σωφροσύνη is control of lusts and desires, cf. 4 Macc. 1:31.

order politically, Thuc., III, 37, 3; VIII, 64, 5, also h. as "wisdom" as opp. to, e.g., ἄβουλος, Hdt., III, 71, 3, cf. esp. σοφίην... σωφρόνως, IV, 77, 1, also Thuc., I, 79, 2; IV, 18, 4. The σώφρων is also contrasted with the ἄφρων and νήπιος in Theogn., 431, 483, 497, 665.

2. σωφροσύνη in the Greek Hellenistic World.

This attempt to establish the chief meaning of the group has not really embraced its main content in class. and post-class. Gk. The difficulty of precise transl. in many passages makes it imperative to try to grasp more accurately the basic meaning. [5] Already in class. lit. we find attempts at definition, e.g., Plat. Charm., 159-176, which often hark back to the pre-philosophical understanding, ibid., 161b, 164b, cf. Heracl. Fr., 116 (Diels, I, 176, 12). [6] The ref in σωφροσύνη is to a basic attitude which alone makes possible certain concrete modes of conduct and in which these continue to have their root. [7] What kind of an attitude this is may be seen already in the one instance of the group in Hom. Il. There Apollo refuses to fight with Poseidon his uncle: ἐννοσίγαι᾽, οὐκ ἄν με σαόφρονα μυθήσαιο ἔμμεναι, εἰ δὴ σοί γε βροτῶν ἕνεκα πτολεμίξω δειλῶν..., 21, 462-4. The reason given is: αἴδετο γάρ ῥα πατροκασιγνήτοιο μιγήμεναι ἐν παλάμῃσι, 21, 468 f. If Apollo as σώφρων does not accept battle, it is on the basic of his αἰδώς. This connection with αἰδώς is constitutive for σωφροσύνη. [8] Proper conduct rooted in αἰδώς is marked by restraint or modesty expressed primarily in relation to someone else. Cf. Hom. Od., 4, 158: When Telemachos comes to Menelaos he does not dare to speak. The reason: ἀλλὰ σαόφρων ἐστί, νεμεσσᾶται δ᾽ἐνὶ θυμῷ. Here νέμεσις, which is complementary to αἰδώς, leads to the modest restraint. [9] The fact that σωφροσύνη embraces modesty and restraint may also be seen in the fact that it is an anton. of ὕβρις, Plat. Resp., III, 399b. [10] It is in ὕβρις against the gods that man oversteps the boundaries which are set for him and which he ought to know and observe, Aesch. Pers., 820, 825, 827; Soph. Ai., 118-133. [11] The gods come to earth to test men for ὕβρις and εὐνομία, Hom. Od., 17, 485-7. [12] Thus σωφροσύνη can be called ἡ Εὐσεβίης γείτων, Critias Fr., 6, 22 (Diels, II, 379, 14). [13] Life in the divinely established order of the polis is included in proper conduct vis-à-vis the gods. [14] Only as σώφρων can man live in the given order; with δικαιοσύνη, σωφροσύνη is thus the main πολιτικὴ ἀρετή which every citizen must have a part in, Plat. Prot., 323a.

σωφροσύνη, then, is very early demanded of man. It is attested gnomically in the seven sages; Pittacus Fr., 13 (Diels, I, 64, 18), cf. Plat. Prot., 343a-b; [15] Democr. Fr., 210,

---

[5] So Weitlich, 2: σωφροσύνη vere Graeca virtus est, quae neque Germanico nec Latino uno nomine sigificari potest. Cf. H. Gauss, Philosophischer Handkomm. zu den Dialogen, Plat., I, 2 (1954), 94.

[6] These def., of course, restrict the meaning. Plat. Charm., 159-176 saw this.

[7] Nägelsbach, 32 speaks of a "basic virtue." Kollmann, 22 finds in the individual modes of conduct "effects and manifestations of sophrosyne."

[8] Cf. also Thuc., I, 84, 3: αἰδὼς σωφροσύνης πλεῖστον μετέχει, furthermore Plat. Charm., 160e; Leg., II, 665e. On the Kleidemos stele in the Athenian cemetery before the Dipylon (middle of the 4th cent. B.C.) we read: πότνια σωφροσύνη, θύγατερ μεγαλόφρονος Αἰδοῦς, Katolog d. Skulpturen zu Athen, 3334, ed. L. Sybel (1881), 240; Türk, 1106. Here there are other examples of personified Sophrosyne → I, 169, 38 ff.

[9] On the connection between αἰδώς and νέμεσις cf. Hes. Op., 197-200; on this cf. Dirlmeier Apollon, 284; K. Kerényi, Die antike Religion² (1952), 90-97.

[10] Cf. Theogn., 379, 754; Aesch. Pers., 829-831; Nägelsbach, 231.

[11] In Soph. Ai., 118-133 Athene shows Odysseus how hubris ends in madness: τοὺς δὲ σώφρονας θεοὶ φιλοῦσιν καὶ στυγοῦσιν τοὺς κακούς, 132 f.

[12] Hubris can be avoided by recognising the might and superiority of the gods, cf. on this U. v. Wilamowitz-Moellendorff, Der Glaube d. Hellenen, II (1932), 123.

[13] Cf. Soph. El., 307 f., 464 f.; Isoc. Or., 8, 63; Türk, 1106 f.

[14] Cf. Xenoph. Mem., IV, 3, 16 and the Protagoras myth, Plat. Prot., 322c; Nägelsbach, 231.

[15] On the sayings on the porch of the temple at Delphi (Μηδὲν ἄγαν — Γνῶθι σαυτόν) cf. Plat. Prot., 343b; Charm., 164-165a, v. also U. v. Wilamowitz-Moellendorff, op. cit., II, 123.

211 (Diels, II, 188, 3-6); Fr., 54 (II, 157, 5); Fr. 208 (187, 16); Fr., 294 (II, 206, 12); Fr., 67 (II, 158, 17). In pre-philosophic days σωφροσύνη is already a constituent part of the canon of cardinal virtues. [16] Its central significance esp. for an aristocratic mode of life may be seen in Theogn., 431, 453 f., 483, 497, 665, 699-701, 753-756. [17] It is already part of the common legacy of the Attic tragedians, Aesch. Ag., 351, 1664; Sept. c. Theb., 568, 610; Eum., 136; Soph. Ai., 586, 677; 1259; 1264 f.; El., 365; Eur. Med., 635; Hipp., 1365; Iph. Aul., 544. [18] The oldest known def. seems to come from the ancient aristocratic ethic; it runs: τὰ ἑαυτοῦ πράττειν, Plat. Charm., 161b. This def. can be expounded in different ways. [19] Another def. is gnomic in origin: γνῶθι σαυτόν, Plat. Charm., 164d; cf. Heracl. Fr., 116 (Diels, I, 176, 12); Ps.-Plat. Amat., 138a. Plat. adopts an "etym." explanation in Crat., 411e: σωφροσύνη is the σωτηρία ("keeping") of φρόνησις. [20] Yet, as Charm., 159-176 shows, Plat. did not fix on any one def. He accepts those commonly given (Charm., 160e, 161b, 164b d; Crat., 411e), but all of them prove too narrow in the question as to the nature of σωφροσύνη, so that any attempts at def. ends negatively: Our concern in respect of σωφροσύνη is not with the knowledge of something but with the knowledge of knowledge itself. For Plato, however, this knowledge cannot be without content (Charm., 172c), so that it is impossible to give a final def. of σωφροσύνη. [21] In the Platonic tradition discussion of σωφροσύνη remained important in the framework of the anthropologically grounded doctrine of the state, Plat. Resp., IV, 427d-434c. Man's being is controlled by the relation of the parts of the soul to one another. Special virtues attach to the individual parts: σοφία to the λογιστικόν, cf. IV, 428a-429a; 439d; 441c-d, ἀνδρεία to the θυμοειδές, cf. IV, 429a-430c; 440e-441e; 442b-c. The third part, the ἐπιθυμητικόν, has no specific virtue, for σωφροσύνη, which is properly appropriate to it, has the task of leaving leadership to the leading part, the λογιστικόν, IV, 442c-d. [22] Plato's idea of society corresponds to the picture of the human soul. In analogy to the three parts of the soul there is made up of three classes: the ἄρχοντες, the φύλακες and the γεωργοὶ καὶ δημιουργοί, → lines 18 ff. σωφροσύνη is the agreement of these three classes as to who should rule, IV, 430d-432a. It is reached by the restraint of the lower classes which makes it possible for each part to do its own job, IV, 433a-434c. [23] τὰ ἑαυτοῦ πράττειν itself is then δικαιοσύνη, IV, 433b. The Platonic tradition then understood σωφροσύνη as a virtue of restraint in respect of the ἐπιθυμητικόν: σώφρων ὁ μετρίας ἐπιθυμίας ἔχων, Ps.-Plat. Def., 415d, and in this regard it could appeal to Plat., cf. Leg., IV, 710a; 717d; Resp., IV, 430e; Symp., 196c. The following statements are important for Plat. The σώφρων is friendly with deity, for he is like deity, Leg., IV, 716d. Where gt. power, reason and σωφροσύνη meet we have the premises for the best constitution and laws, Leg., IV, 712a. Aristot. follows Plat. when he sees in σωφροσύνη the μεσότης between licence and stupidity, Eth. Eud., II, 3, p. 1221a, 2, cf. Plat. Resp., III, 399b. σωφροσύνη relates to the ἐπιθυμητικόν, Topica, V, 8, p. 138b, 2-5. Thus it is only one of the various μεσότητες, which in Eth. Nic., III, 8-18 are defined in terms of the true mean, III, 13, p. 1117b, 23-15, p. 1119b, 18. [24] As in the case of bravery women have less σωφροσύνη, Aristot. Pol., III, 4, p. 1277b, 21-25.

In Stoicism and popular philosophy σωφροσύνη occurs esp. as one of the cardinal virtues

---

[16] The oldest example is Aesch. Sept. c. Theb., 610. But the cardinal virtues go back to the 6th cent. B.C.; cf. R. Harder, *Eigenart d. Griechen. Einführung in d. griech. Kultur* (1962), 154; Schwartz, 52-56.

[17] Cf. Weitlich, 10. In Thuc., VIII, 53, 3; 64, 5 the group again reflects the political consciousness of the aristocracy [Krämer].

[18] For a good survey of the material cf. de Vries, 85-88; also Kollmann, 20-26; Wyss, *op. cit.* (→ n. 2), 41 and 66.

[19] Original meaning: to act as the situation demands [Dihle]. Cf. the def.: τὰ δέοντα πράττειν, Plat. Charm., 164b.

[20] This def. is also used by Aristot. in Eth. Nic., VI, 5, p. 1140b, 11-12.

[21] Gauss, *op. cit.*, 102.

[22] Hirzel, 379-411.

[23] P. Friedländer, *Platon,* III² (1960), 88-92.

[24] For σωφροσύνη in Aristot. cf. Dirlmeier Aristoteles, 347-350.

which are an established and central part of ethical teaching. [25] By way of Hell. Judaism (→ lines 25 ff.) these had an influence in the early Church, → 1103, 31 ff. The pt. of the cardinal virtues is to relate the perceived unity of virtue to the many manifestations worked out in the ethical traditions. [26] All virtues have a single goal: ὁμολογουμένως τῇ φύσει ζῆν. [27] In detail σωφροσύνη can be called ἐπιστήμη αἱρετῶν καὶ φευκτῶν καὶ οὐδετέρων, Stob. Ecl., II, 59, 8 f. [28] The cardinal virtues are sub-divided to bring man under the schema of virtue in concrete situations. Τὸ σωφροσύνη belong εὐταξία, κοσμιότης, αἰδημοσύνη, ἐγκράτεια, Stob. Ecl., II, 60, 20 f. In popular philosophy with its practical ethical purpose there arise extended lists of virtues and vices on the basis of the cardinal virtues. Here, too, σωφροσύνη has an established place. [29] In the pictures of sovereigns it is one of the virtues of the ruler, Muson. Fr., 8 (33, 7-39, 13); cf. Phil. Vit. Mos., I, 152-154; Dio Chrys. Or., 3, 7 and 10. [30] It is also a basic requirement in professional life, Onosander Strategicus, [31] 1, 1; Soranus Gynaecia, I, 1, 3 - 2, 4. [32] Though woman is not man's equal in virtue (Aristot. Pol., III, 4, p. 1277b, 21-25, cf. Muson. Fr., 3 [10, 10-14]), σωφροσύνη is one of her special virtues, Plut. Praec. Coniug., 9 f. (II, 139c). 17 (II, 140c); Amat., 21 (II, 767e). 23 (II, 769b); cf. in the inscr. CIG, I, 2, 1452 and 1453; II, 1, 2384. [33] Here σωφροσύνη is understood esp. as the restraint and control of sexual desires; [34] it thus takes on the sense of "chastity," → 1097, 25 f. But the way was prepared for this sense much earlier. Thus in Eur. one finds a noteworthy restriction to sexual moderation in Med., 635; Hipp., 1365; Iph. Aul., 544 and 1159. The word probably acquired this narrow sense quite soon esp. in popular usage, cf. Anth. Graec., 8, 31; 9, 132 and 166; 10, 56. [35] But the broad sense lived on in the philosophical tradition, as may be seen from its use in Plot. Enn., I, 6, 6. In contemplation man should work on himself until he sees σωφροσύνη, which already has a transcendent character as "virtue," I, 6, 9.

B. The Word Group in the Septuagint and Hellenistic Judaism.

1. If one seeks a Hbr. equivalent, the main candidate is מוּסָר, which is esp. common in Prv. and which LXX almost always renders παιδεία, → V, 604, 30 ff. The LXX saw the profound distinction between מוּסָר and the concept of σωφροσύνη which was so widespread in popular Hell. philosophy, and it thus avoided this Gk. word and its derivates. In the discipline denoted by מוּסָר the issue is not moderation or modesty on the basis of correct self-evaluation but the work of the teacher, whether father in e.g., Prv. 1:8; 15:5; 19:20 or God in, e.g., Dt. 11:2; Is. 26:16; Jer. 30:14; Prv. 15:10. Only in texts extant in Gk. alone or giving clear evidence of Hell. influence do we find the group. In Wis. 9:11 the cardinal virtues σωφροσύνη, φρόνησις and δικαιοσύνη are brought into association and traced back to the wisdom which lives with God in symbiosis (8:3 f.). In 4 Macc., properly a

---

[25] E.g., in Zeno, cf. Plut. Stoic. Rep., 7 (II, 1034c) and v. Arnim Fr., 255-294 (III, 59-72).

[26] F. Überweg, Grundriss d. Gesch. d. Philosophie, I: "Die Philosophie des Altertums," ed. K. Praechter[13] (1953), 427 f.

[27] Acc. to Diog. L., VII, 87 Zeno in περὶ ἀνθρώπου φύσεως proposed ὁμολογουμένως τῇ φύσει ζῆν as the goal of right action, cf. Praechter, op. cit., 426; M. Pohlenz, Die Stoa (1948), 126 and 203.

[28] Cf. also v. Arnim Fr., 265-280 (III, 65-9) for a collection of examples, similarly A. Bonhöffer, Epict. u. d. Stoa (1890), 254.

[29] J. Stelzenberger, Die Beziehungen d. frühchr. Sittenlehre zur Ethik d. Stoa (1933), 439 f.; Wendland Hell. Kultur, 84; Vögtle, 62-73, 136. Cf. also Muson. Fr., 17 (90, 7 f.), 9 (50, 10 f.), 11 (60, 17 f.); Epict. Fr., 14, 3; Ceb. Tab., 20, 3.

[30] Cf. Vögtle, 73-78.

[31] Ed. W. A. Oldfather (1923), 374.

[32] Ed. J. Ilberg, CMG, IV (1927), 4, 13 - 6, 3; Vögtle, 78-81.

[33] Other examples: Deissmann LO, 267, n. 5-8; Vögtle, 92; cf. also Ant. Christ., III, (1932), 133.

[34] Cf. Plut. Amat., 21 (II, 767e): ἐγκρατεία for σωφροσύνη.

[35] Cf. Wyss, op. cit., 41 and 66.

diatribe with the theme περὶ αὐτοκράτορος λογισμοῦ, [36] the education received in the Law gives men ability for the Stoic cardinal virtues, so that is can be said: βασιλεύσει βασιλείαν σώφρονά τε καὶ δικαίαν καὶ ἀγαθὴν καὶ ἀνδρείαν, 4 Macc. 2:23. Further examples are 4 Macc. 2:16, 18; 3:17: σώφρων νοῦς, or 3:19: σώφρων λογισμός.

2. The situation is different in Test. XII. Here one sees the influence of the Stoic doctrine of virtue in the demand for σωφρονεῖν. The ref. in Jud. 16:3 is to abstinence from wine, in Jos. 4:2; 9:2; 10:2, 3 to chastity, and in B. 4:4 to purity gen. There are ascetic and dualistic tendencies which go beyond mere exhortation. [37]

3. Jos. has the group in the usual sense, Ant., 4, 184; 6, 308; 7, 211; 11, 277; 14, 374; 17, 361; Bell., 6, 234; Ap., 2, 195; Vit., 178. The schema of virtue occurs here, but piety is not a virtue; the virtues are constituent parts of piety: οὐ γὰρ μέρος ἀρετῆς ἐποίησεν τὴν εὐσέβειαν, ἀλλὰ ταύτης μέρη τἆλλα, λέγω δὲ τὴν δικαιοσύνην, τὴν σωφροσύνην, τὴν καρτερίαν, τὴν τῶν πολιτῶν πρὸς ἀλλήλους ἐν ἅπασι συμφωνίαν (said of Moses), Ap., 2, 170. [38]

4. Philo follows the normal Hell. use of the group. [39] σωφροσύνη is one of the classical virtues and is often associated with others, esp. the cardinal virtues → 1099, 2 f. [40] Once Philo can adopt the Aristot, view (→ 1099, 36 ff.) that σωφροσύνη is μεσότης between excessive frivolity and covetousness, Deus. Imm., 164. [41] He can also define the distinctiveness of σωφροσύνη in terms of the Platonic division of the soul into three parts (→ 1099, 20 ff.), Leg. All., I, 69-71. Though these virtues are subordinate to εὐσέβεια, as in Jos. (→ lines 9 ff.), σωφροσύνη is accorded special significance [42] to the degree that it battles against man's chief foes, desire and sensual lust, Leg. All., I, 86; II, 99. It is the main instrument against ἀκολασία, Agric., 98 and 109; Mut. Nom., 197, also against lasciviousness, Leg. All., II, 105 f. Here one may see the underlying reasons why more profound significance is attached to σωφροσύνη and the other virtues, [43] namely, asceticism and dualism. With the other cardinal virtues σωφροσύνη has its source in Paradise in the main river of ἀγαθότης, Leg. All., I, 63-73. [44] This origin shows that the virtues are of transcendent derivation. The rootage of σωφροσύνη in the transcendent world may be seen again in the allegorical interpretation of Nu. 21:6 ff. The brazen serpent made by Moses is σωφροσύνη and those bitten by the serpent of Eve, ἡδονή, must look on this (κατιδεῖν ψυχικῶς) to live. In looking on the brazen serpent, i.e., σωφροσύνη, they see God Himself, Leg. All., II, 81. [45] In relation to the understanding of the present word group one sees here the last horizon of Philo's thought: σωφροσύνη as the basis of the possibility of the vision of God stands contrasted with ἀφροσύνη, Som., II, 100. The ἄφρων is the one who remains trapped in the drunkenness of the world, Ebr., 95; Som., II, 168 and 200. [46] Thus the term σωφροσύνη is filled with a totally new content. [47] In

---

36 O. Eissfeldt, *Einl. in d. AT*³ (1964), 832-4; J. Freudenthal, *Die Flavius Josephus beigelegte Schrift "Über die Herrschaft der Vernunft" (IV Makkabäerbuch). Eine Predigt aus dem ersten nachchr. Jhdt.* (1869), esp. 50-55, 93; U. Luck, Art. "Makkabäerbücher," RGG³, IV, 622 f.

37 Dualism permeates exhortation here and is not restricted to the eschatological tradition.

38 συμφωνία here replaces φρόνησις in the framework of the cardinal virtues.

39 On Philo's relation to popular Hell. philosophy cf. P. Wendland, *Philo u. die kynischstoische Diatribe* (1895).

40 With φρόνησις, ἀνδρεία, δικαιοσύνη, Leg. All., I, 63; Cher., 5; Sacr. AC, 84; Poster. C., 128; Ebr., 23; Abr., 219; Praem. Poen., 52; Congr., 2 etc.

41 Cf. Aristot. Eth. Nic., II, 7, p. 1107b, 5 f.; Eth. Eud., II, 3, p. 1221a, 2.

42 In Som., II, 182 σωφροσύνη is set alongside εὐσέβεια.

43 Cf. with Corp. Herm., 9, 4, where ἀρετή, σωφροσύνη, εὐσέβεια are called σπέρματα τοῦ θεοῦ. In Op. Mund., I, 73 the virtues and their opposites are traced back to the fact that man is a "mixed being."

44 Cf. Wis. 9:11.

45 Cf. Plot. Enn., I, 6, 9.

46 Cf. also Lewy, *op. cit.,* 51 f., 130 f. → IV, 938, 19 ff.

47 On the dissolution of the ancient concept of ἀρετή in the Gnostic sphere cf. Jonas Gnosis, II, 1, 24-29, on Philo cf. *ibid.,* 38-43.

distinction from Gnosticism, however, the relation to God stays within life in the world. The one who is obedient to God is also the seed of virtue. But the virtues, esp. σωφρο-σύνη, are not man's attitude; they are strictly God's gift, cf. Leg. All., I, 63-73; II, 81.

C. The Word Group in the New Testament and the Post-Apostolic Fathers.

In the NT this group, which is so important in the Greek and Hell. world, occurs only 14 times, 8 being in the Past. Materially, too, it plays a comparatively minor role. This corresponds to our findings in respect of the LXX → 1100, 26 ff. It is worth noting, however, that the group is not avoided in principle. Within the framework of what was possible and necessary it could be used uninhibitedly to serve the material exposition of faith in the world.

1. In Mk. 5:15 (par. Lk. 8:35) the healing of the demoniac by Jesus is confirmed by the observation that he was seen ἱματισμένον καὶ σωφρονοῦντα.[48] He had been liberated from μανία. In Ac. 26:25 Paul answers the charge of μανία (→ IV, 361, 33 ff.) by arguing that he speaks "true and rational words" which can be understood and tested, and which bear no relation to ecstasy. [49]

2. Paul uses σωφρονέω in a play on words when he admonishes the Romans μὴ ὑπερφρονεῖν παρ' ὃ δεῖ φρονεῖν, ἀλλὰ φρονεῖν εἰς τὸ σωφρονεῖν, R. 12:3. Τὸ ὑπερφρονέω he opposes σωφρονέω. He is using the term in its classical sense: "to observe the proper measure," "not to transgress the set laws" → 1098, 18 ff. But Paul defines this measure as the μέτρον πίστεως which God gives and which is exhibited in integration into the community and concrete service within it, [50] → VI, 851, 35 ff. R. 12:16 offers an exposition of σωφρονεῖν: μὴ τὰ ὑψηλὰ φρονοῦντες ἀλλὰ τοῖς ταπεινοῖς συναπαγόμενοι. The σωφροσύνη of the Christian is ταπεινοφροσύνη (Phil. 2:3), cf. Col. 3:12 f. with its list of Christian virtues. In such lists σωφροσύνη is obviously avoided, as may be seen from 1 Th. 2:10, cf. later Tt. 2:12. In 2 C. 5:13 Paul sets the conduct of the pneumatics (→ 131, n. 261) in contrast to σωφρονέω. Here, too, the concern for the community which faith imposes is illustrated by the example of the apostle. Sober devotion to one's brother corresponds to ecstasy before God. For this puts into effect the love of Christ which consists in His self-sacrifice and which at the same time demands sacrifice from Christians, 2 C. 5:14.

3. In 1 Pt. 4:7 a concluding exhortation demands: σωφρονήσατε οὖν καὶ νήψατε εἰς προσευχάς. Faced by the imminent end of all things the community must not give way to eschatological frenzy. In such excess it would fall victim precisely to this world. [51] The proper attitude in this situation is soberness and moderation. Thus being in the world is sustained by faith. That the reference is to more than an attitude on the part of Christians is clearly shown by the fact that σωφρονεῖν and

---

[48] Cf. Loh. Mk., ad loc. Mt. does not use the term.

[49] The ref. here is not to the virtue of discretion (Haench. Ag., ad loc.) but simply to "being rational, in one's right mind," cf. the examples → 1097, 14; the answering of similar accusations in Just. Apol., 13, 2-4.

[50] Cf. E. Käsemann, "Gottesdienst im Alltag d. Welt," Festschr. f. J. Jeremias, Beih. z. ZNW, 26 (1960), 168 f.; G. Bornkamm, "Glaube u. Vernunft bei Pls." Stud. z. Antike u. Urchr. (1959), 137.

[51] 1 Pt. is not just attacking pagan vices but is trying to prevent relapse into paganism by pneumatic excess. The Spirit works in a holy life (1:15 f.), in integration into the community as οἶκος πνευματικός (2:5). Cf. νήφω and γρηγορέω in 1 Th. 5:6; 1 Pt. 5:8; σωφρονέω is the mode of watching in expectation of the coming day.

νήφειν (→ IV, 938, 44 ff.) ought to lead to prayer and consequently to the surrender of the whole man in his historical existence to the coming Lord. In the community mutual love is the necessary result of such σωφρονεῖν καὶ νήφειν, 1 Pt. 4:8.

4. The influence of popular Hellenistic philosophy with its ethical traditions does not make itself felt until we reach the Pastorals, which in this respect are to be grouped with the post-apostolic fathers. Here the word group is chiefly used to characterise Christian life in the world, whose goal can be described as σωφρόνως καὶ δικαίως καὶ εὐσεβῶς ζῆν (Tt. 2:12). [52] The link with Hellenistic tradition is especially plain in the household tables and lists of virtues and vices. [53] In Tt. 2:2 Christian virtues are denoted by νηφάλιος, σεμνός, σώφρων, ὑγιαίνων τῇ πίστει, τῇ ἀγάπῃ, τῇ ὑπομονῇ. As distinct from Gnostic scorn for the world Christian faith manifests itself in a proper attitude to it and its goods, 1 Tm. 4:3-5. [54] This correct relation is marked by moderation and contentedness, 1 Tm. 6:6-10, 17-19. αἰδώς and σωφροσύνη (1 Tm. 2:9), i.e., a suitable restraint in every respect is expected of women, cf. 1 Tm. 2:15; 1 Cl., 1, 3. In Tt. 2:5 the reference is especially to chastity (→ 1100, 17 ff.) and a disciplined life. According to Tt. 2:6 young men should be summoned to σωφρονεῖν, i.e., a measured and orderly life. If σώφρονα εἶναι is in the list of requirements for a bishop (1 Tm. 3:2; Tt. 1:8) the reference is not just to conduct appropriate to faith but also to presuppositions necessary for the discharge of a leading office, → 1100, 10 ff. The adoption of the group in the Past. should not be regarded as the intrusion of a Christian respectability originally alien to the Gospel. Many motifs must be considered if one is to understand the acceptance of Greek and Hellenistic ethical traditions into primitive Christianity and the early Church. To the degree that faith is concerned with the life of Christians in the world, the ethical traditions with their developed concepts help to ward off a pneumatic-ecstatic misunderstanding of faith. Also warded off are dualistic tendencies which, with ascetic or libertinistic consequences, might view life in the world as no longer life before God. Finally the waning of imminent expectation forced the Church to consider as concretely as possible the relation of Christians to the world in the spheres of life in which they were set. [55]

D. The Early Church.

In acc. with a widespread understanding (→ 1100, 17 ff.) σωφροσύνη is "chastity" and a seemly life in the moral sense, Just. Apol., 14, 2; 15, 1; Tat. Or. Graec., 32, 2. [56] How much the word group had become a common legacy of the Chr. tradition in this sense may be seen from the exposition of Lk. 5:32 in Just. Apol., 15, 7: Christ did not call the δίκαιοι and σώφρονες to repentance but the ἀσεβεῖς, ἀκόλαστοι and ἄδικοι. Just. then uses the group to show the rational character of Chr. faith. He ref. to rational teaching as distinct from μανία in Apol., 13, 2-4; cf. Ac. 26:24 f. Chr. doctrine and the practices of Christians are not poor from the rational standpt. but are exalted above all

---

[52] Dib. Past.³, 32 f.; cf. also 1 Cl., 62, 1; an ἐνάρετος βίος is part of Christian faith.

[53] O. Zöckler, *Die Tugendlehre d. Christentums* (1904), 7-12; K. Weidinger, *Die Haustafeln, ein Stück urchr. Paränese* (1928), 51-73; Vögtle, *passim*.

[54] Cf. also Ign. Eph., 10, 3; Act. Thom. 150; Act. Joh. 59 and esp. 1 Cl., 62, 2, where πίστις, μετάνοια, ἀγάπη, ἐγκράτεια, σωφροσύνη and ὑπομονή are mentioned. Of interest here is the ref. to ἐγκράτεια and σωφροσύνη along with the true Chr. virtues. The way of Chr. ethics clearly leads to Chr. mastery over the world rather than Gnostic contempt for it.

[55] Cf. H. Conzelmann in Dib. Past., 33; W. Foerster, "Εὐσέβεια in d. Past.," NTSt, 5 (1959), 213-218.

[56] Cf. Athenag. Suppl., 32, 2; 34, 2; Tat. Or. Graec., 33, 2.

wisdom, Apol., 15, 3; cf. Tat. Or. Graec., 33, 1. Hence in Just. Apol., 17, 3 prayer for kings and rulers is characterised as prayer for their σώφρων λογισμός, i.e., that they, too, might occupy themselves aright with Christianity and — this is the underlying thought — become Christians. On the other side only he who has a σώφρων λογισμός can be kept from error and apostasy. [57]

† σωφρονίζω.

1. σωφρονίζω "to make someone a σώφρων," i.e., "to bring him to reason," [1] Thrasymachus Fr., 1 (Diels, II, 323, 8); Thuc., VI, 78, 2; Plat. Gorg., 478d; Resp., V, 471a; Dio Chrys. Or., 8, 12; 60, 4; 60, 5; 75, 5; cf. Jos. Bell., 3, 445; 4, 119, also Xenoph. An., VII, 7, 24; also "to bring back to duty." Xenoph. Cyrop., VIII, 6, 16. Philo in Congr., 172 associates παιδεύω, νοιθετέω and σωφρονίζω and thereby shows how the meaning can move off in the direction of "to exhort", "to spur on." An infin. of aim or result then states the purpose of the admonition. [2]

2. In Tt. 2:4 a worthy walk is demanded of older women ἵνα σωφρονίζωσιν τὰς νέας, i.e., that they spur on the younger women to a similar walk, which is then set forth in detail.

3. In Just. Apol. App., 1, 2 the pass. means "to be set right" in respect of a fault, and then in 2, 2 "to attain to a morally suitable life." The call to repentance issued to a world sunk in vice runs: μετάθεσθε, σωφρονίσθητε, 12, 8.

† σωφρονισμός.

1. This word, found only from the imperial period, has a definite act. sence in secular lit.: "Making to understand," "making wise." Inasmuch as understanding is the basis of virtue and an upright life (Plat. Charm., 164d) it also means "admonition to do better," Strabo, 1, 2, 3; Plut. Cato Maior, 5, 1 (I, 338 f.); Jos. Bell., 2, 9; Ant., 17, 210; 18, 128; Philo Leg. All., III, 193. More rarely it can mean "discretion" in the sense of "moderation," "discipline," Plut. Quaestionum Convivalium, VII, 8, 3 (II, 712c); Iambl. Vit. Pyth., 30, 174.

2. In 2 Tm. 1:7 the πνεῦμα given by God is expounded as πνεῦμα δυνάμεως καὶ ἀγάπης καὶ σωφρονισμοῦ. [1] There is probably a link here with R. 8:15. [2] But the orientation in 2 Tm. 1:7 is quite different. The issue is not the φόβος θεοῦ (R. 8:15) but δειλία in the world which does not permit unhampered entry of the charismata. Thus the Spirit is the πνεῦμα υἱοθεσίας (R. 8:15), not in relation to God, but over against the world. With δύναμις and ἀγάπη, wholly along the lines of the Past., we find σωφρονισμός. Hereby the πνεῦμα is related to the regulated life demanded, just as ethical demands, even though they bear a Hellenistic tinge, are understood in terms of the πνεῦμα. [3]

Luck

---

[57] Cf. already the Past. with ὑγιαίνουσα διδασκαλία, 1 Tm. 1:10; 2 Tm. 4:3; Tt. 1:9; 2:1 etc. (→ ὑγιαίνω).

σωφρονίζω. [1] Cf. Debr. Griech. Wortb. § 265: The factitive sense of verbs in -ίζω.
[2] Apart from Tt. 2:4 there is no instance of this usage, cf. Liddell-Scott, Thes. Steph., s.v. G. A. Gerhard, *Phoinix v. Kolophon* (1909), 35 f., 125, 274 is quoted by Pr.-Bauer, s.v. and Dib. Past., ad loc., but does not offer any par. for the construction with the infin.

σωφρονισμός. [1] In spite of v. 6 πνεῦμα is not to be understood here as a grace of office, so inter al. J. E. Belser, *Die Briefe d. Ap. Pls. an Tm. u. Tt.* (1907), ad loc.
[2] Dib. Past., ad loc.
[3] The act. character of the term is to be seen here too, and is brought out by the translation "discipline," but cf. Pr.-Bauer, s.v.